OSL
OFFICIAL SCRABBLE® LISTS

OSL

OFFICIAL SCRABBLE® LISTS

Comprehensive lists, plus hints and strategies

Compiled by
Allan Simmons and **Darryl Francis**

Chambers

Scrabble® is a registered trade mark owned in the USA by
Hasbro, Inc., in Canada by Hasbro International, Inc.,
in Australia by Murfett Regency Pty Ltd, Victoria, and elsewhere
by J W Spear & Sons PLC, Enfield, England.

Published 1991 by W & R Chambers Ltd,
43-45 Annandale Street, Edinburgh EH7 4AZ.

This paperback edition published 1992 by W & R Chambers Ltd.

British Library Cataloguing in Publication Data

A catalogue record for this book is
available from the British Library.

ISBN 0-550-19027 9

Printed in England by Clays Ltd, St Ives plc.

Preface

Scrabble® players already have the support of OSW (*Official Scrabble® Words*) in helping their games and minimizing their arguments. Now another ally is at hand – *Official Scrabble® Lists* (OSL) – which adds to the players' skills and strategies.

Based on OSW, and ultimately on *Chambers English Dictionary*, this vast collection of lists of words, specifically structured for most Scrabble situations, is the Scrabble player's ideal companion. As well as the lists, there are explanatory hints on such subtleties as Rack Balancing, Fours Feeding and Looking at Hooks.

OSL now takes its place along with OSW in ensuring that you enjoy making the most of every game of Scrabble.

> Francis A Spear
> *Chairman*
> J W Spear & Sons PLC

Contents

Introduction

Official Scrabble® Lists is a complete companion to *Official Scrabble® Words* (OSW) itself hailed as the definitive authority for all Scrabble players. *Official Scrabble Lists* (OSL) is a unique and thorough collection derived from the wealth of words within OSW and categorized into sections according to usefulness and interest as recommended by two of the country's top Scrabble players. Whether you are a casual or regular Scrabble player, the lists are an invaluable aid, acting as a convenient vocabulary-building guide for the newcomer and a specialist reference for the more experienced.

The starter section serves as a quick introduction to an armoury of essential vocabulary, supplying all valid two, three and four-letter words plus complete lists of every high-scoring word containing J Q X or Z. There are lists to help players out of awkward situations: words with many consonants; words containing two B's, two C's, two F's etc.; words containing multiple A's, E's, I's, O's or U's. There is a section that concentrates on word endings and a section featuring sóme 200 specially selected combinations of letters unique to Scrabble playing, yielding thousands of likely seven- and eight-letter 'bonus-scoring' words.

And then there's the specialist 'hook' section, detailing every possible single-letter extension of words from two to seven letters to form valid longer words. As well as 'everyday' examples such as BROAD to ABROAD and ABLE to TABLE there are fascinating novelties to be unearthed such as HOMELY to HOMELYN, HAROSET to CHAROSET, and common but often unthought of extensions such as FLAMING to FLAMINGO and UNFAIR to FUNFAIR. This particular section is a delight in itself.

Of course no Scrabble book is complete without anagrams. OSL is no exception, listing every valid

seven and eight-letter word according to its constituent letters arranged in alphabetical order. Here are thousands of anagrams at your fingertips, from the exotic KURSAAL/RUSKALA to the surprising CUSPATE/TEACUPS, and ready solutions for jumbles of letters such as HLPRSUU (SULPHUR of course) and AAAGMNR (what else but ANAGRAM!).

What more could the Scrabble-player want? How about advice on learning words and tips on strategic play? OSL provides the answer here too, with over twenty-five hints offering sound advice to help improve your vocabulary and revealing a few strategic secrets of success.

Official Scrabble Lists is the ultimate single-volume Scrabble players' ready-reckoner.

Allan Simmons

Hints

SECTION ONE

STARTER LISTS

Introduction

This section contains a variety of so-called 'starter lists'.
There are the basic words – a complete listing of all valid
two-letter, three-letter and four-letter words. There are lists
of words with many vowels and words with many consonants – ammunition for helping you discard disproportionate
numbers of vowels or consonants. There are lists of words
with multiple numbers of the same vowel or same consonant
– the awkward vowel dumps and the awkward consonant
dumps. And there are complete lists of words up to eight
letters long with a J, Q, X or Z. Each of the various lists is
described in more detail in its accompanying introductory
text.

BASIC WORDS

The following lists contain all the two-letter, three-letter and four-letter words. There are almost 6000 words in these three lists, and while it is not essential to know all of them, it will certainly help your game to know as many as possible.

There are 106 two-letter words listed here. Two-letter words can be considered as the backbone words of any Scrabble game. They are very important, not necessarily for the scores which they themselves achieve, but also for the scores of other words whose play they facilitate, either at the same time or later in a game.

The two-letter words provide a means of playing words parallel to other words already on the board, resolving surplus vowel problems (for example, AA, EE and OO), squeezing scores out of tight board situations, or opening the board for future scoring opportunities. Many of the two-letter words can have letters added before or after them, in order to make valid three-letter words – see the Hooks section for these.

Make a list of the two-letter words that you are not familiar with and try to introduce them into your games. You might find it additionally helpful to know what your words mean. It really can help to cement the words into your mind if you know roughly what they mean. But you will have to check *Chambers English Dictionary* for meanings. Top-flight Scrabble players will know *all* 106 of these words, and will also be able to define most of them!

There are just over 1000 three-letter words listed here. These are important as they provide a means of discarding unwanted letters, a means of squeezing scores out of difficult board situations, and a means of playing higher-scoring words (perhaps bonuses) by turning two-letter words into three-letter words. Try to familiarize yourself with some of those which are unknown to you, and see if you can play them in your games. Leading Scrabble players will be aware of most of the three-letter words and will be able to call on them when they are needed. But most of the top players will occasionally be uncertain of a three-letter specimen. For example, a Scrabble player may well recall FAY and FEY, but will be unsure of FOY, a player might know HAH and HOH, but will be uncertain about HEH and HUH.

There are approximately 4600 four-letter words here. Their importance is less than that of the two and three-letter words, but they do still provide a useful pool of words to dip into for scoring or rack balancing purposes.

2-LETTER WORDS

AA	AX	EE	GI	IS	MI	OE	OW	TA	WE
AD	AY	EF	GO	IT	MO	OF	OX	TE	WO
AE	BA	EH	GU	JO	MU	OH	OY	TI	XI
AH	BE	EL	HA	KA	MY	OI	PA	TO	YE
AI	BO	EM	HE	KO	NA	OM	PI	UG	YO
AM	BY	EN	HI	KY	NE	ON	PO	UM	YU
AN	CH	ER	HO	LA	NO	OO	RE	UN	ZO
AR	DA	ES	ID	LI	NU	OP	SH	UP	
AS	DI	EX	IF	LO	NY	OR	SI	UR	
AT	DO	FA	IN	MA	OB	OS	SO	US	
AW	EA	FY	IO	ME	OD	OU	ST	UT	

HINT

Two's Company

There are 106 two-letter words and they are all fundamental to the game. The importance of knowing all the two-letter words can't be emphasized enough. They are vital for parallel word play and maximizing scoring on tight boards and should be learnt off by heart. Write out the complete list over and over again. Play a few solo games allowing yourself to 'cheat' by referring to the list but don't rely on the lists for too long. If you don't exercise your memory you won't recall them during actual play.

HINT

Score or Strategy?

The highest-scoring move is not always the best play. Always consider lower-scoring alternatives that might be better for your strategy. A lower-scoring move might not give so many points away to your opponent, or might leave you with a better balance of letters on your rack, or might enable you to set yourself up for a good score the next turn. Losing 10 points one turn may provide an extra 20 points the following turn or, if your emphasis had been on rack balance rather than score, it may even yield a 50-point bonus play.

3-LETTER WORDS

AAS	BAH	CHI	DOR	EWT	GAY	HID	JIB	LES	MAC	MOD
ABA	BAM	CIG	DOS	EYE	GED	HIE	JIG	LET	MAD	MOE
ABB	BAN	CIT	DOT	FAB	GEE	HIM	JIZ	LEU	MAE	MOG
ABY	BAP	CLY	DOW	FAD	GEL	HIN	JOB	LEV	MAG	MOO
ACE	BAR	COB	DRY	FAH	GEM	HIP	JOE	LEW	MAK	MOP
ACT	BAS	COD	DSO	FAN	GEN	HIS	JOG	LEX	MAL	MOR
ADD	BAT	COG	DUB	FAP	GEO	HIT	JOR	LEY	MAM	MOT
ADO	BAY	COL	DUD	FAR	GET	HOA	JOT	LEZ	MAN	MOU
ADS	BED	CON	DUE	FAS	GEY	HOB	JOW	LIB	MAP	MOW
AFT	BEE	COO	DUG	FAT	GHI	HOC	JOY	LID	MAR	MOY
AGA	BEG	COP	DUN	FAW	GIB	HOD	JUD	LIE	MAS	MOZ
AGE	BEL	COR	DUO	FAX	GID	HOE	JUG	LIG	MAT	MUD
AGO	BEN	COS	DUP	FAY	GIE	HOG	JUS	LIN	MAW	MUG
AHA	BET	COT	DUX	FED	GIF	HOH	JUT	LIP	MAX	MUM
AIA	BEY	COW	DYE	FEE	GIG	HOI	KAE	LIS	MAY	MUN
AID	BEZ	COX	DZO	FEN	GIN	HON	KAI	LIT	MEL	MUS
AIL	BIB	COY	EAN	FET	GIO	HOO	KAM	LOB	MEN	MUX
AIM	BID	COZ	EAR	FEU	GIP	HOP	KAS	LOG	MES	NAB
AIN	BIG	CRU	EAS	FEW	GIS	HOS	KAT	LOO	MET	NAE
AIR	BIN	CRY	EAT	FEY	GIT	HOT	KAW	LOP	MEU	NAG
AIS	BIO	CUB	EAU	FEZ	GJU	HOW	KAY	LOR	MEW	NAM
AIT	BIS	CUD	EBB	FIB	GNU	HOX	KEA	LOS	MHO	NAN
AKE	BIT	CUE	ECH	FID	GOA	HOY	KEB	LOT	MID	NAP
ALA	BIZ	CUM	ECU	FIE	GOB	HUB	KED	LOW	MIL	NAS
ALB	BOA	CUP	EDH	FIG	GOD	HUE	KEF	LOX	MIM	NAT
ALE	BOB	CUR	EEK	FIL	GOE	HUG	KEG	LOY	MIR	NAY
ALL	BOD	CUT	EEL	FIN	GOG	HUH	KEN	LUD	MIS	NEB
ALP	BOG	CUZ	EEN	FIR	GON	HUM	KEP	LUG	MIX	NED
ALS	BOH	CWM	EFF	FIT	GOO	HUP	KET	LUM	MIZ	NEE
ALT	BOK	DAB	EFS	FIX	GOS	HUT	KEX	LUR	MNA	NEF
AMI	BON	DAD	EFT	FIZ	GOT	HYE	KEY	LUX	MOA	NEK
AMP	BOO	DAG	EGG	FLU	GOV	HYP	KID	LUZ	MOB	NEP
ANA	BOP	DAH	EGO	FLY	GOY	ICE	KIF	LYE		NET
ANT	BOR	DAK	EHS	FOB	GUB	ICH	KIN	LYM		NEW
ANY	BOS	DAL	EIK	FOE	GUE	ICY	KIP			NIB
APE	BOT	DAM	EKE	FOG	GUM	IDE	KIR			NID
APT	BOW	DAN	ELD	FOH	GUN	IDS	KIT			NIE
ARC	BOX	DAP	ELF	FON	GUP	IFF	KOA			NIL
ARE	BOY	DAS	ELK	FOP	GUR	IFS	KOB			NIM
ARK	BRA	DAW	ELL	FOR	GUS	ILK	KON			NIP
ARM	BRO	DAY	ELM	FOU	GUT	ILL	KOP			NIS
ARS	BUB	DEB	ELS	FOX	GUY	IMP	KOS			NIT
ART	BUD	DEE	ELT	FOY	GYM	INK	KOW			NIX
ARY	BUG	DEI	EME	FRA	GYP	INN	KYE			NOB
ASH	BUM	DEL	EMS	FRO	HAD	INS	LAB			NOD
ASK	BUN	DEN	EMU	FRY	HAE	ION	LAC			NOG
ASP	BUR	DEW	END	FUB	HAG	IOS	LAD			NOH
ASS	BUS	DEY	ENE	FUD	HAH	IRE	LAG			NOM
ATE	BUT	DIB	ENG	FUG	HAJ	IRK	LAH			NON
AUF	BUY	DID	ENS	FUM	HAM	ISH	LAM			NOR
AUK	BYE	DIE	EON	FUN	HAN	ISM	LAP			NOT
AVA	BYS	DIG	ERA	FUR	HAP	ITA	LAR			NOW
AVE	CAB	DIM	ERE	GAB	HAS	ITS	LAS			NOY
AWA	CAD	DIN	ERF	GAD	HAT	IVY	LAT			NTH
AWE	CAM	DIP	ERG	GAE	HAW	JAB	LAV			NUB
AWL	CAN	DIT	ERK	GAG	HAY	JAG	LAW			NUN
AWN	CAP	DIV	ERN	GAL	HEM	JAK	LAX			NUR
AXE	CAR	DOB	ERR	GAM	HEN	JAM	LAY			NUS
AYE	CAT	DOC	ERS	GAN	HEP	JAP	LEA			NUT
AYU	CAW	DOD	ESS	GAP	HER	JAR	LED			NYE
BAA	CAY	DOE	ETA	GAR	HES	JAW	LEE			NYS
BAD	CEE	DOG	ETH	GAS	HET	JAY	LEG			OAF
BAG	CEL	DOH	EUK	GAT	HEW	JEE	LEI			OAK
	CEP	DON	EVE	GAU	HEX	JET	LEK			OAR
	CHA	DOO	EWE		HEY	JEU	LEP			
	CHE	DOP	EWK		HIC					

OAT	OWE	POH	REF	SAG	SOH	TEE	UEY	WAP	YEP
OBI	OWL	POI	REH	SAI	SOL	TEF	UFO	WAR	YES
OBS	OWN	POM	REM	SAL	SON	TEG	UGH	WAS	YET
OCA	OWT	POO	REN	SAM	SOP	TEL	UGS	WAT	YEW
OCH	OYE	POP	REP	SAN	SOS	TEN	ULE	WAW	YEX
ODA	OYS	POS	RES	SAP	SOT	TES	UNI	WAX	YGO
ODD		POT	RET	SAR	SOU	TEW	UNS	WAY	YIN
ODE	PAD	POW	REV	SAT	SOV	THE	UPS	WEB	YIP
ODS	PAH	POX	REW	SAW	SOW	THO	URD	WED	YOB
OES	PAL	POZ	REX	SAX	SOX	THY	URE	WEE	YOD
OFF	PAM	PRE	RHO	SAY	SOY	TIC	URN	WEM	YOK
OFT	PAN	PRO	RHY	SAZ	SPA	TID	USE	WEN	YON
OHM	PAP	PRY	RIA	SEA	SPY	TIE	UTE	WET	YOS
OHO	PAR	PSI	RIB	SEC	STY	TIG	UTS	WEX	YOU
OIK	PAS	PST	RID	SED	SUB	TIL	UTU	WEY	YOW
OIL	PAT	PUB	RIG	SEE	SUD	TIN	UVA	WHO	YUG
OKE	PAW	PUD	RIM	SEG	SUE	TIP		WHY	YUK
OLD	PAX	PUG	RIN	SEI	SUI	TIS	VAC	WIG	YUP
OLE	PAY	PUH	RIP	SEL	SUK	TIT	VAE	WIN	YUS
OLM	PEA	PUN	RIT	SEN	SUM	TOD	VAN	WIS	
OMS	PEC	PUP	RIZ	SET	SUN	TOE	VAS	WIT	ZAG
ONE	PED	PUR	ROB	SEW	SUP	TOG	VAT	WOE	ZAP
ONS	PEE	PUS	ROC	SEX	SUQ	TOM	VAU	WOG	ZAX
OOF	PEG	PUT	ROD	SEY	SUR	TON	VEE	WOK	ZEA
OOH	PEN	PUY	ROE	SEZ	SUS	TOO	VEG	WON	ZED
OOM	PEP	PYE	ROK	SHE	SWY	TOP	VET	WOO	ZEE
OON	PER	PYX	ROM	SHY	SYE	TOR	VEX	WOP	ZEK
OOP	PET		ROO	SIB		TOT	VIA	WOS	ZEL
OOR	PEW	QAT	ROT	SIC	TAB	TOW	VIE	WOT	ZHO
OOS	PHI	QUA	ROW	SIM	TAD	TOY	VIM	WOW	ZIG
OPE	PHO		RUB	SIN	TAE	TRY	VIN	WOX	ZIP
OPS	PIA	RAD	RUC	SIP	TAG	TUB	VIS	WRY	ZIT
OPT	PIC	RAG	RUD	SIR	TAI	TUG	VLY	WUD	ZIZ
ORB	PIE	RAH	RUE	SIS	TAJ	TUI	VOE	WYE	ZOA
ORC	PIG	RAJ	RUG	SIT	TAK	TUM	VOL	WYN	ZOO
ORD	PIN	RAM	RUM	SIX	TAM	TUN	VOR		ZOS
ORE	PIP	RAN	RUN	SKA	TAN	TUP	VOW	XIS	ZUZ
ORF	PIR	RAP	RUT	SKI	TAP	TUT	VOX		
ORS	PIS	RAS	RYA	SKY	TAR	TWA	VUG		
ORT	PIT	RAT	RYE	SLY	TAT	TWO	VUM		
OUK	PIU	RAW		SMA	TAU	TYE			
OUP	PIX	RAX	SAB	SOB	TAW	TYG		WAD	YAH
OUR	PLY	RAY	SAC	SOC	TAX			WAE	YAK
OUT	POA	RED	SAD	SOD	TEA	UDO		WAG	YAM
OVA	POD	REE	SAE	SOG	TED	UDS		WAN	YAP
									YAW
									YEA
									YEN

HINT _____

Tackling the Threes

To the uninitiated the number of allowable three-letter words is quite daunting. However, if you ignore the everyday words the lists begin to become a little more manageable. Pay particular attention to those that can be made by extending two-letter words (see the Hooks section) and those containing tiles worth three points or more. Write out those you don't know and play a few solo games, going out of your way to play some of your newly learnt three-letter words. By actually playing the more obscure words on the board you will find that they soon begin to stick. Many players also find it helpful to know the definitions. These you will find in *Chambers English Dictionary*. Once you can picture what the words mean this too will help them become firmer in your memory.

HINT

Open Play

Most people play Scrabble to win, which is natural and should not be discouraged. However, if you are keen to improve your scoring power and vocabulary, try playing the occasional more open game. This will enable you to concentrate on strengthening your rack-balancing, bonus-spotting and hook-word skills. Here are a few tips on open play:

- Try to ensure vowels are next to premium squares to provide scoring opportunities for high-scoring consonants.
- Experiment with playing the first word to the left of the board to enable easier access to the otherwise awkward top left.
- Play conservatively and consider points per tile gained each move rather than points per move.
- Don't be afraid to open up the triple-word squares and equally don't think you have to take a triple-word square as soon as it is available.
- Change tiles if your rack gets imbalanced and the only moves available block the openings on the board.
- Whenever you get the opportunity start a game with a three-letter word consisting of vowel-consonant-vowel played centrally to open up all four areas of the board, eg ADO, EGO, IRE, OCA, UDO etc.

HINT

Knowing Non-Words

Much time can be wasted in a game when you have a promising-looking set of seven letters on your rack but can't remember whether they make a seven-letter word or not. Therefore it is also beneficial to be familiar with those common sets of seven letters that *don't* make a seven-letter word. Some examples are: ENRAISE, IRELAND, and TAILEND. Note that by forming 'non-words' with these racks they can be more easily recognized during play. Having armed yourself with a selection of non-words the next task is to learn the possible eight-letter plays so that you can be aware of possible bonus plays using available letters on the board. The IRELAND set makes eight-letter words with the letters B F G H N S. These words and those of the other non-words mentioned above can be readily unearthed from the Eight-Letter Anagram lists.

4-LETTER WORDS

ABAC	AKIN	ARAK	AYUS	BEAM	BISH	BORA	BUNK	CART	CILL
ABAS	ALAE	ARAR	AZAN	BEAN	BISK	BORD	BUNS	CASA	CION
ABBA	ALAP	ARBA	AZYM	BEAR	BITE	BORE	BUNT	CASE	CIRE
ABBE	ALAR	ARCH		BEAT	BITO	BORN	BUOY	CASH	CIRL
ABBS	ALAS	ARCO	BAAS	BEAU	BITS	BORS	BURD	CASK	CIST
ABED	ALAY	ARCS	BABA	BECK	BITT	BORT	BURG	CAST	CITE
ABET	ALBE	ARED	BABE	BEDE	BLAB	BOSH	BURK	CATE	CITO
ABID	ALBS	ARES	BABU	BEDS	BLAD	BOSK	BURL	CATS	CITS
ABLE	ALEE	ARET	BABY	BEEF	BLAE	BOSS	BURN	CAUF	CITY
ABLY	ALES	AREW	BACH	BEEN	BLAG	BOTH	BURP	CAUK	CIVE
ABUT	ALEW	ARIA	BACK	BEEP	BLAH	BOTS	BURR	CAUM	CLAD
ABYE	ALFA	ARID	BADE	BEER	BLAT	BOTT	BURS	CAUP	CLAG
ACED	ALGA	ARIL	BAEL	BEES	BLAY	BOUK	BURY	CAWK	CLAM
ACES	ALIT	ARIS	BAFF	BEET	BLEB	BOUN	BUSH	CAWS	CLAN
ACHE	ALLS	ARKS	BAFT	BEGO	BLED	BOUT	BUSK	CAYS	CLAP
ACHY	ALLY	ARMS	BAGS	BEGS	BLEE	BOWL	BUSS	CEAS	CLAT
ACID	ALMA	ARMY	BAHT	BEIN	BLET	BOWR	BUST	CECA	CLAW
ACME	ALME	ARNA	BAIL	BELL	BLIN	BOWS	BUSY	CEDE	CLAY
ACNE	ALMS	AROW	BAIT	BELS	BLIP	BOXY	BUTE	CEDI	CLEF
ACRE	ALOD	ARSE	BAKE	BELT	BLOB	BOYG	BUTS	CEES	CLEG
ACTA	ALOE	ARTS	BALD	BEMA	BLOC	BOYO	BUTT	CEIL	CLEM
ACTS	ALOW	ARTY	BALE	BEND	BLOT	BOYS	BUYS	CELL	CLEW
ACYL	ALPS	ARUM	BALK	BENE	BLOW	BRAD	BUZZ	CELS	CLIP
ADAW	ALSO	ARVO	BALL	BENI	BLUB	BRAE	BYES	CELT	CLOD
ADDS	ALTO	ARYL	BALM	BENJ	BLUE	BRAG	BYKE	CENT	CLOG
ADIT	ALTS	ASAR	BALU	BENS	BLUR	BRAN	BYRE	CEPS	CLOP
ADOS	ALUM	ASCI	BAMS	BENT	BOAK	BRAS	BYTE	CERE	CLOT
ADRY	AMAH	ASHY	BANC	BERE	BOAR	BRAT		CERT	CLOU
ADZE	AMBO	ASKS	BAND	BERG	BOAS	BRAW	CABA	CESS	CLOW
AEON	AMEN	ASPS	BANE	BERK	BOAT	BRAY	CABS	CETE	CLOY
AERY	AMID	ATAP	BANG	BERM	BOBA	BRED	CADE	CHAD	CLUB
AESC	AMIE	ATOC	BANI	BEST	BOBS	BREE	CADI	CHAI	CLUE
AFAR	AMIR	ATOK	BANK	BETA	BOCK	BREN	CADS	CHAL	COAL
AFFY	AMIS	ATOM	BANS	BETE	BODE	BRER	CAFE	CHAM	COAT
AFRO	AMLA	ATOP	BANT	BETH	BODS	BREW	CAFF	CHAP	COAX
AGAR	AMMO	AUFS	BAPS	BETS	BODY	BRIG	CAGE	CHAR	COBB
AGAS	AMOK	AUKS	BAPU	BEVY	BOFF	BRIM	CAGY	CHAS	COBS
AGED	AMPS	AULA	BARB	BEYS	BOGS	BRIO	CAIN	CHAT	COCA
AGEE	AMYL	AULD	BARD	BHEL	BOGY	BRIT	CAKE	CHAW	COCH
AGEN	ANAL	AUNT	BARE	BIAS	BOIL	BROD	CAKY	CHAY	COCK
AGES	ANAN	AURA	BARF	BIBS	BOKE	BROG	CALF	CHEF	COCO
AGHA	ANAS	AUTO	BARK	BICE	BOKO	BROO	CALK	CHER	CODA
AGIN	ANCE	AVAL	BARM	BIDE	BOKS	BROS	CALL	CHEW	CODE
AGIO	ANDS	AVAS	BARN	BIDS	BOLD	BROW	CALM	CHEZ	CODS
AGMA	ANES	AVER	BARP	BIEN	BOLE	BRUT	CALP	CHIC	COED
AGOG	ANEW	AVES	BARS	BIER	BOLL	BUAT	CALX	CHID	COFF
AGON	ANIL	AVID	BASE	BIFF	BOLO	BUBA	CAME	CHIK	COFT
AGUE	ANKH	AVOW	BASH	BIGA	BOLT	BUBO	CAMP	CHIN	COGS
AHEM	ANNA	AWAY	BASK	BIGG	BOMA	BUBS	CAMS	CHIP	COHO
AHOY	ANNO	AWDL	BASS	BIGS	BOMB	BUCK	CANE	CHIS	COIF
AIAS	ANNS	AWED	BAST	BIKE	BONA	BUDO	CANG	CHIT	COIL
AIDE	ANOA	AWES	BATE	BILE	BOND	BUDS	CANN	CHIV	COIN
AIDS	ANON	AWLS	BATH	BILK	BONE	BUFF	CANS	CHOC	COIR
AILS	ANOW	AWNS	BATS	BILL	BONG	BUFO	CANT	CHOP	COKE
AIMS	ANTA	AWNY	BATT	BIND	BONK	BUGS	CANY	CHOU	COKY
AINE	ANTE	AWRY	BAUD	BINE	BONY	BUHL	CAPA	CHOW	COLA
AIRN	ANTI	AXED	BAUK	BING	BOOB	BUIK	CAPE	CHUB	COLD
AIRS	ANTS	AXEL	BAUR	BINK	BOOH	BUKE	CAPO	CHUG	COLE
AIRT	ANUS	AXES	BAWD	BINS	BOOK	BULB	CAPS	CHUM	COLL
AIRY	APAY	AXIL	BAWL	BINT	BOOM	BULK	CARB	CHUT	COLS
AITS	APED	AXIS	BAWN	BIOG	BOON	BULL	CARD	CIAO	COLT
AITU	APES	AXLE	BAWR	BIOS	BOOR	BUMF	CARE	CIDE	COMA
AJAR	APEX	AXON	BAYE	BIRD	BOOS	BUMP	CARK	CIEL	COMB
AJEE	APOD	AYAH	BAYS	BIRK	BOOT	BUMS	CARL	CIGS	COME
AKED	APSE	AYES	BAYT	BIRL	BOPS	BUNA	CARP		COMP
AKEE	APTS	AYRE	BEAD	BIRR		BUND	CARR		COMS
AKES	AQUA		BEAK	BISE		BUNG	CARS		COND

CONE	CULT	DEAD	DIRK	DOUT	DWAM	EMES	EYRE	FETS	FOBS
CONK	CUNT	DEAF	DIRL	DOVE	DYAD	EMEU	EYKY	FETT	FOCI
CONN	CUPS	DEAL	DIRT	DOWD	DYED	EMIR		FEUD	FOEN
CONS	CURB	DEAN	DISA	DOWF	DYER	EMIT	FACE	FEUS	FOES
CONY	CURD	DEAR	DISC	DOWL	DYES	EMMA	FACT	FEYS	FOGS
COOF	CURE	DEAW	DISH	DOWN	EMUS	FADE	FIAR	FOGY
COOK	CURL	DEBS	DISK	DOWP	DYKE	EMYS	FADO	FIAT	FOHN
COOL	CURN	DECK	DISS	DOWS	DYNE	ENDS	FADS	FIBS	FOIL
COOM	CURR	DECO	DITA	DOWT	DZOS	ENEW	FADY	FICO	FOIN
COON	CURS	DEED	DITE	DOXY		ENES	FAFF	FIDS	FOLD
COOP	CURT	DEEM	DITS	DOZE	EACH	ENGS	FAGS	FIEF	FOLK
COOS	CUSH	DEEN	DITT	DOZY	EALE	ENOW	FAHS	FIFE	FOND
COOT	CUSK	DEEP	DIVA	DRAB	EANS	ENVY	FAIK	FIGO	FONE
COPE	CUSP	DEER	DIVE	DRAD	EARD	EOAN	FAIL	FIGS	FONS
COPS	CUSS	DEES	DIVI	DRAG	EARL	EONS	FAIN	FIKE	FONT
COPY	CUTE	DEEV	DIVS	DRAM	EARN	EORL	FAIR	FIKY	FOOD
CORD	CUTS	DEFT	DIXI	DRAP	EARS	EPEE	FAIX	FILE	FOOL
CORE	CWMS	DEFY	DIXY	DRAT	EASE	EPHA	FAKE	FILL	FOOT
CORF		DEID	DOAB	DRAW	EAST	EPIC	FALL	FILM	FOPS
CORK	CYAN	DEIL	DOAT	DRAY	EASY	EPOS	FALX	FILS	FORA
CORM	CYMA	DELE	DOBS	DREE	EATH	ERAS	FAME	FIND	FORD
CORN	CYME	DELF	DOCK	DREW	EATS	ERED	FAND	FINE	FORE
CORS	CYST	DELI	DOCS	DREY	EAUS	ERES	FANG	FINK	FORK
COSE	CYTE	DELL	DODO	DRIB	EAUX	ERGO	FANK	FINO	FORM
COSH	CZAR	DELS	DODS	DRIP	EBBS	ERGS	FANS	FINS	FORT
COSS		DEME	DOEN	DROP	EBON	ERIC	FARD	FIRE	FOSS
COST	DABS	DEMO	DOER	DROW	ECAD	ERKS	FARE	FIRK	FOUD
COSY	DACE	DEMY	DOES	DRUB	ECCE	ERNE	FARL	FIRM	FOUL
COTE	DADO	DENE	DOFF	DRUG	ECCO	ERNS	FARM	FIRN	FOUR
COTH	DADS	DENS	DOGE	DRUM	ECHE	ERRS	FARO	FIRS	FOUS
COTS	DAFF	DENT	DOGS	DSOS	ECHO	ERST	FARS	FISC	FOWL
COTT	DAFT	DENY	DOGY	DUAD	ECHT	ESKY	FART	FISH	FOXY
COUP	DAGO	DERE	DOHS	DUAL	ECRU	ESNE	FASH	FISK	FOYS
COUR	DAGS	DERM	DOIT	DUAN	ECUS	ESPY	FAST	FIST	FOZY
COVE	DAHL	DERN	DOJO	DUAR	EDDO	ESSE	FATE	FITS	FRAB
COWL	DAHS	DERV	DOLE	DUBS	EDDY	ETAS	FATS	FITT	FRAE
COWP	DAIS	DESK	DOLL	DUCE	EDGE	ETAT	FAUN	FIVE	FRAP
COWS	DAKS	DEUS	DOLT	DUCK	EDGY	ETCH	FAUX	FIZZ	FRAS
COXA	DALE	DEVA	DOME	DUCT	EDHS	ETEN	FAWN	FLAB	FRAU
COXY	DALI	DEWS	DOMY	DUDE	EDIT	ETHE	FAWS	FLAG	FRAY
COYS	DALS	DEWY	DONA	DUDS	EECH	ETHS	FAYS	FLAK	FREE
COZE	DALT	DEYS	DONE	DUED	EELS	ETNA	FAZE	FLAM	FRET
COZY	DAME	DHAK	DONG	DUEL	EELY	ETUI	FEAL	FLAN	FRIG
CRAB	DAMN	DHAL	DONS	DUES	EERY	EUGE	FEAR	FLAP	FRIS
CRAG	DAMP	DHOW	DOOB	DUET	EEVN	EUGH	FEAT	FLAT	FRIT
CRAM	DANG	DIAL	DOOK	DUFF	EFFS	EUKS	FECK	FLAW	FRIZ
CRAN	DANK	DIBS	DOOL	DUGS	EFTS	EUOI	FEDS	FLAX	FROG
CRAP	DANS	DICE	DOOM	DUKE	EGAD	EURO	FEED	FLAY	FROM
CRAW	DANT	DICH	DOOR	DULE	EGAL	EVEN	FEEL	FLEA	FROW
CREE	DAPS	DICK	DOOS	DULL	EGER	EVER	FEER	FLED	FUBS
CREW	DARE	DICT	DOPA	DULY	EGGS	EVES	FEES	FLEE	FUCI
CRIB	DARG	DIDO	DOPE	DUMA	EGGY	EVET	FEET	FLEG	FUCK
CRIT	DARI	DIEB	DOPS	DUMB	EGIS	EVIL	FEGS	FLEW	FUDS
CROC	DARK	DIED	DOPY	DUMP	EGMA	EVOE	FEHM	FLEX	FUEL
CROP	DARN	DIES	DORM	DUNE	EGOS	EVOE	FEIS	FLEY	FUFF
CROW	DART	DIET	DORP	DUNG	EHED	EWER	FEIS	FLIC	FUGS
CRUD	DASH	DIGS	DORR	DUNK	EIKS	EWES	FELL	FLIP	FULL
CRUE	DATA	DIKA	DORS	DUNS	EILD	EWKS	FELT	FLIT	FUME
CRUS	DATE	DIKE	DORT	DUNT	EINE	EWTS	FEME	FLIX	FUMS
CRUX	DAUB	DILL	DORY	DUOS	EKED	EXAM	FEND	FLOE	FUMY
CUBE	DAUD	DIME	DOSE	DUPE	EKES	EXES	FENS	FLOG	FUND
CUBS	DAUR	DIMS	DOSS	DUPS	EKKA	EXIT	FENT	FLOP	FUNG
CUDS	DAUT	DINE	DOST	DURA	ELAN	EXON	FEOD	FLOR	FUNK
CUED	DAWD	DING	DOTE	DURE	ELDS	EXPO	FERE	FLOW	FUNS
CUES	DAWK	DINK	DOTH	DURN	ELFS	EXUL	FERM	FLUB	FURL
CUFF	DAWN	DINS	DOTS	DURO	ELKS	EYAS	FERN	FLUE	FURR
CUIF	DAWS	DINT	DOTY	DUSH	ELLS	EYED	FESS	FLUS	FURS
CUIT	DAWT	DIPS	DOUC	DUSK	ELMS	EYES	FEST	FLUX	FURY
CULL	DAYS	DIRE	DOUP	DUST	ELMY	EYNE	FETA	FOAL	FUSC
CULM	DAZE	DIRL	DOUR	DUTY	ELTS	EYRA	FETE	FOAM	FUSE

FUSS	GEES	GLUE	GROW	HAMS	HETS	HORS	IDLY	JEED	JUTS
FUST	GEIT	GLUG	GRUB	HAND	HEWN	HOSE	IDOL	JEEL	JYNX
FUZE	GELD	GLUM	GRUE	HANG	HEWS	HOSS	IDYL	JEEP	
FUZZ	GELS	GLUT	GRUM	HANK	HEYS	HOST	IDYL	JEER	KADE
FYKE	GELT	GNAR	GUAN	HAPS	HICK	HOTE	IFFY	JEES	KADI
FYLE	GEMS	GNAT	GUAR	HARD	HIDE	HOTS	IGAD	JEFF	KAED
FYRD	GENA	GNAW	GUBS	HARK	HIED	HOUF	IKAT	JELL	KAES
	GENE	GNUS	GUCK	HARL	HIES	HOUT	IKON	JESS	KAGO
GABS	GENS	GOAD	GUDE	HARM	HIGH	HOVE	ILEA	JEST	KAID
GABY	GENT	GOAF	GUES	HARN	HIKE	HOWE	ILEX	JETE	KAIE
GADE	GENU	GOAL	GUFF	HARO	HILA	HOWF	ILIA	JETS	KAIF
GADI	GEOS	GOAS	GUID	HARP	HILD	HOWK	ILKA	JEUX	KAIL
GADS	GERE	GOAT	GULA	HART	HILI	HOWL	ILKS	JIAO	KAIM
GAED	GERM	GOBO	GULE	HASH	HILL	HOWS	ILLS	JIBE	KAIN
GAES	GEST	GOBS	GULF	HASK	HILT	HOYA	ILLY	JIBS	KAIS
GAFF	GETA	GOBY	GULL	HASP	HIND	HOYS	IMAM	JIFF	KAKA
GAGA	GETS	GODS	GULP	HAST	HING	HUBS	IMPI	JIGS	KAKI
GAGE	GEUM	GOEL	GULY	HATE	HINS	HUCK	IMPS	JILL	KALE
GAGS	GHAT	GOER	GUMP	HATH	HINT	HUED	INBY	JILT	KALI
GAID	GHEE	GOES	GUMS	HATS	HIPS	HUER	INCH	JIMP	KAME
GAIN	GHIS	GOEY	GUNK	HAUD	HIPT	HUES	INFO	JINK	KAMI
GAIR	GIBE	GOFF	GUNS	HAUL	HIRE	HUFF	INGO	JINN	KANA
GAIT	GIBS	GOGO	GUPS	HAUT	HISH	HUGE	INIA	JINX	KANG
GAJO	GIDS	GOGS	GURL	HAVE	HISN	HUGS	INKS	JIRD	KANS
GALA	GIED	GOLD	GURN	HAWK	HISS	HUGY	INKY	JISM	KANT
GALE	GIEN	GOLE	GURS	HAWM	HIST	HUIA	INLY	JIVE	KAON
GALL	GIES	GOLF	GURU	HAWS	HITS	HULA	INNS	JIZZ	KARA
GALS	GIFT	GOLP	GUSH	HAYS	HIVE	HULE	INRO	JOBE	KART
GAMB	GIGA	GONE	GUST	HAZE	HIYA	HULK	INTO	JOBS	KATI
GAME	GIGS	GONG	GUTS	HAZY	HIZZ	HULL	IONS	JOCK	KATS
GAMP	GILA	GONK	GUYS	HEAD	HOAR	HUMA	IOTA	JOCO	KAVA
GAMS	GILD	GONS	GYAL	HEAL	HOAS	HUMF	IRES	JOES	KAWS
GAMY	GILL	GOOD	GYBE	HEAP	HOAX	HUMP	IRID	JOEY	KAYO
GANE	GILT	GOOF	GYMP	HEAR	HOBO	HUMS	IRIS	JOGS	KAYS
GANG	GIMP	GOOK	GYMS	HEAT	HOBS	HUNG	IRKS	JOHN	KAZI
GAOL	GING	GOOL	GYNY	HEBE	HOCK	HUNK	IRON	JOIN	KEAS
GAPE	GINK	GOON	GYPS	HECH	HODS	HUNT	ISLE	JOKE	KEBS
GAPO	GINN	GOOP	GYRE	HECK	HOED	HUPS	ISMS	JOKY	KECK
GAPS	GINS	GOOR	GYRI	HEED	HOER	HURL	ISMY	JOLE	KEDS
GARB	GIOS	GOOS	GYRO	HEEL	HOES	HURT	ITAS	JOLL	KEEK
GARE	GIPS	GORE	GYTE	HEFT	HOGG	HUSH	ITCH	JOLT	KEEL
GARS	GIRD	GORM	GYVE	HEID	HOGH	HUSK	ITEM	JOMO	KEEN
GART	GIRL	GORY		HEIL	HOGS	HUSO	IWIS	JOOK	KEEP
GASH	GIRN	GOSH	HAAF	HEIR	HOHS	HUSS	IXIA	JORS	KEFS
GASP	GIRO	GOUK	HAAR	HELD	HOIK	HUTS	JABS	JOSH	KEGS
GAST	GIRR	GOUT	HACK	HELE	HOKE	HWYL	JACK	JOSS	KEIR
GATE	GIRT	GOVS	HADE	HELL	HOLD	HYED	JADE	JOTA	KELL
GATH	GISM	GOWD	HADJ	HELM	HOLE	HYEN	JAGS	JOTS	KELP
GATS	GIST	GOWF	HADS	HELP	HOLM	HYES	JAIL	JOUK	KELT
GAUD	GITE	GOWK	HAEM	HEME	HOLP	HYKE	JAKE	JOUR	KEMB
GAUM	GITS	GOWL	HAET	HEMP	HOLS	HYLE	JAKS	JOWL	KEMP
GAUN	GIVE	GOWN	HAFF	HEMS	HOLT	HYMN	JAMB	JOWS	KENS
GAUP	GIZZ	GRAB	HAFT	HEND	HOLY	HYPE	JAMS	JOYS	KENT
GAUR	GJUS	GRAM	HAGG	HENS	HOME	HYPO	JANE	JUBA	KEPI
GAUS	GLAD	GRAN	HAGS	HENT	HOMO	HYPS	JANN	JUBE	KEPS
GAVE	GLAM	GRAT	HAIK	HEPS	HOMY		JAPE	JUDO	KEPT
GAWD	GLED	GRAY	HAIL	HEPT	HOND	IAMB	JAPS	JUDS	KERB
GAWK	GLEE	GREE	HAIN	HERB	HONE	IBEX	JARK	JUGA	KERF
GAWP	GLEG	GREN	HAIR	HERD	HONG	IBIS	JARL	JUGS	KERN
GAYS	GLEI	GREW	HAJI	HERE	HONK	ICED	JARS	JUJU	KESH
GAZE	GLEN	GREY	HAJJ	HERL	HONS	ICER	JASP	JUKE	KEST
GAZY	GLEY	GRID	HAKA	HERM	HOOD	ICES	JASY	JUMP	KETA
GEAL	GLIA	GRIG	HAKE	HERN	HOOF	ICKY	JATO	JUNK	KETS
GEAN	GLIB	GRIM	HALE	HERO	HOOK	ICON	JAUP	JURA	KEYS
GEAR	GLID	GRIN	HALF	HERS	HOOP	IDEA	JAWS	JURE	KHAN
GEAT	GLIM	GRIP	HALL	HERY	HOOT	IDEE	JAYS	JURY	KHAT
GECK	GLIT	GRIS	HALM	HESP	HOPE	IDEM	JAZY	JUST	KHOR
GEDS	GLOB	GRIT	HALO	HEST	HOPS	IDES	JAZZ	JUTE	KHUD
GEED	GLOM	GROG	HALT	HETE	HORE	IDLE	JEAN		KIBE
	GLOW	GROT	HAME		HORN		JEAT		KICK

KIDS	LABS	LEET	LITH	LUGS	MART	MILK	MORA	NANA	NODI
KIER	LACE	LEFT	LIVE	LUIT	MASE	MILL	MORE	NANS	NODS
KIFS	LACK	LEGS	LOAD	LUKE	MASH	MILO	MORN	NAOI	NOEL
KIKE	LACS	LEHR	LOAF	LULL	MASK	MILS	MORS	NAOS	NOES
KILD	LACY	LEIR	LOAM	LULU	MASS	MILT	MORT	NAPA	NOGS
KILL	LADE	LEIS	LOAN	LUMP	MAST	MIME	MOSE	NAPE	NOIL
KILN	LADY	LEKE	LOBE	LUMS	MASU	MINA	MOSS	NAPS	NOLE
KILO	LAER	LEKS	LOBI	LUNE	MATE	MIND	MOST	NARD	NOLL
KILP	LAGS	LEME	LOBO	LUNG	MATH	MINE	MOTE	NARE	NOMA
KILT	LAHS	LEND	LOBS	LUNT	MATS	MING	MOTH	NARK	NOME
KINA	LAIC	LENG	LOCH	LURE	MATT	MINI	MOTS	NARY	NOMS
KIND	LAID	LENO	LOCI	LURK	MATY	MINK	MOTT	NATS	NONE
KINE	LAIK	LENS	LOCK	LURS	MAUD	MINO	MOUE	NAVE	NONG
KING	LAIN	LENT	LOCO	LUSH	MAUL	MINT	MOUP	NAVY	NOOK
KINK	LAIR	LEPS	LODE	LUSK	MAUN	MINX	MOUS	NAYS	NOON
KINO	LAKE	LERE	LOFT	LUST	MAWK	MINY	MOVE	NAZE	NOOP
KINS	LAKH	LESS	LOGE	LUTE	MAWR	MIRE	MOVY	NEAL	NOPE
KIPE	LAKY	LEST	LOGO	LUTZ	MAWS	MIRK	MOWA	NEAP	NORI
KIPP	LAMA	LETS	LOGS	LUXE	MAXI	MIRS	MOWN	NEAR	NORK
KIPS	LAMB	LEVA	LOID	LYAM	MAYA	MIRY	MOWS	NEAT	NORM
KIRI	LAME	LEVE	LOIN	LYES	MAYS	MISE	MOXA	NEBS	NOSE
KIRK	LAMP	LEVY	LOIR	LYME	MAZE	MISO	MOYA	NECK	NOSH
KIRN	LAMS	LEWD	LOKE	LYMS	MAZY	MISS	MOYL	NEDS	NOSY
KIRS	LANA	LEYS	LOLL	LYNE	MEAD	MIST	MOYS	NEED	NOTE
KISH	LAND	LEZZ	LOMA	LYNX	MEAL	MITE	MOZE	NEEM	NOTT
KISS	LANE	LIAR	LOME	LYRE	MEAN	MITT	MOZZ	NEEP	NOUL
KIST	LANG	LIBS	LONE	LYSE	MEAT	MITY	MUCH	NEFS	NOUN
KITE	LANK	LICE	LONG	LYTE	MEED	MIXT	MUCK	NEIF	NOUP
KITH	LANT	LICH	LOOF		MEEK	MIXY	MUDS	NEKS	NOUS
KITS	LANX	LICK	LOOK	MAAR	MEER	MIZZ	MUFF	NEMN	NOUT
KIWI	LAPS	LIDO	LOOM	MACE	MEET	MNAS	MUGS	NENE	NOVA
KNAG	LARD	LIDS	LOON	MACK	MEIN	MOAN	MUID	NEON	NOWL
KNAP	LARE	LIED	LOOP	MACS	MELD	MOAS	MUIL	NEPS	NOWN
KNAR	LARK	LIEF	LOOR	MADE	MELL	MOAT	MUIR	NERD	NOWS
KNEE	LARN	LIEN	LOOS	MADS	MELS	MOBS	MULE	NESH	NOWT
KNEW	LASE	LIER	LOOT	MAGE	MELT	MOCK	MULL	NESS	NOWY
KNIT	LASH	LIES	LOPE	MAGG	MEMO	MODE	MUMM	NEST	NOYS
KNOB	LASS	LIEU	LOPS	MAGI	MEND	MODI	MUMP	NETE	NUBS
KNOP	LAST	LIFE	LORD	MAGS	MENE	MODS	MUMS	NETS	NUDE
KNOT	LATE	LIFT	LORE	MAID	MENG	MOES	MUON	NETT	NUKE
KNOW	LATH	LIGS	LORN	MAIK	MENT	MOGS	MURE	NEUK	NULL
KNUB	LATS	LIKE	LORY	MAIL	MENU	MOHR	MURK	NEUM	NUMB
KNUR	LAUD	LILL	LOSE	MAIM	MEOW	MOIL	MURL	NEVE	NUNS
KNUT	LAUF	LILO	LOSH	MAIN	MERC	MOIT	MUSE	NEWS	NURD
KOAN	LAVA	LILT	LOSS	MAKE	MERE	MOKE	MUSH	NEWT	NURL
KOAS	LAVE	LILY	LOST	MAKO	MERI	MOKI	MUSK	NEXT	NURR
KOBS	LAVS	LIMA	LOTA	MAKS	MERK	MOKO	MUSS	NIBS	NURS
KOFF	LAWK	LIMB	LOTE	MALE	MERL	MOLD	MUST	NICE	NUTS
KOHL	LAWN	LIME	LOTH	MALI	MESA	MOLE	MUTE	NICK	NYAS
KOLA	LAWS	LIMN	LOTO	MALL	MESE	MOLL	MUTT	NIDE	NYED
KOLO	LAYS	LIMP	LOTS	MALM	MESH	MOLT	MYAL	NIDI	NYES
KOND	LAZE	LIMY	LOUD	MALS	MESS	MOLY	MYNA	NIDS	
KONK	LAZY	LIND	LOUN	MALT	METE	MOME	MYTH	NIED	
KONS	LEAD	LINE	LOUP	MAMA	MEUS	MOMS		NIEF	OAFS
KOOK	LEAF	LING	LOUR	MAMS	MEVE		NAAM	NIES	OAKS
KOPS	LEAK	LINK	LOUT	MANA	MEWL	MONA	NAAN	NIFE	OAKY
KORA	LEAL	LINN	LOVE	MAND	MEWS	MONG	NABK	NIFF	OARS
KOSS	LEAM	LINO	LOWE	MANE	MEZE	MONK	NABS	NIGH	OARY
KOTO	LEAN	LINS	LOWN	MANS	MHOS	MONO	NACH	NILL	OAST
KOWS	LEAP	LINT	LOWS	MANY	MICA	MONY	NADA	NILS	OATH
KRIS	LEAR	LINY	LOWT	MAPS	MICE	MOOD	NAFF	NIMS	OATS
KSAR	LEAS	LION	LUAU	MARA	MICK	MOOI	NAGA	NINE	OBEY
KUDU	LEAT	LIPS	LUCE	MARC	MICO	MOOL	NAGS	NIPS	OBIA
KUKU	LECH	LIRA	LUCK	MARD	MIDI	MOON	NAIF	NIRL	OBIS
KYAT	LEED	LIRE	LUDO	MARE	MIDS	MOOP	NAIK	NISI	OBIT
KYLE	LEEK	LIRK	LUDS	MARG	MIEN	MOOR	NAIL	NITS	OBOE
KYND	LEEP	LISK	LUES	MARK	MIFF	MOOS	NAIN	NIXY	OBOL
KYNE	LEER	LISP	LUFF	MARL	MIKE	MOOT	NALA	NOBS	OCAS
KYTE	LEES	LIST	LUGE	MARM	MILD	MOPE	NAME	NOCK	OCHE
		LITE		MARS	MILE	MOPY	NAMS	NODE	ODAL
									ODAS

ODDS	ORTS	PASH	PHUT	POKY	PRYS	RACK	REHS	ROCH	RUNG
ODEA	ORYX	PASS	PIAS	POLE	PSIS	RACY	REIF	ROCK	RUNS
ODES	OSSA	PAST	PICA	POLK	PSST	RADE	REIK	ROCS	RUNT
ODIC	OTIC	PATE	PICE	POLL	PUBS	RADS	REIN	RODE	RURP
ODOR	OTTO	PATH	PICK	POLO	PUCE	RAFF	REIS	RODS	RUSA
ODSO	OUCH	PATS	PICS	POLT	PUCK	RAFT	REKE	ROED	RUSE
ODYL	OUKS	PAUA	PIED	POLY	PUER	RAGA	RELY	ROES	RUSH
OFAY	OULK	PAUL	PIER	POME	PUFF	RAGE	REMS	ROIL	RUSK
OFFS	OUPH	PAVE	PIES	POMP	PUGH	RAGG	REND	ROIN	RUST
OGAM	OUPS	PAWA	PIET	POMS	PUGS	RAGI	RENS	ROKE	RUTH
OGEE	OURN	PAWK	PIGS	POND	PUIR	RAGS	RENT	ROKS	RUTS
OGLE	OURS	PAWL	PIKA	PONE	PUJA	RAHS	RENY	ROKY	RYAL
OGRE	OUST	PAWN	PIKE	PONG	PUKE	RAID	REPP	ROLE	RYAS
OHMS	OUTS	PAWS	PILI	PONK	PULE	RAIK	REPS	ROLL	RYES
OHOS	OUZO	PAYS	PILL	PONS	PULK	RAIL	REST	ROMA	RYFE
OIKS	OVAL	PEAG	PIMP	PONY	PULL	RAIN	RETE	RONE	RYKE
OILS	OVEN	PEAK	PINA	POOD	PULP	RAIT	RETS	RONG	RYND
OILY	OVER	PEAL	PINE	POOF	PULU	RAJA	REVS	RONT	RYOT
OINT	OVUM	PEAN	PING	POOH	PULY	RAKE	REWS	ROOD	RYPE
OKAY	OWED	PEAR	PINK	POOK	PUMA	RAKI	RHEA	ROOF	RYVE
OKES	OWER	PEAS	PINS	POOL	PUMP	RALE	RHOS	ROOK	
OKRA	OWES	PEAT	PINT	POON	PUMY	RAMI	RHUS	ROOM	SABS
OLDS	OWLS	PEBA	PINY	POOP	PUNA	RAMP	RIAL	ROON	SACK
OLDY	OWLY	PECH	PION	POOR	PUNK	RAMS	RIAS	ROOP	SACS
OLEO	OWNS	PECK	PIPA	POOS	PUNS	RANA	RIBS	ROOS	SAFE
OLID	OWRE	PECS	PIPE	POOT	PUNT	RAND	RICE	ROOT	SAGA
OLIO	OWTS	PEDS	PIPI	POPE	PUNY	RANG	RICH	ROPE	SAGE
OLLA	OXEN	PEED	PIPS	POPS	PUPA	RANI	RICK	ROPY	SAGO
OLMS	OXER	PEEK	PIPY	PORE	PUPS	RANK	RICY	RORE	SAGS
OLPE	OYER	PEEL	PIRL	PORK	PURE	RANT	RIDE	RORT	SAGY
OMBU	OYES	PEEN	PIRN	PORN	PURI	RAPE	RIDS	RORY	SAIC
OMEN	OYEZ	PEEP	PIRS	PORT	PURL	RAPS	RIEL	ROSE	SAID
OMER	PACA	PEER	PISE	PORY	PURR	RAPT	RIEM	ROST	SAIL
OMIT	PACE	PEES	PISH	POSE	PURS	RARE	RIFE	ROSY	SAIM
ONCE	PACK	PEGH	PISS	POSH	PUSH	RASE	RIFF	ROTA	SAIN
ONER	PACO	PEGS	PITA	POSS	PUSS	RASH	RIFT	ROTE	SAIR
ONES	PACT	PEIN	PITH	POST	PUTS	RASP	RIGG	ROTI	SAIS
ONLY	PACY	PEKE	PITS	POSY	PUTT	RAST	RIGS	ROTL	SAKE
ONST	PADS	PELA	PITY	POTE	PUTZ	RATA	RILE	ROTS	SAKI
ONTO	PAGE	PELE	PIUM	POTS	PUYS	RATE	RILL	ROUE	SALE
ONUS	PAHS	PELF	PIXY	POTT	PYAT	RATH	RIMA	ROUL	SALP
ONYX	PAID	PELL	PIZE	POUF	PYES	RATS	RIME	ROUM	SALS
OOFS	PAIK	PELT	PLAN	POUK	PYET	RATU	RIMS	ROUP	SALT
OOHS	PAIL	PEND	PLAP	POUR	PYNE	RAUN	RIMU	ROUT	SAME
OOMS	PAIN	PENE	PLAT	POUT	PYOT	RAVE	RIMY	ROUX	SAMP
OONT	PAIR	PENI	PLAY	POWN	PYRE	RAWN	RIND	ROVE	SAND
OOPS	PAIS	PENK	PLEA	POWS	PYRO	RAWS	RINE	ROWS	SANE
OOSE	PALE	PENS	PLEB	POXY		RAYS	RING	ROWT	SANG
OOSY	PALL	PENT	PLED	POZZ	QADI	RAZE	RINK		SANK
OOZE	PALM	PEON	PLIE	PRAD	QATS	RAZZ	RINS		SANS
OOZY	PALP	PEPO	PLIM	PRAM	QUAD	READ	RIOT		SAPS
OPAH	PALS	PEPS	PLOD	PRAT	QUAG	REAK	RIPE		SARD
OPAL	PALY	PERE	PLOP	PRAU	QUAT	REAL	RIPP		SARI
OPED	PAMS	PERI	PLOT	PRAY	QUAY	REAM	RIPS		SARK
OPEN	PAND	PERK	PLOW	PREE	QUEP	REAN	RIPT		SARS
OPES	PANE	PERM	PLOY	PREP	QUEY	REAP	RISE		SASH
OPTS	PANG	PERN	PLUG	PREX	QUID	REAR	RISK		SASS
OPUS	PANS	PERT	PLUM	PREY	QUIM	RECK	RISP		SATE
ORAL	PANT	PERV	PLUS	PRIG	QUIN	REDD	RITE		SATI
ORBS	PAPA	PESO	POAS	PRIM	QUIP	REDE	RITS		SAUL
ORBY	PAPE	PEST	POCK	PROA	QUIT	REDO	RITT		SAUT
ORCS	PAPS	PETS	POCO	PROD	QUIZ	REDS	RIVA		SAVE
ORDS	PARA	PEWS	PODS	PROF	QUOD	REED	RIVE		SAWN
ORES	PARD	PHEW	POEM	PROG	QUOP	REEF	RIVO		SAWS
ORFE	PARE	PHIS	POET	PROM		REEK	ROAD		SAYS
ORFS	PARK	PHIZ	POIS	PROO	RABI	REEL	ROAM		SCAB
ORGY	PARR	PHOH	POKE	PROP	RACA	REEN	ROAN		SCAD
ORLE	PARS	PHON		PROS	RACE	REES	ROAR		SCAG
ORRA	PART	PHOS		PROW	RACH	REFS	ROBE		SCAM
		PHOT		PRUH		REFT	ROBS		SCAN

SCAR	SHAW	SKEO	SOAP	SPIK	SWEE	TATH	THUG	TONG	TUFT
SCAT	SHAY	SKEP	SOAR	SPIN	SWIG	TATS	THUS	TONK	TUGS
SCAW	SHEA	SKER	SOBS	SPIT	SWIM	TATT	TIAR	TONS	TUIS
SCOG	SHED	SKEW	SOCK	SPIV	SWIZ	TATU	TICE	TONY	TULE
SCOT	SHES	SKID	SOCS	SPOT	SWOB	TAUS	TICH	TOOK	TUMP
SCOW	SHET	SKIM	SODA	SPRY	SWOP	TAUT	TICK	TOOL	TUMS
SCRY	SHEW	SKIO	SODS	SPUD	SWOT	TAWS	TIDE	TOOM	TUNA
SCUD	SHIM	SKIP	SOFA	SPUE	SWUM	TAWT	TIDS	TOON	TUND
SCUG	SHIN	SKIS	SOFT	SPUN	SYBO	TAXA	TIED	TOOT	TUNE
SCUL	SHIP	SKIT	SOGS	SPUR	SYCE	TEAD	TIER	TOPE	TUNS
SCUM	SHIR	SKOL	SOHS	STAB	SYED	TEAK	TIFF	TOPI	TUNY
SCUP	SHIT	SKRY	SOIL	STAG	SYEN	TEAL	TIFT	TOPS	TUPS
SCUR	SHIV	SKUA	SOJA	STAP	SYES	TEAM	TIGE	TORC	TURD
SCUT	SHOD	SKUG	SOKE	STAR	SYKE	TEAR	TIGS	TORE	TURF
SCYE	SHOE	SKYR	SOLA	STAW	SYNC	TEAS	TIKA	TORI	TURM
SEAL	SHOG	SLAB	SOLD	STED	SYND	TEAT	TIKE	TORN	TURN
SEAM	SHOO	SLAE	SOLE	STEM	SYNE	TECH	TIKI	TORR	TUSH
SEAN	SHOP	SLAG	SOLI	STEN	SYPE	TEDS	TILE	TORS	TUSK
SEAR	SHOT	SLAM	SOLO	STEP	TAAL	TEDY	TILL	TORT	TUTS
SEAS	SHUL	SLAP	SOLS	STET	TABS	TEED	TILS	TOSE	TUTU
SEAT	SHUN	SLAT	SOMA	STEW	TABU	TEEL	TILT	TOSH	TUZZ
SECS	SHUT	SLAW	SOME	STEY	TACE	TEEM	TIME	TOSS	TWAE
SECT	SHWA	SLAY	SONE	STIE	TACH	TEEN	TIND	TOST	TWAL
SEED	SIAL	SLED	SONG	STIR	TACK	TEER	TINE	TOTE	TWAS
SEEK	SIBB	SLEE	SONS	STOA	TACO	TEES	TING	TOTS	TWAT
SEEL	SIBS	SLEW	SOOK	STOB	TADS	TEFF	TINK	TOUK	TWAY
SEEM	SICE	SLEY	SOOM	STOP	TAED	TEFS	TINS	TOUN	TWEE
SEEN	SICH	SLID	SOON	STOT	TAEL	TEGG	TINT	TOUR	TWIG
SEEP	SICK	SLIM	SOOP	STOW	TAES	TEGS	TINY	TOUT	TWIN
SEER	SICS	SLIP	SOOT	STUB	TAGS	TEHR	TIPI	TOWN	TWIT
SEES	SIDA	SLIT	SOPH	STUD	TAHA	TEIL	TIPS	TOWS	TWOS
SEGO	SIDE	SLOB	SOPS	STUM	TAHR	TELA	TIPT	TOWT	TYDE
SEGS	SIEN	SLOE	SORA	STUN	TAIL	TELD	TIRE	TOWY	TYED
SEIF	SIFT	SLOG	SORB	STYE	TAIS	TELL	TIRL	TOYS	TYES
SEIL	SIGH	SLOP	SORD	SUBS	TAIT	TELS	TIRO	TOZE	TYGS
SEIS	SIGN	SLOT	SORE	SUCH	TAKA	TELT	TIRR	TRAD	TYKE
SEKT	SIKA	SLOW	SORI	SUCK	TAKE	TEME	TITE	TRAM	TYMP
SELD	SIKE	SLUB	SORN	SUDD	TAKS	TEMP	TITI	TRAP	TYND
SELE	SILD	SLUE	SORT	SUDS	TAKY	TEMS	TITS	TRAY	TYNE
SELF	SILE	SLUG	SOSS	SUED	TALA	TEND	TIZZ	TREE	TYPE
SELL	SILK	SLUM	SOTS	SUER	TALC	TENE	TOAD	TREK	TYPO
SELS	SILL	SLUR	SOUK	SUES	TALE	TENS	TOBY	TRET	TYRE
SEME	SILO	SLUT	SOUL	SUET	TALI	TENT	TOCO	TREW	TYRO
SEMI	SILT	SMEE	SOUM	SUIT	TALK	TERF	TODS	TREY	TYTE
SEND	SIMA	SMEW	SOUP	SUKH	TALL	TERM	TODY	TREZ	TZAR
SENS	SIMI	SMIR	SOUR	SUKS	TAME	TERN	TOED	TRIE	
SENT	SIMP	SMIT	SOUS	SULK	TAMP	TEST	TOES	TRIG	UDAL
SEPS	SIMS	SMOG	SOUT	SUMO	TAMS	TETE	TOFF	TRIM	UDOS
SEPT	SIND	SMUG	SOVS	SUMP	TANA	TEWS	TOFT	TRIN	UEYS
SERA	SINE	SMUR	SOWF	SUMS	TANE	TEXT	TOGA	TRIO	UFOS
SERE	SING	SMUT	SOWL	SUNG	TANG	THAE	TOGE	TRIP	UGHS
SERF	SINK	SNAB	SOWM	SUNK	TANK	THAN	TOGS	TROD	UGLI
SERK	SINS	SNAG	SOWN	SUNN	TANS	THAR	TOHO	TROG	UGLY
SERR	SIPE	SNAP	SOWP	SUNS	TAPA	THAT	TOIL	TRON	ULES
SESE	SIPS	SNAR	SOWS	SUPS	TAPE	THAW	TOKE	TROT	ULEX
SESS	SIRE	SNEB	SOYA	SUQS	TAPS	THEE	TOKO	TROW	ULNA
SETA	SIRI	SNED	SOYS	SURA	TAPU	THEM	TOLA	TROY	UMBO
SETS	SIRS	SNEE	SPAE	SURD	TARA	THEN	TOLD	TRUE	UMPH
SETT	SISS	SNIB	SPAN	SURE	TARE	THEW	TOLE	TRUG	UNAU
SEWN	SIST	SNIG	SPAR	SURF	TARN	THEY	TOLL	TRYE	UNBE
SEWS	SITE	SNIP	SPAS	SUSS	TARO	THIG	TOLT	TRYP	UNCE
SEXT	SITH	SNOB	SPAT	SWAB	TARP	THIN	TOLU	TSAR	UNCI
SEXY	SITS	SNOD	SPAW	SWAD	TARS	THIR	TOMB	TUAN	UNCO
SEYS	SIZE	SNOG	SPAY	SWAG	TART	THIS	TOME	TUBA	UNDE
SHAD	SIZY	SNOT	SPEC	SWAM	TASH	THON	TOMS	TUBE	UNDO
SHAG	SKAS	SNOW	SPED	SWAN	TASK	THOU	TONE	TUBS	UNIS
SHAH	SKAT	SNUB	SPET	SWAP	TASS	THRO		TUCK	UNIT
SHAM	SKAW	SNUG	SPEW	SWAT	TATE	THRU		TUFA	UNTO
SHAN	SKEG	SOAK	SPIC	SWAY		THUD		TUFF	UPAS
SHAT			SPIE						UPBY

UPGO	VATS	VINY	WALE	WEBS	WHIP	WOKE	YANG	YINS	YURT
UPON	VAUS	VIOL	WALI	WEDS	WHIR	WOKS	YANK	YIPS	YWIS
UPSY	VAUT	VIRL	WALK	WEED	WHIT	WOLD	YAPP	YIRD	
URAO	VEAL	VISA	WALL	WEEK	WHIZ	WOLF	YAPS	YIRK	ZACK
URDE	VEER	VISE	WALY	WEEL	WHOA	WOMB	YARD	YITE	ZAGS
URDS	VEES	VITA	WAME	WEEM	WHOM	WONS	YARE	YLEM	ZANY
URDY	VEGA	VITE	WAND	WEEN	WHOP	WONT	YARN	YLKE	ZAPS
UREA	VEHM	VIVA	WANE	WEEP	WHOT	WOOD	YARR	YMPE	ZARF
URES	VEIL	VIVE	WANG	WEER	WHOW	WOOF	YATE	YMPT	ZATI
URGE	VEIN	VIVO	WANK	WEES	WICK	WOOL	YAUD	YOBS	ZEAL
URIC	VELA	VIZY	WANS	WEET	WIDE	WOON	YAUP	YOCK	ZEAS
URNS	VELD	VLEI	WANT	WEFT	WIEL	WOOS	YAWL	YODE	ZEBU
URUS	VELE	VOAR	WANY	WEID	WIFE	WOOT	YAWN	YOGA	ZEDS
URVA	VELL	VOES	WAPS	WEIL	WIGS	WOPS	YAWP	YOGH	ZEES
USED	VENA	VOID	WARD	WEIR	WILD	WORD	YAWS	YOGI	ZEIN
USER	VEND	VOLA	WARE	WEKA	WILE	WORE	YAWY	YOKE	ZEKS
USES	VENT	VOLE	WARK	WELD	WILI	WORK	YBET	YOKS	ZELS
UTAS	VERB	VOLS	WARM	WELK	WILL	WORM	YEAD	YOLD	ZERO
UTES	VERS	VOLT	WARN	WELL	WILT	WORN	YEAH	YOLK	ZEST
UTIS	VERT	VORS	WARP	WELT	WILY	WORT	YEAN	YOMP	ZETA
UTUS	VERY	VOTE	WARS	WEMB	WIMP	WOST	YEAR	YOND	ZEZE
UVAS	VEST	VOWS	WART	WEMS	WIND	WOTS	YEAS	YONI	ZHOS
UVEA	VETO	VRIL	WARY	WEND	WINE	WOVE	YEDE	YONT	ZIFF
	VETS	VUGS	WASE	WENS	WING	WOWF	YEED	YOOP	ZIGS
VACS	VIAE	VULN	WASH	WENT	WINK	WOWS	YEGG	YORE	ZILA
VADE	VIAL	VUMS	WASP	WEPT	WINN	WRAP	YELD	YORK	ZIMB
VAES	VIAS		WAST	WERE	WINO	WREN	YELK	YOUK	ZINC
VAGI	VIBE		WATE	WERT	WINS	WRIT	YELL	YOUR	ZING
VAIL	VIBS	WADD	WATS	WEST	WINY	WUDS	YELM	YOWE	ZIPS
VAIN	VICE	WADE	WATT	WETS	WIPE	WULL	YELP	YOWL	ZITS
VAIR	VIDE	WADI	WAUK	WEXE	WIRE	WYES	YELT	YOWS	ZIZZ
VALE	VIED	WADS	WAUL	WEYS	WIRY	WYND	YENS	YUAN	ZOBO
VALI	VIER	WADY	WAUR	WHAM	WISE	WYNN	YEPS	YUCA	ZOBU
VAMP	VIES	WAES	WAVE	WHAP	WISH	WYNS	YERD	YUCK	ZOEA
VANE	VIEW	WAFF	WAVY	WHAT	WISP	WYTE	YERK	YUFT	ZOIC
VANG	VILD	WAFT	WAWE	WHEE	WIST		YESK	YUGA	ZONA
VANS	VILE	WAGE	WAWL	WHEN	WITE	XYST	YEST	YUGS	ZONE
VANT	VILL	WAGS	WAWS	WHET	WITH		YETI	YUKE	ZOOM
VARA	VIMS	WAID	WAXY	WHEW	WITS	YACK	YETT	YUKS	ZOON
VARE	VINA	WAIF	WAYS	WHEY	WIVE	YAFF	YEUK	YUKY	ZOOS
VARY	VINE	WAIL	WEAK	WHID	WOAD	YAKS	YEVE	YULE	ZULU
VASA	VINO	WAIN	WEAL	WHIG	WOCK	YALD	YEWS	YUMP	ZUPA
VASE	VINS	WAIT	WEAN	WHIM	WOES	YALE	YGOE	YUNX	ZURF
VAST	VINT	WAKE	WEAR	WHIN	WOGS	YAMS	YILL	YUPS	ZYME

HINT _____

Fours Feeding

Very few top players are actually familiar with all the four-letter words. The ones they tend to concentrate on are those that are formed from three-letter words (see the Hooks section), those that contain the higher-scoring consonants, and those that are useful for sorting out those vowel problems. Work through the four-letter list and highlight those you don't know then play a solo game restricting yourself to just four-letter words as far as you are able. Initially consult the list whilst playing but also try to play from memory. After a while oddities such as BAPU, COFT, DHAL and EUOI become second nature to your game, and impress your opponents!

HINT

Managing the Big Four

It is rarely worth holding on to the J Q X or Z in the hope of a very high score later in the game unless you are aware of the letters you are likely to pick up and you are not sacrificing scores in the process. Generally, keeping the high score letters back will hinder future opportunities and rack balance. It is often wiser to score what you can rather than wait for something better. But if you are to hold on to any of the big four the X is probably the safest and most flexible simply because of the two-letter words playable. It is also the one your opponent is most likely to unwittingly provide a scoring opportunity for.

HINT

Suspicious Minds

Don't be suspicious of all your opponent's moves. It is often better to play to the strength of your own rack and think about your scoring potential than worry too much about whether your opponent's play is a set-up for a good score next turn. Even amongst top players there are few occasions when there is a deliberate setup play.

HINT

Tile Turnover

An additional consideration when deciding upon the best move is the number of tiles you use. Although other factors such as the score, the balance of the letters left on your rack, and the openness of the move, are just as important, the basic philosophy that using more tiles than your opponent increases your chances of getting any of the good tiles remaining in the bag cannot be completely ignored.

When faced with a choice of moves with a poor rack, more often than not the play using most tiles is the one to favour. The exception is when the only tiles remaining are the awkward tiles that you would rather avoid (eg the Q and the V's). Keeping track of the tiles played is advantageous in judging the value of a high turnover play but ultimately you are at the mercy of your own discretion.

LIGHT AND HEAVY WORDS

Light words are those with many vowels, excluding Y's. Light words are useful for discarding excessive vowels from one's rack, in an attempt to return to a more balanced rack. The numbers of vowels for words of varying lengths in these lists are given here:

       2-letter words, 2 vowels (eg AE, OI)
       3-letter words, 3 vowels (AIA, EAU)
       4-letter words, 3 vowels or more (eg EUOI, IOTA)
       5-letter words, 4 vowels (eg AUDIO, QUEUE)
       6-letter words, 4 vowels or more (eg COOKIE, LEAGUE)
       7-letter words, 5 vowels or more (eg ANAEMIA, EVACUEE)
       8-letter words, 5 vowels or more (eg ALIENATE, ORATORIO)

In trying to recall words with many vowels, try to think of groups of two and three vowels which do occur together – for example, AE, EA, IA, IAE, IOU and OU.

Heavy words are those with many consonants. These are useful for discarding excessive consonants from one's rack, again in an attempt to return to a more balanced rack. The numbers of vowels for words of varying lengths in these lists are given here:

       2-letter words, no vowels except Y (eg MY, SH)
       3-letter words, no vowels except Y (eg FRY, NTH)
       4-letter words, no vowels except Y (eg HYMN, YMPT)
       5-letter words, no vowels except Y (eg CRWTH, NYMPH)
       6-letter words, 1 vowel (eg CHINTZ, RHYTHM)

To avoid these lists ballooning in size, plurals ending in -S have been omitted. In trying to recall words with many consonants, try to home in on words with frequently occurring clumps of letters – for example, CH, GHT, NCH, PH, SCH, SCR, TCH and TH. Of course, there are many others apart from these.

LIGHT WORDS (Many Vowels)

2-letter words - 2 vowels

AA	AE	AI	EA	EE	IO	OE	OI	OO	OU

3-letter words - 3 vowels

AIA	EAU

4-letter words - 3 vowels or more

AEON	AITU	ANOA	BEAU	EMEU	EVOE	IOTA	MOUE	OLIO	URAO
AGEE	AJEE	AQUA	CIAO	EOAN	HUIA	IXIA	NAOI	OOSE	UREA
AGIO	AKEE	AREA	EALE	EPEE	IDEA	JIAO	OBIA	OOZE	UVEA
AGUE	ALAE	ARIA	EASE	ETUI	IDEE	KAIE	OBOE	OUZO	VIAE
AIAS	ALEE	AULA	EAUS	EUGE	ILEA	LIEU	ODEA	PAUA	ZOEA
AIDE	ALOE	AURA	EAUX	EUOI	ILIA	LUAU	OGEE	ROUE	
AINE	AMIE	AUTO	EINE	EURO	INIA	MOOI	OLEO	UNAU	

5-letter words - 4 vowels

```
ADIEU   AIDOI   AQUAE   AURAE   COOEE   OIDIA   OURIE   ZOOEA
AECIA   AINEE   AUDIO   AUREI   EERIE   OORIE   QUEUE
AERIE   AIOLI   AULOI   AVOUE   IAIDO   OUIJA   ZOEAE
```

6-letter words - 4 vowels or more

```
ABELIA  AMEBAE  AURATE  COOEED  EPUISE  HEAUME  LEIPOA  OOZIER  QUALIA  TIBIAE
ABULIA  AMELIA  AUREUS  COOEES  EQUATE  HEEZIE  LIAISE  OPAQUE  QUELEA  TOORIE
ACACIA  AMOEBA  AURORA  COOKIE  EQUINE  HOODOO  LOONIE  OPIATE  QUEUED  TOUPEE
ACAJOU  AMOOVE  AUROUS  COOLIE  EQUIPE  HOOPOE  MANOAO  OPIOID  QUEUES  TOUTIE
ACEDIA  ANEMIA  AUTEUR  COTEAU  ETOILE  HOOROO  MEALIE  ORARIA  QUINIE  UAKARI
ADAGIO  ANOMIE  AVAILE  COULEE  EUCAIN  IAIDOS  MEANIE  OREIDE  QUINOA  UBIQUE
ADIEUS  ANOXIA  AVENUE  COUPEE  EUOUAE  IDEAED  MEDIAE  ORIOLE  QUOOKE  UNEASE
ADIEUX  ANURIA  AVIATE  CURIAE  EUREKA  IDEATE  MEINIE  OROIDE  REALIA  UNIQUE
AECIUM  AOUDAD  AVOUES  DAIMIO  EURIPI  IGUANA  MILIEU  OTIOSE  REDIAE  URAEUS
AEDILE  APIECE  AVOURE  DAUTIE  EVOLUE  IODATE  MOUSIE  OUGLIE  REEKIE  UREDIA
AEMULE  APNOEA  AZALEA  DEARIE  EVOVAE  IODIDE  NAUSEA  OUIJAS  RESEAU  UREDIE
AERATE  APOGEE  AZIONE  DEAWIE  FAERIE  IODINE  NOOKIE  OURALI  ROADIE  UREMIA
AERIAL  APORIA  BAGUIO  DEEPIE  FAUNAE  IODISE  OAKIER  OURARI  ROARIE  UTOPIA
AERIER  ARAISE  BAILEE  DOOLIE  FEAGUE  IODIZE  OARAGE  OUREBI  ROOKIE  UVULAE
AERIES  ARALIA  BAILIE  DOUANE  FEERIE  IODOUS  OARIER  OURIER  ROUCOU  VAUDOO
AEROBE  AREOLA  BATEAU  EASIER  FOODIE  IOLITE  OCREAE  OUTAGE  SAIKEI  VOIDEE
AGAPAE  AREOLE  BAUERA  EATAGE  FOVEAE  IONISE  ODIOUS  OUTATE  SAIQUE  VOODOO
AGOUTA  ARIOSI  BEANIE  ECURIE  GATEAU  IONIUM  OEDEMA  OUTEAT  SAULIE  VOUDOU
AGOUTI  ARIOSO  BOOBOO  EELIER  GAUCIE  IONIZE  OEUVRE  OUTLIE  SEMEIA  WEEPIE
AGUISE  AROUSE  BOODIE  EERIER  GIAOUR  IONONE  OIDIUM  OUTVIE  SOAPIE  WOODIE
AGUIZE  ATAXIA  BOOGIE  EIDOLA  GOALIE  JEELIE  OILIER  OZAENA  SOIREE  ZOOEAE
AIKIDO  ATOCIA  BOOKIE  EKUELE  GOATEE  KAIKAI  OLEATE  PALEAE  SOOGEE  ZOOEAL
AIKONA  AUBADE  BOOTEE  ELUATE  GOOIER  KEELIE  OOIDAL  PEERIE  SOOGIE  ZOOEAS
AIOLIS  AUCUBA  BOUGIE  ELUVIA  GOOLIE  KIERIE  OOLITE  PEEWEE  SOUARI  ZOOZOO
AIRIER  AUDILE  BUREAU  EMEUTE  GOOROO  KOODOO  OOMIAC  PERAEA  TAENIA
ALALIA  AUDIOS  CADEAU  EPAULE  GUINEA  KOOKIE  OOMIAK  PEREIA  TAUPIE
ALEXIA  AUGITE  CAIQUE  EPEIRA  HAIKAI  LAESIE  OORIAL  PIURIU  TEEHEE
ALOGIA  AUMAIL  COAITA  EPIZOA  HAIQUE  LAMIAE  OORIER  POURIE  TEEPEE
AMADOU  AUNTIE  COATEE  EPOPEE  HEARIE  LEAGUE  OOSIER  QUAERE  TENIAE
```

7-letter words - 5 vowels or more

```
ABOULIA  ALIENEE  AREOLAE  AURORAE  EQUINIA  EUTEXIA  NOUVEAU  ROULEAU  ZOOECIA
AECIDIA  AMOEBAE  AUREATE  AUTOCUE  ETAERIO  EVACUEE  OLEARIA  SAOUARI
AEOLIAN  ANAEMIA  AURELIA  CAMAIEU  EUCAINE  EXUVIAE  OOGONIA  SEQUOIA
AEONIAN  AQUARIA  AUREOLA  DOULEIA  EULOGIA  IPOMOEA  OUABAIN  TAENIAE
AIERIES  AQUEOUS  AUREOLE  EPUISEE  EUOUAES  MOINEAU  OUAKARI  URAEMIA
```

8-letter words - 5 vowels or more

```
ABOIDEAU  AERONAUT  APOLOGIA  AURELIAS  AWEARIED  DOULEIAS  EQUALIZE  EUPHUIZE
ABOITEAU  AGACERIE  APOLOGUE  AUREOLAS  BANLIEUE  DUOLOGUE  EQUATION  EUROPIUM
ABOULIAS  AGIOTAGE  APOSITIA  AUREOLED  BAUHINIA  EARPIECE  EQUINIAS  EUTAXIES
ACADEMIA  AGOUTIES  AQUACADE  AUREOLES  BEAUTIED  EATERIES  EQUIPAGE  EUTAXITE
ACAUDATE  AGUACATE  AQUANAUT  AURICULA  BEAUTIES  EBIONISE  EQUISETA  EUTEXIAS
ACAULINE  AIGUILLE  AQUARIAN  AURIFIED  BEAUXITE  EBIONIZE  EQUITIES  EUXENITE
ACAULOSE  AKINESIA  AQUARIUM  AURIFIES  BOUDERIE  ECAUDATE  EQUIVOKE  EVACUATE
ACIERAGE  ALEURONE  AQUILINE  AUROREAN  BOUTIQUE  EDACIOUS  ERADIATE  EVACUEES
ACIERATE  ALIENAGE  ARACEOUS  AUTACOID  BOUZOUKI  EGOITIES  ERIONITE  EVALUATE
ACOEMETI  ALIENATE  ARANEOUS  AUTOCADE  CAESIOUS  EGOMANIA  ETAERIOS  EXAMINEE
ACTINIAE  ALIENEES  ARAPAIMA  AUTOCUES  CAMAIEUX  EMACIATE  ETIOLATE  EXEQUIAL
ACUITIES  ALLELUIA  AREOLATE  AUTOGIRO  CARIACOU  EMERAUDE  ETOURDIE  EXEQUIES
ACULEATE  ALOPECIA  ASEITIES  AUTOMATA  CAUSERIE  ENCAENIA  EUCAINES  EXIGUOUS
ADEQUATE  AMOEBOID  ASSEGAAI  AUTOMATE  CAUTIOUS  EOLIENNE  EULOGIES  EXIMIOUS
ADULARIA  ANAEMIAS  ATARAXIA  AUTOPSIA  CAVIARIE  EOLIPILE  EULOGISE  EXUVIATE
AECIDIUM  ANAEROBE  AUDIENCE  AUTOSOME  COENOBIA  EPICEDIA  EULOGIUM  FACETIAE
AEGIRINE  ANALOGUE  AUDITION  AUTUNITE  COOEEING  EPIGAEAL  EULOGIZE  FAUTEUIL
AEGIRITE  ANOREXIA  AUDITIVE  AUXILIAR  DAIQUIRI  EPIGAEAN  EUPEPSIA  FEATEOUS
AEGLOGUE  ANOUROUS  AUGURIES  AVIARIES  DETAINEE  EPIGEOUS  EUPHOBIA  FEATUOUS
AERATION  APIARIAN  AULARIAN  AVIATION  DIALOGUE  EPILOGUE  EUPHONIA  FILIOQUE
AEROFOIL  APIARIES  AUMAILED  AVIFAUNA  DIAPAUSE  EPOPOEIA  EUPHORIA  FOEDARIE
AEROLITE  APOGAEIC  AURELIAN  AVOISION  DOUANIER  EQUALISE  EUPHUISE  FORHOOIE
```

GAIETIES	INDUCIAE	MEIONITE	OITICICA	OUTHOUSE	POACEOUS	SAOUARIS	UNIONISE
GUAIACUM	INDUVIAE	METAIRIE	OLEARIAS	OUTVALUE	POULAINE	SAPUCAIA	UNIONIZE
HEMIOLIA	INFERIAE	METANOIA	OOGAMIES	OUTVOICE	QUEASIER	SEAQUAKE	URAEMIAS
HEMIOPIA	INITIATE	MEUNIERE	OOGAMOUS	OUVRIERE	QUEAZIER	SEQUELAE	URAEUSES
HETAERAE	IPOMOEAS	MILIARIA	OOGENIES	OVARIOLE	QUEENITE	SEQUOIAS	UREDINIA
HETAERIA	ISOLOGUE	MINUTIAE	OOGONIAL	OVARIOUS	QUEUEING	SQUEEGEE	USURIOUS
HETAIRAI	JALOUSIE	MOIETIES	OOGONIUM	PAENULAE	QUIETIVE	TAENIATE	UXORIOUS
HETAIRIA	JEALOUSE	MOINEAUS	OOLOGIES	PAEONIES	QUIETUDE	TAENIOID	VIRAEMIA
HOODOOED	KAIKAIED	NAUSEATE	ORAGIOUS	PAHOEHOE	QUILLAIA	TENUIOUS	VOODOOED
IDEALISE	LACINIAE	NAUSEOUS	ORATORIO	PARANOEA	RADIALIA	THIOUREA	VOUDOUED
IDEALIZE	LAUREATE	OBSEQUIE	OSIERIES	PARANOIA	REAROUSE	TOXAEMIA	ZABAIONE
IDEATION	MAIEUTIC	OCEANAUT	OUABAINS	PAROEMIA	RELEASEE	UBIETIES	ZOIATRIA
IDEATIVE	MAIOLICA	ODALIQUE	OUAKARIS	PAROUSIA	RETIARII	UINTAITE	ZOOECIUM
IDIOCIES	MAUVAISE	OEILLADE	OUISTITI	PEEKABOO	ROULEAUS	UNEASIER	ZOOGLOEA
INAURATE	MAUVEINE	OILERIES	OUTEATEN	PERIAGUA	ROULEAUX	UNIAXIAL	ZOONOMIA

HINT _____

Practising with Plates

A convenient way to practise Scrabble vocabulary whilst travelling by car is to find words from car number plates. There are a number of Scrabble games playable (if you're not the driver!):

● Find the shortest word containing the three letters of the number plate (ignoring the letter denoting the year).

● Look for seven-letter words by converting the numerals to letters thus (1=I, 2=Z, 3=E, 4=A, 5=S, 6=G, 7=T, 8=B, 9=G, 0=O)
  eg DGF 105H makes DOGFISH!

● Look for seven-letter words by taking the four letters and adding the letters A E I, or I E S, or similar, to give a good 'rack'.

HINT _____

Vowel Advice

Once you have more than two of any vowel on your rack it is all too easy to accumulate more because of the difficulty in sorting out the initial problem. Try the following exercise to become more familiar with those words that solve your multiple vowel imbalance.

Select three A's and then repeatedly pick up any four consonants and see how many A-words you can think of for the first move. Try to find the highest scoring first move and then consult the Awkward Vowel lists for added inspiration. Do not actually play words on the board but treat each fresh rack as if it were the first move. Repeat the exercise with the O's, I's and U's.

HINT

Valuing the S and Blank

The blank and the S are the most valuable tiles in the Scrabble set. Treat them as if they are worth a potential 50 points each. They are the ingredients of most seven and eight-letter bonus plays and as such should be used wisely. It is rarely worth playing an S for just a few extra points unless the move is essential for blocking the opponent in a game where winning is all important. A blank retained on the rack, even if not utilized in a bonus play, will provide that extra degree of flexibility of choice for endgame strategy.

HINT

ING Addiction

Every Scrabble player has retained ING on their rack at some time or another in the hope of getting an -ING bonus word. The usefulness of this strategy is frequently overrated amongst less experienced players. Although it is a common ending, unless you have the fortune to pick up the right letters for an -ING seven-letter word you will find the G more of a hindrance. Furthermore, if you religiously cling on to the ING you are severely limiting your choice of play for each move and are effectively playing with only four tiles. The advice is to avoid any ING addiction and concentrate on just keeping any subset of the letters RETAIN that you may have. This will be more fruitful.

HINT

Looking at Hooks

The two, three and four-letter hook words are probably the most important of the hook words. Try to learn a few useful ones at a time and attempt to introduce them into your game. An interesting exercise to assist is as follows:

Take each letter of the alphabet and find a two, three and four-letter word that takes that letter before or after as a hook to make a longer word. There may be none for some of the more awkward letters. This will give you a balanced variety of some 100 hook words to study.

Note that, for ruthless blocking strategies, the three and four-letter words that do not take hook letters before or after are just as important.

HEAVY WORDS (Many Consonants) except -S plurals

2-letter words - no vowels except Y

BY	CH	FY	KY	MY	NY	SH	ST

3-letter words - no vowels except Y

CLY	DRY	GYM	LYM	PLY	PYX	SKY	STY	TRY	WHY
CRY	FLY	GYP	NTH	PRY	RHY	SLY	SWY	TYG	WRY
CWM	FRY	HYP	NYS	PST	SHY	SPY	THY	VLY	WYN

4-letter words - no vowels except Y

CYST	GYNY	JYNX	LYNX	RYND	SKYR	SYND	TYND	XYST
FYRD	HWYL	KYND	MYTH	SCRY	SPRY	TRYP	WYND	YMPT
GYMP	HYMN	LYMS	PSST	SKRY	SYNC	TYMP	WYNN	

5-letter words - no vowels except Y

CHYND	DRYLY	GRYPT	GYPSY	LYNCH	PSYCH	SLYLY	THYMY	XYLYL
CRWTH	GHYLL	GYNNY	KYDST	MYRRH	PYGMY	SYLPH	TRYST	
CRYPT	GLYPH	GYPPY	LYMPH	NYMPH	SHYLY	SYNCH	WRYLY	

6-letter words - one vowel

BLANCH	CRANCH	FROWST	PRANCK	SCRIMP	SHTETL	SPHINX	STARCH	STRONG	THRIST
BLENCH	CRATCH	GLITCH	PROMPT	SCRIPT	SHTICK	SPIGHT	STENCH	STROWN	THRONG
BLIGHT	CROTCH	GROWTH	PUTSCH	SCROLL	SHTUCK	SPILTH	STITCH	STRUCK	THROWN
BLINTZ	CRUNCH	GRUMPH	RHYTHM	SCROWL	SHTUMM	SPLASH	STOWND	STRUNG	THRUSH
BLOTCH	CRUTCH	GRUTCH	SCARTH	SCRUFF	SKARTH	SPLENT	STRACK	STRUNT	THRUST
BORSCH	CULTCH	HIGHTH	SCATCH	SCRUMP	SKETCH	SPLIFF	STRAFF	SWARTH	THWACK
BRANCH	DIRNDL	KIRSCH	SCHELM	SCRUNT	SKLENT	SPLINT	STRAMP	SWATCH	THWART
BRIGHT	DRACHM	KITSCH	SCHISM	SCULPT	SKLIFF	SPLOSH	STRAND	SWITCH	TRENCH
BROWST	DRENCH	KLEPHT	SCHIST	SCUTCH	SKRIMP	SPRACK	STRASS	SWOWND	TWIGHT
BRUNCH	FLANCH	KNIGHT	SCHLEP	SHLOCK	SKRUMP	SPRANG	STRATH	TCHICK	TWITCH
CATCHT	FLENCH	KNITCH	SCHORL	SHRANK	SLIGHT	SPRAWL	STRAWN	THATCH	WARMTH
CHINCH	FLETCH	KRANTZ	SCHTIK	SHREWD	SMATCH	SPREDD	STRESS	THETCH	WHILST
CHINTZ	FLIGHT	KVETCH	SCHUSS	SHRIFT	SMIGHT	SPRENT	STREWN	THIRST	WHISHT
CHRISM	FLINCH	LENGTH	SCLAFF	SHRILL	SMIRCH	SPRING	STRICH	THRALL	WRENCH
CHURCH	FLITCH	MENSCH	SCLIFF	SHRIMP	SMUTCH	SPRINT	STRICT	THRANG	WRETCH
CLATCH	FLYSCH	PHLEGM	SCORCH	SHRINK	SNATCH	SPRONG	STRIFT	THRASH	WRIGHT
CLENCH	FRATCH	PLANCH	SCOTCH	SHROFF	SNITCH	SPRUNG	STRING	THRAWN	
CLINCH	FRENCH	PLIGHT	SCOWTH	SHROWD	SPARTH	SPRUSH	STROLL	THRESH	
CLUNCH	FRICHT	PLINTH	SCRAWL	SHRUNK	SPERST	STANCH	STROMB	THRIFT	
CLUTCH	FRIGHT	PLONGD	SCRAWM	SHTCHI	SPETCH	STANCK	STROND	THRILL	

Mind Your Changing

Since it is permissible to change any number of your letters instead of a turn during a game (unless there are fewer than seven tiles in the bag), it can be a wise decision to change some or all of your letters even if you can find a word to play on the board. You should consider changing when:

- You have an imbalance of vowels and consonants and the available dump words do not solve your rack problems, score very little, or provide too many scoring opportunities for your opponent.
- There are no scoring opportunities on the board and you don't wish to block your opponent with a low-scoring play.
- You have a Q with no U and none of the U-less Q words are playable.
- You have a promising six-letter combination that combines well with many other letters to make a seven-letter word but not with the seventh letter on your rack. Changing the odd letter in this situation is often not the best strategic move but the time for such a change may be ripe if you desperately need the bonus to catch up or there are no other worthwhile alternatives.

Bonus Hunting

Faced with a rack of seven letters in any order it is not always easy to spot even common seven-letter words. Moving the tiles around will often enable an otherwise hidden seven-letter word to come to light. But rather than frantic shuffling and reshuffling in the hope of inspiration a more organized approach is recommended. Form beginnings and endings with the letters on your rack and check the remaining tiles to see if they form a word with that beginning or ending. For example, with the rack EEFGLOR making the prefix FORE will lead you to FORELEG. With ACEORTV, the prefix OVER will inspire OVERACT. Similarly with the racks AINOORT, AGEINOS and AEFHLTU it may only be by forming the endings -TION, -ISE and -FUL that you will stumble across ORATION, AGONISE and HATEFUL respectively. Also, splitting your rack into two shorter words may enable you to spot an allowable compound word. For example, the unlikely ADEEESW yields SEA and WEED (SEAWEED) and AADORWY makes ROAD and WAY (ROADWAY).

AWKWARD VOWEL DUMPS

It is often a problem when you are faced with two of the same vowel on your rack, except perhaps when they are two E's; it can be a nightmare when you are confronted with more than two, especially if they are I's or U's. Playing just one of the multiple vowels does not always resolve the problem, and one can be faced with the same problem on subsequent turns. This of course does not help your game, so ideally the problem needs to be resolved in one turn. You should find the following lists of words containing multiple A's, E's, I's, O's or U's will greatly assist you in such situations.

The words in these lists can be summarized as follows:

A words:	4 letters, 2 A's (eg AWAY, LAVA)
	5 letters, 3 A's (eg ABACA, KAAMA)
	6 letters, 3 A's (eg BANANA, BAZAAR)
E words:	4 letters, 3 E's (EPEE)
	5 letters, 3 E's (eg GEESE, MELEE)
	6 letters, 4 E's (eg PEEWEE, TEEPEE)
I words:	4 letters, 2 I's (eg IRIS, KIWI)
	5 letters, 2 I's (eg ICING, RIGID)
	6 letters, 3 I's (eg BIKINI, IRITIC)
O words:	5 letters, 3 O's (OVOLO)
	6 letters, 3 O's or more (eg COCOON, VOODOO)
U words:	4 letters, 2 U's (eg GURU, LUAU)
	5 letters, 2 U's or more (eg AUGUR, QUEUE)
	6 letters, 3 U's (eg MUTUUM, UHURUS)

(Note that there is no list of four-letter words with 2 O's – it is not too difficult to play a couple of O's in a four-letter word. Think of all the words with a double-O in them to begin with.)

AWKWARD VOWEL DUMPS - A's

4-letter words - 2 A's

ABAC	AIAS	AMAH	ARAK	AVAL	DATA	LAMA	NADA	RACA	TANA
ABAS	AJAR	AMLA	ARAR	AVAS	GAGA	LANA	NAGA	RAGA	TAPA
ABBA	ALAE	ANAL	ARBA	AWAY	GALA	LAVA	NALA	RAJA	TARA
ACTA	ALAP	ANAN	AREA	AYAH	HAAF	MAAR	NANA	RANA	TAXA
ADAW	ALAR	ANAS	ARIA	AZAN	HAAR	MAMA	NAPA	RATA	VARA
AFAR	ALAS	ANNA	ARNA	BAAS	HAKA	MANA	PACA	SAGA	VASA
AGAR	ALAY	ANOA	ASAR	BABA	KAKA	MARA	PAPA	TAAL	
AGAS	ALFA	ANTA	ATAP	CABA	KANA	MAYA	PARA	TAHA	
AGHA	ALGA	APAY	AULA	CAPA	KARA	NAAM	PAUA	TAKA	
AGMA	ALMA	AQUA	AURA	CASA	KAVA	NAAN	PAWA	TALA	

5-letter words - 3 A's

ABACA	ABAYA	AFARA	ALAAP	ALAPA	ANANA	ARABA	ASANA	KAAMA

6-letter words - 3 A's

ABACAS	ALALIA	ANARAK	ARMADA	AZALEA	BAZAAR	JATAKA	KARAKA	PALAMA	SAMAAN
ABAYAS	ALAPAS	ANATTA	ASANAS	BAHADA	CABALA	KAAMAS	KATANA	PANADA	SAMARA
ACACIA	ALBATA	ARABAS	ATABAL	BAJADA	CABANA	KABALA	LABARA	PANAMA	SATARA
AFARAS	ALPACA	ARALIA	ATAMAN	BALATA	CANADA	KABAYA	MANANA	PAPAYA	TAMARA
AGAPAE	ANABAS	ARCANA	ATAXIA	BANANA	DAGABA	KAMALA	MARACA	PATACA	ZAPATA
ALAAPS	ANANAS	ARGALA	AVATAR	BATATA	JACANA	KANAKA	NAGANA	SALAAM	

AWKWARD VOWEL DUMPS - E's

4-letter words - 3 E's

EPEE

5-letter words - 3 E's

BELEE	EERIE	EMEER	EXEME	HEEZE	MELEE	PEECE	REEDE	TEHEE
BESEE	EEVEN	EPEES	FEESE	KEEVE	NEELE	PEEPE	REEVE	TEPEE
DEERE	ELPEE	ETWEE	FEEZE	LEESE	NEESE	PEEVE	SEMEE	WEEKE
DEEVE	EMCEE	EXEEM	GEESE	LEVEE	NEEZE	PEWEE	TEENE	WEETE

6-letter words - 4 E's

PEEWEE   TEEHEE   TEEPEE

AWKWARD VOWEL DUMPS - I's

4-letter words - 2 I's

DIVI	IBIS	INIA	IWIS	KIWI	NIDI	PIPI	TIKI	WILI
DIXI	ILIA	IRID	IXIA	MIDI	NISI	SIMI	TIPI	
HILI	IMPI	IRIS	KIRI	MINI	PILI	SIRI	TITI	

5-letter words - 2 I's

ACINI	CIRRI	IAMBI	IMINE	IONIC	LICHI	MINIS	PILIS	SIRIH	VIRID
AIDOI	CIVIC	ICIER	IMMIT	IRIDS	LICIT	MODII	PIPIS	SIRIS	VISIE
AIOLI	CIVIL	ICILY	IMMIX	ISSEI	LIKIN	NIHIL	PIPIT	TIBIA	VISIT
ALIBI	DIGIT	ICING	IMPIS	IVIED	LIMIT	NIMBI	PIRAI	TIKIS	VIVID
BIFID	DILLI	ICTIC	IMSHI	IVIES	LININ	NISEI	PIXIE	TIMID	VIZIR
BIKIE	DINIC	IDIOM	INDRI	IXIAS	LIPID	NITID	RADII	TIPIS	WILIS
BLINI	DIVIS	IDIOT	INFIX	JINNI	LIVID	NIXIE	RICIN	TITIS	ZIMBI
CEILI	DIXIE	ILIAC	INION	KILIM	MEDII	OBIIT	RIGID	TORII	
CHILI	FINIS	ILIUM	INTIL	KININ	MIDIS	OIDIA	RISHI	VIGIA	
CILIA	GENII	IMARI	INWIT	KIRIS	MIMIC	ORIBI	SIGIL	VIGIL	
CIPPI	IAIDO	IMIDE	IODIC	KIWIS	MINIM	PILEI	SIMIS	VILLI	

6-letter words - 3 I's

BIKINI   IRIDIC   IRITIC   IRITIS   MIRITI

AWKWARD VOWEL DUMPS - O's

5-letter words - 3 O's

OVOLO

6-letter words - 3 O's or more

BOOBOO	COROZO	FORHOO	GOOROO	HOOPOE	KOODOO	OOLONG	ROTOLO	ZOOZOO
COCOON	DOOCOT	GOOGOL	HOODOO	HOOROO	OOLOGY	ROCOCO	VOODOO	

AWKWARD VOWEL DUMPS - U's

4-letter words - 2 U's

GURU	KUDU	LUAU	PULU	UNAU	UTUS
JUJU	KUKU	LULU	TUTU	URUS	ZULU

5-letter words - 2 U's or more

AUGUR	DURUM	JUGUM	LUAUS	QUEUE	UNAUS	UNGUM	USURP	ZULUS
BUCHU	FUCUS	JUJUS	LULUS	QUIPU	UNCUS	UPRUN	USURY	
BUCKU	FUGUE	KUDUS	LUPUS	TUQUE	UNCUT	URUBU	UVULA	
BUNDU	GURUS	KUDZU	MUCUS	TUTUS	UNDUE	USUAL	VOULU	
BUSSU	HUMUS	KUKUS	PULUS	UHURU	UNDUG	USURE	WUSHU	

6-letter words - 3 U's

MUTUUM	UHURUS	URUBUS

HINT _____

Triple Tactics

Every player recognizes the need to avoid giving the opponent easy access to the triple-word squares. However it is important not to be obsessive about giving away triple-word scores. Playing a word out to the edge of the board such that the word covers the double-letter square between two triple-word squares with a low-scoring tile, does not make it that easy for the opponent to score highly from the triple-word square. In fact, it may force the opponent to use his best tiles to block your use of the triple-word square next turn.

HINT _____

Flashcards

A popular way of testing Scrabble vocabulary is a system called flashcards. Small index cards are used which have 'questions' on one side and the 'answer words' on the reverse. For example if you were using flashcards to learn two-letter words you may have on one card A=13, with the 13 two-letter words beginning with A on the reverse. On another card B=4, and another C=1, would reveal BA BE BO BY and CH on the reverse respectively. Whenever you get a moment you can quickly flick through the cards and test yourself. The system can be used for many categories such as five-vowelled seven-letter words, words containing J Q X Z and so on. A good use of flashcards is to log every seven-letter word played against you that you didn't know thus naturally building up your personal testing library.

HINT

Fighting Back

Don't trade off catching up with poor rack retention. A more balanced rack will enable a greater choice of strategic plays in subsequent turns. Initially concentrate on not slipping any further behind and be wary of scoring opportunities open only to yourself. Perhaps you have the last S or the last A for an (A)JAR hook, and so on. Try to keep the board open unless you can block and catch up in a single play. If your opponent is in front it is likely their rack is worsening whilst they are blocking. Keeping the board open and maintaining your rack balance will keep your hopes alive whereas playing too defensively will only assist your opponent to keep their lead.

HINT

Passing Thoughts

It is allowable to pass in Scrabble, that is, to not play a word or change any tiles. This is in effect what a player does at the end of the game if stuck with any unplayable tiles. However, it is rarely worth passing during the game in the hope that the opponent will give you that vital opening or letter you need.

An example of an occasion where passing may be of advantage is if you have a good rack such as TAILEND and it is your play first, or your opponent has just changed letters instead of playing first. Since TAILEND combines with one of the four vowels (A E O U) to make an eight-letter word (DENTALIA, ENTAILED or LINEATED, DELATION, UNTAILED), it is likely your opponent may give you a bonus play next turn.

HINT

Learn As You Play

Always have a scrap of paper with you other than the scoresheet. Jot down any promising racks you find yourself with, seven-letter words you played that might have anagrams, and any words you think of playing but are unsure of. After the game spend a few minutes with *Official Scrabble Lists* and check out your words and racks, noting any new discoveries. Going through this exercise after every game will gradually strengthen your vocabulary without too much effort.

AWKWARD CONSONANT DUMPS

The best way to describe the words in the following lists is this: words of three to five letters that contain at least two of any one of the following consonants – B, C, F, H, V, W and Y. (Purists should note that Y is referred to here as a consonant, regardless of whether it is acting as a vowel or a consonant in any individual word.) It is not too difficult usually to dump a single F or an H in an attempt to achieve a reasonable score and balance one's rack. It is more of a problem to dump two F's, two H's and so on. These lists should help with your awkward consonant racks.

The lists are arranged so that all the B words come together, then the C word, and so on. The three-letter B words come before the four-letter B words, which come before the five-letter words. Similarly for the other awkward consonants. Do note that there are no three-letter lists here for the letters C, V and Y, as there are no three-letter words having two C's, or two V's or two Y's.

AWKWARD CONSONANT DUMPS   -   B's

3-letter words - 2 B's

ABB	BIB	BOB	BUB	EBB

4-letter words - 2 B's

ABBA	BABA	BABY	BLAB	BLUB	BOMB	BUBO	COBB
ABBE	BABE	BARB	BLEB	BOBA	BOOB	BUBS	EBBS
ABBS	BABU	BIBS	BLOB	BOBS	BUBA	BULB	SIBB

5-letter words - 2 B's or more

ABBAS	BABUL	BIMBO	BOBAS	BUBAL	COBBS	FUBBY	KEBAB	RIBBY	YOBBO
ABBES	BABUS	BLABS	BOBBY	BUBAS	COBBY	GABBY	KEBOB	SIBBS	ZEBUB
ABBEY	BARBE	BLEBS	BOMBE	BUBBY	CUBBY	GOBBI	LOBBY	SLUBB	
ABBOT	BARBS	BLOBS	BOMBO	BULBS	CUBEB	GOBBO	MOBBY	SYBBE	
BABAS	BEBOP	BLUBS	BOMBS	BUMBO	DEBBY	HOBBY	NABOB	TABBY	
BABEL	BEROB	BLURB	BOOBS	BUSBY	DIBBS	HUBBY	NOBBY	TUBBY	
BABES	BIBLE	BOBAC	BOOBY	CABBY	DOBBY	KABAB	NUBBY	WEBBY	
BABOO	BILBO	BOBAK	BRIBE	CABOB	EBBED	KABOB	RABBI	YABBY	

AWKWARD CONSONANT DUMPS   -   C's

4-letter words - 2 C's

CECA	CHIC	CHOC	COCA	COCH	COCK	COCO	CROC	ECCE	ECCO

5-letter words - 2 C's or more

ACCOY	CACHE	CHACK	CHOCS	CLACK	COCCI	CONCH	CUBIC	CYCLO	SECCO
ACOCK	CACTI	CHACO	CHUCK	CLECK	COCCO	CONIC	CULCH	CYNIC	SUCCI
BACCA	CAECA	CHECK	CINCH	CLICK	COCKS	COUCH	CUMEC	ICTIC	TICCA
BACCO	CASCO	CHICA	CINCT	CLOCK	COCKY	CRACK	CURCH	MUCIC	YACCA
BACCY	CATCH	CHICH	CIRCA	CLUCK	COCOA	CRICK	CUSEC	OCCUR	YUCCA
BOCCA	CECUM	CHICK	CIRCS	COACH	COCOS	CROCK	CUTCH	RECCE	ZOCCO
CABOC	CERCI	CHICS	CISCO	COACT	COLIC	CROCS	CYCAD	RECCO	
CACAO	CHACE	CHOCK	CIVIC	COCAS	COMIC	CRUCK	CYCLE	RECCY	

AWKWARD CONSONANT DUMPS - F's

3-letter words - 2 F's

EFF   IFF   OFF

4-letter words - 2 F's or more

AFFY	CAFF	DUFF	FUFF	HUFF	LUFF	OFFS	TEFF	YAFF
BAFF	COFF	EFFS	GAFF	IFFY	MIFF	PUFF	TIFF	ZIFF
BIFF	CUFF	FAFF	GOFF	JEFF	MUFF	RAFF	TOFF	
BOFF	DAFF	FIEF	GUFF	JIFF	NAFF	RIFF	TUFF	
BUFF	DOFF	FIFE	HAFF	KOFF	NIFF	RUFF	WAFF	

5-letter words - 2 F's or more

AFFIX	BUFFS	DAFFY	FIFES	GOFFS	JEFFS	NIFFS	QUIFF	SKOFF	TIFFS
BAFFS	CAFFS	DOFFS	FIFTH	GRAFF	JIFFS	NIFFY	RAFFS	SNIFF	TOFFS
BAFFY	CHAFF	DRAFF	FIFTY	GRIFF	JIFFY	NYAFF	REFFO	SNUFF	TOFFY
BIFFS	CHUFF	DUFFS	FLAFF	GRUFF	KOFFS	OFFAL	RIFFS	SOWFF	TUFFE
BLUFF	CLIFF	EFFED	FLUFF	GUFFS	LUFFA	OFFED	RUFFE	SPIFF	TUFFS
BOFFS	CLOFF	FAFFS	FUFFS	HAFFS	LUFFS	OFFER	RUFFS	STAFF	WAFFS
BUFFA	COFFS	FEOFF	FUFFY	HOUFF	MIFFS	PLUFF	SCAFF	STIFF	WAUFF
BUFFE	CUFFO	FIEFS	GAFFE	HOWFF	MIFFY	PUFFS	SCOFF	STUFF	WHIFF
BUFFI	CUFFS	FIFED	GAFFS	HUFFS	MUFFS	PUFFY	SCUFF	TAFFY	YAFFS
BUFFO	DAFFS	FIFER	GLIFF	HUFFY	NAFFS	QUAFF	SKIFF	TEFFS	ZIFFS

AWKWARD CONSONANT DUMPS - H's

3-letter words - 2 H's

HAH   HOH   HUH

4-letter words - 2 H's

HASH	HATH	HECH	HIGH	HISH	HOGH	HOHS	HUSH	PHOH	SHAH

5-letter words - 2 H's

AHIGH	HANCH	HAUGH	HEUCH	HIGHT	HOGHS	HOTCH	HUSHY	SHAHS	THIGH
CHICH	HARSH	HEATH	HEUGH	HILCH	HOHED	HOUGH	HUTCH	SHASH	WHICH
EPHAH	HASHY	HECHT	HEWGH	HITCH	HOOCH	HUMPH	HYPHA	SHCHI	WHISH
HAITH	HATCH	HEIGH	HIGHS	HITHE	HOOSH	HUNCH	HYTHE	SHUSH	

AWKWARD CONSONANT DUMPS - V's

4-letter words - 2 V's

VIVA   VIVE   VIVO

5-letter words - 2 V's

BEVVY	CIVVY	NAVVY	VALVE	VERVE	VIVAT	VIVER	VIVID	VOLVE
BIVVY	DIVVY	SAVVY	VARVE	VIVAS	VIVDA	VIVES	VOLVA	VULVA

AWKWARD CONSONANT DUMPS - W's

3-letter words - 2 W's

WAW   WOW

4-letter words - 2 W's

WAWE	WAWL	WAWS	WHEW	WHOW	WOWF	WOWS

5-letter words - 2 W's

| EWHOW | PAWAW | WAWES | WAWLS | WHEWS | WIDOW | WOWED | WOWEE | WRAWL |

AWKWARD CONSONANT DUMPS — Y's

4-letter words - 2 Y's

| EYRY | GYNY | YAWY | YUKY |

5-letter words - 2 Y's

AZYGY	DOYLY	GYNNY	KYLEY	SKYEY	WRYLY	YAWEY	YIPPY	YUKKY
BYWAY	DRYLY	GYPPY	PYGMY	SLYLY	XYLYL	YAWNY	YOLKY	YUMMY
COYLY	DYKEY	GYPSY	SHYLY	THYMY	YABBY	YESTY	YUCKY	YUPPY

HINT

Rack Balancing

Always try to keep a balanced rack of vowels and consonants. The more balanced your rack the more choice of words you will have each turn and the more chance you will have of being able to play a bonus-scoring seven-letter word. It helps to be aware that there are 42 vowels to 56 consonants (and 2 blanks) in the Scrabble set. That's three vowels for every four consonants. Counting how many vowels and consonants already played at any stage of a game will serve as a useful guide as to the vowel/consonant distribution remaining in the bag. If there is a surplus of consonants left you might wish to counteract your likely consonant pickup by retaining vowels on your rack when you play, or vice versa.

See the Awkward Vowel Dumps list and the Light and Heavy Words list for some words that will help you keep a balanced rack.

HINT

Edging the Endgame

In a tight game where the scores are close there is an advantage in being the player to be the first to play out and finish the game, thus gaining any points remaining on the opponent's rack and depriving him of another scoring opportunity. Playing out first is often the difference between winning and losing. A handy tip, whenever you have the opportunity or choice near the end of a game, is to ensure there is a single tile in the bag after your turn. This means that, next turn, you have the first opportunity to play with no tiles remaining in the bag thus giving you an advantage in planning a two-move finish. There is further advantage if you have been keeping track of the tiles since you can then have the benefit of the endgame initiative knowing your opponent's exact tiles.

HINT

Combination Management

If you have one of the promising six-letter combinations given under the Bonus Sets section but unfortunately do not have an appropriate seventh letter to make a bonus word, or the bonus word you have does not fit on the board, then it is wiser not to be overly concerned about holding on to your useful six-letter combinations. Rather than just playing the one letter and hoping for a playable bonus word next turn, play two or three tiles. This will probably enable you to score more whilst still retaining the makings of a bonus word. The skill is in making sure you play off the right letters.

For example, with OILERS and an F on your rack there is no bonus word. Rather than just play the F, in the hope of picking a B for BOILERS or a U for LOUSIER perhaps, it is better to play IF or OF. The retention of OLERS or ILERS with a vowel pickup next turn is likely to produce another good six-letter combination such as AILERS, OILERS or RELIES, and hopefully an obliging seventh letter to make a bonus play. If it doesn't, well at least you've scored some points meanwhile.

HINT

Unusual Clues

In browsing through the Anagram section you will find an abundance of unusual seven and eight-letter words. Some of these are more useful than others depending on their constituent letters. Those consisting of just the one and two-point Scrabble tiles (ie A D E G I L N O R S T U) are more likely to appear on your rack and are the ones to concentrate on. A good way to remember these words is by making up a non-existent anagram that you are more likely to form on your rack and that will act as an aide-mémoire. For example, the likely rack ELNOSTU yields the bonus word LENTOUS which may best be recalled as the anagram of the non-existent OUTLENS. Similarly, SEERING makes GREISEN and LOOTIER makes TROOLIE. Both SEERING and LOOTIER are not actual words but merely the clues to GREISEN and TROOLIE. Where there is a more common anagram of an unusual word then this naturally serves as a clue, eg OUTLINE gives ELUTION and AGAINST gives GITANAS.

HIGH SCORERS

The following lists contain all the words of length two to eight letters which contain any of the four high-scoring letters J, Q, X and Z. While most Scrabble players know the obvious words, such as JUDGE, QUEEN, EXALT and ZEROS, how many know the more obscure POOJA, SQUEG, SIXTE and NIZAM?

Knowing these words will enable you to be more adventurous when it comes to grabbing the odd triple-word-score square for 50-odd points – or perhaps playing a bonus word with six single-point letters and a high-scoring letter, such as NAARTJE, LASQUES, ANOXIAS and LAIRIZE, or even playing a bonus word using a letter on the board with words such as INJURANT, EQUITANT, XENURINE and LAZURITE.

If a word contains two of these four high-scoring letters (such as JAZZY, JYNX, QUIZ and ZOOTAXY), then it will appear in two places.

J-WORDS

J – 2-letter words

JO

J – 3-letter words

GJU	JAG	JAP	JAY	JEU	JIZ	JOG	JOW	JUG	RAJ
HAJ	JAK	JAR	JEE	JIB	JOB	JOR	JOY	JUS	TAJ
JAB	JAM	JAW	JET	JIG	JOE	JOT	JUD	JUT	

J – 4-letter words

AJAR	JADE	JARK	JEAN	JEST	JIMP	JOCO	JOMO	JOYS	JUNK
AJEE	JAGS	JARL	JEAT	JETE	JINK	JOES	JOOK	JUBA	JURA
BENJ	JAIL	JARS	JEED	JETS	JINN	JOEY	JORS	JUBE	JURE
DOJO	JAKE	JASP	JEEL	JEUX	JINX	JOGS	JOSH	JUDO	JURY
GAJO	JAKS	JASY	JEEP	JIAO	JIRD	JOHN	JOSS	JUDS	JUST
GJUS	JAMB	JATO	JEER	JIBE	JISM	JOIN	JOTA	JUDY	JUTE
HADJ	JAMS	JAUP	JEES	JIBS	JIVE	JOKE	JOTS	JUGA	JUTS
HAJI	JANE	JAWS	JEFF	JIFF	JIZZ	JOKY	JOUK	JUGS	JYNX
HAJJ	JANN	JAYS	JELL	JIGS	JOBE	JOLE	JOUR	JUJU	PUJA
JABS	JAPE	JAZY	JERK	JILL	JOBS	JOLL	JOWL	JUKE	RAJA
JACK	JAPS	JAZZ	JESS	JILT	JOCK	JOLT	JOWS	JUMP	SOJA

J – 5-letter words

AFLAJ	GADJE	JAGER	JAPED	JEANS	JERKS	JIFFY	JIVES	JOLED	JOURS
AJWAN	GAJOS	JAGGY	JAPES	JEATS	JERKY	JIGOT	JOBED	JOLES	JOUST
BAJAN	GANJA	JAGIR	JARKS	JEBEL	JERRY	JIHAD	JOBES	JOLLS	JOWAR
BAJRA	GAUJE	JAILS	JARLS	JEELS	JESTS	JILLS	JOCKO	JOLLY	JOWED
BAJRI	HADJI	JAKES	JARTA	JEELY	JESUS	JILTS	JOCKS	JOLTS	JOWLS
BANJO	HAJES	JALAP	JARUL	JEEPS	JETES	JIMMY	JODEL	JOLTY	JOYED
BIJOU	HAJIS	JAMBE	JASEY	JEERS	JETON	JIMPY	JOEYS	JOMOS	JUBAS
BUNJE	HAJJI	JAMBO	JASPE	JEFFS	JETTY	JINGO	JOHNS	JONTY	JUBES
BUNJY	HEJAB	JAMBS	JASPS	JEHAD	JEUNE	JINKS	JOINS	JOOKS	JUDAS
CAJUN	HEJRA	JAMBU	JATOS	JELAB	JEWEL	JINNI	JOINT	JORAM	JUDGE
DJINN	HIJRA	JAMES	JAUNT	JELLO	JHALA	JINNS	JOIST	JORUM	JUDOS
DOJOS	HODJA	JAMMY	JAUPS	JELLS	JIAOS	JIRDS	JOKED	JOTAS	JUGAL
EJECT	JABOT	JANES	JAVEL	JELLY	JIBED	JIRGA	JOKER	JOTUN	JUGUM
ENJOY	JACKS	JANNS	JAWAN	JEMMY	JIBER	JISMS	JOKES	JOUGS	JUICE
FALAJ	JADED	JANTY	JAWED	JENNY	JIBES	JIVED	JOKEY	JOUKS	JUICY
FJORD	JADES	JAPAN	JAZZY	JERID	JIFFS	JIVER	JOKOL	JOULE	JUJUS

JUKED	JUMBY	JUNKY	JURAT	KHOJA	NINJA	PUJAS	REJON	TAJES
JUKES	JUMPS	JUNTA	JUROR	KOPJE	OBJET	RAJAH	SAJOU	THUJA
JULEP	JUMPY	JUNTO	JUSTS	LAPJE	OJIME	RAJAS	SHOJI	UPJET
JUMAR	JUNCO	JUPON	JUTES	MAJOR	OUIJA	RAJES	SOJAS	YOJAN
JUMBO	JUNKS	JURAL	JUTTY	MUJIK	POOJA	REJIG	SUJEE	ZANJA

J - 6-letter words

ABJECT	EVEJAR	JACKET	JAPPED	JEHADS	JIBING	JOCKOS	JOUKED	JUMBAL	LAPJE
ABJURE	FINJAN	JACKSY	JARFUL	JEJUNA	JIGGED	JOCOSE	JOULED	JUMBIE	MAJOR
ACAJOU	FJORDS	JADERY	JARGON	JEJUNE	JIGGER	JOCUND	JOULES	JUMBLE	MASJI
ADJOIN	FRIJOL	JADING	JAROOL	JELABS	JIGGLE	JODELS	JOUNCE	JUMBLY	MOUJI
ADJURE	GADJES	JADISH	JARRAH	JELLED	JIGJIG	JOGGED	JOURNO	JUMBOS	MUJIK
ADJUST	GANJAS	JAEGER	JARRED	JELLOS	JIGOTS	JOGGER	JOUSTS	JUMPED	NINJA
AJOWAN	GARJAN	JAGERS	JARTAS	JEMIMA	JIGSAW	JOGGLE	JOVIAL	JUMPER	OBJEC
AJWANS	GAUJES	JAGGED	JARULS	JENNET	JIHADS	JOHNNY	JOWARI	JUNCOS	OBJET
BAJADA	GIDJEE	JAGGER	JARVEY	JERBIL	JILGIE	JOINED	JOWARS	JUNCUS	OBJUR
BAJANS	GURJUN	JAGHIR	JARVIE	JERBOA	JILLET	JOINER	JOWING	JUNGLE	OJIME
BAJRAS	HADJES	JAGIRS	JASEYS	JEREED	JILTED	JOINTS	JOWLED	JUNGLI	OUIJA
BAJREE	HADJIS	JAGUAR	JASIES	JERIDS	JIMINY	JOISTS	JOWLER	JUNGLY	OUTJE
BAJRIS	HAJJES	JAILED	JASPER	JERKED	JIMJAM	JOJOBA	JOYFUL	JUNIOR	OUTJU
BANJAX	HAJJIS	JAILER	JASPES	JERKER	JIMPER	JOKERS	JOYING	JUNKED	PAJOC
BANJOS	HANJAR	JAILOR	JASPIS	JERKIN	JIMPLY	JOKIER	JOYOUS	JUNKER	POOJA
BEJADE	HEJABS	JALAPS	JATAKA	JERQUE	JINGAL	JOKING	JUBATE	JUNKET	POOJA
BEJANT	HEJIRA	JALOPY	JAUNCE	JERSEY	JINGLE	JOLING	JUBBAH	JUNKIE	POPJO
BENJES	HEJRAS	JAMBEE	JAUNSE	JESSED	JINGLY	JOLLED	JUDDER	JUNTAS	RAJAH
BHAJAN	HIJACK	JAMBER	JAUNTS	JESSES	JINKED	JOLTED	JUDGED	JUNTOS	REJEC
BIJOUX	HIJRAH	JAMBES	JAUNTY	JESSIE	JINKER	JOLTER	JUDGES	JUPATI	REJIG
BUNJEE	HIJRAS	JAMBOK	JAUPED	JESTED	JINNEE	JOOKED	JUDIES	JUPONS	REJOI
BUNJES	HOBJAS	JAMBOS	JAVELS	JESTEE	JINXED	JORAMS	JUDOGI	JURANT	SAJOU
BUNJIE	HODJAS	JAMBUL	JAWANS	JESTER	JINXES	JORDAN	JUDOKA	JURATS	SANJA
CAJOLE	INJECT	JAMBUS	JAWARI	JETONS	JIRBLE	JORUMS	JUGALS	JURIES	SEJAN
COJOIN	INJURE	JAMJAR	JAWBOX	JETSAM	JIRGAS	JOSEPH	JUGATE	JURIST	SHOJI
CONJEE	INJURY	JAMMED	JAWING	JETSOM	JISSOM	JOSHED	JUGFUL	JURORS	SOOJE
DEEJAY	JABBED	JAMMER	JAZIES	JETSON	JITNEY	JOSHER	JUGGED	JUSTED	SUJEE
DEJECT	JABBER	JAMPAN	JAZZED	JETTED	JITTER	JOSHES	JUGGLE	JUSTER	SWARA
DJEBEL	JABBLE	JAMPOT	JAZZES	JETTON	JIVERS	JOSKIN	JUICED	JUSTLE	THUJA
DJINNI	JABERS	JANGLE	JEBELS	JEWELS	JIVING	JOSSER	JUICER	JUSTLY	TINAJ
DONJON	JABIRU	JANGLY	JEEING	JEZAIL	JIZZES	JOSSES	JUICES	JUTTED	UNJUS
EJECTA	JABOTS	JANKER	JEELED	JHALAS	JOANNA	JOSTLE	JUJUBE	JYMOLD	UPJET
EJECTS	JACANA	JANSKY	JEELIE	JIBBAH	JOBBED	JOTTED	JUKING	JYNXES	YOJAN
ENJAMB	JACENT	JANTEE	JEERED	JIBBED	JOBBER	JOTTER	JULEPS	KHODJA	YOJAN
ENJOIN	JACKAL	JAPANS	JEERER	JIBBER	JOBING	JOTUNN	JUMARS	KHOJAS	ZANJA
ENJOYS	JACKED	JAPING	JEFFED	JIBERS	JOCKEY	JOTUNS	JUMART	KOPJES	

J - 7-letter words

ABJECTS	BEJADES	DEJEUNE	HIJACKS	JACKETS	JALAPIC	JAMPOTS	JASPERY	JEELIED
ABJOINT	BEJANTS	DISJECT	HIJINKS	JACKMAN	JALAPIN	JANGLED	JATAKAS	JEELIES
ABJURED	BEJEWEL	DISJOIN	HIJRAHS	JACKMEN	JALOPPY	JANGLER	JAUNCED	JEELIN
ABJURER	BHAJANS	DISJUNE	HOBJOBS	JACKPOT	JALOUSE	JANGLES	JAUNCES	JEEPERS
ABJURES	BONJOUR	DJEBELS	INJECTS	JACKSIE	JAMADAR	JANITOR	JAUNSED	JEEPNE
ACAJOUS	BRINJAL	DJIBBAH	INJELLY	JACOBUS	JAMBEAU	JANIZAR	JAUNSES	JEERERS
ADJOINS	BUNJEES	EJECTED	INJOINT	JACONET	JAMBEES	JANKERS	JAUNTED	JEERING
ADJOINT	BUNJIES	EJECTOR	INJUNCT	JACUZZI	JAMBERS	JANNOCK	JAUNTIE	JEFFING
ADJOURN	CAJEPUT	ENJAMBS	INJURED	JADEDLY	JAMBEUX	JANTIER	JAUPING	JEJUNUM
ADJUDGE	CAJOLED	ENJOINS	INJURER	JADEITE	JAMBIER	JANTIES	JAVELIN	JELLABA
ADJUNCT	CAJOLER	ENJOYED	JABBERS	JAEGERS	JAMBIYA	JAPPING	JAVELIN	JELLIED
ADJURED	CAJOLES	ENJOYER	JABBING	JAGGERS	JAMBOKS	JARFULS	JAWARIS	JELLIES
ADJURES	CAJUPUT	EVEJARS	JABBLED	JAGGERY	JAMBONE	JARGONS	JAWBONE	JELLIFY
ADJUSTS	COJOINS	FINJANS	JABBLES	JAGGIER	JAMBOOL	JARGOON	JAWFALL	JELLING
AJOWANS	CONJECT	FRIJOLE	JABIRUS	JAGGING	JAMBULS	JARKMAN	JAWHOLE	JEMADAR
ALFORJA	CONJEED	FRIJOLE	JACAMAR	JAGHIRE	JAMDANI	JARKMEN	JAWINGS	JEMIDAR
AZULEJO	CONJEES	GARJANS	JACANAS	JAGHIRS	JAMESES	JAROOLS	JAYWALK	JEMIMAS
BAJADAS	CONJOIN	GIDJEES	JACCHUS	JAGUARS	JAMJARS	JARRAHS	JAZZIER	JEMMIER
BAJREES	CONJURE	GOUJONS	JACINTH	JAILERS	JAMMERS	JARRING	JAZZILY	JEMMIES
BANJOES	DEEJAYS	GURJUNS	JACKALS	JAILING	JAMMIER	JARVEYS	JAZZING	JENNETS
BASENJI	DEJECTA	HANDJAR	JACKASS	JAILORS	JAMPANI	JARVIES	JAZZMAN	JENNIES
BEJADED	DEJECTS	HEJIRAS	JACKDAW	JAKESES	JAMPANS	JASPERS	JEALOUS	JEOPARD

JERBILS	JEWELRY	JINGLES	JOINERS	JOSSERS	JUDOKAS	JUNIORS	KHANJAR	PERJURY
JERBOAS	JEWFISH	JINGLET	JOINERY	JOSTLED	JUGFULS	JUNIPER	KHODJAS	POOJAHS
JEREEDS	JEZAILS	JINGOES	JOINING	JOSTLES	JUGGING	JUNKERS	KILLJOY	POPJOYS
JERKERS	JIBBAHS	JINJILI	JOINTED	JOTTERS	JUGGINS	JUNKETS	MAJESTY	PREJINK
JERKIER	JIBBERS	JINKERS	JOINTER	JOTTING	JUGGLED	JUNKIER	MAJORAT	PROJECT
JERKIES	JIBBING	JINKING	JOINTLY	JOTUNNS	JUGGLER	JUNKIES	MAJORED	PYJAMAS
JERKING	JIFFIES	JINXING	JOISTED	JOUKERY	JUGGLES	JUNKING	MANJACK	REJECTS
JERKINS	JIGAJIG	JIRBLED	JOJOBAS	JOUKING	JUGULAR	JUNKMAN	MASJIDS	REJOICE
JERQUED	JIGAJOG	JIRBLES	JOKIEST	JOULING	JUICERS	JUNKMEN	MISJOIN	REJOINS
JERQUER	JIGGERS	JISSOMS	JOLLIED	JOUNCED	JUICIER	JUPATIS	MOUJIKS	REJONEO
JERQUES	JIGGING	JITNEYS	JOLLIER	JOUNCES	JUICING	JURALLY	MUDEJAR	REJONES
JERRIES	JIGGISH	JITTERS	JOLLIES	JOURNAL	JUJUBES	JURANTS	MUNTJAC	REJOURN
JERSEYS	JIGGLED	JITTERY	JOLLIFY	JOURNEY	JUMARTS	JURIDIC	MUNTJAK	REJUDGE
JESSAMY	JIGGLES	JOANNAS	JOLLILY	JOURNOS	JUMBALS	JURISTS	NAARTJE	SANJAKS
JESSANT	JIGJIGS	JOANNES	JOLLING	JOUSTED	JUMBIES	JURYMAN	NARTJIE	SAPAJOU
JESSIES	JIGSAWN	JOBBERS	JOLLITY	JOUSTER	JUMBLED	JURYMEN	OBJECTS	SEJEANT
JESTEES	JIGSAWS	JOBBERY	JOLTERS	JOWARIS	JUMBLER	JUSSIVE	OBJURED	SJAMBOK
JESTERS	JILGIES	JOBBING	JOLTIER	JOWLERS	JUMBLES	JUSTEST	OBJURES	SKYJACK
JESTFUL	JILLETS	JOBLESS	JOLTING	JOWLING	JUMBUCK	JUSTICE	OUTJEST	SOJOURN
JESTING	JILTING	JOCKEYS	JONQUIL	JOYANCE	JUMELLE	JUSTIFY	OUTJETS	SOOJEYS
JETFOIL	JIMJAMS	JOCULAR	JONTIES	JOYLESS	JUMPERS	JUSTING	OUTJUMP	SUBJECT
JETSAMS	JIMMIED	JOGGERS	JOOKERY	JUBBAHS	JUMPIER	JUSTLED	OUTJUTS	SUBJOIN
JETSOMS	JIMMIES	JOGGING	JOOKING	JUBILEE	JUMPILY	JUSTLES	OVERJOY	TINAJAS
JETSONS	JIMPEST	JOGGLED	JORDANS	JUDASES	JUMPING	JUTTIED	PAJAMAS	TRAJECT
JETTIER	JIMPIER	JOGGLES	JOSEPHS	JUDDERS	JUNCATE	JUTTIES	PAJOCKE	UNJADED
JETTIES	JINGALS	JOGTROT	JOSHERS	JUDGING	JUNCOES	JUTTING	PAJOCKS	UNJOINT
JETTING	JINGLED	JOHNNIE	JOSHING	JUDOGIS	JUNGLES	JUVENAL	PERJINK	YOJANAS
JETTONS	JINGLER	JOINDER	JOSKINS	JUDOIST	JUNGLIS	KAJAWAH	PERJURE	ZANJERO

J – 8-letter words

ABJECTED	CARJACOU	HANDJARS	JAMBEAUX	JAUNTING	JETPLANE	JODELLED	JUDICIAL
ABJECTLY	COJOINED	HIGHJACK	JAMBIERS	JAVELINS	JETTIEST	JODHPURS	JUDOISTS
ABJOINTS	CONJECTS	HIJACKED	JAMBIYAH	JAWBONED	JETTISON	JOGGINGS	JUGGLERS
ABJURERS	CONJOINS	HIJACKER	JAMBIYAS	JAWBONES	JEWELLED	JOGGLING	JUGGLERY
ABJURING	CONJOINT	INJECTED	JAMBOLAN	JAWBOXES	JEWELLER	JOGTROTS	JUGGLING
ADJACENT	CONJUGAL	INJECTOR	JAMBONES	JAWFALLS	JIBBERED	JOHANNES	JUGULARS
ADJOINED	CONJUNCT	INJOINTS	JAMBOOLS	JAWHOLES	JIBBINGS	JOHNNIES	JUGULATE
ADJOINTS	CONJURED	INJUNCTS	JAMBOREE	JAYWALKS	JICKAJOG	JOINDERS	JUICIEST
ADJOURNS	CONJURER	INJURANT	JAMDANIS	JAZERANT	JIGAJIGS	JOININGS	JULIENNE
ADJUDGED	CONJURES	INJURERS	JAMMIEST	JAZZIEST	JIGAJOGS	JOINTERS	JUMARRED
ADJUDGES	CONJUROR	INJURIES	JAMPANEE	JEALOUSE	JIGGERED	JOINTING	JUMBLERS
ADJUNCTS	CRACKJAW	INJURING	JAMPANIS	JEALOUSY	JIGGINGS	JOINTURE	JUMBLIER
ADJURING	CUNJEVOI	JABBERED	JANGLERS	JEANETTE	JIGGLING	JOISTING	JUMBLING
ADJUSTED	DEEJAYED	JABBERER	JANGLIER	JEELYING	JIGSAWED	JOKESOME	JUMBOISE
ADJUSTER	DEJECTED	JABBLING	JANGLING	JEEPNEYS	JILLAROO	JOKINGLY	JUMBOIZE
ADJUSTOR	DEJEUNER	JACAMARS	JANITORS	JEERINGS	JIMCRACK	JOLLIEST	JUMBUCKS
ADJUTAGE	DEJEUNES	JACINTHS	JANITRIX	JEJUNELY	JIMMYING	JOLLYING	JUMELLES
ADJUTANT	DEMIJOHN	JACKAROO	JANIZARS	JEJUNITY	JIMPIEST	JOLTHEAD	JUMPIEST
ADJUVANT	DISJECTS	JACKBOOT	JANIZARY	JELLABAS	JIMPNESS	JOLTIEST	JUNCATES
AJUTAGES	DISJOINS	JACKDAWS	JANNOCKS	JELLYING	JINGBANG	JONCANOE	JUNCTION
ALFORJAS	DISJOINT	JACKEROO	JANSKIES	JELUTONG	JINGLERS	JONGLEUR	JUNCTURE
AZULEJOS	DISJUNCT	JACKETED	JANTIEST	JEMADARS	JINGLETS	JONQUILS	JUNCUSES
BANJAXED	DISJUNES	JACKPOTS	JAPANNED	JEMIDARS	JINGLIER	JORDELOO	JUNGLIER
BANJAXES	DJELLABA	JACKSIES	JAPANNER	JEMMIEST	JINGLING	JOSTLING	JUNIPERS
BANJOIST	DJIBBAHS	JACONETS	JAPONICA	JEOFAILS	JINGOISH	JOTTINGS	JUNKANOO
BASENJIS	EJECTING	JACQUARD	JARARACA	JEOPARDS	JINGOISM	JOUNCING	JUNKETED
BEJABERS	EJECTION	JACULATE	JARARAKA	JEOPARDY	JINGOIST	JOURNALS	JUNKIEST
BEJADING	EJECTIVE	JACUZZIS	JARGONED	JEREMIAD	JINJILIS	JOURNEYS	JURATORY
BEJESUIT	EJECTORS	JADEITES	JARGOONS	JERKIEST	JIRBLING	JOUSTERS	JURISTIC
BEJEWELS	ENJAMBED	JADERIES	JAROSITE	JERKINGS	JIRKINET	JOUSTING	JURYMAST
BENJAMIN	ENJOINED	JAGGEDLY	JARRINGS	JEROBOAM	JITTERED	JOVIALLY	JUSSIVES
BIJWONER	ENJOINER	JAGGIEST	JASMINES	JERQUERS	JOBATION	JOYANCES	JUSTICER
BRINJALS	ENJOYERS	JAGHIRES	JASPISES	JERQUING	JOBBINGS	JOYFULLY	JUSTICES
CAJEPUTS	ENJOYING	JALAPINS	JAUNCING	JERRICAN	JOCKETTE	JOYOUSLY	JUSTLING
CAJOLERS	FLAPJACK	JALOPIES	JAUNDICE	JERRYCAN	JOCKEYED	JUBILANT	JUSTNESS
CAJOLERY	FORJUDGE	JALOUSED	JAUNSING	JESTBOOK	JOCOROUS	JUBILATE	JUTTYING
CAJOLING	FRABJOUS	JALOUSES	JAUNTIER	JESTINGS	JOCOSELY	JUBILEES	JUVENALS
CAJUPUTS	FRIJOLES	JALOUSIE	JAUNTIES	JETFOILS	JOCOSITY	JUDDERED	JUVENILE
CARCAJOU	GOUJEERS	JAMADARS	JAUNTILY	JETLINER	JOCUNDLY	JUDGMENT	KABELJOU

KAJAWAHS	MAJORING	NIGHTJAR	PEJORATE	PYJAMAED	REJOICER	SJAMBOKS	TRAJECTS
KHANJARS	MAJORITY	NONJUROR	PERJURED	QUILLAJA	REJOICES	SKIPJACK	UNJOINTS
KILLJOYS	MANJACKS	OBJECTED	PERJURER	RAJASHIP	REJOINED	SKYJACKS	UNJOYFUL
KINKAJOU	MARJORAM	OBJECTOR	PERJURES	READJUST	REJONEOS	SLAPJACK	UNJOYOUS
KOMITAJI	MISJOINS	OBJURING	POPINJAY	REJECTED	REJOURNS	SOJOURNS	UNJUSTER
LOGJUICE	MISJUDGE	OUTJESTS	POPJOYED	REJECTER	REJUDGED	STICKJAW	UNJUSTLY
MAHARAJA	MUNTJACS	OUTJUMPS	PREJUDGE	REJECTOR	REJUDGES	SUBJECTS	UPJETTED
MAJESTIC	MUNTJAKS	OVERJOYS	PROJECTS	REJIGGED	SAPAJOUS	SUBJOINS	VERJUICE
MAJOLICA	NAARTJES	OVERJUMP	PULSEJET	REJIGGER	SCRAMJET	SUCURUJU	WHIPJACK
MAJORATS	NARTJIES	PAJOCKES	PULSOJET	REJOICED	SERJEANT	SWARAJES	ZANJEROS

Q-WORDS

Q - 3-letter words

QAT   QUA   SUQ

Q - 4-letter words

AQUA	QATS	QUAG	QUAY	QUEY	QUIM	QUIP	QUIZ	QUOP
QADI	QUAD	QUAT	QUEP	QUID	QUIN	QUIT	QUOD	SUQS

Q - 5-letter words

AQUAE	QIBLA	QUALE	QUAYS	QUEST	QUILL	QUIPU	QUOIF	QUYTE	SQUIT
AQUAS	QUACK	QUALM	QUEAN	QUEUE	QUILT	QUIRE	QUOIN	ROQUE	TALAQ
BURQA	QUADS	QUANT	QUEEN	QUEYN	QUIMS	QUIRK	QUOIT	SQUAB	TOQUE
EQUAL	QUAFF	QUARK	QUEER	QUEYS	QUINA	QUIRT	QUOLL	SQUAD	TUQUE
EQUIP	QUAGS	QUART	QUELL	QUICH	QUINE	QUIST	QUONK	SQUAT	
MAQUI	QUAIL	QUASH	QUEME	QUICK	QUINS	QUITE	QUOPS	SQUAW	
PIQUE	QUAIR	QUASI	QUENA	QUIDS	QUINT	QUITS	QUOTA	SQUEG	
QADIS	QUAKE	QUATS	QUERN	QUIET	QUIPO	QUOAD	QUOTE	SQUIB	
QANAT	QUAKY	QUAYD	QUERY	QUIFF	QUIPS	QUODS	QUOTH	SQUID	

Q - 6-letter words

ACQUIT	EQUANT	OPAQUE	QUAINT	QUEACH	QUEUED	QUINTA	QUOITS	SACQUE	SQUIDS
ASQUAT	EQUATE	PIQUED	QUAIRS	QUEANS	QUEUES	QUINTE	QUOKKA	SAIQUE	SQUIER
BARQUE	EQUINE	PIQUES	QUAKED	QUEASY	QUEYNS	QUINTS	QUOLLS	SEQUEL	SQUIFF
BASQUE	EQUIPE	PIQUET	QUAKES	QUEAZY	QUICHE	QUINZE	QUONKS	SEQUIN	SQUILL
BISQUE	EQUIPS	PLAQUE	QUALIA	QUEENS	QUICKS	QUIPOS	QUOOKE	SQUABS	SQUINT
BURQAS	EQUITY	PULQUE	QUALMS	QUEERS	QUIDAM	QUIPUS	QUORUM	SQUADS	SQUINY
CAIQUE	EXEQUY	QANATS	QUALMY	QUEEST	QUIETS	QUIRED	QUOTAS	SQUAIL	SQUIRE
CALQUE	FAQUIR	QIBLAS	QUANGO	QUEINT	QUIFFS	QUIRES	QUOTED	SQUALL	SQUIRM
CASQUE	HAIQUE	QIGONG	QUANTA	QUELCH	QUIGHT	QUIRKS	QUOTER	SQUAMA	SQUIRR
CHEQUE	JERQUE	QINTAR	QUANTS	QUELEA	QUILLS	QUIRKY	QUOTES	SQUAME	SQUIRT
CHEQUY	LASQUE	QUACKS	QUARKS	QUELLS	QUILTS	QUIRTS	QUOTHA	SQUARE	SQUISH
CINQUE	LIQUID	QUAERE	QUARRY	QUEMED	QUINAS	QUISTS	QUOTUM	SQUASH	SQUITS
CIRQUE	LIQUOR	QUAFFS	QUARTE	QUEMES	QUINCE	QUITCH	QUYTED	SQUATS	TALAQS
CLAQUE	LOQUAT	QUAGGA	QUARTO	QUENAS	QUINES	QUITED	QUYTES	SQUAWK	TOQUES
CLIQUE	MANQUE	QUAGGY	QUARTS	QUENCH	QUINIC	QUITES	QWERTY	SQUAWS	TORQUE
CLIQUY	MAQUIS	QUAHOG	QUARTZ	QUERNS	QUINIE	QUIVER	REQUIT	SQUEAK	TUQUES
CLOQUE	MARQUE	QUAICH	QUASAR	QUESTS	QUINOA	QUOIFS	RISQUE	SQUEAL	UBIQUE
COQUET	MASQUE	QUAIGH	QUATCH	QUETCH	QUINOL	QUOINS	ROQUES	SQUEGS	UNIQUE
EQUALS	MOSQUE	QUAILS	QUAVER	QUETHE	QUINSY	QUOIST	ROQUET	SQUIBS	

Q - 7-letter words

ACQUEST	AQUAVIT	BEZIQUE	CHARQUI	CONQUER	EQUALLY	FAQUIRS	JERQUES	LOQUATS
ACQUIRE	AQUEOUS	BISQUES	CHEQUER	COQUETS	EQUANTS	GRECQUE	JONQUIL	MACAQUE
ACQUIST	AQUIFER	BOUQUET	CHEQUES	COQUITO	EQUATED	HAIQUES	KUMQUAT	MADOQUA
ACQUITE	AQUIVER	BRIQUET	CINQUES	CROQUET	EQUATES	INQILAB	LACQUER	MARQUEE
ACQUITS	ASQUINT	BRUSQUE	CIRQUES	CROQUIS	EQUATOR	INQUERE	LACQUEY	MARQUES
ALFAQUI	BANQUET	CACIQUE	CLAQUES	CUMQUAT	EQUERRY	INQUEST	LASQUES	MARQUIS
ALIQUOT	BAROQUE	CAIQUES	CLIQUES	DOCQUET	EQUINAL	INQUIET	LIQUATE	MASQUER
ANTIQUE	BARQUES	CALQUED	CLIQUEY	ENQUIRE	EQUINIA	INQUIRE	LIQUEFY	MASQUES
AQUAFER	BASQUED	CALQUES	CLOQUES	ENQUIRY	EQUINOX	INQUIRY	LIQUEUR	MESQUIN
AQUARIA	BASQUES	CASQUES	COEQUAL	EQUABLE	EQUIPES	JERQUED	LIQUIDS	MESQUIT
AQUATIC	BEQUEST	CAZIQUE	COMIQUE	EQUABLY	ESQUIRE	JERQUER	LIQUORS	MOSQUES

OBLIQUE	QUAGGAS	QUASHED	QUETHES	QUILLON	QUITTED	RACQUET	SQUAILS	SQUINNY
OBLOQUY	QUAHAUG	QUASHEE	QUETSCH	QUILTED	QUITTER	RELIQUE	SQUALID	SQUINTS
OBSEQUY	QUAHOGS	QUASHES	QUETZAL	QUILTER	QUITTOR	REPIQUE	SQUALLS	SQUIRED
OPAQUED	QUAICHS	QUASHIE	QUEUING	QUINARY	QUIVERS	REQUERE	SQUALLY	SQUIRES
OPAQUER	QUAIGHS	QUASSIA	QUEYNIE	QUINATE	QUIVERY	REQUEST	SQUALOR	SQUIRMS
OPAQUES	QUAILED	QUAVERS	QUIBBLE	QUINCES	QUIZZED	REQUIEM	SQUAMAE	SQUIRMY
PARQUET	QUAKIER	QUAVERY	QUIBLIN	QUINCHE	QUIZZER	REQUIRE	SQUAMES	SQUIRRS
PERIQUE	QUAKING	QUAYAGE	QUICHED	QUINIES	QUIZZES	REQUITE	SQUARED	SQUIRTS
PICQUET	QUALIFY	QUEACHY	QUICHES	QUININE	QUODDED	REQUITS	SQUARER	SQUISHY
PIQUANT	QUALITY	QUEECHY	QUICKEN	QUINNAT	QUODLIN	REQUOTE	SQUARES	SQUITCH
PIQUETS	QUAMASH	QUEENED	QUICKER	QUINOAS	QUOIFED	RISQUES	SQUASHY	SUBAQUA
PIQUING	QUANGOS	QUEENLY	QUICKIE	QUINOLS	QUOINED	ROCQUET	SQUATTY	TEQUILA
PLAQUES	QUANNET	QUEERED	QUICKLY	QUINONE	QUOISTS	ROQUETS	SQUAWKS	TORQUED
PREQUEL	QUANTAL	QUEERER	QUIDAMS	QUINTAL	QUOITED	RORQUAL	SQUAWKY	TORQUES
PULQUES	QUANTED	QUEERLY	QUIDDIT	QUINTAN	QUOITER	SACQUES	SQUEAKS	TSADDIQ
QIGONGS	QUANTIC	QUEESTS	QUIDDLE	QUINTAS	QUOKKAS	SAIQUES	SQUEAKY	TZADDIQ
QINTARS	QUANTUM	QUELEAS	QUIESCE	QUINTES	QUONDAM	SEQUELA	SQUEALS	UNEQUAL
QUACKED	QUARREL	QUELLED	QUIETED	QUINTET	QUONKED	SEQUELS	SQUEEZE	UNIQUER
QUACKLE	QUARTAN	QUELLER	QUIETEN	QUINTIC	QUOPPED	SEQUENT	SQUEEZY	UNIQUES
QUADDED	QUARTER	QUEMING	QUIETER	QUINZES	QUORATE	SEQUINS	SQUELCH	UNQUEEN
QUADRAT	QUARTES	QUERIED	QUIETLY	QUIPPED	QUORUMS	SEQUOIA	SQUIDGE	UNQUIET
QUADRIC	QUARTET	QUERIES	QUIETUS	QUIRING	QUOTERS	SILIQUA	SQUIDGY	UNQUOTE
QUAERED	QUARTIC	QUERIST	QUIGHTS	QUIRKED	QUOTING	SILIQUE	SQUIERS	VAQUERO
QUAERES	QUARTOS	QUESTED	QUILLAI	QUIRTED	QUOTUMS	SQUABBY	SQUIFFY	
QUAFFED	QUARTZY	QUESTER	QUILLED	QUITING	QUYTING	SQUACCO	SQUILLS	
QUAFFER	QUASARS	QUESTOR	QUILLET	QUITTAL	QWERTYS	SQUADDY	SQUINCH	

Q - 8-letter words

ACQUAINT	CACIQUES	EQUATION	LIQUATES	PETANQUE	QUANTISE	QUEERITY	QUIETENS
ACQUESTS	CALQUING	EQUATORS	LIQUESCE	PHYSIQUE	QUANTITY	QUELCHED	QUIETERS
ACQUIGHT	CAZIQUES	EQUINIAS	LIQUEURS	PICQUETS	QUANTIZE	QUELCHES	QUIETEST
ACQUIRAL	CHARQUIS	EQUINITY	LIQUIDLY	PIQUANCY	QUANTONG	QUELLERS	QUIETING
ACQUIRED	CHEQUERS	EQUIPAGE	LIQUIDUS	PIQUETED	QUARRELS	QUELLING	QUIETISM
ACQUIRES	CHEQUIER	EQUIPPED	LIQUORED	PRATIQUE	QUARRIED	QUENCHED	QUIETIST
ACQUISTS	CINQUAIN	EQUISETA	LOQUITUR	PREQUELS	QUARRIER	QUENCHER	QUIETIVE
ACQUITES	CLAQUEUR	EQUITANT	LUSTIQUE	QALAMDAN	QUARRIES	QUENCHES	QUIETUDE
ADEQUACY	CLINIQUE	EQUITIES	MACAQUES	QUACKERY	QUARTANS	QUENELLE	QUIGHTED
ADEQUATE	CLIQUIER	EQUIVOKE	MADOQUAS	QUACKING	QUARTERN	QUERISTS	QUILLAIA
ALFAQUIS	CLIQUISH	ESQUIRES	MAQUETTE	QUACKLED	QUARTERS	QUERYING	QUILLAIS
ALIQUANT	CLIQUISM	ESQUISSE	MAROQUIN	QUACKLES	QUARTETS	QUESTANT	QUILLAJA
ANTIQUED	COEQUALS	EXEQUIAL	MARQUEES	QUADDING	QUARTETT	QUESTERS	QUILLETS
ANTIQUES	COLLOQUE	EXEQUIES	MARQUESS	QUADRANS	QUARTICS	QUESTING	QUILLING
APPLIQUE	COLLOQUY	FILIOQUE	MARQUISE	QUADRANT	QUARTIER	QUESTION	QUILLMAN
AQUACADE	COMIQUES	FREQUENT	MASQUERS	QUADRATE	QUARTILE	QUESTORS	QUILLMEN
AQUAFERS	CONQUERS	GRECQUES	MESQUINE	QUADRATS	QUARTZES	QUETCHED	QUILLONS
AQUALUNG	CONQUEST	HAQUETON	MESQUITE	QUADRIGA	QUASHEES	QUETCHES	QUILTERS
AQUANAUT	COQUETRY	HENEQUEN	MESQUITS	QUADROON	QUASHIES	QUETHING	QUILTING
AQUARIAN	COQUETTE	HENEQUIN	MISQUOTE	QUAESTOR	QUASHING	QUETZALS	QUINCHED
AQUARIST	COQUILLA	HENIQUIN	MOQUETTE	QUAFFERS	QUASSIAS	QUEUEING	QUINCHES
AQUARIUM	COQUILLE	ILLIQUID	MOSQUITO	QUAFFING	QUATCHED	QUEUINGS	QUINCUNX
AQUATICS	COQUITOS	INEQUITY	MUQADDAM	QUAGGIER	QUATCHES	QUEYNIES	QUINELLA
AQUATINT	COTQUEAN	INIQUITY	MUSQUASH	QUAGMIRE	QUATORZE	QUIBBLED	QUININES
AQUAVITS	CRITIQUE	INQILABS	MYSTIQUE	QUAGMIRY	QUATRAIN	QUIBBLER	QUINNATS
AQUEDUCT	CROQUETS	INQUERED	NARQUOIS	QUAHAUGS	QUAVERED	QUIBBLES	QUINONES
AQUIFERS	CUMQUATS	INQUERES	OBLIQUED	QUAILING	QUAVERER	QUIBLINS	QUINSIED
AQUILINE	DAIQUIRI	INQUESTS	OBLIQUER	QUAINTER	QUAYAGES	QUICHING	QUINSIES
ARQUEBUS	DETRAQUE	INQUIETS	OBLIQUES	QUAINTLY	QUAYSIDE	QUICKENS	QUINTAIN
BANQUETS	DISQUIET	INQUIRED	OBLIQUID	QUAKIEST	QUEACHES	QUICKEST	QUINTALS
BAROQUES	DOCQUETS	INQUIRER	OBSEQUIE	QUAKINGS	QUEASIER	QUICKIES	QUINTETS
BASQUINE	ELOQUENT	INQUIRES	ODALIQUE	QUALMIER	QUEASILY	QUICKSET	QUINTETT
BEQUEATH	EMBUSQUE	JACQUARD	OLDSQUAW	QUALMING	QUEAZIER	QUIDDANY	QUINTILE
BEQUESTS	ENQUIRED	JERQUERS	OPAQUELY	QUALMISH	QUEENDOM	QUIDDITS	QUIPPING
BEZIQUES	ENQUIRER	JERQUING	OPAQUEST	QUANDANG	QUEENING	QUIDDITY	QUIPPISH
BLANQUET	ENQUIRES	JONQUILS	OPAQUING	QUANDARY	QUEENITE	QUIDDLED	QUIPSTER
BOUQUETS	EQUALISE	KUMQUATS	PARAQUAT	QUANDONG	QUEENLET	QUIDDLER	QUIRKIER
BOUTIQUE	EQUALITY	LACQUERS	PAROQUET	QUANNETS	QUEERDOM	QUIDDLES	QUIRKING
BRELOQUE	EQUALIZE	LACQUEYS	PARQUETS	QUANTICS	QUEEREST	QUIDNUNC	QUIRKISH
BRIQUETS	EQUALLED	LIQUABLE	PERIQUES	QUANTIFY	QUEERING	QUIESCED	QUIRTING
BRUSQUER	EQUATING	LIQUATED	PERRUQUE	QUANTING	QUEERISH	QUIESCES	QUISLING

QUITCHED	QUONKING	REQUIRES	SQUABASH	SQUARERS	SQUEEDGE	SQUINTER	TRUQUAGE
QUITCHES	QUOPPING	REQUITAL	SQUABBED	SQUAREST	SQUEEGEE	SQUIRAGE	TRUQUEUR
QUITTALS	QUOTABLE	REQUITED	SQUABBER	SQUARING	SQUEEZED	SQUIREEN	TSADDIQS
QUITTERS	QUOTABLY	REQUITER	SQUABBLE	SQUARISH	SQUEEZER	SQUIRELY	TZADDIQS
QUITTING	QUOTIENT	REQUITES	SQUACCOS	SQUARSON	SQUEEZES	SQUIRESS	UBIQUITY
QUITTORS	QWERTIES	REQUOTED	SQUADRON	SQUASHED	SQUEGGED	SQUIRING	UMQUHILE
QUIVERED	RACQUETS	REQUOTES	SQUAILED	SQUASHER	SQUEGGER	SQUIRMED	UNEQUALS
QUIXOTIC	RAMEQUIN	REQUOYLE	SQUAILER	SQUASHES	SQUELCHY	SQUIRRED	UNIQUELY
QUIXOTRY	RELIQUES	ROCQUETS	SQUALLED	SQUATTED	SQUIBBED	SQUIRREL	UNIQUEST
QUIZZERS	REMARQUE	ROQUETED	SQUALLER	SQUATTER	SQUIDDED	SQUIRTED	UNQUEENS
QUIZZERY	REPIQUED	ROQUETTE	SQUALOID	SQUATTLE	SQUIDGED	SQUIRTER	UNQUIETS
QUIZZIFY	REPIQUES	RORQUALS	SQUALORS	SQUAWKED	SQUIDGES	SQUISHED	UNQUOTED
QUIZZING	REQUERED	SEAQUAKE	SQUAMATE	SQUAWKER	SQUIFFER	SQUISHES	UNQUOTES
QUODDING	REQUERES	SEQUELAE	SQUAMOSE	SQUAWMAN	SQUIGGLE	SUBEQUAL	VANQUISH
QUODLINS	REQUESTS	SEQUENCE	SQUAMOUS	SQUAWMEN	SQUIGGLY	SURQUEDY	VAQUEROS
QUOIFING	REQUIEMS	SEQUENTS	SQUAMULA	SQUEAKED	SQUILGEE	TEQUILAS	VEHMIQUE
QUOINING	REQUIGHT	SEQUOIAS	SQUAMULE	SQUEAKER	SQUINIED	TEQUILLA	VERQUERE
QUOITERS	REQUIRED	SILIQUAS	SQUANDER	SQUEALED	SQUINIES	TORQUATE	VERQUIRE
QUOITING	REQUIRER	SILIQUES	SQUARELY	SQUEALER	SQUINTED	TRANQUIL	

X-WORDS

X – 2-letter words

AX	EX	OX	XI

X – 3-letter words

AXE	FAX	HOX	LOX	MUX	POX	SAX	TAX	WEX	ZAX
BOX	FIX	KEX	LUX	NIX	PYX	SEX	VEX	WOX	
COX	FOX	LAX	MAX	PAX	RAX	SIX	VOX	XIS	
DUX	HEX	LEX	MIX	PIX	REX	SOX	WAX	YEX	

X – 4-letter words

APEX	AXON	DIXI	EXON	FLEX	IXIA	MAXI	ONYX	ROUX	WAXY
AXED	BOXY	DIXY	EXPO	FLIX	JEUX	MINX	ORYX	SEXT	WEXE
AXEL	CALX	DOXY	EXUL	FLUX	JINX	MIXT	OXEN	SEXY	XYST
AXES	COAX	EAUX	FAIX	FOXY	JYNX	MIXY	OXER	TAXA	YUNX
AXIL	COXA	EXAM	FALX	HOAX	LANX	MOXA	PIXY	TAXI	
AXIS	COXY	EXES	FAUX	IBEX	LUXE	NEXT	POXY	TEXT	
AXLE	CRUX	EXIT	FLAX	ILEX	LYNX	NIXY	PREX	ULEX	

X – 5-letter words

ADDAX	BOXER	DUXES	EXPEL	HOXED	MAXES	OXTER	REMEX	TELEX	WEXED
ADMIX	BOXES	EMBOX	EXPOS	HOXES	MAXIM	PANAX	SALIX	TEXAS	WEXES
AFFIX	BRAXY	ENFIX	EXTOL	HYRAX	MAXIS	PAXES	SAXES	TEXTS	WOXEN
ANNEX	BUXOM	EPOXY	EXTRA	IMMIX	MIXED	PHLOX	SEXED	TOXIC	XEBEC
ATAXY	CALIX	EXACT	EXUDE	INDEX	MIXEN	PIXEL	SEXER	TOXIN	XENIA
AUXIN	CALYX	EXALT	EXULS	INFIX	MIXER	PIXES	SEXES	UNBOX	XENON
AXELS	CAREX	EXAMS	EXULT	IXIAS	MIXES	PIXIE	SEXTS	UNFIX	XERIC
AXIAL	CAXON	EXCEL	EXURB	IXTLE	MOXAS	PODEX	SILEX	UNSEX	XYLEM
AXILE	CHOUX	EXEAT	FAXED	KEXES	MOXIE	POXED	SIXER	UNTAX	XYLIC
AXILS	CIMEX	EXEEM	FAXES	KYLIX	MUREX	POXES	SIXES	VARIX	XYLOL
AXING	CODEX	EXEME	FIXED	LATEX	MUXED	PREXY	SIXTE	VEXED	XYLYL
AXIOM	COXAE	EXERT	FIXER	LAXER	MUXES	PROXY	SIXTH	VEXER	XYSTI
AXLES	COXAL	EXIES	FIXES	LAXES	NEXUS	PYXED	SIXTY	VEXES	XYSTS
AXOID	COXED	EXILE	FLAXY	LAXLY	NIXES	PYXES	SOREX	VIBEX	YEXED
AXONS	COXES	EXINE	FOXED	LEXES	NIXIE	PYXIS	TAXED	VITEX	YEXES
BEAUX	CULEX	EXIST	FOXES	LEXIS	NOXAL	RADIX	TAXER	VIXEN	ZAXES
BOLIX	CYLIX	EXITS	HELIX	LIMAX	OXERS	RAXED	TAXES	WAXED	
BORAX	DESEX	EXODE	HEXAD	LOXES	OXIDE	RAXES	TAXIS	WAXEN	
BOXED	DIXIE	EXONS	HEXED	LUXES	OXIME	REDOX	TAXON	WAXER	
BOXEN	DRUXY	EXPAT	HEXES	MALAX	OXLIP	RELAX	TAXOR	WAXES	

X – 6-letter words

ADIEUX	CARFOX	ELIXIR	EXODES	EXUDES	HEXOSE	MENINX	PIXELS	SEXTON	VORTEX
AFFLUX	CAUDEX	EUTAXY	EXODIC	EXULTS	HOAXED	MINXES	PIXIES	SEXUAL	WAXERS
ALEXIA	CAXONS	EXACTS	EXODUS	EXURBS	HOAXER	MIXENS	PLEXOR	SIXERS	WAXIER
ALEXIC	CERVIX	EXALTS	EXOGEN	FAXING	HOAXES	MIXERS	PLEXUS	SIXTES	WAXING
ALEXIN	CHENIX	EXAMEN	EXOMIS	FIXATE	HOXING	MIXIER	POLLEX	SIXTHS	WEXING
ANNEXE	CLIMAX	EXARCH	EXONYM	FIXERS	IBEXES	MIXING	POXIER	SMILAX	WRAXLE
ANOXIA	COAXED	EXCAMB	EXOPOD	FIXING	ICEBOX	MOXIES	POXING	SPADIX	XEBECS
ANOXIC	COAXER	EXCEED	EXOTIC	FIXITY	ILEXES	MUXING	PRAXES	SPHINX	XENIAL
APEXES	COAXES	EXCELS	EXPAND	FIXIVE	IMBREX	MYXOMA	PRAXIS	STORAX	XENIAS
ATAXIA	COCCYX	EXCEPT	EXPATS	FIXURE	IMPLEX	NEXTLY	PREFIX	STYRAX	XENIUM
ATAXIC	COMMIX	EXCESS	EXPECT	FLAXEN	INFLUX	NIXIES	PREMIX	SUFFIX	XENONS
ATWIXT	CONFIX	EXCIDE	EXPELS	FLAXES	IXTLES	ONYXES	PREXES	SURTAX	XEROMA
AUXINS	CONVEX	EXCISE	EXPEND	FLEXED	JAWBOX	OREXIS	PROLIX	SYNTAX	XOANON
AXILLA	CORTEX	EXCITE	EXPERT	FLEXES	JINXED	ORIFEX	PTYXES	SYRINX	XYLEMS
AXIOMS	COWPOX	EXCUSE	EXPIRE	FLEXOR	JINXES	ORYXES	PTYXIS	TAXERS	XYLENE
AXISES	COXIER	EXEATS	EXPIRY	FLIXED	JYNXES	OUTBOX	PYXING	TAXIED	XYLOID
AXOIDS	COXING	EXEDRA	EXPORT	FLIXES	KLAXON	OUTFOX	RAXING	TAXIES	XYLOLS
BANJAX	CRUXES	EXEEMS	EXPOSE	FLUXED	LARNAX	OXALIC	REFLEX	TAXING	XYLOMA
BAXTER	DEFLEX	EXEMED	EXPUGN	FLUXES	LARYNX	OXALIS	REFLUX	TAXMAN	XYLOSE
BIAXAL	DEIXES	EXEMES	EXSECT	FORFEX	LAXEST	OXGANG	RHEXES	TAXMEN	XYLYLS
BIJOUX	DEIXIS	EXEMPT	EXSERT	FORNIX	LAXISM	OXGATE	RHEXIS	TAXORS	XYSTER
BOLLIX	DENTEX	EXEQUY	EXTANT	FOXIER	LAXIST	OXHEAD	SAXAUL	TETTIX	XYSTOI
BOMBAX	DEXTER	EXERTS	EXTASY	FOXING	LAXITY	OXIDES	SAXONY	THORAX	XYSTOS
BONXIE	DIAXON	EXEUNT	EXTEND	FRUTEX	LEXEME	OXIMES	SCOLEX	TOXINS	XYSTUS
BOXCAR	DIOXAN	EXHALE	EXTENT	GALAXY	LUMMOX	OXLAND	SEXERS	TOXOID	YEXING
BOXERS	DIOXIN	EXHORT	EXTERN	HALLUX	LUXATE	OXLIPS	SEXFID	TUTRIX	YUNXES
BOXFUL	DIPLEX	EXHUME	EXTINE	HATBOX	LUXURY	OXSLIP	SEXIER	TUXEDO	
BOXIER	DIXIES	EXILED	EXTIRP	HAYBOX	LYNXES	OXTAIL	SEXING	ULEXES	
BOXING	DOGFOX	EXILES	EXTOLD	HEXACT	MAGNOX	OXTERS	SEXISM	UNISEX	
BOYAUX	DOXIES	EXILIC	EXTOLS	HEXADS	MATRIX	OXYGEN	SEXIST	VERTEX	
CALXES	DUPLEX	EXINES	EXTORT	HEXANE	MAXIMA	OXYMEL	SEXPOT	VEXERS	
CARANX	EARWAX	EXISTS	EXTRAS	HEXENE	MAXIMS	PAXWAX	SEXTAN	VEXING	
CARFAX	EFFLUX	EXITED	EXUDED	HEXING	MAXIXE	PINXIT	SEXTET	VIXENS	

X – 7-letter words

ABAXIAL	AXINITE	CONTEXT	EXALTED	EXECUTE	EXOPODS	EXSERTS	FLEXING	HYRAXES
ABRAXAS	AXOLOTL	COTEAUX	EXAMENS	EXEDRAE	EXORDIA	EXTATIC	FLEXION	IMMIXED
ADAXIAL	BATEAUX	COXCOMB	EXAMINE	EXEEMED	EXOTICA	EXTENDS	FLEXORS	IMMIXES
ADDAXES	BAUXITE	COXIEST	EXAMPLE	EXEGETE	EXOTICS	EXTENSE	FLEXURE	INDEXED
ADMIXED	BAXTERS	CURTAXE	EXARATE	EXEMING	EXPANDS	EXTENTS	FLIXING	INDEXER
ADMIXES	BEESWAX	DESEXED	EXARCHS	EXEMPLA	EXPANSE	EXTERNE	FLUMMOX	INDEXES
AFFIXED	BETWIXT	DESEXES	EXARCHY	EXEMPLE	EXPECTS	EXTERNS	FLUXING	INEXACT
AFFIXES	BIAXIAL	DEXTERS	EXCAMBS	EXEMPTS	EXPENDS	EXTINCT	FLUXION	INFIXED
ALEXIAS	BOLIXES	DEXTRAL	EXCEEDS	EXERGUE	EXPENSE	EXTINES	FLUXIVE	INFIXES
ALEXINS	BONXIES	DEXTRAN	EXCEPTS	EXERTED	EXPERTS	EXTIRPS	FOXHOLE	INVEXED
ANNEXED	BORAXES	DEXTRIN	EXCERPT	EXHALED	EXPIATE	EXTORTS	FOXIEST	JAMBEUX
ANNEXES	BOSTRYX	DIAXONS	EXCHEAT	EXHALES	EXPIRED	EXTRACT	FOXINGS	JINXING
ANOREXY	BOXCARS	DIOXANE	EXCIDED	EXHAUST	EXPIRER	EXTRAIT	FOXSHIP	KLAXONS
ANOXIAS	BOXFULS	DIOXANS	EXCIDES	EXHEDRA	EXPLAIN	EXTREAT	FOXTROT	LATEXES
ANTEFIX	BOXIEST	DIOXIDE	EXCISED	EXHIBIT	EXPLANT	EXTREME	GATEAUX	LAXATOR
ANTHRAX	BOXINGS	DIOXINS	EXCISES	EXHORTS	EXPLODE	EXTRUDE	GEARBOX	LAXISMS
ANXIETY	BOXROOM	DRUXIER	EXCITED	EXHUMED	EXPLOIT	EXUDATE	HELIXES	LAXISTS
ANXIOUS	BOXWOOD	ELIXIRS	EXCITER	EXHUMER	EXPLORE	EXUDING	HEXACTS	LAXNESS
APOPLEX	BRAXIES	EMBOXED	EXCITES	EXHUMES	EXPORTS	EXULTED	HEXADIC	LEXEMES
APRAXIA	BRUXISM	EMBOXES	EXCITON	EXIGENT	EXPOSAL	EXURBAN	HEXAGON	LEXICAL
APTERYX	BUREAUX	ENFIXED	EXCITOR	EXILIAN	EXPOSED	EXURBIA	HEXANES	LEXICON
ASEXUAL	BUXOMER	ENFIXES	EXCLAIM	EXILING	EXPOSER	EXUVIAE	HEXAPLA	LEXISES
ASPHYXY	CACHEXY	EPAXIAL	EXCLAVE	EXILITY	EXPOSES	EXUVIAL	HEXAPOD	LOXYGEN
ATARAXY	CADEAUX	EPITAXY	EXCLUDE	EXISTED	EXPOUND	FIXABLE	HEXARCH	LUXATED
ATAXIAS	CALIXES	EPOXIDE	EXCRETA	EXITING	EXPRESS	FIXATED	HEXENES	LUXATES
ATAXIES	CALYXES	EPOXIES	EXCRETE	EXOCARP	EXPUGNS	FIXATES	HEXINGS	MALAXED
AUXESES	CHOENIX	EQUINOX	EXCUDIT	EXODERM	EXPULSE	FIXEDLY	HEXOSES	MALAXES
AUXESIS	COAXERS	EUTEXIA	EXCURSE	EXODIST	EXPUNCT	FIXINGS	HOAXERS	MAXILLA
AUXETIC	COAXIAL	EXACTED	EXCUSAL	EXOGAMY	EXPUNGE	FIXTURE	HOAXING	MAXIMAL
AXIALLY	COAXING	EXACTER	EXCUSED	EXOGENS	EXPURGE	FIXURES	HYDROXY	MAXIMIN
AXILLAE	COMPLEX	EXACTLY	EXCUSER	EXOMION	EXSCIND	FLAXIER	HYPOXIA	MAXIMUM
AXILLAR	CONFLUX	EXACTOR	EXCUSES	EXONYMS	EXSECTS	FLEXILE	HYPOXIC	MAXIXES

MAXWELL	OXHEADS	PHALANX	PYXIDIA	SEXTETS	TAXICAB	TRIAXON	VITEXES	XEROTIC
MILIEUX	OXIDANT	PHARYNX	REANNEX	SEXTETT	TAXIING	TRIPLEX	VITRAUX	XIPHOID
MIXABLE	OXIDASE	PHLOXES	RECTRIX	SEXTILE	TAXIMAN	TUXEDOS	VIXENLY	XOANONS
MIXEDLY	OXIDATE	PHOENIX	RELAXED	SEXTONS	TAXIMEN	UNBOXED	WAXBILL	XYLENES
MIXIEST	OXIDISE	PICKAXE	RELAXES	SEXTUOR	TAXINGS	UNBOXES	WAXIEST	XYLENOL
MIXTION	OXIDIZE	PLANKTY	RELAXIN	SILEXES	TAXIWAY	UNFIXED	WAXINGS	XYLITOL
MIXTURE	OXLANDS	PLEXORS	RESEAUX	SIMPLEX	TAXYING	UNFIXES	WAXWING	XYLOGEN
MONAXON	OXONIUM	PLEXURE	SALPINX	SIXAINE	TECTRIX	UNMIXED	WAXWORK	XYLOMAS
MUREXES	OXSLIPS	PODEXES	SAXAULS	SIXFOLD	TELETEX	UNSEXED	WRAXLED	XYLONIC
NARTHEX	OXTAILS	POSTFIX	SAXHORN	SIXTEEN	TELEXED	UNSEXES	WRAXLES	XYLOSES
NEXUSES	OXTERED	POXIEST	SEEDBOX	SIXTHLY	TELEXES	UNTAXED	XANTHIC	XYSTERS
NOXIOUS	OXYGENS	PRETEXT	SEXFOIL	SIXTIES	TEXASES	UNTAXES	XANTHIN	ZEUXITE
ORATRIX	OXYMELS	PREXIES	SEXIEST	SOAPBOX	TEXTILE	UNVEXED	XERAFIN	ZOOTAXY
OVERTAX	OXYTONE	PRINCOX	SEXISMS	SOREXES	TEXTUAL	UXORIAL	XERARCH	
OXALATE	PANAXES	PROXIES	SEXISTS	SUBTEXT	TEXTURE	VAUDOUX	XERASIA	
OXAZINE	PANCHAX	PROXIMO	SEXLESS	SYNAXES	TOOLBOX	VEXEDLY	XEROMAS	
OXBLOOD	PARADOX	PYREXIA	SEXPOTS	SYNAXIS	TORTRIX	VEXILLA	XEROSES	
OXGANGS	PAXIUBA	PYREXIC	SEXTANS	TAXABLE	TOXICAL	VEXINGS	XEROSIS	
OXGATES	PERPLEX	PYXIDES	SEXTANT	TAXABLY	TOXOIDS	VICTRIX	XEROTES	

X - 8-letter words

ADMIXING	CARBOXYL	DUPLEXES	EXCITONS	EXHUMERS	EXPERTED	EXTIRPED	GEOTAXES
AFFIXING	CARFAXES	DUXELLES	EXCITORS	EXHUMING	EXPERTLY	EXTOLLED	GEOTAXIS
AFFLUXES	CARFOXES	DYSLEXIA	EXCLAIMS	EXIGEANT	EXPIABLE	EXTOLLER	GIAMBEUX
ANNEXING	CARNIFEX	DYSLEXIC	EXCLAVES	EXIGENCE	EXPIATED	EXTORTED	GLORYBOX
ANNEXION	CATHEXES	EARTHWAX	EXCLUDED	EXIGENCY	EXPIATES	EXTORTER	GLOXINIA
ANNEXURE	CATHEXIS	EARWAXES	EXCLUDEE	EXIGENTS	EXPIATOR	EXTRADOS	HARUSPEX
ANOREXIA	CAUDEXES	EFFLUXES	EXCLUDES	EXIGIBLE	EXPIRANT	EXTRAITS	HATBOXES
ANOREXIC	CERVIXES	EMBOXING	EXCRETED	EXIGUITY	EXPIRIES	EXTREATS	HAYBOXES
ANTEFIXA	CHATEAUX	ENDEIXES	EXCRETES	EXIGUOUS	EXPIRING	EXTREMER	HERITRIX
ANTHELIX	CHENIXES	ENDEIXIS	EXCUBANT	EXIMIOUS	EXPLAINS	EXTREMES	HEXAFOIL
APOMIXES	CICATRIX	ENFIXING	EXCURSED	EXISTENT	EXPLANTS	EXTRORSE	HEXAGLOT
APOMIXIS	CLACKBOX	EPICALYX	EXCURSES	EXISTING	EXPLICIT	EXTRUDED	HEXAGONS
APOPLEXY	CLIMAXED	EPOXIDES	EXCURSUS	EXITANCE	EXPLODED	EXTRUDER	HEXAGRAM
APPENDIX	CLIMAXES	EUTAXIES	EXCUSALS	EXOCARPS	EXPLODER	EXTRUDES	HEXAPLAR
APRAXIAS	COMMIXED	EUTAXITE	EXCUSERS	EXOCRINE	EXPLODES	EXUDATES	HEXAPLAS
APYREXIA	COMMIXES	EUTEXIAS	EXCUSING	EXODERMS	EXPLOITS	EXULTANT	HEXAPODS
ASPHYXIA	CONFIXED	EUXENITE	EXCUSIVE	EXODISTS	EXPLORED	EXULTING	HEXAPODY
ATARAXIA	CONFIXES	EXACTERS	EXECRATE	EXODUSES	EXPLORER	EXURBIAS	HEXYLENE
ATARAXIC	CONTEXTS	EXACTEST	EXECUTED	EXOERGIC	EXPLORES	EXUVIATE	HYDROXYL
AUXETICS	CONVEXED	EXACTING	EXECUTER	EXOGAMIC	EXPONENT	FABLIAUX	HYPOXIAS
AUXILIAR	CONVEXES	EXACTION	EXECUTES	EXOMIONS	EXPORTED	FIXATING	ICEBOXES
AVIATRIX	CONVEXLY	EXACTORS	EXECUTOR	EXOMISES	EXPORTER	FIXATION	IMMIXING
AXILLARY	CORTEXES	EXALTING	EXECUTRY	EXOPHAGY	EXPOSALS	FIXATIVE	IMPLEXES
AXINITES	COWPOXES	EXAMINED	EXEEMING	EXOPLASM	EXPOSERS	FIXATURE	INDEXERS
AXIOLOGY	COXALGIA	EXAMINEE	EXEGESES	EXORABLE	EXPOSING	FIXITIES	INDEXING
AXOLOTLS	COXCOMBS	EXAMINER	EXEGESIS	EXORCISE	EXPOSURE	FIXTURES	INEXPERT
AXOPLASM	COXINESS	EXAMINES	EXEGETES	EXORCISM	EXPOUNDS	FLAXIEST	INFIXING
BANDEAUX	COXSWAIN	EXAMPLAR	EXEGETIC	EXORCIST	EXPRESSO	FLEXIBLE	INFLEXED
BANJAXED	CREATRIX	EXAMPLED	EXEMPLAR	EXORCIZE	EXPUGNED	FLEXIBLY	INFLUXES
BANJAXES	CRUCIFIX	EXAMPLES	EXEMPLES	EXORDIAL	EXPULSED	FLEXIONS	INTERMIX
BANXRING	CURATRIX	EXANTHEM	EXEMPLUM	EXORDIUM	EXPULSES	FLEXUOSE	INTERREX
BAUXITES	CURTAXES	EXCAMBED	EXEMPTED	EXOSMOSE	EXPUNCTS	FLEXUOUS	INTERSEX
BAUXITIC	DEFLEXED	EXCAVATE	EXEQUIAL	EXOSPORE	EXPUNGED	FLEXURAL	JAMBEAUX
BEAUXITE	DEFLEXES	EXCEEDED	EXEQUIES	EXOTERIC	EXPUNGER	FLEXURES	JANITRIX
BERCEAUX	DENTEXES	EXCELLED	EXERCISE	EXOTOXIC	EXPUNGES	FLUXIONS	JAWBOXES
BICONVEX	DESEXING	EXCEPTED	EXERGUAL	EXOTOXIN	EXPURGED	FORFEXES	LARYNXES
BISEXUAL	DETOXIFY	EXCEPTOR	EXERGUES	EXPANDED	EXPURGES	FORNIXES	LAXATIVE
BOLLIXES	DEXTRANS	EXCERPTA	EXERTING	EXPANDER	EXSCINDS	FOXBERRY	LAXATORS
BOMBAXES	DEXTRINE	EXCERPTS	EXERTION	EXPANDOR	EXSECTED	FOXGLOVE	LAXITIES
BOXINESS	DEXTRINS	EXCESSES	EXERTIVE	EXPANSES	EXSERTED	FOXHOLES	LEXICONS
BOXROOMS	DEXTROSE	EXCHANGE	EXHALANT	EXPECTED	EXTASIES	FOXHOUND	LEXIGRAM
BOXWOODS	DEXTROUS	EXCHEATS	EXHALING	EXPECTER	EXTENDED	FOXINESS	LIXIVIAL
BRUXISMS	DIOXANES	EXCIDING	EXHAUSTS	EXPEDITE	EXTENDER	FOXSHARK	LIXIVIUM
BUXOMEST	DIOXIDES	EXCISING	EXHEDRAE	EXPELLED	EXTENSOR	FOXSHIPS	LOXYGENS
CACHEXIA	DISANNEX	EXCISION	EXHIBITS	EXPELLEE	EXTERIOR	FOXTROTS	LUMMOXES
CACODOXY	DOGFOXES	EXCITANT	EXHORTED	EXPENDED	EXTERNAL	GALAXIES	LUXATING
CACOMIXL	DOXOLOGY	EXCITERS	EXHORTER	EXPENDER	EXTERNAT	GENETRIX	LUXATION
CAMAIEUX	DRUXIEST	EXCITING	EXHUMATE	EXPENSES	EXTERNES	GENITRIX	LUXMETER

LUXURIES	ORIFEXES	PARADOXY	QUIXOTIC	SIXAINES	TAXIARCH	TUTRIXES	XANTHOMA
LUXURIST	ORTHODOX	PARALLAX	QUIXOTRY	SIXPENCE	TAXICABS	TUXEDOES	XANTHOUS
MAGNOXES	OUTBOXED	PAROXYSM	REFLEXED	SIXPENNY	TAXIWAYS	UNBOXING	XENOGAMY
MALAXAGE	OUTBOXES	PAXIUBAS	REFLEXES	SIXSCORE	TAXONOMY	UNFIXING	XENOLITH
MALAXATE	OUTFOXED	PAXWAXES	REFLEXLY	SIXTEENS	TEGUEXIN	UNFIXITY	XENOPHYA
MALAXING	OUTFOXES	PEROXIDE	REFLUXED	SIXTIETH	TELETEXT	UNIAXIAL	XENOTIME
MANTEAUX	OXALATES	PHORMINX	REFLUXES	SMALLPOX	TELEXING	UNSEXING	XENURINE
MATCHBOX	OXALISES	PICKAXES	RELAXANT	SMILAXES	TETRAXON	UNSEXIST	XERAFINS
MATRIXES	OXAZINES	PLATEAUX	RELAXING	SNUFFBOX	TETTIXES	UNSEXUAL	XERANSES
MAXILLAE	OXBLOODS	PLEXURES	RELAXINS	SPARAXIS	TEXTBOOK	UNTAXING	XERANSIS
MAXIMINS	OXIDANTS	PLEXUSES	RHEXISES	SPHINXES	TEXTILES	UXORIOUS	XERANTIC
MAXIMISE	OXIDASES	POLYAXON	RONDEAUX	SPINIFEX	TEXTUARY	VEXATION	XERAPHIM
MAXIMIST	OXIDATED	PONCEAUX	ROULEAUX	SPINTEXT	TEXTURAL	VEXATORY	XERASIAS
MAXIMIZE	OXIDATES	PONTIFEX	SARDONYX	STORAXES	TEXTURED	VEXILLUM	XYLENOLS
MAXWELLS	OXIDISED	POXVIRUS	SAXATILE	STYRAXES	TEXTURES	VEXINGLY	XYLITOLS
MIREPOIX	OXIDISER	PREFIXED	SAXHORNS	SUBOXIDE	THORAXES	VIDEOTEX	XYLOCARP
MIXTIONS	OXIDISES	PREFIXES	SAXONIES	SUBTEXTS	THYROXIN	VIXENISH	XYLOGENS
MIXTURES	OXIDIZED	PREMIXED	SAXONITE	SUFFIXAL	TOADFLAX	VORTEXES	XYLOIDIN
MONAXIAL	OXIDIZER	PREMIXES	SEXFOILS	SUFFIXED	TOXAEMIA	WAXBERRY	XYLOLOGY
MONAXONS	OXIDIZES	PRETEXTS	SEXINESS	SUFFIXES	TOXAEMIC	WAXBILLS	XYLONITE
MONOXIDE	OXIMETER	PROLIXLY	SEXOLOGY	SUPERTAX	TOXICANT	WAXINESS	XYSTOSES
MORCEAUX	OXONIUMS	PROXIMAL	SEXTANTS	SURTAXED	TOXICITY	WAXWINGS	XYSTUSES
MYXEDEMA	OXTERING	PTYXISES	SEXTETTE	SURTAXES	TOXOCARA	WAXWORKS	ZEUXITES
MYXOMATA	OXYMORON	PYREXIAL	SEXTETTS	SYNTAXES	TRACTRIX	WRAXLING	ZOOTOXIN
NALOXONE	OXYTOCIC	PYREXIAS	SEXTILES	SYNTEXIS	TRANSFIX	XANTHATE	
NEXTNESS	OXYTOCIN	PYROXENE	SEXTOLET	SYRINXES	TRIAXIAL	XANTHEIN	
NITROXYL	OXYTONES	PYROXYLE	SEXTUORS	TABLEAUX	TRIAXONS	XANTHENE	
OPOPANAX	PANMIXIA	PYXIDIUM	SEXTUPLE	TAXATION	TRIOXIDE	XANTHINE	
OREXISES	PANMIXIS	QUINCUNX	SEXUALLY	TAXATIVE	TRUMEAUX	XANTHINS	

Z-WORDS

Z - 2-letter words

ZO

Z - 3-letter words

BEZ	DZO	LEZ	POZ	ZAG	ZED	ZHO	ZIZ	ZUZ
BIZ	FEZ	LUZ	RIZ	ZAP	ZEE	ZIG	ZOA	
COZ	FIZ	MIZ	SAZ	ZAX	ZEK	ZIP	ZOO	
CUZ	JIZ	MOZ	SEZ	ZEA	ZEL	ZIT	ZOS	

Z - 4-letter words

ADZE	DZOS	HAZY	MAZY	PIZE	TREZ	ZEAL	ZEZE	ZOBO	ZURF
AZAN	FAZE	HIZZ	MEZE	POZZ	TUZZ	ZEAS	ZHOS	ZOBU	ZYME
AZYM	FIZZ	JAZY	MIZZ	PUTZ	TZAR	ZEBU	ZIFF	ZOEA	
BUZZ	FOZY	JAZZ	MOZE	QUIZ	VIZY	ZEDS	ZIGS	ZOIC	
CHEZ	FRIZ	JIZZ	MOZZ	RAZE	WHIZ	ZEES	ZILA	ZONA	
COZE	FUZE	KAZI	NAZE	RAZZ	ZACK	ZEIN	ZIMB	ZONE	
COZY	FUZZ	LAZE	OOZE	SIZE	ZAGS	ZEKS	ZINC	ZOOM	
CZAR	GAZE	LAZY	OOZY	SIZY	ZANY	ZELS	ZING	ZOON	
DAZE	GAZY	LEZZ	OUZO	SWIZ	ZAPS	ZERO	ZIPS	ZOOS	
DOZE	GIZZ	LUTZ	OYEZ	TIZZ	ZARF	ZEST	ZITS	ZULU	
DOZY	HAZE	MAZE	PHIZ	TOZE	ZATI	ZETA	ZIZZ	ZUPA	

Z - 5-letter words

ABUZZ	AZOTE	BEZEL	BUZZY	CROZE	DOZER	FURZE	GAZER	GRAZE	HUZZA
ADZES	AZOTH	BEZES	BWAZI	CZARS	DOZES	FURZY	GAZES	GRIZE	HUZZY
AGAZE	AZURE	BLAZE	CEAZE	DARZI	FAZED	FUZEE	GAZON	HAMZA	IZARD
AIZLE	AZURN	BLITZ	CLOZE	DAZED	FAZES	FUZES	GAZOO	HAZED	IZZET
AMAZE	AZURY	BONZE	COLZA	DAZES	FEEZE	FUZZY	GHAZI	HAZEL	JAZZY
AVIZE	AZYGY	BOOZE	COZED	DIAZO	FEZES	GAUZE	GIZMO	HAZER	KANZU
AVYZE	AZYME	BOOZY	COZEN	DIZEN	FIZZY	GAUZY	GLAZE	HAZES	KARZY
AZANS	AZYMS	BRAZE	COZES	DIZZY	FRIZE	GAZAL	GLAZY	HEEZE	KAZIS
AZIDE	BAIZE	BRIZE	CRAZE	DOZED	FRIZZ	GAZED	GLITZ	HERTZ	KAZOO
AZOIC	BAZAR	BUAZE	CRAZY	DOZEN	FROZE	GAZEL	GLOZE	HIZEN	KLUTZ

KRANZ	MAZUT	OUZOS	RITZY	TIZZY	WEIZE	ZATIS	ZIGAN	ZOBUS	ZOONS
KUDZU	MEZES	OZEKI	ROZET	TOAZE	WHIZZ	ZAXES	ZILAS	ZOCCO	ZOPPO
LAZAR	MEZZO	OZONE	ROZIT	TOPAZ	WINZE	ZEALS	ZILCH	ZOEAE	ZORIL
LAZED	MILTZ	PEAZE	SARZA	TOUZE	WIZEN	ZEBEC	ZIMBI	ZOEAL	ZORRO
LAZES	MIZEN	PEIZE	SAZES	TOWZE	WOOTZ	ZEBRA	ZIMBS	ZOEAS	ZOWIE
LAZZI	MIZES	PIEZO	SEAZE	TOZED	WOOZY	ZEBUB	ZINCO	ZOISM	ZULUS
LAZZO	MOTZA	PIZES	SEIZE	TOZES	ZABRA	ZEBUS	ZINCS	ZOIST	ZUPAN
LEAZE	MOZED	PIZZA	SENZA	TOZIE	ZACKS	ZEINS	ZINCY	ZOMBI	ZUPAS
LEZES	MOZES	PLAZA	SIZAR	TZARS	ZAIRE	ZERDA	ZINEB	ZONAE	ZURFS
LEZZY	MUZZY	POZZY	SIZED	ULZIE	ZAMAN	ZEROS	ZINGS	ZONAL	ZUZES
LOZEN	NAZES	PRIZE	SIZEL	UNZIP	ZAMBO	ZESTS	ZINGY	ZONDA	ZYGAL
MAIZE	NAZIR	PUZEL	SIZER	VEZIR	ZAMIA	ZESTY	ZINKE	ZONED	ZYGON
MATZA	NEEZE	PZAZZ	SIZES	VIZIR	ZANJA	ZETAS	ZINKY	ZONES	ZYMES
MATZO	NIZAM	RAZED	SPITZ	VIZOR	ZANTE	ZEZES	ZIPPY	ZOOEA	ZYMIC
MAZED	OOZED	RAZEE	TAZZA	WALTZ	ZANZE	ZHOMO	ZIZEL	ZOOID	
MAZER	OOZES	RAZES	TAZZE	WANZE	ZAPPY	ZIBET	ZLOTY	ZOOKS	
MAZES	OUZEL	RAZOR	TEAZE	WAZIR	ZARFS	ZIFFS	ZOBOS	ZOOMS	

Z - 6-letter words

ABLAZE	BLAZED	DAZING	FUZZLE	HUZOOR	MEZZOS	PUTZES	SNOOZE	WINZES	ZIGGED
ABRAZO	BLAZER	DAZZLE	GAUZES	HUZZAS	MIZENS	PUZELS	SOZZLE	WIZARD	ZIGZAG
AGAZED	BLAZES	DEFUZE	GAZALS	IODIZE	MIZZEN	PUZZEL	SOZZLY	WIZENS	ZILLAH
AGNIZE	BLAZON	DIAZOS	GAZEBO	IONIZE	MIZZES	PUZZLE	STANZA	WIZIER	ZIMBIS
AGRIZE	BLINTZ	DIZAIN	GAZELS	IZARDS	MIZZLE	QUARTZ	STANZE	WUZZLE	ZIMMER
AGRYZE	BLOWZE	DIZENS	GAZERS	IZZARD	MIZZLY	QUEAZY	STANZO	YAKUZA	ZINCED
AGUIZE	BLOWZY	DONZEL	GAZIER	IZZETS	MOTZAS	QUINZE	SUIVEZ	ZABETA	ZINCKY
AIZLES	BONZER	DORIZE	GAZING	JAZIES	MOZING	RANZEL	SYZYGY	ZABRAS	ZINCOS
ALTEZA	BONZES	DOZENS	GAZONS	JAZZED	MOZZES	RAZEED	TAZZAS	ZADDIK	ZINEBS
AMAZED	BOOZED	DOZERS	GAZOON	JAZZES	MOZZIE	RAZEES	TEAZED	ZAFFER	ZINGED
AMAZES	BOOZER	DOZIER	GAZOOS	JEZAIL	MOZZLE	RAZING	TEAZEL	ZAFFRE	ZINGEL
AMAZON	BOOZES	DOZING	GAZUMP	JIZZES	MUZHIK	RAZORS	TEAZES	ZAGGED	ZINKED
APOZEM	BOOZEY	DRAZEL	GEEZER	KAMEEZ	MUZZLE	RAZURE	TEAZLE	ZAMANG	ZINKES
ASSIZE	BORZOI	DZEREN	GHAZAL	KANZUS	MZUNGU	RAZZED	TENZON	ZAMANS	ZINNIA
AVIZED	BRAIZE	ECZEMA	GHAZEL	KAZOOS	NAZIRS	RAZZES	TIZWAS	ZAMBOS	ZIPPED
AVIZES	BRAZED	ENTREZ	GHAZIS	KIBITZ	NEEZED	RAZZIA	TIZZES	ZAMIAS	ZIPPER
AVYZED	BRAZEN	ENZIAN	GIZMOS	KRANTZ	NEEZES	RAZZLE	TOAZED	ZANDER	ZIPTOP
AVYZES	BRAZES	ENZONE	GIZZEN	KUDZUS	NIZAMS	RHIZIC	TOAZES	ZANIED	ZIRCON
AZALEA	BRAZIL	ENZYME	GIZZES	LAZARS	NOZZLE	RIZARD	TOLZEY	ZANIER	ZITHER
AZIDES	BREEZE	EPIZOA	GLAZED	LAZIER	NUZZER	RIZZAR	TOUZED	ZANIES	ZIZELS
AZIONE	BREEZY	ERSATZ	GLAZEN	LAZILY	NUZZLE	RIZZER	TOUZES	ZANJAS	ZIZZED
AZOLLA	BRIZES	EVZONE	GLAZER	LAZING	NYANZA	RIZZOR	TOUZLE	ZANTES	ZIZZES
AZONAL	BRONZE	FAZING	GLAZES	LEAZES	OOZIER	ROZETS	TOWZED	ZANZES	ZLOTYS
AZONIC	BRONZY	FEEZED	GLITZY	LEZZES	OOZILY	ROZITS	TOWZES	ZAPATA	ZOCCOS
AZOTES	BROUZE	FEEZES	GLOZED	LIZARD	OOZING	ROZZER	TOWZIE	ZAPPED	ZODIAC
AZOTHS	BUAZES	FEZZED	GLOZES	LOZELL	OUZELS	SARZAS	TOZING	ZARAPE	ZOETIC
AZOTIC	BUZZED	FEZZES	GOZZAN	LOZENS	OYEZES	SAZHEN	TREZES	ZAREBA	ZOISMS
AZURES	BUZZER	FIZGIG	GRAZED	LUTZES	OZAENA	SAZZES	TUZZES	ZARIBA	ZOISTS
AZYMES	BUZZES	FIZZED	GRAZER	LUZERN	OZEKIS	SCAZON	TWEEZE	ZARNEC	ZOMBIE
BAIZED	BWAZIS	FIZZEN	GRAZES	LUZZES	OZONES	SCHIZO	ULZIES	ZEALOT	ZOMBIS
BAIZES	BYZANT	FIZZER	GRIZES	MAHZOR	PANZER	SCRUZE	UNZIPS	ZEBECK	ZONARY
BANZAI	CEAZED	FIZZES	GUIZER	MAIZES	PATZER	SEAZED	UPGAZE	ZEBECS	ZONATE
BAZAAR	CEAZES	FIZZLE	GUTZER	MATZAH	PAZAZZ	SEAZES	VEZIRS	ZEBRAS	ZONDAS
BAZARS	CHINTZ	FLOOZY	GUZZLE	MATZAS	PEAZED	SEIZED	VIZARD	ZEBUBS	ZONING
BAZAZZ	CIZERS	FOOZLE	HAMZAH	MATZOH	PEAZES	SEIZER	VIZIER	ZELANT	ZONKED
BEDAZE	COLZAS	FOZIER	HAMZAS	MATZOS	PEIZED	SEIZES	VIZIES	ZELOSO	ZONOID
BENZAL	COROZO	FRANZY	HAZARD	MATZOT	PEIZES	SEIZIN	VIZIRS	ZENANA	ZONULA
BENZIL	CORYZA	FRAZIL	HAZELS	MAZARD	PEZANT	SIZARS	VIZORS	ZENDIK	ZONULE
BENZOL	COZIER	FREEZE	HAZERS	MAZERS	PHEEZE	SIZELS	VIZSLA	ZENITH	ZOOEAE
BENZYL	COZIES	FRENZY	HAZIER	MAZHBI	PHIZOG	SIZERS	VIZZIE	ZEPHYR	ZOOEAL
BEZANT	COZING	FRIEZE	HAZILY	MAZIER	PIAZZA	SIZIER	WANZED	ZERDAS	ZOOEAS
BEZAZZ	COZZES	FRIZES	HAZING	MAZILY	PIZAZZ	SIZING	WANZES	ZEREBA	ZOOIDS
BEZELS	CRAZED	FRIZZY	HEEZED	MAZING	PIZZAS	SIZZLE	WAZIRS	ZERIBA	ZOOMED
BEZOAR	CRAZES	FROWZY	HEEZES	MAZOUT	PIZZLE	SLEAZE	WEAZEN	ZEROED	ZOONAL
BEZZLE	CROZES	FROZEN	HEEZIE	MAZUMA	PLAZAS	SLEAZY	WEIZED	ZEROTH	ZOONIC
BIZAZZ	CUZZES	FURZES	HIZENS	MAZUTS	PODZOL	SLEEZY	WEIZES	ZEUGMA	ZOOZOO
BIZONE	CZAPKA	FUZEES	HIZZED	MEAZEL	PRIZED	SNAZZY	WEZAND	ZHOMOS	ZORILS
BIZZES	DARZIS	FUZZED	HIZZES	MEZAIL	PRIZER	SNEEZE	WHEEZE	ZIBETS	ZORINO
BLAIZE		FUZZES	HOWZAT	MEZUZA	PRIZES	SNEEZY	WHEEZY	ZIGANS	ZORROS

| ZOSTER | ZUFOLI | ZUPANS | ZYGONS | ZYGOTE | ZYMITE | ZYMOME |
| ZOUNDS | ZUFOLO | ZYGOMA | ZYGOSE | ZYMASE | ZYMOID | ZYTHUM |

Z — 7-letter words

ABRAZOS	BEZANTS	CRAZILY	FIZZENS	HAZARDS	MESTIZA	PUZZELS	SNOOZES	WANZING
ADONIZE	BEZIQUE	CRAZING	FIZZERS	HAZELLY	MESTIZO	PUZZLED	SNOOZLE	WEAZAND
AGNIZED	BEZOARS	CROZIER	FIZZGIG	HAZIEST	METAZOA	PUZZLER	SNUZZLE	WEAZENS
AGNIZES	BEZZLED	CYANIZE	FIZZIER	HAZINGS	MEZAILS	PUZZLES	SOZZLED	WEIZING
AGONIZE	BEZZLES	CZAPKAS	FIZZING	HEEZIES	MEZUZAH	PZAZZES	SOZZLES	WEZANDS
AGRIZED	BIZARRE	CZARDAS	FIZZLED	HEEZING	MILTZES	QUARTZY	SPITZES	WHAIZLE
AGRIZES	BIZONAL	CZARDOM	FIZZLES	HEROIZE	MITZVAH	QUETZAL	SPREAZE	WHEEZED
AGRYZED	BIZONES	CZARINA	FLOOZIE	HERTZES	MIZMAZE	QUINZES	SPREEZE	WHEEZES
AGRYZES	BLAZERS	CZARISM	FOOZLED	HIZZING	MIZZENS	QUIZZED	SPULZIE	WHEEZLE
AGUIZED	BLAZING	CZARIST	FOOZLER	HOATZIN	MIZZLED	QUIZZER	SQUEEZE	WHIZZED
AGUIZES	BLAZONS	DAMOZEL	FOOZLES	HORIZON	MIZZLES	QUIZZES	SQUEEZY	WHIZZER
ALCAZAR	BLINTZE	DAZEDLY	FORZATI	HUMBUZZ	MOZETTA	RANZELS	STANZAS	WHIZZES
ALCORZA	BLITZED	DAZZLED	FORZATO	HUZOORS	MOZZIES	RAZURES	STANZES	WIZARDS
ALFEREZ	BLITZES	DAZZLER	FOZIEST	HUZZAED	MOZZLES	RAZZIAS	STANZOS	WIZENED
ALIZARI	BLOWZED	DAZZLES	FRAZILS	HUZZIES	MUEZZIN	RAZZING	STARETZ	WIZIERS
ALTEZAS	BLOWZES	DEFROZE	FRAZZLE	ICONIZE	MUZHIKS	RAZZLES	STYLIZE	WOOTZES
ALTEZZA	BONANZA	DEFUZED	FREEZER	IDOLIZE	MUZZIER	REALIZE	SUBZERO	WOOZIER
AMAZING	BOOZERS	DEFUZES	FREEZES	IODIZED	MUZZILY	REFROZE	SUBZONE	WOOZILY
AMAZONS	BOOZIER	DENIZEN	FRIEZED	IODIZES	MUZZLED	REPRIZE	SWAZZLE	WRIZLED
ANALYZE	BOOZILY	DIALYZE	FRIEZES	IONIZED	MUZZLER	RESEIZE	SWIZZES	WUZZLED
ANODIZE	BOOZING	DIARIZE	FRIZING	IONIZER	MUZZLES	RHIZINE	SWIZZLE	WUZZLES
ANZIANI	BORAZON	DIAZOES	FRIZZED	IONIZES	MYTHIZE	RHIZOID	SWOZZLE	ZABETAS
APOZEMS	BORZOIS	DIZAINS	FRIZZES	IRIDIZE	MZUNGUS	RHIZOME	TAILZIE	ZABTIEH
APPRIZE	BRAIZES	DIZENED	FRIZZLE	IRONIZE	NEEZING	RHIZOPI	TEAZELS	ZADDIKS
ARABIZE	BRAZENS	DIZZARD	FRIZZLY	ITEMIZE	NOZZLES	RIOTIZE	TEAZING	ZAFFERS
ASSIZED	BRAZIER	DIZZIED	FURZIER	IZZARDS	NUZZERS	RITZIER	TEAZLED	ZAFFRES
ASSIZER	BRAZILS	DIZZIER	FUZZIER	JACUZZI	NUZZLED	RIZARDS	TEAZLES	ZAGGING
ASSIZES	BRAZING	DIZZIES	FUZZILY	JANIZAR	NUZZLES	RIZZARS	TENDENZ	ZAKUSKA
ATHEIZE	BREEZED	DIZZILY	FUZZING	JAZZIER	NYANZAS	RIZZART	TENZONS	ZAKUSKI
ATOMIZE	BREEZES	DOCKIZE	FUZZLED	JAZZILY	OBELIZE	RIZZERS	TIZZIES	ZAMANGS
AVIZING	BRITZKA	DONZELS	FUZZLES	JAZZING	ODZOOKS	RIZZORS	TOAZING	ZAMARRA
AVYZING	BRONZED	DORIZED	GALLIZE	JAZZMAN	OOZIEST	ROZELLE	TOLZEYS	ZAMARRO
AZALEAS	BRONZEN	DORIZES	GAUZIER	JAZZMEN	ORGANZA	ROZETED	TOPAZES	ZAMOUSE
AZIMUTH	BRONZES	DOZENED	GAZEBOS	JEZAILS	OUTSIZE	ROZITED	TOUZING	ZANDERS
AZIONES	BROUZES	DOZENTH	GAZEFUL	KARZIES	OXAZINE	ROZZERS	TOUZLED	ZANELLA
AZOLLAS	BRULZIE	DOZIEST	GAZELLE	KIBBUTZ	OXIDIZE	SAZERAC	TOUZLES	ZANIEST
AZOTISE	BUMBAZE	DOZINGS	GAZETTE	KLUTZES	OZAENAS	SAZHENS	TOWZING	ZANJERO
AZOTIZE	BUZZARD	DRAZELS	GAZIEST	KOLKHOZ	OZONISE	SCAZONS	TRAPEZE	ZANYING
AZOTOUS	BUZZERS	DRIZZLE	GAZOOKA	KRANZES	OZONIZE	SCHERZI	TRIZONE	ZANYISM
AZULEJO	BUZZIER	DRIZZLY	GAZOONS	KYANIZE	PALAZZI	SCHERZO	TUILZIE	ZAPPIER
AZUREAN	BUZZING	DZERENS	GAZUMPS	LAICIZE	PALAZZO	SCHIZOS	TWEEZED	ZAPPING
AZURINE	BYZANTS	EBONIZE	GEEZERS	LAIRIZE	PANZERS	SCHMELZ	TWEEZES	ZAPTIAH
AZURITE	CADENZA	ECHOIZE	GENIZAH	LAZARET	PARAZOA	SCRUZED	TWIZZLE	ZAPTIEH
AZYGIES	CALZONE	ECTOZOA	GHAZALS	LAZIEST	PATZERS	SCRUZES	TZADDIK	ZARAPES
AZYGOUS	CALZONI	ECZEMAS	GHAZELS	LEZZIES	PEAZING	SEAZING	TZADDIQ	ZAREBAS
AZYMITE	CANZONA	EGOTIZE	GIZZARD	LIONIZE	PECTIZE	SEIZERS	TZIGANY	ZAREEBA
AZYMOUS	CANZONE	ELEGIZE	GIZZENS	LIZARDS	PEIZING	SEIZING	TZIMMES	ZARIBAS
BAIZING	CANZONI	EMBLAZE	GLAZERS	LOZELLS	PEPTIZE	SEIZINS	UNFAZED	ZARNECS
BAPTIZE	CAPSIZE	ENDOZOA	GLAZIER	LOZENGE	PEZANTS	SEIZURE	UNFROZE	ZARNICH
BAZAARS	CAZIQUE	ENFROZE	GLAZING	LOZENGY	PHEAZAR	SELTZER	UNGAZED	ZEALANT
BAZOOKA	CEAZING	ENTOZOA	GLITZES	LUZERNS	PHEEZED	SHMOOZE	UNITIZE	ZEALFUL
BEDAZED	CHALAZA	ENZIANS	GLOZING	MACHZOR	PHEEZES	SHOWBIZ	UNSIZED	ZEALOTS
BEDAZES	CHINTZY	ENZONED	GOZZANS	MADZOON	PHIZOGS	SIAMEZE	UNZONED	ZEALOUS
BEDIZEN	CHORIZO	ENZONES	GRAZERS	MATZAHS	PHIZZES	SIZABLE	UPGAZED	ZEBECKS
BEMAZED	CITIZEN	ENZYMES	GRAZIER	MATZOON	PIAZZAS	SIZIEST	UPGAZES	ZEBRASS
BENZALS	COALIZE	ENZYMIC	GRAZING	MATZOTH	PIZZLES	SIZINGS	UTILIZE	ZEBRINE
BENZENE	COGNIZE	EPIZOAN	GRIZZLE	MAZARDS	PODZOLS	SIZZLED	VIZARDS	ZEBROID
BENZILS	COROZOS	EPIZOIC	GRIZZLY	MAZEFUL	POETIZE	SIZZLER	VIZIERS	ZEBRULA
BENZINE	CORYZAS	EPIZOON	GUEREZA	MAZHBIS	POLYZOA	SIZZLES	VIZORED	ZEBRULE
BENZOIC	COZENED	EVZONES	GUIZERS	MAZIEST	POZZIES	SLEAZES	VIZSLAS	ZEDOARY
BENZOIN	COZENER	FAHLERZ	GUTZERS	MAZOUTS	PRENZIE	SNEEZED	VIZZIED	ZELANTS
BENZOLE	COZIERS	FANZINE	GUZZLED	MAZUMAS	PRETZEL	SNEEZER	VIZZIES	ZEMSTVO
BENZOLS	COZIEST	FEEZING	GUZZLER	MAZURKA	PREZZIE	SNEEZES	WALTZED	ZENANAS
BENZOYL	CRAZIER	FILAZER	GUZZLES	MAZZARD	PRIZERS	SNOOZED	WALTZER	ZENDIKS
BENZYLS	CRAZIES	FIZGIGS	HAMZAHS	MEAZELS	PRIZING	SNOOZER	WALTZES	ZENITHS

ZEOLITE	ZIFFIUS	ZINCIFY	ZINKIER	ZIZZING	ZONULAS	ZOOLOGY	ZORILLE	ZYGOTIC
ZEPHYRS	ZIGANKA	ZINCING	ZINKIFY	ZOARIUM	ZONULES	ZOOMING	ZORILLO	ZYMASES
ZEREBAS	ZIGGING	ZINCITE	ZINKING	ZOCCOLO	ZONULET	ZOONITE	ZORINOS	ZYMITES
ZERIBAS	ZIGZAGS	ZINCKED	ZINNIAS	ZODIACS	ZOOECIA	ZOONOMY	ZOSTERS	ZYMOGEN
ZEROING	ZILCHES	ZINCODE	ZIPPERS	ZOEFORM	ZOOGAMY	ZOOPERY	ZUFFOLI	ZYMOMES
ZESTFUL	ZILLAHS	ZINCOID	ZIPPIER	ZOISITE	ZOOGENY	ZOOTAXY	ZUFFOLO	ZYMOSES
ZESTIER	ZILLION	ZINCOUS	ZIPPING	ZOMBIES	ZOOGONY	ZOOTOMY	ZYGOMAS	ZYMOSIS
ZETETIC	ZIMMERS	ZINGELS	ZIRCONS	ZONATED	ZOOIDAL	ZOOTYPE	ZYGOSES	ZYMOTIC
ZEUGMAS	ZIMOCCA	ZINGIER	ZITHERN	ZONINGS	ZOOLITE	ZOOZOOS	ZYGOSIS	ZYMURGY
ZEUXITE	ZINCIER	ZINGING	ZITHERS	ZONULAR	ZOOLITH	ZORGITE	ZYGOTES	ZYTHUMS

Z - 8-letter words

ADONIZED	BAROMETZ	CANONIZE	DIMERIZE	FANZINES	GRAZIERS	LAICIZED	MUZZIEST
ADONIZES	BARTIZAN	CANZONAS	DISPRIZE	FARADIZE	GRAZINGS	LAICIZES	MUZZLERS
AGNIZING	BAZAZZES	CANZONET	DISSEIZE	FEMINIZE	GRAZIOSO	LAIRIZED	MUZZLING
AGONIZED	BAZOOKAS	CAPONIZE	DIVINIZE	FILAZERS	GRIZZLED	LAIRIZES	MYTHIZED
AGONIZES	BEDAZING	CAPSIZAL	DIZENING	FINALIZE	GRIZZLER	LAZARETS	MYTHIZES
AGRIZING	BEDAZZLE	CAPSIZED	DIZZARDS	FIZZGIGS	GRIZZLES	LAZINESS	NASALIZE
AGRYZING	BEDIZENS	CAPSIZES	DIZZIEST	FIZZIEST	GUEREZAS	LAZULITE	NEBULIZE
AGUIZING	BENZENES	CATALYZE	DIZZYING	FIZZINGS	GUZZLERS	LAZURITE	NODALIZE
ALBITIZE	BENZINES	CAZIQUES	DOCKIZED	FIZZLING	GUZZLING	LEGALIZE	NOMADIZE
ALCAZARS	BENZOATE	CHALAZAE	DOCKIZES	FLOOZIES	HAZARDED	LIONIZED	NOTARIZE
ALCORZAS	BENZOINS	CHALAZAS	DORIZING	FLUIDIZE	HAZARDRY	LIONIZES	NOVELIZE
ALGUAZIL	BENZOLES	CHINTZES	DOUZEPER	FOCALIZE	HAZELNUT	LOCALIZE	NUZZLING
ALIZARIN	BENZOYLS	CHORIZOS	DOZENING	FOOZLERS	HAZINESS	LOGICIZE	OBELIZED
ALIZARIS	BEZAZZES	CHUTZPAH	DOZENTHS	FOOZLING	HEPATIZE	LOZENGED	OBELIZES
ALKALIZE	BEZIQUES	CITIZENS	DOZINESS	FORZANDI	HEROIZED	LOZENGES	OOZINESS
ALTEZZAS	BEZONIAN	CIVILIZE	DRIZZLED	FORZANDO	HEROIZES	LYSOZYME	OPALIZED
AMAZEDLY	BEZZLING	COALIZED	DRIZZLES	FORZATOS	HOACTZIN	MACARIZE	OPTIMIZE
AMORTIZE	BIZAZZES	COALIZES	DYNAMIZE	FOZINESS	HOATZINS	MADERIZE	ORGANIZE
ANALYZED	BIZCACHA	COENZYME	EBENEZER	FRANZIER	HOLOZOIC	MADZOONS	ORGANZAS
ANALYZER	BLAZONED	COGNIZED	EBIONIZE	FRAZZLED	HORIZONS	MAGAZINE	OUTPRIZE
ANALYZES	BLAZONER	COGNIZES	EBONIZED	FRAZZLES	HOWITZER	MAHZORIM	OUTSIZED
ANNALIZE	BLAZONRY	COLONIZE	EBONIZES	FREEZERS	HUMANIZE	MANZELLO	OUTSIZES
ANODIZED	BLINTZES	COZENAGE	ECHOIZED	FREEZING	HUZZAING	MARZIPAN	OVERSIZE
ANODIZES	BLITZING	COZENERS	ECHOIZES	FRENZIED	HYDROZOA	MATZOONS	OXAZINES
ANTICIZE	BLIZZARD	COZENING	ECTOZOAN	FRENZIES	ICONIZED	MAXIMIZE	OXIDIZED
APHETIZE	BLOWZIER	CRAZIEST	ECTOZOIC	FRIEZING	ICONIZES	MAZARINE	OXIDIZER
APHORIZE	BONANZAS	CREDENZA	ECTOZOON	FRIZZIER	IDEALIZE	MAZEMENT	OXIDIZES
APPETIZE	BOOZIEST	CREUTZER	EGOTIZED	FRIZZING	IDOLIZED	MAZINESS	OZONISED
APPRIZED	BORAZONS	CROZIERS	EGOTIZES	FRIZZLED	IDOLIZER	MAZURKAS	OZONISER
APPRIZER	BOTANIZE	CRUZEIRO	ELEGIZED	FRIZZLES	IDOLIZES	MAZZARDS	OZONISES
APPRIZES	BOUZOUKI	CURARIZE	ELEGIZES	FROWZIER	IMMUNIZE	MELODIZE	OZONIZED
ARABIZED	BOZZETTI	CUTINIZE	EMBEZZLE	FURZIEST	INFAMIZE	MEMORIZE	OZONIZER
ARABIZES	BOZZETTO	CYANIZED	EMBLAZED	FUZZIEST	IODIZING	MESPRIZE	OZONIZES
ARCHAIZE	BRAZENED	CYANIZES	EMBLAZES	FUZZLING	IONIZERS	MESTIZAS	PAGANIZE
ARMOZEEN	BRAZENLY	CZARDOMS	EMBLAZON	GADZOOKS	IONIZING	MESTIZOS	PAPALIZE
ARMOZINE	BRAZENRY	CZAREVNA	EMPERIZE	GALLIZED	IRIDIZED	METAZOAN	PARALYZE
ASSIZERS	BRAZIERS	CZARINAS	ENDOZOIC	GALLIZES	IRIDIZES	METAZOIC	PARAZOAN
ASSIZING	BREEZIER	CZARISMS	ENDOZOON	GARBANZO	IRONIZED	METAZOON	PARAZOON
ATHEIZED	BREEZILY	CZARISTS	ENERGIZE	GAUZIEST	IRONIZES	MEZEREON	PARTIZAN
ATHEIZES	BREEZING	CZARITZA	ENFREEZE	GAZEBOES	ITEMIZED	MEZEREUM	PAZAZZES
ATHETIZE	BRITZKAS	DAMOZELS	ENFROZEN	GAZELLES	ITEMIZES	MEZUZAHS	PECTIZED
ATMOLYZE	BRITZSKA	DAZZLERS	ENTOZOAL	GAZEMENT	JACUZZIS	MEZUZOTH	PECTIZES
ATOMIZED	BRONZIER	DAZZLING	ENTOZOIC	GAZETTED	JANIZARS	MINIMIZE	PENALIZE
ATOMIZER	BRONZIFY	DEFREEZE	ENTOZOON	GAZETTES	JANIZARY	MISPRIZE	PEPTIZED
ATOMIZES	BRONZING	DEFROZEN	ENZONING	GAZOGENE	JAZERANT	MITZVAHS	PEPTIZES
AUTOLYZE	BRONZITE	DEFUZING	ENZOOTIC	GAZOOKAS	JAZZIEST	MITZVOTH	PETUNTZE
AZIMUTHS	BRUILZIE	DEMONIZE	EPIZOANS	GAZPACHO	JUMBOIZE	MIZMAZES	PEZIZOID
AZOTISED	BRULZIES	DENAZIFY	EQUALIZE	GAZUMPED	KAMEEZES	MIZZLIER	PHEAZARS
AZOTISES	BULLDOZE	DENIZENS	ERGOTIZE	GENIZAHS	KAMIKAZE	MIZZLING	PHEAZING
AZOTIZED	BUMBAZED	DEPUTIZE	ERSATZES	GIZZARDS	KAZATZKA	MOBILIZE	PHEEZING
AZOTIZES	BUMBAZES	DIALYZED	ETERNIZE	GIZZENED	KIBITZED	MONAZITE	PIAZZIAN
AZULEJOS	BUZZARDS	DIALYZER	ETHERIZE	GLAZIERS	KIBITZER	MONETIZE	PIROZHKI
AZURINES	BUZZIEST	DIALYZES	ETHICIZE	GLAZIEST	KIBITZES	MORALIZE	PIZAZZES
AZURITES	BUZZINGS	DIARIZED	EULOGIZE	GLAZINGS	KRANTZES	MOTORIZE	PIZZERIA
AZYMITES	CADENZAS	DIARIZES	EUPHUIZE	GLITZIER	KREUTZER	MOZETTAS	POETIZED
BAPTIZED	CALZONES	DIAZEPAM	EXORCIZE	GLOZINGS	KYANIZED	MOZETTES	POETIZES
BAPTIZES	CANALIZE	DIGITIZE	FABULIZE	GOLDSIZE	KYANIZES	MUEZZINS	POLARIZE
							POLEMIZE

POLONIZE	RIGIDIZE	SLEEZIER	SUZERAIN	UNITIZES	ZABAIONE	ZIGZAGGY	ZOOMETRY
POLYZOAN	RIOTIZES	SMORZATO	SWAZZLES	UNMUZZLE	ZABTIEHS	ZIKKURAT	ZOOMORPH
POLYZOIC	RITZIEST	SNAZZIER	SWIZZLED	UNPRIZED	ZADDIKIM	ZILLIONS	ZOONITES
POLYZOON	RIVALIZE	SNEEZERS	SWIZZLES	UNSEIZED	ZAMARRAS	ZIMOCCAS	ZOONITIC
PRETZELS	RIZZARED	SNEEZIER	SWOZZLES	UNVIZARD	ZAMARROS	ZINCIEST	ZOONOMIA
PREZZIES	RIZZARTS	SNEEZING	SYZYGIAL	UNZIPPED	ZAMBOMBA	ZINCITES	ZOONOMIC
PRIZABLE	RIZZERED	SNOOZERS	SYZYGIES	UPGAZING	ZAMINDAR	ZINCKIER	ZOONOSES
PROTOZOA	RIZZORED	SNOOZING	TAILZIES	URBANIZE	ZAMOUSES	ZINCKIFY	ZOONOSIS
PTYALIZE	ROBOTIZE	SNOOZLED	TEAZELED	UTILIZED	ZAMPOGNA	ZINCKING	ZOONOTIC
PUZZLERS	ROYALIZE	SNOOZLES	TEAZLING	UTILIZER	ZANELLAS	ZINCODES	ZOOPATHY
PUZZLING	ROZELLES	SNUZZLED	TERRAZZO	UTILIZES	ZANJEROS	ZINGIBER	ZOOPERAL
PYRITIZE	ROZETING	SNUZZLES	TERZETTA	VALORIZE	ZANYISMS	ZINGIEST	ZOOPHILE
PYROLYZE	ROZITING	SOBERIZE	TERZETTI	VAPORIZE	ZAPPIEST	ZINKIEST	ZOOPHILY
QUANTIZE	RURALIZE	SODOMIZE	TERZETTO	VELARIZE	ZAPTIAHS	ZIPPERED	ZOOPHYTE
QUARTZES	SAMIZDAT	SOLARIZE	TETANIZE	VITALIZE	ZAPTIEHS	ZIPPIEST	ZOOSCOPY
QUATORZE	SANITIZE	SOLECIZE	THEORIZE	VIZAMENT	ZARATITE	ZIRCONIA	ZOOSPERM
QUEAZIER	SARRAZIN	SOLONETZ	THIAZIDE	VIZARDED	ZAREEBAS	ZIRCONIC	ZOOSPORE
QUETZALS	SATIRIZE	SORORIZE	TIZWASES	VIZCACHA	ZARNICHS	ZITHERNS	ZOOTHOME
QUIZZERS	SAZERACS	SOZZLIER	TOPAZINE	VIZIRATE	ZARZUELA	ZOARIUMS	ZOOTOMIC
QUIZZERY	SCHERZOS	SOZZLING	TOTALIZE	VIZIRIAL	ZASTRUGA	ZOCCOLOS	ZOOTOXIN
QUIZZIFY	SCHIZOID	SPETSNAZ	TOUZLING	VIZORING	ZASTRUGI	ZODIACAL	ZOOTROPE
QUIZZING	SCHIZONT	SPETZNAZ	TRAPEZED	VOCALIZE	ZEALANTS	ZOETROPE	ZOOTYPES
RACEMIZE	SCHMALTZ	SPREAZED	TRAPEZES	VOWELIZE	ZEALLESS	ZOIATRIA	ZOOTYPIC
RAZEEING	SCHMOOZE	SPREAZES	TRAPEZIA	WALTZERS	ZEALOTRY	ZOISITES	ZOPILOTE
RAZMATAZ	SCRUZING	SPREEZED	TRIZONAL	WALTZING	ZEBRINNY	ZOMBIISM	ZORGITES
REALIZED	SEIZABLE	SPREEZES	TRIZONES	WEAZANDS	ZEBRULAS	ZOMBORUK	ZORILLES
REALIZER	SEIZINGS	SPRITZER	TUILZIED	WEAZENED	ZEBRULES	ZONATION	ZORILLOS
REALIZES	SEIZURES	SPRITZIG	TUILZIES	WHAIZLED	ZECCHINE	ZONELESS	ZUCCHINI
REFREEZE	SELTZERS	SPUILZIE	TUTORIZE	WHAIZLES	ZECCHINI	ZONULETS	ZUCHETTA
REFROZEN	SFORZATI	SPULZIED	TWEEZERS	WHEEZIER	ZECCHINO	ZOOBLAST	ZUCHETTO
REGULIZE	SFORZATO	SPULZIES	TWEEZING	WHEEZILY	ZEMINDAR	ZOOCHORE	ZUGZWANG
RENDZINA	SHMOOZED	SQUEEZED	TWIZZLED	WHEEZING	ZEMSTVOS	ZOOCHORY	ZYGAENID
REPRIZED	SHMOOZES	SQUEEZER	TWIZZLES	WHEEZLED	ZENITHAL	ZOOCYTIA	ZYGANTRA
REPRIZES	SIAMEZED	SQUEEZES	TZADDIKS	WHEEZLES	ZEOLITES	ZOOECIUM	ZYGODONT
RESEIZED	SIAMEZES	STANZAIC	TZADDIQS	WHIZZERS	ZEOLITIC	ZOOGENIC	ZYLONITE
RESEIZES	SIMILIZE	STANZOES	UNAMAZED	WHIZZING	ZEPPELIN	ZOOGLOEA	ZYMOGENS
RESINIZE	SINICIZE	STRELITZ	UNDAZZLE	WIZARDLY	ZERUMBET	ZOOGRAFT	ZYMOLOGY
RHIZINES	SIZEABLE	STYLIZED	UNFREEZE	WIZARDRY	ZESTIEST	ZOOLATER	ZYMOTICS
RHIZOBIA	SIZINESS	STYLIZES	UNFROZEN	WIZENING	ZETETICS	ZOOLATRY	
RHIZOIDS	SIZZLERS	SUBERIZE	UNGLAZED	WOMANIZE	ZEUXITES	ZOOLITES	
RHIZOMES	SIZZLING	SUBSIZAR	UNGRAZED	WOOZIEST	ZIBELINE	ZOOLITHS	
RHIZOPOD	SLEAZIER	SUBZONAL	UNIONIZE	WURTZITE	ZIGANKAS	ZOOLITIC	
RHIZOPUS	SLEAZILY	SUBZONES	UNITIZED	WUZZLING	ZIGGURAT	ZOOMANCY	

HINT

Q But No U

If you are not familiar with *Official Scrabble Words* you may be unaware that there are several words that contain Q with no U. These are all to be found in the Q lists but it is worth highlighting them separately. Write them down and learn them all. They are so vital in situations that would otherwise necessitate a change.

INQILAB, QADI, QALAMDAN, QANAT, QAT, QIBLA, QIGONG, QINTAR, QWERTY, TALAQ, TSADDIQ, TSADDIQIM, TZADDIQ, TZADDIQIM

Note that plural forms of these are also allowed except for TSADDIQIM and TZADDIQIM which are already plural. Also note BURQA, MUQADDAM and SUQ have a U but not after the Q.

HINT _____

Do-It-Yourself Six-Letter Sets

The 200 six-letter combinations in this book represent those most useful to the Scrabble player. There are many more combinations that are useful to study and, as is nearly always the case, compiling lists yourself not only helps you memorize the words but is also more interesting than simply learning from those readily provided. Try deriving your own six-letter combination lists based on names (SHEILA, ALBERT, etc) or fictitious words (INCORE, POSIER, etc) as mnemonics. The Anagram section will be your ideal hunting-ground for this exercise.

HINT _____

Learning The J Q X Z Words

If you have trouble remembering those useful words containg the J Q X or Z then try the following solo game as a learning exercise. Take the J X Z Q and one U out of the letter bag and put to one side. Take six letters at random from the letter bag and place on your rack. Then give yourself a couple of minutes with each of J Q X and Z to see how many different words you can make by combining them with the six letters on your rack. When playing with the Q, if you haven't also picked a U, utilize the U you you've put to one side. Make a note of the highest scoring play you found with each of J Q X and Z and then check with the lists in this book to see if there was anything you missed. Having completed the exercise with the first rack, play any word from your six letters on the board, keeping the J Q X Z and U to one side, and return any remaining letters to the bag. Select another six letters at random for the second turn. repeat the exercise with the fresh rack and so on.

HINT _____

Tile-Tracking

It is acceptable in tournament Scrabble to have a note of the letter distribution and to use it during play as a checklist of what letters are still to come. Most top players use this method to enable them to work out what tiles their opponents have at the end of the game. Such a checklist, when used skilfully, can also provide mid-game information about likely pickups and enable the right combination of tiles to be kept on the rack to give the greatest possibility of playing a bonus word. If you practise tile-tracking whilst playing you will soon find you are more aware of the letter distribution which in turn will assist you to maintain a balanced rack. Even if you don't track all the tiles, keeping a note of the vowels, the S's and blanks, the J Q X Z and the awkward consonants C V and K, will help improve your rack management.

SECTION TWO

ENDINGS

Introduction

Scrabble players naturally think about beginnings of words when they are looking for a play. Can I find a word beginning with BE- or DIS- or QU- or RE- or UN-? As a player becomes more adept, he or she will consider the more obvious endings, such as -ED and -ER and -IER and -ING, and even the humble -S.

The subsequent lists offer a variety of words arranged according to their endings rather than their beginnings. The first set of lists covers useful suffixes, and the second set of lists addresses words ending with the vowels A, I, O and U.

USEFUL SUFFIXES

The following sets of lists offer seven and eight-letter words ending with these suffixes:

-ABLE	-IBLE	-MAN
-AGE	-INGS	-MEN
-EST	-ISH	-OUS
-FUL	-LY	-TION

Those ending with -INGS, -LY and -EST should be especially useful. There are many times that Scrabble players ponder questions such as:

'I know HOSTING is a word, but does it take an S?'
'I know SULTRY is all right, but what about SULTRILY?'
'I know the adjective OARY, but is the superlative OARIEST
    acceptable?'

Familiarity with the lists here should provide instant answers to these and similar questions. In the case of the -EST words, where these are superlatives, it can be implied that the corresponding comparatives ending in -ER are also acceptable, eg OARIER.

There are naturally many other endings useful to the Scrabble player besides those listed here, -OID, -ISM and -IST for example. Those shown here are meant only as a selection. For easy compilation of lists of other endings consult *Chambers Back-Words*, which shows all words according to alphabetical sequence of endings.

WORDS ENDING IN -ABLE

7-letter words -ABLE

ACCABLE	CURABLE	EFFABLE	HATABLE	MIXABLE	PAYABLE	RULABLE	TAKABLE	VOLABLE
AFFABLE	DATABLE	EQUABLE	HIRABLE	MOVABLE	PLIABLE	SALABLE	TAMABLE	
AMIABLE	DISABLE	ERRABLE	LIKABLE	MUTABLE	POTABLE	SAVABLE	TAXABLE	
ASTABLE	DOWABLE	FADABLE	LIVABLE	NAMABLE	RATABLE	SAYABLE	TENABLE	
BATABLE	DUPABLE	FINABLE	LOSABLE	NOTABLE	RETABLE	SEEABLE	TRIABLE	
BUYABLE	DURABLE	FIXABLE	LOVABLE	PACABLE	RIDABLE	SIZABLE	TUNABLE	
CAPABLE	DYEABLE	FLYABLE	MAKABLE	PAPABLE	ROPABLE	SKIABLE	UNHABLE	
CITABLE	EATABLE	FRIABLE	MIRABLE	PARABLE	ROWABLE	SUEABLE	VOCABLE	

8-letter words -ABLE

ABATABLE	BOOKABLE	ERASABLE	GUIDABLE	ISSUABLE	MAILABLE	PINTABLE	RENTABLE
ADORABLE	CLUBABLE	EVADABLE	GULLABLE	KICKABLE	MAKEABLE	PITIABLE	REUSABLE
AMENABLE	COOKABLE	EVITABLE	GUSTABLE	KISSABLE	MISSABLE	PLACABLE	RIDEABLE
AMICABLE	CULPABLE	EXORABLE	HANGABLE	KNOWABLE	MOCKABLE	PLAYABLE	RINSABLE
AMUSABLE	CURBABLE	EXPIABLE	HATEABLE	LAPSABLE	MOOTABLE	PORTABLE	ROLLABLE
ARGUABLE	DAMNABLE	FELLABLE	HEALABLE	LAUDABLE	MOVEABLE	POSEABLE	ROPEABLE
AVOWABLE	DATEABLE	FILMABLE	HELPABLE	LEASABLE	NAMEABLE	POURABLE	RUINABLE
BAILABLE	DENIABLE	FISHABLE	HIREABLE	LETTABLE	OATHABLE	PRIZABLE	RUNNABLE
BANKABLE	DIGGABLE	FOLDABLE	HUGGABLE	LEVIABLE	OPENABLE	PROBABLE	SAILABLE
BEARABLE	DISHABLE	FORDABLE	HUMMABLE	LIFTABLE	OPERABLE	PROVABLE	SALEABLE
BEATABLE	DRAWABLE	FORMABLE	IMITABLE	LIKEABLE	OPINABLE	QUOTABLE	SALVABLE
BEDDABLE	DRIVABLE	FUNDABLE	INARABLE	LIQUABLE	PALPABLE	RAISABLE	SATIABLE
BIDDABLE	DUTIABLE	GAINABLE	INSTABLE	LIVEABLE	PANTABLE	RATEABLE	SCALABLE
BISTABLE	EDUCABLE	GETTABLE	INVIABLE	LOANABLE	PASSABLE	READABLE	SEIZABLE
BLAMABLE	ENVIABLE	GRADABLE	ISOLABLE	LOVEABLE	PECCABLE	RELIABLE	SELLABLE

SHAKABLE	SOLVABLE	SYLLABLE	TELLABLE	TRADABLE	VARIABLE	WARHABLE	WORKABLE
SHAPABLE	SORTABLE	TAKEABLE	TESTABLE	TUNEABLE	VIEWABLE	WASHABLE	WRITABLE
SINGABLE	SPARABLE	TALKABLE	TILLABLE	UNSTABLE	VIOLABLE	WEARABLE	
SIZEABLE	STATABLE	TAMEABLE	TILTABLE	UNUSABLE	VITIABLE	WELDABLE	
SMOKABLE	STORABLE	TANNABLE	TITHABLE	UNVIABLE	VOIDABLE	WILLABLE	
SOCIABLE	SUITABLE	TASTABLE	TOLLABLE	VALUABLE	WALKABLE	WINNABLE	

WORDS ENDING IN -AGE

7-letter words -AGE

ABUSAGE	BROKAGE	CRANAGE	GUNNAGE	MILEAGE	PLUSAGE	SACKAGE	TANKAGE	VINTAGE
ACREAGE	BUOYAGE	DISCAGE	HAULAGE	MINTAGE	PONDAGE	SALVAGE	TANNAGE	VITRAGE
AJUTAGE	BURGAGE	DOCKAGE	HERBAGE	MOCKAGE	PONTAGE	SAUSAGE	TEENAGE	VOLTAGE
AMENAGE	CABBAGE	DRAYAGE	HOSTAGE	MONTAGE	PORTAGE	SCAVAGE	TENTAGE	WAFTAGE
APANAGE	CARNAGE	DUNNAGE	KEELAGE	MOORAGE	POSTAGE	SCUTAGE	THANAGE	WAINAGE
ARRIAGE	CARTAGE	ESCUAGE	KIPPAGE	MOULAGE	POTTAGE	SEEPAGE	TILLAGE	WANTAGE
ASSUAGE	CENTAGE	ETALAGE	LAIRAGE	OUTRAGE	PRESAGE	SELVAGE	TOLLAGE	WASTAGE
ASSWAGE	COINAGE	FALDAGE	LASTAGE	OUVRAGE	PRIMAGE	SERFAGE	TONNAGE	WATTAGE
AULNAGE	COLLAGE	FARDAGE	LEAFAGE	PACKAGE	PRISAGE	SINKAGE	TRUCAGE	WEFTAGE
AVERAGE	COMPAGE	FLOTAGE	LEAKAGE	PANNAGE	PROPAGE	SOAKAGE	TUNNAGE	WINDAGE
BAGGAGE	CORDAGE	FLOWAGE	LIGNAGE	PASSAGE	QUAYAGE	SOCCAGE	UMBRAGE	WORDAGE
BANDAGE	CORKAGE	FOGGAGE	LINEAGE	PAYSAGE	RAMPAGE	SONDAGE	UPSTAGE	YARDAGE
BARRAGE	CORNAGE	FOLIAGE	LINKAGE	PEERAGE	REMUAGE	SPINAGE	VANTAGE	
BONDAGE	CORSAGE	FOOTAGE	LOCKAGE	PEONAGE	RESTAGE	STORAGE	VENDAGE	
BOSCAGE	COTTAGE	FULLAGE	LUGGAGE	PIERAGE	RIBCAGE	STOWAGE	VENTAGE	
BREWAGE	COURAGE	GARBAGE	MASSAGE	PILLAGE	ROOTAGE	SULLAGE	VIDUAGE	
BROCAGE	COWHAGE	GUIDAGE	MESSAGE	PLUMAGE	RUMMAGE	TALLAGE	VILLAGE	

8-letter words -AGE

ACCORAGE	BLOCKAGE	DIALLAGE	FRONDAGE	MALAXAGE	PUPILAGE	STEERAGE	TUTORAGE
ACIERAGE	BREAKAGE	DISUSAGE	FRONTAGE	MARITAGE	ROUGHAGE	STERNAGE	UMPIRAGE
ADJUTAGE	BROCKAGE	DRAINAGE	FROTTAGE	MARRIAGE	SABOTAGE	STILLAGE	VAULTAGE
AGIOTAGE	CABOTAGE	DRESSAGE	FRUITAGE	MESSUAGE	SEWERAGE	STOPPAGE	VAUNTAGE
ALIENAGE	CARRIAGE	DRIFTAGE	FUSELAGE	METAYAGE	SHORTAGE	STREWAGE	VERBIAGE
ALTARAGE	CARUCAGE	ENALLAGE	GRAINAGE	MISUSAGE	SLIPPAGE	STUMPAGE	VICARAGE
AMPERAGE	CHANTAGE	ENDAMAGE	GRILLAGE	MORTGAGE	SMALLAGE	SUBSTAGE	VICINAGE
APPANAGE	CHUMMAGE	ENSILAGE	GROUPAGE	MUCILAGE	SPILLAGE	SUFFRAGE	WAGONAGE
BADINAGE	CLEARAGE	ENVISAGE	GUARDAGE	OVERPAGE	SPOILAGE	TASSWAGE	WATERAGE
BARONAGE	CLEAVAGE	EQUIPAGE	HELOTAGE	PILOTAGE	SPOUSAGE	THIRLAGE	WEIGHAGE
BERTHAGE	CLOUDAGE	FERRIAGE	HERITAGE	PLANTAGE	SQUIRAGE	TRACKAGE	WHARFAGE
BEVERAGE	COVERAGE	FLOATAGE	LANGRAGE	PLUSSAGE	STAFFAGE	TRUCKAGE	WRAPPAGE
BIRDCAGE	COZENAGE	FOOTPAGE	LANGUAGE	POUNDAGE	STALLAGE	TRUQUAGE	WRECKAGE
BLINDAGE	CRIBBAGE	FRAUTAGE	LEVERAGE	PUCELAGE	STEARAGE	TUTELAGE	

WORDS ENDING IN -EST

7-letter words -EST

ACHIEST	BABIEST	CAMPEST	DANKEST	DOPIEST	EERIEST	FOXIEST	HAZIEST	JOKIEST
ACIDEST	BALDEST	CANIEST	DARKEST	DOTIEST	EGGIEST	FOZIEST	HEPPEST	JUSTEST
ACQUEST	BARGEST	CANTEST	DEADEST	DOUCEST	ELMIEST	FULLEST	HIGHEST	KEENEST
ACUTEST	BASSEST	CHICEST	DEAFEST	DOUREST	EVENEST	FUMIEST	HIPPEST	KINDEST
ADDREST	BEQUEST	CLOSEST	DEAREST	DOVIEST	FABBEST	GABFEST	HOKIEST	LACIEST
AERIEST	BIGGEST	COKIEST	DEEDEST	DOWIEST	FADIEST	GAINEST	HOLIEST	LAKIEST
AGILEST	BLATEST	COLDEST	DEEPEST	DOZIEST	FAINEST	GAMIEST	HOMIEST	LANGEST
AIRIEST	BLUIEST	CONFEST	DEFTEST	DROLEST	FAIREST	GAZIEST	HOTTEST	LANKEST
AMPLEST	BOLDEST	CONGEST	DEIDEST	DUFFEST	FALSEST	GLUIEST	ICKIEST	LARGEST
ANAPEST	BONIEST	CONTEST	DENSEST	DULLEST	FASTEST	GOLDEST	IFFIEST	LAZIEST
ARCHEST	BOSSEST	COOLEST	DEWIEST	DUMBEST	FATTEST	GOOIEST	IMPREST	LEANEST
ARIDEST	BOXIEST	COSIEST	DICIEST	DUNNEST	FELLEST	GORIEST	INANEST	LENGEST
ARTIEST	BRAVEST	COXIEST	DIKIEST	DUSKEST	FIKIEST	GOWDEST	INKIEST	LEWDEST
ASHIEST	BRAWEST	COZIEST	DIMMEST	DYKIEST	FIRMEST	GRAVEST	INLIEST	LIEFEST
AULDEST	BUSIEST	CRUDEST	DINKEST	EARNEST	FITTEST	GRAYEST	INQUEST	LIEVEST
AVIDEST	CAGIEST	CURTEST	DISGEST	EASIEST	FLUIEST	GREYEST	IRATEST	LIMIEST
AWAREST	CAKIEST	DAFTEST	DISNEST	EDGIEST	FONDEST	HARDEST	ISMIEST	LIMPEST
AWNIEST	CALMEST	DAMPEST	DOMIEST	EELIEST	FOULEST	HARVEST	JIMPEST	LINIEST

LITHEST	MIMMEST	NUMBEST	PINIEST	RATHEST	SAIREST	STEYEST	TRITEST	WAVIEST
LONGEST	MINIEST	OAKIEST	PINKEST	REALEST	SALTEST	SUAVEST	TUNIEST	WAXIEST
LOOSEST	MIRIEST	OARIEST	PIPIEST	REDDEST	SAMIEST	SUGGEST	UGLIEST	WEAKEST
LOTHEST	MIRKEST	OBESEST	POKIEST	REQUEST	SEAREST	TAKIEST	UNBLEST	WETTEST
LOUDEST	MITIEST	OILIEST	POOREST	RICHEST	SEXIEST	TALLEST	UNDREST	WHITEST
LOWSEST	MIXIEST	OORIEST	PORIEST	RICIEST	SICKEST	TANNEST	VAGUEST	WILDEST
LUSHEST	MOOTEST	OOSIEST	POSHEST	RIMIEST	SIZIEST	TARTEST	VAINEST	WILIEST
MADDEST	MOPIEST	OOZIEST	POXIEST	ROKIEST	SKEWEST	TAUTEST	VASTEST	WILLEST
MAINEST	MOTIEST	OPENEST	PRONEST	ROPIEST	SKYIEST	TEDIEST	VERIEST	WINIEST
MATIEST	MURKEST	ORBIEST	PROTEST	RORIEST	SLOWEST	TEMPEST	VINIEST	WIRIEST
MAUVEST	NAIFEST	OURIEST	PROWEST	ROSIEST	SNIDEST	TENSEST	VOGIEST	WOTTEST
MAZIEST	NAIVEST	OUTJEST	PUIREST	RUBIEST	SOFTEST	TERSEST	WALIEST	WOWFEST
MEANEST	NEAREST	OWLIEST	PULIEST	RULIEST	SOONEST	TIDIEST	WANIEST	YUKIEST
MEEKEST	NEATEST	OWRIEST	PUNIEST	RUMMEST	SOUREST	TINIEST	WANNEST	ZANIEST
MEETEST	NIGHEST	PACIEST	RACIEST	SADDEST	SPAREST	TONIEST	WARIEST	
MIDDEST	NOBLEST	PALIEST	RANKEST	SAGIEST	SPRYEST	TOOMEST	WARMEST	
MILDEST	NOSIEST	PERTEST	RASHEST	SAIDEST	STALEST	TOWIEST	WATTEST	

8-letter words -EST

ACERBEST	BOOZIEST	COMBIEST	DOTTIEST	FLAMIEST	GENTIEST	HEADIEST	KINKIEST
ACRIDEST	BOSKIEST	COMFIEST	DOTTLEST	FLARIEST	GENTLEST	HEADREST	KITTLEST
ADEPTEST	BOSSIEST	CONQUEST	DOWDIEST	FLASHEST	GIDDIEST	HEAPIEST	KOOKIEST
AFFOREST	BOUSIEST	COOMIEST	DOWNIEST	FLATTEST	GIRNIEST	HEAVIEST	LAIGHEST
ALCAHEST	BRAIDEST	COPSIEST	DRABBEST	FLAWIEST	GLADDEST	HEFTIEST	LAIRIEST
ALERTEST	BRAKIEST	CORKIEST	DREAREST	FLAXIEST	GLADIEST	HEMPIEST	LANKIEST
ALKAHEST	BRASHEST	CORNIEST	DROLLEST	FLEETEST	GLARIEST	HENNIEST	LARDIEST
ANAPAEST	BRENTEST	COUTHEST	DRONIEST	FLIPPEST	GLAZIEST	HERBIEST	LARKIEST
ANGRIEST	BRIEFEST	CRANKEST	DRUNKEST	FLORIEST	GLEGGEST	HILLIEST	LATHIEST
ARBALEST	BRINIEST	CRAPIEST	DRUSIEST	FLUKIEST	GLIBBEST	HIPPIEST	LAWNIEST
ARTSIEST	BRISKEST	CRASSEST	DRUXIEST	FLUSHEST	GLIDDEST	HOARIEST	LEADIEST
ASTUTEST	BROADEST	CRAZIEST	DUCKIEST	FLUTIEST	GLUMMEST	HOARSEST	LEAFIEST
BAGGIEST	BROWNEST	CREPIEST	DUDDIEST	FOAMIEST	GOATIEST	HOOKIEST	LEAKIEST
BALKIEST	BUDDIEST	CRISPEST	DULLIEST	FOGGIEST	GODLIEST	HOOLIEST	LEARIEST
BALMIEST	BULGIEST	CRONKEST	DUMMIEST	FOOTIEST	GOLDIEST	HOPPIEST	LEAVIEST
BANALEST	BULKIEST	CROOKEST	DUMPIEST	FOOTREST	GOODIEST	HORNIEST	LEDGIEST
BANDIEST	BULLIEST	CROSSEST	DUNGIEST	FORKIEST	GOOFIEST	HORSIEST	LEERIEST
BARDIEST	BUMPIEST	CRUMPEST	DUNNIEST	FRAILEST	GOOPIEST	HUFFIEST	LEGGIEST
BARGHEST	BUNTIEST	CURDIEST	DURGIEST	FRANKEST	GOOSIEST	HULKIEST	LEISHEST
BARKIEST	BURLIEST	CURLIEST	DUSKIEST	FRESHEST	GORMIEST	HULLIEST	LICHTEST
BARMIEST	BURRIEST	CURNIEST	DUSTIEST	FROWIEST	GORSIEST	HUMANEST	LIGHTEST
BASSIEST	BUSHIEST	CURVIEST	EARLIEST	FUBBIEST	GOUTIEST	HUMBLEST	LINGIEST
BATTIEST	BUSTIEST	CUSHIEST	EMONGEST	FUBSIEST	GRANDEST	HUMIDEST	LINTIEST
BAWDIEST	BUTCHEST	CUTTIEST	EMPTIEST	FUFFIEST	GRAPIEST	HUMPIEST	LIPPIEST
BEADIEST	BUXOMEST	DAFFIEST	ENFOREST	FUGGIEST	GREATEST	HUNKIEST	LITTLEST
BEAMIEST	BUZZIEST	DAMPIEST	EVILLEST	FUNKIEST	GREENEST	HUSHIEST	LIVIDEST
BEEFIEST	CADGIEST	DANDIEST	EXACTEST	FUNNIEST	GRIMIEST	HUSKIEST	LOAMIEST
BEERIEST	CALMIEST	DAUBIEST	FADDIEST	FURRIEST	GRIMMEST	IMMODEST	LOATHEST
BENDIEST	CAMPIEST	DEBBIEST	FAINTEST	FURTHEST	GRITTEST	IMPUREST	LOFTIEST
BENTIEST	CANNIEST	DEEDIEST	FANCIEST	FURZIEST	GROSSEST	INDIGEST	LOOBIEST
BILGIEST	CANTIEST	DEFOREST	FARTHEST	FUSSIEST	GRUFFEST	INEPTEST	LOONIEST
BIRSIEST	CARNIEST	DEMUREST	FATTIEST	FUSTIEST	GRUMMEST	INERTEST	LOOPIEST
BITSIEST	CATTIEST	DICKIEST	FEEBLEST	FUTILEST	GUCKIEST	INSANEST	LOSSIEST
BITTIEST	CAULDEST	DICTIEST	FEINTEST	FUZZIEST	GULFIEST	INTEREST	LOURIEST
BLACKEST	CHARIEST	DILLIEST	FENDIEST	GABBIEST	GUMMIEST	ITCHIEST	LOUSIEST
BLANDEST	CHASTEST	DINGIEST	FENNIEST	GAMMIEST	GUNGIEST	JAGGIEST	LOWLIEST
BLANKEST	CHEAPEST	DINKIEST	FERLIEST	GAPPIEST	GURLIEST	JAMMIEST	LUCIDEST
BLEAKEST	CHEWIEST	DIPPIEST	FERNIEST	GASPIEST	GUSHIEST	JANTIEST	LUCKIEST
BLEAREST	CHIEFEST	DIRTIEST	FETIDEST	GASSIEST	GUSTIEST	JAZZIEST	LUMMIEST
BLINDEST	CHILLEST	DISHIEST	FICKLEST	GAUCHEST	GUTSIEST	JEMMIEST	LUMPIEST
BLITHEST	CHOICEST	DIVINEST	FIERCEST	GAUCIEST	HAILIEST	JERKIEST	LURIDEST
BLONDEST	CHOKIEST	DIZZIEST	FIERIEST	GAUDIEST	HAIRIEST	JETTIEST	LUSHIEST
BLOWIEST	CISSIEST	DOCILEST	FILMIEST	GAUMIEST	HAMMIEST	JIMPIEST	LUSTIEST
BLUDIEST	CLAYIEST	DODDIEST	FINNIEST	GAUNTEST	HANDIEST	JOLLIEST	MALTIEST
BLUFFEST	CLEANEST	DODGIEST	FIRRIEST	GAUZIEST	HANGNEST	JOLTIEST	MANGIEST
BLUNTEST	CLEAREST	DOGGIEST	FISHIEST	GAWCIEST	HAPPIEST	JUICIEST	MANIFEST
BOGGIEST	COALIEST	DOILTEST	FISTIEST	GAWKIEST	HARDIEST	JUMPIEST	MANKIEST
BONNIEST	COARSEST	DONSIEST	FITLIEST	GAWSIEST	HARSHEST	JUNKIEST	MANLIEST
BOOKIEST	COBBIEST	DOOMIEST	FIZZIEST	GELIDEST	HASHIEST	KEDGIEST	MARDIEST
BOOKREST	COCKIEST	DORTIEST	FLAKIEST	GEMMIEST	HASTIEST	KEDGIEST	MARLIEST

MASHIEST	NETTIEST	PONGIEST	RITZIEST	SHORTEST	SPIRIEST	TEUCHEST	VIVIDEST
MASSIEST	NEWSIEST	POOFIEST	ROARIEST	SHOWIEST	SPRUCEST	TEUGHEST	VOGUIEST
MASTIEST	NIFFIEST	POOVIEST	ROCKIEST	SILKIEST	SPUMIEST	THAWIEST	VUGGIEST
MATUREST	NIFTIEST	PORKIEST	ROILIEST	SILLIEST	SQUAREST	THEWIEST	WACKIEST
MAWKIEST	NIMBLEST	PORTIEST	ROOFIEST	SILTIEST	STABLEST	THICKEST	WALLIEST
MEAGREST	NIPPIEST	POTTIEST	ROOMIEST	SIMPLEST	STAGIEST	THINNEST	WALTIEST
MEALIEST	NIRLIEST	POUTIEST	ROOPIEST	SINKIEST	STAIDEST	THYMIEST	WARBIEST
MEATIEST	NITTIEST	PRICIEST	ROOTIEST	SISSIEST	STARKEST	TICHIEST	WARTIEST
MERRIEST	NOBBIEST	PRIMMEST	RORTIEST	SKIEYEST	STEEPEST	TIDDIEST	WASHIEST
MESHIEST	NOISIEST	PRIVIEST	ROUGHEST	SKINTEST	STEEVEST	TIGHTEST	WASPIEST
MESSIEST	NOOKIEST	PROSIEST	ROUNDEST	SKIVIEST	STERNEST	TILLIEST	WEARIEST
MIFFIEST	NOUNIEST	PROUDEST	ROUPIEST	SLACKEST	STEWIEST	TIMIDEST	WEBBIEST
MIGHTEST	NUBBIEST	PUDGIEST	ROWDIEST	SLATIEST	STIEVEST	TINNIEST	WEEDIEST
MILKIEST	NUTTIEST	PUDSIEST	RUDDIEST	SLEEKEST	STIFFEST	TINTIEST	WEENIEST
MINGIEST	OBTUSEST	PUFFIEST	RUGGIEST	SLICKEST	STILLEST	TIPPIEST	WEEPIEST
MINTIEST	OFTENEST	PUGGIEST	RUMMIEST	SLIMIEST	STIVIEST	TIPSIEST	WEIRDEST
MINUTEST	OPAQUEST	PULPIEST	RUNNIEST	SLIMMEST	STONIEST	TIREDEST	WENNIEST
MIRKIEST	ORANGEST	PURPLEST	RUNTIEST	SLOPIEST	STOUTEST	TOFFIEST	WERSHEST
MIRLIEST	ORNATEST	PURSIEST	RUSHIEST	SLUGFEST	SUBTLEST	TOSHIEST	WHEYIEST
MISSIEST	OUNDIEST	PURTIEST	RUSTIEST	SMALLEST	SUDSIEST	TOSSIEST	WHINIEST
MISTIEST	OUTWREST	PUSHIEST	RUTTIEST	SMARTEST	SUETIEST	TOTTIEST	WHITIEST
MOISTEST	OVERKEST	QUAKIEST	SAGGIEST	SMOKIEST	SULKIEST	TOUGHEST	WIMPIEST
MOODIEST	PALLIEST	QUEEREST	SAILIEST	SMUGGEST	SUNNIEST	TOUSIEST	WINDIEST
MOONIEST	PALMIEST	QUICKEST	SALTIEST	SNAKIEST	SUPPLEST	TOUTIEST	WINGIEST
MOORIEST	PALSIEST	QUIETEST	SANDIEST	SNARIEST	SURFIEST	TOWNIEST	WISPIEST
MOPPIEST	PAPPIEST	RABIDEST	SAPPIEST	SNELLEST	SURGIEST	TOWSIEST	WITHIEST
MOROSEST	PARKIEST	RAGGIEST	SARKIEST	SNIPIEST	SURLIEST	TRIGGEST	WITTIEST
MOSSIEST	PASTIEST	RAINIEST	SASSIEST	SNOWIEST	SVELTEST	TRIMMEST	WONKIEST
MOTHIEST	PAWKIEST	RANDIEST	SAUCIEST	SNUGGEST	SWALIEST	TUBBIEST	WOODIEST
MOTLIEST	PEAKIEST	RANGIEST	SAVAGEST	SOAPIEST	SWANKEST	TUFTIEST	WOOFIEST
MOTTIEST	PEATIEST	RAPIDEST	SCALIEST	SOBEREST	SWEETEST	TURFIEST	WOOZIEST
MOUSIEST	PEERIEST	RASPIEST	SCANTEST	SODDIEST	SWELLEST	TUSKIEST	WORDIEST
MUCKIEST	PEPPIEST	RATTIEST	SCARCEST	SOGGIEST	SWIFTEST	TWINIEST	WORMIEST
MUDDIEST	PERKIEST	RAUCLEST	SCARIEST	SOILIEST	SWIPIEST	UNHONEST	WRONGEST
MUGGIEST	PESKIEST	READIEST	SEAMIEST	SOLIDEST	SWISHEST	UNIQUEST	YAWNIEST
MUMSIEST	PETTIEST	REAMIEST	SECUREST	SOMBREST	TACKIEST	UNPRIEST	YOLKIEST
MURKIEST	PHONIEST	REARREST	SEDATEST	SONGFEST	TALKFEST	UNRIPEST	YOUNGEST
MURLIEST	PICKIEST	REDDIEST	SEDGIEST	SONSIEST	TANGIEST	UNSAFEST	YUCKIEST
MUSHIEST	PIGGIEST	REEDIEST	SEEDIEST	SOOTHEST	TARDIEST	UNSUREST	YUKKIEST
MUSKIEST	PINKIEST	REEKIEST	SEELIEST	SOOTIEST	TARRIEST	UNTRUEST	YUMMIEST
MUSSIEST	PIPPIEST	REINVEST	SEEPIEST	SOPPIEST	TARTIEST	UNWISEST	ZAPPIEST
MUSTIEST	PITHIEST	REMOTEST	SEMPLEST	SORRIEST	TASTIEST	URBANEST	ZESTIEST
MUZZIEST	PLAINEST	RESTIEST	SERENEST	SOUNDEST	TATTIEST	UTTEREST	ZINCIEST
NAGGIEST	PLATIEST	RIBBIEST	SEVEREST	SOUPIEST	TAWNIEST	VAIRIEST	ZINGIEST
NAKEDEST	PLUMIEST	RICHTEST	SHADIEST	SPACIEST	TAWTIEST	VALIDEST	ZINKIEST
NAPPIEST	PLUMPEST	RIDGIEST	SHAKIEST	SPARSEST	TEARIEST	VAPIDEST	ZIPPIEST
NARKIEST	PLUSHEST	RIFTIEST	SHALIEST	SPEWIEST	TECHIEST	VASTIEST	
NASTIEST	POCKIEST	RIGHTEST	SHARPEST	SPICIEST	TEENIEST	VEALIEST	
NATTIEST	PODDIEST	RIGIDEST	SHEEREST	SPICKEST	TENTIEST	VEILIEST	
NEEDIEST	PODGIEST	RINDIEST	SHINIEST	SPIKIEST	TEPIDEST	VEINIEST	
NERVIEST	POLITEST	RISKIEST	SHOALEST	SPINIEST	TESTIEST	VIEWIEST	

WORDS ENDING IN -FUL

7-letter words -FUL

BALEFUL	DIREFUL	FOODFUL	HEEDFUL	LUSTFUL	PESTFUL	RISKFUL	SONGFUL	TUNEFUL
BANEFUL	DISHFUL	FRETFUL	HELPFUL	MASTFUL	PIPEFUL	ROOMFUL	SOULFUL	VIALFUL
BASHFUL	DOLEFUL	GAINFUL	HOPEFUL	MAZEFUL	PITHFUL	RUTHFUL	TACTFUL	WAILFUL
BODEFUL	DOOMFUL	GASHFUL	HORNFUL	MINDFUL	PITIFUL	SACKFUL	TALEFUL	WAKEFUL
BOOKFUL	DUREFUL	GAZEFUL	HURTFUL	MISTFUL	PLAYFUL	SARKFUL	TANKFUL	WAMEFUL
BRIMFUL	DUTIFUL	GLADFUL	JESTFUL	MOANFUL	PLOTFUL	SHIPFUL	TEARFUL	WILEFUL
CAREFUL	EASEFUL	GLEEFUL	LIFEFUL	MUSEFUL	POKEFUL	SHOPFUL	TEEMFUL	WISHFUL
CROPFUL	FATEFUL	GUSTFUL	LISTFUL	NEEDFUL	PREYFUL	SIGHFUL	TENTFUL	WISTFUL
DAREFUL	FEARFUL	HANDFUL	LOCKFUL	PAILFUL	PUSHFUL	SKEPFUL	TOILFUL	WORKFUL
DEEDFUL	FISHFUL	HARMFUL	LOOFFUL	PAINFUL	RAGEFUL	SKILFUL	TRAYFUL	ZEALFUL
DERNFUL	FISTFUL	HATEFUL	LUNGFUL	PALMFUL	RESTFUL	SKINFUL	TUBEFUL	ZESTFUL

8-letter words -FUL

APRONFUL	DOUBTFUL	GHASTFUL	MERCIFUL	PRESSFUL	SPADEFUL	TOOTHFUL	VAUNTFUL
AVAILFUL	DREADFUL	GLASSFUL	MIGHTFUL	PRIDEFUL	SPEEDFUL	TRADEFUL	VENGEFUL
BASINFUL	DREAMFUL	GLOOMFUL	MIRTHFUL	PURSEFUL	SPELLFUL	TRISTFUL	VOICEFUL
BELLYFUL	EVENTFUL	GRACEFUL	MOURNFUL	RIGHTFUL	SPITEFUL	TROTHFUL	WAGONFUL
BLAMEFUL	FAITHFUL	GRATEFUL	MOUTHFUL	SCENTFUL	SPOILFUL	TROUTFUL	WASTEFUL
BLISSFUL	FANCIFUL	GRIEFFUL	NIEVEFUL	SCOOPFUL	SPOONFUL	TRUNKFUL	WATCHFUL
BLUSHFUL	FAULTFUL	GROANFUL	NOISEFUL	SCORNFUL	SPORTFUL	TRUSTFUL	WEARIFUL
BOASTFUL	FEASTFUL	GUILEFUL	PAUSEFUL	SENSEFUL	STARTFUL	TRUTHFUL	WORTHFUL
CHARMFUL	FORCEFUL	HOUSEFUL	PEACEFUL	SHAMEFUL	STICKFUL	UDDERFUL	WRACKFUL
CHEERFUL	FOUNTFUL	LADLEFUL	PLAINFUL	SHELLFUL	STORMFUL	UNARTFUL	WRATHFUL
CHESTFUL	FRAUDFUL	LAUGHFUL	PLATEFUL	SLOTHFUL	SURGEFUL	UNJOYFUL	WREAKFUL
CRIMEFUL	FREAKFUL	LIGHTFUL	POUCHFUL	SMILEFUL	TABLEFUL	UNLAWFUL	WRECKFUL
DEARNFUL	FRISKFUL	LOATHFUL	POWERFUL	SNOOTFUL	TASTEFUL	UNUSEFUL	WRONGFUL
DEATHFUL	FRUITFUL	MENSEFUL	PRANKFUL	SOOTHFUL	THANKFUL	UNWILFUL	YOUTHFUL

WORDS ENDING IN -IBLE

7-letter words -IBLE

AUDIBLE	DELIBLE	DOCIBLE	FUSIBLE	LEGIBLE	PATIBLE	RIBIBLE	RISIBLE	VISIBLE

8-letter words -IBLE

CREDIBLE	ELUDIBLE	FEASIBLE	GULLIBLE	MISCIBLE	RINSIBLE	TANGIBLE	VENDIBLE
CRUCIBLE	EVASIBLE	FENCIBLE	HORRIBLE	PARTIBLE	RUNCIBLE	TENSIBLE	VINCIBLE
EDUCIBLE	EXIGIBLE	FLEXIBLE	INEDIBLE	PASSIBLE	SENSIBLE	TERRIBLE	
ELIGIBLE	FALLIBLE	FORCIBLE	MANDIBLE	POSSIBLE	SUASIBLE	THURIBLE	

WORDS ENDING IN -INGS

7-letter words -INGS

ACHINGS	CAKINGS	DRYINGS	GAPINGS	LAYINGS	NOSINGS	RAWINGS	SPAINGS	ULLINGS
ACTINGS	CANINGS	DYEINGS	GATINGS	LIKINGS	OFFINGS	RIDINGS	SPRINGS	UNKINGS
AGEINGS	CASINGS	EARRINGS	GIVINGS	LIMINGS	OGLINGS	RISINGS	SPYINGS	UPPINGS
AIRINGS	CAVINGS	EATINGS	GORINGS	LININGS	ONDINGS	ROBINGS	STRINGS	URGINGS
ANTINGS	CAWINGS	EDGINGS	HAVINGS	LIVINGS	OUTINGS	RODINGS	TAKINGS	URNINGS
ARCINGS	CODINGS	ELDINGS	HAYINGS	LOBINGS	PAGINGS	ROPINGS	TAMINGS	VEXINGS
AWNINGS	COMINGS	ENDINGS	HAZINGS	LORINGS	PALINGS	ROVINGS	TAWINGS	VIKINGS
BAAINGS	COOINGS	ENRINGS	HEWINGS	LOSINGS	PARINGS	ROWINGS	TAXINGS	WADINGS
BAKINGS	COPINGS	ERRINGS	HEXINGS	LOVINGS	PAVINGS	RUEINGS	TIDINGS	WAKINGS
BESINGS	COVINGS	FACINGS	HIDINGS	LOWINGS	PAYINGS	RULINGS	TILINGS	WANINGS
BIDINGS	CRYINGS	FADINGS	HIRINGS	LUGINGS	PIPINGS	SAVINGS	TIMINGS	WAVINGS
BIKINGS	DARINGS	FILINGS	HOLINGS	LUTINGS	POLINGS	SAWINGS	TIRINGS	WAXINGS
BITINGS	DATINGS	FININGS	HOMINGS	MAKINGS	POSINGS	SAYINGS	TOLINGS	WIPINGS
BLUINGS	DICINGS	FIRINGS	INNINGS	MAYINGS	PRYINGS	SEEINGS	TOWINGS	WIRINGS
BODINGS	DIVINGS	FIXINGS	JAWINGS	MININGS	PULINGS	SEWINGS	TOYINGS	WONINGS
BONINGS	DONINGS	FLYINGS	LACINGS	MOWINGS	RACINGS	SIDINGS	TRYINGS	WOOINGS
BORINGS	DOPINGS	FOXINGS	LADINGS	MUSINGS	RAKINGS	SIZINGS	TUBINGS	YOKINGS
BOXINGS	DOTINGS	FRYINGS	LASINGS	NAMINGS	RATINGS	SKIINGS	TUNINGS	ZONINGS
BUSINGS	DOZINGS	GAMINGS	LAWINGS	NIDINGS	RAVINGS	SOWINGS	TYPINGS	

8-letter words -INGS

ABIDINGS	BANKINGS	BEGGINGS	BOILINGS	BUNTINGS	CARVINGS	COININGS	CURSINGS
AISLINGS	BANTINGS	BELTINGS	BOLTINGS	BURNINGS	CASTINGS	COLLINGS	CUTTINGS
AMBLINGS	BARRINGS	BENDINGS	BONDINGS	BUSKINGS	CATLINGS	COMBINGS	CYCLINGS
ANGLINGS	BASHINGS	BETTINGS	BOOKINGS	BUSSINGS	CEASINGS	CONNINGS	DAFFINGS
ARCKINGS	BASTINGS	BIASINGS	BOOMINGS	BUSTINGS	CEILINGS	CORDINGS	DAMPINGS
AWAKINGS	BATTINGS	BIDDINGS	BOWLINGS	BUZZINGS	CHASINGS	COWLINGS	DANCINGS
BACKINGS	BAWLINGS	BILLINGS	BREWINGS	BYGOINGS	CHIDINGS	CRAVINGS	DARLINGS
BAGGINGS	BEADINGS	BINDINGS	BRIMINGS	CABLINGS	CIELINGS	CUBBINGS	DARNINGS
BAITINGS	BEAMINGS	BIRDINGS	BROKINGS	CALLINGS	CLOSINGS	CULLINGS	DAUBINGS
BALKINGS	BEARINGS	BIRLINGS	BUCKINGS	CANTINGS	COAMINGS	CUNNINGS	DAWNINGS
BALLINGS	BEATINGS	BLUEINGS	BUDDINGS	CAPPINGS	COATINGS	CUPPINGS	DEALINGS
BANDINGS	BEDDINGS	BOATINGS	BUGGINGS	CARPINGS	CODLINGS	CURLINGS	DECKINGS

DEVLINGS	GAININGS	INBRINGS	MAIMINGS	PLATINGS	SAGGINGS	STEWINGS	UPSWINGS
DIGGINGS	GANGINGS	INGOINGS	MALTINGS	POLLINGS	SAILINGS	STONINGS	VAMPINGS
DILLINGS	GASPINGS	INKLINGS	MARKINGS	POSTINGS	SALTINGS	STOPINGS	VANNINGS
DIPPINGS	GASSINGS	INSWINGS	MARLINGS	POURINGS	SALVINGS	STOVINGS	VARYINGS
DISHINGS	GAUGINGS	IRONINGS	MASHINGS	POUTINGS	SANDINGS	STOWINGS	VEERINGS
DOATINGS	GEARINGS	JARRINGS	MATTINGS	PRATINGS	SAPLINGS	SUBBINGS	VEILINGS
DOCKINGS	GELDINGS	JEERINGS	MEANINGS	PRAYINGS	SARKINGS	SUCKINGS	VEININGS
DOGGINGS	GETTINGS	JERKINGS	MEETINGS	PRIMINGS	SCALINGS	SUITINGS	VENTINGS
DOPPINGS	GILDINGS	JESTINGS	MELTINGS	PROSINGS	SCORINGS	SUMMINGS	VERSINGS
DRAWINGS	GIRDINGS	JIBBINGS	MENDINGS	PRUNINGS	SCRYINGS	SURFINGS	VESTINGS
DUBBINGS	GLAZINGS	JIGGINGS	MERLINGS	PUDDINGS	SEALINGS	SURGINGS	VIEWINGS
DUCKINGS	GLIDINGS	JOBBINGS	MESHINGS	PUFFINGS	SEARINGS	SWALINGS	VOICINGS
DUFFINGS	GLOZINGS	JOGGINGS	MICHINGS	PUGGINGS	SEATINGS	SWAYINGS	VOIDINGS
DUNNINGS	GODLINGS	JOININGS	MILKINGS	PUNNINGS	SEEDINGS	SYNDINGS	WADDINGS
EANLINGS	GOLFINGS	JOTTINGS	MILLINGS	PURGINGS	SEELINGS	TABLINGS	WAFTINGS
EARNINGS	GOSLINGS	KARTINGS	MINCINGS	PURLINGS	SEEMINGS	TACKINGS	WAILINGS
EARRINGS	GRATINGS	KEELINGS	MINDINGS	PURRINGS	SEININGS	TAILINGS	WAITINGS
EASTINGS	GRAVINGS	KEENINGS	MISTINGS	PUTTINGS	SEIZINGS	TALKINGS	WALKINGS
EEVNINGS	GRAZINGS	KEEPINGS	MOCKINGS	PYONINGS	SENDINGS	TAMPINGS	WALLINGS
EILDINGS	GRICINGS	KEMPINGS	MOORINGS	QUAKINGS	SENSINGS	TANKINGS	WANTINGS
ENVYINGS	GROWINGS	KENNINGS	MOOTINGS	QUEUINGS	SERVINGS	TANLINGS	WARDINGS
ETCHINGS	GUIDINGS	KIDLINGS	MORLINGS	RACKINGS	SETTINGS	TANNINGS	WARLINGS
EVENINGS	GUMMINGS	KILLINGS	MORNINGS	RAGGINGS	SHADINGS	TAPPINGS	WARMINGS
FABLINGS	GUNNINGS	KIRKINGS	MOSLINGS	RAILINGS	SHAKINGS	TARRINGS	WARNINGS
FAGGINGS	HACKINGS	KITLINGS	MOUSINGS	RAISINGS	SHAPINGS	TASKINGS	WARPINGS
FAILINGS	HAININGS	KNIFINGS	MUGGINGS	RANKINGS	SHARINGS	TASTINGS	WASHINGS
FAIRINGS	HALLINGS	LAGGINGS	MUMMINGS	RAPPINGS	SHAVINGS	TATTINGS	WASTINGS
FALLINGS	HALTINGS	LALLINGS	MUNTINGS	RASPINGS	SHOEINGS	TEAMINGS	WAULINGS
FANNINGS	HANGINGS	LAMMINGS	NAILINGS	RATLINGS	SHORINGS	TEASINGS	WAWLINGS
FARCINGS	HARLINGS	LANDINGS	NECKINGS	RATTINGS	SHOWINGS	TELLINGS	WAXWINGS
FARDINGS	HARPINGS	LAPPINGS	NETTINGS	READINGS	SIBLINGS	TENTINGS	WEARINGS
FARMINGS	HASTINGS	LAPWINGS	NITHINGS	REDDINGS	SIFTINGS	TESTINGS	WEAVINGS
FASTINGS	HATTINGS	LASHINGS	NODDINGS	REDWINGS	SINDINGS	THAWINGS	WEBBINGS
FATLINGS	HAWKINGS	LASTINGS	NOGGINGS	REEDINGS	SINGINGS	TICKINGS	WEDDINGS
FAWNINGS	HEADINGS	LATHINGS	NOONINGS	REEFINGS	SINKINGS	TIFFINGS	WEDGINGS
FEEDINGS	HEALINGS	LEADINGS	NOTHINGS	REELINGS	SITTINGS	TILLINGS	WEEDINGS
FEELINGS	HEARINGS	LEANINGS	NULLINGS	RENNINGS	SKATINGS	TILTINGS	WEEPINGS
FEERINGS	HEATINGS	LEASINGS	NUTTINGS	REPPINGS	SKIVINGS	TINNINGS	WELDINGS
FELTINGS	HEAVINGS	LEAVINGS	OAKLINGS	RESTINGS	SLATINGS	TINTINGS	WELLINGS
FENCINGS	HEDGINGS	LEERINGS	ONGOINGS	RIBBINGS	SLICINGS	TIPPINGS	WESTINGS
FERNINGS	HEELINGS	LEGGINGS	OPENINGS	RIDGINGS	SLIDINGS	TITHINGS	WHALINGS
FEUDINGS	HELPINGS	LEKKINGS	OUTWINGS	RIFLINGS	SLOWINGS	TITLINGS	WHININGS
FILLINGS	HERLINGS	LEMMINGS	PACKINGS	RIGGINGS	SMILINGS	TOILINGS	WHITINGS
FINDINGS	HERRINGS	LENDINGS	PADDINGS	RIGLINGS	SMOKINGS	TOLLINGS	WIGGINGS
FIRRINGS	HIDLINGS	LETTINGS	PAIRINGS	RINGINGS	SNARINGS	TOOLINGS	WILDINGS
FISHINGS	HILDINGS	LICKINGS	PANNINGS	RINSINGS	SNIPINGS	TOPPINGS	WINCINGS
FITTINGS	HIPPINGS	LIGGINGS	PANTINGS	RIOTINGS	SNORINGS	TOSSINGS	WINDINGS
FIZZINGS	HIRLINGS	LIMPINGS	PARKINGS	RISPINGS	SOAKINGS	TOTTINGS	WINKINGS
FLUTINGS	HISSINGS	LISPINGS	PARSINGS	ROADINGS	SOARINGS	TOURINGS	WINNINGS
FLYTINGS	HOGGINGS	LISTINGS	PARTINGS	ROARINGS	SOBBINGS	TOUSINGS	WISHINGS
FOAMINGS	HOLDINGS	LOADINGS	PASSINGS	ROCKINGS	SOGGINGS	TRACINGS	WITLINGS
FOILINGS	HOPPINGS	LOAFINGS	PASTINGS	RODDINGS	SOILINGS	TRADINGS	WITTINGS
FOLDINGS	HORNINGS	LOANINGS	PAUSINGS	ROLLINGS	SOOPINGS	TUBBINGS	WOLFINGS
FOOLINGS	HORSINGS	LODGINGS	PECKINGS	ROOFINGS	SOPPINGS	TUFTINGS	WOLVINGS
FOOTINGS	HOSTINGS	LOGGINGS	PEELINGS	ROOTINGS	SORNINGS	TUGGINGS	WORDINGS
FOPLINGS	HOUSINGS	LONGINGS	PEGGINGS	ROUMINGS	SORTINGS	TUNNINGS	WORKINGS
FORGINGS	HOWLINGS	LOOKINGS	PELTINGS	ROUTINGS	SOSSINGS	TURFINGS	WRITINGS
FORMINGS	HUMMINGS	LOONINGS	PETTINGS	RUBBINGS	SOTTINGS	TURNINGS	YAWNINGS
FOWLINGS	HUNTINGS	LOOPINGS	PICKINGS	RUCHINGS	SOUMINGS	TWININGS	YELLINGS
FRAMINGS	HURLINGS	LOPPINGS	PIGGINGS	RUGGINGS	SOURINGS	UNBEINGS	YELPINGS
FRAYINGS	HUSKINGS	LORDINGS	PIGLINGS	RUININGS	SOUSINGS	UNDOINGS	YOWLINGS
FUCKINGS	HUSTINGS	LOURINGS	PINKINGS	RUNNINGS	SPACINGS	UNITINGS	
FUNDINGS	HUTTINGS	LUGEINGS	PINNINGS	RUSTINGS	SPILINGS	UNSLINGS	
FURRINGS	HYLDINGS	LURKINGS	PIONINGS	RUTTINGS	STAGINGS	UNTYINGS	
GADLINGS	IMAGINGS	MADLINGS	PITTINGS	SACKINGS	STARINGS	UPBRINGS	
GAFFINGS	INBEINGS	MAILINGS	PLACINGS	SACRINGS	STAYINGS	UPGOINGS	

WORDS ENDING IN -ISH

7-letter words -ISH

ABOLISH	CATFISH	DOVEISH	GAMPISH	HOTTISH	MOONISH	POORISH	SADDISH	VAMPIS
ALUMISH	CATTISH	DRONISH	GARFISH	HUFFISH	MOORISH	PRUDISH	SALTISH	VARNIS
ANGUISH	CHERISH	DULLISH	GARNISH	JEWFISH	MOREISH	PUBLISH	SELFISH	VOGUIS
BABYISH	CLAYISH	DUMPISH	GIRLISH	JIGGISH	MUGGISH	PUCKISH	SERFISH	WAGGIS
BADDISH	CODFISH	DUNNISH	GNOMISH	KERNISH	MUMPISH	PUGGISH	SICKISH	WAMPIS
BALDISH	COLDISH	DUSKISH	GOATISH	KNAVISH	MURKISH	PUPFISH	SLAVISH	WANNIS
BEAMISH	COLTISH	EVANISH	GOLDISH	LADYISH	NEBBISH	RAFFISH	SLOWISH	WASPIS
BEARISH	COOLISH	FADDISH	GOODISH	LARGISH	NICEISH	RAMMISH	SNAKISH	WEARIS
BEAUISH	COWFISH	FAIRISH	GREYISH	LARKISH	NOURISH	RATTISH	SNOWISH	WENNIS
BIGGISH	CUBBISH	FALSISH	GUARISH	LOMPISH	NUNNISH	REDDISH	SOFTISH	WETTIS
BLEMISH	CULTISH	FASTISH	GULLISH	LONGISH	OGREISH	REDFISH	SOTTISH	WHEYIS
BOARISH	CURRISH	FATTISH	HAGFISH	LOUDISH	OOFTISH	RELLISH	SOURISH	WHITIS
BOBBISH	DAMPISH	FENNISH	HAGGISH	LOUTISH	PARKISH	RIGGISH	STYLISH	WHORIS
BOOKISH	DANKISH	FILMISH	HARDISH	LUBFISH	PECKISH	ROGUISH	SWINISH	WILDIS
BOORISH	DARKISH	FINEISH	HASHISH	LUMPISH	PEEVISH	ROINISH	TARNISH	WIMPIS
BRINISH	DERVISH	FLEMISH	HAWKISH	LUSKISH	PETTISH	ROMPISH	TARTISH	WOLFIS
BRUTISH	DIMMISH	FOGYISH	HELLISH	MAIDISH	PIEDISH	ROOKISH	TIGRISH	WOLVIS
BUCKISH	DOGFISH	FOOLISH	HIGHISH	MANNISH	PIGGISH	ROYNISH	TOFFISH	WORDIS
BULLISH	DOGGISH	FOPPISH	HIPPISH	MAWKISH	PINFISH	RUBBISH	TONNISH	YOBBIS
BURNISH	DOLLISH	FULLISH	HOBBISH	MISSISH	PINKISH	RUMMISH	TOWNISH	
CADDISH	DOLTISH	FURBISH	HOGGISH	MOBBISH	PLANISH	RUNTISH	TUBBISH	
CARLISH	DONNISH	FURNISH	HORNISH	MONKISH	PLENISH	RUTTISH	TUBFISH	

8-letter words -ISH

ADMONISH	CLANNISH	DRUMFISH	GOLDFISH	POKERISH	SHEEPISH	STARFISH	TOLLDIS
ASTONISH	CLAPDISH	DWARFISH	GREENISH	PRANKISH	SHORTISH	STARTISH	TOUGHIS
BABELISH	CLERKISH	EMPERISH	GRUFFISH	PRIGGISH	SHREWISH	STEEPISH	TOVARIS
BAITFISH	CLIQUISH	ENRAVISH	IDIOTISH	PROUDISH	SKIRMISH	STIFFISH	TRICKIS
BLACKISH	CLODDISH	ESSAYISH	JINGOISH	PSEUDISH	SKITTISH	STILTISH	UNMODIS
BLANDISH	CLOWNISH	FAINTISH	KINGFISH	PUPPYISH	SLANGISH	STOCKISH	UNPOLIS
BLIMPISH	CLUBBISH	FEEBLISH	KNACKISH	PURPLISH	SLIMMISH	STOUTISH	VAGARIS
BLOCKISH	COALFISH	FEVERISH	LANGUISH	QUALMISH	SLUGGISH	SUMPHISH	VANQUIS
BLUEFISH	COARSISH	FIENDISH	LIGHTISH	QUEERISH	SLUTTISH	SWAINISH	VIGORIS
BLUNTISH	COMPLISH	FIFTYISH	LIVERISH	QUIPPISH	SMALLISH	SWEETISH	VIPERIS
BOARFISH	CRAWFISH	FLATFISH	LUMPFISH	QUIRKISH	SNAPPISH	SWELLISH	VIXENIS
BOOBYISH	CRAYFISH	FLATTISH	MILKFISH	ROSEFISH	SNEAKISH	SYLPHISH	WALLFIS
BRACKISH	CROSSISH	FLIRTISH	MONKFISH	ROUGHISH	SNOBBISH	THICKISH	WATERIS
BRAINISH	DANDYISH	FLOURISH	NANNYISH	ROUNDISH	SNUBBISH	THIEVISH	WEAKFIS
BRANDISH	DEALFISH	FORTYISH	NOHOWISH	ROWDYISH	SOLIDISH	THINNISH	WOMANIS
BRATTISH	DEMOLISH	FRAILISH	NOVELISH	SAINTISH	SORRYISH	TICKLISH	YOKELIS
BRISKISH	DEVILISH	FREAKISH	NYMPHISH	SANDYISH	SPARKISH	TIGERISH	YOUNGIS
BROADISH	DIMINISH	FRESHISH	OVERFISH	SCAMPISH	SPOFFISH	TIGHTISH	
BROWNISH	DOWDYISH	FRUMPISH	PAGANISH	SCARFISH	SPOOKISH	TILEFISH	
CAMELISH	DRABBISH	GHOULISH	PIPEFISH	SCOMFISH	SQUARISH	TINGLISH	
CHILDISH	DRAFFISH	GLUMPISH	PLAINISH	SCUMFISH	STABLISH	TOADFISH	
CHURLISH	DROLLISH	GOATFISH	PLUMPISH	SHARPISH	STANDISH	TOADYISH	

WORDS ENDING IN -LY

7-letter words -LY

ACUTELY	APISHLY	BLANDLY	BRIEFLY	CHIEFLY	CRAZILY	DENSELY	DURABLY	FADEDL
AFFABLY	AUDIBLY	BLANKLY	BRISKLY	CHILDLY	CRINKLY	DIRTILY	DUSKILY	FAINTL
AGILELY	AURALLY	BLEAKLY	BRISTLY	CIVILLY	CRISPLY	DISALLY	DUSTILY	FAIRIL
ALERTLY	AWFULLY	BLINDLY	BROADLY	CLEANLY	CROSSLY	DIZZILY	DYINGLY	FALSEL
ALONELY	AXIALLY	BLOWFLY	BUIRDLY	CLEARLY	CRUDELY	DOUCELY	EAGERLY	FATALL
ALOOFLY	BAGGILY	BLUFFLY	BULKILY	CLERKLY	CRUELLY	DOWDILY	EARTHLY	FIERIL
AMIABLY	BAIRNLY	BLUNTLY	CANNILY	CLOSELY	CRUMBLY	DREADLY	ELDERLY	FIFTHL
ANGERLY	BALMILY	BONNILY	CATTILY	COCKILY	DANDILY	DRIBBLY	EMPTILY	FINALL
ANGRILY	BANALLY	BOOZILY	CAVALLY	CORNFLY	DAZEDLY	DRIZZLY	EQUABLY	FIREFL
ANOMALY	BAWDILY	BOSSILY	CHARILY	COURTLY	DEARNLY	DROPFLY	EQUALLY	FIRSTL
APETALY	BEAMILY	BRAMBLY	CHEAPLY	CRACKLY	DEATHLY	DUCALLY	ERECTLY	FIXEDL
APHYLLY	BEASTLY	BRAVELY	CHEERLY	CRASSLY	DEEDILY	DUOPOLY	EXACTLY	FLEETL

FLESHLY	GRISTLY	JUMPILY	MODALLY	PESKILY	RURALLY	SOBERLY	TARDILY	VAGUELY
FOAMILY	GRIZZLY	JURALLY	MOISTLY	PETTILY	RUSTILY	SOGGILY	TASTILY	VALIDLY
FOCALLY	GROSSLY	KNOBBLY	MONTHLY	PIOUSLY	SAINTLY	SOLIDLY	TATTILY	VAPIDLY
FOGGILY	GRUFFLY	KNUBBLY	MOODILY	PITHILY	SALABLY	SOOTHLY	TAXABLY	VENALLY
FRAILLY	GRUMBLY	LADYFLY	MORALLY	PLAINLY	SALTILY	SOOTILY	TENSELY	VERMILY
FRANKLY	GRYESLY	LARGELY	MOVABLY	PLIABLY	SAUCILY	SOPPILY	TENTHLY	VEXEDLY
FRECKLY	GRYSELY	LEGALLY	MUDDILY	PLUMPLY	SCANTLY	SORRILY	TEPIDLY	VISIBLY
FRESHLY	GYRALLY	LEGIBLY	MURKILY	PRICKLY	SCRAWLY	SOUNDLY	TERSELY	VITALLY
FRIARLY	HAMMILY	LICHTLY	MUSHILY	PRIMELY	SEEDILY	SPANGLY	TESTILY	VIVIDLY
FRITFLY	HANDILY	LICITLY	MUSKILY	PRIVILY	SHADILY	SPARELY	THICKLY	VIXENLY
FRIZZLY	HAPPILY	LIGHTLY	MUTABLY	PRONELY	SHAKILY	SPARKLY	THIRDLY	VOCALLY
FUGALLY	HARDILY	LITHELY	MUZZILY	PROSILY	SHAPELY	SPICILY	THISTLY	VOLUBLY
FUNNILY	HARSHLY	LOATHLY	NAIVELY	PROUDLY	SHARPLY	SPIKILY	THRILLY	VOWELLY
FUSSILY	HARTELY	LOCALLY	NAKEDLY	PUFFILY	SHEERLY	SPINDLY	TIGERLY	VYINGLY
FUSTILY	HASTILY	LOFTILY	NARGILY	PULPILY	SHINGLY	SPRAWLY	TIGHTLY	WEARILY
FUZZILY	HAZELLY	LOOBILY	NASALLY	QUEENLY	SHOGGLY	SQUALLY	TIMIDLY	WEEVILY
GAUDILY	HEADILY	LOOSELY	NASTILY	QUEERLY	SHOOGLY	STAGILY	TIPSILY	WEIRDLY
GAUNTLY	HEARTLY	LOUSILY	NATTILY	QUICKLY	SHORTLY	STAIDLY	TOSSILY	WHITELY
GELIDLY	HEAVILY	LOVERLY	NEEDILY	QUIETLY	SHOWILY	STALELY	TOTALLY	WIGHTLY
GHASTLY	HOARILY	LOWLILY	NIGHTLY	RABIDLY	SHRILLY	STARKLY	TOUGHLY	WINDILY
GHOSTLY	HUFFILY	LOYALLY	NINTHLY	RAPIDLY	SIGHTLY	STARTLY	TREACLY	WITTILY
GIANTLY	HUMANLY	LUCIDLY	NOBBILY	RATABLY	SILKILY	STATELY	TREMBLY	WOFULLY
GIDDILY	HUMIDLY	LUCKILY	NOISILY	READILY	SILLILY	STEEPLY	TRICKLY	WOMANLY
GODLILY	HUSKILY	LUMPILY	NOTABLY	REAPPLY	SIXTHLY	STERNLY	TRIFOLY	WOOZILY
GOOFILY	IDEALLY	LURIDLY	NOTEDLY	REGALLY	SLACKLY	STIFFLY	TRITELY	WORDILY
GOUTFLY	IGNOBLY	LUSTILY	NYMPHLY	RIGHTLY	SLANTLY	STONILY	TUMIDLY	WORLDLY
GRADELY	INANELY	LYINGLY	ORDERLY	RIGIDLY	SLEEKLY	STOUTLY	TUNABLY	WRIGGLY
GRANDLY	INAPTLY	MASCULY	OVERFLY	RISKILY	SLICKLY	STUBBLY	TWADDLY	WRINKLY
GRAVELY	INEPTLY	MERRILY	OVERPLY	ROCKILY	SLIMILY	STUMBLY	TWIDDLY	WRONGLY
GRAYFLY	INERTLY	MESALLY	OVERTLY	ROOMILY	SMARTLY	SUAVELY	UNAPTLY	YOUNGLY
GREATLY	INJELLY	MESSILY	PANOPLY	ROUGHLY	SMICKLY	SULKILY	UNFITLY	YOUTHLY
GREENLY	IRATELY	METALLY	PAPALLY	ROUNDLY	SMOKILY	SUNNILY	UNGODLY	
GREISLY	JADEDLY	MILKILY	PAWKILY	ROWDILY	SNAKILY	SURLILY	UNMANLY	
GRIESLY	JAZZILY	MISERLY	PEARTLY	ROYALLY	SNIDELY	SWEETLY	UNTRULY	
GRIMILY	JOINTLY	MISTILY	PENALLY	RUDDILY	SNOWILY	SWIFTLY	USUALLY	
GRISELY	JOLLILY	MIXEDLY	PERKILY	RUMMILY	SOAPILY	TACITLY	UTTERLY	

8-letter words -LY

ABJECTLY	BEGGARLY	CLEVERLY	DEUCEDLY	FATHERLY	FRUGALLY	HOPINGLY	LATTERLY
ABRUPTLY	BEHOVELY	CLOUDILY	DEVOUTLY	FAULTILY	FUTILELY	HORRIBLY	LAUDABLY
ABSENTLY	BENIGNLY	CLUMSILY	DIRECTLY	FEASIBLY	GAPINGLY	HORRIDLY	LAVISHLY
ABSURDLY	BESEEMLY	COARSELY	DISAPPLY	FELLOWLY	GARISHLY	HORSEFLY	LAWFULLY
ACTIVELY	BITCHILY	COGENTLY	DISMALLY	FERVIDLY	GENIALLY	HUMANELY	LAWYERLY
ACTUALLY	BITTERLY	COMMONLY	DISTALLY	FESTALLY	GIBINGLY	HUNGERLY	LEADENLY
ADORABLY	BLAMABLY	CONVEXLY	DIVERSLY	FEUDALLY	GIFTEDLY	HUNGRILY	LETHALLY
ADROITLY	BLITHELY	COOINGLY	DIVINELY	FIERCELY	GINGELLY	IMMANELY	LIMPIDLY
AERIALLY	BLOODILY	COUSINLY	DOCTORLY	FILIALLY	GINGERLY	IMPISHLY	LINEALLY
AGUISHLY	BOUNCILY	COVERTLY	DOGGEDLY	FILTHILY	GLASSILY	IMPURELY	LINEARLY
AMAZEDLY	BOYISHLY	COWARDLY	DORSALLY	FINITELY	GLOBALLY	INFIRMLY	LIQUIDLY
AMENABLY	BRASSILY	COYISHLY	DREAMILY	FITFULLY	GLOOMILY	INNATELY	LITHERLY
AMICABLY	BRAZENLY	CRABBILY	DREARILY	FLASHILY	GLOSSILY	INSANELY	LIVELILY
AMUSEDLY	BREEZILY	CRAFTILY	DROOPILY	FLEXIBLY	GOLDENLY	INTENTLY	LOBLOLLY
ANIMALLY	BRIGHTLY	CRANKILY	DROWSILY	FLIMSILY	GRAITHLY	INWARDLY	LOSINGLY
ANNUALLY	BROKENLY	CRAVENLY	EASTERLY	FLINTILY	GRAVELLY	IREFULLY	LOUCHELY
APICALLY	BRUTALLY	CREAKILY	EFFETELY	FLOPPILY	GREASILY	ISSUABLY	LOVELILY
ARCANELY	CANDIDLY	CREDIBLY	EIGHTHLY	FLORALLY	GREEDILY	JAGGEDLY	LOVINGLY
ARDENTLY	CARNALLY	CROAKILY	ELATEDLY	FLORIDLY	GREENFLY	JAUNTILY	LUBBERLY
ARGUABLY	CASUALLY	CROUSELY	ELIGIBLY	FLUENTLY	GRUMPILY	JEJUNELY	LUMBERLY
ARGUTELY	CATCHFLY	CRUSTILY	ENTIRELY	FORCEDLY	GUILTILY	JOCOSELY	LUMPENLY
ARRANTLY	CAUSABLY	CULPABLY	ENVIABLY	FORCIBLY	HEARTILY	JOCUNDLY	MAIDENLY
ARTFULLY	CAUSALLY	CURSEDLY	EPICALLY	FORKEDLY	HEAVENLY	JOKINGLY	MALIGNLY
ASSEMBLY	CHASTELY	DAINTILY	ERRANTLY	FORMALLY	HECTORLY	JOVIALLY	MANFULLY
ASTUTELY	CHEEKILY	DAMNABLY	ERRINGLY	FORMERLY	HEROICLY	JOYFULLY	MANNERLY
AUGUSTLY	CHEERILY	DAPPERLY	EVANGELY	FOURTHLY	HIDDENLY	JOYOUSLY	MANUALLY
AVERSELY	CHILLILY	DARINGLY	EXPERTLY	FRIENDLY	HITCHILY	KERNELLY	MARKEDLY
AVOWEDLY	CHIRPILY	DECENTLY	FACIALLY	FRIGIDLY	HOARSELY	KINDLILY	MASTERLY
BADGERLY	CHOICELY	DEMISSLY	FACILELY	FRISKILY	HOLLOWLY	KNIGHTLY	MATRONLY
BEARABLY	CHORALLY	DEMURELY	FALLIBLY	FROSTILY	HOMELILY	LABIALLY	MATURELY
BEASTILY	CLAMMILY	DENIABLY	FAMOUSLY	FROTHILY	HONESTLY	LATENTLY	MEAGRELY

MEDIALLY	PALLIDLY	QUEASILY	SCRIGGLY	SMUTTILY	STRAGGLY	TRYINGLY	UVULARI	
MELLOWLY	PALPABLY	QUOTABLY	SCRIMPLY	SNAPPILY	STRAITLY	TUNBELLY	VACANTI	
MENTALLY	PALTRILY	RACIALLY	SCURVILY	SNEAKILY	STRICTLY	TURBIDLY	VALUABI	
MESIALLY	PANDERLY	RADIALLY	SEAMANLY	SNIFFILY	STRONGLY	TURGIDLY	VARIABI	
MIGHTILY	PASSABLY	RAGGEDLY	SECONDLY	SNIVELLY	STUFFILY	UNCOMELY	VARIEDI	
MINUTELY	PASSIBLY	RAGINGLY	SECRETLY	SNOTTILY	STUMPILY	UNCOSTLY	VENDIBI	
MISAPPLY	PASTORLY	RAKISHLY	SECURELY	SOCIABLY	STUPIDLY	UNEASILY	VENIALI	
MODERNLY	PATCHILY	RANDOMLY	SEDATELY	SOCIALLY	STURDILY	UNEVENLY	VERBALI	
MODESTLY	PATENTLY	RASCALLY	SENILELY	SOLEMNLY	SUBTILLY	UNFAIRLY	VERNALI	
MODISHLY	PEDATELY	RATEABLY	SENSIBLY	SOMBRELY	SUDDENLY	UNGAINLY	VEXINGI	
MOLTENLY	PETTEDLY	RAVINGLY	SERENELY	SORDIDLY	SUITABLY	UNGENTLY	VIOLABI	
MOMENTLY	PITIABLY	READABLY	SERIALLY	SOUTERLY	SULLENLY	UNHOLILY	VIRGINI	
MONOPOLY	PLACABLY	RECENTLY	SEVERELY	SPARSELY	SULTRILY	UNHOMELY	VISUALI	
MOPINGLY	PLACIDLY	RECTALLY	SEXUALLY	SPEEDILY	SUMMERLY	UNIQUELY	VULGARI	
MOPISHLY	PLAGUILY	REFLEXLY	SHABBILY	SPIRALLY	SUPERBLY	UNITEDLY	WANTONI	
MORBIDLY	PLIANTLY	RELIABLY	SHAGGILY	SPONGILY	SUPINELY	UNJUSTLY	WEASELI	
MOROSELY	PLUCKILY	REMISSLY	SHAUCHLY	SPOOKILY	SYMPHILY	UNKINDLY	WEEVILI	
MORTALLY	PLURALLY	REMOTELY	SHIFTILY	SPOONILY	TAKINGLY	UNKINGLY	WESTERI	
MOTHERLY	POLITELY	RETRALLY	SHODDILY	SPORTILY	TANGIBLY	UNLIKELY	WHEEZII	
MOVEABLY	POPISHLY	RITUALLY	SHREWDLY	SPOTTILY	TARTARLY	UNLIVELY	WHIMSII	
MOVINGLY	PORTERLY	ROBUSTLY	SICKERLY	SPRITELY	TASSELLY	UNLORDLY	WICKEDI	
MULISHLY	POSINGLY	ROOTEDLY	SICKLILY	SPRUCELY	TAWDRILY	UNLOVELY	WILFULI	
MULTIPLY	POSSIBLY	ROTTENLY	SIGNALLY	SQUARELY	TENDERLY	UNMEETLY	WINGEDI	
MUSINGLY	POTENTLY	ROTUNDLY	SILENTLY	SQUIGGLY	TERRIBLY	UNREALLY	WINTERI	
MUTUALLY	PRETTILY	ROVINGLY	SILVERLY	SQUIRELY	TETCHILY	UNSAFELY	WITTOLI	
NARGHILY	PRIESTLY	RUEFULLY	SISTERLY	STANCHLY	THWARTLY	UNSEEMLY	WIZARDI	
NARGILLY	PRIMALLY	RUGGEDLY	SKIMPILY	STARRILY	TIMOUSLY	UNTIDILY	WOEFULI	
NARROWLY	PRINCELY	RUGOSELY	SLANGILY	STATEDLY	TINSELLY	UNTIMELY	WOODENI	
NATIVELY	PROBABLY	SACREDLY	SLEAZILY	STEADILY	TONISHLY	UNUSABLY	WOOINGI	
NOCENTLY	PROLIXLY	SAILORLY	SLEEPILY	STEAMILY	TORPIDLY	UNWARELY	WORTHII	
NORMALLY	PROMPTLY	SALEABLY	SLIGHTLY	STEEVELY	TOUCHILY	UNWARILY	WOUNDII	
OBTUSELY	PROPERLY	SAVAGELY	SLOPPILY	STICKILY	TOWARDLY	UNWIFELY	WRATHII	
OCCULTLY	PROVABLY	SAVINGLY	SLOVENLY	STIEVELY	TOYISHLY	UNWISELY	WRITERI	
OCULARLY	PRYINGLY	SAVOURLY	SMALMILY	STINGILY	TRASHILY	UPPISHLY	YEOMANI	
ODIOUSLY	PUBLICLY	SCANTILY	SMARMILY	STOCKILY	TREVALLY	UPWARDLY	YONDERI	
ONWARDLY	PULINGLY	SCARCELY	SMEARILY	STODGILY	TRIBALLY	URBANELY	YONGTHI	
OPAQUELY	PUTRIDLY	SCRAGGLY	SMOOTHLY	STOLIDLY	TRICKILY	URGENTLY	ZOOPHII	
ORNATELY	QUAINTLY	SCRIBBLY	SMUDGILY	STORMILY	TRUSTILY	USEFULLY		

WORDS ENDING IN -MAN

7-letter words -MAN

ARTSMAN	CASEMAN	FREEMAN	HOODMAN	LINKMAN	OARSMAN	REELMAN	SPAEMAN	WOODM
BASEMAN	CAVEMAN	FROGMAN	HOSEMAN	LOCKMAN	ODDSMAN	RINGMAN	SURFMAN	WOOLM
BATSMAN	CHAPMAN	GADSMAN	INHUMAN	LOCOMAN	OTTOMAN	ROADMAN	SWAGMAN	WORKM
BEADMAN	CLUBMAN	GLEEMAN	ISLEMAN	MAGSMAN	OVERMAN	RODSMAN	TAPSMAN	YARDM
BEDEMAN	COALMAN	GOODMAN	JACKMAN	MAILMAN	PACKMAN	SAGAMAN	TAXIMAN	YEGGM
BELLMAN	DAYSMAN	GOWNMAN	JARKMAN	MALTMAN	PASSMAN	SANDMAN	TOLLMAN	
BILLMAN	DECUMAN	GUDEMAN	JAZZMAN	MARKMAN	PEATMAN	SHIPMAN	TOOLMAN	
BIRDMAN	DRAYMAN	HANGMAN	JUNKMAN	MASHMAN	PIKEMAN	SHOPMAN	TOPSMAN	
BOATMAN	DUSTMAN	HANUMAN	JURYMAN	MILKMAN	POLLMAN	SHOWMAN	TRUEMAN	
BONDMAN	FACEMAN	HEADMAN	KEELMAN	MOBSMAN	PORTMAN	SICKMAN	TURFMAN	
BOOKMAN	FIREMAN	HELIMAN	KINSMAN	MOORMAN	POSTMAN	SNOWMAN	UNHUMAN	
BUSHMAN	FOOTMAN	HERDMAN	LANDMAN	MOOTMAN	RAFTMAN	SOKEMAN	UNWOMAN	
BYREMAN	FOREMAN	HIGHMAN	LINEMAN	NEWSMAN	RAILMAN	SONGMAN	WAKEMAN	

8-letter words -MAN

AIRWOMAN	BONDSMAN	CLASSMAN	FORGEMAN	HANDYMAN	HUNTSMAN	MARKSMAN	PLAIDM
ALDERMAN	BOTHYMAN	COACHMAN	FREEDMAN	HEADSMAN	ISLESMAN	MERESMAN	PLATEM
BAILSMAN	BRAKEMAN	CRAGSMAN	FRESHMAN	HELMSMAN	LANDSMAN	MERRYMAN	PREHUM
BANDSMAN	BRIDEMAN	DAIRYMAN	FRONTMAN	HENCHMAN	LEADSMAN	MOTORMAN	PRESSM
BANDYMAN	BRINKMAN	DALESMAN	FUGLEMAN	HERDSMAN	LIEGEMAN	NOBLEMAN	PROSEM
BANKSMAN	BUTTYMAN	DOOMSMAN	GANGSMAN	HIELAMAN	LINESMAN	OVERSMAN	PUNTSM
BARGEMAN	CHAIRMAN	DRAGOMAN	GAVELMAN	HOASTMAN	LOCKSMAN	PENWOMAN	QUILLM
BATWOMAN	CHESSMAN	DRAGSMAN	GLASSMAN	HOISTMAN	LODESMAN	PETERMAN	RAFTSM
BEADSMAN	CHOIRMAN	EARTHMAN	GOADSMAN	HORSEMAN	MADWOMAN	PITCHMAN	RAMPSM
BEDESMAN	CLANSMAN	FERRYMAN	GOWNSMAN	HOUSEMAN	MARCHMAN	PLACEMAN	RANCHM

REINSMAN	SEEDSMAN	SPACEMAN	STOREMAN	TACKSMAN	TRACKMAN	WATCHMAN
RIFLEMAN	SHAREMAN	SPADEMAN	STUNTMAN	TALESMAN	TREWSMAN	WATERMAN
RIVERMAN	SHEARMAN	SPEARMAN	SUBHUMAN	TALISMAN	TRIPEMAN	WEALSMAN
ROADSMAN	SHIREMAN	SQUAWMAN	SUPERMAN	TALLYMAN	TRUCHMAN	WHEELMAN
ROUTEMAN	SHOREMAN	STALLMAN	SWAGSMAN	TOWNSMAN	TRUCKMAN	WINCHMAN
SALESMAN	SIDESMAN	STOCKMAN	SWORDMAN	TOYWOMAN	UNDERMAN	WOODSMAN

WORDS ENDING IN -MEN

7-letter words -MEN

ABDOMEN	BONDMEN	DURAMEN	GUDEMEN	JUNKMEN	MASHMEN	PIKEMEN	SANDMEN	TAXIMEN
AGNOMEN	BOOKMEN	DUSTMEN	HANGMEN	JURYMEN	MILKMEN	POLLMEN	SHIPMEN	TOLLMEN
ALBUMEN	BUSHMEN	FACEMEN	HEADMEN	KEELMEN	MOBSMEN	PORTMEN	SHOPMEN	TOOLMEN
ARTSMEN	BYREMEN	FIREMEN	HELIMEN	KINSMEN	MOLIMEN	POSTMEN	SHOWMEN	TOPSMEN
BASEMEN	CACUMEN	FOOTMEN	HERDMEN	LANDMEN	MOORMEN	PUTAMEN	SICKMEN	TRUEMEN
BATSMEN	CASEMEN	FORAMEN	HIGHMEN	LINEMEN	MOOTMEN	RAFTMEN	SNOWMEN	TURFMEN
BEADMEN	CAVEMEN	FOREMEN	HILLMEN	LINKMEN	NEWSMEN	RAILMEN	SOKEMEN	VELAMEN
BEDEMEN	CERUMEN	FREEMEN	HOODMEN	LOCKMEN	OARSMEN	REELMEN	SONGMEN	WAKEMEN
BELLMEN	CHAPMEN	FROGMEN	HOSEMEN	LOCOMEN	ODDSMEN	REGIMEN	SPAEMEN	WOODMEN
BILLMEN	CLUBMEN	GADSMEN	ISLEMEN	MAGSMEN	OVERMEN	RINGMEN	SUDAMEN	WOOLMEN
BIRDMEN	COALMEN	GLEEMEN	JACKMEN	MAILMEN	PACKMEN	ROADMEN	SURFMEN	WORKMEN
BITUMEN	DAYSMEN	GOODMEN	JARKMEN	MALTMEN	PASSMEN	RODSMEN	SWAGMEN	YARDMEN
BOATMEN	DRAYMEN	GOWNMEN	JAZZMEN	MARKMEN	PEATMEN	SAGAMEN	TAPSMEN	YEGGMEN

8-letter words -MEN

AIRWOMEN	CHAIRMEN	FORGEMEN	HOASTMEN	MERRYMEN	RANCHMEN	SPECIMEN	TRIPEMEN
ALDERMEN	CHESSMEN	FREEDMEN	HOISTMEN	MOTORMEN	REINSMEN	SQUAWMEN	TRUCHMEN
BAILSMEN	CHOIRMEN	FRESHMEN	HORSEMEN	NOBLEMEN	RIFLEMEN	STALLMEN	TRUCKMEN
BANDSMEN	CLANSMEN	FRONTMEN	HOUSEMEN	OVERSMEN	RIVERMEN	STOCKMEN	UNDERMEN
BANDYMEN	CLASSMEN	FUGLEMEN	HUNTSMEN	PENWOMEN	ROADSMEN	STOREMEN	WATCHMEN
BANKSMEN	CLINAMEN	GANGSMEN	ISLESMEN	PETERMEN	ROUTEMEN	STUNTMEN	WATERMEN
BARGEMEN	COACHMEN	GAVELMEN	LANDSMEN	PITCHMEN	SALESMEN	SUPERMEN	WEALSMEN
BATWOMEN	COGNOMEN	GLASSMEN	LEADSMEN	PLACEMEN	SEEDSMEN	SWAGSMEN	WHEELMEN
BEADSMEN	CRAGSMEN	GOADSMEN	LIEGEMEN	PLAIDMEN	SHAREMEN	SWORDMEN	WINCHMEN
BEDESMEN	CYCLAMEN	GOWNSMEN	LINESMEN	PLATEMEN	SHEARMEN	TACKSMEN	WOODSMEN
BONDSMEN	DAIRYMEN	GRAVAMEN	LOCKSMEN	PRESSMEN	SHIREMEN	TALESMEN	
BOTHYMEN	DALESMEN	HANDYMEN	LODESMEN	PROSEMEN	SHOREMEN	TALLYMEN	
BRAKEMEN	DOOMSMEN	HEADSMEN	MADWOMEN	PUNTSMEN	SIDESMEN	TOWNSMEN	
BRIDEMEN	DRAGSMEN	HELMSMEN	MARCHMEN	QUILLMEN	SPACEMEN	TOYWOMEN	
BRINKMEN	EARTHMEN	HENCHMEN	MARKSMEN	RAFTSMEN	SPADEMEN	TRACKMEN	
BUTTYMEN	FERRYMEN	HERDSMEN	MERESMEN	RAMPSMEN	SPEARMEN	TREWSMEN	

WORDS ENDING IN -OUS

7-letter words -OUS

ACAJOUS	AZYMOUS	COPIOUS	FUNGOUS	IMPIOUS	OCHROUS	POMPOUS	SPINOUS	VEINOUS
ACEROUS	BADIOUS	CORIOUS	FURIOUS	INVIOUS	ODOROUS	PORTOUS	SPUMOUS	VICIOUS
ACETOUS	BILIOUS	CORMOUS	FUSCOUS	JEALOUS	OMINOUS	PULPOUS	SUCCOUS	VIDUOUS
ACINOUS	BIVIOUS	CUPROUS	GASEOUS	LENTOUS	ONEROUS	RAMEOUS	TALCOUS	VILLOUS
AGAMOUS	BRUMOUS	CURIOUS	GEALOUS	LEPROUS	ONYMOUS	RAUCOUS	TEDIOUS	VISCOUS
AMADOUS	BULBOUS	DEVIOUS	GIBBOUS	LIMBOUS	OPACOUS	RHODOUS	TENUOUS	VOUDOUS
AMOROUS	BURNOUS	DUBIOUS	GLEBOUS	LUTEOUS	OSMIOUS	RIOTOUS	TIMEOUS	ZEALOUS
ANUROUS	CACHOUS	DUTEOUS	GLOBOUS	NACROUS	OSSEOUS	ROUCOUS	TYPHOUS	ZINCOUS
ANXIOUS	CALLOUS	EMULOUS	GRUMOUS	NERVOUS	PAPPOUS	ROUTOUS	UBEROUS	
APODOUS	CARIOUS	ENVIOUS	GUMMOUS	NIMIOUS	PARLOUS	RUBIOUS	UMBROUS	
AQUEOUS	CASEOUS	ESTROUS	HEINOUS	NIOBOUS	PERLOUS	RUINOUS	URANOUS	
ARDUOUS	CEREOUS	FATUOUS	HERBOUS	NITROUS	PETROUS	SANIOUS	URINOUS	
ATHEOUS	CHYMOUS	FEATOUS	HIDEOUS	NIVEOUS	PICEOUS	SARCOUS	USUROUS	
ATOKOUS	CIRROUS	FERROUS	HUGEOUS	NOCUOUS	PILEOUS	SERIOUS	VACUOUS	
AZOTOUS	CITROUS	FIBROUS	HYDROUS	NOXIOUS	PITEOUS	SIMIOUS	VALGOUS	
AZYGOUS	CONGOUS	FULVOUS	IGNEOUS	OBVIOUS	PLUMOUS	SINUOUS	VARIOUS	

8-letter words -OUS

ACARPOUS	CERNUOUS	EXIGUOUS	GRIEVOUS	NEMOROUS	POPULOUS	SIBILOUS	TUBULOU
ADUNCOUS	CHLOROUS	EXIMIOUS	GRISEOUS	NIDOROUS	PORTEOUS	SOMBROUS	TUMOROU
AMBEROUS	CITREOUS	FABULOUS	GYPSEOUS	NODULOUS	PRECIOUS	SONOROUS	ULCEROU
ANOUROUS	CORNEOUS	FACTIOUS	HALITOUS	NUBILOUS	PREVIOUS	SOPOROUS	UNCTUOU
ANTICOUS	COUSCOUS	FASHIOUS	HUMOROUS	NUMEROUS	PYRITOUS	SPACIOUS	UNDULOU
APHONOUS	COVETOUS	FASTUOUS	ICHOROUS	NUMINOUS	PYRRHOUS	SPECIOUS	UNJOYOU
APHTHOUS	COVINOUS	FEATEOUS	INCUBOUS	OCHEROUS	RAMULOUS	SPERMOUS	USURIOU
APTEROUS	CROCEOUS	FEATUOUS	INFAMOUS	OCHREOUS	RAVENOUS	SPURIOUS	UXORIOU
ARACEOUS	CROUPOUS	FELONOUS	JOCOROUS	OESTROUS	RESINOUS	SQUAMOUS	VALOROU
ARANEOUS	CUMBROUS	FERREOUS	KOUSKOUS	OOGAMOUS	RIGOROUS	STANNOUS	VANADOU
ARBOROUS	CUPREOUS	FEVEROUS	LACTEOUS	ORAGIOUS	RUMOROUS	STOTIOUS	VAPOROU
ASPEROUS	DARTROUS	FIDDIOUS	LEAPROUS	ORDUROUS	SABULOUS	STRATOUS	VENOMOU
ASTOMOUS	DECOROUS	FLATUOUS	LIGNEOUS	ORGULOUS	SAPAJOUS	STRUMOUS	VENTROU
ATROPOUS	DESIROUS	FLEXUOUS	LUMINOUS	OVARIOUS	SAPOROUS	STUDIOUS	VERTUOU
BIBULOUS	DEXTROUS	FRABJOUS	LUSCIOUS	PABULOUS	SAVOROUS	SUBEROUS	VIGOROU
BIGAMOUS	DIDYMOUS	GEMINOUS	LUSTROUS	PALUDOUS	SCABIOUS	SUDOROUS	VIPEROU
BIMANOUS	DIGAMOUS	GEMMEOUS	MANITOUS	PAPULOUS	SCABROUS	TEMEROUS	VIRTUOU
BIPAROUS	DIGYNOUS	GENEROUS	MARABOUS	PATULOUS	SCARIOUS	TENUIOUS	VITREOU
CADUCOUS	DIMEROUS	GLABROUS	MELANOUS	PERILOUS	SCIOLOUS	THALLOUS	WAVEROU
CAESIOUS	DIPNOOUS	GLAREOUS	MIASMOUS	PERVIOUS	SCLEROUS	TIMOROUS	WONDROU
CANOROUS	DITOKOUS	GLAUCOUS	MUTICOUS	PETALOUS	SCORIOUS	TINAMOUS	WRONGOU
CAPTIOUS	DOLOROUS	GLORIOUS	MUTINOUS	PLUMBOUS	SEDULOUS	TITANOUS	XANTHOU
CARIBOUS	EDACIOUS	GOITROUS	NACREOUS	PLUVIOUS	SELENOUS	TORTIOUS	YTTRIOU
CARNEOUS	ENORMOUS	GORGEOUS	NAUSEOUS	POACEOUS	SENSUOUS	TORTUOUS	
CAUTIOUS	EPIGEOUS	GRACIOUS	NEBULOUS	POLYPOUS	SEPALOUS	TUBEROUS	

WORDS ENDING IN -TION

7-letter words -TION

AMATION	CAPTION	DICTION	EMOTION	FICTION	MIXTION	PORTION	STATION	UNCTIO
AUCTION	CAUTION	EDITION	EMPTION	LECTION	ORATION	RECTION	SUCTION	UNITIO
BASTION	COCTION	ELATION	ENATION	MENTION	OVATION	RUCTION	TACTION	
CANTION	COITION	ELUTION	FACTION	MICTION	PACTION	SECTION	TUITION	

8-letter words -TION

ABLATION	COACTION	EGESTION	FRICTION	LAVATION	NEGATION	QUESTION	TRACTIO
ABLUTION	COLATION	EJECTION	FRUITION	LEGATION	NIDATION	REACTION	VACATIO
ABORTION	CONATION	ELECTION	FUNCTION	LENITION	NODATION	RELATION	VENATIO
ADAPTION	CREATION	EMICTION	GELATION	LIBATION	NOLITION	REMOTION	VEXATIO
ADDITION	DELATION	ENACTION	GUMPTION	LIGATION	NOTATION	ROGATION	VOCATIO
ADNATION	DELETION	EQUATION	GYRATION	LIMATION	NOVATION	ROTATION	VOLITIO
ADOPTION	DEMOTION	ERECTION	HALATION	LOBATION	NUDATION	SANCTION	VOLUTIO
AERATION	DERATION	ERUPTION	HIMATION	LOCATION	NUTATION	SCONTION	ZONATIO
AGNATION	DEVOTION	EVECTION	IDEATION	LOCUTION	OBLATION	SEDATION	
AMBITION	DILATION	EVICTION	IGNITION	LUNATION	PACATION	SEDITION	
AUDITION	DILUTION	EXACTION	ILLATION	LUXATION	PETITION	SOLATION	
AVIATION	DONATION	EXERTION	INACTION	MONITION	POSITION	SOLUTION	
BIBATION	DOTATION	FIXATION	INUSTION	MUNITION	POTATION	SORPTION	
CIBATION	DURATION	FLECTION	JOBATION	MUTATION	PUNITION	SUDATION	
CITATION	EDUCTION	FRACTION	JUNCTION	NATATION	PUPATION	TAXATION	

UNUSUAL VOWEL ENDINGS

Even when Scrabble players are thinking about the endings of words, they tend to concentrate on the 'obvious' endings – like -ATE, -ISE, -URE, -ED, -ER and -ENT. These tend to end with a fairly restricted group of letters – usually D, E, R, S and T. They do not naturally think of words ending with unusual letters. It takes some effort to start thinking about words ending in A, I, O and U. Yet these four letters make up 30% of the tiles in a Scrabble set. They will frequently appear on your rack, but familiarity with everyday English does not encourage you to think of these letters at the ends of words. They can be very useful for linking on to other letters on the board, making two-letter words which begin or end with A, I, O or U.

The following lists are ammunition for correcting that rather limiting view of word endings. Here are lists of all words of lengths two to eight which end with A, I, O and U.

WORDS ENDING IN -A

2-letter words ending in -A

AA	DA	FA	KA	MA	PA
BA	EA	HA	LA	NA	TA

3-letter words ending in -A

ABA	ANA	BRA	GOA	LEA	OVA	RIA	SPA	YEA
AGA	AVA	CHA	HOA	MNA	PEA	RYA	TEA	ZEA
AHA	AWA	ERA	ITA	MOA	PIA	SEA	TWA	ZOA
AIA	BAA	ETA	KEA	OCA	POA	SKA	UVA	
ALA	BOA	FRA	KOA	ODA	QUA	SMA	VIA	

4-letter words ending in -A

ABBA	BOBA	DONA	HILA	KINA	MOYA	PICA	RUSA	TANA	VITA
ACTA	BOMA	DOPA	HIYA	KOLA	MYNA	PIKA	SAGA	TAPA	VIVA
AGHA	BONA	DUMA	HOYA	KORA	NADA	PILA	SERA	TARA	VOLA
AGMA	BORA	DURA	HUIA	LAMA	NAGA	PINA	SETA	TAXA	WEKA
ALFA	BUBA	EGMA	HULA	LANA	NALA	PIPA	SHEA	TELA	WHOA
ALGA	BUNA	EKKA	HUMA	LAVA	NANA	PITA	SHWA	TIKA	YOGA
ALMA	CABA	EMMA	IDEA	LEVA	NAPA	PLEA	SIDA	TOGA	YUCA
AMLA	CAPA	EPHA	ILEA	LIMA	NOMA	PROA	SIKA	TOLA	YUGA
ANNA	CASA	ETNA	ILIA	LIRA	NOVA	PUJA	SIMA	TUBA	ZETA
ANOA	CECA	EYRA	ILKA	LOMA	OBIA	PUMA	SKUA	TUFA	ZILA
ANTA	COCA	FETA	INIA	LOTA	ODEA	PUNA	SODA	TUNA	ZOEA
AQUA	CODA	FLEA	IOTA	MAMA	OKRA	PUPA	SOFA	ULNA	ZONA
ARBA	COLA	FORA	IXIA	MANA	OLLA	RACA	SOJA	UREA	ZUPA
AREA	COMA	GAGA	JOTA	MARA	ORRA	RAGA	SOLA	URVA	
ARIA	COXA	GALA	JUBA	MAYA	OSSA	RAJA	SOMA	UVEA	
ARNA	CYMA	GENA	JUGA	MESA	PACA	RANA	SORA	VARA	
AULA	DATA	GETA	JURA	MICA	PAPA	RATA	SOYA	VASA	
AURA	DEVA	GIGA	KAKA	MINA	PARA	RHEA	STOA	VEGA	
BABA	DIKA	GILA	KANA	MONA	PAUA	RIMA	SURA	VELA	
BEMA	DISA	GLIA	KARA	MORA	PAWA	RIVA	TAHA	VENA	
BETA	DITA	GULA	KAVA	MOWA	PEBA	ROMA	TAKA	VINA	
BIGA	DIVA	HAKA	KETA	MOXA	PELA	ROTA	TALA	VISA	

5-letter words ending in -A

ABACA	BURSA	DOUMA	HALFA	KRONA	MORIA	PELMA	RUPIA	STIPA	USNEA
ABAYA	BWANA	DOURA	HALMA	KURTA	MORRA	PELTA	RUSMA	STOLA	UVULA
ABUNA	CAECA	DOWNA	HALVA	KWELA	MOTZA	PENNA	SABRA	STOMA	VACUA
ADYTA	CALLA	DRAMA	HAMZA	LABDA	MOWRA	PHOCA	SACRA	STRIA	VARNA
AECIA	CALPA	DULIA	HAOMA	LABIA	MUDRA	PHYLA	SAIGA	STUPA	VEENA
AFARA	CANNA	DUMKA	HASTA	LABRA	MULGA	PICRA	SAKIA	SULFA	VESPA
AGILA	CARTA	DURRA	HEJRA	LAIKA	MURRA	PIETA	SALSA	SUMMA	VESTA
AGORA	CELLA	EDEMA	HENNA	LAMIA	MURVA	PILEA	SAMBA	SURRA	VIFDA
ALAPA	CERIA	ENEMA	HERMA	LARVA	MUSHA	PINNA	SANSA	SUTRA	VIGIA
ALDEA	CHARA	ENTIA	HEVEA	LAURA	MYOMA	PINTA	SARSA	SYLVA	VILLA
ALOHA	CHAYA	ERBIA	HIJRA	LAVRA	NABLA	PITTA	SARZA	TABLA	VINCA
ALPHA	CHEKA	ERICA	HODJA	LEMMA	NAIRA	PIZZA	SAUBA	TAFIA	VIOLA
ALULA	CHELA	ETYMA	HOLLA	LEPRA	NALLA	PLAYA	SAUNA	TAIGA	VIRGA
AMEBA	CHICA	EXTRA	HOOKA	LEPTA	NANNA	PLAZA	SCALA	TAIRA	VISTA
AMNIA	CHINA	FACIA	HOSTA	LIANA	NAPPA	PLICA	SCAPA	TALMA	VITTA
ANANA	CHUFA	FAUNA	HURRA	LIBRA	NERKA	POAKA	SCENA	TALPA	VIVDA
ANIMA	CILIA	FELLA	HUTIA	LIMMA	NINJA	PODIA	SCHWA	TANGA	VODKA
AORTA	CIRCA	FESTA	HUZZA	LINGA	NORIA	POLKA	SCOPA	TANKA	VOILA
APNEA	CNIDA	FETTA	HYDRA	LLAMA	NORMA	POOJA	SCUBA	TANNA	VOLTA
ARABA	COBIA	FETWA	HYENA	LOGIA	NUBIA	POOKA	SCUTA	TAPPA	VOLVA
ARECA	COBRA	FLORA	HYPHA	LONGA	NUCHA	POPPA	SELVA	TAYRA	VULVA
ARENA	COCOA	FLOTA	HYPNA	LOOFA	NULLA	PORTA	SENNA	TAZZA	WALLA
AROBA	COLZA	FOLIA	INFRA	LUBRA	NYALA	PRANA	SENSA	TENIA	WINNA
AROMA	COMMA	FONDA	INTRA	LUFFA	OCREA	PRESA	SENZA	TERRA	WONGA
ASANA	CONGA	FOSSA	INULA	LYSSA	OIDIA	PRIMA	SEPIA	TESLA	XENIA
ATRIA	CONIA	FOVEA	JARTA	LYTTA	OMASA	PSORA	SEPTA	TESTA	YACCA
BACCA	COPRA	FRENA	JHALA	MAFIA	OMEGA	PUCKA	SERRA	TETRA	YAKKA
BAJRA	CORIA	GALEA	JIRGA	MAGMA	OPERA	PUKKA	SESSA	THANA	YARFA
BALSA	COSTA	GAMBA	JUNTA	MAHUA	ORGIA	PULKA	SHAMA	THECA	YARTA
BANIA	COTTA	GAMMA	KAAMA	MAHWA	OSSIA	PUNKA	SHAYA	THEMA	YENTA
BARCA	CRENA	GANJA	KACHA	MALVA	OSTIA	QIBLA	SHEVA	THETA	YERBA
BASTA	CUPPA	GARDA	KALPA	MAMBA	OUIJA	QUENA	SHOLA	THUJA	YUCCA
BATTA	CURIA	GEMMA	KANGA	MAMMA	PACHA	QUINA	SIDHA	TIARA	ZABRA
BELGA	DACHA	GENOA	KAPPA	MANIA	PACTA	QUOTA	SIGLA	TIBIA	ZAMIA
BIGHA	DAGGA	GOMPA	KARMA	MANNA	PADMA	RASTA	SIGMA	TICCA	ZANJA
BIOTA	DARGA	GONIA	KASBA	MANTA	PAISA	REATA	SILVA	TINEA	ZEBRA
BOCCA	DELTA	GONNA	KHAYA	MARIA	PAKKA	RECTA	SOFTA	TONGA	ZERDA
BOHEA	DERMA	GOTTA	KHEDA	MASSA	PALEA	REDIA	SOPHA	TREFA	ZONDA
BRAVA	DICTA	GRAMA	KHOJA	MATZA	PALLA	REGMA	SOPRA	TREMA	ZOOEA
BUFFA	DIOTA	GROMA	KINDA	MEDIA	PAMPA	RENGA	SORDA	TRONA	
BULLA	DOGMA	GUANA	KOALA	MISSA	PANDA	REPLA	SORRA	TSUBA	
BUNIA	DOLIA	GUAVA	KOFTA	MOCHA	PANGA	RHYTA	SPICA	ULEMA	
BUNYA	DOLMA	GUMMA	KOKRA	MOLLA	PARKA	RIATA	SPINA	ULTRA	
BURKA	DONGA	GUSLA	KOPPA	MOMMA	PASHA	ROOSA	SPUTA	UMBRA	
BURQA	DORSA	GUTTA	KORMA	MOOLA	PASTA	RUMBA	STELA	URENA	

6-letter words ending in -A

ABELIA	AMRITA	ARROBA	BERTHA	CESURA	CONIMA	DAGOBA	ESPADA	FUNKIA	HEJIRA
ABOLLA	ANATTA	ASTHMA	BODEGA	CHACMA	CONTRA	DAHLIA	EUREKA	GALENA	HEMINA
ABULIA	ANCORA	ATAXIA	BOSHTA	CHAETA	COPITA	DATURA	EXEDRA	GARRYA	HERNIA
ACACIA	ANEMIA	ATOCIA	BREGMA	CHAKRA	COPULA	DHARMA	FACULA	GARUDA	HOLLOA
ACEDIA	ANGINA	AUCUBA	BROLGA	CHAPKA	CORNEA	DHARNA	FARINA	GEISHA	HOLMIA
AGENDA	ANGORA	AURORA	BUCKRA	CHARTA	CORNUA	DHURRA	FASCIA	GELADA	HYAENA
AGOUTA	ANOXIA	AXILLA	BUNNIA	CHATTA	CORONA	DUENNA	FAVELA	GENERA	HYDRIA
AHIMSA	ANTLIA	AZALEA	BURKHA	CHICHA	CORYZA	ECZEMA	FECULA	GENEVA	IGUANA
AIKONA	ANURIA	AZOLLA	CABALA	CHOREA	COSMEA	EGESTA	FEDORA	GITANA	IMPALA
ALALIA	APHTHA	BAHADA	CABANA	CHORIA	CRANIA	EIDOLA	FEMORA	GLIOMA	INDABA
ALBATA	APNOEA	BAJADA	CAFILA	CHROMA	CRISSA	EJECTA	FERULA	GLORIA	INDUNA
ALEXIA	APORIA	BALATA	CALTHA	CHUKKA	CRISTA	ELUVIA	FIBULA	GLOSSA	INFULA
ALISMA	ARALIA	BALBOA	CAMERA	CICADA	CRUSTA	ELYTRA	FIESTA	GOANNA	INSULA
ALOGIA	ARCANA	BANANA	CANADA	CICALA	CUBICA	EMPUSA	FOOTRA	GOPURA	INTIMA
ALPACA	AREOLA	BARYTA	CAPITA	CICUTA	CUESTA	ENIGMA	FOUSSA	GORGIA	INYALA
ALTEZA	ARGALA	BATATA	CARINA	CINEMA	CUPOLA	ENTERA	FOUTRA	GRAPPA	ISCHIA
ALUMNA	ARISTA	BAUERA	CASSIA	CLOACA	CURARA	EPEIRA	FRAENA	GUINEA	JACANA
AMELIA	ARMADA	BEFANA	CATENA	CLUSIA	CUTCHA	EPIZOA	FRISKA	HALLOA	JATAKA
AMENTA	ARNICA	BELUGA	CEDULA	COAITA	CZAPKA	EPOCHA	FRUSTA	HEBONA	JEJUNA
AMOEBA	AROLLA	BEMATA	CEMBRA	CONCHA	DAGABA	ERRATA	FULCRA	HEGIRA	JEMIMA

JERBOA	LABARA	MARINA	NEBULA	PATACA	PYEMIA	RUSSIA	SISTRA	TANTRA	VALUTA
JOANNA	LACUNA	MARKKA	NOCTUA	PATERA	PYURIA	SAHIBA	SITULA	TAPETA	VARROA
JOJOBA	LAGENA	MASULA	NOMINA	PATINA	QUAGGA	SALINA	SKOLIA	TARSIA	VEDUTA
JUDOKA	LAMBDA	MAUNNA	NOVENA	PAYOLA	QUALIA	SALIVA	SMEGMA	TEGULA	VELETA
KABALA	LAMINA	MAXIMA	NUMINA	PELOTA	QUANTA	SALVIA	SOLERA	TELEGA	VESICA
KABAYA	LATRIA	MAZUMA	NUTRIA	PERAEA	QUELEA	SAMARA	SONATA	TEPHRA	VICUNA
KACCHA	LEIPOA	MEDINA	NYANZA	PEREIA	QUINOA	SAMOSA	SOPHIA	TERATA	VIHARA
KAFILA	LIGULA	MEDUSA	OCHREA	PESETA	QUINTA	SAPOTA	SPIREA	TEREFA	VIMANA
KALMIA	LINGUA	MEGARA	OEDEMA	PESEWA	QUOKKA	SATARA	SQUAMA	TERTIA	VIZSLA
KAMALA	LIPOMA	MEZUZA	OMENTA	PESHWA	QUOTHA	SATYRA	STADDA	THANNA	VOMICA
KAMELA	LITHIA	MGANGA	OMERTA	PETARA	RADULA	SCHEMA	STADIA	THULIA	WHATNA
KAMILA	LOCHIA	MIASMA	ONYCHA	PHOBIA	RAFFIA	SCILLA	STANZA	TINAJA	WOMERA
KANAKA	LOGGIA	MIMOSA	OPTIMA	PIAZZA	RANULA	SCLERA	STATUA	TIPULA	XEROMA
KANGHA	LORCHA	MINIMA	ORARIA	PILULA	RAPHIA	SCORIA	STEMMA	TORANA	XYLOMA
KANTHA	LORICA	MODENA	ORBITA	PINETA	RAZZIA	SCOTIA	STIGMA	TORULA	YAKUZA
KARAKA	LUCUMA	MONERA	ORGANA	PIRANA	REALIA	SEMEIA	STIRRA	TOTARA	YARPHA
KATANA	LUMINA	MOORVA	OSCULA	PIRAYA	REDOWA	SENEGA	STRATA	TRAUMA	YOJANA
KERRIA	LUNULA	MORULA	OTTAVA	PITARA	REGINA	SEROSA	STRIGA	TRIVIA	YTTRIA
KGOTLA	LUSTRA	MOTUCA	OZAENA	PLANTA	REGULA	SHARIA	STROMA	TROIKA	ZABETA
KHANGA	MACOYA	MUCOSA	PAELLA	PLASMA	REMORA	SHEILA	STRUMA	TSAMBA	ZAPATA
KHODJA	MACULA	MUMMIA	PAGODA	PLEURA	REMUDA	SHERIA	SUBSEA	TUNDRA	ZAREBA
KHURTA	MAFFIA	MURENA	PAKEHA	PNEUMA	RESEDA	SHIKSA	SULPHA	ULTIMA	ZARIBA
KINEMA	MALTHA	MURRHA	PAKORA	POSADA	RETAMA	SHIRRA	SUNDRA	UNGULA	ZENANA
KORORA	MANANA	MUTUCA	PALAMA	PREMIA	RETINA	SIDDHA	SYLVIA	UREDIA	ZEREBA
KORUNA	MANILA	MYOPIA	PALLIA	PROTEA	RHUMBA	SIENNA	TABULA	UREMIA	ZERIBA
KUFIYA	MANTRA	MYXOMA	PANADA	PRUINA	ROSTRA	SIERRA	TAENIA	URTICA	ZEUGMA
KUMARA	MANTUA	NAGANA	PANAMA	PTERIA	ROSULA	SIESTA	TAHINA	UTOPIA	ZINNIA
KUTCHA	MANUKA	NATURA	PAPAYA	PULKHA	ROTULA	SIFAKA	TAMARA	VAGINA	ZONULA
KWACHA	MARACA	NAUSEA	PAPULA	PUNCTA	RUMINA	SILICA	TANKIA	VALETA	ZYGOMA

7-letter words ending in -A

ABOMASA	APHAGIA	BEGORRA	CASCARA	CURCUMA	EROTICA	GONDOLA	KATORGA	MAREMMA
ABOULIA	APHASIA	BERGAMA	CASSATA	CURIOSA	EULOGIA	GONIDIA	KEITLOA	MARGOSA
ACANTHA	APHELIA	BIODATA	CASSAVA	CURTANA	EUTEXIA	GORILLA	KERYGMA	MARIMBA
ACAPNIA	APHONIA	BIRETTA	CATALPA	CYATHIA	EXCRETA	GRANDMA	KHALIFA	MARKKAA
ACHARYA	APLASIA	BOMBORA	CATASTA	CZARINA	EXEMPLA	GRANDPA	KHEDIVA	MASCARA
ACTINIA	APRAXIA	BONANZA	CATAWBA	DATARIA	EXHEDRA	GUARANA	KIBITKA	MASTABA
ACUSHLA	APTERIA	BORONIA	CAVALLA	DECIDUA	EXORDIA	GUEREZA	KITHARA	MAXILLA
ADDENDA	AQUARIA	BOTTEGA	CEDILLA	DECURIA	EXOTICA	GUMMATA	KUCHCHA	MAZURKA
ADENOMA	ARABICA	BOURKHA	CELESTA	DEJECTA	EXURBIA	GUNNERA	LABELLA	MEDULLA
ADHARMA	ARAROBA	BRACCIA	CEMENTA	DELENDA	FALBALA	HARMALA	LACINIA	MELISMA
AECIDIA	ARGYRIA	BRAVURA	CHALAZA	DELIRIA	FALCULA	HELLOVA	LAMELLA	MESHUGA
AGRAPHA	ARIETTA	BRECCIA	CHECHIA	DIGAMMA	FARRUCA	HELLUVA	LAMPUKA	MESTIZA
ALAMEDA	ARMILLA	BRITSKA	CHIASMA	DILEMMA	FELUCCA	HEMIOLA	LANGAHA	METAZOA
ALCHERA	ASCIDIA	BRITZKA	CHIKARA	DILUVIA	FERMATA	HETAERA	LANTANA	MICELLA
ALCORZA	ASHRAMA	BRUHAHA	CHIMERA	DIORAMA	FIBROMA	HETAIRA	LASAGNA	MILITIA
ALFALFA	ASPIDIA	BUBINGA	CHOLERA	DIPLOMA	FILARIA	HEUREKA	LAVOLTA	MINEOLA
ALFORJA	ASTERIA	BUCCINA	CIBORIA	DOMATIA	FIMBRIA	HEXAPLA	LEMMATA	MINUTIA
ALGEBRA	ATALAYA	BULIMIA	CIMELIA	DOULEIA	FISTULA	HIDALGA	LEMPIRA	MOMENTA
ALGESIA	ATHLETA	CABBALA	CINEREA	DRACHMA	FLUTINA	HIMATIA	LEUCOMA	MONARDA
ALLUVIA	ATRESIA	CADENZA	CITHARA	DROSERA	FORLANA	HOSANNA	LINGULA	MONILIA
ALTEZZA	ATROPIA	CAESURA	CLARKIA	DUODENA	FORMULA	HYMENIA	LOBELIA	MORPHIA
ALTHAEA	AURELIA	CAFFILA	COCHLEA	DVANDVA	FOSSULA	HYPOGEA	LOCUSTA	MORRHUA
ALUMINA	AUREOLA	CALDERA	CODILLA	DYSPNEA	FOVEOLA	HYPOXIA	LOMENTA	MOUSAKA
AMANITA	BACCARA	CALUMBA	COMITIA	DYSURIA	FREESIA	IKEBANA	MADOQUA	MOZETTA
AMENTIA	BACLAVA	CAMPANA	CONARIA	ECHIDNA	FUCHSIA	IMPRESA	MADRASA	MUDIRIA
AMMONIA	BAKLAVA	CANASTA	CONIDIA	ECTHYMA	FURCULA	INDICIA	MADRONA	MULATTA
AMNESIA	BALISTA	CANDELA	COPAIBA	ECTOPIA	FURLANA	INDUSIA	MAGENTA	MURAENA
AMOROSA	BANDANA	CANDIDA	COPAIVA	ECTOZOA	GALABEA	INERTIA	MAGMATA	MUTANDA
AMPHORA	BANDORA	CANELLA	CORALLA	EMBLEMA	GALABIA	INFANTA	MAHATMA	MYALGIA
AMPULLA	BANDURA	CANNULA	CORDOBA	EMPORIA	GALANGA	INGESTA	MAHONIA	MYCELIA
ANAEMIA	BANKSIA	CANTATA	CORELLA	EMPYEMA	GALATEA	IPOMOEA	MALACIA	MYELOMA
ANESTRA	BARBOLA	CANTINA	COROLLA	ENCOMIA	GANGLIA	ISODOMA	MALARIA	MYRINGA
ANGIOMA	BARILLA	CANZONA	CORPORA	ENDOZOA	GAZOOKA	JAMBIYA	MAMILLA	NAPHTHA
ANNATTA	BASIDIA	CARAMBA	CORRIDA	ENEMATA	GENISTA	JELLABA	MANDALA	NEMESIA
ANONYMA	BATTUTA	CARANNA	COTINGA	ENTOZOA	GERBERA	KABBALA	MANDIRA	NEUROMA
ANOSMIA	BAZOOKA	CARAUNA	CREMONA	EPHEDRA	GLUCINA	KACHCHA	MANDOLA	NIGELLA
ANTENNA	BEFFANA	CARIAMA	CROTALA	EQUINIA	GOBURRA	KACHINA	MANDORA	NIRVANA
APEPSIA	BEGONIA	CARIOCA	CURACOA	EROTEMA	GODETIA	KANTELA	MANILLA	NOTANDA

NOTITIA	PANDORA	PISCINA	PYREXIA	RUBELLA	SERPULA	SUMATRA	TORMINA	VIATICA
NOUMENA	PANDURA	PITUITA	PYXIDIA	RUBEOLA	SESTINA	SYNOVIA	TRACHEA	VIDENDA
NOVALIA	PANOCHA	PLACITA	QUASSIA	RUELLIA	SHASTRA	SYRINGA	TREHALA	VIHUELA
NOVELLA	PAPILLA	PLANULA	RABANNA	RUSALKA	SHEHITA	TAFFETA	TRISULA	VINCULA
OCARINA	PAPRIKA	PLATINA	RAMENTA	SABELLA	SHICKSA	TAKAHEA	TSARINA	VIRANDA
OCTAPLA	PARATHA	PLECTRA	RATAFIA	SABURRA	SIGNORA	TALARIA	TUATARA	VISCERA
OLEARIA	PARAZOA	PLEROMA	REFUGIA	SACELLA	SILESIA	TAMASHA	TUTANIA	VIVARIA
OMMATEA	PAREIRA	PLUMULA	REGALIA	SAGITTA	SILIQUA	TAMBURA	TYMPANA	VOLUSPA
OMNIANA	PARELLA	PODAGRA	REGATTA	SAMBUCA	SILPHIA	TANAGRA	ULNARIA	WALLABA
ONDATRA	PARERGA	PODESTA	REGMATA	SANGRIA	SINOPIA	TANTARA	URAEMIA	WEIGELA
ONYCHIA	PARGANA	POLACCA	REPLICA	SARCOMA	SKIMMIA	TAPIOCA	URETHRA	WOOMERA
OOGONIA	PARTITA	POLENTA	RESIDUA	SARDANA	SOREDIA	TARTARA	VALONEA	WOORARA
OPUNTIA	PATAGIA	POLYNIA	RETSINA	SATSUMA	SPATULA	TAVERNA	VALONIA	XERASIA
ORGANZA	PATELLA	POLYNYA	RHODORA	SAVANNA	SPECTRA	TEDESCA	VALVULA	YAMULKA
OROPESA	PAVLOVA	POLYZOA	RHYTINA	SCAGLIA	SPECULA	TEGMINA	VANESSA	YESHIVA
OSMUNDA	PAXIUBA	POTASSA	RICKSHA	SCAPULA	SPICULA	TEMPERA	VANILLA	ZAKUSKA
OSTEOMA	PEISHWA	PRIMULA	RICOTTA	SCHISMA	SPIRAEA	TEMPURA	VARIOLA	ZAMARRA
OSTRACA	PELORIA	PRONOTA	RIVIERA	SCHOLIA	SPLENIA	TEQUILA	VASCULA	ZANELLA
OSTRAKA	PENTHIA	PROPYLA	ROBINIA	SCOPULA	SRADDHA	TEREBRA	VEDALIA	ZAREEBA
OTALGIA	PEREIRA	PTERYLA	ROBUSTA	SCOTOMA	STAMINA	TESSERA	VELARIA	ZEBRULA
OVERSEA	PERGOLA	PUDENDA	ROMAIKA	SCYBALA	STASIMA	THEMATA	VENTANA	ZIGANKA
PADELLA	PERIDIA	PUNALUA	ROMNEYA	SECRETA	STOMATA	THRIMSA	VERANDA	ZIMOCCA
PAENULA	PERSONA	PUPARIA	ROSACEA	SEDILIA	STRETTA	THRYMSA	VERBENA	ZOOECIA
PALABRA	PETUNIA	PUPUNHA	ROSALIA	SEQUELA	STRIATA	TILAPIA	VERRUCA	
PALMYRA	PINNULA	PURPURA	ROSELLA	SEQUOIA	SUBAQUA	TOCCATA	VERRUGA	
PALOOKA	PIRAGUA	PYAEMIA	ROSEOLA	SERIEMA	SUCCUBA	TOHEROA	VETTURA	
PANACEA	PIRANHA	PYGIDIA	ROTUNDA	SERINGA	SULTANA	TOMBOLA	VEXILLA	

8-letter words ending in -A

ABSCISSA	AUTOMATA	CASTELLA	DEMERARA	FIBRILLA	HYDROZOA	MANUBRIA	PARANOEA
ACADEMIA	AUTOPSIA	CATHEDRA	DENTALIA	FISTIANA	HYPALGIA	MARCELLA	PARANOIA
ACALEPHA	AVIFAUNA	CATHISMA	DENTARIA	FLABELLA	HYPOGAEA	MARCHESA	PARHELIA
ADESPOTA	BABUSHKA	CAVATINA	DIARRHEA	FLAGELLA	HYSTERIA	MARIPOSA	PAROEMIA
ADULARIA	BACTERIA	CERCARIA	DIASPORA	FLOTILLA	IMPLUVIA	MARSUPIA	PAROUSIA
ADYNAMIA	BALLISTA	CHARISMA	DIASTEMA	FORAMINA	INSIGNIA	MASSOOLA	PASHMINA
AGNOMINA	BANDANNA	CHIMAERA	DICENTRA	FUGHETTA	INSOMNIA	MATAMATA	PELLAGRA
AGRAPHIA	BARATHEA	CHINAMPA	DICHASIA	GALABIYA	INTARSIA	MELANOMA	PENUMBRA
AKINESIA	BARRANCA	CHINKARA	DIELYTRA	GALLABEA	ISABELLA	MENSTRUA	PERFECTA
ALGAROBA	BASILICA	CHIRAGRA	DIPLOPIA	GALLABIA	ISCHEMIA	MESHUGGA	PERIAGUA
ALIGARTA	BATTALIA	CHLOASMA	DJELLABA	GALTONIA	ISCHURIA	METANOIA	PETECHIA
ALLELUIA	BAUHINIA	CHURINGA	DULCIANA	GARDENIA	JAPONICA	MIASMATA	PHOTOPIA
ALOPECIA	BERGENIA	CHYLURIA	DYSCHROA	GASTRAEA	JARARACA	MILIARIA	PHYSALIA
AMBROSIA	BERYLLIA	CINCHONA	DYSLEXIA	GASTRULA	JARARAKA	MILTONIA	PIASSABA
AMYGDALA	BETHESDA	CLAUSTRA	DYSMELIA	GEMATRIA	KALYPTRA	MINNEOLA	PIASSAVA
ANACONDA	BISCACHA	CLAUSULA	DYSPNOEA	GEROPIGA	KARATEKA	MONSTERA	PIZZERIA
ANALECTA	BIZCACHA	CLITELLA	DYSTOPIA	GESNERIA	KATAKANA	MONTARIA	PLACENTA
ANAPHORA	BLASTEMA	CNIDARIA	ECCLESIA	GLABELLA	KAZATZKA	MOUSSAKA	PLANURIA
ANASARCA	BLASTULA	COCCIDIA	EFFLUVIA	GLAUCOMA	KHANSAMA	MOZZETTA	PLATANNA
ANATHEMA	BRANCHIA	COENOBIA	EGOMANIA	GLIOMATA	KINAKINA	MRIDANGA	PLATYSMA
ANGELICA	BRASSICA	COLCHICA	ENCAENIA	GLORIOSA	KRAMERIA	MYCETOMA	PLETHORA
ANOESTRA	BREGMATA	COLLEGIA	ENGRAMMA	GLOSSINA	LAVATERA	MYXEDEMA	POLLINIA
ANOREXIA	BRITZSKA	COLLYRIA	EPHEMERA	GLOXINIA	LECANORA	MYXOMATA	POLYGALA
ANTEFIXA	BROMELIA	CONFERVA	EPICEDIA	GLUMELLA	LIPOMATA	NAVICULA	POLYURIA
ANTHELIA	BRONCHIA	CONSULTA	EPITHEMA	GOLFIANA	LODICULA	NUBECULA	PREDELLA
ANTHEMIA	BROUHAHA	CONTINUA	EPOPOEIA	GUERILLA	LONICERA	NYMPHAEA	PRESCUTA
ANTISERA	BUDDLEIA	CONURBIA	EQUISETA	GURDWARA	LYMPHOMA	ODONTOMA	PRESIDIA
APOLOGIA	BURLETTA	COQUILLA	ERYTHEMA	GYMKHANA	MACAHUBA	OITICICA	PROFORMA
APOSITIA	CAATINGA	COXALGIA	ESTANCIA	GYMNASIA	MADRASSA	OMBRELLA	PROGERIA
APYREXIA	CACHEXIA	CREDENDA	ESTHESIA	HABANERA	MAGNESIA	OPERCULA	PROTOZOA
ARAPAIMA	CACHUCHA	CREDENZA	EUPEPSIA	HACIENDA	MAGNOLIA	OPERETTA	PRUNELLA
ARAPONGA	CALDARIA	CRIBELLA	EUPHOBIA	HAMARTIA	MAHARAJA	OPUSCULA	PRYTANEA
ARAPUNGA	CALISAYA	CRITERIA	EUPHONIA	HEARTPEA	MAIOLICA	ORCHELLA	PTERYGIA
ARBORETA	CALYPTRA	CROMORNA	EUPHORIA	HEMIOLIA	MAJOLICA	ORCHILLA	PUTAMINA
ASPHYXIA	CAMELLIA	CUNABULA	EXCERPTA	HEMIOPIA	MALVASIA	PALESTRA	PYCNIDIA
ASTHENIA	CAMPAGNA	CYMBIDIA	FALDETTA	HERBARIA	MAMMILLA	PANDEMIA	QUADRIGA
ASTIGMIA	CAPITULA	CZAREVNA	FANTASIA	HETAERIA	MANDIOCA	PANMIXIA	QUILLAIA
ATARAXIA	CAPYBARA	CZARITZA	FASCIOLA	HETAIRIA	MANDORLA	PANORAMA	QUILLAJA
ATHEROMA	CARACARA	DECENNIA	FASCISTA	HOSPITIA	MANTILLA	PARABEMA	QUINELLA
AURICULA	CARNAUBA	DEMENTIA	FENESTRA	HYDREMIA	MANTISSA	PARABOLA	RACHILLA

RADIALIA	SCHEMATA	SHRADDHA	STOTINKA	SYNECHIA	TOXAEMIA	UREDINIA	VULSELLA
RAKSHASA	SCIATICA	SIDALCEA	STROBILA	SYNEDRIA	TOXOCARA	VACCINIA	WISTARIA
RAPHANIA	SCLEREMA	SIGNORIA	STROMATA	SYNTAGMA	TRACHOMA	VAGINULA	WISTERIA
REDDENDA	SCLEROMA	SILICULA	STRONTIA	SYSSITIA	TRAPEZIA	VALLONIA	XANTHOMA
RENDZINA	SCOLIOMA	SINFONIA	SUBCOSTA	TAKAMAKA	TRAUMATA	VELAMINA	XENOPHYA
RESINATA	SCOTOPIA	SONATINA	SUBPHYLA	TAMANDUA	TRICHINA	VELATURA	YARMULKA
RESPONSA	SCROFULA	SORBARIA	SUBPOENA	TAMBOURA	TRIDACNA	VENDETTA	YERSINIA
RETINULA	SCUTELLA	SPIRILLA	SUBTOPIA	TAPADERA	TRIFECTA	VERONICA	YTTERBIA
REWAREWA	SEMANTRA	SPORIDIA	SUBUCULA	TENTORIA	TRIFORIA	VERTEBRA	ZAMBOMBA
RHIZOBIA	SEMICOMA	SQUAMULA	SUBURBIA	TEQUILLA	TRILEMMA	VESICULA	ZAMPOGNA
RUTABAGA	SEMOLINA	STALAGMA	SUDAMINA	TERATOMA	TRIPUDIA	VESTIGIA	ZARZUELA
SACRARIA	SEMUNCIA	STAPELIA	SVASTIKA	TERRARIA	TRITONIA	VIBRISSA	ZASTRUGA
SALICETA	SENSILLA	STAROSTA	SWASTIKA	TERRELLA	TROCHLEA	VICTORIA	ZIRCONIA
SAPUCAIA	SEPTARIA	STEATOMA	SWEETPEA	TERZETTA	TROPARIA	VIEWDATA	ZOIATRIA
SARMENTA	SEPTLEVA	STEMMATA	SYMPODIA	TESSELLA	TSAREVNA	VIRAEMIA	ZOOCYTIA
SASARARA	SERENATA	STERIGMA	SYMPOSIA	TETRAPLA	TSARITSA	VIRTUOSA	ZOOGLOEA
SASTRUGA	SHAMIANA	STIGMATA	SYNANGIA	THERIACA	ULTIMATA	VISCACHA	ZOONOMIA
SAYONARA	SHECHITA	STOCCATA	SYNAPHEA	THIOUREA	UMBRELLA	VITICETA	ZUCHETTA
SCHAPSKA	SHIGELLA	STOMODEA	SYNCYTIA	TORTILLA	UNDERSEA	VIZCACHA	ZYGANTRA

WORDS ENDING IN -I

2-letter words ending in -I

AI	GI	LI	OI	SI	XI
DI	HI	MI	PI	TI	

3-letter words ending in -I

AMI	DEI	HOI	LEI	PHI	PSI	SEI	SUI	TUI
CHI	GHI	KAI	OBI	POI	SAI	SKI	TAI	UNI

4-letter words ending in -I

ANTI	DELI	GYRI	KAZI	MERI	NODI	RAGI	SIMI	TOPI	WILI
ASCI	DIVI	HAJI	KEPI	MIDI	NORI	RAKI	SIRI	TORI	YETI
BANI	DIXI	HILI	KIRI	MINI	PENI	RAMI	SOLI	UGLI	YOGI
BENI	ETUI	IMPI	KIWI	MODI	PERI	RANI	SORI	UNCI	YONI
CADI	EUOI	KADI	LOBI	MOKI	PILI	ROTI	TALI	VAGI	ZATI
CEDI	FOCI	KAKI	LOCI	MOOI	PIPI	SAKI	TAXI	VALI	
CHAI	FUCI	KALI	MAGI	NAOI	PURI	SARI	TIKI	VLEI	
DALI	GADI	KAMI	MALI	NIDI	QADI	SATI	TIPI	WADI	
DARI	GLEI	KATI	MAXI	NISI	RABI	SEMI	TITI	WALI	

5-letter words ending in -I

ABACI	BASSI	COCCI	FERMI	INDRI	MAQUI	OZEKI	RECTI	SUSHI	URARI
ACARI	BENNI	CORGI	FRATI	ISSEI	MEDII	PAGRI	RISHI	SWAMI	UTERI
ACINI	BLINI	CORNI	FUNDI	JINNI	MODII	PALKI	SALMI	TANTI	VILLI
AGAMI	BRAVI	DARZI	FUNGI	KARRI	MOOLI	PALPI	SAMPI	TARSI	XYSTI
AGGRI	BUFFI	DHOBI	GARNI	KATTI	MUFTI	PAOLI	SCAPI	TEMPI	ZIMBI
AGUTI	BWAZI	DHOTI	GENII	KAURI	NAEVI	PARDI	SCUDI	TERAI	ZOMBI
AIDOI	CACTI	DILLI	GHAZI	KHADI	NIMBI	PARKI	SERAI	THAGI	
AIOLI	CARDI	DUOMI	GOBBI	KHAKI	NISEI	PARTI	SHCHI	THOLI	
ALIBI	CEILI	ELCHI	GUSLI	KUKRI	NOMOI	PERAI	SHOJI	TONDI	
APPUI	CERCI	ELEMI	HADJI	LATHI	OBELI	PILEI	SOLDI	TOPHI	
ARDRI	CHILI	ENNUI	HAJJI	LAZZI	OBOLI	PIRAI	SPAHI	TOPOI	
ASSAI	CHOLI	ENVOI	HOURI	LENTI	OCULI	PUTTI	STOAI	TORII	
AULOI	CIPPI	FARCI	IAMBI	LICHI	OKAPI	QUASI	STYLI	TRAGI	
AUREI	CIRRI	FASCI	IMARI	LUNGI	ORIBI	RABBI	SUCCI	TUTTI	
BAJRI	COATI	FASTI	IMSHI	LURGI	OVOLI	RADII	SULCI	URALI	

6-letter words ending in -I

AGOUTI	ARGALI	AVANTI	BHISTI	BUKSHI	CHICHI	CUMULI	DEWANI	ECHINI	FLOCCI
ALKALI	ARGULI	BAILLI	BIKINI	BURITI	CHILLI	CURARI	DHOOTI	ELTCHI	GARDAI
ALUMNI	ARILLI	BANZAI	BOLETI	CALAMI	CHOWRI	CYATHI	DJINNI	EMBOLI	GELATI
ANNULI	ARIOSI	BHAKTI	BONSAI	CANTHI	CLYPEI	CYTISI	DROMOI	EPHEBI	GEMINI
ARCHEI	ASKARI	BHINDI	BORZOI	CESTUI	COLOBI	DECANI	DUETTI	EURIPI	GHARRI

GILGAI	JAWARI	LOBULI	MUNSHI	OURARI	RENVOI	SATORI	SOLIDI	THYRSI	YOGINI
GLUTEI	JOWARI	LOCULI	NAGARI	OUREBI	RHOMBI	SBIRRI	SONERI	TITOKI	ZUFOLI
GOMUTI	JUDOGI	MALLEI	NEROLI	PAPYRI	RUBATI	SCAMPI	SOUARI	TROCHI	
GRIGRI	JUNGLI	MANATI	NIELLI	PERITI	SACCOI	SCYPHI	STRATI	TROPHI	
GURAMI	JUPATI	MAULVI	NILGAI	PHALLI	SAFARI	SESELI	SUNDRI	TSOTSI	
HAIKAI	KABUKI	MAZHBI	NOSTOI	PITHOI	SAIKEI	SHALLI	TAHINI	TUMULI	
HAMULI	KAIKAI	MILADI	NUCLEI	PITURI	SAKKOI	SHTCHI	TAMARI	UAKARI	
HUMERI	KOWHAI	MIRITI	OCELLI	POLYPI	SALAMI	SHUFTI	TAPETI	UNCINI	
ILLUPI	KUMARI	MISHMI	OCTOPI	PUTELI	SALUKI	SIDDHI	TATAMI	WAKIKI	
INCAVI	LIMULI	MODULI	OCTROI	RAGINI	SANDHI	SIMPAI	THALLI	WAPITI	
INCUBI	LITCHI	MUESLI	OURALI	RAMULI	SANSEI	SMALTI	THOLOI	XYSTOI	

7-letter words ending in -I

ALFAQUI	BOUILLI	DAKOITI	GHILGAI	LAPILLI	OUSTITI	RHONCHI	SOPRANI	TSUNAMI
ALIZARI	BRONCHI	DASHEKI	GINGILI	LECYTHI	PACHISI	RHYTHMI	SORDINI	TYMPANI
ALVEOLI	CADUCEI	DASHIKI	GLUTAEI	MACRAMI	PADRONI	RILIEVI	SPLENII	URCEOLI
AMORINI	CALCULI	DEMENTI	GNOCCHI	MAESTRI	PALAZZI	RIPIENI	STAMNOI	VENTURI
ANESTRI	CALZONI	DENARII	GOURAMI	MAFIOSI	PECCAVI	SACCULI	STICHOI	VITELLI
ANZIANI	CANZONI	DIDAKAI	GRADINI	MARCONI	PENUCHI	SAIMIRI	STIMULI	WISTITI
APPALTI	CAVETTI	DIDAKEI	GUARANI	MARTINI	PINDARI	SAMURAI	STRETTI	WOORALI
ARCHAEI	CHAPATI	DIDICOI	HALLALI	MENISCI	PRELUDI	SAOUARI	SUCCUBI	WOURALI
ASSAGAI	CHARQUI	DOCHMII	HIBACHI	MODIOLI	PRONAOI	SARANGI	SUNDARI	ZAKUSKI
ASSEGAI	CHONDRI	EFFENDI	INTARSI	MOLOSSI	PULVINI	SASHIMI	SURCULI	ZUFFOLI
ASTATKI	CHORAGI	ELENCHI	JACUZZI	NAUPLII	QUILLAI	SCHERZI	SYLLABI	
BACCHII	CHOREGI	EMERITI	JAMDANI	NAUTILI	RABBONI	SECONDI	TERMINI	
BACILLI	CHUPATI	EPIGONI	JAMPANI	NONETTI	RAVIOLI	SENARII	THALAMI	
BAMBINI	CLARINI	ETOURDI	JINJILI	NUCELLI	REMBLAI	SERKALI	THROMBI	
BASENJI	COLIBRI	FAGOTTI	KACHERI	NURAGHI	REVERSI	SHIKARI	TIMPANI	
BILIMBI	COLOSSI	FORZATI	KAMICHI	ORIGAMI	RHIZOPI	SIGNORI	TONDINI	
BIRYANI	CRIMINI	FUMETTI	LAMPUKI	OUAKARI	RHOMBOI	SONDELI	TRIPOLI	

8-letter words ending in -I

ACOEMETI	BROCCOLI	COTHURNI	FEDELINI	LINGUINI	PASTRAMI	SASTRUGI	TEDESCHI
ALBERGHI	CANCELLI	CUNJEVOI	FLOCCULI	LITERATI	PEPERONI	SCALDINI	TEOCALLI
AMORETTI	CANTHARI	DAIQUIRI	FORZANDI	LUMBRICI	PERFECTI	SFORZATI	TERAKIHI
ANOESTRI	CAPITANI	DECUBITI	FUNICULI	MACARONI	PERIBOLI	SHANGHAI	TERIYAKI
ANTENATI	CAPRICCI	DIADOCHI	GINGLYMI	MAHARANI	PERRADII	SIGISBEI	TERZETTI
ASSEGAAI	CASTRATI	DIDDICOI	GLADIOLI	MALLEOLI	PIROSHKI	SOFFIONI	UMBILICI
BANDITTI	CHAPATTI	DIPTEROI	GRAFFITI	MARAVEDI	PIROZHKI	SOLFEGGI	UTRICULI
BERIBERI	CHUPATTI	DIVIDIVI	HETAIRAI	MARCHESI	PRODROMI	STAPEDII	VIRTUOSI
BIMBASHI	CICERONI	DRACHMAI	HYDROSKI	MARIACHI	PULVILLI	STOTINKI	ZASTRUGI
BIRIYANI	CICISBEI	DUPONDII	KACHAHRI	MORBILLI	RENMINBI	STROBILI	ZECCHINI
BONAMANI	CONCEPTI	DURUKULI	KOFTGARI	NARCISSI	RETIARII	SUKIYAKI	ZUCCHINI
BOSTANGI	CONCETTI	DUUMVIRI	KOHLRABI	NUCLEOLI	RISPETTI	SUMOTORI	
BOUZOUKI	CONDUCTI	ESOPHAGI	KOMITAJI	OUISTITI	RYOTWARI	TAGLIONI	
BOZZETTI	CONFETTI	FASCISMI	LEKYTHOI	PARCHESI	SANNYASI	TANDOORI	
BRINDISI	CORNETTI	FASCISTI	LIBRETTI	PASTICCI	SARTORII	TARAKIHI	

WORDS ENDING IN -O

2-letter words ending in -O

| BO | GO | IO | KO | MO | OO | SO | WO | ZO |
| DO | HO | JO | LO | NO | PO | TO | YO | |

3-letter words ending in -O

ADO	BRO	DUO	GEO	LOO	PHO	ROO	UDO	YGO
AGO	COO	DZO	GIO	MHO	POO	THO	UFO	ZHO
BIO	DOO	EGO	GOO	MOO	PRO	TOO	WHO	ZOO
BOO	DSO	FRO	HOO	OHO	RHO	TWO	WOO	

4-letter words ending in -O

AFRO	ALTO	ANNO	AUTO	BOKO	BRIO	BUDO	CIAO	COHO	DECO
AGIO	AMBO	ARCO	BEGO	BOLO	BROO	BUFO	CITO	DADO	DEMO
ALSO	AMMO	ARVO	BITO	BOYO	BUBO	CAPO	COCO	DAGO	DIDO

DODO	FICO	HERO	JOCO	LILO	MINO	PEPO	SILO	TOHO	VETO
DOJO	FIGO	HOBO	JOMO	LINO	MISO	PESO	SKEO	TOKO	VINO
DURO	FINO	HOMO	JUDO	LOBO	MOKO	POCO	SKIO	TRIO	VIVO
ECCO	GAJO	HUSO	KAGO	LOCO	MONO	POLO	SOLO	TYPO	WINO
ECHO	GAPO	HYPO	KAYO	LOGO	ODSO	PROO	SUMO	TYRO	ZERO
EDDO	GIRO	INFO	KILO	LOTO	OLEO	PYRO	SYBO	UMBO	ZOBO
ERGO	GOBO	INGO	KINO	LUDO	OLIO	REDO	TACO	UNCO	
EURO	GOGO	INRO	KOLO	MAKO	ONTO	RIVO	TARO	UNDO	
EXPO	GYRO	INTO	KOTO	MEMO	OTTO	SAGO	THRO	UNTO	
FADO	HALO	JATO	LENO	MICO	OUZO	SEGO	TIRO	UPGO	
FARO	HARO	JIAO	LIDO	MILO	PACO	SHOO	TOCO	URAO	

5-letter words ending in -O

ADDIO	BUNCO	CUFFO	FORGO	HOLLO	LENTO	MUNGO	POTTO	SCHMO	VERSO
AGGRO	BUNKO	CURIO	FUERO	HOWSO	LIMBO	NAPOO	PRIMO	SCUDO	VIDEO
AMIGO	BUROO	CUTTO	GADSO	HULLO	LINGO	NEGRO	PROMO	SECCO	VIREO
AUDIO	BURRO	CYCLO	GARBO	HYDRO	LITHO	NGAIO	PULMO	SEGNO	VISTO
AVISO	CACAO	DANIO	GAZOO	IAIDO	LLANO	ORTHO	PUNTO	SERVO	VULGO
AWETO	CAMEO	DECKO	GECKO	IGAPO	LOTTO	OUTDO	PUTTO	SHAKO	WAHOO
BABOO	CANTO	DEKKO	GESSO	IGLOO	MACHO	OUTGO	QUIPO	SMOKO	WHOSO
BACCO	CARGO	DIAZO	GIPPO	IMAGO	MACRO	OVOLO	RADIO	SOCKO	YAHOO
BALOO	CASCO	DILDO	GISMO	INTRO	MAIKO	PANTO	RATIO	SOLDO	YARTO
BANCO	CELLO	DINGO	GIZMO	IROKO	MAMBO	PAOLO	RECCO	SORBO	YOBBO
BANJO	CENTO	DIPSO	GOBBO	JAMBO	MANGO	PAREO	RECTO	SORDO	ZAMBO
BASSO	CHACO	DISCO	GODSO	JELLO	MANTO	PASEO	REFFO	SORGO	ZHOMO
BASTO	CHIAO	DITTO	GOMBO	JINGO	MATLO	PATIO	REPRO	SPADO	ZINCO
BEANO	CHINO	DOGGO	GREGO	JOCKO	MATZO	PEDRO	RETRO	STYLO	ZOCCO
BILBO	CISCO	DSOBO	GUACO	JUMBO	MESTO	PESTO	RHINO	TABOO	ZOPPO
BIMBO	COCCO	DSOMO	GUANO	JUNCO	METRO	PHOTO	RODEO	TANGO	ZORRO
BINGO	COMBO	DUNNO	GUIRO	JUNTO	MEZZO	PIANO	RONDO	TANTO	
BOMBO	COMMO	DUOMO	GUMBO	KAZOO	MICRO	PIEZO	RONEO	TEMPO	
BONGO	COMPO	ESTRO	GUSTO	KEMBO	MISDO	PINGO	RUMBO	TIMBO	
BORGO	CONGO	FANGO	GYPPO	KENDO	MISGO	PINKO	SALTO	TONDO	
BRAVO	CONTO	FATSO	HALLO	KIMBO	MOLTO	PINTO	SALVO	TORSO	
BUCKO	CORNO	FIBRO	HELLO	LARGO	MORRO	POLIO	SAMBO	TURBO	
BUFFO	CORSO	FOLIO	HILLO	LASSO	MOTTO	PONGO	SANKO	TYPTO	
BUMBO	CREDO	FORDO	HIPPO	LAZZO	MUCRO	PORNO	SARGO	UREDO	

6-letter words ending in -O

ABRAZO	BOLERO	CRYPTO	FRANCO	GRINGO	MANOAO	PHYSIO	ROCOCO	STEREO	VIGORO
ADAGIO	BONITO	CUCKOO	FRESCO	GROTTO	MATICO	POMATO	ROTOLO	STINGO	VIRAGO
AIKIDO	BOOBOO	DAIMIO	FUGATO	HALLOO	MEDICO	POMELO	RUBATO	STUCCO	VOMITO
AKIMBO	BRONCO	DAYGLO	FUMADO	HERETO	MELANO	PONCHO	SAMFOO	STUDIO	VOODOO
ALBEDO	BUMALO	DOMINO	GABBRO	HOODOO	MERINO	POTATO	SANCHO	SUBITO	VORAGO
ALBINO	BURGOO	DORADO	GAUCHO	HOOROO	MIKADO	PRESTO	SAPEGO	TATTOO	WANDOO
ALBUGO	CALICO	DRONGO	GAZEBO	IGNARO	MODULO	PRONTO	SBIRRO	TENUTO	WEIRDO
ANATTO	CALIGO	DUELLO	GELATO	INCAVO	MORPHO	PSEUDO	SCHIZO	TERCIO	WHACKO
ANGICO	CAMSHO	DUETTO	GENTOO	INDIGO	NANDOO	PSYCHO	SCRUTO	TEREDO	WHATSO
APOLLO	CASINO	DYNAMO	GHERAO	JOURNO	NARDOO	PUEBLO	SHIPPO	THICKO	ZELOSO
ARIOSO	CATALO	EMBRYO	GHETTO	KAKAPO	NIELLO	PUMELO	SHIVOO	TOMATO	ZOOZOO
ARISTO	CHEAPO	ENHALO	GIGOLO	KIMONO	NUNCIO	PUNCTO	SISSOO	TORERO	ZORINO
ARROYO	CHEERO	ERINGO	GINGKO	KOODOO	NYMPHO	QUANGO	SKIDOO	TRILLO	ZUFOLO
BAGNIO	CHOCHO	ERYNGO	GINKGO	LANUGO	OCTAVO	QUARTO	SMALTO	TROPPO	
BAGUIO	CHROMO	ESCUDO	GITANO	LAVABO	OVERDO	RABATO	SOLANO	TUPELO	
BAMBOO	CICERO	FASCIO	GIUSTO	LEGATO	OVERGO	RANCHO	SOLITO	TURACO	
BARRIO	COLUGO	FIASCO	GOMBRO	LIBIDO	PALOLO	REBATO	SORGHO	TUXEDO	
BISTRO	COMEDO	FINSKO	GOMUTO	LUCUMO	PARAMO	REGULO	SPEEDO	ULTIMO	
BLANCO	COROZO	FOREGO	GOOROO	MACACO	PEDALO	RIGHTO	STALKO	VAUDOO	
BLOTTO	CRAMBO	FORHOO	GORGIO	MANITO	PHYLLO	ROBALO	STANZO	VIBRIO	

7-letter words ending in -O

AGITATO	ANNATTO	AZULEJO	BOTARGO	BUFFALO	CANTICO	CHAMISO	CORANTO	DIABOLO
AILANTO	APPALTO	BAMBINO	BRACCIO	BUGABOO	CASSINO	CHEERIO	CORNUTO	EIGHTVO
ALBERGO	ARNOTTO	BAROCCO	BRASERO	BUMMALO	CATTALO	CHICANO	CRIOLLO	ELECTRO
ALLEGRO	ARRIERO	BARRICO	BRAVADO	BUSHIDO	CAVETTO	CHORIZO	CRUSADO	EMBARGO
AMORINO	ASINICO	BATTERO	BRONCHO	CALANDO	CEMBALO	CLARINO	CURACAO	ESPARTO
AMOROSO	AVOCADO	BEEFALO	BUDGERO	CALYPSO	CENTAVO	COQUITO	CYMBALO	ETAERIO

FAGOTTO	INFERNO	MORENDO	PASSADO	PORTICO	SAGUARO	SOPRANO	TORNADO	VOLPINO
FARRAGO	LENTIGO	MORISCO	PATRICO	POTOROO	SALTATO	SORDINO	TORPEDO	WENDIGO
FERRUGO	LLANERO	MOROCCO	PEDRERO	PRIMERO	SAMSHOO	SQUACCO	TOURACO	WHERESO
FINNSKO	LUMBAGO	MULATTO	PEEKABO	PRIVADO	SAPSAGO	STRETTO	TREMOLO	WHERETO
FORZATO	MADRONO	NATHEMO	PERSICO	PROVISO	SCALADO	SUBZERO	TROMINO	WINDIGO
FUMETTO	MAESTRO	NAVARHO	PIANINO	PROXIMO	SCHERZO	SUPREMO	TYMPANO	ZAMARRO
FURIOSO	MAFIOSO	NELUMBO	PICCOLO	PRURIGO	SCIOLTO	TANGELO	UNDERDO	ZANJERO
GAMBADO	MAGNETO	NONETTO	PIFFERO	REJONEO	SCORPIO	TEDESCO	UNDERGO	ZEMSTVO
GIOCOSO	MALICHO	OKIMONO	PIMENTO	RELIEVO	SECONDO	TENTIGO	VAQUERO	ZOCCOLO
GRADINO	MARCATO	OLOROSO	PINTADO	REVERSO	SENECIO	TESTUDO	VERISMO	ZORILLO
GUANACO	MEMENTO	OREGANO	PLACEBO	RIDOTTO	SERPIGO	THEORBO	VERTIGO	ZUFFOLO
HIDALGO	MESTIZO	PAISANO	PLENIPO	RILIEVO	SFUMATO	THERETO	VIBRATO	
HISTRIO	MISTICO	PAKAPOO	POINADO	RIPIENO	SHAKUDO	TIMPANO	VILIACO	
HORNITO	MOCKADO	PALAZZO	POMPANO	RISOTTO	SHAMPOO	TOBACCO	VILIAGO	
HUANACO	MONTERO	PAMPERO	POMPELO	RONDINO	SIROCCO	TOMBOLO	VIRANDO	
IMPASTO	MORELLO	PAPILIO	PORRIGO	ROSOLIO	SOLDADO	TONDINO	VOLCANO	

8-letter words ending in -O

ALFRESCO	CASTRATO	EXPRESSO	IMPETIGO	MANZELLO	PIMIENTO	SESTETTO	TUCOTUCO
AMORETTO	CAUDILLO	FALSETTO	INNUENDO	MARTELLO	PLUMBAGO	SFORZATO	TUCUTUCO
ARMIGERO	CHARNECO	FANDANGO	INTAGLIO	MODERATO	POIGNADO	SIGISBEO	TWELVEMO
ARPEGGIO	CHECHAKO	FASCISMO	INTARSIO	MONTANTO	POLITICO	SMORZATO	UMBRELLO
ASSIENTO	CICISBEO	FELLATIO	JACKAROO	MOSQUITO	PRELUDIO	SOMBRERO	VARGUENO
AUTOGIRO	COCKATOO	FINNESKO	JACKEROO	NEUTRINO	PRESIDIO	SPADILLO	VARLETTO
AUTOGYRO	COMMANDO	FINOCHIO	JILLAROO	OCOTILLO	PRUNELLO	SPICCATO	VERDELHO
BALLYHOO	CONCERTO	FLAMENCO	JORDELOO	ORATORIO	PULVILIO	STACCATO	VILLAGIO
BARBASCO	CONCETTO	FLAMINGO	JUNKANOO	OSTINATO	RANCHERO	STAMPEDO	VILLIAGO
BARGELLO	CONTANGO	FORZANDO	KAKEMONO	OTTAVINO	REDDENDO	STICCADO	VINDALOO
BARRANCO	CONTINUO	GALAPAGO	KANGAROO	PACHINKO	RENEGADO	STICCATO	VIRTUOSO
BESOGNIO	CONTORNO	GARBANZO	LENTANDO	PADERERO	RISOLUTO	STILETTO	VITILIGO
BONAMANO	CORAGGIO	GARDYLOO	LIBECCIO	PALAMINO	RISPETTO	STOCCADO	WALLAROO
BORACHIO	CORNETTO	GAZPACHO	LIBRETTO	PALISADO	RITENUTO	SUBIMAGO	WANDEROO
BORDELLO	COROCORO	GILLAROO	LITERATO	PALMETTO	ROSOGLIO	SUPPEAGO	ZECCHINO
BOZZETTO	CRUZEIRO	GRACIOSO	LOCOFOCO	PALOMINO	SALTANDO	TAPACOLO	ZUCHETTO
BUCKAROO	CURCULIO	GRAFFITO	MACHISMO	PARLANDO	SARGASSO	TAPACULO	
BUCKAYRO	DOLOROSO	GRAZIOSO	MAESTOSO	PATERERO	SCALDINO	TAPADERO	
BUCKEROO	DUETTINO	GUACHARO	MAKIMONO	PEDERERO	SCENARIO	TENEBRIO	
CACAFOGO	ESCALADO	HALLALOO	MALGRADO	PEEKABOO	SCIROCCO	TERRAZZO	
CAMISADO	ESCAPADO	HEREUNTO	MALLECHO	PEPERINO	SCORDATO	TERZETTO	
CAPITANO	ESPRESSO	HITHERTO	MAMELUCO	PERDENDO	SEICENTO	TRAPUNTO	
CAPUCCIO	ESPUMOSO	HUBBUBOO	MANCANDO	PERFECTO	SERAGLIO	TRECENTO	

WORDS ENDING IN -U

2-letter words ending in -U

GU	MU	NU	OU	YU

3-letter words ending in -U

AYU	ECU	FLU	GJU	LEU	PIU	UTU
CRU	EMU	FOU	GNU	MEU	SOU	VAU
EAU	FEU	GAU	JEU	MOU	TAU	YOU

4-letter words ending in -U

AITU	BEAU	EMEU	JUJU	LUAU	OMBU	RIMU	THOU	TUTU	ZULU
BABU	CHOU	FRAU	KUDU	LULU	PRAU	TABU	THRU	UNAU	
BALU	CLOU	GENU	KUKU	MASU	PULU	TAPU	TOFU	ZEBU	
BAPU	ECRU	GURU	LIEU	MENU	RATU	TATU	TOLU	ZOBU	

5-letter words ending in -U

ADIEU	BUCHU	CORNU	HOKKU	LASSU	PERDU	QUIPU	SNAFU	VERTU
BAYOU	BUCKU	COYPU	JAMBU	NANDU	PILAU	SADHU	TATOU	VIRTU
BIJOU	BUNDU	FICHU	KANZU	NOYAU	POILU	SAJOU	UHURU	VOULU
BOYAU	BUSSU	HAIKU	KUDZU	PAREU	PRAHU	SAMFU	URUBU	WUSHU

6-letter words ending in -U

ABATTU	BATEAU	CONGOU	GAGAKU	JABIRU	MZUNGU	PILLAU	SADDHU	TELEDU
ACAJOU	BUREAU	COTEAU	GATEAU	KIKUYU	NILGAU	PIUPIU	SAMSHU	VOUDOU
AMADOU	CACHOU	DETENU	GOMOKU	LANDAU	NOGAKU	RESEAU	SUBFEU	YNAMBU
APERCU	CADEAU	EPERDU	INGENU	MILIEU	ORMOLU	ROUCOU	TAMANU	

7-letter words ending in -U

BABASSU	BUNRAKU	CATTABU	FABLIAU	MARABOU	PARVENU	ROULEAU	TINAMOU
BANDEAU	CAMAIEU	CHANOYU	INCONNU	MOINEAU	PLATEAU	SAPAJOU	TONNEAU
BASBLEU	CARDECU	CHAPEAU	JAMBEAU	MORCEAU	PONCEAU	SEPPUKU	TRUMEAU
BEBEERU	CARIBOU	CHATEAU	MANITOU	NOUVEAU	PURLIEU	SHIATSU	
BERCEAU	CATECHU	CORBEAU	MANTEAU	NYLGHAU	RONDEAU	TABLEAU	

8-letter words ending in -U

ABOIDEAU	CARCAJOU	CARJACOU	FLAMBEAU	KABELJOU	PIRARUCU	SUCURUJU
ABOITEAU	CARIACOU	FELDGRAU	HAUSFRAU	KINKAJOU	PYENGADU	SURUCUCU

SECTION THREE

BONUS WORD SETS

Introduction

Since there is a 50-point bonus for playing all seven tiles at one turn, seven-letter words are an essential part of the Scrabble player's vocabulary. As seven tiles can also be played around an existing letter on the board, eight-letter words are also a key part of the Scrabble player's word knowledge. Any word which uses all seven of the letters on your rack is called a bonus word, or just plain bonus. Bonuses usually have seven or eight letters, but could have more. (In the USA and some other parts of the world, words which score a 50-point bonus are called 'bingos'.)

Some seven-letter words are more useful than others, simply because they are more likely to occur, given the distribution of letters in the Scrabble set. For this reason, it is an unnecessary task (and a painstakingly lengthy one!) to attempt to learn all of the seven-letter words. There are over 25,000 seven-letter words, yet it is much more worthwhile (and a lot easier!) to concentrate on some of the 20-25% that are going to be the most useful to you. Such seven-letter words can be arranged conveniently according to common six-letter groups of letters. Each group yields a list of seven-letter words that can be made by the addition of a single seventh letter. These are the '6-plus-1 lists' – six letters plus another one letter to make a variety of seven-letter words. The more different letters of the alphabet that a combination goes with, the higher its utility to the Scrabble player.

There are 200 such six-letter sets in the subsequent 6-plus-1 lists, representing the 200 most fruitful and most likely combinations, based on an algorithm of the probability of the six-letter set occurring and the number of different letters it combines with. The six-letter combinations are listed in alphabetical sequence with their respective position in the top 200 shown alongside. In each case, a mnemonic of the six-letter combination is also provided as an aide-mémoire. It is easier to recall that LADIES plus an O makes DEASOIL, rather than ADEILS plus an O.

These six-letter combinations simplify learning and should assist recollection during an actual game. If the concept is new to you, then just concentrate on two or three of the most fertile sets, such as AEINRT (RETAIN), AENRST (ANTERS) and EGINRS (INGERS). When the seven-letter words associated with these become familiar, move on and tackle other six-letter sets. On the other hand, you may want to expand on the 200 lists here. Just select a group of six letters *not* in the list of 200, and then use the seven-letter anagrams list in Section 5 to search for the seven-letter words which can be made by the addition of a single letter to your chosen group of six.

Eight-letter words also need to be in the Scrabble player's armoury. There will be many occasions when the seven letters on your rack can be added to a single letter already on the board, to make an eight-letter word. Perhaps the seven letters on your rack do not make a bonus word by themselves. Even if they do, perhaps the bonus word won't fit on the board anywhere. These are the occasions when you may need to think bigger – eight-letter words! Of course, the seven-letter word on your rack may go down on the board, but the potential eight-letter word might score quite a few more points. Sometimes an eight-letter word will score a lot more points, if it covers two triple-word-score squares – this is the 'nine-timer' which Scrabble players strive for in high-scoring games!

The eight-letter words are arranged here into the 200 most worthwhile six-letter groups – the same top 200 as used for the seven-letter words. Listed beneath each six-letter group are the two-letter combinations which can be added to create an eight-letter word. So, for example, ABEILS plus AL yields both ISABELLA and SAILABLE; ABEILS plus AR yields RAISABLE; and so on. These, then, are the '6-plus-2 lists'. If you don't feel able to tackle all 200 lists in one go, break them up into smaller groups. Begin by concentrating on the most fertile groups (AEIRST, AEINST, and AEINRS are the top three). Once you feel confident about these, move on to other groups. If your own favourite six-letter groups are not listed here, why not use the Eight Letter Anagrams list in Section 5 to create new 6-plus-2 lists?

7-LETTER SETS
from the top 200 6-letter combinations

ABDEIR 134
(ABRIDE)
C CARB1DE
D BRAIDED
E BEADIER
  BEARDIE
G ABRIDGE
  BRIGADE
L BRAILED
  RIDABLE
M EMBRAID
N BANDIER
  BRAINED
R BARDIER
  BRAIDER
  BRIARED
  RABIDER
S BRAISED
  DARBIES
T TRIBADE
U DAUBIER
W BAWDIER

ABEILS 188
(ISABEL)
A ABELIAS
D DISABLE
E BAILEES
F FAIBLES
I BAILIES
K SKIABLE
M EMBAILS
  LAMBIES
N LESBIAN
R BAILERS
S ABSEILS
  ISABELS
  LABISES
T ALBITES
  ASTILBE
  BESTIAL
  LIBATES
  STABILE
W BEWAILS
Y BAILEYS
Z SIZABLE

ABEORS 144
(ABORES)
B EARBOBS
E AEROBES
G BORAGES
I ISOBARE
J JERBOAS
L LABROSE
N BORANES
P SAPROBE
R BRASERO
T BOASTER
  BOATERS
  BORATES
  SORBATE
U AEROBUS
V BRAVOES
X BORAXES

Z BEZOARS

ABERST 122
(BREAST)
A ABREAST
B BARBETS
  RABBETS
  STABBER
D DABSTER
E BEATERS
  BERATES
  REBATES
G BARGEST
H BATHERS
  BERTHAS
  BREATHS
I BAITERS
  BARITES
L ALBERTS
  BATLERS
  BLASTER
  LABRETS
  STABLER
M TAMBERS
N BANTERS
O BOASTER
  BOATERS
  BORATES
  SORBATE
R BARRETS
  BARTERS
S BASTERS
  BESTARS
  BRASSET
  BREASTS
T BATTERS
  TABRETS
U ARBUTES
  SURBATE
V BRAVEST
W BRAWEST
  WABSTER
X BAXTERS
Y BARYTES
  BETRAYS

ACEILR 121
(LACIER)
B CALIBER
  CALIBRE
D DECRIAL
  RADICEL
  RADICLE
F FILACER
G GLACIER
  GRACILE
H CHARLIE
M CALMIER
  CLAIMER
  MIRACLE
  RECLAIM
N CARLINE
O CALORIE
  CARIOLE
  COALIER

  LORICAE
P CALIPER
  REPLICA
R CERRIAL
S CLARIES
  ECLAIRS
  SCALIER
T ARTICLE
  RECITAL
U AURICLE
V CALIVER
  CLAVIER
  VELARIC
Y CLAYIER

ACEINR 65
(CANIER)
A ACARINE
B CARBINE
D CAIRNED
  CARNIED
E CINEREA
F FANCIER
G GRECIAN
L CARLINE
M CARMINE
N CANNIER
P CAPRINE
R CARNIER
S ARSENIC
  CERASIN
T CANTIER
  CERTAIN
  CRINATE
  NACRITE

ACEINS 119
(INCASE)
D CANDIES
  INCASED
F FANCIES
  FASCINE
  FIANCES
G CEASING
  INCAGES
H INCHASE
L ANCILES
  INLACES
  SANICLE
M AMNESIC
  CINEMAS
N CANINES
  NANCIES
O ACINOSE
P INSCAPE
  PINCASE
R ARSENIC
  CARNIES
  CERASIN
S CASEINS
  INCASES
T CANIEST
  CINEAST
U EUCAINS

V INCAVES
Y CYANISE

ACENRS 175
(CANERS)
C CANCERS
D DANCERS
E CAREENS
  CASERNE
  ENRACES
H CHENARS
  RANCHES
I ARSENIC
  CARNIES
  CERASIN
K CANKERS
L LANCERS
  RANCELS
N CANNERS
  SCANNER
O CARNOSE
  COARSEN
  CORNEAS
P PRANCES
S ANCRESS
  CASERNS
T CANTERS
  CARNETS
  NECTARS
  RECANTS
  SCANTER
  TANRECS
  TRANCES
U SURANCE
V CAVERNS
  CRAVENS
Y CARNEYS
  SCENARY
Z ZARNECS

ACENRT 96
(CANTER)
A CATERAN
D CANTRED
  TRANCED
E CRENATE
F CANTREF
H CHANTER
  TRANCHE
I CANTIER
  CERTAIN
  CRINATE
  NACRITE
L CENTRAL
O ENACTOR
S CANTERS
  CARNETS
  NECTARS
  RECANTS
  SCANTER
  TANRECS
  TRANCES
T TRANECT
U CENTAUR
  UNCRATE

  UNTRACE
Y ENCRATY
  NECTARY

ACENST 149
(STANCE)
A CATENAS
C ACCENTS
D DECANTS
  DESCANT
  SCANTED
E CETANES
  TENACES
H CHASTEN
  NATCHES
I CANIEST
  CINEAST
K NACKETS
L CANTLES
  CENTALS
  LANCETS
  SCANTLE
N NASCENT
O COSTEAN
  OCTANES
P CATNEPS
R CANTERS
  CARNETS
  NECTARS
  RECANTS
  SCANTER
  TANRECS
  TRANCES
S ASCENTS
  SECANTS
  STANCES
T CANTEST
U NUTCASE

ACEORS 103
(ORACES)
A ROSACEA
D SARCODE
E ACEROSE
G CARGOES
  CORSAGE
  SOCAGER
H CHOREAS
  ORACHES
  ROACHES
I ORACIES
  SCORIAE
L COALERS
  ESCOLAR
  ORACLES
M AMORCES
N CARNOSE
  COARSEN
  CORNEAS
R COARSER
S ROSACES
T COASTER
  COATERS
U ACEROUS
  CAROUSE

X COAXERS

ACEOST 146
(ACTOSE)
D COASTED
E ACETOSE
  COATEES
I SOCIATE
L ALECOST
  LACTOSE
  LOCATES
  SCATOLE
  TALCOSE
M COMATES
N COSTEAN
  OCTANES
P CAPOTES
  SCOPATE
  TOECAPS
R COASTER
  COATERS
T COSTATE
U ACETOUS
V AVOCETS
  OCTAVES

ACERST 141
(CATERS)
A ACATERS
D REDACTS
E CERATES
  CREATES
  ECARTES
  SECRETA
H ARCHEST
  CHARETS
  CHASTER
  RATCHES
I CRISTAE
  RACIEST
  STEARIC
K RACKETS
  STACKER
  TACKERS
L CARTELS
  CLARETS
  SCARLET
  TARCELS
M MERCATS
N CANTERS
  CARNETS
  NECTARS
  RECANTS
  SCANTER
  TANRECS
  TRANCES
O COASTER
  COATERS
P CARPETS
  PRECAST
  SPECTRA
R CARTERS
  CRATERS
  TRACERS

S ACTRESS
CASTERS
RECASTS
T SCATTER
U ACTURES
CAUTERS
CRUSTAE
CURATES
Y SECTARY

ADEERS 70
(SEARED)
B DEBASER
SABERED
C CREASED
DECARES
SEARCED
D DEADERS
G DRAGEES
GREASED
H ADHERES
HEADERS
HEARSED
SHEARED
I DEARIES
READIES
K SKEARED
L ARLESED
DEALERS
LEADERS
REDEALS
M REMADES
REMEADS
SMEARED
N DEANERS
ENDEARS
O OREADES
P PREASED
SPEARED
R DREARES
READERS
REDSEAR
REREADS
S RESEDAS
T DEAREST
DERATES
ESTRADE
REASTED
SEDATER
STEARED
V ADVERSE
W DRAWEES

ADEEST 85
(SEATED)
B BESTEAD
DEBATES
C TEDESCA
D DEADEST
SEDATED
STEADED
F DEAFEST
DEFASTE
DEFEATS
FEASTED
H HEADSET
I IDEATES
L DELATES
STEALED
M STEAMED

N STEANED
R DEAREST
DERATES
ESTRADE
REASTED
SEDATER
STEARED
S SEDATES
T ESTATED
U SAUTEED
W SWEATED
Y YEASTED

ADEGLN 197
(DANGLE)
B BANGLED
C CANGLED
CLANGED
GLANCED
D DANGLED
GLADDEN
E GLEANED
F FANGLED
FLANGED
I ALIGNED
DEALING
LEADING
J JANGLED
M MANGLED
N ENDLANG
R DANGLER
GNARLED
S DANGLES
GLANDES
SLANGED
T TANGLED
U LANGUED
W WANGLED

ADEGNR 126
(DANGER)
E ANGERED
DERANGE
ENRAGED
GRANDEE
GRENADE
I AREDING
DEARING
DERAIGN
EARDING
GRADINE
GRAINED
READING
L DANGLER
GNARLED
O GROANED
P PRANGED
R GNARRED
GRANDER
S DANGERS
GANDERS
GARDENS
T GRANTED
U ENGUARD
RAUNGED

ADEILR 19
(RAILED)
A RADIALE
B BRAILED

RIDABLE
C DECRIAL
RADICEL
RADICLE
D DIEDRAL
DRAILED
E LEADIER
G GLADIER
GLAIRED
I DELIRIA
IRIDEAL
L DALLIER
DIALLER
RALLIED
O DARIOLE
P PEDRAIL
PREDIAL
R LARDIER
S DERAILS
SIDERAL
T DILATER
TRAILED
V VALIDER
Y READILY

ADEILS 33
(LADIES)
B DISABLE
C SCAILED
D DAIDLES
LADDIES
E AEDILES
DEISEAL
F DISLEAF
G SILAGED
H HALIDES
I DAILIES
LIAISED
SEDILIA
K SKAILED
L DALLIES
DISLEAL
LALDIES
SALLIED
M MEDIALS
MISDEAL
MISLEAD
N DENIALS
SNAILED
O DEASOIL
P ALIPEDS
PAIDLES
PALSIED
R DERAILS
SIDERAL
S AIDLESS
DEASILS
T DETAILS
DILATES
U AUDILES
DEASIUL
V DEVISAL
Y DIALYSE
EYLIADS

ADEINR 4
(RAINED)
A ARANEID
B BANDIER
BRAINED

C CAIRNED
CARNIED
D DANDIER
DRAINED
F FRIANDE
G AREDING
DEARING
DERAIGN
EARDING
GRADINE
GRAINED
READING
H HANDIER
I DENARII
M ADERMIN
INARMED
O ANEROID
P PARDINE
R DRAINER
RANDIER
S RANDIES
SANDIER
SARDINE
T DETRAIN
TRAINED
U UNAIRED
URANIDE
V INVADER
RAVINED

ADEINS 22
(SANDIE)
A NAIADES
B BANDIES
C CANDIES
INCASED
D DANDIES
SDAINED
E ANISEED
G AGNISED
K KANDIES
L DENIALS
SNAILED
M DEMAINS
MAIDENS
MEDIANS
MEDINAS
O ADONISE
ANODISE
SODAINE
P PANDIES
PANSIED
SPAINED
R RANDIES
SANDIER
SARDINE
S SDAINES
T DETAINS
INSTEAD
SATINED
SAINTED
STAINED
TOADIES
V INVADES
W DEWANIS

ADEIRS 12
(RAISED)
A ARAISED
B BRAISED
DARBIES

C CARDIES
RADICES
SIDECAR
E DEARIES
READIES
F FRAISED
G AGRISED
H SHADIER
I DAIRIES
DIARIES
DIARISE
K DAIKERS
DARKIES
L DERAILS
SIDERAL
M ADMIRES
MARDIES
MISREAD
SIDEARM
N RANDIES
SANDIER
SARDINE
O ROADIES
SOREDIA
P ASPIRED
DESPAIR
DIAPERS
PRAISED
R ARRIDES
RAIDERS
T ARIDEST
ASTERID
ASTRIDE
DIASTER
DISRATE
STAIDER
STAIRED
TARDIES
U RESIDUA
V ADVISER
VARDIES

ADEIST 26
(IDATES)
B BASTIDE
C ACIDEST
DACITES
E IDEATES
F DAFTIES
FADIEST
G AGISTED
L DETAILS
DILATES
M MISDATE
N DETAINS
INSTEAD
SAINTED
SATINED
STAINED
O IODATES
TOADIES
R ARIDEST
ASTERID
ASTRIDE
DIASTER
DISRATE
STAIDER
STAIRED
TARDIES

TIRADES
S DISSEAT
SAIDEST
U DAUTIES
V AVIDEST
DATIVES
VISTAED
W DAWTIES
WAISTED

ADELNR 79
(LANDER)
A ADRENAL
B BLANDER
D DANDLER
E LEARNED
G DANGLER
GNARLED
H HANDLER
K RANKLED
L LANDLER
M MANDREL
O LADRONE
S DARNELS
ENLARDS
LANDERS
SLANDER
SNARLED
U LAUNDER
LURDANE
RUNDALE
Y DEARNLY

ADELNS 137
(ANDLES)
C CALENDS
CANDLES
D DANDLES
E LEADENS
G DANGLES
GLANDES
SLANGED
H HANDLES
HANDSEL
I DENIALS
SNAILED
K KALENDS
O LOADENS
R DARNELS
ENLARDS
LANDERS
SLANDER
SNARLED
S SENDALS
T DENTALS
SLANTED
U UNLADES
UNLEADS

ADELRS 88
(ALDERS)
B BEDRALS
C CRADLES
SCALDER
D LADDERS
RADDLES
SADDLER
E ARLESED
DEALERS
LEADERS

```
      REDEALS           SLANDER      M TANDEMS           STANDER      K DISRANK           BREARES
F FARDELS           N SNARLED      N STANDEN           STARNED      L ALDRINS      C CAREERS
G DARGLES      M MANREDS      O ASTONED      O DOATERS      M MANDIRS      D DREARES
H HARELDS           RANDEMS           DONATES           ROASTED      N INNARDS           READERS
      HERALDS           REMANDS           ONSTEAD           TORSADE      O INROADS           REDSEAR
I DERAILS      P PANDERS      P PEDANTS           TROADES           ORDAINS           REREADS
      SIDERAL      R DARNERS           PENTADS      P DEPARTS      T INDARTS      G GREASER
K DARKLES           ERRANDS      R ENDARTS           DRAPETS      U DURIANS      H HEARERS
M MEDLARS           SNARRED           STANDER           PETARDS           SUNDARI           REHEARS
N DARNELS      S SANDERS           STARNED      R DARTERS      W INWARDS           SHEARER
      ENLARDS           SARSDEN      T ATTENDS           DARTRES                          I REARISE
      LANDERS      T ENDARTS      U SAUNTED           RETARDS      AEELRS  72      M REAMERS
      SLANDER           STANDER           UNSATED           STARRED      (EALERS)      N EARNERS
      SNARLED           STARNED      V ADVENTS           TRADERS      C ALERCES      O REAROSE
O LOADERS      U ASUNDER      Y STAYNED      T STARTED           CEREALS      P REAPERS
      ORDEALS           DANSEUR                             TETRADS           RESCALE      R REARERS
      RELOADS           DAUNERS      ADEORS  48      V ADVERTS      D ARLESED      S ERASERS
P PEDLARS      W DAWNERS      (ADORES)           STARVED           DEALERS      T SERRATE
R LARDERS           WANDERS      C SARCODE      W STEWARD           LEADERS           TEARERS
S SARDELS           WARDENS      D DEODARS           STRAWED           REDEALS      U ERASURE
T DARTLES      Z ZANDERS      E OREADES           WRASTED      E RELEASE      V REAVERS
U LAUDERS                          F FEDORAS      Y STRAYED      G GALERES      W SWEARER
W WARSLED      ADENRU  64      I ROADIES                             REGALES           WEARERS
Z DRAZELS      (AUNDER)           SOREDIA      ADGINR 135      H HEALERS
                   B UNBARED      L LOADERS      (RADING)      I REALISE      AEERST  20
ADELST 110      C DURANCE           ORDEALS      B BARDING      K LEAKERS      (EATERS)
(SALTED)           UNRACED           RELOADS           BRIGAND      M MEALERS      A AERATES
B BALDEST      D DAUNDER      M RADOMES      C CARDING      O AREOLES      B BEATERS
      BLASTED      E UNEARED      R ADORERS      E AREDING      P LEAPERS           BERATES
      STABLED      G ENGUARD           DROSERA           DEARING           PLEASER           REBATES
C CASTLED           RAUNGED      T DOATERS           DERAIGN           RELAPSE      C CERATES
      SCLATED      H UNHEARD           ROASTED           EARDING           REPEALS           CREATES
D STADDLE      I UNAIRED           TORSADE           GRADINE      S ARLESES           ECARTES
E DELATES           URANIDE           TROADES           GRAINED           EARLESS           SECRETA
      STEALED      K UNRAKED      U AROUSED           READING           LEASERS      D DEAREST
I DETAILS      L LAUNDER      V SAVORED      F FARDING           RESALES           DERATES
      DILATES           LURDANE      W REDOWAS      G GRADING           RESEALS           ESTRADE
K SKLATED           RUNDALE                             NIGGARD           SEALERS           REASTED
      STALKED      M DURAMEN      ADERST  49      I GRADINI      T ELATERS           SEDATER
L STALLED           MANURED      (DATERS)           RAIDING           REALEST           STEARED
N DENTALS           MAUNDER      B DABSTER      L DARLING           RELATES      F AFREETS
      SLANTED           UNARMED      C REDACTS           LARDING           STEALER           FEASTER
O SALTOED      O RONDEAU           SCARTED      M MRIDANG      U LEASURE      G ERGATES
P SPALTED      P UNPARED      D ADDREST      N DARNING      V LAVEERS           RESTAGE
      STAPLED      S ASUNDER      E DEAREST           NARDING           REVEALS      H AETHERS
R DARTLES           DANSEUR           DERATES           RANDING           SEVERAL           HEATERS
S DESALTS           DAUNERS           ESTRADE      O ADORING      X RELAXES           REHEATS
T SLATTED      T DAUNTER           REASTED           GRADINO      Y SEALERY      I AERIEST
U AULDEST           NATURED           SEDATER           ROADING                             SERIATE
      SALUTED           UNRATED           STEARED      P DRAPING      AEEPRT 142      K RETAKES
                   UNTREAD      F STRAFED      R DARRING      (REPEAT)           SAKERET
ADENRS  62      Y UNREADY      H DEARTHS      S DARINGS      A PATERAE      L ELATERS
(ANDERS)                           HARDEST           GRADINS      D ADEPTER           REALEST
C DANCERS      ADENST  36           HATREDS      T DARTING           PREDATE           RELATES
D DANDERS      (STANED)           THREADS           TRADING           TAPERED           STEALER
E DEANERS      A ANSATED           TRASHED      U DAURING      H PREHEAT      M STEAMER
      ENDEARS      C DECANTS      I ARIDEST      W DRAWING      I PEATIER           TEAMERS
F FARDENS           DESCANT           ASTERID           WARDING      K PERTAKE      N EARNEST
G DANGERS           SCANTED           ASTRIDE      Y YARDING      L PRELATE           EASTERN
      GANDERS      E STEANED           DIASTER                             M TEMPERA           NEAREST
      GARDENS      G STANGED           DISRATE      ADINRS 105      O OPERATE      O ROSEATE
H HANDERS      H HANDSET           STAIDER      (DRAINS)      R TAPERER      P REPEATS
      HARDENS      I DETAINS           STAIRED      A RADIANS      S REPEATS      R SERRATE
I RANDIES           INSTEAD           TARDIES      B RIBANDS      U EPURATE           TEARERS
      SANDIER           SAINTED           TIRADES      E RANDIES      Y PEATERY      S RESEATS
      SARDINE           SATINED      K DARKEST           SANDIER      Z TRAPEZE           SAETERS
K DARKENS           STAINED           STARKED           SARDINE                             SEAREST
L DARNELS      K DANKEST      L DARTLES      F FRIANDS      AEERRS 162           SEATERS
      ENLARDS      L DENTALS      M SMARTED      G DARINGS      (ERASER)           STEARES
      LANDERS           SLANTED      N ENDARTS           GRADINS      B BEARERS           TEASERS
```

TESSERA
T ESTREAT
RESTATE
U AUSTERE
W SWEATER

AEGILN 55
(EALING)
C ANGELIC
ANGLICE
D ALIGNED
DEALING
LEADING
E LINEAGE
F FEALING
FINAGLE
LEAFING
G GEALING
LIGNAGE
H HEALING
K LEAKING
LINKAGE
L NIGELLA
M LEAMING
MEALING
N ANELING
EANLING
LEANING
NEALING
P LEAPING
PEALING
PLEAING
R ENGRAIL
LEARING
NARGILE
REALIGN
REGINAL
S LEASING
LINAGES
SEALING
T ATINGLE
ELATING
GELATIN
GENITAL
U LINGUAE
V LEAVING
Y ALEYING

AEGINR 15
(EARING)
B BEARING
C GRECIAN
D AREDING
DEARING
DERAIGN
EARDING
GRADINE
GRAINED
READING
E REGINAE
F FEARING
G GEARING
NAGGIER
H HEARING
K REAKING
L ENGRAIL
LEARING
NARGILE
REALIGN
REGINAL

M GERMAIN
MANGIER
REAMING
N AGINNER
EARNING
ENGRAIN
GRANNIE
NEARING
O ORIGANE
P REAPING
R ANGRIER
EARRING
GRAINER
RANGIER
REARING
S ANGRIES
EARINGS
ERASING
GAINERS
GRAINES
REGAINS
REGINAS
SEARING
SERINGA
T GRANITE
INGRATE
TANGIER
TEARING
V REAVING
VINEGAR
W WEARING

AEGLNR 91
(ANGLER)
A ALNAGER
B BRANGLE
C CLANGER
D DANGLER
GNARLED
E ENLARGE
GENERAL
GLEANER
G GANGREL
I ENGRAIL
LEARING
NARGILE
REALIGN
REGINAL
J JANGLER
L LANGREL
M MANGLER
P GRAPNEL
S ANGLERS
LARGENS
T TANGLER
TRANGLE
U GRANULE
W WANGLER
WRANGLE
Y ANGERLY

AEGLNS 170
(ANGLES)
A ALNAGES
ANLAGES
GALENAS
LAGENAS
LASAGNE
B BANGLES
C CANGLES

GLANCES
D DANGLES
GLANDES
SLANGED
F FANGLES
FLANGES
G LAGGENS
I LEASING
LINAGES
SEALING
J JANGLES
L LEGLANS
M MANGELS
MANGLES
O ENGAOLS
P SPANGLE
R ANGLERS
LARGENS
S GLASSEN
T LANGEST
TANGLES
U ANGELUS
LAGUNES
LANGUES
W WANGLES
Y LYNAGES

AEGLNT 118
(TANGLE)
D TANGLED
E ELEGANT
H ALENGTH
I ATINGLE
ELATING
GELATIN
GENITAL
O TANGELO
R TANGLER
TRANGLE
S LANGEST
TANGLES
T GANTLET
U LANGUET
W TWANGLE

AEGLRS 167
(LAGERS)
A ALEGARS
LAAGERS
B GARBLES
D DARGLES
E GALERES
REGALES
F REFLAGS
G GARGLES
LAGGERS
RAGGLES
I GRAILES
K GRAKLES
M MALGRES
N ANGLERS
LARGENS
O GAOLERS
P GRAPLES
S LARGESS
T LARGEST
V GRAVELS
VERGLAS
Y ARGYLES
GRAYLES

Z GLAZERS

AEGLST 187
(GLATES)
A AGELAST
ALGATES
B GABLETS
E EAGLETS
LEGATES
TEAGLES
TELEGAS
H HAGLETS
I AGILEST
AIGLETS
LIGATES
TAIGLES
L GALLETS
N LANGEST
TANGLES
O LEGATOS
R LARGEST
T GESTALT
W TALWEGS

AEGNRS 86
(ANGERS)
B BANGERS
GRABENS
D DANGERS
GANDERS
GARDENS
E ENRAGES
G GANGERS
GRANGES
NAGGERS
H GNASHER
HANGERS
I ANGRIES
EARINGS
ERASING
GAINERS
GRAINES
REGAINS
REGINAS
SEARING
SERINGA
L ANGLERS
LARGENS
M ENGRAMS
GERMANS
MANGERS
O ONAGERS
ORANGES
P ENGRASP
R GARNERS
RANGERS
S SERANGS
T ARGENTS
GARNETS
STRANGE
U RAUNGES
UNGEARS
W GNAWERS

AEGNRT 54
(GANTER)
A TANAGER
D GRANTED
E GRANTEE

GREATEN
REAGENT
F ENGRAFT
I GRANITE
INGRATE
TANGIER
TEARING
L TANGLER
TRANGLE
M GARMENT
MARGENT
RAGMENT
N REGNANT
P TREPANG
R GRANTER
REGRANT
S ARGENTS
GARNETS
STRANGE
U GAUNTER

AEGNST 115
(TANGES)
A AGNATES
D STANGED
E NEGATES
H STENGAH
I EASTING
EATINGS
GAINEST
GENISTA
INGATES
INGESTA
TANGIES
TEASING
TSIGANE
L LANGEST
TANGLES
M MAGNETS
N GANNETS
R ARGENTS
GARNETS
STRANGE
T GESTANT

AEGRST 80
(GATERS)
A AGRASTE
B BARGEST
E ERGATES
RESTAGE
G GAGSTER
GARGETS
STAGGER
TAGGERS
H GATHERS
I AGISTER
GAITERS
STAGIER
STRIGAE
TRIAGES
L LARGEST
N ARGENTS
GARNETS
STRANGE
O ORGEATS
STORAGE
P PARGETS
R GARRETS

GARTERS
GRATERS
S STAGERS
T TARGETS
V GRAVEST
Y GRAYEST
GYRATES
STAGERY

AEHRST 169
(HATERS)
B BATHERS
BERTHAS
BREATHS
C ARCHEST
CHARETS
CHASTER
RATCHES
D DEARTHS
HARDEST
HATREDS
THREADS
TRASHED
E AETHERS
HEATERS
REHEATS
F FATHERS
G GATHERS
H HEARTHS
I HASTIER
SHERIAT
L HALTERS
HARSLET
LATHERS
SLATHER
THALERS
M HAMSTER
N ANTHERS
HARTENS
THENARS
O ASTHORE
HAROSET
P SPARTHE
TEPHRAS
THREAPS
S RASHEST
SHASTER
TRASHES
T HATTERS
RATHEST
SHATTER
THREATS
V HARVEST
W THAWERS
WREATHS

AEILMN 133
(MALINE)
A LAMINAE
C MELANIC
F FEMINAL
INFLAME
G LEAMING
MEALING
H HELIMAN
L MANILLE
M MAILMEN
N LINEMAN

```
    MELANIN          SAILERS          TALKIES      H HAEMINS          SAMPIRE          SEARING
O MINEOLA            SERAILS        L TALLIES        HEMINAS        R MARRIES          SERINGA
P IMPANEL            SERIALS        N EASTLIN      J JASMINE          SIMARRE        H ARSHINE
    MANIPLE        T REALIST          ELASTIN      K KINEMAS        S MASSIER          HERNIAS
R MANLIER            RETAILS          ENTAILS      L ISLEMAN        T MAESTRI        I SENARII
    MARLINE          SALTIER          SALIENT        MENIALS          MAISTER        K SNAKIER
    MINERAL          SALTIRE          SLAINTE        SEMINAL          MASTIER        L NAILERS
    RAILMEN          SLATIER          STANIEL      M MISNAME          MISRATE        M MARINES
S ISLEMAN        V REVISAL            TENAILS      O ANOMIES        U UREMIAS          REMAINS
    MENIALS        W SWALIER        O ISOLATE      R MARINES        W AWMRIES          SEMINAR
    SEMINAL          WAILERS        P APLITES        REMAINS                           SIRNAME
T AILMENT                            PALIEST        SEMINAR                          N INSANER
    ALIMENT      AEILRT  10           TALIPES        SIRNAME      AEIMST  95            INSNARE
                 (RETAIL)           R REALIST      S INSEAMS      (MATIES)           O ERASION
AEILNT  11       B LIBRATE            RETAILS        SAMISEN      C ACMITES          P RAPINES
(ENTAIL)           TRIABLE            SALTIER      T INMATES        ETACISM          R SIERRAN
A ANTLIAE        C ARTICLE            SALTIRE        MAINEST        MICATES            SNARIER
E LINEATE          RECITAL            SLATIER        MANTIES        SEMATIC          S ARSINES
F INFLATE        D DILATER          U SITULAE        TAMINES      D MISDATE            SARNIES
G ATINGLE          TRAILED          V ESTIVAL                     E STEAMIE          T ANESTRI
    ELATING      E ATELIER          W WALIEST      AEIMNT  53     G GAMIEST            NASTIER
    GELATIN          REALTIE        Y TAILYES      (INMATE)         SIGMATE            RATINES
    GENITAL      H LATHIER          Z LAZIEST      A AMENTIA      H ATHEISM            RESIANT
M AILMENT        L LITERAL                           ANIMATE      I AMITIES            RETAINS
    ALIMENT          TALLIER        AEIMNR  61     B AMBIENT        ATIMIES            RETINAS
O ELATION        M LAMITER         (REMAIN)       C EMICANT      K MISTAKE            RETSINA
    TOENAIL          MALTIER        B MIRBANE        NEMATIC      M MISMATE            STAINER
P PANTILE        N ENTRAIL         C CARMINE      D MEDIANT        TAMMIES            STARNIE
R ENTRAIL          LATRINE         D ADERMIN      E MATINEE      N INMATES            STEARIN
    LATRINE          RATLINE          INARMED      G MINTAGE        MAINEST          V AVENIRS
    RATLINE          RELIANT        E REMANIE        TEAMING        MANTIES            RAVINES
    RELIANT          RETINAL        F FIREMAN        TEGMINA        TAMINES
    RETINAL          TRENAIL        G GERMAIN      I INTIMAE      O AMOSITE          AEINRT   1
    TRENAIL        P PLAITER          MANGIER        MINIATE        ATOMIES          (RETAIN)
S EASTLIN          PLATIER            REAMING      L AILMENT        ATOMISE          B ATEBRIN
· ELASTIN        R RETIRAL          H HARMINE        ALIMENT        OSMIATE          C CANTIER
    ENTAILS          RETRIAL        K MANKIER      N MANNITE      P IMPASTE            CERTAIN
    SALIENT          TRAILER          RAMEKIN      R MINARET        PASTIME            CRINATE
    SLAINTE        S REALIST        L MANLIER        RAIMENT      R MAESTRI            NACRITE
    STANIEL          RETAILS          MARLINE      S INMATES        MAISTER          D DETRAIN
    TENAILS          SALTIER          MINERAL        MAINEST        MASTIER            TRAINED
U ALUNITE          SALTIRE          RAILMEN        MANTIES        MISRATE          E RETINAE
V VENTAIL          SLATIER        O MORAINE        TAMINES        SEMITAR            TRAINEE
                 T TERTIAL         R MARINER      X TAXIMEN        SMARTIE          F FAINTER
AEILRS  16       U URALITE         S MARINES      Y AMENITY      S ASTEISM            FENITAR
(SAILER)         W WALTIER           REMAINS        ANYTIME        SAMIEST          G GRANITE
A AERIALS        Y IRATELY           SEMINAR                      SAMITES            INGRATE
B BAILERS          REALITY           SIRNAME      AEIMRS 112       TAMISES            TANGIER
C CLARIES                          T MINARET      (ARMIES)       T MATIEST            TEARING
    ECLAIRS      AEILST  24           RAIMENT      B AMBRIES        MATTIES          H INEARTH
    SCALIER      (ALITES)          V VERMIAN      D ADMIRES      Z MAZIEST          I INERTIA
D DERAILS        B ALBITES                          MARDIES        MESTIZA          J JANTIER
    SIDERAL          ASTILBE        AEIMNS  98       MISREAD                           NARTJIE
E REALISE          BESTIAL        (MANIES)          SIDEARM      AEINRS   6         K KERATIN
G GRAILES          LIBATES        A AMNESIA      E SEAMIER      (SARNIE)           L ENTRAIL
H HAILERS          STABILE          ANEMIAS        SERIEMA      C ARSENIC            LATRINE
    SHALIER      C ASTELIC         C AMNESIC      F MISFARE        CARNIES            RATLINE
I LAIRISE          ELASTIC          CINEMAS      G GISARME        CERASIN            RELIANT
    SAILIER          LACIEST        D DEMAINS        MAIGRES      D RANDIES            RETINAL
J JAILERS          LATICES          MAIDENS        MIRAGES        SANDIER            TRENAIL
K SERKALI          SALICET          MEDIANS      H MASHIER        SARDINE          M MINARET
L RALLIES        D DETAILS          MEDINAS        MISHEAR      F INFARES            RAIMENT
M MAILERS          DILATES        E MEANIES      L MAILERS      G ANGRIES          N ENTRAIN
    REALISM      G AGILEST          NEMESIA        REALISM        EARINGS            TRANNIE
N NAILERS          AIGLETS        F FAMINES      M RAMMIES        ERASING          O OTARINE
P PALSIER          LIGATES          INFAMES      N MARINES        GAINERS          P PAINTER
    PARLIES          TAIGLES        G ENIGMAS        REMAINS        GRAINES            PERTAIN
R RAILERS        H HALITES          GAMINES        SEMINAR        REGAINS            REPAINT
    RERAILS      I LAITIES          MEASING        SIRNAME        REGINAS          R RETRAIN
S AIRLESS        K LAKIEST          SEAMING      P IMPRESA                           TERRAIN
```

TRAINER
S ANESTRI
NASTIER
RATINES
RESIANT
RETAINS
RETINAS
RETSINA
STAINER
STARNIE
STEARIN
T INTREAT
ITERANT
NATTIER
NITRATE
TARTINE
TERTIAN
U RUINATE
TAURINE
URANITE
URINATE
W TAWNIER
TINWARE

AEINST 2
(SATINE)
A TAENIAS
B BASINET
BESAINT
BESTAIN
C CANIEST
CINEAST
D DETAINS
INSTEAD
SAINTED
SATINED
STAINED
E ETESIAN
F FAINEST
NAIFEST
G EASTING
EATINGS
GAINEST
GENISTA
INGATES
INGESTA
SEATING
TANGIES
TEASING
TSIGANE
I ISATINE
J JANTIES
K INTAKES
L EASTLIN
ELASTIN
ENTAILS
SALIENT
SLAINTE
STANIEL
TENAILS
M INMATES
MAINEST
MANTIES
TAMINES
N INANEST
O ATONIES
P PANTIES
PATINES
SAPIENT
SPINATE

R ANESTRI
NASTIER
RATINES
RESIANT
RETAINS
RETINAS
RETSINA
STAINER
STARNIE
STEARIN
S ENTASIS
NASTIES
SESTINA
TANSIES
TISANES
T INSTATE
SATINET
U AUNTIES
SINUATE
V NAIVEST
NATIVES
VAINEST
W AWNIEST
TAWNIES
WANIEST
WANTIES
Z ZANIEST

AEIPRS 75
(PRAISE)
A SPIRAEA
C EPACRIS
SCRAPIE
SPACIER
D ASPIRED
DESPAIR
DIAPERS
PRAISED
E APERIES
EPEIRAS
G GASPIER
PRISAGE
SPAIRGE
H HARPIES
SHARPIE
L PALSIER
PARLIES
M IMPRESA
SAMPIRE
N RAPINES
O SOAPIER
P APPRISE
SAPPIER
R PARRIES
PRAISER
RAPIERS
RASPIER
REPAIRS
S ASPIRES
PARESIS
PRAISES
SPIREAS
T PARTIES
PASTIER
PIASTRE
PIRATES
PRATIES
TRAIPSE
U SPURIAE
UPRAISE

V PARVISE
W WASPIER

AEIRST 3
(SATIRE)
A ARISTAE
ASTERIA
ATRESIA
B BAITERS
BARITES
C CRISTAE
RACIEST
STEARIC
D ARIDEST
ASTERID
ASTRIDE
DIASTER
DISRATE
STAIDER
STAIRED
TARDIES
TIRADES
E AERIEST
SERIATE
F FAIREST
G AGISTER
GAITERS
STAGIER
STRIGAE
TRIAGES
H HASTIER
SHERIAT
I AIRIEST
IRISATE
K ARKITES
KARITES
L REALIST
RETAILS
SALTIER
SALTIRE
SLATIER
M MAESTRI
MAISTER
MASTIER
MISRATE
SEMITAR
SMARTIE
N ANESTRI
NASTIER
RATINES
RESIANT
RETAINS
RETINAS
RETSINA
STAINER
STARNIE
STEARIN
O OARIEST
OTARIES
P PARTIES
PASTIER
PIASTRE
PIRATES
PRATIES
TRAIPSE
R ARTSIER
TARRIES
TARSIER
S SAIREST
SATIRES

TIRASSE
T ARTIEST
ARTISTE
ATTIRES
IRATEST
STRIATE
TASTIER
TERTIAS
T TATTIES
U SITUATE
V STATIVE
W TWAITES
Y SATIETY

AEIRTT 29
(ATTIRE)
A ARIETTA
B BATTIER
BIRETTA
C CATTIER
CITRATE
D ATTIRED
E ARIETTE
ITERATE
F FATTIER
L TERTIAL
N INTREAT
ITERANT
NATTIER
NITRATE
TARTINE
TERTIAN
P PARTITE
R RATTIER
RETRAIT
TARTIER
S ARTIEST
ARTISTE
ATTIRES
IRATEST
STRIATE
TASTIER
TERTIAS
T ATTRITE
TATTIER
TITRATE
V TAIVERT
W TATWIER
X EXTRAIT

AEISTT 83
(TASTIE)
A SATIATE
B BATISTE
C CATTIES
TIETACS
F FATTIES
H ATHEIST
STAITHE
K TAKIEST
M MATIEST
MATTIES
N INSTATE
SATINET
O OSTIATE
TOASTIE
P PATTIES
TAPETIS
R ARTIEST
ARTISTE

ATTIRES
IRATEST
STRIATE
TASTIER
TERTIAS
T TATTIES
U SITUATE
V STATIVE
W TWAITES
Y SATIETY

AELNRS 63
(LANERS)
A ARSENAL
B BRANLES
BRANSLE
C LANCERS
RANCELS
D DARNELS
ENLARDS
LANDERS
SLANDER
SNARLED
F SALFERN
G ANGLERS
LARGENS
I NAILERS
K RANKLES
N ENSNARL
LANNERS
O ORLEANS
P PLANERS
REPLANS
R SNARLER
S RANSELS
SALTERN
T ANTLERS
RENTALS
SALTERN
STERNAL
Z RANZELS

AELNRT 28
(ANTLER)
B BRANTLE
C CENTRAL
E ALTERNE
ENTERAL
ETERNAL
G TANGLER
TRANGLE
H ENTHRAL
I ENTRAIL
LATRINE
RATLINE
RELIANT
RETINAL
TRENAIL
L ENTRALL
N LANTERN
P PANTLER
PLANTER
REPLANT
S ANTLERS
RENTALS
SALTERN
STERNAL
T TRENTAL
U NEUTRAL
V VENTRAL

AELNST 34
(ANTLES)
A SEALANT
C CANTLES
CENTALS
LANCETS
SCANTLE
D DENTALS
SLANTED
E ELANETS
LEANEST
G LANGEST
TANGLES
H HANTLES
I EASTLIN
ELASTIN
ENTAILS
SALIENT
SLAINTE
STANIEL
TENAILS
K ANKLETS
ASKLENT
LANKEST
M LAMENTS
MANTELS
MANTLES
N STANNEL
O ETALONS
P PLANETS
PLATENS
R ANTLERS
RENTALS
SALTERN
STERNAL
T LATTENS
TALENTS
U ELUANTS
UNLASTE
V LEVANTS
Y STANYEL
Z ZELANTS

AELORS 42
(ALORES)
B LABROSE
C COALERS
ESCOLAR
ORACLES
D LOADERS
ORDEALS
RELOADS
E AREOLES
F LOAFERS
SAFROLE
G GAOLERS
H SHOALER
L ROSELLA
M MORALES
O ORLEANS
AEROSOL
ROSEOLA
P PAROLES
REPOSAL
S OARLESS
SOLERAS
T OESTRAL

AELOST 46		
(SOLATE)		
B	BOATELS	
	OBLATES	
C	ALECOST	
	LACTOSE	
	LOCATES	
	SCATOLE	
	TALCOSE	
D	SALTOED	
E	OLEATES	
G	LEGATOS	
H	LOATHES	
I	ISOLATE	
K	SKATOLE	
M	MALTOSE	
N	ETALONS	
P	APOSTLE	
	PELOTAS	
R	OESTRAL	
V	SOLVATE	
Z	ZEALOTS	
AELRST 38		
(ALTERS)		
B	ALBERTS	
	BATLERS	
	BLASTER	
	LABRETS	
	STABLER	
C	CARTELS	
	CLARETS	
	SCARLET	
	TARCELS	
D	DARTLES	
E	ELATERS	
	REALEST	
	RELATES	
	STEALER	
F	FALTERS	
G	LARGEST	
H	HALTERS	
	HARSLET	
	LATHERS	
	SLATHER	
	THALERS	
I	REALIST	
	RETAILS	
	SALTIER	
	SALTIRE	
	SLATIER	
K	STALKER	
	TALKERS	
L	STELLAR	
	TELLARS	
M	ARMLETS	
	MARTELS	
N	ANTLERS	
	RENTALS	
	SALTERN	
	STERNAL	
O	OESTRAL	
P	PALTERS	
	PLASTER	
	PLATERS	
	PSALTER	
	STAPLER	
S	ARTLESS	
	LASTERS	
	SALTERS	

	SLATERS	
	TARSELS	
T	RATTLES	
	SLATTER	
	STARLET	
	STARTLE	
	TATLERS	
U	SALUTER	
V	TRAVELS	
	VARLETS	
	VESTRAL	
W	WASTREL	
Y	RAYLETS	
AEMNST 168		
(STAMEN)		
A	NAMASTE	
B	BATSMEN	
D	TANDEMS	
E	ENTAMES	
	MEANEST	
G	MAGNETS	
H	ANTHEMS	
	HETMANS	
I	INMATES	
	MAINEST	
	MANTIES	
	TAMINES	
L	LAMENTS	
	MANTELS	
O	MANTOES	
P	ENSTAMP	
	TAPSMEN	
R	ARTSMEN	
	MARTENS	
	SARMENT	
	SMARTEN	
S	STAMENS	
U	UNTAMES	
	UNTEAMS	
Y	AMNESTY	
AEMRST 124		
(MATERS)		
A	AMEARST	
	RETAMAS	
B	TAMBERS	
C	MERCATS	
D	SMARTED	
E	STEAMER	
	TEAMERS	
H	HAMSTER	
I	MAESTRI	
	MAISTER	
	MASTIER	
	MISRATE	
	SMARTIE	
K	MARKETS	
L	ARMLETS	
	MARTELS	
M	STAMMER	
N	ARTSMEN	
	MARTENS	
	SARMENT	
	SMARTEN	
O	AMORETS	
	MAESTRO	
	OMERTAS	

P	EMPARTS	
	STAMPER	
	TAMPERS	
R	SMARTER	
S	MASTERS	
	STREAMS	
T	MATTERS	
	SMATTER	
U	MATURES	
	STRUMAE	
W	WARMEST	
Y	MASTERY	
	MAYSTER	
	STREAMY	
AENNST 152		
(ANNETS)		
A	ANNATES	
C	NASCENT	
D	STANDEN	
E	NEATENS	
F	ENFANTS	
G	GANNETS	
I	INANEST	
K	KANTENS	
L	STANNEL	
R	TANNERS	
T	TANNEST	
	TENANTS	
W	WANNEST	
AENPST 185		
(PATENS)		
A	ANAPEST	
	PEASANT	
C	CATNEPS	
D	PEDANTS	
	PENTADS	
E	PENATES	
	PESANTE	
I	PANTIES	
	PATINES	
	SAPIENT	
	SPINATE	
L	PLANETS	
	PLATENS	
M	ENSTAMP	
	TAPSMEN	
R	ARPENTS	
	ENTRAPS	
	PANTERS	
	PARENTS	
	PASTERN	
	PERSANT	
	TREPANS	
S	APTNESS	
	PATNESS	
T	PATENTS	
	PATTENS	
U	PEANUTS	
	PESAUNT	
W	STEWPAN	
Y	SYNAPTE	
Z	PEZANTS	
AENRRT 87		
(RANTER)		
A	NARRATE	
E	TERRANE	

G	GRANTER	
	REGRANT	
I	RETRAIN	
	TERRAIN	
	TRAINER	
O	ORNATER	
P	PARTNER	
S	ERRANTS	
	RANTERS	
T	TRANTER	
Y	TERNARY	
AENRST 8		
(ANTERS)		
A	ANESTRA	
B	BANTERS	
C	CANTERS	
	CARNETS	
	NECTARS	
	RECANTS	
	SCANTER	
	TANRECS	
	TRANCES	
D	ENDARTS	
	STANDER	
	STARNED	
E	EARNEST	
	EASTERN	
	NEAREST	
G	ARGENTS	
	GARNETS	
	STRANGE	
H	ANTHERS	
	HARTENS	
	THENARS	
I	ANESTRI	
	NASTIER	
	RATINES	
	RESIANT	
	RETAINS	
	RETINAS	
	RETSINA	
	STAINER	
	STARNIE	
	STEARIN	
K	RANKEST	
	STARKEN	
	TANKERS	
L	ANTLERS	
	RENTALS	
	SALTERN	
	STERNAL	
M	ARTSMEN	
	MARTENS	
	SARMENT	
	SMARTEN	
N	TANNERS	
O	ATONERS	
	SENATOR	
	TREASON	
P	ARPENTS	
	ENTRAPS	
	PANTERS	
	PARENTS	
	PASTERN	
	PERSANT	
	TREPANS	
R	ERRANTS	
	RANTERS	
S	SARSNET	

	TRANSES	
T	NATTERS	
	RATTENS	
U	AUNTERS	
	NATURES	
	SAUNTER	
V	SERVANT	
	VERSANT	
W	STRAWEN	
	WANTERS	
Y	TRAYNES	
AENRTT 71		
(NATTER)		
A	TARTANE	
C	TRANECT	
D	TRANTED	
E	ENTREAT	
	RATTEEN	
	TERNATE	
I	INTREAT	
	ITERANT	
	NATTIER	
	NITRATE	
	TARTINE	
	TERTIAN	
L	TRENTAL	
N	ENTRANT	
P	PATTERN	
	REPTANT	
R	TRANTER	
S	NATTERS	
	RATTENS	
U	TAUNTER	
Y	NATTERY	
AENSTT 116		
(ATTENS)		
B	BATTENS	
C	CANTEST	
D	ATTENDS	
E	NEATEST	
F	FATTENS	
G	GESTANT	
I	INSTATE	
	SATINET	
L	LATTENS	
	TALENTS	
N	TANNEST	
	TENANTS	
O	ATTONES	
	NOTATES	
P	PATENTS	
	PATTENS	
R	NATTERS	
	RATTENS	
T	ATTENTS	
U	ATTUNES	
	NUTATES	
	TAUTENS	
	TETANUS	
	UNSTATE	
X	SEXTANT	
AEORST 13		
(ORATES)		
B	BOASTER	
	BOATERS	
	BORATES	

	SORBATE	
C	COASTER	
	COATERS	
D	DOATERS	
	ROASTED	
	TORSADE	
	TROADES	
E	ROSEATE	
G	ORGEATS	
	STORAGE	
H	ASTHORE	
	HAROSET	
I	OARIEST	
	OTARIES	
L	OESTRAL	
M	AMORETS	
	MAESTRO	
	OMERTAS	
N	ATONERS	
	SENATOR	
	TREASON	
P	ESPARTO	
	PROTEAS	
	SEAPORT	
R	ROASTER	
T	ROTATES	
	TOASTER	
AEPRST 129		
(PATERS)		
A	PETARAS	
C	CARPETS	
	PRECAST	
	SPECTRA	
D	DEPARTS	
	DRAPETS	
	PETARDS	
E	REPEATS	
G	PARGETS	
H	SPARTHE	
	TEPHRAS	
	THREAPS	
I	PARTIES	
	PASTIER	
	PIASTRE	
	PIRATES	
	PRATIES	
	TRAIPSE	
L	PALTERS	
	PLASTER	
	PLATERS	
	PSALTER	
	STAPLER	
M	EMPARTS	
	STAMPER	
	TAMPERS	
N	ARPENTS	
	ENTRAPS	
	PANTERS	
	PARENTS	
	PASTERN	
	PERSANT	
	TREPANS	
O	ESPARTO	
	PROTEAS	
	SEAPORT	
P	TAPPERS	
R	PARTERS	
	PRATERS	
S	PASTERS	

REPASTS	L RATTLES	LAIRING	M MARGINS	TSIGANE	**ANORST 60**
SPAREST	SLATTER	RAILING	N SNARING	F FASTING	(RATONS)
T PATTERS	STARLET	K LARKING	O IGNAROS	G GASTING	A TORANAS
SPATTER	STARTLE	M MARLING	ORIGANS	GATINGS	B BARTONS
TAPSTER	TATLERS	N LARNING	SIGNORA	STAGING	C CANTORS
U PASTURE	M MATTERS	P PARLING	SOARING	H HASTING	CARTONS
UPRATES	SMATTER	T RATLING	P PARINGS	TASHING	CONTRAS
UPSTARE	N NATTERS	W WARLING	PARSING	K SKATING	CRATONS
UPTEARS	RATTENS	Y ANGRILY	RASPING	STAKING	E ATONERS
Y YAPSTER	O ROTATES	NARGILY	SPARING	TAKINGS	SENATOR
Z PATZERS	TOASTER	RAYLING	T GASTRIN	TASKING	TREASON
	P PATTERS		RATINGS	L ANGLIST	I AROINTS
AERRST 138	SPATTER	**AGILNT 174**	STARING	LASTING	RATIONS
(RATERS)	TAPSTER	(LATING)	V RAVINGS	SALTING	L LATRONS
B BARRETS	R RATTERS	B TABLING	W RAWINGS	SLATING	M MATRONS
BARTERS	RESTART	C CATLING	Y SIGNARY	STALING	TRANSOM
C CARTERS	STARTER	E ATINGLE	SYRINGA	M MASTING	N NATRONS
CRATERS	S ASTERTS	ELATING		TAMINGS	O RATOONS
TRACERS	STARETS	GELATIN	**AGINRT 69**	N ANTINGS	P PARTONS
D DARTERS	STATERS	GENITAL	(RATING)	STANING	PATRONS
DARTRES	TASTERS	F FATLING	C CARTING	O AGONIST	TARPONS
RETARDS	T STRETTA	H HALTING	CRATING	GITANOS	T ATTORNS
STARRED	TARTEST	LATHING	TRACING	P PASTING	RATTONS
TRADERS	TATTERS	I TAILING	D DARTING	R GASTRIN	ROTTANS
E SERRATE	U ASTUTER	K TALKING	TRADING	RATINGS	U ROUSANT
TEARERS	STATURE	M MALTING	E GRANITE	STARING	SANTOUR
F FRATERS	W SWATTER	N TANLING	INGRATE	T STATING	Y AROYNTS
RAFTERS	TEWARTS	O ANTILOG	TANGIER	TASTING	
G GARRETS	Y YATTERS	P PLATING	TEARING	U SAUTING	**BEIRST 184**
GARTERS	Z STARETZ	R RATLING	F FARTING	V STAVING	(TRIBES)
GRATERS		S ANGLIST	INGRAFT	W STAWING	A BAITERS
I ARTSIER	**AERSTW 194**	LASTING	RAFTING	TAWINGS	BARITES
TARRIES	(WATERS)	SALTING	G GRATING	WASTING	D BESTRID
TARSIER	A AWAREST	SLATING	TARGING	X TAXINGS	BISTRED
K STARKER	B BRAWEST	STALING	I AIRTING	Y STAYING	E REBITES
M SMARTER	WABSTER	Y GIANTLY	RAITING		F FIBSTER
N ERRANTS	D STEWARD		K KARTING	**AINRST 40**	H HERBIST
RANTERS	STRAWED	**AGINRS 123**	L RATLING	(TRAINS)	I BITSIER
O ROASTER	WRASTED	(GRAINS)	M MARTING	A ANTIARS	K BRISKET
P PARTERS	E SWEATER	A NAGARIS	MIGRANT	ARTISAN	L BLISTER
PRATERS	F FRETSAW	SANGRIA	N RANTING	TSARINA	BRISTLE
S ARRESTS	WAFTERS	SARANGI	O ORATING	D INDARTS	RIBLETS
RASTERS	H THAWERS	B SABRING	ROATING	E ANESTRI	M BETRIMS
STARERS	WREATHS	C ARCINGS	P PARTING	NASTIER	TIMBERS
T RATTERS	I WAISTER	RACINGS	PRATING	RATINES	TIMBRES
RESTART	WAITERS	SACRING	TRAPING	RESIANT	O ORBIEST
STARTER	WARIEST	SCARING	R TARRING	RETAINS	S BESTIRS
Y STRAYER	L WASTREL	D DARINGS	S GASTRIN	RETINAS	BISTERS
	M WARMEST	GRADINS	RATINGS	RETSINA	BISTRES
AERSTT 97	N STRAWEN	E ANGRIES	STARING	STAINER	T BITTERS
(TASTER)	WANTERS	EARINGS	T RATTING	STARNIE	U BUSTIER
B BATTERS	S WASTERS	ERASING	Y GIANTRY	STEARIN	RUBIEST
TABRETS	T SWATTER	GAINERS		G GASTRIN	
C SCATTER	TEWARTS	GRAINES	**AGINST 108**	RATINGS	**CEINOS 109**
D STARTED	Y WASTERY	REGAINS	(SATING)	STARING	(CONIES)
TETRADS		REGINAS	A AGAINST	H TARNISH	A ACINOSE
E ESTREAT	**AGILNR 199**	SEARING	GITANAS	I INTARSI	C CONCISE
RESTATE	(RALING)	SERINGA	B BASTING	L RATLINS	D SECONDI
G TARGETS	B BLARING	F FARSING	C ACTINGS	M MARTINS	E SENECIO
H HATTERS	D DARLING	G SIRGANG	CASTING	O AROINTS	G COGNISE
RATHEST	LARDING	H GARNISH	D DATINGS	RATIONS	COIGNES
SHATTER	E ENGRAIL	RASHING	E EASTING	P SPIRANT	I ICONISE
THREATS	LEARING	SHARING	EATINGS	SPRAINT	K CONKIES
I ARTIEST	NARGILE	I AIRINGS	GAINEST	Q QINTARS	L CINEOLS
ARTISTE	REALIGN	ARISING	GENISTA	S INSTARS	CONSEIL
ATTIRES	REGINAL	RAGINIS	INGATES	SANTIRS	INCLOSE
IRATEST	F FLARING	RAISING	INGESTA	STRAINS	M INCOMES
STRIATE	G GLARING	SAIRING	SEATING	T STRAINT	MESONIC
TASTIER	H HARLING	K RAKINGS	TANGIES	TRANSIT	N CONINES
TERTIAS	I GLAIRIN	SARKING	TEASING	U NUTRIAS	R COINERS

CRINOSE	INSECTS	COARSEN	G SEDGIER	L DENTELS	SINGLED
CRONIES	Y INSECTY	CORNEAS	L RESILED	NESTLED	T GLINTED
ORCEINS		D CONDERS	M REMEIDS	M DEMENTS	TINGLED
ORCINES	**CEIORS 156**	CORSNED	REMISED	N DENNETS	U ELUDING
SERICON	(COSIER)	SCORNED	N DENIERS	STENNED	INDULGE
S CESSION	A ORACIES	E ENCORES	NEREIDS	O DENOTES	V DELVING
COSINES	SCORIAE	NECROSE	RESINED	R STERNED	DEVLING
T NOTICES	B CORBIES	F CONFERS	O OREIDES	TENDERS	W WELDING
SECTION	C CICEROS	G CONGERS	OSIERED	TENDRES	
V NOVICES	D DISCOER	I COINERS	P PREDIES	S DENSEST	**DEGINR 82**
	H HEROICS	CRINOSE	PRESIDE	T DETENTS	(RINGED)
CEINRS 183	L RECOILS	CRONIES	SPEIRED	STENTED	A AREDING
(INCERS)	N COINERS	ORCEINS	R DERRIES	U DETENUS	DEARING
A ARSENIC	CRINOSE	ORCINES	DESIRER	X EXTENDS	DERAIGN
CARNIES	CRONIES	SERICON	RESIDER		EARDING
CERASIN	ORCEINS	K CONKERS	SERRIED	**DEERST 151**	GRADINE
D CINDERS	ORCINES	RECKONS	S DESIRES	(RESTED)	GRAINED
DISCERN	SERICON	L CORNELS	RESIDES	A DEAREST	READING
RESCIND	P COPIERS	N CONNERS	T DIETERS	DERATES	B BREDING
E CERESIN	COPSIER	O CEROONS	REISTED	ESTRADE	C CRINGED
SCRIENE	PERSICO	P CREPONS	U RESIDUE	REASTED	D GRINDED
SINCERE	R CIRROSE	R CORNERS	UREIDES	SEDATER	REDDING
G CRINGES	CORRIES	SCORNER	V DERIVES	STEARED	E DREEING
H NICHERS	CROSIER	S CENSORS	DEVISER	C CRESTED	ENERGID
RICHENS	S COSIERS	T CONSTER	DIVERSE	D REDDEST	GREINED
I IRENICS	T EROTICS	CORNETS	REVISED	TEDDERS	REEDING
SERICIN	TERCIOS	CRONETS		E REESTED	REIGNED
SIRENIC	U SCOURIE	U ROUNCES	**DEENRS 92**	STEERED	F FRINGED
K NICKERS	V CORSIVE		(ENDERS)	I DIETERS	H HERDING
SNICKER	VOICERS	**DEEINR 43**	A DEANERS	REISTED	I DINGIER
M CREMSIN	W COWRIES	(DENIER)	ENDEARS	N STERNED	N GRINNED
MINCERS	SCOWRIE	B BENDIER	B BENDERS	TENDERS	RENDING
O COINERS	Z COZIERS	INBREED	C DECERNS	TENDRES	O ERODING
CRINOSE		C CEDRINE	SCERNED	O OERSTED	GROINED
CRONIES	**CEIRST 166**	E NEEDIER	D REDDENS	ROSETED	IGNORED
ORCEINS	(CITERS)	F DEFINER	E NEEDERS	TEREDOS	NEGROID
ORCINES	A CRISTAE	ENFIRED	SERENED	P PRESTED	REDOING
SERICON	RACIEST	FENDIER	SNEERED	S DESERTS	R GRINDER
P PINCERS	STEARIC	REFINED	F FENDERS	DESSERT	REGRIND
PRINCES	C CRETICS	G DREEING	G GENDERS	TRESSED	S DINGERS
S SCRINES	D CREDITS	ENERGID	H HERDENS	V STERVED	ENGIRDS
T CISTERN	DIRECTS	GREINED	I DENIERS	VERDETS	U DUNGIER
CRETINS	E CERITES	REEDING	NEREIDS	W STREWED	W REDWING
V CRIVENS	RECITES	REIGNED	RESINED	WRESTED	WRINGED
W WINCERS	TIERCES	H INHERED	L LENDERS	X DEXTERS	Y YERDING
	H CITHERS	L RELINED	SLENDER	Y DYESTER	
CEINST 196	ESTRICH	M ERMINED	M MENDERS		**DEGINS 154**
(INSECT)	RICHEST	O ORDINEE	O ENDORSE	**DEGILN 164**	(SINGED)
A CANIEST	I ERISTIC	P REPINED	P SPENDER	(DINGLE)	A AGNISED
CINEAST	RICIEST	RIPENED	R RENDERS	A ALIGNED	E SDEIGNE
E ENTICES	K RICKETS	R DERNIER	S REDNESS	DEALING	SEEDING
F INFECTS	STICKER	S DENIERS	SENDERS	LEADING	G EDGINGS
H ETHNICS	TICKERS	NEREIDS	T STERNED	B BINGLED	SNIGGED
STHENIC	L RELICTS	RESINED	TENDERS	E DELEING	I DINGIES
I INCITES	M CRETISM	U UREDINE	TENDRES	G GELDING	L DINGLES
J INJECTS	METRICS	W WIDENER	U ENDURES	GINGLED	ELDINGS
K SNICKET	N CISTERN	X INDEXER	ENSURED	NIGGLED	ENGILDS
TICKENS	CRETINS		V VENDERS	H HINDLEG	SINGLED
L CLIENTS	O EROTICS	**DEEIRS 58**	Z DZERENS	I EILDING	M SMIDGEN
LECTINS	TERCIOS	(RESIDE)		ELIDING	N ENDINGS
STENCIL	P TRICEPS	A DEARIES	**DEENST 111**	J JINGLED	SENDING
O NOTICES	T TRISECT	READIES	(NESTED)	M MEDLING	O DINGOES
SECTION	U CUITERS	B DERBIES	A STEANED	MELDING	R DINGERS
P INCEPTS	CURIETS	C DECRIES	C DESCENT	MINGLED	ENGIRDS
INSPECT	ICTERUS	D DERIDES	SCENTED	N LENDING	S DESIGNS
PECTINS	W TWICERS	DESIRED	D STENDED	O GLENOID	T NIDGETS
PEINCTS		DIEDRES	E STEENED	P PINGLED	STEDING
R CISTERN	**CENORS 172**	RESIDED	I DESTINE	S DINGLES	STINGED
CRETINS	(CONERS)	E SEEDIER	ENDITES	ELDINGS	U GUNDIES
S INCESTS	A CARNOSE	F DEFIERS	STEINED	ENGILDS	SUEDING

W SWINDGE
  SWINGED
Y DINGEYS
  DYEINGS

DEILNS 120
(INDLES)
A DENIALS
  SNAILED
D DINDLES
  SLIDDEN
E ENISLED
  ENSILED
  LINSEED
G DINGLES
  ELDINGS
  ENGILDS
  SINGLED
I INISLED
K KINDLES
M MILDENS
N DINNLES
  LINDENS
O INDOLES
  SONDELI
P SPELDIN
  SPINDLE
  SPLINED
T DENTILS
W SWINDLE
  WINDLES
Y SNIDELY

DEILRT 73
(TRIDLE)
A DILATER
  TRAILED
B DRIBLET
D RETILED
E RETILED
F FLIRTED
  TRIFLED
H THIRLED
K KIRTLED
L TRILLED
N TENDRIL
  TRINDLE
O DOILTER
P TRIPLED
U DILUTER
W TWIRLED

DEINOS 41
(ONSIDE)
A ADONISE
  ANODISE
  SODAINE
C SECONDI
D NODDIES
G DINGOES
H HOIDENS
I IODINES
  IONISED
L INDOLES
  SONDELI
M MISDONE
N ONDINES
P DISPONE
  SPINODE
R DONSIER

  INDORSE
  ROSINED
  SORDINE
S ONSIDES
T DITONES
  STONIED

DEINRS 51
(DINERS)
A RANDIES
  SANDIER
  SARDINE
B BINDERS
  REBINDS
C CINDERS
  DISCERN
E DENIERS
  NEREIDS
  RESINED
F FINDERS
  FRIENDS
G DINGERS
  ENGIRDS
H HINDERS
  SHRINED
I INSIDER
K KINREDS
  REDSKIN
M MINDERS
  REMINDS
N DINNERS
O DONSIER
  INDORSE
  ROSINED
  SORDINE
P PINDERS
T TINDERS
U INSURED
W REWINDS
  WINDERS

DEINRU 52
(RUINED)
A UNAIRED
  URANIDE
C INDUCER
D UNDRIED
E UREDINE
F UNFIRED
G DUNGIER
H UNHIRED
I URIDINE
J INJURED
M UNRIMED
N DUNNIER
  INURNED
O DOURINE
  OUNDIER
S INSURED
T INTRUDE
  TURDINE
  UNTIRED
  UNTRIDE
  UNTRIED
W UNWIRED

DEINST 32
(SINTED)
A DETAINS

  INSTEAD
  SAINTED
  SATINED
  STAINED
B BIDENTS
D DISTEND
E DESTINE
  ENDITES
  STEINED
F SNIFTED
G NIDGETS
  STEDING
I INDITES
  TINEIDS
K DINKEST
  KINDEST
L DENTILS
M MINDSET
N DENTINS
  INDENTS
  INTENDS
O DITONES
  STONIED
P STIPEND
R TINDERS
S DISNEST
  DISSENT
  SNIDEST
T DENTIST
  DISTENT
  STINTED
U DISTUNE
  DUNITES
Y DENSITY
  DESTINY

DEIORS 27
(ORIDES)
A ROADIES
  SOREDIA
B BORIDES
  DISROBE
C DISCOER
D DORISED
  SODDIER
E OREIDES
  OSIERED
L SOLDIER
  SOLIDER
M MISDOER
  MOIDERS
N DONSIER
  INDORSE
  ROSINED
  SORDINE
O OROIDES
P PERIODS
S DORISES
  DOSSIER
T EDITORS
  ROISTED
  ROSITED
  SORTIED
  STORIED
  TRIODES
V DEVISOR
  DEVOIRS
  VISORED

  VOIDERS
W DOWRIES
  ROWDIES
  WEIRDOS
Z DORIZES

DEIOST 35
(ODITES)
A IODATES
  TOADIES
C CESTOID
  COTISED
D TODDIES
F FOISTED
H HOISTED
J JOISTED
M DOMIEST
  MODISTE
  MOISTED
N DITONES
  STONIED
O OSTEOID
P DEPOSIT
  DOPIEST
  PODITES
  POSITED
  SOPITED
  TOPSIDE
R EDITORS
  ROISTED
  ROSITED
  SORTIED
  STEROID
  STORIED
  TRIODES
T DOTIEST
  STOITED
U OUTSIDE
  TEDIOUS
V DOVIEST
W DOWIEST
X EXODIST
Z DOZIEST

DEIRST 57
(STRIDE)
A ARIDEST
  ASTERID
  ASTRIDE
  DIASTER
  DISRATE
  STAIDER
  STAIRED
  TARDIES
  TIRADES
B BESTRID
  BISTRED
C CREDITS
  DIRECTS
E DIETERS
  REISTED
F FRISTED
H DITHERS
  SHIRTED
I DIRTIES
K SKIRTED
N TINDERS
O EDITORS
  ROISTED
  ROSITED

  SORTIED
  STEROID
  STORIED
  TRIODES
P SPIRTED
  STRIPED
R STIRRED
S DISSERT
  STRIDES
U DUSTIER
  REDUITS
  STUDIER
V DIVERTS
  STRIVED
  VERDITS

DEIRSU 143
(URDIES)
A RESIDUA
B BRUISED
  BURDIES
C CRUISED
  DISCURE
D RUDDIES
E RESIDUE
  UREIDES
G GUIDERS
H HURDIES
K DUIKERS
  DUSKIER
N INSURED
P PUDSIER
  SIRUPED
Q SQUIRED
R DRUSIER
  DURRIES
S DISEURS
  SUDSIER
T DUSTIER
  REDUITS
  STUDIER

DELNOS 181
(OLDENS)
A LOADENS
B BLONDES
  BOLDENS
D NODDLES
F ENFOLDS
  FONDLES
G DONGLES
  GOLDENS
I INDOLES
  SONDELI
M DOLMENS
O NOODLES
  SNOOLED
R RONDELS
S OLDNESS
U LOUDENS
  NODULES
  NOUSLED
W DOWLNES
Z DONZELS

DELORS 145
(OLDERS)
A LOADERS
  ORDEALS
  RELOADS

B BORDELS
C SCOLDER
E RESOLED
F FOLDERS
G LODGERS
H HOLDERS
I SOLDIER
  SOLIDER
M SMOLDER
N RONDELS
P POLDERS
S DORSELS
  RODLESS
  SOLDERS
T DROLEST
  OLDSTER
  STRODLE
W WELDORS
Y YODLERS

DELORT 100
(DOLTER)
A DELATOR
  LEOTARD
D TODDLER
I DOILTER
L TROLLED
N ENTROLD
O ROOTLED
P DROPLET
S DROLEST
  OLDSTER
  STRODLE
T DOTTLER
  DOTTREL
U TROULED

DENORU 99
(UNDOER)
A RONDEAU
B BOUNDER
  REBOUND
  UNROBED
D REDOUND
  ROUNDED
  UNDERDO
F FOUNDER
  REFOUND
G GUERDON
  UNDERGO
  UNGORED
I DOURINE
  OUNDIER
L LOUNDER
  ROUNDEL
  ROUNDLE
M MOURNED
N ENROUND
P POUNDER
  UNROPED
R RONDURE
  ROUNDER
  UNORDER
S RESOUND
  SOUNDER
  UNDOERS
W REWOUND
  WOUNDER

DENOST 74
(STONED)
A ASTONED
DONATES
ONSTEAD
B OBTENDS
C DOCENTS
E DENOTES
F FONDEST
I DITONES
STONIED
M ENDMOST
N STONNED
TENDONS
O SNOOTED
STOODEN
R RODENTS
SNORTED
T SNOTTED
U DEUTONS
SNOUTED

DENRSU 179
(UNDERS)
A ASUNDER
DANSEUR
DAUNERS
B BURDENS
D DUNDERS
E ENDURES
ENSURED
F FUNDERS
REFUNDS
G GERUNDS
H HURDENS
I INSURED
L LURDENS
NURSLED
RUNDLES
N UNDERNS
O RESOUND
SOUNDER
UNDOERS
P SPURNED
S SUNDERS
UNDRESS
T RETUNDS
UNDREST
U UNSURED

DEORST 50
(SORTED)
A DOATERS
ROASTED
TORSADE
TROADES
B DEBTORS
E OERSTED
ROSETED
TEREDOS
F DEFROST
FROSTED
G STODGER
H DEHORTS
SHORTED
I EDITORS
ROISTED
ROSITED
SORTIED
STEROID

STORIED
TRIODES
K STROKED
L DROLEST
OLDSTER
STRODLE
M STORMED
N RODENTS
SNORTED
O ROOSTED
P DEPORTS
REDTOPS
SPORTED
R DORTERS
RODSTER
T DETORTS
U DETOURS
DOUREST
DOUTERS
OUTREDS
ROUSTED
W STROWED
WORSTED
Y DESTROY
ROYSTED
STROYED

DEOSTU 180
(OUSTED)
C CUSTODE
DOUCEST
DOUCETS
SCOUTED
G DEGOUTS
H SHOUTED
SOUTHED
I OUTSIDE
TEDIOUS
J JOUSTED
L LOUDEST
TOUSLED
M MOUSTED
SMOUTED
N DEUTONS
SNOUTED
O OUTDOES
P SPOUTED
R DETOURS
DOUREST
DOUTERS
OUTREDS
ROUSTED
T DUETTOS
TESTUDO
U DUTEOUS
X TUXEDOS

EEILRS 90
(RELIES)
A REALISE
B BELIERS
D RESILED
E SEELIER
F FERLIES
RELIEFS
G LEIGERS
LIEGERS
H LEISHER
L LEISLER
N LIERNES

RELINES
P REPLIES
SPIELER
R RELIERS
S RESILES
T LEISTER
RETILES
STERILE
U LEISURE
V RELIVES
REVILES
SERVILE

EEILST 89
(ELITES)
C SECTILE
E EELIEST
F FELSITE
LEFTIES
LIEFEST
G ELEGIST
ELEGITS
H SHELTIE
K KELTIES
SLEEKIT
L TELLIES
M ELMIEST
N TENSILE
O ESTOILE
ETOILES
P EPISTLE
PELITES
R LEISTER
RETILES
STERILE
S TELESIS
TIELESS
V LEVITES
LIEVEST
X SEXTILE

EEIMNS 192
(EMINES)
A MEANIES
NEMESIA
D DESMINE
E ENEMIES
G SEEMING
I MEINIES
L ISLEMEN
M IMMENSE
O SEMEION
R ERMINES
S INSEEMS
MISSEEN
NEMESIS
SIEMENS
T EMETINS
W MISWEEN
Y MEINEYS

EEINRT 7
(ENTIRE)
A RETINAE
TRAINEE
B BENTIER
C ENTERIC
ENTICER
E TEENIER
F FEINTER

G GENTIER
INTEGER
TEERING
TREEING
H NEITHER
THEREIN
I ERINITE
NITERIE
K KERNITE
N INTERNE
P INEPTER
R INERTER
REINTER
RENTIER
TERRINE
S ENTIRES
ENTRIES
NERITES
TRENISE
T NETTIER
TENTIER
U NEURITE
RETINUE
REUNITE
UTERINE

EEIRRS 182
(ERRIES)
A REARISE
B BERRIES
D DERRIES
DESIRER
RESIDER
SERRIED
F FERRIES
H HERRIES
J JERRIES
L RELIERS
M MERRIES
N RESINER
O ROSIERE
P PERRIES
REPRISE
RESPIRE
S SERRIES
SIRREES
T ETRIERS
REITERS
RESTIER
RETIRES
RETRIES
TERRIES
V REIVERS
REVERSI
REVISER
RIEVERS
W REWIRES

EEIRST 31
(ESTIER)
A AERIEST
SERIATE
B REBITES
C CERITES
RECITES
TIERCES
D DIETERS
REISTED
E EERIEST
H HEISTER

L LEISTER
RETILES
STERILE
M METIERS
TREMIES
TRISEME
N ENTIRES
ENTRIES
NERITES
TRENISE
P RESPITE
R ETRIERS
REITERS
RESTIER
RETIRES
RETRIES
TERRIES
T TESTIER
U SUETIER
V RESTIVE
SIEVERT
STIEVER
VERIEST
W STEWIER
Z ZESTIER

EELNST 161
(NESTLE)
A ELANETS
LEANEST
D DENTELS
NESTLED
E STELENE
G GENTLES
LENGEST
I TENSILE
P PENTELS
R RELENTS
S NESTLES
T NETTLES
U ELUENTS
UNSTEEL
Y ENSTYLE
TENSELY

EELRST 157
(ELTERS)
A ELATERS
REALEST
RELATES
STEALER
B BELTERS
TREBLES
C TERCELS
F FELTERS
REFLETS
G REGLETS
H SHELTER
I LEISTER
RETILES
STERILE
K KELTERS
KESTREL
SKELTER
L RETELLS
TELLERS
M SMELTER
N RELENTS
P PELTERS
PETRELS

RESPELT
SPELTER
S STREELS
T LETTERS
LETTRES
SETTLER
STERLET
TRESTLE
V SVELTER
W SWELTER
WELTERS
WRESTLE
Y RESTYLE
TERSELY
Z SELTZER

EENRST 56
(ENTERS)
A EARNEST
EASTERN
NEAREST
C CENTERS
CENTRES
TENRECS
D STERNED
TENDERS
TENDRES
E ENTREES
RETENES
G GERENTS
REGENTS
H THRENES
I ENTIRES
ENTRIES
NERITES
L RELENTS
N RENNETS
TENNERS
P PRESENT
REPENTS
SERPENT
R RENTERS
STERNER
S NESTERS
RESENTS
STRENES
T TENTERS
TESTERN
U NEUTERS
RETUNES
TENURES
TUREENS
V VENTERS
VENTRES
W WESTERN
X EXTERNS
Y STYRENE
YESTERN

EERSTT 200
(ETTERS)
A ESTREAT
RESTATE
B BETTERS
C TERCETS
E TEETERS
F FETTERS
G GETTERS

H TETHERS	S GIRNELS	M MELTING	TAIGLES	REGIONS	I IGNITER
I TESTIER	LINGERS	O LENTIGO	B GIBLETS	SIGNORE	TIERING
L LETTERS	SLINGER	P PELTING	E ELEGIST	U IGNEOUS	TIGRINE
LETTRES	T RINGLET	R RINGLET	ELEGITS	W INGOWES	L RINGLET
SETTLER	TINGLER	TINGLER	G GIGLETS	WIGEONS	TINGLER
STERLET	TRINGLE	TRINGLE	H SLEIGHT	Y ISOGENY	TRINGLE
TRESTLE	Y RELYING	S GLISTEN	L GILLETS		M METRING
N TENTERS		LESTING	M GIMLETS	**EGINRS 68**	TERMING
TESTERN	**EGILNS 117**	SINGLET	N GLISTEN	(SINGER)	N RENTING
O ROSETTE	(SINGLE)	TINGLES	LESTING	A ANGRIES	RINGENT
P PERTEST	A LEASING	T ETTLING	SINGLET	EARINGS	TERNING
PETTERS	LINAGES	LETTING	TINGLES	ERASING	O GENITOR
R TERRETS	SEALING	U ELUTING	O ELOGIST	GAINERS	S RESTING
S SETTERS	B BINGLES	W WELTING	P PIGLETS	GRAINES	STINGER
STREETS	D DINGLES	WINGLET	R GLISTER	REGAINS	T GITTERN
TERSEST	ELDINGS		GRISTLE	REGINAS	RETTING
TESTERS	ENGILDS	**EGILOS 132**	S LEGISTS	SEARING	U TRUEING
T STRETTE	SINGLED	(LOGIES)	U GLUIEST	SERINGA	V VERTING
TETTERS	E LEESING	A GOALIES	UGLIEST	B BINGERS	Y RETYING
U TRUSTEE	SEELING	B OBLIGES	Z GLITZES	C CRINGES	
Y STREETY	F SELFING	E ELOGIES		D DINGERS	**EGINST 107**
	G GINGLES	L GOLLIES	**EGINNR 178**	ENGIRDS	(ESTING)
EFIRST 191	NIGGLES	M SEMILOG	(GINNER)	E GREISEN	A EASTING
(STRIFE)	SNIGGLE	N ELOIGNS	A AGINNER	F FINGERS	EATINGS
A FAIREST	H SHINGLE	LEGIONS	EARNING	FRINGES	GAINEST
B FIBSTER	I SEILING	LINGOES	ENGRAIN	G GINGERS	GENISTA
D FRISTED	J JINGLES	O GOOLIES	GRANNIE	NIGGERS	INGATES
F RESTIFF	K KINGLES	OLOGIES	NEARING	SNIGGER	INGESTA
STIFFER	L LEGLINS	R GLOIRES	C CERNING	L GIRNELS	SEATING
H SHIFTER	LINGELS	GLORIES	D GRINNED	LINGERS	TANGIES
I FISTIER	LINGLES	S GLIOSES	RENDING	SLINGER	TEASING
K FRISKET	SELLING	T ELOGIST	E ENGINER	M GERMINS	TSIGANE
L FILTERS	M MINGLES	U OUGLIES	INGENER	N ENRINGS	B BESTING
LIFTERS	N GINNELS		F FERNING	GINNERS	D NIDGETS
STIFLER	O ELOIGNS	**EGILRS 159**	G GERNING	O ERINGOS	STEDING
TRIFLES	LEGIONS	(LIGERS)	I REINING	IGNORES	STINGED
M FIRMEST	LINGOES	A GRAILES	K KERNING	REGIONS	H NIGHEST
FREMITS	P PINGLES	B GERBILS	M RINGMEN	SIGNORE	I IGNITES
N SNIFTER	SPIGNEL	D GILDERS	N RENNING	P PERSING	J JESTING
O FOISTER	R GIRNELS	GIRDLES	R GRINNER	PINGERS	K KESTING
FORTIES	LINGERS	GLIDERS	S ENRINGS	SPRINGE	L GLISTEN
S SIFTERS	SLINGER	GRISLED	GINNERS	R ERRINGS	LESTING
STRIFES	S SINGLES	LIDGERS	T RENTING	RINGERS	SINGLET
T FITTERS	T GLISTEN	RIDGELS	RINGENT	SERRING	TINGLES
TITFERS	LESTING	E LEIGERS	TERNING	S INGRESS	M STEMING
U FUSTIER	SINGLET	LIEGERS	U ENURING	RESIGNS	TEMSING
SURFEIT	TINGLES	G LIGGERS	V NERVING	SIGNERS	N NESTING
W SWIFTER	U LUNGIES	I GIRLIES	Y GINNERY	SINGERS	SENTING
	SLUEING	K KILERGS	RENYING	STINGER	TENSING
EGILNR 125	W SLEWING	L GRILLES		T RESTING	R RESTING
(LINGER)	SWINGLE	N GIRNELS	**EGINOS 78**	STINGER	STINGER
A ENGRAIL	Z ZINGELS	LINGERS	(INGOES)	U REUSING	S INGESTS
LEARING		SLINGER	A AGONIES	RUEINGS	SIGNETS
NARGILE	**EGILNT 66**	O GLOIRES	AGONISE	SIGNEUR	T SETTING
REALIGN	(TINGLE)	GLORIES	B BIOGENS	V SERVING	TESTING
REGINAL	A ATINGLE	S GRILSES	C COGNISE	VERSING	U GUNITES
C CLINGER	ELATING	T GLISTER	COIGNES	W SWINGER	V VESTING
CRINGLE	GELATIN	GRISTLE	D DINGOES	WINGERS	W STEWING
E LEERING	GENITAL	U GUILERS	E SOIGNEE	Y SYRINGE	TWINGES
REELING	B BELTING	LIGURES	H SHOEING		WESTING
F FLINGER	D GLINTED	LURGIES	J JINGOES	**EGINRT 39**	
G NIGGLER	TINGLED	Y GREISLY	L ELOIGNS	(TINGER)	**EGNORS 155**
H HERLING	E GENTILE	GRIESLY	LEGIONS	A GRANITE	(ONGERS)
I LEIRING	F FELTING	GRISELY	LINGOES	INGRATE	A ONAGERS
LINGIER	H ENLIGHT		M MISGONE	TANGIER	ORANGES
J JINGLER	LIGHTEN	**EGILST 190**	P EPIGONS	TEARING	C CONGERS
M GREMLIN	I LIGNITE	(LEGIST)	PIGEONS	E GENTIER	E ENGORES
MERLING	J JINGLET	A AGILEST	PINGOES	INTEGER	NEGROES
MINGLER	K KINGLET	AIGLETS	R ERINGOS	TEERING	I ERINGOS
P PINGLER	L TELLING	LIGATES	IGNORES	TREEING	IGNORES
				H RIGHTEN	

```
REGIONS
SIGNORE
M MONGERS
MORGENS
O ORGONES
OROGENS
P SPONGER
S ENGROSS
U SURGEON
V GOVERNS
Y ERYNGOS
GROYNES

EHIRST 153
(ITHERS)
A HASTIER
SHERIAT
B HERBIST
C CITHERS
ESTRICH
RICHEST
D DITHERS
SHIRTED
E HEISTER
F SHIFTER
G SIGHTER
H HITHERS
I HIRSTIE
L SLITHER
M HERMITS
MITHERS
O HERIOTS
HOISTER
SHORTIE
TOSHIER
P HIPSTER
T HITTERS
TITHERS
U HIRSUTE
V THRIVES
W SWITHER
WITHERS
WRITHES
Z ZITHERS

EHORST 189
(OTHERS)
A ASTHORE
HAROSET
B BOSHTER
BOTHERS
C HECTORS
ROCHETS
ROTCHES
TOCHERS
TORCHES
TROCHES
D DEHORTS
SHORTED
F FOTHERS
I HERIOTS
HOISTER
SHORTIE
TOSHIER
L HOLSTER
HOSTLER
M MOTHERS
SMOTHER
THERMOS
N HORNETS
```

```
SHORTEN
THRENOS
THRONES
O HOOTERS
SHOOTER
SOOTHER
P POTHERS
STROPHE
THORPES
R RHETORS
ROTHERS
SHORTER
S TOSHERS
T HOTTERS
U SHOUTER
SOUTHER
W THROWES
X EXHORTS

EIILST 139
(TILIES)
A LAITIES
C ELICITS
I ILEITIS
K KILTIES
L ILLITES
M ELITISM
LIMIEST
LIMITES
N INLIEST
LINIEST
LINTIES
O IOLITES
OILIEST
P SPILITE
R SILTIER
T ELITIST
U UTILISE
W WILIEST

EIINRT 30
(INTIRE)
A INERTIA
C CITRINE
CRINITE
INCITER
NERITIC
D INDITER
E ERINITE
NITERIE
F NIFTIER
G IGNITER
TIERING
TIGRINE
H INHERIT
L LINTIER
M INTERIM
MINTIER
TERMINI
N TINNIER
T NITRITE
NITTIER
TINTIER
V INVITER
VITRINE
W TWINIER
```

```
EILNOS 47
(OLINES)
C CINEOLS
CONSEIL
INCLOSE
D INDOLES
SONDELI
F OLEFINS
G ELOIGNS
LEGIONS
LINGOES
I ELISION
ISOLINE
L LIONELS
NIELLOS
M MOLINES
O LOONIES
P EPSILON
PINOLES
R NEROLIS
S ESLOINS
INSOLES
LESIONS
LIONESS
T ENTOILS
LIONETS
U ELUSION

EILNRS 77
(LINERS)
A NAILERS
B BERLINS
E LIERNES
RELINES
G GIRNELS
LINGERS
SLINGER
I INLIERS
K SLINKER
M LIMNERS
MERLINS
O NEROLIS
P PILSNER
T LINTERS
SNIRTLE
V SILVERN

EILNST 45
(INTLES)
A EASTLIN
ELASTIN
ENTAILS
SALIENT
SLAINTE
STANIEL
TENAILS
C CLIENTS
LECTINS
STENCIL
D DENTILS
E TENSILE
G GLISTEN
LESTING
SINGLET
TINGLES
I INLIEST
LINIEST
LINTIES
K LENTISK
```

```
TINKLES
L LENTILS
LINTELS
N LINNETS
O ENTOILS
LIONETS
P PINTLES
PLENIST
R LINTERS
SNIRTLE
S ENLISTS
LISTENS
SILENTS
TINSELS
U LUTEINS
UNTILES
UTENSIL
V VENTILS
W WESTLIN
WINTLES

EILORS 37
(OILERS)
B BOILERS
REBOILS
C RECOILS
D SOLDIER
SOLIDER
G GLOIRES
GLORIES
I SOILIER
M MOILERS
N NEROLIS
O ORIOLES
P SLOPIER
SPOILER
R LORRIES
S LORISES
LOSSIER
RISSOLE
T LOITERS
TOILERS
U LOUSIER
SOILURE
V OLIVERS
VIOLERS

EILORT 18
(LOITER)
B TRILOBE
C CORTILE
D DOILTER
E TROELIE
F LOFTIER
TREFOIL
J JOLTIER
M MOTLIER
N RETINOL
O TROOLIE
P POITREL
POLITER
S LOITERS
TOILERS
T TORTILE
TRIOLET
U OUTLIER

EILOST 21
(OILETS)
A ISOLATE
```

```
B BETOILS
C CITOLES
E ESTOILE
ETOILES
G ELOGIST
H EOLITHS
HOLIEST
HOSTILE
I IOLITES
OILIEST
L OILLETS
M MOTILES
N ENTOILS
LIONETS
O OOLITES
OSTIOLE
STOOLIE
P PIOLETS
PISTOLE
R LOITERS
TOILERS
T LITOTES
TOILETS
U OUTLIES
V OLIVETS
VIOLETS
W OWLIEST

EILRST 44
(LITERS)
A REALIST
RETAILS
SALTIER
SALTIRE
SLATIER
B BLISTER
BRISTLE
RIBLETS
C RELICTS
E LEISTER
RETILES
STERILE
F FILTERS
LIFTERS
STIFLER
TRIFLES
G GLISTER
GRISTLE
H SLITHER
I SILTIER
K KILTERS
KIRTLES
L RILLETS
STILLER
TILLERS
TRELLIS
M MILTERS
N LINTERS
SNIRTLE
O LOITERS
TOILERS
P SPIRTLE
TRIPLES
S LISTERS
LITTERS
SLITTER
STILTER
TESTRIL
TILTERS
TITLERS
```

```
U LUSTIER
RULIEST
RUTILES

EILSTU 136
(UTILES)
A SITULAE
B BLUIEST
SUBTILE
D DILUTES
F FLUIEST
G GLUIEST
UGLIEST
I UTILISE
L TUILLES
N LUTEINS
UNTILES
UTENSIL
O OUTLIES
P PULIEST
PUTELIS
STIPULE
R LUSTIER
RULIEST
RUTILES
T TITULES

EIMNOS 131
(MONIES)
A ANOMIES
C INCOMES
MESONIC
D MISDONE
E SEMEION
G MISGONE
L MOLINES
O MOONIES
NOISOME
P IMPONES
PEONISM
R MERINOS
MERSION
S EONISMS
T MOISTEN
W WINSOME

EIMNRS 177
(MINERS)
A MARINES
REMAINS
SEMINAR
SIRNAME
C CREMSIN
MINCERS
D MINDERS
REMINDS
E ERMINES
G GERMINS
H MENHIRS
K MERKINS
L LIMNERS
MERLINS
M NIMMERS
O MERINOS
MERSION
T ENTRISM
MINSTER
MINTERS
MINTERS
U MURINES
NEURISM
```

V VERMINS	T METRIST	IGNORES	REPINES	CRETINS	TAURINE
U MUSTIER	U MUSTIER	REGIONS	G PERSING	D TINDERS	URANITE
EIMOST 150	Y MISTERY	SIGNORE	PINGERS	E ENTIRES	URINATE
(SOMITE)	SMYTRIE	H HEROINS	SPRINGE	ENTRIES	B BUNTIER
A AMOSITE		INSHORE	I INSPIRE	NERITES	TRIBUNE
ATOMIES	**EINNST 113**	I IONISER	PIRNIES	TRENISE	TURBINE
ATOMISE	(SINNET)	IRONIES	SNIPIER	F SNIFTER	D INTRUDE
OSMIATE	A INANEST	IRONISE	SPINIER	G RESTING	TURDINE
D DOMIEST	D DENTINS	NOISIER	K PERKINS	STINGER	UNTIRED
MODISTE	INDENTS	J JOINERS	L PILSNER	K SKINTER	E NEURITE
MOISTED	INTENDS	REJOINS	N PINNERS	STINKER	RETINUE
F FOMITES	E INTENSE	L NEROLIS	SPINNER	TINKERS	REUNITE
G EGOTISM	G NESTING	M MERINOS	O ORPINES	L LINTERS	UTERINE
H HOMIEST	SENTING	MERSION	PIONERS	SNIRTLE	G TRUEING
L MOTILES	TENSING	O EROSION	PROINES	M ENTRISM	M MINUTER
M TOMMIES	I INTINES	P ORPINES	P NIPPERS	MINSTER	O ROUTINE
N MOISTEN	TINNIES	PIONERS	SNIPPER	MINTERS	R RUNTIER
P MOPIEST	L LINNETS	PROINES	S SNIPERS	N INTERNS	S TRIUNES
OPTIMES	O INTONES	R IRONERS	T NIPTERS	TINNERS	UNITERS
R EROTISM	TENSION	S ORNISES	PTERINS	O NORITES	T NUTTIER
MOISTER	P PINNETS	SENIORS	U PRUINES	ORIENTS	V UNRIVET
MORTISE	SPINNET	SONERIS	PURINES	STONIER	VENTURI
TRISOME	TENPINS	SONSIER	UPRISEN	TERSION	W UNWRITE
S MITOSES	R INTERNS	T NORITES	Y INSPYRE	TRIONES	
SOMITES	TINNERS	ORIENTS		P NIPTERS	**EINSTT 160**
T MOTIEST	S SENNITS	STONIER	**EINPST 148**	PTERINS	(INTEST)
TITMOSE	SINNETS	TERSION	(INSTEP)	S INSERTS	A INSTATE
U TIMEOUS	T INTENTS	TRIONES	A PANTIES	SINTERS	SATINET
V MOTIVES	U TUNNIES	V RENVOIS	PATINES	T ENTRIST	D DENTIST
Z MESTIZO	V INVENTS	VERSION	SAPIENT	STINTER	DISTENT
		W SNOWIER	SPINATE	TINTERS	STINTED
EIMRST 140	**EINOPS 130**		C INCEPTS	U TRIUNES	G SETTING
(MITERS)	(PONIES)	**EINOST 14**	INSPECT	UNITERS	TESTING
A MAESTRI	D DISPONE	(TONIES)	PECTINS	V INVERTS	I SITTINE
MAISTER	SPINODE	A ATONIES	PEINCTS	STRIVEN	TINIEST
MASTIER	E PEONIES	B BONIEST	D STIPEND	W TWINERS	K KITTENS
MISRATE	G EPIGONS	EBONIST	E PENTISE	WINTERS	M MITTENS
SEMITAR	PIGEONS	C NOTICES	I PINIEST	Y SINTERY	SMITTEN
SMARTIE	PINGOES	SECTION	PINITES		N INTENTS
B BETRIMS	H PHONIES	D DITONES	K PINKEST	**EINRTT 76**	O TONIEST
TIMBERS	I PIONIES	STONIED	L PINTLES	(TINTER)	TONITES
TIMBRES	K PINKOES	H HISTONE	PLENIST	A INTREAT	P SPITTEN
C CRETISM	L EPSILON	J JONTIES	M PIMENTS	ITERANT	R ENTRIST
METRICS	PINOLES	L ENTOILS	N PINNETS	NATTIER	STINTER
E METIERS	M IMPONES	LIONETS	SPINNET	NITRATE	TINTERS
TREMIES	PEONISM	M MOISTEN	TENPINS	TARTINE	U TUNIEST
TRISEME	N PENSION	N INTONES	O POINTES	TERTIAN	W ENTWIST
F FIRMEST	R ORPINES	TENSION	PONTIES	B BITTERN	Y TENSITY
FREMITS	PIONERS	O ISOTONE	P SNIPPET	C CITTERN	
H HERMITS	PROINES	P POINTES	R NIPTERS	D TRIDENT	**EINSTU 81**
MITHERS	S SPINOSE	PONTIES	PTERINS	E NETTIER	(UNITES)
I MIRIEST	T POINTES	R NORITES	S INSTEPS	TENTIER	A AUNTIES
MISTIER	PONTIES	ORIENTS	SPINETS	G GITTERN	SINUATE
RIMIEST	W POWNIES	STONIER	T SPITTEN	RETTING	D DISTUNE
K MIRKEST	Y PIONEYS	TERSION	U PUNIEST	I NITRITE	DUNITES
L MILTERS		TRIONES	PUNTIES	NITTIER	G GUNITES
M MISTERM	**EINORS 9**	S NOSIEST		TINTIER	I UNITIES
N ENTRISM	(SENIOR)	SONTIES	**EINRST 17**	K KNITTER	UNITISE
MINSTER	A ERASION	STONIES	(INTERS)	TRINKET	L LUTEINS
MINTERS	C COINERS	T TONIEST	A ANESTRI	O TRITONE	UNTILES
O EROTISM	CRINOSE	TONITES	NASTIER	S ENTRIST	UTENSIL
MOISTER	CRONIES	W TOWNIES	RATINES	STINTER	M MINUETS
MORTISE	ORCEINS		RESIANT	TINTERS	MINUTES
TRISOME	ORCINES	**EINPRS 158**	RETAINS	U NUTTIER	MISTUNE
P IMPREST	SERICON	(PINERS)	RETINAS	W TWINTER	MUNITES
PERMITS	D DONSIER	A RAPINES	RETSINA	WRITTEN	MUTINES
R RETRIMS	INDORSE	C PINCERS	STAINER		N TUNNIES
TRIMERS	ROSINED	PRINCES	STARNIE	**EINRTU 25**	P PUNIEST
S MISTERS	SORDINE	D PINDERS	STEARIN	(TUNIER)	
SMITERS	G ERINGOS	E EREPSIN	C CISTERN	A RUINATE	

```
PUNTIES
Q INQUEST
QUINTES
R TRIUNES
UNITERS
S INTUSES
T TUNIEST

EIOPST 101
(SOPITE)
A ATOPIES
OPIATES
C POETICS
D DEPOSIT
DOPIEST
PODITES
POSITED
SOPITED
TOPSIDE
E POETISE
H ETHIOPS
OPHITES
K POKIEST
L PIOLETS
PISTOLE
M MOPIEST
OPTIMES
N POINTES
PONTIES
O ISOTOPE
R PERIOST
PORIEST
REPOSIT
RIPOSTE
ROPIEST
S POSTIES
SEPIOST
SOPITES
T POTTIES
TIPTOES
U PITEOUS
X POXIEST
Y ISOTYPE

EIORST 5
(TORIES)
A OARIEST
OTARIES
B ORBIEST
C EROTICS
TERCIOS
D EDITORS
ROISTED
ROSITED
SORTIED
STEROID
STORIED
TRIODES
F FOISTER
FORTIES
G GOITERS
GOITRES
GORIEST
H HERIOTS
HOISTER
SHORTIE
TOSHIER
I RIOTISE
K ROKIEST
L LOITERS
```

```
TOILERS
M EROTISM
MOISTER
MORTISE
TRISOME
N NORITES
ORIENTS
STONIER
TERSION
TRIONES
O OORIEST
ROOTIES
SOOTIER
TOORIES
P PERIOST
PORIEST
REPOSIT
RIPOSTE
ROPIEST
R RIOTERS
ROISTER
RORIEST
S ROSIEST
SORITES
SORTIES
STORIES
TOSSIER
T STOITER
U OURIEST
TOUSIER
V TORSIVE
W OWRIEST
TOWSIER

EIORSV 127
(VIROSE)
A OVARIES
C CORSIVE
VOICERS
D DEVISOR
DEVOIRS
VISORED
VOIDERS
E EROSIVE
I IVORIES
L OLIVERS
VIOLERS
M VERISMO
N RENVOIS
VERSION
R REVISOR
S VIROSES
T TORSIVE

EIOSTT 93
(OTTIES)
A OSTIATE
TOASTIE
B BOTTIES
C COTTISE
D DOTIEST
STOITED
G EGOTIST
H HOTTIES
L LITOTES
TOILETS
M MOTIEST
TITMOSE
N TONIEST
TONITES
```

```
O TOOTSIE
P POTTIES
TIPTOES
R STOITER
T TOTTIES
U TOUSTIE
W TOWIEST

EIPRST 147
(STRIPE)
A PARTIES
PASTIER
PIASTRE
PIRATES
PRATIES
TRAIPSE
C TRICEPS
D SPIRTED
STRIPED
E RESPITE
H HIPSTER
I PITIERS
TIPSIER
L SPIRTLE
TRIPLES
M IMPREST
PERMITS
N NIPTERS
PTERINS
O PERIOST
PORIEST
REPOSIT
RIPOSTE
ROPIEST
P TIPPERS
S ESPRITS
PERSIST
PRIESTS
SITREPS
SPRITES
STIRPES
STRIPES
TRIPSES
T PITTERS
SPITTER
TIPSTER
U PERITUS
PUIREST
V PRIVETS
X EXTIRPS
Y PYRITES
STRIPEY

EIRRST 165
(TRIERS)
A ARTSIER
TARRIES
TARSIER
D STIRRED
E ETRIERS
REITERS
RESTIER
RETIRES
RETRIES
TERRIES
K SKIRRET
SKIRTER
STRIKER
M RETRIMS
TRIMERS
```

```
O RIOTERS
ROISTER
RORIEST
R STIRRER
S STIRRES
T RITTERS
TERRITS
U RUSTIER
V STRIVER
W WRITERS

EIRSTT 104
(SITTER)
A ARTIEST
ARTISTE
ATTIRES
IRATEST
STRIATE
TASTIER
TERTIAS
B BITTERS
C TRISECT
E TESTIER
F FITTERS
TITFERS
H HITTERS
TITHERS
J JITTERS
K SKITTER
L LITTERS
SLITTER
STILTER
TESTRIL
TILTERS
TITLERS
M METRIST
N ENTRIST
STINTER
TINTERS
O STOITER
P PITTERS
SPITTER
TIPSTER
R RITTERS
TERRITS
S SITTERS
T STRETTI
TITTERS
TRITEST
U TERTIUS
V TRIVETS
W TWISTER
WITTERS

EIRSTV 163
(STRIVE)
A TAIVERS
VASTIER
D DIVERTS
VERDITS
E RESTIVE
SIEVERT
STIEVER
VERIEST
G GRIVETS
H THRIVES
I REVISIT
STIVIER
VISITER
```

```
N INVERTS
STRIVEN
O TORSIVE
P PRIVETS
R STRIVER
S STIVERS
STRIVES
TREVISS
VERISTS
T TRIVETS
U VIRTUES

ELORST 67
(TOLERS)
A OESTRAL
B BOLSTER
BOLTERS
LOBSTER
C COLTERS
CORSLET
COSTREL
LECTORS
D DROLEST
OLDSTER
STRODLE
F FLORETS
LOFTERS
H HOLSTER
HOSTLER
I LOITERS
TOILERS
J JOLTERS
L TOLLERS
N LENTORS
O LOOTERS
RETOOLS
ROOTLES
TOOLERS
P PETROLS
S OSTLERS
STEROLS
TORSELS
T SETTLOR
SLOTTER
TOLTERS
U ELUTORS
OUTLERS
TROULES
V REVOLTS
W TROWELS
WORTLES

ELOSTU 173
(TOUSLE)
B BOLETUS
D LOUDEST
TOUSLED
F FOULEST
I OUTLIES
L OUTSELL
N LENTOUS
O OUTSOLE
P TUPELOS
R ELUTORS
OUTLERS
TROULES
S LOTUSES
SOLUTES
TOUSLES
T OUTLETS
```

```
U LUTEOUS
V VOLUTES
Z TOUZLES

EMNOST 186
(MONETS)
A MANTOES
B ENTOMBS
D ENDMOST
E TEMENOS
TONEMES
F FOMENTS
G EMONGST
H MONETHS
I MOISTEN
L LOMENTS
MELTONS
M MOMENTS
MONTEMS
O MOONSET
P POSTMEN
TOPSMEN
R MENTORS
MONSTER
MONTRES
S STEMSON
U UNSMOTE
Y ETYMONS

EMORST 198
(MOTERS)
A AMORETS
MAESTRO
OMERTAS
B BESTORM
MOBSTER
D STORMED
E METEORS
REMOTES
G GROMETS
H MOTHERS
SMOTHER
THERMOS
I EROTISM
MOISTER
MORTISE
TRISOME
N MENTORS
MONSTER
MONTRES
O MOOTERS
P TROMPES
R TERMORS
TREMORS
S MOTSERS
U MOUTERS
OESTRUM

ENORST 23
(TONERS)
A ATONERS
SENATOR
TREASON
B BRETONS
SORBENT
C CONSTER
CORNETS
CRONETS
D RODENTS
SNORTED
```

H HORNETS	S OUTNESS	N POSTERN	TOURERS	ORIGANS	**GINOST 176**
SHORTEN	TONUSES	PRONEST	V TROVERS	SIGNORA	(OSTING)
THRENOS	T STOUTEN	O POOREST	W STROWER	SOARING	A AGONIST
THRONES	U TENUOUS	POOTERS	Y ROYSTER	B BORINGS	GITANOS
I NORITES		STOOPER		ROBINGS	C COSTING
ORIENTS	**ENRSTU 84**	P STOPPER	**EORSTT 114**	SORBING	GNOSTIC
STONIER	(TUNERS)	TOPPERS	(OTTERS)	C SCORING	D DOTINGS
TERSION	A AUNTERS	R PORTERS	A ROTATES	D RODINGS	F SOFTING
TRIONES	NATURES	REPORTS	TOASTER	E ERINGOS	H HOSTING
K STONKER	SAUNTER	SPORTER	B BETTORS	IGNORES	TOSHING
STROKEN	B BRUNETS	S PORTESS	C COTTERS	REGIONS	K STOKING
TONKERS	BUNTERS	POSTERS	D DETORTS	SIGNORE	L LINGOTS
L LENTORS	BURNETS	PRESTOS	E ROSETTE	G GORINGS	TIGLONS
M MENTORS	BURSTEN	REPOSTS	H HOTTERS	GRINGOS	TOLINGS
MONSTER	C ENCRUST	T POTTERS	I STOITER	H HORSING	M GNOMIST
MONTRES	D RETUNDS	PROTEST	J JOTTERS	SHORING	N STONING
N STONERN	UNDREST	SPOTTER	L SETTLOR	I ORIGINS	O SOOTING
O ENROOTS	E NEUTERS	U PETROUS	SLOTTER	SIGNIOR	P POSTING
P POSTERN	RETUNES	POSTURE	TOLTERS	SIGNORI	STOPING
PRONEST	TENURES	POUTERS	N ROTTENS	L LORINGS	R ROSTING
R SNORTER	TUREENS	PROTEUS	SNOTTER	M SMORING	SORTING
S STONERS	G GUNTERS	SEPTUOR	STENTOR	N SNORING	STORING
TENSORS	GURNETS	SPOUTER	O TOOTERS	SORNING	TRIGONS
T ROTTENS	SURGENT	TROUPES	P POTTERS	O ROOSING	S STINGOS
SNOTTER	H HUNTERS	W POWTERS	PROTEST	P PROIGNS	TOSSING
STENTOR	SHUNTER	PROWEST	SPOTTER	PROSING	T SOTTING
U TENOURS	UNHERST	X EXPORTS	R RETORTS	ROPINGS	U OUSTING
TONSURE	I TRIUNES		ROTTERS	S GRISONS	OUTINGS
Y TYRONES	UNITERS	**EORRST 106**	TORRETS	INGROSS	TOUSING
	L RUNLETS	(SORTER)	T STOTTER	SIGNORS	V STOVING
ENOSTT 195	M MUNSTER	A ROASTER	STRETTO	T ROSTING	W STOWING
(ONTEST)	STERNUM	C RECTORS	TOTTERS	SORTING	TOWINGS
A ATTONES	N RUNNETS	D DORTERS	U STOUTER	STORING	TOWSING
NOTATES	STUNNER	RODSTER	TOOTERS	TRIGONS	Y TOYINGS
C CONTEST	O TENOURS	E RESTORE	W SWOTTER	U ROUSING	
D SNOTTED	TONSURE	G GROSERT	X EXTORTS	SOURING	**INORST 59**
H SHOTTEN	P PUNSTER	H RHETORS	Y ROSETTY	V ROVINGS	(TRIONS)
I TONIEST	PUNTERS	ROTHERS		W ROWINGS	A AROINTS
TONITES	R RETURNS	SHORTER	**GILNOT 171**	WORSING	RATIONS
J JETTONS	TURNERS	I RIOTERS	(TOLING)	Y ROSYING	B RIBSTON
L TONLETS	S UNRESTS	ROISTER	A ANTILOG	SIGNORY	C CISTRON
O TESTOON	T ENTRUST	RORIEST	B BILTONG		CITRONS
P POTENTS	NUTTERS	K STROKER	BOLTING	**GINORT 102**	CORNIST
R ROTTENS		M TERMORS	C COLTING	(ROTING)	E NORITES
SNOTTER	**EOPRST 193**	TREMORS	E LENTIGO	A ORATING	ORIENTS
STENTOR	(POSTER)	N SNORTER	F LOFTING	ROATING	STONIER
S OSTENTS	A ESPARTO	O ROOSTER	H THOLING	D DORTING	TERSION
TESTONS	PROTEAS	ROOTERS	I TOILING	E GENITOR	TRIONES
U STOUTEN	SEAPORT	TOREROS	J JOLTING	F FORTING	F FORINTS
	B BESPORT	P PORTERS	L TOLLING	I RIOTING	G ROSTING
ENOSTU 94	D DEPORTS	SPORTER	M MOLTING	K TROKING	SORTING
(OUTENS)	REDTOPS	R RORTERS	O LOOTING	O ROOTING	STORING
A SOUTANE	SPORTED	TERRORS	TOOLING	P PORTING	TRIGONS
C CONTUSE	F FORPETS	S RESORTS	P POLTING	TROPING	H HORNIST
ECONUTS	H POTHERS	ROSTERS	S LINGOTS	S ROSTING	I IRONIST
D DEUTONS	STROPHE	SORTERS	TIGLONS	SORTING	L NOSTRIL
SNOUTED	THORPES	STORERS	TOLINGS	STORING	N INTRONS
G TONGUES	I PERIOST	T RETORTS	T LOTTING	TRIGONS	O ISOTRON
L LENTOUS	PORIEST	ROTTERS	U LOUTING	T ROTTING	TORSION
M UNSMOTE	REPOSIT	TORRETS	W LOWTING	U ROUTING	T TRITONS
N NEUSTON	RIPOSTE	U RETOURS		TOURING	U NITROUS
O UNSOOTE	ROPIEST	ROUSTER	**GINORS 128**	W ROWTING	TURIONS
R TENOURS	L PETROLS	ROUTERS	(SIGNOR)	TROWING	
TONSURE	M TROMPES		A IGNAROS		

8-LETTER SETS
from the top 200 6-letter combinations

ABDEIR 134
(ABRIDE)
AD ABRAIDED
AS ARABISED
AZ ARABIZED
BR DRABBIER
BT RABBITED
CG BIRDCAGE
   CAGEBIRD
CL CALIBRED
CS ASCRIBED
   CARBIDES
DG ABRIDGED
   BRIGADED
DN BRANDIED
   RIBANDED
DR BRAIRDED
EL RIDEABLE
ES BEARDIES
ET EBRIATED
GN BEARDING
   BREADING
GR ABRIDGER
GS ABRIDGES
   BRIGADES
IT DIATRIBE
KM IMBARKED
LN BILANDER
LT LIBRATED
LV DRIVABLE
LY DIABLERY
MN BRIDEMAN
MO AMBEROID
MR IMBARRED
MS EMBRAIDS
NO DEBONAIR
NS BRANDIES
   BRANDISE
ST BARDIEST
   BRAIDEST
   RABIDEST
   TRIBADES
SW BAWDRIES
   DAWBRIES
TV VIBRATED

ABEILS 188
(ISABEL)
AL ISABELLA
   SAILABLE
AR RAISABLE
AT BALISTAE
   LABIATES
   SATIABLE
BH BABELISH
BM BABELISM
BR SLABBIER
BT BISTABLE
CM ALEMBICS
CO SOCIABLE
CR CALIBERS
   CALIBRES
DD DISABLED
DE ABSEILED
DH DISHABLE

DP PIEBALDS
DS DISABLES
EF FEASIBLE
EM BELAMIES
EV EVASIBLE
EZ SEIZABLE
   SIZEABLE
FG FILABEGS
FH FISHABLE
FR BARFLIES
FU FABULISE
FY FEASIBLY
GN SINGABLE
HR BLASHIER
IL BAILLIES
IR BISERIAL
IT ALBITISE
   SIBILATE
KN BLANKIES
KS KISSABLE
KT BALKIEST
LO ISOLABLE
   LOBELIAS
LR LIBERALS
LT BASTILLE
MN BAILSMEN
MR REMBLAIS
MS MISSABLE
MT BALMIEST
   TIMBALES
NP BIPLANES
NR RINSABLE
NS ALBINESS
   LESBIANS
NT INSTABLE
PS PASSIBLE
PT EPIBLAST
RT LIBRATES
ST ASTILBES
   BESTIALS
   STABILES
SU ISSUABLE
   SUASIBLE
TU SUITABLE
TY BEASTILY
UX BISEXUAL
VV BIVALVES

ABEORS 144
(ABORES)
AD SEABOARD
AT RABATOES
BD ABSORBED
BR ABSORBER
   REABSORB
CD BROCADES
CG BROCAGES
CH BROACHES
CI AEROBICS
CM CRAMBOES
CU CORBEAUS
DD ADSORBED
DN BANDORES
   BROADENS
DR BOARDERS

DT BROADEST
EN SEABORNE
ET REBATOES
FR FORBEARS
GK BROKAGES
   GROSBEAK
GO BARGOOSE
HT BATHORSE
IN BARONIES
IS ISOBARES
IT SABOTIER
KO ABROOKES
LT BLOATERS
   SORTABLE
   STORABLE
LU RUBEOLAS
LV ABSOLVER
MR EMBRASOR
MT BROMATES
MU AMBEROUS
NN BARONNES
NS BARONESS
NT BARONETS
PS SAPROBES
PT PROBATES
QU BAROQUES
RS BRASEROS
RT ARBORETS
   TABORERS
ST BOASTERS
   SORBATES
TT ABETTORS
   BATTEROS
   TABORETS
TU SABOTEUR

ABERST 122
(BREAST)
AC ABREACTS
   CABARETS
AL ARBALEST
AN ANTBEARS
   RATSBANE
AO RABATOES
AT RABATTES
   TABARETS
AU ABATURES
BD DRABBEST
   DRABBETS
BS STABBERS
CE ACERBEST
CH BRACHETS
CK BRACKETS
DE BETREADS
   BREASTED
   DEBATERS
DH BREADTHS
DI BARDIEST
   BRAIDEST
   RABIDEST
   TRIBADES
DN BANDSTER
DO BROADEST
DS DABSTERS
DU SURBATED

DW BEDSTRAW
DY DRYBEATS
EG ABSTERGE
EH BREATHES
   HARTBEES
EK BESTREAK
EL BLEAREST
   BLEATERS
   RETABLES
EO REBATOES
ER REBATERS
   TABRERES
   TEREBRAS
ET ABETTERS
EU SUBERATE
GH BARGHEST
GN BANGSTER
GS BARGESTS
HL BLATHERS
   HALBERTS
HO BATHORSE
HS BRASHEST
IK BARKIEST
   BRAKIEST
   BREASKIT
IL LIBRATES
IM BARMIEST
IN ATEBRINS
   BANISTER
IO SABOTIER
IR ARBITERS
   RAREBITS
IT BIRETTAS
IV VIBRATES
IW WARBIEST
IY BESTIARY
   SYBARITE
KY BASKETRY
LM LAMBERTS
LN BRANTLES
LO BLOATERS
   SORTABLE
   STORABLE
LS BLASTERS
   STABLERS
LT BATTLERS
   BLATTERS
   BRATTLES
LU BALUSTER
LW BLEWARTS
MO BROMATES
NO BARONETS
NU UNBRASTE
   URBANEST
OP PROBATES
OR ARBORETS
   TABORERS
OS BOASTERS
   SORBATES
OT ABETTORS
   BATTEROS
   TABORETS
SS BRASSETS
SU ABSTRUSE

   SURBATES
SW WABSTERS
TU ABUTTERS

ACEILR 121
(LACIER)
AT TAILRACE
AV CAVALIER
BB BARBICEL
BD CALIBRED
BK CRABLIKE
BL CRIBELLA
BO ALBICORE
   CABRIOLE
BS CALIBERS
   CALIBRES
CE CELERIAC
CL CLERICAL
CV CERVICAL
DF FRICADEL
DH HERALDIC
DP PLACIDER
DS DECRIALS
   RADICELS
   RADICLES
DT ARTICLED
DU AURICLED
   RADICULE
EH LEACHIER
EN CINEREAL
   RELIANCE
ES ESCALIER
EV RECEIVAL
FS FILACERS
GG CLAGGIER
GL ALLERGIC
GN CLEARING
GS GLACIERS
GV CLAVIGER
HK CHALKIER
   HACKLIER
HO HALICORE
   HEROICAL
HP PARHELIC
HS CHARLIES
IN IRENICAL
KT TALCKIER
KY CREAKILY
LM MICELLAR
   MILLRACE
LO ROCAILLE
LP CALLIPER
LV CAVILLER
MM CLAMMIER
MS CLAIMERS
   MIRACLES
   RECLAIMS
MT METRICAL
NN ENCRINAL
NO ACROLEIN
   CREOLIAN
   LONICERA
NS CARLINES
NT CLARINET
OP CAPRIOLE

OR CARRIOLE
OS CALORIES
   CARIOLES
OT EROTICAL
   LORICATE
PS CALIPERS
   REPLICAS
   SPIRACLE
PT PARTICLE
   PRELATIC
PU PECULIAR
RT CLARTIER
RW CRAWLIER
SS CLASSIER
ST ALTRICES
   ARTICLES
   RECITALS
   SELICTAR
SU AURICLES
SV CALIVERS
   CLAVIERS
   VISCERAL
TT TRACTILE
TV VERTICAL
TY LITERACY

ACEINR 65
(CANIER)
AB CARABINE
AD CANARIED
   RADIANCE
AG CANAIGRE
AS CANARIES
AT CARINATE
AV VARIANCE
BS CARBINES
CH CHANCIER
   CHICANER
CN CANCRINE
DD CANDIDER
   RIDDANCE
DE DERACINE
DH INARCHED
DI ACRIDINE
DN CRANNIED
DR RANCIDER
DT CRINATED
   DICENTRA
EL CINEREAL
   RELIANCE
ES CINEREAS
   INCREASE
   RESIANCE
ET CENTIARE
   CREATINE
   INCREATE
   ITERANCE
FG REFACING
FS FANCIERS
FX CARNIFEX
GH REACHING
GK CREAKING
GL CLEARING
GM AMERCING
   CREAMING

GN	ENRACING	DO	DIOCESAN	PS	INSCAPES	HS	ARCHNESS		UNTRACED	AR	CANASTER

GN ENRACING
GP CAPERING
   PEARCING
   PREACING
GS CREASING
   GRECIANS
   SEARCING
GT CATERING
   CITRANGE
   CREATING
   REACTING
HM CHAIRMEN
HS INARCHES
HV VACHERIN
IL IRENICAL
IS RIANCIES
JR JERRICAN
KK KNACKIER
KR CRANKIER
LN ENCRINAL
LO ACROLEIN
   CREOLIAN
   LONICERA
LS CARLINES
LT CLARINET
MO CORAMINE
MS CARMINES
MU MANICURE
NS CRANNIES
OP APOCRINE
   CAPONIER
   PROCAINE
OS SCENARIO
OT ANORETIC
   CHANTIES
   CREATION
   REACTION
OV VERONICA
OX ANOREXIC
RU CURARINE
RY CINERARY
SS ARSENICS
   CERASINS
   RACINESS
ST CANISTER
   CARNIEST
   NACRITES
   SCANTIER
TT NAVICERT
TV NAVICERT
TX XERANTIC
VY VICENARY

ACEINS 119
(INCASE)
AD AIDANCES
AL CANALISE
AM AMNESIAC
AR CANARIES
AT ESTANCIA
BR CARBINES
BT CABINETS
CG ACCINGES
CH CHICANES
CL CALCINES
   SCENICAL
CO COCAINES
CV VACCINES
DH ECHIDNAS
   INCHASED
DI SCIAENID

DO DIOCESAN
   OCEANIDS
DT DISTANCE
DY CYANIDES
   CYANISED
EF FAIENCES
   FIANCEES
EG AGENCIES
EL SALIENCE
EP SAPIENCE
ER CINEREAS
   INCREASE
   RESIANCE
ET CINEASTE
EU EUCAINES
FN FINANCES
FR FANCIERS
FS FASCINES
FT FANCIEST
GN ENCASING
GO COINAGES
GP ESCAPING
GR CREASING
   GRECIANS
   SEARCING
GS CAGINESS
   CEASINGS
HH HAINCHES
HM MACHINES
HN ENCHAINS
HR INARCHES
HS INCHASES
HT ASTHENIC
HY HYACINES
   SYNECHIA
IL SALICINE
   SILICANE
IP PISCINAE
IR RIANCIES
IT CANITIES
LM MESCALIN
LP CAPELINS
   PANICLES
   PELICANS
LR CARLINES
LS SANICLES
LU AESCULIN
   LUNACIES
LY SALIENCY
MP PEMICANS
MR CARMINES
MS AMNESICS
MT SEMANTIC
MU SEMUNCIA
MY SYCAMINE
NO CANONISE
NP PINNACES
NR CRANNIES
NT ANCIENTS
   CANNIEST
   INSTANCE
NU NUISANCE
NY CYANINES
OP CANOPIES
   CAPONISE
   PAEONICS
OR SCENARIO
OT ACONITES
   CANOEIST

PS INSCAPES
   PINCASES
RS ARSENICS
   CERASINS
   RACINESS
RT CANISTER
   CARNIEST
   NACRITES
   SCANTIER
ST CINEASTS
   SCANTIES
SU ISSUANCE
SY CYANISES
TT CANTIEST
   NICTATES
TV CISTVAEN
   VESICANT
TY CYANITES
YZ CYANIZES

ACENRS 175
(CANERS)
AG CARNAGES
   CRANAGES
AI CANARIES
AP PANCREAS
AT CANASTER
   CATERANS
BH BRANCHES
BI CARBINES
BK BRACKENS
BU UNBRACES
CE CREANCES
CH CHANCERS
   CHANCRES
   CRANCHES
CO CONACRES
DE ASCENDER
   REASCEND
DO DRACONES
   ENDOSARC
DT CANTREDS
DU DURANCES
EE ENCREASE
EG ENGRACES
EH ENARCHES
EI CINEREAS
   INCREASE
   RESIANCE
EL CLEANERS
   CLEANSER
EM MENACERS
ES CASERNES
ET REASCENT
   SARCENET
FI FANCIERS
FT CANTREFS
FU FURNACES
GH CHANGERS
GI CREASING
   GRECIANS
   SEARCING
GL CLANGERS
GM CRAGSMEN
GO ACROGENS
   CORNAGES
HI INARCHES
HL CHARNELS
HM ENCHARMS
HR RANCHERS

HS ARCHNESS
HT CHANTERS
   SNATCHER
   STANCHER
   TRANCHES
HU RAUNCHES
II RIANCIES
IL CARLINES
IM CARMINES
IN CRANNIES
IO SCENARIO
IS ARSENICS
   CERASINS
   RACINESS
IT CANISTER
   CARNIEST
   NACRITES
   SCANTIER
KK KNACKERS
KL CRANKLES
KP PRANCKES
KT CRANKEST
LN SCRANNEL
LU LUCARNES
MO CREMONAS
   ROMANCES
NS SCANNERS
OS COARSENS
   NARCOSES
OT ANCESTOR
   ENACTORS
   SARCONET
   SORTANCE
OU CARNEOUS
   NACREOUS
PR PRANCERS
PU ENCARPUS
   PRAUNCES
ST CRANTSES
SU SURANCES
TT TRANECTS
   TRANSECT
TU CENTAURS
   RECUSANT
   UNCRATES
   UNTRACES
TY ANCESTRY

ACENRT 96
(CANTER)
AC CARCANET
AI CARINATE
AL LACERANT
AS CANASTER
   CATERANS
AT REACTANT
AY CATENARY
CO ACCENTOR
DE CANTERED
   CRENATED
   DECANTER
   NECTARED
   RECANTED
DI CRINATED
   DICENTRA
DO CARTONED
DS CANTREDS
DU UNCARTED
   UNCRATED
   UNDERACT

   UNTRACED
EI CENTIARE
   CREATINE
   INCREATE
   ITERANCE
EN ENTRANCE
EO CAROTENE
EP PERCEANT
ER RECANTER
   RECREANT
ES REASCENT
   SARCENET
EU ENACTURE
   UNCREATE
FP PENCRAFT
FS CANTREFS
GI CATERING
   CITRANGE
   CREATING
   REACTING
HH ETHNARCH
HM MERCHANT
HO ANCHORET
HP PENTARCH
HS CHANTERS
   SNATCHER
   STANCHER
   TRANCHES
HT TRANCHET
HU CHAUNTER
IL CLARINET
IO ANORETIC
   CREATION
   REACTION
IS CANISTER
   CARNIEST
   NACRITES
   SCANTIER
IT INTERACT
IV NAVICERT
IX XERANTIC
KM TRACKMEN
KS CRANKEST
OO CORONATE
OP PORTANCE
OS ANCESTOR
   ENACTORS
   SARCONET
   SORTANCE
OT CONTRATE
OU COURANTE
   OUTRANCE
SS CRANTSES
ST TRANECTS
   TRANSECT
SU CENTAURS
   RECUSANT
   UNCRATES
   UNTRACES
SY ANCESTRY
TU TRUNCATE
UY CENTAURY
   CYANURET

ACENST 149
(STANCE)
AI ESTANCIA
AL ANALECTS
AM CAMSTANE
AP PASTANCE

AR CANASTER
   CATERANS
AT CANTATES
AY CYANATES
BI CABINETS
CE ACESCENT
CO COSECANT
DH SNATCHED
   STANCHED
DI DISTANCE
DL SCANTLED
DN SCANDENT
DP PANDECTS
DR CANTREDS
DS DESCANTS
EG CENTAGES
EI CINEASTE
EL CLEANEST
   LATENCES
EM CASEMENT
EN CANTEENS
EO ACETONES
ER REASCENT
   SARCENET
FI FANCIEST
FR CANTREFS
GO COGNATES
HI ASTHENIC
   CHANTIES
HL STANCHEL
HM MANCHETS
HN ENCHANTS
HR CHANTERS
   SNATCHER
   STANCHER
   TRANCHES
HS CHASTENS
   SNATCHES
   STANCHES
HT ETCHANTS
HU NAUTCHES
   UNCHASTE
HY CHANTEYS
II CANITIES
IM SEMANTIC
IN ANCIENTS
   CANNIEST
   INSTANCE
IO ACONITES
   CANOEIST
IR CANISTER
   CARNIEST
   NACRITES
   SCANTIER
IS CINEASTS
   SCANTIES
IT CANTIEST
   NICTATES
IV CISTVAEN
   VESICANT
IY CYANITES
JO JACONETS
JU JUNCATES
KM TACKSMEN
KR CRANKEST
LO LACTONES
LP CLAPNETS
LS SCANTLES
LT CANTLETS
MO CAMSTONE

```
OP CAPSTONE     IL CALORIES     GN COGNATES     BH BRACHETS     IM CERAMIST     BL BEDERALS
OR ANCESTOR        CARIOLES     GR ESCARGOT     BK BRACKETS        MATRICES     BM EMBREADS
   ENACTORS     IN SCENARIO     GT COTTAGES     CE ACCRETES     IN CANISTER     BP BESPREAD
   SARCONET     IV COVARIES     HI TOISEACH     CH CATCHERS        CARNIEST     BS DEBASERS
   SORTANCE        VARICOSE     HL ESCHALOT        CRATCHES        NACRITES     BT BETREADS
OS COSTEANS     JL CAJOLERS     HR CHAROSET     CO ECTOSARC        SCANTIER        BREASTED
OT CONSTATE     KL EARLOCKS        THORACES     CR CARRECTS     IP CRAPIEST     CC ACCEDERS
OV CENTAVOS     KR CROAKERS     HU OATCACHE     CS SCARCEST        CRISPATE     CE DECREASE
PT PENTACTS     LL CORELLAS        SOUTACHE     DE CEDRATES        PICRATES     CF DEFACERS
RS CRANTSES     LM CAROMELS     HY CHAYOTES     DH STARCHED        PRACTISE        FRESCADE
RT TRANECTS        SCLEROMA     IL ALOETICS     DI ACRIDEST     IR ERRATICS     CH SEARCHED
   TRANSECT     LP PARCLOSE        COALIEST     DN CANTREDS     IS SCARIEST     CI DECIARES
RU CENTAURS        POLACRES        SOCIETAL     DO REDCOATS     IT CITRATES     CK SCREAKED
   RECUSANT     LS ESCOLARS     IN ACONITES     DT DETRACTS        CRISTATE     CL DECLARES
   UNCRATES        LACROSSE        CANOEIST        SCRATTED        SCATTIER        RESCALED
   UNTRACES     LT SECTORAL     IP ECTOPIAS     DU TRADUCES     IU SURICATE     CM SCREAMED
RY ANCESTRY     LU CAROUSEL     IS SOCIATES     EH CHEATERS     IZ CRAZIEST     CN ASCENDER
ST SCANTEST     LY CALOYERS     IT OSCITATE        HECTARES     JM SCRAMJET        REASCEND
SU NUTCASES        COARSELY     JN JACONETS        RECHATES     JT TRAJECTS     CP ESCARPED
SW NEWSCAST     MN CREMONAS     LL COLLATES        RECHEATS     KL TACKLERS     CR SCAREDER
                   ROMANCES     LM CAMELOTS        TEACHERS     KN CRANKEST     CS CARESSED
ACEORS 103      MP COMPARES        MOLECAST     EL CLEAREST     KR TRACKERS     CT CEDRATES
(ORACES)           COMPEARS     LN LACTONES        SCELERAT     KS STACKERS     DG DEGRADES
AS ROSACEAS        MESOCARP     LP POLECATS        TREACLES     KT RACKETTS     DR DREADERS
AU ARACEOUS     MY SYCAMORE     LR SECTORAL     EM CERAMETS     LO SECTORAL     DW SAWDERED
BD BROCADES     NS COARSENS     LS ALECOSTS        CREMATES     LP SCEPTRAL     EG DEGREASE
BG BROCAGES        NARCOSES        COATLESS        MEERCATS        SPECTRAL     EL RELEASED
BH BROACHES     NT ANCESTOR        LACTOSES     EN REASCENT     LS SCARLETS        RESEALED
BI AEROBICS        ENACTORS        SCATOLES        SARCENET     LT CLATTERS     EN ENSEARED
BM CRAMBOES        SARCONET     LT CALOTTES     EO CREASOTE        SCRATTLE        SERENADE
BU CORBEAUS        SORTANCE     LU LACTEOUS     ER CATERERS     LU RAUCLEST     ER ARREEDES
CH CAROCHES     NU CARNEOUS        LOCUSTAE        RETRACES     MP CRAMPETS     ET RESEATED
   COACHERS        NACREOUS        OSCULATE        TERRACES     NO ANCESTOR     FI FEDARIES
CL CORACLES     PP COPPERAS     LY ACOLYTES     ES CATERESS        ENACTORS     FL FEDERALS
CN CONACRES     PX EXOCARPS     MN CAMSTONE        CERASTES        SARCONET     FP PREFADES
CS ARCCOSES     RT ACROTERS     MO COMATOSE     EU SECATEUR        SORTANCE     FT DRAFTEES
CT ECTOSARC        CREATORS     NP CAPSTONE     EX EXACTERS     NS CRANTSES     GI DISAGREE
CW CRACOWES        REACTORS     NR ANCESTOR     FH FRATCHES     NT TRANECTS     GN DERANGES
DG CORDAGES     RU CAROUSER        ENACTORS     FN CANTREFS        TRANSECT        GRANDEES
DI IDOCRASE     ST COARSEST        SARCONET     FO FORECAST     NU CENTAURS        GRENADES
DM COMRADES        COASTERS        SORTANCE     FR REFRACTS        RECUSANT     GP ASPERGED
DN DRACONES     SU CAROUSES     NS COSTEANS     FU FACTURES        UNCRATES        PRESAGED
   ENDOSARC     TT SECTATOR     NT CONSTATE     GI AGRESTIC        UNTRACES     GR REGRADES
DR CORRADES     TU OUTRACES     NV CENTAVOS     GO ESCARGOT     NY ANCESTRY     GS DRESSAGE
DS SARCODES     TV OVERACTS     PU OUTPACES     GU TRUCAGES     OR ACROTERS     GT RESTAGED
DT REDCOATS        OVERCAST     RR ACROTERS     HH HATCHERS        CREATORS     GU GUARDEES
DU CAROUSED     TX EXACTORS        CREATORS     HI CHARIEST        REACTORS     GW RAGWEEDS
EL ESCAROLE                        REACTORS        THERIACS     OS COARSEST     HH REHASHED
EM RACEMOSE     ACEOST 146      RS COARSEST     HL ARCHLETS        COASTERS     HL ASHLERED
ET CREASOTE     (ACTOSE)           COASTERS     HM MATCHERS     OT SECTATOR     HO SOREHEAD
FF AFFORCES     AK OATCAKES     RT SECTATOR     HN CHANTERS     OU OUTRACES     HP EPHEDRAS
FL ALFRESCO     AL CATALOES     RU OUTRACES        SNATCHER     OV OVERACTS        RESHAPED
FR FORECARS     AS SEACOAST     RV OVERACTS        STANCHER        OVERCAST     HR ADHERERS
FT FORECAST     BL OBSTACLE        OVERCAST        TRANCHES     OX EXACTORS        REDSHARE
FX CARFOXES     CD ACCOSTED     RX EXACTORS     HO CHAROSET     PU CAPTURES     HT HEADREST
GK CORKAGES     CL CACOLETS        CREATORS        THORACES        PRESCUTA     HW WASHERED
GM SCARMOGE     CN COSECANT        REACTORS     HP CHAPTERS     QU RACQUETS     IJ JADERIES
GN ACROGENS     CR ECTOSARC     TU OUTCASTE        PATCHERS     RT RETRACTS     IL REALISED
   CORNAGES     DH CATHODES     UU AUTOCUES     HR CHARTERS     SS CRASSEST        SIDEREAL
GO CARGOOSE     DK STOCKADE                        RECHARTS     ST SCATTERS     IM MADERISE
GS CORSAGES     DR REDCOATS     ACERST 141         STARCHER     TT TETRACTS     IN ARSENIDE
   SOCAGERS     DT COSTATED     (CATERS)        HS STARCHES     TU CRUSTATE        DENARIES
GT ESCARGOT     EN ACETONES     AB ABREACTS     HT CHATTERS     TX EXTRACTS        DRAISENE
GU COURAGES     ER CREASOTE        CABARETS        RATCHETS     TY SCATTERY        NEARSIDE
HL CHOLERAS     ET ECOSTATE     AD CADASTRE     HW WATCHERS     UX CURTAXES     IT READIEST
   CHORALES     EV EVOCATES     AF SEACRAFT     HY YACHTERS                        SERIATED
HP POACHERS     FP POSTFACE     AG CARTAGES     IL ALTRICES     ADEERS 70          STEADIER
HR HORSECAR     FR FORECAST     AN CANASTER        ARTICLES     (SEARED)        IV READVISE
HT CHAROSET     FU OUTFACES        CATERANS        RECITALS     AP PASEARED     KN KNEADERS
   THORACES     GL CATELOGS     AT CASTRATE        SELICTAR     BI BEARDIES
                                BE ACERBEST
```

KT STREAKED	DL DESALTED	BR BRANGLED	IL DEARLING	IP PERIDIAL	ER REALISED
LL SARDELLE	DO DEODATES	DE DANEGELD	DRAGLINE	IS LAIRISED	SIDEREAL
LM DEMERSAL	EL TEASELED	DS GLADDENS	MARGINED	IZ LAIRIZED	ES DEISEALS
EMERALDS	ER RESEATED	EO ENGAOLED	IM DREAMING	LO ARILLODE	IDEALESS
LP PLEADERS	FL DEFLATES	ER ENLARGED	IO ORGANDIE	LP PALLIDER	ET LEADIEST
RELAPSED	FN FASTENED	LARGENED	IR DREARING	LS DALLIERS	EV DISLEAVE
LT TREADLES	FR DRAFTEES	ET DANEGELT	IS DERAIGNS	DIALLERS	EY EYELIADS
LV SLAVERED	GO DOGEATES	FI FINAGLED	GRADINES	LV RIVALLED	FG GADFLIES
LW LEEWARDS	GR RESTAGED	HI HEALDING	READINGS	MP IMPARLED	FH DEALFISH
LY DELAYERS	GT GESTATED	HO HEADLONG	IT DERATING	MY DREAMILY	FI LADIFIES
MN AMENDERS	HH HASTENED	II GLIADINE	GRADIENT	NN INLANDER	SALIFIED
MEANDERS	HI ATHEISED	IM MALIGNED	TREADING	NS ISLANDER	FS DISLEAFS
REAMENDS	HEADIEST	IO GALENOID	IY DERAYING	OS DARIOLES	FY LADYFIES
MO SEADROME	HN HASTENED	IP PLEADING	YEARDING	SOLIDARE	GL GALLISED
MR DREAMERS	HR HEADREST	IR DEARLING	JO JARGONED	SOREDIAL	GN DEALINGS
MT MASTERED	HS HEADSETS	DRAGLINE	LS DANGLERS	OT IDOLATER	LEADINGS
STREAMED	IJ JADEITES	IS DEALINGS	GLANDERS	TAILORED	GO GOLIASED
MU MEASURED	IL LEADIEST	LEADINGS	LW WRANGLED	OV OVERLAID	GR SLAIRGED
NN ENSNARED	IM MEDIATES	IT DELATING	MS DRAGSMEN	OX EXORDIAL	GS GLISSADE
NO REASONED	IN ANDESITE	IY DELAYING	NO ANDROGEN	PS PEDRAILS	GT GLADIEST
NS DEARNESS	IR READIEST	LU GLANDULE	DRAGONNE	PREDIALS	GV DISGAVEL
NU UNDERSEA	SERIATED	UNGALLED	OT DRAGONET	PT DIPTERAL	HP HELIPADS
NW ANSWERED	STEADIER	OY GONDELAY	RU GRANDEUR	TRIPEDAL	HV LAVISHED
OW OARWEEDS	IS STEADIES	PS SPANGLED	ST GRANDEST	PU EPIDURAL	HW WHAISLED
PR SPREADER	IV DEVIATES	RS DANGLERS	SU ENGUARDS	PV DEPRIVAL	IM IDEALISM
PS ASPERSED	SEDATIVE	GLANDERS	UU UNARGUED	RY DREARILY	MILADIES
PREASSED	KN NAKEDEST	RW WRANGLED	UZ UNGRAZED	ST DILATERS	IR LAIRISED
REPASSED	KR STREAKED	SS GLADNESS		LARDIEST	IT IDEALIST
PT PREDATES	LM MEDALETS	TW TWANGLED	**ADEILR 19**	SU RESIDUAL	KW SIDEWALK
REPASTED	LO DESOLATE	UZ UNGLAZED	(RAILED)	SY DIALYSER	LP ILLAPSED
TRAPESSED	LP PEDESTAL		AH HEADRAIL	TT DETRITAL	SPADILLE
PU PERSUADE	LR TREADLES	**ADEGNR 126**	AP PRAEDIAL	TY DIELYTRA	LR DALLIERS
PV DEPRAVES	LS DATELESS	(DANGER)	AS SALARIED	VY VARIEDLY	DIALLERS
PERVADES	LY SEDATELY	AI AREADING	BC CALIBRED	YZ DIALYZER	MM DILEMMAS
PW PERSWADE	MN STAMENED	DRAINAGE	BE RIDEABLE		MO DAMOISEL
PZ SPREAZED	MP STAMPEDE	GARDENIA	BN BILANDER	**ADEILS 33**	MP IMPLEADS
RT ARRESTED	STEPDAME	AR ARRANGED	BT LIBRATED	(LADIES)	MISPLEAD
DREAREST	MR MASTERED	BI BEARDING	BV DRIVABLE	AC ALCAIDES	MS MAIDLESS
RETREADS	STREAMED	BREADING	BY DIABLERY	SIDALCEA	MISDEALS
SERRATED	MW MATWEEDS	BL BRANGLED	CF FRICADEL	AD ALIDADES	MISLEADS
TREADERS	NS ASSENTED	BO BONDAGER	CH HERALDIC	AM MALADIES	MT MISDEALT
RV ADVERSER	NU UNSEATED	CE ENGRACED	CP PLACIDER	AP PALISADE	MY DYSMELIA
ST ASSERTED	PR PREDATES	CU UNGRACED	CS DECRIALS	AR SALARIED	NN ANNELIDS
ESTRADES	REPASTED	DE DANGERED	RADICLES	AS ASSAILED	LINDANES
TT ASTERTED	PS STAPEDES	DERANGED	CT ARTICLED	AV VEDALIAS	NO NODALISE
RESTATED	PT ADEPTEST	GARDENED	CU AURICLED	BD DISABLED	NR ISLANDER
TW DEWATERS	RR ARRESTED	DI DREADING	RADICULE	BE ABSEILED	NU UNSAILED
TARWEEDS	DREAREST	DU UNGRADED	DE DEADLIER	BH DISHABLE	NV ANDVILES
WASTERED	RETREADS	EE RENEGADE	DERAILED	BP PIEBALDS	OP EPISODAL
TY ESTRAYED	SERRATED	EI REGAINED	DH DIHEDRAL	BS DISABLES	OPALISED
	TREADERS	EL ENLARGED	DS DIEDRALS	CI LAICISED	SEPALOID
ADEEST 85	RS ASSERTED	LARGENED	EL REALLIED	CL CEDILLAS	OR DARIOLES
(SEATED)	ESTRADES	EM GENDARME	EM REMEDIAL	DECIMALS	SOLIDARE
AC ESTACADE	RT ASTERTED	EN ENDANGER	EP PEDALIER	CM CAMELIDS	SOREDIAL
BD BEDSTEAD	RESTATED	ENRANGED	ER DERAILER	DECLAIMS	OS ASSOILED
BESTADDE	RW DEWATERS	EO RENEGADO	RERAILED	MEDICALS	DEASOILS
BH BETHESDA	TARWEEDS	ER GARDENER	ES REALISED	CO COALISED	OT DIASTOLE
BI BEADIEST	WASTERED	GARNERED	SIDEREAL	CP DISPLACE	ISOLATED
DIABETES	RY ESTRAYED	ES DERANGES	ET RETAILED	CR DECRIALS	SODALITE
BN ABSENTED	ST SEDATEST	GRANDEES	EZ REALIZED	RADICELS	SOLIDATE
BR BETREADS	TT ATTESTED	GRENADES	FI AIRFIELD	RADICLES	OU DOULEIAS
BREASTED	UX EXUDATES	EU DUNGAREE	FN FILANDER	CT CITADELS	PR PEDRAILS
DEBATERS		RENAGUED	FO FORELAID	DIALECTS	PREDIALS
BS BASSETED	**ADEGLN 197**	UNGEARED	GL GRILLADE	DG GLADDIES	PS DESPISAL
BESTEADS	(DANGLE)	EV ENGRAVED	GN DEARLING	DN ISLANDED	PT TALIPEDS
CH DETACHES	AH DANELAGH	FO FRONDAGE	DRAGLINE	DR DIEDRALS	QU SQUAILED
CP ASPECTED	AM MAGDALEN	HI ADHERING	GS SLAIRGED	DY DIALYSED	RT DILATERS
CR CEDRATES	AS SELADANG	HEADRING	HN HARDLINE	EH DEISHEAL	LARDIEST
CU EDUCATES	BI BLINDAGE	HT THRANGED		EI IDEALISE	RU RESIDUAL
DI STEADIED		IK DAKERING		EN DELAINES	

RY DIALYSER		CT DISTANCE	SEDATION	DT DISRATED	SARDINES
SU DEASIULS	GY DERAYING	CY CYANIDES	OX DIOXANES	DW SIDEWARD	NT DETRAINS
SV DEVISALS	READYING	CYANISED	OZ ADONIZES	EF FEDARIES	RANDIEST
SY DIALYSES	YEARDING	DL ISLANDED	ANODIZES	EG DISAGREE	STRAINED
TV VALIDEST	HL HARDLINE	DO ADENOIDS	PR SPRAINED	EJ JADERIES	NU DENARIUS
TY DIASTYLE	HU UNHAIRED	ADONISED	PT DEPAINTS	EL REALISED	UNRAISED
STEADILY	IM MERIDIAN	ANODISED	PV SPAVINED	SIDEREAL	URANIDES
UV DISVALUE	IS DRAISINE	DT DANDIEST	RR DRAINERS	EM MADERISE	NV INVADERS
XY DYSLEXIA	IT DAINTIER	EL DELAINES	SERRANID	EN ARSENIDE	SANDIVER
YZ DIALYZES	IU UREDINIA	EM DEMAINES	RS ARIDNESS	DENARIES	NY SYNEDRIA
	LN INLANDER	EN ADENINES	SARDINES	DRAISENE	OP DIASPORE
ADEINR 4	LS ISLANDER	ANDESINE	RT DETRAINS	NEARSIDE	PARODIES
(RAINED)	MR MANRIDER	ER ARSENIDE	RANDIEST	ET READIEST	OT ASTEROID
AC CANARIED	MS ADERMINS	DENARIES	STRAINED	SERIATED	PP APPRISED
RADIANCE	SIRNAMED	DRAISENE	RU DENARIUS	STEADIER	DRAPPIES
AG AREADING	MY DAIRYMEN	NEARSIDE	UNRAISED	EV READVISE	PR DRAPIERS
DRAINAGE	MZ ZEMINDAR	ES ANISEEDS	URANIDES	FM MISFARED	PS DESPAIRS
GARDENIA	NS INSNARED	ET ANDESITE	RV INVADERS	FN FRIANDES	PT RAPIDEST
AM MARINADE	NZ RENDZINA	FI SANIFIED	SANDIVER	FO FORESAID	SPIRATED
AR DARRAINE	OR ORDAINER	FR FRIANDES	RY SYNEDRIA	GH GARISHED	TRAIPSED
AS ARANEIDS	REORDAIN	GH HEADINGS	ST SANDIEST	HEADRIGS	PU UPRAISED
AT DENTARIA	OS ANEROIDS	SHEADING	SW WINDASES	GL SLAIRGED	RW SWARDIER
BD BRANDIED	DONARIES	GL DEALINGS	TT INSTATED	GN DERAIGNS	ST ASTERIDS
RIBANDED	OT AROINTED	LEADINGS	TU AUDIENTS	GRADINES	DIASTERS
BG BEARDING	ORDINATE	GO AGONISED	SINUATED	READINGS	DISASTER
BREADING	RATIONED	DIAGNOSE	TV DEVIANTS	GP SPAIRGED	DISRATES
BL BILANDER	OU DOUANIER	GR DERAIGNS	TY DESYATIN	HM MISHEARD	SU RADIUSES
BM BRIDEMAN	PS SPRAINED	GRADINES		HP RAPHIDES	SUDARIES
BO DEBONAIR	PT DIPTERAN	READINGS	**ADEIRS 12**	HS RADISHES	SV ADVISERS
BS BRANDIES	PU UNPAIRED	GS ASSIGNED	(RAISED)	HT HAIRSTED	TT STRAITED
BRANDISE	UNREPAID	GT SEDATING	AB ARABISED	HARDIEST	STRIATED
CD CANDIDER	RS DRAINERS	STEADING	AF FARADISE	HV RAVISHED	TARDIEST
RIDDANCE	SERRANID	GW WINDAGES	SAFARIED	HW RAWHIDES	TW TAWDRIES
CE DERACINE	SS ARIDNESS	HK SKINHEAD	AL SALARIED	IL LAIRISED	
CH INARCHED	SARDINES	HO ADHESION	AN ARANEIDS	IN DRAISINE	**ADEIST 26**
CI ACRIDINE	ST DETRAINS	HP DEANSHIP	AP PARADISE	IP PRESIDIA	(IDATES)
CN CRANNIED	RANDIEST	PINHEADS	AT DATARIES	IS DIARISES	AM DIASTEMA
CR RANCIDER	STRAINED	HS SHANDIES	RADIATES	IT IRISATED	AR DATARIES
CT CRINATED	SU DENARIUS	HT HANDIEST	BC ASCRIBED	IZ DIARIZES	RADIATES
DICENTRA	UNRAISED	HV VANISHED	CARBIDES	JM JEMIDARS	AS DIASTASE
DG DREADING	URANIDES	IN SANIDINE	BE BEARDIES	KT STRAIKED	AT SATIATED
DO ORDAINED	SV INVADERS	IR DRAISINE	BG ABRIDGES	LL DALLIERS	BE BEADIEST
DT INDARTED	SANDIVER	IT ADENITIS	BRIGADES	DIALLERS	DIABETES
EF FREDAINE	SY SYNEDRIA	DAINTIES	BM EMBRAIDS	LN ISLANDER	BN BANDIEST
EG REGAINED	TT NITRATED	KY KYANISED	BN BRANDIES	LO DARIOLES	BP BAPTISED
EM REMAINED	TU DATURINE	LN ANNELIDS	BRANDISE	SOLIDARE	BR BARDIEST
EP PINDAREE	INDURATE	LINDANES	BT BARDIEST	SOREDIAL	BRAIDEST
ES ARSENIDE	RUINATED	LO NODALISE	BRAIDEST	LP PEDRAILS	RABIDEST
DENARIES	URINATED	LR ISLANDER	RABIDEST	PREDIALS	TRIBADES
DRAISENE	UV UNVARIED	LU UNSAILED	TRIBADES	LT DILATERS	BS BASTIDES
NEARSIDE	VY VINEYARD	LV ANDVILES	BW BAWDRIES	LARDIEST	BU DAUBIEST
ET DETAINER		MM MISNAMED	DAWBRIES	LU RESIDUAL	BW BAWDIEST
RETAINED	**ADEINS 22**	MO NOMADIES	CE DECIARES	LY DIALYSER	CG CADGIEST
FL FILANDER	(SANDIE)	NOMADISE	CG DISGRACE	MM MERMAIDS	CH SCAITHED
FS FRIANDES	AC AIDANCES	MR ADERMINS	CH RACHIDES	MN ADERMINS	CL CITADELS
FU UNFAIRED	AR ARANEIDS	SIRNAMED	CL DECRIALS	SIRNAMED	DIALECTS
GH ADHERING	BG BEADINGS	MS SIDESMAN	RADICELS	MR ADMIRERS	CN DISTANCE
HEADRING	DEBASING	MT MEDIANTS	RADICLES	DISARMER	CP SPICATED
GK DAKERING	BH BANISHED	MU MAUNDIES	CO IDOCRASE	MS MISREADS	CR ACRIDEST
GL DEARLING	BR BRANDIES	MY DYNAMISE	CP EPACRIDS	SIDEARMS	CT DICTATES
DRAGLINE	BRANDISE	NN NANDINES	CS SIDECARS	MT MARDIEST	DE STEADIED
GM DREAMING	BT BANDIEST	NR INSNARED	CT ACRIDEST	MISRATED	DF FADDIEST
MARGINED	BU UNBIASED	NU UNSAINED	CU DECURIAS	READMITS	DM MISDATED
GO ORGANDIE	BW BEDAWINS	NX DISANNEX	DG DISGRADE	NN INSNARED	DN DANDIEST
GR DREARING	CH ECHIDNAS	OR ANEROIDS	DI DIARISED	NO ANEROIDS	DR DISRATED
GS DERAIGNS	INCHASED	DONARIES	DL DIEDRALS	DONARIES	EH ATHEISED
GRADINES	CI SCIAENID	OS ADONISES	DM DISARMED	SERRANID	HEADIEST
READINGS	CO DIOCESAN	ANODISES	MISDREAD	NR DRAINERS	EJ JADEITES
GT DERATING	OCEANIDS	OT ASTONIED	DO ROADSIDE	SERRANID	EL LEADIEST
GRADIENT			DP DISPREAD	NS ARIDNESS	EM MEDIATES

EN ANDESITE	DISASTER	RUNDALES	RS SLANDERS	PREDIALS	IV VALIDEST
ER READIEST	DISRATES	TY ARDENTLY	RU LAUNDERS	IT DILATERS	IY DIASTYLE
SERIATED	RT STRAITED	UY UNDERLAY	LURDANES	LARDIEST	STEADILY
STEADIER	STRIATED		RUNDALES	IU RESIDUAL	NU UNSALTED
ES STEADIES	TARDIEST	**ADELNS 137**	TU UNSALTED	IY DIALYSER	NW WETLANDS
EV DEVIATES	RW TAWDRIES	(ANDLES)	TW WETLANDS	KP SPARKLED	OP TADPOLES
SEDATIVE	SS ASSISTED	AC CANDELAS		LN LANDLERS	OR DELATORS
FF DAFFIEST	DISSEATS	AG SELADANG	**ADELRS 88**	LO ODALLERS	LEOTARDS
GL GLADIEST	ST DISTASTE	AM DALESMAN	(ALDERS)	LU UDALLERS	LODESTAR
GM SIGMATED	STAIDEST	LEADSMAN	AB BASELARD	MN MANDRELS	OV SOLVATED
GN SEDATING	TU SITUATED	AR ADRENALS	AC CALDERAS	MO EARLDOMS	PT SPLATTED
STEADING		AT EASTLAND	AH ASHLARED	NO LADRONES	PU PULSATED
GO GODETIAS	**ADELNR 79**	AW DANELAWS	AI SALARIED	SOLANDER	RT STARTLED
GU GAUDIEST	(LANDER)	AY ANALYSED	AN ADRENALS	NP SPANDREL	TY STATEDLY
HK SKAITHED	AC CALENDAR	BB SNABBLED	AP PARDALES	NS SLANDERS	
HN HANDIEST	LANDRACE	BS BALDNESS	BB DABBLERS	NU LAUNDERS	**ADENRS 62**
HP PITHEADS	AH ANHEDRAL	BT BLANDEST	DRABBLES	LURDANES	(ANDERS)
HR HAIRSTED	AK KALENDAR	CE CLEANSED	BD BLADDERS	RUNDALES	AI ARANEIDS
HARDIEST	AM ALDERMAN	CO CELADONS	BE BEDERALS	OP LEOPARDS	AL ADRENALS
HS SHADIEST	MALANDER	CT SCANTLED	BG BELGARDS	OS ROADLESS	AV VERANDAS
IL IDEALIST	AS ADRENALS	CU UNSCALED	BH HALBERDS	OT DELATORS	BI BRANDIES
IN ADENITIS	BG BRANGLED	DG GLADDENS	BR DRABLERS	LEOTARDS	BRANDISE
DAINTIES	BI BILANDER	DI ISLANDED	BU DURABLES	LODESTAR	BO BANDORES
IP STAPEDII	BO BANDEROL	DR DANDLERS	CD CLADDERS	OU ROULADES	BROADENS
IR IRISATED	BY BYLANDER	DU UNSADDLE	CE DECLARES	PW SPRAWLED	BR BRANDERS
KR STRAIKED	CE CALENDER	EE ENSEALED	RESCALED	RU RUDERALS	BS DRABNESS
LM MISDEALT	ENCRADLE	EI DELAINES	CH CHALDERS	RW DRAWLERS	BT BANDSTER
LO DIASTOLE	CH CHANDLER	EM DALESMEN	CI DECRIALS	TT STARTLED	CE ASCENDER
ISOLATED	CK CRANKLED	EMENDALS	RADICELS	ZZ DAZZLERS	REASCEND
SODALITE	CO COLANDER	LEADSMEN	RADICLES		CO DRACONES
SOLIDATE	CY CALENDRY	EP DEPLANES	CS SCALDERS	**ADELST 110**	ENDOSARC
LP TALIPEDS	DE ENLARDED	EU UNLEASED	CW SCRAWLED	(SALTED)	CT CANTREDS
LR DILATERS	DS DANDLERS	UNSEALED	CY SACREDLY	AN EASTLAND	CU DURANCES
LARDIEST	EG ENLARGED	EV ENSLAVED	DI DIEDRALS	AT SALTATED	DL DANDLERS
LV VALIDEST	LARGENED	FF SNAFFLED	DN DANDLERS	AU ADULATES	DT STRANDED
LY DIASTYLE	EH REHANDLE	FL ELFLANDS	DP PADDLERS	AY DAYTALES	DU DAUNDERS
STEADILY	EM ALDERMEN	FN FENLANDS	DS SADDLERS	BN BLANDEST	EE ENSEARED
MM MISMATED	EO OLEANDER	GI DEALINGS	DT STRADDLE	BU SUBLATED	SERENADE
MN MEDIANTS	ET ANTLERED	LEADINGS	DW DAWDLERS	CI CITADELS	EG DERANGES
MO ATOMISED	EV LAVENDER	GP SPANGLED	SWADDLER	DIALECTS	GRANDEES
MP DAMPIEST	FI FILANDER	GR DANGLERS	DY SADDLERY	CN SCANTLED	GRENADES
IMPASTED	FO FORELAND	GLANDERS	EE RELEASED	CU CAULDEST	EI ARSENIDE
MR MARDIEST	FU DEARNFUL	GS GLADNESS	RESEALED	SULCATED	DENARIES
MISRATED	DRAGLINE	HR HANDLERS	EF FEDERALS	DE DESALTED	DRAISENE
READMITS	GI DEARLING	HS HANDLESS	EH ASHLERED	DG GLADDEST	NEARSIDE
MS MISDATES	GS DANGLERS	HANDSELS	EI REALISED	DR STRADDLE	EK KNEADERS
MU TAEDIUMS	GLANDERS	HT SHETLAND	SIDEREAL	DS STADDLES	EM AMENDERS
MY DAYTIMES	GW WRANGLED	HU UNHALSED	EL SARDELLE	DW TWADDLES	MEANDERS
NO ASTONIED	HI HARDLINE	UNLASHED	EM DEMERSAL	EE TEASELED	REAMENDS
SEDATION	HS HANDLERS	UNSHALED	EMERALDS	EF DEFLATES	EN ENSNARED
NP DEPAINTS	IN INLANDER	IN ANNELIDS	EP PLEADERS	EI LEADIEST	EO REASONED
NR DETRAINS	IS ISLANDER	LINDANES	RELAPSED	EM MEDALETS	ES DEARNESS
RANDIEST	KP PRANKLED	IO NODALISE	ET TREADLES	EO DESOLATE	EU UNDERSEA
STRAINED	LS LANDLERS	IR ISLANDER	EV SLAVERED	EP. PEDESTAL	EW ANSWERED
NS SANDIEST	MS MANDRELS	IU UNSAILED	EW LEEWARDS	ER TREADLES	FI FRIANDES
NT INSTATED	OP PONDERAL	IV ANDVILES	EY DELAYERS	ES DATELESS	GI DERAIGNS
NU AUDIENTS	OS LADRONES	KU UNSLAKED	FP FELDSPAR	EY SEDATELY	GRADINES
SINUATED	SOLANDER	LP SPENDALL	GG DRAGGLES	FU DEFAULTS	READINGS
NV DEVIANTS	OU UNLOADER	LR LANDLERS	GI SLAIRGED	SULFATED	GL DANGLERS
NY DESYATIN	URODELAN	LS LANDLESS	GN DANGLERS	GI GLADIEST	GLANDERS
OP DIOPTASE	OV OVERLAND	LW ELLWANDS	GLANDERS	HN SHETLAND	GM DRAGSMEN
OR ASTEROID	RONDAVEL	WALLSEND	HN HANDLERS	II IDEALIST	GT GRANDEST
OX OXIDATES	PS SPANDREL	MN LANDSMEN	II LAIRISED	IM MISDEALT	GU ENGUARDS
OZ AZOTISED	PU PENDULAR	MO LODESMAN	IL DALLIERS	IL DIASTOLE	HK REDSHANK
PR RAPIDEST	UNDERLAP	MR MANDRELS	DIALLERS	ISOLATED	HL HANDLERS
SPIRATED	UPLANDER	OR LADRONES	IN ISLANDER	SODALITE	HM HERDSMAN
TRAIPSED	PY PANDERLY	SOLANDER	IO DARIOLES	SOLIDATE	HS HARDNESS
PV VAPIDEST	SS SLANDERS	OY YEALDONS	SOLIDARE	IP TALIPEDS	HU UNSHARED
RS ASTERIDS	SU LAUNDERS	PR SPANDREL	SOREDIAL	IR DILATERS	HW SWANHERD
DIASTERS	LURDANES	PY DYSPNEAL	IP PEDRAILS	LARDIEST	II DRAISINE

IL ISLANDER	UNTRACED	RT UNTARRED	UNTASTED	RS DROSERAS	EW DEWATERS
IM ADERMINS	DD DEUDDARN	SS DANSEURS	UW UNWASTED	RT ROADSTER	TARWEEDS
SIRNAMED	DE DAUNERED	ST DAUNTERS	UY UNSTAYED	ST ASSORTED	WASTERED
IN INSNARED	DG UNGRADED	TRANSUDE	UNSTEADY	TORSADES	EY ESTRAYED
IO ANEROIDS	DO UNADORED	UNTREADS		TU OUTDARES	FF STRAFFED
DONARIES	DP UNDRAPED	SY UNDERSAY	**ADEORS 48**	TX EXTRADOS	FR REDRAFTS
IP SPRAINED	DS DAUNDERS	TT TRUANTED	(ADORES)	UV SAVOURED	REDRAFTS
IR DRAINERS	DT DRAUNTED	WY UNDERWAY	AB SEABOARD	WY RODEWAYS	GN GRANDEST
SERRANID	UNTRADED		ABSORBED		GO GOADSTER
IS ARIDNESS	DW UNWARDED	**ADENST 36**	BC BROCADES	**ADERST 49**	GR DRAGSTER
SARDINES	EF UNFEARED	(STANED)	BD ADSORBED	(DATERS)	HH THRASHED
IT DETRAINS	EG DUNGAREE	AK ASKANTED	BN BANDORES	AC CADASTRE	HI HAIRSTED
RANDIEST	RENAGUED	AL EASTLAND	BROADENS	AG GRADATES	HARDIEST
STRAINED	UNGEARED	AM MANDATES	BR BROADERS	AI DATARIES	HY HYDRATES
IU DENARIUS	EN UNEARNED	AN ANDANTES	BT BROADEST	RADIATES	II IRISATED
UNRAISED	EP UNREAPED	BE ABSENTED	CG CORDAGES	AP ADAPTERS	IK STRAIKED
URANIDES	ES UNDERSEA	BI BANDIEST	CI IDOCRASE	READAPTS	IL DILATERS
IV INVADERS	ET DENATURE	BL BLANDEST	CM COMRADES	AS ASSARTED	LARDIEST
SANDIVER	EV UNREAVED	BR BANDSTER	CN DRACONES	AT ASTARTED	IM MARDIEST
IY SYNEDRIA	FL DEARNFUL	CH SNATCHED	ENDOSARC	AW EASTWARD	MISRATED
KS DARKNESS	FM UNFRAMED	STANCHED	CR CORRADES	BB DRABBEST	READMITS
LL LANDLERS	GR GRANDEUR	CI DISTANCE	CS SARCODES	DRABBETS	IN DETRAINS
LM MANDRELS	GS ENGUARDS	CL SCANTLED	CT REDCOATS	BE BETREADS	RANDIEST
LO LADRONES	GU UNARGUED	CN SCANDENT	CU CAROUSED	BREASTED	STRAINED
SOLANDER	GZ UNGRAZED	CP PANDECTS	DD ADDORSED	DEBATERS	IO ASTEROID
LP SPANDREL	HI UNHAIRED	CR CANTREDS	DI ROADSIDE	BH BREADTHS	IP RAPIDEST
LS SLANDERS	HM UNHARMED	CS DESCANTS	EH SOREHEAD	BI BARDIEST	SPIRATED
LU LAUNDERS	HS UNSHARED	DI DANDIEST	EM SEADROME	BRAIDEST	TRAIPSED
LURDANES	HT UNTHREAD	DR STRANDED	EN REASONED	RABIDEST	IS ASTERIDS
RUNDALES	II UREDINIA	EF FASTENED	EW OARWEEDS	TRIBADES	DIASTERS
MO RANSOMED	IO DOUANIER	EH HASTENED	FI FORESAID	BN BANDSTER	DISASTER
ROADSMEN	IP UNPAIRED	EI ANDESITE	GM ORGASMED	BO BROADEST	DISRATES
MU DURAMENS	UNREPAID	EK NAKEDEST	GT GOADSTER	BS DABSTERS	IT STRAITED
MAUNDERS	URINATED	EM STAMENED	GW DOWAGERS	BU SURBATED	STRIATED
SURNAMED	IS DENARIUS	ES ASSENTED	WORDAGES	BW BEDSTRAW	TARDIEST
OP OPERANDS	UNRAISED	EU UNSEATED	HK HARDOKES	BY DRYBEATS	IW TAWDRIES
PANDORES	URANIDES	FS DAFTNESS	HM HADROMES	CE CEDRATES	JU ADJUSTER
OT TORNADES	IT DATURINE	GI SEDATING	HP RHAPSODE	CH STARCHED	READJUST
PP PARPENDS	INDURATE	STEADING	HR HOARDERS	CI ACRIDEST	LO DELATORS
PR PARDNERS	RUINATED	GR GRANDEST	HW SHADOWER	CN CANTREDS	LEOTARDS
PU UNSPARED	URINATED	HI HANDIEST	IL DARIOLES	CO REDCOATS	LODESTAR
QU SQUANDER	IV UNVARIED	HL SHETLAND	SOLIDARE	CT DETRACTS	LT STARTLED
RY REYNARDS	KM UNMARKED	HS HANDSETS	SOREDIAL	SCRATTED	MO STROAMED
SS SARSDENS	LO UNLOADER	II ADENITIS	IN ANEROIDS	CU TRADUCES	MP STRAMPED
ST STANDERS	URODELAN	DAINTIES	DONARIES	DI DISRATED	NO TORNADES
SU DANSEURS	LP PENDULAR	IM MEDIANTS	IP DIASPORE	DL STRADDLE	NS STANDERS
TU DAUNTERS	UNDERLAP	IO ASTONIED	PARODIES	DN STRANDED	NU DAUNTERS
TRANSUDE	UPLANDER	SEDATION	IT ASTEROID	EE RESEATED	TRANSUDE
UNTREADS	LS LAUNDERS	IP DEPAINTS	JP JEOPARDS	EF DRAFTEES	UNTREADS
TX DEXTRANS	LURDANES	IR DETRAINS	KM DARKSOME	EG RESTAGED	NX DEXTRANS
UY UNDERSAY	RUNDALES	RANDIEST	LL ODALLERS	EH HEADREST	OP ADOPTERS
	LY UNDERLAY	STRAINED	LM EARLDOMS	EI READIEST	ASPORTED
ADENRU 64	MN MUNDANER	IS SANDIEST	LN LADRONES	SERIATED	READOPTS
(AUNDER)	UNDERMAN	IT INSTATED	SOLANDER	STEADIER	OR ROADSTER
BB UNBARBED	MR UNDERARM	IU AUDIENTS	LP LEOPARDS	EK STREAKED	OS ASSORTED
BC UNBRACED	UNMARRED	SINUATED	LS ROADLESS	EL TREADLES	TORSADES
BF FABURDEN	MS DURAMENS	IV DEVIANTS	LT DELATORS	EM MASTERED	OU OUTDARES
BK UNBARKED	MAUNDERS	IY DESYATIN	LEOTARDS	STREAMED	OX EXTRADOS
BR UNBARNED	SURNAMED	LU UNSALTED	LODESTAR	EP PREDATES	PP STRAPPED
BT BREADNUT	MT UNDREAMT	LW WETLANDS	LU ROULADES	REPASTED	PU PASTURED
TURBANED	MW UNWARMED	NP PENDANTS	MN RANSOMED	TRAPESED	UPSTARED
CF FURNACED	NR UNDERRAN	NU ASTUNNED	ROADSMEN	ER ARRESTED	RT REDSTART
CG UNGRACED	NW UNWARNED	OR TORNADES	MT STROAMED	DREAREST	SW STEWARDS
CH RAUNCHED	OX RONDEAUX	OS ONSTEADS	NP OPERANDS	RETREADS	TU STATURED
CK UNRACKED	PS UNSPARED	RS STANDERS	PANDORES	SERRATED	UX SURTAXED
CP PRAUNCED	PT DEPURANT	RU DAUNTERS	NT TORNADES	TREADERS	WW WESTWARD
CS DURANCES	PW UNWARPED	TRANSUDE	PR EARDROPS	ES ASSERTED	
CT UNCARTED	PY UNDERPAY	UNTREADS	PT ADOPTERS	ESTRADES	**ADGINR 135**
UNCRATED	UNPRAYED	RX DEXTRANS	ASPORTED	ET ASTERTED	(RADING)
UNDERACT	QS SQUANDER	TU UNSTATED	READOPTS	RESTATED	AB ABRADING

AC ARCADING
   CARANGID
   CARDIGAN
AE AREADING
   DRAINAGE
   GARDENIA
AM MRIDANGA
AP PARADING
AR DARRAIGN
AU GUARDIAN
AW AWARDING
BB DRABBING
BE BEARDING
   BREADING
BH HANGBIRD
BI BRAIDING
BL BARDLING
BN BRANDING
BO ABORDING
   BOARDING
BS BRIGANDS
CL CRADLING
DE DREADING
DL RADDLING
EE REGAINED
EH ADHERING
   HEADRING
EK DAKERING
EL DEARLING
   DRAGLINE
EM DREAMING
   MARGINED
EO ORGANDIE
ER DREARING
ES DERAIGNS
   GRADINES
   READINGS
ET DERATING
   GRADIENT
   TREADING
EY DERAYING
   READYING
   YEARDING
FS FARDINGS
FT DRAFTING
FW DWARFING
GG DRAGGING
GS NIGGARDS
GU GUARDING
HO HOARDING
HP HANDGRIP
IL DRAILING
IM ADMIRING
IN DRAINING
IO RADIOING
IR ARRIDING
IY DAIRYING
JU ADJURING
KL DARKLING
LS DARLINGS
LT DARTLING
LW DRAWLING
LY DARINGLY
MM DRAMMING
MS MRIDANGS
MY MARDYING
NO ADORNING
NS DARNINGS
NT DRANTING
OO RIGADOON

OS ROADINGS
PP DRAPPING
ST TRADINGS
SW DRAWINGS
   SWARDING
   WARDINGS
TY TARDYING

ADINRS 105
(DRAINS)
AE ARANEIDS
AL LANIARDS
AM MANDIRAS
AR DARRAINS
AT RADIANTS
AV VIRANDAS
BB RIBBANDS
BE BRANDIES
   BRANDISE
BG BRIGANDS
BH BRANDISH
CI ACRIDINS
CO SARDONIC
DO ANDROIDS
   DISADORN
EE ARSENIDE
   DENARIES
   DRAISENE
   NEARSIDE
EF FRIANDES
EG DERAIGNS
   GRADINES
   READINGS
EI DRAISINE
EL ISLANDER
EM ADERMINS
   SIRNAMED
EN INSNARED
EO ANEROIDS
   DONARIES
EP SPRAINED
ER DRAINERS
   SERRANID
ES ARIDNESS
   SARDINES
ET DETRAINS
   RANDIEST
   STRAINED
EU DENARIUS
   UNRAISED
   URANIDES
EV INVADERS
   SANDIVER
EY SYNEDRIA
FG FARDINGS
FM FINDRAMS
FT INDRAFTS
GG NIGGARDS
GL DARLINGS
GM MRIDANGS
GN DARNINGS
GO ROADINGS
GT TRADINGS
GW DRAWINGS
   SWARDING
   WARDINGS
IP PINDARIS
IT DISTRAIN
KS DISRANKS
KT STINKARD

LM MANDRILS
LO ORDINALS
LP SPANDRIL
LU DIURNALS
MW MISDRAWN
MY MISANDRY
NO ANDIRONS
NY INNYARDS
OP PONIARDS
OR ORDINARS
OT INTRADOS
OU DINOSAUR
OV VIRANDOS
RT TRIDARNS
SU SUNDARIS

AEELRS 72
(EALERS)
AB ERASABLE
AT LAETARES
BD BEDERALS
BG BEAGLERS
BN ENABLERS
BP BEPEARLS
BT BLEAREST
   BLEATERS
   RETABLES
BU REUSABLE
BV BESLAVER
CD DECLARES
   RESCALED
CH RELACHES
CI ESCALIER
CM RECLAMES
   SCLEREMA
CN CLEANERS
   CLEANSER
CO ESCAROLE
CP PERCALES
   REPLACES
CR CLEARERS
CS CARELESS
   RESCALES
CT CLEAREST
   SCELERAT
   TREACLES
DE RELEASED
   RESEALED
DF FEDERALS
DH ASHLERED
DI REALISED
   SIDEREAL
DL SARDELLE
DM DEMERSAL
   EMERALDS
DP PLEADERS
   RELAPSED
DT TREADLES
DV SLAVERED
DW LEEWARDS
DY DELAYERS
EE RELEASE
EF EELFARES
ER RELEASER
ES RELEASES
ET TEASELER
EW WEASELER
FI SERAFILE
FS FEARLESS

FT REFLATES
FW WELFARES
GG GREGALES
GI GASELIER
GL ALLEGERS
GN ENLARGES
   GENERALS
   GLEANERS
GP PEREGALS
GS EELGRASS
   GEARLESS
   LARGESSE
GU LEAGUERS
HI SHIRALEE
HO ARSEHOLE
HT HALTERES
   LEATHERS
HV HAVERELS
IL REALLIES
IM ALMERIES
   MEASLIER
IP ESPALIER
   PEARLIES
IR REALISER
IS REALISES
IT ATELIERS
   EARLIEST
   LEARIEST
   REALTIES
IV VELARISE
IY YEARLIES
IZ REALIZES
   SLEAZIER
LP PARELLES
MT LAMETERS
NR LEARNERS
NS REALNESS
NT ALTERNES
NV ENSLAVER
NW RENEWALS
OP PAROLEES
OR RELEASOR
OT OLEASTER
OU AUREOLES
PR PEARLERS
   RELAPSER
PS PLEASERS
   RELAPSES
PT PRELATES
PU PLEASURE
   SERPULAE
PV VESPERAL
QU SQUEALER
RT RELATERS
RV REVERSAL
   SLAVERER
ST STEALERS
   TEARLESS
   TESSERAL
SU LEASURES
SV SEVERALS
SW WARELESS
TT ALERTEST
TU RESALUTE
TY EASTERLY
UV REVALUES
VY AVERSELY

AEEPRT 142
(REPEAT)
AH HEARTPEA
AK PARAKEET
AN PARANETE
AS ASPERATE
   SEPARATE
CC ACCEPTER
CD CARPETED
CF PERFECTA
   PRAEFECT
CH ETHERCAP
CN PERCEANT
CT ETTERCAP
CU PERACUTE
CX EXCERPTA
DD DEPARTED
   PREDATED
DE REPEATED
DG PARGETED
DL PALTERED
DM EMPARTED
   TAMPERED
DN PARENTED
DO OPERATED
DR DEPARTER
DS PREDATES
   REPASTED
   TRAPESED
DT PATTERED
DU DEPURATE
   EPURATED
DZ TRAPEZED
EM PERMEATE
ER REPARTEE
   REPEATER
GR PARGETER
HS PREHEATS
   SPREATHE
IL PEARLITE
IN APERIENT
IS PETARIES
IV PERVIATE
JO PEJORATE
KN PERTAKEN
KS PERTAKES
LR PALTERER
LS PRELATES
LY PTERYLAE
MN PETERMAN
MR TAMPERER
MS TEMPERAS
MT ATTEMPER
OR PATERERO
   PERORATE
OS OPERATES
   PROTEASE
OT OPERETTA
RR PARTERRE
RS TAPERERS
RT PATTERER
RU APERTURE
SS TRAPESES
SU EPURATES
   SUPERATE
SZ TRAPEZES

AEERRS 162
(ERASER)
AF SEAFARER

AN ARRASENE
BC REBRACES
BG GERBERAS
BK BREAKERS
BT REBATERS
   TABRERES
   TEREBRAS
BY SEABERRY
CD SCAREDER
CH REACHERS
   RESEARCH
   SEARCHER
CI CARIERES
   CREASIER
CL CLEARERS
CM CREAMERS
   SCREAMER
CP CAPERERS
CT CATERERS
   RETRACES
   TERRACES
CU ECRASEUR
DD DREADERS
DE ARREEDES
DG REGRADES
DH ADHERERS
   REDSHARE
DM DREAMERS
DP SPREADER
DT ARRESTED
   DREAREST
   RETREADS
DV ADVERSER
EH REHEARSE
EL RELEASER
ET ARRESTEE
FI RAREFIES
FM REFRAMES
FT FERRATES
GI GREASIER
GP ASPERGER
   PRESAGER
GS GREASERS
GT REGRATES
GW WAGERERS
HI HEARSIER
HP REPHRASE
HS SHEARERS
IK RAKERIES
   SKEARIER
IL REALISER
IM SMEARIER
IN REARISEN
IP PEREIRAS
   SPEARIER
IS REARISES
IT ARTERIES
   REASTIER
KT RETAKERS
   STREAKER
KW WREAKERS
LN LEARNERS
LO RELEASOR
LP PEARLERS
   RELAPSER
LT RELATERS
LV REVERSAL
   SLAVERER

MT	STREAMER	
MU	MEASURER	
NO	REASONER	
NS	RARENESS	
NT	TERRANES	
NV	RAVENERS	
NW	ANSWERER	
	REANSWER	
OU	REAROUSE	
OW	SOWARREE	
PP	PAPERERS	
	PREPARES	
	REPAPERS	
PT	TAPERERS	
RT	ARRESTER	
	REARREST	
ST	ASSERTER	
	REASSERT	
	SERRATES	
	TERRASES	
SU	ERASURES	
	REASSURE	
SW	SWEARERS	
TT	RETRATES	
	RETREATS	
	TREATERS	
TU	AUSTERER	
	TREASURE	
TV	TRAVERSE	
TW	WATERERS	
VW	WAVERERS	

AEERST 20
(EATERS)

AG	STEARAGE
AH	HETAERAS
AL	LAETARES
AN	ARSENATE
	SERENATA
AP	ASPERATE
	SEPARATE
AT	STEARATE
BC	ACERBEST
BD	BETREADS
	BREASTED
	DEBATERS
BG	ABSTERGE
BH	BREATHES
	HARTBEES
BK	BESTREAK
BL	BLEAREST
	BLEATERS
	RETABLES
BO	REBATOES
BR	REBATERS
	TABRERES
	TEREBRAS
BT	ABETTERS
BU	SUBERATE
CC	ACCRETES
CD	CEDRATES
CH	CHEATERS
	HECTARES
	RECHATES
	RECHEATS
	TEACHERS
CL	CLEAREST
	SCELERAT
	TREACLES
CM	CERAMETS

	CREMATES
	MEERCATS
CN	REASCENT
	SARCENET
CO	CREASOTE
CR	CATERERS
	RETRACES
	TERRACES
CS	CATERESS
	CERASTES
CU	SECATEUR
CX	EXACTERS
DE	RESEATED
DF	DRAFTEES
DG	RESTAGED
DH	HEADREST
DI	READIEST
	SERIATED
	STEADIER
DK	STREAKED
DL	TREADLES
DM	MASTERED
	STREAMED
DP	PREDATES
	REPASTED
	TRAPESED
DR	ARRESTED
	DREAREST
	RETREADS
	SERRATED
	TREADERS
DS	ASSERTED
	ESTRADES
DT	ASTERTED
	RESTATED
DW	DEWATERS
	TARWEEDS
	WASTERED
DY	ESTRAYED
EG	ETAGERES
	STEERAGE
EI	EATERIES
EL	TEASELER
EN	SERENATE
ER	ARRESTEE
ES	TESSERAE
FH	FEATHERS
FL	REFLATES
FN	FASTENER
	FENESTRA
FR	FERRATES
FS	FEASTERS
FU	FEATURES
GM	GAMESTER
	MEAGREST
GN	ESTRANGE
	GRANTEES
	GREATENS
	REAGENTS
	SEGREANT
	SERGEANT
	STERNAGE
GR	REGRATES
GS	RESTAGES
GT	GREATEST
GU	TREAGUES
GW	STREWAGE
HH	HEATHERS
HI	HEARTIES
HL	HALTERES

	LEATHERS
HM	ERATHEMS
HN	HASTENER
	HEARTENS
HP	PREHEATS
	SPREATHE
HT	THEATERS
	THEATRES
HV	THREAVES
HW	WEATHERS
	WREATHES
IL	ATELIERS
	EARLIEST
	LEARIEST
	REALTIES
IM	EMIRATES
	REAMIEST
	STEAMIER
IN	ARSENITE
	RESINATE
	STEARINE
	TRAINEES
IO	ETAERIOS
IP	PETARIES
IR	ARTERIES
	REASTIER
IS	SERIATES
IT	ARIETTES
	ITERATES
	TEARIEST
	TREATIES
	TREATISE
IV	EVIRATES
IW	SWEATIER
	TAWERIES
	WEARIEST
IY	YEASTIER
JN	SERJEANT
KM	MEERKATS
KO	KERATOSE
	KREASOTE
KP	PERTAKES
KR	RETAKERS
	STREAKER
KS	SAKERETS
LM	LAMETERS
LN	ALTERNES
LO	OLEASTER
LP	PRELATES
LR	RELATERS
LS	STEALERS
	TEARLESS
	TESSERAL
LT	ALERTEST
LU	RESALUTE
LY	EASTERLY
MM	AMMETERS
	METAMERS
MN	REMANETS
MO	EROTEMAS
MP	TEMPERAS
MR	STREAMER
MS	MASSETER
	SEAMSTER
	STEAMERS
MT	TEAMSTER
MY	METAYERS
NO	RESONATE
NR	TERRANES
NS	ASSENTER

	EARNESTS
	SARSENET
NT	ENTREATS
	RATTEENS
NV	AVENTRES
	VETERANS
OP	OPERATES
	PROTEASE
PR	TAPERERS
PS	TRAPESES
PU	EPURATES
	SUPERATE
PZ	TRAPEZES
RR	ARRESTER
	REARREST
RS	ASSERTER
	REASSERT
	SERRATES
	TERRASES
RT	RETRATES
	RETREATS
	TREATERS
RU	AUSTERER
	TREASURE
RV	TRAVERSE
RW	WATERERS
ST	ESTREATS
	RESTATES
SW	SWEATERS
SZ	ERSATZES
TT	ATTESTER
TX	EXTREATS

AEGILN 55
(EALING)

AB	GAINABLE
AC	ANGELICA
AE	ALIENAGE
AP	PELAGIAN
AR	REGALIAN
AT	AGENTIAL
	ALGINATE
BC	BELACING
BD	BLINDAGE
BG	BEAGLING
BM	EMBALING
BN	ENABLING
BR	BLEARING
BS	SINGABLE
BT	BELATING
	BLEATING
	TANGIBLE
BY	BELAYING
CG	CAGELING
	GLACEING
CH	LEACHING
CN	CLEANING
	ELANCING
	ENLACING
CR	CLEARING
CT	CLEATING
CV	CLEAVING
DF	FINAGLED
DH	HEALDING
DI	GLIADINE
DM	MALIGNED
DO	GALENOID
DP	PLEADING
DR	DEARLING

	DRAGLINE
DS	DEALINGS
	LEADINGS
DT	DELATING
DY	DELAYING
EM	LIEGEMAN
ER	ALGERINE
ES	ENSILAGE
	LINEAGES
ET	GALENITE
	GELATINE
	LEGATINE
EV	INVEAGLE
FS	FINAGLES
GG	ALEGGING
GL	ALLEGING
GM	GLEAMING
GN	GLEANING
GR	GANGLIER
	REGALING
GS	LIGNAGES
GT	TEAGLING
GU	LEAGUING
HR	NARGHILE
	NARGILEH
HS	HEALINGS
	LEASHING
	SHEALING
HT	ATHELING
HX	EXHALING
IN	ALIENING
IR	GAINLIER
JR	JANGLIER
KS	LINKAGES
KW	WEAKLING
LS	NIGELLAS
LU	LINGULAE
LY	GENIALLY
MP	EMPALING
MR	GERMINAL
	MALIGNER
	MALINGER
MS	MEASLING
MT	LIGAMENT
MU	AEMULING
MY	YEALMING
NR	LEARNING
NS	EANLINGS
	LEANINGS
NT	GANTLINE
	LATENING
NU	UNGENIAL
NW	WEANLING
NY	YEANLING
OR	GERANIOL
	REGIONAL
OS	GASOLINE
OT	GELATION
	LEGATION
PR	PEARLING
PS	ELAPSING
	PLEASING
PT	PLEATING
RR	GNARLIER
RS	ARLESING
	ENGRAILS
	NARGILES
	REALIGNS
	SLANGIER

RT	ALERTING
	ALTERING
	INTEGRAL
	RELATING
	TANGLIER
	TRIANGLE
RX	RELAXING
RY	LAYERING
	RELAYING
	YEARLING
SS	GAINLESS
	GLASSINE
	LEASINGS
	SEALINGS
ST	EASTLING
	GELATINS
	GENITALS
	STEALING
SV	LEAVINGS
	SLEAVING
SW	SWEALING
TV	VALETING
TX	EXALTING
TZ	TEAZLING
UV	VAGINULE

AEGINR 15
(EARING)

AB	ABEARING
AC	CANAIGRE
AD	AREADING
	DRAINAGE
AF	AFEARING
AG	GRAINAGE
AL	REGALIAN
AN	ANEARING
AS	ANGARIES
AT	AERATING
BD	BEARDING
	BREADING
BE	BAREGINE
	BERGENIA
BK	BREAKING
BL	BLEARING
BM	BREAMING
BO	ABORIGEN
BS	BEARINGS
	SABERING
BT	BERATING
	REBATING
BW	BEWARING
BY	BERAYING
CF	REFACING
CH	REACHING
CK	CREAKING
CL	CLEARING
CM	AMERCING
	CREAMING
CN	ENRACING
CP	CAPERING
	PEARCING
	PREACING
CS	CREASING
	GRECIANS
	SEARCING
CT	CATERING
	CITRANGE
	CREATING
	REACTING

DD DREADING
DE REGAINED
DH ADHERING
   HEADRING
DK DAKERING
DL DEARLING
   DRAGLINE
DM DREAMING
   MARGINED
DO ORGANDIE
DR DREARING
DS DERAIGNS
   GRADINES
   READINGS
DT DERATING
   GRADIENT
   TREADING
DY DERAYING
   READYING
   YEARDING
EG AGREEING
EI ALGERINE
EL ALGERINE
EM GERMAINE
EP PEREGIAN
ER REGAINER
ES GESNERIA
EZ RAZEEING
FH HANGFIRE
FK FREAKING
FW WAFERING
FY AREFYING
GK KNAGGIER
GL GANGLIER
   REGALING
GN ANGERING
   ENRAGING
GS GEARINGS
   GREASING
   SNAGGIER
GV GREAVING
GW WAGERING
HL NARGHILE
   NARGILEH
HS HEARINGS
   HEARSING
   SHEARING
HT EARTHING
   HEARTING
HV HAVERING
IL GAINLIER
IM IMAGINER
   MIGRAINE
IN ARGININE
IR GRAINIER
JL JANGLIER
KM REMAKING
KS SKEARING
KT RETAKING
KW WREAKING
LM GERMINAL
   MALIGNER
   MALINGER
LN LEARNING
LO GERANIOL
   REGIONAL
LP PEARLING
LR GNARLIER
LS ARLESING
   ENGRAILS

NARGILES
REALIGNS
SANGLIER
SLANGIER
LT ALERTING
   ALTERING
   INTEGRAL
   RELATING
   TANGLIER
   TRIANGLE
LX RELAXING
LY LAYERING
   RELAYING
   YEARLING
MN ENARMING
   RENAMING
MP EMPARING
MR REARMING
MS GERMAINS
   SMEARING
MT EMIGRANT
MU GERANIUM
NS AGINNERS
   EARNINGS
   ENGRAINS
   GRANNIES
NV RAVENING
NY RENAYING
   YEARNING
OS IGNAROES
   ORGANISE
   ORIGANES
OZ ORGANIZE
PP PAPERING
PS PREASING
   SPEARING
PT TAPERING
PY REPAYING
RS EARRINGS
   GRAINERS
RV AVERRING
SS REASSIGN
   SEARINGS
   SERINGAS
ST ANGRIEST
   ASTRINGE
   GANISTER
   GANTRIES
   GRANITES
   INGRATES
   RANGIEST
   REASTING
   STEARING
SV VINEGARS
SW SWEARING
   WEARINGS
SY RESAYING
TT ARETTING
   TREATING
TV AVERTING
   TAVERING
   VINTAGER
TW TWANGIER
   WATERING
VW WAVERING
VY VINEGARY
WY WEARYING

AEGLNR 91
(ANGLER)
AG LANGRAGE
AI REGALIAN
AS ALNAGERS
AU AULNAGER
BD BRANGLED
BI BLEARING
BS BRANGLES
CI CLEARING
CS CLANGERS
DE ENLARGED
   LARGENED
DI DEARLING
   DRAGLINE
   GLANDERS
DW WRANGLED
EI ALGERINE
EN ENLARGEN
ER ENLARGER
ES ENLARGES
   GENERALS
   GLEANERS
GI GANGLIER
HI NARGHILE
   NARGILEH
II GAINLIER
IJ JANGLIER
IM GERMINAL
   MALIGNER
   MALINGER
IN LEARNING
IO GERANIOL
   REGIONAL
IP PEARLING
IR GNARLIER
IS ARLESING
   ENGRAILS
   NARGILES
   REALIGNS
   SANGLIER
   SLANGIER
IT ALTERING
   ALTERING
   INTEGRAL
   RELATING
   TANGLIER
   TRIANGLE
IX RELAXING
IY LAYERING
   RELAYING
   YEARLING
JS JANGLERS
LS LANGRELS
MS MANGLERS
OY YEARLONG
PS GRAPNELS
   SPANGLER
   SPRANGLE
RW WRANGLER
ST STRANGLE
   TANGLERS
   TRANGLES
SU GRANULES
SW WANGLERS

WRANGLES
SY LARYNGES
UY GUNLAYER

AEGLNS 170
(ANGLES)
AD SELADANG
AM GAMELANS
AR ALNAGERS
AS LASAGNES
AU AULNAGES
BI SINGABLE
BR BRANGLES
CO CONGEALS
CR CLANGERS
DD GLADDENS
DI DEALINGS
   LEADINGS
DP SPANGLED
DR DANGLERS
   GLANDERS
DS GLADNESS
EI ENSILAGE
   LINEAGES
EM MELANGES
EO GASOLENE
ER ENLARGES
   GENERALS
   GLEANERS
EV EVANGELS
FI FINAGLES
FS FANGLESS
GI LIGNAGES
GR GANGRELS
HI HEALINGS
   LEASHING
   SHEALING
HO HALOGENS
IK LINKAGES
IL NIGELLAS
IM MEASLING
IN EANLINGS
   LEANINGS
IO GASOLINE
IP ELAPSING
   PLEASING
IR ARLESING
   ENGRAILS
   NARGILES
   REALIGNS
   SANGLIER
   SLANGIER
IS GAINLESS
   GLASSINE
   LEASINGS
   SEALINGS
IT EASTLING
   GELATINS
   GENITALS
   STEALING
IV LEAVINGS
   SLEAVING
IW SWEALING
JR JANGLERS
LO ALLONGES
   GALLEONS
LP LANGSPEL
LR LANGRELS
MR MANGLERS
MS GLASSMEN

OT TANGELOS
PR GRAPNELS
   SPANGLER
   SPRANGLE
PS PANGLESS
   SPANGLES
PT SPANGLET
RT STRANGLE
   TANGLERS
   TRANGLES
RU GRANULES
RW WANGLERS
   WRANGLES
RY LARYNGES
TT GANTLETS
TU LANGUETS
TW TWANGLES
UW GUNWALES

AEGLNT 118
(TANGLE)
AI AGENTIAL
   ALGINATE
AP PLANTAGE
AU ANGULATE
BI BELATING
   BLEATING
CI CLEATING
DE DANEGELT
DI DELATING
DW TWANGLED
EI GALENITE
   GELATINE
   LEGATINE
EN ENTANGLE
EO ELONGATE
GI TEAGLING
HI ATHELING
IM LIGAMENT
IN GANTLINE
   LATENING
IO GELATION
   LEGATION
IP PLEATING
IR ALERTING
   ALTERING
   INTEGRAL
   RELATING
   TANGLIER
   TRIANGLE
IS EASTLING
   GELATINS
   GENITALS
   STEALING
IV VALETING
IX EXALTING
IZ TEAZLING
MU GUNMETAL
NP PLANGENT
NU UNTANGLE
OP GANTLOPE
OS TANGELOS
PS SPANGLET
RS STRANGLE
   TANGLERS
   TRANGLES
ST GANTLETS
SU LANGUETS
SW TWANGLES

TU GAUNTLET
UU UNGULATE

AEGLRS 167
(LAGERS)
AB ALGEBRAS
AI GASALIER
   LAIRAGES
   REGALIAS
AN ALNAGERS
AR REALGARS
   RESALGAR
AT AGRESTAL
BB GABBLERS
   GRABBLES
BD BELGARDS
BE BEAGLERS
BM GAMBLERS
   GAMBRELS
BN BRANGLES
BR GARBLERS
CH SCHLAGER
CI GLACIERS
CK GRACKLES
CN CLANGERS
DG DRAGGLES
DI SLAIRGED
DN DANGLERS
   GLANDERS
EG GREGALES
EI GASELIER
EL ALLEGERS
EN ENLARGES
   GENERALS
   GLEANERS
EP PEREGALS
ES EELGRASS
   GEARLESS
   LARGESSE
EU LEAGUERS
GH HAGGLERS
GI SLAGGIER
GN GANGRELS
GT STRAGGLE
HU LAUGHERS
IM GREMIALS
   LAMIGERS
   REGALISM
IN ARLESING
   ENGRAILS
   NARGILES
   REALIGNS
   SANGLIER
   SLANGIER
IO GASOLIER
   GIRASOLE
   SERAGLIO
IS GLASSIER
IT GLARIEST
   REGALIST
IY GREASILY
IZ GLAZIERS
JN JANGLERS
LN LANGRELS
LO ALLEGROS
MN MANGLERS
MO GOMERALS
MU MAULGERS
NP GRAPNELS
   SPANGLER

	SPRANGLE	UV VULGATES	ENGRAILS	BI BERATING	RAGSTONE	STEARING
NT STRANGLE		NARGILES	REBATING	OT TETRAGON	IS EASTINGS
TANGLERS	**AEGNRS 86**	REALIGNS	BS BANGSTER	OY NEGATORY	GENISTAS
TRANGLES	(ANGERS)	SANGLIER	BU BURGANET	PS TREPANGS	GIANTESS
NU GRANULES	AC CARNAGES	SLANGIER	CI CATERING	RS GRANTERS	SEATINGS
NW WANGLERS	CRANAGES	IM GERMAINS	CITRANGE	REGRANTS	TEASINGS
WRANGLES	AE SANGAREE	SMEARING	CREATING	STRANGER	TSIGANES
NY LARYNGES	AI ANGARIES	IN AGINNERS	REACTING	SU STRAUNGE	IT ESTATING
OP PERGOLAS	AL ALNAGERS	EARNINGS	DH THRANGED		TANGIEST
OT LEGATORS	AM MANAGERS	ENGRAINS	DI DERATING	**AEGNST 115**	IU SAUTEING
OU GLAREOUS	AR ARRANGES	GRANNIES	GRADIENT	(TANGES)	IV VINTAGES
PP GRAPPLES	AT STARAGEN	IO IGNAROES	TREADING	AH THANAGES	IW SWEATING
PU EARPLUGS	TANAGERS	ORGANISE	DO DRAGONET	AI SAGINATE	IY YEASTING
GRAUPELS	BI BEARINGS	ORIGANES	DS GRANDEST	AK TANKAGES	LO TANGELOS
RU REGULARS	SABERING	IP PREASING	EE GENERATE	AM MAGENTAS	LP SPANGLET
TU GAULTERS	BL BRANGLES	SPEARING	RENEGATE	MAGNATES	LR STRANGLE
GESTURAL	BT BANGSTER	IR EARRINGS	TEENAGER	AN TANNAGES	TANGLERS
TRAGULES	CE ENGRACES	GRAINERS	EM AGREMENT	AP PAGEANTS	TRANGLES
	CH CHANGERS	IS REASSIGN	EN GENERANT	AR STARAGEN	LT GANTLETS
AEGLST 187	CI CREASING	SEARINGS	ER ETRANGER	TANAGERS	LU LANGUETS
(GLATES)	GRECIANS	SERINGAS	ES ESTRANGE	AT STAGNATE	LW TWANGLES
AA GALATEAS	SEARCING	IT ANGRIEST	GRANTEES	AV VANTAGES	MO MAGNETOS
AE ETALAGES	CL CLANGERS	ASTRINGE	GREATENS	AW WANTAGES	MEGATONS
AL GALLATES	CM CRAGSMEN	GANISTER	REAGENTS	BI BEATINGS	MONTAGES
STALLAGE	CO ACROGENS	GANTRIES	SEGREANT	BN BANTENGS	MR GARMENTS
TALLAGES	CORNAGES	GRANITES	SERGEANT	BR BANGSTER	MARGENTS
AR AGRESTAL	DE DERANGES	INGRATES	STERNAGE	BU SUBAGENT	RAGMENTS
AS AGELASTS	GRANDEES	RANGIEST	EU GAUNTREE	CE CENTAGES	MU AUGMENTS
LASTAGES	GRENADES	REASTING	FM FRAGMENT	CO COGNATES	MUTAGENS
BU GUSTABLE	DI DERAIGNS	STEARING	FO FRONTAGE	DI SEDATING	NO TONNAGES
CI GELASTIC	GRADINES	IV VINEGARS	FS ENGRAFTS	DR GRANDEST	NT TANGENTS
CO CATELOGS	READINGS	IW SWEARING	GS GANGSTER	EF FANTEEGS	NU TUNNAGES
DD GLADDEST	DL DANGLERS	WEARINGS	HI EARTHING	EI SAGENITE	OP PONTAGES
DI GLADIEST	GLANDERS	IY RESAYING	HEARTING	ER ESTRANGE	OR ORANGEST
EE LEGATEES	DM DRAGSMEN	JL JANGLERS	IK RETAKING	GRANTEES	RAGSTONE
EI ELEGIAST	DT GRANDEST	LL LANGRELS	IL ALERTING	GREATENS	PR TREPANGS
EO SEGOLATE	DU ENGUARDS	LM MANGLERS	ALTERING	REAGENTS	RR GRANTERS
ES GATELESS	EG ENGAGERS	LP GRAPNELS	INTEGRAL	SEGREANT	REGRANTS
EV VEGETALS	EH SHAGREEN	SPANGLER	RELATING	SERGEANT	STRANGER
FO FLOTAGES	EI GESNERIA	SPRANGLE	TRIANGLE	STERNAGE	RU STRAUNGE
GR STRAGGLE	EL ENLARGES	LT STRANGLE	IM EMIGRANT	ET TENTAGES	SS GASTNESS
HI LAIGHEST	GENERALS	TANGLERS	IP TAPERING	EV VENTAGES	TU GAUNTEST
HW THALWEGS	GLEANERS	TRANGLES	IS ANGRIEST	FI FEASTING	TUTENAGS
IL LEGALIST	EM AGREMENS	LU GRANULES	ASTRINGE	FR ENGRAFTS	
STILLAGE	EN ENRANGES	LW WANGLERS	GANISTER	GI NAGGIEST	**AEGRST 80**
TILLAGES	ET ESTRANGE	WRANGLES	GANTRIES	GR GANGSTER	(GATERS)
IN EASTLING	GRANTEES	LY LARYNGES	GRANITES	HI GAHNITES	AA GASTRAEA
GELATINS	GREATENS	MO MEGARONS	INGRATES	HEATINGS	AC CARTAGES
GENITALS	REAGENTS	MT GARMENTS	RANGIEST	HN HANGNEST	AD GRADATES
STEALING	SEGREANT	MARGENTS	REASTING	HS STENGAHS	AE STEARAGE
IO OTALGIES	SERGEANT	RAGMENTS	STEARING	IL EASTLING	AG AGGRATES
IR GLARIEST	STERNAGE	NU GUNNERAS	IT ARETTING	GELATINS	AL AGRESTAL
REGALIST	EU RENAGUES	OO OREGANOS	TREATING	GENITALS	AN STARAGEN
IZ GLAZIEST	EV AVENGERS	OR GROANERS	IV AVERTING	STEALING	TANAGERS
LO TOLLAGES	ENGRAVES	OT ORANGEST	TAVERING	IM MANGIEST	AT REGATTAS
NO TANGELOS	FF ENGRAFFS	RAGSTONE	VINTAGER	MINTAGES	BE ABSTERGE
NP SPANGLET	FR GRANFERS	OW WAGONERS	IW TWANGIER	STEAMING	BH BARGHEST
NR STRANGLE	FT ENGRAFTS	PS ENGRASPS	WATERING	TEAMINGS	BN BANGSTER
TANGLERS	GI GEARINGS	PT TREPANGS	LS STRANGLE	IN ANTIGENS	BS BARGESTS
TRANGLES	GREASING	RT GRANTERS	TANGLERS	GENTIANS	CI AGRESTIC
NT GANTLETS	GL GANGRELS	REGRANTS	TRANGLES	STEANING	CO ESCARGOT
NU LANGUETS	GR GRANGERS	STRANGER	MS GARMENTS	IR ANGRIEST	CU TRUCAGES
NW TWANGLES	GT GANGSTER	TU STRAUNGE	MARGENTS	ASTRINGE	DE RESTAGED
OR LEGATORS	HI HEARINGS		RAGMENTS	GANISTER	DN GRANDEST
OV VOLTAGES	HEARSING	**AEGNRT 54**	MU ARGUMENT	GANTRIES	DO GOADSTER
RU GAULTERS	SHEARING	(GANTER)	NO NEGATRON	GRANITES	DR DRAGSTER
GESTURAL	HS GNASHERS	AI AERATING	NP PREGNANT	INGRATES	EE ETAGERES
TRAGULES	IK SKEARING	AS STARAGEN	NY GANNETRY	RANGIEST	STEERAGE
ST GESTALTS	IL ARLESING	TANAGERS	OS ORANGEST	REASTING	EM GAMESTER
UU GLUTAEUS		AU RUNAGATE			MEAGREST

EN ESTRANGE
   GRANTEES
   GREATENS
   REAGENTS
   SEGREANT
   SERGEANT
   STERNAGE
ER REGRATES
ES RESTAGES
ET GREATEST
EU TREAGUES
EW STREWAGE
FI FRIGATES
FN ENGRAFTS
FR GRAFTERS
GI RAGGIEST
GL STRAGGLE
GN GANGSTER
GS GAGSTERS
   STAGGERS
HO SHORTAGE
IL GLARIEST
   REGALIST
IM MAGISTER
   MIGRATES
   RAGTIMES
   STERIGMA
IN ANGRIEST
   ASTRINGE
   GANISTER
   GANTRIES
   GRANITES
   INGRATES
   RANGIEST
   REASTING
   STEARING
IP GRAPIEST
IS AGISTERS
IT STRIGATE
IV VIRGATES
   VITRAGES
LN STRANGLE
   TANGLERS
   TRANGLES
LO LEGATORS
LU GAULTERS
   GESTURAL
   TRAGULES
MN GARMENTS
   MARGENTS
   RAGMENTS
NO ORANGEST
   RAGSTONE
NP TREPANGS
NR GRANTERS
   REGRANTS
   STRANGER
NU STRAUNGE
OO ROOTAGES
OP PORTAGES
OR GARROTES
OS STORAGES
OT GAROTTES
OU OUTRAGES
TY STRATEGY
UU AUGUSTER

AEHRST 169
(HATERS)
AE HETAERAS

AL TREHALAS
BC BRACHETS
BD BREADTHS
BE BREATHES
   HARTBEES
BG BARGHEST
BL BLATHERS
   HALBERTS
BO BATHORSE
BS BRASHEST
CC CATCHERS
   CRATCHES
CD STARCHED
CE CHEATERS
   HECTARES
   RECHATES
   RECHEATS
   TEACHERS
CF FRATCHES
CH HATCHERS
CI CHARIEST
   THERIACS
CL ARCHLETS
CM MATCHERS
CN CHANTERS
   SNATCHER
   STANCHER
   TRANCHES
CO CHAROSET
   THORACES
CP CHAPTERS
   PATCHERS
CR CHARTERS
   RECHARTS
   STARCHER
CS STARCHES
CT CHATTERS
CW WATCHERS
CY YACHTERS
DE HEADREST
DH THRASHED
DI HAIRSTED
   HARDIEST
DY HYDRATES
EF FEATHERS
EH HEATHERS
EI HEARTIES
EL HALTERES
   LEATHERS
EM ERATHEMS
EN HASTENER
   HEARTENS
EP PREHEATS
   SPREATHE
ET THEATERS
   THEATRES
EV THREAVES
EW WEATHERS
   WREATHES
FL FARTHELS
FS SHAFTERS
FT FARTHEST
GO SHORTAGE
HO HAROSETH
HR THRASHER
HS HARSHEST
   THRASHES
II HAIRIEST
IN INEARTHS

IO HOARIEST
IR TRASHIER
IS SHERIATS
IW SWATHIER
   WATERISH
IY HYSTERIA
KN THANKERS
LM THERMALS
LN ENTHRALS
LO LOATHERS
LS HARSLETS
   SLATHERS
MP HAMPSTER
MS HAMSTERS
MU MAUTHERS
MW MAWTHERS
NP PANTHERS
NU HAUNTERS
   UNEARTHS
   UNHEARTS
   URETHANS
OO TOHEROAS
OS ASTHORES
   HAROSETS
   HOARSEST
OT RHEOSTAT
OX THORAXES
PS SHARPEST
   SPARTHES
RU URETHRAS
RY TRASHERY
SS SHASTERS
ST SHATTERS
SV HARVESTS
TY SHATTERY
UU HAUTEURS

AEILMN 133
(MALINE)
AC ANALCIME
   CALAMINE
AH HIELAMAN
AT ALAIMENT
   LAMINATE
AV VELAMINA
BD MANDIBLE
BG EMBALING
BS BAILSMEN
BT BAILMENT
CE CAMELINE
CH INCHMEAL
CI LIMACINE
CN CLINAMEN
CP MANCIPLE
CS MESCALIN
DE ENDEMIAL
DF INFLAMED
DG MALIGNED
DI LIMNAEID
DP PLAIDMEN
DU UNMAILED
DY MAIDENLY
EG LIEGEMAN
EM MELAMINE
ET MELANITE
FR INFLAMER
   RIFLEMAN
FS FLAMINES
   INFLAMES
   MISFALNE

FT FILAMENT
GG GLEAMING
GP EMPALING
GR GERMINAL
   MALIGNER
   MALINGER
GS MEASLING
GT LIGAMENT
GU AEMULING
GY YEALMING
HY HYMENIAL
IN MAINLINE
IS ALIENISM
LS MANILLES
MS MELANISM
MT IMMANTLE
MY IMMANELY
NO MINNEOLA
NP IMPANNEL
NS LINESMAN
   MELANINS
OS MINEOLAS
   SEMOLINA
PS IMPANELS
   MANIPLES
RS MARLINES
   MINERALS
RT TERMINAL
RU LEMURIAN
SS ISLESMAN
ST AILMENTS
   ALIMENTS
   MANLIEST

AEILNT 11
(ENTAIL)
AC ANALCITE
   LAITANCE
AD DENTALIA
AE ALIENATE
AG AGENTIAL
   ALGINATE
AH ANTHELIA
AM ALAIMENT
   LAMINATE
AP PALATINE
AT ANTLIATE
AV AVENTAIL
BD BIDENTAL
BG BELATING
   BLEATING
   TANGIBLE
BM BAILMENT
BP PINTABLE
BS INSTABLE
BV BIVALENT
CC CANTICLE
CG CLEATING
CH CHAINLET
   ETHNICAL
CL CLIENTAL
CP ICEPLANT
   PECTINAL
   PLANETIC
CR CLARINET
DE ENTAILED
   LINEATED
DF INFLATED
DG DELATING
DO DELATION

DP PANTILED
DU UNTAILED
DV DIVALENT
EG GALENITE
   GELATINE
   LEGATINE
EL TENAILLE
EM MELANITE
EP PETALINE
   TAPELINE
ER ELATERIN
   ENTAILER
   TREENAIL
EV ELVANITE
   VENTAILE
FM FILAMENT
FO OLEFIANT
FS INFLATES
GG TEAGLING
GH ATHELING
GM LIGAMENT
GN GANTLINE
   LATENING
GO GELATION
   LEGATION
GP PLEATING
GR ALERTING
   ALTERING
   INTEGRAL
   RELATING
   TANGLIER
   TRIANGLE
GS EASTLING
   GELATINS
   GENITALS
   STEALING
GV VALETING
GX EXALTING
GZ TEAZLING
HL THALLINE
HX ANTHELIX
HZ ZENITHAL
IK KALINITE
IR INERTIAL
IS ALIENIST
   LITANIES
KS LANKIEST
MM IMMANTLE
MR TERMINAL
MS AILMENTS
   ALIMENTS
   MANLIEST
NR INTERNAL
NY INNATELY
OP ANTIPOLE
OR ORIENTAL
   RELATION
OS ELATIONS
   INSOLATE
   TOENAILS
OT TONALITE
PR TRIPLANE
PS PANTILES
   PLAINEST
RS ENTRAILS
   LATRINES
   RATLINES
   TRENAILS
RT RATTLINE
RU RETINULA

   TENURIAL
RV INTERVAL
RY INTERLAY
SS EASTLINS
   ELASTINS
   SALIENTS
   STANIELS
SU ALUNITES
   INSULATE
SV VENTAILS
SW LAWNIEST
VY NATIVELY
   VENALITY

AEILRS 16
(SAILER)
AB RAISABLE
AD SALARIED
AG GASALIER
   LAIRAGES
   REGALIAS
AO OLEARIAS
AS SALARIES
AU AURELIAS
BB SLABBIER
BC CALIBERS
   CALIBRES
BF BARFLIES
BH BLASHIER
BI BISERIAL
BL LIBERALS
BM REMBLAIS
BN RINSABLE
BT LIBRATES
CD DECRIALS
   RADICELS
   RADICLES
CE ESCALIER
CF FILACERS
CG GLACIERS
CH CHARLIES
CM CLAIMERS
   MIRACLES
   RECLAIMS
CN CARLINES
CO CALORIES
CP CALIPERS
   REPLICAS
   SPIRACLE
CS CLASSIER
CT ALTRICES
   ARTICLES
   RECITALS
   SELICTAR
CU AURICLES
CV CALIVERS
   CLAVIERS
   VISCERAL
DD DIEDRALS
DE REALISED
   SIDEREAL
DG SLAIRGED
DI LAIRISED
DL DALLIERS
   DIALLERS
DN ISLANDER
DO DARIOLES
   SOLIDARE
   SOREDIAL

DP PEDRAILS
 PREDIALS
DT DILATERS
 LARDIEST
DU RESIDUAL
DY DIALYSER
EF SERAFILE
EG GASELIER
EH SHIRALEE
EL REALLIES
EM ALMERIES
 LEMPIRAS
 MEASLIER
EP ESPALIER
 PEARLIES
ER REALISER
ES REALISES
ET ATELIERS
 EARLIEST
 LEARIEST
 REALTIES
EV VELARISE
EY YEARLIES
EZ REALIZES
 SLEAZIER
FH FLASHIER
FO FORESAIL
FT FLARIEST
 FRAILEST
FU FAILURES
FV FAVRILES
FZ FILAZERS
GG SLAGGIER
GM GREMIALS
 LAMIGERS
 REGALISM
GN ARLESING
 ENGRAILS
 NARGILES
 REALIGNS
 SANGLIER
 SLANGIER
GO GASOLIER
 GIRASOLE
 SERAGLIO
GS GLASSIER
GT GLARIEST
 REGALIST
GY GREASILY
GZ GLAZIERS
HN INHALERS
HO AIRHOLES
 SHOALIER
HP PLASHIER
HS HAIRLESS
HU HAULIERS
HV LAVISHER
 SHRIEVAL
IL RAILLIES
IN AIRLINES
 SNAILIER
IS LAIRISES
IT LAIRIEST
IV RIVALISE
IZ LAIRIZES
KS SERKALIS
KT LARKIEST
 STALKIER
 STARLIKE
KV KLAVIERS
LR RALLIERS

LS RAILLESS
LT LITERALS
 TALLIERS
LU RUELLIAS
LY SERIALLY
MM SMALMIER
MN MARLINES
 MINERALS
MO MORALISE
MP IMPEARLS
 LEMPIRAS
MR LARMIERS
MS REALISMS
MT LAMITERS
 MARLIEST
MY SMEARILY
NO AILERONS
 ALERIONS
 ALIENORS
NP PEARLINS
 PRALINES
NR SNARLIER
NS RAINLESS
NT ENTRAILS
 LATRINES
 RATLINES
 TRENAILS
NU LUNARIES
NV RAVELINS
NX RELAXINS
NY INLAYERS
 SNAILERY
OP PELORIAS
 POLARISE
OS SOLARISE
OT SOTERIAL
OV OVERSAIL
 VALORISE
 VARIOLES
 VOLARIES
OY ROYALISE
OZ SOLARIZE
PP APPERILS
PR REPRISAL
PT PILASTER
 PLAISTER
 PLAITERS
PV PREVAILS
PW SLIPWARE
QU SQUAILER
RT RETIRALS
 RETRIALS
 TRAILERS
RU RURALISE
ST REALISTS
 SALTIERS
 SALTIRES
 SLAISTER
SV REVISALS
 RIVALESS
TT TERTIALS
TU URALITES
VV REVIVALS
VY VIRELAYS

AEILRT 10
(RETAIL)
AC TAILRACE
AL ARILLATE
AM MATERIAL

AP PARIETAL
AR ARTERIAL
AV VARIETAL
BD LIBRATED
BE LIBERATE
BP PARTIBLE
BS LIBRATES
BW WRITABLE
CD ARTICLED
CK TALCKIER
CM METRICAL
CN CLARINET
CO EROTICAL
 LORICATE
CP PARTICLE
 PRELATIC
CR CLARTIER
CS ALTRICES
 ARTICLES
 RECITALS
 SELICTAR
CT TRACTILE
CV VERTICAL
CY LITERACY
DE RETAILED
DO IDOLATER
 TAILORED
DP DIPTERAL
 TRIPEDAL
DS DILATERS
DT DETRITAL
DY DIELYTRA
EF FRAILTEE
EH ETHERIAL
EM EREMITAL
 MATERIEL
 REALTIME
EN ELATERIN
 ENTAILER
 TREENAIL
EO AEROLITE
EP PEARLITE
ER RETAILER
ES ATELIERS
 EARLIEST
 LEARIEST
 REALTIES
ET LATERITE
 LITERATE
 RELATIVE
FO FLOATIER
FS FLARIEST
 FRAILEST
FT FILTRATE
FU FAULTIER
 FILATURE
GH LITHARGE
 THIRLAGE
GN ALERTING
 ALTERING
 INTEGRAL
 RELATING
 TANGLIER
 TRIANGLE
GS GLARIEST
 REGALIST
GT AGLITTER
GU LIGATURE

GY REGALITY
HO AEROLITH
 LOATHIER
HY HEARTILY
IN INERTIAL
IP LIPARITE
IS LAIRIEST
IT LITERATI
KS LARKIEST
 STALKIER
LS LITERALS
 TALLIERS
LU TAILLEUR
MM TRILEMMA
MN TERMINAL
MS LAMITERS
 MARLIEST
MT REMITTAL
NN INTERNAL
NO ORIENTAL
 RELATION
NP TRIPLANE
NS ENTRAILS
 LATRINES
 RATLINES
 TRENAILS
NT RATTLINE
NU RETINULA
 TENURIAL
NV INTERVAL
 SALICETS
NY INTERLAY
OP EPILATOR
 PETIOLAR
OS SOTERIAL
OT LITERATO
PR PALTRIER
PS PILASTER
 PLAISTER
 PLAITERS
QU QUARTILE
 REQUITAL
RS RETIRALS
 RETRIALS
 TRAILERS
RY LITERARY
SS REALISTS
 SALTIERS
 SALTIRES
 SLAISTER
ST TERTIALS
SU URALITES
TY ALTERITY
UZ LAZURITE
VV TRIVALVE

AEILST 24
(ALITES)
AB BALISTAE
 LABIATES
 SATIABLE
AC SALICETA
AP STAPELIA
AV AESTIVAL
 SALIVATE
AX SAXATILE
BB BISTABLE
BI ALBITISE
 SIBILATE
BK BALKIEST

BL BASTILLE
BM BALMIEST
 TIMBALES
BN INSTABLE
BP EPIBLAST
BR LIBRATES
BS ASTILBES
 BESTIALS
 STABILES
BU SUITABLE
BY BEASTILY
CC CALCITES
CD CITADELS
 DIALECTS
CG GELASTIC
CH ETHICALS
CI SILICATE
CM CALMIEST
 CLEMATIS
 CLIMATES
 METICALS
CO ALOETICS
 COALIEST
 SOCIETAL
CP PLICATES
CR ALTRICES
 ARTICLES
 RECITALS
 SELICTAR
CS ELASTICS
 SALICETS
 SCALIEST
CT LATTICES
CY CLAYIEST
DE LEADIEST
DG GLADIEST
DI IDEALIST
DM MISDEALT
DO DIASTOLE
 ISOLATED
 SODALITE
 SOLIDATE
DP TALIPEDS
DR DILATERS
 LARDIEST
DV VALIDEST
DY DIASTYLE
 STEADILY
EF FEALTIES
 LEAFIEST
EG ELEGIAST
EK LEAKIEST
EL LEALTIES
EM MEALIEST
EP EPILATES
ER ATELIERS
 EARLIEST
 LEARIEST
 REALTIES
ES ASTELIES
ET AILETTES
EV ELATIVES
 LEAVIEST
 VEALIEST
FI FILIATES
FK FLAKIEST
FM FLAMIEST
FN INFLATES
FO FOLIATES
FR FLARIEST

 FRAILEST
FU FISTULAE
FV FESTIVAL
FW FLATWISE
 FLAWIEST
FX FLAXIEST
GH LAIGHEST
GL LEGALIST
 STILLAGE
 TILLAGES
GN EASTLING
 GELATINS
 GENITALS
 STEALING
GO OTALGIES
GR GLARIEST
 REGALIST
GZ GLAZIEST
HI HAILIEST
HS SHALIEST
HT LATHIEST
 LITHATES
HY HYALITES
IL TAILLIES
IN ALIENIST
 LITANIES
IR LAIRIEST
IS SAILIEST
IV VITALISE
IX LAXITIES
IZ TAILZIES
KN LANKIEST
KO KEITLOAS
KR LARKIEST
 STALKIER
 STARLIKE
LP PALLIEST
 PASTILLE
LR LITERALS
 TALLIERS
LS TAILLESS
LW WALLIEST
MN AILMENTS
 ALIMENTS
 MANLIEST
MO LOAMIEST
MP IMPLATES
 PALMIEST
 PALMIETS
 PETALISM
 SEPTIMAL
MR LAMITERS
 MARLIEST
MT MALTIEST
 SMALTITE
MU SIMULATE
MY LAYTIMES
NO ELATIONS
 INSOLATE
 TOENAILS
NP PANTILES
 PLAINEST
NR ENTRAILS
 LATRINES
 RATLINES
 TRENAILS
NS EASTLINS
 ELASTINS
 SALIENTS

STANIELS	GP EMPARING	INFAMISE	AS AMENTIAS	CG GRIMACES	LP IMPEARLS
NU ALUNITES	GR REARMING	FL FLAMINES	ANIMATES	CH CHASMIER	LEMPIRAS
INSULATE	GS GERMAINS	INFLAMES	BL BAILMENT	CHIMERAS	LR LARMIERS
NV VENTAILS	SMEARING	MISFALNE	BS AMBIENTS	MARCHESI	LS REALISMS
NW LAWNIEST	GT EMIGRANT	FT MANIFEST	CG MAGNETIC	CK KERAMICS	LT LAMITERS
OP SPOLIATE	GU GERANIUM	GI IMAGINES	CS SEMANTIC	CL CLAIMERS	MARLIEST
OR SOTERIAL	HS HARMINES	GL MEASLING	DE DEMENTIA	MIRACLES	LY SMEARILY
OS ISOLATES	SHIREMAN	GN MEANINGS	DI MINIATED	RECLAIMS	MP SPAMMIER
OT TOTALISE	KS RAMEKINS	GR GERMAINS	DO DOMINATE	CM RACEMISM	MR SMARMIER
OV VIOLATES	LS MARLINES	SMEARING	NEMATOID	CN CARMINES	MT MARMITES
PR PILASTER	MINERALS	GT MANGIEST	DS MEDIANTS	CT CERAMIST	NN REINSMAN
PLAISTER	LT TERMINAL	MINTAGES	DY DYNAMITE	MATRICES	NO MORAINES
PLAITERS	LU LEMURIAN	STEAMING	EG GEMINATE	DD DISARMED	NR MARINERS
PS PALSIEST	NS MARINERS	TEAMINGS	EL MELANITE	MISDREAD	NS SEMINARS
PT PLATIEST	OS MORAINES	GV VEGANISM	EM MEANTIME	DE MADERISE	SIRNAMES
PY PTYALISE	OW AIRWOMEN	HR HARMINES	ES MATINEES	DF MISFARED	NT MINARETS
QU LIQUATES	OZ ARMOZINE	SHIREMAN	SEMINATE	DH MISHEARD	RAIMENTS
TEQUILAS	PT TRIPEMAN	HS SHAMISEN	FL FILAMENT	DJ JEMIDARS	NU ANEURISM
RR RETIRALS	QU RAMEQUIN	HU HUMANISE	FS MANIFEST	DM MERMAIDS	NY SEMINARY
RETRIALS	RS MARINERS	IL ALIENISM	GL LIGAMENT	DN ADERMINS	OR ARMOIRES
TRAILERS	RV RIVERMAN	IT MINIATES	GN ENTAMING	SIRNAMED	ARMORIES
RS REALISTS	SS SEMINARS	JS JASMINES	GR EMIGRANT	DR ADMIRERS	OT AMORTISE
SALTIERS	SIRNAMES	KR RAMEKINS	GS MANGIEST	DISARMER	ATOMISER
SALTIRES	ST MINARETS	KT MANKIEST	MINTAGES	DS MISREADS	PR RAMPIRES
SLAISTER	RAIMENTS	MISTAKEN	STEAMING	SIDEARMS	PS IMPRESAS
RT TERTIALS	SU ANEURISM	LL MANILLES	TEAMINGS	DT MARDIEST	SAMPIRES
RU URALITES	SY SEMINARY	LM MELANISM	HI THIAMINE	MISRATED	PT PRIMATES
ST SALTIEST	TT MARTINET	LN LINESMAN	HU INHUMATE	READMITS	PV VAMPIRES
SLATIEST	TU RUMINATE	LO MINEOLAS	IS MINIATES	EG GAMESIER	PW SWAMPIER
SW SWALIEST	TW WARIMENT	SEMOLINA	IT INTIMATE	EL ALMERIES	QU MARQUISE
TW WALTIEST	TY TYRAMINE	LP IMPANELS	IU MINUTIAE	MEASLIER	RR MARRIERS
VY VILAYETS		MANIPLES	IV VITAMINE	EN REMANIES	RS SIMARRES
	AEIMNS 98	LR MARLINES	KS MANKIEST	EP EMPAIRES	ST ASTERISM
AEIMNR 61	(MANIES)	MINERALS	MISTAKEN	ER SMEARIER	MAISTERS
(REMAIN)	AA ANAEMIAS	LS ISLESMAN	LM IMMANTLE	ES SERIEMAS	MISRATES
AD MARINADE	AC AMNESIAC	LT AILMENTS	LR TERMINAL	ET EMIRATES	SEMITARS
AP PEARMAIN	AG MAGNESIA	ALIMENTS	LS AILMENTS	REAMIEST	SMARTIES
AT MARINATE	AS AMNESIAS	MANLIEST	ALIMENTS	STEAMIER	SY EMISSARY
AZ MAZARINE	AT AMENTIAS	MS MISNAMES	MANLIEST	FI RAMIFIES	TT MISTREAT
BD BRIDEMAN	ANIMATES	NR REINSMAN	MN IMMANENT	FR FIREARMS	TERATISM
BG BREAMING	BG BEAMINGS	NT MANNITES	MO AMMONITE	FS MISFARES	TU MURIATES
BS MIRBANES	EMBASING	OR MORAINES	NO NOMINATE	GL GREMIALS	SEMITAUR
CG AMERCING	BL BAILSMEN	OU MOINEAUS	NS MANNITES	LAMIGERS	TW WARTIMES
CREAMING	BR MIRBANES	OW WOMANISE	OP PTOMAINE	REGALISM	TX MATRIXES
CH CHAIRMEN	BT AMBIENTS	RR MARINERS	OZ MONAZITE	GN GERMAINS	TY SYMITARE
CO CORAMINE	CH MACHINES	RS SEMINARS	PR TRIPEMAN	SMEARING	WW SWIMWEAR
CS CARMINES	CL MESCALIN	SIRNAMES	RS MINARETS	GO GORAMIES	
CU MANICURE	CP PEMICANS	RT MINARETS	RAIMENTS	GP EPIGRAMS	**AEIMST 95**
DE REMAINED	CR CARMINES	RAIMENTS	RT MARTINET	PRIMAGES	(MATIES)
DG DREAMING	CS AMNESICS	RU ANEURISM	RU RUMINATE	GR ARMIGERS	AD DIASTEMA
MARGINED	CT SEMANTIC	RY SEMINARY	RW WARIMENT	GS GISARMES	AM IMAMATES
DI MERIDIAN	CU SEMUNCIA	SS SAMISENS	RY TYRAMINE	GT MAGISTER	AN AMENTIAS
DR MANRIDER	CY SYCAMINE	ST MANTISES	SS MANTISES	MIGRATES	ANIMATES
DS ADERMINS	DE DEMAINES	SU ANIMUSES	TU MATUTINE	RAGTIMES	BC BETACISM
SIRNAMED	INSEAMED	SZ MAZINESS	VZ VIZAMENT	STERIGMA	BE BEAMIEST
DY DAIRYMEN	DM MISNAMED	UV MAUVEINS		HN HARMINES	BG MEGABITS
DZ ZEMINDAR	DO NOMADIES	MAUVINES	**AEIMRS 112**	SHIREMAN	BH IMBATHES
EG GERMAINE	NOMADISE		(ARMIES)	HP SAMPHIRE	BL BALMIEST
ES REMANIES	DR ADERMINS	**AEIMNT 53**	AC MACARISE	SERAPHIM	TIMBALES
EX EXAMINER	SIRNAMED	(INMATE)	MESARAIC	HR MARSHIER	BN AMBIENTS
FL INFLAMER	DS SIDESMAN	AD ANIMATED	AU URAEMIAS	HS MARISHES	BR BARMIEST
RIFLEMAN	DT MEDIANTS	DIAMANTE	BD EMBRAIDS	MISHEARS	CE EMICATES
GI IMAGINER	DU MAUNDIES	AH ANTHEMIA	BG GAMBIERS	IT AIRTIMES	CH MISTEACH
MIGRAINE	DY DYNAMISE	HAEMATIN	BJ JAMBIERS	SERIATIM	TACHISME
GK REMAKING	ER REMANIES	AL ALAIMENT	BL REMBLAIS	KN RAMEKINS	CJ MAJESTIC
GL GERMINAL	ES NEMESIAS	LAMINATE	BN MIRBANES	KP RAMPIKES	CL CALMIEST
MALIGNER	ET MATINEES	AO METANOIA	BT BARMIEST	LM SMALMIER	CLEMATIS
MALINGER	SEMINATE	AP IMPANATE	BU AUMBRIES	LN MARLINES	CLIMATES
GN ENARMING	EX EXAMINES	AR MARINATE	CC CERAMICS	MINERALS	METICALS
RENAMING	FI INFAMIES		CE RACEMISE	LO MORALISE	CN SEMANTIC

CP CAMPIEST	PETALISM	INCREASE	SNAGGIER	PRALINES	VV VERVAINS
CAMPSITE	SEPTIMAL	RESIANCE	GH HEARINGS	LR SNARLIER	ZZ SNAZZIER
CR CERAMIST	LR LAMITERS	CF FANCIERS	HEARSING	LS RAINLESS	
MATRICES	MARLIEST	CG CREASING	SHEARING	LT ENTRAILS	**AEINRT 1**
CS ETACISMS	LT MALTIEST	GRECIANS	GK SKEARING	LATRINES	(RETAIN)
DD MISDATED	SMALTITE	SEARCING	GL ARLESING	RATLINES	AB RABATINE
DE MEDIATES	LU SIMULATE	CH INARCHES	ENGRAILS	TRENAILS	AC CARINATE
DG SIGMATED	LY LAYTIMES	CI RIANCIES	NARGILES	LU LUNARIES	AD DENTARIA
DL MISDEALT	STEAMILY	CL CARLINES	REALIGNS	LV RAVELINS	AG AERATING
DM MISMATED	MP PSAMMITE	CM CARMINES	SANGLIER	LX RELAXINS	AM MARINATE
DN MEDIANTS	MR MARMITES	CN CRANNIES	GM GERMAINS	LY INLAYERS	AO AERATION
DO ATOMISED	MS MISMATES	CO SCENARIO	SMEARING	SNAILERY	AS ANTISERA
DP DAMPIEST	NN MANNITES	CS ARSENICS	GN AGINNERS	MN REINSMAN	ARTESIAN
IMPASTED	NR MINARETS	CERASINS	EARNINGS	MO MORAINES	RESINATA
DR MARDIEST	RAIMENTS	RACINESS	ENGRAINS	MR MARINERS	AT REATTAIN
MISRATED	OR AMORTISE	CT CANISTER	GRANNIES	MS SEMINARS	AU INAURATE
READMITS	OS AMITOSES	CARNIEST	GO IGNAROES	SIRNAMES	BG BERATING
DS MISDATES	AMOSITES	NACRITES	ORGANISE	MT MINARETS	REBATING
DU TAEDIUMS	ATOMISES	SCANTIER	ORIGANES	RAIMENTS	BO BARITONE
DY DAYTIMES	OSMIATES	DE ARSENIDE	GP PREASING	MU ANEURISM	OBTAINER
EL MEALIEST	OZ ATOMIZES	DENARIES	SPEARING	MY SEMINARY	BS ATEBRINS
EN MATINEES	PR PRIMATES	DRAISENE	GR EARRINGS	NO RAISONNE	BU URBANITE
SEMINATE	PS IMPASTES	NEARSIDE	GRAINERS	NP PANNIERS	CD CRINATED
ER EMIRATES	PASTIMES	DF FRIANDES	GS REASSIGN	NS INSNARES	DICENTRA
REAMIEST	RS ASTERISM	DG DERAIGNS	SEARINGS	NT ENTRAINS	CE CENTIARE
STEAMIER	MAISTERS	GRADINES	SERINGAS	TRANNIES	CREATINE
ES SEAMIEST	MISRATES	READINGS	GT ANGRIEST	NU ANEURINS	INCREATE
STEAMIES	SEMITARS	DI DRAISINE	ASTRINGE	UNARISEN	ITERANCE
ET ESTIMATE	SMARTIES	DL ISLANDER	GANISTER	NW SWANNIER	CG CATERING
ETATISME	RT MISTREAT	DM ADERMINS	GANTRIES	OS ERASIONS	CITRANGE
MEATIEST	TERATISM	SIRNAMED	GRANITES	OT ANOESTRI	CREATING
TEATIMES	RU MURIATES	DN INSNARED	INGRATES	ARSONITE	REACTING
EW TEAMWISE	SEMITAUR	DO ANEROIDS	RANGIEST	NOTARIES	CL CLARINET
FL FLAMIEST	RW WARTIMES	DONARIES	REASTING	NOTARISE	CO ANORETIC
FN MANIFEST	RX MATRIXES	DP SPRAINED	STEARING	ROSINATE	CREATION
FO FOAMIEST	RY SYMITARE	DR DRAINERS	GV VINEGARS	OV AVERSION	REACTION
GM GAMMIEST	SS ASTEISMS	SERRANID	GW SWEARING	PP SNAPPIER	CS CANISTER
GN MANGIEST	MASSIEST	DS ARIDNESS	WEARINGS	PT PAINTERS	CARNIEST
MINTAGES	ST MASTIEST	SARDINES	GY RESAYING	PANTRIES	NACRITES
STEAMING	MISSTATE	DT DETRAINS	HL INHALERS	PERTAINS	SCANTIER
TEAMINGS	SZ MESTIZAS	RANDIEST	HM HARMINES	PINASTER	CT INTERACT
GP PIGMEATS	YZ AZYMITES	STRAINED	SHIREMAN	REPAINTS	CV NAVICERT
GR MAGISTER		DU DENARIUS	HP HEPARINS	PU UNPRAISE	CX XERANTIC
MIGRATES	**AEINRS 6**	UNRAISED	PARISHEN	RT RESTRAIN	DD INDARTED
RAGTIMES	(SARNIE)	URANIDES	SERAPHIN	RETRAINS	DE DETAINER
STERIGMA	AC CANARIES	DV INVADERS	HR SHARNIER	TERRAINS	RETAINED
GS SIGMATES	AD ARANEIDS	SANDIVER	HS ARSHINES	TRAINERS	DG DERATING
GU GAUMIEST	AG ANGARIES	DY SYNEDRIA	HT INEARTHS	ST RESIANTS	GRADIENT
HM HAMMIEST	AP PANARIES	EG GESNERIA	HV ENRAVISH	RETSINAS	TREADING
HP MATESHIP	AT ANTISERA	EH INHEARSE	VANISHER	SNARIEST	DI DAINTIER
SHIPMATE	ARTESIAN	EK SNEAKIER	IK KAISERIN	STAINERS	DO AROINTED
HS ATHEISMS	RESINATA	EM REMANIES	IL AIRLINES	STARNIES	DERATION
MASHIEST	BC CARBINES	EN ANSERINE	SNAILIER	STEARINS	ORDINATE
MATHESIS	BD BRANDIES	EP NAPERI'S	IN SIRENIAN	SU SENARIUS	RATIONED
IN MINIATES	BRANDISE	ER REARISEN	IS AIRINESS	SW WARINESS	DP DIPTERAN
IR AIRTIMES	BG BEARINGS	ES SENARIES	IT INERTIAS	SX XERANSIS	DS DETRAINS
SERIATIM	SABERING	ET ARSENITE	RAINIEST	TT INTREATS	RANDIEST
IT IMITATES	BI BINARIES	RESINATE	IY YERSINIA	NITRATES	STRAINED
JM JAMMIEST	BK BEARSKIN	STEARINE	JT NARTJIES	STRAITEN	DT NITRATED
KN MANKIEST	INBREAKS	TRAINEES	KM RAMEKINS	TARTINES	DU DATURINE
MISTAKEN	BL RINSABLE	EU UNEASIER	KT KERATINS	TERTIANS	INDURATE
KS MISTAKES	BM MIRBANES	FO FARINOSE	NARKIEST	TU RUINATES	RUINATED
KW MAWKIEST	BO BARONIES	FP FIREPANS	KW SWANKIER	URANITES	URINATED
LN AILMENTS	BT ATEBRINS	FR REFRAINS	LM MARLINES	URINATES	EH ATHERINE
ALIMENTS	BANISTER	FS FAIRNESS	MINERALS	TW TINWARES	EK ANKERITE
MANLIEST	BU ANBURIES	SANSERIF	LO AILERONS	UV VAURIENS	KREATINE
LO LOAMIEST	URBANISE	FT FENITARS	ALERIONS	UZ AZURINES	EL ELATERIN
LP IMPLATES	CE CINEREAS	FX XERAFINS	ALIENORS	SUZERAIN	ENTAILER
PALMIEST		GG GEARINGS	LP PEARLINS		TREENAIL
PALMIETS		GREASING			

```
EP APERIENT      NR INERRANT      BO BOTANIES      FN INFANTES         ALIMENTS         URANITES
ER RETAINER      NS ENTRAINS         BOTANISE      FR FENITARS         MANLIEST         URINATES
ES ARSENITE         TRANNIES         NIOBATES      FT FAINTEST      LO ELATIONS      RW TINWARES
   RESINATE      OP ATROPINE         OBEISANT      GG NAGGIEST         INSOLATE      SS SAINTESS
   STEARINE      OR ANTERIOR      BP BEPAINTS      GH GAHNITES         TOENAILS         SESTINAS
   TRAINEES      OS ANOESTRI      BR ATEBRINS         HEATINGS      LP PANTILES      ST INSTATES
FI FAINTIER         ARSONITE         BANISTER      GL EASTLING         PLAINEST         NASTIEST
FS FENITARS         NOTARIES      BS BASINETS         GELATINS      LR ENTRAILS         SATINETS
GH EARTHING         NOTARISE         BASSINET         GENITALS         LATRINES      TT NATTIEST
   HEARTING         ROSINATE         BESAINTS         STEALING         RATLINES      TV TASTEVIN
GK RETAKING      OT TENTORIA         BESTAINS      GM MANGIEST         TRENAILS      TW TAWNIEST
GL ALERTING      OZ NOTARIZE      BT TABINETS         MINTAGES      LS EASTLINS      WY YAWNIEST
   ALTERING      PR TERRAPIN      CD DISTANCE         STEAMING         ELASTINS
   INTEGRAL      PS PAINTERS      CE CINEASTE         TEAMINGS         SALIENTS      AEIPRS  75
   RELATING         PANTRIES      CF FANCIEST      GN ANTIGENS         STANIELS      (PRAISE)
   TANGLIER         PERTAINS      CH ASTHENIC         GENTIANS      LU ALUNITES      AC AIRSPACE
   TRIANGLE         PINASTER         CHANTIES         STEANING      LV VENTAILS      AD PARADISE
GM EMIGRANT         REPAINTS      CI CANITIES      GR ANGRIEST      LW LAWNIEST      AG IGARAPES
GP TAPERING      PT TRIPTANE      CM SEMANTIC         ASTRINGE      MN MANNITES      AI APIARIES
GS ANGRIEST      PU PAINTURE      CN ANCIENTS         GANISTER      MR MINARETS      AN PANARIES
   ASTRINGE      PX EXPIRANT         CANNIEST         GANTRIES         RAIMENTS      AP APPRAISE
   GANISTER      QU QUAINTER         INSTANCE         GRANITES      MS MANTISES      AR PAREIRAS
   GANTRIES      RS RETAINS       CO ACONITES         INGRATES      NO ENATIONS      AS SPIRAEAS
   GRANITES         RETRAINS         CANOEIST         RANGIEST      NP PANTINES      AT ASPIRATE
   INGRATES         STRAINER      CR CANISTER         REASTING      NR ENTRAINS         PARASITE
   RANGIEST         TERRAINS         CARNIEST         STEARING         TRANNIES         SEPTARIA
   REASTING         TRAINERS         NACRITES      GS EASTINGS      NS INSANEST      BE BEPRAISE
   STEARING         TRANSIRE         SCANTIER         GENISTAS      NT ANTIENTS      CC CAPRICES
GT ARETTING      RV VERATRIN      CS CINEASTS         GIANTESS         STANNITE      CD EPACRIDS
   TREATING      RW INTERWAR         SCANTIES         SEATINGS      OP SAPONITE      CG SPAGERIC
GV AVERTING      SS RESIANTS      CT CANTIEST         TEASINGS      OR ANOESTRI      CH CHARPIES
   TAVERING         RETSINAS         NICTATES         TSIGANES         ARSONITE         PARCHESI
   VINTAGER         SNARIEST      CV CISTVAEN      GT ESTATING         NOTARIES         SERAPHIC
GW TWANGIER         STAINERS         VESICANT         TANGIEST         NOTARISE      CI PIRACIES
   WATERING         STARNIES      CY CYANITES      GU SAUTEING         ROSINATE      CK EARPICKS
HP PERIANTH         STEARINS      DD DANDIEST      GV VINTAGES      OS ASSIENTO      CL CALIPERS
HS INEARTHS      ST INTREATS      DE ANDESITE      GW SWEATING         ASTONIES         REPLICAS
HU HAURIENT         NITRATES      DG SEDATING      GY YEASTING      OV STOVAINE         SPIRACLE
HW TARWHINE         STRAITEN         STEADING      HP PENTHIAS      OX SAXONITE      CP EPICARPS
IL INERTIAL         TARTINES      DH HANDIEST         THESPIAN      PP NAPPIEST      CR PERISARC
IP PAINTIER         TERTIANS      DI ADENITIS      HR INEARTHS      PR PAINTERS      CS SCRAPIES
IS INERTIAS      SU RUINATES         DAINTIES      HS ANTHESIS         PANTRIES         CRAPIEST
   RAINIEST         URANITES      DM MEDIANTS         SHANTIES         PERTAINS         CRISPATE
JS NARTJIES         URINATES      DO ASTONIED      HT HESITANT         PINASTER         PICRATES
JU JAUNTIER      SW TINWARES         SEDATION      HW INSWATHE         REPAINTS         PRACTISE
KS KERATINS      TU TAINTURE      DP DEPAINTS      IK KAINITES      PT PATIENTS      DD DISPREAD
   NARKIEST                       DR DETRAINS      IL ALIENIST      PU PETUNIAS      DG SPAIRGED
KW KNITWEAR      AEINST   2          RANDIEST         LITANIES         SUPINATE      DH RAPHIDES
LM TERMINAL      (SATINE)            STRAINED      IM MINIATES      PY EPINASTY      DI PRESIDIA
LN INTERNAL      AB BASANITE      DS SANDIEST      IP PIANISTE      QU ANTIQUES      DL PEDRAILS
LO ORIENTAL      AC ESTANCIA      DT INSTATED      IR INERTIAS         QUANTISE         PREDIALS
   RELATION      AG SAGINATE      DU AUDIENTS         RAINIEST      RR RESTRAIN      DN SPRAINED
LP TRIPLANE      AH ASTHENIA         SINUATED      IS ISATINES         RETRAINS      DO DIASPORE
LS ENTRAILS      AM AMENTIAS      DV DEVIANTS         SANITIES         STRAINER         PARODIES
   LATRINES         ANIMATES      DY DESYATIN         SANITISE         TERRAINS      DP APPRISED
   RATLINES      AR ANTISERA      EG SAGENITE      IV VANITIES         TRAINERS         DRAPPIES
   TRENAILS         ARTESIAN      EM MATINEES      IX AXINITES         TRANSIRE      DR DRAPIERS
LT RATTLINE         RESINATA      ER ARSENITE      IZ SANITIZE      RS RESIANTS      DS DESPAIRS
LU RETINULA      AT ASTATINE         RESINATE      JR NARTJIES         RETSINAS      DT RAPIDEST
   TENURIAL         SANITATE         STEARINE      JT JANTIEST         SNARIEST         SPIRATED
LV INTERVAL         TANAISTE         TRAINEES      JU JAUNTIES         STAINERS         TRAIPSED
LY INTERLAY      AV SANATIVE      ET ANISETTE      KL LANKIEST         STARNIES      DU UPRAISED
MP TRIPEMAN      BC CABINETS         TETANIES      KM MANKIEST         STEARINS      EG PIERAGES
MS MINARETS      BD BANDIEST         TETANISE         MISTAKEN      RT INTREATS      EL ESPALIER
   RAIMENTS      BE BETAINES      EV NAIVETES      KR KERATINS         NITRATES         PEARLIES
MT MARTINET      BG BEATINGS      FG FEASTING         NARKIEST         STRAITEN      EM EMPAIRES
MU RUMINATE      BH ABSINTHE      FI FAINITES      KS SNAKIEST         TARTINES      EN NAPERIES
MW WARIMENT      BK BEATNIKS      FL INFLATES      KV KISTVAEN         TERTIANS      ER PEREIRAS
MY TYRAMINE      BL INSTABLE      FM MANIFEST      KY KYANITES      RU RUINATES         SPEARIER
NO INORNATE      BM AMBIENTS                       LM AILMENTS                       ET PETARIES
```

FF PIAFFERS	VY VESPIARY	DL DILATERS	GP GRAPIEST	SEMITAUR	VY VESTIARY
FN FIREPANS	XY PYREXIAS	LARDIEST	GS AGISTERS	MW WARTIMES	
GK GARPIKES		DM MARDIEST	GT STRIGATE	MX MATRIXES	**AEIRTT 29**
GM EPIGRAMS	**AEIRST 3**	MISRATED	GV VIRGATES	MY SYMITARE	(ATTIRE)
PRIMAGES	(SATIRE)	READMITS	VITRAGES	NN ENTRAINS	AN REATTAIN
GN PREASING	AD DATARIES	DN DETRAINS	HI HAIRIEST	TRANNIES	AP PATRIATE
SPEARING	RADIATES	RANDIEST	HN INEARTHS	NO ANOESTRI	AS ARIETTAS
GS PRISAGES	AN ANTISERA	STRAINED	HO HOARIEST	ARSONITE	ARISTATE
SPAIRGES	ARTESIAN	DO ASTEROID	HR TRASHIER	NOTARIES	AZ ZARATITE
GT GRAPIEST	RESINATA	DP RAPIDEST	HS SHERIATS	NOTARISE	BC BRATTICE
HL PLASHIER	AP ASPIRATE	SPIRATED	HW SWATHIER	ROSINATE	BE BATTERIE
HM SAMPHIRE	PARASITE	TRAIPSED	WATERISH	NP PAINTERS	BR BRATTIER
SERAPHIM	SEPTARIA	DS ASTERIDS	HY HYSTERIA	PANTRIES	BS BIRETTAS
HN HEPARINS	AS ASTERIAS	DIASTERS	IL LAIRIEST	PERTAINS	BY YTTERBIA
PARISHEN	ATRESIAS	DISASTER	IM AIRTIMES	PINASTER	CD TETRACID
SERAPHIN	AT ARIETTAS	DISRATES	SERIATIM	REPAINTS	TETRADIC
HO APHORISE	ARISTATE	DT STRAITED	IN INERTIAS	NR RESTRAIN	CF TRIFECTA
HP PAPISHER	AV VARIATES	STRIATED	RAINIEST	RETRAINS	CH CHATTIER
SAPPHIRE	BD BARDIEST	TARDIEST	IP PARITIES	STRAINER	THEATRIC
HR PHRASIER	BRAIDEST	DW TAWDRIES	IR RARITIES	TERRAINS	CL TRACTILE
HS PARISHES	RABIDEST	EE EATERIES	IS IRISATES	TRAINERS	CM TREMATIC
SHARPIES	TRIBADES	EH HEARTIES	SATIRISE	TRANSIRE	CN INTERACT
IR PRAIRIES	BK BARKIEST	EL ATELIERS	IV VAIRIEST	NS RESIANTS	CR RETRAICT
IT PARITIES	BRAKIEST	EARLIEST	IW WISTERIA	RETSINAS	CS CITRATES
IW PAIRWISE	BREASKIT	LEARIEST	IZ SATIRIZE	SNARIEST	CRISTATE
KM RAMPIKES	BL LIBRATES	REALTIES	JN NARTJIES	STAINERS	SCATTIER
KT PARKIEST	BM BARMIEST	EM EMIRATES	JO JAROSITE	STARNIES	CU URTICATE
LM IMPEARLS	BN ATEBRINS	REAMIEST	KL LARKIEST	STEARINS	CV TRACTIVE
LEMPIRAS	BANISTER	STEAMIER	STALKIER	NT INTREATS	DE ITERATED
LN PEARLINS	BO SABOTIER	EN ARSENITE	STARLIKE	NITRATES	DL DETRITAL
PRALINES	BR ARBITERS	RESINATE	KN KERATINS	STRAITEN	DN NITRATED
LO PELORIAS	RAREBITS	STEARINE	NARKIEST	TARTINES	DO TERATOID
POLARISE	BT BIRETTAS	TRAINEES	KP PARKIEST	TERTIANS	DS STRAITED
LP APPERILS	BV VIBRATES	EO ETAERIOS	KS ASTERISK	NU RUINATES	STRIATED
LR REPRISAL	BW WARBIEST	EP PETARIES	SARKIEST	URANITES	DT TITRATED
LT PILASTER	BY BESTIARY	ER ARTERIES	LL LITERALS	URINATES	EG AIGRETTE
PLAISTER	SYBARITE	REASTIER	TALLIERS	NW TINWARES	EL LATERITE
PLAITERS	CD ACRIDEST	ES SERIATES	LM LAMITERS	OR ROARIEST	LITERATE
LV PREVAILS	CG AGRESTIC	ET ARIETTES	MARLIEST	ROTARIES	ER RETRAITE
LW SLIPWARE	CH CHARIEST	ITERATES	LN ENTRAILS	OV VOTARIES	ES ARIETTES
MM SPAMMIER	THERIACS	TEARIEST	LATRINES	PP PERIAPTS	ITERATES
MR RAMPIRES	CL ALTRICES	TREATIES	RATLINES	PS PASTRIES	TEARIEST
MS IMPRESAS	ARTICLES	TREATISE	TRENAILS	PIASTRES	TREATIES
SAMPIRES	RECITALS	EV EVIRATES	LO SOTERIAL	RASPIEST	TREATISE
MT PRIMATES	SELICTAR	EW SWEATIER	LP PILASTER	TRAIPSES	FL FILTRATE
MV VAMPIRES	CM CERAMIST	TAWERIES	PLAISTER	PV PRIVATES	GL AGLITTER
MW SWAMPIER	MATRICES	WEARIEST	PLAITERS	PW WIRETAPS	GN ARETTING
NN PANNIERS	CN CANISTER	EY YEASTIER	LR RETIRALS	PY ASPERITY	TREATING
NP SNAPPIER	CARNIEST	FG FRIGATES	RETRIALS	RR STARRIER	GS STRIGATE
NT PAINTERS	NACRITES	FI RATIFIES	TRAILERS	RS TARSIERS	HP THREAPIT
PANTRIES	SCANTIER	FL FLARIEST	LS REALISTS	RT RETRAITS	IL LITERATI
PERTAINS	CP CRAPIEST	FRAILEST	SALTIERS	STRAITER	IR IRRITATE
PINASTER	CRISPATE	FN FENITARS	SALTIRES	TARRIEST	IT TITRIATE
REPAINTS	PICRATES	FR FRATRIES	SLAISTER	RW STRAWIER	LM REMITTAL
NU UNPRAISE	PRACTISE	GG RAGGIEST	LT TERTIALS	SWARTIER	LN RATTLINE
OV VAPORISE	CR ERRATICS	GL GLARIEST	LU URALITES	SS TIRASSES	LO LITERATO
PS APPRISES	CS SCARIEST	REGALIST	MM MARMITES	ST ARTISTES	LS TERTIALS
PT PERIAPTS	CT CITRATES	GM MAGISTER	MN MINARETS	ARTSIEST	LY ALTERITY
PZ APPRIZES	CRISTATE	MIGRATES	RAIMENTS	STRIATES	MN MARTINET
RS PRAISERS	SCATTIER	RAGTIMES	MO AMORTISE	SV TRAVISES	MO AMORETTI
RY SPRAYIER	CU SURICATE	STERIGMA	ATOMISER	SW WAISTERS	MS MISTREAT
ST PASTRIES	CZ CRAZIEST	GN ANGRIEST	MP PRIMATES	WAITRESS	TERATISM
PIASTRES	DD DISRATED	ASTRINGE	MS ASTERISM	WASTRIES	NO TENTORIA
RASPIEST	DE READIEST	GANISTER	MAISTERS	TT RATTIEST	NP TRIPTANE
TRAIPSES	SERIATED	GANTRIES	MISRATES	TARTIEST	NS INTREATS
SU UPRAISES	STEADIER	GRANITES	SEMITARS	TITRATES	NITRATES
SV PARVISES	DH HAIRSTED	INGRATES	SMARTIES	TW WARTIEST	STRAITEN
TV PRIVATES	HARDIEST	RANGIEST	MT MISTREAT	TX EXTRAITS	TARTINES
TW WIRETAPS	DI IRISATED	REASTING	TERATISM	UZ AZURITES	TERTIANS
TY ASPERITY	DK STRAIKED	STEARING	MU MURIATES		

NU	TAINTURE		STEATITE	**AELNRS 63**	HP SHRAPNEL	ES ALTERNES	BY ABSENTLY

NU TAINTURE
OV ROTATIVE
RS RETRAITS
   STRAITER
   TARRIEST
RT RETRAITT
RY TERTIARY
SS ARTISTES
   ARTSIEST
   STRIATES
ST RATTIEST
   TARTIEST
   TITRATES
SW WARTIEST
SX EXTRAITS

AEISTT 83
(TASTIE)
AD SATIATED
AG AGITATES
AN ASTATINE
   SANITATE
   TANAISTE
AP APATITES
AR ARIETTAS
   ARISTATE
AS SATIATES
BN TABINETS
BR BIRETTAS
BS BATISTES
BT BATTIEST
CC ECSTATIC
CD DICTATES
CH CHATTIES
   TACHISTE
CK TACKIEST
   TIETACKS
CL LATTICES
CN CANTIEST
   NICTATES
CO OSCITATE
CR CITRATES
   CRISTATE
   SCATTIER
CT CATTIEST
CU EUSTATIC
DN INSTATED
DR STRAITED
   STRIATED
   TARDIEST
DS DISTASTE
   STAIDEST
DU SITUATED
EH ATHETISE
   HESITATE
EL AILETTES
EM ESTIMATE
   ETATISME
   MEATIEST
   TEATIMES
EN ANISETTE
   TETANIES
   TETANISE
EP PEATIEST
ER ARIETTES
   ITERATES
   TEARIEST
   TREATIES
   TREATISE
ET ETATISTE

   STEATITE
EV AVIETTES
   ESTIVATE
   EVITATES
FN FAINTEST
FT FATTIEST
GN ESTATING
   TANGIEST
GO GOATIEST
GR STRIGATE
GS STAGIEST
HL LATHIEST
   LITHATES
HN HESITANT
HS ATHEISTS
   HASTIEST
   STAITHES
HW THAWIEST
   THWAITES
IM IMITATES
IV VITIATES
JN JANTIEST
LM MALTIEST
   SMALTITE
LO TOTALISE
LP PLATIEST
LR TERTIALS
LS SALTIEST
   SLATIEST
LW WALTIEST
MR MISTREAT
   TERATISM
MS MASTIEST
   MISSTATE
NN ANTIENTS
   STANNITE
NP PATIENTS
NR INTREATS
   NITRATES
   STRAITEN
   TARTINES
   TERTIANS
NS INSTATES
   NASTIEST
   SATINETS
NT NATTIEST
NV TASTEVIN
NW TAWNIEST
OS TOASTIES
PS PASTIEST
RR RETRAITS
   STRAITER
   TARRIEST
RS ARTISTES
   ARTSIEST
   STRIATES
RT RATTIEST
   TARTIEST
   TITRATES
RW WARTIEST
RX EXTRAITS
ST TASTIEST
SU SITUATES
SV VASTIEST
TT TATTIEST
TU ATTUITES
TW TAWTIEST

AELNRS 63
(LANERS)
AD ADRENALS
AG ALNAGERS
AK LARNAKES
AP PRENASAL
AS ARSENALS
AY ANALYSER
BE ENABLERS
BG BRANGLES
BI RINSABLE
BS BRANSLES
BT BRANTLES
BY BLARNEYS
CE CLEANERS
   CLEANSER
CG CLANGERS
CH CHARNELS
CI CARLINES
CK CRANKLES
CN SCRANNEL
CU LUCARNES
DD DANDLERS
DG DANGLERS
   GLANDERS
DH HANDLERS
DI ISLANDER
DL LANDLERS
DM MANDRELS
DO LADRONES
   SOLANDER
DP SPANDREL
DS SLANDERS
DU LAUNDERS
   LURDANES
   RUNDALES
EG ENLARGES
   GENERALS
   GLEANERS
ER LEARNERS
ES REALNESS
ET ALTERNES
EV ENSLAVER
EW RENEWALS
FK FLANKERS
FO FARNESOL
FS SALFERNS
FU FLANEURS
   FUNERALS
GG GANGRELS
GI ARLESING
   ENGRAILS
   NARGILES
   REALIGNS
   SANGLIER
   SLANGIER
GJ JANGLERS
GL LANGRELS
GM MANGLERS
GP GRAPNELS
   SPANGLER
   SPRANGLE
GT STRANGLE
   TANGLERS
   TRANGLES
GU GRANULES
GW WANGLERS
   WRANGLES
GY LARYNGES
HI INHALERS

HP SHRAPNEL
HT ENTHRALS
II AIRLINES
   SNAILIER
IM MARLINES
   MINERALS
IO AILERONS
   ALERIONS
   ALIENORS
IP PEARLINS
   PRALINES
IR SNARLIER
IS RAINLESS
IT ENTRAILS
   LATRINES
   RATLINES
   TRENAILS
IU LUNARIES
IV RAVELINS
IX RELAXINS
IY INLAYERS
   SNAILERY
KP PRANKLES
LO LLANEROS
MO ALMONERS
MP LAMPERNS
MU MENSURAL
   NUMERALS
NP PLANNERS
NS ENSNARLS
NT LANTERNS
NU UNLEARNS
OP PERSONAL
OU ALEURONS
OV VERONALS
PT PANTLERS
   PLANTERS
   REPLANTS
PU PURSLANE
   SUPERNAL
RS SNARLERS
ST SALTERNS
TT SLATTERN
   TRENTALS
TU NEUTRALS
TV VENTRALS
UV UNRAVELS
VY SYLVANER
XY LARYNXES

AELNRT 28
(ANTLER)
AC LACERANT
AM MATERNAL
AP PARENTAL
   PATERNAL
   PRENATAL
AT ALTERANT
   ALTERNAT
AX RELAXANT
BE RENTABLE
BS BRANTLES
CI CLARINET
DE ANTLERED
DY ARDENTLY
EH LEATHERN
EI ELATERIN
   ENTAILER
   TREENAIL
EN LANNERET

ES ALTERNES
EV LEVANTER
   RELEVANT
EX EXTERNAL
FU FLAUNTER
GI ALERTING
   ALTERING
   INTEGRAL
   RELATING
   TANGLIER
   TRIANGLE
GS STRANGLE
   TANGLERS
HL ENTHRALL
HS ENTHRALS
II INERTIAL
IM TERMINAL
IN INTERNAL
IO ORIENTAL
   RELATION
IP TRIPLANE
IS ENTRAILS
   LATRINES
   RATLINES
   TRENAILS
IT RATTLINE
IU RETINULA
   TENURIAL
IV INTERVAL
IY INTERLAY
NS LANTERNS
NU UNLEARNT
OT TETRONAL
   TOLERANT
OU OUTLEARN
OY ORNATELY
PS PANTLERS
   PLANTERS
   REPLANTS
PY PLENARTY
RY ERRANTLY
SS SALTERNS
ST SLATTERN
   TRENTALS
SU NEUTRALS
SV VENTRALS

AELNST 34
(ANTLES)
AB BANALEST
AC ANALECTS
AD EASTLAND
AK ALKANETS
   KANTELAS
AM TALESMAN
AP PLATANES
   PLEASANT
AS SEALANTS
AZ ZEALANTS
BD BLANDEST
BI INSTABLE
BK BLANKEST
   BLANKETS
BL NETBALLS
BM SEMBLANT
BO NEOBLAST
   NOTABLES
BR BRANTLES
BU UNSTABLE

BY ABSENTLY
CD SCANTLED
CE CLEANEST
   LATENCES
CH STANCHEL
CO LACTONES
CP CLAPNETS
CS SCANTLES
CT CANTLETS
DH SHETLAND
DU UNSALTED
DW WETLANDS
EE SELENATE
EK KANTELES
EM MANTEELS
   TALESMEN
ER ALTERNES
ES LATENESS
EY ENTAYLES
FI INFLATES
FS FLATNESS
FT FLATTENS
GI EASTLING
   GELATINS
   GENITALS
   STEALING
GO TANGELOS
GP SPANGLET
GR STRANGLE
   TANGLERS
GT GANTLETS
GU LANGUETS
GW TWANGLES
HO ETHANOLS
HR ENTHRALS
HS NATHLESS
HY NAYTHLES
II ALIENIST
   LITANIES
IK LANKIEST
IM AILMENTS
   ALIMENTS
   MANLIEST
IO ELATIONS
   INSOLATE
   TOENAILS
IP PANTILES
   PLAINEST
IR ENTRAILS
   LATRINES
   RATLINES
   TRENAILS
IS EASTLINS
   ELASTINS
   SALIENTS
   STANIELS
IU ALUNITES
   INSULATE
IV VENTAILS
IW LAWNIEST
LM STALLMEN
LS TALLNESS
LT TALLENTS
MO SALMONET
MT MANTLETS
MU NUTMEALS
NR LANTERNS
NS STANNELS
NU ANNULETS

OP LAPSTONE
PLEONAST
POLENTAS
OV VOLANTES
PR PANTLERS
PLANTERS
REPLANTS
PX EXPLANTS
RS SALTERNS
RT SLATTERN
TRENTALS
RU NEUTRALS
RV VENTRALS
SS SALTNESS
SY STANYELS
UV ENVAULTS

AELORS 42
(ALORES)
AI OLEARIAS
AU AUREOLAS
BT BLOATERS
SORTABLE
STORABLE
BU RUBEOLAS
BV ABSOLVER
CC CORACLES
CE ESCAROLE
CF ALFRESCO
CH CHOLERAS
CHORALES
CI CALORIES
CARIOLES
CJ CAJOLERS
CK EARLOCKS
CL CORELLAS
CM CAROMELS
SCLEROMA
CP PARCLOSE
POLACRES
CS ESCOLARS
LACROSSE
CT SECTORAL
CU CAROUSEL
CY CALOYERS
COARSELY
DI DARIOLES
SOLIDARE
SOREDIAL
DL ODALLERS
DM EARLDOMS
DN LADRONES
SOLANDER
DP LEOPARDS
DS ROADLESS
DT DELATORS
LEOTARDS
LODESTAR
DU ROULADES
EH ARSEHOLE
EP PAROLEES
ER RELEASOR
ET OLEASTER
EU AUREOLES
FH FAHLORES
FI FORESAIL
FN FARNESOL
FS SAFROLES
FT FLOATERS
FORESTAL

REFLOATS
FU FUSAROLE
FY FORELAYS
GI GASOLIER
GIRASOLE
SERAGLIO
GL ALLEGROS
GM GOMERALS
GP PERGOLAS
GT LEGATORS
GU GLAREOUS
HI AIRHOLES
SHOALIER
HM ARMHOLES
HT LOATHERS
HY HOARSELY
IM MORALISE
IN AILERONS
ALERIONS
ALIENORS
IP PELORIAS
POLARISE
IS SOLARISE
IT SOTERIAL
IV OVERSAIL
VALORISE
VARIOLES
VOLARIES
IY ROYALISE
IZ SOLARIZE
KW SALEWORK
KY ROKELAYS
LN LLANEROS
LP REPOSALL
LS ROSELLAS
LT REALLOTS
LV OVERALLS
LW SALLOWER
MN ALMONERS
MP PLEROMAS
MT MOLERATS
MU RAMULOSE
NP PERSONAL
NU ALEURONS
NV VERONALS
OS AEROSOLS
ROSEOLAS
PP PROLAPSE
PROPALES
SAPROPEL
PS REPOSALS
PT PETROSAL
PROLATES
PU LEAPROUS
PV OVERLAPS
RT REALTORS
RELATORS
TU ROSULATE
TV LEVATORS
TY ROYALETS
UU ROULEAUS
VY OVERLAYS

AELOST 46
(SOLATE)
AC CATALOES
AM OATMEALS
AX OXALATES
BC OBSTACLE

BN NEOBLAST
NOTABLES
BP POTABLES
BR BLOATERS
SORTABLE
STORABLE
BU ABSOLUTE
BW BESTOWAL
CC CACOLETS
CG CATELOGS
CH ESCHALOT
CI ALOETICS
COALIEST
SOCIETAL
CL COLLATES
CM CAMELOTS
MOLECAST
CN LACTONES
CP POLECATS
CR SECTORAL
CS ALECOSTS
COATLESS
LACTOSES
SCATOLES
CT CALOTTES
LOCUSTAE
OSCULATE
CY ACOLYTES
DE DESOLATE
DI DIASTOLE
ISOLATED
SODALITE
SOLIDATE
DP TADPOLES
DR DELATORS
LEOTARDS
LODESTAR
DV SOLVATED
EG SEGOLATE
ER OLEASTER
FG FLOTAGES
FI FOLIATES
FL FLOATELS
FR FLOATERS
FORESTAL
REFLOATS
FT FALSETTO
GI OTALGIES
GL TOLLAGES
GN TANGELOS
GR LEGATORS
GV VOLTAGES
HN ETHANOLS
HR LOATHERS
HS SHOALEST
HT LOATHEST
IK KEITLOAS
IM LOAMIEST
IN ELATIONS
INSOLATE
TOENAILS
IP SPOLIATE
IR SOTERIAL
IS ISOLATES
IT TOTALISE
IV VIOLATES
KS SKATOLES
LR REALLOTS

MN SALMONET
MR MOLERATS
MS MALTOSES
MT MATELOTS
MY ATMOLYSE
NP LAPSTONE
PLEONAST
POLENTAS
PR PETROSAL
PROLATES
PS APOSTLES
PT PALETOTS
PU OUTLEAPS
PETALOUS
RR REALTORS
RELATORS
RU ROSULATE
RV LEVATORS
RY ROYALETS
SV SOLVATES
SY ASYSTOLE
TU TOLUATES
UV OVULATES
UY AUTOLYSE

AELRST 38
(ALTERS)
AB ARBALEST
AE LAETARES
AG AGRESTAL
AH TREHALAS
AL LATERALS
AP PALESTRA
AZ LAZARETS
BE BLEAREST
BLEATERS
RETABLES
BH BLATHERS
HALBERTS
BI LIBRATES
BM LAMBERTS
BN BRANTLES
BO BLOATERS
SORTABLE
STORABLE
BS BLASTERS
STABLERS
BT BATTLERS
BLATTERS
BRATTLES
BU BALUSTER
BW BLEWARTS
CE CLEAREST
SCELERAT
TREACLES
CH ARCHLETS
CI ALTRICES
ARTICLES
RECITALS
SELICTAR
CK TACKLERS
CO SECTORAL
CP SCEPTRAL
SPECTRAL
CS SCARLETS
CT CLATTERS
SCRATTLE
CU RAUCLEST
DD STRADDLE

DE TREADLES
DI DILATERS
LARDIEST
DO DELATORS
LEOTARDS
LODESTAR
DT STARTLED
EE TEASELER
EF REFLATES
EH HALTERES
LEATHERS
EI ATELIERS
EARLIEST
LEARIEST
REALTIES
EM LAMETERS
EN ALTERNES
EO OLEASTER
EP PRELATES
ER RELATERS
ES STEALERS
TEARLESS
TESSERAL
ET ALERTEST
EU RESALUTE
EY EASTERLY
FH FARTHELS
FI FLARIEST
FRAILEST
FO FLOATERS
FORESTAL
REFLOATS
FT FATTRELS
FU REFUTALS
GG STRAGGLE
GI GLARIEST
REGALIST
GN STRANGLE
TANGLERS
GO LEGATORS
GU GAULTERS
GESTURAL
TRAGULES
HM THERMALS
HN ENTHRALS
HO LOATHERS
HS HARSLETS
II LAIRIEST
IK LARKIEST
STALKIER
STARLIKE
IL LITERALS
TALLIERS
IM LAMITERS
MARLIEST
IN ENTRAILS
LATRINES
RATLINES
IO SOTERIAL
IP PILASTER
PLAISTER
PLAITERS
IR RETIRALS
RETRIALS
TRAILERS
IS REALISTS

SALTIERS
SALTIRES
SLAISTER
IT TERTIALS
KP SPARKLET
KS STALKERS
LO REALLOTS
MM STRAMMEL
TRAMMELS
MO MOLERATS
MP TRAMPLES
MT MALTSTER
MARTLETS
MY MASTERLY
NN LANTERNS
NP PANTLERS
PLANTERS
REPLANTS
NS SALTERNS
NT SLATTERN
TRENTALS
NU NEUTRALS
NV VENTRALS
OP PETROSAL
PROLATES
OR REALTORS
RELATORS
OU ROSULATE
OV LEVATORS
OY ROYALETS
PS PLASTERS
PSALTERS
PT PARTLETS
PLATTERS
PRATTLES
SPLATTER
SPRATTLE
PU APLUSTRE
PY PLASTERY
PSALTERY
RT RATTLERS
STARTLER
RW TRAWLERS
SS STARLESS
ST SLATTERS
STARLETS
STARTLES
SU SALUTERS
SW WARTLESS
WASTRELS
TT TARTLETS
TATTLERS
TU LUSTRATE
TUTELARS
TY SLATTERY
UV VAULTERS
VESTURAL
WZ WALTZERS

AEMNST 168
(STAMEN)
AC CAMSTANE
AD MANDATES
AE EMANATES
MANATEES
AG MAGENTAS
MAGNATES
AI AMENTIAS

	ANIMATES	RV	VARMENTS	IO	AMORTISE	EP	PENTANES	IR	PAINTERS	ST	TRANTERS
AL	TALESMAN	RW	TRANSMEW		ATOMISER	ES	NEATNESS		PANTRIES		
AR	SARMENTA		TREWSMAN	IP	PRIMATES	FI	INFANTES		PERTAINS	**AENRST**	**8**
	SEMANTRA	WY	WAYMENTS	IS	ASTERISM	FU	UNFASTEN		PINASTER		(ANTERS)
AS	NAMASTES				MAISTERS	GH	HANGNEST		REPAINTS	AB	ANTBEARS
AU	MANTEAUS	**AEMRST**	**124**		MISRATES	GI	ANTIGENS	IT	PATIENTS		RATSBANE
BE	BASEMENT		(MATERS)		SEMITARS		GENTIANS	IU	PETUNIAS	AC	CANASTER
BI	AMBIENTS	AF	FERMATAS		SMARTIES		STEANING		SUPINATE		CATERANS
BL	SEMBLANT	AN	SARMENTA	IT	MISTREAT	GO	TONNAGES	IY	EPINASTY	AE	ARSENATE
CE	CASEMENT		SEMANTRA		TERATISM	GT	TANGENTS	LO	LAPSTONE		SERENATA
CH	MANCHETS	AU	AMATEURS	IU	MURIATES	GU	TUNNAGES		PLEONAST	AG	STARAGEN
CI	SEMANTIC	BI	BARMIEST		SEMITAUR	IM	MANNITES		POLENTAS		TANAGERS
CK	TACKSMEN	BL	LAMBERTS	IW	WARTIMES	IO	ENATIONS	LR	PANTLERS	AI	ANTISERA
CO	CAMSTONE	BO	BROMATES	IX	MATRIXES	IP	PANTINES		PLANTERS		ARTESIAN
DE	STAMENED	CE	CERAMETS	IY	SYMITARE	IR	ENTRAINS		REPLANTS		RESINATA
DI	MEDIANTS		CREMATES	LM	STRAMMEL		TRANNIES	LX	EXPLANTS	AJ	NAARTJES
EE	EASEMENT		MEERCATS		TRAMMELS	IS	INSANEST	MS	ENSTAMPS	AM	SARMENTA
EH	METHANES	CH	MATCHERS	LO	MOLERATS	IT	ANTIENTS		PASSMENT		SEMANTRA
EI	MATINEES	CI	CERAMIST	LP	TRAMPLES		STANNITE	MY	PAYMENTS	AO	ANOESTRA
	SEMINATE		MATRICES	LT	MALTSTER	LR	LANTERNS	NN	PENNANTS	AR	NARRATES
EL	MANTEELS	CJ	SCRAMJET		MARTLETS	LS	STANNELS	NO	PENTOSAN	AT	TARTANES
	TALESMEN	CP	CRAMPETS	LY	MASTERLY	LU	ANNULETS	OO	TEASPOON	AV	TAVERNAS
ER	REMANETS	DE	MASTERED	MO	MARMOSET	MR	MANRENTS	OR	OPERANTS		TSAREVNA
ES	TAMENESS		STREAMED	MS	STAMMERS		REMNANTS		PRONATES	BD	BANDSTER
EU	MANSUETE	DI	MARDIEST	NN	MANRENTS	NP	PENNANTS	PR	PARPENTS	BG	BANGSTER
FI	MANIFEST		MISRATED		REMNANTS	OP	PENTOSAN	RR	PARTNERS	BI	ATEBRINS
FR	RAFTSMEN		READMITS	NO	MONSTERA	OR	RESONANT	RS	PASTERNS		BANISTER
GI	MANGIEST	DO	STROAMED		STOREMAN	OU	TONNEAUS	RT	PATTERNS	BL	BRANTLES
	MINTAGES	DP	STRAMPED	NS	SARMENTS	QU	QUANNETS		TRANSEPT	BO	BARONETS
	STEAMING	EG	GAMESTER		SMARTENS	RT	ENTRANTS	RU	PERSAUNT	BU	UNBRASTE
	TEAMINGS		MEAGREST	NU	ANESTRUM	RY	TYRANNES	SU	PESAUNTS		URBANEST
GO	MAGNETOS	EH	ERATHEMS		MENSTRUA			SW	STEWPANS	CD	CANTREDS
	MEGATONS	EI	EMIRATES		TRANSUME	**AENPST**	**185**	SY	SYNAPTES	CE	REASCENT
	MONTAGES		REAMIEST	NV	VARMENTS		(PATENS)	SZ	SPETSNAZ		SARCENET
GR	GARMENTS		STEAMIER	NW	TRANSMEW	AA	ANAPAEST	ZZ	SPETZNAZ	CF	CANTREFS
	MARGENTS	EK	MEERKATS		TREWSMAN	AC	PASTANCE			CH	CHANTERS
	RAGMENTS	EL	LAMETERS	OR	REARMOST	AG	PAGEANTS	**AENRRT**	**87**		SNATCHER
GU	AUGMENTS	EM	AMMETERS	OS	MAESTROS	AH	PHEASANT		(RANTER)		STANCHER
	MUTAGENS		METAMERS	OV	OVERMAST	AL	PLATANES	AB	ABERRANT		TRANCHES
HO	HOASTMEN	EN	REMANETS	PR	TRAMPERS		PLEASANT	AD	NARRATED	CI	CANISTER
HU	HUMANEST	EO	EROTEMAS	PS	STAMPERS	AS	ANAPESTS	AS	NARRATES		CARNIEST
II	MINIATES	EP	TEMPERAS	PT	TRAMPETS		PEASANTS	BE	BANTERER		NACRITES
IK	MANKIEST	ER	STREAMER	PU	TEMPURAS	AT	ANTEPAST	CE	RECANTER		SCANTIER
	MISTAKEN	ES	MASSETER		UPSTREAM	AY	PEASANTY		RECREANT	CK	CRANKEST
IL	AILMENTS		SEAMSTER	ST	MATTRESS	BI	BEPAINTS	DU	UNTARRED	CO	ANCESTOR
	ALIMENTS		STEAMERS		SMARTEST	CD	PANDECTS	EG	ETRANGER		ENACTORS
	MANLIEST	ET	TEAMSTER		SMATTERS	CL	CLAPNETS	EI	RETAINER		SARCONET
IN	MANNITES	EY	METAYERS	SY	MAYSTERS	CO	CAPSTONE	ES	TERRANES		SORTANCE
IR	MINARETS	FN	RAFTSMEN	TU	MATUREST	CT	PENTACTS	EV	TAVERNER	CS	CRANTSES
	RAIMENTS	FO	FOREMAST		TESTAMUR	DI	DEPAINTS	FS	TRANSFER	CT	TRANECTS
IS	MANTISES		FORMATES			DN	PENDANTS	GS	GRANTERS		TRANSECT
LL	STALLMEN	GI	MAGISTER	**AENNST**	**152**	EH	HEPTANES		REGRANTS	CU	CENTAURS
LO	SALMONET		MIGRATES		(ANNETS)		PHENATES		STRANGER		RECUSANT
LT	MANTLETS		RAGTIMES	AD	ANDANTES		STEPHANE	IN	INERRANT		UNCRATES
LU	NUTMEALS		STERIGMA	AG	TANNAGES	EN	PENTANES	IO	ANTERIOR		UNTRACES
NR	MANRENTS	GN	GARMENTS	AN	ANTENNAS	GL	SPANGLET	IP	TERRAPIN	CY	ANCESTRY
	REMNANTS		MARGENTS	AT	STANNATE	GO	PONTAGES	IS	RESTRAIN	DD	STRANDED
OR	MONSTERA		RAGMENTS		TANNATES	GR	TREPANGS		RETRAINS	DG	GRANDEST
	STOREMAN	HL	THERMALS	AU	NAUSEANT	HI	PENTHIAS		STRAINER	DI	DETRAINS
OU	NOTAEUMS	HP	HAMPSTER	AV	VENTANAS		THESPIAN		TERRAINS		RANDIEST
	OUTNAMES	HS	HAMSTERS	BG	BANTENGS	HO	PHAETONS		TRAINERS		STRAINED
	SEAMOUNT	HU	MAUTHERS	CD	SCANDENT		PHONATES		TRANSIRE	DO	TORNADES
PS	ENSTAMPS	HW	MAWTHERS	CE	CANTEENS		STANHOPE	IV	VERATRIN	DS	STANDERS
	PASSMENT	II	AIRTIMES	CH	ENCHANTS	HR	PANTHERS	IW	INTERWAR	DU	DAUNTERS
PY	PAYMENTS	IL	LAMITERS	CI	ANCIENTS	II	PIANISTE	LY	ERRANTLY		TRANSUDE
RS	SARMENTS		MARLIEST		CANNIEST	IL	PANTILES	OO	RATOONER		UNTREADS
	SMARTENS	IM	MARMITES		INSTANCE		PLAINEST	OS	ANTRORSE	DX	DEXTRANS
RU	ANESTRUM	IN	MINARETS	DP	PENDANTS	IN	PANTINES	PS	PARTNERS	EE	SERENATE
	MENSTRUA		RAIMENTS	DU	ASTUNNED	IO	SAPONITE	QU	QUARTERN	EF	FASTENER
	TRANSUME			EO	NEONATES	IP	NAPPIEST	RY	ERRANTRY		FENESTRA

EG ESTRANGE	IM MINARETS	PR PARTNERS	OS ORNATEST	OR ORNATEST	DU OUTDARES
GRANTEES	RAIMENTS	PS PASTERNS	OX TETRAXON	PR PATTERNS	DX EXTRADOS
GREATENS	IN ENTRAINS	PT PATTERNS	OY ATTORNEY	TRANSEPT	EI ETAERIOS
REAGENTS	TRANNIES	TRANSEPT	PS PATTERNS	QU QUESTANT	EK KERATOSE
SEGREANT	IO ANOESTRI	PU PERSAUNT	TRANSEPT	RR TRANTERS	KREASOTE
SERGEANT	ARSONITE	RT TRANTERS	RS TRANTERS	RS TARTNESS	EL OLEASTER
STERNAGE	NOTARIES	SS SARSNETS	SS TARTNESS	RU TAUNTERS	EM EROTEMAS
EH HASTENER	NOTARISE	ST TARTNESS	SU TAUNTERS	SU TAUTNESS	EN RESONATE
HEARTENS	ROSINATE	SU ANESTRUS		UNSTATES	EP OPERATES
EI ARSENITE	IP PAINTERS	SAUNTERS	**AENSTT 116**	SX SEXTANTS	PROTEASE
RESINATE	PANTRIES	SV SERVANTS	(ATTENS)		EV OVEREATS
STEARINE	PERTAINS	VERSANTS	AC CANTATES	**AEORST 13**	FF AFFOREST
TRAINEES	PINASTER	TU TAUNTERS	AG STAGNATE	(ORATES)	FL FLOATERS
EJ SERJEANT	REPAINTS	UV UNSAVERS	AI ASTATINE	AB RABATOES	FORESTAL
EL ALTERNES	IR RESTRAIN	UW UNWATERS	SANITATE	AN ANOESTRA	REFLOATS
EM REMANETS	RETRAINS	WY STERNWAY	TANAISTE	AR AERATORS	FM FOREMAST
EO RESONATE	STRAINER		TANNATES	AT AEROSTAT	FORMATES
ER TERRANES	TERRAINS	**AENRTT 71**	AP ANTEPAST	BD BROADEST	FP FOREPAST
ES ASSENTER	TRAINERS	(NATTER)	AR TARTANES	BE REBATOES	FW FORWASTE
EARNESTS	TRANSIRE	AC REACTANT	BI TABINETS	BH BATHORSE	SOFTWARE
SARSENET	IS RESIANTS	AD TARTANED	CH ETCHANTS	BI SABOTIER	FY FORESTAY
ET ENTREATS	RETSINAS	AI REATTAIN	CI CANTIEST	SORTABLE	GH SHORTAGE
RATTEENS	SNARIEST	AL ALTERANT	NICTATES	STORABLE	GL LEGATORS
EV AVENTRES	STAINERS	ALTERNAT	CL CANTLETS	BM BROMATES	GN ORANGEST
VETERANS	STARNIES	AM ATRAMENT	CO CONSTATE	BN BARONETS	RAGSTONE
FG ENGRAFTS	IT INTREATS	AS TARTANES	CP PENTACTS	BP PROBATES	GO ROOTAGES
FI FENITARS	NITRATES	BO BETATRON	CR TRANECTS	BR ARBORETS	GP PORTAGES
FK FRANKEST	STRAITEN	CH TRANCHET	TRANSECT	TABORERS	GR GARROTES
FM RAFTSMEN	TARTINES	CI INTERACT	CS SCANTEST	BS BOASTERS	GS STORAGES
FR TRANSFER	TERTIANS	CO CONTRATE	DI INSTATED	SORBATES	GT GAROTTES
GG GANGSTER	IU RUINATES	CS TRANECTS	DU UNSTATED	TABORETS	GU OUTRAGES
GI ANGRIEST	URANITES	TRANSECT	UNTASTED	BT ABETTORS	HH HAROSETH
ASTRINGE	URINATES	CU TRUNCATE	EG TENTAGES	BATTEROS	HI HOARIEST
GANISTER	IW TINWARES	DE ATTENDER	EI ANISETTE	TABORETS	HL LOATHERS
GANTRIES	KS STARKENS	NATTERED	TETANIES	BU SABOTEUR	HO TOHEROAS
GRANITES	KZ KRANTZES	RATTENED	TETANISE	CC ECTOSARC	HS ASTHORES
INGRATES	LN LANTERNS	DI NITRATED	ER ENTREATS	CD REDCOATS	HAROSETS
RANGIEST	LP PANTLERS	DO ATTORNED	RATTEENS	CE CREASOTE	HOARSEST
REASTING	PLANTERS	DU TRUANTED	FI FAINTEST	CF FORECAST	HT RHEOSTAT
STEARING	LS SALTERNS	DY TYRANTED	FL FLATTENS	CG ESCARGOT	HX THORAXES
GL STRANGLE	LT SLATTERN	EE ENTERATE	GI ESTATING	CH CHAROSET	IJ JAROSITE
TANGLERS	TRENTALS	EF FATTENER	TANGIEST	THORACES	IL SOTERIAL
TRANGLES	LU NEUTRALS	EH HATERENT	GL GANTLETS	CL SECTORAL	IM AMORTISE
GM GARMENTS	LV VENTRALS	THREATEN	GN TANGENTS	CN ANCESTOR	ATOMISER
MARGENTS	MN MANRENTS	ES ENTREATS	GU GAUNTEST	ENACTORS	IN ANOESTRI
RAGMENTS	REMNANTS	RATTEENS	TUTENAGS	SARCONET	ARSONITE
GO ORANGEST	MO MONSTERA	EV ANTEVERT	HI HESITANT	SORTANCE	NOTARIES
RAGSTONE	STOREMAN	EX EXTERNAT	HS THATNESS	CR ACROTERS	NOTARISE
GP TREPANGS	MS SARMENTS	EY ENTREATY	IJ JANTIEST	CREATORS	ROSINATE
GR GRANTERS	SMARTENS	GI ARETTING	IN ANTIENTS	REACTORS	IR ROARIEST
REGRANTS	MU ANESTRUM	TREATING	STANNITE	CS COARSEST	ROTARIES
STRANGER	MENSTRUA	GO TETRAGON	IP PATIENTS	COASTERS	IV VOTARIES
GU STRAUNGE	TRANSUME	IL RATTLINE	IR INTREATS	CT SECTATOR	KV OVERTASK
HI INEARTHS	MV VARMENTS	IO TENTORIA	NITRATES	CU OUTRACES	LL REALLOTS
HK THANKERS	MW TRANSMEW	IP TRIPTANE	STRAITEN	CV OVERACTS	LM MOLERATS
HL ENTHRALS	TREWSMAN	IS INTREATS	TARTINES	OVERCAST	LP PETROSAL
HP PANTHERS	NO RESONANT	NITRATES	TERTIANS	CX EXACTORS	LR REALTORS
HU HAUNTERS	NT ENTRANTS	STRAITEN	IS INSTATES	DG GOADSTER	RELATORS
UNEARTHS	NY TYRANNES	TARTINES	NASTIEST	DI ASTEROID	LU ROSULATE
UNHEARTS	OP OPERANTS	TERTIANS	SATINETS	DL DELATORS	LV LEVATORS
URETHANS	PRONATES	IU TAINTURE	IT NATTIEST	LEOTARDS	LY ROYALETS
II INERTIAS	OR ANTRORSE	LO TETRONAL	IV TASTEVIN	LODESTAR	MM MARMOSET
RAINIEST	OS ASSENTOR	TOLERANT	IW TAWNIEST	DM STROAMED	MN MONSTERA
IJ NARTJIES	SENATORS	LS SLATTERN	LL TALLENTS	DN TORNADES	STOREMAN
IK KERATINS	OT ORNATEST	TRENTALS	LM MANTLETS	DP ADOPTERS	MR REARMOST
NARKIEST	TREASONS	MO MARTENOT	LR SLATTERN	ASPORTED	MS MAESTROS
IL ENTRAILS	OV VENATORS	NS ENTRANTS	TRENTALS	READOPTS	MV OVERMAST
LATRINES	PP PARPENTS	NY TENANTRY	NR ENTRANTS	DR ROADSTER	NN RESONANT
RATLINES		OP PATENTOR		DS ASSORTED	NP OPERANTS
TRENAILS				TORSADES	

```
      PRONATES
NR  ANTRORSE
NS  ASSENTOR
      SENATORS
      TREASONS
NT  ORNATEST
NV  VENATORS
OR  SORORATE
PR  PRAETORS
      PRORATES
PS  ESPARTOS
      PORTASES
      PROTASES
      SEAPORTS
PT  PROSTATE
PU  APTEROUS
PV  OVERPAST
QU  EQUATORS
      QUAESTOR
RR  ARRESTOR
RS  ASSERTOR
      ASSORTER
      ORATRESS
      ROASTERS
RT  ROSTRATE
ST  STRATOSE
      TOASTERS
SV  VOTARESS
SX  STORAXES
TT  ATTESTOR
      TESTATOR
TU  OUTRATES
      OUTSTARE
UW  OUTSWEAR
      OUTWEARS
VY  OVERSTAY

AEPRST  129
(PATERS)
AC  CAPRATES
AD  ADAPTERS
      READAPTS
AE  ASPERATE
      SEPARATE
AI  ASPIRATE
      PARASITE
      SEPTARIA
AK  PARTAKES
AL  PALESTRA
AP  PARAPETS
BO  PROBATES
CH  CHAPTERS
      PATCHERS
CI  CRAPIEST
      CRISPATE
      PICRATES
      PRACTISE
CL  SCEPTRAL
      SPECTRAL
CM  CRAMPETS
CU  CAPTURES
      PRESCUTA
DE  PREDATES
      REPASTED
      TRAPESED
DI  RAPIDEST
      SPIRATED
      TRAIPSED
DM  STRAMPED
DO  ADOPTERS
```


```
      ASPORTED
      READOPTS
DP  STRAPPED
DU  PASTURED
      UPSTARED
EH  PREHEATS
      SPREATHE
EI  PETARIES
EK  PERTAKES
EL  PRELATES
EM  TEMPERAS
EO  OPERATES
      PROTEASE
ER  TAPERERS
ES  TRAPESES
EU  EPURATES
      SUPERATE
EZ  TRAPEZES
FO  FOREPAST
FS  PRESSFAT
GI  GRAPIEST
GN  TREPANGS
GO  PORTAGES
HM  HAMPSTER
HN  PANTHERS
HS  SHARPEST
      SPARTHES
II  PARITIES
IK  PARKIEST
IL  PILASTER
      PLAISTER
      PLAITERS
IM  PRIMATES
IN  PAINTERS
      PANTRIES
      PERTAINS
      PINASTER
      REPAINTS
IP  PERIAPTS
IS  PASTRIES
      PIASTRES
      RASPIEST
      TRAIPSES
IV  PRIVATES
IW  WIRETAPS
IY  ASPERITY
KL  SPARKLET
LM  TRAMPLES
LN  PANTLERS
      PLANTERS
      REPLANTS
LO  PETROSAL
LS  PLASTERS
      PSALTERS
      STAPLERS
LT  PARTLETS
      PLATTERS
      PRATTLES
      SPLATTER
      SPRATTLE
LU  APLUSTRE
LY  PLASTERY
      PSALTERY
MR  TRAMPERS
MS  STAMPERS
MT  TRAMPETS
MU  TEMPURAS
      UPSTREAM
NO  OPERANTS
```


```
      PRONATES
NP  PARPENTS
NR  PARTNERS
NS  PASTERNS
NT  PATTERNS
      TRANSEPT
NU  PERSAUNT
OR  PRAETORS
      PRORATES
OS  ESPARTOS
      PORTASES
      PROTASES
      SEAPORTS
OT  PROSTATE
OU  APTEROUS
OV  OVERPAST
PR  STRAPPER
      TRAPPERS
QU  PARQUETS
RU  PARTURES
      RAPTURES
SS  SPARSEST
ST  SPATTERS
SU  PASTURES
      UPSTARES
SY  YAPSTERS
TU  STUPRATE
TY  TAPESTRY
UX  SUPERTAX

AERRST  138
(RATERS)
AN  NARRATES
AO  AERATORS
AS  TARRASES
AT  TARTARES
BE  REBATERS
      TABRERES
      TEREBRAS
BI  ARBITERS
BO  ARBORETS
      TABORERS
CC  CARRECTS
CE  CATERERS
      RETRACES
      TERRACES
CF  REFRACTS
CH  CHARTERS
      RECHARTS
      STARCHER
CI  ERRATICS
CK  TRACKERS
CO  ACROTERS
      CREATORS
      REACTORS
CT  RETRACTS
DE  ARRESTED
      DREAREST
      RETREADS
      SERRATED
      TREADERS
DF  DRAFTERS
      REDRAFTS
DG  DRAGSTER
DO  ROADSTER
DT  REDSTART
EE  ARRESTEE
```


```
EF  FERRATES
EG  REGRATES
EI  ARTERIES
      ROASTERS
      REASTIER
EK  RETAKERS
      STREAKER
EL  RELATERS
EM  STREAMER
EN  TERRANES
EP  TAPERERS
ER  ARRESTER
      REARREST
ES  ASSERTER
      REASSERT
      SERRATES
      TERRASES
ET  RETRATES
      RETREATS
      TREATERS
EU  AUSTERER
      TREASURE
EV  TRAVERSE
EW  WATERERS
FG  GRAFTERS
FI  FRATRIES
FN  TRANSFER
GN  GRANTERS
      REGRANTS
GO  GARROTES
HH  THRASHER
HI  TRASHIER
HU  URETHRAS
HY  TRASHERY
II  RARITIES
IL  RETIRALS
      RETRIALS
      TRAILERS
IN  RESTRAIN
      RETRAINS
      STRAINER
      TERRAINS
      TRAINERS
      TRANSIRE
IO  ROARIEST
      ROTARIES
IR  STARRIER
      TARRIERS
IS  TARSIERS
IT  RETRAITS
      STRAITER
      TARRIEST
IW  STRAWIER
      SWARTIER
KS  STARKERS
LO  REALTORS
      RELATORS
LT  RATTLERS
      STARTLER
LW  TRAWLERS
MO  REARMOST
MP  TRAMPERS
NO  ANTRORSE
NP  PARTNERS
NT  TRANTERS
OO  SORORATE
OP  PRAETORS
      PRORATES
OR  ARRESTOR
OS  ASSERTOR
```


```
      ASSORTER
      ORATRESS
      ROASTERS
OT  ROSTRATE
PP  STRAPPER
      TRAPPERS
PU  PARTURES
      RAPTURES
QU  QUARTERS
ST  RESTARTS
      STARTERS
      TREATERS
SU  SERRATUS
SY  STRAYERS
UY  TREASURY

AERSTT  97
(TASTER)
AB  RABATTES
      TABARETS
AC  CASTRATE
AD  ASTARTED
AE  STEARATE
AG  REGATTAS
AI  ARIETTAS
      ARISTATE
AN  TARTANES
AO  AEROSTAT
AR  TARTARES
AU  SATURATE
BE  ABETTERS
BI  BIRETTAS
BL  BATTLERS
      BLATTERS
      BRATTLES
BO  ABETTORS
      BATTEROS
      TABORETS
BU  ABUTTERS
CD  DETRACTS
      SCRATTED
CH  CHATTERS
      RATCHETS
CI  CITRATES
      CRISTATE
      SCATTIER
CJ  TRAJECTS
CK  RACKETTS
CL  CLATTERS
      SCRATTLE
CN  TRANECTS
      TRANSECT
CO  SECTATOR
CR  RETRACTS
CS  SCATTERS
CT  TETRACTS
CU  CRUSTATE
CX  EXTRACTS
CY  SCATTERY
DE  ASTERTED
      RESTATED
DI  STRAITED
      STRIATED
DL  STARTLED
DR  REDSTART
DU  STATURED
EG  GREATEST
EH  THEATERS
      THEATRES
EI  ARIETTES
```


```
      ASSORTER
      TEARIEST
      TREATIES
OT  ROSTRATE
PP  STRAPPER
      TRAPPERS
EM  TEAMSTER
EN  ENTREATS
      RATTEENS
ER  RETRATES
      RETREATS
      TREATERS
ES  ESTREATS
      RESTATES
ET  ATTESTER
EX  EXTREATS
FH  FARTHEST
FL  FATTRELS
      FLATTERS
GI  STRIGATE
GO  GAROTTES
GY  STRATEGY
HO  RHEOSTAT
HS  SHATTERS
HY  SHATTERY
IL  TERTIALS
IM  MISTREAT
      TERATISM
IN  INTREATS
      NITRATES
      STRAITEN
      TARTINES
      TERTIANS
IR  RETRAITS
      STRAITER
      TARRIEST
IS  ARTISTES
      ARTSIEST
      STRIATES
IT  RATTIEST
      TARTIEST
      TITRATES
IW  WARTIEST
IX  EXTRAITS
KS  STARKEST
LM  MALTSTER
      MARTLETS
LN  SLATTERN
      TRENTALS
LP  PARTLETS
      PLATTERS
      PRATTLES
      SPLATTER
      SPRATTLE
LR  RATTLERS
      STARTLER
LS  SLATTERS
      STARLETS
      STARTLES
LT  TARTLETS
      TATTLERS
LU  LUSTRATE
      TUTELARS
LY  SLATTERY
MP  TRAMPETS
MS  MATTRESS
      SMARTEST
      SMATTERS
MU  MATUREST
      TESTAMUR
NN  ENTRANTS
```

NO	ORNATEST	MN	TRANSMEW		RELAYING
NP	PATTERNS		TREWSMAN		YEARLING
	TRANSEPT	NU	UNWATERS	FF	RAFFLING
NR	TRANTERS	NY	STERNWAY	GG	GARGLING
NS	TARTNESS	OU	OUTSWEAR		RAGGLING
NU	TAUNTERS		OUTWEARS	GI	GLAIRING
OP	PROSTATE	ST	SWATTERS	GN	GNARLING
OR	ROSTRATE			GY	GRAYLING
OS	STRATOSE	**AGILNR 199**			RAGINGLY
	TOASTERS	(RALING)		HS	HARLINGS
OT	ATTESTOR	AE	REGALIAN		RINGHALS
	TESTATOR	AG	GANGLIAR	HY	NARGHILY
OU	OUTRATES	AK	KRAALING	IO	ORIGINAL
	OUTSTARE	AM	ALARMING	IS	GLAIRINS
PS	SPATTERS		MARGINAL		RAILINGS
	TAPSTERS	AR	LARRIGAN	IT	RINGTAIL
PU	STUPRATE	BB	RABBLING		TRAILING
PY	TAPESTRY	BD	BARDLING	IV	VIRGINAL
QU	QUARTETS	BE	BLEARING	KN	RANKLING
RS	RESTARTS	BG	GARBLING	LU	ALLURING
	STARTERS	BI	BRAILING		LINGULAR
SU	STATURES	BM	MARBLING	LY	NARGILLY
SW	SWATTERS	BO	LABORING		RALLYING
UV	VETTURAS	BT	BRATLING	MS	MARLINGS
VY	TRAVESTY	BW	BRAWLING	NS	SNARLING
			WARBLING	OP	PAROLING
AERSTW 194		CD	CRADLING	OT	TRIGONAL
(WATERS)		CE	CLEARING	PS	SPARLING
AD	EASTWARD	CO	ORACLING		SPRINGAL
BD	BEDSTRAW	CT	CLARTING	ST	RATLINGS
BI	WARBIEST	CW	CRAWLING		STARLING
BL	BLEWARTS	DD	RADDLING	SU	SINGULAR
BS	WABSTERS	DE	DEARLING	SW	WARLINGS
CH	WATCHERS		DRAGLINE	TT	RATTLING
DE	DEWATERS	DI	DRAILING	TW	TRAWLING
	TARWEEDS	DK	DARKLING	VY	RAVINGLY
	WASTERED	DS	DARLINGS	WW	WRAWLING
DI	TAWDRIES	DT	DARTLING	WX	WRAXLING
DS	STEWARDS	DW	DRAWLING		
DW	WESTWARD	DY	DARINGLY	**AGILNT 174**	
EG	STREWAGE	EE	ALGERINE	(LATING)	
EH	WEATHERS	EG	GANGLIER	AB	ABLATING
	WREATHES		REGALING	AE	AGENTIAL
EI	SWEATIER	EH	NARGHILE		ALGINATE
	TAWERIES		NARGILEH	AO	GALTONIA
	WEARIEST	EI	GAINLIER	AP	PALATING
ER	WATERERS	EJ	JANGLIER	BE	BELATING
ES	SWEATERS	EM	GERMINAL		BLEATING
FO	FORWASTE		MALIGNER		TANGIBLE
	SOFTWARE		MALINGER	BI	LIBATING
FS	FRETSAWS	EN	LEARNING	BN	BANTLING
FU	WAFTURES	EO	GERANIOL	BO	BLOATING
HI	SWATHIER		REGIONAL		OBLIGANT
	WATERISH	EP	PEARLING	BR	BRATLING
HM	MAWTHERS	ER	GNARLIER	BS	BLASTING
II	WISTERIA	ES	ARLESING		STABLING
IM	WARTIMES		ENGRAILS		TABLINGS
IN	TINWARES		NARGILES	BT	BATTLING
IP	WIRETAPS		REALIGNS		BLATTING
IR	STRAWIER		SANGLIER	BY	TANGIBLY
	SWARTIER		SLANGIER	CE	CLEATING
IS	WAISTERS	ET	ALERTING	CH	LATCHING
	WAITRESS		ALTERING	CK	TACKLING
	WASTRIES		INTEGRAL	CN	CANTLING
IT	WARTIEST		RELATING	CO	LOCATING
LR	TRAWLERS		TANGLIER	CR	CLARTING
LS	WARTLESS		TRIANGLE	CS	CASTLING
	WASTRELS	EX	RELAXING		CATLINGS
LZ	WALTZERS	EY	LAYERING		SCLATING

CT	CLATTING	PS	PLATINGS		GREASING
CU	CLAUTING		SPALTING		SNAGGIER
DE	DELATING		STAPLING	EH	HEARINGS
DI	DILATING	PT	PLATTING		HEARSING
DR	DARTLING	RS	RATLINGS		SHEARING
EE	GALENITE		STARLING	EK	SKEARING
	GELATINE	RT	RATTLING	EL	ARLESING
EG	TEAGLING	RW	TRAWLING		ENGRAILS
EH	ATHELING	SS	ANGLISTS		NARGILES
EM	LIGAMENT		LASTINGS		REALIGNS
EN	GANTLINE		SALTINGS		SANGLIER
	LATENING		SLATINGS		SLANGIER
EO	GELATION	ST	SLATTING	EM	GERMAINS
	LEGATION	SU	SALUTING		SMEARING
EP	PLEATING	TT	TATTLING	EN	AGINNERS
ER	ALERTING	TW	WATTLING		EARNINGS
	ALTERING	UV	VAULTING		ENGRAINS
	INTEGRAL	UX	LUXATING		GRANNIES
	RELATING	WZ	WALTZING	EO	IGNAROES
	TANGLIER				ORGANISE
	TRIANGLE	**AGINRS 123**			ORIGANES
ES	EASTLING	(GRAINS)		EP	PREASING
	GELATINS	AB	BARGAINS		SPEARING
	GENITALS	AE	ANGARIES	ER	EARRINGS
	STEALING	AI	ARAISING		GRAINERS
EV	VALETING	AR	ARRAIGNS	ES	REASSIGN
EX	EXALTING	AS	SANGRIAS		SEARINGS
EZ	TEAZLING		SARANGIS		SERINGAS
FH	FANLIGHT	AY	ARAYSING	ET	ANGRIEST
FL	FLATLING	BD	BRIGANDS		ASTRINGE
FO	FLOATING	BE	BEARINGS		GANISTER
FS	FATLINGS		SABERING		GANTRIES
FT	FLATTING	BH	BRASHING		GRANITES
FU	FAULTING	BI	BRAISING		INGRATES
GI	LIGATING	BR	BARRINGS		RANGIEST
	TAIGLING	BT	BRASTING		REASTING
GN	GNATLING	CE	CREASING		STEARING
	TANGLING		GRECIANS	EV	VINEGARS
GO	GLOATING		SEARCING	EW	SWEARING
	GOATLING	CF	FARCINGS		WEARINGS
HL	ALLNIGHT		SCARFING	EY	RESAYING
HO	LOATHING	CH	CHAGRINS	FI	FAIRINGS
HS	HALTINGS		CRASHING		FRAISING
	LATHINGS	CK	ARCKINGS	FM	FARMINGS
IO	INTAGLIO		RACKINGS		FRAMINGS
	LIGATION	CP	CARPINGS	FT	INGRAFTS
	TAGLIONI		SCARPING		STRAFING
IP	PLAITING		SCRAPING	FW	SWARFING
IR	RINGTAIL	CR	SCARRING	FY	FRAYINGS
	TRAILING	CS	SACRINGS	GG	RAGGINGS
IS	TAILINGS	CT	SCARTING	GI	AGRISING
IT	LITIGANT		TRACINGS	GP	GRASPING
IV	VIGILANT	CU	SCAURING		SPARGING
KS	SKLATING	CV	CARVINGS	GS	GRASSING
	STALKING		CRAVINGS		SIRGANGS
	TALKINGS	DE	DERAIGNS	GT	GRATINGS
KY	TAKINGLY	DF	FARDINGS	GU	SUGARING
LS	STALLING	DG	NIGGARDS	GV	GRAVINGS
LY	TALLYING	DL	DARLINGS	GZ	GRAZINGS
MN	MANTLING	DM	MRIDANGS	HK	SHARKING
MS	MALTINGS	DN	DARNINGS	HL	HARLINGS
NP	PLANTING	DO	ROADINGS		RINGHALS
NS	SLANTING	DT	TRADINGS	HP	HARPINGS
	TANLINGS	DW	DRAWINGS		PHRASING
OP	PLOATING		SWARDING		SHARPING
OR	TRIGONAL		WARDINGS	HS	SHARINGS
OS	ANTILOGS	EE	GESNERIA	HT	TRASHING
	SALTOING	EG	GEARINGS	IL	GLAIRINS
OY	ANTILOGY				RAILINGS
				IN	INGRAINS

```
IO SIGNORIA
IP ASPIRING
   PAIRINGS
   PRAISING
IS RAISINGS
JR JARRINGS
KM MARKINGS
KN RANKINGS
KP PARKINGS
   SPARKING
KS SARKINGS
KT KARTINGS
   STARKING
LM MARLINGS
LN SNARLING
LP SPARLING
   SPRINGAL
LT RATLINGS
   STARLING
LU SINGULAR
LW WARLINGS
   WARSLING
MM SMARMING
MO ORGANISM
MT MIGRANTS
   SMARTING
MW SWARMING
   WARMINGS
MY MYRINGAS
NR SNARRING
NS SNARINGS
NT STARNING
NW WARNINGS
OR GARRISON
   ROARINGS
OS ASSIGNOR
   SIGNORAS
   SOARINGS
OT ORGANIST
   ROASTING
OU AROUSING
OV SAVORING
PP RAPPINGS
PR SPARRING
PS PARSINGS
   RASPINGS
PT PARTINGS
   PRATINGS
PW WARPINGS
PY PRAYINGS
   SPRAYING
QU SQUARING
RT STARRING
   TARRINGS
ST GASTRINS
   STARINGS
SU ASSURING
SY SYRINGAS
TT RATTINGS
   STARTING
TV STARVING
TW STRAWING
   WRASTING
TY STRAYING
VW SWARVING
VY VARYINGS
WY RINGWAYS
```


```
AGINRT 69
(RATING)
AE AERATING
BE BERATING
   REBATING
BL BRATLING
BO ABORTING
   TABORING
BS BRASTING
CE CATERING
   CITRANGE
   CREATING
   REACTING
CF CRAFTING
   FRACTING
CH CHARTING
CI GRANITIC
CK TRACKING
CL CLARTING
CN TRANCING
CS SCARTING
   TRACINGS
CT TRACTING
DE DERATING
   GRADIENT
   TREADING
DF DRAFTING
DL DARTLING
DN DRANTING
DS TRADINGS
DY TARDYING
EH EARTHING
   HEARTING
EK RETAKING
EL ALERTING
   ALTERING
   INTEGRAL
   RELATING
   TANGLIER
   TRIANGLE
EM EMIGRANT
EP TAPERING
ES ANGRIEST
   ASTRINGE
   GANISTER
   GRANITES
   INGRATES
   RANGIEST
   REASTING
   STEARING
ET ARETTING
   TREATING
EV AVERTING
EW TWANGIER
   WATERING
FG GRAFTING
FH FARTHING
FS INGRAFTS
   STRAFING
FU FIGURANT
GN GRANTING
GS GRATINGS
GY GYRATING
HJ NIGHTJAR
HS TRASHING
HW THRAWING
   WRATHING
```


```
IK TRAIKING
IL RINGTAIL
   TRAILING
IN TRAINING
IP PIRATING
IT ATTIRING
KS KARTINGS
   STARKING
LO TRIGONAL
LS RATLINGS
   STARLING
LT RATTLING
LW TRAWLING
MP TRAMPING
MS MIGRANTS
   SMARTING
MU MATURING
NO IGNORANT
NS STARNING
NT TRANTING
NU NATURING
NY TRAYNING
   TYRANING
OO ROGATION
OS ORGANIST
   ROASTING
OT ROTATING
   TROATING
OV GRAVITON
OY GYRATION
   ORGANITY
PP TRAPPING
PS PARTINGS
   PRATINGS
PT PRATTING
PU UPRATING
PY PARTYING
RS STARRING
   TARRINGS
RY TARRYING
SS GASTRINS
   STARINGS
ST RATTINGS
   STARTING
SV STARVING
SW STRAWING
   WRASTING
SY STRAYING

AGINST 108
(SATING)
AE SAGINATE
AS ASSIGNAT
BB STABBING
BD DINGBATS
BE BEATINGS
BI BAITINGS
BL BLASTING
   STABLING
   TABLINGS
BN BANTINGS
BO BOASTING
   BOATINGS
   BOSTANGI
BR BRASTING
BS BASTINGS
BT BATTINGS
BW BATSWING
CH SCATHING
CK STACKING
```


```
   TACKINGS
CL CASTLING
   CATLINGS
   SCLATING
CN CANTINGS
CO AGNOSTIC
   COASTING
   COATINGS
   COTINGAS
CR SCARTING
   TRACINGS
CS CASTINGS
CT SCATTING
DE SEDATING
   STEADING
DN STANDING
DO DOATINGS
DR TRADINGS
DU ADUSTING
   SUDATING
EE SAGENITE
EF FEASTING
EG NAGGIEST
EH GAHNITES
   HEATINGS
EL EASTLING
   GELATINS
   GENITALS
   STEALING
EM MANGIEST
   MINTAGES
   STEAMING
   TEAMINGS
EN ANTIGENS
   GENTIANS
   STEANING
ER ANGRIEST
   ASTRINGE
   GANISTER
   GANTRIES
   GRANITES
   INGRATES
   RANGIEST
   REASTING
   STEARING
ES EASTINGS
   GENISTAS
   GIANTESS
   SEATINGS
   TEASINGS
   TSIGANES
ET ESTATING
   TANGIEST
EU SAUTEING
EV VINTAGES
EW SWEATING
EY YEASTING
FF STAFFING
FH SHAFTING
FL FATLINGS
FR INGRAFTS
   STRAFING
FS FASTINGS
FW WAFTINGS
GG STAGGING
GH GHASTING
GI AGISTING
GN STANGING
GR GRATINGS
```


```
GS STAGINGS
HL HALTINGS
   LATHINGS
HN TANGHINS
HO HOASTING
HR TRASHING
HS HASTINGS
   STASHING
HT HATTINGS
HW SWATHING
   THAWINGS
IL TAILINGS
IM GIANTISM
IN SAINTING
   SATINING
   STAINING
IV VISTAING
IW WAITINGS
KL SKLATING
   STALKING
   TALKINGS
KN TANKINGS
KO GOATSKIN
KR KARTINGS
   STARKING
KS SKATINGS
   TASKINGS
LL STALLING
LM MALTINGS
LN SLANTING
   TANLINGS
LO ANTILOGS
   SALTOING
LP PLATINGS
   SPALTING
   STAPLING
LR RATLINGS
   STARLING
LS ANGLISTS
   LASTINGS
   SALTINGS
   SLATINGS
LT SLATTING
LU SALUTING
MP STAMPING
   TAMPINGS
MR MIGRANTS
   SMARTING
MT MATTINGS
NN TANNINGS
NO ASTONING
NP PANTINGS
NR STARNING
NU SAUNTING
   UNSATING
NW WANTINGS
NY STAYNING
OR ORGANIST
   ROASTING
OS AGONISTS
OT TANGOIST
   TOASTING
PP STAPPING
   TAPPINGS
PR PARTINGS
   PRATINGS
PS PASTINGS
PT SPATTING
RR STARRING
   TARRINGS
```


```
RS GASTRINS
   STARINGS
RT RATTINGS
   STARTING
RV STARVING
RW STRAWING
   WRASTING
RY STRAYING
ST TASTINGS
SW WASTINGS
SY STAYINGS
TT TATTINGS
TW SWATTING

AINRST 40
(TRAINS)
AB ATABRINS
   BARTISAN
AC ARCANIST
AD RADIANTS
AE ANTISERA
   ARTESIAN
   RESINATA
AI INTARSIA
AM TAMARINS
AP ASPIRANT
   PARTISAN
AS ARTISANS
   TSARINAS
AV VARIANTS
AY SANITARY
BE ATEBRINS
   BANISTER
BG BRASTING
BO TABORINS
CE CANISTER
   CARNIEST
   NACRITES
   SCANTIER
CF INFARCTS
   INFRACTS
CG SCARTING
   TRACINGS
CO CANTORIS
   CAROTINS
CP CANTRIPS
CU CURTAINS
   SATURNIC
   TURACINS
DE DETRAINS
   RANDIEST
   STRAINED
DF INDRAFTS
DG TRADINGS
DI DISTRAIN
DK STINKARD
DO INTRADOS
DR TRIDARNS
EE ARSENITE
   RESINATE
   STEARINE
   TRAINEES
EF FENITARS
EG ANGRIEST
   ASTRINGE
   GANISTER
   GANTRIES
   GRANITES
   INGRATES
   RANGIEST
```

```
      REASTING
      STEARING
EH INEARTHS
EI INERTIAS
      RAINIEST
EJ NARTJIES
EK KERATINS
EL ENTRAILS
      LATRINES
      RATLINES
      TRENAILS
EM MINARETS
      RAIMENTS
EN ENTRAINS
      TRANNIES
EO ANOESTRI
      ARSONITE
      NOTARIES
      NOTARISE
      ROSINATE
EP PAINTERS
      PANTRIES
      PERTAINS
      PINASTER
      REPAINTS
ER RESTRAIN
      RETRAINS
      STRAINER
      TERRAINS
      TRAINERS
      TRANSIRE
ES RESIANTS
      RETSINAS
      SNARIEST
      STAINERS
      STARNIES
      STEARINS
ET INTREATS
      NITRATES
      STRAITEN
      TARTINES
      TERTIANS
EU RUINATES
      URANITES
      URINATES
EW TINWARES
FG INGRAFTS
      STRAFING
FK RATFINKS
FX TRANSFIX
GG GRATINGS
GH TRASHING
GK KARTINGS
      STARKING
GL RATLINGS
      STARLING
GM MIGRANTS
      SMARTING
GN RANTINGS
GO ORGANIST
      ROASTING
GP PARTINGS
      PRATINGS
GR STARRING
      TARRINGS
GS GASTRINS
      STARINGS
GT RATTINGS
      STARTING
```


```
GV STARVING
GW STRAWING
      WRASTING
GY STRAYING
HL INTHRALS
HO TRAHISON
HP TRANSHIP
HY RHYTINAS
IM MARTINIS
IO INTARSIO
IV VITRAINS
JO JANITORS
KO SKIATRON
LT RATTLINS
LU LUNARIST
MT TRANSMIT
MU NATRIUMS
      NATURISM
MV VARMINTS
NT INTRANTS
NU INSURANT
NY TYRANNIS
OO ORATIONS
OP ATROPINS
OS ARSONIST
OT STRONTIA
OU SUTORIAN
OX TRIAXONS
PS SPIRANTS
      SPRAINTS
PU PURITANS
      UPTRAINS
ST STRAINTS
      TRANSITS
TU NATURIST
TY TANISTRY

ANORST  60
  (RATONS)
AD ONDATRAS
AE ANOESTRA
AH ATHANORS
AY SANTOURS
BE BARONETS
BI TABORINS
BY BARYTONS
CE ANCESTOR
      ENACTORS
      SARCONET
      SORTANCE
CH CHANTORS
CI CANTORIS
      CAROTINS
CO CARTOONS
      CORANTOS
CT CONTRAST
CU COURANTS
DE TORNADES
DI INTRADOS
DM DORMANTS
      MORDANTS
DO DONATORS
DU ROTUNDAS
DW SANDWORT
EE RESONATE
EG ORANGEST
      RAGSTONE
EI ANOESTRI
      ARSONITE
```


```
      NOTARIES
      NOTARISE
      ROSINATE
EM MONSTERA
      STOREMAN
EN RESONANT
EP OPERANTS
      PRONATES
ER ANTRORSE
ES ASSENTOR
      SENATORS
      TREASONS
ET ORNATEST
EV VENATORS
FF AFFRONTS
FL FRONTALS
FM FORMANTS
GH STAGHORN
GI ORGANIST
      ROASTING
GM ANGSTROM
GR GRANTORS
HI TRAHISON
HL ALTHORNS
II INTARSIO
IJ JANITORS
IK SKIATRON
IO ORATIONS
IP ATROPINS
IS ARSONIST
IT STRONTIA
IU SUTORIAN
IX TRIAXONS
KO OSTRAKON
KU OUTRANKS
LO ORTOLANS
LP PLASTRON
MS TRANSOMS
MU ROMAUNTS
NO SONORANT
OP PATROONS
OT ARNOTTOS
SU SANTOURS
VY SOVRANTY

BEIRST  184
  (TRIBES)
AD BARDIEST
      BRAIDEST
      RABIDEST
      TRIBADES
AK BARKIEST
      BRAKIEST
      BREASKIT
AL LIBRATES
AM BARMIEST
AN ATEBRINS
      BANISTER
AO SABOTIER
AR ARBITERS
      RAREBITS
AT BIRETTAS
AV VIBRATES
AW WARBIEST
AY BESTIARY
      SYBARITE
BI RIBBIEST
BL STIBBLER
BU STUBBIER
```


```
      SUBTRIBE
CH BRITCHES
CO BISECTOR
CU BRUCITES
DE BEDRITES
      BESTRIDE
DL BRISTLED
      DRIBLETS
DO DEBITORS
EE BEERIEST
EF BRIEFEST
EH HERBIEST
EU UBERTIES
FL FILBERTS
FS FIBSTERS
GL GILBERTS
HL BLITHERS
HR REBIRTHS
HS HERBISTS
IL TRILBIES
IN BRINIEST
IO ORBITIES
IS BIRSIEST
KS BRISKEST
      BRISKETS
LM TIMBRELS
LO STROBILE
      TRILOBES
LS BLISTERS
      BRISTLES
LT BRITTLES
      TRIBLETS
LU BURLIEST
      SUBTILER
LY BLISTERY
MU IMBRUTES
      TERBIUMS
NO BORNITES
      RIBSTONE
NT BITTERNS
NU TRIBUNES
      TURBINES
OO ROBOTISE
OR ORBITERS
OY SOBRIETY
QU BRIQUETS
RU BURRIEST
SU BUSTIERS
TU TRIBUTES
TY TREYBITS

CEINOS  109
  (CONIES)
AC COCAINES
AD DIOCESAN
      OCEANIDS
AG COINAGES
AN CANONISE
AP CANOPIES
      CAPONISE
      PAEONICS
AR SCENARIO
AT ACONITES
      CANOEIST
BL BINOCLES
BM COMBINES
CD CONCISED
CH CONCHIES
CN INSCONCE
```


```
CR CONCISER
      CORNICES
CS CONCISES
CT CONCEITS
DE CODEINES
DF CONFIDES
DG COGNISED
DH HEDONICS
DI DECISION
      ICONISED
DL INCLOSED
DO COOSINED
DR CONSIDER
DT DEONTICS
DU DOUCINES
DZ ZINCODES
EL CINEOLES
ES SENECIOS
ET SEICENTO
FN CONFINES
FR CONIFERS
      FORENSIC
      FORINSEC
      INFORCES
FX CONFIXES
GL ECLOSING
GS COGNISES
GZ COGNIZES
HL CHOLINES
HO COHESION
HP CHOPINES
HR CHORINES
HY HYOSCINE
IL ISOCLINE
      SILICONE
IN CONIINES
      OSCININE
IP EPINOSIC
IR RECISION
IS ICONISES
IV INVOICES
IX EXCISION
IZ ICONIZES
LL LIONCELS
LO COLONIES
      COLONISE
      ECLOSION
LP PINOCLES
LR INCLOSER
      LICENSOR
LS CONSEILS
      INCLOSES
LT LECTIONS
LX LEXICONS
MN MECONINS
MR CREMOSIN
      INCOMERS
      SERMONIC
NR INCENSOR
NV CONNIVES
OT COONTIES
PR CONSPIRE
      INCORPSE
RR RESORCIN
RS NECROSIS
      SERICONS
RT CORNIEST
      RECTIONS
RU NOURICES
```


```
      ROUNCIES
SS CESSIONS
      COSINESS
ST SECTIONS
SX COXINESS
TT CENTOIST
      STENOTIC
TU COUNTIES
TX EXCITONS
TY CYTOSINE
UV UNVOICES
VV CONVIVES

CEINRS  183
  (INCERS)
AA CANARIES
AB CARBINES
AE CINEREAS
      INCREASE
AF FANCIERS
AG CREASING
      GRECIANS
      SEARCING
AH INARCHES
AI RIANCIES
AL CARLINES
AM CARMINES
AN CRANNIES
AO SCENARIO
AS ARSENICS
      CERASINS
      RACINESS
AT CANISTER
      CARNIEST
      NACRITES
      SCANTIER
BI INSCRIBE
BU BRUCINES
CO CONCISER
      CORNICES
DO CONSIDER
DP PRESCIND
DS DISCERNS
      RESCINDS
DU INDUCERS
EE CERESINE
EG CREESING
      GENERICS
EH ENRICHES
      INHERCES
EK SICKENER
EL LICENSER
      RECLINES
      SILENCER
EN INCENSER
ER SINCERER
ES CERESINS
      SCRIENES
ET CENTRIES
      ENTERICS
      ENTICERS
EU INSECURE
      SINECURE
FO CONIFERS
      FORENSIC
      FORINSEC
      INFORCES
```

GL CLINGERS
   CRINGLES
GN SCERNING
GR CRINGERS
GT CRESTING
GU RECUSING
   RESCUING
   SCUNGIER
   SECURING
GW SCREWING
GY SYNERGIC
HO CHORINES
HP PINCHERS
HS RICHNESS
HT CHRISTEN
   CITHERNS
   SNITCHER
IO RECISION
   SORICINE
IS SERICINS
IT CITRINES
   CRINITES
   INCITERS
IU INCISURE
   SCIURINE
KK KNICKERS
KL CLINKERS
   CRINKLES
KS SNICKERS
KT STRICKEN
KU UNSICKER
LO INCLOSER
   LICENSOR
MO CREMOSIN
   INCOMERS
   SERMONIC
MT CENTRISM
NO INCENSOR
OP CONSPIRE
   INCORPSE
OR RESORCIN
OS NECROSIS
   SERICONS
OT CORNIEST
   RECTIONS
OU NOURICES
   ROUNCIES
PS PRINCESS
ST CISTERNS
TT CENTRIST
   CITTERNS
TU CURNIEST
UV INCURVES
VV CRIVVENS

CEINST 196
(INSECT)
AA ESTANCIA
AB CABINETS
AD DISTANCE
AE CINEASTE
AF FANCIEST
AH ASTHENIC
   CHANTIES
AI CANITIES
AM SEMANTIC
AN ANCIENTS
   CANNIEST
   INSTANCE
AO ACONITES

   CANOEIST
AR CANISTER
   CARNIEST
   NACRITES
   SCANTIER
AS CINEASTS
   SCANTIES
AT CANTIEST
   NICTATES
AV CISTVAEN
   VESICANT
AY CYANITES
CH TECHNICS
CO CONCEITS
CY SYNECTIC
DH SNITCHED
DO DEONTICS
DY SYNDETIC
EG GENETICS
EH SITHENCE
EI NICETIES
EK NECKTIES
EM CENTIMES
EN NESCIENT
EO SEICENTO
EP PECTINES
   PENTICES
ER CENTRIES
   ENTERICS
   ENTICERS
   SCIENTER
   SECRETIN
ES CENTESIS
FL INFLECTS
GH ETCHINGS
GN SCENTING
GR CRESTING
HI ICHNITES
HK KITCHENS
   KNITCHES
   THICKENS
HL LINCHETS
   TINCHELS
HR CHRISTEN
   CITHERNS
   SNITCHER
HS SNITCHES
HW WITCHENS
HZ CHINTZES
IK KINETICS
IN INSCIENT
IR CITRINES
   CRINITES
   INCITERS
IU CUTINISE
IY CYTISINE
   SYENITIC
IZ CITIZENS
   ZINCIEST
   ZINCITES
KR STRICKEN
KS SNICKETS
LO LECTIONS
LS STENCILS
LU CUTLINES
   TUNICLES
MR CENTRISM
OO COONTIES
OR CORNIEST
   RECTIONS

OS SECTIONS
OT CENTOIST
   STENOTIC
OU COUNTIES
OX EXCITONS
OY CYTOSINE
PS INSPECTS
PY PYCNITES
RS CISTERNS
RT CENTRIST
   CITTERNS
RU CURNIEST

CEIORS 156
(COSIER)
AB AEROBICS
AD IDOCRASE
AL CALORIES
   CARIOLES
AN SCENARIO
AV COVARIES
   VARICOSE
BH BRIOCHES
BL BRICOLES
   CORBEILS
BM CROMBIES
   MICROBES
BR CRIBROSE
CK COCKSIER
CN CONCISER
   CORNICES
CT CORTICES
DL SCLEROID
DN CONSIDER
DO CORODIES
DS DISCOERS
DT CORDITES
DU DISCOURE
DV DISCOVER
   DIVORCES
DW CROWDIES
DY DECISORY
EH CHEERIOS
EJ REJOICES
ET COTERIES
   ESOTERIC
EX EXORCISE
FF OFFICERS
FI ORIFICES
FN CONIFERS
   FORENSIC
   FORINSEC
   INFORCES
FP FORCIPES
GG GEORGICS
   SCROGGIE
HM MORICHES
HN CHORINES
HO CHOOSIER
   ISOCHORE
HP SOPHERIC
HS CHORISES
   ORCHESIS
   ORCHISES
HT ROTCHIES
   THEORICS
HW CHOWRIES
IM ISOMERIC
IN RECISION

   SORICINE
IP IRISCOPE
KM OCKERISM
KR ROCKIERS
KT CORKIEST
   ROCKIEST
   STOCKIER
LL COLLIERS
   ORSELLIC
LN INCLOSER
   LICENSOR
LT CLOISTER
   COISTREL
   CORTILES
   COSTLIER
   CREOLIST
MN CREMOSIN
   INCOMERS
   SERMONIC
MP COMPRISE
MR MORRICES
MT MORTICES
MX EXORCISM
MY ISOCRYME
NN INCENSOR
NP CONSPIRE
   INCORPSE
NR RESORCIN
NS NECROSIS
   SERICONS
NT CORNIEST
   RECTIONS
NU NOURICES
   ROUNCIES
OP OPORICES
PP CROPPIES
PS PERSICOS
PT PERSICOT
PU PRECIOUS
RS CROSIERS
RU COURIERS
RZ CROZIERS
SU SCOURIES
SV CORSIVES
SW SCOWRIES
SX SIXSCORE
TT COTTIERS
TU CITREOUS
   OUTCRIES
TV EVICTORS
   VORTICES
TX EXCITORS
   EXORCIST
VY VICEROYS

CEIRST 166
(CITERS)
AD ACRIDEST
AG AGRESTIC
AH CHARIEST
   THERIACS
AL ALTRICES
   ARTICLES
   RECITALS
   SELICTAR
AM CERAMIST
   MATRICES
AN CANISTER
   CARNIEST
   NACRITES

   SCANTIER
AP CRAPIEST
   CRISPATE
   PICRATES
   PRACTISE
AR ERRATICS
AS SCARIEST
AT CITRATES
   CRISTATE
   SCATTIER
AU SURICATE
AZ CRAZIEST
BH BRITCHES
BO BISECTOR
BU BRUCITES
CI ICTERICS
CK CRICKETS
CL CIRCLETS
CO CORTICES
DE DISCREET
   DISCRETE
DH DITCHERS
DO CORDITES
DP PREDICTS
   SCRIPTED
DU CRUDITES
   CURDIEST
   CURTSIED
DV VERDICTS
EF FIERCEST
EH CHESTIER
   HERETICS
EI SERICITE
EL RETICLES
   SCLERITE
   TIERCELS
EN CENTRIES
   ENTERICS
   ENTICERS
   SCIENTER
   SECRETIN
EO COTERIES
   ESOTERIC
EP CREPIEST
   RECEIPTS
ER RECITERS
EU CERUSITE
   CUTESIER
   EUCRITES
EV VERTICES
EX EXCITERS
FU FRUTICES
GN CRESTING
GU SCUTIGER
HH HITCHERS
HI CHRISTIE
HN CHRISTEN
   CITHERNS
   SNITCHER
HO ROTCHIES
   THEORICS
HP PITCHERS
   SPITCHER
HS STRICHES
HT CHITTERS
   RICHTEST
   STITCHER
HY HYSTERIC
IK STICKIER
IM MERISTIC

   TRISEMIC
IN CITRINES
   CRINITES
   INCITERS
IP PICRITES
   PRICIEST
   RECTITIS
IV VERISTIC
JU JUSTICER
KL STICKLER
   STRICKLE
   TICKLERS
   TRICKLES
KN STRICKEN
KO CORKIEST
   ROCKIEST
   STOCKIER
KP PRICKETS
KR TRICKERS
KS STICKERS
LO CLOISTER
   COISTREL
   CORTILES
   COSTLIER
   CREOLIST
LT CLITTERS
LU CURLIEST
   UTRICLES
MN CENTRISM
MO MORTICES
MS CRETISMS
NO CORNIEST
   RECTIONS
NS CISTERNS
NT CENTRIST
   CITTERNS
NU CURNIEST
OP PERSICOT
OT COTTIERS
OU CITREOUS
   OUTCRIES
OV EVICTORS
   VORTICES
OX EXCITORS
   EXORCIST
PR RESCRIPT
PS CRISPEST
PU CREPITUS
   CUPRITES
   PICTURES
   PIECRUST
RT CRITTERS
   RESTRICT
   STRICTER
RU CRUSTIER
   RECRUITS
ST TRISECTS
SU CITRUSES
   CURTSIES
   RICTUSES
SV VICTRESS
TU TUTRICES
UV CURVIEST
UY SECURITY

CENORS 172
(CONERS)
AC CONACRES
AD DRACONES
   ENDOSARC

```
AG ACROGENS      MU CONSUMER         REEDLING        BESTRIDE     MP DEMIREPS      AS DEARNESS
   CORNAGES         MUCRONES      GN ENRINGED     CD DECIDERS        PREMISED      AU UNDERSEA
AI SCENARIO      OR CORONERS      GS DESIGNER        DESCRIED        SIMPERED      AW ANSWERED
AM CREMONAS         CROONERS         ENERGIDS     CL SCLEREID      MS DERMISES     BI INBREEDS
   ROMANCES      OT CORONETS         REDESIGN     CM MISCREED      MT DEMERITS     BL BLENDERS
AS COARSENS      OU CORNEOUS         REEDINGS     CP PRECISED         DEMISTER     BP PREBENDS
   NARCOSES      PY NECROPSY         RESIGNED     CR DECRIERS         DIMETERS     CE RECENSED
AT ANCESTOR      QU CONQUERS      HR HINDERER     CS DESCRIES         MISTERED        SCREENED
   ENACTORS      RS SCORNERS      HS DRISHEEN     CT DISCREET      NN SINNERED        SECERNED
   SARCONET      RW CROWNERS      JO REJOINED        DISCRETE      NO ORDINEES     CH DRENCHES
   SORTANCE      ST CONSTERS      KL REKINDLE     CU DECURIES      NT INSERTED     CK REDNECKS
AU CARNEOUS      TT CORNETTS      KS DEERSKIN     CV DESCRIVE         RESIDENT     CO CENSORED
   NACREOUS      TU CONSTRUE      KT TINKERED        SCRIEVED        SINTERED        NECROSED
BE OBSCENER         CORNUTES      LU UNDERLIE        SERVICED        TRENDIES        SECONDER
BU BOUNCERS         COUNTERS      MO DOMINEER     DP PRESIDED      NU UREDINES     CU CENSURED
CI CONCISER         RECOUNTS      MR REMINDER     DR DERIDERS      NV INVERSED     DO ENDORSED
   CORNICES         TROUNCES      MV VERMINED     DT REDDIEST      NW WIDENERS     DP SPREDDEN
CN CONCERNS      TV CONVERTS      NS SINNERED     DV DIVERSED      NX INDEXERS     DU SUNDERED
CT CONCERTS      TW CROWNETS      NT INDENTER     EM REMEDIES      OV OVERSIDE     EL NEEDLERS
CW CONCREWS      UU CERNUOUS      NU UNREINED     EP SPEEDIER      PR REPRISED     EO ENDORSEE
DE CENSORED      UV UNCOVERS      NV INNERVED     ES DIERESES         RESPIRED     ET RESENTED
   NECROSED      UY CYNOSURE      OS ORDINEES     ET REEDIEST      PS DESPISER     FI DEFINERS
   SECONDER                       OT ORIENTED     EZ RESEIZED         DISPERSE     GI DESIGNER
DH CHONDRES      DEEINR  43       PP NIPPERED     FI DEIFIERS         PRESIDES        ENERGIDS
DI CONSIDER       (DENIER)        QU ENQUIRED        EDIFIERS      PT PRIESTED        REDESIGN
DS CORSNEDS      AC DERACINE         INQUERED        FIRESIDE         RESPITED        REEDINGS
DW DECROWNS      AF FREDAINE      RT INTERRED     FL DEFILERS      PU DUPERIES        RESIGNED
EF ENFORCES      AG REGAINED         TRENDIER        FIELDERS      PV DEPRIVES     HI DRISHEEN
EG COGENERS      AM REMAINED      RV REDRIVEN     FN DEFINERS         PREVISED     HM HERDSMEN
   CONGREES      AP PINDAREE      ST INSERTED     FO FORESIDE      RS DERRISES     HP PREHENDS
EL ENCLOSER      AS ARSENIDE         RESIDENT     GL LEIDGERS         DESIRERS     IK DEERSKIN
ES NECROSES         DENARIES         SINTERED     GN DESIGNER         DRESSIER     IN SINNERED
EV CONSERVE         DRAISENE         TRENDIES        ENERGIDS         RESIDERS     IO ORDINEES
   CONVERSE         NEARSIDE      SU UREDINES        REDESIGN     RT DESTRIER     IT INSERTED
EZ COZENERS      AT DETAINER      SV INVERSED        REEDINGS     RU RUDERIES        RESIDENT
FI CONIFERS         RETAINED      SW WIDENERS        RESIGNED     RV REDRIVES        SINTERED
   FORENSIC      BD REBIDDEN      SX INDEXERS     GO GEORDIES      ST EDITRESS        TRENDIES
   FORINSEC      BF BEFRIEND      TU REUNITED     GT DIGESTER         RESISTED     IU UREDINES
   INFORCES      BG BREEDING      TV INVERTED        ESTRIDGE         SISTERED     IV INVERSED
FU FROUNCES      BM BRIDEMEN      TW WINTERED     GU GUDESIRE      SU DIURESES     IW WIDENERS
GH GROSCHEN      BS INBREEDS      TX DEXTRINE     GV DIVERGES         REISSUED     IX INDEXERS
GS CONGRESS      CG RECEDING                      HK SHREIKED         RESIDUES     LP RESPLEND
GU CONGRUES      CH ENRICHED      DEEIRS  58         SHRIEKED     SV DEVISERS     MO SERMONED
   SCROUNGE         INHERCED       (RESIDE)       HL RELISHED         DISSERVE     NO ENDERONS
GY CRYOGENS         NICHERED      AB BEARDIES        SHIELDER         DISSEVER     OR ENDORSER
HI CHORINES         RICHENED      AC DECIARES     HN DRISHEEN         DIVERSES     OS ENDORSES
HO COEHORNS      CK NICKERED      AF FEDARIES     HO HEROISED      TT TIREDEST     OT ERODENTS
   SCHOONER      CL RECLINED      AG DISAGREE     HP HESPERID      TU ERUDITES     OW ENDOWERS
HV CHEVRONS      CM ENDERMIC      AJ JADERIES        PERISHED         SURETIED        WORSENED
II RECISION      CP PINCERED      AL REALISED     HR REDSHIRE      TW WEIRDEST     PP PERPENDS
   SORICINE      DF FRIENDED         SIDEREAL     HV SHIVERED                      PS SPENDERS
IL INCLOSER      DG ENRIDGED      AM MADERISE        SHRIEVED      DEENRS  92      PT PRETENDS
   LICENSOR      DH HINDERED      AN ARSENIDE     IM DIMERISE       (ENDERS)       RU ENDURERS
IM CREMOSIN      DM REMINDED         DENARIES     IP EPEIRIDS      AC ASCENDER        SUNDERER
   INCOMERS      DN DINNERED         DRAISENE     IS DIERESIS         REASCEND     SU RUDENESS
   SERMONIC      DT DENDRITE         NEARSIDE     IT SIDERITE      AE ENSEARED     TU DENTURES
IN INCENSOR      EF FINEERED      AT READIEST     IV DERISIVE         SERENADE        SEDERUNT
IP CONSPIRE         REDEFINE         SERIATED     IW WEIRDIES      AG DERANGES        UNDERSET
   INCORPSE      EL NEEDLIER         STEADIER     KN DEERSKIN         GRANDEES        UNDESERT
IR RESORCIN      ER REINDEER      AV READVISE     KU DUKERIES         GRENADES     UU UNDERUSE
IS NECROSIS      FF NIFFERED      BC DESCRIBE     KV SKIVERED      AI ARSENIDE     UV UNVERSED
   SERICONS      FG FINGERED         ESCRIBED     LU LEISURED         DENARIES
IT CORNIEST      FR INFERRED      BD BIRDSEED     LV DELIVERS         DRAISENE     DEENST  111
   RECTIONS      FS DEFINERS         DEBRIDES        DESILVER         NEARSIDE      (NESTED)
IU NOURICES      FZ FRENZIED      BF DEBRIEFS        SILVERED     AK KNEADERS     AB ABSENTED
   ROUNCIES      GG GINGERED      BK KERBSIDE        SLIVERED     AM AMENDERS     AF FASTENED
JU CONJURES         NIGGERED      BN INBREEDS     LW WIELDERS         MEANDERS     AH HASTENED
KK KNOCKERS         RENIGGED      BT BEDRITES     LY YIELDERS         REAMENDS     AI ANDESITE
KT CRONKEST      GL ENGIRDLE                      MM IMMERSED      AN ENSNARED     AK NAKEDEST
LO CONSOLER         LINGERED                         SIMMERED     AO REASONED     AM STAMENED
```

AS ASSENTED
AU UNSEATED
BI BENDIEST
BL BENDLETS
CH STENCHED
CS DESCENTS
CY ENCYSTED
DI DESTINED
EF ENFESTED
EI NEEDIEST
ER RESENTED
ET DETENTES
EU DETENUES
EX DENTEXES
FI FENDIEST
   INFESTED
FO SOFTENED
FS DEFTNESS
GI INGESTED
   SIGNETED
   STEEDING
HI DISTHENE
HU ENTHUSED
II DIETINES
IL ENLISTED
   LINTSEED
   LISTENED
IM DEMENTIS
   SEDIMENT
IN DENTINES
   DESINENT
IP PENTISED
IR INSERTED
   RESIDENT
   SINTERED
   TRENDIES
IS DESTINES
IT DINETTES
IU DETINUES
IV EVIDENTS
   INVESTED
KL SKLENTED
LP SPLENTED
LY ENSTYLED
NO SONNETED
NP PENDENTS
NU UNNESTED
OP PENTODES
OR ERODENTS
OS STENOSED
PR PRETENDS
RU DENTURES
   SEDERUNT
   UNDERSET
   UNDESERT
TU UNTESTED

DEERST 151
(RESTED)
AB BETREADS
   BREASTED
   DEBATERS
AC CEDRATES
AE RESEATED
AF DRAFTEES
AG RESTAGED
AH HEADREST
AI READIEST
   SERIATED
   STEADIER

AK STREAKED
AL TREADLES
AM MASTERED
   STREAMED
AP PREDATES
   REPASTED
   TRAPESED
AR ARRESTED
   DREAREST
   RETREADS
   SERRATED
   TREADERS
AS ASSERTED
   ESTRADES
AT ASTERTED
   RESTATED
AW DEWATERS
   TARWEEDS
   WASTERED
AY ESTRAYED
BI BEDRITES
BO BESORTED
   BESTRIDE
   BESTRODE
CE DECREETS
   RESECTED
   SECRETED
CI DISCREET
   DISCRETE
CO CORSETED
   ESCORTED
   SECTORED
CP SCEPTRED
DE DESERTED
DI REDDIEST
DL TREDDLES
DU DETRUDES
EF FESTERED
EG DETERGES
EI REEDIEST
EK STREEKED
EL DEERLETS
   STREELED
EM DEEMSTER
EN RESENTED
EO STEREOED
EP ESTREPED
   PESTERED
ER DESERTER
ET RESETTED
   SETTERED
   STREETED
EV REVESTED
EW WESTERED
EX EXSERTED
FO DEFOREST
   FORESTED
   FOSTERED
GI DIGESTER
   ESTRIDGE
GU GESTURED
HH THRESHED
II SIDERITE
IM DEMERITS
   DEMISTER
   DIMETERS
   MISTERED
IN INSERTED
   RESIDENT
   SINTERED

   TRENDIES
IP PRIESTED
   RESPITED
IR DESTRIER
IS EDITRESS
   RESISTED
   SISTERED
IT TIREDEST
IU ERUDITES
   SURETIED
IW WEIRDEST
LU LUSTERED
   RESULTED
   ULSTERED
LW LEWDSTER
   WRESTLED
LY RESTYLED
MO MODESTER
MP DEMPSTER
MU DEMUREST
   MUSTERED
NO ERODENTS
NP PRETENDS
NU DENTURES
   SEDERUNT
   UNDERSET
   UNDESERT
OP POSTERED
   REEDSTOP
   REPOSTED
OR RESORTED
   RESTORED
   ROSTERED
OS OERSTEDS
OT ROSETTED
   TETRODES
OX DEXTROSE
OY STOREYED
PU PERTUSED
SS DESSERTS
   STRESSED
SU RUSSETED
SY DYESTERS
UV VESTURED
UX EXTRUDES

DEGILN 164
(DINGLE)
AB BLINDAGE
AF FINAGLED
AH HEALDING
AI GLIADINE
AM MALIGNED
AO GALENOID
AP PLEADING
AR DEARLING
   DRAGLINE
AS DEALINGS
   LEADINGS
AT DELATING
AY DELAYING
BE BLEEDING
BN BLENDING
BO IGNOBLED
   INGLOBED
DE ENGILDED
DH HEDDLING
DM MEDDLING
DP PEDDLING
DR REDDLING

DS SLEDDING
DU DELUDING
   INDULGED
   UNGILDED
EN NEEDLING
EO ELOIGNED
   LEGIONED
ER ENGIRDLE
   LINGERED
   REEDLING
ES SEEDLING
ET DELETING
FG FLEDGING
FI DEFILING
   FIELDING
FU INGULFED
GG GLEDGING
GP PLEDGING
GS GELDINGS
   SLEDGING
   SNIGGLED
GU DELUGING
HS HINDLEGS
   SHINGLED
IR GRIDELIN
IS EILDINGS
   SIDELING
IT DILIGENT
IV DEVILING
IW WIELDING
IY YIELDING
KU DUKELING
LU DUELLING
LW DWELLING
NO OLDENING
NS LENDINGS
OP PLODGINE
OS GLENOIDS
   SIDELONG
PS SPELDING
RU INDULGER
RY YELDRING
SU INDULGES
SV DEVLINGS
SW SWINGLED
   WELDINGS
WY WINGEDLY

DEGINR 82
(RINGED)
AA AREADING
   DRAINAGE
   GARDENIA
AB BEARDING
   BREADING
AD DREADING
AE REGAINED
AH ADHERING
   HEADRING
AK DAKERING
AL DEARLING
   DRAGLINE
AM DREAMING
   MARGINED
AO ORGANDIE
AR DREARING
AS DERAIGNS
   GRADINES
   READINGS
AT DERATING

   GRADIENT
   TREADING
AY DERAYING
   READYING
   YEARDING
BE BREEDING
CE RECEDING
CU REDUCING
CY DECRYING
DE ENRIDGED
DG DREDGING
DI DERIDING
DL REDDLING
DS REDDINGS
DU UNGIRDED
EF FINGERED
EG GINGERED
   RENIGGED
EL ENGIRDLE
   LINGERED
   REEDLING
EN ENRINGED
ES DESIGNER
   ENERGIDS
   REDESIGN
   RESIGNED
GU UNRIGGED
IL GRIDELIN
IN NIDERING
IS DESIRING
   RESIDING
IT DIRIGENT
IV DERIVING
   VIRGINED
IW WEIRDING
LU INDULGER
LY YELDRING
MU DEMURING
NT TRENDING
NU ENDURING
   UNRINGED
OP PROIGNED
OR ORDERING
OS NEGROIDS
OU GUERIDON
OV DOVERING
OW DOWERING
PS SPRINGED
PY PREDYING
RS GRINDERS
   REGRINDS
RY GRINDERY
SS DRESSING
ST STRINGED
SW REDWINGS
SY SYNERGID
   SYRINGED

DEGINS 154
(SINGED)
AB BEADINGS
   DEBASING
AH HEADINGS
   SHEADING
AL DEALINGS
   LEADINGS
AO AGONISED

   DIAGNOSE
AR DERAIGNS
   GRADINES
   READINGS
AS ASSIGNED
AT SEDATING
   STEADING
AW WINDAGES
BD BEDDINGS
BN BENDINGS
BO OBSIGNED
CE SECEDING
CK DECKINGS
CN SCENDING
CO COGNISED
CU SEDUCING
CY DYSGENIC
DE DESIGNED
   SDEIGNED
DH SHEDDING
DL SLEDDING
DN SNEDDING
DR REDDINGS
DT STEDDING
DW SWINGED
   WEDDINGS
EF FEEDINGS
EL SEEDLING
EN ENSIGNED
EP SPEEDING
ER DESIGNER
   ENERGIDS
   REDESIGN
   READINGS
   RESIGNED
ES DINGESES
   EDGINESS
   SDEIGNES
   SEEDINGS
ET INGESTED
   SIGNETED
   STEEDING
EW WEEDINGS
EX DESEXING
FU DEFUSING
   FEUDINGS
GH HEDGINGS
GL GELDINGS
   SLEDGING
   SNIGGLED
GW WEDGINGS
HI DINGHIES
HL HINDLEGS
   SHINGLED
HN SHENDING
IL EILDINGS
   SIDELING
IM DEMISING
IN DESINING
   SDEINING
IO INDIGOES
IR DESIRING
   RESIDING
   RINGSIDE
IT DINGIEST
   INDIGEST
IV DEVISING
LN LENDINGS
LO GLENOIDS
   SIDELONG

LP SPELDING	FI INFIDELS	DI TIDDLIER	EP DISPONEE	AG DERAIGNS	IRONISED
LU INDULGES	INFIELDS	DN TRINDLED	ER ORDINEES	GRADINES	RESINOID
LV DEVLINGS	FR FLINDERS	DS STRIDDLE	GI INDIGOES	READINGS	IP INSPIRED
LW SWINGLED	GG GELDINGS	TIDDLERS	GL GLENOIDS	AI DRAISINE	IS INDRISES
WELDINGS	SLEDGING	DW TWIDDLER	SIDELONG	AL ISLANDER	INSIDERS
MN MENDINGS	SNIGGLED	EF FILTERED	GM SMIDGEON	AM ADERMINS	IT DISINTER
MO SMIDGEON	GH HINDLEGS	EL TILLERED	GP DEPOSING	SIRNAMED	INDITERS
MS SMIDGENS	SHINGLED	TREDILLE	DISPONGE	AN INSNARED	NITRIDES
NP SPENDING	GI EILDINGS	EO DOLERITE	PIDGEONS	AO ANEROIDS	RINDIEST
NS SENDINGS	SIDELING	LOITERED	GR NEGROIDS	DONARIES	IU DISINURE
NT STENDING	GN LENDINGS	ET LITTERED	GW WENDIGOS	AP SPRAINED	URIDINES
NU UNSIGNED	GO GLENOIDS	RETITLED	WIDGEONS	AR DRAINERS	IV DIVINERS
NY DESYNING	SIDELONG	HL THRILLED	HM HEDONISM	SERRANID	JO JOINDERS
OP DEPOSING	GP SPELDING	HW WRITHLED	HP DIPHONES	AS ARIDNESS	KL KINDLERS
DISPONGE	GU INDULGES	IP TRIPLIED	SIPHONED	SARDINES	KR DRINKERS
PIDGEONS	GV DEVLINGS	IS REDISTIL	SPHENOID	AT DETRAINS	KS REDSKINS
OR NEGROIDS	GW SWINGLED	NS SNIRTLED	HR HORDEINS	RANDIEST	LO DISENROL
OW WENDIGOS	WELDINGS	TENDRILS	HT HEDONIST	STRAINED	LP SPELDRIN
WIDGEONS	IK DISLIKEN	TRINDLES	IL LIONISED	AU DENARIUS	LS RINDLESS
PR SPRINGED	IO LIONISED	OS STOLIDER	IM DOMINIES	UNRAISED	LT SNIRTLED
PU DISPUNGE	KR KINDLERS	PP TRIPPLED	IR DERISION	URANIDES	TENDRILS
RR GRINDERS	KS KINDLESS	SU DILUTERS	IRONISED	AV INVADERS	TRINDLES
REGRINDS	LW INDWELLS	LURIDEST	RESINOID	SANDIVER	LW SWINDLER
RS DRESSING	MS MILDNESS	VY DEVILTRY	IT EDITIONS	AY SYNEDRIA	NO ENDIRONS
RT STRINGED	MINDLESS		SEDITION	BE INBREEDS	OP DISPONER
RW REDWINGS	MU MUSLINED	**DEINOS 41**	IV VISIONED	BL BLINDERS	POINDERS
RY SYNERGID	OO SOLENOID	(ONSIDE)	JR JOINDERS	BRINDLES	PRISONED
SYRINGED	OR DISENROL	AC DIOCESAN	LO SOLENOID	BU BURNSIDE	OS INDORSES
SU DINGUSES	OS SONDELIS	OCEANIDS	LR DISENROL	CO CONSIDER	SORDINES
SW SWINDGES	OU DELUSION	AD ADENOIDS	LS SONDELIS	CP PRESCIND	OT DRONIEST
TU DUNGIEST	INSOULED	ADONISED	LU DELUSION	CS DISCERNS	OU DOURINES
	UNSOILED	ANODISED	INSOULED	RESCINDS	SOURDINE
DEILNS 120	PR SPELDRIN	AG AGONISED	UNSOILED	CU INDUCERS	OW WINDORES
(INDLES)	PS SPELDINS	DIAGNOSE	MM DEMONISM	DG REDDINGS	WINDROSE
AD ISLANDED	SPINDLES	AH ADHESION	MN MISDONNE	DK KINDREDS	PT SPRINTED
AE DELAINES	PT SPLINTED	AL NODALISE	MO DOMINOES	DO INDORSED	PY INSPYRED
AG DEALINGS	RS RINDLESS	AM NOMADIES	MONODIES	DT STRIDDEN	SU SUNDRIES
LEADINGS	RT SNIRTLED	NOMADISE	MT DEMONIST	EF DEFINERS	TT STRIDENT
AN ANNELIDS	TENDRILS	AR ANEROIDS	NR ENDIRONS	EG DESIGNER	TRIDENTS
LINDANES	TRINDLES	DONARIES	OP POISONED	ENERGIDS	TU INTRUDES
AO NODALISE	RW SWINDLER	AS ADONISES	OZ OZONISED	REDESIGN	TX DEXTRINS
AR ISLANDER	SV VILDNESS	ANODISES	PR DISPONER	REEDINGS	
AU UNSAILED	SW SWINDLES	AT ASTONIED	POINDERS	RESIGNED	**DEINRU 52**
AV ANDVILES	WILDNESS	SEDATION	PRISONED	EH DRISHEEN	(RUINED)
BR BLINDERS	WINDLESS	AX DIOXANES	PS DISPONES	EK DEERSKIN	AF UNFAIRED
BRINDLES	TU DILUENTS	AZ ADONIZES	SPINODES	EN SINNERED	AH UNHAIRED
BT BLINDEST	INSULTED	ANODIZES	PU UNPOISED	EO ORDINEES	AI UREDINIA
CE DECLINES	UNLISTED	BE EBONISED	RS INDORSES	ET INSERTED	AO DOUANIER
LICENSED		BG OBSIGNED	SORDINES	RESIDENT	AP UNPAIRED
SILENCED	**DEILRT 73**	BO NOBODIES	RT DRONIEST	SINTERED	UNREPAID
CO INCLOSED	(TRIDLE)	BU BEDOUINS	RU DOURINES	TRENDIES	AS DENARIUS
CU INCLUDES	AB LIBRATED	CC CONCISED	SOURDINE	EU UREDINES	UNRAISED
NUCLIDES	AC ARTICLED	CE CODEINES	RW WINDORES	EV INVERSED	URANIDES
DG SLEDDING	AE RETAILED	CF CONFIDES	WINDROSE	EW WIDENERS	AT DATURINE
DP SPINDLED	AO IDOLATER	CG COGNISED	ST DONSIEST	EX INDEXERS	INDURATE
SPLENDID	TAILORED	CH HEDONICS	SV VOIDNESS	FL FLINDERS	RUINATED
DW DWINDLES	AP DIPTERAL	CI DECISION	SZ DOZINESS	GI DESIRING	URINATED
SWINDLED	TRIPEDAL	ICONISED	TU OUNDIEST	RESIDING	AV UNVARIED
EE SELENIDE	AS DILATERS	CL INCLOSED	TW DOWNIEST	RINGSIDE	BB UNRIBBED
EG SEEDLING	LARDIEST	CO COOSINED		GO NEGROIDS	BD UNDERBID
EH ENSHIELD	AT DETRITAL	CR CONSIDER	**DEINRS 51**	GP SPRINGED	BL UNBRIDLE
EK SILKENED	AY DIELYTRA	CT DEONTICS	(DINERS)	GR GRINDERS	BS BURNSIDE
EO ESLOINED	BB DRIBBLET	CU DOUCINES	AA ARANEIDS	REGRINDS	BT TURBINED
ES IDLENESS	BO TRILOBED	CZ ZINCODES	AB BRANDIES	GS DRESSING	UNDERBIT
LINSEEDS	BS BRISTLED	DP DISPONED	BRANDISE	GT STRINGED	BU UNBURIED
ET ENLISTED	DRIBLETS	DR INDORSED	AE ARSENIDE	GW REDWINGS	CG REDUCING
LINTSEED	CE DERELICT	DW DISENDOW	DENARIES	GY SYNERGID	CO DECURION
LISTENED	CH ELDRITCH	DISOWNED	DRAISENE	SYRINGED	CP UNPRICED
EY DYELINES	CK TRICKLED	EL ESLOINED	NEARSIDE	HO HORDEINS	CR INCURRED
FF SNIFFLED	CY DIRECTLY	EM DEMONISE	AF FRIANDES	IO DERISION	CS INDUCERS

CV INCURVED
DD UNDERDID
DG UNGIRDED
DL UNRIDDLE
DN UNRIDDEN
DT INTRUDED
EL UNDERLIE
EN UNREINED
EQ ENQUIRED
   INQUERED
ES UREDINES
ET REUNITED
FL UNRIFLED
   URNFIELD
FN REINFUND
   UNFRIEND
GG UNRIGGED
GL INDULGER
GM DEMURING
GN ENDURING
   UNRINGED
GO GUERIDON
IQ INQUIRED
IS DISINURE
   URIDINES
IT UNTIDIER
KN UNKINDER
LP UNDERLIP
MP UNPRIMED
MT RUDIMENT
NO UNIRONED
NP UNDERPIN
NU UNINURED
NV UNDRIVEN
OS DOURINES
   SOURDINE
PP UNRIPPED
PT TURNIPED
PZ UNPRIZED
RT INTRUDER
SS SUNDRIES
ST INTRUDES
TW UNDERWIT

DEINST 32
(SINTED)
AB BANDIEST
AC DISTANCE
AD DANDIEST
AE ANDESITE
AG SEDATING
   STEADING
AH HANDIEST
AI ADENITIS
   DAINTIES
AM MEDIANTS
AO ASTONIED
   SEDATION
AP DEPAINTS
AR DETRAINS
   RANDIEST
   STRAINED
AS SANDIEST
AT INSTATED
AU AUDIENTS
   SINUATED
AV DEVIANTS
AY DESYATIN
BE BENDIEST
BL BLINDEST

CH SNITCHED
CO DEONTICS
CY SYNDETIC
DE DESTINED
DG STEDDING
DR STRIDDEN
DS DISTENDS
DU DISTUNED
EE NEEDIEST
EF FENDIEST
EG INGESTED
   SIGNETED
   STEDDING
EH DISTHENE
EI DIETINES
EL ENLISTED
   LINTSEED
   LISTENED
EM DEMENTIS
   SEDIMENT
EN DENTINES
   DESINENT
EP PENTISED
ER INSERTED
   RESIDENT
   SINTERED
   TRENDIES
ES DESTINES
ET DINETTES
EU DETINUES
EV EVIDENTS
   INVESTED
FU UNSIFTED
GI DINGIEST
   INDIGEST
GN STENDING
GR STRINGED
GU DUNGIEST
HO HEDONIST
IK DINKIEST
IO EDITIONS
   SEDITION
IR DISINTER
   INDITERS
   NITRIDES
   RINDIEST
   TIDINESS
IS INSISTED
IU DISUNITE
   NUDITIES
   UNITISED
   UNTIDIES
IV DIVINEST
IW WINDIEST
LP SPLINTED
LR SNIRTLED
   TENDRILS
   TRINDLES
LU DILUENTS
   INSULTED
   UNLISTED
MO DEMONIST
MS MINDSETS
MU MISTUNED
NU DUNNIEST
   DUNNITES
OR DRONIEST
OS DONSIEST
OU OUNDIEST

OW DOWNIEST
PR SPRINTED
PS STIPENDS
QU SQUINTED
RT STRIDENT
   TRIDENTS
RU INTRUDES
RX DEXTRINS
SS DISNESTS
   DISSENTS
ST DENTISTS
SU DISTUNES
UU UNSUITED

DEIORS 27
(ORIDES)
AC IDOCRASE
AD ROADSIDE
AF FORESAID
AL DARIOLES
   SOLIDARE
   SOREDIAL
AN ANEROIDS
   DONARIES
AP DIASPORE
   PARODIES
AT ASTEROID
BD DISORBED
BF FIBROSED
BM BROMIDES
BR BROIDERS
BS DISROBES
BT DEBITORS
BV OVERBIDS
CL SCLEROID
CN CONSIDER
CO CORODIES
CS DISCOERS
CT CORDITES
CU DISCOURE
CV DISCOVER
   DIVORCES
CW CROWDIES
CY DECISORY
DH SHODDIER
DM DERMOIDS
DN INDORSED
DP DROPSIED
DR DISORDER
   SORDIDER
EF FORESIDE
EG GEORDIES
EH HEROISED
EN ORDINEES
EV OVERSIDE
FF OFFSIDER
FG FIREDOGS
FU FOUDRIES
GG DISGORGE
GN NEGROIDS
GO GOODSIRE
GT STODGIER
HM HEIRDOMS
HN HORDEINS
HP SPHEROID
HS DISHORSE
   HIDROSES
IL IDOLISER
IN DERISION

   IRONISED
   RESINOID
IP PRESIDIO
IT DIORITES
IX OXIDISER
JN JOINDERS
KS DROSKIES
LL DOLLIERS
LN DISENROL
LS SOLDIERS
LT SOLDIER
LU SOULDIER
LY SOLDIERY
MO MOIDORES
MP PROMISED
MR MISORDER
   MORRISED
MS MISDOERS
MT MORTISED
MU DIMEROUS
   ERODIUMS
   SOREDIUM
NN ENDIRONS
NP DISPONER
   POINDERS
   PRISONED
NS INDORSES
   SORDINES
NT DRONIEST
NU DOURINES
   SOURDINE
NW WINDORES
   WINDROSE
OW DOWNIEST
PS DISPOSER
   DROPSIES
PT DIOPTERS
   DIOPTRES
   DIPTEROS
   PERIDOTS
   PROTEIDS
   RIPOSTED
PV DISPROVE
   PROVIDES
PW DROPWISE
RS DROSSIER
RW DROWSIER
RY DERISORY
SS DOSSIERS
ST STEROIDS
SU DESIROUS
SV DEVISORS
TT DORTIEST
TU IODURETS
   OUTRIDES
   OUTSIDER
   SUITORED
TW ROWDIEST
   WORDIEST
WW WIDOWERS

DEIOST 35
(ODITES)
AG GODETIAS
AL DIASTOLE
   ISOLATED
   SODALITE
   SOLIDATE
AM ATOMISED
AN ASTONIED

   SEDATION
AP DIOPTASE
AR ASTEROID
AX OXIDATES
AZ AZOTISED
BR DEBITORS
CL DOCILEST
CM DOMESTIC
CN DEONTICS
CP DESPOTIC
CR CORDITES
CS CESTOIDS
CT COTTISED
DD DODDIEST
DG DODGIEST
DI ODDITIES
DP PODDIEST
DS SODDIEST
DW DOWDIEST
EG EGOTISED
EM TEDISOME
EP EPIDOTES
   POETISED
GG DOGGIEST
GL GODLIEST
   GOLDIEST
GO GOODIEST
GP PODGIEST
GR STODGIER
HN HEDONIST
HU HIDEOUTS
IN EDITIONS
   SEDITION
IR DIORITES
LM MELODIST
LR STOLIDER
LS SOLIDEST
LT DOILTEST
LU SOLITUDE
MM IMMODEST
MN DEMONIST
MO DOOMIEST
   MOODIEST
   SODOMITE
MR MORTISED
MS MODISTES
MT DEMOTIST
NR DRONIEST
NS DONSIEST
NU OUNDIEST
NW DOWNIEST
OW WOODIEST
PR DIOPTERS
   DIOPTRES
   DIPTEROS
   PERIDOTS
   PROTEIDS
   RIPOSTED
PS DEPOSITS
   TOPSIDES
RS STEROIDS
RT DORTIEST
RU IODURETS
   OUTRIDES
   OUTSIDER
   SUITORED
RW ROWDIEST
   WORDIEST
SU OUTSIDES
SX EXODISTS

TT DOTTIEST
UZ OUTSIZED

DEIRST 57
(STRIDE)
AA DATARIES
   RADIATES
AB BARDIEST
   BRAIDEST
   RABIDEST
AC ACRIDEST
AD DISRATED
AE READIEST
   SERIATED
   STEADIER
AH HAIRSTED
   HARDIEST
AI IRISATED
AK STRAIKED
AL DILATERS
   LARDIEST
AM MARDIEST
   MISRATED
   READMITS
AN DETRAINS
   RANDIEST
AO ASTEROID
AP RAPIDEST
   SPIRATED
   TRAIPSED
AS ASTERIDS
   DIASTERS
   DISASTER
   DISRATES
AT STRAITED
   STRIATED
   TARDIEST
AW TAWDRIES
BE BEDRITES
   BESTRIDE
BL BRISTLED
BO DEBITORS
CE DISCREET
   DISCRETE
CH DITCHERS
CO CORDITES
CP PREDICTS
   SCRIPTED
CU CRUDITES
   CURDIEST
   CURTSIED
CV VERDICTS
DE REDDIEST
DL STRIDDLE
   TIDDLERS
DN STRIDDEN
DU RUDDIEST
   STURDIED
EE REEDIEST
EG DIGESTER
   ESTRIDGE
EI SIDERITE
EM DEMERITS
   DEMISTER
   DIMETERS
   MISTERED
EN INSERTED

```
   RESIDENT
   SINTERED
   TRENDIES
EP PRIESTED
   RESPITED
ER DESTRIER
ES EDITRESS
   RESISTED
   SISTERED
ET TIREDEST
EU ERUDITES
   SURETIED
EW WEIRDEST
FR DRIFTERS
GG STRIGGED
GI RIDGIEST
   RIGIDEST
GN STRINGED
GO STODGIER
GU DURGIEST
HI DISHERIT
HT THIRSTED
   THRISTED
IL REDISTIL
IN DISINTER
   INDITERS
   NITRIDES
   RINDIEST
IO DIORITES
IP RIPTIDES
   SPIRITED
IT DIRTIEST
   TRITIDES
LN SNIRTLED
   TENDRILS
   TRINDLES
LO STOLIDER
LU DILUTERS
   LURIDEST
MO MORTISED
MP DIREMPTS
NO DRONIEST
NP SPRINTED
NT STRIDENT
   TRIDENTS
NU INTRUDES
NX DEXTRINS
OP DIOPTERS
   DIOPTRES
   DIPTEROS
   PERIDOTS
   PROTEIDS
   RIPOSTED
OS STEROIDS
OT DORTIEST
OU IODURETS
   OUTRIDES
   OUTSIDER
   SUITORED
OW ROWDIEST
   WORDIEST
PP STRIPPED
PU DISPUTER
   STUPIDER
QU SQUIRTED
RU STURDIER
SS DISSERTS
   DISTRESS
SU DIESTRUS
   DRUSIEST
```


```
   STUDIERS
   STURDIES
TU DETRITUS
UX DRUXIEST

DEIRSU 143
(URDIES)
AC DECURIAS
AL RESIDUAL
AN DENARIUS
   UNRAISED
   URANIDES
AP UPRAISED
AS RADIUSES
   SUDARIES
BL BUILDERS
   REBUILDS
BM IMBURSED
BN BURNSIDE
BS DISBURSE
CD DISCURED
CE DECURIES
CN INDUCERS
CO DISCOURE
CR SCURRIED
CS DISCURES
CT CRUDITES
   CURDIEST
   CURTSIED
DP SPUDDIER
DS DRUIDESS
DT RUDDIEST
   STURDIED
EG GUDESIRE
EK DUKERIES
EL LEISURED
EN UREDINES
EP DUPERIES
ER RUDERIES
ES DIURESES
   REISSUED
ET ERUDITES
   SURETIED
FF DIFFUSER
FO FOUDRIES
FS FISSURED
GL GUILDERS
GM SMUDGIER
GT DURGIEST
HR DHURRIES
IN DISINURE
   URIDINES
IS DIURESIS
KP SPRUIKED
KR SKURRIED
LM MISRULED
LO SOULDIER
LT DILUTERS
   LURIDEST
MO DIMEROUS
   ERODIUMS
   SOREDIUM
MQ SQUIRMED
MS SURMISED
MU RESIDUUM
NO DOURINES
   SOURDINE
NS SUNDRIES
```


```
NT INTRUDES
OS DESIROUS
OT IODURETS
   OUTRIDES
   OUTSIDER
   SUITORED
PS DISPURSE
   SUSPIRED
PT DISPUTER
   STUPIDER
QR SQUIRED
QT SQUIRTED
RT STURDIER
ST DIESTRUS
   DRUSIEST
   STUDIERS
   STURDIES
SY DYSURIES
TT DETRITUS
TX DRUXIEST
VV SURVIVED

DELNOS 181
(OLDENS)
AC CELADONS
AI NODALISE
AM LODESMAN
   SOLANDER
AY YEALDONS
BS BOLDNESS
BT BLONDEST
CE ENCLOSED
CI INCLOSED
CO CONDOLES
   CONSOLED
CS COLDNESS
CU ENCLOUDS
   UNCLOSED
CY CONDYLES
   SECONDLY
EI ESLOINED
EK SLOKENED
EM LODESMEN
EO LOOSENED
ES LESSONED
EU ENSOULED
EY ESLOYNED
FP PENFOLDS
FR FONDLERS
   FORLENDS
GI GLENOIDS
   SIDELONG
II LIONISED
IO SOLENOID
IR DISENROL
IS SONDELIS
IU DELUSION
   INSOULED
   UNSOILED
MU UNSELDOM
OU NODULOSE
   UNLOOSED
OZ SNOOZLED
PR SPLENDOR
RU LOUNDERS
   NOURSLED
   ROUNDELS
   ROUNDLES
   UNSOLDER
```


```
SU LOUDNESS
UU UNDULOSE
   UNSOULED
UV UNSOLVED

DELORS 145
(OLDERS)
AI DARIOLES
   SOLIDARE
   SOREDIAL
AL ODALLERS
AM EARLDOMS
AN LADRONES
   SOLANDER
AP LEOPARDS
AS ROADLESS
AT DELATORS
   LEOTARDS
   LODESTAR
AU ROULADES
BU BOULDERS
   DOUBLERS
BW BOWLDERS
CE RECLOSED
CI SCLEROID
CL SCROLLED
CO CROODLES
   DECOLORS
CS CORDLESS
   SCOLDERS
CU CLOSURED
CW CLOWDERS
   SCROWLED
DE SOLDERED
DO DOODLERS
DP PLODDERS
DT STRODDLE
   STRODLED
   TODDLERS
EM REMODELS
EP DEPLORES
ER SOLDERER
EU URODELES
EV RESOLVED
FN FONDLERS
   FORLENDS
FO FORSLOED
FU FOULDERS
GG DOGGRELS
GP PLEDGORS
HU SHOULDER
II IDOLISER
IL DOLLIERS
IN DISENROL
IS SOLDIERS
IT STOLIDER
IU SOULDIER
IY SOLDIERY
LP REDPOLLS
LS LORDLESS
LT DROLLEST
   STROLLED
MS SMOLDERS
MU MOULDERS
   REMOULDS
   SMOULDER
NP SPLENDOR
NU LOUNDERS
   NOURSLED
   ROUNDELS
```


```
   ROUNDLES
   UNSOLDER
OS LORDOSES
OV OVERSOLD
OW WOOLDERS
PP DROPPLES
PT DROPLETS
PU POULDERS
   POULDRES
ST OLDSTERS
   STRODLES
SW WORDLESS
TT DOTTRELS
UY DELUSORY

DELORT 100
(DOLTER)
AF DEFLATOR
AI IDOLATER
   TAILORED
AP PROLATED
AS DELATORS
   LEOTARDS
   LODESTAR
BI TRILOBED
BU TROUBLED
CH CHORTLED
CU CLOTURED
DS STRODDLE
   STRODLED
   TODDLERS
EI DOLERITE
   LOITERED
EN REDOLENT
EO RETOOLED
ET DOTTEREL
   TOLTERED
EV REVOLTED
EY DELETORY
FO FORETOLD
IS STOLIDER
LS DROLLEST
   STROLLED
NU ROUNDLET
OY ROOTEDLY
PS DROPLETS
SS OLDSTERS
   STRODLES
ST DOTTRELS

DENORU 99
(UNDOER)
AD UNADORED
AI DOUANIER
AL UNLOADER
   URODELAN
AX RONDEAUX
BS BOUNDERS
   REBOUNDS
   SUBORNED
CD UNCORDED
CF FROUNCED
CG CONGRUED
CI DECURION
CJ CONJURED
CK UNCORKED
CT CORNUTED
   TROUNCED
DG GROUNDED
```


```
   UNDERDOG
DL UNLORDED
DS REDOUNDS
DT ROTUNDED
DW UNWORDED
ET DEUTERON
FG UNFORGED
FL FLOUNDER
   UNFOLDER
FM UNFORMED
FO UNROOFED
FR FRONDEUR
FS FOUNDERS
   REFOUNDS
FT FORTUNED
GG UNGORGED
GI GUERIDON
GN GROUNDEN
GR GROUNDER
   REGROUND
GS GUERDONS
GT TRUDGEON
GU UNROUGED
HO HONOURED
HS ENSHROUD
   UNHORSED
IN UNIRONED
IS DOURINES
   SOURDINE
KW UNWORKED
LL UNROLLED
LS LOUNDERS
   NOURSLED
   ROUNDELS
   ROUNDLES
   UNSOLDER
LT ROUNDLET
MO UNMOORED
MW UNWORMED
NS ENROUNDS
OT UNROOTED
PS POUNDERS
PV UNPROVED
RS RONDURES
   ROUNDERS
   UNORDERS
RT ROTUNDER
RU ROUNDURE
SS DOURNESS
   RESOUNDS
   SOUNDERS
ST ROUNDEST
   TONSURED
   UNSORTED
SU UNROUSED
   UNSOURED
SW WOUNDERS
TT UNROTTED
TW UNDERTOW

DENOST 74
(STONED)
AI ASTONIED
   SEDATION
AR TORNADES
AS ONSTEADS
BL BLONDEST
CI DEONTICS
CN CONTENDS
CO SECODONT
```

CU CONTUSED
DM ODDMENTS
DU STOUNDED
DW STOWNDED
EF SOFTENED
EN SONNETED
EP PENTODES
ER ERODENTS
ES STENOSED
GO STEGODON
HI HEDONIST
HZ DOZENTHS
II EDITIONS
   SEDITION
IM DEMONIST
IR DRONIEST
IS DONSIEST
IU OUNDIEST
IW DOWNIEST
MR MORDENTS
MU DEMOUNTS
   MUDSTONE
NR TENDRONS
OU DUOTONES
PR PORTENDS
   PROTENDS
PU OUTSPEND
   UNPOSTED
PW STEWPOND
RU ROUNDEST
   TONSURED
   UNSORTED
SU SOUNDEST
UW UNSTOWED

DENRSU 179
(UNDERS)
AC DURANCES
AD DAUNDERS
AE UNDERSEA
AG ENGUARDS
AH UNSHARED
AI DENARIUS
   UNRAISED
   URANIDES
AL LAUNDERS
   LURDANES
   RUNDALES
AM DURAMENS
   MAUNDERS
   SURNAMED
AP UNSPARED
AQ SQUANDER
AS DANSEURS
AT DAUNTERS
   TRANSUDE
   UNTREADS
AY UNDERSAY
BI BURNSIDE
BL BLUNDERS
BO BOUNDERS
   REBOUNDS
   SUBORNED
BU UNBRUSED
CE CENSURED
CH CHUNDERS
CI INDUCERS
CU UNCURSED
DE SUNDERED
DH HUNDREDS

DO REDOUNDS
EI UREDINES
ER ENDURERS
   SUNDERER
ES RUDENESS
ET DENTURES
   SEDERUNT
   UNDERSET
   UNDESERT
EU UNDERUSE
EV UNVERSED
FO FOUNDERS
   REFOUNDS
GO GUERDONS
GT TRUDGENS
HO ENSHROUD
   UNHORSED
HT THUNDERS
II DISINURE
   URIDINES
IO DOURINES
   SOURDINE
IS SUNDRIES
IT INTRUDES
KT DRUNKEST
KY UNDERSKY
LO LOUNDERS
   NOURSLED
   ROUNDELS
   ROUNDLES
   UNSOLDER
LP PLUNDERS
LT RUNDLETS
   TRUNDLES
NO ENROUNDS
OP POUNDERS
OR RONDURES
   ROUNDERS
   UNORDERS
OS DOURNESS
   RESOUNDS
   SOUNDERS
OT ROUNDEST
   TONSURED
   UNSORTED
OU UNROUSED
   UNSOURED
OW WOUNDERS
PT UPTRENDS
PU UNPURSED
TT STRUNTED

DEORST 50
(SORTED)
AB BROADEST
AC REDCOATS
AG GOADSTER
AI ASTEROID
AL DELATORS
   LEOTARDS
   LODESTAR
AM STROAMED
AN TORNADES
AP ADOPTERS
   ASPORTED
   READOPTS
AR ROADSTER
AS ASSORTED
   TORSADES
AU OUTDARES

AX EXTRADOS
BE BESORTED
   BESTRODE
BI DEBITORS
BU DOUBTERS
   OBTRUDES
   REDOUBTS
CE CORSETED
   ESCORTED
   SECTORED
CI CORDITES
CS DOCTRESS
CU EDUCTORS
   SEDUCTOR
DL STRODDLE
   STRODLED
   TODDLERS
EE STEREOED
EF DEFOREST
   FORESTED
   FOSTERED
EM MODESTER
EN ERODENTS
EP POSTERED
   REEDSTOP
   REPOSTED
ER RESORTED
   RESTORED
   ROSTERED
ES OERSTEDS
ET ROSETTED
   TETRODES
EX DEXTROSE
EY STOREYED
FS DEFROSTS
FW FROWSTED
GI STODGIER
GS STODGERS
GU DROGUETS
HP POTSHERD
HR REDSHORT
II DIORITES
IL STOLIDER
IM MORTISED
IN DRONIEST
IP DIOPTERS
   DIOPTRES
   DIPTEROS
   PERIDOTS
   PROTEIDS
   RIPOSTED
IS STEROIDS
IT DORTIEST
IU IODURETS
   OUTRIDES
   OUTSIDER
   SUITORED
IW ROWDIEST
   WORDIEST
LL DROLLEST
LP DROPLETS
LS OLDSTERS
LT DOTTRELS
MN MORDENTS
MO DOOMSTER
NN TENDRONS
NP PORTENDS
   PROTENDS

NU ROUNDEST
   TONSURED
   UNSORTED
OP DOORSTEP
   TORPEDOS
PP STROPPED
PU POSTURED
   PROUDEST
   SPROUTED
RS RODSTERS
SW WORSTEDS
SY DESTROYS
TU STROUTED
UU OUTDURES
UV OVERDUST
UX DEXTROUS

DEOSTU 180
(OUSTED)
AB BOUTADES
AR OUTDARES
AT OUTDATES
BL DOUBLETS
BR DOUBTERS
   OBTRUDES
   REDOUBTS
CC STUCCOED
CL LOCUSTED
CM COSTUMED
   CUSTOMED
CN CONTUSED
CQ DOCQUETS
CR EDUCTORS
   SEDUCTOR
CS CUSTODES
DN STOUNDED
EG OUTEDGES
EW OUTWEEDS
EX TUXEDOES
GR DROGUETS
HI HIDEOUTS
HS STOUSHED
IL SOLITUDE
IN OUNDIEST
IR IODURETS
   OUTRIDES
   OUTSIDER
   SUITORED
IS OUTSIDES
IZ OUTSIZED
LP POSTLUDE
MN DEMOUNTS
   MUDSTONE
MO OUTMODES
NO DUOTONES
NP OUTSPEND
   UNPOSTED
NR ROUNDEST
   TONSURED
   UNSORTED
NS SOUNDEST
NW UNSTOWED
PR POSTURED
   PROUDEST
   SPROUTED
RT STROUTED
RU OUTDURES
RV OVERDUST
RX DEXTROUS
ST TESTUDOS

EEILRS 90
(RELIES)
AC ESCALIER
AD REALISED
   SIDEREAL
AF SERAFILE
AG GASELIER
AH SHIRALEE
AL REALLIES
AM ALMERIES
   MEASLIER
AP ESPALIER
   PEARLIES
AR REALISED
AS REALISES
AT ATELIERS
   EARLIEST
   LEARIEST
   REALTIES
AV VELARISE
AY YEARLIES
AZ REALIZES
   SLEAZIER
BF BELFRIES
BN BERLINES
BU BLUESIER
CD SCLEREID
CE CELERIES
CG CLERGIES
CN LICENSER
   RECLINES
   SILENCER
CT RETICLES
   SCLERITE
   TIERCELS
CU CISELEUR
   CISELURE
   RECUILES
CV VERSICLE
DF DEFILERS
   FIELDERS
DG LEIDGERS
DH RELISHED
   SHIELDER
DU LEISURED
DV DELIVERS
   DESILVER
   SILVERED
   SLIVERED
DW WIELDERS
DY YIELDERS
EK SKEELIER
   SLEEKIER
EM SEEMLIER
EP SLEEPIER
ET LEERIEST
   SLEETIER
   STEELIER
EV RELIEVES
EZ SLEEZIER
FH FLESHIER
   SHELFIER
FO FORELIES
FS FIRELESS
FT FERLIEST
FU FUSILEER
GN LEERINGS
   REELINGS
GU REGULISE
GV VELIGERS

HL HELLIERS
   SHELLIER
HS HEIRLESS
   RELISHES
HV SHELVIER
IO OILERIES
IT TILERIES
IV LIVERIES
KL SKELLIER
KO ROSELIKE
KT TRISKELE
LM SMELLIER
LO ORSEILLE
LS LEISLERS
LT TREILLES
MN ERMELINS
MT TERMLIES
MV VERMEILS
NO ELOINERS
NP PILSENER
NS REINLESS
NT LISTENER
   SILENTER
OP PELORIES
OT LITEROSE
   TROELIES
OV OVERLIES
   RELIEVOS
   VOLERIES
OW OWLERIES
PR REPLIERS
PS SPIELERS
PT EPISTLER
   PELTRIES
   PERLITES
   REPTILES
QU RELIQUES
RV RELIVERS
   REVILERS
ST LEISTERS
   RITELESS
   TIRELESS
SU LEISURES
SV SERVILES
SW WIRELESS
TT RETITLES

EEILST 89
(ELITES)
AD LEADIEST
AF FEALTIES
   LEAFIEST
AG ELEGIAST
AK LEAKIEST
AL LEALTIES
AM MEALIEST
AP EPILATES
AR ATELIERS
   EARLIEST
   LEARIEST
   REALTIES
AS ASTELIES
AT AILETTES
AV ELATIVES
   LEAVIEST
   VEALIEST
BN STILBENE
   TENSIBLE
BT BETITLES
CR RETICLES

	SCLERITE	SW	WITELESS		ENTAILER	HT	THIRTEEN	BU	REBURIES	QU	REQUIRES
	TIERCELS	SX	SEXTILES		TREENAIL	HW	WHITENER	BV	BREVIERS	RT	RETIRERS
CT	TELESTIC	TX	TEXTILES	AP	APERIENT	IO	ERIONITE	CD	DECRIERS		TERRIERS
	TESTICLE	VY	STIEVELY	AR	RETAINER	IS	ERINITES	CH	CHERRIES	ST	TRESSIER
CU	LEUCITES			AS	ARSENITE		NITERIES	CN	SINCERER	SV	REVERSIS
DG	GELIDEST	**EEIMNS 192**		RESINATE	IT	INTERTIE	CP	PIERCERS	TV	REVERIST
	LEDGIEST	(EMINES)		STEARINE		RETINITE		PRECISER		REVISERS
DN	ENLISTED	AD	DEMAINES		TRAINEES	JL	JETLINER	CS	CERRISES		RIVERETS
	LINTSEED		INSEAMED	BI	BENITIER	KS	KERNITES		CRESSIER		RIVETERS
	LISTENED	AR	REMANIES	BO	TENEBRIO	LS	LISTENER	CT	RECITERS	TW	REWRITES
DP	EPISTLED	AS	NEMESIAS	BT	REBITTEN		SILENTER	CW	SCREWIER	VV	REVIVERS
DS	TIDELESS	AT	MATINEES	CF	FRENETIC	LY	ENTIRELY	DD	DERIDERS		
DU	DILUTEES		SEMINATE	CG	ERECTING		LIENTERY	DH	REDSHIRE	**EEIRST 31**	
DV	DEVILETS	AX	EXAMINES		GENTRICE	MO	TIMONEER	DP	REPRISED	(ESTIER)	
EN	SELENITE	CD	ENDEMICS	CI	ICTERINE	MP	TRIPEMEN		RESPIRED	AD	READIEST
ER	LEERIEST	CG	MISCEGEN	CN	INCENTRE	MR	TERMINER	DS	DERRISES		SERIATED
	SLEETIER	CP	SPECIMEN	CO	ERECTION	MU	MUTINEER		DESIRERS		STEADIER
	STEELIER	CT	CENTIMES		NEOTERIC	MV	VIREMENT		DRESSIER	AE	EATERIES
ES	SEELIEST	DE	INSEEMED	CP	PRENTICE	NS	INTENSER		RESIDERS	AH	HEARTIES
EV	TELEVISE	DH	INMESHED	CS	CENTRIES	NT	RENITENT	DT	DESTRIER	AL	ATELIERS
FM	FISTMELE	DM	ENDEMISM		ENTERICS	OR	REORIENT	DU	RUDERIES		EARLIEST
FR	FERLIEST	DO	DEMONISE		ENTICERS	OS	SEROTINE	DV	REDRIVES		LEARIEST
FS	FELSITES	DS	DESMINES		SCIENTER	OT	TENORITE	EK	SKEERIER		REALTIES
GG	LEGGIEST		SIDESMEN		SECRETIN	OX	EXERTION	EM	MISERERE	AM	EMIRATES
GN	GENTILES	DT	DEMENTIS	CT	RETICENT	PX	INEXPERT	EN	SNEERIER		REAMIEST
	SLEETING		SEDIMENT	CU	CEINTURE	RS	INSERTER	ET	REESTIER		STEAMIER
	STEELING	ET	EMETINES		ENURETIC		REINSERT		RETIREES	AN	ARSENITE
GS	ELEGISTS	FI	FEMINISE	DD	DENDRITE		REINTERS	EV	REREVISE		RESINATE
HS	LEISHEST	GI	GEMINIES	DK	TINKERED		RENTIERS		REVERIES		STEARINE
	SHELTIES	GK	SMEEKING	DN	INDENTER		TERRINES	FN	REFINERS		TRAINEES
IN	LENITIES	GN	MENINGES		INTENDER	RV	INVERTER	FT	FERRITES	AO	ETAERIOS
IR	TILERIES	GR	REGIMENS		INTERNED	RX	INTERREX	GN	RESIGNER	AP	PETARIES
IV	LEVITIES	GS	SEEMINGS	DO	ORIENTED	SS	INTERESS	GT	REGISTER	AR	ARTERIES
	VEILIEST	GT	MEETINGS	DR	INTERRED		SENTRIES	GV	GRIEVERS		REASTIER
IW	LEWISITE		STEEMING		TRENDIER	ST	INERTEST	HK	SHRIEKER	AS	SERIATES
KP	PIKELETS	GU	EUGENISM	DS	INSERTED		INTEREST	HN	ERRHINES	AT	ARIETTES
	SPIKELET	HO	HEMIONES		RESIDENT		STERNITE	HP	PERISHER		ITERATES
KR	TRISKELE	HR	SHIREMEN		SINTERED	SU	ESURIENT		SPHERIER		TEARIEST
LM	MELLITES	HS	INMESHES		TRENDIES		NEURITES	HS	SHERRIES		TREATIES
LR	TREILLES	IT	ENMITIES	DU	REUNITED		RETINUES	HW	WHERRIES		TREATISE
LV	EVILLEST	LN	LINESMEN	DV	INVERTED		REUNITES	IT	REISTIER	AV	EVIRATES
MO	MESOLITE	LR	ERMELINS	DW	WINTERED	SV	NERVIEST	IV	RIVIERES	AW	SWEATIER
	MISLETOE	LS	ISLESMEN	DX	DEXTRINE		REINVEST	KS	SKERRIES		TAWERIES
MP	IMPLETES	LU	SELENIUM	EN	INTERNEE		SERVIENT	LP	REPLIERS		WEARIEST
MR	TERMLIES		SEMILUNE	ES	ETERNISE		SIRVENTE	LV	RELIVERS	AY	YEASTIER
MS	TIMELESS	MR	IMMENSER	ET	REINETTE	SX	INTERSEX		REVILERS	BD	BEDRITES
NN	LENIENTS	NO	NOMINEES		TEENTIER	SY	SERENITY	MP	PREMIERS	BE	BEERIEST
	SENTINEL	NR	REINSMEN	EZ	ETERNIZE	TY	ENTIRETY		REPRIMES	BF	BRIEFEST
NO	NOSELITE	OP	EPISEMON	FS	FERNIEST		ETERNITY		SIMPERER	BH	HERBIEST
NP	PLENTIES	OR	EMERSION	GG	GREETING			MT	MERRIEST	BU	UBERTIES
NR	LISTENER	OT	MONETISE	GM	METERING	**EEIRRS 182**			TRIREMES	CD	DISCREET
	SILENTER		SEMITONE		REGIMENT	(ERRIES)		NP	REPINERS		DISCRETE
NT	ENTITLES	PT	SEPIMENT	GN	ENTERING	AC	CARIERES	NS	RESINERS	CF	FIERCEST
NV	VEINLETS	QU	MESQUINE	GP	PETERING		CREASIER	NT	INSERTER	CH	CHESTIER
OP	PETIOLES	RV	MINEVERS	GS	GENTRIES	AF	RAREFIES		REINSERT		HERETICS
OR	LITEROSE	SW	MISWEENS		INTEGERS	AG	GREASIER		REINTERS	CI	SERICITE
	TROELIES	TT	MINETTES		REESTING	AH	HEARSIER		RENTIERS	CL	RETICLES
OS	ESTOILES				STEERING	AK	RAKERIES		TERRINES		SCLERITE
OW	OWELTIES	**EEINRT 7**			STREIGNE		SKEARIER	NU	REINSURE		TIERCELS
OZ	ZEOLITES	(ENTIRE)		GU	GENITURE	AL	REALISER	NV	VERNIERS	CN	CENTRIES
PR	EPISTLER	AC	CENTIARE	GV	EVERTING	AM	SMEARIER	OP	ROPERIES		ENTERICS
	PELTRIES		CREATINE	GW	TWEERING	AN	REARISEN	OR	ORRERIES		ENTICERS
	PERLITES		INCREATE	GX	EXERTING	AP	PEREIRAS	OS	ROSERIES		SCIENTER
	REPTILES		ITERANCE		GENETRIX		SPEARIER		ROSIERES		SECRETIN
PS	EPISTLES	AD	DETAINER	HN	INHERENT	AS	REARISES	PP	PERSPIRE	CO	ESOTERIC
PY	EPISTYLE		RETAINED	HO	ETHERION	AT	ARTERIES	PR	PERRIERS	CP	CREPIEST
RS	LEISTERS	AH	ATHERINE	HP	NEPHRITE		REASTIER	PS	REPRISES		RECEIPTS
	RITELESS	AK	ANKERITE		PREHNITE	BB	BERBERIS		RESPIRES	CR	RECITERS
	TIRELESS	AL	ELATERIN		TREPHINE			PV	REPRIVES		
RT	RETITLES							PZ	REPRIZES		

```
CU CERUSITE
   CUTESIER
   EUCRITES
CV VERTICES
CX EXCITERS
DD REDDIEST
DE REEDIEST
DG DIGESTER
   ESTRIDGE
DI SIDERITE
DM DEMERITS
   DEMISTER
   DIMETERS
   MISTERED
DN INSERTED
   RESIDENT
   SINTERED
   TRENDIES
DP PRIESTED
   RESPITED
DR DESTRIER
DS EDITRESS
   RESISTED
   SISTERED
DT TIREDEST
DU ERUDITES
   SURETIED
DW WEIRDEST
EH ETHERISE
   SHEETIER
EK REEKIEST
EL LEERIEST
   SLEETIER
   STEELIER
EM EREMITES
EN ETERNISE
   TEENSIER
EP PEERIEST
   STEEPIER
ER REESTIER
   RETIREES
ES STEERIES
FI FEISTIER
   FERITIES
   FIERIEST
FL FERLIEST
FM FEMITERS
FN FERNIEST
FR FERRITES
FT FRISETTE
FY ESTERIFY
GN GENTRIES
   INTEGERS
   REESTING
   STEERING
   STREIGNE
GO ERGOTISE
GP PRESTIGE
GR REGISTER
GT GRISETTE
   TERGITES
HM ERETHISM
   ETHERISM
HO ISOTHERE
   THEORIES
   THEORISE
HP TREESHIP
HS HEISTERS
HT ETHERIST
IL TILERIES
```


```
IN ERINITES
   NITERIES
IR REISTIER
IV VERITIES
JK JERKIEST
KL TRISKELE
KN KERNITES
KP PERKIEST
LL TREILLES
LM TERMLIES
LN LISTENER
   SILENTER
LO LITEROSE
   TROELIES
LP EPISTLER
   PELTRIES
   PERLITES
   REPTILES
LS LEISTERS
   RITELESS
   TIRELESS
LT RETITLES
MM MERISTEM
   MIMESTER
   MISMETRE
MO TIRESOME
MP EMPTIERS
MR MERRIEST
   TRIREMES
MS TRISEMES
MT TERMITES
MU EMERITUS
NN INTENSER
   INTERNES
NO SEROTINE
NR INSERTER
   REINSERT
   REINTERS
   RENTIERS
   TERRINES
NS INTERESS
   SENTRIES
   TRENISES
NT INERTEST
   INTEREST
   STERNITE
NU ESURIENT
   NEURITES
   RETINUES
   REUNITES
NV NERVIEST
   REINVEST
   SERVIENT
   SIRVENTE
NX INTERSEX
NY SERENITY
OP POETRIES
OS EROTESIS
PT PRETTIES
PY PERSEITY
QU QUIETERS
   REQUITES
QW QWERTIES
RR RETIRERS
   TERRIERS
RS TRESSIER
RV REVERIST
   RIVERETS
   RIVETERS
```


```
RW REWRITES
ST RESTIEST
SU SURETIES
SV SIEVERTS
   TREVISES
   VESTRIES
VV VETIVERS
VY SEVERITY

EELNST 161
(NESTLE)
AC CLEANEST
   LATENCES
AE SELENATE
AK KANTELES
AM MANTELES
   TALESMEN
AR ALTERNES
AS LATENESS
AY ENTAYLES
BD BENDLETS
BI STILBENE
   TENSIBLE
CG NEGLECTS
CK NECKLETS
CR LECTERNS
CU ESCULENT
DI ENLISTED
   LINTSEED
   LISTENED
DK SKLENTED
DP SPLENTED
DY ENSTYLED
EI SELENITE
EM ELEMENTS
FO FELSTONE
GI GENTILES
   SLEETING
   STEELING
GT GENTLEST
II LENITIES
IN LENIENTS
   SENTINEL
IO NOSELITE
IP PLENTIES
IR LISTENER
   SILENTER
IV VEINLETS
KO SKELETON
LS SNELLEST
LU ENTELLUS
OR ENTRESOL
OS NOTELESS
   TONELESS
OT NOTELETS
OU TOLUENES
RT LETTERNS
SU TUNELESS
   UNSTEELS
SY ENSTYLES
TU LUNETTES
   UNSETTLE

EELRST 157
(ELTERS)
AA LAETARES
AB BLEAREST
   BLEATERS
   RETABLES
```


```
AC CLEAREST
   SCELERAT
   TREACLES
AD TREADLES
AE TEASELER
AF REFLATES
AH HALTERES
AI ATELIERS
   EARLIEST
   LEARIEST
   REALTIES
AM LAMETERS
AN ALTERNES
AO OLEASTER
AP PRELATES
AR RELATERS
AS STEALERS
   TEARLESS
   TESSERAL
AT ALERTEST
AU RESALUTE
AY EASTERLY
BH BLETHERS
   HERBLETS
BM TREMBLES
CE RESELECT
CF REFLECTS
CI RETICLES
   SCLERITE
   TIERCELS
CN LECTERNS
CO CORSELET
   ELECTORS
   ELECTROS
   SELECTOR
CP PLECTRES
   PRELECTS
CS LECTRESS
CU LECTURES
CY SECRETLY
DD TREDDLES
DE DEERLETS
   STREELED
DU LUSTERED
   RESULTED
   ULSTERED
DW LEWDSTER
   WRESTLED
DY RESTYLED
EI LEERIEST
   SLEETIER
   STEELIER
EO SLOETREE
EP REPLETES
ES TREELESS
ET RESETTLE
EV LEVERETS
   VERSELET
FI FERLIEST
FT FETTLERS
FU FLEURETS
HH THRESHEL
HO HOSTELER
HP TELPHERS
HS SHELTERS
HY SHELTERY
II TILERIES
IK TRISKELE
IL TREILLES
```


```
IM TERMLIES
IN LISTENER
   SILENTER
IO LITEROSE
   TROELIES
IP EPISTLER
   PELTRIES
   PERLITES
   REPTILES
IS LEISTERS
   RITELESS
   TIRELESS
IT RETITLES
KS KESTRELS
   SKELTERS
LO SOLLERET
MO MOLESTER
MS SMELTERS
   TERMLESS
MY SMELTERY
NO ENTRESOL
NT LETTERNS
OT LORETTES
OU RESOLUTE
PS SPELTERS
PZ PRETZELS
RW WRESTLER
SS RESTLESS
   TRESSELS
ST SETTLERS
   STERLETS
   TRESTLES
SW SWELTERS
   WRESTLES
SY RESTYLES
   TYRELESS
SZ SELTZERS
WY WESTERLY

EENRST 56
(ENTERS)
AA ARSENATE
   SERENATA
AC REASCENT
   SARCENET
AE SERENATE
AF FASTENER
   FENESTRA
AG ESTRANGE
   GRANTEES
   GREATENS
   REAGENTS
   SEGREANT
   SERGEANT
   STERNAGE
AH HASTENER
   HEARTENS
AI ARSENITE
   RESINATE
   STEARINE
   TRAINEES
AJ SERJEANT
AL ALTERNES
AM REMANETS
AO RESONATE
AR TERRANES
AS ASSENTER
   EARNESTS
   SARSENET
AT ENTREATS
```


```
   RATTEENS
AV AVENTRES
   VETERANS
BP BESPRENT
BT BRENTEST
BW BESTREWN
CC CRESCENT
CH TRENCHES
CI CENTRIES
   ENTERICS
   ENTICERS
   SCIENTER
   SECRETIN
CL LECTERNS
CN CENTNERS
CU UNSECRET
DE RESENTED
DI INSERTED
   RESIDENT
   SINTERED
   TRENDIES
DO ERODENTS
DP PRETENDS
DU DENTURES
   SEDERUNT
   UNDERSET
   UNDESERT
EG GREENEST
EI ETERNISE
   TEENSIER
EM ENTREMES
EN ETRENNES
EP PRETENSE
   TERPENES
ER ENTERERS
   RESENTER
   TERREENS
   TERRENES
ES SERENEST
EV EVENTERS
EX EXTERNES
EY YESTREEN
FI FERNIEST
FM FERMENTS
FO ENFOREST
   SOFTENER
GH GREENTHS
GI GENTRIES
   INTEGERS
   REESTING
   STEERING
   STREIGNE
GO ESTROGEN
HO HONESTER
II ERINITES
   NITERIES
IK KERNITES
IL LISTENER
   SILENTER
IN INTENSER
   INTERNES
IO SEROTINE
IR INSERTER
   REINSERT
   REINTERS
   RENTIERS
   TERRINES
IS INTERESS
   SENTRIES
   TRENISES
```

IT INERTEST	**DI** TIREDEST	**IN** SNIFTIER	YEARLING	**SW** NEWSGIRL	**DW** SWINGLED
INTEREST	**DO** ROSETTED	**IP** SPITFIRE	**BM** REMBLING	**UV** VELURING	WELDINGS
STERNITE	TETRODES	**IR** FIRRIEST	**BO** IGNOBLER		**EF** FEELINGS
IU ESURIENT	**EL** RESETTLE	**IT** RIFTIEST	**BT** TREBLING	**EGILNS 117**	**EG** NEGLIGES
NEURITES	**ER** RESETTER	**KO** FORKIEST	**CI** CLINGIER	(SINGLE)	**EH** HEELINGS
RETINUES	**EW** TWEETERS	**KS** FRISKETS	**CK** CLERKING	**AB** SINGABLE	SHEELING
REUNITES	**FI** FRISETTE	**LO** FLORIEST	RECKLING	**AD** DEALINGS	**EK** KEELINGS
IV NERVIEST	**FL** FETTLERS	TREFOILS	**CS** CLINGERS	LEADINGS	SLEEKING
REINVEST	**GI** GRISETTE	**LR** TRIFLERS	CRINGLES	**AE** ENSILAGE	**EP** PEELINGS
SERVIENT	TERGITES	**LS** RIFTLESS	**CU** RECULING	LINEAGES	SLEEPING
SIRVENTE	**HI** ETHERIST	STIFLERS	ULCERING	**AF** FINAGLES	SPELING
IX INTERSEX	**HW** WHETTERS	**LT** FLITTERS	**CY** GLYCERIN	**AG** LIGNAGES	**ER** LEERINGS
IY SERENITY	**IL** RETITLES	**LW** FEWTRILS	**DD** REDDLING	**AH** HEALINGS	REELINGS
LO ENTRESOL	**IM** TERMITES	**MU** FREMITUS	**DE** ENGIRDLE	LEASHING	**ES** SEELINGS
LT LETTERNS	**IN** INERTEST	**NS** SNIFTERS	LINGERED	SHEALING	**ET** GENTILES
MO SERMONET	INTEREST	**OO** ROOFIEST	REDDLING	**AK** LINKAGES	SLEETING
STOREMEN	STERNITE	**OP** FIREPOTS	**DI** GRIDELIN	**AL** NIGELLAS	STEELING
MW TREWSMEN	**IP** PRETTIES	**OR** FROSTIER	**DU** INDULGER	**AM** MEASLING	**EV** SLEEVING
NO TENONERS	**IS** RESTIEST	ROTIFERS	**DY** YELDRING	**AN** EANLINGS	**EW** SWEELING
OO ROESTONE	**LN** LETTERNS	**OS** FOISTERS	**EF** FLEERING	LEANINGS	**FH** FLESHING
OP PROTENSE	**LO** LORETTES	**OW** FROWIEST	**EG** LEGERING	**AO** GASOLINE	SHELFING
OT ONSETTER	**LS** SETTLERS	**RT** FRITTERS	**EI** LINGERIE	**AP** ELAPSING	**FN** FLENSING
OV OVERNETS	STERLETS	**RU** FRITURES	**EO** ELOIGNER	PLEASING	**FR** FLINGERS
OX EXTENSOR	TRESTLES	FRUITERS	**ER** LINGERER	**AR** ARLESING	**FT** FELTINGS
PP PERPENTS	**MO** REMOTEST	FURRIEST	**ES** LEERINGS	ENGRAILS	**GG** LEGGINGS
PS PERTNESS	**MP** TEMPTERS	**SU** SURFEITS	REELINGS	NARGILES	**GR** NIGGLERS
PRESENTS	**NO** ONSETTER	SURFIEST	**EU** REGULINE	REALIGNS	SNIGGLER
SERPENTS	**NP** STREPENT	**SW** SWIFTERS	**EV** LEVERING	SANGLIER	**GS** SNIGGLES
PT STREPENT	**NS** STERNEST	**TU** TURFIEST	**FO** FLORIGEN	SLANGIER	**GU** LUGEINGS
PV PREVENTS	TESTERNS	TURFITES	**FS** FLINGERS	**AS** GAINLESS	**HI** SHEILING
RV RENVERST	**OP** TREETOPS	**UX** FIXTURES	**FY** FERLYING	GLASSINE	SHIELING
ST STERNEST	**OS** ROSETTES	**UZ** FURZIEST	**GI** NIGGLIER	LEASINGS	**HL** SHELLING
TESTERNS	**PU** UPSETTER		**GS** NIGGLERS	SEALINGS	**HP** HELPINGS
SU TRUENESS	**PX** PRETEXTS	**EGILNR 125**	SNIGGLER	**AT** EASTLING	**HR** HERLINGS
SW WESTERNS	**RU** REUTTERS	(LINGER)	**GY** GINGERLY	GELATINS	SHINGLER
SY STYRENES	UTTERERS	**AA** REGALIAN	**HI** HIRELING	GENITALS	**HS** SHINGLES
UV VENTURES	**SU** TRUSTEES	**AB** BLEARING	**HS** HERLINGS	STEALING	**HT** ENLIGHTS
	TU UTTEREST	**AC** CLEARING	SHINGLER	SLEAVING	LIGHTENS
EERSTT 200	**UX** TEXTURES	**AD** DEARLING	**IJ** JINGLIER	**AV** LEAVINGS	**HV** SHELVING
(ETTERS)		DRAGLINE	**IK** KINGLIER	SWEALING	**HW** WELSHING
AA STEARATE	**EFIRST 191**	**AE** ALGERINE	**IN** RELINING	**AW** SWEALING	**IN** ENISLING
AB ABETTERS	(STRIFE)	**AG** GANGLIER	**IO** RELIGION	**BM** SEMBLING	ENSILING
AD ASTERTED	**AG** FRIGATES	REGALING	**IS** RESILING	**BO** IGNOBLES	**IP** SPIELING
RESTATED	**AI** RATIFIES	**AH** NARGHILE	**IT** GIRTLINE	INGLOBES	**IR** RESILING
AG GREATEST	**AL** FLARIEST	NARGILEH	RETILING	**BS** BLESSING	**IT** LIGNITES
AH THEATERS	FRAILEST	**AI** GAINLIER	TINGLIER	GLIBNESS	LINGIEST
THEATRES	**AN** FENITARS	**AJ** JANGLIER	TIRELING	**BT** BELTINGS	**IV** VEILINGS
AI ARIETTES	**AR** FRATRIES	**AM** GERMINAL	**IV** RELIVING	**BU** BLUEINGS	**IW** WISELING
ITERATES	**BE** BRIEFEST	MALIGNER	REVILING	BULGINES	**JR** JINGLERS
TEARIEST	**BL** FILBERTS	MALINGER	**JS** JINGLERS	**CI** CEILINGS	**JT** JINGLETS
TREATIES	**BS** FIBSTERS	**AN** LEARNING	**JU** JUNGLIER	CIELINGS	**KK** LEKKINGS
TREATISE	**CE** FIERCEST	**AO** GERANIOL	**MS** GREMLINS	**CO** ECLOSING	**KP** SKELPING
AL ALERTEST	**CU** FRUTICES	REGIONAL	MERLINGS	**CR** CLINGERS	**KS** KINGLESS
AM TEAMSTER	**DR** DRIFTERS	**AP** PEARLING	MINGLERS	CRINGLES	**KT** KINGLETS
AN ENTREATS	**EI** FEISTIER	**AR** GNARLIER	**MU** RELUMING	**CU** LUCIGENS	**LM** SMELLING
RATTEENS	FERITIES	**AS** ARLESING	**OS** RESOLING	**CY** GLYCINES	**LN** SNELLING
AR RETRATES	FIERIEST	ENGRAILS	**OW** LOWERING	**DD** SLEDDING	**LO** LOGLINES
RETREATS	**EL** FERLIEST	NARGILES	**PS** PINGLERS	**DE** SEEDLING	**LP** SPELLING
TREATERS	**EM** FEMITERS	REALIGNS	SPERLING	**DG** GELDINGS	**LT** STELLING
AS ESTREATS	**EN** FERNIEST	SANGLIER	SPRINGLE	SLEDGING	TELLINGS
RESTATES	**ER** FERRITES	SLANGIER	**PY** REPLYING	SNIGGLED	**LW** SWELLING
AT ATTESTER	**ET** FRISETTE	**AT** ALERTING	**RU** RULERING	**DH** HINDLEGS	WELLINGS
AX EXTREATS	**EY** ESTERIFY	ALTERING	**RY** ERRINGLY	SHINGLED	**LY** YELLINGS
BE BESETTER	**FO** FORFEITS	INTEGRAL	**SS** RINGLESS	**DI** EILDINGS	**MM** LEMMINGS
BN BRENTEST	**FU** STUFFIER	RELATING	SLINGERS	SIDELING	**MR** GREMLINS
BU BURETTES	**GH** FIGHTERS	TANGLIER	**ST** LINGSTER	**DN** LENDINGS	MERLINGS
CU CURETTES	FREIGHTS	TRIANGLE	RINGLETS	**DO** GLENOIDS	MINGLERS
DE RESETTED	**GR** GRIFTERS	**AX** RELAXING	STERLING	SIDELONG	**MT** MELTINGS
SETTERED	**HI** SHIFTIER	**AY** LAYERING	TINGLERS	**DP** SPELDING	SMELTING
STREETED	**HS** SHIFTERS	RELAYING	TRINGLES	**DU** INDULGES	**MU** LEGUMINS
				DV DEVLINGS	

NT NESTLING
OR RESOLING
OU LIGNEOUS
OW LONGWISE
PR PINGLERS
   SPERLING
   SPRINGLE
PS SPIGNELS
PT PELTINGS
   PESTLING
PY YELPINGS
RS RINGLESS
   SLINGERS
RT LINGSTER
   RINGLETS
   STERLING
   TINGLERS
   TRINGLES
RW NEWSGIRL
SS SIGNLESS
ST GLISTENS
   SINGLETS
SU UGLINESS
SW SWINGLES
   WINGLESS
TT LETTINGS
   SETTLING
TW SWELTING
   WINGLETS
UV EVULSING

EGILNT 66
(TINGLE)
AA AGENTIAL
   ALGINATE
AB BELATING
   BLEATING
   TANGIBLE
AC CLEATING
AD DELATING
AE GALENITE
   GELATINE
   LEGATINE
AG TEAGLING
AH ATHELING
AM LIGAMENT
AN GANTLINE
   LATENING
AO GELATION
   LEGATION
AP PLEATING
AR ALERTING
   ALTERING
   INTEGRAL
   RELATING
   TANGLIER
   TRIANGLE
AS EASTLING
   GELATINS
   GENITALS
   STEALING
AV VALETING
AX EXALTING
AZ TEAZLING
BE BEETLING
BR TREBLING
BS BELTINGS
BT BLETTING
CE ELECTING
CH LETCHING

CI GENTILIC
CU CULTIGEN
DE DELETING
DI DILIGENT
EF FLEETING
EG GLEETING
ES GENTILES
   SLEETING
EW TWEELING
EX TELEXING
FS FELTINGS
FT FETTLING
GN GENTLING
   GLENTING
HP PENLIGHT
HS ENLIGHTS
   LIGHTENS
IR GIRTLINE
   RETILING
   TINGLIER
   TIRELING
IS LIGNITES
JS JINGLETS
KS KINGLETS
LS STELLING
LU GLUTELIN
MS MELTINGS
   SMELTING
NS NESTLING
NT NETTLING
PS PELTINGS
   PESTLING
PT PETTLING
RS LINGSTER
   RINGLETS
   STERLING
   TINGLERS
   TRINGLES
SS GLISTENS
   SINGLETS
ST LETTINGS
   SETTLING
SW SWELTING
   WINGLETS
UX EXULTING

EGILOS 132
(LOGIES)
AC CALIGOES
AD GOLIASED
AF FOLIAGES
AN GASOLINE
AP SPOILAGE
AR GASOLIER
   GIRASOLE
   SERAGLIO
AS GOLIASES
AT OTALGIES
BE OBLIGIES
BN IGNOBLES
   INGLOBES
CI LOGICISE
CN ECLOSING
DD DISLODGE
DN GLENOIDS
   SIDELONG
DT GODLIEST

   GOLDIEST
DZ GOLDSIZE
ES GELOSIES
EU EULOGIES
   EULOGISE
FG SOLFEGGI
GO GOOGLIES
HU OUGHLIES
LN LOGLINES
MR GOMERILS
MU ELOGIUMS
NR RESOLING
NU LIGNEOUS
NW LONGWISE
OO OOLOGIES
OU ISOLOGUE
RS GLOSSIER
SS GLOSSIES
ST ELOGISTS
TU EULOGIST

EGILRS 159
(LIGERS)
AA GASALIER
   LAIRAGES
   REGALIAS
AC GLACIERS
AD SLAIRGED
AE GASELIER
AG SLAGGIER
AM GREMIALS
   LAMIGERS
   REGALISM
AN ARLESING
   ENGRAILS
   NARGILES
   REALIGNS
   SANGLIER
   SLANGIER
AO GASOLIER
   GIRASOLE
   SERAGLIO
AS GLASSIER
AT GLARIEST
   REGALIST
AY GREASILY
AZ GLAZIERS
BB GRIBBLES
BT GILBERTS
CE CLERGIES
CG SCRIGGLE
CN CLINGERS
   CRINGLES
DD GRIDDLES
DE LEIDGERS
DR GIRDLERS
DU GUILDERS
   SLUDGIER
DW WERGILDS
EN LEERINGS
   REELINGS
EU REGULISE
EV VELIGERS
FN FLINGERS
GG GIGGLERS
GH HIGGLERS
GN NIGGLERS
   SNIGGLER
GW WIGGLERS
   WRIGGLES

HN HERLINGS
   SHINGLER
HT LIGHTERS
   RELIGHTS
   SLIGHTER
IN RESILING
IR GRISLIER
JN JINGLERS
MM GLIMMERS
MN GREMLINS
   MERLINGS
   MINGLERS
MO GOMERILS
NO RESOLING
NP PINGLERS
   SPERLING
   SPRINGLE
NS RINGLESS
   SLINGERS
NT LINGSTER
   RINGLETS
   STERLING
   TINGLERS
   TRINGLES
NW NEWSGIRL
OS GLOSSIER
PP GRIPPLES
ST GLISTERS
   GRISTLES
TT GLITTERS
TU GURLIEST
UV VIRGULES
ZZ GRIZZLES

EGILST 190
(LEGIST)
AC GELASTIC
AD GLADIEST
AE ELEGIAST
AH LAIGHEST
AL LEGALIST
   STILLAGE
   TILLAGES
AN EASTLING
   GELATINS
   GENITALS
   STEALING
AO OTALGIES
AR GLARIEST
   REGALIST
AZ GLAZIEST
BB GLIBBEST
BI BILGIEST
BN BELTINGS
BR GILBERTS
BU BULGIEST
CH GLITCHES
DD GLIDDEST
DE GELIDEST
DH DELIGHTS
   SLIGHTED
DO GODLIEST
   GOLDIEST
EG LEGGIEST
EN GENTILES
   SLEETING
   STEELING
ES ELEGISTS
FN FELTINGS

FU GULFIEST
HN ENLIGHTS
   LIGHTENS
HP PIGHTLES
HR LIGHTERS
   RELIGHTS
   SLIGHTER
HS SLEIGHTS
HT LIGHTEST
IM LEGITIMS
IN LIGNITES
   LINGIEST
JN JINGLETS
KN KINGLETS
LN STELLING
   TELLINGS
MN MELTINGS
   SMELTING
NN NESTLING
NP PELTINGS
   PESTLING
NR LINGSTER
   RINGLETS
   STERLING
   TINGLERS
   TRINGLES
NS GLISTENS
   SINGLETS
NT LETTINGS
   SETTLING
NW SWELTING
   WINGLETS
OS ELOGISTS
OU EULOGIST
RS GLISTERS
   GRISTLES
RT GLITTERS
RU GURLIEST

EGINNR 178
(GINNER)
AA ANEARING
AC ENRACING
AG ANGERING
   ENRAGING
AI ARGININE
AL LEARNING
AM ENARMING
   RENAMING
AS AGINNERS
   EARNINGS
   ENGRAINS
   GRANNIES
AV RAVENING
AY RENAYING
   YEARNING
BE BEGINNER
   BENIGNER
BN BRENNING
BO ENROBING
   RINGBONE
CO ENCORING
CS SCERNING
CT CENTRING
DE ENRINGED
DI NIDERING
DT TRENDING
DU ENDURING
   UNRINGED
EE ENGINEER

EG GREENING
   RENEGING
EP PREENING
ES ENGINERS
   INGENERS
   SERENING
   SNEERING
ET ENTERING
EV ENERVING
EW RENEWING
EY ENGINERY
   RENEYING
FI ENFIRING
   INFRINGE
   REFINING
FS FERNINGS
GI GREINING
   REIGNING
GN GRENNING
GO ENGORING
HI INHERING
IL RELINING
IP REPINING
IS RESINING
NS RENNINGS
OO RONEOING
OP REPONING
OT NITROGEN
OV VIGNERON
RS GRINNERS
RU UNERRING
ST STERNING
SU ENSURING
TU RETUNING
TV VENTRING

EGINOS 78
(INGOES)
AB BEGONIAS
AC COINAGES
AD AGONISED
   DIAGNOSE
AG GASOLINE
AR IGNAROES
   ORGANISE
   ORIGANES
AS AGONISES
AZ AGONIZES
BD OBSIGNED
BL IGNOBLES
   INGLOBES
BO BESOGNIO
BR SOBERING
CD COGNISED
CL ECLOSING
CS COGNISES
CZ COGNIZES
DI INDIGOES
DL GLENOIDS
   SIDELONG
DM SMIDGEON
DP DEPOSING
   DISPONGE
   PIDGEONS
DR NEGROIDS
DW WENDIGOS
   WIDGEONS
EO OOGENIES
EP EPIGONES

ER ERINGOES
ET EGESTION
GK GINGKOES
   GINGKOES
HS SHOEINGS
HT HISTOGEN
HU GINHOUSE
IM IGNOMIES
IR SEIGNIOR
LL LOGLINES
LR RESOLING
LU LIGNEOUS
LW LONGWISE
MR NEGROISM
MT MITOGENS
MU GEMINOUS
MY MOSEYING
NP OPENINGS
PR PERIGONS
   REPOSING
   SPONGIER
PT PONGIEST
PX EXPOSING
PY POESYING
RR IGNORERS
RS SIGNORES
RT GENITORS
   ROSETING
RY SEIGNORY
TT TENTIGOS

EGINRS 68
(SINGER)
AA ANGARIES
AB BEARINGS
   SABERING
AC CREASING
   GRECIANS
   SEARCING
AD DERAIGNS
   GRADINES
   READINGS
AE GESNERIA
AG GEARINGS
   GREASING
   SNAGGIER
AH HEARINGS
   HEARSING
   SHEARING
AK SKEARING
AL ARLESING
   ENGRAILS
   NARGILES
   REALIGNS
   SANGLIER
   SLANGIER
AM GERMAINS
   SMEARING
AN AGINNERS
   EARNINGS
   ENGRAINS
   GRANNIES
AO IGNAROES
   ORGANISE
   ORIGANES
AP PREASING
   SPEARING
AR EARRINGS
   GRAINERS
AS REASSIGN

   SEARINGS
   SERINGAS
AT ANGRIEST
   ASTRINGE
   GANISTER
   GANTRIES
   GRANITES
   INGRATES
   RANGIEST
   REASTING
   STEARING
AV VINEGARS
AW SWEARING
   WEARINGS
AY RESAYING
BE BIGENERS
BO SOBERING
BR BRINGERS
BW BREWINGS
CE CREESING
   GENERICS
CL CLINGERS
   CRINGLES
CN SCERNING
CR CRINGERS
CT CRESTING
CU RECUSING
   RESCUING
   SCUNGIER
   SECURING
CW SCREWING
CY SYNERGIC
DD REDDINGS
DE DESIGNER
   ENERGIDS
   REDESIGN
   REEDINGS
   RESIGNED
DI DESIRING
   RESIDING
   RINGSIDE
DO NEGROIDS
DP SPRINGED
DR GRINDERS
   REGRINDS
DS DRESSING
DT STRINGED
DW REDWINGS
DY SYNERGID
   SYRINGED
EE ENERGIES
   ENERGISE
EF FEERINGS
   REEFINGS
EG GREESING
EH GREENISH
   SHEERING
EJ JEERINGS
EK KREESING
   SKEERING
EL LEERINGS
   REELINGS
EM REGIMENS
EN ENGINERS
   INGENERS
   SERENING
   SNEERING
EO ERINGOES
EP SPEERING
   SPREEING

ER RESIGNER
ES GREISENS
ET GENTRIES
   INTEGERS
   REESTING
   STEERING
   STREIGNE
EU SEIGNEUR
EV SEVERING
   VEERINGS
EW SEWERING
FH FRESHING
FL FLINGERS
FN FERNINGS
FU GUNFIRES
   REFUSING
FW SWERFING
GL NIGGLERS
   SNIGGLER
GS GRESSING
   SNIGGERS
HK GHERKINS
HL HERLINGS
   SHINGLER
HP SPHERING
HR HERRINGS
HT RIGHTENS
HU USHERING
HW SHREWING
   WHINGERS
IL RESILING
IM REMISING
IN RESINING
IO SEIGNIOR
IP SPEIRING
IT GIRNIEST
   IGNITERS
   REISTING
   STINGIER
   STRIGINE
IU SIGNIEUR
IV REVISING
IW RINGWISE
JK JERKINGS
JL JINGLERS
KR SKERRING
KU RESKUING
LM GREMLINS
   MERLINGS
   MINGLERS
LO RESOLING
LP PINGLERS
   SPERLING
   SPRINGLE
LS RINGLESS
   SLINGERS
LT LINGSTER
   RINGLETS
   STERLING
   TINGLERS
   TRINGLES
LW NEWSGIRL
MO NEGROISM
MP IMPREGNS
MS GRIMNESS
MU RESUMING
NN RENNINGS
NR GRINNERS
NT STERNING
NU ENSURING

OP PERIGONS
   REPOSING
   SPONGIER
OR IGNORERS
OS SIGNORES
OT GENITORS
   ROSETING
OY SEIGNORY
PP REPPINGS
PR SPERRING
PS PRESSING
   SPERSING
   SPRINGES
PT PRESTING
PU PERSUING
   PERUSING
   SUPERING
RT RESTRING
   RINGSTER
   STRINGER
   TRESSING
   TRIGNESS
RW WRINGERS
RY SERRYING
ST RESTINGS
   STINGERS
   TRESSING
   TRIGNESS
SV SERVINGS
   VERSINGS
SW SWINGERS
SY SYRINGES
TT GITTERNS
TV STERVING
TW STREWING
   WRESTING
VW SWERVING

EGINRT 39
(TINGER)
AA AERATING
AB BERATING
   REBATING
AC CATERING
   CITRANGE
   CREATING
   REACTING
AD DERATING
   GRADIENT
   TREADING
AH EARTHING
   HEARTING
AK RETAKING
AL ALERTING
   ALTERING
   INTEGRAL
   RELATING
   TANGLIER
   TRIANGLE
AM EMIGRANT
AP TAPERING
AS ANGRIEST
   ASTRINGE
   GANISTER
   GANTRIES
   GRANITES
   INGRATES
   RANGIEST
   REASTING
   STEARING
AT ARETTING

   TREATING
AV AVERTING
   REPOSING
   SPONGIER
   TAVERING
   VINTAGER
AW TWANGIER
   WATERING
BH BERTHING
   BRIGHTEN
BI REBITING
BL TREBLING
CE ERECTING
   GENTRICE
CH RETCHING
CI RECITING
CK TRECKING
CN CENTRING
CO GERONTIC
CS CRESTING
CU ERUCTING
DI DIRIGENT
DN TRENDING
DS STRINGED
EG GREETING
EM METERING
   REGIMENT
EN ENTERING
EP PETERING
ES GENTRIES
   INTEGERS
   REESTING
   STEERING
   STREIGNE
EU GENITURE
EV EVERTING
EW TWEERING
EX EXERTING
   GENETRIX
FH FRIGHTEN
FT FRETTING
FU FEUTRING
   REFUTING
FY GENTRIFY
HI THINGIER
HO THROEING
HS RIGHTENS
HW WRETHING
IL GIRTLINE
   RETILING
   TINGLIER
   TIRELING
IM MERITING
   MITERING
IR RETIRING
IS GIRNIEST
   IGNITERS
   REISTING
   STINGIER
   STRIGINE
IU INTRIGUE
IV RIVETING
IX GENITRIX
KK TREKKING
LS LINGSTER
   RINGLETS
   STERLING
   TINGLERS
   TRINGLES
NO NITROGEN
NS STERNING
NU RETUNING

NV VENTRING
OS GENITORS
   ROSETING
OT OTTERING
OU OUTREIGN
OW TOWERING
OX OXTERING
OZ ROZETING
PS PRESTING
PU ERUPTING
   REPUTING
RS RESTRING
   RINGSTER
   STRINGER
RY RETRYING
SS RESTINGS
   STINGERS
ST GITTERNS
SV STERVING
SW STREWING
   WRESTING
TU UTTERING

EGINST 107
(ESTING)
AA SAGINATE
AB BEATINGS
AD SEDATING
   STEADING
AE SAGENITE
AF FEASTING
AG NAGGIEST
AH GAHNITES
   HEATINGS
AL EASTLING
   GELATINS
   GENITALS
   STEALING
AM MANGIEST
   MINTAGES
   STEAMING
   TEAMINGS
AN ANTIGENS
   GENTIANS
   STEANING
AR ANGRIEST
   ASTRINGE
   GANISTER
   GANTRIES
   GRANITES
   INGRATES
   RANGIEST
   REASTING
   STEARING
AS EASTINGS
   GENISTAS
   GIANTESS
   SEATINGS
   TEASINGS
   TSIGANES
AT ESTATING
   TANGIEST
AU SAUTEING
AV VINTAGES
AW SWEATING
AY YEASTING
BE BEIGNETS

BH	BENIGHTS
BL	BELTINGS
BT	BETTINGS
CE	GENETICS
CH	ETCHINGS
CN	SCENTING
CR	CRESTING
DD	STEDDING
DE	INGESTED
	SIGNETED
	STEEDING
DI	DINGIEST
	INDIGEST
DN	STENDING
DR	STRINGED
DU	DUNGIEST
EG	EGESTING
EH	SEETHING
	SHEETING
EK	STEEKING
EL	GENTILES
	SLEETING
	STEELING
EM	MEETINGS
	STEEMING
EN	STEENING
EO	EGESTION
EP	STEEPING
ER	GENTRIES
	INTEGERS
	REESTING
	STEERING
	STREIGNE
ET	GENTIEST
EU	EUGENIST
EV	STEEVING
	VENTIGES
EW	SWEETING
EX	EXIGENTS
FL	FELTINGS
FM	FIGMENTS
GT	GETTINGS
GU	GUESTING
	GUNGIEST
HI	HEISTING
	NIGHTIES
	THINGIES
HL	ENLIGHTS
	LIGHTENS
HN	SENNIGHT
HR	RIGHTENS
HT	SHETTING
	TIGHTENS
IL	LIGNITES
	LINGIEST
IM	MINGIEST
IN	STEINING
IR	GIRNIEST
	IGNITERS
	REISTING
	STINGIER
	STRIGINE
IW	WINGIEST
IX	EXISTING
IZ	ZINGIEST
JL	JINGLETS
JS	JESTINGS
KL	KINGLETS
LL	STELLING

	TELLINGS
LM	MELTINGS
	SMELTING
LN	NESTLING
LP	PELTINGS
	PESTLING
LR	LINGSTER
	RINGLETS
	STERLING
	TINGLERS
	TRINGLES
LS	GLISTENS
	SINGLETS
LT	LETTINGS
LW	SWELTING
	WINGLETS
MM	STEMMING
MO	MITOGENS
MP	PIGMENTS
NN	STENNING
NR	STERNING
NT	NETTINGS
	STENTING
	TENTINGS
NV	VENTINGS
OP	PONGIEST
OR	GENITORS
	ROSETING
OT	TENTIGOS
PP	STEPPING
PR	PRESTING
PT	PETTINGS
QU	QUESTING
RR	RESTRING
	RINGSTER
	STRINGER
RS	RESTINGS
	STINGERS
	TRESSING
	TRIGNESS
RT	GITTERNS
RV	STERVING
RW	STREWING
	WRESTING
ST	SETTINGS
	TESTINGS
SV	VESTINGS
SW	STEWINGS
	WESTINGS
TT	STETTING

EGNORS 155
(ONGERS)

AC	ACROGENS
	CORNAGES
AI	IGNAROES
	ORGANISE
	ORIGANES
AM	MEGARONS
AO	OREGANOS
AR	GROANERS
AT	ORANGEST
	RAGSTONE
AW	WAGONERS
BI	SOBERING
BU	BURGEONS
CE	COGENERS
	CONGREES

CH	GROSCHEN
CS	CONGRESS
CU	CONGRUES
	SCROUNGE
CY	CRYOGENS
DI	NEGROIDS
DO	DRONGOES
DU	GUERDONS
EG	ENGORGES
EI	ERINGOES
EK	KEROGENS
ET	ESTROGEN
EU	GENEROUS
EY	ERYNGOES
GT	GONGSTER
HL	LEGHORNS
HU	ENROUGHS
	ROUGHENS
II	SEIGNIOR
IL	RESOLING
IM	NEGROISM
IP	PERIGONS
	REPOSING
IR	IGNORERS
IS	SIGNORES
IT	GENITORS
	ROSETING
IY	SEIGNORY
LM	MONGRELS
LU	LOUNGERS
MU	MURGEONS
NT	RONTGENS
PS	SPONGERS
PY	PYROGENS
RT	STRONGER
RW	WRONGERS
ST	SONGSTER
SU	SURGEONS
TU	STURGEON
TW	WRONGEST

EHIRST 153
(ITHERS)

AC	CHARIEST
	THERIACS
AD	HAIRSTED
	HARDIEST
AE	HEARTIES
AI	HAIRIEST
AN	INEARTHS
AO	HOARIEST
AR	TRASHIER
AS	SHERIATS
AW	SWATHIER
	WATERISH
AY	HYSTERIA
BC	BRITCHES
BE	HERBIEST
BL	BLITHERS
BR	REBIRTHS
BS	HERBISTS
CD	DITCHERS
CE	CHESTIER
	HERETICS
CH	HITCHERS
CI	CHRISTIE
CN	CHRISTEN
	CITHERNS
	SNITCHER

CO	ROTCHIES
	THEORICS
CP	PITCHERS
	SPITCHER
CS	STRICHES
CT	CHITTERS
	RICHTEST
	STITCHER
CY	HYSTERIC
DI	DISHERIT
DT	THIRSTED
	THRISTED
EE	ETHERISE
EM	ERETHISM
	ETHERISM
EO	ISOTHERE
	THEORIES
	THEORISE
EP	TREESHIP
ES	HEISTERS
ET	ETHERIST
FG	FIGHTERS
	FREIGHTS
FI	SHIFTIER
FS	SHIFTERS
GG	THIGGERS
GI	TIGERISH
GL	LIGHTERS
	RELIGHTS
	SLIGHTER
GN	RIGHTENS
GO	GHOSTIER
GR	RIGHTERS
GS	SIGHTERS
GT	RIGHTEST
	STREIGHT
HW	WHITHERS
IN	INHERITS
IR	SHIRTIER
IT	SHITTIER
	THIRTIES
KN	RETHINKS
	THINKERS
LL	THILLERS
LP	PHILTERS
	PHILTRES
LS	SLITHERS
	THRISSEL
LT	THRISTLE
LU	LUTHIERS
LW	WHIRTLES
	WHISTLER
LY	SLITHERY
MO	ISOTHERM
	MOITHERS
MS	SMITHERS
MY	SMITHERY
NN	THINNERS
NZ	ZITHERNS
OP	TROPHIES
OR	HERITORS
OS	HOISTERS
	HORSIEST
	HOSTRIES
	SHORTIES
OT	THEORIST
	THORITES
OU	OUTHIRES

OV	OVERHITS
OW	WORTHIES
PS	HIPSTERS
	THRIPSES
PW	WHIPSTER
RT	THIRSTER
RV	THRIVERS
RW	WHIRRETS
SU	RUSHIEST
SW	SWITHERS
TW	WHITRETS
	WHITHER
	WHITTERS

EHORST 189
(OTHERS)

AB	BATHROSE
AC	CHAROSET
	THORACES
AG	SHORTAGE
AH	HAROSETH
AI	HOARIEST
AL	LOATHERS
AO	TOHEROAS
AS	ASTHORES
	HAROSETS
	HOARSEST
AT	RHEOSTAT
AX	THORAXES
BC	BOTCHERS
BL	BROTHELS
BO	THEORBOS
BR	BROTHERS
BT	BETROTHS
CC	CROCHETS
	CROTCHES
CE	TROCHEES
CI	ROTCHIES
	THEORICS
CL	CHORTLES
CO	CHEROOTS
CP	POTCHERS
CR	TORCHERS
CU	SCOUTHER
	TOUCHERS
CW	SCOWTHER
DP	POTSHERD
DR	REDSHORT
EI	ISOTHERE
	THEORIES
	THEORISE
EL	HOSTELER
EM	THEOREMS
EN	HONESTER
FN	FORHENTS
GI	GHOSTIER
GU	ROUGHEST
HU	SHOUTHER
IM	ISOTHERM
IN	HORNIEST
IP	TROPHIES
IR	HERITORS
IS	HOISTERS
	HORSIEST
	HOSTRIES
	SHORTIES
IT	THEORIST
	THORITES
IU	OUTHIRES

IV	OVERHITS
IW	WORTHIES
LN	HORNLETS
LS	HOLSTERS
	HOSTLERS
LT	THROSTLE
LY	HOSTELRY
MO	SMOOTHER
MS	SMOTHERS
MU	MOUTHERS
MY	SMOTHERY
NR	NORTHERS
NS	SHORTENS
NT	THORNSET
NU	SOUTHERN
OS	ORTHOSES
	SHOOTERS
	SOOTHERS
OV	OVERSHOT
PP	PROPHETS
PS	STROPHES
PU	POUTHERS
PY	TROPHESY
RW	THROWERS
ST	SHORTEST
SU	SHOUTERS
	SOUTHERS
UY	OUTHYRES

EIILST 139
(TILIES)

AB	ALBITISE
	SIBILATE
AC	SILICATE
AD	IDEALIST
AF	FILIATES
AH	HAILIEST
AL	TAILLIES
AN	ALIENIST
	LITANIES
AR	LAIRIEST
AS	SAILIEST
AV	VITALISE
AX	LAXITIES
AZ	TAILZIES
BG	BILGIEST
BR	TRILBIES
BT	STILBITE
CC	SCILICET
CF	FELSITIC
DD	TIDDLIES
DL	DILLIEST
DM	DELIMITS
	LIMITEDS
DR	REDISTIL
DU	UTILISED
DV	LIVIDEST
EN	LENITIES
ER	TILERIES
EV	LEVITIES
	VEILIEST
EW	LEWISITE
FH	TILEFISH
FM	FILMIEST
FT	FITLIEST
GM	LEGITIMS
GN	LIGNITES
	LINGIEST
HL	HILLIEST
HT	LITHITES

```
KM MILKIEST      ET INTERTIE      CH CHOLINES      TV NOVELIST      FF SNIFFLER      AS EASTLINS
KS SILKIEST         RETINITE      CI ISOCLINE         VIOLENTS      FG FLINGERS         ELASTINS
LN NIELLIST      FL FLINTIER         SILICONE      TW TOWLINES      GG NIGGLERS         SALIENTS
LR STILLIER         INFILTER      CL LIONCELS      UV EVULSION         SNIGGLER         STANIELS
LS SILLIEST      FO NOTIFIER      CO COLONIES      VV INVOLVES      GH HERLINGS      AU ALUNITES
LT TILLIEST      FS SNIFTIER         COLONISE                         SHINGLER         INSULATE
   TILLITES      GH THINGIER         ECLOSION      EILNRS 77       GI RESILING      AV VENTAILS
LW TWILLIES      GL GIRTLINE      CP PINOCLES      (LINERS)        GJ JINGLERS      AW LAWNIEST
MP LIMEPITS         RETILING      CR INCLOSER      AB RINSABLE      GM GREMLINS      BD BLINDEST
MR LIMITERS         TINGLIER         LICENSOR      AC CARLINES         MERLINGS      BE STILBENE
   MIRLIEST         TIRELING      CS CONSEILS      AD ISLANDER         MINGLERS         TENSIBLE
MS ELITISMS      GM MERITING         INCLOSES      AG ARLESING      GO RESOLING      BG BELTINGS
   SLIMIEST         MITERING      CT LECTIONS         ENGRAILS      GP PINGLERS      BM NIMBLEST
MT MISTITLE      GR RETIRING      CX LEXICONS         NARGILES         SPERLING      BZ BLINTZES
MY MYELITIS      GS GIRNIEST      DE ESLOINED         REALIGNS         SPRINGLE      CF INFLECTS
NO ETIOLINS         IGNITERS      DG GLENOIDS         SANGLIER      GS RINGLESS      CH LINCHETS
NR NIRLIEST         REISTING      DI LIONISED         SLANGIER         SLINGERS      CO LECTIONS
   NITRILES         STINGIER      DO SOLENOID      AH INHALERS      GT LINGSTER      CS STENCILS
NT LINTIEST         STRIGINE      DR DISENROL      AI AIRLINES         RINGLETS      CU CUTLINES
NY SENILITY      GU INTRIGUE      DS SONDELIS         SNAILIER         STERLING         TUNICLES
OP PISOLITE      GV RIVETING      DU DELUSION      AM MARLINES         TINGLERS      DE ENLISTED
   POLITIES      GX GENITRIX         INSOULED         MINERALS         TRINGLES         LINTSEED
OR ROILIEST      HR HIRRIENT         UNSOILED      AO AILERONS      GW NEWSGIRL         LISTENED
OS SOILIEST      HS INHERITS      EF FELONIES         ALERIONS      IK SLINKIER      DP SPLINTED
PP LIPPIEST      JK JIRKINET         OLEFINES         ALIENORS      IT NIRLIEST      DR SNIRTLED
PR TRIPLIES      KL TINKLIER      ER ELOINERS      AP PEARLINS         NITRILES         TENDRILS
PS PITILESS      LS NIRLIEST      ET NOSELITE         PRALINES      KK KLINKERS         TRINDLES
   SPILITES         NITRILES      EV NOVELISE      AR SNARLIER      KM KREMLINS      DU DILUENTS
PY PYELITIS      MO MINORITE      FU NOISEFUL      AS RAINLESS      KP SPRINKLE         INSULTED
RT STILTIER      MS INTERIMS      FX FLEXIONS      AT ENTRAILS      KS SLINKERS         UNLISTED
RU UTILISER         MINISTER      GL LOGLINES         LATRINES      KT LINKSTER      EE SELENITE
ST ELITISTS      MT INTERMIT      GR RESOLING         RATLINES         STRINKLE      EG GENTILES
   SILTIEST      MX INTERMIX      GU LIGNEOUS         TRENAILS         TINKLERS         SLEETING
SU ULITISES      NV INVERTIN      GW LONGWISE      AU LUNARIES      KW WINKLERS         STEELING
   UTILISES      OP POINTIER      HL HELLIONS      AV RAVELINS         WRINKLES      EI LENITIES
UY TUILYIES      OR INTERIOR      HP PINHOLES      AX RELAXINS      MT MINSTREL      EN LENIENTS
UZ TUILZIES      PS PRISTINE      HS HOLINESS      AY INLAYERS      OP PROLINES         SENTINEL
   UTILIZES      RW WINTRIER      HT NEOLITHS         SNAILERY      OR LORINERS      EO NOSELITE
                 SS SINISTER      HV NOVELISH      BB NIBBLERS      OT RETINOLS      EP PLENTIES
EIINRT 30       ST NITRITES      IS ELISIONS      BD BLINDERS      PS PILSNERS      ER LISTENER
(INTIRE)           STINTIER         ISOLINES         BRINDLES      PT SPLINTER         SILENTER
AD DAINTIER      SU NEURITIS         LIONISES      BE BERLINES      PU PURLINES      ET ENTITLES
AF FAINTIER      SV INVITERS         OILINESS      BI RINSIBLE      ST SNIRTLES      EV VEINLETS
AL INERTIAL         VINTRIES      IT ETIOLINS      BK BLINKERS      TU INSULTER      FG FELTINGS
AP PAINTIER         VITRINES      IV OLIVINES      CE LICENSER         LUSTRINE      GH ENLIGHTS
AS INERTIAS                       IZ LIONIZES         RECLINES      TY TINSELRY         LIGHTENS
   RAINIEST      EILNOS 47        KM MOLESKIN         SILENCER                      GI LIGNITES
BE BENITIER      (OLINES)         KW SNOWLIKE      CG CLINGERS      EILNST 45          LINGIEST
BG REBITING      AD NODALISE      LT STELLION         CRINGLES      (INTLES)        GJ JINGLETS
BS BRINIEST      AG GASOLINE      MM MOLIMENS      CK CLINKERS      AB INSTABLE      GK KINGLETS
CD INDIRECT      AK KAOLINES      MU EMULSION         CRINKLES      AF INFLATES      GL STELLING
CE ICTERINE      AM MINEOLAS      MV NOVELISM      CO INCLOSER      AG EASTLING         TELLINGS
CG RECITING         SEMOLINA      NT INSOLENT         LICENSOR         GELATINS      GM MELTINGS
CN INTRINCE      AN SOLANINE      NW SNOWLINE      DF FLINDERS         GENITALS         SMELTING
CS CITRINES      AP OPALINES      OP POLONIES      DK KINDLERS         STEALING      GN NESTLING
   CRINITES      AR AILERONS         POLONISE      DO DISENROL      AI ALIENIST      GP PELTINGS
   INCITERS         ALIENORS      OT LOONIEST      DP SPELDRIN         LITANIES      GR LINGSTER
CU NEURITIC      AT ELATIONS         OILSTONE      DS RINDLESS      AK LANKIEST         RINGLETS
DD NITRIDED         INSOLATE      OV VIOLONES      DT SNIRTLED      AM AILMENTS         STERLING
DG DIRIGENT         TOENAILS      PP PLENIPOS         TENDRILS         ALIMENTS         TINGLERS
DM DIRIMENT      BC BINOCLES      PR PROLINES         TRINDLES         MANLIEST         TRINGLES
DP INTREPID      BG IGNOBLES      PS EPSILONS      DW SWINDLER      AO ELATIONS      GS GLISTENS
DS DISINTER         INGLOBES      PT POINTELS      EG LEERINGS         INSOLATE         SINGLETS
   INDITERS      BO OBELIONS      RR LORINERS         REELINGS         TOENAILS      GT LETTINGS
   NITRIDES      BP BONSPIEL      RT RETINOLS      EM ERMELINS      AP PANTILES         SETTLING
   RINDIEST      BW BOWLINES      SU ELUSIONS      EO ELOINERS         PLAINEST      GW SWELTING
DU UNTIDIER      CD INCLOSED      SW LEWISSON      EP PILSENER      AR ENTRAILS         WINGLETS
EO ERIONITE      CE CINEOLES      TU ELUTIONS      ES REINLESS         LATRINES      HO NEOLITHS
ES ERINITES      CG ECLOSING         OUTLINES      ET LISTENER         RATLINES
   NITERIES                                           SILENTER         TRENAILS
```

IL NIELLIST
IO ETIOLINS
IR NIRLIEST
   NITRILES
IT LINTIEST
IY SENILITY
KR LINKSTER
   STRINKLE
   TINKLERS
KS LENTISKS
KT KNITTLES
KW TWINKLES
LO STELLION
LY SILENTLY
   TINSELLY
MR MINSTREL
MU MUSLINET
NO INSOLENT
OO LOONIEST
   OILSTONE
OP POINTELS
OR RETINOLS
OU ELUTIONS
   OUTLINES
OV NOVELIST
   VIOLENTS
OW TOWLINES
PR SPLINTER
PS PLENISTS
RS SNIRTLES
RU INSULTER
   LUSTRINE
RY TINSELRY
ST TINTLESS
SU UTENSILS
TU LUTENIST

EILORS 37
(OILERS)
AA OLEARIAS
AC CALORIES
   CARIOLES
AD DARIOLES
   SOLIDARE
   SOREDIAL
AF FORESAIL
AG GASOLIER
   GIRASOLE
   SERAGLIO
AH AIRHOLES
   SHOALIER
AM MORALISE
AN AILERONS
   ALERIONS
   ALIENORS
AP PELORIAS
   POLARISE
AS SOLARISE
AT SOTERIAL
AV OVERSAIL
   VALORISE
   VARIOLES
   VOLARIES
AY ROYALISE
AZ SOLARIZE
BB SLOBBIER
BC BRICOLES
   CORBEILS
BH BOLSHIER
BL BROLLIES

BM EMBROILS
BR BROILERS
BT STROBILE
   TRILOBES
BW BLOWSIER
CD SCLEROID
CL COLLIERS
   ORSELLIC
CN INCLOSER
   LICENSOR
CT CLOISTER
   COISTREL
   CORTILES
   COSTLIER
   CREOLIST
DI IDOLISER
DL DOLLIERS
DN DISENROL
DS SOLDIERS
DT STOLIDER
DU SOULDIER
DY SOLDIERY
EF FORELIES
EI OILERIES
EK ROSELIKE
EL ORSEILLE
EN ELOINERS
EP PELORIES
ET LITEROSE
   TROELIES
EV OVERLIES
   RELIEVOS
   VOLERIES
EW OWLERIES
FJ FRIJOLES
FK FOLKSIER
FP PROFILES
FS FLOSSIER
FT FLORIEST
   TREFOILS
GM GOMERILS
GN RESOLING
GS GLOSSIER
HP PILHORSE
   POLISHER
HS SLOSHIER
IT ROILIEST
LT TRILLOES
   TROLLIES
LZ ZORILLES
MO SLOOMIER
MP IMPLORES
   PELORISM
MR LORIMERS
NP PROLINES
NR LORINERS
NT RETINOLS
OT TROOLIES
PP SLOPPIER
PS SPOILERS
PT POITRELS
PU PERILOUS
PV OVERSLIP
SS RISSOLES
SU SOILURES
TT TRIOLETS
TU LOURIEST
   OUTLIERS
ZZ SOZZLIER

EILORT 18
(LOITER)
AC EROTICAL
   LORICATE
AD IDOLATER
   TAILORED
AE AEROLITE
AF FLOATIER
AH AEROLITH
   LOATHIER
AN ORIENTAL
   RELATION
AP EPILATOR
   PETIOLAR
AS SOTERIAL
AT LITERATO
BD TRILOBED
BS STROBILE
   TRILOBES
BT BLOTTIER
   LIBRETTO
CH CHLORITE
   CLOTHIER
CI ELICITOR
CP PETROLIC
CS CLOISTER
   COISTREL
   CORTILES
   COSTLIER
   CREOLIST
CT CLOTTIER
CY CRYOLITE
DE DOLERITE
   LOITERED
DS STOLIDER
EH HOTELIER
EK LORIKEET
EM MOTELIER
ER LOITERER
ES LITEROSE
   TROELIES
FF FORELIFT
   TREFOILS
FU FLUORITE
GH REGOLITH
HP HELIPORT
HY RHYOLITE
IS ROILIEST
IT TROILITE
KO ROOTLIKE
LS TRILLOES
   TROLLIES
NR RITORNEL
NS RETINOLS
NT TROTLINE
OS TROOLIES
OV OVERTOIL
PR PORTLIER
PS POITRELS
PW PILEWORT
RU ULTERIOR
ST TRIOLETS
SU LOURIEST
   OUTLIERS
TY TOILETRY

EILOST 21
(OILETS)
AC ALOETICS

   COALIEST
   SOCIETAL
AD DIASTOLE
   ISOLATED
   SODALITE
   SOLIDATE
AF FOLIATES
AG OTALGIES
AK KEITLOAS
AM LOAMIEST
AN ELATIONS
   INSOLATE
   TOENAILS
AP SPOLIATE
AR SOTERIAL
AS ISOLATES
AT TOTALISE
AV VIOLATES
BB BIBELOTS
BF BOTFLIES
BO LOOBIEST
BR STROBILE
   TRILOBES
BW BLOWIEST
CD DOCILEST
CN LECTIONS
CP TOECLIPS
CR CLOISTER
   COISTREL
   CORTILES
   COSTLIER
   CREOLIST
CS SOLECIST
   SOLSTICE
DG GODLIEST
   GOLDIEST
DM MELODIST
DR STOLIDER
DS SOLIDEST
DT DOILTEST
DU SOLITUDE
EM MESOLITE
   MISLETOE
EN NOSELITE
EP PETIOLES
ER LITEROSE
   TROELIES
ES ESTOILES
EW OWELTIES
EZ ZEOLITES
FJ JETFOILS
FM FILEMOTS
FR FLORIEST
   TREFOILS
FT LOFTIEST
FU OUTFLIES
GS ELOGISTS
GU EULOGIST
HM HELOTISM
HN NEOLITHS
HO HOOLIEST
HP HELISTOP
   HOPLITES
   ISOPLETH
IN ETIOLINS
IP PISOLITE
   POLITIES
IR ROILIEST
IS SOILIEST
JL JOLLIEST

JT JOLTIEST
KY YOLKIEST
LM MELILOTS
LN STELLION
LR TRILLOES
   TROLLIES
LS TOILLESS
LW LOWLIEST
MO TOILSOME
MP POLEMIST
MT MOTLIEST
NN INSOLENT
NO LOONIEST
   OILSTONE
NP POINTELS
NR RETINOLS
NU ELUTIONS
   OUTLINES
NV NOVELIST
   VIOLENTS
NW TOWLINES
OP LOOPIEST
OR TROOLIES
OS OSTIOLES
   STOOLIES
OZ ZOOLITES
PR POITRELS
PS PISTOLES
   PTILOSES
   SLOPIEST
PT PISTOLET
   PLOTTIES
   POLITEST
PX EXPLOITS
RT TRIOLETS
RU LOURIEST
   OUTLIERS
SS LOSSIEST
SU LOUSIEST
TT STILETTO
UV OUTLIVES
   SOLUTIVE

EILRST 44
(LITERS)
AB LIBRATES
AC ALTRICES
   ARTICLES
   RECITALS
   SELICTAR
AD DILATERS
AE ATELIERS
   EARLIEST
   LEARIEST
   REALTIES
AF FLARIEST
   FRAILEST
AG GLARIEST
   REGALIST
AI LAIRIEST
AK LARKIEST
   STALKIER
   STARLIKE
AL LITERALS
   TALLIERS
AM LAMITERS
   MARLIEST
AN ENTRAILS
   LATRINES

   RATLINES
   TRENAILS
AO SOTERIAL
AP PILASTER
   PLAISTER
   PLAITERS
AR RETIRALS
   RETRIALS
   TRAILERS
AS REALISTS
   SALTIERS
   SALTIRES
   SLAISTER
AT TERTIALS
AU URALITES
BB STIBBLER
   TRIBBLES
BD BRISTLED
   DRIBLETS
BF FILBERTS
BG GILBERTS
BH BLITHERS
BI TRILBIES
BM TIMBRELS
BO STROBILE
   TRILOBES
BS BLISTERS
   BRISTLES
BT BRITTLES
   TRIBLETS
BU BURLIEST
   SUBTILER
BY BLISTERY
CC CIRCLETS
CE RETICLES
   SCLERITE
   TIERCELS
CK STICKLER
   STRICKLE
   TICKLERS
   TRICKLES
CO CLOISTER
   COISTREL
   CORTILES
   COSTLIER
   CREOLIST
   CLITTERS
CU CURLIEST
   UTRICLES
DD STRIDDLE
   TIDDLERS
DI REDISTIL
DN SNIRTLED
   TENDRILS
   TRINDLES
DO STOLIDER
DU DILUTERS
   LURIDEST
EE LEERIEST
   SLEETIER
   STEELIER
EF FERLIEST
EI TILERIES
EK TRISKELE
EL TREILLES
EM TERMLIES
EN LISTENER
   SILENTER
EO LITEROSE
   TROELIES

```
EP EPISTLER        TRIPPLES     HR LUTHIERS        SEMITONE   CT CENTRISM   DM IMMODEST
   PELTRIES     PS SPIRTLES     HS LUSHIEST     FI FISNOMIE   EG REGIMENS   DN DEMONIST
   PERLITES     PT SPLITTER     HT THULITES        OMNIFIES   EH SHIREMEN   DO DOOMIEST
   REPTILES        TRIPLETS     IR UTILISER     FR ENSIFORM   EL ERMELINS      MOODIEST
ES LEISTERS     PY PRIESTLY     IS ULITISES        FERMIONS   EM IMMENSER      SODOMITE
   RITELESS        SPRITELY     IY TUILYIES     GI IGNOMIES   EN REINSMEN   DR MORTISED
   TIRELESS        UTILISES     IZ TUILZIES     GR NEGROISM   EO EMERSION   DS MODISTES
ET RETITLES     QU QUILTERS        UTILIZES     GT MITOGENS   EV MINEVERS   DT DEMOTIST
FO FLORIEST     RU SULTRIER     KS SULKIEST     GU GEMINOUS   FO ENSIFORM   EI MOIETIES
   TREFOILS     RW TWIRLERS     LQ QUILLETS     GY MOSEYING      FERMIONS   EL MESOLITE
FR TRIFLERS     SS STIRLESS     LV VITELLUS     HI HOMINIES   FS FIRMNESS      MISLETOE
FS RIFTLESS     ST SLITTERS     MM LUMMIEST     HT HOISTMEN   GI REMISING   EM SOMETIME
   STIFLERS        STILTERS     MN MUSLINET     HU HEMIONUS   GL GREMLINS   EN MONETISE
FT FLITTERS        TESTRILS     MP LUMPIEST     IS EMISSION      MERLINGS      SEMITONE
FW FEWTRILS     SU SURLIEST        PLUMIEST        SIMONIES      MINGLERS   EP EPITOMES
GH LIGHTERS     SY SISTERLY     MR MURLIEST     IV VISNOMIE   GO NEGROISM      EPSOMITE
   RELIGHTS     TU SURTITLE     MS LITMUSES     KL MOLESKIN   GP IMPREGNS   ER TIRESOME
   SLIGHTER     TW WRISTLET     NO ELUTIONS     KR MONIKERS   GS GRIMNESS   FL FILEMOTS
GN LINGSTER     TZ STRELITZ        OUTLINES     KT TOKENISM   GU RESUMING   FT OFTTIMES
   RINGLETS     UV RIVULETS     NR INSULTER     KU MOUSEKIN   HP PHRENISM   GN MITOGENS
   STERLING                        LUSTRINE     LM MOLIMENS   HU RHENIUMS   GR ERGOTISM
   TINGLERS     EILSTU 136      NS UTENSILS     LU EMULSION   IP PRIMINES      GORMIEST
   TRINGLES     (UTILES)        NT LUTENIST     LV NOVELISM   IS MIRINESS   GS EGOTISMS
GS GLISTERS     AB SUITABLE     OR LOURIEST     MR MISNOMER   IT INTERIMS   GW TWIGSOME
   GRISTLES     AF FISTULAE        OUTLIERS     NT MENTIONS      MINISTER   HL HELOTISM
GT GLITTERS     AM SIMULATE     OS LOUSIEST     OP EMPOISON   IV MINIVERS   HN HOISTMEN
GU GURLIEST     AN ALUNITES     OV OUTLIVES     OR IONOMERS   KL KREMLINS   HO SMOOTHIE
HL THILLERS        INSULATE        SOLUTIVE        MOONRISE   KO MONIKERS   HR ISOTHERM
HP PHILTERS     AQ LIQUATES     PP PULPIEST     OS MONOSIES   LT MINSTREL      MOITHERS
   PHILTRES        TEQUILAS     PS STIPULES     OT EMOTIONS   MO MISNOMER   HT MOTHIEST
HS SLITHERS     AR URALITES     QR QUILLERS        MOONIEST   OO IONOMERS   IP OPTIMISE
   THRISSEL     BD BLUDIES      QU LUSTIQUE     OX EXOMIONS      MOONRISE   IY MOYITIES
HT THRISTLE     BG BULGIEST     RR SULTRIER     PS PEONISMS   OS MERSIONS   KN TOKENISM
HU LUTHIERS     BK BULKIEST     RS SURLIEST     PT EMPTIONS   OW WINSOMER   KS SMOKIEST
HW WHIRTLES     BL BULLIEST     RT SURTITLE        NEPOTISM   PS PRIMNESS   LL MELILOTS
   WHISTLER     BR BURLIEST     RV RIVULETS        PIMENTOS   ST ENTRISMS   LO TOILSOME
HY SLITHERY        SUBTILER     ST LUSTIEST     RS MERSIONS      MINSTERS   LP POLEMIST
IL STILLIER     BT SUBTITLE     SU LITUUSES        MINORESS      TRIMNESS   LT MOTLIEST
IM LIMITERS     CC CUTICLES                     RU MONSIEUR   SU NEURISMS   MP METOPISM
   MIRLIEST     CD DULCITES     EIMNOS 131      RW WINSOMER   TU TERMINUS   MT TOTEMISM
IN NIRLIEST        LUCIDEST     (MONIES)        ST MOISTENS   TY ENTRYISM   NN MENTIONS
   NITRILES     CE LEUCITES     AD NOMADIES     TU MOUNTIES      MISENTRY   NO EMOTIONS
IO ROILIEST     CK LUCKIEST        NOMADISE                                    MOONIEST
IP TRIPLIES     CN CUTLINES     AL MINEOLAS     EIMNRS 177    EIMOST 150    NP EMPTIONS
IT STILTIER        TUNICLES        SEMOLINA     (MINERS)      (SOMITE)         NEPOTISM
IU UTILISER        UTRICLES     AR MORAINES     AB MIRBANES   AD ATOMISED      PIMENTOS
KN LINKSTER     CR CURLIEST     AU MOINEAUS     AC CARMINES   AF FOAMIEST   NS MOISTENS
   STRINKLE     CT CUITTLES     AW WOMANISE     AD ADERMINS   AL LOAMIEST   NU MOUNTIES
   TINKLERS     DE DILUTEES     BC COMBINES        SIRNAMED   AR AMORTISE   OR MOORIEST
LO TRILLOES     DI UTILISED     BI EBIONISM     AE REMANIES      ATOMISER      MOTORISE
   TROLLIES     DL DUELLIST     BR BROMINES     AG GERMAINS   AS AMITOSES   PP MOPPIEST
LS STILLERS        DULLIEST     CN MECONINS        SMEARING      AMOSITES   PR IMPOSTER
LT TESTRILL     DN DILUENTS     CR CREMOSIN     AH HARMINES      ATOMISES   PY PEYOTISM
MN MINSTREL        INSULTED        INCOMERS        SHIREMAN      OSMIATES   QU MISQUOTE
MU MURLIEST        UNLISTED        SERMONIC     AK RAMEKINS   AZ ATOMIZES   RR MORTISER
MY LYMITERS     DO SOLITUDE     DE DEMONISE     AL MARLINES   BB BOMBSITE      STORMIER
NO RETINOLS     DP STIPULED     DG SMIDGEON        MINERALS   BC COMBIEST   RS EROTISMS
NP SPLINTER     DR DILUTERS     DH HEDONISM     AN REINSMAN   BG MISBEGOT      MORTISES
NS SNIRTLES        LURIDEST     DI DOMINIES     AO MORAINES   CC COSMETIC      TRISOMES
NU INSULTER     DY SEDULITY     DM DEMONISM     AR MARINERS   CD DOMESTIC   RT OMITTERS
   LUSTRINE     FG GULFIEST     DN MISDONNE     AS SEMINARS   CF COMFIEST   RU MOISTURE
NY TINSELRY     FK FLUKIEST     DO DOMINOES        SIRNAMES   CI COMITIES   RW MISWROTE
OO TROOLIES     FO OUTFLIES        MONODIES     AT MINARETS      SEMIOTIC      WORMIEST
OP POITRELS     FP SPITEFUL     DT DEMONIST        RAIMENTS   CO COOMIEST   RY ISOMETRY
OT TRIOLETS     FT FLUTIEST     EH HEMIONES     AU ANEURISM   CR MORTICES   SS MOSSIEST
OU LOURIEST        FUTILEST     EN NOMINEES     AY SEMINARY   CV VICOMTES   ST MOISTEST
   OUTLIERS     GO EULOGIST     EP EPISEMON     BO BROMINES   DE TEDISOME   SU MOUSIEST
PP RIPPLETS     GR GURLIEST     ER EMERSION     CO CREMOSIN   DL MELODIST   SZ MESTIZOS
   STIPPLER     HK HULKIEST     ET MONETISE        INCOMERS                 TT MOTTIEST
   TIPPLERS     HL HULLIEST                        SERMONIC
                HP SULPHITE
```

```
        TOTEMIST      FU FREMITUS          TRANNIES     BL BONSPIEL     AC SCENARIO        SOURDINE
TU TITMOUSE           GI GRIMIEST       AS INSANEST     CH CHOPINES     AD ANEROIDS     DW WINDORES
                         TIGERISM       AT ANTIENTS     CI EPINOSIC        DONARIES        WINDROSE
EIMRST 140            GM GRIMMEST          STANNITE     CL PINOCLES     AF FARINOSE     EG ERINGOES
(MITERS)             GO ERGOTISM      BO BONNIEST     CR CONSPIRE     AG IGNAROES     EH HEROINES
AB BARMIEST              GORMIEST      CE NESCIENT        INCORPSE        ORGANISE     EK KEROSINE
AC CERAMIST          HO ISOTHERM      CG SCENTING     DD DISPONED        ORIGANES     EL ELOINERS
   MATRICES             MOITHERS      CI INSCIENT     DE DISPONEE     AL AILERONS     EM EMERSION
AD MARDIEST          HS SMITHERS      DE DENTINES     DG DEPOSING        ALERIONS     EP ISOPRENE
   MISRATED          HY SMITHERY         DESINENT        DISPONGE        ALIENORS        PIONEERS
   READMITS          IK MIRKIEST      DG STENDING        PIDGEONS     AM MORAINES     ES ESSOINER
AE EMIRATES          IL LIMITERS      DU DUNNIEST     DH DIPHONES     AN RAISONNE     ET SEROTINE
   REAMIEST             MIRLIEST         DUNNITES        SIPHONED     AS ERASIONS     EV EVERSION
   STEAMIER          IN INTERIMS      EF FENNIEST        SPHENOID     AT ANOESTRI     FK FORESKIN
AG MAGISTER          IT METRITIS      EG STEENING     DO POISONED        ARSONITE     FM ENSIFORM
   MIGRATES          IW MISWRITE      EH HENNIEST     DR DISPONER        NOTARIES        FERMIONS
   RAGTIMES          KU MURKIEST      EI NINETIES        POINDERS        NOTARISE     FN INFERNOS
   STERIGMA          LN MINSTREL      EL LENIENTS        PRISONED        ROSINATE     FP FORPINES
AI AIRTIMES          LU MURLIEST         SENTINEL     DS DISPONES     AV AVERSION     FU REFUSION
   SERIATIM          LY LYMITERS      ER INTENSER        SPINODES     BB SNOBBIER     FX FORNIXES
AL LAMITERS          MP PRIMMEST         INTERNES     DU UNPOISED     BF BONFIRES     GI SEIGNIOR
   MARLIEST          MR TRIMMERS      ES TENNISES     EG EPIGONES     BG SOBERING     GL RESOLING
AM MARMITES          MS MISTERMS      ET SENTIENT     EM EPISEMON     BI BRIONIES     GM NEGROISM
AN MINARETS          MT TRIMMEST      EW ENTWINES     ER ISOPRENE     BM BROMINES     GP PERIGONS
   RAIMENTS          MU RUMMIEST         WENNIEST        PIONEERS     BT BORNITES        REPOSING
AO AMORTISE          NS ENTRISMS      FI FINNIEST     FR FORPINES        RIBSTONE        SPONGIER
   ATOMISER             MINSTERS      FU FUNNIEST     GN OPENINGS     BW BROWNIES     GR IGNORERS
AP PRIMATES          NU TERMINUS      GH SENNIGHT     GR PERIGONS     BY BRYONIES     GS SIGNORES
AS ASTERISM          NY ENTRYISM      GI STEINING        REPOSING     CC CONCISER     GT GENITORS
   MAISTERS             MISENTRY      GL NESTLING        SPONGIER        CORNICES        ROSETING
   MISRATES          OO MOORIEST      GN STENNING     GT PONGIEST     CD CONSIDER     GY SEIGNORY
   SEMITARS             MOTORISE      GR STERNING     GX EXPOSING     CF CONIFERS     HS HERISSON
   SMARTIES          OP IMPOSTER      GT NETTINGS     GY POESYING        FORENSIC     HT HORNIEST
AT MISTREAT          OR MORTISER         STENTING     HL PINHOLES        FORINSEC     IP RIPIENOS
   TERATISM             STORMIER         TENTINGS     HT PHONIEST        INFORCES     IS IONISERS
AU MURIATES          OS EROTISMS      GV VENTINGS        SIPHONET     CH CHORINES        IRONISES
   SEMITAUR             MORTISES      HR THINNERS     IR RIPIENOS     CI RECISION     IV REVISION
AW WARTIMES          OT OMITTERS      HS THINNESS     IT SINOPITE        SORICINE        VISIONER
AX MATRIXES          OU MOISTURE      HT THINNEST     LO POLONIES     CL INCLOSER     IZ IONIZERS
AY SYMITARE          OW MISWROTE      IS TININESS     LP PLENIPOS        LICENSOR        IRONIZES
BL TIMBRELS             WORMIEST      IT TINNIEST     LR PROLINES     CM CREMOSIN     JT JOINTERS
BU IMBRUTES          OY ISOMETRY      IW INTWINES     LS EPSILONS        INCOMERS     KM MONIKERS
   RESUBMIT          PS IMPRESTS      KO INKSTONE     LT POINTELS        SERMONIC     KO ROOINEKS
   TERBIUMS          PU IMPUREST      LO INSOLENT     MO EMPOISON     CN INCENSOR     LP PROLINES
CI MERISTIC             IMPUTERS      MO MENTIONS     MS PEONISMS     CP CONSPIRE     LR LORINERS
   TRISEMIC             STUMPIER      OR INTONERS     MT EMPTIONS        INCORPSE     LT RETINOLS
CN CENTRISM          SS MISTRESS         TERNIONS        NEPOTISM     CR RESORCIN     MM MISNOMER
CO MORTICES          ST METRISTS      OS TENSIONS        PIMENTOS     CS NECROSIS     MO IONOMERS
CS CRETISMS          SY SMYTRIES      OT TINSTONE     NS PENSIONS        SERICONS        MOONRISE
DE DEMERITS          TU SMUTTIER         TONTINES     OR POISONER     CT CORNIEST     MS MERSIONS
   DEMISTER          UV VITREUMS      OU NOUNIEST        SPOONIER        RECTIONS     MU MONSIEUR
   DIMETERS          UX MIXTURES      PR ENPRINTS     OS SPOONIES     CU NOURICES     MW WINSOMER
   MISTERED                           PS SPINNETS     PR POPERINS        ROUNCIES     NT INTONERS
DO MORTISED          EINNST 113       RU RUNNIEST        PROPINES     DD INDORSED        TERNIONS
DP DIREMPTS          (SINNET)            STURNINE     RR PRISONER     DE ORDINEES     NU REUNIONS
EE EREMITES          AC ANCIENTS      RV VINTNERS     RS PORINESS     DG NEGROIDS     NV ENVIRONS
EF FEMITERS             CANNIEST      SU SUNNIEST        PRESSION     DH HORDEINS     OP POISONER
EH ERETHISM             INSTANCE      UW UNTWINES        ROPINESS     DI DERISION        SPOONIER
   ETHERISM          AF INFANTES                      RT POINTERS        IRONISED     OS EROSIONS
EL TERMLIES          AG ANTIGENS      EINOPS 130          PROTEINS        RESINOID     OT SNOOTIER
EM MERISTEM             GENTIANS      (PONIES)            REPOINTS     DJ JOINDERS     OZ OZONISER
   MIMESTER             STEANING      AC CANOPIES     RU PRUINOSE     DL DISENROL     PP POPERINS
   MISMETRE          AM MANNITES         CAPONISE     RV OVERSPIN     DN ENDIRONS        PROPINES
EO TIRESOME          AO ENATIONS         PAEONICS        PROVINES     DP DISPONER     PR PRISONER
EP EMPTIERS          AP PANTINES      AE PAEONIES     TT NEPOTIST        POINDERS     PS PORINESS
ER MERRIEST          AZ EPIZOANS      AH APHONIES                        PRISONED        PRESSION
   TRIREMES          AR ENTRAINS      AL OPALINES     EINORS 9        DS INDORSES        ROPINESS
ES TRISEMES                           AT SAPONITE     (SENIOR)           SORDINES     PT POINTERS
ET TERMITES                           AZ EPIZOANS     AB BARONIES     DT DRONIEST        PROTEINS
EU EMERITUS                           BH HOPBINES                     DU DOURINES
```

```
      REPOINTS          SEDITION      QU QUESTION     GH SPHERING     AN PANTINES        ARTESIAN
PU PRUINOSE       DM DEMONIST      RR INTRORSE     GI SPEIRING     AO SAPONITE        RESINATA
PV OVERSPIN       DR DRONIEST         SNORTIER     GL PINGLERS     AP NAPPIEST     AB ATEBRINS
   PROVINES       DS DONSIEST      RS TERSIONS        SPERLING     AR PAINTERS        BANISTER
RT INTRORSE       DU OUNDIEST      RT SNOTTIER        SPRINGLE        PANTRIES     AC CANISTER
   SNORTIER       DW DOWNIEST         TENORIST     GM IMPREGNS        PERTAINS        CARNIEST
SS ROSINESS       EG EGESTION         TRITONES     GO PERIGONS        PINASTER        NACRITES
ST TERSIONS       EL NOSELITE      RU ROUTINES        REPOSING        REPAINTS        SCANTIER
SU NEUROSIS       EM MONETISE         SNOUTIER        SPONGIER     AT PATIENTS     AD DETRAINS
   RESINOUS          SEMITONE      RV INVESTOR     GP REPPINGS     AU PETUNIAS        RANDIEST
SV VERSIONS       ER SEROTINE      RY TYROSINE     GR SPERRING        SUPINATE        STRAINED
TT SNOTTIER       ES ESSONITE      RZ TRIZONES        SPRINGER     AY EPINASTY     AE ARSENITE
   TENORIST       ET NOISETTE      SS SONSIEST     GS PRESSING     CE PECTINES        RESINATE
   TRITONES          TEOSINTE         STENOSIS        SPERSING        PENTICES        STEARINE
TU ROUTINES       FI NOTIFIES      ST SNOTTIES        SPRINGES     CS INSPECTS        TRAINEES
   SNOUTIER       GH HISTOGEN         STONIEST     GT PRESTING     CY PYCNITES     AF FENITARS
TV INVESTOR       GM MITOGENS      SW SNOWIEST     GU PERSUING     DE PENTISED     AG ANGRIEST
TY TYROSINE       GP PONGIEST      TT TOTIENTS        PERUSING     DL SPLINTED        ASTRINGE
TZ TRIZONES       GR GENITORS      TW TOWNIEST        SUPERING     DR SPRINTED        GANISTER
UV SOUVENIR          ROSETING      UU TENUIOUS     HM PHRENISM     DS STIPENDS        GANTRIES
                  GT TENTIGOS      VY VENOSITY     HU PUNISHER     EG STEEPING        GRANITES
EINOST 14         HL NEOLITHS                      IM PRIMINES     EL PLENTIES        INGRATES
(TONIES)          HM HOISTMEN      EINPRS 158       IO RIPIENOS    EM SEPIMENT        RANGIEST
AB BOTANIES       HP PHONIEST      (PINERS)         IP SNIPPIER    ES PENTISES        REASTING
   BOTANISE          SIPHONET      AA PANARIES      IR INSPIRER    ET INEPTEST        STEARING
   NIOBATES       HR HORNIEST      AD SPRAINED      IS INSPIRES       SPINETTE     AH INEARTHS
   OBEISANT       HS HISTONES      AE NAPERIES      IT PRISTINE    GL PELTINGS     AI INERTIAS
AC ACONITES       HU OUTSHINE      AF FIREPANS      JU JUNIPERS       PESTLING        RAINIEST
   CANOEIST       IL ETIOLINS      AG PREASING      KL SPRINKLE    GM PIGMENTS     AJ NARTJIES
AD ASTONIED       IP SINOPITE         SPEARING      KU SPUNKIER    GO PONGIEST     AK KERATINS
   SEDATION       IS NOISIEST      AH HEPARINS      LO PROLINES    GP STEPPING        NARKIEST
AL ELATIONS       IV NOVITIES         PARISHEN      LS PILSNERS    GR PRESTING     AL ENTRAILS
   INSOLATE       JR JOINTERS         SERAPHIN      LT SPLINTER    GT PETTINGS        LATRINES
   TOENAILS       JT JETTISON      AL PEARLINS      LU PURLINES       SPETTING        RATLINES
AN ENATIONS       KM TOKENISM         PRALINES      MS PRIMNESS    HM SHIPMENT        TRENAILS
AP SAPONITE       KN INKSTONE      AN PANNIERS      NS SPINNERS    HO PHONIEST     AM MINARETS
AR ANOESTRI       KO NOOKIEST      AP SNAPPIER      NT ENPRINTS       SIPHONET        RAIMENTS
   ARSONITE       KW WONKIEST      AT PAINTERS      NY SPINNERY    IK PINKIEST     AN ENTRAINS
   NOTARIES       LL STELLION         PANTRIES      OO POISONER    IO SINOPITE        TRANNIES
   NOTARISE       LN INSOLENT         PERTAINS         SPOONIER    IP NIPPIEST     AO ANOESTRI
   ROSINATE       LO LOONIEST         PINASTER      OP POPERINS    IR PRISTINE        ARSONITE
AS ASSIENTO          OILSTONE         REPAINTS         PROPINES    IS SNIPIEST        NOTARIES
   ASTONIES       LP POINTELS      AU UNPRAISE      OR PRISONER       SPINIEST        NOTARISE
AV STOVAINE       LR RETINOLS      BE PEBRINES      OS PORINESS    LO POINTELS        ROSINATE
AX SAXONITE       LU ELUTIONS      CD PRESCIND         ROPINESS    LR SPLINTER     AP PAINTERS
·BB NOBBIEST         OUTLINES      CH PINCHERS      OT POINTERS    LS PLENISTS        PANTRIES
BE BETONIES       LV NOVELIST      CO CONSPIRE         PROTEINS    MO EMPTIONS        PERTAINS
   EBONITES          VIOLENTS         INCORPSE         REPOINTS       NEPOTISM        PINASTER
BI NIOBITES       LW TOWLINES      CS PRINCESS      OU PRUINOSE       PIMENTOS        REPAINTS
BN BONNIEST       MN MENTIONS      DG SPRINGED      OV OVERSPIN    MS MISSPENT     AR RESTRAIN
BR BORNITES       MO EMOTIONS      DI INSPIRED         PROVINES    NR ENPRINTS        RETRAINS
   RIBSTONE          MOONIEST      DL SPELDRIN      PS SNIPPERS    NS SPINNETS        STRAINER
BS EBONISTS       MP EMPTIONS      DO DISPONER      RT PRINTERS    OR POINTERS        TERRAINS
BT BOTTINES          NEPOTISM         POINDERS         REPRINTS       PROTEINS        TRAINERS
BU BOUNTIES          PIMENTOS         PRISONED         SPRINTER       REPOINTS        TRANSIRE
CC CONCEITS       MS MOISTENS      DT SPRINTED      SY INSPYRES    OT NEPOTIST     AS RESIANTS
CD DEONTICS       MU MOUNTIES      DY INSPYRED      TU UNPRIEST    PS SNIPPETS        RETSINAS
CE SEICENTO       NR INTONERS      EG SPEERING         UNRIPEST    PY SNIPPETY        SNARIEST
CL LECTIONS          TERNIONS         SPREEING                     RR PRINTERS        STAINERS
CO COONTIES       NS TENSIONS      EH INSPHERE      EINPST 148        REPRINTS        STARNIES
CR CORNIEST       NT TINSTONE      EI PINERIES      (INSTEP)          SPRINTER        STEARINS
   RECTIONS          TONTINES      EL PILSENER      AB BEPAINTS    RS SPINSTER     AT INTREATS
CS SECTIONS       NU NOUNIEST      EO ISOPRENE      AD DEPAINTS    RU UNPRIEST        NITRATES
CT CENTOIST       OR SNOOTIER         PIONEERS      AH PENTHIAS       UNRIPEST        STRAITEN
   STENOTIC       OS ISOTONES      ER REPINERS         THESPIAN    TX SPINTEXT        TARTINES
CU COUNTIES       OZ ZOONITES      ES EREPSINS      AI PIANISTE    TY TINTYPES        TERTIANS
CX EXCITONS       PR POINTERS         RIPENESS      AL PANTILES                    AU RUINATES
CY CYTOSINE          PROTEINS      EU PENURIES         PLAINEST    EINRST 17          URANITES
DH HEDONIST          REPOINTS         RESUPINE                     (INTERS)           URINATES
DI EDITIONS       PT NEPOTIST      FO FORPINES                     AA ANTISERA     AW TINWARES
```

BI BRINIEST	INTEREST	LUSTRINE	CU INTERCUT	CH RUTHENIC	AG ESTATING
BO BORNITES	STERNITE	LY TINSELRY	TINCTURE	CI NEURITIC	TANGIEST
RIBSTONE	EU ESURIENT	MS ENTRISMS	DO INTORTED	CL LINCTURE	AH HESITANT
BT BITTERNS	NEURITES	MINSTERS	DS STRIDENT	CO NEUROTIC	AJ JANTIEST
BU TRIBUNES	RETINUES	TRIMNESS	TRIDENTS	CS CURNIEST	AN ANTIENTS
TURBINES	REUNITES	MU TERMINUS	EE REINETTE	CT INTERCUT	STANNITE
CE CENTRIES	EV NERVIEST	MY ENTRYISM	TEENTIER	TINCTURE	AP PATIENTS
ENTERICS	REINVEST	MISENTRY	EH THIRTEEN	DD INTRUDED	AR INTREATS
ENTICERS	SERVIENT	NO INTONERS	EI INTERTIE	DE REUNITED	NITRATES
SCIENTER	SIRVENTE	TERNIONS	RETINITE	DI UNTIDIER	STRAITEN
CG CRESTING	EX INTERSEX	NP ENPRINTS	EN RENITENT	DM RUDIMENT	TARTINES
CH CHRISTEN	EY SERENITY	NU RUNNIEST	EO TENORITE	DP TURNIPED	TERTIANS
CITHERNS	FI SNIFTIER	STURNINE	ES INERTEST	DR INTRUDER	AS INSTATES
SNITCHER	FS SNIFTERS	NV VINTNERS	STERNITE	DS INTRUDES	NASTIEST
CI CITRINES	GH RIGHTENS	OO SNOOTIER	INTEREST	DW UNDERWIT	SATINETS
CRINITES	GI GIRNIEST	OP POINTERS	EY ENTIRETY	EG GENITURE	AT NATTIEST
INCITERS	IGNITERS	PROTEINS	ETERNITY	EM MUTINEER	AV TASTEVIN
CK STRICKEN	REISTING	REPOINTS	FG FRETTING	ES ESURIENT	AW TAWNIEST
CM CENTRISM	STINGIER	OR INTRORSE	FL FLITTERN	NEURITES	BE BENTIEST
STRIGINE	FU UNFITTER	OS TERSIONS	RETINUES	BG BETTINGS
CO CORNIEST	GL LINGSTER	OT SNOTTIER	GO OTTERING	REUNITES	BI STIBNITE
RECTIONS	RINGLETS	TENORIST	GS GITTERNS	FG FEUTRING	BO BOTTINES
CS CISTERNS	STERLING	TRITONES	GU UTTERING	REFUTING	BR BITTERNS
CT CENTRIST	TINGLERS	OU ROUTINES	IM INTERMIT	FT UNFITTER	BU BUNTIEST
CITTERNS	TRINGLES	SNOUTIER	IS NITRITES	GI INTRIGUE	CO CENTOIST
CU CURNIEST	GN STERNING	OV INVESTOR	STINTIER	GN RETUNING	STENOTIC
DD STRIDDEN	GO GENITORS	OY TYROSINE	KO KNOTTIER	GO OUTREIGN	CR CENTRIST
DE INSERTED	ROSETING	OZ TRIZONES	KS KNITTERS	ROUTEING	CITTERNS
RESIDENT	GP PRESTING	PR PRINTERS	TRINKETS	GP ERUPTING	DE DINETTES
SINTERED	GR RESTRING	REPRINTS	LO TROTLINE	REPUTING	DR STRIDENT
TRENDIES	RINGSTER	SPRINTER	NO TONTINER	GT UTTERING	DS DENTISTS
DG STRINGED	STRINGER	PS SPINSTER	NU NUTRIENT	IS NEURITIS	EE TEENIEST
DI DISINTER	GS RESTINGS	PU UNPRIEST	OS SNOTTIER	JO JOINTURE	EF FEINTEST
INDITERS	STINGERS	UNRIPEST	TENORIST	KP TURNPIKE	EG GENTIEST
NITRIDES	TRESSING	QU SQUINTER	TRITONES	LS INSULTER	EI ENTITIES
RINDIEST	TRIGNESS	SS INSTRESS	OU RITENUTO	LUSTRINE	EL ENTITLES
DL SNIRTLED	GT GITTERNS	ST ENTRISTS	PU INPUTTER	MS TERMINUS	EM MINETTES
TENDRILS	GV STERVING	STINTERS	SS ENTRISTS	NO NEUTRINO	EN SENTIENT
TRINDLES	GW STREWING	TU RUNTIEST	STINTERS	NS RUNNIEST	EO NOISETTE
DO DRONIEST	WRESTING	TW TWINTERS	SU RUNTIEST	STURNINE	TEOSINTE
DP SPRINTED	HI INHERITS	TY ENTRYIST	SW TWINTERS	NT NUTRIENT	EP INEPTEST
DT STRIDENT	HK RETHINKS	UV UNRIVETS	SY ENTRYIST	OP ERUPTION	SPINETTE
TRIDENTS	THINKERS	VENTURIS		OS ROUTINES	ER INERTEST
DU INTRUDES	HN THINNERS	UW UNWRITES	**EINRTU 25**	SNOUTIER	INTEREST
DX DEXTRINS	HO HORNIEST		(TUNIER)	OT RITENUTO	ET NETTIEST
EE ETERNISE	HZ ZITHERNS	**EINRTT 76**	AA INAURATE	PR PRURIENT	TENTIEST
TEENSIER	IL NIRLIEST	(TINTER)	AB URBANITE	PS UNPRIEST	EW TENTWISE
EF FERNIEST	NITRILES	AA REATTAIN	AD DATURINE	UNRIPEST	TWENTIES
EG GENTRIES	IM INTERIMS	AC INTERACT	INDURATE	PT INPUTTER	EX EXISTENT
INTEGERS	MINISTER	AD NITRATED	RUINATED	QS SQUINTER	FI NIFTIEST
REESTING	IP PRISTINE	AG ARETTING	URINATED	ST RUNTIEST	FM FITMENTS
STEERING	IS SINISTER	TREATING	AH HAURIENT	SV UNRIVETS	GG GETTINGS
STREIGNE	IT NITRITES	AL RATTLINE	AJ JAUNTIER	VENTURIS	GH SHETTING
EI ERINITES	IU NEURITIS	AM MARTINET	AL RETINULA	SW UNWRITES	TIGHTENS
NITERIES	IV INVITERS	AO TENTORIA	TENURIAL	UV UNVIRTUE	GL LETTINGS
EK KERNITES	VINTRIES	AP TRIPTANE	AM RUMINATE		SETTLING
EL LISTENER	VITRINES	AS INTREATS	AP PAINTURE	**EINSTT 160**	GN NETTINGS
SILENTER	JO JOINTERS	NITRATES	AQ QUAINTER	(INTEST)	STENTING
EN INTENSER	KL LINKSTER	STRAITEN	AS RUINATES	AA ASTATINE	TENTINGS
INTERNES	STRINKLE	TARTINES	URANITES	SANITATE	GO TENTIGOS
EO SEROTINE	TINKLERS	TERTIANS	URINATES	TANAISTE	GP PETTINGS
ER INSERTER	KS STINKERS	AU TAINTURE	AT TAINTURE	AB TABINETS	SPETTING
REINSERT	KT KNITTERS	BE REBITTEN	BD TURBINED	AC CANTIEST	GR GITTERNS
REINTERS	TRINKETS	BS BITTERNS	UNDERBIT	NICTATES	GS SETTINGS
RENTIERS	LM MINSTREL	CE RETICENT	BS TRIBUNES	AD INSTATED	TESTINGS
TERRINES	LO RETINOLS	CO CONTRITE	TURBINES	AE ANISETTE	GT STETTING
ES INTERESS	LP SPLINTER	CORNETTI	CC CINCTURE	TETANIES	HN THINNEST
SENTRIES	LS SNIRTLES	CS CENTRIST	CE CEINTURE	TETANISE	IL LINTIEST
TRENISES	LU INSULTER	CITTERNS	ENURETIC	AF FAINTEST	
ET INERTEST			CG ERUCTING		

```
IM MINTIEST        UNTIDIES   AD DIOPTASE      PROTEINS      CORTILES    HORSIEST
IN TINNIEST     DL DILUENTS   AL SPOLIATE      REPOINTS      COSTLIER    HOSTRIES
IR NITRITES        INSULTED   AN SAPONITE   NT NEPOTIST      CREOLIST    SHORTIES
   STINTIER        UNLISTED   AP APPOSITE   OP OPPOSITE   CM MORTICES HT THEORIST
IT NITTIEST     DM MISTUNED   AS SOAPIEST   OR PORTOISE   CN CORNIEST    THORITES
   TINTIEST     DN DUNNIEST   BY BIOTYPES      ROOPIEST      RECTIONS HU OUTHIRES
IW TWINIEST        DUNNITES   CD DESPOTIC   OS ISOTOPES   CP PERSICOT HV OVERHITS
JO JETTISON     DO OUNDIEST   CE ECTOPIES   OV POOVIEST   CT COTTIERS HW WORTHIES
KL KNITTLES     DQ SQUINTED      PICOTEES   PS SOPPIEST   CU CITREOUS IL ROILIEST
KR KNITTERS     DR INTRUDES   CH POSTICHE   RR PIERROTS      OUTCRIES IR RIOTRIES
   TRINKETS     DS DISTUNES      POTICHES      SPORTIER   CV EVICTORS IS RIOTISES
KS SKINTEST     DU UNSUITED   CK POCKIEST   RS PERIOSTS      VORTICES IZ RIOTIZES
LS TINTLESS     EG EUGENIST   CL TOECLIPS      PROSIEST   CX EXCITORS JN JOINTERS
LU LUTENIST     EQ QUIETENS   CR PERSICOT      REPOSITS      EXORCIST KP PORKIEST
MU MINUTEST     ER ESURIENT   CS COPSIEST      RIPOSTES   DG STODGIER LL TRILLOES
NO TINSTONE        NEURITES   DD PODDIEST      TRIPOSES   DI DIORITES    TROLLIES
   TONTINES        RETINUES   DE EPIDOTES   RT PORTIEST   DL STOLIDER LN RETINOLS
OP NEPOTIST        REUNITES      POETISED      RISPETTO   DM MORTISED LO TROOLIES
OR SNOTTIER     FK FUNKIEST   DG PODGIEST   RU ROUPIEST   DN DRONIEST LP POITRELS
   TENORIST     FN FUNNIEST   DR DIOPTERS      SPOUTIER   DP DIOPTERS LT TRIOLETS
   TRITONES     GG GUESTING      DIOPTRES   RV PIVOTERS      DIOPTRES LU LOURIEST
OS SNOTTIES        GUNGIEST      DIPTEROS      SPORTIVE      DIPTEROS    OUTLIERS
   STONIEST     GQ QUESTING      PERIDOTS   SS SEPIOSTS      PERIDOTS MO MOORIEST
OT TOTIENTS     HK HUNKIEST      PROTEIDS   SU SOUPIEST      PROTEIDS    MOTORISE
OW TOWNIEST     HO OUTSHINE      RIPOSTED   SY ISOTYPES      RIPOSTED    ROOMIEST
PX SPINTEXT     IM MUTINIES   DS DEPOSITS   TT POTTIEST   DS STEROIDS MP IMPOSTER
PY TINTYPES     IQ INQUIETS      TOPSIDES   TU POUTIEST   DT DORTIEST MR MORTISER
QU QUINTETS     IR NEURITIS   EL PETIOLES   TY PEYOTIST   DU IODURETS    STORMIER
RS ENTRISTS     IS UNITISES   EM EPITOMES   UW WIPEOUTS      OUTRIDES MS EROTISMS
   STINTERS     IZ UNITIZES      EPSOMITE                    OUTSIDER    MORTISES
RU RUNTIEST     JK JUNKIEST   ER POETRIES   EIORST   5       SUITORED    TRISOMES
RW TWINTERS     LM MUSLINET   ES POETISES   (TORIES)      DW ROWDIEST MT OMITTERS
RY ENTRYIST     LO ELUTIONS   EZ POETIZES   AB SABOTIER      WORDIEST MU MOISTURE
SW ENTWISTS        OUTLINES   FO POOFIEST   AD ASTEROID   EG ERGOTISE MW MISWROTE
TU NUTTIEST     LR INSULTER   FR FIREPOTS   AE ETAERIOS   EH ISOTHERE    WORMIEST
TW TWITTENS        LUSTRINE   GN PONGIEST   AH HOARIEST      THEORIES MY ISOMETRY
                LS UTENSILS   GO GOOPIEST   AJ JAROSITE      THEORISE NN INTONERS
EINSTU 81       LT LUTENIST   HL HELISTOP   AL SOTERIAL   EL LITEROSE NO SNOOTIER
(UNITES)        MO MOUNTIES      HOPLITES   AM AMORTISE      TROELIES NP POINTERS
AD AUDIENTS     MR TERMINUS      ISOPLETH      ATOMISER   EM TIRESOME    PROTEINS
   SINUATED     MS MISTUNES   HN PHONIEST   AN ANOESTRI   EN SEROTINE    REPOINTS
AG SAUTEING     MT MINUTEST      SIPHONET      ARSONITE   EP POETRIES NR INTRORSE
AJ JAUNTIES     NO NOUNIEST   HP HOPPIEST      NOTARIES   ES EROTESIS    SNORTIER
AL ALUNITES     NR RUNNIEST      POETSHIP      NOTARISE   FF FORFEITS NS TERSIONS
   INSULATE        STURNINE   HR TROPHIES      ROSINATE   FK FORKIEST NT SNOTTIER
AP PETUNIAS     NS SUNNIEST   IL PISOLITE   AR ROARIEST   FL FLORIEST    TENORIST
   SUPINATE     NW UNTWINES      POLITIES      ROTARIES      TREFOILS    TRITONES
AQ ANTIQUES     OQ QUESTION   IM OPTIMISE   AV VOTARIES   FO ROOFIEST NU ROUTINES
   QUANTISE     OR ROUTINES   IN SINOPITE   BC BISECTOR   FP FIREPOTS    SNOUTIER
AR RUINATES        SNOUTIER   IV POSITIVE   BD DEBITORS   FR FROSTIER NV INVESTOR
   URANITES     OU TENUIOUS   KR PORKIEST   BI ORBITIES      ROTIFERS NY TYROSINE
   URINATES     PR UNPRIEST   LM POLEMIST   BL STROBILE   FS FOISTERS NZ TRIZONES
BB NUBBIEST        UNRIPEST   LN POINTELS      TRILOBES   FW FROWIEST OP PORTOISE
BM BITUMENS     QR SQUINTER   LO LOOPIEST   BN BORNITES   GH GHOSTIER    ROOPIEST
BO BOUNTIES     QS INQUESTS   LR POITRELS      RIBSTONE   GM ERGOTISM OT ROOTIEST
BR TRIBUNES     QT QUINTETS   LS PISTOLES   BO ROBOTISE      GORMIEST    TORTOISE
   TURBINES     QU UNIQUEST      PTILOSES   BR ORBITERS   GN GENITORS PR PIERROTS
BT BUNTIEST        UNQUIETS      SLOPIEST   BY SOBRIETY      ROSETING    SPORTIER
CI CUTINISE     RT RUNTIEST   LT PISTOLET   CC CORTICES   GS GORSIEST PS PERIOSTS
CL CUTLINES     RV UNRIVETS      PLOTTIES   CD CORDITES      STRIGOSE    PROSIEST
   TUNICLES        VENTURIS      POLITEST   CE COTERIES   GU GOUSTIER    REPOSITS
CO COUNTIES     RW UNWRITES   LX EXPLOITS      ESOTERIC   GV VERTIGOS    RIPOSTES
CR CURNIEST     SS SENSUIST   MM METOPISM   CH ROTCHIES   GY OYSTRIGE    TRIPOSES
DD DISTUNED     SW UNWISEST   MN EMPTIONS      THEORICS   GZ ZORGITES PT PORTIEST
DE DETINUES     SX UNSEXIST      NEPOTISM   CK CORKIEST   HM ISOTHERM    RISPETTO
DF UNSIFTED     TT NUTTIEST      PIMENTOS      ROCKIEST      MOITHERS    SPOTTIER
DG DUNGIEST                   MP MOPPIEST      STOCKIER   HN HORNIEST PU ROUPIEST
DI DISUNITE     EIOPST 101    MR IMPOSTER   CL CLOISTER   HP TROPHIES    SPOUTIER
   NUDITIES     (SOPITE)      MY PEYOTISM      COISTREL   HR HERITORS PV PIVOTERS
   UNITISED     AC ECTOPIAS   NR POINTERS                 HS HOISTERS
```

SPORTIVE	VIPEROUS	OS SOOTIEST	SPIRITED	UNRIPEST	DF DRIFTERS
QU QUOITERS	RS REVISORS	TOOTSIES	DM DIREMPTS	OO PORTOISE	DU STURDIER
RR ERRORIST	RT SERVITOR	PR PORTIEST	DN SPRINTED	ROOPIEST	EE REESTIER
RS RESISTOR	RU OUVRIERS	RISPETTO	DO DIOPTERS	OR PIERROTS	RETIREES
ROISTERS	RV REVIVORS	SPOTTIER	DIOPTRES	SPORTIER	EF FERRITES
SORRIEST	RY REVISORY	PT POTTIEST	DIPTEROS	OS PERIOSTS	EG REGISTER
RT RORTIEST	TT VIRETOTS	PU POUTIEST	PERIDOTS	PROSIEST	EI REISTIER
RU STOURIER	TU VIRTUOSE	PY PEYOTIST	PROTEIDS	REPOSITS	EM MERRIEST
RV SERVITOR	VITREOUS	RR RORTIEST	RIPOSTED	RIPOSTES	EN INSERTER
ST STOITERS	VOITURES	RS STOITERS	DP STRIPPED	TRIPOSES	REINSERT
SY SEROSITY		RU TUTORISE	DU DISPUTER	OT PORTIEST	REINTERS
TU TUTORISE	**EIOSTT 93**	RV VIRETOTS	EE PEERIEST	RISPETTO	RENTIERS
TV VIRETOTS	(OTTIES)	SS TOSSIEST	STEEPIER	SPOTTIER	TERRINES
UV VIRTUOSE	AC OSCITATE	SU TOUSIEST	EG PRESTIGE	OU ROUPIEST	ER RETIRERS
VITREOUS	AG GOATIEST	SW TOWSIEST	EH TREESHIP	SPOUTIER	TERRIERS
VOITURES	AL TOTALISE	TT TOTTIEST	EK PERKIEST	OV PIVOTERS	ES TRESSIER
	AS TOASTIES	TU TOUTIEST	EL EPISTLER	SPORTIVE	EV REVERIST
EIORSV 127	BI BIOTITES		PELTRIES	PR STRIPPER	RIVERETS
(VIROSE)	BN BOTTINES	**EIPRST 147**	PERLITES	TRIPPERS	RIVETERS
AC COVARIES	CD COTTISED	(STRIPE)	REPTILES	PT TRIPPETS	EW REWRITES
VARICOSE	CN CENTOIST	AA ASPIRATE	EM EMPTIERS	QU QUIPSTER	FG GRIFTERS
AG VIRAGOES	STENOTIC	PARASITE	EO POETRIES	RZ SPRITZER	FI FIRRIEST
AL OVERSAIL	CR COTTIERS	SEPTARIA	ES RESPITES	SS PERSISTS	FL TRIFLERS
VALORISE	CS COTTISES	AC CRAPIEST	ET PRETTIES	ST SPITTERS	FO FROSTIER
VARIOLES	DL DOILTEST	CRISPATE	EY PERSEITY	TIPSTERS	ROTIFERS
VOLARIES	DM DEMOTIST	PICRATES	FI SPITFIRE	SU PURSIEST	FT FRITTERS
AN AVERSION	DR DORTIEST	PRACTISE	FO FIREPOTS	TU PURTIEST	FU FRITURES
AP VAPORISE	DT DOTTIEST	AD RAPIDEST	GN PRESTING	PUTTIERS	FRUITERS
AS SAVORIES	EN NOISETTE	SPIRATED	HL PHILTERS		FURRIEST
AT VOTARIES	TEOSINTE	TRAIPSED	PHILTRES	**EIRRST 165**	GG TRIGGERS
AW AVOWRIES	FF TOFFIEST	AE PETARIES	HO TROPHIES	(TRIERS)	GH RIGHTERS
BD OVERBIDS	FL LOFTIEST	AG GRAPIEST	HS HIPSTERS	AB ARBITERS	GN RESTRING
CD DISCOVER	FM OFFTIMES	AI PARITIES	THRIPSES	RAREBITS	RINGSTER
DIVORCES	FO FOOTIEST	AK PARKIEST	HW WHIPSTER	AC ERRATICS	STRINGER
CS CORSIVES	GH GOTHITES	AL PILASTER	IL TRIPLIES	AE ARTERIES	GT GRITTERS
CT EVICTORS	GN TENTIGOS	PLAISTER	IN PRISTINE	REASTIER	GY REGISTRY
VORTICES	GS EGOTISTS	PLAITERS	IR STRIPIER	AF FRATRIES	HI SHIRTIER
CY VICEROYS	GU GOUTIEST	AM PRIMATES	IS SPIRIEST	AH TRASHIER	HO HERITORS
DE OVERSIDE	HM MOTHIEST	AN PAINTERS	IT RISPETTI	AI RARITIES	HT THIRSTER
DP DISPROVE	HR THEORIST	PANTRIES	IU PURITIES	AL RETRIALS	HV THRIVERS
PROVIDES	THORITES	PERTAINS	IV PRIVIEST	RETRIALS	HW WHIRRETS
DS DEVISORS	HS TOSHIEST	PINASTER	IY PYRITISE	TRAILERS	IO RIOTRIES
EL OVERLIES	IS OSTEITIS	REPAINTS	KO PORKIEST	AN RESTRAIN	IP STRIPIER
RELIEVOS	OTITISES	AP PERIAPTS	LN SPLINTER	RETRAINS	IW WRISTIER
VOLERIES	JL JOLTIEST	AS PASTRIES	LO POITRELS	STRAINER	KS SKIRRETS
EN EVERSION	JN JETTISON	PIASTRES	LP RIPPLETS	TRAINERS	SKIRTERS
EW OVERWISE	LM MOTLIEST	RASPIEST	STIPPLER	TRANSIRE	STRIKERS
EZ OVERSIZE	LP PISTOLET	TRAIPSES	TIPPLERS	AO ROARIEST	LU SULTRIER
FG FORGIVES	PLOTTIES	AV PRIVATES	TRIPPLES	ROTARIES	LW TWIRLERS
FH OVERFISH	POLITEST	AW WIRETAPS	LS SPIRTLES	AR STARRIER	MM TRIMMERS
GT VERTIGOS	LR TRIOLETS	AY ASPERITY	LT SPLITTER	TARRIERS	MO MORTISER
GU GRIEVOUS	LT STILETTO	CD PREDICTS	TRIPLETS	AS TARSIERS	STORMIER
HT OVERHITS	MM TOTEMISM	SCRIPTED	LY PRIESTLY	AT RETRAITS	NO INTRORSE
IN REVISION	MR OMITTERS	CE CREPIEST	SPRITELY	STRAITER	SNORTIER
VISIONER	MS MOISTEST	RECEIPTS	MM PRIMMEST	TARRIEST	NP PRINTERS
KP OVERSKIP	MT MOTTIEST	SPITCHER	MO IMPOSTER	AW STRAWIER	REPRINTS
LP OVERSLIP	TOTEMIST	CH PITCHERS	MS IMPRESTS	SWARTIER	SPRINTER
MP IMPROVES	MU TITMOUSE	CI PICRITES	MU IMPUREST	BH REBIRTHS	OP PIERROTS
MS VERISMOS	NN TINSTONE	PRICIEST	IMPUTERS	BO ORBITERS	SPORTIER
MW OVERSWIM	TONTINES	CK PRICKETS	STUMPIER	BU BURRIEST	OR ERRORIST
NN ENVIRONS	NP NEPOTIST	CO PERSICOT	NN ENPRINTS	CE RECITERS	OS RESISTOR
NP OVERSPIN	NR SNOTTIER	CR RESCRIPT	NO POINTERS	CK TRICKERS	ROISTERS
PROVINES	TENORIST	CS CRISPEST	PROTEINS	CP RESCRIPT	SORRIEST
NS VERSIONS	TRITONES	CU CREPITUS	REPOINTS	CT CRITTERS	OT RORTIEST
NT INVESTOR	NS SNOTTIES	CUPRITES	NR PRINTERS	RESTRICT	OU STOURIER
NU SOUVENIR	STONIEST	PICTURES	REPRINTS	STRICTER	OV SERVITOR
PT PIVOTERS	NT TOTIENTS	PIECRUST	SPRINTER	CU CRUSTIER	PP STRIPPER
SPORTIVE	NW TOWNIEST	DE PRIESTED	NS SPINSTER	RECRUITS	TRIPPERS
PU PERVIOUS	OR ROOTIEST	RESPITED	NU UNPRIEST	DE DESTRIER	PZ SPRITZER
PREVIOUS	TORTOISE	DI RIPTIDES			

```
QU SQUIRTER
RS STIRRERS
SV STRIVERS
TU TRUSTIER

EIRSTT 104
(SITTER)
AA ARIETTAS
   ARISTATE
AB BIRETTAS
AC CITRATES
   CRISTATE
   SCATTIER
AD STRAITED
   STRIATED
   TARDIEST
AE ARIETTES
   ITERATES
   TEARIEST
   TREATIES
   TREATISE
AG STRIGATE
AL TERTIALS
AM MISTREAT
   TERATISM
AN INTREATS
   NITRATES
   STRAITEN
   TARTINES
   TERTIANS
AR RETRAITS
   STRAITER
   TARRIEST
AS ARTISTES
   ARTSIEST
   STRIATES
AT RATTIEST
   TARTIEST
   TITRATES
AW WARTIEST
AX EXTRAITS
BL BRITTLES
   TRIBLETS
BN BITTERNS
BU TRIBUTES
BY TREYBITS
CH CHITTERS
   RICHTEST
   STITCHER
CI RECTITIS
CL CLITTERS
CN CENTRIST
   CITTERNS
CO COTTIERS
CR CRITTERS
   RESTRICT
   STRICTER
CS TRISECTS
CU TUTRICES
DE TIREDEST
DH THIRSTED
   THRISTED
DI DIRTIEST
   TRITIDES
DN STRIDENT
   TRIDENTS
DO DORTIEST
DU DETRITUS
EF FRISETTE
EG GRISETTE
```

```
   TERGITES
EH ETHERIST
EL RETITLES
EM TERMITES
EN INERTEST
   INTEREST
   STERNITE
EP PRETTIES
ES RESTIEST
FI RIFTIEST
FL FLITTERS
FR FRITTERS
FU TURFIEST
   TURFITES
GG TRIGGEST
GH RIGHTEST
   STREIGHT
GL GLITTERS
GN GITTERNS
GR GRITTERS
GT GRITTEST
HI SHITTIER
   THIRTIES
HL THRISTLE
HO THEORIST
   THORITES
HR THIRSTER
HW WHITRETS
   WHITSTER
   WHITTERS
IL STILTIER
IM METRITIS
IN NITRITES
   STINTIER
IP RISPETTI
IU UTERITIS
IW TWISTIER
IZ RITZIEST
KN KNITTERS
   TRINKETS
KS SKITTERS
LL TESTRILL
LO TRIOLETS
LP SPLITTER
   TRIPLETS
LS SLITTERS
   STILTERS
   TESTRILS
LU SURTITLE
LW WRISTLET
LZ STRELITZ
MM TRIMMEST
MO OMITTERS
MS METRISTS
MU SMUTTIER
NO SNOTTIER
   TENORIST
   TRITONES
NS ENTRISTS
   STINTERS
NU RUNTIEST
NW TWINTERS
NY ENTRYIST
OO ROOTIEST
   TORTOISE
OP PORTIEST
   RISPETTO
   SPOTTIER
OR RORTIEST
OS STOITERS
```

```
OU TUTORISE
OV VIRETOTS
PP TRIPPETS
PS SPITTERS
   TIPSTERS
PU PURTIEST
   PUTTIERS
QU QUITTERS
RU TRUSTIER
SU RUSTIEST
   TRUSTIES
SW TWISTERS
TU RUTTIEST
TW TWITTERS
UX TUTRIXES

EIRSTV 163
(STRIVE)
AA VARIATES
AB VIBRATES
AE EVIRATES
AG VIRGATES
   VITRAGES
AI VAIRIEST
AO VOTARIES
AP PRIVATES
AS TRAVISES
AY VESTIARY
CD VERDICTS
CE VERTICES
CI VERISTIC
CO EVICTORS
   VORTICES
CS VICTRESS
CU CURVIEST
EI VERITIES
EN NERVIEST
   REINVEST
   SERVIENT
   SIRVENTE
ER REVERIST
   RIVERETS
   RIVETERS
ES SIEVERTS
   TREVISES
   VESTRIES
EV VETIVERS
EY SEVERITY
GN STERVING
GO VERTIGOS
HO OVERHITS
HR THRIVERS
IN INVITERS
   VINTRIES
   VITRINES
IP PRIVIEST
IS REVISITS
LU RIVULETS
MU VITREUMS
NN VINTNERS
NO INVESTOR
NU UNRIVETS
   VENTURIS
OP PIVOTERS
   SPORTIVE
OR SERVITOR
OT VIRETOTS
OU VIRTUOSE
   VITREOUS
```

```
   VOITURES
RS STRIVERS

ELORST 67
(TOLERS)
AB BLOATERS
   SORTABLE
   STORABLE
AC SECTORAL
AD DELATORS
   LEOTARDS
   LODESTAR
AE OLEASTER
AF FLOATERS
   FORESTAL
   REFLOATS
AG LEGATORS
AH LOATHERS
AI SOTERIAL
AL REALLOTS
AM MOLERATS
AP PETROSAL
   PROLATES
AR REALTORS
   RELATORS
AU ROSULATE
AV LEVATORS
AY ROYALETS
BH BROTHELS
BI STROBILE
   TRILOBES
BS BOLSTERS
   LOBSTERS
BT BLOTTERS
   BOTTLERS
BU BOULTERS
   TROUBLES
CE CORSELET
   ELECTORS
   ELECTROS
   SELECTOR
CH CHORTLES
CI CLOISTER
   COISTREL
   CORTILES
   COSTLIER
   CREOLIST
CS CORSLETS
   COSTRELS
   CROSSLET
CT CLOTTERS
   CROTTLES
CU CLOTURES
   CLOUTERS
   COULTERS
CY COYSTREL
DD STRODDLE
   STRODLED
   TODDLERS
DI STOLIDER
DL DROLLEST
   STROLLED
DP DROPLETS
DS OLDSTERS
   STRODLES
DT DOTTRELS
EE SLOETREE
EH HOSTELER
EI LITEROSE
   TROELIES
```

```
EL SOLLERET
EM MOLESTER
EN ENTRESOL
ET LORETTES
EU RESOLUTE
FG FROGLETS
FI FLORIEST
   TREFOILS
FT FORTLETS
   VELOUTES
FW FELWORTS
HN HORNLETS
HS HOLSTERS
   HOSTLERS
HT THROSTLE
HY HOSTELRY
II ROILIEST
IL TRILLOES
   TROLLIES
IN RETINOLS
IO TROOLIES
IP POITRELS
IT TRIOLETS
IU LOURIEST
   OUTLIERS
LP POLLSTER
LR STROLLER
   TROLLERS
LY TROLLEYS
MM TROMMELS
MO TREMOLOS
NU TURNSOLE
OS ROOTLESS
OT ROOTLETS
OU TORULOSE
PT PLOTTERS
PU PLOUTERS
   POULTERS
PW PLOWTERS
PY PROSTYLE
   PROTYLES
ST SETTLORS
   SLOTTERS
UY SOUTERLY
   UROSTYLE

ELOSTU 173
(TOUSLE)
AB ABSOLUTE
AC LACTEOUS
   LOCUSTAE
   OSCULATE
AP OUTLEAPS
   PETALOUS
AR ROSULATE
AT TOLUATES
AV OVULATES
AY AUTOLYSE
BD DOUBLETS
BR BOULTERS
BY OBTUSELY
CD LOCUSTED
CE ELOCUTES
CH SELCOUTH
CN NOCTULES
CP COUPLETS
   OCTUPLES
CR CLOTURES
   CLOUTERS
   COULTERS
```

```
CT CULOTTES
DI SOLITUDE
DP POSTLUDE
EN TOLUENES
EP EELPOUTS
   OUTSLEEP
ER RESOLUTE
EV EVOLUTES
FI OUTFLIES
GI EULOGIST
IN ELUTIONS
   OUTLINES
IR LOURIEST
   OUTLIERS
IS LOUSIEST
IV OUTLIVES
   SOLUTIVE
JP PULSOJET
LP POLLUTES
LS OUTSELLS
LT OUTTELLS
LW OUTSWELL
   OUTWELLS
NR TURNSOLE
NZ ZONULETS
OR TORULOSE
OS OUTSOLES
PR PLOUTERS
   POULTERS
PT OUTSLEPT
RY SOUTERLY
   UROSTYLE

EMNOST 186
(MONETS)
AC CAMSTONE
AG MAGNETOS
   MEGATONS
   MONTAGES
AH HOASTMEN
AL SALMONET
AR MONSTERA
   STOREMAN
AU NOTAEUMS
   OUTNAMES
   SEAMOUNT
CK STOCKMEN
CM COMMENTS
CN CONTEMNS
DD ODDMENTS
DI DEMONIST
DR MORDENTS
DU DEMOUNTS
   MUDSTONE
EG EMONGEST
   GEMSTONE
EI MONETISE
   SEMITONE
EM MEMENTOS
ER SERMONET
   STOREMEN
GI MITOGENS
HI HOISTMEN
HL MENTHOLS
HO SMOOTHEN
IK TOKENISM
IN MENTIONS
IO EMOTIONS
   MOONIEST
```

```
IP EMPTIONS
   NEPOTISM
   PIMENTOS
IS MOISTENS
IU MOUNTIES
LO MOONLETS
MY METONYMS
NW TOWNSMEN
OP METOPONS
OR MESOTRON
   MONTEROS
OS MOONSETS
RS MONSTERS
RT SORTMENT
   TORMENTS
RU MONTURES
   MOUNTERS
   REMOUNTS
SS STEMSONS

EMORST 198
  (MOTERS)
AB BROMATES
AD STROAMED
AE EROTEMAS
AF FOREMAST
   FORMATES
AI AMORTISE
   ATOMISER
AL MOLERATS
AM MARMOSET
AN MONSTERA
   STOREMAN
AR REARMOST
AS MAESTROS
AV OVERMAST
BS BESTORMS
   MOBSTERS
   SOMBREST
CI MORTICES
CP COMPTERS
CU COSTUMER
   CUSTOMER
DE MODESTER
DI MORTISED
DN MORDENTS
DO DOOMSTER
EE EROTEMES
   STEREOME
EH THEOREMS
EI TIRESOME
EL MOLESTER
EN SERMONET
   STOREMEN
ES SOMERSET
ET REMOTEST
EU TEMEROUS
FO FOREMOST
FP POMFRETS
GI ERGOTISM
   GORMIEST
GM GROMMETS
GU GOURMETS
HI ISOTHERM
   MOITHERS
HO SMOOTHER
HS SMOTHERS
HU MOUTHERS
HY SMOTHERY
IO MOORIEST
```


```
   MOTORISE
   ROOMIEST
IP IMPOSTER
IR MORTISER
   STORMIER
IS EROTISMS
   MORTISES
   TRISOMES
IT OMITTERS
IU MOISTURE
IW MISWROTE
   WORMIEST
IY ISOMETRY
LM TROMMELS
LO TREMOLOS
NO MESOTRON
   MONTEROS
NS MONSTERS
NT SORTMENT
   TORMENTS
NU MONTURES
   MOUNTERS
   REMOUNTS
OP PROMOTES
OS MOROSEST
SU OESTRUMS
   STRUMOSE

ENORST 23
 (TONERS)
AA ANOESTRA
AB BARONETS
AC ANCESTOR
   ENACTORS
   SARCONET
   SORTANCE
AD TORNADES
AE RESONATE
AG ORANGEST
   RAGSTONE
AI ANOESTRI
   ARSONITE
   NOTARIES
   NOTARISE
   ROSINATE
AM MONSTERA
   STOREMAN
AN RESONANT
AP OPERANTS
   PRONATES
AR ANTRORSE
AS ASSENTOR
   SENATORS
   TREASONS
AT ORNATEST
AV VENATORS
BI BORNITES
   RIBSTONE
BS SORBENTS
BU RUBSTONE
BW BESTROWN
   BROWNEST
BY RENTBOYS
CC CONCERTS
CI CORNIEST
   RECTIONS
CK CRONKEST
CO CORONETS
CS CONSTERS
CT CORNETTS
```


```
CU CONSTRUE
   CORNUTES
   COUNTERS
   RECOUNTS
   TROUNCES
CV CONVERTS
CW CROWNETS
DE ERODENTS
DI DRONIEST
DM MORDENTS
DN TENDRONS
DP PORTENDS
   PROTENDS
DU ROUNDEST
   TONSURED
   UNSORTED
EF ENFOREST
   SOFTENER
EG ESTROGEN
EH HONESTER
EI SEROTINE
EL ENTRESOL
EM SERMONET
   STOREMEN
EN TENONERS
EO ROESTONE
EP PROTENSE
ET ONSETTER
EV OVERNETS
EX EXTENSOR
FH FORHENTS
FN FORNENST
FP FORSPENT
FR RENFORST
FU FORTUNES
GG GONGSTER
GI GENITORS
   ROSETING
GN RONTGENS
GR STRONGER
GS SONGSTER
GU STURGEON
GW WRONGEST
HI HORNIEST
HL HORNLETS
HR NORTHERS
HS SHORTENS
HT THORNSET
HU SOUTHERN
IJ JOINTERS
IL RETINOLS
IN INTONERS
   TERNIONS
IO SNOOTIER
IP POINTERS
   PROTEINS
   REPOINTS
IR INTRORSE
   SNORTIER
IS TERSIONS
IT SNOTTIER
   TENORIST
   TRITONES
IU ROUTINES
   SNOUTIER
IV INVESTOR
IY TYROSINE
IZ TRIZONES
KO STROOKEN
KS STONKERS
```


```
KT KNOTTERS
KW NETWORKS
LU TURNSOLE
MO MESOTRON
   MONTEROS
MS MONSTERS
MT SORTMENT
   TORMENTS
MU MONTURES
   MOUNTERS
   REMOUNTS
NS STERNSON
NU NEUTRONS
NY SONNETRY
PS POSTERNS
PT PORTENTS
RS SNORTERS
RT TORRENTS
ST SNOTTERS
   STENTORS
SU TONSURES
TU STENTOUR
TY SNOTTERY
UV VENTROUS
UY TOURNEYS

ENOSTT 195
 (ONTEST)
AC CONSTATE
AR ORNATEST
BI BOTTINES
CI CENTOIST
   STENOTIC
CN CONTENTS
CR CORNETTS
CS CONTESTS
CX CONTEXTS
EF OFTENEST
EI NOISETTE
   TEOSINTE
EL NOTELETS
EN NONETTES
ER ONSETTER
FL FLETTONS
   FONTLETS
GI TENTIGOS
HR THORNSET
IJ JETTISON
IN TINSTONE
   TONTINES
IP NEPOTIST
IR SNOTTIER
   TENORIST
   TRITONES
IS SNOTTIES
   STONIEST
IT TOTIENTS
IW TOWNIEST
KR KNOTTERS
MR SORTMENT
   TORMENTS
NO NONETTOS
OP POTSTONE
OS TESTOONS
PR PORTENTS
PU OUTSPENT
RR TORRENTS
RS SNOTTERS
   STENTORS
RU STENTOUR
```


```
RY SNOTTERY
SU STOUTENS

ENOSTU 94
 (OUTENS)
AM NOTAEUMS
   OUTNAMES
   SEAMOUNT
AN TONNEAUS
AS SOUTANES
BI BOUNTIES
BR RUBSTONE
CD CONTUSED
CF CONFUTES
CI COUNTIES
CK UNSOCKET
CL NOCTULES
CP POUNCETS
CQ CONQUEST
CR CONSTRUE
   CORNUTES
   COUNTERS
   RECOUNTS
   TROUNCES
CS CONTUSES
   COUNTESS
DD STOUNDED
DI OUNDIEST
DM DEMOUNTS
   MUDSTONE
DO DUOTONES
DP OUTSPEND
   UNPOSTED
DR ROUNDEST
   TONSURED
   UNSORTED
DS SOUNDEST
DW UNSTOWED
EL TOLUENES
FR FORTUNES
GH TOUGHENS
GN GUNSTONE
GR STURGEON
GY YOUNGEST
HI OUTSHINE
HN UNHONEST
HO OUTSHONE
HR SOUTHERN
HU NUTHOUSE
IL ELUTIONS
   OUTLINES
IM MOUNTIES
IN NOUNIEST
IQ QUESTION
IR ROUTINES
   SNOUTIER
IU TENUIOUS
LR TURNSOLE
LZ ZONULETS
MR MONTURES
   MOUNTERS
   REMOUNTS
NR NEUTRONS
NS NEUSTONS
   SUNSTONE
PT OUTSPENT
QU UNQUOTES
RS TONSURES
RT STENTOUR
RV VENTROUS
```


```
RY TOURNEYS
ST STOUTENS

ENRSTU 84
 (TUNERS)
AB UNBRASTE
   URBANEST
AC CENTAURS
   RECUSANT
   UNCRATES
   UNTRACES
AD DAUNTERS
   TRANSUDE
   UNTREADS
AG STRAUNGE
AH HAUNTERS
   UNEARTHS
   UNHEARTS
   URETHANS
AI RUINATES
   URANITES
   URINATES
AL NEUTRALS
AM ANESTRUM
   MENSTRUA
   TRANSUME
AP PERSAUNT
AS ANESTRUS
   SAUNTERS
AT TAUNTERS
AV VAUNTERS
AW UNWATERS
BH BURTHENS
BI TRIBUNES
   TURBINES
BO RUBSTONE
CE UNSECRET
CH CHUNTERS
CI CURNIEST
CK STRUCKEN
CL LECTURNS
CM CENTRUMS
CO CONSTRUE
   CORNUTES
   COUNTERS
   RECOUNTS
   TROUNCES
CR CURRENTS
CS CURTNESS
   ENCRUSTS
DE DENTURES
   SEDERUNT
   UNDERSET
   UNDESERT
DG TRUDGENS
DH THUNDERS
DI INTRUDES
DK DRUNKEST
DL RUNDLETS
   TRUNDLES
DO ROUNDEST
   TONSURED
   UNSORTED
DP UPTRENDS
DT STRUNTED
EI ESURIENT
   NEURITES
   RETINUES
   REUNITES
ES TRUENESS
```

EV	VENTURES
FO	FORTUNES
GL	GRUNTLES
GO	STURGEON
GR	GRUNTERS
	RESTRUNG
HL	LUTHERNS
HO	SOUTHERN
HS	HUNTRESS
	SHUNTERS
II	NEURITIS
IL	INSULTER
	LUSTRINE
IM	TERMINUS
IN	RUNNIEST
	STURNINE
IO	ROUTINES
	SNOUTIER
IP	UNPRIEST
	UNRIPEST
IQ	SQUINTER
IT	RUNTIEST
IV	UNRIVETS
	VENTURIS
IW	UNWRITES
JU	UNJUSTER
KY	TURNKEYS
LO	TURNSOLE
MO	MONTURES
	MOUNTERS
	REMOUNTS
MS	MUNSTERS
	STERNUMS
NO	NEUTRONS
NS	STUNNERS
OS	TONSURES
OT	STENTOUR
OV	VENTROUS
OY	TOURNEYS
PS	PUNSTERS
RU	NURTURES
ST	ENTRUSTS
SU	UNSUREST
TU	UNTRUEST

EOPRST 193
(POSTER)

AB	PROBATES
AD	ADOPTERS
	ASPORTED
	READOPTS
AE	OPERATES
	PROTEASE
AF	FOREPAST
AG	PORTAGES
AL	PETROSAL
	PROLATES
AN	OPERANTS
	PRONATES
AR	PRAETORS
	PRORATES
AS	ESPARTOS
	PORTASES
	PROTASES
	SEAPORTS
AT	PROSTATE
AU	APTEROUS
AV	OVERPAST
BS	BESPORTS
CH	POTCHERS

CI	PERSICOT
CJ	PROJECTS
CK	SPROCKET
CM	COMPTERS
CP	PROSPECT
CR	PORRECTS
CT	PROTECTS
CW	SCREWTOP
DE	POSTERED
	REEDSTOP
	REPOSTED
DH	POTSHERD
DI	DIOPTERS
	DIOPTRES
	DIPTEROS
	PERIDOTS
	PROTEIDS
	RIPOSTED
DL	DROPLETS
DN	PORTENDS
	PROTENDS
DO	DOORSTEP
	TORPEDOS
DP	STROPPED
DU	POSTURED
	SPROUTED
EG	PROTEGES
EI	POETRIES
EN	PROTENSE
ES	PORTESSE
ET	TREETOPS
EU	OUTPEERS
EV	OVERSTEP
EY	SEROTYPE
FI	FIREPOTS
FM	POMFRETS
FN	FORSPENT
FO	FORETOPS
FU	POUFTERS
HI	TROPHIES
HP	PROPHETS
HS	STROPHES
HU	POUTHERS
HY	TROPHESY
IK	PORKIEST
IL	POITRELS
IM	IMPOSTER
IN	POINTERS
	PROTEINS
	REPOINTS
IO	PORTOISE
	ROOPIEST
IR	PIERROTS
	SPORTIER
IS	PERIOSTS
	PROSIEST
	REPOSITS
	RIPOSTES
	TRIPOSES
IT	PORTIEST
	RISPETTO
	SPOTTIER
IU	ROUPIEST
	SPOUTIER
IV	PIVOTERS
	SPORTIVE
KU	UPSTROKE
LL	POLLSTER

LT	PLOTTERS
LU	PLOUTERS
	POULTERS
LW	PLOWTERS
LY	PROSTYLE
	PROTYLES
MO	PROMOTES
NS	POSTERNS
NT	PORTENTS
OR	TROOPERS
OS	STOOPERS
OU	OUTROPES
	PORTEOUS
OV	OVERPOST
OW	TOWROPES
PS	STOPPERS
RS	PORTRESS
	SPORTERS
RU	POSTURER
	TROUPERS
ST	PROTESTS
	SPOTTERS
SU	POSTURES
	SEPTUORS
	SPOUTERS

EORRST 106
(SORTER)

AA	AERATORS
AB	ARBORETS
	TABORERS
AC	ACROTERS
	CREATORS
	REACTORS
AD	ROADSTER
AG	GARROTES
AI	ROARIEST
	ROTARIES
AL	REALTORS
	RELATORS
AM	REARMOST
AN	ANTRORSE
AO	SORORATE
AP	PRAETORS
	PRORATES
AR	ARRESTOR
AS	ASSERTOR
	ASSORTER
	ORATRESS
	ROASTERS
AT	ROSTRATE
BH	BROTHERS
BI	ORBITERS
BU	ROBUSTER
CC	CORRECTS
CE	ERECTORS
CF	CROFTERS
CH	TORCHERS
CP	PORRECTS
CY	CORSETRY
DE	RESORTED
	RESTORED
	ROSTERED
DH	REDSHORT
DS	RODSTERS
EF	FORESTER
	FOSTERER
EG	OSTREGER
ER	RESORTER

	RESTORER
	RETRORSE
ES	RESTORES
EU	REROUTES
EX	EXTRORSE
FI	FROSTIER
	ROTIFERS
FN	RENFORST
FS	FORTRESS
FW	FROWSTER
FY	FORESTRY
GN	STRONGER
GS	GROSERTS
HI	HERITORS
HN	NORTHERS
HW	THROWERS
II	RIOTRIES
IM	MORTISER
	STORMIER
IN	INTRORSE
	SNORTIER
IP	PIERROTS
	SPORTIER
IR	ERRORIST
IS	RESISTOR
	ROISTERS
	SORRIEST
IT	RORTIEST
IU	STOURIER
IV	SERVITOR
KS	STROKERS
LL	STROLLER
	TROLLERS
NS	SNORTERS
NT	TORRENTS
OP	TROOPERS
OS	ROOSTERS
PS	PORTRESS
	SPORTERS
PU	POSTURER
	TROUPERS
SS	STRESSOR
	TROSSERS
SU	ROUSTERS
	TROUSERS
SW	STROWERS
	TROWSERS
SY	ROYSTERS
TT	TROTTERS
TU	TORTURES
	TROUTERS

EORSTT 114
(OTTERS)

AA	AEROSTAT
AB	ABETTORS
	BATTEROS
	TABORETS
AC	SECTATOR
AG	GAROTTES
AH	RHEOSTAT
AN	ORNATEST
AP	PROSTATE
AR	ROSTRATE
AS	STRATOSE
	TOASTERS
AT	ATTESTOR
	TESTATOR
AU	OUTRATES
	OUTSTARE

BH	BETROTHS
BL	BLOTTERS
	BOTTLERS
CI	COTTIERS
CL	CLOTTERS
	CROTTLES
CN	CORNETTS
CP	PROTECTS
DE	ROSETTED
	TETRODES
DI	DORTIEST
DL	DOTTRELS
DU	STROUTED
EL	LORETTES
EM	REMOTEST
EN	ONSETTER
EP	TREETOPS
ES	ROSETTES
FL	FORTLETS
FO	FOOTREST
GO	GROTTOES
HI	THEORIST
	THORITES
HL	THROSTLE
HN	THORNSET
HS	SHORTEST
IL	TRIOLETS
IM	OMITTERS
IN	SNOTTIER
	TENORIST
	TRITONES
IO	ROOTIEST
	TORTOISE
IP	PORTIEST
	RISPETTO
	SPOTTIER
IR	RORTIEST
IS	STOITERS
IU	TUTORISE
IV	VIRETOTS
KN	KNOTTERS
LO	ROOTLETS
LP	PLOTTERS
LS	SETTLORS
	SLOTTERS
MN	SORTMENT
	TORMENTS
NP	PORTENTS
NR	TORRENTS
NS	SNOTTERS
	STENTORS
NU	STENTOUR
NY	SNOTTERY
PS	PROTESTS
	SPOTTERS
RT	TROTTERS
RU	TORTURES
	TROUTERS
ST	STOTTERS
SU	TUTORESS
SW	SWOTTERS
UW	OUTWREST

GILNOT 171
(TOLING)

AA	GALTONIA
AB	BLOATING
	OBLIGANT
AC	LOCATING
AE	GELATION

	LEGATION
AF	FLOATING
AG	GLOATING
	GOATLING
AH	LOATHING
AI	INTAGLIO
	LIGATION
	TAGLIONI
AP	PLOATING
AR	TRIGONAL
AS	ANTILOGS
	SALTOING
AY	ANTILOGY
BS	BILTONGS
BT	BLOTTING
	BOTTLING
BU	BOULTING
CH	CLOTHING
CT	CLOTTING
CU	CLOUTING
DD	TODDLING
FO	FOOTLING
FS	SOFTLING
FU	FLOUTING
	OUTFLING
GG	TOGGLING
GU	GLOUTING
HS	SLOTHING
IP	PILOTING
IS	TOILINGS
JS	JOSTLING
LR	TROLLING
LS	TOLLINGS
MR	MORTLING
MT	MOTTLING
MU	MOULTING
NW	TOWNLING
OR	ROOTLING
OS	STOOLING
	TOOLINGS
OT	TOOTLING
PP	TOPPLING
PT	PLOTTING
RU	TROULING
ST	SLOTTING
SU	TOUSLING
UY	OUTLYING
UZ	TOUZLING

GINORS 128
(SIGNOR)

AD	ROADINGS
AE	IGNAROES
	ORGANISE
	ORIGANES
AI	SIGNORIA
AM	ORGANISM
AR	GARRISON
	ROARINGS
AS	ASSIGNOR
	SIGNORAS
	SOARINGS
AT	ORGANIST
	ROASTING
AU	AROUSING
AV	SAVORING
BD	SONGBIRD
BE	SOBERING
BH	BIGHORNS

BK BROKINGS	MU ROUMINGS	THROWING	EP PONGIEST	SIGNPOST	ROSETING
BM SOMBRING	NS SNORINGS	WORTHING	ER GENITORS	STOPINGS	EH HORNIEST
BW BROWSING	SORNINGS	IN IGNITRON	ROSETING	PT SPOTTING	EJ JOINTERS
CD CORDINGS	NT SNORTING	IS RIOTINGS	ET TENTIGOS	PU POUTINGS	EL RETINOLS
CK ROCKINGS	NU GRUNIONS	ROISTING	FI FOISTING	SPOUTING	EN INTONERS
CN SCORNING	OP SPOORING	ROSITING	FL SOFTLING	RS SORTINGS	TERNIONS
CP CORPSING	OT ROOSTING	IZ ROZITING	FO FOOTINGS	RU ROUSTING	EO SNOOTIER
CS CROSSING	ROOTINGS	KS STROKING	FR FROSTING	ROUTINGS	EP POINTERS
SCORINGS	PS PROSINGS	LL TROLLING	GH GHOSTING	TOURINGS	PROTEINS
SCORSING	PT SPORTING	LM MORTLING	GO STOOGING	RW STROWING	REPOINTS
CU COURSING	PU INGROUPS	LO ROOTLING	HI HOISTING	WORSTING	ER INTRORSE
SCOURING	POURINGS	LU TROULING	HL SLOTHING	RY ROYSTING	SNORTIER
SOURCING	ST SORTINGS	MO MOTORING	HN NOTHINGS	STORYING	ES TERSIONS
DD RODDINGS	SU SOURINGS	MS STORMING	HO SHOOTING	STROYING	ET SNOTTIER
DE NEGROIDS	TU ROUSTING	NS SNORTING	SOOTHING	SS TOSSINGS	TENORIST
DI DORISING	ROUTINGS	OP TROOPING	HR SHORTING	ST SOTTINGS	TRITONES
DL GIRLONDS	TOURINGS	OS ROOSTING	HS HOSTINGS	SU TOUSINGS	EU ROUTINES
LORDINGS	TW STROWING	ROOTINGS	HT SHOTTING	SV STOVINGS	SNOUTIER
DW DROWSING	WORSTING	OW WROOTING	TONIGHTS	SW STOWINGS	EV INVESTOR
SWORDING	TY ROYSTING	PS SPORTING	HU SHOUTING	TT STOTTING	EY TYROSINE
WORDINGS	STORYING	PU TROUPING	SOUTHING	TOTTINGS	EZ TRIZONES
EE ERINGOES	STROYING	SS SORTINGS	HW SOWTHING	TW SWOTTING	FG FROSTING
EI SEIGNIOR		SU ROUSTING	IJ JINGOIST	UW OUTSWING	GH SHORTING
EL RESOLING	**GINORT 102**	ROUTINGS	JOISTING	OUTWINGS	GI RIOTINGS
EM NEGROISM	(ROTING)	TOURINGS	IL TOILINGS		ROISTING
EP PERIGONS	AB ABORTING	SW STROWING	IM MOISTING	**INORST 59**	ROSITING
REPOSING	TABORING	WORSTING	IP POSITING	(TRIONS)	GK STROKING
SPONGIER	AL TRIGONAL	SY ROYSTING	SOPITING	AB TABORINS	GM STORMING
ER IGNORERS	AN IGNORANT	STORYING	IR RIOTINGS	AC CANTORIS	GN SNORTING
ES SIGNORES	AO ROGATION	STROYING	ROISTING	CAROTINS	GO ROOSTING
ET GENITORS	AS ORGANIST	TT TROTTING	ROSITING	AD INTRADOS	ROOTINGS
ROSETING	ROASTING	TU TROUTING	IT STOITING	AE ANOESTRI	GP SPORTING
EY SEIGNORY	AT ROTATING	TUTORING	JL JOSTLING	ARSONITE	GS SORTINGS
FF GRIFFONS	TROATING		JT JOTTINGS	NOTARIES	GU ROUSTING
FG FORGINGS	AV GRAVITON	**GINOST 176**	JU JOUSTING	NOTARISE	ROUTINGS
FM FORMINGS	AY GYRATION	(OSTING)	KO STOOKING	ROSINATE	TOURINGS
FO ROOFINGS	ORGANITY	AB BOASTING	KP KINGPOST	AG ORGANIST	GW STROWING
FT FROSTING	BI ORBITING	BOATINGS	KR STROKING	ROASTING	WORSTING
GP PROGGINS	CE GERONTIC	BOSTANGI	LO STOOLING	AH TRAHISON	GY ROYSTING
GS GROSSING	CF CROFTING	AC AGNOSTIC	TOOLINGS	AI INTARSIO	STORYING
GU GROUSING	CH TORCHING	COASTING	LT SLOTTING	AJ JANITORS	STROYING
GW GROWINGS	CI TRIGONIC	COATINGS	LU TOUSLING	AK SKIATRON	HI HISTRION
HN HORNINGS	CK TROCKING	COTINGAS	MO MOOTINGS	AO ORATIONS	HN TINHORNS
HS HORSINGS	CU COURTING	AD DOATINGS	SMOOTING	AP ATROPINS	HO HORNITOS
SHORINGS	EH THROEING	AH HOASTING	MP STOMPING	AS ARSONIST	HS HORNISTS
HT SHORTING	EN NITROGEN	AK GOATSKIN	MR STORMING	AT STRONTIA	IS IRONISTS
HV SHROVING	ES GENITORS	AL ANTILOGS	MS GNOMISTS	AU SUTORIAN	IT INTROITS
HW SHROWING	ROSETING	SALTOING	MU MOUSTING	AX TRIAXONS	KK KIRKTONS
IL LIGROINS	ET OTTERING	AN ASTONING	SMOUTING	BE BORNITES	LS NOSTRILS
IN IRONINGS	EU OUTREIGN	AR ORGANIST	NN STONNING	RIBSTONE	LU TORULINS
ROSINING	ROUTEING	ROASTING	NO SNOOTING	BO ISOBRONT	MO MONITORS
IS SIGNIORS	EW TOWERING	AS AGONISTS	NR SNORTING	BS RIBSTONS	TROMINOS
IT RIOTINGS	EX OXTERING	AT TANGOIST	NS STONINGS	CE CORNIEST	MY TRIONYMS
ROISTING	EZ ROZETING	TOASTING	NT SNOTTING	RECTIONS	NO NOTORNIS
ROSITING	FH FROTHING	BL BILTONGS	NU SNOUTING	CR TRICORNS	OP PORTIONS
IV VISORING	FN FRONTING	BOLTINGS	STOUNING	CS CISTRONS	POSITRON
KT STROKING	FS FROSTING	BO BOOSTING	NY STONYING	CORNISTS	SORPTION
KW WORKINGS	GG TROGGING	CI COTISING	OP STOOPING	CT CONTRIST	OS ISOTRONS
LL ROLLINGS	GU GROUTING	CK STOCKING	OR ROOSTING	CU RUCTIONS	TORSIONS
LM MORLINGS	HN NORTHING	CO SCOOTING	ROOTINGS	DE DRONIEST	OY SONORITY
LU LOURINGS	THORNING	CU SCOUTING	PP STOPPING	DO TORDIONS	
MN MORNINGS	THRONING	DG STODGING	TOPPINGS	DU STURNOID	
MO MOORINGS	HS SHORTING	EE EGESTION	PR SPORTING	TURDIONS	
SMOORING	HT TROTHING	EH HISTOGEN	PS POSTINGS	EE SEROTINE	
MT STORMING	HW INGROWTH	EM MITOGENS		EG GENITORS	

SECTION FOUR

THE HOOKS

Introduction

Which two-letter words can be transformed into which three-letter words by the addition of a single letter at either the front or the end? An example is HI to CHI, GHI and PHI (by adding a letter at the front of HI), and HIC, HID, HIE, HIM, HIN, HIP, HIS and HIT (by adding a letter at the end). Words which can add a letter at the front or back are called hooks, as they provide places for other words to hook on to. All the two-letter hooks such as these appear in the following lists. Of course, it is also helpful to be able to see at a glance which two-letter words *don't* add a letter at either end. All these hooks (and non-hooks!) are shown in the following lists.

Subsequent lists show all the three-letter and four-letter words, along with their hooks and non-hooks.

For longer words, of five, six and seven letters, only actual hooks are shown. Non-hooks have been omitted.

In actual play, it can be very useful to play a three-letter word, (BAP, say), which has an obscure extension to four letters (BAPU). If all the S's and blanks have already been played, the chances are your opponent won't know BAPU, so the opening will likely be safe until you want to put a U on the end of BAP. One other particularly neat hook is PAYS to PAYSD. Chances are that your opponent won't think to extend PAYS by the addition of a D!

PART A: 2-letter word hooks
including all root words

AA	SAM	ASK	PAY	DAP	REF	LES	GUY	**ID**	FIT
BAA	TAM	ASP	RAY	DAS	TEF	MES	**HA**	AID	GIT
AAS	YAM	ASS	SAY	DAW	EFF	OES	AHA	BID	HIT
AD	AMI	**AT**	WAY	DAY	EFS	RES	CHA	DID	KIT
BAD	AMP	BAT	AYE	**DI**	EFT	TES	HAD	FID	LIT
CAD	**AN**	CAT	AYU	DIB	**EH**	YES	HAE	GID	NIT
DAD	BAN	EAT	**BA**	DID	REH	ESS	HAG	HID	PIT
FAD	CAN	FAT	ABA	DIE	EHS	**EX**	HAH	KID	RIT
GAD	DAN	GAT	BAA	DIG	**EL**	HEX	HAJ	LID	SIT
HAD	EAN	HAT	BAD	DIM	BEL	KEX	HAM	MID	TIT
LAD	FAN	KAT	BAG	DIN	CEL	LEX	HAN	NID	WIT
MAD	GAN	LAT	BAH	DIP	DEL	REX	HAP	RID	ZIT
PAD	HAN	MAT	BAM	DIT	EEL	SEX	HAS	TID	ITA
RAD	MAN	NAT	BAN	DIV	GEL	VEX	HAT	IDE	ITS
SAD	NAN	OAT	BAP	**DO**	MEL	WEX	HAW	IDS	**JO**
TAD	PAN	PAT	BAR	ADO	SEL	YEX	HAY	**IF**	JOB
WAD	RAN	QAT	BAS	UDO	TEL	**FA**	**HE**	GIF	JOE
ADD	SAN	RAT	BAT	DOB	ZEL	FAB	CHE	IFF	JOG
ADO	TAN	SAT	BAY	DOC	ELD	FAD	SHE	KIF	JOR
ADS	VAN	TAT	**BE**	DOD	ELF	FAG	THE	IFS	JOT
AE	WAN	VAT	BED	DOE	ELK	FAH	HEM	**IN**	JOW
GAE	ANA	WAT	BEE	DOG	ELL	FAN	HEN	AIN	JOY
HAE	AND	ATE	BEG	DOH	ELM	FAP	HEP	BIN	**KA**
KAE	ANE	**AW**	BEL	DON	ELS	FAR	HER	DIN	SKA
MAE	ANN	CAW	BEN	DOO	ELT	FAS	HES	FIN	KAE
NAE	ANT	DAW	BET	DOP	**EM**	FAT	HET	GIN	KAI
SAE	ANY	FAW	BEY	DOR	GEM	FAW	HEW	HIN	KAS
TAE	**AR**	HAW	BEZ	DOS	HEM	FAX	HEX	KIN	KAT
VAE	BAR	JAW	**BO**	DOT	REM	FAY	HEY	LIN	KAW
WAE	CAR	KAW	BOA	DOW	WEM	**FY**	**HI**	PIN	KAY
AH	EAR	LAW	BOB	**EA**	EME	**GI**	CHI	RIN	**KO**
BAH	FAR	MAW	BOD	KEA	EMS	GIB	GHI	SIN	KOA
DAH	GAR	PAW	BOG	LEA	EMU	GID	PHI	TIN	KOB
FAH	JAR	RAW	BOH	PEA	**EN**	GIE	HIC	VIN	KON
HAH	LAR	SAW	BOK	SEA	BEN	GIF	HID	WIN	KOP
LAH	MAR	TAW	BON	TEA	DEN	GIG	HIE	YIN	KOS
PAH	OAR	WAW	BOO	YEA	EEN	GIN	HIM	INK	KOW
RAH	PAR	YAW	BOP	ZEA	FEN	GIO	HIN	INN	**KY**
YAH	SAR	AWA	BOR	EAN	GEN	GIP	HIP	INS	SKY
AHA	TAR	AWE	BOS	EAR	HEN	GIS	HIS	**IO**	KYE
AI	WAR	AWN	BOT	EAS	KEN	GIT	HIT	BIO	**LA**
KAI	ARC	**AX**	BOW	EAT	MEN	**GO**	**HO**	GIO	ALA
SAI	ARE	FAX	BOX	EAU	PEN	AGO	MHO	ION	LAB
TAI	ARK	LAX	BOY	**EE**	REN	EGO	OHO	IOS	LAC
AIA	ARM	MAX	**BY**	BEE	SEN	YGO	PHO	**IS**	LAD
AID	ARS	PAX	ABY	CEE	TEN	GOA	RHO	AIS	LAG
AIL	ARY	RAX	BYE	DEE	WEN	GOB	THO	BIS	LAH
AIM	**AS**	SAX	BYS	FEE	YEN	GOD	WHO	GIS	LAM
AIN	AAS	TAX	**CH**	GEE	END	GOE	ZHO	HIS	LAP
AIR	BAS	WAX	ECH	JEE	ENE	GOG	HOA	LIS	LAR
AIS	DAS	ZAX	ICH	LEE	ENG	GON	HOB	MIS	LAS
AIT	EAS	AXE	OCH	NEE	ENS	GOO	HOC	NIS	LAT
AM	FAS	**AY**	CHA	PEE	**ER**	GOS	HOD	PIS	LAV
BAM	GAS	BAY	CHE	REE	HER	GOT	HOE	SIS	LAW
CAM	HAS	CAY	CHI	SEE	PER	GOV	HOG	TIS	LAX
DAM	KAS	DAY	**DA**	TEE	ERA	GOY	HOH	VIS	LAY
GAM	LAS	FAY	ODA	VEE	ERE	**GU**	HOI	WIS	**LI**
HAM	MAS	GAY	DAB	WEE	ERF	GUB	HON	XIS	LIB
JAM	NAS	HAY	DAD	ZEE	ERG	GUE	HOO	ISH	LID
KAM	PAS	JAY	DAG	EEK	ERK	GUM	HOP	ISM	LIE
LAM	RAS	KAY	DAH	EEL	ERN	GUN	HOS	**IT**	LIG
MAM	VAS	LAY	DAK	EEN	ERR	GUP	HOT	AIT	LIN
NAM	WAS	MAY	DAL	EF	ERS	GUR	HOW	BIT	LIP
PAM	ASH	NAY	DAM	KEF	**ES**	GUS	HOX	CIT	LIS
RAM			DAN	NEF	HES	GUT	HOY	DIT	

LIT	MUG	ROB	CON	VOR	BOY	REN	TEA	NUN	WET
LO	MUM	SOB	DON	ORB	COY	REP	TED	PUN	WEX
LOB	MUN	YOB	EON	ORC	FOY	RES	TEE	RUN	WEY
LOG	MUS	OBI	FON	ORD	GOY	RET	TEF	SUN	**WO**
LOO	MUX	OBS	GON	ORE	HOY	REV	TEG	TUN	TWO
LOP	**MY**	**OD**	HON	ORF	JOY	REW	TEL	UNI	WOE
LOR	**NA**	BOD	ION	ORS	LOY	REX	TEN	UNS	WOG
LOS	ANA	COD	KON	ORT	MOY	**SH**	TES	**UP**	WOK
LOT	MNA	DOD	NON	**OS**	NOY	ASH	TEW	CUP	WON
LOW	NAB	GOD	WON	BOS	SOY	ISH	**TI**	DUP	WOO
LOX	NAE	HOD	YON	COS	TOY	SHE	TIC	GUP	WOP
LOY	NAG	MOD	ONE	DOS	OYE	SHY	TID	HUP	WOS
MA	NAM	NOD	ONS	GOS	OYS	**SI**	TIE	OUP	WOT
SMA	NAN	POD	**OO**	HOS	**PA**	PSI	TIG	PUP	WOW
MAC	NAP	ROD	BOO	IOS	SPA	SIB	TIL	SUP	WOX
MAD	NAS	SOD	COO	KOS	PAD	SIC	TIN	TUP	**XI**
MAE	NAT	TOD	DOO	LOS	PAH	SIM	TIP	YUP	XIS
MAG	NAY	YOD	GOO	OOS	PAL	SIN	TIS	UPS	**YE**
MAK	**NE**	ODA	HOO	POS	PAM	SIP	TIT	**UR**	AYE
MAL	ANE	ODD	LOO	SOS	PAN	SIR	**TO**	BUR	BYE
MAM	ENE	ODE	MOO	WOS	PAP	SIS	TOD	CUR	DYE
MAN	ONE	ODS	POO	YOS	PAR	SIT	TOE	FUR	EYE
MAP	NEB	**OE**	ROO	ZOS	PAS	SIX	TOG	GUR	HYE
MAR	NED	DOE	TOO	**OU**	PAT	**SO**	TOM	LUR	KYE
MAS	NEE	FOE	WOO	FOU	PAW	DSO	TON	NUR	LYE
MAT	NEF	GOE	ZOO	MOU	PAX	SOB	TOO	OUR	NYE
MAW	NEK	HOE	OOF	SOU	PAY	SOC	TOP	PUR	OYE
MAX	NEP	JOE	OOH	YOU	**PI**	SOD	TOR	SUR	PYE
MAY	NET	MOE	OOM	OUK	PIA	SOG	TOT	URD	RYE
ME	NEW	ROE	OON	OUP	PIC	SOH	TOW	URE	SYE
EME	**NO**	TOE	OOP	OUR	PIE	SOL	TOY	URN	TYE
MEL	NOB	VOE	OOR	OUT	PIG	SON	**UG**	**US**	WYE
MEN	NOD	WOE	OOS	**OW**	PIN	SOP	BUG	BUS	YEA
MES	NOG	OES	**OP**	BOW	PIP	SOS	DUG	GUS	YEN
MET	NOH	**OF**	BOP	COW	PIR	SOT	FUG	JUS	YEP
MEU	NOM	OFF	COP	DOW	PIS	SOU	HUG	MUS	YES
MEW	NON	OFT	DOP	HOW	PIT	SOV	JUG	NUS	YET
MI	NOR	**OH**	FOP	JOW	PIU	SOW	LUG	PUS	YEW
AMI	NOT	BOH	HOP	KOW	PIX	SOX	MUG	SUS	YEX
MID	NOW	DOH	KOP	LOW	**PO**	SOY	PUG	USE	**YO**
MIL	NOY	FOH	LOP	MOW	POA	**ST**	RUG	**UT**	YOB
MIM	**NU**	HOH	MOP	NOW	POD	PST	TUG	BUT	YOD
MIR	GNU	NOH	OOP	POW	POH	STY	VUG	CUT	YOK
MIS	NUB	OOH	POP	ROW	POI	**TA**	YUG	GUT	YON
MIX	NUN	POH	SOP	SOW	POM	ETA	UGH	HUT	YOS
MIZ	NUR	SOH	TOP	TOW	POO	ITA	UGS	JUT	YOU
MO	NUS	OHM	WOP	VOW	POP	TAB	**UM**	NUT	YOW
MOA	NUT	OHO	**OR**	WOW	POS	TAD	BUM	OUT	**YU**
MOB	**NY**	**OI**	BOR	YOW	POT	TAE	CUM	PUT	AYU
MOD	ANY	HOI	COR	OWE	POW	TAG	FUM	RUT	YUG
MOE	NYE	POI	DOR	OWL	POX	TAI	GUM	TUT	YUK
MOG	NYS	OIK	FOR	OWN	POZ	TAJ	HUM	UTE	YUP
MOM	**OB**	OIL	JOR	OWT	**RE**	TAK	LUM	UTS	YUS
MOO	BOB	**OM**	LOR	**OX**	ARE	TAM	MUM	UTU	**ZO**
MOP	COB	MOM	MOR	BOX	ERE	TAN	RUM	**WE**	DZO
MOR	DOB	NOM	NOR	COX	IRE	TAP	SUM	AWE	ZOA
MOT	FOB	OOM	OOR	FOX	ORE	TAR	TUM	EWE	ZOS
MOU	GOB	POM	TOR	HOX	PRE	TAT	VUM	OWE	
MOW	HOB	ROM		LOX	URE	TAU	**UN**	WEB	
MOY	JOB	TOM		POX	RED	TAW	BUN	WED	
MOZ	KOB	OMS		SOX	REE	TAX	DUN	WEE	
MU	LOB	**ON**		VOX	REF	**TE**	FUN	WEM	
EMU	MOB	BON		WOX	REH	ATE	GUN	WEN	
MUD	NOB			**OY**	REM	UTE	MUN		

PART A: 3-letter word hooks
including all root words

AAS	GAGE	AINE	TALE	AND	APTS	FART	WATE	BAG	BENI
BAAS	MAGE	AIR	VALE	BAND	ARC	GART	YATE	BAGS	BENJ
ABA	PAGE	FAIR	WALE	FAND	MARC	HART	AUF	BAH	BENS
BABA	RAGE	GAIR	YALE	HAND	ARCH	KART	CAUF	BAHT	BENT
CABA	SAGE	HAIR	ALEE	LAND	ARCO	MART	LAUF	BAM	BET
ABAC	WAGE	LAIR	ALES	MAND	ARCS	PART	AUFS	BAMS	ABET
ABAS	AGED	PAIR	ALEW	PAND	ARE	TART	AUK	BAN	YBET
ABB	AGEE	SAIR	ALL	RAND	BARE	WART	BAUK	BANC	BETA
ABBA	AGEN	VAIR	BALL	SAND	CARE	ARTS	CAUK	BAND	BETE
ABBE	AGES	AIRN	CALL	WAND	DARE	ARTY	WAUK	BANE	BETH
ABBS	AGO	AIRS	FALL	ANDS	FARE	ARY	AUKS	BANG	BETS
ABY	DAGO	AIRT	GALL	ANE	GARE	NARY	AVA	BANI	BEY
BABY	KAGO	AIRY	HALL	BANE	HARE	VARY	KAVA	BANK	OBEY
GABY	SAGO	AIS	MALL	CANE	LARE	WARY	LAVA	BANS	BEYS
ABYE	AGOG	DAIS	PALL	FANE	MARE	ARYL	AVAL	BANT	BEZ
ACE	AGON	KAIS	TALL	GANE	NARE	ASH	AVAS	BAP	BIB
DACE	AHA	PAIS	WALL	JANE	PARE	BASH	AVE	BAPS	BIBS
FACE	TAHA	SAIS	ALLS	LANE	RARE	CASH	CAVE	BAPU	BID
LACE	AIA	TAIS	ALLY	MANE	TARE	DASH	GAVE	BAR	ABID
MACE	AIAS	AIT	ALP	PANE	VARE	FASH	HAVE	BARB	BIDE
PACE	AID	BAIT	CALP	SANE	WARE	GASH	LAVE	BARD	BIDS
RACE	GAID	GAIT	PALP	TANE	YARE	HASH	NAVE	BARE	BIG
TACE	KAID	RAIT	SALP	VANE	AREA	LASH	PAVE	BARK	BIGA
ACED	LAID	TAIT	ALPS	WANE	ARED	MASH	RAVE	BARM	BIGG
ACES	MAID	WAIT	ALS	ANES	ARES	PASH	SAVE	BARN	BIGS
ACT	PAID	AITS	DALS	ANEW	ARET	RASH	WAVE	BARP	BIN
FACT	RAID	AITU	GALS	ANN	AREW	SASH	AVER	BARS	BIND
PACT	SAID	AKE	MALS	CANN	ARK	TASH	AVES	BAS	BINE
TACT	WAID	BAKE	PALS	JANN	BARK	WASH	AWA	ABAS	BING
ACTA	AIDE	CAKE	SALS	ANNA	CARK	ASHY	PAWA	BASE	BINK
ACTS	AIDS	FAKE	ALSO	ANNO	DARK	ASK	AWAY	BASH	BINS
ADD	AIL	HAKE	ALT	ANNS	HARK	BASK	AWE	BASK	BINT
WADD	BAIL	JAKE	DALT	ANT	JARK	CASK	WAWE	BASS	BIO
ADDS	FAIL	LAKE	HALT	BANT	LARK	HASK	AWED	BAST	BIOG
ADO	HAIL	MAKE	MALT	CANT	MARK	MASK	AWES	BAT	BIOS
DADO	JAIL	RAKE	SALT	DANT	NARK	TASK	AWL	BATE	BIS
FADO	KAIL	SAKE	ALTO	GANT	PARK	ASKS	BAWL	BATH	IBIS
ADOS	MAIL	TAKE	ALTS	KANT	SARK	ASP	PAWL	BATS	OBIS
ADS	NAIL	WAKE	AMI	LANT	WARK	GASP	WAWL	BATT	BISE
CADS	PAIL	AKED	KAMI	PANT	ARKS	HASP	YAWL	BAY	BISH
DADS	RAIL	AKEE	RAMI	RANT	ARM	JASP	AWLS	BAYE	BISK
FADS	SAIL	AKES	AMID	VANT	BARM	RASP	AWN	BAYS	BIT
GADS	TAIL	ALA	AMIE	WANT	FARM	WASP	BAWN	BAYT	OBIT
HADS	VAIL	GALA	AMIR	ANTA	HARM	ASPS	DAWN	BED	BITE
LADS	WAIL	NALA	AMIS	ANTE	MARM	ASS	FAWN	ABED	BITO
MADS	AILS	TALA	AMP	ANTI	WARM	BASS	LAWN	BEDE	BITS
PADS	AIM	ALAE	CAMP	ANTS	ARMS	LASS	PAWN	BEDS	BITT
RADS	KAIM	ALAP	DAMP	ANY	ARMY	MASS	RAWN	BEE	BIZ
TADS	MAIM	ALAR	GAMP	CANY	ARS	PASS	SAWN	BEEF	BOA
WADS	SAIM	ALAS	LAMP	MANY	BARS	SASS	YAWN	BEEN	BOAK
AFT	AIMS	ALAY	RAMP	WANY	CARS	TASS	AWNS	BEEP	BOAR
BAFT	AIN	ALB	SAMP	ZANY	EARS	ATE	AWNY	BEER	BOAS
DAFT	CAIN	ALBE	TAMP	APE	FARS	BATE	AXE	BEET	BOAT
HAFT	FAIN	ALBS	VAMP	CAPE	GARS	CATE	AXED	BEG	BOB
RAFT	GAIN	ALE	AMPS	GAPE	JARS	DATE	AXEL	BEGO	BOBA
WAFT	HAIN	BALE	ANA	JAPE	MARS	FATE	AXES	BEGS	BOBS
AGA	KAIN	DALE	KANA	NAPE	OARS	GATE	AYE	BEL	BOD
GAGA	LAIN	EALE	LANA	PAPE	PARS	HATE	BAYE	BELL	BODE
NAGA	MAIN	GALE	MANA	RAPE	SARS	LATE	AYES	BELS	BODS
RAGA	NAIN	HALE	NANA	TAPE	TARS	MATE	AYU	BELT	BODY
SAGA	PAIN	KALE	RANA	APED	WARS	PATE	AYUS	BEN	BOG
AGAR	RAIN	MALE	TANA	APES	ARSE	RATE	BAA	BEND	BOGS
AGAS	SAIN	PALE	ANAL	APEX	ART	SATE	BAAS	BENE	BOGY
AGE	VAIN	RALE	ANAN	APT	CART	TATE	BAD	BEN	BOH
CAGE	WAIN	SALE	ANAS	RAPT	DART		BADE		BOK

BOKE	BUGS	CARD	SCOG	SCRY	DAWK	DIVS	**DUD**	EASY	REFS
BOKO	**BUM**	CARE	COGS	**CUB**	DAWN	**DOB**	DUDE	**EAT**	TEFS
BOKS	BUMF	CARK	**COL**	CUBE	DAWS	DOBS	DUDS	BEAT	**EFT**
BON	BUMP	CARL	COLA	CUBS	DAWT	**DOC**	**DUE**	FEAT	DEFT
EBON	BUMS	CARP	COLD	**CUD**	**DAY**	DOCK	DUED	GEAT	HEFT
BONA	**BUN**	CARR	COLE	SCUD	DAYS	DOCS	DUEL	HEAT	LEFT
BOND	BUNA	CARS	COLL	CUDS	**DEB**	**DOD**	DUES	JEAT	REFT
BONE	BUND	CART	COLS	**CUE**	DEBS	DODO	DUET	LEAT	WEFT
BONG	BUNG	**CAT**	COLT	CUED	DEBT	DODS	**DUG**	MEAT	EFTS
BONK	BUNK	SCAT	**CON**	CUES	**DEE**	**DOE**	DUGS	NEAT	**EGG**
BONY	BUNS	CATE	ICON	**CUM**	IDEE	DOEN	**DUN**	PEAT	TEGG
BOO	BUNT	CATS	COND	SCUM	DEED	DOER	DUNE	SEAT	YEGG
BOOB	**BUR**	**CAW**	CONE	**CUP**	DEEM	DOES	DUNG	TEAT	EGGS
BOOH	BURD	SCAW	CONK	SCUP	DEEN	**DOG**	DUNK	EATH	EGGY
BOOK	BURG	CAWK	CONN	CUPS	DEEP	DOGE	DUNS	EATS	**EGO**
BOOM	BURK	CAWS	CONS	**CUR**	DEER	DOGS	DUNT	**EAU**	BEGO
BOON	BURL	**CAY**	CONY	CURB	DEES	DOGY	**DUO**	BEAU	SEGO
BOOR	BURN	CAYS	**COO**	CURD	DEEV	**DOH**	DUOS	EAUS	EGOS
BOOS	BURP	**CEE**	COOF	CURE	**DEI**	DOHS	**DUP**	EAUX	**EHS**
BOOT	BURR	CEES	COOK	CURL	DEID	**DON**	DUPE	**EBB**	REHS
BOP	BURS	**CEL**	COOL	CURN	DEIL	DONA	DUPS	EBBS	**EIK**
BOPS	BURY	CELL	COOM	CURR	**DEL**	DONE	**DUX**	**ECH**	REIK
BOR	**BUS**	CELS	COON	CURS	DELE	DONG	**DYE**	ECHE	EIKS
BORA	BUSH	CELT	COOP	CURT	DELF	DONS	DYED	HECH	**EKE**
BORD	BUSK	**CEP**	COOS	**CUT**	DELI	**DOO**	DYER	LECH	LEKE
BORE	BUSS	CEPS	COOT	CUTE	DELL	DOOB	DYES	PECH	PEKE
BORN	BUST	**CHA**	**COP**	CUTS	DELS	DOOK	**DZO**	TECH	REKE
BORS	BUSY	CHAD	SCOP	SCUT	**DEN**	DOOL	DZOS	ECHE	EKED
BORT	**BUT**	CHAI	COPE	**CUZ**	DENE	DOOM	**EAN**	ECHO	EKES
BOS	ABUT	CHAL	COPS	**CWM**	DENS	DOOR	BEAN	ECHT	**ELD**
BOSH	BUTE	CHAM	COPY	CWMS	DENT	DOOS	DEAN	**ECU**	GELD
BOSK	BUTS	CHAP	**COR**	**DAB**	DENY	**DOP**	GEAN	ECUS	HELD
BOSS	BUTT	CHAR	CORD	DABS	**DEW**	DOPA	JEAN	**EDH**	MELD
BOT	**BUY**	CHAS	CORF	**DAD**	DEWS	DOPE	LEAN	EDHS	SELD
BOTH	BUYS	CHAT	CORK	DADA	DEWY	DOPS	MEAN	**EEK**	TELD
BOTS	**BYE**	CHAW	CORM	DADO	**DEY**	DOPY	PEAN	KEEK	VELD
BOTT	ABYE	CHAY	CORN	DADS	DEYS	**DOR**	REAN	LEEK	WELD
BOW	BYES	**CHE**	CORS	**DAG**	**DIB**	DORE	SEAN	MEEK	YELD
BOWL	**BYS**	ACHE	**COS**	DAGO	DIBS	DORK	WEAN	PEEK	ELDS
BOWR	**CAB**	ECHE	COSE	DAGS	**DID**	DORM	YEAN	REEK	**ELF**
BOWS	SCAB	OCHE	COSH	**DAH**	DIDO	DORP	EANS	SEEK	DELF
BOX	CABA	CHEF	COSS	DAHL	**DIE**	DORR	**EAR**	WEEK	PELF
BOXY	CABS	CHER	COST	DAHS	DIEB	DORS	BEAR	**EEL**	SELF
BOY	**CAD**	CHEW	COSY	**DAK**	DIED	DORT	DEAR	FEEL	ELFS
BOYG	ECAD	CHEZ	**COT**	DAKS	DIES	DORY	FEAR	HEEL	**ELK**
BOYO	SCAD	**CHI**	SCOT	**DAL**	DIET	**DOS**	GEAR	JEEL	ELKS
BOYS	CADE	CHIC	COTE	ODAL	**DIG**	ADOS	HEAR	KEEL	WELK
BRA	CADI	CHID	COTH	UDAL	DIGS	UDOS	LEAR	PEEL	YELK
BRAD	CADS	CHIK	COTS	DALE	**DIM**	DOSE	NEAR	REEL	**ELL**
BRAE	**CAM**	CHIN	COTT	DALI	DIME	DOSS	PEAR	SEEL	BELL
BRAG	SCAM	CHIP	**COW**	DALS	DIMS	DOST	REAR	TEEL	CELL
BRAN	CAME	CHIS	SCOW	DALT	**DIN**	**DOT**	SEAR	WEEL	DELL
BRAS	CAMP	CHIT	COWL	**DAM**	DINE	DOTE	TEAR	EELS	FELL
BRAT	CAMS	CHIV	COWP	DAME	DING	DOTH	WEAR	EELY	HELL
BRAW	**CAN**	**CIG**	COWS	DAMN	DINK	DOTS	YEAR	**EEN**	JELL
BRAY	SCAN	CIGS	**COX**	DAMP	DINS	DOTY	EARD	BEEN	KELL
BRO	CANE	**CIT**	COXA	DAMS	DINT	**DOW**	EARL	DEEN	MELL
BROD	CANG	CITE	COXY	**DAN**	**DIP**	DOWD	EARN	KEEN	PELL
BROG	CANN	CITO	**COY**	DANG	DIPS	DOWF	EARS	PEEN	SELL
BROO	CANS	CITS	COYS	DANK	**DIT**	DOWL	**EAS**	REEN	TELL
BROS	CANT	CITY	**COZ**	DANS	ADIT	DOWN	CEAS	SEEN	VELL
BROW	CANY	**CLY**	COZE	DANT	EDIT	DOWP	KEAS	TEEN	WELL
BUB	**CAP**	**COB**	COZY	**DAP**	DITA	DOWS	LEAS	WEEN	YELL
BUBA	CAPA	COBB	**CRU**	DAPS	DITE	DOWT	PEAS	**EFF**	ELLS
BUBO	CAPE	COBS	ECRU	**DAS**	DITS	**DRY**	SEAS	JEFF	**ELM**
BUBS	CAPO	**COD**	CRUD	ODAS	DITT	**DSO**	TEAS	TEFF	HELM
BUD	CAPS	CODA	CRUE	DASH	**DIV**	ODSO	YEAS	EFFS	YELM
BUDO	**CAR**	CODE	CRUS	**DAW**	DIVA	DSOS	ZEAS	**EFS**	ELMS
BUDS	SCAR	CODS	CRUX	ADAW	DIVE	**DUB**	EASE	KEFS	ELMY
BUG	CARB	**COG**	**CRY**	DAWD	DIVI	DUBS	EAST	NEFS	**ELS**

BELS	GENS	NESS	FATE	FLY	GAD	GEM	GOEY	HAGS	HERL
CELS	HENS	SESS	FATS	FOB	EGAD	GEMS	GOG	HAH	HERM
DELS	KENS	ESSE	FAW	FOBS	IGAD	GEN	AGOG	SHAH	HERN
EELS	LENS	ETA	FAWN	FOE	GADE	AGEN	GOGO	HAJ	HERO
GELS	PENS	BETA	FAWS	FOEN	GADI	GENA	GOGS	HAJI	HERS
MELS	RENS	FETA	FAX	FOES	GADS	GENE	GON	HAJJ	HERY
SELS	SENS	GETA	FAY	FOG	GAE	GENS	AGON	HAM	HES
TELS	TENS	KETA	OFAY	FOGY	GAED	GENT	GONE	CHAM	SHES
ZELS	WENS	SETA	FAYS	FOH	GAES	GENU	GONG	SHAM	HESP
ELSE	YENS	ZETA	FED	FOHN	GAG	GEO	GONK	WHAM	HEST
ELT	EON	ETAS	FEDS	FON	GAGA	GEOS	GONS	HAME	HET
BELT	AEON	ETAT	FEE	FOND	GAGE	GET	GOO	HAMS	SHET
CELT	NEON	ETH	FEED	FONE	GAGS	GETA	GOOD	HAN	WHET
FELT	PEON	BETH	FEEL	FONS	GAL	GETS	GOOF	KHAN	HETE
GELT	EONS	ETHE	FEER	FONT	GALA	GEY	GOOK	SHAN	HETS
KELT	ERA	ETHS	FEES	FOP	GALE	GHI	GOOL	THAN	HEW
MELT	SERA	EUK	FEET	FOPS	GALL	GHIS	GOON	HAND	CHEW
PELT	ERAS	NEUK	FEN	FOR	GALS	GIB	GOOP	HANG	PHEW
TELT	ERE	YEUK	FEND	FORA	GAM	GIBE	GOOR	HANK	THEW
WELT	BERE	EUKS	FENS	FORD	OGAM	GIBS	GOOS	HAP	WHEW
YELT	CERE	EVE	FENT	FORE	GAMB	GID	GOS	CHAP	HEWN
ELTS	DERE	LEVE	FET	FORK	GAME	GIDS	EGOS	WHAP	HEWS
EME	FERE	MEVE	FETA	FORM	GAMP	GIE	GOSH	HAPS	HEX
DEME	GERE	NEVE	FETE	FORT	GAMS	GIED	GOT	HAS	HEY
FEME	HERE	YEVE	FETS	FOU	GAMY	GIEN	GOV	HASH	HEYS
HEME	LERE	EVEN	FETT	FOUD	GAN	GIES	GOVS	HASK	HIC
LEME	MERE	EVER	FEU	FOUL	GANE	GIF	GOY	HASP	CHIC
SEME	PERE	EVES	FEUD	FOUR	GANG	GIFT	GOYS	HAST	HICK
TEME	SERE	EVET	FEUS	FOUS	GANT	GIG	GUB	HAT	HID
EMES	WERE	EWE	FEW	FOX	GAP	GIGA	GUBS	CHAT	WHID
EMEU	ERED	EWER	FEY	FOXY	GAPE	GIGS	GUE	GHAT	HIDE
EMS	ERES	EWES	FEYS	FOY	GAPO	GIN	GUES	THAT	HIE
GEMS	ERF	EWK	FEZ	FOYS	GAPS	AGIN	GUM	WHAT	HIED
HEMS	KERF	EWKS	FIB	FRA	GAR	GING	GUMP	HATE	HIES
REMS	SERF	EWT	FIBS	FRAB	AGAR	GINK	GUMS	HATH	HIM
TEMS	TERF	EWTS	FID	FRAE	GARB	GINN	GUN	HATS	SHIM
WEMS	ERG	NEWT	FIDS	FRAP	GARE	GINS	GUNK	HAW	WHIM
EMU	BERG	EYE	FIE	FRAS	GARS	GIO	GUNS	CHAW	HIN
EMUS	ERGO	EYED	FIEF	FRAU	GART	AGIO	GUP	SHAW	CHIN
END	ERGS	EYES	FIG	FRAY	GAS	GIOS	GUPS	THAW	SHIN
BEND	ERK	FAB	FIGO	FRO	AGAS	GIP	GUR	HAWK	THIN
FEND	BERK	FAD	FIGS	AFRO	GASH	GIPS	GURL	HAWM	WHIN
HEND	JERK	FADE	FIL	FROG	GASP	GIS	GURN	HAWS	HIND
LEND	MERK	FADO	FILE	FROM	GAST	EGIS	GURS	HAY	HING
MEND	PERK	FADS	FILL	FROW	GAT	GISM	GURU	CHAY	HINS
PEND	SERK	FADY	FILM	FRY	GATE	GIST	GUS	SHAY	HINT
REND	YERK	FAG	FILS	FUB	GATH	GIT	GUSH	HAYS	HIP
SEND	ERKS	FAGS	FIN	FUBS	GATS	GITE	GUST	HEM	CHIP
TEND	ERN	FAH	FIND	FUD	GAU	GITS	GUT	THEM	SHIP
VEND	BERN	FAHS	FINE	FUDS	GAUD	GJU	GUTS	HEME	WHIP
WEND	DERN	FAN	FINK	FUG	GAUM	GJUS	GUY	HEMP	HIPS
ENDS	FERN	FAND	FINO	FUGS	GAUN	GNU	GUYS	HEMS	HIPT
ENE	HERN	FANE	FINS	FUM	GAUP	GNUS	GYM	HEN	HIS
BENE	KERN	FANG	FIR	FUME	GAUR	GOA	GYMP	THEN	CHIS
DENE	PERN	FANK	FIRE	FUMS	GAUS	GOAD	GYMS	HEND	GHIS
GENE	TERN	FANS	FIRK	FUMY	GAY	GOAF	GYP	HENS	PHIS
MENE	ERNE	FAP	FIRM	FUN	GAYS	GOAL	GYPS	HENT	THIS
NENE	ERNS	FAR	FIRN	FUND	GED	GOAS	HAD	HEP	HISH
PENE	ERR	AFAR	FIRS	FUNG	AGED	GOAT	CHAD	HEPS	HISN
TENE	SERR	FARD	FIT	FUNK	GEDS	GOB	SHAD	HEPT	HISS
ENES	ERRS	FARE	FITS	FUNS	GEE	GOBO	HADE	HER	HIST
ENEW	ERS	FARL	FITT	FUR	AGEE	GOBS	HADJ	CHER	HIT
ENG	HERS	FARM	FIX	FURL	OGEE	GOBY	HADS	HERB	CHIT
LENG	VERS	FARO	FIZ	FURR	GEED	GOD	HAE	HERD	SHIT
MENG	ERST	FARS	FIZZ	FURS	GEES	GODS	HAEM	HERE	WHIT
ENGS	ESS	FART	FLU	FURY	GEL	GOE	HAET		HITS
ENS	CESS	FAS	FLUB	GAB	GELD	YGOE	HAG		
BENS	FESS	FASH	FLUE	GABS	GELS	GOEL	SHAG		
DENS	JESS	FAST	FLUS	GABY	GELT	GOER	HAGG		
FENS	MESS	FAT	FLUX	GABY	GELT	GOES	HAGG	HERE	HITS

HOA	HOWE	CIDE	INK	KISH	JIZZ	KEG	LACE	FLAX	ALEW
WHOA	HOWF	HIDE	BINK	PISH	JOB	SKEG	LACK	LAY	BLEW
HOAR	HOWK	NIDE	DINK	WISH	JOBE	KEGS	LACS	ALAY	CLEW
HOAS	HOWL	RIDE	FINK	ISM	JOBS	KEN	LACY	BLAY	FLEW
HOAX	HOWS	SIDE	GINK	GISM	JOE	KENS	LAD	PLAY	SLEW
HOB	HOX	TIDE	JINK	JISM	JOES	KENT	BLAD	CLAY	LEWD
HOBO	HOY	VIDE	KINK	ISMS	JOEY	KEP	CLAD	SLAY	LEX
HOBS	AHOY	WIDE	LINK	ISMY	JOG	SKEP	GLAD	LAYS	FLEX
HOC	HOYA	IDEA	MINK	ITA	JOGS	KEPI	LADE	LEA	ILEX
CHOC	HOYS	IDEE	PINK	DITA	JOR	KEPS	LADS	PLEA	ULEX
HOCK	HUB	IDEM	RINK	PITA	JORS	KEPT	LADY	LEAD	LEY
HOD	HUBS	IDES	SINK	VITA	JOT	KET	LAG	LEAF	BLEY
SHOD	HUE	AIDS	TINK	ITAS	JOTA	KETA	BLAG	LEAK	FLEY
HODS	HUED	BIDS	WINK	ITS	JOTS	KETE	CLAG	LEAL	GLEY
HOE	HUER	FIDS	INKS	AITS	JOW	KETS	FLAG	LEAM	SLEY
SHOE	HUES	GIDS	INKY	BITS	JOWL	KEX	SLAG	LEAN	LEYS
HOED	HUG	KIDS	INN	CITS	JOWS	KEY	LAGS	LEAP	LEZ
HOER	CHUG	LIDS	GINN	DITS	JOY	KEYS	LAH	LEAR	LEZZ
HOES	THUG	MIDS	JINN	FITS	JOYS	KID	BLAH	LEAS	LIB
HOG	HUGE	NIDS	LINN	GITS	JUBE	SKID	LAHS	LEAT	GLIB
SHOG	HUGS	RIDS	WINN	HITS	JUD	KIDS	LAM	LECH	LIBS
HOGG	HUGY	TIDS	INNS	KITS	JUDO	KIFS	CLAM	LED	LID
HOGH	HUH	YIDS	INS	NITS	JUDS	KIN	FLAM	BLED	GLID
HOGS	HUI	IFF	BINS	PITS	JUDY	AKIN	GLAM	FLED	OLID
HOH	HUM	BIFF	DINS	RITS	JUG	SKIN	LAMA	GLED	SLID
PHOH	CHUM	JIFF	FINS	SITS	JUGA	KINA	LAMB	PLED	LIDO
HOHS	HUMA	MIFF	GINS	TITS	JUGS	KIND	LAME	SLED	LIDS
HOI	HUMF	NIFF	HINS	WITS	JUS	KINE	LAMP	LEE	LIE
HOIK	HUMP	RIFF	KINS	ZITS	GJUS	KING	LAMS	ALEE	PLIE
HON	HUMS	TIFF	LINS	IVY	JUST	KINK	LAP	BLEE	LIED
PHON	HUP	ZIFF	PINS	JAB	JUT	KINO	ALAP	FLEE	LIEF
THON	HUPS	IFFY	RINS	JABS	JUTE	KINS	CLAP	GLEE	LIEN
HOND	HUT	IFS	SINS	JAG	JUTS	KIP	FLAP	SLEE	LIER
HONE	CHUT	ILK	TINS	JAGS	KAE	SKIP	PLAP	LEED	LIES
HONG	PHUT	ILKA	VINS	JAK	KAED	KIPE	SLAP	LEEK	LIEU
HONK	SHUT	ILKS	WINS	JAKE	KAES	KIPP	LAPS	LEEP	LIG
HONS	HUTS	BILK	YINS	JAKS	KAID	KIPS	LAR	LEER	LIGS
HOO	HYE	MILK	ION	JAM	KAIE	KIR	ALAR	LEES	LIN
SHOO	HYED	SILK	CION	JAMB	KAIF	KIRI	LARD	LEET	BLIN
HOOD	HYEN	ILL	LION	JAMS	KAIL	KIRK	LARE	LEG	LIND
HOOF	HYES	BILL	PION	JAP	KAIM	KIRN	LARK	CLEG	LINE
HOOK	HYP	CILL	IONS	JAPE	KAIN	KIRS	LARN	FLEG	LING
HOOP	HYPE	DILL	IOS	JAPS	KAIS	KIT	LAS	GLEG	LINK
HOOT	HYPO	FILL	BIOS	JAR	KAM	SKIT	ALAS	LEGS	LINN
HOP	HYPS	GILL	GIOS	AJAR	KAME	KITE	LASE	LEI	LINO
CHOP	ICE	HILL	IRE	JARK	KAMI	KITH	LASH	VLEI	LINS
SHOP	BICE	JILL	CIRE	JARL	KAS	KITS	LASS	VLEIS	LINT
WHOP	DICE	KILL	DIRE	JARS	SKAS	KOA	LAST	LEIR	LINY
HOPE	LICE	LILL	FIRE	JAW	KAT	KOAN	LAT	LEIS	LIP
HOPS	MICE	MILL	HIRE	JAWS	SKAT	KOAS	BLAT	LEK	BLIP
HOS	NICE	NILL	LIRE	JAY	IKAT	KOB	CLAT	LEKE	CLIP
MHOS	PICE	PILL	MIRE	JAYS	KATI	KOBS	FLAT	LEKS	FLIP
OHOS	RICE	RILL	SIRE	JEE	KATS	KON	PLAT	LEP	SLIP
PHOS	SICE	SILL	TIRE	AJEE	KAW	IKON	SLAT	LEPS	LIPS
RHOS	TICE	TILL	WIRE	JEED	SKAW	KOND	LATE	LEPT	LIS
ZHOS	VICE	VILL	IRES	JEEL	KAWS	KONK	LATH	LES	LISK
HOSE	ICED	WILL	IRK	JEEP	KAY	KONS	LATS	ALES	LISP
HOSS	ICER	YILL	BIRK	JEER	KAYS	KOP	LAV	ULES	LIST
HOST	ICES	ZILL	DIRK	JEES	KAYO	KOPS	LAVA	LESS	LIT
HOT	ICH	ILLS	FIRK	JET	OKAY	KOS	LAVE	LEST	ALIT
PHOT	DICH	ILLY	KIRK	JETE	KEA	KOSS	LAVS	LET	FLIT
SHOT	LICH	IMP	LIRK	JETS	KEAS	KOW	LAW	BLET	GLIT
WHOT	RICH	GIMP	MIRK	JEU	KEB	KOWS	BLAW	LETS	SLIT
HOTE	SICH	JIMP	YIRK	JEUX	KEBS	KYE	CLAW	LEU	LITE
HOTS	TICH	LIMP	IRKS	JIB	KED	LAB	FLAW	LEUD	LITH
HOW	ICY	PIMP	ISH	JIBE	AKED	BLAB	SLAW	LEV	LOB
CHOW	RICY	SIMP	BISH	JIBS	EKED	FLAB	LAWK	LEVA	BLOB
DHOW	IDE	WIMP	DISH	JIG	KEDS	SLAB	LAWN	LEVE	GLOB
SHOW	AIDE	IMPI	FISH	JIGS	KEF	LABS	LAWS	LEVY	SLOB
WHOW	BIDE	IMPS	HISH	JIZ	KEFS	LAC	LAX	LEW	LOBE

LOBI	SLUG	MARS	EMIR	MOYA	NEKS	NOTE	COBS	OFFS	OLMS
LOBO	LUGE	MART	SMIR	MOYL	NEP	NOTT	DOBS	OFT	OMS
LOBS	LUGS	MAS	MIRE	MOYS	NEPS	NOW	FOBS	COFT	COMS
LOG	LUM	MASE	MIRK	MOZ	NET	ANOW	GOBS	LOFT	MOMS
CLOG	ALUM	MASH	MIRS	MOZE	NETE	ENOW	HOBS	SOFT	NOMS
FLOG	GLUM	MASK	MIRY	MOZZ	NETS	KNOW	JOBS	TOFT	OOMS
SLOG	PLUM	MASS	MIS	MUD	NETT	SNOW	KOBS	OHM	POMS
LOGE	SLUM	MAST	AMIS	MUDS	NEW	NOWL	LOBS	OHMS	TOMS
LOGO	LUMP	MASU	MISE	MUG	ANEW	NOWN	MOBS	OHO	ONE
LOGS	LUMS	MAT	MISO	SMUG	ENEW	NOWS	NOBS	COHO	BONE
LOO	LUR	MATE	MISS	MUGS	KNEW	NOWT	ROBS	TOHO	CONE
LOOF	BLUR	MATH	MIST	MUM	NEWS	NOWY	SOBS	OHOS	DONE
LOOK	SLUR	MATS	MIX	MUMM	NEWT	NOY	YOBS	OIK	FONE
LOOM	LURE	MATT	MIXT	MUMP	NIB	NOYS	OCA	HOIK	GONE
LOON	LURK	MATY	MIXY	MUMS	SNIB	NTH	OCAS	OIKS	HONE
LOOP	LURS	MAW	MIZ	MUN	NIBS	NUB	OCH	OIL	LONE
LOOR	LUX	MAWK	MIZZ	MUS	NID	KNUB	COCH	BOIL	NONE
LOOS	FLUX	MAWR	MNA	EMUS	NIDE	SNUB	LOCH	COIL	PONE
LOOT	LUXE	MAWS	MNAS	MUSE	NIDI	NUBS	ROCH	FOIL	RONE
LOP	LUZ	MAX	MOA	MUSH	NIDS	NUN	OCHE	MOIL	SONE
CLOP	LYE	MAXI	MOAN	MUSK	NIE	NUNS	ODA	NOIL	TONE
FLOP	LYES	MAY	MOAS	MUSS	NIED	NUR	CODA	ROIL	ZONE
PLOP	LYM	MAYA	MOAT	MUST	NIEF	KNUR	SODA	SOIL	ONER
SLOP	LYME	MAYO	MOB	MUX	NIES	NURD	ODAL	TOIL	ONES
LOPE	LYMS	MAYS	MOBS	NAB	NIL	NURL	ODAS	OILS	ONS
LOPS	MAC	MEL	MOD	SNAB	ANIL	NURR	ODD	OILY	CONS
LOR	MACE	MELD	MODE	NABK	NILL	NURS	ODDS	OKE	DONS
FLOR	MACK	MELL	MODI	NABS	NILS	NUS	ODE	BOKE	EONS
LORD	MACS	MELS	MODS	NAE	NIM	GNUS	BODE	COKE	FONS
LORE	MAD	MELT	MOE	NAG	NIMS	ONUS	CODE	HOKE	GONS
LORN	MADE	MEN	MOES	KNAG	NIP	NUT	LODE	JOKE	HONS
LORY	MADS	AMEN	MOG	SNAG	SNIP	KNUT	MODE	LOKE	IONS
LOS	MAE	OMEN	SMOG	NAGA	NIPS	NUTS	NODE	MOKE	KONS
LOSE	MAG	MEND	MOGS	NAGS	NIS	NYE	RODE	POKE	OONS
LOSH	MAGE	MENE	MOM	NAM	NISI	NYED	YODE	ROKE	PONS
LOSS	MAGG	MENG	MOME	NAME	NIT	NYES	ODEA	SOKE	SONS
LOST	MAGI	MENT	MOMS	NAMS	KNIT	NYS	ODES	TOKE	TONS
LOT	MAGS	MENU	MOO	NAN	UNIT	OAF	ODS	WOKE	WONS
BLOT	MAK	MES	MOOD	ANAN	NITE	GOAF	BODS	YOKE	ONST
CLOT	MAKE	EMES	MOOI	NANA	NITS	LOAF	CODS	OKES	OOF
PLOT	MAKO	MESA	MOOL	NANS	NIX	OAFS	DODS	OLD	COOF
SLOT	MAKS	MESE	MOON	NAP	NIXY	OAK	GODS	BOLD	GOOF
LOTA	MAL	MESH	MOOP	KNAP	NOB	BOAK	HODS	COLD	HOOF
LOTE	MALA	MESS	MOOR	SNAP	KNOB	SOAK	MODS	FOLD	LOOF
LOTH	MALE	MET	MOOS	NAPA	SNOB	OAKS	NODS	GOLD	POOF
LOTO	MALI	METE	MOOT	NAPE	NOBS	OAKY	PODS	HOLD	ROOF
LOTS	MALL	MEU	MOP	NAPS	NOD	OAR	RODS	MOLD	WOOF
LOW	MALM	MEUS	MOPE	NAS	NODE	BOAR	SODS	SOLD	OOFS
ALOW	MALS	MEW	MOPS	ANAS	NODI	HOAR	TODS	TOLD	OOH
BLOW	MALT	SMEW	MOPY	NAT	NODS	ROAR	YODS	WOLD	BOOH
CLOW	MAM	MEWL	MOR	GNAT	NOG	SOAR	ODSO	YOLD	POOH
FLOW	MAMA	MEWS	MORA	NATS	SNOG	VOAR	OES	OLDS	OOHS
GLOW	MAMS	MHO	MORE	NAY	NOGS	OARS	DOES	OLDY	OOM
PLOW	MAN	MHOS	MORN	NAYS	NOH	OARY	FOES	OLE	BOOM
SLOW	MANA	MID	MORS	NEB	NOM	OAT	GOES	BOLE	COOM
LOWE	MAND	AMID	MORT	SNEB	NOMA	BOAT	HOES	COLE	DOOM
LOWN	MANE	MIDI	MOTE	NEBS	NOME	COAT	JOES	DOLE	LOOM
LOWS	MANS	MIDS	MOTH	NED	NOMS	DOAT	MOES	GOLE	ROOM
LOWT	MANY	MIL	MOTS	SNED	NON	GOAT	NOES	HOLE	SOOM
LOX	MAP	MILD	MOTT	NEDS	ANON	MOAT	ROES	JOLE	TOOM
LOY	MAPS	MILE	MOU	NEE	NONA	OATH	TOES	MOLE	ZOOM
CLOY	MAR	MILK	MOUE	KNEE	NONE	OATS	VOES	NOLE	OOMS
PLOY	MARA	MILL	MOUP	SNEE	NONG	OBA	WOES	POLE	OON
LOYS	MARC	MILO	MOUS	NEED	NOR	OBI	OFF	ROLE	BOON
LUD	MARD	MILS	MOW	NEEM	NORI	OBIA	BOFF	SOLE	COON
LUDO	MARE	MILT	MOWA	NEEP	NORK	OBIS	COFF	TOLE	GOON
LUDS	MARG	MIM	MOWN	NEES	NORM	OBIT	DOFF	VOLE	LOON
LUG	MARK	MIME	MOWS	NEF	NOT	OBS	GOFF	OLEO	MOON
GLUG	MARL	MIR	MOY	NEFS	KNOT	OBS	KOFF	OLM	NOON
PLUG	MARM	AMIR	MOY	NEK	SNOT	BOBS	TOFF	HOLM	POON

ROON	ORBS	OUPS	**OYS**	PEAG	PICS	EPOS	PUTS	RASH	**RES**
SOON	ORBY	**OUR**	BOYS	PEAK	**PIE**	POSE	PUTT	RASP	ARES
TOON	**ORC**	COUR	COYS	PEAL	SPIE	POSH	PUTZ	RAST	ERES
WOON	TORC	DOUR	FOYS	PEAN	PIED	POSS	**PUY**	**RAT**	IRES
ZOON	ORCS	FOUR	HOYS	PEAR	PIER	POST	PUYS	BRAT	ORES
OONS	**ORD**	HOUR	JOYS	PEAS	PIES	POSY	**PYE**	DRAT	URES
OONT	BORD	JOUR	LOYS	PEAT	PIET	**POT**	PYET	GRAT	REST
OOP	CORD	LOUR	MOYS	**PEC**	**PIG**	POTE	**PYX**	PRAT	**RET**
COOP	FORD	POUR	NOYS	PECH	PIGS	POTS	**QAT**	RATA	ARET
GOOP	LORD	SOUR	SOYS	PECK	**PIN**	POTT	QATS	RATE	FRET
HOOP	SORD	TOUR	TOYS	PECS	SPIN	**POW**	**QUA**	RATH	TRET
LOOP	WORD	YOUR	**PAD**	**PED**	PINA	POWN	AQUA	RATS	RETE
MOOP	ORDS	OURN	PADS	APED	PINE	POWS	QUAD	RATU	RETS
NOOP	**ORE**	OURS	**PAH**	OPED	PING	**POX**	QUAG	**RAW**	**REV**
POOP	BORE	**OUT**	OPAH	SPED	PINK	POXY	QUAT	RAWN	REVS
ROOP	CORE	BOUT	PAHS	PEDS	PINS	POZZ	QUAY	RAWS	**REW**
SOOP	FORE	DOUT	**PAL**	**PEE**	PINT	**PRE**	**RAD**	BRAW	AREW
YOOP	GORE	GOUT	OPAL	EPEE	PINY	PREE	BRAD	CRAW	BREW
OOPS	HORE	HOUT	PALE	PEED	**PIP**	PREP	DRAD	DRAW	CREW
OOR	LORE	LOUT	PALL	PEEK	PIPA	PREX	PRAD	**RAX**	DREW
BOOR	MORE	NOUT	PALM	PEEL	PIPE	PREY	TRAD	**RAY**	GREW
DOOR	PORE	POUT	PALP	PEEN	PIPI	**PRO**	RADE	BRAY	TREW
GOOR	RORE	ROUT	PALS	PEEP	PIPS	PROA	RADS	DRAY	REWS
LOOR	SORE	SOUT	PALY	PEER	PIPY	PROD	**RAG**	FRAY	**REX**
MOOR	TORE	TOUT	**PAM**	PEES	**PIR**	PROF	BRAG	GRAY	PREX
POOR	WORE	OUTS	PAMS	**PEG**	PIRL	PROG	CRAG	PRAY	**RHO**
OOS	YORE	**OVA**	**PAN**	PEGH	PIRN	PROM	DRAG	TRAY	RHOS
BOOS	ORES	NOVA	SPAN	PEGS	PIRS	PROO	RAGA	RAYS	**RHY**
COOS	**ORF**	OVAL	PAND	**PEN**	**PIS**	PROP	RAGE	**RED**	**RIA**
DOOS	CORF	**OWE**	PANE	OPEN	PISE	PROS	RAGG	ARED	ARIA
GOOS	ORFE	HOWE	PANG	PEND	PISH	PROW	RAGI	BRED	RIAL
LOOS	ORFS	LOWE	PANS	PENE	PISS	**PRY**	RAGS	ERED	RIAS
MOOS	**ORS**	OWER	PANT	PENI	**PIT**	SPRY	**RAH**	REDD	**RIB**
POOS	BORS	OWES	**PAP**	PENK	SPIT	PRYS	RAHS	REDE	CRIB
ROOS	CORS	**OWL**	PAPA	PENS	PITA	**PSI**	**RAJ**	REDO	DRIB
WOOS	DORS	BOWL	PAPE	PENT	PITH	PSIS	RAJA	REDS	RIBS
ZOOS	HORS	COWL	PAPS	**PEP**	PITS	**PST**	**RAM**	**REE**	**RID**
OOSE	JORS	DOWL	**PAR**	PEPO	PITY	**PUB**	CRAM	BREE	ARID
OOSY	MORS	FOWL	SPAR	PEPS	**PIU**	PUBS	DRAM	CREE	GRID
OPE	TORS	GOWL	PARA	**PER**	PIUM	**PUD**	GRAM	DREE	IRID
COPE	VORS	HOWL	PARD	PERE	**PLY**	SPUD	PRAM	FREE	RIDE
DOPE	**ORT**	JOWL	PARE	PERI	**POA**	PUDS	TRAM	GREE	RIDS
HOPE	BORT	NOWL	PARK	PERK	POAS	**PUG**	RAMI	PREE	**RIG**
LOPE	DORT	SOWL	PARR	PERM	**POD**	PUGH	RAMP	TREE	BRIG
MOPE	FORT	YOWL	PARS	PERN	APOD	PUGS	RAMS	REED	FRIG
NOPE	MORT	OWLS	PART	PERT	PODS	**PUH**	**RAN**	REEF	GRIG
POPE	PORT	OWLY	**PAS**	PERV	**POH**	PUN	BRAN	REEK	PRIG
ROPE	RORT	**OWN**	SPAS	**PET**	**POI**	SPUN	CRAN	REEL	TRIG
TOPE	SORT	DOWN	UPAS	SPET	POIS	PUNA	GRAN	REEN	RIGG
OPED	TORT	GOWN	PASH	PETS	**POM**	PUNK	RANA	REES	RIGS
OPEN	WORT	LOWN	PASS	**PEW**	POME	PUNS	RAND	**REF**	**RIM**
OPES	ORTS	MOWN	PAST	SPEW	POMP	PUNT	RANG	TREF	BRIM
OPS	**OUK**	NOWN	**PAT**	PEWS	POMS	PUNY	RANI	REFS	GRIM
BOPS	BOUK	POWN	SPAT	**PHI**	**POO**	**PUP**	RANK	REFT	PRIM
COPS	GOUK	SOWN	PATE	PHIS	POOD	PUPA	RANT	**REH**	TRIM
DOPS	JOUK	TOWN	PATH	PHIZ	POOH	PUPS	**RAP**	REHS	RIMA
FOPS	POUK	OWNS	PATS	**PHO**	POOK	**PUR**	CRAP	**REM**	RIMS
HOPS	SOUK	**OWT**	**PAW**	PHOH	POOL	SPUR	DRAP	REMS	RIMU
KOPS	TOUK	DOWT	PAWA	PHON	POON	PURE	FRAP	**REN**	RIMY
LOPS	YOUK	LOWT	PAWK	PHOS	POOP	PURI	TRAP	BREN	**RIN**
MOPS	OUKS	NOWT	PAWL	PHOT	POOR	PURL	WRAP	GREN	GRIN
OOPS	**OUP**	ROWT	PAWN	**PIA**	POOS	PURR	RAPE	WREN	TRIN
POPS	COUP	TOWT	PAWS	PIAS	POOT	PURS	RAPS	REND	RIND
SOPS	DOUP	OWTS	**PAX**	**PIC**	**POP**	**PUS**	RAPT	RENS	RINE
TOPS	LOUP	**OYE**	**PAY**	EPIC	POPE	OPUS	**RAS**	RENT	RING
WOPS	MOUP	OYER	APAY	SPIC	POPS	PUSH	BRAS	RENY	RINK
OPT	NOUP	OYES	SPAY	PICA	**POS**	PUSS	ERAS	**REP**	RINS
OPTS	ROUP	OYEZ	PAYS	PICE		**PUT**	FRAS	PREP	**RIP**
ORB	SOUP		**PEA**	PICK			RASE	REPP	DRIP
SORB	OUPH							REPS	

GRIP	TROW	SAIS	SEND	SKIT	**SUB**	TANG	TEND	TOGE	TUPS
TRIP	ROWS	**SAL**	SENS	**SKY**	SUBS	TANK	TENE	TOGS	**TUT**
RIPE	ROWT	SALE	SENT	SKYR	**SUD**	TANS	TENS	**TOM**	TUTS
RIPP	**RUB**	SALP	ESKY	**SLY**	SUDD	**TAP**	TENT	ATOM	TUTU
RIPS	DRUB	SALS	**SET**	**SMA**	SUDS	ATAP	**TES**	TOMB	**TWA**
RIPT	GRUB	SALT	SETA	**SOB**	**SUE**	TAPA	UTES	TOME	TWAE
RIT	RUBE	**SAM**	SETS	SOBS	SUED	TAPE	TEST	TOMS	TWAL
BRIT	RUBS	SAME	SETT	**SOC**	SUER	TAPS	**TEW**	**TON**	TWAS
CRIT	RUBY	SAMP	**SEW**	SOCK	SUES	TAPU	STEW	TONE	TWAT
FRIT	**RUC**	**SAN**	SEWN	SOCS	SUET	**TAR**	TEWS	TONG	TWAY
GRIT	RUCK	SAND	SEWS	**SOD**	**SUI**	TARA	**THE**	TONK	**TWO**
WRIT	RUCS	SANE	**SEX**	SODA	SUIT	TARE	ETHE	TONS	TWOS
RITE	**RUD**	SANG	SEXT	SODS	**SUK**	TARN	THEE	TONY	**TYE**
RITS	CRUD	SANK	SEXY	**SOG**	SUKH	TARO	THEM	**TOO**	STYE
RITT	RUDD	SANS	**SEY**	SOGS	SUKS	TARP	THEN	TOOK	TYED
RIZ	RUDE	**SAP**	SEYS	**SOH**	**SUM**	TARS	THEW	TOOL	TYES
FRIZ	RUDS	SAPS	**SHE**	SOHS	SUMO	TART	THEY	TOOM	**TYG**
ROB	RUE	**SAR**	SHEA	**SOL**	SUMP	**TAT**	**THO**	TOON	TYGS
ROBE	CRUE	ASAR	SHED	SOLA	SUMS	TATE	THON	TOOT	**UDO**
ROBS	GRUE	KSAR	SHES	SOLD	**SUN**	TATH	THOU	**TOP**	BUDO
ROC	RUED	TSAR	SHET	SOLE	SUNG	TATS	**THY**	ATOP	JUDO
CROC	RUES	SARD	SHEW	SOLI	SUNK	TATT	**TIC**	TOPE	LUDO
ROCH	**RUG**	SARI	**SHY**	SOLO	SUNN	TATU	OTIC	TOPI	UDOS
ROCK	DRUG	SARK	ASHY	SOLS	SUNS	**TAU**	TICE	TOPS	**UDS**
ROCS	RUGS	SARS	**SIB**	**SON**	**SUP**	TAUS	TICH	**TOR**	BUDS
ROD	**RUM**	**SAT**	SIBB	SONE	SUPS	TAUT	TICK	TORC	CUDS
BROD	ARUM	SATE	SIBS	SONG	**SUQ**	**TAW**	TICS	TORE	DUDS
PROD	DRUM	SATI	**SIC**	SONS	SUQS	TAWS	**TID**	TORI	FUDS
TROD	GRUM	**SAW**	SICE	**SOP**	**SUR**	TAWT	TIDE	TORN	JUDS
RODE	RUME	SAWN	SICH	SOPH	SURA	**TAX**	TIDS	TORR	LUDS
RODS	RUMP	SAWS	SICK	SOPS	SURD	TAXA	**TIE**	TORS	MUDS
ROE	RUMS	**SAX**	SICS	**SOS**	SURE	TAXI	TIED	TORT	PUDS
ROED	**RUN**	**SAY**	**SIM**	DSOS	SURF	**TEA**	TIER	**TOT**	RUDS
ROES	RUND	SAYS	SIMA	SOSS	**SUS**	TEAD	TIES	STOT	SUDS
ROK	RUNE	**SAZ**	SIMI	**SOT**	SUSS	TEAK	**TIG**	TOTE	WUDS
ROKE	RUNG	**SEA**	SIMP	SOTS	**SWY**	TEAL	TIGE	TOTS	**UEY**
ROKS	RUNS	SEAL	SIMS	**SOU**	**SYE**	TEAM	TIGS	**TOW**	QUEY
ROKY	RUNT	SEAM	**SIN**	SOUK	SYED	TEAR	**TIL**	STOW	UEYS
ROM	**RUT**	SEAN	SIND	SOUL	SYEN	TEAS	TILE	TOWN	**UFO**
FROM	RUTH	SEAR	SINE	SOUM	SYES	TEAT	TILL	TOWS	BUFO
PROM	RUTS	SEAS	SING	SOUP	**TAB**	**TED**	TILS	TOWT	UFOS
ROMA	**RYA**	SEAT	SINK	SOUR	STAB	STED	TILT	TOWY	**UGH**
ROMP	RYAL	**SEC**	SINS	SOUS	TABS	TEDS	**TIN**	**TOY**	EUGH
ROO	RYAS	SECS	**SIP**	SOUT	TABU	TEDY	TIND	TOYS	PUGH
BROO	**RYE**	SECT	SIPE	**SOV**	**TAD**	**TEE**	TINE	**TRY**	UGHS
PROO	TRYE	**SED**	SIPS	SOVS	TADS	TEED	TING	TRYE	**UGS**
ROOD	RYES	**SEE**	**SIR**	**SOW**	**TAE**	TEEL	TINK	TRYP	BUGS
ROOF	**SAB**	SEED	SIRE	SOWF	TAED	TEEM	TINS	**TUB**	DUGS
ROOK	SABS	SEEK	SIRI	SOWL	TAEL	TEEN	TINT	STUB	FUGS
ROOM	**SAC**	SEEL	SIRS	SOWM	TAES	TEES	TINY	TUBA	HUGS
ROON	SACK	SEEM	**SIS**	SOWN	**TAG**	**TEF**	**TIP**	TUBE	JUGS
ROOP	SACS	SEEN	PSIS	SOWP	TAGS	TEFF	TIPI	TUBS	LUGS
ROOS	**SAD**	SEEP	SISS	SOWS	**TAI**	TEFS	TIPS	**TUG**	MUGS
ROOT	**SAE**	SEER	SIST	**SOX**	TAIL	**TEG**	TIPT	TUGS	PUGS
ROT	**SAG**	SEES	**SIT**	**SOY**	TAIS	TEGG	**TIS**	**TUI**	RUGS
GROT	SAGA	**SEG**	SITE	SOYA	TAIT	TEGS	UTIS	TUIS	TUGS
TROT	SAGE	SEGO	SITH	SOYS	**TAJ**	**TEL**	**TIT**	**TUM**	VUGS
ROTA	SAGO	SEGS	SITS	**SPA**	**TAK**	TELA	TITE	STUM	YUGS
ROTE	SAGS	**SEI**	**SIX**	SPAE	TAKA	TELD	TITI	TUMP	**ULE**
ROTI	SAGY	SEIF	**SKA**	SPAN	TAKE	TELL	TITS	TUMS	DULE
ROTL	**SAI**	SEIL	SKAS	SPAR	TAKS	TELS	**TOD**	**TUN**	GULE
ROTS	SAIC	SEIS	SKAT	SPAS	TAKY	TELT	TODS	STUN	HULE
ROW	SAID	**SEL**	SKAW	SPAT	**TAM**	**TEN**	TODY	TUND	MULE
AROW	SAIM	SELD	**SKI**	SPAW	TAME	ETEN	**TOE**	TUNE	PULE
BROW	SAIN	SELE	SKID	SPAY	TAMP	STEN	TOED	TUNS	RULE
CROW	SAIR	SELF	SKIM	**SPY**	TAMS		TOES	TUNY	TULE
DROW		SELL	SKIN	ESPY	**TAN**		**TOG**	**TUP**	YULE
FROW		SELS	SKIO	**STY**	TANA		TOGA		ULES
GROW		**SEN**	SKIP	STYE	TANE				ULEX
PROW			SKIS						**UNI**

UNIS	CURN	VANT	**VOE**	WAPS	WEEK	YWIS	**WYE**	OYES	YUKE
UNIT	DURN	**VAS**	EVOE	**WAR**	WEEL	WISE	WYES	PYES	YUKS
UNS	GURN	AVAS	VOES	WARD	WEEM	WISH	**WYN**	RYES	YUKY
BUNS	OURN	UVAS	**VOL**	WARE	WEEN	WISP	WYND	SYES	**YUP**
DUNS	TURN	VASA	VOLA	WARK	WEEP	WIST	WYNN	TYES	YUPS
FUNS	URNS	VASE	VOLE	WARM	WEER	**WIT**	WYNS	WYES	**YUS**
GUNS	**USE**	VAST	VOLS	WARN	WEES	TWIT	**XIS**	YESK	AYUS
NUNS	FUSE	**VAT**	VOLT	WARP	WEET	WITE	AXIS	YEST	**ZAG**
PUNS	MUSE	VATS	**VOR**	WARS	**WEM**	WITH	**YAH**	**YET**	ZAGS
RUNS	RUSE	**VAU**	VORS	WART	WEMB	WITS	AYAH	PYET	**ZAP**
SUNS	USED	VAUS	**VOW**	WARY	WEMS	**WOE**	**YAK**	YETI	ZAPS
TUNS	USER	VAUT	AVOW	**WAS**	**WEN**	WOES	YAKS	YETT	**ZAX**
UPS	USES	**VEE**	VOWS	TWAS	WEND	**WOG**	**YAM**	**YEW**	**ZEA**
CUPS	**UTE**	VEER	VOX	WASE	WENS	WOGS	YAMS	YEWS	ZEAL
DUPS	BUTE	VEES	**VUG**	WASH	WENT	**WOK**	**YAP**	**YEX**	ZEAS
GUPS	CUTE	**VEG**	VUGS	WASP	**WET**	WOKE	YAPP	**YGO**	**ZED**
HUPS	JUTE	VEGA	**VUM**	WAST	WETS	WOKS	YAPS	YGOE	ZEDS
OUPS	LUTE	**VET**	VUMS	**WAT**	**WEX**	**WON**	**YAW**	**YIN**	**ZEE**
PUPS	MUTE	EVET	**WAD**	SWAT	WEXE	WONS	YAWL	YINS	ZEES
SUPS	UTES	VETO	WADD	TWAT	**WEY**	WONT	YAWN	**YIP**	**ZEK**
TUPS	**UTS**	VETS	WADE	WATE	WEYS	**WOO**	YAWP	YIPS	ZEKS
YUPS	BUTS	**VEX**	WADI	WATS	**WHO**	WOOD	YAWS	**YOB**	**ZEL**
UPSY	CUTS	**VIA**	WADS	WATT	WHOA	WOOF	**YEA**	YOBS	ZELS
URD	GUTS	VIAE	WADY	**WAW**	WHOM	WOOL	YEAD	**YOD**	**ZHO**
BURD	HUTS	VIAL	**WAE**	WAWE	WHOP	WOON	YEAH	YODE	ZHOS
CURD	JUTS	VIAS	TWAE	WAWL	WHOT	WOOS	YEAN	**YOK**	**ZIG**
NURD	NUTS	**VIE**	WAES	WAWS	WHOW	WOOT	YEAR	YOKE	ZIGS
SURD	OUTS	VIED	**WAG**	**WAX**	**WHY**	**WOP**	YEAS	YOKS	**ZIP**
TURD	PUTS	VIER	SWAG	WAXY	**WIG**	SWOP	**YEN**	**YON**	ZIPS
URDE	RUTS	VIES	WAGE	**WAY**	SWIG	WOPS	HYEN	YOND	**ZIT**
URDS	TUTS	VIEW	WAGS	AWAY	TWIG	**WOS**	**YEP**	YONT	ZITS
URDY	**UTU**	**VIM**	**WAN**	SWAY	WIGS	TWOS	YEPS	**YOS**	**ZIZ**
URE	TUTU	VIMS	SWAN	TWAY	**WIN**	WOST	**YES**	**YOU**	ZIZZ
CURE	UTUS	**VIN**	WAND	WAYS	TWIN	**WOT**	AYES	YOUK	**ZOA**
DURE	**UVA**	VINA	WANE	**WEB**	WIND	SWOT	BYES	YOUR	**ZOO**
JURE	UVAS	VINE	WANG	WEBS	WINE	WOTS	DYES	YOWE	ZOOM
LURE	**VAC**	VINO	WANK	**WED**	WING	**WOW**	EYES	YOWL	ZOON
MURE	VACS	VINS	WANS	AWED	WINK	WOWF	HYES	YOWS	ZOOS
PURE	**VAE**	VINT	WANT	OWED	WINN	WOWS	LYES	**YUG**	**ZOS**
SURE	VAES	VINY	WANY	WEDS	WINO	**WOX**	NYES	YUGA	DZOS
UREA	**VAN**	**VIS**	**WAP**	**WEE**	WINS	**WRY**		YUGS	**ZUZ**
URES	VANE	VISA	SWAP	SWEE	WINY	AWRY		**YUK**	
URN	VANG	VISE		TWEE	**WIS**	**WUD**			
BURN	VANS	**VLY**		WEED	IWIS	WUDS			

PART A: 4-letter word hooks
including all root words

ABAC	ACMES	SAGES	AIRS	GALAS	HALMS	SAMPS	ANOAS	LARCH	PARKS
ABACA	ACNE	WAGES	FAIRS	NALAS	MALMS	TAMPS	ANON	MARCH	SARKS
ABACI	ACNES	AGHA	GAIRS	PALAS	PALMS	VAMPS	CANON	PARCH	WARKS
ABACK	ACRE	AGHAS	HAIRS	TALAS	ALOD	AMYL	FANON	ARCO	ARMS
ABACS	NACRE	AGIN	LAIRS	ALAY	ALODS	AMYLS	ANOW	ARCS	BARMS
ABAS	ACRED	AGING	PAIRS	PALAY	ALOE	ANAL	ANTA	MARCS	FARMS
BABAS	ACRES	AGIO	SAIRS	ALAYS	ALOED	BANAL	MANTA	AREA	HARMS
CABAS	ACTA	AGIOS	VAIRS	ALBE	ALOES	CANAL	ANTAE	AREAD	MARMS
ABASE	PACTA	AGMA	AIRT	ALBEE	ALOW	FANAL	ANTAR	AREAL	WARMS
ABASH	ACTS	MAGMA	AIRTS	ALBS	ALOWE	ANAN	ANTE	AREAR	ARMY
ABASK	FACTS	AGMAS	AIRY	ALEE	ALPS	ANANA	ZANTE	AREAS	BARMY
ABBA	PACTS	AGOG	DAIRY	ALES	CALPS	ANAS	ANTED	ARED	ARNA
ABBAS	TACTS	AGOGE	FAIRY	BALES	PALPS	KANAS	ANTES	BARED	VARNA
ABBE	ACYL	AGON	HAIRY	DALES	SALPS	LANAS	ANTI	CARED	ARNAS
ABBES	ACYLS	WAGON	LAIRY	EALES	ALSO	MANAS	TANTI	DARED	AROW
ABBEY	ADAW	AGONE	VAIRY	GALES	ALTO	NANAS	ANTIC	EARED	ARSE
ABBS	ADAWS	AGONS	AITS	HALES	SALTO	RANAS	ANTIS	FARED	CARSE
ABED	ADDS	AGONY	BAITS	KALES	ALTOS	TANAS	ANTS	HARED	FARSE
ABET	WADDS	AGUE	GAITS	MALES	ALTS	ANCE	BANTS	OARED	PARSE
ABETS	ADIT	VAGUE	RAITS	PALES	DALTS	DANCE	CANTS	PARED	ARSES
ABID	ADITS	AGUED	TAITS	RALES	HALTS	HANCE	DANTS	SARED	ARTS
RABID	ADOS	AGUES	WAITS	SALES	MALTS	LANCE	GANTS	TARED	CARTS
TABID	DADOS	AHEM	AITU	TALES	SALTS	NANCE	KANTS	WARED	DARTS
ABIDE	FADOS	AHOY	AITUS	VALES	ALUM	PANCE	LANTS	AREDD	FARTS
ABLE	ADRY	AIAS	AJAR	WALES	ALUMS	RANCE	PANTS	AREDE	HARTS
CABLE	ADZE	AIDE	AJEE	YALES	AMAH	ANDS	RANTS	ARES	KARTS
FABLE	ADZES	WAIDE	AKED	ALEW	AMAHS	BANDS	VANTS	BARES	MARTS
GABLE	AEON	AIDED	BAKED	ALEWS	AMBO	FANDS	WANTS	CARES	PARTS
HABLE	PAEON	AIDER	CAKED	ALFA	JAMBO	HANDS	ANUS	DARES	TARTS
SABLE	AEONS	AIDES	FAKED	HALFA	MAMBO	LANDS	MANUS	FARES	WARTS
TABLE	AERY	AIDS	LAKED	ALFAS	SAMBO	PANDS	APAY	HARES	ARTSY
ABLED	FAERY	GAIDS	NAKED	ALGA	ZAMBO	RANDS	APAYD	LARES	ARTY
ABLER	AESC	KAIDS	RAKED	ALGAE	AMBOS	SANDS	APAYS	MARES	PARTY
ABLES	AFAR	LAIDS	WAKED	ALGAL	AMEN	WANDS	APED	NARES	TARTY
ABLET	AFARA	MAIDS	AKEE	ALIT	SAMEN	ANES	CAPED	PARES	WARTY
ABLY	AFFY	RAIDS	RAKEE	ALLS	YAMEN	BANES	GAPED	TARES	ARUM
ABUT	BAFFY	SAIDS	AKES	BALLS	AMEND	CANES	JAPED	VARES	GARUM
ABUTS	DAFFY	AILS	BAKES	CALLS	AMENE	FANES	RAPED	WARES	LARUM
ABYE	TAFFY	BAILS	CAKES	FALLS	AMENS	JANES	TAPED	ARET	ARUMS
ABYES	AFRO	FAILS	FAKES	GALLS	AMENT	LANES	APES	CARET	ARVO
ACED	AFROS	HAILS	HAKES	HALLS	AMID	MANES	CAPES	ARETE	ARVOS
FACED	AGAR	JAILS	JAKES	MALLS	AMIDE	PANES	GAPES	ARETS	ARYL
LACED	AGARS	KAILS	LAKES	PALLS	AMIE	VANES	JAPES	ARETT	ARYLS
MACED	AGAS	MAILS	MAKES	WALLS	RAMIE	WANES	NAPES	AREW	ASAR
PACED	NAGAS	NAILS	RAKES	ALLY	AMIES	ANEW	PAPES	ARIA	TASAR
RACED	RAGAS	PAILS	SAKES	BALLY	AMIR	ANIL	RAPES	MARIA	ASCI
ACES	SAGAS	RAILS	TAKES	DALLY	AMIRS	ANILE	TAPES	ARIAS	FASCI
DACES	AGAST	SAILS	WAKES	GALLY	AMIS	ANILS	APEX	ARID	ASHY
FACES	AGED	TAILS	AKIN	PALLY	CAMIS	ANKH	APOD	MARID	HASHY
LACES	CAGED	VAILS	LAKIN	RALLY	KAMIS	ANKHS	APODE	ARIL	MASHY
MACES	GAGED	WAILS	TAKIN	SALLY	RAMIS	ANNA	APODS	ARILS	WASHY
PACES	PAGED	AIMS	AKING	TALLY	TAMIS	CANNA	APSE	ARIS	ASKS
RACES	RAGED	KAIMS	ALAE	WALLY	AMISS	MANNA	LAPSE	DARIS	BASKS
TACES	WAGED	MAIMS	ALAP	ALLYL	AMLA	NANNA	APSES	SARIS	CASKS
ACHE	AGEE	SAIMS	JALAP	ALMA	AMLAS	TANNA	APTS	ARISE	HASKS
CACHE	RAGEE	AINE	SALAP	HALMA	AMMO	ANNAL	AQUA	ARISH	MASKS
NACHE	AGEN	DAINE	ALAPA	TALMA	AMMON	ANNAS	AQUAE	ARKS	TASKS
RACHE	AGENE	FAINE	ALAPS	ALMAH	AMMOS	ANNAT	AQUAS	BARKS	ASPS
TACHE	AGENT	RAINE	ALAR	ALMAS	AMOK	ANNO	ARAK	CARKS	GASPS
ACHED	AGES	SAINE	MALAR	ALMEH	AMPS	ANNOY	ARAKS	DARKS	HASPS
ACHES	CAGES	AINEE	TALAR	ALME	CAMPS	ANNS	ARAR	HARKS	JASPS
ACHY	GAGES	AIRN	ALARM	ALMES	DAMPS	BANNS	ARARS	JARKS	RASPS
ACID	MAGES	BAIRN	ALARY	ALMS	GAMPS	CANNS	ARBA	LARKS	WASPS
ACIDS	PAGES	CAIRN	ALAS	BALMS	LAMPS	JANNS	ARBAS	MARKS	ATAP
ACME	RAGES	AIRNS	BALAS	CALMS	RAMPS	ANOA	ARCH	NARKS	ATAPS

ATOC	AVID	AYAHS	BANDY	BATTS	BEING	BIGGY	BLATT	BOFF	ABORD
ATOCS	PAVID	AYES	BANE	BATTY	BELL	BIGS	BLAY	BOFFS	BORDE
ATOK	AVOW	BAYES	BANED	BAUD	BELLE	BIKE	BLAYS	BOGS	BORDS
ATOKE	AVOWS	AYRE	BANES	BAUDS	BELLS	BIKED	BLEB	BOGY	BORE
ATOKS	AWAY	AYRES	BANG	BAUK	BELLY	BIKER	BLEBS	BOIL	ABORE
ATOM	AWAYS	AYUS	OBANG	BAUKS	BELS	BIKES	BLED	ABOIL	YBORE
ATOMS	AWDL	AZAN	BANGS	BAUR	BELT	BILE	ABLED	BOILS	BORED
ATOMY	AWDLS	AZANS	BANI	BAURS	BELTS	BILES	BLEE	BOKE	BOREE
ATOP	AWED	AZYM	BANIA	BAWD	BEMA	BILK	BLEED	BOKED	BOREL
ATOPY	CAWED	AZYME	BANK	BAWDS	BEMAD	BILKS	BLEEP	BOKES	BORER
AUFS	DAWED	AZYMS	BANKS	BAWDY	BEMAS	BILL	BLEES	BOKO	BORES
LAUFS	HAWED	BAAS	BANS	BAWL	BEND	BILLS	BLET	BOKOS	BORN
AUKS	JAWED	BABA	BANT	BAWLS	BENDS	BILLY	BLETS	BOKS	BORNE
BAUKS	KAWED	BABAS	BANTS	BAWN	BENDY	BIND	BLEW	BOLD	BORS
CAUKS	LAWED	BABE	BAPS	BAWNS	BENE	BINDS	BLEY	BOLE	BORT
WAUKS	PAWED	BABEL	BAPU	BAWR	BENES	BINE	BLIN	BOLES	ABORT
AULA	SAWED	BABES	BAPUS	BAWRS	BENET	BING	BLIND	BOLL	BORTS
AULAS	TAWED	BABU	BARB	BAYE	BENI	BINGE	BLINI	BOLLS	BOSH
AULD	YAWED	BABUL	BARBE	BAYED	BENIS	BINGO	BLINK	BOLO	BOSK
CAULD	AWES	BABUS	BARBS	BAYES	BENJ	BINGS	BLINS	BOLOS	BOSKS
HAULD	WAWES	BABY	BARD	BAYS	BENS	BINK	BLIP	BOLT	BOSKY
TAULD	AWLS	BACH	BARDS	BAYT	BENT	BINKS	BLIPS	BOLTS	BOSS
YAULD	BAWLS	BACK	BARDY	BAYTS	BENTS	BINS	BLOB	BOMA	BOSSY
AUNT	PAWLS	ABACK	BARE	BEAD	BENTY	BINT	BLOBS	BOMAS	BOTH
DAUNT	WAWLS	BACKS	BARED	BEADS	BERE	BINTS	BLOC	BOMB	BOTHY
GAUNT	YAWLS	BADE	BARER	BEADY	BERES	BIOG	BLOCK	BOMBE	BOTS
HAUNT	AWNS	BAEL	BARES	BEAK	BERET	BIOGS	BLOCS	BOMBO	BOTT
JAUNT	BAWNS	BAELS	BARF	BEAKS	BERG	BIOS	BLOT	BOMBS	BOTTE
NAUNT	DAWNS	BAFF	BARFS	BEAM	BERGS	BIRD	BLOTS	BONA	BOTTS
SAUNT	FAWNS	BAFFS	BARK	ABEAM	BERK	BIRDS	BLOW	BOND	BOTTY
TAUNT	LAWNS	BAFFY	BARKS	BEAMS	BERKS	BIRK	ABLOW	BONDS	BOUK
VAUNT	PAWNS	BAFT	BARKY	BEAMY	BERM	BIRKS	BLOWN	BONE	BOUKS
AUNTS	RAWNS	ABAFT	BARM	BEAN	BERMS	BIRL	BLOWS	BONED	BOUN
AUNTY	YAWNS	BAGS	BARMS	BEANO	BEST	BIRLE	BLOWY	BONER	BOUND
AURA	AWNY	BAHT	BARMY	BEANS	BESTS	BIRLS	BLUB	BONES	BOUNS
LAURA	LAWNY	BAHTS	BARN	BEAR	BETA	BIRR	BLUBS	BONG	BOUT
AURAE	TAWNY	BAIL	BARNS	ABEAR	BETAS	BIRRS	BLUE	BONGO	ABOUT
AURAL	YAWNY	BAILS	BARP	BEARD	BETE	BISE	BLUED	BONGS	BOUTS
AURAS	AWRY	BAIT	BARPS	BEARE	BETED	BISH	BLUER	BONK	BOWL
AUTO	AXED	BAITS	BARS	BEARS	BETES	BISK	BLUES	BONKS	BOWLS
AUTOS	FAXED	BAKE	BASE	BEAT	BETEL	BISKS	BLUEY	BONY	BOWR
AVAL	RAXED	BAKED	ABASE	BEATH	BETH	BITE	BLUR	BOOB	BOWRS
NAVAL	TAXED	BAKEN	BASED	BEATS	BETHS	BITER	BLURB	BOOBS	BOWS
AVALE	WAXED	BAKER	BASER	BEAU	BETS	BITES	BLURS	BOOBY	BOWSE
AVAS	AXEL	BAKES	BASES	BEAUT	ABETS	BITO	BLURT	BOOH	BOXY
KAVAS	AXELS	BALD	BASH	BEAUX	BEVY	BITOS	BOAK	BOOK	BOYG
LAVAS	AXES	BALE	ABASH	BECK	BEYS	BITS	BOAKS	BOOKS	BOYGS
AVAST	FAXES	BALED	ABASK	BECKE	OBEYS	OBITS	BOAR	BOOKY	BOYO
AVER	LAXES	BALER	BASKS	BECKS	BHEL	BITSY	BOARD	BOOM	BOYOS
CAVER	MAXES	BALES	BASS	BEDE	BHELS	BITT	BOARS	BOOMS	BOYS
HAVER	PAXES	BALK	BASSE	BEDEL	BIAS	BITTE	BOART	BOON	BRAD
LAVER	RAXES	BALKS	BASSI	BEDES	OBIAS	BITTS	BOAS	BOONG	BRADS
PAVER	SAXES	BALKY	BASSO	BEDEW	BIBS	BITTY	BOAST	BOONS	BRAE
RAVER	TAXES	BALL	BASSY	BEDS	BICE	BLAB	BOAT	BOOR	BRAES
SAVER	WAXES	BALLS	BAST	BEEF	BICES	BLABS	BOATS	BOORD	BRAG
TAVER	ZAXES	BALLY	BASTA	BEEFS	BIDE	BLAD	BOBA	BOORS	BRAGS
WAVER	AXIL	BALM	BASTE	BEEFY	ABIDE	BLADE	BOBAC	BOOS	BRAN
AVERS	AXILE	BALMS	BASTO	BEEN	BIDED	BLADS	BOBAK	BOOSE	BRAND
AVERT	AXILS	BALMY	BASTS	BEEP	BIDES	BLAE	BOBAS	BOOST	BRANK
AVES	AXIS	BALU	BATE	BEEPS	BIDET	BLAER	BOBS	BOOT	BRANS
CAVES	MAXIS	BALUS	ABATE	BEER	BIDS	BLAES	BOCK	BOOTH	BRAS
EAVES	TAXIS	BAMS	BATED	BEERS	BIEN	BLAG	BOCKS	BOOTS	BRASH
HAVES	AXLE	BANC	BATES	BEERY	BIER	BLAGS	BODE	BOOTY	BRASS
LAVES	AXLES	BANCO	BATH	BEES	BIERS	BLAH	BODED	BOPS	BRAST
NAVES	AXON	BANCS	BATHE	BEET	BIFF	BLAHS	ABODE	BORA	BRAT
OAVES	CAXON	BAND	BATHS	BEETS	BIFFS	BLAT	BODES	BORAS	BRATS
PAVES	TAXON	ABAND	BATS	BEGO	BIGA	BLATE	BODS	BORAX	BRAW
RAVES	AXONS	BANDH	BATT	BEGOT	BIGAE	BLATS	BODY	BORD	BRAWL
SAVES	AYAH	BANDS	BATTA	BEGS	BIGG				BRAWN
WAVES	RAYAH			BEIN	BIGGS				BRAWS

BRAY	BUIK	BUSSU	CALPS	CART	CERES	CHIT	CLAPS	CODAS	CONK
ABRAY	BUIKS	BUST	CALX	SCART	CERT	CHITS	CLAT	CODE	CONKS
BRAYS	BUKE	BUSTS	CAME	CARTA	CERTS	CHIV	ECLAT	CODED	CONKY
BRED	BUKES	BUSTY	CAMEL	CARTE	CESS	CHIVE	CLATS	CODES	CONN
BREDE	BULB	BUSY	CAMEO	CARTS	CESSE	CHIVS	CLAW	CODEX	CONNE
BREE	BULBS	BUTE	CAMES	CASA	CETE	CHIVY	CLAWS	CODS	CONNS
BREED	BULK	BUTES	SCAMP	CASAS	CETES	CHOC	CLAY	COED	CONS
BREEM	BULKS	SCAMP	CAMP	CASE	CHAD	CHOCK	CLAYS	COEDS	ICONS
BREER	BULKY	BUTT	CAMPS	CASED	CHADS	CHOCS	CLEF	COFF	CONY
BREES	ABUTS	BUTTE	CAMPY	CASES	CHAI	CHOP	CLEFS	SCOFF	COOF
BREN	BULL	BUTTS	CAMS	CASH	CHAIN	CHOPS	CLEFT	COFFS	COOFS
BRENS	BULLA	BUTTY	SCAMS	CASK	CHAIR	CHOU	CLEG	COFT	COOK
BRENT	BULLS	BUYS	CANE	CASKS	CHAIS	CHOUT	CLEGS	COGS	COOKS
BRER	BULLY	BUZZ	CANED	CAST	CHAL	CHOUX	CLEM	COHO	COOKY
BRERE	BUMF	ABUZZ	CANEH	CASTE	CHALK	CHOW	CLEMS	COHOE	COOL
BRERS	BUMFS	BUZZY	CANES	CASTS	CHALS	CHOWS	CLEW	COHOG	COOLS
BREW	ABUZZ	BYES	CANG	SCATS	CHAM	CHUB	CLEWS	COHOS	COOLY
BREWS	BUMP	BYKE	CANGS	CATE	CHAMP	CHUBS	CLIP	COIF	COOM
BRIG	BUMPH	BYKED	CANN	CATER	CHAMS	CHUG	CLIPE	COIL	COOMB
BRIGS	BUMPS	BYKES	CANNA	CATES	CHAP	CHUGS	CLIPS	COILS	COOMS
BRIM	BUMPY	BYRE	CANNS	CATS	CHAPE	CHUM	CLIPT	COIN	COOMY
ABRIM	BUNA	BYRES	CANS	SCATS	CHAPS	CHUMP	CLOD	COINS	COON
BRIMS	BUNAS	BYTE	SCANS	CAUF	CHAR	CHUMS	CLOG	COIR	COONS
BRIO	BUND	BYTES	CANST	CAUK	CHARA	CHUT	CLOGS	COIRS	COOP
BRIOS	BUNDS	CANT	CANT	CAUKS	CHARD	CHUTE	CLOP	COKE	SCOOP
BRIT	BUNDU	CABA	SCANT	CAUL	CHARE	CIAO	CLOPS	COKED	COOPS
BRITS	BUNG	CABAL	CANTO	CAULD	CHARK	CIAOS	CLOT	COKES	COOS
BROD	BUNGS	CABAS	CANTS	CAULK	CHARM	CIDE	CLOTE	COKY	COOST
BRODS	BUNGY	CABS	CANTY	CAULS	CHARR	CIDED	CLOTH	COLA	COOT
BROG	BUNK	SCABS	CANY	CAUM	CHARS	CIDER	CLOTS	COLAS	SCOOT
BROGH	BUNKO	CADE	CAPA	CAUMS	CHART	CIDES	CLOU	COLD	COOTS
BROGS	BUNKS	CADES	CAPAS	CAUP	CHARY	CIEL	CLOUD	COLDS	COPE
BROO	SCABS	CADET	CAPE	SCAUP	CHAS	CIELS	CLOUR	COLE	SCOPE
BROOD	BUNS	CADI	SCAPE	CAUPS	CHASE	CIGS	CLOUS	COLES	COPED
BROOK	BUNT	CADIE	CAPED	CAVE	CHASM	CILL	CLOUT	COLEY	COPER
BROOL	BUNTS	CADIS	CAPER	CAVED	CHAT	CILLS	CLOW	COLL	COPES
BROOM	BUNTY	CADS	CAPES	CAVEL	CHATS	CION	CLOWN	COLLS	COPSE
BROOS	BUOY	ECADS	CAPO	CAVER	CHAW	CIONS	CLOWS	COLLY	COPSY
BROS	BUOYS	SCADS	CAPON	CAVES	CHAWS	CIRE	CLOY	COLS	COPY
BROSE	BURD	CAFE	CAPOS	CAVY	CHAY	CIRES	CLOYE	COLT	CORD
BROW	BURDS	CAFES	CAPOT	CAWK	CHAYA	CIRL	CLOYS	COLTS	CORDS
BROWN	BURG	CAFF	CAPS	CAWKS	CHAYS	CIRLS	CLUB	COMA	CORE
BROWS	BURGH	SCAFF	CARB	CAWS	CHEF	CIST	CLUBS	COMAE	CORED
BRUT	BURGS	CAFFS	CARBS	SCAWS	CHEFS	CISTS	CLUE	COMAL	CORER
BRUTE	BURK	CAGE	CARD	CAYS	CHER	CITE	CLUED	COMAS	CORES
BUAT	BURKA	CAGED	CARDI	CEAS	OCHER	CITED	CLUES	COMB	CORF
BUATS	BURKE	CAGES	CARDS	CEASE	CHERE	CITER	COAL	COMBE	CORK
BUBA	BURKS	CAGEY	CARDY	CECA	CHERT	CITES	COALS	COMBO	CORKS
BUBAL	BURL	CAGY	CARE	CEDE	CHEW	CITO	COALY	COMBS	CORKY
BUBAS	BURLS	CAIN	SCARE	CEDED	CHEWS	CITS	COAT	COMBY	CORM
BUBO	BURLY	CAINS	CARED	CEDES	CHEWY	CITY	COATE	COME	CORMS
BUBS	BURN	CAKE	CARER	CEDI	CHEZ	CIVE	COATI	COMER	CORN
BUCK	BURNS	CAKED	CARES	CEDIS	CHIC	CIVES	COATS	COMES	ACORN
BUCKO	BURNT	CAKES	CARET	CEES	CHICA	CIVET	COAX	COMET	SCORN
BUCKS	BURP	CAKY	CAREX	CEIL	CHICH	CLAD	COBB	COMP	CORNI
BUCKU	BURPS	CALF	CARK	CEILI	CHICK	CLADE	COBBS	COMPO	CORNO
BUDO	BURR	CALFS	CARKS	CEILS	CHICS	CLADS	COBBY	COMPS	CORNS
BUDOS	BURRO	CALK	CARL	CELL	YCLAD	CLAG	COBS	COMPT	CORNU
BUDS	BURRS	CALKS	CARLS	CELLA	CHID	CLAGS	COCA	COMS	CORNY
BUFF	BURRY	CALL	CARP	CELLO	CHIDE	CLAM	COCAS	COND	CORS
BUFFA	BURS	SCALL	SCARP	CELLS	CHIK	CLAME	COCH	YCOND	CORSE
BUFFE	BURSA	CALLA	CARPS	CELS	CHIKS	CLAMP	COCK	CONE	CORSO
BUFFI	BURSE	CALLS	CARR	CELT	CHIN	CLAMS	COCKS	SCONE	COSE
BUFFO	BURST	CALM	CARRS	CELTS	CHINA	CLAN	COCKY	CONED	COSED
BUFFS	BURY	CALMS	CARRY	CENT	CHINE	CLANG	COCO	CONES	COSES
BUFO	BUSH	CALMY	CARS	SCENT	CHINK	CLANK	COCOA	CONEY	COSH
BUFOS	BUSHY	CALP	SCARS	CENTO	CHINO	CLANS	COCOS		COSS
BUGS	BUSK	SCALP	CARSE	CENTS	CHINS	CLAP	CODA		COST
BUHL	BUSKS	CALPA		CEPS	CHIP				
BUHLS	BUSKY			CERE	CHIPS				
	BUSS			CERED	CHIS				

COSTA	CRAPY	CULTS	DAHLS	DAWS	DEMES	DIKEY	DIXIE	DOPEY	DRAM
COSTE	CRAW	CUNT	DAHS	ADAWS	DEMO	DILL	DIXY	DOPS	DRAP
COSTS	SCRAW	CUNTS	DAIS	DAWT	DEMOB	DILLI	DOAB	DOPY	DRAT
COSY	CRAWL	CUPS	DAISY	DAWTS	DEMON	DILLS	DOABS	DORM	ADRAD
COTE	CRAWS	SCUPS	DAKS	DAYS	DEMOS	DILLY	DOAT	DORMS	YDRAD
COTED	CREE	CURB	DALE	ADAYS	DEMY	DIME	DOATS	DORMY	DRAC
COTES	SCREE	CURBS	DALES	DAZE	DENE	DIMER	DOBS	DORP	DRAW
COTH	CREED	CURD	DALI	DAZED	DENES	DIMES	DOCK	DORPS	DRAM
COTHS	CREEK	CURDS	DALIS	DAZES	DENS	DIMS	DOCKS	DORR	DRAW
COTS	CREEL	CURDY	DALS	DEAD	DENSE	DINE	DOCS	DORRS	DRAM
SCOTS	CREEP	CURE	ODALS	DEADS	DENT	DINED	DODO	DORS	DRAT
COTT	CREES	CURED	UDALS	DEAF	DENTS	DINER	DODOS	ODORS	DRAM
COTTA	CREW	CURER	DALT	DEAL	DERE	DINES	DODS	DORSA	DRAW
COTTS	SCREW	CURES	DALTS	IDEAL	DERED	DING	DOEN	DORSE	DRAT
COUP	CREWE	CURL	DAME	DEALS	DERES	DINGE	DOER	DORT	DRAW
SCOUP	CREWS	CURLS	DAMES	DEALT	DERM	DINGO	DOERS	DORTS	DRAW
COUPE	CRIB	CURLY	DAMN	DEAN	DERMA	DINGS	DOES	DORTY	DRAW
COUPS	CRIBS	CURN	DAMNS	DEANS	DERMS	DINGY	DOEST	DORY	DRAW
COUR	CRIT	CURNS	DAMP	DEAR	DERN	DINK	DOFF	DOSE	DRAW
SCOUR	CRITH	CURNY	DAMPS	DEARE	DERNS	DINKS	DOFFS	DOSED	DRAY
COURB	CRITS	CURR	DAMPY	DEARN	DERV	DINKY	DOGE	DOSEH	DRED
COURD	CROC	CURRS	DAMS	DEARS	DERVS	DINS	DOGES	DOSES	DREG
COURE	CROCK	CURRY	DANG	DEARY	DESK	DINT	DOGS	DOSS	DREK
COURS	CROCS	CURS	DANGS	DEAW	DESKS	DINTS	DOGY	DOST	DREW
COURT	CROP	SCURS	DANK	DEAWY	DEUS	DIPS	DOHS	DOTE	DREY
COVE	CROPS	CURSE	DANKS	DEBS	DEVA	DIPSO	DOIT	DOTED	DREG
COVED	CROW	CURST	DANS	DEBT	DEVAS	DIRE	DOITS	DOTER	DREY
COVEN	SCROW	CURT	DANT	DEBTS	DEWS	DIRER	DOJO	DOTES	DRIB
COVER	CROWD	CUSH	DANTS	DECK	DEWY	DIRK	DOJOS	DOTH	DRIB
COVES	CROWN	CUSHY	DAPS	DECKO	DEYS	DIRKE	DOLE	DOTS	DRIP
COVET	CROWS	CUSK	DARE	DECKS	DHAK	DIRKS	DOLED	DOTY	DRIP
COVEY	CRUD	CUSKS	DARED	DECO	DHAKS	DIRL	DOLES	DOUC	DROB
COWL	CRUDE	CUSP	DARES	DECOR	DHAL	DIRLS	DOLL	DOUCE	DROIL
SCOWL	CRUDS	CUSPS	DARG	DECOY	DHALS	DIRT	DOLLS	DOUCS	DROW
COWLS	CRUDY	CUSS	DARGA	DEED	DHOW	DIRTS	DOLLY	DOUP	DROW
COWP	CRUE	CUTE	DARGS	DEEDS	DHOWS	DIRTY	DOLT	DOUPS	DROW
SCOWP	CRUEL	ACUTE	DARI	DEEDY	DIAL	DISA	DOLTS	DOUR	DRUB
COWPS	CRUES	SCUTE	DARIC	DEEM	DIALS	DISAS	DOME	DOURA	DRUM
COWS	CRUET	CUTER	DARIS	ADEEM	DIBS	DISC	DOMED	DOUT	DRUG
SCOWS	CRUS	CUTES	DARK	DEEMS	DICE	DISCO	DOMES	DOUTS	DSOS
COXA	CRUSE	CUTEY	DARKS	DEEN	DICED	DISCS	DOMY	DOVE	ODSOS
COXAE	CRUSH	CUTS	DARKY	DEENS	DICER	DISH	DONA	DOVED	DUAD
COXAL	CRUST	SCUTS	DARN	DEEP	DICES	DISHY	DONAH	DOVER	DUAL
COXY	CRUSY	CWMS	DARNS	DEEPS	DICEY	DISK	DONAS	DOVES	DUAN
COYS	CRUX	CYAN	DART	DEER	DICH	DISKS	DONE	DOWD	DUAL
COZE	CUBE	CYMA	DARTS	DEERE	DICHT	DISS	DONEE	DOWDS	DUAL
COZED	CUBEB	CYMAR	DASH	DEES	DICK	DITA	DONG	DOWDY	DUAN
COZEN	CUBED	CYMAS	DATA	DEEV	DICKS	DITAL	DONGA	DOWF	DUAL
COZES	CUBES	CYME	DATAL	DEEVE	DICKY	DITAS	DONGS	DOWL	DUAN
COZY	CUBS	CYMES	DATE	DEEVS	DICT	DITE	DONS	DOWLE	DUAL
CRAB	CUDS	CYST	DATED	DEFT	DICTA	DITED	DOOB	DOWLS	DUBS
SCRAB	SCUDS	CYSTS	DATER	DEFY	DICTS	DITES	DOOBS	DOWN	DUCE
CRABS	CUED	CYTE	DATES	EDICT	ADITS	DITS	DOOK	ADOWN	EDUCE
CRAG	CUES	CZAR	DAUB	DEID	DIDO	DITT	DOOKS	DOWNA	DUCK
SCRAG	CUFF	CZARS	DAUBE	DEIDS	DIDOS	DITTO	DOOL	DOWNS	DUCK
CRAGS	SCUFF	DABS	DAUBS	DEIL	DIEB	DITTS	DOOLE	DOWNY	DUCK
CRAM	CUFFO	DACE	DAUBY	DEILS	DIEBS	DITTY	DOOM	DOWP	DUCK
SCRAM	CUFFS	DACES	DAUD	DELE	DIED	DIVA	DOOMS	DOWPS	DUCT
CRAME	CUIF	DADO	DAUDS	DELED	DIES	DIVAN	DOOMY	DOWS	EDUCT
CRAMP	CUIFS	DADOS	DAUR	DELES	DIET	DIVAS	DOOR	DOWSE	DUCT
CRAMS	CUIT	DADS	DAURS	DELF	DIETS	DIVE	DOORN	DOWT	DUDE
CRAN	CUITS	DAFF	DAUT	DELFS	DIGS	DIVED	DOORS	DOWTS	DUDS
SCRAN	CULL	DAFFS	DAUTS	DELFT	DIKA	DIVER	DOOS	DOXY	DUDS
CRANE	SCULL	DAFFY	DAWD	DELI	DIKAS	DIVES	DOPA	DOZE	DUEL
CRANK	CULLS	DAFT	DAWDS	DELIS	DIKE	DIVI	DOPAS	DOZED	DUEL
CRANS	CULLY	DAGO	DAWK	DELL	DIKED	DIVIS	DOPE	DOZEN	DUEL
CRAP	CULM	DAGS	DAWKS	DELLS	DIKER	DIVS	DOPED	DOZER	DUES
SCRAP	CULMS	DAHL	DAWN	DELS	DIKES	DIXI	DOPER	DOZES	DUET
CRAPE	CULT	DAHL	DAWNS	DEME	DIKES	DIXI	DOPES	DOZY	DUET

DUETT	DYNES	EASY	LEECH	VELDS	WENDS	MERKS	EURO	EYRY	FASTS
DUFF	DZOS	EATH	REECH	WELDS	ENES	PERKS	EUROS	FACE	FATE
DUFFS	EACH	BEATH	EELS	ELFS	BENES	SERKS	EVEN	FACED	FATED
DUGS	BEACH	DEATH	DEELS	DELFS	DENES	YERKS	EEVEN	FACER	FATES
DUKE	LEACH	HEATH	FEELS	PELFS	GENES	ERNE	SEVEN	FACES	FATSO
DUKED	PEACH	MEATH	HEELS	SELFS	LENES	CERNE	YEVEN	FACET	FATS
DUKES	REACH	NEATH	JEELS	ELKS	MENES	GERNE	EVENS	FACT	FAUN
DULE	TEACH	EATHE	KEELS	YELKS	NENES	KERNE	EVENT	FACTS	FAUNA
DULES	EALE	EATS	MEELS	ELLS	PENES	TERNE	EVER	FADE	FAUNS
DULL	VEALE	BEATS	PEELS	BELLS	TENES	ERNED	BEVER	FADED	FAUX
DULLS	EALES	FEATS	REELS	CELLS	ENEW	ERNES	FEVER	FADES	FAWN
DULY	EANS	GEATS	SEELS	DELLS	RENEW	ERNS	LEVER	FADO	FAWNS
DUMA	BEANS	HEATS	TEELS	FELLS	ENEWS	DERNS	NEVER	FADOS	FAWS
DUMAS	DEANS	JEATS	WEELS	HELLS	ENGS	HERNS	SEVER	FADS	FAYS
DUMB	GEANS	LEATS	EELY	JELLS	LENGS	KERNS	EVERT	FADY	OFAYS
DUMBS	JEANS	MEATS	JEELY	KELLS	MENGS	PERNS	EVERY	FAFF	FAZE
DUMP	LEANS	PEATS	SEELY	MELLS	ENOW	TERNS	EVES	FAFFS	FAZED
DUMPS	PEANS	SEATS	EERY	PELLS	ENVY	ERRS	EVET	FAGS	FAZES
DUMPY	REANS	TEATS	BEERY	SELLS	SENVY	SERRS	EVETS	FAHS	FEAL
DUNE	SEANS	EAUS	LEERY	TELLS	EOAN	ERST	YEVES	FAIK	FEALS
DUNES	WEANS	EAUX	PEERY	VELLS	EONS	PERST	REVET	FAIKS	FEAR
DUNG	YEANS	BEAUX	VEERY	WELLS	AEONS	VERST	EVIL	FAIL	AFEAR
DUNGS	EARD	EBBS	EEVN	YELLS	NEONS	ESKY	DEVIL	FAILS	FEARE
DUNGY	BEARD	EFFS	EEVNS	ELMS	PEONS	PESKY	EVILS	FAIN	FEARS
DUNK	HEARD	JEFFS	EFTS	HELMS	EORL	ESNE	EVOE	FAINE	FEAT
DUNKS	YEARD	TEFFS	HEFTS	YELMS	CEORL	MESNE	EWER	FAINS	FEATS
DUNS	EARDS	EBON	LEFTS	ELMY	EORLS	ESPY	FEWER	FAINT	FECK
DUNSH	EARL	EBONS	WEFTS	ELSE	EPEE	ESSE	HEWER	FAIR	FECKS
DUNT	PEARL	EBONY	EGAD	ELTS	TEPEE	CESSE	NEWER	FAIRS	FEDS
DUNTS	EARLS	ECAD	BEGAD	BELTS	EPEES	DESSE	SEWER	FAIRY	FEED
DUOS	EARLY	ECADS	EGAL	CELTS	EPHA	FESSE	EWERS	FAIX	FEEDS
DUPE	EARN	DECAD	LEGAL	FELTS	EPHAH	GESSE	EWES	FAKE	FEEL
DUPED	DEARN	ECCE	REGAL	GELTS	EPHAS	ESSES	EWEST	FAKED	FEELS
DUPER	LEARN	RECCE	EGER	KELTS	EPIC	ETAS	EWKS	FAKES	FEER
DUPES	YEARN	ECCO	LEGER	MELTS	EPICS	BETAS	EWTS	FAKER	FEERS
DUPS	EARNS	RECCO	EGERS	PELTS	EPOS	GETAS	NEWTS	FALL	FEES
DURA	EARS	ECHE	EGGS	WELTS	PEPOS	KETAS	EXAM	FALLS	FEESE
DURAL	BEARS	ECHED	TEGGS	YELTS	ERAS	ZETAS	EXAMS	FALX	FEET
DURAS	DEARS	ECHES	YEGGS	EMES	TERAS	ETAT	EXES	FAME	FEGS
DURE	FEARS	ECHT	EGGY	DEMES	ERASE	ETATS	HEXES	FAMED	FEHM
DURED	GEARS	FECHT	LEGGY	FEMES	ERED	ETCH	KEXES	FAMES	FEHME
DURES	HEARS	HECHT	PEGGY	HEMES	CERED	FETCH	LEXES	FAND	FEIS
DURN	LEARS	ECRU	EGIS	LEMES	DERED	KETCH	SEXES	FANDS	FELL
DURNS	NEARS	ECRUS	AEGIS	TEMES	MERED	LETCH	VEXES	FANE	FELLA
DURO	PEARS	ECUS	EGMA	EMEU	SERED	RETCH	WEXES	FANES	FELLS
DUROS	REARS	EDDO	REGMA	EMEUS	ERES	VETCH	YEXES	FANG	FELLY
DUROY	SEARS	EDDY	EGMAS	EMIR	BERES	ETEN	EXIT	FANGO	FELT
DUSH	TEARS	NEDDY	EGOS	EMIRS	CERES	ETENS	EXITS	FANGS	FELTS
DUSK	WEARS	REDDY	SEGOS	EMIT	DERES	ETHE	EXON	FANK	FEME
DUSKS	YEARS	TEDDY	EHED	DEMIT	FERES	ETHER	EXONS	FANKS	FEMES
DUSKY	EARST	EDGE	EIKS	REMIT	GERES	ETHS	EXPO	FANS	FEND
DUST	EASE	HEDGE	REIKS	EMITS	LERES	BETHS	EXPOS	FARD	FENDS
ADUST	CEASE	KEDGE	EILD	EMMA	MERES	METHS	EXUL	FARDS	FENDY
DUSTS	LEASE	LEDGE	EILDS	GEMMA	PERES	ETNA	EXULS	FARE	FENS
DUSTY	MEASE	SEDGE	EINE	LEMMA	SERES	ETNAS	EXULT	FARED	FENT
DUTY	PEASE	WEDGE	SEINE	EMMAS	ERGO	ETUI	EYAS	FARES	FENTS
DWAM	SEASE	EDGED	EKED	EMUS	ERGON	ETUIS	EYED	FARL	FEOD
DWAMS	TEASE	EDGER	REKED	EMYS	ERGOT	EUGE	DEYED	FARLE	FEODS
DYAD	EASED	EDGES	EKES	ENDS	ERGS	EUGH	FEYED	FARLS	FERE
DYADS	EASEL	EDGY	PEKES	BENDS	BERGS	HEUGH	KEYED	FARM	YFERE
DYED	EASES	HEDGY	REKES	FENDS	ERIC	LEUGH	HEYED	FARMS	FERER
DYER	EAST	KEDGY	EKKA	HENDS	SERIC	TEUGH	EYES	FARO	FERES
DYERS	BEAST	LEDGY	EKKAS	LENDS	XERIC	EUGHS	DEYES	FAROS	FERM
DYES	FEAST	SEDGY	ELAN	MENDS	ERICA	EUKS	EYNE	FARS	FERMI
DYKE	HEAST	EDHS	ELAND	PENDS	ERICK	NEUKS	EYOT	FARSE	FERMS
DYKED	LEAST	EDIT	ELANS	RENDS	ERICS	YEUKS	EYOTS	FART	FERN
DYKES	REAST	EDITS	ELDS	SENDS	ERKS	EUOI	EYRA	FARTS	FERNS
DYKEY	YEAST	EECH	GELDS	TENDS	BERKS		EYRAS	FASH	FERNY
DYNE	EASTS	BEECH	MELDS	VENDS	FERKS		EYRE	FAST	FESS
		KEECH			JERKS		EYRES	FASTI	FESSE

Column 1: FEST, FESTA, FESTS, FETA, FETAL, FETAS, FETE, FETED, FETES, FETS, FETT, FETTA, FETTS, FEUD, FEUDS, FEUS, FEYS, FIAR, FIARS, FIAT, FIATS, FIBS, FICO, FICOS, FIDS, FIEF, FIEFS, FIFE, FIFED, FIFER, FIFES, FIGO, FIGOS, FIGS, FIKE, FIKED, FIKES, FIKY, FILE, FILED, FILER, FILES, FILET, FILL, FILLE, FILLS, FILLY, FILM, FILMS, FILMY, FILS, FIND, FINDS, FINE, FINED, FINER, FINES, FINK, FINKS, FINO, FINOS, FINS, FIRE, AFIRE, FIRED, FIRER, FIRES, FIRK, FIRKS, FIRM

Column 2: FIRMS, FIRN, FIRNS, FIRS, FIRST, FISC, FISCS, FISH, FISHY, FISK, FISKS, FIST, FISTS, FISTY, FITS, FITT, FITTE, FITTS, FIVE, FIVER, FIVES, FIZZ, FIZZY, FLAB, FLABS, FLAG, FLAGS, OFLAG, FLAK, FLAKE, FLAKS, FLAKY, FLAM, FLAME, FLAMM, FLAMS, FLAMY, FLAN, FLANK, FLANS, FLAP, FLAPS, FLAT, FLATS, FLAW, FLAWN, FLAWS, FLAWY, FLAX, FLAXY, FLAY, FLAYS, FLEA, FLEAM, FLEAS, FLED, FLEE, FLEER, FLEES, FLEET, FLEG, FLEGS, FLEW, FLEWS, FLEX, FLEY, FLEYS, FLIC, FLICK, FLICS

Column 3: FLIP, FLIPS, FLIT, FLITE, FLITS, FLITT, FLIX, FLOE, FLOES, FLOG, FLOGS, FLOP, FLOPS, FLOR, FLORA, FLORS, FLORY, FLOW, FLOWN, FLOWS, FLUB, FLUBS, FLUE, FLUES, FLUEY, FLUS, FLUSH, FLUX, FOAL, FOALS, FOAM, FOAMS, FOAMY, FOBS, FOCI, FOEN, FOES, FOGS, FOGY, FOHN, FOHNS, FOIL, FOILS, FOIN, FOINS, FOLD, FOLDS, FOLK, FOLKS, FOND, FONDA, FONDS, FONE, FONS, FONT, FONTS, FOOD, FOODS, FOOL, FOOLS, FOOT, AFOOT, FOOTS, FOOTY, FOPS, FORA, FORAY, FORD, FORDO, FORDS

Column 4: FORE, AFORE, FOREL, FORES, FORK, FORKS, FORKY, FORM, FORME, FORMS, FORT, FORTE, FORTH, FORTS, FORTY, FOSS, FOSSA, FOSSE, FOUD, FOUL, AFOUL, FOULE, FOULS, FOUR, FOURS, FOUS, FOWL, FOWLS, FOXY, FOYS, FOZY, FRAB, FRABS, FRAE, FRAP, FRAPS, FRAS, FRAU, FRAUD, FRAUS, FRAY, FRAYS, FREE, FREED, FREER, FREES, FREET, FRET, FRETS, FRIG, FRIGS, FRIS, FRISK, FRIST, FRIT, FRITH, FRITS, AFRIT, FRIZ, FRIZE, FRIZZ, FROG, FROGS, FROM, FROW, FROWN, FROWS, FROWY

Column 5: FUBS, FUBSY, FUCI, FUCK, FUCKS, FUDS, FUEL, FUELS, FUFF, FUFFS, FUFFY, FUGS, FULL, FULLS, FULLY, FUME, FUMED, FUMES, FUMET, FUMS, FUMY, FUND, FUNDI, FUNDS, FUNG, FUNGI, FUNGS, FUNK, FUNKS, FUNKY, FUNS, FURL, FURLS, FURR, FURRS, FURS, FURRY, FURY, FUSC, FUSE, FUSED, FUSEE, FUSES, FUSS, FUSSY, FUST, FUSTS, FUSTY, FUZE, FUZEE, FUZES, FUZZ, FUZZY, FYKE, FYKED, FYKES, FYLE, FYLES, FYRD, FYRDS, GABS, GABY, GADE, GADI, GADIS, GADS, GADSO, GAED, GAES

Column 6: GAFF, GAFFE, GAFFS, GAGA, GAGE, GAGED, GAGES, GAGS, GAID, GAIDS, GAIN, GAINS, AGAIN, GAIR, GAIRS, GAIT, GAITS, GAITT, GAJO, GAJOS, GALA, GALAH, GALAS, GALEA, GALE, GALES, GALL, GALLS, GALLY, GALS, GAMB, GAMBA, GAMBS, GAME, GAMED, GAMER, GAMES, GAMP, GAMPS, GAMS, OGAMS, GAMY, GANE, GANG, GANGS, GANT, GANTS, GAOL, GAOLS, GAPE, GAPED, GAPER, GAPES, AGAPE, GAPO, IGAPO, GAPOS, GAPS, GARB, GARBE, GARBO, GARBS, GARE, GARS, GART, GARTH, GASH, GASP, GASPS

Column 7: GASPY, GAST, AGAST, GATE, AGATE, GATED, GATES, GATH, GATHS, GATS, GAUD, GAUDS, GAUDY, GAUM, GAUMS, GAUMY, GAUN, GAUP, GAUPS, GAUR, GAURS, GAUS, GAUSS, GAVE, AGAVE, GAVEL, GAWD, GAWDS, GAWK, GAWKS, GAWKY, GAWP, GAWPS, GAYS, GAZE, AGAZE, GAZED, GAZEL, GAZER, GAZES, GAZY, GEAL, GEALS, GEAN, GEANS, GEAR, GEARE, GEARS, GEAT, GEATS, GECK, GECKO, GECKS, GEDS, GEED, GEES, OGEES, GEIT, GEITS, GELD, GELDS, GELS, GELT, GELTS, GEMS, GENA, GENAL

Column 8: GENAS, GENE, GENES, GENET, AGENE, GENS, GENT, AGENT, GENTS, GENTY, GENU, GENUS, GEOS, GERE, GERES, GERM, GERMS, GEST, GESTE, GESTS, EGEST, GETA, GETAS, GETS, GEUM, GEUMS, GHAT, GHATS, GHEE, GHEES, GHIS, GJUS, GIBE, GIBED, GIBEL, GIBER, GIBES, GIBS, GIDS, GIED, GIEN, GIES, GIFT, GIFTS, GIGA, GIGAS, GIGS, GILA, GILAS, AGILA, GILD, GILDS, GILL, GILLS, GILLY, GILT, GILTS, GIMP, GIMPS, GING, GINGS, AGING, GINK, GINKS, GINN, GINS, GIOS, GIPS, GIPSY, GIRD

Column 9: GIRDS, GIRL, GIRLS, GIRLY, GIRN, GIRNS, GIRO, GIRON, GIROS, GIRR, GIRRS, GIRT, GIRTH, GIRTS, GISM, GISMO, GISMS, GIST, GISTS, AGIST, GITE, GITES, GITS, GIVE, GIVED, GIVEN, GIVER, GIVES, OGIVE, GIZZ, GLAD, GLADE, GLADS, GLADY, GLAM, GLED, GLEDE, GLEDS, OGLED, GLEE, GLEED, GLEEK, GLEES, GLEET, AGLEE, GLEG, GLEI, GLEIS, GLEN, GLENS, GLENT, GLEY, GLEYS, AGLEY, GLIA, GLIAL, GLIAS, GLIB, GLIBS, GLID, GLIDE, GLIM, GLIMS, GLIT, GLITS, GLITZ, GLOB, GLOBE, GLOBS

Column 10: GLOBY, GLOM, GLOMS, GLOW, AGLOW, GLOWS, GLUE, GLUED, GLUER, GLUES, GLUEY, GLUG, GLUGS, GLUM, GLUME, GLUT, GLUTS, GNARL, GNARR, GNARS, GNAT, GNATS, GNAW, GNAWN, GNAWS, GNUS, GOAD, GOADS, GOAF, GOAFS, GOAL, GOALS, GOAS, GOAT, GOATS, GOATY, GOBO, GOBOS, GOBS, GOBY, GODS, GODSO, GOEL, GOELS, GOER, GOERS, GOES, GOEY, GOFF, GOFFS, GOGO, GOGS, GOLD, GOLDS, GOLDY, GOLE, GOLEM, GOLES, GOLF, GOLFS, GOLP, GOLPE, GOLPS, GONE, AGONE, GONER, GONG, GONGS, GONK

GONKS	GREN	GULF	HADED	HAMES	HATE	HEATS	THERE	HILLO	SHOER
GONS	GRENS	GULFS	HADES	HAMS	HATED	HEBE	WHERE	HILLS	HOERS
AGONS	GREW	HADJ	CHAMS	HATER	HEBEN	HERL		HILLY	HOES
GOOD	GREWS	GULL	HADS	SHAMS	HATES	HEBES	HERM	HILT	SHOES
AGOOD	GREY	GULLS	CHADS	WHAMS	HATH	HECH	THERM	HILTS	HOGG
GOODS	GREYS	GULLY	SHADS	HAND	HATS	HECHT	HIND		HOGGS
GOODY	GRID	GULP	SHADS	SHAND	CHATS	HECK	AHIND	HING	HOGH
GOOF	GRIDE	GULPH	HADST	HANDS	GHATS	HECKS	HINDS	HINGS	HOGHS
GOOFS	GRIDS	GULPS	HAEM	HANDY	KHATS	HECKS	EHING	HING	HOGS
GOOFY	GRIG	GULY	HAEMS	HANG	WHATS	HEED	THING	HINGE	SHOGS
GOOK	GRIGS	GUMP	HAET	BHANG	HAUD	HEEDS	HERO	HINGS	HOHS
GOOKS	GRIM	GUMPS	HAETS	PHANG	HAUDS	HEEDY	HEROE	HINS	HOIK
GOOL	GRIME	GUMS	HAFF	WHANG	HAUL	HEEL	HERON	CHINS	HOIKS
GOOLD	GRIMY	GUNK	CHAFF	HANGS	HAULM	SHEEL	HERSE	SHINS	HOKE
GOOLS	GRIN	GUNKS	HAFFS	HANK	HAULS	WHEEL	HERY	WHINS	HOKED
GOOLY	AGRIN	GUNS	HAFT	CHANK	HAULT	HEELS	HERYE	AHINT	HOKES
GOON	GRIND	GUPS	CHAFT	SHANK	HAUT	HEFT	THINS	HINT	HOKEY
GOONS	GRINS	GURL	SHAFT	THANK	HAUTE	THEFT	WHINS	HINTS	HOLD
GOOP	GRIP	GURLS	HAFTS	HANKS	WHEFT	HEFTE	AHINT	HIPS	HOLDS
GOOPS	GRIPE	GURLY	HAGG	HANKY	HEFTE	HEFTS	CHEST	SHIPS	HOLE
GOOPY	GRIPS	GURN	HAGGS	HAPS	HEFTS	HEFTY	GHEST	CHIPS	HOLED
GOOR	GRIS	GURNS	HAIK	CHAPS	HAVE	HEID	HESTS	WHIPS	HOLES
GOORS	GRISE	GURS	HAIKS	SHAPS	CHAVE	HEIDS	HETE	WHIPT	HOLEY
GOOS	GRIST	GURU	HAIKU	SHAPS	SHAVE	HEIL	THETE	SHIPS	HOLM
GOOSE	GRISY	GURUS	HARD	WHAPS	HAVEN	HEIDS	HETES	WHIPS	HOLES
GOOSY	GRIT	GUSH	SHARD	CHAPS	HAVER	HEIR	HIPT	WHIPT	HOLEY
GORE	GRITH	GUSHY	HAILS	CHARD	HAVES	HEIRS	HETS	HIRE	HOLM
GORED	GRITS	GUST	HAILY	HARDS	HAWK	THEIR	HIRE	HIRED	HOLMS
GORES	GROG	GUSTO	HAILY	HARDY	HAWK	SHETS	WHETS	HIRER	HOLP
GORM	GROGS	GUSTS	CHAIN	HARE	HAWM	HELD	HEWN	HIRES	HOLS
GORMS	GROT	GUSTS	HAINS	CHARE	HAWMS	HELE	HEWS	HISH	HOLT
GORMY	GROTS	GUTS	CHAIN	PHARE	HAWS	HELED	CHEWS	HISN	HOLY
GORY	GROW	GUTSY	CHAIR	SHARE	CHAWS	HELES	THEWS	HISS	HOME
GOSH	GROWL	GUYS	WHARE	WHARE	SHAWS	HELL	WHEWS	HIST	HOMED
GOUK	GROWN	GUYSE	HAIRS	HARED	THAWS	SHELL	HEYS	HISTS	HOMER
GOUKS	GROWS	GYAL	HAIRY	HAREM	HAWSE	HELLO	WHEYS	HITS	HOMES
GOUT	GRUB	GYALS	HAJI	HARES	HAYS	HELLS	WHEYS	CHITS	HOMEY
GOUTS	GRUBS	GYBE	HAJIS	CHAYS	HAZE	HELM	WHEYS	SHITS	HOMO
GOUTY	GRUE	GYBED	HAJJ	SHARK	HAZED	WHELM	THICK	WHITS	ZHOMO
GOVS	GRUED	GYBES	HAJJI	CHARK	HAZEL	HELMS	CHICK	HITS	HOMOS
GOWD	GRUEL	GYMP	HAKA	SHARK	HAZER	HELP	HICKS	CHITS	HOMY
GOWDS	GRUES	GYMPS	HAKAM	HARKS	HAZES	HELPS	HIDE	SHITS	HOND
GOWF	GRUM	GYMS	HAKAS	HARLS	HAZY	HEME	CHIDE	WHITS	HONDS
GOWFS	GRUME	GYNY	HAKE	CHARM	HEAD	HEMES	HIDED	HIVE	HOMY
GOWK	GUAN	GYPS	SHAKE	HARMS	AHEAD	HEMP	HIDES	CHIVE	HOND
GOWKS	GUANA	GYPSY	HAKES	SHARN	HEADS	HEMPS	HIED	SHIVE	HONDS
GOWL	GUANO	GYRE	HALE	HARNS	HEADY	HEMPY	HIES	HIVED	OHONE
GOWLS	GUANS	GYRED	SHALE	SHARP	HEAL	HEMS	RHIES	HIVER	PHONE
GOWN	GUAR	GYRES	WHALE	HAROS	SHEAL	HEND	HIGH	HIVES	RHONE
GOWNS	GUARD	GYRI	HALED	HARP	WHEAL	SHEND	THIGH	HIYA	SHONE
GRAB	GUARS	GYRO	HALER	HAROS	HEALD	HENDS	HIGHS	HIZZ	HONED
GRABS	GUBS	GYRON	HALES	HARPS	HEALS	HENS	HIGHT	WHIZZ	HONES
GRAM	GUCK	GYROS	HALF	HARPY	HEAP	THENS	HOAR	HOAR	HONEY
GRAMA	GUCKS	GYTE	HALFA	HART	HEAPS	WHENS	HOARD	HOARD	HONG
GRAME	GUCKY	GYTES	HALL	HARTS	HEAPY	SHENT	HOARS	HOARS	HONGS
GRAMS	GUDE	GYVE	HALLO	CHART	HEAR	HENT	HOARY	HOARY	THONG
GRAN	GUES	GYVED	HALLS	HARTS	AHEAP	THENS	HIKE	HOAS	HONK
GRAND	AGUES	GYVES	SHALL	HASH	CHEAP	HENTS	HIKED	HOAST	HONKS
GRANS	GUESS	HAAF	HALM	SHASH	HEAPS	HEPS	HIKER	HOAX	HONKY
GRANT	GUEST	HAAFS	SHALM	HASK	HEALS	SHENT	HIKES	HOBO	HONS
GRAT	GUFF	HAAR	HALMA	HASKS	HEAR	HEPT	HILA	HOBS	PHONS
GRATE	GUFFS	HAARS	HALMS	HASP	SHEAR	HERB	HILAR	HOBO	PHONS
GRAY	GUID	HACK	HALO	HASPS	HEARD	HERBS	HILD	HOBS	HOOD
GRAYS	GUIDE	CHACK	HALOS	HAST	HEARE	HERBY	CHILD	HOCK	HOODS
GREE	GULA	SHACK	HALT	GHAST	HEARS	HERD	CHILI	CHOCK	HOOF
AGREE	GULAR	THACK	SHALT	HASTA	HEART	SHERD	CHILI	SHOCK	HOOFS
GREED	GULAS	WHACK	HALTS	HASTE	HEAT	HERDS	HILL	HOCKS	HOOK
GREEN	GULE	HACKS	HAME	HASHY	HERE	HERE	CHILL	HODS	CHOOK
GREES	GULES	HADE	SHAME	HASTE	CHERE	CHILL	SHILL	HOED	SHOOK
GREET	GULES	SHADE	HAMED	HASTY	WHEAT	SHERE	THILL	HOER	HOOKA

HOOKS
HOOKY
HOOP
WHOOP
HOOPS
HOOT
SHOOT
WHOOT
HOOTS
HOPE
SHOPE
HOPED
HOPER
HOPES
HOPS
CHOPS
SHOPS
WHOPS
HORE
CHORE
SHORE
WHORE
HORN
SHORN
THORN
HORNS
HORNY
HORS
KHORS
HORSE
HORST
HORSY
HOSE
CHOSE
THOSE
WHOSE
HOSED
HOSEN
HOSES
HOSS
HOST
GHOST
HOSTA
HOSTS
HOTE
SHOTE
HOTEL
HOTEN
HOTS
PHOTS
SHOTS
HOUF
HOUFF
HOUFS
HOUR
HOURI
HOURS
HOUT
CHOUT
SHOUT
HOUTS
HOVE
SHOVE
HOVED
HOVEL
HOVEN
HOVER
HOVES
HOWE
HOWES

HOWF
HOWFF
HOWFS
HOWK
HOWKS
HOWL
THOWL
HOWLS
HOWS
CHOWS
DHOWS
SHOWS
HOWSO
HOYA
HOYAS
HOYS
HUBS
CHUBS
HUCK
CHUCK
SHUCK
HUCKS
HUED
HUER
HUERS
HUES
HUFF
CHUFF
HUFFS
HUFFY
HUGE
HUGER
HUGS
CHUGS
THUGS
HUGY
HUIA
HUIAS
HULA
HULAS
HULE
HULES
HULK
HULKS
HULKY
HULL
AHULL
HULLO
HULLS
HULLY
HUMA
HUMAN
HUMAS
HUMF
HUMFS
HUMP
CHUMP
THUMP
HUMPH
HUMPS
HUMPY
HUMS
CHUMS
HUNG
HUNK
CHUNK
HUNKS
HUNKY
HUNT
SHUNT

HUNTS
HUPS
HURL
CHURL
HURLS
HURLY
HURT
HURTS
HUSH
SHUSH
HUSHY
HUSK
HUSKS
HUSKY
HUSO
HUSOS
HUSS
HUSSY
HUTS
PHUTS
SHUTS
HWYL
HWYLS
HYED
HYEN
HYENA
HYENS
HYES
HYKE
HYKES
HYLE
CHYLE
PHYLE
HYLEG
HYLES
HYMN
HYMNS
HYPE
HYPED
HYPER
HYPES
HYPO
HYPOS
HYPS
IAMB
IAMBI
IAMBS
IBEX
VIBEX
IBIS
ICED
DICED
RICED
TICED
VICED
ICER
DICER
NICER
RICER
ICERS
ICES
BICES
DICES
RICES
SICES
TICES
VICES
ICKY
DICKY
MICKY

PICKY
TICKY
WICKY
ICON
ICONS
IDEA
IDEAL
IDEAS
IDEE
IDEES
IDEM
IDES
AIDES
BIDES
CIDES
HIDES
NIDES
RIDES
SIDES
TIDES
WIDES
IDLE
SIDLE
IDLED
IDLER
IDLES
IDLY
IDOL
IDOLS
IDYL
IDYLL
IDYLS
IFFY
JIFFY
MIFFY
NIFFY
IGAD
IKAT
IKATS
IKON
EIKON
IKONS
ILEA
PILEA
ILEAC
ILEX
SILEX
ILIA
CILIA
ILIAC
ILKA
ILKS
BILKS
MILKS
SILKS
ILLS
BILLS
CILLS
DILLS
FILLS
GILLS
HILLS
JILLS
KILLS
LILLS
MILLS
NILLS
PILLS
RILLS
SILLS

TILLS
VILLS
WILLS
YILLS
ILLY
BILLY
DILLY
FILLY
GILLY
HILLY
SILLY
TILLY
WILLY
IMAM
IMAMS
IMPI
IMPIS
IMPS
GIMPS
LIMPS
PIMPS
SIMPS
TIMPS
WIMPS
INBY
INBYE
INCH
CINCH
FINCH
LINCH
PINCH
WINCH
INFO
INFOS
INGO
BINGO
DINGO
JINGO
LINGO
PINGO
INGOT
INIA
INKS
BINKS
DINKS
FINKS
GINKS
JINKS
KINKS
LINKS
MINKS
PINKS
RINKS
SINKS
TINKS
WINKS
INKY
DINKY
KINKY
PINKY
SINKY
ZINKY
INLY
INNS
JINNS
LINNS
WINNS
INRO
INTO
PINTO

IONS
CIONS
LIONS
PIONS
IOTA
BIOTA
DIOTA
IOTAS
IRES
CIRES
FIRES
HIRES
MIRES
SIRES
TIRES
VIRES
WIRES
IRID
VIRID
IRIDS
IRIS
KIRIS
SIRIS
IRKS
BIRKS
DIRKS
FIRKS
KIRKS
LIRKS
MIRKS
YIRKS
IRON
GIRON
IRONS
IRONY
ISLE
AISLE
LISLE
ISLED
ISLES
ISLET
ISMS
GISMS
JISMS
ISMY
ITAS
DITAS
PITAS
ITCH
AITCH
BITCH
DITCH
FITCH
HITCH
MITCH
PITCH
TITCH
WITCH
ITCHY
ITEM
ITEMS
IWIS
KIWIS
IXIA
IXIAS
JABS
JACK
JACKS
JADE
JADED

JADES
JAGS
JAIL
JAILS
JAKE
JAKES
JAKS
JAMB
JAMBE
JAMBO
JAMBS
JAMBU
JAMS
JANE
JANES
JANN
JANNS
JAPE
JAPED
JAPES
JAPS
JARK
JARKS
JARL
JARLS
JARS
JASP
JASPE
JASPS
JASY
JATO
JATOS
JAUP
JAUPS
JAWS
JAYS
JAZY
JAZZ
JAZZY
JEAN
JEANS
JEAT
JEATS
JEED
JEEL
JEELS
JEELY
JEEP
JEEPS
JEER
JEERS
JEES
JEFF
JEFFS
JELL
JELLO
JELLS
JELLY
JERK
JERKS
JERKY
JESS
JEST
JESTS
JETE
JETES
JETS
JEUX
JIAO
JIAOS

JIBE
JIBED
JIBER
JIBES
JIBS
JIFF
JIFFS
JIFFY
JIGS
JILL
JILLS
JILT
JILTS
JIMP
JIMPY
JINK
JINKS
JINN
DJINN
JINNI
JINNS
JINX
JIRD
JIRDS
JISM
JISMS
JIVE
JIVED
JIVER
JIVES
JIZZ
JOBE
JOBED
JOBES
JOBS
JOCK
JOCKO
JOCKS
JOCO
JOES
JOEY
JOEYS
JOGS
JOHN
JOHNS
JOIN
JOINS
JOINT
JOKE
JOKED
JOKER
JOKES
JOKEY
JOKY
JOLE
JOLED
JOLES
JOLL
JOLLS
JOLLY
JOLT
JOLTS
JOLTY
JOMO
JOMOS
JOOK
JOOKS
JORS
JOSH
JOSS

JOTA
JOTAS
JOTS
JOUK
JOUKS
JOUR
JOURS
JOWL
JOWLS
JOWS
JOYS
JUBA
JUBAS
JUBE
JUBES
JUDO
JUDOS
JUDS
JUDY
JUGA
JUGAL
JUGS
JUJU
JUJUS
JUKE
JUKED
JUKES
JUMP
JUMPS
JUMPY
JUNK
JUNKS
JUNKY
JURA
JURAL
JURAT
JURE
JURY
JUST
JUSTS
JUTE
JUTES
JUTS
JYNX
KADE
KADES
KADI
KADIS
KAED
KAES
KAGO
KAGOS
KAID
KAIDS
KAIE
KAIES
KAIF
KAIFS
KAIL
SKAIL
KAILS
KAIM
KAIMS
KAIN
KAING
KAINS
KAIS
KAKA
KAKAS
KAKI

KAKIS
KALE
KALES
KALI
KALIF
KALIS
KAME
KAMES
KAMI
KAMIK
KAMIS
KANA
KANAS
KANG
KANGA
KANGS
KANS
KANT
KANTS
KAON
KAONS
KARA
KARAS
KARAT
KART
SKART
KARTS
KATI
KATIS
KATS
IKATS
SKATS
KAVA
KAVAS
KAWS
SKAWS
KAYO
KAYOE
KAYOS
KAYS
OKAYS
KAZI
KAZIS
KEAS
KEBS
KECK
KECKS
KEDS
KEEK
KEEKS
KEEL
KEELS
KEEN
KEENS
KEEP
KEEPS
KEFS
KEGS
SKEGS
KEIR
KEIRS
KELL
KELLS
KELLY
KELP
SKELP
KELPS
KELPY
KELT
KELTS

KELTY	EKING	KOAN	BLADE	FLAMS	PLAST	LEAKS	CLEGS	CLICK	LIMY
KEMB	KINGS	KOANS	CLADE	SLAMS	LASTS	LEAKY	FLEGS	FLICK	BLIMY
KEMBO	KINK	KOAS	GLADE	LANA	LATE	LEAL	LEHR	SLICK	SLIMY
KEMBS	SKINK	KOBS	SLADE	LANAS	ALATE	LEAM	LEHRS	LICKS	LIND
KEMP	KINKS	KOFF	LADED	LAND	BLATE	FLEAM	LEIR	LIDO	BLIND
KEMPS	KINKY	SKOFF	LADEN	ALAND	ELATE	GLEAM	LEIRS	LIDOS	LINDS
KEMPT	KINO	KOFFS	LADES	BLAND	PLATE	LEAMS	LEIS	LIDS	LINE
KENS	KINOS	KOHL	LADS	ELAND	SLATE	LEAN	GLEIS	LIED	ALINE
KENT	KINS	KOHLS	BLADS	GLAND	LATED	LEANS	VLEIS	CLIED	CLINE
KENTS	SKINS	KOLA	CLADS	LANDE	LATEN	GLEAN	LEISH	PLIED	LINED
KEPI	KIPE	KOLAS	GLADS	LANDS	LATER	LEANT	LEKE	LIEF	LINEN
KEPIS	KIPES	KOLO	LADY	LANE	LATEX	LEANY	LEKS	LIEFS	LINER
KEPS	KIPP	KOLOS	GLADY	PLANE	LATH	LEAP	LEME	LIEN	LINES
SKEPS	KIPPS	KOND	LAER	SLANE	LATHE	FLEME	LEMED	LIENS	LINEY
KEPT	KIPS	KONK	BLAER	LANES	LATHI	LEAPS	LEMEL	LIER	LING
KERB	SKIPS	KONKS	LAERS	LANG	LATHS	LEAPT	LEMES	FLIER	CLING
KERBS	KIRI	KONS	LAGS	ALANG	LATHY	LEAR	LEND	PLIER	FLING
KERF	KIRIS	IKONS	BLAGS	CLANG	LATS	BLEAR	LENDS	SLIER	SLING
KERFS	KIRK	KOOK	CLAGS	KLANG	BLATS	CLEAR	BLEND	LIERS	LINGA
KERN	KIRKS	KOOKS	FLAGS	SLANG	CLATS	LEARE	LENDS	CLIES	LINGO
KERNE	KIRN	KOOKY	SLAGS	LANK	FLATS	LEARN	LENG	LIES	LINGS
KERNS	KIRNS	KOPS	LAHS	LANKS	PLATS	LEARS	LENGS	FLIES	LINGY
KESH	KIRS	KORA	BLAHS	LANKY	SLATS	LEARY	LENO	PLIES	LINK
KEST	KISH	KORAS	LAIC	BLANK	LAUD	LEAS	LENOS	VLIES	BLINK
KESTS	KISS	KOSS	LAICS	PLANK	BLAUD	PLEAS	LENS	LIEU	CLINK
KETA	KIST	KOTO	LAID	SLAID	LAUDS	LEASE	GLENS	LIEUS	PLINK
KETAS	KISTS	KOTOS	PLAID	LANT	LAUF	LEASH	GLENT	LIFE	SLINK
KETS	KITE	KOTOW	SLAID	LANTS	LAUFS	LEAST	LENT	LIFER	LINN
KEYS	SKITE	KOWS	LAIDS	PLANT	LAVA	LEAT	OLENT	LIFT	LINNS
KHAN	KITED	KRIS	LAIK	SLANT	LAVAS	BLEAT	LENTI	CLIFT	LINNY
KHANS	KITES	KSAR	LAIKS	LANX	LAVE	CLEAT	LENTO	GLIFT	LINO
KHAT	KITH	KSARS	LAIKA	LAPS	CLAVE	PLEAT	LEPS	LIFTS	LINOS
KHATS	KITHE	KUDU	LAIN	ALAPS	SLAVE	LEATS	LERE	LIGS	LINS
KHOR	KITHS	KUDUS	ALAPS	CLAPS	LAVED	LECH	LERED	LIKE	BLINS
KHORS	KITS	KUKU	BLAIN	FLAPS	LAVER	LEED	LERES	ALIKE	LINT
KHUD	SKITS	KUKUS	PLAIN	PLAPS	LAVES	BLEED	LESS	GLIKE	CLINT
KHUDS	KIWI	KYAT	SLAIN	SLAPS	LAVS	GLEED	LEST	YLIKE	FLINT
KIBE	KIWIS	KYATS	LAIR	LAWK	LAWK	LEEK	LESTS	LIKED	GLINT
KIBES	KNAG	KYLE	FLAIR	LAWKS	LAWN	CLEEK	BLEST	LIKEN	LINTS
KICK	KNAGS	KYLES	GLAIR	LARD	FLAWN	GLEEK	BLEST	LIKER	LINTY
KICKS	KNAP	KYLEY	LAIRD	LARDS	LAWNS	SLEEK	LESTS	LIKES	LINY
KIDS	KNAPS	KYND	LAIRS	LARDY	LAWNY	LEEP	LETS	LILL	LION
SKIDS	KNAR	KYNDE	LAIRY	LARE	LAWS	BLEEP	LEVA	LILLS	LIONS
KIER	KNARL	KYNDS	LAKE	BLARE	CLAWS	CLEEP	LEVE	LILO	LIPS
SKIER	KNARS	KYNE	FLAKE	FLARE	FLAWS	SLEEP	LEVEE	LILOS	BLIPS
KIERS	KNEE	KYTE	SLAKE	GLARE	SLAWS	LEEPS	CLEVE	LILT	CLIPS
KIFS	KNEED	SKYTE	LAKED	LARES	LAYS	LEER	LEVEL	LILTS	FLIPS
KIKE	KNEEL	KYTES	LAKER	LARK	LAYS	LEES	LEVER	LILY	SLIPS
KIKES	KNEES	LABS	LAKES	LARKS	ALAYS	LEES	LEVEE	LILY	LIRA
KILD	KNEW	BLABS	LAKH	LARN	BLAYS	LEESE	LEWD	SLILY	LIRAS
KILL	KNIT	FLABS	LAKHS	LARNS	CLAYS	LEET	LEYS	LIMA	LIRE
SKILL	KNITS	SLABS	LAKY	LASE	FLAYS	FLEET	BLEYS	LIMAS	LIRK
KILLS	KNOB	LACE	LAMA	BLASE	PLAYS	GLEET	FLEYS	LIMAX	LIRKS
KILN	KNOBS	GLACE	LAMAS	LASED	SLAYS	SLEET	GLEYS	LIMB	LISK
KILNS	KNOP	PLACE	LLAMA	LASER	BLAZE	LEETS	SLEYS	CLIMB	FLISK
KILO	KNOPS	LACED	LAMAS	LASES	GLAZE	FLEES	LEZZ	LIMBO	GLISK
KILOS	KNOT	LACES	LAMB	LASH	GLAZE	GLEES	LEZZY	LIMBS	LISKS
KILP	KNOTS	LACET	LAMBS	LASH	LAZED	LEESE	LIME	LIME	LISP
KILPS	KNOW	LACEY	LAME	BLASH	LAZES	LEET	LIAR	CLIME	LISPS
KILT	KNOWE	LACK	BLAME	CLASH	LAZY	FLEET	LIARD	SLIME	LIST
KILTS	KNOWN	ALACK	CLAME	FLASH	GLAZY	GLEET	LIARS	LIMED	BLIST
KILTY	KNOWS	BLACK	FLAME	PLASH	LEAD	SLEET	LIART	LIMEN	LISTS
KINA	KNUB	CLACK	LAMED	SLASH	PLEAD	LEADS	ALEFT	LICE	LITE
KINAS	KNUBS	FLACK	LAMER	LASS	LEADS	CLEFT	LICH	LIMEY	BLITE
KIND	KNUR	PLACK	LAMES	CLASS	LEADY	ALEFT	SLICE	LIMN	ELITE
KINDA	KNURL	SLACK	LAMP	GLASS	LEAF	LEFTE	LICH	LIMNS	FLITE
KINDS	KNURR	LACKS	LAMPS	LASSO	LEAFS	LEFTS	LICHI	LIMP	LITED
KINE	KNURS	SLACK	LAMS	LASSU	LEAFY	LEFTY	LICHT	FLIMP	-LITED
KING	KNUT	LACS	LAMS	LAST	LEAK	LEGS	LICK	LIMPS	LITER
AKING	KNUTS	LADE	CLAMS	BLAST	BLEAK	LEGS	LICK	LIMPS	LITES

LITH	LOKE	LOREL	LOWER	PLUMS	MACKS	MARD	MAYST	MERES	MILOR
LITHE	BLOKE	LORES	LOWES	SLUMS	MACS	MARDY	MAZE	MERI	MILOS
LITHO	CLOKE	LORN	LOWN	LUNE	MADE	MARE	AMAZE	MERIL	MILS
LITHS	LOKES	LORY	BLOWN	LUNES	MADS	MARES	MAZED	MERIS	MILT
LIVE	LOLL	FLORY	CLOWN	LUNG	MAGE	MARG	MAZER	MERIT	MILTS
ALIVE	LOLLS	GLORY	FLOWN	CLUNG	IMAGE	MARGE	MAZES	MERK	MILTZ
BLIVE	LOLLY	LOSE	LOWND	FLUNG	MAGES	MARGS	MAZY	MERKS	MIME
OLIVE	LOMA	CLOSE	LOWNE	SLUNG	MAGG	MARK	MEAD	MERL	MIMED
SLIVE	LOMAS	LOSED	LOWNS	LUNGE	MAGGS	MARKS	MEADS	MERLE	MIMER
LIVED	LOME	LOSEL	LOWS	LUNGI	MAGI	MARL	MEAL	MERLS	MIMES
LIVEN	LOMES	LOSEN	BLOWS	LUNGS	MAGIC	MARLE	MEALS	MESA	MINA
LIVER	LONE	LOSER	CLOWS	LUNT	MAGS	MARLS	MEALY	MESAL	MINAE
LIVES	ALONE	LOSES	FLOWS	LUNTS	MAID	MARLY	MEAN	MESAS	MINAR
LOAD	CLONE	LOSH	GLOWS	LURE	MAIDS	MARM	MEANE	MESE	MINAS
LOADS	LONER	FLOSH	PLOWS	LURES	MAIK	SMARM	MEANS	MESEL	MIND
LOAF	LONG	FLOSS	SLOWS	LURED	SMAIK	MARMS	MEANT	MESES	MINDS
LOAFS	ALONG	SLOSH	LOWSE	LURES	MAIKO	MARS	MEANY	MESH	MINE
LOAM	FLONG	FLOSS	LOWT	LURK	MAIKS	MARSH	MEAT	MESHY	AMINE
CLOAM	PLONG	GLOSS	LOWTS	LURKS	MAIL	SMART	MEATH	MESS	IMINE
LOAMS	LONGA	LOSSY	LOYS	LURS	MAILE	MART	MEATS	MESSY	MINED
LOAMY	LONGE	LOST	CLOYS	LURS	MAILS	MARTS	MEATY	METE	MINER
LOAN	LONGS	LOTA	PLOYS	BLURS	MAIM	MASE	MEED	METED	MINES
SLOAN	LOOF	FLOTA	LUAU	SLURS	MAIMS	MASED	MEEDS	METER	MING
LOANS	ALOOF	LOTAH	LUAUS	LUSH	MAIN	MASER	MEEK	METES	MINGS
LOBE	KLOOF	LOTAS	LUCE	BLUSH	MAINS	MASES	SMEEK	MEUS	MINGY
GLOBE	LOOFA	LOTE	LUCES	FLUSH	MAKE	SMASH	MEER	EMEUS	MINI
LOBED	LOOFS	CLOTE	LUCK	PLUSH	MAKER	AMEER	EMEER	MEVE	MINIM
LOBES	LOOK	FLOTE	CLUCK	SLUSH	MAKES	MASHY	MEERS	MEVED	MINIS
LOBI	PLOOK	LOTES	PLUCK	LUSHY	MAKES	MASK	MEET	MEVES	MINK
LOBO	LOOKS	LOTH	LUCKS	LUSK	MAKO	MASKS	MEETS	MEWL	MINKE
LOBOS	LOOM	CLOTH	LUCKY	LUSKS	MAKOS	MASS	MEIN	MEWLS	MINKS
LOBS	BLOOM	SLOTH	LUDO	LUST	MAKS	AMASS	MEINS	SMEWS	MINO
BLOBS	GLOOM	LOTO	LUDOS	LUSTS	MALE	MASSA	MEINT	MEZE	MINOR
GLOBS	SLOOM	LOTOS	LUDS	LUSTY	MALES	MASSE	MEINY	MEZES	MINOS
SLOBS	LOOMS	LOTS	LUES	LUTE	MALI	MASSY	MAST	MHOS	MINT
LOCH	LOON	BLOTS	LUES	ELUTE	MALIC	MAST	MELD	MICA	MINTS
LOCHS	LOONS	CLOTS	CLUES	FLUTE	MALIS	MASTS	MELDS	MICAS	MINTY
LOCI	LOONY	PLOTS	FLUES	LUTED	MALL	MASTY	MELL	MICE	MINX
LOCK	LOOP	SLOTS	GLUES	LUTER	SMALL	MASU	MELLS	AMICE	MINY
BLOCK	BLOOP	SLOTS	SLUES	LUTES	MALLS	MASUS	SMELL	MICE	MIRE
CLOCK	SLOOP	ALOUD	LUFF	KLUTZ	MALM	MATE	MELS	MICK	MIRED
FLOCK	CLOUD	CLOUD	BLUFF	LUTZ	SMALM	AMATE	MELT	MICKS	MIRES
LOCKS	LOOPS	LOUN	FLUFF	LUXE	MALS	MATED	SMELT	MICKY	MIRK
LOCO	LOOPY	LOUND	PLUFF	LUXES	MALT	MATER	MELTS	MICO	MIRKS
LOCOS	LOOR	LOUP	LUFFA	LYAM	SMALT	MATES	MEMO	MICOS	MIRKY
LODE	FLOOR	LOUPE	LUFFS	LYAMS	MALTS	MATEY	MEMOS	MIDI	MIRS
GLODE	LOORD	LOUPS	LUGE	LYES	MALTY	MATH	MEND	MIDIS	AMIRS
LODEN	LOOS	LOUR	LUGED	LYME	MAUD	AMEND	MIDS	MIDS	EMIRS
LODES	LOOSE	LOURE	LUGES	LYMES	MAUDS	MENES	EMEND	MIDST	SMIRS
LOFT	LOOT	CLOUR	LUGS	LYMS	MAUL	MATTE	MENDS	MIEN	MIRY
ALOFT	CLOOT	FLOUR	GLUGS	LYNE	MAULS	MATY	AMENE	MIENS	MISE
LOFTS	SLOOT	LOURE	PLUGS	LYNES	MAUN	MAUD	MENED	MIFF	MISER
LOFTY	LOOTS	LOURS	SLUGS	LYNX	MAUND	MAUDS	MENES	MIFFS	MISES
LOGE	LOPE	LOURY	LUIT	LYRE	MAWK	MAUL	MENG	MIFFY	MISO
ELOGE	ELOPE	LOUT	SLUIT	LYRES	MAWKS	MAULS	MENGE	MIKE	MISOS
LOGES	SLOPE	CLOUT	LUKE	LYSE	MAWKY	MAUN	MENGS	MIKES	MISS
LOGO	LOPED	FLOUT	FLUKE	LYSED	MAWR	MAUND	MENT	MILD	AMISS
LOGOS	LOPER	GLOUT	LULL	LYSES	MAWRS	AMENT	MENU	MILDS	MISSA
LOGS	LOPES	LOUTS	LULLS	LYTE	MAWS	MAWKS	MENUS	MILE	MISSY
CLOGS	LOPS	LOVE	LULU	FLYTE	MAXI	MAWKY	SMILE	MILER	MIST
FLOGS	CLOPS	CLOVE	LULUS	LYTED	MAXIM	MAWR	MEOW	MILES	MISTS
SLOGS	ELOPS	GLOVE	LUMP	LYTES	MAXIS	MAWRS	MEOWS	MILK	MISTY
LOID	FLOPS	SLOVE	CLUMP	MAAR	MARA	MAWS	MERC	MILKS	MITE
SLOID	PLOPS	LOVED	FLUMP	MAARS	MARAH	MAXI	MERCS	MILKY	SMITE
LOIDS	SLOPS	LOVER	PLUMP	MACE	MARAS	MAXIM	MERCY	MILL	MITER
LOIN	LORD	LOVEY	SLUMP	MACED	MARC	MAXIS	MERE	MILLE	MITES
ELOIN	LORDS	LOWE	LUMPS	MACER	MARCH	MAYA	MERED	MILLS	MITT
LOINS	LORDY	ALOWE	LUMPY	MACES	MARCS	MAYAS	MEREL	MILO	MITTS
LOIR	LORE	LOWED	LUMS	MACK	MARA	MAYS	MERER	MILO	MITY
LOIRS	BLORE	LOWED	ALUMS	SMACK	MARCS	MAYS	MERER	MILO	MITY

AMITY	MOODY	MOTTY	MURKS	NANA	NEONS	KNITS	NOTT	ROARS	ODYLE
MIXT	MOOI	MOUE	MURKY	ANANA	NEPS	UNITS	NOUL	SOARS	ODYLS
MIXY	MOOL	MOUES	MURL	NANAS	NERD	NIXY	NOULD	VOARS	OFAY
MIZZ	MOOLA	MOUP	MURLS	NANS	NERDS	NOBS	NOULE	OARY	OFAYS
MNAS	MOOLI	MOUPS	MURLY	NAOI	NESH	KNOBS	NOULS	GOARY	OFFS
MOAN	MOOLS	MOUS	MUSE	NAOS	NESS	SNOBS	NOUN	HOARY	BOFFS
MOANS	MOOLY	SMOUS	AMUSE	NAPA	NEST	NOCK	NOUNS	ROARY	COFFS
MOAS	MOON	MOUSE	MUSED	NAPAS	NESTS	KNOCK	NOUNY	OAST	DOFFS
MOAT	MOONS	MOUST	MUSER	NAPE	NETE	NOCKS	NOUP	BOAST	GOFFS
MOATS	MOONY	MOUSY	MUSES	NAPES	NETES	NODE	NOUPS	COAST	KOFFS
MOBS	MOOP	MOVE	MUSET	NAPS	NETS	ANODE	NOUS	HOAST	TOFFS
MOCK	MOOPS	AMOVE	MUSH	KNAPS	NETT	NODES	NOUT	LOAST	OGAM
SMOCK	MOOR	EMOVE	MUSHA	SNAPS	NETTS	KNOUT	NOVA	ROAST	OGAMS
MOCKS	SMOOR	MOVED	MUSHY	NARD	NETTY	NODI	NOVAE	TOAST	OGEE
MODE	MOORS	MOVER	MUSK	NARDS	NEUK	NODS	NOVAS	OASTS	OGEES
MODEL	MOORY	MOVES	MUSKS	NARE	NEUKS	SNODS	NOWL	OATH	OGLE
MODEM	MOOS	MOVY	MUSKY	NARES	NEUM	NOEL	NOWLS	LOATH	BOGLE
MODES	MOOSE	MOWA	MUSS	NARK	NEUME	NOELS	NOWN	OATHS	FOGLE
MODI	MOOT	MOWAS	MUSSE	NARKS	NEUMS	NOES	NOWS	OATS	OGLED
MODII	SMOOT	MOWN	MUSSY	NARKY	NEVE	NOGS	NOWT	BOATS	OGLER
MODS	MOOTS	MOWS	MUST	NARY	NEVEL	SNOGS	NOWTS	COATS	OGLES
MOES	MOPE	MOXA	MUSTH	SNARE	NEVER	NOIL	NOWY	DOATS	OGRE
MOGS	MOPED	MOXAS	MUSTS	SNARK	NEVES	NOILS	NOYS	GOATS	OGRES
SMOGS	MOPER	MOYA	MUSTY	SNARY	NEWS	NOLE	NUBS	MOATS	OHMS
MOHR	MOPES	MOYAS	MUTE	NATS	NEWSY	NOLES	KNUBS	OBEY	COHOS
MOHRS	MOPS	MOYL	MUTED	GNATS	NEWT	NOLL	SNUBS	OBEYS	OHOS
MOIL	MOPSY	MOYLE	MUTER	NAVE	NEWTS	NOLLS	NUDE	OBIA	TOHOS
MOILS	MOPY	MOYLS	MUTES	NAVEL	NIBS	NOMA	NUDER	OBIAS	OIKS
MOIT	MORA	MOYS	MUTT	NAVES	NICE	NOMAD	NUDES	OBIS	HOIKS
MOITS	MORAL	MOZE	MUTTS	NAVEW	NICER	NOMAS	NUKE	OBIT	OILS
MOKE	MORAS	MOZED	MYAL	NAVY	NICK	NOME	NUKED	OOBIT	BOILS
SMOKE	MORAT	MOZES	MYALL	NAYS	NICKS	NOMEN	NUKES	OBITS	COILS
MOKES	MORAY	MOZZ	MYNA	NAZE	NIDE	NOMES	NULL	OBOE	FOILS
MOKI	MORE	MUCH	MYNAH	NAZES	NIDES	NOMS	NULLA	OBOES	MOILS
MOKIS	SMORE	MUCK	MYNAS	NEAL	NIDI	NONA	NULLS	OBOL	NOILS
MOKO	MOREL	AMUCK	MYTH	NEALS	NIDS	NONAS	NUMB	OBOLI	ROILS
SMOKO	MORES	MUCKS	MYTHS	NEAP	NIED	NONE	NUMBS	OBOLS	SOILS
MOKOS	MORN	MUCKY	NAAM	NEAPS	NIEF	NONES	NUNS	OCAS	TOILS
MOLD	MORNE	MUDS	NAAN	NEAR	NIEFS	NONET	NURD	COCAS	OILY
MOLDS	MORNS	MUFF	NAANS	NEARS	NIES	NONG	NURDS	OCHE	DOILY
MOLE	MORS	MUFFS	NABK	ANEAR	NIFE	NONGS	NURL	BOCHE	ROILY
MOLES	MORSE	MUGS	NABKS	NEAT	NIFES	NOOK	NURLS	OCHER	SOILY
MOLL	MORT	SMUGS	NABS	NEATH	NIFF	NOOKS	NURR	OCHES	OINT
MOLLA	AMORT	MUID	SNABS	NEBS	NIFFS	NOOKY	NURRS	ODAL	JOINT
MOLLS	MORTS	MUIDS	NACH	NECK	NIFFY	NOON	NURS	MODAL	NOINT
MOLLY	MOSE	MUIL	NACHE	NECKS	NIGH	NOONS	NURSE	NODAL	POINT
MOLT	MOSED	MUILS	NADA	NEDS	NIGHS	NOOP	NUTS	PODAL	OINTS
SMOLT	MOSES	MUIR	NADAS	NEED	NIGHT	NOOPS	NYAS	ODALS	OKAY
YMOLT	MOSEY	MUIRS	NAFF	KNEED	NILL	NOPE	NYED	ODAS	OKAYS
MOLTO	MOSS	MULE	NAFFS	SNEED	NILLS	NORI	NYES	CODAS	OKES
MOLTS	MOSSY	MULES	NAGA	NEEDS	NILS	NORIA	OAFS	SODAS	BOKES
MOLY	MOST	MULEY	NAGAS	NEEDY	NIMS	NORIS	GOAFS	ODDS	COKES
MOME	MOSTS	MULL	NAGS	NEEM	NINE	NORK	OAKS	ODEA	HOKES
MOMES	MOTE	MULLS	KNAGS	NEEMS	NINES	NORKS	BOAKS	ODES	JOKES
MOMS	MOTED	MUMM	SNAGS	NEEP	NIPS	NORM	SOAKS	BODES	LOKES
MONA	MOTEL	MUMMS	NAIF	NEEPS	NIRL	NORMA	OAKY	CODES	MOKES
MONAD	MOTEN	MUMMY	NAIK	NEFS	NIRLS	NORMS	OARS	LODES	POKES
MONAL	MOTES	MUMP	NAIKS	NEIF	NIRLY	NOSE	BOARS	MODES	ROKES
MONAS	MOTET	MUMPS	NAIL	NEIFS	NISI	NOSED	HOARS	NODES	SOKES
MONG	MOTEY	MUMS	NAILS	NEKS	NITS	NOSER		RODES	TOKES
AMONG	MOTH	MUMSY	NAIN	NEMN		NOSES		ODIC	YOKES
EMONG	MOTHS	MUON	NALA	NEMNS		NOSEY		IODIC	OKRA
MONGS	MOTHY	MUONS	NALAS	NENE		NOSH		SODIC	KOKRA
MONK	MOTS	MURE	NAME	NENES		NOSY		ODOR	OKRAS
MONKS	MOTT	MURED	NAMED	NEON		NOTE		ODORS	OLDS
MONO	MOTTE	MURES	NAMER			NOTED		GODSO	COLDS
MONOS	MOTTO	MUREX	NAMES			NOTER		ODSO	FOLDS
MONY	MOTTS	MURK	NAMS			NOTES		ODYL	GOLDS
MOOD									HOLDS
MOODS									MOLDS

SOLDS	GOOFS	MOPED	SORTS	OUZO	OWRES	PALET	PART	PEARE	PENKS
WOLDS	HOOFS	OOPED	TORTS	OUZOS	OWTS	PALL	APART	PEARL	PENS
OLDY	LOOFS	ROPED	WORTS	OVAL	DOWTS	SPALL	SPART	PEARS	OPENS
GOLDY	POOFS	TOPED	ORYX	OVALS	LOWTS	PALLA	PARTI	PEART	PENT
OLEO	ROOFS	OPEN	OSSA	OVEN	NOWTS	PALLS	PARTS	PEAS	SPENT
OLEOS	WOOFS	OPENS	FOSSA	COVEN	ROWTS	PALLY	PARTY	PEASE	PENTS
OLID	OOHS	OPES	OTIC	HOVEN	TOWTS	PALM	PASH	PEAT	PEON
SOLID	BOOHS	COPES	LOTIC	WOVEN	OXEN	PALMS	PASHA	SPEAT	PEONS
OLIO	OOMS	DOPES	OTTO	OVENS	WOXEN	PALMY	PASHM	PEATS	PEONY
FOLIO	BOOMS	HOPES	LOTTO	OVER	BOXEN	PALP	PASS	PEATY	PEPO
POLIO	COOMS	LOPES	MOTTO	COVER	OXER	PALPI	PASSE	PEBA	PEPOS
OLIOS	DOOMS	MOPES	POTTO	DOVER	BOXER	PALPS	PAST	PEBAS	PEPS
OLLA	LOOMS	POPES	OTTOS	HOVER	OXERS	PALS	PASTA	PECH	PERE
HOLLA	ROOMS	ROPES	OUCH	LOVER	OPALS	PALSY	PASTE	PECHS	PERES
MOLLA	SOOMS	TOPES	COUCH	MOVER	OYER	PALY	PASTS	PECK	PERI
OLLAS	TOOMS	OPTS	MOUCH	ROVER	COYER	PAMS	PASTY	SPECK	PERIL
OLLAV	ZOOMS	OPUS	POUCH	OVERS	FOYER	PAND	PATE	PECKE	PERIS
OLMS	OONS	MOPUS	TOUCH	OVERT	TOYER	PANDA	SPATE	PECKS	PERK
HOLMS	BOONS	ORAL	VOUCH	OVUM	OYERS	PANDS	PATED	PECS	PERKS
OLPE	COONS	CORAL	OUCHT	NOVUM	OYES	PANDY	PATEN	SPECS	PERKY
GOLPE	GOONS	GORAL	OUKS	OWED	OYEZ	PANE	PATER	PEDS	PERM
OLPES	LOONS	HORAL	BOUKS	BOWED	NOYES	SPANE	PATES	PEED	SPERM
OMBU	MOONS	LORAL	GOUKS	COWED	PACA	PANED	PATH	SPEED	PERMS
OMBUS	NOONS	MORAL	JOUKS	DOWED	PACAS	PANEL	PATHS	PEEK	PERN
OMEN	POONS	PORAL	POUKS	JOWED	PACE	PANES	PATIN	APEEK	PERNS
NOMEN	ROONS	RORAL	SOUKS	LOWED	APACE	PANG	PATINS	PEEKS	PERT
WOMEN	TOONS	SORAL	TOUKS	MOWED	SPACE	SPANG	PATS	PEEL	APERT
OMENS	WOONS	ORALS	YOUKS	NOWED	PACED	PANGA	SPATS	SPEEL	PERTS
OMER	ZOONS	ORBS	OULK	ROWED	PACER	PANGS	PATSY	PEELS	PERV
COMER	OONT	SORBS	OULKS	SOWED	PACES	PANS	PAUA	PEEN	PERVE
HOMER	OONTS	ORBY	OUPH	TOWED	PACEY	SPANS	PAUAS	PEENS	PERVS
VOMER	OOPS	FORBY	OUPHE	VOWED	PACK	PANSY	PAUL	PEEP	PESO
OMERS	COOPS	ORCS	OUPHS	WOWED	PACKS	PANT	SPAUL	PEEPE	PESOS
OMIT	GOOPS	TORCS	OUPS	OWER	PACO	PANTO	PAULS	PEEPS	PEST
VOMIT	HOOPS	ORDS	COUPS	BOWER	PACOS	PANTS	PAVE	PEER	PESTO
OMITS	LOOPS	BORDS	DOUPS	COWER	PACT	PAPA	PAVED	SPEER	PESTS
ONCE	MOOPS	CORDS	LOUPS	DOWER	EPACT	PAPAL	PAVEN	PEERS	PETS
BONCE	NOOPS	FORDS	MOUPS	LOWER	PACTA	PAPAS	PAVER	PEERY	SPETS
NONCE	POOPS	LORDS	NOUPS	MOWER	PACTS	PAPAW	PAVES	PEES	PEWS
PONCE	ROOPS	SORDS	ROUPS	POWER	PACY	PAPE	PAWA	EPEES	SPEWS
SONCE	SOOPS	WORDS	SOUPS	ROWER	SPACY	PAPER	PAWAS	PEGH	PHEW
ONCER	WOOPS	ORES	OURN	SOWER	PADS	PAPES	PAWAW	PEGHS	PHIS
ONCES	YOOPS	BORES	BOURN	TOWER	PAGE	PAPS	PAWK	PEGS	APHIS
ONER	OOSE	CORES	MOURN	OWES	APAGE	PARA	PAWKS	PEIN	PHIZ
BONER	BOOSE	FORES	YOURN	BOWES	PAGED	PARAS	PAWKY	PEINS	PHOH
GONER	GOOSE	GORES	OURS	HOWES	PAGER	PARD	PAWL	PEKE	PHON
LONER	LOOSE	LORES	COURS	LOWES	PAGES	PARDI	PAWLS	PEKES	PHONE
MONER	MOOSE	MORES	FOURS	YOWES	PAHS	PARDIE	PAWN	PELA	PHONS
ONERS	NOOSE	PORES	HOURS	OWLS	OPAHS	PARDS	SPAWN	PELAS	PHONY
ONES	ROOSE	RORES	JOURS	BOWLS	PAID	PARDY	PAWNS	PELE	PHOS
BONES	OOSES	SORES	LOURS	COWLS	APAID	PARE	PAWS	PELES	PHOT
CONES	OOSY	TORES	POURS	DOWLS	PAIK	SPARE	PAYS	PELF	PHOTO
HONES	GOOSY	YORES	SOURS	FOWLS	PAIKS	PARED	APAYS	PELFS	PHOTS
NONES	OOZE	ORFE	TOURS	GOWLS	PAIL	PAREO	SPAYS	PELL	PHUT
PONES	OOZED	ORFES	YOURS	HOWLS	PAILS	PAREOS	PAYSD	SPELL	PHUTS
RONES	OOZES	ORFS	OUST	JOWLS	PAIN	PARER	PEAG	PELLS	PIAS
SONES	OOZY	ORGY	JOUST	NOWLS	SPAIN	PARES	PEAGS	PELT	PICA
TONES	BOOZY	PORGY	MOUST	SOWLS	PAINS	PAREU	PEAK	SPELT	PICAS
ZONES	WOOZY	ORLE	ROUST	YOWLS	PAINT	PARK	APEAK	PELTA	PICE
ONLY	OPAH	ORLES	OUSTS	OWLY	PAIR	SPARK	SPEAK	PELTS	SPICA
FONLY	OPAHS	ORRA	OUTS	LOWLY	PAIRS	PARKA	PEAKS	PEND	SPICE
ONST	OPAL	MORRA	BOUTS	OWNS	PAIS	PARKI	PEAKY	SPEND	PICK
ONTO	COPAL	SORRA	DOUTS	DOWNS	PAISA	PARKS	PEAL	PENDS	SPICK
CONTO	NOPAL	ORTS	GOUTS	GOWNS	PAISE	PARKY	SPEAL	PENE	PICKS
ONUS	OPALS	BORTS	HOUTS	LOWNS	PALE	PARR	PEALS	PENED	PICKY
BONUS	OPED	DORTS	LOUTS	POWNS	SPALE	PARRS	PEAN	PENES	PICS
TONUS	COPED	FORTS	POUTS	TOWNS	PALEA	PARRY	SPEAN	PENI	EPICS
ONYX	DOPED	MORTS	ROUTS	OWRE	PALED	PARS	PEANS	PENIE	SPICS
OOFS	HOPED	PORTS	SOUTS	HOWRE	PALER	SPARS	PEAR	PENIS	PIED
COOFS	LOPED	RORTS	TOUTS	POWRE	PALES	PARSE	SPEAR	PENK	SPIED

PIER	PIPE	PLOW	POODS	POUKE	PROS	PUPAE	QUIMS	RAGG	GRAND
PIERS	PIPED	PLOWS	POOF	POUKS	PROSE	PUPAL	QUIN	RAGGS	RANDS
PIERT	PIPER	PLOY	SPOOF	POUR	PROSY	PUPAS	QUINA	RAGGY	RANDY
PIES	PIPES	PLOYS	POOFS	POURS	PROW	PUPS	QUINE	RAGI	RANG
SPIES	PIPI	PLUG	POOFY	POUT	PROWL	PURE	QUINS	TRAGI	KRANG
PIET	PIPIS	PLUGS	POOH	SPOUT	PROWS	PURED	QUINT	RAGIS	ORANG
PIETA	PIPIT	PLUM	POOK	POUTS	PRUH	PUREE	QUIP	RAGS	PRANG
PIETS	PIPS	PLUMB	SPOOK	POUTY	PRYS	PURER	EQUIP	BRAGS	RANGE
PIETY	PIPY	PLUME	POOKA	POWN	PRYSE	PURES	QUIPO	CRAGS	RANGY
PIGS	PIRL	PLUMP	POOKS	POWND	PSIS	PURI	QUIPS	DRAGS	RANI
PIKA	PIRLS	PLUMS	POOL	POWNS	APSIS	PURIM	QUIPU	RAHS	RANIS
PIKAS	PIRN	PLUMY	SPOOL	POWNY	PSST	PURIN	QUIT	RAID	RANK
PIKE	PIRNS	PLUS	POOLS	POWS	PUBS	PURIS	SQUIT	RAIDS	BRANK
SPIKE	PIRS	PLUSH	POON	POXY	PUCE	PURL	QUITE	RAIK	CRANK
PIKED	PISE	POAS	SPOON	EPOXY	PUCES	PURLS	QUITS	RAIKS	DRANK
PIKER	PISES	POCK	SPOOR	POZZ	PUCK	PURR	QUIZ	TRAIK	FRANK
PIKES	PISH	POCKS	POONS	POZZY	PUCKA	PURRS	QUOD	RAIL	PRANK
PILA	APISH	POCKY	POONS	PRAD	PUCKS	PURS	QUODS	BRAIL	RANKE
PILAU	PISS	POCO	POO	SPRAD	PUDS	PURSE	QUOP	DRAIL	RANKS
PILAW	PITA	PODS	APOOP	PRAM	PUDSY	PURSY	QUOPS	FRAIL	RANT
PILE	PITAS	APODS	POOS	PRAMS	PUER	PUSH	RABI	GRAIL	DRANT
SPILE	PITH	POEM	POOT	PRAT	PUERS	PUSHY	RABIC	TRAIL	GRANT
PILEA	PITHS	POEMS	POOTS	SPRAT	PUFF	PUSS	RABID	RAILE	ORANT
PILED	PITHY	POET	POOP	PRATE	PUFFS	PUSSY	RABIS	RAILS	TRANT
PILEI	PITS	POETS	POOPS	PRATS	PUFFY	PUTS	RACA	RAIN	RANTS
PILER	SPITS	POIS	POOR	PRATY	PUGH	PUTT	RACE	BRAIN	RAPE
PILES	PITY	POISE	POORT	PRAU	PUGS	PUTTI	BRACE	DRAIN	CRAPE
PILI	PIUM	POKE	POPE	PRAUS	PUIR	PUTTO	GRACE	GRAIN	DRAPE
PILIS	OPIUM	SPOKE	POPES	PRAY	PUJA	PUTTS	TRACE	TRAIN	GRAPE
PILL	PIUMS	POKED	POPS	SPRAY	PUJAS	PUTTY	RACED	RAINE	TRAPE
SPILL	PIXY	POKER	POPSY	PRAYS	PUKE	PUTZ	RACER	RAINS	RAPED
PILLS	PIZE	POKES	PORE	PREE	PUKED	PUYS	RACES	RAINY	RAPER
PIMP	PIZES	POKY	PORED	SPREE	PUKER	PYA	BRACES	RAIT	RAPES
PIMPS	PLAN	POLE	PORER	PREED	PUKES	PYAS	GRACES	RAITS	RAPS
PINA	PLANE	POLED	PORES	PREEN	PUKKA	PYAT	TRACES	RAJA	CRAPS
SPINA	PLANK	POLER	PORK	PREES	PULE	PYATS	RACH	RAJAH	DRAPS
PINAS	PLANS	POLES	PORKS	PREP	PULED	PYES	RACHE	RAJAS	FRAPS
PINE	PLANT	POLEY	PORKY	PREPS	PULER	PYET	ORACH	RAKE	TRAPS
OPINE	PLAP	POLK	PORN	PREX	PULES	PYETS	RACK	BRAKE	WRAPS
SPINE	PLAPS	POLKA	PORNO	PREXY	SPULE	PYNE	BRACK	CRAKE	RAPT
PINED	PLAT	POLKS	PORNS	PREY	PULK	PYNED	CRACK	DRAKE	WRAPT
PINES	SPLAT	POLL	PORT	PREYS	PULKA	PYNES	FRACK	RAKED	YRAPT
PINEY	PLATS	POLLS	SPORT	PRIG	PULKS	PYOT	TRACK	RAKEE	RARE
PING	PLATY	POLLY	APORT	SPRIG	PULL	PYOTS	WRACK	RAKER	CRARE
APING	PLAY	POLO	PORTA	PRIGS	PULLS	PYRE	RACKS	RAKES	RARER
OPING	SPLAY	POLOS	PORTS	PRIM	PULP	PYRES	RACY	RAKI	RASE
PINGO	UPLAY	POLT	PORTY	PRIMA	PULPS	PYRO	ORACY	RAKIS	ERASE
PINGS	PLAYA	POLTS	POSE	PRIME	PULPY	PYROS	RADE	RALE	PRASE
PINK	PLAYS	POLY	POSED	PRIMO	PULU	QADI	RADS	RALES	RASED
SPINK	PLEA	POLYP	POSER	PRIMP	PULUS	QADIS	BRADS	RAMEN	RASES
PINKO	PLEAD	POLYS	POSES	PRIMS	PULY	QATS	PRADS	RAMENS	RASH
PINKS	PLEAS	POME	POSH	PRIMY	PUMA	QUAD	TRADS	RAMI	BRASH
PINKY	PLEAT	POMES	SPOSH	PROA	PUMAS	QUADS	RAFF	RAMIE	CRASH
PINS	PLEB	POMP	POSS	PROAS	PUMP	SQUAD	RAFFS	RAMIS	TRASH
SPINS	PLEBS	POMPS	POSSE	PROD	PUMPS	QUAG	DRAFF	RAMP	RASP
PINT	PLED	POMS	POST	SPROD	PUMY	QUAGS	GRAFF	CRAMP	GRASP
PINTA	UPLED	POND	POSTS	PRODS	PUNA	QUAT	RAFT	TRAMP	RASPS
PINTO	PLIE	PONDS	POSY	PROF	PUNAS	QUATS	CRAFT	RAMPS	RASPY
PINTS	PLIED	PONE	POTE	PROFS	PUNK	QUAY	DRAFT	RAMS	RAST
PINY	PLIER	PONES	POTED	PROG	SPUNK	QUAYD	GRAFT	CRAMS	BRAST
SPINY	PLIES	PONEY	POTES	SPROG	PUNKA	QUAYS	KRAFT	DRAMS	WRAST
PION	PLIM	PONG	POTIN	PROGS	PUNKAH	QUEAN	RAFTS	GRAMS	RASTA
PIONS	PLIMS	PONGO	POTS	PROM	PUNKS	QUEP	RAGA	PRAMS	RATA
PIONY	PLOD	PONGS	SPOTS	PROMO	PUNS	QUEY	RAGAS	TRAMS	RATAN
PIOY	PLODS	PONGY	POTT	PROMS	PUNT	QUEYN	RAGE	RANA	RATAS
PIOYE	PLOP	PONK	POTTO	PROO	PUNTO	QUEYS	RAGED	PRANA	RATE
PIOYS	PLOPS	PONKS	POTTS	PROOF	PUNTS	QUID	RAGEE	RANAS	CRATE
PIPA	PLOT	PONS	POTTY	PROOFS	PUNTY	QUIDS	RAGER	RANCE	FRATE
PIPAL	PLOTS	PONY	POUF	PROP	PUNY	SQUID	RAGES	RAND	GRATE
PIPAS	PLOTS	POOD	POUFS	POUK	PROPS	PUPA	QUIM	RAGES	BRAND	IRATE

ORATE	UREAL	REEST	ARIAS	TRILL	RISEN	RODES	CROOK	**ROTS**	GRUFF
PRATE	REALM	**REFS**	**RIBS**	RILLE	RISER	**RODS**	DROOK	GROTS	RUFFE
URATE	REALS	**REFT**	CRIBS	RILLS	RISES	BRODS	ROOKS	TROTS	RUFFS
WRATE	**REAM**	REHS	DRIBS	**RIMA**	**RISK**	PRODS	ROOKY	**ROUE**	**RUGS**
RATED	BREAM	**REIF**	RICE	PRIMA	BRISK	**ROED**	**ROOM**	ROUES	DRUGS
RATEL	CREAM	PREIF	GRICE	RIMAE	FRISK	ROES	BROOM	ROUL	TRUGS
RATER	DREAM	REIFS	PRICE	**RIME**	RISKS	**ROES**	GROOM	PROUL	**RUIN**
RATES	REAME	REIFY	TRICE	CRIME	RISKY	**ROIL**	VROOM	ROULE	RUING
RATH	REAMS	**REIK**	RICED	GRIME	**RISP**	BROIL	ROOMS	ROULS	RUINS
WRATH	REAMY	REIKS	RICER	PRIME		DROIL	ROOMY	**ROUM**	**RUKH**
RATHE	**REAN**	**REIN**	RICES	RIMED	CRISP	DROIL	**ROON**	ROUMS	RUKHS
RATHS	REANS	GREIN	RICEY	RIMER	RISPS	ROILS	ROONS	**ROUP**	**RULE**
RATS	**REAP**	REINS	**RICH**	RIMES	**RITE**	ROILY	**ROOP**	ROUPS	RULED
BRATS	REAPS	**REIS**	RICHT	**RIMS**	**RITS**	GROIN	ROOPS	ROUPY	RULER
PRATS	**REAR**	REIST	**RICK**	RITES	URITE	PROIN	**ROOS**	**ROUT**	RULES
RATU	AREAR	**REKE**	BRICK	PRIMS	**RITS**	**ROIN**	TROOP	CROUT	**RULY**
RATUS	DREAR	REKED	CRICK	TRIMS	BRITS	ROINS	ROOPS	GROUT	**RUME**
RAUN	REARM	REKES	ERICK	**RIMU**	CRITS	**ROKE**	**ROOS**	TROUT	RUMEN
RAUNS	REARS	**RELY**	PRICK	RIMUS	FRITS	BROKE	BROOS	ROUTE	RUMES
RAVE	**RECK**	**REMS**	TRICK	**RIMY**	GRITS	PROKE	ROOSA	ROUTH	**RUMP**
BRAVE	DRECK	**REND**	WRICK	GRIMY	WRITS	TROKE	ROOSE	ROUTS	CRUMP
CRAVE	TRECK	TREND	RICKS	PRIMY	ROKED	WROKE	ROOST	**ROUX**	FRUMP
DRAVE	WRECK	RENDS	**RICY**	**RIND**	**RITT**	ROKER	WROOT	**ROVE**	TRUMP
GRAVE	RECKS	**RENS**	PRICY	GRIND	RITTS	ROKES	**ROOT**	DROVE	RUMPS
TRAVE	**REDD**	BRENS	**RIDE**	RINDS	**RIVA**	**ROKS**	ROOTS	GROVE	**RUMS**
RAVED	REDDS	GRENS	BRIDE	RINDY	RIVAS	**ROKY**	ROOTY	PROVE	**RUND**
RAVEL	REDDY	WRENS	GRIDE	**RINE**	**RIVE**	**ROLE**	**ROOT**	ROVED	RUNDS
RAVEN	**REDE**	**RENT**	PRIDE	BRINE	RIVED	ROLES	ROKER	ROVER	**RUNE**
RAVER	REDES	RENTE	TRIDE	CRINE	RIVEL	PROLE	ROKES	ROVES	RUNED
RAVES	**REDO**	PRENT	RIDER	DRIVE	RIVEN	PROLL	ROKS	**ROWS**	**RUND**
RAWN	CREDO	RENTE	RIDES	URINE	RIVER	DROLL	WROOT	BROWS	RUNDS
BRAWN	UREDO	RENTS	**RIDS**	**RING**	RIVES	TROLL	PROLL	CROWS	**RUNE**
DRAWN	**REDO**	YRENT	GRIDS	BRING	RIVET	**ROLL**	DROLL	DROWS	PRUNE
PRAWN	CREDO	**RENY**	IRIDS	ERING	**RIVO**	ROLLS	**ROMA**	**RORE**	RUNED
RAWNS	UREDO	**REPP**	**RIEL**	WRING	RIVOS	**ROMA**	AROMA	CRORE	RUNES
RAWS	REDOX	REPPS	ARIEL	RINGS	**ROAD**	GROMA	CRORE	FRORE	RUNES
BRAWS	**REDS**	**REPS**	ORIEL	**RINK**	BROAD	ROMAL	EROSE	FRORE	**RUNG**
CRAWS	**REED**	PREPS	RIELS	BRINK	TROAD	ROMAN	BROSE	**ROWT**	RUNGS
DRAWS	BREED	**REST**	**RIEM**	DRINK	ROADS	ROMAS	EROSE	ROWTH	**RUNS**
RAYS	CREED	RESTY	RIEMS	PRINK	**ROAM**	**ROMP**	PROSE	ROWTS	**RUNT**
BRAYS	DREED	**REST**	**RIFE**	RINKS	ROAMS	TROMP	ROSED	**RUBE**	BRUNT
DRAYS	FREED	CREST	RIFER	**RINS**	**ROAN**	ROMPS	ROSES	RUBES	GRUNT
FRAYS	GREED	DREST	**RIFF**	GRINS	ROANS	**RONE**	ROSET	**RUBS**	PRUNT
GRAYS	PREED	PREST	GRIFF	TRINS	**ROAR**	CRONE	**ROST**	DRUBS	RUNTS
PRAYS	TREED	WREST	RIFFS	RINSE	ROARS	DRONE	CROST	GRUBS	RUNTY
TRAYS	REEDE	RESTS	**RIFT**	**RIOT**	ROARY	GRONE	FROST	**RUCK**	**RURP**
RAZE	REEDS	RESTY	DRIFT	ARIOT	**ROBE**	KRONE	ROSTS	CRUCK	RURPS
BRAZE	REEDY	**RETE**	GRIFT	GRIOT	PROBE	PRONE	**ROSY**	RUCKS	RURPS
CRAZE	**REEF**	ARETE	RIFTE	RIOTS	ROBED	TRONE	PROSY	**RUSA**	RUSAS
GRAZE	REEFS	RETES	RIFTS	**ROBE**	ROBES	RONEO	PRUDE	RUSAS	**RUSE**
RAZED	**REEK**	**RETS**	RIFTY	PROBE	**ROBS**	RONES	RUDER	**RUSE**	CRUSE
RAZEE	CREEK	FRETS	**RIGG**	GRIPE	**ROCH**	RONG	**RODA**	**RUCS**	CRUSE
RAZES	REEKS	TRETS	RIGGS	TRIPE	BROCH	RONTE	ROTAL	**RUDD**	DRUSE
RAZZ	REEKY	**RETS**	**RIGS**	RIPED	**ROCK**	RONTS	ROTAS	RUDDS	RUSES
READ	**REEL**	**REVS**	BRIGS	RIPEN	BROCK	**RONG**	CRUDS	RUDDY	RUSES
AREAD	CREEL	**REWS**	FRIGS	RIPER	CROCK	WRONG	BROOD	**RUDE**	**RUSH**
BREAD	REELS	BREWS	GRIGS	RIPES	FROCK	FRONT	ROODS	CRUDE	BRUSH
DREAD	**REEN**	CREWS	PRIGS	**RIPP**	TROCK	RONTE	ROTAL	PRUDE	CRUSH
OREAD	PREEN	GREWS	TRIGS	RIPPS	ROCKS	RONTS	ROTAS	RUDER	FRUSH
TREAD	TREEN	TREWS	**RILE**	RIPS	ROCKY	**ROOD**	**ROTA**	**RUDS**	RUSHY
READS	REENS	**RHEA**	RILED	DRIPS	**ROCS**	BROOD	ROTAL	CRUDS	**RUSK**
READY	**REES**	RHEAS	RILES	GRIPS	CROCS	ROODS	ROTAS	**RUED**	RUSKS
REAK	BREES	**RHOS**	RILEY	TRIPS	**RODE**	**ROOF**	**ROTE**	**RUES**	**RUST**
BREAK	CREES	**RHUS**	**RILL**	**RIPT**	ERODE	ROOFS	ROTED	CRUES	BRUST
CREAK	DREES	**RIAL**	BRILL	**RISE**	TRODE	ROOFY	ROTES	GRUES	CRUST
FREAK	FREES	PRIAL	DRILL	ARISE	RODED	**ROOK**	**ROTI**	TRUES	FRUST
WREAK	GREES	TRIAL	FRILL	BRISE	RODEO	BROOK	ROTIS	**RUFF**	TRUST
REAKS	GREES	URIAL	GRILL	CRISE	**RODE**	**ROOK**	**ROTL**		RUSTS
REAL	PREES	RIALS	KRILL	GRISE	RODED	BROOK	ROTLS	**RUFF**	RUSTY
AREAL	TREES	**RIAS**	PRILL	PRISE	RODED	BROOK	ROTLS	RUFF	**RUTH**

TRUTH	SALPS	SCAG	SEAT	SERF	SHINY	SIFTS	SITES	SLAW	SMITE
RUTHS	SALS	SCAGS	SEATS	SERFS	SHIP	SIGH	SITH	SLAWS	SMITH
RUTS	SALSA	SCAM	SECS	SERK	SHIPS	SIGHS	SITHE	SLAY	SMITS
RYAL	SALSE	SCAMP	SECT	SERKS	SHIR	SIGHT	SITS	SLAYS	SMOG
RYALS	SALT	SCAMS	SECTS	SERR	SHIRE	SIGN	SIZE	SLED	SMOGS
RYAS	SALTO	SCAN	SEED	SERRA	SHIRK	SIGNS	SIZED	SLEDS	SMUG
RYES	SALTS	SCAND	SEEDS	SERRE	SHIRR	SIKA	SIZEL	ISLED	SMUGS
RYFE	SALTY	SCANS	SEEDY	SERRS	SHIRS	SIKAS	SIZER	SLEE	SMUR
RYKE	SAME	SCANT	SEEK	SERRY	SHIRT	SIKE	SIZES	SLEEK	SMURS
GRYKE	YSAME	SCAR	SEEKS	SESE	SHIT	SIKES	SIZY	SLEEP	SMUT
RYKED	SAMEL	SCARE	SEEL	SESEY	SHITE	SILD	SKAS	SLEET	SMUTS
RYKES	SAMEN	SCARF	SEELD	SESS	SHITS	SILDS	SKAT	SLEW	SNAB
RYND	SAMES	SCARP	SEELS	SESSA	SHIV	SILE	SKATE	SLEWS	SNABS
RYNDS	SAMEY	SCARS	SEELY	SETA	SHIVE	ESILE	SKATS	SLEY	SNAG
RYOT	SAMP	SCART	SEEM	SETAE	SHIVS	SILED	SKATT	SLEYS	SNAGS
RYOTS	SAMPI	SCARY	SEEMS	SETS	SHOD	SILEN	SKAW	SLID	SNAP
RYPE	SAMPS	SCAT	SEEN	SETT	SHOED	SILER	SKAWS	SLIDE	SNAPS
GRYPE	SAND	SCATH	SEEP	SETTS	SHOER	SILES	SKEG	SLIM	SNAR
RYPER	SANDS	SCATS	SEEPS	SEWN	SHOES	SILEX	SKEGS	SLIME	SNARE
RYVE	SANDY	SCATT	SEEPY	SEWS	SHOG	SILK	SKEO	SLIMS	SNARK
RYVED	SANE	SCAW	SEER	SEXT	SHOGS	SILKS	SKEOS	SLIMY	SNARL
RYVES	SANER	SCAWS	SEERS	SEXTS	SHOO	SILKY	SKEP	SLIP	SNARS
SABS	SANG	SCOG	SEES	SEXY	SHOOK	SILL	SKEPS	SLIPE	SNARY
SACK	SANGS	SCOGS	SEGO	SEYS	SHOOL	SILLS	SKER	SLIPS	SNEB
SACKS	SANK	SCOT	SEGOL	SHAD	SHOON	SILLY	ASKER	SLIPT	SNEBS
SACS	SANKO	ASCOT	SEGOS	SHADE	SHOOS	SILO	ESKER	SLIT	SNED
SAFE	SANS	ESCOT	SEGS	SHADS	SHOOT	SILOS	SKERS	SLITS	SNEDS
SAFED	SANSA	SCOTS	SEIF	SHADY	SHOP	SILT	SKEW	SLOB	SNEE
SAFER	SAPS	SCOW	SEIFS	SHAG	SHOPE	SILTS	SKEWS	SLOBS	SNEED
SAFES	SARD	SCOWL	SEIL	SHAGS	SHOPS	SILTY	ASKEW	SLOE	SNEER
SAGA	SARDS	SCOWP	SEILS	SHAH	SHOT	SIMA	SKID	SLOES	SNEES
SAGAS	SARI	SCOWS	SEIS	SHAHS	SHOTE	SIMAR	SKIDS	SLOG	SNIB
SAGE	SARIN	SCRY	SEISE	SHAM	SHOTS	SIMAS	SKIM	SLOGS	SNIBS
USAGE	SARIS	SCUD	SEISM	SHAMA	SHOTT	SIMI	SKIMP	SLOP	SNIG
SAGER	SARK	SCUDI	SEKT	SHAME	SHOW	SIMIS	SKIMS	SLOPE	SNIGS
SAGES	SARKS	SCUDO	SEKTS	SHAMS	SHOWN	SIMP	SKIN	SLOPS	SNIP
SAGO	SARKY	SCUDS	SELD	SHAN	SHOWS	SIMPS	SKINK	SLOPY	SNIPE
SAGOS	SARS	SCUG	SELE	SHAND	SHOWY	SIMS	SKINS	SLOT	SNIPS
SAGS	KSARS	SCUGS	SELES	SHANK	SHUL	SIND	SKINT	SLOTH	SNIPY
SAGY	TSARS	SCUL	SELF	SHANS	SHULS	SINDS	SKIO	SLOTS	SNOB
SAIC	SARSA	SCULK	SELFS	SHAT	SHUN	SINE	SKIOS	SLOW	SNOBS
SAICE	SASH	SCULL	SELL	SHAW	SHUNS	SINED	SKIP	SLOWS	SNOD
SAICK	SASS	SCULP	SELLE	PSHAW	SHUNT	SINES	SKIPS	SLUB	SNODS
SAICS	SASSE	SCULS	SELLS	SHAWL	SHUT	SINEW	SKIS	SLUBB	SNOG
SAID	SASSY	SCUM	SELS	SHAWM	SHUTS	SING	SKIT	SLUBS	SNOGS
SAIDS	SATE	SCUMS	SEME	SHAWS	SHWA	USING	SKITE	SLUE	SNOT
SAIL	SATED	SCUP	SEMEE	SHAY	SHWAS	SINGE	SKITS	SLUED	SNOTS
SAILS	SATES	SCUPS	SEMEN	SHAYA	SIAL	SINGS	SKOL	SLUES	SNOW
SAILY	SATI	SCUR	SEMI	SHAYS	SIALS	SINK	SKRY	SLUG	SNOWK
SAIM	SATIN	SCURF	SEMIE	SHEA	SIBB	SINKS	SKUA	SLUGS	SNOWS
SAIMS	SATIS	SCURS	SEMIS	SHEAF	SIBBS	SINKY	SKUAS	SLUM	SNOWY
SAIN	SAUL	SCUT	SEND	SHEAL	SIBS	SINS	SKUG	SLUMP	SNUB
SAINE	SAULS	SCUTA	SENDS	SHEAR	SICE	SIPE	SKUGS	SLUMS	SNUBS
SAINS	SAULT	SCUTE	SENS	SHEAS	SICES	SIPED	SKYR	SLUR	SNUG
SAINT	SAUT	SCUTS	SENSA	SHED	SICH	SIPES	SKYRE	SLURB	SNUGS
SAIR	SAUTE	SCYE	SENSE	SHEDS	SICK	SIPS	SKYRS	SLURP	SOAK
SAIRS	SAUTS	SCYES	SENT	SHES	SICKS	SIRE	SLAB	SLURS	SOAKS
SAIS	SAVE	SEAL	SENTS	ASHES	SICS	SIRED	SLABS	SLUT	SOAP
SAIST	SAVED	SEALS	SEPS	ISHES	SIDA	SIREN	SLAE	SLUTS	SOAPS
SAKE	SAVER	SEAM	SEPT	SHET	SIDAS	SIRES	SLAES	SMEE	SOAPY
SAKER	SAVES	SEAME	SEPTA	ASHET	SIDE	SIRI	SLAG	SMEEK	SOAR
SAKES	SAVEY	SEAMS	SEPTS	SHETS	SIDED	SIRIH	SLAGS	SMEES	SOARE
SAKI	SAWN	SEAMY	SERA	SHEW	SIDER	SIRIS	SLAM	SMEW	SOARS
SAKIA	SAWS	SEAN	SERAC	SHEWN	SIDES	SIRS	SLAMS	SMEWS	SOBS
SAKIS	SAYS	SEANS	SERAI	SHEWS	SIEN	SISS	SLAP	SMIR	SOCK
SALE	SAYST	SEAR	SERAL	SHIM	SIENS	SISSY	SLAPS	SMIRK	SOCKO
SALEP	SCAB	SEARE	SERE	SHIMS	SIENT	SIST	SLAT	SMIRR	SOCKS
SALES	SCABS	SEARS	SERED	SHIN	SIFT	SISTS	SLATS	SMIRS	SOCS
SALET	SCAD	SEAS	SERER	SHINE		SITE	SLATE	SMIT	SODA
SALP	SCADS	SEASE	SERES	SHINS		SITED	SLATY		SODAS

SODS	SORBS	SPASM	STAR	STUNT	SWAN	TACHE	TANK	TAXA	STEME
SOFA	SORD	SPAT	STARE	STYE	SWANG	TACK	STANK	TAXI	TEMED
SOFAR	SORDA	SPATE	STARK	STYED	SWANK	TACKS	TANKA	TAXIS	TEMES
SOFAS	SORDO	SPATS	STARN	STYES	SWANS	TACKY	TANKS	TEAD	TEMP
SOFT	SORDS	SPAW	STARR	SUBS	SWAP	TACO	TANS	TEADE	TEMPI
SOFTA	SORE	SPAWL	STARS	SUCH	SWAPS	TACOS	TANSY	TEADS	TEMPO
SOFTS	SORED	SPAWN	START	SUCK	SWAPT	TACT	TAPA	TEAK	TEMPS
SOFTY	SOREE	SPAWS	STAW	SUCKS	SWAT	TACTS	TAPAS	TEAKS	TEMPT
SOGS	SOREL	SPAY	STAWS	SUDD	SWATH	TADS	TAPE	STEAK	TEMS
SOHS	SORER	SPAYD	STAY	SUDDS	SWATS	TAED	TAPED	ETAPE	ITEMS
SOIL	SORES	SPAYS	STAYD	SUDS	SWAY	TAEL	TAPEN	TEAL	STEMS
SOILS	SOREX	SPEC	STAYS	SUDSY	ASWAY	TAELS	TAPER	TEALS	TEMSE
SOILY	SORI	SPECK	STED	SUED	SWAYL	TAES	TAPES	TEAM	TEND
SOJA	SORN	SPECS	STEDD	SUEDE	SWAYS	TAGS	TAPET	STEAM	STEND
SOJAS	SORNS	SPED	STEDE	SUER	SWEE	STAGS	TAPS	TEAMS	TENDS
SOKE	SORT	SPET	STEDS	SUERS	SWEED	TAHA	ATAPS	TEAR	TENE
SOKEN	SORTS	SPETS	STEM	SUES	SWEEL	TAHAS	STAPS	STEAR	CTENE
SOKES	SOSS	SPEW	STEME	SUET	SWEEP	TAHR	TAPU	TEARS	TENES
SOLA	SOTS	SPEWS	STEMS	SUETS	SWEER	TAHRS	TAPUS	TEARY	TENET
SOLAH	SOUK	SPEWY	STEN	SUETY	SWEES	TAIL	TARA	TEAS	TENS
SOLAN	SOUKS	SPIC	STEND	SUIT	SWEET	TAILS	TARAS	TEAT	ETENS
SOLAR	SOUL	ASPIC	STENS	SUITE	SWIG	TAIS	TARE	TEATS	TENSE
SOLAS	SOULS	SPICA	STENT	SUITS	SWIGS	TAISH	STARE	TECH	STENS
SOLD	SOUM	SPICE	STEP	SUKH	SWIM	TAIT	TARED	TECHS	TENT
SOLDE	SOUMS	SPICK	STEPS	SUKHS	ASWIM	TAITS	TARES	TECHY	STENT
SOLDI	SOUP	SPICS	STEPT	SUKS	SWIMS	TAKA	TARN	TEDS	TENTH
SOLDO	SOUPS	SPICY	STET	SULK	SWIZ	TAKAS	STARN	TEDY	TENTS
SOLDS	SOUPY	SPIE	STETS	SULKS	SWOB	TAKE	TARNS	TEED	TENTY
SOLE	SOUR	SPIED	STEW	SULKY	SWOBS	TAKEN	TARO	STEED	TERF
SOLED	SOURS	SPIEL	STEWS	SUMO	SWOP	TAKER	TAROC	TEEL	TERFE
SOLEN	SOUS	SPIES	STEWY	SUMOS	SWOPS	TAKES	TAROK	STEEL	TERFS
SOLER	SOUSE	SPIK	STEY	SUMP	SWOPT	TAKS	TAROS	TEELS	TERM
SOLES	SOUT	SPIKE	STIE	SUMPH	SWOT	TAKY	TAROT	TEEM	TERMS
SOLI	SOUTH	SPIKS	STIED	SUMPS	SWOTS	TALA	TARP	TEEMS	TERN
SOLID	SOUTS	SPIKY	STIES	SUMS	SWUM	TALAK	TARPS	TEEN	TERNE
SOLO	SOVS	SPIN	STIR	SUNG	SYBO	TALAQ	TARS	STEEN	TERNS
SOLOS	SOWF	SPINA	ASTIR	SUNK	SYBOE	TALAR	STARS	TEEND	STERN
SOLS	SOWFF	SPINE	STIRE	SUNKS	SYBOW	TALAS	TARSI	TEENE	TEST
SOMA	SOWFS	SPINK	STIRK	SUNN	SYCE	TALC	TART	TEENS	TESTA
SOMAS	SOWL	SPINS	STIRP	SUNNS	SYCEE	TALCS	START	TEENY	TESTE
SOME	SOWLE	SPINY	STIRS	SUNNY	SYCES	TALE	TARTS	TEER	TESTS
SONE	SOWLS	SPIT	STOA	SUNS	SYED	STALE	STARTS	STEER	TESTY
SONES	SOWM	SPITE	STOAE	SUPS	SYEN	TALES	TARTY	TEERS	TETE
SONG	SOWMS	SPITS	STOAI	SUQS	SYENS	STALES	TASH	TEES	TETES
SONGS	SOWN	SPITZ	STOAS	SURA	SYES	TALI	STASH	TEFF	TEWS
SONS	SOWND	SPIV	STOAT	SURAH	SYKE	TALK	TASK	TEFFS	STEWS
SONSE	SOWNE	SPIVS	STOB	SURAL	SYKER	STALK	TASKS	TEGG	TEXT
SONSY	SOWP	SPOT	STOBS	SURAS	SYKES	TALKS	TASS	TEGGS	TEXTS
SOOK	SOWPS	SPOTS	STOP	SURAT	SYLI	STALKS	TASSE	TEGS	THAE
SOOKS	SOWS	SPRY	STOPE	SURD	SYNC	TALL	TATE	TEHR	THAN
SOOM	SOWSE	SPUD	STOPS	SURDS	SYNCH	STALL	STATE	TEHRS	THANA
SOOMS	SOYA	SPUDS	STOT	SURE	SYNCS	TALLY	TATER	TEIL	THANE
SOON	SOYAS	SPUE	STOTS	USURE	SYND	TAME	TATES	STEIL	THANK
SOOP	SOYS	SPUED	STOW	SURED	SYNDS	TAMED	TATH	TEILS	THAR
SOOPS	SPAE	SPUES	STOWN	SURER	SYNE	TAMER	TATHS	TELA	THARS
SOOT	SPAED	SPUN	STOWS	SURES	SYNED	TAMES	TATS	STELA	THAT
SOOTE	SPAER	SPUNK	STUB	SURF	SYNES	TAMP	ETATS	TELAE	THAW
SOOTH	SPAES	SPUR	STUBS	SURFS	SYPE	STAMP	TATT	TELD	THAWS
SOOTS	SPAN	SPURN	STUD	SURFY	SYPED	TAMPS	TATTS	TELE	THAWY
SOOTY	SPANE	SPURS	STUDS	SUSS	SYPES	STAMPS	TATTY	STELE	THEE
SOPH	SPANG	SPURT	STUDY	SWAB	TAAL	TAMS	TATU	TELES	THEED
SOPHA	SPANK	STAB	STUM	SWABS	TAALS	TANA	TATUS	STELES	THEEK
SOPHS	SPANS	STABS	STUMM	SWAD	TABS	TANAS	TAUS	TELL	THEES
SOPS	SPAR	STAG	STUMP	SWADS	TABU	TANE	TAUT	STELL	THEM
SORA	SPARD	STAGE	STUMS	SWAG	TABUN	TANG	TAUTS	TELLS	THEMA
PSORA	SPARE	STAGS	STUN	SWAGE	TABUS	STANG	TAWS	TELLY	THEME
SORAL	SPARK	STAGY	ASTUN	SWAGS	TACE	TANGA	STAWS	TELS	THEN
SORAS	SPARS	STAP	STUNG	SWAM	TACES	TANGO	TAWSE	TELT	THENS
SORB	SPART	STAPH	STUNK	SWAMI	TACET	TANGS	TAWT	TELTS	THEW
SORBO	SPAS	STAPS	STUNS	SWAMP	TACH	TANGY	TAWTS	TEME	THEWS

THEWY	STILE	TOES	TOOM	TOWSE	TROTH	TURDS	TZARS	ZUPAS	LUTES
THEY	UTILE	TOFF	TOOMS	TOWSY	TROTS	TURF	UDAL	UPBY	MUTES
THIG	TILED	TOFFS	TOON	TOWT	TROW	TURFS	UDALS	UPBYE	UTIS
THIGH	TILER	TOFFY	TOONS	TOWTS	STROW	TURFY	UDOS	UPGO	CUTIS
THIGS	TILES	TOFT	TOOT	TOWY	TROWS	TURM	BUDOS	UPON	UTUS
THIN	TILL	TOFTS	TOOTH	TOYS	TROY	TURME	JUDOS	JUPON	TUTUS
THINE	TILLS	TOFU	TOOTS	TOZE	STROY	TURMS	KUDOS	YUPON	UVAS
THING	TILLY	TOFUS	TOPE	TOZED	TROYS	TURN	LUDOS	UPSY	UVEA
THINK	TILS	TOGA	STOPE	TOZES	TRUE	TURNS	UEYS	URAO	UVEAL
THINS	TILT	TOGAS	TOPED	TRAD	TRUED	TUSH	UFOS	URDE	VACS
THIR	ATILT	TOGE	TOPEE	STRAD	TRUER	TUSK	UGHS	URDEE	VADE
THIRD	STILT	TOGED	TOPEK	TRADE	TRUES	TUSKS	BUFOS	URDS	EVADE
THIRL	TILTH	TOGES	TOPER	TRADS	TRUG	TUSKY	EUGHS	BURDS	VADED
THIS	TILTS	TOGS	TOPES	TRAM	TRUGS	TUTS	UGLI	CURDS	VADES
THON	TIME	TOHO	TOPI	TRAMP	TRYE	TUTU	UGLIS	HURDS	VAES
THONG	STIME	TOHOS	TOPIC	TRAMS	TRYER	TUTUS	UGLY	NURDS	VAGI
THOU	TIMED	TOIL	TOPIS	TRAP	TRYP	TWAE	ULES	SURDS	VAIL
THOUS	TIMER	TOILE	TOPS	STRAP	TRYPS	TWAES	DULES	TURDS	AVAIL
THRO	TIMES	TOILS	STOPS	TRAPE	TSAR	TWAL	GULES	URDY	VAILS
THROB	TIND	TOKE	TORC	TRAPS	TSARS	TWALS	HULES	CURDY	VAIN
THROE	TINDS	ATOKE	TORCH	TRAY	TUAN	TWAS	MULES	UREA	VAIR
THROW	TINE	STOKE	TORCS	TRAYS	TUANS	TWAT	PULES	UREAL	VAIRE
THRU	TINED	TOKED	TORE	STRAY	TUBA	TWATS	RULES	UREAS	VAIRS
THRUM	TINES	TOKEN	STORE	TREE	TUBAE	TWAY	TULES	URES	VAIRY
THUD	TING	TOKES	TORES	TREED	TUBAL	TWAYS	YULES	CURES	VALE
THUDS	STING	TOKO	TORI	TREEN	TUBAR	TWEE	ULEX	DURES	AVALE
THUG	TINGE	TOKOS	TORIC	TREES	TUBAS	ETWEE	CULEX	LURES	VALES
THUGS	TINGS	TOLA	TORII	TREF	TUBE	TWEED	ULNA	MURES	VALET
THUS	TINK	STOLA	TORN	TREFA	TUBED	TWEEL	ULNAE	PURES	VALI
TIAR	TINKS	TOLAS	TORO	TREK	TUBER	TWEER	ULNAR	SURES	VALID
TIARA	STINK	TOLD	TOROS	TREKS	TUBES	TWEET	UMBO	URGE	VALIS
TIARS	TINS	TOLE	TORR	TRET	TUBS	TWIG	BUMBO	GURGE	VAMP
TICE	TINT	STOLE	TORRS	TRETS	STUBS	TWIGS	GUMBO	PURGE	VAMPS
TICED	STINT	TOLED	TORS	TREW	TUCK	TWIN	JUMBO	SURGE	VANE
TICES	TINTS	TOLES	TORSE	TREWS	STUCK	TWINE	RUMBO	URGED	VANED
TICH	TINTY	TOLL	TORSK	STREW	TUCKS	TWINK	UMBOS	URGER	VANES
STICH	TINY	ATOLL	TORSO	TREY	TUFA	TWINS	UMPH	URGES	VANG
TICHY	TIPI	TOLLS	TORT	TREYS	TUFAS	TWINY	BUMPH	URIC	VANGS
TICK	TIPIS	TOLT	TORTE	TREZ	TUFF	TWIT	HUMPH	AURIC	VANS
STICK	TIPS	TOLU	TORTS	TRIE	TUFFE	TWITE	SUMPH	URNS	VANT
TICKS	TIPSY	TOLUS	TOSE	TRIED	TUFFS	TWITS	UNAU	BURNS	AVANT
TICKY	TIPT	TOMB	TOSED	TRIER	TUFT	TWOS	UNBE	CURNS	VANTS
TICS	TIRE	TOMBS	TOSES	TRIES	TUFTS	TYDE	UNBED	DURNS	VARA
TIDE	TIRED	TOME	TOSH	TRIG	TUFTY	STYE	UNCE	GURNS	VARAN
TIDED	TIRES	TOMES	TOSHY	STRIG	TUGS	TYED	BUNCE	TURNS	VARAS
TIDES	STIRE	TOMO	TOSS	TRIGS	TUIS	STYED	DUNCE	URUS	VARE
TIDS	TIRL	TOMS	TOSSY	TRIM	ETUIS	TYES	OUNCE	GURUS	VAREC
TIDY	TIRLS	ATOMS	TOST	TRIMS	TUISM	STYES	PUNCE	URVA	VARES
TIED	TIRO	TONE	YTOST	TRIN	TULE	TYGS	UNCES	MURVA	VARY
STIED	TIROS	ATONE	TOTE	TRINE	TULES	TYKE	UNCI	URVAS	OVARY
TIER	TIRR	STONE	TOTED	TRINS	TUMP	TYKES	UNCO	USED	VASA
TIERS	TIRRS	TONED	TOTEM	TRIO	TUMPS	TYMP	BUNCO	BUSED	VASAL
TIES	TITE	TONES	TOTES	TRIOR	TUMPY	TYMPS	JUNCO	FUSED	VASE
STIES	TITER	TONEY	TOTS	TRIOS	TUMS	TYND	UNCOS	MUSED	VASES
TIFF	TITI	TONG	STOTS	TRIP	STUM	TYNDE	UNDE	MUSER	VAST
STIFF	TITIS	TONGA	TOUK	ATRIP	STUMS	TYNE	UNDEE	USER	AVAST
TIFFS	TITS	STONG	TOUKS	STRIP	TUNA	TYNED	UNDER	USERS	VASTS
TIFT	TIVY	TONGS	TOUN	TRIPE	TUNAS	TYNES	UNDO	USES	VASTY
TIFTS	TIZZ	TONK	STOUN	TRIPS	TUND	TYPE	UNDY	BUSES	VATS
TIGE	TIZZY	STONK	TOUNS	TROD	TUNDS	TYPED	UNIS	FUSES	VAUS
TIGER	TOAD	TONKS	TOUR	TRODE	TUNE	TYPES	UNIT	MUSES	VAUT
TIGES	TOADS	TONS	TOURS	TRODS	TUNED	TYPO	UNITE	PUSES	VAUTE
TIGS	TOADY	TONY	TOUT	TROG	TUNER	TYPOS	UNITS	RUSES	VAUTS
TIKA	TOBY	ATONY	TOUTS	TROGS	TUNES	TYRE	UNITY	SUSES	VEAL
TIKAS	TOCO	STONY	TOWN	TRON	TUNS	TYRED	UNTO	UTAS	UVEAL
TIKE	TOCOS	TOOK	STOWN	TRONA	STUN	TYRES	JUNTO	UTES	VEALE
TIKES	TODS	STOOK	TOWNS	TRONC	STUNS	STYRE	PUNTO	BUTES	VEALS
TIKI	TODY	TOOL	TOWNY	TRONE	TUNY	TYRO	UPAS	CUTES	VEALS
TIKIS	TOEA	STOOL	TOWS	TRONS	TUPS	TYTE	JUPAS	BUTES	VEALY
TILE	TOED	TOOLS	STOWS	TROT	TURD	TZAR	PUPAS	JUTES	VEER

VEERS	VIES	VOLED	DWALE	SWASH	WEENY	WHEEL	WIMP	WIVED	WRITE
VEERY	IVIES	VOLES	SWALE	WASHY	WEEP	WHEEN	WIMPS	WIVES	WRITS
VEES	VIEW	VOLET	WALED	WASP	SWEEP	WHEN	WIND	WOAD	WUDS
VEGA	VIEWS	VOLS	WALER	WASPS	WEEPS	WHENS	WINDS	WOADS	WULL
VEGAN	VIEWY	VOLT	WALES	WASPY	WEEPY	WHET	WINDY	WOCK	WULLS
VEGAS	VILD	VOLTA	WALI	WAST	WEER	WHETS	WINE	WOCKS	WYES
VEHM	VILDE	VOLTE	WALIS	WASTE	SWEER	WHEW	WINED	WOES	WYND
VEHME	VILE	VOLTS	WALK	WASTS	TWEER	WHEWS	WINES	WOGS	WYNDS
VEIL	VILER	VORS	WALKS	WATE	WEES	WHEY	WINEY	WOKE	WYNN
VEILS	VILL	VOTE	WALL	WATER	WEEST	WHEYS	WING	WOKEN	WYNNS
VEILY	VILLA	VOTED	WALLA	WATS	WEET	WHID	WINGE	AWOKE	WYNS
VEIN	VILLI	VOTER	WALLS	SWATS	WEETE	WHIDS	WINGS	WOKS	WYTE
VEINS	VILLS	VOTES	WALLY	TWATS	WEFT	WHIG	WINGY	WOLD	WYTED
VEINY	VIMS	VOWS	WALY	WATT	WEFTE	WHIGS	WINK	WOLDS	WYTES
VELA	VINA	AVOWS	SWALY	WATTS	WEFTS	WHIM	WINKS	WOLF	XYST
VELAR	VINAL	VRIL	WAME	WAUK	WEID	WHIMS	WINN	WOLFS	XYSTI
VELD	VINAS	VRILS	WAMED	WAUKS	WEIDS	WHIN	WINNA	WOMB	XYSTS
VELDS	VINE	VUGS	WAMES	WAUL	WEIL	WHINE	WINNS	WOMBS	YACK
VELDT	AVINE	VULN	WAND	WAULK	WEILS	WHINS	WINO	WOMBY	YACKS
VELE	OVINE	VULNS	WANDS	WAULS	WEIR	WHINY	WINOS	WONS	YAFF
VELES	VINED	VUMS	WANED	WAUR	WEIRS	WHIP	WINS	WONT	YAFFS
VELL	VINER	WADD	WANES	WAURS	WEKA	WHIPS	WINY	WONTS	LYAMS
VELLS	VINES	WADDS	WANEY	WAVE	WEKAS	WHIPT	WIPE	WOOD	YANG
VENA	VINEW	WADDY	WANG	AWAVE	WELD	WHIR	WIPED	WOODS	KYANG
VENAE	VINO	WADE	SWANG	WAVED	WELDS	WHIRL	WIPER	WOODY	YANGS
VENAL	VINOS	WADED	TWANG	WAVER	WELK	WHIRR	WIPES	WOOF	YANK
VEND	VINS	WADER	WANGS	WAVES	WELKE	WHIRS	WIRE	WOOFS	YANKS
VENDS	VINT	WADES	WANK	WAVEY	WELKS	WHIT	WIRED	WOOFY	YAPP
VENT	VINTS	WADI	SWANK	WAVY	WELKT	WHITE	WIRER	WOOL	YAPPS
EVENT	VINY	WADIS	TWANK	WAWE	WELL	WHITS	WIRES	WOOLD	YAPS
VENTS	VINYL	WADS	WANKS	WAWES	WELLS	WHITY	WIRY	WOOLS	YARD
VERB	VIOL	SWADS	WANS	WAWL	WELT	WHIZ	WISE	WOON	YARDS
VERBS	VIOLA	WADY	SWANS	WAWLS	WELTS	WHIZZ	WISED	WOONS	YARE
VERS	VIOLD	WAES	WANT	WAWS	WEMB	WHOA	WISER	WOOS	YARER
AVERS	VIOLS	TWAES	WANTS	WAXY	WEMBS	WHOM	WISES	WOOSH	YARN
OVERS	VIRL	WAFF	WANTY	WAYS	WEMS	WHOP	WISH	WOOT	YARNS
VERSE	VIRLS	WAFFS	WANY	AWAYS	WEND	WHOPS	WISP	WOOTZ	YARR
VERSO	VISA	WAFT	WARD	SWAYS	WENDS	WHOT	WISPS	WOPS	YARRS
VERST	VISAS	WAFTS	AWARD	TWAYS	WENS	WHOW	WISPY	SWOPS	YATE
VERT	VISE	WAGE	SWARD	WEAK	WENT	WICK	WIST	WORD	YATES
AVERT	VISED	SWAGE	WARDS	TWEAK	WENTS	WICKS	TWIST	SWORD	YAUD
EVERT	VISES	WAGED	WARE	WEAL	WEPT	WICKY	WITE	WORDS	YAUDS
OVERT	VITA	WAGER	SWARE	SWEAL	SWEPT	WIDE	WITED	WORDY	YAUP
VERTS	VITAE	WAGES	AWARE	WEALD	WERE	WIDEN	WITES	WORE	YAWL
VERTU	VITAL	WAGS	WARED	WEALS	WERT	WIDER	WITH	SWORE	YAWLS
VERY	VITE	WAID	WARES	WEAN	WEST	WIDES	SWITH	AWORK	YAWN
EVERY	EVITE	WAIDE	WARK	WEANS	WESTS	WIEL	WITHE	WORK	YAWNS
VEST	VITEX	WAIF	WARKS	WEAR	EWEST	WIELD	WITHS	WORKS	YAWNY
VESTA	VIVA	WAIFS	WARM	SWEAR	WETS	WIELS	WITHY	WORM	YAWP
VESTS	VIVAS	WAIFT	SWARM	WEARS	WEXE	WIFE	WITS	WORMS	YAWPS
VETO	VIVAT	WAIL	WARMS	WEARY	WEXED	WIGS	TWITS	WORMY	YAWS
VETS	VIVE	WAILS	WARN	WEBS	WEXES	SWIGS	WIVE	WORN	YAWY
EVETS	VIVER	WAIN	AWARN	WEDS	WEYS	TWIGS		SWORN	YBET
VIAE	VIVES	SWAIN	WARNS	WEED	WHAM	WILD		WORT	YEAD
VIAL	VIVO	TWAIN	WARP	TWEED	WHAMS	WILDS		WORTH	YEADS
VIALS	VIZY	WAINS	WARPS	WEEDS	WHAP	WILE		WORTS	YEAH
VIAS	VLEI	WAIT	WARS	WEEDY	WHAPS	WILED		WOST	YEAN
VIBE	VLEIS	AWAIT	SWART	WEEK	WHAT	WILES		WOTS	YEANS
VIBES	VOAR	WAITE	WARST	WEEKE	WHATS	WILI		SWOTS	YEAR
VIBEX	VOARS	WAITS	WART	WEEKS	WHEE	WILIS		WOVE	YEARD
VIBS	VOES	WAKE	WARTS	WEEL		WILL		WOVEN	YEARN
VICE	VOID	AWAKE	WARTY	AWEEL		SWILL		WOWF	YEARS
VICED	AVOID	WAKED	WARY	SWEEL		TWILL		WOWS	YEAS
VICES	OVOID	WAKEN	WASE	TWEEL		WILLS		WRAP	YEAST
VIDE	VOIDS	WAKER	WASES	WEEM		WILLY		WRAPS	
VIDEO	VOLA	WAKES	WASH	WEEMS		WILT		WRAPT	
VIED	VOLAE	WALD	AWASH	WEEN		TWILT		WREN	
IVIED	VOLAR	WALDS		TWEEN		WILTS		WRENS	
VIER	VOLE	WALE		WEENS		WILY		WRIT	
VIERS									

YEDE	YEPS	YILLS	YOGAS	AYONT	YUCKS	ZACKS	ZEST	ZINGY	ZOOMS
YEDES	YERD	YINS	YOGH	YOOP	YUCKY	ZAGS	ZESTS	ZIPS	ZOON
YEED	YERDS	YIPS	YOGHS	YOOPS	YUFT	ZANY	ZESTY	ZITS	ZOONS
YEEDS	YERK	YIRD	YOGI	YORE	YUFTS	ZAPS	ZETA	ZIZZ	ZOOS
YEGG	YERKS	YIRDS	YOGIC	YORES	YUGA	ZARF	ZETAS	ZOBO	ZULU
YEGGS	YESK	YIRK	YOGIN	YORK	YUGAS	ZARFS	ZEZE	ZOBOS	ZULUS
YELD	YESKS	YIRKS	YOGIS	YORKS	YUGS	ZATI	ZEZES	ZOBU	ZUPA
GYELD	YEST	YITE	YOKE	YOUK	YUKE	ZATIS	ZHOS	ZOEA	ZUPAN
YELK	YESTS	YITES	YOKED	YOUKS	YUKED	ZEAL	ZIFF	ZOEAE	ZUPAS
YELKS	YESTY	YLEM	YOKEL	YOUR	YUKES	ZEALS	ZIFFS	ZOEAL	ZURF
YELL	YETI	XYLEM	YOKES	YOURN	YUKS	ZEAS	ZIGS	ZOEAS	ZURFS
YELLS	YETIS	YLEMS	YOKS	YOURS	YUKY	ZEBU	ZILA	ZOIC	ZYME
YELM	YETT	YLKE	YOLD	YOURT	YULE	ZEBUB	ZILAS	AZOIC	AZYME
YELMS	YETTS	YMPE	YOLK	YOWE	YULES	ZEBUS	ZIMB	ZONA	ZYMES
YELP	YEUK	YMPES	YOLKS	YOWES	YUMP	ZEDS	ZIMBS	ZONAE	
AYELP	YEUKS	YMPT	YOLKY	YOWL	YUMPS	ZEES	ZIMBI	ZONAL	
YELPS	YEVE	YOBS	YOMP	YOWLS	YUNX	ZEIN	ZINC	ZONE	
YELT	YEVEN	YOCK	YOMPS	YOWS	YUPS	ZEINS	ZINCO	OZONE	
YELTS	YEVES	YOCKS	YOND	YUAN	YURT	ZEKS	ZINCS	ZONED	
YENS	YEWS	YODE	YONI	YUCA	YURTS	ZELS	ZINCY	ZONES	
HYENS	YGOE	YODEL	YONIS	YUCAS	YWIS	ZERO	ZING	ZOOM	
SYENS	YILL	YOGA	YONT	YUCK	ZACK	ZEROS	ZINGS		

PART B: 5-letter word hooks
extensible words only

ABACA
ABACAS
ABAND
ABANDS
ABASE
ABASED
ABASES
ABATE
ABATED
ABATES
ABAYA
KABAYA
ABAYAS
ABBES
ABBESS
ABBEY
ABBEYS
ABBOT
ABBOTS
ABCEE
ABCEES
ABEAR
ABEARS
ABELE
KABELE
ABELES
ABHOR
ABHORS
ABIDE
ABIDED
ABIDES
ABIES
BABIES
GABIES
RABIES
ABLED
CABLED
FABLED
GABLED
SABLED
TABLED
ABLER
FABLER
ABLES
CABLES
FABLES
GABLES
SABLES
TABLES
ABLEST
ABLET
GABLET
TABLET
ABLETS
ABODE
ABODED
ABODES
ABORD
ABORDS
ABORT
ABORTS
ABOUT
ABOUTS
ABRAY
ABRAYS
ABRIN
ABRINS
ABSEY
ABSEYS
ABSIT
ABSITS
ABUNA
ABUNAS
ABUSE
ABUSED
ABUSER
ABUSES
ABYSM
ABYSMS
ACARI
ACARID
ACCOY
ACCOYS
ACHED
BACHED
CACHED
ACHES
BACHES
CACHES
LACHES
NACHES
RACHES
TACHES
ACING
FACING
LACING
MACING
PACING
RACING
ACKEE
HACKEE
ACKEES
ACORN
ACORNS
ACRED
SACRED
ACRES
NACRES
ACTIN
ACTING
ACTINS
ACTON
ACTONS
ACTOR
FACTOR
ACTORS
ACUTE
ACUTER
ACUTES
ADAGE
ADAGES
ADAPT
ADAPTS
ADDED
DADDED
GADDED
MADDED
PADDED
WADDED
ADDER
GADDER
LADDER
MADDER
PADDER
SADDER
ADDERS
ADDIO
ADDIOS
ADDLE
DADDLE
FADDLE
PADDLE
RADDLE
SADDLE
WADDLE
ADDLED
ADDLES
ADEEM
ADEEMS
ADEPT
ADEPTS
ADIEU
ADIEUS
ADIEUX
ADIOS
RADIOS
ADMIN
ADMINS
ADMIT
ADMITS
ADOBE
ADOBES
ADOPT
ADOPTS
ADORE
ADORED
ADORER
ADORES
ADORN
ADORNS
ADULT
ADULTS
ADUST
ADUSTS
ADVEW
ADVEWS
AEONS
PAEONS
AERIE
FAERIE
AERIER
AERIES
AFARA
AFARAS
AFEAR
AFEARD
AFEARS
AFRIT
AFRITS
AFTER
DAFTER
RAFTER
WAFTER
AFTERS
AGAMI
AGAMIC
AGAMID
AGAMIS
AGATE
AGATES
AGAVE
AGAVES
AGAZE
AGAZED
AGENE
SAGENE
AGENES
AGENT
AGENTS
AGGER
DAGGER
GAGGER
JAGGER
LAGGER
NAGGER
SAGGER
TAGGER
YAGGER
AGGERS
AGGRO
AGGROS
AGHAS
AGHAST
AGILA
AGILAS
AGILE
VAGILE
AGILER
AGING
CAGING
GAGING
PAGING
RAGING
WAGING
AGINGS
AGIST
AGISTS
AGLET
EAGLET
HAGLET
AGLETS
AGMAS
MAGMAS
AGOGE
AGOGES
AGONS
WAGONS
AGORA
AGORAS
AGREE
AGREED
AGREES
AGUED
VAGUED
AGUES
VAGUES
AGUTI
AGUTIS
AIDED
LAIDED
MAIDED
RAIDED
AIDER
RAIDER
AIDERS
AIDOS
IAIDOS
AILED
BAILED
FAILED
HAILED
JAILED
MAILED
NAILED
RAILED
SAILED
TAILED
VAILED
WAILED
AIMED
MAIMED
AIOLI
AIOLIS
AIRED
FAIRED
HAIRED
LAIRED
PAIRED
SAIRED
AIRER
FAIRER
SAIRER
AIRERS
AIRNS
BAIRNS
CAIRNS
AISLE
AISLED
AISLES
AIZLE
AIZLES
AJWAN
AJWANS
AKEES
RAKEES
AKENE
AKENES
AKING
BAKING
CAKING
FAKING
LAKING
MAKING
RAKING
TAKING
WAKING
AKKAS
YAKKAS
ALAAP
ALAAPS
ALANG
LALANG
ALANGS
ALAPA
ALAPAS
ALAPS
JALAPS
ALARM
ALARMS
ALARY
SALARY
ALATE
MALATE
PALATE
ALATED
ALAYS
PALAYS
ALBUM
ALBUMS
ALDEA
ALDEAS
ALDER
BALDER
ALDERN
ALDERS
ALEPH
ALEPHS
ALERT
ALERTS
ALEYE
ALEYED
ALEYES
ALFAS
HALFAS
ALGIN
ALGINS
ALGUM
ALGUMS
ALIBI
ALIBIS
ALIEN
ALIENS
ALIGN
MALIGN
ALIGNS
ALINE
SALINE
VALINE
ALINED
ALINES
ALKYD
ALKYDS
ALKYL
ALKYLS
ALLAY
ALLAYS
ALLEE
MALLEE
SALLEE
ALLEES
ALLEL
ALLELE
ALLELS
ALLEY
GALLEY
VALLEY
ALLEYS
ALLOD
ALLODS
ALLOT
BALLOT
TALLOT
ALLOTS
ALLOW
BALLOW
CALLOW
FALLOW
GALLOW
HALLOW
MALLOW
SALLOW
TALLOW
WALLOW
ALLOWS
ALLOY
ALLOYS
ALLYL
ALLYLS
ALMAH
ALMAHS
ALMAS
HALMAS
TALMAS
ALMEH
ALMEHS
ALMUG
ALMUGS
ALOED
HALOED
ALOES
HALOES
ALOHA
ALOHAS
ALONG
KALONG
ALPHA
ALPHAS
ALTAR
ALTARS
ALTER
FALTER
HALTER
PALTER
SALTER
ALTERN
ALTERS
ALTOS
SALTOS
ALULA
ALULAS
ALURE
ALURES
ALWAY
ALWAYS
AMASS
CAMASS
AMATE
HAMATE
RAMATE
AMATED
AMATES
AMAZE
AMAZED
AMAZES
AMBAN
AMBANS
AMBER
CAMBER
JAMBER
LAMBER
TAMBER
AMBERS
AMBERY
AMBIT
GAMBIT
AMBITS
AMBLE
GAMBLE
HAMBLE
RAMBLE
WAMBLE
AMBLED
AMBLER
AMBLES
AMBOS
JAMBOS
MAMBOS
SAMBOS
ZAMBOS
AMEBA
AMEBAE
AMEBAS
AMEER
AMEERS
AMEND
AMENDE
AMENDS
AMENE
AMENED
AMENS
YAMENS
AMENT
LAMENT
AMENTA
AMENTS
AMICE
AMICES
AMIDE
AMIDES
AMIES
RAMIES
AMIGO
AMIGOS
AMINE
FAMINE
GAMINE
TAMINE
AMINES
AMMAN
AMMANS
AMMON
GAMMON
MAMMON
AMMONS
AMOUR
AMOURS
AMOVE
AMOVED
AMOVES
AMPLE
CAMPLE
SAMPLE
AMPLER
AMPLY
DAMPLY
AMPUL
AMPULE
AMPULS
AMRIT
AMRITA
AMRITS
AMUSE
AMUSED
AMUSER
AMUSES
ANANA
BANANA
MANANA
ANANAS
ANCLE
ANCLES
ANEAR
ANEARS
ANELE
ANELED
ANELES
ANENT
MANENT
ANGEL
MANGEL
ANGELS
ANGER
BANGER
DANGER
GANGER
HANGER
LANGER
MANGER
RANGER
ANGERS
ANGLE
BANGLE
CANGLE
DANGLE
FANGLE
JANGLE
MANGLE
TANGLE
WANGLE
ANGLED
ANGLER
ANGLES
ANGST
ANGSTS
ANIGH
ANIGHT
ANIMA
ANIMAL
ANIMAS
ANIME
ANIMES
ANION
FANION
ANIONS
ANISE

ANISES
ANKER
BANKER
CANKER
DANKER
HANKER
JANKER
LANKER
RANKER
TANKER
WANKER
YANKER
ANKERS
ANKLE
FANKLE
RANKLE
WANKLE
ANKLED
ANKLES
ANKLET
ANNAL
ANNALS
ANNAS
CANNAS
MANNAS
NANNAS
TANNAS
ANNAT
ANNATS
ANNEX
ANNEXE
ANNOY
ANNOYS
ANNUL
ANNULI
ANNULS
ANODE
ANODES
ANTAR
CANTAR
KANTAR
ANTARS
ANTED
BANTED
CANTED
DANTED
GANTED
KANTED
PANTED
RANTED
WANTED
ANTES
ZANTES
ANTIC
MANTIC
ANTICK
ANTICS
ANTIS
MANTIS
ANTRE
ANTRES
ANVIL
ANVILS
AORTA
AORTAL
AORTAS
APERY
NAPERY
PAPERY
APHID

APHIDS
APHIS
RAPHIS
APING
CAPING
GAPING
JAPING
RAPING
TAPING
APIOL
APIOLS
APISH
PAPISH
APISM
PAPISM
APISMS
APNEA
APNEAS
APODE
APODES
APPAL
APPALS
APPAY
APPAYD
APPAYS
APPLE
DAPPLE
APPLES
APPUI
APPUIS
APPUY
APPUYS
APRON
NAPRON
APRONS
APSES
LAPSES
ARABA
ARABAS
ARAME
ARAMES
ARBOR
HARBOR
ARBORS
ARCED
FARCED
ARDEB
ARDEBS
ARDRI
ARDRIS
AREAD
AREADS
ARECA
ARECAS
AREDE
AREDES
AREFY
RAREFY
ARENA
ARENAS
ARETE
ARETES
ARETS
CARETS
ARETT
ARETTS
ARGAL
ARGALA
ARGALI
ARGAN

ARGAND
ARGANS
ARGIL
ARGILS
ARGOL
ARGOLS
ARGON
JARGON
ARGONS
ARGOT
ARGOTS
ARGUE
ARGUED
ARGUER
ARGUES
ARGUS
SARGUS
ARIEL
ARIELS
ARISE
ARISEN
ARISES
ARISH
BARISH
GARISH
HARISH
MARISH
PARISH
ARKED
BARKED
CARKED
HARKED
LARKED
MARKED
NARKED
PARKED
ARLES
FARLES
MARLES
PARLES
ARMED
FARMED
HARMED
WARMED
ARMET
ARMETS
ARMIL
ARMILS
ARMOR
ARMORS
ARMORY
ARNAS
VARNAS
ARNUT
ARNUTS
AROBA
AROBAS
AROID
LAROID
AROIDS
AROMA
AROMAS
ARRAH
JARRAH
ARRAS
NARRAS
TARRAS
ARRAY
WARRAY
ARRAYS

ARRET
BARRET
GARRET
ARRETS
ARRIS
KARRIS
ARRISH
ARROW
BARROW
FARROW
HARROW
MARROW
NARROW
TARROW
YARROW
ARROWS
ARROWY
ARSES
CARSES
FARSES
PARSES
ARSON
PARSON
ARSONS
ARTAL
HARTAL
ARTEL
CARTEL
MARTEL
ARTELS
ARTIC
ARTICS
ARUMS
GARUMS
LARUMS
ARVAL
LARVAL
ASANA
ASANAS
ASCOT
MASCOT
ASCOTS
ASHEN
WASHEN
ASHES
BASHES
CASHES
DASHES
FASHES
GASHES
HASHES
LASHES
MASHES
PASHES
RASHES
SASHES
TASHES
WASHES
ASHET
ASHETS
ASIDE
ASIDES
ASKED
BASKED
CASKED
MASKED
TASKED
ASKER
MASKER
TASKER

ASKERS
ASPEN
ASPENS
ASPER
GASPER
JASPER
RASPER
ASPERS
ASPIC
ASPICK
ASPICS
ASSAI
ASSAIL
ASSAIS
ASSAY
ASSAYS
ASSES
BASSES
GASSES
LASSES
MASSES
PASSES
RASSES
SASSES
TASSES
ASSESS
ASSET
BASSET
TASSET
ASSETS
ASSOT
ASSOTS
ASSOTT
ASTER
BASTER
CASTER
EASTER
FASTER
LASTER
MASTER
PASTER
RASTER
TASTER
VASTER
WASTER
ASTERN
ASTERS
ASTERT
ASTUN
ASTUNS
ATMAN
BATMAN
VATMAN
ATMANS
ATOKE
ATOKES
ATOLL
ATOLLS
ATONE
ATONED
ATONER
ATONES
ATRIA
LATRIA
ATRIAL
ATTAP
ATTAPS
ATTAR
ATTARS
ATTIC

ATTICS
AUDIO
AUDIOS
AUDIT
AUDITS
AUGER
GAUGER
SAUGER
AUGERS
AUGHT
CAUGHT
HAUGHT
NAUGHT
RAUGHT
TAUGHT
WAUGHT
AUGHTS
AUGUR
AUGURS
AUGURY
AUMIL
AUMILS
AUNTS
DAUNTS
GAUNTS
HAUNTS
JAUNTS
NAUNTS
SAUNTS
TAUNTS
VAUNTS
AUNTY
JAUNTY
AURAS
LAURAS
AURIC
TAURIC
AUXIN
AUXINS
AVAIL
AVAILE
AVAILS
AVALE
AVALED
AVALES
AVANT
SAVANT
AVANTI
AVENS
HAVENS
PAVENS
RAVENS
AVERS
CAVERS
HAVERS
LAVERS
PAVERS
RAVERS
SAVERS
TAVERS
WAVERS
AVERSE
AVERT
TAVERT
AVERTS
AVINE
RAVINE
SAVINE
AVION
AVIONS

AVISE
PAVISE
AVISED
AVISES
AVISO
AVISOS
AVIZE
AVIZED
AVIZES
AVOID
AVOIDS
AVOUE
AVOUES
AVYZE
AVYZED
AVYZES
AWAIT
AWAITS
AWAKE
AWAKED
AWAKEN
AWAKES
AWARD
VAWARD
AWARDS
AWARE
AWARER
AWARN
AWARNS
AWETO
AWETOS
AWFUL
LAWFUL
AWING
CAWING
DAWING
HAWING
JAWING
KAWING
LAWING
PAWING
RAWING
SAWING
TAWING
YAWING
AWNED
DAWNED
FAWNED
PAWNED
YAWNED
AWNER
DAWNER
FAWNER
PAWNER
AWNERS
AWOKE
AWOKEN
AXING
FAXING
RAXING
TAXING
WAXING
AXIOM
AXIOMS
AXOID
AXOIDS
AXONS
CAXONS
AYAHS
RAYAHS

AYRIE
AYRIES
AZIDE
AZIDES
AZOTE
AZOTES
AZOTH
AZOTHS
AZURE
RAZURE
AZURES
AZYME
AZYMES
BABEL
BABELS
BABOO
BABOON
BABOOS
BABUL
BABULS
BACCA
BACCAE
BACCAS
BACCO
BACCOS
BACON
BACONS
BADGE
BADGER
BADGES
BAGEL
BAGELS
BAIRN
BAIRNS
BAIZE
BAIZED
BAIZES
BAJAN
BAJANS
BAJRA
BAJRAS
BAJRI
BAJRIS
BAKER
BAKERS
BAKERY
BALER
BALERS
BALOO
BALOOS
BALSA
BALSAM
BALSAS
BANCO
BANCOS
BANDH
BANDHS
BANDS
ABANDS
BANGS
OBANGS
BANIA
BANIAN
BANIAS
BANJO
BANJOS
BARBE
BARBED
BARBEL
BARBER

BARBES
BARBET
BARCA
BARCAS
BARES
BAREST
BARGE
BARGED
BARGEE
BARGES
BARON
BARONS
BARONY
BARRE
BARRED
BARREL
BARREN
BARRES
BARRET
BARYE
BARYES
BASAL
BASALT
BASAN
BASANS
BASED
ABASED
BASES
ABASES
BASEST
BASIC
BASICS
BASIL
BASILS
BASIN
BASING
BASINS
BASON
BASONS
BASSE
BASSED
BASSER
BASSES
BASSET
BASSO
BASSOS
BASTE
BASTED
BASTER
BASTES
BASTO
BASTOS
BATED
ABATED
BATES
ABATES
BATHE
BATHED
BATHER
BATHES
BATIK
BATIKS
BATON
BATONS
BATTA
BATTAS
BAULK
BAULKS
BAVIN
BAVINS

BAYLE	BELEES	BIBLES	BLACK	BLITES	BODLE	BORNE	BRACED	BREVE
BAYLES	BELGA	BICES	BLACKS	BLOAT	BODLES	ABORNE	BRACER	BREVES
BAYOU	BELGAS	IBICES	BLADE	BLOATS	BOGAN	BORON	BRACES	BREVET
BAYOUS	BELIE	BIDED	BLADED	BLOCK	BOGANS	BORONS	BRACK	BRIAR
BAZAR	BELIED	ABIDED	BLADES	BLOCKS	BOGEY	BORTS	BRACKS	BRIARS
BAZARS	BELIEF	ABIDES	BLAES	BLOCKY	BOGEYS	ABORTS	BRACT	BRIBE
BEACH	BELIER	BIDES	BLAEST	BLOKE	BOGIE	BOSOM	BRACTS	BRIBED
BEACHY	BELIES	BIDET	BLAIN	BLOKES	BOGIES	BOSOMS	BRAID	BRIBER
BEANO	BELLE	BIDETS	BLAINS	BLOND	BOGLE	BOSOMY	ABRAID	BRIBES
BEANOS	BELLED	BIDON	BLAME	BLONDE	BOGLES	BOSON	BRAIDE	BRICK
BEARD	BELLES	BIDONS	BLAMED	BLONDS	BOHEA	BOSONS	BRAIDS	BRICKS
BEARDS	BEMAD	BIELD	BLAMES	BLOOD	BOHEAS	BOSUN	BRAIL	BRICKY
BEARE	BEMADS	BIELDS	BLAND	BLOODS	BOING	BOSUNS	BRAILS	BRIDE
BEARED	BEMUD	BIELDY	BLANK	BLOODY	BOINGS	BOTCH	BRAIN	BRIDED
BEARER	BEMUDS	BIGHA	BLANKS	BLOOM	BOINK	BOTCHY	BRAINS	BRIDES
BEARES	BENET	BIGHAS	BLANKY	ABLOOM	BOINKS	BOTEL	BRAINY	BRIEF
BEARS	BENETS	BIGHT	BLARE	BLOOMS	BOLUS	BOTELS	BRAKE	BRIEFS
ABEARS	BENNE	BIGHTS	BLARED	BLOOMY	OBOLUS	BOTTE	BRAKED	BRIER
BEAST	BENNES	BIGOT	BLARES	BLOOP	BOMBE	BOTTED	BRAKES	BRIERS
BEASTS	BENNET	BIGOTS	BLASH	BLOOPS	BOMBED	BOTTES	BRAME	BRIERY
BEATH	BENNI	BIJOU	BLASHY	BLORE	BOMBER	BOUGE	BRAMES	BRILL
BEATHS	BENNIS	BIJOUX	BLAST	BLORES	BOMBES	BOUGED	BRAND	BRILLS
BEAUT	BEPAT	BIKER	OBLAST	BLOWS	BOMBO	BOUGES	BRANDS	BRINE
BEAUTS	BEPATS	BIKERS	BLASTS	BLOWSE	BOMBOS	BOUGET	BRANDY	BRINED
BEAUTY	BERAY	BIKIE	BLATE	BLOWSY	BONCE	BOUGH	BRANK	BRINES
BEBOP	BERAYS	BIKIES	ABLATE	BLUDE	BONCES	BOUGHS	BRANKS	BRING
BEBOPS	BERET	BILBO	OBLATE	BLUDES	BONER	BOUGHT	BRANKY	BRINGS
BECKE	BERETS	BILBOS	BLATER	BLUES	BONERS	BOULE	BRASH	BRINK
BECKED	BEROB	BILGE	BLATT	BLUEST	BONGO	BOULES	BRASHY	BRINKS
BECKES	BEROBS	BILGED	BLATTS	BLUESY	BONGOS	BOULT	BRASS	BRISE
BECKET	BERTH	BILGES	BLAUD	BLUEY	BONIE	BOULTS	BRASSY	BRISES
BEDEL	BERTHA	BIMBO	BLAUDS	BLUEYS	BONIER	BOUND	BRAST	BRISK
BEDELL	BERTHE	BIMBOS	BLAZE	BLUFF	BONNE	ABOUND	BRASTS	BRISKS
BEDELS	BERTHS	BINGE	BLAZED	BLUFFS	BONNES	YBOUND	BRAVE	BRISKY
BEDEW	BERYL	BINGED	BLAZER	BLUID	BONNET	BOURD	BRAVED	BROAD
BEDEWS	BERYLS	BINGES	BLAZES	BLUIDS	BONZE	BOURDS	BRAVER	ABROAD
BEDIM	BESEE	BINGO	BLEAK	BLUIDY	BONZER	BOURG	BRAVES	BROADS
BEDIMS	BESEEM	BINGOS	BLEAKS	BLUNK	BONZES	BOURGS	BRAVO	BROCH
BEDYE	BESEEN	BIOME	BLEAKY	BLUNKS	BOOKS	BOURN	BRAVOS	BROCHE
BEDYED	BESEES	BIOMES	BLEAR	BLUNT	BOOKSY	BOURNE	BRAWL	BROCHS
BEDYES	BESET	BIONT	BLEARS	BLUNTS	BOONG	BOURNS	BRAWLS	BROCK
BEFIT	BESETS	BIONTS	BLEARY	BLURB	BOONGS	BOUSE	BRAWLY	BROCKS
BEFITS	BESIT	BIOTA	BLEAT	BLURBS	BOORD	BOUSED	BRAWN	BROGH
BEFOG	BESITS	BIOTAS	BLEATS	BLURT	BOORDE	BOUSES	BRAWNS	BROGHS
BEFOGS	BESOM	BIPED	BLEED	BLURTS	BOORDS	BOUTS	BRAWNY	BROIL
BEGAR	BESOMS	BIPEDS	BLEEDS	BLUSH	BOOSE	BOWAT	BRAYS	BROILS
BEGARS	BESOT	BIPOD	BLEEP	ABLUSH	BOOSED	BOWATS	ABRAYS	BROKE
BEGEM	BESOTS	BIPODS	BLEEPS	BOARD	BOOSES	BOWEL	BRAZE	BROKED
BEGEMS	BETEL	BIRLE	BLEND	ABOARD	BOOST	BOWELS	BRAZED	BROKEN
BEGET	BETELS	BIRLED	BLENDE	BOARDS	BOOSTS	BOWER	BRAZEN	BROKER
BEGETS	BETID	BIRLES	BLENDS	BOART	BOOTH	BOWERS	BRAZES	BROKES
BEGIN	BETIDE	BIRSE	BLENT	BOARTS	BOOTHS	BOWERY	BREAD	BROND
BEGINS	BETON	BIRSES	YBLENT	BOAST	BOOZE	BOWES	BREADS	BRONDS
BEGUM	BETONS	BIRTH	BLEST	BOASTS	BOOZED	BOWET	BREAK	BROOD
BEGUMS	BETONY	BIRTHS	ABLEST	BOBAC	BOOZER	BOWETS	BREAKS	BROODS
BEGUN	BEVEL	BISES	BLETS	BOBACS	BOOZES	BOWNE	BREAM	BROODY
BEGUNK	BEVELS	IBISES	ABLETS	BOBAK	BOOZEY	BOWNED	BREAMS	BROOK
BEIGE	BEVER	BISON	BLIMP	BOBAKS	BORDE	BOWNES	BREDE	BROOKS
BEIGEL	BEVERS	BISONS	BLIMPS	BOCCA	BORDEL	BOWSE	BREDED	BROOL
BEIGES	BEVUE	BITCH	BLIND	BOCCAS	BORDER	BOWSED	BREDES	BROOLS
BEING	BEVUES	BITCHY	BLINDS	BOCHE	BORDES	BOWSER	BREED	BROOM
BEINGS	BEWET	BITER	BLINI	BOCHES	BORDS	BOWSES	BREEDS	BROOMS
BEKAH	BEWETS	OBITER	BLINIS	BODED	ABORDS	BOXER	BREER	BROOMY
BEKAHS	BEWIG	BITERS	BLINK	ABODED	BOREE	BOXERS	BREERS	BROOS
BELAH	BEWIGS	BITTE	BLINKS	BODES	BOREEN	BOYAR	BREES	BROOSE
BELAHS	BEZEL	BITTED	BLINS	ABODES	BOREES	BOYARS	BREESE	BROSE
BELAY	BEZELS	BITTEN	ABLINS	BODGE	BORER	BOYAU	BRENT	BROSES
BELAYS	BHANG	BITTER	BLITE	BODGED	BORERS	BOYAUX	YBRENT	BROSE
BELEE	BHANGS			BODGER	BORGO	BRERE	BRERES	BROTH
BELEED	BIBLE			BODGES	BORGOS	BRACE		BROTH

BROTHS	BUNIA	CABOB	CANOE	CARVEL	SCENTS	CHARTS	CHIMED	CHUMPS
BROWN	BUNIAS	CABOBS	CANOED	CARVEN	CEORL	CHASE	CHIMER	CHUNK
BROWNS	BUNJE	CABOC	CANOES	CARVER	CEORLS	CHASED	CHIMES	CHUNKS
BROWNY	BUNJEE	CABOCS	CANON	CARVES	CERGE	CHASER	CHIMP	CHUNKY
BROWS	BUNJES	CACAO	CANONS	CASCO	CERGES	CHASES	CHIMPS	CHURL
BROWSE	BUNKO	CACAOS	CANTO	CASCOS	CERIA	CHASM	CHINA	CHURLS
BROWST	BUNKOS	CACHE	CANTON	CASTE	CERIAS	CHASMS	CHINAR	CHURN
BRUIT	BUNYA	CACHED	CANTOR	CASTED	CERNE	CHASY	CHINAS	CHURNS
BRUITS	BUNYAS	CACHES	CANTOS	CASTER	SCERNE	CHASMS	CHINE	CHURR
BRUME	BURAN	CACHET	CANTS	CASTES	CERNED	CHAYA	CHINED	CHURRS
BRUMES	BURANS	CADET	SCANTS	CERNES	CHAYAS	CHUSE		
BRUNT	BURGH	CADETS	CANTY	CATCH	CESSE	CHEAP	CHINES	CHUSES
BRUNTS	BURGHS	CADGE	SCANTY	SCATCH	CESSED	CHEAPO	CHINK	CHUTE
BRUSH	BURIN	CADGED	CAPAS	CATCHT	CESSER	CHEAPS	CHINKS	CHUTES
BRUSHY	BURINS	CADGER	SCAPAS	CATCHY	CESSES	CHEAPY	CHINKY	CHYLE
BRUST	BURKA	CADGES	CAPED	CATER	CETYL	CHEAT	CHINO	CHYLES
BRUSTS	BURKAS	CADIE	SCAPED	ACATER	ACETYL	CHEATS	CHINOS	CHYME
BRUTE	BURKE	CADIES	CAPER	CATES	CETYLS	CHECK	CHIRK	CHYMES
BRUTED	BURKED	CADRE	CAPERS	ACATES	CHACE	CHECKS	CHIRKS	CIBOL
BRUTES	BURKES	CADRES	CAPES	CATTY	CHACED	CHECKY	CHIRL	CIBOLS
BUAZE	BUROO	CAECA	SCAPES	SCATTY	CHACES	CHEEK	CHIRLS	CIDER
BUAZES	BUROOS	CAECAL	CAPLE	CAULD	CHACK	CHEEKS	CHIRM	ACIDER
BUBAL	BURQA	CAFFS	CAPLES	CAULDS	CHACKS	CHEEKY	CHIRMS	CIDERS
BUBALS	BURQAS	SCAFFS	CAPON	CAULK	CHACO	CHEEP	CHIRP	CIDERY
BUCHU	BURRO	CAGOT	CAPONS	CAULKS	CHACOS	CHEEPS	CHIRPS	CIGAR
BUCHUS	BURROS	CAGOTS	CAPOT	CAUPS	CHAFE	CHEER	CHIRR	CIGARS
BUCKU	BURROW	CAIRD	CAPOTE	SCAUPS	CHAFED	CHEERO	CHIRRS	CIMAR
BUCKUS	BURSA	CAIRDS	CAPOTS	CAUSE	CHAFER	CHEERS	CHIRT	CIMARS
BUDGE	BURSAE	CAIRN	CAPUL	CAUSED	CHAFES	CHEERY	CHIRTS	CIONS
BUDGED	BURSAL	CAIRNS	CAPULS	CAUSEN	CHAFF	CHEKA	CHIVE	SCIONS
BUDGER	BURSAR	CALIF	CARAP	CAUSER	CHAFFS	CHEKAS	CHIVED	CIRCA
BUDGES	BURSE	CALIFS	CARAPS	CAUSES	CHAFFY	CHELA	CHIVES	CIRCAR
BUDGET	BURSES	CALLA	CARAT	CAUSEY	CHAFT	CHELAE	CHOCK	CISCO
BUFFE	BURST	CALLAS	CARATS	CAVEL	CHAFTS	CHELAS	CHOCKS	CISCOS
BUFFED	ABURST	CALLS	CARDI	CAVELS	CHAIN	CHERT	CHOIR	CITAL
BUFFER	BURSTS	SCALLS	CARDIS	CAVER	CHAINS	CHERTS	CHOIRS	CITALS
BUFFET	BUSED	CALPA	CARED	CAVERN	CHAIR	CHERTY	CHOKE	CITER
BUGLE	ABUSED	CALPAC	SCARED	CAVERS	CHAIRS	CHEST	CHOKED	CITERS
BUGLED	BUSES	CALPAS	CARER	CAVIE	CHAIS	CHESTS	CHOKER	CITES
BUGLER	ABUSES	CALPS	CARERS	CAVIER	CHAISE	CHESTY	CHOKES	CITESS
BUGLES	BUSSU	SCALPS	CARES	CAVIES	CHICA	CHICA	CHOKEY	CIVET
BUGLET	BUSSUS	CALVE	SCARES	CAVIL	CHICAS	CHICH	CHOLI	CIVETS
BUILD	BUTTE	CALVED	CARESS	CAVILS	CHICH	CHICHA	CHOLIC	CIVIC
BUILDS	BUTTED	CALVER	CARET	CAXON	CHICHA	CHICHI	CHOLIS	CIVICS
BUIST	BUTTER	CALVES	CARETS	CAXONS	CHICHI	CHICK	CHOMP	CLACK
BUISTS	BUTTES	CAMAN	CAROB	CEASE	CHICK	TCHICK	CHOMPS	CLACKS
BULGE	BUTYL	CAMANS	CAROBS	CEASED	CHANK	CHICKS	CHOOK	CLADE
BULGED	BUTYLS	CAMAS	CAROL	CEASES	CHANKS	CHIDE	CHOOKS	CLADES
BULGER	BUYER	CAMASH	CAROLS	CEAZE	CHANT	CHIDED	CHOOM	CLAIM
BULGES	BUYERS	CAMASS	CAROM	CEAZED	CHANTS	CHIDER	CHOOMS	CLAIMS
BULLA	BWANA	CAMEL	CAROMS	CEAZES	CHANTY	CHIEF	CHORD	CLAME
BULLAE	BWANAS	SCAMEL	CARPS	CEDAR	CHAPE	CHIEFS	CHORDS	CLAMES
BULLAS	BWAZI	CAMELS	SCARPS	CEDARN	CHAPEL	CHIEL	CHORE	CLAMP
BULSE	BWAZIS	CAMEO	SCARPS	CEDARS	CHAPES	CHIELD	CHOREA	CLAMPS
BULSES	BYLAW	CAMEOS	CARRY	CEILI	CHARA	CHIELS	CHOREE	CLANG
BUMBO	BYLAWS	CAMES	SCARRY	CEILIS	CHARAS	CHILD	CHORES	CLANGS
BUMBOS	BYWAY	CAMESE	CARSE	CELLA	CHARD	CHILDE	CHOSE	CLANK
BUMPH	BYWAYS	CAMIS	CARSES	CELLAE	CHARDS	CHILDS	CHOSEN	CLANKS
BUMPHS	CABAL	CAMISE	CARTA	CELLAR	CHARE	CHILE	CHOSES	CLART
BUNAS	CABALA	CAMPS	CARTAS	CELLO	CHARED	CHILES	CHOUT	CLARTS
ABUNAS	CABALS	SCAMPS	CARTE	CELLOS	CHARES	CHILE	SCHOUT	CLARTY
BUNCE	CABBY	CANAL	ECARTE	CELOM	CHARET	CHILI	CHOUTS	CLASP
BUNCED	SCABBY	CANALS	CARTED	CELOMS	CHARK	CHILIS	CHUCK	CLASPS
BUNCES	CABER	CANEH	CARTEL	CENSE	CHARKS	CHILL	CHUCKS	CLASS
BUNCH	CABERS	CANEHS	CARTER	CENSED	CHARM	CHILLI	CHUFA	CLASSY
BUNCHY	CABIN	CANID	CARTES	CENSER	CHARMS	CHILLS	CHUFAS	CLATS
BUNCO	CABINS	CANIDS	CARTS	CENSES	CHARR	CHILLY	CHUFF	ECLATS
BUNCOS	CABLE	CANNA	SCARTS	CENTO	CHARRS	CHIMB	CHUFFS	CLAUT
BUNDU	CABLED	CANNAE	CARVE	CENTOS	CHARRY	CHIMBS	CHUFFY	CLAUTS
BUNDUS	CABLES	CANNAS	CARVED	CENTS	CHARTA	CHIME	CHUMP	CLAVE

SCLAVE	**CLOSE**	**COCOA**	CONGES	COSTAL	CRAIGS	CREESH	CROUPE	**CURAT**
CLAVER	ECLOSE	COCOAS	**CONGO**	**COSTE**	**CRAKE**	**CREME**	CROUPS	CURATE
CLAVES	CLOSED	**CODON**	CONGOS	COSTED	CRAKED	CREMES	CROUPY	CURATS
CLEAN	CLOSER	CODONS	CONGOU	COSTER	CRAKES	**CRENA**	**CROUT**	**CURER**
CLEANS	CLOSES	**COFFS**	**CONIA**	COSTES	**CRAME**	CRENAS	CROUTE	CURERS
CLEAR	CLOSET	SCOFFS	CONIAS	**COTTA**	CRAMES	**CREPE**	CROUTS	**CURIA**
CLEARS	**CLOTE**	**COGIE**	**CONIC**	COTTAR	**CRAMP**	CREPED	**CROWD**	CURIAE
CLEAT	CLOTES	COGIES	CONICS	COTTAS	CRAMPS	CREPES	CROWDS	CURIAS
CLEATS	**CLOTH**	**COGUE**	ICONIC	**COUCH**	CRAMPY	**CRESS**	**CROWN**	**CURIE**
CLECK	CLOTHE	COGUES	**CONNE**	COUCHE	**CRAMS**	CRESSY	CROWNS	ECURIE
CLECKS	CLOTHS	**COHOE**	CONNED	**COUGH**	SCRAMS	**CREST**	SCROWS	CURIES
CLEEK	**CLOUD**	COHOES	CONNER	COUGHS	**CRANE**	CRESTS	**CROZE**	CURIET
CLEEKS	CLOUDS	**COHOG**	CONNES	**COUNT**	CRANED	**CREWE**	CROZES	**CURIO**
CLEEP	CLOUDY	COHOGS	**CONTE**	COUNTS	CRANES	CREWED	**CRUCK**	CURIOS
CLEEPS	**CLOUR**	**COIGN**	CONTES	COUNTY	**CRANK**	CREWEL	CRUCKS	**CURRY**
CLEFT	CLOURS	COIGNE	**CONTO**	**COUPE**	CRANKS	CREWES	**CRUDE**	SCURRY
CLEFTS	**CLOUT**	COIGNS	CONTOS	COUPED	CRANKY	**CREWS**	CRUDER	**CURSE**
CLEPE	CLOUTS	**COLDS**	**COOEE**	COUPEE	**CRANS**	SCREWS	CRUDES	CURSED
CLEPED	**CLOVE**	SCOLDS	COOEED	COUPER	SCRANS	**CRICK**	**CRUEL**	CURSER
CLEPES	CLOVEN	**COLEY**	COOEES	COUPES	**CRAPE**	CRICKS	CRUELS	CURSES
CLERK	CLOVER	COLEYS	**COOEY**	**COUPS**	CRAPED	CRICKY	**CRUET**	**CURVE**
CLERKS	CLOVES	**COLIC**	COOEYS	SCOUPS	CRAPES	**CRIED**	CRUETS	CURVED
CLEVE	CLOYED	COLICS	**COOMB**	**COURB**	**CRAPS**	**CRIER**	**CRUMB**	CURVES
CLEVER	CLOYES	**COLIN**	COOMBS	COURBS	SCRAPS	CRIERS	CRUMBS	CURVET
CLEVES	**CLUCK**	COLINS	**COOPS**	**COURE**	**CRARE**	**CRIES**	CRUMBY	**CURVY**
CLICK	CLUCKS	**COLON**	SCOOPS	COURED	CRARES	**CRIME**	**CRUMP**	SCURVY
CLICKS	CLUCKY	COLONS	**COOTS**	COURES	**CRATE**	CRIMED	CRUMPS	**CUSEC**
CLIFF	**CLUMP**	COLONY	SCOOTS	COURS	CRATED	CRIMES	CRUMPY	CUSECS
SCLIFF	CLUMPS	**COLOR**	**COPAL**	SCOURS	CRATER	**CRIMP**	**CRUOR**	**CUTCH**
CLIFFS	CLUMPY	COLORS	COPALS	COURSE	CRATES	CRIMPS	CRUORS	SCUTCH
CLIFFY	**CLUNK**	**COLZA**	**COPER**	**COURT**	**CRAVE**	CRIMPY	**CRUSE**	CUTCHA
CLIFT	CLUNKS	COLZAS	COPERS	COURTS	CRAVED	**CRINE**	CRUSET	**CUTER**
CLIFTS	**CLYPE**	**COMBE**	**COPES**	**COUTH**	CRAVEN	SCRINE	**CRUST**	ACUTER
CLIFTY	CLYPED	COMBED	SCOPES	COUTHY	CRAVER	CRINED	CRUSTA	ACUTES
CLIMB	CLYPEI	COMBER	**COPRA**	**COVEN**	CRAVES	CRINES	CRUSTS	**CUTES**
CLIMBS	CLYPES	COMBES	COPRAS	COVENS	**CRAWL**	**CRISE**	CRUSTY	CUTEST
CLIME	**CNIDA**	**COMBO**	**COPSE**	COVENT	ACRAWL	CRISES	**CRUVE**	CUTESY
CLIMES	CNIDAE	COMBOS	COPSED	**COVER**	SCRAWL	**CRISP**	CRUVES	**CUTEY**
CLINE	**COACH**	**COMER**	COPSES	COVERS	CRAWLS	CRISPS	**CRWTH**	CUTEYS
CLINES	COACHY	COMERS	**CORAL**	COVERT	CRAWLY	CRISPY	CRWTHS	**CUTIE**
CLING	**COACT**	**COMET**	CORALS	**COVET**	**CRAWS**	**CRITH**	**CRYPT**	CUTIES
CLINGS	COACTS	COMETS	**CORBE**	COVETS	SCRAWS	CRITHS	CRYPTS	**CUTIN**
CLINGY	**COAPT**	**COMIC**	CORBEL	**COVEY**	**CRAZE**	**CROAK**	CRYPTO	CUTINS
CLINK	COAPTS	COMICS	CORBES	COVEYS	CRAZED	CROAKS	**CTENE**	**CUTTO**
CLINKS	**COARB**	**COMMA**	**CORED**	**COVIN**	CRAZES	CROAKY	CTENES	CUTTOE
CLINT	COARBS	COMMAS	SCORED	COVING	**CREAK**	**CROCK**	**CUBEB**	**CUVEE**
CLINTS	**COAST**	**COMMO**	**CORER**	COVINS	CREAKS	CROCKS	CUBEBS	CUVEES
CLIPE	COASTS	COMMON	SCORER	COWAN	CREAKY	**CROFT**	**CUBIC**	**CYCAD**
CLIPED	**COATE**	COMMOS	CORERS	COWANS	**CREAM**	CROFTS	CUBICA	CYCADS
CLIPES	COATED	COMMOT	**CORES**	**COWER**	CREAMS	**CROMB**	**CUBIT**	**CYCLE**
CLOAK	COATEE	**COMPO**	SCORES	COWERS	CREAMY	CROMBS	CUBITS	CYCLED
CLOAKS	COATER	COMPOS	**CORGI**	**COWLS**	**CREDO**	**CROME**	**CUFFS**	CYCLER
CLOAM	COATES	COMPOT	CORGIS	SCOWLS	CREDOS	CROMED	SCUFFS	CYCLES
CLOAMS	**COATI**	**COMPT**	**CORIA**	COWPS	**CREED**	CROMES	**CULET**	**CYCLO**
CLOCK	COATIS	COMPTS	SCORIA	SCOWPS	CREEDS	**CRONE**	CULETS	CYCLOS
CLOCKS	**COBIA**	**CONCH**	**CORNS**	**COYPU**	**CREEK**	CRONES	**CULLS**	**CYDER**
CLOFF	COBIAS	CONCHA	ACORNS	COYPUS	CREEKS	CRONET	SCULLS	CYDERS
CLOFFS	**COBLE**	CONCHE	SCORNS	**COZEN**	CREEKY	**CROOK**	**CUMEC**	**CYMAR**
CLOKE	COBLES	CONCHS	**CORNU**	COZENS	**CREEL**	CROOKS	CUMECS	CYMARS
CLOKED	**COBRA**	CONCHY	CORNUA	**CRABS**	CREELS	**CROON**	**CUMIN**	**CYNIC**
CLOKES	COBRAS	**CONES**	**CORPS**	SCRABS	**CREEP**	CROONS	CUMINS	CYNICS
CLONE	**COCCI**	SCONES	CORPSE	**CRACK**	CREEPS	**CRORE**	**CUPEL**	**CYTON**
CLONED	COCCID	**CONEY**	**CORSE**	CRACKS	CREEPY	CRORES	CUPELS	CYTONS
CLONES	**COCCO**	CONEYS	SCORSE	**CRAFT**	**CREES**	**CROSS**	**CUPID**	**DACHA**
CLONK	COCCOS	**CONGA**	CORSES	CRAFTS	SCREES	ACROSS	CUPIDS	DACHAS
CLONKS	**COCKS**	CONGAS	CORSET	CRAFTY	**CREESE**	CROSSE	**CUPPA**	**DAGGA**
CLOOP	COCKSY	**CONGE**	**CORSO**	**CRAGS**		**CROUP**	CUPPAS	DAGGAS
CLOOPS		CONGED	CORSOS	SCRAGS				**DAINE**
CLOOT		CONGEE	**COSTA**	**CRAIG**				SDAINE
CLOOTS		CONGER	COSTAE					

DAINED	DEBELS	DEPOTS	DINGEY	DONUTS	DRAFFY	DROOK	DURUM	DEARTH
DAINES	DEBIT	DEPTH	DINIC	DOOLE	DRAFT	DROOKS	DURUMS	HEARTH
DAINT	DEBITS	DEPTHS	DINICS	DOOLES	DRAFTS	DROOL	DUSTS	EARTHS
DAINTY	DEBUG	DERAY	DIODE	DOORN	DRAIL	DROOLS	ADUSTS	EARTHY
DAKER	DEBUGS	DERAYS	DIODES	DOORNS	DRAILS	DROOP	DUVET	EASED
DAKERS	DEBUT	DERMA	DIOTA	DOORS	DRAIN	DROOPS	DUVETS	CEASED
DALLE	DEBUTS	DERMAL	DIOTAS	ADOORS	DRAINS	DROOPY	DWALE	LEASED
DALLES	DECAD	DERMAS	DIPSO	DOPER	DRAKE	DROPS	DWALES	MEASED
DAMAN	DECADE	DERTH	DIPSOS	DOPERS	DRAKES	DROPSY	DWALM	PEASED
DAMANS	DECADS	DERTHS	DIRGE	DORAD	DRAMA	DROSS	DWALMS	SEASED
DAMAR	DECAL	DESSE	DIRGES	DORADO	DRAMAS	DROSSY	DWARF	TEASED
DAMARS	DECALS	DESSES	DIRKE	DORADS	DRANT	DROUK	DWARFS	EASEL
DAMME	DECAY	DETER	DIRKED	DOREE	DRANTS	DROUKS	DWAUM	TEASEL
DAMMED	DECAYS	DETERS	DIRKES	DOREES	DRAPE	DROVE	DWAUMS	WEASEL
DAMMER	DECKO	DEUCE	DISCO	DORSA	DRAPED	DROVER	DWELL	EASELS
DANCE	DECKOS	DEUCED	DISCOS	DORSAL	DRAPER	DROVES	DWELLS	EASES
DANCED	DECOR	DEUCES	DISME	DORSE	DRAPES	DROWN	DWINE	CEASES
DANCER	DECORS	DEVEL	DITAL	DORSEL	DRAPET	DROWNS	DWINED	LEASES
DANCES	DECOY	DEVELS	DITALS	DORSER	DRAWL	DROWSE	DWINES	MEASES
DANIO	DECOYS	DEVIL	DITED	DOSEH	DRAWLS	DROWSY	DYING	PEASES
DANIOS	DEEMS	DEVILS	DITTO	DOSEHS	ADREAD	DRUID	DYINGS	SEASES
DANTS	ADEEMS	DEVOT	DITTOS	DOTER	DREAD	DRUIDS	EAGER	TEASES
IDANTS	DEEVE	DEVOTE	DIVAN	DOTERS	DREADS	DRUNK	EAGERS	EASLE
DARAF	DEEVED	DEVOTS	DIVANS	DOUAR	DREAM	DRUNKS	EAGLE	MEASLE
DARAFS	DEEVES	DEWAN	DIVER	DOUARS	DREAMS	DRUPE	BEAGLE	EASLES
DARGA	DEFAT	DEWANI	DIVERS	DOUBT	DREAMT	DRUPEL	TEAGLE	EASTS
DARGAS	DEFATS	DEWANS	DIVERT	DOUBTS	DREAMY	DRUPES	EAGLES	BEASTS
DARIC	DEFER	DHOBI	DIVES	DOUCE	DREAR	DRUSE	EAGLET	FEASTS
DARICS	DEFERS	DHOBIS	DIVEST	DOUCER	DREARE	DRUSES	EAGRE	HEASTS
DARRE	DEGUM	DHOLE	DIVOT	DOUCET	DREARS	DRYAD	MEAGRE	LEASTS
DARRED	DEGUMS	DHOLES	DIVOTS	DOUGH	DREARY	DRYADS	VEALES	REASTS
DARRES	DEIGN	DHOLL	DIWAN	DOUGHS	DRECK	DRYER	EALES	YEASTS
DARZI	DEIGNS	DHOLLS	DIWANS	DOUGHT	DRECKS	DRYERS	EANED	EATEN
DARZIS	DEISM	DHOTI	DIXIE	DOUGHY	DRERE	DSOBO	BEANED	BEATEN
DATAL	DEISMS	DHOTIS	DIXIES	DOUMA	DRERES	DSOBOS	LEANED	NEATEN
DATALS	DEIST	DIAZO	DIZEN	DOUMAS	DRESS	DSOMO	MEANED	EATER
DATER	DEISTS	DIAZOS	DIZENS	DOURA	DRESSY	DSOMOS	PEANED	BEATER
DATERS	DEKKO	DICER	DJINN	DOURAS	DRIER	DUCAT	SEANED	HEATER
DAUBE	DEKKOS	DICERS	DJINNI	DOUSE	DRIERS	DUCATS	WEANED	NEATER
DAUBED	DELAY	DICHT	DODGE	DOUSED	DRIES	DUCES	YEANED	SEATER
DAUBER	DELAYS	DICHTS	DODGED	DOUSER	DRIEST	EDUCES	EARDS	EATERS
DAUBES	DELFT	DICOT	DODGEM	DOUSES	DRIFT	DUCTS	BEARDS	EATERY
DAULT	DELFTS	DICOTS	DODGER	DOVER	ADRIFT	EDUCTS	HEARDS	EATHE
DAULTS	DELPH	DICTS	DODGES	DOVERS	DRIFTS	DUETT	YEARDS	MEATHE
DAUNT	DELPHS	EDICTS	DOGIE	DOVIE	DRIFTY	DUETTO	EARED	EAVES
DAUNTS	DELTA	DIENE	DOGIES	DOVIER	DRILL	DUETTS	BEARED	DEAVES
DAVIT	DELTAS	DIENES	DOGMA	DOWAR	DRILLS	DULIA	DEARED	HEAVES
DAVITS	DELVE	DIGHT	DOGMAS	DOWARS	DRINK	DULIAS	FEARED	LEAVES
DAWED	DELVED	DIGHTS	DOING	DOWEL	DRINKS	DULSE	GEARED	REAVES
ADAWED	DELVER	DIGIT	DOINGS	DOWELS	DRIVE	DULSES	LEARED	WEAVES
DEALS	DELVES	DIGITS	DOLCE	DOWER	DRIVEL	DUNCE	NEARED	EBBED
IDEALS	DEMAN	DIKAS	DOLCES	DOWERS	DRIVEN	DUNCES	REARED	KEBBED
DEARE	DEMAND	DIKAST	DOLMA	DOWIE	DRIVER	DUOMO	SEARED	NEBBED
DEARED	DEMANS	DIKER	DOLMAN	DOWIER	DRIVES	DUOMOS	WEARED	WEBBED
DEARER	DEMIT	DIKERS	DOLMAS	DOWLE	DROIL	DUPER	EARLS	ECADS
DEARES	DEMITS	DILDO	DONAH	DOWLES	DROILS	DUPERS	PEARLS	DECADS
DEARN	DEMOB	DILDOE	DONAHS	DOWSE	DROIT	DUPERY	EARLY	ECHED
DEARNS	DEMOBS	DILDOS	DONEE	DOWSED	ADROIT	DUPLE	DEARLY	LECHED
DEATH	DEMON	DILLI	DONEES	DOWSER	DROITS	DUPLET	NEARLY	PECHED
DEATHS	DEMONS	DILLIS	DONGA	DOWSES	DROLE	DUPLEX	PEARLY	ECHES
DEATHY	DEMUR	DIMER	DONGAS	DOWSET	DROLER	DURAL	REARLY	EECHES
DEAVE	DEMURE	DIMERS	DONNE	DOYEN	DROLES	DURALS	YEARLY	LECHES
DEAVED	DEMURS	DINAR	DONNED	DOYENS	DROLL	DURES	EARNS	ECLAT
DEAVES	DENAY	DINARS	DONNEE	DOZEN	DROLLS	DURESS	DEARNS	ECLATS
DEBAG	DENAYS	DINER	DONNES	DOZENS	DROLLY	DUROY	LEARNS	EDEMA
DEBAGS	DENIM	DINERS	DONOR	DOZER	DROME	DUROYS	YEARNS	OEDEMA
DEBAR	DENIMS	DINGE	DONORS	DOZERS	DROMES	DURRA	EARST	EDEMAS
DEBARK	DENSE	DINGED	DONUT	DRAFF	DRONE	DURRAS	PEARST	EDGED
DEBARS	DENSER	DINGER		DRAFFS	DRONED		EARTH	HEDGED
DEBEL	DEPOT	DINGES			DRONES			

KEDGED	EIKONS	ELUTED	ENDED	EPHOD	ESCOT	ETUDE	EXISTS	FARCE
SEDGED	EISEL	ELUTES	BENDED	EPHODS	ESCOTS	ETUDES	EXODE	FARCED
WEDGED	EISELL	ELVAN	FENDED	EPHOR	ESILE	ETWEE	EXODES	FARCES
EDGER	EISELS	ELVANS	HENDED	EPHORS	RESILE	ETWEES	EXPAT	FARCI
HEDGER	EJECT	ELVER	MENDED	EPOCH	ESILES	EUGHS	EXPATS	FARCIN
KEDGER	DEJECT	DELVER	PENDED	EPOCHA	ESKAR	HEUGHS	EXPEL	FARLE
LEDGER	REJECT	ELVERS	SENDED	EPOCHS	ESKARS	EUKED	EXPELS	FARLES
EDGERS	EJECTA	DELVES	TENDED	EPODE	ESKER	YEUKED	EXPOS	FARSE
EDGES	EJECTS	ELVES	VENDED	EPODES	ESKERS	EUPAD	EXPOSE	FARSED
HEDGES	EKING	HELVES	WENDED	EPOPT	ESSAY	EUPADS	EXTOL	FARSES
KEDGES	REKING	PELVES	ENDEW	EPOPTS	ESSAYS	EUSOL	EXTOLD	FASCI
LEDGES	ELAND	SELVES	ENDEWS	EPRIS	ESSES	EUSOLS	EXTOLS	FASCIA
SEDGES	ELANDS	EMBAR	ENDOW	EPRISE	CESSES	EVADE	EXTRA	FASCIO
WEDGES	ELATE	EMBARS	ENDOWS	EQUAL	DESSES	EVADED	EXTRAS	FATSO
EDICT	BELATE	EMBARK	VENDUE	EQUALS	FESSES	EVADES	EXUDE	FATSOS
EDICTS	DELATE	EMBAY	ENDUE	EQUIP	GESSES	EVENS	EXUDED	FAULT
EDILE	RELATE	EMBAYS	ENDUED	EQUIPE	JESSES	EEVENS	EXUDES	FAULTY
AEDILE	VELATE	EMBED	ENDUES	EQUIPS	LESSES	SEVENS	EXULT	FAUNA
SEDILE	ELATED	KEMBED	ENEMA	ERASE	MESSES	EVENT	EXULTS	FAUNAE
EDILES	ELATER	EMBEDS	ENEMAS	ERASED	NESSES	EVENTS	EXURB	FAUNAL
EDUCE	ELATES	EMBER	ENEWS	ERASER	SESSES	EVERT	EXURBS	FAUNAS
DEDUCE	ELBOW	MEMBER	RENEWS	ERASES	YESSES	REVERT	EYING	FAVEL
REDUCE	ELBOWS	EMBERS	ENIAC	ERBIA	ESTER	REVERY	FEYING	FAVELA
SEDUCE	ELCHI	EMBOG	ENIACS	ERBIAS	FESTER	SEVERY	HEYING	FAVELL
EDUCED	ELCHIS	EMBOGS	ENJOY	ERECT	JESTER	EVETS	KEYING	FAVOR
EDUCES	ELDER	EMBOW	ENJOYS	ERECTS	NESTER	EVICT	EYRIE	FAVORS
EDUCT	GELDER	EMBOWS	ENMEW	ERICA	PESTER	EVICTS	EYRIES	FAYNE
DEDUCT	MELDER	EMBUS	ENMEWS	ERICAS	RESTER	EVILS	FABLE	FAYNED
EDUCTS	WELDER	EMBUSY	ENNUI	ERICK	TESTER	DEVILS	FABLED	FAYNES
EERIE	ELDERS	EMCEE	ENNUIS	ERICKS	WESTER	EVITE	FABLER	FEARE
FEERIE	ELDIN	EMCEED	ENROL	ERING	YESTER	LEVITE	FABLES	FEARED
PEERIE	ELDING	EMCEES	ENROLL	CERING	ESTERS	EVITED	FACER	FEARES
EERIER	ELDINS	EMEER	ENROLS	DERING	ESTOC	EVITES	FACERS	FEARS
EEVEN	ELECT	EMEERS	ENSEW	LERING	ESTOCS	EVOKE	FACET	AFEARS
EEVENS	SELECT	EMEND	ENSEWS	MERING	ESTOP	EVOKED	FACETE	FEAST
EFFED	ELECTS	DEMITS	ENSUE	SERING	ESTOPS	EVOKES	FACETS	FEASTS
JEFFED	ELEMI	REMITS	ENSUED	ERINGO	ESTRO	EWERS	FACIA	FECHT
REFFED	ELEMIS	EMMAS	ENSUES	ERNED	ESTROS	HEWERS	FACIAL	FECHTS
EGERS	ELFED	LEMMAS	ENTER	CERNED	ETAGE	SEWERS	FACIAS	FEESE
LEGERS	SELFED	EMMER	CENTER	GERNED	ETAGES	EWEST	FADGE	FEESED
EGEST	ELFIN	EMMERS	RENTER	KERNED	ETAPE	FEWEST	FADGED	FEESES
REGEST	ELFING	EMMET	TENTER	TERNED	ETAPES	NEWEST	FADGES	FEEZE
EGESTA	ELFINS	EMMETS	VENTER	ERNES	ETHAL	EXACT	FAGOT	FEEZED
EGESTS	ELIAD	EMMEW	ENTERA	CERNES	LETHAL	EXACTS	FAGOTS	FEEZES
EGGAR	ELIADS	EMMEWS	ENTERS	GERNES	ETHALS	EXALT	FAINE	FEIGN
BEGGAR	ELIDE	EMOTE	CENTRY	KERNES	ETHER	EXALTS	FAINED	FEIGNS
SEGGAR	RELIDE	DEMOTE	GENTRY	TERNES	AETHER	EXCEL	FAINER	FEINT
EGGARS	ELIDED	REMOTE	SENTRY	ERODE	HETHER	EXCELS	FAINES	FEINTS
EGGED	ELIDES	EMOTED	ENURE	ERODED	NETHER	EXEAT	FAINT	FELLA
BEGGED	ELITE	EMOTES	TENURE	ERODES	PETHER	EXEATS	FAINTS	FELLAH
LEGGED	PELITE	EMOVE	ENURED	ERRED	TETHER	EXEEM	FAITH	FELLAS
PEGGED	ELITES	EMOVED	ENURES	SERRED	WETHER	EXEEMS	FAITHS	FELON
EGGER	ELOGE	EMOVES	ENVOI	ERROR	ETHERS	EXEME	FAKER	FELONS
LEGGER	ELOGES	EMULE	RENVOI	TERROR	ETHIC	LEXEME	FAKERS	FELONY
EGGERS	ELOIN	AEMULE	ENVOIS	ERRORS	ETHICS	EXEMED	FAKERY	FEMAL
EGGERY	ELOINS	EMULED	ENVOY	ERSES	ETHYL	EXEMES	FAKIR	FEMALE
EGRET	ELOPE	EMULES	LENVOY	HERSES	METHYL	EXERT	FAKIRS	FEMALS
REGRET	ELOPED	EMURE	RENVOY	MERSES	ETHYLS	EXERTS	FALSE	FEMME
EGRETS	ELOPER	DEMURE	ENVOYS	PERSES	LEXEME	EXILE	FALSED	FEMMES
EIDER	ELOPES	EMURED	EORLS	VERSES	ETTIN	EXILED	FALSER	FEMUR
DEIDER	ELPEE	EMURES	CEORLS	ERSES	ETTINS	EXILES	FALSES	FEMURS
EIDERS	ELPEES	ENACT	EOSIN	HERSES	ETTLE	EXINE	FANAL	FENCE
EIGHT	ELSIN	ENACTS	EOSINS	MERSES	KETTLE	EXINES	FANALS	FENCED
HEIGHT	ELSINS	ENARM	EPACT	ERUCT	METTLE	EXIST	FANGO	FENCER
KEIGHT	ELUDE	ENARMS	EPACTS	ERUCTS	NETTLE	SEXIST	FANGOS	FENCES
WEIGHT	DELUDE	ENATE	EPEES	ERUPT	PETTLE		FANON	FEOFF
EIGHTH	ELUDED	SENATE	TEPEES	ERUPTS	SETTLE		FANONS	FEOFFS
EIGHTS	ELUDER		EPHAH	ERVEN	ETTLED		FARAD	FERES
EIGHTY	ELUDES		EPHAHS	VERVEN	ETTLES		FARADS	FEREST
EIKON	ELUTE							

FERMI	FIORDS	FLIMPS	FLYER	FOUND	FRISKS	FUROLS	IGAPOS	GENIP
FERMIS	FIRER	FLING	FLYERS	FOUNDS	FRISKY	FUROR	GARBE	GENIPS
FESSE	FIRERS	FLINGS	FLYPE	FOUNT	FRIST	FURORE	GARBED	GENOA
FESSES	FIRST	FLINT	FLYPED	FOUNTS	FRISTS	FURORS	GARBES	GENOAS
FESTA	FIRSTS	FLINTS	FLYPES	FOUTH	FRITH	FURZE	GARBO	GENOM
FESTAL	FIRTH	FLINTY	FLYTE	FOUTHS	FRITHS	FURZES	GARBOS	GENOME
FESTAS	FIRTHS	FLIRT	FLYTED	FOVEA	FRITS	FUSEE	GARDA	GENOMS
FETOR	FITCH	FLIRTS	FLYTES	FOVEAE	AFRITS	FUSEES	GARDAI	GENRE
FETORS	FITCHE	FLIRTY	FOEHN	FOVEAL	FRIZE	FUSIL	GARRE	GENRES
FETTA	FITCHY	FLISK	FOEHNS	FOWTH	FRIZES	FUSILE	GARRED	GENTS
FETTAS	FITTE	FLISKS	FOGEY	FOWTHS	FRIZZ	FUSILS	GARRES	AGENTS
FETWA	FITTED	FLISKY	FOGEYS	FOYER	FRIZZY	FUTON	GARRET	GEODE
FETWAS	FITTER	FLITE	FOGLE	FOYLE	FROCK	FUTONS	GARTH	GEODES
FEUAR	FITTES	FLITED	FOGLES	FOYLED	FROCKS	FUZEE	GARTHS	GEOID
FEUARS	FIVER	FLITES	FOIST	FOYLES	FROND	FUZEES	GARUM	GEOIDS
FEVER	FIVERS	FLOAT	FOISTS	FOYNE	FRONDS	FYTTE	GARUMS	GERAH
FEVERS	FIXER	AFLOAT	FOLIA	FOYNED	FRONT	FYTTES	GATES	GERAHS
FIBER	FIXERS	FLOATS	FOLIAR	FOYNES	AFRONT	GABLE	AGATES	GERBE
FIBERS	FJORD	FLOATY	FOLIE	FRACT	FRONTS	GABLED	GAUGE	GERBES
FIBRE	FJORDS	FLOCK	FOLIES	FRACTS	FRORE	GABLES	GAUGED	GERLE
FIBRED	FLACK	FLOCKS	FOLIO	FRAIL	FROREN	GABLET	GAUGER	GERLES
FIBRES	FLACKS	FLONG	FOLIOS	FRAILS	FRORN	GADGE	GAUGES	GERNE
FIBRO	FLAFF	FLONGS	FOLKS	FRAIM	FRORNE	GADGES	GAUJE	GERNED
FIBROS	FLAFFS	FLOOD	FOLKSY	FRAIMS	FROST	GADGET	GAUJES	GERNES
FICHE	FLAGS	FLOODS	FONDA	FRAME	FROSTS	GADJE	GAULT	GESSE
FICHES	OFLAGS	FLOOR	FONDAS	FRAMED	FROSTY	GADSO	GAULTS	GESSED
FICHU	FLAIL	FLOORS	FORAY	FRAMER	FROTH	GADSOS	GAUNT	GESSES
FICHUS	FLAILS	FLORA	FORAYS	FRAMES	FROTHS	GAFFE	GAUNTS	GESTE
FIDGE	FLAIR	FLORAE	FORBY	FRANC	FROTHY	GAFFED	GAUZE	GESTES
FIDGED	FLAIRS	FLORAL	FORBYE	FRANCO	FROWN	GAFFER	GAUZES	GESTS
FIDGES	FLAKE	FLORAS	FORCE	FRANCS	FROWNS	GAFFES	GAVEL	EGESTS
FIDGET	FLAKED	FLOSS	FORCED	FRANK	FROWS	GAITT	GAVELS	GHAST
FIELD	FLAKES	FLOSSY	FORCER	FRANKS	FROWST	GAITTS	GAYAL	AGHAST
AFIELD	FLAME	FLOTA	FORCES	FRATE	FROWSY	GALAH	GAYALS	GHAUT
FIELDS	AFLAME	FLOTAS	FOREL	FRATER	FROZE	GALAHS	GAZAL	GHAUTS
FIEND	FLAMED	FLOTE	FORELS	FRAUD	FROZEN	GALEA	GAZALS	GHAZI
FIENDS	FLAMEN	FLOTEL	FORES	FRAUDS	FRUIT	GALEAS	GAZED	GHAZIS
FIENT	FLAMES	FLOTES	FOREST	FREAK	FRUITS	GALLY	AGAZED	GHOST
FIENTS	FLAMM	FLOUR	FORGE	FREAKS	FRUITY	GALOP	GAZEL	GHOSTS
FIERE	FLAMMS	FLOURS	FORGED	FREAKY	FRUMP	GALOPS	GAZELS	GHOSTY
FIERES	FLANK	FLOURY	FORGER	FREER	FRUMPS	GALUT	GAZER	GHOUL
FIFER	FLANKS	FLOUT	FORGES	FREES	FRUMPY	GALUTH	GAZERS	GHOULS
FIFERS	FLARE	FLOUTS	FORGET	FREEST	FRUST	GALUTS	GAZON	GHYLL
FIFTH	FLARED	FLUFF	FORGO	FREET	FRUSTA	GAMBA	GAZONS	GHYLLS
FIFTHS	FLARES	FLUFFS	FORGOT	AFREET	FRUSTS	GAMBAS	GAZOO	GIANT
FIGHT	FLASH	FLUFFY	FORME	FREETS	FRYER	GAMES	GAZOOS	GIANTS
FIGHTS	FLASHY	FLUID	FORMED	FREETY	FRYERS	GAMEST	GEARE	GIBEL
FILER	FLASK	FLUIDS	FORMER	FREIT	FUDGE	GAMESY	GEARED	GIBELS
FILERS	FLASKS	FLUKE	FORMES	FREITS	FUDGED	GAMIC	GEARES	GIBER
FILET	FLAWN	FLUKED	FORTE	FREITY	FUDGES	AGAMIC	GEBUR	GIBERS
FILETS	FLAWNS	FLUKES	FORTED	FREMD	FUERO	OGAMIC	GEBURS	GIGOT
FILLE	FLEAM	FLUKEY	FORTES	FREMDS	FUEROS	GAMIN	GECKO	GIGUE
FILLED	FLEAMS	FLUME	FORTH	FREON	FUGIE	GAMINE	GECKOS	GIGUES
FILLER	FLECK	FLUMES	FORTHY	FREONS	FUGIES	GAMINS	GEIST	GILAS
FILLES	FLECKS	FLUMP	FORUM	FRERE	FUGLE	GAMING	AGEIST	AGILAS
FILLET	FLEER	FLUMPS	FORUMS	FRERES	FUGLED	GEISTS	GILET	
FILTH	FLEERS	FLUNK	FOSSA	FRESH	FUGLES	GAMMA	GEMEL	GILETS
FILTHS	FLEET	FLUNKS	FOSSAE	AFRESH	FUGUE	GAMMAS	GEMELS	GIMME
FILTHY	FLEETS	FLUNKY	FOSSAS	FRIAR	FUGUES	GAMMED	GEMMA	GIMMER
FINAL	FLEME	FLUOR	FOSSE	FRIARS	FUMET	GAMMER	GEMMAE	GIMMES
FINALE	FLEMES	FLUORS	FOSSED	FRIARY	FUMETS	GAMMES	GEMMAN	GINGS
FINALS	FLESH	FLURR	FOSSES	FRIER	FUNDI	GAMUT	GEMOT	AGINGS
FINER	FLESHY	FLURRS	FOUAT	FRIERS	FUNDIS	GAMUTS	GEMOTS	GIPPO
FINERS	FLICK	FLURRY	FOUATS	FRILL	FURAL	GANJA	GENES	GIPPOS
FINERY	FLICKS	FLUSH	FOUET	FRILLS	FURALS	GANJAS	AGENES	GIRON
FINES	FLIER	FLUSHY	FOUETS	FRILLY	FURAN	GAPER	GENET	GIRONS
FINEST	FLIERS	FLUTE	FOULE	FRISK	FURANE	GAPERS	GENETS	GIRTH
FINIS	FLIEST	FLUTED	FOULED	FRISKA	FURANS	GAPOS	GENIE	GIRTHS
FINISH	FLIMP	FLUTER	FOULER		FUROL	GENIES		
FIORD		FLUTES	FOULES		FUROLE			

GISMO	GLISKS	GORAL	GRAVEN	GRISTS	GUIDES	SHADED	HAMZAS	HAULMS
GISMOS	GLITZ	GORALS	GRAVER	GRITH	GUILD	HADES	HANAP	HAULS
GISTS	GLITZY	GORGE	GRAVES	GRITHS	GUILE	SHADES	HANCE	HAULST
AGISTS	GLOAT	GORGED	GREAT	GRIZE	GUILED	HADJI	CHANCE	HAUNT
GIUST	GLOATS	GORGES	GREATS	AGRIZE	GUILER	HAFFS	HANCES	HAUNTS
GIUSTO	GLOBE	GORGET	GREBE	GRIZES	GUILES	HAFTS	HANDS	HAUSE
GIUSTS	GLOBED	GORSE	GREBES	GROAN	GUILT	CHAFFS	SHANDS	HAUSED
GIVER	GLOBES	GOSSE	GRECE	GROANS	GUILTS	HAFTS	HANDY	HAUSES
GIVERS	GLOGG	GOSSES	GRECES	GROAT	GUILTY	SHAFTS	SHANDY	HAVEN
GIVES	GLOGGS	GOUGE	GREED	GROATS	GUIMP	HAICK	HANGS	SHAVEN
OGIVES	GLOOM	GOUGED	GREEDS	GROIN	GUIMPE	HAICKS	BHANGS	HAVENS
GIZMO	GLOOMS	GOUGES	GREEDY	GROINS	GUIMPS	HAINS	PHANGS	HAVER
GIZMOS	GLOOMY	GOURD	GREEN	GROMA	GUIRO	CHAINS	WHANGS	HAVERS
GLACE	GLOSS	GOURDE	GREENS	GROMAS	GUIROS	HAIRS	HANKS	HAVES
GLACES	GLOSSA	GOURDS	GREENY	GRONE	GUISE	CHAIRS	CHANKS	SHAVER
GLADE	GLOSSY	GOURDY	GREES	GRONED	GUISED	HAIRST	SHANKS	HAVOC
GLADES	GLOUT	GOUTY	AGREES	GRONES	GUISER	THANKS	THANKS	HAVOCS
GLAIK	GLOUTS	GOWAN	GREESE	GROOF	GUISES	HAJJI	HAOMA	HAWED
GLAIKS	GLOVE	GOWANS	GREET	GROOFS	GULAG	HAJJIS	HAOMAS	CHAWED
GLAIR	AGOUTY	GOWANY	GREETE	GROOM	GULAGS	HAKAM	HAPPY	SHAWED
GLAIRS	GLOVED	GRAAL	GREETS	GROOMS	GULPH	HAKAMS	CHAPPY	THAWED
GLAIRY	GLOVER	GRAALS	GREGE	GROPE	GULPHS	HAKIM	HARAM	HAWMS
GLAND	GLOVES	GRACE	AGREGE	GROPED	GUMBO	HAKIMS	HARAMS	SHAWMS
GLANDS	GLOZE	GRACED	GREGO	GROPER	GUMBOS	HALAL	HARDS	HAWSE
GLARE	GLOZED	GRACES	GREGOS	GROPES	GUNGE	HALALS	CHARDS	HAWSED
GLARED	GLOZES	GRADE	GREIN	GROUF	GUNGES	HALED	SHARDS	HAWSER
GLARES	GLUER	GRADED	GREINS	GROUFS	GURGE	HALER	CHARED	HAWSES
GLASS	GLUERS	GRADER	GRESE	GROUP	GURGES	THALER	SHARED	HAYLE
GLASSY	GLUME	GRADES	GRESES	GROUPS	GUSLA	HALERS	HAREM	HAYLES
GLAUM	GLUMES	GRAFF	GREVE	GROUPY	GUSLAR	HALEST	HAREMS	HAZEL
GLAUMS	GLUON	GRAFFS	GREVES	GROUT	GUSLAS	HALFA	HARES	GHAZEL
GLAUR	GLUONS	GRAFT	GRICE	GROUTS	GUSLE	HALFAS	PHARES	HAZELS
GLAURS	GLYPH	GRAFTS	GRICER	GROUTY	GUSLES	HALLO	HARIM	HAZER
GLAURY	GLYPHS	GRAIL	GRICES	GROVE	GUSLI	HALLOA	HARIMS	HAZERS
GLAZE	GNARL	GRAILE	GRIDE	GROVEL	GUSLIS	HALLOO	HARKS	HEALD
GLAZED	GNARLS	GRAILS	GRIDED	GROVES	GUSTO	HALLOS	CHARKS	HEALDS
GLAZEN	GNARLY	GRAIN	GRIDES	GROWL	GUSTOS	HALLOW	SHARKS	HEALS
GLAZER	GNARR	GRAINE	GRIEF	GROWLS	GUTTA	HALMA	CHARMS	SHEALS
GLAZES	GNARRS	GRAINS	GRIEFS	GROWLY	GUTTAE	HALMAS	SHARNS	WHEALS
GLEAM	GNOME	GRAINY	GRIFF	GRUEL	GUTTAS	HALMS	HAROS	HEAPS
GLEAMS	GNOMES	GRAIP	GRIFFE	GRUELS	GUYLE	SHALMS	PHAROS	CHEAPS
GLEAMY	GODET	GRAIPS	GRIFFS	GRUME	GUYLED	HALSE	HARPS	HEAPY
GLEAN	GODETS	GRAMA	GRIFT	GRUMES	GUYLER	HALSED	SHARPS	CHEAPY
GLEANS	GODSO	GRAMAS	GRIFTS	GRUNT	GUYLES	HALSER	HARRY	HEARD
GLEBE	GODSON	GRAME	GRIKE	GRUNTS	GUYOT	HALSES	CHARRY	HEARDS
GLEBES	GODSOS	GRAMES	GRIKES	GRYCE	GUYOTS	HALVA	GHARRY	HEARE
GLEDE	GOFER	GRAND	GRILL	GRYCES	GUYSE	HALVAH	HARTS	WHEARE
GLEDES	GOFERS	GRANDE	GRILLE	GRYDE	GUYSES	HALVAS	CHARTS	HEARER
GLEED	GOING	GRANDS	GRILLS	GRYDED	GYELD	HALVE	HASTE	HEARES
GLEEDS	AGOING	GRANT	GRIME	GRYDES	GYELDS	HALVED	CHASTE	HEARS
GLEEK	GOINGS	GRANTS	GRIMED	GRYKE	GYNAE	HALVER	HASTED	SHEARS
GLEEKS	GOLEM	GRAPE	GRIMES	GRYKES	GYNAES	HALVES	HASTEN	HEARSY
GLEET	GOLEMS	GRAPED	GRIND	GRYPE	GYPPO	HAMAL	HASTES	HEART
GLEETS	GOLPE	GRAPES	GRINDS	GRYPES	GYPPOS	HAMALS	HATCH	HEARTH
GLEETY	GOLPES	GRAPEY	GRIOT	GUACO	GYRON	HAMED	THATCH	HEARTS
GLENT	GOMBO	GRAPH	GRIOTS	GUACOS	GYRONS	HAMES	HATER	HEARTY
GLENTS	GOMBOS	GRAPHS	GRIPE	GUANA	GYROS	SHAMES	HATERS	HEAST
GLIDE	GOMPA	GRASP	GRIPED	IGUANA	GYROSE	HAMMY	HAUGH	HEASTE
GLIDED	GOMPAS	GRASPS	GRIPER	GUANAS	HABIT	SHAMMY	HAUGHS	HEASTS
GLIDER	GONAD	GRASS	GRIPES	GUANO	HABITS	HAMZA	HAUGHT	HEATH
GLIDES	GONADS	GRASSY	GRISE	GUANOS	HACEK	HAMZAH	HAULD	SHEATH
GLIFF	GONER	GRATE	AGRISE	GUARD	HACEKS		HAULDS	HEATHS
GLIFFS	GONERS	GRATED	GRISED	GUARDS	HACKS		HAULM	HEATHY
GLIFT	GOOLD	GRATER	GRISES	GUAVA	CHACKS			HEATS
GLIFTS	GOOLDS	GRATES	GRIST	GUAVAS	SHACKS			CHEATS
GLIKE	GOOSE	GRAVE		GUEST	THACKS			WHEATS
GLIKES	GOOSED	GRAVED		GUESTS	WHACKS			HEAVE
GLINT	GOOSES	GRAVEL		GUIDE	HADED			
GLINTS	GOOSEY			GUIDED				
GLISK	GOPAK			GUIDER				
	GOPAKS							

SHEAVE THEAVE HEAVED HEAVEN HEAVER HEAVES HEBEN HEBENS HECHT HECHTS HECKS CHECKS HEDGE HEDGED HEDGER HEDGES HEELS SHEELS WHEELS HEEZE PHEEZE WHEEZE HEEZED HEEZES HEFTE HEFTED HEFTS THEFTS WHEFTS HEIGH HEIGHT HEIRS THEIRS HEIST THEIST HEISTS HEJAB HEJABS HEJRA HEJRAS HELLO HELLOS HELLS SHELLS HELMS WHELMS HELOT HELOTS HELPS WHELPS HELVE SHELVE HELVED HELVES HEMES THEMES HENCE THENCE WHENCE HENDS SHENDS HENGE HENGES HENNA HENNAS HENRY HENRYS HEPAR HEPARS HERDS

SHERDS HERMA HERMAE HERMS THERMS HEROE HEROES HERON HERONS HERRY CHERRY SHERRY WHERRY HERSE HERSED HERSES HERYE HERYED HERYES HESTS CHESTS HETES HEUCH SHEUCH HEUCHS HEUGH SHEUGH WHEUGH HEUGHS HEVEA HEVEAS HEWED CHEWED SHEWED THEWED WHEWED HEWER HEWERS HEXAD HEXADS HEXES RHEXES HICKS CHICKS THICKS HIDED CHIDED HIDES CHIDES HIGHS THIGHS HIGHT HIGHTH HIGHTS HIJRA HIJRAH HIJRAS HIKER HIKERS HILLO HILLOS HILLS CHILLS SHILLS THILLS HILLY CHILLY WHILLY HINGE

WHINGE HINGED HINGES HINGS HINNY SHINNY WHINNY SHIPPO HIPPO HIPPOS HIPPY CHIPPY WHIPPY HIRER HIRERS HIRES SHIRES HISTS WHISTS HITCH HITCHY HITHE HITHER HITHES HIVED CHIVED HIVER SHIVER HIVERS CHIVES SHIVES HIZEN HIZENS HOARD HOARDS HOARS HOARSE HOAST HOASTS HOCKS SHOCKS CHOCKS HODJA KHODJA HODJAS HOERS SHOERS HOGAN HOGANS HOGEN HOGENS HOICK HOICKS HOISE HOISED HOISES HOIST HOISTS HOKED HOKES HOKEY HOKUM HOKUMS HOLED THOLED

HOLES DHOLES THOLES WHOLES HOLLA HOLLAS HOLLO HOLLOA HOLLOS HOLLOW HOLLY WHOLLY HOMER HOMERS HOMME HOMMES HOMOS ZHOMOS HONED PHONED HONES PHONES RHONES HONEST HONEY HONEYS HONGS HONOR HONORS HOOEY HOOEYS HOOKA HOOKAH HOOKAS HOOKS CHOOKS SHOOKS HOOLY DHOOLY HOOPS WHOOPS HOORD HOORDS HOOSH WHOOSH HOOTS SHOOTS WHOOTS HOOVE HOOVED HOOVEN HOOVER HOOVES HOPER HOPERS HOPPY CHOPPY SHOPPY HORAL CHORAL HORDE HORDED HORDES HORME HORMES HORNS THORNS

HORNY THORNY HORSE AHORSE HORSED HORSES HORSTS CHOSEN HOSEN HOSES CHOSES HOSTA HOSTAS HOSTS GHOSTS HOTEL HOTELS HOUFF HOUFFS HOUGH CHOUGH SHOUGH THOUGH HOUGHS HOUND HOUNDS HOURI HOURIS HOUSE HOUSED HOUSEL HOUSES CHOUSE HOUTS CHOUTS SHOUTS HOVED SHOVED HOVEL HOVELS HOVER HOVERS HOVES SHOVES HOWFF HOWFFS HOWLS THOWLS HOWRE HOWRES HUBBY CHUBBY HUCKS CHUCKS SHUCKS HUFFS CHUFFS CHUFFY HULLO HULLOS HUMAN HUMANE HUMANS HUMOR HUMORS HUMPH

HUMPHS HUMPS CHUMPS THUMPS HUMUS HUMUSY HUNKS HUNKY HUNTS SHUNTS CHURLS DHURRA HURRAH HURRAS HURRAY HURST HURSTS HUTIA HUTIAS HUZZA HUZZAS HYDRA HYDRAS HYDRO HYDROS HYENA HYENAS HYING SHYING HYLEG HYLEGS HYLES CHYLES PHYLES HYMEN HYMENS HYNDE HYNDES HYPER HYPERS HYPHA HYPHAE HYPHAL HYSON HYSONS HYTHE HYTHES IAIDO IAIDOS IAMBI IAMBIC ICERS DICERS RICERS ICHED MICHED NICHED RICHED ICHES FICHES LICHES MICHES NICHES RICHES TICHES ICHOR

ICHORS ICIER DICIER RICIER ICING DICING RICING TICING VICING ICINGS BICKER DICKER KICKER LICKER NICKER PICKER RICKER SICKER TICKER WICKER YICKER ICKERS ICTAL RICTAL ICTUS RICTUS IDANT AIDANT IDANTS IDEAL IDEALS IDIOM IDIOMS IDIOT IDIOTS IDLED SIDLED IDLER IDLERS IDLES SIDLES IDLEST IDYLL IDYLLS IDYLS IGAPO IGAPOS IGLOO IGLOOS IHRAM IHRAMS IKONS EIKONS ILEUM ILEUS PILEUM PILEUS ILIUM CILIUM ILLTH ILLTHS IMAGE IMAGED IMAGES IMAGO IMAGOS IMARI IMARIS IMAUM IMAUMS

IMBAR MIMBAR IMBARK IMBARS IMBED LIMBED NIMBED IMBEDS IMBUE IMBUED IMBUES IMIDE IMIDES IMINE IMINES IMMEW IMMEWS IMMIT IMMITS IMPED GIMPED LIMPED PIMPED IMPEDE IMPEL IMPELS IMPIS IMPISH IMPLY DIMPLY JIMPLY PIMPLY SIMPLY IMPOT IMPOTS INANE INANER INANES INARM INARMS INCLE INCUR INCURS INCUS INCUSE INDEW INDEWS INDOL INDOLE INDOLS INDRI INDRIS INDUE INDUED INDUES INFER INFERE INFERS INGAN FINGAN INGANS INGLE BINGLE DINGLE GINGLE JINGLE KINGLE LINGLE MINGLE

PINGLE SINGLE TINGLE INGLES INGOT LINGOT INGOTS INION MINION PINION INKED DINKED FINKED JINKED KINKED LINKED PINKED RINKED TINKED WINKED ZINKED INKER DINKER JINKER PINKER SINKER TINKER WINKER INKERS INKLE KINKLE TINKLE WINKLE INKLED INKLES INLAY INLAYS INLET INLETS INNED BINNED DINNED FINNED GINNED LINNED PINNED SINNED TINNED INNER DINNER FINNER GINNER PINNER SINNER TINNER WINNER INNERS INORB INORBS INPUT INPUTS INSET INSETS INTER LINTER MINTER SINTER TINTER WINTER INTERN

INTERS	IXTLES	JINNI	SKAILS	SKELPS	KNACK	KRENG	LADLE	GLANDS
INTRO	IZARD	DJINNI	KALIF	KEMBO	KNACKS	KRENGS	LADLED	LANES
INTRON	LIZARD	JIRGA	KALIFS	KEMBOS	KNACKY	KRILL	LADLES	PLANES
INTROS	RIZARD	JIRGAS	KALPA	KENAF	KNARL	KRILLS	LAGAN	SLANES
INULA	VIZARD	JIVER	KALPAK	KENAFS	KNARLS	KRONE	LAGANS	LANKS
INULAS	WIZARD	JIVERS	KALPAS	KENDO	KNAVE	KRONEN	LAGER	BLANKS
INURE	IZARDS	JOCKO	KAMIK	KENDOS	KNAVES	KRONER	LAGERS	CLANKS
INURED	IZZET	JOCKOS	KAMIKS	KERNE	KNEAD	KRONES	LAHAR	FLANKS
INURES	IZZETS	JODEL	KANEH	KERNED	KNEADS	KUDZU	LAHARS	PLANKS
INURN	JABOT	JODELS	KANEHS	KERNEL	KNEEL	KUDZUS	LAIDS	LANKY
INURNS	JABOTS	JOINT	KANGA	KERNES	KNEELS	KUKRI	PLAIDS	BLANKY
INWIT	JACKS	JOINTS	KANGAS	KERVE	KNELL	KUKRIS	LAIGH	LANTS
INWITH	JACKSY	JOIST	KANZU	KERVED	KNELLS	KULAK	LAIGHS	PLANTS
INWITS	JAGER	JOISTS	KANZUS	KERVES	KNIFE	KULAKS	LAIKA	SLANTS
IONIC	JAGIR	JOKER	KAPOK	KESAR	KNIFED	KULAN	LAIKAS	LAPEL
BIONIC	JAGIRS	JOKERS	KAPOKS	KESARS	KNIFES	KULANS	LAIKS	LAPELS
PIONIC	JALAP	JORAM	KAPPA	KETCH	KNIVE	KURRE	GLAIKS	LAPJE
IOTAS	JALAPS	JORAMS	KAPPAS	SKETCH	KNIVED	KURRES	LAIRD	LAPSE
BIOTAS	JAMBE	JORUM	KAPUT	KEVEL	KNIVES	KURTA	LAIRDS	ELAPSE
DIOTAS	JAMBEE	JORUMS	KAPUTT	KEVELS	KNOCK	KURTAS	LAIRS	LAPSED
IRADE	JAMBER	JOTUN	KARAT	KHADI	KNOCKS	KUTCH	FLAIRS	LAPSES
TIRADE	JAMBES	JOTUNN	KARATE	KHADIS	KNOLL	KUTCHA	GLAIRS	LARES
IRADES	JAMBO	JOTUNS	KARATS	KHAKI	KNOLLS	KWELA	GLAIRY	BLARES
IRATE	JAMBOK	JOULE	KARMA	KHAKIS	KNOSP	KWELAS	LAIRY	FLARES
PIRATE	JAMBOS	JOULED	KARMAS	KHAYA	KNOSPS	KYANG	LAKED	GLARES
IRATER	JAMBU	JOULES	KARRI	KHAYAS	KNOUT	KYANGS	FLAKED	LARGE
IRKED	JAMBUL	JOUST	KARRIS	KHEDA	KNOUTS	KYLEY	SLAKED	LARGEN
DIRKED	JAMBUS	JOUSTS	KARST	KHEDAS	KNOWE	KYLEYS	LAKER	LARGER
FIRKED	JAPAN	JOWAR	KARSTS	KHOJA	KNOWER	KYLIE	LAKERS	LARGES
KIRKED	JAPANS	JOWARI	KARTS	KHOJAS	KNOWES	KYLIES	LAKES	LARGO
LIRKED	JARTA	JOWARS	SKARTS	KIANG	KNURL	KYLIN	FLAKES	LARGOS
YIRKED	JARTAS	JUDGE	KASBA	KIANGS	KNURLS	KYLINS	SLAKES	ALARUM
IROKO	JARUL	JUDGED	KASBAH	KIDEL	KNURR	KYLOE	LAKIN	LARUMS
IROKOS	JARULS	JUDGES	KASBAS	KIDELS	KNURRS	KYLOES	LAKING	LARVA
IRONS	JASEY	JUGAL	KATTI	KIERS	KOALA	KYNDE	LAKINS	LARVAE
GIRONS	JASEYS	JUGALS	KATTIS	SKIERS	KOALAS	KYNDED	LAMAS	LARVAL
ISHES	JASPE	JUICE	KAUGH	KIEVE	KOBAN	KYNDES	LLAMAS	LASER
BISHES	JASPER	JUICED	KAUGHS	KIEVES	KOBANG	KYTES	LAMED	LASERS
DISHES	JASPES	JUICER	KAURI	KIGHT	KOBANS	SKYTES	BLAMED	LASSO
FISHES	JAUNT	JUICES	KAURIS	KIGHTS	KOFFS	KYTHE	LAMES	LASSOS
HISHES	JAUNTS	JULEP	KAVAS	KILEY	SKOFFS	KYTHED	BLAMES	LASSU
KISHES	JAUNTY	JULEPS	KAVASS	KILEYS	KOFTA	KYTHES	CLAMES	LASSUS
PISHES	JAVEL	JUMAR	KAYAK	KILIM	KOFTAS	LABDA	FLAMES	LASTS
WISHES	JAVELS	JUMARS	KAYAKS	KILIMS	KOINE	LABDAS	LAMEST	BLASTS
ISLED	JAWAN	JUMART	KAYLE	KILLS	KOINES	LABEL	LAMIA	LATCH
AISLED	JAWANS	JUMBO	KAYLES	SKILLS	KOKRA	LABELS	LAMIAE	CLATCH
MISLED	DJEBEL	JUMBOS	KAYOE	KIMBO	KOKRAS	LABIA	LAMIAS	LATED
ISLES	JEBEL	JUNCO	KAYOED	KIMBOS	KOKUM	LABIAL	LAMMY	ALATED
AISLES	JEBELS	JUNCOS	KAYOES	KINAS	KOKUMS	LABOR	CLAMMY	ELATED
LISLES	JEHAD	JUNTA	KAZOO	KINASE	KOPJE	LABORS	LAMPS	PLATED
ISLET	JEHADS	JUNTAS	KAZOOS	KININ	KOPJES	LACED	CLAMPS	SLATED
ISLETS	JELAB	JUNTO	KEBAB	KININS	KOPPA	LACES	LANCE	LATEN
ISSEI	JELABS	JUNTOS	KEBABS	KINKS	KOPPAS	GLACES	GLANCE	PLATEN
ISSEIS	JELLO	JUPON	KEBOB	SKINKS	KORMA	PLACES	LANCED	LATENS
ISSUE	JELLOS	JUPONS	KEBOBS	KIOSK	KORMAS	LACET	LANCER	LATENT
TISSUE	JERID	JURAT	KECKS	KIOSKS	KOTOW	PLACET	LANCES	LATER
ISSUED	JERIDS	JURATS	KECKSY	KISAN	KOTOWS	LACETS	LANCET	BLATER
ISSUER	JETON	JUROR	KEDGE	KISANS	KRAAL	LACKS	LANCH	ELATER
ISSUES	JETONS	JURORS	KEDGED	KITED	KRAALS	BLACKS	BLANCH	PLATER
ISTLE	JEWEL	KAAMA	KEDGER	KITES	KRAFT	CLACKS	FLANCH	SLATER
MISTLE	JEWELS	KAAMAS	KEDGES	KITHE	KRAFTS	FLACKS	PLANCH	LATHE
ISTLES	JHALA	KABAB	KEEVE	KITHED	KRAIT	PLACKS	LANDE	LATHED
ITCHY	JHALAS	KABABS	KEEVES	KITHES	KRAITS	SLACKS	LANDED	LATHEE
BITCHY	JIBER	KABOB	KEFIR	KLANG	KRANG	LADED	LANDER	LATHEN
FITCHY	JIBERS	KABOBS	KEFIRS	KLANGS	KRANGS	BLADED	LANDES	LATHER
HITCHY	JIGOT	KAHAL	KELIM	KLOOF	KRANS	LADES	LANDS	LATHES
PITCHY	JIGOTS	KAHALS	KELIMS	KLOOFS	SKRANS	BLADES	BLANDS	LATHI
IVIED	JIHAD	KAIAK	KELLY		KRAUT	CLADES	ELANDS	
DIVIED	JIHADS	KAIAKS	SKELLY		KRAUTS	GLADES		
IXTLE		KAILS	KELPS			SLADES		

LATHIS	CLEARS	LEMELS	LICKS	BLIMPS	LIVEN	LOIPES	LOSERS	GLOWER
LATKE	LEARY	LEMES	CLICKS	FLIMPS	SLIVEN	LOKES	LOSES	SLOWER
LATKES	BLEARY	FLEMES	FLICKS	LINCH	LIVENS	BLOKES	CLOSES	LOWERS
LAUCH	LEASE	LEMMA	SLICKS	CLINCH	LIVER	CLOKES	ULOSES	LOWERY
LAUCHS	PLEASE	LEMMAS	LIEGE	FLINCH	OLIVER	LOLOG	LOSSY	LOWES
LAUDS	LEASED	LEMON	LIEGER	LINDS	SLIVER	LOLOGS	FLOSSY	LOWEST
BLAUDS	LEASER	LEMONS	LIEGES	BLINDS	LIVERS	LONER	GLOSSY	LOWLY
LAUGH	LEASES	LEMONY	LIENS	LINED	LIVERY	LONERS	LOTAH	SLOWLY
LAUGHS	LEAST	LEMUR	ALIENS	ALINED	LIVES	LONGA	LOTAHS	LOWND
LAUGHY	LEASTS	LEMURS	LIERS	LINEN	OLIVES	LONGAN	LOTAS	LOWNDS
LAUND	LEATS	LENDS	FLIERS	LINENS	SLIVES	LONGAS	FLOTAS	LOWNE
LAUNDS	BLEATS	BLENDS	PLIERS	LINER	LIVOR	LONGE	LOTES	LOWNED
LAURA	CLEATS	LENTI	LIEVE	LINERS	LIVORS	LONGED	CLOTES	LOWNES
LAURAS	PLEATS	LENTIC	LIEVER	LINES	LIVRE	LONGER	FLOTES	LOWNS
LAVED	LEAVE	LENTIL	LIFER	ALINES	LIVRES	LONGES	LOTTO	LOWSE
SLAVED	CLEAVE	LENTO	LIFERS	CLINES	LLAMA	LONGS	BLOTTO	LOWSER
LAVER	GLEAVE	LENTOR	LIFTS	LINGA	LLAMAS	FLONGS	LOTTOS	BLOWSE
CLAVER	SLEAVE	LENTOS	CLIFTS	LINGAM	LLANO	PLONGS	LOUGH	LOWSES
SLAVER	LEAVED	LEONE	GLIFTS	LINGAS	LLANOS	LOOFA	CLOUGH	LOZEN
LAVERS	LEAVEN	LEONES	LIGAN	LINGO	LOAMS	LOOFAH	PLOUGH	LOZENS
CLAVES	LEAVES	LEPER	LIGAND	LINGOT	CLOAMS	LOOFAS	SLOUGH	LUBRA
SLAVES	LEAZE	LEPERS	LIGANS	LINGS	LOANS	LOOFS	LOUGHS	LUBRAS
LAVRA	SLEAZE	LEPRA	LIGER	CLINGS	SLOANS	KLOOFS	LOUND	LUCKS
LAVRAS	LEAZES	LEPRAS	LIGERS	SLINGS	LOATH	LOOKS	LOUNDS	CLUCKS
LAWED	LEDGE	LETCH	LIGGE	LINGY	LOATHE	PLOOKS	LOUPE	LUCKY
CLAWED	FLEDGE	LEUCH	LIGGED	CLINGY	LOATHY	LOOMS	LOUPED	CLUCKY
FLAWED	GLEDGE	CLEUCH	LIGGEN	LININ	LOAVE	BLOOMS	LOUPEN	PLUCKY
LAWNS	PLEDGE	PLEUCH	LIGGER	LINING	LOAVED	GLOOMS	LOUPES	LUCRE
FLAWNS	SLEDGE	CLEUGH	LIGGES	LININS	LOAVES	SLOOMS	LOURE	LUCRES
LAXES	LEDGER	PLEUGH	LIGHT	LINKS	LOBBY	LOOPS	LOURED	LUFFA
FLAXES	LEDGES	LEVEE	ALIGHT	BLINKS	LOBED	SLOOPS	LOURES	LUFFAS
LAXEST	FLEDGY	LEVEED	BLIGHT	CLINKS	LOBES	LOORD	LOURS	LUFFS
LAYER	LEDGY	LEVEES	FLIGHT	SLINKS	GLOBES	LOORDS	LOURY	BLUFFS
PLAYER	LEDUM	LEVEL	PLIGHT	LINTS	LOBOS	LOOSE	LOUSE	FLUFFS
SLAYER	LEDUMS	LEVELS	SLIGHT	CLINTS	LOBOSE	LOOSED	LOUSED	PLUFFS
LAYERS	LEEAR	LEVER	LIGHTS	FLINTS	LOCAL	LOOSEN	LOUSES	LUMEN
LAZAR	LEEARS	LEVERS	LIGNE	GLINTS	LOCALE	LOOSER	LOUTS	LUMENS
LAZARS	LEECH	LEVIN	LIGNES	LINTY	LOCALS	LOOSES	CLOUTS	LUMMY
LAZED	FLEECH	LEVINS	LIKEN	FLINTY	LOCKS	LOOTS	FLOUTS	PLUMMY
BLAZED	SLEECH	LEVIS	LIKENS	LIPID	BLOCKS	CLOOTS	GLOUTS	SLUMMY
GLAZED	LEEKS	ALEVIN	LIKER	LIPIDE	CLOCKS	SLOOTS	SLOUTS	LUMPS
LAZES	CLEEKS	LEXES	LIKERS	LIPIDS	FLOCKS	LOPED	LOVAT	CLUMPS
BLAZES	GLEEKS	FLEXES	LIKES	LIPPY	LOCUM	ELOPED	LOVATS	FLUMPS
GLAZES	SLEEKS	ILEXES	GLIKES	LISKS	LOCUMS	LOPER	LOVED	PLUMPS
LEACH	LEEPS	ULEXES	LIKIN	LISLE	LOCUS	ELOPER	GLOVED	SLUMPS
BLEACH	BLEEPS	LIANA	LIKING	LISLES	LOCUST	LOPERS	LOVER	LUMPY
PLEACH	CLEEPS	LIANAS	LIKINS	LITED	LODEN	ELOPES	CLOVER	CLUMPY
LEACHY	SLEEPS	LIANE	LILAC	FLITED	LODENS	LOPES	GLOVER	GLUMPY
LEADS	LEERS	LIANES	LILACS	LITER	LODGE	SLOPED	PLOVER	PLUMPY
PLEADS	FLEERS	LIANG	LIMAX	LITERS	LODGED	SLOPES	LOVERS	SLUMPY
LEAKS	LEESE	LIANGS	CLIMAX	LITES	LODGER	LORAL	CLOVES	LUNAR
BLEAKS	LEESES	LIARD	LIMBO	BLITES	LODGES	LORAN	GLOVES	LUNARS
LEAKY	LEETS	LIARDS	LIMBOS	ELITES	LOGAN	LORANS	LOVEY	LUNARY
BLEAKY	FLEETS	LIBEL	LIMBS	FLITES	SLOGAN	LOREL	LOVEYS	LUNCH
LEAMS	GLEETS	LIBELS	CLIMBS	LITHE	LOGANS	LORES	LOWAN	CLUNCH
FLEAMS	SLEETS	LIBER	LIMED	BLITHE	LOGES	LORIC	LOWANS	LUNGE
GLEAMS	LEFTS	LIBERS	SLIMED	LITHED	ELOGES	LORICA	LOWED	BLUNGE
LEANS	CLEFTS	LIBRA	LIMEN	LITHER	LOGIA	LORICS	BLOWED	PLUNGE
CLEANS	LEGER	LIBRAE	LIMENS	LITHES	ALOGIA	LOSED	FLOWED	LUNGED
GLEANS	LEGERS	LIBRAS	LIMES	LITHO	LOGIC	LOSEL	GLOWED	LUNGES
LEARE	LEGGE	LICHI	CLIMES	LITHOS	LOGICS	LOSELS	PLOWED	LUNGIE
LEARED	ALEGGE	LICHIS	SLIMES	LITRE	LOGIE	LOSER	SLOWED	LUNGIS
LEARES	LEGGED	LICHT	LIMEY	LITRES	LOGIES		LOWER	LUNTS
LEARN	LEGGER	LICHTS	BLIMEY	LIVED	LOIDS		BLOWER	BLUNTS
LEARNS	LEGGES	LICIT	LIMEYS	SLIVED	SLOIDS		CLOSER	LUPIN
LEARNT	LEGIT	ELICIT	LIMIT		LOINS		FLOWER	LUPINE
LEARS	ELEGIT		LIMITS		ELOINS			
BLEARS	LEMAN		LIMMA		LOIPE			
	LEMANS		LIMMAS					
	LEMEL		LIMPS					

LUPINS	MAFIAS	MANORS	MAVIN	MENSES	MIDGES	SMITES	MOOLA	MOUCH
LURES	MAGES	MANSE	MAVINS	MEREL	MIDGET	MITRE	MOOLAH	SMOUCH
ALURES	IMAGES	MANSES	MAXIM	MERELL	MIDST	MITRED	MOOLAS	MOULD
LURGI	MAGIC	MANTA	MAXIMA	MERELS	AMIDST	MITRES	MOOLI	MOULDS
LURGIS	MAGICS	MANTAS	MAXIMS	MERELY	MIDSTS	MIXEN	MOOLIS	MOULDY
LURRY	MAGMA	MANTO	MAYBE	MERES	MIEVE	MIXENS	MOORS	MOULT
FLURRY	MAGMAS	MANTOS	MAYBES	MEREST	MIEVED	MIXER	SMOORS	MOULTS
SLURRY	MAGOT	MANUL	MAYOR	MERGE	MIEVES	MIXERS	MOOTS	MOUND
LUSHY	MAGOTS	MANULS	MAYORS	MERGED	MIGHT	MIZEN	SMOOTS	MOUNDS
FLUSHY	MAHOE	MAPLE	MAZED	MERGER	SMIGHT	MIZENS	MOOVE	MOUNT
PLUSHY	MAHOES	MAPLES	AMAZED	MERGES	MIGHTS	MNEME	AMOOVE	AMOUNT
SLUSHY	MAHUA	MAQUI	MAZER	EMERGE	MIGHTY	MNEMES	MOOVED	MOUNTS
LUTED	MAHUAS	MAQUIS	MAZERS	MERIL	MILER	MOBLE	MOOVES	MOUNTY
ELUTED	MAHWA	MARAH	MAZES	MERILS	MILERS	MOBLED	MOPED	MOURN
FLUTED	MAHWAS	MARAHS	AMAZES	MERIS	MILES	MOBLES	MOPEDS	MOURNS
LUTER	MAIKO	MARGE	MAZUT	MERISM	SMILER	MOCHA	MOPER	MOUSE
FLUTER	MAIKOS	MARGES	MAZUTS	MERIT	SMILES	MOCHAS	MOPERS	SMOUSE
LUTERS	MAIKS	MARID	MEANE	MERITS	MILLE	MOCKS	MORAL	MOUSED
LUTES	SMAIKS	MARIDS	MEANED	MERLE	MILLED	SMOCKS	AMORAL	MOUSER
ELUTES	MAILE	MARLE	MEANER	MERLES	MILLER	MODEL	MORALE	MOUSES
FLUTES	MAILED	MARLED	MEANES	MERSE	MILLES	MODELS	MORALL	MOUSEY
LUXES	MAILER	MARLES	MEARE	MERSES	MILLET	MODEM	MORALS	MOUST
FLUXES	MAILES	MARMS	MEARES	MESEL	MILOR	MODEMS	MORAS	MOUSTS
LYCEE	MAIRE	SMARMS	MEASE	MESELS	MILORD	MODES	MORASS	MOUTH
LYCEES	MAIRES	MAROR	MEASED	MESES	MILORS	MODEST	MORAT	MOUTHS
LYING	MAISE	MARORS	MEASES	EMESES	MIMER	MOGGY	MORATS	MOUTHY
CLYING	MAISES	MARSH	MEATH	TMESES	MIMERS	SMOGGY	MORAY	MOVED
FLYING	MAIZE	MARSHY	SMEATH	MESON	MIMIC	MOGUL	MORAYS	AMOVED
PLYING	MAIZES	MARTS	MEATHE	MESONS	MIMICS	MOGULS	MOREL	EMOVED
LYINGS	MAJOR	SMARTS	MEATHS	METAL	MINAR	MOHEL	MORELS	MOVER
LYMPH	MAJORS	MASER	MEDAL	METALS	MINARS	MOHELS	MORES	MOVERS
LYMPHS	MAKAR	MASERS	MEDALS	METER	MINCE	MOHUR	SMORES	MOVES
LYRIC	MAKARS	MASON	MEDIA	METERS	MINCED	MOHURS	MORIA	EMOVES
LYRICS	MAKER	MASONS	MEDIAE	METIC	MINCER	MOIRE	MORIAS	MOVIE
LYSIN	MAKERS	MASSA	MEDIAL	METICS	MINCES	MOIRES	MORNE	MOVIES
LYSINE	MALAR	MASSAS	MEDIAN	METIF	MINER	MOIST	MORNED	MOWER
LYSING	MALARS	MASSE	MEDIC	METIFS	MINERS	MOISTS	MORNES	MOWERS
LYSINS	MALIC	MASSED	MEDICK	METOL	MINES	MOKES	MORON	MOWRA
LYSOL	MALICE	MASSES	MEDICO	METOLS	AMINES	SMOKES	MORONS	MOWRAS
LYSOLS	MALIS	MATCH	MEDICS	METRE	IMINES	MOKOS	MORPH	MOXIE
LYSSA	MALIST	SMATCH	MEDLE	METRED	MINIM	SMOKOS	MORPHO	MOXIES
LYSSAS	MALLS	MATED	MEDLED	METRES	MINIMA	MOLAR	MORPHS	MOYLE
LYTED	SMALLS	AMATED	MEDLES	METRO	MINIMS	MOLARS	MORRA	SMOYLE
FLYTED	MALMS	MATER	MEDLEY	METROS	MINIS	MOLES	MORRAS	MOYLED
LYTES	SMALMS	MATERS	MEERS	MEUSE	MINISH	MOLEST	MORRO	MOYLES
FLYTES	MALTS	MATES	AMEERS	MEUSED	MINKE	MOLLA	MORROS	MPRET
LYTHE	SMALTS	AMATES	EMEERS	MEUSES	MINKES	MOLLAH	MORROW	MPRETS
LYTHES	MALVA	MATIN	MEITH	MEZZO	MINOR	MOLLAS	MORSE	MUCIN
LYTTA	MALVAS	MATING	MEITHS	MEZZOS	MINORS	MOLTS	MORSEL	MUCINS
LYTTAS	MAMBA	MATINS	MELEE	MHORR	MIRKS	SMOLTS	MORSES	MUCOR
MACAW	MAMBAS	MATLO	MELEES	MHORRS	SMIRKS	MOMMA	MOSEY	MUCORS
MACAWS	MAMBO	MATLOS	MELIC	MIAOW	MIRKY	MOMMAS	MOSEYS	MUCRO
MACER	MAMBOS	MATLOW	MELICS	MIAOWS	MIRTH	MONAD	MOTED	MUCROS
MACERS	MAMMA	MATTE	MELLS	MIASM	MIRTHS	MONADS	EMOTED	MUDIR
MACHO	MAMMAE	MATTED	SMELLS	MIASMA	MISER	MONAL	MOTEL	MUDIRS
MACHOS	MAMMAL	MATTER	MELON	MIASMS	MISERE	MONALS	MOTELS	MUDRA
MACKS	MAMMAS	MATTES	MELONS	MIAUL	MISERS	MONER	MOTES	MUDRAS
SMACKS	MANEH	MATZA	MELTS	MIAULS	MISES	MONERA	EMOTES	MUFTI
MACLE	MANEHS	MATZAH	SMELTS	MICHE	AMISES	MONERS	MOTET	MUFTIS
MACLED	MANGE	MATZAS	MENDS	MICHED	MISSA	MONEY	MOTETS	MUIST
MACLES	MANGEL	MATZO	AMENDS	MICHER	MISSAL	MONEYS	MOTETT	MUISTS
MACRO	MANGER	MATZOH	EMENDS	MICHES	MISSAS	MONOS	MOTIF	MUJIK
MACRON	MANGES	MATZOS	MENED	MICRO	MISSAY	MONOSY	MOTIFS	MUJIKS
MACROS	MANGEY	MATZOT	MENGE	MICRON	MITER	MONTE	MOTOR	MULCT
MADAM	MANIA	MAUND	MENGED	MICROS	MITERS	MONTEM	MOTORS	MULCTS
MADAME	MANIAC	MAUNDS	MENGES	MIDDY	MITES	MONTES	MOTORY	MULES
MADAMS	MANIAS	MAUNDY	MENSE	SMIDDY	SMITER	MONTH	MOTTE	EMULES
MADGE	MANNA	MAUVE	MENSED	MIDGE	MITERS	MONTHS	MOTTES	MULEY
MADGES	MANNAS	MAUVER				MOOCH	MOTZA	MULEYS
MAFIA	MANOR	MAUVES				SMOOCH	MOTZAS	

MULGA	NADIRS	ANEARS	SNIFFS	NOOKS	NURSER	MOCKER	COILED	OMERS
MULGAS	NAEVE	NEATH	NIFFY	SNOOKS	NURSES	ROCKER	DOILED	COMERS
MULSE	NAEVES	ANEATH	SNIFFY	NOOPS	NYAFF	SOCKER	FOILED	HOMERS
MULSES	NAGGY	SNEATH	NIFTY	SNOOPS	NYAFFS	OCKERS	MOILED	VOMERS
MUNGO	KNAGGY	UNEATH	SNIFTY	NOOSE	NYALA	OCREA	ROILED	OMITS
MUNGOS	SNAGGY	NEBEK	NIGER	NOOSED	INYALA	OCREAE	SOILED	VOMITS
MURAL	NAGOR	NEBEKS	NIGERS	NOOSES	NYALAS	OCTAD	TOILED	OMLAH
MURALS	NAGORS	NEBEL	NIGHT	NOPAL	NYLON	OCTADS	OILER	OMLAHS
MURED	NAHAL	NEBELS	ANIGHT	NOPALS	NYLONS	OCTET	BOILER	OMRAH
EMURED	NAHALS	NECKS	KNIGHT	NORIA	NYMPH	OCTETS	MOILER	OMRAHS
MURES	NAIAD	SNECKS	NIGHTS	NORIAS	NYMPHO	OCTETT	TOILER	ONCER
EMURES	NAIADS	NEELD	NIGHTY	NORMA	NYMPHS	OCULI	OILERS	ONCERS
MURRA	NAILS	NEELDS	NIHIL	NORMAL	OAKEN	LOCULI	OILERY	ONCES
MURRAM	SNAILS	NEELE	NIHILS	NORMAN	SOAKEN	ODDER	OINTS	BONCES
MURRAS	NAIRA	NEELES	NINJA	NORMAS	OAKER	DODDER	JOINTS	NONCES
MURRAY	NAIRAS	NEESED	NINJAS	NORTH	SOAKER	FODDER	NOINTS	PONCES
MURRE	NAIVE	NEESE	NINON	NORTHS	OAKERS	NODDER	POINTS	SONCES
MURREN	NAIVER	NEESED	NINONS	NOSER	OAKUM	ODEON	OJIME	ONELY
MURRES	NAKED	NEESES	NINTH	NOSERS	OAKUMS	ODEONS	OJIMES	LONELY
MURREY	NAKERS	NEEZE	NINTHS	NOSES	OARED	ODEUM	OKAPI	ONERS
MURRY	NAKER	NEEZED	NIPPY	ENOSES	HOARED	ODEUMS	OKAPIS	BONERS
SMURRY	SNAKED	NEEZES	SNIPPY	GNOSES	ROARED	ODISM	OKRAS	GONERS
MURVA	NALLA	NEIGH	NISEI	NOSEY	SOARED	IODISM	KOKRAS	LONERS
MURVAS	NALLAH	NEIGHS	NISEIS	NOSEYS	OASTS	ODISMS	OLDEN	MONERS
MUSED	NALLAS	NEIVE	NISSE	NOTCH	OAST	ODIST	BOLDEN	ONION
AMUSED	NAMER	NEIVES	NISSES	NOTCHY	COAST	CODIST	GOLDEN	GONION
MUSER	NAMERS	NELLY	NITON	NOTER	COASTS	MODIST	HOLDEN	ONIONS
AMUSER	NANAS	SNELLY	NITONS	NOTERS	HOASTS	ODISTS	OLDENS	ONIONY
MUSERS	ANANAS	NEPER	NITRE	NOTUM	ROASTS	ODIUM	OLDER	ONNED
MUSES	NANCE	NEPERS	NITRES	NOTUMS	TOASTS	PODIUM	BOLDER	CONNED
AMUSES	NANCES	NEPIT	NITRY	NOULD	LOAVES	SODIUM	COLDER	DONNED
MUSET	NANDU	NEPITS	NITRYL	NOULDE	OBANG	ODIUMS	FOLDER	FONNED
MUSETS	NANDUS	NERKA	NIXIE	NOULE	GOBANG	ODOUR	GOLDER	WONNED
MUSIC	NANNA	NERKAS	NIXIES	NOULES	KOBANG	ODOURS	HOLDER	ONSET
MUSICS	NANNAS	NERVE	NIZAM	NOVEL	OBANGS	ODSOS	POLDER	ONSETS
MUSIT	NAPOO	ENERVE	NIZAMS	NOVELS	OBEAH	GODSOS	SOLDER	OOBIT
MUSITS	NAPOOS	NERVED	NOBBY	NOVUM	OBEAHS	ODYLE	OLDIE	OOBITS
MUSSE	NAPPA	NERVER	KNOBBY	NOVUMS	OBESE	ODYLES	OLDIES	OOHED
MUSSED	NAPPAS	NERVES	SNOBBY	NOWAY	OBESER	OFFAL	OLEIN	BOOHED
MUSSEL	NAPPE	NEUME	NOBLE	NOWAYS	OBIAS	OFFALS	SOLEIN	OOMPH
MUSSES	NAPPED	NEUMES	NOBLER	NOWED	COBIAS	OFFED	OLEINS	OOMPHS
MUSTH	NAPPER	NEVEL	NOBLES	SNOWED	OBITS	BOFFED	OLENT	OOPED
MUSTHS	NAPPES	NEVELS	NOCKS	UNOWED	OOBITS	DOFFED	DOLENT	COOPED
MUTCH	NAPPY	NEWED	KNOCKS	NOYAU	OBJET	GOFFED	OLEUM	HOOPED
SMUTCH	SNAPPY	ENEWED	NODAL	NOYAUS	OBJETS	OFFER	OLEUMS	LOOPED
MUTES	NARES	NEWEL	ANODAL	NUBBY	OBOES	COFFER	OLIOS	MOOPED
MUTEST	SNARES	NEWELL	ENODAL	KNUBBY	GOBOES	DOFFER	FOLIOS	POOPED
MUTON	NARKS	NEWELS	ANODES	SNUBBY	HOBOES	GOFFER	POLIOS	ROOPED
MUTONS	SNARKS	NGAIO	NOINT	NUBIA	OCCUR	OFFERS	OLIVE	SOOPED
MVULE	NASAL	NGAIOS	ANOINT	NUBIAS	OCCURS	OFLAG	SOLIVE	OORIE
MVULES	NASALS	NICHE	NOINTS	NUCHA	OCEAN	OFLAGS	OLIVER	TOORIE
MYALL	NATCH	NICHED	NOISE	NUCHAL	OCEANS	OFTEN	OLIVES	OORIER
MYALLS	SNATCH	NICHER	NOISED	NUCHAS	OCHER	SOFTEN	OLIVET	OOSES
MYNAH	NAUNT	NICHES	NOISES	NUDES	TOCHER	OGGIN	OLLAS	BOOSES
MYNAHS	NAUNTS	NICKS	KNICKS	NUDEST	OCHERS	HOGGIN	HOLLAS	GOOSES
MYOMA	NAVEL	KNICKS	SNICKS	NUDGE	OCHERY	NOGGIN	MOLLAS	LOOSES
MYOMAS	NAVELS	SNICKS	KNOLLS	SNUDGE	OCHES	OGGINS	OLLAV	NOOSES
MYOPE	NAVEW	NICOL	NOMAD	NUDGED	BOCHES	OGHAM	OLLAVS	ROOSES
MYOPES	NAVEWS	NICOLS	NOMADE	NUDGES	COCHES	OGHAMS	OLOGY	OOZED
MYRRH	KNAVE	NIDE	NOMADS	NUDIE	ROCHES	OGIVE	OOLOGY	BOOZED
MYRRHS	KNAVES	NIDES	SNIDES	NUDIES	OCHRE	OGIVES	OLPES	OOZES
NABLA	NAWAB	NIDOR	NOMES	NULLA	OCHREA	OGLER	GOLPES	BOOZES
NABLAS	NAWABS	NIDORS	GNOMES	NULLAH	OCHRED	OGLERS	OMASA	OPALS
NABOB	NAZIR	NIECE	NOMIC	NULLAS	OCHRES	OGLES	OMASAL	COPALS
NABOBS	NAZIRS	NIECES	ANOMIC	NURLS	OCHREY	BOGLES	OMBRE	NOPALS
NACHE	NEAFE	NIEVE	GNOMIC	NURRS	OCKER	FOGLES	HOMBRE	OPERA
NACHES	NEAFES	NIEVES	NONCE	NURSE	COCKER	OGRES	SOMBRE	OPERAS
NACRE	NEAPS	NIFES	NONCES	NURSED	DOCKER	OGRESS	OMBRES	OPINE
NACRES	SNEAPS	KNIFES	NONET	NURSE	HOCKER	OILED	OMEGA	OPINED
NADIR	NEARS	NIFFS	NONETS	NURSED	LOCKER	BOILED	OMEGAS	OPINES

OPING	ORTHOS	LOUPED	JOWING	PACTS	PANICK	PASSER	SPEALS	PENCES
COPING	ORVAL	MOUPED	LOWING	EPACTS	PANICS	PASSES	PEANS	PENDS
DOPING	ORVALS	POUPED	MOWING	PADLE	PANIM	PASTA	SPEANS	SPENDS
HOPING	OSHAC	ROUPED	ROWING	PADLES	PANIMS	PASTAS	PEARE	PENED
LOPING	OSHACS	OUPHE	SOWING	PADMA	PANNE	PASTE	PEARES	OPENED
MOPING	OSIER	OUPHES	TOWING	PADMAS	PANNED	PASTED	PEARL	PENIE
OOPING	COSIER	OURIE	VOWING	PADRE	PANNES	PASTEL	PEARLS	PENIES
ROPING	HOSIER	POURIE	WOWING	PADRES	PANTO	PASTER	PEARLY	PENNA
TOPING	NOSIER	OURIER	OWLED	PAEAN	PANTON	PASTES	PEARS	PENNAE
OPIUM	OOSIER	OUSEL	BOWLED	PAEANS	PANTOS	PATCH	SPEARS	PENNAL
OPIUMS	ROSIER	HOUSEL	COWLED	PAEON	PAPAW	PATCHY	PEARST	PENNE
OPTIC	OSIERS	OUSELS	FOWLED	PAEONS	PAPAWS	PATEN	PEASE	PENNED
OPTICS	OSIERY	OUSTS	GOWLED	PAEONY	PAPER	PATENS	PEASED	PENNER
ORACH	OSMIC	JOUSTS	HOWLED	PAGAN	PAPERS	PATENT	PEASES	PENNES
ORACHE	COSMIC	MOUSTS	JOWLED	PAGANS	PAPERY	PATER	PEATS	PERAI
ORALS	OSTIA	ROUSTS	SOWLED	PAGER	PARCH	PATERA	SPEATS	PERAIS
CORALS	OSTIAL	OUTBY	YOWLED	PAGERS	EPARCH	PATERS	PEAZE	PERCE
GORALS	OTARY	OUTBYE	OWLER	PAGLE	PARDI	PATES	PEAZED	PERCED
MORALS	NOTARY	OUTED	BOWLER	PAGLES	PARDIE	SPATES	PEAZES	PERCEN
ORANG	ROTARY	DOUTED	FOWLER	PAGOD	PARED	PATIN	PECAN	PERCES
ORANGE	VOTARY	LOUTED	HOWLER	PAGODA	SPARED	PATINA	PECANS	PERDU
ORANGS	OTHER	POUTED	JOWLER	PAGODS	PAREO	PATINE	PECKE	EPERDU
ORANT	BOTHER	ROUTED	OWLERS	PAGRI	PAREOS	PATINS	PECKED	PERDUE
VORANT	FOTHER	TOUTED	OWLERY	PAGRIS	PARER	PATIO	PECKER	PERDUS
ORANTS	LOTHER	OUTER	OWLET	PAINS	PARERS	PATIOS	PECKES	PERIL
ORATE	MOTHER	COUTER	HOWLET	SPAINS	PARES	PATTE	PECKS	PERILS
BORATE	POTHER	DOUTER	OWLETS	PAINT	SPARES	PATTED	SPECKS	PERIS
LORATE	ROTHER	FOUTER	OWNED	PAINTS	PAREU	PATTEN	PEDAL	PERISH
ORATED	TOTHER	MOUTER	BOWNED	PAINTY	PAREUS	PATTER	PEDALO	PERMS
ORATES	OTHERS	POUTER	DOWNED	PAIRE	PARGE	PATTES	PEDALS	SPERMS
ORBED	OTTAR	ROUTER	GOWNED	PAIRED	PARGED	PAULS	PEDRO	PERSE
SORBED	COTTAR	SOUTER	LOWNED	PAIRES	PARGES	SPAULS	PEDROS	SPERSE
ORBIT	OTTARS	TOUTER	OWNER	PAISA	PARGET	PAUSE	PEECE	PERSES
ORBITA	OTTER	OUTERS	DOWNER	PAISAS	PARKA	PAUSED	PEECES	PERST
ORBITS	COTTER	OUTRED	OWNERS	PALAY	PARKAS	PAUSER	PEELS	SPERST
ORBITY	HOTTER	OUZEL	OWRES	PALAYS	PARKI	PAUSES	SPEELS	PERVE
ORCIN	JOTTER	OUZELS	HOWRES	PALEA	PARKIN	PAVAN	PEEOY	PERVED
ORCINE	POTTER	OVARY	POWRES	PALEAE	PARKIS	PAVANE	PEEOYS	PERVES
ORCINS	ROTTER	COVARY	OWRIE	PALED	PARKS	PAVANS	PEEPE	PESTO
ORDER	TOTTER	OVATE	COWRIE	OPALED	SPARKS	PAVEN	PEEPED	PESTOS
BORDER	OTTERS	BOVATE	OWRIER	PALES	PARLE	PAVENS	PEEPER	PETAL
ORDERS	OTTOS	OVATED	OXERS	SPALES	PARLED	PAVER	PEEPES	PETALS
OREAD	LOTTOS	OVATES	BOXERS	PALEST	PARLES	PAVERS	PEERS	PETAR
OREADS	POTTOS	OVENS	OXIDE	PALET	PARLEY	PAVIN	SPEERS	PETARA
ORGAN	OUBIT	COVENS	OXIDES	PALETS	PAROL	SPAVIN	PEEVE	PETARD
ORGANA	WOUBIT	OVERS	OXIME	PALKI	PAROLE	PAVING	PEEVED	PETARS
ORGANS	OUBITS	COVERS	OXIMES	PALKIS	PARRY	PAVINS	PEEVER	PETARY
ORGIA	OUCHT	DOVERS	OXLIP	PALLA	SPARRY	PAVIS	PEEVES	PETER
GORGIA	OUCHTS	HOVERS	OXLIPS	PALLAE	PARSE	PAVISE	PEISE	PETERS
ORGIAS	OUGHT	LOVERS	OXTER	PALLAH	SPARSE	PAWAW	PEISED	PETIT
ORGUE	BOUGHT	MOVERS	OXTERS	PALLS	PARSEC	PAWAWS	PEISES	PETITE
MORGUE	DOUGHT	ROVERS	OYERS	SPALLS	PARSED	PAWLS	PEIZE	PETRE
ORGUES	FOUGHT	OVERT	FOYERS	PAMPA	PARSER	SPAWLS	PEIZED	PETREL
ORIBI	MOUGHT	COVERT	TOYERS	PAMPAS	PARSES	PAWNS	PEIZES	PETRES
ORIBIS	NOUGHT	OVINE	OZEKI	PANCE	PARTI	SPAWNS	PEKAN	PEWEE
ORIEL	ROUGHT	BOVINE	OZEKIS	PANCES	PARTIM	PAYED	PEKANS	PEWEES
ORIELS	SOUGHT	OVIST	OZONE	PANDA	PARTIS	SPAYED	PEKOE	PEWIT
ORLOP	OUGHTS	OVISTS	OZONES	PANDAR	PARTS	PAYEE	PEKOES	PEWITS
ORLOPS	OUIJA	OVOID	PACED	PANDAS	SPARTS	PAYEES	PELLS	PEYSE
ORMER	OUIJAS	OVOIDS	PACER	PANEL	PASEO	PAYER	SPELLS	PEYSED
DORMER	OUNCE	OVULE	SPACED	PANELS	PASEOS	PAYERS	PELMA	PEYSES
FORMER	BOUNCE	OVULES	SPACER	PANES	PASHA	PEACE	PELMAS	PHAGE
WORMER	JOUNCE	OWCHE	PACES	SPANES	PASHAS	PEACED	PELTA	PHAGES
ORMERS	POUNCE	OWCHES	SPACES	PANGA	PASHM	PEACES	PELTAE	PHANG
ORPIN	ROUNCE	OWING	PACEY	PANGAS	PASHMS	PEACH	PELTAS	UPHANG
ORPINE	OUNCES	BOWING	SPACEY	PANGS	PASSE	PEACHY	PELTS	PHANGS
ORPINS	OUNDY	COWING	PACHA	SPANGS	PASSED	PEAKS	SPELTS	PHARE
ORRIS	WOUNDY	DOWING	PACHAK	PANIC	PASSEE	SPEAKS	PENCE	PHARES
MORRIS	OUPED		PACHAS			PEALS	SPENCE	PHASE
ORTHO	COUPED						PENCEL	PHASED

PHASES	PILAWS	PIXIES	PLOATS	POLIOS	POTTOS	**PREIF**	PRIZER	PSALMS
PHEER	**PILED**	**PIZZA**	**PLONG**	**POLKA**	**POTTY**	PREIFE	PRIZES	**PSEUD**
PHEERE	SPILED	PIZZAS	PLONGD	POLKAS	SPOTTY	PREIFS	**PROBE**	PSEUDO
PHEERS	**PILER**	**PLACE**	PLONGE	**POLYP**	**POUCH**	**PRENT**	PROBED	PSEUDS
PHENE	PILERS	PLACED	PLONGS	POLYPE	POUCHY	SPRENT	PROBES	**PSHAW**
SPHENE	**PILES**	PLACER	**PLONK**	POLYPI	**POUKE**	PRENTS	**PRODS**	PSHAWS
PHENES	SPILES	PLACES	PLONKS	POLYPS	POUKES	**PRESE**	SPRODS	**PSORA**
PHEON	**PILLS**	PLACET	**PLOOK**	**POMBE**	**POULE**	PRESES	**PROEM**	PSORAS
PHEONS	SPILLS	**PLACK**	UPLOOK	POMBES	POULES	PRESET	PROEMS	**PSYCH**
PHESE	**PILOT**	PLACKS	PLOOKS	**PONCE**	**POULP**	**PREST**	**PROGS**	PSYCHE
PHESED	PILOTS	**PLAGE**	**PLOUK**	PONCED	POULPE	UPREST	**PROIN**	PSYCHO
PHESES	**PILOW**	PLAGES	PLOUKS	PONCES	POULPS	PRESTO	PROINE	PSYCHS
PHIAL	PILOWS	**PLAID**	**PLUCK**	**PONEY**	**POULT**	PRESTS	PROINS	**PSYOP**
PHIALS	**PINAS**	UPLAID	PLUCKS	PONEYS	POULTS	**PREVE**	**PROKE**	PSYOPS
PHOCA	SPINAS	PLAIDS	PLUCKY	**PONGO**	**POUND**	PREVED	PROKED	**PUDDY**
PHOCAE	**PINED**	**PLAIN**	**PLUFF**	PONGOS	POUNDS	PREVES	PROKER	SPUDDY
PHOCAS	OPINED	PLAINS	PLUFFS	**PONGY**	**POUPE**	**PRIAL**	PROKES	**PUDGE**
PHONE	SPINED	PLAINT	PLUFFY	SPONGY	POUPED	PRIALS	**PROLE**	PUDGES
PHONED	**PINES**	**PLAIT**	**PLUMB**	**POOFS**	POUPES	**PRICE**	PROLED	**PUDOR**
PHONES	OPINES	PLAITS	PLUMBS	SPOOFS	**POUTS**	PRICED	PROLEG	PUDORS
PHONEY	SPINES	**PLANE**	**PLUME**	**POOJA**	SPOUTS	PRICER	PROLES	**PUGIL**
PHONY	**PINGO**	PLANED	PLUMED	POOJAH	**POUTY**	PRICES	**PROLL**	PUGILS
APHONY	PINGOS	PLANER	PLUMES	POOJAS	SPOUTY	PRICEY	UPROLL	**PUKER**
PHOTO	**PINKO**	PLANES	**PLUMP**	**POOKA**	**POWAN**	**PRICK**	PROLLS	PUKERS
PHOTON	PINKOS	PLANET	PLUMPS	POOKAS	POWANS	PRICKS	**PROMO**	**PULER**
PHOTOS	**PINKS**	**PLANK**	PLUMPY	**POOKS**	**POWER**	**PRIDE**	PROMOS	PULERS
PHYLA	SPINKS	PLANKS	**PLUNK**	SPOOKS	POWERS	PRIDED	**PRONE**	**PULES**
PHYLAE	**PINNA**	**PLANT**	PLUNKS	**POOLS**	**POWIN**	PRIDES	PRONER	SPULES
PHYLE	PINNAE	PLANTA	**PLUSH**	SPOOLS	POWINS	**PRIEF**	PRONES	**PULKA**
PHYLES	**PINNY**	PLANTS	PLUSHY	**POONS**	**POWND**	PRIEFE	**PRONG**	PULKAS
PIANO	**PINON**	**PLASH**	**POACH**	SPOONS	POWNDS	PRIEFS	SPRONG	**PULSE**
PIANOS	SPINNY	PLASHY	POACHY	**POORT**	**POWRE**	**PRIER**	PRONGS	PULSED
PICAS	PINONS	SPLASH	**POAKA**	POORTS	POWRED	PRIERS	**PROOF**	PULSES
SPICAS	**PINOT**	**PLASM**	POAKAS	**POOVE**	POWRES	**PRIES**	PROOFS	**PULUS**
PICKS	PINOTS	PLASMA	**POAKE**	POOVES	**POYNT**	PRIEST	**PRORE**	OPULUS
SPICKS	**PINTA**	PLASMS	POAKES	**POPPA**	POYNTS	**PRIGS**	PRORES	**PUMIE**
PICOT	**PINTO**	**PLAST**	**PODAL**	POPPAS	**POYSE**	SPRIGS	**PROSE**	PUMIES
PICOTE	PINTOS	YPLAST	**PODGE**	**PORER**	POYSED	**PRILL**	UPROSE	**PUNCE**
PICOTS	**PIOYE**	PLASTE	PODGES	PORERS	POYSES	PRILLS	PROSED	PUNCES
PICRA	PIOYES	**PLATE**	**PODIA**	**PORES**	**PRAAM**	**PRIMA**	PROSER	**PUNCH**
PICRAS	**PIPAL**	PLATED	PODIAL	SPORES	PRAAMS	PRIMAL	PROSES	PUNCHY
PICUL	PIPALS	PLATEN	**POGGE**	**PORGE**	**PRAHU**	**PRIME**	**PROUL**	**PUNKA**
PICULS	**PIPER**	PLATER	POGGES	PORGED	PRAHUS	PRIMED	PROULS	PUNKAH
PIECE	PIPERS	PLATES	**POILU**	PORGES	**PRANA**	PRIMER	**PROVE**	PUNKAS
APIECE	**PIPIT**	**PLATS**	POILUS	**PORNO**	PRANAS	PRIMES	PROVED	**PUNKS**
PIECED	PIPITS	SPLATS	**POIND**	PORNOS	**PRANG**	**PRIMO**	PROVEN	SPUNKS
PIECEN	**PIPUL**	**PLAYA**	POINDS	**PORTA**	SPRANG	PRIMOS	PROVER	**PUNTO**
PIECER	PIPULS	PLAYAS	**POINT**	PORTAL	**PRANK**	**PRIMP**	PROVES	PUNTOS
PIECES	**PIQUE**	**PLAYS**	POINTE	PORTAS	PRANKS	PRIMPS	**PROWL**	**PUPIL**
PIEND	PIQUED	SPLAYS	POINTS	**PORTS**	PRANKY	**PRINK**	PROWLS	PUPILS
PIENDS	PIQUES	UPLAYS	**POISE**	SPORTS	**PRASE**	PRINKS	**PROYN**	**PUREE**
PIERS	PIQUET	**PLAZA**	POISED	**PORTY**	PRASES	**PRINT**	PROYNE	PUREED
PIERST	**PIRAI**	PLAZAS	POISER	SPORTY	**PRATE**	SPRINT	PROYNS	PUREES
PIETA	PIRAIS	**PLEAD**	POISES	**POSER**	PRATED	PRINTS	**PRUDE**	PUREST
PIETAS	**PISTE**	UPLEAD	**POKAL**	POSERS	PRATER	**PRION**	PRUDES	**PURGE**
PIGHT	PISTES	PLEADS	POKALS	**POSES**	PRATES	PRIONS	**PRUNE**	SPURGE
SPIGHT	**PITCH**	**PLEAS**	**POKER**	**POSIT**	**PRATS**	**PRIOR**	PRUNED	PURGED
YPIGHT	PITCHY	PLEASE	POKERS	POSITS	SPRATS	PRIORS	PRUNER	PURGER
PIGHTS	**PITON**	**PLEAT**	**POKES**	**POSSE**	**PRAWN**	PRIORY	PRUNES	PURGES
PIKED	PITONS	PLEATS	SPOKES	POSSED	PRAWNS	**PRISE**	**PRUNT**	**PURIM**
SPIKED	**PITTA**	**PLEON**	**POLAR**	POSSER	**PRAYS**	EPRISE	PRUNTS	PURIMS
PIKER	PITTAS	PLEONS	POLARS	POSSES	SPRAYS	UPRISE	**PRYER**	**PURIN**
PIKERS	**PIUMS**	**PLICA**	**POLER**	POSSET	PRISED	PRISED	SPRYER	PURINE
PIKES	OPIUMS	PLICAE	POLERS	**POTCH**	**PREED**	PRISER	**PRYSE**	PURING
SPIKES	**PIVOT**	PLICAL	**POLEY**	POTCHE	SPREED	PRISES	PRYSED	PURINS
PIKUL	PIVOTS	**PLIER**	POLEYN	**POTIN**	**PREEN**	**PRISM**	PRYSES	**PURIS**
PIKULS	**PIXEL**	PLIERS	POLEYS	POTING	PREENS	PRISMS	PRIZED	PURISM
PILAU	PIXELS	**PLINK**	**POLIO**	POTINS	**PREES**	PRISMY	**PRIZE**	PURIST
PILAUS	**PIXIE**	PLINKS	POLIOS	**POTTO**	SPREES	**PRIZE**	PRIZED	**PURSE**
PILAW		**PLOAT**					**PSALM**	

PURSED	QUEST	QUOTE	BRAILS	BRANDS	FRATER	TRAYNE	REBELS	REESTY
PURSER	QUESTS	QUOTED	DRAILS	GRANDS	GRATER	RAYNES	REBID	REEVE
PURSES	QUEUE	QUOTER	FRAILS	RANDY	IRATER	RAYON	REBIDS	PREEVE
PURSEW	QUEUED	QUOTES	GRAILS	BRANDY	PRATER	CRAYON	REBIT	REEVED
PUSES	QUEUES	QUOTH	TRAILS	RANEE	RATERS	RAYONS	REBITE	REEVES
OPUSES	QUEYN	QUOTHA	RAINE	RANEES	RATES	RAZED	REBUT	REFEL
PUSLE	QUEYNS	QUYTE	GRAINE	RANGE	CRATES	BRAZED	REBUTS	REFELS
PUSLED	QUICH	QUYTED	RAINED	GRANGE	GRATES	CRAZED	RECAL	REFER
PUSLES	QUICHE	QUYTES	RAINES	ORANGE	ORATES	GRAZED	RECALL	PREFER
PUTTI	QUICK	RABAT	RAINS	RANGED	PRATES	RAZEE	RECALS	REFERS
PUTTIE	QUICKS	RABATO	BRAINS	RANGER	URATES	RAZEED	RECAP	REFFO
PUZEL	QUIDS	RABATS	DRAINS	RANGES	RATHE	RAZEES	RECAPS	REFFOS
PUZELS	SQUIDS	RABBI	GRAINS	RANKE	RATHER	RAZES	RECCE	REFIT
PYGAL	QUIET	RABBIN	TRAINS	RANKED	RATHS	BRAZES	RECCED	REFITS
PYGALS	QUIETS	RABBIS	BRAINY	RANKER	WRATHS	CRAZES	RECCES	REGAL
PYLON	QUIFF	RABBIT	GRAINY	RANKES	RATIO	GRAZES	RECCO	REGALE
PYLONS	SQUIFF	RACED	BRAIRD	RANKS	RATION	RAZOR	RECCOS	REGALS
PYRES	QUIFFS	BRACED	RAIRD	BRANKS	RATIOS	RAZORS	RECIT	REGAR
SPYRES	QUILL	GRACED	RAIRDS	CRANKS	RATTY	REACH	RECITE	REGARD
QANAT	SQUILL	TRACED	RAISE	FRANKS	BRATTY	AREACH	RECITS	REGARS
QANATS	QUILLS	RACER	ARAISE	PRANKS	RAVED	BREACH	RECKS	REGIE
QIBLA	QUILT	BRACER	BRAISE	RANTS	BRAVED	CREACH	DRECKS	REGIES
QIBLAS	QUILTS	TRACER	FRAISE	CRANTS	CRAVED	PREACH	TRECKS	REGMA
QUACK	QUINA	RACERS	PRAISE	DRANTS	GRAVED	REACT	WRECKS	BREGMA
QUACKS	QUINAS	RACES	RAISED	GRANTS	RAVEL	REACTS	RECTA	REGUR
QUADS	QUINE	BRACES	RAISER	ORANTS	RAVELS	RECTA	RECTAL	REGURS
SQUADS	EQUINE	GRACES	RAISES	TRANTS	RAVEN	READS	RECTO	REIFS
QUAFF	QUINES	TRACES	RAITS	RAPED	CRAVEN	AREADS	RECTOR	PREIFS
QUAFFS	QUINS	RACHE	KRAITS	CRAPED	GRAVEN	BREADS	RECTOS	REIGN
QUAIL	QUINSY	ORACHE	TRAITS	DRAPED	RAVENS	DREADS	RECUR	REIGNS
SQUAIL	QUINT	RACHES	RAJAH	GRAPED	RAVER	OREADS	RECURS	GREINS
QUAILS	SQUINT	RACKS	RAJAHS	TRAPED	BRAVER	TREADS	REDAN	REIRD
QUAIR	QUINTA	BRACKS	RAKED	RAPER	CRAVER	REAKS	REDANS	REIRDS
QUAIRS	QUINTE	CRACKS	BRAKED	DRAPER	GRAVER	BREAKS	REDES	REIST
QUAKE	QUINTS	TRACKS	CRAKED	RAPERS	RAVERS	CREAKS	AREDES	REISTS
QUAKED	QUIPO	WRACKS	RAKEE	RAPES	RAVES	FREAKS	BREDES	REISTY
QUAKES	QUIPOS	RACON	RAKEES	CRAPES	BRAVES	WREAKS	REDIA	REIVE
QUALM	QUIPS	RACONS	RAKER	DRAPES	CRAVES	REALM	UREDIA	REIVER
QUALMS	EQUIPS	RADAR	RAKERS	GRAPES	GRAVES	REALMS	REDIAE	REIVES
QUALMY	QUIPU	RADARS	RAKERY	TRAPES	TRAVES	REAME	REDIP	REJIG
QUANT	QUIPUS	RADIO	RAKES	RAPHE	RAVIN	REAMED	REDIPS	REJIGS
EQUANT	QUIRE	RADIOS	BRAKES	RAPHES	RAVINE	REAMER	REECH	RELAY
QUANTA	SQUIRE	RADON	CRAKES	RAPID	RAVING	REAMES	BREECH	RELAYS
QUANTS	QUIRED	RADONS	DRAKES	RAPIDS	RAVINS	REAMS	REECHY	RELET
QUARK	QUIRES	RAFFS	RAKIS	RASED	RAWER	BREAMS	REEDE	RELETS
QUARKS	QUIRK	DRAFFS	RAKISH	ERASED	RAWLY	CREAMS	REEDED	RELIC
QUART	QUIRKS	GRAFFS	ORALLY	RASES	BRAWLY	DREAMS	REEDEN	RELICS
QUARTE	QUIRKY	RAFTS	RALLY	BRASES	CRAWLY	REAMY	REEDER	RELICT
QUARTO	QUIRT	CRAFTS	RALLYE	CRASES	RAWNS	CREAMY	REEDES	RELIE
QUARTS	SQUIRT	DRAFTS	RAMEE	ERASES	BRAWNS	DREAMY	REEDS	RELIED
QUARTZ	QUIRTS	GRAFTS	RAMEES	RASPS	PRAWNS	REARM	BREEDS	RELIEF
QUASH	QUIST	KRAFTS	RAMIE	GRASPS	RAXES	REARMS	CREEDS	RELIER
SQUASH	QUISTS	RAGEE	RAMIES	WRASSE	PRAXES	REARS	GREEDS	RELIES
QUATS	QUITE	DRAGEE	RAMPS	RASSE	RAYAH	REAST	REEDY	REMAN
SQUATS	QUITED	RAGEES	CRAMPS	RASSES	RAYAHS	REASTS	GREEDY	REMAND
QUEAN	QUITES	RAGER	TRAMPS	RATAN	RAYED	REATA	REEKS	REMANS
QUEANS	QUITS	RAGERS	RANAS	RATANS	BRAYED	REATAS	BREEKS	REMEN
QUEEN	SQUITS	RAGGY	PRANAS	RATCH	FRAYED	REATE	CREEKS	REMENS
QUEENS	QUOIF	CRAGGY	RANCE	CRATCH	GRAYED	REATES	REEKY	REMIT
QUEER	QUOIFS	DRAGGY	PRANCE	FRATCH	PRAYED	REAVE	CREEKY	FREMIT
QUEERS	QUOIN	RAIDS	TRANCE	RATED	RAYLE	REAVER	REELS	REMITS
QUELL	QUOINS	BRAIDS	RANCED	CRATED	GRAYLE	REAVES	CREELS	RENAY
QUELLS	QUOIT	RAIKS	RANCEL	GRATED	RAYLED	REBEC	REENS	RENAYS
QUEME	QUOITS	RAILE	RANCES	ORATED	RAYLES	REBECS	PREENS	RENDS
QUEMED	QUOLL	GRAILE	RANCH	PRATED	RAYLET	REBEL	REEST	TRENDS
QUEMES	QUOLLS	RAILED	BRANCH	RATEL	RAYNE		FREEST	RENEW
QUENA	QUONK	RAILER	CRANCH	RATELS			REESTS	RENEWS
QUENAS	QUONKS	RAILES	RANCHO	RATER				RENEY
QUERN	QUOTA	RAILS	RANDS	CRATER				RENEYS
QUERNS	QUOTAS							

RENGA	REWTHS	RIDGEL	CRINES	GRIVET	ROLAGS	GROPER	ROUSED	CRUCKS
RENGAS	RHEUM	RIDGES	TRINES	PRIVET	ROLES	PROPER	ROUSER	TRUCKS
RENIG	RHEUMS	RIELS	URINES	TRIVET	DROLES	ROPERS	ROUSES	RUDDY
RENIGS	RHEUMY	ARIELS	RINGS	RIVETS	PROLES	ROPERY	ROUST	CRUDDY
RENIN	RHIME	ORIELS	BRINGS	RIYAL	ROLLS	ROPES	ROUSTS	RUDER
RENINS	RHIMES	RIEVE	WRINGS	RIYALS	DROLLS	GROPES	ROUTE	CRUDER
RENNE	RHINE	GRIEVE	RINKS	ROACH	PROLLS	TROPES	CROUTE	RUDERY
BRENNE	RHINES	PRIEVE	DRINKS	BROACH	TROLLS	ROQUE	ROUTED	RUFFE
FRENNE	RHINO	RIEVER	BRINKS	ROADS	ROMAL	ROQUES	ROUTER	RUFFED
RENNED	RHINOS	RIEVES	PRINKS	BROADS	ROMALS	ROQUET	ROUTES	RUFFES
RENNES	RHOMB	RIFFS	RINSE	TROADS	ROMAN	RORES	ROUTH	RUING
RENNET	RHOMBI	GRIFFS	RINSED	ROANS	ROMANS	CRORES	ROUTHS	GRUING
RENTE	RHOMBS	RIFLE	RINSER	GROANS	ROMAS	PRORES	DROUTH	TRUING
RENTED	RHONE	TRIFLE	RINSES	ROAST	AROMAS	RORIE	ROUTS	RUINGS
RENTER	RHONES	RIFLED	RIOTS	ROASTS	GROMAS	RORIER	CROUTS	RULER
RENTES	RHUMB	RIFLER	GRIOTS	ROATE	ROMPS	ROSED	GROUTS	RULERS
RENTS	RHUMBA	RIFLES	RIPED	ROATED	RONDE	PROSED	TROUTS	RUMAL
PRENTS	RHUMBS	RIFTE	GRIPED	ROATES	RONDES	ROSES	UROSES	BRUMAL
REPAY	RHYME	RIFTED	RIPEN	ROBED	RONDEL	BROSES	PROVED	RUMALS
PREPAY	RHYMED	RIFTS	RIPENS	PROBED	RONDES	PROSES	PROVER	RUMBA
REPAYS	RHYMER	DRIFTS	RIPER	ROBES	RONDO	ROSET	TROVER	RUMBAS
REPEL	RHYMES	GRIFTS	RIPERS	PROBES	RONDOS	GROSET	ROVED	RUMBO
REPELS	RHYNE	DRIFTY	RIPES	ROBIN	RONEO	ROSETS	DROVER	RUMBOS
REPLA	RHYNES	RIGHT	CRIPES	ROBING	RONES	ROSETY	ROVER	RUMEN
REPLAN	RIALS	ARIGHT	GRIPES	ROBINS	RONTE	ROSIN	ROVERS	CRUMEN
REPLAY	PRIALS	BRIGHT	TRIPES	ROBLE	RONTES	ROSING	ROVES	RUMES
REPOT	TRIALS	FRIGHT	RIPEST	ROBLES	RONTS	ROSINS	DROVES	BRUMES
REPOTS	URIALS	WRIGHT	RISEN	ROBOT	ROODS	ROSINY	GROVES	GRUMES
REPRO	RIANT	RIGHTO	ARISEN	ROBOTS	ROOFS	ROSIT	PROVES	RUMLY
REPROS	CRIANT	RIGHTS	RISER	ROCKS	GROOFS	ROSITS	ROWAN	DRUMLY
RERUN	RIATA	RIGID	PRISER	BROCKS	PROOFS	ROSTS	ROWANS	GRUMLY
RERUNS	RIATAS	FRIGID	RISERS	CROCKS	ROOKS	FROSTS	ROWED	RUMMY
RESAY	RICED	RIGIDS	RISES	FROCKS	BROOKS	ROTAL	CROWED	CRUMMY
RESAYS	PRICED	RIGOL	ARISES	TROCKS	CROOKS	CROTAL	TROWED	RUMOR
RESET	TRICED	RIGOLL	BRISES	RODED	DROOKS	ROTCH	ROWEL	RUMORS
PRESET	RICER	RIGOLS	CRISES	ERODED	ROOMS	CROTCH	TROWEL	RUMPS
RESETS	GRICER	RIGOR	FRISES	RODEO	BROOMS	ROTCHE	ROWELS	CRUMPS
RESIN	PRICER	RIGORS	GRISES	RODEOS	GROOMS	ROTOR	ROWEN	FRUMPS
RESINS	RICES	RILLE	IRISES	RODES	VROOMS	ROTORS	ROWENS	TRUMPS
RESIT	GRICES	GRILLE	KRISES	ERODES	ROOMY	ROUGE	ROWER	RUNCH
RESITS	PRICES	RILLED	PRISES	TRODES	BROOMY	ROUGED	ROWERS	BRUNCH
RESTS	TRICES	RILLES	RISHI	ROGER	ROONS	ROUGES	ROWME	CRUNCH
CRESTS	RICEY	RILLET	RISHIS	DROGER	CROONS	ROUGH	ROWMES	RUNED
PRESTS	PRICEY	RILLS	RISKS	ROGERS	ROOPS	BROUGH	ROWND	PRUNED
WRESTS	RICHT	BRILLS	BRISKS	ROGUE	DROOPS	TROUGH	ROWNDS	RUNES
RETCH	FRICHT	DRILLS	FRISKS	ROGUED	TROOPS	ROUGHS	ROWTH	PRUNES
WRETCH	RICHTS	FRILLS	RISKY	ROGUES	ROOPY	ROUGHT	GROWTH	RUNTS
RETES	RICIN	GRILLS	BRISKY	ROILS	DROOPY	ROUGHY	ROWTHS	BRUNTS
ARETES	RICING	KRILLS	FRISKY	BROILS	ROOSA	ROULE	ROYAL	GRUNTS
RETIE	RICINS	PRILLS	RISPS	DROILS	ROOSAS	TROULE	ROYALS	PRUNTS
RETIED	RICKS	TRILLS	RITES	ROINS	ROOSE	ROULES	ROYNE	RUPEE
RETIES	BRICKS	RIMED	TRITES	GROINS	BROOSE	ROULS	GROYNE	RUPEES
RETRO	CRICKS	CRIMED	URITES	PROINS	ROOSED	PROULS	PROYNE	RUPIA
RETROD	ERICKS	GRIMED	WRITES	ROIST	ROOSES	ROUND	ROYNED	RUPIAH
RETROS	PRICKS	PRIMED	RIVAL	ROISTS	ROOST	AROUND	ROYNES	RUPIAS
REUSE	TRICKS	RIMER	RIVALS	ROKED	ROOSTS	GROUND	ROYST	RURAL
REUSED	WRICKS	PRIMER	RIVEL	BROKED	ROOTS	ROUNDS	ROYSTS	CRURAL
REUSES	RIDER	TRIMER	DRIVEL	PROKED	WROOTS	ROUPS	ROZET	RURALS
REVEL	ARIDER	RIMES	RIVELS	TROKED	ROPED	CROUPS	ROZETS	RUSES
REVELS	RIDERS	CRIMES	RIVEN	ROKER	GROPED	GROUPS	ROZIT	CRUSES
REVET	RIDES	GRIMES	DRIVEN	BROKER	TROPED	ROUPY	ROZITS	DRUSES
BREVET	BRIDES	PRIMES	RIVER	PROKER	ROPER	CROUPY	RUBIN	URUSES
REVETS	GRIDES	RIMUS	DRIVER	ROKERS		GROUPY	RUBINE	RUSHY
REVIE	IRIDES	PRIMUS	RIVERS	ROKES		ROUSE	RUBINS	BRUSHY
REVIED	PRIDES	RINDS	RIVERY	BROKES		CROUSE	RUBLE	RUSMA
REVIES	RIDGE	GRINDS	RIVES	PROKES		GROUSE	RUBLES	RUSMAS
REVIEW	BRIDGE	RINES	DRIVES	TROKES		TROUSE	RUCHE	RUSTS
REVUE	FRIDGE	BRINES	RIVET	ROLAG	ROPED	ROUSE	RUCHED	BRUSTS
REVUES	RIDGED				GROPED	CROUSE	RUCHES	CRUSTS
REWTH					ROPER	TROUSE	RUCKS	FRUSTS

TRUSTS	SALEP	SASINS	SCALLS	SCOOP	SCROWS	SEGUES	SERVED	SHARK
RUSTY	SALEPS	SASSE	SCALP	SCOOPS	SCRUB	SEINE	SERVER	SHARKS
CRUSTY	SALET	SASSED	SCALPS	SCOOT	SCRUBS	SEINED	SERVES	SHARN
TRUSTY	SALETS	SASSES	SCAMP	SCOOTS	SCRUM	SEINER	SETON	SHARNS
RUTHS	SALLE	SATIN	SCAMPI	SCOPA	SCRUMP	SEINES	SETONS	SHARNY
TRUTHS	SALLEE	ISATIN	SCAMPS	SCOPAE	SCRUMS	SEISE	SEVEN	SHARP
RUTIN	SALLES	SATING	SCANT	SCOPE	SCUBA	SEISED	SEVENS	SHARPS
RUTINS	SALLET	SATINS	SCANTS	SCOPES	SCUBAS	SEISER	SEVER	SHAVE
RYBAT	SALMI	SATINY	SCANTY	SCORE	SCUDO	SEISES	SEVERE	SHAVED
RYBATS	SALMIS	SATYR	SCAPA	SCORED	ESCUDO	SEISM	SEVERS	SHAVEN
RYKES	SALON	SATYRA	SCAPAS	SCORER	SCUFF	SEISMS	SEVERY	SHAVER
GRYKES	SALONS	SATYRS	SCAPE	SCORES	SCUFFS	SEIZE	SEWEL	SHAVES
RYMME	SALOP	SAUBA	ESCAPE	SCORN	SCUFFY	SEIZED	SEWELS	SHAWL
RYMMED	SALOPS	SAUBAS	SCAPED	SCORNS	SCUFT	SEIZER	SEWEN	SHAWLS
RYMMES	SALSA	SAUCE	SCAPES	SCOTS	SCUFTS	SEIZES	SEWENS	SHAWM
SABER	SALSAS	SAUCED	SCARE	ASCOTS	SCULK	SELAH	SEWER	SHAWMS
SABERS	SALSE	SAUCER	SCARED	ESCOTS	SCULKS	SELAHS	SEWERS	SHAWS
SABIN	SALSES	SAUCES	SCARER	SCOUG	SCULL	SELLE	SEWIN	PSHAWS
SABINS	SALTO	SAUCH	SCARES	SCOUGS	SCULLE	SELLER	SEWING	SHAYA
SABLE	SALTOS	SAUCHS	SCAREY	SCOUP	SCULLS	SELLES	SEWINS	SHAYAS
USABLE	SALUE	SAUGH	SCARF	SCOUPS	SCULP	SELVA	SEXER	SHCHI
SABLED	SALUED	SAUGHS	SCARFS	SCOUR	SCULPS	SELVAS	SEXERS	SHCHIS
SABLES	SALUES	SAULT	SCARP	SCOURS	SCULPT	SEMEN	SEYEN	SHEAF
SABOT	SALVE	SAULTS	ESCARP	SCOUT	SCURF	SEMENS	SEYENS	SHEAFS
SABOTS	SALVED	SAUNA	SCARPS	SCOUTS	SCURFS	SEMIE	SHACK	SHEAFY
SABRA	SALVER	SAUNAS	SCART	SCOWL	SCURFY	SEMIES	SHACKS	SHEAL
SABRAS	SALVES	SAUNT	SCARTH	SCOWLS	SCUSE	SENNA	SHADE	SHEALS
SABRE	SALVO	SAUNTS	SCARTS	SCOWP	SCUSED	SENNAS	SHADED	SHEAR
SABRED	SALVOR	SAUTE	SCATH	SCOWPS	SCUSES	SENSE	SHADES	SHEARS
SABRES	SALVOS	SAUTED	SCATHE	SCRAB	SCUTA	SENSED	SHAFT	SHEEL
SACRA	SAMAN	SAUTES	SCATHS	SCRABS	SCUTAL	SENSES	SHAFTS	SHEELS
SACRAL	SAMANS	SAVER	SCATT	SCRAE	SCUTE	SEPAD	SHAKE	SHEEN
SADHU	SAMBA	SAVERS	SCATTS	SCRAES	SCUTES	SEPADS	SHAKEN	SHEENS
SADHUS	TSAMBA	SAVEY	SCATTY	SCRAG	SDAYN	SEPAL	SHAKER	SHEENY
SAFES	SAMBAL	SAVEYS	SCAUD	SCRAGS	SDAYNS	SEPALS	SHAKES	SHEEP
SAFEST	SAMBAR	SAVIN	SCAUDS	SCRAM	SDEIN	SEPIA	SHAKO	SHEEPY
SAGER	SAMBAS	SAVINE	SCAUP	SCRAMS	SDEINS	SEPIAS	SHAKOS	SHEER
USAGER	SAMBO	SAVING	SCAUPS	SCRAN	SEAME	SEPOY	SHALE	SHEERS
SAGES	SAMBOS	SAVINS	SCAUR	SCRANS	SEAMED	SEPOYS	SHALED	SHEET
USAGES	SAMEL	SAVOR	SCAURS	SCRAP	SEAMEN	SEPTA	SHALES	SHEETS
SAGEST	SAMELY	SAVORS	SCAURY	SCRAPS	SEAMER	SEPTAL	SHALL	SHEETY
SAHIB	SAMFU	SAVORY	SCEAT	SCRAT	SEAMES	SERAC	SHALLI	SHEIK
SAHIBA	SAMFUS	SAVOY	SCEATT	SCRATS	SEARE	SERACS	SHALM	SHEIKH
SAHIBS	SAMPI	SAVOYS	SCEND	SCRAW	SEARED	SERAI	SHALMS	SHEIKS
SAICE	SAMPIS	SAWAH	SCENDS	SCRAWL	SEARER	SERAIL	SHAMA	SHELF
SAICES	SANKO	SAWAHS	SCENE	SCRAWS	SEASE	SERAIS	SHAMAN	SHELFS
SAICK	SANKOS	SAWER	SCENED	SCRAY	SEASED	SERES	SHAMAS	SHELFY
SAICKS	SANSA	SAWERS	SCENES	SCRAYE	SEASES	SEREST	SHAME	SHELL
SAIDS	SANSAS	SAYED	SCENT	SCRAYS	SEAZE	SERGE	ASHAME	SHELLS
SAIDST	SAPAN	SAYEDS	ASCENT	SCREE	SEAZED	SERGES	SHAMED	SHELLY
SAIGA	SAPANS	SAYER	SCENTS	SCREED	SEAZES	SERIF	SHAMER	SHEND
SAIGAS	SAPOR	SAYERS	SCHMO	SCREEN	SEBUM	SERIFS	SHAMES	YSHEND
SAINE	SAPORS	SAYID	SCHMOE	SCREES	SEBUMS	SERIN	SHAND	SHENDS
SAINED	SAREE	SAYIDS	SCHUL	SCREW	SECCO	SERING	SHANDS	SHENT
SAINT	SAREES	SAYON	SCHULS	SCREWS	SECCOS	SERINS	SHANK	YSHENT
SAINTS	SARGE	SAYONS	SCHWA	SCREWY	SEDAN	SERON	SHANKS	SHERD
SAITH	SARGES	SCAFF	SCHWAS	SCRIM	SEDANS	SERONS	SHAPE	SHERDS
SAITHE	SARGO	SCAFFS	SCION	SCRIMP	SEDGE	SEROW	SHAPED	SHETS
SAITHS	SARGOS	SCAIL	SCIONS	SCRIMS	SEDGED	SEROWS	SHAPEN	ASHETS
SAJOU	SARIN	SCAILS	SCLIM	SCRIP	SEDGES	SERRA	SHAPER	SHEVA
SAJOUS	SARING	SCALA	SCLIMS	SCRIPS	SEDUM	SERRAE	SHAPES	SHEVAS
SAKER	SARINS	SCALAE	SCOFF	SCRIPT	SEDUMS	SERRAN	SHARD	SHIEL
SAKERS	SAROD	SCALAR	SCOFFS	SCROG	SEGAR	SERRAS	SHARDS	SHIELD
SAKIA	SARODS	SCALD	SCOLD	SCROGS	SEGARS	SERRE	SHARE	SHIELS
SAKIAS	SARSA	SCALDS	SCOLDS	SCROW	SEGNO	SERRED	SHARED	SHIER
SALAD	SARSAS	SCALE	SCONE	ESCROW	SEGNOS	SERRES	SHARER	ASHIER
SALADE	SARZA	SCALED	SCONES	SCROWL	SEGOL	SERUM	SHARES	SHIERS
SALADS	SARZAS	SCALER	SCOOG		SEGOLS	SERUMS		SHIES
SALAL	SASIN	SCALES	SCOOGS		SEGUE	SERVE		SHIEST
SALALS	SASINE	SCALL			SEGUED			SHIFT

SHIFTS	SHROWD	**SIRUP**	SKIMPS	SLEEPY	SLUSHY	SMOUSE	**SNOOL**	**SONNE**
SHIFTY	SHROWS	SIRUPS	SKIMPY	**SLEET**	**SLYPE**	SMOUT	SNOOLS	**SONNES**
SHILL	**SHRUB**	**SISAL**	**SKINK**	SLEETS	SLYPES	SMOUTS	**SNOOP**	**SONNET**
SHILLS	**SHRUBS**	SISALS	SKINKS	SLEETY	**SMACK**	SMOWT	SNOOPS	**SONSE**
SHINE	**SHRUG**	**SITAR**	**SKIRL**	**SLICE**	SMACKS	SMOWTS	**SNOOT**	SONSES
ASHINE	SHRUGS	SITARS	SKIRLS	SLICED	**SMAIK**	**SNACK**	SNOOTS	**SOOLE**
SHINED	SHTUM	**SITHE**	**SKIRR**	SLICER	SMAIKS	SNACKS	SNOOTY	SOOLED
SHINER	SHTUMM	SITHED	SKIRRS	SLICES	**SMALL**	**SNAFU**	**SNORE**	SOOLES
SHINES	**SHUCK**	SITHEN	**SKIRT**	**SLICK**	SMALLS	SNAFUS	SNORED	**SOOTE**
SHIRE	SHUCKS	SITHES	SKIRTS	SLICKS	**SMALM**	**SNAIL**	SNORER	SOOTED
SHIRES	**SHUNT**	**SIVER**	**SKITE**	**SLIDE**	SMALMS	SNAILS	SNORES	SOOTES
SHIRK	SHUNTS	SIVERS	SKITED	SLIDED	SMALMY	SNAILY	**SNORT**	**SOOTH**
SHIRKS	**SHYER**	**SIXER**	SKITES	SLIDER	**SMALT**	**SNAKE**	SNORTS	**SOOTHE**
SHIRR	SHYERS	SIXERS	**SKIVE**	SLIDES	SMALTI	SNAKED	SNORTY	SOOTHS
SHIRRA	**SIBYL**	**SIXTE**	SKIVED	**SLIME**	SMALTO	SNAKES	**SNOUT**	**SOPHA**
SHIRRS	SIBYLS	SIXTES	SKIVER	SLIMED	SMALTS	**SNARE**	SNOUTS	SOPHAS
SHIRT	SIDER	**SIXTH**	SKIVES	SLIMES	**SMARM**	SNARED	SNOUTY	**SOPOR**
SHIRTS	SIDERS	SIXTHS	**SKLIM**	SLIMS	SMARMS	SNARER	**SNOWK**	SOPORS
SHIRTY	SIDES	**SIZAR**	SKLIMS	SLIMSY	SMARMY	SNARES	SNOWKS	**SORAS**
SHITE	ASIDES	SIZARS	**SKOFF**	**SLING**	**SMART**	SNARK	**SNUFF**	PSORAS
SHITES	**SIDHA**	**SIZEL**	SKOFFS	ISLING	SMARTS	SNARKS	SNUFFS	**SORBO**
SHIVE	SIDHAS	SIZELS	**SKRAN**	SLINGS	SMARTY	**SNARL**	SNUFFY	SORBOS
SHIVER	**SIDLE**	**SIZER**	SKRANS	**SLINK**	**SMEAR**	SNARLS	**SOARE**	**SORDO**
SHIVES	SIDLED	SIZERS	**SKRIK**	SLINKS	ASMEAR	SNARLY	SOARED	SORDOR
SHLEP	SIDLES	**SKAIL**	SKRIKS	SLINKY	SMEARS	SNATH	SOARES	**SOREE**
SHLEPS	**SIEGE**	SKAILS	**SKULK**	**SLIPE**	SMEARY	SNATHE	**SOBER**	SOREES
SHOAL	SIEGED	**SKALD**	SKULKS	SLIPES	**SMEEK**	SNATHS	SOBERS	**SOREL**
SHOALS	SIEGER	SKALDS	**SKULL**	**SLIVE**	SMEEKS	**SNEAD**	**SOCLE**	SORELL
SHOALY	SIEGES	**SKART**	SKULLS	SLIVED	**SMELL**	SNEADS	SOCLES	SORELS
SHOAT	**SIENT**	SKARTH	**SKUNK**	SLIVEN	SMELLS	**SNEAK**	**SOFAR**	SORELY
SHOATS	SIENTS	SKARTS	SKUNKS	SLIVER	SMELLY	SNEAKS	SOFARS	**SORES**
SHOCK	**SIETH**	**SKATE**	**SKYER**	SLIVES	**SMELT**	SNEAKY	**SOFTA**	SOREST
SHOCKS	SIETHS	SKATED	SKYERS	SLOAN	SMELTS	**SNEAP**	SOFTAS	**SORGO**
SHOER	**SIEVE**	SKATER	**SKYRE**	SLOANS	**SMILE**	SNEAPS	**SOGER**	SORGOS
SHOERS	SIEVED	SKATES	SKYRED	**SLOID**	SMILED	**SNECK**	SOGERS	**SORRA**
SHOJI	SIEVES	**SKATT**	SKYRES	SLOIDS	SMILER	SNECKS	**SOKEN**	SORRAS
SHOJIS	**SIGHT**	SKATTS	**SKYTE**	**SLOOM**	SMILES	**SNEER**	SOKENS	**SOUCE**
SHOLA	SIGHTS	**SKEAN**	SKYTED	SLOOMS	SMILET	SNEERS	**SOLAH**	SOUCED
SHOLAS	**SIGIL**	SKEANS	SKYTES	SLOOMY	**SMIRK**	SNEERY	SOLAHS	SOUCES
SHOOK	SIGILS	**SKEAR**	**SLACK**	**SLOOP**	SMIRKS	SNEES	**SOLAN**	**SOUGH**
SHOOKS	**SIGMA**	SKEARS	SLACKS	SLOOPS	SMIRKY	SNEESH	SOLAND	SOUGHS
SHOOL	SIGMAS	**SKEER**	**SLADE**	**SLOOT**	**SMIRR**	**SNELL**	SOLANO	SOUGHT
SHOOLS	**SILEN**	SKEERS	SLADES	SLOOTS	SMIRRS	SNELLS	SOLANS	**SOUND**
SHOOT	SILENE	SKEERY	**SLAKE**	**SLOPE**	SMIRRY	SNELLY	**SOLAR**	SOUNDS
SHOOTS	SILENS	**SKEET**	ASLAKE	ASLOPE	**SMITE**	**SNICK**	SOLARS	**SOURS**
SHORE	SILENT	SKEETS	SLAKED	SLOPED	SMITER	SNICKS	**SOLDE**	SOURSE
ASHORE	**SILER**	**SKEIN**	SLAKES	SLOPES	SMITES	**SNIDE**	SOLDER	**SOUSE**
SHORED	SILERS	SKEINS	**SLANE**	**SLOSH**	**SMITH**	SNIDER	SOLDES	SOUSED
SHORER	SILES	**SKELF**	SLANES	SLOSHY	SMITHS	SNIDES	**SOLEN**	SOUSES
SHORES	ESILES	SKELFS	**SLANG**	**SLOTH**	SMITHY	**SNIFF**	SOLENS	**SOUTH**
SHORT	**SILVA**	**SKELM**	SLANGS	SLOTHS	**SMOCK**	SNIFFS	**SOLER**	SOUTHS
SHORTS	SILVAE	SKELMS	SLANGY	**SLOVE**	SMOCKS	SNIFFY	SOLERS	**SOWAR**
SHORTY	SILVAN	**SKELP**	**SLANT**	SLOVEN	**SMOKE**	**SNIFT**	**SOLID**	SOWARS
SHOTE	SILVAS	SKELPS	ASLANT	**SLOYD**	SMOKED	SNIFTS	SOLIDI	**SOWCE**
SHOTES	**SIMAR**	**SKENE**	SLANTS	SLOYDS	SMOKER	SNIFTY	SOLIDS	SOWCED
SHOTT	SIMARS	SKENES	**SLATE**	**SLUBB**	SMOKES	**SNIPE**	**SOLUM**	SOWCES
SHOTTS	**SINEW**	SKERS	SLATED	SLUBBS	SMOKO	SNIPED	SOLUMS	**SOWER**
SHOUT	SINEWS	ASKERS	SLATER	SLUBBY	SMOKOS	SNIPER	**SOLVE**	SOWERS
SHOUTS	SINEWY	ESKERS	SLATES	**SLUIT**	**SMOLT**	SNIPES	SOLVED	**SOWFF**
SHOVE	**SINGE**	**SKIER**	**SLAVE**	SLUITS	SMOLTS	**SNIRT**	SOLVER	SOWFFS
SHOVED	SINGED	SKIERS	SLAVED	**SLUMP**	**SMOOR**	SNIRTS	SOLVES	**SOWLE**
SHOVEL	SINGER	**SKIES**	SLAVER	SLUMPS	SMOORS	**SNOEK**	**SONAR**	SOWLED
SHOVER	SINGES	ESKIES	SLAVES	SLUMPY	**SMOOT**	SNOEKS	SONARS	SOWLES
SHOVES	**SIREN**	**SKIFF**	SLAVEY	**SLURB**	SMOOTH	**SNOKE**	**SONCE**	**SOWND**
SHRED	SIRENE	SKIFFS	**SLEEK**	SLURBS	SMOOTS	SNOKED	SONCES	SOWNDS
SHREDS	SIRENS	**SKILL**	SLEEKS	**SLURP**	**SMORE**	SNOKES	**SONDE**	**SOWNE**
SHREW	**SIRIH**	SKILLS	SLEEKY	SLURPS	SMORED	**SNOOD**	SONDES	SOWNES
SHREWD	SIRIHS	SKILLY	**SLEEP**	**SLUSE**	SMORES	SNOODS	**SONIC**	**SOWSE**
SHREWS	**SIROC**	**SKIMP**	ASLEEP	SLUSES	**SMOUS**	**SNOOK**	SONICS	SOWSED
SHROW	SIROCS		SLEEPS	**SLUSH**	OSMOUS	SNOOKS		SOWSES

SOWTH	SPEAR	ASPINE	SPRIGS	STALER	STEDES	STINGS	STOPED	STROWS
SOWTHS	SPEARS	SPINED	SPRIT	STALES	STEED	STINGY	STOPES	STROY
SOYLE	SPEARY	SPINEL	ESPRIT	STALK	STEEDS	STINK	STOPS	STROYS
SOYLED	SPEAT	SPINES	SPRITE	STALKO	STEEDY	STINKS	ESTOPS	STRUM
SOYLES	SPEATS	SPINET	SPRITS	STALKS	STEEK	STINT	STORE	ESTRUM
SPACE	SPECK	SPINK	SPROD	STALKY	STEEKS	STINTS	STORED	STRUMA
SPACED	SPECKS	SPINKS	SPRODS	STALL	STEEL	STINTY	STORER	STRUMS
SPACER	SPECKY	SPIRE	SPROG	STALLS	STEELD	STIPA	STORES	STRUT
SPACES	SPEED	ASPIRE	SPROGS	STAMP	STEELS	STIPAS	STOREY	STRUTS
SPACEY	SPEEDO	SPIREA	SPRUE	STAMPS	STEELY	STIPE	STORK	ASTRUT
SPADE	SPEEDS	SPIRED	SPRUES	STAND	STEEM	STIPEL	STORKS	STUCK
SPADED	SPEEDY	SPIRES	SPRUG	STANDS	STEEMS	STIPES	STORM	STUCKS
SPADER	SPEEL	SPIRT	SPRUGS	STANE	ESTEEM	STIRE	STORMS	STUFF
SPADES	SPEELS	SPIRTS	SPULE	STANED	STEEN	STIRED	STORMY	STUFFS
SPADO	SPEER	SPITE	SPULES	STANES	STEENS	STIRES	STOUN	STUFFY
SPADOS	SPEERS	SPITED	SPUME	STANG	STEEP	STIRK	STOUND	STULL
SPAER	SPEIR	SPITES	SPUMED	STANGS	STEEPS	STIRKS	STOUNS	STULLS
SPAERS	SPEIRS	SPLAT	SPUMES	STANK	STEEPY	STIRP	STOUP	STULM
SPAHI	SPELD	SPLATS	SPUNK	STANKS	STEER	STIRPS	STOUPS	STULMS
SPAHIS	SPELDS	SPLAY	SPUNKS	STAPH	STEERS	STIRS	STOUR	STUMP
SPAIN	SPELK	SPLAYS	SPUNKY	STAPHS	STEERY	STIVE	STOURS	STUMPS
SPAING	SPELKS	SPLIT	SPURN	STARE	STEIL	STIVED	STOURY	STUMPY
SPAINS	SPELL	SPLITS	SPURNE	ASTARE	STEILS	STIVER	STOUT	STUNS
SPALD	SPELLS	SPODE	SPURNS	STARED	STEIN	STIVES	STOUTH	ASTUNS
SPALDS	SPELT	SPODES	SPURT	STARER	STEINS	STOAT	STOUTS	STUNT
SPALE	SPELTS	SPOIL	SPURTS	STARES	STELA	STOATS	STOVE	STUNTS
SPALES	SPEND	SPOILS	SPYAL	STARK	STELAE	STOCK	STOVED	STUPA
SPALL	SPENDS	SPOILT	SPYALS	STARKS	STELAR	STOCKS	STOVER	STUPAS
SPALLE	SPERM	SPOKE	SPYRE	STARN	STELE	STOCKY	STOVES	STUPE
SPALLS	SPERMS	SPOKEN	SPYRES	STARNS	STELES	STOEP	STOWN	STUPED
SPALT	SPIAL	SPOKES	SQUAB	STARR	STELL	STOEPS	STOWND	STUPES
SPALTS	SPIALS	SPOOF	SQUABS	STARRS	STELLS	STOIT	STRAD	STURT
SPANE	SPICA	SPOOFS	SQUAD	STARRY	STEME	STOITS	STRADS	STURTS
SPANED	SPICAS	SPOOK	SQUADS	START	STEMED	STOKE	STRAE	STYLE
SPANES	SPICE	SPOOKS	SQUAT	ASTART	STEMES	STOKED	STRAES	STYLED
SPANG	SPICED	SPOOKY	ASQUAT	STARTS	STEND	STOKER	STRAG	STYLES
SPANGS	SPICER	SPOOL	SQUATS	STATE	STENDS	STOKES	STRAGS	STYLET
SPANK	SPICES	SPOOLS	SQUAW	ESTATE	STENT	STOLA	STRAK	STYLO
SPANKS	SPICK	SPOOM	SQUAWK	STATED	OSTENT	STOLAS	STRAKE	STYLOS
SPARE	ASPICK	SPOOMS	SQUAWS	STATER	STENTS	STOLE	STRAP	STYME
SPARED	SPICKS	SPOON	SQUEG	STATES	STERE	STOLED	STRAPS	STYMED
SPARER	SPICS	SPOONS	SQUEGS	STAVE	STEREO	STOLEN	STRAW	STYMES
SPARES	ASPICS	SPOONY	SQUIB	STAVED	STERES	STOLES	STRAWN	STYRE
SPARK	SPIDE	SPOOR	SQUIBS	STAVES	STERN	STOMP	STRAWS	STYRED
SPARKE	SPIDER	SPOORS	SQUID	STEAD	STERNS	STOMPS	STRAWY	STYRES
SPARKS	SPIED	SPORE	SQUIDS	STEADS	ASTERN	STOND	STRAY	SUAVE
SPARS	ESPIED	SPORES	SQUIT	STEADY	STICH	STONDS	ASTRAY	SUAVER
SPARSE	SPIEL	SPORT	SQUITS	STEAK	STICHS	STONE	ESTRAY	SUBAH
SPART	SPIELS	ASPORT	STACK	STEAKS	STICK	ASTONE	STRAYS	SUBAHS
SPARTH	SPIES	SPORTS	STACKS	STEAL	STICKS	STONED	STREP	SUBER
SPARTS	ESPIES	SPORTY	STADE	OSTEAL	STICKY	STONER	STREPS	SUBERS
SPASM	SPIFF	SPOSH	STADES	STEALE	STIFF	STONES	STREW	SUCRE
SPASMS	SPIFFY	SPOSHY	STAFF	STEALS	STIFFS	STONK	STREWN	SUCRES
SPATE	SPIKE	SPOUT	STAFFS	STEALT	STILB	STONKS	STREWS	SUDOR
SPATES	SPIKED	SPOUTS	STAGE	STEAM	STILBS	STONN	STRIA	SUDORS
SPAUL	SPIKES	SPOUTY	STAGED	STEAMS	STILE	STONNE	STRIAE	SUEDE
SPAULD	SPILE	SPRAG	STAGER	STEAMY	STILED	STONNS	STRID	SUEDED
SPAULS	SPILED	SPRAGS	STAGES	STEAN	STILES	STONY	STRIDE	SUEDES
SPAWL	SPILES	SPRAT	STAGEY	STEANE	STILET	ASTONY	STRIDS	SUGAR
SPAWLS	SPILL	SPRATS	STAIG	STEANS	STILL	STOOK	STRIG	SUGARS
SPAWN	SPILLS	SPRAY	STAIGS	STEAR	STILLS	STOOKS	STRIGA	SUGARY
SPAWNS	SPILT	SPRAYS	STAIN	STEARD	STILLY	STOOL	STRIGS	SUING
SPAYD	SPILTH	SPRED	STAINS	STEARE	STILT	STOOLS	STRIP	SUINGS
SPAYDS	SPINA	SPREDD	STAIR	STEARS	STILTS	STOOP	STRIPE	SUINT
SPEAK	SPINAE	SPREDS	STAIRS	STEDD	STILTY	ASTOOP	STRIPS	SUINTS
SPEAKS	SPINAL	SPREE	STAKE	STEDDE	STIME	STOOPE	STRIPY	SUITE
SPEAL	SPINAR	SPREED	STAKED	STEDDS	STIMED	STOOPS	STROP	SUITED
SPEALS	SPINAS	SPREES	STAKES	STEDDY	STIMES	STOOR	STROPS	SUITES
SPEAN	SPINE	SPRIG	STALE	STEDE	STING	STOORS	STROW	SUJEE
SPEANS			STALED	STEDED	STINGO	STOPE	STROWN	SUJEES

SUMAC	SWEAL	SYBOW	ETALON	STARRY	TEAZEL	TENUES	THEMED	THUJA
SUMACH	SWEALS	SYBOWS	TALONS	TARSI	TEAZES	TEPAL	THEMES	THUJAS
SUMACS	SWEAR	SYCEE	TALPA	TARSIA	TEDDY	TEPALS	THEOW	THUMB
SUMMA	SWEARD	SYCEES	TALPAE	TARTS	STEDDY	TEPEE	THEOWS	THUMBS
SUMMAE	SWEARS	SYLPH	TALPAS	STARTS	TEELS	TEPEES	THERE	THUMBY
SUMMAR	SWEAT	SYLPHS	TALUK	TASAR	STEELS	TERAI	THERES	THUMP
SUMMAT	SWEATS	SYLVA	TALUKS	TASARS	TEEMS	TERAIS	THERM	THUMPS
SUMPH	SWEATY	SYLVAE	TAMAL	TASSE	STEEMS	TERCE	THERMS	THYME
SUMPHS	SWEDE	SYLVAN	TAMALE	TASSEL	TEEND	TERCEL	THESE	THYMES
SUPER	SWEDES	SYLVAS	TAMALS	TASSES	TEENDS	TERCES	THESES	TIARA
SUPERB	SWEEL	SYMAR	TAMER	TASSET	TEENE	TERCET	THETA	TIARAS
SUPERS	SWEELS	SYMARS	TAMERS	TASTE	TEENED	TEREK	THETAS	TIBIA
SURAH	SWEEP	SYNCH	TAMES	TASTED	TEENES	TEREKS	THETE	TIBIAE
SURAHS	SWEEPS	SYNCHS	TAMEST	TASTER	TEENS	TERFE	THETES	TIBIAL
SURAT	SWEEPY	SYNOD	TAMIN	TASTES	STEENS	TERFES	THICK	TIBIAS
SURATS	SWEER	SYNODS	TAMINE	TATER	TEENSY	TERNE	THICKO	TICAL
SURED	SWEERT	SYREN	TAMING	TATERS	TEERS	TERNED	THICKS	TICALS
USURED	SWEET	SYRENS	TAMINS	TATES	STEERS	TERNES	THICKY	TICKS
SURER	SWEETS	SYRUP	TAMIS	TATIE	TEETH	TERNS	THIGH	TICKY
USURER	SWEETY	SYRUPS	TAMISE	TATIES	TEETHE	STERNS	THIGHS	STICKS
SURES	SWEIR	SYRUPY	TAMPS	TATOU	TEHEE	TERRA	THILL	STICKY
USURES	SWEIRT	SYTHE	STAMPS	TATOUS	TEHEED	TERRAE	THILLS	TIFFS
SUREST	SWELL	SYTHES	TANGA	TATUS	TEHEES	TERRAS	THING	STIFFS
SURGE	SWELLS	SYVER	TANGAS	STATUS	TEILS	TERSE	THINGS	TIGER
SURGED	SWELT	SYVERS	TANGO	TAUBE	STEILS	TERSER	THINGY	TIGERS
SURGES	SWELTS	TABLA	TANGOS	TAUBES	TEIND	TESLA	THINK	TIGERY
SURRA	SWERF	TABLAS	TANGS	TAUNT	TEINDS	TESLAS	THINKS	TIGHT
SURRAS	SWERFS	TABLE	STANGS	TAUNTS	TELAE	TESTA	THIOL	TIGHTS
SUSHI	SWIFT	TABLED	TANKA	TAUPE	TELAS	TESTAS	THIOLS	TIGON
SUSHIS	SWIFTS	TABLES	TANKAS	TAUPES	STELAE	TESTE	THIRD	TIGONS
SUTOR	SWILL	TABLET	TANKS	TAVER	TELLS	TESTED	THIRDS	TILDE
SUTORS	SWILLS	TABOO	STANKS	TAVERN	STELLS	TESTEE	THIRL	TILDES
SUTRA	SWING	TABOOS	TANNA	TAVERS	TEMED	TESTER	THIRLS	TILED
SUTRAS	SWINGE	TABOR	TANNAH	TAVERT	ITEMED	TESTES	THOFT	STILED
SWAGE	SWINGS	TABORS	TANNAS	TAWED	TEMES	TETRA	THOFTS	TILER
SWAGED	SWINK	TABUN	TAPER	STAWED	TEMPO	TETRAD	THOLE	TILERS
SWAGES	SWINKS	TABUNS	TAPERS	TAWER	TEMPOS	TETRAS	THOLED	TILERY
SWAIN	SWIPE	TACHE	TAPES	TAWERS	TEMPS	TEWED	THOLES	TILES
SWAINS	SWIPED	TACHES	STAPES	TAWERY	TEMPT	TEWEL	THONG	STILES
SWALE	SWIPER	TACKS	TAPET	TAWSE	TEMPTS	TEWELS	THONGS	TILLS
SWALED	SWIPES	STACKS	TAPETA	TAWSES	TEMSE	TEWIT	THORN	STILLS
SWALES	SWIPEY	TAFIA	TAPETI	TAXER	TEMSED	TEWITS	THORNS	TILLY
SWAMI	SWIRE	TAFIAS	TAPETS	TAXERS	TEMSES	THACK	THORNY	STILLY
SWAMIS	SWIRES	TAIGA	TAPIR	TAXOR	TENCH	THACKS	THORP	TILTH
SWAMP	SWIRL	TAIGAS	TAPIRS	TAXORS	STENCH	THAGI	THORPE	TILTHS
SWAMPS	ASWIRL	TAINT	TAPIS	TAYRA	TENDS	THAGIS	THORPS	TILTS
SWAMPY	SWIRLS	TAINTS	TAPIST	TAYRAS	STENDS	THANA	THOWL	STILTS
SWANK	SWIRLY	TAIRA	TAPPA	TAZZA	TENES	THANAH	THOWLS	TIMBO
SWANKS	SWISH	TAIRAS	TAPPAS	TAZZAS	CTENES	THANAS	THRAW	TIMBOS
SWANKY	SWISHY	TAKER	TARED	TEADE	TENET	THANE	THRAWN	TIMED
SWARD	SWONE	TAKERS	TARES	TEADES	TENETS	THANES	THRAWS	STIMED
USWARD	SWONES	TAKES	STARES	TEADS	TENIA	ETHANE	THREE	TIMER
SWARDS	SWOON	STAKES	TARGE	STEADS	TENIAE	THANK	THREEP	TIMERS
SWARDY	SWOONS	TAKIN	TARGED	TEAKS	TENIAS	THANKS	THREES	TIMES
SWARF	SWOOP	TAKING	TARGES	STEAKS	TENNE	THECA	THRID	STIMES
SWARFS	SWOOPS	TAKINS	TARGET	TEALS	TENNER	THECAE	THRIDS	TIMON
SWARM	SWORD	TALAK	TARNS	STEALS	TENNES	THECAL	THRIP	TIMONS
ASWARM	SWORDS	TALAKS	STARNS	TEAMS	TENON	THEEK	THRIPS	TINCT
SWARMS	SWOUN	TALAQ	TAROC	STEAMS	TENONS	THEEKS	THROB	TINCTS
SWART	SWOUND	TALAQS	TAROCS	TEARS	TENOR	THEFT	ATHROB	TINEA
SWARTH	SWOUNE	TALAR	TAROK	STEARS	TENORS	THEFTS	THROBS	TINEAS
SWARTY	SWOUNS	TALARS	TAROKS	TEASE	TENSE	THEGN	THROE	TINGE
SWASH	SYBBE	TALES	TAROT	TEASED	TENSED	THEGNS	THROED	TINGED
SWASHY	SYBBES	STALES	TAROTS	TEASEL	TENSER	THEIC	THROES	TINGES
SWATH	SYBIL	TALKS	TARRE	TEASER	TENSES	THEICS	THROW	TINGS
SWATHE	SYBILS	STALKS	TARRED	TEASES	TENTH	THEIR	THROWE	STINGS
SWATHS	SYBOE	TALMA	TARRES	TEAZE	TENTHS	THEIRS	THROWN	TINKS
SWATHY	SYBOES	TALMAS	TARRY	TEAZED	TENTS	THEME	THROWS	STINKS
SWAYL		TALON			STENTS		THRUM	TINTS
SWAYLS					TENUE		THRUMS	STINTS

TINTY	ATONED	TOUSED	STRASS	TROADE	TUBBY	TWIERS	UKASES	UNDAMS
STINTY	STONED	TOUSER	TRAVE	TROADS	STUBBY	TWILL	ULCER	UNDER
TIRED	TONES	TOUSES	TRAVEL	TROAT	TUBER	TWILLS	ULEMA	DUNDER
STIRED	ATONES	TOUTS	TRAVES	TROATS	TUBERS	TWILLY	ULEMAS	FUNDER
TIRES	STONES	STOUTS	TRAWL	TROCK	TUCKS	TWILT	ULMIN	SUNDER
STIRES	TONGA	TOUZE	TRAWLS	TROCKS	STUCKS	TWINE	ULMINS	UNDERN
TITAN	TONGAS	TOUZED	TRAYS	TRODE	TUFFE	TWINED	ULNAR	UNFIT
TITANS	TONIC	TOUZES	STRAYS	TRODES	TUFFES	TWINER	ULNARE	UNFITS
TITCH	TONICS	TOWED	TREAD	TROKE	TUFFET	TWINES	ULTRA	UNGET
STITCH	ATONIC	STOWED	TREADS	STROKE	TUFFS	TWINK	ULTRAS	UNGETS
TITER	TONKS	TOWEL	TREAT	TROKED	STUFFS	TWINKS	ULYIE	UNGOD
TITERS	STONKS	TOWELS	TREATS	TROKES	TUISM	TWIRE	ULYIES	UNGODS
TITHE	TONNE	TOWER	TREATY	TROLL	TUISMS	TWIRED	ULZIE	UNGUM
TITHED	STONNE	STOWER	TRECK	STROLL	TULIP	TWIRES	ULZIES	UNGUMS
TITHER	TONNES	TOWERS	TRECKS	TROLLS	TULIPS	TWIRL	UMBEL	UNHAT
TITHES	TOOLS	TOWERY	TREEN	TROLLY	TULLE	TWIRLS	UMBELS	SUNHAT
TITIS	STOOLS	TOWSE	TREENS	TROMP	TULLES	TWIRLY	UMBER	UNHATS
OTITIS	TOOTH	TOWSED	TREMA	TROMPE	TUMOR	TWIRP	CUMBER	UNIFY
TITLE	TOOTHS	TOWSER	TREMAS	TROMPS	TUMORS	TWIRPS	DUMBER	MUNIFY
TITLED	TOOTHY	TOWSES	TREND	TRONA	TUMPS	TWIST	LUMBER	UNION
TITLER	TOOTS	TOWZE	TRENDS	TRONAS	STUMPS	TWISTS	NUMBER	BUNION
TITLES	TOOTSY	TOWZED	TRENDY	TRONC	TUMPY	TWISTY	UMBERS	UNIONS
TITRE	TOPED	TOWZES	TRESS	TRONCS	STUMPY	TWITE	UMBERY	UNITE
TITRES	STOPED	TOXIN	STRESS	TRONE	TUNER	TWITES	UMBOS	DUNITE
TITUP	TOPEE	TOXINS	TRESSY	TRONES	TUNERS	TWOER	BUMBOS	GUNITE
TITUPS	TOPEES	TOYER	TREWS	TROOP	TUNIC	TWOERS	GUMBOS	MUNITE
TITUPY	TOPEK	TOYERS	STREWS	TROOPS	TUNICS	TWYER	RUMBOS	UNITED
TOAST	TOPEKS	TOZIE	TRIAD	TROPE	TUPEK	TWYERE	UMBRA	UNITER
TOASTS	TOPER	TOZIES	TRIADS	TROPED	TUPEKS	TWYERS	UMBRAE	UNITES
TOASTY	TOPERS	TRACE	TRIAL	TROPES	TUPIK	TYING	UMBRAL	UNKED
TOAZE	TOPES	TRACED	ATRIAL	TROTH	TUPIKS	STYING	UMBRAS	BUNKED
TOAZED	STOPES	TRACER	TRIALS	TROTHS	TUQUE	TYLER	UMBRE	DUNKED
TOAZES	TOPIC	TRACES	TRIBE	TROUT	TUQUES	TYLERS	UMBREL	FUNKED
TODAY	ATOPIC	TRACK	TRIBES	TROUTS	TURBO	TYPIC	UMBRES	JUNKED
TODAYS	TOPICS	TRACKS	TRICE	TROUTY	TURBOS	ETYPIC	UMIAK	UNKET
TODDE	TOQUE	TRACT	TRICED	TROWS	TURBOT	TYPTO	UMIAKS	JUNKET
TODDED	TOQUES	TRACTS	TRICES	STROWS	TURME	TYPTOS	UMPTY	SUNKET
TODDES	TORAN	TRADE	TRICK	TROYS	TURMES	TYRAN	HUMPTY	UNLAW
TOGUE	TORANA	TRADED	TRICKS	STROYS	TUTEE	TYRANS	UNARM	UNLAWS
TOGUES	TORANS	TRADER	TRICKY	TRUCE	TUTEES	TYRANT	UNARMS	UNLAY
TOILE	TORES	TRADES	TRIDE	TRUCES	TUTOR	TYRED	UNBAG	UNLAYS
ETOILE	STORES	TRADS	TRIER	TRUCK	TUTORS	STYRED	UNBAGS	UNLET
TOILED	TORII	STRADS	ETRIER	TRUCKS	TUTTI	TYRES	UNBAR	RUNLET
TOILER	TORIIS	TRAGI	TRIERS	TRUES	TUTTIS	STYRES	UNBARE	UNLID
TOILES	TORSE	TRAGIC	TRIGS	TRUEST	TWAIN	TYTHE	UNBARK	UNLIDS
TOILET	TORSEL	TRAIK	STRIGS	TRULL	ATWAIN	TYTHED	UNBARS	UNLIT
TOISE	TORSES	TRAIKS	TRIKE	TRULLS	TWAINS	TYTHES	UNBED	SUNLIT
TOISES	TORSK	TRAIL	TRIKED	TRUMP	TWANG	UDDER	SUNBED	UNMAN
TOKED	TORSKS	TRAILS	TRIKES	TRUMPS	TWANGS	DUDDER	UNBEDS	GUNMAN
STOKED	TORSO	TRAIN	TRILL	TRUNK	TWANGY	JUDDER	UNCAP	UNMANS
TOKEN	TORSOS	STRAIN	TRILLO	TRUNKS	TWANK	PUDDER	UNCAPE	UNMEW
TOKENS	TORTE	TRAINS	TRILLS	TRUST	TWANKS	RUDDER	UNCAPS	UNMEWS
TOKES	TORTEN	TRAIT	TRINE	TRUSTS	TWEAK	SUDDER	UNCES	UNPAY
ATOKES	TORTES	STRAIT	TRINED	TRUSTY	TWEAKS	UDDERS	BUNCES	UNPAYS
STOKES	TOSES	TRAITS	TRINES	TRUTH	TWEED	UGGED	DUNCES	UNPEG
TOLAS	PTOSES	TRAMP	TRIOR	TRUTHS	TWEEDS	BUGGED	OUNCES	UNPEGS
STOLAS	TOTAL	STRAMP	TRIORS	TRUTHY	TWEEDY	FUGGED	PUNCES	UNPEN
TOLED	TOTALS	TRAMPS	TRIPE	TRYER	TWEEL	HUGGED	UNCLE	UNPENS
STOLED	TOTEM	TRANT	STRIPE	TRYERS	ATWEEL	JUGGED	NUNCLE	UNPENT
TOLES	TOTEMS	TRANTS	TRIPES	TRYST	TWEELS	LUGGED	UNCLED	UNPIN
STOLES	TOUCH	TRAPE	TRIPS	TRYSTS	TWEELY	MUGGED	UNCLES	UNPINS
TOLLS	TOUCHE	TRAPED	STRIPS	TSUBA	TWEER	PUGGED	UNCLEW	UNRIG
ATOLLS	TOUCHY	TRAPES	TRIST	TSUBAS	TWEERS	RUGGED	UNCOS	RUNRIG
TOMAN	TOUGH	TRAPS	TRISTE	TUART	TWEET	TUGGED	BUNCOS	UNRIGS
TOMANS	TOUGHS	STRAPS	TRITE	TUARTS	TWEETS	UHLAN	JUNCOS	UNRIP
TONAL	TOUNS	TRASH	TRITER	TUATH	TWERP	UHLANS	UNCUS	UNRIPE
ATONAL	STOUNS	TRASHY	TRITES	TUATHS	TWERPS	UHURU	JUNCUS	UNRIPS
TONDO	TOURS	TRASS	TROAD		TWICE	UHURUS	UNDAM	UNSAY
TONDOS	STOURS				TWICER	UKASE		UNSAYS
TONED	TOUSE				TWIER			UNSET

SUNSET	BURGER	UVULAE	**VELDT**	VIGORS	VOGIER	**WAIFT**	**WATER**	**WEIRD**
UNSETS	PURGER	UVULAR	VELDTS	**VILLA**	**VOGUE**	WAIFTS	WATERS	WEIRDO
UNSEW	URGERS	UVULAS	**VENEY**	VILLAN	VOGUED	**WAINS**	WATERY	WEIRDS
UNSEWN	**URGES**	VADED	VENEYS	VILLAR	VOGUES	SWAINS	**WAUFF**	**WEISE**
UNSEWS	GURGES	EVADED	**VENGE**	VILLAS	VOGUEY	TWAINS	WAUFFS	WEISED
UNTIE	PURGES	**VADES**	AVENGE	**VINCA**	**VOICE**	**WAIST**	**WAUGH**	WEISES
AUNTIE	SURGES	EVADES	VENGED	VINCAS	VOICED	WAISTS	WAUGHS	**WEIZE**
UNTIED	**URIAL**	**VAGUE**	VENGER	**VINER**	VOICER	**WAITE**	WAUGHT	WEIZED
UNTIES	BURIAL	VAGUED	VENGES	VINERS	VOICES	TWAITE	**WAULK**	WEIZES
UNTIL	URIALS	VAGUER	**VENIN**	VINERY	**VOIDS**	WAITED	WAULKS	**WELKE**
UNTILE	MURINE	VAGUES	VENINS	**VINEW**	AVOIDS	WAITER	**WAVER**	WELKED
UNTIN	PURINE	**VAILS**	**VENOM**	VINEWS	OVOIDS	WAITES	WAVERS	WELKES
MUNTIN	**URINE**	AVAILS	VENOMS	**VINYL**	**VOILE**	**WAITS**	WAVERY	**WELLS**
UNTINS	URINED	**VAKIL**	**VENTS**	VINYLS	VOILES	AWAITS	**WAVEY**	DWELLS
UNWIT	URINES	VAKILS	EVENTS	**VIOLA**	**VOLAR**	WAKED	WAVEYS	SWELLS
UNWITS	**URITE**	**VALES**	**VENUE**	VIOLAS	VOLARY	**WAKEN**	**WAXER**	**WELTS**
UNWON	URITES	AVALES	AVENUE	**VIPER**	**VOLET**	AWAKEN	WAXERS	SWELTS
UNWONT	**URMAN**	**VALET**	VENUES	VIPERS	VOLETS	WAKENS	**WAYED**	**WHACK**
UNZIP	URMANS	VALETA	**VERGE**	**VIREO**	**VOLTE**	**WAKER**	SWAYED	WHACKO
UNZIPS	**URNED**	VALETE	VERGED	VIREOS	VOLTES	**WAKES**	**WAZIR**	WHACKS
UPJET	BURNED	VALETS	VERGER	**VIRGA**	**VOLVA**	AWAKES	WAZIRS	WHACKY
UPJETS	GURNED	**VALIS**	VERGES	VIRGAS	VOLVAS	WALED	**WEALD**	**WHALE**
UPLAY	TURNED	VALISE	**VERSE**	**VIRGE**	**VOLVE**	SWALED	WEALDS	WHALED
UPLAYS	**URSON**	**VALOR**	VERSED	VIRGER	VOLVED	**WALER**	**WEALS**	WHALER
UPPED	URSONS	VALORS	VERSER	VIRGES	VOLVES	WALERS	SWEALS	WHALES
CUPPED	**URUBU**	**VALSE**	VERSES	**VIRTU**	**VOMER**	**WALES**	**WEAMB**	**WHANG**
DUPPED	URUBUS	VALSED	VERSET	VIRTUE	VOMERS	DWALES	WEAMBS	WHANGS
HUPPED	**URVAS**	VALSES	**VERSO**	VIRTUS	**VOMIT**	SWALES	**WEARS**	**WHARE**
PUPPED	MURVAS	**VALUE**	VERSOS	**VISED**	VOMITO	**WALIS**	SWEARS	WHARES
SUPPED	**USAGE**	VALUED	**VERST**	AVISED	VOMITS	WALISE	**WEARY**	**WHARF**
TUPPED	USAGER	VALUER	VERSTS	**VISES**	**VOTER**	**WALLA**	AWEARY	WHARFS
UPPER	USAGES	VALUES	VERTS	AVISES	VOTERS	WALLAH	**WEAVE**	**WHATS**
CUPPER	**USERS**	**VALVE**	AVERTS	**VISIE**	**VOUCH**	WALLAS	WEAVED	WHATSO
SUPPER	MUSERS	VALVED	EVERTS	VISIED	AVOUCH	**WANGS**	WEAVER	**WHAUP**
UPPERS	**USHER**	VALVES	**VERTU**	VISIER	**VOUGE**	TWANGS	WEAVES	WHAUPS
UPRUN	USHERS	**VAPOR**	VERTUE	VISIES	VOUGES	**WANKS**	**WEBER**	**WHAUR**
UPRUNS	GUSHER	VAPORS	VERTUS	**VISIT**	**VROOM**	SWANKS	WEBERS	WHAURS
UPSEE	HUSHER	**VARAN**	**VERVE**	VISITE	VROOMS	TWANKS	**WECHT**	**WHEAL**
UPSEES	LUSHER	VARANS	VERVEL	VISITS	**VROUW**	**WANZE**	WECHTS	WHEALS
UPSET	MUSHER	**VAREC**	VERVEN	**VISNE**	VROUWS	WANZED	**WEDGE**	**WHEAR**
UPSETS	PUSHER	VARECH	VERVES	VISNES	**VULVA**	WANZES	WEDGED	WHEARE
UPSEY	RUSHER	VARECS	VERVET	**VISON**	VULVAL	**WARDS**	WEDGES	**WHEAT**
UPSEYS	**USING**	**VARNA**	**VESPA**	VISONS	VULVAR	AWARDS	**WEEDS**	WHEATS
UPTAK	BUSING	VARNAS	VESPAS	**VISOR**	VULVAS	SWARDS	TWEEDS	**WHEEL**
UPTAKE	FUSING	**VARVE**	**VESTA**	VISORS	**WACKE**	**WARMS**	**WEEDY**	AWHEEL
UPTAKS	MUSING	VARVED	VESTAL	**VISTA**	WACKES	SWARMS	TWEEDY	WHEELS
UPTIE	**USNEA**	VARVEL	VESTAS	VISTAL	**WADDY**	**WARNS**	**WEEKE**	WHEELY
UPTIED	USNEAS	VARVES	**VETCH**	VISTAS	SWADDY	AWARNS	WEEKES	**WHEEN**
UPTIES	**USUAL**	**VAULT**	KVETCH	**VISTO**	**WADER**	**WARRE**	**WEETE**	WHEENS
URALI	USUALS	VAULTS	VETCHY	VISTOS	WADERS	WARRED	WEETEN	**WHEFT**
OURALI	**USURE**	VAULTY	**VEXER**	**VITAL**	**WAFER**	WARREN	**WEFTE**	WHEFTS
URALIS	USURED	**VAUNT**	VEXERS	AVITAL	WAFERS	WARREY	WEFTED	**WHELK**
URARI	USURER	AVAUNT	**VEZIR**	VITALS	WAFERY	**WARTY**	WEFTES	WHELKS
CURARI	USURES	VAUNTS	VEZIRS	**VITTA**	**WAGED**	SWARTY	**WEIGH**	WHELKY
OURARI	**USURP**	**VAUTE**	**VIAND**	VITTAE	SWAGED	**WASHY**	WEIGHS	**WHELM**
URARIS	USURPS	VAUTED	VIANDS	**VIVDA**	**WAGER**	SWASHY	WEIGHT	WHELMS
URATE	**UTILE**	VAUTES	**VICAR**	VIVDAS	WAGERS	**WASTE**		**WHELP**
AURATE	FUTILE	**VAWTE**	VICARS	**VIVER**	**WAGES**	WASTED		WHELPS
CURATE	RUTILE	VAWTED	VICARY	VIVERS	SWAGES	WASTEL		**WHERE**
URATES	SUTILE	VAWTES	**VIDEO**	**VIXEN**	**WAGON**	WASTER		WHERES
URBAN	**UTTER**	**VEALE**	VIDEOS	VIXENS	WAGONS	WASTES		**WHIFF**
TURBAN	BUTTER	VEALES	**VIFDA**	**VIZIR**	**WATCH**			WHIFFS
URBANE	CUTTER	**VEENA**	VIFDAS	VIZIRS	AWATCH			WHIFFY
URENA	GUTTER	VEENAS	**VIGIA**	**VIZOR**	SWATCH			**WHIFT**
MURENA	MUTTER	**VEGAN**	VIGIAS	VIZORS				WHIFTS
URENAS	NUTTER	VEGANS	**VIGIL**	**VOCAL**				**WHILE**
URGED	PUTTER	**VEGIE**	VIGILS	VOCALS				AWHILE
PURGED	RUTTER	VEGIES	**VIGOR**	**VODKA**				WHILED
SURGED	UTTERS	**VELAR**	VIGORO	VODKAS				WHILES
URGER	**UVULA**	VELARS		**VOGIE**				**WHIMS**

WHIMSY	WIDOWS	WINZES	WONGAS	WREAK	XYLEMS	YEASTY	YUCCA	ZINEBS
WHINE	WIDTH	WIPED	WOODS	WREAKE	XYLOL	YENTA	YUCCAS	ZINKE
WHINED	WIDTHS	WIPER	WOODSY	WREAKS	XYLOLS	YENTAS	YULAN	ZINKED
WHINER	WIELD	SWIPED	WOOER	WRECK	XYLYL	YERBA	YULANS	ZINKES
WHINES	WIELDS	SWIPER	WOOERS	WRECKS	XYLYLS	YERBAS	YUPON	ZIZEL
WHIRL	WIELDY	WIPERS	WOOLD	WREST	YACCA	YESES	YUPONS	ZIZELS
WHIRLS	WIGAN	WIPES	WOOLDS	WRESTS	YACCAS	CYESES	ZABRA	ZLOTY
WHIRR	WIGANS	SWIPES	WOONS	WRICK	YACHT	OYESES	ZABRAS	ZLOTYS
WHIRRS	WIGHT	WIRED	SWOONS	WRICKS	YACHTS	YIELD	ZAMAN	ZOCCO
WHIRRY	TWIGHT	WIRER	WOOSH	WRIER	YAFFS	YIELDS	ZAMANG	ZOCCOS
WHISH	WIGHTS	WIRERS	SWOOSH	OWRIER	YAGER	YLEMS	ZAMANS	ZOISM
WHISHT	WILLS	WIRES	WORDS	WRIES	YAGERS	XYLEMS	ZAMBO	ZOISMS
WHISK	SWILLS	SWIRES	SWORDS	WRIEST	YAHOO	YOBBO	ZAMBOS	ZOIST
WHISKS	TWILLS	WISES	WORLD	WRING	YAHOOS	YOBBOS	ZAMIA	ZOISTS
WHISKY	WILLY	WISEST	WORLDS	WRINGS	YAKKA	YODEL	ZAMIAS	ZOMBI
WHIST	TWILLY	WISTS	WORSE	WRIST	YAKKAS	YODELS	ZANJA	ZOMBIE
WHISTS	WILTS	TWISTS	WORSED	WRISTS	YAMEN	YODLED	ZANJAS	ZOMBIS
WHITE	TWILTS	WITCH	WORSEN	WRISTY	YAMENS	YODLER	ZANTE	ZONAL
WHITED	WINCE	SWITCH	WORSER	WRITE	YANGS	YODLES	ZANTES	AZONAL
WHITEN	WINCED	TWITCH	WORSES	WRITER	KYANGS	YOGIN	ZANZE	ZONDA
WHITER	WINCER	WITES	WORST	WRITES	YAPOK	YOGINI	ZANZES	ZONDAS
WHITES	WINCES	TWITES	WORSTS	WROKE	YAPOKS	YOGINS	ZEBEC	ZONES
WHITEY	WINCEY	WITHE	WORTH	YWROKE	YAPON	YOGIS	ZEBECK	OZONES
WHOLE	WINED	WITHED	WORTHS	WROKEN	YAPONS	YOGISM	ZEBECS	ZOOEA
WHOLES	DWINED	WITHER	WORTHY	AWRONG	YARFA	YOICK	ZEBRA	ZOOEAE
WHOOP	TWINED	WITHES	WOULD	WRONG	YARFAS	YOICKS	ZEBRAS	ZOOEAL
WHOOPS	WINES	WIZEN	WOULDS	WRONGS	YARTA	YOJAN	ZEBUB	ZOOID
WHOOT	DWINES	WIZENS	WOUND	WROOT	YARTAS	YOJANA	ZEBUBS	ZOOIDS
WHOOTS	TWINES	WODGE	SWOUND	WROOTS	YARTO	YOJANS	ZERDA	ZORIL
WHORE	WINGE	WODGES	WOUNDS	WURST	YARTOS	YOKEL	ZERDAS	ZORILS
WHORED	SWINGE	WOKEN	WOUNDY	WURSTS	YCLED	YOKELS	ZHOMO	ZORRO
WHORES	TWINGE	AWOKEN	WRACK	WUSHU	CYCLED	YOUNG	ZHOMOS	ZORROS
WHORL	WINGED	WOLVE	WRACKS	WUSHUS	YEALM	YOUNGS	ZIBET	ZUPAN
WHORLS	WINGER	WOLVED	AWRACK	XEBEC	YEALMS	YOURT	ZIBETS	ZUPANS
WHORT	WINGES	WOLVER	WRAST	XEBECS	YEARD	YOURTS	ZIGAN	ZYGON
WHORTS	WINGS	WOLVES	WRASTS	XENIA	YEARDS	YOUTH	ZIGANS	ZYGONS
WIDEN	SWINGS	WOMAN	WRATH	XENIAL	YEARN	YOUTHS	ZIMBI	ZYMES
WIDENS	WINKS	WOMANS	WRATHS	XENIAS	YEARNS	YOUTHY	ZIMBIS	AZYMES
WIDES	SWINKS	WONGA	WRATHY	XENON	YEAST	YOWIE	ZINCO	
WIDEST	TWINKS		WRAWL	XENONS	YEASTS	YOWIES	ZINCOS	
WIDOW	WINZE		WRAWLS	XYLEM			ZINEB	

PART B: 6-letter word hooks
extensible words only

ABATOR	BABYING	HACKERS	WADDLED	**AERIES**	**AGINGS**	WAILING	**ALEXIN**
ABATORS	**ACACIA**	LACKERS	**ADDLES**	FAERIES	PAGINGS	**AIMING**	ALEXINS
ABAYAS	ACACIAS	PACKERS	DADDLES	AERIEST	**AGLETS**	MAIMING	**ALGATE**
KABAYAS	**ACAJOU**	RACKERS	FADDLES	**AEROBE**	EAGLETS	**AIRGAP**	ALGATES
ABDABS	ACAJOUS	TACKERS	PADDLES	AEROBES	HAGLETS	AIRGAPS	**ALIDAD**
HABDABS	**ACANTH**	YACKERS	RADDLES	**AETHER**	**AGNAIL**	**AIRIER**	ALIDADE
ABDUCE	ACANTHA	**ACKNOW**	SADDLES	AETHERS	AGNAILS	HAIRIER	ALIDADS
ABDUCED	ACANTHS	ACKNOWN	WADDLES	**AFFAIR**	**AGNAME**	LAIRIER	**ALIGHT**
ABDUCES	**ACARID**	ACKNOWS	**ADDOOM**	AFFAIRE	AGNAMED	VAIRIER	ALIGHTS
ABDUCT	ACARIDS	**ACMITE**	ADDOOMS	AFFAIRS	AGNAMES	**AIRILY**	**ALIGNS**
ABDUCTS	**ACATER**	ACMITES	**ADDUCE**	**AFFEAR**	**AGNISE**	FAIRILY	MALIGNS
ABELES	**ACATES**	**ACQUIT**	ADDUCED	AFFEARD	AGNISED	**AIRING**	**ALINES**
KABELES	VACATES	ACQUITE	ADDUCER	AFFEARE	AGNISES	HAIRING	SALINES
ABELIA	**ACCEDE**	ACQUITS	ADDUCES	AFFEARS	**AGNIZE**	FAIRING	VALINES
ABELIAS	ACCEDED	**ACTING**	**ADDUCT**	**AFFECT**	AGNIZED	LAIRING	**ALIPED**
ABJECT	ACCEDER	ACTINGS	ADDUCTS	AFFECTS	AGNIZES	PAIRING	TALIPED
ABJECTS	ACCEDES	**ACTION**	**ADHERE**	**AFFEER**	**AGOGIC**	SAIRING	ALIPEDS
ABJURE	**ACCEND**	FACTION	ADHERED	AFFEERS	AGOGICS	AIRINGS	**ALISMA**
ABJURED	ACCENDS	PACTION	ADHERER	**AFFIES**	**AGOUTA**	**AIRNED**	ALISMAS
ABJURER	**ACCENT**	TACTION	ADHERES	BAFFIES	AGOUTAS	CAIRNED	**ALKALI**
ABJURES	ACCENTS	ACTIONS	**ADJOIN**	DAFFIES	**AGOUTI**	**AIRWAY**	ALKALIS
ABLATE	**ACCEPT**	**ACTIVE**	ADJOINS	TAFFIES	AGOUTIS	FAIRWAY	**ALKANE**
ABLATED	ACCEPTS	FACTIVE	ADJOINT	**AFFINE**	**AGREGE**	AIRWAYS	ALKANES
ABLATES	**ACCITE**	**ACTORS**	ADJURE	AFFINED	AGREGES	**AJOWAN**	**ALKANET**
ABLAUT	ACCITED	FACTORS	ADJURED	AFFINES	**AGRISE**	AJOWANS	**ALKENE**
ABLAUTS	ACCITES	**ACTUAL**	ADJURES	**AFFIRM**	AGRISED	**AKEDAH**	ALKENES
ABLETS	**ACCLOY**	FACTUAL	**ADJUST**	AFFIRMS	AGRISES	AKEDAHS	**ALKYNE**
GABLETS	ACCLOYS	TACTUAL	ADJUSTS	**AFFORD**	**AGRIZE**	**ALALIA**	ALKYNES
TABLETS	**ACCOIL**	**ACTURE**	**ADMIRE**	AFFORDS	AGRIZED	ALALIAS	**ALLEES**
ABLING	ACCOILS	FACTURE	ADMIRED	**AFFRAP**	AGRIZES	**ALANGS**	MALLEES
CABLING	**ACCORD**	ACTURES	ADMIRER	AFFRAPS	**AGRYZE**	LALANGS	SALLEES
FABLING	ACCORDS	VACUITY	ADMIRES	**AFFRAY**	AGRYZED	**ALARUM**	**ALLEGE**
SABLING	**ACCOST**	**ACUMEN**	**ADORER**	AFFRAYS	AGRYZES	ALARUMS	ALLEGED
TABLING	ACCOSTS	CACUMEN	ADORERS	**AFFRET**	**AGUISE**	**ALATED**	ALLEGER
ABOLLA	**ACCREW**	ACUMENS	**ADREAD**	AFFRETS	AGUISED	PALATED	ALLEGES
ABOLLAE	ACCREWS	**ACUTES**	ADREADS	**AFGHAN**	AGUISES	**ALBATA**	**ALLELE**
ABOLLAS	**ACCRUE**	ACUTEST	**ADSORB**	AFGHANS	**AGUIZE**	ALBATAS	ALLELES
ABOUND	ACCRUED	**ADAGIO**	ADSORBS	**AFREET**	AGUIZED	**ALBEDO**	**ALLEYS**
ABOUNDS	ACCRUES	ADAGIOS	**ADVENE**	AFREETS	AGUIZES	ALBEDOS	GALLEYS
ABRADE	**ACCUSE**	**ADDEEM**	ADVENED	**AFTERS**	**AHIMSA**	**ALBERT**	VALLEYS
ABRADED	ACCUSED	ADDEEMS	ADVENES	RAFTERS	AHIMSAS	HALBERT	**ALLICE**
ABRADES	ACCUSER	**ADDEND**	**ADVENT**	WAFTERS	**AIDERS**	ALBERTS	ALLICES
ABRAID	ACCUSES	ADDENDA	ADVENTS	**AGAMID**	RAIDERS	**ALBINO**	**ALLIED**
ABRAIDS	**ACEDIA**	ADDENDS	**ADVERB**	AGAMIDS	RAIDERS	ALBINOS	DALLIED
ABRAZO	ACEDIAS	**ADDERS**	ADVERBS	**AGARIC**	**AIDING**	**ALBITE**	GALLIED
ABRAZOS	**ACETAL**	GADDERS	**ADVERT**	AGARICS	LAIDING	ALBITES	RALLIED
ABREGE	ACETALS	LADDERS	ADVERTS	**AGEING**	MAIDING	**ALBUGO**	SALLIED
ABREGES	**ACETYL**	MADDERS	**ADVICE**	AGEINGS	RAIDING	ALBUGOS	TALLIED
ABROAD	ACETYLS	PADDERS	ADVICES	**AGEISM**	MAIDING	**ALCOVE**	**ALLIES**
ABROADS	**ACHAGE**	**ADDICT**	**ADVISE**	AGEISMS	RAIDING	ALCOVES	DALLIES
ABRUPT	ACHAGES	ADDICTS	ADVISED	**AGEIST**	**AIGLET**	**ALDOSE**	GALLIES
ABRUPTS	**ACHENE**	**ADDING**	ADVISER	AGEISTS	AIGLETS	ALDOSES	RALLIES
ABSEIL	ACHENES	DADDING	ADVISES	**AGENDA**	**AIKIDO**	**ALDRIN**	SALLIES
ABSEILS	**ACHING**	GADDING	**ADWARD**	AGENDAS	AIKIDOS	ALDRINS	TALLIES
ABSENT	BACHING	HADDING	ADWARDS	**AGENES**	**AILING**	**ALEGAR**	WALLIES
ABSENTS	CACHING	MADDING	**AEDILE**	SAGENES	BAILING	ALEGARS	**ALLONS**
ABSORB	ACHINGS	PADDING	AEDILES	**AGGERS**	FAILING	**ALEGGE**	BALLONS
ABSORBS	**ACHKAN**	WADDING	**AEMULE**	DAGGERS	HAILING	ALEGGED	GALLONS
ABULIA	ACHKANS	**ADDLED**	AEMULED	GAGGERS	JAILING	ALEGGES	**ALLOTS**
ABULIAS	**ACKEES**	DADDLED	AEMULES	JAGGERS	MAILING	**ALERCE**	BALLOTS
ABUSER	HACKEES	FADDLED	**AERATE**	LAGGERS	NAILING	ALERCES	TALLOTS
ABUSERS	**ACKERS**	PADDLED	AERATED	NAGGERS	RAILING	**ALEVIN**	**ALLOWS**
ABVOLT	BACKERS	RADDLED	AERATES	SAGGERS	SAILING	ALEVINS	BALLOWS
ABVOLTS	DACKERS	SADDLED	**AERIAL**	TAGGERS	TAILING	**ALEXIA**	CALLOWS
ABYING			AERIALS	YAGGERS	VAILING	ALEXIAS	FALLOWS

GALLOWS	**AMBLES**	**ANANAS**	BANKERS	TANTRUM	ARALIAS	**ARKING**	ARRIVES
HALLOWS	GAMBLES	BANANAS	CANKERS	ANTRUMS	**ARAYSE**	BARKING	**ARROBA**
MALLOWS	HAMBLES	MANANAS	HANKERS	**ANURIA**	ARAYSED	CARKING	ARROBAS
SALLOWS	RAMBLES	**ANANKE**	JANKERS	ANURIAS	ARAYSES	HARKING	**ARROWS**
TALLOWS	WAMBLES	ANANKES	RANKERS	**ANYONE**	**ARBORS**	LARKING	BARROWS
WALLOWS	**AMELIA**	**ANARAK**	TANKERS	ANYONES	HARBORS	MARKING	FARROWS
ALLUDE	AMELIAS	ANARAKS	WANKERS	**ANYWAY**	**ARBOUR**	NARKING	HARROWS
ALLUDED	**AMENDE**	**ANARCH**	YANKERS	ANYWAYS	HARBOUR	PARKING	MARROWS
ALLUDES	AMENDED	ANARCHS	**ANKLED**	**AORIST**	ARBOURS	SARKING	NARROWS
ALLURE	AMENDER	ANARCHY	FANKLED	AORISTS	**ARBUTE**	**ARKITE**	TARROWS
ALLURED	AMENDES	**ANATTA**	RANKLED	**AOUDAD**	ARBUTES	ARKITES	YARROWS
ALLURER	**AMENTA**	ANATTAS	**ANKLES**	AOUDADS	**ARCADE**	**ARKOSE**	**ARROWY**
ALLURES	RAMENTA	**ANATTO**	FANKLES	**APACHE**	ARCADED	ARKOSES	MARROWY
ALMAIN	**AMENTS**	ANATTOS	RANKLES	APACHES	ARCADES	**ARMADA**	**ARROYO**
ALMAINS	AMENTAL	**ANCHOR**	**ANKLET**	**APEDOM**	MARCHED	ARMADAS	ARROYOS
ALMOND	LAMENTS	ANCHORS	ANKLETS	APEDOMS	PARCHED	**ARMFUL**	**ARSHIN**
ALMONDS	**AMERCE**	**ANCILE**	**ANLACE**	**APERCU**	**ARCHER**	HARMFUL	ARSHINE
ALNAGE	AMERCED	ANCILES	ANLACES	APERCUS	MARCHER	ARMFULS	ARSHINS
ALNAGER	AMERCES	**ANCOME**	**ANLAGE**	**APHTHA**	ARCHERS	**ARMING**	**ARSINE**
ALNAGES	**AMINES**	ANCOMES	ANLAGES	NAPHTHA	ARCHERY	FARMING	ARSINES
ALOGIA	FAMINES	**ANEMIA**	**ANNEAL**	APHTHAE	**ARCHES**	HARMING	**ARSONS**
ALOGIAS	GAMINES	ANEMIAS	ANNEALS	**APISMS**	LARCHES	WARMING	PARSONS
ALPACA	TAMINES	**ANGELS**	**ANNEXE**	PAPISMS	MARCHES	**ARMLET**	**ARTELS**
ALPACAS	**AMISES**	MANGELS	ANNEXED	**APLITE**	PARCHES	ARMLETS	CARTELS
ALPEEN	CAMISES	**ANGERS**	ANNEXES	APLITES	**ARCHEST**	**ARMOUR**	MARTELS
ALPEENS	KAMISES	DANGERS	**ANNUAL**	**APLOMB**	**ARCHIL**	ARMOURS	**ARTIER**
ALPINE	TAMISES	GANGERS	ANNUALS	APLOMBS	ARCHILS	ARMOURY	TARTIER
ALPINES	**AMMONS**	HANGERS	**ANOINT**	**APNOEA**	**ARCHON**	**ARMPIT**	WARTIER
ALSIKE	GAMMONS	MANGERS	ANOINTS	APNOEAS	ARCHONS	ARMPITS	**ARTIST**
ALSIKES	MAMMONS	RANGERS	**ANOMIE**	**APOGEE**	**ARCING**	**ARMURE**	ARTISTE
ALSOON	**AMOEBA**	**ANGICO**	ANOMIES	APOGEES	ARCINGS	ARMURES	ARTISTS
ALSOONE	AMOEBAE	ANGICOS	**ANONYM**	**APOLLO**	FARCING	**ARNICA**	**ASARUM**
ALTERN	AMOEBAS	**ANGINA**	ANONYMA	APOLLOS	ARCINGS	ARNICAS	ASARUMS
SALTERN	**AMOMUM**	ANGINAL	ANONYMS	**APORIA**	**ARCSIN**	**AROINT**	**ASCEND**
ALTERNE	AMOMUMS	ANGINAS	**ANORAK**	APORIAS	ARCSINS	AROINTS	ASCENDS
ALTERS	**AMOOVE**	ANGLED	ANORAKS	**APOZEM**	**ARCTAN**	**AROLLA**	**ASCENT**
FALTERS	AMOOVED	BANGLED	**ANOXIA**	APOZEMS	ARCTANS	AROLLAS	ASCENTS
HALTERS	**AMOOVES**	CANGLED	ANOXIAS	**APPAIR**	**ARCTIC**	**AROUSE**	NASCENT
PALTERS	**AMORCE**	DANGLED	**ANSATE**	APPAIRS	ARCTICS	AROUSED	ASCENTS
SALTERS	AMORCES	FANGLED	ANSATED	**APPEAL**	**ARDOUR**	AROUSER	**ASCIAN**
ALTEZA	**AMORET**	JANGLED	**ANSWER**	APPEALS	ARDOURS	AROUSES	ASCIANS
ALTEZAS	AMORETS	MANGLED	ANSWERS	**APPEAR**	AREOLAE	**AROYNT**	**ASCOTS**
ALUDEL	**AMOUNT**	TANGLED	**ANTARS**	APPEARS	AREOLAR	AROYNTS	MASCOTS
ALUDELS	AMOUNTS	WANGLED	CANTARS	WAPPEND	**AREOLE**	**ARPENT**	**ASEITY**
ALUMNA	**AMPERE**	**ANGLER**	KANTARS	**APPEND**	AREOLES	ARPENTS	GASEITY
ALUMNAE	AMPERES	DANGLER	**ANTHEM**	APPENDS	**ARGALA**	**ARRACK**	**ASHAME**
AMADOU	**AMPLER**	JANGLER	ANTHEMS	**APPLES**	ARGALAS	BARRACK	ASHAMED
AMADOUS	SAMPLER	MANGLER	**ANTHER**	DAPPLES	**ARGALI**	CARRACK	ASHAMES
AMATOL	**AMPULE**	TANGLER	PANTHER	SAPPLES	ARGALIS	ARRACKS	**ASHERY**
AMATOLS	AMPULES	WANGLER	ANTHERS	**APPORT**	**ARGAND**	**ARRANT**	FASHERY
AMAZON	**AMRITA**	ANGLERS	**ANTIAR**	RAPPORT	ARGANDS	FARRANT	WASHERY
AMAZONS	AMRITAS	**ANGLES**	ANTIARS	APPORTS	**ARGENT**	WARRANT	**ASHIER**
AMBAGE	**AMTMAN**	BANGLES	**ANTICK**	**APPOSE**	ARGENTS	**ARRAYS**	CASHIER
AMBAGES	AMTMANS	CANGLES	ANTICKE	APPOSED	**ARGHAN**	WARRAYS	HASHIER
AMBERS	**AMULET**	DANGLES	**ANTING**	APPOSER	ARGHANS	**ARREAR**	MASHIER
CAMBERS	AMULETS	FANGLES	BANTING	**APPOSES**	**ARGONS**	ARREARS	WASHIER
JAMBERS	**AMUSER**	JANGLES	CANTING	**APRONS**	JARGONS	**ARRECT**	**ASHLAR**
LAMBERS	**AMUSES**	MANGLES	DANTING	NAPRONS	**ARGUER**	CARRECT	ASHLARS
TAMBERS	CAMUSES	TANGLES	GANTING	**APTOTE**	ARGUERS	**ARREST**	**ASHLER**
AMBITS	WAMUSES	WANGLES	KANTING	APTOTES	**ARGYLE**	ARRESTS	ASHLERS
GAMBITS	**AMYLUM**	**ANGORA**	PANTING	ARABIN	ARGYLES	**ARRETS**	**ASHRAM**
AMBLED	AMYLUMS	ANGORAS	RANTING	**ARABIN**	**ARIOSO**	BARRETS	ASHRAMA
GAMBLED	**ANADEM**	**ANICUT**	WANTING	CARABIN	ARIOSOS	GARRETS	ASHRAMS
HAMBLED	ANADEMS	ANICUTS	ANTINGS	ARABINS	**ARISTA**	**ARRIDE**	**ASKANT**
RAMBLED	**ANALLY**	**ANIMAL**	**ANTLER**	**ARABLE**	ARISTAE	ARRIDED	ASKANTS
WAMBLED	BANALLY	ANIMALS	PANTLER	PARABLE	ARISTAS	ARRIDES	**ASKARI**
AMBLER	**ANALOG**	**ANIONS**	ANTLERS	**ARAISE**	**ARISTO**	**ARRIVE**	ASKARIS
GAMBLER	ANALOGS	FANIONS	ANTLIAE	ARAISED	ARISTAS	ARRIVED	**ASKERS**
RAMBLER	ANALOGY	**ANKERS**	ANTLIAE	ARAISES	ARISTOS	**ARRIVE**	MASKERS
AMBLERS			**ANTRUM**	**ARALIA**	ARISTOS	ARRIVED	TASKERS
							ASKING

BASKING	WASTERS	AUGERS	AVOSET	BADDIES	BALSAMY	BARRAT	BATTLES
CASKING	ASTERT	GAUGERS	AVOSETS	BADGER	BAMBOO	BARRATS	BATTUE
MASKING	ASTERTS	SAUGERS	AVOURE	BADGERS	BAMBOOS	BARREL	BATTUES
TASKING	ASTHMA	AUGHTS	AVOURES	BAETYL	BAMMER	BARRELS	BAUBLE
ASLAKE	ASTHMAS	NAUGHTS	AVOWAL	BAETYLS	BAMMERS	BARRET	BAUBLES
ASLAKED	ASTONE	WAUGHTS	AVOWALS	BAFFLE	BAMPOT	BARRETS	BAUERA
ASLAKES	ASTONED	AUGITE	AVOYER	BAFFLED	BAMPOTS	BARRIO	BAUERAS
ASPECT	ASTONES	AUGITES	AVOYERS	BAFFLER	BANANA	BARRIOS	BAWBEE
ASPECTS	ASTRAL	AUGUST	AVULSE	BAFFLES	BANANAS	BARROW	BAWBLE
ASPERS	CASTRAL	AUGUSTE	AVULSED	BAGFUL	BANDAR	BARROWS	BAWBLES
GASPERS	ASTUTE	AUGUSTS	AVULSES	BAGFULS	BANDARS	BARTER	BAWLER
JASPERS	ASTUTER	AUKLET	AWAKEN	BAGGIT	BANDED	BARTERS	BAWLERS
RASPERS	ASYLUM	AUKLETS	AWAKENS	BAGGITS	ABANDED	BARTON	BAWLEY
ASPERSE	ASYLUMS	AULDER	AWARDS	BAGNIO	BANDIT	BARTONS	BAWLEYS
ASPICK	ATABAL	CAULDER	VAWARDS	BAGNIOS	BANDITS	BARYON	BAXTER
ASPICKS	ATABALS	AUMAIL	AWHAPE	BAGUIO	BANDOG	BARYONS	BAXTERS
ASPINE	ATABEG	AUMAILS	AWHAPED	BAGUIOS	BANDOGS	BARYTA	BAYARD
ASPINES	ATABEGS	AUNTER	AWHAPES	BAGWIG	BANGER	BARYTAS	BAYARDS
ASPIRE	ATABEK	DAUNTER	AWHEEL	BAGWIGS	BANGERS	BASALT	BAZAAR
ASPIRED	ATABEKS	GAUNTER	AWHEELS	BAHADA	BANGLE	BASALTS	BAZAARS
ASPIRES	ATAMAN	HAUNTER	AWMRIE	BAHADAS	BANGLED	BASHAW	BEACON
ASPORT	ATAMANS	SAUNTER	AWMRIES	BAILEE	BANGLES	BASHAWS	BEACONS
ASPORTS	ATAXIA	TAUNTER	AWNERS	BAILEES	BANIAN	BASHED	BEADLE
ASSAIL	ATAXIAS	VAUNTER	DAWNERS	BAILER	BANIANS	BASHER	BEADLES
VASSAIL	ATOCIA	AUNTERS	FAWNERS	BAILERS	BANKER	BASHERS	BEAGLE
WASSAIL	ATOCIAS	AUNTIE	PAWNERS	BAILEY	BANKERS	BASHES	BEAGLED
ASSAILS	ATONED	AUNTIES	LAWNIER	BAILEYS	BANKET	ABASHED	BEAGLER
ASSART	ATONER	JAUNTIE	TAWNIER	BAILIE	BANKETS	ABASHES	BEAGLES
ASSARTS	ATONERS	AURATE	YAWNIER	BAILIES	BANNER	BASING	BEAKER
ASSENT	ATRIAL	AURATED	AWNIER	BAILLI	BANNERS	ABASING	BEAKERS
ASSENTS	PATRIAL	AURATES	DAWNING	BAILLIE	BANTAM	BASKET	BEAMER
ASSERT	ATRIUM	AURIST	FAWNING	BAILLIS	BANTAMS	BASKETS	BEAMERS
ASSERTS	NATRIUM	AURISTS	PAWNING	BAILOR	BANTER	BASNET	BEANIE
ASSETS	ATTACH	AURORA	YAWNING	BAILORS	BANTERS	BASNETS	BEANIES
BASSETS	ATTACHE	AURORAE	AWNINGS	BAININ	BANYAN	BASQUE	BEARER
TASSETS	ATTACK	AURORAL	AXILLA	BAININS	BANYANS	BASQUED	BEARERS
ASSIGN	ATTACKS	AURORAS	MAXILLA	BAITER	BAOBAB	BASQUES	BEATER
ASSIGNS	ATTAIN	AUTEUR	AXILLAE	BAITERS	BAOBABS	BASSES	BEATERS
ASSIST	ATTAINS	HAUTEUR	AXILLAR	BAJADA	BARBEL	BASSEST	BEAVER
BASSIST	ATTAINT	AUTEURS	AYWORD	BAJADAS	BARBELS	BASSET	BEAVERS
ASSISTS	ATTASK	AUTHOR	NAYWORD	BAJREE	BARBER	BASSETS	BEAVERY
ASSIZE	ATTASKS	AUTHORS	AYWORDS	BAJREES	BARBERS	BASTER	BEBUNG
ASSIZED	ATTASKT	AUTISM	AZALEA	BAKING	BARBET	BASTERS	BEBUNGS
ASSIZER	ATTEND	AUTISMS	AZALEAS	BAKINGS	BARBETS	BASTLE	BECALL
ASSIZES	ATTENDS	AUTUMN	AZIONE	BALATA	BARBIE	BASTLES	BECALLS
ASSOIL	ATTENT	AUTUMNS	AZIONES	BALATAS	BARBIES	BATATA	BECALM
ASSOILS	ATTENTS	AUTUMNY	AZOLLA	BALBOA	BAREGE	BATATAS	BECALMS
ASSORT	ATTEST	AVAILE	AZOLLAS	BALBOAS	BAREGES	BATEAU	BECKET
ASSORTS	FATTEST	AVAILED	AZURES	BALEEN	BARGEE	BATEAUX	BECKETS
ASSUME	WATTEST	AVAILES	RAZURES	BALEENS	BARGEES	BATHER	BECKON
ASSUMED	ATTESTS	AVATAR	BAAING	BALKER	BARGES	BATHERS	BECKONS
ASSUMES	ATTIRE	AVATARS	BAAINGS	BALKERS	BARGEST	BATING	BECOME
ASSURE	ATTIRED	AVAUNT	BABBLE	BALLAD	BARITE	ABATING	BECOMES
ASSURED	ATTIRES	AVAUNTS	BABBLED	BALLADE	BARITES	BATLER	BECURL
ASSURER	ATTONE	AVENGE	BABBLER	BALLADS	BARIUM	BATLERS	BECURLS
ASSURES	ATTONES	AVENGED	BABBLES	BALLAN	BARIUMS	BATLET	BEDAUB
ASTART	ATTORN	AVENGER	BABIES	BALLANS	BARKAN	BATLETS	BEDAUBS
ASTARTS	ATTORNS	AVENGES	BABIEST	BALLANT	BARKANS	BATOON	BEDAZE
ASTERN	ATTRAP	AVENIR	BABLAH	BALLAT	BARKEN	BATOONS	BEDAZED
EASTERN	ATTRAPS	AVENIRS	BABLAHS	BALLATS	BARKENS	BATTEL	BEDAZES
PASTERN	ATTUNE	AVENUE	BABOON	BALLET	BARKER	BATTELS	BEDBUG
ASTERS	ATTUNED	AVENUES	BABOONS	BALLETS	BARKERS	BATTEN	BEDBUGS
BASTERS	ATTUNES	AVIATE	BABOOS	BALLON	BARLEY	BATTENS	BEDDER
CASTERS	AUBADE	AVIATED	BABOOSH	BALLONS	BARLEYS	BATTER	BEDDERS
FASTERS	AUBADES	AVIATES	BACKER	BALLOT	BARNEY	BATTERO	BEDECK
LASTERS	AUCUBA	AVISES	BACKERS	BALLOTS	BARNEYS	BATTERS	BEDECKS
MASTERS	AUCUBAS	MAVISES	BACKET	BALLOW	BAROCK	BATTERY	BEDELL
PASTERS	AUDILE	PAVISES	BACKETS	BALLOWS	BAROCKS	BATTLE	BEDELLS
RASTERS	AUDILES	AVOCET	BADDIE	BALSAM	BARQUE	BATTLED	BEDLAM
TASTERS		AVOCETS		BALSAMS	BARQUES	BATTLER	

BEDLAMS	BEHOVES	BENZOLE	BETRAYS	BILIAN	BITTORS	BOBCATS	BONSAI
BEDPAN	BEHOWL	BENZOLS	BETRIM	BILIANS	BITTUR	BOBWIG	BONSAIS
BEDPANS	BEHOWLS	BENZYL	BETRIMS	BILKER	BITTURS	BOBWIGS	BONXIE
BEDRAL	BEIGEL	BENZYLS	BETTED	BILKERS	BIVIUM	BOCAGE	BONXIES
BEDRALS	BEIGELS	BEPELT	ABETTED	BILLET	BIVIUMS	BOCAGES	BOOBOO
BEDROP	BEJADE	BEPELTS	BETTER	BILLETS	BIZONE	BODACH	BOOBOOK
BEDROPS	BEJADED	BEPUFF	ABETTER	BILLIE	BIZONES	BODACHS	BOOBOOS
BEDROPT	BEJADES	BEPUFFS	BETTERS	BILLIES	BLAGUE	BODDLE	BOODIE
BEDUCK	BEJANT	BERATE	BETTOR	BILLON	BLAGUES	BODDLES	BOODIED
BEDUCKS	BEJANTS	BERATED	ABETTOR	BILLONS	BLANCO	BODEGA	BOODIES
BEDUIN	BELACE	BERATES	BEURRE	BILLOW	BLANCOS	BODEGAS	BOODLE
BEDUINS	BELACED	BERLEY	BEURRES	BILLOWS	BLASTS	BODGER	BOODLES
BEDUNG	BELACES	BERLEYS	BEWAIL	BILLOWY	OBLASTS	BODGERS	BOOGIE
BEDUNGS	BELATE	BERLIN	BEWAILS	BINDER	BLAZER	BODGIE	BOOGIED
BEDUST	BELATED	BERLINE	BEWARE	BINDERS	BLAZERS	BODGIES	BOOGIES
BEDUSTS	BELATES	BERLINS	BEWARED	BINDERY	BLAZON	BODICE	BOOKIE
BEEGAH	BELAUD	BERRET	BEWARES	BINGER	BLAZONS	BODICES	BOOKIER
BEEGAHS	BELAUDS	BERRETS	BEWEEP	BINGERS	BLENDE	BODING	BOOKIES
BEENAH	BELDAM	BERTHA	BEWEEPS	BINGLE	BLENDED	BODINGS	BOOMER
BEENAHS	BELDAME	BERTHAS	BEWRAY	BINGLED	BLENDER	ABODING	BOOMERS
BEEPER	BELDAMS	BERTHE	BEWRAYS	BINGLES	BLENDES	BODKIN	BOORDE
BEEPERS	BELIEF	BERTHED	BEYOND	BIOGEN	BLIGHT	BODKINS	BOORDES
BEETLE	BELIEFS	BERTHES	BEYONDS	BIOGENS	BLIGHTS	BODRAG	BOOTEE
BEETLED	BELIER	BESEEM	BEZANT	BIOGENY	BLIGHTY	BODRAGS	BOOTEES
BEETLES	BELIERS	BESEEMS	BEZANTS	BIONIC	BLINTZ	BOFFIN	BOOZER
BEFALL	BELLOW	BESIDE	BEZOAR	BIONICS	BLINTZE	BOFFING	BOOZERS
BEFALLS	BELLOWS	BESIDES	BEZOARS	BIOPIC	BLITHE	BOFFINS	BOPPER
BEFANA	BELONG	BESIGH	BEZZLE	BIOPICS	BLITHER	BOGGLE	BOPPERS
BEFANAS	BELONGS	BESIGHS	BEZZLED	BIOTIC	BLONDE	BOGGLED	BORAGE
BEFLUM	BELOVE	BESING	BEZZLES	ABIOTIC	BLONDER	BOGGLER	BORAGES
BEFLUMS	BELOVED	BESINGS	BHAJAN	BIOTIN	BLONDES	BOGGLES	BORANE
BEFOAM	BELOVES	BESMUT	BHAJANS	BIOTINS	BLOTCH	BOGOAK	BORANES
BEFOAMS	BELTER	BESMUTS	BHAKTI	BIRDER	BLOTCHY	BOGOAKS	BORATE
BEFOOL	BELTERS	BESOIN	BHAKTIS	BIRDERS	BLOUSE	BOGONG	BORATES
BEFOOLS	BELUGA	BESOINS	BHARAL	BIRDIE	BLOUSED	BOGONGS	BORDAR
BEFOUL	BELUGAS	BESORT	BHARALS	BIRDIED	BLOUSES	BOHUNK	BORDARS
BEFOULS	BEMAUL	BESORTS	BHINDI	BIRDIES	BLOWER	BOHUNKS	BORDEL
BEGGAR	BEMAULS	BESPAT	BHINDIS	BIREME	BLOWERS	BOILER	BORDELS
BEGGARS	BEMEAN	BESPATE	BHISTI	BIREMES	BLOWIE	BOILERS	BORDER
BEGGARY	BEMEANS	BESPIT	BHISTIS	BIRKIE	BLOWIER	BOILERY	BORDERS
BEGIFT	BEMEANT	BESPITS	BIBBER	BIRKIES	BLOWIES	BOLDEN	BOREEN
BEGIFTS	BEMETE	BESPOT	BIBBERS	BIRLER	BLOWSE	BOLDENS	BOREENS
BEGILD	BEMETED	BESPOTS	BICARB	BIRLERS	BLOWSED	BOLERO	BORIDE
BEGILDS	BEMETES	BESTAR	BICARBS	BIRSLE	BLOWSES	BOLEROS	BORIDES
BEGIRD	BEMIRE	BESTARS	BICKER	BIRSLED	BLOWZE	BOLIDE	BORING
BEGIRDS	BEMIRED	BESTIR	BICKERS	BIRSLES	BLOWZED	BOLIDES	BORINGS
BEGNAW	BEMIRES	BESTIRS	BIDDEN	BISECT	BLOWZES	BOLTER	BORREL
BEGNAWS	BEMOAN	BESTOW	ABIDDEN	BISECTS	BLUDGE	BOLTERS	BORRELL
BEGUIN	BEMOANS	BESTOWS	BIDDER	BISHOP	BLUDGED	BOMBER	BORROW
BEGUINE	BEMOCK	BESTUD	BIDDERS	BISHOPS	BLUDGER	BOMBERS	BORROWS
BEGUINS	BEMOCKS	BESTUDS	BIDENT	BISMAR	BLUDGES	BONBON	BORSCH
BEGUNK	BEMOIL	BETAKE	BIDENTS	BISMARS	BLUDIE	BONBONS	BORSCHT
BEGUNKS	BEMOILS	BETAKEN	BIDING	BISQUE	BLUDIER	BONDER	BORZOI
BEHAVE	BEMUSE	BETAKES	ABIDING	BISQUES	BLUING	BONDERS	BORZOIS
BEHAVED	BEMUSED	BETEEM	BIDINGS	BISTER	BLUINGS	BONDUC	BOSBOK
BEHAVES	BEMUSES	BETEEME	BIFFIN	BISTERS	BLUNGE	BONDUCS	BOSBOKS
BEHEAD	BENAME	BETEEMS	BIFFING	BISTRE	BLUNGED	BONING	BOSCHE
BEHEADS	BENAMED	BETHEL	BIFFINS	BISTRED	BLUNGER	BONINGS	BOSCHES
BEHEST	BENAMES	BETHELS	BIGGIE	BISTRES	BLUNGES	BONISM	BOSKET
BEHESTS	BENDER	BETIDE	BIGGIES	BISTRO	BOATEL	BONISMS	BOSKETS
BEHIND	BENDERS	BETIDED	BIGGIN	BISTROS	BOATELS	BONIST	BOSSES
BEHINDS	BENNET	BETIDES	BIGGING	BITING	BOATER	EBONIST	BOSSEST
BEHOLD	BENNETS	BETIME	BIGGINS	BITINGS	BOATERS	BONISTS	BOSTON
BEHOLDS	BENUMB	BETIMED	BIGWIG	BITTER	BOBBIN	BONITO	BOSTONS
BEHOOF	BENUMBS	BETIMES	BIGWIGS	BITTERN	BOBBING	BONITOS	BOTHAN
BEHOOFS	BENZAL	BETISE	BIKING	BITTERS	BOBBINS	BONNET	BOTHANS
BEHOTE	BENZALS	BETISES	BIKINGS	BITTIE	BOBBLE	BONNETS	BOTHER
BEHOTES	BENZIL	BETOIL	BIKINI	BITTIER	BOBBLED	BONNIE	BOTHERS
BEHOVE	BENZILS	BETOILS	BIKINIS	BITTIES	BOBBLES	BONNIER	BOTHIE
BEHOVED	BENZOL	BETRAY		BITTOR	BOBCAT	BONNIES	BOTHIES

BOTTLE	BRAIZES	BROGUES	BUGLERS	BURDIES	BUTLERS	CAESARS	CAMLET
BOTTLED	BRANCH	BROKER	BUGLET	BUREAU	BUTLERY	CAFARD	CAMLETS
BOTTLER	BRANCHY	BROKERS	BUGLETS	BUREAUS	BUTTED	CAFARDS	CAMPED
BOTTLES	BRANLE	BROKERY	BUGONG	BUREAUX	ABUTTED	CAFILA	SCAMPED
BOTTOM	BRANLES	BROLGA	BUGONGS	BURGEE	BUTTER	CAFILAS	CAMPER
BOTTOMS	BRAVER	BROLGAS	BUKSHI	BURGEES	ABUTTER	CAFTAN	SCAMPER
BOUCHE	BRAVERY	BRONCO	BUKSHIS	BURGER	BUTTERS	CAFTANS	CAMPERS
BOUCHEE	BRAVES	BRONCOS	BULBIL	BURGERS	BUTTERY	CAGOUL	CAMPLED
BOUCHES	BRAVEST	BRONZE	BULBILS	BURGLE	BUTTLE	CAGOULE	CAMPLES
BOUCLE	BRAYED	BRONZED	BULBUL	BURGLED	BUTTLED	CAGOULS	CANADA
BOUCLES	ABRAYED	BRONZEN	BULBULS	BURGLES	BUTTLES	CAHIER	CANADAS
BOUGET	BRAYER	BRONZES	BULGER	BURGOO	BUTTON	CAHIERS	CANAPE
BOUGETS	BRAYERS	BROOSE	BULGERS	BURGOOS	BUTTONS	CAHOOT	CANAPES
BOUGHT	BRAZEN	BROOSES	BULKER	BURHEL	BUTTONY	CAHOOTS	CANARD
ABOUGHT	BRAZENS	BROUGH	BULKERS	BURHELS	BUZZER	CAIMAC	CANARDS
BOUGHTS	BRAZIL	BROUGHS	BULLER	BURIAL	BUZZERS	CAIMACS	CANCAN
BOUGIE	BRAZILS	BROUGHT	BULLERS	BURIALS	BYGONE	CAIMAN	CANCANS
BOUGIES	BREARE	BROUZE	BULLET	BURITI	BYGONES	CAIMANS	CANCEL
BOULLE	BREARES	BROUZES	BULLETS	BURITIS	BYLINE	CAIQUE	CANCELS
BOULLES	BREAST	BROWSE	BUMBLE	BURKHA	BYLINES	CAIQUES	CANCER
BOUNCE	ABREAST	BROWSED	BUMBLED	BURKHAS	BYPATH	CAJOLE	CANCERS
BOUNCED	BREASTS	BROWSES	BUMBLES	BURLAP	BYPATHS	CAJOLED	CANDID
BOUNCER	BREATH	BROWST	BUMKIN	BURLAPS	BYRLAW	CAJOLER	CANDIDA
BOUNCES	BREATHE	BROWSTS	BUMKINS	BURLER	BYRLAWS	CAJOLES	CANDIE
BOUNDS	BREATHS	BRUISE	BUMMEL	BURLERS	BYRNIE	CAKING	CANDIED
ABOUNDS	BREATHY	BRUISED	BUMMELS	BURLEY	BYRNIES	CAKINGS	CANDIES
BOURNE	BREESE	BRUISER	BUMMER	BURLEYS	BYROAD	CALCAR	CANDLE
BOURNES	BREESES	BRUISES	BUMMERS	BURNER	BYROADS	CALCARS	CANDLED
BOURSE	BREEZE	BRUNET	BUMMLE	BURNERS	BYROOM	CALICO	CANDLES
BOURSES	BREEZED	BRUNETS	BUMMLED	BURNET	BYROOMS	CALICOS	CANDOR
BOUTON	BREEZES	BUBBLE	BUMMLES	BURNETS	BYSSAL	CALIGO	CANDORS
BOUTONS	BREHON	BUBBLED	BUMPER	BURREL	ABYSSAL	CALIGOS	CANFUL
BOVATE	BREHONS	BUBBLES	BUMPERS	BURRELL	BYWORD	CALIPH	CANFULS
OBOVATE	BRENNE	BUCKER	BUNDLE	BURRELS	BYWORDS	CALIPHS	CANGLE
BOVATES	BRENNES	BUCKERS	BUNDLED	BURROW	BYWORK	CALKER	CANGLED
BOVVER	BRETON	BUCKET	BUNDLES	BURROWS	BYWORKS	CALKERS	CANGLES
BOVVERS	BRETONS	BUCKETS	BUNGEE	BURSAR	BYZANT	CALKIN	CANGUE
BOWFIN	BREVET	BUCKIE	BUNGEES	BURSARS	BYZANTS	CALKING	CANGUES
BOWFINS	BREVETE	BUCKIES	BUNGEY	BURSARY	CABALA	CALKINS	CANINE
BOWGET	BREVETS	BUCKLE	BUNGEYS	BURTON	CABALAS	CALLED	CANINES
BOWGETS	BREWER	BUCKLED	BUNGIE	BURTONS	CABANA	SCALLED	CANING
BOWLER	BREWERS	BUCKLER	BUNGIES	BUSBOY	CABANAS	CALLER	CANINGS
BOWLERS	BREWERY	BUCKLES	BUNGLE	BUSBOYS	CABBIE	CALLERS	CANKER
BOWPOT	BRIBER	BUCKRA	BUNGLED	BUSHEL	CABBIES	CALLET	CANKERS
BOWPOTS	BRIBERS	BUCKRAM	BUNGLER	BUSHELS	CABRIE	CALLETS	CANKERY
BOWSER	BRIBERY	BUCKRAS	BUNGLES	BUSIES	CABRIES	CALLOW	CANNED
BOWSERS	BRIDAL	BUDDLE	BUNION	BUSIEST	CABRIT	CALLOWS	SCANNED
BOWWOW	BRIDALS	BUDDLED	BUNIONS	BUSING	CABRITS	CALPAC	CANNEL
BOWWOWS	BRIDGE	BUDDLES	BUNJEE	ABUSING	CACHET	CALPACK	CANNELS
BOWYER	ABRIDGE	BUDGER	BUNJEES	BUSINGS	CACHETS	CALPACS	CANNER
BOWYERS	BRIDGED	BUDGERO	BUNJIE	BUSKER	CACHOU	CALQUE	SCANNER
BOXCAR	BRIDGES	BUDGERS	BUNJIES	BUSKERS	CACHOUS	CALQUED	CANNERS
BOXCARS	BRIDIE	BUDGET	BUNKER	BUSKET	CACKLE	CALQUES	CANNERY
BOXFUL	BRIDIES	BUDGETS	BUNKERS	BUSKETS	CACKLED	CALTHA	CANNON
BOXFULS	BRIDLE	BUDGIE	BUNKUM	BUSKIN	CACKLER	CALTHAS	CANNONS
BOXING	BRIDLED	BUDGIES	BUNKUMS	BUSKING	CACKLES	CALVER	CANTAR
BOXINGS	BRIDLER	BUFFER	BUNNIA	BUSKINS	CACOON	CALVERS	CANTARS
BRACER	BRIDLES	BUFFERS	BUNNIAS	BUSTEE	CACOONS	CAMBER	CANTED
BRACERS	BRIGUE	BUFFET	BUNTER	BUSTEES	CADDIE	CAMBERS	SCANTED
BRAIDE	BRIGUED	BUFFETS	BUNTERS	BUSTER	CADDIED	CAMELS	CANTER
BRAIDED	BRIGUES	BUGGAN	BUNYIP	BUSTERS	CADDIES	SCAMELS	SCANTER
BRAIDER	BROACH	BUGGANS	BUNYIPS	BUSTLE	CADDIS	CAMERA	CANTERS
BRAIDS	ABROACH	BUGGER	BURBLE	BUSTLED	CADDISH	CAMERAL	CANTLE
ABRAIDS	BROADS	BUGGERS	BURBLED	BUSTLER	CADEAU	CAMERAS	SCANTLE
BRAIRD	ABROADS	BUGGERY	BURBLES	BUSTLES	CADEAUX	CAMESE	CANTLED
BRAIRDS	BROCHE	BUGGIN	BURBOT	BUTANE	CADGER	CAMESES	CANTLES
BRAISE	BROCHES	BUGGING	BURBOTS	BUTANES	CADGERS	CAMION	CANTLET
BRAISED	BROGAN	BUGGINS	BURDEN	BUTENE	CADUAC	CAMIONS	CANTON
BRAISES	BROGANS	BUGLER	BURDENS	BUTENES	CADUACS	CAMISE	CANTONS
BRAIZE	BROGUE		BURDIE	BUTLER	CAESAR	CAMISES	

CANTOR	CARPERS	CATKIN	CENTERS	CHANGER	CHICHIS	CHOUSES	CITRIN
CANTORS	CARPET	CATKINS	CENTRE	CHANGES	CHICKS	CHOUTS	CITRINE
CANVAS	CARPETS	CATNAP	CENTRED	CHAPEL	TCHICKS	SCHOUTS	CITRINS
CANVASS	CARRAT	CATNAPS	CENTRES	CHAPELS	CHICLE	CHOWRI	CITRON
CANYON	CARRATS	CATNEP	CENTUM	CHAPES	CHICLES	CHOWRIS	CITRONS
CANYONS	CARREL	CATNEPS	CENTUMS	CHAPESS	CHICON	CHRISM	CIVISM
CAPING	CARRELL	CATNIP	CERATE	CHAPKA	CHICONS	CHRISMS	CIVISMS
SCAPING	CARRELS	CATNIPS	CERATED	CHAPKAS	CHIDER	CHROMA	CLAMBE
CAPITA	CARROT	CATSUP	CERATES	CHARET	CHIDERS	CHROMAS	CLAMBER
CAPITAL	CARROTS	CATSUPS	CEREAL	CHARETS	CHIELD	CHROME	CLAMOR
CAPITAN	CARROTY	CATTED	CEREALS	CHARGE	CHIELDS	CHROMED	CLAMORS
CAPLIN	CARTED	SCATTED	CERIPH	CHARGED	CHIGOE	CHROMES	CLAQUE
CAPLINS	SCARTED	CAUDAL	CERIPHS	CHARGER	CHIGOES	CHROMO	CLAQUES
CAPOTE	CARTEL	ACAUDAL	CERISE	CHARGES	CHIGRE	CHROMOS	CLARET
CAPOTES	CARTELS	CAUDLE	CERISES	CHARTA	CHIGRES	CHUKAR	CLARETS
CAPPER	CARTER	CAUDLED	CERITE	CHARTAS	CHIKOR	CHUKARS	CLAUSE
CAPPERS	CARTERS	CAUDLES	CERITES	CHASER	CHIKORS	CHUKKA	CLAUSES
CAPRIC	CARTES	CAUKER	CERIUM	CHASERS	CHILDE	CHUKKAS	CLAVER
CAPRICE	ECARTES	CAUSER	CERIUMS	CHASSE	CHILDED	CHUKOR	CLAVERS
CAPRID	CARTON	CAUSERS	CERMET	CHASSES	CHILDER	CHUKORS	CLAVES
CAPRIDS	CARTONS	CAUSEY	CERMETS	CHASTE	CHILLI	CHURCH	SCLAVES
CAPSID	CARVEL	CAUSEYS	CERNED	CHASTEN	CHILLIS	CHURCHY	CLAVIE
CAPSIDS	CARVELS	CAUTEL	SCERNED	CHASTER	CHIMER	CHYACK	CLAVIER
CAPTAN	CARVER	CAUTELS	CERNES	CHATON	CHIMERA	CHYACKS	CLAVIES
CAPTANS	CARVERS	CAUTER	SCERNES	CHATONS	CHIMERE	CHYPRE	CLEANS
CAPTOR	CARVES	CAUTERS	CEROON	CHATTA	CHIMERS	CHYPRES	CLEANSE
CAPTORS	SCARVES	CAUTERY	CEROONS	CHATTAS	CHINAR	CICADA	CLEAVE
CARACK	CASBAH	CAVEAT	CERUSE	CHAUFE	CHINARS	CICADAS	CLEAVED
CARACKS	CASBAHS	CAVEATS	CERUSES	CHAUFED	CHINES	CICALA	CLEAVER
CARACT	CASEIN	CAVERN	CESIUM	CHAUFES	CHINESE	CICALAS	CLEAVES
CARACTS	CASEINS	CAVERNS	CESIUMS	CHAUFF	CHINTZ	CICERO	CLEEVE
CARAFE	CASERN	CAVIAR	CESSER	CHAUFFS	CHINTZY	CICEROS	CLEEVES
CARAFES	CASERNE	CAVIARS	CESSERS	CHAUNT	CHISEL	CICUTA	CLEPED
CARBON	CASERNS	CAVIARE	CESTUI	CHAUNTS	CHISELS	CICUTAS	YCLEPED
CARBONS	CASHAW	CAVIARES	CESTUIS	CHEERO	CHITAL	CIERGE	CLERIC
CARBOY	CASHAWS	CAVIER	CESURA	CHEEROS	CHITALS	CIERGES	CLERICS
CARBOYS	CASHEW	CAVIERS	CESURAS	CHEESE	CHITIN	CIGGIE	CLEUCH
CARDER	CASHEWS	CAVING	CESURE	CHEESED	CHITINS	CIGGIES	CLEUCHS
CARDERS	CASING	CAVINGS	CESURES	CHEESES	CHITON	CILICE	CLEUGH
CAREEN	CASINGS	CAVORT	CETANE	CHENAR	CHITONS	CILICES	CLEUGHS
CAREENS	CASINO	CAVORTS	CETANES	CHENARS	CHOCHO	CIMIER	CLICHE
CAREER	CASINOS	CAWING	CETYLS	CHENET	CHOCHOS	CIMIERS	CLICHED
CAREERS	CASKET	CAWINGS	ACETYLS	CHENETS	CHOICE	CINDER	CLICHES
CAREME	CASKETS	CAWKER	CHACMA	CHEQUE	CHOICER	CINDERS	CLIENT
CAREMES	CASQUE	CAWKERS	CHACMAS	CHEQUER	CHOICES	CINDERY	CLIENTS
CARERS	CASQUES	CAYMAN	CHADAR	CHEQUES	CHOKER	CINEMA	CLIFFS
SCARERS	CASSIA	CAYMANS	CHADARS	CHERUB	CHOKERS	CINEMAS	SCLIFFS
CARIBE	CASSIAS	CAYUSE	CHADOR	CHERUBS	CHOKEY	CINEOL	CLINIC
CARIBES	CASTER	CAYUSES	CHADORS	CHERUP	CHOKEYS	CINEOLE	ACLINIC
CARINA	CASTERS	CEDULA	CHAETA	CHERUPS	CHOLER	CINEOLS	CLINICS
OCARINA	CASTLE	CEDULAS	CHAETAE	CHESIL	CHOLERA	CINQUE	CLIQUE
CARINAS	CASTLED	CELIAC	CHAFER	CHESILS	CHOLERS	CINQUES	CLIQUES
CARING	CASTLES	CELIACS	CHAFERS	CHEVEN	CHOOSE	CIPHER	CLIQUEY
SCARING	CASTOR	CELLAR	CHAGAN	CHEVENS	CHOOSER	CIPHERS	CLITIC
CARLOT	CASTORS	OCELLAR	CHAGANS	CHEVIN	CHOOSES	CIRCAR	CLITICS
CARLOTS	CASTORY	CELLARS	CHAISE	CHEVINS	CHOOSEY	CIRCARS	CLOACA
CARNAL	CASUAL	CEMBRA	CHAISES	CHEWET	CHOPIN	CIRCLE	CLOACAE
CARNALS	CASUALS	CEMBRAS	CHAKRA	CHEWETS	CHOPINE	CIRCLED	CLOACAL
CARNET	CATALO	CEMENT	CHAKRAS	CHIACK	CHOPINS	CIRCLER	CLOCHE
CARNETS	CATALOG	CEMENTA	CHALAN	CHIACKS	CHORAL	CIRCLES	CLOCHES
CARNEY	CATALOS	CEMENTS	CHALANS	CHIASM	CHORALE	CIRCLET	CLOQUE
CARNEYS	CATENA	CENOTE	CHALET	CHIASMA	CHORALS	CIRCUS	CLOQUES
CARPAL	CATENAE	CENOTES	CHALETS	CHIASMS	CHOREA	CIRCUSY	CLOSED
CARPALS	CATENAS	CENSER	CHANCE	CHIBOL	CHOREAS	CIRQUE	ECLOSED
CARPED	CATERS	CENSERS	CHANCED	CHIBOLS	CHOREE	CIRQUES	CLOSER
SCARPED	ACATERS	CENSOR	CHANCEL	CHICHA	CHOREES	CITHER	CLOSERS
CARPEL	CATGUT	CENSORS	CHANCER	CHICHI	CHOUGH	CITHERN	CLOSES
CARPELS	CATGUTS	CENTAL	CHANCES		CHOUGHS	CITHERS	ECLOSES
CARPER	CATION	CENTALS	CHANGE		CHOUSE	CITOLE	CLOSEST
SCARPER	CATIONS	CENTER	CHANGED		CHOUSED	CITOLES	CLOSET

CLOSETS	COFFEES	**COMBLE**	**CONSUL**	**CORIUM**	**COTEAU**	SCOWLED	CREATED
CLOTHE	**COFFER**	COMBLES	CONSULS	CORIUMS	COTEAUX	**COWPAT**	**CREATES**
CLOTHED	SCOFFER	**COMEDO**	CONSULT	**CORKER**	**COTING**	COWPATS	**CRECHE**
CLOTHES	COFFERS	COMEDOS	**CONTES**	CORKERS	COTINGA	**COWPED**	CRECHES
CLOUGH	**COFFIN**	**COMFIT**	CONTEST	**CORKIR**	**COTISE**	SCOWPED	**CREDIT**
CLOUGHS	COFFING	COMFITS	**CONTRA**	CORKIRS	COTISED	**COWRIE**	CREDITS
CLOVER	COFFINS	**COMING**	CONTRAS	**CORNEA**	COTISES	SCOWRIE	**CREEDS**
CLOVERS	**COFFLE**	COMINGS	**CONVEY**	CORNEAL	COTTAR	COWRIES	**CREESE**
CLOVERY	COFFLES	**COMMER**	CONVEYS	CORNEAS	COTTARS	**COYOTE**	CREESED
CLUSIA	**COGGED**	COMMERE	**CONVOY**	**CORNED**	**COTTER**	COYOTES	CREESES
CLUSIAS	SCOGGED	COMMERS	CONVOYS	ACORNED	COTTERS	**COZIER**	**CREESH**
COAITA	**COGGER**	**COMMIE**	**COOING**	SCORNED	**COTTON**	COZIERS	CREESHY
COAITAS	COGGERS	COMMIES	COOINGS	**CORNEL**	COTTONS	**COZIES**	**CREMOR**
COALER	**COGGIE**	**COMMIT**	**COOKER**	CORNELS	COTTONY	COZIEST	CREMORS
COALERS	COGGIES	COMMITS	COOKERS	**CORNER**	**COTWAL**	**CRADLE**	**CREMSON**
COARSE	**COGGLE**	**COMMON**	COOKERY	SCORNER	COTWALS	CRADLED	**CRENEL**
COARSEN	COGGLED	COMMONS	**COOKIE**	CORNERS	**COTYLE**	CRADLES	CRENELS
COARSER	COGGLES	**COMMOT**	COOKIES	**CORNET**	COTYLES	**CRAGGY**	**CREOLE**
COATEE	**COHERE**	COMMOTE	**COOLER**	CORNETS	**COUCAL**	SCRAGGY	CREOLES
COATEES	COHERED	COMMOTS	COOLERS	CORNETT	COUCALS	**CRAMES**	**CREPON**
COATER	COHERER	**COMPEL**	**COOLIE**	**CORNUA**	**COUCHE**	CRAMESY	CREPONS
COATERS	COHERES	COMPELS	COOLIES	CORNUAL	COUCHED	**CRANCH**	**CRESOL**
COAXER	**COHORN**	**COMPOS**	**COOLTH**	**CORONA**	COUCHEE	SCRANCH	CRESOLS
COAXERS	COHORNS	COMPOSE	COOLTHS	CORONAE	COUCHES	**CRANIA**	**CRETIC**
COBALT	**COHORT**	COMPOST	**COOPED**	CORONAL	**COUGAR**	CRANIAL	CRETICS
COBALTS	COHORTS	COMPOTE	**COOPER**	CORONAS	COUGARS	**CRANNY**	**CRETIN**
COBBER	**COHUNE**	COMPOTS	SCOOPER	**COROZO**	**COULEE**	SCRANNY	CRETINS
COBBERS	COHUNES	**CONCHA**	COOPERS	COROZOS	COULEES	**CRAPED**	**CREWED**
COBBLE	**COIGNE**	CONCHAE	COOPERY	**CORPSE**	**COUPED**	SCRAPED	SCREWED
COBBLED	COIGNED	**CONCHE**	**COOSEN**	CORPSED	**COUPEE**	**CRAPES**	**CREWEL**
COBBLER	COIGNES	CONCHED	COOSENS	CORPSES	COUPEES	SCRAPES	CREWELS
COBBLES	**COINER**	CONCHES	**COOSER**	**CORRAL**	**COUPER**	**CRAPLE**	**CRIMPS**
COBNUT	COINERS	**CONCUR**	COOSERS	CORRALS	COUPERS	CRAPLES	SCRIMPS
COBNUTS	**COJOIN**	CONCURS	**COOSIN**	**CORRIE**	**COUPLE**	**CRATCH**	**CRIMPY**
COBURG	COJOINS	**CONDER**	COOSINS	CORRIES	COUPLED	SCRATCH	SCRIMPY
COBURGS	**COLDER**	CONDERS	**CORSES**	**CORSES**	COUPLER	**CRATER**	**CRINES**
COBWEB	SCOLDER	**CONDOM**	SCORSES	SCORSES	COUPLES	CRATERS	SCRINES
COBWEBS	**COLLAR**	CONDOMS	**COPECK**	**CORSET**	COUPLET	**CRATON**	**CRINGE**
COCCID	COLLARD	**CONDOR**	COPECKS	CORSETS	**COUPON**	CRATONS	CRINGED
COCCIDS	COLLARS	CONDORS	**COPIER**	**CORVEE**	COUPONS	**CRATUR**	CRINGER
COCKER	**COLLET**	CONDERS	COPIERS	CORVEES	CRATURS	CRINGES
COCKERS	COLLETS	**CONFAB**	**COPING**	**CORVET**	CRATURS	**CRINUM**
COCKET	**COLLIE**	CONFABS	COPINGS	CORVETS	**CRAVAT**	CRINUMS
COCKETS	COLLIED	**CONFER**	**COPITA**	**CORVID**	CRAVATS	**CRISTA**
COCKLE	COLLIER	CONFERS	COPITAS	CORVIDS	**CRAVEN**	CRISTAE
COCKLED	COLLIES	**CONFIT**	**COPPER**	**CORYMB**	CRAVENS	**CRITIC**
COCKLES	**COLLOP**	CONFITS	COPPERS	CORYMBS	**CRAVER**	CRITICS
COCOON	SCOLLOP	**CONGEE**	COPPERY	**CORYZA**	CRAVERS	**CROCHE**
COCOONS	COLLOPS	CONGEED	**COPPIN**	CORYZAS	**CRAWLS**	CROCHES
CODDLE	**COLOUR**	CONGEES	COPPINS	**COSECH**	SCRAWLS	CROCHET
CODDLED	COLOURS	**CONGER**	**COPPLE**	COSECHS	**CRAWLY**	**CRONET**
CODDLES	COLOURY	CONGERS	COPPLES	**COSHER**	SCRAWLY	CRONETS
CODGER	**COLTER**	CONGERY	**COPULA**	COSHERS	**CRAYER**	**CROSSE**
CODGERS	COLTERS	**CONGES**	SCOPULA	COSHERY	CRAYERS	CROSSED
CODING	**COLUGO**	CONGEST	COPULAR	**COSIER**	**CRAYON**	CROSSER
CODINGS	COLUGOS	**CONGOU**	COPULAS	COSIERS	CRAYONS	CROSSES
CODIST	**COLUMN**	CONGOUS	**COQUET**	COSIEST	**CREACH**	**CROTAL**
CODISTS	COLUMNS	**CONIMA**	COQUETS	**COSINE**	CREACHS	SCROTAL
CODLIN	**COLURE**	CONIMAS	**CORBAN**	COSINES	**CREAGH**	CROTALA
CODLING	COLURES	**CONINE**	CORBANS	**COSMEA**	CREAGHS	CROTALS
CODLINS	**COMARB**	CONINES	**CORBEL**	COSMEAS	**CREAKS**	**CROTON**
COELOM	COMARBS	**CONJEE**	CORBELS	**COVYNE**	SCREAKS	CROTONS
COELOME	**COMART**	CONJEED	**CORBIE**	**COSSET**	COVYNES	SCREAKY	**CROUPE**
COELOMS	COMARTS	CONJEES	CORBIES	COSSETS	**COWAGE**	SCREAKY	CROUPED
COERCE	**COMATE**	**CONKER**	**CORDON**	**COSSIE**	COWAGES	**CREAMS**	CROUPER
COERCED	COMATES	CONKERS	CORDONS	COSSIES	**COWARD**	SCREAMS	CROUPES
COERCES	**COMBAT**	**CONNER**	**CORERS**	**COSTAL**	COWARDS	**CREASE**	**CROUTE**
COEVAL	COMBATS	CONNERS	SCORERS	COSTALS	**COWBOY**	CREASED	CROUTES
COEVALS	**COMBER**	**CONOID**	**CORING**	**COSTER**	COWBOYS	CREASES	**CRUDES**
COFFEE	COMBERS	CONOIDS	SCORING	COSTERS	**COWLED**	**CREATE**	CRUDEST
						OCREATE	

CRUISE	CUISSES	CURRIES	DACOITS	DANDLED	DAZZLED	DECOCTS	DEGUST
CRUISED	CUITER	CURSER	DACOITY	DANDLER	DAZZLER	DECODE	DEGUSTS
CRUISER	CUITERS	CURSERS	DACTYL	DANDLES	DAZZLES	DECODED	DEHORN
CRUISES	CULLED	CURSOR	DACTYLS	DANGER	DEACON	DECODER	DEHORNS
CRUIVE	SCULLED	CURSORS	DADDLE	DANGERS	DEACONS	DECODES	DEHORT
CRUIVES	CULLER	CURSORY	DADDLED	DANGLE	DEADEN	DECOKE	DEHORTS
CRUMEN	SCULLER	CURTAL	DADDLES	DANGLED	DEADENS	DECOKED	DEJECT
CRUMENS	CULLERS	CURVET	DAEDAL	DANGLER	DEADER	DECOKES	DEJECTA
CRUMMY	CULLETS	CURVETS	DAEDALE	DANGLES	DEADERS	DECREE	DEJECTS
SCRUMMY	CULMEN	CUSHAT	DAEMON	DANTON	DEAFEN	DECREED	DELATE
CRUMPS	CULMENS	CUSHATS	DAEMONS	DANTONS	DEAFENS	DECREES	DELATED
SCRUMPS	CULTER	CUSHAW	DAFTAR	DAPHNE	DEALER	DECREET	DELATES
CRUMPY	CULTERS	CUSHAWS	DAFTARS	DAPHNES	DEALERS	DECREW	DELETE
SCRUMPY	CULVER	CUSSER	DAFTIE	DAPPER	DEANER	DECREWS	DELETED
CRUNCH	CULVERS	CUSSERS	DAFTIES	DAPPERS	DEANERS	DECTET	DELETES
SCRUNCH	CULVERT	CUSTOM	DAGABA	DAPPLE	DEANERY	DECTETS	DELICE
CRUNCHY	CUMBER	CUSTOMS	DAGABAS	DAPPLED	DEARES	DEDUCE	DELICES
CRUSET	SCUMBER	CUTEST	DAGGER	DAPPLES	DEAREST	DEDUCED	DELICT
CRUSETS	CUMBERS	ACUTEST	DAGGERS	DARGLE	DEARIE	DEDUCES	DELICTS
CRUSIE	CUMMER	CUTLER	DAGGLE	DARGLES	DEARIES	DEDUCT	DELUDE
CRUSIES	SCUMMER	CUTLERS	DAGGLED	DARING	DEARTH	DEDUCTS	DELUDED
CRUSTA	CUMMERS	CUTLERY	DAGGLES	DARINGS	DEARTHS	DEEJAY	DELUDER
CRUSTAE	CUMMIN	CUTLET	DAGOBA	DARKEN	DEASIL	DEEJAYS	DELUDES
CRUSTAL	CUMMINS	CUTLETS	DAGOBAS	DARKENS	DEASILS	DEEMED	DELUGE
CRYING	CUNNER	SCUTTER	DAHLIA	DARKEY	DEBARK	ADEEMED	DELUGED
SCRYING	SCUNNER	CUTTLE	DAHLIAS	DARKEYS	DEBARKS	DEEPEN	DELUGES
CRYINGS	CUPFUL	CUTTLES	DAIDLE	DARKIE	DEBASE	DEEPENS	DELVER
CRYPTO	CUPFULS	SCUTTLE	DAIDLED	DARKIES	DEBASED	DEEPIE	DELVERS
CRYPTON	CUPOLA	CUTTOE	DAIDLES	DARKLE	DEBASER	DEEPIES	DEMAIN
CRYPTOS	CUPOLAR	CUTTOES	DAIKER	DARKLED	DEBASES	DEFACE	DEMAINE
CUBAGE	CUPOLAS	CYANIN	DAIKERS	DARKLES	DEBATE	DEFACED	DEMAINS
CUBAGES	CUPPER	CYANINE	DAIKON	DARNEL	DEBATED	DEFACER	DEMAND
CUBICA	CUPPERS	CYANINS	DAIKONS	DARNELS	DEBATER	DEFACES	DEMANDS
CUBICAL	CUPULE	CYATHI	DAIMIO	DARNER	DEBATES	DEFAME	DEMARK
CUBICAS	GUPULES	CYATHIA	DAIMIOS	DARNERS	DEBTEE	DEFAMED	DEMARKS
CUBISM	CURARA	CYCLER	DAIMON	DARTER	DEBTEES	DEFAMES	DEMEAN
CUBISMS	CURARAS	CYCLERS	DAIMONS	DARTERS	DEBTOR	DEFAST	DEMEANE
CUBIST	CURARE	CYCLIC	DAINED	DARTLE	DEBTORS	DEFASTE	DEMEANS
CUBISTS	CURARES	ACYCLIC	SDAINED	DARTLED	DECADE	DEFEAT	DEMENT
CUBOID	CURARI	CYGNET	DAINES	DARTLES	DECADES	DEFEATS	DEMENTI
CUBOIDS	CURARIS	CYGNETS	SDAINES	DARTRE	DECAMP	DEFECT	DEMENTS
CUCKOO	CURATE	CYMBAL	DAKOIT	DARTRES	DECAMPS	DEFECTS	DEMISE
CUCKOOS	CURATES	CYMBALO	DAKOITI	DASHER	DECANE	DEFEND	DEMISED
CUDDEN	CURDLE	CYMBALS	DAKOITS	DASHERS	DECANES	DEFENDS	DEMISES
CUDDENS	CURDLED	CYPHER	DALLOP	DASSIE	DECANT	DEFIER	DEMIST
CUDDIE	CURDLES	CYPHERS	DALLOPS	DASSIES	DECANTS	DEFIERS	DEMISTS
CUDDIES	CURFEW	CYPRID	DALTON	DATING	DECARB	DEFILE	DEMODE
CUDDIN	CURFEWS	CYPRIDS	DALTONS	DATINGS	DECARBS	DEFILED	DEMODED
CUDDINS	CURIES	CYSTID	DAMAGE	DATIVE	DECARE	DEFILER	DEMOTE
CUDDLE	ECURIES	CYSTIDS	DAMAGED	DATIVES	DECARES	DEFILES	DEMOTED
SCUDDLE	CURIET	CYTASE	DAMAGES	DATURA	DECCIE	DEFINE	DEMOTES
CUDDLED	CURIETS	CYTASES	DAMASK	DATURAS	DECCIES	DEFINED	DEMURE
CUDDLES	CURIOS	CYTODE	DAMASKS	DAUBER	DECEIT	DEFINER	DEMURED
CUDGEL	CURIOSA	CYTODES	DAMMAR	DAUBERS	DECEITS	DEFINES	DEMURER
CUDGELS	CURIUM	CZAPKA	DAMMARS	DAUBERY	DECERN	DEFORM	DEMURES
CUEIST	CURIUMS	CZAPKAS	DAMMER	DAUNER	DECERNS	DEFORMS	DENGUE
CUEISTS	CURLER	DABBER	DAMMERS	DAUNERS	DECIDE	DEFOUL	DENGUES
CUESTA	CURLERS	DABBERS	DAMPEN	DAUTIE	DECIDED	DEFOULS	DENIAL
CUESTAS	CURLEW	DABBLE	DAMPENS	DAUTIES	DECIDER	DEFRAY	DENIALS
CUFFED	CURLEWS	DABBLED	DAMPER	DAWDLE	DECIDES	DEFRAYS	DENIER
SCUFFED	CURPEL	DABBLER	DAMPERS	DAWDLED	DECIME	DEFUSE	DENIERS
CUFFIN	CURPELS	DABBLES	DAMSEL	DAWDLER	DECIMES	DEFUSED	DENNET
CUFFING	CURRED	DACITE	DAMSELS	DAWDLES	DECKER	DEFUSES	DENNETS
CUFFINS	SCURRED	DACITES	DAMSON	DAWING	DECKERS	DEFUZE	DENOTE
CUFFLE	CURRIE	DACKER	DAMSONS	DAWNER	DECKLE	DEFUZED	DENOTED
SCUFFLE	CURRIED	DACKERS	ADAWING	DAWNERS	DECKLED	DEFUZES	DENOTES
CUFFLED	CURRIER	DACOIT	DANCER	DAWTIE	DECKLES	DEGOUT	DENTAL
CUFFLES			DANCERS	DAWTIES	DECOCT	DEGOUTS	DENTALS
CUISSE			DANDER	DAZZLE	DECOCTS	DEGREE	DENTEL
CUISSER			DANDERS			DEGREES	EDENTAL
			DANDLE				

DENTELS	DESYNED	DIARCHY	DINGERS	**DITHER**	**DOGGERY**	DORIZES	DRAGONS
DENTIL	DESYNES	**DIATOM**	**DINGEY**	DITHERS	**DOGGIE**	**DORMER**	**DRAPER**
DENTILS	**DETAIL**	DIATOMS	DINGEYS	DITHERY	DOGGIER	DORMERS	DRAPERS
DENTIN	DETAILS	**DIAXON**	**DINGLE**	**DITING**	DOGGIES	**DORSAL**	DRAPERY
DENTINE	**DETAIN**	DIAXONS	DINGLES	EDITING	**DOLLAR**	DORSALS	**DRAPET**
DENTING	DETAINS	**DIBBER**	**DINNER**	**DITONE**	DOLLARS	**DORSEL**	DRAPETS
DENTINS	**DETECT**	DIBBERS	DINNERS	DITONES	**DOLLOP**	DORSELS	**DRAUNT**
DENUDE	DETECTS	**DIBBLE**	**DINNLE**	**DITTAY**	DOLLOPS	**DORSER**	DRAUNTS
DENUDED	**DETENT**	DIBBLED	DINNLED	DITTAYS	**DOLMAN**	DORSERS	**DRAWEE**
DENUDES	DETENTE	DIBBLER	DINNLES	**DIVERS**	DOLMANS	**DORTER**	DRAWEES
DEODAR	DETENTS	DIBBLES	DIOXAN	DIVERSE	**DOLMEN**	DORTERS	**DRAWER**
DEODARS	**DETENU**	**DICAST**	DIOXANE	**DIVERT**	DOLMENS	**DOSAGE**	DRAWERS
DEPART	DETENUE	DICASTS	DIOXANS	DIVERTS	**DOLOUR**	DOSAGES	**DRAZEL**
DEPARTS	DETENUS	**DICING**	DIOXIN	**DIVEST**	DOLOURS	**DOSSAL**	DRAZELS
DEPEND	**DETEST**	DICINGS	DIOXINS	DIVESTS	**DOMAIN**	DOSSALS	**DREADS**
DEPENDS	DETESTS	**DICKER**	**DIPLOE**	**DIVIDE**	DOMAINS	**DOSSEL**	ADREADS
DEPICT	**DETORT**	DICKERS	DIPLOES	DIVIDED	**DOMETT**	DOSSELS	**DREARE**
DEPICTS	DETORTS	**DICKEY**	**DIPLON**	DIVIDER	DOMETTS	**DOSSER**	DREARER
DEPLOY	**DETOUR**	DICKEYS	DIPLONS	DIVIDES	**DOMINO**	DOSSERS	DREARES
DEPLOYS	DETOURS	**DICKIE**	DIPLONT	**DIVINE**	DOMINOS	**DOSSIL**	**DREDGE**
DEPONE	**DEUTON**	DICKIER	**DIPOLE**	DIVINED	**DONATE**	DOSSILS	DREDGED
DEPONED	DEUTONS	DICKIES	DIPOLES	DIVINER	DONATED	**DOTAGE**	DREDGER
DEPONES	**DEVALL**	**DIDDER**	**DIPPER**	DIVINES	DONATES	DOTAGES	DREDGES
DEPORT	DEVALLS	DIDDERS	DIPPERS	**DIVING**	**DONGLE**	**DOTANT**	**DRIVEL**
DEPORTS	**DEVEST**	**DIDDLE**	**DIRDAM**	DIVINGS	DONGLES	DOTANTS	DRIVELS
DEPOSE	DEVESTS	DIDDLED	DIRDAMS	**DIZAIN**	**DONING**	**DOTARD**	**DRIVER**
DEPOSED	**DEVICE**	DIDDLER	**DIRDUM**	DIZAINS	DONINGS	DOTARDS	DRIVERS
DEPOSER	DEVICES	DIDDLES	DIRDUMS	**DJEBEL**	**DONJON**	**DOTING**	**DROGER**
DEPOSES	**DEVISE**	**DIEDRE**	**DIRECT**	DJEBELS	DONJONS	DOTINGS	DROGERS
DEPUTE	DEVISED	DIEDRES	DIRECTS	**DOATER**	**DONKEY**	**DOTTLE**	**DROGUE**
DEPUTED	DEVISEE	**DIESEL**	**DIRHAM**	DOATERS	DONKEYS	DOTTLED	DROGUES
DEPUTES	DEVISER	DIESELS	DIRHAMS	**DOBBER**	**DONNAT**	DOTTLER	**DROGUET**
DERAIL	DEVISES	**DIETER**	**DIRHEM**	DOBBERS	DONNATS	DOTTLES	**DROICH**
DERAILS	**DEVOIR**	DIETERS	DIRHEMS	**DOBBIE**	**DONNEE**	**DOUANE**	DROICHS
DERATE	DEVOIRS	**DIFFER**	**DIRIGE**	DOBBIES	DONNEES	DOUANES	DROICHY
DERATED	**DEVOTE**	DIFFERS	DIRIGES	**DOBBIN**	**DONNOT**	**DOUBLE**	DROLES
DERATES	DEVOTED	**DIGEST**	**DIRNDL**	DOBBING	DONNOTS	DOUBLED	DROLEST
DERHAM	DEVOTEE	DIGESTS	DIRNDLS	DOBBINS	**DONSIE**	DOUBLER	**DROMON**
DERHAMS	DEVOTES	**DIGGER**	**DISARM**	**DOCENT**	DONSIER	DOUBLES	DROMOND
DERIDE	**DEVOUR**	DIGGERS	DISARMS	DOCENTS	**DONZEL**	DOUBLET	DROMONS
DERIDED	DEVOURS	**DIGLOT**	**DISBAR**	**DOCILE**	DONZELS	**DOUCET**	**DRONGO**
DERIDER	**DEVVEL**	DIGLOTS	DISBARK	DOCILER	**DOOCOT**	DOUCETS	DRONGOS
DERIDES	DEVVELS	**DIKAST**	DISBARS	**DOCKEN**	DOOCOTS	**DOUCHE**	**DROOME**
DERIVE	**DEWANI**	DIKASTS	**DISBUD**	DOCKENS	**DOODAD**	DOUCHED	DROOMES
DERIVED	DEWANIS	**DIKTAT**	DISBUDS	**DOCKER**	DOODADS	DOUCHES	**DROUTH**
DERIVES	**DEWITT**	DIKTATS	**DISCUS**	DOCKERS	**DOODAH**	**DOUGHT**	DROUTHS
DESALT	DEWITTS	**DILATE**	DISCUSS	**DOCKET**	DOODAHS	DOUGHTY	DROUTHY
DESALTS	**DEWLAP**	DILATED	**DISEUR**	DOCKETS	**DOODLE**	**DOUSER**	**DROVER**
DESERT	DEWLAPS	DILATER	DISEURS	**DOCTOR**	DOODLED	DOUSERS	DROVERS
DESERTS	DEWLAPT	DILATES	**DISMAL**	DOCTORS	DOODLER	**DOUTER**	**DROWSE**
DESIGN	**DEXTER**	**DILDOE**	DISMALS	**DODDER**	DOODLES	DOUTERS	DROWSED
DESIGNS	DEXTERS	DILDOES	**DISMAN**	DODDERY	**DOOKET**	**DOWLNE**	DROWSES
DESINE	**DHARMA**	**DILUTE**	DISMANS	**DODDLE**	DOOKETS	DOWLNES	**DRUDGE**
DESINED	ADHARMA	DILUTED	**DISMAY**	DODDLES	**DOOLIE**	DOWLNEY	DRUDGED
DESINES	DHARMAS	DILUTER	DISMAYD	**DODGEM**	DOOLIES	**DOWNER**	DRUDGER
DESIRE	**DHARNA**	DILUTES	DISMAYL	DODGEMS	**DOPANT**	DOWNERS	DRUDGES
DESIRED	DHARNAS	**DIMBLE**	DISMAYS	**DODGER**	DOPANTS	**DOWSER**	**DRUPEL**
DESIRER	**DHOOTI**	DIMBLES	**DISOWN**	DODGERS	**DOPING**	DOWSERS	DRUPELS
DESIRES	DHOOTIS	**DIMMER**	DISOWNS	DODGERY	DOPINGS	**DOWSET**	**DRYING**
DESIST	**DHURRA**	DIMMERS	**DISPEL**	**DODKIN**	**DOPPER**	DOWSETS	DRYINGS
DESISTS	DHURRAS	**DIMPLE**	DISPELS	DODKINS	DOPPERS	**DOYLEY**	**DUALIN**
DESMAN	**DIADEM**	DIMPLED	**DISPLE**	**DODMAN**	**DOPPIE**	DOYLEYS	DUALINS
DESMANS	DIADEMS	DIMPLES	DISPLED	DODMANS	DOPPIES	**DOZING**	**DUBBIN**
DESMID	**DIALOG**	**DIMWIT**	DISPLES	**DOFFER**	**DORADO**	DOZINGS	DUBBING
DESMIDS	DIALOGS	DIMWITS	**DISTIL**	DOFFERS	DORADOS	**DRACHM**	DUBBINS
DESORB	**DIAPER**	**DINDLE**	DISTILL	**DOGATE**	**DORISE**	DRACHMA	**DUCKER**
DESORBS	DIAPERS	DINDLED	DISTILS	DOGATES	DORISED	DRACHMS	DUCKERS
DESPOT	**DIAPIR**	DINDLES	**DISUSE**	**DOGGER**	DORISES	**DRAGEE**	**DUDDER**
DESPOTS	DIAPIRS	DINDLES	DISUSED	DOGGERS	**DORIZE**	DRAGEES	DUDDERS
DESYNE	**DIARCH**	**DINGER**	DISUSES	DOGGERS	DORIZED	**DRAGON**	DUDDERY

Column 1: DUDDIE, DUDDIER, DUDEEN, DUDEENS, DUDISM, DUDISMS, DUELLO, DUELLOS, DUENNA, DUENNAS, DUETTO, DUETTOS, DUFFEL, DUFFELS, DUFFER, DUFFERS, DUFFLE, DUFFLES, DUGONG, DUGONGS, DUGOUT, DUGOUTS, DUIKER, DUIKERS, DUMDUM, DUMDUMS, DUMPER, DUMPERS, DUMPLE, DUMPLED, DUMPLES, DUNDER, DUNDERS, DUNITE, DUNITES, DUNLIN, DUNLINS, DUPION, DUPIONS, DUPLET, DUPLETS, DURANT, DURANTS, DURBAR, DURBARS, DURDUM, DURDUMS, DURESS, DURESSE, DURGAN, DURGANS, DURIAN, DURIANS, DURION, DURIONS, DURRIE, DURRIES, DUSKEN, DUSKENS, DUSTED, ADUSTED, DUSTER, DUSTERS, DUYKER, DUYKERS, DYBBUK, DYBBUKS, DYEING, DYEINGS, DYNAMO

Column 2: DYNAMOS, DYNAST, DYNASTS, DYNASTY, DYNODE, DYNODES, DYVOUR, DYVOURS, DZEREN, DZERENS, EAGLES, EAGLET, EAGLETS, EAGRES, MEAGRES, EANING, BEANING, LEANING, MEANING, PEANING, SEANING, WEANING, YEANING, EARBOB, EARBOBS, EARDED, BEARDED, YEARDED, EARFUL, FEARFUL, TEARFUL, EARFULS, EARING, BEARING, DEARING, FEARING, GEARING, HEARING, LEARING, NEARING, REARING, SEARING, TEARING, WEARING, EARINGS, EARLAP, EARLAPS, EARNED, LEARNED, YEARNED, EARNER, EARNERS, EARTHS, DEARTHS, HEARTHS, EARWIG, EARWIGS, EASELS, TEASELS, WEASELS, EASING, CEASING, LEASING, MEASING, PEASING, SEASING

Column 3: TEASING, EASLES, MEASLES, EASTED, FEASTED, REASTED, YEASTED, EASTER, FEASTER, EASTERN, EATAGE, EATAGES, EATCHE, EATCHES, EATERS, BEATERS, HEATERS, SEATERS, EATERY, PEATERY, EATHLY, DEATHLY, EATING, BEATING, FEATING, HEATING, SEATING, EATINGS, EBBING, KEBBING, NEBBING, WEBBING, ECARTE, ECARTES, ECBOLE, ECBOLES, ECHING, EECHING, LECHING, PECHING, ECHOER, ECHOERS, ECLAIR, ECLAIRS, ECLOSE, RECLOSE, ECLOSED, ECLOSES, ECONUT, ECONUTS, ECTYPE, ECTYPES, ECURIE, ECURIES, ECZEMA, ECZEMAS, EDDIES, NEDDIES, TEDDIES, REDDISH, EDEMAS, OEDEMAS, EDGERS, HEDGERS, KEDGERS, LEDGERS, EDGIER, HEDGIER, KEDGIER

Column 4: LEDGIER, SEDGIER, EDGING, HEDGING, KEDGING, WEDGING, EDGINGS, EDIBLE, EDIBLES, EDILES, AEDILES, EDITOR, EDITORS, EDUCED, DEDUCED, REDUCED, SEDUCED, EDUCES, DEDUCES, REDUCES, SEDUCES, EDUCTS, DEDUCTS, EECHED, LEECHED, REECHED, EECHES, KEECHES, LEECHES, REECHES, EELIER, SEELIER, EERIER, BEERIER, LEERIER, PEERIER, EFFACE, EFFACED, EFFACES, EFFECT, EFFECTS, EFFEIR, EFFEIRS, EFFERE, EFFERED, EFFERES, EFFING, JEFFING, REFFING, EFFORT, EFFORTS, EFFRAY, EFFRAYS, EFFUSE, EFFUSED, EFFUSES, EFTEST, DEFTEST, EGALLY, LEGALLY, REGALLY, EGENCE, REGENCE, EGENCES, EGENCY, REGENCY, EGESTS, REGESTS, EGGARS

Column 5: BEGGARS, SEGGARS, EGGCUP, EGGCUPS, EGGERS, LEGGERS, EGGIER, EGGING, LEGGING, PEGGING, EGGLER, EGGLERS, EGGNOG, EGGNOGS, EGISES, AEGISES, EGOISM, EGOISMS, EGOIST, EGOISTS, EGRESS, NEGRESS, REGRESS, EGRETS, REGRETS, EIGHTH, EIGHTHS, EIGHTS, HEIGHTS, WEIGHTS, EIGHTY, WEIGHTY, EIRACK, EIRACKS, EISELL, EISELLS, EITHER, NEITHER, EJECTA, DEJECTA, EJECTS, DEJECTS, REJECTS, ELANCE, ELANCED, ELANCES, ELANET, ELANETS, ELAPSE, DELAPSE, RELAPSE, ELAPSED, ELAPSES, ELATED, BELATED, DELATED, RELATED, VELATED, ELATER, RELATER, ELATERS, ELATES, BELATES, DELATES, RELATES, ELCHEE, ELCHEES, ELDERS

Column 6: GELDERS, MELDERS, WELDERS, ELDING, GELDING, MELDING, WELDING, ELDINGS, ELECTS, SELECTS, ELEGIT, ELEGITS, ELENCH, ELENCHI, ELENCHS, ELEVEN, ELEVENS, ELEVON, ELEVONS, ELFING, SELFING, ELFISH, SELFISH, ELICIT, ELICITS, ELIXIR, ELIXIRS, ELOIGN, ELOIGNS, ELOPER, ELOPERS, ELSHIN, ELSHINS, ELTCHI, ELTCHIS, ELUANT, ELUANTS, ELUATE, ELUATES, ELUDED, DELUDED, ELUDER, DELUDER, ELUDERS, ELUDES, DELUDES, ELUENT, ELUENTS, ELUTOR, ELUTORS, ELUVIA, ELUVIAL, ELVERS, DELVERS, ELYTRA, ELYTRAL, EMBACE, EMBACES, EMBAIL, EMBAILS, EMBALE, EMBALED, EMBALES, EMBALL, EMBALLS, EMBALM, EMBALMS, EMBANK

Column 7: EMBANKS, EMBARK, EMBARKS, EMBASE, EMBASED, EMBASES, EMBERS, MEMBERS, EMBLEM, EMBLEMA, EMBLEMS, EMBLIC, EMBLICS, EMBOIL, EMBOILS, EMBOLI, EMBOLIC, EMBRUE, EMBRUED, EMBRUES, EMBRYO, EMBRYON, EMBRYOS, EMERGE, DEMERGE, REMERGE, EMERGED, EMERGES, EMESES, NEMESES, EMESIS, NEMESIS, EMETIC, EMETICS, EMETIN, EMETINE, EMETINS, EMEUTE, EMEUTES, EMIGRE, EMIGRES, EMMOVE, EMMOVED, EMMOVES, EMOTED, DEMOTED, EMOTES, DEMOTES, REMOTES, EMOVED, REMOVED, EMOVES, REMOVES, EMPALE, EMPALED, EMPALES, EMPARE, EMPARED, EMPARES, EMPART, EMPARTS, EMPIRE, EMPIRES, EMPLOY, EMPLOYS, EMPUSA, EMPUSAS, EMPUSE, EMPUSES, EMULED

Column 8: AEMULED, EMULES, AEMULES, EMULGE, EMULGED, EMULGES, EMUNGE, EMUNGED, EMUNGES, EMURED, DEMURED, EMURES, DEMURES, LEMURES, ENABLE, TENABLE, ENABLED, ENABLER, ENABLES, ENAMEL, ENAMELS, ENAMOR, ENAMORS, ENCAGE, ENCAGED, ENCAGES, ENCALM, ENCALMS, ENCAMP, ENCAMPS, ENCASE, ENCASED, ENCASES, ENCAVE, ENCAVED, ENCAVES, ENCODE, ENCODED, ENCODES, ENCORE, ENCORED, ENCORES, ENCYST, ENCYSTS, ENDART, ENDARTS, ENDEAR, ENDEARS, ENDING, BENDING, FENDING, HENDING, LENDING, MENDING, PENDING, RENDING, SENDING, TENDING, VENDING, WENDING, ENDINGS, ENDITE, ENDITED, ENDITES, ENDIVE, ENDIVES, ENDUES, VENDUES, ENDURE, ENDURED

ENDURER	ENLOCKS	ENTICER	EPOPEES	ESCROWS	ETHNICS	EVZONES	EXPOSER
ENDURES	ENMOVE	ENTICES	EPOSES	ESCUDO	ETHYLS	EXACTS	EXPOSES
ENERVE	ENMOVED	ENTIRE	DEPOSES	ESCUDOS	METHYLS	HEXACTS	EXPUGN
ENERVED	ENMOVES	ENTIRES	REPOSES	ESILES	ETHYNE	EXAMEN	EXPUGNS
ENERVES	ENNEAD	ENTOIL	EPRISE	RESILES	ETHYNES	EXAMENS	EXSECT
ENEWED	ENNEADS	ENTOILS	REPRISE	ESLOIN	ETOILE	EXARCH	EXSECTS
RENEWED	ENNUYE	ENTOMB	EPUISE	ESLOINS	ETOILES	HEXARCH	EXSERT
ENFACE	ENNUYED	ENTOMBS	EPUISEE	ESPADA	ETRIER	EXARCHS	EXSERTS
ENFACED	ENOSES	ENTRAP	EQUANT	ESPADAS	ETRIERS	EXARCHY	EXTANT
ENFACES	KENOSES	ENTRAPS	EQUANTS	ESPIAL	ETTLED	EXCAMB	SEXTANT
ENFANT	ENOSIS	ENTREE	EQUATE	ESPIALS	FETTLED	EXCAMBS	EXTEND
ENFANTS	KENOSIS	ENTREES	EQUATED	ESPRIT	METTLED	EXCEED	EXTENDS
ENFIRE	ENOUGH	ENURES	EQUATES	ESPRITS	NETTLED	EXCEEDS	EXTENT
ENFIRED	ENOUGHS	TENURES	EQUIPE	ESSIVE	PETTLED	EXCEPT	EXTENTS
ENFIRES	ENRACE	ENVIER	EQUIPES	ESSIVES	SETTLED	EXCEPTS	EXTERN
ENFOLD	ENRACED	ENVIERS	ERASER	ESSOIN	ETTLES	EXCIDE	EXTERNE
PENFOLD	ENRACES	ENVIES	ERASERS	ESSOINS	KETTLES	EXCIDED	EXTERNS
TENFOLD	ENRAGE	ENVOIS	ERBIUM	ESTATE	METTLES	EXCIDES	EXTINE
ENFOLDS	ENRAGED	SENVIES	TERBIUM	GESTATE	NETTLES	EXCISE	EXTINES
ENFORM	ENRAGES	RENVOIS	ERBIUMS	RESTATE	PETTLES	EXCISED	EXTIRP
ENFORMS	ENRANK	ENVOYS	ERGATE	TESTATE	SETTLES	EXCISES	EXTIRPS
ENFREE	ENRANKS	LENVOYS	ERGATES	ESTATED	ETYMON	EXCITE	EXTORT
ENFREED	ENRING	RENVOYS	ERIACH	ESTATES	ETYMONS	EXCITED	EXTORTS
ENFREES	ENRINGS	ENWALL	ERIACHS	ESTEEM	EUCAIN	EXCITER	EYALET
ENGAGE	ENROBE	ENWALLS	ERINGO	ESTEEMS	EUCAINE	EXCITES	EYALETS
ENGAGED	ENROBED	ENWIND	ERINGOS	ESTERS	EUCAINS	EXCUSE	EYEFUL
ENGAGER	ENROBES	ENWINDS	ERMINE	FESTERS	EUCHRE	EXCUSED	EYEFULS
ENGAGES	ENROLL	ENWOMB	ERMINED	JESTERS	EUCHRED	EXCUSER	EYELET
ENGAOL	ENROLLS	ENWOMBS	ERMINES	NESTERS	EUCHRES	EXCUSES	EYELETS
ENGAOLS	ENROOT	ENWRAP	ERNING	PESTERS	EUGHEN	EXEDRA	EYELID
ENGILD	ENROOTS	ENWRAPS	CERNING	RESTERS	LEUGHEN	EXEDRAE	EYELIDS
ENGILDS	ENSEAL	ENZIAN	FERNING	TESTERS	EUKING	EXEMES	EYLIAD
ENGINE	ENSEALS	ENZIANS	GERNING	WESTERS	YEUKING	LEXEMES	EYLIADS
ENGINED	ENSEAM	ENZONE	KERNING	ESTRAL	EUNUCH	EXEMPT	FABLER
ENGINER	ENSEAMS	ENZONED	TERNING	OESTRAL	EUNUCHS	EXEMPTS	FABLERS
ENGINES	ENSEAR	ENZONES	EROTIC	VESTRAL	EUOUAE	EXHALE	FABRIC
ENGIRD	ENSEARS	ENZYME	XEROTIC	ESTRAY	EUOUAES	EXHALED	FABRICS
ENGIRDS	ENSIGN	ENZYMES	EROTICA	ESTRAYS	EUPHON	EXHALES	FACADE
ENGLUT	ENSIGNS	EOLITH	EROTICS	ESTRUM	EUPHONS	EXHORT	FACADES
ENGLUTS	ENSILE	NEOLITH	ERRAND	OESTRUM	EUPHONY	EXHORTS	FACETE
ENGOBE	PENSILE	EOLITHS	ERRANDS	ESTRUMS	EUREKA	EXHUME	FACETED
ENGOBES	SENSILE	EONISM	ERRANT	ESTRUS	EUREKAS	EXHUMED	FACIAL
ENGORE	TENSILE	PEONISM	ERRANTS	OESTRUS	HEUREKA	EXHUMER	FACIALS
ENGORED	ENSILED	EONISMS	ERRING	ETAGES	EVEJAR	EXHUMES	FACING
ENGORES	ENSILES	EPARCH	HERRING	METAGES	EVEJARS	EXISTS	FACINGS
ENGRAM	ENSOUL	EPARCHS	SERRING	ETALON	EVERTS	SEXISTS	FACTOR
ENGRAMS	ENSOULS	EPARCHY	ERRINGS	ETALONS	REVERTS	EXOGEN	FACTORS
ENGULF	ENSURE	EPAULE	ERRORS	ETCHED	EVINCE	EXOGENS	FACTORY
ENGULFS	CENSURE	EPAULES	TERRORS	FETCHED	EVINCED	EXONYM	FACTUM
ENHALO	ENSURED	EPAULET	ERYNGO	LETCHED	EVINCES	EXONYMS	FACTUMS
ENHALOS	ENSURER	EPEIRA	ERYNGOS	RETCHED	EVITES	EXOPOD	FACULA
ENIGMA	ENSURES	EPEIRAS	ESCAPE	ETCHER	LEVITES	EXOPODS	FACULAE
ENIGMAS	ENTAIL	EPERDU	ESCAPED	ETCHERS	EVOKED	EXOTIC	FACULAR
ENISLE	VENTAIL	EPHEBI	ESCAPEE	ETCHES	REVOKED	EXOTICA	FADDLE
ENISLED	ENTAILS	EPHEBIC	ESCAPER	FETCHES	EVOKES	EXOTICS	FADDLED
ENISLES	ENTAME	EPIGON	ESCAPES	KETCHES	REVOKES	EXPAND	FADDLES
ENJAMB	ENTAMED	EPIGONE	ESCARP	LETCHES	EVOLUE	EXPANDS	FADEUR
ENJAMBS	ENTAMES	EPIGONI	ESCARPS	RETCHES	EVOLUES	EXPECT	FADEURS
ENJOIN	ENTERA	EPIGONS	ESCHAR	VETCHES	EVOLVE	EXPECTS	FADING
ENJOINS	ENTERAL	EPIMER	ESCHARS	ETHANE	DEVOLVE	EXPEND	FADINGS
ENLACE	ENTERS	EPIMERS	ESCHEW	METHANE	REVOLVE	EXPENDS	FAERIE
ENLACED	CENTERS	EPIZOA	ESCHEWS	ETHANES	EVOLVED	EXPERT	FAERIES
ENLACES	RENTERS	EPIZOAN	ESCORT	ETHENE	EVOLVES	EXPERTS	FAGGOT
ENLARD	TENTERS	EPOCHA	ESCORTS	ETHENES	EVOVAE	EXPIRE	FAGGOTS
ENLARDS	VENTERS	EPOCHAL	ESCROC	ETHERS	EVOVAES	EXPIRED	FAIBLE
ENLINK	ENTETE	EPOCHAS	ESCROCS	AETHERS	EVULSE	EXPIRES	FAIBLES
ENLINKS	ENTETEE	EPONYM	ESCROL	PETHERS	EVULSED	EXPORT	FAILLE
ENLIST	ENTICE	EPONYMS	ESCROLL	TETHERS	EVULSES	EXPORTS	FAILLES
ENLISTS	PENTICE	EPOPEE	ESCROLS	WETHERS	EVZONE	EXPOSE	FAINES
ENLOCK	ENTICED		ESCROW	ETHNIC		EXPOSED	FAINEST

FAITOR	FAUCET	FESTALS	FILTER	FIZZEN	FODDERS	FORMER	FRICHTS
FAITORS	FAUCETS	FESTER	FILTERS	FIZZENS	FOETOR	FORMERS	FRIDGE
FALCON	FAUTOR	FESTERS	FIMBLE	FIZZER	FOETORS	FORMOL	FRIDGED
FALCONS	FAUTORS	FETICH	FIMBLES	FIZZERS	FOGGER	FORMOLS	FRIDGES
FALLAL	FAVELA	FETICHE	FINALE	FIZZLE	FOGGERS	FORPET	FRIEND
FALLALS	FAVELAS	FETTER	FINALES	FIZZLED	FOGLESS	FORPETS	FRIENDS
FALLOW	FAVISM	FETTERS	FINDER	FIZZLES	FOGRAM	FORPIT	FRIEZE
FALLOWS	FAVISMS	FETTLE	FINDERS	FLACON	FOGRAMS	FORPITS	FRIEZED
FALSER	FAVOUR	FETTLED	FINEER	FLACONS	FOIBLE	FORRAY	FRIEZES
FALSERS	FAVOURS	FETTLER	FINEERS	FLAGON	FOIBLES	FORRAYS	FRIGHT
FALSES	FAWNER	FETTLES	FINGAN	FLAGONS	FOISON	FORSAY	FRIGHTS
FALSEST	FAWNERS	FEUTRE	FINGANS	FLAMEN	FOISONS	FORSAYS	FRIGOT
FALSIE	FEAGUE	FEUTRED	FINGER	FLAMENS	FOLDER	FOSSIL	FRIGOTS
FALSIES	FEAGUED	FEUTRES	FINGERS	FLANGE	FOLDERS	FOSSILS	FRIJOL
FALTER	FEAGUES	FEWMET	FINIAL	FLANGED	FOLIOS	FOSSOR	FRIJOLE
FALTERS	FEARED	FEWMETS	FINIALS	FLANGES	FOLIOSE	FOSSORS	FRINGE
FAMINE	AFEARED	FEWTER	FINING	FLASER	FOLLOW	FOSTER	FRINGED
FAMINES	FECULA	FEWTERS	FININGS	FLASERS	FOLLOWS	FOSTERS	FRINGES
FANDOM	FECULAS	FIACRE	FINJAN	FLAUNE	FOMENT	FOTHER	FRIPON
FANDOMS	FEDORA	FIACRES	FINJANS	FLAUNES	FOMENTS	FOTHERS	FRIPONS
FANGLE	FEDORAS	FIANCE	FINNAC	FLAUNT	FONDLE	FOUGHT	FRISKA
FANGLED	FEEBLE	FIANCEE	FINNACK	FLAUNTS	FONDLED	FOUGHTY	FRISKAS
FANGLES	FEEBLED	FIANCES	FINNACS	FLAUNTY	FONDLER	FOULES	FRIVOL
FANION	FEEBLER	FIASCO	FINNAN	FLAVIN	FONDLES	FOULEST	FRIVOLS
FANIONS	FEEBLES	FIASCOS	FINNANS	FLAVINE	FONDUE	FOURTH	FROISE
FANKLE	FEEDER	FIAUNT	FINNER	FLAVINS	FONDUES	FOURTHS	FROISES
FANKLED	FEEDERS	FIAUNTS	FINNERS	FLAYER	FOODIE	FOUSSA	FROLIC
FANKLES	FEELER	FIBBER	FIORIN	FLAYERS	FOODIES	FOUSSAS	FROLICS
FANNEL	FEELERS	FIBBERS	FIORINS	FLECHE	FOOTER	FOUTER	FROWIE
FANNELL	FEERIE	FIBBERY	FIPPLE	FLECHES	FOOTERS	FOUTERS	FROWIER
FANNELS	FEERIES	FIBRIL	FIPPLES	FLEDGE	FOOTIE	FOUTRA	FROWST
FANNER	FEERIN	FIBRILS	FIRING	FLEDGED	FOOTLE	FOUTRAS	FROWSTS
FANNERS	FEERING	FIBRIN	FIRINGS	FLEDGES	FOOTLED	FOUTRE	FROWSTY
FANTAD	FEERINS	FIBRINS	FIRKIN	FLEECE	FOOTLES	FOUTRES	FRUICT
FANTADS	FELINE	FIBROS	FIRKING	FLEECED	FOOTRA	FOWLER	FRUICTS
FANTOD	FELINES	FIBROSE	FIRKINS	FLEECER	FOOTRAS	FOWLERS	FRYING
FANTODS	FELLAH	FIBULA	FIRLOT	FLEECES	FOOZLE	FOXING	FRYINGS
FANTOM	FELLAHS	FIBULAR	FIRLOTS	FLENSE	FOOZLED	FOXINGS	FUCKER
FANTOMS	FELLER	FIBULAS	FIRMAN	FLENSED	FOOZLER	FRAGOR	FUCKERS
FAQUIR	FELLERS	FICKLE	FIRMANS	FLENSES	FOOZLES	FRAGORS	FUCOID
FAQUIRS	FELLOE	FICKLED	FIRMER	FLEXOR	FORAGE	FRAISE	FUCOIDS
FARCIN	FELLOES	FICKLER	FIRMERS	FLEXORS	FORAGED	FRAISED	FUDDLE
FARCING	FELLOW	FICKLES	FISCAL	FLIGHT	FORAGER	FRAISES	FUDDLED
FARCINS	FELLOWS	FICTOR	FISCALS	FLIGHTS	FORAGES	FRAMER	FUDDLER
FARDEL	FELTER	FICTORS	FISGIG	FLIGHTY	FORBAD	FRAMERS	FUDDLES
FARDELS	FELTERS	FIDDLE	FISGIGS	FLORET	FORBADE	FRAPPE	FUGATO
FARDEN	FEMALE	FIDDLED	FISHER	FLORETS	FORBID	FRAPPED	FUGATOS
FARDENS	FEMALES	FIDDLER	FISHERS	FLORIN	FORBIDS	FRAPPEE	FULFIL
FARINA	FEMORA	FIDDLES	FISHERY	FLORINS	FORCAT	FRATCH	FULFILS
FARINAS	FEMORAL	FIDDLEY	FISSLE	FLOTEL	FORCATS	FRATCHY	FULGOR
FARMER	FENCER	FIDGET	FISSLED	FLOTELS	FORCER	FRATER	FULGORS
FARMERS	FENCERS	FIDGETS	FISSLES	FLOUSE	FORCERS	FRATERS	FULHAM
FARMERY	FENDER	FIDGETY	FITCHE	FLOUSED	FOREST	FRATERY	FULHAMS
FARREN	FENDERS	FIERCE	FITCHEE	FLOUSES	FORESTS	FRAZIL	FULLAM
FARRENS	FENNEC	FIERCER	FITCHES	FLOWER	FORGER	FRAZILS	FULLAMS
FARROW	FENNECS	FIESTA	FITCHET	FLOWERS	FORGERS	FREETS	FULLAN
FARROWS	FENNEL	FIESTAS	FITCHEW	FLOWERY	FORGERY	AFREETS	FULLANS
FASCIA	FENNELS	FIGURE	FITTER	FLUATE	FORGET	FREEZE	FULLER
FASCIAL	FERREL	FIGURED	FITTERS	FLUATES	FORGETS	FREEZER	FULLERS
FASCIAS	FERRELS	FIGURES	FITTES	FLUENT	FORHOO	FREEZES	FULMAR
FASTEN	FERRET	FILFOT	FITTEST	FLUENTS	FORHOOS	FREMIT	FULMARS
FASTENS	FERRETS	FILFOTS	FIXATE	FLUGEL	FORHOW	FREMITS	FUMADO
FASTER	FERRETY	FILING	FIXATED	FLUGELS	FORHOWS	FRENNE	FUMADOS
FASTERS	FERULA	FILINGS	FIXATES	FLUTER	FORINT	FRENNES	FUMAGE
FATHER	FERULAS	FILLER	FIXING	FLUTERS	FORINTS	FRESCO	FUMAGES
FATHERS	FERULE	FILLERS	FIXINGS	FLYING	FORKER	FRESCOS	FUMBLE
FATHOM	FERULES	FILLET	FIXURE	FLYINGS	FORKERS	FRIAND	FUMBLED
FATHOMS	FESCUE	FILLETS	FIXURES	FLYWAY	FORMAT	FRIANDE	FUMBLER
FATTEN	FESCUES	FILLIP	FIZGIG	FLYWAYS	FORMATE	FRIANDS	FUMBLES
FATTENS	FESTAL	FILLIPS	FIZGIGS	FODDER	FORMATS	FRICHT	FUNDER

FUNDERS	GAITER	GARCONS	GAWPER	GHETTOS	GIRDERS	GOATEE	GOOSEY
FUNKIA	GAITERS	GARDEN	GAWPERS	GIAOUR	GIRDLE	GOATEED	GOOSEYS
FUNKIAS	GALAGE	GARDENS	GAZEBO	GIAOURS	GIRDLED	GOATEES	GOPHER
FUNNEL	GALAGES	GARGET	GAZEBOS	GIBBER	GIRDLER	GOBANG	GOPHERS
FUNNELS	GALENA	GARGETS	GAZOON	GIBBERS	GIRDLES	GOBANGS	GOPURA
FURANE	GALENAS	GARGLE	GAZOONS	GIBBET	GIRKIN	GOBBET	GOPURAM
FURANES	GALERE	GARGLED	GAZUMP	GIBBETS	GIRKINS	GOBBETS	GOPURAS
FUREUR	GALERES	GARGLES	GAZUMPS	GIBBON	GIRLIE	GOBBLE	GORGET
FUREURS	GALIOT	GARIAL	GEEZER	GIBBONS	GIRLIES	GOBBLED	GORGETS
FURFUR	GALIOTS	GARIALS	GEEZERS	GIBLET	GIRNEL	GOBBLER	GORGIA
FURFURS	GALLET	GARJAN	GEISHA	GIBLETS	GIRNELS	GOBBLES	GORGIAS
FUROLE	GALLETS	GARJANS	GEISHAS	GIDGEE	GIRNIE	GOBLET	GORGIO
FUROLES	GALLEY	GARLIC	GEISTS	GIDGEES	GIRNIER	GOBLETS	GORGIOS
FURORE	GALLEYS	GARLICS	AGEISTS	GIDJEE	GITANA	GOBLIN	GORGON
FURORES	GALLON	GARNER	GELADA	GIDJEES	GITANAS	GOBLINS	GORGONS
FURROW	GALLONS	GARNERS	GELADAS	GIGGIT	GITANO	GODDAM	GORING
FURROWS	GALLOP	GARNET	GELATI	GIGGITS	GITANOS	GODDAMN	GORINGS
FURROWY	GALLOPS	GARNETS	GELATIN	GIGGLE	GIVING	GODOWN	GOSLET
FUSAIN	GALLOW	GARRAN	GELDER	GIGGLED	GIVINGS	GODOWNS	GOSLETS
FUSAINS	GALLOWS	GARRANS	GELDERS	GIGGLER	GIZZEN	GODSON	GOSPEL
FUSION	GALOOT	GARRET	GENDER	GIGGLES	GIZZENS	GODSONS	GOSPELS
FUSIONS	GALOOTS	GARRETS	GENDERS	GIGLET	GLAIVE	GODWIT	GOSSAN
FUSSER	GALUTH	GARRON	GENERA	GIGLETS	GLAIVED	GODWITS	GOSSANS
FUSSERS	GALUTHS	GARRONS	GENERAL	GIGLOT	GLAIVES	GOFFER	GOSSIB
FUSTET	GAMBET	GARROT	GENEVA	GIGLOTS	GLAMOR	GOFFERS	GOSSIBS
FUSTETS	GAMBETS	GARROTE	GENEVAS	GIGOLO	GLAMORS	GOGGLE	GOSSIP
FUSTIC	GAMBIR	GARROTS	GENNET	GIGOLOS	GLANCE	GOGGLED	GOSSIPS
FUSTICS	GAMBIRS	GARRYA	GENNETS	GILCUP	GLANCED	GOGGLER	GOSSIPY
FUSTOC	GAMBIT	GARRYAS	GENOME	GILCUPS	GLANCES	GOGGLES	GOURDE
FUSTOCS	GAMBITS	GARTER	GENOMES	GILDER	GLAZER	GOGLET	GOURDES
FUTILE	GAMBLE	GARTERS	GENTLE	GILDERS	GLAZERS	GOGLETS	GOUTTE
FUTILER	GAMBLED	GARUDA	GENTLED	GILGAI	GLEAVE	GOITER	GOUTTES
FUTURE	GAMBLER	GARUDAS	GENTLER	GILGAIS	GLEAVES	GOITERS	GOVERN
FUTURES	GAMBLES	GARVIE	GENTLES	GILGIE	GLEDGE	GOITRE	GOVERNS
FUZZLE	GAMBOL	GARVIES	GENTOO	GILGIES	GLEDGED	GOITRED	GOWFER
FUZZLED	GAMBOLS	GASCON	GENTOOS	GILLET	GLEDGES	GOITRES	GOWFERS
FUZZLES	GAMETE	GASCONS	GEODES	GILLETS	GLIDER	GOLDEN	GOWPEN
FYLFOT	GAMETES	GASKET	GEODESY	GILLIE	GLIDERS	GOLDENS	GOWPENS
FYLFOTS	GAMINE	GASKETS	GERBIL	GILLIED	GLIOMA	GOLFER	GOZZAN
GABBER	GAMINES	GASKIN	GERBILS	GILLIES	GLIOMAS	GOLFERS	GOZZANS
GABBERS	GAMING	GASKINS	GERENT	GILPEY	GLOBIN	GOLLAN	GRABEN
GABBLE	GAMINGS	GASPER	GERENTS	GILPEYS	GLOBINS	GOLLAND	GRABENS
GABBLED	GAMMER	GASPERS	GERMAN	GIMBAL	GLOIRE	GOLLANS	GRADER
GABBLER	GAMMERS	GATEAU	GERMANE	GIMBALS	GLOIRES	GOLLAR	GRADERS
GABBLES	GAMMON	GATEAUS	GERMANS	GIMLET	GLORIA	GOLLARS	GRADIN
GABBRO	GAMMONS	GATEAUX	GERMEN	GIMLETS	GLORIAS	GOLLOP	GRADINE
GABBROS	GANDER	GATHER	GERMENS	GIMMAL	GLOSSA	GOLLOPS	GRADING
GABION	GANDERS	GATHERS	GERMIN	GIMMALS	GLOSSAE	GOMBRO	GRADINI
GABIONS	GANGER	GATING	GERMING	GIMMER	GLOSSAL	GOMBROS	GRADINO
GABLET	GANGERS	GATINGS	GERMINS	GIMMERS	GLOSSAS	GOMOKU	GRADINS
GABLETS	GANGUE	GAUCHE	GERUND	GIMMOR	GLOVER	GOMOKUS	GRAILE
GADDER	GANGUES	GAUCHER	GERUNDS	GIMMORS	GLOVERS	GOMUTI	GRAILES
GADDERS	GANNET	GAUCHO	GETTER	GINGAL	GLOWER	GOMUTIS	GRAINE
GADGET	GANNETS	GAUCHOS	GETTERS	GINGALL	GLOWERS	GOMUTO	GRAINED
GADGETS	GANOID	GAUCIE	GEWGAW	GINGALS	GLUTEN	GOMUTOS	GRAINER
GADGIE	GANOIDS	GAUCIER	GEWGAWS	GINGER	GLUTENS	GOOBER	GRAINES
GADGIES	GANOIN	GAUFER	GEYSER	GINGERS	GLYCIN	GOOBERS	GRAITH
GADOID	GANOINS	GAUFERS	GEYSERS	GINGERY	GLYCINS	GOOGLE	GRAITHS
GADOIDS	GAOLER	GAUFRE	GHARRI	GINGLE	GLYCOL	GOOGLED	GRAKLE
GAFFER	GAOLERS	GAUFRES	GHARRIS	GINGLED	GLYCOLS	GOOGLES	GRAKLES
GAFFERS	GAPING	GAUGER	GHAZAL	GINGLES	GNAWER	GOOGOL	GRAMAS
GAGAKU	GAPINGS	GAUGERS	GHAZALS	GINNEL	GNAWERS	GOOGOLS	GRAMASH
GAGAKUS	GARAGE	GAUPER	GHAZEL	GINNELS	GNOMON	GOOLEY	GRAMME
GAGGER	GARAGED	GAUPERS	GHAZELS	GINNER	GNOMONS	GOOLEYS	GRAMMES
GAGGERS	GARAGES	GAVAGE	GHERAO	GINNERS	GOALIE	GOOLIE	GRANDE
GAGGLE	GARBLE	GAVAGES	GHERAOS	GINNERY	GOALIES	GOOLIES	GRANDEE
GAGGLED	GARBLED	GAVIAL	GHESSE	GIPSEN	GOANNA	GOONEY	GRANDER
GAGGLES	GARBLER	GAVIALS	GHESSED	GIPSENS	GOANNAS	GOONEYS	GRANGE
GAINER	GARBLES	GAWKER	GHESSES	GIRDER	GOANNAS	GOOROO	GRANGER
GAINERS	GARCON	GAWKERS	GHETTO	GIRDER		GOOROOS	GRANGES

GRAPLE	GROCERS	GUISER	GYMBALS	HAIQUES	HANGARS	HARTENS	HEALER
GRAPLES	GROCERY	GUISERS	GYMMAL	HAIRED	HANGED	HASHES	HEALERS
GRAPPA	GROMET	GUISES	GYMMALS	CHAIRED	CHANGED	SHASHES	HEALTH
GRAPPAS	GROMETS	AGUISES	GYNNEY	HAIRST	PHANGED	HASLET	HEALTHS
GRASTE	GROOVE	GUITAR	GYNNEYS	HALERS	WHANGED	HASLETS	HEALTHY
AGRASTE	GROOVED	GUITARS	GYPPIE	THALERS	HANGER	HASSAR	HEARER
GRATER	GROOVES	GUIZER	GYPPIES	HALIDE	CHANGER	HASSARS	SHEARER
GRATERS	GROPER	GUIZERS	GYPSUM	HALIDES	HANGERS	HASSLE	HEARERS
GRAVEL	GROPERS	GULDEN	GYPSUMS	HALING	HANJAR	HASSLED	HEARSE
GRAVELS	GROSER	GULDENS	GYRATE	SHALING	KHANJAR	HASSLES	HEARSED
GRAVELY	GROSERS	GULLER	GYRATED	WHALING	HANJARS	HASTED	HEARSES
GRAVER	GROSERT	GULLERY	GYRATES	HALITE	HANKED	GHASTED	HEARTH
GRAVERS	GROSET	GULLET	HABOOB	HALITES	SHANKED	HASTEN	HEARTHS
GRAVES	GROSETS	GULLETS	HABOOBS	HALLAL	THANKED	CHASTEN	HEASTE
GRAVEST	GROTTO	GULLEY	HACHIS	HALLALI	HANKER	HASTENS	HEASTES
GRAYLE	GROTTOS	GULLEYS	RHACHIS	HALLALS	THANKER	HATFUL	HEATED
GRAYLES	GROUCH	GULPER	HACKED	HALLAN	HANKERS	HATFULS	CHEATED
GRAZER	GROUCHY	GULPERS	CHACKED	HALLANS	HANSEL	HATPEG	HEATER
GRAZERS	GROUND	GUMNUT	WHACKED	HALLOA	HANSELS	HATPEGS	CHEATER
GREASE	AGROUND	GUMNUTS	HACKEE	HALLOAS	HANSOM	HATPIN	THEATER
GREASED	GROUNDS	GUNITE	HACKEES	HALLOO	HANSOMS	HATPINS	HEATERS
GREASER	GROUSE	GUNITES	HACKER	HALLOOS	HANTLE	HATRED	HEATHS
GREASES	GROUSED	GUNNEL	WHACKER	HALLOW	HANTLES	HATREDS	HEATHY
GREAVE	GROUSER	GUNNELS	HACKERS	SHALLOW	HAPPED	HATTED	HEAUME
GREAVED	GROUSES	GUNNER	HACKERY	HALLOWS	CHAPPED	CHATTED	HEAUMES
GREAVES	GROVEL	GUNNERA	HACKLE	HALOID	WHAPPED	HATTER	HEAVED
GREECE	GROVELS	GUNNERS	SHACKLE	HALOIDS	HAPPEN	CHATTER	SHEAVED
GREECES	GROWER	GUNNERY	HACKLED	HALSER	HAPPENS	HATTERS	HEAVEN
GREESE	GROWERS	GUNSEL	HACKLES	HALSERS	HAPTIC	HAUGHT	HEAVENS
GREESES	GROWTH	GUNSELS	HACKLET	HALTER	HAPTICS	HAUGHTY	HEAVER
GREETE	GROWTHS	GUNTER	HADDIE	HALTERS	HARBOR	HAULER	HEAVERS
GREETED	GROYNE	GUNTERS	HADDIES	HALVAH	HARBORS	HAULERS	HEAVES
GREETES	GROYNES	GUNYAH	HADING	HALVAHS	HARDEN	HAUNTS	SHEAVES
GRICER	GRUDGE	GUNYAHS	SHADING	HALVER	HARDENS	CHAUNTS	THEAVES
GRICERS	GRUDGED	GURAMI	HADITH	HALVERS	HAREEM	HAUYNE	HEBONA
GRIECE	GRUDGES	GURAMIS	HADITHS	HAMBLE	HAREEMS	HAUYNES	HEBONAS
GRIECED	GRUMPH	GURGLE	HADRON	SHAMBLE	HARELD	HAVERS	HECKLE
GRIECES	GRUMPHS	GURGLED	HADRONS	HAMBLED	HARELDS	SHAVERS	HECKLED
GRIEVE	GRYFON	GURGLES	HAEMIN	HAMBLES	HARING	HAVING	HECKLER
GRIEVED	GRYFONS	GURJUN	HAEMINS	HAMING	CHARING	HAVINGS	HECKLES
GRIEVER	GUANAS	GURJUNS	HAFFET	SHAMING	SHARING	HAWING	HECTIC
GRIEVES	IGUANAS	GURLET	HAFFETS	HAMLET	HARKED	CHAWING	HECTICS
GRIFFE	GUANIN	GURLETS	HAFFIT	CHAMLET	SHARKED	SHAWING	HECTOR
GRIFFES	GUANINE	GURNET	HAFFITS	HAMLETS	HARKEN	THAWING	HECTORS
GRIGRI	GUANINS	GURNETS	HAFTED	HAMMAL	HARKENS	HAWKER	HEDDLE
GRIGRIS	GUBBAH	GURNEY	SHAFTED	HAMMALS	HARLOT	HAWKERS	HEDDLED
GRILLE	GUBBAHS	GURNEYS	HAGBUT	HAMMAM	HARLOTS	HAWKEY	HEDDLES
GRILLED	GUDDLE	GURRAH	HAGBUTS	HAMMAMS	HARMAN	HAWKEYS	HEDGER
GRILLES	GUDDLED	GURRAHS	HAGDEN	HAMMED	HARMANS	HAWKIE	HEDGERS
GRILSE	GUDDLES	GUSHER	HAGDENS	SHAMMED	HARMED	HAWKIES	HEEHAW
GRILSES	GUENON	GUSHERS	HAGDON	WHAMMED	CHARMED	HAWSER	HEEHAWS
GRINGO	GUENONS	GUSLAR	HAGDONS	HAMMER	HARMEL	HAWSERS	HEELED
GRINGOS	GUFFAW	GUSLARS	HAGGED	SHAMMER	HARMELS	HAYING	SHEELED
GRIPER	GUFFAWS	GUSSET	SHAGGED	HAMMERS	HARMIN	HAYINGS	WHEELED
GRIPERS	GUGGLE	GUSSETS	HAGGIS	HAMPER	HARMINE	HAYMOW	HEELER
GRIPPE	GUGGLED	GUTTER	HAGGISH	HAMPERS	HARMING	HAYMOWS	WHEELER
GRIPPED	GUGGLES	GUTTERS	HAGGLE	HAMZAH	HARMINS	HAYSEL	HEELERS
GRIPPER	GUIDER	GUTTLE	HAGGLED	HAMZAHS	HARPED	HAYSELS	HEEZED
GRIPPES	GUIDERS	GUTTLED	HAGGLER	HANCES	SHARPED	HAZARD	PHEEZED
GRISED	GUIDON	GUTTLES	HAGGLES	CHANCES	HARPER	HAZARDS	WHEEZED
AGRISED	GUIDONS	GUTZER	HAGLET	HANDER	SHARPER	HAZELS	HEEZES
GRISES	GUILER	GUTZERS	HAGLETS	HANDERS	HARPERS	GHAZELS	PHEEZES
AGRISES	GUILERS	GUYLER	HAIDUK	HANDLE	HARROW	HAZING	WHEEZES
GRISON	GUIMPE	GUYLERS	HAIDUKS	HANDLED	HARROWS	HAZINGS	HEEZIE
GRISONS	GUIMPED	GUZZLE	HAILER	HANDLER	HARTAL	HEADER	HEEZIES
GRIVET	GUIMPES	GUZZLED	HAILERS	HANDLES	HARTALS	HEADERS	HEGIRA
GRIVETS	GUINEA	GUZZLER	HAINED	HANGAR	HARTEN	HEALED	HEGIRAS
GRIZES	GUINEAS	GUZZLES	CHAINED			SHEALED	HEIFER
AGRIZES	GUISED	GYMBAL	HAIQUE				
GROCER	AGUISED						

HEIFERS
HEIGHT
AHEIGHT
HEIGHTS
HEISTS
THEISTS
HEJIRA
HEJIRAS
HELIUM
HELIUMS
HELLED
SHELLED
HELLER
SHELLER
HELLERS
HELMED
WHELMED
HELMET
HELMETS
HELPED
WHELPED
HELPER
HELPERS
HELVED
SHELVED
HELVES
SHELVES
THELVES
HEMINA
HEMINAS
HENNER
HENNERS
HENNERY
HENNIN
HENNING
HENNINS
HEPTAD
HEPTADS
HERALD
HERALDS
HERBAL
HERBALS
HERBAR
HERBARS
HERBARY
HERDEN
HERDENS
HERDIC
HERDICS
HEREAT
THEREAT
WHEREAT
HEREBY
THEREBY
WHEREBY
HEREIN
THEREIN
WHEREIN
HEREOF
THEREOF
WHEREOF
HEREON
THEREON
WHEREON
HERETO
THERETO
WHERETO
HERIOT
HERIOTS
HERMAE

THERMAE
HERMIT
HERMITS
HERNIA
HERNIAL
HERNIAS
HEROIC
HEROICS
HEROIN
HEROINE
HEROINS
HEROON
HEROONS
HETHER
THETHER
WHETHER
HETMAN
HETMANS
HEUCHS
SHEUCHS
HEUGHS
SHEUGHS
WHEUGHS
CHEWING
SHEWING
WHEWING
HEWINGS
HEXACT
HEXACTS
HEXANE
HEXANES
HEXENE
HEXENES
HEXING
HEXINGS
HEXOSE
HEXOSES
HEYDAY
HEYDAYS
HICCUP
HICCUPS
HICCUPY
HICKEY
HICKEYS
HIDAGE
HIDAGES
HIDDEN
CHIDDEN
HIDDER
SHIDDER
WHIDDER
HIDDERS
HIDING
CHIDING
HIDINGS
HIGGLE
HIGGLED
HIGGLER
HIGGLES
HIGHER
HIGHERS
HIGHTH
HIGHTHS
HIJACK
HIJACKS
HIJRAH
HIJRAHS
HILLED
CHILLED

SHILLED
HINDER
HINDERS
HINGED
WHINGED
HINGES
WHINGES
HIPPED
CHIPPED
SHIPPED
WHIPPED
HIPPER
CHIPPER
SHIPPER
WHIPPER
HIPPIE
CHIPPIE
HIPPIER
HIPPIES
HIPPOS
SHIPPOS
HIRING
HIRINGS
HIRPLE
HIRPLED
HIRPLES
HIRSEL
HIRSELS
HIRSLE
HIRSLED
HIRSLES
HISHED
WHISHED
HISHES
WHISHES
HISSED
WHISSED
HISSES
WHISSES
HISTED
WHISTED
THITHER
WHITHER
HITHERS
HITTER
CHITTER
WHITTER
HITTERS
SHIVERS
HIVING
CHIVING
HIZZED
WHIZZED
HIZZES
PHIZZES
WHIZZES
HOARSE
HOARSEN
HOARSER
HOAXER
HOAXERS
HOBBIT
HOBBITS
HOBBLE
HOBBLED
HOBBLER
HOBBLES
HOBDAY

HOBDAYS
HOBJOB
HOBJOBS
HOBNOB
HOBNOBS
HOCKED
CHOCKED
SHOCKED
HOCKER
CHOCKER
SHOCKER
HOCKERS
HOCKEY
HOCKEYS
HODDEN
HODDENS
HODDLE
HODDLED
HODDLES
HODJAS
KHODJAS
HOEING
SHOEING
HOGGED
SHOGGED
HOGGER
HOGGERS
HOGGERY
HOGGET
HOGGETS
HOGGIN
HOGGING
HOGGINS
HOGTIE
HOGTIED
HOGTIES
HOIDEN
HOIDENS
HOKIER
CHOKIER
HOKING
CHOKING
HOLDER
HOLDERS
HOLIES
HOLIEST
HOLING
THOLING
HOLINGS
HOLISM
WHOLISM
HOLISMS
HOLIST
HOLISTS
HOLLER
HOLLERS
HOLLOA
HOLLOAS
HOLLOW
HOLLOWS
HOLMIA
HOLMIAS
HOMAGE
HOMAGED
HOMAGER
HOMAGES
HOMELY
HOMELYN

HOMING
HOMINGS
HONEST
HONESTY
HONEYS
HONIED
PHONIED
HONING
PHONING
HONKER
HONKERS
HONKIE
HONKIES
HONOUR
HONOURS
HOODOO
HOODOOS
HOOFER
HOOFERS
HOOKAH
HOOKAHS
HOOKER
HOOKERS
HOOKEY
HOOKEYS
HOOLEY
HOOLEYS
HOOPED
WHOOPED
HOOPER
WHOOPER
HOOPERS
HOOPOE
HOOPOES
HOORAH
HOORAHS
HOORAY
HOORAYS
HOOTED
WHOOTED
HOOTER
HOOTERS
HOOVER
HOOVERS
HOPDOG
HOPDOGS
HOPPED
CHOPPED
SHOPPED
WHOPPED
HOPPER
CHOPPER
SHOPPER
WHOPPER
HOPPERS
HORKEY
HORKEYS
HORNED
THORNED
HORNER
HORNERS
HORNET
HORNETS
HORROR
HORRORS

HORSON
HORSONS
HOSIER
HOSIERS
HOSIERY
HOSTED
PHONEYS
GHOSTED
HOSTEL
HOSTELS
HOTBED
HOTBEDS
HOTPOT
HOTPOTS
SHOTTED
HOTTER
HOTTERS
HOTTIE
HOTTIES
HOUDAH
HOUDAHS
HOUDAN
HOUDANS
HOUGHS
CHOUGHS
SHOUGHS
HOUSED
CHOUSED
HOUSEL
HOUSELS
HOUSES
CHOUSES
SHOVELS
HOVERS
SHOVERS
HOVING
SHOVING
HOWDAH
HOWDAHS
HOWDIE
HOWDIES
HOWKER
HOWKERS
HOWLER
HOWLERS
HOWLET
HOWLETS
HOYDEN
HOYDENS
HUBBUB
HUBBUBS
HUCKLE
CHUCKLE
HUCKLES
HUDDLE
HUDDLED
HUDDLES
HUFFED
CHUFFED
HUGGED
CHUGGED
HUMANE
HUMANER
HUMBLE
HUMBLED
HUMBLER
HUMBLES
HUMBUG
HUMBUGS

HUMECT
HUMECTS
HUMHUM
HUMHUMS
HUMITE
HUMITES
HUMLIE
HUMLIES
HUMMED
CHUMMED
HUMMEL
HUMMELS
HUMMER
HUMMERS
HUMMUM
HUMMUMS
HUMOUR
HUMOURS
HUMPED
THUMPED
HUMPEN
HUMPENS
HUNGER
HUNGERS
AHUNGRY
HUNGRY
HUNKER
HUNKERS
HUNTED
SHUNTED
HUNTER
SHUNTER
HUNTERS
CHUNTER
SHUNTER
HUNTERS
HURDEN
HURDENS
HURDLE
HURDLED
HURDLER
HURDLES
HURLER
HURLERS
HURLEY
HURLEYS
HURRAH
HURRAHS
HURRAS
DHURRAS
HURRAY
HURRAYS
HURTER
HURTERS
HURTLE
HURTLED
HURTLES
HUSHED
SHUSHED
HUSHER
HUSHERS
HUSHES
SHUSHES
HUSKER
HUSKERS
HUSSAR
HUSSARS
HUSSIF
HUSSIFS
HUSTLE
HUSTLED
HUSTLER

HUSTLES
HUZOOR
HUZOORS
HYAENA
HYAENAS
HYBRID
HYBRIDS
HYDRIA
HYDRIAE
HYDRIAS
HYDYNE
HYDYNES
HYLISM
HYLISMS
HYLIST
HYLISTS
HYMNAL
HYMNALS
HYPATE
HYPATES
HYPHEN
HYPHENS
HYPNIC
HYPNICS
HYPNUM
HYPNUMS
HYSSOP
HYSSOPS
IAMBIC
IAMBICS
IBICES
VIBICES
ICHING
MICHING
NICHING
RICHING
ICICLE
ICICLES
ICIEST
DICIEST
RICIEST
ICINGS
DICINGS
ICKERS
BICKERS
DICKERS
KICKERS
LICKERS
NICKERS
PICKERS
RICKERS
TICKERS
WICKERS
YICKERS
ICKIER
DICKIER
PICKIER
IDEATE
IDEATED
IDEATES
IDLING
HIDLING
KIDLING
SIDLING
IFFIER
MIFFIER
NIFFIER
IGNARO
IGNAROS
IGNITE

LIGNITE	IMPAVES	ZINCITE	INFORMS	ZINKIER	INSIDER	INVENTS	MIRITIS
IGNITED	IMPAWN	INCITED	INFULA	INKING	INSIDES	INVERT	IRKING
IGNITER	IMPAWNS	INCITER	INFULAE	DINKING	INSIST	INVERTS	DIRKING
IGNITES	IMPEDE	INCITES	INFUSE	FINKING	INSISTS	INVEST	FIRKING
IGNORE	IMPEDED	INCLIP	INFUSED	JINKING	INSOLE	INVESTS	KIRKING
SIGNORE	IMPEDES	INCLIPS	INFUSER	KINKING	INSOLES	INVITE	LIRKING
IGNORED	IMPEND	INCOME	INFUSES	LINKING	INSOUL	INVITED	YIRKING
IGNORER	IMPENDS	INCOMER	FINGANS	PINKING	INSOULS	INVITEE	IRONER
IGNORES	IMPING	INCOMES	INGANS	RINKING	INSPAN	INVITER	IRONERS
IGUANA	GIMPING	INCUSE	INGATE	SINKING	INSPANS	INVITES	IRRUPT
IGUANAS	LIMPING	INCUSED	INGATES	TINKING	INSTAL	INVOKE	IRRUPTS
ILEXES	PIMPING	INCUSES	INGENU	WINKING	INSTALL	INVOKED	ISABEL
SILEXES	IMPINGE	INDABA	INGENUE	ZINKING	INSTALS	INVOKES	ISABELS
ILICES	IMPISH	INDABAS	INGENUS	INKLED	INSTAR	INWALL	ISATIN
CILICES	WIMPISH	INDART	INGEST	TINKLED	INSTARS	INWALLS	ISATINE
ILLIAD	IMPLEX	INDARTS	INGESTA	INKLES	INSTEP	INWARD	ISATINS
ILLIADS	SIMPLEX	INDENE	INGESTS	KINKLES	INSTEPS	INWARDS	ISCHIA
ILLIPE	IMPONE	INDENES	INGINE	TINKLES	INSTIL	INWICK	ISCHIAL
ILLIPES	IMPONED	INDENT	INGINES	WINKLES	INSTILL	INWICKS	ISLAND
ILLITE	IMPONES	INDENTS	INGLES	INKPOT	INSTILS	INWIND	ISLANDS
TILLITE	IMPORT	INDICT	BINGLES	INKPOTS	INSULA	INWINDS	ISLING
ILLITES	IMPORTS	INDICTS	DINGLES	INLACE	INSULAE	INWORK	AISLING
ILLUDE	IMPOSE	INDIGO	GINGLES	INLACED	INSULAR	INWORKS	ISOBAR
ILLUDED	IMPOSED	INDIGOS	JINGLES	INLACES	INSULAS	INWOVE	ISOBARE
ILLUDES	IMPOSER	WINDIGO	KINGLES	INLAND	INSULT	INWOVEN	ISOBARS
ILLUME	IMPOSES	INDITE	LINGLES	INLANDS	INSULTS	INWRAP	ISOGON
ILLUMED	IMPOST	INDITED	MINGLES	INLIER	INSURE	INWRAPS	ISOGONS
ILLUMES	IMPOSTS	INDITER	PINGLES	INLIERS	INSURED	INYALA	ISOHEL
ILLUPI	IMPUGN	INDITES	SINGLES	INLOCK	INSURER	INYALAS	ISOHELS
ILLUPIS	IMPUGNS	INDIUM	TINGLES	INLOCKS	INSURES	IODATE	ISOMER
IMBARK	IMPURE	INDIUMS	INGOES	INMATE	INTAKE	IODATES	ISOMERE
IMBARKS	IMPURER	INDOLE	DINGOES	INMATES	INTAKES	IODIDE	ISOMERS
IMBARS	IMPUTE	INDOLES	JINGOES	INNATE	INTEND	IODIDES	ISOPOD
MIMBARS	IMPUTED	INDOOR	LINGOES	PINNATE	INTENDS	IODINE	ISOPODS
IMBASE	IMPUTER	INDOORS	PINGOES	INNERS	INTENT	IODINES	ISSUED
IMBASED	IMPUTES	INDUCE	INGOTS	DINNERS	INTENTS	IODISE	ISSUER
IMBASES	INANES	INDUCED	LINGOTS	FINNERS	INTERN	IODISED	ISSUERS
IMBIBE	INANEST	INDUCER	INGULF	GINNERS	INTERNE	IODISES	ISSUES
IMBIBED	INCAGE	INDUCES	INGULFS	PINNERS	INTERNS	IODISM	TISSUED
IMBIBER	INCAGED	INDUCT	INHALE	SINNERS	INTERS	IODISMS	TISSUES
IMBIBES	INCAGES	INDUCTS	INHALED	TINNERS	LINTERS	IODIZE	ISTLES
IMBOSK	INCASE	INDULT	INHALER	WINNERS	MINTERS	IODIZED	MISTLES
IMBOSKS	PINCASE	INDULTS	INHALES	INNING	SINTERS	IODIZES	ITALIC
IMBRUE	INCASED	INDUNA	INHERE	BINNING	TINTERS	IOLITE	ITALICS
IMBRUED	INCASES	INDUNAS	INHERED	DINNING	WINTERS	IOLITES	ITCHED
IMBRUES	INCAVE	INFALL	INHERES	GINNING	INTIMA	IONISE	BITCHED
IMMASK	INCAVED	INFALLS	INHOOP	LINNING	INTIMAE	LIONISE	DITCHED
IMMASKS	INCAVES	INFAME	INHOOPS	PINNING	INTINE	IONISED	HITCHED
IMMUNE	INCEDE	INFAMED	INHUME	RINNING	INTINES	IONISER	MITCHED
IMMUNES	INCEDED	INFAMES	INHUMED	SINNING	INTOMB	IONISES	PITCHED
IMMURE	INCEDES	INFANT	INHUMES	TINNING	INTOMBS	IONIUM	WITCHED
IMMURED	INCEPT	INFANTA	INISLE	WINNING	INTONE	IONIUMS	ITCHES
IMMURES	INCEPTS	INFANTE	INISLED	INNINGS	INTONED	IONIZE	AITCHES
IMPACT	INCEST	INFANTS	INISLES	INROAD	INTONER	LIONIZE	BITCHES
IMPACTS	INCESTS	INFARE	INJECT	INROADS	INTONES	IONIZED	DITCHES
IMPAIR	INCHED	INFARES	INJECTS	INSANE	INTRON	IONIZER	FITCHES
IMPAIRS	CINCHED	INFECT	INJURE	INSANER	INTRONS	IONIZES	HITCHES
IMPALA	FINCHED	INFECTS	INJURED	INSEAM	INTUIT	IONONE	MITCHES
IMPALAS	PINCHED	INFEFT	INJURER	INSEAMS	INTUITS	IONONES	PITCHES
IMPALE	WINCHED	INFEFTS	INJURES	INSECT	INTUSE	IPECAC	TITCHES
IMPALED	INCHES	INFEST	INKERS	INSECTS	INTUSES	IPECACS	WITCHES
IMPALES	CINCHES	INFESTS	JINKERS	INSECTY	INULAS	IRADES	IZARDS
IMPARK	FINCHES	INFILL	SINKERS	INSEEM	INULASE	TIRADES	LIZARDS
IMPARKS	LINCHES	INFILLS	TINKERS	INSEEMS	INULIN	IREFUL	RIZARDS
IMPARL	PINCHES	INFLOW	WINKERS	INSERT	INULINS	DIREFUL	VIZARDS
IMPARLS	WINCHES	INFLOWS	INKIER	INSERTS	INVADE	IRENIC	WIZARDS
IMPART	INCISE	INFOLD	DINKIER	INSHIP	INVADED	EIRENIC	IZZARD
IMPARTS	INCISED	PINFOLD	KINKIER	KINSHIP	INVADER	SIRENIC	DIZZARD
IMPAVE	INCISES	INFOLDS	PINKIER	INSHIPS	INVADES	IRENICS	GIZZARD
IMPAVED	INCITE	INFORM	SINKIER	INSIDE	INVENT	IRITIS	IZZARDS

JABBER	JAUNCES	JILLETS	JUDDERS	**KAISER**	**KEELER**	**KHODJA**	KIPPERS
JABBERS	**JAUNSE**	JIMJAM	**JUDOGI**	KAISERS	KEELERS	KHODJAS	**KIRBEH**
JABBLE	JAUNSED	JIMJAMS	JUDOGIS	**KAKAPO**	**KEELIE**	**KHURTA**	KIRBEHS
JABBLED	JAUNSES	**JINGAL**	**JUDOKA**	KAKAPOS	KEELIES	KHURTAS	**KIRPAN**
JABBLES	**JAWARI**	JINGALS	JUDOKAS	**KALIAN**	**KEENER**	KIAUGHS	KIRPANS
JABIRU	JAWARIS	**JINGLE**	**JUGFUL**	KALIANS	KEENERS	**KIRTLE**
JABIRUS	**JAWING**	JINGLED	JUGFULS	**KALIUM**	**KEEPER**	**KIBBLE**	KIRTLED
JACANA	JAWINGS	JINGLER	**JUGGLE**	KALIUMS	KEEPERS	KIBBLED	KIRTLES
JACANAS	**JEBELS**	JINGLES	JUGGLED	**KALMIA**	**KEFFEL**	KIBBLES	**KISMET**
JACKAL	DJEBELS	JINGLET	JUGGLER	KALMIAS	KEFFELS	**KIBLAH**	KISMETS
JACKALS	**JEELIE**	**JINKER**	JUGGLES	**KALONG**	**KEKSYE**	KIBLAHS	**KISSER**
JACKET	JEELIED	JINKERS	**JUICER**	KALONGS	KEKSYES	**KICKER**	KISSERS
JACKETS	JEELIES	**JIRBLE**	JUICERS	**KALPAK**	**KELOID**	KICKERS	**KITING**
JAEGER	**JEERER**	JIRBLED	**JUJUBE**	KALPAKS	KELOIDS	SKIDDED	SKITING
JAEGERS	JEERERS	JIRBLES	JUJUBES	**KAMALA**	**KELPER**	**KIDDER**	**KITSCH**
JAGGER	**JEMIMA**	**JISSOM**	**JUMART**	KAMALAS	KELPERS	KIDDERS	KITSCHY
JAGGERS	JEMIMAS	JISSOMS	JUMARTS	**KAMELA**	**KELPIE**	**KIDDLE**	**KITTEN**
JAGGERY	**JENNET**	**JITNEY**	**JUMBAL**	KAMELAS	KELPIES	KIDDLES	KITTENS
JAGHIR	JENNETS	JITNEYS	JUMBALS	**KAMILA**	**KELSON**	**KIDNAP**	KITTENY
JAGHIRE	**JERBIL**	**JITTER**	**JUMBIE**	KAMILAS	KELSONS	KIDNAPS	**KITTLE**
JAGHIRS	JERBILS	JITTERS	JUMBIES	**KAMSIN**	**KELTER**	**KIDNEY**	SKITTLE
JAGUAR	**JERBOA**	JITTERY	**JUMBLE**	KAMSINS	SKELTER	KIDNEYS	KITTLED
JAGUARS	JERBOAS	**JOANNA**	JUMBLED	**KANAKA**	KELTERS	KITTLER
JAILER	**JEREED**	JOANNAS	JUMBLER	KANAKAS	**KELTIE**	**KIERIE**	KITTLES
JAILERS	JEREEDS	**JOBBER**	JUMBLES	**KANGHA**	KELTIES	KIERIES	**KITTUL**
JAILOR	**JERKER**	JOBBERS	**JUMPER**	KANGHAS	**KELVIN**	**KIKUYU**	KITTULS
JAILORS	JERKERS	JOBBERY	JUMPERS	**KANTAR**	KELVINS	KIKUYUS	**KLAXON**
JAMBEE	**JERKIN**	**JOCKEY**	**JUNGLE**	KANTARS	**KEMPER**	**KILERG**	KLAXONS
JAMBEES	JERKING	JOCKEYS	JUNGLES	**KANTEN**	KEMPERS	KILERGS	**KLEPHT**
JAMBER	JERKINS	**JOGGER**	**JUNGLI**	KANTENS	**KEMPLE**	**KILLED**	KLEPHTS
JAMBERS	**JERQUE**	JOGGERS	JUNGLIS	**KANTHA**	KEMPLES	KILLER	**KLUDGE**
JAMBOK	JERQUED	**JOGGLE**	**JUNIOR**	KANTHAS	SKILLED	KILLERS	KLUDGES
SJAMBOK	JERQUER	JOGGLED	JUNIORS	**KAOLIN**	**KENNEL**	KILLER	**KNAWEL**
JAMBOKS	JERQUES	JOGGLES	**JUNKER**	KAOLINE	KENNELS	KILLERS	KNAWELS
JAMBUL	**JERSEY**	**JOINER**	JUNKERS	KAOLINS	**KENNER**	**KILLUT**	**KNIGHT**
JAMBULS	JERSEYS	JOINERS	**JUNKET**	**KARAIT**	KENNERS	KILLUTS	KNIGHTS
JAMJAR	**JESSIE**	JOINERY	JUNKETS	KARAITS	**KENNET**	**KILTER**	**KNOWER**
JAMJARS	JESSIES	**JOJOBA**	**JUNKIE**	**KARAKA**	KENNETS	KILTERS	KNOWERS
JAMMER	**JESTEE**	JOJOBAS	JUNKIER	KARAKAS	**KEPHIR**	**KILTIE**	**KOBANG**
JAMMERS	JESTEES	**JOLTER**	JUNKIES	**KARATE**	KEPHIRS	KILTIES	KOBANGS
JAMPAN	**JESTER**	JOLTERS	**JUPATI**	KARATES	**KERMES**	**KIMMER**	**KOBOLD**
JAMPANI	JESTERS	**JORDAN**	JUPATIS	**KARITE**	KERMESS	KIMMERS	KOBOLDS
JAMPANS	**JETSAM**	JORDANS	**JURANT**	KARITES	**KERNEL**	SKIMMER	**KONFYT**
JAMPOT	**JETSOM**	**JOSEPH**	JURANTS	**KARSEY**	KERNELS	KIMMONO	KONFYTS
JAMPOTS	JETSOMS	JOSEPHS	**JURIST**	KARSEYS	**KERRIA**	KIMONO	**KOODOO**
JANGLE	**JETSON**	**JOSHER**	JURISTS	**KASBAH**	KERRIAS	OKIMONO	KOODOOS
JANGLED	JETSONS	JOSHERS	**JUSTLE**	KASBAHS	**KERSEY**	KIMONOS	**KOOKIE**
JANGLER	**JETTON**	**JOSKIN**	JUSTLED	**KATANA**	KERSEYS	**KINASE**	KOOKIER
JANGLES	JETTONS	JOSKINS	JUSTLES	KATANAS	**KETONE**	KINASES	**KOOLAH**
JANKER	**JEZAIL**	JOSSER	**JOSSER**	**KABALA**	**KATHAK**	**KINCOB**	KOOLAHS
JANKERS	JEZAILS	JOSSERS	KABALAS	KATHAKS	**KETOSE**	KINCOBS	**KOPECK**
JARFUL	**JIBBAH**	**JOSTLE**	KABAYA	**KATION**	KETOSES	**KINDLE**	KOPECKS
JARFULS	DJIBBAH	JOSTLED	KABAYAS	KATIONS	**KETTLE**	KINDLED	**KOPPIE**
JARGON	JIBBAHS	JOSTLES	**KABELE**	**KEASAR**	KETTLES	KINDLER	KOPPIES
JARGONS	**JIBBER**	**JOTTER**	KABELES	KEASARS	**KGOTLA**	KINDLES	**KORKIR**
JAROOL	JIBBERS	JOTTERS	**KABUKI**	**KEBBIE**	KGOTLAS	**KINGLE**	KORKIRS
JAROOLS	**JIGGER**	**JOTUNN**	KABUKIS	KEBBIES	**KHALAT**	KINGLES	**KORORA**
JARRAH	JIGGERS	JOTUNNS	**KACCHA**	**KEBELE**	KHALATS	KINGLET	KORORAS
JARRAHS	**JIGGLE**	**JOUNCE**	KACCHAS	KEBELES	**KHALIF**	**KINKED**	**KORUNA**
JARVEY	JIGGLED	JOUNCED	**KAFILA**	**KEBLAH**	KHALIFA	SKINKED	KORUNAS
JARVEYS	JIGGLES	JOUNCES	KAFILAS	KEBLAHS	KHALIFS	**KINKLE**	**KOSHER**
JARVIE	**JIGJIG**	**JOURNO**	**KAFTAN**	**KECKLE**	**KHANGA**	KINKLES	KOSHERS
JARVIES	JIGJIGS	JOURNOS	KAFTANS	KECKLED	KHANGAS	**KINONE**	**KOTWAL**
JASPER	**JIGSAW**	**JOWARI**	**KAGOOL**	KECKLES	**KHANUM**	KINONES	KOTWALS
JASPERS	JIGSAWN	JOWARIS	KAGOOLS	**KEDDAH**	KHANUMS	**KINRED**	**KOULAN**
JASPERY	JIGSAWS	**JOWLER**	**KAGOUL**	KEDDAHS	**KHARIF**	KINREDS	KOULANS
JATAKA	**JILGIE**	JOWLERS	KAGOULS	**KEDGER**	KHARIFS	**KIPPED**	**KOWHAI**
JATAKAS	JILGIES	**JUBBAH**	KAGOULE	KEDGERS	**KHILAT**	SKIPPED	KOWHAIS
JAUNCE	**JILLET**	JUBBAHS	KAGOULS	**KEEKER**	KHILATS	**KIPPER**	**KOWTOW**
JAUNCED	JILLETS	**JUDDER**	**KAIKAI**	KEEKERS	**KHILIM**	SKIPPER	KOWTOWS

KRAKEN	LADING	LANCERS	LARGESS	PLATTER	GLEAMED	LEFTIE	LETHEE
KRAKENS	LADINGS	LANCES	LARGEST	SLATTER	LEANED	LEFTIES	LETHEES
KREESE	LAGENA	ELANCES	LARIAT	LAUDED	CLEANED	LEGATE	LETTED
KREESED	LAGENAS	GLANCES	LARIATS	BLAUDED	GLEANED	LEGATEE	BLETTED
KREESES	LAGGED	LANCET	LARKER	LAUDER	LEANER	LEGATES	LETTER
KUFIAH	BLAGGED	LANCETS	LARKERS	LAUDERS	CLEANER	LEGATO	LETTERN
KUFIAHS	CLAGGED	LANDAU	LARRUP	LAUNCE	GLEANER	LEGATOR	LETTERS
KUFIYA	FLAGGED	LANDAUS	LARRUPS	LAUNCED	LEANLY	LEGATOS	LETTRE
KUFIYAH	SLAGGED	LANDER	LARUMS	LAUNCES	CLEANLY	LEGEND	LETTRES
KUFIYAS	LAGGEN	SLANDER	ALARUMS	LAUNCH	LEAPER	LEGENDS	LEUCIN
KUMARA	LAGGENS	LANDERS	LASCAR	FLAUNCH	LEAPERS	LEGGED	LEUCINE
KUMARAS	LAGGER	LANDES	LASCARS	LAUREL	LEARED	ALEGGED	LEUCINS
KUMARI	LAGGERS	BLANDER	LASERS	LAURELS	BLEARED	FLEGGED	LEVANT
KUMARIS	LAGGIN	LANGER	FLASERS	LAVABO	CLEARED	LEGGER	LEVANTS
KUMMEL	LAGGING	CLANGER	LASHED	LAVABOS	LEASED	GLEGGER	LEVINS
KUMMELS	LAGGINS	LANGUE	CLASHED	LAVAGE	PLEASED	LEGGERS	ALEVINS
KUNKAR	LAGOON	LANGUED	FLASHED	LAVAGES	LEASER	ALEGGES	LEVITE
KUNKARS	LAGOONS	LANGUES	PLASHED	LAVEER	PLEASER	LEGION	LEVITES
KUNKUR	LAGUNE	LANGUET	SLASHED	LAVEERS	LEASERS	LEGIONS	LEXEME
KUNKURS	LAGUNES	LANGUR	LASHER	CLAVERS	LEASES	LEGIST	LEXEMES
KURGAN	LAIDED	LANGURS	LASHERS	SLAVERS	PLEASES	LEGISTS	LIABLE
KURGANS	PLAIDED	LANKED	LASHES	LAVING	LEASOW	LEGLAN	PLIABLE
KURVEY	LAIRED	BLANKED	BLASHES	SLAVING	LEASOWE	LEGLANS	LIAISE
KURVEYS	GLAIRED	CLANKED	CLASHES	LAVISH	LEASOWS	LEGLEN	LIAISED
KWACHA	LAISSE	FLANKED	FLASHES	SLAVISH	LEAVED	LEGLENS	LIAISES
KWACHAS	LAISSES	PLANKED	PLASHES	LAVOLT	CLEAVED	LEGLET	LIBATE
LAAGER	LAKIER	LANKER	SLASHES	LAVOLTA	SLEAVED	LEGLETS	LIBATED
LAAGERS	FLAKIER	BLANKER	LASING	LAVOLTS	LEAVEN	LEGLIN	LIBATES
LABIAL	LAKING	FLANKER	LASINGS	LAWING	LEAVENS	LEGLINS	LIBBED
LABIALS	FLAKING	LANKLY	LASKET	LAWINGS	LEAVES	LEGUME	GLIBBED
LABLAB	LALANG	BLANKLY	LASKETS	LAWYER	CLEAVES	LEGUMES	LIBBER
LABLABS	LALANGS	LANNER	LASQUE	LAWYERS	GLEAVES	LEIGER	GLIBBER
LABOUR	LALDIE	PLANNER	LASQUES	LAXISM	SLEAVES	LEIGERS	LIBBERS
LABOURS	LALDIES	LANNERS	LASSES	LAXISMS	LEAZES	LEIPOA	LIBIDO
LABRET	LALLAN	LANUGO	CLASSES	LAXIST	SLEAZES	LEIPOAS	LIBIDOS
LABRETS	LALLANS	LANUGOS	GLASSES	LAXISTS	LEBBEK	LEMING	LIBKEN
LABRID	LAMBDA	LAPDOG	LASSIE	LAYERS	LEBBEKS	FLEMING	LIBKENS
LABRIDS	LAMBDAS	LAPDOGS	LASSIES	FLAYERS	LECHER	LENDER	LICHEE
LACETS	LAMBER	LAPFUL	LASTED	PLAYERS	LECHERS	BLENDER	LICHEES
PLACETS	CLAMBER	LAPFULS	BLASTED	SLAYERS	LECHERY	SLENDER	LICHEN
LACIER	LAMBERS	LAPPED	LASTER	LAYING	LECHES	LENDERS	LICHENS
GLACIER	LAMBERT	CLAPPED	BLASTER	ALAYING	FLECHES	LENGTH	LICHES
LACING	LAMBIE	FLAPPED	LASTERS	CLAYING	LECHWE	ALENGTH	CLICHES
PLACING	LAMBIES	PLAPPED	LATENS	FLAYING	LECHWES	LENGTHS	LICKED
LACINGS	LAMENT	SLAPPED	PLATENS	PLAYING	LECTIN	LENGTHY	CLICKED
LACKED	LAMENTS	LAPPEL	LATEST	SLAYING	LECTINS	LENSES	FLICKED
BLACKED	LAMINA	LAPPELS	LATESTS	LAYINGS	LECTOR	FLENSES	SLICKED
CLACKED	LAMINAE	LAPPER	LATHEE	LAZIER	LECTORS	LENTIL	LICKER
SLACKED	LAMINAR	CLAPPER	LATHEES	GLAZIER	LEDDEN	LENTILS	CLICKER
LACKER	LAMING	FLAPPER	LATHER	LAZING	LEDDENS	LENTOR	FLICKER
BLACKER	FLAMING	SLAPPER	BLATHER	BLAZING	LEDGER	LENTORS	SLICKER
CLACKER	LAMMED	LAPPERS	LATHERS	GLAZING	PLEDGER	LENVOY	LICKERS
FLACKER	CLAMMED	LAPPET	LATHERY	LEADED	LEDGERS	LENVOYS	LICTOR
SLACKER	FLAMMED	LAPPETS	LATRIA	PLEADED	LEDGES	LEPTON	LICTORS
LACKERS	SLAMMED	LAPPIE	LATRIAS	LEADEN	FLEDGES	LEPTONS	LIDGER
LACKEY	LAMMER	LAPPIES	LATRON	LEADENS	GLEDGES	LESION	LIDGERS
LACKEYS	SLAMMER	LAPSED	LATRONS	LEADER	PLEDGES	LESIONS	LIEGER
LACUNA	LAMMERS	ELAPSED	LATTEN	PLEADER	SLEDGES	LESSEE	LIEGERS
LACUNAE	LAMMIE	LAPSES	LATTENS	LEADERS	LEEING	LESSEES	LIERNE
LACUNAL	LAMMIES	ELAPSES	LATTER	LEAGUE	FLEEING	LESSEN	LIERNES
LACUNAR	LAMPAD	LAPTOP	BLATTER	LEAGUED	GLEEING	LESSENS	LIFTED
LADDER	LAMPADS	LAPTOPS	CLATTER	LEAGUER	LEEPED	LESSES	CLIFTED
BLADDER	LAMPED	LARDER	FLATTER	LEAGUES	BLEEPED	BLESSES	LIFTER
CLADDER	CLAMPED	LARDERS		LEAKER	CLEEPED	LESSON	LIFTERS
GLADDER	LANCED	LARDON		BLEAKER	LEERED	LESSONS	LIGAND
LADDERS	ELANCED	LARDONS		LEAKERS	FLEERED	LESSOR	LIGANDS
LADDERY	GLANCED	LARGEN		LEAMED	LEEWAY	PLESSOR	LIGATE
LADDIE	LANCER	LARGENS			LEEWAYS	LESSORS	LIGATED
GLADDIE		LARGES					LIGATES
LADDIES							LIGGER

Column 1: LIGGERS, LIGHTS, ALIGHTS, BLIGHTS, FLIGHTS, PLIGHTS, SLIGHTS, LIGNIN, LIGNINS, LIGNUM, LIGNUMS, LIGULA, LIGULAE, LIGULAR, LIGULAS, LIGULE, LIGULES, LIGURE, LIGURES, LIKING, LIKINGS, LIMAIL, LIMAILS, LIMBEC, LIMBECK, LIMBECS, LIMBED, CLIMBED, LIMBER, CLIMBER, LIMBERS, LIMIER, SLIMIER, LIMING, SLIMING, LIMINGS, LIMMER, GLIMMER, SLIMMER, LIMMERS, LIMNER, LIMNERS, LIMPED, FLIMPED, LIMPET, LIMPETS, LINAGE, LINAGES, LINDEN, LINDENS, LINGAM, LINGAMS, LINGEL, LINGELS, LINGER, CLINGER, FLINGER, SLINGER, LINGERS, LINGLE, LINGLES, LINGOT, LINGOTS, LINGUA, LINGUAE, LINGUAL, LINGUAS, LINHAY, LINHAYS, LINING

Column 2: ALINING, LININGS, LINKED, BLINKED, CLINKED, PLINKED, BLINNED, LINNET, LINNETS, LINNEY, LINNEYS, LINSEY, LINSEYS, LINTEL, LINTELS, LINTER, LINTERS, LINTIE, LINTIER, LINTIES, LIONEL, LIONELS, LIONET, LIONETS, LIPASE, LIPASES, LIPIDE, LIPIDES, LIPOID, LIPOIDS, LIPPED, BLIPPED, CLIPPED, FLIPPED, SLIPPED, LIPPEN, LIPPENS, LIPPIE, CLIPPIE, LIPPIER, LIPPIES, LIQUID, LIQUIDS, LIQUOR, LIQUORS, LISPER, LISPERS, LISSES, BLISSES, LISSOM, LISSOME, LISTEL, LISTELS, LISTEN, GLISTEN, LISTENS, LISTER, BLISTER, GLISTER, LISTERS, LITCHI, LITCHIS, LITHER, BLITHER, SLITHER, LITHES, LITHEST, LITHIA, LITHIAS

Column 3: LITING, FLITING, CLITTER, FLITTER, GLITTER, SLITTER, LITTERS, LITTERY, LITTLE, LITTLER, LITTLES, LIVERS, CLIVERS, OLIVERS, SLIVERS, LIVING, SLIVING, LIVINGS, LIZARD, LIZARDS, LOADEN, LOADENS, LOADER, LOADERS, LOAFER, LOAFERS, LOATHE, LOATHED, LOATHER, LOATHES, LOBATE, GLOBATE, LOBBED, LOBBING, GLOBING, LOBINGS, LOBOSE, GLOBOSE, LOBULE, GLOBULE, LOBULES, LOCALE, LOCALES, LOCATE, LOCATED, LOCATES, LOCHAN, LOCHANS, LOCHIA, LOCHIAL, LOCKED, BLOCKED, CLOCKED, FLOCKED, LOCKER, BLOCKER, CLOCKER, LOCKERS, LOCKET, LOCKETS, LOCULE, LOCULES, LOCUST, LOCUSTA, LOCUSTS, LODGER, LODGERS, LOFTER

Column 4: LOFTERS, LOGANS, SLOGANS, LOGGAT, LOGGATS, LOGGED, FLOGGED, SLOGGED, LOGGER, CLOGGER, SLOGGER, LOGGERS, LOGGIA, LOGGIAS, LOGIES, ELOGIES, OLOGIES, LOGLOG, LOGLOGS, LOITER, LOITERS, LOLLER, LOLLERS, LOLLOP, LOLLOPS, LOMENT, LOMENTA, LOMENTS, LONELY, ALONELY, LONGAN, LONGANS, LONGED, PLONGED, LONGES, LONGEST, LOOFAH, LOOFAHS, LOOKER, LOOKERS, LOOMED, BLOOMED, GLOOMED, SLOOMED, LOONIE, LOONIER, LOONIES, LOOPED, BLOOPED, BLOOPER, LOOPER, LOOPERS, LOOSEN, LOOSENS, LOOSES, LOOSEST, LOOTER, LOOTERS, LOPERS, ELOPERS, LOPING, ELOPING, SLOPING, LOPPED, CLOPPED, FLOPPED, PLOPPED, SLOPPED

Column 5: LOPPER, LOPPERS, LOQUAT, LOQUATS, LORCHA, LORCHAS, LORICA, LORICAE, LORIES, LORING, LORINGS, LORIOT, LORIOTS, LOSERS, CLOSERS, LOSING, CLOSING, LOSINGS, LOSSES, GLOSSES, FLOSSES, LOTION, LOTIONS, LOTTED, BLOTTED, PLOTTED, SLOTTED, LOUDEN, LOUDENS, LOUGHS, CLOUGHS, PLOUGHS, SLOUGHS, LOUNGE, LOUNGED, LOUNGER, LOUNGES, LOURED, FLOURED, CLOURED, LOUSED, BLOUSED, FLOUSED, LOUSES, BLOUSES, FLOUSES, LOUTED, CLOUTED, FLOUTED, GLOUTED, LOUVER, LOUVERS, LOUVRE, LOUVRED, LOUVRES, LOVAGE, LOVAGES, LOVERS, CLOVERS, GLOVERS, PLOVERS, LOVING, GLOVING, LOVINGS, LOWBOY, LOWBOYS, LOWERS, BLOWERS

Column 6: FLOWERS, GLOWERS, LOWERY, FLOWERY, LOWEST, SLOWEST, LOWING, BLOWING, FLOWING, GLOWING, PLOWING, SLOWING, LOWINGS, LOWNED, CLOWNED, LOWNES, LOWNESS, LOWSES, LOWSEST, LOZELL, LOZELLS, LUBBER, BLUBBER, SLUBBER, LUBBERS, LUCERN, LUCERNE, LUCERNS, LUCKIE, LUCKIER, LUCKIES, LUCUMA, LUCUMAS, LUCUMO, LUCUMOS, LUFFED, BLUFFED, FLUFFED, PLUFFED, LUGGED, GLUGGED, PLUGGED, SLUGGED, LUGGER, PLUGGER, SLUGGER, LUGGERS, LUGGIE, LUGGIES, LUGING, LUGINGS, LUMBER, CLUMBER, PLUMBER, SLUMBER, LUMBERS, LUMINA, ALUMINA, LUMINAL, LUMINE, LUMINED, LUMINES, LUMMOX, FLUMMOX, LUMPED, CLUMPED, FLUMPED, PLUMPED, SLUMPED

Column 7: LUMPEN, PLUMPEN, LUMPER, PLUMPER, LUMPERS, LUNATE, LUNATED, LUNGED, BLUNGED, PLUNGED, BLUNGES, PLUNGES, LUNGIE, LUNGIES, LUNKER, BLUNKER, LUNKERS, LUNTED, BLUNTED, LUNULA, LUNULAR, LUNULAS, LUNULE, LUNULES, LUNYIE, LUNYIES, LUPINE, LUPINES, LURDAN, LURDANE, LURDANS, LURDEN, LURDENS, LURKER, LURKERS, LUSHED, BLUSHED, FLUSHED, SLUSHED, LUSHER, BLUSHER, FLUSHER, PLUSHER, LUSHERS, LUSHES, BLUSHES, FLUSHES, PLUSHES, SLUSHES, LUSHEST, LUSTER, BLUSTER, CLUSTER, FLUSTER, LUSTERS, LUSTRA, LUSTRAL, LUSTRE, LUSTRED, LUSTRES, LUTEAL, GLUTEAL, PLUTEAL, LUTEIN, LUTEINS, LUTERS, FLUTERS, LUTING

Column 8: ELUTING, FLUTING, LUTINGS, LUTIST, FLUTIST, LUTISTS, LUTZES, KLUTZES, LUXATE, LUXATED, LUXATES, LUZERN, LUZERNS, LYCEUM, LYCEUMS, LYCHEE, LYCHEES, LYINGS, FLYINGS, LYNAGE, LYNAGES, LYRATE, LYRATED, LYRISM, LYRISMS, LYRIST, LYRISTS, LYSINE, LYSINES, LYTING, FLYTING, MACACO, MACACOS, MACHAN, MACHANS, MACKLE, MACKLED, MACKLES, MACOYA, MACOYAS, MACRON, MACRONS, MACULA, MACULAE, MACULAR, MACULE, MACULES, MADAME, MADAMED, MADCAP, MADCAPS, MADDEN, MADDENS, MADDER, MADDERS, MADRAS, MADRASA, MAENAD, MAENADS, MAFFIA, MAFFIAS, MAGGOT, MAGGOTS, MAGGOTY, MAGIAN, MAGIANS, MAGILP, MAGILPS, MAGISM, IMAGISM

MAGISMS	MANATIS	**MARCEL**	MASJIDS	**MAYING**	MEGOHMS	**MERINO**	MIDDLES
MAGNET	**MANCHE**	MARCELS	MAYINGS	**MEGRIM**	MERINOS	**MIDGET**
MAGNETO	MANCHES	**MARGAY**	MASKER	MAYINGS	MEGRIMS	**MERISM**	MIDGETS
MAGNETS	MANCHET	MARGAYS	MASKERS	**MAZARD**	MEGRIMS	MERISMS	**MIDRIB**
MAGNUM	**MANDIR**	**MARGIN**	**MASLIN**	MAZARDS	**MEINEY**	**MERKIN**	MIDRIBS
MAGNUMS	MANDIRA	MARGINS	MASLINS	**MAZHBI**	MEINEYS	MERKINS	**MIDWAY**
MAGPIE	MANDIRS	**MARINA**	**MASQUE**	MAZHBIS	**MEINIE**	**MERLIN**	MIDWAYS
MAGPIES	**MANDOM**	MARINAS	MASQUES	**MAZING**	MEINIES	MERLING	**MIGHTS**
MAGUEY	MANDOMS	**MARINE**	MASQUER	AMAZING	**MELANO**	MERLINS	SMIGHTS
MAGUEYS	**MANEGE**	MARINER	MASQUES	**MAZOUT**	MELANOS	**MERLON**	MIGHTST
MAHMAL	MANEGED	MARINES	**MASSED**	MAZOUTS	**MELDER**	MERLONS	**MIHRAB**
MAHMALS	MANEGES	**MARKER**	MASSES	**MAZUMA**	MELDERS	**MEROME**	MIHRABS
MAHOUT	MANGAL	MARKERS	AMASSES	MAZUMAS	MELLAY	MEROMES	**MIKADO**
MAHOUTS	MANGALS	**MARKET**	**MASSIF**	**MEADOW**	MELLAYS	MESAIL	MIKADOS
MAHSIR	**MANGEL**	MARKETS	MASSIFS	MEADOWS	**MELLED**	MESAILS	**MIKRON**
MAHSIRS	MANGELS	**MARKKA**	**MASTER**	MEADOWY	SMELLED	**MESCAL**	MIKRONS
MAIDAN	**MANGER**	MARKKAA	MASTERS	**MEAGRE**	**MELLOW**	MESCALS	**MILADI**
MAIDANS	MANGERS	MARKKAS	MASTERY	MEAGRER	MELLOWS	**MESSAN**	MILADIS
MAIDEN	**MANGLE**	**MARLIN**	**MASTIC**	MEAGRES	MELLOWY	MESSANS	**MILAGE**
MAIDENS	MANGLED	MARLINE	MASTICH	**MEALER**	**MELTED**	**MESTEE**	MILAGES
MAIGRE	MANGLER	MARLING	MASTICS	MEALERS	**MELTON**	MESTEES	**MILDEN**
MAIGRES	MANGLES	MARLINS	**MASULA**	**MEALIE**	MELTONS	**METAGE**	MILDENS
MAILER	**MANIAC**	**MARMOT**	MASULAS	MEALIER	**MEMBER**	METAGES	**MILDEW**
MAILERS	MANIACS	MARMOTS	**MATICO**	MEALIES	MEMBERS	**METEOR**	MILDEWS
MAINOR	**MANILA**	**MAROON**	MATICOS	**MEANES**	**MEMOIR**	METEORS	MILDEWY
MAINORS	MANILAS	MAROONS	**MATING**	MEANEST	MEMOIRS	**METHOD**	**MILERS**
MAKING	**MANIOC**	**MARQUE**	**MATLOW**	MEANIE	**MENACE**	METHODS	SMILERS
MAKINGS	MANIOCS	MARQUEE	MATLOWS	**MEASLE**	MENACED	**METHYL**	**MILIEU**
MALATE	**MANITO**	MARQUES	**MATRIC**	MEASLED	MENACER	METHYLS	MILIEUS
MALATES	MANITOS	**MARRAM**	MATRICE	MEASLES	MENACES	**METICS**	MILIEUX
MALGRE	MANITOU	MARRAMS	MATRICS	**MEATHE**	**MENAGE**	EMETICS	**MILKER**
MALGRES	**MANNER**	**MARROW**	**MATRON**	MEATHES	AMENAGE	**METIER**	MILKERS
MALICE	MANNERS	MARROWS	MATRONS	**MEATHS**	MENAGES	METIERS	**MILLER**
MALICED	**MANOAO**	MARROWY	**MATTER**	SMEATHS	**MENDED**	**METOPE**	MILLERS
MALICES	MANOAOS	**MARRUM**	MATTERS	**MEAZEL**	AMENDED	METOPES	**MILLET**
MALIGN	**MANRED**	MARRUMS	MATTERY	MEAZELS	EMENDED	**METRIC**	MILLETS
MALIGNS	MANREDS	**MARTED**	**MEDDLE**	MEDDLE	**MENDER**	METRICS	**MILORD**
MALKIN	**MANTEL**	SMARTED	MEDDLED	MEDDLED	MENDERS	**METTLE**	MILORDS
MALKINS	MANTELS	**MARTEL**	MEDDLER	**MEDIAL**	**MENEER**	METTLED	**MILSEY**
MALLAM	**MANTID**	MARTELS	MEDDLES	MEDIALS	MENEERS	METTLES	MILSEYS
MALLAMS	MANTIDS	**MARTEN**	**MATURE**	**MEDIAN**	**MENHIR**	**MEUSES**	**MILTER**
MALLED	**MANTLE**	SMARTEN	MATURED	MEDIANS	MENHIRS	SMEUSES	MILTERS
SMALLED	MANTLED	MARTENS	MATURER	MEDIANT	**MENIAL**	**MEZAIL**	**MIMBAR**
MALLEE	MANTLES	**MARTIN**	MATURES	**MEDICK**	MENIALS	MEZAILS	MIMBARS
MALLEES	MANTLET	MARTING	**MATZAH**	MEDICKS	**MENING**	**MEZUZA**	**MIMOSA**
MALLET	**MANTRA**	MARTINI	MATZAHS	**MEDICO**	AMENING	MEZUZAH	MIMOSAS
MALLETS	MANTRAM	MARTINS	**MATZOT**	MEDICOS	OMENING	**MGANGA**	**MINBAR**
MALLOW	MANTRAP	**MARTYR**	MATZOTH	**MEDINA**	**MENTAL**	MGANGAS	MINBARS
MALLOWS	MANTRAS	MARTYRS	**MAUGRE**	MEDINAS	AMENTAL	**MIASMA**	**MINCER**
MALMAG	**MANTUA**	MARTYRY	MAUGRES	**MEDIUM**	OMENTAL	MIASMAL	MINCERS
MALMAGS	MANTUAS	**MARVEL**	**MAULVI**	MEDIUMS	**MENTOR**	MIASMAS	**MINDER**
MALTHA	**MANUAL**	MARVELS	MAULVIS	**MEDLAR**	MENTORS	**MICATE**	MINDERS
MALTHAS	MANUALS	**MASCLE**	**MAUMET**	MEDLARS	**MENTUM**	EMICATE	**MINGLE**
MAMMAL	**MANUKA**	MASCLED	MAUMETS	**MEDLEY**	AMENTUM	MICATED	MINGLED
MAMMALS	MANUKAS	MASCLES	**MAUVES**	MEDLEYS	OMENTUM	MICATES	MINGLER
MAMMEE	**MANURE**	**MASCON**	MAUVEST	**MEDUSA**	**MERCAT**	**MICHER**	MINGLES
MAMMEES	MANURED	MASCONS	**MAUVIN**	MEDUSAE	MERCATS	MICHERS	**MINIMA**
MAMMER	MANURER	**MASCOT**	MAUVINE	MEDUSAN	**MERCER**	**MICKEY**	MINIMAL
MAMMERS	MANURES	MASCOTS	MAUVINS	MEDUSAS	MERCERS	MICKEYS	**MINING**
MAMMET	**MAPPER**	**MASHED**	**MAWKIN**	**MEEKEN**	MERCERY	**MICKLE**	MININGS
MAMMETS	MAPPERS	SMASHED	MAWKINS	MEEKENS	**MERCAT**	MICKLES	**MINION**
MAMMON	MAPPERY	**MASHER**	**MAWMET**	**MEGARA**	**MERELL**	**MICRON**	MINIONS
MAMMONS	**MARACA**	SMASHER	MAWMETS	MEGARAD	MERELLS	OMICRON	**MINIUM**
MANAGE	MARACAS	MASHERS	**MAXIMA**	**MEGARA**	**MERGED**	MICRONS	MINIUMS
MANAGED	**MARAUD**	**MASHES**	MAXIMAL	MEGARAD	EMERGED	**MIDDAY**	**MINNIE**
MANAGER	MARAUDS	SMASHES	MAXIIXE	**MEGASS**	**MERGER**	MIDDAYS	MINNIES
MANAGES	**MARBLE**	**MASHIE**	MAXIXES	MEGASSE	MERGERS	**MIDDEN**	**MINNOW**
MANANA	MARBLED	MASHIER	**MAYDAY**	**MEGILP**	**MERGES**	MIDDENS	MINNOWS
MANANAS	MARBLER	MASHIES	MAYDAYS	MEGILPS	EMERGES	**MIDDLE**	**MINTER**
MANATI	MARBLES	**MASJID**	**MAYHEM**	**MEGOHM**	EMERGES	MIDDLED	MINTERS

MINUET	MIZZENS	MONGER	MORTAL	MOUTONS	MUMMERY	MUSKLES	NAGARI
MINUETS	MIZZLE	MONGERS	MORTALS	MOVING	MUMMIA	MUSLIN	NAGARIS
MINUTE	MIZZLED	MONGERY	MORTAR	AMOVING	MUMMIAS	MUSLINS	NAGGED
MINUTED	MIZZLES	MONGOL	MORTARS	EMOVING	MUMPER	MUSMON	SNAGGED
MINUTER	MNEMON	MONGOLS	MORULA	MOWING	MUMPERS	MUSMONS	NAGGER
MINUTES	MNEMONS	MONIAL	MORULAR	MOWINGS	MUNDIC	MUSROL	NAGGERS
MINYAN	MOANER	MONIALS	MORULAS	MOYLED	MUNDICS	MUSROLS	NAILED
MINYANS	MOANERS	MONISM	MOSAIC	SMOYLED	MUNITE	MUSSEL	SNAILED
MIRAGE	MOBBIE	MONISMS	MOSAICS	MOYLES	MUNITED	MUSSELS	NAILER
MIRAGES	MOBBIES	MONIST	MOSQUE	SMOYLES	MUNITES	MUSTEE	NAILERS
MIRITI	MOBBLE	MONISTS	MOSQUES	MOZZIE	MUNSHI	MUSTEES	NAILERY
MIRITIS	MOBBLED	MONKEY	MOSSIE	MOZZIES	MUNSHIS	MUSTER	NALLAH
MIRROR	MOBBLES	MONKEYS	MOSSIER	MOZZLE	MUNTIN	MUSTERS	NALLAHS
MIRRORS	MOBILE	MONTEM	MOSSIES	MOZZLES	MUNTINS	MUTANT	NAMING
MISAIM	MOBILES	MONTEMS	MOTETT	MUCATE	MURAGE	MUTANTS	NAMINGS
MISAIMS	MOCKED	MONTRE	MOTETTS	MUCATES	MURAGES	MUTATE	NANDOO
MISCUE	SMOCKED	MONTRES	MOTHER	MUCHEL	MURDER	MUTATED	NANDOOS
MISCUED	MOCKER	MOOLAH	SMOTHER	MUCHELL	MURDERS	MUTATES	NANISM
MISCUES	MOCKERS	MOOLAHS	MOTHERS	MUCHELS	MURENA	MUTINE	ONANISM
MISERE	MOCKERY	MOONER	MOTHERY	MUCKER	MURENAS	MUTINED	NANISMS
MISERES	MOCOCK	MOONERS	MOTILE	MUCKERS	MURINE	MUTINES	NANKIN
MISFIT	MOCOCKS	MOORED	MOTILES	MUCKLE	MURINES	MUTISM	NANKINS
MISFITS	MOCUCK	SMOORED	MOTION	MUCKLES	MURING	MUTISMS	NAPALM
MISHAP	MOCUCKS	MOORVA	EMOTION	MUCLUC	EMURING	MUTTER	NAPALMS
MISHAPS	MODENA	MOORVAS	MOTIONS	MUCLUCS	MURLAN	MUTTERS	NAPKIN
MISHAPT	MODENAS	MOOTED	MOTIVE	MUCOSA	MURLANS	MUTTON	NAPKINS
MISHIT	MODERN	SMOOTED	EMOTIVE	MUCOSAE	MURLIN	MUTTONS	NAPPED
MISHITS	MODERNS	MOOTER	MOTIVED	MUDDLE	MURLINS	MUTTONY	KNAPPED
MISHMI	MODEST	MOOTERS	MOTIVES	MUDDLED	MURMUR	MUTUCA	SNAPPED
MISHMIS	MODESTY	MOOVED	MOTLEY	MUDDLER	MURMURS	MUTUCAS	NAPPER
MISKEN	MODIST	MOOVES	MOTLEYS	MUDDLES	MURRAM	MUTULE	KNAPPER
MISKENS	MODISTE	AMOOVED	MOTMOT	MUESLI	MURRAMS	MUTULES	SNAPPER
MISKENT	MODISTS	AMOOVES	MOTMOTS	MUESLIS	MURRAY	MUTUUM	NAPPERS
MISLAY	MODULE	MOPANE	MOTSER	MUFFIN	MURRAYS	MUTUUMS	NAPRON
MISLAYS	MODULES	MOPANES	MOTSERS	MUFFINS	MURREN	MUZHIK	NAPRONS
MISSAL	MOGGAN	MOPOKE	MOTTLE	MUFFLE	MURRENS	MUZHIKS	NARDOO
MISSALS	MOGGANS	MOPOKES	MOTTLED	MUFFLED	MURREY	MUZZLE	NARDOOS
MISSAY	MOGGIE	MOPPER	MOTTLES	MUFFLER	MURREYS	MUZZLED	NARROW
MISSAYS	MOGGIES	MOPPERS	MOTUCA	MUFFLES	MURRHA	MUZZLER	NARROWS
MISSEE	MOHAIR	MOPPET	MOTUCAS	MUFLON	MURRHAS	MUZZLES	NASARD
MISSEEM	MOHAIRS	MOPPETS	MOUJIK	MUFLONS	MURRIN	MYELIN	NASARDS
MISSEEN	MOHAWK	MORALE	MOUJIKS	MUGFUL	MURRINE	MYELINS	NASION
MISSEES	MOHAWKS	MORALES	MOULIN	MUGFULS	MURRINS	MYELON	NASIONS
MISSEL	MOIDER	MORALL	MOULINS	MUGGED	MUSANG	MYELONS	NASUTE
MISSELS	MOIDERS	MORALLS	MOUNTS	SMUGGED	MUSANGS	MYGALE	NASUTES
MISSES	MOILED	MORALLY	AMOUNTS	MUGGER	MUSCAT	MYGALES	NATION
AMISSES	SMOILED	MORASS	MOUSED	MUGGERS	MUSCATS	MYOGEN	ENATION
MISSET	MOILER	MORASSY	SMOUSED	MUKLUK	MUSCID	MYOGENS	NATIONS
MISSETS	MOILERS	MOREEN	MOUSER	MUKLUKS	MUSCIDS	MYOPIA	NATIVE
MISSIS	MOLEST	MOREENS	SMOUSER	MULLAH	MUSCLE	MYOPIAS	NATIVES
MISSISH	MOLESTS	MORGAY	MOUSERS	MULLAHS	MUSCLED	MYOPIC	NATRON
MISTER	MOLINE	MORGAYS	MOUSERY	MULLER	MUSCLES	MYOPICS	NATRONS
MISTERM	MOLINES	MORGEN	MOUSES	MULLERS	MUSERS	MYOSIN	NATTER
MISTERS	MOLLAH	MORGENS	SMOUSES	MULLET	AMUSERS	MYOSINS	NATTERS
MISTERY	MOLLAHS	MORGUE	MOUSIE	MULLETS	MUSEUM	MYOTIC	NATTERY
MISTLE	MOLLIE	MORGUES	MOUSIER	MULLEY	MUSEUMS	MYOTICS	NATURA
MISTLED	MOLLIES	MORION	MOUSIES	MULLEYS	MUSHER	MYRIAD	NATURAE
MISTLES	MOLOCH	MORIONS	MOUSLE	MULMUL	MUSHERS	MYRIADS	NATURAL
MISUSE	MOLOCHS	MORKIN	MOUSLED	MULMULL	MUSING	MYRTLE	NATURE
MISUSED	MOLTEN	MORKINS	MOUSLES	MULMULS	AMUSING	MYRTLES	NATURED
MISUSER	YMOLTEN	MORNAY	MOUSME	MULTUM	MUSINGS	MYSTIC	NATURES
MISUSES	MOMENT	MORNAYS	MOUSMEE	MULTUMS	MUSIVE	MYSTICS	NAUGHT
MITERS	MOMENTA	MOROSE	MOUSMES		AMUSIVE	MZUNGU	NAUGHTS
SMITERS	MOMENTS	MOROSER	MOUSSE		MUSKEG	MZUNGUS	NAUGHTY
MITHER	MOMMET	MORPHO	MOUSSES		MUSKEGS	NABBER	NAUSEA
MITHERS	MOMMETS	MORPHOS	MOUTAN		MUSKET	NABBERS	NAUSEAS
MITTEN	MONAUL	MORROW	MOUTANS		MUSKETS	NACKET	NAUTIC
SMITTEN	MONAULS	MORROWS	MOUTER		MUSKLE	NACKETS	NAUTICS
MITTENS	MONETH	MORSEL	MOUTERS			NAGANA	NAVAID
MIZZEN	MONETHS	MORSELS	MOUTON			NAGANAS	NAVAIDS

NEAFFE
NEAFFES
NEAPED
SNEAPED
NEARED
ANEARED
UNEARED
NEATEN
UNEATEN
NEATENS
NEBBED
SNEBBED
NEBBUK
NEBBUKS
NEBECK
NEBECKS
NEBULA
NEBULAE
NEBULAR
NEBULE
NEBULES
NECKED
SNECKED
NECTAR
NECTARS
NECTARY
NEEDER
NEEDERS
NEEDLE
NEEDLED
NEEDLER
NEEDLES
NEEZED
SNEEZED
NEEZES
SNEEZES
NEGATE
NEGATED
NEGATES
NEKTON
NEKTONS
NELSON
NELSONS
NEPHEW
NEPHEWS
NEREID
NEREIDS
NERINE
NERINES
NERITE
NERITES
NEROLI
NEROLIS
NERVED
ENERVED
NERVER
NERVERS
NERVES
ENERVES
NESTER
NESTERS
NESTLE
NESTLED
NESTLES
NETFUL
NETFULS
NETTLE
NETTLED
NETTLES
NEURON

NEURONE
NEURONS
NEUTER
NEUTERS
NEWELL
NEWELLS
NEWING
ENEWING
NEWTON
NEWTONS
NIACIN
NIACINS
NIBBED
SNIBBED
NIBBLE
NIBBLED
NIBBLER
NIBBLES
NICHER
NICHERS
NICKAR
NICKARS
NICKED
SNICKED
NICKEL
NICKELS
NICKER
KNICKER
SNICKER
NICKERS
NICKUM
NICKUMS
NIDGET
NIDGETS
NIDING
NIDINGS
NIELLO
NIELLOS
NIFFED
NIFFER
SNIFFED
SNIFFER
NIFFERS
NIGGER
SNIGGER
NIGGERS
NIGGERY
NIGGLE
SNIGGLE
NIGGLED
NIGGLER
NIGGLES
NIGHTS
KNIGHTS
NILGAI
NILGAIS
NILGAU
NILGAUS
NIMBLE
NIMBLER
NIMMER
NIMMERS
NINCOM
NINCOMS
NINCUM
NINCUMS
NIPPED
SNIPPED
NIPPER
SNIPPER

NIPPERS
NIPPLE
NIPPLED
NIPPLES
NIPTER
NIPTERS
NIRLIE
NIRLIER
NITRYL
NITRYLS
NITWIT
NITWITS
NOBBLE
KNOBBLE
NOBBLED
NOBBLER
NOBBLES
NOBLES
NOBLEST
NOCAKE
NOCAKES
NOCENT
NOCENTS
NOCHEL
NOCHELS
NOCKED
KNOCKED
NOCKET
NOCKETS
NOCTUA
NOCTUAS
NODDED
SNODDED
NODDER
NODDERS
NODDLE
NODDLED
NODDLES
NODULE
NODULED
NODULES
NOESES
NOESIS
NOETIC
ANOETIC
NOGGIN
NOGGING
NOGGINS
NOINTS
ANOINTS
NOMADE
NOMADES
NOMINA
NOMINAL
NOMISM
NOMISMS
NONAGE
NONAGED
NONAGES
NONANE
NONANES
NOODLE
NOODLED
NOODLES
NOOKIE
NOOKIER
NOOKIES
NORITE

NORITES
NORMAL
NORMALS
NORMAN
NORMANS
NORSEL
NORSELS
NOSEAN
NOSEANS
NOSIES
NOSIEST
NOSING
NOSINGS
NOSTOC
NOSTOCS
NOTATE
NOTATED
NOTATES
NOTICE
NOTICED
NOTICES
NOTION
NOTIONS
NOUGAT
NOUGATS
NOUGHT
NOUGHTS
NOUSLE
NOUSLED
NOUSLES
NOVENA
NOVENAS
NOVICE
NOVICES
NOYADE
NOYADES
NOZZLE
NOZZLED
NOZZLES
NUANCE
NUANCED
NUANCES
NUBBED
SNUBBED
NUBBIN
NUBBING
NUBBINS
NUBBLE
KNUBBLE
NUBBLED
NUBBLES
NUBBLY
KNUBBLY
NUCLEI
NUCLEIN
NUCULE
NUCULES
NUDGED
SNUDGED
NUDGES
SNUDGES
NUDISM
NUDISMS
NUDIST
NUDISTS
NUGGAR
NUGGARS
NUGGET
NUGGETS
NUGGETY
NULLAH

NULLAHS
NUMBAT
NUMBATS
NUMBER
NUMBERS
NUMDAH
NUMDAHS
NUMNAH
NUMNAHS
NUNCIO
NUNCIOS
NUNCLE
NUNCLES
NURHAG
NURHAGS
NURLED
KNURLED
NURSER
NURSERS
NURSERY
NURSLE
NURSLED
NURSLES
NUTATE
NUTATED
NUTATES
NUTLET
NUTLETS
NUTMEG
NUTMEGS
NUTRIA
NUTRIAS
NUTTER
NUTTERS
NUTTERY
NUZZER
NUZZERS
NUZZLE
NUZZLED
NUZZLES
NYALAS
INYALAS
NYANZA
NYANZAS
NYMPHO
NYMPHOS
OAKERS
SOAKERS
OARAGE
OARAGES
OARIER
HOARIER
ROARIER
OARING
HOARING
ROARING
SOARING
OBANGS
GOBANGS
KOBANGS
OBDURE
OBDURED
OBDURES
OBECHE
OBECHES
OBEISM
OBEISMS
OBEYER
OBEYERS

OBIISM
OBIISMS
OBJECT
OBJECTS
OBJURE
OBJURED
OBJURES
OBLAST
OBLASTS
OBLATE
OBLATES
OBLIGE
OBLIGED
OBLIGES
OBLONG
OBLONGS
OBOIST
OBOISTS
OBSIGN
OBSIGNS
OBTAIN
OBTAINS
OBTEND
OBTENDS
OBTEST
OBTESTS
OBTUND
OBTUNDS
OBTUSE
OBTUSER
OBVERT
OBVERTS
OCCULT
OCCULTS
OCELOT
OCELOTS
OCHERS
TOCHERS
OCHREA
OCHREAE
OCKERS
COCKERS
DOCKERS
HOCKERS
LOCKERS
MOCKERS
ROCKERS
SOCKERS
OCTANE
OCTANES
OCTANT
OCTANTS
OCTAVE
OCTAVES
OCTAVO
OCTAVOS
OCTETT
OCTETTS
OCTROI
OCTROIS
OCTUOR
OCTUORS
OCULAR
JOCULAR
LOCULAR
VOCULAR
OCULARS
OCULUS

LOCULUS
ODISMS
ODISTS
IODISMS
MODISTS
ODIUMS
OECIST
OECISTS
OEDEMA
OEDEMAS
OEUVRE
OEUVRES
OFFCUT
OFFCUTS
OFFEND
OFFENDS
OFFERS
COFFERS
DOFFERS
GOFFERS
OFFICE
OFFICER
OFFICES
OFFING
BOFFING
COFFING
DOFFING
GOFFING
OFFINGS
OFFISH
TOFFISH
OFFPUT
OFFPUTS
OFFSET
OFFSETS
OGDOAD
OGDOADS
OGGINS
HOGGINS
NOGGINS
OGLING
OGLINGS
OIKIST
OIKISTS
OILCAN
OILCANS
OILERS
BOILERS
MOILERS
TOILERS
OILERY
BOILERY
OILIER
ROILIER
SOILIER
OILING
BOILING
COILING
FOILING
MOILING
ROILING
SOILING
TOILING
OILLET
OILLETS
OILNUT
OILNUTS
OINTED

JOINTED
NOINTED
POINTED
OLDENS
BOLDENS
GOLDENS
OLDEST
BOLDEST
COLDEST
GOLDEST
OLDISH
COLDISH
GOLDISH
OLEATE
OLEATES
OLEFIN
OLEFINE
OLEFINS
OLFACT
OLFACTS
OLIVER
OLIVERS
OLIVES
SOLIVES
OLIVET
OLIVETS
OLLAMH
OLLAMHS
OMBRES
HOMBRES
OMELET
OMELETS
OMENTA
LOMENTA
MOMENTA
OMENTAL
OMERTA
OMERTAS
OMNIUM
OMNIUMS
ONAGER
ONAGERS
ONCOME
ONCOMES
ONCOST
ONCOSTS
ONDINE
ONDINES
ONDING
BONDING
FONDING
PONDING
ONDINGS
ONEYER
MONEYER
ONEYERS
ONEYRE
ONEYRES
ONFALL
ONFALLS
ONFLOW
ONFLOWS
ONNING
CONNING
DONNING
FONNING
KONNING
RONNING
WONNING

ONSIDE	OPIATED	GORGIAS	BOTHERS	**OUTAGE**	OUTTOPS	OXYMELS	SPALLED
ONSIDES	OPIATES	ORGIAST	FOTHERS	OUTAGES	**OUTVIE**	**OYESES**	**PALLET**
ONUSES	**OPPOSE**	**ORGIES**	MOTHERS	**OUTBAR**	OUTVIED	**OYSTER**	PALLETS
BONUSES	OPPOSED	PORGIES	POTHERS	OUTBARS	OUTVIES	NOYESES	**PALLIA**
TONUSES	OPPOSER	**ORGONE**	ROTHERS	**OUTBID**	**OUTWIN**	ROYSTER	PALLIAL
ONWARD	OPPOSES	ORGONES	COTTARS	OUTBIDS	OUTWIND	OYSTERS	**PALLOR**
ONWARDS	**OPPUGN**	FORGONE	**OTTARS**	**OUTEAT**	OUTWING	**OZAENA**	PALLORS
ONYCHA	OPPUGNS	**ORGUES**	**OTTAVA**	OUTEATS	OUTWINS	OZAENAS	PALMARY
ONYCHAS	**OPTANT**	MORGUES	OTTAVAS	**OUTERS**	**OUTWIT**	OZAENAS	**PALMER**
OOCYTE	OPTANTS	**ORIENT**	**OTTERS**	COUTERS	OUTWITH	PACERS	PALMERS
OOCYTES	**OPTIMA**	ORIENTS	COTTERS	DOUTERS	OUTWITS	SPACERS	**PALMIE**
OODLES	OPTIMAL	**ORIGAN**	HOTTERS	FOUTERS	**OUVERT**	**PACHAK**	PALMIER
BOODLES	**OPTIME**	ORIGANE	JOTTERS	MOUTERS	OUVERTE	PACHAKS	PALMIES
DOODLES	OPTIMES	ORIGANS	POTTERS	POUTERS	COUVERT	**PACIER**	PALMIET
NOODLES	**OPTION**	**ORIGIN**	ROTTERS	ROUTERS	**OVATES**	SPACIER	**PALOLO**
POODLES	OPTIONS	ORIGINS	TOTTERS	SOUTERS	BOVATES	**PACING**	PALOLOS
OOGAMY	**OPUSES**	ORIOLE	**OUBITS**	TOUTERS	**OVATOR**	PACKER	**PALTER**
ZOOGAMY	MOPUSES	ORIOLES	WOUBITS	**OUTFIT**	OVATORS	PACKERS	PALTERS
OOGENY	**ORACHE**	**ORISON**	**OUCHES**	OUTFITS	**OVERED**	**PACKET**	**PAMPER**
ZOOGENY	ORACHES	ORISONS	BOUCHES	**OUTFLY**	COVERED	PACKETS	PAMPERO
OOHING	**ORACLE**	**ORMERS**	COUCHES	GOUTFLY	DOVERED	**PADANG**	PAMPERS
BOOHING	CORACLE	DORMERS	DOUCHES	**OUTGUN**	HOVERED	PADANGS	**PANADA**
OOIDAL	ORACLED	FORMERS	MOUCHES	OUTGUNS	LOVERED	**PADAUK**	PANADAS
ZOOIDAL	ORACLES	WORMERS	POUCHES	**OUTHER**	**OVERGO**	PADAUKS	**PANAMA**
OOLITE	**ORALLY**	ORMOLU	TOUCHES	COUTHER	OVERGOT	**PADDER**	PANAMAS
ZOOLITE	MORALLY	ORMOLUS	VOUCHES	MOUTHER	**OVERLY**	PADDERS	**PANDAR**
OOLITES	**ORANGE**	**ORNATE**	**OUGHLY**	POUTHER	LOVERLY	**PADDLE**	PANDARS
OOLOGY	ORANGER	ORNATER	ROUGHLY	SOUTHER	**OVISAC**	PADDLED	**PANDER**
NOOLOGY	ORANGES	**OROGEN**	TOUGHLY	**OUTHIT**	OVISACS	PADDLER	PANDERS
ZOOLOGY	**ORARIA**	OROGENS	**OUGHTS**	OUTHITS	**OWLERS**	PADDLES	**PANDIT**
OOLONG	ORARIAN	OROGENY	BOUGHTS	**OUTING**	BOWLERS	**PADOUK**	PANDITS
OOLONGS	**ORATES**	**OROIDE**	NOUGHTS	DOUTING	FOWLERS	PADOUKS	**PANFUL**
OOMIAC	BORATES	OROIDES	**OUGLIE**	LOUTING	HOWLERS	**PAELLA**	PANFULS
OOMIACK	**ORATOR**	**ORPHAN**	OUGLIED	POUTING	JOWLERS	PAELLAS	**PANGED**
OOMIACS	ORATORS	ORPHANS	OUGLIES	ROUTING	**OWLETS**	**PAGING**	SPANGED
OOMIAK	ORATORY	**ORPINE**	**OULONG**	TOUTING	**OWLIER**	PAGINGS	**PANGEN**
OOMIAKS	**ORBING**	FORPINE	OULONGS	OUTINGS	LOWLIER	**PAGODA**	PANGENE
OOMPAH	SORBING	ORPINES	**OUNCES**	**OUTJET**	**OWLING**	PAGODAS	PANGENS
OOMPAHS	**ORBITA**	PORTHOS	BOUNCES	OUTJETS	BOWLING	**PAIDLE**	**PANICK**
OOPING	ORBITAL	**OSCULA**	POUNCES	**OUTJUT**	COWLING	PAIDLES	PANICKS
COOPING	ORBITAS	OSCULAR	ROUNCES	OUTJUTS	FOWLING	**PAIGLE**	PANICKY
HOOPING	**ORCEIN**	**OSCULE**	**OUPING**	**OUTLAW**	GOWLING	PAIGLES	**PANING**
LOOPING	ORCEINS	OSCULES	COUPING	OUTLAWS	HOWLING	**PAINED**	SPANING
MOOPING	**ORCHAT**	**OSIERS**	LOUPING	**OUTLAY**	JOWLING	SPAINED	**PANISC**
POOPING	ORCHATS	COSIERS	MOUPING	OUTLAYS	SOWLING	**PAINIM**	**PANISK**
ROOPING	**ORCHEL**	HOSIERS	POUPING	**OUTLER**	YOWLING	PAINIMS	PANISKS
SOOPING	ORCHELS	ROSIERS	ROUPING	OUTLERS	**OWNERS**	**PAIOCK**	**PANNED**
OORIAL	**ORCHID**	HOSIERY	**OURALI**	**OUTLET**	DOWNERS	PAIOCKE	SPANNED
OORIALS	ORCHIDS	**OSMATE**	WOURALI	OUTLETS	**OWNING**	PAIOCKS	**PANTER**
OORIER	**ORCHIL**	OSMATES	OURALIS	**OUTLIE**	BOWNING	**PAJOCK**	PANTERS
MOORIER	ORCHILS	**OSMIUM**	**OURARI**	OUTLIED	DOWNING	PAJOCKE	**PANTON**
OOSIER	**ORCINE**	OSMIUMS	OURARIS	OUTLIER	GOWNING	PAJOCKS	PANTONS
GOOSIER	PORCINE	**OSMOSE**	**OUREBI**	OUTLIES	LOWNING	**PAKEHA**	**PANTUN**
OOZIER	ORCINES	OSMOSED	OUREBIS	**OUTMAN**	**OXGANG**	PAKEHAS	PANTUNS
BOOZIER	**ORDAIN**	OSMOSES	**OURIER**	OUTMANS	OXGANGS	**PAKORA**	**PANZER**
WOOZIER	ORDAINS	**OSMUND**	COURIER	**OUTPUT**	**OXGATE**	PAKORAS	PANZERS
OOZILY	**ORDEAL**	OSMUNDA	LOURIER	OUTPUTS	OXGATES	**PALACE**	**PAPAIN**
BOOZILY	ORDEALS	OSMUNDS	**OUSELS**	**OUTRAN**	**OXHEAD**	PALACES	PAPAINS
WOOZILY	**ORDERS**	**OSPREY**	HOUSELS	OUTRANK	OXHEADS	**PALAMA**	**PAPAYA**
OOZING	BORDERS	OSPREYS	**OUSTED**	**OUTRED**	**OXLAND**	PALAMAE	PAPAYAS
BOOZING	**ORDURE**	**OSSEIN**	JOUSTED	OUTREDS	OXLANDS	**PALATE**	**PAPISM**
OPAQUE	BORDURE	OSSEINS	MOUSTED	**OUTRUN**	**OXSLIP**	PALATED	PAPISMS
OPAQUED	ORDURES	**OSTENT**	ROUSTED	OUTRUNS	OXSLIPS	PALATES	**PAPIST**
OPAQUER	**OREIDE**	OSTENTS	**OUSTER**	**OUTSET**	**OXTAIL**	**PALING**	PAPISTS
OPAQUES	OREIDES	**OSTLER**	JOUSTER	OUTSETS	OXTAILS	PALINGS	**PAPULA**
OPENER	**ORGASM**	HOSTLER	ROUSTER	**OUTSIT**	**OXYGEN**	**PALKEE**	PAPULAE
OPENERS	ORGASMS	OSTLERS	OUSTERS	OUTSITS	LOXYGEN	PALKEES	PAPULAR
OPHITE	**ORGEAT**	**OTHERS**	**OUTACT**	**OUTSUM**	OXYGENS	**PALLAH**	**PAPULE**
OPHITES	ORGEATS		OUTACTS	OUTSUMS	**OXYMEL**	PALLAHS	
OPIATE	ORGIAS			**OUTTOP**		PALLED	

PAPULES	PARSER	PAUNCHY	PEDLAR	PENSUM	PETHER	PHYLLOS	PILFER
PARADE	SPARSER	PAUPER	PEDLARS	PENSUMS	PETHERS	PHYSIC	PILFER
PARADED	PARSERS	PAUPERS	PEDLARY	PENTAD	PETREL	PHYSICS	PILING
PARADES	PARSON	PAUSER	PEELED	PENTADS	PETRELS	PHYSIO	SPILING
PARAGE	PARSONS	PAUSERS	SPEELED	PENTEL	PETROL	PHYSIOS	PILLAR
PARAGES	PARTAN	PAVAGE	PEELER	PENTELS	PETROLS	PHYTON	PILLAR
PARAMO	SPARTAN	PAVAGES	PEELERS	PENULT	PETTER	PHYTONS	PILLAU
PARAMOS	PARTANS	PAVANE	SPEELER	PENULTS	PETTERS	PIAFFE	PILLAU
PARANG	PARTER	PAVANES	PEENGE	PEOPLE	PETTLE	PIAFFED	PILLED
PARANGS	PARTERS	PAVING	PEENGED	PEOPLED	PETTLED	PIAFFER	SPILLED
PARAPH	PARTON	PAVINGS	PEENGES	PEOPLES	PETTLES	PIAFFES	PILLOW
PARAPHS	PARTONS	PAVINS	PEEPER	PEPLUM	PEWTER	PIAZZA	PILLOW
PARCEL	PARURE	SPAVINS	PEEPERS	PEPLUMS	PEWTERS	PIAZZAS	PILULA
PARCELS	PARURES	PAVIOR	PEEPUL	PEPPER	PEYOTE	PICENE	PILULA
PARDAL	PARVIS	PAVIORS	PEEPULS	PEPPERS	PEYOTES	EPICENE	PILULE
PARDALE	PARVISE	PAVISE	PEERED	PEPPERY	PEZANT	PICENES	PILULE
PARDALS	PASCAL	PAVISES	SPEERED	PEPSIN	PEZANTS	PICKER	PIMENT
PARDON	PASCALS	PAVONE	PEERIE	PEPSINE	PHALLI	SPICKER	PIMENT
PARDONS	PASEAR	PAVONES	PEERIER	PEPSINS	PHALLIC	PICKERS	PIMENT
PARENT	PASEARS	PAWNCE	PEERIES	PEPTIC	PHALLIN	PICKERY	PIMPLE
PARENTS	PASHIM	PAWNCES	PEEVER	PEPTICS	PHANGS	PICKET	PIMPLE
PARERS	PASHIMS	PAWNED	PEEVERS	PERDUE	UPHANGS	PICKETS	PIMPLE
SPARERS	PASSER	SPAWNED	PEEWEE	EPERDUE	PHASIC	PICKLE	PINCER
PARGED	PASSERS	PAWNEE	PEEWEES	PERDUES	APHASIC	PICKLED	PINCER
SPARGED	PASTEL	PAWNEES	PEEWIT	PERIOD	PHEERE	PICKLER	PINDER
PARGES	PASTELS	PAWNER	PEEWITS	PERIODS	PHEERES	PICKLES	PINDER
SPARGES	PASTER	SPAWNER	PEINCT	PERKIN	PHEESE	PICNIC	PINGER
PARGET	PASTERN	PAWNERS	PEINCTS	PERKING	PHEESED	PICNICS	PINGER
PARGETS	PASTERS	PAWPAW	PELAGE	PERKINS	PHEESES	PICOTE	PINGER
PARIAH	PASTIL	PAWPAWS	PELAGES	PERMIT	PHEEZE	PICOTED	PINGLE
PARIAHS	PASTILS	PAYING	PELHAM	PERMITS	PHEEZED	PICOTES	PINGLE
PARIAL	PASTOR	APAYING	PELHAMS	PERONE	PHEEZES	PIDDLE	PINGLE
PARIALS	PASTORS	PAYINGS	PELITE	PERONES	PHENES	PIDDLED	PINIER
PARING	PATACA	SPAYING	PELITES	PERRON	SPHENES	PIDDLER	SPINIER
SPARING	PATACAS	PAYNIM	PELLET	PERRONS	PHENIC	PIDDLES	PINIES
PARINGS	PATENT	PAYNIMS	PELLETS	PERSES	SPHENIC	PIDGIN	PINIES
PARKED	PATENTS	PAYOLA	PELMET	SPERSES	PHENOL	PIDGINS	PINING
SPARKED	PATERA	PAYOLAS	PELMETS	PERSON	PHENOLS	PIECEN	OPINING
PARKEE	PATERAE	PEACOD	PELOID	PERSONA	PHENYL	PIECENS	PINION
PARKEES	PATHED	PEACODS	PELOIDS	PERSONS	PHENYLS	PIECER	PINION
PARKER	SPATHED	PEANED	PELOTA	PERSUE	PHESES	PIECERS	PINION
PARKERS	PATHIC	SPEANED	PELOTAS	PERSUED	APHESES	PIERCE	PINITE
PARKIN	SPATHIC	PEANUT	PELTAS	PERSUES	PHIZOG	PIERCED	PINITE
PARKING	PATHICS	PEANUTS	PELTAST	PERUKE	PHIZOGS	PIERCER	PINKIE
PARKINS	PATINA	PEAPOD	PELTER	PERUKED	PHLEGM	PIERCES	PINKIE
PARKIS	PATINAS	PEAPODS	SPELTER	PERUKES	PHLEGMS	PIERID	PINKIE
PARKISH	PATINE	PEARCE	PELTERS	PERUSE	PHLEGMY	PIERIDS	PINNER
PARKLY	PATINED	PEARCED	PENCEL	PERUSED	PHLOEM	PIFFLE	SPINNER
SPARKLY	PATINES	PEARCES	PENCELS	PERUSER	PHLOEMS	PIFFLED	PINNER
PARLAY	PATROL	PEAVEY	PENCES	PERUSES	PHOBIA	PIFFLER	PINNET
PARLAYS	PATROLS	PEAVEYS	SPENCES	PESADE	PHOBIAS	PIFFLES	SPINNET
PARLEY	PATRON	PEBBLE	PENCIL	PESADES	PHOEBE	PIGEON	PINNET
PARLEYS	PATRONS	PEBBLED	PENCILS	PESANT	PHOEBES	PIGEONS	PINNIE
PAROLE	PATTED	PEBBLES	PENFUL	PESANTE	PHONEY	PIGGIE	PINNIE
PAROLED	SPATTED	PECKED	PENFULS	PESANTS	PHONEYS	PIGGIER	PINOLE
PAROLEE	PATTEE	SPECKED	PENING	PESETA	PHONIC	PIGGIES	PINOLES
PAROLES	SPATTEE	PECKER	OPENING	PESETAS	APHONIC	PIGGIN	PINTLE
PARPEN	PATTEN	PECKERS	PENNAL	PESEWA	PHONICS	PIGGING	PINTLES
PARPEND	PATTENS	PECTIN	PENNALS	PESEWAS	PHONON	PIGGINS	PIOLET
PARPENS	PATTER	PECTINS	PENNER	PESHWA	PHONONS	PIGHTS	PIOLET
PARPENT	SPATTER	PEDALO	PENNERS	PESHWAS	PHOTIC	SPIGHTS	PIONER
PARRAL	PATTERN	PEDALOS	PENNON	PESTER	APHOTIC	PIGLET	PIONERS
PARRALS	PATTERS	PEDANT	PENNONS	PESTERS	PHOTICS	PIGLETS	PIONEY
PARREL	PATTLE	PEDANTS	PENSEE	PESTLE	PHOTON	PIGPEN	PIONEYS
PARRELS	PATTLES	PEDDER	PENSEES	PESTLED	PHOTONS	PIGPENS	PIPAGE
PARROT	PATZER	PEDDERS	PENSEL	PESTLES	PHRASE	PIKING	PIPAGES
PARROTS	PATZERS	PEDDLE	PENSELS	PETARA	PHRASED	SPIKING	PIPING
PARROTY	PAUNCE	PEDDLED	PENSIL	PETARAS	PHRASER	PILAFF	PIPINGS
PARSEC	PAUNCES	PEDDLER	PENSILE	PETARD	PHRASES	PILAFFS	
PARSECS	PAUNCH	PEDDLES	PENSILS	PETARDS	PHYLLO	PILFER	

PIPKIN	PLASTER	**PODIUM**	PONGEES	**POSSES**	POUTERS	PRESETS	**PROTYL**
PIPKINS	**PLATAN**	SPODIUM	**PONGID**	POSSESS	**POWDER**	**PRESTO**	PROTYLE
PIPPIN	PLATANE	**PODLEY**	PONGIDS	**POSSET**	POWDERS	PRESTOS	PROTYLS
PIPPING	PLATANS	PODLEYS	**PONTIE**	POSSETS	POWDERY	**PRESTS**	**PROVEN**
PIPPINS	**PLATEN**	**PODSOL**	PONTIES	**POSSIE**	**POWNEY**	UPRESTS	PROVEND
PIQUET	PLATENS	PODSOLS	**PONTIL**	POSSIES	POWNEYS	**PREWYN**	**PROVER**
PIQUETS	**PLATER**	**PODZOL**	PONTILE	**POSSUM**	**POWNIE**	PREWYNS	PROVERB
PIRANA	PLATERS	PODZOLS	PONTILS	OPOSSUM	POWNIES	**PRICER**	PROVERS
PIRANAS	**PLAYED**	**POETIC**	**PONTON**	POSSUMS	**POWTER**	PRICERS	**PROYNE**
PIRATE	SPLAYED	POETICS	PONTONS	**POSTAL**	POWTERS	**PRIEFE**	PROYNED
PIRATED	**PLAYER**	**POFFLE**	**POODLE**	POSTALS	**POWWOW**	PRIEFES	PROYNES
PIRATES	PLAYERS	POFFLES	POODLES	**POSTER**	POWWOWS	**PRIEST**	**PRUINA**
PIRAYA	**PLEADS**	**POGROM**	**POOGYE**	POSTERN	**POYSON**	PRIESTS	PRUINAS
PIRAYAS	UPLEADS	POGROMS	POOGYEE	POSTERS	POYSONS	**PRIEVE**	**PRUINE**
PIRNIE	**PLEASE**	**POINTE**	POOGYES	**POSTIE**	**PRAISE**	PRIEVED	PRUINES
PIRNIES	PLEASED	POINTED	**POOJAH**	POSTIES	UPRAISE	PRIEVES	**PRUNER**
PISTIL	PLEASER	POINTEL	POOJAHS	**POSTIL**	PRAISED	**PRIMER**	PRUNERS
PISTILS	PLEASES	POINTER	**POOLED**	APOSTIL	PRAISER	PRIMERO	**PRYING**
PISTOL	**PLEDGE**	POINTES	SPOOLED	POSTILS	PRAISES	PRIMERS	PRYINGS
PISTOLE	PLEDGED	**POISER**	**POONAC**	**POTAGE**	**PRANCE**	**PRINCE**	**PSYCHE**
PISTOLS	PLEDGEE	POISERS	POONACS	POTAGES	PRANCED	PRINCED	PSYCHED
PISTON	PLEDGER	**POISON**	**POORER**	**POTASS**	PRANCER	PRINCES	PSYCHES
PISTONS	PLEDGES	POISONS	SPOORER	POTASSA	PRANCES	**PRINTS**	**PSYCHO**
PITARA	PLEDGET	**POLDER**	**POOTER**	**POTCHE**	**PRANCK**	SPRINTS	PSYCHOS
PITARAH	**PLENTY**	POLDERS	POOTERS	POTCHED	PRANCKE	**PRISER**	**PSYWAR**
PITARAS	APLENTY	**POLEYN**	**POPJOY**	POTCHER	PRANCKS	PRISERS	PSYWARS
PITIER	**PLENUM**	POLEYNS	POPJOYS	POTCHES	**PRATED**	**PRISES**	**PTERIA**
PITIERS	PLENUMS	**POLICE**	**POPLAR**	**POTEEN**	**PRATER**	UPRISES	APTERIA
PITTED	**PLEUCH**	POLICED	POPLARS	POTEENS	PRATERS	**PRISON**	**PTERIN**
SPITTED	PLEUCHS	POLICES	**POPLIN**	**POTENT**	**PRATES**	PRISONS	PTERINS
PITTEN	**PLEUGH**	**POLING**	POPLINS	POTENTS	UPRATES	**PRIVET**	**PTISAN**
SPITTEN	PLEUGHS	POLINGS	**POPPER**	**POTFUL**	**PRATIE**	PRIVETS	PTISANS
PITTER	**PLEURA**	**POLITE**	POPPERS	POTFULS	PRATIES	**PRIZER**	**PUBLIC**
SPITTER	PLEURAE	POLITER	**POPPET**	**POTGUN**	**PRAWLE**	PRIZERS	PUBLICS
PITTERS	PLEURAL	**POLLAN**	POPPETS	POTGUNS	PRAWLES	**PROBIT**	**PUCKER**
PITURI	**PLEXOR**	POLLANS	**POPPIT**	**POTHER**	**PRAYED**	PROBITS	PUCKERS
PITURIS	PLEXORS	**POLLEN**	POPPITS	POTHERS	**PRAYER**	PROBITY	PUCKERY
PIUPIU	**PLIGHT**	POLLENS	**POPPLE**	POTHERY	PRAYERS	**PROFIT**	**PUDDEN**
PIUPIUS	YPLIGHT	POLLENT	POPPLED	**POTION**	**PREACE**	PROFITS	PUDDENS
PIZZLE	PLIGHTS	**POLLER**	POPPLES	POTIONS	PREACED	**PROIGN**	**PUDDER**
PIZZLES	**PLINTH**	POLLERS	**POPRIN**	**POTTED**	PREACES	PROIGNS	PUDDERS
PLACER	PLINTHS	**POLYPE**	POPRINS	SPOTTED	**PREACH**	**PROINE**	**PUDDLE**
PLACERS	**PLONGE**	POLYPES	**PORGIE**	**POTTER**	PREACHY	PROINED	PUDDLED
PLACET	PLONGED	**POMACE**	PORGIES	SPOTTER	**PREASE**	PROINES	PUDDLER
PLACETS	PLONGES	POMACES	**PORISM**	POTTERS	PREASED	**PROKER**	PUDDLES
PLACIT	**PLOOKS**	**POMADE**	PORISMS	POTTERY	PREASES	PROKERS	**PUEBLO**
PLACITA	UPLOOKS	POMADED	**PORKER**	**POTTLE**	**PRECIS**	**PROLEG**	PUEBLOS
PLACITS	**PLOUGH**	POMADES	PORKERS	POTTLES	PRECISE	PROLEGS	**PUFFER**
PLAGUE	PLOUGHS	**POMELO**	**POROSE**	**POUDER**	**PREEVE**	**PROLER**	PUFFERS
PLAGUED	**PLOVER**	POMELOS	POROSES	**POUDRE**	PREEVED	PROLERS	PUFFERY
PLAGUES	PLOVERS	**POMMEL**	**PORTAL**	POUDRES	PREEVES	**PROLLS**	**PUFFIN**
PLAGUEY	PLOVERY	POMMELE	PORTALS	**POUFFE**	**PREFAB**	UPROLLS	PUFFING
PLAICE	**PLUNGE**	POMMELS	**PORTED**	POUFFES	PREFABS	**PROMPT**	PUFFINS
PLAICES	PLUNGED	**POMPEY**	SPORTED	**POULPE**	**PREFER**	PROMPTS	**PUISNE**
PLAINT	PLUNGER	POMPEYS	**PORTER**	POULPES	PREFERS	**PRONES**	PUISNES
PLAINTS	PLUNGES	**POMPOM**	SPORTER	**POUNCE**	**PREIFE**	PRONEST	**PULING**
PLANER	**PLURAL**	POMPOMS	PORTERS	POUNCED	PREIFES	**PROPEL**	PULINGS
PLANERS	PLURALS	**POMPON**	**POSADA**	POUNCES	**PRELIM**	PROPELS	**PULKHA**
PLANET	**PLUTON**	POMPONS	POSADAS	POUNCET	PRELIMS	**PROPER**	PULKHAS
PLANETS	PLUTONS	**POMROY**	**POSEUR**	**POURER**	**PREMED**	PROPERS	**PULLER**
PLANTA	**PLYING**	POMROYS	POSEURS	POURERS	PREMEDS	**PROPYL**	PULLERS
PLANTAR	UPLYING	**PONCHO**	**POSHES**	**POURIE**	**PREMIE**	PROPYLA	**PULLET**
PLANTAS	**PNEUMA**	PONCHOS	SPOSHES	POURIES	PREMIER	PROPYLS	PULLETS
PLAQUE	PNEUMAS	**PONDER**	POSHEST	**POUSSE**	PREMIES	**PROSER**	**PULLEY**
PLAQUES	**POCHAY**	PONDERS	**POSING**	POUSSES	**PREPAY**	PROSERS	PULLEYS
PLASHY	POCHAYS	**PONDOK**	POSINGS	**POUTED**	PREPAYS	**PROTEA**	**PULPER**
SPLASHY	**POCKET**	PONDOKS	**POSNET**	SPOUTED	**PRESET**	PROTEAN	PULPERS
PLASMA	POCKETS	**PONGED**	POSNETS	**POUTER**		PROTEAS	**PULPIT**
PLASMAS	**PODITE**	SPONGED	**POSSER**	SPOUTER		**PROTON**	PULPITS
PLASTE	PODITES	**PONGEE**	POSSERS			PROTONS	**PULQUE**

PULQUES	**PURRED**	**QUAIGH**	AQUIVER	**RADIAL**	FRAILLY	RANDANS	GRAPING
PULSAR	SPURRED	QUAIGHS	QUIVERS	RADIALE	**RAINED**	**RANDED**	TRAPING
PULSARS	**PURSER**	**QUAILS**	QUIVERY	RADIALS	BRAINED	BRANDED	**RAPIST**
PULTAN	PURSERS	SQUAILS	**QUOIST**	**RADIAN**	DRAINED	**RANDEM**	RAPISTS
PULTANS	**PURSEW**	**QUANGO**	QUOISTS	RADIANS	GRAINED	RANDEMS	**RAPPED**
PULTON	PURSEWS	QUANGOS	**QUOKKA**	RADIANT	TRAINED	**RANDIE**	CRAPPED
PULTONS	**PURSUE**	**QUANTA**	QUOKKAS	**RADIUM**	**RAINES**	RANDIER	DRAPPED
PULTUN	PURSUED	QUANTAL	**QUORUM**	RADIUMS	GRAINES	RANDIES	FRAPPED
PULTUNS	PURSUER	**QUANTS**	QUORUMS	**RADOME**	**RAIRDS**	**RANDOM**	TRAPPED
PULVER	PURSUES	EQUANTS	**QUOTER**	RADOMES	BRAIRDS	RANDOMS	WRAPPED
PULVERS	**PURVEY**	**QUARTE**	QUOTERS	**RADULA**	**RAISED**	**RANDON**	**RAPPEE**
PULVIL	PURVEYS	QUARTER	**QUOTUM**	RADULAE	ARAISED	RANDONS	FRAPPEE
PULVILS	**PUSHER**	QUARTES	QUOTUMS	RADULAR	BRAISED	**RANGED**	**RAPPEL**
PULWAR	PUSHERS	QUARTET	**QWERTY**	**RAFALE**	FRAISED	**RANGER**	RAPPELS
PULWARS	**PUSSEL**	**QUARTO**	QWERTYS	RAFALES	PRAISED	GRANGER	**RAPPER**
PUMELO	PUSSELS	QUARTOS	**RABBET**	**RAFFIA**	**RAISER**	ORANGER	TRAPPER
PUMELOS	**PUTEAL**	**QUARTZ**	DRABBET	RAFFIAS	PRAISER	RANGERS	WRAPPER
PUMICE	PUTEALS	QUARTZY	RABBETS	**RAFFLE**	RAISERS	RANGES	RAPPERS
PUMICED	**PUTELI**	**QUASAR**	**RABBIN**	RAFFLED	ARAISES	GRANGES	**RAPTOR**
PUMICES	PUTELIS	QUASARS	RABBINS	RAFFLER	BRAISES	ORANGES	RAPTORS
PUMMEL	**PUTLOG**	**QUAVER**	**RABBIT**	RAFFLES	FRAISES	**RANKED**	**RASCAL**
PUMMELS	PUTLOGS	QUAVERS	FRABBIT	**RAFTED**	PRAISES	BRANKED	RASCALS
PUMPER	**PUTTEE**	QUAVERY	RABBITS	CRAFTED	**RAISIN**	CRANKED	**RASHED**
PUMPERS	PUTTEES	**QUEACH**	RABBITY	DRAFTED	RAISING	FRANKED	BRASHED
PUNCTO	**PUTTER**	QUEACHY	**RABBLE**	GRAFTED	RAISINS	PRANKED	CRASHED
PUNCTOS	SPUTTER	**QUEEST**	BRABBLE	**RAFTER**	**RAIYAT**	**RANKER**	TRASHED
PUNDIT	PUTTERS	QUEESTS	DRABBLE	DRAFTER	RAIYATS	FRANKER	**RASHER**
PUNDITS	**PUTTIE**	**QUELCH**	GRABBLE	GRAFTER	**RAKING**	RANKERS	RASHERS
PUNKAH	PUTTIED	SQUELCH	PRABBLE	RAFTERS	BRAKING	RANKEST	BRASHES
PUNKAHS	PUTTIER	**QUELEA**	RABBLED	**RAGEES**	CRAKING	**RANKLE**	CRASHES
PUNNER	PUTTIES	QUELEAS	RABBLER	DRAGEES	RAKINGS	CRANKLE	TRASHES
PUNNERS	**PUTURE**	**QUETHE**	RABBLES	**RAGGED**	**RALLYE**	PRANKLE	RASHEST
PUNNET	PUTURES	QUETHES	**RACEME**	BRAGGED	RALLYES	RANKLED	**RASING**
PUNNETS	**PUZZEL**	**QUICHE**	RACEMED	CRAGGED	**RAMBLE**	RANKLES	ERASING
PUNTEE	PUZZELS	QUICHED	RACEMES	DRAGGED	RAMBLED	**RANKLY**	**RASPED**
PUNTEES	**PUZZLE**	QUICHES	**RACERS**	RAGGEDY	RAMBLER	FRANKLY	GRASPED
PUNTER	PUZZLED	**QUIDAM**	BRACERS	**RAGGEE**	RAMBLES	**RANSEL**	**RASPER**
PUNTERS	PUZZLER	QUIDAMS	TRACERS	RAGGEES	**RAMCAT**	RANSELS	GRASPER
PUPATE	PUZZLES	**QUIGHT**	**RACHES**	**RAGGLE**	RAMCATS	**RANSOM**	RASPERS
PUPATED	**PYCNON**	QUIGHTS	BRACHES	RAGGLED	**RAMMED**	TRANSOM	**RASSES**
PUPATES	PYCNONS	**QUILLS**	ORACHES	RAGGLES	CRAMMED	RANSOMS	BRASSES
PUPPET	**PYEMIA**	SQUILLS	**RACHIS**	**RAGINI**	DRAMMED	**RANTED**	FRASSES
PUPPETS	PYEMIAS	**QUINCE**	ARACHIS	RAGINIS	**RAMMER**	DRANTED	GRASSES
PURDAH	**PYGARG**	QUINCES	**RACING**	**RAGLAN**	CRAMMER	GRANTED	TRASSES
PURDAHS	PYGARGS	**QUINIE**	BRACING	RAGLANS	RAMMERS	TRANTED	WRASSES
PURFLE	**PYONER**	QUINIES	GRACING	**RAGMAN**	**RAMPED**	**RANTER**	**RASTER**
PURFLED	PYONERS	**QUINOA**	TRACING	RAGMANS	TRAMPED	GRANTER	RASTERS
PURFLES	**PYRENE**	QUINOAS	RACINGS	**RAGMEN**	**RAMPER**	TRANTER	**RASURE**
PURGER	PYRENES	**QUINOL**	**RACISM**	RAGMENT	TRAMPER	RANTERS	ERASURE
PURGERS	**PYRITE**	QUINOLS	RACISMS	**RAGOUT**	RAMPERS	**RANULA**	RASURES
PURGES	PYRITES	**QUINTA**	**RACIST**	RAGOUTS	**RAMROD**	RANULAS	**RATBAG**
SPURGES	**PYROPE**	QUINTAL	RACISTS	**RAIDED**	RAMRODS	**RANZEL**	RATBAGS
PURINE	PYROPES	QUINTAN	**RACKED**	BRAIDED	**RAMSON**	RANZELS	**RATERS**
PURINES	**PYTHON**	QUINTAS	CRACKED	**RAIDER**	RAMSONS	**RAPERS**	CRATERS
PURISM	PYTHONS	**QUINTE**	TRACKED	BRAIDER	**RANCED**	DRAPERS	FRATERS
PURISMS	**PYURIA**	QUINTES	WRACKED	RAIDERS	PRANCED	**RAPHIA**	GRATERS
PURIST	PYURIAS	QUINTET	**RACKER**	**RAIKED**	TRANCED	RAPHIAS	PRATERS
PURISTS	**QIGONG**	**QUINTS**	CRACKER	**RAILED**	**RANCEL**	**RAPIER**	**RATIFY**
PURLER	QIGONGS	SQUINTS	RACKERS	BRAILED	RANCELS	CRAPIER	GRATIFY
PURLERS	**QINTAR**	**QUINZE**	**RACKET**	DRAILED	**RANCES**	DRAPIER	**RATINE**
PURLIN	QINTARS	QUINZES	BRACKET	TRAILED	PRANCES	GRAPIER	RATINES
PURLINE	**QUAERE**	**QUIRED**	RACKETS	**RAILER**	TRANCES	RAPIERS	**RATING**
PURLING	QUAERED	QUIRES	RACKETT	BRAILER	**RANCHO**	**RAPINE**	CRATING
PURLINS	QUAERES	SQUIRED	RACKETY	FRAILER	RANCHOS	RAPINES	GRATING
PURPIE	**QUAGGA**	SQUIRES	**RACOON**	TRAILER	**RANCOR**	**RAPING**	ORATING
PURPIES	QUAGGAS	**QUIRTS**	RACOONS	RAILERS	RANCORS	CRAPING	PRATING
PURPLE	**QUAHOG**	SQUIRTS	**RADDLE**	RAILES	**RANDAN**	DRAPING	RATINGS
PURPLED	QUAHOGS	**QUITCH**	RADDLED	**RAILLY**			
PURPLER	**QUAICH**	SQUITCH	RADDLES				
PURPLES	QUAICHS	**QUIVER**					

RATION	GRAYLES	REBUKE	AREDING	REFUTE	RELINE	RENNET	RERAIL
ORATION	RAYLESS	REBUKED	BREDING	REFUTED	RELINED	RENNETS	RERAILS
RATIONS	RAYLET	REBUKER	REDLEG	REFUTER	RELINES	RENNIN	REREAD
RATLIN	RAYLETS	REBUKES	REDLEGS	REFUTES	RELIVE	RENNING	REREADS
RATLINE	RAYNES	RECALL	REDOWA	REGAIN	RELIVED	RENNINS	RESALE
RATLING	TRAYNES	RECALLS	REDOWAS	REGAINS	RELIVER	RENOWN	RESALES
RATLINS	RAYONS	RECANT	REDRAW	REGALE	RELIVES	RENOWNS	RESCUE
RATOON	CRAYONS	RECANTS	REDRAWN	GREGALE	RELOAD	RENTAL	RESCUED
RATOONS	RAZING	RECAST	REDRAWS	REGALED	RELOADS	TRENTAL	RESCUER
RATTAN	BRAZING	PRECAST	REDTOP	REGALES	RELUCT	RENTALS	RESCUES
RATTANS	CRAZING	RECASTS	REDTOPS	REGARD	RELUCTS	RENTER	RESEAL
RATTED	GRAZING	RECEDE	REDUCE	REGARDS	RELUME	BRENTER	RESEALS
DRATTED	RAZURE	PRECEDE	REDUCED	REGENT	RELUMED	RENTERS	RESEAT
PRATTED	RAZURES	RECEDED	REDUCER	REGENTS	RELUMES	RENVOI	RESEATS
RATTEN	RAZZIA	RECEDES	REDUCES	REGEST	REMADE	RENVOIS	RESEAU
RATTENS	RAZZIAS	RECEPT	REDUIT	REGESTS	REMADES	RENVOY	RESEAUS
RATTER	RAZZLE	PRECEPT	REDUITS	REGGAE	REMAIN	RENVOYS	RESEAUX
RATTERS	RAZZLES	RECEPTS	REEBOK	REGGAES	REMAINS	REOPEN	RESECT
RATTERY	READER	RECESS	REEBOKS	REGIME	REMAKE	REOPENS	RESECTS
RATTLE	READERS	PRECESS	REEDER	REGIMEN	REMAKES	REPACK	RESEDA
BRATTLE	REAKED	RECIPE	BREEDER	REGIMES	REMAND	REPACKS	RESEDAS
PRATTLE	CREAKED	RECIPES	REEDERS	REGINA	REMANDS	REPAID	RESELL
RATTLED	FREAKED	RECITE	REEFER	REGINAE	REMARK	PREPAID	RESELLS
RATTLER	WREAKED	RECITED	REEFERS	REGINAL	REMARKS	REPAIR	RESENT
RATTLES	REAMED	RECITER	REEKIE	REGINAS	REMBLE	REPAIRS	PRESENT
RATTON	BREAMED	RECITES	REEKIER	REGION	TREMBLE	REPAST	RESENTS
RATTONS	CREAMED	RECKED	REELER	REGIONS	REMBLED	REPASTS	RESETS
RAUCLE	DREAMED	TRECKED	REELERS	REGIVE	REMBLES	REPAYS	PRESETS
RAUCLER	REAMER	WRECKED	REEVED	REGIVEN	REMEAD	PREPAYS	RESHIP
RAUGHT	CREAMER	RECKON	PREEVED	REGIVES	REMEADS	REPEAL	RESHIPS
DRAUGHT	DREAMER	RECKONS	REEVES	REGLET	REMEDE	REPEALS	RESIDE
FRAUGHT	REAMERS	RECOIL	PREEVES	REGLETS	REMEDES	REPEAT	PRESIDE
RAUNCH	REAPER	RECOILS	REFACE	REGRET	REMEID	REPEATS	RESIDED
BRAUNCH	REAPERS	RECORD	REFACED	REGRETS	REMEIDS	REPENT	RESIDER
CRAUNCH	REARER	RECORDS	REFACES	REGULA	REMIND	REPENTS	RESIDES
RAUNCHY	DREARER	RECOUP	REFECT	REGULAE	REMINDS	REPINE	RESIGN
RAUNGE	REARERS	RECOUPS	PREFECT	REGULAR	REMISE	REPINED	RESIGNS
RAUNGED	REASON	RECTOR	REFECTS	REGULO	PREMISE	REPINER	RESILE
RAUNGES	TREASON	ERECTOR	REFERS	REGULOS	REMISED	REPINES	RESILED
RAVAGE	REASONS	RECTORS	PREFERS	REHEAR	REMISES	REPLAN	RESILES
RAVAGED	REASTS	RECTORY	REFILL	REHEARD	REMISS	REPLANS	RESIST
RAVAGER	BREASTS	RECTUM	REFILLS	REHEARS	PREMISS	REPLANT	RESISTS
RAVAGES	REATES	RECTUMS	REFINE	REHEAT	REMITS	REPLAY	RESKEW
RAVELS	CREATES	RECULE	REFINED	PREHEAT	FREMITS	REPLAYS	RESKEWS
GRAVELS	REAVER	RECULED	REFINER	REHEATS	REMORA	REPONE	RESKUE
TRAVELS	REAVERS	RECULES	REFINES	REHEEL	REMORAS	REPONED	RESKUED
RAVENS	REAVES	RECURE	REFLAG	REHEELS	REMOTE	REPONES	RESKUES
CRAVENS	GREAVES	RECURED	REFLAGS	REINED	REMOTER	REPORT	RESOLE
RAVERS	REBACK	RECURES	REFLET	GREINED	REMOTES	REPORTS	RESOLED
CRAVERS	REBACKS	RECUSE	REFLETS	REITER	REMOVE	REPOSE	RESOLES
GRAVERS	REBATE	RECUSED	REFLOW	REITERS	PREMOVE	REPOSED	RESORB
RAVINE	REBATED	RECUSES	REFLOWS	REIVER	REMOVED	REPOSES	RESORBS
RAVINED	REBATER	REDACT	REFOOT	REIVERS	REMOVER	REPOST	RESORT
RAVINES	REBATES	REDACTS	REFOOTS	REJECT	REMOVES	REPOSTS	RESORTS
RAVING	REBECK	REDDEN	REFORM	REJECTS	REMUDA	REPPED	RESTED
BRAVING	REBECKS	REDDENS	PREFORM	REJOIN	REMUDAS	PREPPED	CRESTED
CRAVING	REBIND	REDDER	REFORMS	REJOINS	RENAME	REPUGN	PRESTED
GRAVING	REBINDS	REDDERS	REFUEL	RELATE	RENAMED	REPUGNS	WRESTED
RAVINGS	REBITE	REDDLE	REFUELS	PRELATE	RENAMES	REPULP	RESTEM
RAWEST	REBITES	TREDDLE	REFUGE	RELATED	RENDER	REPULPS	RESTEMS
BRAWEST	REBOIL	REDDLED	REFUGED	RELATER	RENDERS	REPURE	RESTER
RAWING	REBOILS	REDDLES	REFUGEE	RELATES	RENEGE	REPURED	WRESTER
DRAWING	REBORE	REDEAL	REFUGES	RELENT	RENEGED	REPURES	RESTERS
RAWINGS	REBORED	REDEALS	REFUND	RELENTS	RENEGER	REPUTE	RESULT
RAYING	REBORES	REDEALT	REFUNDS	RELICT	RENEGES	REPUTED	RESULTS
BRAYING	REBUFF	REDEEM	REFUSE	RELICTS	RENNED	REPUTES	RESUME
FRAYING	REBUFFS	REDEEMS	REFUSED	RELIEF	GRENNED	REQUIT	PRESUME
GRAYING		REDEYE	REFUSER	RELIEFS	RENNES	REQUITE	RESUMED
PRAYING		REDEYES	REFUSES	RELIER	BRENNES	REQUITS	RESUMES
RAYLES		REDING		RELIERS	FRENNES		RETAIL

```
RETAILS    REVESTS    RIBOSE     TRIFLED    RINSERS    DRIVING    BROILED    ROSACE
RETAIN     REVETS     RIBOSES    RIFLER     RIOTER     RIVLIN     DROILED    ROSACEA
RETAINS    BREVETS    RICERS     TRIFLER    RIOTERS    RIVLINS    ROINED     ROSACES
RETAKE     REVEUR     GRICERS    RIFLERS    RIPECK     RIZARD     GROINED    ROSETS
RETAKEN    REVEURS    PRICERS    RIFLES     RIPECKS    RIZARDS    PROINED    GROSETS
RETAKER    REVIEW     RICHEN     TRIFLES    RIPERS     RIZZAR     ROKERS     ROSIER
RETAKES    PREVIEW    RICHENS    RIFTED     GRIPERS    RIZZARS    BROKERS    CROSIER
RETAMA     REVIEWS    RICHES     DRIFTED    RIPING     RIZZART    PROKERS    PROSIER
RETAMAS    REVILE     RICHEST    GRIFTED    GRIPING    RIZZER     ROKING     ROSIERE
RETARD     REVILED    RICHTS     RIGGED     RIPPED     RIZZERS    BROKING    ROSIERS
RETARDS    REVILER    FRICHTS    GRIGGED    DRIPPED    RIZZOR     PROKING    ROSIES
RETELL     REVILES    RICIER     PRIGGED    GRIPPED    RIZZORS    TROKING    ROSIEST
RETELLS    REVISE     PRICIER    TRIGGED    TRIPPED    ROADIE     ROLLED     ROSILY
RETENE     PREVISE    RICING     RIGGER     RIPPER     ROADIES    DROLLED    PROSILY
RETENES    REVISED    GRICING    FRIGGER    FRIPPER    ROAMER     PROLLED    ROSING
RETILE     REVISER    PRICING    PRIGGER    GRIPPER    ROAMERS    TROLLED    PROSING
RETILED    REVISES    TRICING    TRIGGER    TRIPPER    ROARER     ROLLER     ROSSER
RETILES    REVIVE     RICKED     RIGGERS    RIPPERS    ROARERS    DROLLER    CROSSER
RETINA     REVIVED    BRICKED    RIGHTO     RIPPLE     ROARIE     PROLLER    GROSSER
RETINAE    REVIVER    CRICKED    RIGHTOS    ARIPPLE    ROATED     TROLLER    ROSSERS
RETINAL    REVIVES    PRICKED    RIGHTS     CRIPPLE    TROATED    ROLLERS    ROSTED
RETINAS    REVOKE     TRICKED    FRIGHTS    GRIPPLE    ROBALO     ROMAGE     FROSTED
RETIRE     REVOKED    WRICKED    WRIGHTS    TRIPPLE    ROBALOS    ROMAGES    ROSTER
RETIRED    REVOKES    RICKER     RIGLIN     RIPPLED    ROBBER     ROMPER     ROSTERS
RETIREE    REVOLT     PRICKER    RIGLING    RIPPLER    ROBBERS    ROMPERS    ROSTRA
RETIRER    REVOLTS    TRICKER    RIGLINS    RIPPLES    ROBBERY    RONDEL     ROSTRAL
RETIRES    REWARD     RICKERS    RIGOLL     RIPPLET    ROBING     RONDELS    ROSULA
RETOOL     REWARDS    RICKLE     RIGOLLS    RIPRAP     ROBINGS    RONYON     ROSULAS
RETOOLS    REWIND     BRICKLE    RIGOUR     RIPRAPS    PROBING    RONYONS    ROTATE
RETORT     REWINDS    PRICKLE    RIGOURS    RISERS     ROBINGS    ROOFED     ROTATED
RETORTS    REWIRE     TRICKLE    RILLED     PRISERS    ROBUST     PROOFED    ROTATES
RETOUR     REWIRED    RICKLES    DRILLED    RISING     ROBUSTA    ROOFER     ROTCHE
RETOURS    REWIRES    RICKLY     FRILLED    ARISING    ROCHES     ROOFERS    ROTCHES
RETREE     REWORD     PRICKLY    GRILLED    GRISING    BROCHES    ROOKED     ROTGUT
RETREES    REWORDS    TRICKLY    PRILLED    IRISING    CROCHES    BROOKED    ROTGUTS
RETRIM     REWORK     RIDDER     TRILLED    KRISING    TROCHES    CROOKED    ROTHER
RETRIMS    REWORKS    RIDDERS    RILLES     PRISING    ROCHET     DROOKED    BROTHER
RETTED     REWRAP     RIDDLE     GRILLES    RISINGS    ROCHETS    ROOKIE     ROTHERS
ARETTED    REWRAPS    GRIDDLE    RILLET     RISKED     ROCKED     ROOKIES    ROTOLO
FRETTED    RHAPHE     RIDDLED    RILLETS    BRISKED    BROCKED    ROOMED     ROTOLOS
RETUND     RHAPHES    RIDDLER    RIMERS     FRISKED    CROCKED    BROOMED    ROTTAN
RETUNDS    RHETOR     RIDDLES    PRIMERS    RISKER     FROCKED    GROOMED    ROTTANS
RETUNE     RHETORS    RIDENT     TRIMERS    BRISKER    TROCKED    VROOMED    ROTTED
RETUNED    RHOMBI     TRIDENT    RIMIER     FRISKER    ROCKER     ROOMER     TROTTED
RETUNES    RHOMBIC    RIDGED     GRIMIER    RISKERS    ROCKERS    ROOMERS    ROTTEN
RETURF     RHUMBA     BRIDGED    RIMING     RISPED     ROCKERY    ROOPED     ROTTENS
RETURFS    RHUMBAS    FRIDGED    BRIMING    CRISPED    ROCKET     DROOPED    ROTTER
RETURN     RHYMER     RIDGEL     CRIMING    RISQUE     BROCKET    TROOPED    TROTTER
RETURNS    RHYMERS    RIDGELS    GRIMING    RISQUES    CROCKET    ROOSES     ROTTERS
REURGE     RHYTHM     RIDGES     PRIMING    RITTED     ROCKETS    BROOSES    ROTULA
REURGED    RHYTHMI    BRIDGES    RIMMED     FRITTED    ROCOCO     ROOTED     ROTULAS
REURGES    RHYTHMS    FRIDGES    BRIMMED    GRITTED    ROCOCOS    WROOTED    ROTUND
REVAMP     RIBALD     RIDGIL     PRIMMED    RITTER     RODDED     ROOTER     OROTUND
REVAMPS    RIBALDS    RIDGILS    TRIMMED    CRITTER    BRODDED    ROOTERS    ROTUNDA
REVEAL     RIBAND     RIDING     RINDED     FRITTER    PRODDED    ROOTLE     ROTUNDS
REVEALS    RIBANDS    BRIDING    BRINDED    GRITTER    RODENT     ROOTLED    ROUBLE
REVERB     RIBAUD     GRIDING    GRINDED    RITTERS    ERODENT    ROOTLES    TROUBLE
PREVERB    RIBAUDS    PRIDING    RINGED     RITUAL     RODENTS    ROOTLET    ROUBLES
REVERBS    RIBBED     RIDINGS    CRINGED    RITUALS    RODING     ROPERS     ROUCOU
REVERE     CRIBBED    RIEVER     FRINGED    RIVAGE     ERODING    GROPERS    ROUCOUS
REVERED    DRIBBED    GRIEVER    WRINGED    RIVAGES    RODINGS    PROPERS    ROUGHS
REVERER    RIBBON     RIEVERS    RINGER     RIVELS     ROEMER     ROPING     BROUGHS
REVERES    RIBBONS    RIEVES     BRINGER    RIVERS     ROEMERS    GROPING    TROUGHS
REVERS     RIBBONY    GRIEVES    CRINGER    DRIVELS    ROGERS     TROPING    ROUGHT
REVERSE    RIBIBE     PRIEVES    WRINGER    RIVETS     DROGERS    ROPINGS    BROUGHT
REVERSI    RIBIBES    RIFFLE     RINGERS    GRIVETS    ROGUES     ROQUET     DROUGHT
REVERSO    RIBLET     RIFFLED    PRINKED    PRIVETS    DROGUES    ROQUETS    WROUGHT
REVERT     TRIBLET    RIFFLER    RINKED     TRIVETS    ROILED     RORTER     ROUGHY
REVERTS                RIFFLES    PRINKED                                   FROUGHY
REVEST     RIBLETS    RIFLED     RINSER     RIVING     ROILED     RORTERS    ROULES
```

TROULES
ROUNCE
FROUNCE
TROUNCE
ROUNCES
ROUNDS
GROUNDS
ROUPED
CROUPED
GROUPED
TROUPED
ROUSED
AROUSED
GROUSED
ROUSER
AROUSER
GROUSER
ROUSERS
ROUSES
AROUSES
GROUSES
TROUSES
ROUTED
GROUTED
ROUTER
TROUTER
ROUTERS
ROUTES
CROUTES
ROUTHS
DROUTHS
ROVERS
DROVERS
PROVERS
TROVERS
ROVING
PROVING
ROVINGS
ROWELS
TROWELS
ROWERS
GROWERS
ROWING
CROWING
GROWING
TROWING
ROWINGS
ROWTHS
GROWTHS
ROYNED
PROYNED
ROYNES
GROYNES
PROYNES
ROZZER
ROZZERS
RUBATO
RUBATOS
RUBBED
DRUBBED
GRUBBED
RUBBER
GRUBBER
RUBBERS
RUBBERY
RUBBLE
GRUBBLE
RUBBLES
RUBIES
RUBIEST

RUBINE
RUBINES
RUBRIC
RUBRICS
RUCKED
TRUCKED
BRUCKLE
TRUCKLE
RUCKLED
RUCKLES
RUDDER
RUDDERS
RUDDLE
CRUDDLE
RUDDLED
RUDDLES
RUDELY
CRUDELY
RUDERY
PRUDERY
RUDEST
CRUDEST
RUDISH
PRUDISH
RUEING
GRUEING
TRUEING
RUEINGS
RUELLE
RUELLES
RUFFIN
RUFFING
RUFFINS
RUFFLE
TRUFFLE
RUFFLED
RUFFLER
RUFFLES
RUGGED
DRUGGED
RUGGER
DRUGGER
RUGGERS
RUINER
RUINERS
RULING
RULINGS
RUMBLE
CRUMBLE
DRUMBLE
GRUMBLE
RUMBLED
RUMBLER
RUMBLES
RUMBLY
CRUMBLY
GRUMBLY
RUMKIN
RUMKINS
RUMMER
BRUMMER
DRUMMER
GRUMMER
RUMMERS
RUMOUR
RUMOURS
RUMPED
CRUMPED
FRUMPED

TRUMPED
RUMPLE
CRUMPLE
FRUMPLE
RUMPLED
RUMPLES
RUNDLE
TRUNDLE
RUNDLED
RUNDLES
RUNDLET
RUNKLE
CRUNKLE
RUNKLED
RUNKLES
RUNLET
RUNLETS
RUNNEL
RUNNELS
RUNNER
RUNNERS
RUNNET
RUNNETS
RUNRIG
RUNRIGS
RUNTED
BRUNTED
GRUNTED
PRUNTED
RUNWAY
RUNWAYS
RUPIAH
RUPIAHS
RUSHED
BRUSHED
CRUSHED
FRUSHED
RUSHER
RUSHERS
RUSHES
BRUSHES
CRUSHES
FRUSHES
RUSSEL
RUSSELS
RUSSET
RUSSETS
RUSSETY
RUSSIA
RUSSIAS
RUSTED
CRUSTED
TRUSTED
RUSTIC
RUSTICS
RUSTLE
RUSTLED
RUSTLER
RUSTLES
RUSTRE
RUSTRED
RUSTRES
RUTILE
RUTILES
RUTTER
RUTTERS
RYOKAN
RYOKANS

RYPECK
RYPECKS
RYTHME
RYTHMED
RYTHMES
SABBAT
SABBATS
SACHEM
SACHEMS
SACHET
SACHETS
SACQUE
SACQUES
SADDEN
SADDENS
SADDHU
SADDHUS
SADDLE
SADDLED
SADDLER
SADDLES
SADISM
SADISMS
SADIST
SADISTS
SAETER
SAETERS
SAFARI
SAFARIS
SAGENE
SAGENES
SAGGAR
SAGGARD
SAGGARS
SAGGER
SAGGERS
SAGOIN
SAGOINS
SAGUIN
SAGUINS
SAHIBA
SAHIBAH
SAHIBAS
SAIKEI
SAIKEIS
SAILER
SAILERS
SAILOR
SAILORS
SAIQUE
SAIQUES
SAITHE
SAITHES
SAKIEH
SAKIEHS
SALAAM
SALAAMS
SALADE
SALADES
SALAMI
SALAMIS
SALINA
SALINAS
SALINE
SALINES
SALIVA
SALIVAL
SALIVAS
SALLAD
SALLADS

SALLAL
SALLALS
SALLEE
SALLEES
SALLET
SALLETS
SALLOW
SALLOWS
SALLOWY
SALMON
SALMONS
SALOON
SALOONS
SALOOP
SALOOPS
SALTER
SALTERN
SALTERS
SALUKI
SALUKIS
SALUTE
SALUTED
SALUTER
SALUTES
SALVER
SALVERS
SALVIA
SALVIAS
SALVOR
SALVORS
SAMAAN
SAMAANS
SAMARA
SAMARAS
SAMBAL
SAMBALS
SAMBAR
SAMBARS
SAMBAS
TSAMBAS
SAMBUR
SAMBURS
SAMFOO
SAMFOOS
SAMIEL
SAMIELS
SAMITE
SAMITES
SAMLET
SAMLETS
SAMLOR
SAMLORS
SAMOSA
SAMOSAS
SAMPAN
SAMPANS
SAMPLE
SAMPLED
SAMPLER
SAMPLES
SAMSHU
SAMSHUS
SANCHO
SANCHOS
SANDAL
SANDALS
SANDER
SANDERS
SANDHI

SANDHIS
SANGAR
SANGARS
SANJAK
SANJAKS
SANNUP
SANNUPS
SANPAN
SANPANS
SANSEI
SANSEIS
SANTAL
SANTALS
SANTIR
SANTIRS
SANTON
SANTONS
SANTUR
SANTURS
SAPELE
SAPELES
SAPOTA
SAPOTAS
SAPPAN
SAPPANS
SAPPER
SAPPERS
SARDEL
SARDELS
SARNEY
SARNEYS
SARNIE
SARNIES
SARONG
SARONGS
SARSEN
SARSENS
SARTOR
SARTORS
SASHAY
SASHAYS
SASINE
SASINES
SATARA
SATARAS
SATEEN
SATEENS
SATINS
ISATINS
SATIRE
SATIRES
SATORI
SATORIS
SATRAP
SATRAPS
SATRAPY
SATYRA
SATYRAL
SATYRAS
SAUCER
SAUCERS
SAUGER
SAUGERS
SAULGE
SAULGES
SAULIE
SAULIES
SAUREL
SAURELS
SAVAGE

SAVAGED
SAVAGER
SAVAGES
SAVANT
SAVANTS
SAVATE
SAVATES
SAVINE
SAVINES
SAVING
SAVINGS
SAVOUR
SAVOURS
SAVOURY
SAVVEY
SAVVEYS
SAWDER
SAWDERS
SAWING
SAWINGS
SAWNEY
SAWNEYS
SAWPIT
SAWPITS
SAWYER
SAWYERS
SAXAUL
SAXAULS
SAYING
SAYINGS
SAYYID
SAYYIDS
SAZHEN
SAZHENS
SCAITH
SCAITHS
SCALAR
SCALARS
SCALER
SCALERS
SCAMEL
SCAMELS
SCAMPI
SCAMPIS
SCAPED
ESCAPED
SCAPES
ESCAPES
SCARAB
SCARABS
SCARCE
SCARCER
SCARER
SCARERS
SCARPS
ESCARPS
SCARRE
SCARRED
SCARRES
SCARTH
SCARTHS
SCATHE
SCATHED
SCATHES
SCAZON
SCAZONS
SCENDS
ASCENDS
SCENTS
ASCENTS

SCERNE
SCERNED
SCERNES
SCHELM
SCHELMS
SCHEME
SCHEMED
SCHEMER
SCHEMES
SCHISM
SCHISMA
SCHISMS
SCHIST
SCHISTS
SCHIZO
SCHIZOS
SCHLEP
SCHLEPP
SCHLEPS
SCHMOE
SCHMOES
SCHOOL
SCHOOLE
SCHOOLS
SCHORL
SCHORLS
SCHOUT
SCHOUTS
SCHTIK
SCHTIKS
SCHUIT
SCHUITS
SCHUYT
SCHUYTS
SCILLA
SCILLAS
SCIROC
SCIROCS
SCLAFF
SCLAFFS
SCLATE
SCLATED
SCLATES
SCLAVE
SCLAVES
SCLERA
SCLERAL
SCLERAS
SCLERE
SCLERES
SCLIFF
SCLIFFS
SCONCE
SCONCED
SCONCES
SCORER
SCORERS
SCORIA
SCORIAC
SCORIAE
SCORSE
SCORSED
SCORSER
SCORSES
SCOTER
SCOTERS
SCOTIA
SCOTIAS
SCOURS

SCOURSE **SCOUSE** SCOUSES **SCOUTH** SCOUTHS **SCOWTH** SCOWTHS **SCRAPE** SCRAPED SCRAPER SCRAPES **SCRAWL** SCRAWLS SCRAWLY **SCRAWM** SCRAWMS **SCRAYE** SCRAYES **SCREAK** SCREAKS SCREAKY **SCREAM** SCREAMS **SCREED** SCREEDS **SCREEN** SCREENS **SCRIBE** ASCRIBE ESCRIBE SCRIBED SCRIBER SCRIBES **SCRIKE** SCRIKED SCRIKES **SCRIMP** SCRIMPS SCRIMPY **SCRINE** SCRINES **SCRIPT** SCRIPTS **SCRIVE** SCRIVED SCRIVES **SCROBE** SCROBES **SCROLL** ESCROLL SCROLLS **SCROOP** SCROOPS **SCROWL** SCROWLE SCROWLS **SCROWS** ESCROWS **SCRUFF** SCRUFFS SCRUFFY **SCRUMP** SCRUMPS SCRUMPY **SCRUNT** SCRUNTS SCRUNTY **SCRUTO** SCRUTOS **SCRUZE**

SCRUZED SCRUZES **SCRYER** SCRYERS **SCRYNE** SCRYNES **SCULLE** SCULLED SCULLER SCULLES **SCULPT** SCULPTS **SCUNGE** SCUNGED SCUNGES **SCYTHE** SCYTHED SCYTHER SCYTHES **SDAINE** SDAINED SDAINES **SEABED** SEABEDS **SEALCH** SEALCHS **SEALER** SEALERS SEALERY **SEALGH** SEALGHS **SEAMER** SEAMERS **SEANCE** SEANCES **SEARAT** SEARATS **SEARCE** SEARCED SEARCES **SEASON** SEASONS **SEATER** SEATERS **SEAWAY** SEAWAYS **SEBATE** SEBATES **SECANT** SECANTS **SECEDE** SECEDED SECEDER SECEDES **SECERN** SECERNS **SECKEL** SECKELS **SECOND** SECONDE SECONDI SECONDO SECONDS **SECRET** SECRETA SECRETE SECRETS **SECTOR** SECTORS **SECURE**

SECURED SECURER SECURES **SEDATE** SEDATED SEDATER SEDATES **SEDUCE** SEDUCED SEDUCER SEDUCES **SEEDER** SEEDERS **SEEING** SEEINGS **SEEKER** SEEKERS **SEEMER** SEEMERS **SEESAW** SEESAWS **SEETHE** SEETHED SEETHER SEETHES **SEGGAR** SEGGARS **SEGHOL** SEGHOLS **SEICHE** SEICHES **SEINER** SEINERS **SEISIN** SEISING SEISINS **SEIZER** SEIZERS **SEIZIN** SEIZING SEIZINS **SELECT** SELECTS **SELKIE** SELKIES **SELLER** SELLERS **SEMBLE** SEMBLED SEMBLES **SEMEME** SEMEMES **SEMMIT** SEMMITS **SEMPLE** SEMPLER **SEMSEM** SEMSEMS **SENATE** SENATES **SENDAL** SENDALS **SENDER** SENDERS **SENEGA** SENEGAS **SENIOR** SENIORS **SENNET** SENNETS

SENNIT SENNITS **SENSOR** SENSORS SENSORY **SEPHEN** SEPHENS **SEPIUM** SEPIUMS **SEPSES** SEPSIS ASEPSES ASEPSIS **SEPTET** SEPTETS SEPTETT **SEPTIC** ASEPTIC **SEQUEL** SEQUELA SEQUELS **SEQUIN** SEQUINS **SERAIL** SERAILS **SERANG** SERANGS **SERAPE** SERAPES **SERAPH** SERAPHS **SERDAB** SERDABS **SEREIN** SEREINS **SERENE** SERENED SERENER SERENES **SERIAL** SERIALS **SERING** SERINGA **SERIPH** SERIPHS **SERMON** SERMONS **SEROON** SEROONS **SEROSA** SEROSAE SEROSAS **SERRAN** SERRANS **SERVAL** SERVALS **SERVER** SERVERS SERVERY **SESAME** SESAMES **SESELI** SESELIS **SESTET** SESTETS SESTETT **SESTON** SESTONS **SETTEE** SETTEES

SETTER SETTERS **SETTLE** SETTLED SETTLER SETTLES **SEVERE** SEVERED SEVERER **SEWAGE** SEWAGES **SEWING** SEWINGS **SEXISM** SEXISMS **SEXIST** SEXISTS **SEXPOT** SEXPOTS **SEXTAN** SEXTANS SEXTANT **SEXTET** SEXTETS SEXTETT **SEXTON** SEXTONS **SEXUAL** ASEXUAL **SHADOW** SHADOWS SHADOWY **SHADUF** SHADUFS **SHAIKH** SHAIKHS **SHAIRN** SHAIRNS **SHAKER** SHAKERS **SHALLI** SHALLIS **SHALOT** SHALOTS **SHAMAN** SHAMANS **SHAMED** ASHAMED **SHAMER** SHAMERS **SHAMES** ASHAMES **SHAMOY** SHAMOYS **SHAPER** SHAPERS **SHARER** SHARERS **SHARIA** SHARIAS SHARIAT **SHAVER** SHAVERS **SHAVIE** SHAVIES **SHAWED** PSHAWED **SHEATH** SHEATHE SHEATHS

SHEATHY **SHEAVE** SHEAVED SHEAVES **SHEIKH** SHEIKHS **SHEILA** SHEILAS **SHEKEL** SHEKELS **SHELVE** SHELVED SHELVES **SHENDS** YSHENDS **SHERIA** SHERIAS SHERIAT **SHERIF** SHERIFF SHERIFS **SHEUCH** SHEUCHS **SHEUGH** SHEUGHS **SHEWEL** SHEWELS **SHIELD** SHIELDS **SHIEST** ASHIEST **SHIKAR** SHIKARI SHIKARS **SHIKSA** SHIKSAS **SHIKSE** SHIKSES **SHINER** SHINERS **SHINES** SHINESS **SHINNE** SHINNED SHINNES **SHIPPO** SHIPPON SHIPPOS **SHIRRA** SHIRRAS **SHIVER** ASHIVER SHIVERS SHIVERY **SHIVOO** SHIVOOS **SHLOCK** SHLOCKS **SHODER** SHODERS **SHOFAR** SHOFARS **SHOGUN** SHOGUNS **SHORAN** SHORANS **SHORER** SHORERS **SHOUGH** SHOUGHS

SHOVEL SHOVELS **SHOVER** SHOVERS **SHOWER** SHOWERS SHOWERY **SHREEK** SHREEKS **SHREIK** SHREIKS **SHRIEK** SHRIEKS **SHRIFT** SHRIFTS **SHRIKE** SHRIKES **SHRILL** SHRILLS SHRILLY **SHRIMP** SHRIMPS **SHRINE** SHRINED SHRINES **SHRINK** SHRINKS **SHRIVE** SHRIVED SHRIVEL SHRIVEN SHRIVER SHRIVES **SHROFF** SHROFFS **SHROUD** SHROUDS SHROUDY **SHROVE** SHROVED SHROVES **SHTCHI** SHTCHIS **SHTETL** SHTETLS **SHTOOK** SHTOOKS **SHTUCK** SHTUCKS **SHUFTI** SHUFTIS **SIALON** SIALONS **SICKEN** SICKENS **SICKIE** SICKIES **SICKLE** SICKLED SICKLES **SIDDHA** SIDDHAS **SIDDHI** SIDDHIS **SIDING** SIDINGS **SIEGER**

SIEGERS **SIENNA** SIENNAS **SIERRA** SIERRAN SIERRAS **SIESTA** SIESTAS **SIFAKA** SIFAKAS **SIFFLE** SIFFLED SIFFLES **SIFTER** SIFTERS **SIGHER** SIGHERS **SIGNAL** SIGNALS **SIGNER** SIGNERS **SIGNET** SIGNETS **SIGNOR** SIGNORA SIGNORE SIGNORI SIGNORS SIGNORY **SILAGE** SILAGED SILAGES **SILANE** SILANES **SILENE** SILENES **SILENT** SILENTS **SILICA** SILICAS **SILKEN** SILKENS **SILKIE** SILKIER SILKIES **SILLER** SILLERS **SILVAN** SILVANS **SILVER** SILVERN SILVERS SILVERY **SIMIAN** SIMIANS **SIMILE** SIMILES **SIMKIN** SIMKINS **SIMMER** SIMMERS **SIMNEL** SIMNELS **SIMOOM** SIMOOMS **SIMOON** SIMOONS **SIMORG** SIMORGS **SIMPAI**

SIMPAIS	SIZZLED	SLEECHY	SMUDGES	**SOIGNE**	**SORELL**	SPARRED	**SPIRAL**
SIMPER	SIZZLER	**SLEEVE**	**SNARER**	SOIGNEE	SORELLS	SPARRER	SPIRALS
SIMPERS	SIZZLES	SLEEVED	SNARERS	**SOIREE**	**SORGHO**	SPARRES	**SPIREA**
SIMPLE	**SKAITH**	SLEEVER	**SNASTE**	SOIREES	SORGHOS	**SPARSE**	SPIREAS
SIMPLED	SKAITHS	SLEEVES	SNASTES	**SOLACE**	**SORNER**	SPARSER	**SPIRED**
SIMPLER	**SKARTH**	**SLEIGH**	**SNATCH**	SOLACED	SORNERS	**SPARTH**	ASPIRED
SIMPLES	SKARTHS	SLEIGHS	SNATCHY	SOLACES	**SORREL**	SPARTHE	**SPIRES**
SIMPLEX	**SKATER**	SLEIGHT	**SNATHE**	**SOLAND**	SORRELS	SPARTHS	ASPIRES
SIMURG	SKATERS	**SLEUTH**	SNATHES	SOLANDS	**SORROW**	**SPATHE**	**SPIRIC**
SIMURGH	**SKETCH**	SLEUTHS	**SNEATH**	**SOLANO**	SORROWS	SPATHED	SPIRICS
SIMURGS	SKETCHY	**SLICER**	SNEATHS	SOLANOS	**SORTER**	SPATHES	**SPIRIT**
SINDON	**SKEWER**	SLICERS	**SNEBBE**	**SOLDAN**	SORTERS	**SPAULD**	SPIRITS
SINDONS	SKEWERS	**SLIDER**	SNEBBED	SOLDANS	**SORTIE**	SPAULDS	SPIRITY
SINGER	**SKIDOO**	SLIDERS	SNEBBES	**SOLDER**	SORTIED	**SPAVIE**	**SPITAL**
SINGERS	SKIDOOS	**SLIGHT**	**SNEEZE**	SOLDERS	SORTIES	SPAVIES	SPITALS
SINGLE	**SKIING**	SLIGHTS	SNEEZED	**SOLERA**	**SOUARI**	**SPAVIN**	**SPLASH**
SINGLED	SKIINGS	**SLIVER**	SNEEZER	SOLERAS	SOUARIS	SPAVINS	SPLASHY
SINGLES	**SKIVER**	SLIVERS	SNEEZES	**SOLITO**	**SOUPER**	**SPAYAD**	**SPLEEN**
SINGLET	SKIVERS	**SLOGAN**	**SNIDES**	SOLITON	SOUPERS	SPAYADS	SPLEENS
SINKER	**SKIVIE**	SLOGANS	SNIDEST	**SOLIVE**	**SOUPLE**	**SPECIE**	SPLEENY
SINKERS	SKIVIER	**SLOKEN**	**SNIPER**	SOLIVES	SOUPLED	SPECIES	**SPLENT**
SINNER	**SKLATE**	SLOKENS	SNIPERS	**SOLLAR**	SOUPLES	**SPEEDO**	SPLENTS
SINNERS	SKLATED	**SLOUCH**	**SNIVEL**	SOLLARS	**SOURCE**	SPEEDOS	**SPLICE**
SINNET	SKLATES	SLOUCHY	SNIVELS	**SOLLER**	SOURCED	**SPENCE**	SPLICED
SINNETS	**SKLENT**	**SLOUGH**	**SNOOZE**	SOLLERS	SOURCES	SPENCER	SPLICES
SINTER	ASKLENT	SLOUGHS	SNOOZED	**SOLUTE**	**SOURSE**	SPENCES	**SPLIFF**
SINTERS	SKLENTS	SLOUGHY	SNOOZER	SOLUTES	SOURSES	**SPERRE**	SPLIFFS
SINTERY	**SKLIFF**	**SLOVEN**	SNOOZES	**SOLVER**	**SOUTAR**	SPERRED	**SPLINE**
SIPHON	SKLIFFS	SLOVENS	**SNORER**	SOLVERS	SOUTARS	SPERRES	SPLINED
SIPHONS	**SKREEN**	**SLUDGE**	SNORERS	**SOMBRE**	**SOUTER**	**SPERSE**	SPLINES
SIPPER	SKREENE	SLUDGES	**SNUBBE**	SOMBRED	SOUTERS	ASPERSE	**SPLINT**
SIPPERS	SKREENS	**SLUICE**	SNUBBED	SOMBRER	**SOVIET**	SPERSED	SPLINTS
SIPPET	**SKRIMP**	SLUICED	SNUBBER	SOMBRES	SOVIETS	SPERSES	**SPLORE**
SIPPETS	SKRIMPS	SLUICES	SNUBBES	**SOMITE**	**SOVRAN**	**SPEWER**	SPLORES
SIPPLE	**SKRUMP**	**SMALTO**	**SNUDGE**	SOMITES	SOVRANS	SPEWERS	**SPONGE**
SIPPLED	SKRUMPS	SMALTOS	SNUDGED	**SONANT**	**SOWING**	**SPHAER**	SPONGED
SIPPLES	**SKRYER**	**SMEATH**	SNUDGES	SONANTS	SOWINGS	SPHAERE	SPONGER
SIRCAR	SKRYERS	SMEATHS	**SOAKER**	**SONATA**	**SOWSSE**	SPHAERS	SPONGES
SIRCARS	**SKYLAB**	**SMEETH**	SOAKERS	SONATAS	SOWSSED	**SPHEAR**	**SPORTS**
SIRDAR	SKYLABS	SMEETHS	**SOAPIE**	**SONERI**	SOWSSES	SPHEARE	ASPORTS
SIRDARS	**SKYWAY**	**SMEGMA**	SOAPIER	SONERIS	**SOWTER**	SPHEARS	**SPOTTE**
SIRENE	SKYWAYS	SMEGMAS	SOAPIES	**SONNET**	SOWTERS	**SPHENE**	SPOTTED
SIRENES	**SLAIRG**	**SMEUSE**	**SOBOLE**	SONNETS	**SOZZLE**	SPHENES	SPOTTER
SIRKAR	SLAIRGS	SMEUSES	SOBOLES	**SONSIE**	SOZZLED	**SPHERE**	SPOTTES
SIRKARS	**SLAKED**	**SMIGHT**	**SOCAGE**	SONSIER	SOZZLES	SPHERED	**SPOUSE**
SIRRAH	ASLAKED	SMIGHTS	SOCAGER	**SONTAG**	**SPACER**	SPHERES	ESPOUSE
SIRRAHS	YSLAKED	**SMILER**	SOCAGES	SONTAGS	SPACERS	**SPIALS**	SPOUSED
SIRREE	**SLAKES**	SMILERS	**SOCCER**	**SOOGEE**	**SPADER**	ESPIALS	SPOUSES
SIRREES	ASLAKES	**SMILET**	SOCCERS	SOOGEED	SPADERS	**SPICER**	**SPRAIN**
SISKIN	**SLALOM**	SMILETS	**SOCIAL**	SOOGEES	**SPAHEE**	SPICERS	SPRAINS
SISKINS	SLALOMS	**SMITER**	ASOCIAL	**SOOGIE**	SPAHEES	**SPICKS**	SPRAINT
SISSOO	**SLATER**	SMITERS	SOCIALS	SOOGIED	**SPAING**	ASPICKS	**SPRAWL**
SISSOOS	SLATERS	**SMOILE**	**SOCKER**	SOOGIES	SPAINGS	**SPIDER**	ASPRAWL
SISTER	**SLAVER**	SMOILED	SOCKERS	**SOOJEY**	**SPALLE**	SPIDERS	SPRAWLS
SISTERS	SLAVERS	SMOILES	**SOCKET**	SOOJEYS	SPALLED	SPIDERY	SPRAWLY
SITCOM	SLAVERY	**SMOKER**	SOCKETS	**SOOTHE**	SPALLES	**SPIGHT**	**SPREAD**
SITCOMS	**SLAVEY**	SMOKERS	**SODAIN**	SOOTHED	**SPARER**	SPIGHTS	ASPREAD
SITHEN	SLAVEYS	**SMOOTH**	SODAINE	SOOTHER	SPARERS	**SPIGOT**	SPREADS
SITHENS	**SLAYER**	SMOOTHE	**SODDEN**	SOOTHES	**SPARES**	SPIGOTS	**SPREDD**
SITREP	SLAYERS	SMOOTHS	SODDENS	**SOPHIA**	SPAREST	**SPILTH**	SPREDDE
SITREPS	**SLEAVE**	**SMOUSE**	**SODGER**	SOPHIAS	**SPARGE**	SPILTHS	SPREDDS
SITTAR	SLEAVED	SMOUSED	SODGERS	**SOPITE**	SPARGED	**SPINAR**	**SPRING**
SITTARS	SLEAVES	SMOUSER	**SODIUM**	SOPITED	SPARGER	SPINARS	SPRINGE
SITTER	**SLEAZE**	SMOUSES	SODIUMS	SOPITES	SPARGES	**SPINEL**	SPRINGS
SITTERS	SLEAZES	**SMOYLE**	**SOFFIT**	**SORAGE**	**SPARID**	SPINELS	SPRINGY
SITULA	**SLEDGE**	SMOYLED	SOFFITS	SORAGES	SPARIDS	**SPINES**	**SPRINT**
SITULAE	SLEDGED	SMOYLES	**SOFTEN**	**SORBET**	**SPARKE**	ASPINES	SPRINTS
SIZING	SLEDGER	**SMUDGE**	SOFTENS	SORBETS	SPARKED	**SPINET**	**SPRITE**
SIZINGS	SLEDGES	SMUDGED	**SOFTIE**	**SORDOR**	SPARKES	SPINETS	SPRITES
SIZZLE	**SLEECH**	SMUDGER	SOFTIES	SORDORS	**SPARRE**		**SPRITS**

ESPRITS	SQUISHY	STEALED	STODGE	STRAYS	STRUMAE	SUDDER	SURFER
SPROUT	STABLE	STEALER	STODGED	ESTRAYS	STRUMS	SUDDERS	SURFERS
ASPROUT	ASTABLE	STEALES	STODGER	STREAK	ESTRUMS	SUDSER	SURING
SPROUTS	STABLED	STEALT	STODGES	STREAKS	STRUNT	SUDSERS	USURING
SPRUCE	STABLER	STEANE	STOGEY	STREAKY	STRUNTS	SUFFER	SURREY
SPRUCED	STABLES	STEANED	STOGEYS	STREAM	STUCCO	SUFFERS	SURREYS
SPRUCER	STACTE	STEANES	STOGIE	STREAMS	STUCCOS	SUITOR	SURVEW
SPRUCES	STACTES	STEARE	STOGIES	STREAMY	STUDIO	SUITORS	SURVEWE
SPRUIK	STADDA	STEARED	STOKER	STREEK	STUDIOS	SULFUR	SURVEWS
SPRUIKS	STADDAS	STEARES	STOKERS	STREEKS	STUMER	SULFURS	SURVEY
SPRUIT	STADIA	STEDDE	STOLON	STREEL	STUMERS	SULLEN	SURVEYS
SPRUITS	STADIAL	STEDDED	STOLONS	STREELS	STUPID	SULLENS	SUSLIK
SPULYE	STADIAS	STEDDES	STONED	STREET	STUPIDS	SULTAN	SUSLIKS
SPULYED	STAGER	STEEMS	STONER	STREETS	STUPOR	SULTANA	SUTLER
SPULYES	STAGERS	ESTEEMS	STONERN	STREETY	STUPORS	SULTANS	SUTLERS
SPUNGE	STAGERY	STEEVE	STONERS	STRENE	STYLAR	SUMACH	SUTLERY
SPUNGES	STAITH	STEEVED	ASTONES	STRENES	ASTYLAR	SUMACHS	SUTTEE
SPURGE	STAITHE	STEEVER	STONNE	STRICH	STYLET	SUMMAR	SUTTEES
SPURGES	STAITHS	STEEVES	STONNED	ESTRICH	STYLETS	SUMMARY	SUTTLE
SPURNE	STALAG	STEMME	STONNES	OSTRICH	STYMIE	SUMMAT	SUTTLED
SPURNED	STALAGS	STEMMED	STOOGE	STRICT	STYMIED	SUMMATE	SUTTLES
SPURNER	STALES	STEMMES	STOOGED	ASTRICT	STYMIES	SUMMATS	SUTURE
SPURNES	STALEST	STENCH	STOOGES	STRIDE	SUBACT	SUMMER	SUTURED
SPYING	STAMEN	STENCHY	STOOPE	ASTRIDE	SUBACTS	SUMMERS	SUTURES
ESPYING	STAMENS	STENTS	STOOPED	STRIDES	SUBDEW	SUMMERY	SVELTE
SPYINGS	STANCE	OSTENTS	STOOPER	STRIFE	SUBDEWS	SUMMIT	SVELTER
SQUAIL	STANCES	STEPPE	STOOPES	STRIFES	SUBDUE	SUMMITS	SWARDS
SQUAILS	STANZA	STEPPED	STORER	STRIFT	SUBDUED	SUMMON	USWARDS
SQUALL	STANZAS	STEPPER	STORERS	STRIFTS	SUBDUER	SUMMONS	SWARTH
SQUALLS	STANZE	STEPPES	STOREY	STRIGA	SUBDUES	SUMPIT	SWARTHS
SQUALLY	STANZO	STEREO	STOREYS	STRIGAE	SUBFEU	SUMPITS	SWARTHY
SQUAMA	STANZOS	STEREOS	STORGE	STRIKE	SUBFEUS	SUNBED	SWARVE
SQUAMAE	STAPLE	STEROL	STORGES	STRIKER	SUBLET	SUNBEDS	SWARVED
SQUAME	STAPLED	STEROLS	STOUND	STRIKES	SUBLETS	SUNBOW	SWARVES
SQUAMES	STAPLER	STERVE	ASTOUND	STRING	SUBMIT	SUNBOWS	SWATHE
SQUARE	STAPLES	STERVED	STOUNDS	STRINGS	SUBMITS	SUNDAE	SWATHED
SQUARED	STARCH	STERVES	STOUTH	STRINGY	SUBORN	SUNDAES	SWATHES
SQUARER	STARCHY	STEVEN	STOUTHS	STRIPE	SUBORNS	SUNDER	SWAYER
SQUARES	STARER	STEVENS	STOVER	STRIPED	SUBSET	ASUNDER	SWAYERS
SQUASH	STARERS	STEWER	STOVERS	STRIPES	SUBSETS	SUNDERS	SWEARD
SQUASHY	STARTS	STEWERS	ESTOVER	STRIPEY	SUBTIL	SUNDRA	SWEARDS
SQUAWK	ASTARTS	STIEVE	STOWER	STRIVE	SUBTILE	SUNDRAS	SWERVE
SQUAWKS	STARVE	STIEVER	STOWERS	STRIVED	SUBTLE	SUNDRI	SWERVED
SQUAWKY	STARVED	STIFLE	STOWND	STRIVEN	SUBTLER	SUNDRIS	SWERVER
SQUEAK	STARVES	STIFLED	STOWNDS	STRIVER	SUBURB	SUNGAR	SWERVES
SQUEAKS	STATED	STIFLER	STOWRE	STRIVES	SUBURBS	SUNGARS	SWEVEN
SQUEAKY	ESTATED	STIFLES	STOWRES	STROAM	SUBWAY	SUNHAT	SWEVENS
SQUEAL	STATER	STIGMA	STRAFE	STROAMS	SUBWAYS	SUNHATS	SWINGE
SQUEALS	STATERS	STIGMAS	STRAFED	STROBE	SUCCES	SUNKET	SWINGED
SQUIER	STATES	STIGME	STRAFES	STROBES	SUCCESS	SUNKETS	SWINGER
SQUIERS	ESTATES	STIGMES	STRAFF	STROKE	SUCCOR	SUNKIE	SWINGES
SQUIFF	STATIC	STILET	STRAFFS	STROKED	SUCCORS	SUNKIES	SWIPER
SQUIFFY	ASTATIC	STILETS	STRAIK	STROKEN	SUCCORY	SUNRAY	SWIPERS
SQUILL	STATICS	STIMIE	STRAIKS	STROKER	SUCCUS	SUNRAYS	SWITCH
SQUILLS	STATOR	STIMIED	STRAIN	STROKES	SUCCUSS	SUNSET	SWITCHY
SQUINT	STATORS	STIMIES	STRAINS	STROLL	SUCKEN	SUNSETS	SWIVEL
ASQUINT	STATUA	STINGO	STRAINT	STROLLS	SUCKENS	SUNTAN	SWIVELS
SQUINTS	STATUAS	STINGOS	STRAIT	STROMB	SUCKER	SUNTANS	SWIVET
SQUIRE	STATUE	STIPEL	STRAITS	STROMBS	SUCKERS	SUPAWN	SWIVETS
ESQUIRE	STATUED	STIPELS	STRAKE	STROND	SUCKET	SUPAWNS	SWOUND
SQUIRED	STATUES	STIRRA	STRAKES	STRONDS	SUCKETS	SUPINE	SWOUNDS
SQUIRES	STAYER	STIRRAH	STRAMP	STROOK	SUCKLE	SUPINES	SWOUNE
SQUIRM	STAYERS	STIRRAS	STRAMPS	STROOKE	SUCKLED	SUPPER	SWOUNES
SQUIRMS	STAYNE	STIRRE	STRAND	STROUD	SUCKLER	SUPPERS	SWOWND
SQUIRMY	STAYNED	STIRRED	ASTRAND	STROUDS	SUCKLES	SUPPLE	SWOWNDS
SQUIRR	STAYNES	STIRRER	STRANDS	STROUP	SUDATE	SUPPLED	SWOWNE
SQUIRRS	STAYRE	STIRRES	STRATH	STROUPS	SUDATED	SUPPLER	SWOWNES
SQUIRT	STAYRES	STIVER	STRATHS	STROUT	SUDATES	SUPPLES	SYLVAN
SQUIRTS	STEALE	STIVERS		STROUTS	SUDDEN	SURBED	SYLVANS
SQUISH				STRUMA	ASUDDEN	SURBEDS	

SYLVIA	TAIGLES	**TANDEM**	TARSIAS	ATAXIES	**TELLER**	STERNED	**THIRAM**
SYLVIAS	**TAILOR**	TANDEMS	**TARTAN**	**TAXING**	TELLERS	**TERRET**	THIRAMS
SYMBOL	TAILORS	**TANGED**	TARTANA	TAXINGS	**TELSON**	TERRETS	**THIRST**
SYMBOLE	**TAILYE**	STANGED	TARTANE	**TCHICK**	TELSONS	**TERRIT**	ATHIRST
SYMBOLS	TAILYES	**TANGIE**	TARTANS	TCHICKS	**TEMPER**	TERRITS	THIRSTS
SYNDET	**TAIPAN**	TANGIER	**TARTAR**	**TEACUP**	TEMPERA	**TERROR**	THIRSTY
SYNDETS	TAIPANS	TANGIES	TARTARE	TEACUPS	TEMPERS	TERRORS	**THIVEL**
SYNDIC	**TAIVER**	**TANGLE**	TARTARS	**TEAGLE**	**TEMPLE**	**TERTIA**	THIVELS
SYNDICS	TAIVERS	TANGLED	STARTER	TEAGLED	STEMPLE	TERTIAL	**THORON**
SYNROC	TAIVERT	TANGLER	**TARTLY**	TEAGLES	TEMPLED	TERTIAN	THORONS
SYNROCS	**TAKAHE**	TANGLES	STARTLY	**TEAMED**	TEMPLES	TERTIAS	**THORPE**
SYNTAN	TAKAHEA	**TANGUN**	**TASHED**	STEAMED	TEMPLET	**TESTEE**	THORPES
SYNTANS	TAKAHES	TANGUNS	STASHED	**TEAMER**	**TENACE**	TESTEES	**THOUGH**
SYPHON	**TAKING**	**TANIST**	**TASHES**	TEAMERS	TENACES	**TESTER**	THOUGHT
SYPHONS	STAKING	TANISTS	STASHES	**TEAPOT**	**TENAIL**	TESTERN	**THOWEL**
SYSTEM	TAKINGS	**TANKER**	**TASKER**	TEAPOTS	TENAILS	TESTERS	THOWELS
SYSTEMS	**TALANT**	TANKERS	TASKERS	**TEAPOY**	**TENANT**	**TESTON**	**THRALL**
TABARD	TALANTS	**TANKIA**	**TASLET**	TEAPOYS	TENANTS	TESTONS	THRALLS
TABARDS	**TALBOT**	TANKIAS	TASLETS	**TEARER**	**TENDED**	**TETHER**	**THRANG**
TABBED	TALBOTS	**TANNAH**	**TASSEL**	TEARERS	STENDED	TETHERS	THRANGS
STABBED	**TALCUM**	TANNAHS	TASSELL	**TEASEL**	**TENDER**	**TETRAD**	**THRAVE**
TABLED	TALCUMS	**TANNER**	TASSELS	TEASELS	TENDERS	TETRADS	THRAVES
STABLED	**TALENT**	TANNERS	**TASSET**	**TEASER**	**TENDON**	**TETRYL**	**THREAD**
TABLES	TALENTS	TANNERY	TASSETS	TEASERS	TENDONS	TETRYLS	THREADS
STABLES	**TALION**	**TANNIC**	**TASSIE**	**TEAZEL**	**TENDRE**	**TETTER**	THREADY
TABLET	TALIONS	STANNIC	TASSIES	TEAZELS	TENDRES	TETTERS	**THREAP**
TABLETS	**TALKED**	**TANNIN**	**TASTER**	**TEAZLE**	**TENNER**	**TEWART**	THREAPS
TABOUR	STALKED	TANNING	TASTERS	TEAZLED	TENNERS	TEWARTS	**THREAT**
TABOURS	**TALKER**	TANNINS	**TATAMI**	TEAZLES	**TENOUR**	**TEWHIT**	THREATS
TABRET	STALKER	**TANREC**	TATAMIS	**TEBBAD**	TENOURS	TEWHITS	**THREEP**
TABRETS	TALKERS	TANRECS	**TATERS**	TEBBADS	**TENREC**	**TEWING**	THREEPS
TABULA	**TALKIE**	**TANTRA**	STATERS	**TECKEL**	TENRECS	STEWING	**THRENE**
TABULAE	TALKIES	TANTRAS	**TATLER**	TECKELS	**TENSES**	**THAIRM**	THRENES
TABULAR	**TALLAT**	**TAPETA**	TATLERS	**TEDDED**	TENSEST	THAIRMS	**THRIFT**
TACKED	TALLATS	TAPETAL	**TATTER**	STEDDED	**TENSON**	**THALER**	THRIFTS
STACKED	**TALLET**	TAPETI	TATTERS	**TEDDER**	TENSONS	THALERS	THRIFTY
TACKER	TALLETS	TAPETIS	TATTERY	TEDDERS	**TENSOR**	**THALLI**	**THRILL**
STACKER	**TALLOT**	**TAPIST**	**TATTIE**	**TEDIUM**	TENSORS	THALLIC	ATHRILL
TACKERS	TALLOTS	TAPISTS	TATTIER	TEDIUMS	**TENTED**	**THANAH**	THRILLS
TACKET	**TALLOW**	**TAPPED**	TATTIES	**TEEHEE**	STENTED	THANAHS	THRILLY
STACKET	TALLOWS	STAPPED	**TATTLE**	TEEHEED	**TENTER**	**THANES**	**THRIST**
TACKETS	TALLOWY	**TAPPER**	TATTLED	TEEHEES	TENTERS	ETHANES	THRISTS
TACKETY	**TALONS**	TAPPERS	TATTLER	**TEEMED**	**TENTIE**	**THANNA**	THRISTY
TACKLE	ETALONS	**TAPPET**	TATTLES	STEEMED	TENTIER	THANNAH	**THRIVE**
TACKLED	**TALWEG**	TAPPETS	**TATTOO**	**TEEMER**	**TENURE**	THANNAS	THRIVED
TACKLER	TALWEGS	**TARAND**	TATTOOS	TEEMERS	TENURES	**THATCH**	THRIVEN
TACKLES	**TAMALE**	TARANDS	**TATTOW**	**TEENED**	**TENZON**	THATCHT	THRIVER
TACTIC	TAMALES	**TARCEL**	TATTOWS	STEENED	TENZONS	**THAWER**	THRIVES
ATACTIC	**TAMANU**	TARCELS	**TATUED**	**TEEPEE**	**TEPHRA**	THAWERS	**THROAT**
TACTICS	TAMANUS	**TARGET**	STATUED	TEEPEES	TEPHRAS	**THEAVE**	THROATS
TAENIA	**TAMARA**	TARGETS	**TAUPIE**	**TEERED**	**TERCEL**	THEAVES	THROATY
TAENIAE	TAMARAS	**TARIFF**	TAUPIES	STEERED	TERCELS	**THEINE**	**THRONE**
TAENIAS	**TAMARI**	TARIFFS	**TAUTEN**	**TEETER**	**TERCET**	THEINES	THRONED
TAGGED	TAMARIN	**TARING**	TAUTENS	TEETERS	TERCETS	**THEISM**	THRONES
STAGGED	TAMARIS	STARING	**TAUTOG**	**TEETHE**	**TERCIO**	ATHEISM	**THRONG**
TAGGER	**TAMBER**	**TARMAC**	TAUTOGS	TEETHED	TERCIOS	THEISMS	THRONGS
STAGGER	TAMBERS	TARMACS	**TAVERN**	TEETHES	**TEREDO**	**THEIST**	**THROWE**
TAGGERS	**TAMINE**	**TARPAN**	TAVERNA	**TEGULA**	TEREDOS	ATHEIST	THROWER
TAGRAG	TAMINES	TARPANS	TAVERNS	TEGULAE	**TEREFA**	THEISTS	THROWES
TAGRAGS	**TAMING**	**TARPON**	**TAWING**	TEGULAR	TEREFAH	**THENAR**	**THRUST**
TAGUAN	TAMINGS	TARPONS	STAWING	**TELEDU**	**TERGUM**	THENARS	THRUSTS
TAGUANS	**TAMISE**	**TARRED**	TAWINGS	TELEDUS	TERGUMS	**THIBET**	**THULIA**
TAHINA	TAMISES	STARRED	**TAWNEY**	**TELEGA**	**TERMER**	THIBETS	THULIAS
TAHINAS	**TAMPED**	**TARROW**	TAWNEYS	TELEGAS	TERMERS	**THIBLE**	**THWACK**
TAHINI	STAMPED	TARROWS	**TAWPIE**	**TELESM**	**TERMOR**	THIBLES	THWACKS
TAHINIS	**TAMPER**	**TARSAL**	TAWPIES	TELESMS	TERMORS	**THICKO**	**THWART**
TAHSIL	STAMPER	TARSALS	**TAWTIE**	**TELLAR**	**TERNAL**	THICKOS	ATHWART
TAHSILS	TAMPERS	**TARSEL**	TAWTIER	STELLAR	ETERNAL	**THIEVE**	THWARTS
TAIGLE	**TAMPON**	TARSELS	**TAXIES**	TELLARS	STERNAL	THIEVED	**THYMOL**
TAIGLED	TAMPONS	**TARSIA**			**TERNED**	THIEVES	THYMOLS

THYRSE	TINAJA	TISICK	TOMBACS	TOREROS	TOWMON	TRIGON	TROUSE
THYRSES	TINAJAS	TISICKS	TOMBAK	TOROID	TOWMOND	TRIGONS	TROUSES
TIBIAL	TINCAL	TISSUE	TOMBAKS	TOROIDS	TOWMONS	TRIKES	TROUTS
STIBIAL	TINCALS	TISSUED	TOMBOC	TORPID	TOWMONT	STRIKES	STROUTS
TICKED	TINDAL	TISSUES	TOMBOCS	TORPIDS	TOWNEE	TRILBY	TROVER
STICKED	TINDALS	TITBIT	TOMBOY	TORPOR	TOWNEES	TRILBYS	TROVERS
TICKEN	TINDER	TITBITS	TOMBOYS	TORPORS	TOWNIE	TRIMER	TROWED
TICKENS	TINDERS	TITFER	TOMIUM	TORQUE	TOWNIER	TRIMERS	STROWED
TICKER	TINDERY	TITFERS	TOMIUMS	TORQUED	TOWNIES	TRIODE	TROWEL
STICKER	TINEID	TITHER	TOMPON	TORQUES	TOWSER	TRIODES	TROWELS
TICKERS	TINEIDS	TITHERS	TOMPONS	TORRET	TOWSERS	TRIPES	TRUANT
TICKET	TINFUL	TITIAN	TOMTIT	TORRETS	TOXOID	STRIPES	TRUANTS
TICKETS	TINFULS	TITIANS	TOMTITS	TORSEL	TOXOIDS	TRIPLE	TRUDGE
TICKEY	TINGED	TITLER	TONEME	TORSELS	TOYING	TRIPLED	TRUDGED
TICKEYS	STINGED	TITLERS	TONEMES	TORULA	TOYINGS	TRIPLES	TRUDGEN
TICKLE	TINGLE	TITOKI	TONGUE	TORULAS	TRACER	TRIPLET	TRUDGER
STICKLE	ATINGLE	TITOKIS	TONGUED	TOSHER	TRACERS	TRIPLEX	TRUDGES
TICKLED	TINGLED	TITTER	TONGUES	TOSHERS	TRACERY	TRIPOD	TRUISM
TICKLER	TINGLER	TITTERS	STONIER	TOSSER	TRADER	TRIPODS	TRUISMS
TICKLES	TINGLES	TITTLE	TONIES	TOSSERS	TRADERS	TRIPODY	TRYING
TIDBIT	TINKER	TITTLED	STONIES	TOTARA	TRAIKS	TRISUL	TRYINGS
TIDBITS	STINKER	TITTLES	TONIEST	TOTARAS	STRAIKS	TRISULA	TSAMBA
TIDDLE	TINKERS	TITTUP	TONING	TOTTED	TRAINS	TRISULS	TSAMBAS
TIDDLED	TINKLE	TITTUPS	ATONING	STOTTED	STRAINS	TRITES	TSETSE
TIDDLER	TINKLED	TITTUPY	STONING	TOTTER	TRAITS	TRITEST	TSETSES
TIDDLES	TINKLER	TITULE	TONITE	STOTTER	STRAITS	TRITON	TSOTSI
TIDDLEY	TINKLES	TITULED	TONITES	TOTTERS	TRAMPS	TRITONE	TSOTSIS
TIDIES	TINNER	TITULES	TONKER	TOTTERY	STRAMPS	TRITONS	TUBAGE
TIDIEST	TINNERS	TOCHER	STONKER	TOTTIE	TRANCE	TRIUNE	TUBAGES
TIDING	TINNIE	TOCHERS	TONKERS	TOTTIER	TRANCED	TRIUNES	TUBBED
TIDINGS	TINNIER	TOCSIN	TONLET	TOTTIES	TRANCES	TRIVET	STUBBED
TIERCE	TINNIES	TOCSINS	TONLETS	TOUCAN	TRANSE	TRIVETS	TUBBER
TIERCEL	TINPOT	TODDLE	TONNAG	TOUCANS	TRANSES	TRIVIA	TUBBERS
TIERCES	TINPOTS	TODDLED	TONNAGE	TOUCHE	TRAPAN	TRIVIAL	TUBFUL
TIETAC	TINSEL	TODDLER	TONNAGS	TOUCHED	TRAPANS	TROADE	TUBFULS
TIETACK	TINSELS	TODDLES	TONNES	TOUCHER	TRAPPY	TROADES	TUBING
TIETACS	TINSEY	TOECAP	STONNES	TOUCHES	STRAPPY	TROCAR	TUBINGS
TIFFED	TINSEYS	TOECAPS	TONSIL	TOUPEE	TRAUMA	TROCARS	TUBULE
STIFFED	TINTED	TOFFEE	TONSILS	TOUPEES	TRAUMAS	TROCHE	TUBULES
TIFFIN	STINTED	TOFFEES	TONSOR	TOUPET	TRAVEL	TROCHEE	TUCHUN
TIFFING	TINTER	TOGATE	TONSORS	TOUPETS	TRAVELS	TROCHES	TUCHUNS
TIFFINS	STINTER	TOGATED	TOOART	TOURER	TRAYNE	TROGON	TUCKER
TIGLON	TINTERS	TOGGLE	TOOARTS	TOURERS	TRAYNED	TROGONS	TUCKERS
TIGLONS	TIPPER	TOGGLED	TOOLED	TOUSER	TRAYNES	TROIKA	TUCKET
TILING	TIPPERS	TOGGLES	STOOLED	TOUSERS	TREBLE	TROIKAS	TUCKETS
STILING	TIPPET	TOILER	TOOLER	TOUSLE	TREBLED	TROKED	TUFFET
TILINGS	TIPPETS	TOILERS	TOOLERS	TOUSLED	TREBLES	STROKED	TUFFETS
TILLED	TIPPLE	TOILES	TOORIE	TOUSLES	TREMIE	TROKES	TUFTER
STILLED	TIPPLED	ETOILES	TOORIES	TOUTER	TREMIES	STROKES	TUFTERS
TILLER	TIPPLER	TOILET	TOOTER	STOUTER	TREMOR	TROLLS	TUGGER
STILLER	TIPPLES	TOILETS	TOOTERS	TOUTERS	TREMORS	STROLLS	TUGGERS
TILLERS	TIPTOE	TOISON	TOOTLE	TOUTIE	TREPAN	TROMPE	TUGRIK
TILTED	TIPTOED	TOISONS	TOOTLED	TOUTIER	TREPANG	TROMPES	TUGRIKS
STILTED	TIPTOES	TOKING	TOOTLES	TOUZLE	TREPANS	TROPHI	TUILLE
TILTER	TIPTOP	STOKING	TOPING	TOUZLED	TREVIS	TROPHIC	TUILLES
STILTER	TIPTOPS	TOLING	STOPING	TOUZLES	TREVISS	TROPHY	TULBAN
TILTERS	TIPULA	TOLINGS	TOPPED	TOWAGE	TRIAGE	ATROPHY	TULBANS
TIMBAL	TIPULAS	TOLLER	STOPPED	TOWAGES	TRIAGES	TROPIC	TULWAR
TIMBALE	TIRADE	TOLLERS	TOPPER	TOWARD	TRICAR	TROPICS	TULWARS
TIMBALS	TIRADES	TOLSEL	TOPPERS	TOWARDS	TRICARS	TROTYL	TUMBLE
TIMBER	TIRING	TOLSELS	TOPPLE	TOWBAR	TRICKS	TROTYLS	STUMBLE
TIMBERS	STIRING	TOLSEY	TOPPLED	TOWBARS	TRICKSY	TROUGH	TUMBLED
TIMBRE	TIRINGS	TOLSEYS	TOPPLES	TOWERS	TRICOT	TROUGHS	TUMBLER
TIMBREL	TIRRED	TOLTER	STOPPLE	STOWERS	TRICOTS	TROULE	TUMBLES
TIMBRES	STIRRED	TOLTERS	TOPPLED	TOWHEE	TRIERS	TROULED	TUMOUR
TIMING	TIRRIT	TOLUOL	TOPPLES	TOWHEES	ETRIERS	TROULES	TUMOURS
STIMING	TIRRITS	TOLUOLS	TORANA	TOWING	TRIFLE	TROUPE	TUMPED
TIMINGS	TISANE	TOLZEY	TORANAS	TOWINGS	TRIFLED	TROUPED	STUMPED
TIMIST	TISANES	TOLZEYS	TORERO		TRIFLER	TROUPER	TUMULT
TIMISTS		TOMBAC			TRIFLES	TROUPES	TUMULTS

TUNDRA	TWICER	ULLAGED	UNBOLTS	UNEDGES	UNIQUE	UNPACK	UNSHUT
TUNDRAS	TWICERS	ULLAGES	UNBONE	UNFACT	UNIQUER	UNPACKS	UNSHUTS
TUNDUN	TWIGHT	ULLING	UNBONED	UNFACTS	UNIQUES	UNPICK	UNSNAP
TUNDUNS	TWIGHTS	BULLING	UNBONES	UNFAIR	UNISON	UNPICKS	UNSNAPS
TUNING	TWINER	CULLING	UNBOOT	FUNFAIR	UNISONS	UNPLUG	UNSOUL
TUNINGS	TWINERS	DULLING	UNBOOTS	UNFAIRS	UNITED	UNPLUGS	UNSOULS
TUNNED	TWINGE	FULLING	UNBORN	UNFOLD	MUNITED	UNPOPE	UNSPAR
STUNNED	TWINGED	GULLING	UNBORNE	UNFOLDS	UNITER	UNPOPED	UNSPARS
TUNNEL	TWINGES	HULLING	UNCAGE	UNFOOL	UNITERS	UNPOPES	UNSTEP
TUNNELS	TWITCH	LULLING	UNCAGED	UNFOOLS	UNITES	UNPRAY	UNSTEPS
TUPELO	TWITCHY	MULLING	UNCAGES	UNFORM	DUNITES	UNPRAYS	UNSTOP
TUPELOS	TWYERE	NULLING	UNCAPE	UNFORMS	GUNITES	UNPROP	UNSTOPS
TURACO	TWYERES	PULLING	UNCAPED	UNFURL	MUNITES	UNPROPS	UNSTOW
TURACOS	TYCOON	WULLING	UNCAPES	UNFURLS	UNKING	UNRAKE	UNSTOWS
TURBAN	TYCOONS	ULLINGS	UNCART	UNGEAR	BUNKING	UNRAKED	UNSUIT
TURBAND	TYLOTE	ULOSES	UNCARTS	UNGEARS	DUNKING	UNRAKES	SUNSUIT
TURBANS	TYLOTES	DULOSES	UNCASE	UNGILD	FUNKING	UNREAD	UNSUITS
TURBANT	TYMBAL	ULOSIS	UNCASED	UNGILDS	JUNKING	UNREADY	UNSURE
TURBIT	TYMBALS	DULOSIS	UNCASES	UNGIRD	UNKINGS	UNREEL	UNSURED
TURBITH	TYMPAN	ULSTER	UNCATE	UNGIRDS	UNKNIT	UNREELS	UNSURER
TURBITS	TYMPANA	ULSTERS	UNCIAL	UNGIRT	UNKNITS	UNREIN	UNTACK
TURBOT	TYMPANI	ULTIMA	UNCIALS	UNGIRTH	UNKNOT	UNREINS	UNTACKS
TURBOTS	TYMPANO	ULTIMAS	UNCLES	UNGLUE	UNKNOTS	UNREST	UNTAME
TUREEN	TYMPANS	ULTION	NUNCLES	UNGLUED	UNLACE	UNRESTS	UNTAMED
TUREENS	TYMPANY	ULTIONS	UNCLEW	UNGLUES	UNLACED	UNRIGS	UNTAMES
TURGOR	TYPHON	UMBERS	UNCLEWS	UNGOWN	UNLACES	RUNRIGS	UNTEAM
TURGORS	TYPHONS	CUMBERS	UNCLOG	UNGOWNS	UNLADE	UNRIPE	UNTEAMS
TURION	TYPING	LUMBERS	UNCLOGS	UNGULA	UNLADED	UNRIPER	UNTENT
TURIONS	TYPINGS	NUMBERS	UNCOCK	UNGULAE	UNLADEN	UNROBE	UNTENTS
TURKEY	TYPIST	UMBLES	UNCOCKS	UNGYVE	UNLADES	UNROBED	UNTENTY
TURKEYS	TYPISTS	BUMBLES	UNCOIL	UNGYVED	UNLAST	UNROBES	UNTHAW
TURNER	TYRANT	FUMBLES	UNCOILS	UNGYVES	UNLASTE	UNROLL	UNTHAWS
TURNERS	TYRANTS	HUMBLES	UNCOLT	UNHAIR	UNLEAD	UNROLLS	UNTIES
TURNERY	TYSTIE	JUMBLES	UNCOLTS	UNHAIRS	UNLEADS	UNROOF	AUNTIES
TURNIP	TYSTIES	MUMBLES	UNCOPE	UNHAND	UNLESS	UNROOFS	PUNTIES
TURNIPS	UAKARI	NUMBLES	UNCOPED	UNHANDS	SUNLESS	UNROOT	UNTILE
TURRET	OUAKARI	RUMBLES	UNCOPES	UNHANDY	UNLIKE	UNROOTS	UNTILED
TURRETS	UAKARIS	TUMBLES	UNCORD	UNHANG	SUNLIKE	UNROPE	UNTILES
TURTLE	UBERTY	UMBREL	UNCORDS	UNHANGS	UNLIKES	UNROPED	UNTINS
TURTLED	PUBERTY	UMBRELS	UNCORK	UNHASP	UNLIME	UNROPES	MUNTINS
TURTLER	UBIETY	UMBRIL	UNCORKS	UNHASPS	UNLIMED	UNRULE	UNTOMB
TURTLES	DUBIETY	UMBRILS	UNCOWL	UNHATS	UNLIMES	UNRULED	UNTOMBS
TUSCHE	UDDERS	UMLAUT	UNCOWLS	SUNHATS	UNLINE	UNRULES	UNTRIM
TUSCHES	DUDDERS	UMLAUTS	UNCURL	UNHEAD	UNLINED	UNSAFE	UNTRIMS
TUSKAR	JUDDERS	UMPIRE	UNCURLS	UNHEADS	UNLINES	UNSAFER	UNTRUE
TUSKARS	PUDDERS	UMPIRED	UNDATE	UNHEAL	UNLINK	UNSEAL	UNTRUER
TUSKER	RUDDERS	UMPIRES	UNDATED	UNHEALS	UNLINKS	UNSEALS	UNTUCK
TUSKERS	SUDDERS	UNABLE	UNDEAF	UNHELE	UNLIVE	UNSEAM	UNTUCKS
TUSSAH	UGGING	TUNABLE	UNDECK	UNHELED	UNLIVED	UNSEAMS	UNTUNE
TUSSAHS	BUGGING	UNBARE	UNDECKS	UNHELES	UNLIVES	UNSEAT	UNTUNED
TUSSEH	FUGGING	UNBARED	UNDERN	UNHELM	UNLOAD	UNSEATS	UNTUNES
TUSSEHS	HUGGING	UNBARES	UNDERNS	UNHELMS	UNLOADS	UNSEEL	UNTURF
TUSSER	JUGGING	UNBARK	UNDIES	UNHIVE	UNLOCK	UNSEELS	UNTURFS
TUSSERS	LUGGING	UNBARKS	GUNDIES	UNHIVES	UNLOCKS	UNSEEN	UNTURN
TUSSLE	MUGGING	UNBEAR	UNDINE	UNHIVED	UNLORD	UNSEENS	UNTURNS
TUSSLED	PUGGING	UNBEARS	NUNDINE	UNHOOD	UNLORDS	UNSELF	UNVAIL
TUSSLES	RUGGING	UNBEDS	UNDINES	NUNHOOD	UNLOVE	UNSELFS	UNVAILE
TUTSAN	TUGGING	SUNBEDS	UNDOCK	UNHOODS	UNLOVED	UNSETS	UNVAILS
TUTSANS	UGLIED	UNBELT	UNDOCKS	UNHOOK	UNLOVES	SUNSETS	UNVEIL
TUXEDO	OUGLIED	SUNBELT	UNDOER	UNHOOKS	UNMAKE	UNSHED	UNVEILS
TUXEDOS	UGLIES	UNBELTS	UNDOERS	UNHOOP	UNMAKES	DUNSHED	UNWARE
TUYERE	OUGLIES	UNBEND	UNDRAW	UNHOOPS	UNMASK	UNSHIP	UNWARES
TUYERES	UGLIEST	UNBENDS	UNDRAWN	UNHUSK	UNMASKS	NUNSHIP	UNWEAL
TWAITE	ULICON	UNBIND	UNDRAWS	UNHUSKS	UNMOOR	UNSHIPS	UNWEALS
TWAITES	ULICONS	UNBINDS	UNEASE	UNIONS	UNMOORS	UNSHOE	UNWILL
TWEEZE	ULIKON	UNBITT	UNEASES	BUNIONS	UNNAIL	UNSHOED	UNWILLS
TWEEZED	ULIKONS	UNBITTS	UNEDGE	UNIPED	UNNAILS	UNSHOES	UNWIND
TWEEZES	ULLAGE	UNBOLT	UNEDGED	UNIPEDS	UNNEST	UNSHOT	UNWINDS
TWELVE	FULLAGE			UNIPOD	UNNESTS	GUNSHOT	UNWIRE
TWELVES	SULLAGE			UNIPODS	DUNNEST		UNWIRED

UNWIRES	UPHURL	UPTILTS	USANCES	VALUER	VENDISS	VERTUE	VIROSES
UNWISE	UPHURLS	UPTOWN	USEFUL	VALUERS	VENDOR	VERTUES	VIRTUE
SUNWISE	UPKEEP	UPTOWNS	MUSEFUL	VALUTA	VENDORS	VERVEL	VIRTUES
UNWISER	UPKEEPS	UPTURN	USHERS	VALUTAS	VENDUE	VERVELS	VISAGE
UNWIVE	UPKNIT	UPTURNS	GUSHERS	VAMOSE	VENDUES	VERVEN	VISAGED
UNWIVED	UPKNITS	UPWAFT	HUSHERS	VAMOSED	VENEER	VERVENS	VISAGES
UNWIVES	UPLAND	UPWAFTS	LUSHERS	VAMOSES	VENEERS	VERVET	VISCIN
UNWORK	UPLANDS	UPWARD	MUSHERS	VAMPER	VENENE	VERVETS	VISCINS
UNWORKS	UPLEAD	UPWARDS	PUSHERS	VAMPERS	VENEWE	VESICA	VISCUM
UNWOVE	UPLEADS	UPWELL	RUSHERS	VANDAL	VENEWES	VESICAE	VISCUMS
UNWOVEN	UPLEAN	UPWELLS	USTION	VANDALS	VENGED	VESICAL	VISIER
UNWRAP	UPLEANS	UPWIND	USTIONS	VANISH	AVENGED	VESPER	VISIERS
UNWRAPS	UPLEANT	UPWINDS	USURER	EVANISH	VENGER	VESPERS	VISILE
UNYOKE	UPLEAP	URACIL	USURERS	VANNER	AVENGER	VESSEL	VISILES
UNYOKED	UPLEAPS	URACILS	USURES	VANNERS	VENGES	VESSELS	VISING
UNYOKES	UPLEAPT	URALIS	USURESS	VAPOUR	AVENGES	VESTAL	AVISING
UPBEAR	UPLIFT	OURALIS	USWARD	VAPOURS	VENIRE	VESTALS	VISION
UPBEARS	UPLIFTS	URANIN	USWARDS	VAPOURY	VENIRES	VEXING	VISIONS
UPBIND	UPLOCK	URANINS	UTISES	VARECH	VENITE	VEXINGS	VISITE
UPBINDS	UPLOCKS	URANYL	CUTISES	VARECHS	VENITES	VIATOR	VISITED
UPBLOW	UPLOOK	URANYLS	UTMOST	VARIER	VENNEL	VIATORS	VISITEE
UPBLOWN	UPLOOKS	URARIS	OUTMOST	VARIERS	VENNELS	VIBIST	VISITER
UPBLOWS	UPMAKE	OURARIS	UTMOSTS	VARIES	VENTER	VIBISTS	VISITES
UPBOIL	UPMAKER	URATES	UTOPIA	OVARIES	EVENTER	VIBRIO	VISUAL
UPBOILS	UPMAKES	AURATES	UTOPIAN	VARLET	VENTERS	VIBRIOS	VISUALS
UPBRAY	UPPERS	CURATES	UTOPIAS	VARLETS	VENTIL	VICTIM	VITRIC
UPBRAYS	CUPPERS	URBANE	UTTERS	VARROA	VENTILS	VICTIMS	VITRICS
UPCAST	SUPPERS	URBANER	BUTTERS	VARROAS	VENTRE	VICTOR	VITTLE
UPCASTS	UPPING	URCHIN	CUTTERS	VARVEL	AVENTRE	EVICTOR	VITTLES
UPCOIL	CUPPING	URCHINS	GUTTERS	VARVELS	VENTRED	VICTORS	VIZARD
UPCOILS	DUPPING	UREIDE	MUTTERS	VASSAL	VENTRES	VICTORY	VIZARDS
UPCOME	HUPPING	UREIDES	NUTTERS	VASSALS	VENUES	VICUNA	VIZIER
UPCOMES	PUPPING	UREMIA	PUTTERS	VATFUL	AVENUES	VICUNAS	VIZIERS
UPCURL	TUPPING	UREMIAS	RUTTERS	VATFULS	VENULE	VIDAME	VIZSLA
UPCURLS	UPPINGS	URENAS	VACATE	VAUDOO	VENULES	VIDAMES	VIZSLAS
UPDATE	UPRATE	MURENAS	VACATED	VAUDOOS	VERBAL	VIELLE	VIZZIE
UPDATED	UPRATED	URETER	VACATES	VAUNCE	VERBALS	VIELLES	VIZZIED
UPDATES	UPRATES	URETERS	VACUUM	VAUNCED	VERDET	VIEWER	VIZZIES
UPDRAG	UPREAR	URGENT	VACUUMS	VAUNCES	VERDETS	VIGORO	VOCULE
UPDRAGS	UPREARS	SURGENT	VADING	VAUNTS	VERDIT	VIGOROS	VOCULES
UPDRAW	UPREST	TURGENT	EVADING	AVAUNTS	VERDITS	VIGOUR	VOICER
UPDRAWN	UPRESTS	URGERS	VAGINA	VAWARD	VERGER	VIGOURS	VOICERS
UPDRAWS	UPRISE	BURGERS	VAGINAE	VAWARDS	VERGERS	VIHARA	VOIDED
UPFILL	UPRISEN	PURGERS	VAGINAL	VECTOR	VERISM	VIHARAS	AVOIDED
UPFILLS	UPRISES	URGING	VAGINAS	VECTORS	VERISMO	VIKING	VOIDEE
UPFLOW	UPRIST	PURGING	VAGUES	VEGGIE	VERISMS	VIKINGS	VOIDEES
UPFLOWS	UPRISTS	SURGING	VAGUEST	VEGGIES	VERIST	VILLAN	VOIDER
UPFURL	UPROAR	URGINGS	VAHINE	VELATE	VERISTS	VILLANS	VOIDERS
UPFURLS	UPROARS	URIALS	VAHINES	VELATED	VERMIL	VILLANY	VOLANT
UPGANG	UPROLL	BURIALS	VAILED	VELETA	VERMILS	VIMANA	VOLANTE
UPGANGS	UPROLLS	URINAL	AVAILED	VELETAS	VERMILY	VIMANAS	VOLLEY
UPGAZE	UPROOT	URINALS	VAKEEL	VELLET	VERMIN	VIOLER	VOLLEYS
UPGAZED	UPROOTS	URINES	VAKEELS	VELLETS	VERMINS	VIOLERS	VOLOST
UPGAZES	UPSEND	MURINES	VALETA	VELLON	VERMINY	VIOLET	VOLOSTS
UPGROW	UPSENDS	PURINES	VALETAS	VELLONS	VERREL	VIOLETS	VOLUME
UPGROWN	UPSHOT	URNFUL	VALETE	VELLUM	VERRELS	VIOLIN	VOLUMED
UPGROWS	UPSHOTS	URNFULS	VALETED	VELLUMS	VERSAL	VIOLINS	VOLUMES
UPHANG	UPSIDE	URNING	VALETES	VELOUR	VERSALS	VIRAGO	VOLUTE
UPHANGS	UPSIDES	BURNING	VALINE	VELOURS	VERSER	VIRAGOS	EVOLUTE
UPHAUD	UPSTAY	GURNING	VALINES	VELURE	VERSERS	VIRGER	VOLUTED
UPHAUDS	UPSTAYS	TURNING	VALISE	VELURED	VERSET	VIRGERS	VOLUTES
UPHEAP	UPSWAY	URNINGS	VALISES	VELURES	OVERSET	VIRGIN	VOLVED
UPHEAPS	UPSWAYS	UROPOD	VALLAR	VELVET	VERSETS	VIRGINS	EVOLVED
UPHILL	UPTAKE	UROPODS	VALLARY	VELVETS	VERSIN	VIRION	VOLVES
UPHILLS	UPTAKEN	URTICA	VALLEY	VENDEE	VERSINE	VIRIONS	EVOLVES
UPHOLD	UPTAKES	URTICAS	VALLEYS	VENDEES	VERSING	VIROID	VOMICA
UPHOLDS	UPTEAR	USAGER	VALLUM	VENDER	VERSINS	VIROIDS	VOMICAS
UPHROE	UPTEARS	USAGERS	VALLUMS	VENDERS	VERTED	VIROID	VOMITO
EUPHROE	UPTILT	USANCE	VALOUR	VENDIS	AVERTED	VIROSE	VOMITOS
UPHROES			VALOURS		EVERTED		VOODOO

VOODOOS	WAIVERS	**WARBLE**	WAXINGS	WESANDS	WIGWAGS	**WINNLE**	**WOMERA**
VOTEEN	WAKENS	WARBLED	**WAYING**	**WESTER**	**WIGWAM**	WINNLES	WOMERAS
VOTEENS	AWAKENS	WARBLER	SWAYING	WESTERN	WIGWAMS	**WINNOW**	**WONDER**
VOUDOU	AWAKENS	WARBLES	**WAYLAY**	WESTERS	**WILDER**	WINNOWS	WONDERS
VOUDOUS	WAKIKI	**WARDED**	WAYLAYS	**WETHER**	WILDERS	**WINSEY**	WONINGS
VOULGE	WAKIKIS	AWARDED	WAYLAYS	WETHERS	**WILLED**	WINSEYS	**WOOBUT**
VOULGES	**WAKING**	SWARDED	**WEAKEN**	**WEZAND**	SWILLED	**WINTER**	WOOBUTS
VOWING	AWAKING	**WARDEN**	WEAKENS	WEZANDS	TWILLED	TWINTER	**WOODIE**
AVOWING	WAKINGS	WARDENS	**WEALTH**	WHACKO	**WILLER**	WINTERS	WOODIER
VOYAGE	**WALIER**	**WARDER**	WEALTHS	WHACKOS	SWILLER	WINTERY	WOODIES
VOYAGED	SWALIER	WARDERS	WEALTHY	**WHALER**	WILLERS	**WINTLE**	**WOOFER**
VOYAGER	**WALIES**	**WARDOG**	**WEANEL**	WHALERS	**WILLET**	WINTLED	WOOFERS
VOYAGES	WALIEST	WARDOGS	WEANELS	WHALERY	WILLETS	WINTLES	**WOOING**
VOYEUR	**WALING**	**WARMED**	**WEANER**	**WHARVE**	WILLEY	**WIPERS**	WOOINGS
VOYEURS	SWALING	SWARMED	WEANERS	WHARVES	WILLEYS	**WIPING**	**WOONED**
VULCAN	**WALISE**	**WARMER**	**WEAPON**	**WHEECH**	WILLIE	SWIPING	SWOONED
VULCANS	WALISES	WARMERS	WEAPONS	WHEECHS	WILLIED	WIPINGS	**WOOSEL**
VULGAR	**WALKER**	**WARMTH**	**WEARER**	**WHEELS**	WILLIES	**WIRING**	WOOSELS
VULGARS	WALKERS	WARMTHS	SWEARER	AWHEELS	**WILLOW**	WIRINGS	WOOSELS
WABAIN	**WALLAH**	**WARNED**	WEARERS	**WHEEZE**	WILLOWS	TWIRING	WOOSELS
WABAINS	WALLAHS	AWARNED	**WEASEL**	WHEEZED	WILLOWY	**WISARD**	**WOPPED**
WABBLE	**WALLER**	**WARNER**	WEASELS	WHEEZES	**WILTED**	WISARDS	SWOPPED
WABBLED	WALLERS	WARNERS	**WEAVER**	**WHENCE**	TWILTED	**WISDOM**	**WORDED**
WABBLER	SWALLET	**WARPER**	WEAVERS	WHENCES	**WIMBLE**	WISDOMS	SWORDED
WABBLES	WALLETS	WARPERS	**WEAZEN**	**WHERES**	WIMBLED	**WISENT**	**WORKER**
WABOOM	**WALLOP**	**WARRAN**	WEAZENS	WHERESO	WIMBLES	WISENTS	WORKERS
WABOOMS	WALLOPS	WARRAND	**WEDELN**	**WHEUGH**	**WIMPLE**	**WISHED**	**WORMER**
WADDIE	**WALLOW**	WARRANS	**WEDGIE**	WHEUGHS	WIMPLED	SWISHED	WORMERS
WADDIED	SWALLOW	WARRANT	WEDGIES	**WHIDAH**	WIMPLES	**WISHER**	WORMERY
WADDIES	WALLOWS	**WARRAY**	**WEEDER**	WHIDAHS	**WINCER**	SWISHER	**WORRAL**
WADDLE	**WALNUT**	WARRAYS	WEEDERS	**WHINER**	WINCERS	WISHERS	WORRALS
SWADDLE	WALNUTS	**WARREN**	WEEDERY	WHINERS	**WINCEY**	**WISHES**	**WORREL**
TWADDLE	**WAMBLE**	WARRENS	**WEEING**	**WHINGE**	WINCEYS	SWISHES	WORRELS
WADDLED	WAMBLED	**WARREY**	SWEEING	WHINGED	**WINDAC**	**WISKET**	**WORRIT**
WADDLES	WAMBLES	WARREYS	**WEEPER**	WHINGER	WINDACS	WISKETS	WORRITS
WADING	**WAMPEE**	**WARSLE**	WEEPERS	WHINGES	**WINDER**	**WISTED**	**WORSEN**
WADINGS	WAMPEES	WARSLED	**WEEPIE**	**WHISHT**	WINDERS	TWISTED	WORSENS
WADMAL	**WAMPUM**	WARSLES	WEEPIES	WHISHTS	**WINDLE**	**WITGAT**	**WORTLE**
WADMALS	WAMPUMS	**WASHED**	**WEETEN**	**WHITEN**	DWINDLE	WITGATS	WORTLES
WADMOL	**WANDER**	SWASHED	SWEETEN	WHITENS	SWINDLE	**WITHER**	**WOTTED**
WADMOLL	WANDERS	**WASHER**	**WEEVER**	**WHITES**	WINDLES	SWITHER	SWOTTED
WADMOLS	**WANDOO**	SWASHER	WEEVERS	WHITEST	**WINDOW**	WITHERS	**WOUBIT**
WADSET	WANDOOS	SWASHER	**WHITEY**	WINDOWS	**WITHIN**	WOUBITS
WADSETS	**WANGAN**	WASHERS	**WEEVIL**	WHITEYS	**WINERY**	**WITHING**	**WOULDS**
WADSETT	WANGANS	WASHERY	WEEVILS	**WHYDAH**	SWINERY	**WITTED**	WOULDST
WAFFLE	**WANGLE**	**WASHES**	WEEVILY	WHYDAHS	**WINGED**	TWITTED	**WOUNDS**
WAFFLED	TWANGLE	SWASHES	**WEIGHT**	**WICKEN**	SWINGED	**WITTER**	SWOUNDS
WAFFLES	WANGLED	**WASPIE**	WEIGHTS	WICKENS	TWINGED	TWITTER	**WOWSER**
WAFTER	WANGLER	WASPIER	WEIGHTY	**WICKER**	**WINGER**	WITTERS	WOWSERS
WAFTERS	WANGLES	WASPIES	**WEIRDO**	WICKERS	SWINGER	**WITTOL**	**WRAITH**
WAGGED	**WANGUN**	**WASTEL**	WEIRDOS	**WICKET**	WINGERS	WITTOLS	WRAITHS
SWAGGED	WANGUNS	WASTELS	**WELDER**	WICKETS	**WINGES**	**WIVERN**	**WRASSE**
WAGGLE	**WANING**	**WASTER**	WELDERS	**WIDDLE**	SWINGES	WIVERNS	WRASSES
WAGGLED	WANINGS	WASTERS	**WELDOR**	WIDDLED	TWINGES	**WRAXLE**
WAGGLES	**WANKED**	WASTERY	WELDORS	WIDDLES	**WINIER**	**WIZARD**	WRAXLED
WAGGON	SWANKED	**WATTER**	**WELKIN**	WIDGET	DWINING	WIZARDS	WRAXLES
WAGGONS	**WANKER**	SWATTER	WELKING	**WIDGET**	TWINIER	**WIZIER**	**WREAKE**
WAGING	SWANKER	**WATTLE**	WELKINS	WIDGETS	**WINING**	WIZIERS	WREAKED
SWAGING	WANKERS	TWATTLE	DWELLED	**WIGEON**	TWINING	**WOBBLE**	WREAKER
WAHINE	**WANTER**	WATTLED	**WELLED**	WIGEONS	**WINKED**	WOBBLED	WREAKES
WAHINES	WANTERS	WATTLES	WIGGED	SWINKED	WOBBLER	**WREATH**
WAILER	**WANTON**	**WAUCHT**	SWELLED	**WIGGED**	TWINKED	WOBBLES	WREATHE
WAILERS	WANTONS	WAUCHTS	SWIGGED	**WINKER**	**WOGGLE**	WREATHS
WAITED	**WAPITI**	**WAUGHT**	**WELLIE**	TWIGGED	WINKERS	WOGGLES	WREATHY
AWAITED	WAPITIS	WAUGHTS	WELLIES	**WIGGLE**	**WINKLE**	**WOLFER**	**WRETHE**
WAITER	**WAPPED**	**WAVIES**	**WELTED**	WIGGLED	TWINKLE	WOLFERS	WRETHED
WAITERS	SWAPPED	WAVIEST	SWELTED	WIGGLER	WINKLER	**WOLVER**	WRETHES
WAITES	**WAPPER**	**WAVING**	**WELTER**	WIGGLES	WINKLES	WOLVERS	**WRIEST**
TWAITES	SWAPPER	WAVINGS	WELTERS	**WIGHTS**	**WINNER**	**WOMBAT**	OWRIEST
WAIVER	WAPPERS	**WAXING**	**WESAND**	**WIGWAG**	WINNERS	WOMBATS	**WRIGHT**

WRIGHTS	**XYLOMA**	**YAPOCK**	**YNAMBU**	**YUCKER**	ZARIBAS	ZILLAHS	**ZOOZOO**
WRITER	XYLOMAS	YAPOCKS	YNAMBUS	YUCKERS	**ZARNEC**	**ZIMMER**	ZOOZOOS
WRITERS	**XYLOSE**	**YAPPER**	**YODLER**	**YUMPIE**	ZARNECS	ZIMMERS	**ZORINO**
WRITHE	XYLOSES	YAPPERS	YODLERS	YUMPIES	**ZEALOT**	ZINGEL	ZORINOS
WRITHED	**XYSTER**	**YARPHA**	**YOGINI**	**YUPPIE**	ZEALOTS	ZINGELS	**ZOSTER**
WRITHEN	XYSTERS	YARPHAS	YOGINIS	YUPPIES	**ZEBECK**	**ZINNIA**	ZOSTERS
WRITHES	**YABBER**	**YARROW**	**YOGISM**	**YWROKE**	ZEBECKS	ZINNIAS	**ZYGOMA**
WROATH	YABBERS	YARROWS	YOGISMS	YWROKEN	**ZEBRAS**	**ZIPPER**	ZYGOMAS
WROATHS	**YABBIE**	**YATTER**	**YOGURT**	**ZABETA**	ZEBRASS	ZIPPERS	**ZYGOSE**
WROKEN	YABBIES	YATTERS	YOGURTS	ZABETAS	**ZELANT**	**ZIRCON**	ZYGOSES
YWROKEN	**YACKER**	**YAUPON**	**YOJANA**	**ZADDIK**	ZELANTS	ZIRCONS	**ZYGOTE**
WUNNER	YACKERS	YAUPONS	YOJANAS	ZADDIKS	**ZENANA**	**ZITHER**	ZYGOTES
WUNNERS	**YAFFED**	**YAWPER**	**YOKING**	TZADDIK	ZENANAS	ZITHERN	**ZYMASE**
WURLEY	NYAFFED	YAWPERS	YOKINGS	**ZAFFER**	**ZENDIK**	ZITHERS	ZYMASES
WURLEYS	**YAFFLE**	**YELLOW**	**YONKER**	ZAFFERS	**ZENITH**	**ZODIAC**	**ZYMITE**
WUTHER	YAFFLES	YELLOWS	YONKERS	**ZAFFRE**	ZENITHS	ZODIACS	AZYMITE
WUTHERS	**YAGGER**	YELLOWY	**YOPPER**	ZAFFRES	**ZEPHYR**	**ZOMBIE**	ZYMITES
WUZZLE	YAGGERS	**YELPER**	YOPPERS	**ZAMANG**	ZEPHYRS	ZOMBIES	**ZYMOME**
WUZZLED	**YAKKER**	YELPERS	**YORKER**	ZAMANGS	**ZONATE**	**ZONING**	ZYMOMES
WUZZLES	YAKKERS	**YESTER**	YORKERS	**ZANDER**	ZEREBA	ZONINGS	**ZYTHUM**
WYVERN	**YAMMER**	DYESTER	**YORKIE**	ZANDERS	ZEREBAS	**ZONULA**	ZYTHUMS
WYVERNS	YAMMERS	YESTERN	YORKIES	**ZANIES**	**ZERIBA**	ZONULAR	
XEROMA	**YANKER**	**YICKER**	**YOWLEY**	ZANIEST	ZERIBAS	ZONULAS	
XEROMAS	YANKERS	YICKERS	YOWLEYS	**ZARAPE**	**ZEUGMA**	**ZONULE**	
XOANON	**YANKIE**	**YIKKER**	**YSHEND**	ZARAPES	ZEUGMAS	ZONULES	
XOANONS	YANKIES	YIKKERS	YSHENDS	**ZAREBA**	**ZIGZAG**	ZONULET	
XYLENE	**YAOURT**	**YMPING**	**YTTRIA**	ZAREBAS	ZIGZAGS		
XYLENES	YAOURTS	GYMPING	YTTRIAS	**ZARIBA**	**ZILLAH**		

PART B: 7-letter word hooks
extensible words only

ABACTOR	ABUTTALS	ACQUIRE	ADHARMAS	AFFRONTS	AIRINGS	ALERION
ABACTORS	ABUTTER	ACQUIRED	ADHERER	AGACANT	FAIRINGS	ALERIONS
ABALONE	ABUTTERS	ACQUIRES	ADHERERS	AGACANTE	PAIRINGS	ALEURON
ABALONES	ACADEME	ACQUIST	ADHIBIT	AGAMOID	AIRLESS	ALEURONE
ABANDON	ACADEMES	ACQUISTS	ADHIBITS	AGAMOIDS	HAIRLESS	ALEURONS
ABANDONS	ACALEPH	ACQUITE	ADJOINT	AGELAST	AIRLIFT	ALFALFA
ABATURE	ACALEPHA	ACQUITES	ADJOINTS	AGELASTS	AIRLIFTS	ALFALFAS
ABATURES	ACALEPHE	ACREAGE	ADJOURN	AGELESS	AIRLINE	ALFAQUI
ABDOMEN	ACALEPHS	ACREAGES	ADJOURNS	WAGELESS	AIRLINER	ALFAQUIS
ABDOMENS	ACANTHA	ACRIDIN	ADJUDGE	AGGRACE	AIRLINES	ALFORJA
ABETTER	ACANTHAS	ACRIDINE	ADJUDGED	AGGRACED	AIRMAIL	ALFORJAS
ABETTERS	ACAPNIA	ACRIDINS	ADJUDGES	AGGRACES	AIRMAILS	ALGEBRA
ABETTOR	ACAPNIAS	ACROBAT	ADJUNCT	AGGRADE	AIRPORT	ALGEBRAS
ABETTORS	ACATOUR	ACROBATS	ADJUNCTS	AGGRADED	AIRPORTS	ALGESIA
ABIDING	ACATOURS	ACROGEN	ADMIRAL	AGGRADES	AIRSHIP	ALGESIAS
ABIDINGS	ACCEDER	ACROGENS	ADMIRALS	AGGRATE	AIRSHIPS	ALICANT
ABIGAIL	ACCEDERS	ACRONYM	ADMIRER	AGGRATED	AIRSTOP	ALICANTS
ABIGAILS	ACCIDIE	ACRONYMS	ADMIRERS	AGGRATES	AIRSTOPS	ALIDADE
ABILITY	ACCIDIES	ACROTER	ADONISE	AGILITY	AIRTIME	ALIDADES
LABILITY	ACCINGE	ACROTERS	ADONISED	VAGILITY	AIRTIMES	ALIENEE
ABJOINT	ACCINGED	ACRYLIC	ADONISES	AGINNER	AIRWARD	ALIENEES
ABJOINTS	ACCINGES	ACRYLICS	ADONIZE	AGINNERS	AIRWARDS	ALIENOR
ABJURER	ACCLAIM	ACTINIA	ADONIZED	AGISTER	AIRWAVE	ALIENORS
ABJURERS	ACCLAIMS	ACTINIAE	ADONIZES	MAGISTER	AIRWAVES	ALIFORM
ABLATOR	ACCOAST	ACTINIAN	ADOPTER	AGISTERS	AIRWAYS	PALIFORM
ABLATORS	ACCOASTS	ACTINIAS	ADOPTERS	AGISTOR	FAIRWAYS	ALIGNED
ABOULIA	ACCOMPT	ACTINON	ADRENAL	AGISTORS	AISLING	MALIGNED
ABOULIAS	ACCOMPTS	ACTINONS	ADRENALS	AGITATE	AISLINGS	ALIMENT
ABREACT	ACCOUNT	ACTIONS	ADULATE	AGITATED	AJUTAGE	ALIMENTS
ABREACTS	ACCOUNTS	FACTIONS	RADULATE	AGITATES	AJUTAGES	ALIMONY
ABRIDGE	ACCOURT	PACTIONS	ADULATED	AGITATO	AKVAVIT	PALIMONY
ABRIDGED	ACCOURTS	TACTIONS	ADULATES	MAGNATES	AKVAVITS	ALIPEDS
ABRIDGER	ACCRETE	ACTUATE	ADVANCE	AGNATES	ALAMEDA	TALIPEDS
ABRIDGES	ACCRETED	ACTUATED	TADVANCE	AGNOMEN	ALAMEDAS	ALIZARI
ABROOKE	ACCRETES	ACTUATES	ADVANCED	AGNOMENS	ALAMODE	ALIZARIN
ABROOKED	ACCRUAL	ACTURES	ADVANCES	AGONISE	ALAMODES	ALIZARIS
ABROOKES	ACCRUALS	FACTURES	ADVERSE	AGONISED	ALANNAH	ALKALIS
ABSCIND	ACCURSE	ACUMENS	ADVERSER	AGONISES	ALANNAHS	ALKALISE
ABSCINDS	ACCURSED	CACUMENS	ADVISER	AGONIST	ALBERTS	ALKANET
ABSCISE	ACCURSES	ACUSHLA	ADVISERS	AGONISTS	HALBERTS	ALKANETS
ABSCISED	ACCUSAL	ACUSHLAS	ADVISOR	AGONIZE	ALBUMEN	ALLAYER
ABSCISES	ACCUSALS	ADAMANT	ADVISORS	AGONIZED	ALBUMENS	ALLAYERS
ABSCISSA	ACCUSER	ADAMANTS	ADVISORY	AGONIZES	ALBUMIN	ALLEDGE
ABSCISSE	ACCUSERS	ADAPTER	AERATOR	AGRAFFE	ALBUMINS	ALLEDGED
ABSCOND	ACETATE	ADAPTERS	AERATORS	AGRAFFES	ALCAIDE	ALLEDGES
ABSCONDS	ACETATES	ADAPTOR	AEROBIC	AIDANCE	ALCAIDES	ALLEGER
ABSENCE	ACETONE	ADAPTORS	AEROBICS	AIDANCES	ALCALDE	ALLEGERS
ABSENCES	ACETONES	ADDLING	AEROSOL	AIDLESS	ALCALDES	ALLEGGE
ABSINTH	ACHARYA	DADDLING	AEROSOLS	MAIDLESS	ALCAYDE	ALLEGGED
ABSINTHE	ACHARYAS	FADDLING	AFFAIRE	AILANTO	ALCAYDES	ALLEGGES
ABSINTHS	ACHIEVE	PADDLING	AFFAIRES	AILANTOS	ALCAZAR	ALLEGRO
ABSOLVE	ACHIEVED	RADDLING	AFFEARE	AILERON	ALCAZARS	ALLEGROS
ABSOLVED	ACHIEVER	SADDLING	AFFEARED	AILERONS	ALCHERA	ALLHEAL
ABSOLVER	ACHIEVES	WADDLING	AFFEARES	AILETTE	ALCHERAS	ALLHEALS
ABSOLVES	ACKNOWN	ADDUCER	AFFICHE	AILETTES	ALCOHOL	ALLISES
ABSTAIN	ACKNOWNE	ADDUCERS	AFFICHES	AILMENT	ALCOHOLS	GALLISES
ABSTAINS	ACOLYTE	ADENINE	AFFLICT	BAILMENT	ALCORZA	ALLNESS
ABTHANE	ACOLYTES	ADENINES	AFFLICTS	AILMENTS	ALCORZAS	TALLNESS
ABTHANES	ACOLYTH	ADENOID	AFFOORD	AIRHOLE	ALECOST	ALLONGE
ABUSAGE	ACOLYTHS	ADENOIDS	AFFOORDS	AIRHOLES	ALECOSTS	ALLONGES
ABUSAGES	ACONITE	ADENOMA	AFFORCE	AIRIEST	ALEMBIC	ALLONYM
ABUSION	TACONITE	ADENOMAS	AFFORCED	HAIRIEST	ALEMBICS	ALLONYMS
ABUSIONS	ACONITES	ADERMIN	AFFORCES	LAIRIEST	ALEPINE	ALLOWED
ABUTTAL	ACQUEST	ADERMINS	AFFRONT	VAIRIEST	ALEPINES	FALLOWED
	ACQUESTS	ADHARMA	AFFRONTE			GALLOWED

HALLOWED	AMBIENTS	**ANAEMIA**	**ANILINE**	**ANTRUMS**	APPROVES	ARIETTAS
SALLOWED	**AMBLERS**	ANAEMIAS	ANILINES	TANTRUMS	**APPULSE**	**ARIETTE**
TALLOWED	GAMBLERS	**ANAGOGE**	**ANIMATE**	**APAGOGE**	APPULSES	ARIETTES
WALLOWED	RAMBLERS	ANAGOGES	ANIMATED	APAGOGES	**APRAXIA**	**ARISHES**
ALLSEED	**AMBLING**	**ANAGRAM**	ANIMATES	**APANAGE**	APRAXIAS	GARISHES
ALLSEEDS	GAMBLING	ANAGRAMS	**ANIMISM**	APANAGED	**APRICOT**	MARISHES
ALLURER	HAMBLING	**ANALYSE**	ANIMISMS	APANAGES	APRICOTS	PARISHES
ALLURERS	LAMBLING	ANALYSED	**ANIMIST**	**APATITE**	**AQUAFER**	**ARMBAND**
ALLUVIA	RAMBLING	ANALYSER	ANIMISTS	APATITES	AQUAFERS	ARMBANDS
ALLUVIAL	WAMBLING	ANALYSES	**ANISEED**	**APEHOOD**	**AQUARIA**	**ARMHOLE**
ALLYING	AMBLINGS	**ANALYST**	ANISEEDS	APEHOODS	AQUARIAN	ARMHOLES
DALLYING	**AMBONES**	ANALYSTS	**ANNATES**	**APEPSIA**	**AQUATIC**	**ARMIGER**
GALLYING	JAMBONES	**ANALYZE**	TANNATES	APEPSIAS	AQUATICS	ARMIGERO
RALLYING	**AMBROID**	ANALYZED	**ANNATTA**	**APERIES**	**AQUAVIT**	ARMIGERS
SALLYING	AMBROIDS	ANALYZER	ANNATTAS	NAPERIES	AQUAVITS	**ARMILLA**
TALLYING	**AMENAGE**	ANALYZES	**ANNATTO**	**APHAGIA**	**AQUIFER**	ARMILLAE
ALMANAC	AMENAGED	**ANAPEST**	ANNATTOS	APHAGIAS	AQUIFERS	ARMILLAS
ALMANACS	AMENAGES	ANAPESTS	**ANNELID**	**APHASIA**	**ARABICA**	**ARMLESS**
ALMIRAH	**AMENDER**	**ANATASE**	ANNELIDS	APHASIAC	ARABICAS	HARMLESS
ALMIRAHS	AMENDERS	ANATASES	**ANNICUT**	APHASIAS	**ARABINS**	**ARMLOCK**
ALMONER	**AMENTIA**	**ANCIENT**	ANNICUTS	**APHELIA**	CARABINS	ARMLOCKS
ALMONERS	AMENTIAS	ANCIENTS	**ANNULAR**	APHELIAN	**ARABISE**	**ARMOIRE**
ALNAGER	**AMENTUM**	**ANDANTE**	ANNULARS	**APHIDES**	ARABISED	ARMOIRES
ALNAGERS	RAMENTUM	ANDANTES	**ANNULET**	**APHONIA**	ARABISES	**ARNOTTO**
ALODIUM	**AMILDAR**	**ANDIRON**	ANNULETS	APHONIAS	**ARABIZE**	ARNOTTOS
ALODIUMS	AMILDARS	ANDIRONS	**ANODISE**	APHONIAS	ARABIZED	**AROUSAL**
ALOETIC	**AMMETER**	**ANDROID**	ANODISED	**APLANAT**	ARABIZES	AROUSALS
ALOETICS	AMMETERS	ANDROIDS	ANODISES	APLANATS	**ARANEID**	**AROUSED**
ALPHORN	**AMMIRAL**	**ANDVILE**	**ANODIZE**	**APLASIA**	ARANEIDS	CAROUSED
ALPHORNS	AMMIRALS	ANDVILES	ANODIZED	APLASIAS	**ARAROBA**	**AROUSER**
ALTERED	**AMMONAL**	**ANELACE**	ANODIZES	**APOCOPE**	ARAROBAS	AROUSERS
FALTERED	AMMONALS	ANELACES	**ANODYNE**	APOCOPES	**ARBITER**	**AROUSES**
HALTERED	**AMMONIA**	**ANEMONE**	ANODYNES	**APOPLEX**	ARBITERS	CAROUSES
PALTERED	AMMONIAC	ANEMONES	**ANONYMA**	APOPLEXY	**ARBLAST**	**ARPENTS**
ALTERNE	AMMONIAS	**ANEROID**	ANONYMAS	**APOSTIL**	ARBLASTS	PARPENTS
ALTERNES	**AMNESIA**	ANEROIDS	**ANOSMIA**	APOSTILS	**ARBORET**	**ARRACKS**
ALTESSE	AMNESIAC	**ANEURIN**	ANOSMIAS	**APOSTLE**	ARBORETA	BARRACKS
ALTESSES	AMNESIAS	ANEURINS	**ANTACID**	APOSTLES	ARBORETS	CARRACKS
ALTEZZA	**AMNESIC**	**ANGEKOK**	ANTACIDS	**APOTHEM**	**ARBOURS**	**ARRAIGN**
ALTEZZAS	AMNESICS	ANGEKOKS	**ANTBEAR**	APOTHEMS	HARBOURS	DARRAIGN
ALTHAEA	**AMORISM**	**ANGELIC**	ANTBEARS	**APPARAT**	**ARCHERS**	ARRAIGNS
ALTHAEAS	AMORISMS	ANGELICA	**ANTEFIX**	APPARATS	MARCHERS	**ARRANGE**
ALTHORN	**AMORIST**	**ANGERED**	ANTEFIXA	**APPAREL**	**ARCHING**	ARRANGED
ALTHORNS	AMORISTS	DANGERED	**ANTENNA**	APPARELS	MARCHING	ARRANGER
ALUMINA	**AMOROSA**	**ANGIOMA**	ANTENNAE	**APPEASE**	PARCHING	ARRANGES
ALUMINAS	AMOROSAS	ANGIOMAS	ANTENNAL	APPEASED	**ARCHIVE**	**ARRASES**
ALUMIUM	**AMOROSO**	**ANGLERS**	ANTENNAS	APPEASES	ARCHIVES	NARRASES
ALUMIUMS	AMOROSOS	DANGLERS	**ANTHERS**	**APPERIL**	**ARCHLET**	TARRASES
ALUNITE	**AMOSITE**	JANGLERS	PANTHERS	APPERILL	ARCHLETS	**ARRAYED**
ALUNITES	AMOSITES	MANGLERS	**ANTICKE**	APPERILS	**ARCHWAY**	WARRAYED
ALVEOLE	**AMPHORA**	TANGLERS	ANTICKED	**APPLAUD**	ARCHWAYS	**ARREEDE**
ALVEOLES	AMPHORAE	WANGLERS	**ANTIENT**	APPLAUDS	**ARCINGS**	ARREEDES
ALYSSUM	**AMPOULE**	**ANGLING**	ANTIENTS	**APPOINT**	FARCINGS	**ARRIAGE**
ALYSSUMS	AMPOULES	CANGLING	**ANTIGEN**	APPOINTS	**ARCKING**	ARRIAGES
AMALGAM	**AMPULLA**	DANGLING	ANTIGENS	**APPORTS**	ARCKINGS	CARRIAGE
AMALGAMS	AMPULLAE	FANGLING	**ANTILOG**	RAPPORTS	**ARCUATE**	MARRIAGE
AMANITA	**AMPUTEE**	GANGLING	ANTILOGS	**APPOSER**	ARCUATED	**ARRIERO**
AMANITAS	AMPUTEES	JANGLING	ANTILOGY	APPOSERS	**ARDRIGH**	ARRIEROS
AMARANT	**AMTRACK**	MANGLING	**ANTINGS**	**APPRISE**	ARDRIGHS	**ARRIVAL**
AMARANTH	AMTRACKS	TANGLING	BANTINGS	APPRISED	**AREFIED**	ARRIVALS
AMARANTS	**AMYGDAL**	WANGLING	CANTINGS	APPRISES	RAREFIED	**ARROWED**
AMASSES	AMYGDALA	**ANGLIST**	PANTINGS	**APPRIZE**	**AREFIES**	FARROWED
CAMASSES	AMYGDALE	ANGLISTS	WANTINGS	APPRIZED	RAREFIES	HARROWED
AMATEUR	AMYGDALS	**ANGRIES**	**ANTIQUE**	APPRIZER	**ARGENTS**	MARROWED
AMATEURS	**AMYLASE**	ANGRIEST	ANTIQUED	APPRIZES	MARGENTS	NARROWED
AMATION	AMYLASES	**ANGUINE**	ANTIQUES	**APPROOF**	**ARGUSES**	TARROWED
AMATIONS	**AMYLENE**	SANGUINE	**ANTLERS**	APPROOFS	SARGUSES	**ARSENAL**
AMBERED	AMYLENES	**ANGUISH**	PANTLERS	**APPROVE**	**ARGYRIA**	ARSENALS
CAMBERED	**AMYLOID**	LANGUISH	**ANTONYM**	APPROVED	ARGYRIAS	
AMBIENT	AMYLOIDS		ANTONYMS	APPROVER	**ARIETTA**	

ARSENIC	ASSEVERS	ATOMISE	AURELIAS	AXOLOTLS	BAILLIE	BANTENG
ARSENICS	ASSHOLE	ATOMISED	AUREOLA	AYWORDS	BAILLIES	BANTENGS
ARSHEEN	ASSHOLES	ATOMISER	AUREOLAS	NAYWORDS	BAITING	BANTING
ARSHEENS	ASSIEGE	ATOMISES	AUREOLE	AZIMUTH	BAITINGS	BANTINGS
ARSHINE	ASSIEGED	ATOMISM	AUREOLED	AZIMUTHS	BAKLAVA	BAPTISE
ARSHINES	ASSIEGES	ATOMISMS	AUREOLES	AZOTISE	BAKLAVAS	BAPTISED
ARTICLE	ASSISTS	ATOMIST	AURICLE	AZOTISED	BALADIN	BAPTISES
PARTICLE	BASSISTS	ATOMISTS	AURICLED	AZOTISES	BALADINE	BAPTISM
ARTICLED	ASSIZER	ATOMIZE	AURICLES	AZOTIZE	BALADINS	BAPTISMS
ARTICLES	ASSIZERS	ATOMIZED	AUSPICE	AZOTIZED	BALANCE	BAPTIST
ARTIEST	ASSUAGE	ATOMIZER	AUSPICES	AZOTIZES	BALANCED	BAPTISTS
TARTIEST	ASSUAGED	ATOMIZES	AUSTERE	AZULEJO	BALANCER	BAPTIZE
WARTIEST	ASSUAGES	ATONING	AUSTERER	AZULEJOS	BALANCES	BAPTIZED
ARTISAN	ASSURED	BATONING	AUTEURS	AZURINE	BALDRIC	BAPTIZES
BARTISAN	ASSUREDS	ATRESIA	HAUTEURS	AZURINES	BALDRICK	BARACAN
PARTISAN	ASSURER	ATRESIAS	AUTOCAR	AZURITE	BALDRICS	BARACANS
ARTISANS	ASSURERS	ATROPIA	AUTOCARP	LAZURITE	BALISTA	BARBATE
ARTISTE	ASSWAGE	ATROPIAS	AUTOCARS	AZURITES	BALISTAE	BARBATED
ARTISTES	TASSWAGE	ATROPIN	AUTOCUE	AZYMITE	BALISTAS	BARBOLA
ARTLESS	ASSWAGED	ATROPINE	AUTOCUES	AZYMITES	BALKING	BARBOLAS
WARTLESS	ASSWAGES	ATROPINS	AUTOMAT	BABASSU	BALKINGS	BARBULE
ARTWORK	ASTABLE	ATTACHE	AUTOMATA	BABASSUS	BALLADE	BARBULES
PARTWORK	ASTATKI	ATTACHED	AUTOMATE	BABBITT	BALLADED	BARCHAN
ARTWORKS	ASTATKIS	ATTACHES	AUTOMATS	BABBITTS	BALLADES	BARCHANE
ASCARID	ASTEISM	ATTAINT	AUTONYM	BABBLER	BALLANT	BARCHANS
ASCARIDS	ASTEISMS	ATTAINTS	TAUTONYM	BABBLERS	BALLANTS	BARGAIN
ASCETIC	ASTERIA	ATTEMPT	AUTONYMS	BABICHE	BALLAST	BARGAINS
ASCETICS	ASTERIAS	ATTEMPTS	AUTOVAC	BABICHES	BALLASTS	BARGEES
ASCIDIA	ASTERID	ATTRACT	AUTOVACS	BABUCHE	BALLING	BARGEESE
ASCIDIAN	ASTERIDS	ATTRACTS	AUXETIC	BABUCHES	BALLINGS	BARGEST
ASCRIBE	ASTHORE	ATTRIST	AUXETICS	BABUDOM	BALLIUM	BARGESTS
ASCRIBED	ASTHORES	ATTRISTS	AVARICE	BABUDOMS	BALLIUMS	BARILLA
ASCRIBES	ASTILBE	ATTUITE	AVARICES	BABUISM	BALLOON	BARILLAS
ASEPTIC	ASTILBES	ATTUITED	AVENGER	BABUISMS	BALLOONS	BARKHAN
ASEPTICS	ASTOUND	ATTUITES	AVENGERS	BACCARA	BALONEY	BARKHANS
ASHIEST	ASTOUNDS	AUBERGE	AVENTRE	BACCARAS	BALONEYS	BARMAID
HASHIEST	ASTRICT	AUBERGES	AVENTRED	BACCARAT	BAMBINO	BARMAIDS
MASHIEST	ASTRICTS	AUCTION	AVENTRES	BACKBIT	BAMBINOS	BARMKIN
WASHIEST	ASTROID	AUCTIONS	AVERAGE	BACKBITE	BANDAGE	BARMKINS
ASHRAMA	ASTROIDS	AUDIENT	AVERAGED	BACKHOE	BANDAGED	BAROCCO
ASHRAMAS	ATABRIN	AUDIENTS	AVERAGES	BACKHOES	BANDAGES	BAROCCOS
ASINICO	ATABRINS	AUDITOR	AVIATOR	BACKING	BANDANA	BARONET
ASINICOS	ATAGHAN	AUDITORS	AVIATORS	BACKINGS	BANDANAS	BARONETS
ASKANCE	YATAGHAN	AUDITORY	AVIETTE	BACKLOG	BANDEAU	BARONNE
ASKANCED	ATAGHANS	AUFGABE	AVIETTES	BACKLOGS	BANDEAUX	BARONNES
ASKANCES	ATALAYA	AUFGABES	AVIONIC	BACKPAY	BANDIES	BAROQUE
ASPERGE	ATALAYAS	AUGMENT	AVIONICS	BACKPAYS	BANDIEST	BAROQUES
ASPERGED	ATAVISM	AUGMENTS	AVOCADO	BACKSAW	BANDING	BARRACE
ASPERGER	ATAVISMS	AUGURER	AVOCADOS	BACKSAWS	ABANDING	BARRACES
ASPERGES	ATEBRIN	AUGURERS	AWAKING	BACKSET	BANDINGS	BARRACK
ASPERSE	ATEBRINS	AUGUSTE	AWAKINGS	BACKSETS	BANDOOK	BARRACKS
ASPERSED	ATELIER	AUGUSTER	AWFULLY	BACKSEY	BANDOOKS	BARRAGE
ASPERSES	ATELIERS	AUGUSTES	LAWFULLY	BACKSEYS	BANDORA	BARRAGES
ASPHALT	ATHANOR	AULDEST	AWLBIRD	BACLAVA	BANDORAS	BARRICO
ASPHALTS	ATHANORS	CAULDEST	AWLBIRDS	BACLAVAS	BANDORE	BARRICOS
ASPIRIN	ATHEISE	AULNAGE	AWNIEST	BAFFLER	BANDORES	BARRIER
ASPIRING	ATHEISED	AULNAGER	LAWNIEST	BAFFLERS	BANDROL	BARRIERS
ASPIRINS	ATHEISES	AULNAGES	TAWNIEST	BAGARRE	BANDROLS	BARRING
ASSAGAI	ATHEISM	AUNTERS	YAWNIEST	BAGARRES	BANDURA	BARRINGS
ASSAGAIS	ATHEISMS	DAUNTERS	AWNINGS	BAGASSE	BANDURAS	BARWOOD
ASSAILS	ATHEIST	HAUNTERS	DAWNINGS	BAGASSES	BANKING	BARWOODS
VASSAILS	ATHEISTS	SAUNTERS	FAWNINGS	BAGGAGE	BANKINGS	BARYTON
WASSAILS	ATHEIZE	TAUNTERS	YAWNINGS	BAGGAGES	BANKSIA	BARYTONE
ASSAULT	ATHEIZED	VAUNTERS	AXILLAE	BAGGING	BANKSIAS	BARYTONS
ASSAULTS	ATHEIZES	AUNTIES	MAXILLAE	BAGGINGS	BANNOCK	BASBLEU
ASSAYER	ATHLETA	JAUNTIES	AXILLAR	BAGPIPE	BANNOCKS	BASBLEUS
ASSAYERS	ATHLETAS	AUREATE	AXILLARY	BAGPIPER	BANQUET	BASCULE
ASSEGAI	ATHLETE	LAUREATE	AXINITE	BAGPIPES	BANQUETS	BASCULES
ASSEGAIS	ATHLETES	AURELIA	AXINITES	BAILIFF	BANSHEE	BASEMEN
ASSEVER		AURELIAN	AXOLOTL	BAILIFFS	BANSHEES	BASEMENT

BASENJI	BEARINGS	**BEGORRA**	BEPAINTS	BESTREWS	**BINOCLE**	**BLEEPER**
BASENJIS	**BEASTIE**	BEGORRAH	**BEPEARL**	**BESTRID**	BINOCLES	BLEEPERS
BASHING	BEASTIES	**BEGRIME**	BEPEARLS	BESTRIDE	**BIOCIDE**	**BLENDER**
ABASHING	**BEATING**	BEGRIMED	**BEPROSE**	**BETAINE**	BIOCIDES	BLENDERS
BASHINGS	BEATINGS	BEGRIMES	BEPROSED	BETAINES	**BIOPHOR**	**BLESBOK**
BASHLYK	**BEATNIK**	**BEGUILE**	BEPROSES	**BETEEME**	BIOPHORE	BLESBOKS
BASHLYKS	BEATNIKS	BEGUILED	**BEQUEST**	BETEEMED	BIOPHORS	**BLETHER**
BASIDIA	**BEAUFET**	BEGUILER	BEQUESTS	BETEEMES	**BIOTITE**	BLETHERS
BASIDIAL	**BEAUFETS**	BEGUILES	**BERCEAU**	**BETHINK**	BIOTITES	**BLEWART**
BASINET	**BEAUFIN**	**BEGUINE**	BERCEAUX	BETHINKS	**BIOTYPE**	BLEWARTS
BASINETS	BEAUFINS	BEGUINES	**BEREAVE**	**BETHUMB**	BIOTYPES	**BLINDER**
BASOCHE	**BEBEERU**	**BEHIGHT**	BEREAVED	BETHUMBS	**BIPLANE**	BLINDERS
BASOCHES	BEBEERUS	BEHIGHTS	BEREAVEN	**BETHUMP**	BIPLANES	**BLINKER**
BASSIST	**BECASSE**	**BEHOOVE**	BEREAVES	BETHUMPS	**BIRDING**	BLINKERS
BASSISTS	BECASSES	BEHOOVED	**BERGAMA**	**BETITLE**	BIRDINGS	**BLINTZE**
BASSOON	**BECHARM**	BEHOOVES	BERGAMAS	BETITLED	**BIRETTA**	BLINTZES
BASSOONS	BECHARMS	**BEIGNET**	**BERGYLT**	BETITLES	BIRETTAS	**BLISTER**
BASTARD	**BECLOUD**	BEIGNETS	BERGYLTS	**BETOKEN**	**BIRLING**	BLISTERS
BASTARDS	BECLOUDS	**BEJEWEL**	**BERLINE**	BETOKENS	BIRLINGS	BLISTERY
BASTARDY	**BEDAWIN**	BEJEWELS	BERLINES	**BETREAD**	**BIRLINN**	**BLITHER**
BASTIDE	BEDAWINS	**BEKNAVE**	**BERSERK**	BETREADS	BIRLINNS	BLITHERS
BASTIDES	**BEDDING**	BEKNAVED	BERSERKS	**BETROTH**	**BIRYANI**	**BLOATER**
BASTING	BEDDINGS	BEKNAVES	**BESAINT**	BETROTHS	BIRYANIS	BLOATERS
BASTINGS	**BEDERAL**	**BELCHER**	BESAINTS	**BETTERS**	**BISCUIT**	**BLOCKER**
BASTION	BEDERALS	BELCHERS	**BESEEKE**	ABETTERS	BISCUITS	BLOCKERS
BASTIONS	**BEDEVIL**	**BELDAME**	BESEEKES	**BETTING**	BISCUITY	**BLONDES**
BATABLE	BEDEVILS	BELDAMES	**BESHAME**	ABETTING	**BISMUTH**	BLONDEST
ABATABLE	**BEDIGHT**	**BELGARD**	BESHAMED	**BETTORS**	BISMUTHS	**BLOOMER**
BATHTUB	BEDIGHTS	BELGARDS	**BESHAMES**	ABETTORS	**BISTORT**	BLOOMERS
BATHTUBS	**BEDIZEN**	**BELIEVE**	**BESHINE**	**BETWEEN**	BISTORTS	BLOOMERY
BATISTE	BEDIZENS	BELIEVED	BESHINES	BETWEENS	**BITTERN**	**BLOOPER**
BATISTES	**BEDOUIN**	BELIEVER	**BESHREW**	**BEWHORE**	BITTERNS	BLOOPERS
BATTERO	BEDOUINS	BELIEVES	BESHREWS	BEWHORED	**BITTIES**	**BLOOSME**
BATTEROS	**BEDPOST**	**BELLHOP**	**BESIEGE**	BEWHORES	**BITTIEST**	BLOOSMED
BATTING	BEDPOSTS	BELLHOPS	BESIEGED	**BEZIQUE**	**BITTOCK**	BLOOSMES
BATTINGS	**BEDRITE**	**BELOVED**	BESIEGER	BEZIQUES	BITTOCKS	**BLOSSOM**
BATTLER	BEDRITES	BELOVEDS	BESIEGES	**BHISTEE**	**BITTOUR**	BLOSSOMS
BATTLERS	**BEDROCK**	**BELTING**	**BESLAVE**	BHISTEES	BITTOURS	BLOSSOMY
BATTUTA	BEDROCKS	BELTINGS	BESLAVED	**BIASING**	**BITUMEN**	**BLOTTER**
BATTUTAS	**BEDROOM**	**BELTWAY**	BESLAVER	BIASINGS	BITUMENS	BLOTTERS
BAUCHLE	BEDROOMS	BELTWAYS	BESLAVES	**BIVALVE**	**BLOUBOK**
BAUCHLED	**BEDSIDE**	**BEMEDAL**	**BESMEAR**	**BIBCOCK**	BIVALVES	BLOUBOKS
BAUCHLES	BEDSIDES	BEMEDALS	BESMEARS	BIBCOCKS	**BIVOUAC**	**BLOUSON**
BAUDRIC	**BEDSORE**	**BEMOUTH**	**BESPEAK**	**BIBELOT**	BIVOUACS	BLOUSONS
BAUDRICK	BEDSORES	BEMOUTHS	BESPEAKS	BIBELOTS	**BLABBER**	**BLOWGUN**
BAUDRICS	**BEDTICK**	**BENCHER**	**BESPEED**	**BIBLIST**	BLABBERS	BLOWGUNS
BAUXITE	BEDTICKS	BENCHERS	BESPEEDS	BIBLISTS	**BLACKEN**	**BLOWIES**
BAUXITES	**BEDTIME**	**BENDING**	**BESPICE**	**BICYCLE**	BLACKENS	BLOWIEST
BAWCOCK	BEDTIMES	BENDINGS	BESPICED	BICYCLED	**BLADDER**	**BLUBBER**
BAWCOCKS	**BEDWARD**	**BENDLET**	BESPICES	BICYCLES	BLADDERS	BLUBBERS
BAWDIES	BEDWARDS	BENDLETS	**BESPOKE**	**BIDDING**	BLADDERY	**BLUCHER**
BAWDIEST	**BEDWARF**	**BENEFIC**	BESPOKEN	BIDDINGS	**BLANKET**	BLUCHERS
BAWDKIN	BEDWARFS	BENEFICE	**BESPORT**	**BIDINGS**	BLANKETS	**BLUDGER**
BAWDKINS	**BEEFALO**	**BENEFIT**	BESPORTS	ABIDINGS	BLANKETY	BLUDGERS
BAWLING	BEEFALOS	BENEFITS	**BESPOUT**	**BIFOCAL**	**BLARNEY**	**BLUECAP**
BAWLINGS	**BEEHIVE**	**BENIGHT**	BESPOUTS	BIFOCALS	BLARNEYS	BLUECAPS
BAYONET	BEEHIVES	BENIGHTS	**BESTAIN**	**BIGENER**	**BLASTER**	**BLUEING**
BAYONETS	**BEFFANA**	**BENISON**	BESTAINS	BIGENERS	BLASTERS	BLUEINGS
BAZOOKA	BEFFANAS	BENISONS	**BESTEAD**	**BIGHORN**	**BLATHER**	**BLUETTE**
BAZOOKAS	**BEGGING**	**BENZENE**	BESTEADS	BIGHORNS	BLATHERS	BLUETTES
BEADING	BEGGINGS	BENZENES	**BESTIAL**	**BILIMBI**	**BLATTER**	**BLUFFER**
BEADINGS	**BEGHARD**	**BENZINE**	BESTIALS	BILIMBIS	BLATTERS	BLUFFERS
BEAGLER	BEGHARDS	BENZINES	**BESTICK**	**BILLING**	**BLAUBOK**	**BLUNDER**
BEAGLERS	**BEGINNE**	**BENZOIN**	BESTICKS	BILLINGS	BLAUBOKS	BLUNDERS
BEAMING	BEGINNER	BENZOINS	**BESTILL**	**BILLION**	**BLAWORT**	**BLUNGER**
BEAMINGS	BEGINNES	**BENZOLE**	BESTILLS	BILLIONS	BLAWORTS	BLUNGERS
BEARDIE	**BEGLOOM**	BENZOLES	**BESTORM**	**BILTONG**	**BLEATER**	**BLUNKER**
BEARDIES	BEGLOOMS	**BENZOYL**	BESTORMS	BILTONGS	BLEATERS	BLUNKERS
BEARING	**BEGONIA**	BENZOYLS	**BESTREW**	**BINDING**	**BLEEDER**	**BLUSHER**
ABEARING	BEGONIAS	**BEPAINT**	BESTREWN	BINDINGS	BLEEDERS	BLUSHERS

BLUSHET	BOOKIEST	BOURDERS	BRAVURAS	BRISURES	BRUMMERS	BULWARK
BLUSHETS	BOOKING	BOURDON	BRAWLER	BRITSKA	BRUSHER	BULWARKS
BLUSTER	BOOKINGS	BOURDONS	BRAWLERS	BRITSKAS	BRUSHERS	BUMBAZE
BLUSTERS	BOOKLET	BOURKHA	BRAYING	BRITTLE	BRUSQUE	BUMBAZED
BLUSTERY	BOOKLETS	BOURKHAS	ABRAYING	BRITTLER	BRUSQUER	BUMBAZES
BOARDER	BOOKSIE	BOURLAW	BRAZIER	BRITTLES	BRUXISM	BUMMOCK
BOARDERS	BOOKSIER	BOURLAWS	BRAZIERS	BRITZKA	BRUXISMS	BUMMOCKS
BOASTER	BOOMING	BOURREE	BREADTH	BRITZKAS	BUBINGA	BUMPKIN
BOASTERS	BOOMINGS	BOURREES	BREADTHS	BROADEN	BUBINGAS	BUMPKINS
BOATING	BOOSTER	BOUTADE	BREAKER	BROADENS	BUBUKLE	BUNDOOK
BOATINGS	BOOSTERS	BOUTADES	BREAKERS	BROCADE	BUBUKLES	BUNDOOKS
BOBSLED	BOOTLEG	BOWHEAD	BREATHE	BROCADED	BUCCINA	BUNGLER
BOBSLEDS	BOOTLEGS	BOWHEADS	BREATHED	BROCADES	BUCCINAS	BUNGLERS
BOBTAIL	BORAZON	BOWLDER	BREATHER	BROCAGE	BUCKEEN	BUNRAKU
BOBTAILS	BORAZONS	BOWLDERS	BREATHES	BROCAGES	BUCKEENS	BUNRAKUS
BODIKIN	BORDURE	BOWLINE	BRECCIA	BROCARD	BUCKING	BUNTING
BODIKINS	BORDURES	BOWLINES	BRECCIAS	BROCARDS	BUCKINGS	BUNTINGS
BOGBEAN	BOREDOM	BOWLING	BRECHAM	BROCHAN	BUCKLER	BUOYAGE
BOGBEANS	BOREDOMS	BOWLINGS	BRECHAMS	BROCHANS	BUCKLERS	BUOYAGES
BOGGARD	BORNITE	BOWSHOT	BREEDER	BROCKET	BUCKRAM	BURDOCK
BOGGARDS	BORNITES	BOWSHOTS	BREEDERS	BROCKETS	BUCKRAMS	BURDOCKS
BOGGART	BORONIA	BOXROOM	BREVETE	BRODKIN	BUCKSAW	BURETTE
BOGGARTS	BORONIAS	BOXROOMS	BREVIER	BRODKINS	BUCKSAWS	BURETTES
BOGGLER	BOROUGH	BOXWOOD	BREVIERS	BROIDER	BUCOLIC	BURGAGE
BOGGLERS	BOROUGHS	BOXWOODS	BREWAGE	BROIDERS	BUCOLICS	BURGAGES
BOGLAND	BORSCHT	BOYCOTT	BREWAGES	BROIDERY	BUDDIES	BURGEON
BOGLANDS	BORSCHTS	BOYCOTTS	BREWING	BROILER	BUDDIEST	BURGEONS
BOGYISM	BORSTAL	BOYHOOD	BREWINGS	BROILERS	BUDDING	BURGHER
BOGYISMS	BORSTALL	BOYHOODS	BRICKIE	BROKAGE	BUDDINGS	BURGHERS
BOILING	BORSTALS	BRABBLE	BRICKIER	BROKAGES	BUDGERO	BURGLAR
BOILINGS	BORTSCH	BRABBLED	BRICKIES	BROKING	BUDGEROS	BURGLARS
BOLIVAR	BORTSCHT	BRABBLES	BRICOLE	BROKINGS	BUDGEROW	BURGLARY
BOLIVARS	BOSCAGE	BRACHET	BRIDGED	BROMATE	BUFFOON	BURNING
BOLLARD	BOSCAGES	BRACHETS	ABRIDGED	BROMATES	BUFFOONS	BURNINGS
BOLLARDS	BOTARGO	BRACKEN	BRIDGES	BROMIDE	BUGABOO	BURNOUS
BOLLOCK	BOTARGOS	BRACKENS	ABRIDGES	BROMIDES	BUGABOOS	BURNOUSE
BOLLOCKS	BOTCHER	BRACKET	BRIDLER	BROMINE	BUGBANE	BURRELL
BOLONEY	BOTCHERS	BRACKETS	BRIDLERS	BROMINES	BUGBANES	BURRELLS
BOLONEYS	BOTCHERY	BRADAWL	BRIDOON	BROMMER	BUGBEAR	BURRHEL
BOLSHIE	BOTHOLE	BRADAWLS	BRIDOONS	BROMMERS	BUGBEARS	BURRHELS
BOLSHIER	BOTHOLES	BRAIDED	BRIGADE	BRONCHI	BUGGANE	BURSTER
BOLSHIES	BOTTEGA	ABRAIDED	BRIGADED	BRONCHIA	BUGGANES	BURSTERS
BOLSTER	BOTTEGAS	BRAMBLE	BRIGADES	BRONCHO	BUGGING	BURTHEN
BOLSTERS	BOTTINE	BRAMBLES	BRIGAND	BRONCHOS	BUGGINGS	BURTHENS
BOLTING	BOTTINES	BRANDER	BRIGANDS	BROODER	BUGWORT	BURWEED
BOLTINGS	BOTTLER	BRANDERS	BRIMING	BROODERS	BUGWORTS	BURWEEDS
BOMBARD	BOTTLERS	BRANGLE	BRIMINGS	BROOKED	BUILDER	BUSGIRL
BOMBARDS	BOUCHEE	BRANGLED	BRIMMER	ABROOKED	BUILDERS	BUSGIRLS
BOMBAST	BOUCHEES	BRANGLES	BRIMMERS	BROTHEL	BUKSHEE	BUSHIDO
BOMBASTS	BOUDOIR	BRANSLE	BRINDLE	BROTHELS	BUKSHEES	BUSHIDOS
BOMBORA	BOUDOIRS	BRANSLES	BRINDLED	BROTHER	BULGINE	BUSHIES
BOMBORAS	BOUILLI	BRANTLE	BRINDLES	BROTHERS	BULGINES	BUSHIEST
BONANZA	BOUILLIS	BRANTLES	BRINGER	BROWNIE	BULIMIA	BUSKING
BONANZAS	BOULDER	BRASERO	BRINGERS	BROWNIER	BULIMIAS	BUSKINGS
BONDAGE	BOULDERS	BRASEROS	BRINJAL	BROWNIES	BULIMIC	BUSSING
BONDAGER	BOULTER	BRASHES	BRINJALS	BRUCHID	BULIMICS	BUSSINGS
BONDAGES	BOULTERS	BRASHEST	BRIOCHE	BRUCHIDS	BULLACE	BUSTARD
BONDING	BOUNCER	BRASIER	BRIOCHES	BRUCINE	BULLACES	BUSTARDS
BONDINGS	BOUNCERS	BRASIERS	BRIQUET	BRUCINES	BULLBAT	BUSTIER
BONESET	BOUNDED	BRASSET	BRIQUETS	BRUCITE	BULLBATS	BUSTIERS
BONESETS	ABOUNDED	BRASSETS	BRISKEN	BRUCITES	BULLDOG	BUSTING
BONFIRE	BOUNDEN	BRASSIE	BRISKENS	BRUHAHA	BULLDOGS	BUSTINGS
BONFIRES	YBOUNDEN	BRASSIER	BRISKET	BRUHAHAS	BULLIES	BUSTLER
BONISTS	BOUNDER	BRASSIES	BRISKETS	BRUISER	BULLIEST	BUSTLERS
EBONISTS	BOUNDERS	BRATTLE	BRISTLE	BRUISERS	BULLION	BUTANOL
BONNIES	BOUQUET	BRATTLED	BRISTLED	BRULYIE	BULLIONS	BUTANOLS
BONNIEST	BOUQUETS	BRATTLES	BRISTLES	BRULYIES	BULLOCK	BUTCHER
BOOBOOK	BOURBON	BRAVADO	BRISURE	BRULZIE	BULLOCKS	BUTCHERS
BOOBOOKS	BOURBONS	BRAVADOS		BRULZIES	BULRUSH	BUTCHERY
BOOKIES	BOURDER	BRAVURA		BRUMMER	BULRUSHY	BUTCHES

BUTCHEST	CAISSONS	CAMAIEUX	CANTICOY	CARABINS	CAROUSEL	CATASTA
BUTMENT	CAITIFF	CAMARON	CANTIER	CARACAL	CAROUSER	CATASTAS
ABUTMENT	CAITIFFS	CAMARONS	SCANTIER	CARACALS	CAROUSES	CATAWBA
BUTMENTS	CAITIVE	CAMBISM	CANTINA	CARACOL	CARPARK	CATAWBAS
BUTTERS	CAITIVES	CAMBISMS	CANTINAS	CARACOLE	CARPARKS	CATBIRD
ABUTTERS	CAJEPUT	CAMBIST	CANTING	CARACOLS	CARPERS	CATBIRDS
BUTTING	CAJEPUTS	CAMBISTS	SCANTING	CARACUL	SCARPERS	CATBOAT
ABUTTING	CAJOLER	CAMBIUM	CANTINGS	CARACULS	CARPING	CATBOATS
BUTTOCK	CAJOLERS	CAMBIUMS	CANTION	CARAMEL	SCARPING	CATCALL
BUTTOCKS	CAJOLERY	CAMBOGE	CANTIONS	CARAMELS	CARPINGS	CATCALLS
BUVETTE	CALCINE	CAMBOGES	CANTLED	CARANNA	CARPORT	CATCHER
BUVETTES	CALCINED	CAMBREL	SCANTLED	CARANNAS	CARPORTS	CATCHERS
BUYABLE	CALCINES	CAMBRELS	CANTLES	CARAUNA	CARRACK	CATCHES
BUYABLES	CALCITE	CAMBRIC	SCANTLES	CARAUNAS	CARRACKS	SCATCHES
BUZZARD	CALCITES	CAMBRICS	CANTLET	CARAVAN	CARRACT	CATCHUP
BUZZARDS	CALCIUM	CAMELID	CANTLETS	CARAVANS	CARRACTS	CATCHUPS
BUZZING	CALCIUMS	CAMELIDS	CANTRED	CARAVEL	CARRECT	CATECHU
BUZZINGS	CALDERA	CAMELOT	CANTREDS	CARAVELS	CARRECTS	CATECHUS
BYCOKET	CALDERAS	CAMELOTS	CANTREF	CARAWAY	CARRELL	CATELOG
BYCOKETS	CALDRON	CAMPANA	CANTREFS	CARAWAYS	CARRELLS	CATELOGS
BYGOING	CALDRONS	CAMPANAS	CANTRIP	CARBIDE	CARRIER	CATERAN
BYGOINGS	CALIBER	CAMPERS	CANTRIPS	CARBIDES	CARRIERS	CATERANS
BYPLACE	CALIBERS	SCAMPERS	CANZONA	CARBINE	CARRION	CATERER
BYPLACES	CALIBRE	CAMPHOR	CANZONAS	CARBINES	CARRIONS	CATERERS
BYWONER	CALIBRED	CAMPHORS	CANZONE	CARCAKE	CARTAGE	CATHEAD
BYWONERS	CALIBRES	CAMPING	CANZONET	CARCAKES	CARTAGES	CATHEADS
CABARET	CALICHE	SCAMPING	CAPABLE	CARCASE	CARTING	CATHODE
CABARETS	CALICHES	CAMPION	CAPABLER	CARCASED	SCARTING	CATHODES
CABBAGE	CALIPEE	CAMPIONS	CAPELET	CARCASES	CARTOON	CATHOOD
CABBAGED	CALIPEES	CANAKIN	CAPELETS	CARDECU	CARTOONS	CATHOODS
CABBAGES	CALIPER	CANAKINS	CAPELIN	CARDECUE	CARTWAY	CATLING
CABBALA	CALIPERS	CANASTA	CAPELINE	CARDECUS	CARTWAYS	CATLINGS
CABBALAS	CALIVER	CANASTAS	CAPELINS	CARDIAC	CARVING	CATMINT
CABINET	CALIVERS	CANDELA	CAPERER	CARDIACS	CARVINGS	CATMINTS
CABINETS	CALLANT	CANDELAS	CAPERERS	CARDOON	SCARTING	CATSKIN
CABLING	CALLANTS	CANDENT	CAPITAL	CARDOONS	CASCADE	CATSKINS
CABLINGS	CALLING	SCANDENT	CAPITALS	CARIAMA	CASCADED	CATSUIT
CABOOSE	CALLINGS	CANDIDA	CAPITAN	CARIAMAS	CASCADES	CATSUITS
CABOOSES	CALMANT	CANDIDAS	CAPITANI	CARIBOU	CASCARA	CATTABU
CACIQUE	CALMANTS	CANDOCK	CAPITANO	CARIBOUS	CASCARAS	CATTABUS
CACIQUES	CALOMEL	CANDOCKS	CAPITANS	CARIERE	CASEMEN	CATTALO
CACKLER	CALOMELS	CANDOUR	CAPORAL	CARIERES	CASEMENT	CATTALOS
CACKLERS	CALORIC	CANDOURS	CAPORALS	CARINAS	CASERNE	CATTERY
CACODYL	CALORICS	CANELLA	CAPPING	OCARINAS	CASERNES	SCATTERY
CACODYLS	CALORIE	CANELLAS	CAPPINGS	CARIOCA	CASHIER	CATTIER
CACOLET	CALORIES	CANIKIN	CAPRATE	CARIOCAS	CASHIERS	SCATTIER
CACOLETS	CALOTTE	CANIKINS	CAPRATES	CARIOLE	CASSATA	CATTIES
CACUMEN	CALOTTES	CANNACH	CAPRICE	CARIOLES	CASSATAS	CATTIEST
CACUMENS	CALOYER	CANNACHS	CAPRICES	CARIOUS	CASSAVA	CATTING
CADAVER	CALOYERS	CANNERS	CAPSIZE	SCARIOUS	CASSAVAS	SCATTING
CADAVERS	CALPACK	SCANNERS	CAPSIZED	CARLINE	CASSINO	CAUDATE
CADDICE	CALPACKS	CANNING	CAPSIZES	CARLINES	CASSINOS	ACAUDATE
CADDICES	CALTRAP	SCANNING	CAPSTAN	CARLOAD	CASSOCK	ECAUDATE
CADENCE	CALTRAPS	CANNULA	CAPSTANS	CARLOADS	CASSOCKS	CAUDATED
CADENCED	CALTROP	CANNULAE	CAPSULE	CARLOCK	CASSONE	CAUDRON
CADENCES	CALTROPS	CANNULAS	CAPSULES	CARLOCKS	CASSONES	CAUDRONS
CADENZA	CALUMBA	CANTATA	CAPTAIN	CARMINE	CASTING	CAULINE
CADENZAS	CALUMBAS	CANTATAS	CAPTAINS	CARMINES	CASTINGS	ACAULINE
CADMIUM	CALUMET	CANTATE	CAPTION	CARNAGE	CASTOCK	CAULKER
CADMIUMS	CALUMETS	CANTATES	CAPTIONS	CARNAGES	CASTOCKS	CAULKERS
CAESIUM	CALYCLE	CANTDOG	CAPTIVE	CARNIES	CASUIST	CAULOME
CAESIUMS	CALYCLED	CANTDOGS	CAPTIVED	CARNIEST	CASUISTS	CAULOMES
CAESURA	CALYCLES	CANTEEN	CAPTIVES	CAROCHE	CATALOG	CAUSTIC
CAESURAL	CALYPSO	CANTEENS	CAPTURE	CAROCHES	CATALOGS	CAUSTICS
CAESURAS	CALYPSOS	CANTEST	CAPTURED	CAROMEL	CATALPA	CAUTION
CAFFILA	CALZONE	SCANTEST	CAPTURES	CAROMELS	CATALPAS	CAUTIONS
CAFFILAS	CALZONES	CANTHUS	CAPUCHE	CAROTIN	CATAPAN	CAVALLA
CAGOULE	CAMAIEU	ACANTHUS	CAPUCHES	CAROTINS	CATAPANS	CAVALLAS
CAGOULES	CAMAIEU	CANTICO	CARABIN	CAROUSE	CATARRH	CAVIARE
CAISSON	CAMAIEU	CANTICOS	CARABINE	CAROUSED	CATARRHS	CAVIARES

CAYENNE	CHADDAR	CHARACT	CHELATE	CHINKIER	CHUCKLED	CLABBERS
CAYENNED	CHADDARS	CHARACTS	CHELATED	CHINKIES	CHUCKLES	CLACHAN
CAYENNES	CHAFFER	CHARADE	CHELATES	CHINOOK	CHUDDAH	CLACHANS
CAZIQUE	CHAFFERS	CHARADES	CHELOID	CHINOOKS	CHUDDAHS	CLACKER
CAZIQUES	CHAFFERY	CHARGER	CHELOIDS	CHINWAG	CHUDDAR	CLACKERS
CEASING	CHAGRIN	CHARGERS	CHEMISE	CHINWAGS	CHUDDARS	CLADDER
CEASINGS	CHAGRINS	CHARIOT	CHEMISES	CHIPPIE	CHUKKER	CLADDERS
CEDILLA	CHALAZA	CHARIOTS	CHEMISM	CHIPPIER	CHUKKERS	CLADISM
CEDILLAS	CHALAZAE	CHARISM	CHEMISMS	CHIPPIES	CHUMLEY	CLADISMS
CEDRATE	CHALAZAS	CHARISMA	CHEMIST	CHIRPER	CHUMLEYS	CLADIST
CEDRATES	CHALDER	CHARISMS	CHEMISTS	CHIRPERS	CHUNDER	CLADISTS
CEILIDH	CHALDERS	CHARLEY	CHEQUER	CHIRRUP	CHUNDERS	CLADODE
CEILIDHS	CHALICE	CHARLEYS	CHEQUERS	CHIRRUPS	CHUNNEL	CLADODES
CEILING	CHALICED	CHARLIE	CHEROOT	CHIRRUPY	CHUNNELS	CLAIMER
CEILINGS	CHALICES	CHARLIES	CHEROOTS	CHITTER	CHUNNER	CLAIMERS
CELADON	CHALLAN	CHARMER	CHERVIL	CHITTERS	CHUNNERS	CLAMBER
CELADONS	CHALLANS	CHARMERS	CHERVILS	CHLORAL	CHUNTER	CLAMBERS
CELESTA	CHALONE	CHARNEL	CHESNUT	CHLORALS	CHUNTERS	CLAMOUR
CELESTAS	CHALONES	CHARNELS	CHESNUTS	CHOBDAR	CHUPATI	CLAMOURS
CELESTE	CHAMADE	CHARPIE	CHESSEL	CHOBDARS	CHUPATIS	CLAMPER
CELESTES	CHAMADES	CHARPIES	CHESSELS	CHOCTAW	CHUTIST	CLAMPERS
CELLIST	CHAMBER	CHARPOY	CHEVRON	CHOCTAWS	CHUTISTS	CLANGER
CELLISTS	CHAMBERS	CHARPOYS	CHEVRONS	CHOICES	CHUTNEY	CLANGERS
CELLULE	CHAMFER	CHARQUI	CHEVRONY	CHOICEST	CHUTNEYS	CLANGOR
CELLULES	CHAMFERS	CHARQUIS	CHEWINK	CHOKIES	CICHLID	CLANGORS
CEMBALO	CHAMISE	CHARTER	CHEWINKS	CHOKIEST	CICHLIDS	CLAPNET
CEMBALOS	CHAMISES	CHARTERS	CHIASMA	CHOLERA	CIELING	CLAPNETS
CENACLE	CHAMISO	CHASING	CHIASMAS	CHOLERAS	CIELINGS	CLAPPER
CENACLES	CHAMISOS	CHASINGS	CHIBOUK	CHOLINE	CILIATE	CLAPPERS
CENSURE	CHAMLET	CHASTEN	CHIBOUKS	CHOLINES	CILIATED	CLARINO
CENSURED	CHAMLETS	CHASTENS	CHICANE	CHONDRE	CINEAST	CLARINOS
CENSURES	CHAMPAC	CHATEAU	CHICANED	CHONDRES	CINEASTE	CLARION
CENTAGE	CHAMPACS	CHATEAUX	CHICANER	CHONDRI	CINEASTS	CLARIONS
CENTAGES	CHAMPAK	CHATTEL	CHICANES	CHONDRIN	CINEOLE	CLARKIA
CENTAUR	CHAMPAKS	CHATTELS	CHICANO	CHOOKIE	CINEOLES	CLARKIAS
CENTAURS	CHANCEL	CHATTER	CHICANOS	CHOOKIES	CINEREA	CLASPER
CENTAURY	CHANCELS	CHATTERS	CHICKEN	CHOOSER	CINEREAL	CLASPERS
CENTAVO	CHANCER	CHAUMER	CHICKENS	CHOOSERS	CINEREAS	CLASSIC
CENTAVOS	CHANCERS	CHAUMERS	CHIDING	CHOPINE	CISSIES	CLASSICS
CENTIME	CHANCRE	CHAUNCE	CHIDINGS	CHOPINES	CISSIEST	CLATTER
CENTIMES	CHANCRES	CHAUNCED	CHIEFER	CHOPPER	CISSOID	CLATTERS
CENTNER	CHANGER	CHAUNCES	CHIEFERY	CHOPPERS	CISSOIDS	CLAUCHT
CENTNERS	CHANGERS	CHAUNGE	CHIFFON	CHORAGI	CISTERN	CLAUCHTS
CENTRUM	CHANNEL	CHAUNGED	CHIFFONS	CHORAGIC	CISTERNS	CLAUGHT
CENTRUMS	CHANNELS	CHAUNGES	CHIGGER	CHORALE	CISTRON	CLAUGHTS
CEPHEID	CHANOYU	CHAUVIN	CHIGGERS	CHORALES	CISTRONS	CLAVATE
CEPHEIDS	CHANOYUS	CHAUVINS	CHIGNON	CHOREGI	CIRCUIT	CLAVATED
CERAMET	CHANSON	CHAYOTE	CHIGNONS	CHOREGIC	CIRCUITS	CLAVIER
CERAMETS	CHANSONS	CHAYOTES	CHIKARA	CHORINE	CIRCUITY	CLAVIERS
CERAMIC	CHANTER	CHEAPEN	CHIKARAS	CHORINES	CISSIES	CLAYPAN
CERAMICS	CHANTERS	CHEAPENS	CHIKHOR	CHORIST	CISSIEST	CLAYPANS
CERASIN	CHANTEY	CHEAPIE	CHIKHORS	CHORISTS	CISSOID	CLEANER
CERASINS	CHANTEYS	CHEAPIES	CHILIAD	CHORIZO	CISSOIDS	CLEANERS
CERESIN	CHANTIE	CHEATER	CHILIADS	CHORIZOS	CISTERN	CLEANSE
CERESINE	CHANTIES	CHEATERS	CHILLER	CHOROID	CISTERNS	CLEANSED
CERESINS	CHANTOR	CHEATERY	SCHILLER	CHOROIDS	CISTRON	CLEANSER
CERNING	CHANTORS	CHECHIA	CHILLERS	CHORTLE	CISTRONS	CLEANSES
SCERNING	CHAPATI	CHECHIAS	CHILLUM	CHORTLED	CITADEL	CLEARER
CERUMEN	CHAPATIS	CHECKER	CHILLUMS	CHORTLES	CITADELS	CLEARERS
CERUMENS	CHAPEAU	CHECKERS	CHIMERA	CHOWDER	CITHARA	CLEAVER
CESSION	CHAPEAUS	CHEEPER	CHIMERAS	CHOWDERS	CITHARAS	CLEAVERS
CESSIONS	CHAPLET	CHEEPERS	CHIMERE	CHRISOM	CITHERN	CLERUCH
CESSPIT	CHAPLETS	CHEERER	CHIMERES	CHRISOMS	CITHERNS	CLERUCHS
CESSPITS	CHAPPED	CHEERERS	CHIMLEY	CHRONIC	CITIZEN	CLERUCHY
CESTODE	SCHAPPED	CHEERIO	CHIMLEYS	CHRONICS	CITIZENS	CLICKER
CESTODES	CHAPPIE	CHEERIOS	CHIMNEY	CHRONON	CITRATE	CLICKERS
CESTOID	CHAPPIER	CHEETAH	CHIMNEYS	CHRONONS	CITRATES	CLICKET
CESTOIDS	CHAPPIES	CHEETAHS	CHINDIT	CHUCKIE	CITRINE	CLICKETS
CHABOUK	CHAPTER	CHEKIST	CHINDITS	CHUCKIES	CITRINES	CLIMATE
CHABOUKS	CHAPTERS	CHEKISTS	CHINKIE	CHUCKLE	CITTERN	CLIMATED

CLIMATES	COBBLERS	COINAGES	**COMMODE**	**CONCEAL**	CONGEALS	CONTENDS
CLIMBER	COBBLERY	**COINING**	COMMODES	CONCEALS	**CONGEST**	**CONTENT**
CLIMBERS	**COCAINE**	COININGS	**COMMOTE**	**CONCEDE**	CONGESTS	CONTENTS
CLINGER	COCAINES	**COITION**	COMMOTES	CONCEDED	**CONGREE**	**CONTEST**
CLINGERS	**COCHLEA**	COITIONS	**COMMOVE**	CONCEDER	CONGREED	CONTESTS
CLINKER	COCHLEAE	**COLIBRI**	COMMOVED	CONCEDES	CONGREES	**CONTEXT**
CLINKERS	COCHLEAR	COLIBRIS	COMMOVES	**CONCEIT**	CONGREET	CONTEXTS
CLIPPER	COCHLEAS	**COLLAGE**	**COMMUNE**	CONCEITS	**CONGRUE**	**CONTORT**
CLIPPERS	**COCKADE**	COLLAGEN	COMMUNED	CONCEITY	CONGRUED	CONTORTS
CLIPPIE	COCKADES	COLLAGES	COMMUNES	**CONCENT**	CONGRUES	**CONTOUR**
CLIPPIES	**COCKEYE**	**COLLARD**	**COMMUTE**	CONCENTS	**CONIDIA**	CONTOURS
CLITTER	COCKEYED	COLLARDS	COMMUTED	**CONCEPT**	CONIDIAL	**CONTRAS**
CLITTERS	COCKEYES	**COLLATE**	COMMUTER	CONCEPTI	**CONIFER**	CONTRAST
CLOBBER	**COCKIES**	COLLATED	COMMUTES	CONCEPTS	CONIFERS	**CONTROL**
CLOBBERS	COCKIEST	COLLATES	**COMPACT**	**CONCERN**	CONIINE	CONTROLS
CLOCKER	**COCKNEY**	**COLLECT**	COMPACTS	CONCERNS	CONIINES	**CONTUND**
CLOCKERS	COCKNEYS	COLLECTS	**COMPAGE**	**CONCERT**	**CONJECT**	CONTUNDS
CLOGGER	**COCKPIT**	**COLLEEN**	COMPAGES	CONCERTO	CONJECTS	**CONTUSE**
CLOGGERS	COCKPITS	COLLEENS	**COMPARE**	CONCERTS	**CONJOIN**	CONTUSED
CLOISON	**COCONUT**	**COLLEGE**	COMPARED	**CONCHIE**	CONJOINS	CONTUSES
CLOISONS	COCONUTS	COLLEGER	COMPARES	CONCHIES	CONJOINT	**CONVENE**
CLOSING	**COCOTTE**	COLLEGES	**COMPART**	**CONCISE**	**CONJURE**	CONVENED
ECLOSING	COCOTTES	**COLLIDE**	COMPARTS	CONCISED	CONJURED	CONVENER
CLOSINGS	**COCTION**	COLLIDED	**COMPEAR**	CONCISER	CONJURER	CONVENES
CLOSURE	COCTIONS	COLLIDES	COMPEARS	CONCISES	CONJURES	**CONVENT**
CLOSURED	**CODEINE**	**COLLIER**	**COMPEER**	**CONCOCT**	**CONNECT**	CONVENTS
CLOSURES	CODEINES	COLLIERS	COMPEERS	CONCOCTS	CONNECTS	**CONVERT**
CLOTBUR	**CODICIL**	COLLIERY	**COMPEND**	**CONCORD**	**CONNING**	CONVERTS
CLOTBURS	CODICILS	**COLLING**	COMPENDS	CONCORDS	CONNINGS	**CONVICT**
CLOTTER	**CODILLA**	COLLINGS	**COMPERE**	**CONCREW**	**CONNIVE**	CONVICTS
CLOTTERS	CODILLAS	**COLLOID**	COMPERED	CONCREWS	CONNIVED	**CONVIVE**
CLOTURE	**CODILLE**	COLLOIDS	COMPERES	**CONDEMN**	CONNIVER	CONVIVED
CLOTURED	CODILLES	**COLLOPS**	**COMPETE**	CONDEMNS	CONNIVES	CONVIVES
CLOTURES	**CODLING**	SCOLLOPS	COMPETED	**CONDOLE**	**CONNOTE**	**CONVOKE**
CLOUTER	CODLINGS	**COLLUDE**	COMPETES	CONDOLED	CONNOTED	CONVOKED
CLOUTERS	**COEHORN**	COLLUDED	**COMPILE**	CONDOLES	CONNOTES	CONVOKES
CLOWDER	COEHORNS	COLLUDER	COMPILED	**CONDONE**	**CONQUER**	**COOKOUT**
CLOWDERS	**COELIAC**	COLLUDES	COMPILER	CONDONED	CONQUERS	COOKOUTS
CLUDGIE	COELIACS	**COLONEL**	COMPILES	CONDONES	**CONSEIL**	**COOLANT**
CLUDGIES	**COELOME**	COLONELS	**COMPLIN**	**CONDUCE**	CONSEILS	COOLANTS
CLUMBER	COELOMES	**COLONIC**	COMPLINE	CONDUCED	**CONSENT**	**COONTIE**
CLUMBERS	**COEQUAL**	COLONICS	COMPLINS	CONDUCES	CONSENTS	COONTIES
CLUPEID	COEQUALS	**COLUBER**	**COMPLOT**	**CONDUCT**	**CONSIGN**	**COOPERS**
CLUPEIDS	**COFFERS**	COLUBERS	COMPLOTS	CONDUCTI	CONSIGNS	SCOOPERS
CLUSTER	SCOFFERS	**COLUMEL**	**COMPORT**	CONDUCTS	**CONSIST**	**COOPING**
CLUSTERS	**COFFING**	COLUMELS	COMPORTS	**CONDUIT**	CONSISTS	SCOOPING
CLUSTERY	SCOFFING	**COMBINE**	**COMPOSE**	CONDUITS	**CONSOLE**	**COPAIBA**
CLUTTER	**COFFRET**	COMBINED	COMPOSED	**CONDYLE**	CONSOLED	COPAIBAS
CLUTTERS	COFFRETS	COMBINES	COMPOSER	CONDYLES	CONSOLER	**COPAIVA**
CLYSTER	**COGENCE**	**COMBING**	COMPOSES	**CONFECT**	CONSOLES	COPAIVAS
CLYSTERS	COGENCES	COMBINGS	**COMPOST**	CONFECTS	**CONSORT**	**COPEPOD**
COACHEE	**COGENER**	**COMBLES**	COMPOSTS	**CONFIDE**	CONSORTS	COPEPODS
COACHEES	COGENERS	COMBLESS	**COMPOTE**	CONFIDED	**CONSTER**	**COPILOT**
COACHER	**COGGING**	**COMBUST**	COMPOTES	CONFIDER	CONSTERS	COPILOTS
COACHERS	SCOGGING	COMBUSTS	**COMPTER**	CONFIDES	**CONSULT**	**COPPICE**
COALISE	**COGNATE**	**COMFORT**	COMPTERS	**CONFINE**	CONSULTA	COPPICED
COALISED	COGNATES	COMFORTS	**COMPUTE**	CONFINED	CONSULTS	COPPICES
COALISES	**COGNISE**	**COMFREY**	COMPUTED	CONFINER	**CONSUME**	**COPULAS**
COALIZE	COGNISED	COMFREYS	COMPUTER	CONFINES	CONSUMED	SCOPULAS
COALIZED	COGNISES	**COMIQUE**	COMPUTES	**CONFIRM**	CONSUMER	**COPYISM**
COALIZES	**COGNIZE**	COMIQUES	**COMRADE**	CONFIRMS	CONSUMES	COPYISMS
COAMING	COGNIZED	**COMMAND**	COMRADES	**CONFORM**	**CONTACT**	**COPYIST**
COAMINGS	COGNIZES	COMMANDO	**CONACRE**	CONFORMS	CONTACTS	COPYISTS
COARSEN	**COHABIT**	COMMANDS	CONACRED	**CONFUSE**	**CONTAIN**	**COQUITO**
COARSENS	COHABITS	**COMMEND**	CONACRES	CONFUSED	CONTAINS	COQUITOS
COASTER	**COHERER**	COMMENDS	**CONARIA**	CONFUSES	**CONTECK**	**CORACLE**
COASTERS	COHERERS	**COMMENT**	CONARIAL	**CONFUTE**	CONTECKS	CORACLES
COATING	**COHIBIT**	COMMENTS	**CONCAVE**	CONFUTED	**CONTEMN**	**CORANTO**
COATINGS	COHIBITS	**COMMERE**	CONCAVED	CONFUTES	CONTEMNS	CORANTOS
COBBLER	**COINAGE**	COMMERES	CONCAVES	**CONGEAL**	**CONTEND**	**CORBEAU**

CORBEAUS	**CORSNED**	COUNTERS	**COWSHED**	CREMATES	CROMBIES	CRUSADOS
CORBEIL	CORSNEDS	**COUPING**	COWSHEDS	**CREMONA**	**CROODLE**	**CRUSHER**
CORBEILS	**CORTEGE**	SCOUPING	**COWSLIP**	CREMONAS	CROODLED	CRUSHERS
CORDAGE	CORTEGES	**COUPLER**	COWSLIPS	**CRENATE**	CROODLES	**CRUSIAN**
CORDAGES	**CORTILE**	COUPLERS	**COXCOMB**	CRENATED	**CROONER**	CRUSIANS
CORDIAL	CORTILES	**COUPLET**	COXCOMBS	**CRESSET**	CROONERS	**CRYINGS**
CORDIALS	**CORYPHE**	COUPLETS	**COZENER**	CRESSETS	**CROPFUL**	SCRYINGS
CORDING	CORYPHEE	**COUPURE**	COZENERS	**CRETISM**	CROPFULL	**CRYOGEN**
CORDINGS	CORYPHES	COUPURES	**CRABBED**	CRETISMS	CROPFULS	CRYOGENS
CORDITE	**COSINES**	**COURAGE**	SCRABBED	**CREVICE**	**CROPPER**	CRYOGENY
CORDITES	COSINESS	COURAGES	**CRACKER**	CREVICES	CROPPERS	**CRYONIC**
CORDOBA	**COSMISM**	**COURANT**	CRACKERS	**CREWING**	**CROQUET**	CRYONICS
CORDOBAS	ACOSMISM	COURANTE	**CRACKLE**	SCREWING	CROQUETS	**CRYPTON**
CORELLA	COSMISMS	COURANTS	CRACKLED	**CRIBBLE**	**CROSIER**	CRYPTONS
CORELLAS	**COSMIST**	**COURIER**	CRACKLES	CRIBBLED	CROSIERS	**CRYSTAL**
CORIOUS	ACOSMIST	COURIERS	**CRACOWE**	CRIBBLES	**CROSSES**	CRYSTALS
SCORIOUS	COSMISTS	**COURING**	CRACOWES	**CRICKET**	CROSSEST	**CUBBING**
CORKAGE	**COSTARD**	SCOURING	**CRAGGED**	CRICKETS	**CROTTLE**	CUBBINGS
CORKAGES	COSTARDS	**COURLAN**	SCRAGGED	**CRICOID**	CROTTLES	**CUBHOOD**
CORNAGE	**COSTATE**	COURLANS	**CRAMMED**	CRICOIDS	**CROUPER**	CUBHOODS
CORNAGES	ECOSTATE	**COURSED**	SCRAMMED	**CRIMMER**	CROUPERS	**CUBICLE**
CORNERS	COSTATED	SCOURSED	**CRAMMER**	CRIMMERS	**CROUPON**	CUBICLES
SCORNERS	**COSTEAN**	**COURSER**	CRAMMERS	**CRIMPED**	CROUPONS	**CUCKOLD**
CORNETT	COSTEANS	COURSERS	**CRAMPET**	SCRIMPED	**CROUTON**	CUCKOLDS
CORNETTI	**COSTREL**	**COURSES**	CRAMPETS	**CRIMPER**	CROUTONS	CUCKOLDY
CORNETTO	COSTRELS	SCOURSES	**CRAMPIT**	CRIMPERS	**CROWDER**	**CUDBEAR**
CORNETTS	**COSTUME**	**COUTERS**	CRAMPITS	**CRIMPLE**	CROWDERS	CUDBEARS
CORNICE	COSTUMED	SCOUTERS	**CRAMPON**	CRIMPLED	**CROWDIE**	**CUDDLED**
CORNICED	**COSTUMER**	**COUTHER**	CRAMPONS	CRIMPLES	CROWDIES	SCUDDLED
CORNICES	COSTUMES	SCOUTHER	**CRANAGE**	**CRIMSON**	**CROWNER**	**CUDDLES**
CORNING	**COTERIE**	**COUTHIE**	CRANAGES	CRIMSONS	CROWNERS	SCUDDLES
SCORNING	COTERIES	COUTHIER	**CRANIUM**	**CRINATE**	**CROWNET**	**CUDWEED**
CORNIST	**COTHURN**	**COUTURE**	CRANIUMS	CRINATED	CROWNETS	CUDWEEDS
CORNISTS	COTHURNI	COUTURES	**CRANKLE**	**CRINGER**	**CROZIER**	**CUFFING**
CORNUTE	COTHURNS	**COUVADE**	CRANKLED	CRINGERS	CROZIERS	SCUFFING
CORNUTED	**COTINGA**	COUVADES	CRANKLES	**CRINGLE**	**CRUBEEN**	**CUFFLED**
CORNUTES	COTINGAS	**COUVERT**	**CRANNOG**	CRINGLES	CRUBEENS	SCUFFLED
CORNUTO	**COTLAND**	COUVERTS	CRANNOGS	**CRINITE**	**CRUCIAN**	**CUFFLES**
CORNUTOS	COTLANDS	**COVELET**	**CRAPING**	CRINITES	CRUCIANS	SCUFFLES
COROLLA	**COTTAGE**	COVELETS	SCRAPING	**CRINKLE**	**CRUDDLE**	**CUISINE**
COROLLAS	COTTAGED	**COWBANE**	**CRAPPED**	CRINKLED	CRUDDLED	CUISINES
CORONAL	COTTAGER	COWBANES	SCRAPPED	CRINKLES	CRUDDLES	**CUISSER**
CORONALS	COTTAGES	**COWBELL**	**CRAVING**	**CRINOID**	**CRUISER**	CUISSERS
CORONER	COTTAGEY	COWBELLS	CRAVINGS	CRINOIDS	CRUISERS	**CUITTLE**
CORONERS	**COTTIER**	**COWBIRD**	**CRAWLED**	**CRIOLLO**	**CRUISIE**	CUITTLED
CORONET	COTTIERS	COWBIRDS	SCRAWLED	CRIOLLOS	CRUISIES	CUITTLES
CORONETS	**COTTISE**	**COWGIRL**	**CRAWLER**	**CRIPPLE**	**CRULLER**	**CULICID**
CORPORA	COTTISED	COWGIRLS	SCRAWLER	CRIPPLED	CRULLERS	CULICIDS
CORPORAL	COTTISES	**COWHAGE**	CRAWLERS	CRIPPLES	**CRUMBLE**	**CULLERS**
CORPORAS	**COTTOID**	COWHAGES	**CRAZIES**	**CRISPER**	CRUMBLED	SCULLERS
CORRADE	COTTOIDS	**COWHAND**	CRAZIEST	CRISPERS	CRUMBLES	**CULLING**
CORRADED	**COTTOWN**	COWHANDS	**CREAKED**	**CRISPIN**	**CRUMPED**	SCULLING
CORRADES	COTTOWNS	**COWHEEL**	SCREAKED	CRISPING	SCRUMPED	CULLINGS
CORRECT	**COUCHEE**	COWHEELS	**CREAMED**	CRISPINS	**CRUMPET**	**CULLION**
CORRECTS	COUCHEES	**COWHERD**	SCREAMED	**CRITTER**	CRUMPETS	SCULLION
CORRIDA	**COUGHER**	COWHERDS	**CREAMER**	CRITTERS	**CRUMPLE**	CULLIONS
CORRIDAS	COUGHERS	**COWHIDE**	SCREAMER	**CRITTUR**	CRUMPLED	**CULOTTE**
CORRODE	**COUGUAR**	COWHIDED	CREAMERS	CRITTURS	CRUMPLES	CULOTTES
CORRODED	COUGUARS	COWHIDES	CREAMERY	**CROAKER**	**CRUNCHY**	**CULPRIT**
CORRODES	**COULOIR**	**COWLICK**	**CREANCE**	CROAKERS	SCRUNCHY	CULPRITS
CORRUPT	COULOIRS	COWLICKS	CREANCES	**CROCHET**	**CRUNKLE**	**CULTISM**
CORRUPTS	**COULOMB**	**COWLING**	**CREATOR**	CROCHETS	CRUNKLED	CULTISMS
CORSAGE	COULOMBS	SCOWLING	CREATORS	**CROCKET**	CRUNKLES	**CULTIST**
CORSAGES	**COULTER**	COWLINGS	**CREEPER**	CROCKETS	**CRUPPER**	CULTISTS
CORSAIR	COULTERS	**COWPING**	CREEPERS	**CROMACK**	CRUPPERS	**CULTURE**
CORSAIRS	**COUNCIL**	SCOWPING	**CREEPIE**	CROMACKS	**CRUSADE**	CULTURED
CORSIVE	COUNCILS	**COWPOKE**	CREEPIER	**CROMBIE**	CRUSADED	CULTURES
CORSIVES	**COUNSEL**	COWPOKES	CREEPIES		CRUSADER	**CULVERT**
CORSLET	COUNSELS	**COWRIES**	**CREMATE**		CRUSADES	CULVERTS
CORSLETS	**COUNTER**	SCOWRIES	CREMATED		**CRUSADO**	**CUMARIN**

CUMARINS	CURTSEYS	CZARDOMS	**DASTARD**	DECEIVED	**DEFINER**	DEMENTIS
CUMBERS	**CURVATE**	**CZARINA**	DASTARDS	DECEIVER	DEFINERS	**DEMERGE**
SCUMBERS	CURVATED	CZARINAS	DASTARDY	DECEIVES	**DEFLATE**	DEMERGED
CUMMERS	**CURVIER**	**CZARISM**	**DASYPOD**	**DECIARE**	DEFLATED	DEMERGER
SCUMMERS	SCURVIER	CZARISMS	DASYPODS	DECIARES	DEFLATER	DEMERGES
CUMQUAT	**CUSHION**	**CZARIST**	**DASYURE**	**DECIBEL**	DEFLATES	**DEMERIT**
CUMQUATS	CUSHIONS	CZARISTS	DASYURES	DECIBELS	**DEFLECT**	DEMERITS
CUMSHAW	CUSHIONY	**DABBLER**	**DATARIA**	**DECIDER**	DEFLECTS	**DEMERSE**
CUMSHAWS	**CUSTARD**	DABBLERS	DATARIAS	DECIDERS	**DEFORCE**	DEMERSED
CUNETTE	CUSTARDS	**DABSTER**	DATARIES	**DECIDUA**	DEFORCED	DEMERSES
CUNETTES	**CUSTOCK**	DABSTERS	**DAUBING**	DECIDUAL	DEFORCES	**DEMESNE**
CUNNERS	CUSTOCKS	**DADDOCK**	DAUBINGS	DECIDUAS	**DEFRAUD**	DEMESNES
SCUNNERS	**CUSTODE**	DADDOCKS	**DAUNDER**	**DECIMAL**	DEFRAUDS	**DEMIGOD**
CUNNING	CUSTODES	**DAFFIES**	DAUNDERS	DECIMALS	**DEFROCK**	DEMIGODS
CUNNINGS	**CUSTREL**	DAFFIEST	**DAUNTER**	**DECKING**	DEFROCKS	**DEMIREP**
CUPGALL	CUSTRELS	**DAFFING**	DAUNTERS	DECKINGS	**DEFROST**	DEMIREPS
CUPGALLS	**CUTAWAY**	DAFFINGS	**DAUNTON**	**DECLAIM**	DEFROSTS	**DEMOUNT**
CUPHEAD	CUTAWAYS	**DAGLOCK**	DAUNTONS	DECLAIMS	**DEFROZE**	DEMOUNTS
CUPHEADS	**CUTBACK**	DAGLOCKS	**DAUPHIN**	**DECLARE**	DEFROZEN	**DEMURES**
CUPPERS	CUTBACKS	**DAGWOOD**	DAUPHINS	DECLARED	**DEFUNCT**	DEMUREST
SCUPPERS	**CUTCHES**	DAGWOODS	**DAWCOCK**	DECLARER	DEFUNCTS	**DENDRON**
CUPPING	SCUTCHES	**DAINING**	DAWCOCKS	DECLARES	**DEGRADE**	DENDRONS
CUPPINGS	**CUTICLE**	SDAINING	**DAWDLER**	**DECLASS**	DEGRADED	**DENIZEN**
CUPRITE	CUTICLES	**DAKOITI**	DAWDLERS	DECLASSE	DEGRADES	DENIZENS
CUPRITES	**CUTIKIN**	DAKOITIS	**DAWNING**	**DECLINE**	**DEHISCE**	**DENTATE**
CURACAO	CUTIKINS	**DALLIER**	DAWNINGS	DECLINED	DEHISCED	EDENTATE
CURACAOS	**CUTLINE**	DALLIERS	**DAYMARK**	DECLINES	DEHISCES	DENTATED
CURACOA	CUTLINES	**DAMBROD**	DAYMARKS	**DECODER**	**DEICIDE**	**DENTINE**
CURACOAS	**CUTTERS**	DAMBRODS	**DAYSTAR**	DECODERS	DEICIDES	DENTINES
CURARIS	SCUTTERS	**DAMOSEL**	DAYSTARS	**DECOLOR**	**DEICTIC**	**DENTIST**
CURARISE	**CUTTIES**	DAMOSELS	**DAYTALE**	DECOLORS	DEICTICS	DENTISTS
CURATOR	CUTTIEST	**DAMOZEL**	DAYTALER	**DECORUM**	**DEIFIER**	**DENTURE**
CURATORS	**CUTTING**	DAMOZELS	DAYTALES	DECORUMS	DEIFIERS	DENTURES
CURATORY	CUTTINGS	**DAMPING**	**DAYTIME**	**DECREET**	**DEIGNED**	**DEODAND**
CURCUMA	**CUTTLES**	DAMPINGS	DAYTIMES	DECREETS	SDEIGNED	DEODANDS
CURCUMAS	SCUTTLES	**DANCING**	**DAZZLER**	**DECRIAL**	**DEISEAL**	**DEODATE**
CURETTE	**CUTWORM**	DANCINGS	DAZZLERS	DECRIALS	DEISEALS	DEODATES
CURETTED	CUTWORMS	**DANDIES**	**DEADPAN**	**DECRIER**	**DEJEUNE**	**DEONTIC**
CURETTES	**CUVETTE**	DANDIEST	DEADPANS	DECRIERS	DEJEUNER	DEONTICS
CURLING	CUVETTES	**DANDLER**	**DEALING**	**DECROWN**	DEJEUNES	**DEPAINT**
CURLINGS	**CYANATE**	DANDLERS	DEALINGS	DECROWNS	**DELAINE**	DEPAINTS
CURRACH	CYANATES	**DANELAW**	**DEASIUL**	**DECRYPT**	DELAINES	**DEPECHE**
CURRACHS	**CYANIDE**	DANELAWS	DEASIULS	DECRYPTS	**DELAPSE**	DEPECHES
CURRAGH	CYANIDED	**DANGLER**	**DEASOIL**	**DECUMAN**	DELAPSED	**DEPLANE**
CURRAGHS	CYANIDES	DANGLERS	DEASOILS	DECUMANS	DELAPSES	DEPLANED
CURRANT	CYANINE	**DANSEUR**	**DEBACLE**	**DECUPLE**	**DELATOR**	DEPLANES
CURRANTS	CYANINES	DANSEURS	DEBACLES	DECUPLED	DELATORS	**DEPLETE**
CURRANTY	**CYANISE**	**DAPHNID**	**DEBASER**	DECUPLES	**DELAYER**	DEPLETED
CURRENT	CYANISED	DAPHNIDS	DEBASERS	**DECURIA**	DELAYERS	DEPLETES
CURRENTS	CYANISES	**DAPSONE**	**DEBATER**	DECURIAS	**DELIGHT**	**DEPLORE**
CURRIED	**CYANITE**	DAPSONES	DEBATERS	**DECURVE**	DELIGHTS	DEPLORED
SCURRIED	CYANITES	**DARIOLE**	**DEBBIES**	DECURVED	**DELIMIT**	DEPLORES
CURRIER	CYANIZE	DARIOLES	DEBBIEST	DECURVES	DELIMITS	**DEPLUME**
SCURRIER	CYANIZED	**DARLING**	**DEBITOR**	**DEEMING**	**DELIVER**	DEPLUMED
CURRIERS	CYANIZES	DARLINGS	DEBITORS	ADEEMING	DELIVERS	DEPLUMES
CURRIES	**CYCLING**	**DARNING**	**DEBOUCH**	**DEERLET**	DELIVERY	**DEPOSAL**
SCURRIES	CYCLINGS	DARNINGS	DEBOUCHE	DEERLETS	**DELOUSE**	DEPOSALS
CURRING	**CYCLIST**	**DARRAIN**	**DEBRIDE**	**DEFACER**	DELOUSED	**DEPOSER**
SCURRING	CYCLISTS	DARRAINE	DEBRIDED	DEFACERS	DELOUSES	DEPOSERS
CURSING	**CYCLOID**	DARRAINS	DEBRIDES	**DEFAULT**	**DELUDER**	**DEPOSIT**
CURSINGS	CYCLOIDS	**DARRAYN**	**DEBRIEF**	DEFAULTS	DELUDERS	DEPOSITS
CURTAIL	**CYCLONE**	DARRAYNS	DEBRIEFS	**DEFENCE**	**DEMAINE**	**DEPRAVE**
CURTAILS	CYCLONES	**DARSHAN**	**DECAGON**	DEFENCED	DEMAINES	DEPRAVED
CURTAIN	**CYMBALO**	DARSHANS	DECAGONS	DEFENCES	**DEMAYNE**	DEPRAVES
CURTAINS	CYMBALOS	**DASHEEN**	**DECAPOD**	**DEFENSE**	DEMAYNES	**DEPRIVE**
CURTANA	**CYPRIAN**	DASHEENS	DECAPODS	DEFENSES	**DEMEANE**	DEPRIVED
CURTANAS	CYPRIANS	**DASHEKI**	**DECEASE**	**DEFICIT**	DEMEANED	DEPRIVES
CURTAXE	**CYSTOID**	DASHEKIS	DECEASED	DEFICITS	DEMEANES	**DEPSIDE**
CURTAXES	CYSTOIDS	**DASHIKI**	DECEASES	**DEFILER**	**DEMENTI**	DEPSIDES
CURTSEY	**CZARDOM**	DASHIKIS	**DECEIVE**	DEFILERS	DEMENTIA	**DERAIGN**

DERAIGNS	**DEVIANT**	DIARIZED	DIMETERS	DISCERNS	DISMAYLS	**DISTURB**
DERANGE	DEVIANTS	DIARIZES	**DIMORPH**	**DISCERP**	**DISNEST**	DISTURBS
DERANGED	**DEVIATE**	**DIASTER**	DIMORPHS	DISCERPS	DISNESTS	**DISTYLE**
DERANGES	DEVIATED	DIASTERS	**DINETTE**	**DISCIDE**	**DISOBEY**	DISTYLES
DERIDER	DEVIATES	**DIBBLER**	DINETTES	DISCIDED	DISOBEYS	**DISYOKE**
DERIDERS	**DEVILET**	DIBBLERS	**DINGBAT**	DISCIDES	**DISPACE**	DISYOKED
DERMOID	DEVILETS	**DICHORD**	DINGBATS	**DISCOER**	DISPACED	DISYOKES
DERMOIDS	**DEVISAL**	DICHORDS	**DINGIES**	DISCOERS	DISPACES	**DITCHER**
DERRICK	DEVISALS	**DICKIES**	DINGIEST	**DISCORD**	**DISPARK**	DITCHERS
DERRICKS	**DEVISEE**	DICKIEST	**DINKIES**	DISCORDS	DISPARKS	**DIURNAL**
DESCALE	DEVISEES	**DICTATE**	DINKIEST	**DISCURE**	**DISPART**	DIURNALS
DESCALED	**DEVISER**	DICTATED	**DINMONT**	DISCURED	DISPARTS	**DIVERGE**
DESCALES	DEVISERS	DICTATES	DINMONTS	DISCURES	**DISPEND**	DIVERGED
DESCANT	**DEVISOR**	**DICTION**	**DIOCESE**	**DISDAIN**	DISPENDS	DIVERGES
DESCANTS	DEVISORS	DICTIONS	DIOCESES	DISDAINS	**DISPLAY**	**DIVERSE**
DESCEND	**DEVLING**	**DIDAKAI**	**DIOPTER**	**DISEASE**	DISPLAYS	DIVERSED
DESCENDS	DEVLINGS	DIDAKAIS	DIOPTERS	DISEASED	**DISPONE**	DIVERSES
DESCENT	**DEVOICE**	**DIDAKEI**	**DIOPTRE**	DISEASES	DISPONED	**DIVIDER**
DESCENTS	DEVOICED	DIDAKEIS	DIOPTRES	**DISEDGE**	DISPONER	DIVIDERS
DESERVE	DEVOICES	**DIDDLER**	**DIORAMA**	DISEDGED	DISPONES	**DIVINER**
DESERVED	**DEVOLVE**	DIDDLERS	DIORAMAS	DISEDGES	**DISPORT**	DIVINERS
DESERVER	DEVOLVED	**DIDICOI**	**DIORISM**	**DISEUSE**	DISPORTS	**DIVINES**
DESERVES	DEVOLVES	DIDICOIS	DIORISMS	DISEUSES	**DISPOSE**	DIVINEST
DESIRER	**DEVOTEE**	**DIDICOY**	**DIORITE**	**DISFAME**	DISPOSED	**DIVISOR**
DESIRERS	DEVOTEES	DIDICOYS	DIORITES	DISFAMES	DISPOSER	DIVISORS
DESKILL	**DEWATER**	**DIEBACK**	**DIOXANE**	**DISFORM**	DISPOSES	**DIVORCE**
DESKILLS	DEWATERS	DIEBACKS	DIOXANES	DISFORMS	**DISPOST**	DIVORCED
DESMINE	**DEXTRAN**	**DIEDRAL**	**DIOXIDE**	**DISGEST**	DISPOSTS	DIVORCER
DESMINES	DEXTRANS	DIEDRALS	DIOXIDES	DISGESTS	**DISPRED**	DIVORCES
DESPAIR	**DEXTRIN**	**DIETINE**	**DIPHONE**	**DISGOWN**	DISPREDS	**DIVULGE**
DESPAIRS	DEXTRINE	DIETINES	DIPHONES	DISGOWNS	**DISPUTE**	DIVULGED
DESPISE	DEXTRINS	**DIETIST**	**DIPLOID**	**DISGUST**	DISPUTED	DIVULGES
DESPISED	**DHARMAS**	DIETISTS	DIPLOIDY	DISGUSTS	DISPUTER	**DIZZARD**
DESPISER	ADHARMAS	**DIFFUSE**	**DIPLOMA**	**DISHELM**	DISPUTES	DIZZARDS
DESPISES	**DHURRIE**	DIFFUSED	DIPLOMAS	DISHELMS	**DISRANK**	**DIZZIES**
DESPITE	DHURRIES	DIFFUSER	DIPLOMAT	**DISHFUL**	DISRANKS	DIZZIEST
DESPITES	**DIABASE**	DIFFUSES	**DIPLONT**	DISHFULS	**DISRATE**	**DJIBBAH**
DESPOIL	DIABASES	**DIGAMMA**	DIPLONTS	**DISHING**	DISRATED	DJIBBAHS
DESPOILS	**DIABOLO**	DIGAMMAS	**DIPNOAN**	DISHINGS	DISRATES	**DOATING**
DESPOND	DIABOLOS	**DIGGING**	DIPNOANS	**DISHOME**	**DISROBE**	DOATINGS
DESPONDS	**DIADROM**	DIGGINGS	**DIPPING**	DISHOMED	DISROBED	**DOCKAGE**
DESSERT	DIADROMS	**DIGITAL**	DIPPINGS	DISHOMES	DISROBES	DOCKAGES
DESSERTS	**DIAGRAM**	DIGITALS	**DIPTYCH**	**DISHORN**	**DISROOT**	**DOCKING**
DESTINE	DIAGRAMS	**DIGLYPH**	DIPTYCHS	DISHORNS	DISROOTS	DOCKINGS
DESTINED	**DIAGRID**	DIGLYPHS	**DIREMPT**	**DISJECT**	**DISRUPT**	**DOCKISE**
DESTINES	DIAGRIDS	**DIGRAPH**	DIREMPTS	DISJECTS	DISRUPTS	DOCKISED
DESTROY	**DIALECT**	DIGRAPHS	**DIRTIES**	**DISJOIN**	**DISSEAT**	DOCKISES
DESTROYS	DIALECTS	**DILATER**	DIRTIEST	DISJOINS	DISSEATS	**DOCKIZE**
DETENTE	**DIALIST**	DILATERS	**DISABLE**	DISJOINT	**DISSECT**	DOCKIZED
DETENTES	DIALISTS	**DILATOR**	DISABLED	**DISJUNE**	DISSECTS	DOCKIZES
DETENUE	**DIALLER**	DILATORS	DISABLES	DISJUNES	**DISSENT**	**DOCQUET**
DETENUES	DIALLERS	DILATORY	**DISAVOW**	**DISLEAF**	DISSENTS	DOCQUETS
DETERGE	**DIALYSE**	**DILEMMA**	DISAVOWS	DISLEAFS	**DISSERT**	**DODDIES**
DETERGED	DIALYSED	DILEMMAS	**DISBAND**	**DISLIKE**	DISSERTS	DODDIEST
DETERGES	DIALYSER	**DILLIES**	DISBANDS	DISLIKED	**DISTAFF**	**DOGBANE**
DETINUE	DIALYSES	DILLIEST	**DISBARK**	DISLIKEN	DISTAFFS	DOGBANES
DETINUES	**DIALYZE**	**DILLING**	DISBARKS	DISLIKES	**DISTAIN**	**DOGBOLT**
DETRACT	DIALYZED	DILLINGS	**DISCAGE**	**DISLIMB**	DISTAINS	DOGBOLTS
DETRACTS	DIALYZER	**DILUENT**	DISCAGED	DISLIMBS	**DISTEND**	**DOGCART**
DETRAIN	DIALYZES	DILUENTS	DISCAGES	**DISLIMN**	DISTENDS	DOGCARTS
DETRAINS	**DIAMOND**	**DILUTEE**	**DISCANT**	DISLIMNS	**DISTICH**	**DOGEATE**
DETRUDE	DIAMONDS	DILUTEES	DISCANTS	**DISLINK**	DISTICHS	DOGEATES
DETRUDES	**DIAPASE**	**DILUTER**	**DISCARD**	DISLINKS	**DISTILL**	**DOGGIES**
DEVALUE	DIAPASES	DILUTERS	DISCARDS	**DISLOAD**	DISTILLS	DOGGIEST
DEVALUED	**DIARISE**	**DILUTOR**	**DISCASE**	DISLOADS	**DISTORT**	**DOGGING**
DEVALUES	DIARISED	DILUTORS	DISCASED	**DISMASK**	DISTORTS	DOGGINGS
DEVELOP	DIARISES	**DILUVIA**	DISCASES	DISMASKS	**DISTUNE**	**DOGGONE**
DEVELOPE	**DIARIST**	DILUVIAL	**DISCEPT**	**DISMAST**	DISTUNED	DOGGONED
DEVELOPS	DIARISTS	DILUVIAN	DISCEPTS	DISMASTS	DISTUNES	**DOGGREL**
	DIARIZE	**DIMETER**	**DISCERN**	**DISMAYL**		

DOGGRELS	DOULEIAS	DREAREST	**DUCHESS**	DVANDVAS	**EASTING**	**ECTOZOA**
DOGHOLE	**DOURINE**	**DREDGER**	DUCHESSE	**DVORNIK**	FEASTING	ECTOZOAN
DOGHOLES	DOURINES	DREDGERS	**DUCKIES**	DVORNIKS	REASTING	**ECUELLE**
DOGSHIP	**DOVECOT**	**DRESSER**	DUCKIEST	**DWELLER**	YEASTING	ECUELLES
DOGSHIPS	DOVECOTE	DRESSERS	**DUCKING**	DWELLERS	EASTINGS	**ECURIES**
DOGSKIN	DOVECOTS	**DREVILL**	DUCKINGS	**DWINDLE**	**EASTLIN**	DECURIES
DOGSKINS	**DOVEKIE**	DREVILLS	**DUDGEON**	DWINDLED	EASTLING	**EDGIEST**
DOGTOWN	DOVEKIES	**DRIBBER**	DUDGEONS	DWINDLES	EASTLINS	HEDGIEST
DOGTOWNS	**DOVELET**	DRIBBERS	**DUDHEEN**	**DYELINE**	**EATABLE**	KEDGIEST
DOGTROT	DOVELETS	**DRIBBLE**	DUDHEENS	DYELINES	BEATABLE	LEDGIEST
DOGTROTS	**DOWAGER**	DRIBBLED	**DUELLER**	**DYESTER**	EATABLES	SEDGIEST
DOGVANE	DOWAGERS	DRIBBLER	DUELLERS	DYESTERS	**EATINGS**	**EDGINGS**
DOGVANES	**DOWDIES**	DRIBBLES	**DUFFING**	**DYNAMIC**	BEATINGS	HEDGINGS
DOGWOOD	DOWDIEST	DRIBBLET	DUFFINGS	DYNAMICS	HEATINGS	WEDGINGS
DOGWOODS	**DOWNBOW**	**DRIBLET**	**DUKEDOM**	ADYNAMIC	SEATINGS	**EDIFICE**
DOITKIN	DOWNBOWS	DRIBLETS	DUKEDOMS	**DYSODIL**	**EBAUCHE**	EDIFICES
DOITKINS	**DOYENNE**	**DRIFTER**	**DULCIAN**	DYSODILE	EBAUCHES	**EDIFIER**
DOLLDOM	DOYENNES	DRIFTERS	DULCIANA	DYSODILS	**EBBTIDE**	EDIFIERS
DOLLDOMS	**DOZENTH**	**DRILLER**	DULCIANS	**DYSPNEA**	EBBTIDES	**EDITION**
DOLLIER	DOZENTHS	DRILLERS	**DULCITE**	DYSPNEAL	**EBONISE**	SEDITION
DOLLIERS	**DRABBER**	DRINKER	DULCITES	DYSPNEAS	EBONISED	**EDITIONS**
DOLPHIN	DRABBERS	DRINKERS	**DULCOSE**	**DYSURIA**	EBONISES	**EDUCATE**
DOLPHINS	**DRABBET**	**DRIZZLE**	DULCOSES	DYSURIAS	**EBONIST**	EDUCATED
DOMICIL	DRABBETS	DRIZZLED	**DULLARD**	**EANLING**	EBONISTS	EDUCATES
DOMICILE	**DRABBLE**	DRIZZLES	DULLARDS	WEANLING	**EBONITE**	**EDUCING**
DOMICILS	DRABBLED	**DROGHER**	**DUMAIST**	YEANLING	EBONITES	DEDUCING
DOMINIE	DRABBLER	DROGHERS	DUMAISTS	EANLINGS	**EBONIZE**	REDUCING
DOMINIES	DRABBLES	**DROGUET**	**DUMMIES**	**EARACHE**	EBONIZED	SEDUCING
DONATOR	**DRABLER**	DROGUETS	DUMMIEST	EARACHES	EBONIZES	**EDUCTOR**
DONATORS	DRABLERS	**DROLLER**	**DUMPBIN**	**EARDING**	**EBRIATE**	EDUCTORS
DONATORY	**DRACHMA**	DROLLERY	DUMPBINS	BEARDING	EBRIATED	**EECHING**
DONNISM	DRACHMAE	**DROMOND**	**DUMPIES**	YEARDING	**ECBOLIC**	LEECHING
DONNISMS	DRACHMAI	DROMONDS	DUMPIEST	**EARDROP**	ECBOLICS	REECHING
DONSHIP	DRACHMAS	**DROPLET**	**DUNGEON**	EARDROPS	**ECHAPPE**	**EELFARE**
DONSHIPS	**DRACONE**	DROPLETS	DUNGEONS	**EARDRUM**	ECHAPPES	EELFARES
DOODLER	DRACONES	**DROPPER**	**DUNNAGE**	EARDRUMS	**ECHELON**	**EELIEST**
DOODLERS	**DRAFTEE**	DROPPERS	DUNNAGES	**EARFLAP**	ECHELONS	SEELIEST
DOORMAT	DRAFTEES	**DROPPLE**	**DUNNIES**	EARFLAPS	**ECHIDNA**	**EELPOUT**
DOORMATS	**DRAFTER**	DROPPLES	DUNNIEST	**EARINGS**	ECHIDNAS	EELPOUTS
DOORWAY	DRAFTERS	**DROSERA**	**DUNNING**	BEARINGS	**ECHOISE**	**EELWORM**
DOORWAYS	**DRAGGLE**	DROSERAS	DUNNINGS	GEARINGS	ECHOISED	EELWORMS
DOPPING	DRAGGLED	**DROSTDY**	**DUNNITE**	HEARINGS	ECHOISES	**EERIEST**
DOPPINGS	DRAGGLES	DROSTDYS	DUNNITES	SEARINGS	**ECHOISM**	BEERIEST
DORHAWK	**DRAGOON**	**DROUGHT**	**DUNNOCK**	WEARINGS	ECHOISMS	LEERIEST
DORHAWKS	DRAGOONS	DROUGHTS	DUNNOCKS	**EARLDOM**	**ECHOIST**	PEERIEST
DORLACH	**DRAINER**	DROUGHTY	**DUODENA**	EARLDOMS	ECHOISTS	**EEVNING**
DORLACHS	DRAINERS	**DROWNER**	DUODENAL	**EARLESS**	**ECHOIZE**	EEVNINGS
DORMANT	**DRAPIER**	DROWNERS	**DUOTONE**	FEARLESS	ECHOIZED	**EFFENDI**
DORMANTS	DRAPIERS	**DRUDGER**	DUOTONES	GEARLESS	ECHOIZES	EFFENDIS
DORNICK	**DRAPPIE**	DRUDGERS	**DURABLE**	TEARLESS	**ECLIPSE**	**EFFORCE**
DORNICKS	DRAPPIES	DRUDGERY	DURABLES	**EARLIER**	ECLIPSED	EFFORCED
DORTOUR	**DRASTIC**	**DRUGGER**	**DURAMEN**	PEARLIER	ECLIPSES	EFFORCES
DORTOURS	DRASTICS	DRUGGERS	DURAMENS	**EARLOCK**	**ECLOGUE**	**EFFULGE**
DOSSIER	**DRAUGHT**	**DRUGGET**	**DURANCE**	EARLOCKS	ECLOGUES	EFFULGED
DOSSIERS	DRAUGHTS	DRUGGETS	DURANCES	**EARMARK**	**ECLOSED**	EFFULGES
DOTTLES	DRAUGHTY	**DRUMBLE**	**DURESSE**	EARMARKS	RECLOSED	**EGALITY**
DOTTLEST	**DRAWING**	DRUMBLED	DURESSES	**EARNERS**	**ECLOSES**	LEGALITY
DOTTREL	DRAWINGS	DRUMBLES	**DURMAST**	LEARNERS	RECLOSES	REGALITY
DOTTRELS	**DRAWLER**	**DRUMLIN**	DURMASTS	**EARNEST**	**ECOCIDE**	**EGENCES**
DOUBLER	DRAWLERS	DRUMLINS	**DUSTBIN**	EARNESTS	ECOCIDES	REGENCES
DOUBLERS	**DRAYAGE**	**DRUMMER**	DUSTBINS	**EARNING**	**ECOLOGY**	**EGGHEAD**
DOUBLET	DRAYAGES	DRUMMERS	**DUSTING**	LEARNING	OECOLOGY	EGGHEADS
DOUBLETS	**DREADED**	**DRYBEAT**	ADUSTING	YEARNING	**ECORCHE**	**EGGIEST**
DOUBTER	ADREADED	DRYBEATS	**DUUMVIR**	EARNINGS	ECORCHES	LEGGIEST
DOUBTERS	**DREADER**	**DUALISM**	DUUMVIRI	**EARPICK**	**ECOTYPE**	**EGOTISE**
DOUCEUR	DREADERS	DUALISMS	DUUMVIRS	EARPICKS	ECOTYPES	EGOTISED
DOUCEURS	**DREAMER**	**DUALIST**	**DUVETYN**	**EARPLUG**	**ECTHYMA**	EGOTISES
DOUCINE	DREAMERS	DUALISTS	DUVETYNE	EARPLUGS	ECTHYMAS	**EGOTISM**
DOUCINES	DREAMERY	**DUBBING**	DUVETYNS	**EARRING**	**ECTOPIA**	EGOTISMS
DOULEIA	**DREARES**	DUBBINGS	**DVANDVA**	EARRINGS	ECTOPIAS	EGOTISMS

EGOTIST	ELEVATED	EMBRAIDS	EMPLUMED	**ENDGAME**	**ENGRAVE**	CENSURES
EGOTISTS	ELEVATES	**EMBRAVE**	EMPLUMES	ENDGAMES	ENGRAVED	**ENSWEEP**
EGOTIZE	**ELFHOOD**	EMBRAVED	**EMPOWER**	**ENDINGS**	ENGRAVEN	ENSWEEPS
EGOTIZED	SELFHOOD	EMBRAVES	EMPOWERS	BENDINGS	ENGRAVER	**ENTAILS**
EGOTIZES	ELFHOODS	**EMBREAD**	**EMPRESS**	LENDINGS	ENGRAVES	VENTAILS
EIDETIC	**ELFLAND**	EMBREADS	EMPRESSE	MENDINGS	**ENGUARD**	**ENTAYLE**
EIDETICS	ELFLANDS	**EMBREWE**	**EMPRISE**	SENDINGS	ENGUARDS	VENTAYLE
EIGHTVO	**ELISION**	EMBREWED	EMPRISES	**ENDIRON**	**ENGULPH**	ENTAYLED
EIGHTVOS	ELISIONS	EMBREWES	**EMPTIER**	ENDIRONS	ENGULPHS	ENTAYLES
EILDING	**ELITISM**	**EMBROIL**	EMPTIERS	**ENDOGEN**	**ENHANCE**	**ENTENTE**
EILDINGS	ELITISMS	EMBROILS	**EMPTIES**	ENDOGENS	ENHANCED	ENTENTES
EJECTED	**ELITIST**	**EMBROWN**	EMPTIEST	ENDOGENY	ENHANCES	**ENTERED**
DEJECTED	ELITISTS	EMBROWNS	**EMPTION**	**ENDORSE**	**ENJOYER**	CENTERED
REJECTED	**ELLIPSE**	**EMBRUTE**	EMPTIONS	ENDORSED	ENJOYERS	TENTERED
EJECTOR	ELLIPSES	EMBRUTED	**EMPYEMA**	ENDORSEE	**ENLARGE**	**ENTERER**
REJECTOR	**ELLWAND**	EMBRUTES	EMPYEMAS	ENDORSER	ENLARGED	ENTERERS
EJECTORS	ELLWANDS	**EMBRYON**	**EMULATE**	ENDORSES	ENLARGEN	**ENTERIC**
EKISTIC	**ELMWOOD**	EMBRYONS	EMULATED	**ENDOWER**	ENLARGER	ENTERICS
EKISTICS	ELMWOODS	**EMERALD**	EMULATES	ENDOWERS	ENLARGES	**ENTHRAL**
EKPWELE	**ELOCUTE**	EMERALDS	**EMULING**	**ENDSHIP**	**ENLIGHT**	ENTHRALL
EKPWELES	ELOCUTED	**EMERGED**	AEMULING	ENDSHIPS	PENLIGHT	ENTHRALS
ELAPSED	ELOCUTES	DEMERGED	**EMULSIN**	**ENDURER**	ENLIGHTS	**ENTHUSE**
DELAPSED	**ELOGIST**	REMERGED	EMULSINS	ENDURERS	**ENLIVEN**	ENTHUSED
RELAPSED	ELOGISTS	**EMERGES**	**EMULSOR**	**ENDWISE**	ENLIVENS	ENTHUSES
ELAPSES	**ELOGIUM**	DEMERGES	EMULSORS	BENDWISE	**ENNOBLE**	**ENTICED**
DELAPSES	ELOGIUMS	REMERGES	**EMURING**	**ENERGID**	ENNOBLED	PENTICED
RELAPSES	**ELOINER**	**EMERSED**	DEMURING	ENERGIDS	ENNOBLES	**ENTICER**
ELASTIC	ELOINERS	DEMERSED	**ENABLER**	**ENEWING**	**ENOUNCE**	ENTICERS
GELASTIC	**ELUDERS**	**EMETINE**	ENABLERS	RENEWING	DENOUNCE	**ENTICES**
ELASTICS	DELUDERS	EMETINES	**ENACTOR**	**ENFELON**	RENOUNCE	PENTICES
ELASTIN	**ELUDING**	**EMICATE**	ENACTORS	ENFELONS	ENOUNCED	**ENTITLE**
ELASTINS	DELUDING	EMICATED	**ENAMOUR**	**ENFEOFF**	ENOUNCES	ENTITLED
ELATERS	**ELUSION**	EMICATES	ENAMOURS	ENFEOFFS	**ENPRINT**	ENTITLES
RELATERS	DELUSION	**EMIRATE**	**ENATION**	**ENFOLDS**	ENPRINTS	**ENTOMIC**
ELATING	ELUSIONS	EMIRATES	VENATION	PENFOLDS	**ENQUIRE**	PENTOMIC
BELATING	**ELUSIVE**	**EMITTED**	ENATIONS	**ENFORCE**	ENQUIRED	**ENTOZOA**
DELATING	DELUSIVE	DEMITTED	**ENCHAFE**	RENFORCE	ENQUIRER	ENTOZOAL
RELATING	**ELUSORY**	REMITTED	ENCHAFED	ENFORCED	ENQUIRES	**ENTRAIL**
ELATION	DELUSORY	**EMONGES**	ENCHAFES	ENFORCES	**ENRANGE**	ENTRAILS
DELATION	**ELUTION**	EMONGEST	**ENCHAIN**	**ENFRAME**	ENRANGED	**ENTRAIN**
GELATION	ELUTIONS	**EMOTING**	ENCHAINS	ENFRAMED	ENRANGES	ENTRAINS
RELATION	**ELUVIUM**	DEMOTING	**ENCHANT**	ENFRAMES	**ENRHEUM**	**ENTRANT**
ELATIONS	ELUVIUMS	**EMOTION**	PENCHANT	**ENFROZE**	ENRHEUMS	ENTRANTS
ELATIVE	**EMANATE**	DEMOTION	ENCHANTS	ENFROZEN	**ENROUGH**	**ENTREAT**
RELATIVE	EMANATED	REMOTION	**ENCHARM**	**ENGAGER**	ENROUGHS	ENTREATS
ELATIVES	EMANATES	EMOTIONS	ENCHARMS	ENGAGERS	**ENROUND**	ENTREATY
ELDINGS	**EMBATHE**	**EMOVING**	**ENCHASE**	**ENGINER**	ENROUNDS	**ENTRIES**
GELDINGS	EMBATHED	REMOVING	ENCHASED	ENGINERS	**ENSHELL**	CENTRIES
WELDINGS	EMBATHES	**EMPAIRE**	ENCHASES	ENGINERY	ENSHELLS	GENTRIES
ELECTED	**EMBLAZE**	EMPAIRED	**ENCHEER**	**ENGLOBE**	**ENSLAVE**	SENTRIES
SELECTED	EMBLAZED	EMPAIRES	ENCHEERS	ENGLOBED	ENSLAVED	**ENTRISM**
ELECTOR	EMBLAZES	**EMPANEL**	**ENCLASP**	ENGLOBES	ENSLAVER	CENTRISM
SELECTOR	**EMBLOOM**	EMPANELS	ENCLASPS	**ENGLOOM**	ENSLAVES	ENTRISMS
ELECTORS	EMBLOOMS	**EMPAYRE**	**ENCLAVE**	ENGLOOMS	**ENSNARE**	**ENTRIST**
ELECTRO	**EMBOGUE**	EMPAYRED	ENCLAVED	**ENGORGE**	ENSNARED	CENTRIST
ELECTRON	EMBOGUED	EMPAYRES	ENCLAVES	ENGORGED	ENSNARES	ENTRISTS
ELECTROS	EMBOGUES	**EMPERCE**	**ENCLOSE**	ENGORGES	**ENSNARL**	**ENTRUST**
ELEGIAC	**EMBOSOM**	EMPERCED	ENCLOSED	**ENGRACE**	ENSNARLS	ENTRUSTS
ELEGIACS	EMBOSOMS	EMPERCES	ENCLOSER	ENGRACED	**ENSTAMP**	**ENTWINE**
ELEGISE	**EMBOUND**	**EMPEROR**	ENCLOSES	ENGRACES	ENSTAMPS	ENTWINED
ELEGISED	EMBOUNDS	EMPERORS	**ENCLOUD**	**ENGRAFF**	**ENSTEEP**	ENTWINES
ELEGISES	**EMBOWEL**	**EMPIRIC**	ENCLOUDS	ENGRAFFS	ENSTEEPS	**ENTWIST**
ELEGIST	EMBOWELS	EMPIRICS	**ENCRUST**	**ENGRAFT**	**ENSTYLE**	ENTWISTS
ELEGISTS	**EMBOWER**	**EMPLACE**	ENCRUSTS	ENGRAFTS	ENSTYLED	**ENVAULT**
ELEGIZE	EMBOWERS	EMPLACED	**ENCRYPT**	**ENGRAIL**	ENSTYLES	ENVAULTS
ELEGIZED	**EMBRACE**	EMPLACES	ENCRYPTS	ENGRAILS	**ENSURED**	**ENVELOP**
ELEGIZES	EMBRACED	**EMPLANE**	**ENDEMIC**	**ENGRAIN**	CENSURED	ENVELOPE
ELEMENT	EMBRACER	EMPLANED	ENDEMICS	ENGRAINS	**ENSURER**	ENVELOPS
ELEMENTS	EMBRACES	EMPLANES	**ENDERON**	**ENGRASP**	ENSURERS	**ENVENOM**
ELEVATE	**EMBRAID**	**EMPLUME**	ENDERONS	ENGRASPS	**ENSURES**	ENVENOMS

ENVIRON
ENVIRONS
ENVYING
ENVYINGS
ENWHEEL
ENWHEELS
EOLITHS
NEOLITHS
EONISMS
PEONISMS
EPACRID
EPACRIDS
EPAGOGE
EPAGOGES
EPAULET
EPAULETS
EPEIRID
EPEIRIDS
EPERGNE
EPERGNES
EPHEDRA
EPHEDRAS
EPICARP
EPICARPS
EPICEDE
EPICEDES
EPICENE
EPICENES
EPICIER
EPICIERS
EPICISM
EPICISMS
EPICIST
EPICISTS
EPICURE
EPICURES
EPIDOTE
LEPIDOTE
EPIDOTES
EPIGONE
EPIGONES
EPIGRAM
EPIGRAMS
EPILATE
DEPILATE
EPILATED
EPILATES
EPISODE
EPISODES
EPISOME
EPISOMES
EPISTLE
EPISTLED
EPISTLER
EPISTLES
EPITAPH
EPITAPHS
EPITHEM
EPITHEMA
EPITHEMS
EPITHET
EPITHETS
EPITOME
EPITOMES
EPIZOAN
EPIZOANS
EPOXIDE
EPOXIDES
EPSILON
EPSILONS

EPURATE
DEPURATE
EPURATED
EPURATES
EQUATOR
EQUATORS
EQUINIA
EQUINIAS
ERASION
ERASIONS
ERASURE
ERASURES
ERATHEM
ERATHEMS
ERBIUMS
TERBIUMS
ERECTER
ERECTERS
ERECTOR
ERECTORS
EREMITE
EREMITES
EREPSIN
EREPSINS
ERINITE
ERINITES
ERISTIC
MERISTIC
VERISTIC
ERMELIN
ERMELINS
ERMINED
VERMINED
ERODENT
ERODENTS
ERODIUM
ERODIUMS
EROSION
EROSIONS
EROTEMA
EROTEMAS
EROTEME
EROTEMES
EROTICA
EROTICAL
EROTISM
EROTISMS
ERRATIC
ERRATICS
ERRHINE
ERRHINES
ERRINGS
HERRINGS
ERUDITE
ERUDITES
ESCALOP
ESCALOPE
ESCALOPS
ESCAPEE
ESCAPEES
ESCAPER
ESCAPERS
ESCHEAT
ESCHEATS
ESCOLAR
ESCOLARS
ESCRIBE
DESCRIBE
ESCRIBED
ESCRIBES

ESCROLL
ESCROLLS
ESCUAGE
ESCUAGES
ESLOYNE
ESLOYNED
ESLOYNES
ESPARTO
ESPARTOS
ESPOUSE
ESPOUSED
ESPOUSER
ESPOUSES
ESQUIRE
ESQUIRES
ESSAYER
ESSAYERS
ESSENCE
ESSENCES
ESSOYNE
ESSOYNES
ESTATED
GESTATED
RESTATED
ESTATES
GESTATES
RESTATES
ESTHETE
AESTHETE
ESTHETES
ESTIVAL
AESTIVAL
FESTIVAL
ESTOILE
ESTOILES
ESTOVER
ESTOVERS
ESTRADE
ESTRADES
ESTREAT
ESTREATS
ESTREPE
ESTREPED
ESTREPES
ESTROUS
OESTROUS
ESTRUMS
OESTRUMS
ETACISM
BETACISM
ETACISMS
ETAERIO
ETAERIOS
ETAGERE
ETAGERES
ETALAGE
ETALAGES
ETCHANT
ETCHANTS
ETCHING
FETCHING
KETCHING
LETCHING
RETCHING
ETCHINGS
ETHANES
METHANES
ETHANOL
METHANOL
ETHANOLS

ETHICAL
ETHICALS
ETIOLIN
ETIOLINS
ETOURDI
ETOURDIE
ETRENNE
ETRENNES
ETTLING
FETTLING
NETTLING
PETTLING
SETTLING
EUCAINE
EUCAINES
EUCLASE
EUCLASES
EUCRITE
EUCRITES
EUGENIC
EUGENICS
EUGENOL
EUGENOLS
EUPHROE
EUPHROES
EUREKAS
HEUREKAS
EUSTYLE
EUSTYLES
EUTEXIA
EUTEXIAS
EVACUEE
EVACUEES
EVANGEL
EVANGELS
EVANGELY
EVASION
EVASIONS
EVENING
EVENINGS
EVENTER
EVENTERS
EVERTED
REVERTED
EVICTOR
EVICTORS
EVIDENT
EVIDENTS
EVIRATE
EVIRATED
EVIRATES
EVITATE
LEVITATE
EVITATED
EVITATES
EVOCATE
EVOCATED
EVOCATES
EVOKING
REVOKING
EVOLUTE
REVOLUTE
EVOLUTED
EVOLUTES
EVOLVED
DEVOLVED
REVOLVED
EVOLVES
DEVOLVES

REVOLVES
EXACTER
EXACTERS
EXACTOR
EXACTORS
EXAMINE
EXAMINED
EXAMINEE
EXAMINER
EXAMINES
EXAMPLE
EXAMPLED
EXAMPLES
EXCERPT
EXCERPTA
EXCERPTS
EXCHEAT
EXCHEATS
EXCITER
EXCITERS
EXCITON
EXCITONS
EXCITOR
EXCITORS
EXCLAIM
EXCLAIMS
EXCLAVE
EXCLAVES
EXCLUDE
EXCLUDED
EXCLUDEE
EXCLUDES
EXCRETE
EXCRETED
EXCRETES
EXCURSE
EXCURSED
EXCURSES
EXCUSAL
EXCUSALS
EXCUSER
EXCUSERS
EXECUTE
EXECUTED
EXECUTER
EXECUTES
EXEGETE
EXEGETES
EXEMPLA
EXEMPLAR
EXEMPLE
EXEMPLES
EXERGUE
EXERGUES
EXHAUST
EXHAUSTS
EXHEDRA
EXHEDRAE
EXHIBIT
EXHIBITS
EXHUMER
EXHUMERS
EXIGENT
EXIGENTS
EXOCARP
EXOCARPS
EXODERM
EXODERMS
EXODIST
EXODISTS

EXOMION
EXOMIONS
EXORDIA
EXORDIAL
EXPANSE
EXPANSES
EXPENSE
EXPENSES
EXPIATE
EXPIATED
EXPIATES
EXPLAIN
EXPLAINS
EXPLANT
EXPLANTS
EXPLODE
EXPLODED
EXPLODER
EXPLODES
EXPLOIT
EXPLOITS
EXPLORE
EXPLORED
EXPLORER
EXPLORES
EXPOSAL
EXPOSALS
EXPOSER
EXPOSERS
EXPOUND
EXPOUNDS
EXPRESS
EXPRESSO
EXPULSE
EXPULSED
EXPULSES
EXPUNCT
EXPUNCTS
EXPUNGE
EXPUNGED
EXPUNGER
EXPUNGES
EXPURGE
EXPURGED
EXPURGES
EXSCIND
EXSCINDS
EXTERNE
EXTERNES
EXTRACT
EXTRACTS
EXTRAIT
EXTRAITS
EXTREAT
EXTREATS
EXTREME
EXTREMER
EXTREMES
EXTRUDE
EXTRUDED
EXTRUDER
EXTRUDES
EXUDATE
EXUDATES
EXURBIA
EXURBIAS
EYEBALL
EYEBALLS
EYEBOLT
EYEBOLTS

EYEBROW
EYEBROWS
EYEHOOK
EYEHOOKS
EYELIAD
EYELIADS
EYESORE
EYESORES
FABLIAU
FABLIAUX
FABLING
FABLINGS
FACONNE
FACONNES
FACTION
FACTIONS
FACTOID
FACTOIDS
FACTURE
FACTURES
FADAISE
FADAISES
FADDISM
FADDISMS
FADDIST
FADDISTS
FAGGING
FAGGINGS
FAHLORE
FAHLORES
FAIENCE
FAIENCES
FAILING
FAILINGS
FAILURE
FAILURES
FAIRING
FAIRINGS
FAIRWAY
FAIRWAYS
FAITOUR
FAITOURS
FALAFEL
FALAFELS
FALBALA
FALBALAS
FALCADE
FALCADES
FALCATE
FALCATED
FALCULA
FALCULAS
FALDAGE
FALDAGES
FALLING
FALLINGS
FALSISM
FALSISMS
FANATIC
FANATICS
FANCIER
FANCIERS
FANCIEST
FANCIES
FANFARE
FANFARED
FANFARES
FANGLES
FANGLESS
FANNELL

FANNELLS	FEATHERS	**FERRULE**	**FILIATE**	**FIVEPIN**	FLINDERS	**FLYTRAP**
FANNING	**FEATHERY**	FERRULES	FILIATED	FIVEPINS	**FLINGER**	FLYTRAPS
FANNINGS	**FEATURE**	**FERTILE**	FILIATES	**FIXTURE**	FLINGERS	**FOAMING**
FANTAIL	FEATURED	FERTILER	**FILIBEG**	FIXTURES	**FLIPPER**	FOAMINGS
FANTAILS	**FEATURES**	**FERVOUR**	FILIBEGS	**FIZZGIG**	FLIPPERS	**FOGGAGE**
FANTASM	**FECHTER**	FERVOURS	**FILLING**	FIZZGIGS	**FLITTER**	FOGGAGED
FANTASMS	FECHTERS	**FESTOON**	FILLINGS	**FIZZING**	FLITTERN	FOGGAGES
FANTAST	**FEDARIE**	FESTOONS	**FILMDOM**	FIZZINGS	**FLIVVER**	**FOGHORN**
FANTASTS	FEDARIES	**FETICHE**	FILMDOMS	**FLACKER**	FLIVVERS	FOGHORNS
FANTEEG	**FEDAYEE**	FETICHES	**FILMSET**	FLACKERS	**FLOATEL**	**FOGYDOM**
FANTEEGS	FEDAYEEN	**FETLOCK**	FILMSETS	**FLACKET**	FLOATELS	FOGYDOMS
FANZINE	**FEDERAL**	FETLOCKS	**FIMBRIA**	FLACKETS	**FLOATER**	**FOGYISM**
FANZINES	FEDERALS	**FETTLER**	FIMBRIAS	**FLAFFER**	FLOATERS	FOGYISMS
FARADAY	**FEEBLES**	FETTLERS	**FINAGLE**	FLAFFERS	**FLOORER**	**FOILING**
FARADAYS	FEEBLEST	**FEUDING**	FINAGLED	**FLAMFEW**	FLOORERS	FOILINGS
FARAWAY	**FEEDING**	FEUDINGS	FINAGLES	FLAMFEWS	**FLOOSIE**	**FOISTER**
FARAWAYS	FEEDINGS	**FEUDIST**	**FINANCE**	**FLAMING**	FLOOSIES	FOISTERS
FARCEUR	**FEEDLOT**	FEUDISTS	FINANCED	FLAMINGO	**FLOOZIE**	**FOLACIN**
FARCEURS	FEEDLOTS	**FIANCEE**	FINANCES	**FLANEUR**	FLOOZIES	FOLACINS
FARCING	**FEELING**	FIANCEES	**FINBACK**	FLANEURS	**FLORIST**	**FOLDING**
FARCINGS	FEELINGS	**FIBROID**	FINBACKS	**FLANKER**	FLORISTS	FOLDINGS
FARDAGE	**FEERING**	FIBROIDS	**FINDING**	FLANKERS	**FLORUIT**	**FOLIAGE**
FARDAGES	FEERINGS	**FIBROIN**	FINDINGS	**FLANNEL**	FLORUITS	FOLIAGED
FARDING	**FELAFEL**	FIBROINS	**FINDRAM**	FLANNELS	**FLOTAGE**	FOLIAGES
FARDINGS	FELAFELS	**FIBROMA**	FINDRAMS	**FLANNEN**	FLOTAGES	**FOLIATE**
FARMING	**FELLATE**	FIBROMAS	**FINESSE**	FLANNENS	**FLOTSAM**	FOLIATED
FARMINGS	FELLATED	**FIBROSE**	FINESSED	**FLAPPER**	FLOTSAMS	FOLIATES
FARRIER	FELLATES	FIBROSED	FINESSER	FLAPPERS	**FLOUNCE**	**FOLIOLE**
FARRIERS	**FELSITE**	FIBROSES	FINESSES	**FLASHER**	FLOUNCED	FOLIOLES
FARRIERY	FELSITES	**FIBSTER**	**FINNACK**	FLASHERS	FLOUNCES	**FOLKWAY**
FARRUCA	**FELSPAR**	FIBSTERS	FINNACKS	**FLASHES**	**FLOWAGE**	FOLKWAYS
FARRUCAS	FELSPARS	**FICKLES**	**FINNOCK**	FLASHEST	FLOWAGES	**FONDANT**
FARTHEL	**FELTING**	FICKLEST	FINNOCKS	**FLASKET**	**FLUENCE**	FONDANTS
FARTHELS	FELTINGS	**FICTION**	**FIREARM**	FLASKETS	FLUENCES	**FONDLER**
FASCINE	**FELUCCA**	FICTIONS	FIREARMS	**FLATLET**	**FLUIDIC**	FONDLERS
FASCINES	FELUCCAS	**FIDDLER**	**FIREBUG**	FLATLETS	FLUIDICS	**FONTLET**
FASCISM	**FELWORT**	FIDDLERS	FIREBUGS	**FLATTEN**	**FLUNKEY**	FONTLETS
FASCISMI	FELWORTS	**FIDDLEY**	**FIREDOG**	FLATTENS	FLUNKEYS	**FOOLING**
FASCISMO	**FEMITER**	FIDDLEYS	FIREDOGS	**FLATTER**	**FLUSHER**	FOOLINGS
FASCISMS	FEMITERS	**FIDEISM**	**FIREPAN**	FLATTERS	FLUSHERS	**FOOTAGE**
FASCIST	**FENCING**	FIDEISMS	FIREPANS	FLATTERY	**FLUSHES**	FOOTAGES
FASCISTA	FENCINGS	**FIELDER**	**FIREPOT**	**FLAUGHT**	FLUSHEST	**FOOTBAR**
FASCISTI	**FENITAR**	FIELDERS	FIREPOTS	FLAUGHTS	**FLUSTER**	FOOTBARS
FASCISTS	FENITARS	**FIFTEEN**	**FIRRING**	**FLAVINE**	FLUSTERS	**FOOTBOY**
FASHION	**FENLAND**	FIFTEENS	FIRRINGS	FLAVINES	FLUSTERY	FOOTBOYS
FASHIONS	FENLANDS	**FIGHTER**	**FISHEYE**	**FLAVONE**	**FLUTINA**	**FOOTING**
FASTING	**FEOFFEE**	FIGHTERS	FISHEYES	FLAVONES	FLUTINAS	FOOTINGS
FASTINGS	FEOFFEES	**FIGMENT**	**FISHGIG**	**FLAVOUR**	**FLUTING**	**FOOTLES**
FATIGUE	**FEOFFER**	FIGMENTS	FISHGIGS	FLAVOURS	FLUTINGS	FOOTLESS
FATIGUED	FEOFFERS	**FIGWORT**	**FISHING**	**FLECKER**	**FLUTIST**	**FOOTPAD**
FATIGUES	**FEOFFOR**	FIGWORTS	FISHINGS	FLECKERS	FLUTISTS	FOOTPADS
FATLING	FEOFFORS	**FILABEG**	**FISSION**	**FLEECER**	**FLUTTER**	**FOOTROT**
FATLINGS	**FERLIES**	FILABEGS	FISSIONS	FLEECERS	FLUTTERS	FOOTROTS
FATTIES	FERLIEST	**FILACER**	**FISSURE**	**FLEERER**	**FLUXION**	**FOOTWAY**
FATTIEST	**FERMATA**	FILACERS	FISSURED	FLEERERS	FLUXIONS	FOOTWAYS
FAUCHON	FERMATAS	**FILARIA**	FISSURES	**FLESHER**	**FLYBANE**	**FOOZLER**
FAUCHONS	**FERMENT**	FILARIAL	**FISTFUL**	FLESHERS	FLYBANES	FOOZLERS
FAUNIST	FERMENTS	FILARIAS	FISTFULS	**FLETTON**	**FLYBELT**	**FOPLING**
FAUNISTS	**FERMION**	**FILASSE**	**FISTULA**	FLETTONS	FLYBELTS	FOPLINGS
FAVRILE	FERMIONS	FILASSES	FISTULAE	**FLEURET**	**FLYBLOW**	**FORAGER**
FAVRILES	**FERMIUM**	**FILAZER**	FISTULAR	FLEURETS	FLYBLOWS	FORAGERS
FAWNING	FERMIUMS	FILAZERS	FISTULAS	**FLEURON**	**FLYBOAT**	**FORAYER**
FAWNINGS	**FERNING**	**FILBERD**	**FITCHET**	FLEURONS	FLYBOATS	FORAYERS
FAYENCE	FERNINGS	FILBERDS	FITCHETS	**FLEXION**	**FLYBOOK**	**FORBEAR**
FAYENCES	**FERRATE**	**FILBERT**	**FITCHEW**	FLEXIONS	FLYBOOKS	FORBEARS
FEARING	FERRATES	FILBERTS	FITCHEWS	**FLEXURE**	**FLYOVER**	**FORBODE**
AFEARING	**FERRITE**	**FILCHER**	**FITMENT**	FLEXURES	FLYOVERS	FORBODES
FEASTER	FERRITES	FILCHERS	FITMENTS	**FLICKER**	**FLYTING**	**FOREARM**
FEASTERS	**FERRUGO**	**FILEMOT**	**FITTING**	FLICKERS	FLYTINGS	FOREARMS
FEATHER	FERRUGOS	FILEMOTS	FITTINGS	**FLINDER**	FLYTINGS	**FORECAR**

FORECARS	FORTUNES	**FREIGHT**	FUDDLERS	**FUTTOCK**	**GALUMPH**	GAUGINGS
FOREGUT	**FORWARD**	FREIGHTS	**FUELLER**	FUTTOCKS	GALUMPHS	**GAULTER**
FOREGUTS	FORWARDS	**FRESHEN**	FUELLERS	**GABBARD**	**GAMBADO**	GAULTERS
FORELAY	**FORWARN**	FRESHENS	**FUGUIST**	GABBARDS	GAMBADOS	**GAVOTTE**
FORELAYS	FORWARNS	**FRESHER**	FUGUISTS	**GABBART**	**GAMBIER**	GAVOTTES
FORELEG	FORZATI	FRESHERS	**FULCRUM**	GABBARTS	GAMBIERS	**GAWKIES**
FORELEGS	SFORZATI	**FRESHES**	FULCRUMS	**GABBLER**	**GAMBIST**	GAWKIEST
FORELIE	**FORZATO**	**FRESHEST**	**FULGOUR**	GABBLERS	GAMBISTS	**GAZELLE**
FORELIES	SFORZATO	**FRESHET**	FULGOURS	**GABELLE**	**GAMBLER**	GAZELLES
FOREPAW	FORZATOS	FRESHETS	**FULLAGE**	GABELLER	GAMBLERS	**GAZETTE**
FOREPAWS	**FOSSICK**	**FRETSAW**	FULLAGES	GABELLES	**GAMBOGE**	GAZETTED
FORERUN	FOSSICKS	FRETSAWS	**FULMINE**	**GABFEST**	GAMBOGES	GAZETTES
FORERUNS	**FOSSULA**	**FRIANDE**	FULMINED	GABFESTS	**GAMBREL**	**GAZOOKA**
FORESAY	FOSSULAS	FRIANDES	FULMINES	**GADLING**	GAMBRELS	GAZOOKAS
FORESAYS	**FOUDRIE**	**FRIBBLE**	**FULSOME**	GADLINGS	**GAMELAN**	**GEALOUS**
FORESEE	FOUDRIES	FRIBBLED	FULSOMER	**GADROON**	GAMELANS	GEALOUSY
FORESEEN	**FOUETTE**	FRIBBLER	**FUMBLER**	GADROONS	**GAMMOCK**	**GEARING**
FORESEES	FOUETTES	FRIBBLES	FUMBLERS	**GADWALL**	GAMMOCKS	GEARINGS
FORETOP	**FOUGADE**	**FRIGATE**	**FUMETTE**	GADWALLS	**GANGING**	**GEEBUNG**
FORETOPS	FOUGADES	FRIGATES	FUMETTES	**GAFFING**	GANGINGS	GEEBUNGS
FOREVER	**FOULARD**	**FRIGGER**	**FUNDING**	GAFFINGS	**GANGLIA**	**GELATIN**
FOREVERS	FOULARDS	FRIGGERS	FUNDINGS	**GAGSTER**	GANGLIAR	GELATINE
FORFAIR	**FOULDER**	**FRIJOLE**	**FUNERAL**	GAGSTERS	**GANGREL**	GELATINS
FORFAIRN	FOULDERS	FRIJOLES	FUNERALS	**GAHNITE**	GANGRELS	**GELDING**
FORFAIRS	**FOUMART**	**FRIPPER**	**FUNFAIR**	GAHNITES	**GANGWAY**	GELDINGS
FORFEIT	FOUMARTS	FRIPPERS	FUNFAIRS	**GAINING**	GANGWAYS	**GEMMATE**
FORFEITS	**FOUNDER**	FRIPPERY	**FUNICLE**	GAININGS	**GANTLET**	GEMMATED
FORFEND	FOUNDERS	**FRISEUR**	FUNICLES	**GAINSAY**	GANTLETS	GEMMATES
FORFENDS	**FOURGON**	FRISEURS	**FUNNIES**	GAINSAYS	**GARBAGE**	**GEMMULE**
FORGING	FOURGONS	**FRISKER**	FUNNIEST	**GALABEA**	GARBAGES	GEMMULES
FORGINGS	**FOVEOLA**	FRISKERS	**FURCATE**	GALABEAH	**GARBLER**	**GEMSBOK**
FORGIVE	FOVEOLAS	**FRISKET**	FURCATED	GALABEAS	GARBLERS	GEMSBOKS
FORGIVEN	**FOVEOLE**	FRISKETS	**FURCULA**	GALABIA	**GARBOIL**	**GENAPPE**
FORGIVES	FOVEOLES	**FRISSON**	FURCULAR	GALABIAH	GARBOILS	GENAPPES
FORHENT	**FOWLING**	FRISSONS	FURCULAS	GALABIAS	**GARDANT**	**GENERAL**
FORHENTS	FOWLINGS	**FRISURE**	**FURFAIR**	**GALANGA**	GARDANTS	GENERALE
FORLANA	**FOXHOLE**	FRISURES	FURFAIRS	GALANGAL	**GARIGUE**	GENERALS
FORLANAS	FOXHOLES	**FRITTER**	**FURIOSO**	GALANGAS	GARIGUES	**GENERIC**
FORLEND	**FOXSHIP**	FRITTERS	FURIOSOS	**GALATEA**	**GARLAND**	GENERICS
FORLENDS	FOXSHIPS	**FRITURE**	**FURLANA**	GALATEAS	GARLANDS	**GENETIC**
FORLESE	**FOXTROT**	FRITURES	FURLANAS	**GALEATE**	**GARMENT**	GENETICS
FORLESES	FOXTROTS	**FRIZZLE**	**FURLONG**	GALEATED	GARMENTS	**GENETTE**
FORLORN	**FRAGILE**	FRIZZLED	FURLONGS	**GALILEE**	**GAROTTE**	GENETTES
FORLORNS	FRAGILER	FRIZZLES	**FURNACE**	GALILEES	GAROTTED	**GENIPAP**
FORMANT	**FRAMING**	**FROGBIT**	FURNACED	**GALIPOT**	GAROTTER	GENIPAPS
FORMANTS	FRAMINGS	FROGBITS	FURNACES	GALIPOTS	GAROTTES	**GENISTA**
FORMATE	**FRANION**	**FROGLET**	**FURRIER**	**GALLANT**	**GARPIKE**	GENISTAS
FORMATED	FRANIONS	FROGLETS	FURRIERS	GALLANTS	GARPIKES	**GENITAL**
FORMATES	**FRAUGHT**	**FRONTAL**	FURRIERY	**GALLATE**	**GARROTE**	GENITALS
FORMING	FRAUGHTS	FRONTALS	**FURRING**	GALLATES	GARROTED	**GENITOR**
FORMINGS	**FRAYING**	**FRONTON**	FURRINGS	**GALLEON**	GARROTES	GENITORS
FORMULA	FRAYINGS	FRONTONS	**FURTHER**	GALLEONS	**GARVOCK**	**GENIZAH**
FORMULAE	**FRAZZLE**	**FROUNCE**	FURTHERS	**GALLIOT**	GARVOCKS	GENIZAHS
FORMULAR	FRAZZLED	FROUNCED	**FURTIVE**	GALLIOTS	**GASAHOL**	**GENTIAN**
FORMULAS	FRAZZLES	FROUNCES	FURTIVER	**GALLISE**	GASAHOLS	GENTIANS
FORPINE	**FRECKLE**	**FROWARD**	**FUSAROL**	GALLISED	**GASOHOL**	**GENTILE**
FORPINED	FRECKLED	FROWARDS	FUSAROLE	GALLISES	GASOHOLS	GENTILES
FORPINES	FRECKLES	**FRUITER**	FUSAROLS	**GALLIUM**	**GASPING**	**GENTLES**
FORSAKE	**FREEBEE**	FRUITERS	**FUSHION**	GALLIUMS	GASPINGS	GENTLEST
FORSAKEN	FREEBEES	FRUITERY	FUSHIONS	**GALLIZE**	**GASSING**	**GEORDIE**
FORSAKES	**FREEBIE**	**FRUMPLE**	**FUSTIAN**	GALLIZED	GASSINGS	GEORDIES
FORSLOE	FREEBIES	FRUMPLED	FUSTIANS	GALLIZES	**GASTRIN**	**GEORGIC**
FORSLOED	**FREEDOM**	FRUMPLES	**FUTCHEL**	**GALLOON**	GASTRINS	GEORGICS
FORSLOES	FREEDOMS	**FRUSTUM**	FUTCHELS	GALLOONS	**GATEWAY**	**GERBERA**
FORSLOW	**FREESIA**	FRUSTUMS	**FUTHARK**	**GALOCHE**	GATEWAYS	GERBERAS
FORSLOWS	FREESIAS	**FUCHSIA**	FUTHARKS	GALOCHED	**GAUDGIE**	**GERENUK**
FORTLET	**FREEWAY**	FUCHSIAS	**FUTHORC**	GALOCHES	GAUDGIES	GERENUKS
FORTLETS	FREEWAYS	**FUCKING**	FUTHORCS	**GALOPIN**	**GAUDIES**	**GERMAIN**
FORTUNE	**FREEZER**	FUCKINGS	**FUTHORK**	GALOPING	GAUDIEST	GERMAINE
FORTUNED	FREEZERS	**FUDDLER**	FUTHORKS	GALOPINS	**GAUGING**	GERMAINS

GESTALT	GLACIERS	GLYPTIC	GOSHAWKS	GRANULE	GRIMACES	GUANINES
GESTALTS	GLADDEN	GLYPTICS	GOSLING	GRANULES	GRINDER	GUARANA
GESTATE	GLADDENS	GNASHER	GOSLINGS	GRAPHIC	GRINDERS	GUARANAS
GESTATED	GLADDIE	GNASHERS	GOSSOON	AGRAPHIC	GRINDERY	GUARDEE
GESTATES	GLADDIES	GNOCCHI	GOSSOONS	GRAPHICS	GRINNER	GUARDEES
GESTURE	GLADDON	GNOCCHIS	GOTHITE	GRAPNEL	GRINNERS	GUAYULE
GESTURED	GLADDONS	GNOMIST	GOTHITES	GRAPNELS	GRIPPER	GUAYULES
GESTURES	GLAIRIN	GNOMISTS	GOUACHE	GRAPPLE	GRIPPERS	GUDGEON
GETAWAY	GLAIRINS	GNOSTIC	GOUACHES	GRAPPLED	GRIPPLE	GUDGEONS
GETAWAYS	GLAMOUR	AGNOSTIC	GOUGERE	GRAPPLES	GRIPPLES	GUERDON
GETTING	GLAMOURS	GOBBLER	GOUGERES	GRASPER	GRISING	GUERDONS
GETTINGS	GLAZIER	GOBBLERS	GOURAMI	GRASPERS	AGRISING	GUEREZA
GHARIAL	GLAZIERS	GOBURRA	GOURAMIS	GRASSER	GRISKIN	GUEREZAS
GHARIALS	GLAZING	GOBURRAS	GOURMET	GRASSERS	GRISKINS	GUESSER
GHERKIN	GLAZINGS	GODETIA	GOURMETS	GRASSUM	GRISTLE	GUESSERS
GHERKINS	GLEANER	GODETIAS	GOWLAND	GRASSUMS	GRISTLES	GUESTEN
GHILGAI	GLEANERS	GODHEAD	GOWLANDS	GRATING	GRITTER	GUESTENS
GHILGAIS	GLENOID	GODHEADS	GOWNBOY	GRATINGS	GRITTERS	GUICHET
GHILLIE	GLENOIDS	GODHOOD	GOWNBOYS	GRAUPEL	GRIZZLE	GUICHETS
GHILLIED	GLIADIN	GODHOODS	GRABBER	GRAUPELS	GRIZZLED	GUIDAGE
GHILLIES	GLIADINS	GODLING	GRABBERS	GRAVING	GRIZZLER	GUIDAGES
GIDDIES	GLIBBER	GODLINGS	GRABBLE	GRAVINGS	GRIZZLES	GUIDING
GIDDIEST	GLIBBERY	GODROON	GRABBLED	GRAVURE	GROANER	GUIDINGS
GIGGLER	GLIDDER	GODROONS	GRABBLER	GRAVURES	GROANERS	GUILDER
GIGGLERS	GLIDDERY	GODSEND	GRABBLES	GRAZIER	GROCKLE	GUILDERS
GILBERT	GLIDING	GODSENDS	GRACKLE	GRAZIERS	GROCKLES	GUIPURE
GILBERTS	GLIDINGS	GODSHIP	GRACKLES	GRAZING	GROGRAM	GUIPURES
GILDING	GLIMMER	GODSHIPS	GRADATE	GRAZINGS	GROGRAMS	GUISARD
GILDINGS	AGLIMMER	GODWARD	GRADATED	GREASER	GROMMET	GUISARDS
GILLION	GLIMMERS	GODWARDS	GRADATES	GREASERS	GROMMETS	GUISING
GILLIONS	GLIMMERY	GOGGLER	GRADDAN	GREATEN	GROSERT	AGUISING
GILTCUP	GLIMPSE	GOGGLERS	GRADDANS	GREATENS	GROSERTS	GUMBOIL
GILTCUPS	GLIMPSED	GOLDEYE	GRADINE	GRECIAN	GROSSES	GUMBOILS
GIMMICK	GLIMPSES	GOLDEYES	GRADINES	GRECIANS	GROSSEST	GUMBOOT
GIMMICKS	GLISTEN	GOLFING	GRADUAL	GRECQUE	GROUPER	GUMBOOTS
GIMMICKY	GLISTENS	GOLFINGS	GRADUALS	GRECQUES	GROUPERS	GUMDROP
GINGALL	GLISTER	GOLIARD	GRAFTER	GREEING	GROUPIE	GUMDROPS
GINGALLS	GLISTERS	GOLIARDS	GRAFTERS	AGREEING	GROUPIES	GUMMING
GINGHAM	GLITTER	GOLIARDY	GRAINER	GREENER	GROUSER	GUMMINGS
GINGHAMS	AGLITTER	GOLLAND	GRAINERS	GREENERY	GROUSERS	GUMMITE
GINGILI	GLITTERS	GOLLANDS	GRAMARY	GREENTH	GROWING	GUMMITES
GINGILIS	GLITTERY	GOMBEEN	GRAMARYE	GREENTHS	GROWINGS	GUMSHOE
GINNERS	GLOBATE	GOMBEENS	GRAMMAR	GREGALE	GROWLER	GUMSHOED
AGINNERS	GLOBATED	GOMERAL	GRAMMARS	GREGALES	GROWLERS	GUMSHOES
GINSENG	GLOBOID	GOMERALS	GRANDAD	GREISEN	GROWLERY	GUNBOAT
GINSENGS	GLOBOIDS	GOMERIL	GRANDADS	GREISENS	GRUBBER	GUNBOATS
GINSHOP	GLOBOSE	GOMERILS	GRANDAM	GREMIAL	GRUBBERS	GUNFIRE
GINSHOPS	GLOBOSES	GONDOLA	GRANDAMS	GREMIALS	GRUBBLE	GUNFIRES
GIRAFFE	GLOBULE	GONDOLAS	GRANDEE	GREMLIN	GRUBBLED	GUNNAGE
GIRAFFES	GLOBULES	GONIDIA	GRANDEES	GREMLINS	GRUBBLES	GUNNAGES
GIRASOL	GLOBULET	GONIDIAL	GRANDMA	GRENADE	GRUMBLE	GUNNERA
GIRASOLE	GLONOIN	GOODIES	GRANDMAS	GRENADES	GRUMBLED	GUNNERAS
GIRASOLS	GLONOINS	GOODIEST	GRANDPA	GREYHEN	GRUMBLER	GUNNING
GIRDING	GLOSSER	GOOSIES	GRANDPAS	GREYHENS	GRUMBLES	GUNNINGS
GIRDINGS	GLOSSERS	GOOSIEST	GRANFER	GRIBBLE	GRUMMET	GUNPLAY
GIRDLER	GLOZING	GOPURAM	GRANFERS	GRIBBLES	GRUMMETS	GUNPLAYS
GIRDLERS	GLOZINGS	GOPURAMS	GRANGER	GRICING	GRUNION	GUNPORT
GIRLOND	GLUCINA	GORCOCK	GRANGERS	GRICINGS	GRUNIONS	GUNPORTS
GIRLONDS	GLUCINAS	GORCOCKS	GRANITE	GRIDDLE	GRUNTER	GUNROOM
GIROSOL	GLUCOSE	GORCROW	GRANITES	GRIDDLES	GRUNTERS	GUNROOMS
GIROSOLS	GLUCOSES	GORCROWS	GRANNAM	GRIEVER	GRUNTLE	GUNSHIP
GISARME	GLUTTON	GORILLA	GRANNAMS	GRIEVERS	GRUNTLED	GUNSHIPS
GISARMES	GLUTTONS	GORILLAS	GRANNIE	GRIFFIN	GRUNTLES	GUNSHOT
GITTERN	GLUTTONY	GORMAND	GRANNIES	GRIFFINS	GRYPHON	GUNSHOTS
GITTERNS	GLYCINE	GORMANDS	GRANTEE	GRIFFON	GRYPHONS	GUNWALE
GIZZARD	GLYCINES	GORSEDD	GRANTEES	GRIFFONS	GRYSBOK	GUNWALES
GIZZARDS	GLYCOSE	GORSEDDS	GRANTER	GRIFTER	GRYSBOKS	GURNARD
GLACIAL	GLYCOSES	GORSOON	GRANTERS	GRIFTERS	GUANACO	GURNARDS
GLACIALS		GORSOONS	GRANTOR	GRIMACE	GUANACOS	GURUDOM
GLACIER		GOSHAWK	GRANTORS	GRIMACED	GUANINE	GURUDOMS

GURUISM	**HAIRING**	HANDJARS	**HAROSET**	CHAUNTER	**HEAVIES**	**HERBAGE**
GURUISMS	CHAIRING	**HANDLER**	CHAROSET	HAUNTERS	HEAVIEST	HERBAGED
GUTCHER	**HAIRPIN**	CHANDLER	HAROSETH	**HAUTBOY**	**HEAVING**	HERBAGES
GUTCHERS	HAIRPINS	HANDLERS	HAROSETS	HAUTBOYS	SHEAVING	**HERBIST**
GUTTATE	**HALAVAH**	HANDLESS	**HARPERS**	**HAUTEUR**	HEAVINGS	HERBISTS
GUTTATED	HALAVAHS	**HANDOUT**	SHARPERS	HAUTEURS	**HEBENON**	**HERBLET**
GUTTATES	**HALBERD**	HANDOUTS	**HARPIES**	**HAVEOUR**	HEBENONS	HERBLETS
GUZZLER	HALBERDS	**HANDSAW**	SHARPIES	HAVEOURS	**HECKLER**	**HERDBOY**
GUZZLERS	**HALBERT**	HANDSAWS	**HARPING**	**HAVEREL**	HECKLERS	HERDBOYS
GWINIAD	HALBERTS	**HANDSEL**	SHARPING	HAVERELS	**HECTARE**	**HERETIC**
GWINIADS	**HALCYON**	HANDSELS	HARPINGS	**HAVINGS**	HECTARES	HERETICS
GWYNIAD	HALCYONS	**HANDSET**	**HARPIST**	SHAVINGS	**HEDGING**	**HERITOR**
GWYNIADS	**HALFLIN**	HANDSETS	HARPISTS	**HAVIOUR**	HEDGINGS	HERITORS
GYMNAST	HALFLING	**HANGDOG**	**HARPOON**	HAVIOURS	**HEDONIC**	**HERLING**
GYMNASTS	HALFLINS	HANGDOGS	HARPOONS	**HAWBUCK**	HEDONICS	HERLINGS
GYROCAR	**HALIBUT**	**HANGERS**	**HARRIER**	HAWBUCKS	**HEELERS**	**HEROINE**
GYROCARS	HALIBUTS	CHANGERS	HARRIERS	**HAWKBIT**	WHEELERS	HEROINES
HABITAT	**HALIDOM**	**HANGING**	**HARRIES**	HAWKBITS	**HEELING**	**HEROISE**
HABITATS	HALIDOMS	CHANGING	GHARRIES	**HAWKING**	SHEELING	HEROISED
HABITUE	**HALIMOT**	PHANGING	**HARSHEN**	HAWKINGS	WHEELING	HEROISES
HABITUES	HALIMOTE	WHANGING	HARSHENS	**HAYBAND**	HEELINGS	**HEROISM**
HACHURE	HALIMOTS	HANGINGS	**HARSLET**	HAYBANDS	**HEEZING**	HEROISMS
HACHURED	**HALLALI**	**HANGOUT**	HARSLETS	**HAYCOCK**	PHEEZING	**HEROIZE**
HACHURES	HALLALIS	HANGOUTS	**HARVEST**	HAYCOCKS	WHEEZING	HEROIZED
HACKBUT	**HALLANS**	KHANJARS	HARVESTS	**HAYFORK**	**HEIRDOM**	HEROIZES
HACKBUTS	CHALLANS	**HANKERS**	**HASSOCK**	HAYFORKS	HEIRDOMS	**HERRIED**
HACKERS	**HALLIAN**	THANKERS	HASSOCKS	**HAYLOFT**	**HEISTER**	CHERRIED
WHACKERS	HALLIANS	**HANKING**	HASSOCKY	HAYLOFTS	HEISTERS	**HERRIES**
HACKING	**HALLING**	SHANKING	**HASTATE**	**HAYRICK**	**HELIPAD**	CHERRIES
CHACKING	HALLINGS	THANKING	HASTATED	HAYRICKS	HELIPADS	SHERRIES
WHACKING	**HALLION**	**HANUMAN**	**HASTENS**	**HAYSEED**	**HELLERS**	WHERRIES
HACKINGS	HALLIONS	HANUMANS	CHASTENS	HAYSEEDS	SHELLERS	**HERRING**
HACKLED	**HALLOWS**	**HAPLESS**	**HASTING**	**HAYWARD**	**HELLIER**	HERRINGS
SHACKLED	SHALLOWS	CHAPLESS	GHASTING	HAYWARDS	SHELLIER	**HERSALL**
HACKLER	**HALLWAY**	**HAPLOID**	HASTINGS	**HAYWIRE**	HELLIERS	HERSALLS
HACKLERS	HALLWAYS	HAPLOIDY	**HATBAND**	HAYWIRES	**HELLING**	**HERSHIP**
HACKLES	**HALLYON**	**HAPPIER**	HATBANDS	**HEADING**	SHELLING	HERSHIPS
SHACKLES	HALLYONS	CHAPPIER	**HATCHED**	SHEADING	**HELLION**	**HESSIAN**
HACKLET	**HALOGEN**	**HAPPIES**	THATCHED	HEADINGS	HELLIONS	HESSIANS
HACKLETS	HALOGENS	CHAPPIES	**HATCHEL**	**HEADRIG**	**HELMING**	**HETAERA**
HACKNEY	**HALTING**	HAPPIEST	HATCHELS	HEADRIGS	WHELMING	HETAERAE
HACKNEYS	HALTINGS	**HAPPING**	**HATCHER**	**HEADSET**	**HELPING**	HETAERAS
HADDOCK	**HALYARD**	CHAPPING	THATCHER	HEADSETS	WHELPING	**HETAIRA**
SHADDOCK	HALYARDS	WHAPPING	HATCHERS	**HEADWAY**	HELPINGS	HETAIRAI
HADDOCKS	**HAMBLED**	**HARBOUR**	HATCHERY	HEADWAYS	**HELVING**	**HEUREKA**
HADROME	SHAMBLED	HARBOURS	**HATCHES**	**HEALING**	SHELVING	**HEURISM**
HADROMES	**HAMBLES**	**HARDOKE**	THATCHES	SHEALING	**HEMIOLA**	HEURISMS
HAFFLIN	SHAMBLES	HARDOKES	**HATCHET**	HEALINGS	HEMIOLAS	**HEXAGON**
HAFFLINS	**HAMLETS**	**HARDTOP**	HATCHETS	**HEARERS**	**HEMIONE**	HEXAGONS
HAFNIUM	CHAMLETS	HARDTOPS	HATCHETY	SHEARERS	HEMIONES	**HEXAPLA**
HAFNIUMS	**HAMMERS**	**HARICOT**	**HATRACK**	**HEARING**	**HEMLOCK**	HEXAPLAR
HAFTING	SHAMMERS	HARICOTS	HATRACKS	SHEARING	HEMLOCKS	HEXAPLAS
SHAFTING	**HAMMING**	**HARKING**	**HATTERS**	HEARINGS	**HEMPIES**	**HEXAPOD**
HAGBOLT	SHAMMING	CHARKING	CHATTERS	**HEARKEN**	HEMPIEST	HEXAPODS
HAGBOLTS	WHAMMING	SHARKING	SHATTERS	HEARKENS	**HENBANE**	HEXAPODY
HAGDOWN	**HAMMOCK**	**HARLING**	**HATTING**	**HEARSAY**	HENBANES	**HEYDUCK**
HAGDOWNS	HAMMOCKS	HARLINGS	CHATTING	HEARSAYS	**HENDING**	HEYDUCKS
HAGGARD	**HAMPERS**	**HARMALA**	**HATTOCK**	**HEARTEN**	SHENDING	**HIBACHI**
HAGGARDS	CHAMPERS	HARMALAS	HATTOCKS	HEARTENS	**HENNIES**	HIBACHIS
HAGGING	**HAMSTER**	**HARMFUL**	**HAUBERK**	**HEATERS**	HENNIEST	**HICATEE**
SHAGGING	HAMSTERS	CHARMFUL	HAUBERKS	CHEATERS	**HENPECK**	HICATEES
HAGGLER	**HANAPER**	**HARMINE**	**HAULAGE**	THEATERS	HENPECKS	**HIDALGA**
HAGGLERS	HANAPERS	HARMINES	HAULAGES	**HEATHEN**	**HEPARIN**	HIDALGAS
HAHNIUM	**HANDBAG**	**HARMING**	**HAULIER**	HEATHENS	HEPARINS	**HIDALGO**
HAHNIUMS	HANDBAGS	CHARMING	HAULIERS	**HEATHER**	**HEPATIC**	HIDALGOS
HAINING	**HANDCAR**	**HARMOST**	**HAUNTED**	HEATHERS	HEPATICS	**HIDDERS**
CHAINING	HANDCARS	HARMOSTS	CHAUNTED	HEATHERY	**HEPSTER**	SHIDDERS
HAININGS	**HANDFUL**	HARMOSTY	**HAUNTER**	**HEATING**	HEPSTERS	WHIDDERS
HAIRCUT	HANDFULS			HEATINGS	**HEPTANE**	**HIDEOUT**
HAIRCUTS	**HANDJAR**				HEPTANES	

HIDEOUTS	CHITTERS	**HOMOLOG**	HORNINGS	HUNKIEST	HYPOXIAS	IMAGINER
HIDINGS	WHITTERS	HOMOLOGS	**HORNIST**	**HUNTERS**	**IAMBIST**	IMAGINES
CHIDINGS	**HITTING**	HOMOLOGY	HORNISTS	CHUNTERS	IAMBISTS	**IMAGING**
HIDLING	CHITTING	HOMONYM	SHUNTERS	SHUNTERS	**ICEBERG**	IMAGINGS
HIDLINGS	SHITTING	HOMONYMS	HORNITO	**HUNTING**	ICEBERGS	**IMAGISM**
HIGGLER	**HIZZING**	HOMONYMY	HORNITOS	SHUNTING	**ICEPACK**	IMAGISMS
HIGGLERS	WHIZZING	**HONEYED**	**HORNLET**	HUNTINGS	ICEPACKS	**IMAGIST**
HIGHBOY	**HOARDER**	PHONEYED	HORNLETS	**HURDLER**	**ICHNITE**	IMAGISTS
HIGHBOYS	HOARDERS	**HOODLUM**	**HORSING**	HURDLERS	ICHNITES	**IMAMATE**
HIGHWAY	**HOARSEN**	HOODLUMS	HORSINGS	**HURLING**	**ICKIEST**	IMAMATES
HIGHWAYS	HOARSENS	**HOOFROT**	**HOSANNA**	HURLINGS	**ICONISE**	**IMBATHE**
HILDING	**HOATZIN**	HOOFROTS	HOSANNAS	**HURRIES**	ICONISED	IMBATHED
CHILDING	HOATZINS	**HOOKIES**	**HOSPICE**	DHURRIES	ICONISES	IMBATHES
HILDINGS	**HOBBLER**	CHOOKIES	HOSPICES	**HURTLES**	**ICONIZE**	**IMBIBER**
HILLIER	HOBBLERS	HOOKIEST	**HOSTAGE**	HURTLESS	ICONIZED	IMBIBERS
CHILLIER	**HOBNAIL**	**HOOLOCK**	HOSTAGES	**HUSBAND**	ICONIZES	**IMBOSOM**
HILLING	HOBNAILS	HOOLOCKS	**HOSTING**	HUSBANDS	**ICTERIC**	IMBOSOMS
CHILLING	**HOBODOM**	**HOOPERS**	GHOSTING	**HUSHING**	ICTERICS	**IMBOWER**
SHILLING	HOBODOMS	WHOOPERS	HOSTINGS	SHUSHING	**ICTUSES**	IMBOWERS
HILLOCK	**HOBOISM**	**HOOPING**	**HOSTLER**	**HUSKIES**	RICTUSES	**IMBROWN**
HILLOCKS	HOBOISMS	WHOOPING	HOSTLERS	HUSKIEST	**IDLESSE**	IMBROWNS
HILLOCKY	**HOCKERS**	**HOOSGOW**	**HOTHEAD**	**HUSKING**	IDLESSES	**IMBRUTE**
HILLTOP	SHOCKERS	HOOSGOWS	**HOTSHOT**	HUSKINGS	**IDOLISE**	IMBRUTED
HILLTOPS	**HOCKING**	**HOOSHED**	HOTSHOTS	**HUSTLER**	IDOLISED	IMBRUTES
HINDLEG	CHOCKING	WHOOSHED	**HOTTING**	HUSTLERS	IDOLISER	**IMBURSE**
HINDLEGS	SHOCKING	**HOOSHES**	SHOTTING	**HUTMENT**	IDOLISES	IMBURSED
HINNIED	**HOEDOWN**	WHOOSHES	**HOUSING**	HUTMENTS	**IDOLISM**	IMBURSES
SHINNIED	HOEDOWNS	**HOOTERS**	CHOUSING	**HUTTING**	IDOLISMS	**IMITANT**
WHINNIED	**HOGBACK**	SHOOTERS	HOUSINGS	HUTTINGS	**IDOLIST**	IMITANTS
HINNIES	HOGBACKS	**HOOTING**	**HOWLING**	**HYACINE**	IDOLISTS	**IMITATE**
SHINNIES	**HOGGING**	SHOOTING	HOWLINGS	HYACINES	**IDOLIZE**	IMITATED
WHINNIES	SHOGGING	WHOOTING	WHOOTING	**HYALINE**	IDOLIZED	IMITATES
HIPPIER	HOGGINGS	**HOPBIND**	HUANACOS	HYALINES	IDOLIZER	**IMMENSE**
CHIPPIER	**HOGHOOD**	HOPBINDS	**HUCKLES**	**HYALITE**	IDOLIZES	IMMENSER
WHIPPIER	HOGHOODS	**HOPBINE**	CHUCKLES	HYALITES	**IFFIEST**	**IMMERGE**
HIPPIES	**HOGWARD**	HOPBINES	**HUFFIER**	**HYDATID**	MIFFIEST	IMMERGED
CHIPPIES	HOGWARDS	**HOPEFUL**	CHUFFIER	HYDATIDS	NIFFIEST	IMMERGES
HIPPIEST	**HOGWEED**	HOPEFULS	**HUFFKIN**	HYDRANT	**IGARAPE**	**IMMERSE**
HIPPING	HOGWEEDS	**HOPLITE**	HUFFKINS	HYDRANTH	IGARAPES	IMMERSED
CHIPPING	**HOISTER**	HOPLITES	**HUGGING**	HYDRANTS	**IGNEOUS**	IMMERSES
SHIPPING	HOISTERS	**HOPPERS**	CHUGGING	**HYDRATE**	LIGNEOUS	**IMPAINT**
WHIPPING	**HOKIEST**	CHOPPERS	**HUITAIN**	HYDRATED	**IGNITER**	IMPAINTS
HIPPINGS	CHOKIEST	SHOPPERS	HUITAINS	HYDRATES	IGNITERS	**IMPANEL**
HIPSTER	**HOLDING**	WHOPPERS	**HUMBLES**	**HYDRIDE**	**IGNITES**	IMPANELS
WHIPSTER	HOLDINGS	**HOPPIER**	HUMBLEST	HYDRIDES	LIGNITES	**IMPASSE**
HIPSTERS	**HOLESOM**	CHOPPIER	**HUMDRUM**	**HYDROID**	**IGNOBLE**	IMPASSES
HIRLING	HOLESOME	SHOPPIER	HUMDRUMS	HYDROIDS	IGNOBLED	**IMPASTE**
CHIRLING	**HOLIBUT**	**HOPPING**	**HUMERAL**	**HYDROXY**	IGNOBLER	IMPASTED
THIRLING	HOLIBUTS	CHOPPING	HUMERALS	HYDROXYL	IGNOBLES	IMPASTES
WHIRLING	**HOLIDAY**	SHOPPING	**HUMIDOR**	**HYGIENE**	**IGNORER**	**IMPASTO**
HIRLINGS	HOLIDAYS	WHOPPING	HUMIDORS	HYGIENES	IGNORERS	IMPASTOS
HIRUDIN	**HOLISMS**	HOPPINGS	**HUMMAUM**	**IGNORES**	**IGNORES**	**IMPEARL**
HIRUDINS	WHOLISMS	**HOPSACK**	HUMMAUMS	**HYLDING**	SIGNORES	IMPEARLS
HISHING	**HOLLAND**	HOPSACKS	**HUMMING**	HYLDINGS	**IGUANID**	**IMPERIL**
WHISHING	HOLLANDS	**HORDEIN**	CHUMMING	**HYLOIST**	IGUANIDS	IMPERILS
HISSING	**HOLMIUM**	HORDEINS	HUMMINGS	HYLOISTS	**IKEBANA**	**IMPINGE**
WHISSING	HOLMIUMS	**HORDOCK**	**HUMMOCK**	HYMENIA	IKEBANAS	IMPINGED
HISSINGS	**HOLSTER**	HORDOCKS	HUMMOCKS	HYMENIAL	**ILKADAY**	IMPINGES
HISTING	HOLSTERS	**HORIZON**	HUMMOCKY	HYMNIST	ILKADAYS	**IMPLANT**
WHISTING	**HOLYDAM**	HORIZONS	**HUMOGEN**	HYMNISTS	**ILLAPSE**	IMPLANTS
HISTONE	HOLYDAME	**HORMONE**	HUMOGENS	**HYPERON**	ILLAPSED	**IMPLATE**
HISTONES	HOLYDAMS	HORMONES	**HUMPIES**	HYPERONS	ILLAPSES	IMPLATED
HISTRIO	**HOMAGER**	**HORNBUG**	HUMPIEST	**HYPNONE**	**ILLITES**	IMPLATES
HISTRION	HOMAGERS	HORNBUGS	**HUMPING**	HYPNONES	TILLITES	**IMPLEAD**
HISTRIOS	**HOMELYN**	**HORNFUL**	THUMPING	**HYPOGEA**	**ILLOGIC**	IMPLEADS
HITCHER	HOMELYNS	HORNFULS	**HUNDRED**	HYPOGEAL	ILLOGICS	**IMPLETE**
HITCHERS	**HOMINID**	**HORNIER**	HUNDREDS	HYPOGEAN	**IMAGINE**	IMPLETED
HITHERS	HOMINIDS	THORNIER	**HUNKIER**	**HYPONYM**	IMAGINED	IMPLETES
WHITHERS	**HOMMOCK**	**HORNING**	CHUNKIER	HYPONYMS		**IMPLODE**
HITTERS	HOMMOCKS	THORNING	**HUNKIES**	**HYPOXIA**		IMPLODED

IMPLODES	INCLOSES	INFORCED	TINNINGS	**INTERIM**	VIRIDIAN	HITCHIER
IMPLORE	**INCLUDE**	INFORCES	WINNINGS	INTERIMS	**IRIDISE**	PITCHIER
IMPLORED	INCLUDED	**INFRACT**	INNYARD	**INTERNE**	IRIDISED	**ITCHING**
IMPLORER	INCLUDES	INFRACTS	INNYARDS	INTERNED	IRIDISES	BITCHING
IMPLORES	**INCOMER**	**INFUSER**	INQILAB	INTERNEE	**IRIDIUM**	DITCHING
IMPOSER	INCOMERS	INFUSERS	INQILABS	INTERNES	IRIDIUMS	HITCHING
IMPOSERS	**INCONNU**	**INGENER**	**INQUERE**	**IRIDIZE**	MITCHING
IMPOUND	INCONNUE	INGENERS	INQUERED	INTHRALL	IRIDIZED	PITCHING
IMPOUNDS	INCONNUS	**INGENUE**	INQUERES	INTHRALS	IRIDIZES	WITCHING
IMPREGN	**INCRUST**	INGENUES	**INQUEST**	**INTONER**	**IRISATE**	**ITEMISE**
IMPREGNS	INCRUSTS	**INGLOBE**	INQUESTS	INTONERS	IRISATED	ITEMISED
IMPRESA	**INCURVE**	INGLOBED	**INQUIET**	**INTRANT**	IRISATES	ITEMISES
IMPRESAS	INCURVED	INGLOBES	INQUIETS	INTRANTS	**IRKSOME**	**ITEMIZE**
IMPRESE	INCURVES	**INGOING**	**INQUIRE**	**INTREAT**	MIRKSOME	ITEMIZED
IMPRESES	**INDEXER**	INGOINGS	INQUIRED	INTREATS	**IRONING**	ITEMIZES
IMPRESS	INDEXERS	**INGRAFT**	INQUIRER	**INTROIT**	IRONINGS	**ITERATE**
IMPRESSE	**INDICAN**	INGRAFTS	INQUIRES	INTROITS	**IRONISE**	LITERATE
IMPREST	INDICANS	**INGRAIN**	**INSANIE**	**INTRUDE**	IRONISED	ITERATED
IMPRESTS	INDICANT	INGRAINS	INSANIES	INTRUDED	IRONISES	ITERATES
IMPRINT	**INDIGOS**	**INGRATE**	**INSCAPE**	INTRUDER	**IRONIST**	**IVORIST**
IMPRINTS	WINDIGOS	INGRATES	INSCAPES	INTRUDES	IRONISTS	IVORISTS
IMPROVE	**INDITER**	**INGROUP**	**INSCULP**	**INTRUST**	**IRONIZE**	**IVRESSE**
IMPROVED	INDITERS	INGROUPS	INSCULPS	INTRUSTS	IRONIZED	IVRESSES
IMPROVER	**INDORSE**	**INGULPH**	INSCULPT	**INTWINE**	IRONIZES	**IZZARDS**
IMPROVES	INDORSED	INGULPHS	**INSHELL**	INTWINED	**ISAGOGE**	DIZZARDS
IMPULSE	INDORSES	**INHABIT**	INSHELLS	INTWINES	ISAGOGES	GIZZARDS
IMPULSES	**INDRAFT**	INHABITS	**INSHIPS**	**INTWIST**	**ISATINE**	**JACAMAR**
IMPUTER	INDRAFTS	**INHALER**	KINSHIPS	INTWISTS	ISATINES	JACAMARS
IMPUTERS	**INDUCER**	INHALERS	**INSIDER**	**INULASE**	**ISOBARE**	**JACINTH**
INBEING	INDUCERS	**INHAUST**	INSIDERS	INULASES	ISOBARES	JACINTHS
INBEINGS	INDUCES	INHAUSTS	**INSIGHT**	**INVADER**	ISOBASES	**JACKDAW**
INBREAK	**INDULGE**	**INHERCE**	INSIGHTS	INVADERS	**ISOBASE**	JACKDAWS
INBREAKS	INDULGED	INHERCED	**INSIGNE**	**INVALID**	ISOBASES	**JACKPOT**
INBREED	INDULGER	INHERCES	INSIGNES	INVALIDS	**ISOBATH**	JACKPOTS
INBREEDS	INDULGES	**INHERIT**	**INSINEW**	**INVEIGH**	ISOBATHS	**JACKSIE**
INBRING	**INDUSIA**	INHERITS	INSINEWS	INVEIGHS	**ISOCHOR**	JACKSIES
INBRINGS	INDUSIAL	INHIBIT	**INSNARE**	**INVERSE**	ISOCHORS	**JACONET**
INBURST	**INDWELL**	INHIBITS	INSNARED	INVERSED	**ISODONT**	JACONETS
INBURSTS	INDWELLS	**INHUMAN**	INSNARES	INVERSES	ISODONTS	**JACUZZI**
INCASES	**INEARTH**	INHUMANE	**INSPECT**	**INVITEE**	**ISOGAMY**	JACUZZIS
PINCASES	INEARTHS	**INITIAL**	INSPECTS	INVITEES	MISOGAMY	**JADEITE**
INCENSE	**INERTIA**	INITIALS	**INSPIRE**	**INVITER**	**ISOGRAM**	JADEITES
INCENSED	INERTIAL	**INJOINT**	INSPIRED	INVITERS	ISOGRAMS	**JAGHIRE**
INCENSER	INERTIAS	INJOINTS	INSPIRER	**INVOICE**	**ISOHYET**	JAGHIRES
INCENSES	**INFANTA**	**INJUNCT**	INSPIRES	INVOICED	ISOHYETS	**JALAPIN**
INCHASE	INFANTAS	INJUNCTS	**INSPYRE**	INVOICES	**ISOKONT**	JALAPINS
INCHASED	**INFANTE**	**INJURER**	INSPYRED	**INVOLVE**	ISOKONTS	**JALOUSE**
INCHASES	INFANTED	INJURERS	INSPYRES	INVOLVED	**ISOLATE**	JALOUSED
INCHING	INFANTES	**INKHORN**	**INSTALL**	INVOLVES	ISOLATED	JALOUSES
CINCHING	**INFARCT**	INKHORNS	INSTALLS	**INWEAVE**	ISOLATES	**JAMADAR**
PINCHING	INFARCTS	INKIEST	**INSTANT**	INWEAVES	**ISOLINE**	JAMADARS
WINCHING	**INFERNO**	**INKIEST**	INSTANTS	**IODURET**	ISOLINES	**JAMBEAU**
INCHPIN	INFERNOS	DINKIEST	**INSTATE**	IODURETS	**ISOMERE**	JAMBEAUX
LINCHPIN	**INFIDEL**	KINKIEST	INSTATED	**IONISED**	ISOMERES	**JAMBIER**
INCHPINS	INFIDELS	PINKIEST	INSTATES	LIONISED	**ISOSPIN**	JAMBIERS
INCISOR	**INFIELD**	SINKIEST	**INSTILL**	**IONISER**	ISOSPINS	**JAMBIYA**
INCISORS	INFIELDS	ZINKIEST	INSTILLS	IONISERS	**ISOTONE**	JAMBIYAH
INCISORY	**INFLAME**	**INKLING**	**INSULIN**	IONISES	ISOTONES	JAMBIYAS
INCITER	INFLAMED	TINKLING	INSULINS	LIONISES	**ISOTOPE**	**JAMBOKS**
INCITERS	INFLAMER	INKLINGS	**INSURER**	**IONIZED**	ISOTOPES	SJAMBOKS
INCITES	INFLAMES	**INKSPOT**	INSURERS	LIONIZED	**ISOTRON**	**JAMBONE**
ZINCITES	**INFLATE**	INKSPOTS	**INSWING**	**IONIZER**	ISOTRONS	JAMBONES
INCLASP	INFLATED	**INKWELL**	INSWINGS	IONIZERS	**ISOTYPE**	**JAMBOOL**
INCLASPS	INFLATES	INKWELLS	**INTARSI**	**IONIZES**	ISOTYPES	JAMBOOLS
INCLINE	**INFLECT**	**INLAYER**	INTARSIA	LIONIZES	**ISSUING**	**JAMDANI**
INCLINED	INFLECTS	INLAYERS	INTARSIO	**IONOMER**	TISSUING	JAMDANIS
INCLINES	**INFLICT**	**INNERVE**	**INTEGER**	IONOMERS	**ITACISM**	**JAMPANI**
INCLOSE	INFLICTS	INNERVED	INTEGERS	**IPOMOEA**	ITACISMS	JAMPANIS
INCLOSED	**INFOLDS**	INNERVES	**INTENSE**	IPOMOEAS	**ITCHIER**	**JANGLER**
INCLOSER	**INFORCE**	**INNINGS**	INTENSER	**IRIDIAN**	BITCHIER	JANGLERS

JANITOR	JIGGING	KACHINAS	KERATINS	KILOBITS	KNAPPLED	LACINIAE
JANITORS	JIGGINGS	KAGOULE	KERMESS	KILOTON	KNAPPLES	LACKERS
JANIZAR	JINGLER	KAGOULES	KERMESSE	KILOTONS	KNEADER	CLACKERS
JANIZARS	JINGLERS	KAINITE	KERNITE	KIMMERS	KNEADERS	FLACKERS
JANIZARY	JINGLET	KAINITES	KERNITES	SKIMMERS	KNEELER	SLACKERS
JANNOCK	JINGLETS	KAJAWAH	KEROGEN	KIMONOS	KNEELERS	LACKING
JANNOCKS	JINJILI	KAJAWAHS	KEROGENS	OKIMONOS	KNEVELL	BLACKING
JANTIES	JINJILIS	KAKODYL	KERYGMA	KINCHIN	KNEVELLS	CLACKING
JANTIEST	JOBBING	KAKODYLS	KERYGMAS	KINCHINS	KNICKER	SLACKING
JARGOON	JOBBINGS	KAMERAD	KESTREL	KINDLER	KNICKERS	LACQUER
JARGOONS	JOGGING	KAMERADS	KESTRELS	KINDLERS	KNIFING	LACQUERS
JARRING	JOGGINGS	KAMICHI	KETCHES	KINDLES	KNIFINGS	LACQUEY
JARRINGS	JOGTROT	KAMICHIS	SKETCHES	KINDLESS	KNITTER	LACQUEYS
JASMINE	JOGTROTS	KAMPONG	KETCHUP	KINDRED	KNITTERS	LACTASE
JASMINES	JOHNNIE	KAMPONGS	KETCHUPS	KINDREDS	KNITTLE	LACTASES
JAUNTIE	JOHNNIES	KAMSEEN	KEYHOLE	KINESES	KNITTLES	LACTATE
JAUNTIER	JOINDER	KAMSEENS	KEYHOLES	AKINESES	KNITTLES	LACTATED
JAUNTIES	JOINDERS	KANTELA	KEYNOTE	KINESIS	KNOBBER	LACTATES
JAVELIN	JOINING	KANTELAS	KEYNOTED	AKINESIS	KNOBBERS	LACTEAL
JAVELINS	JOININGS	KANTELE	KEYNOTES	KINETIC	KNOBBLE	LACTEALS
JAWBONE	JOINTER	KANTELES	KHADDAR	KINETICS	KNOBBLED	LACTONE
JAWBONED	JOINTERS	KAOLINE	KHADDARS	KINFOLK	KNOBBLES	LACTONES
JAWBONES	JOLLIES	KAOLINES	KHALIFA	KINFOLKS	KNOCKER	LACTOSE
JAWFALL	JOLLIEST	KARAISM	KHALIFAH	KINGCUP	KNOCKERS	LACTOSES
JAWFALLS	JONQUIL	KARAISMS	KHALIFAS	KINGCUPS	KNOTTER	LACUNAR
JAWHOLE	JONQUILS	KARAKUL	KHALIFAT	KINGDOM	KNOTTERS	LACUNARS
JAWHOLES	JOTTING	KARAKULS	KHAMSIN	KINGDOMS	KNUBBLE	LACUNARY
JAYWALK	JOTTINGS	KARTING	KHAMSINS	KINGLES	KNUBBLED	LADANUM
JAYWALKS	JOURNAL	KARTINGS	KHANATE	KINGLESS	KNUBBLES	LADANUMS
JEALOUS	JOURNALS	KASHMIR	KHANATES	KINGLET	KNUCKLE	LADDERS
JEALOUSE	JOURNEY	KASHMIRS	KHANJAR	KINGLETS	KNUCKLED	BLADDERS
JEALOUSY	JOURNEYS	KATHODE	KHANJARS	KINKING	KNUCKLES	BLADDERY
JEEPNEY	JOUSTER	KATHODES	KHEDIVA	SKINKING	KOFTGAR	CLADDERS
JEEPNEYS	JOUSTERS	KATORGA	KHEDIVAL	KINLESS	KOFTGARI	LADDERY
JEERING	JOYANCE	KATORGAS	KHEDIVAS	SKINLESS	KOFTGARS	LADDIES
JEERINGS	JOYANCES	KATYDID	KHEDIVE	KINSHIP	KREMLIN	GLADDIES
JELLABA	JUBILEE	KATYDIDS	KHEDIVES	KINSHIPS	KREMLINS	LADRONE
DJELLABA	JUBILEES	KEBBOCK	KHOTBAH	KIPPAGE	KRIMMER	LADRONES
JELLABAS	JUDOIST	KEBBOCKS	KHOTBAHS	KIPPAGES	KRIMMERS	LADYBUG
JEMADAR	JUDOISTS	KEBBUCK	KHOTBEH	KIPPERS	KRYPTON	LADYBUGS
JEMADARS	JUGGLER	KEBBUCKS	KHOTBEHS	SKIPPERS	KRYPTONS	LADYCOW
JEMIDAR	JUGGLERS	KEELAGE	KHUTBAH	KIPPING	KUFFIAH	LADYCOWS
JEMIDARS	JUGGLERY	KEELAGES	KHUTBAHS	SKIPPING	KUFFIAHS	LADYISM
JEMMIES	JUGULAR	KEELING	KIBITKA	KIRIMON	KUFFIEH	LADYISMS
JEMMIEST	JUGULARS	KEELINGS	KIBITKAS	KIRIMONS	KUFFIEHS	LADYKIN
JEOFAIL	JUMBLER	KEELSON	KIDDIER	KIRKING	KUFIYAH	LADYKINS
JEOFAILS	JUMBLERS	KEELSONS	KIDDIERS	KIRKINGS	KUFIYAHS	LAETARE
JEOPARD	JUMBUCK	KEENING	KIDDING	KIRKTON	KUMQUAT	LAETARES
JEOPARDS	JUMBUCKS	KEENINGS	SKIDDING	KIRKTONS	KUMQUATS	LAGGARD
JEOPARDY	JUMELLE	KEEPING	KIDLING	KITCHEN	KURSAAL	LAGGARDS
JERKIES	JUMELLES	KEEPINGS	KIDLINGS	KITCHENS	KURSAALS	LAGGING
JERKIEST	JUNCATE	KEEPNET	KIKUMON	KITHARA	KYANISE	BLAGGING
JERKING	JUNCATES	KEEPNETS	KIKUMONS	KITHARAS	KYANISED	CLAGGING
JERKINGS	JUNIPER	KEITLOA	KILLCOW	KITLING	KYANISES	FLAGGING
JERQUER	JUNIPERS	KEITLOAS	KILLCOWS	KITLINGS	KYANITE	SLAGGING
JERQUERS	JUNKIES	KELLAUT	KILLDEE	KITTLED	KYANITES	LAGGINGS
JESTING	JUNKIEST	KELLAUTS	KILLDEES	KITTLES	KYANIZE	LAICISE
JESTINGS	JUSSIVE	KELLIES	KILLICK	SKITTLED	KYANIZED	LAICISED
JETFOIL	JUSSIVES	SKELLIES	KILLICKS	KITTLEST	KYANIZES	LAICISES
JETFOILS	JUSTICE	KELTERS	KILLING	KLAVIER	LABARUM	LAICIZE
JETTIES	JUSTICER	SKELTERS	SKILLING	KLAVIERS	LABARUMS	LAICIZED
JETTIEST	JUSTICES	KEMPING	KILLINGS	KLINKER	LABELLA	LAICIZES
JIBBAHS	JUVENAL	KEMPINGS	KILLJOY	KLINKERS	FLABELLA	LAIDING
DJIBBAHS	JUVENALS	KENNING	KILLJOYS	KNACKER	GLABELLA	PLAIDING
JIBBING	KABBALA	KENNINGS	KILLOCK	KNACKERS	LABIATE	LAIRAGE
JIBBINGS	KABBALAH	KEPPING	KILLOCKS	KNACKERY	LABIATES	LAIRAGES
JIGAJIG	KABBALAS	SKEPPING	KILOBAR	KNAPPER	LABROID	LAIRIER
JIGAJIGS	KACHERI	KERAMIC	KILOBARS	KNAPPERS	LABROIDS	GLAIRIER
JIGAJOG	KACHERIS	KERAMICS	KILOBIT	KNAPPLE	LACINGS	LAIRING
JIGAJOGS	KACHINA	KERATIN	KILOBITS		PLACINGS	GLAIRING

LAIRISE	LANDLERS	LASHKAR	LAZARETS	LECTURER	BLENDING	SLICKING
LAIRISED	LANEWAY	LASHKARS	LAZIEST	LECTURES	LENDINGS	LICKINGS
LAIRISES	LANEWAYS	LASKETS	GLAZIEST	LECTURN	LENIENT	LIGGING
LAIRIZE	LANGAHA	FLASKETS	LEACHED	LECTURNS	LENIENTS	LIGGINGS
LAIRIZED	LANGAHAS	LASSOCK	BLEACHED	LEDGERS	LENTISK	LIGHTED
LAIRIZES	LANGREL	LASSOCKS	PLEACHED	PLEDGERS	LENTISKS	ALIGHTED
LAKELET	LANGRELS	LASTAGE	LEACHES	SLEDGERS	LEOPARD	BLIGHTED
LAKELETS	LANGUET	LASTAGES	BLEACHES	LEDGIER	LEOPARDS	FLIGHTED
LAKIEST	LANGUETS	LASTERS	PLEACHES	FLEDGIER	LEOTARD	PLIGHTED
FLAKIEST	LANGUOR	BLASTERS	LEADERS	LEECHED	LEOTARDS	SLIGHTED
LALLING	LANGUORS	LASTING	PLEADERS	FLEECHED	LEPTOME	LIGHTEN
LALLINGS	LANIARD	LASTINGS	LEADING	LEECHEE	LEPTOMES	LIGHTENS
LAMBAST	LANIARDS	LATCHED	PLEADING	LEECHEES	LESBIAN	LIGHTER
LAMBASTE	LANKEST	CLATCHED	LEADINGS	LEECHES	LESBIANS	BLIGHTER
LAMBASTS	BLANKEST	LATCHES	LEAFAGE	FLEECHES	LESSORS	PLIGHTER
LAMBERS	LANKING	CLATCHES	LEAFAGES	SLEECHES	PLESSORS	SLIGHTER
CLAMBERS	BLANKING	LATCHET	LEAFBUD	LEEPING	LETCHED	LIGHTERS
LAMBERT	CLANKING	LATCHETS	LEAFBUDS	BLEEPING	FLETCHED	LIGHTLY
LAMBERTS	FLANKING	LATENCE	LEAFLET	CLEEPING	LETCHES	SLIGHTLY
LAMBKIN	PLANKING	LATENCES	LEAFLETS	SLEEPING	FLETCHES	LIGNAGE
LAMBKINS	LANNERS	LATERAL	LEAGUER	LEERING	LETTERN	LIGNAGES
LAMELLA	PLANNERS	LATERALS	LEAGUERS	FLEERING	LETTERNS	LIGNITE
LAMELLAE	LANOLIN	LATHERS	LEAKAGE	LEERINGS	LETTING	LIGNITES
LAMELLAR	LANOLINE	BLATHERS	LEAKAGES	LEEWARD	BLETTING	LIGROIN
LAMETER	LANOLINS	SLATHERS	LEAKIER	LEEWARDS	LETTINGS	LIGROINS
LAMETERS	LANTANA	LATHING	LEAMING	LEFTISM	LETTUCE	LIMACEL
LAMIGER	LANTANAS	LATHINGS	GLEAMING	LEFTISMS	LETTUCES	LIMACELS
LAMIGERS	LANTERN	LATITAT	LEANEST	LEFTIST	LEUCINE	LIMACON
LAMINAR	LANTERNS	LATITATS	CLEANEST	LEFTISTS	LEUCINES	LIMACONS
LAMINARY	LANYARD	LATRINE	LEANING	LEGATEE	LEUCITE	LIMBECK
LAMITER	LANYARDS	LATRINES	CLEANING	LEGATEES	LEUCITES	LIMBECKS
LAMITERS	LAPPERS	LATTENS	GLEANING	LEGATOR	LEUCOMA	LIMBERS
LAMMERS	CLAPPERS	FLATTENS	LEANINGS	LEGATORS	LEUCOMAS	CLIMBERS
SLAMMERS	FLAPPERS	LATTICE	LEARIER	LEGGING	LEVATOR	LIMBING
LAMMING	SLAPPERS	LATTICED	BLEARIER	ALEGGING	LEVATORS	BLIMBING
CLAMMING	LAPPING	LATTICES	LEARING	FLEGGING	ELEVATOR	CLIMBING
FLAMMING	CLAPPING	LAUDING	BLEARING	LEGGINGS	LEVATORS	LIMEPIT
SLAMMING	FLAPPING	BLAUDING	LEARNER	LEGGISM	LEVERET	LIMEPITS
LAMMINGS	PLAPPING	LAUGHER	LEARNERS	LEGGISMS	LEVERETS	LIMIEST
LAMPERN	SLAPPING	LAUGHERS	LEASERS	LEGHORN	LEXICON	SLIMIEST
LAMPERNS	LAPPINGS	LAUNDER	PLEASERS	LEGHORNS	LEXICONS	LIMITED
LAMPING	LAPSANG	LAUNDERS	LEASING	LEGISTS	LIAISON	LIMITEDS
CLAMPING	LAPSANGS	LAUWINE	PLEASING	ELEGISTS	LIAISONS	LIMITER
LAMPION	LAPSING	LAUWINES	LEASINGS	LEGITIM	LIBBARD	LIMITERS
LAMPIONS	ELAPSING	LAVOLTA	LEASOWE	LEGITIMS	LIBBARDS	LIMMERS
LAMPOON	LAPWING	LAVOLTAS	LEASOWED	LEGROOM	LIBBING	GLIMMERS
LAMPOONS	LAPWINGS	LAWLAND	LEASOWES	LEGROOMS	GLIBBING	SLIMMERS
LAMPREY	LAPWORK	LAWLANDS	LEASURE	LEGUMIN	LIBERAL	LIMPING
LAMPREYS	LAPWORKS	LAWLESS	LEASURES	LEGUMINS	LIBERALS	FLIMPING
LAMPUKA	LARDOON	CLAWLESS	LEASURE	LEGWORK	LIBRATE	LIMPINGS
LAMPUKAS	LARDOONS	FLAWLESS	PLEASURE	LEGWORKS	LIBRATED	LIMPKIN
LAMPUKI	LARGESS	LAWSUIT	LEASURES	LEIDGER	LIBRATES	LIMPKINS
LAMPUKIS	LARGESSE	LAWSUITS	LEATHER	LEIDGERS	LICENCE	LINCHES
LANCHED	LARMIER	LAXATOR	LEATHERN	LEISLER	LICENCED	CLINCHES
BLANCHED	LARMIERS	LAXATORS	LEATHERS	LEISLERS	LICENCES	FLINCHES
FLANCHED	LARVATE	LAYAWAY	LEATHERY	LEISTER	LICENSE	LINCHET
PLANCHED	LARVATED	LAYAWAYS	LEAVING	LEISTERS	LICENSED	LINCHETS
LANCHES	LASAGNA	LAYBACK	CLEAVING	LEISURE	LICENSEE	LINDANE
BLANCHES	LASAGNAS	PLAYBACK	SLEAVING	LEISURED	LICENSER	LINDANES
FLANCHES	LASAGNE	LAYBACKS	LEAVINGS	LEISURES	LICENSES	LINEAGE
PLANCHES	LASAGNES	LAYETTE	LECTERN	LEKKING	LICHTER	LINEAGES
LANCING	LASHERS	LAYETTES	LECTERNS	LEKKINGS	FLICHTER	LINEATE
ELANCING	FLASHERS	LAYLOCK	LECTION	LEMMING	LICHWAY	LINEATED
GLANCING	SLASHERS	LAYLOCKS	ELECTION	CLEMMING	LICHWAYS	LINGERS
LANDERS	LASHING	LAYTIME	FLECTION	LEMMINGS	LICKERS	CLINGERS
GLANDERS	CLASHING	PLAYTIME	LECTIONS	LEMPIRA	CLICKERS	FLINGERS
SLANDERS	FLASHING	LAYTIMES	LECTORS	LEMPIRAS	FLICKERS	SLINGERS
LANDING	PLASHING	PLAYTIME	ELECTORS	LENDERS	SLICKERS	LINGIER
LANDINGS	SLASHING	LAYTIMES	LECTURE	BLENDERS	LICKING	CLINGIER
LANDLER	LASHINGS	LAZARET	LECTURED	LENDING	CLICKING	LINGULA

LINGULAE
LINGULAR
LINGULAS
LINKAGE
LINKAGES
LINKBOY
LINKBOYS
LINKING
BLINKING
CLINKING
PLINKING
SLINKING
LINNING
BLINNING
LINOCUT
LINOCUTS
LINSANG
LINSANGS
LINSEED
LINSEEDS
LINTIER
FLINTIER
LINTIES
LINTIEST
LIONCEL
LIONCELS
LIONISE
LIONISED
LIONISES
LIONISM
LIONISMS
LIONIZE
LIONIZED
LIONIZES
LIPPIER
SLIPPIER
LIPPIES
CLIPPIES
LIPPIEST
LIPPING
BLIPPING
CLIPPING
FLIPPING
SLIPPING
LIQUATE
LIQUATED
LIQUATES
LIQUEUR
LIQUEURS
LISPING
LISPINGS
LISPUND
LISPUNDS
LISTENS
GLISTENS
LISTERS
BLISTERS
GLISTERS
LISTING
LISTINGS
LITERAL
LITERALS
LITHATE
LITHATES
LITHELY
BLITHELY
LITHEST
BLITHEST
LITHITE
LITHITES

LITHIUM
LITHIUMS
LITTERS
CLITTERS
FLITTERS
GLITTERS
SLITTERS
LITTERY
GLITTERY
LITTLES
LITTLEST
LITTLIN
LITTLING
LITTLINS
LIVELOD
LIVELODS
LLANERO
LLANEROS
LOADING
LOADINGS
LOAFING
LOAFINGS
LOAMING
GLOAMING
LOANING
LOANINGS
LOATHER
LOATHERS
LOATHES
LOATHEST
LOBBING
BLOBBING
LOBBYER
LOBBYERS
LOBELET
LOBELETS
LOBELIA
LOBELIAS
LOBSTER
LOBSTERS
LOBULAR
GLOBULAR
LOBULES
GLOBULES
LOBWORM
LOBWORMS
BLOCKAGE
LOCKAGES
LOCKERS
BLOCKERS
CLOCKERS
LOCKFUL
LOCKFULS
LOCKING
BLOCKING
CLOCKING
FLOCKING
LOCKOUT
LOCKOUTS
LOCKRAM
LOCKRAMS
LOCUSTA
LOCUSTAE
LODGING
LODGINGS
LOGGERS
CLOGGERS
SLOGGERS
LOGGING

CLOGGING
FLOGGING
SLOGGING
LOGGINGS
LOGICAL
ALOGICAL
LOGLINE
LOGLINES
LOGWOOD
LOGWOODS
LONGBOW
LONGBOWS
LONGING
LONGINGS
LOOBIES
LOOBIEST
LOOFFUL
LOOFFULS
LOOKING
LOOKINGS
LOOKOUT
LOOKOUTS
LOOMING
LOONIES
LOONIEST
LOONING
LOONINGS
LOOPERS
BLOOPERS
LOOPING
LOOPINGS
CLOPPING
FLOPPING
PLOPPING
SLOPPING
LOPPINGS
LORDING
LORDINGS
LORDKIN
LORDKINS
LORETTE
LORETTES
LORIMER
LORIMERS
LORINER
LORINERS
LORRELL
LORRELLS
LOSINGS
CLOSINGS
LOSSIER
FLOSSIER
GLOSSIER
LOTTING
BLOTTING
CLOTTING
PLOTTING
SLOTTING
LOUNDER
FLOUNDER
LOUNDERS
LOUNGER

LOUNGERS
LOURIER
FLOURIER
CLOURING
FLOURING
LOURING
LOURINGS
LOUSING
BLOUSING
FLOUSING
LOUTING
CLOUTING
FLOUTING
GLOUTING
PLONGING
LOVERED
CLOVERED
LOWERED
FLOWERED
GLOWERED
LOWINGS
SLOWINGS
LOWLAND
LOWLANDS
LOWNESS
SLOWNESS
LOWNING
CLOWNING
LOWVELD
LOWVELDS
LOXYGEN
LOXYGENS
LOZENGE
LOZENGED
LOZENGES
LUBBARD
LUBBARDS
LUBBERS
BLUBBERS
SLUBBERS
LUCARNE
LUCARNES
LUCERNE
LUCERNES
LUCIFER
LUCIFERS
LUCIGEN
LUCIGENS
LUCKIER
CLUCKIER
PLUCKIER
LUCKIES
LUCKIEST
LUCKILY
PLUCKILY
LUDSHIP
LUDSHIPS
LUFFING
BLUFFING
FLUFFING
PLUFFING
LUGEING
LUGEINGS
LUGGAGE
LUGGAGES
LUGGERS
PLUGGERS
SLUGGERS
LUGGING
GLUGGING
PLUGGING

SLUGGING
LUGSAIL
LUGSAILS
LUGWORM
LUGWORMS
LUMBAGO
PLUMBAGO
LUMBANG
LUMBANGS
LUMBERS
CLUMBERS
PLUMBERS
SLUMBERS
LUMMIER
PLUMMIER
SLUMMIER
LUMPERS
PLUMPERS
LUMPIER
CLUMPIER
SLUMPIER
LUMPING
CLUMPING
FLUMPING
PLUMPING
SLUMPING
LUMPISH
GLUMPISH
PLUMPISH
LUMPKIN
LUMPKINS
LUNATIC
LUNATICS
LUNCHER
LUNCHERS
LUNCHES
CLUNCHES
LUNETTE
LUNETTES
LUNGFUL
LUNGFULS
LUNGING
BLUNGING
PLUNGING
LUNKERS
BLUNKERS
PLUNKERS
LUNTING
BLUNTING
LUPULIN
LUPULINE
LUPULINS
LURCHER
LURCHERS
LURDANE
LURDANES
LURKING
LURKINGS
LURRIES
FLURRIES
SLURRIES
LUSHERS
BLUSHERS
FLUSHERS
LUSHEST
FLUSHEST
PLUSHEST
LUSHIER

FLUSHIER
PLUSHIER
SLUSHIER
LUSHING
BLUSHING
FLUSHING
SLUSHING
LUSTERS
BLUSTERS
CLUSTERS
FLUSTERS
LUTHERN
LUTHERNS
LUTHIER
LUTHIERS
LUTINGS
FLUTINGS
LUTISTS
FLUTISTS
LYCOPOD
LYCOPODS
LYDDITE
LYDDITES
LYMITER
LYMITERS
LYMPHAD
LYMPHADS
LYNCHET
LYNCHETS
LYOPHIL
LYOPHILE
MACADAM
MACADAMS
MACAQUE
MACAQUES
MACHAIR
MACHAIRS
MACHETE
MACHETES
MACHINE
MACHINED
MACHINES
MACHREE
MACHREES
MACRAME
MACRAMES
MACRAMI
MACRAMIS
MADLING
MADLINGS
MADOQUA
MADOQUAS
MADRASA
MADRASAH
MADRASAS
MADRONA
MADRONAS
MADRONO
MADRONOS
MADWORT
MADWORTS
MADZOON
MADZOONS
MAESTRO
MAESTROS
MAFFICK
MAFFICKS
MAFFLIN

MAFFLING
MAFFLINS
MAGENTA
MAGENTAS
MAGISMS
IMAGISMS
MAGNATE
MAGNATES
MAGNETO
MAGNETON
MAGNETOS
MAHATMA
MAHATMAS
MAHONIA
MAHONIAS
MAHSEER
MAHSEERS
MAIDISM
MAIDISMS
MAILING
MAILINGS
MAILLOT
MAILLOTS
MAIMING
MAIMINGS
MAINOUR
MAINOURS
MAINTOP
MAINTOPS
MAISTER
MAISTERS
MAJORAT
MAJORATS
MALACIA
MALACIAS
MALAISE
MALAISES
MALARIA
MALARIAL
MALARIAN
MALARIAS
MALEATE
MALEATES
MALEFIC
MALEFICE
MALEFICES
MALICHO
MALICHOS
MALISON
MALISONS
MALLARD
MALLARDS
MALLING
SMALLING
MALMSEY
MALMSEYS
MALTASE
MALTASES
MALTING
MALTINGS
MALTOSE
MALTOSES
MAMELON
MAMELONS
MAMILLA
MAMILLAE
MAMILLAR
MAMMOCK
MAMMOCKS
MAMMOTH
MAMMOTHS

MANACLE	MANTEAUX	SMARTING	MATZOONS	MEERKATS	MERSIONS	MIDNOONS
MANACLED	**MANTEEL**	**MARTINI**	**MAULGRE**	**MEETING**	**MESHING**	**MIDRIFF**
MANACLES	MANTEELS	MARTINIS	MAULGRES	MEETINGS	MESHINGS	MIDRIFFS
MANAGER	**MANTLET**	**MARTLET**	**MAUNDER**	**MEGABAR**	**MESQUIN**	**MIDSHIP**
MANAGERS	MANTLETS	MARTLETS	MAUNDERS	MEGABARS	MESQUINE	MIDSHIPS
MANAKIN	**MANTRAM**	**MARYBUD**	**MAUTHER**	**MEGABIT**	**MESQUIT**	**MIDWIFE**
MANAKINS	MANTRAMS	MARYBUDS	MAUTHERS	MEGABITS	MESQUITE	MIDWIFED
MANATEE	**MANTRAP**	**MASCARA**	**MAUVAIS**	**MEGAFOG**	MESQUITS	MIDWIFES
MANATEES	MANTRAPS	MASCARAS	MAUVAISE	MEGAFOGS	**MESSAGE**	**MIDWIVE**
MANCHET	**MANUMIT**	**MASHERS**	**MAUVEIN**	**MEGARAD**	MESSAGED	MIDWIVED
MANCHETS	MANUMITS	SMASHERS	MAUVEINE	MEGARADS	MESSAGES	MIDWIVES
MANDALA	**MANURER**	**MASHIES**	MAUVEINS	**MEGARON**	**MESTIZA**	**MIGRANT**
MANDALAS	MANURERS	MASHIEST	**MAUVINE**	MEGARONS	MESTIZAS	EMIGRANT
MANDATE	**MAORMOR**	**MASHING**	MAUVINES	**MEGASSE**	**MESTIZO**	MIGRANTS
MANDATED	MAORMORS	SMASHING	**MAWSEED**	MEGASSES	MESTIZOS	**MIGRATE**
MANDATES	**MAPPIST**	MASHINGS	MAWSEEDS	**MEGATON**	**METAMER**	EMIGRATE
MANDIOC	MAPPISTS	**MASHLAM**	**MAWTHER**	MEGATONS	METAMERE	MIGRATED
MANDIOCA	**MARABOU**	MASHLAMS	MAWTHERS	**MELANGE**	METAMERS	MIGRATES
MANDIOCS	MARABOUS	**MASHLIM**	**MAXILLA**	MELANGES	**METAYER**	**MILEAGE**
MANDIRA	MARABOUT	MASHLIMS	MAXILLAE	**MELANIN**	METAYERS	MILEAGES
MANDIRAS	**MARBLER**	**MASHLIN**	**MAXIMIN**	MELANINS	**METAZOA**	**MILFOIL**
MANDOLA	MARBLERS	MASHLINS	MAXIMINS	**MELILOT**	METAZOAN	MILFOILS
MANDOLAS	**MARCHER**	**MASHLUM**	**MAXWELL**	MELILOTS	**METCAST**	**MILITAR**
MANDORA	MARCHERS	MASHLUMS	MAXWELLS	**MELISMA**	METCASTS	MILITARY
MANDORAS	**MARCHES**	**MASQUER**	**MAYPOLE**	MELISMAS	**METHANE**	**MILITIA**
MANDREL	MARCHESA	MASQUERS	MAYPOLES	**MELLING**	METHANES	MILITIAS
MANDRELS	MARCHESE	**MASSAGE**	**MAYSTER**	SMELLING	**METHINK**	**MILKING**
MANDRIL	MARCHESI	MASSAGED	MAYSTERS	**MELLITE**	METHINKS	MILKINGS
MANDRILL	**MARCONI**	MASSAGES	**MAYWEED**	MELLITES	**METICAL**	**MILLDAM**
MANDRILS	MARCONIS	**MASSEUR**	MAYWEEDS	**MELODIC**	EMETICAL	MILLDAMS
MANGLER	**MARDIES**	MASSEURS	**MAZURKA**	MELODICS	METICALS	**MILLIME**
MANGLERS	MARDIEST	**MASSING**	MAZURKAS	**MELTING**	**METISSE**	MILLIMES
MANGOLD	**MAREMMA**	AMASSING	**MAZZARD**	SMELTING	METISSES	**MILLING**
MANGOLDS	MAREMMAS	**MASTABA**	MAZZARDS	MELTINGS	**METONYM**	MILLINGS
MANHOLE	**MARGENT**	MASTABAS	**MEACOCK**	**MELTITH**	METONYMS	**MILLION**
MANHOLES	MARGENTS	**MASTICH**	MEACOCKS	MELTITHS	METONYMY	MILLIONS
MANHOOD	**MARGOSA**	MASTICHS	**MEAGRES**	**MEMENTO**	**METOPON**	**MIMMICK**
MANHOODS	MARGOSAS	**MASTIFF**	MEAGREST	MEMENTOS	METOPONS	MIMMICKS
MANHUNT	**MARIMBA**	MASTIFFS	**MEALIES**	**MENACER**	**METRIST**	**MINARET**
MANHUNTS	MARIMBAS	**MASTOID**	MEALIEST	MENACERS	METRISTS	MINARETS
MANIHOC	**MARINER**	MASTOIDS	**MEANDER**	**MENAGES**	**MEZUZAH**	**MINCING**
MANIHOCS	MARINERS	**MATADOR**	MEANDERS	AMENAGES	MEZUZAHS	MINCINGS
MANIKIN	**MARKHOR**	MATADORE	**MEANING**	**MENDERS**	**MICATED**	**MINDING**
MANIKINS	MARKHORS	MATADORS	MEANINGS	AMENDERS	EMICATED	MINDINGS
MANILLA	**MARKING**	**MATCHED**	**MEASURE**	**MENDING**	**MICATES**	**MINDSET**
MANILLAS	MARKINGS	SMATCHED	MEASURED	AMENDING	EMICATES	MINDSETS
MANILLE	**MARLINE**	**MATCHER**	MEASURER	EMENDING	**MICELLA**	**MINEOLA**
MANILLES	MARLINES	MATCHERS	MEASURES	MENDINGS	MICELLAS	MINEOLAS
MANIPLE	**MARLING**	**MATCHES**	**MECONIN**	**MENFOLK**	**MICELLE**	**MINERAL**
MANIPLES	MARLINGS	SMATCHES	MECONINS	MENFOLKS	MICELLES	MINERALS
MANITOU	**MARMITE**	**MATELOT**	**MEDALET**	**MENORAH**	**MICHING**	**MINETTE**
MANITOUS	MARMITES	MATELOTE	MEDALETS	MENORAHS	MICHINGS	MINETTES
MANJACK	**MARMOSE**	MATELOTS	**MEDDLER**	**MENTHOL**	**MICROBE**	**MINEVER**
MANJACKS	MARMOSES	**MATINEE**	MEDDLERS	MENTHOLS	MICROBES	MINEVERS
MANKIND	MARMOSET	MATINEES	**MEDIANT**	**MENTION**	**MICRONS**	**MINGLER**
MANKINDS	**MARPLOT**	**MATRICE**	MEDIANTS	MENTIONS	OMICRONS	MINGLERS
MANNITE	MARPLOTS	MATRICES	**MEDIATE**	**MERCHET**	**MICTION**	**MINIATE**
MANNITES	**MARQUEE**	**MATTERS**	MEDIATED	MERCHETS	MICTIONS	MINIATED
MANNOSE	MARQUEES	SMATTERS	MEDIATES	**MERFOLK**	**MIDDIES**	MINIATES
MANNOSES	**MARQUES**	**MATTING**	**MEDICAL**	MERFOLKS	SMIDDIES	**MINICAB**
MANPACK	MARQUESS	MATTINGS	MEDICALS	**MERGING**	**MIDIRON**	MINICABS
MANPACKS	**MARQUIS**	**MATTOCK**	**MEDULLA**	EMERGING	MIDIRONS	**MINICAR**
MANRENT	MARQUISE	MATTOCKS	MEDULLAE	SMIDGING	**MIDLAND**	MINICARS
MANRENTS	**MARRIER**	**MATTOID**	MEDULLAR	**MERLING**	MIDLANDS	**MINIKIN**
MANSARD	MARRIERS	MATTOIDS	MEDULLAS	MERLINGS	MIDLANDS	MINIKINS
MANSARDS	**MARSHAL**	**MATURES**	**MEDUSAN**	**MERMAID**	**MIDMOST**	**MINISUB**
MANSION	MARSHALS	MATUREST	MEDUSANS	MERMAIDS	AMIDMOST	MINISUBS
MANSIONS	**MARTENS**	**MATWEED**	**MEERCAT**	**MERRIES**	MIDMOSTS	**MINIVER**
MANTEAU	SMARTENS	MATWEEDS	MEERCATS	MERRIEST	**MIDNOON**	MINIVERS
MANTEAUS	**MARTING**	**MATZOON**	**MEERKAT**	**MERSION**	MIDNOONS	**MINIVET**
				EMERSION		

MINIVETS
MINNICK
MINNICKS
MINNOCK
MINNOCKS
MINSTER
MINSTERS
MINTAGE
MINTAGES
MINUEND
MINUENDS
MINUTES
MINUTEST
MINUTIA
MINUTIAE
MIRACLE
MIRACLES
MIRADOR
MIRADORS
MIRBANE
MIRBANES
MIRKIER
SMIRKIER
MISCALL
MISCALLS
MISCAST
MISCASTS
MISDATE
MISDATED
MISDATES
MISDEAL
MISDEALS
MISDEALT
MISDEED
MISDEEDS
MISDEEM
MISDEEMS
MISDIET
MISDIETS
MISDOER
MISDOERS
MISDRAW
MISDRAWN
MISDRAWS
MISEASE
MISEASES
MISFALL
MISFALLS
MISFARE
MISFARED
MISFARES
MISFILE
MISFILED
MISFILES
MISFIRE
MISFIRED
MISFIRES
MISFORM
MISFORMS
MISGIVE
MISGIVEN
MISGIVES
MISHEAR
MISHEARD
MISHEARS
MISHMEE
MISHMEES
MISJOIN
MISJOINS
MISKNOW

MISKNOWN
MISKNOWS
MISLEAD
MISLEADS
MISLIKE
MISLIKED
MISLIKER
MISLIKES
MISLIVE
MISLIVED
MISLIVES
MISLUCK
MISLUCKS
MISMAKE
MISMAKES
MISMATE
MISMATED
MISMATES
MISNAME
MISNAMED
MISNAMES
MISPLAY
MISPLAYS
MISRATE
MISRATED
MISRATES
MISREAD
MISREADS
MISRULE
MISRULED
MISRULES
MISSEEM
MISSEEMS
MISSEND
MISSENDS
MISSIES
MISSIEST
MISSILE
EMISSILE
MISSILES
MISSING
AMISSING
MISSION
EMISSION
MISSIONS
MISSIVE
EMISSIVE
OMISSIVE
MISSIVES
MISSTEP
MISSTEPS
MISSUIT
MISSUITS
MISTAKE
MISTAKEN
MISTAKES
MISTELL
MISTELLS
MISTERM
MISTERMS
MISTICO
MISTICOS
MISTIME
MISTIMED
MISTIMES
MISTING
MISTINGS
MISTRAL
MISTRALS

MISTUNE
MISTUNED
MISTUNES
MISUSER
MISUSERS
MISWEEN
MISWEENS
MISWEND
MISWENDS
MISWORD
MISWORDS
MISYOKE
MISYOKED
MISYOKES
MITHERS
SMITHERS
MITOGEN
MITOGENS
MITOSES
AMITOSES
AMITOSIS
MITOTIC
AMITOTIC
MITZVAH
MITZVAHS
MIXTION
MIXTIONS
MIXTURE
MIXTURES
MIZMAZE
MIZMAZES
MOBSTER
MOBSTERS
MOCHELL
MOCHELLS
MOCKAGE
MOCKAGES
MOCKING
MOCKINGS
SMOCKING
MODICUM
MODICUMS
MODISTE
MODISTES
MOELLON
MOELLONS
MOFETTE
MOFETTES
MOIDORE
MOIDORES
MOILING
SMOILING
MOINEAU
MOINEAUS
MOISTEN
MOISTENS
MOITHER
MOITHERS
MOLERAT
MOLERATS
MOLIMEN
MOLIMENS
MOLLUSC
MOLLUSCS
MOLLUSK
MOLLUSKS
MONARCH
MONARCHS
MONARCHY

MONARDA
MONARDAS
MONAXON
MONAXONS
MONDAIN
MONDAINE
MONDAINS
MONEYER
MONEYERS
MONGREL
MONGRELS
MONIKER
MONIKERS
MONILIA
MONILIAS
MONITOR
MONITORS
MONITORY
MONOCLE
MONOCLED
MONOCLES
MONOCOT
MONOCOTS
MONOFIL
MONOFILS
MONOMER
MONOMERS
MONSOON
MONSOONS
MONSTER
MONSTERA
MONSTERS
MONTAGE
MONTAGES
MONTANT
MONTANTO
MONTANTS
MONTERO
MONTEROS
MONTURE
MONTURES
MOOCHED
MOOCHER
MOOCHERS
MOOCHES
SMOOCHES
MOODIES
MOODIEST
MOOKTAR
MOOKTARS
MOONEYE
MOONEYES
MOONIES
MOONIEST
MOONLET
MOONLETS
MOONSET
MOONSETS
MOORAGE
MOORAGES
MOORHEN
MOORHENS
MOORILL
MOORILLS
MOORING
MOORINGS
SMOORING
MOORLOG
MOORLOGS

MOOTING
SMOOTING
MOOTINGS
MOOVING
AMOOVING
MORAINE
MORAINES
MORCEAU
MORCEAUX
MORDANT
MORDENT
MORDENTS
MORELLO
MORELLOS
MORICHE
MORICHES
MORISCO
MORISCOS
MORLING
MORLINGS
MORMAOR
MORMAORS
MORNING
MORNINGS
MOROCCO
MOROCCOS
MORPHEW
MORPHEWS
MORPHIA
MORPHIAS
MORRHUA
MORRHUAS
MORRICE
MORRICES
MORRION
MORRIONS
MORSURE
MORSURES
MORTICE
MORTICED
MORTICER
MORTICES
MORTISE
MORTISED
MORTISER
MORTISES
MORWONG
MORWONGS
MOSSIES
MOSSIEST
MOTHERS
SMOTHERS
MOTHERY
SMOTHERY
MOTIONS
EMOTIONS
MOUCHED
SMOUCHED
MOUCHER
MOUCHERS
MOUCHES
SMOUCHES
MOUFLON
MOUFLONS
MOULAGE
MOULAGES
MOULDER
SMOULDER

MOULDERS
SMOULDERS
MOUNTED
AMOUNTED
MOUNTER
MOUNTERS
MOUNTIE
MOUNTIES
MOURNER
MOURNERS
MOUSAKA
MOUSAKAS
MOUSERS
SMOUSERS
MOUSIES
MOUSIEST
MOUSING
SMOUSING
MOUSINGS
MOUSMEE
MOUSMEES
MOUTHER
MOUTHERS
MOVABLE
MOVABLES
MOWBURN
MOWBURNS
MOWBURNT
MOYLING
SMOYLING
MOZETTA
MOZETTAS
MRIDANG
MRIDANGA
MRIDANGS
MUCHELL
MUCHELLS
MUCIGEN
MUCIGENS
MUDDIES
MUDDIEST
MUDDLER
MUDDLERS
MUDIRIA
MUDIRIAS
MUDLARK
MUDLARKS
MUDPACK
MUDPACKS
MUDSCOW
MUDSCOWS
MUDWORT
MUDWORTS
MUEDDIN
MUEDDINS
MUEZZIN
MUEZZINS
MUFFLER
MUFFLERS
MUGGING
MUGGINGS
MUGSHOT
MUGSHOTS
MUGWORT
MUGWORTS
MUGWUMP
MUGWUMPS
MUKHTAR
MUKHTARS
MULATTA

MULATTAS
MULATTO
MULATTOS
MULLEIN
MULLEINS
MULLION
MULLIONS
MULLOCK
MULLOCKS
MULMULL
MULMULLS
MULTURE
MULTURED
MULTURER
MULTURES
MUMBLER
MUMBLERS
MUMMING
MUMMINGS
MUMMOCK
MUMMOCKS
MUNCHER
MUNCHERS
MUNDANE
MUNDANER
MUNNION
MUNNIONS
MUNSTER
MUNSTERS
MUNTING
MUNTINGS
MUNTJAC
MUNTJACS
MUNTJAK
MUNTJAKS
MUONIUM
MUONIUMS
MURAENA
MURAENAS
MURGEON
MURGEONS
MURIATE
MURIATED
MURIATES
MURLAIN
MURLAINS
MURRAIN
MURRAINS
MURRION
MURRIONS
MURTHER
MURTHERS
MUSCONE
MUSCONES
MUSETTE
AMUSETTE
MUSETTES
MUSICAL
MUSICALE
MUSICALS
MUSIMON
MUSIMONS
MUSKONE
MUSKONES
MUSTANG
MUSTANGS
MUSTARD
MUSTARDS
MUTAGEN
MUTAGENS

MUTCHES	NANKEENS	NEEDLES	SNICKERS	NOCKING	NOTITIAS	NYMPHAE
SMUTCHES	NAPHTHA	NEEDLESS	NICKING	KNOCKING	NOUMENA	NYMPHAEA
MUZZLER	NAPHTHAS	NEEZING	SNICKING	NOCTUID	NOUMENAL	NYMPHET
MUZZLERS	NAPPERS	SNEEZING	NICTATE	NOCTUIDS	NOURICE	NYMPHETS
MYALGIA	KNAPPERS	NEGLECT	NICTATED	NOCTULE	NOURICES	OAKLING
MYALGIAS	SNAPPERS	NEGLECTS	NICTATES	NOCTULES	NOURSLE	OAKLINGS
MYALISM	NAPPIER	NEGLIGE	NIFFERS	NOCTURN	NOURSLED	OARIEST
MYALISMS	SNAPPIER	NEGLIGEE	SNIFFERS	NOCTURNE	NOURSLES	HOARIEST
MYCELIA	NAPPIES	NEGLIGES	NIFFIER	NOCTURNS	NOUSELL	ROARIEST
MYCELIAL	NAPPIEST	NEGROID	SNIFFIER	NODDING	NOUSELLS	OARWEED
MYELOMA	NAPPING	NEGROIDS	NIFFING	SNODDING	NOVELLA	OARWEEDS
MYELOMAS	KNAPPING	NELUMBO	SNIFFING	NODDINGS	NOVELLAE	OATCAKE
MYLODON	SNAPPING	NELUMBOS	NIFTIER	NOGGING	NOVELLAS	OATCAKES
MYLODONS	NARGILE	NEMESIA	SNIFTIER	SNOGGING	NOWHERE	OATMEAL
MYLODONT	NARGILEH	NEMESIAS	NIGELLA	NOGGINGS	NOWHERES	OATMEALS
MYNHEER	NARGILES	NEOLITH	NIGELLAS	NOINTED	NOYANCE	OBELION
MYNHEERS	NARRATE	NEOLITHS	NIGGARD	ANOINTED	NOYANCES	OBELIONS
MYOGRAM	NARRATED	NEONATE	NIGGARDS	NOMARCH	NUBBIER	OBELISE
MYOGRAMS	NARRATES	NEONATES	NIGGERS	NOMARCHS	KNUBBIER	OBELISED
MYOSOTE	NARTJIE	NEPHRON	SNIGGERS	NOMARCHY	SNUBBIER	OBELISES
MYOSOTES	NARTJIES	NEPHRONS	NIGGLED	NOMBRIL	NUBBING	OBELISK
MYOTUBE	NARWHAL	NERVATE	SNIGGLED	NOMBRILS	SNUBBING	OBELISKS
MYOTUBES	NARWHALS	ENERVATE	NIGGLER	NOMINAL	NUBBLED	OBELIZE
MYRBANE	NASHGAB	NERVINE	SNIGGLER	NOMINALS	KNUBBLED	OBELIZED
MYRBANES	NASHGABS	NERVINES	NIGGLERS	NOMINEE	NUBBLES	OBELIZES
MYRINGA	NASTIES	NERVING	NIGGLES	NOMINEES	KNUBBLES	OBLIGEE
MYRINGAS	NASTIEST	ENERVING	SNIGGLES	NONAGON	NUCLEAR	OBLIGEES
MYRRHOL	NATCHES	NERVULE	NIGHTED	NONAGONS	NUCLEARY	OBLIGOR
MYRRHOLS	SNATCHES	NERVULES	KNIGHTED	NONETTE	NUCLEIN	OBLIGORS
MYTHISE	NATIONS	NERVURE	NIGHTIE	NONETTES	NUCLEINS	OBLIQUE
MYTHISED	ENATIONS	NERVURES	NIGHTIES	NONETTO	NUCLEON	OBLIQUER
MYTHISES	NATRIUM	NETBALL	NIGHTLY	NONETTOS	NUCLEONS	OBLIQUES
MYTHISM	NATRIUMS	NETBALLS	KNIGHTLY	NONSUIT	NUCLIDE	OBSCENE
MYTHISMS	NATURAL	NETSUKE	NIOBATE	NONSUITS	NUCLIDES	OBSCENER
MYTHIST	NATURALS	NETSUKES	NIOBATES	NONUPLE	NUDGING	OBSCURE
MYTHISTS	NAVARCH	NETTING	NIOBITE	NONUPLET	SNUDGING	OBSCURED
MYTHIZE	NAVARCHS	NETTINGS	NIOBITES	NOOKIES	NULLING	OBSCURER
MYTHIZED	NAVARCHY	NETWORK	NIOBIUM	NOOKIEST	NULLINGS	OBSCURES
MYTHIZES	NAVARHO	NETWORKS	NIOBIUMS	NOONDAY	NUMERAL	OBSERVE
NAARTJE	NAVARHOS	NEURINE	NIPPERS	NOONDAYS	NUMERALS	OBSERVED
NAARTJES	NAVARIN	NEURINES	SNIPPERS	NOONING	NUNATAK	OBSERVER
NACARAT	NAVARINS	NEURISM	NIPPIER	NOONINGS	NUNATAKS	OBSERVES
NACARATS	NAVETTE	ANEURISM	SNIPPIER	NORIMON	NUNDINE	OBTRUDE
NACELLE	NAVETTES	NEURISMS	NIPPING	NORIMONS	NUNDINES	OBTRUDED
NACELLES	NAYWARD	NEURITE	SNIPPING	NORLAND	NUNHOOD	OBTRUDER
NACRITE	NAYWARDS	NEURITES	NIRVANA	NORLANDS	NUNHOODS	OBTRUDES
NACRITES	NAYWORD	NEUROMA	NIRVANAS	NORTHER	NUNSHIP	OBVERSE
NAGAPIE	NAYWORDS	NEUROMAS	NITERIE	NORTHERN	NUNSHIPS	OBVERSES
NAGAPIES	NEAPING	NEURONE	NITERIES	NORTHERS	NUPTIAL	OBVIATE
NAGGIER	SNEAPING	NEURONES	NITHING	NORWARD	NUPTIALS	OBVIATED
KNAGGIER	NEARING	NEUSTON	NITHINGS	NORWARDS	NURAGHI	OBVIATES
SNAGGIER	ANEARING	NEUSTONS	NITRATE	NOSEBAG	NURAGHIC	OCARINA
NAGGING	NEBBICH	NEUTRAL	NITRATED	NOSEBAGS	NURLING	OCARINAS
SNAGGING	NEBBICHS	NEUTRALS	NITRATES	NOSEGAY	KNURLING	OCCIPUT
NAGMAAL	NEBBING	NEUTRON	NITRIDE	NOSEGAYS	NURTURE	OCCIPUTS
NAGMAALS	SNEBBING	NEUTRONS	NITRIDED	NOSTRIL	NURTURED	OCCLUDE
NAILERY	NEBBISH	NEWCOME	NITRIDES	NOSTRILS	NURTURER	OCCLUDED
SNAILERY	NEBBISHE	NEWCOMER	NITRILE	NOSTRUM	NURTURES	OCCLUDES
NAILING	NECKING	NEWSBOY	NITRILES	NOSTRUMS	NUTCASE	OCEANID
SNAILING	SNECKING	NEWSBOYS	NITRITE	NOTABLE	NUTCASES	OCEANIDS
NAILINGS	NECKINGS	NEWSIES	NITRITES	NOTABLES	NUTMEAL	OCHERED
NAIVETE	NECKLET	NEWSIEST	NOBBIER	NOTAEUM	NUTMEALS	TOCHERED
NAIVETES	NECKLETS	NIBBING	SNOBBIER	NOTAEUMS	NUTTING	OCTAGON
NAMASTE	NECKTIE	SNIBBING	NOBBLED	NOTCHEL	NUTTINGS	OCTAGONS
NAMASTES	NECKTIES	NIBBLER	KNOBBLED	NOTCHELS	NUZZLED	OCTAPLA
NANDINE	NECROSE	NIBBLERS	NOBBLER	NOTELET	SNUZZLED	OCTAPLAS
NANDINES	NECROSED	NIBLICK	NOBBLERS	NOTELETS	NUZZLES	OCTETTE
NANISMS	NECROSES	NIBLICKS	NOBBLES	NOTHING	SNUZZLES	OCTETTES
ONANISMS	NEEDLER	NICKERS	KNOBBLES	NOTHINGS	NYLGHAU	OCTOPOD
NANKEEN	NEEDLERS	KNICKERS		NOTITIA	NYLGHAUS	

OCTOPODS	COLDNESS	**OOSPORE**	ORDINEES	OUAKARIS	**OUTHYRE**	OUTROARS
OCTUPLE	**OLDSTER**	ZOOSPORE	**ORDURES**	**OULAKAN**	OUTHYRED	**OUTROOP**
OCTUPLED	OLDSTERS	OOSPORES	BORDURES	OULAKANS	OUTHYRES	OUTROOPS
OCTUPLES	**OLEARIA**	**OOZIEST**	**OREGANO**	**OURALIS**	**OUTINGS**	**OUTROOT**
OCTUPLET	OLEARIAS	BOOZIEST	OREGANOS	WOURALIS	POUTINGS	OUTROOTS
OCULATE	**OLEFINE**	WOOZIEST	**OREWEED**	**OURIEST**	ROUTINGS	**OUTROPE**
LOCULATE	OLEFINES	**OPALINE**	OREWEEDS	LOURIEST	**OUTJEST**	OUTROPER
OCULATED	**OLIGIST**	OPALINES	**ORGANZA**	**OURSELF**	OUTJESTS	OUTROPES
OCULIST	OLIGISTS	**OPAQUES**	ORGANZAS	YOURSELF	**OUTJUMP**	**OUTSAIL**
OCULISTS	**OLIVINE**	OPAQUEST	**ORGIAST**	**OUSTERS**	OUTJUMPS	OUTSAILS
ODALISK	OLIVINES	**OPENING**	ORGIASTS	JOUSTERS	**OUTLAND**	**OUTSELL**
ODALISKS	**OLOGIES**	OPENINGS	**ORIFICE**	ROUSTERS	OUTLANDS	OUTSELLS
ODALLER	OOLOGIES	**OPERAND**	ORIFICES	**OUSTING**	**OUTLAST**	**OUTSHOT**
ODALLERS	**OLOROSO**	OPERANDS	ORIGAMI	JOUSTING	OUTLASTS	OUTSHOTS
ODDBALL	DOLOROSO	**OPERANT**	ORIGAMIS	MOUSTING	**OUTLEAP**	**OUTSIDE**
ODDBALLS	OLOROSOS	OPERANTS	**ORIGANE**	ROUSTING	OUTLEAPS	OUTSIDER
ODDMENT	DOLOROSOS	**OPERATE**	ORIGANES	OUSTITI	OUTLEAPT	OUTSIDES
ODDMENTS	**OLYCOOK**	OPERATED	**OROLOGY**	OUSTITIS	**OUTLIER**	**OUTSIZE**
ODYLISM	OLYCOOKS	OPERATES	HOROLOGY	**OUTBACK**	OUTLIERS	OUTSIZED
ODYLISMS	**OLYKOEK**	**OPINION**	**OROPESA**	OUTBACKS	**OUTLINE**	OUTSIZES
ODYSSEY	OLYKOEKS	OPINIONS	OROPESAS	**OUTBRAG**	OUTLINED	**OUTSOAR**
ODYSSEYS	**OMENTUM**	**OPORICE**	**ORPHREY**	OUTBRAGS	OUTLINES	OUTSOARS
OENOMEL	LOMENTUM	OPORICES	ORPHREYS	**OUTBURN**	**OUTLIVE**	**OUTSOLE**
OENOMELS	MOMENTUM	**OPOSSUM**	ORPINES	OUTBURNS	OUTLIVED	OUTSOLES
OERSTED	TOMENTUM	OPOSSUMS	FORPINES	OUTBURNT	OUTLIVES	**OUTSPAN**
OERSTEDS	**OMICRON**	**OPPIDAN**	**ORRISES**	**OUTCAST**	**OUTLOOK**	OUTSPANS
OESTRUM	OMICRONS	OPPIDANS	MORRISES	OUTCASTE	OUTLOOKS	**OUTSTAY**
OESTRUMS	**OMITTER**	**OPPOSER**	**ORTOLAN**	OUTCASTS	**OUTMODE**	OUTSTAYS
OFFENCE	OMITTERS	OPPOSERS	PORTOLAN	**OUTCOME**	OUTMODED	**OUTSTEP**
OFFENCES	**OMNIFIC**	**OPSONIN**	ORTOLANS	OUTCOMES	OUTMODES	OUTSTEPS
OFFENSE	SOMNIFIC	OPSONINS	**OSCULUM**	**OUTCROP**	**OUTMOVE**	**OUTTAKE**
OFFENSES	**ONANISM**	**OPUNTIA**	OSCULUMS	OUTCROPS	OUTMOVED	OUTTAKEN
OFFERED	ONANISMS	OPUNTIAS	**OSMIATE**	**OUTDARE**	OUTMOVES	OUTTAKES
COFFERED	**ONANIST**	**OPUSCLE**	OSMIATES	OUTDARED	**OUTNAME**	**OUTTALK**
GOFFERED	ONANISTS	OPUSCLES	**OSMOSES**	OUTDARES	OUTNAMED	OUTTALKS
OFFEREE	**ONCOGEN**	**ORACLES**	COSMOSES	**OUTDATE**	OUTNAMES	**OUTTELL**
OFFEREES	ONCOGENE	CORACLES	KOSMOSES	OUTDATED	**OUTPACE**	OUTTELLS
OFFERER	ONCOGENS	**ORANGER**	**OSMUNDA**	OUTDATES	OUTPACED	**OUTTURN**
OFFERERS	**ONDATRA**	ORANGERY	OSMUNDAS	**OUTDOOR**	OUTPACES	OUTTURNS
OFFEROR	ONDATRAS	**ORANGES**	**OSSELET**	OUTDOORS	**OUTPART**	**OUTVOTE**
OFFERORS	**ONDINGS**	ORANGEST	OSSELETS	**OUTDURE**	OUTPARTS	OUTVOTED
OFFICER	BONDINGS	**ORARIAN**	**OSSETER**	OUTDURED	**OUTPEEP**	OUTVOTER
OFFICERS	**ONENESS**	ORARIANS	OSSETERS	OUTDURES	OUTPEEPS	OUTVOTES
OFFLOAD	DONENESS	**ORARION**	**OSSICLE**	**OUTEDGE**	**OUTPEER**	**OUTWALK**
OFFLOADS	GONENESS	ORARIONS	OSSICLES	OUTEDGES	OUTPEERS	OUTWALKS
OFFSCUM	LONENESS	**ORARIUM**	**OSTEOMA**	**OUTFACE**	**OUTPLAY**	**OUTWARD**
OFFSCUMS	**ONEYERS**	ORARIUMS	OSTEOMAS	OUTFACED	OUTPLAYS	OUTWARDS
OFFSIDE	MONEYERS	**ORATION**	**OSTIOLE**	OUTFACES	**OUTPORT**	**OUTWEAR**
OFFSIDER	**ONGOING**	ORATIONS	OSTIOLES	**OUTFALL**	OUTPORTS	OUTWEARS
OFFSIDES	ONGOINGS	**ORATORY**	**OSTLERS**	OUTFALLS	**OUTPOST**	OUTWEARY
OFFTAKE	**ONSTEAD**	MORATORY	HOSTLERS	**OUTFLOW**	OUTPOSTS	**OUTWEED**
OFFTAKES	ONSTEADS	**ORBITAL**	**OTALGIA**	OUTFLOWN	**OUTPOUR**	GOUTWEED
OFTENER	**ONYCHIA**	ORBITALS	OTALGIAS	OUTFLOWS	OUTPOURS	OUTWEEDS
SOFTENER	ONYCHIAS	**ORBITER**	**OTARIES**	**OUTFOOT**	**OUTPRAY**	**OUTWEEP**
OILIEST	**OOGONIA**	ORBITERS	NOTARIES	OUTFOOTS	OUTPRAYS	OUTWEEPS
ROILIEST	OOGONIAL	**ORCHARD**	ROTARIES	**OUTGATE**	**OUTRACE**	**OUTWELL**
SOILIEST	**OOLAKAN**	ORCHARDS	VOTARIES	OUTGATES	OUTRACED	OUTWELLS
OILSKIN	OOLAKANS	**ORCINOL**	**OTOCYST**	**OUTGIVE**	OUTRACES	**OUTWICK**
OILSKINS	**OOLITES**	ORCINOLS	OTOCYSTS	OUTGIVEN	**OUTRAGE**	OUTWICKS
OINTING	ZOOLITES	**ORDERED**	**OTOLITH**	OUTGIVES	OUTRAGED	**OUTWIND**
JOINTING	**OOLITIC**	BORDERED	OTOLITHS	**OUTGOER**	OUTRAGES	OUTWINDS
NOINTING	ZOOLITIC	**ORDERER**	**OTTERED**	OUTGOERS	**OUTRANK**	**OUTWING**
POINTING	**OOMIACK**	ORDERERS	HOTTERED	**OUTGROW**	OUTRANKS	OUTWINGS
OKIMONO	OOMIACKS	**ORDINAL**	POTTERED	OUTGROWN	**OUTRATE**	**OUTWORK**
OKIMONOS	**OOPHYTE**	ORDINALS	TOTTERED	OUTGROWS	OUTRATED	OUTWORKS
OLDENED	ZOOPHYTE	**ORDINAR**	**OTTOMAN**	**OUTHAUL**	OUTRATES	**OUVRAGE**
BOLDENED	OOPHYTES	ORDINARS	OTTOMANS	OUTHAULS	**OUTRIDE**	OUVRAGES
GOLDENED	**OORIEST**	**ORDINARY**	**OUABAIN**	**OUTHIRE**	OUTRIDER	**OUVRIER**
OLDNESS	MOORIEST	ORDINARY	OUABAINS	OUTHIRED	OUTRIDES	OUVRIERE
BOLDNESS	GOOSIEST	**ORDINEE**	OUAKARI	OUTHIRES	**OUTROAR**	OUVRIERS

OVARIES	OVERTLY	PADDINGS	PALMIST	PAPILLA	PARONYMY	PATAGIAL
COVARIES	COVERTLY	PADDLER	PALMISTS	PAPILLAE	PAROTID	PATAMAR
OVATION	OVERTOP	PADDLERS	PALMYRA	PAPILLAR	PAROTIDS	PATAMARS
NOVATION	OVERTOPS	PADDOCK	PALMYRAS	PAPOOSE	PARPANE	PATBALL
OVATIONS	OVERUSE	PADDOCKS	PALOOKA	PAPOOSES	PARPANES	PATBALLS
OVERACT	OVERUSED	PADELLA	PALOOKAS	PAPPIES	PARPEND	PATCHER
OVERACTS	OVERUSES	PADELLAS	PALPATE	PAPPIEST	PARPENDS	PATCHERS
OVERALL	OVICIDE	PADLOCK	PALPATED	PAPRIKA	PARPENT	PATCHERY
COVERALL	OVICIDES	PADLOCKS	PALPATES	PAPRIKAS	PARPENTS	PATELLA
OVERALLS	OVIDUCT	PAENULA	PALSIES	PARABLE	PARQUET	PATELLAE
OVERAWE	OVIDUCTS	PAENULAE	PALSIEST	SPARABLE	PARQUETS	PATELLAR
OVERAWED	OVULATE	PAENULAS	PAMPERO	PARABLED	PARROCK	PATELLAS
OVERAWES	OVULATED	PAEONIC	PAMPEROS	PARABLES	PARROCKS	PATHWAY
OVERBID	OVULATES	PAEONICS	PANACEA	PARACME	PARSING	PATHWAYS
OVERBIDS	OWLIEST	PAGEANT	PANACEAN	PARACMES	PARSINGS	PATIENT
OVERBUY	LOWLIEST	PAGEANTS	PANACEAS	PARADOX	PARSLEY	PATIENTS
OVERBUYS	OXALATE	PAGURID	PANACHE	PARADOXY	PARSLEYS	PATRIAL
OVERDYE	OXALATES	PAGURIDS	PANACHES	PARAFLE	PARSNEP	PATRIALS
OVERDYED	OXAZINE	PAILFUL	PANCAKE	PARAFLES	PARSNEPS	PATRICK
OVERDYES	OXAZINES	PAILFULS	PANCAKED	PARAGON	PARSNIP	PATRICKS
OVEREAT	OXBLOOD	PAILLON	PANCAKES	PARAGONS	PARSNIPS	PATRIOT
OVEREATS	OXBLOODS	PAILLONS	PANDECT	PARANYM	PARTAKE	PATRIOTS
OVEREYE	OXIDANT	PAINING	PANDECTS	PARANYMS	PARTAKEN	PATROON
OVEREYED	OXIDANTS	SPAINING	PANDOOR	PARAPET	PARTAKER	PATROONS
OVEREYES	OXIDASE	PAINTER	PANDOORS	PARAPETS	PARTAKES	PATTERN
OVERGET	OXIDASES	PAINTERS	PANDORA	PARASOL	PARTIAL	PATTERNS
OVERGETS	OXIDATE	PAIOCKE	PANDORAS	PARASOLS	PARTIALS	PATTERS
OVERHIT	OXIDATED	PAIOCKES	PANDORE	PARATHA	PARTING	SPATTERS
OVERHITS	OXIDATES	PAIRIAL	PANDORES	PARATHAS	PARTINGS	PATTING
OVERING	OXIDISE	PAIRIALS	PANDOUR	PARAZOA	PARTITA	SPATTING
COVERING	OXIDISED	PAIRING	PANDOURS	PARAZOAN	PARTITAS	PATULIN
DOVERING	OXIDISER	PAIRINGS	PANDURA	PARBOIL	PARTLET	PATULINS
HOVERING	OXIDISES	PAISANO	PANDURAS	PARBOILS	PARTLETS	PAUSING
OVERJOY	OXIDIZE	PAISANOS	PANGENE	PARCHES	PARTNER	PAUSINGS
OVERJOYS	OXIDIZED	PAISLEY	PANGENES	PARCHESI	PARTNERS	PAVIOUR
OVERLAP	OXIDIZER	PAISLEYS	PANGING	PARDALE	PARTURE	PAVIOURS
OVERLAPS	OXIDIZES	PAJOCKE	SPANGING	PARDALES	PARTURES	PAVLOVA
OVERLAY	OXONIUM	PAJOCKES	PANGRAM	PARDNER	PARVENU	PAVLOVAS
OVERLAYS	OXONIUMS	PAKAPOO	PANGRAMS	PARDNERS	PARVENUS	PAWNERS
OVERLIE	OXYGENS	PAKAPOOS	PANICLE	PAREIRA	PARVISE	SPAWNERS
OVERLIER	LOXYGENS	PAKFONG	PANICLED	PAREIRAS	PARVISES	PAWNING
OVERLIES	OXYTONE	PAKFONGS	PANICLES	PARELLA	PASSADE	SPAWNING
OVERMAN	OXYTONES	PAKTONG	PANNAGE	PARELLAS	PASSADES	PAXIUBA
OVERMANS	OYSTERS	PAKTONGS	PANNAGES	PARELLE	PASSADO	PAXIUBAS
OVERNET	ROYSTERS	PALABRA	PANNICK	PARELLES	PASSADOS	PAYMENT
OVERNETS	OZONISE	PALABRAS	PANNICKS	PARFAIT	PASSAGE	PAYMENTS
OVERPAY	OZONISED	PALADIN	PANNIER	PARFAITS	PASSAGED	PAYROLL
OVERPAYS	OZONISER	PALADINS	PANNIERS	PARGANA	PASSAGES	PAYROLLS
OVERRAN	OZONISES	PALATAL	PANNING	PARGANAS	PASSING	PAYSAGE
OVERRANK	OZONIZE	PALATALS	SPANNING	PARGING	PASSINGS	PAYSAGES
OVERRED	OZONIZED	PALAVER	PANNINGS	SPARGING	PASSION	PEACHER
OVERREDS	OZONIZER	PALAVERS	PANOCHA	PARISON	PASSIONS	PEACHERS
OVERREN	OZONIZES	PALETOT	PANOCHAS	PARISONS	PASSIVE	PEACOCK
OVERRENS	PABULUM	PALETOTS	PANTHER	PARITOR	PASSIVES	PEACOCKS
OVERRUN	PABULUMS	PALETTE	PANTHERS	PARITORS	PASSKEY	PEACOCKY
OVERRUNS	PACHISI	PALETTES	PANTILE	PARKING	PASSKEYS	PEAKING
OVERSEA	PACHISIS	PALFREY	PANTILED	PARKINGS	PASSMEN	SPEAKING
OVERSEAS	PACIEST	PALFREYS	PANTILES	PARKISH	PASSMENT	PEANING
OVERSEE	SPACIEST	PALLING	PANTINE	SPARKISH	PASTERN	SPEANING
OVERSEEN	PACKAGE	SPALLING	PANTINES	PARKWAY	PASTERNS	PEARLER
OVERSEER	PACKAGED	PALLONE	PANTING	PARKWAYS	PASTIES	PEARLERS
OVERSEES	PACKAGER	PALLONES	PANTINGS	PARLING	PASTIEST	PEARLIN
OVERSET	PACKAGES	PALMATE	PANTLER	SPARLING	PASTIME	PEARLING
OVERSETS	PACKING	PALMATED	PANTLERS	PARLOUR	PASTIMES	PEARLINS
OVERSEW	PACKINGS	PALMFUL	PANTOUM	PARLOURS	PASTING	PEASANT
OVERSEWN	PACKWAY	PALMFULS	PANTOUMS	PAROLEE	PASTINGS	PEASANTS
OVERSEWS	PACKWAYS	PALMIES	PAPERER	PAROLEES	PASTURE	PEASANTY
OVERSOW	PACTION	PALMIEST	PAPERERS	PARONYM	PASTURED	PEASCOD
OVERSOWN	PACTIONS	PALMIET	PAPILIO	PARONYMS	PASTURES	PEASCODS
OVERSOWS	PADDING	PALMIETS	PAPILIOS	PARONYMS	PATAGIA	PEBRINE

PEBRINES	PENDANTS	PERFECTI	PERUSERS	APIARIST	PIGLINGS	PINNACES
PECCAVI	PENDENT	PERFECTO	PERVADE	PIARISTS	PIGMEAT	PINNATE
PECCAVIS	PENDENTS	PERFECTS	PERVADED	PIASTRE	PIGMEATS	PINNATED
PECKING	PENDING	PERFORM	PERVADES	PIASTRES	PIGMENT	PINNERS
SPECKING	SPENDING	PERFORMS	PERVERT	PIBROCH	PIGMENTS	SPINNERS
PECKINGS	PENFOLD	PERFUME	PERVERTS	PIBROCHS	PIGSKIN	PINNETS
PECTISE	PENFOLDS	PERFUMED	PESAUNT	PICADOR	PIGSKINS	SPINNETS
PECTISED	PENGUIN	PERFUMER	PESAUNTS	PICADORS	PIGSNEY	PINNIES
PECTISES	PENGUINS	PERFUMES	PETCOCK	PICAMAR	PIGSNEYS	PINNIES
PECTIZE	PENNANT	PERFUSE	PETCOCKS	PICCOLO	PIGSNIE	PINNING
PECTIZED	PENNANTS	PERFUSED	PETIOLE	PICCOLOS	PIGSNIES	SPINNING
PECTIZES	PENNINE	PERFUSES	PETIOLED	PICENES	PIGTAIL	PINNINGS
PECTOSE	PENNINES	PERGOLA	PETIOLES	EPICENES	PIGTAILS	PINNOCK
PECTOSES	PENSION	PERGOLAS	PETTIES	PICKAXE	PIGWEED	PINNOCKS
PEDDLER	PENSIONS	PERIAPT	PETTIEST	PICKAXES	PIGWEEDS	PINNULA
PEDDLERS	PENTACT	PERIAPTS	PETTING	PICKEER	PIKELET	PINNULAS
PEDICAB	PENTACTS	PERIDIA	SPETTING	PICKEERS	SPIKELET	PINNULE
PEDICABS	PENTANE	PERIDIAL	PETTINGS	PICKING	PIKELETS	PINNULES
PEDICEL	PENTANES	PERIDOT	PETUNIA	PICKINGS	PILCHER	PINOCLE
PEDICELS	PENTENE	PERIDOTE	PETUNIAS	PICKLER	PILCHERS	PINOCLES
PEDICLE	PENTENES	PERIDOTS	PFENNIG	PICKLERS	PILCORN	PINTADO
PEDICLED	PENTHIA	PERIGEE	PFENNIGE	PICKMAW	PILCORNS	PINTADOS
PEDICLES	PENTHIAS	PERIGON	PFENNIGS	PICKMAWS	PILCROW	PINTAIL
PEDRAIL	PENTICE	PERIGONE	PHAEISM	PICOTEE	PILCROWS	PINTAILS
PEDRAILS	PENTICED	PERIGONS	PHAEISMS	PICOTEES	PILEATE	PIONEER
PEDRERO	PENTICES	PERIOST	PHAETON	PICQUET	PILEATED	PIONEERS
PEDREROS	PENTISE	PERIOSTS	PHAETONS	PICQUETS	PILGRIM	PIONING
PEEKABO	PENTISED	PERIQUE	PHALLIN	PICRATE	PILGRIMS	PIONINGS
PEEKABOO	PENTISES	PERIQUES	PHALLINS	PICRATES	PILLAGE	PIPEFUL
PEEKABOS	PENTODE	PERIWIG	PHANTOM	PICRITE	SPILLAGE	PIPEFULS
PEELERS	PENTODES	PERIWIGS	PHANTOMS	PICRITES	PILLAGED	PIPETTE
SPEELERS	PENTOSE	PERJURE	PHANTOMY	PICTURE	PILLAGER	PIPETTED
PEELING	PENTOSES	PERJURED	PHASMID	PICTURED	PILLAGES	PIPETTES
SPEELING	PENUCHE	PERJURER	PHASMIDS	PICTURES	PILLING	PIRAGUA
PEELINGS	PENUCHES	PERJURES	PHEAZAR	PIDDLER	SPILLING	PIRAGUAS
PEERAGE	PENUCHI	PERLITE	PHEAZARS	PIDDLERS	PILLION	PIRANHA
PEERAGES	PENUCHIS	PERLITES	PHELLEM	PIDDOCK	PILLIONS	PIRANHAS
PEERIES	PEONAGE	PERMUTE	PHELLEMS	PIDDOCKS	PILLOCK	PIRATED
PEERIEST	PEONAGES	PERMUTED	PHENATE	PIDGEON	PILLOCKS	SPIRATED
PEERING	PEONISM	PERMUTES	PHENATES	PIDGEONS	PILSNER	PIROGUE
SPEERING	PEONISMS	PERPEND	PHILTER	PIEBALD	PILSNERS	PIROGUES
PEGGING	PEPSINE	PERPENDS	PHILTERS	PIEBALDS	PIMENTO	PISCINA
PEGGINGS	PEPSINES	PERPENT	PHILTRE	PIERAGE	PIMENTOS	PISCINAE
PEISHWA	PEPTIDE	PERPENTS	PHILTRES	PIERAGES	PINBALL	PISCINAS
PEISHWAH	PEPTIDES	PERRIER	PHOBISM	PIERCER	PINBALLS	PISCINE
PEISHWAS	PEPTISE	PERRIERS	PHOBISMS	PIERCERS	PINCASE	PISCINES
PELICAN	PEPTISED	PERSICO	PHOBIST	PIERROT	PINCASES	PISMIRE
PELICANS	PEPTISES	PERSICOS	PHOBISTS	PIERROTS	PINCHER	PISMIRES
PELISSE	PEPTIZE	PERSICOT	PHONATE	PIETISM	PINCHERS	PISSOIR
PELISSES	PEPTIZED	PERSING	PHONATED	PIETISMS	PINDARI	PISSOIRS
PELLACH	PEPTIZES	SPERSING	PHONATES	PIETIST	PINDARIS	PISTOLE
PELLACHS	PEPTONE	PERSIST	PHONEME	PIETISTS	PINFOLD	PISTOLES
PELLACK	PEPTONES	PERSISTS	PHONEMES	PIFFERO	PINFOLDS	PISTOLET
PELLACKS	PERAEON	PERSONA	PHONIES	PIFFEROS	PINGLER	PITAPAT
PELLOCK	PERAEONS	PERSONAE	APHONIES	PIFFLER	PINGLERS	PITAPATS
PELLOCKS	PERCALE	PERSONAL	PHONIEST	PIFFLERS	PINGUIN	PITARAH
PELORIA	PERCALES	PERSONAS	PHOTISM	PIGBOAT	PINGUINS	PITARAHS
PELORIAS	PERCEPT	PERTAIN	PHOTISMS	PIGBOATS	PINHEAD	PITCHER
PELTAST	PERCEPTS	PERTAINS	PHRASER	PIGFEED	PINHEADS	SPITCHER
PELTASTS	PERCHER	PERTAKE	PHRASERS	PIGFEEDS	PINHOLE	PITCHERS
PELTERS	PERCHERS	PERTAKEN	PIAFFER	PIGGIES	PINHOLES	PITFALL
SPELTERS	PERDURE	PERTAKES	PIAFFERS	PIGGIEST	PINIEST	PITFALLS
PELTING	PERDURED	PERTURB	PIANINO	PIGGING	SPINIEST	PITHEAD
PELTINGS	PERDURES	PERTURBS	PIANINOS	PIGGINGS	PINIONS	PITHEADS
PEMICAN	PEREGAL	PERTUSE	PIANISM	PIGHTED	OPINIONS	PITTERS
PEMICANS	PEREGALS	PERTUSED	PIANISMS	SPIGHTED	PINKIES	SPITTERS
PENANCE	PEREIRA	PERUSAL	PIANIST	PIGHTLE	PINKIEST	PITTING
PENANCED	PEREIRAS	PERUSALS	PIANISTE	PIGHTLES	PINKING	SPITTING
PENANCES	PERFECT	PERUSER	PIANISTS	PIGLING	PINKINGS	PITTINGS
PENDANT	PERFECTA	PERUSER	PIARIST	PIGLING	PINNACE	PITTITE

PITTITES	PLAUDITS	PLUMBERY	POLACRES	PONIARD	POSTEEN	POUTHER
PITUITA	PLAYBOY	PLUMBUM	POLARON	PONIARDS	POSTEENS	POUTHERS
PITUITAS	PLAYBOYS	PLUMBUMS	POLARONS	PONTAGE	POSTERN	POUTIER
PITUITE	PLAYING	PLUMCOT	POLECAT	PONTAGES	POSTERNS	SPOUTIER
PITUITES	SPLAYING	PLUMCOTS	POLECATS	PONTIFF	POSTILS	POUTING
PIVOTER	UPLAYING	PLUMIST	POLEMIC	PONTIFFS	APOSTILS	SPOUTING
PIVOTERS	PLAYLET	PLUMISTS	POLEMICS	PONTOON	POSTING	POUTINGS
PLACARD	PLAYLETS	PLUMMET	POLENTA	SPONTOON	POSTINGS	PRABBLE
PLACARDS	PLEADER	PLUMMETS	POLENTAS	PONTOONS	POSTURE	PRABBLES
PLACATE	PLEADERS	PLUMPEN	POLITIC	POOFTAH	POSTURED	PRACTIC
PLACATED	PLEASER	PLUMPENS	POLITICK	POOFTAHS	POSTURER	PRACTICE
PLACATES	PLEASERS	PLUMPER	POLITICO	POOFTER	POSTURES	PRACTICK
PLACCAT	PLECTRE	PLUMPERS	POLITICS	POOFTERS	POTABLE	PRACTICS
PLACCATS	PLECTRES	PLUMULA	POLLACK	POOGYEE	POTABLES	PRAETOR
PLACEBO	PLEDGEE	PLUMULAE	POLLACKS	POOGYEES	POTASSA	PRAETORS
PLACEBOS	PLEDGEES	PLUMULAR	POLLARD	POOKING	POTASSAS	PRAIRIE
PLACING	PLEDGER	PLUMULE	POLLARDS	SPOOKING	POTCHER	PRAIRIED
PLACINGS	PLEDGERS	PLUMULES	POLLING	POOLING	POTCHERS	PRAIRIES
PLACKET	PLEDGET	PLUNDER	POLLINGS	SPOOLING	POTENCE	PRAISED
PLACKETS	PLEDGETS	PLUNDERS	POLLOCK	POPADUM	POTENCES	UPRAISED
PLAFOND	PLEDGOR	PLUNGER	POLLOCKS	POPADUMS	POTHEEN	PRAISER
PLAFONDS	PLEDGORS	PLUNGERS	POLLUTE	POPCORN	POTHEENS	PRAISERS
PLAGIUM	PLENIPO	PLUNKER	POLLUTED	POPCORNS	POTHOLE	PRAISES
PLAGIUMS	PLENIPOS	PLUNKERS	POLLUTER	POPEDOM	POTHOLER	UPRAISES
PLAITER	PLENIST	PLUSAGE	POLLUTES	POPEDOMS	POTHOLES	PRALINE
PLAITERS	PLENISTS	PLUSAGES	POLOIST	POPERIN	POTHOOK	PRALINES
PLANNER	PLEOPOD	PLUSHES	POLOISTS	POPERINS	POTHOOKS	PRANCER
PLANNERS	PLEOPODS	PLUSHEST	POLONIE	POPOVER	POTICHE	PRANCERS
PLANTER	PLEROMA	PLUVIAL	POLONIES	POPOVERS	POTICHES	PRANCKE
PLANTERS	PLEROMAS	PLUVIALS	POLYGAM	POPULAR	POTOROO	PRANCKED
PLANULA	PLEROME	PLYWOOD	POLYGAMS	POPULARS	POTOROOS	PRANCKES
PLANULAE	PLEROMES	PLYWOODS	POLYGAMY	PORIFER	POTTAGE	PRANKLE
PLANULAR	PLESSOR	POACHER	POLYGON	PORIFERS	POTTAGES	PRANKLED
PLASHED	PLESSORS	POACHERS	POLYGONS	PORPESS	POTTERS	PRANKLES
SPLASHED	PLEXURE	POCHARD	POLYGONY	PORPESSE	SPOTTERS	PRATING
PLASHES	PLEXURES	POCHARDS	POLYMER	PORRECT	POTTIER	UPRATING
SPLASHES	PLICATE	POCHOIR	POLYMERS	PORRECTS	SPOTTIER	PRATINGS
PLASHET	PLICATED	POCHOIRS	POLYMERY	PORRIGO	POTTIES	PRATTLE
PLASHETS	PLICATES	POCKARD	POLYNIA	PORRIGOS	POTTIEST	SPRATTLE
PLASMID	PLISKIE	POCKARDS	POLYNIAS	PORTAGE	POTTING	PRATTLED
PLASMIDS	PLISKIES	POCKPIT	POLYNYA	PORTAGES	SPOTTING	PRATTLER
PLASMIN	PLODDER	POCKPITS	POLYNYAS	PORTEND	POUFTAH	PRATTLES
PLASMINS	PLODDERS	PODAGRA	POLYPOD	PORTENDS	POUFTAHS	PRAUNCE
PLASTER	PLONKER	PODAGRAL	POLYPODS	PORTENT	POUFTER	PRAUNCED
PLASTERS	PLONKERS	PODAGRAS	POLYPODY	PORTENTS	POUFTERS	PRAUNCES
PLASTERY	PLOOKIE	PODESTA	POLYZOA	PORTERS	POULARD	PRAWLIN
PLASTIC	PLOOKIER	PODESTAS	POLYZOAN	SPORTERS	POULARDS	PRAWLINS
APLASTIC	PLOSION	POETISE	POMATUM	PORTESS	POULDER	PRAYERS
PLASTICS	PLOSIONS	POETISED	POMATUMS	PORTESSE	POULDERS	SPRAYERS
PLASTID	PLOSIVE	POETISES	POMEROY	PORTICO	POULDRE	PRAYING
PLASTIDS	PLOSIVES	POETIZE	POMEROYS	PORTICOS	POULDRES	SPRAYING
PLATANE	PLOTTER	POETIZED	POMFRET	PORTIER	POULTER	PRAYINGS
PLATANES	PLOTTERS	POETIZES	POMFRETS	SPORTIER	POULTERS	PREASSE
PLATEAU	PLOTTIE	POINADO	POMPANO	PORTIERE	POUNCET	PREASSED
PLATEAUS	PLOTTIES	POINADOS	POMPANOS	PORTING	POUNCETS	PREASSES
PLATEAUX	PLOUKIE	POINDER	POMPELO	SPORTING	POUNDAL	PREBEND
PLATINA	PLOUKIER	POINDERS	POMPELOS	PORTION	POUNDALS	PREBENDS
PLATINAS	PLOUTER	POINTEL	POMPION	PORTIONS	POUNDER	PRECEDE
PLATING	PLOUTERS	POINTELS	POMPIONS	PORTRAY	POUNDERS	PRECEDED
PLATINGS	PLOWTER	POINTER	POMPOON	PORTRAYS	POURING	PRECEDES
PLATOON	PLOWTERS	POINTERS	POMPOONS	POSAUNE	POURINGS	PRECEPT
PLATOONS	PLUCKER	POISSON	PONCEAU	POSAUNES	POURSEW	PRECEPTS
PLATTED	PLUCKERS	POISSONS	PONCEAUS	POSEUSE	POURSEWS	PRECISE
SPLATTED	PLUGGER	POITREL	PONCEAUX	POSEUSES	POURSUE	PRECISED
PLATTER	PLUGGERS	POITRELS	PONDAGE	POSITON	POURSUED	PRECISER
SPLATTER	PLUMAGE	POKEFUL	PONDAGES	POSITONS	POURSUES	PRECISES
PLATTERS	PLUMAGED	POKEFULS	PONGIER	POSSUMS	POUSSIN	PRECOOK
PLAUDIT	PLUMAGES	POLACCA	PONGING	OPOSSUMS	POUSSINS	PRECOOKS
PLAUDITE	PLUMBERS	POLACCAS	SPONGING	POSTAGE	POUTERS	PREDATE
		POLACRE		POSTAGES	SPOUTERS	PREDATED

PREDATES	PRETEND	PROBANGS	PROPAGE	PROVISO	PUPARIA	PYRAMIDS
PREDIAL	PRETENDS	PROBATE	PROPAGED	PROVISOR	PUPARIAL	PYRETIC
PREDIALS	PRETEXT	PROBATED	PROPAGES	PROVISOS	PUPUNHA	APYRETIC
PREDICT	PRETEXTS	PROBATES	PROPALE	PROVOKE	PUPUNHAS	PYREXIA
PREDICTS	PRETZEL	PROBLEM	PROPALED	PROVOKED	PURGING	APYREXIA
PREDOOM	PRETZELS	PROBLEMS	PROPALES	PROVOKER	PURGINGS	PYREXIAL
PREDOOMS	PREVAIL	PROCEED	PROPANE	PROVOKES	PURITAN	PYREXIAS
PREEING	PREVAILS	PROCEEDS	PROPANES	PROVOST	PURITANS	PYROGEN
SPREEING	PREVENE	PROCTOR	PROPEND	PROVOSTS	PURLIEU	PYROGENS
PREEMIE	PREVENED	PROCTORS	PROPENDS	PROWLER	PURLIEUS	PYRRHIC
PREEMIES	PREVENES	PROCURE	PROPENE	PROWLERS	PURLINE	PYRRHICS
PREFACE	PREVENT	PROCURED	PROPENES	PRUNING	PURLINES	PYRROLE
PREFACED	PREVENTS	PROCURER	PROPHET	PRUNINGS	PURLING	PYRROLES
PREFACES	PREVERB	PROCURES	PROPHETS	PRURIGO	PURLINGS	PYTHIUM
PREFADE	PREVERBS	PRODUCE	PROPINE	PRURIGOS	SPURLING	PYTHIUMS
PREFADED	PREVIEW	PRODUCED	PROPINED	PRURITUS	PURLOIN	QUACKLE
PREFADES	PREVIEWS	PRODUCER	PROPINES	PSALTER	PURLOINS	QUACKLED
PREFECT	PREVISE	PRODUCES	PROPONE	PSALTERS	PURPLES	QUACKLES
PREFECTS	PREVISED	PRODUCT	PROPONED	PSALTERY	PURPLEST	QUADRAT
PREFORM	PREVISES	PRODUCTS	PROPONES	PSYCHIC	PURPORT	QUADRATE
PREFORMS	PREZZIE	PROFANE	PROFANE	PSYCHICS	PURPORTS	QUADRATS
PREHEAT	PREZZIES	PROFANED	PROPOSE	PTARMIC	PURPOSE	QUAFFER
PREHEATS	PRIBBLE	PROFANER	PROPOSED	PTARMICS	PURPOSED	QUAFFERS
PREHEND	PRIBBLES	PROFANES	PROPOSER	PTERYLA	PURPOSES	QUAHAUG
PREHENDS	PRICKER	PROFFER	PROPOSES	PTERYLAE	PURPURA	QUAHAUGS
PRELATE	PRICKERS	PROFFERS	PRORATE	PTYALIN	PURPURAS	QUAILED
PRELATES	PRICKET	PROFILE	PRORATED	PTYALINS	PURPURE	SQUAILED
PRELECT	PRICKETS	PROFILED	PRORATES	PUCCOON	PURPURES	QUAKING
PRELECTS	PRICKLE	PROFILER	PROSING	PUCCOONS	PURRING	QUAKINGS
PRELUDE	PRICKLED	PROFILES	PROSINGS	PUCELLE	SPURRING	QUALITY
PRELUDED	PRICKLES	PROFUSE	PROSPER	PUCELLES	PURRINGS	EQUALITY
PRELUDES	PRIGGED	PROFUSER	PROSPERS	PUDDING	PURSUAL	QUANNET
PRELUDI	SPRIGGED	PROGRAM	PROTEAS	SPUDDING	PURSUALS	QUANNETS
PRELUDIO	PRIGGER	PROGRAMS	PROTEASE	PUDDINGS	PURSUER	QUANTIC
PREMIER	PRIGGERS	PROJECT	PROTECT	PUDDINGY	PURSUERS	QUANTICS
PREMIERE	PRIGGERY	PROJECTS	PROTECTS	PUDDLER	PURSUIT	QUARREL
PREMIERS	PRIMAGE	PROLATE	PROTEGE	PUDDLERS	PURSUITS	QUARRELS
PREMISE	PRIMAGES	PROLATED	PROTEGEE	PUDDOCK	PURVIEW	QUARTAN
PREMISED	PRIMATE	PROLATES	PROTEGES	PUDDOCKS	PURVIEWS	QUARTANS
PREMISES	PRIMATES	PROLINE	PROTEID	PUDENDA	PUSHROD	QUARTER
PREMIUM	PRIMERO	PROLINES	PROTEIDS	PUDENDAL	PUSHRODS	QUARTERN
PREMIUMS	PRIMEROS	UPROLLED	PROTEIN	PUFFING	PUSTULE	QUARTERS
PREMOVE	PRIMEUR	PROLLER	PROTEINS	PUFFINGS	PUSTULES	QUARTET
PREMOVED	PRIMEURS	PROLLERS	PROTEND	PUGGIES	PUTCHER	QUARTETS
PREMOVES	PRIMINE	PROLONG	PROTENDS	PUGGIEST	PUTCHERS	QUARTETT
PREPACK	PRIMINES	PROLONGE	PROTEST	PUGGING	PUTCHUK	QUARTIC
PREPACKS	PRIMING	PROLONGS	PROTESTS	PUGGINGS	PUTCHUKS	QUARTICS
PREPARE	PRIMINGS	PROMISE	PROTHYL	PUGGREE	PUTLOCK	QUASHED
PREPARED	PRIMULA	PROMISED	PROTHYLE	PUGGREES	PUTLOCKS	SQUASHED
PREPARER	PRIMULAS	PROMISEE	PROTHYLS	PULDRON	PUTTERS	QUASHEE
PREPARES	PRINCES	PROMISER	PROTIST	PULDRONS	SPUTTERS	QUASHEES
PREPUCE	PRINCESS	PROMISES	PROTISTS	PULSATE	PUTTIER	QUASHES
PREPUCES	PRINTED	PROMMER	PROTIUM	PULSATED	PUTTIERS	QUASHIE
PREQUEL	SPRINTED	PROMMERS	PROTIUMS	PULSATES	PUTTING	QUASHIES
PREQUELS	PRINTER	PROMOTE	PROTYLE	PULTOON	PUTTINGS	QUASSIA
PRESAGE	SPRINTER	PROMOTED	PROTYLES	PULTOONS	PUTTOCK	QUASSIAS
PRESAGED	PRINTERS	PROMOTER	PROULER	PULTURE	PUTTOCKS	QUAYAGE
PRESAGER	PRISAGE	PROMOTES	PROULERS	PULTURES	PUZZLER	QUAYAGES
PRESAGES	PRISAGES	PRONATE	PROVAND	PUMPION	PUZZLERS	QUELLER
PRESENT	PRISING	PRONATED	PROVANDS	PUMPIONS	PYAEMIA	QUELLERS
PRESENTS	UPRISING	PRONATES	PROVEND	PUMPKIN	PYAEMIAS	QUERIST
PRESIDE	PRIVADO	PRONEUR	PROVENDS	PUMPKINS	PYCNITE	QUERISTS
PRESIDED	PRIVADOS	PRONEURS	PROVERB	PUNALUA	PYCNITES	QUESTER
PRESIDES	PRIVATE	PRONOTA	PROVERBS	PUNALUAN	PYEBALD	QUESTERS
PRESSER	PRIVATES	PRONOTAL	PROVIDE	PUNALUAS	PYEBALDS	QUESTOR
PRESSERS	PRIVIES	PRONOUN	PROVIDED	PUNCHER	PYGIDIA	QUESTORS
PRESUME	PRIVIEST	PRONOUNS	PROVIDER	PUNCHERS	PYGIDIAL	QUETZAL
PRESUMED	PROBAND	PROOTIC	PROVIDES	PUNNING	PYRALID	QUETZALS
PRESUMER	PROBANDS	PROOTICS	PROVINE	PUNNINGS	PYRALIDS	QUEUING
PRESUMES	PROBANG		PROVINED	PUNSTER	PYRAMID	
			PROVINES	PUNSTERS		

QUEUINGS	QUOITERS	**RAGBOLT**	RAMBLERS	RANSACKS	**RATPACK**	**READING**
QUEYNIE	**RABANNA**	RAGBOLTS	**RAMBLES**	RANSOMS	RATPACKS	AREADING
QUEYNIES	RABANNAS	**RAGGIER**	BRAMBLES	TRANSOMS	**RATTEEN**	BREADING
QUIBBLE	**RABATTE**	CRAGGIER	**RAMEKIN**	**RANTERS**	RATTEENS	DREADING
QUIBBLED	RABATTED	DRAGGIER	RAMEKINS	GRANTERS	**RATTIER**	TREADING
QUIBBLER	RABATTES	**RAGGIES**	**RAMMERS**	TRANTERS	BRATTIER	READINGS
QUIBBLES	**RABBETS**	RAGGIEST	CRAMMERS	**RANTING**	**RATTING**	**READMIT**
QUIBLIN	DRABBETS	**RAGGING**	**RAMMING**	DRANTING	PRATTING	READMITS
QUIBLINS	**RABBLED**	BRAGGING	CRAMMING	GRANTING	RATTINGS	**READOPT**
QUICKEN	BRABBLED	DRAGGING	DRAMMING	TRANTING	**RATTISH**	READOPTS
QUICKENS	DRABBLED	RAGGINGS	**RAMPAGE**	**RAPHIDE**	BRATTISH	**REAGENT**
QUICKIE	GRABBLED	**RAGGLED**	RAMPAGED	RAPHIDES	**RATTLED**	REAGENTS
QUICKIES	**RABBLER**	DRAGGLED	RAMPAGES	**RAPIERS**	BRATTLED	**REAKING**
QUIDDIT	DRABBLER	RAGGLES	**RAMPART**	DRAPIERS	PRATTLED	BREAKING
QUIDDITS	GRABBLER	DRAGGLES	RAMPARTS	**RAPLOCH**	**RATTLER**	CREAKING
QUIDDITY	**RABBLERS**	**RAGMENT**	**RAMPERS**	RAPLOCHS	PRATTLER	FREAKING
QUIDDLE	**RABBLES**	FRAGMENT	TRAMPERS	**RAPPERS**	RATTLERS	WREAKING
QUIDDLED	BRABBLES	RAGMENTS	**RAMPICK**	TRAPPERS	**RATTLES**	**REALGAR**
QUIDDLER	DRABBLES	**RAGTIME**	RAMPICKS	WRAPPERS	BRATTLES	REALGARS
QUIDDLES	GRABBLES	RAGTIMER	**RAMPIKE**	**RAPPING**	PRATTLES	**REALIGN**
QUIESCE	PRABBLES	RAGTIMES	RAMPIKES	CRAPPING	PRATTLIN	REALIGNS
QUIESCED	**RABBONI**	**RAGWEED**	**RAMPING**	DRAPPING	**RATTLINE**	**REALISE**
QUIESCES	RABBONIS	RAGWEEDS	CRAMPING	FRAPPING	RATTLING	REALISED
QUIETEN	**RACCOON**	**RAGWORK**	TRAMPING	TRAPPING	RATTLINS	REALISER
QUIETENS	RACCOONS	RAGWORKS	**RAMPION**	WRAPPING	**RAVAGER**	REALISES
QUIETER	**RACEWAY**	**RAGWORM**	RAMPIONS	RAPPINGS	RAVAGERS	**REALISM**
QUIETERS	RACEWAYS	RAGWORMS	**RAMPIRE**	**RAPPORT**	**RAVELIN**	REALISMS
QUILLAI	**RACHIAL**	**RAGWORT**	RAMPIRED	RAPPORTS	RAVELINS	**REALIST**
QUILLAIA	BRACHIAL	RAGWORTS	RAMPIRES	**RAPTURE**	**RAVENED**	REALISTS
QUILLAIS	**RACINGS**	**RAIDING**	**RANCHED**	RAPTURED	CRAVENED	**REALIZE**
QUILLET	TRACINGS	BRAIDING	BRANCHED	RAPTURES	**RAVENER**	REALIZED
QUILLETS	**RACKERS**	**RAIKING**	CRANCHED	**RAREBIT**	RAVENERS	REALIZER
QUILLON	CRACKERS	TRAIKING	**RANCHER**	RAREBITS	**RAVINGS**	REALIZES
QUILLONS	TRACKERS	**RAILERS**	BRANCHER	**RASCHEL**	CRAVINGS	**REALLIE**
QUILTER	**RACKETS**	**RAILING**	RANCHERO	RASCHELS	GRAVINGS	REALLIED
QUILTERS	BRACKETS	BRAILING	RANCHERS	**RASHEST**	**RAVIOLI**	REALLIES
QUINCHE	**RACKETT**	DRAILING	**RANCHES**	BRASHEST	RAVIOLIS	**REALLOT**
QUINCHED	RACKETTS	TRAILING	BRANCHES	**RASHING**	**RAWBONE**	REALLOTS
QUINCHES	**RACKING**	TRAILERS	CRANCHES	BRASHING	RAWBONED	**REALTIE**
QUINIES	CRACKING	RAILINGS	TRANCHES	CRASHING	**RAWHEAD**	REALTIES
SQUINIES	TRACKING	**RAILWAY**	**RANCING**	TRASHING	RAWHEADS	**REALTOR**
QUININE	WRACKING	RAILWAYS	PRANCING	**RASPERS**	**RAWHIDE**	REALTORS
QUININES	**RACKINGS**	**RAIMENT**	TRANCING	GRASPERS	RAWHIDES	**REAMEND**
QUINNAT	**RACLOIR**	RAIMENTS	**RANCOUR**	**RASPING**	**RAWINGS**	REAMENDS
QUINNATS	RACLOIRS	**RAINBOW**	RANCOURS	GRASPING	DRAWINGS	**REAMERS**
QUINONE	**RACQUET**	RAINBOWS	**RANDIES**	RASPINGS	**RAYLING**	CREAMERS
QUINONES	RACQUETS	RAINBOWY	BRANDIES	**RASTRUM**	GRAYLING	DREAMERS
QUINTAL	**RADIANT**	**RAINIER**	RANDIEST	RASTRUMS	**RAZZLES**	**REAMIER**
QUINTALS	RADIANTS	BRAINIER	**RANDING**	**RASURES**	FRAZZLES	CREAMIER
QUINTET	**RADIATE**	GRAINIER	BRANDING	ERASURES	**REACHED**	DREAMIER
QUINTETS	ERADIATE	**RAINING**	**RANGERS**	**RATAFIA**	AREACHED	**REAMING**
QUINTETT	RADIATED	BRAINING	GRANGERS	RATAFIAS	BREACHED	BREAMING
QUIPPED	RADIATES	DRAINING	**RANGING**	**RATCHES**	PREACHED	CREAMING
EQUIPPED	**RADICAL**	GRAINING	PRANGING	CRATCHES	**REACHER**	DREAMING
QUIRING	RADICALS	TRAINING	**RANKEST**	FRATCHES	PREACHER	**REARING**
SQUIRING	**RADICEL**	**RAISERS**	CRANKEST	**RATCHET**	TREACHER	DREARING
QUIRTED	**RADICLE**	PRAISERS	FRANKEST	BRATCHET	REACHERS	**REARISE**
SQUIRTED	RADICLES	**RAISING**	**RANKING**	RATCHETS	**REACHES**	REARISEN
QUITTAL	ARAISING	BRANKING	**RATFINK**	AREACHES	**REASONS**
QUITTALS	**RAFFISH**	BRAISING	CRANKING	RATFINKS	BREACHES	TREASONS
QUITTER	DRAFFISH	FRAISING	FRANKING	**RATINGS**	PREACHES	**REASTED**
QUITTERS	**RAFFLER**	PRAISING	PRANKING	GRATINGS	**REACTOR**	BREASTED
QUITTOR	RAFFLERS	RAISINGS	RANKINGS	PRATINGS	REACTORS	**REAVING**
QUITTORS	**RAFTERS**	**RAKSHAS**	**RANKLED**	**RATIONS**	**READAPT**	GREAVING
QUIZZER	DRAFTERS	RAKSHASA	CRANKLED	ORATIONS	READAPTS	**REAWAKE**
QUIZZERS	GRAFTERS	**RALLIER**	PRANKLED	**RATLINE**	**READERS**	REAWAKED
QUIZZERY	**RAFTING**	RALLIERS	**RANKLES**	RATLINES	DREADERS	REAWAKEN
QUODLIN	CRAFTING	**RAMAKIN**	CRANKLES	**RATLING**	**READIES**	REAWAKES
QUODLINS	DRAFTING	RAMAKINS	PRANKLES	BRATLING	READIEST	**REAWOKE**
QUOITER	GRAFTING	**RAMBLER**	**RANSACK**	RATLINGS	**TREADERS**	

REAWOKEN	RECOWERS	**REEVING**	REGRATER	RELIVERS	REORDERS	**REQUIRE**
REBATER	**RECOYLE**	PREEVING	REGRATES	**REMANET**	**REPACKS**	REQUIRED
REBATERS	RECOYLED	**REFACED**	**REGREDE**	REMANETS	PREPACKS	REQUIRER
REBIRTH	RECOYLES	PREFACED	REGREDED	**REMANIE**	**REPAINT**	REQUIRES
REBIRTHS	**RECRUIT**	**REFACES**	REGREDES	REMANIES	REPAINTS	**REQUITE**
REBLOOM	RECRUITS	PREFACES	**REGREET**	**REMBLAI**	**REPAPER**	REQUITED
REBLOOMS	**RECTION**	**REFECTS**	REGREETS	REMBLAIS	REPAPERS	REQUITER
REBOUND	ERECTION	PREFECTS	**REGRIND**	**REMBLED**	**REPINER**	REQUITES
REBOUNDS	RECTIONS	**REFEREE**	REGRINDS	TREMBLED	REPINERS	**REQUOTE**
REBRACE	**RECTORS**	REFEREED	**REGROUP**	**REMBLES**	**REPIQUE**	REQUOTED
REBRACED	ERECTORS	REFEREES	REGROUPS	TREMBLES	REPIQUED	REQUOTES
REBRACES	**RECUILE**	**REFINER**	**REGULAR**	**REMERGE**	REPIQUES	**REROUTE**
REBUILD	RECUILED	REFINERS	REGULARS	REMERGED	**REPLACE**	REROUTED
REBUILDS	RECUILES	REFINERY	**REHEARS**	REMERGES	REPLACED	REROUTES
REBUKER	**RECURVE**	**REFLATE**	REHEARSE	**REMISED**	REPLACER	**RESCALE**
REBUKERS	RECURVED	REFLATED	**REHEATS**	PREMISED	REPLACES	RESCALED
RECEDED	RECURVES	REFLATES	PREHEATS	**REMISES**	**REPLANT**	RESCALES
PRECEDED	**RECYCLE**	**REFLECT**	**REHOUSE**	PREMISES	REPLANTS	**RESCIND**
RECEDES	RECYCLED	REFLECTS	REHOUSED	**REMNANT**	**REPLETE**	RESCINDS
PRECEDES	RECYCLES	**REFLOAT**	REHOUSES	REMNANTS	REPLETED	PRESCIND
RECEIPT	**REDBACK**	REFLOATS	**REINING**	**REMODEL**	REPLETES	**RESCORE**
RECEIPTS	REDBACKS	**REFORMS**	GREINING	REMODELS	**REPLICA**	RESCORED
RECEIVE	**REDCOAT**	PREFORMS	**REINTER**	**REMORSE**	REPLICAS	RESCORES
RECEIVED	REDCOATS	**REFOUND**	REINTERS	PREMORSE	**REPLIER**	**RESCUER**
RECEIVER	**REDDING**	REFOUNDS	**REISSUE**	**REMOTES**	REPLIERS	RESCUERS
RECEIVES	REDDINGS	**REFRACT**	REISSUED	REMOTEST	**REPOINT**	**RESEIZE**
RECENSE	**REDDLED**	REFRACTS	REISSUES	**REMOULD**	REPOINTS	RESEIZED
RECENSED	TREDDLED	**REFRAIN**	**REJOICE**	REMOULDS	**REPOSAL**	RESEIZES
RECENSES	**REDDLES**	REFRAINS	REJOICED	**REMOUNT**	REPOSALL	**RESENTS**
RECEPTS	TREDDLES	**REFRAME**	REJOICER	REMOUNTS	REPOSALS	PRESENTS
PRECEPTS	**REDNECK**	REFRAMED	REJOICES	**REMOVAL**	**REPOSIT**	**RESERVE**
RECHART	REDNECKS	REFRAMES	**REJONEO**	REMOVALS	REPOSITS	PRESERVE
RECHARTS	**REDOUBT**	**REFROZE**	REJONEOS	**REMOVED**	**REPPING**	RESERVED
RECHATE	REDOUBTS	REFROZEN	**REJOURN**	PREMOVED	PREPPING	RESERVES
RECHATES	**REDOUND**	**REFUGEE**	REJOURNS	**REMOVER**	REPPINGS	**RESHAPE**
RECHEAT	REDOUNDS	REFUGEES	**REJUDGE**	REMOVERS	**REPRIME**	RESHAPED
RECHEATS	**REDPOLL**	**REFUSAL**	PREJUDGE	**REMOVES**	REPRIMED	RESHAPES
RECHECK	REDPOLLS	REFUSALS	REJUDGED	PREMOVES	REPRIMES	**RESIANT**
RECHECKS	**REDRAFT**	**REFUSER**	REJUDGES	**REMUAGE**	**REPRINT**	RESIANTS
RECITAL	REDRAFTS	REFUSERS	**RELACHE**	REMUAGES	REPRINTS	**RESIDED**
RECITALS	**REDRIVE**	**REFUTAL**	RELACHES	**REMUEUR**	**REPRISE**	PRESIDED
RECITER	REDRIVEN	REFUTALS	**RELAPSE**	REMUEURS	REPRISED	**RESIDER**
RECITERS	REDRIVES	**REFUTER**	RELAPSED	**RENAGUE**	REPRISES	RESIDERS
RECKING	**REDSKIN**	REFUTERS	RELAPSER	RENAGUED	**REPRIVE**	**RESIDES**
TRECKING	REDSKINS	**REGALES**	RELAPSES	RENAGUES	REPRIVED	PRESIDES
WRECKING	**REDUCER**	GREGALES	**RELATER**	**RENDING**	REPRIVES	**RESIDUA**
RECLAIM	REDUCERS	**REGALIA**	RELATERS	TRENDING	**REPRIZE**	RESIDUAL
RECLAIMS	**REDWING**	REGALIAN	**RELATES**	**RENEGER**	REPRIZED	**RESIDUE**
RECLAME	REDWINGS	REGALIAS	PRELATES	RENEGERS	REPRIZES	RESIDUES
RECLAMES	**REDWOOD**	**REGATTA**	**RELATOR**	**RENEGUE**	**REPROOF**	**RESINER**
RECLIMB	REDWOODS	REGATTAS	RELATORS	RENEGUED	REPROOFS	RESINERS
RECLIMBS	**REECHED**	**REGENCE**	**RELAXIN**	RENEGUER	**REPROVE**	**RESOLVE**
RECLINE	BREECHED	REGENCES	RELAXING	RENEGUES	REPROVED	RESOLVED
RECLINED	**REECHES**	**REGIMEN**	RELAXINS	**RENEWAL**	REPROVER	RESOLVER
RECLINER	BREECHES	REGIMENS	**RELEASE**	RENEWALS	REPROVES	RESOLVES
RECLINES	**REECHIE**	**REGIMENT**	RELEASED	**RENEWER**	**REPRYVE**	**RESOUND**
RECLOSE	REECHIER	**REGMATA**	RELEASEE	RENEWERS	REPRYVED	RESOUNDS
RECLOSED	**REEDERS**	BREGMATA	RELEASER	**RENNING**	REPRYVES	**RESPEAK**
RECLOSES	BREEDERS	**REGNANT**	RELEASES	BRENNING	**REPTILE**	RESPEAKS
RECLUSE	**REEDIER**	PREGNANT	**RELIEVE**	GRENNING	REPTILES	**RESPECT**
RECLUSES	GREEDIER	**REGORGE**	RELIEVED	RENNINGS	**REPULSE**	RESPECTS
RECOUNT	**REEDING**	REGORGED	RELIEVER	**RENTALS**	REPULSED	**RESPELL**
RECOUNTS	BREEDING	REGORGES	RELIEVES	TRENTALS	REPULSES	RESPELLS
RECOURE	REEDINGS	**REGRADE**	**RELIEVO**	**RENTBOY**	**REQUERE**	**RESPIRE**
RECOURED	**REEFING**	REGRADED	RELIEVOS	RENTBOYS	REQUERED	RESPIRED
RECOURES	REEFINGS	REGRADES	**RELIGHT**	**RENTIER**	REQUERES	RESPIRES
RECOVER	**REEKIER**	**REGRANT**	RELIGHTS	RENTIERS	**REQUEST**	**RESPITE**
RECOVERS	CREEKIER	REGRANTS	**RELIQUE**	**REORDER**	REQUESTS	RESPITED
RECOVERY	**REELING**	**REGRATE**	RELIQUES	PREORDER	**REQUIEM**	RESPITES
RECOWER	REELINGS	REGRATED	**RELIVER**		REQUIEMS	**RESPOKE**

RESPOKEN	**RETRAIT**	REVIVALS	PRICKETS	FRIGIDER	CRIPPLED	ROBUSTAS
RESPOND	RETRAITE	**REVIVER**	**RICKING**	FRIGIDLY	TRIPPLED	**ROCHETS**
RESPONDS	RETRAITS	REVIVERS	BRICKING	**RIGIDLY**	**RIPPLER**	CROCHETS
RESPRAY	RETRAITT	**REVIVOR**	CRICKING	**RIGLING**	TRIPPLER	**ROCKERY**
RESPRAYS	**RETRATE**	REVIVORS	PRICKING	RIGLINGS	RIPPLERS	CROCKERY
RESTAFF	RETRATED	**REVOLVE**	TRICKING	RILLING	CRIPPLES	**ROCKETS**
RESTAFFS	RETRATES	REVOLVED	WRICKING	DRILLING	GRIPPLES	BROCKETS
RESTAGE	**RETREAD**	REVOLVER	**RICKLES**	FRILLING	TRIPPLES	CROCKETS
RESTAGED	RETREADS	REVOLVES	PRICKLES	GRILLING	**RIPPLET**	**ROCKIER**
RESTAGES	**RETREAT**	**REWEIGH**	TRICKLES	PRILLING	RIPPLETS	ROCKIERS
RESTART	RETREATS	REWEIGHS	**RICKSHA**	TRILLING	**RIPTIDE**	**ROCKING**
RESTARTS	**RETRIAL**	**REWRITE**	RICKSHAS	**RIMIEST**	RIPTIDES	CROCKING
RESTATE	RETRIALS	REWRITES	RICKSHAW	GRIMIEST	**RISKERS**	FROCKING
RESTATED	**RETSINA**	**REYNARD**	**RICOTTA**	**RIMLESS**	FRISKERS	TROCKING
RESTATES	RETSINAS	REYNARDS	RICOTTAS	BRIMLESS	**RISKFUL**	ROCKINGS
RESTERS	**RETTING**	**RHABDOM**	**RIDDLER**	**RIMMING**	FRISKFUL	**ROCKLAY**
WRESTERS	ARETTING	RHABDOMS	RIDDLERS	BRIMMING	**RISKIER**	ROCKLAYS
RESTING	**FRETTING**	**RHENIUM**	**RIDDLES**	PRIMMING	FRISKIER	**ROCQUET**
CRESTING	**REUNION**	RHENIUMS	GRIDDLES	TRIMMING	**RISKILY**	ROCQUETS
PRESTING	REUNIONS	**RHIZINE**	**RIDGING**	**RINDING**	FRISKILY	**RODDING**
WRESTING	**REUNITE**	RHIZINES	BRIDGING	GRINDING	**RISKING**	BRODDING
RESTINGS	REUNITED	**RHIZOID**	FRIDGING	**RINGBIT**	BRISKING	PRODDING
RESTOCK	REUNITES	RHIZOIDS	RIDGINGS	RINGBITS	FRISKING	RODDINGS
RESTOCKS	**REUTTER**	**RHIZOME**	**RIDOTTO**	**RINGERS**	**RISOTTO**	**RODENTS**
RESTORE	REUTTERS	RHIZOMES	RIDOTTOS	BRINGERS	RISOTTOS	ERODENTS
RESTORED	**REVALUE**	**RHODIUM**	**RIEMPIE**	CRINGERS	**RISPING**	**RODEWAY**
RESTORER	REVALUED	RHODIUMS	RIEMPIES	WRINGERS	CRISPING	RODEWAYS
RESTORES	REVALUES	**RHODORA**	**RIEVERS**	**RINGGIT**	RISPINGS	**RODSTER**
RESTYLE	**REVENGE**	RHODORAS	GRIEVERS	RINGGITS	**RISSOLE**	RODSTERS
RESTYLED	REVENGED	**RHOMBOI**	**RIEVING**	**RINGING**	RISSOLES	**ROEBUCK**
RESTYLES	REVENGER	RHOMBOID	GRIEVING	BRINGING	**RITTERS**	ROEBUCKS
RESUMED	REVENGES	**RHUBARB**	PRIEVING	CRINGING	CRITTERS	**ROILING**
PRESUMED	**REVENUE**	RHUBARBS	**RIFFLER**	FRINGING	FRITTERS	BROILING
RESUMES	REVENUED	RHUBARBY	RIFFLERS	WRINGING	GRITTERS	DROILING
PRESUMES	REVENUES	**RHYMIST**	**RIFLERS**	RINGINGS	**RITTING**	**ROINING**
RESURGE	**REVERBS**	RHYMISTS	TRIFLERS	**RINGLET**	FRITTING	GROINING
RESURGED	PREVERBS	**RHYTHMI**	**RIFLING**	RINGLETS	GRITTING	PROINING
RESURGES	**REVERER**	RHYTHMIC	TRIFLING	**RINGWAY**	GRITTING	**ROISTER**
RETABLE	REVERERS	**RHYTINA**	RIFLINGS	RINGWAYS	**RIVERET**	ROISTERS
RETABLES	**REVERIE**	RHYTINAS	**RIFTIER**	**RINKING**	RIVERETS	**ROKELAY**
RETAKER	REVERIES	**RIBBAND**	DRIFTIER	DRINKING	**RIVETER**	ROKELAYS
RETAKERS	**REVERSE**	RIBBANDS	**RIFTING**	PRINKING	RIVETERS	**ROLLERS**
RETCHED	REVERSED	**RIBBING**	DRIFTING	**RINNING**	**RIVIERA**	PROLLERS
WRETCHED	REVERSER	CRIBBING	GRIFTING	GRINNING	RIVIERAS	TROLLERS
RETCHES	REVERSES	DRIBBING	**RIGGALD**	**RINSING**	**RIVIERE**	**ROLLICK**
WRETCHES	**REVERSI**	RIBBINGS	RIGGALDS	RINSINGS	RIVIERES	ROLLICKS
RETHINK	REVERSIS	**RIBCAGE**	**RIGGERS**	**RIOTING**	**RIVULET**	**ROLLING**
RETHINKS	**REVERSO**	RIBCAGES	FRIGGERS	RIOTINGS	RIVULETS	DROLLING
RETICLE	REVERSOS	**RIBIBLE**	PRIGGERS	**RIOTISE**	**RIZZART**	PROLLING
RETICLES	**REVEUSE**	RIBIBLES	TRIGGERS	RIOTISES	RIZZARTS	TROLLING
RETINOL	REVEUSES	**RIBLETS**	**RIGGING**	**RIOTIZE**	**ROACHED**	ROLLINGS
RETINOLS	**REVIEWS**	DRIBLETS	FRIGGING	RIOTIZES	BROACHED	**ROLLMOP**
RETINUE	PREVIEWS	TRIBLETS	GRIGGING	**RIPIENO**	**ROACHES**	ROLLMOPS
RETINUES	**REVILER**	**RIBSTON**	PRIGGING	RIPIENOS	BROACHES	**ROLLOCK**
RETIRAL	REVILERS	RIBSTONE	TRIGGING	**RIPOSTE**	**ROADING**	ROLLOCKS
RETIRALS	**REVISAL**	RIBSTONS	RIGGINGS	RIPOSTED	ROADINGS	ROMAIKA
RETIREE	REVISALS	**RIBWORK**	**RIGGISH**	RIPOSTES	**ROADWAY**	ROMAIKAS
RETIREES	**REVISED**	CRIBWORK	PRIGGISH	**RIPPERS**	BROADWAY	**ROMANCE**
RETIRER	PREVISED	RIBWORKS	**RIGHTED**	FRIPPERS	ROADWAYS	ROMANCED
RETIRERS	**REVISER**	**RIBWORT**	FRIGHTED	GRIPPERS	**ROARING**	ROMANCER
RETITLE	REVISERS	RIBWORTS	**RIGHTEN**	TRIPPERS	ROARINGS	ROMANCES
RETITLED	**REVISES**	**RICHTED**	BRIGHTEN	**RIPPIER**	**ROASTER**	**ROMAUNT**
RETITLES	PREVISES	FRICHTED	FRIGHTEN	GRIPPIER	ROASTERS	ROMAUNTS
RETRACE	TREVISES	**RICIEST**	RIGHTENS	**RIPPING**	**ROATING**	**ROMNEYA**
RETRACED	**REVISIT**	PRICIEST	**RIGHTER**	DRIPPING	TROATING	ROMNEYAS
RETRACES	REVISITS	**RICKERS**	RIGHTERS	GRIPPING	**ROBINIA**	**RONDEAU**
RETRACT	**REVISOR**	PRICKERS	**RIGHTLY**	TRIPPING	ROBINIAS	RONDEAUX
RETRACTS	REVISORS	TRICKERS	BRIGHTLY	**RIPPLED**	**ROBOTIC**	**RONDINO**
RETRAIN	**REVISORY**	**RICKETS**	**RIGIDER**		ROBOTICS	RONDINOS
RETRAINS	**REVIVAL**	CRICKETS			**ROBUSTA**	**RONDURE**

RONDURES	FROSTING	GROUTING	RUFFLERS	**RUNKLES**	SADDLERS	SALUTERS
RONTGEN	**ROSTRUM**	TROUTING	**RUFFLES**	CRUNKLES	SADDLERY	**SALVAGE**
RONTGENS	ROSTRUMS	ROUTINGS	TRUFFLES	**RUNNING**	**SAFFIAN**	SALVAGED
ROOFING	**ROTATOR**	**ROWBOAT**	**RUGGERS**	RUNNINGS	SAFFIANS	SALVAGES
PROOFING	ROTATORS	ROWBOATS	DRUGGERS	**RUNNION**	**SAFFRON**	**SALVETE**
ROOFINGS	ROTATORY	CROWDIES	**RUGGING**	TRUNNION	SAFFRONS	SALVETES
ROOINEK	**ROTCHES**	ROWDIEST	RUGGINGS	RUNNIONS	SAFFRONY	**SALVING**
ROOINEKS	CROTCHES	**ROWINGS**	DRUGGING	**RUPTURE**	**SAFROLE**	SALVINGS
ROOKING	**ROTCHIE**	GROWINGS	RUINATE	RUPTURED	SAFROLES	**SAMBUCA**
BROOKING	ROTCHIES	**ROWLOCK**	RUINATED	RUPTURES	**SAGENES**	SAMBUCAS
CROOKING	**ROTHERS**	ROWLOCKS	RUINATES	**RUSALKA**	SAGENESS	**SAMISEN**
DROOKING	BROTHERS	**ROWNDED**	**RUINING**	RUSALKAS	**SAGGARD**	SAMISENS
ROOMFUL	**ROTIFER**	DROWNDED	RUININGS	**RUSHERS**	SAGGARDS	**SAMOVAR**
ROOMFULS	ROTIFERS	**ROYALET**	**RULLION**	BRUSHERS	**SAGGING**	SAMOVARS
ROOMIER	**ROTTERS**	ROYALETS	RULLIONS	CRUSHERS	SAGGINGS	**SAMPIRE**
BROOMIER	TROTTERS	**ROYNING**	**RULLOCK**	**RUSHIER**	**SAGITTA**	SAMPIRES
ROOMING	**ROTTING**	PROYNING	RULLOCKS	BRUSHIER	SAGITTAL	**SAMPLER**
BROOMING	TROTTING	**ROYSTER**	**RUMBLED**	**RUSHING**	SAGITTAS	SAMPLERS
GROOMING	**ROTUNDA**	ROYSTERS	CRUMBLED	BRUSHING	**SAGOUIN**	SAMPLERY
VROOMING	ROTUNDAS	**ROZELLE**	DRUMBLED	CRUSHING	SAGOUINS	**SAMSHOO**
ROOPIER	ROTUNDS	ROZELLES	GRUMBLED	FRUSHING	**SAGUARO**	SAMSHOOS
DROOPIER	**ROUBLES**	**RUBBERS**	**RUMBLER**	**RUSTIER**	SAGUAROS	**SANCTUM**
ROOPING	TROUBLES	GRUBBERS	GRUMBLER	CRUSTIER	**SAHIBAH**	SANCTUMS
DROOPING	**ROUGHEN**	**RUBBING**	RUMBLERS	TRUSTIER	SAHIBAHS	**SANDBAG**
TROOPING	ROUGHENS	GRUBBING	**RUMBLES**	**RUSTILY**	**SAILING**	SANDBAGS
ROOSTER	**ROUGHER**	RUBBINGS	CRUMBLES	CRUSTILY	SAILINGS	**SANDING**
ROOSTERS	ROUGHERS	DRUBBING	DRUMBLES	TRUSTILY	**SAIMIRI**	SANDINGS
ROOTAGE	**ROUGHIE**	**RUBBISH**	GRUMBLES	**RUSTING**	SAIMIRIS	**SANGRIA**
ROOTAGES	ROUGHIES	RUBBISHY	**RUMMAGE**	BRUSTING	**SAKERET**	SANGRIAS
ROOTIES	**ROULADE**	**RUBBLES**	RUMMAGED	CRUSTING	SAKERETS	**SANICLE**
ROOTIEST	ROULADES	GRUBBLES	RUMMAGER	TRUSTING	**SAKIYEH**	SANICLES
ROOTING	**ROULEAU**	**RUBDOWN**	RUMMAGES	RUSTINGS	SAKIYEHS	**SANTOUR**
WROOTING	ROULEAUS	RUBDOWNS	**RUMMERS**	**RUSTLER**	**SAKSAUL**	SANTOURS
ROOTINGS	ROULEAUX	**RUBELLA**	BRUMMERS	RUSTLERS	SAKSAULS	**SAOUARI**
ROOTLES	**ROUMING**	RUBELLAN	DRUMMERS	**RUSTLES**	**SALAMON**	SAOUARIS
ROOTLESS	ROUMINGS	RUBELLAS	**RUMMEST**	RUSTLESS	SALAMONS	**SAPAJOU**
ROOTLET	**ROUNCES**	**RUBEOLA**	GRUMMEST	**RUTHFUL**	**SALBAND**	SAPAJOUS
ROOTLETS	TROUNCES	RUBEOLAS	**RUMMIER**	TRUTHFUL	SALBANDS	**SAPHEAD**
ROPEWAY	**ROUNDED**	**RUBICON**	CRUMMIER	**RUTTING**	**SALCHOW**	SAPHEADS
ROPEWAYS	GROUNDED	RUBICONS	**RUMMIES**	RUTTINGS	SALCHOWS	**SAPLING**
ROQUETS	**ROUNDEL**	**RUCHING**	CRUMMIES	**RYBAULD**	**SALFERN**	SAPLINGS
CROQUETS	ROUNDELS	RUCHINGS	RUMMIEST	RYBAULDS	SALFERNS	**SAPONIN**
RORQUAL	**ROUNDER**	**RUCKING**	**RUMPING**	**RYEPECK**	**SALICET**	SAPONINS
RORQUALS	GROUNDER	TRUCKING	CRUMPING	RYEPECKS	SALICETA	**SAPPHIC**
ROSACEA	ROUNDERS	**RUCKLED**	FRUMPING	**SABATON**	SALICETS	SAPPHICS
ROSACEAS	**ROUNDLE**	TRUCKLED	TRUMPING	SABATONS	**SALICIN**	**SAPROBE**
ROSAKER	ROUNDLES	**RUCKLES**	**RUMPLED**	**SABELLA**	SALICINE	SAPROBES
ROSAKERS	ROUNDLET	TRUCKLES	CRUMPLED	ISABELLA	SALICINS	**SAPSAGO**
ROSALIA	**ROUPIER**	**RUCTION**	FRUMPLED	SABELLAS	**SALIENT**	SAPSAGOS
ROSALIAS	CROUPIER	RUCTIONS	**RUMPLES**	**SABURRA**	SALIENTS	**SAPWOOD**
ROSELLA	**ROUPING**	**RUDDIER**	CRUMPLES	SABURRAL	**SALIGOT**	SAPWOODS
ROSELLAS	CROUPING	CRUDDIER	FRUMPLES	SABURRAS	SALIGOTS	**SARAFAN**
ROSELLE	GROUPING	**RUDDIES**	RUMPLESS	**SACCADE**	**SALPIAN**	SARAFANS
ROSELLES	TROUPING	RUDDIEST	**RUNAWAY**	SACCADES	SALPIANS	**SARANGI**
ROSEOLA	**ROUSERS**	**RUDDLED**	RUNAWAYS	**SACCULE**	**SALTANT**	SARANGIS
ROSEOLAS	AROUSERS	CRUDDLED	**RUNCHES**	SACCULES	SALTANTS	**SARCASM**
ROSETTE	GROUSERS	**RUDDLES**	BRUNCHES	**SACKAGE**	**SALTATE**	SARCASMS
ROSETTED	**ROUSING**	CRUDDLES	CRUNCHES	SACKAGES	SALTATED	**SARCODE**
ROSETTES	AROUSING	**RUDDOCK**	**RUNDALE**	**SACKBUT**	SALTATES	SARCODES
ROSIERE	GROUSING	RUDDOCKS	RUNDALES	SACKBUTS	**SALTERN**	**SARCOID**
ROSIERES	**ROUSTER**	**RUDERAL**	**RUNDLED**	**SACKFUL**	SALTERNS	SARCOIDS
ROSIERS	ROUSTERS	RUDERALS	TRUNDLED	SACKFULS	**SALTERS**	**SARCOMA**
CROSIERS	**ROUTERS**	**RUELLIA**	**RUNDLES**	**SACKING**	PSALTERS	SARCOMAS
ROSIEST	TROUTERS	RUELLIAS	TRUNDLES	SACKINGS	**SALTIER**	**SARDANA**
PROSIEST	**ROUTHIE**	**RUFFIAN**	**RUNDLET**	**SACRING**	SALTIERS	SARDANAS
ROSOLIO	ROUTHIER	RUFFIANS	RUNDLETS	SACRINGS	**SALTING**	**SARDINE**
ROSOLIOS	**ROUTINE**	**RUFFLED**	**RUNDOWN**	**SACRIST**	SALTINGS	SARDINES
ROSSERS	ROUTINES	TRUFFLED	RUNDOWNS	SACRISTS	**SALTIRE**	**SARKFUL**
TROSSERS	**ROUTING**	**RUFFLER**	**RUNKLED**	SACRISTY	SALTIRES	SARKFULS
ROSTING			CRUNKLED	**SADDLER**	**SALUTER**	**SARKING**

SARKINGS	**SCALLOP**	**SCHLOCK**	SCOURSES	SCRUPLER	SEASURES	**SEMINAR**
SARMENT	ESCALLOP	SCHLOCKS	**SCOUTER**	SCRUPLES	**SEATING**	SEMINARS
SARMENTA	SCALLOPS	**SCHMOCK**	SCOUTERS	**SCRYING**	SEATINGS	SEMINARY
SARMENTS	**SCALPEL**	SCHMOCKS	**SCOWDER**	SCRYINGS	**SEAWARD**	**SEMIPED**
SARSDEN	SCALPELS	**SCHMUCK**	SCOWDERS	**SCUCHIN**	SEAWARDS	SEMIPEDS
SARSDENS	**SCALPER**	SCHMUCKS	**SCOWRER**	SCUCHINS	**SEAWEED**	**SEMITAR**
SARSNET	SCALPERS	**SCHNOOK**	**SCOWRIE**	**SCUDDER**	SEAWEEDS	SEMITARS
SARSNETS	**SCAMBLE**	SCHNOOKS	SCOWRIES	SCUDDERS	**SECEDER**	**SENATOR**
SASHIMI	SCAMBLED	**SCHNORR**	**SCRAICH**	**SCUDDLE**	SECEDERS	SENATORS
SASHIMIS	**SCAMBLER**	SCHNORRS	SCRAICHS	SCUDDLED	**SECLUDE**	**SENDING**
SATCHEL	SCAMBLES	**SCHOLAR**	**SCRAIGH**	SCUDDLES	SECLUDED	SENDINGS
SATCHELS	**SCAMPER**	SCHOLARS	SCRAIGHS	**SCUDLER**	SECLUDES	**SENECIO**
SATIATE	SCAMPERS	**SCHOOLE**	**SCRAPER**	SCUDLERS	**SECONDE**	SENECIOS
SATIATED	**SCAMPIS**	SCHOOLED	SCRAPERS	**SCUFFLE**	SECONDED	**SENSING**
SATIATES	SCAMPISH	SCHOOLES	**SCRAPIE**	SCUFFLED	SECONDEE	SENSINGS
SATINET	**SCANDAL**	**SCHTICK**	SCRAPIES	SCUFFLER	SECONDER	**SENSISM**
SATINETS	SCANDALS	SCHTICKS	**SCRATCH**	SCUFFLES	SECONDES	SENSISMS
SATSUMA	**SCANNER**	**SCHTOOK**	SCRATCHY	**SCULLER**	**SECRETE**	**SENSIST**
SATSUMAS	SCANNERS	SCHTOOKS	**SCRAUCH**	SCULLERS	SECRETED	SENSISTS
SATYRAL	**SCANTLE**	**SCHTUCK**	SCRAUCHS	SCULLERY	SECRETES	**SEPIOST**
SATYRALS	SCANTLED	SCHTUCKS	**SCRAUGH**	**SCULPIN**	**SECTION**	SEPIOSTS
SATYRID	SCANTLES	**SCIARID**	SCRAUGHS	SCULPINS	SECTIONS	**SEPPUKU**
SATYRIDS	**SCAPING**	SCIARIDS	**SCREECH**	**SCUMBAG**	**SECULAR**	SEPPUKUS
SAUNTER	ESCAPING	**SCIATIC**	**SCREEVE**	SCUMBAGS	SECULARS	**SEPTATE**
SAUNTERS	**SCAPPLE**	SCIATICA	SCREEVED	**SCUMBER**	**SECULUM**	ASEPTATE
SAURIAN	SCAPPLED	**SCIENCE**	**SCREEVER**	SCUMBERS	SECULUMS	**SEPTETT**
SAURIANS	SCAPPLES	SCIENCED	SCREEVES	**SCUMBLE**	**SECURER**	SEPTETTS
SAUSAGE	**SCAPULA**	SCIENCES	**SCREICH**	SCUMBLED	SECURERS	**SEPTIME**
SAUSAGES	SCAPULAE	**SCISSEL**	SCREICHS	SCUMBLES	**SECURES**	SEPTIMES
SAUTOIR	**SCAPULAR**	SCISSELS	**SCREIGH**	**SCUMMER**	SECUREST	**SEPTUOR**
SAUTOIRS	SCAPULAS	**SCISSIL**	SCREIGHS	SCUMMERS	**SEDATES**	SEPTUORS
SAVAGER	**SCARLET**	SCISSILE	**SCREWER**	**SCUNNER**	SEDATEST	**SEQUELA**
SAVAGERY	SCARLETS	SCISSILS	SCREWERS	SCUNNERS	**SEDUCER**	SEQUELAE
SAVAGES	**SCARPED**	**SCISSOR**	**SCRIBED**	**SCUPPER**	SEDUCERS	**SEQUENT**
SAVAGEST	ESCARPED	SCISSORS	ASCRIBED	SCUPPERS	**SEEDBED**	SEQUENTS
SAVANNA	**SCARPER**	**SCOFFER**	ESCRIBED	**SCURRIL**	SEEDBEDS	**SEQUOIA**
SAVANNAH	SCARPERS	SCOFFERS	**SCRIBER**	SCURRILE	**SEEDING**	SEQUOIAS
SAVANNAS	**SCATOLE**	**SCOLDER**	SCRIBERS	**SCUTAGE**	SEEDINGS	**SERENES**
SAVARIN	SCATOLES	SCOLDERS	**SCRIBES**	SCUTAGES	**SEEDLIP**	SERENESS
SAVARINS	**SCATTER**	**SCOLLOP**	ASCRIBES	**SCUTTER**	SEEDLIPS	SERENEST
SAVELOY	SCATTERS	SCOLLOPS	ESCRIBES	SCUTTERS	**SEELING**	**SERFAGE**
SAVELOYS	**SCAUPER**	**SCOOPER**	**SCRIECH**	**SCUTTLE**	SEELINGS	SERFAGES
SAVIOUR	SCAUPERS	SCOOPERS	SCRIECHS	SCUTTLED	**SEEMING**	**SERFDOM**
SAVIOURS	**SCAVAGE**	**SCOOTER**	**SCRIENE**	SCUTTLER	SEEMINGS	SERFDOMS
SAWDUST	**SCAVAGER**	SCOOTERS	SCRIENES	SCUTTLES	**SEEPAGE**	**SERIATE**
SAWDUSTS	SCAVAGES	**SCOPULA**	**SCRIEVE**	**SCYTALE**	SEEPAGES	SERIATED
SAWDUSTY	**SCEDULE**	SCOPULAS	SCRIEVED	SCYTALES	**SEETHER**	SERIATES
SAXHORN	SCEDULES	**SCORING**	SCRIEVES	**SCYTHER**	SEETHERS	**SERICIN**
SAXHORNS	SCENDED	SCORINGS	**SCROLLS**	SCYTHERS	**SEGMENT**	SERICINS
SAZERAC	ASCENDED	**SCORNER**	ESCROLLS	**SDEIGNE**	SEGMENTS	**SERICON**
SAZERACS	**SCEPTIC**	SCORNERS	**SCROOGE**	SDEIGNED	**SEINING**	SERICONS
SCABBLE	SCEPTICS	**SCORPER**	SCROOGED	SDEIGNES	SEININGS	**SERIEMA**
SCABBLED	**SCEPTRE**	SCORPERS	SCROOGES	**SEAFOOD**	**SEISMIC**	SERIEMAS
SCABBLES	SCEPTRED	**SCORPIO**	**SCROTUM**	SEAFOODS	ASEISMIC	**SERINGA**
SCAFFIE	SCEPTRES	SCORPION	SCROTUMS	**SEAGULL**	**SEITIES**	SERINGAS
SCAFFIES	**SCHAPPE**	SCORPIOS	**SCROUGE**	SEAGULLS	ASEITIES	**SERKALI**
SCAGLIA	SCHAPPED	**SCORSER**	SCROUGED	**SEALANT**	**SEIZING**	SERKALIS
SCAGLIAS	SCHAPPES	SCORSERS	**SCROUGER**	SEALANTS	SEIZINGS	**SERPENT**
SCALADE	**SCHEMER**	**SCOTOMA**	SCROUGES	**SEALING**	**SEIZURE**	SERPENTS
ESCALADE	SCHEMERS	SCOTOMAS	**SCROWLE**	SEALINGS	SEIZURES	**SERPULA**
SCALADES	**SCHERZO**	**SCOURER**	SCROWLED	**SEAMARK**	**SELFISM**	SERPULAE
SCALADO	SCHERZOS	SCOURERS	SCROWLES	SEAMARKS	SELFISMS	**SERRATE**
ESCALADO	**SCHISMA**	**SCOURGE**	**SCROYLE**	**SEAPORT**	**SELFIST**	SERRATED
SCALADOS	SCHISMAS	SCOURGED	SCROYLES	SEAPORTS	SELFISTS	SERRATES
SCALDER	**SCHLEPP**	**SCOURGER**	**SCRUNCH**	**SEARING**	**SELTZER**	**SERUEWE**
SCALDERS	SCHLEPPS	SCOURGES	SCRUNCHY	SEARINGS	SELTZERS	SERUEWED
SCALIER	SCHLEPPY	**SCOURIE**	**SCRUPLE**	**SEASIDE**	**SELVAGE**	SERUEWES
ESCALIER	**SCHLICH**	SCOURIES	SCRUPLED	SEASIDES	SELVAGED	**SERVANT**
SCALING	SCHLICHS	**SCOURSE**		**SEASURE**	SELVAGEE	SERVANTS
SCALINGS		SCOURSED			SELVAGES	

SERVEWE	SHALLOP	SHERIATS	SHORINGS	SIGNIORS	SIRNAMES	SKITTLE
SERVEWED	SHALLOPS	SHERIFF	SHORTEN	SIGNORA	SIROCCO	SKITTLED
SERVEWES	SHALLOT	SHERIFFS	SHORTENS	SIGNORAS	SIROCCOS	SKITTLES
SERVICE	SHALLOTS	SHIATSU	SHORTIE	SIGNORE	SISSIES	SKIVING
SERVICED	SHALLOW	SHIATSUS	SHORTIES	SIGNORES	SISSIEST	SKIVINGS
SERVICES	SHALLOWS	SHICKER	SHOTGUN	SIGNORI	SITDOWN	SKOLLIE
SERVILE	SHALWAR	SHICKERS	SHOTGUNS	SIGNORIA	SITDOWNS	SKOLLIES
SERVILES	SHALWARS	SHICKSA	SHOTTLE	SILENCE	SITFAST	SKREENE
SERVING	SHAMBLE	SHICKSAS	SHOTTLES	SILENCED	SITFASTS	SKREENES
SERVINGS	SHAMBLED	SHIDDER	SHOUTER	SILENCER	SITTING	SKREIGH
SESSION	SHAMBLES	SHIDDERS	SHOUTERS	SILENCES	SITTINGS	SKREIGHS
SESSIONS	SHAMING	SHIFTER	SHOWGHE	SILESIA	SITUATE	SKRIECH
SESTETT	ASHAMING	SHIFTERS	SHOWGHES	SILESIAS	SITUATED	SKRIECHS
SESTETTE	SHAMMER	SHIKARI	SHOWING	SILICLE	SITUATES	SKRIEGH
SESTETTO	SHAMMERS	SHIKARIS	SHOWINGS	SILICLES	SIXAINE	SKRIEGHS
SESTETTS	SHAMPOO	SHIMMER	SHRIEVE	SILICON	SIXAINES	SKUDLER
SESTINA	SHAMPOOS	SHIMMERS	SHRIEVED	SILICONE	SIXTEEN	SKUDLERS
SESTINAS	SHAPING	SHIMMERY	SHRIEVES	SILICONS	SIXTEENS	SKULKER
SESTINE	SHAPINGS	SHINDIG	SHRIGHT	SILIQUA	SIZZLER	SKULKERS
SESTINES	SHARIAT	SHINDIGS	SHRIGHTS	SILIQUAS	SIZZLERS	SKULPIN
SETBACK	SHARIATS	SHINGLE	SHRIVEL	SILIQUE	SJAMBOK	SKULPINS
SETBACKS	SHARING	SHINGLED	SHRIVELS	SILIQUES	SJAMBOKS	SKUMMER
SETTING	SHARINGS	SHINGLER	SHRIVER	SILKIES	SKATING	SKUMMERS
SETTINGS	SHARKER	SHINGLES	SHRIVERS	SILKIEST	SKATINGS	SKUTTLE
SETTLER	SHARKERS	SHIPFUL	SHUCKER	SILLIES	SKATOLE	SKUTTLED
SETTLERS	SHARPEN	SHIPFULS	SHUCKERS	SILLIEST	SKATOLES	SKUTTLES
SETTLOR	SHARPENS	SHIPLAP	SHUDDER	SILLOCK	SKEETER	SKYJACK
SETTLORS	SHARPER	SHIPLAPS	SHUDDERS	SILLOCKS	SKEETERS	SKYJACKS
SETUALE	SHARPERS	SHIPMEN	SHUDDERY	SILURID	SKEGGER	SKYLARK
SETUALES	SHARPIE	SHIPMENT	SHUFFLE	SILURIDS	SKEGGERS	SKYLARKS
SETWALL	SHARPIES	SHIPPEN	SHUFFLED	SIMARRE	SKELDER	SKYLINE
SETWALLS	SHASTER	SHIPPENS	SHUFFLER	SIMARRES	SKELDERS	SKYLINES
SEVENTH	SHASTERS	SHIPPER	SHUFFLES	SIMILOR	SKELLIE	SKYSAIL
SEVENTHS	SHASTRA	SHIPPERS	SHUNTER	SIMILORS	SKELLIED	SKYSAILS
SEVERAL	SHASTRAS	SHIPPON	SHUNTERS	SIMITAR	SKELLIER	SKYWARD
SEVERALS	SHATTER	SHIPPONS	SHUTTER	SIMITARS	SKELLIES	SKYWARDS
SEXFOIL	SHATTERS	SHIRKER	SHUTTERS	SIMPKIN	SKELLUM	SLABBER
SEXFOILS	SHATTERY	SHIRKERS	SHUTTLE	SIMPKINS	SKELLUMS	SLABBERS
SEXTANT	SHAVING	SHITTAH	SHUTTLED	SIMPLER	SKELTER	SLABBERY
SEXTANTS	SHAVINGS	SHITTAHS	SHUTTLES	SIMPLERS	SKELTERS	SLACKEN
SEXTETT	SHAWING	SHITTIM	SHYSTER	SIMPLES	SKEPFUL	SLACKENS
SEXTETTE	PSHAWING	SHITTIMS	SHYSTERS	SIMPLEST	SKEPFULS	SLACKER
SEXTETTS	SHEARER	SHMOOSE	SIAMANG	SIMULAR	SKEPTIC	SLACKERS
SEXTILE	SHEARERS	SHMOOSED	SIAMANGS	SIMULARS	SKEPTICS	SLADANG
SEXTILES	SHEATHE	SHMOOSES	SIAMESE	SIMURGH	SKIDPAN	SLADANGS
SEXTUOR	SHEATHED	SHMOOZE	SIAMESED	SIMURGHS	SKIDPANS	SLAKING
SEXTUORS	SHEATHES	SHMOOZED	SIAMESES	SINCERE	SKIFFLE	ASLAKING
SEYSURE	SHEBANG	SHMOOZES	SIAMEZE	SINCERER	SKIFFLES	SLAMMER
SEYSURES	SHEBANGS	SHOCKER	SIAMEZED	SINDING	SKILLET	SLAMMERS
SFUMATO	SHEBEEN	SHOCKERS	SIAMEZES	SINGING	SKILLETS	SLANDER
SFUMATOS	SHEBEENS	SHOEING	SIBLING	SINGINGS	SKIMMER	ISLANDER
SHABBLE	SHEDDER	SHOEINGS	SIBLINGS	SINGLET	SKIMMERS	SLANDERS
SHABBLES	SHEDDERS	SHOGGLE	SIBSHIP	SINGLETS	SKIMMIA	SLAPPER
SHACKLE	SHEHITA	SHOGGLED	SIBSHIPS	SINGULT	SKIMMIAS	SLAPPERS
SHACKLED	SHEHITAH	SHOGGLES	SIDEARM	SINGULTS	SKINFUL	SLASHER
SHACKLES	SHEHITAS	SHOOGIE	SIDEARMS	SINKAGE	SKINFULS	SLASHERS
SHADING	SHELLAC	SHOOGIED	SIDECAR	SINKAGES	SKINKER	SLATHER
SHADINGS	SHELLACS	SHOOGIES	SIDECARS	SINKING	SKINKERS	SLATHERS
SHADOOF	SHELLER	SHOOGLE	SIDEWAY	SINKINGS	SKINNER	SLATING
SHADOOFS	SHELLERS	SHOOGLED	SIDEWAYS	SINOPIA	SKINNERS	SLATINGS
SHAFTER	SHELTER	SHOOGLES	SIEVERT	SINOPIAS	SKIPPER	SLATTER
SHAFTERS	SHELTERS	SHOOTER	SIEVERTS	SINUATE	SKIPPERS	SLATTERN
SHAITAN	SHELTERY	SHOOTERS	SIFTING	SINUATED	SKIPPET	SLATTERS
SHAITANS	SHELTIE	SHOPFUL	SIFTINGS	SINUATES	SKIPPETS	SLATTERY
SHAKING	SHELTIES	SHOPFULS	SIGHTER	SIRGANG	SKIRRET	SLEDGER
SHAKINGS	SHERBET	SHOPHAR	SIGHTERS	SIRGANGS	SKIRRETS	SLEDGERS
SHAKUDO	SHERBETS	SHOPHARS	SIGMATE	SIRLOIN	SKIRTER	SLEEKEN
SHAKUDOS	SHEREEF	SHOPPER	SIGMATED	SIRLOINS	SKIRTERS	SLEEKENS
SHALLON	SHEREEFS	SHOPPERS	SIGMATES	SIRNAME	SKITTER	SLEEKER
SHALLONS	SHERIAT	SHORING	SIGNIOR	SIRNAMED	SKITTERS	SLEEKERS

SLEEPER	**SMELTER**	SNIGGLED	SOILINGS	**SORNING**	**SPARTHE**	SPIGNELS
SLEEPERS	SMELTERS	SNIGGLER	**SOILURE**	SORNINGS	SPARTHES	**SPILING**
SLEEPERY	**SMELTERY**	SNIGGLES	SOILURES	**SOROBAN**	**SPASTIC**	SPILINGS
SLEEVER	**SMICKER**	**SNIPING**	**SOJOURN**	SOROBANS	SPASTICS	**SPILITE**
SLEEVERS	SMICKERS	SNIPINGS	SOJOURNS	**SOROCHE**	**SPATTEE**	SPILITES
SLEIGHT	**SMICKET**	**SNIPPER**	**SOLANUM**	SOROCHES	SPATTEES	**SPILLER**
SLEIGHTS	SMICKETS	SNIPPERS	SOLANUMS	**SORTING**	**SPATTER**	SPILLERS
SLICING	**SMIDGEN**	**SNIPPET**	**SOLDADO**	SORTINGS	SPATTERS	**SPINAGE**
SLICINGS	SMIDGENS	SNIPPETS	SOLDADOS	**SOSSING**	**SPATULA**	SPINAGES
SLICKEN	**SMIDGIN**	**SNIPPETY**	**SOLDIER**	SOSSINGS	SPATULAR	**SPINDLE**
SLICKENS	SMIDGINS	**SNIRTLE**	SOLDIERS	**SOTTING**	SPATULAS	SPINDLED
SLICKER	**SMILING**	SNIRTLED	SOLDIERY	SOTTINGS	**SPATULE**	SPINDLES
SLICKERS	SMILINGS	SNIRTLES	**SOLICIT**	**SOUBISE**	SPATULES	**SPINNER**
SLIDDER	**SMOKIES**	**SNOOKER**	SOLICITS	SOUBISES	**SPAWNER**	SPINNERS
SLIDDERS	**SMOKIEST**	SNOOKERS	SOLICITY	**SOUFFLE**	SPAWNERS	**SPINNERY**
SLIDDERY	**SMOKING**	**SNOOPER**	**SOLIDUM**	SOUFFLES	**SPEAKER**	**SPINNET**
SLIDING	SMOKINGS	SNOOPERS	SOLIDUMS	**SOULDAN**	SPEAKERS	SPINNETS
SLIDINGS	**SMOLDER**	**SNOOZER**	**SOLIPED**	SOULDANS	**SPECIAL**	**SPINNEY**
SLIMMER	SMOLDERS	SNOOZERS	SOLIPEDS	**SOUMING**	ESPECIAL	SPINNEYS
SLIMMERS	**SMOOTHE**	**SNOOZLE**	**SOLITON**	SOUMINGS	SPECIALS	**SPINODE**
SLINGER	SMOOTHED	SNOOZLED	SOLITONS	**SOUNDER**	**SPECKLE**	SPINODES
SLINGERS	**SMOOTHEN**	SNOOZLES	**SOLOIST**	SOUNDERS	SPECKLED	**SPINOUT**
SLINKER	**SMOOTHER**	**SNORING**	SOLOISTS	**SOUPCON**	SPECKLES	SPINOUTS
SLINKERS	SMOOTHES	SNORINGS	**SOLVATE**	SOUPCONS	**SPECTER**	**SPINULE**
SLIPPER	**SMOTHER**	**SNORKEL**	SOLVATED	**SOURING**	SPECTERS	SPINULES
SLIPPERS	SMOTHERS	SNORKELS	SOLVATES	SOURINGS	**SPECTRA**	**SPIRAEA**
SLIPPERY	**SMOTHERY**	**SNORTER**	**SOLVENT**	**SOUROCK**	SPECTRAL	SPIRAEAS
SLIPWAY	**SMOUSER**	SNORTERS	SOLVENTS	SOUROCKS	**SPECTRE**	**SPIRANT**
SLIPWAYS	SMOUSERS	**SNOTTER**	**SOMBRER**	**SOUSING**	SPECTRES	ASPIRANT
SLITHER	**SMUDGER**	SNOTTERS	SOMBRERO	SOUSINGS	**SPECULA**	SPIRANTS
SLITHERS	SMUDGERS	**SNOTTERY**	**SOMBRES**	**SOUSLIK**	SPECULAR	**SPIREME**
SLITHERY	**SMUGGLE**	**SNOWCAP**	SOMBREST	SOUSLIKS	**SPEEDER**	SPIREMES
SLITTER	SMUGGLED	SNOWCAPS	**SOMEONE**	**SOUTANE**	SPEEDERS	**SPIRING**
SLITTERS	**SMUGGLER**	**SNUBBER**	SOMEONES	SOUTANES	**SPEELER**	ASPIRING
SLOBBER	SMUGGLES	SNUBBERS	**SOMEWAY**	**SOUTHER**	SPEELERS	**SPIRTLE**
SLOBBERS	**SMYTRIE**	**SNUFFER**	SOMEWAYS	SOUTHERN	**SPELDER**	SPIRTLES
SLOBBERY	SMYTRIES	SNUFFERS	**SONANCE**	SOUTHERS	SPELDERS	**SPITTER**
SLOCKEN	**SNABBLE**	**SNUFFLE**	SONANCES	**SPACING**	**SPELDIN**	SPITTERS
SLOCKENS	SNABBLED	SNUFFLED	**SONDAGE**	SPACINGS	SPELDING	**SPITTLE**
SLOGGER	SNABBLES	**SNUFFLER**	SONDAGES	**SPADGER**	SPELDINS	SPITTLES
SLOGGERS	**SNAFFLE**	SNUFFLES	**SONDELI**	SPADGERS	**SPELLER**	**SPLENIA**
SLOTTER	SNAFFLED	**SNUGGER**	SONDELIS	**SPAIRGE**	SPELLERS	SPLENIAL
SLOTTERS	SNAFFLES	**SNUGGERY**	**SONSHIP**	SPAIRGED	**SPELTER**	**SPLODGE**
SLOWING	**SNAPPER**	**SNUGGLE**	SONSHIPS	SPAIRGES	SPELTERS	SPLODGES
SLOWINGS	SNAPPERS	SNUGGLED	**SOOPING**	**SPANCEL**	**SPENCER**	**SPLOTCH**
SLUBBER	**SNARING**	SNUGGLES	SOOPINGS	SPANCELS	SPENCERS	SPLOTCHY
SLUBBERS	SNARINGS	**SNUZZLE**	**SOOTHER**	**SPANGLE**	**SPENDER**	**SPLURGE**
SLUGGER	**SNARLER**	SNUZZLED	SOOTHERS	SPANGLED	SPENDERS	SPLURGED
SLUGGERS	SNARLERS	SNUZZLES	**SOOTHES**	**SPANGLER**	**SPERSED**	SPLURGES
SLUMBER	**SNEAKER**	**SOAKAGE**	SOOTHEST	SPANGLES	ASPERSED	**SPODIUM**
SLUMBERS	SNEAKERS	SOAKAGES	**SOPHISM**	SPANGLET	**SPERSES**	SPODIUMS
SLUMBERY	**SNEERER**	**SOAKING**	SOPHISMS	**SPANIEL**	ASPERSES	**SPOILER**
SLUMMER	SNEERERS	SOAKINGS	**SOPHIST**	SPANIELS	**SPERTHE**	SPOILERS
SLUMMERS	**SNEEZER**	**SOAPIES**	SOPHISTS	**SPANKER**	SPERTHES	**SPONDEE**
SMACKER	SNEEZERS	**SOAPIEST**	**SOPPING**	SPANKERS	**SPHAERE**	SPONDEES
SMACKERS	**SNICKER**	**SOARING**	SOPPINGS	**SPANNER**	SPHAERES	**SPONDYL**
SMARAGD	SNICKERS	SOARINGS	**SOPRANO**	SPANNERS	**SPHEARE**	SPONDYLS
SMARAGDS	**SNICKET**	**SOBBING**	SOPRANOS	**SPARGER**	SPHEARES	**SPONGER**
SMARTEN	SNICKETS	SOBBINGS	**SORBATE**	SPARGERS	**SPHERIC**	SPONGERS
SMARTENS	**SNIFFER**	**SOCAGER**	SORBATES	**SPARKLE**	SPHERICS	**SPONGIN**
SMARTIE	SNIFFERS	SOCAGERS	**SORBENT**	SPARKLED	**SPICATE**	SPONGING
SMARTIES	**SNIFFLE**	**SOCCAGE**	SORBENTS	**SPARKLER**	SPICATED	SPONGINS
SMASHER	SNIFFLED	SOCCAGES	**SORDINE**	SPARKLES	**SPICULA**	**SPONSON**
SMASHERS	**SNIFFLER**	**SOCIATE**	SORDINES	SPARKLET	SPICULAR	SPONSONS
SMATTER	SNIFFLES	SOCIATES	**SOREDIA**	**SPAROID**	SPICULAS	**SPONSOR**
SMATTERS	**SNIFTER**	**SOCKEYE**	SOREDIAL	SPAROIDS	**SPICULE**	SPONSORS
SMEDDUM	SNIFTERS	SOCKEYES	**SOREHON**	**SPARRER**	SPICULES	**SPOOFER**
SMEDDUMS	**SNIGGER**	**SOGGING**	SOREHONS	SPARRERS	**SPIELER**	SPOOFERS
SMELLER	SNIGGERS	SOGGINGS	**SORGHUM**	**SPARROW**	SPIELERS	SPOOFERY
SMELLERS	**SNIGGLE**	**SOILING**	SORGHUMS	SPARROWS	**SPIGNEL**	

SPOOLER	SQUACCO	STANYEL	STEMBOK	STINTERS	STRANGE	STYLITE
SPOOLERS	SQUACCOS	STANYELS	STEMBOKS	STIPEND	ESTRANGE	STYLITES
SPOONEY	SQUALOR	STAPLER	STEMLET	STIPENDS	STRANGER	STYLIZE
SPOONEYS	SQUALORS	STAPLERS	STEMLETS	STIPPLE	STRAYED	STYLIZED
SPOORER	SQUARER	STAPPLE	STEMPEL	STIPPLED	ESTRAYED	STYLIZES
SPOORERS	SQUARERS	STAPPLES	STEMPELS	STIPPLER	STRAYER	STYLOID
SPORRAN	SQUARES	STARDOM	STEMPLE	STIPPLES	STRAYERS	STYLOIDS
SPORRANS	SQUAREST	STARDOMS	STEMPLES	STIPULE	STRETCH	STYPTIC
SPORTED	SQUEEZE	STARING	STEMSON	STIPULED	STRETCHY	STYPTICS
ASPORTED	SQUEEZED	STARINGS	STEMSONS	STIPULES	STREWER	STYRENE
SPORTER	SQUEEZER	STARKEN	STENCIL	STIRRAH	STREWERS	STYRENES
SPORTERS	SQUEEZES	STARKENS	STENCILS	STIRRAHS	STRIATE	SUASION
SPORULE	SQUELCH	STARKER	STENGAH	STIRRER	STRIATED	SUASIONS
SPORULES	SQUELCHY	STARKERS	STENGAHS	STIRRERS	STRIATES	SUBADAR
SPOTTER	SQUIDGE	STARLET	STENTOR	STIRRUP	STRIDOR	SUBADARS
SPOTTERS	SQUIDGED	STARLETS	STENTORS	STIRRUPS	STRIDORS	SUBATOM
SPOUSAL	SQUIDGES	STARNIE	STEPNEY	STISHIE	STRIGIL	SUBATOMS
ESPOUSAL	SQUIRES	STARNIES	STEPNEYS	STISHIES	STRIGILS	SUBBING
SPOUSALS	ESQUIRES	STARTED	STEPPER	STODGER	STRIKER	SUBBINGS
SPOUSED	SQUIRESS	ASTARTED	STEPPERS	STODGERS	STRIKERS	SUBDEAN
ESPOUSED	SRADDHA	STARTER	STEPSON	STOITER	STRIVER	SUBDEANS
SPOUSES	SRADDHAS	STARTERS	STEPSONS	STOITERS	STRIVERS	SUBDUAL
ESPOUSES	STABBER	STARTLE	STERLET	STOMACH	STRODLE	SUBDUALS
SPOUTER	STABBERS	STARTLED	STERLETS	STOMACHS	STRODLED	SUBDUCE
SPOUTERS	STABILE	STARTLER	STERNUM	STOMACHY	STRODLES	SUBDUCED
SPRAINT	STABILES	STARTLES	STERNUMS	STOMATA	STROKER	SUBDUCES
SPRAINTS	STABLER	STASHIE	STEROID	STOMATAL	STROKERS	SUBDUCT
SPRAYER	STABLERS	STASHIES	STEROIDS	STONIED	STROOKEN	SUBDUCTS
SPRAYERS	STABLES	STATING	ASTEROID	ASTONIED	STROOKES	SUBDUER
SPREAGH	STABLEST	ESTATING	STEWARD	STONIES	STROPHE	SUBDUERS
SPREAGHS	STACKER	STATION	STEWARDS	ASTONIES	STROPHES	SUBEDAR
SPREAZE	STACKERS	STATIONS	STEWING	STONIEST	STROWER	SUBEDARS
SPREAZED	STACKET	STATISM	STEWINGS	STONING	STROWERS	SUBEDIT
SPREAZES	STACKETS	STATISMS	STEWPAN	ASTONING	STRUDEL	SUBEDITS
SPREDDE	STADDLE	STATIST	STEWPANS	STONINGS	STRUDELS	SUBERIN
SPREDDEN	STADDLES	STATISTS	STEWPOT	STONKER	STUBBLE	SUBERINS
SPREDDES	STADIAL	STATURE	STEWPOTS	STONKERS	STUBBLED	SUBFUSC
SPREEZE	STADIALS	STATURED	STHENIC	STOOKER	STUBBLES	SUBFUSCS
SPREEZED	STADIUM	STATURES	ASTHENIC	STOOKERS	STUDDLE	SUBFUSK
SPREEZES	STADIUMS	STATUTE	STIBBLE	STOOLIE	STUDDLES	SUBFUSKS
SPRIGHT	STAFFER	STATUTES	STIBBLER	STOOLIES	STUDENT	SUBJECT
SPRIGHTS	STAFFERS	STAYING	STIBBLES	STOOPER	STUDENTS	SUBJECTS
SPRINGE	STAGGER	STAYINGS	STIBINE	STOOPERS	STUDIER	SUBJOIN
SPRINGED	STAGGERS	STEALER	STIBINES	STOPING	STUDIERS	SUBJOINS
SPRINGER	STAGING	STEALERS	STIBIUM	STOPINGS	STUFFER	SUBLATE
SPRINGES	STAGINGS	STEALTH	STIBIUMS	STOPPED	STUFFERS	SUBLATED
SPRUCES	STAINER	STEALTHS	STICKER	ESTOPPED	STUMBLE	SUBLIME
SPRUCEST	STAINERS	STEALTHY	STICKERS	STOPPER	STUMBLED	SUBLIMED
SPULYIE	STAITHE	STEAMER	STICKLE	STOPPERS	STUMBLER	SUBLIMER
SPULYIED	STAITHES	STEAMERS	STICKLED	STOPPLE	STUMBLES	SUBLIMES
SPULYIES	STALKER	STEAMIE	STICKLER	STOPPLED	STUMMEL	SUBPLOT
SPULZIE	STALKERS	STEAMIER	STICKLES	STOPPLES	STUMMELS	SUBPLOTS
SPULZIED	STAMINA	STEAMIES	STICKUP	STORAGE	STUMPER	SUBSERE
SPULZIES	STAMINAL	STEARIN	STICKUPS	STORAGES	STUMPERS	SUBSERES
SPUNKIE	STAMINAS	STEARINE	STIDDIE	STOTTER	STUNNED	SUBSIDE
SPUNKIER	STAMMEL	STEARING	STIDDIED	STOTTERS	ASTUNNED	SUBSIDED
SPUNKIES	STAMMELS	STEARINS	STIDDIES	STOUNDS	STUNNER	SUBSIDES
SPURNER	STAMMER	STEEMED	STIFFEN	ASTOUNDS	STUNNERS	SUBSIST
SPURNERS	STAMMERS	ESTEEMED	STIFFENS	STOUTEN	STURMER	SUBSISTS
SPURRER	STAMPED	STEEPEN	STIFLER	STOUTENS	STURMERS	SUBSOIL
SPURRERS	STAMPEDE	STEEPENS	STIFLERS	STOVERS	STUSHIE	SUBSOILS
SPURREY	STAMPEDO	STEEPER	STILLER	ESTOVERS	STUSHIES	SUBSUME
SPURREYS	STAMPER	STEEPERS	STILLERS	STOVING	STUTTER	SUBSUMED
SPURTLE	STAMPERS	STEEPLE	STILTER	STOVINGS	STUTTERS	SUBSUMES
SPURTLES	STANDER	STEEPLED	STILTERS	STOWAGE	STYLISE	SUBTACK
SPUTNIK	STANDERS	STEEPLES	STINGER	STOWAGES	STYLISED	SUBTACKS
SPUTNIKS	STANIEL	STEERER	STINGERS	STOWING	STYLISES	SUBTEEN
SPUTTER	STANIELS	STEERERS	STINKER	STOWINGS	STYLIST	SUBTEENS
SPUTTERS	STANNEL	STEEVES	STINKERS	STRAINT	STYLISTS	SUBTEND
SPUTTERY	STANNELS	STEEVEST	STINTER	STRAINTS		

SUBTENDS	SUMMATED	**SURGEON**	**SWEATER**	**SYMBION**	**TACHIST**	TAMARIND
SUBTEXT	SUMMATES	SURGEONS	SWEATERS	SYMBIONS	TACHISTE	TAMARINS
SUBTEXTS	**SUMMING**	**SURGING**	**SWEENEY**	SYMBIONT	TACHISTS	**TAMARIS**
SUBTILE	SUMMINGS	SURGINGS	SWEENEYS	**SYMBOLE**	**TACHYON**	TAMARISK
SUBTILER	**SUMMIST**	**SURLOIN**	**SWEEPER**	SYMBOLES	TACHYONS	**TAMASHA**
SUBTYPE	SUMMISTS	SURLOINS	SWEEPERS	**SYMITAR**	**TACKERS**	TAMASHAS
SUBTYPES	**SUMPTER**	**SURMISE**	**SWEETEN**	SYMITARE	STACKERS	**TAMBOUR**
SUBUNIT	SUMPTERS	SURMISED	SWEETENS	SYMITARS	**TACKETS**	TAMBOURA
SUBUNITS	**SUNBATH**	SURMISER	**SWEETIE**	**SYMPTOM**	STACKETS	TAMBOURS
SUBVERT	SUNBATHE	SURMISES	SWEETIES	SYMPTOMS	**TACKIES**	**TAMBURA**
SUBVERTS	SUNBATHS	**SURNAME**	**SWELLER**	**SYNAPSE**	TACKIEST	TAMBURAS
SUBZONE	**SUNBEAM**	SURNAMED	SWELLERS	SYNAPSES	**TACKING**	**TAMPERS**
SUBZONES	SUNBEAMS	SURNAMES	**SWELTER**	**SYNAPTE**	TACKINGS	**TAMPING**
SUCCADE	SUNBEAMY	**SURTOUT**	SWELTERS	SYNAPTES	STACKING	STAMPING
SUCCADES	**SUNBELT**	SURTOUTS	**SWERVER**	**SYNCARP**	**TACKLER**	**TAMPINGS**
SUCCEED	SUNBELTS	**SURVEWE**	SWERVERS	SYNCARPS	TACKLERS	TAMPION
SUCCEEDS	**SUNBURN**	SURVEWED	**SWIDDEN**	SYNCARPY	**TACTION**	TAMPIONS
SUCCOUR	SUNBURNS	SURVEWES	SWIDDENS	**SYNCOPE**	TACTIONS	**TANADAR**
SUCCOURS	SUNBURNT	**SURVIEW**	**SWIFTER**	SYNCOPES	**TACTISM**	TANADARS
SUCCUBA	**SUNDARI**	SURVIEWS	SWIFTERS	**SYNDING**	TACTISMS	**TANAGER**
SUCCUBAE	SUNDARIS	**SURVIVE**	**SWIGGER**	SYNDINGS	**TADPOLE**	TANAGERS
SUCCUBAS	**SUNDIAL**	SURVIVED	SWIGGERS	**SYNFUEL**	TADPOLES	**TANAGRA**
SUCCUMB	SUNDIALS	SURVIVES	**SWILLER**	SYNFUELS	**TAEDIUM**	TANAGRAS
SUCCUMBS	**SUNDOWN**	**SUSPECT**	SWILLERS	**SYNODAL**	TAEDIUMS	**TANGELO**
SUCKING	SUNDOWNS	SUSPECTS	**SWIMMER**	SYNODALS	**TAFFETA**	TANGELOS
SUCKINGS	**SUNGLOW**	**SUSPEND**	SWIMMERS	**SYNONYM**	TAFFETAS	**TANGENT**
SUCKLER	SUNGLOWS	SUSPENDS	**SWINDGE**	SYNONYMS	**TAGGERS**	TANGENTS
SUCKLERS	**SUNRISE**	**SUSPENS**	SWINDGED	SYNONYMY	STAGGERS	**TANGHIN**
SUCRASE	SUNRISES	SUSPENSE	SWINDGES	**SYNOVIA**	**TAGGING**	TANGHINS
SUCRASES	**SUNSPOT**	**SUSPIRE**	**SWINDLE**	SYNOVIAL	STAGGING	**TANGIES**
SUCRIER	SUNSPOTS	SUSPIRED	SWINDLED	SYNOVIAS	**TAGMEME**	TANGIEST
SUCRIERS	**SUNSUIT**	SUSPIRES	SWINDLER	**SYRINGA**	TAGMEMES	**TANGING**
SUCROSE	SUNSUITS	**SUSTAIN**	SWINDLES	SYRINGAS	**TAILARD**	STANGING
SUCROSES	**SUNTRAP**	SUSTAINS	**SWINGER**	**SYRINGE**	TAILARDS	**TANGLER**
SUCTION	SUNTRAPS	**SWABBER**	SWINGERS	SYRINGED	**TAILING**	TANGLERS
SUCTIONS	**SUNWARD**	SWABBERS	**SWINGLE**	SYRINGES	TAILINGS	**TANGRAM**
SUFFETE	SUNWARDS	**SWADDLE**	SWINGLED	**SYRPHID**	**TAILLIE**	TANGRAMS
SUFFETES	**SUPPAWN**	SWADDLED	SWINGLES	SYRPHIDS	TAILLIES	**TANKAGE**
SUFFICE	SUPPAWNS	SWADDLER	**SWIPPLE**	**SYSTOLE**	TAILZIE	TANKAGES
SUFFICED	**SUPPLES**	SWADDLES	SWIPPLES	ASYSTOLE	TAILZIES	**TANKARD**
SUFFICER	SUPPLEST	**SWAGGER**	**SWISHER**	SYSTOLES	**TAKAHEA**	TANKARDS
SUFFICES	**SUPPORT**	SWAGGERS	SWISHERS	**SYSTYLE**	TAKAHEAS	**TANKFUL**
SUFFUSE	SUPPORTS	**SWAGGIE**	**SWISHES**	SYSTYLES	**TALAUNT**	TANKFULS
SUFFUSED	**SUPPOSE**	SWAGGIES	SWISHEST	**TABANID**	TALAUNTS	**TANKING**
SUFFUSES	SUPPOSED	**SWALING**	**SWITHER**	TABANIDS	**TALAYOT**	TANKINGS
SUGGEST	SUPPOSER	SWALINGS	SWITHERS	**TABARET**	TALAYOTS	**TANLING**
SUGGESTS	SUPPOSES	**SWALLET**	**SWIZZLE**	TABARETS	**TALIPAT**	TANLINGS
SUICIDE	**SUPREME**	SWALLETS	SWIZZLED	**TABBING**	TALIPATS	**TANNAGE**
SUICIDES	SUPREMER	**SWALLOW**	SWIZZLES	STABBING	**TALIPED**	TANNAGES
SUITING	SUPREMES	SWALLOWS	**SWOBBER**	**TABINET**	TALIPEDS	STANNATE
SUITINGS	**SUPREMO**	**SWAMPER**	SWOBBERS	TABINETS	**TALIPOT**	**TANNATE**
SULCATE	SUPREMOS	SWAMPERS	**SWOPPER**	**TABLEAU**	TALIPOTS	TANNATES
SULCATED	**SURANCE**	**SWANKER**	SWOPPERS	TABLEAUX	**TALKERS**	**TANNING**
SULFATE	SURANCES	SWANKERS	**SWORDER**	**TABLING**	STALKERS	TANNINGS
SULFATED	**SURBASE**	**SWANKEY**	SWORDERS	STABLING	**TALKING**	**TANTARA**
SULFATES	SURBASED	SWANKEYS	**SWOTTER**	TABLINGS	STALKING	TANTARAS
SULKIES	SURBASES	**SWAPPER**	SWOTTERS	**TABLOID**	TALKINGS	**TANTRUM**
SULKIEST	**SURBATE**	SWAPPERS	**SWOZZLE**	TABLOIDS	**TALLAGE**	TANTRUMS
SULLAGE	SURBATED	**SWARMER**	SWOZZLES	**TABORER**	STALLAGE	**TANYARD**
SULLAGES	SURBATES	SWARMERS	**SYENITE**	TABORERS	TALLAGED	TANYARDS
SULPHUR	**SURCOAT**	**SWASHER**	SYENITES	**TABORET**	TALLAGES	**TAPERER**
SULPHURS	SURCOATS	SWASHERS	**SYLLABI**	TABORETS	**TALLBOY**	TAPERERS
SULPHURY	**SURFACE**	**SWATTER**	SYLLABIC	**TABORIN**	TALLBOYS	**TAPIOCA**
SULTANA	SURFACED	SWATTERS	**SYLPHID**	TABORING	**TALLENT**	TAPIOCAS
SULTANAS	SURFACER	**SWAYING**	SYLPHIDE	TABORINS	TALLENTS	**TAPPICE**
SUMATRA	SURFACES	SWAYINGS	SYLPHIDS	**TABRERE**	**TALLIER**	TAPPICED
SUMATRAS	**SURFEIT**	**SWAZZLE**	**SYLVINE**	TABRERES	TALLIERS	TAPPICES
SUMMAND	SURFEITS	SWAZZLES	SYLVINES	**TACHISM**	**TALLITH**	**TAPPING**
SUMMANDS	**SURFING**	**SWEARER**	**SYLVITE**	TACHISME	TALLITHS	STAPPING
SUMMATE	SURFINGS	SWEARERS	SYLVITES	TACHISMS	**TAMARIN**	

TAPPINGS	**TEASING**	TEREBRAE	**THEATER**	THUNDERY	**TINGLER**	TOFFIEST
TAPROOM	TEASINGS	TEREBRAS	**THEATERS**	**THWAITE**	TINGLERS	**TOHEROA**
TAPROOMS	**TEATIME**	**TERGITE**	**THEATRE**	THWAITES	**TINHORN**	TOHEROAS
TAPROOT	TEATIMES	TERGITES	**THEATRES**	**THYLOSE**	TINHORNS	**TOILING**
TAPROOTS	**TECHNIC**	TERMITE	**THEISMS**	THYLOSES	**TINKERS**	TOILINGS
TAPSTER	TECHNICS	TERMITES	ATHEISMS	**THYMINE**	STINKERS	**TOISECH**
TAPSTERS	**TEDDIES**	**TERNING**	**THEISTS**	THYMINES	**TINKING**	TOISECHS
TARDIES	STEDDIES	STERNING	ATHEISTS	**THYROID**	STINKING	**TOKAMAK**
TARDIEST	**TEDDING**	**TERNION**	**THEORBO**	THYROIDS	**TINKLER**	TOKAMAKS
TARRIER	STEDDING	TERNIONS	THEORBOS	**TICKERS**	TINKLERS	**TOLLAGE**
STARRIER	**TEEMING**	**TERPENE**	**THEOREM**	STICKERS	**TINNIES**	TOLLAGES
TARRIERS	STEEMING	TERPENES	THEOREMS	**TICKIES**	TINNIEST	**TOLLING**
TARRIES	**TEENAGE**	**TERRACE**	**THEORIC**	STICKIES	**TINNING**	TOLLINGS
TARRIEST	TEENAGED	TERRACED	THEORICS	**TICKING**	TINNINGS	**TOLUATE**
TARRING	TEENAGER	TERRACES	**THERIAC**	STICKING	**TINTERS**	TOLUATES
STARRING	**TEENING**	**TERRAIN**	THERIACA	**TICKINGS**	STINTERS	**TOLUENE**
TARRINGS	STEENING	TERRAINS	THERIACS	**TICKLED**	STINTIER	TOLUENES
TARROCK	**TEERING**	**TERRANE**	**THERMAL**	STICKLED	STINTIER	**TOMBOLA**
TARROCKS	STEERING	TERRANES	THERMALS	**TICKLER**	**TINTING**	TOMBOLAS
TARSIER	**TEKTITE**	**TERREEN**	**THIAMIN**	STICKLER	TINTINGS	**TOMBOLO**
TARSIERS	TEKTITES	TERREENS	THIAMINE	TICKLERS	**TINTIER**	TOMBOLOS
TARTANA	**TELECOM**	**TERRENE**	THIAMINS	**TICKLES**	**TINTYPE**	**TOMFOOL**
TARTANAS	TELECOMS	TERRENES	**THICKEN**	STICKLES	TINTYPES	TOMFOOLS
TARTANE	**TELEOST**	**TERRIER**	THICKENS	**TIDDIES**	**TINWARE**	**TOMPION**
TARTANED	TELEOSTS	TERRIERS	**THICKET**	STIDDIES	TINWARES	TOMPIONS
TARTANES	**TELETEX**	**TERRINE**	THICKETS	TIDDIEST	**TIPPING**	**TONDINO**
TARTARE	TELETEXT	TERRINES	THICKETY	**TIDDLER**	TIPPINGS	TONDINOS
TARTARES	**TELLING**	**TERSION**	**THIGGER**	TIDDLERS	**TIPPLED**	**TONIEST**
TARTINE	STELLING	TERSIONS	THIGGERS	**TIDDLEY**	STIPPLED	STONIEST
TARTINES	TELLINGS	**TERTIAL**	**THILLER**	TIDDLEYS	**TIPPLER**	**TONIGHT**
TARTISH	**TELPHER**	TERTIALS	THILLERS	**TIERCEL**	STIPPLER	TONIGHTS
STARTISH	TELPHERS	**TERTIAN**	**THIMBLE**	TIERCELS	**TIPPLES**	**TONKERS**
TARTLET	**TEMPERA**	TERTIANS	THIMBLED	**TIETACK**	STIPPLES	STONKERS
TARTLETS	TEMPERAS	**TESSERA**	THIMBLES	TIETACKS	**TIPSTER**	**TONNAGE**
TARWEED	**TEMPEST**	TESSERAE	**THINKER**	**TIFFING**	TIPSTERS	TONNAGES
TARWEEDS	TEMPESTS	TESSERAL	THINKERS	STIFFING	**TIRASSE**	**TONNEAU**
TASHING	**TEMPLES**	**TESTERN**	**THINNER**	TIFFINGS	TIRASSES	TONNEAUS
STASHING	STEMPLES	TESTERNS	THINNERS	**TIGHTEN**	**TIRRING**	**TONNELL**
TASKING	**TEMPLET**	**TESTING**	**THISTLE**	TIGHTENS	STIRRING	TONNELLS
TASKINGS	TEMPLETS	TESTINGS	THISTLES	**TILAPIA**	**TITCHES**	**TONSURE**
TASSELL	**TEMPTER**	**TESTOON**	**THORITE**	TILAPIAS	STITCHES	TONSURED
TASSELLS	TEMPTERS	TESTOONS	THORITES	**TILLAGE**	**TITHING**	TONSURES
TASSELLY	**TEMPURA**	**TESTRIL**	**THORIUM**	STILLAGE	TITHINGS	**TONTINE**
TASTING	TEMPURAS	TESTRILL	THORIUMS	TILLAGES	**TITLARK**	TONTINER
TASTINGS	**TENCHES**	TESTRILS	**THOUGHT**	**TILLERS**	TITLARKS	TONTINES
TATTIES	STENCHES	**TESTUDO**	THOUGHTS	STILLERS	**TITLING**	**TOOLBAG**
TATTIEST	**TENDING**	TESTUDOS	**THREAVE**	**TILLIER**	TITLINGS	TOOLBAGS
TATTING	STENDING	**TETRACT**	THREAVES	STILLIER	**TITRATE**	**TOOLING**
TATTINGS	**TENDRIL**	TETRACTS	**THRIMSA**	**TILLING**	TITRATED	STOOLING
TATTLER	TENDRILS	**TETRODE**	THRIMSAS	STILLING	TITRATES	TOOLINGS
TATTLERS	**TENDRON**	TETRODES	**THRIVER**	TILLINGS	**TITULAR**	**TOOLKIT**
TAUNTER	TENDRONS	**TEUCHAT**	THRIVERS	**TILLITE**	TITULARY	TOOLKITS
TAUNTERS	**TENONER**	TEUCHATS	**THROMBI**	TILLITES	TITULARY	**TOOTSIE**
TAVERNA	TENONERS	**TEXTILE**	THROMBIN	**TILTERS**	TITULARY	TOOTSIES
TAVERNAS	**TENSION**	TEXTILES	**THROWER**	STILTERS	**TOASTER**	**TOPARCH**
TAWNIES	TENSIONS	**TEXTURE**	THROWERS	**TILTING**	TOASTERS	TOPARCHS
TAWNIEST	**TENTAGE**	TEXTURED	**THRUWAY**	STILTING	**TOASTIE**	TOPARCHY
TAXICAB	TENTAGES	TEXTURES	THRUWAYS	TILTINGS	TOASTIES	**TOPCOAT**
TAXICABS	**TENTFUL**	**THALAMI**	**THRYMSA**	**TIMBALE**	**TOBACCO**	TOPCOATS
TAXIWAY	TENTFULS	THALAMIC	THRYMSAS	TIMBALES	TOBACCOS	**TOPKNOT**
TAXIWAYS	**TENTIGO**	**THALWEG**	**THUGGEE**	**TIMBREL**	**TOCCATA**	TOPKNOTS
TEACHER	TENTIGOS	THALWEGS	THUGGEES	TIMBRELS	STOCCATA	**TOPLESS**
TEACHERS	**TENTING**	**THANAGE**	**THULITE**	**TINAMOU**	TOCCATAS	STOPLESS
TEAMERS	STENTING	THANAGES	THULITES	TINAMOUS	**TODDLER**	**TOPMAST**
STEAMERS	TENTINGS	**THANKER**	**THULIUM**	**TINCHEL**	TODDLERS	TOPMASTS
TEAMING	**TEQUILA**	THANKERS	THULIUMS	TINCHELS	**TOECLIP**	**TOPONYM**
STEAMING	TEQUILAS	**THANNAH**	**THUMPER**	**TINFOIL**	TOECLIPS	TOPONYMS
TEAMINGS	**TERBIUM**	THANNAHS	THUMPERS	TINFOILS	**TOENAIL**	TOPONYMY
TEARING	TERBIUMS	**THAWING**	**THUNDER**	**TINGING**	TOENAILS	**TOPPERS**
STEARING	**TEREBRA**	THAWINGS	THUNDERS	STINGING	**TOFFIES**	STOPPERS

TOPPING	TOURISTS	**TRAMPLE**	**TREKKER**	**TRIGGER**	**TROCHEE**	**TRUSSER**
STOPPING	TOURISTY	TRAMPLED	TREKKERS	TRIGGERS	TROCHEES	TRUSSERS
TOPPINGS	**TOURNEY**	TRAMPLER	**TREMBLE**	TRIGLOT	**TROELIE**	**TRUSTEE**
TOPPLED	TOURNEYS	TRAMPLES	ATREMBLE	TRIGLOTS	TROELIES	TRUSTEES
STOPPLED	**TOUSING**	TRAMWAY	TREMBLED	**TRIGRAM**	**TROKING**	**TRUSTER**
TOPPLES	TOUSINGS	TRAMWAYS	TREMBLER	TRIGRAMS	STROKING	TRUSTERS
STOPPLES	**TOWAGES**	**TRANCHE**	TREMBLES	**TRIKING**	**TROLLED**	**TRYPSIN**
TOPSAIL	STOWAGES	TRANCHES	**TREMOLO**	STRIKING	STROLLED	TRYPSINS
TOPSAILS	**TOWINGS**	TRANCHET	TREMOLOS	**TRILITH**	**TROLLER**	**TRYSAIL**
TOPSIDE	STOWINGS	**TRANECT**	**TRENAIL**	TRILITHS	STROLLER	TRYSAILS
TOPSIDES	**TOWLINE**	TRANECTS	TRENAILS	**TRILOBE**	TROLLERS	**TRYSTER**
TOPSPIN	TOWLINES	**TRANGAM**	**TRENISE**	TRILOBED	**TROLLEY**	TRYSTERS
TOPSPINS	**TOWMOND**	TRANGAMS	TRENISES	TRILOBES	**TROLLEY**	**TSADDIK**
TORCHER	TOWMONDS	**TRANGLE**	**TRENTAL**	TRILOBES	TROLLEYS	TSADDIKS
TORCHERE	**TOWMONT**	STRANGLE	TRENTALS	**TRIMMER**	**TROLLOP**	**TSADDIQ**
TORCHERS	TOWMONTS	TRANGLES	**TREPANG**	TRIMMERS	TROLLOPS	TSADDIQS
TORCHON	**TOWNIES**	**TRANKUM**	TREPANGS	**TRIMTAB**	TROLLOPY	**TSARDOM**
TORCHONS	TOWNIEST	TRANKUMS	**TRESSED**	TRIMTABS	**TROMINO**	TSARDOMS
TORDION	**TOWPATH**	**TRANNIE**	STRESSED	**TRINDLE**	TROMINOS	**TSARINA**
TORDIONS	TOWPATHS	TRANNIES	**TRESSEL**	TRINDLED	**TROMMEL**	TSARINAS
TORGOCH	**TOWROPE**	**TRANSIT**	TRESSELS	TRINDLES	TROMMELS	**TSARISM**
TORGOCHS	TOWROPES	TRANSITS	**TRESSES**	**TRINGLE**	**TROOLIE**	TSARISMS
TORMENT	**TOYSHOP**	**TRANSOM**	STRESSES	TRINGLES	TROOLIES	**TSARIST**
TORMENTS	TOYSHOPS	TRANSOMS	**TRESTLE**	**TRINKET**	**TROOPER**	TSARISTS
TORMINA	**TRACHEA**	**TRANTER**	TRESTLES	TRINKETS	TROOPERS	**TSIGANE**
TORMINAL	TRACHEAE	TRANTERS	**TREYBIT**	**TRINKUM**	**TROPHIC**	TSIGANES
TORNADE	TRACHEAL	**TRAPEZE**	TREYBITS	TRINKUMS	STROPHIC	**TSUNAMI**
TORNADES	**TRACING**	TRAPEZED	**TRIARCH**	**TRIOLET**	**TROPISM**	TSUNAMIS
TORPEDO	TRACINGS	TRAPEZES	TRIARCHS	TRIOLETS	TROPISMS	**TUATARA**
TORPEDOS	**TRACKER**	**TRAPPED**	TRIARCHY	ATROPISM	**TROPIST**	TUATARAS
TORRENT	TRACKERS	STRAPPED	**TRIATIC**	TRIONYM	TROPISTS	**TUBBIER**
TORRENTS	**TRACTOR**	**TRAPPER**	TRIATICS	TRIONYMS	**TROTTER**	STUBBIER
TORSADE	TRACTORS	STRAPPER	**TRIAXON**	**TRIPLET**	TROTTERS	**TUBBING**
TORSADES	**TRADING**	TRAPPERS	TRIAXONS	TRIPLETS	**TROUBLE**	STUBBING
TORSION	TRADINGS	**TRASSES**	**TRIBADE**	**TRIPOLI**	TROUBLED	**TUBEFUL**
TORSIONS	**TRADUCE**	STRASSES	TRIBADES	TRIPOLIS	TROUBLER	TUBEFULS
TORTURE	TRADUCED	**TRAVAIL**	**TRIBBLE**	**TRIPPED**	TROUBLES	**TUBFAST**
TORTURED	TRADUCER	TRAVAILS	TRIBBLES	STRIPPED	**TROUNCE**	TUBFASTS
TORTURER	TRADUCES	**TRAWLER**	**TRIBLET**	**TRIPPER**	TROUNCER	**TUFTING**
TORTURES	**TRAFFIC**	TRAWLERS	TRIBLETS	STRIPPER	TROUNCES	TUFTINGS
TORULIN	TRAFFICS	**TRAYBIT**	**TRIBUNE**	TRIPPERS	**TROUPER**	**TUGGING**
TORULINS	**TRAGULE**	TRAYBITS	TRIBUNES	**TRIPPET**	TROUPERS	TUGGINGS
TOSHACH	TRAGULES	**TRAYFUL**	**TRIBUTE**	TRIPPETS	**TROUTER**	**TUILYIE**
TOSHACHS	**TRAIKED**	TRAYFULS	TRIBUTER	**TRIPPLE**	TROUTERS	TUILYIED
TOSSING	STRAIKED	**TREACLE**	TRIBUTES	TRIPPLED	**TROWING**	TUILYIES
TOSSINGS	**TRAILER**	TREACLED	**TRICKER**	TRIPPLER	STROWING	**TUILZIE**
TOSSPOT	TRAILERS	TREACLES	TRICKERS	TRIPPLES	**TRUCAGE**	TUILZIED
TOSSPOTS	**TRAINED**	**TREADER**	TRICKERY	**TRIREME**	TRUCAGES	TUILZIES
TOTIENT	STRAINED	TREADERS	**TRICKLE**	TRIREMES	**TRUCKER**	**TUITION**
TOTIENTS	**TRAINEE**	**TREADLE**	STRICKLE	**TRISECT**	TRUCKERS	TUITIONS
TOTTERS	TRAINEES	TREADLED	TRICKLED	TRISECTS	**TRUCKLE**	**TULCHAN**
STOTTERS	**TRAINER**	TREADLER	TRICKLES	**TRISEME**	TRUCKLED	TULCHANS
TOTTIES	TRAINERS	TREADLES	TRICKLET	TRISEMES	TRUCKLER	**TUMBLED**
TOTTIEST	STRAINER	**TREAGUE**	**TRICORN**	**TRISHAW**	TRUCKLES	STUMBLED
TOTTING	TRAINERS	TREAGUES	TRICORNE	TRISHAWS	**TRUDGEN**	**TUMBLER**
STOTTING	**TRAIPSE**	**TREASON**	TRICORNS	**TRISOME**	TRUDGENS	STUMBLER
TOTTINGS	TRAIPSED	TREASONS	**TRIDARN**	TRISOMES	**TRUDGER**	TUMBLERS
TOUCHER	TRAIPSES	**TREATER**	TRIDARNS	**TRISULA**	TRUDGERS	**TUMBLES**
TOUCHERS	**TRAITOR**	TREATERS	**TRIDENT**	TRISULAS	**TRUFFLE**	STUMBLES
TOUGHEN	TRAITORS	**TREDDLE**	STRIDENT	**TRITIDE**	TRUFFLED	**TUMBREL**
TOUGHENS	**TRAJECT**	TREDDLED	TRIDENTS	TRITIDES	TRUFFLES	TUMBRELS
TOUGHIE	TRAJECTS	TREDDLES	**TRIDUUM**	**TRITIUM**	**TRUMEAU**	**TUMBRIL**
TOUGHIES	**TRAMMEL**	**TREETOP**	TRIDUUMS	TRITIUMS	TRUMEAUS	TUMBRILS
TOURACO	STRAMMEL	TREETOPS	**TRIFFID**	**TRITONE**	TRUMEAUX	**TUMESCE**
TOURACOS	TRAMMELS	**TREFOIL**	TRIFFIDS	TRITONES	**TRUMPET**	TUMESCED
TOURING	**TRAMPED**	TREFOILS	TRIFFIDY	**TRIUMPH**	STRUMPET	TUMESCES
TOURINGS	STRAMPED	**TREHALA**	**TRIFLER**	TRIUMPHS	TRUMPETS	**TUMPING**
TOURISM	**TRAMPER**	TREHALAS	TRIFLERS	**TRIVIUM**	**TRUNDLE**	STUMPING
TOURISMS	TRAMPERS	**TREILLE**	**TRIGGED**	TRIVIUMS	TRUNDLED	**TUMULAR**
TOURIST	**TRAMPET**	TREILLES	STRIGGED	**TRIZONE**	TRUNDLES	
	TRAMPETS			TRIZONES		

TUMULARY	TWATTLER	**UDDERED**	UNCLOAKS	UNIFIERS	UNQUOTES	**UNSTRAP**
TUNICIN	TWATTLES	JUDDERED	**UNCLOSE**	**UNIFIES**	**UNRAVEL**	UNSTRAPS
TUNICINS	**TWEEDLE**	PUDDERED	UNCLOSED	MUNIFIES	UNRAVELS	**UNSTRIP**
TUNICLE	TWEEDLED	**UKELELE**	UNCLOSES	**UNIFORM**	**UNREAVE**	UNSTRIPS
TUNICLES	TWEEDLES	UKELELES	**UNCLOUD**	UNIFORMS	UNREAVED	**UNSUITS**
TUNNAGE	**TWEETER**	**UKULELE**	UNCLOUDS	**UNIQUES**	UNREAVES	SUNSUITS
TUNNAGES	TWEETERS	UKULELES	UNCLOUDY	UNIQUEST	**UNREEVE**	**UNSWEAR**
TUNNING	**TWELFTH**	**ULICHON**	UNCOVER	**UNITING**	UNREEVED	UNSWEARS
STUNNING	TWELFTHS	ULICHONS	UNCOVERS	MUNITING	UNREEVES	**UNTHINK**
TUNNINGS	**TWIBILL**	**ULLAGES**	**UNCRATE**	UNITINGS	**UNRIGHT**	UNTHINKS
TURACIN	TWIBILLS	FULLAGES	UNCRATED	**UNITION**	UNRIGHTS	**UNTRACE**
TURACINS	**TWIDDLE**	SULLAGES	UNCRATES	MUNITION	**UNRIVET**	UNTRACED
TURBAND	TWIDDLED	**ULLINGS**	**UNCROWN**	PUNITION	UNRIVETS	UNTRACES
TURBANDS	TWIDDLER	CULLINGS	UNCROWNS	UNITIONS	**UNROOST**	**UNTREAD**
TURBANT	TWIDDLES	NULLINGS	**UNCTION**	**UNITISE**	UNROOSTS	UNTREADS
TURBANTS	**TWIGGER**	**ULULATE**	FUNCTION	UNITISED	**UNROUND**	**UNTRUST**
TURBINE	TWIGGERS	ULULATED	JUNCTION	UNITISES	UNROUNDS	UNTRUSTS
TURBINED	**TWINING**	ULULATES	UNCTIONS	**UNITIVE**	**UNSAINT**	UNTRUSTY
TURBINES	TWININGS	**UMBERED**	**UNCURSE**	PUNITIVE	UNSAINTS	**UNTRUTH**
TURBITH	**TWINKLE**	CUMBERED	UNCURSED	**UNITIZE**	**UNSCALE**	UNTRUTHS
TURBITHS	TWINKLED	LUMBERED	UNCURSES	UNITIZED	UNSCALED	**UNTWINE**
TURBOND	TWINKLER	NUMBERED	**UNDERDO**	UNITIZES	UNSCALES	UNTWINED
TURBONDS	TWINKLES	**UMBRAGE**	UNDERDOG	UNJOINT	**UNSCREW**	UNTWINES
TURDION	**TWINTER**	UMBRAGED	**UNDIGHT**	UNJOINTS	UNSCREWS	**UNTWIST**
TURDIONS	TWINTERS	UMBRAGES	UNDIGHTS	**UNKNOWN**	**UNSENSE**	UNTWISTS
TURFING	**TWIRLER**	**UMBRELS**	**UNDINES**	UNKNOWNS	UNSENSED	**UNTYING**
TURFINGS	TWIRLERS	TUMBRELS	NUNDINES	**UNLEARN**	UNSENSES	UNTYINGS
TURFITE	**TWISCAR**	**UMBRERE**	**UNDOING**	UNLEARNS	**UNSHALE**	**UNVAILE**
TURFITES	TWISCARS	UMBRERES	UNDOINGS	UNLEARNT	UNSHALED	UNVAILED
TURMOIL	**TWISTER**	**UMBRILS**	**UNEARTH**	**UNLOOSE**	UNSHALES	UNVAILES
TURMOILS	TWISTERS	TUMBRILS	UNEARTHS	UNLOOSED	**UNSHAPE**	**UNVISOR**
TURNDUN	**TWITTEN**	**UMBROUS**	**UNEQUAL**	UNLOOSEN	UNSHAPED	UNVISORS
TURNDUNS	TWITTENS	CUMBROUS	UNEQUALS	UNLOOSES	UNSHAPEN	**UNVOICE**
TURNING	**TWITTER**	**UNALIST**	**UNFAIRS**	**UNMOULD**	UNSHAPES	UNVOICED
TURNINGS	TWITTERS	UNALISTS	FUNFAIRS	UNMOULDS	**UNSHELL**	UNVOICES
TURNKEY	TWITTERY	**UNAWARE**	**UNFAITH**	**UNMOUNT**	UNSHELLS	**UNWARIE**
TURNKEYS	**TWIZZLE**	UNAWARES	UNFAITHS	UNMOUNTS	**UNSHIPS**	UNWARIER
TURNOFF	TWIZZLED	**UNBEGET**	**UNFROCK**	**UNNERVE**	GUNSHIPS	**UNWATER**
TURNOFFS	TWIZZLES	UNBEGETS	UNFROCKS	UNNERVED	NUNSHIPS	UNWATERS
TURPETH	**TWOSOME**	**UNBEING**	**UNFROZE**	UNNERVES	**UNSHOOT**	UNWATERY
TURPETHS	TWOSOMES	UNBEINGS	UNFROZEN	**UNNOBLE**	UNSHOOTS	**UNWEAVE**
TURTLER	**TYCHISM**	**UNBELTS**	**UNGIRTH**	UNNOBLED	**UNSHOUT**	UNWEAVES
TURTLERS	TYCHISMS	SUNBELTS	UNGIRTHS	UNNOBLES	UNSHOUTS	**UNWOMAN**
TUSSOCK	**TYLOPOD**	**UNBLIND**	**UNGLOVE**	**UNORDER**	**UNSINEW**	UNWOMANS
TUSSOCKS	TYLOPODS	UNBLINDS	UNGLOVED	UNORDERS	UNSINEWS	**UNWORTH**
TUSSOCKY	**TYMPANA**	**UNBLOCK**	UNGLOVES	**UNPAINT**	**UNSLING**	UNWORTHS
TUSSORE	TYMPANAL	SUNBLOCK	**UNGUARD**	UNPAINTS	UNSLINGS	UNWORTHY
TUSSORES	**TYMPANI**	UNBLOCKS	UNGUARDS	**UNPANEL**	**UNSNARL**	**UNWRITE**
TUTANIA	TYMPANIC	**UNBOSOM**	**UNGUENT**	UNPANELS	UNSNARLS	UNWRITES
TUTANIAS	**TYPHOID**	UNBOSOMS	UNGUENTS	**UNPAPER**	**UNSNECK**	**UPBRAID**
TUTELAR	TYPHOIDS	**UNBRACE**	**UNHEART**	UNPAPERS	UNSNECKS	UPBRAIDS
TUTELARS	**TYPHOON**	UNBRACED	UNHEARTS	**UNPLACE**	**UNSPEAK**	**UPBREAK**
TUTELARY	TYPHOONS	UNBRACES	**UNHINGE**	UNPLACED	UNSPEAKS	UPBREAKS
TUTENAG	**TYPICAL**	**UNBROKE**	UNHINGED	UNPLACES	**UNSPELL**	**UPBRING**
TUTENAGS	ATYPICAL	UNBROKEN	UNHINGES	**UNPLAIT**	UNSPELLS	UPBRINGS
TUTWORK	ETYPICAL	**UNBUILD**	**UNHOARD**	UNPLAITS	**UNSPOKE**	**UPBROKE**
TUTWORKS	**TYRANNE**	UNBUILDS	UNHOARDS	**UNPLUMB**	UNSPOKEN	UPBROKEN
TWADDLE	TYRANNED	**UNBURNT**	**UNHOODS**	UNPLUMBS	**UNSTACK**	**UPBUILD**
TWADDLED	TYRANNES	SUNBURNT	NUNHOODS	UNPLUME	UNSTACKS	UPBUILDS
TWADDLER	**TZADDIK**	**UNCHAIN**	**UNHORSE**	UNPLUMED	**UNSTATE**	**UPBURST**
TWADDLES	TZADDIKS	UNCHAINS	UNHORSED	UNPLUMES	UNSTATED	UPBURSTS
TWANGLE	**TZADDIQ**	**UNCHARM**	UNHORSES	**UNPURSE**	UNSTATES	**UPCHEER**
TWANGLED	TZADDIQS	UNCHARMS	**UNHOUSE**	UNPURSED	**UNSTEEL**	UPCHEERS
TWANGLES	**UAKARIS**	**UNCHECK**	UNHOUSED	UNPURSES	UNSTEELS	**UPCLIMB**
TWANKAY	OUAKARIS	UNCHECKS	UNHOUSES	**UNQUEEN**	**UNSTICK**	UPCLIMBS
TWANKAYS	**UBEROUS**	**UNCHILD**	**UNICORN**	UNQUEENS	GUNSTICK	**UPCLOSE**
TWASOME	SUBEROUS	UNCHILDS	UNICORNS	**UNQUIET**	UNSTICKS	UPCLOSED
TWASOMES	TUBEROUS	**UNCLASP**	**UNIFIED**	UNQUIETS	**UNSTOCK**	UPCLOSES
TWATTLE	**UDALLER**	UNCLASPS	MUNIFIED	**UNQUOTE**	GUNSTOCK	**UPGOING**
TWATTLED	UDALLERS	**UNCLOAK**	**UNIFIER**	UNQUOTED	UNSTOCKS	UPGOINGS

UPGRADE	UPVALUE	UTOPIANS	VANILLA	VENDAGES	VERSING	VILIAGO
UPGRADED	UPVALUED	UTOPIAS	VANILLAS	VENERER	VERSINGS	VILIAGOS
UPGRADES	UPVALUES	UTOPIAST	VANNING	VENERERS	VERSION	VILLAGE
UPHEAVE	UPWHIRL	UTOPISM	VANNINGS	VENGERS	AVERSION	VILLAGER
UPHEAVED	UPWHIRLS	UTOPISMS	VANTAGE	AVENGERS	EVERSION	VILLAGES
UPHEAVES	URAEMIA	UTOPIST	VANTAGED	VENGING	VERSIONS	VILLAIN
UPHOARD	URAEMIAS	UTOPISTS	VANTAGES	AVENGING	VERTIGO	VILLAINS
UPHOARDS	URALITE	UTRICLE	VAQUERO	VENISON	VERTIGOS	VILLAINY
UPHOIST	URALITES	UTRICLES	VAQUEROS	VENISONS	VERTING	VILLEIN
UPHOISTS	URANIDE	UTTERED	VAREUSE	VENTAGE	AVERTING	VILLEINS
UPHOORD	URANIDES	BUTTERED	VAREUSES	VENTAGES	EVERTING	VINASSE
UPHOORDS	URANISM	GUTTERED	VARIANT	VENTAIL	VERVAIN	VINASSES
UPHROES	URANISMS	MUTTERED	VARIANTS	AVENTAIL	VERVAINS	VINEGAR
EUPHROES	URANITE	PUTTERED	VARIATE	VENTAILE	VESICLE	VINEGARS
UPLYING	URANITES	UTTERER	VARIATED	VENTAILS	VESICLES	VINEGARY
DUPLYING	URANIUM	UTTERERS	VARIATES	VENTANA	VESSAIL	VINTAGE
UPMAKER	URANIUMS	VACANCE	AVARICES	VENTANAS	VESSAILS	VINTAGED
UPMAKERS	UREDINE	VACANCES	VARIOLA	VENTERS	VESTIGE	VINTAGER
UPPINGS	UREDINES	VACATUR	VARIOLAR	EVENTERS	VESTIGES	VINTAGES
CUPPINGS	URETHAN	VACATURS	VARIOLAS	VENTIGE	VESTING	VINTNER
UPRAISE	URETHANE	VACCINE	VARIOLE	VENTIGES	VESTINGS	VINTNERS
UPRAISED	URETHANS	VACCINES	OVARIOLE	VENTING	VESTURE	VIOLATE
UPRAISES	URETHRA	VACCINES	VARIOLES	EVENTING	VESTURED	VIOLATED
UPRIGHT	URETHRAE	VACUATE	VARIOUS	VENTINGS	VESTURER	VIOLATES
UPRIGHTS	URETHRAL	EVACUATE	OVARIOUS	VENTRAL	VESTURES	VIOLENT
UPRISAL	URETHRAS	VACUATED	VARMENT	VENTRALS	VETCHES	VIOLENTS
UPRISALS	URGENCE	VACUATES	VARMENTS	VENTRED	KVETCHES	VIOLIST
UPROUSE	URGENCES	VACUIST	VARMINT	AVENTRED	VETERAN	VIOLISTS
UPROUSED	URGINGS	VACUISTS	VARMINTS	VENTRES	VETERANS	VIOLONE
UPROUSES	PURGINGS	VACUOLE	VARYING	AVENTRES	VETIVER	VIOLONES
UPSHOOT	SURGINGS	VACUOLES	VARYINGS	VENTURE	VETIVERS	VIRANDA
UPSHOOTS	URICASE	VAGRANT	VASCULA	VENTURED	VETKOEK	VIRANDAS
UPSILON	URICASES	VAGRANTS	VASCULAR	VENTURER	VETKOEKS	VIRANDO
UPSILONS	URIDINE	VAILING	VASSAIL	VENTURES	VETTURA	VIRANDOS
UPSPEAK	URIDINES	AVAILING	VASSAILS	VENTURI	VETTURAS	VIRELAY
UPSPEAKS	URINATE	VAIVODE	VAULTER	VENTURIS	VIADUCT	VIRELAYS
UPSPEAR	URINATED	VAIVODES	VAULTERS	VERANDA	VIADUCTS	VIRETOT
UPSPEARS	URINATES	VALANCE	VAUNTED	VERANDAH	VIALFUL	VIRETOTS
UPSPOKE	URNINGS	VALANCED	AVAUNTED	VERANDAS	VIALFULS	VIRGATE
UPSPOKEN	BURNINGS	VALANCES	VAUNTER	VERBENA	VIATORS	VIRGATES
UPSTAGE	TURNINGS	VALENCE	VAUNTERS	VERBENAS	AVIATORS	VIRGULE
UPSTAGED	URODELE	VALENCES	VAUNTERY	VERBOSE	VIBRATE	VIRGULES
UPSTAGES	URODELES	VALIANT	VAURIEN	VERBOSER	VIBRATED	VISCERA
UPSTAIR	UROLITH	VALIANTS	VAURIENS	VERDICT	VIBRATES	VISCERAL
UPSTAIRS	UROLITHS	VALONEA	VEDALIA	VERDICTS	VIBRATO	VISCOSE
UPSTAND	UROLOGY	VALONEAS	VEDALIAS	VERDURE	VIBRATOR	VISCOSES
UPSTANDS	OUROLOGY	VALONIA	VEDETTE	VERDURED	VIBRATOS	VISIBLE
UPSTARE	UROMERE	VALONIAS	VEDETTES	VERDURES	VICEROY	VISIBLES
UPSTARED	UROMERES	VALUATE	VEERING	VERISMO	VICEROYS	VISITEE
UPSTARES	UROSOME	EVALUATE	VEERINGS	VERISMOS	VICIATE	VISITEES
UPSTART	UROSOMES	VALUATED	VEGETAL	VERMEIL	VICIATED	VISITER
UPSTARTS	USHERED	VALUATES	VEGETALS	VERMEILS	VICIATES	VISITERS
UPSURGE	HUSHERED	VALVULA	VEHICLE	VERMELL	VICOMTE	VISITOR
UPSURGED	USUCAPT	VALVULAE	VEHICLES	VERMELLS	VICOMTES	VISITORS
UPSURGES	USUCAPTS	VALVULAR	VEILING	VERNIER	VICTORS	VITAMIN
UPSWARM	USURPER	VALVULE	VEILINGS	VERNIERS	VICTUAL	VITAMINE
UPSWARMS	USURPERS	VALVULES	VEINING	VERONAL	VICTUALS	VITAMINS
UPSWEEP	UTENSIL	VAMOOSE	VEININGS	VERONALS	VIDETTE	VITELLI
UPSWEEPS	UTENSILS	VAMOOSED	VEINLET	VERRUCA	VIDETTES	VITELLIN
UPSWELL	UTILISE	VAMPING	VEINLETS	VERRUCAE	VIDUAGE	VITIATE
UPSWELLS	UTILISED	VAMPINGS	VELIGER	VERRUCAS	VIDUAGES	VITIATED
UPSWING	UTILISER	VAMPIRE	VELIGERS	VERRUGA	VIEWING	VITIATES
UPSWINGS	UTILISES	VAMPIRED	VELOUTE	VERRUGAS	VIEWINGS	VITRAGE
UPTHROW	UTILITY	VAMPIRES	VELOUTES	VERSANT	VIHUELA	VITRAGES
UPTHROWN	FUTILITY	VANDYKE	VENATOR	VERSANTS	VIHUELAS	VITRAIN
UPTHROWS	UTILIZE	VANDYKED	VENATORS	VERSETS	VILAYET	VITRAINS
UPTRAIN	UTILIZED	VANDYKES	VENDACE	OVERSETS	VILAYETS	VITREUM
UPTRAINS	UTILIZER	VANESSA	VENDACES	VERSINE	VILIACO	VITREUMS
UPTREND	UTILIZES	VANESSAS	VENDAGE	VERSINES	VILIACOS	VITRINE
UPTRENDS	UTOPIAN					VITRINES

VITRIOL	WAFTING	AWANTING	WASTREL	WEDLOCKS	WHAIZLES	WHIRLERS
VITRIOLS	WAFTINGS	WANTINGS	WASTRELS	WEEDIER	WHALING	WHIRRET
VOCABLE	WAFTURE	WAPPERS	WATCHER	WEEDING	WHAMPLE	WHIRRETS
VOCABLES	WAFTURES	SWAPPERS	WATCHERS	WEEDINGS	WHAMPLES	WHIRTLE
VOCODER	WAGERER	WAPPING	WATCHES	WEEKDAY	WHANGAM	WHIRTLES
VOCODERS	WAGERERS	SWAPPING	SWATCHES	WEEKDAYS	WHANGAMS	WHISKER
VOICING	WAGGING	WARATAH	WATCHET	WEEKEND	WHANGEE	WHISKERS
VOICINGS	SWAGGING	WARATAHS	WATCHETS	WEEKENDS	WHANGEES	WHISKERY
VOIDING	WAGONER	WARBLER	WATERER	WEEPERS	WHATNOT	WHISKET
AVOIDING	WAGONERS	WARBLERS	WATERERS	SWEEPERS	WHATNOTS	WHISKETS
VOIDINGS	WAGTAIL	WARDING	WATTAGE	WEEPIER	WHATSIT	WHISKEY
VOITURE	WAGTAILS	AWARDING	WATTAGES	SWEEPIER	WHATSITS	WHISKEYS
VOITURES	WAILING	SWARDING	WATTLED	WEEPIES	WHEEDLE	WHISPER
VOIVODE	WAILINGS	WARDINGS	TWATTLED	WEEPIEST	WHEEDLED	WHISPERS
VOIVODES	WAINAGE	WARDROP	WATTLES	WEEPING	WHEEDLER	WHISPERY
VOLANTE	WAINAGES	WARDROPS	TWATTLES	SWEEPING	WHEEDLES	WHISTLE
VOLANTES	WAINING	WARFARE	WAULING	WEEPINGS	WHEELER	WHISTLED
VOLPINO	SWAINING	WARFARED	WAULINGS	WEETING	WHEELERS	WHISTLER
VOLPINOS	WAISTER	WARFARER	WAVELET	SWEETING	WHEELIE	WHISTLES
VOLTAGE	WAISTERS	WARFARES	WAVELETS	TWEETING	WHEELIER	WHITHER
VOLTAGES	WAITING	WARHEAD	WAVERER	WEFTAGE	WHEELIES	WHITHERS
VOLUSPA	AWAITING	WARHEADS	WAVERERS	WEFTAGES	WHEENGE	WHITIES
VOLUSPAS	WAITINGS	WARISON	WAVESON	WEIGELA	WHEENGED	WHITIEST
VOLUTED	WAIVODE	WARISONS	WAVESONS	WEIGELAS	WHEENGES	WHITING
EVOLUTED	WAIVODES	WARLING	WAWLING	WEIGHER	WHEEPLE	WHITINGS
VOLUTES	WAIWODE	WARLINGS	WAWLINGS	WEIGHERS	WHEEPLED	WHITLOW
EVOLUTES	WAIWODES	WARLOCK	WAXBILL	WEIRDIE	WHEEPLES	WHITLOWS
VOLUTIN	WAKENED	WARLOCKS	WAXBILLS	WEIRDIES	WHEESHT	WHITRET
VOLUTINS	AWAKENED	WARLORD	WAXWING	WELCHER	WHEESHTS	WHITRETS
VOLVING	WAKENER	WARLORDS	WAXWINGS	WELCHERS	WHEEZLE	WHITTAW
EVOLVING	WAKENERS	WARMERS	WAXWORK	WELCOME	WHEEZLED	WHITTAWS
VOUCHED	WAKINGS	SWARMERS	WAXWORKS	WELCOMED	WHEEZLES	WHITTER
AVOUCHED	AWAKINGS	WARMING	WAYFARE	WELCOMER	WHEMMLE	WHITTERS
VOUCHEE	WALIEST	SWARMING	WAYFARED	WELCOMES	WHEMMLED	WHITTLE
VOUCHEES	SWALIEST	WARMINGS	WAYFARER	WELDING	WHEMMLES	WHITTLED
VOUCHER	WALKING	WARNING	WAYFARES	WELDINGS	WHERRET	WHITTLER
VOUCHERS	WALKINGS	AWARNING	WAYMARK	WELFARE	WHERRETS	WHITTLES
VOUCHES	WALKWAY	WARNINGS	WAYMARKS	WELFARES	WHETTER	WHIZZER
AVOUCHES	WALKWAYS	WARPATH	WAYMENT	WELLING	WHETTERS	WHIZZERS
VOYAGER	WALLABA	WARPATHS	WAYMENTS	DWELLING	WHICKER	WHOLISM
VOYAGERS	WALLABAS	WARPING	WAYSIDE	SWELLING	WHICKERS	WHOLISMS
VULGATE	WALLETS	WARPINGS	WAYSIDES	WELLINGS	WHIDDER	WHOMBLE
EVULGATE	SWALLETS	WARRAND	WEARERS	WELSHER	WHIDDERS	WHOMBLED
VULGATES	WALLIES	WARRANDS	SWEARERS	WELSHERS	WHIFFER	WHOMBLES
VULTURE	WALLIEST	WARRANT	WEARIED	WELTERS	WHIFFET	WHOMMLE
VULTURES	WALLING	WARRANTS	AWEARIED	SWELTERS	WHIFFETS	WHOMMLED
VULTURN	WALLINGS	WARRANTY	WEARIES	WELTING	WHIFFLE	WHOMMLES
VULTURNS	WALLOWS	WARRIOR	WEARIEST	SWELTING	WHIFFLED	WHOOBUB
WABBLER	SWALLOWS	WARRIORS	WEARING	WENCHER	WHIFFLER	WHOOBUBS
WABBLERS	WALTZER	WARSHIP	SWEARING	WENCHERS	WHIFFLES	WHOOPEE
WABSTER	WALTZERS	WARSHIPS	WEARINGS	WENDIGO	WHIMPER	WHOOPEES
WABSTERS	WAMEFUL	WARTIER	WEASAND	WENDIGOS	WHIMPERS	WHOOPER
WADDIES	WAMEFULS	SWARTIER	WEASANDS	WERGILD	WHIMPLE	WHOOPERS
SWADDIES	WANGLED	WARTIME	WEATHER	WERGILDS	WHIMPLED	WHOPPER
WADDING	TWANGLED	WARTIMES	WEATHERS	WESTERN	WHIMPLES	WHOPPERS
WADDINGS	WANGLER	WASHERS	WEAVING	WESTERNS	WHIMSEY	WHUMMLE
WADDLED	WANGLERS	SWASHERS	WEAVINGS	WESTING	WHIMSEYS	WHUMMLED
SWADDLED	WANGLES	WASHIER	WEAZAND	WESTINGS	WHINGER	WHUMMLES
TWADDLED	TWANGLES	SWASHIER	WEAZANDS	WETBACK	WHINGERS	WIDDLED
WADDLES	WANHOPE	WASHING	WEBBING	WETBACKS	WHINING	TWIDDLED
SWADDLES	WANHOPES	SWASHING	WEBBINGS	WETLAND	WHININGS	WIDDLES
TWADDLES	WANIGAN	WASHINGS	WEBSTER	WETLANDS	WHIPCAT	TWIDDLES
WADMAAL	WANIGANS	WASPIES	WEBSTERS	WHACKER	WHIPCATS	WIDENER
WADMAALS	WANKERS	WASPIEST	WEBWORM	WHACKERS	WHIPPER	WIDENERS
WADMOLL	SWANKERS	WASSAIL	WEBWORMS	WHAISLE	WHIPPERS	WIDGEON
WADMOLLS	WANKING	WASSAILS	WEDDING	WHAISLED	WHIPPET	WIDGEONS
WADSETT	SWANKING	WASTAGE	WEDDINGS	WHAISLES	WHIPPETS	WIDOWER
WADSETTS	WANTAGE	WASTAGES	WEDGING	WHAIZLE	WHIRLER	WIDOWERS
WAFTAGE	WANTAGES	WASTING	WEDGINGS	WHAIZLED		WIELDER
WAFTAGES	WANTING	WASTINGS	WEDLOCK			WIELDERS

WIGGING	WINIEST	WITLOOFS	WORDING	WRINKLE	YELPING	ZEMSTVOS
SWIGGING	TWINIEST	WITTERS	SWORDING	WRINKLED	YELPINGS	ZEOLITE
TWIGGING	WINKING	TWITTERS	WORDINGS	WRINKLES	YESHIVA	ZEOLITES
WIGGINGS	SWINKING	WITTING	WORKING	WRITING	YESHIVAH	ZETETIC
WIGGLER	TWINKING	TWITTING	WORKINGS	WRITINGS	YESHIVAS	ZETETICS
WIGGLERS	WINKINGS	WITTINGS	WORKTOP	WRONGER	YIELDER	ZEUXITE
WIGHTED	WINKLER	WITWALL	WORKTOPS	WRONGERS	YIELDERS	ZEUXITES
TWIGHTED	TWINKLER	WITWALLS	WORRIER	WRYBILL	YOGHURT	ZIGANKA
WILDCAT	WINKLERS	WOBBLER	WORRIERS	WRYBILLS	YOGHURTS	ZIGANKAS
WILDCATS	WINKLES	WOBBLERS	WORSHIP	WRYNECK	YOUNGTH	ZILLION
WILDING	TWINKLES	WOIWODE	WORSHIPS	WRYNECKS	YOUNGTHS	ZILLIONS
WILDINGS	WINNING	WOIWODES	WORSTED	XANTHIN	YOUNKER	ZIMOCCA
WILDOAT	TWINNING	WOLFING	WORSTEDS	XANTHINE	YOUNKERS	ZIMOCCAS
WILDOATS	WINNINGS	WOLFINGS	WOSBIRD	XANTHINS	YOWLING	ZINCITE
WILLERS	WINNOCK	WOLFKIN	WOSBIRDS	XERAFIN	YOWLINGS	ZINCITES
SWILLERS	WINNOCKS	WOLFKINS	WOTTING	XERAFINS	YPSILON	ZINCODE
WILLIES	WINSOME	WOLFRAM	SWOTTING	XERASIA	YPSILONS	ZINCODES
TWILLIES	WINSOMER	WOLFRAMS	WOUNDED	XERASIAS	YTTRIUM	ZITHERN
WILLING	WINTERS	WOLVING	SWOUNDED	XYLENOL	YTTRIUMS	ZITHERNS
SWILLING	TWINTERS	WOLVINGS	WOUNDER	XYLENOLS	ZABTIEH	ZOARIUM
TWILLING	WIPEOUT	WOODCUT	WOUNDERS	XYLITOL	ZABTIEHS	ZOARIUMS
WILTING	WIPEOUTS	WOODCUTS	WOURALI	XYLITOLS	ZADDIKS	ZOCCOLO
TWILTING	WIRETAP	WOODIES	WOURALIS	XYLOGEN	TZADDIKS	ZOCCOLOS
WIMBREL	WIRETAPS	WOODIEST	WRANGLE	XYLOGENS	ZAMARRA	ZOISITE
WIMBRELS	WISHERS	WOOLDER	WRANGLED	YACHTER	ZAMARRAS	ZOISITES
WINCING	SWISHERS	WOOLDERS	WRANGLER	YACHTERS	ZAMARRO	ZONULET
WINCINGS	WISHING	WOOLFAT	WRANGLES	YAFFING	ZAMARROS	ZONULETS
WINDAGE	SWISHING	WOOLFATS	WRAPPER	NYAFFING	ZAMOUSE	ZOOLITE
WINDAGES	WISHINGS	WOOLLEN	WRAPPERS	YAKHDAN	ZAMOUSES	ZOOLITES
WINDIGO	WISSING	WOOLLENS	WREAKER	YAKHDANS	ZANELLA	ZOOLITH
WINDIGOS	SWISSING	WOOLSEY	WREAKERS	YAMULKA	ZANELLAS	ZOOLITHS
WINDING	WISTING	WOOLSEYS	WREATHE	YAMULKAS	ZANJERO	ZOONITE
WINDINGS	TWISTING	WOOMERA	WREATHED	YAPSTER	ZANJEROS	ZOONITES
WINDLES	WISTITI	WOOMERAS	WREATHEN	YAPSTERS	ZANYISM	ZOOTYPE
DWINDLES	WISTITIS	WOONING	WREATHER	YARDAGE	ZANYISMS	ZOOTYPES
SWINDLES	WITCHED	SWOONING	WREATHES	YARDAGES	ZAPTIAH	ZORGITE
WINDLESS	SWITCHED	WOORALI	WRECKER	YARDANG	ZAPTIAHS	ZORGITES
WINDOCK	TWITCHED	WOORALIS	WRECKERS	YARDANGS	ZAPTIEH	ZORILLE
WINDOCKS	WITCHEN	WOORARA	WRESTER	YASHMAK	ZAPTIEHS	ZORILLO
WINDORE	WITCHENS	WOORARAS	WRESTERS	YASHMAKS	ZAREEBA	ZORILLOS
WINDORES	WITCHES	WOOSELL	WRESTLE	YATAGAN	ZAREEBAS	ZYMITES
WINDROW	SWITCHES	WOOSELLS	WRESTLED	YATAGANS	ZARNICH	AZYMITES
WINDROWS	TWITCHES	WOOSHED	WRESTLER	YAWNING	ZARNICHS	ZYMOGEN
WINGERS	WITHERS	SWOOSHED	WRESTLES	YAWNINGS	ZEALANT	ZYMOGENS
SWINGERS	SWITHERS	WOOSHES	WRIGGLE	YEALDON	ZEALANTS	ZYMOTIC
WINGING	WITHIES	SWOOSHES	WRIGGLED	YEALDONS	ZEBRULA	ZYMOTICS
SWINGING	WITHIEST	WOPPING	WRIGGLER	YELLING	ZEBRULAS	
TWINGING	WITLING	SWOPPING	WRIGGLES	YELLINGS	ZEBRULE	
WINGLET	WITLINGS	WORDAGE	WRINGER	YELLOCH	ZEBRULES	
WINGLETS	WITLOOF	WORDAGES	WRINGERS	YELLOCHS	ZEMSTVO	

SECTION FIVE

ANAGRAMS

Introduction

This final substantial section contains all valid seven-letter and eight-letter words arranged in alphabetical order of their constituent letters.

Suppose you have the seven letters THORCES on your rack. You are convinced that there must be a valid 7-letter word there. Just arrange the letters in alphabetical order (CEHORST), then look for CEHORST in the following seven-letter lists, where it appears alphabetically ordered between CEHORSS and CEHORSU. You will find that there are six valid anagrams of your seven letters! Perhaps you have the seven letters CORLINE, and you cannot see a valid seven-letter word. Arrange the letters into alphabetical order (CEILNOR) and check the list here. Lo and behold! The list goes from CEILNOP to CEILNOS, confirming that there is no valid anagram of those seven letters.

The same theory applies to eight-letter words. All valid eight-letter words have been reduced to their alphabetically ordered forms, and these have then been arranged themselves into alphabetical order. What anagrams, if any, are there for the eight letters THROUCES? Easy! Put the letters into alphabetical order, check CEHORSTU in the eight-letter list, and find that SCOUTHER and TOUCHERS are both valid words!

The Seven-Letter Anagrams list contains over 25 000 words, and the Eight-Letter list has over 29 000 words. Happy anagram searching!

7-LETTER ANAGRAMS

AAAALTY	ATALAYA	AAACPST	PATACAS	AAAIQRU	AQUARIA	AABCINR	CARABIN
AAABBCL	CABBALA	AAACRWY	CARAWAY	AAAISTX	ATAXIAS	AABCIOP	COPAIBA
AAABBKL	KABBALA	AAACSST	CASSATA	AAAJKST	JATAKAS	AABCITX	TAXICAB
AAABCCR	BACCARA	AAACSSV	CASSAVA	AAAJMPS	PAJAMAS	AABCKLY	LAYBACK
AAABCIR	ARABICA	AAACSTT	CATASTA	AAAKKMR	MARKKAA	AABCKPY	BACKPAY
AAABCLS	CABALAS	AAADELM	ALAMEDA	AAAKKNS	KANAKAS	AABCKRR	BARRACK
AAABCLV	BACLAVA	AAADFRY	FARADAY	AAAKKRS	KARAKAS	AABCKSW	BACKSAW
AAABCMR	CARAMBA	AAADHMR	ADHARMA	AAAKLMS	KAMALAS	AABCLMU	CALUMBA
AAABCNR	BARACAN	AAADILX	ADAXIAL	AAAKNRS	ANARAKS	AABCLSY	SCYBALA
AAABCNS	CABANAS	AAADIRT	DATARIA	AAAKNST	KATANAS	AABCMSU	SAMBUCA
AAABCTW	CATAWBA	AAADJMR	JAMADAR	AAALLPT	PALATAL	AABCORT	ABACTOR
AAABDGS	DAGABAS	AAADLMN	MANDALA	AAALMSS	SALAAMS		ACROBAT
AAABDHS	BAHADAS	AAADLMW	WADMAAL	AAALNNT	LANTANA	AABCOTT	CATBOAT
AAABDJS	BAJADAS	AAADMNT	ADAMANT	AAALNPT	APLANAT	AABCRSS	SCARABS
AAABDNN	BANDANA	AAADMRS	ARMADAS	AAALWYY	LAYAWAY	AABCSUU	AUCUBAS
AAABEGL	GALABEA		MADRASA	AAAMNNS	MANANAS	AABCTTU	CATTABU
AAABFLL	FALBALA	AAADNPS	PANADAS	AAAMNPS	PANAMAS	AABDDEN	ABANDED
AAABGIL	GALABIA	AAADNRS	SARDANA	AAAMNRT	AMARANT	AABDDER	ABRADED
AAABILX	ABAXIAL	AAADNRT	TANADAR	AAAMNSS	SAMAANS	AABDEFL	FADABLE
AAABKLS	KABALAS	AAAEGLT	GALATEA	AAAMNST	ATAMANS	AABDEGN	BANDAGE
AAABKLV	BAKLAVA	AAAEGNP	APANAGE	AAAMPRT	PATAMAR	AABDEHS	ABASHED
AAABKSY	KABAYAS	AAAEHKT	TAKAHEA	AAAMRRZ	ZAMARRA	AABDEIS	DIABASE
AAABLLW	WALLABA	AAAEHLT	ALTHAEA	AAAMRSS	SAMARAS	AABDELL	BALLADE
AAABLPR	PALABRA	AAAEIMN	ANAEMIA	AAAMRST	TAMARAS	AABDELT	ABLATED
AAABLST	ALBATAS	AAAELMP	PALAMAE	AAANNSV	SAVANNA		DATABLE
	ATABALS	AAAELSZ	AZALEAS	AAANNTT	ANNATTA	AABDEMN	BEADMAN
	BALATAS	AAAENST	ANATASE	AAANRTT	TANTARA	AABDENU	BANDEAU
AAABMOS	ABOMASA	AAAFFLL	ALFALFA		TARTANA	AABDERS	ABRADES
AAABMST	MASTABA	AAAFIRT	RATAFIA	AAANSTT	ANATTAS	AABDERY	ABRAYED
AAABNNR	RABANNA	AAAFNRS	SARAFAN	AAAOPRZ	PARAZOA	AABDESU	AUBADES
AAABNNS	BANANAS	AAAFRWY	FARAWAY	AAAPPRT	APPARAT	AABDGHN	HANDBAG
AAABORR	ARAROBA	AAAGGLN	GALANGA	AAAPPSY	PAPAYAS	AABDGMO	GAMBADO
AAABRSX	ABRAXAS	AAAGHIP	APHAGIA	AAARSST	SATARAS	AABDGNS	SANDBAG
AAABRSZ	BAZAARS	AAAGHLN	LANGAHA	AAARSTV	AVATARS	AABDGOS	DAGOBAS
AAABSTT	BATATAS	AAAGHNT	ATAGHAN	AAARTTU	TUATARA	AABDHMS	BADMASH
AAACCIS	ACACIAS	AAAGHPR	AGRAPHA	AAARTXY	ATARAXY	AABDHNT	HATBAND
AAACCLR	CARACAL	AAAGIPT	PATAGIA	AABBBOS	BAOBABS	AABDHNY	HAYBAND
AAACCRS	CASCARA	AAAGISS	ASSAGAI	AABBCEG	CABBAGE	AABDHRS	BARDASH
AAACDLU	ACAUDAL	AAAGLMM	AMALGAM	AABBCGY	CABBAGY	AABDIIS	BASIDIA
AAACDMM	MACADAM	AAAGLMN	NAGMAAL	AABBDGR	GABBARD	AABDILN	BALADIN
AAACDNS	CANADAS	AAAGLNS	LASAGNA	AABBDHS	HABDABS	AABDIMR	BARMAID
AAACENP	PANACEA	AAAGLRS	ARGALAS	AABBELT	BATABLE	AABDINS	INDABAS
AAACGNT	AGACANT	AAAGMMT	MAGMATA	AABBERT	BARBATE	AABDINT	TABANID
AAACHLZ	CHALAZA	AAAGMNR	ANAGRAM	AABBGRT	GABBART	AABDIOT	BIODATA
AAACHNT	ACANTHA	AAAGMNS	SAGAMAN	AABBHLS	BABLAHS	AABDIRS	ABRAIDS
AAACHRY	ACHARYA	AAAGNNS	NAGANAS	AABBLLS	LABLABS	AABDLLS	BALLADS
AAACILM	MALACIA	AAAGNPR	PARGANA	AABBLOR	BARBOLA	AABDLMS	LAMBDAS
AAACIMR	CARIAMA	AAAGNRT	TANAGRA	AABBLOS	BALBOAS	AABDLNS	SALBAND
AAACINP	ACAPNIA	AAAGNRU	GUARANA	AABBSST	SABBATS	AABDLRW	BRADAWL
AAACINR	ACARIAN	AAAGNTY	YATAGAN	AABBSSU	BABASSU	AABDMNR	ARMBAND
AAACJMR	JACAMAR	AAAHHLV	HALAVAH	AABCCEL	ACCABLE	AABDNNO	ABANDON
AAACJNS	JACANAS	AAAHIPS	APHASIA	AABCCER	BACCARE	AABDNOR	BANDORA
AAACLLV	CAVALLA	AAAHJKW	KAJAWAH	AABCCET	BACCATE	AABDNRS	BANDARS
AAACLMN	ALMANAC	AAAHLMR	HARMALA	AABCCIR	BRACCIA	AABDNRU	BANDURA
AAACLPS	ALPACAS	AAAHLNN	ALANNAH	AABCEKR	BACKARE	AABDORS	ABROADS
AAACLPT	CATALPA	AAAHMMT	MAHATMA	AABCELN	BALANCE	AABDORV	BRAVADO
AAACLRZ	ALCAZAR	AAAHMRS	ASHRAMA	AABCELP	CAPABLE	AABDRST	BASTARD
AAACMNP	CAMPANA	AAAHMST	TAMASHA		PACABLE		TABARDS
AAACMRS	MARACAS	AAAHPRT	PARATHA	AABCEMR	MACABRE	AABDRSU	SUBADAR
	MASCARA	AAAHRTW	WARATAH	AABCERR	BARRACE	AABDRSY	BAYARDS
AAACNNR	CARANNA	AAAILLS	ALALIAS	AABCERT	ABREACT	AABDSTU	DATABUS
AAACNPT	CATAPAN	AAAILMR	MALARIA		CABARET	AABEELT	EATABLE
AAACNRT	NACARAT	AAAILPS	APLASIA	AABCHMT	AMBATCH	AABEEMO	AMOEBAE
AAACNRU	CARAUNA	AAAILRS	ARALIAS	AABCHNR	BARCHAN	AABEERZ	ZAREEBA
AAACNRV	CARAVAN	AAAILRT	TALARIA	AABCHOR	ABROACH	AABEFFL	AFFABLE
AAACNST	CANASTA	AAAIMNT	AMANITA	AABCHSS	CASBAHS	AABEFFN	BEFFANA
AAACNTT	CANTATA	AAAIPRX	APRAXIA	AABCILM	CAMBIAL	AABEFGU	AUFGABE

AABEFNS	BEFANAS		BAAINGS	AABMSSY	AMBASSY	AACDEHT	CATHEAD
AABEGGG	BAGGAGE	AABGINT	ABATING	AABNNOZ	BONANZA	AACDEII	AECIDIA
AABEGGR	GARBAGE	AABGRST	RATBAGS	AABNNSY	BANYANS	AACDEIL	ALCAIDE
AABEGLR	ALGEBRA	AABHHIS	SAHIBAH	AABNOST	SABATON	AACDEIN	AIDANCE
AABEGMR	BERGAMA	AABHHRU	BRUHAHA	AABORRS	ARROBAS	AACDEIS	ACEDIAS
	MEGABAR	AABHISS	SAHIBAS	AABORST	ABATORS	AACDELL	ALCALDE
AABEGMS	AMBAGES	AABHITT	HABITAT	AABORSZ	ABRAZOS	AACDELN	CANDELA
AABEGRR	BAGARRE	AABHJNS	BHAJANS	AABOTTY	ATTABOY		DECANAL
	BARRAGE	AABHKNR	BARKHAN	AABQSUU	SUBAQUA	AACDELR	CALDERA
AABEGSS	BAGASSE	AABHKSS	KASBAHS	AABRRST	BARRATS	AACDELS	SCALADE
AABEGST	ATABEGS	AABHLRS	BHARALS	AABRRSU	SABURRA	AACDELY	ALCAYDE
AABEGSU	ABUSAGE	AABHLTY	BATHYAL	AABRRUV	BRAVURA	AACDEMY	ACADEMY
AABEHLT	HATABLE	AABHSSW	BASHAWS	AABRSTY	BARYTAS	AACDENV	ADVANCE
AABEHNT	ABTHANE	AABIILX	BIAXIAL	AABSSSY	SASSABY	AACDENZ	CADENZA
AABEHRS	EARBASH	AABIJMY	JAMBIYA	AABTTTU	BATTUTA	AACDEPS	SCAPAED
AABEHSS	ABASHES	AABIKNS	BANKSIA	AACCDES	CASCADE	AACDERS	ARCADES
AABEIKN	IKEBANA	AABILLR	BARILLA		SACCADE	AACDERV	CADAVER
AABEILM	AMABILE	AABILLS	LABIALS	AACCDIR	CARDIAC	AACDETU	CAUDATE
	AMIABLE	AABILMN	BIMANAL	AACCDIS	CICADAS	AACDEUX	CADEAUX
AABEILS	ABELIAS	AABILMY	AMIABLY	AACCDSU	CADUACS	AACDFIR	FARADIC
AABEILT	LABIATE	AABILOU	ABOULIA	AACCEKR	CARCAKE	AACDFRS	CAFARDS
AABEIRS	ARABISE	AABILRS	BASILAR	AACCELO	CLOACAE	AACDHMR	DRACHMA
AABEIRZ	ARABIZE	AABILST	BALISTA	AACCENV	VACANCE	AACDHNR	HANDCAR
AABEJLL	JELLABA	AABILSU	ABULIAS	AACCERS	CARCASE	AACDHRS	CHADARS
AABEJMU	JAMBEAU	AABIMMR	MARIMBA	AACCEST	SACCATE	AACDIIS	ASCIDIA
AABEKLM	MAKABLE	AABINNS	BANIANS	AACCHHK	KACHCHA	AACDILR	RADICAL
AABEKLT	TAKABLE	AABINOU	OUABAIN	AACCHIR	ARCHAIC	AACDINT	ANTACID
AABEKST	ATABEKS	AABINRS	ARABINS	AACCHKS	KACCHAS	AACDINV	VANADIC
AABELLL	LABELLA	AABINRT	ATABRIN	AACCHLN	CLACHAN	AACDIOR	ACAROID
AABELLN	BALNEAL	AABINST	ABSTAIN	AACCHMP	CHAMPAC	AACDIRS	ACARIDS
AABELLO	ABOLLAE	AABINSW	WABAINS	AACCHMS	CHACMAS		ASCARID
AABELLS	SABELLA	AABIPUX	PAXIUBA	AACCHNN	CANNACH	AACDJKW	JACKDAW
	SALABLE	AABIRSZ	ZARIBAS	AACCHRT	CHARACT	AACDLNO	CALANDO
AABELMN	NAMABLE	AABISTT	ABATTIS	AACCILM	ACCLAIM	AACDLNS	SCANDAL
AABELMT	TAMABLE	AABKNRS	BARKANS	AACCILS	CICALAS	AACDLOR	CARLOAD
AABELNO	ABALONE	AABKOOZ	BAZOOKA	AACCIMS	CAIMACS	AACDLOS	SCALADO
AABELNR	BANALER	AABLLNS	BALLANS	AACCIOR	CARIOCA	AACDLPR	PLACARD
AABELPP	PAPABLE	AABLLNT	BALLANT	AACCITT	ATACTIC	AACDMPS	MADCAPS
AABELPR	PARABLE	AABLLNY	BANALLY	AACCKLP	CALPACK	AACDNRS	CADRANS
AABELPY	PAYABLE	AABLLOS	ABOLLAS	AACCKRR	CARRACK		CANARDS
AABELRT	RATABLE	AABLLPT	PATBALL	AACCKRS	CARACKS	AACDOOV	AVOCADO
AABELSS	BALASES	AABLLST	BALLAST	AACCLLO	CLOACAL	AACDRSS	CSARDAS
AABELST	ABLATES		BALLATS	AACCLLT	CATCALL	AACDRSZ	CZARDAS
	ASTABLE	AABLLSY	SALABLY	AACCLOP	POLACCA	AACEEGR	ACREAGE
AABELSV	SAVABLE	AABLLWY	WALLABY	AACCLOR	CARACOL	AACEEHR	EARACHE
AABELSY	SAYABLE	AABLMRU	LABARUM	AACCLPS	CALPACS	AACEEHT	CHAETAE
AABELTU	TABLEAU	AABLMSS	BALSAMS	AACCLPT	PLACCAT	AACEELN	ANELACE
	TABULAE		SAMBALS	AACCLRS	CALCARS	AACEENT	CATENAE
AABELTX	TAXABLE	AABLMST	LAMBAST	AACCLRU	ACCRUAL	AACEETT	ACETATE
AABEMNS	BASEMAN	AABLMSY	ABYSMAL		CARACUL	AACEFLT	FALCATE
AABEMOS	AMOEBAS		BALSAMY	AACCLSU	ACCUSAL	AACEFLU	FACULAE
AABENRT	ANTBEAR	AABLNTT	BLATANT	AACCMOS	MACACOS	AACEFMN	FACEMAN
AABENTY	ABEYANT	AABLORT	ABLATOR	AACCNNS	CANCANS	AACEFRS	CARAFES
AABERST	ABREAST	AABLOSV	LAVABOS	AACCNVY	VACANCY	AACEGGR	AGGRACE
AABERSU	BAUERAS	AABLPRU	PABULAR	AACCORU	CURACAO	AACEGHS	ACHAGES
AABERSZ	ZAREBAS	AABLRST	ARBLAST		CURACOA	AACEGKP	PACKAGE
AABERTT	RABATTE	AABLRTU	TABULAR	AACCOST	ACCOAST	AACEGKS	SACKAGE
	TABARET	AABLRTY	RATABLY	AACCOTT	TOCCATA	AACEGNR	CARNAGE
AABERTU	ABATURE	AABLSST	BASALTS	AACCRRT	CARRACT		CRANAGE
AABESTZ	ZABETAS	AABLSSY	ABYSSAL	AACCRSS	CARCASS	AACEGRT	CARTAGE
AABETUX	BATEAUX	AABLSTU	ABLAUTS	AACCRST	CARACTS	AACEGSV	SCAVAGE
AABFFLY	AFFABLY	AABLTTU	ABUTTAL	AACDDEL	DECADAL	AACEHIR	ARCHAEI
AABFILU	FABLIAU	AABLTXY	TAXABLY	AACDDER	ARCADED	AACEHLP	ACALEPH
AABFLRU	FABULAR	AABMNOT	BOATMAN	AACDDHR	CHADDAR	AACEHLR	ALCHERA
AABGHNS	GABNASH	AABMNST	BANTAMS	AACDDIN	CANDIDA	AACEHNP	PANACHE
	NASHGAB		BATSMAN	AACDEEM	ACADEME	AACEHNR	ACHARNE
AABGHSW	BAGWASH	AABMORU	MARABOU	AACDEFL	FALCADE	AACEHPP	APPEACH
AABGIIL	ABIGAIL	AABMRSS	SAMBARS	AACDEFS	FACADES	AACEHPS	APACHES
AABGINR	BARGAIN	AABMRTU	TAMBURA	AACDEHM	CHAMADE	AACEHPU	CHAPEAU
AABGINS	ABASING	AABMSST	TSAMBAS	AACDEHR	CHARADE		

AACEHRT	TRACHEA	AACGINT	AGNATIC	AACIOPV	COPAIVA		CAPTANS
AACEHST	ACHATES	AACGIRS	AGARICS	AACIOST	ATOCIAS		CATNAPS
AACEHTT	ATTACHE	AACGIRV	AGRAVIC		COAITAS	AACNRST	ARCTANS
AACEHTU	CHATEAU	AACGLOT	CATALOG	AACIQTU	AQUATIC		CANTARS
AACEIMN	ANAEMIC	AACGNOU	GUANACO	AACIRSS	ASCARIS	AACNRTU	CURTANA
AACEIMU	CAMAIEU	AACHIKN	KACHINA	AACIRST	CARITAS	AACNSSV	CANVASS
AACEINR	ACARINE	AACHIKR	CHIKARA	AACIRSV	CAVIARS	AACNSTU	ASCAUNT
AACEIRV	AVARICE	AACHILR	RACHIAL	AACISSS	CASSIAS	AACORST	OSTRACA
	CAVIARE	AACHIMR	MACHAIR	AACISTT	ASTATIC	AACORTU	ACATOUR
AACEKNP	PANCAKE	AACHIMS	CHIASMA	AACJKLS	JACKALS		AUTOCAR
AACEKNS	ASKANCE	AACHIPS	APHASIC	AACJKMN	JACKMAN	AACOTUV	AUTOVAC
AACEKOT	OATCAKE	AACHIPT	CHAPATI		MANJACK	AACRRST	CARRATS
AACELLN	CANELLA	AACHIRS	ARACHIS	AACJKSS	JACKASS	AACRRSU	CURARAS
AACELLS	SACELLA	AACHIRT	CITHARA	AACJOSU	ACAJOUS	AACRSTV	CRAVATS
AACELLT	LACTEAL	AACHITY	CYATHIA	AACKMNP	MANPACK	AACRTTT	ATTRACT
AACELMN	MANACLE	AACHKMP	CHAMPAK		PACKMAN	AACRTUV	VACATUR
AACELMR	CAMERAL	AACHKNS	ACHKANS	AACKMRT	AMTRACK	AACRTUY	ACTUARY
	CARAMEL	AACHKPS	CHAPKAS	AACKNRS	RANSACK	AACRTWY	CARTWAY
AACELMU	MACULAE		PACHAKS	AACKPRR	CARPARK	AACTUWY	CUTAWAY
AACELNS	ANLACES	AACHKRS	CHAKRAS	AACKPRT	RATPACK	AADDDEN	ADDENDA
AACELNU	LACUNAE	AACHKRT	HATRACK	AACKPSZ	CZAPKAS	AADDEEL	DAEDALE
AACELNV	VALANCE	AACHKSW	KWACHAS	AACKPWY	PACKWAY	AADDEGM	DAMAGED
AACELPS	PALACES	AACHLLN	CHALLAN	AACKRRS	ARRACKS	AADDEIL	ALIDADE
AACELPT	PLACATE	AACHLNS	CHALANS	AACKSTT	ATTACKS	AADDEMM	MADAMED
AACELRV	CARAVEL	AACHLPS	PASCHAL	AACLLNT	CALLANT	AADDENP	DEADPAN
AACELST	ACETALS	AACHLST	CALTHAS	AACLLNU	LACUNAL	AADDEPR	PARADED
	LACTASE	AACHLSU	ACUSHLA	AACLLOR	CORALLA	AADDEPT	ADAPTED
AACELTT	LACTATE	AACHMNP	CHAPMAN	AACLLSU	CLAUSAL	AADDERS	ADREADS
AACELTV	CLAVATE	AACHMNS	MACHANS	AACLLVY	CAVALLY	AADDERW	AWARDED
AACEMMR	MACRAME	AACHNOP	PANOCHA	AACLMNO	COALMAN	AADDESX	ADDAXES
AACEMNS	CASEMAN	AACHNOU	HUANACO	AACLMNT	CALMANT	AADDGNR	GRADDAN
AACEMNV	CAVEMAN	AACHNPX	PANCHAX		CLAMANT		GRANDAD
AACEMPR	PARACME	AACHNRS	ANARCHS	AACLMRU	MACULAR	AADDHKR	KHADDAR
AACEMQU	MACAQUE	AACHNRV	NAVARCH	AACLMSU	CALAMUS	AADDHRS	SRADDHA
AACEMRS	CAMERAS	AACHNRY	ANARCHY	AACLNNU	CANNULA	AADDIIK	DIDAKAI
AACEMSS	CAMASES	AACHNST	ACANTHS	AACLNPY	CLAYPAN	AADDILS	ALIDADS
AACENPS	CANAPES	AACHRRT	CATARRH	AACLNRS	CARNALS	AADDNVV	DVANDVA
AACENRT	CATERAN	AACHRST	CHARTAS	AACLNRU	LACUNAR	AADDOSU	AOUDADS
AACENST	CATENAS	AACHRWY	ARCHWAY	AACLOPR	CAPORAL	AADDRST	DASTARD
AACENTT	CANTATE	AACHSSW	CASHAWS	AACLOPT	OCTAPLA	AADDRSW	ADWARDS
AACENTY	CYANATE	AACHSTT	CHATTAS	AACLORT	CROTALA	AADDSST	STADDAS
AACEORS	ROSACEA	AACIILN	LACINIA	AACLORZ	ALCORZA	AADEEFR	AFEARED
AACEPRT	CAPRATE	AACIINT	ACTINIA	AACLOST	CATALOS	AADEENR	ANEARED
AACERSS	CAESARS	AACIITV	VIATICA		COASTAL	AADEERT	AERATED
AACERST	ACATERS	AACIJLP	JALAPIC	AACLOTT	CATTALO	AADEFFR	AFFEARD
AACERSU	CAESURA	AACIKLR	CLARKIA	AACLOTV	OCTAVAL	AADEFFR	AFFEARD
AACERSZ	SAZERAC	AACIKNN	CANAKIN	AACLPRS	CARPALS	AADEFGR	FARDAGE
AACERTU	ARCUATE	AACILNR	CRANIAL	AACLPRT	CALTRAP	AADEFIS	FADAISE
AACERWY	RACEWAY	AACILNT	ACTINAL	AACLPSS	PASCALS	AADEFLU	AEFAULD
AACESTV	CAVEATS		ALICANT	AACLPSU	PASCUAL	AADEFLW	AEFAWLD
	VACATES	AACILOS	ASOCIAL		SCAPULA	AADEGGR	AGGRADE
AACETTU	ACTUATE	AACILOX	COAXIAL	AACLRSS	LASCARS		GARAGED
AACETUV	VACUATE	AACILPS	SPACIAL		RASCALS	AADEGLS	GELADAS
AACFFIL	CAFFILA	AACILPT	CAPITAL		SCALARS	AADEGMN	AGNAMED
AACFILS	CAFILAS		PLACITA	AACLRST	CASTRAL		MANAGED
	FACIALS	AACIMMR	MACRAMI	AACLRVY	CAVALRY	AADEGMR	MEGARAD
	FASCIAL	AACIMNS	CAIMANS	AACLSSU	CASUALS	AADEGMS	DAMAGES
AACFILU	FAUCIAL		MANIACS	AACLSUV	VASCULA	AADEGNS	AGENDAS
AACFINT	FANATIC	AACIMPR	PICAMAR	AACLTTU	TACTUAL	AADEGRT	GRADATE
AACFISS	FASCIAS	AACINNT	CANTINA	AACMNOR	CAMARON	AADEGRV	RAVAGED
AACFLLU	FALCULA	AACINOR	CONARIA	AACMNRU	ARCANUM	AADEGRY	DRAYAGE
AACFLLY	FALLACY		OCARINA	AACMNSY	CAYMANS		YARDAGE
AACFLRU	FACULAR	AACINPT	CAPITAN	AACMORS	SARCOMA	AADEGSV	SAVAGED
AACFLTU	FACTUAL		CAPTAIN	AACMORT	MARCATO	AADEHKS	AKEDAHS
AACFNST	CAFTANS	AACINRS	ARNICAS	AACMOSY	MACOYAS	AADEHMN	HEADMAN
AACFRRU	FARRUCA		CARINAS	AACMRSS	SARCASM	AADEHMS	ASHAMED
AACGHNS	CHAGANS	AACINRZ	CZARINA	AACMRST	RAMCATS	AADEHPS	SAPHEAD
AACGILL	GLACIAL	AACINSS	ASCIANS		TARMACS	AADEHPW	AWHAPED
AACGILM	MAGICAL	AACINST	SATANIC	AACNNOZ	CANZONA	AADEHRW	RAWHEAD
AACGILS	SCAGLIA	AACIOPT	TAPIOCA	AACNPST	CAPSTAN		WARHEAD

AADEHWY	HEADWAY	AADGLNR	GARLAND	AADLPPU	APPLAUD	AAEFFGR	AGRAFFE
AADEILR	RADIALE	AADGLNS	SLADANG	AADLPRS	PARDALS	AAEFFIR	AFFAIRE
AADEILV	AVAILED	AADGLRU	GRADUAL	AADLRRU	RADULAR	AAEFFLL	FALAFEL
	VEDALIA	AADGMNR	GRANDAM	AADMMRS	DAMMARS	AAEFFNR	FANFARE
AADEINR	ARANEID		GRANDMA	AADMNNS	SANDMAN	AAEFFRS	AFFEARS
AADEINS	NAIADES	AADGMNS	GADSMAN	AADMNOR	MADRONA	AAEFFTT	TAFFETA
AADEIPS	DIAPASE	AADGMRS	SMARAGD		MANDORA	AAEFGTW	WAFTAGE
AADEIRS	ARAISED	AADGNPR	GRANDPA		MONARDA	AAEFLPR	EARFLAP
AADEIRT	RADIATE	AADGNPS	PADANGS		ROADMAN		PARAFLE
	TIARAED	AADGNRS	ARGANDS	AADMNRS	MANSARD	AAEFLRS	RAFALES
AADEITV	AVIATED	AADGNRT	GARDANT	AADMNRY	DRAYMAN	AAEFLSV	FAVELAS
AADEITW	AWAITED	AADGNRY	YARDANG		YARDMAN	AAEFMRT	FERMATA
AADEJMR	JEMADAR	AADGOPR	PODAGRA	AADMNSY	DAYSMAN	AAEFQRU	AQUAFER
AADEKLR	KRAALED	AADGOPS	PAGODAS	AADMNTU	MUTANDA	AAEFRRW	WARFARE
AADEKMR	KAMERAD	AADGRSU	GARUDAS	AADMOQU	MADOQUA	AAEFRWY	WAYFARE
AADELLP	PADELLA	AADHILS	DAHLIAS	AADMORT	MATADOR	AAEGGLS	GALAGES
AADELLY	ALLAYED	AADHJNR	HANDJAR	AADMOSU	AMADOUS	AAEGGNO	ANAGOGE
AADELMO	ALAMODE	AADHLRY	HALYARD	AADMRSU	MARAUDS	AAEGGOP	APAGOGE
AADELMR	ALARMED	AADHMRS	DHARMAS	AADMRSZ	MAZARDS	AAEGGRS	GARAGES
AADELMX	MALAXED		DHARNAS	AADMRZZ	MAZZARD	AAEGGRT	AGGRATE
AADELNR	ADRENAL	AADHNRS	DARSHAN	AADMSYY	MAYDAYS	AAEGGSV	GAVAGES
AADELNW	DANELAW	AADHNSW	HANDSAW	AADNNOT	NOTANDA	AAEGHLU	HAULAGE
AADELPR	PARDALE	AADHRSZ	HAZARDS	AADNNRS	RANDANS	AAEGHNT	THANAGE
AADELPT	PALATED	AADHRWY	HAYWARD	AADNOPR	PANDORA	AAEGILR	LAIRAGE
AADELRU	RADULAE	AADIILR	DIARIAL	AADNORT	ONDATRA		REGALIA
AADELRY	ALREADY	AADIINR	DIARIAN	AADNORY	ANYROAD	AAEGILS	ALGESIA
AADELSS	SALADES	AADIIPS	ASPIDIA	AADNPRS	PANDARS	AAEGINP	NAGAPIE
	SALSAED	AADIJMN	JAMDANI	AADNPRU	PANDURA	AAEGINV	VAGINAE
AADELTU	ADULATE	AADIKLY	ILKADAY	AADNRRW	WARRAND	AAEGINW	WAINAGE
AADELTY	DAYTALE	AADILLO	ALODIAL	AADNRRY	DARRAYN	AAEGIPR	IGARAPE
AADEMNO	ADENOMA	AADILMR	ADMIRAL	AADNRSS	NASARDS	AAEGIRR	ARRIAGE
AADEMNS	ANADEMS		AMILDAR	AADNRST	ASTRAND	AAEGISS	ASSEGAI
	MAENADS	AADILNP	PALADIN		TARANDS	AAEGITT	AGITATE
AADEMNT	MANDATE	AADILNR	LANIARD	AADNRTY	TANYARD	AAEGJTU	AJUTAGE
AADEMSS	AMASSED	AADILPS	APSIDAL	AADNRVW	VANWARD	AAEGKNT	TANKAGE
AADENNT	ANDANTE	AADILRS	RADIALS	AADNRWY	NAYWARD	AAEGKOS	SOAKAGE
AADENRV	VERANDA	AADILRT	TAILARD	AADOPRS	PARADOS	AAEGLLR	GLAREAL
AADENRW	AWARNED	AADILST	STADIAL	AADOPRT	ADAPTOR	AAEGLLT	GALLATE
AADENST	ANSATED	AADILTV	DATIVAL	AADOPRX	PARADOX		TALLAGE
AADENSW	WEASAND	AADILWY	WAYLAID	AADOPSS	PASSADO	AAEGLMN	GAMELAN
AADENWZ	WEAZAND	AADIMNR	MANDIRA		POSADAS	AAEGLMT	GAMETAL
AADEPRS	ASPREAD	AADIMNS	MAIDANS	AADORWY	ROADWAY	AAEGLNR	ALNAGER
	PARADES	AADIMOR	DIORAMA	AADPSSY	SPAYADS	AAEGLNS	ALNAGES
AADEPRT	ADAPTER	AADIMOT	DOMATIA	AADQRTU	QUADRAT		ANLAGES
	READAPT	AADINRR	DARRAIN	AADRSTU	DATURAS		GALENAS
AADEPSS	ESPADAS	AADINRS	RADIANS	AADRSTY	DAYSTAR		LAGENAS
	PASSADE	AADINRT	RADIANT	AADRSVW	VAWARDS		LASAGNE
AADERRS	ARRASED	AADINRV	VIRANDA	AADRWWY	WAYWARD	AAEGLNU	AULNAGE
AADERRY	ARRAYED	AADINSV	NAVAIDS	AAEEFFR	AFFEARE	AAEGLOP	APOGEAL
AADERSW	SEAWARD	AADIRRW	AIRWARD	AAEEFGL	LEAFAGE	AAEGLRR	REALGAR
AADERSY	ARAYSED	AADISST	STADIAS	AAEEGKL	LEAKAGE	AAEGLRS	ALEGARS
AADERTU	AURATED	AADKMRY	DAYMARK	AAEEGLT	ETALAGE		LAAGERS
AADESSY	ASSAYED	AADKMSS	DAMASKS		GALEATE	AAEGLST	AGELAST
AADFLTW	TWAFALD	AADKNRT	TANKARD	AAEEGMN	AMENAGE		ALGATES
AADFNRR	FARRAND	AADKPSU	PADAUKS	AAEEGRV	AVERAGE		LASTAGE
AADFNST	FANTADS	AADKRWW	AWKWARD	AAEEGST	EATAGES	AAEGLSV	LAVAGES
AADFRST	DAFTARS	AADLLMR	MALLARD	AAEEHRT	HETAERA		SALVAGE
AADGGHR	HAGGARD	AADLLNW	LAWLAND	AAEEINT	TAENIAE	AAEGMNR	MANAGER
AADGGLR	LAGGARD	AADLLPU	PALUDAL	AAEEKRW	REAWAKE	AAEGMNS	AGNAMES
AADGGRS	SAGGARD	AADLLSS	SALLADS	AAEELMT	MALEATE		MANAGES
AADGHIL	HIDALGA	AADLMMN	LANDMAN	AAEELOR	AREOLAE		SAGAMEN
AADGIMM	DIGAMMA	AADLMNO	MANDOLA	AAEELRT	LAETARE	AAEGMNT	MAGENTA
AADGIMO	AGAMOID	AADLMNU	LADANUM	AAEEMNT	EMANATE		MAGNATE
AADGIMR	DIAGRAM	AADLMPS	LAMPADS		ENEMATA	AAEGMPR	RAMPAGE
AADGIMS	AGAMIDS	AADLMSW	WADMALS		MANATEE	AAEGMRT	REGMATA
AADGINW	ADAWING	AADLNRY	LANYARD	AAEEPPS	APPEASE	AAEGMSS	MASSAGE
AADGIOS	ADAGIOS	AADLNSS	SANDALS	AAEEPRT	PATERAE	AAEGNNP	PANNAGE
AADGLLW	GADWALL	AADLNSU	LANDAUS	AAEERST	AERATES	AAEGNNT	TANNAGE
AADGLMY	AMYGDAL	AADLNSV	VANDALS	AAEERTU	AUREATE	AAEGNOP	APOGEAN
				AAEERTX	EXARATE	AAEGNPT	PAGEANT

AAEGNRR	ARRANGE	AAEIPPS	APEPSIA	AAELPTT	TAPETAL	AAERSTU	AURATES
AAEGNRT	TANAGER	AAEIPRR	PAREIRA	AAELPTU	PLATEAU	AAERSTW	AWAREST
AAEGNST	AGNATES	AAEIPRS	SPIRAEA	AAELPTY	APETALY	AAESSTV	SAVATES
AAEGNTV	VANTAGE	AAEIPRT	APTERIA	AAELRTV	LARVATE	AAESSWY	SEAWAYS
AAEGNTW	WANTAGE	AAEIPTT	APATITE	AAELRTZ	LAZARET	AAFFINS	MAFFIAS
AAEGORS	OARAGES	AAEIRSS	ARAISES	AAELRVY	ALVEARY	AAFFINS	SAFFIAN
AAEGPRR	PARERGA	AAEIRST	ARISTAE	AAELSST	ATLASES	AAFFIRS	AFFAIRS
AAEGPRS	PARAGES		ASTERIA	AAELSTT	SALTATE		RAFFIAS
AAEGPSS	PASSAGE		ATRESIA	AAELSTV	VALETAS	AAFFPRS	AFFRAPS
AAEGPSV	PAVAGES	AAEIRSX	XERASIA	AAELSTZ	ALTEZAS	AAFFRSY	AFFRAYS
AAEGPSY	PAYSAGE	AAEIRTT	ARIETTA	AAELSUX	ASEXUAL	AAFGHNS	AFGHANS
AAEGQUY	QUAYAGE	AAEIRTV	VARIATE	AAELTUV	VALUATE	AAFGORR	FARRAGO
AAEGRRV	RAVAGER	AAEIRVW	AIRWAVE	AAELTVV	VALVATE	AAFHIKL	KHALIFA
AAEGRST	AGRASTE	AAEISTT	SATIATE	AAELTZZ	ALTEZZA	AAFHLWY	HALFWAY
AAEGRSV	RAVAGES	AAEISTV	AVIATES	AAELWWY	WELAWAY	AAFIILR	FILARIA
	SAVAGER	AAEISTX	ATAXIES	AAEMMMR	MAREMMA	AAFIKLS	KAFILAS
AAEGRTT	REGATTA	AAEJNRT	NAARTJE	AAEMMMT	MAMMATE	AAFIKSS	SIFAKAS
AAEGSSU	ASSUAGE	AAEKLMS	KAMELAS	AAEMMOT	OMMATEA	AAFILNT	FANTAIL
	SAUSAGE	AAEKLNS	ALKANES	AAEMNNT	EMANANT	AAFILQU	ALFAQUI
AAEGSSV	AVGASES	AAEKLNT	ALKANET	AAEMNPP	PAMPEAN	AAFINNT	INFANTA
	SAVAGES		KANTELA	AAEMNPS	SPAEMAN	AAFINRS	FARINAS
AAEGSSW	ASSWAGE	AAEKLSS	ASLAKES	AAEMNPT	PEATMAN	AAFIPRT	PARFAIT
AAEGSTU	GATEAUS	AAEKMNW	WAKEMAN	AAEMNRT	RAMENTA	AAFIRSS	SAFARIS
AAEGSTW	WASTAGE	AAEKMRR	EARMARK	AAEMNRU	MURAENA	AAFIRWY	FAIRWAY
AAEGTTW	WATTAGE	AAEKMRS	SEAMARK	AAEMNST	NAMASTE	AAFJLLW	JAWFALL
AAEGTUX	GATEAUX	AAEKNNS	ANANKES	AAEMNTU	MANTEAU	AAFJLOR	ALFORJA
AAEGTWY	GATEWAY	AAEKNSW	AWAKENS	AAEMOTZ	METAZOA	AAFKNST	KAFTANS
	GETAWAY	AAEKPRT	PARTAKE	AAEMQSU	SQUAMAE	AAFLLLS	FALLALS
AAEHHPT	APHTHAE	AAEKRSS	KEASARS	AAEMRST	AMEARST	AAFLLTY	FATALLY
AAEHILP	APHELIA	AAEKRST	KARATES		RETAMAS	AAFLMPR	FRAMPAL
AAEHIRT	HETAIRA	AAELLLM	LAMELLA	AAEMRTU	AMATEUR	AAFLNOR	FORLANA
AAEHKNT	KHANATE	AAELLNZ	ZANELLA	AAEMSSS	AMASSES	AAFLNRU	FURLANA
AAEHKPS	PAKEHAS	AAELLPR	PARELLA	AAENNNT	ANTENNA	AAFLSSY	SALSAFY
AAEHKST	TAKAHES	AAELLPS	PAELLAS	AAENNST	ANNATES	AAFLWYY	FLYAWAY
AAEHLLL	ALLHEAL	AAELLPT	PATELLA	AAENNSZ	ZENANAS	AAFMNRT	RAFTMAN
AAEHLPX	HEXAPLA	AAELLRT	LATERAL	AAENNTT	TANNATE	AAFMNST	FANTASM
AAEHLRT	TREHALA	AAELLRY	ALLAYER	AAENNTV	VENTANA	AAFNRRT	FARRANT
AAEHLTT	ATHLETA	AAELMMT	LEMMATA	AAENOPS	APNOEAS	AAFNSTT	FANTAST
AAEHMSS	ASHAMES	AAELMNT	AMENTAL	AAENOSZ	OZAENAS	AAFNSTY	FANTASY
AAEHMTT	THEMATA	AAELMNU	ALUMNAE	AAENPPR	PARPANE	AAGGILN	GANGLIA
AAEHNPR	HANAPER	AAELMOT	OATMEAL	AAENPST	ANAPEST	AAGGKSU	GAGAKUS
AAEHNSY	HYAENAS	AAELMPT	PALMATE		PEASANT	AAGGMNS	MGANGAS
AAEHPRZ	PHEAZAR	AAELMST	MALATES	AAENPSV	PAVANES	AAGGNOY	ANAGOGY
AAEHPSW	AWHAPES		MALTASE	AAENPSX	PANAXES	AAGGNWY	GANGWAY
AAEHRSY	HEARSAY		TAMALES	AAENPTT	EPATANT	AAGGQSU	QUAGGAS
AAEHSTT	HASTATE	AAELMSX	MALAXES	AAENRRT	NARRATE	AAGGRSS	SAGGARS
AAEILLX	AXILLAE	AAELMSY	AMYLASE	AAENRSS	NARASES	AAGGRST	TAGRAGS
AAEILMN	LAMINAE	AAELNNS	ANNEALS	AAENRST	ANESTRA	AAGHILR	GHARIAL
AAEILMS	AMELIAS	AAELNOV	VALONEA	AAENRTT	TARTANE	AAGHKNS	KANGHAS
	MALAISE	AAELNPT	PLATANE	AAENRTU	NATURAE		KHANGAS
AAEILNO	AEOLIAN	AAELNPU	PAENULA		TAUREAN	AAGHLNT	GNATHAL
AAEILNT	ANTLIAE	AAELNRS	ARSENAL	AAENRTV	TAVERNA	AAGHLOS	GASAHOL
AAEILOR	OLEARIA	AAELNST	SEALANT	AAENRUW	UNAWARE	AAGHLSZ	GHAZALS
AAEILPX	EPAXIAL	AAELNSY	ANALYSE	AAENRUZ	AZUREAN	AAGHMNN	HANGMAN
AAEILRS	AERIALS	AAELNTT	TETANAL	AAENSSU	NAUSEAS	AAGHMNW	WHANGAM
AAEILRU	AURELIA	AAELNTZ	ZEALANT	AAENSSV	VANESSA	AAGHMRS	GRAMASH
AAEILRV	VELARIA	AAELNWY	LANEWAY	AAEORRT	AERATOR	AAGHNRS	ARGHANS
AAEILSS	ALIASES	AAELNYZ	ANALYZE	AAEORRU	AURORAE		HANGARS
AAEILSV	AVAILES	AAELORR	AREOLAR	AAEPPRS	APPEARS	AAGHQUU	QUAHAUG
AAEILSX	ALEXIAS	AAELORU	AUREOLA	AAEPPRT	PARAPET	AAGHSTY	SAGATHY
AAEIMMT	IMAMATE	AAELOTX	OXALATE	AAEPRSS	PASEARS	AAGIKNW	AWAKING
AAEIMNS	AMNESIA	AAELPPR	APPAREL	AAEPRST	PETARAS	AAGIKNZ	ZIGANKA
	ANEMIAS	AAELPPS	APPEALS	AAEPRSZ	ZARAPES	AAGILMY	MYALGIA
AAEIMNT	AMENTIA	AAELPPT	PALPATE	AAEPRTY	PEATARY	AAGILNN	ANGINAL
	ANIMATE	AAELPPU	PAPULAE	AAERRRS	ARREARS	AAGILNP	PAGINAL
AAEIMPY	PYAEMIA	AAELPRS	EARLAPS	AAERRSS	ARRASES	AAGILNS	AGNAILS
AAEIMRU	URAEMIA	AAELPRT	APTERAL	AAERRTT	TARTARE	AAGILNV	AVALING
AAEIMTV	AMATIVE	AAELPRV	PALAVER	AAERSST	SEARATS		VAGINAL
AAEINNO	AEONIAN	AAELPSS	PALASES	AAERSSY	ARAYSES	AAGILNY	ALAYING
AAEINST	TAENIAS	AAELPST	PALATES		ASSAYER	AAGILOS	ALOGIAS

AAGILOT	OTALGIA	AAGOPSS	SAPSAGO	AAHNNOS	HOSANNA	AAILMSU	AUMAILS
AAGILRS	ARGALIS	AAGORSU	SAGUARO	AAHNNST	TANNAHS	AAILNOT	AILANTO
	GARIALS	AAGOSTU	AGOUTAS		THANNAS	AAILNOV	NOVALIA
AAGILSV	GAVIALS	AAGPPRS	GRAPPAS	AAHNORT	ATHANOR		VALONIA
AAGILTW	WAGTAIL	AAGRRSY	GARRYAS	AAHNORV	NAVARHO	AAILNPS	SALPIAN
AAGIMNO	ANGIOMA	AAHHLSV	HALVAHS	AAHNRTX	ANTHRAX	AAILNPT	PLATINA
AAGIMNS	MAGIANS	AAHHMSZ	HAMZAHS	AAHNRTY	RHATANY	AAILNRU	ULNARIA
	SIAMANG	AAHHNNT	THANNAH	AAHPPRS	PARAPHS	AAILNRY	LANIARY
AAGIMNT	AMATING	AAHHNPT	NAPHTHA	AAHPRSY	YARPHAS	AAILNSS	SALINAS
AAGIMNZ	AMAZING	AAHHNST	THANAHS	AAHPRTW	WARPATH	AAILNSY	INYALAS
AAGINNS	ANGINAS	AAHIIMT	HIMATIA	AAHPTWY	PATHWAY	AAILNTV	VALIANT
AAGINNW	WANIGAN	AAHIKRT	KITHARA	AAHRSSS	HASSARS	AAILORS	ROSALIA
AAGINPY	APAYING	AAHILMR	ALMIRAH	AAHRSST	SHASTRA	AAILORV	VARIOLA
AAGINRR	ARRAIGN	AAHILMT	THALAMI	AAHRTTW	ATHWART	AAILPPT	APPALTI
AAGINRS	NAGARIS	AAHILNT	THALIAN	AAHSSSY	SASHAYS	AAILPZZ	PALAZZI
	SANGRIA	AAHIMNO	MAHONIA	AAIIKKS	KAIKAIS	AAILPRS	PARIALS
	SARANGI	AAHIMSS	AHIMSAS	AAIILMR	AIRMAIL	AAILPRT	PARTIAL
AAGINRU	GUARANI	AAHINOP	APHONIA	AAIILPR	PAIRIAL		PATRIAL
AAGINST	AGAINST	AAHINPR	PIRANHA	AAIILPT	TILAPIA	AAILPST	SPATIAL
	GITANAS	AAHINST	SHAITAN	AAIILRZ	ALIZARI	AAILPTT	TALIPAT
AAGINSU	IGUANAS		TAHINAS	AAIINNZ	ANZIANI	AAILRRV	ARRIVAL
AAGINSV	VAGINAS	AAHIPRS	PARIAHS	AAIIRVV	VIVARIA	AAILRST	LARIATS
AAGINSY	GAINSAY		RAPHIAS	AAIJLNP	JALAPIN		LATRIAS
AAGIOTT	AGITATO	AAHIPRT	PITARAH	AAIJMNP	JAMPANI	AAILRTV	TRAVAIL
AAGIPRS	AIRGAPS	AAHIPTZ	ZAPTIAH	AAIJNRZ	JANIZAR	AAILRWY	RAILWAY
AAGIPRU	PIRAGUA	AAHIRSS	SHARIAS	AAIJNST	TINAJAS	AAILSSS	ASSAILS
AAGIRRY	ARGYRIA	AAHIRST	SHARIAT	AAIJRSW	JAWARIS	AAILSSV	SALIVAS
AAGISTT	SAGITTA	AAHIRSV	VIHARAS	AAIKLLS	ALKALIS		VASSAIL
AAGJNRS	GARJANS	AAHJKNR	KHANJAR	AAIKLMS	KALMIAS	AAILSSW	WASSAIL
AAGJRSU	JAGUARS	AAHJNRS	HANJARS		KAMILAS	AAILTTT	LATITAT
AAGKOOZ	GAZOOKA	AAHJRRS	JARRAHS	AAIKLNS	KALIANS	AAIMMNO	AMMONIA
AAGKORT	KATORGA	AAHKKST	KATHAKS	AAIKMNN	MANAKIN	AAIMMSS	MIASMAS
AAGLLNS	LALANGS	AAHKLRS	LASHKAR	AAIKMNR	RAMAKIN	AAIMMNO	OMNIANA
AAGLLNT	GALLANT	AAHKLST	KHALATS	AAIKMOR	ROMAIKA	AAIMNOS	ANOSMIA
AAGLMMS	MALMAGS	AAHKMSY	YASHMAK	AAIKMRS	KARAISM	AAIMNOT	AMATION
AAGLMNS	MANGALS	AAHKNST	KANTHAS	AAIKNST	TANKIAS	AAIMNRS	MARINAS
AAGLNOS	ANALOGS	AAHKRSS	RAKSHAS	AAIKORU	OUAKARI	AAIMNRT	TAMARIN
AAGLNOY	ANALOGY	AAHLLLS	HALLALS	AAIKPPR	PAPRIKA	AAIMNST	MANATIS
AAGLNPS	LAPSANG		NALLAHS	AAIKRSS	ASKARIS		STAMINA
AAGLNRS	RAGLANS	AAHLLOS	HALLOAS	AAIKRST	KARAITS	AAIMNSV	VIMANAS
AAGLNRU	ANGULAR	AAHLLPS	PALLAHS	AAIKRSU	UAKARIS	AAIMNTX	TAXIMAN
AAGLRUU	AUGURAL	AAHLLSW	WALLAHS	AAIKSTT	ASTATKI	AAIMRST	AMRITAS
AAGLSST	STALAGS	AAHLLWY	HALLWAY	AAIKTVV	AKVAVIT		TAMARIS
AAGMMNS	MAGSMAN	AAHLMMS	HAMMALS	AAILLLP	PALLIAL	AAIMRSU	SAMURAI
AAGMMRR	GRAMMAR		MAHMALS	AAILLMM	MAMILLA	AAIMSST	STASIMA
AAGMMTU	GUMMATA		MASHLAM	AAILLMN	MANILLA	AAIMSTT	TATAMIS
AAGMNNR	GRANNAM	AAHLMRS	MARSHAL	AAILLMR	ARMILLA	AAIMSTV	ATAVISM
AAGMNPR	PANGRAM	AAHLMRU	HAMULAR	AAILLMX	MAXILLA	AAIMSUV	MAUVAIS
AAGMNPY	PANGAMY	AAHLMST	MALTHAS	AAILLNV	VANILLA	AAINNRU	URANIAN
AAGMNRS	RAGMANS	AAHLNPX	PHALANX	AAILLPP	PAPILLA	AAINNRV	NAVARIN
AAGMNRT	TANGRAM	AAHLNRW	NARWHAL	AAILLRX	AXILLAR		NIRVANA
	TRANGAM	AAHLPRS	PHRASAL	AAILLSV	SALIVAL	AAINOPS	PAISANO
AAGMNSW	SWAGMAN	AAHLPST	ASPHALT	AAILLUV	ALLUVIA	AAINORR	ORARIAN
AAGMNSZ	ZAMANGS		TAPLASH	AAILLXY	AXIALLY	AAINORV	OVARIAN
AAGMOPY	APOGAMY	AAHLRSS	ASHLARS	AAILMMN	MAILMAN	AAINOSX	ANOXIAS
AAGMORS	MARGOSA	AAHLRST	HARTALS	AAILMMR	AMMIRAL	AAINPPS	PAPAINS
AAGMOSU	AGAMOUS	AAHLRSW	SHALWAR	AAILMMS	MIASMAL	AAINPRS	PIRANAS
AAGMRRY	GRAMARY	AAHMMMS	HAMMAMS	AAILMMX	MAXIMAL	AAINPST	PATINAS
AAGMRSY	MARGAYS	AAHMMNS	MASHMAN	AAILMNR	LAMINAR		TAIPANS
AAGNNOS	GOANNAS	AAHMNNU	HANUMAN		RAILMAN	AAINRST	ANTIARS
AAGNNSW	WANGANS	AAHMNRS	HARMANS	AAILMNS	ALMAINS		ARTISAN
AAGNOPR	PARAGON	AAHMNSS	SHAMANS		ANIMALS		TSARINA
AAGNORS	ANGORAS	AAHMOPR	AMPHORA		MANILAS	AAINRSU	ANURIAS
AAGNORZ	ORGANZA	AAHMQSU	QUAMASH	AAILMNT	MATINAL		SAURIAN
AAGNPRS	PARANGS	AAHMRSS	ASHRAMS	AAILMNU	ALUMINA	AAINRSV	SAVARIN
AAGNRRS	GARRANS	AAHMSST	ASTHMAS	AAILMPS	IMPALAS	AAINRTV	VARIANT
AAGNRRY	GRANARY	AAHMSTZ	MATZAHS	AAILMRT	MARITAL	AAINSTT	ATTAINS
AAGNRSS	SANGARS				MARTIAL	AAINSTV	VANITAS
AAGNRTV	VAGRANT			AAILMSS	ALISMAS	AAINTTT	ATTAINT
AAGNSTU	TAGUANS				SALAMIS		

AAINTTU	TUTANIA	AALLMPU	AMPULLA
AAIOPRS	APORIAS	AALLNPU	PLANULA
AAIOPRT	ATROPIA	AALLNSY	NASALLY
AAIORSU	SAOUARI	AALLORS	AROLLAS
AAIORTV	AVIATOR	AALLOSZ	AZOLLAS
AAIPPRS	APPAIRS	AALLOTV	LAVOLTA
AAIPPRU	PUPARIA	AALLPPY	PAPALLY
AAIPPTT	PITAPAT	AALLRUY	AURALLY
AAIPRST	PITARAS	AALLRVY	VALLARY
AAIPRSY	PIRAYAS	AALLSTT	TALLATS
AAIPRTT	PARTITA	AALLUVV	VALVULA
AAIPSZZ	PIAZZAS	AALMMMS	MAMMALS
AAIQSSU	QUASSIA	AALMMNO	AMMONAL
AAIQTUV	AQUAVIT	AALMMNT	MALTMAN
AAIRSST	ARISTAS	AALMNOS	SALAMON
	TARSIAS	AALMNOY	ANOMALY
AAIRSTT	STRIATA	AALMNPS	NAPALMS
AAIRSTY	RAIYATS	AALMNSU	MANUALS
AAIRSWY	AIRWAYS	AALMORT	ALAMORT
AAIRSZZ	RAZZIAS	AALMORY	MAYORAL
AAITWXY	TAXIWAY	AALMOST	AMATOLS
AAJJMRS	JAMJARS	AALMPRY	PALMARY
AAJKLWY	JAYWALK		PALMYRA
AAJKMNR	JARKMAN	AALMPSS	PLASMAS
AAJKNSS	SANJAKS	AALMRRU	RAMULAR
AAJMNPS	JAMPANS	AALMRSU	ALARUMS
AAJMNZZ	JAZZMAN	AALMSSU	MASULAS
AAJMORT	MAJORAT	AALMTTU	MULATTA
AAJMPSY	PYJAMAS	AALNNRU	ANNULAR
AAJNNOS	JOANNAS	AALNNSU	ANNUALS
AAJNOSW	AJOWANS	AALNPRT	PLANTAR
AAJNOSY	YOJANAS	AALNPST	PLANTAS
AAJOPSU	SAPAJOU		PLATANS
AAKKLPS	KALPAKS	AALNPUU	PUNALUA
AAKKLRU	KARAKUL	AALNQTU	QUANTAL
AAKKMOT	TOKAMAK	AALNRSU	RANULAS
AAKKMRS	MARKKAS	AALNRTT	LATRANT
AAKKOPS	KAKAPOS	AALNRTU	NATURAL
AAKKSUZ	ZAKUSKA	AALNSST	SANTALS
AAKLMPU	LAMPUKA	AALNSTT	SALTANT
AAKLMRY	MALARKY		TALANTS
AAKLMUY	YAMULKA	AALNSTU	SULTANA
AAKLNOO	OOLAKAN	AALNSTY	ANALYST
AAKLNOU	OULAKAN	AALNTTU	TALAUNT
AAKLOOP	PALOOKA	AALOPPT	APPALTO
AAKLRSU	KURSAAL	AALOPRS	PARASOL
	RUSALKA	AALOPSY	PAYOLAS
AAKLSSU	SAKSAUL	AALOPVV	PAVLOVA
AAKLWWY	WALKWAY	AALOPZZ	PALAZZO
AAKMMNR	MARKMAN	AALORRU	AURORAL
AAKMNSU	MANUKAS	AALORSU	AROUSAL
AAKMOSU	MOUSAKA	AALORTX	LAXATOR
AAKMRSU	KUMARAS	AALOSTT	SALTATO
AAKMRUZ	MAZURKA	AALOSVW	AVOWALS
AAKMRWY	WAYMARK	AALOTTY	TALAYOT
AAKNNTU	NUNATAK	AALPPRU	PAPULAR
AAKNORS	ANORAKS	AALPRRS	PARRALS
AAKNRST	KANTARS	AALPRSW	ASPRAWL
AAKNSST	ASKANTS	AALPRSY	PARLAYS
AAKNTWY	TWANKAY	AALPSTU	SPATULA
AAKOOPP	PAKAPOO	AALRSST	TARSALS
AAKOPRS	PAKORAS	AALRSTU	AUSTRAL
AAKORST	OSTRAKA	AALRSTY	ASTYLAR
AAKPRWY	PARKWAY		SATYRAL
AAKRTUY	AUTARKY	AALSSSV	VASSALS
AAKSSTT	ATTASKS	AALSSTU	ASSAULT
AAKSTTT	ATTASKT	AALSSUX	SAXAULS
AALLLNS	LALLANS	AALSTUV	VALUTAS
AALLLSS	SALLALS	AALSWYY	WAYLAYS
AALLMMS	MALLAMS	AAMMMRY	MAMMARY

AAMMNRT	MANTRAM	AAPRSTT	ATTRAPS
AAMMNST	AMTMANS	AAPRSTY	SATRAPY
AAMMRRS	MARRAMS	AAQRSSU	QUASARS
AAMMRST	RAMSTAM	AARRSTT	TARTARS
AAMMSUZ	MAZUMAS	AARRSWY	WARRAYS
AAMNNOY	ANONYMA	AARSSST	ASSARTS
AAMNOOS	MANOAOS	AARSSTT	ASTARTS
AAMNORS	OARSMAN	AARSSTY	SATYRAS
AAMNOSZ	AMAZONS	AASSTTU	STATUAS
AAMNOTY	ANATOMY	ABBBDEL	BABBLED
AAMNPRT	MANTRAP		BLABBED
	RAMPANT	ABBBELR	BABBLER
AAMNPRY	PARANYM		BLABBER
AAMNPSS	PASSMAN		BRABBLE
	SAMPANS	ABBBELS	BABBLES
AAMNPST	TAPSMAN	ABBBITT	BABBITT
AAMNPTY	TYMPANA	ABBCDER	CRABBED
AAMNRST	ARTSMAN	ABBCDES	SCABBED
	MANTRAS	ABBCEHI	BABICHE
AAMNSTU	MANTUAS	ABBCEHU	BABUCHE
	TAMANUS	ABBCEIS	CABBIES
AAMOORS	AMOROSA	ABBCELR	CLABBER
AAMOPRS	PARAMOS	ABBCELS	SCABBLE
AAMORRZ	ZAMARRO	ABBCIKT	BACKBIT
AAMORSV	SAMOVAR	ABBCIRS	BICARBS
AAMORTY	AMATORY	ABBCOST	BOBCATS
AAMOSSS	SAMOSAS	ABBDDEL	DABBLED
AAMOSTT	STOMATA	ABBDDER	DRABBED
AAMOTTU	AUTOMAT	ABBDEFR	FRABBED
AAMPRRT	RAMPART	ABBDEGL	GABBLED
AAMPSSY	AMPASSY	ABBDEGR	GRABBED
AAMRSST	MATRASS	ABBDEIT	TABBIED
AAMRSSU	ASARUMS	ABBDEJL	JABBLED
AAMRSTU	SUMATRA	ABBDELR	DABBLER
	TRAUMAS		DRABBLE
AAMRTWY	TRAMWAY		RABBLED
AAMSSTU	SATSUMA	ABBDELS	DABBLES
AANNOTT	ANNATTO		SLABBED
AANNPSS	SANPANS	ABBDELW	WABBLED
AANNSYZ	NYANZAS	ABBDERR	DRABBER
AANORST	TORANAS	ABBDERS	DABBERS
AANOSST	SONATAS	ABBDERT	DRABBET
AANOSTT	ANATTOS	ABBDEST	STABBED
AANPPSS	SAPPANS		TEBBADS
AANPRST	PARTANS	ABBDESU	BEDAUBS
	SPARTAN	ABBDESW	SWABBED
	TARPANS	ABBDGIN	DABBING
	TRAPANS	ABBDHIJ	DJIBBAH
AANPSST	PASSANT	ABBDILR	LIBBARD
AANQRTU	QUARTAN	ABBDINR	RIBBAND
AANRRSW	WARRANS	ABBDITY	DABBITY
AANRRTW	WARRANT	ABBDLRU	LUBBARD
AANRSTT	RATTANS	ABBDMOR	BOMBARD
	TANTRAS	ABBDMOU	BABUDOM
	TARTANS	ABBEESW	BAWBEES
AANRUWY	RUNAWAY	ABBEFST	FABBEST
AANSSTV	SAVANTS	ABBEGIR	GABBIER
AANSSTZ	STANZAS	ABBEGLR	GABBLER
AANSTTT	STATANT		GRABBLE
AANSTUV	AVAUNTS	ABBEGLS	GABBLES
AANSWYY	ANYWAYS	ABBEGNO	BOGBEAN
AAOORRW	WOORARA	ABBEGNU	BUGBANE
AAOPSST	POTASSA	ABBEGRR	GRABBER
	SAPOTAS	ABBEGRS	GABBERS
AAORRSU	AURORAS	ABBEGRU	BUGBEAR
AAORRSV	VARROOS	ABBEHLS	SHABBLE
AAORSTT	TOTARAS	ABBEIRS	BARBIES
AAOSTTV	OTTAVAS	ABBEIST	BABIEST
AAPPSWW	PAWPAWS		TABBIES
AAPRSST	SATRAPS	ABBEISY	YABBIES

ABBEJLS	JABBLES	ABCCIMR	CAMBRIC
ABBEJRS	JABBERS	ABCCINU	BUCCINA
ABBELMR	BRAMBLE	ABCCIOR	BORACIC
ABBELNS	SNABBLE		BRACCIO
ABBELPR	PRABBLE	ABCCISU	CUBICAS
ABBELRR	RABBLER	ABCCKOW	BAWCOCK
ABBELRS	BARBELS	ABCCKTU	CUTBACK
	RABBLES	ABCCOOR	BAROCCO
	SLABBER	ABCCOOT	TOBACCO
ABBELRU	BARBULE	ABCCSUU	SUCCUBA
ABBELRW	WABBLER	ABCDEEH	BEACHED
ABBELSU	BASBLEU	ABCDEEL	BELACED
	BAUBLES		DEBACLE
ABBELSW	BAWBLES	ABCDEHT	BATCHED
	WABBLES	ABCDEHU	DEBAUCH
ABBELUY	BUYABLE	ABCDEIK	DIEBACK
ABBEMUZ	BUMBAZE	ABCDEIN	CABINED
ABBENRS	NABBERS	ABCDEIP	PEDICAB
ABBEORS	EARBOBS	ABCDEIR	CARBIDE
ABBERRS	BARBERS	ABCDEKL	BLACKED
ABBERST	BARBETS	ABCDEKR	REDBACK
	RABBETS	ABCDEOR	BROCADE
	STABBER	ABCDERS	DECARBS
ABBERSW	SWABBER	ABCDERU	CUDBEAR
ABBERSY	YABBERS	ABCDESU	ABDUCES
ABBFIRT	FRABBIT	ABCDHIO	ICHABOD
ABBGGIN	GABBING	ABCDHOR	CHOBDAR
ABBGHSU	GUBBAHS	ABCDHOS	BODACHS
ABBGIJN	JABBING	ABCDIIS	DIBASIC
ABBGINN	NABBING	ABCDILR	BALDRIC
ABBGINR	BARBING	ABCDINS	ABSCIND
ABBGINT	TABBING	ABCDIRS	SCABRID
ABBGINU	BUBINGA	ABCDIRT	CATBIRD
ABBGINY	BABYING	ABCDIRU	BAUDRIC
ABBGOOU	BUGABOO	ABCDISU	SUBACID
ABBGORS	GABBROS	ABCDNOS	ABSCOND
ABBHIJS	JIBBAHS	ABCDOOR	CORDOBA
ABBHISY	BABYISH	ABCDORR	BROCARD
ABBHJSU	JUBBAHS	ABCDSTU	ABDUCTS
ABBHOOS	BABOOSH	ABCEEHS	BEACHES
	HABOOBS	ABCEEHU	EBAUCHE
ABBHRRU	RHUBARB	ABCEELS	BELACES
ABBHTTU	BATHTUB	ABCEEMR	EMBRACE
ABBIIMN	BAMBINI	ABCEEMS	EMBACES
ABBILOR	BILOBAR	ABCEENS	ABSENCE
ABBILOT	BOBTAIL	ABCEERR	ACERBER
ABBILSU	BUBALIS		REBRACE
ABBIMNO	BAMBINO	ABCEERU	BERCEAU
ABBIMSU	BABUISM	ABCEESS	BECASSE
ABBINOR	RABBONI	ABCEESU	BECAUSE
ABBINRS	RABBINS	ABCEGIR	RIBCAGE
ABBIRST	RABBITS	ABCEGMO	CAMBOGE
ABBIRTY	RABBITY	ABCEGOR	BROCAGE
ABBKLOU	BLAUBOK	ABCEGOS	BOCAGES
ABBLLTU	BULLBAT		BOSCAGE
ABBLMRY	BRAMBLY	ABCEGSU	CUBAGES
ABBMOOR	BOMBORA	ABCEHKO	BACKHOE
ABBMOOS	BAMBOOS	ABCEHLU	BAUCHLE
ABBMOST	BOMBAST	ABCEHMR	BECHARM
ABBNOOS	BABOONS		BRECHAM
ABBORSS	ABSORBS		CHAMBER
ABBQSUY	SQUABBY		CHAMBRE
ABCCEIR	ACERBIC	ABCEHOS	BASOCHE
	BRECCIA	ABCEHRS	BRACHES
ABCCEIS	BACCIES	ABCEHRT	BRACHET
	SEBACIC	ABCEHST	BATCHES
ABCCEOS	BACCOES	ABCEILM	ALEMBIC
ABCCHII	BACCHII	ABCEILR	CALIBER
ABCCHTY	BYCATCH		CALIBRE
ABCCILU	CUBICAL		

ABCEILT	CITABLE	ABCIIOR	CIBORIA
ABCEIMO	AMOEBIC	ABCIIOT	ABIOTIC
ABCEINR	CARBINE	ABCILRS	SCRIBAL
ABCEINT	CABINET	ABCILTU	CUBITAL
ABCEIOR	AEROBIC	ABCIMMS	CAMBISM
ABCEIRS	ASCRIBE	ABCIMMU	CAMBIUM
	CABRIES	ABCIMST	CAMBIST
	CARIBES	ABCINOT	BOTANIC
ABCEISS	ABSCISE	ABCIORR	BARRICO
	SCABIES	ABCIORU	CARIBOU
ABCEITT	TABETIC	ABCIOUV	BIVOUAC
ABCEJST	ABJECTS	ABCIRST	CABRITS
ABCEKLN	BLACKEN	ABCIRTY	BARYTIC
ABCEKLR	BLACKER	ABCISSS	ABSCISS
ABCEKNR	BRACKEN	ABCJOSU	JACOBUS
ABCEKRS	BACKERS	ABCKMRU	BUCKRAM
	REBACKS	ABCKNNO	BANNOCK
ABCEKRT	BRACKET	ABCKORS	BAROCKS
ABCEKST	BACKETS	ABCKOTU	OUTBACK
	BACKSET	ABCKRSU	BUCKRAS
	SETBACK	ABCKSTU	SACKBUT
ABCEKSY	BACKSEY		SUBTACK
ABCEKTW	WETBACK	ABCKSUW	BUCKSAW
ABCELLS	BECALLS	ABCLMNU	CLUBMAN
ABCELLU	BULLACE	ABCLMOY	CYMBALO
ABCELMO	CEMBALO	ABCLMSY	CYMBALS
ABCELMR	CAMBREL	ABCLNOS	BLANCOS
	CLAMBER	ABCLNOY	BALCONY
ABCELMS	BECALMS	ABCLOST	COBALTS
	SCAMBLE	ABCMORS	COMARBS
ABCELOP	PLACEBO	ABCMOST	COMBATS
ABCELOV	VOCABLE		TOMBACS
ABCELPU	BLUECAP	ABCNORS	CARBONS
ABCELPY	BYPLACE		CORBANS
ABCELRU	CURABLE	ABCORSX	BOXCARS
ABCELSU	BASCULE	ABCORSY	CARBOYS
ABCEMRS	CAMBERS	ABCSSTU	SUBACTS
	CEMBRAS	ABDDDEL	BLADDED
ABCEMSX	EXCAMBS	ABDDEEJ	BEJADED
ABCENOS	BEACONS	ABDDEER	BEARDED
ABCENOW	COWBANE		BREADED
ABCENRU	UNBRACE	ABDDEES	DEBASED
ABCEOOS	CABOOSE	ABDDEET	DEBATED
ABCEORU	CORBEAU	ABDDEEZ	BEDAZED
ABCERRS	BRACERS	ABDDEHN	BANDHED
ABCESSS	ABSCESS	ABDDEIN	ABIDDEN
ABCFIKN	FINBACK		BANDIED
ABCFILO	BIFOCAL	ABDDEIR	BRAIDED
ABCFIRS	FABRICS	ABDDEIS	BADDIES
ABCFLOO	COBLOAF	ABDDELR	BLADDER
ABCFNOS	CONFABS	ABDDELU	BLAUDED
ABCGHIN	BACHING	ABDDENR	BRANDED
ABCGHKO	HOGBACK	ABDDEOR	ABORDED
ABCGIKN	BACKING		BOARDED
ABCGILN	CABLING	ABDDERW	BEDWARD
ABCGINR	BRACING	ABDDHIS	BADDISH
ABCGKLO	BACKLOG	ABDDINS	DISBAND
ABCGMSU	SCUMBAG	ABDDLLO	ODDBALL
ABCHHII	HIBACHI	ABDDMOR	DAMBROD
ABCHIMT	BATHMIC	ABDEEGL	BEAGLED
ABCHIOT	COHABIT	ABDEEHO	OBEAHED
ABCHKOU	CHABOUK	ABDEEHS	BEHEADS
ABCHKTU	HACKBUT	ABDEEHT	BEATHED
ABCHKUW	HAWBUCK	ABDEEHV	BEHAVED
ABCHNOR	BROCHAN	ABDEEIR	BEADIER
ABCHNRU	BRAUNCH		BEARDIE
ABCHNRY	BRANCHY	ABDEEJS	BEJADES
ABCIILL	BACILLI	ABDEELM	BELDAME
ABCIIMN	MINICAB		BEMEDAL
ABCIIMS	IAMBICS		EMBALED

ABDEELN ENABLED	BRAIDER	ABDETTU ABUTTED	ABDRUZZ BUZZARD
ABDEELR BEDERAL	BRIARED	ABDGGOR BOGGARD	ABEEELS SEEABLE
BLEARED	RABIDER	ABDGIIN ABIDING	ABEEERV BEREAVE
ABDEELS BEADLES	ABDEIRS BRAISED	ABDGILN BALDING	ABEEFFL EFFABLE
ABDEELT BELATED	DARBIES	ABDGINN BANDING	ABEEFLO BEEFALO
BLEATED	ABDEIRT TRIBADE	ABDGINO ABODING	ABEEFTU BEAUFET
ABDEELY DYEABLE	ABDEIRU DAUBIER	ABDGINR BARDING	ABEEGHR HERBAGE
ABDEEMN BEADMEN	ABDEIRW BAWDIER	BRIGAND	ABEEGHS BEEGAHS
BEDEMAN	ABDEISS BIASSED	ABDGINT DINGBAT	ABEEGLL GABELLE
BENAMED	ABDEIST BASTIDE	ABDGINU DAUBING	ABEEGLR BEAGLER
ABDEEMR AMBERED	ABDEISW BAWDIES	ABDGLNO BOGLAND	ABEEGLS BEAGLES
BREAMED	ABDEJRU ABJURED	ABDGLUY LADYBUG	ABEEGRR GERBERA
EMBREAD	ABDEKLN BLANKED	ABDGNOS BANDOGS	ABEEGRS ABREGES
ABDEEMS EMBASED	ABDEKLU BAULKED	ABDGORS BODRAGS	BAREGES
ABDEEMY EMBAYED	ABDEKNR BRANKED	ABDHHOS DOBHASH	BARGEES
ABDEEMZ BEMAZED	ABDEKNU UNBAKED	ABDHIIT ADHIBIT	ABEEGRU AUBERGE
ABDEERS DEBASER	ABDEKRS DEBARKS	ABDHILS BALDISH	ABEEGRW BREWAGE
SABERED	ABDELMR MARBLED	ABDHMOR RHABDOM	ABEEHMS BESHAME
ABDEERT BERATED	RAMBLED	ABDHMSU BUDMASH	ABEEHMT EMBATHE
BETREAD	ABDELMS BEDLAMS	ABDHNSU HUSBAND	ABEEHNN HENBANE
DEBATER	BELDAMS	ABDHOSY HOBDAYS	ABEEHNS BANSHEE
REBATED	ABDELMW WAMBLED	ABDHRSU BURDASH	BEENAHS
ABDEERW BEWARED	ABDELMY EMBAYLD	RHABDUS	ABEEHNT BENEATH
ABDEERY BERAYED	ABDELNR BLANDER	ABDIKNW BAWDKIN	ABEEHRT BREATHE
ABDEESS DEBASES	ABDELOR LABORED	ABDIKRS DISBARK	ABEEHSV BEHAVES
SEABEDS	ABDELOS ALBEDOS	ABDILOO DIABOLO	ABEEILS BAILEES
ABDEEST BESTEAD	ABDELOT BLOATED	ABDILOR LABROID	ABEEIMR BEAMIER
DEBATES	ABDELOW DOWABLE	ABDILOT TABLOID	ABEEINS BEANIES
ABDEESZ BEDAZES	ABDELPU DUPABLE	ABDILRS BRIDALS	ABEEINT BETAINE
ABDEETT ABETTED	ABDELPY PYEBALD	LABRIDS	ABEEIRT EBRIATE
ABDEFFL BAFFLED	ABDELRR DRABLER	RIBALDS	ABEEIST BEASTIE
ABDEFLU LEAFBUD	ABDELRS BEDRALS	ABDILRW AWLBIRD	ABEEJMS JAMBEES
ABDEFOR FORBADE	ABDELRU DURABLE	ABDILRY RABIDLY	ABEEJRS BAJREES
ABDEFRW BEDWARF	ABDELRW BRAWLED	ABDILUY AUDIBLY	ABEEKLR BLEAKER
ABDEFST BEDFAST	WARBLED	ABDILWY BAWDILY	ABEEKLS KABELES
ABDEGGL BLAGGED	ABDELST BALDEST	ABDIMNR BIRDMAN	ABEEKNT BETAKEN
ABDEGGR BRAGGED	BLASTED	ABDIMOR AMBROID	ABEEKNV BEKNAVE
ABDEGHR BEGHARD	STABLED	ABDINOR INBOARD	ABEEKOP PEEKABO
ABDEGIN BEADING	ABDELSU BELAUDS	ABDINRS RIBANDS	ABEEKPS BESPAKE
ABDEGIR ABRIDGE	ABDELTT BATTLED	ABDINST BANDITS	BESPEAK
BRIGADE	BLATTED	ABDIOSU BADIOUS	ABEEKRR BREAKER
ABDEGLM GAMBLED	ABDEMMO MAMBOED	ABDIPRU UPBRAID	ABEEKRS BEAKERS
ABDEGLN BANGLED	ABDEMNO ABDOMEN	ABDIRRS BRAIRDS	ABEEKST BETAKES
ABDEGLR BELGARD	ABDEMRU RUMBAED	ABDIRSS DISBARS	ABEELLY EYEBALL
GARBLED	ABDENOR BANDORE	ABDIRSU RIBAUDS	ABEELMM EMBLEMA
ABDEGNO BONDAGE	BROADEN	SUBARID	ABEELMS EMBALES
DOGBANE	ABDENOT BATONED	ABDIRTY TRIBADY	ABEELMZ EMBLAZE
ABDEGOS BODEGAS	ABDENOY NAEBODY	ABDKNOO BANDOOK	ABEELNP PLEBEAN
ABDEGRS BADGERS	ABDENPS BEDPANS	ABDLLNY BLANDLY	ABEELNR ENABLER
ABDEHIT HABITED	ABDENRR BRANDER	ABDLLOR BOLLARD	ABEELNS BALEENS
ABDEHLM HAMBLED	ABDENRU UNBARED	ABDLNOR BANDROL	ENABLES
ABDEHLR HALBERD	ABDENRW BRAWNED	ABDLORY BROADLY	ABEELNT TENABLE
ABDEHOW BOWHEAD	ABDENSS BADNESS	ABDLRUY DURABLY	ABEELNU NEBULAE
ABDEHRS BERDASH	ABDENSU SUBDEAN	RYBAULD	ABEELPR BEPEARL
BRASHED	ABDENTU UNBATED	ABDLRYY BYRLADY	ABEELQU EQUABLE
ABDEHRT BREADTH	ABDEOOT TABOOED	ABDLSUU SUBDUAL	ABEELRR BLEARER
ABDEILP BIPEDAL	ABDEORR BOARDER	ABDMNNO BONDMAN	ERRABLE
PIEBALD	BROADER	ABDMRUY MARYBUD	ABEELRT BLEATER
ABDEILR BRAILED	ABDEORT ABORTED	ABDNOOR ONBOARD	RETABLE
RIDABLE	TABORED	ABDNOPR PROBAND	ABEELST BELATES
ABDEILS DISABLE	ABDEOST BOASTED	ABDNOSU ABOUNDS	ABEELSU SUEABLE
ABDEILT LIBATED	ABDEOTU BOUTADE	BAUSOND	ABEELSV BESLAVE
ABDEILU AUDIBLE	ABDEQSU BASQUED	ABDNOYY ANYBODY	ABEEMNS BASEMEN
ABDEIMR EMBRAID	ABDERSS SERDABS	ABDNRTU TURBAND	BEMEANS
ABDEIMS IMBASED	ABDERST DABSTER	ABDOORW BARWOOD	BENAMES
ABDEINR BANDIER	ABDERSU DAUBERS	ABDORRS BORDARS	ABEEMNT BEMEANT
BRAINED	SUBEDAR	ABDORSS ADSORBS	ABEEMRS BEAMERS
ABDEINS BANDIES	ABDERSV ADVERBS	ABDORSY BYROADS	BESMEAR
ABDEINW BEDAWIN	ABDERTY DRYBEAT	ABDRRSU DURBARS	ABEEMRV EMBRAVE
ABDEIRR BARDIER	ABDERUY DAUBERY	ABDRSTU BUSTARD	ABEEMSS EMBASES

ABEEMST EMBASTE	ABEGMRU UMBRAGE	TRIABLE
ABEENRV VERBENA	ABEGMST GAMBETS	ABEILSS ABSEILS
ABEEORS AEROBES	ABEGNNT BANTENG	ISABELS
ABEEPST BESPATE	ABEGNOS NOSEBAG	LABISES
ABEERRS BEARERS	ABEGNRS BANGERS	ABEILST ALBITES
BREARES	GRABENS	ASTILBE
ABEERRT REBATER	ABEGNSW BEGNAWS	BESTIAL
TABRERE	ABEGORR BEGORRA	LIBATES
TEREBRA	ABEGORS BORAGES	STABILE
ABEERST BEATERS	ABEGORX GEARBOX	ABEILSW BEWAILS
BERATES	ABEGOSZ GAZEBOS	ABEILSY BAILEYS
REBATES	ABEGOTT BOTTEGA	ABEILSZ SIZABLE
ABEERSV BEAVERS	ABEGOUY BUOYAGE	ABEILVV BIVALVE
ABEERSW BEWARES	ABEGRST BARGEST	ABEIMNR MIRBANE
ABEERSZ ZEREBAS	ABEGSTU TUBAGES	ABEIMNT AMBIENT
ABEERTT ABETTER	ABEHILR HIRABLE	ABEIMRR BARMIER
ABEERVY BEAVERY	ABEHIMS BEAMISH	ABEIMRS AMBRIES
ABEESST SEBATES	ABEHIMT IMBATHE	ABEIMSS IMBASES
ABEESWX BEESWAX	ABEHIRS BEARISH	ABEINOT NIOBATE
ABEFFIS BAFFIES	ABEHISU BEAUISH	ABEINPT BEPAINT
ABEFFLR BAFFLER	ABEHITU HABITUE	ABEINRT ATEBRIN
ABEFFLS BAFFLES	ABEHITZ ZABTIEH	ABEINST BASINET
ABEFFOT OFFBEAT	ABEHKLS KEBLAHS	BESAINT
ABEFGIL FILABEG	ABEHKRU HAUBERK	BESTAIN
ABEFGST GABFEST	ABEHLMS HAMBLES	ABEINTT TABINET
ABEFILN FINABLE	SHAMBLE	ABEIORS ISOBARE
ABEFILR FRIABLE	ABEHLNU UNHABLE	ABEIOSS ABIOSES
ABEFILS FAIBLES	ABEHLRS HERBALS	ISOBASE
ABEFILX FIXABLE	ABEHLRT BLATHER	ABEIOTV OBVIATE
ABEFINU BEAUFIN	HALBERT	ABEIPST BAPTISE
ABEFITY BEATIFY	ABEHLSS BLASHES	ABEIPTZ BAPTIZE
ABEFLLS BEFALLS	ABEHNOS HEBONAS	ABEIRRR BARRIER
ABEFLLU BALEFUL	ABEHRRS BRASHER	ABEIRRS BRASIER
ABEFLLY FLYABLE	HERBARS	ABEIRRT ARBITER
ABEFLNU BANEFUL	ABEHRRY HERBARY	RAREBIT
ABEFLNY FLYBANE	ABEHRSS BASHERS	ABEIRRW WARBIER
ABEFLRS FABLERS	BRASHES	ABEIRRZ BIZARRE
ABEFMOS BEFOAMS	ABEHRST BATHERS	BRAZIER
ABEFORR FORBEAR	BERTHAS	ABEIRSS BASSIER
ABEFPRS PREFABS	BREATHS	BRAISES
ABEGGIR BAGGIER	ABEHRTY BREATHY	BRASSIE
ABEGGMO GAMBOGE	ABEIILL BAILLIE	ABEIRST BAITERS
ABEGGNU BUGGANE	ABEIILS BAILIES	BARITES
ABEGGRS BEGGARS	ABEIJMR JAMBIER	ABEIRSX BRAXIES
ABEGGRU BURGAGE	ABEIJNS BASENJI	ABEIRSZ BRAIZES
ABEGGRY BEGGARY	ABEIKLL LIKABLE	ZERIBAS
ABEGHNS SHEBANG	ABEIKLR BALKIER	ABEIRTT BATTIER
ABEGIMN BEAMING	ABEIKLS SKIABLE	BIRETTA
ABEGIMR GAMBIER	ABEIKNR INBREAK	ABEIRTV VIBRATE
ABEGIMT MEGABIT	ABEIKNT BEATNIK	ABEIRUX EXURBIA
ABEGINN BEANING	ABEIKRR BARKIER	ABEISSS BIASSES
ABEGINO BEGONIA	BRAKIER	ABEISTT BATISTE
ABEGINR BEARING	ABEILLO LOBELIA	ABEISUV ABUSIVE
ABEGINT BEATING	ABEILLP PLIABLE	ABEITUX BAUXITE
ABEGINY ABYEING	ABEILLR LIBERAL	ABEJMNO JAMBONE
ABEGIPP BAGPIPE	ABEILLV LIVABLE	ABEJMNS ENJAMBS
ABEGKOR BROKAGE	ABEILMR BALMIER	ABEJMRS JAMBERS
ABEGLMR GAMBLER	MIRABLE	ABEJMUX JAMBEUX
GAMBREL	REMBLAI	ABEJNOS BANJOES
ABEGLMS GAMBLES	ABEILMS EMBAILS	ABEJNOW JAWBONE
ABEGLNR BRANGLE	LAMBIES	ABEJNST BEJANTS
ABEGLNS BANGLES	ABEILMT LIMBATE	ABEJORS JERBOAS
ABEGLOR ALBERGO	TIMBALE	ABEJRRU ABJURER
ABEGLOT GLOBATE	ABEILMX MIXABLE	ABEJRSU ABJURES
ABEGLRR GARBLER	ABEILMY BEAMILY	ABEKLLY BLEAKLY
ABEGLRS GARBLES	ABEILNP BIPLANE	ABEKLNR BLANKER
ABEGLST GABLETS	ABEILNS LESBIAN	ABEKLNT BLANKET
ABEGLSU BELUGAS	ABEILPT PATIBLE	ABEKLRS BALKERS
BLAGUES	ABEILRS BAILERS	ABEKMNS EMBANKS
ABEGMOR EMBARGO	ABEILRT LIBRATE	ABEKMRS EMBARKS

ABEKNRS BANKERS
BARKENS
ABEKNST BANKETS
ABEKOOR ABROOKE
ABEKPRU UPBREAK
ABEKRRS BARKERS
ABEKSST BASKETS
ABELLMN BELLMAN
ABELLMS EMBALLS
ABELLNT NETBALL
ABELLOS LOSABLE
ABELLOV LOVABLE
VOLABLE
ABELLRU RUBELLA
RULABLE
ABELLST BALLETS
ABELLTU BULLATE
ABELMMR MEMBRAL
ABELMMS EMBALMS
ABELMNT LAMBENT
ABELMNU ALBUMEN
ABELMOV MOVABLE
ABELMRR MARBLER
RAMBLER
ABELMRS AMBLERS
LAMBERS
MARBLES
RAMBLES
ABELMRT LAMBERT
ABELMSU BEMAULS
ABELMSW WAMBLES
ABELMTU MUTABLE
ABELNOT NOTABLE
ABELNOY BALONEY
ABELNRS BRANLES
BRANSLE
ABELNRT BRANTLE
ABELNRU NEBULAR
ABELNRY BLARNEY
ABELNSZ BENZALS
ABELNTU TUNABLE
ABELOPR ROPABLE
ABELOPT POTABLE
ABELORS LABROSE
ABELORT BLOATER
ABELORU RUBEOLA
ABELORW ROWABLE
ABELOSS BOLASES
ABELOST BOATELS
OBLATES
ABELOSV ABSOLVE
ABELPRU PUBERAL
ABELQUY EQUABLY
ABELRRS BARRELS
ABELRRW BRAWLER
WARBLER
ABELRSS BRALESS
ABELRST ALBERTS
BATLERS
BLASTER
LABRETS
STABLER
ABELRSV VERBALS
ABELRSW BAWLERS
WARBLES
ABELRSY BARLEYS
ABELRSZ BLAZERS
ABELRTT BATTLER
BLATTER
BRATTLE

ABELRTW	BLEWART
ABELRUZ	ZEBRULA
ABELRVY	BRAVELY
ABELSST	BASTLES
	STABLES
ABELSTT	BATLETS
	BATTELS
	BATTLES
	BLATEST
	TABLETS
ABELSTU	SUBLATE
ABELSTY	BAETYLS
	BEASTLY
ABELSWY	BAWLEYS
ABELTWY	BELTWAY
ABEMMRS	BAMMERS
ABEMNOS	AMBONES
	BEMOANS
ABEMNOT	BOATMEN
ABEMNRY	BYREMAN
	MYRBANE
ABEMNST	BATSMEN
ABEMNSU	SUNBEAM
ABEMORT	BROMATE
ABEMRST	TAMBERS
ABEMSSY	EMBASSY
ABENNOR	BARONNE
ABENNRS	BANNERS
ABENORS	BORANES
ABENORT	BARONET
	REBOANT
ABENORW	RAWBONE
ABENOTY	BAYONET
ABENQTU	BANQUET
ABENRRU	URBANER
ABENRST	BANTERS
ABENRSU	UNBARES
	UNBEARS
ABENRSY	BARNEYS
ABENRSZ	BRAZENS
ABENRUX	EXURBAN
ABENSST	ABSENTS
	BASNETS
ABENSTT	BATTENS
ABENSTU	BUTANES
ABENSTZ	BEZANTS
ABEOOTV	OBOVATE
ABEOPRS	SAPROBE
ABEOPRT	PROBATE
ABEOQRU	BAROQUE
ABEORRS	BRASERO
ABEORRT	ARBORET
	TABORER
ABEORST	BOASTER
	BOATERS
	BORATES
	SORBATE
ABEORSU	AEROBUS
ABEORSV	BRAVOES
ABEORSX	BORAXES
ABEORSZ	BEZOARS
ABEORTT	ABETTOR
	BATTERO
	TABORET
ABEOSTV	BOVATES
ABEPRSU	UPBEARS
ABEQRSU	BARQUES
ABEQSSU	BASQUES
ABERRST	BARRETS
	BARTERS

ABERRSY	BRAYERS
ABERRVY	BRAVERY
ABERSSS	BRASSES
ABERSST	BASTERS
	BESTARS
	BRASSET
	BREASTS
ABERSSU	ABUSERS
	SURBASE
ABERSSZ	ZEBRASS
ABERSTT	BATTERS
	TABRETS
ABERSTU	ARBUTES
	SURBATE
ABERSTV	BRAVEST
ABERSTW	BRAWEST
	WABSTER
ABERSTX	BAXTERS
ABERSTY	BARYTES
	BETRAYS
ABERSUU	BUREAUS
ABERSWY	BEWRAYS
ABERTTU	ABUTTER
ABERTTY	BATTERY
ABERUUX	BUREAUX
ABESSST	BASSEST
	BASSETS
ABESSSY	ABYSSES
ABESTTU	BATTUES
ABFFGIN	BAFFING
ABFFIIL	BAILIFF
ABFFLOU	BUFFALO
ABFGILN	FABLING
ABFGINR	BARFING
ABFGLSU	BAGFULS
ABFHLSU	BASHFUL
ABFIILR	BIFILAR
ABFIIMR	FIMBRIA
ABFILRU	FIBULAR
ABFILSU	FIBULAS
ABFIMOR	FIBROMA
ABFLOTY	FLYBOAT
ABFOORT	FOOTBAR
ABFSTTU	TUBFAST
ABGGGIN	BAGGING
ABGGILY	BAGGILY
ABGGINN	BANGING
ABGGINR	BARGING
	GARBING
ABGGIST	BAGGITS
ABGGISW	BAGWIGS
ABGGNOS	GOBANGS
ABGGNSU	BUGGANS
ABGGORT	BOGGART
ABGHILN	BLAHING
ABGHINS	BASHING
ABGHINT	BATHING
ABGHLOT	HAGBOLT
ABGHLRU	BURGHAL
ABGHOTU	ABOUGHT
ABGHSTU	HAGBUTS
ABGIILN	BAILING
ABGIINS	BIASING
ABGIINT	BAITING
ABGIINZ	BAIZING
ABGIKLN	BALKING
ABGIKNN	BANKING
ABGIKNO	BOAKING
ABGIKNR	BARKING
	BRAKING

ABGIKNS	BAKINGS
	BASKING
ABGIKNU	BAUKING
ABGILLN	BALLING
ABGILMN	AMBLING
	BALMING
	BLAMING
	LAMBING
ABGILMS	GIMBALS
ABGILNR	BLARING
ABGILNS	SABLING
ABGILNT	TABLING
ABGILNW	BAWLING
ABGILNZ	BLAZING
ABGILOR	GARBOIL
ABGIMMN	BAMMING
ABGIMRS	GAMBIRS
ABGIMST	GAMBIST
	GAMBITS
ABGINNN	BANNING
ABGINNR	BARNING
ABGINNT	BANTING
ABGINOS	BAGNIOS
	GABIONS
ABGINOT	BOATING
ABGINRR	BARRING
ABGINRS	SABRING
ABGINRV	BRAVING
ABGINRY	BRAYING
ABGINRZ	BRAZING
ABGINSS	BASSING
ABGINST	BASTING
ABGINSU	ABUSING
ABGINTT	BATTING
ABGINTU	TABUING
ABGINTY	BAYTING
ABGIOPT	PIGBOAT
ABGIOSU	BAGUIOS
ABGKNOS	KOBANGS
ABGKOOS	BOGOAKS
ABGLMNU	LUMBANG
ABGLMOS	GAMBOLS
ABGLMOU	LUMBAGO
ABGLMSY	GYMBALS
ABGLOOT	TOOLBAG
ABGLORS	BROLGAS
ABGLORT	RAGBOLT
ABGLOSU	ALBUGOS
ABGLRRU	BURGLAR
ABGNOPR	PROBANG
ABGNORS	BROGANS
ABGNOTU	GUNBOAT
ABGOORT	BOTARGO
ABGORRU	GOBURRA
ABGORTU	OUTBRAG
ABHHKOT	KHOTBAH
ABHHKTU	KHUTBAH
ABHHSUY	HUSHABY
ABHIINT	INHABIT
ABHIKLS	KIBLAHS
ABHIKST	BHAKTIS
ABHIKTW	HAWKBIT
ABHILNO	HOBNAIL
ABHILOS	ABOLISH
ABHILTU	HALIBUT
ABHIMRS	MIHRABS
ABHIMSZ	MAZHBIS
ABHINST	ABSINTH
ABHIOPS	PHOBIAS
ABHIORS	BOARISH

ABHIOST	ISOBATH
ABHISTU	HABITUS
ABHKLSY	BASHLYK
ABHKORU	BOURKHA
ABHKRSU	BURKHAS
	KURBASH
ABHMNSU	BUSHMAN
ABHMRSU	RHUMBAS
ABHNOST	BOTHANS
ABHNSTU	SUNBATH
ABHORRS	HARBORS
ABHORRU	HARBOUR
ABHOTUY	HAUTBOY
ABHPSTY	BYPATHS
ABHRSTU	TARBUSH
ABIIKKT	KIBITKA
ABIILLS	BAILLIS
ABIILMU	BULIMIA
ABIILNQ	INQILAB
ABIILNS	AIBLINS
	BILIANS
ABIILRY	BILIARY
ABIILST	STIBIAL
ABIILTY	ABILITY
ABIIMST	IAMBIST
ABIINNS	BAININS
ABIINOR	ROBINIA
ABIINRY	BIRYANI
ABIIOSS	ABIOSIS
ABIJLNR	BRINJAL
ABIJNOT	ABJOINT
ABIJRSU	JABIRUS
ABIKKSU	KABUKIS
ABIKLMN	LAMBKIN
ABIKLOR	KILOBAR
ABIKMNR	BARMKIN
ABIKMRS	IMBARKS
ABIKRST	BRITSKA
ABIKRTZ	BRITZKA
ABILLMN	BILLMAN
ABILLMU	BALLIUM
ABILLMY	BALMILY
ABILLNP	PINBALL
ABILLPY	PLIABLY
ABILLSY	SYLLABI
ABILLTT	BATTILL
ABILLWX	WAXBILL
ABILMNU	ALBUMIN
ABILMST	TIMBALS
ABILNOS	ALBINOS
ABILNOT	BITONAL
ABILNOZ	BIZONAL
ABILNRY	BAIRNLY
ABILOPR	BIPOLAR
	PARBOIL
ABILORS	BAILORS
ABILORT	ORBITAL
ABILORV	BOLIVAR
ABILOTU	OBITUAL
ABILRRY	LIBRARY
ABILRSU	BURIALS
	RAILBUS
ABILRSZ	BRAZILS
ABIMMRS	MIMBARS
ABIMNRS	MINBARS
ABIMOSS	BIOMASS
ABIMPST	BAPTISM
ABIMRSS	BISMARS
ABIMRST	IMBRAST
ABIMRSU	BARIUMS

ABIMRTT	TRIMTAB	ABMNSUY	YNAMBUS	ACCDORS	ACCORDS	ACCENPT	PECCANT
ABIMTTY	AMBITTY	ABMOOSW	WABOOMS	ACCEEHO	COACHEE	ACCENRS	CANCERS
ABINNSU	BUNNIAS	ABMOPST	BAMPOTS	ACCEELN	CENACLE	ACCENST	ACCENTS
ABINOOR	BORONIA	ABMORTU	TAMBOUR	ACCEENR	CREANCE	ACCEOPY	CACOEPY
ABINORT	TABORIN	ABMOSTU	SUBATOM	ACCEERT	ACCRETE	ACCEORW	CRACOWE
ABINORW	RAINBOW	ABMOSTW	WOMBATS	ACCEFLU	FELUCCA	ACCEPRY	PECCARY
ABINOSS	BONSAIS	ABMRSSU	SAMBURS	ACCEGIN	ACCINGE	ACCEPST	ACCEPTS
ABINOST	BASTION	ABNOORS	SOROBAN	ACCEGOS	SOCCAGE	ACCERRS	SCARCER
	OBTAINS	ABNOORZ	BORAZON	ACCEHHI	CHECHIA	ACCERRT	CARRECT
ABINOSU	ABUSION	ABNOOSS	BASSOON	ACCEHIL	CALICHE	ACCERSU	ACCRUES
ABINRTV	VIBRANT	ABNOOST	BATOONS		CHALICE		ACCURSE
ABIORRS	BARRIOS	ABNORST	BARTONS	ACCEHIM	MACCHIE		ACCUSER
ABIORSS	ISOBARS	ABNORSY	BARYONS	ACCEHIN	CHICANE	ACCERSW	ACCREWS
ABIORST	ORBITAS	ABNORTY	BARYTON	ACCEHLN	CHANCEL	ACCESSU	ACCUSES
ABIORTV	VIBRATO	ABNOSSU	BONASUS	ACCEHLO	COCHLEA	ACCFIIP	PACIFIC
ABIPSTT	BAPTIST	ABNOTUY	BUOYANT	ACCEHNO	CONCHAE	ACCFILY	CALCIFY
ABIRTTY	TRAYBIT	ABNRSTU	TURBANS	ACCEHNR	CHANCER	ACCGHIN	CACHING
ABISSST	BASSIST	ABNRTTU	TURBANT		CHANCRE		CHACING
ABJJOOS	JOJOBAS	ABNSTYZ	BYZANTS	ACCEHNS	CHANCES	ACCHHIS	CHICHAS
ABJKMOS	JAMBOKS	ABOOPSX	SOAPBOX	ACCEHNT	CATCHEN	ACCHHKU	KUCHCHA
	SJAMBOK	ABOORTW	ROWBOAT	ACCEHNU	CHAUNCE	ACCHIKS	CHIACKS
ABJLMOO	JAMBOOL	ABORRSU	ARBOURS	ACCEHOR	CAROCHE	ACCHIMS	CHASMIC
ABJLMSU	JAMBULS	ABORRSW	BARROWS		COACHER	ACCHINO	CHICANO
	JUMBALS	ABORSTU	OUTBARS	ACCEHOS	CHACOES	ACCHIOT	CHAOTIC
ABKLLNY	BLANKLY		ROBUSTA		COACHES	ACCHIRS	SCRAICH
ABKLRUW	BULWARK		RUBATOS	ACCEHPU	CAPUCHE	ACCHJSU	JACCHUS
ABKLSSY	SKYLABS		TABOURS	ACCEHRS	CREACHS	ACCHKOY	HAYCOCK
ABKMNOO	BOOKMAN	ABORSTW	TOWBARS	ACCEHRT	CATCHER	ACCHKSY	CHYACKS
ABKMOST	TOMBAKS	ABOSTUU	AUTOBUS		RECATCH	ACCHLTU	CLAUCHT
ABKNRSU	UNBARKS	ABPRSTU	ABRUPTS	ACCEHST	CACHETS	ACCHNRS	SCRANCH
ABKNRUU	BUNRAKU		UPBRAST		CATCHES	ACCHNRU	CRAUNCH
ABLLLUY	LULLABY	ABPRSUY	UPBRAYS	ACCEHTU	CATECHU	ACCHOSU	CACHOUS
ABLLNOO	BALLOON	ABRRSSU	BURSARS	ACCEHXY	CACHEXY	ACCHOTW	CHOCTAW
ABLLNOS	BALLONS	ABRRSSY	BURSARY	ACCEIKP	ICEPACK	ACCHOUY	ACOUCHY
ABLLOPR	PROBALL	ABRRTUY	TURBARY	ACCEILN	CALCINE	ACCHPTU	CATCHUP
ABLLORU	LOBULAR	ABRSTUU	ARBUTUS	ACCEILO	COELIAC		UPCATCH
ABLLOST	BALLOTS	ABSSUWY	SUBWAYS	ACCEILS	CALICES	ACCHRRU	CURRACH
ABLLOSW	BALLOWS	ACCCILY	ACYCLIC		CELIACS	ACCHRST	SCRATCH
ABLLOTY	TALLBOY	ACCDDEE	ACCEDED	ACCEILT	CALCITE	ACCHRSU	SCRAUCH
ABLLRUY	BULLARY	ACCDDEI	CADDICE	ACCEIMR	CERAMIC	ACCIILN	ACLINIC
ABLMMOU	BUMMALO	ACCDEEN	CADENCE		RACEMIC	ACCIINT	ACTINIC
ABLMNOU	UMBONAL	ACCDEER	ACCEDER	ACCEINO	COCAINE	ACCIIST	ASCITIC
ABLMOOT	TOMBOLA	ACCDEES	ACCEDES		OCEANIC		SCIATIC
ABLMOPS	APLOMBS	ACCDEHK	CHACKED	ACCEINV	VACCINE	ACCILLU	CALCULI
ABLMOSY	LAMBOYS	ACCDEHN	CHANCED	ACCEIPR	CAPRICE	ACCILMO	COMICAL
ABLMOVY	MOVABLY	ACCDEHO	COACHED	ACCEIPS	IPECACS	ACCILMU	CALCIUM
ABLMPUU	PABULUM	ACCDEHT	CATCHED	ACCEIPV	PECCAVI	ACCILNO	CONICAL
ABLMSTY	TYMBALS	ACCDEII	ACCIDIE	ACCEIQU	CACIQUE		LACONIC
ABLMTUY	MUTABLY	ACCDEIO	ACCOIED	ACCEIRS	CARICES	ACCILNY	CYNICAL
ABLNOSZ	BLAZONS	ACCDEIT	ACCITED	ACCEIRT	CREATIC	ACCILOR	CALORIC
ABLNOTU	BUTANOL	ACCDEIU	CADUCEI	ACCEIST	ACCITES	ACCILOS	ACCOILS
ABLNOTY	NOTABLY	ACCDEKL	CACKLED		ASCETIC		CALICOS
ABLNSTU	TULBANS		CLACKED	ACCEKLR	CACKLER	ACCILOV	VOCALIC
ABLNTUY	TUNABLY	ACCDEKO	COCKADE		CLACKER	ACCILRU	CRUCIAL
ABLOORS	ROBALOS	ACCDEKR	CRACKED		CRACKLE	ACCILRY	ACRYLIC
ABLOORY	OBOLARY	ACCDENS	ACCENDS	ACCEKLS	CACKLES	ACCILSS	CLASSIC
ABLOPYY	PLAYBOY	ACCDENY	CADENCY	ACCEKMO	MEACOCK	ACCILST	CLASTIC
ABLORST	BORSTAL	ACCDEOT	COACTED	ACCEKOP	PEACOCK	ACCILSU	SACCULI
ABLORSU	LABOURS	ACCDEOY	ACCOYED	ACCEKRR	CRACKER	ACCIMOZ	ZIMOCCA
ABLORTW	BLAWORT	ACCDERU	ACCRUED	ACCELLY	CALYCLE	ACCINNO	CANONIC
ABLORUW	BOURLAW		CARDECU	ACCELNO	CONCEAL	ACCINOT	CANTICO
ABLOSST	OBLASTS	ACCDESU	ACCUSED	ACCELNS	CANCELS	ACCINRU	CRUCIAN
ABLOSTT	TALBOTS		SUCCADE	ACCELOR	CORACLE	ACCIOPR	CAPROIC
ABLOSTV	ABVOLTS	ACCDFIL	FLACCID	ACCELOT	CACOLET	ACCIORS	SCORIAC
ABLPRSU	BURLAPS	ACCDILS	SCALDIC	ACCELSU	SACCULE	ACCIPRT	PRACTIC
ABLPSUY	PLAYBUS	ACCDIOT	OCTADIC	ACCELSY	CALYCES	ACCIRRS	CIRCARS
ABLRSWY	BYRLAWS	ACCDKNO	CANDOCK	ACCEMNU	CACUMEN	ACCIRST	ARCTICS
ABLRTUU	TUBULAR	ACCDKOW	DAWCOCK	ACCENOR	CONACRE	ACCISTT	TACTICS
ABMMNOS	MOBSMAN	ACCDLOY	ACCOYLD	ACCENOS	ASCONCE	ACCISTU	CAUSTIC
ABMNSTU	NUMBATS		CACODYL	ACCENOV	CONCAVE		CICUTAS

ACCKLOR CARLOCK	CREEDAL	ACDEHMP CHAMPED	ACDEKNR CRANKED
ACCKLRY CRACKLY	DECLARE	ACDEHMR CHARMED	ACDEKNS SNACKED
ACCKMOR CROMACK	ACDEELS DESCALE	MARCHED	ACDEKOR CROAKED
ACCKOSS CASSOCK	ACDEELT CLEATED	ACDEHMS CHASMED	ACDEKQU QUACKED
ACCKOST CASTOCK	ACDEELV CLEAVED	ACDEHMT MATCHED	ACDEKRS DACKERS
ACCLOSU COUCALS	ACDEEMN MENACED	ACDEHNR ENDARCH	ACDEKRT TRACKED
ACCLOSY ACCLOYS	ACDEEMR AMERCED	RANCHED	ACDEKRW WRACKED
ACCMOPT ACCOMPT	CREAMED	ACDEHNT CHANTED	ACDEKST STACKED
COMPACT	RACEMED	ACDEHOP POACHED	ACDELLS SCALLED
ACCMRUU CURCUMA	ACDEENR ENRACED	ACDEHOR ROACHED	ACDELMM CLAMMED
ACCNOOR RACCOON	ACDEENS DECANES	ACDEHOT CATHODE	ACDELMP CAMPLED
ACCNOOS CACOONS	ENCASED	ACDEHPP CHAPPED	CLAMPED
ACCNOTT CONTACT	ACDEENT ENACTED	ACDEHPR PARCHED	ACDELMS MASCLED
ACCNOTU ACCOUNT	ACDEENV ENCAVED	ACDEHPT PATCHED	ACDELNO CELADON
ACCOQSU SQUACCO	VENDACE	ACDEHPU CUPHEAD	ACDELNS CALENDS
ACCORSS CORCASS	ACDEEPR CAPERED	ACDEHRR CHARRED	CANDLES
ACCORTU ACCOURT	PEARCED	ACDEHRS CRASHED	ACDELNT CANTLED
ACCOSST ACCOSTS	PREACED	ACDEHRT CHARTED	ACDELNU LAUNCED
ACCRSTU ACCURST	ACDEEPS ESCAPED	ACDEHST SCATHED	UNLACED
ACDDDEI CADDIED	ACDEERS CREASED	ACDEHTT CHATTED	ACDELOR ORACLED
ACDDDEL CLADDED	DECARES	ACDEHTW WATCHED	ACDELOS SOLACED
ACDDDEU ADDUCED	SEARCED	ACDEHTY YACHTED	ACDELOT LOCATED
ACDDDKO DADDOCK	ACDEERT CATERED	ACDEILL CEDILLA	ACDELPP CLAPPED
ACDDEEF DEFACED	CEDRATE	ACDEILM CAMELID	ACDELPS CLASPED
ACDDEER CEDARED	CERATED	CLAIMED	SCALPED
ACDDEES DECADES	CREATED	DECIMAL	ACDELQU CALQUED
ACDDEEY DECAYED	REACTED	DECLAIM	ACDELRS CRADLES
ACDDEIN CANDIED	ACDEEST TEDESCA	MALICED	SCALDER
ACDDEIS CADDIES	ACDEETU EDUCATE	MEDICAL	ACDELRT CLARTED
ACDDEIU DECIDUA	ACDEETX EXACTED	ACDEILN INLACED	ACDELRU CAULDER
ACDDELN CANDLED	ACDEFFH CHAFFED	ACDEILR DECRIAL	ACDELRW CRAWLED
ACDDELO CLADODE	ACDEFHU CHAUFED	RADICEL	ACDELSS CLASSED
ACDDELR CLADDER	ACDEFIN FANCIED	RADICLE	DECLASS
CRADLED	ACDEFIR FARCIED	ACDEILS SCAILED	ACDELST CASTLED
ACDDELS SCALDED	ACDEFRS SCARFED	ACDEILT CITADEL	SCLATED
ACDDELU CAUDLED	ACDEFRT CRAFTED	DELTAIC	ACDELSU CAUDLES
ACDDEMU DUCDAME	FRACTED	DIALECT	CEDULAS
ACDDEOP DECAPOD	ACDEGGL CLAGGED	EDICTAL	ACDELTT CLATTED
ACDDERU ADDUCER	ACDEGGR CRAGGED	ACDEIMT MICATED	ACDELTU CLAUTED
ACDDESU ADDUCES	ACDEGHN CHANGED	ACDEIMY MEDIACY	ACDEMMR CRAMMED
SCAUDED	GANCHED	ACDEINO OCEANID	ACDEMNU DECUMAN
ACDDHHU CHUDDAH	ACDEGHR CHARGED	ACDEINR CAIRNED	ACDEMOR CAROMED
ACDDHIS CADDISH	ACDEGIN INCAGED	CARNIED	COMRADE
ACDDHKO HADDOCK	ACDEGIR CADGIER	ACDEINS CANDIES	ACDEMPR CRAMPED
ACDDHRU CHUDDAR	ACDEGIS DISCAGE	INCASED	ACDEMPS DECAMPS
ACDDIRS DISCARD	ACDEGKO DOCKAGE	ACDEINV INCAVED	SCAMPED
ACDDIST ADDICTS	ACDEGLN CANGLED	ACDEINY CYANIDE	ACDENNS SCANNED
ACDDKOP PADDOCK	CLANGED	ACDEIPR EPACRID	ACDENNT CANDENT
ACDDSSY CADDYSS	GLANCED	ACDEIPS DISPACE	ACDENNU NUANCED
ACDDSTU ADDUCTS	ACDEGNO CONGAED	ACDEIRR ACRIDER	ACDENOR ACORNED
ACDEEES DECEASE	DECAGON	CARRIED	DRACONE
ACDEEFF EFFACED	ACDEGNU UNCAGED	ACDEIRS CARDIES	ACDENOS DEACONS
ACDEEFN ENFACED	ACDEGOR CARGOED	RADICES	ACDENPR PRANCED
ACDEEFR DEFACER	CORDAGE	SIDECAR	ACDENPT PANDECT
REFACED	ACDEGRS CADGERS	ACDEIRU DECURIA	ACDENPU UNCAPED
ACDEEFS DEFACES	ACDEHHN HANCHED	ACDEISS DISCASE	ACDENRS DANCERS
ACDEEFT FACETED	ACDEHHT HATCHED	ACDEIST ACIDEST	ACDENRT CANTRED
ACDEEGL GLACEED	ACDEHIN CHAINED	DACITES	TRANCED
ACDEEGN ENCAGED	ECHIDNA	ACDEISV ADVICES	ACDENRU DURANCE
ACDEEHL LEACHED	ACDEHIP EDAPHIC	ACDEITT DICTATE	UNRACED
ACDEEHP PEACHED	ACDEHIR CHAIRED	ACDEITY EDACITY	ACDENRY ARDENCY
ACDEEHR REACHED	ACDEHIX HEXADIC	ACDEJLO CAJOLED	ACDENSS ASCENDS
ACDEEHT CHEATED	ACDEHKL CHALKED	ACDEJNU JAUNCED	ACDENST DECANTS
ACDEEIR DECIARE	HACKLED	ACDEKLM MACKLED	DESCANT
ACDEEJT DEJECTA	ACDEHKR CHARKED	ACDEKLN CLANKED	SCANTED
ACDEEKR CREAKED	ACDEHKW WHACKED	ACDEKLO CLOAKED	ACDENSU UNCASED
ACDEELN CLEANED	ACDEHLN LANCHED	ACDEKLS SLACKED	ACDENTU UNACTED
ELANCED	ACDEHLR CHALDER	ACDEKLT TACKLED	ACDENUV VAUNCED
ENLACED	ACDEHLS CLASHED	ACDEKLU CAULKED	ACDEOPS PEACODS
ACDEELR CLEARED	ACDEHLT LATCHED	ACDEKMS SMACKED	PEASCOD

ACDEOPT	COAPTED	ACDINST	DISCANT
ACDEORR	CORRADE	ACDINSU	SUDANIC
ACDEORS	SARCODE	ACDINSW	WINDACS
ACDEORT	CORDATE	ACDIOPR	PARODIC
	REDCOAT		PICADOR
ACDEOST	COASTED	ACDIORR	CORRIDA
ACDEOUV	COUVADE	ACDIORS	SARCOID
ACDEPPR	CRAPPED	ACDIORT	ARCTOID
ACDEPRS	SCARPED		CAROTID
	SCRAPED	ACDIOST	DACOITS
ACDERRS	CARDERS	ACDIOSZ	ZODIACS
	SCARRED	ACDIOTY	DACOITY
ACDERST	REDACTS	ACDIPRS	CAPRIDS
	SCARTED	ACDIPSS	CAPSIDS
ACDERSU	CRUSADE	ACDIQRU	QUADRIC
	SCAURED	ACDIRST	DRASTIC
ACDERTT	DETRACT	ACDISST	DICASTS
	TRACTED	ACDITUV	VIADUCT
ACDERTU	TRADUCE	ACDJNTU	ADJUNCT
ACDESTT	SCATTED	ACDKLOP	PADLOCK
ACDFIIY	ACIDIFY	ACDKLSY	SKYCLAD
ACDFIOT	FACTOID	ACDKMOO	MOCKADO
ACDGGIN	CADGING	ACDKMPU	MUDPACK
ACDGINN	DANCING	ACDKOPR	POCKARD
ACDGINO	GONADIC	ACDLLOR	COLLARD
ACDGINR	CARDING	ACDLLUY	DUCALLY
ACDGKLO	DAGLOCK	ACDLNOR	CALDRON
ACDGNOT	CANTDOG	ACDLNOT	COTLAND
ACDGORT	DOGCART	ACDLOWY	LADYCOW
ACDHIIL	CHILIAD	ACDLSTY	DACTYLS
ACDHIOP	PHACOID	ACDMMNO	COMMAND
ACDHIRY	DIARCHY	ACDMORZ	CZARDOM
ACDHLOR	CHORDAL	ACDNOOR	CARDOON
	DORLACH	ACDNORS	CANDORS
ACDHMRS	DRACHMS	ACDNORU	CANDOUR
ACDHNOW	COWHAND		CAUDRON
ACDHOOT	CATHOOD	ACDORST	COSTARD
ACDHOPR	POCHARD	ACDORSU	CRUSADO
ACDHORR	ORCHARD	ACDORSW	COWARDS
ACDHORS	CHADORS	ACDRSTU	CUSTARD
ACDHRUY	DUARCHY	ACDRSUU	CARDUUS
ACDHRYY	DYARCHY	ACEEEPS	ESCAPEE
ACDIIIN	INDICIA	ACEEEUV	EVACUEE
ACDIINN	INDICAN	ACEEFFS	EFFACES
ACDIINO	CONIDIA	ACEEFHN	ENCHAFE
ACDIINR	ACRIDIN	ACEEFIN	FAIENCE
ACDIIRS	CIDARIS		FIANCEE
	SCIARID	ACEEFMN	FACEMEN
ACDIIRT	TRIACID	ACEEFNS	ENFACES
	TRIADIC	ACEEFNY	FAYENCE
ACDIITY	ACIDITY	ACEEFPR	PREFACE
ACDIKLS	SKALDIC	ACEEFRS	REFACES
ACDILLO	CODILLA	ACEEGIL	ELEGIAC
ACDILMO	DOMICAL	ACEEGNR	ENGRACE
ACDILMS	CLADISM	ACEEGNS	ENCAGES
ACDILNO	NODICAL	ACEEGNT	CENTAGE
ACDILNU	DULCIAN	ACEEGSU	ESCUAGE
ACDILOP	PLACOID	ACEEHHT	CHEETAH
	PODALIC	ACEEHIP	CHEAPIE
ACDILOR	CORDIAL	ACEEHIT	HICATEE
ACDILPU	PALUDIC		TEACHIE
ACDILST	CLADIST	ACEEHIV	ACHIEVE
ACDILTW	WILDCAT	ACEEHKS	HACKEES
ACDIMMU	CADMIUM	ACEEHLR	RELACHE
ACDIMNO	MANDIOC	ACEEHLS	LEACHES
	MONACID	ACEEHLT	CHELATE
	MONADIC	ACEEHMP	EMPEACH
	NOMADIC	ACEEHMR	MACHREE
ACDIMNY	DYNAMIC	ACEEHMT	MACHETE
ACDINRU	IRACUND	ACEEHNN	ENHANCE

ACEEHNP	CHEAPEN		CASERNE
ACEEHNS	ACHENES		ENRACES
	ENCHASE	ACEENRT	CRENATE
ACEEHOR	OCHREAE	ACEENSS	ENCASES
ACEEHPP	ECHAPPE		SEANCES
ACEEHPR	CHEAPER	ACEENST	CETANES
	PEACHER		TENACES
ACEEHPS	PEACHES	ACEENSV	ENCAVES
ACEEHRR	REACHER	ACEENTU	CUNEATE
ACEEHRS	REACHES	ACEEORS	ACEROSE
ACEEHRT	CHEATER	ACEEORT	OCREATE
	HECTARE	ACEEOST	ACETOSE
	RECHATE		COATEES
	RECHEAT	ACEEOTV	EVOCATE
	TEACHER	ACEEPRR	CAPERER
ACEEHST	EATCHES	ACEEPRS	ESCAPER
	ESCHEAT		PEARCES
	TEACHES		PERCASE
ACEEHTT	THECATE		PREACES
ACEEHTX	EXCHEAT	ACEEPSS	ESCAPES
ACEEILP	CALIPEE	ACEERRS	CAREERS
ACEEIMT	EMICATE	ACEERRT	CATERER
ACEEINR	CINEREA		RETRACE
ACEEINU	EUCAINE		TERRACE
ACEEIRR	CARIERE	ACEERSS	CREASES
ACEEISV	VESICAE		SEARCES
ACEELLN	NACELLE	ACEERST	CERATES
ACEELMP	EMPLACE		CREATES
ACEELMR	RECLAME		ECARTES
ACEELNR	CLEANER		SECRETA
ACEELNS	CLEANSE	ACEERTX	EXACTER
	ELANCES		EXCRETA
	ENLACES	ACEESSS	ASCESES
	SCALENE	ACEESST	ECTASES
ACEELNT	LATENCE	ACEFFHI	AFFICHE
ACEELNV	ENCLAVE	ACEFFHR	CHAFFER
	VALENCE	ACEFFIS	SCAFFIE
ACEELPR	PERCALE	ACEFFOR	AFFORCE
	REPLACE	ACEFFST	AFFECTS
ACEELPT	CAPELET	ACEFHMR	CHAMFER
ACEELRR	CLEARER	ACEFHRS	CHAFERS
ACEELRS	ALERCES	ACEFHSU	CHAUFES
	CEREALS	ACEFILM	MALEFIC
	RESCALE	ACEFILR	FILACER
ACEELRT	TREACLE	ACEFINN	FINANCE
ACEELRU	CAERULE	ACEFINR	FANCIER
ACEELRV	CLEAVER	ACEFINS	FANCIES
ACEELST	CELESTA		FASCINE
ACEELSU	EUCLASE		FIANCES
ACEELSV	CLEAVES	ACEFIRS	FARCIES
ACEELVX	EXCLAVE		FIACRES
ACEEMNR	MENACER	ACEFITV	FACTIVE
ACEEMNS	CASEMEN	ACEFITY	ACETIFY
	MENACES	ACEFKLR	FLACKER
ACEEMNT	CEMENTA	ACEFKLT	FLACKET
ACEEMNV	CAVEMEN	ACEFLRU	CAREFUL
ACEEMRR	CREAMER	ACEFLSU	FECULAS
ACEEMRS	AMERCES	ACEFNNO	FACONNE
	CAREMES	ACEFNRT	CANTREF
	RACEMES	ACEFNRU	FURNACE
ACEEMRT	CERAMET	ACEFOPR	PROFACE
	CREMATE	ACEFORR	FORECAR
	MEERCAT	ACEFOTU	OUTFACE
ACEEMSS	CAMESES	ACEFRRT	REFRACT
ACEEMSZ	ECZEMAS	ACEFRRU	FARCEUR
ACEENNP	PENANCE	ACEFRSU	SURFACE
ACEENNT	CANTEEN	ACEFRTU	FACTURE
ACEENNY	CAYENNE		FURCATE
ACEENOT	ACETONE	ACEFSTU	FAUCETS
ACEENRS	CAREENS	ACEGHLO	GALOCHE

ACEGHNR	CHANGER	ACEHINN	ENCHAIN		RANCHES	ACEIKSS	SEASICK
ACEGHNS	CHANGES	ACEHINS	INCHASE	ACEHNRT	CHANTER	ACEIKST	CAKIEST
	GANCHES	ACEHINT	CHANTIE		TRANCHE		TACKIES
ACEGHNU	CHAUNGE	ACEHINY	HYACINE	ACEHNST	CHASTEN	ACEIKTT	TIETACK
ACEGHOU	GOUACHE	ACEHIPP	CHAPPIE		NATCHES	ACEILLM	LIMACEL
ACEGHOW	COWHAGE	ACEHIPR	CHARPIE	ACEHNTT	ETCHANT		MICELLA
ACEGHRR	CHARGER	ACEHIPT	APHETIC	ACEHNTU	UNTEACH	ACEILLS	ALLICES
ACEGHRS	CHARGES		HEPATIC	ACEHNTY	CHANTEY	ACEILLX	LEXICAL
	CREAGHS	ACEHIRR	CHARIER	ACEHOPR	POACHER	ACEILMN	MELANIC
ACEGHRU	GAUCHER	ACEHIRS	CAHIERS	ACEHOPS	EPOCHAS	ACEILMR	CALMIER
ACEGILL	ELLAGIC		CASHIER		POACHES		CLAIMER
ACEGILN	ANGELIC		ERIACHS	ACEHORS	CHOREAS		MIRACLE
	ANGLICE	ACEHIRT	THERIAC		ORACHES		RECLAIM
ACEGILP	PELAGIC	ACEHIRV	ARCHIVE		ROACHES	ACEILMS	LIMACES
ACEGILR	GLACIER	ACEHISS	CHAISES	ACEHOSS	CHAOSES		MALICES
	GRACILE	ACEHIST	ACHIEST	ACEHOTY	CHAYOTE	ACEILMT	CLIMATE
ACEGIMR	GRIMACE		AITCHES	ACEHPPS	SCHAPPE		METICAL
ACEGIMT	GAMETIC	ACEHKLR	HACKLER	ACEHPRS	EPARCHS	ACEILMX	EXCLAIM
ACEGINO	COINAGE	ACEHKLS	HACKLES		PARCHES	ACEILMY	MYCELIA
ACEGINP	PEACING		SHACKLE	ACEHPRT	CHAPTER	ACEILNP	CAPELIN
ACEGINR	GRECIAN	ACEHKLT	HACKLET		PATCHER		PANICLE
ACEGINS	CEASING	ACEHKNY	HACKNEY	ACEHPRY	EPARCHY		PELICAN
	INCAGES	ACEHKRS	HACKERS		PREACHY	ACEILNR	CARLINE
ACEGINV	VEGANIC	ACEHKRW	WHACKER	ACEHPSS	CHAPESS	ACEILNS	ANCILES
ACEGINZ	CEAZING	ACEHKRY	HACKERY	ACEHPST	PATCHES		INLACES
ACEGIRU	GAUCIER	ACEHLLP	PELLACH	ACEHQUY	QUEACHY		SANICLE
ACEGIRW	GAWCIER	ACEHLLS	SHELLAC	ACEHRRS	ARCHERS	ACEILNU	CAULINE
ACEGIST	CAGIEST	ACEHLMT	CHAMLET	ACEHRRT	CHARTER	ACEILOR	CALORIE
ACEGKLO	LOCKAGE	ACEHLMY	ALCHEMY		RECHART		CARIOLE
ACEGKLR	GRACKLE	ACEHLNN	CHANNEL	ACEHRRX	XERARCH		COALIER
ACEGKMO	MOCKAGE	ACEHLNO	CHALONE	ACEHRRY	ARCHERY		LORICAE
ACEGKOR	CORKAGE	ACEHLNR	CHARNEL	ACEHRSS	CHASERS	ACEILOS	COALISE
ACEGLLO	COLLAGE		LARCHEN		CRASHES	ACEILOT	ALOETIC
ACEGLNO	CONGEAL	ACEHLNS	LANCHES		ESCHARS	ACEILOZ	COALIZE
ACEGLNR	CLANGER	ACEHLOP	EPOCHAL	ACEHRST	ARCHEST	ACEILPR	CALIPER
ACEGLNS	CANGLES	ACEHLOR	CHOLERA		CHARETS		REPLICA
	GLANCES		CHORALE		CHASTER	ACEILPS	PLAICES
ACEGLOT	CATELOG	ACEHLOS	LOACHES		RATCHES		SPECIAL
ACEGLOU	CAGOULE		OSCHEAL	ACEHRSU	ARCHEUS	ACEILPT	PLICATE
ACEGMOP	COMPAGE	ACEHLPS	CHAPELS	ACEHRSV	VARECHS	ACEILRR	CERRIAL
ACEGNOR	ACROGEN	ACEHLPT	CHAPLET	ACEHRSX	EXARCHS	ACEILRS	CLARIES
	CORNAGE	ACEHLPY	CHEAPLY	ACEHRSY	HYRACES		ECLAIRS
ACEGNOT	COGNATE	ACEHLRS	LARCHES	ACEHRTT	CHATTER		SCALIER
ACEGNSU	CANGUES		RASCHEL		RATCHET	ACEILRT	ARTICLE
	UNCAGES	ACEHLRT	ARCHLET	ACEHRTW	WATCHER		RECITAL
ACEGORS	CARGOES	ACEHLRY	CHARLEY	ACEHRTY	YACHTER	ACEILRU	AURICLE
	CORSAGE	ACEHLSS	CLASHES	ACEHRXY	EXARCHY	ACEILRV	CALIVER
	SOCAGER		SEALCHS	ACEHSSS	CHASSES		CLAVIER
ACEGORU	COURAGE	ACEHLST	CHALETS	ACEHSST	SACHETS		VELARIC
ACEGOSS	SOCAGES		LATCHES		SCATHES	ACEILRY	CLAYIER
ACEGOSW	COWAGES		SATCHEL	ACEHSSW	CASHEWS	ACEILSS	SALICES
ACEGOTT	COTTAGE	ACEHLTT	CHATTEL	ACEHSTW	WATCHES	ACEILST	ASTELIC
ACEGRTU	TRUCAGE		LATCHET	ACEHSTX	HEXACTS		ELASTIC
ACEGSTU	SCUTAGE	ACEHMNP	CHAPMEN	ACEHTTU	TEUCHAT		LACIEST
ACEHHLT	HATCHEL	ACEHMNR	ENCHARM	ACEHTTW	WATCHET		LATICES
ACEHHNS	HANCHES	ACEHMNS	MANCHES	ACEIILM	CIMELIA		SALICET
ACEHHRT	HATCHER	ACEHMNT	MANCHET	ACEIILS	LAICISE	ACEILSV	CLAVIES
ACEHHRU	HACHURE	ACEHMRR	CHARMER	ACEIILT	CILIATE		VESICAL
ACEHHRX	HEXARCH		MARCHER	ACEIILZ	LAICIZE	ACEILSX	CALIXES
ACEHHST	HATCHES	ACEHMRS	MARCHES	ACEIITV	CAITIVE	ACEILTT	LATTICE
ACEHHTT	HATCHET		MESARCH		VICIATE		TACTILE
ACEHIKR	KACHERI	ACEHMRT	MATCHER	ACEIJKS	JACKSIE	ACEIMNO	ENCOMIA
ACEHILL	HELICAL		REMATCH	ACEIKMR	KERAMIC	ACEIMNP	PEMICAN
ACEHILP	APHELIC	ACEHMRU	CHAUMER	ACEIKNT	ANTICKE	ACEIMNR	CARMINE
ACEHILR	CHARLIE	ACEHMSS	SACHEMS	ACEIKOP	PAIOCKE	ACEIMNS	AMNESIC
ACEHILT	ETHICAL	ACEHMST	MATCHES	ACEIKPR	EARPICK		CINEMAS
ACEHIMN	MACHINE	ACEHMTY	ECTHYMA	ACEIKPX	PICKAXE	ACEIMNT	EMICANT
ACEHIMP	IMPEACH	ACEHNNT	ENCHANT	ACEIKRS	EIRACKS		NEMATIC
ACEHIMR	CHIMERA	ACEHNRR	RANCHER	ACEIKRT	TACKIER	ACEIMPR	CAMPIER
ACEHIMS	CHAMISE	ACEHNRS	CHENARS	ACEIKRW	WACKIER	ACEIMPY	PYAEMIC

ACEIMRT	MATRICE	ACEIRRT	CIRRATE	ACEKRSY	SCREAKY	ACELOPS	ESCALOP
ACEIMRU	URAEMIC		ERRATIC		YACKERS	ACELOPT	POLECAT
ACEIMSS	CAMISES	ACEIRRZ	CRAZIER	ACEKRTT	RACKETT	ACELOQU	COEQUAL
ACEIMST	ACMITES	ACEIRST	CRISTAE	ACEKRTY	RACKETY	ACELORS	COALERS
	ETACISM		RACIEST	ACEKSST	CASKETS		ESCOLAR
	MICATES		STEARIC	ACEKSTT	STACKET		ORACLES
	SEMATIC	ACEIRSU	SAUCIER		TACKETS	ACELORY	CALOYER
ACEIMSU	CAESIUM		URICASE	ACEKTTY	TACKETY	ACELOSS	SOLACES
ACEINNP	PINNACE	ACEIRSV	CARVIES	ACELLMO	CALOMEL	ACELOST	ALECOST
ACEINNR	CANNIER		CAVIERS	ACELLNU	NUCLEAL		LACTOSE
ACEINNS	CANINES		VARICES	ACELLNY	CLEANLY		LOCATES
	NANCIES		VISCERA	ACELLOR	CORELLA		SCATOLE
ACEINNT	ANCIENT	ACEIRSZ	CRAZIES		OCELLAR		TALCOSE
ACEINNY	CYANINE	ACEIRTT	CATTIER	ACELLOS	LOCALES	ACELOSV	ALCOVES
ACEINOP	PAEONIC		CITRATE	ACELLOT	COLLATE		COEVALS
ACEINOS	ACINOSE	ACEISSS	ASCESIS	ACELLPS	SCALPEL	ACELOTT	CALOTTE
ACEINOT	ACONITE	ACEISST	ASCITES	ACELLPY	CLYPEAL	ACELOTU	OCULATE
	ANOETIC		ECTASIS	ACELLRR	CARRELL	ACELOTY	ACOLYTE
ACEINPR	CAPRINE	ACEISTT	CATTIES	ACELLRS	CALLERS		COTYLAE
ACEINPS	INSCAPE		TIETACS		CELLARS	ACELOUV	VACUOLE
	PINCASE	ACEITTV	CAVETTI		RECALLS	ACELPPR	CLAPPER
ACEINRR	CARNIER	ACEITTX	EXTATIC		SCLERAL	ACELPPS	SCAPPLE
ACEINRS	ARSENIC	ACEITUX	AUXETIC	ACELLRY	CLEARLY	ACELPRS	CARPELS
	CARNIES	ACEJKMN	JACKMEN	ACELLST	CALLETS		CLASPER
	CERASIN	ACEJKOP	PAJOCKE	ACELMNO	COALMEN		CRAPLES
ACEINRT	CANTIER	ACEJKST	JACKETS	ACELMNS	ENCALMS		PARCELS
	CERTAIN	ACEJLOR	CAJOLER	ACELMOR	CAROMEL		PLACERS
	CRINATE	ACEJLOS	CAJOLES	ACELMOT	CAMELOT		SCALPER
	NACRITE	ACEJNOT	JACONET	ACELMOU	CAULOME	ACELPRT	PLECTRA
ACEINSS	CASEINS	ACEJNOY	JOYANCE		LEUCOMA	ACELPRY	PRELACY
	INCASES	ACEJNSU	JAUNCES	ACELMPR	CLAMPER	ACELPST	PLACETS
ACEINST	CANIEST	ACEJNTU	JUNCATE	ACELMPS	CAMPLES	ACELPSU	CAPSULE
	CINEAST	ACEJPTU	CAJEPUT	ACELMRS	MARCELS		SPECULA
ACEINSU	EUCAINS	ACEJRTT	TRAJECT	ACELMRY	CAMELRY	ACELPTY	ECTYPAL
ACEINSV	INCAVES	ACEKKNR	KNACKER	ACELMSS	MASCLES	ACELQRU	LACQUER
ACEINSY	CYANISE	ACEKLLP	PELLACK		MESCALS	ACELQSU	CALQUES
ACEINTT	NICTATE	ACEKLMS	MACKLES		SCAMELS		CLAQUES
	TETANIC	ACEKLNR	CRANKLE	ACELMST	CALMEST	ACELQUY	LACQUEY
ACEINTV	VENATIC	ACEKLNS	SLACKEN		CAMLETS	ACELRRS	CARRELS
ACEINTX	INEXACT	ACEKLOR	EARLOCK	ACELMSU	MACULES	ACELRRU	RAUCLER
ACEINTY	CYANITE	ACEKLPT	PLACKET	ACELMTU	CALUMET	ACELRRW	CRAWLER
ACEINYZ	CYANIZE	ACEKLQU	QUACKLE	ACELNNS	CANNELS	ACELRSS	SCALERS
ACEIOOZ	ZOOECIA	ACEKLRS	CALKERS	ACELNNU	UNCLEAN		SCLERAS
ACEIOPT	ECTOPIA		LACKERS	ACELNNY	LYNCEAN	ACELRST	CARTELS
ACEIORS	ORACIES		SLACKER	ACELNOR	CORNEAL		CLARETS
	SCORIAE	ACEKLRT	TACKLER	ACELNOT	LACTONE		SCARLET
ACEIORT	EROTICA	ACEKLRU	CAULKER	ACELNOZ	CALZONE		TARCELS
ACEIOST	SOCIATE	ACEKLST	TACKLES	ACELNPS	ENCLASP	ACELRSU	SECULAR
ACEIOTX	EXOTICA	ACEKLSY	LACKEYS		SPANCEL	ACELRSV	CALVERS
ACEIPPR	EPICARP	ACEKMNP	PACKMEN	ACELNPT	CLAPNET		CARVELS
ACEIPPT	TAPPICE	ACEKMRS	SMACKER	ACELNPU	UNPLACE		CLAVERS
ACEIPRR	CRAPIER	ACEKNOS	NOCAKES	ACELNRS	LANCERS	ACELRTT	CLATTER
ACEIPRS	EPACRIS	ACEKNPR	PRANCKE		RANCELS	ACELRTY	TREACLY
	SCRAPIE	ACEKNRR	CRANKER	ACELNRT	CENTRAL	ACELSSS	CLASSES
	SPACIER	ACEKNRS	CANKERS	ACELNRU	LUCARNE		SACLESS
ACEIPRT	PARETIC	ACEKNRY	CANKERY		NUCLEAR	ACELSST	CASTLES
	PICRATE	ACEKNST	NACKETS		UNCLEAR		SCLATES
ACEIPST	ASEPTIC	ACEKORR	CROAKER	ACELNRY	LARCENY	ACELSSU	CLAUSES
	PACIEST	ACEKPPR	PREPACK	ACELNST	CANTLES	ACELSSV	SCLAVES
	SPICATE	ACEKPRS	PACKERS		CENTALS	ACELSTU	CAUTELS
ACEIPSU	AUSPICE		REPACKS		LANCETS		SULCATE
ACEIPSZ	CAPSIZE	ACEKPST	PACKETS		SCANTLE	ACELSTY	ACETYLS
ACEIPTV	CAPTIVE	ACEKRRS	RACKERS	ACELNSU	CENSUAL		SCYTALE
ACEIQRU	ACQUIRE	ACEKRRT	TRACKER		LAUNCES	ACELSUX	EXCUSAL
ACEIQSU	CAIQUES	ACEKRSS	SCREAKS		UNLACES	ACELSXY	CALYXES
ACEIQTU	ACQUITE	ACEKRST	RACKETS		UNSCALE	ACELTUY	ACUTELY
ACEIQUZ	CAZIQUE		STACKER	ACELNTT	CANTLET	ACELTXY	EXACTLY
ACEIRRR	CARRIER		TACKERS	ACELNTY	LATENCY	ACEMMRR	CRAMMER
ACEIRRS	CARRIES	ACEKRSU	CAUKERS	ACELNVY	VALENCY	ACEMNOR	CREMONA
	SCARIER	ACEKRSW	CAWKERS	ACELOPR	POLACRE		ROMANCE

ACEMNOS	ANCOMES
ACEMNPS	ENCAMPS
ACEMNSU	ACUMENS
ACEMOPR	COMPARE
	COMPEAR
ACEMOPS	POMACES
ACEMORS	AMORCES
ACEMORU	MORCEAU
ACEMOSS	COSMEAS
ACEMOST	COMATES
ACEMOSU	MUCOSAE
ACEMPRS	CAMPERS
	SCAMPER
ACEMPRT	CRAMPET
ACEMPST	CAMPEST
ACEMRSS	SCREAMS
ACEMRST	MERCATS
ACEMRSY	CRAMESY
ACEMSSU	CAMUSES
ACEMSTT	METCAST
ACEMSTU	MUCATES
ACENNOS	ANCONES
	SONANCE
ACENNOT	CONNATE
ACENNOY	NOYANCE
ACENNOZ	CANZONE
ACENNRS	CANNERS
	SCANNER
ACENNRY	CANNERY
ACENNST	NASCENT
ACENNSU	NUANCES
ACENNTY	TENANCY
ACENOOR	CORONAE
ACENOPT	PATONCE
ACENOPU	PONCEAU
ACENORS	CARNOSE
	COARSEN
	CORNEAS
	OCTANES
ACENORT	ENACTOR
ACENOSS	CASSONE
ACENOST	COSTEAN
	OCTANES
ACENOTT	ATTONCE
ACENOTV	CENTAVO
ACENPRR	PRANCER
ACENPRS	PRANCES
ACENPRU	PRAUNCE
ACENPST	CATNEPS
ACENPSU	PAUNCES
	UNCAPES
ACENPSW	PAWNCES
ACENPTT	PENTACT
ACENPTY	PATENCY
ACENRSS	ANCRESS
	CASERNS
ACENRST	CANTERS
	CARNETS
	NECTARS
	RECANTS
	SCANTER
	TANRECS
	TRANCES
ACENRSU	SURANCE
ACENRSV	CAVERNS
	CRAVENS
ACENRSY	CARNEYS
	SCENARY
ACENRSZ	ZARNECS
ACENRTT	TRANECT
ACENRTU	CENTAUR
	UNCRATE
	UNTRACE
ACENRTY	ENCRATY
	NECTARY
ACENSST	ASCENTS
	SECANTS
	STANCES
ACENSSU	UNCASES
	USANCES
ACENSTT	CANTEST
ACENSTU	NUTCASE
ACENSUV	VAUNCES
ACEOOPP	APOCOPE
ACEOOTZ	ECTOZOA
ACEOPRX	EXOCARP
ACEOPST	CAPOTES
	SCOPATE
	TOECAPS
ACEOPTU	OUTPACE
ACEORRS	COARSER
ACEORRT	ACROTER
	CREATOR
	REACTOR
ACEORSS	ROSACES
ACEORST	COASTER
	COATERS
ACEORSU	ACEROUS
	CAROUSE
ACEORSX	COAXERS
ACEORTU	OUTRACE
ACEORTV	OVERACT
ACEORTX	EXACTOR
ACEOSSU	CASEOUS
ACEOSTT	COSTATE
ACEOSTU	ACETOUS
ACEOSTV	AVOCETS
	OCTAVES
ACEOTTV	CAVETTO
ACEOTUU	AUTOCUE
ACEOTUX	COTEAUX
ACEPPRS	CAPPERS
ACEPRRS	CARPERS
	SCARPER
	SCRAPER
ACEPRSS	ESCARPS
	PARSECS
	SCRAPES
	SPACERS
ACEPRST	CARPETS
	PRECAST
	SPECTRA
ACEPRSU	APERCUS
	SCAUPER
ACEPRTU	CAPTURE
ACEPSST	ASPECTS
ACEPSTU	CUSPATE
	TEACUPS
ACEQRTU	RACQUET
ACEQSSU	CASQUES
	SACQUES
ACEQSTU	ACQUEST
ACERRSS	CRASSER
	SCARERS
	SCARRES
ACERRST	CARTERS
	CRATERS
	TRACERS
ACERRSU	CURARES
ACERRSV	CARVERS
	CRAVERS
ACERRSY	CRAYERS
ACERRTT	RETRACT
ACERRTY	TRACERY
ACERRUV	VERRUCA
ACERSST	ACTRESS
	CASTERS
	RECASTS
ACERSSU	ARCUSES
	CAUSERS
	CESURAS
	SAUCERS
	SUCRASE
ACERSSV	SCARVES
ACERSSY	SCRAYES
ACERSTT	SCATTER
ACERSTU	ACTURES
	CAUTERS
	CRUSTAE
	CURATES
ACERSTY	SECTARY
ACERTTT	TETRACT
ACERTTU	CURTATE
ACERTTX	EXTRACT
ACERTTY	CATTERY
ACERTUV	CURVATE
ACERTUX	CURTAXE
ACERTUY	CAUTERY
ACESSTT	STACTES
ACESSTU	CAESTUS
	CUESTAS
ACESSTY	CYTASES
	ECSTASY
ACESSUY	CAUSEYS
	CAYUSES
ACESTTU	ACUTEST
	SCUTATE
ACESTTY	TESTACY
ACESTUY	EUSTACY
ACFFHSU	CHAUFFS
ACFFIIT	CAITIFF
ACFFIKM	MAFFICK
ACFFILT	AFFLICT
ACFFIRT	TRAFFIC
ACFFIRY	FARCIFY
ACFFLSS	SCLAFFS
ACFGHIN	CHAFING
ACFGINR	FARCING
ACFGINS	FACINGS
ACFHIST	CATFISH
ACFHISU	FUCHSIA
ACFHLNU	FLAUNCH
ACFHNOU	FAUCHON
ACFHRTY	FRATCHY
ACFIILN	FINICAL
ACFIKNN	FINNACK
ACFILNO	FOLACIN
ACFILRY	CLARIFY
ACFILSS	FISCALS
ACFIMOR	ACIFORM
ACFIMSS	FASCISM
ACFINNS	FINNACS
ACFINNY	INFANCY
ACFINOT	FACTION
ACFINRS	FARCINS
ACFINRT	FRANTIC
	INFARCT
	INFRACT
ACFIOSS	FIASCOS
ACFIPRY	CAPRIFY
ACFIRSY	SACRIFY
	SCARIFY
ACFISST	FASCIST
ACFKLSU	SACKFUL
ACFLLOY	FOCALLY
ACFLNOS	FALCONS
	FLACONS
ACFLNSU	CANFULS
ACFLOST	OLFACTS
ACFLRUU	FURCULA
ACFLTTU	TACTFUL
ACFLTUY	FACULTY
ACFMSTU	FACTUMS
ACFNSTU	UNFACTS
ACFORST	FACTORS
	FORCATS
ACFORTY	FACTORY
ACGGINR	GRACING
ACGGIOS	AGOGICS
ACGGRSY	SCRAGGY
ACGHIKN	HACKING
ACGHIMO	OGHAMIC
ACGHINR	ARCHING
	CHAGRIN
	CHARING
ACGHINS	ACHINGS
	CASHING
	CHASING
ACGHINT	GNATHIC
ACGHINW	CHAWING
	CHINWAG
ACGHIOR	CHORAGI
ACGHIPR	GRAPHIC
ACGHIRS	SCRAIGH
ACGHLTU	CLAUGHT
ACGHOSU	GAUCHOS
ACGHRRU	CURRAGH
ACGHRSU	SCRAUGH
ACGIILN	ALGINIC
ACGIITU	AUGITIC
ACGIJKN	JACKING
ACGIKLN	CALKING
	LACKING
ACGIKNP	PACKING
ACGIKNR	ARCKING
	CARKING
	CRAKING
	RACKING
ACGIKNS	CAKINGS
	CASKING
	SACKING
ACGIKNT	TACKING
ACGIKNV	VACKING
ACGIKNY	YACKING
ACGILLN	CALLING
ACGILLO	LOGICAL
ACGILMN	CALMING
ACGILMY	MYALGIC
ACGILNN	LANCING
ACGILNO	COALING
ACGILNP	PLACING
ACGILNS	LACINGS
	SCALING
ACGILNT	CATLING
ACGILNU	GLUCINA
ACGILNV	CALVING
ACGILNW	CLAWING
ACGILNY	CLAYING
ACGILOS	CALIGOS
ACGILRS	GARLICS
ACGIMMN	CAMMING

ACGIMNO	COAMING	ACHILRY	CHARILY	ACHMSSU	SUMACHS	ACIKNPY	PANICKY
ACGIMNP	CAMPING	ACHILST	CHITALS	ACHMSUW	CUMSHAW	ACIKNRS	NICKARS
ACGIMNU	CAUMING	ACHILSY	CLAYISH	ACHNNOS	CHANSON	ACIKNST	CATKINS
ACGINNN	CANNING	ACHILWY	LICHWAY	ACHNORS	ANCHORS		CATSKIN
ACGINNR	CRANING	ACHIMNO	MANIHOC		ARCHONS	ACIKOPS	PAIOCKS
	RANCING	ACHIMOS	CHAMISO		RANCHOS	ACIKPRT	PATRICK
ACGINNS	CANINGS		CHAMOIS	ACHNORT	CHANTOR	ACIKPSS	ASPICKS
ACGINNT	CANTING	ACHIMRS	CHARISM	ACHNOSS	SANCHOS	ACILLMS	MISCALL
ACGINOR	ORGANIC	ACHIMSS	CHIASMS	ACHNOST	CHATONS	ACILLRY	LYRICAL
ACGINOS	ANGICOS		SCHISMA	ACHNOSY	ONYCHAS	ACILLSS	SCILLAS
ACGINOT	COATING	ACHIMST	MASTICH	ACHNOTY	TACHYON	ACILMNO	LIMACON
	COTINGA		TACHISM	ACHNOUY	CHANOYU	ACILMOT	COMITAL
ACGINOX	COAXING	ACHINNU	UNCHAIN	ACHNOVY	ANCHOVY	ACILMPS	PLASMIC
ACGINPP	CAPPING	ACHINOP	APHONIC	ACHNPSS	SCHNAPS	ACILMSU	MUSICAL
ACGINPR	CARPING	ACHINOY	ONYCHIA	ACHNPUY	PAUNCHY	ACILNNY	CANNILY
	CRAPING	ACHINPS	SPINACH	ACHNRTY	CHANTRY	ACILNOR	CLARINO
ACGINPS	SCAPING	ACHINRS	CHINARS	ACHNRUY	RAUNCHY		CLARION
	SPACING	ACHINRZ	ZARNICH		UNCHARY	ACILNOS	OILCANS
ACGINRS	ARCINGS	ACHINTX	XANTHIC	ACHNSTU	CANTHUS	ACILNOZ	CALZONI
	RACINGS	ACHINUV	CHAUVIN		CHAUNTS	ACILNPS	CAPLINS
	SACRING	ACHIOPT	APHOTIC		STAUNCH		INCLASP
	SCARING	ACHIORT	CHARIOT	ACHNSTY	SNATCHY	ACILNPY	PLIANCY
ACGINRT	CARTING		HARICOT	ACHOOST	CAHOOTS	ACILNST	TINCALS
	CRATING	ACHIPPS	SAPPHIC	ACHOPRT	TOPARCH	ACILNSU	UNCIALS
	TRACING	ACHIPST	HAPTICS	ACHOPRY	CHARPOY	ACILNTU	LUNATIC
ACGINRV	CARVING		PATHICS	ACHOPSY	POCHAYS	ACILNUV	VINCULA
	CRAVING		SPATHIC	ACHORST	ORCHATS	ACILOPT	OPTICAL
ACGINRZ	CRAZING	ACHIPTU	CHUPATI	ACHORSU	AUROCHS		TOPICAL
ACGINSS	CASINGS	ACHIPTW	WHIPCAT	ACHRSST	SCARTHS	ACILORR	RACLOIR
ACGINST	ACTINGS	ACHIQRU	CHARQUI	ACHRSTY	STARCHY	ACILOSS	SOCIALS
	CASTING	ACHIQSU	QUAICHS	ACHRSUU	URACHUS	ACILOST	STOICAL
ACGINSU	CAUSING	ACHIRRT	TRIARCH	ACHSSTU	CUSHATS	ACILOTV	VOLATIC
	SAUCING	ACHIRTU	HAIRCUT	ACHSSUW	CUSHAWS		VOLTAIC
ACGINSV	CAVINGS	ACHIRTY	CHARITY	ACHSTUW	WAUCHTS	ACILOTX	TOXICAL
ACGINSW	CAWINGS	ACHISSS	CHASSIS	ACHSTUY	CYATHUS	ACILPST	PLACITS
ACGINTT	CATTING	ACHISST	SCAITHS	ACIIKNN	CANIKIN		PLASTIC
ACGIRST	GASTRIC	ACHISTT	CATTISH	ACIIKRS	AIRSICK	ACILPSU	SPICULA
ACGKMMO	GAMMOCK		TACHIST	ACIILMM	MIMICAL	ACILPTY	TYPICAL
ACGKORV	GARVOCK	ACHKKSU	CHUKKAS	ACIILNR	CLARINI	ACILRSU	URACILS
ACGLLPU	CUPGALL	ACHKMMO	HAMMOCK	ACIILNS	SALICIN	ACILRTU	CURTAIL
ACGLNOR	CLANGOR	ACHKOPS	HOPSACK		SINICAL		TRUCIAL
ACGLOSU	CAGOULS	ACHKOSS	HASSOCK	ACIILNV	VICINAL	ACILRTY	CLARITY
ACGNNOR	CRANNOG	ACHKOSW	WHACKOS	ACIILOV	VILIACO	ACILRYZ	CRAZILY
ACGNOOT	OCTAGON	ACHKOTT	HATTOCK	ACIILRY	CILIARY	ACILSSS	CLASSIS
ACGNORS	GARCONS	ACHKRSU	CHUKARS	ACIILSS	SILICAS	ACILSSU	CLUSIAS
ACGNOSS	GASCONS	ACHKSTW	THWACKS	ACIILST	ITALICS	ACILSUY	SAUCILY
ACGORRY	GYROCAR	ACHLLOO	ALCOHOL	ACIILTY	LAICITY	ACILTTY	CATTILY
ACGORSU	COUGARS	ACHLLOR	CHLORAL	ACIIMMS	MIASMIC		TACITLY
ACGORUU	COUGUAR	ACHLMSY	CHLAMYS	ACIIMNR	MINICAR	ACILTUV	VICTUAL
ACGSTTU	CATGUTS	ACHLMYY	ALCHYMY	ACIIMOT	COMITIA	ACIMNOP	CAMPION
ACHHIRS	RHACHIS	ACHLNOS	LOCHANS	ACIIMST	ISMATIC	ACIMNOR	MARCONI
ACHHOST	TOSHACH	ACHLNOY	HALCYON		ITACISM	ACIMNOS	CAMIONS
ACHHTTT	THATCHT	ACHLNTU	TULCHAN	ACIINNO	ANIONIC		CONIMAS
ACHIIKM	KAMICHI		UNLATCH	ACIINNS	NIACINS		MANIOCS
ACHIILS	ISCHIAL	ACHLOPR	RAPLOCH	ACIINOS	ASINICO		MASONIC
ACHIIPS	PACHISI	ACHLOPT	POTLACH	ACIINOV	AVIONIC	ACIMNRU	CRANIUM
ACHIJKS	HIJACKS	ACHLORS	CHORALS	ACIINPS	PISCINA		CUMARIN
ACHIJNT	JACINTH		LORCHAS	ACIINTT	TITANIC	ACIMNTT	CATMINT
ACHIKRS	RICKSHA		SCHOLAR	ACIIPPR	PRIAPIC	ACIMOOS	OOMIACS
ACHIKRY	HAYRICK	ACHLORT	TROCHAL	ACIIPRT	PIRATIC	ACIMOPT	POTAMIC
ACHIKSS	SHICKSA	ACHLOSW	SALCHOW	ACIIRST	SATIRIC	ACIMOSS	MOSAICS
ACHILLO	LOCHIAL	ACHLOTY	ACOLYTH	ACIIRTT	TRIATIC	ACIMOST	MATICOS
ACHILLP	PHALLIC	ACHLPST	SPLATCH	ACIJUZZ	JACUZZI		SOMATIC
ACHILLS	CHALLIS	ACHMNOR	MONARCH	ACIKLNS	CALKINS	ACIMOSV	VOMICAS
ACHILLT	THALLIC		NOMARCH	ACIKMNS	SICKMAN	ACIMPRT	CRAMPIT
ACHILMO	MALICHO	ACHMNRU	UNCHARM	ACIKMOO	OOMIACK		PTARMIC
ACHILOS	SCHOLIA	ACHMOPR	CAMPHOR	ACIKMPR	RAMPICK	ACIMPRY	PRIMACY
ACHILPS	CALIPHS	ACHMORS	CHROMAS	ACIKMPW	PICKMAW	ACIMPSS	SCAMPIS
ACHILRS	ARCHILS	ACHMORZ	MACHZOR	ACIKNNP	PANNICK		SPASMIC
	CARLISH	ACHMOST	STOMACH	ACIKNPS	PANICKS	ACIMPST	IMPACTS

ACIMRSS RACISMS	ACIRSTZ CZARIST	CROTALS	ACOOPSU OPACOUS
ACIMRST MATRICS	ACISSTT STATICS	SCROTAL	ACOOPTT TOPCOAT
ACIMRSZ CZARISM	ACISSTU CASUIST	ACLORSU OCULARS	ACOORTU TOURACO
ACIMSST MASTICS	ACISTTU CATSUIT	OSCULAR	ACOOSTV OCTAVOS
MISCAST	ACISTUV VACUIST	ACLORUV VOCULAR	ACOPRRT CARPORT
ACIMSTT TACTISM	ACITUVY VACUITY	ACLOSST COSTALS	ACOPRST CAPTORS
ACINNOT ACTINON	ACJKKSY SKYJACK	ACLOSTU LOCUSTA	ACOPSTU UPCOAST
CANTION	ACJKNNO JANNOCK	TALCOUS	ACOPSTW COWPATS
CONTAIN	ACJKOPS PAJOCKS	ACLOSTW COTWALS	ACORRST CARROTS
ACINNOZ CANZONI	ACJKOPT JACKPOT	ACLPRTY CRYPTAL	TROCARS
ACINNST STANNIC	ACJLORU JOCULAR	ACLPRUU CUPULAR	ACORRTT TRACTOR
ACINNSY CYANINS	ACJMNTU MUNTJAC	ACLRSSW SCRAWLS	ACORRTU CURATOR
ACINNTU ANNICUT	ACJPTUU CAJUPUT	ACLRSSY CRASSLY	ACORRTY CARROTY
ACINOPT CAPTION	ACKLLOP POLLACK	ACLRSTU CRUSTAL	ACORSST CASTORS
PACTION	ACKLLOY LAYLOCK	CURTALS	ACORSSU SARCOUS
ACINORR CARRION	ACKLLSY SLACKLY	ACLRSTY CRYSTAL	ACORSTT COTTARS
ACINORS SARONIC	ACKLMNO LOCKMAN	ACLRSWY SCRAWLY	ACORSTU SURCOAT
ACINORT CAROTIN	ACKLMOR ARMLOCK	ACLSSTU CUTLASS	TURACOS
ACINOSS CAISSON	LOCKRAM	ACMNOPR CRAMPON	ACORSTV CAVORTS
CASINOS	ACKLNOU UNCLOAK	ACMNOPY COMPANY	ACORSTY CASTORY
CASSINO	ACKLORW WARLOCK	ACMNORS MACRONS	ACORSUU RAUCOUS
ACINOST ACTIONS	ACKLORY ROCKLAY	ACMNORY ACRONYM	ACORSYZ CORYZAS
CATIONS	ACKLOSS LASSOCK	ACMNOSS MASCONS	ACOSTTU OUTACTS
·ACINOSU ACINOUS	ACKMMMO MAMMOCK	ACMNSTU SANCTUM	OUTCAST
ACINOTT TACTION	ACKMOTT MATTOCK	ACMOOST SCOTOMA	ACOSUUV VACUOUS
ACINOTU AUCTION	ACKNNOW ACKNOWN	ACMOPRT COMPART	ACPPRSY SCRAPPY
CAUTION	ACKNOSW ACKNOWS	ACMOPSS COMPASS	ACPSSTU CATSUPS
ACINPRT CANTRIP	ACKNPRS PRANCKS	ACMOPST COMPAST	UPCASTS
ACINPRY CYPRIAN	ACKNPSU UNPACKS	ACMORST COMARTS	ACPSTUU USUCAPT
ACINPSS PANISCS	ACKNSTU UNSTACK	ACMOSST MASCOTS	ACRRSTU CRATURS
ACINPST CATNIPS	UNTACKS	ACMOSTU MOTUCAS	ACRSTTU TRACTUS
ACINQTU QUANTIC	ACKOPRR PARROCK	ACMQTUU CUMQUAT	ADDDDEL DADDLED
ACINRSS ARCSINS	ACKOPSY YAPOCKS	ACMRSSW SCRAWMS	ADDDDOR DODDARD
ACINRSU CRUSIAN	ACKORRT TARROCK	ACMSSTU MUSCATS	ADDDEER DREADED
ACINRTT TANTRIC	ACLLLOY LOCALLY	ACMSTUU MUTUCAS	ADDDEFL FADDLED
ACINRTU CURTAIN	ACLLOOR COROLLA	ACMSUUV VACUUMS	ADDDEGL GLADDED
TURACIN	ACLLOPS SCALLOP	ACNNNOS CANNONS	ADDDEIL DAIDLED
ACINSTU ANICUTS	ACLLORS COLLARS	ACNNNUY UNCANNY	ADDDEIS DADDIES
NAUTICS	ACLLORU LOCULAR	ACNNORY CANONRY	ADDDEIW WADDIED
ACINSUV VICUNAS	ACLLOSU CALLOUS	ACNNOST CANTONS	ADDDELN DANDLED
ACIOPRS PROSAIC	ACLLOSW CALLOWS	ACNNOSY CANYONS	ADDDELP PADDLED
ACIOPRT APRICOT	ACLLOVY VOCALLY	SONANCY	ADDDELR RADDLED
PAROTIC	ACLMNOO LOCOMAN	ACNNRSY SCRANNY	ADDDELS DADDLES
PATRICO	ACLMNUY CALUMNY	ACNOOPS POONACS	SADDLED
ACIOPST COPITAS	ACLMORS CLAMORS	ACNOORS CORONAS	ADDDELW DAWDLED
ACIOPTT APTOTIC	ACLMORU CLAMOUR	RACOONS	WADDLED
ACIOPTY OPACITY	ACLMSTU TALCUMS	ACNOORT CARTOON	ADDDENO DEODAND
ACIORRS CORSAIR	ACLMSUU LUCUMAS	CORANTO	ADDDENS ADDENDS
ACIORSU CARIOUS	ACLMSUY MASCULY	ACNOPSW SNOWCAP	ADDDEQU QUADDED
CURIOSA	ACLNOOR CORONAL	ACNORRS RANCORS	ADDDGIN DADDING
ACIORTT RICOTTA	ACLNOOT COOLANT	ACNORRU RANCOUR	ADDDOOS DOODADS
ACIOSST SCOTIAS	ACLNOOV VOLCANO	ACNORST CANTORS	ADDEEEM ADEEMED
ACIOSSV OVISACS	ACLNORU CORNUAL	CARTONS	ADDEEFM DEFAMED
ACIPRSY PISCARY	COURLAN	CONTRAS	ADDEEGR DEGRADE
ACIPRVY PRIVACY	ACLNOUV UNVOCAL	CRATONS	ADDEEHL HEALDED
ACIPSST SPASTIC	ACLNPSU UNCLASP	ACNORSU NACROUS	ADDEEHR ADHERED
ACIPTUY PAUCITY	ACLNRTU TRUNCAL	ACNORSY CRAYONS	ADDEEIR READIED
ACIQRTU QUARTIC	ACLNSTY SCANTLY	ACNORTU COURANT	ADDEEIT IDEATED
ACIQSTU ACQUIST	ACLNSUV VULCANS	ACNOSSZ SCAZONS	ADDEEKN KNEADED
ACQUITS	ACLOPRT CALTROP	ACNOSTT OCTANTS	ADDEEKR DAKERED
ACIRRSS SIRCARS	PROCTAL	ACNOSTU CONATUS	ADDEELN DELENDA
ACIRRST TRICARS	ACLOPRU COPULAR	NOCTUAS	ADDEELP PLEADED
ACIRRSU CURARIS	CUPOLAR	TOUCANS	ADDEELT DELATED
ACIRSST RACISTS	ACLOPSU COPULAS	ACNPRSY SYNCARP	ADDEELY DELAYED
SACRIST	CUPOLAS	ACNRRTU CURRANT	ADDEEMN AMENDED
ACIRSSU CUIRASS	SCOPULA	ACNRSTU UNCARTS	ADDEEMR DREAMED
ACIRSTT ASTRICT	ACLOPSY CALYPSO	ACNRSUY UNSCARY	ADDEEMS ADDEEMS
ACIRSTU URTICAS	ACLOPTY POLYACT	ACNRSWY SCRAWNY	ADDEENS DEADENS
ACIRSTW TWISCAR	ACLORRS CORRALS	ACNRTUY TRUANCY	ADDEENV ADVENED
ACIRSTY SATYRIC	ACLORST CARLOTS	ACOOPRR CORPORA	ADDEENY DENAYED

ADDEEOT	DEODATE	ADDELMW	DWALMED	ADDGINW	DAWDING		ALLEGED
ADDEERR	DREADER	ADDELNR	DANDLER		WADDING	ADEEGLM	GLEAMED
ADDEERS	DEADERS	ADDELNS	DANDLES	ADDGIOS	GADOIDS	ADEEGLN	GLEANED
ADDEERT	DERATED	ADDELNU	UNLADED	ADDGLNO	GLADDON	ADEEGLR	REGALED
ADDEERY	DERAYED	ADDELPP	DAPPLED	ADDGMNO	GODDAMN	ADEEGLT	TEAGLED
	YEARDED	ADDELPR	PADDLER	ADDGOOS	OGDOADS	ADEEGLU	LEAGUED
ADDEEST	DEADEST	ADDELPS	PADDLES	ADDGOOW	DAGWOOD	ADEEGMN	ENDGAME
	SEDATED	ADDELRS	LADDERS	ADDGORW	GODWARD		MANEGED
	STEADED		RADDLES	ADDGOSY	DOGDAYS	ADEEGNR	ANGERED
ADDEEVW	ADVEWED		SADDLER	ADDHINP	DAPHNID		DERANGE
ADDEFIR	FADDIER	ADDELRT	DARTLED	ADDHISS	SADDISH		ENRAGED
ADDEFLS	FADDLES	ADDELRW	DAWDLER		SIDDHAS		GRANDEE
ADDEFLY	FADEDLY		DRAWLED	ADDHITY	HYDATID		GRENADE
ADDEFNU	UNFADED	ADDELRY	DREADLY	ADDHOOS	DOODAHS	ADEEGNT	AGENTED
ADDEFRT	DRAFTED		LADDERY	ADDHSSU	SADDHUS		NEGATED
ADDEFRU	DEFRAUD	ADDELSS	SADDLES	ADDIINS	DISDAIN	ADEEGNV	AVENGED
ADDEFRW	DWARFED	ADDELST	STADDLE	ADDIKST	TSADDIK		VENDAGE
ADDEGGL	DAGGLED	ADDELSW	DAWDLES	ADDIKSZ	ZADDIKS	ADEEGOT	DOGEATE
ADDEGGR	DRAGGED		SWADDLE	ADDIKTY	KATYDID		GOATEED
ADDEGHO	GODHEAD		WADDLES	ADDIKTZ	TZADDIK	ADEEGRR	REGRADE
ADDEGIL	GLADDIE	ADDELTW	TWADDLE	ADDILMN	MIDLAND	ADEEGRS	DRAGEES
ADDEGIN	DEADING	ADDELYZ	DAZEDLY	ADDILNY	DANDILY		GREASED
ADDEGJU	ADJUDGE	ADDELZZ	DAZZLED	ADDILOS	DISLOAD	ADEEGRU	GUARDEE
ADDEGLN	DANGLED	ADDEMMR	DRAMMED	ADDIMNO	DIAMOND	ADEEGRV	GREAVED
	GLADDEN		MADDENS	ADDIMOR	DIADROM	ADEEGRW	RAGWEED
ADDEGLR	GLADDER	ADDEMNU	MAUNDED	ADDIMRS	DIRDAMS		WAGERED
ADDEGRS	GADDERS	ADDEMOP	POMADED	ADDIMSY	DISMAYD	ADEEHIR	HEADIER
ADDEGRU	GUARDED	ADDEMRS	MADDERS		MIDDAYS	ADEEHLR	HEDERAL
ADDEHIS	HADDIES	ADDEMST	MADDEST	ADDINOR	ANDROID	ADEEHLS	LEASHED
ADDEHKS	KEDDAHS	ADDEMUW	DWAUMED	ADDINRY	DIANDRY		SHEALED
ADDEHLN	HANDLED	ADDENOR	ADORNED	ADDIPRS	DISPRAD	ADEEHLX	EXHALED
ADDEHOR	HOARDED	ADDENOT	DONATED	ADDIQST	TSADDIQ	ADEEHMN	HEADMEN
ADDEHRS	SHARDED		NODATED	ADDIRZZ	DIZZARD	ADEEHNN	HENNAED
ADDEIIK	DIDAKEI	ADDENOU	DUODENA	ADDLLRU	DULLARD	ADEEHNS	DASHEEN
ADDEIIS	DAISIED	ADDENPU	PUDENDA	ADDLOOS	SOLDADO	ADEEHNV	HAVENED
ADDEILL	DALLIED	ADDENRS	DANDERS	ADDLTWY	TWADDLY	ADEEHPR	EPHEDRA
	DIALLED	ADDENRT	DRANTED	ADDMNOS	DODMANS	ADEEHRR	ADHERER
ADDEILP	PLAIDED	ADDENRU	DAUNDER		ODDSMAN		REHEARD
ADDEILR	DIEDRAL	ADDENSS	SADDENS	ADDMOOS	ADDOOMS	ADEEHRS	ADHERES
	DRAILED	ADDENSU	ASUDDEN	ADDNNOR	DONNARD		HEADERS
ADDEILS	DAIDLES	ADDENSY	SDAYNED	ADDOORS	DORADOS		HEARSED
	LADDIES	ADDENTU	DAUNTED	ADDOPSY	DASYPOD		SHEARED
ADDEILT	DILATED		UNDATED	ADDORST	DOTARDS	ADEEHRT	EARTHED
ADDEIMR	ADMIRED	ADDEOPT	ADOPTED	ADDQSUY	SQUADDY		HEARTED
	MARDIED	ADDEORS	DEODARS	ADEEEFY	FEDAYEE	ADEEHRV	HAVERED
ADDEIMS	DIADEMS	ADDEPPR	DRAPPED	ADEEEMN	DEMEANE	ADEEHRX	EXHEDRA
ADDEIMX	ADMIXED	ADDEPRS	PADDERS	ADEEERR	ARREEDE	ADEEHST	HEADSET
ADDEINO	ADENOID	ADDEPTU	UPDATED	ADEEERX	EXEDRAE	ADEEHSV	SHEAVED
ADDEINP	PANDIED	ADDERSS	ADDRESS	ADEEESW	SEAWEED	ADEEHSY	HAYSEED
ADDEINR	DANDIER	ADDERST	ADDREST	ADEEFGU	FEAGUED	ADEEIJT	JADEITE
	DRAINED	ADDERSW	SWARDED	ADEEFHS	SHEAFED	ADEEILN	ALIENED
	SDAINED	ADDERSY	DRYADES	ADEEFIR	AREFIED		DELAINE
ADDEINS	DANDIES	ADDERTT	DRATTED		FEDARIE	ADEEILR	LEADIER
ADDEINU	UNAIDED	ADDESST	SADDEST	ADEEFKR	FREAKED	ADEEILS	AEDILES
ADDEINV	INVADED	ADDESTU	ADUSTED	ADEEFLR	FEDERAL		DEISEAL
	VIDENDA		SUDATED	ADEEFLT	DEFLATE	ADEEILY	EYELIAD
ADDEIOR	RADIOED	ADDFHIS	FADDISH	ADEEFMS	DEFAMES	ADEEIMN	DEMAINE
ADDEIOT	TOADIED	ADDFIMS	FADDISM	ADEEFNS	DEAFENS	ADEEIMT	MEDIATE
ADDEIOV	AVOIDED	ADDFINY	DANDIFY	ADEEFPR	PREFADE	ADEEINN	ADENINE
ADDEIPS	PADDIES	ADDFIST	FADDIST	ADEEFRT	DRAFTEE	ADEEINS	ANISEED
ADDEIRR	ARRIDED	ADDGGIN	GADDING	ADEEFRW	WAFERED	ADEEIRR	READIER
ADDEIRT	TARDIED	ADDGHIN	HADDING	ADEEFST	DEAFEST	ADEEIRS	DEARIES
ADDEISV	ADVISED	ADDGIIR	DIAGRID		DEFASTE		READIES
ADDEISW	WADDIES	ADDGILN	ADDLING		DEFEATS	ADEEIRW	WEARIED
ADDEITU	AUDITED	ADDGIMN	MADDING		FEASTED	ADEEISS	DISEASE
ADDEJLY	JADEDLY	ADDGINO	DADOING	ADEEGGH	EGGHEAD		SEASIDE
ADDEJNU	UNJADED	ADDGINP	PADDING	ADEEGGL	ALEGGED	ADEEIST	IDEATES
ADDEJRU	ADJURED	ADDGINU	DAUDING	ADEEGGN	ENGAGED	ADEEITV	DEVIATE
ADDEKLR	DARKLED			ADEEGLL	ALLEDGE	ADEEJSY	DEEJAYS
ADDELLU	ALLUDED					ADEEKNR	KNEADER

	NAKEDER	ADEENNS	ENNEADS	ADEFFNY	NYAFFED	ADEGGNS	SNAGGED
ADEEKNS	SNEAKED	ADEENNX	ANNEXED	ADEFFQU	QUAFFED	ADEGGRS	DAGGERS
ADEEKNW	WAKENED	ADEENPS	SNEAPED	ADEFFST	STAFFED	ADEGGRY	RAGGEDY
ADEEKRS	SKEARED		SPEANED	ADEFFUW	WAUFFED	ADEGGST	GADGETS
ADEEKRW	WREAKED	ADEENRS	DEANERS	ADEFGGL	FLAGGED		STAGGED
ADEEKTW	TWEAKED		ENDEARS	ADEFGLN	FANGLED	ADEGGSW	SWAGGED
ADEEKWY	WEEKDAY	ADEENRU	UNEARED		FLANGED	ADEGHIN	HEADING
ADEELLS	ALLSEED	ADEENRV	RAVENED	ADEFGOR	FORAGED	ADEGHIR	HEADRIG
ADEELLY	ALLEYED	ADEENRY	DEANERY	ADEFGOT	FAGOTED	ADEGHIS	HIDAGES
ADEELMP	EMPALED		RENAYED	ADEFGOU	FOUGADE	ADEGHLU	LAUGHED
ADEELMR	EMERALD		YEARNED	ADEFGRT	GRAFTED	ADEGHMO	HOMAGED
ADEELMS	MEASLED	ADEENST	STEANED	ADEFHIT	FAITHED	ADEGHNP	PHANGED
ADEELMT	MEDALET	ADEENSV	ADVENES	ADEFHLS	FLASHED	ADEGHNS	GNASHED
ADEELMU	AEMULED	ADEENTT	DENTATE	ADEFHRW	WHARFED		HAGDENS
ADEELMY	YEALMED	ADEEORS	OREADES	ADEFHST	SHAFTED	ADEGHNW	WHANGED
ADEELNP	DEPLANE	ADEEORW	OARWEED	ADEFILL	FLAILED	ADEGHPR	GRAPHED
ADEELNR	LEARNED	ADEEPPR	PAPERED	ADEFILS	DISLEAF	ADEGHST	GHASTED
ADEELNS	LEADENS	ADEEPRS	PREASED	ADEFIMN	INFAMED	ADEGHUW	WAUGHED
ADEELNT	EDENTAL		SPEARED	ADEFIMS	DISFAME	ADEGILL	GALLIED
	LATENED	ADEEPRT	ADEPTER	ADEFINR	FRIANDE	ADEGILN	ALIGNED
ADEELPR	PEARLED		PREDATE	ADEFINT	DEFIANT		DEALING
	PLEADER		TAPERED		FAINTED		LEADING
ADEELPS	DELAPSE	ADEEPRV	DEPRAVE	ADEFIRS	FRAISED	ADEGILO	GEOIDAL
	ELAPSED		PERVADE	ADEFIST	DAFTIES	ADEGILR	GLADIER
	PLEASED	ADEEPSS	PESADES		FADIEST		GLAIRED
ADEELPT	PLEATED	ADEEQRU	QUAERED		FIXATED	ADEGILS	SILAGED
ADEELRS	ARLESED	ADEEQTU	EQUATED	ADEFITX	FIXATED	ADEGILT	LIGATED
	DEALERS	ADEERRR	DREARER	ADEFKLN	FANKLED		TAIGLED
	LEADERS	ADEERRS	DREARES		FLANKED	ADEGILV	GLAIVED
	REDEALS		READERS	ADEFKNR	FRANKED	ADEGINR	AREDING
ADEELRT	ALERTED		REDSEAR	ADEFLLN	ELFLAND		DEARING
	ALTERED		REREADS	ADEFLMM	FLAMMED		DERAIGN
	REDEALT	ADEERRT	RETREAD	ADEFLNN	FENLAND		EARDING
	RELATED		TREADER	ADEFLOT	FLOATED		GRADINE
	TREADLE	ADEERRV	AVERRED	ADEFLPP	FLAPPED		GRAINED
ADEELRW	LEEWARD	ADEERSS	RESEDAS	ADEFLRS	FARDELS		READING
ADEELRX	RELAXED	ADEERST	DEAREST	ADEFLRU	DAREFUL	ADEGINS	AGNISED
ADEELRY	DELAYER		DERATES	ADEFLTT	FLATTED	ADEGINV	DEAVING
	LAYERED		ESTRADE	ADEFLTU	DEFAULT		EVADING
	RELAYED		REASTED		FAULTED	ADEGINW	WINDAGE
ADEELST	DELATES		SEDATER	ADEFMNU	UNFAMED	ADEGINY	YEADING
	STEALED		STEARED	ADEFNRS	FARDENS	ADEGINZ	AGNIZED
ADEELSV	SLEAVED	ADEERSV	ADVERSE	ADEFNSU	UNDEAFS	ADEGIOT	GODETIA
ADEELSW	SWEALED	ADEERSW	DRAWEES	ADEFNUZ	UNFAZED	ADEGIRS	AGRISED
ADEELTV	VALETED	ADEERTT	ARETTED	ADEFOOS	SEAFOOD	ADEGIRU	GAUDIER
	VELATED		TREATED	ADEFORS	FEDORAS	ADEGIRZ	AGRIZED
ADEELTX	EXALTED	ADEERTV	AVERTED	ADEFORV	FAVORED	ADEGIST	AGISTED
ADEELTZ	TEAZLED		TREATED	ADEFORY	FEODARY	ADEGISU	AGUISED
ADEELUV	DEVALUE	ADEERTW	DEWATER		FORAYED		GAUDIES
ADEEMNR	AMENDER		TARWEED	ADEFPPR	FRAPPED	ADEGISV	VISAGED
	ENARMED		WATERED	ADEFPRR	PREFARD	ADEGIUV	VIDUAGE
	MEANDER	ADEERVW	WAVERED	ADEFRRT	DRAFTER	ADEGIUZ	AGUIZED
	REAMEND	ADEESST	SEDATES		REDRAFT	ADEGJLN	JANGLED
	RENAMED	ADEESSY	ESSAYED	ADEFRST	STRAFED	ADEGLLU	ULLAGED
ADEEMNS	AMENDES	ADEESTT	ESTATED	ADEFRSU	FADEURS	ADEGLMN	MANGLED
	DEMEANS	ADEESTU	SAUTEED	ADEFRSW	SWARFED	ADEGLMU	GLAUMED
ADEEMNT	ENTAMED	ADEESTW	SWEATED	ADEFRSY	DEFRAYS	ADEGLNN	ENDLANG
ADEEMNY	DEMAYNE	ADEESTY	YEASTED	ADEFRUY	FEUDARY	ADEGLNR	DANGLER
ADEEMOS	OEDEMAS	ADEESVY	SAVEYED	ADEFSTT	DAFTEST		GNARLED
ADEEMPR	EMPARED	ADEETUX	EXUDATE	ADEGGGL	GAGGLED	ADEGLNS	GLANDES
ADEEMRR	DREAMER	ADEFFFL	FLAFFED	ADEGGHL	HAGGLED		SLANGED
	REARMED	ADEFFGR	GRAFFED	ADEGGHS	SHAGGED	ADEGLNT	TANGLED
ADEEMRS	REMADES	ADEFFIN	AFFINED	ADEGGIS	GADGIES	ADEGLNU	LANGUED
	REMEADS	ADEFFIP	PIAFFED	ADEGGIU	GAUDGIE	ADEGLNW	WANGLED
	SMEARED	ADEFFIR	DAFFIER		GUIDAGE	ADEGLOP	GALOPED
ADEEMST	STEAMED	ADEFFIS	DAFFIES	ADEGGLR	DRAGGLE	ADEGLOT	GLOATED
ADEEMSU	MEDUSAE	ADEFFIX	AFFIXED		GARGLED	ADEGLPU	PLAGUED
ADEEMSW	MAWSEED	ADEFFLM	MAFFLED		RAGGLED	ADEGLRS	DARGLES
ADEEMTW	MATWEED	ADEFFLR	RAFFLED	ADEGGLS	DAGGLES	ADEGLRU	RAGULED
ADEEMWY	MAYWEED	ADEFFLW	WAFFLED	ADEGGLW	WAGGLED		

ADEGLRY	GRADELY	ADEHKNT	THANKED	ADEIJMR	JEMIDAR	ADEIMOW	MIAOWED
ADEGLSS	GLASSED	ADEHKOR	HARDOKE	ADEIKLS	SKAILED	ADEIMPR	DAMPIER
ADEGMNS	GADSMEN	ADEHKOT	KATHODE	ADEIKNS	KANDIES	ADEIMPV	IMPAVED
ADEGMNU	GUDEMAN	ADEHKRS	SHARKED	ADEIKRS	DAIKERS	ADEIMRR	ADMIRER
ADEGNNO	NONAGED	ADEHLLO	HALLOED		DARKIES		MARDIER
ADEGNNU	DUNNAGE	ADEHLNR	HANDLER	ADEIKRT	TRAIKED		MARRIED
ADEGNOP	PONDAGE	ADEHLNS	HANDLES	ADEILLR	DALLIER	ADEIMRS	ADMIRES
ADEGNOR	GROANED		HANDSEL		DIALLER		MARDIES
ADEGNOS	SONDAGE	ADEHLOS	SHOALED		RALLIED		MISREAD
ADEGNOT	TANGOED	ADEHLOT	LOATHED	ADEILLS	DALLIES		SIDEARM
ADEGNOV	DOGVANE	ADEHLPS	PLASHED		DISLEAL	ADEIMRT	READMIT
ADEGNOW	GOWANED	ADEHLRS	HARELDS		LALDIES	ADEIMST	MISDATE
	WAGONED		HERALDS		SALLIED	ADEIMSV	VIDAMES
ADEGNPR	PRANGED	ADEHLSS	HASSLED	ADEILLT	TALLIED	ADEIMSX	ADMIXES
ADEGNPS	SPANGED		SLASHED	ADEILLV	VIALLED	ADEIMTU	TAEDIUM
ADEGNPU	UNPAGED	ADEHLSW	SHAWLED	ADEILLY	IDEALLY	ADEIMTY	DAYTIME
ADEGNRR	GNARRED	ADEHLTY	DEATHLY	ADEILMM	DILEMMA	ADEINNN	NANDINE
	GRANDER	ADEHMMS	SHAMMED	ADEILMP	IMPALED		NANNIED
ADEGNRS	DANGERS	ADEHMMW	WHAMMED		IMPLEAD	ADEINOR	ANEROID
	GANDERS	ADEHMNR	HERDMAN	ADEILMS	MEDIALS	ADEINOS	ADONISE
	GARDENS	ADEHMOR	HADROME		MISDEAL		ANODISE
ADEGNRT	GRANTED	ADEHMRS	DERHAMS		MISLEAD		SODAINE
ADEGNRU	ENGUARD	ADEHMSS	SMASHED	ADEILMU	MIAULED	ADEINOV	NAEVOID
	RAUNGED	ADEHNPS	DAPHNES	ADEILNN	ANNELID	ADEINOX	DIOXANE
ADEGNST	STANGED	ADEHNRS	HANDERS		LINDANE	ADEINOZ	ADONIZE
ADEGNTU	GAUNTED		HARDENS	ADEILNP	PLAINED		ANODIZE
ADEGNTW	TWANGED	ADEHNRU	UNHEARD	ADEILNS	DENIALS	ADEINPR	PARDINE
ADEGNUW	UNWAGED	ADEHNSS	SNASHED		SNAILED	ADEINPS	PANDIES
ADEGNUZ	UNGAZED	ADEHNST	HANDSET	ADEILNU	ALIUNDE		PANSIED
ADEGORW	DOWAGER	ADEHNSU	UNHEADS		UNIDEAL		SPAINED
	WORDAGE	ADEHNTU	HAUNTED	ADEILNV	ANDVILE	ADEINPT	DEPAINT
ADEGOSS	DOSAGES	ADEHOOP	APEHOOD	ADEILOR	DARIOLE		PAINTED
ADEGOST	DOGATES	ADEHOPX	HEXAPOD	ADEILOS	DEASOIL		PATINED
	DOTAGES	ADEHORR	HOARDER	ADEILOU	DOULEIA	ADEINRR	DRAINER
ADEGOTT	TOGATED	ADEHOST	HOASTED	ADEILPP	APPLIED		RANDIER
ADEGOVY	VOYAGED	ADEHOSX	OXHEADS	ADEILPR	PEDRAIL	ADEINRS	RANDIES
ADEGPRS	GRASPED	ADEHPPW	WHAPPED		PREDIAL		SANDIER
	SPADGER	ADEHPRS	PHRASED	ADEILPS	ALIPEDS		SARDINE
	SPARGED		SHARPED		PAIDLES	ADEINRT	DETRAIN
ADEGPRU	UPGRADE	ADEHPST	HEPTADS		PALSIED		TRAINED
ADEGPUZ	UPGAZED		SPATHED	ADEILPT	PLAITED	ADEINRU	UNAIRED
ADEGRRS	GRADERS	ADEHPSW	PSHAWED		TALIPED		URANIDE
	REGARDS	ADEHQSU	QUASHED	ADEILQU	QUAILED	ADEINRV	INVADER
ADEGRSS	GRASSED	ADEHRRU	HURRAED	ADEILRR	LARDIER		RAVINED
ADEGRSU	SUGARED	ADEHRSS	DASHERS	ADEILRS	DERAILS	ADEINSS	SDAINES
ADEGRTY	GYRATED	ADEHRST	DEARTHS		SIDERAL	ADEINST	DETAINS
	TRAGEDY		HARDEST	ADEILRT	DILATER		INSTEAD
ADEGRUU	AUGURED		HATREDS		TRAILED		SAINTED
ADEGRUY	GAUDERY		THREADS	ADEILRV	VALIDER		SATINED
ADEGRYZ	AGRYZED		TRASHED	ADEILRY	READILY		STAINED
ADEGSSU	DEGAUSS	ADEHRTW	WRATHED	ADEILSS	AIDLESS	ADEINSV	INVADES
ADEHHOT	HOTHEAD	ADEHRTY	HYDRATE		DEASILS	ADEINSW	DEWANIS
ADEHIKS	DASHEKI		THREADY	ADEILST	DETAILS	ADEINTT	TAINTED
ADEHIKV	KHEDIVA	ADEHSST	STASHED		DILATES	ADEINTU	AUDIENT
ADEHILN	INHALED	ADEHSSW	SWASHED	ADEILSU	AUDILES	ADEINTV	DEVIANT
ADEHILP	HELIPAD	ADEHSTW	SWATHED		DEASIUL	ADEINVV	NAVVIED
ADEHILS	HALIDES	ADEHSYY	HEYDAYS	ADEILSV	DEVISAL	ADEIOPS	ADIPOSE
ADEHILY	HEADILY	ADEHUZZ	HUZZAED	ADEILSY	DIALYSE	ADEIOPT	OPIATED
ADEHINP	PINHEAD	ADEIILR	DELIRIA		EYLIADS	ADEIORS	ROADIES
ADEHINR	HANDIER		IRIDEAL	ADEILYZ	DIALYZE		SOREDIA
ADEHIPP	HAPPIED	ADEIILS	DAILIES	ADEIMMR	MERMAID	ADEIORX	EXORDIA
ADEHIPR	RAPHIDE		LIAISED	ADEIMMS	MISMADE	ADEIOST	IODATES
ADEHIPS	APHIDES		SEDILIA	ADEIMNR	ADERMIN		TOADIES
ADEHIPT	PITHEAD	ADEIINR	DENARII		INARMED	ADEIOSX	OXIDASE
ADEHIRR	HARDIER	ADEIIPR	PERIDIA	ADEIMNS	DEMAINS	ADEIOSZ	DIAZOES
	HARRIED	ADEIIRS	DAIRIES		MAIDENS	ADEIOTX	OXIDATE
ADEHIRS	SHADIER		DIARIES		MEDIANS	ADEIOVV	VAIVODE
ADEHIRW	RAWHIDE		DIARISE		MEDINAS	ADEIOVW	WAIVODE
ADEHIRY	HYDRIAE	ADEIIRZ	DIARIZE	ADEIMNT	MEDIANT	ADEIOWW	WAIWODE
ADEHKNS	SHANKED	ADEIISS	DAISIES	ADEIMNU	UNAIMED	ADEIPPR	DRAPPIE

```
        PREPAID
ADEIPPU APPUIED
ADEIPRR DRAPIER
        PARRIED
        RAPIDER
ADEIPRS ASPIRED
        DESPAIR
        DIAPERS
        PRAISED
ADEIPRT PARTIED
        PIRATED
ADEIPRV VAPIDER
ADEIPSS APSIDES
ADEIRRS ARRIDES
        RAIDERS
ADEIRRT TARDIER
        TARRIED
ADEIRRV ARRIVED
ADEIRST ARIDEST
        ASTERID
        ASTRIDE
        DIASTER
        DISRATE
        STAIDER
        STAIRED
        TARDIES
        TIRADES
ADEIRSU RESIDUA
ADEIRSV ADVISER
        VARDIES
ADEIRTT ATTIRED
ADEIRTV TARDIVE
ADEIRTY DIETARY
ADEISSS DASSIES
ADEISST DISSEAT
        SAIDEST
ADEISSV ADVISES
ADEISSZ ASSIZED
ADEISTU DAUTIES
ADEISTV AVIDEST
        DATIVES
        VISTAED
ADEISTW DAWTIES
        WAISTED
ADEISVV SAVVIED
ADEISWY SIDEWAY
        WAYSIDE
ADEJMOR MAJORED
ADEJMRU MUDEJAR
ADEJNSU JAUNSED
ADEJNTU JAUNTED
ADEJOPR JEOPARD
ADEJRSU ADJURES
ADEJSSU JUDASES
ADEKLNP PLANKED
ADEKLNR RANKLED
ADEKLNS KALENDS
ADEKLNY NAKEDLY
ADEKLRS DARKLES
ADEKLST SKLATED
        STALKED
ADEKLSY YSLAKED
ADEKLUW WAULKED
ADEKMRS DEMARKS
ADEKNPP KNAPPED
ADEKNPR PRANKED
ADEKNPS SPANKED
ADEKNRR KNARRED
ADEKNRS DARKENS
ADEKNRU UNRAKED

ADEKNST DANKEST
ADEKNSU UNASKED
ADEKNSW SWANKED
ADEKNUW UNWAKED
ADEKNVY VANDYKE
ADEKPRS SPARKED
ADEKRST DARKEST
        STARKED
ADEKRSY DARKEYS
ADELLMS SMALLED
ADELLMU MEDULLA
ADELLNR LANDLER
ADELLNW ELLWAND
ADELLOR ODALLER
ADELLOW ALLOWED
ADELLOY ALLOYED
ADELLPS SPALLED
ADELLRU ALLURED
        UDALLER
ADELLST STALLED
ADELLSU ALLUDES
        ALUDELS
ADELLSV DEVALLS
ADELMMS SLAMMED
        SMALLED
ADELMNN LANDMEN
ADELMNR MANDREL
ADELMNT MANTLED
ADELMOR EARLDOM
ADELMOS DAMOSEL
ADELMOZ DAMOZEL
ADELMPS SAMPLED
ADELMRS MEDLARS
ADELMSS DAMSELS
ADELNNP PLANNED
ADELNNU UNLADEN
ADELNOR LADRONE
ADELNOS LOADENS
ADELNOT TALONED
ADELNOY YEALDON
ADELNPT PLANTED
ADELNRS DARNELS
        ENLARDS
        LANDERS
        SLANDER
        SNARLED
ADELNRU LAUNDER
        LURDANE
        RUNDALE
ADELNRY DEARNLY
ADELNSS SENDALS
ADELNST DENTALS
        SLANTED
ADELNSU UNLADES
        UNLEADS
ADELNTU LUNATED
        UNDEALT
ADELNTW WETLAND
ADELNUW UNLAWED
ADELOPR LEOPARD
        PAROLED
ADELOPS DEPOSAL
        PEDALOS
ADELOPT PLOATED
        TADPOLE
ADELORS LOADERS
        ORDEALS
        RELOADS
ADELORT DELATOR
        LEOTARD

ADELORU ROULADE
ADELOSS ALDOSES
        LASSOED
ADELOST SALTOED
ADELPPP PLAPPED
ADELPPS DAPPLES
        SLAPPED
ADELPRS PEDLARS
ADELPRY PEDLARY
ADELPST SPALTED
        STAPLED
ADELPSU UPLEADS
ADELPSW DEWLAPS
        SPAWLED
ADELPSY SPLAYED
ADELPTT PLATTED
ADELPTW DEWLAPT
ADELRRS LARDERS
ADELRRU RUDERAL
ADELRRW DRAWLER
ADELRSS SARDELS
ADELRST DARTLES
ADELRSU LAUDERS
ADELRSW WARSLED
ADELRSZ DRAZELS
ADELRTT RATTLED
ADELRTW TRAWLED
ADELRTX DEXTRAL
ADELRTY LYRATED
ADELRWW WRAWLED
ADELRWX WRAXLED
ADELRZZ DAZZLER
ADELSST DESALTS
ADELSTT SLATTED
ADELSTU AULDEST
        SALUTED
ADELSUV AVULSED
ADELSWY SWAYLED
ADELSZZ DAZZLES
ADELTTT TATTLED
ADELTTW WATTLED
ADELTUV VAULTED
ADELTUX LUXATED
ADELTWZ WALTZED
ADEMMRS DAMMERS
        SMARMED
ADEMNNS SANDMEN
ADEMNNU MUNDANE
        UNNAMED
ADEMNOR ROADMEN
ADEMNOS DAEMONS
        MASONED
        MODENAS
        MONADES
        NOMADES
ADEMNOW WOMANED
ADEMNPS DAMPENS
ADEMNRS MANREDS
        RANDEMS
        REMANDS
ADEMNRU DURAMEN
        MANURED
        MAUNDER
        UNARMED
ADEMNRY DRAYMEN
        YARDMEN
ADEMNSS DESMANS
        MADNESS
ADEMNST TANDEMS
ADEMNSU MEDUSAN

        SUDAMEN
ADEMNSY DAYSMEN
ADEMNTU UNMATED
        UNTAMED
ADEMOOV AMOOVED
ADEMOPS APEDOMS
        POMADES
ADEMORS RADOMES
ADEMOSV VAMOSED
ADEMOSW MEADOWS
ADEMOSY SOMEDAY
ADEMOWY MEADOWY
ADEMPRS DAMPERS
ADEMPRT TRAMPED
ADEMPSS SPASMED
ADEMPST DAMPEST
        STAMPED
ADEMPSW SWAMPED
ADEMRRU EARDRUM
ADEMRST SMARTED
ADEMRSU REMUDAS
ADEMRSW SWARMED
ADEMRTU MATURED
ADEMSSU ASSUMED
        MEDUSAS
ADEMTTU MUTATED
ADENNOY ANNOYED
        ANODYNE
ADENNPS SPANNED
ADENNPT PENDANT
ADENNST STANDEN
ADENNSU DUENNAS
ADENNWY DEWANNY
ADENOOP NAPOOED
ADENOOZ ENDOZOA
ADENOPR APRONED
        OPERAND
        PADRONE
        PANDORE
ADENOPS DAPSONE
ADENORT TORNADE
ADENORU RONDEAU
ADENOST ASTONED
        DONATES
        ONSTEAD
ADENOSU DOUANES
ADENOSY NOYADES
ADENOTT NOTATED
ADENOTZ ZONATED
ADENPPR PARPEND
ADENPPS APPENDS
        SNAPPED
ADENPPW WAPPEND
ADENPRR PARDNER
ADENPRS PANDERS
ADENPRU UNPARED
ADENPRW PRAWNED
ADENPST PEDANTS
        PENTADS
ADENPSW SPAWNED
ADENPSX EXPANDS
ADENPSY DYSPNEA
ADENPUV UNPAVED
ADENQTU QUANTED
ADENRRS DARNERS
        ERRANDS
        SNARRED
ADENRRW REDRAWN
ADENRRY REYNARD
ADENRSS SANDERS
```

	SARSDEN	ADEPPSW SWAPPED	ADFLMOO DAMFOOL	ADGINOT DOATING
ADENRST	ENDARTS	ADEPPTU PUPATED	ADFLNOP PLAFOND	ADGINPP DAPPING
	STANDER	ADEPPUY APPUYED	ADFLORU FOULARD	ADGINPR DRAPING
	STARNED	ADEPRRS DRAPERS	ADFMNOS FANDOMS	ADGINPS SPADING
ADENRSU	ASUNDER	SPARRED	ADFMOSU FUMADOS	ADGINRR DARRING
	DANSEUR	ADEPRRY DRAPERY	ADFNNOT FONDANT	ADGINRS DARINGS
	DAUNERS	ADEPRSS ADPRESS	ADFNOST FANTODS	GRADINS
ADENRSW	DAWNERS	SPADERS	ADFOOPT FOOTPAD	ADGINRT DARTING
	WANDERS	SPREADS	ADFORRW FORWARD	TRADING
	WARDENS	ADEPRST DEPARTS	FROWARD	ADGINRU DAURING
ADENRSZ	ZANDERS	DRAPETS	ADGGGIN DAGGING	ADGINRW DRAWING
ADENRTT	TRANTED	PETARDS	ADGGHNO HANGDOG	WARDING
ADENRTU	DAUNTER	ADEPRSY SPRAYED	ADGGILN GADLING	ADGINRY YARDING
	NATURED	ADEPRTT PRATTED	ADGGILR RIGGALD	ADGINST DATINGS
	UNRATED	ADEPRTU UPRATED	ADGGINN DANGING	ADGINSW WADINGS
	UNTREAD	ADEPSTT SPATTED	ADGGINO GOADING	ADGINTU DAUTING
ADENRTV	VERDANT	ADEPSTU UPDATES	ADGGINR GRADING	ADGINTW DAWTING
ADENRTX	DEXTRAN	ADEQRSU SQUARED	NIGGARD	ADGINWY GWYNIAD
ADENRTY	DENTARY	ADERRST DARTERS	ADGGINU GAUDING	ADGIPRU PAGURID
	TRAYNED	DARTRES	ADGHILO HIDALGO	ADGIRSU GUISARD
	TYRANED	RETARDS	ADGHINN HANDING	ADGIRZZ GIZZARD
ADENRUY	UNREADY	STARRED	ADGHINS DASHING	ADGLLNO GOLLAND
ADENSSS	SADNESS	TRADERS	SHADING	ADGLMNO MANGOLD
ADENSSU	SUNDAES	ADERRSW DRAWERS	ADGHINU HAUDING	ADGLNOO GONDOLA
ADENSSW	WESANDS	REDRAWS	ADGHIPR DIGRAPH	ADGLNOR GOLDARN
ADENSTT	ATTENDS	REWARDS	ADGHIRR ARDRIGH	ADGLNOW GOWLAND
ADENSTU	SAUNTED	WARDERS	ADGHNOS HAGDONS	ADGLNOY DAYLONG
	UNSATED	ADERSSU ASSURED	ADGHNOW HAGDOWN	ADGLNRY GRANDLY
ADENSTV	ADVENTS	RUDASES	ADGHORW HOGWARD	ADGLOPS LAPDOGS
ADENSTY	STAYNED	ADERSSW SAWDERS	ADGHRTU DRAUGHT	ADGMNOO GOODMAN
ADENSUV	UNSAVED	SWEARDS	ADGIILN GLIADIN	ADGMNOR GORMAND
ADENSWY	ENDWAYS	ADERSTT STARTED	LAIDING	ADGNOOR DRAGOON
ADENSWZ	WEZANDS	TETRADS	ADGIILT DIGITAL	GADROON
ADENTTU	ATTUNED	ADERSTV ADVERTS	ADGIIMN MAIDING	ADGNORS DRAGONS
	NUTATED	STARVED	ADGIINN DAINING	ADGNORU AGROUND
	TAUNTED	ADERSTW STEWARD	ADGIINO GONIDIA	ADGNRRU GURNARD
ADENTUV	VAUNTED	STRAWED	ADGIINR GRADINI	ADGNRSU DURGANS
ADENTUX	UNTAXED	WRASTED	RAIDING	ADGNRUU UNGUARD
ADENUWY	UNWAYED	ADERSTY STRAYED	ADGIINU IGUANID	ADGORSW WARDOGS
ADEOORT	ODORATE	ADERSUY DASYURE	ADGIINW GWINIAD	ADGPRSU UPDRAGS
ADEOPPS	APPOSED	ADERSVW DWARVES	ADGIIPY PYGIDIA	ADHHIRS HARDISH
	PEAPODS	SWARVED	ADGILLN LADLING	ADHHIST HADITHS
ADEOPQU	OPAQUED	ADERWWY WEYWARD	ADGILMN MADLING	ADHHISW WHIDAHS
ADEOPRR	EARDROP	ADESSTU SUDATES	ADGILNN LANDING	ADHHOSU HOUDAHS
ADEOPRT	ADOPTER	ADESSTW WADSETS	ADGILNO DIGONAL	ADHHOSW HOWDAHS
	READOPT	ADESTTU STATUED	LOADING	ADHHSWY WHYDAHS
ADEOPRV	VAPORED	ADESTTW SWATTED	ADGILNR DARLING	ADHIIKS DASHIKI
ADEOPSS	SPADOES	WADSETT	LARDING	ADHIIMS MAIDISH
ADEORRS	ADORERS	ADFFGIN DAFFING	ADGILNS LADINGS	ADHIKNS DANKISH
	DROSERA	ADFFHNO OFFHAND	LIGANDS	ADHIKRS DARKISH
ADEORRW	ARROWED	ADFFIST DISTAFF	ADGILNU LANGUID	ADHIKSU HAIDUKS
ADEORST	DOATERS	ADFFLNO FANFOLD	LAUDING	ADHILMO HALIDOM
	ROASTED	ADFFLOO OFFLOAD	ADGILOR GOLIARD	ADHILNY HANDILY
	TORSADE	ADFFOOR AFFOORD	ADGILOS DIALOGS	ADHILOP HAPLOID
	TROADES	ADFFORS AFFORDS	ADGILSU GLADIUS	ADHILOS HALOIDS
ADEORSU	AROUSED	ADFGGIN FADGING	ADGILUY GAUDILY	ADHILOY HOLIDAY
ADEORSV	SAVORED	ADFGINN FANDING	ADGIMMN DAMMING	HYALOID
ADEORSW	REDOWAS	ADFGINR FARDING	ADGIMNN DAMNING	ADHILRY HARDILY
ADEORTT	ROTATED	ADFGINS FADINGS	ADGIMNP DAMPING	ADHILSY LADYISH
	TROATED	ADFGLLU GLADFUL	ADGIMNR MRIDANG	SHADILY
ADEORTU	OUTDARE	ADFHLNU HANDFUL	ADGINNR DARNING	ADHIMPS DAMPISH
ADEORWY	RODEWAY	ADFHOOS SHADOOF	NARDING	PHASMID
ADEORYZ	ZEDOARY	ADFHSSU SHADUFS	RANDING	ADHIMRS DIRHAMS
ADEOSTT	TOASTED	ADFILLU FLUIDAL	ADGINNS SANDING	ADHINOT ANTHOID
ADEOTTU	OUTDATE	ADFIMNR FINDRAM	ADGINNT DANTING	ADHINPU DAUPHIN
ADEPPRS	DAPPERS	ADFIMNY DAMNIFY	ADGINNW DAWNING	ADHINSS SANDHIS
ADEPPRT	TRAPPED	ADFINRS FRIANDS	ADGINOR ADORING	ADHIRSY HYDRIAS
ADEPPRW	WRAPPED	ADFINRT INDRAFT	GRADINO	ADHJKOS KHODJAS
ADEPPST	STAPPED	ADFIORS FORSAID	ROADING	ADHKORW DORHAWK
		ADFLLYY LADYFLY	ADGINOS GANOIDS	ADHKOSU SHAKUDO

```
ADHLLNO HOLLAND        ADILLVY VALIDLY                PONIARD       ADLNOSY SYNODAL
ADHLMOY HOLYDAM        ADILMNO MONDIAL        ADINOPT PINTADO       ADLNOTU OUTLAND
ADHLMPY LYMPHAD        ADILMNR MANDRIL        ADINORR ORDINAR       ADLNPSU UPLANDS
ADHMNOO HOODMAN        ADILMNU MAUDLIN        ADINORS INROADS       ADLNRSU LURDANS
        MANHOOD       ADILMOP DIPLOMA                ORDAINS       ADLNRUY LAUNDRY
ADHMNSU NUMDAHS        ADILMOU ALODIUM        ADINORV VIRANDO       ADLOPRU POULARD
ADHNNSU UNHANDS        ADILMOY AMYLOID        ADINOSX DIAXONS       ADLORRW WARLORD
ADHNNUY UNHANDY        ADILMPS PLASMID                DIOXANS       ADLORSS DORSALS
ADHNORS HADRONS        ADILMSS DISMALS        ADINOTX OXIDANT       ADLORSU SUDORAL
ADHNORU UNHOARD        ADILMSU DUALISM        ADINPST PANDITS       ADLOSSS DOSSALS
ADHNOSU HOUDANS        ADILMSY DISMAYL        ADINRRT TRIDARN       ADLPSSU SPAULDS
ADHNOTU HANDOUT                LADYISM        ADINRST INDARTS       ADMMNOS MANDOMS
ADHNRSY SHANDRY        ADILNNS INLANDS        ADINRSU DURIANS       ADMMNSU SUMMAND
ADHNRTY HYDRANT        ADILNOR ORDINAL                SUNDARI       ADMNOOR MADRONO
ADHNRUY UNHARDY        ADILNRS ALDRINS        ADINRSW INWARDS       ADMNOOW WOODMAN
ADHOORR RHODORA        ADILNRU DIURNAL        ADINRTU TRIDUAN       ADMNOOZ MADZOON
ADHOPRT HARDTOP        ADILNSS ISLANDS        ADINSTT DISTANT       ADMNOQU QUONDAM
ADHOPRU UPHOARD        ADILNST TINDALS        ADINSTU UNSTAID       ADMNORS RANDOMS
ADHOSSW SHADOWS        ADILNSU DUALINS        ADINTTY DITTANY               RODSMAN
ADHOSWY SHADOWY                SUNDIAL        ADIOPRS SPAROID       ADMNORT DORMANT
ADHPRSU PURDAHS        ADILOOV OVOIDAL        ADIOPRT PAROTID               MORDANT
ADHPSUU UPHAUDS        ADILOOZ ZOOIDAL        ADIOPRV PRIVADO       ADMNOSS DAMSONS
ADHRRSS DHURRAS        ADILOPR DIPOLAR        ADIORST ASTROID       ADMNOSU OSMUNDA
ADIIILR IRIDIAL        ADILORT DILATOR        ADIORSU SAUROID       ADMNOSY DYNAMOS
ADIIINR IRIDIAN        ADILOTU OUTLAID        ADIORSV ADVISOR       ADMNSTU DUSTMAN
ADIIKOS AIKIDOS        ADILOTW WILDOAT        ADIORTU AUDITOR       ADMOORT DOORMAT
ADIIKOT DAKOITI        ADILPRY PYRALID        ADIOSVW DISAVOW       ADMOPPU POPADUM
ADIILLS ILLIADS                RAPIDLY        ADIPRSS SPARIDS       ADMORRS RAMRODS
ADIILMS MILADIS        ADILPST PLASTID        ADIPRST DISPART       ADMORST STARDOM
        MISLAID       ADILPSY DISPLAY        ADIRRSS SIRDARS               TSARDOM
ADIILNO LIANOID        ADILPTU PLAUDIT        ADIRRSZ RIZARDS       ADMORTW MADWORT
ADIILNV INVALID        ADILPVY VAPIDLY        ADIRSSU SARDIUS       ADMRSTU DURMAST
ADIILOS SIALOID        ADILQSU SQUALID        ADIRSSW WISARDS               MUSTARD
ADIILST DIALIST        ADILRSZ LIZARDS        ADIRSTY SATYRID       ADNNOOS NANDOOS
ADIILUV DILUVIA        ADILRTY TARDILY        ADIRSUY DYSURIA       ADNNOOY NOONDAY
ADIIMMS MAIDISM        ADILSTU DUALIST        ADIRSVZ VIZARDS       ADNNORS RANDONS
ADIIMOS DAIMIOS        ADILSTY STAIDLY        ADIRSWZ WIZARDS       ADNNORT DONNART
ADIIMPV IMPAVID        ADILTUY DUALITY        ADIRSZZ IZZARDS       ADNNOST DANTONS
ADIIMRU MUDIRIA        ADIMNNO MONDAIN        ADISSST SADISTS               DONNATS
ADIIMSS MISSAID        ADIMNOS DAIMONS        ADISSYY SAYYIDS       ADNNOTU DAUNTON
ADIINPR PINDARI                DOMAINS        ADISTTY DITTAYS       ADNNRUW UNDRAWN
        PRIDIAN       ADIMNRS MANDIRS        ADJKOSU JUDOKAS       ADNOOPR PANDOOR
ADIINST DISTAIN        ADIMNSS DISMANS        ADJNORS JORDANS       ADNOORS NARDOOS
ADIINSU INDUSIA        ADIMNST MANTIDS        ADJNORU ADJOURN       ADNOORT DONATOR
        SUIDIAN       ADIMOOS ISODOMA        ADJSSTU ADJUSTS               ODORANT
ADIINSZ DIZAINS        ADIMORR MIRADOR        ADKKLOY KAKODYL               TORNADO
ADIIPRS DIAPIRS        ADIMOST DIATOMS        ADKLMRU MUDLARK       ADNOOSW WANDOOS
ADIIPXY PYXIDIA                MASTOID        ADKOPSU PADOUKS       ADNOPRS PARDONS
ADIIRST DIARIST        ADIMOTT MATTOID        ADKRSWY SKYWARD       ADNOPRU PANDOUR
ADIIRTY ARIDITY        ADIMPRY PYRAMID        ADLLMOW WADMOLL       ADNOPRV PROVAND
ADIITVY AVIDITY        ADIMQSU QUIDAMS        ADLLMOY MODALLY       ADNOPST DOPANTS
ADIJMSS MASJIDS        ADIMRSS DISARMS        ADLLNOW LOWLAND       ADNORRW NORWARD
ADIJNOS ADJOINS        ADIMRSU RADIUMS        ADLLOPR POLLARD       ADNORSW ONWARDS
ADIJNOT ADJOINT        ADIMRSW MISDRAW        ADLLOPS DALLOPS       ADNORTU ROTUNDA
ADIKLNY LADYKIN        ADIMRSY MYRIADS        ADLLORS DOLLARS       ADNORWY NAYWORD
ADIKLOS ODALISK        ADIMSSS SADISMS        ADLMNOS ALMONDS       ADNOSTT DOTANTS
ADIKLPS KLIPDAS        ADIMSST DISMAST                DOLMANS       ADNOSTU ASTOUND
ADIKMNN MANKIND        ADIMSSY DISMAYS        ADLMORU MODULAR       ADNPRUW UPDRAWN
ADIKMOS MIKADOS        ADIMSTU DUMAIST        ADLMOSW WADMOLS       ADNPSTU UPSTAND
ADIKMSS DISMASK                STADIUM        ADLNNOR NORLAND       ADNRSST STRANDS
ADIKNOS DAIKONS        ADIMSWY MIDWAYS        ADLNOOR LARDOON       ADNRSSU SUNDRAS
ADIKNPS KIDNAPS        ADINNOP DIPNOAN        ADLNOPU POUNDAL       ADNRSTU DRAUNTS
        SKIDPAN       ADINNOR ANDIRON        ADLNORS LARDONS               DURANTS
ADIKNRS DISRANK        ADINNRS INNARDS        ADLNORU NODULAR               TUNDRAS
ADIKOST DAKOITS        ADINNRW INDRAWN        ADLNOSS SOLANDS       ADNRSUW SUNWARD
ADIKPRS DISPARK        ADINNRY INNYARD                SOLDANS               UNDRAWS
ADIKSST DIKASTS        ADINNSU INDUNAS        ADLNOST DALTONS       ADNSSTY DYNASTS
ADIKSTT DIKTATS        ADINOOP POINADO        ADLNOSU SOULDAN       ADNSTYY DYNASTY
ADILLMM MILLDAM        ADINOPP OPPIDAN                UNLOADS       ADOOPSU APODOUS
ADILLSY DISALLY        ADINOPR PADRONI        ADLNOSX OXLANDS       ADOOPSW SAPWOOD
```

ADOORWY	DOORWAY	AEEGILW	WEIGELA	AEEGRRT	GREATER
ADOOSUV	VAUDOOS	AEEGINP	EPIGEAN		REGRATE
ADOPRRW	WARDROP	AEEGINR	REGINAE	AEEGRRW	WAGERER
ADORRSU	ARDOURS	AEEGIPR	PIERAGE	AEEGRSS	GREASES
ADORSTW	TOWARDS	AEEGISS	AEGISES	AEEGRST	ERGATES
ADORSUU	ARDUOUS		ASSIEGE		RESTAGE
ADORSWY	AYWORDS	AEEGJRS	JAEGERS	AEEGRSV	GREAVES
ADORTUW	OUTWARD	AEEGLLR	ALLEGER	AEEGRTU	TREAGUE
ADOUUVX	VAUDOUX	AEEGLLS	ALLEGES	AEEGRUZ	GUEREZA
ADPRSUW	UPDRAWS	AEEGLLZ	GAZELLE	AEEGSSW	SEWAGES
	UPWARDS	AEEGLMN	GLEEMAN	AEEGSTT	GESTATE
ADRSSUW	USWARDS		MELANGE		TAGETES
ADSSTUW	SAWDUST	AEEGLNR	ENLARGE	AEEGTTZ	GAZETTE
AEEEFLR	EELFARE		GENERAL	AEEHHNT	HEATHEN
AEEEGKL	KEELAGE		GLEANER	AEEHHRT	HEATHER
AEEEGLT	LEGATEE	AEEGLNT	ELEGANT	AEEHHST	SHEATHE
AEEEGNT	TEENAGE	AEEGLNV	EVANGEL	AEEHHSW	HEEHAWS
AEEEGPR	PEERAGE	AEEGLPR	PEREGAL	AEEHIPR	HEAPIER
AEEEGPS	SEEPAGE	AEEGLPS	PELAGES	AEEHIRV	HEAVIER
AEEEGRT	ETAGERE	AEEGLRS	GALERES	AEEHIST	ATHEISE
AEEEILN	ALIENEE		REGALES	AEEHISV	HEAVIES
AEEELRS	RELEASE	AEEGLRU	LEAGUER	AEEHITZ	ATHEIZE
AEEELTV	ELEVATE		REGULAE	AEEHKNR	HEARKEN
AEEEFLL	FELAFEL	AEEGLRY	EAGERLY	AEEHKNT	THANKEE
AEEEFNS	NEAFFES	AEEGLSS	AGELESS	AEEHKRU	HEUREKA
AEEEFRS	AFFEERS		ALGESES	AEEHLNT	LETHEAN
AEEFGNT	FANTEEG	AEEGLST	EAGLETS	AEEHLRS	HEALERS
AEEFGRS	SERFAGE		LEGATES	AEEHLRT	LEATHER
AEEFGSU	FEAGUES		TEAGLES	AEEHLRV	HAVEREL
AEEFGTW	WEFTAGE		TELEGAS	AEEHLSS	LEASHES
AEEFHRT	FEATHER	AEEGLSU	LEAGUES	AEEHLST	LATHEES
	TEREFAH	AEEGLSV	GLEAVES	AEEHLSW	AWHEELS
AEEFILR	LEAFIER		SELVAGE	AEEHLSX	EXHALES
AEEFILW	ALEWIFE	AEEGLTU	TEGULAE	AEEHLSY	EYELASH
AEEFIRS	AREFIES	AEEGLTV	VEGETAL	AEEHLTT	ATHLETE
	FAERIES	AEEGMMT	GEMMATE	AEEHMNT	METHANE
	FREESIA		TAGMEME	AEEHMRS	HAREEMS
AEEFLLT	FELLATE	AEEGMNR	GERMANE		MAHSEER
	LEAFLET	AEEGMNS	MANEGES	AEEHMRT	ERATHEM
AEEFLMS	FEMALES		MENAGES		THERMAE
AEEFLRT	REFLATE	AEEGMRR	MEAGRER	AEEHMST	MEATHES
AEEFLRW	WELFARE	AEEGMRS	MEAGRES	AEEHMSU	HEAUMES
AEEFLRY	LEAFERY	AEEGMRU	REMUAGE	AEEHNPT	HEPTANE
AEEFLRZ	ALFEREZ	AEEGMSS	MEGASSE		PHENATE
AEEFLSU	EASEFUL		MESSAGE	AEEHNRS	ARSHEEN
AEEFMNR	ENFRAME	AEEGMST	GAMETES	AEEHNRT	EARTHEN
	FREEMAN		METAGES		HEARTEN
AEEFMRR	REFRAME	AEEGNNP	PANGENE	AEEHNST	ETHANES
AEEFOTV	FOVEATE	AEEGNNR	ENRANGE	AEEHNSV	HEAVENS
AEEFPPR	FRAPPEE	AEEGNOP	PEONAGE	AEEHNSX	HEXANES
AEEFRRT	FERRATE	AEEGNPP	GENAPPE	AEEHNTW	WHEATEN
AEEFRST	AFREETS	AEEGNRS	ENRAGES	AEEHPRS	RESHAPE
	FEASTER	AEEGNRT	GRANTEE		SPHAERE
AEEFRTU	FEATURE		GREATEN		SPHEARE
AEEFRWY	FREEWAY		REAGENT	AEEHPRT	PREHEAT
AEEGGLL	ALLEGGE	AEEGNRU	RENAGUE	AEEHPSS	APHESES
AEEGGLR	GREGALE	AEEGNRV	AVENGER		SPAHEES
AEEGGLS	ALEGGES		ENGRAVE	AEEHPUV	UPHEAVE
AEEGGLT	GATELEG	AEEGNSS	SAGENES	AEEHQSU	QUASHEE
AEEGGNR	ENGAGER		SENEGAS	AEEHRRS	HEARERS
AEEGGNS	ENGAGES	AEEGNST	NEGATES		REHEARS
AEEGGOP	EPAGOGE	AEEGNSV	AVENGES		SHEARER
AEEGGRS	AGREGES		GENEVAS	AEEHRSS	HEARSES
	RAGGEES	AEEGNTT	TENTAGE	AEEHRST	AETHERS
	REGGAES	AEEGNTV	VENTAGE		HEATERS
AEEGHNW	WHANGEE	AEEGOPS	APOGEES		REHEATS
AEEGILL	GALILEE	AEEGOST	GOATEES	AEEHRSV	HEAVERS
AEEGILM	MILEAGE	AEEGPRS	ASPERGE	AEEHRSW	WHEREAS
AEEGILN	LINEAGE		PRESAGE	AEEHRTT	THEATER
AEEGILP	EPIGEAL	AEEGRRS	GREASER		THEATRE

	THEREAT
AEEHRTV	THREAVE
AEEHRTW	WEATHER
	WHEREAT
	WREATHE
AEEHSST	HEASTES
AEEHSSV	SHEAVES
AEEHSTV	THEAVES
AEEIIRS	AIERIES
AEEIKLR	LEAKIER
AEEIKPR	PEAKIER
AEEILLR	REALLIE
AEEILMR	MEALIER
AEEILMS	MEALIES
AEEILNP	ALEPINE
AEEILNT	LINEATE
AEEILPT	EPILATE
	PILEATE
AEEILRR	EARLIER
	LEARIER
AEEILRS	REALISE
AEEILRT	ATELIER
	REALTIE
AEEILRV	LEAVIER
	VEALIER
AEEILRZ	REALIZE
AEEILTT	AILETTE
AEEILTV	ELATIVE
AEEIMNR	REMANIE
AEEIMNS	MEANIES
	NEMESIA
AEEIMNT	MATINEE
AEEIMNX	EXAMINE
AEEIMPR	EMPAIRE
AEEIMRR	REAMIER
AEEIMRS	SEAMIER
	SERIEMA
AEEIMRT	EMIRATE
	MEATIER
AEEIMSS	MISEASE
	SIAMESE
AEEIMST	STEAMIE
AEEIMSZ	SIAMEZE
AEEIMTT	TEATIME
AEEINRT	RETINAE
	TRAINEE
AEEINST	ETESIAN
AEEINTV	NAIVETE
AEEINVW	INWEAVE
AEEIORT	ETAERIO
AEEIPRR	PEREIRA
AEEIPRS	APERIES
	EPEIRAS
AEEIPRT	PEATIER
AEEIPSV	PEAVIES
AEEIPTX	EXPIATE
AEEIRRR	ARRIERE
AEEIRRS	REARISE
AEEIRRT	TEARIER
AEEIRRW	WEARIER
AEEIRST	AERIEST
	SERIATE
AEEIRSW	WEARIES
AEEIRTT	ARIETTE
	ITERATE
AEEIRTV	EVIRATE
AEEISST	EASIEST
AEEISVV	EVASIVE
AEEITTV	AVIETTE
	EVITATE

Letters	Word(s)
AEEITUX	EUTEXIA
AEEIUVX	EXUVIAE
AEEJKSS	JAKESES
AEEJMSS	JAMESES
AEEJNST	SEJEANT
AEEJNTU	JAUNTEE
AEEJRSV	EVEJARS
AEEKLLT	LAKELET
AEEKLMN	KEELMAN
AEEKLNS	ALKENES
AEEKLNT	KANTELE
AEEKLPS	PALKEES
AEEKLRS	LEAKERS
AEEKLSV	VAKEELS
AEEKMNS	KAMSEEN
AEEKMNW	WAKEMEN
AEEKMRS	REMAKES
AEEKMRT	MEERKAT
AEEKNNN	NANKEEN
AEEKNRS	SNEAKER
AEEKNRT	RETAKEN
AEEKNRW	WAKENER
AEEKNSW	WEAKENS
AEEKORW	REAWOKE
AEEKPRS	PARKEES
	RESPEAK
	SPEAKER
AEEKPRT	PERTAKE
AEEKRRT	RETAKER
AEEKRRW	WREAKER
AEEKRST	RETAKES
	SAKERET
AEEKRSU	EUREKAS
AEEKRSW	WREAKES
AEEKSSS	ASKESES
AEEKSTW	WEAKEST
AEELLLS	ALLELES
AEELLMS	MALLEES
AEELLOV	ALVEOLE
AEELLPR	PARELLE
AEELLSS	SALLEES
AEELMNP	EMPANEL
	EMPLANE
AEELMNR	REELMAN
AEELMNS	ENAMELS
AEELMNT	MANTEEL
AEELMNV	VELAMEN
AEELMNY	AMYLENE
AEELMPS	EMPALES
AEELMPX	EXAMPLE
	EXEMPLA
AEELMRS	MEALERS
AEELMRT	LAMETER
AEELMSS	MEASLES
AEELMSU	AEMULES
AEELMSZ	MEAZELS
AEELMTU	EMULATE
AEELNNR	LERNEAN
AEELNPS	ALPEENS
	SPELEAN
AEELNRR	LEARNER
AEELNRT	ALTERNE
	ENTERAL
	ETERNAL
AEELNRW	RENEWAL
AEELNSS	ENSEALS
AEELNST	ELANETS
	LEANEST
AEELNSV	ENSLAVE
	LEAVENS
AEELNSW	WEANELS
AEELNTY	ENTAYLE
AEELOPR	PAROLEE
AEELORS	AREOLES
AEELORU	AUREOLE
AEELOST	OLEATES
AEELOSW	LEASOWE
AEELPRR	PEARLER
AEELPRS	LEAPERS
	PLEASER
	RELAPSE
	REPEALS
AEELPRT	PRELATE
AEELPRU	PLEURAE
AEELPSS	ELAPSES
	PLEASES
	SAPELES
AEELPSU	EPAULES
AEELPTT	PALETTE
	PELTATE
AEELPTU	EPAULET
AEELQSU	QUELEAS
	SEQUELA
AEELRRT	ALERTER
	RELATER
AEELRSS	ARLESES
	EARLESS
	LEASERS
	RESALES
	RESEALS
	SEALERS
AEELRST	ELATERS
	REALEST
	RELATES
	STEALER
AEELRSU	LEASURE
AEELRSV	LAVEERS
	REVEALS
	SEVERAL
AEELRSX	RELAXES
AEELRSY	SEALERY
AEELRUV	REVALUE
AEELSST	ALTESSE
	STEALES
	TEASELS
AEELSSV	SLEAVES
AEELSSW	AWELESS
	WEASELS
AEELSSZ	SLEAZES
AEELSTU	ELUATES
	SETUALE
AEELSTV	SALVETE
	VALETES
	VELETAS
AEELSTX	LATEXES
AEELSTY	EYALETS
AEELSTZ	TEAZELS
	TEAZLES
AEELSWY	LEEWAYS
AEELTTY	LAYETTE
AEELTVW	WAVELET
AEEMMMS	MAMMEES
AEEMMPY	EMPYEMA
AEEMMRT	AMMETER
	METAMER
AEEMNNO	ANEMONE
AEEMNPS	SPAEMEN
AEEMNPT	PEATMEN
AEEMNRS	RENAMES
AEEMNRT	REMANET
AEEMNSS	ENSEAMS
AEEMNST	ENTAMES
	MEANEST
AEEMNSX	EXAMENS
AEEMORT	EROTEMA
AEEMOSW	AWESOME
	WAESOME
AEEMPRS	AMPERES
	EMPARES
AEEMPRT	TEMPERA
AEEMPRY	EMPAYRE
AEEMPSW	WAMPEES
AEEMPTU	AMPUTEE
AEEMQRU	MARQUEE
AEEMRRS	REAMERS
AEEMRSS	SEAMERS
AEEMRST	STEAMER
	TEAMERS
AEEMRSU	MEASURE
AEEMRTY	METAYER
AEEMSSS	SESAMES
AEENNOT	NEONATE
AEENNPT	PENNATE
	PENTANE
AEENNRS	ENSNARE
AEENNRX	REANNEX
AEENNST	NEATENS
AEENNSX	ANNEXES
AEENNTU	UNEATEN
AEENOPR	PERAEON
AEENOSS	ANOESES
AEENPST	PENATES
	PESANTE
AEENPSW	PAWNEES
AEENPSX	EXPANSE
AEENRRS	EARNERS
AEENRRT	TERRANE
AEENRRV	RAVENER
AEENRSS	ENSEARS
AEENRST	EARNEST
	EASTERN
	NEAREST
AEENRSW	WEANERS
AEENRTT	ENTREAT
	RATTEEN
	TERNATE
AEENRTV	AVENTRE
	NERVATE
	VETERAN
AEENRUV	UNREAVE
AEENSST	ENTASES
	SATEENS
	SENATES
	STEANES
AEENSSU	UNEASES
AEENSSV	AVENSES
AEENSSW	WAENESS
AEENSTT	NEATEST
AEENSUV	AVENUES
AEENSWZ	WEAZENS
AEENTTV	NAVETTE
AEENUVW	UNWEAVE
AEEOPRT	OPERATE
AEEORRS	REAROSE
AEEORSS	SEROSAE
AEEORST	ROSEATE
AEEORSV	OVERSEA
AEEORTV	OVERATE
	OVEREAT
AEEORVW	OVERAWE
AEEOSUU	EUOUAES
AEEOSVV	EVOVAES
AEEPPRR	PAPERER
	PREPARE
	REPAPER
AEEPPRS	RAPPEES
AEEPRRS	REAPERS
AEEPRRT	TAPERER
AEEPRSS	ASPERSE
	PARESES
	PRAESES
	PREASES
	PREASSE
	SERAPES
AEEPRST	REPEATS
AEEPRSZ	SPREAZE
AEEPRTU	EPURATE
AEEPRTY	PEATERY
AEEPRTZ	TRAPEZE
AEEPSSS	ASEPSES
AEEPSST	PESETAS
AEEPSSW	PESEWAS
AEEPSTT	SEPTATE
	SPATTEE
AEEPSVY	PEAVEYS
AEEQRSU	QUAERES
AEEQSTU	EQUATES
AEERRRS	REARERS
AEERRSS	ERASERS
AEERRST	SERRATE
	TEARERS
AEERRSU	ERASURE
AEERRSV	REAVERS
AEERRSW	SWEARER
	WEARERS
AEERRTT	RETRATE
	RETREAT
	TREATER
AEERRTW	WATERER
AEERRVW	WAVERER
AEERSST	RESEATS
	SAETERS
	SEAREST
	SEATERS
	STEARES
	TEASERS
	TESSERA
AEERSSU	RESEAUS
	SEASURE
AEERSSV	ASSEVER
AEERSSY	ESSAYER
AEERSTT	ESTREAT
	RESTATE
AEERSTU	AUSTERE
AEERSTW	SWEATER
AEERSUV	VAREUSE
AEERSUX	RESEAUX
AEERSVW	WEAVERS
AEERTTX	EXTREAT
AEESSSW	SEESAWS
AEESSTT	ESTATES
AEESSTX	TEXASES
AEESSUX	AUXESES
AEESTTT	TESTATE
AEFFFLR	FLAFFER
AEFFGIR	GIRAFFE
AEFFGNR	ENGRAFF
AEFFGRS	GAFFERS
AEFFHST	HAFFETS
AEFFINS	AFFINES

```
AEFFIPR PIAFFER     AEFILMN FEMINAL             SAFROLE             LIGNAGE
AEFFIPS PIAFFES             INFLAME     AEFLORT FLOATER     AEGGINR GEARING
AEFFIST TAFFIES     AEFILMR FLAMIER             FLOREAT             NAGGIER
AEFFISX AFFIXES     AEFILNS FINALES             REFLOAT     AEGGINS AGEINGS
AEFFKOP OFFPEAK     AEFILNT INFLATE     AEFLORY FORELAY     AEGGIOS ISAGOGE
AEFFKOT OFFTAKE     AEFILNU INFULAE     AEFLPPR FLAPPER     AEGGIRR RAGGIER
AEFFLLY FLYLEAF     AEFILOT FOLIATE     AEFLPRS FELSPAR     AEGGIRS RAGGIES
AEFFLMW FLAMFEW     AEFILRR FLARIER     AEFLPRY PALFREY             SAGGIER
AEFFLNS SNAFFLE             FRAILER     AEFLRSS FALSERS     AEGGIRU GARIGUE
AEFFLRR RAFFLER     AEFILRU FAILURE             FLASERS     AEGGISW SWAGGIE
AEFFLRS RAFFLES     AEFILRV FAVRILE     AEFLRST FALTERS     AEGGJRS JAGGERS
AEFFLRU FEARFUL     AEFILRW FLAWIER     AEFLRSU EARFULS     AEGGJRY JAGGERY
AEFFLSW WAFFLES     AEFILRX FLAXIER             FERULAS     AEGGLNO AGELONG
AEFFLSY YAFFLES     AEFILRZ FILAZER             REFUSAL     AEGGLNR GANGREL
AEFFLTU FATEFUL     AEFILSS FALSIES     AEFLRSY FLAYERS     AEGGLNS LAGGENS
AEFFQRU QUAFFER             FILASSE     AEFLRTT FLATTER     AEGGLRS GARGLES
AEFFRST AFFRETS     AEFIMNR FIREMAN     AEFLRTU REFUTAL             LAGGERS
        RESTAFF     AEFIMNS FAMINES             TEARFUL             RAGGLES
        STAFFER             INFAMES     AEFLRZZ FRAZZLE     AEGGLSW WAGGLES
AEFFRSY EFFRAYS     AEFIMOR FOAMIER     AEFLSST FALSEST     AEGGMNY YEGGMAN
AEFFRSZ ZAFFERS     AEFIMRR FIREARM             FESTALS     AEGGMSS EGGMASS
        ZAFFRES     AEFIMRS MISFARE     AEFLSTU FLUATES     AEGGNNU GUNNAGE
AEFFTTY TAFFETY     AEFINNS FANNIES             SULFATE     AEGGNRR GRANGER
AEFGGGO FOGGAGE     AEFINNT INFANTE     AEFMNOR FORAMEN     AEGGNRS GANGERS
AEFGGMO MEGAFOG     AEFINNZ FANZINE             FOREMAN             GRANGES
AEFGGRY FAGGERY     AEFINPR FIREPAN     AEFMNRT RAFTMEN             NAGGERS
AEFGILN FEALING     AEFINRR REFRAIN     AEFMNRU FRAENUM     AEGGNSU GANGUES
        FINAGLE     AEFINRS INFARES     AEFMOOR FOREARM     AEGGRRY RAGGERY
        LEAFING     AEFINRT FAINTER     AEFMORT FORMATE     AEGGRSS AGGRESS
AEFGILO FOLIAGE             FENITAR     AEFMRRS FARMERS             SAGGERS
AEFGILR FRAGILE     AEFINRX XERAFIN             FRAMERS             SEGGARS
AEFGINR FEARING     AEFINST FAINEST     AEFMRRY FARMERY     AEGGRST GAGSTER
AEFGINT FEATING             NAIFEST     AEFNNRS FANNERS             GARGETS
AEFGIRT FRIGATE     AEFINTX ANTEFIX     AEFNRSS FARNESS             STAGGER
AEFGIRU REFUGIA     AEFIQRU AQUIFER     AEFNRSU FURANES             TAGGERS
AEFGITU FATIGUE     AEFIRRR FARRIER             UNSAFER     AEGGRSU GAUGERS
AEFGLLU FULLAGE     AEFIRSS FRAISES     AEFNRSW FAWNERS     AEGGRSW SWAGGER
AEFGLNS FANGLES     AEFIRST FAIREST     AEFNSST FASTENS     AEGGRSY YAGGERS
        FLANGES     AEFIRTT FATTIER             FATNESS     AEGGRWY WAGGERY
AEFGLOT FLOTAGE     AEFISST FIESTAS     AEFNSTT FATTENS     AEGGSWW GEWGAWS
AEFGLOW FLOWAGE     AEFISTT FATTIES     AEFOPRW FOREPAW     AEGHHIT AHEIGHT
AEFGLRS REFLAGS     AEFISTX FIXATES     AEFORRV OVERFAR     AEGHIJR JAGHIRE
AEFGLRU RAGEFUL     AEFKLNR FLANKER     AEFORRY FORAYER     AEGHILN HEALING
AEFGLUZ GAZEFUL     AEFKLNS FANKLES     AEFORSW FORESAW     AEGHILR LAIGHER
AEFGMSU FUMAGES     AEFKLST FLASKET     AEFORSY FORESAY     AEGHINP HEAPING
AEFGNRR GRANFER     AEFKLUW WAKEFUL     AEFOSST FATSOES     AEGHINR HEARING
AEFGNRT ENGRAFT     AEFKNRR FRANKER     AEFOSTU FEATOUS     AEGHINT GAHNITE
AEFGOOT FOOTAGE     AEFKORS FORSAKE     AEFRRST FRATERS             HEATING
AEFGORR FORAGER     AEFLLNN FANNELL             RAFTERS     AEGHINV HEAVING
AEFGORS FORAGES             FLANNEL     AEFRRTY FRATERY     AEGHINZ GENIZAH
AEFGORV FORGAVE     AEFLLOT FLOATEL     AEFRSSS FRASSES     AEGHIRS HEGIRAS
AEFGRRT GRAFTER     AEFLLSY FALSELY     AEFRSST FASTERS     AEGHISS GEISHAS
AEFGRSU GAUFERS     AEFLLTT FLATLET             STRAFES     AEGHLNO HALOGEN
        GAUFRES     AEFLLTU TALEFUL     AEFRSTW FRETSAW     AEGHLNT ALENGTH
AEFHLLS FELLAHS     AEFLLUZ ZEALFUL             WAFTERS     AEGHLRU LAUGHER
AEFHLOR FAHLORE     AEFLMNS FLAMENS     AEFRTUW WAFTURE     AEGHLSS SEALGHS
AEFHLRS FLASHER     AEFLMOR FEMORAL     AEFSSTT FASTEST     AEGHLST HAGLETS
AEFHLRT FARTHEL     AEFLMUW WAMEFUL     AEFSSUV FAVUSES     AEGHLSZ GHAZELS
AEFHLRZ FAHLERZ     AEFLMUZ MAZEFUL     AEFSTTT FATTEST     AEGHLTW THALWEG
AEFHLSS FLASHES     AEFLNNN FLANNEN     AEGGGLS GAGGLES     AEGHMNN HANGMEN
AEFHLTU HATEFUL     AEFLNNS FANNELS     AEGGGLU LUGGAGE     AEGHMOR HOMAGER
AEFHRRT FARTHER     AEFLNOV FLAVONE     AEGGGRS GAGGERS     AEGHMOS HOMAGES
AEFHRST FATHERS     AEFLNRS SALFERN     AEGGHLR HAGGLER     AEGHMSU MESHUGA
        SHAFTER     AEFLNRU FLANEUR     AEGGHLS HAGGLES     AEGHNOX HEXAGON
AEFHRSY FASHERY             FUNERAL     AEGGIJR JAGGIER     AEGHNRS GNASHER
AEFIILT FILIATE     AEFLNSU FLAUNES     AEGGILN GEALING             HANGERS
AEFIIRS FAIRIES     AEFLNTT FLATTEN                         AEGHNRU NURAGHE
AEFIJLO JEOFAIL     AEFLOOV FOVEOLA                         AEGHNSS GNASHES
AEFIKLR FLAKIER     AEFLORS LOAFERS                         AEGHNST STENGAH
AEFILLS FAILLES                                             AEGHOPY HYPOGEA
```

AEGHORS	GHERAOS		MEANING		TANGIER	AEGLLOT	TOLLAGE
AEGHOST	HOSTAGE	AEGIMNP	PIGMEAN		TEARING	AEGLLRY	ALLERGY
AEGHPRS	SPREAGH	AEGIMNR	GERMAIN	AEGINRV	REAVING		GALLERY
AEGHPST	HATPEGS		MANGIER		VINEGAR		LARGELY
AEGHRST	GATHERS		REAMING	AEGINRW	WEARING		REGALLY
AEGIIMN	IMAGINE	AEGIMNS	ENIGMAS	AEGINSS	AGNISES	AEGLLST	GALLETS
AEGIKLN	LEAKING		GAMINES		SEASING	AEGLLSU	SEAGULL
	LINKAGE		MEASING	AEGINST	EASTING		SULLAGE
AEGIKLT	GLAIKET		SEAMING		EATINGS		ULLAGES
AEGIKNP	PEAKING	AEGIMNT	MINTAGE		GAINEST	AEGLLSY	GALLEYS
AEGIKNR	REAKING		TEAMING		GENISTA	AEGLLTU	GLUTEAL
AEGIKNS	SINKAGE		TEGMINA		INGATES	AEGLMNR	MANGLER
AEGIKPP	KIPPAGE	AEGIMOS	IMAGOES		INGESTA	AEGLMNS	MANGELS
AEGIKPR	GARPIKE	AEGIMPR	EPIGRAM		SEATING		MANGLES
AEGIKRW	GAWKIER		PRIMAGE		TANGIES	AEGLMOR	GOMERAL
AEGIKSW	GAWKIES	AEGIMPS	MAGPIES		TEASING	AEGLMOU	MOULAGE
AEGILLL	ILLEGAL	AEGIMPT	PIGMEAT		TSIGANE	AEGLMPU	PLUMAGE
AEGILLN	NIGELLA	AEGIMRR	ARMIGER	AEGINSU	GUINEAS	AEGLMRS	MALGRES
AEGILLP	PILLAGE	AEGIMRS	GISARME	AEGINSZ	AGNIZES	AEGLMRU	MAULGRE
AEGILLS	GALLIES		MAIGRES	AEGINTV	VINTAGE	AEGLMSY	MYGALES
	GALLISE		MIRAGES	AEGINTZ	TEAZING	AEGLNOS	ENGAOLS
AEGILLT	TILLAGE	AEGIMRT	MIGRATE	AEGINVW	WEAVING	AEGLNOT	TANGELO
AEGILLU	LIGULAE		RAGTIME	AEGIORT	GOATIER	AEGLNPR	GRAPNEL
AEGILLV	VILLAGE	AEGIMRU	GAUMIER	AEGIPPR	GAPPIER	AEGLNPS	SPANGLE
AEGILLY	AGILELY	AEGIMRY	IMAGERY	AEGIPPS	PIPAGES	AEGLNRS	ANGLERS
AEGILLZ	GALLIZE	AEGIMSS	AGEISMS	AEGIPRR	GRAPIER		LARGENS
AEGILMN	LEAMING	AEGIMST	GAMIEST	AEGIPRS	GASPIER	AEGLNRT	TANGLER
	MEALING		SIGMATE		PRISAGE		TRANGLE
AEGILMR	GREMIAL	AEGIMSV	MISGAVE		SPAIRGE	AEGLNRU	GRANULE
	LAMIGER	AEGINNP	NEAPING	AEGIRRZ	GRAZIER	AEGLNRW	WANGLER
AEGILMS	MILAGES		PEANING	AEGIRSS	AGRISES		WRANGLE
AEGILNN	ANELING	AEGINNR	AGINNER		GASSIER	AEGLNRY	ANGERLY
	EANLING		EARNING	AEGIRST	AGISTER	AEGLNSS	GLASSEN
	LEANING		ENGRAIN		GAITERS	AEGLNST	LANGEST
	NEALING		GRANNIE		STAGIER		TANGLES
AEGILNP	LEAPING		NEARING		STRIGAE	AEGLNSU	ANGELUS
	PEALING	AEGINNS	SEANING		TRIAGES		LAGUNES
	PLEAING	AEGINNT	ANTEING	AEGIRSV	GARVIES		LANGUES
AEGILNR	ENGRAIL		ANTIGEN		GRAVIES	AEGLNSW	WANGLES
	LEARING		GENTIAN		RIVAGES	AEGLNSY	LYNAGES
	NARGILE	AEGINNU	ANGUINE	AEGIRSW	EARWIGS	AEGLNTT	GANTLET
	REALIGN		GUANINE		GAWSIER	AEGLNTU	LANGUET
	REGINAL	AEGINNW	WEANING	AEGIRSZ	AGRIZES	AEGLNTW	TWANGLE
AEGILNS	LEASING	AEGINNY	YEANING	AEGIRTV	VIRGATE	AEGLNUU	UNGULAE
	LINAGES	AEGINOR	ORIGANE		VITRAGE	AEGLNUW	GUNWALE
	SEALING	AEGINOS	AGONIES	AEGIRUZ	GAUZIER	AEGLOPR	PERGOLA
AEGILNT	ATINGLE		AGONISE	AEGISST	AGEISTS	AEGLORS	GAOLERS
	ELATING	AEGINOZ	AGONIZE		SAGIEST	AEGLORT	LEGATOR
	GELATIN	AEGINPP	GENIPAP	AEGISSU	AGUISES	AEGLOSS	GLOSSAE
	GENITAL	AEGINPR	REAPING	AEGISSV	VISAGES	AEGLOST	LEGATOS
AEGILNU	LINGUAE	AEGINPS	PEASING	AEGISTU	AUGITES	AEGLOSU	GEALOUS
AEGILNV	LEAVING		SPAEING	AEGISTY	GASEITY	AEGLOSV	LOVAGES
AEGILNY	ALEYING		SPINAGE	AEGISTZ	GAZIEST	AEGLOTV	VOLTAGE
AEGILOS	GOALIES	AEGINPZ	PEAZING	AEGISUZ	AGUIZES	AEGLPPR	GRAPPLE
AEGILOU	EULOGIA	AEGINRR	ANGRIER	AEGISYZ	AZYGIES	AEGLPRS	GRAPLES
AEGILPS	PAIGLES		EARRING	AEGJLNR	JANGLER	AEGLPRU	EARPLUG
AEGILRR	GLARIER		GRAINER	AEGJLNS	JANGLES		GRAUPEL
AEGILRS	GRAILES		RANGIER	AEGKKNO	ANGEKOK	AEGLPSU	PLAGUES
AEGILRZ	GLAZIER		REARING	AEGKLOU	KAGOULE		PLUSAGE
AEGILSS	ALGESIS	AEGINRS	ANGRIES	AEGKLRS	GRAKLES	AEGLPUY	PLAGUEY
	SILAGES		EARINGS	AEGKMRY	KERYGMA	AEGLRRU	REGULAR
AEGILST	AGILEST		ERASING	AEGKRSW	GAWKERS	AEGLRSS	LARGESS
	AIGLETS		GAINERS	AEGKSST	GASKETS	AEGLRST	LARGEST
	LIGATES		GRAINES	AEGLLLY	LEGALLY	AEGLRSV	GRAVELS
	TAIGLES		REGAINS	AEGLLNO	ALLONGE		VERGLAS
AEGILSV	GLAIVES		REGINAS		GALLEON	AEGLRSY	ARGYLES
AEGILTU	GLUTAEI		SEARING	AEGLLNR	LANGREL		GRAYLES
AEGILTY	EGALITY		SERINGA	AEGLLNS	LEGLANS	AEGLRSZ	GLAZERS
AEGIMMR	GAMMIER	AEGINRT	GRANITE	AEGLLOR	ALLEGRO	AEGLRTU	GAULTER
AEGIMNN	AMENING		INGRATE				TEGULAR

	TRAGULE	AEGNRTU GAUNTER	AEHHRST HEARTHS
AEGLRTY GREATLY	AEGNSSY GAYNESS	AEHHSSS SHASHES
AEGLRVY GRAVELY	AEGNSTT GESTANT	AEHHSST SHEATHS
AEGLSSS GLASSES	AEGNTTU TUTENAG	AEHHSTY SHEATHY
AEGLSSU SAULGES	AEGOORT ROOTAGE	AEHIILR HAILIER
AEGLSTT GESTALT	AEGOPPR PROPAGE	AEHIIRR HAIRIER
AEGLSTW TALWEGS	AEGOPRT PORTAGE	AEHIJRS HEJIRAS
AEGLTUV VULGATE	AEGOPST POSTAGE	AEHIKNS HANKIES
AEGLUUY GUAYULE	POTAGES	AEHIKRS SHAKIER
AEGLUVY VAGUELY	AEGOPTT POTTAGE	AEHIKSS SAKIEHS
AEGMMNS MAGSMEN	AEGORRT GARROTE	AEHIKSW HAWKIES
AEGMMRS GAMMERS	AEGORSS SORAGES	AEHIKSY SAKIYEH
GRAMMES	AEGORST ORGEATS	AEHILMN HELIMAN
AEGMMRU RUMMAGE	STORAGE	AEHILMO HEMIOLA
AEGMMSS SMEGMAS	AEGORTT GAROTTE	AEHILNR HERNIAL
AEGMNNO AGNOMEN	AEGORTU OUTRAGE	INHALER
AEGMNOR MEGARON	AEGORUV OUVRAGE	AEHILNS INHALES
AEGMNOS MANGOES	AEGORVY VOYAGER	AEHILNY HYALINE
AEGMNOT MAGNETO	AEGOSSU GASEOUS	AEHILOR AIRHOLE
MEGATON	AEGOSTU OUTAGES	AEHILRS HAILERS
MONTAGE	AEGOSTW STOWAGE	SHALIER
AEGMNPY PYGMEAN	TOWAGES	AEHILRT LATHIER
AEGMNRS ENGRAMS	AEGOSTX OXGATES	AEHILRU HAULIER
GERMANS	AEGOSVY VOYAGES	AEHILSS SHEILAS
MANGERS	AEGOTTU OUTGATE	AEHILST HALITES
AEGMNRT GARMENT	AEGOTTV GAVOTTE	AEHILSW WHAISLE
MARGENT	AEGOTUV OUTGAVE	AEHILTT LITHATE
RAGMENT	AEGPRRS GRASPER	AEHILTY HYALITE
AEGMNST MAGNETS	SPARGER	AEHILUV VIHUELA
AEGMNSW SWAGMEN	AEGPRRY GRAPERY	AEHILVY HEAVILY
AEGMNTU AUGMENT	AEGPRSS GASPERS	AEHILWZ WHAIZLE
MUTAGEN	SPARGES	AEHIMMR HAMMIER
AEGMOOR MOORAGE	AEGPRST PARGETS	AEHIMNR HARMINE
AEGMORS ROMAGES	AEGPRSU GAUPERS	AEHIMNS HAEMINS
AEGMOSY GAYSOME	AEGPRSW GAWPERS	HEMINAS
AEGMOXY EXOGAMY	AEGPSSU PEGASUS	AEHIMNY HYMENIA
AEGMRSU MAUGRES	AEGPSTU UPSTAGE	AEHIMPS PHAEISM
MURAGES	AEGPSUZ UPGAZES	AEHIMRS MASHIER
AEGMSUY MAGUEYS	AEGRRSS GRASSER	MISHEAR
AEGMSUZ ZEUGMAS	AEGRRST GARRETS	AEHIMSS MASHIES
AEGNNOS NONAGES	GARTERS	AEHIMST ATHEISM
AEGNNOT TONNAGE	GRATERS	AEHINPR HEPARIN
AEGNNPS PANGENS	AEGRRSU ARGUERS	AEHINPS INPHASE
AEGNNRT REGNANT	AEGRRSV GRAVERS	AEHINPT PENTHIA
AEGNNRU GUNNERA	AEGRRSZ GRAZERS	AEHINRS ARSHINE
AEGNNST GANNETS	AEGRRUU AUGURER	HERNIAS
AEGNNTT TANGENT	AEGRRUV GRAVURE	AEHINRT INEARTH
AEGNNTU TUNNAGE	VERRUGA	AEHINSS HESSIAN
AEGNOOR OREGANO	AEGRSSS GRASSES	AEHINSV EVANISH
AEGNOPT PONTAGE	AEGRSST STAGERS	VAHINES
AEGNORR GROANER	AEGRSSU ARGUSES	AEHINSW WAHINES
ORANGER	SAUGERS	AEHIORR HOARIER
AEGNORS ONAGERS	USAGERS	AEHIPPR HAPPIER
ORANGES	AEGRSTT TARGETS	AEHIPPS HAPPIES
AEGNORW WAGONER	AEGRSTV GRAVEST	AEHIPPT EPITAPH
AEGNOSY NOSEGAY	AEGRSTY GRAYEST	AEHIPRS HARPIES
AEGNOWY WAYGONE	GYRATES	SHARPIE
AEGNPRS ENGRASP	STAGERY	AEHIPSS APHESIS
AEGNPRT TREPANG	AEGRSYZ AGRYZES	AEHIPSW PEISHWA
AEGNRRS GARNERS	AEGSSSU GAUSSES	AEHIPTZ ZAPTIEH
RANGERS	AEGSTUU AUGUSTE	AEHIQSU HAIQUES
AEGNRRT GRANTER	AEGSTUV VAGUEST	QUASHIE
REGRANT	AEGTTTU GUTTATE	AEHIRRR HARRIER
AEGNRSS SERANGS	AEHHIRS HASHIER	AEHIRRS HARRIES
AEGNRST ARGENTS	AEHHIST SHEHITA	AEHIRSS ARISHES
GARNETS	AEHHLST HEALTHS	SHERIAS
STRANGE	AEHHLTY HEALTHY	AEHIRST HASTIER
AEGNRSU RAUNGES	AEHHNRS HARSHEN	SHERIAT
UNGEARS	AEHHPRS RHAPHES	AEHIRSV ASHIVER
AEGNRSW GNAWERS	AEHHRRS HARSHER	AEHIRSW WASHIER

WEARISH
AEHIRTW THAWIER
AEHIRWY HAYWIRE
AEHISST ASHIEST
SAITHES
STASHIE
TAISHES
AEHISSV SHAVIES
AEHISTT ATHEIST
STAITHE
AEHISTZ HAZIEST
AEHISVY YESHIVA
AEHITTW THWAITE
AEHJLOW JAWHOLE
AEHKNRS HANKERS
HARKENS
AEHKNRT THANKER
AEHKOSS SHAKOES
AEHKRRS SHARKER
AEHKRSS SHAKERS
AEHKRSW HAWKERS
AEHKSWY HAWKEYS
AEHLLOS HALLOES
AEHLLOV HELLOVA
AEHLLRS HERSALL
AEHLLUV HELLUVA
AEHLLYZ HAZELLY
AEHLMNO MANHOLE
AEHLMNY HYMENAL
AEHLMOR ARMHOLE
AEHLMPS PELHAMS
AEHLMPW WHAMPLE
AEHLMRS HARMELS
AEHLMRT THERMAL
AEHLMRU HUMERAL
AEHLMST HAMLETS
AEHLNOS ENHALOS
AEHLNOT ETHANOL
AEHLNRT ENTHRAL
AEHLNSS HANSELS
AEHLNST HANTLES
AEHLNSU UNHEALS
UNLEASH
UNSHALE
AEHLORS SHOALER
AEHLORT LOATHER
AEHLOSS ASSHOLE
AEHLOST LOATHES
AEHLPRS SPHERAL
AEHLPSS HAPLESS
PLASHES
AEHLPST PLASHET
AEHLPSY SHAPELY
AEHLRSS ASHLERS
HALSERS
LASHERS
SLASHER
AEHLRST HALTERS
HARSLET
LATHERS
SLATHER
THALERS
AEHLRSU HAULERS
AEHLRSV HALVERS
AEHLRSW WHALERS
AEHLRTY EARTHLY
HARTELY
HEARTLY
LATHERY
AEHLRWY WHALERY

AEHLSSS	HASSLES		
	SLASHES		
AEHLSST	HASLETS		
	HATLESS		
AEHLSSY	HAYSELS		
AEHLSTT	STEALTH		
AEHLSTW	WEALTHS		
AEHLTWY	WEALTHY		
AEHMMNS	MASHMEN		
AEHMMRS	HAMMERS		
	SHAMMER		
AEHMMSY	MAYHEMS		
AEHMNOR	MENORAH		
AEHMNOS	HOSEMAN		
AEHMNOT	NATHEMO		
AEHMNOY	HAEMONY		
AEHMNPY	NYMPHAE		
AEHMNRU	HUMANER		
AEHMNST	ANTHEMS		
	HETMANS		
AEHMOPT	APOTHEM		
AEHMPRS	HAMPERS		
AEHMPTY	EMPATHY		
AEHMRSS	MARSHES		
	MASHERS		
	SHAMERS		
	SMASHER		
AEHMRST	HAMSTER		
AEHMRTU	MAUTHER		
AEHMRTW	MAWTHER		
AEHMSSS	SMASHES		
AEHMSST	SMEATHS		
AEHMUZZ	MEZUZAH		
AEHNNTU	UNNEATH		
AEHNNWY	ANYWHEN		
AEHNOPT	PHAETON		
	PHONATE		
AEHNOPW	WANHOPE		
AEHNORS	HOARSEN		
AEHNORT	ANOTHER		
AEHNPPS	HAPPENS		
AEHNPRS	SHARPEN		
AEHNPRT	PANTHER		
AEHNPSU	UNSHAPE		
AEHNRSS	HARNESS		
AEHNRST	ANTHERS		
	HARTENS		
	THENARS		
AEHNRTU	HAUNTER		
	UNEARTH		
	UNHEART		
	URETHAN		
AEHNRTX	NARTHEX		
AEHNSSS	SNASHES		
AEHNSST	HASTENS		
	SNATHES		
	SNEATHS		
AEHNSSZ	SAZHENS		
AEHNSUY	HAUYNES		
AEHNTTW	WHATTEN		
AEHOORT	TOHEROA		
AEHORRS	HOARSER		
AEHORST	ASTHORE		
	HAROSET		
AEHORSX	HOAXERS		
AEHORUV	HAVEOUR		
AEHOSTU	ATHEOUS		
AEHPPRS	PERHAPS		
AEHPPSU	UPHEAPS		
AEHPRRS	HARPERS		

	PHRASER	AEIINTX	AXINITE
	SHARPER	AEIIPRR	PRAIRIE
AEHPRSS	PHRASES	AEIIRRV	RIVIERA
	SERAPHS		VAIRIER
	SHAPERS	AEIIRST	AIRIEST
	SPHAERS		IRISATE
	SPHEARS	AEIITTV	VITIATE
AEHPRST	SPARTHE	AEIJLNV	JAVELIN
	TEPHRAS	AEIJLRS	JAILERS
	THREAPS	AEIJLSZ	JEZAILS
AEHPRTY	THERAPY	AEIJMMR	JAMMIER
AEHPSST	SPATHES	AEIJMMS	JEMIMAS
AEHPSSW	PESHWAS	AEIJMNS	JASMINE
AEHPSTY	HYPATES	AEIJNRT	JANTIER
AEHQSSU	QUASHES		NARTJIE
AEHRRSS	RASHERS	AEIJNST	JANTIES
	SHARERS	AEIJNTU	JAUNTIE
AEHRRTU	URETHRA	AEIJRSV	JARVIES
AEHRSST	RASHEST	AEIJRZZ	JAZZIER
	SHASTER	AEIKLNO	KAOLINE
	TRASHES	AEIKLNR	LANKIER
AEHRSSV	SHAVERS	AEIKLNU	UNALIKE
AEHRSSW	HAWSERS	AEIKLOT	KEITLOA
	SWASHER	AEIKLRR	LARKIER
	WASHERS	AEIKLRS	SERKALI
AEHRSTT	HATTERS	AEIKLRV	KLAVIER
	RATHEST	AEIKLRW	WARLIKE
	SHATTER	AEIKLSS	ALSIKES
	THREATS	AEIKLST	LAKIEST
AEHRSTV	HARVEST		TALKIES
	THRAVES	AEIKMMS	MISMAKE
AEHRSTW	THAWERS	AEIKMNP	PIKEMAN
	WREATHS	AEIKMNR	MANKIER
AEHRSVW	WHARVES		RAMEKIN
AEHRSWY	WASHERY	AEIKMNS	KINEMAS
AEHRSXY	HYRAXES	AEIKMPR	RAMPIKE
AEHRTUU	HAUTEUR	AEIKMRW	MAWKIER
AEHRTWY	WREATHY	AEIKMSS	KAMISES
AEHSSST	STASHES	AEIKMST	MISTAKE
AEHSSSW	SWASHES	AEIKNRR	NARKIER
AEHSSTW	SWATHES	AEIKNRS	SNAKIER
AEHSTUX	EXHAUST	AEIKNRT	KERATIN
AEIIKNT	KAINITE	AEIKNSS	KINASES
AEIIKSS	SAIKEIS	AEIKNST	INTAKES
AEIILLT	TAILLIE	AEIKNSY	KYANISE
AEIILNN	ANILINE		YANKIES
AEIILNR	AIRLINE	AEIKNTY	KYANITE
AEIILNX	EXILIAN	AEIKNYZ	KYANIZE
AEIILRR	LAIRIER	AEIKOST	OAKIEST
AEIILRS	LAIRISE	AEIKPRR	PARKIER
	SAILIER	AEIKPRW	PAWKIER
AEIILRZ	LAIRIZE	AEIKQRU	QUAKIER
AEIILSS	LIAISES	AEIKRRS	KERRIAS
	SILESIA		SARKIER
AEIILST	LAITIES	AEIKRSS	KAISERS
AEIILTZ	TAILZIE		KARSIES
AEIIMNT	INTIMAE	AEIKRST	ARKITES
	MINIATE		KARITES
AEIIMRT	AIRTIME	AEIKRSZ	KARZIES
AEIIMST	AMITIES	AEIKSSS	ASKESIS
	ATIMIES	AEIKSTT	TAKIEST
AEIIMTT	IMITATE	AEILLMN	MANILLE
AEIINNS	ASININE	AEILLNR	RALLINE
	INSANIE	AEILLOV	ALVEOLI
AEIINQU	EQUINIA	AEILLPR	PALLIER
AEIINRR	RAINIER	AEILLPS	ILLAPSE
AEIINRS	SENARII	AEILLRR	RALLIER
AEIINRT	INERTIA	AEILLRS	RALLIES
AEIINST	ISATINE	AEILLRT	LITERAL
AEIINSX	SIXAINE		TALLIER

AEILLRU	RUELLIA		
AEILLRW	WALLIER		
AEILLSS	ALLISES		
	SALLIES		
AEILLST	TALLIES		
AEILLSW	WALLIES		
AEILLUV	ELUVIAL		
AEILLVX	VEXILLA		
AEILMMN	MAILMEN		
AEILMMS	LAMMIES		
	MELISMA		
AEILMNN	LINEMAN		
	MELANIN		
AEILMNO	MINEOLA		
AEILMNP	IMPANEL		
	MANIPLE		
AEILMNR	MARLINE		
	MINERAL		
	RAILMEN		
AEILMNS	ISLEMAN		
	MENIALS		
	SEMINAL		
AEILMNT	AILMENT		
	ALIMENT		
AEILMOR	LOAMIER		
AEILMPR	IMPEARL		
	LEMPIRA		
	PALMIER		
AEILMPS	IMPALES		
	PALMIES		
AEILMPT	IMPLATE		
	PALMIET		
AEILMRR	MARLIER		
AEILMRS	MAILERS		
	REALISM		
AEILMRT	LAMITER		
	MALTIER		
AEILMSS	AIMLESS		
	MESAILS		
	SAMIELS		
	SEISMAL		
AEILMSZ	MEZAILS		
AEILMTY	LAYTIME		
AEILNNY	INANELY		
AEILNOP	OPALINE		
AEILNOR	AILERON		
	ALERION		
	ALIENOR		
AEILNOT	ELATION		
	TOENAIL		
AEILNPR	PEARLIN		
	PLAINER		
	PRALINE		
AEILNPS	ALPINES		
	SPANIEL		
	SPLENIA		
AEILNPT	PANTILE		
AEILNPX	EXPLAIN		
AEILNQU	EQUINAL		
AEILNRS	NAILERS		
AEILNRT	ENTRAIL		
	LATRINE		
	RATLINE		
	RELIANT		
	RETINAL		
	TRENAIL		
AEILNRV	RAVELIN		
AEILNRW	LAWNIER		

```
AEILNRX RELAXIN      AEILRVY VIRELAY              MASTIER              NASTIER
AEILNRY INLAYER      AEILRWY WEARILY              MISRATE              RATINES
        NAILERY     AEILSSS LAISSES              SEMITAR              RESIANT
AEILNSS SALINES              LASSIES              SMARTIE              RETAINS
        SILANES     AEILSSU SAULIES      AEIMRSU UREMIAS              RETINAS
AEILNST EASTLIN      AEILSSV VALISES      AEIMRSW AWMRIES              RETSINA
        ELASTIN              VESSAIL      AEIMRTU MURIATE              STAINER
        ENTAILS     AEILSSW WALISES      AEIMRTW WARTIME              STARNIE
        SALIENT     AEILSTU SITULAE      AEIMSSS AMISSES              STEARIN
        SLAINTE     AEILSTV ESTIVAL      AEIMSST ASTEISM      AEINRSV AVENIRS
        STANIEL     AEILSTW WALIEST              SAMIEST              RAVINES
        TENAILS     AEILSTY TAILYES              SAMITES      AEINRTT INTREAT
AEILNSU INSULAE      AEILSTZ LAZIEST              TAMISES              ITERANT
        INULASE     AEILTVY VILAYET      AEIMSSV MASSIVE              NATTIER
AEILNSV ALEVINS      AEILUVX EXUVIAL              MAVISES              NITRATE
        VALINES     AEIMMMS MAMMIES      AEIMSSY MYIASES              TARTINE
AEILNSX ALEXINS      AEIMMNS MISNAME      AEIMSTT MATIEST              TARTINE
AEILNTU ALUNITE      AEIMMRS RAMMIES              MATTIES              TERTIAN
AEILNTV VENTAIL      AEIMMRT MARMITE      AEIMSTZ MAZIEST      AEINRTU RUINATE
AEILNUV UNALIVE      AEIMMST MISMATE              MESTIZA              TAURINE
        UNVAILE              TAMMIES      AEIMSUV AMUSIVE              URANITE
AEILNUW LAUWINE      AEIMMZZ MIZMAZE      AEIMSXX MAXIXES              URINATE
AEILNVY NAIVELY      AEIMNNT MANNITE      AEIMTYZ AZYMITE      AEINRTW TAWNIER
AEILOPR PELORIA      AEIMNOR MORAINE      AEINNNS NANNIES              TINWARE
AEILOPS LEIPOAS      AEIMNOS ANOMIES      AEINNOT ENATION      AEINRUV VAURIEN
AEILORV VARIOLE      AEIMNOU MOINEAU      AEINNPR PANNIER              UNWARIE
AEILOST ISOLATE      AEIMNRR MARINER      AEINNPT PANTINE      AEINRUZ AZURINE
AEILOTV VIOLATE      AEIMNRS MARINES              PINNATE      AEINRVV VERVAIN
AEILPPR APPERIL              REMAINS      AEINNRS INSANER      AEINRWY YAWNIER
        ARIPPLE              SEMINAR              INSNARE      AEINSSS SANSEIS
AEILPPS APPLIES              SIRNAME      AEINNRT ENTRAIN              SASINES
        LAPPIES     AEIMNRT MINARET              TRANNIE      AEINSST ENTASIS
AEILPRS PALSIER              RAIMENT      AEINNRU ANEURIN              NASTIES
        PARLIES     AEIMNRV VERMIAN      AEINNSS SIENNAS              SESTINA
AEILPRT PLAITER      AEIMNSS INSEAMS      AEINNST INANEST              TANSIES
        PLATIER              SAMISEN      AEINNSZ ENZIANS              TISANES
AEILPRV PREVAIL      AEIMNST INMATES      AEINNTT ANTIENT      AEINSSV SAVINES
AEILPSS ESPIALS              MAINEST              ANTIENT              VINASSE
        LAPISES              MANTIES      AEINOPZ EPIZOAN      AEINSTT INSTATE
        LIPASES              TAMINES      AEINORS ERASION              SATINET
        PALSIES     AEIMNTX TAXIMEN      AEINORT OTARINE      AEINSTU AUNTIES
AEILPST APLITES      AEIMNTY AMENITY      AEINOSS ANOESIS              SINUATE
        PALIEST              ANYTIME      AEINOST ATONIES      AEINSTV NAIVEST
        TALIPES     AEIMNUV MAUVEIN      AEINOSV EVASION              NATIVES
AEILPSY PAISLEY              MAUVINE      AEINOSZ AZIONES              VAINEST
AEILQTU LIQUATE      AEIMOOP IPOMOEA      AEINOXZ OXAZINE      AEINSTW AWNIEST
        TEQUILA     AEIMOPR EMPORIA      AEINPPR NAPPIER              TAWNIES
AEILRRS RAILERS      AEIMORR ARMOIRE      AEINPPS NAPPIES              WANIEST
        RERAILS     AEIMOST AMOSITE      AEINPRS RAPINES              WANTIES
AEILRRT RETIRAL              ATOMIES      AEINPRT PAINTER      AEINSTZ ZANIEST
        RETRIAL              ATOMISE              PERTAIN      AEINSVV NAVVIES
        TRAILER              OSMIATE              REPAINT      AEINSWY ANYWISE
AEILRSS AIRLESS      AEIMOTZ ATOMIZE      AEINPSS ASPINES      AEINTVY NAIVETY
        SAILERS     AEIMPRR RAMPIRE              PANSIES      AEINTXY ANXIETY
        SERAILS     AEIMPRS IMPRESA      AEINPST PANTIES      AEIOPRS SOAPIER
        SERIALS              SAMPIRE              PATINES      AEIOPSS SOAPIES
AEILRST REALIST      AEIMPRT PRIMATE              SAPIENT      AEIOPST ATOPIES
        RETAILS     AEIMPRV VAMPIRE              SPINATE              OPIATES
        SALTIER     AEIMPSS IMPASSE      AEINPTT PATIENT      AEIOQSU SEQUOIA
        SALTIRE     AEIMPST IMPASTE      AEINPTU PETUNIA      AEIORRR ARRIERO
        SLATIER              PASTIME      AEINPTY PANEITY              ROARIER
AEILRSV REVISAL      AEIMPSV IMPAVES      AEINQTU ANTIQUE      AEIORST OARIEST
AEILRSW SWALIER      AEIMPSW MAPWISE              QUINATE              OTARIES
        WAILERS     AEIMPSY PYEMIAS      AEINRRS SIERRAN      AEIORSV OVARIES
AEILRTT TERTIAL      AEIMRRR MARRIER              SNARIER      AEIOSTT OSTIATE
AEILRTU URALITE      AEIMRRS MARRIES      AEINRRT RETRAIN              TOASTIE
AEILRTW WALTIER              SIMARRE              TERRAIN      AEIOSTZ AZOTISE
AEILRTY IRATELY      AEIMRSS MASSIER              TRAINER      AEIOTZZ AZOTIZE
        REALITY     AEIMRST MAESTRI      AEINRSS ARSINES      AEIPPPR PAPPIER
AEILRVV REVIVAL              MAISTER              SARNIES      AEIPPPS PAPPIES
                                         AEINRST ANESTRI      AEIPPRS APPRISE
```

	SAPPIER	AEIRSTV	TAIVERS	AEKMMNR	MARKMEN	AELLPPS	LAPPELS
AEIPPRT	PERIAPT		VASTIER	AEKMNOS	SOKEMAN	AELLPRU	PLEURAL
AEIPPRZ	APPRIZE	AEIRSTW	WAISTER	AEKMNSU	UNMAKES	AELLPSS	SPALLES
	ZAPPIER		WAITERS	AEKMPRU	UPMAKER	AELLPST	PALLETS
AEIPPSS	PASPIES		WARIEST	AEKMPSU	UPMAKES	AELLPTU	PLUTEAL
AEIPRRS	PARRIES	AEIRSVW	WAIVERS	AEKMRRS	MARKERS	AELLPTY	PLAYLET
	PRAISER	AEIRTTT	ATTRITE		REMARKS	AELLQUY	EQUALLY
	RAPIERS		TATTIER	AEKMRSS	MASKERS	AELLRRU	ALLURER
	RASPIER		TITRATE	AEKMRST	MARKETS	AELLRST	STELLAR
	REPAIRS	AEIRTTV	TAIVERT	AEKNNRS	ENRANKS		TELLARS
AEIPRSS	ASPIRES	AEIRTTW	TAWTIER	AEKNNST	KANTENS	AELLRSU	ALLURES
	PARESIS	AEIRTTX	EXTRAIT	AEKNNTU	UNTAKEN		LAURELS
	PRAISES	AEIRTUY	AUREITY	AEKNPPR	KNAPPER	AELLRSW	WALLERS
	SPIREAS	AEIRTUZ	AZURITE	AEKNPRS	SPANKER	AELLRSY	RALLYES
AEIPRST	PARTIES	AEIRTVY	VARIETY	AEKNPSU	UNSPEAK	AELLRTY	ALERTLY
	PASTIER	AEISSST	SIESTAS	AEKNPTU	UPTAKEN		ELYTRAL
	PIASTRE		TASSIES	AEKNRRS	RANKERS	AELLSST	SALLETS
	PIRATES	AEISSSZ	ASSIZES	AEKNRSS	KRANSES		TASSELL
	PRATIES	AEISSUV	SUASIVE	AEKNRST	RANKEST	AELLSSW	LAWLESS
	TRAIPSE	AEISSUX	AUXESIS		STARKEN	AELLSTT	TALLEST
AEIPRSU	SPURIAE	AEISSVV	SAVVIES		TANKERS		TALLETS
	UPRAISE	AEISTTT	TATTIES	AEKNRSU	UNRAKES	AELLSTW	SETWALL
AEIPRSV	PARVISE	AEISTTU	SITUATE	AEKNRSW	SWANKER		SWALLET
AEIPRSW	WASPIER	AEISTTV	STATIVE		WANKERS		WALLETS
AEIPRTT	PARTITE	AEISTTW	TWAITES	AEKNRSY	YANKERS	AELLSTY	STALELY
AEIPRTV	PRIVATE	AEISTTY	SATIETY	AEKNRSZ	KRANZES	AELLSVY	VALLEYS
AEIPRTW	WIRETAP	AEISTVW	WAVIEST	AEKNRVY	KNAVERY	AELLTUU	ULULATE
AEIPRXY	PYREXIA	AEISTWX	WAXIEST	AEKNSSU	ANKUSES	AELLUVV	VALVULE
AEIPSSS	ASEPSIS	AEITTTU	ATTUITE	AEKNSWY	SWANKEY	AELMMNO	MAMELON
AEIPSST	PASTIES	AEITTTV	VITTATE	AEKORRS	ROSAKER	AELMMNT	MALTMEN
	PATSIES	AEJKMNR	JARKMEN	AEKORSS	ARKOSES	AELMMOY	MYELOMA
	TAPISES	AEJKNRS	JANKERS		SOAKERS	AELMMRS	LAMMERS
AEIPSSV	PASSIVE	AEJLNUV	JUVENAL	AEKOTTU	OUTTAKE		SLAMMER
	PAVISES	AEJLOSU	JALOUSE	AEKPPSU	UPSPAKE	AELMMRT	TRAMMEL
	SPAVIES		JEALOUS		UPSPEAK	AELMMST	STAMMEL
AEIPSSW	WASPIES	AEJLOUZ	AZULEJO	AEKPRRS	PARKERS	AELMMSY	MALMSEY
AEIPSTT	PATTIES	AEJMMRS	JAMMERS	AEKPRSS	SPARKES	AELMNOR	ALMONER
	TAPETIS	AEJMNZZ	JAZZMEN	AEKPSSY	PASSKEY		NEMORAL
AEIPSTU	TAUPIES	AEJMSST	JETSAMS	AEKPSTU	UPTAKES	AELMNOS	MELANOS
AEIPSTW	TAWPIES	AEJMSSY	JESSAMY	AEKQSSU	SQUEAKS	AELMNOT	LOMENTA
AEIPTXY	EPITAXY	AEJMSTY	MAJESTY	AEKQSUY	SQUEAKY		OMENTAL
AEIQRUV	AQUIVER	AEJNNOS	JOANNES	AEKRRST	STARKER		TELAMON
AEIQSSU	SAIQUES	AEJNORZ	ZANJERO	AEKRSST	SKATERS	AELMNPR	LAMPERN
AEIRRRT	TARRIER	AEJNSST	JESSANT		STRAKES	AELMNRU	NUMERAL
AEIRRSS	ARRISES	AEJNSSU	JAUNSES		STREAKS	AELMNST	LAMENTS
	RAISERS	AEJPRSS	JASPERS		TASKERS		MANTELS
	SIERRAS	AEJPRSY	JASPERY	AEKRSSY	KARSEYS		MANTLES
AEIRRST	ARTSIER	AEJRSVY	JARVEYS	AEKRSTY	STREAKY	AELMNSU	MENSUAL
	TARRIES	AEKKNRS	KRAKENS	AEKSSSV	KVASSES	AELMNTT	MANTLET
	TARSIER	AEKKRSY	SKREAKY	AELLMNU	LUMENAL	AELMNTU	NUTMEAL
AEIRRSV	ARRIVES		YAKKERS	AELLMRS	SMALLER	AELMOPR	PLEROMA
	VARIERS	AEKLLTU	KELLAUT	AELLMST	MALLETS	AELMOPU	AMPOULE
AEIRRTT	RATTIER	AEKLNPP	KNAPPLE	AELLMSU	MALLEUS	AELMOPY	MAYPOLE
	RETRAIT	AEKLNPR	PRANKLE	AELLMSY	MELLAYS	AELMORS	MORALES
	TARTIER	AEKLNRS	RANKLES		MESALLY	AELMORT	MOLERAT
AEIRRTW	WARTIER	AEKLNST	ANKLETS	AELLMTY	METALLY	AELMORV	REMOVAL
AEIRRTY	RETIARY		ASKLENT	AELLMWX	MAXWELL	AELMOST	MALTOSE
AEIRSSS	SASSIER		LANKEST	AELLNOP	PALLONE	AELMOTT	MATELOT
AEIRSST	SAIREST	AEKLNSW	KNAWELS	AELLNOR	LLANERO	AELMPRS	PALMERS
	SATIRES	AEKLNSY	ALKYNES	AELLNOV	NOVELLA		SAMPLER
	TIRASSE	AEKLORY	ROKELAY	AELLNOY	ALONELY	AELMPRT	TEMPLAR
AEIRSSU	SAURIES	AEKLOST	SKATOLE	AELLNPY	PENALLY		TRAMPLE
AEIRSSZ	ASSIZER	AEKLPRS	SPARKLE	AELLNRT	ENTRALL	AELMPRY	LAMPREY
AEIRSTT	ARTIEST	AEKLRRS	LARKERS	AELLNSS	ALLNESS	AELMPSS	SAMPLES
	ARTISTE	AEKLRST	STALKER	AELLNSW	ENWALLS	AELMPST	AMPLEST
	ATTIRES		TALKERS	AELLNTT	TALLENT	AELMPSU	AMPULES
	IRATEST	AEKLRSW	WALKERS	AELLNVY	VENALLY	AELMPTU	PLUMATE
	STRIATE	AEKLSST	LASKETS	AELLORS	ROSELLA	AELMRRS	MARRELS
	TASTIER		SKLATES	AELLORT	REALLOT	AELMRSS	ARMLESS
	TERTIAS	AEKLSTU	AUKLETS	AELLORV	OVERALL	AELMRST	ARMLETS

	MARTELS	AELOPST APOSTLE	AELRRSU SURREAL	SUMMATE
AELMRSU	MAULERS	PELOTAS	AELRRTT RATTLER	AEMMSTW MAWMETS
AELMRSV	MARVELS	AELOPSX EXPOSAL	AELRRTW TRAWLER	AEMNNOS MANNOSE
AELMRTT	MARTLET	AELOPTT PALETOT	AELRSST ARTLESS	AEMNNOT MONTANE
AELMSST	SAMLETS	AELOPTU OUTLEAP	LASTERS	AEMNNOU NOUMENA
AELMSTU	AMULETS	AELORRT REALTOR	SALTERS	AEMNNRS MANNERS
AELNNPR	PLANNER	RELATOR	SLATERS	AEMNNRT MANRENT
AELNNPS	PENNALS	AELORSS OARLESS	TARSELS	REMNANT
AELNNPU	UNPANEL	SOLERAS	AELRSSU SAURELS	AEMNNSW NEWSMAN
AELNNRS	ENSNARL	AELORST OESTRAL	AELRSSV SALVERS	AEMNNTU UNMEANT
	LANNERS	AELORTV LEVATOR	SERVALS	AEMNOPS MOPANES
AELNNRT	LANTERN	AELORTY ROYALET	SLAVERS	AEMNORS ENAMORS
AELNNRU	UNLEARN	AELORUU ROULEAU	VERSALS	MOANERS
AELNNST	STANNEL	AELORVY OVERLAY	AELRSSW WARSLES	OARSMEN
AELNNTU	ANNULET	AELOSSS LASSOES	AELRSSY RAYLESS	AEMNORU ENAMOUR
AELNOOS	ALSOONE	AELOSSV SALVOES	SLAYERS	NEUROMA
AELNOPT	POLENTA	AELOSSW LEASOWS	AELRSTT RATTLES	AEMNORV OVERMAN
AELNORS	ORLEANS	AELOSTV SOLVATE	SLATTER	AEMNORY ROMNEYA
AELNORU	ALEURON	AELOSTZ ZEALOTS	STARLET	AEMNOSS MONASES
AELNORV	VERONAL	AELOSUZ ZEALOUS	STARTLE	AEMNOST MANTOES
AELNOST	ETALONS	AELOSVY SAVELOY	TATLERS	AEMNOTU NOTAEUM
AELNOTV	VOLANTE	AELOTTU TOLUATE	AELRSTU SALUTER	OUTNAME
AELNPRS	PLANERS	AELOTUV OVULATE	AELRSTV TRAVELS	AEMNPSS PASSMEN
	REPLANS	AELOTVV VOLVATE	VARLETS	AEMNPST ENSTAMP
AELNPRT	PANTLER	AELPPRS LAPPERS	VESTRAL	TAPSMEN
	PLANTER	RAPPELS	AELRSTW WASTREL	AEMNPSU PNEUMAS
	REPLANT	SLAPPER	AELRSTY RAYLETS	AEMNPTU PUTAMEN
AELNPRY	PLENARY	AELPPRY REAPPLY	AELRSUV VALUERS	AEMNPTY PAYMENT
AELNPSS	NAPLESS	AELPPSS SAPPLES	AELRSVV VARVELS	AEMNRRU MANURER
AELNPST	PLANETS	AELPPST LAPPETS	AELRSVY SLAVERY	AEMNRST ARTSMEN
	PLATENS	STAPPLE	AELRSWX WRAXLES	MARTENS
AELNPSU	UPLEANS	AELPPSU APPULSE	AELRSWY LAWYERS	SARMENT
AELNPTU	UPLEANT	PAPULES	AELRSZZ RAZZLES	SMARTEN
AELNPTX	EXPLANT	UPLEAPS	AELRTTT TARTLET	AEMNRSU MANURES
AELNPTY	APLENTY	AELPPTU UPLEAPT	TATTLER	MURENAS
	PENALTY	AELPQSU PLAQUES	AELRTTU TUTELAR	SURNAME
AELNQUU	UNEQUAL	AELPRRS PARRELS	AELRTUV VAULTER	AEMNRTU TRUEMAN
AELNRRS	SNARLER	AELPRST PALTERS	AELRTWZ WALTZER	AEMNRTV VARMENT
AELNRSS	RANSELS	PLASTER	AELSSST TASSELS	AEMNSSS MESSANS
AELNRST	ANTLERS	PLATERS	AELSSTT LATESTS	AEMNSST STAMENS
	RENTALS	PSALTER	SALTEST	AEMNSSU UNSEAMS
	SALTERN	STAPLER	STALEST	AEMNSTU UNTAMES
	STERNAL	AELPRSU PERUSAL	TASLETS	UNTEAMS
AELNRSZ	RANZELS	SERPULA	AELSSTU SALUTES	AEMNSTY AMNESTY
AELNRTT	TRENTAL	AELPRSW PRAWLES	TALUSES	AEMNTWY WAYMENT
AELNRTU	NEUTRAL	AELPRSY PARLEYS	AELSSTV VESTALS	AEMOORW WOOMERA
AELNRTV	VENTRAL	PARSLEY	AELSSTW WASTELS	AEMOOST OSTEOMA
AELNRUV	UNRAVEL	PLAYERS	AELSSUV AVULSES	AEMOOSV AMOOVES
AELNSSU	SENSUAL	REPLAYS	AELSSVY SLAVEYS	VAMOOSE
	UNSEALS	SPARELY	AELSSWY WAYLESS	AEMOPPR PAMPERO
AELNSSW	AWNLESS	AELPRTT PARTLET	AELSTTT TATTLES	AEMOPSZ APOZEMS
AELNSSX	LAXNESS	PLATTER	AELSTTW WATTLES	AEMORRS REMORAS
AELNSTT	LATTENS	PRATTLE	AELSTTY STATELY	ROAMERS
	TALENTS	AELPRTY PEARTLY	STYLATE	AEMORRV OVERARM
AELNSTU	ELUANTS	PRELATY	AELSTUX LUXATES	AEMORST AMORETS
	UNLASTE	PTERYLA	AELSTWZ WALTZES	MAESTRO
AELNSTV	LEVANTS	AELPRUY EPULARY	AELSUVY SUAVELY	OMERTAS
AELNSTY	STANYEL	AELPSSS SAPLESS	AELSWZZ SWAZZLE	AEMORSU RAMEOUS
AELNSTZ	ZELANTS	AELPSST PASTELS	AELTTTW TWATTLE	AEMORSW WOMERAS
AELNSUW	UNWEALS	STAPLES	AELTTUX TEXTUAL	AEMORSX XEROMAS
AELNTUV	ENVAULT	AELPSTT PATTLES	AELTUVV VULVATE	AEMOSST OSMATES
AELOORS	AEROSOL	PELTAST	AEMMMRS MAMMERS	AEMOSSV VAMOSES
	ROSEOLA	AELPSTU PULSATE	AEMMMST MAMMETS	AEMOSTW TWASOME
AELOPPR	PROPALE	PUTEALS	AEMMNNT MOMENTA	AEMOSUZ ZAMOUSE
AELOPPX	APOPLEX	SPATULE	AEMMNTU AMENTUM	AEMOSWY SOMEWAY
AELOPRR	PREORAL	AELPUUV UPVALUE	AEMMORS MARMOSE	AEMOTTZ MOZETTA
AELOPRS	PAROLES	AELQRRU QUARREL	AEMMRRS RAMMERS	AEMPPRS MAPPERS
	REPOSAL	AELQSSU LASQUES	AEMMRST STAMMER	PAMPERS
AELOPRT	PROLATE	SQUEALS	AEMMRSY YAMMERS	AEMPPRY MAPPERY
AELOPRV	OVERLAP	AELQTUZ QUETZAL	AEMMSTU MAUMETS	AEMPRRS RAMPERS

AEMPRRT	TRAMPER
AEMPRST	EMPARTS
	STAMPER
	TAMPERS
AEMPRSV	REVAMPS
	VAMPERS
AEMPRSW	SWAMPER
AEMPRTT	TRAMPET
AEMPRTU	TEMPURA
AEMPSSU	EMPUSAS
AEMPTTT	ATTEMPT
AEMPTTU	TAPETUM
AEMQRSU	MARQUES
	MASQUER
AEMQSSU	MASQUES
	SQUAMES
AEMRRRY	REMARRY
AEMRRST	SMARTER
AEMRRSU	ARMURES
AEMRRSW	SWARMER
	WARMERS
AEMRRTU	ERRATUM
	MATURER
AEMRSST	MASTERS
	STREAMS
AEMRSSU	AMUSERS
	MASSEUR
AEMRSTT	MATTERS
	SMATTER
AEMRSTU	MATURES
	STRUMAE
AEMRSTW	WARMEST
AEMRSTY	MASTERY
	MAYSTER
	STREAMY
AEMRTTY	MATTERY
AEMRTUU	TRUMEAU
AEMSSSU	ASSUMES
AEMSSUW	WAMUSES
AEMSSYZ	ZYMASES
AEMSTTU	MUTATES
AEMSTUV	MAUVEST
AENNNOS	NONANES
AENNNPT	PENNANT
AENNOPS	PANNOSE
AENNOSS	NOSEANS
AENNOSV	NOVENAS
AENNOSY	ANYONES
AENNOTU	TONNEAU
AENNPRS	SPANNER
AENNQTU	QUANNET
AENNRST	TANNERS
AENNRSV	VANNERS
AENNRTT	ENTRANT
AENNRTV	VERNANT
AENNRTY	TANNERY
	TYRANNE
AENNSSW	WANNESS
AENNSTT	TANNEST
	TENANTS
AENNSTW	WANNEST
AENOOTZ	ENTOZOA
AENOPPR	PROPANE
AENOPRS	PERSONA
AENOPRT	OPERANT
	PRONATE
	PROTEAN
AENOPSU	POSAUNE
AENOPSV	PAVONES
AENOPSW	WEAPONS
AENORRT	ORNATER
AENORRV	OVERRAN
AENORSS	REASONS
AENORST	ATONERS
	SENATOR
	TREASON
AENORTV	VENATOR
AENORXY	ANOREXY
AENOSSS	SEASONS
AENOSST	ASTONES
AENOSTT	ATTONES
	NOTATES
AENOSTU	SOUTANE
AENOSUV	WAVESON
AENOUUV	NOUVEAU
AENPPRS	NAPPERS
	PARPENS
	PARSNEP
	SNAPPER
AENPPRT	PARPENT
AENPPRU	UNPAPER
AENPRRT	PARTNER
AENPRST	ARPENTS
	ENTRAPS
	PANTERS
	PARENTS
	PASTERN
	PERSANT
	TREPANS
AENPRSW	ENWRAPS
	PAWNERS
	SPAWNER
AENPRSZ	PANZERS
AENPRTT	PATTERN
	REPTANT
AENPRUV	PARVENU
AENPSST	APTNESS
	PATNESS
	PESANTS
AENPSTT	PATENTS
	PATTENS
AENPSTU	PEANUTS
	PESAUNT
AENPSTW	STEWPAN
AENPSTY	SYNAPTE
AENPSTZ	PEZANTS
AENQSTU	EQUANTS
AENRRSS	SERRANS
	SNARERS
AENRRST	ERRANTS
	RANTERS
AENRRSW	WARNERS
	WARRENS
AENRRTT	TRANTER
AENRRTY	TERNARY
AENRSSS	SARSENS
AENRSST	SARSNET
	TRANSES
AENRSSW	ANSWERS
	RAWNESS
AENRSSY	SARNEYS
AENRSTT	NATTERS
	RATTENS
AENRSTU	AUNTERS
	NATURES
	SAUNTER
AENRSTV	SERVANT
	TAVERNS
	VERSANT
AENRSTW	STRAWEN
	WANTERS
AENRSTY	TRAYNES
AENRSUW	UNSWEAR
	UNWARES
AENRTTU	TAUNTER
AENRTTY	NATTERY
AENRTUV	VAUNTER
AENRTUW	UNWATER
AENRUWY	UNWEARY
AENSSST	ASSENTS
	SNASTES
AENSSTU	NASUTES
	UNSEATS
AENSSTX	SEXTANS
AENSSTY	STAYNES
AENSSTZ	STANZES
AENSSWY	SAWNEYS
AENSSXY	SYNAXES
AENSTTT	ATTENTS
AENSTTU	ATTUNES
	NUTATES
	TAUTENS
	TETANUS
	UNSTATE
AENSTTX	SEXTANT
AENSTUX	UNTAXES
AENSTWY	TAWNEYS
AENTTTU	ATTUENT
AEOOPPS	PAPOOSE
AEOOPRS	OROPESA
AEOPPPS	PAPPOSE
AEOPPRS	APPOSER
AEOPPRV	APPROVE
AEOPPSS	APPOSES
AEOPQRU	OPAQUER
AEOPQSU	OPAQUES
AEOPRRT	PRAETOR
	PRORATE
AEOPRST	ESPARTO
	PROTEAS
	SEAPORT
AEOPRTT	PORTATE
AEOPRVY	OVERPAY
AEOPRWY	ROPEWAY
AEOPSSS	PSOASES
AEOPSTT	APTOTES
	TEAPOTS
AEOPSTY	TEAPOYS
AEOPSTZ	TOPAZES
AEOQRTU	EQUATOR
	QUORATE
AEOQRUV	VAQUERO
AEOQSUU	AQUEOUS
AEORRRS	ROARERS
AEORRST	ROASTER
AEORRSU	AROUSER
AEORSSS	SAROSES
	SEROSAS
AEORSSU	AROUSES
AEORSTT	ROTATES
	TOASTER
AEORSUV	AVOURES
AEORSVW	OVERSAW
AEORSVY	AVOYERS
AEORTTU	OUTRATE
AEORTUW	OUTWEAR
AEORTVX	OVERTAX
AEOSSTV	AVOSETS
AEOSTTU	OUTEATS
AEPPRRS	RAPPERS
AEPPRRT	TRAPPER
AEPPRRW	WRAPPER
AEPPRSS	APPRESS
	SAPPERS
	TAPPERS
AEPPRST	TAPPERS
AEPPRSU	PAUPERS
	UPSPEAR
AEPPRSW	SWAPPER
	WAPPERS
AEPPRSY	PREPAYS
	YAPPERS
AEPPSTT	TAPPETS
AEPPSTU	UPSTEP
AEPQRTU	PARQUET
AEPRRRS	SPARRER
AEPRRSS	PARSERS
	RASPERS
	SPARERS
	SPARRES
	SPARSER
AEPRRST	PARTERS
	PRATERS
AEPRRSU	PARURES
	UPREARS
AEPRRSW	REWRAPS
	WARPERS
AEPRRSY	PRAYERS
	RESPRAY
	SPRAYER
AEPRRTU	PARTURE
	RAPTURE
AEPRRTY	PETRARY
AEPRSSS	PASSERS
AEPRSST	PASTERS
	REPASTS
	SPAREST
AEPRSSU	PAUSERS
AEPRSSY	PESSARY
AEPRSTT	PATTERS
	SPATTER
	TAPSTER
AEPRSTU	PASTURE
	UPRATES
	UPSTARE
	UPTEARS
AEPRSTY	YAPSTER
AEPRSTZ	PATZERS
AEPRSWY	YAWPERS
AEPRSYY	SPRAYEY
AEPRTXY	PTERYAX
AEPSSTU	PETASUS
AEPSTTU	UPSTATE
AEPSZZZ	PZAZZES
AEQRRSU	SQUARER
AEQRRTU	QUARTER
AEQRSSU	SQUARES
AEQRSTU	QUARTES
AEQRSUV	QUAVERS
AEQRTTU	QUARTET
AEQRUVY	QUAVERY
AERRSST	ARRESTS
	RASTERS
	STARERS
AERRSSU	ASSURER
	RASURES
AERRSTT	RATTERS
	RESTART
	STARTER
AERRSTY	STRAYER

AERRSUZ	RAZURES	AFGGGIN	FAGGING	AFHKORY	HAYFORK	AFKLRSU	SARKFUL
AERRSWY	WARREYS	AFGGINN	FANGING	AFHKRTU	FUTHARK	AFLLMPU	PALMFUL
AERRTTY	RATTERY	AFGGOST	FAGGOTS	AFHLMRU	HARMFUL	AFLLMSU	FULLAMS
AERSSST	ASSERTS	AFGHHIS	HAGFISH	AFHLMSU	FULHAMS	AFLLNOS	ONFALLS
	TRASSES	AFGHINS	FASHING	AFHLOOS	LOOFAHS	AFLLNSU	FULLANS
AERSSSU	ASSURES	AFGHINT	HAFTING	AFHLOTY	HAYLOFT	AFLLOOY	ALOOFLY
	SARUSES	AFGHIRS	GARFISH	AFHLSTU	HATFULS	AFLLOSW	FALLOWS
AERSSSW	WRASSES	AFGHLSU	GASHFUL	AFHMOST	FATHOMS	AFLLOTU	OUTFALL
AERSSTT	ASTERTS	AFGHLTU	FLAUGHT	AFHOOPT	POOFTAH	AFLLPSU	LAPFULS
	STARETS	AFGHRTU	FRAUGHT	AFHOPTU	POUFTAH	AFLLPUY	PLAYFUL
	STATERS	AFGIIKN	FAIKING	AFHORSS	SHOFARS	AFLLUWY	AWFULLY
	TASTERS	AFGIILN	FAILING	AFIILNS	FINIALS	AFLMNOU	MOANFUL
AERSSTV	STARVES	AFGIINN	FAINING	AFIILRT	AIRLIFT	AFLMORU	FORMULA
AERSSTW	WASTERS	AFGIINR	FAIRING	AFIILRY	FAIRILY	AFLMORW	WOLFRAM
AERSSTY	ESTRAYS	AFGIINT	FIATING	AFIIMOS	MAFIOSI	AFLMOST	FLOTSAM
	STAYERS	AFGIINW	WAIFING	AFIJNNS	FINJANS	AFLMRSU	ARMFULS
	STAYRES	AFGIKLN	FLAKING	AFIKNRT	RATFINK		FULMARS
AERSSUV	VARUSES	AFGILLN	FALLING	AFIKNSU	FUNKIAS	AFLMSTU	MASTFUL
AERSSVW	SWARVES	AFGILMN	FLAMING	AFIKRSS	FRISKAS	AFLMSUU	FAMULUS
AERSSWY	SAWYERS	AFGILNO	FOALING	AFIKSUY	KUFIYAS	AFLNORT	FRONTAL
	SWAYERS		LOAFING	AFILLMS	MISFALL	AFLNOTT	FLOTANT
AERSTTT	STRETTA	AFGILNR	FLARING	AFILLNS	INFALLS	AFLNPSU	PANFULS
	TARTEST	AFGILNS	FALSING	AFILLNY	FINALLY	AFLNRTU	RUNFLAT
	TATTERS	AFGILNT	FATLING	AFILLPT	PITFALL	AFLNSTU	FLAUNTS
AERSTTU	ASTUTER	AFGILNU	GAINFUL	AFILLPU	PAILFUL	AFLNTUY	FLAUNTY
	STATURE	AFGILNW	FLAWING	AFILLRY	FRAILLY	AFLOOTW	WOOLFAT
AERSTTW	SWATTER	AFGILNY	ANGLIFY	AFILLUV	FLUVIAL	AFLORSU	FUSAROL
	TEWARTS		FLAYING		VIALFUL	AFLORUV	FLAVOUR
AERSTTY	YATTERS	AFGILRU	FIGURAL	AFILLUW	WAILFUL	AFLORWW	WARWOLF
AERSTTZ	STARETZ	AFGIMNO	FOAMING	AFILMOR	ALIFORM	AFLOSSU	FOSSULA
AERSTUU	AUTEURS	AFGIMNR	FARMING	AFILMOY	FOAMILY	AFLPRTY	FLYTRAP
AERSTUY	ESTUARY		FRAMING	AFILMPY	AMPLIFY	AFLRTUY	TRAYFUL
AERTTTY	TATTERY	AFGIMNY	MAGNIFY	AFILMSS	FALSISM	AFLSTUV	VATFULS
AERTTUV	VETTURA	AFGINNN	FANNING	AFILNPU	PAINFUL	AFLSWYY	FLYWAYS
AESSSTT	TASSETS	AFGINNW	FAWNING	AFILNSV	FLAVINS	AFMNOOT	FOOTMAN
AESSTTT	ATTESTS	AFGINNY	FAYNING	AFILNTU	FLUTINA	AFMNORT	FORMANT
AESSTTU	STATUES	AFGINRR	FARRING	AFILNTY	FAINTLY	AFMNOST	FANTOMS
AESSTTV	VASTEST	AFGINRS	PARSING	AFILQUY	QUALIFY	AFMNRSU	SURFMAN
AESSTUV	SUAVEST	AFGINRT	FARTING	AFILRRY	FRIARLY	AFMNRTU	TURFMAN
AESSTUY	EUSTASY		INGRAFT	AFILRSZ	FRAZILS	AFMOOSS	SAMFOOS
AESSVVY	SAVVEYS		RAFTING	AFILRTY	FRAILTY	AFMORST	FARMOST
AESTTTU	STATUTE	AFGINRY	FRAYING	AFILSSY	SALSIFY		FORMATS
	TAUTEST	AFGINST	FASTING	AFILSTU	FISTULA	AFMORTU	FOUMART
AESTTTW	WATTEST	AFGINTT	FATTING	AFILSTY	FALSITY	AFMOSTT	AFTMOST
AFFFGIN	FAFFING	AFGINTW	WAFTING	AFIMNRS	FIRMANS	AFMOSTU	SFUMATO
AFFGGIN	GAFFING	AFGIOTT	FAGOTTI	AFIMOOS	MAFIOSO	AFNORRW	FORWARN
AFFGINN	NAFFING	AFGIRTY	GRATIFY	AFIMORV	AVIFORM	AFNSSTU	SUNFAST
AFFGINW	WAFFING	AFGKNOP	PAKFONG	AFIMSSS	MASSIFS	AFOOPPR	APPROOF
AFFGINY	AFFYING	AFGKORT	KOFTGAR	AFIMSSV	FAVISMS	AFOORST	FOOTRAS
	YAFFING	AFGLLUY	FUGALLY	AFINNNS	FINNANS	AFOORTZ	FORZATO
AFFGSUW	GUFFAWS	AFGLNOS	FLAGONS	AFINNOR	FRANION	AFOOTWY	FOOTWAY
AFFHIKU	KUFFIAH	AFGLRYY	GRAYFLY	AFINNOS	FANIONS	AFORRSW	FARROWS
AFFHILN	HAFFLIN	AFGMNOR	FROGMAN	AFINNST	INFANTS	AFORRSY	FORRAYS
AFFHIRS	RAFFISH	AFGMORS	FOGRAMS	AFINRSU	UNFAIRS	AFORSSY	FORSAYS
AFFHIST	HAFFITS	AFGOOTT	FAGOTTO	AFINSSU	FUSAINS	AFORSTU	FAUTORS
AFFILMN	MAFFLIN	AFGORRS	FRAGORS	AFINSTU	FAUNIST		FOUTRAS
AFFILPS	PILAFFS	AFGOSTU	FUGATOS		FIAUNTS	AFORSUV	FAVOURS
AFFILSY	FALSIFY	AFHIIRS	FAIRISH		FUSTIAN	AFOSSSU	FOUSSAS
AFFIMRS	AFFIRMS	AFHIKLS	KHALIFS		INFAUST	AFOSTUU	FATUOUS
AFFIMST	MASTIFF	AFHIKRS	KHARIFS	AFIORST	FAITORS	AFPSTUW	UPWAFTS
AFFINRU	FUNFAIR	AFHIKSU	KUFIAHS	AFIORTU	FAITOUR	AGGGGIN	GAGGING
	RUFFIAN	AFHIKUY	KUFIYAH	AFIORTZ	FORZATI	AGGGHIN	HAGGING
AFFINTY	TIFFANY	AFHILLN	HALFLIN	AFIQRSU	FAQUIRS	AGGGIJN	JAGGING
AFFIORR	FURFAIR	AFHILSS	FALSISH	AFISSTT	SITFAST	AGGGILN	LAGGING
AFFIRRU	FURFAIR	AFHIMNU	HAFNIUM	AFISSTY	SATISFY	AGGGIMN	MAGGING
AFFIRST	TARIFFS	AFHINOS	FASHION	AFITTUY	FATUITY	AGGGINN	GANGING
AFFNORS	SAFFRON	AFHINTU	UNFAITH	AFJLRSU	JARFULS		NAGGING
AFFNORT	AFFRONT	AFHISST	FASTISH	AFKLNRY	FRANKLY	AGGGINR	RAGGING
AFFRSST	STRAFFS	AFHISTT	FATTISH	AFKLNTU	TANKFUL	AGGGINS	SAGGING
				AFKLOWY	FOLKWAY	AGGGINT	TAGGING

AGGGINU	GAUGING	AGHHIWY	HIGHWAY	AGHLOOS	GASOHOL		JIGSAWN
AGGGINW	WAGGING	AGHHOSW	HOGWASH	AGHLOSU	GOULASH	AGIJNZZ	JAZZING
AGGGINZ	ZAGGING	AGHHTUY	HAUGHTY	AGHLSTU	GALUTHS	AGIJSSW	JIGSAWS
AGGHHIS	HAGGISH	AGHIILN	HAILING	AGHLSTY	GHASTLY	AGIKKNY	YAKKING
AGGHIIL	GHILGAI	AGHIINN	HAINING	AGHNNSU	UNHANGS	AGIKLNN	LANKING
AGGHIMN	GINGHAM	AGHIINR	HAIRING	AGHNOTU	HANGOUT	AGIKLNO	OAKLING
AGGHINN	HANGING	AGHIJRS	JAGHIRS	AGHNPSU	UPHANGS	AGIKLNR	LARKING
AGGHINS	GASHING	AGHIKNN	HANKING	AGHNRST	THRANGS	AGIKLNS	SLAKING
AGGHISW	WAGGISH	AGHIKNR	HARKING	AGHNRSU	NURHAGS	AGIKLNT	TALKING
AGGIIJJ	JIGAJIG	AGHIKNS	SHAKING	AGHNRUY	AHUNGRY	AGIKLNW	WALKING
AGGIILS	GILGAIS	AGHIKNW	HAWKING	AGHNSTU	NAUGHTS	AGIKMNR	MARKING
AGGIIMN	IMAGING	AGHIKSU	KIAUGHS	AGHNSUY	GUNYAHS	AGIKMNS	MAKINGS
AGGIINN	GAINING	AGHILLN	HALLING	AGHNTUY	NAUGHTY		MASKING
AGGIJJO	JIGAJOG	AGHILNO	HALOING	AGHOQSU	QUAHOGS	AGIKNNR	NARKING
AGGIKNW	GAWKING	AGHILNR	HARLING	AGHPTUY	PAUGHTY		RANKING
AGGILLN	GALLING	AGHILNS	HALSING	AGHRRSU	GURRAHS	AGIKNNS	SNAKING
	GINGALL		LASHING	AGHRSTY	GYTRASH	AGIKNNT	KANTING
AGGILNN	ANGLING		SHALING	AGHSTUW	WAUGHTS		TANKING
AGGILNO	GAOLING	AGHILNT	HALTING	AGIIJLN	JAILING	AGIKNNU	UNAKING
	GOALING		LATHING	AGIIKLN	LAIKING	AGIKNNW	WANKING
AGGILNR	GLARING	AGHILNU	HAULING	AGIIKLT	GLAIKIT	AGIKNNY	YANKING
AGGILNS	GINGALS	AGHILNV	HALVING	AGIIKNP	PAIKING	AGIKNOS	SOAKING
	LAGGINS	AGHILNW	WHALING	AGIIKNR	RAIKING	AGIKNOY	KAYOING
AGGILNZ	GLAZING	AGHILRS	LARGISH	AGIILMN	MAILING		OKAYING
AGGILOS	LOGGIAS	AGHILRT	ALRIGHT	AGIILNN	ALINING	AGIKNPR	PARKING
AGGIMMN	GAMMING	AGHILST	ALIGHTS		NAILING	AGIKNQU	QUAKING
AGGIMNS	GAMINGS	AGHIMMN	HAMMING	AGIILNR	GLAIRIN	AGIKNRS	RAKINGS
AGGIMNU	GAUMING	AGHIMNR	HARMING		LAIRING		SARKING
AGGINNP	PANGING	AGHIMNS	MASHING		RAILING	AGIKNRT	KARTING
AGGINNR	RANGING		SHAMING	AGIILNS	AISLING	AGIKNSS	GASKINS
AGGINNT	GANTING	AGHIMNW	HAWMING		NILGAIS	AGIKNST	SKATING
	TANGING	AGHIMPS	GAMPISH		SAILING		STAKING
AGGINNW	GNAWING	AGHINNT	TANGHIN	AGIILNT	TAILING		TAKINGS
AGGINPP	GAPPING	AGHINOR	HOARING	AGIILNV	VAILING		TASKING
AGGINPR	GRAPING	AGHINOX	HOAXING	AGIILNW	WAILING	AGIKNSW	WAKINGS
	PARGING	AGHINPP	HAPPING	AGIILOV	VILIAGO	AGIKNUW	WAUKING
AGGINPS	GAPINGS	AGHINPR	HARPING	AGIILPT	PIGTAIL	AGILLLN	LALLING
	GASPING	AGHINPS	HASPING	AGIILTY	AGILITY	AGILLMN	MALLING
	PAGINGS		PASHING	AGIIMMN	MAIMING	AGILLMU	GALLIUM
AGGINPU	GAUPING		PHASING	AGIIMMS	IMAGISM	AGILLNP	PALLING
AGGINPW	GAWPING		SHAPING	AGIIMMN	MAINING	AGILLNU	LINGUAL
AGGINRR	GARRING	AGHINPT	PATHING	AGIIMOR	ORIGAMI		LINGULA
AGGINRS	SIRGANG	AGHINRS	GARNISH	AGIIMST	IMAGIST	AGILLNW	WALLING
AGGINRT	GRATING		RASHING	AGIINNP	PAINING	AGILLNY	ALLYING
	TARGING		SHARING	AGIINNR	AIRNING	AGILLOR	GORILLA
AGGINRU	ARGUING	AGHINRU	NURAGHI		INGRAIN	AGILLOT	GALLIOT
AGGINRV	GRAVING	AGHINSS	SASHING		RAINING	AGILLRU	LIGULAR
AGGINRY	GRAYING	AGHINST	HASTING	AGIINNS	SAINING	AGILLSU	LIGULAS
AGGINRZ	GRAZING		TASHING	AGIINNW	WAINING		LUGSAIL
AGGINSS	GASSING	AGHINSU	ANGUISH	AGIINPR	PAIRING	AGILMMN	LAMMING
AGGINST	GASTING		HAUSING	AGIINRS	AIRINGS	AGILMMS	GIMMALS
	GATINGS	AGHINSV	HAVINGS		ARISING	AGILMNO	LOAMING
	STAGING		SHAVING		RAGINIS	AGILMNP	LAMPING
AGGINSW	SWAGING	AGHINSW	HAWSING		RAISING		PALMING
AGGINUV	VAGUING		SHAWING		SAIRING	AGILMNR	MARLING
AGGIORS	GORGIAS		WASHING	AGIINRT	AIRTING	AGILMNS	LINGAMS
AGGISWW	WIGWAGS	AGHINSY	HAYINGS		RAITING		MALIGNS
AGGISZZ	ZIGZAGS	AGHINSZ	HAZINGS	AGIINSV	AVISING	AGILMNT	MALTING
AGGLOST	LOGGATS	AGHINTT	HATTING		VISAING	AGILMNU	MAULING
AGGMNOS	MOGGANS		TATHING	AGIINTW	WAITING	AGILMOS	GLIOMAS
AGGMORR	GROGRAM	AGHIOST	GOATISH	AGIINTX	TAXIING	AGILMPS	MAGILPS
AGGMOST	MAGGOTS	AGHIPSW	PIGWASH	AGINNVV	VIVAING	AGILMPU	PLAGIUM
AGGMOTY	MAGGOTY	AGHIQSU	QUAIGHS	AGIINVW	WAIVING	AGILNNO	LOANING
AGGNOSW	WAGGONS	AGHIRRS	GHARRIS	AGIINVZ	AVIZING	AGILNNP	PLANING
AGGNOSX	OXGANGS	AGHIRST	GRAITHS	AGIJLNS	JINGALS	AGILNNR	LARNING
AGGNPSU	UPGANGS	AGHIRSU	GUARISH	AGIJMMN	JAMMING	AGILNNS	LINSANG
AGGNRSU	NUGGARS	AGHKOSW	GOSHAWK	AGIJNPP	JAPPING	AGILNNT	TANLING
AGGPRSY	PYGARGS	AGHLMPU	GALUMPH	AGIJNPU	JAUPING	AGILNOP	GALOPIN
AGHHIMN	HIGHMAN	AGHLNUY	NYLGHAU	AGIJNRR	JARRING	AGILNOT	ANTILOG
AGGHINS	HASHING			AGIJNSW	JAWINGS	AGILNOV	LOAVING

AGILNPP	LAPPING	AGIMORU	GOURAMI
	PALPING	AGIMOSY	ISOGAMY
AGILNPR	PARLING	AGIMRRT	TRIGRAM
AGILNPS	LAPSING	AGIMRSU	GURAMIS
	PALINGS	AGIMRTY	TRIGAMY
	SAPLING	AGIMSST	STIGMAS
AGILNPT	PLATING	AGIMSWW	WIGWAMS
AGILNPW	LAPWING	AGINNNP	PANNING
AGILNPY	PLAYING	AGINNNT	TANNING
AGILNRT	RATLING	AGINNNV	VANNING
AGILNRW	WARLING	AGINNNW	WANNING
AGILNRY	ANGRILY	AGINNOS	GANOINS
	NARGILY	AGINNOT	ATONING
	RAYLING	AGINNPP	NAPPING
AGILNSS	LASINGS	AGINNPS	SPANING
	SIGNALS	AGINNPT	PANTING
AGILNST	ANGLIST	AGINNPW	PAWNING
	LASTING	AGINNRS	SNARING
	SALTING	AGINNRT	RANTING
	SLATING	AGINNRW	WARNING
	STALING	AGINNRY	YARNING
AGILNSU	LINGUAS	AGINNST	ANTINGS
	NILGAUS		STANING
	SALUING	AGINNSU	GUANINS
AGILNSV	SALVING	AGINNSW	AWNINGS
	SLAVING		WANINGS
	VALSING	AGINNTW	WANTING
AGILNSW	LAWINGS	AGINNWY	YAWNING
	SWALING	AGINNWZ	WANZING
AGILNSY	LAYINGS	AGINNYZ	ZANYING
	SLAYING	AGINOOO	OOGONIA
AGILNTY	GIANTLY	AGINOPS	SOAPING
AGILNUV	VALUING	AGINORR	ROARING
AGILNUW	WAULING	AGINORS	IGNAROS
AGILNVV	VALVING		ORIGANS
AGILNWW	WAWLING		SIGNORA
AGILNWY	YAWLING		SOARING
AGILOPT	GALIPOT	AGINORT	ORATING
AGILORS	GIRASOL		ROATING
	GLORIAS	AGINOSS	SAGOINS
AGILOST	GALIOTS	AGINOST	AGONIST
	SALIGOT		GITANOS
AGILRSS	SLAIRGS	AGINOSU	SAGOUIN
AGILSTY	STAGILY	AGINOTV	OVATING
AGIMMNR	RAMMING	AGINOTZ	TOAZING
AGIMMSS	MAGISMS	AGINOVW	AVOWING
AGIMNNN	MANNING	AGINPPP	PAPPING
AGIMNNO	MOANING	AGINPPR	RAPPING
AGIMNNR	RINGMAN	AGINPPS	SAPPING
AGIMNNS	NAMINGS	AGINPPT	TAPPING
AGIMNOR	ROAMING	AGINPPW	WAPPING
AGIMNOT	MOATING	AGINPPY	YAPPING
AGIMNOV	AMOVING	AGINPPZ	ZAPPING
AGIMNPP	MAPPING	AGINPRS	PARINGS
AGIMNPR	RAMPING		PARSING
AGIMNPT	TAMPING		RASPING
AGIMNPV	VAMPING		SPARING
AGIMNRR	MARRING	AGINPRT	PARTING
AGIMNRS	MARGINS		PRATING
AGIMNRT	MARTING		TRAPING
	MIGRANT	AGINPRW	WARPING
AGIMNRW	WARMING	AGINPRY	PRAYING
AGIMNRY	MYRINGA	AGINPSS	PASSING
AGIMNSS	MASSING		SPAINGS
AGIMNST	MASTING	AGINPST	PASTING
	TAMINGS	AGINPSU	PAUSING
AGIMNSU	AMUSING	AGINPSV	PAVINGS
AGIMNSY	MAYINGS	AGINPSY	PAYINGS
AGIMNTT	MATTING	AGINPTT	PATTING
AGIMORS	ISOGRAM		

AGINPWY	YAWPING	AGLLOSS	GLOSSAL
AGINRRT	TARRING	AGLLOSW	GALLOWS
AGINRRW	WARRING	AGLLOTT	GLOTTAL
AGINRST	GASTRIN	AGLLRYY	GYRALLY
	RATINGS	AGLMMSY	GYMMALS
	STARING	AGLMOPY	POLYGAM
AGINRSV	RAVINGS	AGLMORS	GLAMORS
AGINRSW	RAWINGS	AGLMORU	GLAMOUR
AGINRSY	SIGNARY	AGLNNOS	LONGANS
	SYRINGA	AGLNOOS	LAGOONS
AGINRTT	RATTING	AGLNORU	LANGUOR
AGINRTY	GIANTRY	AGLNOSS	SLOGANS
AGINRUW	WAURING	AGLNOST	ALONGST
AGINRVY	VARYING	AGLNOSU	LANUGOS
AGINRWY	RINGWAY	AGLNPSY	SPANGLY
AGINRZZ	RAZZING	AGLNPUY	GUNPLAY
AGINSSS	ASSIGNS	AGLNRSU	LANGURS
	SASSING	AGLNTUY	GAUNTLY
AGINSSU	SAGUINS	AGLOOPY	APOLOGY
AGINSSV	SAVINGS	AGLOOST	GALOOTS
AGINSSW	SAWINGS	AGLOSSS	GLOSSAS
AGINSSY	SAYINGS	AGLOSUV	VALGOUS
AGINSTT	STATING	AGLRSSU	GUSLARS
	TASTING	AGLRSUU	ARGULUS
AGINSTU	SAUTING	AGLRSUV	VULGARS
AGINSTV	STAVING	AGMMNOS	GAMMONS
AGINSTW	STAWING	AGMMNSU	MAGNUMS
	TAWINGS	AGMMORY	MYOGRAM
	WASTING	AGMNNOS	SONGMAN
AGINSTX	TAXINGS	AGMNNOW	GOWNMAN
AGINSTY	STAYING	AGMNORU	ORGANUM
AGINSVW	WAVINGS	AGMNOST	AMONGST
AGINSWX	WAXINGS	AGMNSSU	MUSANGS
AGINSWY	SWAYING	AGMNSTU	MUSTANG
AGINTTT	TATTING	AGMNSTY	GYMNAST
AGINTTU	TATUING	AGMNSYY	SYNGAMY
	TAUTING	AGMOOYZ	ZOOGAMY
AGINTTV	VATTING	AGMOPRR	PROGRAM
AGINTTW	TAWTING	AGMOPRU	GOPURAM
AGINTUV	VAUTING	AGMORRW	RAGWORM
AGINTVW	VAWTING	AGMORSS	ORGASMS
AGINTXY	TAXYING	AGMORSY	MORGAYS
AGINTYZ	TZIGANY	AGMOSYZ	ZYGOMAS
AGINVYZ	AVYZING	AGMPRSU	GRAMPUS
AGINWWX	WAXWING	AGMPSUZ	GAZUMPS
AGIORST	AGISTOR	AGMRSSU	GRASSUM
	ORGIAST	AGNNNOO	NONAGON
AGIORSU	GIAOURS	AGNNOOR	ORGANON
AGIORSV	VIRAGOS	AGNNOST	TONNAGS
AGIOSTU	AGOUTIS	AGNNSTU	TANGUNS
AGIRSTU	GUITARS	AGNNSUW	WANGUNS
AGIRTVY	GRAVITY	AGNOOSZ	GAZOONS
AGISTTW	WITGATS	AGNOQSU	QUANGOS
AGISTUV	VAGITUS	AGNORRS	GARRONS
AGJLRUU	JUGULAR	AGNORRT	GRANTOR
AGJNOOR	JARGOON	AGNORSS	SARONGS
AGJNORS	JARGONS	AGNOSSS	GOSSANS
AGKLNOS	KALONGS	AGNOSST	SONTAGS
AGKLOOS	KAGOOLS	AGNOSTU	NOUGATS
AGKLOST	KGOTLAS	AGNOSZZ	GOZZANS
AGKLOSU	KAGOULS	AGNRSSU	SUNGARS
AGKMNOP	KAMPONG	AGNRTUY	GAUNTRY
AGKNOPT	PAKTONG	AGOPRSU	GOPURAS
AGKNRSU	KURGANS	AGORRST	GARROTS
AGKORRW	RAGWORK	AGORRTW	RAGWORT
AGLLNOO	GALLOON	AGORSTU	RAGOUTS
AGLLNOS	GALLONS	AGOSTTU	TAUTOGS
	GOLLANS	AGOSUYZ	AZYGOUS
AGLLOPS	GALLOPS	AGSSTUU	AUGUSTS
AGLLORS	GOLLARS	AHHHISS	HASHISH

AHHIJRS HIJRAHS	AHIMPSW WAMPISH	AHLMNSY HYMNALS	AIIILMT MILITIA
AHHIKSS SHAIKHS	AHIMRSS MAHSIRS	AHLMNUY HUMANLY	AIIILNT INITIAL
AHHIKSW HAWKISH	AHIMRST THAIRMS	AHLMOOS MOOLAHS	AIIIMRS SAIMIRI
AHHIMNU HAHNIUM	THIRAMS	AHLMORU HUMORAL	AIIKKSW WAKIKIS
AHHIPRS RHAPHIS	THRIMSA	AHLMSUU HAMULUS	AIIKMMS SKIMMIA
AHHISTT SHITTAH	AHIMTUZ AZIMUTH	AHLNOPR ALPHORN	AIIKMNN MANIKIN
AHHKOOS HOOKAHS	AHIMTVZ MITZVAH	AHLNORT ALTHORN	AIIKRTT TRAIKIT
AHHLRSY HARSHLY	AHINNSW WANNISH	AHLORST HARLOTS	AIILLLP LAPILLI
AHHOORS HOORAHS	AHINNTX XANTHIN	AHLOSST SHALOTS	AIILLMN LIMINAL
AHHOPRS SHOPHAR	AHINORT ORTHIAN	AHLOSTU OUTLASH	AIILLMS LIMAILS
AHHRRSU HURRAHS	AHINOTZ HOATZIN	AHLOTUU OUTHAUL	AIILLNV VILLAIN
AHIIKRS SHIKARI	AHINPST HATPINS	AHLPRSY SHARPLY	AIILLQU QUILLAI
AHIILPS SILPHIA	AHINRSS ARSHINS	AHLPRUY HYPURAL	AIILMMN MINIMAL
AHIILST LITHIAS	SHAIRNS	AHLPSSY SPLASHY	AIILMNO MONILIA
AHIIMNT THIAMIN	AHINRST TARNISH	AHMMMOT MAMMOTH	AIILMRS SIMILAR
AHIIMSS SASHIMI	AHINRSU UNHAIRS	AHMMMUU HUMMAUM	AIILMRT MILITAR
AHIINPR HAIRPIN	AHINRSV VARNISH	AHMNNSU NUMNAHS	AIILMRY MILIARY
AHIINST TAHINIS	AHINRTY RHYTINA	AHMNNTU MANHUNT	AIILNOS LIAISON
AHIINTU HUITAIN	AHINSTU INHAUST	AHMNNUU UNHUMAN	AIILNPT PINTAIL
AHIIPRS AIRSHIP	AHIOPSS SOPHIAS	AHMNOPS SHOPMAN	AIILNPU NAUPLII
AHIKLRS LARKISH	AHIOPXY HYPOXIA	AHMNOPT PHANTOM	AIILNTU NAUTILI
AHIKLST KHILATS	AHIORUV HAVIOUR	AHMNORY HARMONY	AIILNTY ANILITY
AHIKLSY SHAKILY	AHIPRST HARPIST	AHMNOSS HANSOMS	AIILOPP PAPILIO
AHIKMNS KHAMSIN	AHIPRSU RUPIAHS	AHMNOSW SHOWMAN	AIILORV RAVIOLI
AHIKMRS KASHMIR	AHIPRSW WARSHIP	AHMNRYY HYMNARY	AIILQSU SILIQUA
AHIKMSW MAWKISH	AHIPSSW WASPISH	AHMOOPS OOMPAHS	AIILRTV TRIVIAL
AHIKNSS SNAKISH	AHIRRSS SHIRRAS	SHAMPOO	VITRAIL
AHIKNSV KNAVISH	SIRRAHS	AHMOOSS SAMSHOO	AIIMMNS ANIMISM
AHIKOSW KOWHAIS	AHIRRST STIRRAH	AHMORRU MORRHUA	AIIMMNX MAXIMIN
AHIKPRS PARKISH	AHIRSST HAIRSTS	AHMORST HARMOST	AIIMMSS MISAIMS
AHIKRSS SHIKARS	AHIRSTT ATHIRST	AHMOSSY SHAMOYS	AIIMNOR AMORINI
AHIKSSS SHIKSAS	RATTISH	AHMOSTU MAHOUTS	AIIMNPS PAINIMS
AHIKSST SKAITHS	TARTISH	AHMOSWY HAYMOWS	PIANISM
AHILLNO HALLION	AHIRSTW TRISHAW	AHMOTTZ MATZOTH	AIIMNPT IMPAINT
AHILLNP PHALLIN	WRAITHS	AHMRRSU MURRHAS	TIMPANI
AHILLRT ATHRILL	AHISSTT STAITHS	AHMRSTW WARMTHS	AIIMNRT MARTINI
AHILLSS SHALLIS	AHISSTU SHIATSU	AHMRSTY THRYMSA	AIIMNSS SIMIANS
AHILLSZ ZILLAHS	THIASUS	AHMSSSU SAMSHUS	AIIMNST ANIMIST
AHILLTT TALLITH	AHISSTW WHATSIS	AHNOOPR HARPOON	AIIMNTT IMITANT
AHILMMS MASHLIM	AHISTTW WHATSIT	AHNOPRS ORPHANS	AIIMNTU MINUTIA
AHILMMY HAMMILY	AHITTWW WHITTAW	AHNORSS SHORANS	AIIMNTV VITAMIN
AHILMNS MASHLIN	AHJOOPS POOJAHS	AHNORSX SAXHORN	AIIMPRS IMPAIRS
AHILMOS HOLMIAS	AHKLOOS KOOLAHS	AHNOTTW WHATNOT	AIIMPSS SIMPAIS
AHILMOT HALIMOT	AHKLPSU PULKHAS	AHNPPUU PUPUNHA	AIIMRST SIMITAR
AHILMSU ALUMISH	AHKMNSU KHANUMS	AHNPPUY UNHAPPY	AIIMSSY MYIASIS
AHILNPS PLANISH	AHKMORR MARKHOR	AHNPRXY PHARYNX	AIINNOP PIANINO
AHILNRT INTHRAL	AHKMOSW MOHAWKS	AHNPSSU UNHASPS	AIINNSZ ZINNIAS
AHILNSY LINHAYS	AHKMRTU MUKHTAR	AHNSSTU SUNHATS	AIINNTY INANITY
AHILORY HOARILY	AHKNPSU PUNKAHS	AHNSTUW UNTHAWS	AIINOPS SINOPIA
AHILPPS SHIPLAP	AHKRSST SKARTHS	AHNSTUY UNHASTY	AIINOTT NOTITIA
AHILPPY HAPPILY	AHKRSTU KHURTAS	AHOORSY HOORAYS	AIINPRS ASPIRIN
AHILPSY APISHLY	AHLLMOS MOLLAHS	AHOPRTY ATROPHY	AIINPST PIANIST
AHILSST SALTISH	OLLAMHS	AHOPTTW TOWPATH	AIINRSS RAISINS
TAHSILS	AHLLMSU MULLAHS	AHORRSW HARROWS	AIINRST INTARSI
AHILSSV SLAVISH	AHLLNOS SHALLON	AHORSTT THROATS	AIINRTV VITRAIN
AHILSTU HALITUS	AHLLNOY HALLYON	AHORSTU AUTHORS	AIINSST ISATINS
THULIAS	AHLLNSU NULLAHS	AHORSTW WROATHS	AIINSTT TITIANS
AHILSTY HASTILY	AHLLOOS HALLOOS	AHORTTY THROATY	AIIPRST PIARIST
AHIMMRS RAMMISH	HOLLOAS	AHPRRTY PHRATRY	AIIPSTW WAPITIS
AHIMNNS MANNISH	AHLLOPS SHALLOP	AHPRSST SPARTHS	AIIPTTU PITUITA
AHIMNNU INHUMAN	AHLLOST SHALLOT	AHPSXYY ASPHYXY	AIJJMMS JIMJAMS
AHIMNPS SHIPMAN	AHLLOSW HALLOWS	AHQQSUY SQUASHY	AIJLORS JAILORS
AHIMNRS HARMINS	SHALLOW	AHRRSUY HURRAYS	AIJLYZZ JAZZILY
AHIMOPR MORPHIA	AHLLOTY LOATHLY	AHRSSSU HUSSARS	AIJNORT JANITOR
AHIMORS MOHAIRS	AHLLPSU PHALLUS	AHRSSTT STRATHS	AIJORSW JOWARIS
AHIMPSS MISHAPS	AHLLPYY APHYLLY	AHRSSTW SWARTHS	AIJPSTU JUPATIS
PASHIMS	AHLLRST THRALLS	AHRSTTW THWARTS	AIKKSUZ ZAKUSKI
AHIMPST MISHAPT	AHLLSTU THALLUS	AHRSTWY SWARTHY	AIKLMMN MILKMAN
AHIMPSV VAMPISH	AHLMMSU MASHLUM	AHRTUWY THRUWAY	AIKLMNN LINKMAN
	AHLMNPY NYMPHAL	AHSSSTU TUSSAHS	AIKLMNS MALKINS

AIKLMPU	LAMPUKI	AILNNPU	PINNULA	AILSTUW	LAWSUIT	AINNSTU	UNSAINT
AIKLMSU	KALIUMS	AILNNSU	UNNAILS	AILTTTY	TATTILY	AINNTUY	ANNUITY
AIKLNOS	KAOLINS		UNSLAIN	AIMMMSU	MUMMIAS	AINOOPR	PRONAOI
AIKLNSY	SNAKILY	AILNOPY	POLYNIA	AIMMMUX	MAXIMUM	AINOORR	ORARION
AIKLPWY	PAWKILY	AILNOSS	SIALONS	AIMMNTU	MANUMIT	AINOORT	ORATION
AIKLRTT	TITLARK	AILNOST	TALIONS	AIMMORS	AMORISM	AINOOTV	OVATION
AIKLSSU	SALUKIS	AILNOTU	OUTLAIN	AIMMOSS	MIMOSAS	AINOPPT	APPOINT
AIKLSSY	SKYSAIL	AILNPRW	PRAWLIN	AIMMOST	ATOMISM	AINOPRS	PARISON
AIKMMSS	IMMASKS	AILNPST	PLAINTS	AIMNNOS	MANSION		SOPRANI
AIKMNNS	KINSMAN	AILNPSX	SALPINX		ONANISM	AINOPRT	ATROPIN
AIKMNSS	KAMSINS	AILNPTU	NUPTIAL	AIMNNSS	NANISMS	AINOPSS	PASSION
AIKMNSW	MAWKINS		PATULIN	AIMNNSY	MINYANS	AINOPTU	OPUNTIA
AIKMOOS	OOMIAKS		UNPLAIT	AIMNOOR	AMORINO		UTOPIAN
AIKMPRS	IMPARKS	AILNPTY	INAPTLY	AIMNOPR	RAMPION	AINOQSU	QUINOAS
AIKMRSU	KUMARIS		PTYALIN	AIMNOPT	MAINTOP	AINORST	AROINTS
AIKNNNS	NANKINS	AILNQTU	QUINTAL		TAMPION		RATIONS
AIKNNPS	NAPKINS	AILNRST	RATLINS		TIMPANO	AINORSW	WARISON
AIKNOST	KATIONS	AILNRSU	INSULAR	AIMNORS	MAINORS	AINORTX	TRIAXON
AIKNPRS	KIRPANS		URINALS	AIMNORT	TORMINA	AINOSSU	SANIOUS
	PARKINS	AILNRTT	RATTLIN	AIMNORU	MAINOUR		SUASION
AIKNPSS	PANISKS	AILNSST	INSTALS	AIMNOST	MANITOS	AINOSTT	STATION
AIKORST	TROIKAS	AILNSSU	INSULAS		STAMNOI	AINOSUX	ANXIOUS
AIKRRSS	SIRKARS	AILNSSV	SILVANS	AIMNOTU	MANITOU	AINOSVY	SYNOVIA
AIKRSST	STRAIKS	AILNSTU	UNALIST		TINAMOU	AINPPRS	PARSNIP
AILLMNU	LUMINAL	AILNSTY	NASTILY	AIMNPSW	IMPAWNS	AINPQTU	PIQUANT
AILLMOT	MAILLOT		SAINTLY	AIMNPSY	PAYNIMS	AINPRSS	SPINARS
AILLMPU	PALLIUM	AILNSUV	UNVAILS	AIMNPTY	TYMPANI		SPRAINS
AILLNNO	LANOLIN	AILNTTY	NATTILY	AIMNRRU	MURRAIN	AINPRST	SPIRANT
AILLNOP	PAILLON	AILNTUV	UNVITAL	AIMNRSU	URANISM		SPRAINT
AILLNPY	PLAINLY	AILOORS	OORIALS	AIMNRTU	NATRIUM	AINPRSU	PRUINAS
AILLNST	INSTALL	AILOORW	WOORALI	AIMNRTV	VARMINT	AINPRSW	INWRAPS
AILLNSV	VILLANS	AILOPST	APOSTIL	AIMNRUU	URANIUM	AINPRTU	PURITAN
AILLNSW	INWALLS		TOPSAIL	AIMNSTT	MATTINS		UPTRAIN
AILLNVY	VILLANY	AILOPSY	SOAPILY	AIMNSTU	TSUNAMI	AINPSST	PTISANS
AILLPRS	PILLARS	AILOPTT	TALIPOT	AIMNSUV	MAUVINS	AINPSSV	SPAVINS
AILLPRU	PILULAR	AILOPTV	PIVOTAL	AIMNSYZ	ZANYISM	AINQRST	QINTARS
AILLPSU	PILLAUS	AILOQTU	ALIQUOT	AIMOPST	IMPASTO	AINQRUY	QUINARY
	PILULAS	AILORSS	SAILORS	AIMOPSY	MYOPIAS	AINQSTU	ASQUINT
AILLPUV	PLUVIAL	AILORST	TAILORS	AIMORRU	ORARIUM		QUINTAS
AILLRSU	ARILLUS	AILORSU	OURALIS	AIMORST	AMORIST	AINRRTY	TRINARY
AILLSTY	SALTILY	AILORUW	WOURALI	AIMORUZ	ZOARIUM	AINRRUY	URINARY
AILLTVY	VITALLY	AILORUX	UXORIAL	AIMOSTT	ATOMIST	AINRSST	SANTIRS
AILLTWW	WITWALL	AILORVY	OLIVARY	AIMPPSS	PAPISMS		STRAINS
AILMMOR	IMMORAL	AILOSSS	ASSOILS	AIMPPST	MAPPIST	AINRSTT	STRAINT
AILMMSY	MYALISM	AILOSTU	OUTSAIL	AIMPRRY	PRIMARY		TRANSIT
AILMMUU	ALUMIUM	AILOSTX	OXTAILS	AIMPRST	ARMPITS	AINRSTU	NUTRIAS
AILMNNO	NOMINAL	AILPRSS	SPIRALS		IMPARTS	AINRTUY	UNITARY
AILMNOP	LAMPION	AILPRSU	PARULIS	AIMPRSY	PYRAMIS	AINSSTT	TANISTS
AILMNOS	MALISON		UPRISAL	AIMQRSU	MARQUIS	AINSSTU	ISSUANT
	MONIALS	AILPRSY	PYRALIS	AIMRSST	TSARISM		SUSTAIN
	SOMNIAL	AILPSST	PASTILS	AIMRSTY	MAISTRY	AINSSXY	SYNAXIS
AILMNOY	ALIMONY		SPITALS		SYMITAR	AINTTVY	TANTIVY
AILMNPS	PLASMIN	AILPSTU	TIPULAS	AIMSSSY	MISSAYS	AIOORSS	ARIOSOS
AILMNPT	IMPLANT	AILPSWY	SLIPWAY	AIMSSTT	STATISM	AIOPRRT	AIRPORT
AILMNRS	MARLINS	AILQSSU	SQUAILS	AIMSSTU	AUTISMS		PARITOR
AILMNRU	MURLAIN	AILQTTU	QUITTAL	AINNNST	TANNINS	AIOPRST	AIRSTOP
AILMNSS	MASLINS	AILQTUY	QUALITY	AINNOPS	SAPONIN		PAROTIS
AILMOPT	OPTIMAL	AILRRVY	RIVALRY	AINNOSS	NASIONS	AIOPRSV	PAVIORS
AILMOST	SOMITAL	AILRSTT	STARLIT	AINNOST	ANOINTS	AIOPRTT	PATRIOT
AILMPRS	IMPARLS	AILRSTU	RITUALS		NATIONS	AIOPRTY	TOPIARY
AILMPRU	PRIMULA		TRISULA		ONANIST	AIOPRUV	PAVIOUR
AILMPST	PALMIST	AILRSTY	TRYSAIL	AINNPSS	INSPANS	AIOPSTU	UTOPIAS
AILMPSY	MISPLAY	AILRTTU	TITULAR	AINNPTU	UNPAINT	AIORRRW	WARRIOR
AILMRST	MISTRAL	AILRTUV	VIRTUAL	AINNQTU	QUINNAT	AIORRSU	OURARIS
AILMRSU	SIMULAR		VITULAR		QUINTAN	AIORRTT	TRAITOR
AILMSSS	MISSALS	AILSSTX	LAXISTS	AINNRSU	URANINS	AIORRTX	ORATRIX
AILMSSX	LAXISMS	AILSSUV	VISUALS	AINNRTT	INTRANT	AIORSST	ARIOSTS
AILMSSY	MISLAYS	AILSSVY	SYLVIAS	AINNRTU	URINANT		ARISTOS
AILMSTU	ULTIMAS	AILSSVZ	VIZSLAS	AINNSTT	INSTANT		SATORIS
AILMSUV	MAULVIS	AILSTTY	TASTILY				

AIORSSU	SOUARIS	ALLLOYY	LOYALLY
AIORSSU	SAUTOIR	ALLMNOP	POLLMAN
AIORSTV	TRAVOIS	ALLMNOT	TOLLMAN
	VIATORS	ALLMNOY	ALLONYM
AIORSTY	OSTIARY	ALLMORS	MORALLS
AIORSUV	SAVIOUR	ALLMORY	MORALLY
	VARIOUS	ALLMOSS	SLALOMS
AIPPRRS	RIPRAPS	ALLMOSW	MALLOWS
AIPPSST	PAPISTS	ALLMPUU	PLUMULA
AIPRSST	RAPISTS	ALLMSUV	VALLUMS
AIPRSTU	UPSTAIR	ALLNOPS	POLLANS
AIPRSUY	PYURIAS	ALLNRUU	LUNULAR
AIPRTVY	PRAVITY	ALLNSTY	SLANTLY
AIPSSTT	TAPISTS	ALLNSUU	LUNULAS
AIPSSTW	SAWPITS	ALLNTUU	ULULANT
AIRRSST	STIRRAS	ALLOOPS	APOLLOS
AIRRSZZ	RIZZARS		PALOLOS
AIRRTZZ	RIZZART	ALLOOTX	AXOLOTL
AIRSSSU	RUSSIAS	ALLOPRS	PALLORS
AIRSSTT	ARTISTS	ALLOPRY	PAYROLL
	SITTARS	ALLOPSW	WALLOPS
	STRAITS	ALLORSS	SOLLARS
	TSARIST	ALLORYY	ROYALLY
AIRSSTU	AURISTS	ALLOSSW	SALLOWS
AIRSTTT	ATTRIST	ALLOSTT	TALLOTS
AIRSTTY	YTTRIAS	ALLOSTV	LAVOLTS
AIRSTVY	VARSITY	ALLOSTW	TALLOWS
AIRTUVX	VITRAUX	ALLOSWW	SWALLOW
AISSSST	ASSISTS		WALLOWS
AISSTTT	STATIST	ALLOSWY	SALLOWY
AISTTVY	VASTITY	ALLOTTY	TOTALLY
AISTUVY	SUAVITY	ALLOTWY	TALLOWY
AJKMNNU	JUNKMAN	ALLOTYY	LOYALTY
AJKMNTU	MUNTJAK	ALLPRSU	PLURALS
AJLLRUY	JURALLY	ALLQSSU	SQUALLS
AJLNORU	JOURNAL	ALLQSUY	SQUALLY
AJLOORS	JAROOLS	ALLRRUY	RURALLY
AJLOPPY	JALOPPY	ALLRSTU	LUSTRAL
AJMNRUY	JURYMAN	ALLSUUY	USUALLY
AJMOPST	JAMPOTS	ALMMSUY	AMYLUMS
AJMRSTU	JUMARTS	ALMNNUY	UNMANLY
AJNRSTU	JURANTS	ALMNOOP	LAMPOON
AKKLRSY	SKYLARK	ALMNOOT	TOOLMAN
AKKNRSU	KUNKARS	ALMNOOW	WOOLMAN
AKKOQSU	QUOKKAS	ALMNORS	NORMALS
AKLNOSU	KOULANS	ALMNORU	UNMORAL
AKLNOSX	KLAXONS	ALMNORY	ALMONRY
AKLOPRW	LAPWORK	ALMNOSS	SALMONS
AKLOSTW	KOTWALS	ALMNOSU	MONAULS
AKLOTTU	OUTTALK		SOLANUM
AKLOTUW	OUTWALK	ALMNOWY	WOMANLY
AKLPRSY	SPARKLY	ALMNRSU	MURLANS
AKLRSTY	STARKLY	ALMNSUU	ALUMNUS
AKMNORW	WORKMAN	ALMOPRT	MARPLOT
AKMNRTU	TRANKUM	ALMORRU	MORULAR
AKMNSSU	UNMASKS	ALMORSS	SAMLORS
AKMOORT	MOOKTAR	ALMORST	MORTALS
AKMQTUU	KUMQUAT	ALMORSU	MORULAS
AKNORSU	KORUNAS	ALMOSST	SMALTOS
AKNORSY	RYOKANS	ALMOSTW	MATLOWS
AKNORTU	OUTRANK	ALMOSXY	XYLOMAS
AKOOPRT	PARTOOK	ALMOTTU	MULATTO
AKOORRS	KORORAS	ALMRSTY	SMARTLY
AKOOSTU	ATOKOUS	ALMRSUU	RAMULUS
AKORRTW	ARTWORK	ALMRTUU	TUMULAR
AKORWWX	WAXWORK	ALMSSUY	ALYSSUM
AKQSSUW	SQUAWKS		ASYLUMS
AKQSUWY	SQUAWKY	ALMSTUU	UMLAUTS
AKRSSTU	TUSKARS	ALNNRSU	UNSNARL
AKSSWYY	SKYWAYS	ALNNSUU	ANNULUS

ALNOOPR	POLARON		MURRAMS
ALNOOPT	PLATOON	AMMRSUY	SUMMARY
ALNOORT	ORTOLAN	AMMSSTU	SUMMATS
ALNOOSS	SALOONS	AMNNOOX	MONAXON
	SOLANOS	AMNNORS	NORMANS
ALNOPPY	PANOPLY	AMNNOSW	SNOWMAN
ALNOPSS	SPONSAL	AMNNOSY	ANONYMS
ALNOPYY	POLYNYA	AMNNOTT	MONTANT
ALNORST	LATRONS	AMNNOTY	ANTONYM
ALNORUY	UNROYAL	AMNNOUW	UNWOMAN
ALNORUZ	ZONULAR	AMNOOPP	POMPANO
ALNOSUZ	ZONULAS	AMNOORS	MAROONS
ALNPRUY	PLANURY	AMNOOTT	OTTOMAN
ALNPSTU	PULTANS	AMNOOTZ	MATZOON
ALNPTUY	UNAPTLY	AMNOPRT	PORTMAN
ALNPTXY	PLANXTY	AMNOPRY	PARONYM
ALNRSUY	URANYLS	AMNOPST	POSTMAN
ALNSSTU	SULTANS		TAMPONS
ALNSSVY	SYLVANS		TOPSMAN
ALNSTUW	WALNUTS	AMNOPTU	PANTOUM
ALNSUUU	UNUSUAL	AMNOPTY	TYMPANO
ALOOPSS	SALOOPS	AMNORSS	RAMSONS
ALOOPYZ	POLYZOA		RANSOMS
ALOORRS	SORORAL	AMNORST	MATRONS
ALOPPRS	POPLARS		TRANSOM
ALOPPRU	POPULAR	AMNORSY	MASONRY
ALOPPRY	PROPYLA		MORNAYS
ALOPPST	LAPTOPS	AMNORTU	ROMAUNT
ALOPRRU	PARLOUR	AMNOSST	STAMNOS
ALOPRST	PATROLS	AMNOSTU	AMOUNTS
	PORTALS		MOUTANS
ALOPRSU	PARLOUS		OUTMANS
ALOPSST	POSTALS	AMNOTUY	AUTONYM
ALOPSSU	SPOUSAL	AMNPSTY	TYMPANS
ALOPSUV	VOLUSPA	AMNPTYY	TYMPANY
ALOPTUY	OUTPLAY	AMNQTUU	QUANTUM
ALOQRRU	RORQUAL	AMNRRUY	UNMARRY
ALOQRSU	SQUALOR	AMNRSTU	ANTRUMS
ALOQSTU	LOQUATS		UNSMART
ALORRST	ROSTRAL	AMNRTTU	TANTRUM
ALORRSW	WORRALS	AMNSTTU	MUTANTS
ALORSSU	ROSULAS	AMNSTUU	AUTUMNS
ALORSSV	SALVORS	AMNTUUY	AUTUMNY
ALORSTU	ROTULAS	AMOOORS	AMOROSO
	TORULAS	AMOOPRT	TAPROOM
ALORSUV	VALOURS	AMOORSU	AMOROUS
ALORTYY	ROYALTY	AMOORSW	MOORVAS
ALOSTTU	OUTLAST	AMOPSTT	TOPMAST
ALOSTUW	OUTLAWS	AMORRST	MORTARS
ALOSTUY	OUTLAYS	AMORRSU	ARMOURS
ALPRRSU	LARRUPS	AMORRSW	MARROWS
ALPRSSU	PULSARS	AMORRUY	ARMOURY
ALPRSSW	SPRAWLS	AMORRWY	MARROWY
ALPRSUU	PURSUAL	AMORSST	MATROSS
ALPRSUW	PULWARS		STROAMS
ALPRSWY	SPRAWLY	AMORSSY	MORASSY
ALRSTTY	STARTLY	AMOSTUZ	MAZOUTS
ALRSTUU	SUTURAL	AMOSUYZ	AZYMOUS
ALRSTUW	TULWARS	AMPRSST	STRAMPS
AMMMNOS	MAMMONS	AMPRSUW	UPSWARM
AMMMOSU	AMOMUMS	AMRRSTU	RASTRUM
AMMNOOR	MOORMAN	AMRRSTY	MARTYRS
AMMNOOT	MOOTMAN	AMRRSUY	MURRAYS
AMMNRUY	NUMMARY	AMRRTYY	MARTYRY
AMMOORR	MAORMOR	AMRSTTU	STRATUM
	MORMAOR	ANNOOSX	XOANONS
AMMOPTU	POMATUM	ANNOPRS	NAPRONS
AMMORST	MARMOTS	ANNOPST	PANTONS
AMMPSUW	WAMPUMS	ANNOPTY	POYNANT
AMMRRSU	MARRUMS	ANNORST	NATRONS

ANNOSST	SANTONS	AOPRRTY	PARROTY
	SONANTS		PORTRAY
ANNOSTW	WANTONS	AOPRSST	ASPORTS
ANNOTTY	TANTONY		PASTORS
ANNPSSU	SANNUPS	AOPRSTU	ASPROUT
	UNSNAPS	AOPRSUV	VAPOURS
ANNPSTU	PANTUNS	AOPRTTU	OUTPART
ANNRTYY	TYRANNY	AOPRTUY	OUTPRAY
ANNSSTU	SUNTANS	AOPRUVY	VAPOURY
ANNSSTY	SYNTANS	AOPSSTU	PASSOUT
ANOOPRS	PRONAOS	AOPSTUY	AUTOPSY
	SOPRANO	AOQRSTU	QUARTOS
ANOOPRT	PATROON	AORRSST	SARTORS
	PRONATA	AORRSTW	TARROWS
ANOORST	RATOONS	AORRSWY	SOWARRY
ANOORTT	ARNOTTO		YARROWS
ANOPRRS	SPORRAN	AORSSST	ASSORTS
ANOPRSS	PARSONS	AORSSTT	STATORS
ANOPRST	PARTONS	AORSSTU	SOUTARS
	PATRONS	AORSSUV	SAVOURS
	TARPONS	AORSSUY	OSSUARY
ANOPRTV	PROVANT		SUASORY
ANOPSTT	OPTANTS	AORSTUY	YAOURTS
ANOPSTU	OUTSPAN	AORSUVY	SAVOURY
ANOPSUY	YAUPONS	AORTUVY	AVOUTRY
ANORRSW	NARROWS	AOSTTTW	TATTOWS
ANORSSV	SOVRANS	AOSTTUY	OUTSTAY
ANORSTT	ATTORNS	APPRRUU	PURPURA
	RATTONS	APPRSTY	STRAPPY
	ROTTANS	APPRSUY	PAPYRUS
ANORSTU	ROUSANT	APRSSSU	SURPASS
	SANTOUR	APRSSWY	PSYWARS
ANORSTY	AROYNTS	APRSTTU	UPSTART
ANORSUU	ANUROUS	APRSTTY	TAPSTRY
	URANOUS	APSSTUY	UPSTAYS
ANORWWY	WAYWORN	APSSUWY	UPSWAYS
ANOSSTZ	STANZOS	AQRTUYZ	QUARTZY
ANPPSUW	SUPPAWN	AQSTTUY	SQUATTY
ANPRSSU	UNSPARS	ARSSTTU	STRATUS
ANPRSTU	SUNTRAP	BBBDELO	BLOBBED
	UNSTRAP		BOBBLED
ANPRSUW	UNWRAPS	BBBDELU	BLUBBED
ANPRSUY	UNPRAYS		BUBBLED
ANPSSUW	SUPAWNS	BBBEIOS	BOBBIES
ANRSSTU	SANTURS	BBBEIRS	BIBBERS
ANRSSUY	SUNRAYS	BBBEISU	BUBBIES
ANRSTTU	TRUANTS	BBBELRU	BLUBBER
ANRSTTY	TYRANTS	BBBELSU	BUBBLES
ANRSUWY	RUNWAYS	BBBEORY	BOBBERY
ANSSTTU	TUTSANS	BBBGIIN	BIBBING
AOOPPRS	APROPOS	BBBGINO	BOBBING
AOOPRTT	TAPROOT	BBBHIOS	BOBBISH
AOORRST	ORATORS	BBBHSUU	HUBBUBS
AOORRSY	ARROYOS	BBBINOS	BOBBINS
AOORRTT	ROTATOR	BBCCIKO	BIBCOCK
AOORRTU	OUTROAR	BBCDEHU	CHUBBED
AOORRTY	ORATORY	BBCDEIR	CRIBBED
AOORSTT	TOOARTS	BBCDELO	COBBLED
AOORSTU	OUTSOAR	BBCDELU	CLUBBED
AOORSTV	OVATORS	BBCEHIN	NEBBICH
AOOSTTT	TATTOOS	BBCEILR	CRIBBLE
AOOSTUZ	AZOTOUS	BBCEKKO	KEBBOCK
AOOTXYZ	ZOOTAXY	BBCEKKU	KEBBUCK
AOPPPSU	PAPPOUS	BBCELOR	CLOBBER
AOPPRRT	RAPPORT		COBBLER
AOPPRST	APPORTS	BBCELOS	COBBLES
AOPRRST	PARROTS	BBCEORS	COBBERS
	RAPTORS		
AOPRRSU	UPROARS		
AOPRRSW	SPARROW		

BBCEOSW	COBWEBS	BBEGIRS	GIBBERS
BBCGINO	COBBING	BBEGIST	GIBBETS
BBCGINU	CUBBING	BBEGLOR	GOBBLER
BBCHISU	CUBBISH	BBEGLOS	GOBBLES
BBCINOU	BUBONIC	BBEGLRU	GRUBBLE
BBCRSUY	SCRUBBY	BBEGNSU	BEBUNGS
BBDDEIL	DIBBLED	BBEGOST	GOBBETS
BBDDEIR	DRIBBED	BBEGRRU	GRUBBER
BBDDERU	DRUBBED	BBEHINS	NEBBISH
BBDEEIR	DEBBIER	BBEHIOS	HOBBIES
BBDEEIS	DEBBIES	BBEHISU	HUBBIES
BBDEEIT	EBBTIDE	BBEHLOR	HOBBLER
BBDEELP	PEBBLED	BBEHLOS	HOBBLES
BBDEENS	SNEBBED	BBEHMTU	BETHUMB
BBDEFLU	FLUBBED	BBEIILR	RIBIBLE
BBDEGIL	GLIBBED	BBEIIMR	IMBIBER
BBDEGLO	GOBBLED	BBEIIMS	IMBIBES
BBDEGRU	GRUBBED	BBEIIRR	RIBBIER
BBDEGSU	BEDBUGS	BBEIIRS	RIBIBES
BBDEHLO	HOBBLED	BBEIJRS	JIBBERS
BBDEIIM	IMBIBED	BBEIKLS	KIBBLES
BBDEIKL	KIBBLED	BBEILNR	NIBBLER
BBDEILN	NIBBLED	BBEILNS	NIBBLES
BBDEILO	BILOBED	BBEILOS	BILBOES
	LOBBIED		LOBBIES
BBDEILR	DIBBLER	BBEILOT	BIBELOT
	DRIBBLE	BBEILPR	PRIBBLE
BBDEILS	DIBBLES	BBEILQU	QUIBBLE
BBDEINS	SNIBBED	BBEILRS	LIBBERS
BBDEIRR	DRIBBER	BBEILRT	TRIBBLE
BBDEIRS	DIBBERS	BBEILST	STIBBLE
BBDEKNO	KNOBBED	BBEILSY	YIBBLES
BBDELMO	MOBBLED	BBEIMOS	MOBBIES
BBDELMU	BUMBLED	BBEINOR	NOBBIER
BBDELNO	NOBBLED	BBEINRU	NUBBIER
BBDELNU	NUBBLED	BBEIOOS	BOOBIES
BBDELOS	BOBSLED	BBEIRRS	BRIBERS
BBDELOW	WOBBLED	BBEIRRY	BRIBERY
BBDELRU	BURBLED	BBEIRTU	TUBBIER
BBDELSU	SLUBBED	BBEISSU	BUSBIES
BBDENSU	SNUBBED	BBEJORS	JOBBERS
BBDEORS	DOBBERS	BBEJORY	JOBBERY
BBDEOSW	SWOBBED	BBEKLNO	KNOBBLE
BBDESTU	STUBBED	BBEKLNU	KNUBBLE
BBDGIIN	DIBBING	BBEKLOS	BLESBOK
BBDGINO	DOBBING	BBEKLUU	BUBUKLE
BBDGINU	DUBBING	BBEKNOR	KNOBBER
BBDILRY	DRIBBLY	BBEKNSU	NEBBUKS
BBDINOS	DOBBINS	BBELMOS	MOBBLES
BBDINSU	DUBBINS	BBELMSU	BUMBLES
BBDKSUY	DYBBUKS	BBELNOR	NOBBLER
BBEEERU	BEBEERU	BBELNOS	NOBBLES
BBEEIKS	KEBBIES	BBELNSU	NUBBLES
BBEEIRW	WEBBIER	BBELORS	SLOBBER
BBEEKLS	LEBBEKS	BBELORW	WOBBLER
BBEELPS	PEBBLES	BBELORY	LOBBYER
BBEELSS	EBBLESS	BBELOSW	WOBBLES
BBEENSS	SNEBBES	BBELRSU	BURBLES
BBEFILR	FRIBBLE		LUBBERS
BBEFIRS	FIBBERS		RUBBLES
BBEFIRU	FUBBIER		SLUBBER
BBEFIRY	FIBBERY	BBELSTU	STUBBLE
BBEFRUY	FUBBERY	BBEMNSU	BENUMBS
BBEGIKN	KEBBING	BBEMORS	BOMBERS
BBEGILR	GLIBBER	BBENOTW	BOWBENT
	GRIBBLE	BBENRSU	SNUBBER
BBEGINN	NEBBING	BBENSSU	SNUBBES
BBEGINW	WEBBING	BBEOOSY	YOBBOES
BBEGIOS	GIBBOSE	BBEORRS	ROBBERS
		BBEORRY	ROBBERY

BBEORSW	SWOBBER	BCDEEHN	BENCHED	BCEHOSS	BOSCHES	BCGIKNU	BUCKING
BBERRSU	RUBBERS	BCDEEIL	DECIBEL	BCEHOST	BOTCHES	BCGIMNO	COMBING
BBERRUY	RUBBERY	BCDEEKS	BEDECKS	BCEHOSU	BOUCHES	BCGINNU	BUNCING
BBERSTU	TUBBERS	BCDEHIR	BIRCHED	BCEHRSU	CHERUBS	BCGINRU	CURBING
BBFGIIN	FIBBING	BCDEHIT	BITCHED	BCEHRTU	BUTCHER	BCGORSU	COBURGS
BBFGINO	FOBBING	BCDEHNU	BUNCHED	BCEHSTU	BUTCHES	BCHIIOT	COHIBIT
BBFGINU	FUBBING	BCDEHOT	BOTCHED	BCEIIKR	BRICKIE	BCHIKOU	CHIBOUK
BBGGIIN	GIBBING	BCDEHOU	DEBOUCH	BCEIISV	VIBICES	BCHIKSU	BUCKISH
BBGIIJN	JIBBING	BCDEIIO	BIOCIDE	BCEIKLM	LIMBECK	BCHILOS	CHIBOLS
BBGIILN	LIBBING	BCDEIKR	BRICKED	BCEIKLR	BRICKLE	BCHIMOR	RHOMBIC
BBGIINN	NIBBING	BCDEIKT	BEDTICK	BCEIKNR	BRICKEN	BCHINOR	BRONCHI
BBGIINR	BRIBING	BCDEILM	CLIMBED	BCEIKRS	BICKERS	BCHIOPR	PIBROCH
	RIBBING	BCDEILO	DOCIBLE	BCEIKST	BESTICK	BCHLOTY	BLOTCHY
BBGIJNO	JOBBING	BCDEIOS	BODICES	BCEIKSU	BUCKIES	BCHNOOR	BRONCHO
BBGILNO	LOBBING	BCDEIRS	SCRIBED	BCEILMO	EMBOLIC	BCHORST	BORSCHT
BBGILNU	BULBING	BCDEKLO	BLOCKED	BCEILMR	CLIMBER		BORTSCH
BBGIMNO	BOMBING	BCDEKLU	BUCKLED		RECLIMB	BCIIKLN	NIBLICK
	MOBBING	BCDEKOR	BEDROCK	BCEILMS	EMBLICS	BCIILMU	BULIMIC
BBGINNU	NUBBING		BROCKED		LIMBECS	BCIILOR	COLIBRI
BBGINOO	BOOBING	BCDEKSU	BEDUCKS	BCEILNO	BINOCLE	BCIINOS	BIONICS
BBGINOR	ROBBING	BCDELOU	BECLOUD	BCEILOR	BRICOLE	BCIINOT	BIONTIC
BBGINOS	GIBBONS	BCDEMOR	CROMBED		CORBEIL	BCIIOPS	BIOPICS
	SOBBING	BCDEMRU	CRUMBED	BCEIMNO	COMBINE	BCIISTU	BISCUIT
BBGINRU	RUBBING	BCDENOU	BOUNCED	BCEIMOR	COMBIER	BCIKNOS	KINCOBS
BBGINSU	GUBBINS		BUNCOED		CROMBIE	BCIKORT	BROCKIT
	SUBBING	BCDEORU	COURBED		MICROBE	BCIKOTT	BITTOCK
BBGINTU	TUBBING	BCDESUU	SUBDUCE	BCEINOZ	BENZOIC	BCILMPU	PLUMBIC
BBGIOSU	GIBBOUS	BCDHIOR	BICHORD	BCEINRU	BRUCINE		UPCLIMB
BBGIOSW	BOBWIGS	BCDHIRU	BRUCHID	BCEIORS	CORBIES	BCILPSU	PUBLICS
BBHHIOS	HOBBISH	BCDHOOU	CUBHOOD	BCEIRRS	SCRIBER	BCIMSSU	CUBISMS
BBHIMOS	MOBBISH	BCDIORW	COWBIRD	BCEIRSS	SCRIBES	BCINORU	RUBICON
BBHIOST	HOBBITS	BCDIOSU	CUBOIDS	BCEIRSU	SUBERIC	BCINSUU	INCUBUS
BBHIOSY	YOBBISH	BCDKORU	BURDOCK	BCEIRTU	BRUCITE	BCIOORT	ROBOTIC
BBHIRSU	RUBBISH	BCDNOSU	BONDUCS	BCEISST	BISECTS	BCIORST	STROBIC
BBHISTU	TUBBISH	BCDSTUU	SUBDUCT	BCEJOST	OBJECTS	BCIOSTY	SYBOTIC
BBHJOOS	HOBJOBS	BCEEEHN	BEECHEN	BCEJSTU	SUBJECT	BCIRRSU	RUBRICS
BBHNOOS	HOBNOBS	BCEEEHS	BEECHES	BCEKLOR	BLOCKER	BCIRTUY	BUTYRIC
BBHOOUW	WHOOBUB		BESEECH	BCEKLRU	BRUCKLE	BCISSTU	CUBISTS
BBHRSUY	SHRUBBY	BCEEFIN	BENEFIC		BUCKLER	BCISTUU	CUBITUS
BBIIILM	BILIMBI	BCEEGIR	ICEBERG	BCEKLSU	BUCKLES	BCJKMUU	JUMBUCK
BBIILST	BIBLIST	BCEEHIP	EPHEBIC	BCEKMOS	BEMOCKS	BCKLLOO	BOLLOCK
BBIKTUZ	KIBBUTZ	BCEEHLR	BELCHER	BCEKNOS	BECKONS	BCKLLOU	BULLOCK
BBILLSU	BULBILS	BCEEHLS	BELCHES	BCEKORT	BROCKET	BCKLNOU	UNBLOCK
BBILNOY	NOBBILY	BCEEHNR	BENCHER	BCEKORU	ROEBUCK	BCKMMOU	BUMMOCK
BBINNSU	NUBBINS	BCEEHNS	BENCHES	BCEKOSU	BUCKOES	BCKMOSU	BUCKSOM
BBINORS	RIBBONS	BCEEHOS	OBECHES	BCEKOTY	BYCOKET	BCKOTTU	BUTTOCK
BBINORY	RIBBONY	BCEEHOU	BOUCHEE	BCEKRSU	BUCKERS	BCLMOOU	COULOMB
BBKLNOY	KNOBBLY	BCEEIPS	BESPICE	BCEKSTU	BESTUCK	BCLMRUY	CRUMBLY
BBKLNUY	KNUBBLY	BCEEIRS	ESCRIBE		BUCKETS	BCLOOSU	COLOBUS
BBKLOOU	BLOUBOK	BCEEKNS	NEBECKS	BCELLOW	COWBELL	BCLORTU	CLOTBUR
BBKOOOO	BOOBOOK	BCEEKNU	BUCKEEN	BCELMNU	CLUBMEN	BCMOOST	TOMBOCS
BBKOOSS	BOSBOKS	BCEEKRS	REBECKS	BCELMOS	COMBLES	BCMORSY	CORYMBS
BBLLSUU	BULBULS	BCEEKST	BECKETS	BCELMRU	CLUMBER	BCMOSTU	COMBUST
BBLOSUU	BULBOUS	BCEEKSZ	ZEBECKS		CRUMBLE	BCNOORS	BRONCOS
BBLSTUY	STUBBLY	BCEELOS	ECBOLES	BCELMSU	SCUMBLE	BCNOSTU	COBNUTS
BBNNOOS	BONBONS	BCEEMOS	BECOMES	BCELORS	CORBELS	BCOOSWY	COWBOYS
BBNOORU	BOURBON	BCEENOS	OBSCENE	BCELORU	COLUBER	BCOOTTY	BOYCOTT
BBOOOOS	BOOBOOS	BCEENRU	CRUBEEN	BCELOSU	BOUCLES	BDDDELU	BUDDLED
BBORSTU	BURBOTS	BCEFIIS	SEBIFIC	BCELRSU	BECURLS	BDDDEOR	BRODDED
BBOSSUY	BUSBOYS	BCEGIKN	BECKING	BCELSSU	CUBLESS	BDDEEES	SEEDBED
BBRSSUU	SUBURBS	BCEHINR	BIRCHEN	BCEMNTU	CUMBENT	BDDEEEW	BEDEWED
BCCEILO	ECBOLIC	BCEHINT	BENTHIC	BCEMORS	COMBERS	BDDEEIR	DEBRIDE
BCCEILU	CUBICLE	BCEHIOR	BRIOCHE	BCEMRSU	CUMBERS	BDDEEIS	BEDSIDE
BCCEILY	BICYCLE	BCEHIRS	BIRCHES		SCUMBER	BDDEEIT	BETIDED
BCCILOU	BUCOLIC	BCEHIST	BITCHES	BCENORU	BOUNCER		DEBITED
BCCINOO	OBCONIC	BCEHITW	BEWITCH	BCENOSU	BOUNCES	BDDEELN	BLENDED
BCCISUU	SUCCUBI	BCEHLRU	BLUCHER	BCEORSS	SCROBES	BDDEERS	BEDDERS
BCCMOOX	COXCOMB	BCEHNSU	BUNCHES	BCEORSU	OBSCURE	BDDEGIN	BEDDING
BCCMSUU	SUCCUMB	BCEHORS	BROCHES	BCFSSUU	SUBFUSC	BDDEGIR	BRIDGED
BCDEEHL	BELCHED	BCEHORT	BOTCHER	BCGIKNO	BOCKING	BDDEGLU	BLUDGED

BDDEIIR	BIRDIED	BDEELSS	BLESSED	BDEILOP	LOBIPED		DOUBLES
BDDEIIS	BIDDIES	BDEELTT	BLETTED	BDEILOR	BROILED	BDELOSW	BLOWSED
BDDEILN	BLINDED	BDEELZZ	BEZZLED	BDEILOS	BOLIDES	BDELOTT	BLOTTED
BDDEILR	BRIDLED	BDEEMOW	EMBOWED	BDEILPP	BLIPPED		BOTTLED
BDDEILU	BUILDED	BDEEMOX	EMBOXED	BDEILRR	BRIDLER	BDELOTU	BOULTED
BDDEINR	BRINDED	BDEEMRU	EMBRUED	BDEILRS	BIRSLED		DOUBLET
BDDEIOO	BOODIED		UMBERED		BRIDLES	BDELOWZ	BLOWZED
BDDEIRS	BIDDERS	BDEEMSU	BEMUSED	BDEILRT	DRIBLET	BDELRRU	BLURRED
BDDEIRU	BUDDIER	BDEENOR	ENROBED	BDEILRU	BLUDIER	BDELRTU	BLURTED
BDDEISU	BUDDIES	BDEENPR	PREBEND		BUILDER	BDELSSU	BUDLESS
BDDELNU	BUNDLED	BDEENRS	BENDERS		REBUILD	BDELSTU	BUSTLED
BDDELOO	BLOODED	BDEEORR	REBORED	BDEILTZ	BLITZED	BDELSWY	LEWDSBY
BDDELOS	BODDLES	BDEEORS	BEDSORE	BDEIMMR	BRIMMED	BDELTTU	BUTTLED
BDDELOU	DOUBLED		SOBERED	BDEIMNR	BIRDMEN	BDEMNNO	BONDMEN
BDDELSU	BUDDLES	BDEEORW	BOWERED	BDEIMOR	BROMIDE	BDEMNOU	EMBOUND
BDDENOU	BOUNDED	BDEEOSX	SEEDBOX	BDEIMRU	IMBRUED	BDEMOOR	BEDROOM
BDDEOOR	BROODED	BDEERUW	BURWEED	BDEIMTU	BITUMED		BOREDOM
BDDEORU	OBDURED	BDEFFLU	BLUFFED	BDEINOR	INORBED		BROOMED
BDDEOTU	DOUBTED	BDEFILR	FILBERD	BDEINOU	BEDOUIN	BDEMOOS	BOSOMED
BDDESUU	SUBDUED	BDEFLMU	FUMBLED	BDEINRS	BINDERS	BDEMORS	SOMBRED
BDDGIIN	BIDDING	BDEFLOU	BODEFUL		REBINDS	BDEMSTU	DUMBEST
BDDGINU	BUDDING	BDEFOOR	FORBODE	BDEINRY	BINDERY	BDENNOU	BOUNDEN
BDDISSU	DISBUDS	BDEGGLO	BOGGLED	BDEINST	BIDENTS		UNBONED
BDEEEFL	FEEBLED	BDEGGOR	BROGGED	BDEINSU	BEDUINS	BDENNSU	UNBENDS
BDEEELL	DELEBLE	BDEGHIT	BEDIGHT	BDEIOOS	BOODIES	BDENORS	BONDERS
BDEEELP	BLEEPED	BDEGILN	BINGLED	BDEIORR	BROIDER	BDENORU	BOUNDER
BDEEELR	BLEEDER	BDEGILO	OBLIGED	BDEIORS	BORIDES		REBOUND
BDEEELT	BEETLED	BDEGILS	BEGILDS		DISROBE		UNROBED
BDEEEMN	BEDEMEN	BDEGINN	BENDING	BDEIORT	DEBITOR	BDENORW	BROWNED
BDEEEMT	BEMETED	BDEGINO	BOINGED		ORBITED	BDENORZ	BRONZED
BDEEEPS	BESPEED	BDEGINR	BREDING	BDEIORV	OVERBID	BDENOST	OBTENDS
BDEEERR	BREEDER	BDEGIOO	BOOGIED	BDEIORZ	ZEBROID	BDENOSY	BEYONDS
	BREERED	BDEGIOS	BODGIES	BDEIOSY	DISOBEY	BDENOUW	UNBOWED
BDEEERZ	BREEZED	BDEGIOT	BIGOTED	BDEIRRS	BIRDERS	BDENOUX	UNBOXED
BDEEEST	DEBTEES	BDEGIRS	BEGIRDS	BDEIRST	BESTRID	BDENRSU	BURDENS
BDEEFIR	BRIEFED		BRIDGES		BISTRED	BDENRTU	BRUNTED
	DEBRIEF	BDEGIRU	BRIGUED	BDEIRSU	BRUISED	BDENSSU	SUNBEDS
BDEEGOR	BEGORED	BDEGISU	BUDGIES		BURDIES	BDENSTU	SUBTEND
BDEEHOV	BEHOVED	BDEGLNU	BLUNGED	BDEIRTU	BRUITED	BDENSUY	SEBUNDY
BDEEHRT	BERTHED	BDEGLRU	BLUDGER	BDEISSU	SUBSIDE	BDEOORR	BROODER
BDEEIKN	BEINKED		BURGLED	BDEISTU	BUISTED	BDEOORS	BOORDES
BDEEILL	BELLIED	BDEGLSU	BLUDGES		SUBEDIT	BDEOOST	BOOSTED
	DELIBLE	BDEGNSU	BEDUNGS	BDEITUY	DUBIETY	BDEOPRS	BEDROPS
BDEEILS	EDIBLES	BDEGORS	BODGERS	BDEJLMU	JUMBLED	BDEOPRT	BEDROPT
BDEEILV	BEDEVIL	BDEGORU	BUDGERO	BDEJORU	OBJURED	BDEOPST	BEDPOST
BDEEIMR	BEMIRED	BDEGRSU	BUDGERS	BDEKLNU	BLUNKED	BDEORRS	BORDERS
BDEEIMT	BEDTIME	BDEGSTU	BUDGETS	BDEKNOU	BUNKOED	BDEORRU	BORDURE
	BETIMED	BDEHINS	BEHINDS	BDEKNSU	DEBUNKS		BOURDER
BDEEINR	BENDIER	BDEHLMU	HUMBLED	BDEKOOR	BROOKED	BDEORSS	DESORBS
	INBREED	BDEHLOS	BEHOLDS	BDELMMU	BUMMLED	BDEORST	DEBTORS
BDEEINZ	BEDIZEN	BDEHLSU	BLUSHED		MUMBLED	BDEORSU	OBDURES
BDEEIRR	BERRIED	BDEHMTU	THUMBED	BDELMOO	BLOOMED	BDEORSW	BROWSED
	BRIERED	BDEHORY	HERDBOY	BDELMPU	PLUMBED	BDEORTU	DOUBTER
BDEEIRS	DERBIES	BDEHOST	HOTBEDS	BDELMRU	DRUMBLE		OBTRUDE
BDEEIRT	BEDRITE	BDEHRSU	BRUSHED		RUMBLED		OUTBRED
BDEEISS	BESIDES	BDEIIRS	BIRDIES	BDELMTU	TUMBLED		REDOUBT
BDEEIST	BETIDES		BRIDIES	BDELNOR	BLONDER	BDERSSU	SURBEDS
BDEEIVV	BEVVIED	BDEIIVV	BIVVIED	BDELNOS	BLONDES	BDERSTU	BURSTED
BDEEJLS	DJEBELS	BDEIJLR	JIRBLED		BOLDENS	BDERSUU	SUBDUER
BDEEKMO	KEMBOED	BDEIKLN	BLINKED	BDELNRU	BLUNDER	BDERSUY	RUDESBY
BDEEKRU	REBUKED	BDEIKMO	KIMBOED	BDELNSU	BUNDLES	BDESSTU	BEDUSTS
BDEELLS	BEDELLS	BDEIKNO	BOINKED	BDELNTU	BLUNTED		BESTUDS
BDEELMR	REMBLED	BDEIKRS	BRISKED	BDELOOP	BLOOPED	BDESSUU	SUBDUES
BDEELMS	SEMBLED	BDEILLU	BULLIED	BDELOOS	BOODLES	BDESSUW	SUBDEWS
BDEELNR	BLENDER	BDEILMS	DIMBLES	BDELORS	BORDELS	BDFIIOR	FIBROID
BDEELNS	BLENDES	BDEILMW	WIMBLED	BDELORU	BOULDER	BDFIISU	FIDIBUS
BDEELNT	BENDLET	BDEILNN	BLINNED		DOUBLER	BDFIORS	FORBIDS
BDEELOV	BELOVED	BDEILNR	BLINDER	BDELORW	BOWLDER	BDGGINO	BODGING
BDEELOW	ELBOWED		BRINDLE	BDELOST	BOLDEST	BDGGINU	BUDGING
BDEELRT	TREBLED			BDELOSU	BLOUSED	BDGIINN	BINDING

BDGIINR	BIRDING	BEEEKLS	KEBELES	BEEILTT	BETITLE		SOBERER
	BRIDING	BEEELPR	BLEEPER	BEEIMRS	BEMIRES	BEEORRU	BOURREE
BDGIINS	BIDINGS	BEEELST	BEETLES		BIREMES	BEEORSV	OBSERVE
BDGIIOO	GOBIOID	BEEEMOS	BEESOME	BEEIMST	BETIMES		OBVERSE
BDGILOO	GLOBOID	BEEEMRW	EMBREWE	BEEINNS	BENNIES		VERBOSE
BDGIMNU	DUMBING	BEEEMSS	BESEEMS	BEEINNZ	BENZINE	BEEORSY	OBEYERS
BDGINNO	BONDING	BEEEMST	BEMETES	BEEINOS	EBONIES	BEEORWY	EYEBROW
BDGINNU	BUNDING		BETEEMS		EBONISE	BEEOSST	OBESEST
BDGINOS	BODINGS	BEEENNZ	BENZENE	BEEINOT	EBONITE	BEEPRRV	PREVERB
BDGINOY	BODYING	BEEENTW	BETWEEN	BEEINOZ	EBONIZE	BEEQSTU	BEQUEST
BDGLLOU	BULLDOG	BEEEPRS	BEEPERS	BEEINPR	PEBRINE	BEERRST	BERRETS
BDGLOOT	DOGBOLT	BEEEPSW	BEWEEPS	BEEINRT	BENTIER	BEERRSU	BEURRES
BDHIINS	BHINDIS	BEEERSS	BREESES	BEEINRZ	ZEBRINE	BEERRSV	REVERBS
BDHINOP	HOPBIND	BEEERSZ	BREEZES	BEEIORS	EBRIOSE	BEERRSW	BREWERS
BDHIOSU	BUSHIDO	BEEERTV	BREVETE	BEEIQUZ	BEZIQUE	BEERRWY	BREWERY
BDHIRSY	HYBRIDS	BEEFGIN	BEEFING	BEEIRRS	BERRIES	BEERSSU	REBUSES
BDHMOOO	HOBODOM	BEEFILR	FEBRILE	BEEIRRV	BREVIER		SUBSERE
BDHOOOY	BOYHOOD	BEEFILS	BELIEFS	BEEIRST	REBITES	BEERSTT	BETTERS
BDIIKNO	BODIKIN	BEEFINT	BENEFIT	BEEIRTY	EBRIETY	BEERSTV	BREVETS
BDIILMS	DISLIMB	BEEFIRR	BRIEFER	BEEISST	BETISES	BEERSTW	BESTREW
BDIILOS	LIBIDOS	BEEFNRU	FUNEBRE	BEEISTT	BETTIES		WEBSTER
BDIIMRS	MIDRIBS	BEEGGNU	GEEBUNG	BEEISVV	BEVVIES	BEERTTU	BURETTE
BDIISTT	TIDBITS	BEEGILL	LEGIBLE	BEEJNSU	BUNJEES	BEESSTU	BUSTEES
BDIKNOR	BRODKIN	BEEGILO	OBLIGEE	BEEKNOT	BETOKEN	BEETTUV	BUVETTE
BDIKNOS	BODKINS	BEEGILS	BEIGELS	BEEKOPS	BESPOKE	BEFFLRU	BLUFFER
BDILLNY	BLINDLY	BEEGILU	BEGUILE	BEEKORS	REEBOKS	BEFFPSU	BEPUFFS
BDILNNU	UNBLIND	BEEGIMR	BEGRIME	BEEKRRS	BERSERK	BEFFRSU	BUFFERS
BDILNUU	UNBUILD	BEEGINN	BEGINNE	BEEKRRU	REBUKER		REBUFFS
BDILPUU	UPBUILD	BEEGINP	BEEPING	BEEKRSU	REBUKES	BEFFSTU	BUFFETS
BDILRUY	BUIRDLY	BEEGINR	BIGENER	BEELLMN	BELLMEN	BEFGIIL	FILIBEG
BDILTUY	DIBUTYL	BEEGINT	BEETING	BEELLOT	LOBELET	BEFGIRU	FIREBUG
BDIMNPU	DUMPBIN		BEIGNET	BEELMMS	EMBLEMS	BEFGIST	BEGIFTS
BDINNSU	UNBINDS	BEEGINU	BEGUINE	BEELMOW	EMBOWEL	BEFHOOS	BEHOOFS
BDINOOR	BRIDOON	BEEGLNO	ENGLOBE	BEELMRS	REMBLES	BEFILMS	FIMBLES
BDINPSU	UPBINDS	BEEGMNO	GOMBEEN	BEELMRT	TREMBLE	BEFILOS	FOIBLES
BDINSTU	DUSTBIN	BEEGMOU	EMBOGUE	BEELMSS	SEMBLES	BEFILPY	PLEBIFY
BDIOOOV	OBOVOID	BEEGNOS	ENGOBES	BEELNNO	ENNOBLE	BEFILRT	FILBERT
BDIOORU	BOUDOIR	BEEGNSU	BUNGEES	BEELNOZ	BENZOLE	BEFILRY	BRIEFLY
BDIORSW	WOSBIRD	BEEGNTU	UNBEGET	BEELNSU	NEBULES	BEFILSU	FUSIBLE
BDIOSSY	BYSSOID	BEEGRSU	BURGEES	BEELOSV	BELOVES	BEFINOR	BONFIRE
BDIOSTU	OUTBIDS	BEEHINS	BESHINE	BEELOTY	EYEBOLT	BEFIORS	FIBROSE
BDIOSUU	DUBIOUS	BEEHIRR	HERBIER	BEELPST	BEPELTS	BEFIRST	FIBSTER
BDIRSTU	DISTURB	BEEHIST	BHISTEE	BEELRST	BELTERS	BEFIRSU	FUBSIER
BDISSUY	SUBSIDY	BEEHKSU	BUKSHEE		TREBLES	BEFLLTY	FLYBELT
BDKLOOS	KOBOLDS	BEEHLRT	BLETHER	BEELRSY	BERLEYS	BEFLMRU	FUMBLER
BDKNOOU	BUNDOOK		HERBLET	BEELRUZ	ZEBRULE	BEFLMSU	BEFLUMS
BDLOOOX	OXBLOOD	BEEHLST	BETHELS	BEELSSS	BLESSES		FUMBLES
BDNNOUU	UNBOUND	BEEHNNO	HEBENON	BEELSZZ	BEZZLES	BEFLOOS	BEFOOLS
BDNOORU	BOURDON	BEEHNOS	BESHONE	BEELTTU	BLUETTE	BEFLOSU	BEFOULS
BDNOOWW	DOWNBOW	BEEHOOV	BEHOOVE	BEEMMRS	MEMBERS	BEFLTUU	TUBEFUL
BDNOPUU	UPBOUND	BEEHOPS	EPHEBOS	BEEMNPT	BENEMPT	BEFOORR	FORBORE
BDNORTU	TURBOND		PHOEBES	BEEMNRY	BYREMEN	BEFSSUU	SUBFEUS
BDNORUW	RUBDOWN	BEEHORS	HERBOSE	BEEMORW	EMBOWER	BEGGGIN	BEGGING
BDNOSTU	OBTUNDS	BEEHORW	BEWHORE	BEEMOSS	MEBOSES	BEGGIIS	BIGGIES
BDOOOWX	BOXWOOD	BEEHOST	BEHOTES	BEEMOSX	EMBOXES	BEGGINO	BEGOING
BDORSWY	BYWORDS	BEEHOSV	BEHOVES	BEEMRRU	UMBRERE	BEGGIOR	BOGGIER
BEEEEFR	FREEBEE	BEEHPSU	EPHEBUS	BEEMRSU	EMBRUES	BEGGIST	BIGGEST
BEEEEKS	BESEEKE	BEEHRST	BERTHES	BEEMRTU	EMBRUTE	BEGGISU	BUGGIES
BEEEEMT	BETEEME		SHERBET	BEEMSSU	BEMUSES	BEGGLOR	BOGGLER
BEEEFIR	BEEFIER	BEEHRSW	BESHREW	BEENNRS	BRENNES	BEGGLOS	BOGGLES
	FREEBIE	BEEHRTY	THEREBY	BEENNST	BENNETS	BEGGRSU	BUGGERS
BEEEFLR	FEEBLER	BEEHRWY	WHEREBY	BEENORS	BOREENS	BEGGRUY	BUGGERY
BEEEFLS	FEEBLES	BEEHSST	BEHESTS		ENROBES	BEGHHIT	BEHIGHT
BEEEGIS	BESIEGE	BEEHSTY	BHEESTY	BEENOST	BONESET	BEGHINT	BENIGHT
BEEEGRR	BERGERE	BEEIJLU	JUBILEE	BEENRRT	BRENTER	BEGHISS	BESIGHS
BEEEHIV	BEEHIVE	BEEILLS	BELLIES	BEENSTU	BUTENES	BEGHIST	BETIGHT
BEEEHNS	SHEBEEN	BEEILNR	BERLINE		SUBTEEN	BEGHRRU	BURGHER
BEEEILV	BELIEVE	BEEILOS	OBELISE	BEEOOST	BOOTEES	BEGIILR	BILGIER
BEEEIRR	BEERIER	BEEILOZ	OBELIZE	BEEOPRS	BEPROSE	BEGIINN	INBEING
BEEEJLW	BEJEWEL	BEEILRS	BELIERS	BEEORRS	REBORES	BEGIKMN	KEMBING

BEGILLN BELLING	BEHILST THIBLES	BEILLST BESTILL	BEINORT BORNITE
BEGILLY LEGIBLY	BEHILSU HELIBUS	BILLETS	BEINORW BROWNIE
BEGILNO IGNOBLE	BEHINOP HOPBINE	BEILLSU BULLIES	BEINOSS BESOINS
INGLOBE	BEHIOST BOTHIES	BEILMNR NIMBLER	BEINOST BONIEST
BEGILNS BINGLES	BEHIOTW HOWBEIT	BEILMOR EMBROIL	EBONIST
BEGILNT BELTING	BEHIRRT REBIRTH	BEILMOS BEMOILS	BEINOSX BONXIES
BEGILNU BLUEING	BEHIRST HERBIST	EMBOILS	BEINOSZ BIZONES
BULGINE	BEHIRSU BUSHIER	MOBILES	BEINOTT BOTTINE
BEGILNY BELYING	BEHISSU BUSHIES	BEILMRS LIMBERS	BEINRSU RUBINES
BEGILOS OBLIGES	BEHISTT THIBETS	BEILMRT TIMBREL	SUBERIN
BEGILRS GERBILS	BEHLLOP BELLHOP	BEILMRW WIMBREL	BEINRSY BYRNIES
BEGILRT GILBERT	BEHLMOW WHOMBLE	BEILMSU SUBLIME	BEINRTT BITTERN
BEGILRU BULGIER	BEHLMRU HUMBLER	BEILMSW WIMBLES	BEINRTU BUNTIER
BEGILST GIBLETS	BEHLMSU HUMBLES	BEILNOO OBELION	TRIBUNE
BEGINNU UNBEING	BEHLOOT BOTHOLE	BEILNOW BOWLINE	TURBINE
BEGINOS BIOGENS	BEHLORT BROTHEL	BEILNRS BERLINS	BEINSSY BYSSINE
BEGINOY BIOGENY	BEHLOSW BEHOWLS	BEILNSY BYLINES	BEIOORZ BOOZIER
OBEYING	BEHLRRU BURRHEL	BEILNSZ BENZILS	BEIOOST BOOTIES
BEGINRR BRINGER	BEHLRSU BLUSHER	BEILNTZ BLINTZE	BEIOPTY BIOTYPE
BEGINRS BINGERS	BURHELS	BEILOOR LOOBIER	BEIORRT ORBITER
BEGINRW BREWING	BEHLSSU BLUSHES	BEILOOS LOOBIES	BEIORSS BOSSIER
BEGINSS BESINGS	BUSHELS	BEILOQU OBLIQUE	RIBOSES
BIGNESS	BEHLSTU BLUSHET	BEILORR BROILER	BEIORST ORBIEST
BEGINST BESTING	BEHMNSU BUSHMEN	BEILORS BOILERS	BEIORSU BOUSIER
BEGINSU BEGUINS	BEHMORS HOMBRES	REBOILS	OUREBIS
BUNGIES	BEHMOTU BEMOUTH	BEILORT TRILOBE	BEIOSSU SOUBISE
BEGINTT BETTING	BEHMPTU BETHUMP	BEILORW BLOWIER	BEIOSTT BOTTIES
BEGIOOS BOOGIES	BEHNORS BREHONS	BEILORY BOILERY	BEIOSTX BOXIEST
BEGIOSU BOUGIES	BEHNOST BENTHOS	BEILOST BETOILS	BEIOSTY OBESITY
BEGIRSU BRIGUES	BEHNRTU BURTHEN	BEILOSW BLOWIES	BEIPSST BESPITS
RUGBIES	BEHOORT THEORBO	BEILOSX BOLIXES	BEIPSSU PUBISES
BEGISSU GIBUSES	BEHORRT BROTHER	BEILRRS BIRLERS	BEIQRTU BRIQUET
BEGKMOS GEMSBOK	BEHORST BOSHTER	BEILRRU BURLIER	BEIQSSU BISQUES
BEGKNSU BEGUNKS	BOTHERS	BEILRSS BIRSLES	BEIRRRU BURRIER
BEGLLOU GLOBULE	BEHORSU HERBOUS	RIBLESS	BEIRRSU BRISURE
BEGLMOO BEGLOOM	BEHORTT BETROTH	BEILRST BLISTER	BRUISER
BEGLMRU GRUMBLE	BEHRRSU BRUSHER	BRISTLE	BEIRSST BESTIRS
BEGLNOS BELONGS	BEHRSSU BRUSHES	RIBLETS	BISTERS
BEGLNRU BLUNGER	BEIIKLR RIBLIKE	BEILRTT BRITTLE	BISTRES
BUNGLER	BEIIKRS BIRKIES	TRIBLET	BEIRSSU BRUISES
BEGLNSU BLUNGES	BEIILLS BILLIES	BEILRTU REBUILT	BEIRSTT BITTERS
BUNGLES	BEIILRS RISIBLE	BEILRTY LIBERTY	BEIRSTU BUSTIER
BEGLOOS GLOBOSE	BEIILSV VISIBLE	BEILRUY BRULYIE	RUBIEST
BEGLOOT BOOTLEG	BEIINOT NIOBITE	BEILRUZ BRULZIE	BEIRTTU TRIBUTE
BEGLOST GOBLETS	BEIINRR BRINIER	BEILSSS BLISSES	BEIRTTY TREYBIT
BEGLOSU GLEBOUS	BEIINST STIBINE	BEILSTU BLUIEST	BEIRTVY BREVITY
BEGLRSU BUGLERS	BEIIOTT BIOTITE	SUBTILE	BEIRUZZ BUZZIER
BULGERS	BEIIRRS BIRSIER	BEILSTW BLEWITS	BEISSTU BUSIEST
BURGLES	BEIIRST BITSIER	BEILSTZ BLITZES	BEISTTU BUTTIES
BEGLRTY BERGYLT	BEIIRTT BITTIER	BEIMMRR BRIMMER	BEITTWX BETWIXT
BEGLSTU BUGLETS	BEIISTT BITTIES	BEIMNOR BROMINE	BEJJSUU JUJUBES
BEGNNUU UNBEGUN	BEIISVV BIVVIES	BEIMNTU BITUMEN	BEJLMRU JUMBLER
BEGNORU BURGEON	BEIJLRS JERBILS	BEIMORW IMBOWER	BEJLMSU JUMBLES
BEGNOSY BYGONES	JIRBLES	BEIMOSS OBEISMS	BEJLOSS JOBLESS
BEGNOTU UNBEGOT	BEIJMSU JUMBIES	BEIMOSZ ZOMBIES	BEJORSU OBJURES
BEGNSUY BUNGEYS	BEIJNSU BUNJIES	BEIMPRU BUMPIER	BEKLNRU BLUNKER
BEGOORS GOOBERS	BEIKLNR BLINKER	BEIMRST BETRIMS	BEKLOOT BOOKLET
BEGORSU BROGUES	BEIKLNS LIBKENS	TIMBERS	BEKLRSU BULKERS
BEGOSTU BOUGETS	BEIKLOS OBELISK	TIMBRES	BEKMNOO BOOKMEN
BEGOSTW BOWGETS	BEIKLRS BILKERS	BEIMRSU ERBIUMS	BEKMOST STEMBOK
BEGRRSU BURGERS	BEIKLRU BULKIER	IMBRUES	BEKNNOW BEKNOWN
BEGRSSU BURGESS	BEIKNRS BRISKEN	IMBURSE	BEKNORS BONKERS
BEHHKOT KHOTBEH	BEIKOOR BOOKIER	BEIMRTU IMBRUTE	BEKNORU UNBROKE
BEHIITX EXHIBIT	BEIKOOS BOOKIES	TERBIUM	BEKNRSU BUNKERS
BEHIKNT BETHINK	BOOKSIE	BEINNOR BONNIER	BEKOPRU UPBROKE
BEHIKRS KIRBEHS	BEIKORS BOSKIER	BEINNOS BENISON	BEKORRS BROKERS
BEHILMS BLEMISH	BEIKRRS BRISKER	BONNIES	BEKORRY BROKERY
BEHILMT THIMBLE	BEIKRST BRISKET	BEINNOZ BENZOIN	BEKOSST BOSKETS
BEHILOS BOLSHIE	BEILLMN BILLMEN	BEINNSU BUNNIES	BEKRSSU BUSKERS
BEHILRT BLITHER	BEILLRU BULLIER	BEINOOS BOONIES	BEKSSTU BUSKETS

BELLORR	BORRELL		BUSTLER	BEORSST	BESORTS	BGGINOY	BYGOING

```
BELLORR  BORRELL           BUSTLER      BEORSST  BESORTS      BGGINOY  BYGOING
BELLOSU  BOULLES           BUTLERS               SORBETS      BGGINSU  BUGGINS
         LOBULES           SUBTLER               STROBES      BGGNOOS  BOGONGS
         SOLUBLE   BELRSUY  BURLEYS      BEORSSU  BOURSES      BGGNOSU  BUGONGS
BELLOSW  BELLOWS   BELRTUY  BUTLERY      BEORSSW  BOWSERS      BGHHIOY  HIGHBOY
BELLOUV  VOLUBLE   BELSSTU  BUSTLES               BROWSES      BGHILST  BLIGHTS
BELLRRU  BURRELL            SUBLETS      BEORSTT  BETTORS      BGHILTY  BLIGHTY
BELLRSU  BULLERS   BELSTTU  BUTTLES      BEORSTU  OBTUSER      BGHINOO  BOOHING
BELLSTU  BULLETS   BELSTUU  TUBULES      BEORSTV  OBVERTS               HOBOING
BELMMOO  EMBLOOM   BEMMNOS  MOBSMEN      BEORSUU  UBEROUS      BGHINOR  BIGHORN
BELMMRU  MUMBLER   BEMMOOS  EMBOSOM      BEORSUZ  BROUZES      BGHINSU  BUSHING
BELMMSU  BUMMELS   BEMMORR  BROMMER               SUBZERO      BGHMSUU  HUMBUGS
         BUMMLES   BEMMRRU  BRUMMER      BEORSVV  BOVVERS      BGHNORU  HORNBUG
         MUMBLES   BEMMRSU  BUMMERS      BEORSWY  BOWYERS      BGHOORU  BOROUGH
BELMNOU  NELUMBO   BEMNORW  EMBROWN      BEORUVY  OVERBUY      BGHORSU  BROUGHS
BELMNSU  NUMBLES   BEMNORY  EMBRYON      BEOSSST  BOSSEST      BGHORTU  BROUGHT
BELMOOR  BLOOMER   BEMNOST  ENTOMBS      BEOSSTT  OBTESTS      BGHOSTU  BOUGHTS
         REBLOOM   BEMNOSU  UMBONES      BEOSSTW  BESTOWS      BGIIKLN  BILKING
BELMOOS  BLOOSME   BEMNOSW  ENWOMBS      BEPRRTU  PERTURB      BGIIKNS  BIKINGS
BELMOPR  PROBLEM   BEMNPTY  BYNEMPT      BEPRTUY  PUBERTY      BGIILLN  BILLING
BELMORT  TEMBLOR   BEMNRSU  NUMBERS      BEPSTUY  SUBTYPE      BGIILMN  LIMBING
BELMOSU  EMBOLUS   BEMNSTU  NUMBEST      BEQRSUU  BRUSQUE      BGIILNO  BOILING
BELMOSY  SYMBOLE   BEMNTTU  BUTMENT      BERRSTU  BURSTER      BGIILNR  BIRLING
BELMPRU  PLUMBER   BEMOORS  BOOMERS      BERSSTU  BUSTERS      BGIILNS  SIBLING
BELMRRU  RUMBLER   BEMORRS  SOMBRER      BERSTTU  BUTTERS      BGIIMNR  BRIMING
BELMRSU  LUMBERS   BEMORSS  SOMBRES      BERSTUV  SUBVERT      BGIIMNU  IMBUING
         RUMBLES   BEMORST  BESTORM      BERSUZZ  BUZZERS      BGIINNN  BINNING
         SLUMBER            MOBSTER      BERTTUY  BUTTERY      BGIINNR  BRINING
         UMBRELS   BEMORSU  UMBROSE      BESSSTU  SUBSETS               INBRING
BELMRTU  TUMBLER   BEMORSY  EMBRYOS      BESTTUX  SUBTEXT      BGIINRT  RINGBIT
         TUMBREL   BEMORUX  BUXOMER      BFFGIIN  BIFFING      BGIINST  BITINGS
BELMRTY  TREMBLY   BEMORWW  WEBWORM      BFFGINO  BOFFING      BGIINTT  BITTING
BELMSTU  STUMBLE   BEMOTUY  MYOTUBE      BFFGINU  BUFFING      BGIKLNU  BULKING
         TUMBLES   BEMPRSU  BUMPERS      BFFIINS  BIFFINS      BGIKNNO  BONKING
BELNNOU  UNNOBLE   BEMSSTU  BESMUTS      BFFINOS  BOFFINS      BGIKNNU  BUNKING
BELNNTU  UNBLENT   BEMSSUU  SUBSUME      BFFLLUY  BLUFFLY      BGIKNOO  BOOKING
BELNOOY  BOLONEY   BENNORU  UNBORNE      BFFNOOU  BUFFOON      BGIKNOR  BROKING
BELNOST  NOBLEST   BENNORW  NEWBORN      BFGIORT  FROGBIT      BGIKNRU  BURKING
BELNOSZ  BENZOLS   BENNORZ  BRONZEN      BFHILSU  LUBFISH      BGIKNSU  BUSKING
BELNOYZ  BENZOYL   BENNOST  BONNETS      BFHIRSU  FURBISH      BGILLNO  BOLLING
BELNRTU  BLUNTER   BENNOSU  UNBONES      BFHISTU  TUBFISH      BGILLNU  BULLING
BELNSSU  UNBLESS   BENOPRU  UPBORNE      BFIILRS  FIBRILS      BGILMNO  MOBLING
BELNSTU  SUNBELT   BENORRW  BROWNER      BFIINOR  FIBROIN      BGILMOU  GUMBOIL
         UNBELTS   BENORST  BRETONS      BFIINRS  FIBRINS      BGILNOS  GLOBINS
         UNBLEST            SORBENT      BFILMRU  BRIMFUL               LOBINGS
BELNSYZ  BENZYLS   BENORSU  BOURNES      BFINOSW  BOWFINS      BGILNOT  BILTONG
BELOOPR  BLOOPER            UNROBES      BFIORSU  FIBROUS               BOLTING
BELOORS  BOLEROS   BENORSZ  BRONZES      BFIRTUY  BRUTIFY      BGILNOW  BLOWING
BELOOSS  SOBOLES   BENORTY  RENTBOY      BFKLOOU  BOOKFUL               BOWLING
BELOPSU  PUEBLOS   BENORWY  BYWONER      BFKLOOY  FLYBOOK      BGILNOY  IGNOBLY
BELORST  BOLSTER   BENOSSU  BONUSES      BFKSSUU  SUBFUSK      BGILNRU  BURLING
         BOLTERS   BENOSUX  UNBOXES      BFLLOWY  BLOWFLY      BGILNSU  BLUINGS
         LOBSTER   BENOSUZ  SUBZONE               FLYBLOW      BGILOOR  OBLIGOR
BELORSU  ROUBLES   BENOSWY  NEWSBOY      BFLOSUX  BOXFULS      BGILOOY  BIOLOGY
BELORSW  BLOWERS   BENRRSU  BURNERS      BFLSTUU  TUBFULS      BGILRSU  BUSGIRL
         BOWLERS   BENRSTU  BRUNETS      BFOOOTY  FOOTBOY      BGIMMNU  BUMMING
BELORSY  SOBERLY            BUNTERS      BGGGIIN  BIGGING      BGIMNNU  NUMBING
BELORTT  BLOTTER            BURNETS      BGGGINO  BOGGING      BGIMNOO  BOOMING
         BOTTLER            BURSTEN      BGGGINU  BUGGING      BGIMNOT  TOMBING
BELORTU  BOULTER   BEOORSS  BROOSES      BGGHIIS  BIGGISH      BGIMNOW  WOMBING
         TROUBLE   BEOORST  BOOSTER      BGGIILN  BILGING      BGIMNPU  BUMPING
BELOSSU  BLOUSES   BEOORSZ  BOOZERS      BGGIINN  BINGING      BGIMOSY  BOGYISM
         BOLUSES   BEOPPRS  BOPPERS      BGGIINS  BIGGINS      BGINNOS  BONINGS
BELOSSW  BLOWSES   BEOPRRV  PROVERB      BGGIISW  BIGWIGS      BGINNOU  BOUNING
BELOSTT  BOTTLES   BEOPRST  BESPORT      BGGILNO  GLOBING      BGINNOW  BOWNING
BELOSTU  BOLETUS   BEOPSST  BESPOTS      BGGILNU  BUGLING      BGINNRU  BURNING
BELOSWZ  BLOWZES   BEOPSTU  BESPOUT               BULGING      BGINNTU  BUNTING
BELRRSU  BURLERS   BEOQSUY  OBSEQUY      BGGINNO  BONGING      BGINOOS  BOOSING
         BURRELS   BEOQTUU  BOUQUET      BGGINNU  BUNGING      BGINOOT  BOOTING
BELRSTU  BLUSTER   BEORRSS  RESORBS      BGGINOU  BOUGING
```

BGINOOZ BOOZING	BIILLNO BILLION	BIOORSZ BORZOIS	BPRSTUU UPBURST
BGINOPP BOPPING	BIILLOU BOUILLI	BIOOSST OBOISTS	CCCDIOO COCCOID
BGINOPR PROBING	BIILLTW TWIBILL	BIOOSUV OBVIOUS	CCCDIOS COCCIDS
BGINORS BORINGS	BIILNNR BIRLINN	BIOPRST PROBITS	CCCNOOT CONCOCT
ROBINGS	BIILNQU QUIBLIN	BIOPRTY PROBITY	CCDEEER RECCEED
SORBING	BIILOSU BILIOUS	BIORRTW RIBWORT	CCDEEHK CHECKED
BGINOSS BOSSING	BIILSVY VISIBLY	BIORSST BISTROS	CCDEEIO ECOCIDE
OBSIGNS	BIIMNOU NIOBIUM	BIORSTT BISTORT	CCDEEIR RECCIED
BGINOSU BOUSING	BIIMNSU MINIBUS	BITTORS	CCDEEIS DECCIES
BGINOSW BOWSING	MINISUB	BIORSUU RUBIOUS	CCDEEKL CLECKED
BGINOSX BOXINGS	BIIMOSS OBIISMS	BIORTTU BITTOUR	CCDEENO CONCEDE
BGINOTT BOTTING	BIIMSTU STIBIUM	BIOSTUW WOUBITS	CCDEENY DECENCY
BGINOUY BUOYING	BIIMSUV BIVIUMS	BIRSTTU BITTURS	CCDEEOR COERCED
BGINPRU BURPING	BIINOST BIOTINS	TURBITS	CCDEESU SUCCEED
UPBRING	BIIORSV VIBRIOS	BISSSTU SUBSIST	CCDEHIL CLICHED
BGINRRU BURRING	BIIOSUV BIVIOUS	BJNOORU BONJOUR	CCDEHIN CINCHED
BGINRTU BRUTING	BIIRSTU BURITIS	BKMNSUU BUNKUMS	CCDEHKO CHOCKED
BGINRUY BURYING	BIISSTV VIBISTS	BKNORSY SKYBORN	CCDEHKU CHUCKED
RUBYING	BIISTTT TITBITS	BKORSWY BYWORKS	CCDEHNO CONCHED
BGINSSU BUSINGS	BIJNOSU SUBJOIN	BLLNTUY BLUNTLY	CCDEHOU COUCHED
BUSSING	BIKLLUY BULKILY	BLLOSUU LOBULUS	CCDEIIT DEICTIC
BGINSTU BUSTING	BIKLNOY LINKBOY	BLLOUVY VOLUBLY	CCDEIKL CLICKED
TUBINGS	BIKLRSY BRISKLY	BLMMPUU PLUMBUM	CCDEIKR CRICKED
BGINSUY BUSYING	BIKMNPU BUMPKIN	BLMNPUU UNPLUMB	CCDEILR CIRCLED
BGINTTU BUTTING	BIKMNSU BUMKINS	BLMOOOT TOMBOLO	CCDEIMO COMEDIC
BGINUZZ BUZZING	BIKMOSS IMBOSKS	BLMOORW LOBWORM	CCDEIOS CODICES
BGIORTY BIGOTRY	BIKNSSU BUSKINS	BLMOOSS BLOSSOM	CCDEKLO CLOCKED
BGIOSSS GOSSIBS	BIKORRW RIBWORK	BLMOSSY SYMBOLS	COCKLED
BGKORSY GRYSBOK	BILLNOS BILLONS	BLMRSUY SLUMBRY	CCDEKLU CLUCKED
BGLMRUY GRUMBLY	BILLNOU BULLION	BLMSTUY STUMBLY	CCDEKOR CROCKED
BGLNOOS OBLONGS	BILLOOY LOOBILY	BLNNOUW UNBLOWN	CCDELOU OCCLUDE
BGLNOOW LONGBOW	BILLOSW BILLOWS	BLNOOSU BLOUSON	CCDENOS SCONCED
BGLNOUW BLOWGUN	BILLOUV VOLUBIL	BLNOPUW UPBLOWN	CCDENOU CONDUCE
BGLOOSU GLOBOUS	BILLOWY BILLOWY	BLNOSTU UNBOLTS	CCDEOST DECOCTS
BGLOSSU BUGLOSS	BILLRWY WRYBILL	BLOOOTX TOOLBOX	CCDHIIL CICHLID
BGMOORS GOMBROS	BILMNOR NOMBRIL	BLOOQUY OBLOQUY	CCDIILO CODICIL
BGMOOTU GUMBOOT	BILMOSU LIMBOUS	BLOOSWY LOWBOYS	CCDIILU CULICID
BGNOOWY GOWNBOY	BILMRSU UMBRILS	BLOPSTU SUBPLOT	CCDIIOR CRICOID
BGOORSU BURGOOS	BILMRTU TUMBRIL	BLOPSUW UPBLOWS	CCDILOY CYCLOID
BGORTUW BUGWORT	BILMSUU BULIMUS	BMNOOSU UNBOSOM	CCDKLOU CUCKOLD
BHIIINT INHIBIT	BILNNOY BONNILY	BMNORUW MOWBURN	CCDNOOR CONCORD
BHIINKS BRINISH	BILNTUU UNBUILT	BMNOSTU UNTOMBS	CCDNOTU CONDUCT
BHIIPSS SIBSHIP	BILOOYZ BOOZILY	BMOOORX BOXROOM	CCEEGNO COGENCE
BHIISST BHISTIS	BILOPSU UPBOILS	BMOORSY BYROOMS	CCEEHKR CHECKER
BHIKOOS BOOKISH	BILOSSU SUBSOIL	BMOOSTT BOTTOMS	RECHECK
BHIKSSU BUKSHIS	BILOSSY BOSSILY	BMOOSTY TOMBOYS	CCEEHOR ECORCHE
BHILLSU BULLISH	BILPTUU UPBUILT	BMORSST STROMBS	CCEEHOU COUCHEE
BHILOTU HOLIBUT	BILRSTY BRISTLY	BMORSUU BRUMOUS	CCEEHRS CRECHES
BHILPSU PUBLISH	TRILBYS	UMBROUS	SCREECH
BHIMOOR RHOMBOI	BILRTUY TILBURY	BNNRSUU SUNBURN	CCEEILN LICENCE
BHIMOOS HOBOISM	BIMMOOS IMBOSOM	BNNRTUU UNBURNT	CCEEINR ECCRINE
BHIMOPS PHOBISM	BIMNORS MISBORN	BNOOSST BOSTONS	CCEEINS SCIENCE
BHIMORT THROMBI	BIMNORW IMBROWN	BNOOSTU BOUTONS	CCEEIRS RECCIES
BHIMSTU BISMUTH	BIMNOSS BONISMS	UNBOOTS	CCEEIRV CREVICE
BHINRSU BURNISH	BIMNOST INTOMBS	BNOOTTY BOTTONY	CCEEKOY COCKEYE
BHIOOPR BIOPHOR	BIMNOSU OMNIBUS	BNORSSU SUBORNS	CCEELRY RECYCLE
BHIOORS BOORISH	BIMNOSY SYMBION	BNORSTU BURTONS	CCEENRY RECENCY
BHIOPSS BISHOPS	BIMRSUX BRUXISM	BNORSUU BURNOUS	CCEEORS COERCES
BHIOPST PHOBIST	BIMSSSU SUBMISS	BNORTUU OUTBURN	CCEERSY SECRECY
BHIOSWZ SHOWBIZ	BIMSSTU SUBMITS	BNOSSUW SUNBOWS	CCEFNOT CONFECT
BHIRSTU BRUTISH	BINNOSU BUNIONS	BNOSTTU BUTTONS	CCEGNOY COGENCY
BHIRTTU TURBITH	BINOORS BONSOIR	BNOTTUY BUTTONY	CCEHHIS CHICHES
BHKNOSU BOHUNKS	BINOOST BONITOS	BOOPSTW BOWPOTS	CCEHIKN CHICKEN
BHLRSUU BULRUSH	BINOOSU NIOBOUS	BOORRSW BORROWS	CCEHIKU CHUCKIE
BHMOORS RHOMBOS	BINORST RIBSTON	BOOSTUW WOOBUTS	CCEHILS CHICLES
BHMORSU RHOMBUS	BINOSST BONISTS	BOOSWWW BOWWOWS	CLICHES
BHMUUZZ HUMBUZZ	BINPSUY BUNYIPS	BORRSUW BURROWS	CCEHIMS CHEMICS
BHOOSTW BOWSHOT	BINRSTU INBURST	BORSSTW BROWSTS	CCEHINO CONCHIE
BIIIKNS BIKINIS	BINSTTU UNBITTS	BORSTTU TURBOTS	CCEHINS CINCHES
BIIKLOT KILOBIT	BINSTUU SUBUNIT	BORSTXY BOSTRYX	CCEHINT TECHNIC

Key	Word(s)
CCEHIOR	CHOICER
CCEHIOS	CHOICES
CCEHIRS	SCREICH
	SCRIECH
CCEHIST	CHICEST
	HECTICS
CCEHKLU	CHUCKLE
CCEHKNU	UNCHECK
CCEHKOR	CHOCKER
CCEHLOS	CLOCHES
CCEHLRU	CLERUCH
CCEHLSU	CLEUCHS
	CULCHES
CCEHNOS	CONCHES
CCEHORS	CROCHES
CCEHORT	CROCHET
CCEHOSS	COSECHS
CCEHOSU	COUCHES
CCEHRSU	CURCHES
CCEHSTU	CUTCHES
CCEIILS	CILICES
	ICICLES
CCEIIMS	CIMICES
CCEIIRT	ICTERIC
CCEIKLR	CLICKER
CCEIKLT	CLICKET
CCEIKOR	COCKIER
CCEIKOS	COCKIES
CCEIKRT	CRICKET
CCEIKRY	CRICKEY
CCEILOT	COCTILE
CCEILRR	CIRCLER
CCEILRS	CIRCLES
	CLERICS
CCEILRT	CIRCLET
CCEILSU	CULICES
CCEILSY	CYLICES
CCEILTU	CUTICLE
CCEIMNO	MECONIC
CCEIMOT	COMETIC
CCEIMST	SMECTIC
CCEINOR	CORNICE
CCEINOS	CONCISE
CCEINOT	CONCEIT
CCEINRT	CENTRIC
CCEIOPP	COPPICE
CCEIOPT	ECTOPIC
CCEIORS	CICEROS
CCEIORT	ORECTIC
CCEIOSS	CISCOES
CCEIPST	SCEPTIC
CCEIRST	CRETICS
CCEJNOT	CONJECT
CCEKLOR	CLOCKER
CCEKLOS	COCKLES
CCEKNOT	CONTECK
CCEKNOY	COCKNEY
CCEKOPS	COPECKS
CCEKOPT	PETCOCK
CCEKORS	COCKERS
CCEKORT	CROCKET
CCEKOST	COCKETS
CCELLOT	COLLECT
CCELNOY	CYCLONE
CCELNUY	LUCENCY
CCELRSY	CYCLERS
CCENNOR	CONCERN
CCENNOT	CONCENT
	CONNECT
CCENOPT	CONCEPT
CCENORT	CONCERT
CCENORW	CONCREW
CCENOSS	SCONCES
CCEOOTT	COCOTTE
CCEOPRT	PERCOCT
CCEORRT	CORRECT
CCEORSS	ESCROCS
	SOCCERS
CCEOSSU	SUCCOSE
CCESSSU	SUCCESS
CCFIRUY	CRUCIFY
CCFLOSU	FLOCCUS
CCGHINO	GNOCCHI
CCGIINS	SICCING
CCGIKNO	COCKING
CCGILNY	CYCLING
CCGKOOR	GORCOCK
CCHHIIS	CHICHIS
CCHHIIT	ICHTHIC
CCHHILS	SCHLICH
CCHHOOS	CHOCHOS
CCHHRUY	CHURCHY
CCHIIST	STICHIC
CCHIKST	SCHTICK
	TCHICKS
CCHILOR	CHLORIC
CCHIMOR	CHROMIC
CCHINOR	CHRONIC
CCHINOS	CHICONS
CCHINSU	SCUCHIN
CCHIORY	CHICORY
CCHIOTW	COWITCH
CCHIPSU	HICCUPS
CCHIPSY	PSYCHIC
CCHIPUY	HICCUPY
CCHIRST	SCRITCH
CCHKLOS	SCHLOCK
CCHKMOS	SCHMOCK
CCHKMSU	SCHMUCK
CCHKOSY	COCKSHY
CCHKSTU	SCHTUCK
CCHNRSU	SCRUNCH
CCHNRUY	CRUNCHY
CCIIILS	SILICIC
CCIILNS	CLINICS
CCIILST	CLITICS
CCIINPS	PICNICS
CCIIRST	CRITICS
CCIIRTU	CIRCUIT
CCIISTY	SICCITY
CCIKLOW	COWLICK
CCIKLOY	COCKILY
	COLICKY
CCIKOPT	COCKPIT
CCILNOO	COLONIC
CCILNOU	COUNCIL
CCILOOP	PICCOLO
CCILSTY	CYCLIST
CCIMOTY	MYCOTIC
CCINOOT	COCTION
CCINORY	CRYONIC
CCINOTV	CONVICT
CCIOORS	SIROCCO
CCIOPTU	OCCIPUT
CCIORSS	SCIROCS
CCIPRTY	CRYPTIC
CCIRSUY	CIRCUSY
CCKMOOS	MOCOCKS
CCKMOSU	MOCUCKS
CCKNOSU	UNCOCKS
CCKOOSU	CUCKOOS
CCKOSTU	CUSTOCK
CCLMSUU	MUCLUCS
CCLOOOZ	ZOCCOLO
CCLOPSY	CYCLOPS
CCLOSTU	OCCULTS
CCMOOOR	MOROCCO
CCNOOOS	COCOONS
CCNOOPU	PUCCOON
CCNOOTU	COCONUT
CCNOPUY	CONCUPY
CCNORSU	CONCURS
CCNOSSU	CONCUSS
CCOOORS	ROCOCOS
CCORSSU	SUCCORS
CCORSUU	SUCCOUR
CCORSUY	SUCCORY
CCOSSTU	STUCCOS
CCSSSUU	SUCCUSS
CDDDEEI	DECIDED
CDDDEEO	DECODED
CDDDEEU	DEDUCED
	CODDLED
CDDDELO	CLODDED
CDDDELU	CUDDLED
CDDDESU	SCUDDED
CDDEEER	DECREED
	RECEDED
CDDEEES	SECEDED
CDDEEII	DEICIDE
CDDEEIN	INCEDED
CDDEEIR	DECIDER
	DECRIED
CDDEEIS	DECIDES
CDDEEIX	EXCIDED
CDDEEKL	DECKLED
CDDEEKO	DECKOED
	DECOKED
CDDEENO	ENCODED
CDDEEOR	DECODER
CDDEEOS	DECODES
CDDEEOY	DECOYED
CDDEERU	REDUCED
CDDEESU	DEDUCES
	SEDUCED
CDDEEUW	CUDWEED
CDDEHIL	CHILDED
CDDEHIN	CHIDDEN
CDDEHIT	DICHTED
	DITCHED
CDDEHNU	DUNCHED
CDDEHOU	DOUCHED
CDDEIIS	DISCIDE
CDDEINU	INDUCED
CDDEISU	CUDDIES
CDDELOS	CODDLES
	SCOLDED
CDDELOU	CLOUDED
CDDELRU	CRUDDLE
	CURDLED
CDDELSU	CUDDLES
	SCUDDLE
CDDENSU	CUDDENS
CDDEORW	CROWDED
CDDERSU	SCUDDER
CDDESTU	DEDUCTS
CDDGINO	CODDING
CDDHIOR	DICHORD
CDDIIIO	DIDICOI
CDDIIOS	DISCOID
CDDIIOY	DIDICOY
CDDIIRU	DRUIDIC
CDDIKOP	PIDDOCK
CDDINSU	CUDDINS
CDDIORS	DISCORD
CDDKOPU	PUDDOCK
CDDKORU	RUDDOCK
CDEEEFL	FLEECED
CDEEEFN	DEFENCE
CDEEEHK	CHEEKED
CDEEEHL	LEECHED
CDEEEHP	CHEEPED
	DEPECHE
CDEEEHR	CHEERED
	REECHED
CDEEEHS	CHEESED
CDEEEIP	EPICEDE
CDEEEIV	DECEIVE
CDEEEJT	EJECTED
CDEEEKL	CLEEKED
CDEEELP	CLEEPED
CDEEELT	ELECTED
CDEEEPR	PRECEDE
CDEEERS	CREESED
	DECREES
	RECEDES
	SECEDER
CDEEERT	DECREET
	ERECTED
CDEEESS	SECEDES
CDEEESX	EXCEEDS
CDEEFHT	FETCHED
CDEEFII	EDIFICE
CDEEFKL	FLECKED
CDEEFLT	DEFLECT
CDEEFOR	DEFORCE
CDEEFST	DEFECTS
CDEEGIR	GRIECED
CDEEGNO	CONGEED
CDEEHIP	CEPHEID
CDEEHIS	DEHISCE
CDEEHIV	CHEVIED
CDEEHKL	HECKLED
CDEEHLT	LETCHED
CDEEHLW	WELCHED
CDEEHMS	SCHEMED
CDEEHNW	WENCHED
CDEEHOR	COHERED
	OCHERED
CDEEHPR	PERCHED
CDEEHRT	RETCHED
CDEEHRU	EUCHRED
CDEEHST	CHESTED
CDEEIIT	EIDETIC
CDEEILN	DECLINE
CDEEILP	PEDICEL
	PEDICLE
CDEEILS	DELICES
CDEEIMN	ENDEMIC
CDEEIMS	DECIMES
CDEEINO	CODEINE
CDEEINR	CEDRINE
CDEEINS	INCEDES
CDEEINT	ENTICED
CDEEINV	EVINCED
CDEEIOS	DIOCESE
CDEEIOV	DEVOICE

CDEEIPR	PIERCED	CDEFFLU	CUFFLED
CDEEIPT	PEDETIC	CDEFFOS	SCOFFED
CDEEIRR	DECRIER	CDEFFSU	SCUFFED
CDEEIRS	DECRIES	CDEFHIL	FILCHED
CDEEIRT	RECITED	CDEFHIN	FINCHED
CDEEIST	DECEITS	CDEFIIT	DEFICIT
CDEEISV	DEVICES	CDEFIKL	FICKLED
CDEEISX	EXCIDES		FLICKED
	EXCISED	CDEFILT	CLIFTED
CDEEITV	EVICTED	CDEFINO	CONFIDE
CDEEITX	EXCITED	CDEFKLO	FLOCKED
CDEEJNO	CONJEED	CDEFKOR	DEFROCK
CDEEJST	DEJECTS		FROCKED
CDEEKKL	KECKLED	CDEFNTU	DEFUNCT
CDEEKLR	CLERKED	CDEFOSU	FOCUSED
CDEEKLS	DECKLES	CDEFRTU	FRUCTED
CDEEKNR	REDNECK	CDEFSUU	FUCUSED
CDEEKNS	SNECKED	CDEGGHU	CHUGGED
CDEEKOS	DECOKES	CDEGGLO	CLOGGED
CDEEKPS	SPECKED		COGGLED
CDEEKRS	DECKERS	CDEGGOS	SCOGGED
CDEEKRT	TRECKED	CDEGGSU	SCUGGED
CDEEKRW	WRECKED	CDEGHLU	GULCHED
CDEELMM	CLEMMED	CDEGHOU	COUGHED
CDEELOS	ECLOSED	CDEGIKN	DECKING
CDEELPU	DECUPLE	CDEGILU	CLUDGIE
CDEELPY	YCLEPED	CDEGINO	COIGNED
CDEELRU	RECULED	CDEGINR	CRINGED
	ULCERED	CDEGINU	EDUCING
CDEELSU	SCEDULE	CDEGIOR	ERGODIC
	SECLUDE	CDEGLSU	CUDGELS
CDEELUX	EXCLUDE	CDEGNSU	SCUNGED
CDEENOR	ENCORED	CDEGOOS	SCOOGED
CDEENOS	ENCODES	CDEGORS	CODGERS
	SECONDE	CDEGOSU	SCOUGED
CDEENOZ	COZENED	CDEHHIL	HILCHED
CDEENRS	DECERNS	CDEHHIT	HITCHED
	SCERNED	CDEHHNU	HUNCHED
CDEENRT	CENTRED	CDEHHOT	HOTCHED
	CREDENT	CDEHHTU	HUTCHED
CDEENST	DESCENT	CDEHIIL	CEILIDH
	SCENTED	CDEHIIV	CHIVIED
CDEEOOY	COOEYED	CDEHIKN	CHINKED
CDEEOPR	COPERED	CDEHIKO	HOICKED
	PROCEED	CDEHIKR	CHIRKED
CDEEORV	COVERED	CDEHIKT	THICKED
CDEEORW	COWERED	CDEHILL	CHILLED
CDEEOST	CESTODE	CDEHILO	CHELOID
	TEDESCO		HELCOID
CDEEOTV	COVETED	CDEHILP	DELPHIC
CDEERRU	RECURED	CDEHILR	CHILDER
	REDUCER		CHIRLED
CDEERSS	SCREEDS	CDEHILS	CHIELDS
CDEERST	CRESTED	CDEHILT	LICHTED
CDEERSU	RECUSED	CDEHIMR	CHIRMED
	REDUCES	CDEHIMT	MITCHED
	RESCUED	CDEHINO	HEDONIC
	SECURED	CDEHINP	PINCHED
	SEDUCER	CDEHINW	WINCHED
CDEERSW	DECREWS	CDEHIOR	CHOIRED
	SCREWED	CDEHIOW	COWHIDE
CDEERTU	ERUCTED	CDEHIPP	CHIPPED
CDEERUV	DECURVE	CDEHIPR	CHIRPED
CDEESSU	SEDUCES	CDEHIPT	PITCHED
CDEESSY	ECDYSES	CDEHIQU	QUICHED
CDEESTT	DECTETS	CDEHIRR	CHIRRED
	DETECTS	CDEHIRS	CHIDERS
CDEESUX	EXCUSED		HERDICS
CDEFFHU	CHUFFED	CDEHIRT	CHIRTED
CDEFFIL	CLIFFED		DITCHER

	RICHTED	CDEIKOZ	DOCKIZE
CDEHIST	DITCHES	CDEIKPR	PRICKED
CDEHISU	DUCHIES	CDEIKRR	DERRICK
CDEHITT	CHITTED	CDEIKRS	DICKERS
CDEHITW	WITCHED		SCRIKED
CDEHIVV	CHIVVED	CDEIKRT	TRICKED
CDEHKOS	SHOCKED	CDEIKRU	DUCKIER
CDEHKSU	SHUCKED	CDEIKRW	WRICKED
CDEHKUY	HEYDUCK	CDEIKST	STICKED
CDEHLMU	MULCHED	CDEIKSU	DUCKIES
CDEHLNU	LUNCHED	CDEIKSY	DICKEYS
CDEHLNY	LYNCHED	CDEILLO	CODILLE
CDEHLOT	CLOTHED		COLLIDE
CDEHLRU	LURCHED		COLLIED
CDEHMMU	CHUMMED	CDEILLU	CULLIED
CDEHMNU	MUNCHED	CDEILMO	MELODIC
CDEHMOO	MOOCHED	CDEILNU	INCLUDE
CDEHMOP	CHOMPED		NUCLIDE
CDEHMOR	CHROMED	CDEILOO	OCELOID
CDEHMOU	MOUCHED	CDEILOP	POLICED
CDEHNOR	CHONDRE	CDEILOR	DOCILER
CDEHNOT	NOTCHED	CDEILPP	CLIPPED
CDEHNPU	PUNCHED	CDEILPS	SPLICED
CDEHNRU	CHUNDER	CDEILPU	CLUPEID
	CHURNED	CDEILRU	LUCIDER
CDEHNSU	DUNCHES	CDEILST	DELICTS
CDEHNSY	SYNCHED	CDEILSU	SLUICED
CDEHOPP	CHOPPED	CDEILTU	DUCTILE
CDEHOPT	POTCHED		DULCITE
CDEHOPU	POUCHED	CDEIMNO	DEMONIC
CDEHORT	TORCHED	CDEIMOR	DORMICE
CDEHORW	CHOWDER	CDEIMOS	MEDICOS
	COWHERD	CDEIMOT	DEMOTIC
CDEHOSU	CHOUSED	CDEIMPR	CRIMPED
	DOUCHES	CDEIMPU	PUMICED
	HOCUSED	CDEIMSU	MISCUED
CDEHOSW	COWSHED	CDEINOS	SECONDI
CDEHOTU	TOUCHED	CDEINOT	CTENOID
CDEHOUV	VOUCHED		DEONTIC
CDEHPSY	PSYCHED		NOTICED
CDEHRRU	CHURRED	CDEINOU	DOUCINE
CDEHRSU	CRUSHED	CDEINOZ	ZINCODE
CDEHSSU	DUCHESS	CDEINPR	PRINCED
CDEHSTU	DUTCHES	CDEINRS	CINDERS
CDEHSTY	SCYTHED		DISCERN
CDEIIKR	DICKIER		RESCIND
CDEIIKS	DICKIES	CDEINRU	INDUCER
CDEIIMR	DIMERIC	CDEINRY	CINDERY
CDEIINS	INCISED	CDEINSU	INCUDES
	INDICES		INCUSED
CDEIINT	IDENTIC		INDUCES
	INCITED	CDEINSX	EXSCIND
CDEIIOR	ERICOID	CDEINTT	TINCTED
CDEIIOV	OVICIDE	CDEIOPR	PERCOID
CDEIIRT	DICTIER	CDEIOPT	PICOTED
	DICIEST	CDEIORS	DISCOER
CDEIISU	SUICIDE	CDEIORT	CORDITE
CDEIJST	DISJECT	CDEIORV	DIVORCE
CDEIKLN	CLINKED	CDEIORW	CROWDIE
CDEIKLP	PICKLED	CDEIOST	CESTOID
CDEIKLS	SICKLED		COTISED
	SLICKED	CDEIPRS	CRISPED
CDEIKLT	TICKLED		DISCERP
CDEIKMS	MEDICKS	CDEIPRT	PREDICT
CDEIKNS	DICKENS	CDEIPST	DEPICTS
	SNICKED		DISCEPT
CDEIKNZ	ZINCKED	CDEIRRU	CURDIER
CDEIKOS	DOCKISE		CURRIED
CDEIKOY	YOICKED	CDEIRST	CREDITS
			DIRECTS

CDEIRSU	CRUISED
	DISCURE
CDEIRSV	SCRIVED
CDEIRTV	VERDICT
CDEISST	DISSECT
CDEISSY	ECDYSIS
CDEITUX	EXCUDIT
CDEJNOU	JOUNCED
CDEKKNO	KNOCKED
CDEKLNO	CLONKED
CDEKLNU	CLUNKED
CDEKLOW	WEDLOCK
CDEKLPU	PLUCKED
CDEKLRU	RUCKLED
CDEKLSU	SCULKED
	SUCKLED
CDEKMOS	SMOCKED
CDEKNOS	DOCKENS
CDEKNRU	DRUCKEN
CDEKNSU	UNDECKS
CDEKOOR	CROOKED
CDEKORS	DOCKERS
CDEKORT	TROCKED
CDEKOST	DOCKETS
	STOCKED
CDEKRSU	DUCKERS
CDEKRTU	TRUCKED
CDELLOU	COLLUDE
CDELLSU	SCULLED
CDELMPU	CLUMPED
CDELMSU	MUSCLED
CDELMTU	MULCTED
CDELNOO	CONDOLE
CDELNOU	ENCLOUD
CDELNOW	CLOWNED
CDELNOY	CONDYLE
CDELOOR	COLORED
	CROODLE
	DECOLOR
CDELOPP	CLOPPED
CDELOPU	COUPLED
CDELORS	SCOLDER
CDELORU	CLOURED
CDELORW	CLOWDER
CDELOST	COLDEST
CDELOSU	DULCOSE
CDELOSW	SCOWLED
CDELOTT	CLOTTED
CDELOTU	CLOUTED
CDELOUY	DOUCELY
CDELPSU	SCULPED
CDELRSU	CURDLES
	SCUDLER
CDELRUY	CRUDELY
CDEMMNO	COMMEND
CDEMMOO	COMMODE
CDEMMSU	SCUMMED
CDEMNNO	CONDEMN
CDEMNOP	COMPEND
CDEMOOS	COMEDOS
CDEMOPT	COMPTED
CDEMORU	DECORUM
CDEMPRU	CRUMPED
CDENNOO	CONDONE
CDENNOT	CONTEND
CDENOOR	CROONED
CDENOOS	SECONDO
CDENOPU	POUNCED
	UNCOPED
CDENORS	CONDERS
	CORSNED
	SCORNED
CDENORW	CROWNED
	DECROWN
CDENOSS	SECONDS
CDENOST	DOCENTS
CDENOTU	COUNTED
CDENPUY	PUDENCY
CDENRUU	UNCURED
CDENRUY	DUNCERY
CDEOOPP	COPEPOD
CDEOOPS	SCOOPED
CDEOORR	CORRODE
CDEOORV	VOCODER
CDEOOST	SCOOTED
CDEOOTV	DOVECOT
CDEOPPR	CROPPED
CDEOPRS	CORPSED
CDEOPRU	CROUPED
	PRODUCE
CDEOPSU	SCOUPED
CDEOPSW	SCOWPED
CDEOQTU	DOCQUET
CDEORRS	RECORDS
CDEORRW	CROWDER
CDEORSS	CROSSED
	SCORSED
CDEORSU	COURSED
	SCOURED
	SOURCED
CDEORSW	SCOWDER
CDEORTU	COURTED
	EDUCTOR
CDEORUU	DOUCEUR
CDEOSSU	ESCUDOS
CDEOSTU	CUSTODE
	DOUCEST
	DOUCETS
	SCOUTED
CDEOSTY	CYTODES
CDEPRSU	SPRUCED
CDEPRTY	DECRYPT
CDERRSU	SCURRED
CDERSTU	CRUDEST
	CRUSTED
CDERSUZ	SCRUZED
CDFHIOS	CODFISH
CDFIILU	FLUIDIC
CDFILUY	DULCIFY
CDFIOOT	OCTOFID
CDFIOSU	FUCOIDS
CDGHIIN	CHIDING
CDGIINO	GONIDIC
CDGIINS	DICINGS
	DISCING
CDGIINT	DICTING
CDGIKNO	DOCKING
CDGIKNU	DUCKING
CDGILNO	CODLING
CDGINNO	CONDIGN
CDGINOR	CORDING
CDGINOS	CODINGS
CDGINRU	CURDING
CDGINTU	DUCTING
CDHIIMO	DOCHMII
CDHIINT	CHINDIT
CDHIIST	DISTICH
CDHILLY	CHILDLY
CDHILNU	UNCHILD
CDHILOS	COLDISH
CDHINOR	CHONDRI
CDHIOOR	CHOROID
	OCHROID
CDHIORS	DROICHS
	ORCHIDS
CDHIORY	DROICHY
CDHIPTY	DIPTYCH
CDHKOOR	HORDOCK
CDIIIOT	IDIOTIC
CDIIJRU	JURIDIC
CDIILLY	IDYLLIC
CDIILMO	DOMICIL
CDIINOR	CRINOID
CDIINOT	DICTION
CDIINOZ	ZINCOID
CDIINST	INDICTS
CDIIOSS	CISSOID
CDIIOTY	IDIOTCY
CDIKNOR	DORNICK
CDIKNOW	WINDOCK
CDILLOO	COLLOID
CDILLUY	LUCIDLY
CDILNOS	CODLINS
CDILOTU	DULOTIC
CDIMMOU	MODICUM
CDIMNOO	MONODIC
CDIMNSU	MUNDICS
CDIMOSU	MUSCOID
CDIMSSU	MUSCIDS
CDINOOS	CONOIDS
CDINOOT	ODONTIC
CDINOSY	SYNODIC
CDINOTU	CONDUIT
	NOCTUID
CDINSSY	SYNDICS
CDINSTU	INDUCTS
CDIOOTT	COTTOID
CDIORSV	CORVIDS
CDIOSST	CODISTS
CDIOSTY	CYSTOID
CDIOTUV	OVIDUCT
CDIPRSY	CYPRIDS
CDIRSUY	DYSURIC
CDIRTUY	CRUDITY
CDISSSU	DISCUSS
CDISSTY	CYSTIDS
CDKNNOU	DUNNOCK
CDKNOSU	UNDOCKS
CDLNOUU	UNCLOUD
CDLOOPY	LYCOPOD
CDMNOOS	CONDOMS
CDMOSUW	MUDSCOW
CDNNOTU	CONTUND
CDNOORS	CONDORS
	CORDONS
CDNORSU	UNCORDS
CDOOOPT	OCTOPOD
CDOOOST	DOOCOTS
CDOORRY	CORRODY
CDOORST	DOCTORS
CDOOTUW	WOODCUT
CDOPRTU	PRODUCT
CDOSTUY	CUSTODY
CEEEEHL	LEECHEE
CEEEFLR	FLEECER
CEEEFLS	FLEECES
CEEEGNR	REGENCE
CEEEGNS	EGENCES
CEEEGRS	GREECES
CEEEHIR	REECHIE
CEEEHKS	KEECHES
CEEEHLS	ELCHEES
	LEECHES
CEEEHNR	ENCHEER
CEEEHPR	CHEEPER
CEEEHRR	CHEERER
CEEEHRS	REECHES
CEEEHSS	CHEESES
CEEEINP	EPICENE
CEEEIPR	CREEPIE
CEEEIRV	RECEIVE
CEEELLU	ECUELLE
CEEELPY	YCLEEPE
CEEELST	CELESTE
CEEELSV	CLEEVES
CEEEMPR	EMPERCE
CEEENRS	RECENSE
CEEENSS	ESSENCE
CEEEPRR	CREEPER
CEEERRT	ERECTER
CEEERSS	CREESES
CEEERST	SECRETE
CEEERSV	SCREEVE
CEEERTX	EXCRETE
CEEETUX	EXECUTE
CEEFFNO	OFFENCE
CEEFFOR	EFFORCE
CEEFFOS	COFFEES
CEEFFST	EFFECTS
CEEFHIR	CHIEFER
CEEFHIT	FETICHE
	FITCHEE
CEEFHLS	FLECHES
CEEFHRT	FECHTER
CEEFHST	FETCHES
CEEFINV	VENEFIC
CEEFIRR	FIERCER
CEEFKLR	FLECKER
	FRECKLE
CEEFLNU	FLUENCE
CEEFLRT	REFLECT
CEEFNNS	FENNECS
CEEFNOR	ENFORCE
CEEFNRS	FENCERS
CEEFPRT	PERFECT
	PREFECT
CEEFRST	REFECTS
CEEFSSU	FESCUES
CEEGHIN	EECHING
CEEGINR	CREEING
	ENERGIC
CEEGINT	GENETIC
CEEGINU	EUGENIC
CEEGIRS	CIERGES
	GRIECES
CEEGKOS	GECKOES
CEEGLLO	COLLEGE
CEEGLNT	NEGLECT
CEEGLOU	ECLOGUE
CEEGNOR	COGENER
	CONGREE
CEEGNOS	CONGEES
CEEGNRU	URGENCE
CEEGNRY	REGENCY
CEEGORT	CORTEGE
CEEGQRU	GRECQUE
CEEHHSW	WHEECHS
CEEHILN	ELENCHI
CEEHILS	HELICES

	LICHEES
CEEHILV	VEHICLE
CEEHIMR	CHIMERE
CEEHIMS	CHEMISE
CEEHINR	INHERCE
CEEHINS	CHINESE
CEEHIOR	CHEERIO
CEEHIOS	ECHOISE
CEEHIOZ	ECHOIZE
CEEHIRT	ETHERIC
	HERETIC
	TECHIER
CEEHIRW	CHEWIER
CEEHISS	SEICHES
CEEHISV	CHEVIES
CEEHKLR	HECKLER
CEEHKLS	HECKLES
CEEHKNP	HENPECK
CEEHKST	KETCHES
CEEHLNO	ECHELON
CEEHLNS	ELENCHS
CEEHLNU	LEUCHEN
CEEHLOW	COWHEEL
CEEHLRS	LECHERS
CEEHLRW	WELCHER
CEEHLRY	CHEERLY
	LECHERY
CEEHLSS	CHESSEL
CEEHLST	LETCHES
CEEHLSW	LECHWES
	WELCHES
CEEHLSY	LYCHEES
	SLEECHY
CEEHMRS	SCHEMER
CEEHMRT	MERCHET
CEEHMSS	SCHEMES
CEEHNPU	PENUCHE
CEEHNRW	WENCHER
CEEHNST	CHENETS
	TENCHES
CEEHNSV	CHEVENS
CEEHNSW	WENCHES
	WHENCES
CEEHORR	COHERER
CEEHORS	CHEEROS
	CHOREES
	COHERES
	ECHOERS
CEEHORT	TROCHEE
CEEHOUV	VOUCHEE
CEEHPRR	PERCHER
CEEHPRS	PERCHES
CEEHPRU	UPCHEER
CEEHQRU	CHEQUER
CEEHQSU	CHEQUES
CEEHQUY	QUEECHY
CEEHRST	ETCHERS
	RETCHES
CEEHRSU	EUCHRES
CEEHRSY	CREESHY
CEEHRTU	TEUCHER
CEEHSSS	CHESSES
CEEHSSW	ESCHEWS
CEEHSTV	VETCHES
CEEHSTW	CHEWETS
CEEIINR	EIRENIC
CEEIIPR	EPICIER
CEEIJOR	REJOICE
CEEIKLT	CLEEKIT
CEEIKNT	NECKTIE
CEEIKPR	PICKEER
CEEILLM	MICELLE
CEEILNO	CINEOLE
CEEILNR	RECLINE
CEEILNS	LICENSE
	SELENIC
	SILENCE
CEEILNU	LEUCINE
CEEILPS	ECLIPSE
CEEILRT	RETICLE
	TIERCEL
CEEILRU	RECUILE
CEEILST	SECTILE
CEEILSV	VESICLE
CEEILTU	LEUCITE
CEEIMNT	CENTIME
CEEIMRS	MERCIES
CEEIMST	EMETICS
CEEINNS	INCENSE
CEEINOS	SENECIO
CEEINPR	PERCINE
CEEINPS	PICENES
	PIECENS
CEEINPT	PENTICE
CEEINRS	CERESIN
	SCRIENE
	SINCERE
CEEINRT	ENTERIC
	ENTICER
CEEINRV	CERVINE
CEEINST	ENTICES
CEEINSV	EVINCES
CEEIOPT	PICOTEE
CEEIORT	COTERIE
CEEIPRR	CREPIER
	PIERCER
CEEIPRS	PIECERS
	PIERCES
	PRECISE
	RECIPES
CEEIPRT	RECEIPT
CEEIPRU	EPICURE
CEEIPSS	SPECIES
CEEIPST	PECTISE
CEEIPTZ	PECTIZE
CEEIQSU	QUIESCE
CEEIRRT	RECITER
CEEIRSS	CERISES
CEEIRST	CERITES
	RECITES
	TIERCES
CEEIRSU	ECURIES
CEEIRSV	SCRIEVE
	SERVICE
CEEIRTU	EUCRITE
CEEIRTX	EXCITER
CEEISSX	EXCISES
CEEISTX	EXCITES
CEEITTZ	ZETETIC
CEEJNOS	CONJEES
CEEJORT	EJECTOR
CEEJRST	REJECTS
CEEKKLS	KECKLES
CEEKKSS	KECKSES
CEEKLNT	NECKLET
CEEKLPS	SPECKLE
CEEKLSS	SECKELS
CEEKLST	TECKELS
CEEKOOS	COKESES
CEEKOSY	SOCKEYE
CEEKPRS	PECKERS
CEEKPRY	RYEPECK
CEEKRRW	WRECKER
CEELLLU	CELLULE
CEELLNO	COLLEEN
CEELLPU	PUCELLE
CEELMNT	CLEMENT
CEELMOO	COELOME
CEELMOT	TELECOM
CEELMOW	WELCOME
CEELNOS	ENCLOSE
CEELNPS	PENCELS
CEELNRS	CRENELS
CEELNRT	LECTERN
CEELNRU	LUCERNE
CEELORS	CREOLES
	RECLOSE
CEELORT	ELECTOR
	ELECTRO
CEELORY	RECOYLE
CEELOSS	ECLOSES
CEELOSU	COULEES
CEELOTU	ELOCUTE
CEELOTV	COVELET
CEELPRT	PLECTRE
	PRELECT
CEELRSS	SCLERES
CEELRST	TERCELS
CEELRSU	RECLUSE
	RECULES
CEELRSW	CREWELS
CEELRTU	LECTURE
CEELRTY	ERECTLY
CEELSST	SELECTS
CEELTTU	LETTUCE
CEEMMOR	COMMERE
CEEMNOW	NEWCOME
CEEMNRU	CERUMEN
CEEMNST	CEMENTS
CEEMOPR	COMPEER
	COMPERE
CEEMOPT	COMPETE
CEEMRRS	MERCERS
CEEMRRY	MERCERY
	REMERCY
CEEMRST	CERMETS
CEEMSTU	TUMESCE
CEEMSTY	MYCETES
CEENNOU	ENOUNCE
CEENNOV	CONVENE
CEENNRT	CENTNER
CEENOPT	POTENCE
CEENORS	ENCORES
	NECROSE
CEENORZ	COZENER
CEENOST	CENOTES
CEENPRS	SPENCER
CEENPSS	SPENCES
CEENRSS	CENSERS
	SCERNES
	SCREENS
	SECERNS
CEENRST	CENTERS
	CENTRES
	TENRECS
CEENRSU	CENSURE
CEENRSY	SCENERY
CEENTTU	CUNETTE
CEEOPST	PECTOSE
CEEOPSU	COUPEES
CEEOPTY	ECOTYPE
CEEORRS	RESCORE
CEEORRT	ERECTOR
CEEORRU	RECOURE
CEEORRV	RECOVER
CEEORRW	RECOWER
CEEORSU	CEREOUS
CEEORSV	CORVEES
CEEOTTT	OCTETTE
CEEPPRT	PERCEPT
	PRECEPT
CEEPPRU	PREPUCE
CEEPRSS	PRECESS
CEEPRST	RECEPTS
	RESPECT
	SCEPTRE
	SPECTER
	SPECTRE
CEEPRTX	EXCERPT
CEEPSTX	EXCEPTS
	EXPECTS
CEEPSTY	ECTYPES
CEERRSU	RECURES
	RESCUER
	SECURER
CEERRSW	SCREWER
CEERRUV	RECURVE
CEERSSS	CESSERS
	CRESSES
CEERSST	CRESSET
	RESECTS
	SECRETS
CEERSSU	CERUSES
	CESURES
	RECUSES
	RESCUES
	SECURES
CEERSTT	TERCETS
CEERSUX	EXCURSE
	EXCUSER
CEERTTU	CURETTE
CEESSTX	EXSECTS
CEESSUX	EXCUSES
CEETTUV	CUVETTE
CEFFIOR	OFFICER
CEFFIOS	OFFICES
CEFFISU	SUFFICE
CEFFLOS	COFFLES
CEFFLSU	CUFFLES
	SCUFFLE
CEFFORS	COFFERS
	SCOFFER
CEFFORT	COFFRET
CEFGINN	FENCING
CEFHILR	FILCHER
CEFHILS	FILCHES
CEFHILY	CHIEFLY
CEFHINS	FINCHES
CEFHIRY	CHIEFRY
CEFHIST	FITCHES
CEFHITT	FITCHET
CEFHITW	FITCHEW
CEFHLTU	FUTCHEL
CEFIILT	FICTILE
CEFIIOR	ORIFICE
CEFIITV	FICTIVE
CEFIKLR	FICKLER
	FLICKER
CEFIKLS	FICKLES
CEFILNT	INFLECT

CEFILNU	FUNICLE	CEGINNR	CERNING		TINCHEL		HOCKERS
CEFILRU	LUCIFER	CEGINNS	CENSING	CEHILPR	PILCHER		SHOCKER
CEFIMOR	COMFIER		SCENING	CEHILPS	PILCHES	CEHKOSY	CHOKEYS
CEFIMRY	MERCIFY	CEGINOS	COGNISE	CEHILRT	LICHTER		HOCKEYS
CEFINNO	CONFINE		COIGNES	CEHILRV	CHERVIL	CEHKPTU	KETCHUP
CEFINOR	CONIFER	CEGINOZ	COGNIZE	CEHILSS	CHESILS	CEHKRSU	SHUCKER
	INFORCE	CEGINPR	CREPING		CHISELS	CEHKSTU	KUTCHES
CEFINST	INFECTS		PERCING	CEHILST	ELTCHIS	CEHKSTY	SKETCHY
CEFIPSY	SPECIFY	CEGINRR	CRINGER	CEHILSZ	ZILCHES	CEHLLMO	MOCHELL
CEFIRSS	SFERICS	CEGINRS	CRINGES	CEHILTY	LECYTHI	CEHLLMU	MUCHELL
CEFIRTY	CERTIFY	CEGINRW	CREWING	CEHIMMS	CHEMISM	CEHLLNS	SCHNELL
	RECTIFY	CEGINSS	CESSING	CEHIMNY	CHIMNEY	CEHLLOY	YELLOCH
CEFKLOT	FETLOCK	CEGIRRS	GRICERS	CEHIMOR	MORICHE	CEHLMSS	SCHELMS
CEFKLRY	FRECKLY	CEGKLOR	GROCKLE	CEHIMOS	ECHOISM	CEHLMSU	MUCHELS
CEFKRSU	FUCKERS	CEGLOOY	ECOLOGY	CEHIMRS	CHIMERS		MULCHES
CEFLNOU	FLOUNCE	CEGLOSU	GLUCOSE		MICHERS	CEHLMSZ	SCHMELZ
CEFLNUY	FLUENCY	CEGLOSY	GLYCOSE	CEHIMRT	THERMIC	CEHLMUY	CHUMLEY
CEFMORY	COMFREY	CEGNNOO	ONCOGEN	CEHIMST	CHEMIST	CEHLNNU	CHUNNEL
CEFNORS	CONFERS	CEGNORS	CONGERS		MITCHES	CEHLNOS	NOCHELS
CEFNORU	FROUNCE	CEGNORU	CONGRUE	CEHINOP	CHOPINE	CEHLNOT	NOTCHEL
CEFNOSS	CONFESS	CEGNORY	CONGERY		PHOCINE	CEHLNRU	LUNCHER
CEFNOST	CONFEST		CRYOGEN	CEHINOR	CHORINE	CEHLNSU	LUNCHES
CEFNOSU	CONFUSE	CEGNOST	CONGEST	CEHINOT	HENOTIC	CEHLNSY	LYNCHES
CEFNOTU	CONFUTE	CEGNRUY	URGENCY	CEHINOX	CHOENIX	CEHLNTY	LYNCHET
CEFOPRS	FORCEPS	CEGNSSU	SCUNGES	CEHINPR	NEPHRIC	CEHLOOS	SCHOOLE
CEFORRS	FORCERS	CEGNSTY	CYGNETS		PHRENIC	CEHLORS	CHOLERS
CEFORRT	CROFTER	CEGOORS	SCROOGE		PINCHER		ORCHELS
CEFORSS	FRESCOS	CEGORRS	GROCERS	CEHINPS	PINCHES	CEHLORT	CHORTLE
CEFOSSU	FOCUSES	CEGORRY	GROCERY		SPHENIC	CEHLOST	CLOTHES
CEFRSUW	CURFEWS	CEGORSU	SCOURGE	CEHINPU	PENUCHI	CEHLPPS	SCHLEPP
CEFSSUU	FUCUSES		SCROUGE	CEHINQU	QUINCHE	CEHLPSS	SCHLEPS
CEGGHIR	CHIGGER	CEHHILS	HILCHES	CEHINRS	NICHERS	CEHLPSU	PLEUCHS
CEGGIIS	CIGGIES	CEHHIRS	CHERISH		RICHENS	CEHLQSU	SQUELCH
CEGGIKN	GECKING		SHRIECH	CEHINRT	CITHERN	CEHLRRU	LURCHER
CEGGIOR	GEORGIC	CEHHIRT	HITCHER	CEHINST	ETHNICS	CEHLRSU	LURCHES
CEGGIOS	COGGIES	CEHHIST	HITCHES		STHENIC	CEHMNRU	MUNCHER
CEGGLOR	CLOGGER	CEHHNSU	HUNCHES	CEHINSU	ECHINUS	CEHMNSU	MUNCHES
CEGGLOS	COGGLES	CEHHOOS	HOOCHES	CEHINSV	CHEVINS	CEHMOOR	MOOCHER
CEGGORS	COGGERS	CEHHOST	HOTCHES	CEHINSW	WINCHES	CEHMOOS	MOOCHES
CEGGPSU	EGGCUPS		SHOCHET	CEHINTW	WITCHEN	CEHMORS	CHROMES
CEGHILN	LECHING	CEHHSSU	SHEUCHS	CEHIOPS	HOSPICE	CEHMORU	MOUCHER
CEGHINO	ECHOING	CEHHSTU	HUTCHES	CEHIOPT	POTICHE	CEHMOSS	SCHMOES
CEGHINP	PECHING	CEHIIKN	CHINKIE	CEHIORS	HEROICS	CEHMOSU	MOUCHES
CEGHINT	ETCHING	CEHIINR	HIRCINE	CEHIORT	ROTCHIE	CEHMSTU	HUMECTS
CEGHINW	CHEWING	CEHIINS	NICEISH		THEORIC		MUTCHES
CEGHIOR	CHOREGI	CEHIINT	ICHNITE	CEHIOST	ECHOIST	CEHNNRU	CHUNNER
CEGHIOS	CHIGOES	CEHIIPP	CHIPPIE		TOISECH	CEHNOOR	COEHORN
CEGHIRS	CHIGRES	CEHIIRT	ITCHIER	CEHIOTU	COUTHIE	CEHNORV	CHEVRON
	SCREIGH		TICHIER	CEHIPPR	CHIPPER	CEHNOST	NOTCHES
CEGHITU	GUICHET	CEHIISV	CHIVIES	CEHIPRR	CHIRPER	CEHNOSU	COHUNES
CEGHLSU	CLEUGHS	CEHIKNT	KITCHEN	CEHIPRS	CERIPHS	CEHNPRU	PUNCHER
	GULCHES		THICKEN		CIPHERS		UNPERCH
CEGHORU	COUGHER	CEHIKNW	CHEWINK		SPHERIC	CEHNPSU	PUNCHES
CEGHRTU	GUTCHER	CEHIKOO	CHOOKIE	CEHIPRT	PITCHER	CEHNRSU	RUNCHES
CEGIILN	CEILING	CEHIKOR	CHOKIER	CEHIPST	PITCHES	CEHNRTU	CHUNTER
	CIELING	CEHIKOS	CHOKIES	CEHIQSU	QUICHES	CEHNSTU	CHESNUT
CEGIINP	PIECING	CEHIKPS	PECKISH	CEHIRRT	RICHTER	CEHNSTY	STENCHY
CEGIKKN	KECKING	CEHIKRS	SHICKER	CEHIRST	CITHERS	CEHNSUU	EUNUCHS
CEGIKNN	NECKING		SKRIECH		ESTRICH	CEHNTUY	CHUTNEY
CEGIKNP	PECKING	CEHIKRT	THICKER		RICHEST	CEHOOPS	POOCHES
CEGIKNR	RECKING	CEHIKRW	WHICKER	CEHIRSU	CUSHIER	CEHOORS	CHOOSER
CEGIKRU	GUCKIER	CEHIKST	CHEKIST	CEHIRSZ	SCHERZI		SOROCHE
CEGILNP	CLEPING	CEHIKSY	HICKEYS	CEHIRTT	CHITTER	CEHOORT	CHEROOT
CEGILNR	CLINGER	CEHIKTT	THICKET	CEHISSU	CUISHES	CEHOOSS	CHOOSES
	CRINGLE	CEHILLR	CHILLER	CEHISTT	TITCHES	CEHOOSY	CHOOSEY
CEGILNU	CLUEING	CEHILMY	CHIMLEY	CEHISTW	WITCHES	CEHOPPR	CHOPPER
	LUCIGEN	CEHILNO	CHOLINE	CEHKKRU	CHUKKER	CEHOPRS	PORCHES
CEGILNW	CLEWING	CEHILNS	LICHENS	CEHKLMO	HEMLOCK	CEHOPRT	POTCHER
CEGILNY	GLYCINE		LINCHES	CEHKLSU	HUCKLES	CEHOPRY	CORYPHE
CEGIMNU	MUCIGEN	CEHILNT	LINCHET	CEHKORS	CHOKERS	CEHOPST	POTCHES

CEHOPSU	POUCHES		CRINITE
CEHORRT	TORCHER		INCITER
CEHORSS	COSHERS		NERITIC
CEHORST	HECTORS	CEIINRZ	ZINCIER
	ROCHETS	CEIINSS	ICINESS
	ROTCHES		INCISES
	TOCHERS	CEIINST	INCITES
	TORCHES	CEIINSU	CUISINE
	TROCHES	CEIINTZ	CITIZEN
CEHORSU	CHOREUS		ZINCITE
CEHORSY	COSHERY	CEIIOPZ	EPIZOIC
CEHORSZ	SCHERZO	CEIIPPR	PIPERIC
CEHORTU	COUTHER	CEIIPRR	PRICIER
	RETOUCH	CEIIPRS	SPICIER
	TOUCHER	CEIIPRT	PICRITE
CEHORTW	WOTCHER	CEIIPST	EPICIST
CEHORUV	VOUCHER	CEIIRSS	CISSIER
CEHOSSU	CHOUSES	CEIIRST	ERISTIC
	HOCUSES		RICIEST
CEHOSTU	TOUCHES	CEIIRSU	CRUISIE
CEHOSUV	VOUCHES	CEIISSS	CISSIES
CEHPRSU	CHERUPS	CEIISVV	CIVVIES
CEHPRSY	CHYPRES	CEIJNST	INJECTS
	CYPHERS	CEIJRSU	JUICERS
CEHPRTU	PUTCHER	CEIJSTU	JUSTICE
CEHPSSY	PSYCHES	CEIKKNR	KNICKER
CEHQSTU	QUETSCH	CEIKKRS	KICKERS
CEHRRSU	CRUSHER	CEIKLMS	MICKLES
CEHRSSU	CRUSHES	CEIKLNR	CLINKER
CEHRSTT	STRETCH		CRINKLE
CEHRSTY	SCYTHER	CEIKLNS	NICKELS
CEHSSTU	TUSCHES		SLICKEN
CEHSSTY	SCYTHES	CEIKLPR	PICKLER
CEIIJRU	JUICIER		PRICKLE
CEIIKLS	SICLIKE	CEIKLPS	PICKLES
CEIIKMS	MICKIES	CEIKLRS	LICKERS
CEIIKNT	KINETIC		RICKLES
CEIIKPR	PICKIER		SLICKER
CEIIKQU	QUICKIE	CEIKLRT	TICKLER
CEIIKSS	SICKIES		TRICKLE
CEIIKST	EKISTIC	CEIKLRU	LUCKIER
	ICKIEST	CEIKLSS	SICKLES
	TICKIES	CEIKLST	STICKLE
CEIIKSW	WICKIES		TICKLES
CEIILLS	SILICLE	CEIKLSU	LUCKIES
CEIILNN	INCLINE	CEIKLSY	KYLICES
CEIILPP	CLIPPIE	CEIKMRS	SMICKER
CEIILPT	PELITIC	CEIKMRU	MUCKIER
CEIILST	ELICITS	CEIKMST	SMICKET
CEIILTV	LEVITIC	CEIKMSY	MICKEYS
CEIIMMT	MIMETIC	CEIKNOS	CONKIES
CEIIMNR	CRIMINE	CEIKNOT	KENOTIC
CEIIMNS	MENISCI	CEIKNQU	QUICKEN
CEIIMOT	MEIOTIC	CEIKNRS	NICKERS
CEIIMPR	EMPIRIC		SNICKER
CEIIMPS	EPICISM	CEIKNSS	SICKENS
CEIIMRS	CIMIERS	CEIKNST	SNICKET
CEIIMSS	SEISMIC		TICKENS
CEIIMTT	TITMICE	CEIKNSW	WICKENS
CEIINNO	CONIINE	CEIKOOS	COOKIES
	INCONIE	CEIKOPR	POCKIER
CEIINOR	ONEIRIC	CEIKORR	CORKIER
CEIINOS	ICONISE		ROCKIER
CEIINOV	INVOICE	CEIKOST	COKIEST
CEIINOZ	ICONIZE	CEIKPRR	PRICKER
CEIINPS	PISCINE	CEIKPRS	PICKERS
CEIINRS	IRENICS		RIPECKS
	SERICIN		SPICKER
	SIRENIC	CEIKPRT	PRICKET
CEIINRT	CITRINE		

CEIKPRY	PICKERY	CEIMNOR	INCOMER
CEIKPST	PICKETS	CEIMNOS	INCOMES
	SKEPTIC		MESONIC
CEIKQRU	QUICKER	CEIMNOT	ENTOMIC
CEIKRRS	RICKERS		TONEMIC
CEIKRRT	TRICKER	CEIMNRS	CREMSIN
CEIKRSS	SCRIKES		MINCERS
CEIKRST	RICKETS	CEIMNRU	NUMERIC
	STICKER	CEIMNYZ	ENZYMIC
	TICKERS	CEIMOOR	COOMIER
CEIKRSW	WICKERS	CEIMOPT	METOPIC
CEIKRSY	YICKERS	CEIMOQU	COMIQUE
CEIKRTY	RICKETY	CEIMORR	MORRICE
CEIKRUY	YUCKIER	CEIMORT	MORTICE
CEIKSST	SICKEST	CEIMOTT	TOTEMIC
CEIKSTT	TICKETS	CEIMOTV	VICOMTE
CEIKSTW	WICKETS	CEIMPPR	CRIMPER
CEIKSTY	TICKEYS	CEIMPRS	SPERMIC
CEILLNO	LIONCEL	CEIMPSU	PUMICES
CEILLNU	NUCELLI	CEIMRST	CRETISM
CEILLOR	COLLIER		METRICS
CEILLOS	COLLIES	CEIMRSU	CERIUMS
CEILLST	CELLIST		MURICES
CEILLSU	CULLIES	CEIMSSU	CESIUMS
CEILMOP	COMPILE		MISCUES
	POLEMIC	CEINNOS	CONINES
CEILMPR	CRIMPLE	CEINNOV	CONNIVE
CEILNNU	NUCLEIN	CEINOOT	COONTIE
CEILNOP	PINOCLE	CEINOPR	PERICON
CEILNOS	CINEOLS		PORCINE
	CONSEIL	CEINOPT	ENTOPIC
	INCLOSE		NEPOTIC
CEILNOT	LECTION	CEINORR	CORNIER
CEILNOX	LEXICON	CEINORS	COINERS
CEILNPS	PENCILS		CRINOSE
	SPLENIC		CRONIES
CEILNST	CLIENTS		ORCEINS
	LECTINS		ORCINES
	STENCIL		SERICON
CEILNSU	LEUCINS	CEINORT	RECTION
CEILNTU	CUTLINE	CEINORU	NOURICE
	TUNICLE	CEINORV	CORVINE
CEILOOS	COOLIES	CEINORY	ORIENCY
CEILOPR	PELORIC	CEINOSS	CESSION
CEILOPS	POLICES		COSINES
CEILOPT	TOECLIP	CEINOST	NOTICES
CEILORS	RECOILS		SECTION
CEILORT	CORTILE	CEINOSV	NOVICES
CEILORU	URCEOLI	CEINOTT	ENTOTIC
CEILOSS	OSSICLE		TONETIC
CEILOST	CITOLES	CEINOTX	EXCITON
CEILPPR	CLIPPER	CEINOUV	UNVOICE
	CRIPPLE	CEINOVV	CONNIVE
CEILPSS	SPLICES	CEINPRS	PINCERS
CEILPSU	SPICULE		PRINCES
CEILQSU	CLIQUES	CEINPRY	CYPRINE
CEILQUY	CLIQUEY	CEINPST	INCEPTS
CEILRRU	CURLIER		INSPECT
CEILRSS	SLICERS		PECTINS
CEILRST	RELICTS		PEINCTS
CEILRSV	CLIVERS	CEINPTY	PYCNITE
CEILRSY	CLERISY	CEINQSU	CINQUES
CEILRTT	CLITTER		QUINCES
CEILRTU	UTRICLE	CEINRRU	CURNIER
CEILSSS	SCISSEL	CEINRSS	SCRINES
CEILSSU	SLUICES	CEINRST	CISTERN
CEILTTU	CUITTLE		CRETINS
CEIMMOS	COMMIES	CEINRSV	CRIVENS
CEIMMRR	CRIMMER	CEINRSW	WINCERS
CEIMNNO	MECONIN	CEINRTT	CITTERN

CEINRUV	INCURVE	CEIRSSV	SCRIVES	CEKSTTU	TUCKETS	CELOSTY	COTYLES
CEINSST	INCESTS	CEIRSTT	TRISECT	CELLMOU	COLUMEL	CELOSUV	VOCULES
	INSECTS	CEIRSTU	CUITERS	CELLNOO	COLONEL	CELOTTU	CULOTTE
CEINSSU	INCUSES		CURIETS	CELLNOS	ESCROLL	CELPRSU	CURPELS
CEINSTY	INSECTY		ICTERUS	CELLOST	COLLETS		SCRUPLE
CEINSWY	WINCEYS	CEIRSTW	TWICERS	CELLOSU	CUPULES	CELPSUU	CUPULES
CEINTTX	EXTINCT	CEIRSUV	CRUIVES		OCELLUS	CELPSUY	CLYPEUS
CEINVVY	VIVENCY		CURSIVE	CELLOSY	CLOSELY	CELRRSU	CURLERS
CEIOOPR	OPORICE	CEIRTTU	CUTTIER	CELLRRU	CRULLER	CELRSTU	CLUSTER
CEIOPPS	COPPIES	CEIRTTX	TECTRIX	CELLRSU	CRUELLS		CULTERS
CEIOPRS	COPIERS	CEISSSU	CUISSES		CULLERS		CUSTREL
	COPSIER	CEISSTU	CESTUIS		SCULLER		CUTLERS
	PERSICO		CUEISTS	CELLRUY	CRUELLY		RELUCTS
CEIOPST	POETICS		CUTISES	CELLSSU	SCULLES	CELRSTY	CLYSTER
CEIOPSU	PICEOUS		ICTUSES	CELLSTU	CULLETS	CELRSUV	CULVERS
CEIORRS	CIRROSE	CEISTTU	CUTTIES	CELMNOO	LOCOMEN	CELRSUW	CURLEWS
	CORRIES	CEJKOSY	JOCKEYS		MONOCLE	CELRTTU	CLUTTER
	CROSIER	CEJNORU	CONJURE	CELMNSU	CULMENS	CELRTUU	CULTURE
CEIORRU	COURIER	CEJNOSU	JOUNCES	CELMOOS	COELOMS	CELRTUV	CULVERT
CEIORRZ	CROZIER		JUNCOES	CELMOPS	COMPELS	CELRTUY	CRUELTY
CEIORSS	COSIERS	CEJOPRT	PROJECT	CELMOPX	COMPLEX		CUTLERY
CEIORST	EROTICS	CEKKLNU	KNUCKLE	CELMPRU	CRUMPLE	CELSTTU	CUTLETS
	TERCIOS	CEKKNOR	KNOCKER	CELMSSU	MUSCLES		CUTTLES
CEIORSU	SCOURIE	CEKKOPS	KOPECKS	CELMSUU	SECULUM		SCUTTLE
CEIORSV	CORSIVE	CEKLLOP	PELLOCK	CELMSUY	LYCEUMS	CEMMNOT	COMMENT
	VOICERS	CEKLLRY	CLERKLY	CELNNOU	NUCLEON	CEMMNOU	COMMUNE
CEIORSW	COWRIES	CEKLMNO	LOCKMEN	CELNNSU	NUNCLES	CEMMOOT	COMMOTE
	SCOWRIE	CEKLMSU	MUCKLES	CELNOOS	COLONES	CEMMOOV	COMMOVE
CEIORSZ	COZIERS	CEKLNOS	ENLOCKS		CONSOLE	CEMMORS	COMMERS
CEIORTT	COTTIER		SLOCKEN	CELNORS	CORNELS	CEMMOTU	COMMUTE
CEIORTV	EVICTOR	CEKLNRU	CRUNKLE	CELNOSU	COUNSEL	CEMMRSU	CUMMERS
CEIORTX	EXCITOR	CEKLORS	LOCKERS		UNCLOSE		SCUMMER
	XEROTIC	CEKLOST	LOCKETS	CELNOTU	NOCTULE	CEMNNOT	CONTEMN
CEIORVY	VICEROY	CEKLPRU	PLUCKER	CELNRSU	LUCERNS	CEMNOOP	COMPONE
CEIOSSS	COSSIES	CEKLRSU	RUCKLES	CELNRTU	LECTURN	CEMNOOS	ONCOMES
CEIOSST	COSIEST		SUCKLER	CELNSUU	NUCLEUS	CEMNOOY	ECONOMY
	COTISES	CEKLRTU	TRUCKLE		NUCULES	CEMNOSU	CONSUME
	OECISTS	CEKLSSU	SUCKLES	CELNSUW	UNCLEWS		MUSCONE
CEIOSSV	VISCOSE	CEKMORS	MOCKERS	CELOORS	COOLERS	CEMNRSU	CRUMENS
CEIOSTT	COTTISE	CEKMORY	MOCKERY	CELOOST	COOLEST	CEMNRTU	CENTRUM
CEIOSTV	COSTIVE	CEKMRSU	MUCKERS		OCELOTS	CEMNSTU	CENTUMS
CEIOSTX	COXIEST	CEKNNSU	UNSNECK	CELOPPS	COPPLES	CEMOOPS	COMPOSE
	EXOTICS	CEKNOOV	CONVOKE	CELOPRU	COUPLER	CEMOOPT	COMPOTE
CEIOSTY	SOCIETY	CEKNORR	CRONKER	CELOPSU	COUPLES	CEMOOTU	OUTCOME
CEIOSTZ	COZIEST	CEKNORS	CONKERS		OPUSCLE	CEMOPRT	COMPTER
CEIPPST	PEPTICS		RECKONS		UPCLOSE	CEMOPSU	UPCOMES
CEIPQTU	PICQUET	CEKNOST	NOCKETS	CELOPTU	COUPLET	CEMOPTU	COMPUTE
CEIPRRS	CRISPER	CEKNRWY	WRYNECK		OCTUPLE	CEMORRS	CREMORS
	PRICERS	CEKNSSU	SUCKENS	CELOQSU	CLOQUES	CEMOSSU	COMUSES
CEIPRSS	SPICERS	CEKOOPR	PRECOOK	CELORSS	CLOSERS		MUSCOSE
CEIPRST	TRICEPS	CEKOOPW	COWPOKE		CRESOLS	CEMOSSY	MYCOSES
CEIPRSY	SPICERY	CEKOORR	CROOKER		ESCROLS	CEMOSTU	COSTUME
CEIPRTU	CUPRITE	CEKOORS	COOKERS	CELORST	COLTERS	CEMPRRU	CRUMPER
	PICTURE	CEKOORY	COOKERY		CORSLET	CEMPRTU	CRUMPET
CEIPRTY	PYRETIC	CEKOPST	POCKETS		COSTREL	CEMRRUY	MERCURY
CEIPRXY	PYREXIC	CEKORRS	CORKERS		LECTORS	CEMRSTU	RECTUMS
CEIPSSS	SCEPSIS		ROCKERS	CELORSU	CLOSURE	CEMSSUU	MUCUSES
CEIPSST	CESSPIT	CEKORRY	ROCKERY		COLURES	CENNOOT	CONNOTE
CEIQRSU	CIRQUES	CEKORSS	SOCKERS	CELORSV	CLOVERS	CENNORS	CONNERS
CEIRRRU	CURRIER	CEKORST	RESTOCK	CELORSW	SCROWLE	CENNOST	CONSENT
CEIRRSU	CRUISER		ROCKETS	CELORSY	SCROYLE		NOCENTS
	CURRIES	CEKPRSU	PUCKERS	CELORTT	CLOTTER	CENNOTT	CONTENT
	SUCRIER	CEKPRSY	RYPECKS		CROTTLE	CENNOTV	CONVENT
CEIRRTT	CRITTER	CEKPRUY	PUCKERY	CELORTU	CLOTURE	CENNRSU	CUNNERS
CEIRRTU	RECRUIT	CEKRRTU	TRUCKER		CLOUTER		SCUNNER
CEIRRTX	RECTRIX	CEKRSSU	SUCKERS		COULTER	CENOORR	CORONER
CEIRRUV	CURVIER	CEKRSTU	TUCKERS	CELORVY	CLOVERY		CROONER
CEIRSSU	CRUISES	CEKRSUY	YUCKERS	CELOSST	CLOSEST	CENOORS	CEROONS
	CRUSIES	CEKSSTU	SUCKETS		CLOSETS	CENOORT	CORONET
	CUISSER			CELOSSU	OSCULES	CENOOSS	COOSENS

CENOPRS	CREPONS		SCOURER	CFIIMNO	OMNIFIC	CGIINNZ	ZINCING
CENOPSU	POUNCES	CEORRSW	SCOWRER	CFIINOT	FICTION	CGIINOV	VOICING
	UNCOPES	CEORRSY	SORCERY	CFIINYZ	ZINCIFY	CGIINPR	PRICING
CENOPSY	SYNCOPE	CEORRTY	RECTORY	CFIIOSS	OSSIFIC	CGIINPS	SPICING
CENOPTU	POUNCET	CEORSSS	CROSSES	CFIKNNO	FINNOCK	CGIINRT	TRICING
CENOPTY	POTENCY		SCORSES	CFIKOSS	FOSSICK	CGIKLNO	CLOKING
CENOQRU	CONQUER	CEORSST	CORSETS	CFILORS	FROLICS		LOCKING
CENORRS	CORNERS		COSTERS	CFILORU	FLUORIC	CGIKMNO	MOCKING
	SCORNER		ESCORTS	CFIMNOR	CONFIRM	CGIKMNU	MUCKING
CENORRW	CROWNER		SCOTERS	CFIMOST	COMFITS	CGIKNNO	CONKING
CENORSS	CENSORS		SECTORS	CFINOST	CONFITS		NOCKING
CENORST	CONSTER	CEORSSU	COURSES	CFIORST	FICTORS	CGIKNOO	COOKING
	CORNETS		SCOURSE	CFIORSY	SCORIFY	CGIKNOR	CORKING
	CRONETS		SOURCES	CFIRSTU	FRUICTS		ROCKING
CENORSU	ROUNCES		SUCROSE	CFISSTU	FUSTICS	CGIKNOS	SOCKING
CENORTT	CORNETT	CEORSSW	ESCROWS	CFKLLOU	LOCKFUL	CGIKNOY	YOCKING
CENORTU	CORNUTE	CEORSTT	COTTERS	CFKNORU	UNFROCK	CGIKNPU	KINGCUP
	COUNTER	CEORSTU	COUTERS	CFKOTTU	FUTTOCK	CGIKNRU	RUCKING
	RECOUNT		CROUTES	CFLMRUU	FULCRUM	CGIKNSU	SUCKING
	TROUNCE		SCOUTER	CFLNORY	CORNFLY	CGIKNTU	TUCKING
CENORTV	CONVERT	CEORSTV	CORVETS	CFLNOUX	CONFLUX	CGIKNUY	YUCKING
CENORTW	CROWNET		COVERTS	CFLOPRU	CROPFUL	CGILLNO	COLLING
CENORUV	UNCOVER		VECTORS	CFLPSUU	CUPFULS	CGILLNU	CULLING
CENOSSY	COYNESS	CEORTUU	COUTURE	CFMNOOR	CONFORM	CGILMNU	CULMING
CENOSTT	CONTEST	CEORTUV	COUVERT	CFMOORT	COMFORT	CGILNNO	CLONING
CENOSTU	CONTUSE	CEOSSST	COSSETS	CFOSSTU	FUSTOCS	CGILNNU	UNCLING
	ECONUTS	CEOSSSU	SCOUSES	CFOSSUU	FUSCOUS	CGILNOO	COOLING
CENOSTV	COVENTS	CEOSSSY	SYCOSES	CGGGINO	COGGING	CGILNOS	CLOSING
CENOSVY	CONVEYS	CEOSTTT	OCTETTS	CGGIINR	GRICING	CGILNOT	COLTING
	COVYNES	CEOSTTU	CUTTOES	CGGORSY	SCROGGY	CGILNOW	COWLING
CENOTTX	CONTEXT	CEPPRRU	CRUPPER	CGHHOSU	CHOUGHS	CGILNOY	CLOYING
CENPRTY	ENCRYPT	CEPPRSU	CUPPERS	CGHIIMN	CHIMING	CGILNPY	CLYPING
CENPTUX	EXPUNCT		SCUPPER		MICHING	CGILNRU	CURLING
CENRRTU	CURRENT	CEPRRSU	SPRUCER	CGHIINN	CHINING	CGILNSY	GLYCINS
CENRSSY	SCRYNES	CEPRSSU	PERCUSS		INCHING	CGILORW	COWGIRL
CENRSTU	ENCRUST		SPRUCES		NICHING	CGILOTT	GLOTTIC
CENRSUU	UNCURSE	CEPRSSY	CYPRESS	CGHIINR	RICHING	CGILPSU	GILCUPS
CENRSUW	UNSCREW	CEPRSTY	SCEPTRY	CGHIINT	ITCHING	CGILPTU	GILTCUP
CENRTUY	CENTURY	CEPSSTU	SUSPECT	CGHIINV	CHIVING	CGILPTY	GLYPTIC
CENSSTY	ENCYSTS	CERRSSU	CURSERS	CGHIKNO	CHOKING	CGIMNOO	COOMING
CEOOPRS	COOPERS	CERRSSY	SCRYERS		HOCKING	CGIMNOR	CROMING
	SCOOPER	CERSSSU	CUSSERS	CGHILPY	GLYPHIC	CGIMNOS	COMINGS
CEOOPRY	COOPERY	CERSSTU	CRUSETS	CGHINNO	CHIGNON	CGINNNO	CONNING
CEOORSS	COOSERS	CERSSUZ	SCRUZES	CGHINOR	OCHRING	CGINNNU	CUNNING
CEOORST	SCOOTER	CERSTTU	CURTEST	CGHINOS	COSHING	CGINNOP	PONCING
CEOOSTY	COYOTES		CUTTERS	CGHINRU	RUCHING	CGINNOR	CORNING
	OOCYTES		SCUTTER	CGHINSU	CHUSING	CGINNOS	CONSIGN
CEOPPRR	CROPPER	CERSTUV	CURVETS	CGHIOSY	GOYISCH	CGINNSY	SYNCING
CEOPPRS	COPPERS	CERSTUY	CURTSEY	CGHLOSU	CLOUGHS	CGINOOP	COOPING
CEOPPRY	COPPERY	CFFGINO	COFFING	CGHOORT	TORGOCH	CGINOOS	COOINGS
CEOPRRS	SCORPER	CFFGINU	CUFFING	CGHORUY	GROUCHY	CGINOPP	COPPING
CEOPRRT	PORRECT	CFFHINO	CHIFFON	CGIIJNU	JUICING	CGINOPS	COPINGS
CEOPRRU	CROUPER	CFFILSS	SCLIFFS	CGIIKKN	KICKING		COPSING
	PROCURE	CFFINOS	COFFINS	CGIIKLN	LICKING	CGINOPU	COUPING
CEOPRSS	CORPSES	CFFINSU	CUFFINS	CGIIKMM	GIMMICK	CGINOPW	COWPING
	PROCESS	CFFMOSU	OFFSCUM	CGIIKNN	NICKING	CGINOPY	COPYING
CEOPRSU	COUPERS	CFFOSTU	OFFCUTS	CGIIKNP	PICKING	CGINORS	SCORING
	CROUPES	CFFRSSU	SCRUFFS	CGIIKNR	RICKING	CGINORU	COURING
	RECOUPS	CFFRSUY	SCRUFFY	CGIIKNS	SICKING	CGINORW	CROWING
CEOPRTT	PROTECT	CFGIINO	COIFING	CGIIKNT	TICKING	CGINOST	COSTING
CEOPRUU	COUPURE	CFGIKNU	FUCKING	CGIIKNW	WICKING		GNOSTIC
CEOQRTU	CROQUET	CFGINOR	FORCING	CGIILLO	ILLOGIC	CGINOSU	SOUCING
	ROCQUET	CFHIMYY	CHYMIFY	CGIILNO	COILING	CGINOSV	COVINGS
CEOQSTU	COQUETS	CFHIOSW	COWFISH	CGIILNP	CLIPING	CGINOSW	SOWCING
CEORRSS	CROSSER	CFHIRST	FRICHTS	CGIILNS	SLICING	CGINPPU	CUPPING
	RECROSS	CFHORTU	FUTHORC	CGIIMNN	MINCING	CGINRRU	CURRING
	SCORERS	CFIIIMR	MIRIFIC	CGIIMNR	CRIMING	CGINRSU	CURSING
	SCORSER	CFIIIVV	VIVIFIC	CGIINNO	COINING	CGINRSY	CRYINGS
CEORRST	RECTORS	CFIIKNY	FINICKY	CGIINNR	CRINING		SCRYING
CEORRSU	COURSER	CFIILNT	INFLICT	CGIINNW	WINCING	CGINRUV	CURVING

CGINSSU	CUSSING	CHIOSST	STICHOS
	SCUSING	CHIOSSZ	SCHIZOS
CGINTTU	CUTTING	CHIPRRU	CHIRRUP
CGIOOOS	GIOCOSO	CHIPRRY	PYRRHIC
CGIOTYZ	ZYGOTIC	CHIPSSY	PHYSICS
CGLLOSY	GLYCOLS	CHIQSTU	SQUITCH
CGLNOSU	UNCLOGS	CHIRRSU	CURRISH
CGLOOSU	COLUGOS	CHIRSTY	CHRISTY
CGNOOSU	CONGOUS	CHISSST	SCHISTS
CGOORRW	GORCROW	CHISSTU	SCHUITS
CHHIKOR	CHIKHOR	CHISTTU	CHUTIST
CHHINOR	RHONCHI	CHISTWY	SWITCHY
CHHINTU	UNHITCH	CHITTWY	TWITCHY
CHHIRST	SHRITCH	CHKLOOO	HOOLOCK
CHHISST	SHTCHIS	CHKLOSS	SHLOCKS
CHHISTY	ICHTHYS	CHKMMOO	HOMMOCK
CHHRTTU	THRUTCH	CHKMMOU	HUMMOCK
CHIIKNN	KINCHIN	CHKNOOS	SCHNOOK
CHIIKSS	SICKISH	CHKOOST	SCHTOOK
CHIILLS	CHILLIS	CHKORSU	CHUKORS
CHIILST	LITCHIS	CHKPTUU	PUTCHUK
CHIIMSU	ISCHIUM	CHKSSTU	SHTUCKS
CHIINNP	INCHPIN	CHLMOOS	MOLOCHS
CHIINST	CHITINS	CHLOOSS	SCHOOLS
CHIIOPT	OPHITIC	CHLOOST	COOLTHS
CHIIOST	STICHOI	CHLOPST	SPLOTCH
CHIKLLO	HILLOCK	CHLORSS	SCHORLS
CHIKLTY	THICKLY	CHLORTY	CHOLTRY
CHIKNOO	CHINOOK	CHLOSSS	SCHLOSS
CHIKORS	CHIKORS	CHLOSUY	SLOUCHY
CHIKORY	HICKORY	CHMOORS	CHROMOS
CHIKOST	THICKOS	CHMOOST	SCHTOOM
CHIKPSU	PUCKISH	CHMOSUY	CHYMOUS
CHIKSST	SCHTICK	CHNNOOR	CHRONON
	SHTICKS	CHNNOSU	NONSUCH
CHIKSTY	KITSCHY	CHNOOPS	PONCHOS
CHILLMU	CHILLUM	CHNOORS	COHORNS
CHILLTY	LICHTLY	CHNOORT	TORCHON
CHILNOU	ULICHON	CHNORRS	SCHNORR
CHILNSY	LYCHNIS	CHNORTU	COTHURN
CHILOOS	COOLISH	CHNOTUU	UNCOUTH
CHILORS	ORCHILS	CHNSTUU	TUCHUNS
CHILOST	COLTISH	CHOORST	COHORTS
CHILSTU	CULTISH	CHOORSU	OCHROUS
CHIMNPY	NYMPHIC	CHOPSSY	PSYCHOS
CHIMOPR	MORPHIC	CHORSTU	TROCHUS
CHIMORS	CHRISOM	CHOSSTU	SCHOUTS
CHIMRRY	MYRRHIC		SCOUTHS
CHIMRSS	CHRISMS	CHOSSTW	SCOWTHS
CHIMSSS	SCHISMS	CHPSSUY	SCYPHUS
CHIMSTY	TYCHISM	CHRRSUU	CHURRUS
CHINOOR	CHORION	CHSSTUY	SCHUYTS
CHINOPS	CHOPINS	CIIILLT	ILLICIT
	PHONICS	CIIILNV	INCIVIL
CHINOST	CHITONS	CIIIMNR	CRIMINI
CHINOSU	CUSHION	CIIINPT	INCIPIT
CHINPSY	HYPNICS	CIIKKLL	KILLICK
CHINQSU	SQUINCH	CIIKMMM	MIMMICK
CHINRSU	URCHINS	CIIKMNN	MINNICK
CHINTUW	UNWITCH	CIIKNSW	INWICKS
CHINTYZ	CHINTZY	CIIKNTU	CUTIKIN
CHIOOPR	POCHOIR	CIIKSST	TISICKS
CHIOORS	ISOCHOR	CIIKSTT	STICKIT
CHIOORZ	CHORIZO	CIILLTY	LICITLY
CHIOPRT	TROPHIC	CIILLVY	CIVILLY
CHIOPST	PHOTICS	CIILNOP	CIPOLIN
CHIOPXY	HYPOXIC	CIILNOS	SILICON
CHIORST	CHORIST	CIILNPS	INCLIPS
	OSTRICH	CIILNUV	UNCIVIL
CHIORSW	CHOWRIS	CIILOOT	OOLITIC
CIILOPT	POLITIC	CILNOXY	XYLONIC
CIILOST	COLITIS	CILNPSU	INSCULP
	SOLICIT		SCULPIN
CIILPSY	SPICILY	CILNPTU	UNCLIPT
CIILSSS	SCISSIL	CILNSTU	LINCTUS
CIIMMRY	MIMICRY	CILOOPT	COPILOT
CIIMNNO	NIMONIC	CILOORU	COULOIR
CIIMNOT	MICTION	CILOOSS	COLOSSI
CIIMOST	MISTICO	CILOOST	SCIOLTO
	SOMITIC	CILOPRW	PILCROW
CIIMOTT	MITOTIC	CILOPRY	PYLORIC
CIIMOTV	MOTIVIC	CILOPSU	UPCOILS
CIIMSSV	CIVISMS	CILOPSW	COWSLIP
CIIMSTV	VICTIMS	CILORST	LICTORS
CIINNTU	TUNICIN	CILOSTU	COUTILS
CIINOOT	COITION		OCULIST
CIINOPS	PSIONIC	CILPRSY	CRISPLY
CIINORS	INCISOR	CILPRTU	CULPRIT
CIINPRS	CRISPIN	CILRRSU	SCURRIL
CIINQTU	QUINTIC	CILRSUU	SURCULI
CIINRST	CITRINS	CILSTTU	CULTIST
CIINSSV	VISCINS	CIMMNSU	CUMMINS
CIINTUY	UNICITY	CIMMOSS	COSMISM
CIIORST	SORITIC	CIMMOST	COMMITS
CIIOSUV	VICIOUS	CIMNNOS	NINCOMS
CIIPRSS	SPIRICS	CIMNNSU	NINCUMS
CIIPRTY	PYRITIC	CIMNOOR	MORONIC
CIIRSTV	VITRICS		OMICRON
CIIRTVX	VICTRIX	CIMNORS	CRIMSON
CIJNNOO	CONJOIN		MICRONS
CIJNNTU	INJUNCT	CIMNRSU	CRINUMS
CIJNOOS	COJOINS	CIMOORS	MORISCO
CIKKLLO	KILLOCK	CIMOOST	OSMOTIC
CIKLLOP	PILLOCK	CIMOPSY	COPYISM
CIKLLOR	ROLLICK		MISCOPY
CIKLLOS	SILLOCK		MYOPICS
CIKLLOW	KILLCOW	CIMORSU	CORIUMS
CIKLLSY	SLICKLY	CIMOSST	COSMIST
CIKLLUY	LUCKILY		SITCOMS
CIKLMSU	MISLUCK	CIMOSSY	MYCOSIS
CIKLMSY	SMICKLY	CIMOSTY	MYOTICS
CIKLNOS	INLOCKS	CIMOTYZ	ZYMOTIC
CIKLNRY	CRINKLY	CIMPRSS	SCRIMPS
CIKLORY	ROCKILY	CIMPRSY	SCRIMPY
CIKLPRY	PRICKLY	CIMRSSU	CRISSUM
CIKLQUY	QUICKLY	CIMRSUU	CURIUMS
CIKLRTY	TRICKLY	CIMSSTY	MYSTICS
CIKLSTU	LUSTICK	CIMSSUV	VISCUMS
CIKMNNO	MONNICK	CINNNOU	INCONNU
CIKMNSU	NICKUMS	CINNORU	UNICORN
CIKNNOP	PINNOCK	CINNOSU	NUNCIOS
CIKNNOW	WINNOCK	CINNOTU	UNCTION
CIKNPSU	UNPICKS	CINNSSU	UNCINUS
CIKNSTU	UNSTICK	CINOOPS	OPSONIC
CIKOPPT	POCKPIT	CINOORS	CORONIS
CIKORRS	CORKIRS	CINOOSS	COOSINS
CIKOTUW	OUTWICK	CINOPPS	COPPINS
CIKPSTU	STICKUP	CINOPRX	PRINCOX
CIKRSTY	TRICKSY	CINORRT	TRICORN
CILLNOU	CULLION	CINORSS	INCROSS
CILLOOR	CRIOLLO	CINORST	CISTRON
CILLOPY	POLLICY		CITRONS
CILMNOP	COMPLIN		CORNIST
CILMSTU	CULTISM	CINORSZ	ZIRCONS
CILNOOR	ORCINOL	CINORTU	RUCTION
CILNOOS	CLOISON	CINOSST	CONSIST
CILNOPR	PILCORN		TOCSINS
CILNOSU	ULICONS	CINOSSU	COUSINS
	UNCOILS	CINOSTU	SUCTION
CILNOTU	LINOCUT	CINOSUZ	ZINCOUS

CINRSTU	INCRUST
CIOOPRS	SCORPIO
CIOOPRT	PORTICO
	PROOTIC
CIOOPSU	COPIOUS
CIOOQTU	COQUITO
CIOORST	OCTROIS
CIOORSU	CORIOUS
CIOPRST	TROPICS
CIOPSTY	COPYIST
CIOQRSU	CROQUIS
CIORRSU	CIRROUS
CIORSSS	SCISSOR
CIORSTT	TRICOTS
CIORSTU	CITROUS
CIORSTV	VICTORS
CIORSUU	CURIOUS
CIORTVY	VICTORY
CIOSSSY	SYCOSIS
CIOSSUV	VISCOUS
CIPRSST	SCRIPTS
CIPRSSU	PRUSSIC
CIPRTTY	TRYPTIC
CIPSTTY	STYPTIC
CIRRTTU	CRITTUR
CIRSSTU	RUSTICS
CIRTUVY	CURVITY
CISSTUY	CYTISUS
CJNORUY	CONJURY
CKLLMOU	MULLOCK
CKLLOOP	POLLOCK
CKLLOOR	ROLLOCK
CKLLORU	RULLOCK
CKLNOSU	UNLOCKS
CKLNUUY	UNLUCKY
CKLOOOY	OLYCOOK
CKLOORW	ROWLOCK
CKLOOTU	LOCKOUT
CKLOPSU	UPLOCKS
CKLOPTU	PUTLOCK
CKMMMOU	MUMMOCK
CKNORSU	UNCORKS
CKNOSTU	UNSTOCK
	UNTUCKS
CKOOOTU	COOKOUT
CKOORSU	SOUROCK
CKOPTTU	PUTTOCK
CKOSSTU	TUSSOCK
CLLMOSU	MOLLUSC
CLLOOPS	COLLOPS
	SCOLLOP
CLLORSS	SCROLLS
CLLOSUU	LOCULUS
CLMNOSU	COLUMNS
CLMOOPT	COMPLOT
CLMOPTU	PLUMCOT
CLMOSUU	LUCUMOS
	OSCULUM
CLMSUUU	CUMULUS
CLNOORT	CONTROL
CLNOOSS	CONSOLS
CLNOSSU	CONSULS
CLNOSTU	CONSULT
	UNCOLTS
CLNOSUW	UNCOWLS
CLNRSUU	UNCURLS
CLOORSU	COLOURS
CLOORUY	COLOURY
CLORSSW	SCROWLS
CLORSSY	CROSSLY
CLORTUY	COURTLY
CLOSSTU	LOCUSTS
CLPRSUU	UPCURLS
CLPSSTU	SCULPTS
CMMNOOS	COMMONS
CMMOOST	COMMOTS
CMMRSUY	SCRUMMY
CMNOOOT	MONOCOT
CMNOOPY	COMPONY
CMNOPTU	PUNCTUM
CMOOPRT	COMPORT
CMOOPST	COMPOST
	COMPOTS
CMOORSU	CORMOUS
CMOOSTY	SCOTOMY
CMORSTU	SCROTUM
CMORTUW	CUTWORM
CMOSSTU	CUSTOMS
CMPRSSU	SCRUMPS
CMPRSUY	SCRUMPY
CNNOPSY	PYCNONS
CNNORTU	NOCTURN
CNNORUW	UNCROWN
CNOOPPR	POPCORN
CNOOPRU	CROUPON
CNOOPSU	COUPONS
	SOUPCON
CNOORST	CONSORT
	CROTONS
CNOORTT	CONTORT
CNOORTU	CONTOUR
	CORNUTO
	CROUTON
CNOOSST	NOSTOCS
	ONCOSTS
CNOOSTT	COTTONS
CNOOSTY	TYCOONS
CNOOSUU	NOCUOUS
CNOOSVY	CONVOYS
CNOOTTW	COTTOWN
CNOOTTY	COTTONY
CNOPRTY	CRYPTON
CNOPSTU	PUNCTOS
CNORSSU	UNCROSS
CNORSSY	SYNROCS
CNORTUY	COUNTRY
CNRSSTU	SCRUNTS
CNRSTUY	SCRUNTY
COOORSZ	COROZOS
COOPRRT	PROCTOR
COOPRSS	SCROOPS
COOPSTU	OCTOPUS
COORSTU	OCTUORS
COORSUU	ROUCOUS
COOSTTY	OTOCYST
COPRRTU	CORRUPT
COPRSTY	CRYPTOS
COPRSUU	CUPROUS
CORRSSU	CURSORS
CORRSUY	CURSORY
CORSSTU	SCRUTOS
DDDDEIL	DIDDLED
DDDDEGR	DREDGED
DDDEEHL	HEDDLED
DDDEEIR	DERIDED
DDDEELM	MEDDLED
DDDEELP	PEDDLED
DDDEELR	REDDLED
DDDEELS	SLEDDED
DDDEELU	DELUDED
DDDEEMO	DEMODED
DDDEENS	SNEDDED
DDDEENU	DENUDED
DDDEERU	UDDERED
DDDEEST	STEDDED
DDDEFIL	FIDDLED
DDDEFLU	FUDDLED
DDDEGII	GIDDIED
DDDEGLU	GUDDLED
DDDEGRU	DRUDGED
DDDEHIW	WHIDDED
DDDEHLO	HODDLED
DDDEHLU	HUDDLED
DDDEHTU	THUDDED
DDDEIIK	KIDDIED
DDDEIIV	DIVIDED
DDDEIKS	SKIDDED
DDDEILM	MIDDLED
DDDEILN	DINDLED
	RIDDLED
DDDEILP	PIDDLED
DDDEILR	DIDDLER
	RIDDLED
DDDEILS	DIDDLES
DDDEILT	TIDDLED
DDDEILW	WIDDLED
DDDEIMU	MUDDIED
DDDEIOR	DODDIER
DDDEIOS	DODDIES
DDDEIRS	DIDDERS
DDDEIRU	DUDDIER
	RUDDIED
DDDELMU	MUDDLED
DDDELNO	NODDLED
DDDELOO	DOODLED
DDDELOP	PLODDED
DDDELOS	DODDLES
DDDELPU	PUDDLED
DDDELRU	RUDDLED
DDDENOS	SNODDED
DDDEOPR	PRODDED
DDDEOQU	QUODDED
DDDEORS	DODDERS
DDDEORY	DODDERY
DDDEPSU	SPUDDED
DDDERSU	DUDDERS
DDDERUY	DUDDERY
DDDESTU	STUDDED
DDDGINO	DODDING
DDEEEIR	DEEDIER
DDEEELN	NEEDLED
DDEEELT	DELETED
DDEEEMN	EMENDED
DDEEENT	TEENDED
DDEEENW	ENDEWED
DDEEEPS	SPEEDED
DDEEEST	DEEDEST
	STEEDED
DDEEESX	DESEXED
DDEEFGL	FLEDGED
DDEEFII	DEIFIED
	EDIFIED
DDEEFIL	DEFILED
	FIELDED
DDEEFIN	DEFINED
DDEEFLU	DEEDFUL
DDEEFNS	DEFENDS
DDEEFSU	DEFUSED
DDEEFUZ	DEFUZED
DDEEGGL	GLEDGED
DDEEGIN	DEEDING
	DEIGNED
DDEEGIS	DISEDGE
DDEEGLP	PLEDGED
DDEEGLS	SLEDGED
DDEEGLU	DELUGED
DDEEGNU	UNEDGED
DDEEGRR	DREDGER
DDEEGRS	DREDGES
DDEEHLS	HEDDLES
DDEEHNU	DUDHEEN
DDEEHRS	SHEDDER
DDEEILS	SLEIDED
DDEEILW	WIELDED
DDEEILY	DEEDILY
	YIELDED
DDEEIMP	IMPEDED
DDEEIMS	DEMISED
	MISDEED
DDEEINS	DESINED
	NEDDIES
	SDEINED
DDEEINT	ENDITED
	TEINDED
DDEEINW	INDEWED
	WIDENED
DDEEINX	INDEXED
DDEEINZ	DIZENED
DDEEIOV	VIDEOED
DDEEIPR	PREDIED
DDEEIPS	DEPSIDE
DDEEIRR	DERIDER
	REDDIER
	RIDERED
DDEEIRS	DERIDES
	DESIRED
	DIEDRES
	RESIDED
DDEEIRV	DERIVED
DDEEIRW	WEIRDED
DDEEIST	DEIDEST
	TEDDIES
DDEEISV	DEVISED
DDEEKKO	DEKKOED
DDEELLU	DUELLED
DDEELLW	DWELLED
DDEELMR	MEDDLER
DDEELMS	MEDDLES
DDEELNO	OLDENED
DDEELNS	LEDDENS
DDEELPR	PEDDLER
DDEELPS	PEDDLES
	SPELDED
DDEELRS	REDDLES
DDEELRT	TREDDLE
DDEELRU	DELUDER
DDEELSU	DELUDES
DDEEMOT	DEMOTED
DDEEMRU	DEMURED
DDEENOP	DEPONED
DDEENOT	DENOTED
DDEENOW	ENDOWED
DDEENOZ	DOZENED
DDEENPS	DEPENDS
DDEENRS	REDDENS
DDEENRT	TRENDED
DDEENRU	ENDURED
DDEENST	STENDED

DDEENSU	DENUDES	DDEHNRU	HUNDRED	DDEINST	DISTEND	DDENOSW	SOWNDED
	DUDEENS	DDEHNSU	DUNSHED	DDEINSW	SWIDDEN	DDENOSY	DYNODES
DDEENSY	DESYNED	DDEHRSU	SHUDDER	DDEIOPR	PODDIER	DDENOUW	WOUNDED
DDEEOPS	DEPOSED	DDEHRSY	SHREDDY	DDEIORS	DORISED	DDENPSU	PUDDENS
DDEEORR	ORDERED	DDEIIKR	KIDDIER		SODDIER	DDENRSU	DUNDERS
DDEEORV	DOVERED	DDEIIKS	KIDDIES	DDEIORV	OVERDID	DDENSTU	STUDDEN
DDEEORW	DOWERED	DDEIIMS	MIDDIES	DDEIORW	DOWDIER	DDEOOPR	DROOPED
DDEEOTV	DEVOTED	DDEIINT	INDITED	DDEIORZ	DORIZED	DDEOORU	ODOURED
DDEEPRS	PEDDERS	DDEIINV	DIVINED	DDEIOST	TODDIES	DDEOORW	REDWOOD
	SPREDDE	DDEIIOS	IODIDES	DDEIOSW	DOWDIES	DDEOPPR	DROPPED
DDEEPTU	DEPUTED		IODISED	DDEIOTT	DITTOED	DDEORSW	DROWSED
DDEERRS	REDDERS	DDEIIOX	DIOXIDE	DDEIOWW	WIDOWED		SWORDED
DDEERSS	DRESSED	DDEIIOZ	IODIZED	DDEIPPR	DRIPPED	DDEPRSS	SPREDDS
DDEERST	REDDEST	DDEIIRT	DIRTIED	DDEIPRS	DISPRED	DDEPRSU	PUDDERS
	TEDDERS		TIDDIER	DDEIPSU	PUDDIES	DDERRSU	RUDDERS
DDEERTU	DETRUDE	DDEIIRV	DIVIDER	DDEIRRS	RIDDERS	DDERSSU	SUDDERS
DDEESST	STEDDES	DDEIIST	STIDDIE	DDEIRRU	RUDDIER	DDGGINO	DODGING
DDEETTU	DUETTED		TIDDIES	DDEIRSU	RUDDIES		GODDING
DDEFGIR	FRIDGED	DDEIISV	DIVIDES	DDEISSU	DISUSED	DDGHINO	HODDING
DDEFILR	FIDDLER	DDEIISW	WIDDIES	DDEISTU	STUDIED	DDGHOOO	GODHOOD
DDEFILS	FIDDLES	DDEIITT	DITTIED	DDEJRSU	JUDDERS	DDGIILY	GIDDILY
DDEFILY	FIDDLEY	DDEIIVV	DIVVIED	DDEKMOU	DUKEDOM	DDGIINR	RIDDING
DDEFIRT	DRIFTED	DDEIIZZ	DIZZIED	DDEKOOR	DROOKED	DDGIMNU	MUDDING
DDEFLNO	FONDLED	DDEIKLN	KINDLED	DDEKORU	DROUKED	DDGINNO	NODDING
DDEFLOO	FLOODED	DDEIKLS	KIDDLES	DDELLOR	DROLLED	DDGINOP	PODDING
DDEFLRU	FUDDLER	DDEIKNR	KINDRED	DDELMOU	MOULDED	DDGINOR	RODDING
DDEFLSU	FUDDLES	DDEIKRS	KIDDERS	DDELMPU	DUMPLED	DDGINOS	SODDING
DDEFNOR	FRONDED	DDEILLO	DOLLIED	DDELMRU	MUDDLER	DDGINOT	TODDING
DDEFNOU	FOUNDED	DDEILLR	DRILLED	DDELMSU	MUDDLES	DDGINPU	PUDDING
DDEFORS	FODDERS	DDEILLU	ILLUDED	DDELNOO	NOODLED	DDGINRU	RUDDING
DDEGGRU	DRUGGED	DDEILMP	DIMPLED	DDELNOS	NODDLES	DDGINUW	WUDDING
	GRUDGED	DDEILMS	MIDDLES	DDELNOU	LOUNDED	DDGOOOW	DOGWOOD
DDEGHIT	DIGHTED	DDEILNN	DINNLED		NODULED	DDHIISS	SIDDHIS
DDEGIIR	GIDDIER	DDEILNS	DINDLES	DDELNOW	LOWNDED	DDHIKSU	KIDDUSH
DDEGIIS	GIDDIES		SLIDDEN	DDELNRU	RUNDLED	DDHIORY	HYDROID
DDEGILR	GIRDLED	DDEILNW	DWINDLE	DDELOOR	DOODLER	DDIILOP	DIPLOID
	GLIDDER	DDEILOR	DROILED		DROOLED	DDIIQTU	QUIDDIT
	GRIDDLE	DDEILOS	DILDOES	DDELOOS	DOODLES	DDIKNOS	DODKINS
DDEGIMO	DEMIGOD	DDEILOT	DELTOID	DDELOOW	WOOLLED	DDILMUY	MUDDILY
DDEGINR	GRINDED	DDEILPR	PIDDLER	DDELOPR	PLODDER	DDILNRS	DIRNDLS
	REDDING	DDEILPS	DISPLED	DDELORT	TODDLER	DDILOSY	DYSODIL
DDEGINT	TEDDING		PIDDLES	DDELORW	WORLDED	DDILOWY	DOWDILY
DDEGINW	WEDDING	DDEILPU	DUPLIED	DDELOST	TODDLES	DDILRUY	RUDDILY
DDEGINY	EDDYING	DDEILQU	QUIDDLE	DDELOTT	DOTTLED	DDILTWY	TWIDDLY
DDEGIOR	DODGIER	DDEILRR	RIDDLER	DDELPRU	PUDDLER	DDIMRSU	DIRDUMS
DDEGLSU	GUDDLES	DDEILRS	RIDDLES	DDELPSU	PUDDLES	DDIMSSU	DUDISMS
DDEGMOS	DODGEMS		SLIDDER	DDELRSU	RUDDLES	DDINOST	SNODDIT
DDEGMSU	SMUDGED	DDEILRT	TIDDLER	DDELSTU	STUDDLE	DDIORTU	TURDOID
DDEGNOS	GODSEND	DDEILST	TIDDLES	DDEMMRU	DRUMMED	DDLLMOO	DOLLDOM
DDEGNOU	DUDGEON	DDEILSW	WIDDLES	DDEMMSU	SMEDDUM	DDMMSUU	DUMDUMS
DDEGNSU	SNUDGED	DDEILTU	DILUTED	DDEMNOS	ODDSMEN	DDMNOOR	DROMOND
DDEGORS	DODGERS	DDEILTW	TWIDDLE	DDEMNOT	ODDMENT	DDMRSUU	DURDUMS
	GORSEDD	DDEILTY	LYDDITE	DDEMNOU	MOUNDED	DDORSTY	DROSTDY
DDEGORY	DODGERY		TIDDLEY	DDENNOR	DENDRON	DEEEEHT	TEEHEED
DDEGOSS	GODDESS	DDEIMMU	DUMMIED		DONNERD	DEEEEMX	EXEEMED
DDEGOST	STODGED	DDEIMNS	MIDDENS	DDENOOS	SNOODED	DEEEFFR	EFFERED
DDEGRRU	DRUDGER	DDEIMNU	MUEDDIN	DDENOPS	DESPOND	DEEEFLR	FLEERED
DDEGRSU	DRUDGES	DDEIMOO	MOODIED	DDENOPU	POUNDED	DEEEFLT	FLEETED
DDEGRTU	TRUDGED	DDEIMOR	DERMOID	DDENOPW	POWNDED	DEEEFNR	ENFREED
DDEHIRS	HIDDERS	DDEIMOS	DESMOID	DDENORS	NODDERS	DEEEFNS	DEFENSE
	REDDISH	DDEIMRU	MUDDIER	DDENORT	TRODDEN	DEEEFRS	FEEDERS
	SHIDDER	DDEIMSS	DESMIDS	DDENORU	REDOUND	DEEEFRV	FEVERED
DDEHIRT	THIRDED	DDEIMST	MIDDEST		ROUNDED	DEEEGKL	GLEEKED
DDEHIRW	WHIDDER	DDEIMSU	DEDIMUS		UNDERDO	DEEEGLP	PLEDGEE
DDEHIRY	HYDRIDE		MUDDIES	DDENORW	DROWNED	DEEEGLT	GLEETED
DDEHLOS	HODDLES	DDEINOP	POINDED		ROWNDED	DEEEGMR	DEMERGE
DDEHLRU	HURDLED	DDEINOS	NODDIES		WONDRED		EMERGED
DDEHLSU	HUDDLES	DDEINOT	DENTOID	DDENOSS	ODDNESS	DEEEGNP	PEENGED
DDEHNOS	HODDENS	DDEINPS	DISPEND		SODDENS	DEEEGNR	GREENED
DDEHNOU	HOUNDED	DDEINRU	UNDRIED	DDENOSU	SOUNDED		

	RENEGED	DEEENSW	ENSEWED	DEEFIRZ	FRIEZED	DEEGMNU	EMUNGED
DEEEGRR	REGREDE	DEEENSZ	SNEEZED	DEEFLLU	FUELLED		GUDEMEN
DEEEGRS	DEGREES	DEEENTT	DETENTE	DEEFLNS	FLENSED	DEEGNNO	ENDOGEN
DEEEGRT	DETERGE	DEEENTU	DETENUE	DEEFLNU	NEEDFUL	DEEGNNR	GRENNED
	GREETED	DEEEORW	OREWEED	DEEFLOT	FEEDLOT	DEEGNOR	ENGORED
DEEEGST	EGESTED	DEEEOTV	DEVOTEE	DEEFLTT	FETTLED	DEEGNRS	GENDERS
DEEEHKT	THEEKED	DEEEPRS	SPEEDER	DEEFMOR	FREEDOM	DEEGNSU	DENGUES
DEEEHLS	SHEELED		SPEERED	DEEFNRS	FENDERS		UNEDGES
DEEEHLW	WHEEDLE	DEEEPRT	PETERED	DEEFNUU	UNFEUED	DEEGOOS	SOOGEED
	WHEELED	DEEEPRU	EPERDUE	DEEFORV	OVERFED	DEEGORR	ROGERED
DEEEHNS	SHEENED	DEEEPRV	PREEVED	DEEFORZ	DEFROZE	DEEGOSY	GEODESY
DEEEHPS	PHEESED	DEEEPSS	PEDESES	DEEFRSU	REFUSED	DEEGOTU	OUTEDGE
DEEEHPZ	PHEEZED	DEEEPST	DEEPEST	DEEFRSW	SWERFED	DEEGRRU	REURGED
DEEEHRS	SHEERED		STEEPED	DEEFRTT	FRETTED	DEEGSSU	GUESSED
DEEEHST	SEETHED	DEEEQRU	QUEERED	DEEFRTU	FEUTRED	DEEGSTU	GUESTED
	SHEETED	DEEERRS	REEDERS		REFUTED	DEEHIKV	KHEDIVE
DEEEHTT	TEETHED	DEEERRV	REVERED	DEEFSSU	DEFUSES	DEEHILS	SHIELED
DEEEHWZ	WHEEZED	DEEERSS	SEEDERS	DEEFSTT	DEFTEST	DEEHILT	LETHIED
DEEEIJL	JEELIED	DEEERST	REESTED	DEEFSUZ	DEFUZES	DEEHINR	INHERED
DEEEIMR	EMERIED		STEERED	DEEGGIS	GIDGEES	DEEHIRR	HERRIED
DEEEINR	NEEDIER	DEEERSV	DESERVE	DEEGGLS	GLEDGES	DEEHIST	HEISTED
DEEEIPS	DEEPIES		SEVERED	DEEGHIN	HEEDING	DEEHITV	THIEVED
DEEEIRR	REEDIER	DEEERSW	SEWERED		NEIGHED	DEEHKLW	WHELKED
DEEEIRS	SEEDIER		SWEERED	DEEGHIR	HEDGIER	DEEHLLO	HELLOED
DEEEIRW	WEEDIER		WEEDERS	DEEGHIW	WEIGHED	DEEHLLS	SHELLED
DEEEISV	DEVISEE	DEEERSY	REDEYES	DEEGHOW	HOGWEED	DEEHLMW	WHELMED
DEEEJNU	DEJEUNE	DEEERTV	EVERTED	DEEGHRS	HEDGERS	DEEHLNU	UNHELED
DEEEJRS	JEREEDS	DEEERTW	TWEERED	DEEGHSS	GHESSED	DEEHLOV	HOVELED
DEEEKLN	KNEELED	DEEERTX	EXERTED	DEEGIJS	GIDJEES	DEEHLPW	WHELPED
DEEEKLS	SLEEKED	DEEERWY	WEEDERY	DEEGIKR	KEDGIER	DEEHLSV	SHELVED
DEEEKMS	SMEEKED	DEEESSX	DESEXES	DEEGILN	DELEING	DEEHLSW	WELSHED
DEEEKNW	WEEKEND	DEEESTV	STEEVED	DEEGILR	GELIDER	DEEHMNR	HERDMEN
DEEEKRS	KREESED	DEEESTW	SWEETED		LEDGIER	DEEHMNS	MENSHED
	SKEERED	DEEETTV	VEDETTE		LEIDGER	DEEHMRU	RHEUMED
DEEELMS	MESELED	DEEETTW	TWEETED	DEEGIMN	DEEMING	DEEHMUX	EXHUMED
DEEELNR	NEEDLER	DEEETWZ	TWEEZED	DEEGINN	ENGINED	DEEHNOY	HONEYED
DEEELNS	NEEDLES	DEEFFFO	FEOFFED		NEEDING	DEEHNPR	PREHEND
DEEELPS	SPEELED	DEEFFIN	EFFENDI	DEEGINR	DREEING	DEEHNRS	HERDENS
DEEELPT	DEPLETE	DEEFFOR	OFFERED		ENERGID	DEEHNUY	UNHEEDY
DEEELRT	DEERLET	DEEFFSU	EFFUSED		GREINED	DEEHORV	HOVERED
DEEELRV	LEVERED	DEEFGGL	FLEGGED		REEDING	DEEHPRS	SPHERED
DEEELST	DELETES	DEEFGIN	FEEDING		REIGNED	DEEHRSS	HERDESS
	SLEETED		FEIGNED	DEEGINS	SDEIGNE	DEEHRSU	USHERED
	STEELED	DEEFGIP	PIGFEED		SEEDING	DEEHRSW	SHREWED
DEEELSV	SLEEVED	DEEFGLS	FLEDGES	DEEGINV	DEEVING	DEEHRTW	WRETHED
DEEELSW	SWEELED	DEEFGRU	REFUGED	DEEGINW	WEEDING	DEEHTTW	WHETTED
DEEELTW	TWEEDLE	DEEFHLS	FLESHED	DEEGINY	YEEDING	DEEIINT	DIETINE
	TWEELED		SHELFED	DEEGIOR	GEORDIE	DEEIIPR	EPEIRID
DEEELTX	TELEXED	DEEFHLU	HEEDFUL	DEEGIPW	PIGWEED	DEEIIRW	WEIRDIE
DEEEMMW	EMMEWED	DEEFHRS	FRESHED	DEEGIRS	SEDGIER	DEEIIST	DEITIES
DEEEMNS	DEMESNE	DEEFIIR	DEIFIER	DEEGIRV	DIVERGE	DEEIJLL	JELLIED
DEEEMNW	ENMEWED		EDIFIER		GRIEVED	DEEIKLL	KILLDEE
DEEEMRS	DEMERSE		REIFIED	DEEGIST	EDGIEST	DEEIKLN	LIKENED
	EMERSED	DEEFIIS	DEIFIES	DEEGISW	WEDGIES	DEEIKNS	ENSKIED
	REDEEMS		EDIFIES	DEEGJRU	REJUDGE	DEEIKOV	DOVEKIE
	REMEDES	DEEFILN	ENFILED	DEEGKRS	KEDGERS	DEEILNO	ELOINED
DEEEMRT	METERED	DEEFILR	DEFILER	DEEGLMU	EMULGED	DEEILNR	RELINED
DEEEMST	STEEMED		FERLIED	DEEGLNS	LEGENDS	DEEILNS	ENISLED
DEEENPR	PREENED		FIELDER	DEEGLNT	GENTLED		ENSILED
DEEENPS	DEEPENS	DEEFILS	DEFILES		GLENTED		LINSEED
DEEENQU	QUEENED	DEEFINR	DEFINER	DEEGLOY	GOLDEYE	DEEILNV	LIVENED
DEEENRS	NEEDERS		ENFIRED	DEEGLPR	PLEDGER	DEEILNY	DYELINE
	SERENED		FENDIER	DEEGLPS	PLEDGES		NEEDILY
	SNEERED		REFINED	DEEGLPT	PLEDGET	DEEILPR	REPLIED
DEEENRT	ENTERED	DEEFINS	DEFINES	DEEGLRS	GELDERS	DEEILPS	SEEDLIP
DEEENRV	ENERVED	DEEFINT	FEINTED		LEDGERS		SPIELED
DEEENRW	RENEWED	DEEFINX	ENFIXED		REDLEGS	DEEILRS	RESILED
DEEENRY	RENEYED	DEEFIRR	FERRIED		SLEDGER	DEEILRT	RETILED
DEEENST	STEENED	DEEFIRS	DEFIERS	DEEGLSS	SLEDGES	DEEILRV	DELIVER
DEEENSV	VENDEES	DEEFIRT	FETIDER	DEEGLSU	DELUGES		RELIVED

	REVILED	DEEIPSS	DESPISE	DEELNSW	WEDELNS	DEENOST	DENOTES
DEEILRW	WIELDER		PEDESIS	DEELNSY	DENSELY	DEENPPR	PERPEND
DEEILRY	YIELDER	DEEIPST	DESPITE	DEELNTT	NETTLED	DEENPRS	SPENDER
DEEILSS	DIESELS	DEEIQRU	QUERIED	DEELOPP	PEOPLED	DEENPRT	PRETEND
	IDLESSE	DEEIQTU	QUIETED	DEELOPR	DEPLORE	DEENPSX	EXPENDS
DEEILSY	EYELIDS	DEEIRRS	DERRIES	DEELOPV	DEVELOP	DEENRRS	RENDERS
	SEEDILY		DESIRER	DEELOPX	EXPLODE	DEENRRU	ENDURER
DEEILTU	DILUTEE		RESIDER	DEELORS	RESOLED	DEENRSS	REDNESS
DEEILTV	DEVILET		SERRIED	DEELORU	URODELE		SENDERS
DEEIMMS	MISDEEM	DEEIRRT	RETIRED	DEELORV	LOVERED	DEENRST	STERNED
DEEIMMW	IMMEWED		RETRIED	DEELORW	LOWERED		TENDERS
DEEIMNR	ERMINED		TIREDER	DEELOSU	DELOUSE		TENDRES
DEEIMNT	DEMENTI	DEEIRRV	REDRIVE	DEELOTV	DOVELET	DEENRSU	ENDURES
DEEIMPR	DEMIREP		RIVERED	DEELOVV	DEVOLVE		ENSURED
DEEIMPS	IMPEDES	DEEIRRW	REWIRED		EVOLVED	DEENRSV	VENDERS
	SEMIPED		WEIRDER	DEELPRS	SPELDER	DEENRSZ	DZERENS
DEEIMPT	EMPTIED	DEEIRSS	DESIRES	DEELPRU	PRELUDE	DEENRTU	DENTURE
DEEIMRS	REMEIDS		RESIDES	DEELPST	PESTLED		RETUNED
	REMISED	DEEIRST	DIETERS	DEELPTT	PETTLED	DEENRTV	VENTRED
DEEIMRT	DEMERIT		REISTED	DEELRRU	RULERED	DEENSST	DENSEST
	DIMETER	DEEIRSU	RESIDUE	DEELRSU	ELUDERS	DEENSSY	DESYNES
	MERITED		UREIDES	DEELRSV	DELVERS	DEENSTT	DETENTS
	MITERED	DEEIRSV	DERIVES	DEELRSW	WELDERS		STENTED
DEEIMSS	DEMISES		DEVISER	DEELRUV	VELURED	DEENSTU	DETENUS
DEEIMTT	EMITTED		DIVERSE	DEELSTT	SETTLED	DEENSTX	EXTENDS
DEEINNP	PENNIED		REVISED	DEELSTU	TELEDUS	DEENSUV	VENDUES
DEEINNS	INDENES	DEEIRTU	ERUDITE	DEELSTW	LEWDEST	DEENUVX	UNVEXED
DEEINNT	DENTINE	DEEIRTV	RIVETED		SWELTED	DEEOPRR	PEDRERO
DEEINNU	ENNUIED	DEEIRVV	REVIVED	DEELSUV	EVULSED	DEEOPRS	DEPOSER
DEEINNZ	DENIZEN	DEEISSU	DISEUSE	DEELSVV	DEVVELS		REPOSED
DEEINOR	ORDINEE	DEEISSV	DEVISES	DEELTUX	EXULTED	DEEOPRW	POWERED
DEEINPR	REPINED	DEEISTT	TEDIEST	DEELVXY	VEXEDLY	DEEOPSS	DEPOSES
	RIPENED	DEEISTW	DEWIEST	DEEMMOV	EMMOVED		SPEEDOS
DEEINRR	DERNIER	DEEISTX	EXISTED	DEEMMST	STEMMED	DEEOPSX	EXPOSED
DEEINRS	DENIERS	DEEITTV	VIDETTE	DEEMNOV	ENMOVED		PODEXES
	NEREIDS	DEEJNOY	ENJOYED		VENOMED	DEEORRR	ORDERER
	RESINED	DEEJQRU	JERQUED	DEEMNOY	MONEYED		REORDER
DEEINRU	UREDINE	DEEKKRT	TREKKED	DEEMNRS	MENDERS	DEEORRS	REREDOS
DEEINRW	WIDENER	DEEKLLN	KNELLED	DEEMNST	DEMENTS	DEEORRV	OVERRED
DEEINRX	INDEXER	DEEKLPS	SKELPED	DEEMNTU	UNMETED		REDROVE
DEEINSS	DESINES	DEEKLRS	SKELDER	DEEMNUW	UNMEWED	DEEORST	OERSTED
DEEINST	DESTINE	DEEKNOT	TOKENED	DEEMORS	EMERODS		ROSETED
	ENDITES	DEEKORV	REVOKED	DEEMORV	REMOVED		TEREDOS
	STEINED	DEEKPPS	SKEPPED	DEEMORX	EXODERM	DEEORTT	OTTERED
DEEINSV	ENDIVES	DEEKPRU	PERUKED	DEEMOSS	DEMOSES		TETRODE
DEEINSW	ENDWISE	DEEKRRS	SKERRED	DEEMOST	DEMOTES	DEEORTW	TOWERED
	SINEWED	DEEKRSU	RESKUED	DEEMOSY	MOSEYED	DEEORTX	OXTERED
DEEINSX	INDEXES	DEELLMS	SMELLED	DEEMPRS	PREMEDS	DEEORTZ	ROZETED
DEEINTT	DINETTE	DEELLNS	SNELLED	DEEMPTT	TEMPTED	DEEORUV	OVERDUE
DEEINTU	DETINUE	DEELLPS	SPELLED	DEEMRRU	DEMURER	DEEORVY	OVERDYE
DEEINTV	EVIDENT	DEELLQU	QUELLED	DEEMRSU	DEMURES	DEEOSTV	DEVOTES
DEEINVW	VINEWED	DEELLRU	DUELLER		RESUMED	DEEOTUW	OUTWEED
DEEINVX	INVEXED	DEELLRW	DWELLER	DEENNOR	ENDERON	DEEPPPR	PREPPED
DEEINWZ	WIZENED	DEELLRY	ELDERLY	DEENNOS	DONNEES	DEEPPST	STEPPED
DEEIOPS	EPISODE	DEELLST	STELLED	DEENNOT	TENONED	DEEPPRS	SPERRED
	POESIED	DEELLSW	SWELLED	DEENNOY	DOYENNE	DEEPRRU	PERDURE
DEEIOPT	EPIDOTE	DEELMNO	LEMONED	DEENNOZ	ENZONED		REPURED
DEEIOPX	EPOXIDE	DEELMOR	REMODEL	DEENNPT	PENDENT	DEEPRSS	DEPRESS
DEEIORS	OREIDES	DEELMPT	TEMPLED	DEENNST	DENNETS		PRESSED
	OSIERED	DEELMPU	DEPLUME		STENNED		SPERSED
DEEIOSV	VOIDEES	DEELMRS	MELDERS	DEENNTZ	TENDENZ	DEEPRST	PRESTED
DEEIPPT	PEPTIDE	DEELMRU	RELUMED	DEENNUY	ENNUYED	DEEPRSU	PERDUES
DEEIPRS	PREDIES	DEELMST	SMELTED	DEENOOR	RONEOED		PERSUED
	PRESIDE	DEELMSY	MEDLEYS	DEENOPR	REPONED		PERUSED
	SPEIRED	DEELMTT	METTLED	DEENOPS	DEPONES		SUPERED
DEEIPRT	TEPIDER	DEELNRS	LENDERS		SPONDEE	DEEPRTU	ERUPTED
DEEIPRV	DEPRIVE		SLENDER	DEENOPT	PENTODE		REPUTED
	PRIEVED	DEELNSS	ENDLESS	DEENORS	ENDORSE	DEEPSTU	DEPUTES
DEEIPRX	EXPIRED	DEELNST	DENTELS	DEENORT	ERODENT		
			NESTLED	DEENORW	ENDOWER		

DEEQSTU	QUESTED	DEFIIMS	FIDEISM	DEFMORS	DEFORMS	DEGHINN	HENDING

DEEQSTU QUESTED
DEERRSS DRESSER
       REDRESS
DEERRUV VERDURE
DEERSSS DRESSES
DEERSST DESERTS
       DESSERT
       TRESSED
DEERSSU DURESSE
DEERSTV STERVED
       VERDETS
DEERSTW STREWED
       WRESTED
DEERSTX DEXTERS
DEERSTY DYESTER
DEERSVW SWERVED
DEERTTU UTTERED
DEERTUX EXTRUDE
DEESSTT DETESTS
DEESSTV DEVESTS
DEESTTT STETTED
DEFFFLU FLUFFED
DEFFHIW WHIFFED
DEFFHOU HOUFFED
DEFFHOW HOWFFED
DEFFIKS SKIFFED
DEFFILP PIFFLED
DEFFILR RIFFLED
DEFFILS SIFFLED
DEFFINS SNIFFED
DEFFIOS OFFSIDE
DEFFIRS DIFFERS
DEFFIST STIFFED
DEFFISU DIFFUSE
DEFFKOS SKOFFED
DEFFLMU MUFFLED
DEFFLPU PLUFFED
DEFFLRU RUFFLED
DEFFLSU DUFFELS
       DUFFLES
DEFFNOR FORFEND
DEFFNOS OFFENDS
DEFFNSU SNUFFED
DEFFORS DOFFERS
DEFFOSW SOWFFED
DEFFRSU DUFFERS
DEFFSTU DUFFEST
       STUFFED
DEFGGIR FRIGGED
DEFGGLO FLOGGED
DEFGGOR FROGGED
DEFGINN FENDING
DEFGINR FRINGED
DEFGINU FEUDING
DEFGINY DEFYING
DEFGIOR FIREDOG
DEFGIRS FRIDGES
DEFGIRT GRIFTED
DEFGIRU FIGURED
DEFGIST FIDGETS
DEFGITY FIDGETY
DEFGRTU GRUFTED
DEFHIRS REDFISH
DEFHIST SHIFTED
DEFHLOO ELFHOOD
DEFHLSU FLUSHED
DEFHORT FROTHED
DEFHRSU FRUSHED
DEFIILN INFIDEL
       INFIELD

DEFIIMS FIDEISM
DEFIIMW MIDWIFE
DEFIINU UNIFIED
DEFIINX INFIXED
DEFIKLS FLISKED
DEFIKRS FRISKED
DEFILLO FOLLIED
DEFILLR FRILLED
DEFILMP FLIMPED
DEFILNR FLINDER
DEFILNU UNFILDE
       UNFILED
DEFILOO FOLIOED
DEFILPP FLIPPED
DEFILRT FLIRTED
       TRIFLED
DEFILRU DIREFUL
DEFILSS FISSLED
DEFILST STIFLED
DEFILTT FLITTED
DEFILXY FIXEDLY
DEFILZZ FIZZLED
DEFIMOR DEIFORM
DEFINRS FINDERS
       FRIENDS
DEFINRU UNFIRED
DEFINST SNIFTED
DEFINSU INFUSED
DEFINSY DENSIFY
DEFINUX UNFIXED
DEFINUY UNDEIFY
DEFIOOS FOODIES
DEFIOQU QUOIFED
DEFIORU FOUDRIE
DEFIOST FOISTED
DEFIPRY PERFIDY
DEFIRRT DRIFTER
DEFIRST FRISTED
DEFIRTT FRITTED
DEFIRTU FRUITED
DEFIRZZ FRIZZED
DEFISTU FEUDIST
DEFISTW SWIFTED
DEFKLNU FLUNKED
DEFLLOU DOLEFUL
DEFLLUW DEWFULL
DEFLMPU FLUMPED
DEFLNOO ONEFOLD
DEFLNOP PENFOLD
DEFLNOR FONDLER
       FORLEND
DEFLNOS ENFOLDS
       FONDLES
DEFLNOT TENFOLD
DEFLOOR FLOORED
DEFLOOT FOOTLED
DEFLOOZ FOOZLED
DEFLOPP FLOPPED
DEFLORS FOLDERS
DEFLORU FLOURED
       FOULDER
DEFLOSU DEFOULS
       FLOUSED
DEFLOTU FLOUTED
DEFLPRU PURFLED
DEFLRRU FLURRED
DEFLRUU DUREFUL
DEFLUZZ FUZZLED
DEFMNUU UNFUMED

DEFMORS DEFORMS
       SERFDOM
DEFMPRU FRUMPED
DEFNOOR FORDONE
DEFNORT FRONTED
DEFNORU FOUNDER
       REFOUND
DEFNORW FROWNED
DEFNOST FONDEST
DEFNOSU FONDUES
DEFNRSU FUNDERS
       REFUNDS
DEFOOPR PROOFED
DEFOOPS SPOOFED
DEFOORS FORDOES
DEFORST DEFROST
       FROSTED
DEGGGIL GIGGLED
DEGGGIR GRIGGED
DEGGGLO GOGGLED
DEGGGLU GLUGGED
       GUGGLED
DEGGGOR GROGGED
DEGGHIL HIGGLED
DEGGHIN HEDGING
DEGGHIW WHIGGED
DEGGHOS SHOGGED
DEGGIJL JIGGLED
DEGGIKN KEDGING
DEGGILN GELDING
       GINGLED
       NIGGLED
DEGGILW WIGGLED
DEGGINS EDGINGS
       SNIGGED
DEGGINW WEDGING
DEGGIOR DOGGIER
DEGGIOS DOGGIES
DEGGIPR PRIGGED
DEGGIRS DIGGERS
DEGGIRT TRIGGED
DEGGISW SWIGGED
DEGGITW TWIGGED
DEGGJLO JOGGLED
DEGGJLU JUGGLED
DEGGKSU SKUGGED
DEGGLOO GOOGLED
DEGGLOR DOGGREL
DEGGLOS SLOGGED
DEGGLOT TOGGLED
DEGGLPU PLUGGED
DEGGLRU GURGLED
DEGGLSU SLUGGED
DEGGMSU SMUGGED
DEGGNOO DOGGONE
DEGGNOS SNOGGED
DEGGNOU GUDGEON
DEGGNSU SNUGGED
DEGGOPR PROGGED
DEGGORS DOGGERS
DEGGORT TROGGED
DEGGORY DOGGERY
DEGGOSS DOGGESS
DEGGRRU DRUGGER
DEGGRSU GRUDGES
DEGGRTU DRUGGET
DEGHHOU HOUGHED
DEGHILN HINDLEG
DEGHILT DELIGHT
       LIGHTED

DEGHINN HENDING
DEGHINR HERDING
DEGHINT NIGHTED
DEGHINW WHINGED
DEGHIOT HOGTIED
DEGHIPT PIGHTED
DEGHIRT GIRTHED
       RIGHTED
DEGHIST SIGHTED
DEGHITW WIGHTED
DEGHLOO DOGHOLE
DEGHLPU GULPHED
DEGHNOT THONGED
DEGHORR DROGHER
DEGHORU ROUGHED
DEGHOST GHOSTED
DEGHOSU SOUGHED
DEGIILL GILLIED
DEGIILN EILDING
       ELIDING
DEGIINR DINGIER
DEGIINS DINGIES
DEGIINT DIETING
       EDITING
       IGNITED
DEGIIPS GIPSIED
DEGIIRR RIDGIER
       RIGIDER
DEGIIRS DIRIGES
DEGIJLN JINGLED
DEGIKLO GODLIKE
DEGILLR GRILLED
DEGILLU GULLIED
DEGILLY GELIDLY
DEGILMN MEDLING
       MELDING
       MINGLED
DEGILNN LENDING
DEGILNO GLENOID
DEGILNP PINGLED
DEGILNS DINGLES
       ELDINGS
       ENGILDS
       SINGLED
DEGILNT GLINTED
       TINGLED
DEGILNU ELUDING
       INDULGE
DEGILNV DELVING
       DEVLING
DEGILNW WELDING
DEGILOR GLORIED
       GODLIER
       GOLDIER
DEGILOU OUGLIED
DEGILRR GIRDLER
DEGILRS GILDERS
       GIRDLES
       GLIDERS
       GRISLED
       LIDGERS
       RIDGELS
DEGILRU GUILDER
DEGILRW WERGILD
DEGILUV DIVULGE
DEGIMNN MENDING
DEGIMNS SMIDGEN
DEGIMPU GUIMPED
DEGIMST MIDGETS
DEGINNN DENNING

DEGINNP	PENDING	DEGLOPR	PLEDGOR
DEGINNR	GRINNED	DEGLOPS	SPLODGE
	RENDING	DEGLORS	LODGERS
DEGINNS	ENDINGS	DEGLORW	GROWLED
	SENDING	DEGLOSS	GLOSSED
DEGINNT	DENTING		GODLESS
	TENDING	DEGLOST	GOLDEST
DEGINNU	ENDUING	DEGLOTU	GLOUTED
DEGINNV	VENDING	DEGLSSU	SLUDGES
DEGINNW	WENDING	DEGLTTU	GLUTTED
DEGINNY	DENYING		GUTTLED
DEGINOP	PIDGEON	DEGLUZZ	GUZZLED
DEGINOR	ERODING	DEGMNOO	GOODMEN
	GROINED	DEGMOOR	GROOMED
	IGNORED	DEGMRSU	SMUDGER
	NEGROID	DEGMSSU	SMUDGES
	REDOING	DEGNNOU	DUNGEON
DEGINOS	DINGOES	DEGNOPR	PRONGED
DEGINOW	WENDIGO	DEGNOPS	SPONGED
	WIDGEON	DEGNORU	GUERDON
DEGINRR	GRINDER		UNDERGO
	REGRIND		UNGORED
DEGINRS	DINGERS	DEGNORW	WRONGED
	ENGIRDS	DEGNOTU	TONGUED
DEGINRU	DUNGIER	DEGNRSU	GERUNDS
DEGINRW	REDWING	DEGNRTU	GRUNTED
	WRINGED		TRUDGEN
DEGINRY	YERDING	DEGNRUU	UNURGED
DEGINSS	DESIGNS	DEGNSSU	SNUDGES
DEGINST	NIDGETS	DEGNUVY	UNGYVED
	STEDING	DEGOORV	GROOVED
	STINGED	DEGOOST	STOOGED
DEGINSU	GUNDIES	DEGOPRU	GROUPED
	SUEDING	DEGORRS	DROGERS
DEGINSW	SWINDGE	DEGORSS	GROSSED
	SWINGED		SODGERS
DEGINSY	DINGEYS	DEGORST	STODGER
	DYEINGS	DEGORSU	DROGUES
DEGINTW	TWINGED		GOURDES
DEGINUX	EXUDING		GROUSED
DEGIOOR	GOODIER	DEGORTU	DROGUET
DEGIOOS	GOODIES		GROUTED
	SOOGIED	DEGOSST	STODGES
DEGIOPR	PODGIER	DEGOSTU	DEGOUTS
DEGIORT	GOITRED	DEGOSTW	GOWDEST
DEGIPPR	GRIPPED	DEGRRTU	TRUDGER
DEGIPRU	PUDGIER	DEGRSTU	TRUDGES
DEGIPSY	GYPSIED	DEGSSTU	DEGUSTS
DEGIQSU	SQUIDGE	DEHHISW	WHISHED
DEGIRRS	GIRDERS	DEHHMPU	HUMPHED
DEGIRRU	DURGIER	DEHHOOS	HOOSHED
DEGIRSS	DIGRESS	DEHHSSU	SHUSHED
DEGIRSU	GUIDERS	DEHIINN	HINNIED
DEGIRTT	GRITTED	DEHIIPS	PIEDISH
DEGISST	DIGESTS	DEHIIRS	DISHIER
	DISGEST	DEHIKRS	SHIRKED
DEGISTU	GIUSTED		SHRIKED
DEGISTW	WIDGETS	DEHIKSW	WHISKED
DEGKLSU	KLUDGES	DEHILLO	HILLOED
DEGLMMO	GLOMMED	DEHILLS	SHILLED
DEGLMOO	GLOOMED	DEHILMS	DISHELM
DEGLNNO	ENDLONG	DEHILNP	DELPHIN
DEGLNOP	PLONGED	DEHILPR	HIRPLED
DEGLNOS	DONGLES	DEHILRS	HIRSLED
	GOLDENS	DEHILRT	THIRLED
DEGLNOU	LOUNGED	DEHILRW	WHIRLED
DEGLNPU	PLUNGED	DEHILSS	SHIELDS
DEGLNSU	GULDENS	DEHILTY	DIETHYL
DEGLNUU	UNGLUED	DEHIMMW	WHIMMED
	UNGULED	DEHIMNU	INHUMED

DEHIMOR	HEIRDOM		THRONED
DEHIMOS	DISHOME	DEHNOSU	UNSHOED
DEHIMOT	ETHMOID	DEHNOSY	HOYDENS
DEHIMRS	DIRHEMS	DEHNOTZ	DOZENTH
DEHIMRU	HUMIDER	DEHNRSU	HURDENS
DEHIMST	SMITHED	DEHNRTU	THUNDER
DEHINNS	SHINNED	DEHNSSU	DUNSHES
DEHINNT	THINNED		SNUSHED
DEHINOP	DIPHONE	DEHNSSY	YSHENDS
	PHONIED	DEHNSTU	SHUNTED
DEHINOR	HORDEIN	DEHNSYY	HYDYNES
DEHINOS	HOIDENS	DEHOOPT	PHOTOED
DEHINPS	ENDSHIP	DEHOOPW	WHOOPED
DEHINRS	HINDERS	DEHOOST	SOOTHED
	SHRINED	DEHOOSW	WOOSHED
DEHINRU	UNHIRED	DEHOOTT	TOOTHED
DEHINUV	UNHIVED	DEHOOTW	WHOOTED
DEHIORT	THEROID	DEHOPPS	SHOPPED
DEHIOST	HOISTED	DEHOPPW	WHOPPED
DEHIOSU	HIDEOUS	DEHORSS	SHODERS
DEHIOSV	DOVEISH	DEHORST	DEHORTS
DEHIOSW	HOWDIES		SHORTED
DEHIOTU	HIDEOUT	DEHORSV	SHROVED
DEHIPPS	SHIPPED	DEHORSW	SHROWED
DEHIPPW	WHIPPED	DEHORTT	TROTHED
DEHIRRS	SHIRRED	DEHORTW	WORTHED
DEHIRRU	DHURRIE	DEHOSTT	SHOTTED
	HURRIED	DEHOSTU	SHOUTED
DEHIRRW	WHIRRED		SOUTHED
DEHIRST	DITHERS	DEHOSTW	SOWTHED
	SHIRTED	DEIIIRS	IRIDISE
DEHIRSU	HURDIES	DEIIIRZ	IRIDIZE
DEHIRSV	DERVISH	DEIIJMM	JIMMIED
	SHRIVED	DEIIKLS	DISLIKE
DEHIRTV	THRIVED	DEIIKNR	DINKIER
DEHIRTW	WRITHED	DEIIKNS	DINKIES
DEHIRTY	DITHERY	DEIIKST	DIKIEST
DEHISSW	SWISHED	DEIILLR	DILLIER
	WHISSED	DEIILLS	DILLIES
DEHISTW	WHISTED	DEIILLW	WILLIED
DEHISVV	SHIVVED	DEIILMP	IMPLIED
DEHIWZZ	WHIZZED	DEIILMT	DELIMIT
DEHLLOO	HOLLOED		LIMITED
DEHLLOU	HULLOED	DEIILNS	INISLED
DEHLMSU	MULSHED	DEIILOS	DOILIES
DEHLOOS	SHOOLED		IDOLISE
DEHLOPP	HOPPLED	DEIILOZ	IDOLIZE
DEHLORS	HOLDERS	DEIILPS	LIPIDES
DEHLORW	WHORLED	DEIILRV	LIVIDER
DEHLOSS	SLOSHED	DEIIMMX	IMMIXED
DEHLOST	SLOTHED	DEIIMNO	DOMINIE
DEHLRRU	HURDLER	DEIIMRT	TIMIDER
DEHLRSU	HURDLES	DEIIMST	MISDIET
DEHLRTU	HURTLED		STIMIED
DEHLSSU	SLUSHED	DEIIMVW	MIDWIVE
DEHLSTU	HUSTLED	DEIINOS	IODINES
DEHMNOO	HOODMEN		IONISED
DEHMORU	HUMORED	DEIINOT	EDITION
DEHMOST	METHODS		TENIOID
DEHMOTU	MOUTHED	DEIINOZ	IONIZED
DEHMPTU	THUMPED	DEIINRR	RINDIER
DEHMRTY	RYTHMED	DEIINRS	INSIDER
DEHNNSU	SHUNNED	DEIINRT	INDITER
DEHNOOR	HONORED		NITRIDE
DEHNOOW	HOEDOWN	DEIINRU	URIDINE
DEHNOPU	UNHOPED	DEIINRV	DIVINER
DEHNORS	DEHORNS	DEIINRW	WINDIER
DEHNORT	NORTHED	DEIINSS	INSIDES
	THONDER	DEIINST	INDITES
	THORNED		TINEIDS

DEIINSV DIVINES	DEILLOV LIVELOD	SLIPPED	DEIMPRT DIREMPT
DEIINTV INVITED	DEILLPR PRILLED	DEILPPT TIPPLED	DEIMPRU DUMPIER
DEIIORT DIORITE	DEILLPS SPILLED	DEILPPU UPPILED	UMPIRED
DEIIORV IVORIED	DEILLQU QUILLED	DEILPRT TRIPLED	DEIMPSU DUMPIES
DEIIOSS IODISES	DEILLRR DRILLER	DEILPRU PRELUDI	DEIMPTU IMPUTED
DEIIOSX OXIDISE	DEILLRT TRILLED	DEILPSS DISPELS	DEIMRRS SMIRRED
DEIIOSZ IODIZES	DEILLRU DULLIER	DISPLES	DEIMRSW MISDREW
DEIIOXZ OXIDIZE	DEILLRV DREVILL	DEILPSU DUPLIES	DEIMRUU UREDIUM
DEIIPPR DIPPIER	DEILLSS LIDLESS	DEILPTY TEPIDLY	DEIMSST DEMISTS
DEIIPRS PIERIDS	DEILLST STILLED	DEILQTU QUILTED	DEIMSSU MISUSED
DEIIPRT RIPTIDE	DEILLSU ILLUDES	DEILRRU LURIDER	DEIMSTT SMITTED
DEIIRRT DIRTIER	SULLIED	DEILRSS SLIDERS	DEIMSTU MUISTED
DEIIRST DIRTIES	DEILLSW SWILLED	DEILRSV DRIVELS	TEDIUMS
DEIIRTT TRITIDE	DEILLTW TWILLED	DEILRSW SWIRLED	DEIMSTY STYMIED
DEIIRVV VIVIDER	DEILMMP PLIMMED	WILDERS	DEINNNU NUNDINE
DEIIRZZ DIZZIER	DEILMMS SLIMMED	DEILRTU DILUTER	DEINNOO ONIONED
DEIISTT DIETIST	DEILMNS MILDENS	DEILRTW TWIRLED	DEINNOP PINNOED
DITTIES	DEILMNU LUMINED	DEILRVY DEVILRY	DEINNOR ENDIRON
TIDIEST	UNLIMED	DEILRWY WEIRDLY	DEINNOS ONDINES
DEIISTV VISITED	DEILMOP IMPLODE	DEILRWZ WRIZLED	DEINNOT INTONED
DEIISVV DIVVIES	DEILMOS SMOILED	DEILRZZ DRIZZLE	NOINTED
DEIISZZ DIZZIES	DEILMOY MYELOID	DEILSTT STILTED	DEINNRS DINNERS
DEIIVZZ VIZZIED	DEILMPP PIMPLED	DEILSTU DILUTES	DEINNRU DUNNIER
DEIJLLO JOLLIED	DEILMPS DIMPLES	DEILSTW WILDEST	INURNED
DEIJNOR JOINDER	DEILMPW WIMPLED	DEILSTY DISTYLE	DEINNST DENTINS
DEIJNOT JOINTED	DEILMST MILDEST	DEILSZZ SIZZLED	INDENTS
DEIJNRU INJURED	MISTLED	DEILTTT TITTLED	INTENDS
DEIJNSU DISJUNE	DEILMSW MILDEWS	DEILTTU TITULED	DEINNSU DUNNIES
DEIJOST JOISTED	DEILMWY MILDEWY	DEILTTW TWILTED	UNDINES
DEIJTTU JUTTIED	DEILMXY MIXEDLY	DEIMMMU MUMMIED	DEINNSW ENWINDS
DEIKKNS SKINKED	DEILMZZ MIZZLED	DEIMMOT TOMMIED	DEINNTU DUNNITE
DEIKLLS DESKILL	DEILNNS DINNLES	DEIMMPR PRIMMED	DEINNTW TWINNED
SKILLED	LINDENS	DEIMMRS DIMMERS	DEINOPR POINDER
DEIKLNP PLINKED	DEILNNU UNLINED	DEIMMRT TRIMMED	PROINED
DEIKLNR KINDLER	DEILNOO EIDOLON	DEIMMRU DUMMIER	DEINOPS DISPONE
DEIKLNS KINDLES	DEILNOS INDOLES	IMMURED	SPINODE
DEIKLNT TINKLED	SONDELI	DEIMMST DIMMEST	DEINOPT POINTED
DEIKLOR RODLIKE	DEILNOT LENTOID	DEIMMSU DUMMIES	DEINOQU QUOINED
DEIKLOS KELOIDS	DEILNOU UNOILED	MEDIUMS	DEINORR DRONIER
DEIKLRS SKIRLED	DEILNPP NIPPLED	DEIMNNU MINUEND	DEINORS DONSIER
DEIKLRT KIRTLED	DEILNPS SPELDIN	DEIMNOP IMPONED	INDORSE
DEIKLTT KITTLED	SPINDLE	DEIMNOS MISDONE	ROSINED
DEIKMMS SKIMMED	SPLINED	DEIMNPS IMPENDS	SORDINE
DEIKMPS SKIMPED	DEILNRT TENDRIL	DEIMNRS MINDERS	DEINORU DOURINE
DEIKMRS SMIRKED	TRINDLE	REMINDS	OUNDIER
DEIKNNS SKINNED	DEILNST DENTILS	DEIMNRU UNRIMED	DEINORW DOWNIER
DEIKNOV INVOKED	DEILNSW SWINDLE	DEIMNSS DIMNESS	WINDORE
DEIKNPR PRINKED	WINDLES	MISSEND	DEINOSS ONSIDES
DEIKNRR DRINKER	DEILNSY SNIDELY	DEIMNST MINDSET	DEINOST DITONES
DEIKNRS KINREDS	DEILNTU DILUENT	DEIMNSW MISWEND	STONIED
REDSKIN	UNTILED	DEIMNTU MINUTED	DEINPPS SNIPPED
DEIKNST DINKEST	DEILNTW INDWELT	MUNITED	DEINPRS PINDERS
KINDEST	WINTLED	MUTINED	DEINPRT PRINTED
DEIKNSW SWINKED	DEILNUV UNLIVED	DEIMNUX UNMIXED	DEINPST STIPEND
DEIKNSY KIDNEYS	DEILOOS DOOLIES	DEIMOOR DOOMIER	DEINPSU UNIPEDS
DEIKNSZ ZENDIKS	DEILOPS DESPOIL	MOIDORE	UNSPIDE
DEIKNTT KNITTED	DIPLOES	MOODIER	UNSPIED
DEIKNTW TWINKED	DIPOLES	DEIMOOS MOODIES	DEINPUW UNWIPED
DEIKOSY DISYOKE	PELOIDS	DEIMOPS IMPOSED	DEINRST TINDERS
DEIKPPS SKIPPED	SOLIPED	DEIMORS MISDOER	DEINRSU INSURED
DEIKQRU QUIRKED	SPOILED	MOIDERS	DEINRSW REWINDS
DEIKRRS SKIRRED	DEILOPT PILOTED	DEIMORU ERODIUM	WINDERS
DEIKRST SKIRTED	DEILORS SOLDIER	DEIMOSS MISDOES	DEINRTT TRIDENT
DEIKRSU DUIKERS	SOLIDER	DEIMOST DOMIEST	DEINRTU INTRUDE
DUSKIER	DEILORT DOILTER	MODISTE	TURDINE
DEIKSTY DYKIEST	DEILOSY DOYLIES	MOISTED	UNTIRED
DEILLMU ILLUMED	DEILOTU OUTLIED	DEIMOTT OMITTED	UNTRIDE
DEILLNW INDWELL	DEILPPR RIPPLED	DEIMOTV MOTIVED	UNTRIED
DEILLOR DOLLIER	DEILPPS SIPPLED	VOMITED	DEINRTX DEXTRIN
DEILLOS DOLLIES		DEIMPPR PRIMPED	DEINRTY TINDERY

DEINRUW	UNWIRED
DEINSST	DISNEST
	DISSENT
	SNIDEST
DEINSSV	VENDISS
DEINSSW	WINDSES
DEINSTT	DENTIST
	DISTENT
	STINTED
DEINSTU	DISTUNE
	DUNITES
DEINSTY	DENSITY
	DESTINY
DEINSUZ	UNSIZED
DEINUVW	UNWIVED
DEIOORS	OROIDES
DEIOORW	WOODIER
DEIOOST	OSTEOID
DEIOOSW	WOODIES
DEIOOVV	VOIVODE
DEIOOWW	WOIWODE
DEIOPPP	POPPIED
DEIOPPS	DOPPIES
DEIOPRS	PERIODS
DEIOPRT	DIOPTER
	DIOPTRE
	PERIDOT
	PROTEID
DEIOPRV	PROVIDE
DEIOPSS	DISPOSE
DEIOPST	DEPOSIT
	DOPIEST
	PODITES
	POSITED
	SOPITED
	TOPSIDE
DEIOPSV	VESPOID
DEIOPTT	TIPTOED
DEIOPTV	PIVOTED
DEIOQTU	QUOITED
DEIORRT	DORTIER
DEIORRW	ROWDIER
	WORDIER
	WORRIED
DEIORSS	DORISES
	DOSSIER
DEIORST	EDITORS
	ROISTED
	ROSITED
	SORTIED
	STEROID
	STORIED
	TRIODES
DEIORSV	DEVISOR
	DEVOIRS
	VISORED
	VOIDERS
DEIORSW	DOWRIES
	ROWDIES
	WEIRDOS
DEIORSZ	DORIZES
DEIORTT	DOTTIER
DEIORTU	ETOURDI
	IODURET
	OUTRIDE
DEIORTZ	ROZITED
DEIORVZ	VIZORED
DEIORWW	WIDOWER
DEIOSTT	DOTIEST
	STOITED
DEIOSTU	OUTSIDE
	TEDIOUS
DEIOSTV	DOVIEST
DEIOSTW	DOWIEST
DEIOSTX	EXODIST
DEIOSTZ	DOZIEST
DEIOSUV	DEVIOUS
DEIOTUV	OUTVIED
DEIPPPU	PUPPIED
DEIPPQU	QUIPPED
DEIPPRS	DIPPERS
DEIPPRT	TRIPPED
DEIPPSU	DUPPIES
DEIPRSS	SPIDERS
DEIPRST	SPIRTED
	STRIPED
DEIPRSU	PUDSIER
	SIRUPED
DEIPRSY	SPIDERY
DEIPSSU	UPSIDES
DEIPSTT	SPITTED
DEIPSTU	DISPUTE
DEIPSXY	PYXIDES
DEIPTTU	PUTTIED
	TITUPED
DEIQRSU	SQUIRED
DEIQRTU	QUIRTED
DEIQTTU	QUITTED
DEIQUZZ	QUIZZED
DEIRRST	STIRRED
DEIRRSU	DRUSIER
	DURRIES
DEIRRSV	DRIVERS
DEIRRUX	DRUXIER
DEIRSST	DISSERT
	STRIDES
DEIRSSU	DISEURS
	SUDSIER
DEIRSTU	DUSTIER
	REDUITS
	STUDIER
DEIRSTV	DIVERTS
	STRIVED
	VERDITS
DEISSST	DESISTS
DEISSSU	DISUSES
DEISSTU	STUDIES
	TISSUED
DEISSTV	DIVESTS
DEISTTW	DEWITTS
	TWISTED
DEITTTW	TWITTED
DEJLOST	JOSTLED
DEJLSTU	JUSTLED
DEJOSTU	JOUSTED
DEKKLSU	SKULKED
DEKKNSU	SKUNKED
DEKLLNO	KNOLLED
DEKLNOP	PLONKED
DEKLNPU	PLUNKED
DEKLNRU	KNURLED
	RUNKLED
DEKLRSU	SKUDLER
DEKNNRU	DRUNKEN
DEKNOOS	SNOOKED
DEKNOQU	QUONKED
DEKNOSW	SNOWKED
DEKNOSY	DONKEYS
DEKNOTT	KNOTTED
DEKNOTU	KNOUTED
DEKNOUY	UNYOKED
DEKNPSU	SPUNKED
DEKNRRU	DRUNKER
DEKNRTU	TRUNKED
DEKNSSU	DUSKENS
DEKOOPS	SPOOKED
DEKOOST	DOOKETS
	STOOKED
DEKOOTW	KOTOWED
DEKOPST	DESKTOP
DEKORST	STROKED
DEKOSSU	KUDOSES
DEKRSUY	DUYKERS
DEKSSTU	DUSKEST
DELLOOW	WOOLLED
DELLOPR	PROLLED
	REDPOLL
DELLORR	DROLLER
DELLORT	TROLLED
DELLOSU	DUELLOS
DELLOVW	LOWVELD
DELLSTU	DULLEST
DELMMSU	SLUMMED
DELMNOS	DOLMENS
DELMOOS	SLOOMED
DELMOOW	ELMWOOD
DELMORS	SMOLDER
DELMORU	MOULDER
	REMOULD
DELMOSU	MODULES
	MOUSLED
DELMOSY	SMOYLED
DELMOTT	MOTTLED
DELMOTU	MOULTED
DELMOUV	VOLUMED
DELMPPU	PLUMPED
DELMPRU	RUMPLED
DELMPSU	DUMPLES
	SLUMPED
DELMUZZ	MUZZLED
DELNOOS	NOODLES
	SNOOLED
DELNORS	RONDELS
DELNORT	ENTROLD
DELNORU	LOUNDER
	ROUNDEL
	ROUNDLE
DELNOSS	OLDNESS
DELNOSU	LOUDENS
	NODULES
	NOUSLED
DELNOSW	DOWLNES
DELNOSZ	DONZELS
DELNOTY	NOTEDLY
DELNOUV	UNLOVED
DELNOWY	DOWLNEY
DELNPRU	PLUNDER
DELNRSU	LURDENS
	NURSLED
	RUNDLES
DELNRTU	RUNDLET
	TRUNDLE
DELNRUU	UNRULED
DELNSSU	DULNESS
DELNUWY	UNWELDY
DELNUZZ	NUZZLED
DELOOPP	PLEOPOD
DELOOPS	POODLES
	SPOOLED
DELOORT	ROOTLED
DELOORW	WOOLDER
DELOOST	STOOLED
DELOOTT	TOOTLED
DELOPPP	PLOPPED
	POPPLED
DELOPPR	DROPPLE
DELOPPS	SLOPPED
DELOPPT	TOPPLED
DELOPRS	POLDERS
DELOPRT	DROPLET
DELOPRU	POULDER
	POULDRE
	PROULED
DELOPRW	PROWLED
DELOPSU	SOUPLED
DELOPSY	DEPLOYS
	PODLEYS
DELOPTT	PLOTTED
DELORRY	ORDERLY
DELORSS	DORSELS
	RODLESS
	SOLDERS
DELORST	DROLEST
	OLDSTER
	STRODLE
DELORSW	WELDORS
DELORSY	YODLERS
DELORTT	DOTTLER
	DOTTREL
DELORTU	TROULED
DELORUV	LOUVRED
DELOSSS	DOSSELS
DELOSSU	DULOSES
DELOSTT	DOTTLES
	SLOTTED
DELOSTU	LOUDEST
	TOUSLED
DELOSYY	DOYLEYS
DELOSZZ	SOZZLED
DELOTUV	VOLUTED
DELOTUZ	TOUZLED
DELPPRU	PURPLED
DELPPSU	SUPPLED
DELPRSU	DRUPELS
	SLURPED
DELPSSU	PLUSSED
DELPSTU	DUPLETS
DELPSUY	SPULYED
DELPUZZ	PUZZLED
DELRRSU	SLURRED
DELRSTU	LUSTRED
	RUSTLED
	STRUDEL
DELRTTU	TURTLED
DELSSTU	TUSSLED
DELSTTU	SUTTLED
DELUWZZ	WUZZLED
DEMMRRU	DRUMMER
DEMMSTU	STUMMED
DEMNOOR	MORENDO
DEMNOOW	WOODMEN
DEMNORS	MODERNS
	RODSMEN
DEMNORT	MORDENT
DEMNORU	MOURNED
DEMNORY	DEMONRY
DEMNOST	ENDMOST
DEMNOTU	DEMOUNT
	MOUNTED
DEMNOUV	UNMOVED

DEMNSTU	DUSTMEN		SOUNDER		DROWSES	DFLOTWY	TWYFOLD
DEMOOPP	POPEDOM		UNDOERS	DEORSTT	DETORTS	DFNNOUU	UNFOUND
DEMOOPR	PREDOOM	DENORSV	VENDORS	DEORSTU	DETOURS	DFNORUY	FOUNDRY
DEMOOPS	SPOOMED	DENORSW	DOWNERS		DOUREST	DGGGIIN	DIGGING
DEMOORS	DROOMES		WONDERS		DOUTERS	DGGGINO	DOGGING
	SMOORED	DENORUW	REWOUND		OUTREDS	DGGHIOS	DOGGISH
DEMOORT	MOTORED		WOUNDER		ROUSTED	DGGIILN	GILDING
DEMOORV	VROOMED	DENOSTT	SNOTTED	DEORSTW	STROWED		GLIDING
DEMOOSS	OSMOSED	DENOSTU	DEUTONS		WORSTED	DGGIINN	DINGING
DEMOOST	SMOOTED		SNOUTED	DEORSTY	DESTROY	DGGIINR	GIRDING
DEMOOTT	MOTTOED	DENOSUW	SWOUNED		ROYSTED		GRIDING
DEMOOTU	OUTMODE	DENPRSU	SPURNED		STROYED		RIDGING
DEMOPST	STOMPED	DENPRTU	PRUDENT	DEORSUV	DEVOURS	DGGIINU	GUIDING
DEMORRS	DORMERS		PRUNTED	DEORTTT	TROTTED	DGGIJNU	JUDGING
DEMORRU	RUMORED		UPTREND	DEORTTU	TUTORED	DGGILNO	GODLING
DEMORST	STORMED	DENPSSU	SUSPEND	DEORTUU	OUTDURE		LODGING
DEMOSSU	SMOUSED		UPSENDS	DEOSSSW	SOWSSED	DGGINNO	DONGING
DEMOSTT	DOMETTS	DENRSSU	SUNDERS	DEOSSTW	DOWSETS	DGGINNU	DUNGING
DEMOSTU	MOUSTED		UNDRESS	DEOSSYY	ODYSSEY		NUDGING
	SMOUTED	DENRSSY	DRYNESS	DEOSTTT	STOTTED	DGGINRY	GRYDING
DEMOSTY	MODESTY	DENRSTU	RETUNDS	DEOSTTU	DUETTOS	DGGNOSU	DUGONGS
DEMPRSU	DUMPERS		UNDREST		TESTUDO	DGHHOOO	HOGHOOD
DEMPRTU	TRUMPED	DENRSUU	UNSURED	DEOSTTW	SWOTTED	DGHIILN	HIDLING
DEMPSTU	STUMPED	DENSSTY	SYNDETS	DEOSTUU	DUTEOUS		HILDING
DEMRRSU	MURDERS	DENSTTU	STUDENT	DEOSTUX	TUXEDOS	DGHIINS	DISHING
	SMURRED		STUNTED	DEPRRSU	SPURRED		HIDINGS
DEMSTTU	SMUTTED	DENTUVY	DUVETYN	DEPRRUY	PRUDERY		SHINDIG
DENNORT	DONNERT	DEOOPPS	OPPOSED	DEPRSTU	SPURTED	DGHILNO	HOLDING
	TENDRON	DEOOPRS	SPOORED	DEPRSUU	PURSUED	DGHILNY	HYLDING
DENNORU	ENROUND	DEOOPRT	TORPEDO		USURPED	DGHILOS	GOLDISH
DENNOST	STONNED		TROOPED	DEPRSUY	SYRUPED	DGHILPY	DIGLYPH
	TENDONS	DEOOPSW	SWOOPED	DERRSTU	RUSTRED	DGHINOO	HOODING
DENNOTU	UNNOTED	DEOOPSX	EXOPODS	DERSSSU	SUDSERS	DGHINOR	HORDING
	UNTONED	DEOORST	ROOSTED	DERSSTU	DUSTERS	DGHINSU	DUSHING
DENNOUW	ENWOUND	DEOORTU	OUTRODE		TRUSSED	DGHINTU	UNDIGHT
	UNOWNED	DEOORTW	WROOTED	DERSTTU	STURTED	DGHIOOS	GOODISH
DENNOUZ	UNZONED	DEOOSTU	OUTDOES		TRUSTED	DGHIOPS	DOGSHIP
DENNRSU	UNDERNS	DEOPPPR	PROPPED	DERSTTY	TRYSTED		GODSHIP
DENNSTU	DUNNEST	DEOPPQU	QUOPPED	DERSTUU	SUTURED	DGHOPSU	HOPDOGS
	STUNNED	DEOPPRR	DROPPER	DFFGINO	DOFFING	DGHORTU	DROUGHT
DENNTUU	UNTUNED	DEOPPRS	DOPPERS	DFFGINU	DUFFING	DGHOTUY	DOUGHTY
DENOOPS	SNOOPED	DEOPPST	STOPPED	DFFIIMR	MIDRIFF	DGIIINV	DIVIING
	SPOONED	DEOPPSW	SWOPPED	DFFIIRT	TRIFFID	DGIIKLN	KIDLING
DENOOST	SNOOTED	DEOPRRU	PROUDER	DFFIMOR	DIFFORM	DGIIKNN	DINKING
	STOODEN	DEOPRST	DEPORTS	DFFLOOU	FOODFUL		KINDING
DENOOSW	SWOONED		REDTOPS	DFGGIIN	FIDGING	DGIIKNR	DIRKING
DENOOSZ	SNOOZED		SPORTED	DFGGINU	FUDGING	DGIIKNS	DISKING
DENOOTU	DUOTONE	DEOPRSU	POUDERS	DFGHIOS	DOGFISH	DGIILLN	DILLING
	OUTDONE		POUDRES	DFGIINN	FINDING	DGIILNO	LOIDING
DENOOUW	UNWOOED	DEOPRSW	POWDERS	DFGIINY	DIGNIFY	DGIILNR	DIRLING
DENOPPR	PROPEND	DEOPRTU	TROUPED	DFGILNO	FOLDING	DGIILNS	SIDLING
DENOPPU	UNPOPED	DEOPRWY	POWDERY	DFGINNO	FONDING		SLIDING
DENOPRS	PONDERS	DEOPSST	DESPOTS	DFGINNU	FUNDING	DGIILNW	WILDING
	RESPOND	DEOPSSU	SPOUSED	DFGINOR	FORDING	DGIILRS	RIDGILS
DENOPRT	PORTEND	DEOPSTT	SPOTTED	DFGINOU	FUNGOID	DGIILRY	RIGIDLY
	PROTEND	DEOPSTU	SPOUTED	DFGMOOY	FOGYDOM	DGIIMMN	DIMMING
DENOPRU	POUNDER	DEOPTTY	TYPTOED	DFHILSU	DISHFUL	DGIIMNN	MINDING
	UNROPED	DEOQRTU	TORQUED	DFILMMO	FILMDOM	DGIIMNS	SMIDGIN
DENOPRV	PROVEND	DEORRSS	DORSERS	DFILMNU	MINDFUL	DGIIMOS	SIGMOID
DENOPRY	PROYNED	DEORRST	DORTERS	DFILNOP	PINFOLD	DGIINNN	DINNING
DENOPSU	UNPOSED		RODSTER	DFILNOS	INFOLDS	DGIINNR	RINDING
DENOPTY	POYNTED	DEORRSU	ORDURES	DFILOSX	SIXFOLD	DGIINNS	NIDINGS
DENOPUX	EXPOUND	DEORRSV	DROVERS	DFILOTW	TWIFOLD		SINDING
DENORRU	RONDURE	DEORRSW	REWORDS	DFILTUU	DUT1FUL	DGIINNT	DINTING
	ROUNDER		SWORDER	DFIMNUY	MUNDIFY		TINDING
	UNORDER	DEORSSS	DOSSERS	DFIMORS	DISFORM	DGIINNU	INDUING
DENORRW	DROWNER		DROSSES	DFLMOOU	DOOMFUL	DGIINNW	DWINING
DENORST	RODENTS	DEORSSU	DOUSERS	DFLNOSU	UNFOLDS		WINDING
	SNORTED	DEORSSW	DOWSERS	DFLOOTW	TWOFOLD	DGIINOS	INDIGOS
DENORSU	RESOUND			DFLOPRY	DROPFLY	DGIINOV	VOIDING

DGIINOW WINDIGO	DGIOPRY PRODIGY	DHORXYY HYDROXY	DILSTUY DUSTILY
DGIINPP DIPPING	DGIOSTW GODWITS	DIIIMRU IRIDIUM	DIMMOST MIDMOST
DGIINPR PRIDING	DGIQSUY SQUIDGY	DIIIMSV DIVISIM	DIMNNOO MIDNOON
DGIINPS PIDGINS	DGISSTU DISGUST	DIIINPS INSIPID	DIMNNOS DONNISM
DGIINPU PINGUID	DGLNOUY UNGODLY	DIIJNOS DISJOIN	DIMNNOT DINMONT
DGIINRS RIDINGS	DGLOOOW LOGWOOD	DIIKLNS DISLINK	DIMNOOS DOMINOS
DGIINRT DIRTING	DGLOPSY SPLODGY	DIIKNOT DOITKIN	DIMNOPU IMPOUND
DGIINRV DRIVING	DGLOSYY DYSLOGY	DIILLST DISTILL	DIMNSSU NUDISMS
DGIINRY YIRDING	DGMOPRU GUMDROP	DIILMNS DISLIMN	DIMOPSU SPODIUM
DGIINSS SIDINGS	DGMORUU GURUDOM	DIILMOO MODIOLI	DIMORSW MISWORD
DGIINST TIDINGS	DGNOOOR GODROON	DIILMOS IDOLISM	DIMOSST MODISTS
DGIINSV DIVINGS	DGNOORS DRONGOS	DIILMTY TIMIDLY	DIMOSSU SODIUMS
DGIINTT DITTING	DGNOOSS GODSONS	DIILNWY WINDILY	DIMOSSW WISDOMS
DGIINTY DIGNITY	DGNOOSW GODOWNS	DIILOPS LIPOIDS	DIMRTUU TRIDUUM
TIDYING	DGNOOTW DOGTOWN	DIILOST IDOLIST	DIMRUUV DUUMVIR
DGIIORT TIGROID	DGNORSU GROUNDS	DIILQSU LIQUIDS	DINNOOR RONDINO
DGIJOSU JUDOGIS	DGOORTT DOGTROT	DIILRSU SILURID	DINNOOT TONDINO
DGIKMNO KINGDOM	DGOSTUU DUGOUTS	DIILRTY DIRTILY	DINNOSS SINDONS
DGIKNNU DUNKING	DHIILNS HIDLINS	DIILSST DISTILS	DINNOUW INWOUND
DGIKNNY KYNDING	DHIILOT LITHOID	DIILVVY VIVIDLY	DINNSUW UNWINDS
DGIKNOO DOOKING	DHIILSW WILDISH	DIILYZZ DIZZILY	DINOORS INDOORS
DGIKNOS DOGSKIN	DHIIMMS DIMMISH	DIIMNOR MIDIRON	SORDINO
DGIKNSU DUSKING	DHIIMNO HOMINID	DIIMNSU INDIUMS	DINOORT TORDION
DGILLNO DOLLING	DHIIMPS MIDSHIP	DIIMORS DIORISM	DINOOST ISODONT
DGILLNU DULLING	DHIINNU HIRUDIN	DIIMOSS IODISMS	DINOPSU DUPIONS
DGILLOY GODLILY	DHIIOPX XIPHOID	DIIMSSS DISMISS	UNIPODS
DGILMNO MOLDING	DHIIORZ RHIZOID	DIIMSTW DIMWITS	DINORSU DURIONS
DGILNOR GIRLOND	DHIIOST HISTOID	DIIMSUV VIDIMUS	DINORTU TURDION
LORDING	DHIKSSU DUSKISH	DIINNOT TONDINI	DINORWW WINDROW
DGILNOY YODLING	DHILLOS DOLLISH	DIINNSW INWINDS	DINOSSW DISOWNS
DGILNSU UNGILDS	DHILLSU DULLISH	DIINORS SORDINI	DINOSTW SITDOWN
DGILNYY DYINGLY	DHILMUY HUMIDLY	DIINOSX DIOXINS	DINOSWW WINDOWS
DGILOST DIGLOTS	DHILNOP DOLPHIN	DIIOPRS SPIROID	DINOTUW OUTWIND
DGILRUY GUILDRY	DHILOST DOLTISH	DIIORSV DIVISOR	DINPSTU PUNDITS
DGIMNOO DOOMING	DHILOSU LOUDISH	VIROIDS	DINPSUW UPWINDS
DGIMNPU DUMPING	DHILPSU LUDSHIP	DIITUVY VIDUITY	DINRSSU SUNDRIS
DGIMOPY PYGMOID	DHILPSY SYLPHID	DIJOSTU JUDOIST	DINSSTU NUDISTS
DGINNNO DONNING	DHILRTY THIRDLY	DIKLNOR LORDKIN	DIOOPSS ISOPODS
DGINNNU DUNNING	DHIMOPR DIMORPH	DIKLSUY DUSKILY	DIOORST DISROOT
DGINNOP PONDING	DHIMORU HUMIDOR	DIKNORV DVORNIK	TOROIDS
DGINNOR DRONING	RHODIUM	DIKOORT DROOKIT	DIOORTT RIDOTTO
DGINNOS DONINGS	DHIMPSU DUMPISH	DIKOOSS SKIDOOS	DIOOSTX TOXOIDS
ONDINGS	DHINNOS DONNISH	DIKORTU DROUKIT	DIOPRST DISPORT
DGINNOU UNDOING	DHINNSU DUNNISH	DILLOSY SOLIDLY	TORPIDS
DGINNOW DOWNING	DHINOPS DONSHIP	DILLRUY LURIDLY	TRIPODS
DGINNSY SYNDING	DHINOPY HYPNOID	DILMNRU DRUMLIN	DIOPRTY TRIPODY
DGINNTU DUNTING	DHINORS DISHORN	DILMOOY MOODILY	DIOPSST DISPOST
TUNDING	DRONISH	DILMORS MILORDS	DIORRST STRIDOR
DGINNUY UNDYING	DHIOOST DHOOTIS	DILMOST MISTOLD	DIORSTT DISTORT
DGINOOW WOODING	DHIOPTY TYPHOID	DILMOSU SOLIDUM	DIOSSTU STUDIOS
DGINOPP DOPPING	DHIORSW WORDISH	DILMOSY ODYLISM	DIOSUUV VIDUOUS
DGINOPS DOPINGS	DHIORTY THYROID	DILMTUY TUMIDLY	DIPRSTU DISRUPT
PONGIDS	DHIPRSU PRUDISH	DILNNSU DUNLINS	DIPSSTU STUPIDS
DGINORR DORRING	DHIPRSY SYRPHID	DILNOOS OODLINS	DIRSTUY SURDITY
DGINORS RODINGS	DHKORSY DROSHKY	DILNOPS DIPLONS	DJNNOOS DONJONS
DGINORT DORTING	DHLMOOU HOODLUM	DILNOPT DIPLONT	DKNNRUU UNDRUNK
DGINORW WORDING	DHLOPSU UPHOLDS	DILNOQU QUODLIN	DKNOOPS PONDOKS
DGINOSS DOSSING	DHMMRUU HUMDRUM	DILNORT INTROLD	DKOOOOS KOODOOS
DGINOST DOTINGS	DHMNOYY HYMNODY	DILNOSU UNSOLID	DKOOOSZ ODZOOKS
DGINOSU DOUSING	DHNNOOU NUNHOOD	DILNPSU LISPUND	DLLOOPS DOLLOPS
GUIDONS	DHNOOSU UNHOODS	DILNPSY SPINDLY	DLLORWY WORLDLY
DGINOSW DISGOWN	DHOOOOS HOODOOS	DILNSTU INDULTS	DLMNOOY MYLODON
DOWSING	DHOOPRU UPHOORD	DILORTU DILUTOR	DLMNOUU UNMOULD
DGINOSZ DOZINGS	DHOORSU RHODOUS	DILORWY ROWDILY	DLMOSUU MODULUS
DGINOTT DOTTING	DHOPRSU PUSHROD	WORDILY	DLNOPRU PULDRON
DGINOTU DOUTING	DHORSSU SHROUDS	DILOSSS DOSSILS	DLNOPSY SPONDYL
DGINPPU DUPPING	DHORSTU DROUTHS	DILOSSU DULOSIS	DLNORSU UNLORDS
DGINRSU UNGIRDS	DHORSUY HYDROUS	SOLIDUS	DLNORUY ROUNDLY
DGINRSY DRYINGS	SHROUDY	DILOSTY STYLOID	DLNOSUY SOUNDLY
DGINSTU DUSTING	DHORTUY DROUTHY	DILRYZZ DRIZZLY	DLOOPPY POLYPOD

DLOOPSS	PODSOLS	EEEGLNT	GENTEEL	EEEKLNR	KNEELER	EEENRSZ	SNEEZER
DLOOPSZ	PODZOLS	EEEGMRR	REMERGE	EEEKLNS	SLEEKEN	EEENRTV	EVENTER
DLOOPTY	TYLOPOD	EEEGMRS	EMERGES	EEEKLPW	EKPWELE	EEENRTX	EXTERNE
DLOOPUY	DUOPOLY	EEEGNPR	EPERGNE	EEEKLRS	KEELERS	EEENRUV	REVENUE
DLOOPWY	PLYWOOD	EEEGNPS	PEENGES		SLEEKER		UNREEVE
DLOORSU	DOLOURS	EEEGNRR	GREENER	EEEKMNS	MEEKENS	EEENSSZ	SNEEZES
DLOOSTU	OUTSOLD		RENEGER	EEEKMST	MEEKEST	EEENSTV	EVENEST
DLOOTTU	OUTTOLD	EEEGNRS	RENEGES	EEEKNPT	KEEPNET	EEENSTW	SWEETEN
DLOPRUY	PROUDLY	EEEGNRU	RENEGUE	EEEKNRS	KEENERS	EEENSTX	EXTENSE
DLOSTUW	WOULDST	EEEGNRV	REVENGE		SKREENE	EEENSVW	VENEWES
DMNOORS	DROMONS	EEEGNSS	GENESES	EEEKNST	KEENEST	EEENSWY	SWEENEY
DMNOOTW	TOWMOND	EEEGNTT	GENETTE	EEEKPRS	KEEPERS	EEEOPPS	EPOPEES
DMNOSSU	OSMUNDS	EEEGRRT	REGREET	EEEKRSS	KREESES	EEEORSV	OVERSEE
DMORTUW	MUDWORT	EEEGRSS	GREESES		SEEKERS	EEEORSY	EYESORE
DNNOOST	DONNOTS	EEEGRST	GREETES	EEEKRST	SKEETER	EEEORVY	OVEREYE
DNNORUU	UNROUND	EEEGRSZ	GEEZERS			EEEPPRS	PEEPERS
DNNORUW	RUNDOWN	EEEGRUX	EXERGUE	EEELMNR	REELMEN	EEEPRSS	PEERESS
DNNOSUU	UNSOUND	EEEHILW	WHEELIE	EEELMNT	ELEMENT	EEEPRST	ESTREPE
DNNOSUW	SUNDOWN	EEEHISZ	HEEZIES	EEELMPX	EXEMPLE		STEEPER
DNNOUUW	UNWOUND	EEEHLNW	ENWHEEL	EEELMSX	LEXEMES	EEEPRSV	PEEVERS
DNNRTUU	TURNDUN	EEEHLPW	WHEEPLE	EEELNST	STELENE		PREEVES
DNNSTUU	TUNDUNS	EEEHLRS	HEELERS	EEELNSV	ELEVENS	EEEPRSW	SWEEPER
DNOORTU	OROTUND		REHEELS	EEELPRS	PEELERS		WEEPERS
DNOPUUW	UPWOUND	EEEHLRW	WHEELER		SLEEPER	EEEPRSZ	SPREEZE
DNORSST	STRONDS	EEEHLST	LETHEES		SPEELER	EEEQRRU	QUEERER
DNORSTU	ROTUNDS	EEEHLWZ	WHEEZLE	EEELPRT	REPLETE		REQUERE
DNOSSTU	STOUNDS	EEEHNST	ETHENES	EEELPST	STEEPLE	EEEQSUZ	SQUEEZE
DNOSSTW	STOWNDS	EEEHNSX	HEXENES	EEELRRS	REELERS	EEERRRV	REVERER
DNOSSUW	SWOUNDS	EEEHPRS	PHEERES	EEELRSV	SLEEVER	EEERRST	RETREES
DNOSSWW	SWOWNDS	EEEHPSS	PHEESES	EEELRTV	LEVERET		STEERER
DOOOOSV	VOODOOS	EEEHPSZ	PHEEZES	EEELSSS	LESSEES	EEERRSV	RESERVE
DOOORSU	ODOROUS	EEEHRRS	SHEERER	EEELSST	TELESES		REVERES
DOOORTU	OUTDOOR	EEEHRST	SEETHER	EEELSSV	SLEEVES		REVERSE
DOOPRSU	UROPODS	EEEHSST	SEETHES	EEELSSY	EYELESS		SEVERER
DOOPRSY	PROSODY	EEEHSTT	ESTHETE	EEELSTX	TELEXES		SEVERER
DOOPSTU	UPSTOOD		TEETHES	EEELSTY	EYELETS	EEERSSS	SEERESS
DOORRSS	SORDORS	EEEHSWZ	WHEEZES	EEELTTX	TELETEX	EEERSTT	TEETERS
DOORRTU	DORTOUR	EEEIJLS	JEELIES	EEEMMSS	MESEEMS	EEERSTV	STEEVER
DOOSUUV	VOUDOUS	EEEIKLS	KEELIES		SEMEMES	EEERSTW	SWEETER
DORSSTU	STROUDS	EEEIKRR	REEKIER	EEEMNRS	MENEERS	EEERSUV	REVEUSE
DORSUVY	DYVOURS	EEEILRR	LEERIER	EEEMNSS	NEMESES	EEERSUW	SERUEWE
DORUVYY	DYVOURY	EEEILRS	SEELIER	EEEMORT	EROTEME	EEERSVW	SERVEWE
EEEEFRR	REFEREE	EEEILRV	RELIEVE	EEEMRSS	SEEMERS		WEEVERS
EEEEGTX	EXEGETE	EEEILST	EELIEST	EEEMRST	TEEMERS	EEERTTW	TWEETER
EEEEHST	TEEHEES	EEEIMNS	ENEMIES	EEEMRTX	EXTREME	EEESSTT	SETTEES
EEEENTT	ENTETEE	EEEIMNT	EMETINE	EEEMSST	ESTEEMS		TESTEES
EEEEPST	TEEPEES	EEEIMPR	PREEMIE		MESTEES	EEESSTV	STEEVES
EEEEPSW	PEEWEES	EEEIMRS	EMERIES	EEEMSTT	MEETEST	EEESTWZ	TWEEZES
EEEFFFO	FEOFFEE	EEEIMRT	EREMITE	EEENNPT	PENTENE	EEFFFNO	ENFEOFF
EEEFFOR	OFFEREE	EEEINRT	TEENIER	EEENNRT	ETRENNE	EEFFFOR	FEOFFER
EEEFFRS	EFFERES	EEEINRW	WEENIER	EEENNTT	ENTENTE	EEFFGLU	EFFULGE
EEEFGRU	REFUGEE	EEEIPRR	PEERIER	EEENPRT	TERPENE	EEFFINT	FIFTEEN
EEEFHRS	SHEREEF	EEEIPRS	PEERIES	EEENPRV	PREVENE	EEFFIRS	EFFEIRS
EEEFIRS	FEERIES		SEEPIER	EEENPSS	PENSEES	EEFFKLS	KEFFELS
EEEFLRR	FLEERER	EEEIPRW	WEEPIER	EEENPST	ENSTEEP	EEFFNOS	OFFENSE
EEEFLRS	FEELERS	EEEIPSW	WEEPIES		STEEPEN	EEFFORR	OFFERER
EEEFLRT	FLEETER	EEEIRRT	RETIREE	EEENPSW	ENSWEEP	EEFFOST	TOFFEES
EEEFMNR	FREEMEN	EEEIRRV	REVERIE	EEENPSX	EXPENSE	EEFFSSU	EFFUSES
EEEFNRS	ENFREES	EEEIRST	EERIEST	EEENRRS	SERENER	EEFFSTU	SUFFETE
EEEFORS	FORESEE	EEEIRSV	VEERIES		SNEERER	EEFGILN	FEELING
EEEFRRS	REEFERS	EEEIRSZ	RESEIZE	EEENRRT	ENTERER		FLEEING
EEEFRRZ	FREEZER	EEEISTW	SWEETIE		TERREEN	EEFGINR	FEERING
EEEFRSZ	FREEZES	EEEJNPY	JEEPNEY		TERRENE		FREEING
EEEGHNW	WHEENGE	EEEJPRS	JEEPERS	EEENRRV	VENERER		REEFING
EEEGILS	ELEGIES	EEEJRRS	JEERERS	EEENRRW	RENEWER	EEFGINS	FEESING
	ELEGISE	EEEJSST	JESTEES	EEENRSS	SERENES	EEFGINZ	FEEZING
EEEGILZ	ELEGIZE	EEEKKRS	KEEKERS	EEENRST	ENTREES	EEFGLLU	GLEEFUL
EEEGINP	EPIGENE	EEEKLLU	UKELELE		RETENES	EEFGLOR	FORELEG
EEEGIPR	PERIGEE	EEEKLMN	KEELMEN	EEENRSV	ENERVES	EEFGRSU	REFUGES
EEEGLMN	GLEEMEN				VENEERS	EEFHIRS	HEIFERS
						EEFHIRT	HEFTIER

EEFHISY	FISHEYE
EEFHLNS	ENFLESH
EEFHLRS	FLESHER
	HERSELF
EEFHLSS	FLESHES
EEFHNRS	FRESHEN
EEFHORT	THEREOF
EEFHORW	WHEREOF
EEFHRRS	FRESHER
	REFRESH
EEFHRSS	FRESHES
EEFHRST	FRESHET
EEFIIRR	FIERIER
EEFIIRS	REIFIES
EEFILLS	FELLIES
EEFILLX	FLEXILE
EEFILNO	OLEFINE
EEFILNS	FELINES
EEFILOR	FORELIE
EEFILRR	FERLIER
EEFILRS	FERLIES
	RELIEFS
EEFILRT	FERTILE
EEFILST	FELSITE
	LEFTIES
	LIEFEST
EEFIMNR	FIREMEN
EEFIMRT	FEMITER
EEFINNR	FENNIER
EEFINRR	FERNIER
	REFINER
EEFINRS	ENFIRES
	FEERINS
	FINEERS
	REFINES
EEFINRT	FEINTER
EEFINSS	FINESSE
EEFINSX	ENFIXES
EEFIPRS	PREIFES
	PRIEFES
EEFIRRS	FERRIES
EEFIRRT	FERRITE
EEFIRSZ	FRIEZES
EEFISTV	FESTIVE
EEFLLOS	FELLOES
EEFLLRS	FELLERS
EEFLLRU	FUELLER
EEFLLST	FELLEST
EEFLLTY	FLEETLY
EEFLMTU	TEEMFUL
EEFLNNO	ENFELON
EEFLNNS	FENNELS
EEFLNOS	ONESELF
EEFLNSS	FLENSES
EEFLOOV	FOVEOLE
EEFLORS	FORLESE
EEFLRRS	FERRELS
EEFLRRU	FERRULE
EEFLRST	FELTERS
	REFLETS
EEFLRSU	FERULES
	REFUELS
EEFLRTT	FETTLER
EEFLRTU	FLEURET
EEFLRUX	FLEXURE
EEFLSTT	FETTLES
EEFLSUY	EYEFULS
EEFMNOR	FOREMEN
EEFMNRT	FERMENT
EEFMOTT	MOFETTE
EEFMPRU	PERFUME
EEFMSTW	FEWMETS
EEFMTTU	FUMETTE
EEFNNRS	FRENNES
EEFNORT	OFTENER
EEFNORZ	ENFROZE
EEFNRRY	FERNERY
EEFNRTV	FERVENT
EEFNSSW	FEWNESS
EEFORRV	FOREVER
EEFORRZ	REFROZE
EEFOTTU	FOUETTE
EEFPRRS	PREFERS
EEFPRSU	PERFUSE
EEFRRST	FERRETS
EEFRRSU	REFUSER
EEFRRTU	REFUTER
EEFRRTY	FERRETY
EEFRSST	FESTERS
EEFRSSU	REFUSES
EEFRSTT	FETTERS
EEFRSTU	FEUTRES
	REFUTES
EEFRSTW	FEWTERS
EEFSSTU	FETUSES
EEGGGLR	GLEGGER
EEGGHTU	THUGGEE
EEGGILN	GLEEING
	NEGLIGE
EEGGILR	LEGGIER
EEGGINR	GREEING
EEGGIPS	PEGGIES
EEGGISV	VEGGIES
EEGGKRS	SKEGGER
EEGGLRS	EGGLERS
	LEGGERS
EEGGMNY	YEGGMEN
EEGGNOR	ENGORGE
EEGGNOY	GEOGENY
EEGGORR	REGORGE
EEGGORU	GOUGERE
EEGGPRU	PUGGREE
EEGHILN	HEELING
EEGHINT	THEEING
EEGHINY	HYGIENE
EEGHINZ	HEEZING
EEGHIRW	REWEIGH
	WEIGHER
EEGHLNU	LEUGHEN
EEGHNRT	GREENTH
EEGHNRY	GREYHEN
EEGHRTU	TEUGHER
EEGHSSS	GHESSES
EEGIIRS	GRIESIE
EEGIJLN	JEELING
EEGIJNR	JEERING
EEGIKKN	KEEKING
EEGIKLN	KEELING
EEGIKNN	KEENING
	KNEEING
EEGIKNP	KEEPING
	PEEKING
EEGIKNR	REEKING
EEGIKNS	SEEKING
EEGILNP	LEEPING
	PEELING
EEGILNR	LEERING
	REELING
EEGILNS	LEESING
	SEELING
EEGILNT	GENTILE
EEGILOS	ELOGIES
EEGILRS	LEIGERS
	LIEGERS
EEGILRV	VELIGER
EEGILST	ELEGIST
	ELEGITS
EEGIMMR	GEMMIER
	IMMERGE
EEGIMNR	MEERING
	REGIMEN
EEGIMNS	SEEMING
EEGIMNT	MEETING
	TEEMING
EEGIMNX	EXEMING
EEGIMRS	EMIGRES
	REGIMES
	REMIGES
EEGINNP	PEENING
EEGINNR	ENGINER
	INGENER
EEGINNS	ENGINES
	NEESING
	SNEEING
EEGINNT	TEENING
EEGINNU	GENUINE
	INGENUE
EEGINNV	EEVNING
	EVENING
EEGINNW	ENEWING
	WEENING
EEGINNZ	NEEZING
EEGINOP	EPIGONE
EEGINOS	SOIGNEE
EEGINPP	PEEPING
EEGINPR	PEERING
	PREEING
EEGINPS	SEEPING
EEGINPV	PEEVING
EEGINPW	WEEPING
EEGINRS	GREISEN
EEGINRT	GENTIER
	INTEGER
	TEERING
	TREEING
EEGINRV	REEVING
	REGIVEN
	VEERING
EEGINSS	GENESIS
	SEEINGS
EEGINSW	SEEWING
	SWEEING
EEGINTV	VENTIGE
EEGINTW	WEETING
EEGINTX	EXIGENT
EEGIOST	EGOTISE
	GOETIES
EEGIOTZ	EGOTIZE
EEGIRRV	GRIEVER
EEGIRSS	SIEGERS
EEGIRSV	GRIEVES
	REGIVES
EEGIRTT	TERGITE
EEGISTV	VESTIGE
EEGKNOR	KEROGEN
EEGKNRU	GERENUK
EEGLLNS	LEGLENS
EEGLLSS	LEGLESS
EEGLLST	LEGLETS
EEGLMMU	GEMMULE
EEGLMSU	EMULGES
	LEGUMES
EEGLNOR	ERELONG
EEGLNOU	EUGENOL
EEGLNOZ	LOZENGE
EEGLNRT	GENTLER
EEGLNRY	GREENLY
EEGLNST	GENTLES
	LENGEST
EEGLRST	REGLETS
EEGLRTY	TELERGY
EEGMMRY	GEMMERY
EEGMNOS	EMONGES
	GENOMES
EEGMNRS	GERMENS
EEGMNST	SEGMENT
EEGMNSU	EMUNGES
EEGMRRS	MERGERS
EEGNNST	GENNETS
EEGNOPS	PONGEES
EEGNORS	ENGORES
	NEGROES
EEGNOSX	EXOGENS
EEGNPUX	EXPUNGE
EEGNRSS	NEGRESS
EEGNRST	GERENTS
	REGENTS
EEGNRSV	VENGERS
EEGNSSU	GENUSES
	NEGUSES
EEGNSTU	GUESTEN
EEGOOPY	POOGYEE
EEGOOSS	SOOGEES
EEGOPRT	PROTEGE
EEGORTV	OVERGET
EEGOSSS	GESSOES
EEGPRUX	EXPURGE
EEGRRSS	REGRESS
EEGRRST	REGRETS
EEGRRSU	RESURGE
	REURGES
EEGRRSV	VERGERS
EEGRSST	REGESTS
EEGRSSU	GUESSER
EEGRSSY	GEYSERS
EEGRSTT	GETTERS
EEGRSTU	GESTURE
EEGRSTY	GREYEST
EEGSSSU	GUESSES
EEHHRTT	THETHER
EEHHRTW	WHETHER
EEHHSTW	WHEESHT
EEHILLR	HELLIER
EEHILMN	HELIMEN
EEHILPS	EPHELIS
EEHILRS	LEISHER
EEHILST	SHELTIE
EEHILSX	HELIXES
EEHIMMS	MISHMEE
EEHIMNO	HEMIONE
EEHIMPR	HEMPIER
EEHIMPS	HEMPIES
EEHIMPT	EPITHEM
EEHIMRS	MESHIER
EEHINNR	HENNIER
EEHINNS	HENNIES
EEHINOR	HEROINE
EEHINRR	ERRHINE
EEHINRS	HENRIES

INHERES	WHOEVER	EEILLSV VIELLES	MISSEEM
EEHINRT NEITHER	EEHOSST ETHOSES	EEILLSW WELLIES	EEIMNNO NOMINEE
THEREIN	EEHOSSX HEXOSES	EEILMNN LINEMEN	EEIMNNT EMINENT
EEHINRW WHEREIN	EEHOSTW TOWHEES	EEILMNR ERMELIN	EEIMNOS SEMEION
EEHINST THEINES	EEHPPST HEPPEST	EEILMNS ISLEMEN	EEIMNRS ERMINES
EEHIORS HEROISE	EEHPRSS SPHERES	EEILMPT IMPLETE	EEIMNRV MINEVER
EEHIORZ HEROIZE	EEHPRST HEPSTER	EEILMRV VERMEIL	EEIMNSS INSEEMS
EEHIPRT PRITHEE	PETHERS	EEILMST ELMIEST	MISSEEN
EEHIPSV PEEVISH	SPERTHE	EEILNNO LEONINE	NEMESIS
EEHIPTT EPITHET	THREEPS	EEILNNT LENIENT	SIEMENS
EEHIRRS HERRIES	EEHPRTY PRYTHEE	EEILNNV ENLIVEN	EEIMNST EMETINS
EEHIRSS HEIRESS	EEHQSTU QUETHES	EEILNOR ELOINER	EEIMNSW MISWEEN
HERISSE	EEHRRSW WERSHER	EEILNPS PENSILE	EEIMNSY MEINEYS
EEHIRST HEISTER	EEHRRTW WHERRET	EEILNRS LIERNES	EEIMNTT MINETTE
EEHIRSV SHRIEVE	EEHRSTT TETHERS	RELINES	EEIMOPS EPISOME
EEHIRTW THEWIER	EEHRSTW WETHERS	EEILNSS ENISLES	EEIMOPT EPITOME
EEHIRWY WHEYIER	WRETHES	ENSILES	EEIMORS ISOMERE
EEHISTV THIEVES	EEHRSTZ HERTZES	SENSILE	EEIMOSS MEIOSES
EEHKLOY KEYHOLE	EEHRTTW WHETTER	SILENES	EEIMOTV EMOTIVE
EEHKLSS SHEKELS	EEHRVWY WHYEVER	EEILNST TENSILE	EEIMPRR PREMIER
EEHKOOY EYEHOOK	EEIIKRS KIERIES	EEILNTT ENTITLE	REPRIME
EEHKRSS SHREEKS	EEIILRV VEILIER	EEILNTV VEINLET	EEIMPRS EMPIRES
EEHLLMP PHELLEM	EEIIMNS MEINIES	EEILOPT PETIOLE	EMPRISE
EEHLLNS ENSHELL	EEIIMPR RIEMPIE	EEILORT TROELIE	EPIMERS
EEHLLOS HELLOES	EEIIMRT EMERITI	EEILORV OVERLIE	IMPRESE
EEHLLRS HELLERS	EEIIMST ITEMISE	RELIEVO	PREMIES
SHELLER	EEIIMTZ ITEMIZE	EEILOST ESTOILE	PREMISE
EEHLMMW WHEMMLE	EEIINRT ERINITE	ETOILES	SPIREME
EEHLMST HELMETS	NITERIE	EEILOTZ ZEOLITE	EEIMPRT EMPTIER
EEHLNSU UNHELES	EEIINRV VEINIER	EEILPRR REPLIER	EEIMPST EMPTIES
EEHLPRS HELPERS	EEIINTV INVITEE	EEILPRS REPLIES	SEPTIME
EEHLPRT TELPHER	EEIIPST PIETIES	SPIELER	EEIMQRU REQUIEM
EEHLPSS PLESHES	EEIIRRV RIVIERE	EEILPRT PERLITE	EEIMRRR MERRIER
EEHLRST SHELTER	EEIIRVW VIEWIER	REPTILE	EEIMRRS MERRIES
EEHLRSW WELSHER	EEIISST SEITIES	EEILPRU PUERILE	EEIMRRT TRIREME
EEHLRSY SHEERLY	EEIISTV VISITEE	EEILPSS PELISSE	EEIMRSS MESSIER
EEHLSSU HUELESS	EEIJKRR JERKIER	EEILPST EPISTLE	MISERES
EEHLSSV SHELVES	EEIJKRS JERKIES	PELITES	REMISES
EEHLSSW SHEWELS	EEIJLLS JELLIES	EEILQRU RELIQUE	EEIMRST METIERS
WELSHES	EEIJMMR JEMMIER	EEILRRS RELIERS	TREMIES
EEHLSTV THELVES	EEIJMMS JEMMIES	EEILRRV RELIVER	TRISEME
EEHMNOP PHONEME	EEIJNNS JENNIES	REVILER	EEIMRTT TERMITE
EEHMNOS HOSEMEN	EEIJRRS JERRIES	EEILRSS RESILES	EEIMSSS MISSEES
EEHMNRU ENRHEUM	EEIJRTT JETTIER	EEILRST LEISTER	SEMISES
EEHMNRY MYNHEER	EEIJSSS JESSIES	RETILES	EEINNOP PENNINE
EEHMNSS MENSHES	EEIJSTT JETTIES	STERILE	EEINNPS PENNIES
EEHMORT THEOREM	EEIKLLS KELLIES	EEILRSU LEISURE	EEINNRS NERINES
EEHMRUX EXHUMER	SKELLIE	EEILRSV RELIVES	EEINNRT INTERNE
EEHMSST SMEETHS	EEIKLPS KELPIES	REVILES	EEINNRU NEURINE
EEHMSUX EXHUMES	EEIKLPT PIKELET	SERVILE	EEINNRV ENRIVEN
EEHNNRS HENNERS	EEIKLSS SELKIES	EEILRTT RETITLE	INNERVE
EEHNNRY HENNERY	EEIKLST KELTIES	EEILSSS SESELIS	NERVINE
EEHNOPT POTHEEN	SLEEKIT	SESSILE	EEINNRW WENNIER
EEHNORT THEREON	EEIKMNP PIKEMEN	EEILSST TELESIS	EEINNST INTENSE
EEHNORW NOWHERE	EEIKNRT KERNITE	TIELESS	EEINNTW ENTWINE
WHEREON	EEIKNSS ENSKIES	EEILSSU ILEUSES	EEINOPR PEREION
EEHNPSS SEPHENS	KINESES	EEILSSW LEWISES	PIONEER
SPHENES	EEIKPRR PERKIER	EEILSSX LEXISES	EEINOPS PEONIES
EEHNPSW NEPHEWS	EEIKPRS PESKIER	SILEXES	EEINPPS PEPSINE
EEHNRST THRENES	EEIKRSY SKIEYER	EEILSTV LEVITES	EEINPRR REPINER
EEHNSTU ENTHUSE	EEIKSTT STEEKIT	LIEVEST	EEINPRS EREPSIN
EEHNSTV SEVENTH	EEIKTTT TEKTITE	EEILSTX SEXTILE	REPINES
EEHNSTY ETHYNES	EEILLMT MELLITE	EEILSUV ELUSIVE	EEINPRT INEPTER
EEHOOPW WHOOPEE	EEILLNS NELLIES	EEILSVW WEEVILS	EEINPRZ PRENZIE
EEHOPRU EUPHROE	EEILLPS ELLIPSE	EEILSZZ LEZZIES	EEINPSS PENISES
EEHORSU REHOUSE	EEILLRS LEISLER	EEILTTX TEXTILE	EEINPST PENTISE
EEHORSW WHERESO	EEILLRT TREILLE	EEILVWY WEEVILY	EEINPSV PENSIVE
EEHORTT THERETO	EEILLRV EVILLER	EEIMMNS IMMENSE	VESPINE
EEHORTW WHERETO	EEILLSS EISELLS	EEIMMRS IMMERSE	EEINQRU ENQUIRE
EEHORVW HOWEVER	EEILLST TELLIES	EEIMMSS MIMESES	

	INQUERE
EEINQTU	QUIETEN
EEINQUY	QUEYNIE
EEINRRS	RESINER
EEINRRT	INERTER
	REINTER
	RENTIER
	TERRINE
EEINRRV	NERVIER
	VERNIER
EEINRSS	SEINERS
	SEREINS
	SIRENES
EEINRST	ENTIRES
	ENTRIES
	NERITES
	TRENISE
EEINRSV	ENVIERS
	INVERSE
	VENIRES
	VERSINE
EEINRSW	NEWSIER
EEINRTT	NETTIER
	TENTIER
EEINRTU	NEURITE
	RETINUE
	REUNITE
	UTERINE
EEINSST	SESTINE
EEINSSV	SENVIES
EEINSSW	NEWSIES
EEINSTV	TENSIVE
	VENITES
EEINSTX	EXTINES
	SIXTEEN
EEINSTY	SYENITE
EEIOPSS	POESIES
EEIOPST	POETISE
EEIOPSX	EPOXIES
EEIOPTZ	POETIZE
EEIORRS	ROSIERE
EEIORSS	SOIREES
EEIORSV	EROSIVE
EEIOSST	ISOETES
EEIPPPR	PEPPIER
EEIPPST	PEPTISE
EEIPPTT	PIPETTE
EEIPPTZ	PEPTIZE
EEIPQRU	PERIQUE
	REPIQUE
EEIPQSU	EQUIPES
EEIPRRR	PERRIER
EEIPRRS	PERRIES
	REPRISE
	RESPIRE
EEIPRRV	REPRIVE
EEIPRRZ	REPRIZE
EEIPRST	RESPITE
EEIPRSV	PREVISE
	PRIEVES
EEIPRSW	SPEWIER
EEIPRSX	EXPIRES
	PREXIES
EEIPRTT	PETTIER
EEIPRVW	PREVIEW
EEIPRZZ	PREZZIE
EEIPSTT	PETTIES
EEIPSTW	PEEWITS
EEIQRRU	REQUIRE
EEIQRSU	ESQUIRE

	QUERIES
EEIQRTU	QUIETER
	REQUITE
EEIRRRT	RETIRER
	TERRIER
EEIRRSS	SERRIES
	SIRREES
EEIRRST	ETRIERS
	REITERS
	RESTIER
	RETIRES
	RETRIES
	TERRIES
EEIRRSV	REIVERS
	REVERSI
	REVISER
	RIEVERS
EEIRRSW	REWIRES
EEIRRTV	RIVERET
	RIVETER
EEIRRTW	REWRITE
EEIRRVV	REVIVER
EEIRSSU	REISSUE
EEIRSSV	IVRESSE
	REVISES
EEIRSSZ	SEIZERS
EEIRSTT	TESTIER
EEIRSTU	SUETIER
EEIRSTV	RESTIVE
	SIEVERT
	STIEVER
	VERIEST
EEIRSTW	STEWIER
EEIRSTZ	ZESTIER
EEIRSUZ	SEIZURE
EEIRSVV	REVIVES
EEIRSVW	REVIEWS
	VIEWERS
EEIRTVV	VETIVER
EEISSSV	ESSIVES
EEISSTX	SEXIEST
EEISTVX	VITEXES
EEITUXZ	ZEUXITE
EEJKRRS	JERKERS
EEJLLMU	JUMELLE
EEJLRWY	JEWELRY
EEJNNST	JENNETS
EEJNOOR	REJONEO
EEJNORS	REJONES
EEJNORY	ENJOYER
EEJPRRU	PERJURE
EEJQRRU	JERQUER
EEJQRSU	JERQUES
EEJRSST	JESTERS
EEJRSSY	JERSEYS
EEKKOTV	VETKOEK
EEKKRRT	TREKKER
EEKKSSY	KEKSYES
EEKLLNV	KNEVELL
EEKLLSY	SLEEKLY
EEKLLUU	UKULELE
EEKLMPS	KEMPLES
EEKLNNS	KENNELS
EEKLNOS	KEELSON
EEKLNRS	KERNELS
EEKLPRS	KELPERS
	KESTREL
	SKELTER
EEKLSSY	KEYLESS

EEKLSTT	KETTLES
EEKMNOS	SOKEMEN
EEKMPRS	KEMPERS
EEKMRSS	KERMESS
EEKNNRS	KENNERS
EEKNNST	KENNETS
EEKNOSS	KENOSES
EEKNOST	KETONES
EEKNOTY	KEYNOTE
EEKNRSS	SKREENS
EEKNSTU	NETSUKE
EEKOPRS	RESPOKE
EEKOSSS	SEKOSES
EEKOSST	KETOSES
EEKPPSU	UPKEEPS
EEKPRSU	PERUKES
EEKRSST	STREEKS
EEKRSSU	RESKUES
EEKRSSW	RESKEWS
	SKEWERS
EEKRSSY	KERSEYS
EEKSSTW	SKEWEST
EELLMRS	MERELLS
	SMELLER
EELLMRV	VERMELL
EELLNOV	NOVELLE
EELLNRS	SNELLER
EELLNSW	NEWELLS
EELLORS	ROSELLE
EELLORZ	ROZELLE
EELLPRS	RESPELL
	SPELLER
EELLPST	PELLETS
EELLQRU	QUELLER
EELLRSS	RESELLS
	SELLERS
EELLRST	RETELLS
	TELLERS
EELLRSU	RUELLES
EELLRSW	SWELLER
EELLSTV	VELLETS
EELMMOP	POMMELE
EELMMPU	EMPLUME
EELMNOO	OENOMEL
EELMOPR	PLEROME
EELMOPT	LEPTOME
EELMORW	EELWORM
EELMOST	OMELETS
EELMPRS	SEMPLER
EELMPST	PELMETS
	STEMPEL
	STEMPLE
	TEMPLES
EELMPTT	TEMPLET
EELMRST	SMELTER
EELMRSU	LEMURES
	RELUMES
EELMSST	TELESMS
EELMSTT	METTLES
	STEMLET
EELNNSV	VENNELS
EELNOPV	ENVELOP
EELNOSV	ELEVONS
EELNOSY	ESLOYNE
EELNOTT	NOTELET
EELNOTU	TOLUENE
EELNPSS	PENSELS
	SPLEENS
EELNPST	PENTELS

EELNPSY	SPLEENY
EELNQUY	QUEENLY
EELNRST	RELENTS
EELNRSU	UNREELS
EELNRTT	LETTERN
EELNRUV	NERVULE
EELNSSS	LESSENS
EELNSST	NESTLES
EELNSSU	UNSEELS
EELNSTT	NETTLES
EELNSTU	ELUENTS
	UNSTEEL
EELNSTY	ENSTYLE
	TENSELY
EELNSUV	VENULES
EELNSXY	XYLENES
EELNTTU	LUNETTE
EELOPPS	PEOPLES
EELOPRS	ELOPERS
	LEPROSE
EELOPRX	EXPLORE
EELOPSS	ELOPSES
EELOPTU	EELPOUT
EELORSS	RESOLES
EELORSV	RESOLVE
EELORTT	LORETTE
EELORVV	REVOLVE
EELOSSS	LOESSES
EELOSST	OSSELET
	TELOSES
EELOSTT	TELEOST
EELOSUV	EVOLUES
EELOSVV	EVOLVES
EELOTUV	EVOLUTE
	VELOUTE
EELPPRX	PERPLEX
EELPPSU	PEEPULS
EELPQRU	PREQUEL
EELPRST	PELTERS
	PETRELS
	RESPELT
	SPELTER
EELPRSU	REPULSE
EELPRSY	SLEEPRY
	YELPERS
EELPRTZ	PRETZEL
EELPRUX	PLEXURE
EELPRVY	REPLEVY
EELPSST	PESTLES
EELPSTT	PETTLES
EELPSTY	STEEPLY
EELPSUX	EXPULSE
EELQRUY	QUEERLY
EELQSSU	SEQUELS
EELRRSV	VERRELS
EELRRVY	REVELRY
EELRSST	STREELS
	TRESSEL
EELRSSU	RULESSE
EELRSTT	LETTERS
	LETTRES
	SETTLER
	STERLET
	TRESTLE
EELRSTV	SVELTER
EELRSTW	SWELTER
	WELTERS
	WRESTLE
EELRSTY	RESTYLE
	TERSELY

EELRSTZ	SELTZER	EENNOTY	NEOTENY
EELRSUV	VELURES	EENNPRS	PENNERS
EELRSVV	VERVELS	EENNQUU	UNQUEEN
EELSSSU	USELESS	EENNRST	RENNETS
EELSSSV	VESSELS		TENNERS
EELSSSX	SEXLESS	EENNRUV	UNNERVE
EELSSTT	SETTLES	EENNSST	SENNETS
EELSSUV	EVULSES	EENNSSU	UNSEENS
EELSTUY	EUSTYLE		UNSENSE
EELSTVV	VELVETS	EENNSSW	NEWNESS
EELSTVW	TWELVES	EENOPPR	PROPENE
EELSTWY	SWEETLY	EENOPPT	PEPTONE
EELTVVY	VELVETY	EENOPRS	OPENERS
EEMMNOT	MEMENTO		PERONES
EEMMORS	MEROMES		REOPENS
EEMMOSU	MOUSMEE		REPONES
EEMMOSV	EMMOVES	EENOPST	OPENEST
EEMMSSS	SEMSEMS		PENTOSE
EEMMSST	STEMMES		POSTEEN
EEMNNOV	ENVENOM		POTEENS
EEMNNSW	NEWSMEN	EENORRV	OVERREN
EEMNOOS	SOMEONE	EENORSY	ONEYERS
EEMNOOY	MOONEYE		ONEYRES
EEMNORS	MOREENS	EENORTV	OVERNET
EEMNORV	OVERMEN	EENOSSY	ESSOYNE
EEMNORY	MONEYER		NOYESES
EEMNOST	TEMENOS	EENOSTV	VENTOSE
	TONEMES		VOTEENS
EEMNOSV	ENMOVES	EENOSTW	TOWNEES
EEMNPTU	UMPTEEN	EENOSVZ	EVZONES
EEMNRTU	TRUEMEN	EENPPRT	PERPENT
EEMNSYZ	ENZYMES	EENPRST	PRESENT
EEMOOSW	WOESOME		REPENTS
EEMOPRR	EMPEROR		SERPENT
EEMOPRT	TEMPORE	EENPRSY	PYRENES
EEMOPRV	PREMOVE	EENPRTV	PREVENT
EEMOPRW	EMPOWER	EENPSTU	PUNTEES
EEMOPST	METOPES	EENPSTW	ENSWEPT
EEMORRS	REMORSE	EENPSTY	STEPNEY
	ROEMERS	EENQSTU	SEQUENT
EEMORRT	REMOTER	EENRRST	RENTERS
EEMORRU	UROMERE		STERNER
EEMORRV	REMOVER	EENRRSU	ENSURER
EEMORST	METEORS	EENRRSV	NERVERS
	REMOTES	EENRRUV	NERVURE
EEMORSV	REMOVES	EENRSST	NESTERS
EEMPRRT	PRETERM		RESENTS
EEMPRSS	EMPRESS		STRENES
EEMPRST	TEMPERS	EENRSSU	ENSURES
EEMPRSU	PRESUME	EENRSTT	TENTERS
	SUPREME		TESTERN
EEMPRTT	TEMPTER	EENRSTU	NEUTERS
EEMPRTU	PERMUTE		RETUNES
EEMPSSU	EMPUSES		TENURES
EEMPSTT	TEMPEST		TUREENS
EEMPSTX	EXEMPTS	EENRSTV	VENTERS
EEMRRST	TERMERS		VENTRES
EEMRRUU	REMUEUR	EENRSTW	WESTERN
EEMRSST	RESTEMS	EENRSTX	EXTERNS
EEMRSSU	RESUMES	EENRSTY	STYRENE
EEMRSUX	MUREXES		YESTERN
EEMSSSU	SMEUSES	EENRSVV	VERVENS
EEMSSTU	MUSTEES	EENRTUV	VENTURE
EEMSTTU	MUSETTE	EENSSST	SETNESS
EENNORT	ENTERON	EENSSSY	SYNESES
	TENONER	EENSSTT	TENSEST
EENNORU	NEURONE	EENSSTV	STEVENS
EENNOSS	ONENESS	EENSSTW	WETNESS
EENNOSZ	ENZONES	EENSSUV	VENUSES
EENNOTT	NONETTE	EENSSUX	NEXUSES

	UNSEXES	EEPSTTU	PUTTEES
EENSSVW	SWEVENS	EEQRRUY	EQUERRY
EENSTTX	EXTENTS	EEQRSTU	QUESTER
EENSTTY	TEENTSY		REQUEST
EENSTUW	UNSWEET	EEQSSTU	QUEESTS
EENSTVY	SEVENTY	EEQSUYZ	SQUEEZY
EEOOPRS	OPEROSE	EERRSST	RESTERS
EEOPPTU	OUTPEEP	EERRSSV	SERVERS
EEOPRRV	REPROVE		VERSERS
EEOPRSS	REPOSES	EERRSTT	TERRETS
EEOPRSX	EXPOSER	EERRSTU	URETERS
EEOPRTT	TREETOP	EERRSTV	REVERTS
EEOPRTU	OUTPEER	EERRSTW	STREWER
EEOPSSS	SPEOSES		WRESTER
EEOPSSU	ESPOUSE	EERRSUV	REVEURS
	POSEUSE	EERRSVW	SWERVER
EEOPSSX	EXPOSES	EERRSVY	SERVERY
EEOPSTU	TOUPEES	EERRTTU	REUTTER
EEOPSTY	PEYOTES		UTTERER
EEOPTUW	OUTWEEP	EERRTTY	RETTERY
EEOQRTU	REQUOTE	EERSSST	TRESSES
EEORRST	RESTORE	EERSSTT	SETTERS
EEORRSV	REVERSO		STREETS
EEORRTU	REROUTE		TERSEST
EEORRTW	REWROTE		TESTERS
EEORSST	OSSETER	EERSSTV	REVESTS
	STEREOS		STERVES
EEORSSX	SOREXES		VERSETS
	XEROSES	EERSSTW	STEWERS
EEORSTT	ROSETTE		WESTERS
EEORSTV	ESTOVER	EERSSTX	EXSERTS
	OVERSET	EERSSUY	SEYSURE
EEORSTX	XEROTES	EERSSVW	SWERVES
EEORSTY	ESOTERY	EERSTTT	STRETTE
EEORSUV	OEUVRES		TETTERS
	OVERUSE	EERSTTU	TRUSTEE
EEORSVW	OVERSEW	EERSTTY	STREETY
EEORTUV	OUVERTE	EERSTUV	VERSUTE
EEPPPRS	PEPPERS		VERTUES
EEPPPRY	PEPPERY		VESTURE
EEPPRST	STEPPER	EERSTUY	TUYERES
EEPPSST	STEPPES	EERSTVV	VERVETS
EEPPSUW	UPSWEEP	EERSTWY	TWYERES
EEPPSUY	EUPEPSY	EERSUVW	SURVEWE
EEPRRSS	PRESSER	EERTTUX	TEXTURE
	REPRESS	EESSSTT	SESTETS
	SPERRES		TSETSES
EEPRRSU	PERUSER	EESSTTT	SESTETT
	REPURES	EESSTTU	SUTTEES
EEPRRTV	PERVERT	EESSTTX	SEXTETS
EEPRRVY	REPRYVE	EESSTTY	STEYEST
EEPRSSS	PRESSES	EESTTTW	WETTEST
	SPERSES	EESTTTX	SEXTETT
EEPRSST	PESTERS	EFFFIRU	FUFFIER
	PRESETS	EFFFOOR	FEOFFOR
EEPRSSU	PERSUES	EFFGIJN	JEFFING
	PERUSES	EFFGINR	REFFING
EEPRSSV	VESPERS	EFFGIRS	GRIFFES
EEPRSSW	SPEWERS	EFFGORS	GOFFERS
EEPRSSX	EXPRESS	EFFGRRU	GRUFFER
EEPRSTT	PERTEST	EFFHIKU	KUFFIEH
	PETTERS	EFFHILW	WHIFFLE
EEPRSTU	PERTUSE	EFFHIRS	SHERIFF
	REPUTES	EFFHIRU	HUFFIER
EEPRSTW	PEWTERS	EFFHIRW	WHIFFER
EEPRSTX	EXPERTS	EFFHITW	WHIFFET
EEPRTTX	PRETEXT	EFFHLSU	SHUFFLE
EEPSSTT	SEPTETS	EFFIIJS	JIFFIES
EEPSTTT	SEPTETT	EFFIIMR	MIFFIER
		EFFIINR	NIFFIER

EFFIIST	FIFTIES
	IFFIEST
EFFIKLS	SKIFFLE
EFFILLU	LIFEFUL
EFFILNS	SNIFFLE
EFFILPR	PIFFLER
EFFILPS	PIFFLES
EFFILRR	RIFFLER
EFFILRS	RIFFLES
EFFILRY	FIREFLY
EFFILSS	SIFFLES
EFFINRS	NIFFERS
	SNIFFER
EFFINST	INFEFTS
	STIFFEN
EFFIOPR	PIFFERO
EFFIORT	FORFEIT
	TOFFIER
EFFIOST	TOFFIES
EFFIPRU	PUFFIER
EFFIRST	RESTIFF
	STIFFER
EFFLMRU	MUFFLER
EFFLMSU	MUFFLES
EFFLNSU	SNUFFLE
EFFLOPS	POFFLES
EFFLOSU	SOUFFLE
EFFLRRU	RUFFLER
EFFLRSU	RUFFLES
EFFLRTU	FRETFUL
	TRUFFLE
EFFNRSU	SNUFFER
EFFNRUU	UNRUFFE
EFFOORR	OFFEROR
EFFOPRR	PROFFER
EFFOPSU	POUFFES
EFFORST	EFFORTS
EFFOSST	OFFSETS
EFFPRSU	PUFFERS
EFFPRUY	PUFFERY
EFFRSSU	SUFFERS
EFFRSTU	STUFFER
EFFSSUU	SUFFUSE
EFFSTTU	TUFFETS
EFGGIOR	FOGGIER
EFGGIRR	FRIGGER
EFGGIRU	FUGGIER
EFGGIRY	FIGGERY
EFGGORS	FOGGERS
EFGHINT	HEFTING
EFGHIRT	FIGHTER
	FREIGHT
EFGILLN	FELLING
EFGILMN	FLEMING
EFGILNR	FLINGER
EFGILNS	SELFING
EFGILNT	FELTING
EFGILNX	FLEXING
EFGILNY	FLEYING
EFGILRU	GULFIER
EFGIMNT	FIGMENT
EFGINNP	PFENNIG
EFGINNR	FERNING
EFGINOR	FOREIGN
EFGINRS	FINGERS
	FRINGES
EFGINRU	GUNFIRE
EFGINTT	FETTING
EFGINTW	WEFTING
EFGIOOR	GOOFIER
EFGIORV	FORGIVE
EFGIRRT	GRIFTER
EFGIRSU	FIGURES
EFGLLSU	FLUGELS
EFGLNSU	ENGULFS
EFGLNTU	FULGENT
EFGLORS	GOLFERS
EFGLORT	FROGLET
EFGLOSS	FOGLESS
EFGMNOR	FROGMEN
EFGNOOR	FORGONE
EFGOORS	FORGOES
EFGORRS	FORGERS
EFGORRU	FERRUGO
EFGORRY	FORGERY
EFGORST	FORGETS
EFGORSW	GOWFERS
EFGORTU	FOREGUT
EFHIINS	FINEISH
EFHIIRS	FISHIER
EFHIJSW	JEWFISH
EFHILMS	FLEMISH
	HIMSELF
EFHILSS	SELFISH
EFHINNS	FENNISH
EFHIRSS	FISHERS
	SERFISH
	SHERIFS
EFHIRST	SHIFTER
EFHIRSY	FISHERY
EFHISUW	HUSWIFE
EFHLLPU	HELPFUL
EFHLLSY	FLESHLY
EFHLNSU	UNFLESH
EFHLOOX	FOXHOLE
EFHLOPU	HOPEFUL
EFHLOSS	FLOSHES
EFHLRSU	FLUSHER
EFHLRSY	FRESHLY
EFHLSSU	FLUSHES
EFHLSTY	THYSELF
EFHLTTW	TWELFTH
EFHNORT	FORHENT
EFHOORS	HOOFERS
EFHORST	FOTHERS
EFHRRTU	FURTHER
EFHRSSU	FRUSHES
EFIIKST	FIKIEST
EFIILLS	FILLIES
EFIILMR	FILMIER
EFIILMS	MISFILE
EFIILRT	FITLIER
EFIILRY	FIERILY
EFIILSS	FISSILE
EFIINNR	FINNIER
EFIINPV	FIVEPIN
EFIINRT	NIFTIER
EFIINRU	UNIFIER
EFIINSU	UNIFIES
EFIINSX	INFIXES
EFIIRRR	FIRRIER
EFIIRRT	RIFTIER
EFIIRST	FISTIER
EFIIRZZ	FIZZIER
EFIISSV	FISSIVE
EFIJLLY	JELLIFY
EFIJLOR	FRIJOLE
EFIJLOT	JETFOIL
EFIKLRU	FLUKIER
EFIKNRU	FUNKIER
EFIKORR	FORKIER
EFIKRRS	FRISKER
EFIKRST	FRISKET
EFILLMS	MISFELL
EFILLOO	FOLIOLE
EFILLOS	FOLLIES
EFILLRS	FILLERS
	REFILLS
EFILLST	FILLETS
EFILLUW	WILEFUL
EFILMNU	FULMINE
EFILMOT	FILEMOT
EFILMSS	SELFISM
EFILMST	FILMSET
	LEFTISM
EFILNOS	OLEFINS
EFILNOX	FLEXION
EFILNSS	FINLESS
EFILOOS	FLOOSIE
	FOLIOSE
EFILOOZ	FLOOZIE
EFILOPR	PROFILE
EFILORR	FLORIER
EFILORT	LOFTIER
	TREFOIL
EFILOSX	SEXFOIL
EFILPPR	FLIPPER
EFILPPS	FIPPLES
EFILPPU	PIPEFUL
EFILPRS	PILFERS
EFILPRY	PILFERY
EFILQUY	LIQUEFY
EFILRRS	RIFLERS
EFILRRT	TRIFLER
EFILRST	FILTERS
	LIFTERS
	STIFLER
	TRIFLES
EFILRTT	FLITTER
EFILRTU	FLUTIER
	FUTILER
EFILRVV	FLIVVER
EFILRZZ	FRIZZLE
EFILSSS	FISSLES
EFILSST	SELFIST
	STIFLES
EFILSTT	LEFTIST
EFILSTU	FLUIEST
EFILSZZ	FIZZLES
EFILUVX	FLUXIVE
EFIMMRU	FERMIUM
EFIMNOR	FERMION
EFIMNTT	FITMENT
EFIMOST	FOMITES
EFIMRRS	FIRMERS
EFIMRST	FIRMEST
	FREMITS
EFIMSTU	FUMIEST
EFIMTTU	FUMETTI
EFINNOR	INFERNO
EFINNRS	FINNERS
EFINNRU	FUNNIER
EFINNSU	FUNNIES
EFINOPR	FORPINE
EFINRST	SNIFTER
EFINRSU	INFUSER
EFINRUY	REUNIFY
EFINSST	FITNESS
	INFESTS
EFINSSU	INFUSES
EFINSUX	UNFIXES
EFINSZZ	FIZZENS
EFIOOPR	POOFIER
EFIOORR	ROOFIER
EFIOORT	FOOTIER
EFIOORW	WOOFIER
EFIOPRR	PORIFER
EFIOPRT	FIREPOT
EFIORRT	ROTIFER
EFIORRW	FROWIER
EFIORSS	FROISES
EFIORST	FOISTER
	FORTIES
EFIOSST	SOFTIES
EFIOSTX	FOXIEST
EFIOSTZ	FOZIEST
EFIPPRR	FRIPPER
EFIPRTY	PETRIFY
EFIRRRU	FURRIER
EFIRRSU	FRISEUR
	FRISURE
	SURFIER
EFIRRTT	FRITTER
EFIRRTU	FRITURE
	FRUITER
	TURFIER
EFIRRTY	TERRIFY
EFIRRUZ	FURZIER
EFIRSST	SIFTERS
	STRIFES
EFIRSSU	FISSURE
	FUSSIER
EFIRSTT	FITTERS
	TITFERS
EFIRSTU	FUSTIER
	SURFEIT
EFIRSTW	SWIFTER
EFIRSUX	FIXURES
EFIRSVY	VERSIFY
EFIRSZZ	FIZZERS
	FRIZZES
EFIRTTU	TUFTIER
	TURFITE
EFIRTUV	FURTIVE
EFIRTUX	FIXTURE
EFIRUZZ	FUZZIER
EFISTTT	FITTEST
EFISTTY	TESTIFY
EFJLSTU	JESTFUL
EFKLMNO	MENFOLK
EFKLMOR	MERFOLK
EFKLNUY	FLUNKEY
EFKLOPU	POKEFUL
EFKLPSU	SKEPFUL
EFKORRS	FORKERS
EFLLOST	FLOTELS
EFLLOSW	FELLOWS
EFLLRSU	FULLERS
EFLLSTU	FULLEST
EFLMOSU	FULSOME
EFLMPRU	FRUMPLE
EFLMSUU	MUSEFUL
EFLNNSU	FUNNELS
EFLNORT	FORLENT
EFLNORU	FLEURON
EFLNORY	FELONRY
EFLNOTT	FLETTON
	FONTLET
EFLNPSU	PENFULS

EFLNSSU	FULNESS		FOOTERS	EGGIMOS	MOGGIES	EGHIINT	NIGHTIE
	UNSELFS		REFOOTS	EGGIMRU	MUGGIER	EGHIINV	INVEIGH
EFLNSTU	FLUENTS	EFOORSW	WOOFERS	EGGINNR	GERNING	EGHIKNR	GHERKIN
	NETFULS	EFOPPRY	FOPPERY	EGGINNS	GINSENG	EGHIKRS	SKREIGH
EFLNSUY	SYNFUEL	EFOPRSS	PROFESS	EGGINNV	VENGING		SKRIEGH
EFLNTTU	TENTFUL	EFOPRST	FORPETS	EGGINRS	GINGERS	EGHILLN	HELLING
EFLNTUU	TUNEFUL	EFOPRSU	PROFUSE		NIGGERS	EGHILMN	HELMING
EFLOORR	FLOORER	EFOPRTU	POUFTER		SNIGGER	EGHILNP	HELPING
	FORLORE	EFOPRTY	TORPEFY	EGGINRU	GRUEING	EGHILNR	HERLING
EFLOORS	FORSLOE	EFORRSU	FERROUS		GUNGIER	EGHILNS	SHINGLE
EFLOORY	FOOLERY		FURORES	EGGINRV	VERGING	EGHILNT	ENLIGHT
EFLOORZ	FOOZLER	EFORRTY	TORREFY	EGGINRW	GREWING		LIGHTEN
EFLOOST	FOOTLES	EFORRUV	FERVOUR	EGGINRY	GINGERY	EGHILNV	HELVING
EFLOOSZ	FOOZLES	EFORSST	FORESTS		GREYING	EGHILPT	PIGHTLE
EFLORST	FLORETS		FOSTERS		NIGGERY	EGHILRT	LIGHTER
	LOFTERS	EFORSSU	FOURSES	EGGINSS	GESSING		RELIGHT
EFLORSU	FUROLES	EFORSTU	FOUTERS	EGGINTT	GETTING	EGHILSS	SLEIGHS
	OURSELF		FOUTRES	EGGINTW	TWIGGEN	EGHILST	SLEIGHT
EFLORSW	FLOWERS	EFOSSTT	SOFTEST	EGGIORS	SOGGIER	EGHIMMN	HEMMING
	FOWLERS	EFOSTWW	WOWFEST	EGGIPRR	PRIGGER	EGHIMNS	MESHING
	REFLOWS	EFPRTUY	PUTREFY	EGGIPRU	PUGGIER	EGHIMNT	THEMING
	WOLFERS	EFPSTUY	STUPEFY	EGGIPRY	PIGGERY	EGHIMPT	EMPIGHT
EFLORSX	FLEXORS	EFRRSSU	SURFERS	EGGIPSU	PUGGIES	EGHINNN	HENNING
EFLORTT	FORTLET	EFRRSTU	RETURFS	EGGIRRS	RIGGERS	EGHINNT	HENTING
EFLORTW	FELWORT	EFRRSUU	FUREURS	EGGIRRT	TRIGGER	EGHINNU	UNHINGE
EFLORVY	FLYOVER	EFRSSSU	FUSSERS	EGGIRRU	RUGGIER	EGHINOS	SHOEING
	OVERFLY	EFRSTTU	TUFTERS	EGGIRSW	SWIGGER	EGHINPS	HESPING
EFLORWW	WERWOLF	EFRSTUU	FUTURES	EGGIRTW	TWIGGER		PHESING
EFLORWY	FLOWERY	EFSSTTU	FUSTETS	EGGIRUV	VUGGIER	EGHINRR	HERRING
EFLOSSS	FLOSSES	EGGGILN	LEGGING	EGGIRWY	WIGGERY	EGHINRT	RIGHTEN
EFLOSSU	FLOUSES	EGGGILR	GIGGLER	EGGJLOS	JOGGLES	EGHINRW	WHINGER
EFLOSTU	FOULEST	EGGGILS	GIGGLES	EGGJLRU	JUGGLER	EGHINRY	HERYING
EFLOTUW	OUTFLEW	EGGGINP	PEGGING	EGGJLSU	JUGGLES	EGHINST	NIGHEST
EFLPRSU	PURFLES	EGGGLOR	GOGGLER	EGGJORS	JOGGERS	EGHINSW	HEWINGS
EFLPRUY	PREYFUL	EGGGLOS	GOGGLES	EGGLMSU	SMUGGLE		SHEWING
EFLPSTU	PESTFUL	EGGGLSU	GUGGLES	EGGLNSU	SNUGGLE		WHINGES
EFLRSTU	FLUSTER	EGGGNOS	EGGNOGS	EGGLOOS	GOOGLES	EGHINSX	HEXINGS
	FLUTERS	EGGHILR	HIGGLER	EGGLOOY	GEOLOGY	EGHINTT	TIGHTEN
	RESTFUL	EGGHILS	HIGGLES	EGGLORS	LOGGERS	EGHINWW	WHEWING
EFLRTTU	FLUTTER	EGGHINP	PEGHING		SLOGGER	EGHIOOS	SHOOGIE
EFLSTUZ	ZESTFUL	EGGHIRT	THIGGER	EGGLOST	GOGLETS	EGHIORS	OGREISH
EFLSUZZ	FUZZLES	EGGHLOS	SHOGGLE		TOGGLES	EGHIORU	ROUGHIE
EFMNOOT	FOOTMEN	EGGHORS	HOGGERS	EGGLOSW	WOGGLES	EGHIOST	HOGTIES
EFMNORS	ENFORMS	EGGHORY	HOGGERY	EGGLPRU	PLUGGER	EGHIOTT	GOTHITE
EFMNOST	FOMENTS	EGGHOST	HOGGETS	EGGLRSU	GURGLES	EGHIOTU	TOUGHIE
EFMNRSU	SURFMEN	EGGIILS	GILGIES		LUGGERS	EGHIOTV	EIGHTVO
EFMNRTU	TURFMEN	EGGIINS	SIEGING		SLUGGER	EGHIRRT	RIGHTER
EFMOORZ	ZOEFORM	EGGIIPR	PIGGIER	EGGMRSU	MUGGERS	EGHIRSS	SIGHERS
EFMOPRR	PERFORM	EGGIIPS	PIGGIES		SMUGGER	EGHIRST	SIGHTER
	PREFORM	EGGIJLS	JIGGLES	EGGNOOY	GEOGONY	EGHIRSU	GUSHIER
EFMOPRT	POMFRET	EGGIJRS	JIGGERS	EGGNRSU	SNUGGER	EGHIRSY	GREYISH
EFMORRS	FORMERS	EGGILLN	GELLING	EGGNSTU	NUGGETS	EGHIRTT	TIGHTER
	REFORMS	EGGILMS	LEGGISM	EGGNTUY	NUGGETY	EGHISTW	WEIGHTS
EFMOTTU	FUMETTO	EGGILNN	LENGING	EGGORRY	GREGORY	EGHITWY	WEIGHTY
EFMPRUY	PERFUMY	EGGILNR	NIGGLER	EGGORST	GORGETS	EGHLMPS	PHLEGMS
EFMRTUY	FURMETY	EGGILNS	GINGLES	EGGORTY	TOGGERY	EGHLMPY	PHLEGMY
EFNNORT	FORNENT		NIGGLES	EGGPRUY	PUGGERY	EGHLNOR	LEGHORN
EFNNOTU	UNOFTEN		SNIGGLE	EGGRRSU	RUGGERS	EGHLNPU	ENGULPH
EFNOOST	FESTOON	EGGILNU	LUGEING	EGGRSTU	TUGGERS	EGHLNST	LENGTHS
EFNORRU	FORERUN	EGGILNY	GLEYING	EGGSSTU	SUGGEST	EGHLNTY	LENGTHY
EFNORTU	FORTUNE	EGGILRS	LIGGERS	EGHHIMN	HIGHMEN	EGHLOOS	SHOOGLE
EFNORTW	FORWENT	EGGILRW	WIGGLER	EGHHIRS	HIGHERS	EGHLOSS	SEGHOLS
EFNORUZ	UNFROZE		WRIGGLE	EGHHIST	EIGHTHS	EGHLPSU	PLEUGHS
EFNOSST	SOFTENS	EGGILST	GIGLETS		HEIGHTS	EGHMMOS	MEGOHMS
EFOOPRR	REPROOF	EGGILSU	LUGGIES		HIGHEST	EGHMNOU	HUMOGEN
EFOOPRS	SPOOFER	EGGILSW	WIGGLES	EGHHOSW	SHOWGHE	EGHMOSU	GUMSHOE
EFOOPRT	FORETOP	EGGIMMN	GEMMING	EGHHSSU	SHEUGHS	EGHNORU	ENROUGH
	POOFTER	EGGIMNN	MENGING	EGHHSUW	WHEUGHS		ROUGHEN
EFOORRS	ROOFERS	EGGIMNR	GERMING	EGHIILL	GHILLIE	EGHNOSU	ENOUGHS
EFOORST	FOETORS		MERGING	EGHIINR	HEIRING	EGHNOTU	TOUGHEN

EGHNRSU	HUNGERS	EGIKLNW	WELKING	EGILNSU	LUNGIES	MISGOES
EGHOPRS	GOPHERS	EGIKLRS	KILERGS		SLUEING	EGIMOST	EGOTISM
EGHORRU	ROUGHER	EGIKMNP	KEMPING	EGILNSW	SLEWING	EGIMPSU	GUIMPES
EGHORTU	TOUGHER	EGIKNNN	KENNING		SWINGLE	EGIMPSY	PYGMIES
EGHOSTT	GHETTOS	EGIKNNR	KERNING	EGILNSZ	ZINGELS	EGIMSST	STIGMES
EGHOSUU	HUGEOUS	EGIKNNT	KENTING	EGILNTT	ETTLING	EGINNNP	PENNING
EGHRSSU	GUSHERS	EGIKNOV	EVOKING		LETTING	EGINNNR	RENNING
EGHRTUY	THEURGY	EGIKNPP	KEPPING	EGILNTU	ELUTING	EGINNNY	YENNING
EGIIJLS	JILGIES	EGIKNPR	PERKING	EGILNTW	WELTING	EGINNOP	OPENING
EGIILLS	GILLIES	EGIKNRV	KERVING		WINGLET	EGINNPU	PENGUIN
EGIILMT	LEGITIM	EGIKNRY	YERKING	EGILNVY	LEVYING	EGINNRR	GRINNER
EGIILNR	LEIRING	EGIKNST	KESTING	EGILOOS	GOOLIES	EGINNRS	ENRINGS
	LINGIER	EGIKNSW	SKEWING		OLOGIES		GINNERS
EGIILNS	SEILING	EGIKNSY	YESKING	EGILORS	GLOIRES	EGINNRT	RENTING
EGIILNT	LIGNITE	EGIKNUY	YEUKING		GLORIES		RINGENT
EGIILNV	VEILING	EGILLMN	MELLING	EGILOSS	GLIOSES		TERNING
EGIILNX	EXILING	EGILLNO	LOGLINE	EGILOST	ELOGIST	EGINNRU	ENURING
EGIILPS	GILPIES	EGILLNS	LEGLINS	EGILOSU	OUGLIES	EGINNRV	NERVING
EGIILRS	GIRLIES		LINGELS	EGILPPR	GRIPPLE	EGINNRY	GINNERY
EGIIMNN	MEINING		LINGLES	EGILPST	PIGLETS		RENYING
EGIIMNP	IMPINGE		SELLING	EGILPSY	GILPEYS	EGINNSS	ENSIGNS
EGIIMNR	MINGIER	EGILLNT	TELLING	EGILRRU	GURLIER		SENSING
EGIIMNT	ITEMING	EGILLNW	WELLING	EGILRSS	GRILSES	EGINNST	NESTING
EGIIMNV	MIEVING	EGILLNY	YELLING	EGILRST	GLISTER		SENTING
EGIIMPS	PIGMIES	EGILLOS	GOLLIES		GRISTLE		TENSING
EGIIMRR	GRIMIER	EGILLRS	GRILLES	EGILRSU	GUILERS	EGINNSU	ENSUING
EGIIMSV	MISGIVE	EGILLST	GILLETS		LIGURES		GUNNIES
EGIINNP	PEINING	EGILLSU	GULLIES		LURGIES		INGENUS
EGIINNR	REINING		LIGULES	EGILRSY	GREISLY	EGINNSW	NEWSING
EGIINNS	INGINES	EGILMMN	LEMMING		GRIESLY	EGINNSY	GYNNIES
	INSIGNE	EGILMMR	GLIMMER		GRISELY	EGINNTT	NETTING
	SEINING	EGILMNR	GREMLIN	EGILRTT	GLITTER		TENTING
EGIINNV	VEINING		MERLING	EGILRTY	TIGERLY	EGINNTV	VENTING
EGIINOP	EPIGONI		MINGLER	EGILRUV	VIRGULE	EGINNVY	ENVYING
EGIINPS	PEISING	EGILMNS	MINGLES	EGILRZZ	GRIZZLE	EGINOPR	PERIGON
	PIGSNIE	EGILMNT	MELTING	EGILSST	LEGISTS		PONGIER
EGIINPZ	PEIZING	EGILMNU	EMULING	EGILSSW	WIGLESS	EGINOPS	EPIGONS
EGIINRR	GIRNIER		LEGUMIN	EGILSTU	GLUIEST		PIGEONS
EGIINRT	IGNITER	EGILMNW	MEWLING		UGLIEST		PINGOES
	TIERING	EGILMNY	YELMING	EGILSTZ	GLITZES	EGINORR	IGNORER
	TIGRINE	EGILMOR	GOMERIL	EGIMMRR	GRIMMER	EGINORS	ERINGOS
EGIINRV	REIVING	EGILMOS	SEMILOG	EGIMMRS	GIMMERS		IGNORES
	RIEVING	EGILMOU	ELOGIUM		MEGRIMS		REGIONS
EGIINRW	WEIRING	EGILMPS	GLIMPSE	EGIMMRU	GUMMIER		SIGNORE
	WINGIER		MEGILPS	EGIMMTU	GUMMITE	EGINORT	GENITOR
EGIINRZ	ZINGIER	EGILMST	GIMLETS	EGIMNNN	NEMNING	EGINORV	OVERING
EGIINSS	SEISING	EGILNNS	GINNELS	EGIMNNO	OMENING	EGINORZ	ZEROING
EGIINST	IGNITES	EGILNOP	ELOPING	EGIMNNR	RINGMEN	EGINOSU	IGNEOUS
EGIINSV	SIEVING	EGILNOS	ELOIGNS	EGIMNNS	MENSING	EGINOSW	INGOWES
	VISEING		LEGIONS	EGIMNOS	MISGONE		WIGEONS
EGIINSW	WEISING		LINGOES	EGIMNOT	EMOTING	EGINOSY	ISOGENY
EGIINSZ	SEIZING	EGILNOT	LENTIGO		MITOGEN	EGINOTT	TENTIGO
EGIINTV	EVITING	EGILNPP	LEPPING	EGIMNOV	EMOVING	EGINOTV	VETOING
EGIINTX	EXITING	EGILNPR	PINGLER	EGIMNOW	MEOWING	EGINPPP	PEPPING
EGIINVW	VIEWING	EGILNPS	PINGLES	EGIMNPR	IMPREGN	EGINPPR	REPPING
EGIINWZ	WEIZING		SPIGNEL		PERMING	EGINPPS	PIGPENS
EGIIPPS	GIPPIES	EGILNPT	PELTING	EGIMNPT	PIGMENT	EGINPRS	PERSING
EGIIPRW	PERIWIG	EGILNPY	YELPING		TEMPING		PINGERS
EGIIPSS	GIPSIES	EGILNRS	GIRNELS	EGIMNQU	QUEMING		SPRINGE
EGIJKNR	JERKING		LINGERS	EGIMNRS	GERMINS	EGINPRU	PUERING
EGIJLLN	JELLING		SLINGER	EGIMNRT	METRING	EGINPRV	PERVING
EGIJLNR	JINGLER	EGILNRT	RINGLET		TERMING		PREVING
EGIJLNS	JINGLES		TINGLER	EGIMNRU	EMURING	EGINPRY	PREYING
EGIJLNT	JINGLET		TRINGLE	EGIMNSS	MESSING	EGINPSS	GIPSENS
EGIJNOS	JINGOES	EGILNRY	RELYING	EGIMNST	STEMING	EGINPSU	SPUEING
EGIJNST	JESTING	EGILNSS	SINGLES		TEMSING	EGINPSW	SPEWING
EGIJNTT	JETTING	EGILNST	GLISTEN	EGIMNSU	MEUSING	EGINPSY	ESPYING
EGIKKLN	LEKKING		LESTING	EGIMNSW	MEWSING		PEYSING
EGIKLNS	KINGLES		SINGLET	EGIMORR	GORMIER		PIGSNEY
EGIKLNT	KINGLET		TINGLES	EGIMOSS	EGOISMS	EGINPTT	PETTING

EGINPYY	EPIGYNY	EGIPSSY	GYPSIES		MORGENS	EGORSSS	GROSSES
EGINQUU	QUEUING	EGIRRSU	GURRIES	EGMNORU	MURGEON	EGORSST	GROSETS
EGINRRS	ERRINGS		SURGIER	EGMNORY	MONGERY		STORGES
	RINGERS	EGIRRSV	VIRGERS	EGMNOST	EMONGST	EGORSSU	GROUSES
	SERRING	EGIRRTT	GRITTER	EGMNOSY	MYOGENS	EGORTUW	OUTGREW
EGINRRW	WRINGER	EGIRSST	TIGRESS	EGMNOYZ	ZYMOGEN	EGOSSTY	STOGEYS
EGINRSS	INGRESS	EGIRSSU	GUISERS	EGMNSTU	NUTMEGS	EGOSTTU	GOUTTES
	RESIGNS	EGIRSTU	GUSTIER	EGMORST	GROMETS	EGOSTYZ	ZYGOTES
	SIGNERS		GUTSIER	EGMORSU	GRUMOSE		
	SINGERS	EGIRSTV	GRIVETS		MORGUES	EGPRRSU	PURGERS
EGINRST	RESTING	EGIRSUZ	GUIZERS	EGMORTU	GOURMET	EGPRSSU	SPURGES
	STINGER	EGISTTU	GUTTIES	EGMRSTU	TERGUMS	EGPRSUU	UPSURGE
EGINRSU	REUSING	EGJLNSU	JUNGLES	EGNNORT	RONTGEN	EGRRSUY	SURGERY
	RUEINGS	EGKLORW	LEGWORK	EGNNOSU	GUENONS	EGRSSUY	GYRUSES
	SIGNEUR	EGKMSSU	MUSKEGS	EGNNPTU	PUNGENT	EGRSTTU	GUTTERS
EGINRSV	SERVING	EGLLRSU	GULLERS	EGNNRSU	GUNNERS	EGRSTUZ	GUTZERS
	VERSING	EGLLRUY	GULLERY	EGNNRUY	GUNNERY	EGSSSTU	GUSSETS
EGINRSW	SWINGER	EGLLSTU	GULLETS	EGNNSYY	GYNNEYS		
	WINGERS	EGLLSUY	GULLEYS	EGNNTUU	UNGUENT	EHHIKSS	SHEIKHS
EGINRSY	SYRINGE	EGLMMRU	GLUMMER	EGNOOPS	PONGOES	EHHILLS	HELLISH
EGINRTT	GITTERN	EGLMNOO	ENGLOOM	EGNOORS	ORGONES	EHHIPRS	HERSHIP
	RETTING	EGLMNOR	MONGREL		OROGENS	EHHIRST	HITHERS
EGINRTU	TRUEING	EGLMOOR	LEGROOM	EGNOORY	OROGENY	EHHIRSU	HUSHIER
EGINRTV	VERTING	EGLMNSU	GUNNELS	EGNOOST	GENTOOS	EHHIRTT	THITHER
EGINRTY	RETYING	EGLNOOY	NEOLOGY	EGNOOSY	GOONEYS	EHHIRTW	WHITHER
EGINRVV	REVVING	EGLNOPS	PLONGES	EGNOOTU	OUTGONE	EHHISSW	WHISHES
EGINRVY	REVYING	EGLNORU	LOUNGER	EGNOOYZ	ZOOGENY	EHHISWY	WHEYISH
EGINSST	INGESTS	EGLNOST	LONGEST	EGNOPRS	SPONGER	EHHNPSY	HYPHENS
	SIGNETS	EGLNOSU	LOUNGES	EGNOPRY	PROGENY	EHHOOSS	HOOSHES
EGINSSW	SEWINGS	EGLNOUV	UNGLOVE		PYROGEN	EHHORTT	THOTHER
	SWINGES	EGLNOXY	LOXYGEN	EGNOPSS	SPONGES	EHHRSSU	HUSHERS
EGINSTT	SETTING		XYLOGEN	EGNOPSW	GOWPENS	EHHSSSU	SHUSHES
	TESTING	EGLNOYZ	LOZENGY	EGNORRW	WRONGER	EHIILLR	HILLIER
EGINSTU	GUNITES	EGLNPRU	PLUNGER	EGNORSS	ENGROSS	EHIILTT	LITHITE
EGINSTV	VESTING	EGLNPSU	PLUNGES	EGNORSU	SURGEON	EHIINNS	HINNIES
EGINSTW	STEWING	EGLNRTU	GRUNTLE	EGNORSV	GOVERNS	EHIINRS	SHINIER
	TWINGES	EGLNSSU	GUNSELS	EGNORSY	ERYNGOS	EHIINRT	INHERIT
	WESTING	EGLNSTU	ENGLUTS		GROYNES	EHIINRW	WHINIER
EGINSVX	VEXINGS		GLUTENS	EGNORUY	YOUNGER	EHIINRZ	RHIZINE
EGINSZZ	GIZZENS	EGLNSUU	UNGLUES	EGNOSTU	TONGUES	EHIIPPR	HIPPIER
EGINTTV	VETTING	EGLOOSY	GOOLEYS	EGNOSXY	OXYGENS	EHIIPPS	HIPPIES
EGINTTW	WETTING	EGLOPRS	PROLEGS	EGNPRSU	REPUGNS	EHIIPRT	PITHIER
EGIOOPR	GOOPIER	EGLOPSS	GOSPELS	EGNPSSU	SPUNGES	EHIIRST	HIRSTIE
EGIOORS	GOOSIER	EGLORRW	GROWLER	EGNPSUX	EXPUGNS	EHIIRTW	WHITIER
EGIOOSS	GOOSIES	EGLORSS	GLOSSER	EGNRRTU	GRUNTER		WITHIER
	SOOGIES	EGLORSU	REGULOS	EGNRSTU	GUNTERS	EHIISST	STISHIE
EGIOOST	GOOIEST	EGLORSV	GLOVERS		GURNETS	EHIISTW	WHITIES
EGIOPRS	PORGIES		GROVELS		SURGENT		WITHIES
	SERPIGO	EGLORSW	GLOWERS	EGNRSUY	GURNEYS	EHIJNNO	JOHNNIE
EGIOPRU	GROUPIE	EGLOSSS	GLOSSES	EGNRSYY	SYNERGY	EHIKLRU	HULKIER
	PIROGUE	EGLOSST	GOSLETS	EGNRTTU	GRUTTEN	EHIKNOS	HONKIES
EGIORRS	GORSIER	EGLOSUV	VOULGES		TURGENT	EHIKNRS	KERNISH
EGIORST	GOITERS	EGLPRSU	GULPERS	EGNSUVY	UNGYVES	EHIKNRT	RETHINK
	GOITRES		SPLURGE	EGOOPSY	POOGYES		THINKER
	GORIEST	EGLRSTU	GURLETS	EGOORSV	GROOVES	EHIKNRU	HUNKIER
EGIORTU	GOUTIER	EGLRSUU	REGULUS	EGOORSY	GOOSERY	EHIKNSS	KNISHES
EGIORTV	VERTIGO	EGLRSUY	GUYLERS	EGOORTU	OUTGOER	EHIKNSU	HUNKIES
EGIORTZ	ZORGITE	EGLRSYY	GRYESLY	EGOORTV	OVERGOT	EHIKOOR	HOOKIER
EGIORUV	VOGUIER		GRYSELY	EGOOSST	STOOGES	EHIKOOS	HOOKIES
EGIOSST	EGOISTS	EGLRUZZ	GUZZLER	EGOOSSY	GOOSEYS	EHIKOST	HOKIEST
	STOGIES	EGLSSTU	GUTLESS	EGOOSTU	OUTGOES	EHIKPRS	KEPHIRS
EGIOSTT	EGOTIST	EGLSTTU	GUTTLES	EGOPRRS	GROPERS	EHIKRRS	SHIRKER
EGIOSTV	VOGIEST	EGLSTUU	GLUTEUS	EGOPRRU	GROUPER	EHIKRSS	SHREIKS
EGIOTUV	OUTGIVE	EGLSUZZ	GUZZLES		REGROUP		SHRIEKS
EGIPPRR	GRIPPER	EGMMORT	GROMMET	EGORRSS	GROSERS		SHRIKES
EGIPPRS	GRIPPES	EGMMRRU	GRUMMER		GROSSER	EHIKRSU	HUSKIER
EGIPPSU	GUPPIES	EGMMRTU	GRUMMET	EGORRST	GROSERT	EHIKRSW	WHISKER
EGIPPSY	GYPPIES	EGMNNOS	SONGMEN	EGORRSU	GROUSER	EHIKSSS	SHIKSES
EGIPRRS	GRIPERS	EGMNNOW	GOWNMEN	EGORRSW	GROWERS	EHIKSSU	HUSKIES
EGIPRUU	GUIPURE	EGMNORS	MONGERS	EGORRUY	ROGUERY	EHIKSTW	WHISKET

EHIKSWY	WHISKEY	EHIMTYZ	MYTHIZE
EHILLMN	HILLMEN	EHINNNS	HENNINS
EHILLNO	HELLION	EHINNRT	THINNER
EHILLNS	INSHELL	EHINNSS	SHINNES
EHILLOS	HILLOES	EHINOPR	PHONIER
	HOLLIES	EHINOPS	PHONIES
EHILLRS	RELLISH	EHINOPX	PHOENIX
EHILLRT	THILLER	EHINORR	HORNIER
EHILLRU	HULLIER	EHINORS	HEROINS
EHILLTY	LITHELY		INSHORE
EHILMPW	WHIMPLE	EHINOST	HISTONE
EHILMSU	HELIUMS	EHINOSU	HEINOUS
	HUMLIES	EHINPPS	SHIPPEN
EHILMTT	MELTITH	EHINRSS	SHINERS
EHILMUW	UMWHILE		SHRINES
EHILNOP	PINHOLE	EHINRSV	SHRIVEN
EHILNOT	NEOLITH	EHINRSW	WHINERS
EHILNPS	PLENISH	EHINRTV	THRIVEN
EHILNSS	ELSHINS	EHINRTW	WRITHEN
EHILOOR	HOOLIER	EHINRTZ	ZITHERN
EHILOPT	HOPLITE	EHINSSS	SHINESS
EHILOSS	ISOHELS	EHINSST	SITHENS
EHILOST	EOLITHS	EHINSTW	WHITENS
	HOLIEST	EHINSTZ	ZENITHS
	HOSTILE	EHINSUV	UNHIVES
EHILPRS	HIRPLES	EHIOPPR	HOPPIER
EHILPRT	PHILTER	EHIOPST	ETHIOPS
	PHILTRE		OPHITES
EHILRRW	WHIRLER	EHIORRS	HORSIER
EHILRSS	HIRSELS	EHIORRT	HERITOR
	HIRSLES	EHIORSS	HOSIERS
EHILRST	SLITHER	EHIORST	HERIOTS
EHILRSU	HURLIES		HOISTER
	LUSHIER		SHORTIE
EHILRSV	SHRIVEL		TOSHIER
EHILRTU	LUTHIER	EHIORSW	SHOWIER
EHILRTW	WHIRTLE	EHIORSY	HOSIERY
EHILSSS	SLISHES	EHIORTT	THORITE
EHILSTT	LISTETH	EHIORTU	OUTHIRE
	LITHEST		ROUTHIE
	THISTLE	EHIORTV	OVERHIT
EHILSTV	THIVELS	EHIOSTT	HOTTIES
EHILSTW	WHISTLE	EHIOSTY	ISOHYET
EHILTTU	THULITE	EHIPPRS	SHIPPER
EHILTTW	WHITTLE	EHIPPRW	WHIPPER
EHILTWY	WHITELY	EHIPPST	HIPPEST
EHIMMRS	SHIMMER	EHIPPTW	WHIPPET
EHIMNPS	SHIPMEN	EHIPRSS	RESHIPS
EHIMNRS	MENHIRS		SERIPHS
EHIMNRU	RHENIUM	EHIPRST	HIPSTER
EHIMNSU	INHUMES	EHIPRSU	PUSHIER
EHIMNTY	THYMINE	EHIPRSW	WHISPER
EHIMORS	HEROISM	EHIPSTT	PETTISH
	MOREISH	EHIPSZZ	PHIZZES
EHIMORT	MOITHER	EHIRRSS	SHERRIS
	MOTHIER	EHIRRSU	HURRIES
EHIMORZ	RHIZOME		RUSHIER
EHIMOST	HOMIEST	EHIRRSV	SHRIVER
EHIMPRU	HUMPIER	EHIRRTV	THRIVER
EHIMPRW	WHIMPER	EHIRRTW	WHIRRET
EHIMPSU	HUMPIES	EHIRSSV	SHIVERS
EHIMRST	HERMITS		SHRIVES
	MITHERS	EHIRSSW	SWISHER
EHIMRSU	HEURISM		WISHERS
	MUSHIER	EHIRSTT	HITTERS
EHIMRTY	THYMIER		TITHERS
EHIMSST	THEISMS	EHIRSTU	HIRSUTE
EHIMSTU	HUMITES	EHIRSTV	THRIVES
EHIMSTY	MYTHISE	EHIRSTW	SWITHER
EHIMSWY	WHIMSEY		

	WITHERS	EHLRSSU	LUSHERS
	WRITHES	EHLRSTU	HURTLES
EHIRSTZ	ZITHERS		HUSTLER
EHIRSVY	SHIVERY	EHLRSUY	HURLEYS
EHIRTTW	WHITRET	EHLSSSU	SLUSHES
	WHITTER	EHLSSTT	SHTETLS
EHIRWZZ	WHIZZER	EHLSSTU	HUSTLES
EHISSSU	HUSSIES		LUSHEST
EHISSSW	SWISHES		SLEUTHS
	WHISSES	EHLSTTU	SHUTTLE
EHISSTT	THEISTS	EHMMRSU	HUMMERS
EHISSTU	STUSHIE	EHMNOOR	HORMONE
EHISTTW	TEWHITS		MOORHEN
	WETTISH	EHMNOPS	SHOPMEN
	WHITEST	EHMNOST	MONETHS
EHISTWY	WHITEYS	EHMNOSW	SHOWMEN
EHISUZZ	HUZZIES	EHMNPSU	HUMPENS
EHISWZZ	WHIZZES	EHMNPTY	NYMPHET
EHJOPSS	JOSEPHS	EHMNTTU	HUTMENT
EHJORSS	JOSHERS	EHMOOSS	SHMOOSE
EHKLNOS	LOKSHEN	EHMOOST	SMOOTHE
EHKLPST	KLEPHTS	EHMOOSW	SOMEHOW
EHKNORS	HONKERS	EHMOOSZ	SHMOOZE
EHKNRSU	HUNKERS	EHMOPRW	MORPHEW
EHKNSSU	HUNKSES	EHMORST	MOTHERS
EHKOORS	HOOKERS		SMOTHER
EHKOOSY	HOOKEYS		THERMOS
EHKORSS	KOSHERS	EHMORTU	MOUTHER
EHKORSW	HOWKERS	EHMORTY	MOTHERY
EHKORSY	HORKEYS	EHMOSWY	SOMEWHY
EHKRSSU	HUSKERS	EHMPRTU	THUMPER
EHLLNSU	UNSHELL	EHMRRSY	RHYMERS
EHLLOOS	HOLLOES	EHMRRTU	MURTHER
EHLLORS	HOLLERS	EHMRSSU	MUSHERS
EHLLOSU	HULLOES	EHMRSTY	RYTHMES
EHLMMOW	WHOMMLE	EHMRSUU	HUMERUS
EHLMMSU	HUMMELS	EHMSSUU	HUMMUSE
EHLMMUW	WHUMMLE	EHNNOPR	NEPHRON
EHLMNOT	MENTHOL	EHNNOPY	HYPNONE
EHLMNOY	HOMELYN	EHNNSTU	UNSHENT
EHLMNSU	UNHELMS	EHNNSUW	UNSHEWN
EHLMOOS	HOLESOM	EHNOORS	HEROONS
EHLMOPS	PHLOEMS		ONSHORE
EHLMSSU	MULSHES		SOREHON
EHLMSTY	METHYLS	EHNOPRY	HYPERON
EHLNOPS	PHENOLS	EHNOPSU	EUPHONS
EHLNORT	HORNLET	EHNOPSY	PHONEYS
EHLNPSY	PHENYLS	EHNOPUY	EUPHONY
EHLNRTU	LUTHERN	EHNORRS	HORNERS
EHLNTTY	TENTHLY	EHNORRT	HORRENT
EHLOOPT	POTHOLE		NORTHER
EHLOOSY	HOOLEYS	EHNORRY	HERONRY
EHLOPPS	HOPPLES	EHNORST	HORNETS
EHLOPSX	PHLOXES		SHORTEN
EHLORST	HOLSTER		THRENOS
	HOSTLER		THRONES
EHLORSW	HOWLERS	EHNORSU	UNHORSE
EHLORTY	HELOTRY	EHNOSST	HOTNESS
EHLOSSS	SLOSHES	EHNOSSU	UNSHOES
EHLOSST	HOSTELS	EHNOSTT	SHOTTEN
EHLOSSU	HOUSELS	EHNOSTY	HONESTY
EHLOSSV	SHOVELS	EHNOSUU	UNHOUSE
EHLOSTT	LOTHEST	EHNPRSY	PHRENSY
	SHOTTLE	EHNRSTU	HUNTERS
EHLOSTW	HOWLETS		SHUNTER
	THOWELS		UNHERST
EHLOSTY	THYLOSE	EHNRTWY	WRYTHEN
EHLPRSU	PLUSHER	EHNSSSU	SNUSHES
EHLPSSU	PLUSHES	EHNSSSY	SHYNESS
EHLRRSU	HURLERS	EHOOOPS	HOOPOES

```
EHOOPRS HOOPERS
EHOOPRW WHOOPER
EHOOPTY OOPHYTE
EHOORST HOOTERS
        SHOOTER
        SOOTHER
EHOORSV HOOVERS
EHOOSST SOOTHES
EHOOSSW WOOSHES
EHOPPRS HOPPERS
        SHOPPER
EHOPPRT PROPHET
EHOPPRW WHOPPER
EHOPRRY ORPHREY
EHOPRST POTHERS
        STROPHE
        THORPES
EHOPRSU UPHROES
EHOPRTU POUTHER
EHOPRTY POTHERY
EHOPRUY EUPHORY
EHOPSSS SPOSHES
EHOPSST POSHEST
EHORRSS SHORERS
EHORRST RHETORS
        ROTHERS
        SHORTER
EHORRTW THROWER
EHORSST TOSHERS
EHORSSV SHOVERS
        SHROVES
EHORSSW SHOWERS
EHORSTT HOTTERS
EHORSTU SHOUTER
        SOUTHER
EHORSTW THROWES
EHORSTX EXHORTS
EHORSWY SHOWERY
EHORTUY OUTHYRE
EHOSSST HOSTESS
EHOSTTT HOTTEST
EHOTTTW WOTTETH
EHPRSSU PUSHERS
EHPRSYZ ZEPHYRS
EHPRTTU TURPETH
EHPRTUW UPTHREW
EHRRSSU RUSHERS
EHRRSTU HURTERS
EHRSSTY SHYSTER
        THYRSES
EHRSTTU SHUTTER
EHRSTTW STREWTH
EHRSTUW WUTHERS
EHRSTUY TUSHERY
EHRTTTY THRETTY
EHSSSTU TUSSEHS
EIIILRV RILIEVI
EIIILST ILEITIS
EIIINPR RIPIENI
EIIJMMS JIMMIES
EIIJMPR JIMPIER
EIIKKNR KINKIER
EIIKLMR MILKIER
EIIKLMS MISLIKE
EIIKLPS PLISKIE
EIIKLRS SILKIER
EIIKLSS SILKIES
EIIKLST KILTIES
EIIKMRR MIRKIER
EIIKNPR PINKIER

EIIKNPS PINKIES
EIIKNRS SINKIER
EIIKNRZ ZINKIER
EIIKNSS KINESIS
EIIKNST INKIEST
EIIKPRS SPIKIER
EIIKRRS RISKIER
EIIKRSV SKIVIER
EIIKSTT KITTIES
EIILLMM MILLIME
EIILLMT LIMELIT
EIILLNV VILLEIN
EIILLPS ILLIPES
EIILLRS SILLIER
EIILLRT TILLIER
EIILLSS SILLIES
EIILLST ILLITES
EIILLSW WILLIES
EIILLTT TILLITE
EIILLTV VITELLI
EIILMNV MILVINE
EIILMPR IMPERIL
EIILMPS IMPLIES
EIILMPT LIMEPIT
EIILMRR MIRLIER
EIILMRS MILREIS
        SLIMIER
EIILMRT LIMITER
EIILMSS MISSILE
        SIMILES
EIILMST ELITISM
        LIMIEST
        LIMITES
EIILMSU MILIEUS
EIILMSV MISLIVE
EIILMUX MILIEUX
EIILNNS LINNIES
EIILNOS ELISION
        ISOLINE
        LIONISE
EIILNOT ETIOLIN
EIILNOV OLIVINE
EIILNOZ LIONIZE
EIILNPS SPLENII
EIILNRR NIRLIER
EIILNRS INLIERS
EIILNRT LINTIER
        NITRILE
EIILNSS INISLES
EIILNST INLIEST
        LINIEST
        LINTIES
EIILORR ROILIER
EIILORS SOILIER
EIILORV RILIEVO
EIILOST IOLITES
        OILIEST
EIILPPR LIPPIER
EIILPPS LIPPIES
EIILPST SPILITE
EIILQSU SILIQUE
EIILRST SILTIER
EIILRSX ELIXIRS
EIILSSV VISILES
EIILSTT ELITIST
EIILSTU UTILISE
EIILSTW WILIEST
EIILTUY TUILYIE
EIILTUZ TUILZIE

        UTILIZE
EIILTXY EXILITY
EIIMMSS MIMESIS
EIIMMST MISTIME
EIIMMSX IMMIXES
EIIMNNS MINNIES
EIIMNPR PRIMINE
EIIMNRT INTERIM
        MINTIER
        TERMINI
EIIMNRV MINIVER
EIIMNST MINIEST
EIIMNTV MINIVET
EIIMNTY NIMIETY
EIIMOSS MEIOSIS
EIIMPRS PISMIRE
        PRIMSIE
EIIMPRW WIMPIER
EIIMPST PIETISM
EIIMPTY IMPIETY
EIIMRSS MISSIER
EIIMRST MIRIEST
        MISTIER
        RIMIEST
EIIMSSS MISSIES
EIIMSST ISMIEST
        STIMIES
EIIMSSV MISSIVE
EIIMSTT MITIEST
EIIMSTX MIXIEST
EIINNNS NINNIES
EIINNPS PINNIES
EIINNQU QUININE
EIINNRT TINNIER
EIINNST INTINES
        TINNIES
EIINNSW INSINEW
EIINNTV INVENIT
EIINNTW INTWINE
EIINOPR RIPIENO
EIINOPS PIONIES
EIINORS IONISER
        IRONIES
        IRONISE
        NOISIER
EIINORZ IONIZER
        IRONIZE
EIINOSS IONISES
EIINOSZ IONIZES
EIINPPR NIPPIER
EIINPRS INSPIRE
        PIRNIES
        SNIPIER
        SPINIER
EIINPST PINIEST
        PINITES
EIINQRU INQUIRE
EIINQSU QUINIES
EIINQTU INQUIET
EIINRTT NITRITE
        NITTIER
        TINTIER
EIINRTV INVITER
        VITRINE
EIINRTW TWINIER
EIINSSS SEISINS
EIINSSZ SEIZINS
EIINSTT SITTINE
        TINIEST
EIINSTU UNITIES

        UNITISE
        VINIEST
EIINSTV INVITES
        WINIEST
EIINSTW WINIEST
EIINTUV UNITIVE
EIINTUZ UNITIZE
EIIORST RIOTISE
EIIORSV IVORIES
EIIORTZ RIOTIZE
EIIOSTZ ZOISITE
EIIPPPR PIPPIER
EIIPPRR RIPPIER
EIIPPRT TIPPIER
EIIPPRZ ZIPPIER
EIIPPST PIPIEST
EIIPPSY YIPPIES
EIIPRRS SPIRIER
EIIPRRV PRIVIER
EIIPRST PITIERS
        TIPSIER
EIIPRSV PRIVIES
EIIPRSW SWIPIER
        WISPIER
EIIPSTT PIETIST
EIIPTTT PITTITE
EIIPTTU PITUITE
EIIRRTZ RITZIER
EIIRSSS SISSIER
EIIRSSV VISIERS
EIIRSTV REVISIT
        STIVIER
        VISITER
EIIRSTW WIRIEST
EIIRSVZ VIZIERS
EIIRSWZ WIZIERS
EIIRTTW WITTIER
EIISSSS SISSIES
EIISSTV VISITES
EIISSTX SIXTIES
EIISSTZ SIZIEST
EIISTTT TITTIES
EIISTUV UVEITIS
EIISTZZ TIZZIES
EIISVZZ VIZZIES
EIJKNPR PERJINK
        PREJINK
EIJKNRS JERKINS
        JINKERS
EIJKNRU JUNKIER
EIJKNSU JUNKIES
EIJKOST JOKIEST
EIJLLNY INJELLY
EIJLLOR JOLLIER
EIJLLOS JOLLIES
EIJLLST JILLETS
EIJLORT JOLTIER
EIJMPRU JUMPIER
EIJMPST JIMPEST
EIJNNOS ENJOINS
EIJNORS JOINERS
        REJOINS
EIJNORT JOINTER
EIJNORY JOINERY
EIJNOST JONTIES
EIJNPRU JUNIPER
EIJNRRU INJURER
EIJNRSU INJURES
EIJNSTY JITNEYS
EIJRSTT JITTERS
EIJRTTY JITTERY
```

EIJSSUV	JUSSIVE	EIKNOSS	KENOSIS
EIJSTTU	JUTTIES	EIKNOSV	INVOKES
EIKKLNR	KLINKER	EIKNPRS	PERKINS
EIKKLNS	KINKLES	EIKNPST	PINKEST
EIKKNRS	SKINKER	EIKNPSU	SPUNKIE
EIKKOOR	KOOKIER	EIKNRSS	SINKERS
EIKKRSY	YIKKERS	EIKNRST	SKINTER
EIKKRUY	YUKKIER		STINKER
EIKLLNW	INKWELL		TINKERS
EIKLLOS	SKOLLIE	EIKNRSW	WINKERS
EIKLLRS	KILLERS	EIKNRTT	KNITTER
EIKLLST	SKILLET		TRINKET
EIKLMMN	MILKMEN	EIKNSSU	SUNKIES
EIKLMNN	LINKMEN	EIKNSTT	KITTENS
EIKLMNR	KREMLIN	EIKNTTY	KITTENY
EIKLMRS	MILKERS	EIKOORS	ROOKIES
EIKLNNS	ENLINKS	EIKOPPS	KOPPIES
EIKLNRS	SLINKER	EIKOPRR	PORKIER
EIKLNRT	TINKLER	EIKOPST	POKIEST
EIKLNRW	WINKLER	EIKORST	ROKIEST
	WRINKLE	EIKORSY	YORKIES
EIKLNSS	KINLESS	EIKOSST	KETOSIS
	SILKENS	EIKPPRS	KIPPERS
EIKLNST	LENTISK		SKIPPER
	TINKLES	EIKPPST	SKIPPET
EIKLNSU	SUNLIKE	EIKPSSS	SKEPSIS
	UNLIKES	EIKRRSS	RISKERS
EIKLNSV	KELVINS	EIKRRST	SKIRRET
EIKLNSW	WELKINS		SKIRTER
	WINKLES		STRIKER
EIKLNSY	SKYLINE	EIKRSSS	KISSERS
EIKLNTT	KNITTLE	EIKRSST	STRIKES
EIKLNTW	TWINKLE	EIKRSSV	SKIVERS
EIKLOOP	PLOOKIE	EIKRSTT	SKITTER
EIKLOPU	PLOUKIE	EIKRSTU	TURKIES
EIKLORY	YOLKIER		TUSKIER
EIKLPRY	PERKILY	EIKSSTW	WISKETS
EIKLPSY	PESKILY	EIKSSTY	SKYIEST
EIKLRST	KILTERS	EIKSTUY	YUKIEST
	KIRTLES	EILLLOS	LOLLIES
EIKLRSU	SULKIER	EILLMNU	MULLEIN
EIKLRTT	KITTLER	EILLMOS	MOLLIES
EIKLSSU	SULKIES	EILLMOT	MELILOT
EIKLSTT	KITTLES	EILLMOU	MOUILLE
	SKITTLE	EILLMRS	MILLERS
EIKMMRR	KRIMMER	EILLMST	MILLETS
EIKMMRS	KIMMERS		MISTELL
	SKIMMER	EILLMSU	ILLUMES
EIKMNNS	KINSMEN	EILLNNP	PENNILL
EIKMNOR	MONIKER	EILLNOS	LIONELS
EIKMNRS	MERKINS		NIELLOS
EIKMNSS	MISKENS	EILLNSS	ILLNESS
EIKMNST	MISKENT	EILLNST	LENTILS
EIKMNSW	MISKNEW		LINTELS
EIKMORS	IRKSOME	EILLOPS	POLLIES
	SMOKIER	EILLORW	LOWLIER
EIKMOSS	SMOKIES	EILLORZ	ZORILLE
EIKMOSY	MISYOKE	EILLOST	OILLETS
EIKMRRU	MURKIER	EILLOSV	VILLOSE
EIKMRSS	KIRMESS	EILLOSW	WOLLIES
EIKMRST	MIRKEST	EILLPRS	SPILLER
EIKMRSU	MUSKIER	EILLPSS	LIPLESS
EIKMSST	KISMETS	EILLPSU	PILULES
EIKNNOS	KINONES	EILLQTU	QUILLET
EIKNNRS	SKINNER	EILLRSS	SILLERS
EIKNOOR	NOOKIER	EILLRST	RILLETS
	ROOINEK		STILLER
EIKNOOS	NOOKIES		TILLERS
EIKNOPS	PINKOES		TRELLIS
EIKNORW	WONKIER	EILLRSW	SWILLER

	WILLERS	EILNOOR	LOONIER
EILLRTT	LITTLER	EILNOOS	LOONIES
EILLSST	LISTELS	EILNOOV	VIOLONE
EILLSSU	SULLIES	EILNOPP	PLENIPO
EILLSTT	LITTLES	EILNOPR	PROLINE
EILLSTU	TUILLES	EILNOPS	EPSILON
EILLSTW	WILLEST		PINOLES
	WILLETS	EILNOPT	POINTEL
EILLSWY	WILLEYS		PONTILE
EILMMNO	MOLIMEN	EILNORR	LORINER
EILMMRS	LIMMERS	EILNORS	NEROLIS
	SLIMMER	EILNORT	RETINOL
EILMMRU	LUMMIER	EILNOSS	ESLOINS
EILMNOS	MOLINES		INSOLES
EILMNRS	LIMNERS		LESIONS
	MERLINS		LIONESS
EILMNSS	SIMNELS	EILNOST	ENTOILS
EILMNSU	EMULSIN		LIONETS
	LUMINES	EILNOSU	ELUSION
	UNLIMES	EILNOTU	ELUTION
EILMNSY	MYELINS		OUTLINE
EILMOOS	MOOLIES	EILNOTV	VIOLENT
EILMOPR	IMPLORE	EILNOTW	TOWLINE
EILMORR	LORIMER	EILNOVV	INVOLVE
EILMORS	MOILERS	EILNPPS	LIPPENS
EILMORT	MOTLIER		NIPPLES
EILMOSS	LIMOSES	EILNPRS	PILSNER
	LISSOME	EILNPRU	PURLINE
	SMOILES	EILNPSS	PENSILS
EILMOST	MOTILES		SPINELS
EILMPPS	PIMPLES		SPLINES
EILMPPU	PLUMPIE	EILNPST	PINTLES
EILMPRS	PRELIMS		PLENIST
	SIMPLER	EILNPSU	LUPINES
EILMPRU	LUMPIER		SPINULE
	PLUMIER	EILNPTY	INEPTLY
EILMPRY	PRIMELY	EILNPUV	VULPINE
EILMPSS	SIMPLES	EILNRST	LINTERS
EILMPST	LIMPEST		SNIRTLE
	LIMPETS	EILNRSV	SILVERN
EILMPSU	IMPULSE	EILNRTY	INERTLY
EILMPSW	WIMPLES	EILNSSS	SINLESS
EILMPSX	SIMPLEX	EILNSST	ENLISTS
EILMPTY	EMPTILY		LISTENS
EILMRRU	MURLIER		SILENTS
EILMRRY	MERRILY		TINSELS
EILMRSS	RIMLESS	EILNSSU	INSULSE
	SMILERS		SILENUS
EILMRST	MILTERS	EILNSSV	SNIVELS
EILMRSU	MISRULE	EILNSSY	LINSEYS
EILMRSV	VERMILS		LYSINES
EILMRSY	MISERLY	EILNSTU	LUTEINS
EILMRTY	LIMITER		UNTILES
EILMRVY	VERMILY		UTENSIL
EILMSSS	MISSELS	EILNSTV	VENTILS
EILMSST	MISTLES	EILNSTW	WESTLIN
	SMILETS		WINTLES
EILMSSU	MUESLIS	EILNSUV	UNLIVES
EILMSSY	MESSILY		UNVEILS
	MILSEYS	EILNSUY	LUNYIES
EILMSTT	SMITTLE	EILNSVY	SYLVINE
EILMSTZ	MILTZES	EILNVXY	VIXENLY
EILMSZZ	MIZZLES	EILOOPR	LOOPIER
EILMUUV	ELUVIUM	EILOORS	ORIOLES
EILNNPU	PINNULE	EILOORT	TROOLIE
EILNNST	LINNETS	EILOOST	OOLITES
EILNNSU	UNLINES		OSTIOLE
EILNNSW	WINNLES		STOOLIE
EILNNSY	LINNEYS	EILOOTZ	ZOOLITE
EILNOOP	POLONIE	EILOPRS	SLOPIER

	SPOILER		TESTRIL	EIMNPTU	PINETUM	EIMPSTU	IMPETUS
EILOPRT	POITREL		TILTERS	EIMNQSU	MESQUIN		IMPUTES
	POLITER		TITLERS	EIMNRRU	MURRINE	EIMPSUY	YUMPIES
EILOPST	PIOLETS	EILRSTU	LUSTIER	EIMNRST	ENTRISM	EIMQSTU	MESQUIT
	PISTOLE		RULIEST		MINSTER	EIMRRST	RETRIMS
EILOPSU	PILEOUS		RUTILES		MINTERS		TRIMERS
EILOPSV	PLOSIVE			EIMNRSU	MURINES	EIMRRSU	MURRIES
EILOPTT	PLOTTIE	EILRSUW	WURLIES		NEURISM	EIMRSST	MISTERS
EILOPTX	EXPLOIT	EILRSVY	SILVERY	EIMNRSV	VERMINS		SMITERS
EILORRS	LORRIES	EILRSZZ	SIZZLER	EIMNRTU	MINUTER	EIMRSSU	MISUSER
EILORRU	LOURIER	EILRTTY	LITTERY	EIMNRVY	VERMINY		MUSSIER
EILORSS	LORISES		TRITELY	EIMNSSS	SENSISM		SURMISE
	LOSSIER	EILRTUV	RIVULET	EIMNSST	MISSENT	EIMRSSV	VERISMS
	RISSOLE	EILSSTT	STILETS	EIMNSSU	MINUSES	EIMRSTT	METRIST
EILORST	LOITERS	EILSSTW	WITLESS	EIMNSTT	MITTENS	EIMRSTU	MUSTIER
	TOILERS	EILSSTY	STYLISE		SMITTEN	EIMRSTY	MISTERY
EILORSU	LOUSIER	EILSSVW	SWIVELS	EIMNSTU	MINUETS		SMYTRIE
	SOILURE	EILSSZZ	SIZZLES		MINUTES	EIMRTUV	VITREUM
EILORSV	OLIVERS	EILSTTT	TITTLES		MISTUNE	EIMRTUX	MIXTURE
	VIOLERS	EILSTTU	TITULES		MUNITES	EIMRUZZ	MUZZIER
EILORTT	TORTILE	EILSTTV	VITTLES		MUTINES	EIMSSST	MISSETS
	TRIOLET	EILSTTY	STYLITE	EIMNSTW	MISWENT	EIMSSSU	MISUSES
EILORTU	OUTLIER		TESTILY	EIMNSZZ	MIZZENS	EIMSSSX	SEXISMS
EILOSSV	SOLIVES	EILSTVY	SYLVITE	EIMNUZZ	MUEZZIN	EIMSSTY	STYMIES
EILOSTT	LITOTES	EILSTYZ	STYLIZE	EIMOORR	MOORIER	EIMSTYZ	ZYMITES
	TOILETS	EILSWZZ	SWIZZLE		ROOMIER	EINNNOS	NONNIES
EILOSTU	OUTLIES	EILTWZZ	TWIZZLE	EIMOPPR	MOPPIER	EINNNRS	RENNINS
EILOSTV	OLIVETS	EIMMMOS	MOMMIES		POMPIER	EINNOOS	IONONES
	VIOLETS	EIMMMST	MIMMEST	EIMOPRR	PRIMERO	EINNOPS	PENSION
EILOSTW	OWLIEST	EIMMMSU	MUMMIES	EIMOPRS	IMPOSER	EINNOQU	QUINONE
EILOTUV	OUTLIVE	EIMMNRS	NIMMERS		PROMISE	EINNORT	INTONER
EILPPRR	RIPPLER	EIMMNSU	IMMUNES	EIMOPRV	IMPROVE		TERNION
EILPPRS	RIPPLES	EIMMOPS	POMMIES	EIMOPSS	IMPOSES	EINNORU	NOUNIER
	SLIPPER	EIMMORS	MEMOIRS		MOPSIES		REUNION
EILPPRT	RIPPLET	EIMMOST	TOMMIES	EIMOPST	MOPIEST	EINNORV	ENVIRON
	TIPPLER	EIMMPRR	PRIMMER		OPTIMES	EINNOSS	SONNIES
	TRIPPLE	EIMMPRU	PREMIUM	EIMORRW	WORMIER	EINNOST	INTONES
EILPPRU	PULPIER	EIMMRRT	TRIMMER	EIMORSS	ISOMERS		TENSION
EILPPSS	PIPLESS	EIMMRRU	RUMMIER		MOSSIER	EINNOSV	VENISON
	SIPPLES	EIMMRSS	MERISMS	EIMORST	EROTISM	EINNOTT	NONETTI
EILPPST	STIPPLE		SIMMERS		MOISTER		TONTINE
	TIPPLES	EIMMRST	MISTERM		MORTISE	EINNOVW	INWOVEN
EILPPSW	SWIPPLE	EIMMRSU	IMMURES		TRISOME	EINNPRS	PINNERS
EILPRSS	LISPERS		MUMSIER	EIMORSU	MOUSIER		SPINNER
EILPRST	SPIRTLE		RUMMIES	EIMORSV	VERISMO	EINNPRT	ENPRINT
	TRIPLES	EIMMRSW	SWIMMER	EIMORTT	MOTTIER	EINNPST	PINNETS
EILPRTT	TRIPLET	EIMMRSZ	ZIMMERS		OMITTER		SPINNET
EILPRTX	TRIPLEX	EIMMRUY	YUMMIER	EIMOSSS	MOSSIES		TENPINS
EILPRUU	PURLIEU	EIMMSST	SEMMITS	EIMOSST	MITOSES	EINNPSY	SPINNEY
EILPSST	STIPELS	EIMMSTU	TUMMIES		SOMITES	EINNRRU	RUNNIER
EILPSTT	SPITTLE	EIMMSTZ	TZIMMES	EIMOSTT	MOTIEST	EINNRSS	SINNERS
EILPSTU	PULIEST	EIMNNOT	MENTION		TITMOSE	EINNRST	INTERNS
	PUTELIS	EIMNOOR	IONOMER	EIMOSTU	TIMEOUS		TINNERS
	STIPULE		MOONIER	EIMOSTV	MOTIVES	EINNRSU	SUNNIER
EILPSUY	SPULYIE	EIMNOOS	MOONIES	EIMOSTZ	MESTIZO		UNREINS
EILPSUZ	SPULZIE		NOISOME	EIMOSZZ	MOZZIES		UNRISEN
EILPSZZ	PIZZLES	EIMNOOT	EMOTION	EIMPRRS	PRIMERS	EINNRSW	WINNERS
EILPTTY	PETTILY	EIMNOOX	EXOMION	EIMPRRU	IMPURER	EINNRTV	VINTNER
EILQRTU	QUILTER	EIMNOPS	IMPONES		PRIMEUR	EINNRUV	UNRIVEN
EILQRUU	LIQUEUR		PEONISM	EIMPRSS	IMPRESS	EINNSST	SENNITS
EILQTUY	QUIETLY	EIMNOPT	EMPTION		PREMISS		SINNETS
EILRRSU	LURRIES		PIMENTO		SIMPERS	EINNSSY	SINSYNE
	SURLIER	EIMNORS	MERINOS	EIMPRST	IMPREST	EINNSTT	INTENTS
EILRRTW	TWIRLER		MERSION		PERMITS	EINNSTU	TUNNIES
EILRSST	LISTERS	EIMNOSS	EONISMS	EIMPRSU	SPUMIER	EINNSTV	INVENTS
EILRSSV	SILVERS	EIMNOST	MOISTEN		UMPIRES	EINNSUW	UNSINEW
	SLIVERS	EIMNOSW	WINSOME	EIMPRTU	IMPUTER	EINNTUW	UNTWINE
EILRSTT	LITTERS	EIMNOTU	MOUNTIE	EIMPSST	MISSTEP	EINOOPZ	EPIZOON
	SLITTER	EIMNOTY	OMNEITY	EIMPSSU	SEPIUMS	EINOORS	EROSION
	STILTER		OMNIETY			EINOOST	ISOTONE
		EIMNPST	PIMENTS				

EINOOSZ	OZONISE		PUNTIES
EINOOTZ	ZOONITE	EINPTTY	TINTYPE
EINOOZZ	OZONIZE	EINQRUU	UNIQUER
EINOPPR	POPERIN	EINQRUY	ENQUIRY
	PROPINE	EINQSSU	SEQUINS
EINOPRS	ORPINES	EINQSTU	INQUEST
	PIONERS		QUINTES
	PROINES	EINQSUU	UNIQUES
EINOPRT	POINTER	EINQSUZ	QUINZES
	PROTEIN	EINQTTU	QUINTET
	PTERION	EINQTUU	UNQUIET
	REPOINT	EINRRSS	RINSERS
EINOPRV	PROVINE		RUINERS
EINOPSS	SPINOSE	EINRRTU	RUNTIER
EINOPST	POINTES	EINRSST	INSERTS
	PONTIES		SINTERS
EINOPSW	POWNIES	EINRSSU	INSURES
EINOPSY	PIONEYS		SUNRISE
EINOQUX	EQUINOX	EINRSTT	ENTRIST
EINORRS	IRONERS		STINTER
EINORSS	ORNISES		TINTERS
	SENIORS	EINRSTU	TRIUNES
	SONERIS		UNITERS
	SONSIER	EINRSTV	INVERTS
EINORST	NORITES		STRIVEN
	ORIENTS	EINRSTW	TWINERS
	STONIER		WINTERS
	TERSION	EINRSTY	SINTERY
	TRIONES	EINRSUW	UNWIRES
EINORSV	RENVOIS		UNWISER
	VERSION	EINRSVW	WIVERNS
EINORSW	SNOWIER	EINRSWY	SWINERY
EINORTT	TRITONE	EINRTTU	NUTTIER
EINORTU	ROUTINE	EINRTTW	TWINTER
EINORTW	TOWNIER		WRITTEN
EINORTZ	TRIZONE	EINRTUV	UNRIVET
EINOSSS	ESSOINS		VENTURI
	OSSEINS	EINRTUW	UNWRITE
	SESSION	EINRTWY	WINTERY
EINOSST	NOSIEST	EINSSST	SENSIST
	SONTIES	EINSSSU	NISUSES
	STONIES		SINUSES
EINOSSU	SINUOSE	EINSSSY	SYNESIS
EINOSTT	TONIEST	EINSSTU	INTUSES
	TONITES	EINSSTV	INVESTS
EINOSTW	TOWNIES	EINSSTW	WISENTS
EINOSUV	ENVIOUS		WITNESS
	NIVEOUS	EINSSTY	TINSEYS
	VEINOUS	EINSSUW	SUNWISE
EINOTTT	TOTIENT	EINSSWY	WINSEYS
EINPPRS	NIPPERS	EINSTTU	TUNIEST
	SNIPPER	EINSTTW	ENTWIST
EINPPSS	PEPSINS	EINSTTY	TENSITY
EINPPST	SNIPPET	EINSUVW	UNWIVES
EINPRRT	PRINTER	EINTTTW	TWITTEN
	REPRINT	EINTTUY	TENUITY
EINPRRU	UNRIPER	EIOOPRR	ROOPIER
EINPRSS	SNIPERS	EIOOPRV	POOVIER
EINPRST	NIPTERS	EIOOPST	ISOTOPE
	PTERINS	EIOORRT	ROOTIER
EINPRSU	PRUINES	EIOORST	OORIEST
	PURINES		ROOTIES
	UPRISEN		SOOTIER
EINPRSY	INSPYRE		TOORIES
EINPSST	INSTEPS	EIOORWZ	WOOZIER
	SPINETS	EIOOSST	OOSIEST
EINPSSU	PUISNES	EIOOSTT	TOOTSIE
	SUPINES	EIOOSTZ	OOZIEST
EINPSTT	SPITTEN		
EINPSTU	PUNIEST		

EIOPPPS	POPPIES	EIPPRRS	RIPPERS
EIOPPRS	SOPPIER	EIPPRRT	TRIPPER
EIOPPSS	POPSIES	EIPPRSS	SIPPERS
EIOPRRS	PROSIER	EIPPRST	TIPPERS
EIOPRRT	PIERROT	EIPPRSU	PURPIES
	PORTIER	EIPPRSZ	ZIPPERS
EIOPRRU	ROUPIER	EIPPRTT	TRIPPET
EIOPRSS	POISERS	EIPPSST	SIPPETS
EIOPRST	PERIOST	EIPPSTT	TIPPETS
	PORIEST	EIPPSUY	YUPPIES
	REPOSIT	EIPQSTU	PIQUETS
	RIPOSTE	EIPRRSS	PRISERS
	ROPIEST	EIPRRSU	PURSIER
EIOPRSU	POURIES	EIPRRSZ	PRIZERS
	SOUPIER	EIPRRTU	PURTIER
EIOPRSX	PROXIES	EIPRRTY	TRIPERY
EIOPRTT	POTTIER	EIPRRUV	UPRIVER
EIOPRTU	POUTIER	EIPRSST	ESPRITS
EIOPRTV	PIVOTER		PERSIST
EIOPSSS	POSSIES		PRIESTS
EIOPSST	POSTIES		SITREPS
	SEPIOST		SPRITES
	SOPITES		STIRPES
	TIPTOES		STRIPES
EIOPSTT	POTTIES		TRIPSES
EIOPSTU	PITEOUS	EIPRSSU	SUSPIRE
EIOPSTX	POXIEST		UPRISES
EIOPSTY	ISOTYPE	EIPRSSW	SWIPERS
EIOPSZZ	POZZIES	EIPRSTT	PITTERS
EIOPTUW	WIPEOUT		SPITTER
EIOQRTU	QUOITER		TIPSTER
EIORRRS	SORRIER	EIPRSTU	PERITUS
EIORRRT	RORTIER		PUIREST
EIORRRW	WORRIER	EIPRSTV	PRIVETS
EIORRSS	ORRISES	EIPRSTX	EXTIRPS
	ROSIERS	EIPRSTY	PYRITES
EIORRST	RIOTERS		STRIPEY
	ROISTER	EIPRSUU	EURIPUS
	RORIEST	EIPRTTU	PUTTIER
EIORRSV	REVISOR	EIPRUVW	PURVIEW
EIORRSW	WORRIES	EIPSSSU	PUSSIES
EIORRUV	OUVRIER	EIPSSTZ	SPITZES
EIORRVV	REVIVOR	EIPSTTU	PUTTIES
EIORSST	ROSIEST	EIQRSSU	RISQUES
	SORITES		SQUIERS
	SORTIES		SQUIRES
	STORIES	EIQRSTU	QUERIST
	TOSSIER		REQUITS
EIORSSU	SERIOUS	EIQRSUV	QUIVERS
EIORSSV	VIROSES	EIQRTTU	QUITTER
EIORSSX	XEROSIS	EIQRUVY	QUIVERY
EIORSTT	STOITER	EIQRUZZ	QUIZZER
EIORSTU	OURIEST	EIQSTUU	QUIETUS
	TOUSIER	EIQSUZZ	QUIZZES
EIORSTV	TORSIVE	EIRRRST	STIRRER
EIORSTW	OWRIEST	EIRRSST	STIRRES
	TOWSIER	EIRRSTT	RITTERS
EIORTTT	TOTTIER		TERRITS
EIORTTU	TOUTIER	EIRRSTU	RUSTIER
EIORTTV	TORTIVE	EIRRSTV	STRIVER
	VIRETOT	EIRRSTW	WRITERS
EIORTUV	VOITURE	EIRRSZZ	RIZZERS
EIOSSTV	SOVIETS	EIRRTTU	RUTTIER
	STOVIES	EIRSSST	RESISTS
EIOSTTT	TOTTIES		SISTERS
EIOSTTU	TOUSTIE	EIRSSSU	ISSUERS
EIOSTTW	TOWIEST		RISUSES
EIOSTUV	OUTVIES	EIRSSTT	SITTERS
EIOSTUZ	OUTSIZE	EIRSSTV	STIVERS
EIPPPSU	PUPPIES		STRIVES

	TREVISS	EKMNOSU	MUSKONE	ELLOPRR	PROLLER	ELMSTUU	MUTULES
	VERISTS	EKMNOSY	MONKEYS	ELLOPRS	POLLERS	ELMSUZZ	MUZZLES
EIRSSUU	USURIES	EKMNPTU	UNKEMPT	ELLOPTU	POLLUTE	ELNNOPU	NONUPLE
EIRSSUV	VIRUSES	EKMOOPS	MOPOKES	ELLORRS	ROLLERS	ELNNOSS	NELSONS
EIRSTTT	STRETTI	EKMORSS	SMOKERS	ELLORRT	TROLLER	ELNNRSU	RUNNELS
	TITTERS	EKMRSTU	MURKEST	ELLORSS	SOLLERS	ELNNSTU	TUNNELS
	TRITEST	EKMSSTU	MUSKETS		SORELLS	ELNOOSS	LOOSENS
EIRSTTU	TERTIUS	EKNNOST	NEKTONS	ELLORST	TOLLERS	ELNOOSU	UNLOOSE
EIRSTTV	TRIVETS	EKNOORS	SNOOKER	ELLORTY	TROLLEY	ELNOOSZ	SNOOZLE
EIRSTTW	TWISTER	EKNOPSU	UNSPOKE	ELLOSST	TOLSELS	ELNOPRU	PLEURON
	WITTERS	EKNORST	STONKER	ELLOSTU	OUTSELL	ELNOPRY	PRONELY
EIRSTUV	VIRTUES		STROKEN	ELLOSVY	VOLLEYS	ELNOPST	LEPTONS
EIRSUVV	SURVIVE		TONKERS	ELLOSWY	YELLOWS	ELNOPSY	POLEYNS
EIRSUVW	SURVIEW	EKNORSW	KNOWERS	ELLOTTU	OUTTELL	ELNOPTU	OPULENT
EIRTTTW	TWITTER	EKNORSY	YONKERS	ELLOTUW	OUTWELL	ELNORSS	NORSELS
EISSSTU	TISSUES	EKNORTT	KNOTTER	ELLOVWY	VOWELLY	ELNORST	LENTORS
EISSSTW	SWITSES	EKNORTW	NETWORK	ELLOWYY	YELLOWY	ELNORSU	NOURSLE
EISSSTX	SEXISTS	EKNORUY	YOUNKER	ELLPRSU	PULLERS	ELNORTY	ELYTRON
EISSTTY	TYSTIES	EKNORWY	YWROKEN	ELLPSTU	PULLETS	ELNOSSS	LESSONS
EISSTUV	TUSSIVE	EKNOSUY	UNYOKES	ELLPSUW	UPSWELL		SONLESS
EISSTVW	SWIVETS	EKNRTUY	TURNKEY		UPWELLS	ELNOSST	TELSONS
EISSWZZ	SWIZZES	EKNSSTU	SUNKETS	ELLPSUY	PULLEYS	ELNOSSU	ENSOULS
EISTTTU	TUTTIES	EKOOPRT	PERTOOK	ELMMOPS	POMMELS		NOUSLES
EJJMNUU	JEJUNUM	EKOOPRV	PROVOKE	ELMMORT	TROMMEL	ELNOSSV	SLOVENS
EJKMNNU	JUNKMEN	EKOORRY	ROOKERY	ELMMPSU	PUMMELS	ELNOSSW	LOWNESS
EJKNRSU	JUNKERS	EKOORST	STOOKER	ELMMPTU	PLUMMET	ELNOSTT	TONLETS
EJKNSTU	JUNKETS		STROOKE	ELMMRSU	SLUMMER	ELNOSTU	LENTOUS
EJKOORY	JOOKERY	EKOPPSU	UPSPOKE	ELMMSTU	STUMMEL	ELNOSTV	SOLVENT
EJKORUY	JOUKERY	EKOPRRS	PORKERS	ELMNOOT	MOONLET	ELNOSUV	UNLOVES
EJLORST	JOLTERS		PROKERS		TOOLMEN	ELNOSUZ	ZONULES
EJLORSW	JOWLERS	EKORRST	STROKER	ELMNOOW	WOOLMEN	ELNOSVY	LENVOYS
EJLOSST	JOSTLES	EKORRSW	REWORKS	ELMNORS	MERLONS	ELNOSZZ	NOZZLES
EJLOSSY	JOYLESS		WORKERS	ELMNOST	LOMENTS	ELNOTUZ	ZONULET
EJLSSTU	JUSTLES	EKORRSY	YORKERS		MELTONS	ELNOTVY	NOVELTY
EJMNRUY	JURYMEN	EKORSST	STOKERS	ELMNOSY	MYELONS	ELNPSST	SPLENTS
EJMOSST	JETSOMS		STROKES	ELMNOTU	MOULTEN	ELNPSTU	PENULTS
EJMPRSU	JUMPERS	EKPPSUU	SEPPUKU	ELMNOTY	YMOLTEN	ELNRSSU	NURSLES
EJNORRU	REJOURN	EKPRSSY	KRYPSES	ELMNPPU	PLUMPEN	ELNRSTU	RUNLETS
EJNORUY	JOURNEY	EKRRSSY	SKRYERS	ELMNPSU	PLENUMS	ELNRSTY	STERNLY
EJNOSST	JETSONS	EKRSSTU	TUSKERS	ELMNPUU	UNPLUME	ELNRSUU	UNRULES
EJNOSTT	JETTONS	EKRSTUY	TURKEYS	ELMOOPP	POMPELO	ELNRSUZ	LUZERNS
EJOORVY	OVERJOY	EKRSUVY	KURVEYS	ELMOOPS	POMELOS	ELNSSSU	SUNLESS
EJOOSSY	SOOJEYS	ELLLORR	LORRELL	ELMOORT	TREMOLO	ELNSSSY	SLYNESS
EJORSSS	JOSSERS	ELLLORS	LOLLERS	ELMOPRY	POLYMER	ELNSTTU	NUTLETS
EJORSTT	JOTTERS	ELLLOSZ	LOZELLS	ELMOPSU	PLUMOSE	ELNSUZZ	NUZZLES
EJORSTU	JOUSTER	ELLMNOO	MOELLON		PUMELOS		SNUZZLE
EJOSTTU	OUTJEST	ELLMNOP	POLLMEN	ELMOPSY	EMPLOYS	ELOOPRS	LOOPERS
	OUTJETS	ELLMNOT	TOLLMEN	ELMORSS	MORSELS		SPOOLER
EJPRRUY	PERJURY	ELLMOOR	MORELLO	ELMORSU	EMULSOR	ELOORST	LOOTERS
EJSSTTU	JUSTEST	ELLMOSW	MELLOWS	ELMOSST	MOLESTS		RETOOLS
EKKLOOY	OLYKOEK	ELLMOWY	MELLOWY	ELMOSSU	MOUSLES		ROOTLES
EKKLRSU	SKULKER	ELLMPUU	PLUMULE	ELMOSSY	SMOYLES		TOOLERS
EKLLMSU	SKELLUM	ELLMRSU	MULLERS	ELMOSTT	MOTTLES	ELOORTT	ROOTLET
EKLMNSU	KUMMELS	ELLMSTU	MULLETS	ELMOSTY	MOTLEYS	ELOOSST	LOOSEST
EKLMSSU	MUSKLES	ELLMSUV	VELLUMS	ELMOSUU	EMULOUS		LOTOSES
EKLNOPR	PLONKER	ELLMSUY	MULLEYS	ELMOSUV	VOLUMES	ELOOSSW	WOOSELS
EKLNORS	SNORKEL	ELLNNOT	TONNELL	ELMOSXY	OXYMELS	ELOOSTT	TOOTLES
EKLNOSS	KELSONS	ELLNOOW	WOOLLEN	ELMOSZZ	MOZZLES	ELOOSTU	OUTSOLE
	SLOKENS	ELLNOPS	POLLENS	ELMPPRU	PLUMPER	ELOOSWY	WOOLSEY
EKLNPRU	PLUNKER	ELLNOPT	POLLENT	ELMPPSU	PEPLUMS	ELOPPPS	POPPLES
EKLNRSU	LUNKERS	ELLNORS	ENROLLS	ELMPRSU	LUMPERS	ELOPPRS	LOPPERS
	RUNKLES	ELLNOSU	NOUSELL		RUMPLES		PROPELS
EKLNSST	SKLENTS	ELLNOSV	VELLONS	ELMPRUY	PLUMERY	ELOPPST	STOPPLE
EKLOORS	LOOKERS	ELLNOSW	SWOLLEN	ELMRSTY	MYRTLES		TOPPLES
EKLRRSU	LURKERS	ELLNOXY	XYLENOL	ELMRTUU	MULTURE	ELOPPSU	POULPES
EKLSTTU	SKUTTLE	ELLNPSU	UNSPELL	ELMRTUY	ELYTRUM	ELOPPSY	POLYPES
EKLSTUZ	KLUTZES	ELLNSSU	SULLENS	ELMRUZZ	MUZZLER	ELOPRRS	PROLERS
EKMMRSU	SKUMMER	ELLNSUU	LUNULES	ELMSSSU	MUSSELS	ELOPRRU	PROULER
EKMNORW	WORKMEN	ELLOOSW	WOOSELL		SUMLESS	ELOPRRW	PROWLER
EKMNORY	MONKERY	ELLOOSY	LOOSELY			ELOPRRY	PYRROLE

ELOPRSS	PLESSOR	ELPRSTU	SPURTLE
	SPLORES	ELPRSUV	PULVERS
ELOPRST	PETROLS	ELPRTUU	PULTURE
ELOPRSU	LEPROUS	ELPRUZZ	PUZZLER
	PELORUS	ELPSSSU	PLUSSES
	PERLOUS		PUSSELS
	SPORULE	ELPSSUU	LUPUSES
ELOPRSV	PLOVERS	ELPSSUY	SPULYES
ELOPRSX	PLEXORS	ELPSTUU	PLUTEUS
ELOPRSY	LEPROSY		PUSTULE
ELOPRTT	PLOTTER	ELPSUZZ	PUZZELS
ELOPRTU	PLOUTER		PUZZLES
	POULTER	ELRRSTU	RUSTLER
ELOPRTW	PLOWTER	ELRRTTU	TURTLER
ELOPRTY	PROTYLE	ELRSSSU	RUSSELS
ELOPRVY	OVERPLY	ELRSSTU	LUSTERS
	PLOVERY		LUSTRES
ELOPSST	TOPLESS		RESULTS
ELOPSSU	SOUPLES		RUSTLES
ELOPSTT	POTTLES		SUTLERS
ELOPSTU	TUPELOS		ULSTERS
ELORRSS	SORRELS	ELRSTTU	TURTLES
ELORRSW	WORRELS	ELRSTTY	TETRYLS
ELORSSS	LESSORS	ELRSTUY	SUTLERY
ELORSST	OSTLERS	ELRSTWY	SWELTRY
	STEROLS	ELRSUWY	WURLEYS
	TORSELS	ELRTTUY	UTTERLY
ELORSSV	SOLVERS	ELRTUUV	VULTURE
ELORSTT	SETTLOR	ELSSSTU	TUSSLES
	SLOTTER	ELSSTTU	SUTTLES
	TOLTERS	ELSSTTY	STYLETS
ELORSTU	ELUTORS	ELSSTYY	SYSTYLE
	OUTLERS	ELSUWZZ	WUZZLES
	TROULES	EMMMOST	MOMMETS
ELORSTV	REVOLTS	EMMMRSU	MUMMERS
ELORSTW	TROWELS	EMMMRUY	MUMMERY
	WORTLES	EMMNNOS	MNEMONS
ELORSUV	LOUVERS	EMMNOOR	MONOMER
	LOUVRES		MOORMEN
	VELOURS		MOOTMEN
ELORSUY	ELUSORY	EMMNOST	MOMENTS
ELORSVW	WOLVERS		MONTEMS
ELORTTY	LOTTERY	EMMNOTU	OMENTUM
ELORTVY	OVERTLY	EMMNOTY	METONYM
ELOSSTU	LOTUSES	EMMNSTU	MENTUMS
	SOLUTES	EMMOPRR	PROMMER
	TOUSLES	EMMOSSU	MOUSMES
ELOSSTW	LOWSEST	EMMOSYZ	ZYMOMES
	SLOWEST	EMMPRSU	MUMPERS
ELOSSTY	SYSTOLE	EMMRRSU	RUMMERS
	TOLSEYS	EMMRSSU	SUMMERS
	TYLOSES	EMMRSTU	RUMMEST
ELOSSXY	XYLOSES	EMMRSUY	SUMMERY
ELOSSZZ	SOZZLES	EMMSSUU	MUSEUMS
ELOSTTU	OUTLETS	EMNNOOR	MONERON
ELOSTTY	TYLOTES	EMNNOSW	SNOWMEN
ELOSTUU	LUTEOUS	EMNOOPT	METOPON
ELOSTUV	VOLUTES	EMNOORS	MOONERS
ELOSTUZ	TOUZLES	EMNOORT	MONTERO
ELOSTYZ	TOLZEYS	EMNOOSS	MONOSES
ELOSWYY	YOWLEYS	EMNOOST	MOONSET
ELOSWZZ	SWOZZLE	EMNOOSY	NOYSOME
ELPPRRU	PURPLER	EMNOOTY	ENOMOTY
ELPPRSU	PULPERS	EMNOPRT	PORTMEN
	PURPLES	EMNOPST	POSTMEN
	REPULPS		TOPSMEN
	SUPPLER	EMNOPSY	EPONYMS
ELPPSSU	SUPPLES	EMNORRU	MOURNER
ELPQSUU	PULQUES	EMNORSS	SERMONS
ELPRRSU	PURLERS	EMNORST	MENTORS

	MONSTER	ENNORSW	RENOWNS
	MONTRES	ENNORTU	NEUTRON
EMNORTT	TORMENT	ENNOSST	SONNETS
EMNORTU	MONTURE		STONNES
	MOUNTER		TENSONS
	REMOUNT	ENNOSSW	NOWNESS
EMNOSST	STEMSON	ENNOSTU	NEUSTON
EMNOSTU	UNSMOTE	ENNOSTW	NEWTONS
EMNOSTY	ETYMONS	ENNOSTZ	TENZONS
EMNOSXY	EXONYMS	ENNOUVW	UNWOVEN
EMNPSSU	PENSUMS	ENNPRSU	PUNNERS
EMNRRSU	MURRENS	ENNPSTU	PUNNETS
EMNRSTU	MUNSTER		UNSPENT
	STERNUM	ENNRRSU	RUNNERS
EMOOPRT	PROMOTE	ENNRSTU	RUNNETS
EMOOPRY	POMEROY		STUNNER
EMOORRS	MOROSER	ENNRSUW	WUNNERS
	ROOMERS	ENNSSTU	UNNESTS
EMOORST	MOOTERS	ENNSTTU	UNTENTS
EMOORSU	UROSOME	ENNSTUU	UNTUNES
EMOOSSS	OSMOSES	ENNTTUY	UNTENTY
EMOOSTT	MOOTEST	ENOOPPR	PROPONE
	MOTTOES	ENOOPRS	SNOOPER
	TOOMEST	ENOOPSY	SPOONEY
EMOOSTW	TWOSOME	ENOORSS	SEROONS
EMOOSTY	MYOSOTE	ENOORST	ENROOTS
	TOYSOME	ENOORSU	ONEROUS
EMOOTUV	OUTMOVE	ENOORSZ	SNOOZER
EMOPPRS	MOPPERS	ENOOSST	SOONEST
EMOPPST	MOPPETS	ENOOSSZ	SNOOZES
EMOPPSY	POMPEYS	ENOOSTT	TESTOON
EMOPRRS	ROMPERS	ENOOSTU	UNSOOTE
EMOPRST	TROMPES	ENOOTXY	OXYTONE
EMOPRSU	SUPREMO	ENOPPSU	UNPOPES
EMOPSSU	MOPUSES	ENOPRRS	PERRONS
EMOPSSY	MYOPSES	ENOPRRU	PRONEUR
EMOQSSU	MOSQUES	ENOPRSS	PERSONS
EMORRST	TERMORS	ENOPRST	POSTERN
	TREMORS		PRONEST
EMORRSU	MORSURE	ENOPRSU	UNROPES
EMORRSW	WORMERS	ENOPRSY	PROYNES
EMORRWY	WORMERY		PYONERS
EMORSST	MOTSERS	ENOPRTT	PORTENT
EMORSSU	MOUSERS	ENOPRTY	ENTROPY
	SMOUSER	ENOPSST	POSNETS
EMORSTU	MOUTERS		STEPSON
	OESTRUM	ENOPSTT	POTENTS
EMORSUY	MOUSERY	ENOPSWY	POWNEYS
EMOSSSU	MOUSSES	ENOQTUU	UNQUOTE
	SMOUSES	ENORRSS	SNORERS
EMOSSYZ	ZYMOSES		SORNERS
EMOSTTT	MOTETTS	ENORRST	SNORTER
EMOSTVZ	ZEMSTVO	ENORRTT	TORRENT
EMPPRSU	PUMPERS	ENORRUV	OVERRUN
EMPRSTU	STUMPER	ENORSSS	SENSORS
	SUMPTER	ENORSST	STONERS
EMPRTTU	TRUMPET		TENSORS
EMRRSTU	STURMER	ENORSSW	WORSENS
EMRRSUY	MURREYS	ENORSSY	SENSORY
EMRSSTU	ESTRUMS	ENORSTT	ROTTENS
	MUSTERS		SNOTTER
	STUMERS		STENTOR
EMRSTTU	MUTTERS	ENORSTU	TENOURS
EMRSTYY	MYSTERY		TONSURE
EMSSSTY	SYSTEMS	ENORSTY	TYRONES
ENNNOPS	PENNONS	ENORSUV	NERVOUS
ENNNRUY	NUNNERY	ENORSVY	RENVOYS
ENNOOTT	NONETTO	ENORTUW	UNWROTE
ENNORST	STONERN	ENORTUY	TOURNEY
ENNORSU	NEURONS		

ENOSSST	SESTONS
ENOSSTT	OSTENTS
	TESTONS
ENOSSTU	OUTNESS
	TONUSES
ENOSSTW	TWONESS
ENOSSTX	SEXTONS
ENOSSUW	SWOUNES
ENOSSWW	SWOWNES
ENOSTTU	STOUTEN
ENOSTUU	TENUOUS
ENOTTUW	OUTWENT
ENPRRSU	PRUNERS
	SPURNER
ENPRSSU	SPURNES
ENPRSTU	PUNSTER
	PUNTERS
ENPRSUU	UNPURSE
ENPRSWY	PREWYNS
ENPSSSU	SUSPENS
ENPSSTU	UNSTEPS
ENPSTTU	STUPENT
ENPSTUW	UNSWEPT
ENRRSSU	NURSERS
ENRRSTU	RETURNS
	TURNERS
ENRRSUU	UNSURER
ENRRSUY	NURSERY
ENRRTUU	NURTURE
	UNTRUER
ENRRTUY	TURNERY
ENRSSTU	UNRESTS
ENRSSWY	WRYNESS
ENRSTTU	ENTRUST
	NUTTERS
ENRSUZZ	NUZZERS
ENRSVWY	WYVERNS
ENRTTUY	NUTTERY
ENSSSTU	SUNSETS
EOOOPRS	OOSPORE
EOOPPRS	OPPOSER
	PROPOSE
EOOPPRV	POPOVER
EOOPPSS	OPPOSES
EOOPRRS	SPOORER
EOOPRRT	TROOPER
EOOPRSS	POROSES
EOOPRST	POOREST
	POOTERS
	STOOPER
EOOPRTU	OUTROPE
EOOPRTV	OVERTOP
EOOPRTW	TOWROPE
EOOPRVY	POOVERY
EOOPRYZ	ZOOPERY
EOOPSST	STOOPES
EOOPTYZ	ZOOTYPE
EOORRST	ROOSTER
	ROOTERS
	TOREROS
EOORSSS	SOROSES
EOORSVW	OVERSOW
EOORTUW	OUTWORE
EOOSSSU	OSSEOUS
EOOSTWZ	WOOTZES
EOOTTUV	OUTVOTE
EOPPPRS	POPPERS
EOPPPST	POPPETS
EOPPRRS	PROPERS
	PROSPER
EOPPRSS	OPPRESS
	PORPESS
EOPPRST	STOPPER
	TOPPERS
EOPPRSU	PURPOSE
EOPPRSW	SWOPPER
EOPPRSY	PYROPES
	YOPPERS
EOPPSSU	SUPPOSE
EOPRRSS	PRESSOR
	PROSERS
EOPRRST	PORTERS
	REPORTS
	SPORTER
EOPRRSU	POURERS
EOPRRSV	PROVERS
EOPRRTU	TROUPER
EOPRSSS	POSSERS
EOPRSST	PORTESS
	POSTERS
	PRESTOS
	REPOSTS
EOPRSSU	POSEURS
	SOUPERS
EOPRSSW	PROWESS
EOPRSSY	OSPREYS
	PYROSES
EOPRSTT	POTTERS
	PROTEST
	SPOTTER
EOPRSTU	PETROUS
	POSTURE
	POUTERS
	PROTEUS
	SEPTUOR
	SPOUTER
	TROUPES
EOPRSTW	POWTERS
	PROWEST
EOPRSTX	EXPORTS
EOPRSUU	POURSUE
	UPROUSE
EOPRSUW	POURSEW
EOPRTTY	POTTERY
EOPRTUY	EUTROPY
EOPRTVY	POVERTY
EOPSSSS	POSSESS
EOPSSST	POSSETS
EOPSSSU	POUSSES
	SPOUSES
EOPSSTT	SPOTTES
EOPSSTX	SEXPOTS
EOPSTTU	OUTSTEP
	TOUPETS
EOPSTTW	STEWPOT
EOPTTUW	OUTWEPT
EOQRSTU	QUESTOR
	QUOTERS
	ROQUETS
	TORQUES
EORRRST	RORTERS
	TERRORS
EORRSSS	ROSSERS
EORRSST	RESORTS
	ROSTERS
	SORTERS
	STORERS
EORRSSU	ROUSERS
EORRSTT	RETORTS
	ROTTERS
	TORRETS
EORRSTU	RETOURS
	ROUSTER
	ROUTERS
	TOURERS
EORRSTV	TROVERS
EORRSTW	STROWER
EORRSTY	ROYSTER
EORRSZZ	ROZZERS
EORRTTT	TROTTER
EORRTTU	TORTURE
	TROUTER
EORSSST	TOSSERS
EORSSSU	SOURSES
EORSSTU	ESTROUS
	OESTRUS
	OUSTERS
	SOUREST
	SOUTERS
	TOUSERS
	TROUSES
	TUSSORE
EORSSTV	STOVERS
EORSSTW	SOWTERS
	STOWERS
	STOWRES
	TOWSERS
EORSSTZ	ZOSTERS
EORSSWW	WOWSERS
EORSTTT	STOTTER
	STRETTO
	TOTTERS
EORSTTU	STOUTER
	TOUTERS
EORSTTW	SWOTTER
EORSTTX	EXTORTS
EORSTTY	ROSETTY
EORSTUX	SEXTUOR
EORSUVY	VOYEURS
EORTTTY	TOTTERY
EOSSSSW	SOWSSES
EOSTTTW	WOTTEST
EPPPSTU	PUPPETS
EPPRRTU	PRERUPT
EPPRRUU	PURPURE
EPPRSSU	SUPPERS
EPPSTUW	UPSWEPT
EPRRRSU	SPURRER
EPRRSSU	PURSERS
EPRRSUU	PURSUER
	USURPER
EPRRSUY	SPURREY
EPRRTUU	RUPTURE
EPRSSTU	UPRESTS
EPRSSUU	PURSUES
EPRSSUW	PURSEWS
EPRSTTU	SPUTTER
EPRSTUU	PUTURES
EPRSUVY	PURVEYS
EQRSTWY	QWERTYS
ERRSSTU	RUSTRES
	TRUSSER
ERRSSUY	SURREYS
ERRSTTU	RUTTERS
	TRUSTER
	TURRETS
ERRSTTY	TRYSTER
ERSSSTU	RUSSETS
	TRUSSES
	TUSSERS
ERSSSUU	USURESS
ERSSTTU	TUTRESS
ERSSTUU	SUTURES
ERSSTUY	RUSSETY
ERSSTXY	XYSTERS
ERSSUVW	SURVEWS
ERSSUVY	SURVEYS
ERSTTTU	STUTTER
FFFGINU	FUFFING
FFGGINO	GOFFING
FFGHINU	HUFFING
FFGIIMN	MIFFING
FFGIINN	NIFFING
FFGIINR	GRIFFIN
FFGIINT	TIFFING
FFGILNU	LUFFING
FFGIMNU	MUFFING
FFGINOR	GRIFFON
FFGINOS	OFFINGS
FFGINPU	PUFFING
FFGINRU	RUFFING
FFGLRUY	GRUFFLY
FFHHISU	HUFFISH
FFHIISY	FISHIFY
FFHIKNU	HUFFKIN
FFHILSU	FISHFUL
FFHILTY	FIFTHLY
FFHILUY	HUFFILY
FFHIOST	TOFFISH
FFHORSS	SHROFFS
FFIINST	TIFFINS
FFIISUZ	ZIFFIUS
FFIKLSS	SKLIFFS
FFILLSU	FULFILS
FFILOST	FILFOTS
FFILOUZ	ZUFFOLI
FFILPSS	SPLIFFS
FFILPUY	PUFFILY
FFILRTY	FRITFLY
FFILSTU	FISTFUL
FFILSTY	STIFFLY
FFIMNSU	MUFFINS
FFINOPT	PONTIFF
FFINPSU	PUFFINS
FFINRSU	RUFFINS
FFIORTY	FORTIFY
FFIOSST	SOFFITS
FFIQSUY	SQUIFFY
FFIRTUY	FRITUFY
FFLLOOU	LOOFFUL
FFLOOUZ	ZUFFOLO
FFLOSTY	FYLFOTS
FFNORTU	TURNOFF
FFOPSTU	OFFPUTS
FFRRSUU	FURFURS
FGGGIIN	FIGGING
FGGGINO	FOGGING
FGGGINU	FUGGING
FGGHIIS	FISHGIG
FGGIINT	GIFTING
FGGIISS	FISGIGS
FGGIISZ	FIZGIGS
FGGIIZZ	FIZZGIG

FGGILNO	GOLFING	FGIMNOR	FORMING	FIIIKNN	FINIKIN		PROFITS
FGGILNU	FUGLING	FGIMOSY	FOGYISM	FIIKNRS	FIRKINS	FIOPSTX	POSTFIX
	GULFING	FGINNNO	FONNING	FIIKNYZ	ZINKIFY	FIORSUU	FURIOUS
FGGILOY	FOGGILY	FGINNNU	FUNNING	FIILLMO	MILFOIL	FIOSTTU	OUTFITS
FGGINOO	GOOFING	FGINNOY	FOYNING	FIILLNS	INFILLS	FIRSSTT	STRIFTS
FGGINOR	FORGING	FGINOOR	ROOFING	FIILLPS	FILLIPS	FKLORUW	WORKFUL
FGGINOW	GOWFING	FGINOOT	FOOTING	FIILNOT	TINFOIL	FKNOSTY	KONFYTS
FGHIINS	FISHING	FGINORT	FORTING	FIILPTU	PITIFUL	FKOOORS	FORSOOK
FGHILST	FLIGHTS	FGINOST	SOFTING	FIIMSST	MISFITS	FLLOOSW	FOLLOWS
FGHILSU	SIGHFUL	FGINOSW	SOWFING	FIINORS	FIORINS	FLLOPTU	PLOTFUL
FGHILTY	FLIGHTY	FGINOSX	FOXINGS	FIINOSS	FISSION		TOPFULL
FGHIMNU	HUMFING	FGINRRU	FURRING	FIINRTY	NITRIFY	FLLOSUU	SOULFUL
FGHINOO	HOOFING	FGINRSU	SURFING	FIIPSTY	TIPSIFY	FLLOUWY	WOFULLY
FGHINOU	HOUFING	FGINRSY	FRYINGS	FIIRTVY	VITRIFY	FLLSTUU	LUSTFUL
FGHINOW	HOWFING	FGINRTU	TURFING	FIJLLOY	JOLLIFY	FLMMOUX	FLUMMOX
FGHIOSY	FOGYISH	FGINSSU	FUSSING	FIJSTUY	JUSTIFY	FLMNOOU	MOUFLON
FGHIRST	FRIGHTS	FGINSTU	FUSTING	FIKKLNO	KINFOLK	FLMNOSU	MUFLONS
FGHNOOR	FOGHORN	FGINTTU	TUFTING	FIKLLSU	SKILFUL	FLMOOOT	TOMFOOL
FGIIKNN	FINKING	FGINUZZ	FUZZING	FIKLNOW	WOLFKIN	FLMOORS	FORMOLS
	KNIFING	FGIORST	FRIGOTS	FIKLNSU	SKINFUL	FLMOORU	ROOMFUL
FGIIKNR	FIRKING	FGIORTW	FIGWORT	FIKLRSU	RISKFUL	FLNOORR	FORLORN
FGIIKNS	FISKING	FGISTUU	FUGUIST	FIKNNOS	FINNSKO	FLNOOSU	UNFOOLS
FGIILLN	FILLING	FGJLSUU	JUGFULS	FILLMOY	MOLLIFY	FLNOOSW	ONFLOWS
FGIILMN	FILMING	FGLLNUU	LUNGFUL	FILLNUY	NULLIFY	FLNRSUU	UNFURLS
FGIILNO	FOILING	FGLMSUU	MUGFULS	FILLOTU	TOILFUL		URNFULS
FGIILNR	RIFLING	FGLNORU	FURLONG	FILLOTY	LOFTILY	FLOORSW	FORSLOW
FGIILNS	FILINGS	FGLNOSU	SONGFUL	FILLPSU	UPFILLS	FLOOTUW	OUTFLOW
FGIILNT	FLITING	FGLNPUU	UPFLUNG	FILLSTU	LISTFUL	FLOPSTU	POTFULS
	LIFTING	FGLOOUY	UFOLOGY	FILMNOO	MONOFIL	FLOPSUW	UPFLOWS
FGIILNX	FLIXING	FGLORSU	FULGORS	FILMSTU	MISTFUL	FLOSUUV	FULVOUS
FGIILNY	LIGNIFY	FGLORUU	FULGOUR	FILNNUY	FUNNILY	FLPRSUU	UPFURLS
FGIIMNR	FIRMING	FGLOTUY	GOUTFLY	FILNORS	FLORINS	FLRSSUU	SULFURS
FGIINNO	FOINING	FGLSTUU	GUSTFUL	FILNOSW	INFLOWS	FMNORSU	UNFORMS
FGIINNS	FININGS	FGNOORU	FOURGON	FILNOUX	FLUXION	FMRSTUU	FRUSTUM
FGIINRR	FIRRING	FGNORSY	GRYFONS	FILNSTU	TINFULS	FNNNUUY	UNFUNNY
FGIINRS	FIRINGS	FGNOSUU	FUNGOUS	FILNTUY	UNFITLY	FNNOORT	FRONTON
FGIINRT	RIFTING	FHIILMS	FILMISH	FILOOTW	WITLOOF	FNOORRW	FORWORN
FGIINRY	NIGRIFY	FHIINPS	PINFISH	FILORST	FIRLOTS	FNOORSU	UNROOFS
FGIINRZ	FRIZING	FHILLSU	FULLISH		FLORIST	FNOPRTU	UPFRONT
FGIINST	FISTING	FHILOOS	FOOLISH	FILORSV	FRIVOLS	FNRSTUU	UNTURFS
	SIFTING	FHILOSW	WOLFISH	FILORTU	FLORUIT	FNSTTUU	UNSTUFT
FGIINSX	FIXINGS	FHILPSU	SHIPFUL	FILORTY	TRIFOLY	FOOOORTT	FOOTROT
FGIINSY	SIGNIFY	FHILPTU	PITHFUL	FILOSSS	FOSSILS	FOOOTTU	OUTFOOT
FGIINTT	FITTING	FHILSUW	WISHFUL	FILPPUY	PULPIFY	FOORSSS	FOSSORS
	TIFTING	FHINOSU	FUSHION	FILPSTU	UPLIFTS	FOORTTX	FOXTROT
FGIINZZ	FIZZING	FHINRSU	FURNISH	FILRSTY	FIRSTLY	FORRSUW	FURROWS
FGIKLNU	FLUKING	FHIOOST	OOFTISH	FILRYZZ	FRIZZLY	FORRUWY	FURROWY
FGIKNNU	FUNKING	FHIOPPS	FOPPISH	FILSSUY	FUSSILY	FORSSTW	FROWSTS
FGIKNOR	FORKING	FHIOPSX	FOXSHIP	FILSTTU	FLUTIST	FORSTWY	FROWSTY
FGILLNU	FULLING	FHIORRY	HORRIFY	FILSTUW	WISTFUL	GGGGIIN	GIGGING
FGILNOO	FOOLING	FHIOSST	SOFTISH	FILSTUY	FUSTILY	GGGHINO	HOGGING
	LOOFING	FHIPPSU	PUPFISH	FILSTWY	SWIFTLY	GGGHINU	HUGGING
FGILNOP	FOPLING	FHIRSST	SHRIFTS	FIMMMUY	MUMMIFY	GGGIIJN	JIGGING
FGILNOT	LOFTING	FHIRSTT	THRIFTS	FIMMORS	MISFORM	GGGIILN	LIGGING
FGILNOU	FOULING	FHIRTTY	THRIFTY	FIMNORS	INFORMS	GGGIINP	PIGGING
FGILNOW	FLOWING	FHIRTUY	THURIFY	FIMNORU	UNIFORM	GGGIINR	RIGGING
	FOWLING	FHISSSU	HUSSIFS	FIMOORV	OVIFORM	GGGIINT	TIGGING
	WOLFING	FHISSTU	SHUFTIS	FIMORRT	TRIFORM	GGGIINW	WIGGING
FGILNOY	FOYLING	FHKORTU	FUTHORK	FIMORTY	MORTIFY	GGGIINZ	ZIGGING
FGILNPY	FLYPING	FHLNORU	HORNFUL	FIMRTUY	FURMITY	GGGIIST	GIGGITS
FGILNRU	FURLING	FHLNSUU	UNFLUSH	FIMSTYY	MYSTIFY	GGGIJNO	JOGGING
FGILNSU	INGULFS	FHLOPSU	SHOPFUL	FINOOSS	FOISONS	GGGIJNU	JUGGING
FGILNSY	FLYINGS	FHLPSUU	PUSHFUL	FINOPRS	FRIPONS	GGGILNO	LOGGING
FGILNTU	FLUTING	FHLRTUU	HURTFUL	FINOPTY	PONTIFY	GGGILNU	LUGGING
FGILNTY	FLYTING		RUTHFUL	FINORSS	FRISSON	GGGIMNU	MUGGING
FGILNUX	FLUXING	FHOOORS	FORHOOS	FINORST	FORINTS	GGGINNO	GONGING
FGILOOY	GOOFILY	FHOOORT	HOOFROT	FINOSSU	FUSIONS		NOGGING
FGILORY	GLORIFY	FHOORSW	FORHOWS	FIOORSU	FURIOSO	GGGINOR	GORGING
		FHORSTU	FOURTHS	FIOPRST	FORPITS	GGGINOS	SOGGING
						GGGINOT	TOGGING

GGGINOU GOUGING	GGIMNSU MUGGINS	GHIKNOO HOOKING	GHIORST RIGHTOS
GGGINPU PUGGING	GGINNNU GUNNING	GHIKNOW HOWKING	GHIORSU ROGUISH
GGGINRU RUGGING	GGINNOO ONGOING	GHIKNST KNIGHTS	GHIOSUV VOGUISH
GGGINTU TUGGING	GGINNOP PONGING	GHIKNSU HUSKING	GHIPRST SPRIGHT
GGHHIIN HIGHING	GGINNOR GRONING	GHIKNTY KYTHING	GHIPRTU UPRIGHT
GGHHIOS HOGGISH	GGINNOS NOGGINS	GHILLNU HULLING	GHIPSST SPIGHTS
GGHIIJS JIGGISH	GGINNOW GOWNING	GHILLSU GULLISH	GHIPTTU UPTIGHT
GGHIINN HINGING	GGINNRU GURNING	GHILLTY LIGHTLY	GHIQSTU QUIGHTS
NIGHING	GGINOOS GOOSING	GHILNOS HOLINGS	GHIRSTW WRIGHTS
GGHIINS SIGHING	GGINOPR GROPING	LONGISH	GHISTTW TWIGHTS
GGHIIPS PIGGISH	PORGING	GHILNOT THOLING	GHLMOOO HOMOLOG
GGHIIRS RIGGISH	GGINOPU UPGOING	GHILNOW HOWLING	GHLOOSY SHOOGLY
GGHIITT THIGGIT	GGINOQS QIGONGS	GHILNPU INGULPH	GHLOPSU PLOUGHS
GGHIMSU MUGGISH	GGINORS GORINGS	GHILNRU HURLING	GHLORUY ROUGHLY
GGHINNO HONGING	GRINGOS	GHILNSU LUSHING	GHLOSSU SLOUGHS
GGHINOS HOGGINS	GGINORU ROGUING	GHILNSY SHINGLY	GHLOSTY GHOSTLY
GGHINSU GUSHING	ROUGING	GHILNTY NIGHTLY	GHLOSUY SLOUGHY
GGHIPSU PUGGISH	GGINORW GROWING	GHILPST PLIGHTS	GHLOTUY TOUGHLY
GGHLOSY SHOGGLY	GGINOUV VOGUING	GHILPTY YPLIGHT	GHMORSU SORGHUM
GGIIILN GINGILI	GGINPPY GYPPING	GHILRTY RIGHTLY	GHMOSTU MUGSHOT
GGIIJJS JIGJIGS	GGINPRU PURGING	GHILSST SLIGHTS	GHMPRSU GRUMPHS
GGIIKNN KINGING	GGINRSU SURGING	GHILSTY SIGHTLY	GHNOPRY GRYPHON
GGIILLN GILLING	URGINGS	GHILTTY TIGHTLY	GHNORST THRONGS
GGIILNP PIGLING	GGINSTU GUSTING	GHILTWY WIGHTLY	GHNORUU UNROUGH
GGIILNR RIGLING	GGINTTU GUTTING	GHIMMNU HUMMING	GHNOSSU SHOGUNS
GGIILNU GUILING	GGIOORS GORGIOS	GHIMMNY HYMNING	GHNOSTU GUNSHOT
GGIIMNN MINGING	GGIPRSY SPRIGGY	GHIMNOS GNOMISH	NOUGHTS
GGIIMNP GIMPING	GGLLOOS LOGLOGS	HOMINGS	SHOTGUN
GGIIMNR GRIMING	GGLOOOS GOOGOLS	GHIMNPU HUMPING	GHNOTUY YOUNGTH
GGIINNN GINNING	GGNOORS GORGONS	GHIMNRY RHYMING	GHOOOSW HOOSGOW
GGIINNO INGOING	GGHHIIS HIGHISH	GHIMNSU MUSHING	GHOORSS SORGHOS
GGIINNP PINGING	GGHHIST HIGHTHS	GHIMRSU SIMURGH	GHORSTU TROUGHS
GGIINNR GIRNING	GGHIINS HISHING	GHIMSST SMIGHTS	GHORSTW GROWTHS
RINGING	GGHINSU HUSHING	GHIMSTT MIGHTST	GHORTUW WROUGHT
GGIINNS SIGNING	GGHIRST SHRIGHT	GHINNOP PHONING	GHORTUY YOGHURT
SINGING	GGHORTU THROUGH	GHINNOR HORNING	GHOSTUU OUTGUSH
GGIINNT TINGING	GGHOSSU SHOUGHS	GHINNOS NOSHING	GIIINRS IRISING
GGIINNW WINGING	GGHOTTU THOUGHT	GHINNOT NOTHING	GIIJKNN JINKING
GGIINNZ ZINGING	GGHIIKNO HOIKING	GHINNTU HUNTING	GIIJLNT JILTING
GGIINPR GRIPING	GGHIIKNT KITHING	GHINOOP HOOPING	GIIJNNO JOINING
GGIINPS PIGGINS	GGHIILLN HILLING	GHINOOS SHOOING	GIIJNNX JINXING
GGIINRS GRISING	GGHIILNR HIRLING	GHINOOT HOOTING	GIIKKNN KINKING
GGIINRT GIRTING	GGHIILNT HILTING	GHINOOV HOOVING	GIIKKNR KIRKING
RINGGIT	LITHING	GHINOPP HOPPING	GIIKLLN KILLING
GGIINSU GUISING	GGHIILNW WHILING	GHINOPS GINSHOP	GIIKLMN MILKING
GGIINSV GIVINGS	GGHIILRS GIRLISH	POSHING	GIIKLNN INKLING
GGIIRRS GRIGRIS	GGHIINNS SHINING	GHINORS HORSING	KILNING
GGJINSU JUGGINS	GGHIINNT HINTING	SHORING	LINKING
GGILLNU GULLING	NITHING	GHINORW WHORING	GIIKLNR LIRKING
GGILNNO LONGING	GGHIINOS HOISING	GHINOST HOSTING	GIIKLNS LIKINGS
GGILNNU LUNGING	GGHIINPP HIPPING	TOSHING	SILKING
GGILNOS GOSLING	GGHIINPS PISHING	GHINOSU HOUSING	GIIKLNT KILTING
OGLINGS	GGHIINPT PITHING	GHINOSV SHOVING	KITLING
GGILNOV GLOVING	GGHIINRS HIRINGS	GHINOSW SHOWING	GIIKNPP PINKING
GGILNOW GLOWING	GGHIINSS HISSING	GHINOTT HOTTING	GIIKNRR RINKING
GOWLING	GGHIINST HISTING	TONIGHT	GIIKNNS SINKING
GGILNOZ GLOZING	INSIGHT	GHINOTU THOUING	GIIKNNT TINKING
GGILNPU GULPING	SHITING	GHINPPU HUPPING	GIIKNNV KNIVING
GGILNRU GURLING	SITHING	GHINPPY HYPPING	GIIKNNW WINKING
GGILNSU LUGINGS	GGHIINSW WISHING	GHINPSU GUNSHIP	GIIKNNZ ZINKING
GGILNUY GUYLING	GGHIINTT HITTING	PUSHING	GIIKNPP KIPPING
UGLYING	TITHING	GHINRSU RUSHING	GIIKNPS PIGSKIN
GGILOOS GIGOLOS	GGHIINTW WHITING	GHINRTU HURTING	SPIKING
GGILOST GIGLOTS	WITHING	UNGIRTH	GIIKNRS GIRKINS
GGILOSY SOGGILY	GGHIINZZ HIZZING	UNRIGHT	GRISKIN
GGILRWY WRIGGLY	GGHIIRST TIGRISH	GHINSTU TUSHING	KRISING
GGIMMNU GUMMING	GGHIJNOS JOSHING	UNSIGHT	RISKING
GGIMNOR GORMING	GGHIKLNU HULKING	GHINTTU HUTTING	GIIKNRT TRIKING
GGIMNPU GUMPING	GGHIKNNO HONKING	GHINTTY TYTHING	GIIKNRY YIRKING
GGIMNPY GYMPING		GHIOPSZ PHIZOGS	GIIKNSS KISSING

	SKIINGS	GIINNOP	OPINING	GIJLLNO	JOLLING	
GIIKNST	KISTING		PIONING	GIJLNOT	JOLTING	
	SKITING	GIINNOR	IRONING	GIJLNOU	JOULING	
GIIKNSV	SKIVING		ROINING	GIJLNOW	JOWLING	
	VIKINGS	GIINNOS	NOISING	GIJLNSU	JUNGLIS	
GIIKNTT	KITTING	GIINNOT	OINTING	GIJMNPU	JUMPING	
GIILLLN	LILLING	GIINNPP	NIPPING	GIJNOTT	JOTTING	
GIILLMN	MILLING	GIINNPS	SNIPING	GIJNSTU	JUSTING	
GIILLNN	NILLING	GIINNPU	PINGUIN	GIJNTTU	JUTTING	
GIILLNO	GILLION	GIINNRS	RINSING	GIKKNNO	KONKING	
GIILLNP	PILLING	GIINNRT	TRINING	GIKKNOO	KOOKING	
GIILLNR	RILLING	GIINNRU	INURING	GIKKNOY	YOKKING	
GIILLNT	LILTING		RUINING	GIKLNOO	LOOKING	
	TILLING		URINING	GIKLNOP	POLKING	
GIILLNW	WILLING	GIINNSW	INSWING	GIKLNRU	LURKING	
GIILMNN	LIMNING	GIINNTT	TINTING	GIKLNSU	LUSKING	
GIILMNO	MOILING	GIINNTU	UNITING		SULKING	
GIILMNP	LIMPING	GIINNTV	VINTING	GIKMNOS	SMOKING	
GIILMNS	LIMINGS	GIINNTW	TWINING	GIKMNSU	MUSKING	
	SLIMING	GIINOPS	POISING	GIKNNOO	KONNING	
	SMILING	GIINORS	ORIGINS	GIKNNOP	PONKING	
GIILMNT	MILTING		SIGNIOR	GIKNNOS	SNOKING	
GIILMPR	PILGRIM		SIGNORI	GIKNNOT	TONKING	
GIILMRY	GRIMILY	GIINORT	RIOTING	GIKNNOW	KNOWING	
GIILNNN	LINNING	GIINOSY	YOGINIS	GIKNNSU	UNKINGS	
GIILNNR	NIRLING	GIINPPP	PIPPING	GIKNOOP	POOKING	
GIILNNS	LIGNINS	GIINPPR	RIPPING	GIKNOOR	ROOKING	
	LININGS	GIINPPS	PIPINGS	GIKNOPR	PROKING	
GIILNNY	INLYING		SIPPING	GIKNOPU	POUKING	
GIILNOR	LIGROIN	GIINPPT	TIPPING	GIKNORT	TROKING	
	ROILING	GIINPPY	YIPPING	GIKNORW	WORKING	
GIILNOS	SILOING	GIINPPZ	ZIPPING	GIKNORY	YORKING	
	SOILING	GIINPQU	PIQUING	GIKNOST	STOKING	
GIILNOT	TOILING	GIINPRS	PRISING	GIKNOSY	YOKINGS	
GIILNPP	LIPPING		RISPING	GIKNOUY	YOUKING	
GIILNPS	LISPING		SPIRING	GIKNRSY	SKRYING	
	SPILING	GIINPRZ	PRIZING		SKYRING	
GIILNRS	RIGLINS	GIINPSS	PISSING	GIKNSTU	TUSKING	
GIILNRT	TIRLING	GIINPST	SPITING	GIKNSTY	SKYTING	
GIILNST	LISTING	GIINPSW	SWIPING	GIKRSTU	TUGRIKS	
	SILTING		WIPINGS	GILLLNO	LOLLING	
	STILING		WISPING	GILLLNU	LULLING	
	TILINGS	GIINPTT	PITTING	GILLMNU	MULLING	
GIILNSV	LIVINGS	GIINPTY	PITYING	GILLNNU	NULLING	
	SLIVING	GIINQRU	QUIRING	GILLNOP	POLLING	
GIILNTT	TILTING	GIINQTU	QUITING	GILLNOR	ROLLING	
	TITLING	GIINRRS	SIRRING	GILLNOT	TOLLING	
GIILNTW	WILTING	GIINRRT	TIRRING	GILLNPU	PULLING	
	WITLING	GIINRSS	RISINGS	GILLNSU	ULLINGS	
GIILOSS	GLIOSIS	GIINRST	STIRING	GILLNUW	WULLING	
GIILOST	OLIGIST		TIRINGS	GILLNYY	LYINGLY	
GIILRST	STRIGIL	GIINRSV	VIRGINS	GILLORS	RIGOLLS	
GIIMMNN	NIMMING	GIINRSW	WIRINGS	GILMNOO	LOOMING	
GIIMMNR	RIMMING	GIINRTT	RITTING		MOOLING	
GIIMNNS	MININGS	GIINRTW	TWIRING	GILMNOR	MORLING	
GIIMNNT	MINTING		WRITING	GILMNOT	MOLTING	
GIIMNPP	PIMPING	GIINSST	SISTING	GILMNOY	MOYLING	
GIIMNPR	PRIMING	GIINSSU	ISSUING	GILMNPU	LUMPING	
GIIMNRT	MITRING	GIINSSW	WISSING		PLUMING	
GIIMNSS	MISSING	GIINSSZ	SIZINGS	GILMNRU	MURLING	
GIIMNST	MISTING	GIINSTT	SITTING	GILMNSU	LIGNUMS	
	SMITING	GIINSTU	SUITING	GILNNOO	GLONOIN	
	STIMING	GIINSTV	STIVING		LOONING	
	TIMINGS	GIINSTW	WISTING	GILNNOU	LOUNING	
GIINNNP	PINNING	GIINTTT	TITTING	GILNNOW	LOWNING	
GIINNNR	RINNING	GIINTTW	WITTING	GILNNRU	NURLING	
GIINNNS	INNINGS	GIINZZZ	ZIZZING	GILNNSU	UNSLING	
	SINNING	GIJKNNU	JUNKING	GILNNTU	LUNTING	
GIINNNT	TINNING	GIJKNOO	JOOKING	GILNNUV	VULNING	
GIINNNW	WINNING	GIJKNOU	JOUKING	GILNOOP	LOOPING	

	POOLING
GILNOOS	LOOSING
	SOLOING
	SOOLING
GILNOOT	LOOTING
	TOOLING
GILNOPP	LOPPING
GILNOPR	PROLING
GILNOPS	POLINGS
	SLOPING
GILNOPT	POLTING
GILNOPU	LOUPING
GILNOPW	PLOWING
GILNORS	LORINGS
GILNORU	LOURING
GILNOSS	LOSINGS
GILNOST	LINGOTS
	TIGLONS
	TOLINGS
GILNOSU	LOUSING
GILNOSV	LOVINGS
	SOLVING
GILNOSW	LOWINGS
	LOWSING
	SLOWING
	SOWLING
GILNOTT	LOTTING
GILNOTU	LOUTING
GILNOTW	LOWTING
GILNOVV	VOLVING
GILNOVW	WOLVING
GILNOWY	YOWLING
GILNPPU	PULPING
GILNPRU	PURLING
GILNPSU	PLUSING
	PULINGS
	PULSING
	PUSLING
GILNPUY	UPLYING
GILNRSU	RULINGS
GILNSTU	LUSTING
	LUTINGS
	SINGULT
GILNSTY	STYLING
GILNVYY	VYINGLY
GILOORS	GIROSOL
GILORTT	TRIGLOT
GILORTY	TRILOGY
GILOSTT	GLOTTIS
GILRSTY	GRISTLY
GILRTUY	LITURGY
GILRYZZ	GRIZZLY
GIMMMNU	MUMMING
GIMMNPU	MUMPING
GIMMNRY	RYMMING
GIMMNSU	SUMMING
GIMMNUV	VUMMING
GIMMORS	GIMMORS
GIMNNOO	MOONING
GIMNNOR	MORNING
GIMNNTU	MUNTING
GIMNOOP	MOOPING
GIMNOOR	MOORING
	ROOMING
GIMNOOS	SOOMING
GIMNOOT	MOOTING
	TOOMING
GIMNOOV	MOOVING
GIMNOOZ	ZOOMING
GIMNOPP	MOPPING

GIMNOPR	ROMPING
GIMNOPU	MOUPING
GIMNOPY	YOMPING
GIMNORS	SMORING
GIMNORU	ROUMING
GIMNORW	WORMING
GIMNOSS	MOSSING
GIMNOST	GNOMIST
GIMNOSU	MOUSING
	SOUMING
GIMNOSW	MOWINGS
	SOWMING
GIMNPPU	PUMPING
GIMNPRU	RUMPING
GIMNPSU	IMPUGNS
	SPUMING
GIMNPTU	TUMPING
GIMNSSU	MUSINGS
	MUSSING
GIMNSTU	MUSTING
GIMNSTY	STYMING
GIMORSS	SIMORGS
GIMOSSY	YOGISMS
GIMOSTU	GOMUTIS
GIMRSSU	SIMURGS
GIMRSUU	GURUISM
GINNNOO	NOONING
GINNNOR	RONNING
GINNNOW	WONNING
GINNNPU	PUNNING
GINNNRU	RUNNING
GINNNSU	SUNNING
GINNNTU	TUNNING
GINNOOS	NOOSING
GINNOOW	WOONING
GINNOPS	SPONGIN
GINNOPY	PONYING
GINNORS	SNORING
	SORNING
GINNORU	GRUNION
GINNORW	INGROWN
GINNORY	ROYNING
GINNOSS	NOSINGS
GINNOST	STONING
GINNOSW	SNOWING
	WONINGS
GINNOSZ	ZONINGS
GINNOTW	WONTING
GINNPRU	PRUNING
GINNPTU	PUNTING
GINNRSU	NURSING
	URNINGS
GINNRTU	TURNING
GINNSTU	TUNINGS
GINNTTU	NUTTING
GINNTUY	UNTYING
GINOOPP	POOPING
GINOOPR	ROOPING
GINOOPS	SOOPING
GINOOPT	POOTING
GINOORS	ROOSING
GINOORT	ROOTING
GINOOSS	ISOGONS
GINOOST	SOOTING
GINOOSW	WOOINGS
GINOOTT	TOOTING
GINOPPP	POPPING
GINOPPS	SOPPING
GINOPPT	TOPPING
GINOPPU	POUPING

GINOPPW	WOPPING
GINOPRS	PROIGNS
	PROSING
	ROPINGS
GINOPRT	PORTING
	TROPING
GINOPRU	INGROUP
	POURING
	ROUPING
GINOPRV	PROVING
GINOPRW	POWRING
GINOPSS	POSINGS
	POSSING
GINOPST	POSTING
	STOPING
GINOPSY	POYSING
GINOPTT	POTTING
GINOPTU	POUTING
GINOQTU	QUOTING
GINORRV	VORRING
GINORSS	GRISONS
	INGROSS
	SIGNORS
GINORST	ROSTING
	SORTING
	STORING
	TRIGONS
GINORSU	ROUSING
	SOURING
GINORSV	ROVINGS
GINORSW	ROWINGS
	WORSING
GINORSY	ROSYING
	SIGNORY
GINORTT	ROTTING
GINORTU	ROUTING
	TOURING
GINORTW	ROWTING
	TROWING
GINOSSS	SOSSING
GINOSST	STINGOS
	TOSSING
GINOSSU	SOUSING
GINOSSW	SOWINGS
	SOWSING
GINOSTT	SOTTING
GINOSTU	OUSTING
	OUTINGS
	TOUSING
GINOSTV	STOVING
GINOSTW	STOWING
	TOWINGS
	TOWSING
GINOSTY	TOYINGS
GINOTTT	TOTTING
GINOTTU	TOUTING
GINOTTW	TOWTING
	WOTTING
GINOTUW	OUTWING
GINOTUZ	TOUZING
GINOTWZ	TOWZING
GINPPPU	PUPPING
GINPPSU	SUPPING
	UPPINGS
GINPPTU	TUPPING
GINPRRU	PURRING
GINPRSS	SPRINGS
GINPRSU	PURSING
GINPRSY	PRYINGS
	PRYSING

	SPRINGY
GINPSSY	SPYINGS
GINPSTU	STUPING
GINPSTY	TYPINGS
GINPSUW	UPSWING
GINPTTU	PUTTING
GINPTUY	UPTYING
GINQTUY	QUYTING
GINRRSU	RUNRIGS
GINRSST	STRINGS
GINRSTU	RUSTING
GINRSTY	STRINGY
	STYRING
	TRYINGS
GINRSUU	USURING
GINRTTU	RUTTING
GINSSSU	SUSSING
GINTTTU	TUTTING
GIOOPRR	PORRIGO
GIOORSV	VIGOROS
GIOPRRU	PRURIGO
GIOPSSS	GOSSIPS
GIOPSST	SPIGOTS
GIOPSSY	GOSSIPY
GIORRSU	RIGOURS
GIORSUV	VIGOURS
GIOSSYZ	ZYGOSIS
GISWWYY	WYSIWYG
GJNOOSU	GOUJONS
GJNRSUU	GURJUNS
GJOORTT	JOGTROT
GKMOOSU	GOMOKUS
GLLOOPS	GOLLOPS
GLMNOOS	MONGOLS
GLMOOOR	MOORLOG
GLMOOYY	MYOLOGY
GLMORUW	LUGWORM
GLNNOOR	LORGNON
GLNNSUU	UNSLUNG
GLNOOOS	OOLONGS
GLNOOOY	NOOLOGY
GLNOOPR	PROLONG
GLNOOPY	POLYGON
GLNOOSU	OULONGS
GLNORWY	WRONGLY
GLNOSUW	SUNGLOW
GLNOTTU	GLUTTON
GLNOUYY	YOUNGLY
GLNPSUU	UNPLUGS
GLOOORY	OROLOGY
GLOOOTY	OTOLOGY
GLOOOYZ	ZOOLOGY
GLOORUY	UROLOGY
GLOPSTU	PUTLOGS
GLORSSY	GROSSLY
GLPRSUY	SPLURGY
GMMOSUU	GUMMOUS
GMMPUUW	MUGWUMP
GMNNOOS	GNOMONS
GMNOORU	GUNROOM
GMNOORW	MORWONG
GMNSTUU	GUMNUTS
GMNSUUZ	MZUNGUS
GMOOPRS	POGROMS
GMOOSTU	GOMUTOS
GMORSUU	GRUMOUS
GMORTUW	MUGWORT
GMPSSUY	GYPSUMS
GMRUYYZ	ZYMURGY
GNNORUW	UNGROWN

GNNORYY	GYRONNY
GNNOSUW	UNGOWNS
GNNRUUW	UNWRUNG
GNOOORS	GORSOON
GNOOOSS	GOSSOON
GNOOOYZ	ZOOGONY
GNOORST	TROGONS
GNOPPSU	OPPUGNS
GNOPRTU	GUNPORT
GNOPRUW	UPGROWN
GNOPSTU	POTGUNS
GNOSTUU	OUTGUNS
GOOOORS	GOROOOS
GOORSTT	GROTTOS
GOORTUW	OUTGROW
GOPRSUW	UPGROWS
GORRSTU	TURGORS
GORSTTU	ROTGUTS
GORSTUY	YOGURTS
HHIIPPS	HIPPISH
HHIISTW	WHITISH
HHIMRTY	RHYTHMI
HHINORS	HORNISH
HHIORSW	WHORISH
HHIOSTT	HOTTISH
HHISSTW	WHISHTS
HHMMSUU	HUMHUMS
HHMRSTY	RHYTHMS
HHOOSTT	HOTSHOT
HIIJKNS	HIJINKS
HIIKLMS	KHILIMS
HIIKNPS	KINSHIP
	PINKISH
HIILMTU	LITHIUM
HIILPST	SHILPIT
HIILPTY	PITHILY
HIILRTT	TRILITH
HIIMMSS	MISHMIS
HIIMPSW	WIMPISH
HIIMSSS	MISSISH
HIIMSST	MISHITS
HIIMSTT	SHITTIM
HIINORS	ROINISH
HIINPSS	INSHIPS
HIINSSW	SWINISH
HIIOPRZ	RHIZOPI
HIIORST	HISTRIO
HIKLSSU	LUSKISH
HIKLSUY	HUSKILY
HIKMNOS	MONKISH
HIKMRSU	MURKISH
HIKMSUZ	MUZHIKS
HIKNNOR	INKHORN
HIKNNTU	UNTHINK
HIKNRSS	SHRINKS
HIKOORS	ROOKISH
HILLOPT	HILLTOP
HILLOPY	LYOPHIL
HILLPSU	UPHILLS
HILLRRS	SHRILLS
HILLRST	THRILLS
HILLRSY	SHRILLY
HILLRTY	THRILLY
HILMMOU	HOLMIUM
HILMOPS	LOMPISH
	PHLOMIS
HILMOSS	HOLISMS
HILMOSW	WHOLISM
HILMPSU	LUMPISH
HILMSSY	HYLISMS

HILMSUY	MUSHILY	HIQSSUY	SQUISHY
HILMTUU	THULIUM	HIRSSTT	THIRSTS
HILNNTY	NINTHLY		THRISTS
HILNPST	PLINTHS	HIRSTTU	RUTTISH
HILOOTT	OTOLITH	HIRSTTY	THIRSTY
HILOOTZ	ZOOLITH		THRISTY
HILORTU	UROLITH	HKKLOOZ	KOLKHOZ
HILOSST	HOLISTS	HKNOOSU	UNHOOKS
HILOSSW	SLOWISH	HKNSSUU	UNHUSKS
HILOSTU	LOUTISH	HKOOOPT	POTHOOK
HILOSTY	HYLOIST	HKOOSST	SHTOOKS
HILOSVW	WOLVISH	HLLOOSW	HOLLOWS
HILOSWY	SHOWILY	HLLOPSY	PHYLLOS
HILOTWW	WHITLOW	HLMNOTY	MONTHLY
HILPRUW	UPWHIRL	HLMNPYY	NYMPHLY
HILPSST	SPILTHS	HLMORRY	MYRRHOL
HILSSTY	HYLISTS	HLMOSTY	THYMOLS
	STYLISH	HLOOSTY	SOOTHLY
HILSTTY	THISTLY	HLOPRTY	PROTHYL
HILSTXY	SIXTHLY	HLORSTY	SHORTLY
HIMMPSU	MUMPISH	HLOTUYY	YOUTHLY
HIMMRSU	RUMMISH	HLPRSUU	SULPHUR
HIMMSTY	MYTHISM		UPHURLS
HIMNOOS	MOONISH	HMMMSUU	HUMMUMS
HIMNSSU	MUNSHIS	HMMNOOY	HOMONYM
HIMNSTY	HYMNIST	HMMRTUY	THRUMMY
HIMOORS	MOORISH	HMNOPSY	NYMPHOS
HIMOPRS	ROMPISH	HMNOPYY	HYPONYM
HIMOPSS	SOPHISM	HMNPSUY	HYPNUMS
HIMOPST	PHOTISM	HMOOPRS	MORPHOS
HIMORTU	THORIUM	HMOOSST	SMOOTHS
HIMOTTY	TIMOTHY	HMORSUU	HUMOURS
HIMPRSS	SHRIMPS	HMSTUYZ	ZYTHUMS
HIMPRTU	TRIUMPH	HNNOOPS	PHONONS
HIMPTUY	PYTHIUM	HNNORSU	UNSHORN
HIMRSTY	RHYMIST	HNNOSUW	UNSHOWN
HIMSSTU	ISTHMUS	HNOOPST	PHOTONS
HIMSTTY	MYTHIST	HNOOPSU	UNHOOPS
HINNNSU	NUNNISH	HNOOPTY	TYPHOON
HINNORT	TINHORN	HNOORSS	HORSONS
HINNOST	TONNISH	HNOORST	THORONS
HINNPSU	NUNSHIP	HNOORSU	HONOURS
HINOOPS	INHOOPS	HNOOSTU	UNSHOOT
HINOORT	HORNITO	HNOPSSY	SYPHONS
HINOORZ	HORIZON	HNOPSTY	PHYTONS
HINOOST	INSOOTH		PYTHONS
HINOPPS	SHIPPON		TYPHONS
HINOPSS	SIPHONS	HNORTUW	UNWORTH
	SONSHIP	HNOSTUU	UNSHOUT
HINORST	HORNIST	HNRTTUU	UNTRUTH
HINORSU	NOURISH	HNSSTUU	UNSHUTS
HINORSY	ROYNISH	HOOPRST	PORTHOS
HINOSSW	SNOWISH	HOOPSTT	HOTPOTS
HINOSTW	TOWNISH	HOOPSTU	UPSHOOT
HINPSSU	UNSHIPS	HOOPSTY	TOYSHOP
HINPTUW	UNWHIPT	HOORRRS	HORRORS
HINRSTU	RUNTISH	HOORRST	ORTHROS
HIOOPRS	POORISH	HOORSUZ	HUZOORS
HIOOSSV	SHIVOOS	HOOSTTU	OUTSHOT
HIOPPSS	SHIPPOS	HOPRTUW	UPTHROW
HIOPRSW	WORSHIP	HOPSSSY	HYSSOPS
HIOPSST	SOPHIST	HOPSSTU	UPSHOTS
HIOPSSY	PHYSIOS	HOPSTUY	TYPHOUS
HIOPSTU	UPHOIST	HORSTUU	OUTRUSH
HIORSSU	SOURISH	HOSSTTU	STOUTHS
HIORSTY	HISTORY	HRSSTTU	THRUSTS
HIOSSTT	SOTTISH	HRSSTUY	THYRSUS
HIOSTTU	OUTHITS	IIIJJLN	JINJILI
HIOTTUW	OUTWITH	IIIKMNN	MINIKIN
	WITHOUT	IIIMRST	MIRITIS

IIISTTW	WISTITI	IIINOSUV	INVIOUS
IIJMNOS	MISJOIN	IINOTTU	TUITION
IIJNNOT	INJOINT	IINPPPS	PIPPINS
IIKLLMY	MILKILY	IINQRUY	INQUIRY
IIKLLSY	SILKILY	IINRTTY	TRINITY
IIKLMNP	LIMPKIN	IINSSST	INSISTS
IIKLNOS	OILSKIN	IINSTTU	INTUITS
IIKLPSY	SPIKILY	IINSTTW	INTWIST
IIKLRSY	RISKILY		NITWITS
IIKMNOR	KIRIMON	IIOPRSS	PISSOIR
IIKMNPS	SIMPKIN	IIORSSV	VIROSIS
IIKMNSS	SIMKINS	IIORSTV	IVORIST
IIKNPPS	PIPKINS		VISITOR
IIKNSSS	SISKINS	IIOSTTU	OUSTITI
IIKOSST	OIKISTS	IIPPSUU	PIUPIUS
IIKOSTT	TITOKIS	IIPRSST	SPIRITS
IILLLSY	SILLILY		TRIPSIS
IILLMNO	MILLION	IIPRSTU	PITURIS
IILLMSY	SLIMILY	IIPRSTY	SPIRITY
IILLNOP	PILLION	IIPRTVY	PRIVITY
IILLNOZ	ZILLION	IIRRSTT	TIRRITS
IILLNST	INSTILL	IJKLLOY	KILLJOY
IILLNTT	LITTLIN	IJKMOSU	MOUJIKS
IILLPSU	ILLUPIS	IJKNOSS	JOSKINS
IILMNOS	LIONISM	IJLLLOY	JOLLILY
IILMORS	SIMILOR	IJLLOTY	JOLLITY
IILMOSS	LIMOSIS	IJLMPUY	JUMPILY
IILMSTU	STIMULI	IJLNOQU	JONQUIL
IILMSTY	MISTILY	IJLNOTY	JOINTLY
IILNNSU	INSULIN	IJMOSSS	JISSOMS
	INULINS	IJNNOTU	UNJOINT
IILNORS	SIRLOIN	IJNORSU	JUNIORS
IILNOSV	VIOLINS	IJRSSTU	JURISTS
IILNOSY	NOISILY	IKKMNOU	KIKUMON
IILNPUV	PULVINI	IKKNORT	KIRKTON
IILNRSV	RIVLINS	IKKORRS	KORKIRS
IILNSST	INSTILS	IKKSUUY	KIKUYUS
IILOPRT	TRIPOLI	IKLLSTU	KILLUTS
IILORTV	VITRIOL	IKLLSUY	SULKILY
IILOSTV	VIOLIST	IKLMNPU	LUMPKIN
IILPRVY	PRIVILY	IKLMOSY	SMOKILY
IILPSST	PISTILS	IKLMRUY	MURKILY
IILPSTY	TIPSILY	IKLMSUY	MUSKILY
IILTTUY	UTILITY	IKLNNSU	UNLINKS
IILTTWY	WITTILY	IKLNOOS	SKOLION
IIMMMNU	MINIMUM	IKLNOOT	KILOTON
IIMMNSU	MINIMUS	IKLNOSU	ULIKONS
	MINIUMS	IKLNPSU	SKULPIN
IIMNNOS	MINIONS	IKLNRWY	WRINKLY
IIMNOSS	MISSION	IKLOOTT	TOOLKIT
IIMNOSU	IONIUMS	IKLOSSU	SOUSLIK
	NIMIOUS	IKLSSSU	SUSLIKS
IIMNOTX	MIXTION	IKLSTTU	KITTULS
IIMNPRT	IMPRINT	IKMNOOO	OKIMONO
IIMOPSU	IMPIOUS	IKMNOOS	KIMONOS
IIMOSST	MITOSIS	IKMNORS	MIKRONS
IIMOSSU	SIMIOUS		MORKINS
IIMRTTU	TRITIUM	IKMNOSW	MISKNOW
IIMRTUV	TRIVIUM	IKMNPPU	PUMPKIN
IIMSSTT	TIMISTS	IKMNRSU	RUMKINS
IIMSSTU	MISSUIT	IKMNRTU	TRINKUM
IINNOOP	OPINION	IKMOOST	MISTOOK
IINNOPS	PINIONS	IKMOSSU	KOUMISS
IINNOTU	UNITION	IKMPRSS	SKRIMPS
IINOPSS	ISOSPIN	IKNNPTU	UNPINKT
	SINOPIS	IKNNSTU	UNKNITS
IINORST	IRONIST	IKNOOST	ISOKONT
IINORSV	VIRIONS	IKNOPST	INKPOTS
IINORTT	INTROIT		INKSPOT
IINOSSV	VISIONS	IKNORSW	INWORKS

IKNPSTU	SPUTNIK	ILOORTY	OLITORY
	UPKNITS	ILOOSST	SOLOIST
IKPRSSU	SPRUIKS	ILOOSTY	SOOTILY
IKPRSSY	KRYPSIS	ILOOWYZ	WOOZILY
ILLLOWY	LOWLILY	ILOPPSY	SOPPILY
ILLMNOU	MULLION	ILOPRSY	PROSILY
ILLMOOR	MOORILL	ILOPSST	PISTOLS
ILLMPUY	LUMPILY		POSTILS
ILLMSUU	LIMULUS	ILOPSSX	OXSLIPS
ILLNOQU	QUILLON	ILOPSTT	SPOTLIT
ILLNORU	RULLION	ILOPSUY	PIOUSLY
ILLNPUU	LUPULIN	ILOQRSU	LIQUORS
ILLNSUW	UNWILLS	ILORRSY	SORRILY
ILLNTUY	NULLITY	ILOSSTY	TOSSILY
ILLOORZ	ZORILLO		TYLOSIS
ILLOPRY	PILLORY	ILOSTTW	WITTOLS
ILLOPSW	PILLOWS	ILPPSTU	PULPITS
ILLOPWY	PILLOWY	ILPSTTU	UPTILTS
ILLOSUV	VILLOUS	ILRSSTU	TRISULS
ILLOSUY	LOUSILY	ILRSSTY	LYRISTS
ILLOSWW	WILLOWS	ILRSTUY	RUSTILY
ILLOTXY	XYLITOL	ILSSTTU	LUTISTS
ILLOWWY	WILLOWY	ILSSTTY	STYLIST
ILLPPUY	PULPILY	IMMNOSS	MONISMS
ILLPSUV	PULVILS		NOMISMS
ILLQSSU	SQUILLS	IMMNOSU	MUSIMON
ILLRSUY	SURLILY		OMNIUMS
ILLSTUY	LUSTILY	IMMNOUU	MUONIUM
ILMMRUY	RUMMILY	IMMOOSS	SIMOOMS
ILMMSUU	MIMULUS	IMMOPTU	OPTIMUM
ILMNOOT	MOONLIT	IMMOSSU	OSMIUMS
ILMNOSU	MOULINS	IMMOSTU	TOMIUMS
ILMNRSU	MURLINS	IMMSSTU	MUTISMS
ILMNSSU	MUSLINS		SUMMIST
ILMOORY	ROOMILY		SUMMITS
ILMOOSS	MOLOSSI	IMNNNOU	MUNNION
ILMORTU	TURMOIL	IMNNOOR	NORIMON
ILMOSTY	MOISTLY	IMNNOSW	MINNOWS
ILMPSTU	PLUMIST	IMNNSTU	MUNTINS
ILMRSSY	LYRISMS	IMNOOPP	POMPION
ILMUYZZ	MUZZILY	IMNOOPT	TOMPION
ILNNSUY	SUNNILY	IMNOORR	MORRION
ILNOOPS	PLOSION	IMNOORS	MORIONS
ILNOOPV	VOLPINO	IMNOORT	MONITOR
ILNOOST	LOTIONS		TROMINO
	SOLITON	IMNOOSS	MONOSIS
ILNOPPS	POPLINS		SIMOONS
ILNOPRU	PURLOIN	IMNOOST	MOTIONS
ILNOPST	PONTILS	IMNOOSU	OMINOUS
ILNOPSU	UPSILON	IMNOOSY	ISONOMY
ILNOPSY	YPSILON	IMNOOUX	OXONIUM
ILNOQSU	QUINOLS	IMNOPPU	PUMPION
ILNORST	NOSTRIL	IMNORRU	MURRION
ILNORSU	SURLOIN	IMNORTY	TRIONYM
ILNORTU	TORULIN	IMNOSST	MONISTS
ILNOSST	TONSILS	IMNOSSY	MYOSINS
ILNOSSU	INSOULS	IMNOSVY	VISNOMY
ILNOSTU	OILNUTS	IMNRRSU	MURRINS
	ULTIONS	IMNRSTU	UNTRIMS
ILNOSTY	STONILY	IMOOPRX	PROXIMO
ILNOSWY	SNOWILY	IMOOSSS	OSMOSIS
ILNOTUV	VOLUTIN	IMOOSSU	OSMIOUS
ILNPRSU	PURLINS	IMOOSTV	VOMITOS
ILNPSST	SPLINTS	IMOPRSS	PORISMS
ILNPSTU	UNSPILT	IMOPRST	IMPORTS
ILNRSTY	NITRYLS		TROPISM
ILNSSTU	INSULTS	IMOPSST	IMPOSTS
ILOOORS	ROSOLIO	IMOPSTU	UTOPISM
ILOOPST	POLOIST	IMORRRS	MIRRORS
ILOORST	LORIOTS		

IMORSTU	TOURISM		TROPIST
IMORSTY	TRISOMY	IOPSTTU	UTOPIST
IMOSSYZ	ZYMOSIS	IOQRTTU	QUITTOR
IMOSTTT	TOMTITS	IOQSSTU	QUOISTS
IMPRSSU	PURISMS	IORRSTW	WORRITS
IMPSSTU	SUMPITS	IORRSZZ	RIZZORS
IMQRSSU	SQUIRMS	IORRTTX	TORTRIX
IMQRSUY	SQUIRMY	IORSSTU	SUITORS
IMRSSTU	SISTRUM	IORSTTU	TOURIST
	TRISMUS	IOSSSTT	TSOTSIS
	TRUISMS	IOSSTTU	OUTSITS
IMRTTUY	YTTRIUM	IOSTTUW	OUTWITS
INNNORU	RUNNION	IPRRSTU	IRRUPTS
INNOOST	NOTIONS		STIRRUP
INNORST	INTRONS	IPRSSTU	PURISTS
INNOSSU	UNISONS		SPRUITS
INNOSTU	NONSUIT		UPRISTS
INNOSWW	WINNOWS	IPRSTUU	PURSUIT
INNQSUY	SQUINNY	IPSSSTY	STYPSIS
INOOPRT	PORTION	IPSSTTY	TYPISTS
INOOPSS	POISONS	IPSTTTU	TITTUPS
	POISSON	IPTTTUY	TITTUPY
INOOPST	OPTIONS	IQRRSSU	SQUIRRS
	POSITON	IQRSSTU	SQUIRTS
	POTIONS	JMOPTUU	OUTJUMP
INOORSS	ORISONS	JNNOSTU	JOTUNNS
INOORST	ISOTRON	JNOORSU	JOURNOS
	TORSION		SOJOURN
INOORSZ	ZORINOS	JOOPPSY	POPJOYS
INOOSST	TOISONS	JOSTTUU	OUTJUTS
INOOSUX	NOXIOUS	KKLMSUU	MUKLUKS
INOPPRS	POPRINS	KKNRSUU	KUNKURS
INOPPST	TOPSPIN	KLLMOSU	MOLLUSK
INOPRSS	PRISONS	KLOOOTU	LOOKOUT
INOPSST	PISTONS		OUTLOOK
INOPSSU	POUSSIN	KLOOPSU	UPLOOKS
	SPINOUS	KMPRSSU	SKRUMPS
INOPSTT	TINPOTS	KNNNOUW	UNKNOWN
INOPSTU	SPINOUT	KNNOSTU	UNKNOTS
INORSTT	TRITONS	KNOOPTT	TOPKNOT
INORSTU	NITROUS	KNOPRTY	KRYPTON
	TURIONS	KNORSUW	UNWORKS
INORSUU	RUINOUS	KOOOTTU	OUTTOOK
	URINOUS	KOOPRTW	WORKTOP
INORSUV	UNVISOR	KOORTUW	OUTWORK
INOSSTU	USTIONS	KOOSTWW	KOWTOWS
INOSSUU	SINUOUS	KORTTUW	TUTWORK
INOSTUW	OUTWINS	LLLMMUU	MULMULL
INPRSST	SPRINTS	LLLOOPS	LOLLOPS
INPRSTU	TURNIPS	LLMMSUU	MULMULS
	UNSTRIP	LLMOOPR	ROLLMOP
INPRSTY	TRYPSIN	LLMPPUY	PLUMPLY
INQSSTU	SQUINTS	LLNORSU	UNROLLS
INRSTTU	INTRUST	LLOOPRT	TROLLOP
INSSTUU	SUNSUIT	LLOOSTU	TOLUOLS
	UNSUITS	LLOPRSU	UPROLLS
INSTTUW	UNTWIST	LLORSST	STROLLS
INTTUWY	UNWITTY	LMMSTUU	MULTUMS
IOOPRSS	POROSIS	LMOORSU	ORMOLUS
IOOPRSV	PROVISO	LMOOSTY	TOYLSOM
IOOPSTY	ISOTOPY	LMOPSUU	PLUMOUS
IOORSSS	SOROSIS	LMORSSU	MUSROLS
IOORSTT	RISOTTO	LMRSTUU	LUSTRUM
IOORSTU	RIOTOUS	LMSTTUU	TUMULTS
IOOSSSS	SISSOOS	LMSTUUU	TUMULUS
IOPPPST	POPPITS	LNNOPSU	NONPLUS
IOPPSTT	TIPTOPS	LNOOPTU	PULTOON
IOPRSSY	PYROSIS	LNOOSST	STOLONS
IOPRSTT	PROTIST	LNOPSTU	PLUTONS
			PULTONS

LNOSSUU	UNSOULS	MNOOOYZ	ZOONOMY	MOSSTUU	OUTSUMS	NRSTTUU	UNTRUST
LNPSTUU	PULTUNS	MNOOPPS	POMPONS	NNNSUUY	UNSUNNY	OOOOPRT	POTOROO
LNRTUUV	VULTURN	MNOOPST	TOMPONS	NNOOOPT	PONTOON	OOOOSZZ	ZOOZOOS
LNRTUUY	UNTRULY	MNOOPTY	TOPONYM	NNOOPRU	PRONOUN	OOOPRTU	OUTROOP
LOOOORS	OLOROSO	MNOORSU	UNMOORS	NNOOPSS	SPONSON	OOORTTU	OUTROOT
LOOORST	ROTOLOS	MNOOSTU	MOUTONS	NNOOPST	PONTONS	OOPRRST	TORPORS
LOOSSTV	VOLOSTS	MNOOSTW	TOWMONS	NNOORSY	RONYONS	OOPRSTU	PORTOUS
LOPPRSY	PROPYLS	MNOOSUY	ONYMOUS	NNORSUW	UNSWORN		UPROOTS
LOPPSUU	PULPOUS	MNOOTTW	TOWMONT	NNOSSUY	UNSONSY	OOPRSTV	PROVOST
LOPPSUY	POLYPUS	MNORSTU	NOSTRUM	NNOSTYY	SYNTONY	OOPRTTU	OUTPORT
LOPRSTY	PROTYLS	MNOSTTU	MUTTONS	NNRSTUU	UNTURNS	OOPRTUU	OUTPOUR
LOPRSUY	PYLORUS	MNOTTUY	MUTTONY	NOOPRSS	SPONSOR	OOPSSTT	TOSSPOT
LOPRTUY	POULTRY	MOOOTYZ	ZOOTOMY	NOOPRST	PROTONS	OOPSTTU	OUTPOST
LORSTTY	TROTYLS	MOOPPSU	POMPOUS	NOOPSSY	POYSONS		OUTTOPS
LORSTUU	TORULUS	MOOPRSY	POMROYS	NOORSST	TONSORS	OOPSWWW	POWWOWS
LOSTTUY	STOUTLY	MOOPSSU	OPOSSUM	NOORSTU	UNROOST	OORRSSW	SORROWS
LPRSSUU	SURPLUS	MOOPSTT	TOPMOST		UNROOTS	OORSTUU	ROUTOUS
MMNOSSU	MUSMONS	MOORRSW	MORROWS	NOORTUW	OUTWORN	OPPRRTU	PURPORT
	SUMMONS	MOOSTTU	OUTMOST	NOPPRSU	UNPROPS	OPPRSTU	SUPPORT
MMOOPPS	POMPOMS	MOPPRST	PROMPTS	NOPSSTU	SUNSPOT	OPPRSTY	STROPPY
MMOOSTT	MOTMOTS	MOPSSSU	POSSUMS		UNSTOPS	OPPRSUY	PYROPUS
MMOOPSTY	SYMPTOM	MOPSSUU	SPUMOUS	NOPSTUW	UPTOWNS	OPRSSTU	SPROUTS
MMRRSUU	MURMURS	MOQRSUU	QUORUMS	NORSTUU	OUTRUNS		STROUPS
MMSTUUU	MUTUUMS	MOQSTUU	QUOTUMS	NORTTUU	OUTTURN		STUPORS
MNNOOOS	MONSOON	MORRSTU	ROSTRUM	NOSSTUW	UNSTOWS	OPSTTUU	OUTPUTS
MNNOSYY	SYNONYM	MORRSUU	RUMOURS	NPRSTUU	UPTURNS	ORSSTTU	STROUTS
MNNOTUU	UNMOUNT	MORSTUU	TUMOURS	NRSSTTU	STRUNTS	ORSSUUU	USUROUS
MNOOOPP	POMPOON	MOSSTTU	UTMOSTS	NRSSTUU	UNTRUSS	ORSTTUU	SURTOUT

8-LETTER ANAGRAMS

AAAACCRR	CARACARA	AAAACCRTT	CATARACT	AAADHMRS	ADHARMAS	AAAGNOPR	ARAPONGA
AAAACJRR	JARARACA	AAACDEIM	ACADEMIA		MADRASAH	AAAGNPRS	PARASANG
AAAACNRS	ANASARCA	AAACDEQU	AQUACADE	AAADHNRT	THANADAR		PARGANAS
AAAADMTV	AMADAVAT	AAACDETU	ACAUDATE	AAADIILR	RADIALIA	AAAGNPRU	ARAPUNGA
AAAADTVV	AVADAVAT	AAACDILR	CALDARIA	AAADILRU	ADULARIA	AAAGNRST	TANAGRAS
AAAAHJMR	MAHARAJA	AAACDINR	ACARIDAN	AAADIMNY	ADYNAMIA	AAAGNRSU	GUARANAS
AAAAIMPR	ARAPAIMA	AAACDKLY	LACKADAY	AAADIRST	DATARIAS	AAAGNSTY	YATAGANS
AAAAIRTX	ATARAXIA	AAACDMMS	MACADAMS	AAADJMRS	JAMADARS	AAAHHLSV	HALAVAHS
AAAAJKRR	JARARAKA	AAACDNNO	ANACONDA	AAADKLMN	KALAMDAN	AAAHIMNR	MAHARANI
AAAAKKMT	TAKAMAKA	AAACDNRS	SANDARAC	AAADKRRV	AARDVARK	AAAHIMNS	SHAMIANA
AAAAKKNT	KATAKANA	AAACDOTV	ADVOCAAT	AAADLMNQ	QALAMDAN	AAAHIMRT	HAMARTIA
AAAALSTY	ATALAYAS	AAACEGNT	AGACANTE	AAADLMNS	MANDALAS	AAAHINPR	RAPHANIA
AAAAMMTT	MATAMATA	AAACEGTU	AGUACATE	AAADLMSW	WADMAALS	AAAHIPSS	APHASIAS
AAAARRSS	SASARARA	AAACEHLP	ACALEPHA	AAADMNST	ADAMANTS	AAAHJKSW	KAJAWAHS
AAABBCLS	CABBALAS	AAACEHLZ	CHALAZAE	AAADMNTU	TAMANDUA	AAAHKMNS	KHANSAMA
AAABBELT	ABATABLE	AAACELNT	ANALECTA	AAADMRSS	MADRASAS	AAAHKRSS	RAKSHASA
AAABBHKL	KABBALAH	AAACELST	CATALASE		MADRASSA	AAAHLMRS	HARMALAS
AAABBILT	ABBATIAL	AAACENNP	PANACEAN			AAAHLNNS	ALANNAHS
AAABBKLS	KABBALAS	AAACENPS	PANACEAS	AAADNRSS	SARDANAS	AAAHMMST	MAHATMAS
AAABCCRS	BACCARAS	AAACGINT	CAATINGA	AAADNRST	TANADARS	AAAHMNRT	AMARANTH
AAABCCRT	BACCARAT	AAACGLSW	SCALAWAG	AAAEGISS	ASSEGAAI	AAAHMRSS	ASHRAMAS
AAABCHLS	CALABASH	AAACGMNP	CAMPAGNA	AAAEGLMX	MALAXAGE	AAAHMSST	TAMASHAS
AAABCHMU	MACAHUBA	AAACHIPS	APHASIAC	AAAEGLRT	ALTARAGE	AAAHNNSV	SAVANNAH
AAABCINT	ANABATIC	AAACHLNR	ANARCHAL	AAAEGLST	GALATEAS	AAAHNOPR	ANAPHORA
AAABCIRS	ARABICAS	AAACHLSZ	CHALAZAS	AAAEGNPP	APPANAGE	AAAHNSTY	ATHANASY
AAABCLSV	BACLAVAS	AAACHNST	ACANTHAS	AAAEGNPS	APANAGES	AAAHPRST	PARATHAS
AAABCNRR	BARRACAN	AAACHRSY	ACHARYAS	AAAEGRST	GASTRAEA	AAAHRSTW	WARATAHS
	BARRANCA	AAACILMN	MANIACAL	AAAEHKST	TAKAHEAS	AAAHTTWY	THATAWAY
AAABCNRS	BARACANS	AAACILMS	MALACIAS	AAAEHLST	ALTHAEAS	AAAIINPR	APIARIAN
AAABCNRU	CARNAUBA	AAACILSY	CALISAYA	AAAEHMNT	ANATHEMA	AAAIKKMM	KAIMAKAM
AAABCPRY	CAPYBARA	AAACIMRS	CARIAMAS	AAAEHNPS	ANAPHASE	AAAILLMR	MALARIAL
AAABCSTW	CATAWBAS	AAACINPS	ACAPNIAS	AAAEIMNS	ANAEMIAS	AAAILLPT	PALATIAL
AAABDEST	DATABASE	AAACINTV	CAVATINA	AAAEKKRT	KARATEKA	AAAILMNR	MALARIAN
AAABDKNT	DATABANK	AAACIPSU	SAPUCAIA	AAAELMPT	PALAMATE	AAAILMRS	MALARIAS
AAABDNNN	BANDANNA	AAACIRRS	SACRARIA	AAAELMTX	MALAXATE	AAAILMSV	MALVASIA
AAABDNNS	BANDANAS	AAACIRTX	ATARAXIC	AAAELRTV	LAVATERA	AAAILNRU	AULARIAN
AAABDNRS	SARABAND	AAACJMRS	JACAMARS	AAAENOPR	PARANOEA	AAAILPRV	PARAVAIL
AAABDNRT	ABRADANT	AAACKMRT	TAMARACK	AAAENPRV	PARAVANE	AAAILPSS	APLASIAS
AAABEGHL	GALABEAH	AAACLLSV	CAVALLAS	AAAENPST	ANAPAEST	AAAILRST	SALARIAT
AAABEGLL	GALLABEA	AAACLMNS	ALMANACS	AAAENSST	ANATASES	AAAIMMST	MIASMATA
AAABEGLS	GALABEAS	AAACLMRY	CALAMARY	AAAERTWY	TEARAWAY	AAAIMNST	AMANITAS
AAABEHNR	HABANERA	AAACLPST	CATALPAS	AAAFFLLS	ALFALFAS	AAAINNRR	RANARIAN
AAABEHRT	BARATHEA	AAACLRST	ALCATRAS	AAAFINST	FANTASIA	AAAINOPR	PARANOIA
AAABEMPR	PARABEMA	AAACLRSZ	ALCAZARS	AAAFINUV	AVIFAUNA	AAAINQRU	AQUARIAN
AAABENSS	ANABASES	AAACMNPS	CAMPANAS	AAAFIRST	RATAFIAS	AAAIPRSX	APRAXIAS
AAABFLLS	FALBALAS	AAACMRSS	MASCARAS	AAAFNRSS	SARAFANS	AAAIPSSV	PIASSAVA
AAABGHIL	GALABIAH	AAACMRSU	AMARACUS	AAAFRSWY	FARAWAYS	AAAKKTZZ	KAZATZKA
AAABGILL	GALABIA	AAACNNRS	CARANNAS	AAAGGLLN	GALANGAL	AAAKMNRS	NAMASKAR
AAABGILS	GALABIAS	AAACNPST	CATAPANS	AAAGGLNS	GALANGAS	AAAKOSWY	SOAKAWAY
AAABGILY	GALABIYA	AAACNRST	NACARATS	AAAGGLOP	GALAPAGO	AAALLPRX	PARALLAX
AAABGLOR	ALGAROBA	AAACNRSU	CARAUNAS	AAAGHIPR	AGRAPHIA	AAALLPST	PALATALS
AAABGRTU	RUTABAGA	AAACNRSV	CARAVANS	AAAGHIPS	APHAGIAS	AAALNNPT	PLATANNA
AAABILTT	BATTALIA	AAACNSST	CANASTAS	AAAGHLNS	LANGAHAS	AAALNNST	LANTANAS
AAABINSS	ANABASIS	AAACNSTT	CANTATAS	AAAGHNST	ATAGHANS	AAALNPRT	RATAPLAN
AAABIPSS	PIASSABA	AAACRRWY	CARRAWAY	AAAGHNTY	YATAGHAN	AAALNPST	APLANATS
AAABKLSV	BAKLAVAS	AAACRSWY	CARAWAYS	AAAGILPT	PATAGIAL	AAALNRTT	TARLATAN
AAABKPSS	BAASSKAP	AAACSSST	CASSATAS	AAAGILRT	ALIGARTA	AAALPRST	SATRAPAL
AAABLLSW	WALLABAS	AAACSSSV	CASSAVAS	AAAGINRR	AGRARIAN	AAALSWYY	LAYAWAYS
AAABLOPR	PARABOLA	AAACSSTT	CATASTAS	AAAGISSS	ASSAGAIS	AAAMNOPR	PANORAMA
AAABLPRS	PALABRAS	AAACSTWY	CASTAWAY	AAAGLMMS	AMALGAMS	AAAMNRST	AMARANTS
AAABMSST	MASTABAS	AAADEGNP	APANAGED	AAAGLMNS	NAGMAALS	AAAMOTTU	AUTOMATA
AAABNNRS	RABANNAS	AAADELMS	ALAMEDAS	AAAGLMST	STALAGMA	AAAMPRST	PATAMARS
AAABORRS	ARAROBAS		SALAAMED	AAAGLNSS	LASAGNAS	AAAMRRSZ	ZAMARRAS
AAACCEPR	CARAPACE	AAADENTV	VANADATE	AAAGLRRW	WARRAGAL	AAAMRTTU	TRAUMATA
AAACCIMM	CAIMACAM	AAADEPRT	TAPADERA	AAAGLRST	ASTRAGAL	AAAMRTZZ	RAZMATAZ
AAACCLRS	CARACALS	AAADFRSY	FARADAYS	AAAGMNRS	ANAGRAMS	AAANNSSV	SAVANNAS
AAACCRSS	CASCARAS	AAADGLMY	AMYGDALA	AAAGMPRR	PARAGRAM	AAANNSTT	ANNATTAS

AAAANOPRZ	PARAZOAN	AABCEILM	AMICABLE	AABCRSTT	ABSTRACT	AABDKNNS	SANDBANK
AAANORSY	SAYONARA	AABCEIMN	AMBIANCE	AABCSTTU	CATTABUS	AABDLLRY	BALLADRY
AAANPRTV	PARAVANT	AABCEINR	CARABINE	AABDDEGN	BANDAGED	AABDLLUY	LAUDABLY
AAANQTUU	AQUANAUT	AABCEIRT	BACTERIA	AABDDEHN	HEADBAND	AABDLMNU	LABDANUM
AAANRSTT	TANTARAS	AABCEKLM	CLAMBAKE	AABDDEIR	ABRAIDED	AABDLMNY	DAMNABLY
	TARANTAS	AABCEKLR	LACEBARK	AABDDELL	BALLADED	AABDLNPT	PLATBAND
	TARTANAS	AABCELLP	PLACABLE	AABDDENR	BRANDADE	AABDLNSS	SALBANDS
AAAORSWY	SOARAWAY	AABCELLR	CABALLER	AABDDLNS	BADLANDS	AABDLORR	LARBOARD
AAAPPRST	APPARATS	AABCELLS	SCALABLE	AABDDMOR	DAMBOARD	AABDLORY	ADORABLY
AAAPQRTU	PARAQUAT	AABCELNR	BALANCER	AABDEEHL	BEHEADAL	AABDLRSW	BRADAWLS
AAARSTTU	TUATARAS		BARNACLE	AABDEELR	READABLE	AABDMNNS	BANDSMAN
AABBCDEG	CABBAGED	AABCELNS	BALANCES	AABDEELT	DATEABLE	AABDMNNY	BANDYMAN
AABBCDKN	BACKBAND	AABCELOR	ALBACORE		DEALBATE	AABDMNRS	ARMBANDS
AABBCDRS	SCABBARD	AABCELPR	CAPABLER	AABDEELV	EVADABLE	AABDNNOS	ABANDONS
AABBCEGS	CABBAGES	AABCELRT	BRACTEAL	AABDEERY	BAYADERE	AABDNNTU	ABUNDANT
AABBCEIS	ABBACIES	AABCELWY	CABLEWAY	AABDEGIN	BADINAGE	AABDNORS	BANDORAS
AABBCEKR	BAREBACK	AABCEMRV	VAMBRACE	AABDEGLR	GRADABLE	AABDNRSU	BANDURAS
AABBCINR	BARBICAN	AABCENYY	ABEYANCY	AABDEGNS	BANDAGES	AABDORSV	BRAVADOS
AABBCIRR	BARBARIC	AABCEORT	BOATRACE	AABDEHHI	DAHABIEH	AABDORWY	BROADWAY
AABBCIST	SABBATIC	AABCERRS	BARRACES	AABDEHKR	HARDBAKE	AABDRRSS	BRASSARD
AABBCORS	BARBASCO	AABCERST	ABREACTS	AABDEHMR	HARDBEAM	AABDRRSS	BRASSARD
AABBDERT	BARBATED		CABARETS	AABDEILN	BALADINE	AABDRSST	BASTARDS
AABBDGRS	GABBARDS	AABCESSU	ABACUSES	AABDEIOU	ABOIDEAU	AABDRSSU	SUBADARS
AABBEELR	BEARABLE	AABCFIIL	BIFACIAL	AABDEIRS	ARABISED	AABDRSTY	BASTARDY
AABBEELT	BEATABLE	AABCFKLL	BACKFALL	AABDEIRZ	ARABIZED	AABEEGKR	BREAKAGE
AABBEILL	BAILABLE	AABCFKLT	FLATBACK	AABDEISS	DIABASES	AABEEGNT	ABNEGATE
AABBEKLN	BANKABLE	AABCFKST	FASTBACK	AABDEJLL	DJELLABA	AABEEHLL	HEALABLE
AABBELLM	BLAMABLE	AABCHILR	BRACHIAL	AABDEJNX	BANJAXED	AABEEHLT	HATEABLE
AABBELLS	BASEBALL	AABCHINR	BRANCHIA	AABDEKRY	DAYBREAK	AABEEKLM	MAKEABLE
AABBELRY	BEARABLY	AABCHKLS	BACKLASH	AABDELLS	BALLADES	AABEEKLT	TAKEABLE
AABBEORT	BAREBOAT	AABCHKRS	SHABRACK	AABDELLU	LAUDABLE	AABEEKMT	BAKEMEAT
AABBGRST	GABBARTS	AABCHKSW	BACKWASH	AABDELMN	DAMNABLE		MAKEBATE
AABBHKSU	BABUSHKA	AABCHLOO	COOLABAH	AABDELMS	BALSAMED	AABEEKRW	BAKEWARE
AABBIILL	BILABIAL	AABCHNRS	BARCHANS	AABDELOR	ADORABLE	AABEELLS	LEASABLE
AABBILRT	BARBITAL	AABCIILS	BASILICA	AABDELPR	PARABLED		SALEABLE
AABBLLMY	BLAMABLY	AABCIKLT	TAILBACK	AABDELRS	BASELARD	AABEELMN	AMENABLE
AABBLORS	BARBOLAS	AABCILLR	BACILLAR	AABDELRT	TRADABLE		NAMEABLE
AABBLSSU	SUBBASAL	AABCILMS	BALSAMIC	AABDELRW	DRAWABLE	AABEELMT	TAMEABLE
AABBMMOZ	ZAMBOMBA		CABALISM	AABDELRY	READABLY	AABEELRS	ERASABLE
AABBSSSU	BABASSUS	AABCILMY	AMICABLY	AABDEMNS	BEADSMAN	AABEELRT	RATEABLE
AABCCCHI	BACCHIAC	AABCILNN	CANNIBAL	AABDENTU	UNABATED	AABEELRW	WEARABLE
AABCCEHK	BACKACHE	AABCILNO	ANABOLIC	AABDENUX	BANDEAUX	AABEELST	EATABLES
AABCCELS	CASCABEL	AABCILST	BASALTIC	AABDENVW	WAVEBAND	AABEEMPR	ABAMPERE
AABCCERT	BRACCATE		CABALIST	AABDEORS	SEABOARD	AABEENOR	ANAEROBE
AABCCHIS	BISCACHA	AABCINNN	CANNABIN	AABDERRT	TABERDAR	AABEERRT	ABERRATE
AABCCHIZ	BIZCACHA	AABCINNR	CINNABAR	AABDERRW	BEARWARD	AABEERSZ	ZAREEBAS
AABCCHKT	BACKCHAT	AABCINNS	CANNABIS	AABDERWY	WAYBREAD	AABEERTT	TRABEATE
AABCCHNT	BACCHANT	AABCINRS	CARABINS	AABDFHLN	FAHLBAND	AABEFFNS	BEFFANAS
AABCCINN	CANNABIC	AABCINSU	BANAUSIC	AABDGHNS	HANDBAGS	AABEFGSU	AUFGABES
AABCCKKP	BACKPACK	AABCIOPS	COPAIBAS	AABDGINN	ABANDING	AABEFLLL	FLABELLA
AABCCKLP	BLACKCAP	AABCIRSS	BRASSICA	AABDGINR	ABRADING	AABEFLMU	FLAMBEAU
AABCCKLW	CLAWBACK	AABCISSS	ABSCISSA	AABDGMOS	GAMBADOS	AABEGGGS	BAGGAGES
AABCCMOT	CATACOMB	AABCISTX	TAXICABS	AABDGNOV	VAGABOND	AABEGGRS	GARBAGES
AABCDEIN	ABIDANCE	AABCKLPY	PLAYBACK	AABDGNSS	SANDBAGS	AABEGHIL	GALABIEH
AABCDEIT	ABDICATE	AABCKLSY	LAYBACKS	AABDGORR	GARBOARD	AABEGHLN	HANGABLE
AABCDELL	CABALLED	AABCKPSY	BACKPAYS	AABDGOTU	GADABOUT	AABEGHNR	BERGHAAN
AABCDELN	BALANCED	AABCKRRS	BARRACKS	AABDHLLN	HANDBALL	AABEGILN	GAINABLE
AABCDHKN	BACKHAND	AABCKSSW	BACKSAWS	AABDHNST	HATBANDS	AABEGINR	ABEARING
AABCDHKR	HARDBACK	AABCKSWY	SWAYBACK	AABDHNSY	HAYBANDS	AABEGLLL	GLABELLA
AABCDIIS	DIABASIC	AABCLLLO	COALBALL	AABDHRSU	SUBAHDAR	AABEGLRS	ALGEBRAS
AABCDINT	ABDICANT	AABCLLPY	PLACABLY	AABDIILS	BASIDIAL	AABEGLRT	GLABRATE
AABCDKRW	BACKWARD	AABCLMSU	CALUMBAS	AABDILLN	BALLADIN	AABEGLRU	ARGUABLE
	DRAWBACK	AABCLNUU	CUNABULA	AABDILNS	BALADINS	AABEGMNR	BARGEMAN
AABCDKRY	BACKYARD	AABCLOOR	COOLABAR	AABDIMNR	MADBRAIN	AABEGMNY	MANGABEY
AABCDNRR	BRANCARD	AABCLRRY	CARBARYL	AABDIMRS	BARMAIDS	AABEGMRS	BERGAMAS
AABCEENY	ABEYANCE	AABCMSSU	SAMBUCAS	AABDINNR	RAINBAND		MEGABARS
AABCEERS	SCARABEE	AABCNORR	BARRANCO	AABDINST	TABANIDS	AABEGMRT	BREGMATA
AABCEERT	ACERBATE	AABCORST	ABACTORS			AABEGNOR	BARONAGE
AABCEGOT	CABOTAGE		ACROBATS			AABEGORT	ABROGATE
AABCEHNR	BARCHANE	AABCOSTT	CATBOATS			AABEGOST	SABOTAGE

Key	Word	Key	Word
AABEGRRS	BAGARRES	AABELTUX	TABLEAUX
	BARRAGES	AABENRRT	ABERRANT
AABEGSSS	BAGASSES	AABENRST	ANTBEARS
AABEGSSU	ABUSAGES		RATSBANE
AABEHIRR	HERBARIA	AABEORRT	ARBORETA
AABEHKLS	SHAKABLE	AABEORST	RABATOES
AABEHLOT	OATHABLE	AABERSTT	RABATTES
AABEHLPS	SHAPABLE		TABARETS
AABEHLPT	ALPHABET	AABERSTU	ABATURES
AABEHLRW	WARHABLE	AABESZZZ	BAZAZZES
AABEHLSW	WASHABLE	AABFILUX	FABLIAUX
AABEHNST	ABTHANES	AABFLOTT	FALTBOAT
AABEIKNS	IKEBANAS		FLATBOAT
AABEILLM	MAILABLE	AABGGNOT	TABOGGAN
AABEILLS	ISABELLA	AABGGRRT	BRAGGART
	SAILABLE	AABGHINS	ABASHING
AABEILNR	INARABLE	AABGHNSS	NASHGABS
AABEILRS	RAISABLE	AABGIILS	ABIGAILS
AABEILRV	VARIABLE	AABGILNT	ABLATING
AABEILST	BALISTAE	AABGINRS	BARGAINS
	LABIATES	AABGINRY	ABRAYING
	SATIABLE	AABGIRST	BARGAIST
AABEILTV	ABLATIVE	AABGLLRY	BALLYRAG
AABEINOZ	ZABAIONE	AABGLMNU	GALBANUM
AABEINRT	RABATINE	AABGLRUY	ARGUABLY
AABEINST	BASANITE	AABGMORR	BAROGRAM
AABEIOTU	ABOITEAU	AABGNORZ	GARBANZO
AABEIRSS	ARABISES	AABHHISS	SAHIBAHS
AABEIRSV	ABRASIVE	AABHHORU	BROUHAHA
AABEIRSZ	ARABIZES	AABHHRSU	BRUHAHAS
AABEJLLS	JELLABAS	AABHIINU	BAUHINIA
AABEJMUX	JAMBEAUX	AABHIJMY	JAMBIYAH
AABEJNSX	BANJAXES	AABHILTU	HABITUAL
AABEKLLT	TALKABLE	AABHINST	HABITANS
AABEKLLW	WALKABLE	AABHINTT	HABITANT
AABEKMNR	BRAKEMAN	AABHIRST	TABASHIR
AABEKPRR	PARBREAK	AABHISTT	HABITATS
AABEKRRS	BARESARK	AABHKNRS	BARKHANS
AABELLNO	LOANABLE	AABHNOTU	AUTOBAHN
AABELLPP	PALPABLE	AABHQSSU	SQUABASH
AABELLPS	LAPSABLE	AABHRRSU	SURBAHAR
AABELLPY	PLAYABLE	AABIJMSY	JAMBIYAS
AABELLSS	SABELLAS	AABIKNSS	BANKSIAS
AABELLSV	SALVABLE	AABILLLY	LABIALLY
AABELLSY	SALEABLY	AABILLRS	BARILLAS
AABELLUV	VALUABLE	AABILLST	BALLISTA
AABELMNY	AMENABLY	AABILMNS	BAILSMAN
AABELMST	BLASTEMA	AABILNNU	BIANNUAL
	LAMBASTE	AABILNOR	BARONIAL
AABELMSU	AMUSABLE	AABILNOT	ABLATION
AABELMTU	AMBULATE	AABILNRU	BINAURAL
AABELNNT	TANNABLE	AABILNTY	BANALITY
AABELNOS	ABALONES	AABILOSU	ABOULIAS
AABELNPS	ANABLEPS	AABILOTT	BOATTAIL
AABELNPT	PANTABLE	AABILRRT	ARBITRAL
AABELNRY	BALNEARY	AABILRST	ARBALIST
AABELNST	BANALEST	AABILRVY	VARIABLY
AABELOPR	PARABOLE	AABILSST	BALISTAS
AABELORR	ARBOREAL	AABIMMRS	MARIMBAS
AABELOSV	LAVABOES	AABIMNNO	BONAMANI
AABELOVW	AVOWABLE	AABIMNRU	MANUBRIA
AABELPRS	PARABLES	AABIMORS	AMBROSIA
	SPARABLE	AABINNPR	BRAINPAN
AABELPSS	PASSABLE	AABINORS	ABRASION
AABELRST	ARBALEST	AABINOSU	OUABAINS
AABELRTY	BETRAYAL	AABINRST	ATABRINS
	RATEABLY		BARTISAN
AABELSTT	STATABLE	AABINRTZ	BARTIZAN
	TASTABLE	AABINSST	ABSTAINS
AABELTTU	TABULATE	AABIORRS	SORBARIA

Key	Word	Key	Word
AABIORTT	ABATTOIR		CARUCATE
AABIOSSY	BIOASSAY	AACCFGOO	CACAFOGO
AABIPSUX	PAXIUBAS	AACCFILR	FARCICAL
AABIRTUY	RUBAIYAT	AACCGILT	GALACTIC
AABJLMNO	JAMBOLAN	AACCHILL	CAILLACH
AABKLLPR	BALLPARK	AACCHILP	PACHALIC
AABKMNNS	BANKSMAN	AACCHINR	ANARCHIC
AABKOOSZ	BAZOOKAS		CHARACIN
AABLLMOR	BALMORAL	AACCHISV	VISCACHA
AABLLNST	BALLANTS	AACCHIVZ	VIZCACHA
AABLLPPY	PALPABLY	AACCHLNS	CLACHANS
AABLLPST	PATBALLS	AACCHLOR	CHARCOAL
AABLLSST	BALLASTS	AACCHLOT	CACHALOT
AABLLSTU	BLASTULA	AACCHLRS	CLARSACH
AABLLUVY	VALUABLY	AACCHMNO	COACHMAN
AABLMNOR	ABNORMAL	AACCHMPS	CHAMPACS
AABLMNTU	AMBULANT	AACCHNNS	CANNACHS
AABLMRSU	LABARUMS	AACCHNOR	CORANACH
AABLMSST	LAMBASTS	AACCHRST	CHARACTS
AABLNTTT	BLATTANT	AACCIINV	VACCINIA
AABLORST	ABLATORS	AACCIIST	SCIATICA
AABLOTUY	LAYABOUT	AACCILMS	ACCLAIMS
AABLPSSY	PASSABLY	AACCILNV	VACCINAL
AABLRRSU	SABURRAL	AACCILRU	ACICULAR
AABLRSST	ARBLASTS	AACCILTT	TACTICAL
AABLSTTU	ABUTTALS	AACCIORS	CARIOCAS
AABMMOSU	ABOMASUM	AACCIORU	CARIACOU
AABMNNOO	BONAMANO	AACCIRTY	CARYATIC
AABMNOTW	BATWOMAN	AACCJKRW	CRACKJAW
AABMNRTU	RAMBUTAN	AACCJORU	CARCAJOU
AABMORSU	MARABOUS		CARJACOU
AABMORTU	MARABOUT	AACCKLPS	CALPACKS
	TAMBOURA	AACCKORT	COATRACK
AABMOSSU	ABOMASUS	AACCKRRS	CARRACKS
AABMRSTU	TAMBURAS	AACCLLRU	CALCULAR
AABNNOST	ABSONANT	AACCLLST	CATCALLS
AABNNOSZ	BONANZAS	AACCLMNY	CLAMANCY
AABNOSST	SABATONS	AACCLOPS	POLACCAS
AABORRRT	BARRATOR	AACCLORS	CARACOLS
AABORRST	BAROSTAT	AACCLPRS	CALCSPAR
AABRRRTY	BARRATRY	AACCLPST	PLACCATS
AABRRSST	BRASSART	AACCLRSU	ACCRUALS
AABRRSSU	SABURRAS		CARACULS
AABRRSUV	BRAVURAS		SACCULAR
AABSTTTU	BATTUTAS	AACCLSSU	ACCUSALS
AACCCDIS	SACCADIC	AACCORSU	CURACAOS
AACCCHHU	CACHUCHA		CURACOAS
AACCCRUY	ACCURACY	AACCOSST	ACCOASTS
AACCDDES	CASCADED	AACCOSTT	STACCATO
AACCDEIM	ACADEMIC		STOCCATA
AACCDELO	ACCOLADE		TOCCATAS
AACCDENU	CADUCEAN	AACCRRST	CARRACTS
AACCDERS	CARCASED	AACDDEIL	DAEDALIC
AACCDESS	CASCADES	AACDDENV	ADVANCED
	SACCADES	AACDDETU	CAUDATED
AACCDIRS	CARDIACS	AACDDHRS	CHADDARS
AACCDOVY	ADVOCACY	AACDDINS	CANDIDAS
AACCEELT	CALCEATE	AACDEEHH	HEADACHE
AACCEENT	CETACEAN	AACDEEHR	AREACHED
AACCEGOR	ACCORAGE		HEADRACE
AACCEGRU	CARUCAGE	AACDEEHS	HEADCASE
AACCEHIX	CACHEXIA	AACDEELS	ESCALADE
AACCEIRR	CERCARIA	AACDEEMS	ACADEMES
AACCEKRS	CARCAKES	AACDEEPS	ESCAPADE
AACCELOR	CARACOLE	AACDEEST	ESTACADE
AACCELPT	PLACCATE	AACDEETU	ECAUDATE
AACCENRT	CARCANET	AACDEFHR	HARDFACE
AACCENSV	VACANCES	AACDEFLS	FALCADES
AACCERSS	CARCASES	AACDEFLT	FALCATED
AACCERTU	ACCURATE		

AACDEGGR	AGGRACED	AACDIINS	ASCIDIAN	AACEFRSX	CARFAXES	AACEINRS	CANARIES
AACDEGKP	PACKAGED	AACDILLP	PALLADIC	AACEFRTT	ARTEFACT	AACEINRT	CARINATE
AACDEGMR	DECAGRAM	AACDILMT	DALMATIC	AACEGGRS	AGGRACES	AACEINRV	VARIANCE
AACDEHHY	HEADACHY	AACDILNO	DIACONAL	AACEGHNT	CHANTAGE	AACEINST	ESTANCIA
AACDEHIN	HACIENDA	AACDILNR	CARDINAL	AACEGILN	ANGELICA	AACEIPPS	PAPACIES
AACDEHLN	CHALANED	AACDILNU	DULCIANA	AACEGILT	GLACIATE	AACEIPRS	AIRSPACE
AACDEHLP	CEPHALAD	AACDILOZ	ZODIACAL	AACEGINR	CANAIGRE	AACEIPRT	APRICATE
AACDEHMR	DRACHMAE	AACDILRR	RAILCARD	AACEGIOP	APOGAEIC	AACEIPSS	CAPIASES
AACDEHMS	CHAMADES	AACDILRS	RADICALS	AACEGIRR	CARRIAGE	AACEIPTT	APATETIC
AACDEHRS	CHARADES	AACDIMNO	MANDIOCA	AACEGIRV	VICARAGE		CAPITATE
AACDEHRT	CATHEDRA	AACDIMNY	ADYNAMIC	AACEGKPR	PACKAGER	AACEIRSV	AVARICES
AACDEHST	CATHEADS	AACDIMOS	CAMISADO	AACEGKPS	PACKAGES		CAVIARES
AACDEHTT	ATTACHED	AACDIMRS	CAMISARD	AACEGKRT	TRACKAGE	AACEIRTV	VICARATE
AACDEILS	ALCAIDES	AACDIMRT	DRAMATIC	AACEGKSS	SACKAGES	AACEITTV	ACTIVATE
	SIDALCEA	AACDINRT	RADICANT	AACEGLNY	LANCEGAY		CAVITATE
AACDEIMN	MAENADIC		TRIDACNA	AACEGNRS	CARNAGES	AACEJLTU	JACULATE
AACDEIMS	CAMISADE	AACDINRY	RADIANCY		CRANAGES	AACEKKLW	CAKEWALK
AACDEINR	CANARIED	AACDINST	ANTACIDS	AACEGRST	CARTAGES	AACEKNPS	PANCAKES
	RADIANCE	AACDIOTU	AUTACOID	AACEGRSV	SCAVAGER	AACEKNSS	ASKANCES
AACDEINS	AIDANCES	AACDIRSS	ASCARIDS	AACEGSSV	SCAVAGES	AACEKOST	OATCAKES
AACDEIRT	RADICATE	AACDIRTY	CARYATID	AACEHILL	HELIACAL	AACEKRTT	ATTACKER
AACDEJNT	ADJACENT	AACDITUY	AUDACITY	AACEHILN	ACHENIAL	AACELLMR	MARCELLA
AACDEKNP	PANCAKED	AACDJKSW	JACKDAWS	AACEHIMR	CHIMAERA	AACELLNS	CANELLAS
AACDEKNS	ASKANCED	AACDJQRU	JACQUARD	AACEHIMT	HAEMATIC	AACELLOT	ALLOCATE
AACDEKTT	ATTACKED	AACDKLLN	LACKLAND	AACEHIRS	ARCHAISE	AACELLST	CASTELLA
AACDELLS	ALCALDES	AACDLNSS	SCANDALS	AACEHIRT	THERIACA		LACTEALS
AACDELMN	MANACLED	AACDLORS	CARLOADS	AACEHIRZ	ARCHAIZE	AACELMNP	PLACEMAN
AACDELNR	CALENDAR	AACDLORT	CARTLOAD	AACEHLNT	CALANTHE	AACELMNS	MANACLES
	LANDRACE	AACDLOSS	SCALADOS	AACEHLPS	ACALEPHS	AACELMRS	CARAMELS
AACDELNS	CANDELAS	AACDLPRS	PLACARDS	AACEHLRS	ALCHERAS	AACELMTU	MACULATE
AACDELNV	VALANCED	AACDLRTY	DACTYLAR	AACEHLRT	TRACHEAL	AACELNNU	CANNULAE
AACDELOS	ESCALADO	AACDMMOR	CARDAMOM	AACEHLSS	CALASHES	AACELNOR	LECANORA
AACDELPT	PLACATED	AACDMMRU	CARDAMUM	AACEHLST	ALCAHEST	AACELNPR	PARLANCE
AACDELRS	CALDERAS	AACDMNNO	MANCANDO	AACEHMNP	CAMPHANE	AACELNPT	PLACENTA
AACDELSS	SCALADES	AACDMNOR	CARDAMON	AACEHMRS	MARCHESA	AACELNRT	LACERANT
AACDELSY	ALCAYDES	AACDOOSV	AVOCADOS	AACEHMSS	CAMASHES	AACELNRY	ARCANELY
AACDELTT	LACTATED	AACDORRT	CARTROAD	AACEHMST	SCHEMATA	AACELNST	ANALECTS
AACDELTV	CLAVATED	AACEEFIT	FACETIAE	AACEHNPS	PANACHES	AACELNSV	VALANCES
AACDENSV	ADVANCES	AACEEFLP	PALEFACE	AACEHPSU	CHAPEAUS	AACELNTU	LACUNATE
	CANVASED	AACEEGIR	ACIERAGE	AACEHRSS	CHARASES	AACELOST	CATALOES
AACDENSZ	CADENZAS		AGACERIE	AACEHRSU	ARCHAEUS	AACELOSU	ACAULOSE
AACDENTU	ADUNCATE	AACEEGLR	CLEARAGE	AACEHRTT	REATTACH	AACELPST	PLACATES
AACDENTV	TADVANCE	AACEEGLV	CLEAVAGE	AACEHSTT	ATTACHES	AACELPSU	SCAPULAE
AACDEOPS	ESCAPADO	AACEEGRS	ACREAGES	AACEHTUX	CHATEAUX	AACELRSU	CAESURAL
AACDEOTU	AUTOCADE	AACEEHLP	ACALEPHE	AACEIILN	LACINIAE	AACELRSV	CARAVELS
AACDEOTV	ADVOCATE	AACEEHLT	LEACHATE	AACEIINT	ACTINIAE	AACELRWY	CLEARWAY
AACDEQUY	ADEQUACY	AACEEHRS	AREACHES	AACEIIRV	CAVIARIE	AACELSST	LACTASES
AACDERST	CADASTRE		EARACHES	AACEIKMT	KAMACITE	AACELSTT	LACTATES
AACDERSV	CADAVERS			AACEILLM	CAMELLIA	AACELSTY	CATALYSE
AACDERTU	ARCUATED	AACEEHRT	TRACHEAE	AACEILLN	ALLIANCE	AACELTYZ	CATALYZE
AACDETTU	ACTUATED	AACEEIMT	EMACIATE		CANAILLE	AACEMMRS	MACRAMES
AACDETUV	VACUATED	AACEEINN	ENCAENIA	AACEILMN	ANALCIME	AACEMNPS	SPACEMAN
AACDGINR	ARCADING	AACEEIRT	ACIERATE		CALAMINE	AACEMNST	CAMSTANE
	CARANGID	AACEEKRT	CARETAKE	AACEILMT	CALAMITE	AACEMPRS	PARACMES
	CARDIGAN	AACEELNS	ANELACES	AACEILNS	CANALISE	AACEMQSU	MACAQUES
AACDHHKR	HARDHACK	AACEELRT	LACERATE	AACEILNT	ANALCITE	AACEMRSS	MASSACRE
AACDHIIS	DICHASIA	AACEELST	ESCALATE		LAITANCE	AACEMSSS	CAMASSES
AACDHILR	DIARCHAL	AACEELTU	ACULEATE	AACEILNU	ACAULINE	AACENOTU	OCEANAUT
AACDHIMR	DRACHMAI	AACEEMRT	MACERATE	AACEILNV	VALIANCE	AACENPRS	PANCREAS
AACDHINP	HANDICAP		RACEMATE	AACEILNZ	CANALIZE	AACENPST	PASTANCE
AACDHINR	ARACHNID	AACEEMST	CASEMATE	AACEILOP	ALOPECIA	AACENPSU	SAUCEPAN
AACDHKRT	HARDTACK	AACEENTT	CATENATE	AACEILRT	TAILRACE	AACENRST	CANASTER
AACDHLNP	HANDCLAP	AACEEPSS	SEASCAPE	AACEILRV	CAVALIER		CATERANS
AACDHLOT	CATHODAL	AACEERTV	ACERVATE	AACEILST	SALICETA	AACENRTT	REACTANT
AACDHLRY	CHARLADY	AACEESTT	ACETATES	AACEIMNS	AMNESIAC	AACENRTY	CATENARY
AACDHMMR	DRAMMACH	AACEETUV	EVACUATE	AACEIMRS	MACARISE	AACENRVZ	CZAREVNA
AACDHMRS	DRACHMAS	AACEETVX	EXCAVATE		MESARAIC	AACENSSV	CANVASES
AACDHNRS	HANDCARS	AACEFFIN	AFFIANCE	AACEIMRZ	MACARIZE	AACENSTT	CANTATES
AACDHPRS	CRASHPAD	AACEFHLP	HALFPACE	AACEIMTT	CATAMITE	AACENSTY	CYANATES
AACDIINR	CNIDARIA	AACEFIST	FASCIATE	AACEIMUX	CAMAIEUX	AACENTUV	EVACUANT
		AACEFRST	SEACRAFT				

```
AACEOPRT CAPROATE      AACHIMNP CHINAMPA      AACILNRV CARNIVAL      AACLLSUY CASUALLY
AACEORSS ROSACEAS      AACHIMNR CHAIRMAN      AACILNST ALICANTS               CAUSALLY
AACEORSU ARACEOUS      AACHIMNS SHAMANIC      AACILNTT TANTALIC      AACLLTUY ACTUALLY
AACEOSST SEACOAST      AACHIMNT MATACHIN      AACILNTU NAUTICAL      AACLMNNS CLANSMAN
AACEPRST CAPRATES      AACHIMRR ARMCHAIR      AACILNTY ANALYTIC      AACLMNSS CLASSMAN
AACERSSU CAESURAS      AACHIMRS ARCHAISM      AACILNUV NAVICULA      AACLMNST CALMANTS
AACERSSZ SAZERACS               CHARISMA      AACILNVY VALIANCY      AACLMRRU MACRURAL
AACERSTT CASTRATE               MACHAIRS      AACILPRU PIACULAR      AACLNNOT CANTONAL
AACERSWY RACEWAYS      AACHIMSS CHIASMAS      AACILPST APLASTIC      AACLNNSU CANNULAS
AACERTTT TRACTATE      AACHIMST CATHISMA               CAPITALS      AACLNOTT OCTANTAL
AACESSSV CAVASSES      AACHINNT ACANTHIN      AACILPSZ CAPSIZAL      AACLNPSY CLAYPANS
AACESSTT SCEATTAS      AACHINRT CANTHARI      AACILPTU CAPITULA      AACLNRSU LACUNARS
AACESTTU ACTUATES      AACHINSW CHAINSAW      AACILPTY ATYPICAL      AACLNRUY LACUNARY
AACESTUV VACUATES      AACHIPST CHAPATIS      AACILQRU ACQUIRAL      AACLNTVY VACANTLY
AACESUWY CAUSEWAY      AACHIPTT CHAPATTI      AACILRTY ALACRITY      AACLOOPT TAPACOLO
AACFFILS CAFFILAS      AACHIRST ARCHAIST      AACILRUU AURICULA      AACLOPRS CAPORALS
AACFGRST CRAGFAST               CITHARAS      AACILSTT STATICAL      AACLOPST OCTAPLAS
AACFHMST CAMSHAFT      AACHIRTX TAXIARCH      AACILSTY SALACITY      AACLOPTU TAPACULO
AACFILLY FACIALLY      AACHKMPS CHAMPAKS      AACIMMNO AMMONIAC      AACLORRU ORACULAR
AACFILOS FASCIOLA      AACHKPSS SCHAPSKA      AACIMMRS MACARISM      AACLORSU CAROUSAL
AACFINST FANATICS      AACHKRST HATRACKS               MACRAMIS      AACLORSZ ALCORZAS
AACFIRRT AIRCRAFT      AACHKSTY HAYSTACK               MARASMIC      AACLORUV VACUOLAR
AACFIRTT ARTIFACT      AACHLLNS CHALLANS      AACIMNOR MACARONI      AACLOSTT CATTALOS
AACFISST FASCISTA      AACHLMNO MONACHAL               MAROCAIN      AACLPPRT CLAPTRAP
AACFJKLP FLAPJACK      AACHLMOS CHLOASMA      AACIMNOT ANATOMIC      AACLPRST CALTRAPS
AACFLLSU FALCULAS      AACHLSSU ACUSHLAS      AACIMORT AROMATIC      AACLPRSU CAPSULAR
AACFRRSU FARRUCAS      AACHMMNR MARCHMAN      AACIMPRS PICAMARS               SCAPULAR
AACGGINO ANAGOGIC      AACHMMNR RANCHMAN      AACINNST CANTINAS      AACLPRTY CALYPTRA
AACGGIOP APAGOGIC      AACHMNTW WATCHMAN      AACINOPR PARANOIC      AACLPSSU SCAPULAS
AACGHIPR AGRAPHIC      AACHMNUY NAUMACHY      AACINOPT CAPITANO      AACLPTTU CATAPULT
AACGHIRR CHIRAGRA      AACHMORT ACHROMAT               PACATION      AACLRSTU CLAUSTRA
AACGHLLO AGALLOCH               TRACHOMA      AACINORS OCARINAS      AACLRSUV VASCULAR
AACGHOPZ GAZPACHO      AACHMPRT CHAMPART      AACINORT RAINCOAT      AACLSTTY CATALYST
AACGHORU GUACHARO      AACHMPRY PHARMACY      AACINOTV VACATION      AACLSTUY CASUALTY
AACGIIMN MAGICIAN      AACHNOPS PANOCHAS      AACINPST CAPITANS      AACMNOOR MACAROON
AACGILLO ALOGICAL      AACHNOSU HUANACOS               CAPTAINS      AACMNORS CAMARONS
AACGILLS GLACIALS      AACHNPRS SARPANCH      AACINPTY CAPITAYN               MASCARON
AACGILLU ALGUACIL      AACHNRSV NAVARCHS      AACINQTU ACQUAINT      AACMNPRY RAMPANCY
AACGILNO ANALOGIC      AACHNRVY NAVARCHY      AACINRST ARCANIST      AACMORSS SARCOMAS
AACGILNV GALVANIC      AACHNSTU ACANTHUS      AACINRSZ CZARINAS      AACMRSSS SARCASMS
AACGILOX COXALGIA      AACHOPPR APPROACH      AACINSTZ STANZAIC      AACNNOSZ CANZONAS
AACGILRT TRAGICAL      AACHORTU RACAHOUT      AACIOPST TAPIOCAS      AACNOTTY CATATONY
AACGILSS SCAGLIAS      AACHOTTU TACAHOUT      AACIOPSV COPAIVAS      AACNPSST CAPSTANS
AACGIMMT MAGMATIC      AACHRRST CATARRHS      AACIPRST SATRAPIC      AACNRSTT TRANSACT
AACGIMNN MANGANIC      AACHRSWY ARCHWAYS      AACIPRTY RAPACITY      AACNRSTU CURTANAS
AACGIMNP CAMPAIGN      AACHRTUY AUTARCHY      AACIQSTU AQUATICS      AACOORTX TOXOCARA
         PANGAMIC      AACIILMN ANIMALIC      AACIRRTT TARTARIC      AACOPRSU ACARPOUS
AACGIMRR MARGARIC      AACIILMO MAIOLICA      AACIRSTT CASTRATI      AACOPRTU AUTOCARP
AACGIMUU GUAIACUM      AACIILRT IATRICAL      AACIRTZZ CZARITZA      AACORRTV VARACTOR
AACGINPS SCAPAING      AACIILRV VICARIAL      AACJKLPS SLAPJACK      AACORSTT CASTRATO
AACGINTV VACATING      AACIINNT ACTINIAN      AACJKMNS MANJACKS      AACORSTU ACATOURS
AACGISTY SAGACITY      AACIINPR PICARIAN      AACJKOOR JACKAROO               AUTOCARS
AACGLMOU GLAUCOMA      AACIINPT CAPITANI      AACKKNPS KNAPSACK      AACORTTU ACTUATOR
AACGLOST CATALOGS      AACIINST ACTINIAS      AACKLNPS KNAPSCAL               AUTOCRAT
AACGMNRS CRAGSMAN      AACIJLMO MAJOLICA      AACKLOWY LOCKAWAY      AACOSTUV AUTOVACS
AACGNOSU GUANACOS      AACIJNOP JAPONICA      AACKMNPS MANPACKS      AACRSTTT ATTRACTS
AACGNRVY VAGRANCY      AACIKLRS CLARKIAS      AACKMNRT TRACKMAN      AACRSTUV VACATURS
AACHHIKR KACHAHRI      AACIKMNW MACKINAW      AACKMNST TACKSMAN      AACRSTWY CARTWAYS
AACHHTWY HATCHWAY      AACIKNNS CANAKINS      AACKMRST AMTRACKS      AACSTUWY CUTAWAYS
AACHIIMR MARIACHI      AACIKRTU AUTARKIC      AACKNNRS RANSACKS      AADDDEER ADREADED
AACHIKNR CHINKARA      AACILLMR LACRIMAL      AACKORWY ROCKAWAY      AADDDERW ADWARDED
AACHIKNS KACHINAS      AACILLMT CLIMATAL      AACKPRRS CARPARKS      AADDDGNR GRANDDAD
AACHIKRS CHIKARAS      AACILLPY APICALLY      AACKPRST RATPACKS      AADDEGGR AGGRADED
AACHILLP CALIPHAL      AACILLRY RACIALLY      AACKPSWY PACKWAYS      AADDEGRT GRADATED
AACHILLR RACHILLA      AACILMNT CALAMINT      AACKRTWY TRACKWAY      AADDEHHR HARDHEAD
AACHILMS CHAMISAL               CLAIMANT      AACLLMRY LACRYMAL      AADDEHLN HEADLAND
AACHILMT THALAMIC      AACILMOR ACROMIAL      AACLLNRY CARNALLY      AADDEHMN HANDMADE
AACHILNP CHAPLAIN      AACILMOT ATOMICAL      AACLLNST CALLANTS      AADDEHRZ HAZARDED
AACHILPS CALIPASH      AACILMTY CALAMITY      AACLLRSY RASCALLY      AADDEILN DEDALIAN
AACHILRV ARCHIVAL      AACILNOR CONARIAL      AACLLSUU CLAUSULA      AADDEILS ALIDADES
```

AADDEIRT	RADIATED	AADEGILT	GLADIATE
AADDEKMS	DAMASKED	AADEGINR	AREADING
AADDELTU	ADULATED		DRAINAGE
AADDEMNT	MANDATED		GARDENIA
AADDEMRU	MARAUDED	AADEGINT	INDAGATE
AADDEMRY	DAYDREAM	AADEGITT	AGITATED
AADDENPR	PANDARED	AADEGITV	DIVAGATE
AADDENPS	DEADPANS	AADEGJTU	ADJUTAGE
AADDGNRS	GRADDANS	AADEGLLT	TALLAGED
	GRANDADS	AADEGLMN	MAGDALEN
AADDGNRU	GRADUAND	AADEGLMY	AMYGDALE
AADDHHRS	SHRADDHA	AADEGLNS	SELADANG
AADDHIMN	HANDMAID	AADEGLSV	SALVAGED
AADDHKRS	KHADDARS	AADEGMPR	RAMPAGED
AADDHRSS	SRADDHAS	AADEGMSS	MASSAGED
AADDIIKS	DIDAKAIS	AADEGNRR	ARRANGED
AADDILNO	DIANODAL	AADEGNTV	VANTAGED
AADDKMMO	MOKADDAM	AADEGPSS	PASSAGED
AADDLLNY	LANDLADY	AADEGRST	GRADATES
AADDLNRW	LANDWARD	AADEGRSV	SAVEGARD
AADDLNRY	YARDLAND	AADEGRSY	DRAYAGES
AADDMMQU	MUQADDAM		YARDAGES
AADDNRST	STANDARD	AADEGRTU	GRADUATE
AADDNRWY	YARDWAND	AADEGSSU	ASSUAGED
AADDNSVV	DVANDVAS	AADEGSSW	ASSWAGED
AADDRSST	DASTARDS	AADEHHOR	HOARHEAD
AADDRSTY	DASTARDY	AADEHILR	HEADRAIL
AADEEFFR	AFFEARED	AADEHIRR	DIARRHEA
AADEEGHR	HEADGEAR	AADEHKMR	HEADMARK
AADEEGLR	LAAGERED	AADEHLLL	HALALLED
AADEEGLT	GALEATED	AADEHLLO	HALLOAED
AADEEGMN	AMENAGED	AADEHLMP	HEADLAMP
	ENDAMAGE	AADEHLNR	ANHEDRAL
AADEEGRV	AVERAGED	AADEHLRS	ASHLARED
AADEEHMT	MEATHEAD	AADEHMNS	HEADSMAN
AADEEIRT	ERADIATE	AADEHMST	MASTHEAD
AADEEIRW	AWEARIED	AADEHNRV	VERANDAH
AADEEKNW	AWAKENED	AADEHPPR	PARAPHED
AADEEKRW	REAWAKED	AADEHPSS	SAPHEADS
AADEELNN	ANNEALED	AADEHRRW	HARDWARE
AADEELPP	APPEALED	AADEHRSS	HARASSED
AADEELTV	ALVEATED	AADEHRSW	RAWHEADS
AADEEMNT	EMANATED		WARHEADS
AADEEMRR	DEMERARA	AADEHSSY	SASHAYED
AADEENTT	ANTEDATE	AADEHSTT	HASTATED
AADEEPPR	APPEARED	AADEHSWY	HEADWAYS
AADEEPPS	APPEASED	AADEIIKK	KAIKAIED
AADEEPRS	PASEARED	AADEILMS	MALADIES
AADEEQTU	ADEQUATE	AADEILMU	AUMAILED
AADEFFLT	AFFLATED	AADEILNT	DENTALIA
AADEFFNR	FANFARED	AADEILPR	PRAEDIAL
AADEFFRY	AFFRAYED	AADEILPS	PALISADE
AADEFGLS	FALDAGES	AADEILPT	LAPIDATE
AADEFGRS	FARDAGES	AADEILRS	SALARIED
AADEFHLT	FLATHEAD	AADEILSS	ASSAILED
AADEFHST	HEADFAST	AADEILSV	VEDALIAS
AADEFIRS	PARADISE	AADEILTV	VALIDATE
	SAFARIED	AADEIMNN	AMANDINE
AADEFIRZ	FARADIZE	AADEIMNP	PANDEMIA
AADEFISS	FADAISES	AADEIMNR	MARINADE
AADEFLLR	FALDERAL	AADEIMNT	ANIMATED
AADEFLRY	DEFRAYAL		DIAMANTE
AADEFLTT	FALDETTA	AADEIMPZ	DIAZEPAM
AADEFRRW	WARFARED	AADEIMRV	MARAVEDI
AADEFRWY	WAYFARED	AADEIMST	DIASTEMA
AADEGGRS	AGGRADES	AADEINRR	DARRAINE
AADEGGRT	AGGRATED	AADEINRS	ARANEIDS
AADEGGRU	GUARDAGE	AADEINRT	DENTARIA
AADEGHLN	DANELAGH	AADEINTT	ATTAINED
AADEGILL	DIALLAGE		

AADEIPPR	APPAIRED	AADERRWY	WARRAYED
AADEIPRS	PARADISE	AADERSST	ASSARTED
AADEIPSS	DIAPASES	AADERSSW	SEAWARDS
AADEIPSU	DIAPAUSE	AADERSTT	ASTARTED
AADEIPTV	ADAPTIVE	AADERSTW	EASTWARD
AADEIRST	DATARIES	AADFGNNO	FANDANGO
	RADIATES	AADFGRSU	SAUFGARD
AADEIRTV	VARIATED	AADFHNST	HANDFAST
AADEISST	DIASTASE	AADFIMRS	FARADISM
AADEISTT	SATIATED	AADFINRU	UNAFRAID
AADEITVW	VIEWDATA	AADFLLLN	LANDFALL
AADEJMPY	PYJAMAED	AADFLORW	AARDWOLF
AADEJMRS	JEMADARS	AADFLOTX	TOADFLAX
AADEJNPN	JAPANNED	AADFLOWY	FOLDAWAY
AADEKLNR	KALENDAR	AADFMRRY	FARMYARD
AADEKMNR	MANDRAKE	AADGGHRS	HAGGARDS
AADEKMRS	KAMERADS	AADGGIMN	DAMAGING
AADEKNST	ASKANTED	AADGGLNN	GANGLAND
AADEKSTT	ATTASKED	AADGGLRS	LAGGARDS
AADELLPP	APPALLED	AADGGRSS	SAGGARDS
AADELLPS	PADELLAS	AADGGRST	STAGGARD
AADELLRT	DATALLER	AADGHILS	HIDALGAS
AADELLWY	WELLADAY	AADGHIPR	DIAGRAPH
AADELMNR	ALDERMAN	AADGHRTU	HATGUARD
	MALANDER	AADGIINS	GAINSAID
AADELMNS	DALESMAN	AADGILLR	GAILLARD
	LEADSMAN		GALLIARD
AADELMOS	ALAMODES	AADGILMR	MADRIGAL
AADELMPT	PALMATED	AADGILNO	DIAGONAL
AADELMRU	ALARUMED		GONADIAL
AADELMYZ	AMAZEDLY	AADGILNS	SALADING
AADELNRS	ADRENALS	AADGIMMN	MADAMING
AADELNST	EASTLAND	AADGIMMS	DIGAMMAS
AADELNSW	DANELAWS	AADGIMNR	MRIDANGA
AADELNSY	ANALYSED	AADGIMOS	AGAMOIDS
AADELNYZ	ANALYZED	AADGIMPR	PARADIGM
AADELPPT	PALPATED	AADGIMRS	DIAGRAMS
AADELPRS	PARDALES	AADGIMRT	GRADATIM
AADELPRY	PARLAYED	AADGINPR	PARADING
AADELRTU	RADULATE	AADGINPT	ADAPTING
AADELRTV	LARVATED	AADGINRR	DARRAIGN
AADELRTY	DAYTALER	AADGINRU	GUARDIAN
AADELSST	SALTATED	AADGINRW	AWARDING
AADELSTU	ADULATES	AADGIQRU	QUADRIGA
AADELSTY	DAYTALES	AADGLLSW	GADWALLS
AADELTUV	VALUATED	AADGLMOR	MALGRADO
AADEMNOS	ADENOMAS	AADGLMSY	AMYGDALS
AADEMNPS	SPADEMAN	AADGLNRS	GARLANDS
AADEMNST	MANDATES	AADGLNSS	SLADANGS
AADEMNUZ	UNAMAZED	AADGLOPR	PODAGRAL
AADEMORT	MATADORE	AADGLRSU	GRADUALS
AADEMRRU	MARAUDER	AADGMNOR	DRAGOMAN
AADEMRSS	MADRASES	AADGMNOS	GOADSMAN
AADEMSSS	ADMASSES	AADGMNRS	DRAGSMAN
AADENNST	ANDANTES		GRANDAMS
AADENRRT	NARRATED		GRANDMAS
AADENRRW	WARRANED	AADGMRSS	SMARAGDS
AADENRSV	VERANDAS	AADGNNQU	QUANDANG
AADENRTT	TARTANED	AADGNPRS	GRANDPAS
AADENSSW	WEASANDS	AADGNRST	GARDANTS
AADENSWZ	WEAZANDS	AADGNRSY	YARDANGS
AADENTUV	AVAUNTED	AADGNRTU	GUARDANT
AADEOPRT	TAPADERO	AADGNRUV	VANGUARD
AADEOPST	ADESPOTA	AADGOPRS	PODAGRAS
AADEORRT	AERODART	AADHHIPS	PADISHAH
AADEPRST	ADAPTERS	AADHIINP	APHIDIAN
	READAPTS	AADHILLR	HALLIARD
AADEPSSS	PASSADES	AADHILNR	HANDRAIL
AADEQRTU	QUADRATE	AADHILRV	HAVILDAR
AADERRRW	REARWARD		

AADHINRR	HARRIDAN	AADKLMNR	LANDMARK	AAEEGRSV	AVERAGES	AAEFLRTW	FLATWARE
AADHJNRS	HANDJARS	AADKLNPR	PARKLAND	AAEEGRTW	WATERAGE	AAEFMRST	FERMATAS
AADHKNSY	YAKHDANS	AADKLRTU	TALUKDAR	AAEEHIRT	HETAERIA	AAEFQRSU	AQUAFERS
AADHLMOY	DALMAHOY	AADKMNRS	DARKMANS	AAEEHPRT	HEARTPEA	AAEFRRRW	WARFARER
AADHLNPY	HANDPLAY	AADKMRSY	DAYMARKS	AAEEHRST	HETAERAS	AAEFRRSW	WARFARES
AADHLNSW	WASHLAND	AADKNRST	TANKARDS	AAEEHRTW	WHEATEAR	AAEFRRWY	WAYFARER
AADHLRSY	HALYARDS	AADKORWY	WORKADAY	AAEEHRWY	HEREAWAY	AAEFRSWY	WAYFARES
AADHMNNY	HANDYMAN	AADKPRRW	PARKWARD	AAEEILNT	ALIENATE	AAEGGINR	GRAINAGE
AADHMNOU	OMADHAUN	AADLLMRS	MALLARDS	AAEEINTT	TAENIATE	AAEGGIOT	AGIOTAGE
AADHNRSS	DARSHANS	AADLLNSW	LAWLANDS	AAEEJMNP	JAMPANEE	AAEGGLNR	LANGRAGE
AADHNSSW	HANDSAWS	AADLMNNS	LANDSMAN	AAEEKLTW	LATEWAKE	AAEGGLNU	LANGUAGE
AADHNSTT	HATSTAND	AADLMNOR	MANDORLA	AAEEKMNS	NAMESAKE	AAEGGNOS	ANAGOGES
AADHRRTW	THRAWARD	AADLMNOS	MANDOLAS	AAEEKNRW	REAWAKEN	AAEGGNOW	WAGONAGE
AADHRRYZ	HAZARDRY	AADLMNSS	LANDMASS	AAEEKPRT	PARAKEET	AAEGGNRY	GARGANEY
AADHRSWY	HAYWARDS	AADLMNSU	LADANUMS	AAEEKQSU	SEAQUAKE	AAEGGOPR	PARAGOGE
AADIJMNS	JAMDANIS	AADLMNUU	LAUDANUM	AAEEKRSW	REAWAKES	AAEGGOPS	APAGOGES
AADIKLLO	ALKALOID	AADLNOPR	PARLANDO	AAEELLLM	LAMELLAE	AAEGGRST	AGGRATES
AADIKLLR	KILLADAR	AADLNOST	SALTANDO	AAEELLMT	MALLEATE	AAEGHLNP	PHALANGE
AADIKLRY	KAILYARD	AADLNRSY	LANYARDS	AAEELLPT	PATELLAE	AAEGHLSU	HAULAGES
AADIKLSY	ILKADAYS	AADLORST	LOADSTAR	AAEELMST	MALEATES	AAEGHMRX	HEXAGRAM
AADIKMNS	DAMASKIN	AADLORTU	ADULATOR	AAEELNNR	ANNEALER	AAEGHMSS	GAMASHES
AADILLLO	ALLODIAL	AADLPPSU	APPLAUDS		LERNAEAN	AAEGHNRU	HARANGUE
AADILLNR	LANDRAIL	AADMMNOW	MADWOMAN	AAEELNPS	SEAPLANE	AAEGHNST	THANAGES
AADILLPR	PALLIARD	AADMMNSU	MANDAMUS		SPELAEAN	AAEGHOPY	HYPOGAEA
AADILLRS	SILLADAR	AADMNORS	MADRONAS	AAEELNPU	PAENULAE	AAEGILLT	ALLIGATE
AADILLRY	RADIALLY		MANDORAS	AAEELORT	AREOLATE	AAEGILNP	PELAGIAN
AADILMNN	MAINLAND		MONARDAS	AAEELRST	LAETARES	AAEGILNR	REGALIAN
AADILMNO	DOMAINAL		ROADSMAN	AAEELRTU	LAUREATE	AAEGILNT	AGENTIAL
	DOMANIAL	AADMNORT	MANDATOR	AAEELSST	ELASTASE		ALGINATE
AADILMNP	PLAIDMAN	AADMNRSS	MANSARDS	AAEELTUV	EVALUATE	AAEGILRS	GASALIER
AADILMRS	ADMIRALS	AADMOPPP	PAPPADOM	AAEEMNST	EMANATES		LAIRAGES
	AMILDARS	AADMOQSU	MADOQUAS		MANATEES		REGALIAS
AADILNOR	ORDALIAN	AADMORST	MATADORS	AAEEMPRS	PARAMESE	AAEGILSS	ALGESIAS
AADILNPR	PRANDIAL	AADMRSZZ	MAZZARDS	AAEENNNT	ANTENNAE	AAEGILSX	GALAXIES
AADILNPS	PALADINS	AADNOPRS	PANDORAS	AAEENPRT	PARANETE	AAEGIMNO	EGOMANIA
AADILNRS	LANIARDS	AADNORST	ONDATRAS	AAEENRRS	ARRASENE	AAEGIMNS	MAGNESIA
AADILNTT	DILATANT	AADNORTY	DONATARY	AAEENRST	ARSENATE	AAEGIMNZ	MAGAZINE
AADILOPS	PALISADO	AADNOSUV	VANADOUS		SERENATA	AAEGIMRR	MARRIAGE
AADILORR	RAILROAD	AADNOSWY	NOWADAYS	AAEENSTU	NAUSEATE	AAEGIMRT	GEMATRIA
AADILPRS	PARDALIS	AADNQRSU	QUADRANS	AAEEPPRR	APPEARER		MARITAGE
AADILPRY	LAPIDARY	AADNQRTU	QUADRANT		RAPPAREE	AAEGINNR	ANEARING
AADILRRS	RISALDAR	AADNQRUY	QUANDARY		REAPPEAR	AAEGINPS	NAGAPIES
AADILRST	TAILARDS	AADNRRSW	WARRANDS	AAEEPPSS	APPEASES		PAGANISE
AADILSST	STADIALS	AADNRRSY	DARRAYNS	AAEEPRST	ASPERATE	AAEGINPT	PAGINATE
AADIMNNR	MANDARIN	AADNRSTY	TANYARDS		SEPARATE	AAEGINPZ	PAGANIZE
AADIMNRS	MANDIRAS	AADNRSWY	NAYWARDS	AAEEPSTT	ASEPTATE	AAEGINRS	ANGARIES
AADIMNRT	TAMARIND	AADOPPRR	PARADROP	AAEERRWW	REWAREWA	AAEGINRT	AERATING
AADIMNRY	DAIRYMAN	AADOPRST	ADAPTORS	AAEERSTT	STEARATE	AAEGINST	SAGINATE
	MAINYARD	AADOPRXY	PARADOXY	AAEERSWX	EARWAXES	AAEGINSW	WAINAGES
AADIMNRZ	ZAMINDAR	AADOPSSS	PASSADOS	AAEFFGRS	AGRAFFES	AAEGINTV	NAVIGATE
AADIMNSS	DAMASSIN	AADOPSUY	PADUASOY	AAEFFGST	STAFFAGE		VAGINATE
AADIMNSU	SUDAMINA	AADORSWY	ROADWAYS	AAEFFIRS	AFFAIRES	AAEGIPRS	IGARAPES
AADIMNUV	VANADIUM	AADQRSTU	QUADRATS	AAEFFLLS	FALAFELS	AAEGIPRU	PERIAGUA
AADIMORS	DIORAMAS	AADRSSTY	DAYSTARS	AAEFFLPR	PARAFFLE	AAEGIRRS	ARRIAGES
AADIMSTZ	SAMIZDAT	AAEEEHRT	HETAERAE	AAEFFNRS	FANFARES	AAEGIRSV	VAGARIES
AADINNOT	ADNATION	AAEEFFRS	AFFEARES	AAEFFSTT	TAFFETAS	AAEGISSS	ASSEGAIS
AADINOPR	PARANOID	AAEEFGLS	LEAFAGES	AAEFGHRW	WHARFAGE	AAEGISST	AGITATES
AADINOPS	DIAPASON	AAEEFRRS	SEAFARER	AAEFGINR	AFEARING	AAEGIVWY	GIVEAWAY
AADINOPT	ADAPTION	AAEEGILN	ALIENAGE	AAEFGITT	FATIGATE	AAEGJSTU	AJUTAGES
AADINRRS	DARRAINS	AAEEGILP	EPIGAEAL	AAEFGLLL	FLAGELLA	AAEGKNST	TANKAGES
AADINRRW	AIRDRAWN	AAEEGINP	EPIGAEAN	AAEFGLOT	FLOATAGE	AAEGKOSS	SOAKAGES
AADINRST	RADIANTS	AAEEGKLS	LEAKAGES	AAEFGRTU	FRAUTAGE	AAEGLLMS	SMALLAGE
AADINRSV	VIRANDAS	AAEEGLLN	ENALLAGE	AAEFGSTW	WAFTAGES	AAEGLLPR	PELLAGRA
AADIOPRS	DIASPORA	AAEEGLST	ETALAGES	AAEFILTY	FAYALITE	AAEGLLSS	GALLEASS
AADIORRT	RADIATOR	AAEEGMNS	AMENAGES	AAEFIMRR	AIRFRAME	AAEGLLST	GALLATES
AADIPSUY	UPADAISY	AAEEGMPR	AMPERAGE	AAEFINNT	FAINEANT		STALLAGE
AADIRRSW	AIRWARDS	AAEEGMTY	METAYAGE	AAEFINTX	ANTEFIXA		TALLAGES
AADIRRSY	DISARRAY	AAEEGNRS	SANGAREE	AAEFLMTT	FLATMATE	AAEGLLTU	GLUTAEAL
AADJNTTU	ADJUTANT	AAEEGRST	STEARAGE	AAEFLPRS	EARFLAPS	AAEGLMNS	GAMELANS
AADJNTUV	ADJUVANT				PARAFLES	AAEGLMNV	GAVELMAN

AAEGLNOU	ANALOGUE
AAEGLNPT	PLANTAGE
AAEGLNRS	ALNAGERS
AAEGLNRU	AULNAGER
AAEGLNSS	LASAGNES
AAEGLNSU	AULNAGES
AAEGLNTU	ANGULATE
AAEGLOSV	AASVOGEL
AAEGLRRS	REALGARS
	RESALGAR
AAEGLRRW	WARRAGLE
AAEGLRST	AGRESTAL
AAEGLRTY	LEGATARY
AAEGLSST	AGELASTS
	LASTAGES
AAEGLSSV	SALVAGES
AAEGLSVY	SAVAGELY
AAEGLTUV	VAULTAGE
AAEGMMNR	ENGRAMMA
AAEGMNPY	PYGMAEAN
AAEGMNRS	MANAGERS
AAEGMNRV	GRAVAMEN
AAEGMNST	MAGENTAS
	MAGNATES
AAEGMORR	AEROGRAM
AAEGMORS	SAGAMORE
AAEGMPRS	RAMPAGES
AAEGMPRU	RAMPAUGE
AAEGMRRV	MARGRAVE
AAEGMRRY	GRAMARYE
AAEGMSSS	MASSAGES
AAEGMTTW	MEGAWATT
AAEGNNOP	NEOPAGAN
AAEGNNPS	PANNAGES
AAEGNNST	TANNAGES
AAEGNPST	PAGEANTS
AAEGNRRR	ARRANGER
AAEGNRRS	ARRANGES
AAEGNRST	STARAGEN
	TANAGERS
AAEGNRTU	RUNAGATE
AAEGNSTT	STAGNATE
AAEGNSTV	VANTAGES
AAEGNSTW	WANTAGES
AAEGNTUV	VAUNTAGE
AAEGORRT	ARROGATE
AAEGORTT	AEGROTAT
AAEGPPRW	WRAPPAGE
AAEGPSSS	PASSAGES
AAEGPSSY	PAYSAGES
AAEGQSUY	QUAYAGES
AAEGRRSV	RAVAGERS
AAEGRSTT	REGATTAS
AAEGRSVY	SAVAGERY
AAEGSSSU	ASSUAGES
	SAUSAGES
AAEGSSSW	ASSWAGES
AAEGSSTV	SAVAGEST
AAEGSSTW	TASSWAGE
	WASTAGES
AAEGSTTW	WATTAGES
AAEGSTWY	GATEWAYS
	GETAWAYS
AAEHIIRT	HETAIRAI
	HETAIRIA
AAEHILMN	HIELAMAN
AAEHILNP	APHELIAN
AAEHILNT	ANTHELIA
AAEHILPR	PARHELIA
AAEHIMNT	ANTHEMIA
	HAEMATIN
AAEHINPT	APHANITE
AAEHINST	ASTHENIA
AAEHIPST	APATHIES
AAEHKLST	ALKAHEST
AAEHKMRY	HAYMAKER
AAEHKNST	KHANATES
AAEHLLLS	ALLHEALS
AAEHLMSY	SEALYHAM
AAEHLMTU	HAMULATE
AAEHLNTX	EXHALANT
AAEHLPRX	HEXAPLAR
AAEHLPSX	HEXAPLAS
AAEHLPUV	UPHEAVAL
AAEHLRST	TREHALAS
AAEHLRTT	THEATRAL
AAEHLSTT	ATHLETAS
AAEHMNPY	NYMPHAEA
AAEHMNRS	SHAREMAN
	SHEARMAN
AAEHMNRT	EARTHMAN
AAEHMOPR	AMPHORAE
AAEHMORT	ATHEROMA
AAEHNPRS	HANAPERS
AAEHNPST	PHEASANT
AAEHNPSY	SYNAPHEA
AAEHNTTX	XANTHATE
AAEHPRSZ	PHEAZARS
AAEHRRSS	HARASSER
AAEHRSSS	HARASSES
AAEHRSSY	HEARSAYS
AAEHRTWX	EARTHWAX
AAEIIKNS	AKINESIA
AAEIIMRV	VIRAEMIA
AAEIIPRS	APIARIES
AAEIIRSV	AVIARIES
AAEIKKMZ	KAMIKAZE
AAEIKLLN	ALKALINE
AAEIKLLS	ALKALIES
	ALKALISE
AAEIKLLZ	ALKALIZE
AAEIKMRR	KRAMERIA
AAEILLLU	ALLELUIA
AAEILLMM	MAMILLAE
AAEILLMR	ARMILLAE
AAEILLMX	MAXILLAE
AAEILLPP	PAPILLAE
AAEILLPT	PALLIATE
AAEILLRT	ARILLATE
AAEILLRY	AERIALLY
AAEILLTT	TALLIATE
AAEILLTV	ALLATIVE
AAEILMNT	ALAIMENT
	LAMINATE
AAEILMNV	VELAMINA
AAEILMRT	MATERIAL
AAEILMSS	MALAISES
AAEILNNS	ANNALISE
AAEILNNZ	ANNALIZE
AAEILNPR	AIRPLANE
AAEILNPT	PALATINE
AAEILNRU	AURELIAN
AAEILNRV	VALERIAN
AAEILNSS	NASALISE
AAEILNSZ	NASALIZE
AAEILNTT	ANTLIATE
AAEILNTV	AVENTAIL
AAEILORS	OLEARIAS
AAEILPPS	PAPALISE
AAEILPPZ	PAPALIZE
AAEILPRT	PARIETAL
AAEILPST	STAPELIA
AAEILRRT	ARTERIAL
AAEILRSS	SALARIES
AAEILRSU	AURELIAS
AAEILRTV	VARIETAL
AAEILSTV	AESTIVAL
	SALIVATE
AAEILSTX	SAXATILE
AAEILTVX	LAXATIVE
AAEIMMST	IMAMATES
AAEIMNOT	METANOIA
AAEIMNPR	PEARMAIN
AAEIMNPT	IMPANATE
AAEIMNRT	MARINATE
AAEIMNRZ	MAZARINE
AAEIMNSS	AMNESIAS
AAEIMNST	AMENTIAS
	ANIMATES
AAEIMOPR	PAROEMIA
AAEIMOTX	TOXAEMIA
AAEIMPSY	PYAEMIAS
AAEIMRSU	URAEMIAS
AAEIMSUV	MAUVAISE
AAEINNTT	ANTENATI
AAEINORT	AERATION
AAEINORX	ANOREXIA
AAEINPRS	PANARIES
AAEINRST	ANTISERA
	ARTESIAN
	RESINATA
AAEINRTT	REATTAIN
AAEINRTU	INAURATE
AAEINSTT	ASTATINE
	SANITATE
	TANAISTE
AAEINSTV	SANATIVE
AAEINTTT	TITANATE
AAEIPPRS	APPRAISE
AAEIPPSS	APEPSIAS
AAEIPRRS	PAREIRAS
AAEIPRSS	SPIRAEAS
AAEIPRST	ASPIRATE
	PARASITE
	SEPTARIA
AAEIPRTT	PATRIATE
AAEIPRTZ	TRAPEZIA
AAEIPRXY	APYREXIA
AAEIPSTT	APATITES
AAEIRRRT	TERRARIA
AAEIRSST	ASTERIAS
	ATRESIAS
AAEIRSSX	XERASIAS
AAEIRSTT	ARIETTAS
	ARISTATE
AAEIRSTV	VARIATES
AAEIRSVW	AIRWAVES
AAEIRTTZ	ZARATITE
AAEISSTT	SATIATES
AAEITTVX	TAXATIVE
AAEJNNPR	JAPANNER
AAEJNRST	NAARTJES
AAEJNRTZ	JAZERANT
AAEJRSSW	SWARAJES
AAEKLMRY	MALARKEY
AAEKLNRS	LARNAKES
AAEKLNST	ALKANETS
	KANTELOS
AAEKMRRS	EARMARKS
AAEKMRSS	SEAMARKS
AAEKNPRT	PARTAKEN
AAEKPRRT	PARTAKER
AAEKPRST	PARTAKES
AAEKSSSV	KAVASSES
	VAKASSES
AAELLLMR	LAMELLAR
AAELLLPR	PARALLEL
AAELLMPU	AMPULLAE
AAELLNPU	PLANULAE
AAELLNSZ	ZANELLAS
AAELLORV	ALVEOLAR
AAELLPRS	PARELLAS
AAELLPRT	PATELLAR
AAELLPST	PATELLAS
AAELLRST	LATERALS
AAELLRSY	ALLAYERS
AAELLUVV	VALVULAE
AAELLWWY	WELLAWAY
AAELLWYY	ALLEYWAY
AAELMMNO	MELANOMA
AAELMMTU	MALAMUTE
AAELMNOT	MALONATE
AAELMNPT	PLATEMAN
AAELMNRT	MATERNAL
AAELMNSS	SALESMAN
AAELMNST	TALESMAN
AAELMNSW	WEALSMAN
AAELMNSY	SEAMANLY
AAELMOST	OATMEALS
AAELMPRT	MALAPERT
AAELMPRX	EXAMPLAR
AAELMPSS	LAMPASES
	LAMPASSE
AAELMPST	PLATEASM
AAELMPTV	VAMPLATE
AAELMPTY	PLAYMATE
AAELMRSY	LAMASERY
AAELMRTT	MALTREAT
AAELMSST	MALTASES
AAELMSSY	AMYLASES
AAELNNNT	ANTENNAL
AAELNNOT	NEONATAL
AAELNNTU	ANNULATE
AAELNOSS	SEASONAL
AAELNOSV	VALONEAS
AAELNPRS	PRENASAL
AAELNPRT	PARENTAL
	PATERNAL
	PRENATAL
AAELNPRW	WARPLANE
AAELNPST	PLATANES
	PLEASANT
AAELNPSU	PAENULAS
AAELNRSS	ARSENALS
AAELNRSY	ANALYSER
AAELNRTT	ALTERANT
	ALTERNAT
AAELNRTX	RELAXANT
AAELNRYZ	ANALYZER
AAELNSST	SEALANTS
AAELNSSV	ENVASSAL
AAELNSSY	ANALYSES
AAELNSTZ	ZEALANTS
AAELNSWY	LANEWAYS
AAELNSYZ	ANALYZES
AAELORSU	AUREOLAS
AAELORTY	ALEATORY
AAELOSTX	OXALATES
AAELPPRS	APPARELS
AAELPPST	PALPATES

AAELPPSU	APPLAUSE	AAEORTTV	ROTAVATE	AAGGNSWY	GANGWAYS	AAGINNTW	AWANTING
AAELPRST	PALESTRA	AAEPPRST	PARAPETS	AAGHHINS	SHANGHAI	AAGINPPY	APPAYING
AAELPRSV	PALAVERS	AAEPPSTT	APPESTAT	AAGHILNN	HANGNAIL	AAGINPRU	PAGURIAN
AAELPRSY	PARALYSE	AAEPSWXX	PAXWAXES	AAGHILPY	HYPALGIA	AAGINRRS	ARRAIGNS
AAELPRTT	TETRAPLA	AAEPSZZZ	PAZAZZES	AAGHILRS	GHARIALS	AAGINRRY	ARRAYING
AAELPRYZ	PARALYZE	AAERRSST	TARRASES		HARIGALS	AAGINRSS	SANGRIAS
AAELPSTU	PLATEAUS	AAERRSTT	TARTARES	AAGHIMNS	ASHAMING		SARANGIS
AAELPSTV	PALSTAVE	AAERRTTT	TARTRATE	AAGHIMRT	TAGHAIRM	AAGINRSY	ARAYSING
AAELPTUV	VAPULATE	AAERSSSY	ASSAYERS	AAGHINPS	PAGANISH	AAGINSST	ASSIGNAT
AAELPTUX	PLATEAUX	AAERSSTU	SATURATE	AAGHINPW	AWHAPING	AAGINSSU	GAUSSIAN
AAELRSTZ	LAZARETS	AAERTWWY	WATERWAY	AAGHIPRR	AIRGRAPH	AAGINSSY	ASSAYING
AAELRTUV	VELATURA	AAFFILRT	TAFFRAIL	AAGHIRSV	VAGARISH		GAINSAYS
AAELRUZZ	ZARZUELA	AAFFINPR	PARAFFIN	AAGHKMNY	GYMKHANA	AAGIORTT	AGITATOR
AAELRWYY	WAYLAYER	AAFFINSS	SAFFIANS	AAGHLNPY	ANAGLYPH	AAGIPRSU	PIRAGUAS
AAELSSTT	SALTATES	AAFFLPST	PALSTAFF	AAGHLOSS	GASAHOLS	AAGIRRSY	ARGYRIAS
AAELSTUV	VALUATES	AAFFLSTU	AFFLATUS	AAGHMNOY	MAHOGANY	AAGIRSTV	GRAVITAS
AAELSTZZ	ALTEZZAS	AAFFNNOR	FANFARON	AAGHMNSW	WHANGAMS		STRAVAIG
AAEMMMRS	MAREMMAS	AAFGILNO	GOLFIANA	AAGHNOPR	AGRAPHON	AAGISSTT	SAGITTAS
AAEMMNRT	ARMAMENT	AAFGLLNU	LANGLAUF	AAGHOPPR	APOGRAPH	AAGKNOOR	KANGAROO
AAEMMSTT	STEMMATA	AAFGLNRT	FLAGRANT	AAGHQSUU	QUAHAUGS	AAGKOOSZ	GAZOOKAS
AAEMNOTZ	METAZOAN	AAFGNRRT	FRAGRANT	AAGHRRTU	ARRAUGHT	AAGKORST	KATORGAS
AAEMNPRS	SPEARMAN	AAFHHIKL	KHALIFAH	AAGIILMN	IMAGINAL	AAGLLMOY	ALLOGAMY
AAEMNPRT	PARAMENT	AAFHIKLS	KHALIFAS	AAGIILNV	AVAILING	AAGLLNOO	LAGOONAL
AAEMNRST	SARMENTA	AAFHIKLT	KHALIFAT	AAGIIMST	ASTIGMIA	AAGLLNRY	LARYNGAL
	SEMANTRA		KHILAFAT	AAGIINRS	ARAISING	AAGLLNST	GALLANTS
AAEMNRSU	MURAENAS	AAFHIRST	AIRSHAFT	AAGIINTV	AVIATING	AAGLLOPY	POLYGALA
AAEMNRTT	ATRAMENT	AAFHRSUU	HAUSFRAU	AAGIINTW	AWAITING	AAGLMNSS	GLASSMAN
AAEMNRTW	WATERMAN	AAFIILLM	FAMILIAL	AAGIKLNO	KAOLIANG	AAGLNNOO	ANALOGON
AAEMNSST	NAMASTES	AAFIILLR	FILARIAL	AAGIKLNR	KRAALING	AAGLNPSS	LAPSANGS
AAEMNSTU	MANTEAUS	AAFIILMR	FAMILIAR	AAGIKLNS	ASLAKING	AAGLNQUU	AQUALUNG
AAEMNTUX	MANTEAUX	AAFIILRS	FILARIAS	AAGIKMRS	SKIAGRAM	AAGLNRRU	GRANULAR
AAEMORTT	TERATOMA	AAFIINST	FISTIANA	AAGIKNSW	AWAKINGS	AAGLOPRY	PARALOGY
AAEMOSTT	STEATOMA	AAFIKLLY	ALKALIFY	AAGIKNSZ	ZIGANKAS	AAGLRRUW	WARRAGUL
AAEMOTTU	AUTOMATE	AAFILLNW	RAINFALL	AAGILLNY	ALLAYING	AAGLRSTU	GASTRULA
AAEMPPSS	PAMPASES	AAFILLUV	AVAILFUL	AAGILLSS	GALLIASS	AAGMMRRS	GRAMMARS
AAEMPTTU	AMPUTATE	AAFILMST	FATALISM	AAGILLTV	GALLIVAT	AAGMNNOR	NANOGRAM
AAEMQSTU	SQUAMATE	AAFILNST	FANTAILS	AAGILLUZ	ALGUAZIL	AAGMNNRS	GRANNAMS
AAEMRRTU	ARMATURE	AAFILOPR	PARAFOIL	AAGILMNO	MAGNOLIA	AAGMNOPZ	ZAMPOGNA
AAEMRSTU	AMATEURS	AAFILQSU	ALFAQUIS	AAGILMNR	ALARMING	AAGMNORT	MARTAGON
AAEMRTTU	MATURATE	AAFILSTT	FATALIST		MARGINAL	AAGMNPRS	PANGRAMS
AAENNNST	ANTENNAS	AAFILTTY	FATALITY	AAGILMNX	MALAXING	AAGMNRST	TANGRAMS
AAENNOTT	ANNOTATE	AAFIMNOR	FORAMINA	AAGILMOT	GLIOMATA		TRANGAMS
AAENNSTT	STANNATE	AAFINNRS	SAFRANIN	AAGILMSY	MYALGIAS	AAGMNRTU	ARMGAUNT
	TANNATES	AAFINNST	INFANTAS	AAGILNOT	GALTONIA	AAGMNSSW	SWAGSMAN
AAENNSTU	NAUSEANT	AAFINRRW	WARFARIN	AAGILNPT	PALATING	AAGMNSTY	SYNTAGMA
AAENNSTV	VENTANAS	AAFINSTU	FAUSTIAN	AAGILNRR	LARRIGAN	AAGMORSS	MARGOSAS
AAENORRU	AUROREAN	AAFIPRST	PARFAITS	AAGILNSS	SALSAING	AAGMOTUY	AUTOGAMY
AAENORST	ANOESTRA	AAFIRSWY	FAIRWAYS	AAGILNUV	VAGINULA	AAGMRSST	MATGRASS
AAENORSU	ARANEOUS	AAFJLLSW	JAWFALLS	AAGILOOP	APOLOGIA	AAGNNSTT	STAGNANT
AAENORTU	AERONAUT	AAFJLORS	ALFORJAS	AAGILOST	OTALGIAS	AAGNOPRS	PARAGONS
AAENOSST	ASSONATE	AAFLLPRT	PRATFALL	AAGILPRY	PLAGIARY	AAGNOPRT	TRAGOPAN
AAENPPRS	PARPANES	AAFLLPST	SPATFALL	AAGILRRW	WARRIGAL	AAGNORRT	ARROGANT
AAENPPRT	APPARENT	AAFLMORV	LAVAFORM	AAGILSTT	SAGITTAL		TARRAGON
	TRAPPEAN	AAFLNORS	FORLANAS	AAGILSTW	WAGTAILS	AAGNORSZ	ORGANZAS
AAENPRTY	PRYTANEA	AAFLNOTT	FLOATANT	AAGIMMRR	MARIGRAM	AAGNORTU	ARGONAUT
AAENPSST	ANAPESTS	AAFLNRSU	FURLANAS	AAGIMNNO	AGNOMINA	AAGNRSTV	VAGRANTS
	PEASANTS	AAFLSTWY	FLATWAYS	AAGIMNOS	ANGIOMAS	AAGNRTUY	GUARANTY
AAENPSTT	ANTEPAST	AAFMNRST	RAFTSMAN	AAGIMNPS	PAGANISM	AAGNRTYZ	ZYGANTRA
AAENPSTY	PEASANTY	AAFMNSST	FANTASMS	AAGIMNRR	MARGARIN	AAGOPSSS	SAPSAGOS
AAENRRSS	NARRASES	AAFNPPRT	FRAPPANT	AAGIMNSS	AMASSING	AAGORSSS	SARGASSO
AAENRRST	NARRATES	AAFNSSTT	FANTASTS		SIAMANGS	AAGORSSU	SAGUAROS
AAENRSTT	TARTANES	AAGGGINR	GARAGING	AAGIMNSY	GYMNASIA	AAGRSSTU	SASTRUGA
AAENRSTV	TAVERNAS	AAGGILNR	GANGLIAR	AAGIMPTU	PATAGIUM	AAGRSTUZ	ZASTRUGA
	TSAREVNA	AAGGIMNN	MANAGING	AAGIMSSV	SAVAGISM	AAHHNNST	THANNAHS
AAENRSUW	UNAWARES	AAGGIMNR	MARAGING	AAGIMSTT	STIGMATA	AAHHNPST	NAPHTHAS
AAENSSSV	VANESSAS	AAGGINRV	RAVAGING	AAGINNOT	AGNATION	AAHIIKRT	TARAKIHI
AAENTTTT	ATTENTAT	AAGGINSV	SAVAGING	AAGINNRW	AWARNING	AAHIJPRS	RAJASHIP
AAEOPSTT	APOSTATE	AAGGITTW	GIGAWATT	AAGINNSW	WANIGANS	AAHIKLPS	PASHALIK
AAEORRST	AERATORS	AAGGLLLY	LALLYGAG	AAGINNSY	SYNANGIA	AAHIKRST	KITHARAS
AAEORSST	AEROSTAT	AAGGMNNS	GANGSMAN	AAGINNTV	VAGINANT	AAHILLLS	HALLALIS

AAHILLNS	HALLIANS	AAIIRTVX	AVIATRIX	AAILNSSY	ANALYSIS	AAINRSSV	SAVARINS
AAHILMNR	HARMALIN	AAIJLLQU	QUILLAJA	AAILNSTV	VALIANTS	AAINRSTV	VARIANTS
AAHILMRS	ALMIRAHS	AAIJLNPS	JALAPINS	AAILNSTY	NASALITY	AAINRSTY	SANITARY
AAHILNNT	INHALANT	AAIJMNPS	JAMPANIS	AAILNTTT	LATITANT	AAINSSSS	ASSASSIN
AAHILNOT	HALATION	AAIJNRSZ	JANIZARS	AAILNTTY	NATALITY	AAINSTTT	ANTISTAT
AAHILPSY	PHYSALIA	AAIJNRYZ	JANIZARY	AAILORRS	RASORIAL		ATTAINTS
AAHIMNOS	MAHONIAS	AAIKKNOS	SKOKIAAN	AAILORRV	VARIOLAR	AAINSTTU	TUTANIAS
AAHIMNPS	PASHMINA	AAIKLNST	NASTALIK	AAILORSS	ROSALIAS	AAINSTTY	SATANITY
AAHINOPS	APHONIAS	AAIKMNNS	MANAKINS	AAILORSV	VARIOLAS	AAIOPRRT	TROPARIA
AAHINPRS	PIRANHAS	AAIKMNRS	RAMAKINS	AAILPPRU	PUPARIAL	AAIOPRST	ATROPIAS
AAHINRTU	HAURIANT	AAIKMNST	ANTIMASK	AAILPPST	PAPALIST	AAIOPRSU	PAROUSIA
AAHINSST	SHAITANS	AAIKMORS	ROMAIKAS	AAILPRST	PARTIALS	AAIOPSTU	AUTOPSIA
AAHIPRST	PITARAHS	AAIKMRSS	KARAISMS		PATRIALS	AAIORSSU	SAOUARIS
AAHIPSTZ	ZAPTIAHS	AAIKMRST	TAMARISK		TRIAPSAL	AAIORSTV	AVIATORS
AAHIPSXY	ASPHYXIA	AAIKORSU	OUAKARIS	AAILPSTT	TALIPATS	AAIPPSTT	PITAPATS
AAHIRSST	SHARIATS	AAIKPPRS	PAPRIKAS	AAILRRSV	ARRIVALS	AAIPRSSX	SPARAXIS
AAHJKNRS	KHANJARS	AAIKSSTT	ASTATKIS	AAILRSTV	TRAVAILS	AAIPRSTT	PARTITAS
AAHKLLMR	HALLMARK	AAIKSSTV	SVASTIKA	AAILRSVY	SALIVARY	AAIQRSTU	AQUARIST
AAHKLRSS	LASHKARS	AAIKSSTW	SWASTIKA	AAILRSWY	RAILWAYS	AAIQSSSU	QUASSIAS
AAHKMOTW	TOMAHAWK	AAIKSTVV	AKVAVITS	AAILSSSV	VASSAILS	AAIQSTUV	AQUAVITS
AAHKMSSY	YASHMAKS	AAILLLUV	ALLUVIAL	AAILSSSW	WASSAILS	AAIRSSTT	TSARITSA
AAHLLLOO	HALLALOO	AAILLMMM	MAMMILLA	AAILSSTY	STAYSAIL	AAIRSTWY	STAIRWAY
AAHLLOPT	ALLOPATH	AAILLMMR	MAMILLAR	AAILSTTT	LATITATS	AAISTWXY	TAXIWAYS
AAHLLSWY	HALLWAYS	AAILLMNS	MANILLAS	AAIMMNOS	AMMONIAS	AAJKLSWY	JAYWALKS
AAHLMMSS	MASHLAMS	AAILLMNT	MANTILLA	AAIMMNST	MAINMAST	AAJMMORR	MARJORAM
AAHLMOOS	MASOOLAH	AAILLMNY	ANIMALLY	AAIMMRSU	SAMARIUM	AAJMORST	MAJORATS
AAHLMRSS	MARSHALS	AAILLMRS	ARMILLAS	AAIMNORT	ANIMATOR	AAJOPSSU	SAPAJOUS
AAHLMSTU	THALAMUS	AAILLNOV	VALLONIA		MONTARIA	AAKKLRSU	KARAKULS
AAHLNRSW	NARWHALS	AAILLNSV	VANILLAS		TAMANOIR	AAKKMOST	TOKAMAKS
AAHLPSST	ASPHALTS	AAILLPPR	PAPILLAR	AAIMNORW	AIRWOMAN	AAKLMPSU	LAMPUKAS
AAHLRSSW	SHALWARS	AAILLRRY	ARILLARY	AAIMNOSS	ANOSMIAS	AAKLMRUY	YARMULKA
AAHMNNSU	HANUMANS	AAILLRXY	AXILLARY	AAIMNOST	AMATIONS	AAKLMSUY	YAMULKAS
AAHMNORT	MARATHON	AAILMMRS	ALARMISM	AAIMNPRZ	MARZIPAN	AAKLNOOS	OOLAKANS
AAHMNOST	HOASTMAN		AMMIRALS	AAIMNPTU	PUTAMINA	AAKLNOSU	OULAKANS
AAHMNOTX	XANTHOMA	AAILMNNT	LAMANTIN	AAIMNRRT	TRIMARAN	AAKLOOPS	PALOOKAS
AAHMNPST	PHANTASM	AAILMNOP	PALAMINO	AAIMNRRU	RANARIUM	AAKLPRTY	KALYPTRA
AAHMRSST	STRAMASH	AAILMNOR	MANORIAL	AAIMNRST	TAMARINS	AAKLRSSU	KURSAALS
AAHNNOSS	HOSANNAS		MORAINAL	AAIMNSST	MANTISSA		RUSALKAS
AAHNORST	ATHANORS	AAILMNOX	MONAXIAL		SATANISM	AAKLSSSU	SAKSAULS
AAHNORSV	NAVARHOS	AAILMNPS	PANISLAM		STAMINAS	AAKLSWWY	WALKWAYS
AAHNPSTY	PHANTASY	AAILMNRU	MANURIAL	AAIMNSTU	AMIANTUS	AAKMMNRS	MARKSMAN
AAHOPRTU	AUTOHARP	AAILMNRY	LAMINARY	AAIMNSTY	MAINSTAY	AAKMOSSU	MOUSAKAS
AAHPRSTW	WARPATHS	AAILMNST	STAMINAL	AAIMOPRS	MARIPOSA		MOUSSAKA
AAHPSTWY	PATHWAYS		TALISMAN	AAIMPRST	PASTRAMI	AAKMRSUZ	MAZURKAS
AAHRRTTW	THRAWART	AAILMNSU	ALUMINAS	AAIMPRSU	MARSUPIA	AAKMRSWY	WAYMARKS
AAHRSSST	SHASTRAS	AAILMNSV	NAVALISM	AAIMQRUU	AQUARIUM	AAKNNSTU	NUNATAKS
AAIIILMR	MILIARIA	AAILMOPT	LIPOMATA	AAIMRRSY	MISARRAY	AAKNSTWY	TWANKAYS
AAIIKKNN	KINAKINA	AAILMORR	ARMORIAL	AAIMSSTV	ATAVISMS	AAKOOPPS	PAKAPOOS
AAIILLQU	QUILLAIA	AAILMPPS	PAPALISM	AAINNOPV	PAVONIAN	AAKPRSWY	PARKWAYS
AAIILMNS	MAINSAIL	AAILMPRT	PRIMATAL	AAINNOST	SONATINA	AALLLSTY	LAYSTALL
AAIILMRS	AIRMAILS	AAILMRST	ALARMIST	AAINNOTT	NATATION	AALLMNST	STALLMAN
AAIILNRZ	ALIZARIN		ALASTRIM	AAINNRSV	NAVARINS	AALLMNTY	TALLYMAN
AAIILNUX	UNIAXIAL	AAILMTTU	ULTIMATA		NIRVANAS	AALLMNUY	MANUALLY
AAIILPRR	RIPARIAL	AAILNNOT	NATIONAL	AAINNRTU	NUTARIAN	AALLNNUY	ANNUALLY
AAIILPRS	PAIRIALS	AAILNNPT	PLAINANT	AAINNSST	NAISSANT	AALLNPRU	PLANULAR
AAIILPST	TILAPIAS		PLANTAIN	AAINNSSY	SANNYASI	AALLOORW	WALLAROO
AAIILRSZ	ALIZARAS	AAILNNRU	LUNARIAN	AAINOPSS	PAISANOS	AALLORSU	ALLOSAUR
AAIILRTX	TRIAXIAL	AAILNNST	ANNALIST	AAINORRS	ORARIANS	AALLOSTV	LAVOLTAS
AAIILRUX	AUXILIAR		SANTALIN		ROSARIAN	AALLPRST	PLASTRAL
AAIIMNNT	MAINTAIN	AAILNOPS	SALOPIAN	AAINOTTX	TAXATION	AALLRUVV	VALVULAR
AAIIMNPX	PANMIXIA	AAILNOPT	TALAPOIN	AAINPRST	ASPIRANT	AALMMNOS	AMMONALS
AAIINOTV	AVIATION	AAILNORT	NOTARIAL		PARTISAN	AALMMNORT	MATRONAL
AAIINPRR	RIPARIAN		RATIONAL	AAINPRTZ	PARTIZAN	AALMNORU	MONAURAL
AAIINPZZ	PIAZZIAN	AAILNOST	AILANTOS	AAINQRTU	QUATRAIN	AALMNOSS	SALAMONS
AAIINRST	INTARSIA	AAILNOSV	VALONIAS	AAINQTTU	AQUATINT	AALMNPTY	TYMPANAL
AAIIOPST	APOSITIA	AAILNOTV	LAVATION	AAINRRSS	SARRASIN	AALMNTTU	TANTALUM
AAIIORTZ	ZOIATRIA	AAILNPRU	PLANURIA	AAINRRSZ	SARRAZIN	AALMNTUU	AUTUMNAL
AAIIPRST	APIARIST	AAILNPSS	SALPIANS	AAINRSST	ARTISANS	AALMOOSS	MASSOOLA
AAIIRSTV	AVIARIST	AAILNPST	PLATINAS		TSARINAS	AALMOPSX	AXOPLASM
AAIIRSTW	WISTARIA	AAILNQTU	ALIQUANT	AAINRSSU	SAURIANS	AALMOSTT	STOMATAL

AALMPPSU	PASPALUM	AAOPSSST	POTASSAS	ABBDGINR	DRABBING	ABBGILNU	BAUBLING

AALMPPSU PASPALUM
AALMPRSY PALMYRAS
AALMPSTY PLATYSMA
AALMQSUU SQUAMULA
AALMSTTU MULATTAS
AALNNOPT PANTALON
AALNNPUU PUNALUAN
AALNNRSU ANNULARS
AALNNTUU LUNANAUT
AALNOPRT PATRONAL
AALNPSUU PUNALUAS
AALNRRTY ARRANTLY
AALNRSTU NATURALS
AALNSSTT SALTANTS
AALNSSTU SULTANAS
AALNSSTY ANALYSTS
AALNSTTU TALAUNTS
        TANTALUS
AALOPPRV APPROVAL
AALOPRSS PARASOLS
AALOPRST PASTORAL
AALOPSVV PAVLOVAS
AALORSSU AROUSALS
AALORSTX LAXATORS
AALORTUV VALUATOR
AALORTVY LAVATORY
AALOSTTY TALAYOTS
AALPRSTU PASTURAL
        SPATULAR
AALPSSTU SPATULAS
AALRRRTY TARTARLY
AALRSSTY SATYRALS
AALRSSVY VASSALRY
AALRSTTW STALWART
AALRSTUY SALUTARY
AALSSSTU ASSAULTS
AAMMNPRS RAMPSMAN
AAMMNRST MANTRAMS
AAMMOTXY MYXOMATA
AAMMRSSU MARASMUS
AAMNNOSY ANONYMAS
AAMNPRST MANTRAPS
AAMNPRSY PARANYMS
AAMNQSUW SQUAWMAN
AAMOORSS AMOROSAS
AAMOPRRU PARAMOUR
AAMORRSZ ZAMARROS
AAMORSSV SAMOVARS
AAMORSTT STROMATA
AAMOSTTU AUTOMATS
AAMPRRST RAMPARTS
AAMRSSST SMARTASS
AAMRSSTU SUMATRAS
AAMRSTWY TRAMWAYS
AAMSSSTU SATSUMAS
AANNOSST ASSONANT
AANNOSTT ANNATTOS
AANNRSTY STANNARY
AANOOPPX OPOPANAX
AANOOPRZ PARAZOON
AANOPRTY ANATROPY
AANORRRT NARRATOR
AANORSTY SANATORY
AANORTTY NATATORY
AANQRSTU QUARTANS
AANRRSTW WARRANTS
AANRRTWY WARRANTY
AANRSTTU SATURANT
AANRSUWY RUNAWAYS
AAOORRSW WOORARAS

AAOPSSST POTASSAS
AAOPSSTY APOSTASY
AAORSSTT STAROSTA
AAORSUVV VAVASOUR
AAORSVVY VAVASORY
AAOSTWWY STOWAWAY
AARSTTUY STATUARY
ABBBDEEL BEDABBLE
ABBBDELR BRABBLED
ABBBEILR BABBLIER
ABBBELRS BABBLERS
        BLABBERS
        BRABBLES
ABBBGILN BABBLING
        BLABBING
ABBBISTT BABBITTS
ABBCDELS SCABBLED
ABBCDERS SCRABBED
ABBCEERU BARBECUE
ABBCEGIR CRIBBAGE
ABBCEHIS BABICHES
ABBCEHOU BABOUCHE
ABBCEHSU BABUCHES
ABBCEHTU BATHCUBE
ABBCEIKT BACKBITE
ABBCEILR BARBICEL
ABBCEIRR CRABBIER
ABBCEIRS SCABBIER
ABBCEKLU BLUEBACK
ABBCEKNO BACKBONE
ABBCEKNU BUCKBEAN
ABBCELLU CLUBABLE
ABBCELRS CLABBERS
        SCRABBLE
ABBCELRU CURBABLE
ABBCELSS SCABBLES
ABBCGINR CRABBING
ABBCGINS SCABBING
ABBCGIOR GABBROIC
ABBCIILL BIBLICAL
ABBCIINR RABBINIC
ABBCIKRT BRICKBAT
ABBCILRY CRABBILY
ABBCKLOY BLACKBOY
ABBDDEEL BEDDABLE
ABBDDEEU BEDAUBED
ABBDDEIL BIDDABLE
ABBDDELR DRABBLED
ABBDEEJR JABBERED
ABBDEERR BARBERED
ABBDEERT RABBETED
ABBDEERY YABBERED
ABBDEGLR GRABBLED
ABBDEIRR DRABBIER
ABBDEIRT RABBITED
ABBDELMO BABELDOM
ABBDELNS SNABBLED
ABBDELRR DRABBLER
ABBDELRS DABBLERS
        DRABBLES
ABBDEMUZ BUMBAZED
ABBDENRU UNBARBED
ABBDEORS ABSORBED
ABBDEQSU SQUABBED
ABBDERRS DRABBERS
ABBDERST DRABBEST
        DRABBETS
ABBDFOOY BABYFOOD
ABBDGILN DABBLING

ABBDGINR DRABBING
ABBDGIOR GABBROID
ABBDHIJS DJIBBAHS
ABBDHIRS DRABBISH
ABBDHIRT BIRDBATH
ABBDHOOY BABYHOOD
ABBDILNO BAILBOND
ABBDILRS LIBBARDS
ABBDINRS RIBBANDS
ABBDLRSU LUBBARDS
ABBDMORS BOMBARDS
ABBDMOSU BABUDOMS
ABBEEINR BEARBINE
ABBEEJRR JABBERER
ABBEENOR BAREBONE
ABBEERTT BARBETTE
ABBEESSS ABBESSES
ABBEFILR FLABBIER
ABBEGIST GABBIEST
ABBEGLRR GRABBLER
ABBEGLRS GABBLERS
        GRABBLES
ABBEGNOS BOGBEANS
ABBEGNSU BUGBANES
ABBEGRRS GRABBERS
ABBEGRSU BUGBEARS
ABBEHILS BABELISH
ABBEHIRS SHABBIER
ABBEHLSS SHABBLES
ABBEHORT BATHROBE
ABBEILMS BABELISM
ABBEILNU BUBALINE
ABBEILOT BILOBATE
ABBEILRS SLABBIER
ABBEILRW WABBLIER
ABBEILST BISTABLE
ABBEINTT TABBINET
ABBEIRRT RABBITER
ABBEKLOO BOOKABLE
ABBELMRS BRAMBLES
ABBELNSS SNABBLES
ABBELOPR PROBABLE
ABBELORU BELABOUR
ABBELPRS PRABBLES
ABBELQSU SQUABBLE
ABBELRRS RABBLERS
ABBELRSS SLABBERS
ABBELRSW WABBLERS
ABBELRSY SLABBERY
ABBELSSU BARBULES
ABBELSUY BUYABLES
ABBEMOOR AEROBOMB
ABBEMOSX BOMBAXES
ABBEMSUZ BUMBAZES
ABBEORRS ABSORBER
        REABSORB
ABBEORTW BROWBEAT
ABBEQRSU SQUABBER
ABBERRRY BARBERRY
ABBERRYY BAYBERRY
ABBERSST STABBERS
ABBERSSW SWABBERS
ABBFGINR FRABBING
ABBGGILN GABBLING
ABBGGINR GRABBING
ABBGIJLN JABBLING
ABBGILNR RABBLING
ABBGILNS SLABBING

ABBGILNU BAUBLING
ABBGILNW WABBLING
ABBGINST STABBING
ABBGINSU BUBINGAS
ABBGINSW SWABBING
ABBGINTY TABBYING
ABBGOOSU BUGABOOS
ABBHIIMS BIMBASHI
ABBHILSY SHABBILY
ABBHRRSU RHUBARBS
ABBHRRUY RHUBARBY
ABBHSTTU BATHTUBS
ABBIINOT BIBATION
ABBILLOT BOATBILL
ABBILLSU SILLABUB
ABBILOST BIOBLAST
        BOBTAILS
ABBIMNOS BAMBINOS
ABBIMSSU BABUISMS
ABBINORS RABBONIS
ABBIRRTY RABBITRY
ABBIRSUU SUBURBIA
ABBKLOSU BLAUBOKS
ABBLLLOW BLOWBALL
ABBLLSTU BULLBATS
ABBLLSUY SYLLABUB
ABBLOPRY PROBABLY
ABBMOORS BOMBORAS
ABBMOSST BOMBASTS
ABBNRSUU SUBURBAN
ABBOSSTY BOBSTAYS
ABCCDEHO CABOCHED
ABCCDHIK DABCHICK
ABCCEEHN BECHANCE
ABCCEELP PECCABLE
ABCCEILY CELIBACY
ABCCEIRS BRECCIAS
ABCCEIRT BACTERIC
ABCCESUU SUCCUBAE
ABCCHISU BACCHIUS
ABCCHNOO CABOCHON
ABCCIKKK KICKBACK
ABCCIKKP PICKBACK
ABCCIKOR ABRICOCK
ABCCILOR CARBOLIC
ABCCILOT COBALTIC
ABCCIMRS CAMBRICS
ABCCINOR CARBONIC
ABCCINSU BUCCINAS
ABCCIORS ASCORBIC
ABCCKLLO BALLCOCK
ABCCKLOX CLACKBOX
ABCCKOOT COCKBOAT
ABCCKOSW BAWCOCKS
ABCCKRTU BUCKCART
ABCCKSTU CUTBACKS
ABCCOORS BAROCCOS
ABCCOOST TOBACCOS
ABCCSSUU SUCCUBAS
ABCDDEER DECARBED
ABCDDEOR BROCADED
ABCDDETU ABDUCTED
ABCDEEFK FEEDBACK
ABCDEEHL BLEACHED
ABCDEEHR BERDACHE
        BREACHED
ABCDEEJT ABJECTED
ABCDEEKR REBACKED
ABCDEELL BECALLED

ABCDEELM	BECALMED	ABCEEHLS	BLEACHES	ABCEIRSS	ASCRIBES	ABCHILMO	CHOLIAMB
ABCDEELS	DEBACLES	ABCEEHRS	BREACHES	ABCEIRSW	CRABWISE	ABCHILOO	COOLIBAH
ABCDEELU	EDUCABLE	ABCEEHSU	EBAUCHES	ABCEIRTT	BRATTICE	ABCHIMOR	CHORIAMB
ABCDEEMR	CAMBERED	ABCEEILT	CELIBATE	ABCEIRTY	ACERBITY	ABCHINOR	BRONCHIA
	EMBRACED	ABCEEIMN	AMBIENCE	ABCEISSS	ABSCISES	ABCHIOOR	BORACHIO
ABCDEEMX	EXCAMBED	ABCEELRR	CEREBRAL		ABSCISSE	ABCHIOST	COHABITS
ABCDEENO	BEACONED	ABCEELRT	BRACELET	ABCEISST	ASBESTIC	ABCHIRRT	TRIBRACH
ABCDEERR	REBRACED	ABCEEMRR	EMBRACER	ABCEJLTY	ABJECTLY	ABCHKLOT	HACKBOLT
ABCDEETU	ABDUCTEE	ABCEEMRS	EMBRACES	ABCEKLMO	MOCKABLE	ABCHKMPU	HUMPBACK
ABCDEGIR	BIRDCAGE	ABCEENSS	ABSENCES	ABCEKLNS	BLACKENS	ABCHKOOP	CHAPBOOK
	CAGEBIRD	ABCEERRS	REBRACES	ABCEKLOO	COOKABLE	ABCHKOSU	CHABOUKS
ABCDEHLN	BLANCHED	ABCEERST	ACERBEST	ABCEKLPU	PALEBUCK	ABCHKSTU	HACKBUTS
ABCDEHLU	BAUCHLED	ABCEERUX	BERCEAUX	ABCEKLST	BLACKEST	ABCHKSUW	HAWBUCKS
ABCDEHNR	BRANCHED	ABCEESSS	BECASSES	ABCEKNRS	BRACKENS	ABCHMOTX	MATCHBOX
ABCDEHOR	BROACHED	ABCEFIIT	BEATIFIC	ABCEKOOS	BOOKCASE	ABCHNORS	BROCHANS
ABCDEHOS	CABOSHED	ABCEFIKR	BACKFIRE		CASEBOOK	ABCIIMNS	MINICABS
ABCDEIIT	DIABETIC	ABCEFINO	BONIFACE	ABCEKRST	BRACKETS	ABCIINOT	CIBATION
ABCDEIKS	BACKSIDE	ABCEGHIN	BEACHING	ABCEKSST	BACKSETS	ABCIINSS	ABSCISIN
	DIEBACKS	ABCEGILN	BELACING		SETBACKS	ABCIIORS	ISOBARIC
ABCDEILR	CALIBRED	ABCEGIMN	EMBACING	ABCEKSSY	BACKSEYS	ABCIISTT	TRIBASIC
ABCDEIPS	PEDICABS	ABCEGIRS	RIBCAGES	ABCEKSTW	WETBACKS	ABCIISTY	BASICITY
ABCDEIRS	ASCRIBED	ABCEGKLL	BLACKLEG	ABCELLPU	CULPABLE	ABCIITUX	BAUXITIC
	CARBIDES	ABCEGKLO	BLOCKAGE	ABCELLSU	BUCELLAS	ABCIKLST	BACKLIST
ABCDEISS	ABSCISED	ABCEGKOR	BROCKAGE		BULLACES	ABCIKNPS	BACKSPIN
ABCDEKLO	BLOCKADE	ABCEGMOS	CAMBOGES	ABCELMNY	LAMBENCY	ABCILLRU	LUBRICAL
ABCDEKLV	BACKVELD	ABCEGNOR	BONGRACE	ABCELMOS	CEMBALOS	ABCILLSU	BACILLUS
ABCDEKNU	UNBACKED	ABCEGORS	BROCAGES	ABCELMRS	CAMBRELS	ABCILLSY	SYLLABIC
ABCDEKRS	REDBACKS	ABCEGOSS	BOSCAGES		CLAMBERS	ABCILNPU	PUBLICAN
ABCDELMS	SCAMBLED	ABCEHITT	BATHETIC		SCAMBLER	ABCILOOR	COOLIBAR
ABCDELNO	BLANCOED	ABCEHKOS	BACKHOES		SCRAMBLE	ABCILOSY	SOCIABLY
ABCDELOO	CABOODLE	ABCEHKTW	BETHWACK	ABCELMSS	SCAMBLES	ABCILRRU	RUBRICAL
ABCDEMOT	COMBATED	ABCEHLNS	BLANCHES	ABCELNOT	BALCONET	ABCIMMSS	CAMBISMS
ABCDENRU	UNBRACED	ABCEHLOR	BACHELOR	ABCELNUU	NUBECULA	ABCIMMSU	CAMBIUMS
ABCDENTU	ABDUCENT	ABCEHLSU	BAUCHLES	ABCELOOT	BOOTLACE	ABCIMORR	MICROBAR
ABCDEORS	BROCADES		CHASUBLE	ABCELOPS	PLACEBOS	ABCIMRTU	UMBRATIC
ABCDERSU	CUDBEARS	ABCEHMOT	HECATOMB	ABCELORT	BROCATEL	ABCIMSST	CAMBISTS
ABCDESTU	SUBACTED	ABCEHMRS	BECHARMS	ABCELOST	OBSTACLE	ABCINORU	CONURBIA
ABCDGINU	ABDUCING		BRECHAMS	ABCELOSV	VOCABLES	ABCINRVY	VIBRANCY
ABCDHKLO	HOLDBACK		CHAMBERS	ABCELOTU	BLUECOAT	ABCIORRS	BARRICOS
ABCDHORS	CHOBDARS	ABCEHNRR	BRANCHER	ABCELPSU	BLUECAPS	ABCIORSU	CARIBOUS
ABCDIILO	BIOCIDAL	ABCEHNRS	BRANCHES	ABCELPSY	BYPLACES	ABCIOSSU	SCABIOUS
	DIABOLIC	ABCEHOPU	PABOUCHE	ABCELRSW	BESCRAWL	ABCIOSUV	BIVOUACS
ABCDIIMY	CYMBIDIA	ABCEHORR	BROACHER	ABCELRTT	BRACTLET	ABCIRSTT	ABSTRICT
ABCDIIRT	TRIBADIC	ABCEHORS	BROACHES	ABCELSSU	BASCULES	ABCJKOOT	JACKBOOT
ABCDIKLR	BALDRICK	ABCEHOSS	BASOCHES	ABCEMORS	CRAMBOES	ABCKKORW	BACKWORK
ABCDIKLS	BACKSLID	ABCEHRST	BRACHETS	ABCENOSW	COWBANES	ABCKLLOS	BALLOCKS
ABCDIKRU	BAUDRICK	ABCEHRTT	BRATCHET	ABCENOUY	BUOYANCE	ABCKLOPT	BLACKTOP
ABCDILLR	BIRDCALL	ABCEIKKL	KICKABLE	ABCENRSU	UNBRACES	ABCKLOSW	SLOWBACK
ABCDILOU	CUBOIDAL	ABCEIKLR	CRABLIKE	ABCENTUX	EXCUBANT	ABCKLOTU	BLACKOUT
ABCDILRS	BALDRICS	ABCEILLR	CRIBELLA	ABCEOOSS	CABOOSES	ABCKMOOR	BACKROOM
ABCDINSS	ABSCINDS	ABCEILLT	BALLETIC	ABCEORSU	CORBEAUS	ABCKMORR	BROCKRAM
ABCDIRST	CATBIRDS	ABCEIKLR	CRABLIKE	ABCERRTU	CARBURET	ABCKMOST	BACKMOST
ABCDIRSU	BAUDRICS	ABCEILMS	ALEMBICS	ABCERTUU	CUBATURE	ABCKMRSU	BUCKRAMS
	SUBACRID	ABCEILNN	BINNACLE	ABCESTUU	SUBACUTE	ABCKNNOS	BANNOCKS
ABCDKNOW	BACKDOWN	ABCEILNU	BACULINE	ABCFIKLL	BACKFILL	ABCKNRTU	TURNBACK
ABCDKOPR	BACKDROP	ABCEILOR	ALBICORE	ABCFIKNS	FINBACKS	ABCKOORU	BUCKAROO
ABCDKORW	BACKWORD		CABRIOLE	ABCFILOS	BIFOCALS	ABCKOPST	BACKSTOP
ABCDLLNU	CLUBLAND	ABCEILOS	SOCIABLE	ABCFKOST	SOFTBACK	ABCKORUY	BUCKAYRO
ABCDNOSS	ABSCONDS	ABCEILRS	CALIBERS	ABCGGIMO	GAMBOGIC	ABCKOSTU	OUTBACKS
ABCDOORS	CORDOBAS		CALIBRES	ABCGHINT	BATCHING	ABCKSSTU	SACKBUTS
ABCDOPRU	CUPBOARD	ABCEILTT	BITTACLE	ABCGHKOS	HOGBACKS		SUBTACKS
ABCDORRS	BROCARDS	ABCEILTU	BACULITE	ABCGIINN	CABINING	ABCKSSUW	BUCKSAWS
ABCDORTU	ABDUCTOR	ABCEIMST	BETACISM	ABCGIKLN	BLACKING	ABCLLPUY	CULPABLY
ABCDORUY	OBDURACY	ABCEINOO	COENOBIA	ABCGIKNS	BACKINGS	ABCLMOSY	CYMBALOS
ABCEEEFK	BEEFCAKE	ABCEINRS	CARBINES	ABCGILNS	CABLINGS	ABCLMSUY	SCYBALUM
ABCEEFNT	BENEFACT	ABCEINST	CABINETS	ABCGKLOS	BACKLOGS	ABCLNORY	CARBONYL
ABCEEHIR	BEACHIER	ABCEINTU	INCUBATE	ABCGMSSU	SCUMBAGS	ABCLORXY	CARBOXYL
ABCEEHLM	BECHAMEL	ABCEIORS	AEROBICS	ABCHHIIS	HIBACHIS	ABCLSSSU	SUBCLASS
ABCEEHLN	ALEBENCH	ABCEIORT	BORACITE	ABCHIKLS	BLACKISH	ABCLSUUU	SUBUCULA
ABCEEHLR	BLEACHER	ABCEIRRT	CRIBRATE	ABCHIKRS	BRACKISH	ABCMOORT	MOBOCRAT

ABCNNORU	CONURBAN
ABCNORTY	CORYBANT
ABCNOUYY	BUOYANCY
ABCORRSS	CROSSBAR
ABCORRTU	TURBOCAR
ABCORSSU	SCABROUS
ABCOSSTU	SUBCOSTA
ABCOSTTU	COTTABUS
ABCRSTTU	SUBTRACT
ABDDDEEM	BEMADDED
ABDDEEEH	BEHEADED
ABDDEEGG	DEBAGGED
ABDDEEGR	BADGERED
ABDDEEHS	BEDASHED
ABDDEEKR	DEBARKED
ABDDEELU	BELAUDED
ABDDEERR	DEBARRED
ABDDEEST	BEDSTEAD
	BESTADDE
ABDDEGIR	ABRIDGED
	BRIGADED
ABDDEHMO	HEBDOMAD
ABDDEHOY	HOBDAYED
ABDDEILS	DISABLED
ABDDEILU	BUDDLEIA
ABDDEINR	BRANDIED
	RIBANDED
ABDDEIRR	BRAIRDED
ABDDELRS	BLADDERS
ABDDELRY	BLADDERY
ABDDENNU	UNBANDED
ABDDENOU	ABOUNDED
ABDDEORS	ADSORBED
ABDDERSW	BEDWARDS
ABDDGILN	BLADDING
ABDDHIOR	RHABDOID
ABDDILMO	LAMBDOID
ABDDILRY	LADYBIRD
ABDDIMNO	BONDMAID
ABDDINSS	DISBANDS
ABDDLLOS	ODDBALLS
ABDDMORS	DAMBRODS
ABDEEEFN	BEDEAFEN
ABDEEEMN	BEMEANED
ABDEEERV	BEAVERED
	BEREAVED
ABDEEFIT	TABEFIED
ABDEEFLM	FLAMBEED
ABDEEFMO	BEFOAMED
ABDEEGGL	BEDAGGLE
ABDEEGGR	BEGGARED
ABDEEGHR	HERBAGED
ABDEEGNW	BEGNAWED
ABDEEGRU	BEDEGUAR
ABDEEHMS	BESHAMED
ABDEEHMT	EMBATHED
ABDEEHNO	BONEHEAD
ABDEEHRT	BREATHED
ABDEEHSS	BEDASHES
ABDEEHST	BETHESDA
ABDEEHTT	BEHATTED
ABDEEILM	EMBAILED
ABDEEILN	DENIABLE
ABDEEILR	RIDEABLE
ABDEEILS	ABSEILED
ABDEEILT	DELIBATE
ABDEEILW	BEWAILED
ABDEEIRS	BEARDIES
ABDEEIRT	EBRIATED
ABDEEIST	BEADIEST
	DIABETES
ABDEEITU	BEAUTIED
ABDEEJMN	ENJAMBED
ABDEEKMN	EMBANKED
ABDEEKMR	BEDMAKER
	EMBARKED
ABDEEKNR	BARKENED
	BEDARKEN
ABDEEKNV	BEKNAVED
ABDEELLL	LABELLED
ABDEELLM	EMBALLED
ABDEELLW	WELDABLE
ABDEELMM	EMBALMED
ABDEELMS	BELDAMES
	BEMEDALS
ABDEELMU	BEMAULED
ABDEELMZ	EMBLAZED
ABDEELNT	BANDELET
ABDEELRS	BEDERALS
ABDEELSV	BESLAVED
ABDEELTT	BATTELED
	TABLETED
ABDEELZZ	BEDAZZLE
ABDEEMNO	BEMOANED
ABDEEMNS	BEADSMEN
	BEDESMAN
ABDEEMRR	EMBARRED
ABDEEMRS	EMBREADS
ABDEEMRV	EMBRAVED
ABDEENNR	BANNERED
ABDEENNT	BANTERED
ABDEENRZ	BRAZENED
ABDEENST	ABSENTED
ABDEENTT	BATTENED
ABDEEPRS	BESPREAD
ABDEEPTT	BEPATTED
ABDEERRT	BARTERED
ABDEERSS	DEBASERS
ABDEERST	BETREADS
	BREASTED
	DEBATERS
ABDEERTT	BATTERED
	DRABETTE
ABDEERTY	BETRAYED
ABDEERWY	BEWRAYED
ABDEESST	BASSETED
	BESTEADS
ABDEFLLO	FOLDABLE
ABDEFLNU	FUNDABLE
	UNFABLED
ABDEFLOR	FORDABLE
ABDEFLSU	LEAFBUDS
ABDEFNRU	FABURDEN
ABDEFRSW	BEDWARFS
ABDEGGIL	DIGGABLE
ABDEGGNU	UNBAGGED
ABDEGHRS	BEGHARDS
ABDEGIJN	BEJADING
ABDEGILN	BLINDAGE
ABDEGILU	GUIDABLE
ABDEGIMT	GAMBITED
ABDEGINO	GABIONED
ABDEGINR	BEARDING
	BREADING
ABDEGINS	BEADINGS
	DEBASING
ABDEGINT	DEBATING
ABDEGINZ	BEDAZING
ABDEGIRR	ABRIDGER
ABDEGIRS	ABRIDGES
	BRIGADES
ABDEGLNR	BRANGLED
ABDEGLOT	GLOBATED
ABDEGLRS	BELGARDS
ABDEGLRY	BADGERLY
ABDEGMRU	UMBRAGED
ABDEGNOR	BONDAGER
ABDEGNOS	BONDAGES
	DOGBANES
ABDEGOPR	PEGBOARD
ABDEGRSU	SUBGRADE
ABDEHILL	BILLHEAD
ABDEHILS	DISHABLE
ABDEHIMT	IMBATHED
ABDEHINS	BANISHED
ABDEHITU	HABITUDE
ABDEHKLU	BULKHEAD
ABDEHLLN	HANDBELL
ABDEHLLU	BULLHEAD
ABDEHLMS	SHAMBLED
ABDEHLOT	BOLTHEAD
ABDEHLRS	HALBERDS
ABDEHMRU	RHUMBAED
ABDEHMSU	AMBUSHED
ABDEHNTU	UNBATHED
ABDEHORR	ABHORRED
	HARBORED
ABDEHOSW	BESHADOW
	BOWHEADS
ABDEHRST	BREADTHS
ABDEIIRT	DIATRIBE
ABDEIKMR	IMBARKED
ABDEIKNU	BAUDEKIN
ABDEILMN	MANDIBLE
ABDEILNR	BILANDER
ABDEILNT	BIDENTAL
ABDEILNY	DENIABLY
ABDEILOV	VOIDABLE
ABDEILPS	PIEBALDS
ABDEILRT	LIBRATED
ABDEILRV	DRIVABLE
ABDEILRY	DIABLERY
ABDEILSS	DISABLES
ABDEILTU	DUTIABLE
ABDEIMNR	BRIDEMAN
ABDEIMOO	AMOEBOID
ABDEIMOR	AMBEROID
ABDEIMRR	IMBARRED
ABDEIMRS	EMBRAIDS
ABDEINOR	DEBONAIR
ABDEINOT	OBTAINED
ABDEINRS	BRANDIES
	BRANDISE
ABDEINST	BANDIEST
ABDEINSU	UNBIASED
ABDEINTU	UNBAITED
ABDEIOTV	OBVIATED
ABDEIPST	BAPTISED
ABDEIPTZ	BAPTIZED
ABDEIRST	BARDIEST
	BRAIDEST
	RABIDEST
	TRIBADES
ABDEIRSW	BAWDRIES
	DAWBRIES
ABDEIRTV	VIBRATED
ABDEISST	BASTIDES
ABDEISSU	DISABUSE
ABDEISTU	DAUBIEST
ABDEISTW	BAWDIEST
ABDEITTU	DUBITATE
ABDEJNOW	JAWBONED
ABDEKLSW	SKEWBALD
ABDEKNNU	UNBANKED
ABDEKNRU	UNBARKED
ABDEKOOR	ABROOKED
ABDEKORY	KEYBOARD
ABDELLOT	BALLOTED
ABDELMNU	UNBLAMED
ABDELNOR	BANDEROL
ABDELNOZ	BLAZONED
ABDELNRY	BYLANDER
ABDELNSS	BALDNESS
ABDELNST	BLANDEST
ABDELORU	LABOURED
ABDELOSV	ABSOLVED
ABDELPSY	PYEBALDS
ABDELRRS	DRABLERS
ABDELRSU	DURABLES
ABDELRTT	BRATTLED
ABDELSTU	SUBLATED
ABDEMNNS	BANDSMEN
ABDEMNNY	BANDYMEN
ABDEMNOS	ABDOMENS
ABDEMRTU	DRUMBEAT
	UMBRATED
ABDENOOT	BATOONED
ABDENORS	BANDORES
	BROADENS
ABDENORW	RAWBONED
ABDENORY	BONEYARD
ABDENOTW	DOWNBEAT
ABDENRRS	BRANDERS
ABDENRRU	UNBARRED
ABDENRSS	DRABNESS
ABDENRST	BANDSTER
ABDENRTU	BREADNUT
	TURBANED
ABDENSSU	SUBDEANS
ABDENTTU	DEBUTANT
ABDEOPRT	PROBATED
ABDEORRS	BOARDERS
ABDEORRU	ARBOURED
ABDEORRW	WARDROBE
ABDEORST	BROADEST
ABDEORTU	OBDURATE
	TABOURED
ABDEOSTU	BOUTADES
ABDEPRUY	UPBRAYED
ABDEPSSY	BYPASSED
ABDERRSU	ABSURDER
ABDERSST	DABSTERS
ABDERSSU	SUBEDARS
	SURBASED
ABDERSTU	SURBATED
ABDERSTW	BEDSTRAW
ABDERSTY	DRYBEATS
ABDFLOOT	FOLDBOAT
ABDGGORS	BOGGARDS
ABDGHINN	BANDHING
ABDGHINR	HANGBIRD
ABDGIINR	BRAIDING
ABDGIINS	ABIDINGS
ABDGILNR	BARDLING
ABDGILNU	BLAUDING
ABDGIMRU	GUIMBARD
ABDGINNR	BRANDING
ABDGINNS	BANDINGS
ABDGINNY	BANDYING

ABDGINOR	ABORDING	ABEEERRT	TEREBRAE
	BOARDING	ABEEERSV	BEREAVES
ABDGINRS	BRIGANDS	ABEEFFTU	BEAUFFET
ABDGINST	DINGBATS	ABEEFILS	FEASIBLE
ABDGINSU	DAUBINGS	ABEEFIST	TABEFIES
ABDGLNOS	BOGLANDS	ABEEFLLL	FELLABLE
ABDGLOOR	LOGBOARD	ABEEFLLN	BEFALLEN
ABDGLSUY	LADYBUGS	ABEEFLOS	BEEFALOS
ABDHHSSU	SHADBUSH	ABEEFORR	FOREBEAR
ABDHIIST	ADHIBITS	ABEEFSTU	BEAUFETS
	DISHABIT	ABEEGHRS	HERBAGES
ABDHILLN	HANDBILL	ABEEGHRT	BERTHAGE
ABDHILNS	BLANDISH	ABEEGINR	BAREGINE
ABDHINRS	BRANDISH		BERGENIA
ABDHIORS	BROADISH	ABEEGIRV	VERBIAGE
ABDHIPRS	BARDSHIP	ABEEGLLR	GABELLER
ABDHIRTY	BIRTHDAY	ABEEGLLS	GABELLES
ABDHKNOO	HANDBOOK	ABEEGLRS	BEAGLERS
ABDHLORW	BLOWHARD	ABEEGLTT	GETTABLE
ABDHMORS	RHABDOMS	ABEEGMNR	BARGEMEN
ABDHMOTU	BADMOUTH	ABEEGMTY	MEGABYTE
ABDHNSSU	HUSBANDS	ABEEGOSZ	GAZEBOES
ABDIILLR	BILLIARD	ABEEGRRS	GERBERAS
ABDIIMNR	MIDBRAIN	ABEEGRST	ABSTERGE
ABDIIMSU	BASIDIUM	ABEEGRSU	AUBERGES
ABDIINOS	OBSIDIAN	ABEEGRSW	BREWAGES
ABDIINTT	BANDITTI	ABEEGTTU	BAGUETTE
ABDIIRTY	RABIDITY	ABEEHILR	HIREABLE
ABDIKLNR	BLINKARD	ABEEHINT	THEBAINE
ABDIKNSW	BAWDKINS	ABEEHLLP	HELPABLE
ABDIKRSS	DISBARKS	ABEEHLLR	BEERHALL
ABDILOOS	DIABOLOS		HAREBELL
ABDILORS	LABROIDS	ABEEHLSV	BEHALVES
ABDILOST	BLASTOID	ABEEHMSS	BESHAMES
	TABLOIDS	ABEEHMST	EMBATHES
ABDILRRY	RIBALDRY	ABEEHNNS	HENBANES
ABDILRSW	AWLBIRDS	ABEEHNPP	BEHAPPEN
ABDILRZZ	BLIZZARD	ABEEHNSS	BANSHEES
ABDIMORS	AMBROIDS	ABEEHNTT	HEBETANT
ABDINOTY	ANTIBODY	ABEEHQTU	BEQUEATH
ABDINRTY	BANDITRY	ABEEHRRT	BREATHER
ABDIPRSU	UPBRAIDS	ABEEHRST	BREATHES
ABDIRRUY	RIBAUDRY		HARTBEES
ABDKLNOO	BOOKLAND	ABEEIKLL	LIKEABLE
ABDKNOOS	BANDOOKS	ABEEIKLR	BLEAKIER
ABDLLNOS	SLOBLAND	ABEEIKRS	BAKERIES
ABDLLORS	BOLLARDS	ABEEIILLR	RELIABLE
ABDLNORS	BANDROLS	ABEEILLV	LEVIABLE
ABDLRSUY	ABSURDLY		LIVEABLE
	RYBAULDS	ABEEILMS	BELAMIES
ABDLSSUU	SUBDUALS	ABEEILNP	PLEBEIAN
ABDLSTUU	SUBADULT	ABEEILNU	BANLIEUE
ABDMNNOS	BONDSMAN	ABEEILNV	ENVIABLE
ABDMNOUW	MAWBOUND	ABEEILPX	EXPIABLE
ABDMRSUY	MARYBUDS	ABEEILRR	BLEARIER
ABDNOPRS	PROBANDS	ABEEILRT	LIBERATE
ABDNORUY	BOUNDARY	ABEEILSV	EVASIBLE
ABDNRSTU	TURBANDS	ABEEILSZ	SEIZABLE
ABDOORSW	BARWOODS		SIZEABLE
ABDOORTU	OUTBOARD	ABEEILTV	EVITABLE
ABDOOSSW	BASSWOOD	ABEEILVW	VIEWABLE
ABDRSSTU	BUSTARDS	ABEEIMRT	AMBERITE
ABDRSUZZ	BUZZARDS	ABEEIMST	BEAMIEST
ABEEEGRS	BARGEESE	ABEEINST	BETAINES
ABEEEGRV	BEVERAGE	ABEEINTY	AYENBITE
ABEEEHTT	HEBETATE	ABEEIPRS	BEPRAISE
ABEEENRT	TENEBRAE	ABEEIRTT	BATTERIE
ABEEENRV	BEREAVEN	ABEEIRTV	BREVIATE
ABEEENST	ABSENTEE	ABEEISST	BEASTIES
		ABEEISSV	ABESSIVE

ABEEISTU	BEAUTIES	ABEEORST	REBATOES
ABEEITUX	BEAUXITE	ABEEORTV	OVERBEAT
ABEEJMOR	JAMBOREE	ABEEPRRY	PEABERRY
ABEEKLOT	KEELBOAT	ABEERRRT	BARTERER
ABEEKLST	BLEAKEST	ABEERRST	REBATERS
ABEEKMNR	BRAKEMEN		TABRERES
	EMBANKER		TEREBRAS
ABEEKNSV	BEKNAVES	ABEERRSY	SEABERRY
ABEEKOOP	PEEKABOO	ABEERRTT	BARRETTE
ABEEKOPS	PEEKABOS	ABEERRTV	VERTEBRA
ABEEKPSS	BESPEAKS	ABEERRTY	BETRAYER
ABEEKRRS	BREAKERS		TEABERRY
ABEEKRST	BESTREAK	ABEERSTT	ABETTERS
ABEELLLS	SELLABLE	ABEERSTU	SUBERATE
ABEELLLT	TELLABLE	ABEESZZZ	BEZAZZES
ABEELLOT	BALLOTEE	ABEFFLRS	BAFFLERS
ABEELLOV	LOVEABLE	ABEFGILS	FILABEGS
ABEELLSY	EYEBALLS	ABEFGLLR	BERGFALL
ABEELLTT	LETTABLE	ABEFGSST	GABFESTS
ABEELMMR	EMBALMER	ABEFHILS	FISHABLE
	EMMARBLE	ABEFHOOT	HOOFBEAT
ABEELMOV	MOVEABLE	ABEFILLL	FALLIBLE
ABEELMPR	PREAMBLE	ABEFILLM	FILMABLE
ABEELMRT	ATREMBLE	ABEFILLR	FIREBALL
ABEELMSS	ASSEMBLE	ABEFILLT	LIFTABLE
	BEAMLESS	ABEFILOT	LIFEBOAT
ABEELMSZ	EMBLAZES	ABEFILRS	BARFLIES
ABEELMTT	EMBATTLE	ABEFILSU	FABULISE
ABEELNOP	BEANPOLE	ABEFILSY	FEASIBLY
	OPENABLE	ABEFILUZ	FABULIZE
ABEELNRS	ENABLERS	ABEFINSU	BEAUFINS
ABEELNRT	RENTABLE	ABEFIRRT	FIREBRAT
ABEELNTU	TUNEABLE	ABEFITUY	BEAUTIFY
ABEELOPR	OPERABLE	ABEFLLMU	BLAMEFUL
	ROPEABLE	ABEFLLTU	TABLEFUL
ABEELOPS	POSEABLE	ABEFLMOR	FORMABLE
ABEELORX	EXORABLE	ABEFLNRU	FUNEBRAL
ABEELPRS	BEPEARLS	ABEFLNSY	FLYBANES
ABEELRST	BLEAREST	ABEFOORT	BAREFOOT
	BLEATERS	ABEFORRS	FORBEARS
	RETABLES	ABEGGHLU	HUGGABLE
ABEELRSU	REUSABLE	ABEGGILN	BEAGLING
ABEELRSV	BESLAVER	ABEGGIST	BAGGIEST
ABEELRTT	BATTELER	ABEGGLRY	BEGGARLY
ABEELRTU	BATELEUR	ABEGGMOS	GAMBOGES
	BLEUATRE	ABEGGNSU	BUGGANES
ABEELSSS	BASELESS	ABEGGRSU	BURGAGES
ABEELSST	BATELESS	ABEGHILP	PHILABEG
ABEELSSU	SUBLEASE	ABEGHILR	ALBERGHI
ABEELSSV	BESLAVES	ABEGHINO	OBEAHING
ABEELSTT	TESTABLE	ABEGHINT	BEATHING
ABEEMMNR	MEMBRANE	ABEGHINV	BEHAVING
ABEEMMRU	BUMMAREE	ABEGHNSS	SHEBANGS
ABEEMNOR	BEMOANER	ABEGHORR	BEGORRAH
ABEEMNST	BASEMENT	ABEGHRRY	HAGBERRY
ABEEMNTT	ABETMENT	ABEGHRST	BARGHEST
	BATEMENT	ABEGIIMS	BIGAMIES
ABEEMRSS	BESMEARS	ABEGIKNR	BREAKING
ABEEMRSV	EMBRAVES	ABEGIKNT	BETAKING
ABEENNRT	BANNERET	ABEGILMN	EMBALING
ABEENNRU	EBURNEAN	ABEGILNN	ENABLING
ABEENNTU	UNBEATEN	ABEGILNR	BLEARING
ABEENORS	SEABORNE	ABEGILNS	SINGABLE
ABEENOTZ	BENZOATE	ABEGILNT	BELATING
ABEENRRR	BARRENER		BLEATING
ABEENRRT	BANTERER		TANGIBLE
ABEENRSS	BARENESS	ABEGILNY	BELAYING
ABEENRSV	VERBENAS	ABEGILOT	OBLIGATE
ABEENSSS	BASENESS	ABEGIMNN	BENAMING
ABEEOORV	OVERBEAR	ABEGIMNR	BREAMING

ABEGIMNS	BEAMINGS	ABEHMSSU	AMBUSHES	ABEILPRZ	PRIZABLE	ABEIRSTY	BESTIARY
	EMBASING	ABEHNSTU	SUNBATHE	ABEILPSS	PASSIBLE		SYBARITE
ABEGIMNY	EMBAYING	ABEHORRR	ABHORRER	ABEILPST	EPIBLAST	ABEIRSUX	EXURBIAS
ABEGIMRS	GAMBIERS	ABEHORST	BATHORSE	ABEILRRU	REBURIAL	ABEIRTTY	YTTERBIA
ABEGIMST	MEGABITS	ABEHOSST	BATHOSES	ABEILRRW	BRAWLIER	ABEISSST	BASSITES
ABEGIMUX	GIAMBEUX	ABEHOSTX	HATBOXES	ABEILRST	LIBRATES	ABEISSTT	BATISTES
ABEGINOR	ABORIGEN	ABEHOSXY	HAYBOXES	ABEILRTW	WRITABLE	ABEISTTT	BATTIEST
ABEGINOS	BEGONIAS	ABEHRSST	BRASHEST	ABEILSST	ASTILBES	ABEISTUX	BAUXITES
ABEGINRS	BEARINGS	ABEIILLS	BAILLIES		BESTIALS	ABEISZZZ	BIZAZZES
	SABERING	ABEIILMT	IMITABLE		STABILES	ABEITTTU	TITUBATE
ABEGINRT	BERATING	ABEIILMN	BIENNIAL	ABEILSSU	ISSUABLE	ABEJKLOU	KABELJOU
	REBATING	ABEIILNV	INVIABLE		SUASIBLE	ABEJMNOS	JAMBONES
ABEGINRW	BEWARING	ABEIILPT	PITIABLE	ABEILSTU	SUITABLE	ABEJMOOR	JEROBOAM
ABEGINRY	BERAYING	ABEIILRR	LIBRAIRE	ABEILSTY	BEASTILY	ABEJNOSW	JAWBONES
ABEGINST	BEATINGS	ABEIILRS	BISERIAL	ABEILSUX	BISEXUAL	ABEJOSWX	JAWBOXES
ABEGINTT	ABETTING	ABEIILST	ALBITISE	ABEILSVV	BIVALVES	ABEJRRSU	ABJURERS
ABEGINTW	WINGBEAT		SIBILATE	ABEIMNRS	MIRBANES	ABEKLMOS	SMOKABLE
ABEGIOSS	BIOGASES	ABEIILTV	VITIABLE	ABEIMNST	AMBIENTS	ABEKLNOW	KNOWABLE
ABEGIPPR	BAGPIPER	ABEIILTZ	ALBITIZE	ABEIMRST	BARMIEST	ABEKLNST	BLANKEST
ABEGIPPS	BAGPIPES	ABEIINRR	BRAINIER	ABEIMRSU	AUMBRIES		BLANKETS
ABEGKORS	BROKAGES	ABEIINRS	BINARIES	ABEIMRTV	AMBIVERT	ABEKLNTY	BLANKETY
	GROSBEAK	ABEIJLTU	JUBILATE		VERBATIM	ABEKLORW	WORKABLE
ABEGLLLU	GULLABLE	ABEIJMNN	BENJAMIN	ABEIMSSU	IAMBUSES	ABEKLRSS	BARKLESS
ABEGLLOR	BARGELLO	ABEIJMRS	JAMBIERS	ABEINNOZ	BEZONIAN	ABEKMNNS	BANKSMEN
ABEGLMRS	GAMBLERS	ABEIJNSS	BASENJIS	ABEINNRR	BRANNIER	ABEKNSSY	SNEAKSBY
	GAMBRELS	ABEIKLLN	BALKLINE	ABEINNRU	INURBANE	ABEKOORS	ABROOKES
ABEGLNRS	BRANGLES	ABEIKLNS	BLANKIES	ABEINORR	AIRBORNE	ABEKORTU	OUTBREAK
ABEGLRRS	GARBLERS	ABEIKLSS	KISSABLE	ABEINORS	BARONIES	ABEKPRSU	UPBREAKS
ABEGLRUU	BLAGUEUR	ABEIKLST	BALKIEST	ABEINORT	BARITONE	ABEKRSTY	BASKETRY
ABEGLSTU	GUSTABLE	ABEIKNRR	BRANKIER		OBTAINER	ABELLLMU	LABELLUM
ABEGMNOS	GAMBESON	ABEIKNRS	BEARSKIN	ABEINOST	BOTANIES	ABELLLOR	ROLLABLE
ABEGMORT	BERGAMOT		INBREAKS		BOTANISE	ABELLLOT	TOLLABLE
ABEGMRSU	UMBRAGES	ABEIKNST	BEATNIKS		NIOBATES	ABELLLSY	SYLLABLE
ABEGNNST	BANTENGS	ABEIKRST	BARKIEST		OBEISANT	ABELLMOR	OMBRELLA
ABEGNOSS	NOSEBAGS		BRAKIEST	ABEINOTZ	BOTANIZE	ABELLMRU	UMBELLAR
ABEGNRST	BANGSTER		BREASKIT	ABEINPST	BEPAINTS		UMBRELLA
ABEGNRTU	BURGANET	ABEILLLT	TILLABLE	ABEINQSU	BASQUINE	ABELLNOT	BALLONET
ABEGNSTU	SUBAGENT	ABEILLLW	WILLABLE	ABEINRRW	BRAWNIER	ABELLNRU	RUBELLAN
ABEGOORS	BARGOOSE	ABEILLMM	LIMBMEAL	ABEINRST	ATEBRINS	ABELLNST	NETBALLS
ABEGOSTT	BOTTEGAS	ABEILLOS	ISOLABLE		BANISTER	ABELLOSV	SOLVABLE
ABEGOSUY	BUOYAGES		LOBELIAS	ABEINRSU	ANBURIES	ABELLOTU	LOBULATE
ABEGRRUV	BURGRAVE	ABEILLOV	VIOLABLE		URBANISE	ABELLRSU	RUBELLAS
ABEGRSST	BARGESTS	ABEILLQU	LIQUABLE	ABEINRTU	URBANITE	ABELLRVY	VERBALLY
ABEGSSTU	SUBSTAGE	ABEILLRS	LIBERALS	ABEINRUZ	URBANIZE	ABELMNNO	NOBLEMAN
ABEHILLR	HAIRBELL	ABEILLRY	BERYLLIA	ABEINSST	BASINETS	ABELMNOZ	EMBLAZON
ABEHILNR	HIBERNAL		RELIABLY		BASSINET	ABELMNST	SEMBLANT
ABEHILRS	BLASHIER	ABEILLST	BASTILLE		BESAINTS	ABELMNSU	ALBUMENS
ABEHILTT	TITHABLE	ABEILLTT	TILTABLE		BESTAINS	ABELMOOT	MOOTABLE
ABEHIMOS	OBEAHISM	ABEILMNS	BAILSMEN	ABEINSSU	UNBIASES	ABELMOSV	MOVABLES
ABEHIMST	IMBATHES	ABEILMNT	BAILMENT	ABEINSTT	TABINETS	ABELMOVY	MOVEABLY
ABEHINSS	BANISHES	ABEILMOR	BROMELIA	ABEINTTU	INTUBATE	ABELMPTU	PLUMBATE
ABEHINST	ABSINTHE	ABEILMRS	REMBLAIS	ABEIORSS	ISOBARES	ABELMRRS	MARBLERS
ABEHIOPU	EUPHOBIA	ABEILMRW	WAMBLIER	ABEIORST	SABOTIER		RAMBLERS
ABEHIORV	BEHAVIOR	ABEILMSS	MISSABLE	ABEIORTV	ABORTIVE	ABELMRST	LAMBERTS
ABEHIRRS	BRASHIER	ABEILMST	BALMIEST	ABEIOSSS	ISOBASES	ABELMSSY	ASSEMBLY
ABEHISTU	HABITUES		TIMBALES	ABEIOSTV	OBVIATES	ABELNNOR	BANNEROL
ABEHISTZ	ZABTIEHS	ABEILNNW	WINNABLE	ABEIPSST	BAPTISES	ABELNNRU	RUNNABLE
ABEHKLLW	HAWKBELL	ABEILNOP	OPINABLE	ABEIPSTZ	BAPTIZES	ABELNORZ	BLAZONER
ABEHKNOR	HORNBEAK	ABEILNPS	BIPLANES	ABEIRRRS	BARRIERS	ABELNOST	NEOBLAST
ABEHKRSU	HAUBERKS	ABEILNPT	PINTABLE	ABEIRRSS	BRASIERS		NOTABLES
ABEHLLRT	BETHRALL	ABEILNRS	RINSABLE		BRASSIER	ABELNOSY	BALONEYS
ABEHLMMU	HUMMABLE	ABEILNRU	RUINABLE	ABEIRRST	ARBITERS	ABELNQTU	BLANQUET
ABEHLMSS	SHAMBLES	ABEILNSS	ALBINESS		RAREBITS	ABELNRSS	BRANSLES
ABEHLNOT	BENTHOAL		LESBIANS	ABEIRRSZ	BRAZIERS	ABELNRST	BRANTLES
ABEHLOTY	HYLOBATE	ABEILNST	INSTABLE	ABEIRRTT	BRATTIER	ABELNRSY	BLARNEYS
ABEHLRST	BLATHERS	ABEILNTV	BIVALENT	ABEIRRVY	BREVIARY	ABELNRUY	URBANELY
	HALBERTS	ABEILNUV	UNVIABLE	ABEIRSSS	BRASSIES	ABELNRYZ	BRAZENLY
ABEHLSSS	BASHLESS	ABEILNVY	ENVIABLY	ABEIRSTT	BIRETTAS	ABELNSTU	UNSTABLE
ABEHMNOR	HORNBEAM	ABEILPRT	PARTIBLE	ABEIRSTV	VIBRATES	ABELNSTY	ABSENTLY
ABEHMOOR	REHOBOAM			ABEIRSTW	WARBIEST	ABELNSUU	UNUSABLE

ABELOPRT	PORTABLE		TABORETS
ABELOPRU	POURABLE	ABEORSTU	SABOTEUR
ABELOPRV	PROVABLE	ABEORTTU	OBTURATE
ABELOPST	POTABLES		TABOURET
ABELOQTU	QUOTABLE	ABEORTUV	OUTBRAVE
ABELORRU	LABOURER	ABEOSSST	ASBESTOS
ABELORST	BLOATERS	ABEOSTUV	SUBOVATE
	SORTABLE	ABEPRRTU	ABRUPTER
	STORABLE	ABEPSSSY	BYPASSES
ABELORSU	RUBEOLAS	ABEQRSUU	ARQUEBUS
ABELORSV	ABSOLVER	ABERRTYY	TAYBERRY
ABELOSSU	SABULOSE	ABERRWXY	WAXBERRY
ABELOSSV	ABSOLVES	ABERSSST	BRASSETS
ABELOSTU	ABSOLUTE	ABERSSSU	SURBASES
ABELOSTW	BESTOWAL	ABERSSTU	ABSTRUSE
ABELPRTU	PUBERTAL		SURBATES
ABELQSUU	SUBEQUAL	ABERSSTW	WABSTERS
ABELRRSW	BRAWLERS	ABERSTTU	ABUTTERS
	WARBLERS	ABERTTUY	BUTYRATE
ABELRRTU	BARRULET	ABFFGILN	BAFFLING
ABELRSST	BLASTERS	ABFFIILS	BAILIFFS
	STABLERS	ABFFLLPU	PUFFBALL
ABELRSSY	LABRYSES	ABFFNOTU	BOUFFANT
ABELRSTT	BATTLERS	ABFGILNS	FABLINGS
	BLATTERS	ABFGLLOO	GOOFBALL
	BRATTLES	ABFGORUU	FAUBOURG
ABELRSTU	BALUSTER	ABFHIIST	BAITFISH
ABELRSTW	BLEWARTS	ABFHILLS	FISHBALL
ABELRSUZ	ZEBRULAS	ABFHIORS	BOARFISH
ABELRTTU	BURLETTA	ABFIILLR	FIBRILLA
	REBUTTAL	ABFIIMRS	FIMBRIAS
ABELSSTT	STABLEST	ABFILLLY	FALLIBLY
ABELSSTU	SUBLATES	ABFILNSU	BASINFUL
ABELSTUU	SUBULATE	ABFILSTU	FABULIST
ABELSTWY	BELTWAYS	ABFIMORS	FIBROMAS
ABELTTUU	TUBULATE	ABFJORSU	FRABJOUS
ABEMMNOO	MOONBEAM	ABFKLLOR	KORFBALL
ABEMNOTU	UMBONATE	ABFLLOOT	FOOTBALL
ABEMNOTW	BATWOMEN	ABFLLOST	SOFTBALL
ABEMNPRU	PENUMBRA	ABFLOSTU	BOASTFUL
ABEMNRSY	MYRBANES	ABFLOSTY	FLYBOATS
ABEMNSSU	SUNBEAMS	ABFLOSUU	FABULOUS
ABEMNSUY	SUNBEAMY	ABFNORTU	TURBOFAN
ABEMNTTU	ABUTMENT	ABFOORST	FOOTBARS
ABEMORRS	EMBRASOR	ABFSSTTU	TUBFASTS
ABEMORST	BROMATES	ABGGGILN	BLAGGING
ABEMORSU	AMBEROUS	ABGGGINR	BRAGGING
ABEMORTZ	BAROMETZ	ABGGGINS	BAGGINGS
ABENNORS	BARONNES	ABGGIJNN	JINGBANG
ABENOPSU	SUBPOENA	ABGGILMN	GAMBLING
ABENORSS	BARONESS	ABGGILNR	GARBLING
ABENORST	BARONETS	ABGGNOOT	TOBOGGAN
ABENORTT	BETATRON	ABGGORST	BOGGARTS
ABENORTV	BEVATRON	ABGHHILL	HIGHBALL
ABENORTY	BARYTONE	ABGHIINT	HABITING
ABENOSTY	BAYONETS	ABGHILMN	HAMBLING
ABENQSTU	BANQUETS	ABGHINRS	BRASHING
ABENRRYZ	BRAZENRY	ABGHINSS	BASHINGS
ABENRSTU	UNBRASTE	ABGHIOPR	BIOGRAPH
	URBANEST	ABGHLOST	HAGBOLTS
ABEOPRSS	SAPROBES	ABGHMORU	BROUGHAM
ABEOPRST	PROBATES	ABGIILNR	BRAILING
ABEOQRSU	BAROQUES	ABGIILNS	SAIBLING
ABEORRSS	BRASEROS	ABGIILNT	LIBATING
ABEORRST	ARBORETS	ABGIIMNS	IMBASING
	TABORERS	ABGIIMST	BIGAMIST
ABEORSST	BOASTERS	ABGIINNR	BRAINING
	SORBATES	ABGIINOR	ABORIGIN
ABEORSTT	ABETTORS	ABGIINRS	BRAISING
	BATTEROS	ABGIINSS	BIASINGS

	BIASSING	ABGORRSU	GOBURRAS
ABGIINST	BAITINGS	ABGORSTU	OUTBRAGS
ABGIJNRU	ABJURING	ABHHKOST	KHOTBAHS
ABGIKLNN	BLANKING	ABHHKSTU	KHUTBAHS
ABGIKLNS	BALKINGS	ABHHRRSTU	HATBRUSH
ABGIKLNU	BAULKING	ABHIINRS	BRAINISH
ABGIKNNR	BRANKING	ABHIINST	INHABITS
ABGIKNNS	BANKINGS	ABHIIORZ	RHIZOBIA
ABGILLMN	LAMBLING	ABHIKLOR	KOHLRABI
ABGILLNS	BALLINGS	ABHIKSTW	HAWKBITS
ABGILMNR	MARBLING	ABHILLPT	PITHBALL
	RAMBLING	ABHILNOS	HOBNAILS
ABGILMNS	AMBLINGS	ABHILNOT	BIATHLON
ABGILMNW	WAMBLING	ABHILSST	STABLISH
ABGILNNT	BANTLING	ABHILSTU	HALIBUTS
ABGILNOR	LABORING	ABHIMMST	BATHMISM
ABGILNOT	BLOATING	ABHINSST	ABSINTHS
	OBLIGANT	ABHIOSST	ISOBATHS
ABGILNRT	BRATLING	ABHIOSTU	HAUTBOIS
ABGILNRW	BRAWLING	ABHIRSTT	BRATTISH
	WARBLING	ABHKLSSY	BASHLYKS
ABGILNST	BLASTING	ABHKLSUW	BUSHWALK
	STABLING	ABHKORSU	BOURKHAS
	TABLINGS		KOURBASH
ABGILNSW	BAWLINGS	ABHLLMOT	MOTHBALL
ABGILNTT	BATTLING	ABHLLOOY	BALLYHOO
	BLATTING	ABHLPSUY	SUBPHYLA
ABGILNTY	TANGIBLY	ABHMNOTY	BOTHYMAN
ABGILORS	GARBOILS	ABHMNSUU	SUBHUMAN
ABGIMMNO	MAMBOING	ABHMOORT	BATHROOM
ABGIMNRU	RUMBAING	ABHNSSTU	SUNBATHS
ABGIMOSU	BIGAMOUS	ABHOORST	TARBOOSH
	SUBIMAGO	ABHORRSU	HARBOURS
ABGIMSST	GAMBISTS	ABHORSTU	TARBOUSH
ABGINNOT	BATONING	ABHOSTUY	HAUTBOYS
ABGINNRU	UNBARING	ABIIINRY	BIRIYANI
ABGINNRX	BANXRING	ABIIKKST	KIBITKAS
ABGINNST	BANTINGS	ABIIKLSS	BASILISK
ABGINOOT	TABOOING	ABIILLMR	MILLIBAR
ABGINORT	ABORTING	ABIILLTY	LABILITY
	TABORING	ABIILMNO	BINOMIAL
ABGINOST	BOASTING	ABIILMNS	ALBINISM
	BOATINGS	ABIILMSU	BULIMIAS
	BOSTANGI	ABIILNOT	LIBATION
ABGINRRS	BARRINGS	ABIILNQS	INQILABS
ABGINRST	BRASTING	ABIILNST	SIBILANT
ABGINSST	BASTINGS	ABIILPTY	PITIABLY
ABGINSTT	BATTINGS	ABIIMNOT	AMBITION
ABGINSTW	BATSWING	ABIIMSST	IAMBISTS
ABGINTTU	ABUTTING	ABIINORS	ROBINIAS
ABGIOPST	PIGBOATS	ABIINRSY	BIRYANIS
ABGLLLOY	GLOBALLY	ABIIRSSV	VIBRISSA
ABGLLORU	GLOBULAR	ABIJLNRS	BRINJALS
ABGLLRUY	BULLYRAG	ABIJLNTU	JUBILANT
ABGLMNSU	LUMBANGS	ABIJNOOT	JOBATION
ABGLMOPU	PLUMBAGO	ABIJNOST	ABJOINTS
ABGLMOSU	LUMBAGOS		BANJOIST
ABGLNOOT	LONGBOAT	ABIKLMNS	LAMBKINS
ABGLNOUW	BUNGALOW		LAMBSKIN
ABGLOOST	TOOLBAGS	ABIKLNRY	BYRLAKIN
ABGLOOTY	BATOLOGY	ABIKLORS	KILOBARS
ABGLORST	RAGBOLTS	ABIKMNNR	BRINKMAN
ABGLORSU	GLABROUS	ABIKMNRS	BARMKINS
ABGLRRSU	BURGLARS	ABIKNORR	IRONBARK
ABGLRRUY	BURGLARY	ABIKRSST	BRITSKAS
ABGMNOOR	GAMBROON	ABIKRSTZ	BRITZKAS
ABGNOPRS	PROBANGS		BRITZKSA
ABGNORSU	OSNABURG	ABILLLPY	PLAYBILL
ABGNOSTU	GUNBOATS	ABILLMSU	BALLIUMS
ABGOORST	BOTARGOS	ABILLNPS	PINBALLS

ABILLOVY	VIOLABLY
ABILLRTY	TRIBALLY
ABILLSWX	WAXBILLS
ABILMNOU	OLIBANUM
ABILMNSU	ALBUMINS
ABILMOPS	BIOPLASM
ABILNOOT	LOBATION
	OBLATION
ABILNORU	UNILOBAR
ABILNOTU	ABLUTION
	ABUTILON
ABILNRTU	TRIBUNAL
	TURBINAL
ABILOPRS	PARBOILS
ABILOPST	BIOPLAST
ABILORST	ORBITALS
	STROBILA
ABILORSV	BOLIVARS
ABILORTY	LIBATORY
ABILPSSY	PASSIBLY
ABILRSSY	BRASSILY
ABILRSUV	SUBVIRAL
ABILSSUY	ISSUABLY
ABILSTUY	SUITABLY
ABIMMNOO	MAINBOOM
ABIMNOSU	BIMANOUS
ABIMNRTU	TAMBURIN
ABIMPSST	BAPTISMS
ABIMRSST	STRABISM
ABIMRSTT	TRIMTABS
ABINOORS	BORONIAS
ABINOORT	ABORTION
ABINORST	TABORINS
ABINORSW	RAINBOWS
ABINORTU	TABOURIN
ABINORWY	RAINBOWY
ABINOSST	BASTIONS
ABINOSSU	ABUSIONS
ABINOSTT	BOTANIST
ABINRTUY	URBANITY
ABINTTTU	TITUBANT
ABIOPRSU	BIPAROUS
ABIOPSTU	SUBTOPIA
ABIORRST	ARBORIST
ABIORRTV	VIBRATOR
ABIORSTV	VIBRATOS
ABIORTUY	OBITUARY
ABIPSSTT	BAPTISTS
ABIRRSTU	AIRBURST
ABIRSSUZ	SUBSIZAR
ABIRSTTY	TRAYBITS
ABISSSST	BASSISTS
ABJKMOSS	SJAMBOKS
ABJLMOOS	JAMBOOLS
ABKKMOOR	BOOKMARK
ABKLLNOR	BANKROLL
ABKLOOPY	PLAYBOOK
ABKLRSUW	BULWARKS
ABKNPRTU	BANKRUPT
ABKNRSUU	BUNRAKUS
ABKOORTW	WORKBOAT
ABKOOSTT	KOTTABOS
ABLLMOPW	BLOWLAMP
ABLLNOOS	BALLOONS
ABLLNOSW	SNOWBALL
ABLLORST	BORSTALL
ABLLOSTY	TALLBOYS
ABLLRTUY	BRUTALLY
ABLLSSUY	SYLLABUS
ABLMNRUU	ALBURNUM
	LABURNUM
ABLMOOST	TOMBOLAS
ABLMOSTY	MYOBLAST
ABLMPSUU	PABULUMS
ABLNORYZ	BLAZONRY
ABLNOSTU	BUTANOLS
ABLNOSUZ	SUBZONAL
ABLNRSUU	SUBLUNAR
ABLNSUUY	UNUSABLY
ABLOORTY	OBLATORY
ABLOOSTT	BOOTLAST
ABLOOSTZ	ZOOBLAST
ABLOPRVY	PROVABLY
ABLOPSUU	PABULOUS
ABLOPSYY	PLAYBOYS
ABLOQTUY	QUOTABLY
ABLORSST	BORSTALS
ABLORSSU	SUBSOLAR
ABLORSTW	BLAWORTS
ABLORSUW	BOURLAWS
ABLOSSUU	SABULOUS
ABLOSTTU	SUBTOTAL
ABLPRTUY	ABRUPTLY
ABMNTTUY	BUTTYMAN
ABMORSTU	TAMBOURS
ABMOSSTU	SUBATOMS
ABNOORRT	ROBORANT
ABNOORSS	SOROBANS
ABNOORSZ	BORAZONS
ABNOOSSS	BASSOONS
ABNORSTY	BARYTONS
ABNORTUU	RUNABOUT
ABNOSSSU	BONASSUS
ABNRSTTU	TURBANTS
ABOORRSU	ARBOROUS
ABOORSTW	ROWBOATS
ABORSSTU	ROBUSTAS
ACCCDIIO	COCCIDIA
ACCCENPY	PECCANCY
ACCCFIIL	CALCIFIC
ACCCHILO	COLCHICA
ACCCIIPR	CAPRICCI
ACCCILLY	CYCLICAL
ACCCIOPU	CAPUCCIO
ACCDDEEN	ACCENDED
	CADENCED
ACCDDEIS	CADDICES
ACCDDEOR	ACCORDED
ACCDDIIT	DIDACTIC
ACCDEENS	CADENCES
ACCDEENT	ACCENTED
ACCDEERS	ACCEDERS
ACCDEERT	ACCRETED
ACCDEERU	CARDECUE
ACCDEERW	ACCREWED
ACCDEESS	ACCESSED
ACCDEGIN	ACCEDING
	ACCINGED
ACCDEHIK	CHIACKED
ACCDEHIL	CHALICED
ACCDEHIN	CHICANED
ACCDEHKY	CHYACKED
ACCDEHLT	CLATCHED
ACCDEHNR	CRANCHED
ACCDEHNU	CHAUNCED
ACCDEIIS	ACCIDIES
ACCDEILN	CALCINED
ACCDEILU	CAUDICLE
ACCDEILY	DELICACY
ACCDEINT	ACCIDENT
ACCDEIRT	ACCREDIT
ACCDEISU	CAUDICES
ACCDEKLR	CRACKLED
ACCDEKOS	COCKADES
ACCDELLY	CALYCLED
ACCDELOY	ACCLOYED
ACCDENOR	CONACRED
ACCDENOV	CONCAVED
ACCDEORR	ACCORDER
ACCDEOST	ACCOSTED
ACCDERSU	ACCURSED
	CARDECUS
ACCDESSU	SUCCADES
ACCDESUU	CADUCEUS
	CAUCUSED
ACCDGHOO	COACHDOG
ACCDHIIR	DIARCHIC
ACCDHIMO	DOCHMIAC
ACCDHIOT	CATHODIC
ACCDHLOR	CLOCHARD
ACCDIIST	DICASTIC
ACCDIITY	DICACITY
ACCDILOY	CALYCOID
ACCDILTY	DACTYLIC
ACCDINOR	CANCROID
	DRACONIC
ACCDIOOR	CORACOID
ACCDIORS	SARCODIC
ACCDIOST	STICCADO
ACCDITUY	CADUCITY
ACCDKNOS	CANDOCKS
ACCDKOSW	DAWCOCKS
ACCDLOSY	CACODYLS
ACCDOOST	STOCCADO
ACCDOOXY	CACODOXY
ACCDOSUU	CADUCOUS
ACCEEHIT	HICCATEE
ACCEEHLO	COCHLEAE
ACCEEHOS	COACHEES
ACCEEHRT	CETERACH
ACCEEHST	SEECATCH
ACCEEILR	CELERIAC
ACCEEILS	ECCLESIA
ACCEEKLN	NECKLACE
ACCEELNR	CLARENCE
ACCEELNS	CENACLES
ACCEELOS	COALESCE
ACCEENNS	NASCENCE
ACCEENPR	CREPANCE
ACCEENRS	CREANCES
ACCEENST	ACESCENT
ACCEEORT	CROCEATE
ACCEEPRT	ACCEPTER
ACCEERST	ACCRETES
ACCEESSS	ACCESSES
ACCEFFIY	EFFICACY
ACCEFILS	FASCICLE
ACCEFLSU	FELUCCAS
ACCEGINS	ACCINGES
ACCEGOSS	SOCCAGES
ACCEHHIS	CHECHIAS
ACCEHHKO	CHECHAKO
ACCEHILM	ALCHEMIC
	CHEMICAL
ACCEHILP	CEPHALIC
ACCEHILS	CALICHES
	CHALICES
ACCEHILT	HECTICAL
ACCEHIMN	MECHANIC
ACCEHINO	ANECHOIC
ACCEHINR	CHANCIER
	CHICANER
ACCEHINS	CHICANES
ACCEHIOS	COACHIES
ACCEHIRT	CATCHIER
ACCEHLNS	CHANCELS
ACCEHLOR	COCHLEAR
ACCEHLOS	COCHLEAS
ACCEHLOT	CATECHOL
ACCEHLST	CLATCHES
ACCEHMNO	COACHMEN
ACCEHNNO	CHACONNE
ACCEHNNY	CYNANCHE
ACCEHNOR	CHARNECO
	ENCROACH
ACCEHNOT	CONCHATE
ACCEHNRS	CHANCERS
	CHANCRES
	CRANCHES
ACCEHNSU	CHAUNCES
ACCEHORS	CAROCHES
	COACHERS
ACCEHPSU	CAPUCHES
ACCEHRST	CATCHERS
	CRATCHES
ACCEHSST	SCATCHES
ACCEHSTU	CATECHUS
ACCEIKPS	ICEPACKS
ACCEILLI	CANCELLI
ACCEILLR	CLERICAL
ACCEILLU	CAULICLE
ACCEILLV	CLAVICLE
ACCEILNS	CALCINES
	SCENICAL
ACCEILNT	CANTICLE
ACCEILNV	CLAVECIN
ACCEILNY	CALYCINE
ACCEILOS	CALICOES
	COELIACS
ACCEILRV	CERVICAL
ACCEILST	CALCITES
ACCEIMOS	OCCAMIES
ACCEIMRS	CERAMICS
ACCEINNR	CANCRINE
ACCEINOS	COCAINES
ACCEINSV	VACCINES
ACCEINTU	CUNEATIC
ACCEIOTV	COACTIVE
ACCEIPRS	CAPRICES
ACCEIPRT	PRACTICE
ACCEIPSV	PECCAVIS
ACCEIQSU	CACIQUES
ACCEIRRR	RICERCAR
ACCEIRSU	CURACIES
ACCEIRTU	CRUCIATE
ACCEISST	ASCETICS
ACCEISTT	ECSTATIC
ACCEKLNR	CRACKNEL
ACCEKLRS	CACKLERS
	CLACKERS
	CRACKLES
ACCEKMOS	MEACOCKS
ACCEKOPS	PEACOCKS
ACCEKOPY	PEACOCKY
ACCEKRRS	CRACKERS
ACCELLSY	CALYCLES
ACCELLUY	CALYCULE
ACCELMNY	CYCLAMEN
ACCELNOS	CONCEALS

ACCELNOV	CONCLAVE	ACCHRRSU	CURRACHS
ACCELNRU	CARUNCLE	ACCHRSSU	SCRAUCHS
ACCELORS	CORACLES	ACCHRSTY	SCRATCHY
ACCELOST	CACOLETS	ACCIIIOT	OITICICA
ACCELRSY	SCARCELY	ACCIILLN	CLINICAL
ACCELSSU	SACCULES	ACCIILMT	CLIMATIC
ACCELWYY	CYCLEWAY	ACCIILRT	CRITICAL
ACCEMNSU	CACUMENS	ACCIIMNN	CINNAMIC
ACCENNSY	NASCENCY	ACCIINNO	ANICONIC
ACCENORR	CORNACRE	ACCIINNP	PICCANIN
ACCENORS	CONACRES	ACCIINOT	ACONITIC
ACCENORT	ACCENTOR	ACCIIPST	PASTICCI
ACCENOST	COSECANT	ACCIIRTX	CICATRIX
ACCENOSU	CONCAUSE	ACCIJKMR	JIMCRACK
ACCENOSV	CONCAVES	ACCIKLOT	COCKTAIL
ACCEOPRT	ACCEPTOR	ACCIKNST	CANSTICK
ACCEOPTU	OCCUPATE	ACCIKOPR	APRICOCK
ACCEORSS	ARCCOSES	ACCIKPRT	PRACTICK
ACCEORST	ECTOSARC	ACCILMOS	COSMICAL
ACCEORSW	CRACOWES	ACCILMOX	CACOMIXL
ACCEORTU	ACCOUTRE	ACCILMSU	CALCIUMS
ACCEOSSS	SACCOSES	ACCILNOT	CICLATON
ACCERRST	CARRECTS	ACCILNOV	VOLCANIC
ACCERSST	SCARCEST	ACCILNUV	VULCANIC
ACCERSSU	ACCURSES	ACCILORS	CALORICS
	ACCUSERS	ACCILORT	CORTICAL
ACCESSTU	CACTUSES	ACCILPRY	CAPRYLIC
ACCESSUU	CAUCUSES	ACCILRRU	CIRCULAR
ACCFHLTY	CATCHFLY	ACCILRSY	ACRYLICS
ACCFIILT	LACTIFIC	ACCILSSS	CLASSICS
ACCGHIKN	CHACKING	ACCIMNOS	MOCCASIN
ACCGHINN	CHANCING	ACCIMNTU	CANTICUM
ACCGHINO	COACHING	ACCIMORU	COUMARIC
ACCGHINT	CATCHING	ACCIMOSZ	ZIMOCCAS
ACCGHIOR	CHORAGIC	ACCIMPSU	CAPSICUM
ACCGIINT	ACCITING	ACCINOOS	OCCASION
ACCGIKLN	CACKLING	ACCINOOT	COACTION
	CLACKING	ACCINORT	NARCOTIC
ACCGIKMR	GIMCRACK	ACCINORV	CAVICORN
ACCGIKNR	CRACKING	ACCINOST	CANTICOS
ACCGINOT	COACTING	ACCINOTY	CANTICOY
ACCGINOY	ACCOYING		CYANOTIC
ACCGINRU	ACCRUING	ACCINRSU	CRUCIANS
ACCGINSU	ACCUSING	ACCIOPST	SPICCATO
ACCGLOOY	CACOLOGY	ACCIORST	ACROSTIC
ACCHHITT	CHITCHAT	ACCIORSY	ISOCRACY
ACCHHMOS	CAMSHOCH	ACCIOSTT	STICCATO
ACCHIIRT	RACHITIC	ACCIOSTU	ACOUSTIC
ACCHIIST	CHIASTIC	ACCIPRST	PRACTICS
ACCHILNO	CHALONIC	ACCIRSTY	SCARCITY
ACCHILOR	ORICHALC	ACCISSTU	CAUSTICS
ACCHILOT	CATHOLIC	ACCKKRSU	RUCKSACK
ACCHINNO	CINCHONA	ACCKLORS	CARLOCKS
ACCHINOS	CHICANOS	ACCKMMRU	CRUMMACK
ACCHINPU	CAPUCHIN	ACCKMORS	CROMACKS
ACCHIORT	THORACIC	ACCKOOOT	COCKATOO
	TROCHAIC	ACCKOPRT	CRACKPOT
ACCHIRRT	CARRITCH	ACCKOSSS	CASSOCKS
ACCHIRSS	SCRAICHS	ACCKOSST	CASTOCKS
ACCHKLOR	CHARLOCK	ACCLLOSU	OCCLUSAL
ACCHKOSY	HAYCOCKS	ACCLLSUU	CALCULUS
ACCHLOOT	CACHOLOT	ACCLSSUU	SACCULUS
ACCHLSTU	CLAUCHTS	ACCMOPST	ACCOMPTS
ACCHMORS	CASCHROM		COMPACTS
ACCHNNUY	UNCHANCY	ACCMOSTU	ACCUSTOM
ACCHNOOR	CORONACH	ACCMRSUU	CURCUMAS
ACCHNOTU	COUCHANT	ACCNOORS	RACCOONS
ACCHORTU	CARTOUCH	ACCNOOTU	COCOANUT
ACCHOSTW	CHOCTAWS	ACCNOPTU	OCCUPANT
ACCHPSTU	CATCHUPS	ACCNORTT	CONTRACT

ACCNOSTT	CONTACTS	ACDEEESS	DECEASES
ACCNOSTU	ACCOUNTS	ACDEEFFT	AFFECTED
ACCOQSSU	SQUACCOS	ACDEEFHN	ENCHAFED
ACCORRTY	CARRYCOT	ACDEEFIL	CALEFIED
ACCORSTU	ACCOURTS	ACDEEFIN	DEFIANCE
ACDDDEIT	ADDICTED	ACDEEFPR	PREFACED
ACDDDETU	ADDUCTED	ACDEEFRS	DEFACERS
ACDDDKOS	DADDOCKS		FRESCADE
ACDDEEES	DECEASED	ACDEEFRY	FEDERACY
ACDDEEHT	DETACHED	ACDEEGLY	DELEGACY
ACDDEEIT	DEDICATE	ACDEEGNR	ENGRACED
ACDDEEKR	DACKERED	ACDEEHIV	ACHIEVED
ACDDEELR	DECLARED	ACDEEHLP	PLEACHED
ACDDEELS	DESCALED	ACDEEHLT	CHELATED
ACDDEEMP	DECAMPED	ACDEEHMR	DEMARCHE
ACDDEENR	CREDENDA	ACDEEHNN	ENHANCED
ACDDEENS	ASCENDED	ACDEEHNR	ENARCHED
ACDDEENT	DECADENT	ACDEEHNS	ENCASHED
	DECANTED		ENCHASED
ACDDEERT	REDACTED	ACDEEHPR	PREACHED
ACDDEETU	EDUCATED	ACDEEHRS	SEARCHED
ACDDEGIS	DISCAGED	ACDEEHSS	CHASSEED
ACDDEIIL	DEICIDAL	ACDEEHST	DETACHES
ACDDEIIM	MEDICAID	ACDEEIIP	EPICEDIA
ACDDEILU	DECIDUAL	ACDEEILT	DELICATE
ACDDEINR	CANDIDER	ACDEEIMR	MEDICARE
	RIDDANCE	ACDEEIMT	DECIMATE
ACDDEINT	DEDICANT		EMICATED
ACDDEINY	CYANIDED		MEDICATE
ACDDEIPS	DISPACED	ACDEEINN	DECENNIA
ACDDEISS	CADDISES		ENNEADIC
	DISCASED	ACDEEINR	DERACINE
ACDDEISU	DECIDUAS	ACDEEINU	AUDIENCE
ACDDEITT	DICTATED	ACDEEINV	DEVIANCE
ACDDEKLO	DEADLOCK	ACDEEIPS	DISPEACE
ACDDEKOR	RADDOCKE	ACDEEIRS	DECIARES
ACDDELOS	CLADODES	ACDEEJKT	JACKETED
ACDDELRS	CLADDERS	ACDEEKLR	LACKERED
ACDDENTU	ADDUCENT	ACDEEKLY	LACKEYED
ACDDEOPS	DECAPODS	ACDEEKNR	CANKERED
ACDDEORR	CORRADED	ACDEEKPR	REPACKED
ACDDEORW	COWARDED	ACDEEKPT	PACKETED
ACDDERSU	ADDUCERS	ACDEEKRS	SCREAKED
	CRUSADED	ACDEEKRT	RACKETED
ACDDERTU	TRADUCED	ACDEELLR	CELLARED
ACDDGILN	CLADDING		RECALLED
ACDDGINU	ADDUCING	ACDEELMN	ENCALMED
ACDDGINY	CADDYING	ACDEELMP	EMPLACED
ACDDHHSU	CHUDDAHS	ACDEELNR	CALENDER
ACDDHIIO	DIADOCHI		ENCRADLE
ACDDHIMR	DIDRACHM	ACDEELNS	CLEANSED
ACDDHKOS	HADDOCKS	ACDEELNT	LANCETED
	SHADDOCK	ACDEELNV	ENCLAVED
ACDDHRSU	CHUDDARS	ACDEELPR	REPLACED
ACDDIIOR	CARDIOID	ACDEELRR	DECLARER
ACDDILNY	CANDIDLY	ACDEELRS	DECLARES
ACDDILTY	DIDACTYL		RESCALED
ACDDINNU	UNCANDID	ACDEELRT	CLARETED
ACDDINSY	DISCANDY		DECRETAL
ACDDIRSS	DISCARDS		TREACLED
ACDDKLNO	DOCKLAND	ACDEELRV	CALVERED
ACDDKOPS	PADDOCKS		CLAVERED
ACDDKORY	DOCKYARD	ACDEELSS	DECLASSE
ACDDORTU	ADDUCTOR		DESCALES
ACDEEEFT	DEFECATE	ACDEEMNP	ENCAMPED
ACDEEEKS	SEEDCAKE	ACDEEMRS	SCREAMED
ACDEEENR	CAREENED	ACDEEMRT	CREMATED
ACDEEENT	ANTECEDE	ACDEENNP	PENANCED
ACDEEERR	CAREERED	ACDEENNT	TENDANCE
ACDEEERS	DECREASE	ACDEENNY	CAYENNED

ACDEENOT	ANECDOTE	ACDEHILT	DITHECAL
ACDEENRS	ASCENDER	ACDEHIMN	MACHINED
	REASCEND	ACDEHIMS	SCHIEDAM
ACDEENRT	CANTERED	ACDEHINR	INARCHED
	CRENATED	ACDEHINS	ECHIDNAS
	DECANTER		INCHASED
	NECTARED	ACDEHIRS	RACHIDES
	RECANTED	ACDEHIRT	THRIDACE
ACDEENRV	CAVERNED		TRACHEID
	CRAVENED	ACDEHIST	SCAITHED
ACDEENRY	CARNEYED	ACDEHISU	CHIAUSED
ACDEENRZ	CREDENZA	ACDEHKLO	HEADLOCK
ACDEENSV	VENDACES	ACDEHKLS	SHACKLED
ACDEENTT	DANCETTE	ACDEHKNU	UNHACKED
ACDEEOPS	PEASECOD	ACDEHKOV	HAVOCKED
ACDEEORT	DECORATE	ACDEHKRU	ARCHDUKE
ACDEEOTV	EVOCATED	ACDEHKTW	THWACKED
ACDEEPPR	RECAPPED	ACDEHLNP	PLANCHED
ACDEEPRS	ESCARPED	ACDEHLNR	CHANDLER
ACDEEPRT	CARPETED	ACDEHLNU	LAUNCHED
ACDEEPST	ASPECTED	ACDEHLRS	CHALDERS
ACDEERRS	SCAREDER	ACDEHMST	SMATCHED
ACDEERRT	RETRACED	ACDEHNOR	ANCHORED
	TERRACED		RONDACHE
ACDEERSS	CARESSED	ACDEHNPU	PAUNCHED
ACDEERST	CEDRATES	ACDEHNRU	RAUNCHED
ACDEESTU	EDUCATES	ACDEHNST	SNATCHED
ACDEESUX	CAUDEXES		STANCHED
ACDEESUY	CAUSEYED	ACDEHNSU	UNCASHED
ACDEFFHU	CHAUFFED	ACDEHNTU	CHAUNTED
ACDEFFLS	SCLAFFED	ACDEHOPY	POCHAYED
ACDEFFOR	AFFORCED	ACDEHORR	HARDCORE
ACDEFGIN	DEFACING	ACDEHORT	CHORDATE
ACDEFHLN	FLANCHED	ACDEHORW	COWHEARD
ACDEFIIL	DEIFICAL	ACDEHOST	CATHODES
ACDEFIIP	PACIFIED	ACDEHOUV	AVOUCHED
ACDEFILR	FRICADEL	ACDEHPPS	SCHAPPED
ACDEFINN	FINANCED	ACDEHPST	DESPATCH
ACDEFLOT	OLFACTED	ACDEHPSU	CUPHEADS
ACDEFNRU	FURNACED	ACDEHQTU	QUATCHED
ACDEFORT	FACTORED	ACDEHRST	STARCHED
ACDEFOTU	OUTFACED	ACDEHTUW	WAUCHTED
ACDEFRSU	SURFACED	ACDEIILS	LAICISED
ACDEFRTU	FURCATED	ACDEIILT	CILIATED
ACDEGGRS	SCRAGGED	ACDEIILZ	LAICIZED
ACDEGHLO	GALOCHED	ACDEIIMU	AECIDIUM
ACDEGHNU	CHAUNGED	ACDEIINR	ACRIDINE
	GAUNCHED	ACDEIINS	SCIAENID
ACDEGIIL	ALGICIDE	ACDEIINT	ACTINIDE
ACDEGIKM	MAGICKED		DIACTINE
ACDEGIMR	DECIGRAM		INDICATE
	GRIMACED	ACDEIINU	INDUCIAE
ACDEGINU	GUIDANCE	ACDEIITV	CAVITIED
ACDEGINY	DECAYING		VATICIDE
ACDEGIRS	DISGRACE		VICIATED
ACDEGISS	DISCAGES	ACDEIJNU	JAUNDICE
ACDEGIST	CADGIEST	ACDEIKNP	PANICKED
ACDEGKOS	DOCKAGES	ACDEIKNT	ANTICKED
ACDEGLOU	CLOUDAGE	ACDEILLM	MEDALLIC
ACDEGNOS	DECAGONS	ACDEILLN	DECLINAL
ACDEGNRU	UNGRACED	ACDEILLS	CEDILLAS
ACDEGORS	CORDAGES	ACDEILLV	CAVILLED
ACDEGOTT	COTTAGED	ACDEILMO	CAMELOID
ACDEHHIN	HAINCHED	ACDEILMS	CAMELIDS
ACDEHHNU	HAUNCHED		DECIMALS
ACDEHHRU	HACHURED		DECLAIMS
ACDEHHTT	THATCHED		MEDICALS
ACDEHIIP	APHICIDE	ACDEILMT	CLIMATED
ACDEHIJK	HIJACKED		MALEDICT
ACDEHILR	HERALDIC		

ACDEILMX	CLIMAXED	ACDELMOR	CLAMORED
ACDEILNP	PANICLED	ACDELMSU	MUSCADEL
ACDEILOS	COALISED	ACDELNOO	CANOODLE
ACDEILOZ	COALIZED	ACDELNOR	COLANDER
ACDEILPR	PLACIDER	ACDELNOS	CELADONS
ACDEILPS	DISPLACE	ACDELNPU	UNPLACED
ACDEILPT	PLICATED	ACDELNRY	CALENDRY
ACDEILRS	DECRIALS	ACDELNST	SCANTLED
	RADICELS	ACDELNSU	UNSCALED
	RADICLES	ACDELOPT	CLODPATE
ACDEILRT	ARTICLED	ACDELOPU	CUPOLAED
ACDEILRU	AURICLED	ACDELORV	OVERCLAD
	RADICULE	ACDELOTU	OCULATED
ACDEILST	CITADELS	ACDELPPS	SCAPPLED
	DIALECTS	ACDELRSS	SCALDERS
ACDEILTT	LATTICED	ACDELRSW	SCRAWLED
ACDEIMNO	COMEDIAN	ACDELRSY	SACREDLY
	DAEMONIC	ACDELSTU	CAULDEST
	DEMONIAC		SULCATED
ACDEIMNP	PANDEMIC	ACDEMMRS	SCRAMMED
ACDEIMPT	IMPACTED	ACDEMNOR	ROMANCED
ACDEIMRT	DERMATIC	ACDEMNSU	DECUMANS
ACDEINNR	CRANNIED	ACDEMOPR	COMPARED
ACDEINOP	CANOPIED	ACDEMORS	COMRADES
ACDEINOS	DIOCESAN	ACDEMORT	DEMOCRAT
	OCEANIDS	ACDEMRSW	SCRAWMED
ACDEINOV	VOIDANCE	ACDEMUUV	VACUUMED
ACDEINPT	PEDANTIC	ACDENNNO	CANNONED
	PENTADIC	ACDENNOR	ORDNANCE
ACDEINRR	RANCIDER	ACDENNOT	CANTONED
ACDEINRT	CRINATED	ACDENNST	SCANDENT
	DICENTRA	ACDENOPR	ENDOCARP
ACDEINST	DISTANCE	ACDENORS	DRACONES
ACDEINSY	CYANIDES		ENDOSARC
	CYANISED	ACDENORT	CARTONED
ACDEINTT	NICTATED	ACDENORY	CRAYONED
ACDEINVY	DEVIANCY		DEACONRY
ACDEINYZ	CYANIZED	ACDENOSY	CYANOSED
ACDEIOPS	DIASCOPE	ACDENOTU	OUTDANCE
ACDEIORS	IDOCRASE	ACDENPPU	UNCAPPED
ACDEIORT	CERATOID	ACDENPRU	PRAUNCED
ACDEIORV	COVARIED	ACDENPST	PANDECTS
ACDEIOSS	ACIDOSES	ACDENRST	CANTREDS
ACDEIOSU	EDACIOUS	ACDENRSU	DURANCES
ACDEIPPT	TAPPICED	ACDENRTU	UNCRATED
ACDEIPRS	EPACRIDS		UNDERACT
ACDEIPSS	DISPACES		UNTRACED
	SPADICES	ACDENRVY	VERDANCY
ACDEIPST	SPICATED	ACDENSST	DESCANTS
ACDEIPSZ	CAPSIZED	ACDENSUU	UNCAUSED
ACDEIPTV	CAPTIVED	ACDENTTY	DANCETTY
ACDEIQRU	ACQUIRED	ACDEOPRU	CROUPADE
ACDEIRSS	SIDECARS	ACDEOPSS	PEASCODS
ACDEIRST	ACRIDEST	ACDEOPTT	CAPOTTED
ACDEIRSU	DECURIAS	ACDEOPTU	OUTPACED
ACDEIRTT	TETRACID	ACDEORRS	CORRADES
	TETRADIC	ACDEORRT	REDACTOR
ACDEISSS	DISCASES	ACDEORSS	SARCODES
ACDEISTT	DICTATES	ACDEORST	REDCOATS
ACDEKLNR	CRANKLED	ACDEORSU	CAROUSED
ACDEKLQU	QUACKLED	ACDEORTU	EDUCATOR
ACDEKNPR	PRANCKED		OUTRACED
ACDEKNPU	UNPACKED	ACDEORTV	CAVORTED
ACDEKNRU	UNRACKED	ACDEOSTT	COSTATED
ACDEKNTU	UNTACKED	ACDEOSUV	COUVADES
ACDEKOST	STOCKADE	ACDEOTTU	OUTACTED
ACDELLNU	UNCALLED	ACDEPPRS	SCRAPPED
ACDELLOR	CAROLLED	ACDEPRTU	CAPTURED
	COLLARED	ACDEQTUU	AQUEDUCT
ACDELLOT	COLLATED		

ACDERRSU	CRUSADER	ACDIIRST	CARDITIS	ACDNORSU	CANDOURS	ACEEHLSS	LACHESES
ACDERRTU	TRADUCER	ACDIIRTY	ACRIDITY		CAUDRONS	ACEEHLST	CHELATES
ACDERSSU	CRUSADES	ACDIISST	SADISTIC	ACDNOSTW	DOWNCAST	ACEEHLTV	CHEVALET
ACDERSTT	DETRACTS	ACDIKMOO	COOKMAID	ACDNOSUU	ADUNCOUS	ACEEHMNP	CAMPHENE
	SCRATTED	ACDIKRRY	RICKYARD	ACDOOPTY	OCTAPODY	ACEEHMNR	MENARCHE
ACDERSTU	TRADUCES	ACDILLOS	CODILLAS	ACDOORST	OSTRACOD	ACEEHMRS	CASHMERE
ACDERTUV	CURVATED	ACDILLOU	CAUDILLO		SCORDATO		MACHREES
ACDFFHNU	HANDCUFF		LODICULA	ACDOPRST	POSTCARD		MARCHESE
ACDFFIRT	DIFFRACT	ACDILLPY	PLACIDLY	ACDORRWY	COWARDRY	ACEEHMST	MACHETES
ACDFFLOS	SCAFFOLD	ACDILMOR	DROMICAL	ACDORSST	COSTARDS	ACEEHNNS	ENHANCES
ACDFIILU	FIDUCIAL	ACDILMSS	CLADISMS	ACDORSSU	CRUSADOS	ACEEHNPS	CHEAPENS
ACDFILOU	FUCOIDAL	ACDILNOO	CONOIDAL	ACDRSSTU	CUSTARDS	ACEEHNRS	ENARCHES
ACDFIOST	FACTOIDS	ACDILNOS	SCALDINO	ACEEEFRR	CAREFREE	ACEEHNRV	REVANCHE
ACDGIILO	DIALOGIC	ACDILNSU	DULCIANS	ACEEEGLN	ELEGANCE	ACEEHNSS	ENCASHES
ACDGILNN	CANDLING	ACDILNSY	SYNDICAL	ACEEEGRS	CARGEESE		ENCHASES
ACDGILNR	CRADLING	ACDILNUU	NUDICAUL	ACEEEIPR	EARPIECE	ACEEHORT	OCHREATE
ACDGILNS	SCALDING	ACDILOPY	POLYACID	ACEEEKNT	NECKATEE	ACEEHPPS	ECHAPPES
ACDGILNU	CAUDLING	ACDILORS	CORDIALS	ACEEELMR	CAMELEER	ACEEHPRR	PREACHER
ACDGIMOT	DOGMATIC	ACDILOUV	OVIDUCAL	ACEEENRS	ENCREASE	ACEEHPRS	PEACHERS
ACDGINNS	DANCINGS	ACDILPSU	CUSPIDAL	ACEEENSV	EVANESCE		PREACHES
ACDGINNY	CANDYING	ACDILSST	CLADISTS	ACEEEPSS	ESCAPEES	ACEEHPRT	ETHERCAP
ACDGINSU	SCAUDING	ACDILSTW	WILDCATS	ACEEERRT	RECREATE	ACEEHPST	CHEAPEST
ACDGIOPR	PODAGRIC	ACDIMMSU	CADMIUMS	ACEEERTX	EXECRATE	ACEEHQSU	QUEACHES
ACDGKLOS	DAGLOCKS	ACDIMNOO	MONOACID	ACEEESUV	EVACUEES	ACEEHRRS	REACHERS
ACDGNOST	CANTDOGS	ACDIMNOS	MANDIOCS	ACEEFFIN	CAFFEINE		RESEARCH
ACDGORST	DOGCARTS	ACDIMNSU	MUSCADIN	ACEEFFRT	AFFECTER		SEARCHER
ACDHIILS	CHILIADS		SCANDIUM	ACEEFHNS	ENCHAFES	ACEEHRRT	TREACHER
ACDHIKOR	CHOKIDAR	ACDIMNSY	DYNAMICS	ACEEFILM	MALEFICE	ACEEHRSS	SEARCHES
ACDHILPR	PILCHARD	ACDIMOSY	DOCIMASY	ACEEFILS	CALEFIES	ACEEHRST	CHEATERS
ACDHILPS	CLAPDISH	ACDINOPS	SPONDAIC	ACEEFINS	FAIENCES		HECTARES
ACDHINOR	HADRONIC	ACDINORS	SARDONIC		FIANCEES		RECHATES
	RHODANIC	ACDINORT	TORNADIC	ACEEFKOR	ECOFREAK		RECHEATS
ACDHINRY	DINARCHY	ACDINORW	CORDWAIN	ACEEFLPU	PEACEFUL		TEACHERS
ACDHINSW	SANDWICH	ACDINSST	DISCANTS	ACEEFLSS	FACELESS	ACEEHRTT	CATHETER
ACDHIOPS	SCAPHOID	ACDINSTY	DYNASTIC	ACEEFNSY	FAYENCES	ACEEHRTY	CHEATERY
ACDHIORY	HYRACOID	ACDINTUY	ADUNCITY	ACEEFPRS	PREFACES	ACEEHSST	ESCHEATS
ACDHIPST	DISPATCH	ACDIOPRS	PICADORS	ACEEFPRT	PERFECTA	ACEEHSTX	CATHEXES
ACDHLNOR	CHALDRON		SPORADIC		PRAEFECT		EXCHEATS
	CHLORDAN	ACDIORRS	CORRIDAS	ACEEFRSU	FARCEUSE	ACEEIKNP	PEACENIK
	CHONDRAL	ACDIORSS	SARCOIDS	ACEEGHNR	ENCHARGE	ACEEIKRR	CREAKIER
ACDHLORS	DORLACHS	ACDIORTT	DICTATOR	ACEEGHNX	EXCHANGE	ACEEILMN	CAMELINE
ACDHMORU	MOUCHARD	ACDIPRST	ADSCRIPT	ACEEGHRR	RECHARGE	ACEEILMT	EMETICAL
ACDHNORW	CHAWDRON	ACDIRSST	DRASTICS	ACEEGILS	ELEGIACS	ACEEILNP	CAPELINE
ACDHNOSW	COWHANDS	ACDIRSTT	DISTRACT		LEGACIES	ACEEILNR	CINEREAL
ACDHOOST	CATHOODS	ACDISTUV	VIADUCTS	ACEEGINS	AGENCIES		RELIANCE
ACDHOPRS	POCHARDS	ACDJNSTU	ADJUNCTS	ACEEGKNR	NECKGEAR	ACEEILNS	SALIENCE
ACDHORRS	ORCHARDS	ACDKLOPS	PADLOCKS	ACEEGKRW	WRECKAGE	ACEEILPS	CALIPEES
ACDHORSW	SHOWCARD	ACDKMMOR	DRAMMOCK	ACEEGLNY	ELEGANCY		ESPECIAL
ACDHORSY	DYSCHROA	ACDKMPSU	MUDPACKS	ACEEGLPU	PUCELAGE	ACEEILRS	ESCALIER
ACDIIIPR	DIAPIRIC	ACDKOPRS	POCKARDS	ACEEGNOZ	COZENAGE	ACEEILRV	RECEIVAL
ACDIIJLU	JUDICIAL	ACDLLORS	COLLARDS	ACEEGNRS	ENGRACES	ACEEIMOT	ACOEMETI
ACDIILMS	DISCLAIM	ACDLNNOR	CORNLAND	ACEEGNRY	REAGENCY	ACEEIMRR	CREAMIER
ACDIILNO	CONIDIAL	ACDLNOPR	CROPLAND	ACEEGNST	CENTAGES		REARMICE
ACDIILNS	SCALDINI	ACDLNORS	CALDRONS	ACEEGNSV	SCAVENGE	ACEEIMRS	RACEMISE
ACDIILSU	SUICIDAL	ACDLNORU	CAULDRON	ACEEGORR	RACEGOER	ACEEIMRT	CEMITARE
ACDIILTY	CALIDITY	ACDLNORY	CONDYLAR	ACEEGORV	COVERAGE	ACEEIMRZ	RACEMIZE
	DIALYTIC	ACDLNOST	COTLANDS	ACEEGSSU	ESCUAGES	ACEEIMST	EMICATES
ACDIIMNO	DAIMONIC	ACDLOORT	DOCTORAL	ACEEHHST	CHEETAHS	ACEEINPS	SAPIENCE
ACDIIMOR	DIORAMIC	ACDLORWY	COWARDLY	ACEEHILR	LEACHIER	ACEEINPT	PATIENCE
ACDIIMOT	DIATOMIC	ACDLOSWY	LADYCOWS	ACEEHINT	ECHINATE	ACEEINRS	CINEREAS
ACDIIMSU	ASCIDIUM	ACDMMNOO	COMMANDO	ACEEHIPR	PEACHIER		INCREASE
ACDIINNS	INDICANS	ACDMMNOS	COMMANDS	ACEEHIPS	CHEAPIES		RESIANCE
ACDIINNT	INDICANT	ACDMNORY	DORMANCY	ACEEHIPT	PETECHIA	ACEEINRT	CENTIARE
ACDIINOP	PINACOID		MORDANCY	ACEEHIRV	ACHIEVER		CREATINE
ACDIINOT	ACTINOID	ACDMOOPR	MACROPOD	ACEEHIST	HICATEES		INCREATE
	DIATONIC	ACDMORSZ	CZARDOMS	ACEEHISV	ACHIEVES		ITERANCE
ACDIINPY	PYCNIDIA	ACDNOORR	RONCADOR	ACEEHITV	ATCHIEVE	ACEEINST	CINEASTE
ACDIINRS	ACRIDINS	ACDNOORS	CARDOONS	ACEEHKTT	HACKETTE	ACEEINSU	EUCAINES
ACDIIOSS	ACIDOSIS	ACDNOORV	CORDOVAN	ACEEHLPS	PLEACHES	ACEEINTV	ENACTIVE
ACDIIRSS	SCIARIDS	ACDNOOTU	DUCATOON	ACEEHLRS	RELACHES	ACEEINTX	EXITANCE

ACEEIPST	SPECIATE		CREMATES	ACEFILRS	FILACERS	ACEGILNN	CLEANING
ACEEIRRS	CARIERES		MEERCATS	ACEFINNS	FINANCES		ELANCING
	CREASIER	ACEENNPS	PENANCES	ACEFINRS	FANCIERS		ENLACING
ACEEIRSU	CAUSERIE	ACEENNRT	ENTRANCE	ACEFINRX	CARNIFEX	ACEGILNR	CLEARING
ACEEIRSW	WISEACRE	ACEENNST	CANTEENS	ACEFINSS	FASCINES	ACEGILNT	CLEATING
ACEEIRTV	CREATIVE	ACEENNSY	CAYENNES	ACEFINST	FANCIEST	ACEGILNV	CLEAVING
	REACTIVE	ACEENORT	CAROTENE	ACEFIOSS	FIASCOES	ACEGILOS	CALIGOES
ACEEISTV	VESICATE	ACEENOST	ACETONES	ACEFIRRT	CRAFTIER	ACEGILRS	GLACIERS
ACEEKLMR	MACKEREL	ACEENPRR	PARCENER	ACEFIRTT	TRIFECTA	ACEGILRV	CLAVIGER
ACEEKLRW	EELWRACK	ACEENPRT	PERCEANT	ACEFIRTY	FERACITY	ACEGILSS	GLACISES
ACEEKMPT	EMPACKET	ACEENRRT	RECANTER	ACEFKLRS	FLACKERS	ACEGILST	GELASTIC
ACEEKNRW	NECKWEAR		RECREANT	ACEFKLST	FLACKETS	ACEGIMMT	TAGMEMIC
ACEEKRRT	RACKETER	ACEENRSS	CASERNES	ACEFLLSS	CALFLESS	ACEGIMMN	MENACING
ACEELLNS	NACELLES	ACEENRST	REASCENT	ACEFLMNO	FLAMENCO	ACEGIMNR	AMERCING
ACEELLNT	LANCELET		SARCENET	ACEFLNOR	FALCONER		CREAMING
ACEELLOT	OCELLATE	ACEENRTU	ENACTURE	ACEFLNOT	CONFLATE	ACEGIMNT	MAGNETIC
ACEELLPT	CAPELLET		UNCREATE		FALCONET	ACEGIMOX	EXOGAMIC
ACEELLRR	CELLARER	ACEEORST	CREASOTE	ACEFLORS	ALFRESCO	ACEGIMRS	GRIMACES
ACEELLRT	CELLARET	ACEEOSTT	ECOSTATE	ACEFLRTU	FULCRATE	ACEGINNO	CANOEING
ACEELMNO	CAMELEON	ACEEOSTV	EVOCATES	ACEFMNOO	MOONFACE	ACEGINNR	ENRACING
ACEELMNP	PLACEMEN	ACEEPRRS	CAPERERS	ACEFNNOS	FACONNES	ACEGINNS	ENCASING
ACEELMPS	EMPLACES	ACEEPRSS	ESCAPERS	ACEFNORV	CONFERVA	ACEGINNT	ENACTING
ACEELMRS	RECLAMES	ACEEPRTT	ETTERCAP	ACEFNPRT	PENCRAFT	ACEGINNV	ENCAVING
	SCLEREMA	ACEEPRTU	PERACUTE	ACEFNRST	CANTREFS	ACEGINOS	COINAGES
ACEELNPT	PENTACLE	ACEEPRTX	EXCERPTA	ACEFNRSU	FURNACES	ACEGINPR	CAPERING
ACEELNRR	LARCENER	ACEEPSSU	AUCEPSES	ACEFOOPT	FOOTPACE		PEARCING
ACEELNRS	CLEANERS	ACEEPSTT	SPECTATE	ACEFOPST	POSTFACE		PREACING
	CLEANSER	ACEERRST	CATERERS	ACEFORRS	FORECARS	ACEGINPS	ESCAPING
ACEELNRU	CERULEAN		RETRACES	ACEFORST	FORECAST	ACEGINRS	CREASING
ACEELNSS	CLEANSES		TERRACES	ACEFORSX	CARFOXES		GRECIANS
ACEELNST	CLEANEST	ACEERRSU	ECRASEUR	ACEFOSTU	OUTFACES		SEARCING
	LATENCES	ACEERRTU	CREATURE	ACEFRRST	REFRACTS	ACEGINRT	CATERING
ACEELNSU	NUCLEASE	ACEERRUV	VERRUCAE	ACEFRRSU	FARCEURS		CITRANGE
ACEELNSV	ENCLAVES	ACEERSSS	CARESSES		SURFACER		CREATING
	VALENCES	ACEERSST	CATERESS	ACEFRRTU	FRACTURE		REACTING
ACEELNTT	TENTACLE		CERASTES	ACEFRSSU	SURFACES	ACEGINSS	CAGINESS
ACEELNTU	NUCLEATE	ACEERSSU	SURCEASE	ACEFRSTU	FACTURES		CEASINGS
ACEELOPS	ESCALOPE	ACEERSSV	CREVASSE	ACEGGILN	CAGELING	ACEGINTX	EXACTING
ACEELORS	ESCAROLE	ACEERSTU	SECATEUR		GLACEING	ACEGIOTT	COGITATE
ACEELORT	RELOCATE	ACEERSTX	EXACTERS	ACEGGILR	CLAGGIER	ACEGIPRS	SPAGERIC
ACEELPRR	REPLACER	ACEERTTU	ERUCTATE	ACEGGINN	ENGAGING	ACEGIRST	AGRESTIC
ACEELPRS	PERCALES	ACEESSST	ECSTASES	ACEGGIOP	EPAGOGIC	ACEGISTU	GAUCIEST
	REPLACES	ACEESSTT	CASSETTE	ACEGGIRR	CRAGGIER	ACEGISTW	GAWCIEST
ACEELPST	CAPELETS	ACEESTTX	EXACTEST	ACEGHILN	LEACHING	ACEGKLOS	LOCKAGES
ACEELPTU	PECULATE	ACEFFGIN	EFFACING	ACEGHILT	LICHGATE	ACEGKLOV	GAVELOCK
ACEELPTY	CLYPEATE	ACEFFHIR	CHAFFIER	ACEGHINP	PEACHING	ACEGKLRS	GRACKLES
ACEELRRS	CLEARERS	ACEFFHIS	AFFICHES	ACEGHINR	REACHING	ACEGKMOS	MOCKAGES
ACEELRSS	CARELESS	ACEFFHRS	CHAFFERS	ACEGHINT	CHEATING	ACEGKORS	CORKAGES
	RESCALES	ACEFFHRY	CHAFFERY		TEACHING	ACEGKORW	CAGEWORK
ACEELRST	CLEAREST	ACEFFIMS	CAFFEISM	ACEGHLOS	GALOCHES	ACEGKRTU	TRUCKAGE
	SCELERAT	ACEFFISS	SCAFFIES	ACEGHLRS	SCHLAGER	ACEGLLNO	COLLAGEN
	TREACLES	ACEFFORS	AFFORCES	ACEGHLTY	LYCHGATE	ACEGLLOS	COLLAGES
ACEELRSV	CLEAVERS	ACEFGINN	ENFACING	ACEGHMMU	CHUMMAGE	ACEGLNOS	CONGEALS
ACEELRTT	RACLETTE	ACEFGINR	REFACING	ACEGHMOR	ECHOGRAM	ACEGLNRS	CLANGERS
ACEELRTU	ULCERATE	ACEFGINT	FACETING		GRAMOCHE	ACEGLOST	CATELOGS
ACEELRTV	CERVELAT	ACEFGLRU	GRACEFUL	ACEGHNRS	CHANGERS	ACEGLOSU	CAGOULES
ACEELSST	CELESTAS	ACEFHIKS	FISHCAKE	ACEGHNRU	UNCHARGE	ACEGMNOY	GEOMANCY
ACEELSSU	EUCLASES	ACEFHLNS	FLANCHES	ACEGHNSU	CHAUNGES	ACEGMNRS	CRAGSMEN
ACEELSTT	TELECAST	ACEFHMRS	CHAMFERS		GAUNCHES	ACEGMOPS	COMPAGES
ACEELSVX	EXCLAVES	ACEFHORU	FAROUCHE	ACEGHOSU	GOUACHES	ACEGMORS	SCARMOGE
ACEEMNOT	MECONATE	ACEFHRST	FRATCHES	ACEGHOSW	COWHAGES	ACEGMRRY	GRAMERCY
ACEEMNPS	SPACEMEN	ACEFIIPR	PACIFIER	ACEGHRRS	CHARGERS	ACEGNNOY	CYANOGEN
ACEEMNRS	MENACERS	ACEFIIPS	PACIFIES	ACEGHRTU	RECAUGHT	ACEGNNTY	TANGENCY
ACEEMNST	CASEMENT	ACEFIIRT	ARTIFICE	ACEGHSTU	GAUCHEST	ACEGNORS	ACROGENS
ACEEMORS	RACEMOSE	ACEFILLY	FACILELY	ACEGIIMP	EPIGAMIC		CORNAGES
ACEEMORV	OVERCAME	ACEFILOP	EPIFOCAL	ACEGIINV	VICINAGE	ACEGNOST	COGNATES
ACEEMRRS	CREAMERS	ACEFILOS	FASCIOLE	ACEGIKNR	CREAKING	ACEGNSSY	CAGYNESS
	SCREAMER		FOCALISE	ACEGILLO	COLLEGIA	ACEGOORS	CARGOOSE
ACEEMRRY	CREAMERY	ACEFILOZ	FOCALIZE	ACEGILLR	ALLERGIC	ACEGOPRY	GEOCARPY
ACEEMRST	CERAMETS			ACEGILMU	MUCILAGE	ACEGORSS	CORSAGES

	SOCAGERS	ACEHINSY	HYACINES	ACEHLRST	ARCHLETS	ACEHPRTY	PATCHERY
ACEGORST	ESCARGOT		SYNECHIA	ACEHLRSY	CHARLEYS		PETCHARY
ACEGORSU	COURAGES	ACEHIOPR	POACHIER	ACEHLRTU	ARCHLUTE	ACEHQSTU	QUATCHES
ACEGORTT	COTTAGER	ACEHIOST	TOISEACH		TRAUCHLE	ACEHRRST	CHARTERS
ACEGORTY	CATEGORY	ACEHIPPR	CHAPPIER	ACEHLSSS	CASHLESS		RECHARTS
ACEGOSTT	COTTAGES	ACEHIPPS	CHAPPIES	ACEHLSST	SATCHELS		STARCHER
ACEGOTTY	COTTAGEY	ACEHIPRS	CHARPIES	ACEHLSTT	CHATTELS	ACEHRRTT	TETRARCH
ACEGRSTU	TRUCAGES		PARCHESI		LATCHETS	ACEHRSST	STARCHES
ACEGSSTU	SCUTAGES		SERAPHIC	ACEHLSTY	CHASTELY	ACEHRSSU	CHASSEUR
ACEHHINS	HAINCHES	ACEHIPRT	CHAPITER	ACEHMMNR	MARCHMEN	ACEHRSTT	CHATTERS
ACEHHIRR	HIERARCH		PATCHIER	ACEHMNNR	RANCHMEN		RATCHETS
ACEHHIST	SHECHITA		PHREATIC	ACEHMNRS	ENCHARMS	ACEHRSTW	WATCHERS
ACEHHLST	HATCHELS	ACEHIPST	HEPATICS	ACEHMNRT	MERCHANT	ACEHRSTY	YACHTERS
ACEHHLSU	SHAUCHLE		PASTICHE	ACEHMNSS	CHESSMAN	ACEHRTTY	TRACHYTE
ACEHHMNN	HENCHMAN	ACEHIPTT	PATHETIC	ACEHMNST	MANCHETS	ACEHSSSU	CHAUSSES
ACEHHNRT	ETHNARCH	ACEHIPTW	WHITECAP	ACEHMNTW	WATCHMEN	ACEHSSTT	CHASTEST
ACEHHNSU	HAUNCHES	ACEHIRSS	CASHIERS	ACEHMORT	CHROMATE	ACEHSSTW	SWATCHES
ACEHHPRT	HEPTARCH		RACHISES	ACEHMPRS	CHAMPERS	ACEHSTTU	CATHETUS
ACEHHRST	HATCHERS	ACEHIRST	CHARIEST	ACEHMRRS	CHARMERS		TEUCHATS
ACEHHRSU	HACHURES		THERIACS		MARCHERS	ACEHSTTW	WATCHETS
ACEHHRTT	THATCHER	ACEHIRSU	EUCHARIS	ACEHMRST	MATCHERS	ACEHTTUZ	ZUCHETTA
ACEHHRTY	HATCHERY	ACEHIRSV	ARCHIVES	ACEHMRSU	CHAUMERS	ACEIILMN	LIMACINE
	THEARCHY	ACEHIRSW	ARCHWISE	ACEHMSST	SMATCHES	ACEIILNR	IRENICAL
ACEHHSTT	HATCHETS	ACEHIRTT	CHATTIER	ACEHMSTU	MUSTACHE	ACEIILNS	SALICINE
	THATCHES		THEATRIC	ACEHMSTY	ECTHYMAS		SILICANE
ACEHHTTY	HATCHETY	ACEHISST	CHASTISE	ACEHNNOP	PANCHEON	ACEIILSS	LAICISES
ACEHIIMS	ISCHEMIA		TAISCHES	ACEHNNPT	PENCHANT	ACEIILST	SILICATE
ACEHIIRT	HIERATIC	ACEHISSU	CHIAUSES	ACEHNNST	ENCHANTS	ACEIILSZ	LAICIZES
ACEHIJKR	HIJACKER	ACEHISTT	CHATTIES	ACEHNOPR	CANEPHOR	ACEIIMRV	VIRAEMIC
ACEHIKLP	KEPHALIC		TACHISTE		CHAPERON	ACEIIMSS	ASEISMIC
ACEHIKLR	CHALKIER	ACEHISTX	CATHEXIS	ACEHNOPT	CENOTAPH	ACEIIMTU	MAIEUTIC
	HACKLIER	ACEHKLOV	HAVELOCK	ACEHNORR	RANCHERO	ACEIINPS	PISCINAE
ACEHIKLW	LICHWAKE	ACEHKLPR	KREPLACH	ACEHNORT	ANCHORET	ACEIINRS	RIANCIES
ACEHIKRS	KACHERIS	ACEHKLRS	HACKLERS	ACEHNPRT	PENTARCH	ACEIINST	CANITIES
ACEHIKRW	WHACKIER	ACEHKLSS	SHACKLES	ACEHNPSU	PAUNCHES	ACEIINTV	INACTIVE
ACEHILLT	HELLICAT	ACEHKLST	HACKLETS	ACEHNRRS	RANCHERS	ACEIINTZ	ANTICIZE
ACEHILMN	INCHMEAL	ACEHKLTY	LATCHKEY	ACEHNRSS	ARCHNESS	ACEIIPRS	PIRACIES
ACEHILMP	IMPLEACH	ACEHKNSY	HACKNEYS	ACEHNRST	CHANTERS	ACEIIRRT	CRITERIA
ACEHILMS	CAMELISH	ACEHKOSW	WHACKOES		SNATCHER	ACEIIRSV	VICARIES
ACEHILNT	CHAINLET	ACEHKOTU	TUCKAHOE		STANCHER	ACEIISTU	ACUITIES
	ETHNICAL	ACEHKRSW	WHACKERS		TRANCHES	ACEIISTV	CAITIVES
ACEHILOR	HALICORE	ACEHKRTW	THWACKER	ACEHNRSU	RAUNCHES		CAVITIES
	HEROICAL	ACEHLLMO	MALLECHO	ACEHNRTT	TRANCHET		VICIATES
ACEHILPR	PARHELIC	ACEHLLOR	ORCHELLA	ACEHNRTU	CHAUNTER	ACEIITTV	VITICETA
ACEHILRS	CHARLIES	ACEHLLPS	PELLACHS	ACEHNSST	CHASTENS	ACEIJKSS	JACKSIES
ACEHILST	ETHICALS	ACEHLLSS	SHELLACS		SNATCHES	ACEIJMST	MAJESTIC
ACEHILTT	ATHLETIC	ACEHLLSU	HALLUCES		STANCHES	ACEIJNRR	JERRICAN
	THETICAL	ACEHLMOT	CHAMELOT	ACEHNSTT	ETCHANTS	ACEIKKNR	KNACKIER
ACEHIMNP	CAMPHINE	ACEHLMST	CHAMLETS	ACEHNSTU	NAUTCHES	ACEIKLRT	TALCKIER
ACEHIMNR	CHAIRMEN	ACEHLNNS	CHANNELS		UNCHASTE	ACEIKLRY	CREAKILY
ACEHIMNS	MACHINES	ACEHLNOS	CHALONES	ACEHNSTY	CHANTEYS	ACEIKMNN	NICKNAME
ACEHIMNU	ACHENIUM	ACEHLNOU	EULACHON	ACEHOPRR	REPROACH	ACEIKMRS	KERAMICS
ACEHIMPR	CAMPHIRE	ACEHLNPS	PLANCHES	ACEHOPRS	POACHERS	ACEIKMRV	MAVERICK
ACEHIMPT	EMPATHIC	ACEHLNPT	PLANCHET	ACEHORRS	HORSECAR	ACEIKNRR	CRANKIER
	EMPHATIC	ACEHLNRS	CHARNELS	ACEHORRV	OVERARCH	ACEIKOPS	PAIOCKES
ACEHIMRS	CHASMIER	ACEHLNRU	LAUNCHER	ACEHORST	CHAROSET	ACEIKORR	CROAKIER
	CHIMERAS	ACEHLNST	STANCHEL		THORACES	ACEIKPRS	EARPICKS
	MARCHESI	ACEHLNSU	LAUNCHES	ACEHORTT	THEOCRAT	ACEIKPSX	PICKAXES
ACEHIMRT	RHEMATIC	ACEHLORS	CHOLERAS	ACEHORTU	OUTREACH	ACEIKRRV	VRAICKER
ACEHIMSS	CHAMISES		CHORALES	ACEHOSSW	SHOWCASE	ACEIKSTT	TACKIEST
ACEHIMST	MISTEACH	ACEHLORT	CHELATOR	ACEHOSTU	CATHOUSE		TIETACKS
	TACHISME		CHLORATE		SOUTACHE	ACEIKSTW	WACKIEST
ACEHIMTT	THEMATIC		TROCHLEA	ACEHOSTY	CHAYOTES	ACEILLLT	CLITELLA
ACEHINNS	ENCHAINS	ACEHLORU	LEACHOUR	ACEHOSUV	AVOUCHES	ACEILLMR	MICELLAR
ACEHINOT	INCHOATE	ACEHLOST	ESCHALOT	ACEHPPSS	CHAPPESS		MILLRACE
ACEHINRS	INARCHES	ACEHLPRT	CHAPTREL		SCHAPPES	ACEILLMS	LIMACELS
ACEHINRV	VACHERIN	ACEHLPRY	CHAPELRY	ACEHPRST	CHAPTERS		MICELLAS
ACEHINSS	INCHASES	ACEHLPSS	CHAPLESS		PATCHERS	ACEILLMT	METALLIC
ACEHINST	ASTHENIC	ACEHLPST	CHAPLETS	ACEHPRSU	PURCHASE	ACEILLMY	MYCELIAL
	CHANTIES	ACEHLRSS	RASCHELS			ACEILLNT	CLIENTAL

ACEILLOP	CALLIOPE	ACEILPST	PLICATES
ACEILLOR	ROCAILLE	ACEILPTY	ETYPICAL
ACEILLOS	LOCALISE	ACEILPXY	EPICALYX
ACEILLOT	TEOCALLI	ACEILRRT	CLARTIER
ACEILLOZ	LOCALIZE	ACEILRRW	CRAWLIER
ACEILLPR	CALLIPER	ACEILRSS	CLASSIER
ACEILLPS	ALLSPICE	ACEILRST	ALTRICES
ACEILLPY	EPICALLY		ARTICLES
ACEILLRV	CAVILLER		RECITALS
ACEILMMO	CAMOMILE		SELICTAR
ACEILMMR	CLAMMIER	ACEILRSU	AURICLES
ACEILMNN	CLINAMEN	ACEILRSV	CALIVERS
ACEILMNP	MANCIPLE		CLAVIERS
ACEILMNS	MESCALIN		VISCERAL
ACEILMOS	CAMISOLE	ACEILRTT	TRACTILE
ACEILMPS	MISPLACE	ACEILRTV	VERTICAL
ACEILMPT	PELMATIC	ACEILRTY	LITERACY
ACEILMRS	CLAIMERS	ACEILSST	ELASTICS
	MIRACLES		SALICETS
	RECLAIMS		SCALIEST
ACEILMRT	METRICAL	ACEILSTT	LATTICES
ACEILMST	CALMIEST	ACEILSTY	CLAYIEST
	CLEMATIS	ACEILSUV	VESICULA
	CLIMATES	ACEILTVY	ACTIVELY
	METICALS	ACEIMMNP	PEMMICAN
ACEILMSU	MUSICALE	ACEIMMOS	SEMICOMA
ACEILMSX	CLIMAXES	ACEIMMRS	RACEMISM
	EXCLAIMS	ACEIMNOR	CORAMINE
ACEILMTU	AMULETIC	ACEIMNPS	PEMICANS
ACEILNNP	PANNICLE	ACEIMNRS	CARMINES
	PINNACLE	ACEIMNRU	MANICURE
ACEILNNR	ENCRINAL	ACEIMNSS	AMNESICS
ACEILNOR	ACROLEIN	ACEIMNST	SEMANTIC
	CREOLIAN	ACEIMNSU	SEMUNCIA
	LONICERA	ACEIMNSY	SYCAMINE
ACEILNPS	CAPELINS	ACEIMOPT	POEMATIC
	PANICLES	ACEIMOTX	TOXAEMIC
	PELICANS	ACEIMOTZ	METAZOIC
ACEILNPT	ICEPLANT	ACEIMPRR	CRAMPIER
	PECTINAL		MERICARP
	PLANETIC	ACEIMPSS	ESCAPISM
ACEILNRS	CARLINES	ACEIMPST	CAMPIEST
ACEILNRT	CLARINET		CAMPSITE
ACEILNSS	SANICLES	ACEIMPTU	PUMICATE
ACEILNSU	AESCULIN	ACEIMRST	CERAMIST
	LUNACIES		MATRICES
ACEILNSY	SALIENCY	ACEIMRTT	TREMATIC
ACEILOPR	CAPRIOLE	ACEIMRTU	MURICATE
ACEILOPT	POETICAL	ACEIMSST	ETACISMS
ACEILORR	CARRIOLE	ACEIMSSU	CAESIUMS
ACEILORS	CALORIES	ACEINNOS	CANONISE
	CARIOLES	ACEINNOT	ENACTION
ACEILORT	EROTICAL	ACEINNOZ	CANONIZE
	LORICATE	ACEINNPS	PINNACES
ACEILOSS	COALISES	ACEINNRS	CRANNIES
ACEILOST	ALOETICS	ACEINNST	ANCIENTS
	COALIEST		CANNIEST
	SOCIETAL		INSTANCE
ACEILOSV	VOCALISE	ACEINNSU	NUISANCE
ACEILOSZ	COALIZES	ACEINNSY	CYANINES
ACEILOTV	LOCATIVE	ACEINNTU	UNCINATE
ACEILOVZ	VOCALIZE	ACEINOPR	APOCRINE
ACEILPPY	PIPECLAY		CAPONIER
ACEILPRS	CALIPERS		PROCAINE
	REPLICAS	ACEINOPS	CANOPIES
	SPIRACLE		CAPONISE
ACEILPRT	PARTICLE		PAEONICS
	PRELATIC	ACEINOPZ	CAPONIZE
ACEILPRU	PECULIAR	ACEINORS	SCENARIO
ACEILPSS	SPECIALS	ACEINORT	ANORETIC

	CREATION		SCARRIER
	REACTION	ACEIRRST	ERRATICS
ACEINORV	VERONICA	ACEIRRSU	CURARISE
ACEINORX	ANOREXIC	ACEIRRSW	AIRSCREW
ACEINOST	ACONITES	ACEIRRTT	RETRAICT
	CANOEIST	ACEIRRTX	CREATRIX
ACEINOTT	TACONITE	ACEIRRTY	RETIRACY
ACEINOTV	CONATIVE	ACEIRRUZ	CURARIZE
	INVOCATE	ACEIRSST	SCARIEST
ACEINOTX	EXACTION	ACEIRSSU	SCAURIES
ACEINPSS	INSCAPES		URICASES
	PINCASES	ACEIRSSV	VICARESS
ACEINPTT	PITTANCE	ACEIRSTT	CITRATES
ACEINPUY	PICAYUNE		CRISTATE
ACEINRRU	CURARINE		SCATTIER
ACEINRRY	CINERARY	ACEIRSTU	SURICATE
ACEINRSS	ARSENICS	ACEIRSTZ	CRAZIEST
	CERASINS	ACEIRTTU	URTICATE
	RACINESS	ACEIRTTV	TRACTIVE
ACEINRST	CANISTER	ACEIRTUV	CURATIVE
	CARNIEST	ACEIRTVY	VERACITY
	NACRITES	ACEISSSS	CASSISES
	SCANTIER	ACEISSST	ECSTASIS
ACEINRTT	INTERACT	ACEISSSU	SAUCISSE
ACEINRTV	NAVICERT	ACEISSTU	SAUCIEST
ACEINRTX	XERANTIC	ACEISTTT	CATTIEST
ACEINRVY	VICENARY	ACEISTTU	EUSTATIC
ACEINSSV	CINEASTS	ACEISTUX	AUXETICS
	SCANTIES	ACEJKOOR	JACKEROO
ACEINSSU	ISSUANCE	ACEJKOPS	PAJOCKES
ACEINSSY	CYANISES	ACEJLORS	CAJOLERS
ACEINSTT	CANTIEST	ACEJLORY	CAJOLERY
	NICTATES	ACEJMRST	SCRAMJET
ACEINSTV	CISTVAEN	ACEJNNOO	JONCANOE
	VESICANT	ACEJNOST	JACONETS
ACEINSTY	CYANITES	ACEJNOSY	JOYANCES
ACEINSYZ	CYANIZES	ACEJNRRY	JERRYCAN
ACEINTTU	TUNICATE	ACEJNSTU	JUNCATES
ACEINTTX	EXCITANT	ACEJPSTU	CAJEPUTS
ACEINTTY	TENACITY	ACEJRSTT	TRAJECTS
ACEINTUV	UNACTIVE	ACEKKNRS	KNACKERS
ACEIOPRT	OPERATIC	ACEKKNRY	KNACKERY
ACEIOPST	ECTOPIAS	ACEKLLPS	PELLACKS
ACEIORSV	COVARIES	ACEKLNRS	CRANKLES
	VARICOSE	ACEKLNSS	SLACKENS
ACEIOSST	SOCIATES	ACEKLNTU	UNTACKLE
ACEIOSSU	CAESIOUS	ACEKLORS	EARLOCKS
ACEIOSTT	OSCITATE	ACEKLORV	LAVEROCK
ACEIOTVV	VOCATIVE	ACEKLPRS	SPRACKLE
ACEIPPRR	PERICARP	ACEKLPST	PLACKETS
ACEIPPRS	EPICARPS	ACEKLQSU	QUACKLES
ACEIPPST	TAPPICES	ACEKLRSS	SLACKERS
ACEIPPRS	PERISARC	ACEKLRST	TACKLERS
ACEIPRSS	SCRAPIES	ACEKLRSU	CAULKERS
ACEIPRST	CRAPIEST	ACEKLSSS	SACKLESS
	CRISPATE	ACEKLSST	SLACKEST
	PICRATES	ACEKMNRT	TRACKMEN
	PRACTISE	ACEKMNST	TACKSMEN
ACEIPRTV	PRACTIVE	ACEKMRSS	SMACKERS
ACEIPRTY	APYRETIC	ACEKNNOW	ACKNOWNE
ACEIPSST	ASEPTICS	ACEKNPRS	PRANCKES
	ESCAPIST	ACEKNPRU	UNPACKER
	SPACIEST	ACEKNRST	CRANKEST
ACEIPSSU	AUSPICES	ACEKOORT	CARETOOK
ACEIPSSZ	CAPSIZES	ACEKOORW	COOKWARE
ACEIPSTV	CAPTIVES	ACEKORRS	CROAKERS
ACEIQRSU	ACQUIRES	ACEKORRV	OVERRACK
ACEIQSTU	ACQUITES	ACEKPPRS	PREPACKS
ACEIQSUZ	CAZIQUES	ACEKPSSY	SKYSCAPE
ACEIRRRS	CARRIERS	ACEKQRUY	QUACKERY

ACEKRRST	TRACKERS	ACELOPSS	ESCALOPS	ACENNOSS	CANONESS	ACEORSST	COARSEST
ACEKRRTY	RACKETRY	ACELOPST	POLECATS		SONANCES		COASTERS
ACEKRSST	STACKERS	ACELOPTU	COPULATE	ACENNOSU	SONUANCE	ACEORSSU	CAROUSES
ACEKRSTT	RACKETTS	ACELOPTY	CALOTYPE	ACENNOSY	NOYANCES	ACEORSTT	SECTATOR
ACEKSSTT	STACKETS	ACELOQSU	COEQUALS	ACENNOTV	COVENANT	ACEORSTU	OUTRACES
ACEKSSUW	WAESUCKS	ACELORRT	RECTORAL	ACENNOTZ	CANZONET	ACEORSTV	OVERACTS
ACELLLRU	CELLULAR	ACELORSS	ESCOLARS	ACENNPRY	PERNANCY		OVERCAST
ACELLMOS	CALOMELS		LACROSSE	ACENNRSS	SCANNERS	ACEORSTX	EXACTORS
ACELLMSU	SACELLUM	ACELORST	SECTORAL	ACENNSUY	SEACUNNY	ACEORTUY	EUCARYOT
ACELLNRU	NUCELLAR	ACELORSU	CAROUSEL	ACENOORT	CORONATE	ACEOSTTU	OUTCASTE
ACELLOPS	COLLAPSE	ACELORSY	CALOYERS	ACENOOTZ	ECTOZOAN	ACEOSTUU	AUTOCUES
	ESCALLOP		COARSELY	ACENOPRT	PORTANCE	ACEPRRSS	SCARPERS
ACELLORR	CAROLLER	ACELORTU	COLATURE	ACENOPST	CAPSTONE		SCRAPERS
ACELLORS	CORELLAS	ACELOSST	ALECOSTS	ACENOPSU	PONCEAUS	ACEPRSSU	CARPUSES
ACELLORV	COVERALL		COATLESS	ACENOPUX	PONCEAUX		SCAUPERS
	OVERCALL		LACTOSES	ACENOQTU	COTQUEAN	ACEPRSTU	CAPTURES
ACELLORW	CALLOWER		SCATOLES	ACENORRW	CAREWORN		PRESCUTA
ACELLOST	COLLATES	ACELOSTT	CALOTTES	ACENORSS	COARSENS	ACEPSTTY	TYPECAST
ACELLOTU	LOCULATE	ACELOSTU	LACTEOUS		NARCOSES	ACEQRSTU	RACQUETS
ACELLPSS	SCALPELS		LOCUSTAE	ACENORST	ANCESTOR	ACEQSSTU	ACQUESTS
ACELLRRS	CARRELLS		OSCULATE		ENACTORS	ACERRSTT	RETRACTS
ACELLRTY	RECTALLY	ACELOSTY	ACOLYTES		SARCONET	ACERRSUV	VERRUCAS
ACELLSSU	CALLUSES	ACELOSUV	VACUOLES		SORTANCE	ACERSSST	CRASSEST
ACELLSSW	CLAWLESS	ACELPPRS	CLAPPERS	ACENORSU	CARNEOUS	ACERSSSU	SUCRASES
ACELLSTU	SCUTELLA		SCRAPPLE		NACREOUS	ACERSSTT	SCATTERS
ACELLTWY	CETYWALL	ACELPPSS	SCAPPLES	ACENORTT	CONTRATE	ACERSTTT	TETRACTS
ACELMMOU	MAMELUCO	ACELPRSS	CLASPERS	ACENORTU	COURANTE	ACERSTTU	CRUSTATE
ACELMNNS	CLANSMEN		SCALPERS		OUTRANCE	ACERSTTX	EXTRACTS
ACELMNOR	AMELCORN	ACELPRST	SCEPTRAL	ACENORUY	EUCARYON	ACERSTTY	SCATTERY
ACELMNRU	CRUMENAL		SPECTRAL	ACENOSSS	CASSONES	ACERSTUX	CURTAXES
ACELMNSS	CALMNESS	ACELPRSU	SPECULAR	ACENOSST	COSTEANS	ACFFGHIN	CHAFFING
	CLASSMEN	ACELPSSU	CAPSULES	ACENOSSV	CAVESSON	ACFFHNOR	CHAFFRON
ACELMOPT	COMPLEAT	ACELPTUU	CUPULATE	ACENOSSY	CYANOSES	ACFFIILO	OFFICIAL
ACELMORS	CAROMELS	ACELPTUY	EUCALYPT	ACENOSTT	CONSTATE	ACFFIIST	CAITIFFS
	SCLEROMA	ACELQRSU	LACQUERS	ACENOSTV	CENTAVOS	ACFFIKMS	MAFFICKS
ACELMORY	CLAYMORE	ACELQRUU	CLAQUEUR	ACENOTTU	TOUCANET	ACFFILNU	FANCIFUL
ACELMOST	CAMELOTS	ACELQSUY	LACQUEYS	ACENPRRS	PRANCERS	ACFFILST	AFFLICTS
	MOLECAST	ACELRRSW	CRAWLERS	ACENPRSU	ENCARPUS	ACFFIRST	TRAFFICS
ACELMOSU	CAULOMES		SCRAWLER		PRAUNCES	ACFFLOSW	SCOFFLAW
	LEUCOMAS	ACELRSSS	SCARLESS	ACENPSTT	PENTACTS	ACFGHINU	CHAUFING
	MACULOSE	ACELRSST	SCARLETS	ACENPTTU	PUNCTATE	ACFGIIMN	MAGNIFIC
ACELMPRS	CLAMPERS	ACELRSSU	SECULARS	ACENRSST	CRANTSES	ACFGIIPR	CAPRIFIG
ACELMPSY	ECLAMPSY	ACELRSTT	CLATTERS	ACENRSSU	SURANCES	ACFGINNY	FANCYING
ACELMSSU	LACMUSES		SCRATTLE	ACENRSTT	TRANECTS	ACFGINRS	FARCINGS
ACELMSTU	CALUMETS	ACELRSTU	RAUCLEST		TRANSECT		SCARFING
	MUSCATEL	ACELRTTU	CULTRATE	ACENRSTU	CENTAURS	ACFGINRT	CRAFTING
ACELMSSU	SAECULUM	ACELSSTT	TACTLESS		RECUSANT		FRACTING
ACELMTUU	CUMULATE	ACELSSTY	SCYTALES		UNCRATES	ACFGITUY	FUGACITY
ACELNNRS	SCRANNEL	ACELSSUX	EXCUSALS		UNTRACES	ACFGKNOP	PACKFONG
ACELNORV	NOVERCAL	ACEMMOTY	MYCETOMA	ACENRSTY	ANCESTRY	ACFHHINW	HAWFINCH
ACELNOST	LACTONES	ACEMMRRS	CRAMMERS	ACENRTTU	TRUNCATE	ACFHILNO	FALCHION
ACELNOSU	LACUNOSE	ACEMNORR	ROMANCER	ACENRTUY	CENTAURY	ACFHILNU	FAULCHIN
ACELNOSZ	CALZONES	ACEMNORS	CREMONAS		CYANURET	ACFHILOS	COALFISH
ACELNOTV	COVALENT		ROMANCES	ACENSSTT	SCANTEST	ACFHINOU	FAUCHION
ACELNOVY	CONVEYAL	ACEMNOST	CAMSTONE	ACENSSTU	NUTCASES	ACFHIRSS	SCARFISH
ACELNPSS	ENCLASPS	ACEMNRUY	NUMERACY	ACENSSTW	NEWSCAST	ACFHIRSW	CRAWFISH
	SPANCELS	ACEMNSSU	MANCUSES	ACEOOPPS	APOCOPES	ACFHIRSY	CRAYFISH
ACELNPST	CLAPNETS	ACEMOOST	COMATOSE	ACEOOPSU	POACEOUS	ACFHISSU	FUCHSIAS
ACELNPSU	UNPLACES	ACEMOPRS	COMPARES	ACEOORTV	OVERCOAT	ACFHLMRU	CHARMFUL
ACELNRSU	LUCARNES		COMPEARS	ACEOPPRS	COPPERAS	ACFHLTUW	WATCHFUL
ACELNRUY	NUCLEARY		MESOCARP	ACEOPRRT	RECAPTOR	ACFHMNOR	CHAMFRON
ACELNRVY	CRAVENLY	ACEMORRT	CREMATOR	ACEOPRSX	EXOCARPS	ACFHNOSU	FAUCHONS
ACELNSST	SCANTLES	ACEMORSY	SYCAMORE	ACEOPRTT	ATTERCOP	ACFIILST	FISTICAL
ACELNSSU	UNSCALES	ACEMORTY	COMETARY	ACEOPSTU	OUTPACES	ACFIILSV	SALVIFIC
ACELNSTT	CANTLETS	ACEMORUX	MORCEAUX	ACEORRST	ACROTERS	ACFIILTY	FACILITY
ACELOPPU	POPULACE	ACEMPRSS	SCAMPERS		CREATORS	ACFIIMPS	PACIFISM
ACELOPRS	PARCLOSE	ACEMPRST	CRAMPETS		REACTORS	ACFIIMSS	FASCISMI
	POLACRES	ACEMPSSU	CAMPUSES	ACEORRSU	CAROUSER	ACFIIPST	PACIFIST
ACELOPRT	PECTORAL	ACEMSSTT	METCASTS	ACEORRTT	RETROACT	ACFIISST	FASCISTI
ACELOPRU	OPERCULA	ACENNNOU	ANNOUNCE	ACEORRVW	OVERCRAW	ACFIKLNS	CALFSKIN

ACFIKNNS	FINNACKS	ACGHINPR	PARCHING	ACGILNOT	LOCATING	ACGLOSUU	GLAUCOUS
ACFILNOR	FORNICAL	ACGHINPT	NIGHTCAP	ACGILNPP	CLAPPING	ACGNNOOT	CONTANGO
ACFILNOS	FOLACINS		PATCHING	ACGILNPS	CLASPING	ACGNNORS	CRANNOGS
ACFILORT	TRIFOCAL	ACGHINRR	CHARRING		PLACINGS	ACGNOOST	OCTAGONS
ACFILRTY	CRAFTILY	ACGHINRS	CHAGRINS		SCALPING	ACGORRSY	GYROCARS
ACFILSSY	CLASSIFY		CRASHING	ACGILNQU	CALQUING	ACGORSSW	COWGRASS
ACFIMNRU	FRANCIUM	ACGHINRT	CHARTING	ACGILNRT	CLARTING	ACGORSUU	COUGUARS
ACFIMOSS	FASCISMO	ACGHINRU	CHURINGA	ACGILNRW	CRAWLING	ACGPPSUU	SCUPPAUG
ACFIMSSS	FASCISMS		NURAGHIC	ACGILNSS	CLASSING	ACHHILPT	PHTHALIC
ACFINORT	FRACTION	ACGHINSS	CHASINGS		SCALINGS	ACHHINTW	WHINCHAT
ACFINOST	FACTIONS	ACGHINST	SCATHING	ACGILNST	CASTLING	ACHHINTY	HYACINTH
ACFINRST	INFARCTS	ACGHINSW	CHINWAGS		CATLINGS	ACHHIPPR	HIPPARCH
	INFRACTS	ACGHINTT	CHATTING		SCLATING	ACHHLMOS	MASHLOCH
ACFINSTY	SANCTIFY	ACGHINTW	WATCHING	ACGILNSU	GLUCINAS	ACHHLNOR	RHONCHAL
ACFIOSTU	FACTIOUS	ACGHINTY	YACHTING	ACGILNTT	CLATTING	ACHHLPRY	PHYLARCH
ACFIRTUY	FURACITY	ACGHIPRS	GRAPHICS	ACGILNTU	CLAUTING	ACHHLSUY	SHAUCHLY
ACFISSST	FASCISTS	ACGHIQTU	ACQUIGHT	ACGILRSU	SURGICAL	ACHHNTTU	NUTHATCH
ACFKLORS	FORSLACK	ACGHIRSS	SCRAIGHS	ACGIMMNR	CRAMMING		UNTHATCH
ACFKLOST	LOCKFAST	ACGHLLOR	GRALLOCH	ACGIMNOR	CAROMING	ACHHOSST	TOSHACHS
ACFKLRUW	WRACKFUL	ACGHLSTU	CLAUGHTS	ACGIMNOS	COAMINGS	ACHHPTUZ	CHUTZPAH
ACFKLSSU	SACKFULS	ACGHNTUU	UNCAUGHT	ACGIMNPR	CRAMPING	ACHIIKMS	KAMICHIS
ACFKOSTT	FATSTOCK	ACGHORSU	CHORAGUS	ACGIMNPS	SCAMPING	ACHIILMS	CHILIASM
ACFLMNOO	MOONCALF	ACGHPTUU	UPCAUGHT	ACGIMNSY	GYMNASIC	ACHIILST	CHILIAST
ACFLNORY	FALCONRY	ACGHRRSU	CURRAGHS		SYNGAMIC	ACHIINRT	TRICHINA
ACFLOOPS	FOOLSCAP	ACGHRSSU	SCRAUGHS	ACGIMORS	ORGASMIC	ACHIIPSS	PACHISIS
ACFLORSU	SCROFULA	ACGIILMN	CLAIMING	ACGINNNS	SCANNING	ACHIIRST	RACHITIS
ACFLRRUU	FURCULAR		MALICING	ACGINNNU	NUANCING	ACHIIRSU	ISCHURIA
ACFLRSUU	FURCULAS	ACGIILLN	INLACING	ACGINNPR	PRANCING	ACHIJKPW	WHIPJACK
ACFMOTTU	FACTOTUM	ACGIILNO	LOGICIAN	ACGINNPU	UNCAPING	ACHIJNST	JACINTHS
ACGGGILN	CLAGGING	ACGIILNS	SCAILING	ACGINNRT	TRANCING	ACHIKKNS	KNACKISH
ACGGHINN	CHANGING	ACGIIMNT	MICATING	ACGINNRU	UNCARING	ACHIKKSW	KICKSHAW
	GANCHING	ACGIIMOS	ISOGAMIC	ACGINNRY	CARNYING	ACHIKLLW	HICKWALL
ACGGHINR	CHARGING	ACGIIMST	SIGMATIC	ACGINNST	CANTINGS	ACHIKLPT	CHALKPIT
ACGGIINN	INCAGING	ACGIINNS	INCASING		SCANTING	ACHIKNOP	PACHINKO
ACGGIINT	GIGANTIC	ACGIINNV	INCAVING	ACGINNSU	UNCASING	ACHIKRSS	RICKSHAS
ACGGIIOS	ISAGOGIC	ACGIINRT	GRANITIC	ACGINNUV	VAUNCING	ACHIKRSW	RICKSHAW
ACGGILNN	CANGLING	ACGIIPRS	SPAGIRIC	ACGINOPT	COAPTING	ACHIKRSY	HAYRICKS
	CLANGING	ACGIJJKO	JICKAJOG	ACGINORY	CONGIARY	ACHIKSSS	SHICKSAS
	GLANCING	ACGIJLNO	CAJOLING	ACGINOST	AGNOSTIC	ACHILLOR	ORCHILLA
ACGGINNO	CONGAING	ACGIJNNU	JAUNCING		COASTING	ACHILLRT	CLITHRAL
ACGGINNU	UNCAGING	ACGIKLMN	MACKLING		COATINGS	ACHILMOP	OMPHALIC
ACGGINOR	CARGOING	ACGIKLNN	CLANKING		COTINGAS	ACHILMOS	MALICHOS
ACGGIOOR	CORAGGIO	ACGIKLNO	CLOAKING	ACGINPPR	CRAPPING	ACHILMRS	CHRISMAL
ACGGLNOU	GLUCAGON	ACGIKLNS	SLACKING	ACGINPPS	CAPPINGS	ACHILMTY	MYTHICAL
ACGGLRSY	SCRAGGLY	ACGIKLNT	TACKLING	ACGINPRS	CARPINGS	ACHILNNS	CLANNISH
ACGHHIJK	HIGHJACK	ACGIKLNU	CAULKING		SCARPING	ACHILNOO	HOOLICAN
ACGHHINN	HANCHING	ACGIKLRY	GARLICKY		SCRAPING	ACHILNOS	LICHANOS
ACGHHINT	HATCHING	ACGIKMNS	SMACKING	ACGINPSS	SPACINGS	ACHILNPS	CLANSHIP
ACGHIINN	CHAINING	ACGIKNNR	CRANKING	ACGINRRS	SCARRING	ACHILOPR	RHOPALIC
ACGHIINR	CHAIRING	ACGIKNNS	SNACKING	ACGINRRY	CARRYING	ACHILOPS	SOPHICAL
ACGHIKLN	CHALKING	ACGIKNOR	CROAKING	ACGINRSS	SACRINGS	ACHILORT	ACROLITH
	HACKLING	ACGIKNPS	PACKINGS	ACGINRST	SCARTING	ACHILPSY	PHYSICAL
ACGHIKNR	CHARKING	ACGIKNQU	QUACKING		TRACINGS	ACHILPTY	PATCHILY
ACGHIKNS	HACKINGS	ACGIKNRS	ARCKINGS	ACGINRSU	SCAURING	ACHILRUY	CHYLURIA
ACGHIKNW	WHACKING		RACKINGS	ACGINRSV	CARVINGS	ACHILRVY	CHIVALRY
ACGHILNN	LANCHING	ACGIKNRT	TRACKING		CRAVINGS	ACHILSWY	LICHWAYS
ACGHILNS	CLASHING	ACGIKNRW	WRACKING	ACGINRTT	TRACTING	ACHIMMOS	MACHISMO
ACGHILNT	LATCHING	ACGIKNSS	SACKINGS	ACGINSST	CASTINGS	ACHIMMST	MISMATCH
ACGHILNU	LAUCHING	ACGIKNST	STACKING	ACGINSTT	SCATTING	ACHIMNNW	WINCHMAN
ACGHILOR	OLIGARCH		TACKINGS	ACGIOORS	GRACIOSO	ACHIMNOP	CHAMPION
ACGHIMNP	CHAMPING	ACGIKPRS	GRIPSACK	ACGIORST	ORGASTIC	ACHIMNOR	CHOIRMAN
ACGHIMNR	CHARMING	ACGILLNS	CALLINGS	ACGIORSU	GRACIOUS		HARMONIC
	MARCHING	ACGILMMN	CLAMMING	ACGIPRSY	SPAGYRIC	ACHIMNOS	MANIHOCS
ACGHIMNT	MATCHING	ACGILMNP	CAMPLING	ACGJLNOU	CONJUGAL	ACHIMNPT	PITCHMAN
ACGHINNR	RANCHING		CLAMPING	ACGKMMOS	GAMMOCKS	ACHIMOPR	AMPHORIC
ACGHINNT	CHANTING	ACGILNNT	CANTLING	ACGKORSV	GARVOCKS	ACHIMOSS	CHAMISOS
ACGHINNU	UNACHING	ACGILNNU	LAUNCING	ACGLLPSU	CUPGALLS		ISOCHASM
ACGHINOP	POACHING		UNLACING	ACGLMOUU	COAGULUM	ACHIMPSS	SCAMPISH
ACGHINOR	ROACHING	ACGILNOR	ORACLING	ACGLNORS	CLANGORS	ACHIMRSS	CHARISMS
ACGHINPP	CHAPPING	ACGILNOS	SOLACING	ACGLNORU	CLANGOUR	ACHIMRST	CHARTISM

ACHIMSSS	SCHISMAS	ACHNRSYY	SYNARCHY	ACIKLORY	CROAKILY	ACIMNORS	MARCONIS
ACHIMSST	MASTICHS	ACHNRTUY	CHAUNTRY	ACIKMOOS	OOMIACKS	ACIMNORT	ROMANTIC
	TACHISMS	ACHOPRST	TOPARCHS	ACIKMPRS	RAMPICKS	ACIMNORU	CONARIUM
ACHIMSSU	CHIASMUS	ACHOPRSY	CHARPOYS	ACIKMPST	MAPSTICK		COUMARIN
ACHIMTUY	CYATHIUM	ACHOPRTY	TOPARCHY	ACIKMPSW	PICKMAWS	ACIMNORY	ACRIMONY
ACHINNOP	PANCHION	ACHOTTUW	OUTWATCH	ACIKNNPS	PANNICKS	ACIMNOSS	MOCASSIN
ACHINNSU	UNCHAINS	ACHRSTTU	STRAUCHT	ACIKNSST	CATSKINS	ACIMNOST	MONASTIC
ACHINOPR	PAROCHIN	ACIIILMN	INIMICAL	ACIKPRST	PATRICKS	ACIMNOTU	ACONITUM
ACHINORT	ANORTHIC	ACIIILNV	CIVILIAN	ACILLLOP	POLLICAL	ACIMNPTY	TYMPANIC
ACHINOSY	ONYCHIAS	ACIIKNNN	CANNIKIN	ACILLMMY	CLAMMILY	ACIMNRSU	CRANIUMS
ACHINOTZ	HOACTZIN	ACIIKNNS	CANIKINS	ACILLMOS	LOCALISM		CUMARINS
ACHINRSZ	ZARNICHS	ACIIKPRT	PAITRICK	ACILLMSS	MISCALLS	ACIMNSTT	CATMINTS
ACHINSUV	CHAUVINS	ACIILLSU	SILICULA	ACILLNOO	COLONIAL	ACIMORST	ACROTISM
ACHIORSS	COARSISH	ACIILLTV	VILLATIC	ACILLNOR	CARILLON	ACIMORSY	CRAMOISY
ACHIORST	CHARIOTS	ACIILMNR	CRIMINAL	ACILLNOS	SCALLION	ACIMOSST	ACOSMIST
	HARICOTS	ACIILNOR	IRONICAL	ACILLOQU	COQUILLA		MASSICOT
ACHIPPSS	SAPPHICS	ACIILNOT	TALIONIC	ACILLORT	CLITORAL	ACIMOSTT	MASTICOT
ACHIPRRT	PARRITCH	ACIILNPT	PLATINIC	ACILLORY	COLLYRIA		STOMATIC
ACHIPSTU	CHUPATIS	ACIILNSS	SALICINS	ACILLOST	LOCALIST	ACIMPRST	CRAMPITS
ACHIPSTW	WHIPCATS	ACIILOSV	VILIACOS	ACILLOSY	SOCIALLY		PTARMICS
ACHIPTTU	CHUPATTI	ACIILRTT	TRITICAL	ACILLOTY	LOCALITY	ACIMRRSY	MISCARRY
ACHIQRSU	CHARQUIS	ACIILRTU	URALITIC	ACILMNOP	COMPLAIN	ACIMRSSZ	CZARISMS
ACHIRRST	TRIARCHS	ACIILSST	SILASTIC	ACILMNOS	LACONISM	ACIMSSST	MISCASTS
ACHIRRTY	TRIARCHY	ACIILSTV	SILVATIC		LIMACONS	ACIMSSTT	TACTISMS
ACHIRSTT	CHARTIST	ACIIMNOR	MORAINIC	ACILMOOS	SCOLIOMA	ACINNOOT	CONATION
	STRAICHT	ACIIMNOS	SIMONIAC	ACILMOPR	PROCLAIM	ACINNORR	NARICORN
ACHIRSTU	HAIRCUTS	ACIIMNOT	AMNIOTIC	ACILMOPT	COMPITAL	ACINNOSS	SCANSION
ACHISSTT	TACHISTS	ACIIMNRS	MINICARS	ACILMOSV	VOCALISM	ACINNOST	ACTINONS
ACHISTTY	CHASTITY	ACIIMNST	ACTINISM	ACILMPTU	PLACITUM		CANONIST
ACHKMMOS	HAMMOCKS	ACIIMNSU	MUSICIAN	ACILMSSU	MUSICALS		CANTIONS
ACHKMORS	SHAMROCK	ACIIMNTU	ACTINIUM	ACILMSTY	MYSTICAL		CONTAINS
ACHKNOOT	CANTHOOK	ACIIMNTY	IMITANCY	ACILMTUY	ULTIMACY		SANCTION
ACHKOPSS	HOPSACKS		INTIMACY	ACILNOOT	COLATION	ACINNOTU	CONTINUA
ACHKOSSS	HASSOCKS		MINACITY		LOCATION	ACINNRTY	TYRANNIC
ACHKOSSY	HASSOCKY	ACIIMOST	IOTACISM	ACILNOOV	VOCALION	ACINNSTU	ANNICUTS
ACHKOSTT	HATTOCKS	ACIIMOTT	AMITOTIC	ACILNOPS	SALPICON	ACINNSTY	INSTANCY
ACHLLOOS	ALCOHOLS	ACIIMPRT	PRIMATIC	ACILNOPT	PLATONIC	ACINOOPR	PICAROON
ACHLLORS	CHLORALS	ACIIMPRV	VAMPIRIC	ACILNORS	CLARINOS	ACINOOTV	VOCATION
ACHLLORY	CHORALLY	ACIIMRST	SCIMITAR		CLARIONS	ACINOPPT	PANOPTIC
ACHLMSTZ	SCHMALTZ	ACIIMRTU	MURIATIC	ACILNORT	CONTRAIL	ACINOPRS	PARSONIC
ACHLNOOU	OULACHON	ACIIMSST	ITACISMS	ACILNOSU	UNSOCIAL	ACINOPST	CAPTIONS
ACHLNOSY	HALCYONS	ACIIMTUV	VIATICUM	ACILNOUV	UNIVOCAL		PACTIONS
ACHLNSTU	TULCHANS	ACIINNOT	INACTION	ACILNPSS	INCLASPS	ACINORRS	CARRIONS
ACHLNSTY	STANCHLY		NICOTIAN	ACILNRSU	CISLUNAR	ACINORRT	CONTRAIR
ACHLOPRS	RAPLOCHS	ACIINNQU	CINQUAIN	ACILNRUY	CULINARY	ACINORSS	NARCOSIS
ACHLOPRT	CALTHROP	ACIINNTT	INCITANT	ACILNSTU	LUNATICS	ACINORST	CANTORIS
ACHLOPRY	POLYARCH	ACIINNTY	CANINITY		SULTANIC		CAROTINS
ACHLOPTT	POTLATCH	ACIINOPT	OPTICIAN	ACILNSTY	SCANTILY	ACINORTT	TRACTION
ACHLORSS	SCHOLARS	ACIINORZ	ZIRCONIA	ACILOPRT	TROPICAL	ACINOSSS	CAISSONS
ACHLOSSW	SALCHOWS	ACIINOSS	ASINICOS	ACILORRS	RACLOIRS		CASSINOS
ACHLOSTY	ACOLYTHS	ACIINOSV	AVIONICS	ACILORRV	CORRIVAL	ACINOSSY	CYANOSIS
ACHMNORS	MONARCHS	ACIINOTT	CITATION	ACILORST	CALORIST	ACINOSTT	OSCITANT
	NOMARCHS	ACIINPSS	PISCINAS	ACILORTV	VORTICAL		TACTIONS
ACHMNORY	MONARCHY	ACIINRSS	NARCISSI	ACILOSTV	VOCALIST	ACINOSTU	ANTICOUS
	NOMARCHY	ACIINRTU	URANITIC	ACILOTVY	VOCALITY		AUCTIONS
ACHMNRSU	UNCHARMS	ACIIORST	AORISTIC	ACILPRSU	SPICULAR		CAUTIONS
ACHMNRTU	TRUCHMAN	ACIIORTV	VICTORIA	ACILPRTU	PICTURAL	ACINOSTW	WAINSCOT
ACHMOPRS	CAMPHORS	ACIIPPST	PAPISTIC	ACILPSST	PLASTICS	ACINOSWX	COXSWAIN
ACHMORTU	OUTMARCH	ACIIRSTT	ARTISTIC	ACILPSSU	SPICULAS	ACINOTTX	TOXICANT
ACHMOSST	STOMACHS		TRIATICS	ACILRSTU	CURTAILS	ACINPQUY	PIQUANCY
ACHMOSTY	STOMACHY	ACIISTTU	AUTISTIC		RUSTICAL	ACINPRST	CANTRIPS
ACHMOTTU	OUTMATCH	ACIISTTV	ACTIVIST	ACILRTUV	CULTIVAR	ACINPRSY	CYPRIANS
ACHMSSUW	CUMSHAWS	ACIITTVY	ACTIVITY		CURVIRAL	ACINPSTY	SYNAPTIC
ACHNNORU	UNANCHOR	ACIITVVY	VIVACITY	ACILSTUV	VICTUALS	ACINQSTU	QUANTICS
ACHNNOSS	CHANSONS	ACIJKKPS	SKIPJACK	ACILSTVY	SYLVATIC	ACINRSSU	CRUSIANS
ACHNORST	CHANTORS	ACIJKSTW	STICKJAW	ACIMMOSS	ACOSMISM	ACINRSTU	CURTAINS
ACHNOSTY	TACHYONS	ACIJSUZZ	JACUZZIS	ACIMMTUY	CYMATIUM		SATURNIC
ACHNOSUY	CHANOYUS	ACIKLMST	MALSTICK	ACIMNNNO	CINNAMON		TURACINS
ACHNPPSS	SCHNAPPS	ACIKLNRY	CRANKILY	ACIMNOOR	ACROMION	ACINRTTU	TACITURN
ACHNRSTU	UNSTARCH			ACIMNOPS	CAMPIONS		URTICANT

ACINSTTY	SANCTITY
	SCANTITY
ACINSTYY	SYNCYTIA
ACIOOPST	SCOTOPIA
ACIOOTYZ	ZOOCYTIA
ACIOPRST	APRICOTS
	PISCATOR
ACIOPRTT	PROTATIC
ACIOPRTY	POTICARY
ACIOPSST	POTASSIC
ACIOPSSU	SPACIOUS
ACIOPSTU	CAPTIOUS
ACIOPTTU	AUTOPTIC
ACIORRSS	CORSAIRS
ACIORSSU	SCARIOUS
ACIORSTT	RICOTTAS
ACIORTTY	ATROCITY
	CITATORY
ACIORTVY	VORACITY
ACIOSTUU	CAUTIOUS
ACIPRRUU	PIRARUCU
ACIPSSST	SPASTICS
ACIQRSTU	QUARTICS
ACIQSSTU	ACQUISTS
ACIRRTTX	TRACTRIX
ACIRRTUX	CURATRIX
ACIRSSST	SACRISTS
ACIRSSTT	ASTRICTS
ACIRSSTW	TWISCARS
ACIRSSTY	SACRISTY
ACIRSSZT	CZARISTS
ACISSSTU	CASUISTS
ACISSTTU	CATSUITS
ACISSTUV	VACUISTS
ACISTTUY	ASTUCITY
ACJKKSSY	SKYJACKS
ACJKNNOS	JANNOCKS
ACJKOPST	JACKPOTS
ACJMNSTU	MUNTJACS
ACJPSTUU	CAJUPUTS
ACKKMOPR	POCKMARK
ACKKORRW	RACKWORK
ACKLLOPS	POLLACKS
ACKLLOSY	LAYLOCKS
ACKLLPSU	SKULLCAP
ACKLMNOS	LOCKSMAN
ACKLMORS	ARMLOCKS
	LOCKRAMS
ACKLNOSU	UNCLOAKS
ACKLOOSW	WOOLSACK
ACKLORSW	WARLOCKS
ACKLORSY	ROCKLAYS
ACKLOSSS	LASSOCKS
ACKMMMOS	MAMMOCKS
ACKMNOST	STOCKMAN
ACKMNRTU	TRUCKMAN
ACKMOSTT	MATTOCKS
ACKNSSTU	UNSTACKS
ACKOPRRS	PARROCKS
ACKORRST	TARROCKS
ACLLMNOU	COLUMNAL
ACLLMORU	CORALLUM
ACLLOORS	COROLLAS
ACLLOORT	COLLATOR
ACLLOOSS	COLOSSAL
ACLLOPSS	SCALLOPS
ACLLORUY	OCULARLY
ACLLRTUU	CULTURAL
ACLMMNOU	COMMUNAL
ACLMNOOO	COOLAMON
ACLMNORU	COLUMNAR
ACLMNORY	NORMALCY
ACLMORSU	CLAMOURS
ACLMORTU	CROTALUM
ACLMPRSU	SCALPRUM
ACLMRSUU	MUSCULAR
ACLMSUUV	VASCULUM
ACLNOORS	CORONALS
ACLNOORT	COLORANT
ACLNOOST	COOLANTS
ACLNOPSY	SYNCOPAL
ACLNORSU	CONSULAR
	COURLANS
ACLNOSTU	CONSULTA
	OSCULANT
ACLNPSSU	UNCLASPS
ACLNPTUU	PUNCTUAL
ACLNSSUY	UNCLASSY
ACLOOPRR	CORPORAL
ACLOPRST	CALTROPS
ACLOPRXY	XYLOCARP
ACLOPSSU	SCOPULAS
ACLOPSSY	CALYPSOS
ACLOPSUU	OPUSCULA
ACLORRTU	TORCULAR
ACLOSSTU	OUTCLASS
ACLRSSTY	CRYSTALS
ACMMNOSY	SCAMMONY
ACMMNOYY	MYOMANCY
ACMNOOPR	MONOCARP
ACMNOORR	CROMORNA
ACMNOORT	MONOCRAT
ACMNOOYZ	ZOOMANCY
ACMNOPRS	CRAMPONS
ACMNORSY	ACRONYMS
ACMNSSTU	SANCTUMS
ACMOOSST	SCOTOMAS
ACMOPRST	COMPARTS
ACMORSTY	COSTMARY
ACMQSTUU	CUMQUATS
ACNNNORY	CANNONRY
ACNNOSTT	CONSTANT
ACNOOORT	OCTAROON
ACNOORRY	CORONARY
ACNOORST	CARTOONS
	CORANTOS
	OSTRACON
ACNOORSU	CANOROUS
ACNOORTY	OCTONARY
ACNORRSU	RANCOURS
ACNORRTY	CONTRARY
ACNORSTT	CONTRAST
ACNORSTU	COURANTS
ACNORTTU	TURNCOAT
ACNORTUY	NOCTUARY
ACNPRSSY	SYNCARPS
ACNPRSUY	SPRAUNCY
ACNPRSYY	SYNCARPY
ACNRRSTU	CURRANTS
ACNRRTUY	CURRANTY
ACOOPRRS	CORPORAS
ACOOPSTT	TOPCOATS
ACOORSTU	TOURACOS
ACOPRRST	CARPORTS
ACOPRRTT	PROTRACT
ACORRSTT	TRACTORS
ACORRSTU	CURATORS
ACORRTUY	CURATORY
ACORSSTU	SURCOATS
ACORSSUW	CURASSOW
ACORSSWY	CROSSWAY
ACORSTTY	CRYOSTAT
ACOSSTTU	OUTCASTS
ACPSSTUU	USUCAPTS
ADDDEEEM	ADDEEMED
ADDDEEEN	DEADENED
ADDDEEGR	DEGRADED
ADDDEEIM	DIADEMED
ADDDEELR	LADDERED
ADDDEEMN	DEMANDED
	MADDENED
ADDDEENR	DANDERED
	REDDENDA
ADDDEENS	SADDENED
ADDDEEPS	SEPADDED
ADDDEGJU	ADJUDGED
ADDDELSW	SWADDLED
ADDDELTW	TWADDLED
ADDDEMNU	ADDENDUM
ADDDEMOO	ADDOOMED
ADDDENOS	DEODANDS
ADDDENRU	DEUDDARN
ADDDEORS	ADDORSED
ADDDGILN	DADDLING
ADDEEEFN	DEAFENED
ADDEEEFT	DEFEATED
ADDEEEJY	DEEJAYED
ADDEEELN	LEADENED
ADDEEEMN	DEMEANED
ADDEEENR	DEADENER
	ENDEARED
ADDEEFIL	DEFILADE
ADDEEFIM	MADEFIED
ADDEEFLT	DEFLATED
ADDEEFNU	UNDEAFED
ADDEEFPR	PREFADED
ADDEEFRY	DEFRAYED
ADDEEFTT	DEFATTED
ADDEEGLL	ALLEDGED
ADDEEGLN	DANEGELD
ADDEEGNR	DANGERED
	DERANGED
	GARDENED
ADDEEGRR	REGARDED
	REGRADED
ADDEEGRS	DEGRADES
ADDEEGSS	DEGASSED
ADDEEHLR	HERALDED
ADDEEHLY	ALDEHYDE
ADDEEHNR	HARDENED
ADDEEHNU	UNHEADED
ADDEEHRT	THREADED
ADDEEIKR	DAIKERED
ADDEEILN	DEADLINE
ADDEEILR	DEADLIER
	DERAILED
ADDEEILT	DETAILED
ADDEEIMT	MEDIATED
ADDEEINT	DETAINED
ADDEEIPR	DIAPERED
ADDEEISS	DISEASED
ADDEEIST	STEADIED
ADDEEITV	DEVIATED
ADDEEKMR	DEMARKED
ADDEEKNR	DARKENED
ADDEELLM	MEDALLED
ADDEELLP	PEDALLED
ADDEELLV	DEVALLED
ADDEELNO	LOADENED
ADDEELNP	DEPLANED
ADDEELNR	ENLARDED
ADDEELNU	UNLEADED
ADDEELOR	RELOADED
ADDEELPS	DELAPSED
ADDEELRT	TREADLED
ADDEELST	DESALTED
ADDEELUV	DEVALUED
ADDEEMNN	DEMANNED
ADDEEMNP	DAMPENED
ADDEEMNR	DAMNEDER
	DEMANDER
	REMANDED
ADDEENPP	APPENDED
ADDEENPR	PANDERED
ADDEENPX	EXPANDED
ADDEENRR	DARNEDER
ADDEENRT	ENDARTED
ADDEENRU	DAUNERED
ADDEENRW	DAWNERED
	WANDERED
	WARDENED
ADDEENSS	DEADNESS
ADDEENTT	ATTENDED
	DENTATED
ADDEENTU	DENUDATE
ADDEEOST	DEODATES
ADDEEPRT	DEPARTED
	PREDATED
ADDEEPRV	DEPRAVED
	PERVADED
ADDEERRS	DREADERS
ADDEERRT	RETARDED
ADDEERRW	REWARDED
	WARDERED
ADDEERSW	SAWDERED
ADDEERTV	ADVERTED
ADDEFFOR	AFFORDED
ADDEFIIL	LADIFIED
ADDEFILY	LADYFIED
ADDEFIST	FADDIEST
ADDEFLRU	DREADFUL
ADDEFRSU	DEFRAUDS
ADDEGGLR	DRAGGLED
ADDEGHOS	GODHEADS
ADDEGILS	GLADDIES
ADDEGINR	DREADING
ADDEGIRS	DISGRADE
ADDEGJSU	ADJUDGES
ADDEGLNS	GLADDENS
ADDEGLST	GLADDEST
ADDEGNRU	UNGRADED
ADDEGPRU	UPGRADED
ADDEHHIN	HINDHEAD
ADDEHILR	DIHEDRAL
ADDEHMRU	DRUMHEAD
ADDEHNNU	UNHANDED
ADDEHNSU	UNDASHED
	UNSHADED
ADDEHORW	HEADWORD
ADDEHOSW	SHADOWED
ADDEHRTY	HYDRATED
ADDEIIKS	DIDAKEIS
ADDEIIRS	DIARISED
ADDEIIRZ	DIARIZED
ADDEIITV	ADDITIVE
ADDEIJNO	ADJOINED
ADDEILNS	ISLANDED
ADDEILRS	DIEDRALS
ADDEILSY	DIALYSED

ADDEILYZ	DIALYZED	ADDGILNP	PADDLING
ADDEIMOS	SODAMIDE	ADDGILNR	RADDLING
ADDEIMRS	DISARMED	ADDGILNS	SADDLING
	MISDREAD	ADDGILNW	DAWDLING
ADDEIMST	MISDATED		WADDLING
ADDEIMSY	DISMAYED	ADDGINPS	PADDINGS
ADDEIMTT	ADMITTED	ADDGINQU	QUADDING
ADDEINOR	ORDAINED	ADDGINSW	WADDINGS
ADDEINOS	ADENOIDS	ADDGINWY	WADDYING
	ADONISED	ADDGLNOS	GLADDONS
	ANODISED	ADDGOOSW	DAGWOODS
ADDEINOZ	ADONIZED	ADDGORSW	GODWARDS
	ANODIZED	ADDHHLNO	HANDHOLD
ADDEINRT	INDARTED	ADDHIMOO	MAIDHOOD
ADDEINST	DANDIEST	ADDHINPS	DAPHNIDS
ADDEIOPR	PARODIED	ADDHINRW	HINDWARD
ADDEIORS	ROADSIDE	ADDHINSY	DANDYISH
ADDEIOTX	OXIDATED	ADDHIOTY	HYDATOID
ADDEIPPR	DIDAPPER	ADDHISTY	HYDATIDS
ADDEIPRS	DISPREAD	ADDHLOOY	LADYHOOD
ADDEIPSS	DIPSADES	ADDHOORW	HARDWOOD
ADDEIRST	DISRATED	ADDIIKMZ	ZADDIKIM
ADDEIRSW	SIDEWARD	ADDIILUV	DIVIDUAL
ADDEIRVZ	VIZARDED	ADDIINOT	ADDITION
ADDEISSU	DISSUADE	ADDIINTV	DIVIDANT
ADDEISSW	SWADDIES	ADDIKSST	TSADDIKS
ADDEJSTU	ADJUSTED	ADDIKSTY	KATYDIDS
ADDEKNVY	VANDYKED	ADDIKSTZ	TZADDIKS
ADDELLOR	DOLLARED	ADDILMNS	MIDLANDS
ADDELMOS	DOLMADES	ADDILNNW	LANDWIND
ADDELNOU	DUODENAL	ADDILOSS	DISLOADS
	UNLOADED	ADDIMNOS	DIAMONDS
ADDELNPU	PUDENDAL	ADDIMNSY	DANDYISM
ADDELNRS	DANDLERS	ADDIMORS	DIADROMS
ADDELNSU	UNSADDLE	ADDINNOR	ORDINAND
ADDELPRS	PADDLERS	ADDINORS	ANDROIDS
ADDELRSS	SADDLERS		DISADORN
ADDELRST	STRADDLE	ADDINQUY	QUIDDANY
ADDELRSW	DAWDLERS	ADDINRWW	WINDWARD
	SWADDLER	ADDIQSST	TSADDIQS
ADDELRSY	SADDLERY	ADDIQSTZ	TZADDIQS
ADDELRTW	TWADDLER	ADDIRSZZ	DIZZARDS
ADDELSST	STADDLES	ADDKNRRU	DRUNKARD
ADDELSSW	SWADDLES	ADDLLNOR	LANDLORD
ADDELSTW	TWADDLES	ADDLLRSU	DULLARDS
ADDEMMNU	UNDAMMED	ADDLNNOW	DOWNLAND
ADDEMNNU	UNDAMNED	ADDLNOOW	WOODLAND
ADDEMNPU	UNDAMPED	ADDLNORS	LANDDROS
ADDENNOT	DANTONED	ADDLOOSS	SOLDADOS
ADDENOPR	PARDONED	ADDMOOSY	DOOMSDAY
ADDENORU	UNADORED	ADDNOPWY	PANDOWDY
ADDENPRU	UNDRAPED	ADDNORWW	DOWNWARD
ADDENRST	STRANDED	ADDOORWW	WOODWARD
ADDENRSU	DAUNDERS	ADDOORWY	WOODYARD
ADDENRTU	DRAUNTED	ADDOPSSY	DASYPODS
	UNTRADED		
ADDENRUW	UNWARDED	ADEEEFFR	AFFEERED
ADDEORTU	OUTDARED	ADEEEFNY	FEDAYEEN
ADDEOTTU	OUTDATED	ADEEEFRT	FEDERATE
ADDEPRSU	SUPERADD	ADEEEGLT	DELEGATE
ADDFFILO	DAFFODIL	ADEEEGNR	RENEGADE
ADDFFINR	DANDRIFF	ADEEEGNT	TEENAGED
ADDFFNRU	DANDRUFF	ADEEEGPS	GAPESEED
ADDFGILN	FADDLING	ADEEEGRS	DEGREASE
ADDFIMSS	FADDISMS	ADEEEHHW	HEEHAWED
ADDFISST	FADDISTS	ADEEEHRT	REHEATED
ADDGGILN	GLADDING	ADEEEHRX	EXHEDRAE
ADDGIILN	DAIDLING	ADEEEHSY	EYESHADE
ADDGIIRS	DIAGRIDS	ADEEEINT	DETAINEE
ADDGILNN	DANDLING	ADEEEKNW	WEAKENED

ADEEELNS	ENSEALED	ADEEGLLT	GALLETED
ADEEELNV	LEAVENED	ADEEGLNO	ENGAOLED
ADEEELPR	REPEALED	ADEEGLNR	ENLARGED
ADEEELRS	RELEASED		LARGENED
	RESEALED	ADEEGLNT	DANEGELT
ADEEELRV	LAVEERED	ADEEGLSV	SELVAGED
	REVEALED	ADEEGMMT	GEMMATED
ADEEELST	TEASELED	ADEEGMNR	GENDARME
ADEEELSW	WEASELED	ADEEGMNS	ENDGAMES
ADEEELTV	ELEVATED	ADEEGMNY	MEGADYNE
ADEEELTZ	TEAZELED	ADEEGMOP	MEGAPODE
ADEEEMNS	DEMEANES	ADEEGMSS	MESSAGED
	ENSEAMED	ADEEGNNR	ENDANGER
ADEEEMNT	EMENDATE		ENRANGED
ADEEEMRU	EMERAUDE	ADEEGNNV	VENDANGE
ADEEENNT	NEATENED	ADEEGNOR	RENEGADO
ADEEENRS	ENSEARED	ADEEGNRR	GARDENER
	SERENADE		GARNERED
ADEEENTT	ATTENDEE	ADEEGNRS	DERANGES
	EDENTATE		GRANDEES
ADEEENWZ	WEAZENED		GRENADES
ADEEEPRT	REPEATED	ADEEGNRU	DUNGAREE
ADEEERRS	ARREEDES		RENAGUED
ADEEERST	RESEATED		UNGEARED
ADEEESSW	SEAWEEDS	ADEEGNRV	ENGRAVED
	SEESAWED	ADEEGNSS	AGEDNESS
ADEEFFIR	EFFRAIDE	ADEEGNSV	VENDAGES
ADEEFHOR	FOREHEAD	ADEEGORT	DEROGATE
ADEEFHRT	FATHERED	ADEEGOST	DOGEATES
ADEEFILN	ENFILADE	ADEEGOTW	GOATWEED
ADEEFIMS	MADEFIES	ADEEGPRS	ASPERGED
ADEEFINR	FREDAINE		PRESAGED
ADEEFIOR	FOEDARIE	ADEEGPRT	PARGETED
ADEEFIRR	RAREFIED	ADEEGRRR	REGARDER
ADEEFIRS	FEDARIES	ADEEGRRS	REGRADES
ADEEFIRY	REAEDIFY	ADEEGRRT	GARRETED
ADEEFLLT	FELLATED		GARTERED
ADEEFLOR	FREELOAD		REGRATED
ADEEFLRR	DEFERRAL	ADEEGRRU	REDARGUE
ADEEFLRS	FEDERALS	ADEEGRSS	DRESSAGE
ADEEFLRT	DEFLATER	ADEEGRST	RESTAGED
	FALTERED	ADEEGRSU	GUARDEES
	REFLATED	ADEEGRSW	RAGWEEDS
ADEEFLSS	FADELESS	ADEEGRTT	TARGETED
ADEEFLST	DEFLATES	ADEEGSSS	DEGASSES
ADEEFMNR	ENFRAMED	ADEEGSTT	GESTATED
	FREEDMAN	ADEEGSWY	EDGEWAYS
ADEEFMRR	REFRAMED	ADEEGTTZ	GAZETTED
ADEEFNRU	UNFEARED	ADEEHHRS	REHASHED
ADEEFNSS	DEAFNESS	ADEEHHST	SHEATHED
ADEEFNST	FASTENED	ADEEHILN	HEADLINE
ADEEFNTT	FATTENED	ADEEHILS	DEISHEAL
ADEEFORR	FOREREAD	ADEEHIRT	DEATHIER
ADEEFORT	FOREDATE	ADEEHISS	EADISHES
ADEEFPRS	PREFADES	ADEEHIST	ATHEISED
ADEEFRRT	RAFTERED		HEADIEST
ADEEFRRY	DEFRAYER	ADEEHISV	ADHESIVE
	FEDERARY	ADEEHITZ	ATHEIZED
ADEEFRST	DRAFTEES	ADEEHKNR	HANKERED
ADEEFRTU	FEATURED		HARKENED
ADEEGGHS	EGGHEADS	ADEEHKWW	HAWKWEED
ADEEGGLL	ALLEGGED	ADEEHLNO	ENHALOED
ADEEGGRR	RAGGEDER	ADEEHLNR	REHANDLE
ADEEGHOR	GHERAOED	ADEEHLNU	UNHEALED
ADEEGHRT	GATHERED	ADEEHLRS	ASHLERED
ADEEGIMN	ADEEMING	ADEEHLRT	HALTERED
ADEEGINR	REGAINED		LATHERED
ADEEGIRS	DISAGREE	ADEEHLSS	HEADLESS
ADEEGISS	ASSIEGED	ADEEHMMR	HAMMERED
ADEEGLLS	ALLEDGES	ADEEHMNN	MENHADEN

```
ADEEHMNS HEADSMEN
ADEEHMNT ANTHEMED
ADEEHMPR HAMPERED
ADEEHNOT HEADNOTE
ADEEHNPP HAPPENED
ADEEHNRR HARDENER
ADEEHNRT ADHERENT
         HARTENED
         THREADEN
ADEEHNSS DASHEENS
ADEEHNST HASTENED
ADEEHNTU UNHEATED
ADEEHOPR HEADROPE
ADEEHORS SOREHEAD
ADEEHORV OVERHEAD
ADEEHPPU UPHEAPED
ADEEHPRS EPHEDRAS
         RESHAPED
ADEEHPUV UPHEAVED
ADEEHRRS ADHERERS
         REDSHARE
ADEEHRRT THREADER
ADEEHRST HEADREST
ADEEHRSW WASHERED
ADEEHRTT HATTERED
         THREATED
ADEEHRTW WREATHED
ADEEHSST HEADSETS
ADEEHSSY HAYSEEDS
ADEEIILS IDEALISE
ADEEIILZ IDEALIZE
ADEEIITV IDEATIVE
ADEEIJMR JEREMIAD
ADEEIJRS JADERIES
ADEEIJST JADEITES
ADEEILLO OEILLADE
ADEEILLR REALLIED
ADEEILMN ENDEMIAL
ADEEILMR REMEDIAL
ADEEILMV MEDIEVAL
ADEEILNS DELAINES
ADEEILNT ENTAILED
         LINEATED
ADEEILPR PEDALIER
ADEEILPT DEPILATE
         EPILATED
         PILEATED
ADEEILRR DERAILER
         RERAILED
ADEEILRS REALISED
         SIDEREAL
ADEEILRT RETAILED
ADEEILRZ REALIZED
ADEEILSS DEISEALS
         IDEALESS
ADEEILST LEADIEST
ADEEILSV DISLEAVE
ADEEILSY EYELIADS
ADEEIMNR REMAINED
ADEEIMNS DEMAINES
         INSEAMED
ADEEIMNT DEMENTIA
ADEEIMNX EXAMINED
ADEEIMPR EMPAIRED
ADEEIMRR DREAMIER
ADEEIMRS MADERISE
ADEEIMRT DIAMETER
         REMEDIAT
ADEEIMRZ MADERIZE
ADEEIMSS SIAMESED

ADEEIMST MEDIATES
ADEEIMSZ SIAMEZED
ADEEIMTT MEDITATE
ADEEINNS ADENINES
         ANDESINE
ADEEINPR PINDAREE
ADEEINPT DIAPENTE
         NEAPTIDE
ADEEINRS ARSENIDE
         DENARIES
         DRAISENE
         NEARSIDE
ADEEINRT DETAINER
         RETAINED
ADEEINSS ANISEEDS
ADEEINST ANDESITE
ADEEIPRR REPAIRED
ADEEIPTX EXPIATED
ADEEIRRR DREARIER
ADEEIRST READIEST
         SERIATED
         STEADIER
ADEEIRSV READVISE
ADEEIRTT ITERATED
ADEEIRTV DERIVATE
         EVIRATED
         TAIVERED
ADEEISSS DISEASES
         SEASIDES
ADEEISST STEADIES
ADEEISSV ADESSIVE
ADEEISTV DEVIATES
         SEDATIVE
ADEEITTV EVITATED
ADEEKMRR REMARKED
ADEEKMRT MARKETED
ADEEKNNR ENRANKED
ADEEKNPW KNAPWEED
ADEEKNRS KNEADERS
ADEEKNST NAKEDEST
ADEEKQSU SQUEAKED
ADEEKRST STREAKED
ADEEKSWY WEEKDAYS
ADEELLLP LAPELLED
ADEELLMT METALLED
ADEELLMU MEDULLAE
ADEELLNP PANELLED
ADEELLNW ENWALLED
ADEELLNY LEADENLY
ADEELLPR PEDALLER
         PREDELLA
ADEELLPT PALLETED
         PETALLED
ADEELLQU EQUALLED
ADEELLRS SARDELLE
ADEELLRT TELLARED
ADEELLRV RAVELLED
ADEELLSS ALLSEEDS
         LEADLESS
ADEELLTY ELATEDLY
ADEELMNO LEMONADE
ADEELMNP EMPLANED
ADEELMNR ALDERMEN
ADEELMNS DALESMEN
ADEELMNT LAMENTED
ADEELMOS SOMEDEAL
ADEELMPX EXAMPLED
ADEELMRS DEMERSAL

         EMERALDS
ADEELMST MEDALETS
ADEELMTU EMULATED
ADEELNNU UNANELED
ADEELNOR OLEANDER
ADEELNPS DEPLANES
ADEELNPU UPLEANED
ADEELNRT ANTLERED
ADEELNRV LAVENDER
ADEELNSU UNLEASED
         UNSEALED
ADEELNSV ENSLAVED
ADEELNTT TALENTED
ADEELNTU UNELATED
ADEELNTV LEVANTED
ADEELNTY ENTAYLED
ADEELOPS PEDALOES
ADEELORU AUREOLED
ADEELORV OVERLADE
ADEELOST DESOLATE
ADEELOSW LEASOWED
ADEELPPR LAPPERED
ADEELPPT LAPPETED
ADEELPPU UPLEAPED
ADEELPRS PLEADERS
         RELAPSED
ADEELPRT PALTERED
ADEELPRY PARLEYED
         REPLAYED
ADEELPSS DELAPSES
ADEELPST PEDESTAL
ADEELPTY PEDATELY
ADEELQSU SQUEALED
ADEELRRR LARDERER
ADEELRRT TREADLER
ADEELRST TREADLES
ADEELRSV SLAVERED
ADEELRSY DELAYERS
ADEELRUV REVALUED
ADEELSST DATELESS
ADEELSTY SEDATELY
ADEELSUV DEVALUES
ADEEMMMR MAMMERED
ADEEMMRY YAMMERED
ADEEMMSS MESDAMES
ADEEMMXY MYXEDEMA
ADEEMNNR MANNERED
         REMANNED
ADEEMNOR DEMEANOR
         ENAMORED
ADEEMNOT NEMATODE
ADEEMNPS SPADEMEN
ADEEMNRS AMENDERS
         MEANDERS
         REAMENDS
ADEEMNSS SEEDSMAN
ADEEMNST STAMENED
ADEEMNSU UNSEAMED
ADEEMNSY DEMAYNES
ADEEMNTU UNTEAMED
ADEEMNTW METEWAND
ADEEMORS SEADROME
ADEEMORT MODERATE
ADEEMPPR PAMPERED
ADEEMPRT EMPARTED
         TAMPERED
ADEEMPRV REVAMPED
ADEEMPRY EMPAYRED
ADEEMPST STAMPEDE

         STEPDAME
ADEEMRRS DREAMERS
ADEEMRRY DREAMERY
ADEEMRST MASTERED
         STREAMED
ADEEMRSU MEASURED
ADEEMRTT MATTERED
ADEEMRTY METEYARD
ADEEMSSW MAWSEEDS
ADEEMSTW MATWEEDS
ADEEMSWY MAYWEEDS
ADEENNRS ENSNARED
ADEENNRU UNEARNED
ADEENNTT TENANTED
ADEENNUW UNWEANED
ADEENNUY UNYEANED
ADEENOPW WEAPONED
ADEENORS REASONED
ADEENORY AERODYNE
ADEENOSS SEASONED
ADEENOTT DENOTATE
         DETONATE
ADEENPRT PARENTED
ADEENPRU UNREAPED
ADEENPRX EXPANDER
ADEENPTT PATENTED
         PATTENED
ADEENRRW WANDERER
ADEENRSS DEARNESS
ADEENRSU UNDERSEA
ADEENRSW ANSWERED
ADEENRTT ATTENDER
         NATTERED
         RATTENED
ADEENRTU DENATURE
ADEENRTV AVENTRED
ADEENRUV UNREAVED
ADEENSST ASSENTED
ADEENSSU DANSEUSE
ADEENSTU UNSEATED
ADEENTTU TAUTENED
ADEENTTV VENDETTA
ADEEOPRR PADERERO
ADEEOPRT OPERATED
ADEEORRV OVERREAD
ADEEORSW OARWEEDS
ADEEORVW OVERAWED
ADEEPPRR DAPPERER
ADEEPPRW WAPPERED
ADEEPPRS SPREADER
ADEEPRRT DEPARTER
ADEEPRRU UPREARED
ADEEPRSS ASPERSED
         PREASSED
         REPASSED
ADEEPRST PREDATES
         REPASTED
         TRAPESED
ADEEPRSU PERSUADE
ADEEPRSV DEPRAVES
         PERVADES
ADEEPRSW PERSWADE
ADEEPRSZ SPREAZED
ADEEPRTT PATTERED
ADEEPRTU DEPURATE
         EPURATED
ADEEPRTZ TRAPEZED
ADEEPSST STAPEDES
ADEEPSTT ADEPTEST
```

ADEEPSWY	SPEEDWAY	ADEFILMN	INFLAMED	ADEGHIRS	GARISHED	ADEGIOST	GODETIAS
ADEEQRTU	DETRAQUE	ADEFILNR	FILANDER		HEADRIGS	ADEGIPRS	SPAIRGED
ADEEQRUV	QUAVERED	ADEFILNT	INFLATED	ADEGHIRT	GRAITHED	ADEGIRWY	RIDGEWAY
ADEERRRT	RETARDER	ADEFILOR	FORELAID	ADEGHLNO	HEADLONG	ADEGISSU	DISUSAGE
ADEERRRW	REREWARD	ADEFILOT	FOLIATED	ADEGHLOS	GALOSHED	ADEGISTU	GAUDIEST
	REWARDER	ADEFILSS	DISLEAFS	ADEGHNNU	UNHANGED	ADEGISUV	VIDUAGES
ADEERRST	ARRESTED	ADEFILSY	LADYFIES	ADEGHNRT	THRANGED	ADEGJNOR	JARGONED
	DREAREST	ADEFIMPR	FIREDAMP	ADEGHOOP	PAGEHOOD	ADEGKLOY	DEKALOGY
	RETREADS	ADEFIMRS	MISFARED	ADEGHORT	GOATHERD	ADEGLLNU	GLANDULE
	SERRATED	ADEFIMSS	DISFAMES	ADEGHRTU	DAUGHTER		UNGALLED
	TREADERS	ADEFINNT	INFANTED	ADEGHTUW	WAUGHTED	ADEGLLOP	GALLOPED
ADEERRSV	ADVERSER	ADEFINRS	FRIANDES	ADEGIILN	GLIADINE	ADEGLLOR	GOLLARED
ADEERRTT	RETRATED	ADEFINRU	UNFAIRED	ADEGIIMN	IMAGINED	ADEGLLOW	GALLOWED
ADEERRTW	REDWATER	ADEFINYZ	DENAZIFY	ADEGIIMS	DIGAMIES	ADEGLMOR	GLAMORED
ADEERRWY	WARREYED	ADEFIORS	FORESAID	ADEGIINT	IDEATING	ADEGLMOS	GLADSOME
ADEERSST	ASSERTED	ADEFLLLU	LADLEFUL	ADEGIITT	DIGITATE	ADEGLMPU	PLUMAGED
	ESTRADES	ADEFLLNS	ELFLANDS	ADEGIJSW	JIGSAWED	ADEGLMUY	AMYGDULE
ADEERSTT	ASTERTED	ADEFLLOW	FALLOWED	ADEGIKNN	KNEADING	ADEGLNOY	GONDELAY
	RESTATED	ADEFLLUY	FEUDALLY	ADEGIKNR	DAKERING	ADEGLNPS	SPANGLED
ADEERSTW	DEWATERS	ADEFLMRU	DREAMFUL	ADEGILLO	GLADIOLE	ADEGLNRS	DANGLERS
	TARWEEDS	ADEFLNNS	FENLANDS	ADEGILLP	PILLAGED		GLANDERS
	WASTERED	ADEFLNOR	FORELAND	ADEGILLR	GRILLADE	ADEGLNRW	WRANGLED
ADEERSTY	ESTRAYED	ADEFLNRU	DEARNFUL	ADEGILLS	GALLISED	ADEGLNSS	GLADNESS
ADEERTTT	TATTERED	ADEFLNTU	FLAUNTED	ADEGILLZ	GALLIZED	ADEGLNTW	TWANGLED
ADEERTTY	YATTERED	ADEFLNUU	UNFEUDAL	ADEGILMN	MALIGNED	ADEGLNUZ	UNGLAZED
ADEERTWW	WARTWEED	ADEFLNUW	UNFLAWED	ADEGILNO	GALENOID	ADEGLOPP	GALOPPED
ADEERVYY	EVERYDAY	ADEFLORT	DEFLATOR	ADEGILNP	PLEADING	ADEGLPPR	GRAPPLED
ADEESSSS	ASSESSED	ADEFLPRS	FELDSPAR	ADEGILNR	DEARLING	ADEGMMNO	GAMMONED
ADEESSTT	SEDATEST	ADEFLPSU	SPADEFUL		DRAGLINE	ADEGMMRU	RUMMAGED
ADEESTTT	ATTESTED	ADEFLRTU	TRADEFUL	ADEGILNS	DEALINGS	ADEGMNOS	GOADSMEN
ADEESTUX	EXUDATES	ADEFLRTW	LEFTWARD		LEADINGS	ADEGMNOY	ENDOGAMY
ADEESVVY	SAVVEYED	ADEFLRZZ	FRAZZLED	ADEGILNT	DELATING	ADEGMNRS	DRAGSMEN
ADEFFGUW	GUFFAWED	ADEFLSTU	DEFAULTS	ADEGILNY	DELAYING	ADEGMORS	ORGASMED
ADEFFIMR	AFFIRMED		SULFATED	ADEGILOS	GOLIASED	ADEGMPUZ	GAZUMPED
ADEFFIRR	DRAFFIER	ADEFMNRU	UNFRAMED	ADEGILOU	DIALOGUE	ADEGNNOR	ANDROGEN
ADEFFIRT	TARIFFED	ADEFMORT	FORMATED	ADEGILRS	SLAIRGED		DRAGONNE
ADEFFIST	DAFFIEST	ADEFMOSU	FAMOUSED	ADEGILSS	GLISSADE	ADEGNNPU	UNPANGED
ADEFFLNS	SNAFFLED		FUMADOES	ADEGILSV	DISGAVEL	ADEGNNSU	DUNNAGES
ADEFFRST	STRAFFED	ADEFNNNU	UNFANNED	ADEGIMNN	AMENDING	ADEGNOPS	PONDAGES
ADEFGGGO	FOGGAGED	ADEFNOPR	PROFANED	ADEGIMNR	DREAMING	ADEGNOPU	POUNDAGE
ADEFGGOT	FAGGOTED	ADEFNSST	DAFTNESS		MARGINED	ADEGNORT	DRAGONET
ADEFGIIS	GASIFIED	ADEFOOSS	SEAFOODS	ADEGIMOR	IDEOGRAM	ADEGNOSS	SONDAGES
ADEFGILN	FINAGLED	ADEFORRR	FORRADER	ADEGIMRT	MIGRATED	ADEGNOSV	DOGVANES
ADEFGILO	FOLIAGED	ADEFORRW	FARROWED	ADEGIMST	SIGMATED	ADEGNPUY	PYENGADU
ADEFGILS	GADFLIES		FOREWARD	ADEGINNV	ADVENING	ADEGNRRU	GRANDEUR
	GASFIELD	ADEFORRY	FORRAYED	ADEGINNY	DENAYING	ADEGNRST	GRANDEST
ADEFGIMN	DEFAMING	ADEFORUV	FAVOURED	ADEGINOR	ORGANDIE	ADEGNRSU	ENGUARDS
ADEFGIRT	DRIFTAGE	ADEFPTUW	UPWAFTED	ADEGINOS	AGONISED	ADEGNRUU	UNARGUED
ADEFGIRU	ARGUFIED	ADEFRRST	DRAFTERS		DIAGNOSE	ADEGNRUZ	UNGRAZED
ADEFGITU	FATIGUED		REDRAFTS	ADEGINOZ	AGONIZED	ADEGOORY	GOODYEAR
ADEFGLOT	GATEFOLD	ADEFSSTT	STEDFAST	ADEGINPU	ANGUIPED	ADEGOPPR	PROPAGED
ADEFGLRU	FELDGRAU	ADEGGIRR	DRAGGIER	ADEGINRR	DREARING	ADEGOPRR	PROGRADE
ADEFGNOR	FRONDAGE	ADEGGISU	GAUDGIES	ADEGINRS	DERAIGNS	ADEGORRT	GARROTED
ADEFGOSU	FOUGADES		GUIDAGES		GRADINES	ADEGORST	GOADSTER
ADEFHILS	DEALFISH	ADEGGJLY	JAGGEDLY		READINGS	ADEGORSW	DOWAGERS
ADEFHILY	HAYFIELD	ADEGGLRS	DRAGGLES	ADEGINRT	DERATING		WORDAGES
ADEFHIMS	FAMISHED	ADEGGLRY	RAGGEDLY		GRADIENT	ADEGORTT	GAROTTED
ADEFHKOR	FORKHEAD	ADEGGMOY	DEMAGOGY		TREADING	ADEGORTU	OUTRAGED
ADEFHLTU	DEATHFUL	ADEGGNOW	WAGGONED	ADEGINRY	DERAYING		RAGOUTED
ADEFHMOT	FATHOMED	ADEGGNNU	UNGAUGED		READYING	ADEGPRSS	SPADGERS
ADEFHNOR	FOREHAND	ADEGGOPY	PEDAGOGY		YEARDING	ADEGPRSU	UPGRADES
ADEFHOST	SOFTHEAD	ADEGGPRS	SPRAGGED	ADEGINSS	ASSIGNED	ADEGPSTU	UPSTAGED
ADEFIILR	AIRFIELD	ADEGGRTY	GADGETRY	ADEGINST	SEDATING	ADEGRRST	DRAGSTER
ADEFIILS	LADIFIES	ADEGHHOS	HOGSHEAD		STEADING	ADEGRSSU	GRADUSES
	SALIFIED	ADEGHILN	HEALDING	ADEGINSW	WINDAGES	ADEGTTTU	GUTTATED
ADEFIILT	FILIATED	ADEGHILT	ALIGHTED	ADEGINTV	VINTAGED	ADEHHIPR	RHAPHIDE
ADEFIIMR	RAMIFIED	ADEGHINR	ADHERING	ADEGINVW	ADVEWING	ADEHHIPS	HEADSHIP
ADEFIINS	SANIFIED		HEADRING	ADEGINYZ	ZYGAENID	ADEHHNTU	HEADHUNT
ADEFIIRT	RATIFIED	ADEGHINS	HEADINGS	ADEGIORT	ERGATOID	ADEHHOOR	HOORAHED
ADEFIIRU	AURIFIED		SHEADING			ADEHHOST	HOTHEADS

ADEHHRRU	HURRAHED	ADEHMOOR	HEADROOM	VITIATED	DEASOILS
ADEHHRST	THRASHED	ADEHMORS	HADROMES	ADEIITUV AUDITIVE	ADEILOST DIASTOLE
ADEHIITZ	THIAZIDE	ADEHMORW	HOMEWARD	ADEIJMRS JEMIDARS	ISOLATED
ADEHIKLV	KHEDIVAL	ADEHMOST	HEADMOST	ADEIKLLO KELOIDAL	SODALITE
ADEHIKNS	SKINHEAD	ADEHMOSU	MADHOUSE	ADEIKLLP PIKADELL	SOLIDATE
ADEHIKSS	DASHEKIS	ADEHMOSY	SHAMOYED	ADEIKLLY LADYLIKE	ADEILOSU DOULEIAS
ADEHIKST	SKAITHED	ADEHNOPR	ORPHANED	ADEIKLSW SIDEWALK	ADEILOTT DATOLITE
ADEHIKSV	KHEDIVAS	ADEHNOPT	PHONATED	ADEIKMMS IMMASKED	ADEILOTV DOVETAIL
ADEHILLP	PHIALLED	ADEHNORV	HANDOVER	ADEIKMPR IMPARKED	VIOLATED
	PILLHEAD		OVERHAND	ADEIKMRT TIDEMARK	ADEILPPP PEDIPALP
ADEHILNR	HARDLINE	ADEHNPSU	UNHASPED	ADEIKNSY KYANISED	ADEILPRS PEDRAILS
ADEHILNU	UNHAILED		UNSHAPED	ADEIKNYZ KYANIZED	PREDIALS
ADEHILPS	HELIPADS	ADEHNPTU	UNPATHED	ADEIKORT KERATOID	ADEILPRT DIPTERAL
ADEHILSV	LAVISHED	ADEHNRSS	HARDNESS	ADEIKRST STRAIKED	TRIPEDAL
ADEHILSW	WHAISLED	ADEHNRSU	UNSHARED	ADEILLMY MEDIALLY	ADEILPRU EPIDURAL
ADEHILWZ	WHAIZLED	ADEHNRSW	SWANHERD	ADEILLNU UNALLIED	ADEILPRV DEPRIVAL
ADEHIMRS	MISHEARD	ADEHNRTU	UNTHREAD	ADEILLNW INWALLED	ADEILPSS DESPISAL
ADEHIMRY	HYDREMIA	ADEHNSST	HANDSETS	ADEILLOR ARILLODE	ADEILPST TALIPEDS
ADEHINOP	DIAPHONE	ADEHNSSU	UNSASHED	ADEILLPR PALLIDER	ADEILPTU PLAUDITE
ADEHINOS	ADHESION	ADEHNSUV	UNSHAVED	ADEILLPS ILLAPSED	ADEILQSU SQUAILED
ADEHINPS	DEANSHIP	ADEHNSUW	UNWASHED		SPADILLE	ADEILQTU LIQUATED
	PINHEADS	ADEHNTTU	UNHATTED	ADEILLRS DALLIERS	ADEILRRY DREARILY
ADEHINPU	DAUPHINE	ADEHNTUW	UNTHAWED		DIALLERS	ADEILRST DILATERS
ADEHINRU	UNHAIRED	ADEHOOPS	APEHOODS	ADEILLRV RIVALLED	LARDIEST
ADEHINSS	SHANDIES	ADEHOORW	HAREWOOD	ADEILMMS DILEMMAS	ADEILRSU RESIDUAL
ADEHINST	HANDIEST	ADEHOORY	HOORAYED	ADEILMNP PLAIDMEN	ADEILRSY DIALYSER
ADEHINSV	VANISHED	ADEHOPRS	RHAPSODE	ADEILMNU UNMAILED	ADEILRTT DETRITAL
ADEHIOTT	ATHETOID	ADEHOPST	POTASHED	ADEILMNY MAIDENLY	ADEILRTY DIELYTRA
ADEHIPRS	RAPHIDES	ADEHOPSX	HEXAPODS	ADEILMOS DAMOISEL	ADEILRVY VARIEDLY
ADEHIPST	PITHEADS	ADEHOPXY	HEXAPODY	ADEILMPP PALMIPED	ADEILRYZ DIALYZER
ADEHIRSS	RADISHES	ADEHORRS	HOARDERS	ADEILMPR IMPARLED	ADEILSSU DEASIULS
ADEHIRST	HAIRSTED	ADEHORRW	HARROWED	ADEILMPS IMPLEADS	ADEILSSV DEVISALS
	HARDIEST	ADEHORSW	SHADOWER		MISPLEAD	ADEILSSY DIALYSES
ADEHIRSV	RAVISHED	ADEHORTT	THROATED	ADEILMPT IMPLATED	ADEILSTV VALIDEST
ADEHIRSW	RAWHIDES	ADEHORTU	AUTHORED	ADEILMRY DREAMILY	ADEILSTY DIASTYLE
ADEHIRVW	HIVEWARD	ADEHQSSU	SQUASHED	ADEILMSS MAIDLESS	STEADILY
ADEHISST	SHADIEST	ADEHRRUY	HURRAYED		MISDEALS	ADEILSUV DISVALUE
ADEHJLOT	JOLTHEAD	ADEHRSTY	HYDRATES		MISLEADS	ADEILSXY DYSLEXIA
ADEHKLNU	LUNKHEAD	ADEIILMN	LIMNAEID	ADEILMST MISDEALT	ADEILSYZ DIALYZES
ADEHKNRS	REDSHANK	ADEIILMS	IDEALISM	ADEILMSY DYSMELIA	ADEILTTU ALTITUDE
ADEHKNSU	UNSHAKED		MILADIES	ADEILNNR INLANDER	LATITUDE
ADEHKORS	HARDOKES	ADEIILPR	PERIDIAL	ADEILNNS ANNELIDS	ADEIMMNS MISNAMED
ADEHKORW	HEADWORK	ADEIILRS	LAIRISED		LINDANES	ADEIMMNU UNMAIMED
ADEHKOST	KATHODES	ADEIILRZ	LAIRIZED	ADEILNNU UNNAILED	ADEIMMRS MERMAIDS
ADEHLLOO	HALLOOED	ADEIILST	IDEALIST	ADEILNOP PALINODE	ADEIMMST MISMATED
	HOLLOAED	ADEIILTV	DILATIVE	ADEILNOS NODALISE	ADEIMNNO DEMONIAN
ADEHLLOW	HALLOWED	ADEIILTY	IDEALITY	ADEILNOT DELATION	MONDAINE
ADEHLLRT	THRALLED	ADEIIMMS	MISAIMED	ADEILNOZ NODALIZE	ADEIMNOP DOPAMINE
ADEHLLRW	HELLWARD	ADEIIMNR	MERIDIAN	ADEILNPT PANTILED	ADEIMNOS NOMADIES
ADEHLMNO	HOMELAND	ADEIIMNT	MINIATED	ADEILNPU PALUDINE	NOMADISE
ADEHLMOY	HOLYDAME	ADEIIMPR	IMPAIRED	ADEILNRS ISLANDER	ADEIMNOT DOMINATE
ADEHLNRS	HANDLERS	ADEIIMTT	IMITATED	ADEILNRU UNDERLAI	NEMATOID
ADEHLNSS	HANDLESS	ADEIINNS	SANIDINE	ADEILNSU UNSAILED	ADEIMNOZ NOMADIZE
	HANDSELS	ADEIINOT	IDEATION	ADEILNSV ANDVILES	ADEIMNPW IMPAWNED
ADEHLNST	SHETLAND		TAENIOID	ADEILNTU UNTAILED	ADEIMNRR MANRIDER
ADEHLNSU	UNHALSED	ADEIINRS	DRAISINE	ADEILNTV DIVALENT	ADEIMNRS ADERMINS
	UNLASHED	ADEIINRT	DAINTIER	ADEILNUV UNVAILED	SIRNAMED
	UNSHALED	ADEIINRU	UREDINIA	ADEILOPS EPISODAL	ADEIMNRY DAIRYMEN
ADEHLOPS	ASPHODEL	ADEIINST	ADENITIS		OPALISED	ADEIMNRZ ZEMINDAR
	PHOLADES		DAINTIES		SEPALOID	ADEIMNSS SIDESMAN
ADEHLPSS	SPLASHED	ADEIINUV	INDUVIAE	ADEILOPT PETALOID	ADEIMNST MEDIANTS
ADEHLRRY	HERALDRY	ADEIIPRR	PERRADII	ADEILOPZ OPALIZED	ADEIMNSU MAUNDIES
ADEHMNNY	HANDYMEN		PRAIRIED	ADEILOQU ODALIQUE	ADEIMNSY DYNAMISE
ADEHMNOS	HANDSOME	ADEIIPRS	PRESIDIA	ADEILORS DARIOLES	ADEIMNTY DYNAMITE
ADEHMNOT	METHADON	ADEIIPST	STAPEDII		SOLIDARE	ADEIMNYZ DYNAMIZE
	THANEDOM	ADEIIRSS	DIARISES		SOREDIAL	ADEIMORR AIRDROME
ADEHMNRS	HERDSMAN	ADEIIRST	IRISATED	ADEILORT IDOLATER	ADEIMORT MEDIATOR
ADEHMNRU	UNHARMED	ADEIIRSZ	DIARIZES		TAILORED	ADEIMOSS SESAMOID
ADEHMNSU	UNSHAMED	ADEIITTV	TIDIVATE	ADEILORV OVERLAID	ADEIMOST ATOMISED
ADEHMOOP	OOMPAHED			ADEILORX EXORDIAL	ADEIMOTZ ATOMIZED
				ADEILOSS ASSOILED	

ADEIMPRR	RAMPIRED		RUINATED
ADEIMPRT	IMPARTED		URINATED
ADEIMPRV	VAMPIRED	ADEINRUV	UNVARIED
ADEIMPST	DAMPIEST	ADEINRVY	VINEYARD
	IMPASTED	ADEINSST	SANDIEST
ADEIMRRS	ADMIRERS	ADEINSSW	WINDASES
	DISARMER	ADEINSTT	INSTATED
ADEIMRSS	MISREADS	ADEINSTU	AUDIENTS
	SIDEARMS		SINUATED
ADEIMRST	MARDIEST	ADEINSTV	DEVIANTS
	MISRATED	ADEINSTY	DESYATIN
	READMITS	ADEIOPRS	DIASPORE
ADEIMRTU	MURIATED		PARODIES
ADEIMSST	MISDATES	ADEIOPRV	OVERPAID
ADEIMSTU	TAEDIUMS	ADEIOPST	DIOPTASE
ADEIMSTY	DAYTIMES	ADEIOPTV	ADOPTIVE
ADEINNNS	NANDINES	ADEIORRT	ADROITER
ADEINNOT	ANOINTED	ADEIORST	ASTEROID
	ANTINODE	ADEIORTT	TERATOID
ADEINNPT	PINNATED	ADEIORTV	DEVIATOR
ADEINNPU	UNPAINED	ADEIOSSX	OXIDASES
ADEINNRS	INSNARED	ADEIOSTX	OXIDATES
ADEINNRZ	RENDZINA	ADEIOSTZ	AZOTISED
ADEINNSU	UNSAINED	ADEIOSVV	VAIVODES
ADEINNSX	DISANNEX	ADEIOSWV	WAIVODES
ADEINNTU	INUNDATE	ADEIOSWW	WAIWODES
ADEINOPT	ANTIPODE	ADEIOTZZ	AZOTIZED
ADEINORR	ORDAINER	ADEIPPRS	APPRISED
	REORDAIN		DRAPPIES
ADEINORS	ANEROIDS	ADEIPPRZ	APPRIZED
	DONARIES	ADEIPRRS	DRAPIERS
ADEINORT	AROINTED	ADEIPRSS	DESPAIRS
	DERATION	ADEIPRST	RAPIDEST
	ORDINATE		SPIRATED
	RATIONED		TRAIPSED
ADEINORU	DOUANIER	ADEIPRSU	UPRAISED
ADEINOSS	ADONISES	ADEIPRTU	EUPATRID
	ANODISES	ADEIPSTV	VAPIDEST
ADEINOST	ASTONIED	ADEIPTTU	APTITUDE
	SEDATION	ADEIQRRU	QUARRIED
ADEINOSX	DIOXANES	ADEIQSUY	QUAYSIDE
ADEINOSZ	ADONIZES	ADEIRRSW	SWARDIER
	ANODIZES	ADEIRRTW	TAWDRIER
ADEINOTT	ANTIDOTE	ADEIRRWW	WIREDRAW
	TETANOID	ADEIRRZZ	RIZZARED
ADEINOTV	DONATIVE	ADEIRSST	ASTERIDS
ADEINPPX	APPENDIX		DIASTERS
ADEINPRS	SPRAINED		DISASTER
ADEINPRT	DIPTERAN		DISRATES
ADEINPRU	UNPAIRED	ADEIRSSU	RADIUSES
	UNREPAID		SUDARIES
ADEINPST	DEPAINTS	ADEIRSSV	ADVISERS
ADEINPSV	SPAVINED	ADEIRSTT	STRAITED
ADEINQTU	ANTIQUED		STRIATED
ADEINRRS	DRAINERS		TARDIEST
	SERRANID	ADEIRSTW	TAWDRIES
ADEINRSS	ARIDNESS	ADEIRTTT	TITRATED
	SARDINES	ADEIRVWY	DRIVEWAY
ADEINRST	DETRAINS	ADEISSST	ASSISTED
	RANDIEST		DISSEATS
	STRAINED	ADEISSTT	DISTASTE
ADEINRSU	DENARIUS		STAIDEST
	UNRAISED	ADEISSWY	SIDEWAYS
	URANIDES		WAYSIDES
ADEINRSV	INVADERS	ADEISTTU	SITUATED
	SANDIVER	ADEITTTU	ATTITUDE
ADEINRSY	SYNEDRIA		ATTUITED
ADEINRTT	NITRATED	ADEJLOSU	JALOUSED
ADEINRTU	DATURINE	ADEJMRRU	JUMARRED
	INDURATE	ADEJOPRS	JEOPARDS

ADEJOPRY	JEOPARDY	ADELNSTU	UNSALTED
ADEJRSTU	ADJUSTER	ADELNSTW	WETLANDS
	READJUST	ADELNTUU	UNDULATE
ADEKLMRY	MARKEDLY	ADELNUUV	UNVALUED
ADEKLNPP	KNAPPLED	ADELNUZZ	UNDAZZLE
ADEKLNPR	PRANKLED	ADELOORV	OVERLOAD
ADEKLNSU	UNSLAKED	ADELOOWW	WOODWALE
ADEKLPRS	SPARKLED	ADELOPPR	PROPALED
ADEKMNRU	UNMARKED	ADELOPRS	LEOPARDS
ADEKMNSU	UNMASKED	ADELOPRT	PROLATED
ADEKMORS	DARKSOME	ADELOPSS	DEPOSALS
ADEKNRSS	DANKNESS	ADELOPST	TADPOLES
	DARKNESS	ADELOPSU	PALUDOSE
ADEKNSVY	VANDYKES	ADELOPSY	SEPALODY
ADEKQSUW	SQUAWKED	ADELOPTY	PETALODY
ADELLMOR	MORALLED	ADELORRV	OVERLARD
ADELLMOS	SLALOMED	ADELORSS	ROADLESS
ADELLMRU	MEDULLAR	ADELORST	DELATORS
ADELLMSU	MEDULLAS		LEOTARDS
ADELLNNU	ANNULLED	ADELORSU	ROULADES
ADELLNPS	SPENDALL	ADELOSSW	DOWLASES
ADELLNRS	LANDLERS	ADELOSTV	SOLVATED
ADELLNSS	LANDLESS	ADELOTUV	OVULATED
ADELLNSW	ELLWANDS	ADELOTUW	OUTLAWED
	WALLSEND	ADELOVWY	AVOWEDLY
ADELLNUW	UNWALLED	ADELPPRY	DAPPERLY
ADELLOPW	WALLOPED	ADELPRRU	LARRUPED
ADELLORS	ODALLERS	ADELPRSW	SPRAWLED
ADELLOSW	SALLOWED	ADELPRTT	PRATTLED
ADELLOTT	ALLOTTED	ADELPSTT	SPLATTED
	TOTALLED	ADELPSTU	PULSATED
ADELLOTV	LAVOLTED	ADELPUUV	UPVALUED
ADELLOTW	TALLOWED	ADELRRSU	RUDERALS
ADELLOWW	WALLOWED	ADELRRSW	DRAWLERS
ADELLQSU	SQUALLED	ADELRRTU	ULTRARED
ADELLRSU	UDALLERS	ADELRSTT	STARTLED
ADELLTUU	ULULATED	ADELRSZZ	DAZZLERS
ADELMNNS	LANDSMEN	ADELRTUY	ADULTERY
ADELMNOS	LODESMAN	ADELSTTY	STATEDLY
ADELMNRS	MANDRELS	ADELTTTW	TWATTLED
ADELMORS	EARLDOMS	ADEMMNOW	MADWOMEN
ADELMOSS	DAMOSELS	ADEMMSTU	SUMMATED
ADELMOSZ	DAMOZELS	ADEMNNNU	UNMANNED
ADELMOTU	MODULATE	ADEMNNOU	UNMOANED
ADELMPRT	TRAMPLED	ADEMNNRU	MUNDANER
ADELMRRU	DEMURRAL		UNDERMAN
ADELMSUY	AMUSEDLY	ADEMNOOR	MAROONED
ADELMTUU	UMLAUTED	ADEMNOPR	POMANDER
ADELNNNU	UNNANELD	ADEMNOPT	TAMPONED
ADELNOPR	PONDERAL	ADEMNORS	RANSOMED
ADELNORS	LADRONES		ROADSMEN
	SOLANDER	ADEMNOTU	AMOUNTED
ADELNORU	UNLOADER		OUTNAMED
	URODELAN	ADEMNPSS	DAMPNESS
ADELNORV	OVERLAND	ADEMNRRU	UNDERARM
	RONDAVEL		UNMARRED
ADELNOSY	YEALDONS	ADEMNRSU	DURAMENS
ADELNPRS	SPANDREL		MAUNDERS
ADELNPRU	PENDULAR		SURNAMED
	UNDERLAP	ADEMNRTU	UNDREAMT
	UPLANDER	ADEMNRUW	UNWARMED
ADELNPRY	PANDERLY	ADEMNSSU	MEDUSANS
ADELNPSY	DYSPNEAL	ADEMNSUU	UNAMUSED
ADELNRSS	SLANDERS	ADEMOORT	MODERATO
ADELNRSU	LAUNDERS	ADEMOOST	STOMODEA
	LURDANES	ADEMOOSV	VAMOOSED
	RUNDALES	ADEMOPST	STAMPEDO
ADELNRTY	ARDENTLY	ADEMORRT	MORTARED
ADELNRUY	UNDERLAY	ADEMORRU	ARMOURED

ADEMORRW	MARROWED	ADEOPPRV	APPROVED
ADEMORST	STROAMED	ADEOPRRS	EARDROPS
ADEMPRST	STRAMPED	ADEOPRRT	PARROTED
ADEMRRSU	EARDRUMS		PREDATOR
ADEMRRTY	MARTYRED		PRORATED
ADENNNTU	UNTANNED	ADEOPRRU	UPROARED
ADENNOSY	ANODYNES	ADEOPRST	ADOPTERS
ADENNOTU	UNATONED		ASPORTED
ADENNOTW	WANTONED		READOPTS
ADENNPST	PENDANTS	ADEOPRTT	TETRAPOD
ADENNRRU	UNDERRAN	ADEOPRUV	VAPOURED
ADENNRTY	TYRANNED	ADEOPSST	PODESTAS
ADENNRUW	UNWARNED	ADEOPSTT	DESPOTAT
ADENNSTU	ASTUNNED		POSTDATE
ADENNTUW	UNWANTED	ADEORRSS	DROSERAS
ADENOOPS	EPANODOS	ADEORRST	ROADSTER
ADENOORT	RATOONED	ADEORRTW	TARROWED
ADENOORW	WANDEROO	ADEORRVW	OVERDRAW
ADENOPRR	PARDONER	ADEORSST	ASSORTED
ADENOPRS	OPERANDS		TORSADES
	PANDORES	ADEORSTU	OUTDARES
ADENOPRT	PRONATED	ADEORSTX	EXTRADOS
ADENOPRX	EXPANDOR	ADEORSUV	SAVOURED
ADENOPSS	DAPSONES	ADEORSWY	RODEWAYS
	SPADONES	ADEORTTU	OUTRATED
ADENOPSU	UNSOAPED	ADEOSSTT	ASSOTTED
ADENOPSY	DYSPNOEA	ADEOSTTU	OUTDATES
ADENORRW	NARROWED	ADEOTTTW	TATTOWED
ADENORST	TORNADES	ADEPPRST	STRAPPED
ADENORTT	ATTORNED	ADEPRRTU	RAPTURED
ADENORTY	AROYNTED	ADEPRSTU	PASTURED
ADENORUX	RONDEAUX		UPSTARED
ADENOSST	ONSTEADS	ADEPSTUY	UPSTAYED
ADENOTUY	AUTODYNE	ADEPSUWY	UPSWAYED
ADENOUVW	UNAVOWED	ADEQSTTU	SQUATTED
ADENPPRS	PARPENDS	ADERRSSW	WARDRESS
ADENPPSU	UNSAPPED	ADERRSST	REDSTART
ADENPPTU	UNTAPPED	ADERRSSU	ASSUREDS
ADENPRRS	PARDNERS	ADERSSTW	STEWARDS
ADENPRSU	UNSPARED	ADERSSUY	DASYURES
ADENPRTU	DEPURANT	ADERSTTU	STATURED
ADENPRTY	PEDANTRY	ADERSTUX	SURTAXED
ADENPRUW	UNWARPED	ADERSTWW	WESTWARD
ADENPRUY	UNDERPAY	ADESSTTW	WADSETTS
	UNPRAYED	ADFFGIIR	GIRAFFID
ADENPSSY	DYSPNEAS	ADFFGINS	DAFFINGS
ADENQRSU	SQUANDER	ADFFHIRS	DRAFFISH
ADENRRSY	REYNARDS	ADFFISST	DISTAFFS
ADENRRTU	UNTARRED	ADFFLOOS	OFFLOADS
ADENRRWY	WARDENRY	ADFFLRUU	FRAUDFUL
ADENRSSS	SARSDENS	ADFFOORS	AFFOORDS
ADENRSST	STANDERS	ADFGINNU	UNFADING
ADENRSSU	DANSEURS	ADFGINRS	FARDINGS
ADENRSTU	DAUNTERS	ADFGINRT	DRAFTING
	TRANSUDE	ADFGINRW	DWARFING
	UNTREADS	ADFHIOST	TOADFISH
ADENRSTX	DEXTRANS	ADFHIRSW	DWARFISH
ADENRSUY	UNDERSAY	ADFHLNSU	HANDFULS
ADENRTTU	TRUANTED	ADFHLOST	HOLDFAST
ADENRTTY	TYRANTED	ADFHOOSS	SHADOOFS
ADENRUWY	UNDERWAY	ADFIILPY	LAPIDIFY
ADENSTTU	UNSTATED	ADFILLLN	LANDFILL
	UNTASTED	ADFILLMN	FILMLAND
ADENSTUW	UNWASTED	ADFILLNW	WINDFALL
ADENSTUY	UNSTAYED	ADFILMNO	MANIFOLD
	UNSTEADY	ADFIMNRS	FINDRAMS
ADENSUWY	UNSWAYED	ADFIMORY	FAIRYDOM
ADEOOPSS	APODOSES	ADFIMRSW	DWARFISM
ADEOORRT	TOREADOR	ADFINORZ	FORZANDI
ADEOOTTT	TATTOOED	ADFINRST	INDRAFTS

ADFIORSV	DISFAVOR	ADGILLNY	DALLYING
ADFKLLNO	FOLKLAND	ADGILMNS	MADLINGS
ADFLLNOW	DOWNFALL	ADGILMNW	DWALMING
ADFLMNOR	LANDFORM	ADGILMOR	MARIGOLD
ADFLMNOY	MANYFOLD	ADGILNNS	LANDINGS
ADFLMOPR	FRAMPOLD		SANDLING
ADFLNOPS	PLAFONDS	ADGILNNU	UNLADING
ADFLOOWY	FLOODWAY	ADGILNOS	LOADINGS
ADFLORSU	FOULARDS	ADGILNPP	DAPPLING
ADFNNOST	FONDANTS	ADGILNRS	DARLINGS
ADFNOORZ	FORZANDO	ADGILNRT	DARTLING
ADFOOPST	FOOTPADS	ADGILNRW	DRAWLING
ADFORRSW	FORWARDS	ADGILNRY	DARINGLY
	FROWARDS	ADGILNZZ	DAZZLING
ADGGGILN	DAGGLING	ADGILOPR	PRODIGAL
ADGGGINR	DRAGGING	ADGILORS	GOLIARDS
ADGGHNOS	HANGDOGS	ADGILORY	GOLIARDY
ADGGILNN	DANGLING		GYROIDAL
ADGGILNS	GADLINGS	ADGIMMNR	DRAMMING
ADGGILRS	RIGGALDS	ADGIMMNW	DWAMMING
ADGGINRS	NIGGARDS	ADGIMMNU	MAUNDING
ADGGINRU	GUARDING	ADGIMNOP	POMADING
ADGGLRSU	SLUGGARD	ADGIMNPS	DAMPINGS
ADGHHILN	HIGHLAND	ADGIMNRS	MRIDANGS
ADGHHIOR	HIGHROAD	ADGIMNRY	MARDYING
ADGHILNN	HANDLING	ADGIMNUW	DWAUMING
ADGHILOS	HIDALGOS	ADGIMOSU	DIGAMOUS
ADGHILPY	DIAGLYPH	ADGINNOR	ADORNING
ADGHILTY	DAYLIGHT	ADGINNOT	DONATING
ADGHINOR	HOARDING	ADGINNPY	PANDYING
ADGHINPR	HANDGRIP	ADGINNRS	DARNINGS
ADGHINSS	SHADINGS	ADGINNRT	DRANTING
ADGHIPRS	DIGRAPHS	ADGINNSS	SANDINGS
ADGHIRRS	ARDRIGHS	ADGINNST	STANDING
ADGHITTW	TIGHTWAD	ADGINNSW	DAWNINGS
ADGHLNNO	LONGHAND	ADGINNSY	SDAYNING
ADGHNOSW	HAGDOWNS	ADGINNTU	DAUNTING
ADGHOOPR	ODOGRAPH	ADGINOOP	POIGNADO
ADGHORSW	HOGWARDS	ADGINOOR	RIGADOON
ADGHPSYY	DYSPHAGY	ADGINOPT	ADOPTING
ADGHRSTU	DRAUGHTS	ADGINORS	ROADINGS
ADGHRTUY	DRAUGHTY	ADGINOST	DOATINGS
ADGIILLN	DIALLING	ADGINOTY	TOADYING
ADGIILNO	GONIDIAL	ADGINPPR	DRAPPING
ADGIILNP	PLAIDING	ADGINPTU	UPDATING
ADGIILNR	DRAILING	ADGINRST	TRADINGS
ADGIILNS	GLIADINS	ADGINRSW	DRAWINGS
ADGIILNT	DILATING		SWARDING
ADGIILPY	PYGIDIAL		WARDINGS
ADGIILST	DIGITALS	ADGINRTY	TARDYING
ADGIILTY	ALGIDITY	ADGINSTU	ADUSTING
ADGIIMNR	ADMIRING		SUDATING
ADGIIMNX	ADMIXING	ADGINSWY	GWYNIADS
ADGIIMST	DIGAMIST	ADGIPRSU	PAGURIDS
ADGIINNR	DRAINING	ADGIRSSU	GUISARDS
ADGIINNS	SDAINING	ADGIRSZZ	GIZZARDS
ADGIINNV	INVADING	ADGKOOSZ	GADZOOKS
ADGIINNY	DIGYNIAN	ADGLLNOS	GOLLANDS
ADGIINOR	RADIOING	ADGLMNOS	MANGOLDS
ADGIINOV	AVOIDING	ADGLNOOS	GONDOLAS
ADGIINRR	ARRIDING	ADGLNOSW	GOWLANDS
ADGIINRY	DAIRYING	ADGLOORY	GARDYLOO
ADGIINSU	IGUANIDS	ADGMNORS	GORMANDS
ADGIINSV	ADVISING	ADGMNORU	GOURMAND
ADGIINSW	GWINIADS	ADGNNOQU	QUANDONG
ADGIINTU	AUDITING	ADGNNORS	GRANDSON
ADGIJNRU	ADJURING	ADGNNRYY	GYNANDRY
ADGIKLNR	DARKLING	ADGNOORS	DRAGOONS
ADGILLNU	ALLUDING		GADROONS
		ADGNRRSU	GURNARDS

ADGNRSUU	UNGUARDS		INDUVIAL	ADILNOOV	VINDALOO	ADINOPRS	PONIARDS
ADGOOPRS	GOSPODAR	ADIILOPP	DIPLOPIA	ADILNOPY	PALINODY	ADINOPST	PINTADOS
ADGORTUU	OUTGUARD	ADIILSST	DIALISTS	ADILNORS	ORDINALS	ADINORRS	ORDINARS
ADHHIPRS	HARDSHIP	ADIILSSY	DIALYSIS	ADILNOTY	NODALITY	ADINORRY	ORDINARY
ADHHNRTY	HYDRANTH	ADIILTVY	VALIDITY	ADILNPRS	SPANDRIL	ADINORST	INTRADOS
ADHIIKSS	DASHIKIS	ADIIMMSS	MAIDISMS	ADILNPST	DISPLANT	ADINORSU	DINOSAUR
ADHIINOP	OPHIDIAN	ADIIMPSU	ASPIDIUM	ADILNRSU	DIURNALS	ADINORSV	VIRANDOS
ADHIINRW	WHINIARD	ADIIMRSU	MUDIRIAS	ADILNRWY	INWARDLY	ADINORTU	DURATION
ADHILLMO	HOLLIDAM	ADIINNOT	NIDATION	ADILNSSU	SUNDIALS	ADINOSTU	SUDATION
ADHILLOP	PHALLOID	ADIINOTU	AUDITION	ADILNSSW	WINDLASS	ADINOSTX	OXIDANTS
ADHILLOT	THALLOID	ADIINPRS	PINDARIS	ADILOORT	TOROIDAL	ADINRRST	TRIDARNS
ADHILMOO	HOMALOID	ADIINRST	DISTRAIN	ADILOPRT	TRIPODAL	ADINRSSU	SUNDARIS
ADHILMOS	HALIDOMS	ADIINSST	DISTAINS	ADILOPSS	DISPOSAL	ADINRUVZ	UNVIZARD
ADHILNST	HANDLIST	ADIIOPRS	SPORIDIA	ADILOQSU	SQUALOID	ADIOOPSS	APODOSIS
ADHILOPY	HAPLOIDY	ADIIOPRT	TAPIROID	ADILORST	DILATORS	ADIOPRSS	SPAROIDS
ADHILOSY	HOLIDAYS	ADIIORST	TARSIOID	ADILORSY	SOLIDARY	ADIOPRST	PARODIST
ADHILPSY	LADYSHIP	ADIIPRTU	TRIPUDIA	ADILORTY	ADROITLY		PAROTIDS
ADHIMNOS	ADMONISH	ADIIPRTY	RAPIDITY		DILATORY	ADIOPRSV	PRIVADOS
ADHIMNOU	HUMANOID	ADIIPSTY	SAPIDITY		IDOLATRY	ADIOPRTY	PODIATRY
ADHIMOPP	AMPHIPOD	ADIIPTVY	VAPIDITY	ADILOSTW	WILDOATS	ADIOPSTY	DYSTOPIA
ADHIMPSS	PHASMIDS	ADIIRSST	DIARISTS	ADILOSTY	SODALITY	ADIORRTT	TRADITOR
ADHIMRTY	MYRIADTH	ADIIRSTT	DISTRAIT	ADILPPSY	DISAPPLY	ADIORSST	ASTROIDS
ADHINPSU	DAUPHINS		TRIADIST	ADILPRSY	PYRALIDS	ADIORSSV	ADVISORS
ADHINRWY	WHINYARD	ADIJNOST	ADJOINTS	ADILPSST	PLASTIDS	ADIORSTT	STRADIOT
ADHINSST	STANDISH	ADIKKRRW	KIRKWARD	ADILPSSY	DISPLAYS	ADIORSTU	AUDITORS
ADHINSSY	SANDYISH	ADIKKRRY	KIRKYARD	ADILPSTU	PLAUDITS	ADIORSVY	ADVISORY
ADHINSTU	DIANTHUS	ADIKLNPS	LANDSKIP	ADILRTWY	TAWDRILY	ADIORTUY	AUDITORY
ADHIOSTY	TOADYISH	ADIKLNSY	LADYKINS	ADILRWYZ	WIZARDLY	ADIOSSVW	DISAVOWS
ADHIPRSW	WARDSHIP	ADIKLOSS	ODALISKS	ADILSSTU	DUALISTS	ADIPRRTU	PURTRAID
ADHIPRSY	SHIPYARD	ADIKMNNS	MANKINDS	ADIMMNOO	AMMONOID	ADIPRSST	DISPARTS
ADHIPSTY	DISPATHY	ADIKMSSS	DISMASKS	ADIMMNOS	MONADISM	ADIRRWYZ	WIZARDRY
ADHIRTWW	WITHDRAW	ADIKNNNU	DUNNAKIN		NOMADISM	ADIRSSTY	SATYRIDS
ADHKNORW	HANDWORK	ADIKNNST	INKSTAND	ADIMMNSY	DYNAMISM	ADIRSSUY	DYSURIAS
ADHKORSW	DORHAWKS	ADIKNPSS	SKIDPANS	ADIMMOST	AMIDMOST	ADJNORSU	ADJOURNS
ADHKOSSU	SHAKUDOS	ADIKNRSS	DISRANKS	ADIMMOTU	DOMATIUM	ADJORSTU	ADJUSTOR
ADHLLNOS	HOLLANDS	ADIKNRST	STINKARD	ADIMNNOS	MONDAINS	ADKKLOSY	KAKODYLS
ADHLMORT	THRALDOM	ADIKPRSS	DISPARKS	ADIMNNOT	DOMINANT	ADKLMRSU	MUDLARKS
ADHLMOSY	HOLYDAMS	ADILLLPY	PALLIDLY	ADIMNOOR	MAINDOOR	ADKLOORW	WORKLOAD
ADHLMPSY	LYMPHADS	ADILLMMS	MILLDAMS	ADIMNOST	DONATISM	ADKMOORR	DARKROOM
ADHLNORW	WALDHORN	ADILLMNR	MANDRILL		SAINTDOM	ADKNORTU	OUTDRANK
ADHMNOOS	MANHOODS	ADILLMOU	ALLODIUM	ADIMNRSW	MISDRAWN	ADKNRSTU	STUNKARD
ADHNNOOR	HONORAND	ADILLMOV	VILLADOM	ADIMNRSY	MISANDRY	ADKRSSWY	SKYWARDS
ADHNORSU	UNHOARDS	ADILLMSY	DISMALLY	ADIMNSTY	DYNAMIST	ADLLMOSW	WADMOLLS
ADHNOSTU	HANDOUTS	ADILLNPS	LANDSLIP	ADIMOPRY	MYRIAPOD	ADLLNOSW	LOWLANDS
	THOUSAND	ADILLOPS	SPADILLO	ADIMOPSY	SYMPODIA	ADLLOPRS	POLLARDS
ADHNOSUW	UNSHADOW	ADILLOSW	DISALLOW	ADIMORRS	MIRADORS	ADLLORSY	DORSALLY
ADHNRSTY	HYDRANTS	ADILLOSY	DISLOYAL	ADIMOSST	MASTOIDS	ADLMNOOR	MOORLAND
ADHOOPRS	HOSPODAR	ADILLRWY	WILLYARD	ADIMOSTT	MATTOIDS	ADLMNORY	RANDOMLY
ADHOORRS	RHODORAS	ADILLSTY	DISTALLY	ADIMOSTY	TOADYISM	ADLMNOSS	MOSSLAND
ADHOORSW	ROADSHOW	ADILMMOS	MODALISM	ADIMPRSY	PYRAMIDS	ADLMOORU	MALODOUR
ADHOORYZ	HYDROZOA	ADILMNNO	MANDOLIN	ADIMRSSW	MISDRAWS	ADLMOPRW	MOLDWARP
ADHOPRST	HARDTOPS	ADILMNOS	SALMONID	ADIMRSUU	SUDARIUM	ADLMOPSY	PSALMODY
ADHOPRSU	UPHOARDS	ADILMNRS	MANDRILS	ADIMSSST	DISMASTS	ADLNNORS	NORLANDS
ADHOPRSY	RHAPSODY	ADILMOOR	MODIOLAR	ADIMSSTU	DUMAISTS	ADLNNOTW	TOWNLAND
ADHORSTU	TOADRUSH	ADILMOPS	DIPLOMAS		STADIUMS	ADLNNTUU	UNDULANT
ADHPSTYY	DYSPATHY	ADILMOPT	DIPLOMAT	ADINNNTU	INUNDANT	ADLNOORS	LARDOONS
ADIIINRV	VIRIDIAN	ADILMOPY	OLYMPIAD	ADINNOOT	DONATION	ADLNOPRT	PORTLAND
ADIIIQRU	DAIQUIRI	ADILMORU	ORDALIUM		NODATION	ADLNOPRU	PAULDRON
ADIIKLMM	MILKMAID	ADILMOST	MODALIST	ADINNOPS	DIPNOANS	ADLNOPSU	POUNDALS
ADIIKLST	TAILSKID	ADILMOSU	ALODIUMS	ADINNORS	ANDIRONS	ADLNORWY	ONWARDLY
ADIIKNOP	PINAKOID	ADILMOSY	AMYLOIDS	ADINNORT	ORDINANT	ADLNOSSU	SOULDANS
ADIIKOST	DAKOITIS	ADILMOTY	MODALITY	ADINNOTU	NUDATION	ADLNOSSY	SYNODALS
ADIILLMR	MILLIARD	ADILMPSS	PLASMIDS	ADINNRSY	INNYARDS	ADLNOSTU	OUTLANDS
ADIILLNY	IDYLLIAN	ADILMPSU	PALUDISM	ADINOOPS	ISOPODAN	ADLOORWW	WOOLWARD
ADIILLUV	DILUVIAL	ADILMSSU	DUALISMS		POINADOS	ADLOPRSU	POULARDS
ADIILNOT	DILATION	ADILMSSY	DISMAYLS	ADINOOPT	ADOPTION	ADLOPSUU	PALUDOUS
ADIILNSU	INDUSIAL		LADYISMS	ADINOORT	TANDOORI	ADLOQSUW	OLDSQUAW
ADIILNSV	INVALIDS	ADILNNNU	NUNDINAL	ADINOOTT	DOTATION	ADLORRSW	WARLORDS
ADIILNTY	DAINTILY	ADILNNSU	DISANNUL	ADINOPPS	OPPIDANS	ADLORTWY	TOWARDLY
ADIILNUV	DILUVIAN	ADILNOOR	DOORNAIL	ADINOPRR	RAINDROP	ADLPRUWY	UPWARDLY

ADMMNOOS	DOOMSMAN		RENEGATE	AEEFIPSW	SPAEWIFE
ADMMNSSU	SUMMANDS		TEENAGER	AEEFIRRS	RAREFIES
ADMMNTUU	MUTANDUM	AEEEGPRS	PEERAGES	AEEFIRSS	FREESIAS
ADMNNORY	MONANDRY	AEEEGPSS	SEEPAGES	AEEFISST	SAFETIES
ADMNNOTU	NOTANDUM	AEEEGRST	ETAGERES	AEEFKMNT	FAKEMENT
ADMNOOOT	ODONTOMA		STEERAGE	AEEFKOPR	FOREPEAK
ADMNOORS	MADRONOS	AEEEGRSW	SEWERAGE	AEEFLLMR	FEMERALL
ADMNOOST	MASTODON	AEEEGTTV	VEGETATE	AEEFLLMT	FLAMELET
ADMNOOSW	WOODSMAN	AEEEHLRT	ETHEREAL	AEEFLLNV	EVENFALL
ADMNOOSZ	MADZOONS	AEEEHMPR	EPHEMERA	AEEFLLRW	FAREWELL
ADMNORST	DORMANTS	AEEEHNRS	ENHEARSE	AEEFLLSS	LEAFLESS
	MORDANTS	AEEEHRRS	REHEARSE	AEEFLLST	FELLATES
ADMNORSW	SWORDMAN	AEEEHRRT	REHEATER		LEAFLETS
ADMNOSSU	OSMUNDAS	AEEEHSTT	AESTHETE	AEEFLMOS	FLEASOME
ADMOORST	DOORMATS	AEEEILNS	ALIENEES	AEEFLMSS	FAMELESS
ADMOPPPU	POPPADUM	AEEEIMNX	EXAMINEE	AEEFLNRU	FUNEREAL
ADMOPPSU	POPADUMS	AEEEIRST	EATERIES	AEEFLORV	OVERLEAF
ADMORSST	STARDOMS	AEEEJNTT	JEANETTE	AEEFLRRR	REFERRAL
	TSARDOMS	AEEEKKPS	KEEPSAKE	AEEFLRSS	FEARLESS
ADMORSTW	MADWORTS	AEEEKMSS	KAMEESES	AEEFLRST	REFLATES
ADMRSSTU	DURMASTS	AEEEKMSZ	KAMEEZES	AEEFLRSW	WELFARES
	MUSTARDS	AEEEKNRW	WEAKENER	AEEFMNOR	FOREMEAN
ADNNOOSY	NOONDAYS	AEEELLST	TELESALE		FORENAME
ADNNORTY	DYNATRON	AEEELNRV	VENEREAL	AEEFMNRS	ENFRAMES
ADNNOSTU	DAUNTONS	AEEELNST	SELENATE	AEEFMORS	FEARSOME
ADNOOPRS	PANDOORS	AEEELPRR	REPEALER	AEEFMRRS	REFRAMES
	SPADROON	AEEELQSU	SEQUELAE	AEEFMRTY	FEMETARY
ADNOOQRU	QUADROON	AEEELRRS	RELEASER	AEEFNRST	FASTENER
ADNOORST	DONATORS	AEEELRRV	REVEALER		FENESTRA
ADNOORTY	DONATORY	AEEELRSS	RELEASES	AEEFNRTT	FATTENER
ADNOOSVW	ADVOWSON	AEEELRST	TEASELER	AEEFNSSS	SAFENESS
ADNOPRSU	PANDOURS	AEEELRSW	WEASELER	AEEFOSTU	FEATEOUS
ADNOPRSV	PROVANDS	AEEELSTV	ELEVATES	AEEFRRST	FERRATES
ADNOQRSU	SQUADRON	AEEEMMRT	METAMERE	AEEFRSST	FEASTERS
ADNORRSW	NORWARDS	AEEEMNST	EASEMENT	AEEFRSTU	FEATURES
ADNORSTU	ROTUNDAS	AEEEMPRS	PERMEASE	AEEFRSWY	FREEWAYS
ADNORSTW	SANDWORT	AEEEMPRT	PERMEATE	AEEFTTUV	FAUVETTE
ADNORSWY	NAYWORDS	AEEENNRV	VENEREAN	AEEGGHIW	WEIGHAGE
ADNORSXY	SARDONYX	AEEENPTT	PATENTEE	AEEGGINR	AGREEING
ADNORTUW	UNTOWARD	AEEENRST	SERENATE	AEEGGIRV	AGGRIEVE
ADNORWWY	WANWORDY	AEEENRTT	ENTERATE	AEEGGLLS	ALLEGGES
ADNOSSTU	ASTOUNDS	AEEENRTV	ENERVATE	AEEGGLOU	AEGLOGUE
ADNOSTTU	OUTSTAND		VENERATE	AEEGGLRS	GREGALES
ADNPSSTU	UPSTANDS	AEEEPRRT	REPARTEE	AEEGGNNR	GANGRENE
ADNRSSUW	SUNWARDS		REPEATER	AEEGGNOS	GASOGENE
ADOOPRSU	SAUROPOD	AEEEPSTW	SWEETPEA	AEEGGNOZ	GAZOGENE
ADOOPSSW	SAPWOODS	AEEERRST	ARRESTEE	AEEGGNRS	ENGAGERS
ADOORSWY	DOORWAYS	AEEERSST	TESSERAE	AEEGGOPS	EPAGOGES
ADOPRRSW	WARDROPS	AEEFFLLS	FELAFELS	AEEGGPRU	PUGGAREE
ADOPRSSW	PASSWORD	AEEFFLRT	TAFFEREL	AEEGHIRT	HERITAGE
ADORRSTU	DARTROUS	AEEFFNRT	AFFERENT	AEEGHLOT	HELOTAGE
ADORSTUW	OUTWARDS	AEEFGILR	FILAGREE	AEEGHLRW	RAGWHEEL
ADORSTUY	SUDATORY	AEEFGIRR	FERRIAGE	AEEGHMPR	GRAPHEME
ADORTUVY	ADVOUTRY	AEEFGIRS	FEGARIES	AEEGHNRS	SHAGREEN
ADPRRTUY	PURTRAYD	AEEFGLSU	FUSELAGE	AEEGHNSW	WHANGEES
ADSSSTUW	SAWDUSTS	AEEFGNST	FANTEEGS	AEEGHRRT	GATHERER
ADSSTUWY	SAWDUSTY	AEEFGRSS	SERFAGES		REGATHER
AEEEELRS	RELEASEE	AEEFGSTW	WEFTAGES	AEEGIINR	AEGIRINE
AEEEFLRS	EELFARES	AEEFHIRS	SHEAFIER	AEEGIIRT	AEGIRITE
AEEEFRTY	AFTEREYE	AEEFHRST	FEATHERS	AEEGIIST	GAIETIES
AEEEGKLS	KEELAGES	AEEFHRTY	FEATHERY	AEEGILLS	GALILEES
AEEEGLLS	LEGALESE	AEEFIINR	INFERIAE		LEGALISE
AEEEGLNR	GENERALE	AEEFIKRR	FREAKIER	AEEGILLZ	LEGALIZE
AEEEGLRT	EGLATERE	AEEFIKRS	FAKERIES	AEEGILMN	LIEGEMAN
	REGELATE	AEEFIKRW	WAKERIFE	AEEGILMR	GLEAMIER
	RELEGATE	AEEFILNR	FLANERIE	AEEGILMS	MILEAGES
AEEEGLRV	LEVERAGE	AEEFILRS	SERAFILE	AEEGILNR	ALGERINE
AEEEGLST	LEGATEES	AEEFILRT	FRAILTEE	AEEGILNS	ENSILAGE
AEEEGLSV	SELVAGEE	AEEFILST	FEALTIES		LINEAGES
AEEEGNRT	GENERATE		LEAFIEST	AEEGILNT	GALENITE

	GELATINE		
	LEGATINE		
AEEGILNV	INVEAGLE		
AEEGILPR	PERIGEAL		
AEEGILRS	GASELIER		
AEEGILST	ELEGIAST		
AEEGILSW	WEIGELAS		
AEEGILTV	LEVIGATE		
AEEGIMNR	GERMAINE		
AEEGIMNT	GEMINATE		
AEEGIMRS	GAMESIER		
AEEGIMRT	EMIGRATE		
	REMIGATE		
AEEGINPR	PERIGEAN		
AEEGINRR	REGAINER		
AEEGINRS	GESNERIA		
AEEGINRZ	RAZEEING		
AEEGINSS	ASSIGNEE		
AEEGINST	SAGENITE		
AEEGINSV	ENVISAGE		
AEEGINTV	NEGATIVE		
AEEGINTX	EXIGEANT		
AEEGIPQU	EQUIPAGE		
AEEGIPRS	PIERAGES		
AEEGIRRS	GREASIER		
AEEGIRTT	AIGRETTE		
AEEGISSS	ASSIEGES		
AEEGLLNR	ALLERGEN		
AEEGLLRS	ALLEGERS		
AEEGLLSZ	GAZELLES		
AEEGLMNS	MELANGES		
AEEGLMNV	GAVELMEN		
AEEGLMRT	TELEGRAM		
AEEGLMRY	MEAGRELY		
AEEGLNNR	ENLARGEN		
AEEGLNNT	ENTANGLE		
AEEGLNOS	GASOLENE		
AEEGLNOT	ELONGATE		
AEEGLNRR	ENLARGER		
AEEGLNRS	ENLARGES		
	GENERALS		
	GLEANERS		
AEEGLNSV	EVANGELS		
AEEGLNVY	EVANGELY		
AEEGLOST	SEGOLATE		
AEEGLPRS	PEREGALS		
AEEGLRSS	EELGRASS		
	GEARLESS		
	LARGESSE		
AEEGLRSU	LEAGUERS		
AEEGLRTU	REGULATE		
AEEGLRUX	EXERGUAL		
AEEGLSST	GATELESS		
AEEGLSSV	SELVAGES		
AEEGLSSW	WAGELESS		
AEEGLSSY	EYEGLASS		
AEEGLSTV	VEGETALS		
AEEGLTTU	TUTELAGE		
AEEGLTUV	EVULGATE		
AEEGMMOS	GAMESOME		
AEEGMMST	GEMMATES		
	TAGMEMES		
AEEGMNOR	ARGEMONE		
AEEGMNRS	AGREMENS		
AEEGMNRT	AGREMENT		
AEEGMNSS	GAMENESS		
	MAGNESES		
AEEGMNTZ	GAZEMENT		
AEEGMOST	SOMEGATE		
AEEGMRST	GAMESTER		

	MEAGREST	AEEHIPTT HEPATITE	AEEHNSST ANTHESES	AEEILQSU EQUALISE
AEEGMRSU	REMUAGES	AEEHIPTZ APHETIZE	AEEHNSTU UNEATHES	AEEILQUX EXEQUIAL
AEEGMSSS	MEGASSES	HEPATIZE	AEEHNSTW ENSWATHE	AEEILQUZ EQUALIZE
	MESSAGES	AEEHIRRS HEARSIER	AEEHORRV OVERHEAR	AEEILRRS REALISER
AEEGMSSU	MESSUAGE	AEEHIRRT EARTHIER	AEEHORSS SEAHORSE	AEEILRRT RETAILER
AEEGNNNO	ENNEAGON	HEARTIER	SEASHORE	AEEILRRZ REALIZER
AEEGNNPS	PANGENES	AEEHIRSS ASHERIES	AEEHORTV OVERHEAT	AEEILRSS REALISES
AEEGNNRS	ENRANGES	AEEHIRST HEARTIES	AEEHPRRS REPHRASE	AEEILRST ATELIERS
AEEGNNRT	GENERANT	AEEHIRSV SHIVAREE	AEEHPRSS RESHAPES	EARLIEST
AEEGNNRU	ENRAUNGE	AEEHISST ATHEISES	SPHAERES	LEARIEST
AEEGNNRV	ENGRAVEN	ESTHESIA	SPHEARES	REALTIES
AEEGNOPS	PEONAGES	AEEHISTT ATHETISE	AEEHPRST PREHEATS	AEEILRSV VELARISE
AEEGNPPS	GENAPPES	HESITATE	SPREATHE	AEEILRSY YEARLIES
AEEGNRRT	ETRANGER	AEEHISTV HEAVIEST	AEEHPSUV UPHEAVES	AEEILRSZ REALIZES
AEEGNRRV	ENGRAVER	AEEHISTZ ATHEIZES	AEEHQSSU QUASHEES	SLEAZIER
AEEGNRST	ESTRANGE	AEEHITTZ ATHETIZE	AEEHRRSS SHEARERS	AEEILRTT LATERITE
	GRANTEES	AEEHKLLR RAKEHELL	AEEHRRTU URETHRAE	LITERATE
	GREATENS	AEEHKLLU KEELHAUL	AEEHRRTW WREATHER	AEEILRTV LEVIRATE
	REAGENTS	AEEHKNRS HEARKENS	AEEHRSTT THEATERS	RELATIVE
	SEGREANT	AEEHKRSU HEUREKAS	THEATRES	AEEILRVW LIVEWARE
	SERGEANT	AEEHLLSS SEASHELL	AEEHRSTV THREAVES	REVIEWAL
	STERNAGE	AEEHLMNW WHEELMAN	AEEHRSTW WEATHERS	AEEILRVZ VELARIZE
AEEGNRSU	RENAGUES	AEEHLMNY HYMENEAL	WREATHES	AEEILSST ASTELIES
AEEGNRSV	AVENGERS	AEEHLMOS HEALSOME	AEEHRTVW WHATEVER	AEEILSTT AILETTES
	ENGRAVES	AEEHLMPT HELPMATE	AEEIIMRT METAIRIE	AEEILSTV ELATIVES
AEEGNRTU	GAUNTREE	AEEHLNOS ENHALOES	AEEIISST ASEITIES	LEAVIEST
AEEGNSSS	SAGENESS	AEEHLNPT ELEPHANT	AEEIKKLW LIKEWAKE	VEALIEST
AEEGNSTT	TENTAGES	AEEHLNRT LEATHERN	AEEIKLRW WEAKLIER	AEEILSVW ALEWIVES
AEEGNSTV	VENTAGES	AEEHLNSS HALENESS	AEEIKLST LEAKIEST	AEEILTTV LEVITATE
AEEGNTTV	VEGETANT	AEEHLNVY HEAVENLY	AEEIKLVW WAVELIKE	AEEIMMNT MEANTIME
AEEGOPRV	OVERPAGE	AEEHLORS ARSEHOLE	AEEIKMMR MERIMAKE	AEEIMNRS REMANIES
AEEGOPSS	SAPEGOES	AEEHLORV OVERHALE	AEEIKNRS SNEAKIER	AEEIMNRX EXAMINER
AEEGORVV	OVERGAVE	AEEHLPST PLEASETH	AEEIKNRT ANKERITE	AEEIMNSS NEMESIAS
AEEGOSTX	GEOTAXES	AEEHLPTT TELEPATH	KREATINE	AEEIMNST MATINEES
AEEGPRRS	ASPERGER	AEEHLRST HALTERES	AEEIKNSS AKINESES	SEMINATE
	PRESAGER	LEATHERS	AEEIKPST PEAKIEST	AEEIMNSX EXAMINES
AEEGPRRT	PARGETER	AEEHLRSV HAVERELS	AEEIKRRS RAKERIES	AEEIMNUV MAUVEINE
AEEGPRSS	ASPERGES	AEEHLRTT HEARTLET	SKEARIER	AEEIMPRS EMPAIRES
	PRESAGES	AEEHLRTY LEATHERY	AEEILLNT TENAILLE	AEEIMRRS SMEARIER
AEEGRRRT	REGRATER	AEEHLSST HATELESS	AEEILLRS REALLIES	AEEIMRSS SERIEMAS
AEEGRRSS	GREASERS	AEEHLSTT ATHLETES	AEEILLST LEALTIES	AEEIMRST EMIRATES
AEEGRRST	REGRATES	AEEHLTTY ETHYLATE	AEEILMMN MELAMINE	REAMIEST
AEEGRRSW	WAGERERS	AEEHMMRR HAMMERER	AEEILMNT MELANITE	STEAMIER
AEEGRSST	RESTAGES	AEEHMNNY HYMENEAN	AEEILMRS ALMERIES	AEEIMRTV VIAMETER
AEEGRSTT	GREATEST	AEEHMNRS SHAREMEN	MEASLIER	AEEIMSSS MISEASES
AEEGRSTU	TREAGUES	SHEARMEN	AEEILMRT EREMITAL	SIAMESES
AEEGRSTW	STREWAGE	AEEHMNRT EARTHMEN	MATERIEL	AEEIMSST SEAMIEST
AEEGRSUZ	GUEREZAS	AEEHMNST METHANES	REALTIME	STEAMIES
AEEGSSTT	GESTATES	AEEHMNTX EXANTHEM	AEEILMST MEALIEST	AEEIMSSZ SIAMEZES
AEEGSTTZ	GAZETTES	AEEHMPSS EMPHASES	AEEILMSV MALVESIE	AEEIMSTT ESTIMATE
AEEHHHSS	HASHEESH	AEEHMRSS MAHSEERS	AEEILNPR PERINEAL	ETATISME
AEEHHIRT	HEATHIER	AEEHMRST ERATHEMS	AEEILNPS ALEPINES	MEATIEST
AEEHHNST	ENSHEATH	AEEHMRTY ERYTHEMA	PENALISE	TEATIMES
	HEATHENS	AEEHMSST MATHESES	SEPALINE	AEEIMSTW TEAMWISE
AEEHHOOP	PAHOEHOE	AEEHMTUX EXHUMATE	AEEILNPT PETALINE	AEEINNRS ANSERINE
AEEHHRSS	REHASHES	AEEHNNSS SNEESHAN	TAPELINE	AEEINOPS PAEONIES
AEEHHRST	HEATHERS	AEEHNNTX XANTHENE	AEEILNPZ PENALIZE	AEEINPRS NAPERIES
AEEHHRTY	HEATHERY	AEEHNOPR EARPHONE	AEEILNRT ELATERIN	AEEINPRT APERIENT
AEEHHSST	SHEATHES	AEEHNPST HEPTANES	ENTAILER	AEEINPTT PIANETTE
AEEHIKRS	SHIKAREE	PHENATES	TREENAIL	AEEINRRS REARISEN
AEEHILNP	ELAPHINE	STEPHANE	AEEILNTV ELVANITE	AEEINRRT RETAINER
AEEHILRS	SHIRALEE	AEEHNRSS ARSHEENS	VENTAILE	AEEINRSS SANARIES
AEEHILRT	ETHERIAL	AEEHNRST HASTENER	AEEILORT AEROLITE	AEEINRST ARSENITE
AEEHIMPT	EPITHEMA	HEARTENS	AEEILOTT ETIOLATE	RESINATE
AEEHIMTT	HEMATITE	AEEHNRSU UNHEARSE	AEEILPRR PEARLIER	STEARINE
AEEHINRS	INHEARSE	AEEHNRTT HATERENT	AEEILPRS ESPALIER	TRAINEES
AEEHINRT	ATHERINE	THREATEN	PEARLIES	AEEINRSU UNEASIER
AEEHIPST	APHETISE	AEEHNRTU URETHANE	AEEILPRT EPILATES	AEEINSSS EASINESS
	HEAPIEST	AEEHNRTW WREATHEN	AEEILPST EPILATES	AEEINSSV VAINESSE
	HEPATISE	AEEHNRWY ANYWHERE	AEEILPSW PALEWISE	AEEINSTT ANISETTE

```
         TETANIES       AEEKNPSU SNEAKEUP    AEELNRSW RENEWALS    AEEMNPRT PETERMAN
         TETANISE       AEEKNPSW NEWSPEAK    AEELNRTV LEVANTER    AEEMNPRY EMPYREAN
AEEINSTV NAIVETES       AEEKNRSS SNEAKERS             RELEVANT    AEEMNPTV PAVEMENT
AEEINSVW INWEAVES       AEEKNRSW WAKENERS    AEELNRTX EXTERNAL    AEEMNRST REMANETS
AEEINTTZ TETANIZE       AEEKNSSW WEAKNESS    AEELNSST LATENESS    AEEMNRSW MENSWEAR
AEEIOOPP EPOPOEIA       AEEKORRV OVERRAKE    AEELNSSV ENSLAVES    AEEMNRTU NUMERATE
AEEIORST ETAERIOS       AEEKORST KERATOSE             VANELESS    AEEMNRTV AVERMENT
AEEIPPSS APEPSIES                KREASOTE    AEELNSTY ENTAYLES    AEEMNRTW WATERMEN
AEEIPPST APPETISE       AEEKORTV OVERTAKE    AEELNTUV EVENTUAL    AEEMNRUV MANEUVER
AEEIPPSU EUPEPSIA                TAKEOVER    AEELNTVY VENTAYLE    AEEMNSSS SAMENESS
AEEIPPTT APPETITE       AEEKPRSS RESPEAKS    AEELOPRS PAROLEES    AEEMNSST TAMENESS
AEEIPPTZ APPETIZE       AEEKPRST PERTAKES    AEELOPRV OVERLEAP    AEEMNSTU MANSUETE
AEEIPRRR REPAIRER       AEEKQRSU SQUEAKER    AEELORRS RELEASOR    AEEMORST EROTEMAS
AEEIPRRS PEREIRAS       AEEKRRST RETAKERS    AEELORST OLEASTER    AEEMPPRR PAMPERER
         SPEARIER                STREAKER    AEELORSU AUREOLES    AEEMPRRT TAMPERER
AEEIPRST PETARIES       AEEKRRSW WREAKERS    AEELORTT TOLERATE    AEEMPRST TEMPERAS
AEEIPRTV PERVIATE       AEEKRSST SAKERETS    AEELORTV ELEVATOR    AEEMPRSY EMPAYRES
AEEIPSST EPITASES       AEELLLTT TELLTALE    AEELOSSW LEASOWES    AEEMPRTT ATTEMPER
AEEIPSTT PEATIEST       AEELLMMS MAMSELLE    AEELOTTT TEETOTAL    AEEMPSTU AMPUTEES
AEEIPSTX EXPIATES       AEELLNOV NOVELLAE    AEELPRRS PEARLERS    AEEMQRRU REMARQUE
AEEIQRSU QUEASIER       AEELLOSV ALVEOLES             RELAPSER    AEEMQRSU MARQUEES
AEEIQRUZ QUEAZIER       AEELLOTT ALLOTTEE    AEELPRRT PALTERER    AEEMQTTU MAQUETTE
AEEIQSTU EQUISETA       AEELLPRS PARELLES    AEELPRSS PLEASERS    AEEMRRST STREAMER
AEEIRRSS REARISES       AEELLPPT PLATELET             RELAPSES    AEEMRRSU MEASURER
AEEIRRST ARTERIES       AEELLRRT TERRELLA    AEELPRST PRELATES    AEEMRSST MASSETER
         REASTIER       AEELLSST SATELLES    AEELPRSU PLEASURE             SEAMSTER
AEEIRRTT RETRAITE                TESSELLA             SERPULAE             STEAMERS
AEEIRRTW WATERIER       AEELLSSZ ZEALLESS    AEELPRSV VESPERAL    AEEMRSSU REASSUME
AEEIRSST SERIATES       AEELLSTT STELLATE    AEELPRTY PTERYLAE    AEEMRSTT TEAMSTER
AEEIRSTT ARIETTES       AEELLSWY WEASELLY    AEELPSST SPATLESE    AEEMRSTY METAYERS
         ITERATES       AEELLTVV VALVELET             TAPELESS    AEEMSSSU MASSEUSE
         TEARIEST       AEELMMTU MALEMUTE    AEELPSTT PALETTES    AEEMSSTU MEATUSES
         TREATIES       AEELMNPS EMPANELS    AEELPSTU EPAULETS    AEEMSTTU AMUSETTE
         TREATISE                EMPLANES    AEELPSTV SEPTLEVA    AEENNOST NEONATES
AEEIRSTV EVIRATES                ENSAMPLE    AEELQRSU SQUEALER    AEENNPST PENTANES
AEEIRSTW SWEATIER       AEELMNPT PLATEMEN    AEELRRST RELATERS    AEENNRSS ENSNARES
         TAWERIES       AEELMNSS LAMENESS    AEELRRSV REVERSAL             NEARNESS
         WEARIEST                MANELESS             SLAVERER    AEENNRTU ENAUNTER
AEEIRSTY YEASTIER                NAMELESS    AEELRRTU URETERAL    AEENNRTV REVENANT
AEEIRSVV AVERSIVE                SALESMEN    AEELRSST STEALERS    AEENNRUX ANNEXURE
AEEISSTX EXTASIES       AEELMNST MANTEELS             TEARLESS    AEENNSSS SANENESS
AEEISTTT ETATISTE                TALESMEN             TESSERAL    AEENNSST NEATNESS
         STEATITE       AEELMNSW WEALSMEN    AEELRSSU LEASURES    AEENOPRS PERAEONS
AEEISTTV AVIETTES       AEELMNSY AMYLENES    AEELRSSV SEVERALS             PERSONAE
         ESTIVATE       AEELMNTT MANTELET    AEELRSSW WARELESS    AEENORRS REASONER
         EVITATES       AEELMNTV LAVEMENT    AEELRSTT ALERTEST    AEENORST SEASONER
AEEISTUX EUTAXIES       AEELMOTT MATELOTE    AEELRSTU RESALUTE             RESONATE
         EUTEXIAS       AEELMPRX EXEMPLAR    AEELRSTY EASTERLY    AEENORTV OVERNEAT
AEEITTUX EUTAXITE       AEELMPRY EMPYREAL    AEELRSUV REVALUES             RENOVATE
AEEITUVX EXUVIATE       AEELMPSX EXAMPLES    AEELRSVY AVERSELY    AEENORVW OVENWARE
AEEJLNPT JETPLANE       AEELMPTT PALMETTE    AEELSSST ALTESSES    AEENOTTU OUTEATEN
AEEJLOSU JEALOUSE                TEMPLATE             SATELESS    AEENPPTT APPETENT
AEEJNRST SERJEANT       AEELMRST LAMETERS             SEATLESS    AEENPQTU PETANQUE
AEEJOPRT PEJORATE       AEELMSSS SEAMLESS    AEELSSTU SETUALES    AEENPSSX EXPANSES
AEEKKLWY LYKEWAKE       AEELMSST MATELESS    AEELSSTV SALVETES    AEENRRRW WARRENER
AEEKKPSY KEEPSAKY                MEATLESS    AEELSSVW WAVELESS    AEENRRSS RARENESS
AEEKLLST LAKELETS                TAMELESS    AEELSTTY LAYETTES    AEENRRST TERRANES
         SKELETAL       AEELMSTU EMULATES    AEELSTVW WAVELETS    AEENRRSV RAVENERS
AEEKLMRT TELEMARK       AEELNNRT LANNERET    AEEMMNRS MERESMAN    AEENRRSW ANSWERER
AEEKLMSS MAKELESS       AEELNNSS LEANNESS    AEEMMNTZ MAZEMENT             REANSWER
AEEKLNST KANTELES       AEELNOPR PERONEAL    AEEMMPSY EMPYEMAS    AEENRRTV TAVERNER
AEEKLSSW WAKELESS       AEELNOPT ANTELOPE    AEEMMRST AMMETERS    AEENRSSS SEARNESS
AEEKLSTY EYESTALK       AEELNORU ALEURONE             METAMERS    AEENRSST ASSENTER
AEEKMNSS KAMSEENS       AEELNPPS SPALPEEN    AEEMMSST MESSMATE             EARNESTS
AEEKMRRR REMARKER       AEELNPSS PALENESS    AEEMNNOS ANEMONES             SARSENET
AEEKMRRT MARKETER       AEELNRRS LEARNERS    AEEMNNRT REMANENT    AEENRSSX XERANSES
AEEKMRST MEERKATS       AEELNRSS REALNESS    AEEMNNSS MEANNESS    AEENRSTT ENTREATS
AEEKNNNS NANKEENS       AEELNRST ALTERNES    AEEMNORV OVERNAME             RATTEENS
AEEKNORW REAWOKEN       AEELNRSV ENSLAVER    AEEMNORZ ARMOZEEN    AEENRSTV AVENTRES
AEEKNPRT PERTAKEN                            AEEMNPRS SPEARMEN
```

	VETERANS	AEESSSSS	ASSESSES	AEFHIKRS	FREAKISH	AEFILSTU	FISTULAE
AEENRSUV	UNREAVES	AEFFFLRS	FLAFFERS	AEFHIKSW	WEAKFISH	AEFILSTV	FESTIVAL
AEENRTTV	ANTEVERT	AEFFGIRS	GIRAFFES	AEFHILLN	FELLAHIN	AEFILSTW	FLATWISE
AEENRTTX	EXTERNAT	AEFFGNRS	ENGRAFFS	AEFHILOR	FORHAILE		FLAWIEST
AEENRTTY	ENTREATY	AEFFGRSU	SUFFRAGE	AEFHILOX	HEXAFOIL	AEFILSTX	FLAXIEST
AEENRTUV	AVENTURE	AEFFHIKY	KAFFIYEH	AEFHILRS	FLASHIER	AEFILTUU	FAUTEUIL
AEENSTTV	NAVETTES	AEFFILUV	EFFLUVIA	AEFHIMSS	FAMISHES	AEFIMMMR	MAMMIFER
AEENSUVW	UNWEAVES	AEFFIMRR	AFFIRMER	AEFHLMSU	SHAMEFUL	AEFIMNST	MANIFEST
AEEOPRRT	PATERERO		REAFFIRM	AEFHLORS	FAHLORES	AEFIMORR	AERIFORM
	PERORATE	AEFFIPRS	PIAFFERS	AEFHLRSS	FLASHERS	AEFIMORT	FORMIATE
AEEOPRST	OPERATES	AEFFKLRU	FREAKFUL	AEFHLRST	FARTHELS	AEFIMOST	FOAMIEST
	PROTEASE	AEFFKOST	OFFTAKES	AEFHLRTY	FATHERLY	AEFIMRRS	FIREARMS
AEEOPRTT	OPERETTA	AEFFLMSW	FLAMFEWS	AEFHLSST	FLASHEST	AEFIMRRW	FIRMWARE
AEEORRSU	REAROUSE	AEFFLNSS	SNAFFLES	AEFHMNRS	FRESHMAN	AEFIMRSS	MISFARES
AEEORRSW	SOWARREE	AEFFLNTU	AFFLUENT	AEFHNRSW	FERNSHAW	AEFINNSS	FAINNESS
AEEORRTV	OVERRATE	AEFFLRRS	RAFFLERS	AEFHRSST	SHAFTERS	AEFINNST	INFANTES
AEEORRVW	OVERWEAR	AEFFLSTU	FEASTFUL	AEFHRSTT	FARTHEST	AEFINNSZ	FANZINES
AEEORRVY	OVERYEAR		SUFFLATE	AEFIILMS	FAMILIES	AEFINOPR	PINAFORE
AEEORSSV	OVERSEAS	AEFFLSUX	AFFLUXES	AEFIILNS	FINALISE	AEFINORS	FARINOSE
AEEORSTV	OVEREATS	AEFFMRSU	EARMUFFS	AEFIILNZ	FINALIZE	AEFINPRS	FIREPANS
AEEORSVW	OVERAWES	AEFFNORT	AFFRONTE	AEFIILSS	SALIFIES	AEFINRRS	REFRAINS
AEEPPRRR	PREPARER	AEFFORST	AFFOREST	AEFIILST	FILIATES	AEFINRUF	UNFAIRER
AEEPPRRS	PAPERERS	AEFFQRSU	QUAFFERS	AEFIIMNS	INFAMIES	AEFINRRZ	FRANZIER
	PREPARES	AEFFRSST	RESTAFFS		INFAMISE	AEFINRSS	FAIRNESS
	REPAPERS		STAFFERS	AEFIIMNZ	INFAMIZE		SANSERIF
AEEPPRRT	PARTERRE	AEFGGGOS	FOGGAGES	AEFIIMRS	RAMIFIES	AEFINRST	FENITARS
AEEPRRST	TAPERERS	AEFGGILR	FLAGGIER	AEFIINRT	FAINTIER	AEFINRSX	XERAFINS
AEEPRRTT	PATTERER	AEFGGINU	FEAGUING	AEFIINSS	SANIFIES	AEFINSTT	FAINTEST
AEEPRRTU	APERTURE	AEFGGMOS	MEGAFOGS	AEFIINST	FAINITES	AEFIQRSU	AQUIFERS
AEEPRSSS	ASPERSES	AEFGHINR	HANGFIRE	AEFIIPRT	APERITIF	AEFIRRRS	FARRIERS
	PREASSES	AEFGHINS	SHEAFING	AEFIIRRS	FRIARIES	AEFIRRRY	FARRIERY
	REPASSES	AEFGHOSS	FOGASHES	AEFIIRRT	RATIFIER	AEFIRRST	FRATRIES
AEEPRSST	TRAPESES	AEFGHTTU	FUGHETTA	AEFIIRSU	RATIFIES	AEFIRTUX	FIXATURE
AEEPRSSZ	SPREAZES	AEFGIIRS	GASIFIER	AEFIIRSU	AURIFIES	AEFISTTT	FATTIEST
AEEPRSTU	EPURATES	AEFGIISS	GASIFIES	AEFIITVX	FIXATIVE	AEFKLMRY	FLYMAKER
	SUPERATE	AEFGIKNR	FREAKING	AEFIJLOS	JEOFAILS	AEFKLNRS	FLANKERS
AEEPRSTZ	TRAPEZES	AEFGILNS	FINAGLES	AEFIKLST	FLAKIEST	AEFKLRUW	WREAKFUL
AEEPSSTT	SPATTEES	AEFGILOS	FOLIAGES	AEFIKMRR	FIREMARK	AEFKLSST	FLASKETS
AEEQRRUV	QUAVERER	AEFGILRR	FRAGILER	AEFIKRUW	WAUKRIFE	AEFKLSTT	TALKFEST
AEERRRST	ARRESTER	AEFGIMTU	FUMIGATE	AEFILLOT	FELLATIO	AEFKNORS	FORSAKEN
	REARREST	AEFGINRW	WAFERING	AEFILMNR	INFLAMER	AEFKNRST	FRANKEST
AEERRSST	ASSERTER	AEFGINRY	AREFYING		RIFLEMAN	AEFKOPRS	FORSPEAK
	REASSERT	AEFGINST	FEASTING	AEFILMNS	FLAMINES	AEFKORSS	FORSAKES
	SERRATES	AEFGINTU	FANTIGUE		INFLAMES	AEFLLMMU	FLAMMULE
	TERRASES	AEFGIRST	FRIGATES		MISFALNE	AEFLLNNS	FANNELLS
AEERRSSU	ERASURES	AEFGIRSU	ARGUFIES	AEFILMNT	FILAMENT		FLANNELS
	REASSURE	AEFGIRTU	FIGURATE	AEFILMST	FLAMIEST	AEFLLNNU	UNFALLEN
AEERRSSW	SWEARERS		FRUITAGE	AEFILMSY	MAYFLIES	AEFLLORV	OVERFALL
AEERRSTT	RETRATES	AEFGISTU	FATIGUES	AEFILMTY	FEMALITY	AEFLLORW	FALLOWER
	RETREATS	AEFGLLOP	FLAGPOLE	AEFILNNR	INFERNAL	AEFLLOST	FLOATELS
	TREATERS	AEFGLLSU	FULLAGES	AEFILNOR	FORELAIN	AEFLLPRT	PRATFELL
AEERRSTU	AUSTERER	AEFGLNSS	FANGLESS	AEFILNOT	OLEFIANT	AEFLLPTU	PLATEFUL
	TREASURE	AEFGLORW	GAREFOWL	AEFILNPS	LIFESPAN	AEFLLRUW	AWFULLER
AEERRSTV	TRAVERSE	AEFGLOST	FLOTAGES	AEFILNRU	FRAULEIN	AEFLLRUX	FLEXURAL
AEERRSTW	WATERERS	AEFGLOSW	FOWLAGES	AEFILNST	INFLATES	AEFLLSSW	FLAWLESS
AEERRSVW	WAVERERS	AEFGLRTU	GRATEFUL	AEFILNSV	FLAVINES	AEFLLSTT	FLATLETS
AEERSSSS	REASSESS	AEFGMNOR	FORGEMAN	AEFILOOR	AEROFOIL	AEFLLSTY	FESTALLY
AEERSSSU	SEASURES	AEFGMNRT	FRAGMENT	AEFILORS	FORESAIL	AEFLMNOT	MATFELON
AEERSSSV	ASSEVERS	AEFGNNOT	FONTANGE	AEFILORT	FLOATIER	AEFLMORU	FORMULAE
AEERSSSY	ESSAYERS	AEFGNORT	FRONTAGE	AEFILOST	FOLIATES		FUMAROLE
AEERSSTT	ESTREATS	AEFGNRRS	GRANFERS	AEFILRST	FLARIEST	AEFLMOSS	FOAMLESS
	RESTATES	AEFGOOPT	FOOTPAGE		FRAILEST	AEFLMPRR	FRAMPLER
AEERSSTW	SWEATERS	AEFGOORT	FOOTGEAR	AEFILRSU	FAILURES	AEFLMSUW	WAMEFULS
AEERSSTZ	ERSATZES	AEFGOOST	FOOTAGES	AEFILRSV	FAVRILES	AEFLNNNS	FLANNENS
AEERSSUU	URAEUSES	AEFGORRS	FORAGERS	AEFILRSZ	FILAZERS	AEFLNNOT	FONTANEL
AEERSSUV	VAREUSES	AEFGORRT	FROTTAGE	AEFILRTT	FILTRATE	AEFLNOPR	FOREPLAN
AEERSTTT	ATTESTER	AEFGOSSU	FOUGASSE	AEFILRTU	FAULTIER	AEFLNOPT	PANTOFLE
AEERSTTX	EXTREATS	AEFGRRST	GRAFTERS		FILATURE	AEFLNORS	FARNESOL
AEERTTTZ	TERZETTA			AEFILRUW	WEARIFUL	AEFLNOSV	FLAVONES
AEERVWYY	EVERYWAY			AEFILSSS	FILASSES	AEFLNRSS	SALFERNS

AEFLNRSU	FLANEURS	AEGGHMSU	MESHUGGA	AEGHINNV	HAVENING	AEGIKNSS	SINKAGES
	FUNERALS	AEGGHOPY	GEOPHAGY	AEGHINRS	HEARINGS	AEGIKNTW	TWEAKING
AEFLNRTU	FLAUNTER	AEGGHORU	ROUGHAGE		HEARSING	AEGIKPPS	KIPPAGES
AEFLNSST	FLATNESS	AEGGIJST	JAGGIEST		SHEARING	AEGIKPRS	GARPIKES
AEFLNSTT	FLATTENS	AEGGIKNR	KNAGGIER	AEGHINRT	EARTHING	AEGIKSTW	GAWKIEST
AEFLNSUY	UNSAFELY	AEGGILLN	ALLEGING		HEARTING	AEGILLMS	LEGALISM
AEFLOOSV	FOVEOLAS	AEGGILLR	GRILLAGE	AEGHINRV	HAVERING	AEGILLNS	NIGELLAS
AEFLOPRY	FOREPLAY	AEGGILMN	GLEAMING	AEGHINST	GAHNITES	AEGILLNU	LINGULAE
AEFLORSS	SAFROLES	AEGGILNN	GLEANING		HEATINGS	AEGILLNY	GENIALLY
AEFLORST	FLOATERS	AEGGILNR	GANGLIER	AEGHINSV	HEAVINGS	AEGILLPR	PILLAGER
	FORESTAL		REGALING		SHEAVING	AEGILLPS	PILLAGES
	REFLOATS	AEGGILNS	LIGNAGES	AEGHINSZ	GENIZAHS		SPILLAGE
AEFLORSU	FUSAROLE	AEGGILNT	TEAGLING	AEGHINTT	GNATHITE	AEGILLRU	GUERILLA
AEFLORSY	FORELAYS	AEGGILNU	LEAGUING	AEGHIOPS	ESOPHAGI	AEGILLRV	VILLAGER
AEFLOSTT	FALSETTO	AEGGILRS	SLAGGIER	AEGHIPPR	EPIGRAPH	AEGILLSS	GALLISES
AEFLPPRS	FLAPPERS	AEGGILRW	WAGGLIER	AEGHIPRT	GRAPHITE	AEGILLST	LEGALIST
AEFLPPRY	FLYPAPER	AEGGIMNN	MANEGING	AEGHIRRS	GHARRIES		STILLAGE
AEFLPRSS	FELSPARS	AEGGIMRT	GREGATIM	AEGHIRSS	GARISHES		TILLAGES
AEFLPRSY	PALFREYS	AEGGINNR	ANGERING	AEGHLNOS	HALOGENS	AEGILLSV	VILLAGES
AEFLPSUU	PAUSEFUL		ENRAGING	AEGHLOPY	HYPOGEAL	AEGILLSZ	GALLIZES
AEFLRSSU	REFUSALS	AEGGINNT	AGENTING	AEGHLOSS	GALOSHES	AEGILLTU	LIGULATE
AEFLRSTT	FATTRELS		NEGATING	AEGHLOTX	HEXAGLOT	AEGILLTY	LEGALITY
	FLATTERS	AEGGINNV	AVENGING	AEGHLRSU	LAUGHERS	AEGILMMR	AGLIMMER
AEFLRSTU	REFUTALS	AEGGINRS	GEARINGS	AEGHLRTU	LAUGHTER		LAMMIGER
AEFLRSZZ	FRAZZLES		GREASING	AEGHLRTY	LETHARGY	AEGILMNP	EMPALING
AEFLRTTY	FLATTERY		SNAGGIER	AEGHLSTW	THALWEGS	AEGILMNR	GERMINAL
AEFLSSTU	FLATUSES	AEGGINRV	GREAVING	AEGHMNOP	PHENOGAM		MALIGNER
	SULFATES	AEGGINRW	WAGERING	AEGHMOPT	APOTHEGM		MALINGER
AEFLSTTT	FLATTEST	AEGGINST	NAGGIEST	AEGHMORS	HOMAGERS	AEGILMNS	MEASLING
AEFLSTTU	TASTEFUL	AEGGIOPR	ARPEGGIO	AEGHNNST	HANGNEST	AEGILMNT	LIGAMENT
AEFLSTUW	WASTEFUL		GEROPIGA	AEGHNOPT	HEPTAGON	AEGILMNU	AEMULING
AEFMNRRY	FERRYMAN	AEGGIOSS	ISAGOGES		PATHOGEN	AEGILMNY	YEALMING
AEFMNRST	RAFTSMEN	AEGGIQRU	QUAGGIER	AEGHNOPY	HYPOGEAN	AEGILMRS	GREMIALS
AEFMORRS	FOREARMS	AEGGIRRU	GARRIGUE	AEGHNORV	HANGOVER		LAMIGERS
AEFMORST	FOREMAST	AEGGIRST	RAGGIEST		OVERHANG		REGALISM
	FORMATES	AEGGIRSU	GARIGUES	AEGHNOSX	HEXAGONS	AEGILMRX	LEXIGRAM
AEFMORVW	WAVEFORM	AEGGIRWY	EARWIGGY	AEGHNPSW	SPANGHEW	AEGILNNR	LEARNING
AEFMOSSU	FAMOUSES	AEGGISST	SAGGIEST	AEGHNRSS	GNASHERS	AEGILNNS	EANLINGS
AEFNNSTU	UNFASTEN	AEGGISSW	SWAGGIES	AEGHNSST	STENGAHS		LEANINGS
AEFNOPRR	PROFANER	AEGGLNRS	GANGRELS	AEGHOPPY	APOPHYGE	AEGILNNT	GANTLINE
AEFNOPRS	PROFANES	AEGGLORY	GARGOYLE	AEGHOPXY	EXOPHAGY		LATENING
AEFNORRW	FOREWARN	AEGGLRST	STRAGGLE	AEGHORST	SHORTAGE	AEGILNNU	UNGENIAL
AEFNRRST	TRANSFER	AEGGMNNS	GANGSMEN	AEGHOSST	HOSTAGES	AEGILNNW	WEANLING
AEFNRRUY	FUNERARY	AEGGMORR	ERGOGRAM	AEGHPRSS	SPREAGHS	AEGILNNY	YEANLING
AEFNSSST	FASTNESS	AEGGMORT	MORTGAGE	AEGHPRTU	UPGATHER	AEGILNOR	GERANIOL
AEFNSSTU	UNSAFEST	AEGGNNSU	GUNNAGES	AEGIILLU	AIGUILLE		REGIONAL
AEFNSTUY	UNSAFETY	AEGGNORV	OVERGANG	AEGIILMR	REMIGIAL	AEGILNOS	GASOLINE
AEFOORTW	FOOTWEAR	AEGGNORW	WAGGONER	AEGIILNN	ALIENING	AEGILNOT	GELATION
AEFOPRRT	FOREPART	AEGGNRRS	GRANGERS	AEGIILNR	GAINLIER		LEGATION
AEFOPRST	FOREPAST	AEGGNRST	GANGSTER	AEGIILRR	GLAIRIER	AEGILNPR	PEARLING
AEFOPRSW	FOREPAWS	AEGGOPRU	GROUPAGE	AEGIILTT	LITIGATE	AEGILNPS	ELAPSING
AEFORRSW	FORSWEAR	AEGGRSST	GAGSTERS	AEGIIMNR	IMAGINER		PLEASING
AEFORRSY	FORAYERS		STAGGERS		MIGRAINE	AEGILNPT	PLEATING
AEFORRUV	FAVOURER	AEGGRSSW	SWAGGERS	AEGIIMNS	IMAGINES	AEGILNRR	GNARLIER
AEFORRWY	FORWEARY	AEGHIJRS	JAGHIRES	AEGIIMTT	MITIGATE	AEGILNRS	ARLESING
AEFORSSY	FORESAYS	AEGHILLS	SHIGELLA	AEGIINNR	ARGININE		ENGRAILS
AEFORSTW	FORWASTE	AEGHILMT	MEGALITH	AEGIINNR	GRAINIER		NARGILES
	SOFTWARE	AEGHILNR	NARGHILE	AEGIIRRT	IRRIGATE		REALIGNS
AEFORSTY	FORESTAY		NARGILEH	AECIISTV	VESTIGIA		SANGLIER
AEFOSTUU	FEATUOUS	AEGHILNS	HEALINGS	AECIJLNR	JANGLIER		SLANGIER
AEFOSTUV	VOUTSAFE		LEASHING	AEGIKLNS	LINKAGES	AEGILNRT	ALERTING
AEFPRSST	PRESSFAT		SHEALING	AEGIKLNW	WEAKLING		ALTERING
AEFRSSTW	FRETSAWS	AEGHILNT	ATHELING	AEGIKMNR	REMAKING		INTEGRAL
AEFRSTUW	WAFTURES	AEGHILNX	EXHALING	AEGIKNNS	SNEAKING		RELATING
AEGGGILN	ALEGGING	AEGHILRT	LITHARGE	AEGIKNNW	WAKENING		TANGLIER
AEGGGINN	ENGAGING		THIRLAGE	AEGIKNOY	KAYOEING		TRIANGLE
AEGGGLSU	LUGGAGES	AEGHILRU	LAUGHIER	AEGIKNPS	SPEAKING	AEGILNRX	RELAXING
AEGGHIRS	SHAGGIER	AEGHILST	LAIGHEST	AEGIKNRS	SKEARING	AEGILNRY	LAYERING
AEGGHISS	HAGGISES	AEGHIMPS	MAGESHIP	AEGIKNRT	RETAKING		RELAYING
AEGGHLRS	HAGGLERS	AEGHINNT	NAETHING	AEGIKNRW	WREAKING		YEARLING

AEGILNSS	GAINLESS	AEGINNNX	ANNEXING	AEGINSTW	SWEATING	AEGLNPRS	GRAPNELS
	GLASSINE	AEGINNOT	NEGATION	AEGINSTY	YEASTING		SPANGLER
	LEASINGS	AEGINNPS	SNEAPING	AEGINSVW	WEAVINGS		SPRANGLE
	SEALINGS		SPEANING	AEGINSVY	SAVEYING	AEGLNPSS	PANGLESS
AEGILNST	EASTLING	AEGINNRS	AGINNERS	AEGIOPPR	PROGERIA		SPANGLES
	GELATINS		EARNINGS	AEGIORSS	ARGOSIES	AEGLNPST	SPANGLET
	GENITALS		ENGRAINS	AEGIORSV	VIRAGOES	AEGLNRRW	WRANGLER
	STEALING		GRANNIES	AEGIOSTT	GOATIEST	AEGLNRST	STRANGLE
AEGILNSV	LEAVINGS	AEGINNRV	RAVENING	AEGIOSTU	AGOUTIES		TANGLERS
	SLEAVING	AEGINNRY	RENAYING	AEGIOSTX	GEOTAXIS		TRANGLES
AEGILNSW	SWEALING		YEARNING	AEGIPPST	GAPPIEST	AEGLNRSU	GRANULES
AEGILNTV	VALETING	AEGINNST	ANTIGENS	AEGIPRSS	PRISAGES	AEGLNRSW	WANGLERS
AEGILNTX	EXALTING		GENTIANS		SPAIRGES		WRANGLES
AEGILNTZ	TEAZLING		STEANING	AEGIPRST	GRAPIEST	AEGLNRSY	LARYNGES
AEGILNUV	VAGINULE	AEGINNSU	GUANINES	AEGIPRTY	PTERYGIA	AEGLNRUY	GUNLAYER
AEGILOPS	SPOILAGE		SANGUINE	AEGIPSST	GASPIEST	AEGLNSTT	GANTLETS
AEGILOPT	PILOTAGE	AEGINORS	IGNAROES	AEGIQRSU	SQUIRAGE	AEGLNSTU	LANGUETS
AEGILORS	GASOLIER		ORGANISE	AEGIRRSS	GRASSIER	AEGLNSTW	TWANGLES
	GIRASOLE		ORIGANES	AEGIRRSU	SUGARIER	AEGLNSUW	GUNWALES
	SERAGLIO	AEGINORZ	ORGANIZE	AEGIRRSZ	GRAZIERS	AEGLNTTU	GAUNTLET
AEGILOSS	GOLIASES	AEGINOSS	AGONISES	AEGIRRTY	ARGYRITE	AEGLNTUU	UNGULATE
AEGILOST	OTALGIES	AEGINOSZ	AGONIZES		GERIATRY	AEGLOOOZ	ZOOGLOEA
AEGILPPS	SLIPPAGE	AEGINPPR	PAPERING	AEGIRSST	AGISTERS	AEGLOOPU	APOLOGUE
AEGILPPU	PUPILAGE	AEGINPPS	GENIPAPS	AEGIRSTT	STRIGATE	AEGLOORY	AEROLOGY
AEGILPRU	PLAGUIER	AEGINPRS	PREASING	AEGIRSTV	VIRGATES	AEGLOPRS	PERGOLAS
AEGILRRU	GLAURIER		SPEARING		VITRAGES	AEGLORST	LEGATORS
AEGILRSS	GLASSIER	AEGINPRT	TAPERING	AEGIRSUU	AUGURIES	AEGLORSU	GLAREOUS
AEGILRST	GLARIEST	AEGINPRY	REPAYING	AEGISSST	GASSIEST	AEGLORTU	OUTGLARE
	REGALIST	AEGINPSS	SPINAGES	AEGISSTT	STAGIEST	AEGLORTW	WATERLOG
AEGILRSY	GREASILY	AEGINQTU	EQUATING	AEGISSTW	GAWSIEST	AEGLORTY	GEOLATRY
AEGILRSZ	GLAZIERS	AEGINRRS	EARRINGS	AEGISTUZ	GAUZIEST	AEGLOSSW	GALOWSES
AEGILRTT	AGLITTER		GRAINERS	AEGJLNRS	JANGLERS	AEGLOSTV	VOLTAGES
AEGILRTU	LIGATURE	AEGINRRV	AVERRING	AEGJLTUU	JUGULATE	AEGLOSUY	GEALOUSY
AEGILRTY	REGALITY	AEGINRSS	REASSIGN	AEGKKKNO	ANGEKKOK	AEGLPPRS	GRAPPLES
AEGILSTZ	GLAZIEST		SEARINGS	AEGKKNOS	ANGEKOKS	AEGLPRSU	EARPLUGS
AEGIMMST	GAMMIEST		SERINGAS	AEGKLOSU	KAGOULES		GRAUPELS
AEGIMNNR	ENARMING	AEGINRST	ANGRIEST	AEGKMNRU	GUNMAKER	AEGLPSSU	PLUSAGES
	RENAMING		ASTRINGE	AEGKMRSY	KERYGMAS		PLUSSAGE
AEGIMNNS	MEANINGS		GANISTER	AEGLLLMU	GLUMELLA	AEGLRRSU	REGULARS
AEGIMNNT	ENTAMING		GANTRIES	AEGLLNOS	ALLONGES	AEGLRRUV	VULGARER
AEGIMNPR	EMPARING		GRANITES		GALLEONS	AEGLRSTU	GAULTERS
AEGIMNRR	REARMING		INGRATES	AEGLLNOV	LONGEVAL		GESTURAL
AEGIMNRS	GERMAINS		RANGIEST	AEGLLNPS	LANGSPEL		TRAGULES
	SMEARING		REASTING	AEGLLNRS	LANGRELS	AEGLRTUY	ARGUTELY
AEGIMNRT	EMIGRANT		STEARING	AEGLLOPR	GALLOPER	AEGLSSTT	GESTALTS
AEGIMNRU	GERANIUM	AEGINRSV	VINEGARS	AEGLLORS	ALLEGROS	AEGLSSUV	VALGUSES
AEGIMNST	MANGIEST	AEGINRSW	SWEARING	AEGLLORV	OVERGALL	AEGLSTUU	GLUTAEUS
	MINTAGES		WEARINGS	AEGLLORY	ALLEGORY	AEGLSTUV	VULGATES
	STEAMING	AEGINRSY	RESAYING	AEGLLOSS	GOALLESS	AEGLSUUY	GUAYULES
	TEAMINGS	AEGINRTT	ARETTING	AEGLLOST	TOLLAGES	AEGMMNOR	GAMMONER
AEGIMNSV	VEGANISM		TREATING	AEGLLOTT	TOLLGATE	AEGMMRRU	RUMMAGER
AEGIMOOS	OOGAMIES	AEGINRTV	AVERTING	AEGLLRVY	GRAVELLY	AEGMMRSU	RUMMAGES
AEGIMORR	ARMIGERO		TAVERING	AEGLLSSU	GALLUSES	AEGMNNOS	AGNOMENS
AEGIMORS	GORAMIES		VINTAGER		SEAGULLS	AEGMNNOT	MAGNETON
AEGIMORW	WAGMOIRE	AEGINRTW	TWANGIER		SULLAGES	AEGMNORS	MEGARONS
AEGIMPRS	EPIGRAMS		WATERING	AEGLMNNO	MANGONEL	AEGMNORV	MANGROVE
	PRIMAGES	AEGINRVW	WAVERING	AEGLMNRS	MANGLERS	AEGMNOST	MAGNETOS
AEGIMPRU	UMPIRAGE	AEGINRVY	VINEGARY	AEGLMNSS	GLASSMEN		MEGATONS
AEGIMPST	PIGMEATS	AEGINRWY	WEARYING	AEGLMNTU	GUNMETAL		MONTAGES
AEGIMQRU	QUAGMIRE	AEGINSST	EASTINGS	AEGLMORS	GOMERALS	AEGMNOSX	MAGNOXES
AEGIMRRS	ARMIGERS		GENISTAS	AEGLMOSU	MOULAGES	AEGMNOXY	XENOGAMY
AEGIMRRT	RAGTIMER		GIANTESS	AEGLMOTV	MEGAVOLT	AEGMNRST	GARMENTS
AEGIMRSS	GISARMES		SEATINGS	AEGLMPSU	PLUMAGES		MARGENTS
AEGIMRST	MAGISTER		TEASINGS	AEGLMRSU	MAULGRES		RAGMENTS
	MIGRATES		TSIGANES	AEGLMSSU	GAUMLESS	AEGMNRTU	MUTAGENS
	RAGTIMES	AEGINSSY	ESSAYING	AEGLNNPT	PLANGENT	AEGMNSSW	SWAGSMEN
	STERIGMA	AEGINSTT	ESTATING	AEGLNNTU	UNTANGLE	AEGMNSTU	AUGMENTS
AEGIMSST	SIGMATES		TANGIEST	AEGLNOPT	GANTLOPE	AEGMOORS	MOORAGES
AEGIMSSU	MISUSAGE	AEGINSTU	SAUTEING	AEGLNORY	YEARLONG	AEGMOPRW	GAPEWORM
AEGIMSTU	GAUMIEST	AEGINSTV	VINTAGES	AEGLNOST	TANGELOS		

AEGMORSS	GOSSAMER	AEGRSTUU	AUGUSTER
AEGMPSTU	STUMPAGE	AEGSSTUU	AUGUSTES
AEGNNOPT	PENTAGON	AEGSTTTU	GUTTATES
AEGNNORT	NEGATRON	AEHHHIST	SHEHITAH
AEGNNOST	TONNAGES	AEHHIMTW	HAMEWITH
AEGNNPRT	PREGNANT	AEHHIPSW	PEISHWAH
AEGNNRSU	GUNNERAS	AEHHISST	HASHIEST
AEGNNRTY	GANNETRY		SHEHITAS
AEGNNSTT	TANGENTS	AEHHISVY	YESHIVAH
AEGNNSTU	TUNNAGES	AEHHLNTU	UNHEALTH
AEGNOORS	OREGANOS	AEHHNRSS	HARSHENS
AEGNOPRR	PARERGON	AEHHNRSW	HERNSHAW
AEGNOPST	PONTAGES	AEHHORST	HAROSETH
AEGNORRS	GROANERS	AEHHRRST	THRASHER
AEGNORRY	ORANGERY	AEHHRSST	HARSHEST
AEGNORST	ORANGEST		THRASHES
	RAGSTONE	AEHIIKLR	HAIRLIKE
AEGNORSW	WAGONERS	AEHIIKRT	TERAKIHI
AEGNORTT	TETRAGON	AEHIIKST	SHIITAKE
AEGNORTY	NEGATORY	AEHIILMO	HEMIOLIA
AEGNORUV	VARGUENO	AEHIILNR	HAIRLINE
AEGNOSSY	NOSEGAYS	AEHIILST	HAILIEST
AEGNOTUY	AUTOGENY	AEHIIMNT	THIAMINE
AEGNPRSS	ENGRASPS	AEHIIMOP	HEMIOPIA
AEGNPRST	TREPANGS	AEHIINNT	IANTHINE
AEGNPRRY	PANEGYRY	AEHIIRST	HAIRIEST
AEGNRRST	GRANTERS	AEHIKNSS	SNEAKISH
	REGRANTS	AEHIKSST	SHAKIEST
	STRANGER	AEHIKSSY	SAKIYEHS
AEGNRSTU	STRAUNGE	AEHILLNT	THALLINE
AEGNSSST	GASTNESS	AEHILMNY	HYMENIAL
AEGNSTTU	GAUNTEST	AEHILMOS	HEMIOLAS
	TUTENAGS	AEHILMOT	HALIMOTE
AEGOORST	ROOTAGES	AEHILMSW	LIMEWASH
AEGOORSV	VORAGOES	AEHILNOP	APHELION
AEGOOSWY	WAYGOOSE	AEHILNRS	INHALERS
AEGOPPRS	PROPAGES	AEHILNSY	HYALINES
AEGOPPST	STOPPAGE	AEHILNTX	ANTHELIX
AEGOPPSU	SUPPEAGO	AEHILNTZ	ZENITHAL
AEGOPRST	PORTAGES	AEHILORS	AIRHOLES
AEGOPRTU	PORTAGUE		SHOALIER
AEGOPSST	POSTAGES	AEHILORT	AEROLITH
AEGOPSSU	SPOUSAGE		LOATHIER
AEGOPSTT	POTTAGES	AEHILPRS	PLASHIER
AEGORRRT	REGRATOR	AEHILRSS	HAIRLESS
AEGORRST	GARROTES	AEHILRSU	HAULIERS
AEGORRTT	GAROTTER	AEHILRSV	LAVISHER
	GARROTTE		SHRIEVAL
AEGORSST	STORAGES	AEHILRTY	HEARTILY
AEGORSTT	GAROTTES	AEHILSST	SHALIEST
AEGORSTU	OUTRAGES	AEHILSSV	LAVISHES
AEGORSUV	OUVRAGES	AEHILSSW	WHAISLES
AEGORSVY	VOYAGERS	AEHILSTT	LATHIEST
AEGORTTU	TUTORAGE		LITHATES
AEGORUVY	VOYAGEUR	AEHILSTY	HYALITES
AEGOSSTW	STOWAGES	AEHILSUV	VIHUELAS
AEGOSTTU	OUTGATES	AEHILSWZ	WHAIZLES
AEGOSTTV	GAVOTTES	AEHIMMSS	SHAMMIES
AEGPRRSS	GRASPERS	AEHIMMST	HAMMIEST
	SPARGERS	AEHIMNNU	INHUMANE
AEGPSSTU	UPSTAGES	AEHIMNRS	HARMINES
AEGPSSUU	GAUPUSES		SHIREMAN
AEGPSSUW	GAWPUSES	AEHIMNSS	SHAMISEN
AEGQRTUU	TRUQUAGE	AEHIMNSU	HUMANISE
AEGRRSSS	GRASSERS	AEHIMNTU	INHUMATE
AEGRRSUU	AUGURERS	AEHIMNUZ	HUMANIZE
AEGRRSUV	GRAVURES	AEHIMPRS	SAMPHIRE
	VERRUGAS		SERAPHIM
AEGRSSSU	SARGUSES	AEHIMPRT	TERAPHIM
AEGRSTTY	STRATEGY	AEHIMPRX	XERAPHIM

AEHIMPSS	EMPHASIS	AEHISSSW	SIWASHES
	MISSHAPE	AEHISSSY	ESSAYISH
	PHAEISMS	AEHISSTT	ATHEISTS
AEHIMPST	MATESHIP		HASTIEST
	SHIPMATE		STAITHES
AEHIMRRS	MARSHIER	AEHISSTU	HIATUSES
AEHIMRSS	MARISHES	AEHISSTW	WASHIEST
	MISHEARS	AEHISSVY	YESHIVAS
AEHIMSST	ATHEISMS	AEHISTTW	THAWIEST
	MASHIEST		THWAITES
	MATHESIS	AEHJLOSW	JAWHOLES
AEHINNSS	SHANNIES	AEHJNNOS	JOHANNES
AEHINNTX	XANTHEIN	AEHKMOPW	MOPEHAWK
	XANTHINE	AEHKNNSU	UNSHAKEN
AEHINOPS	APHONIES	AEHKNRST	THANKERS
AEHINOPU	EUPHONIA	AEHKNSWW	NEWSHAWK
AEHINPRS	HEPARINS	AEHKRRSS	SHARKERS
	PARISHEN	AEHLLLTY	LETHALLY
	SERAPHIN	AEHLLMOP	LAMPHOLE
AEHINPRT	PERIANTH	AEHLLNRT	ENTHRALL
AEHINPST	PENTHIAS	AEHLLRSS	HERSALLS
	THESPIAN	AEHLMMNS	HELMSMAN
AEHINRRS	SHARNIER	AEHLMNOS	MANHOLES
AEHINRSS	ARSHINES	AEHLMNOT	METHANOL
AEHINRST	INEARTHS	AEHLMNUY	HUMANELY
AEHINRSV	ENRAVISH	AEHLMORS	ARMHOLES
	VANISHER	AEHLMPPT	PAMPHLET
AEHINRTU	HAURIENT	AEHLMPSW	WHAMPLES
AEHINRTW	TARWHINE	AEHLMRSS	HARMLESS
AEHINSSS	HESSIANS	AEHLMRST	THERMALS
AEHINSST	ANTHESIS	AEHLMRSU	HUMERALS
	SHANTIES	AEHLNOST	ETHANOLS
AEHINSSV	VANISHES	AEHLNPRS	SHRAPNEL
AEHINSSZ	HAZINESS	AEHLNPTY	ENTHALPY
AEHINSTT	HESITANT	AEHLNRST	ENTHRALS
AEHINSTW	INSWATHE	AEHLNSST	NATHLESS
AEHINTTT	ANTITHET	AEHLNSSU	UNLASHES
AEHIOPRS	APHORISE		UNSHALES
AEHIOPRU	EUPHORIA	AEHLNSTY	NAYTHLES
AEHIOPRZ	APHORIZE	AEHLNTUZ	HAZELNUT
AEHIORRV	OVERHAIR	AEHLOPRT	PLETHORA
AEHIORST	HOARIEST	AEHLORST	LOATHERS
AEHIORTU	THIOUREA	AEHLORSY	HOARSELY
AEHIPPRS	PAPISHER	AEHLORUV	OVERHAUL
	SAPPHIRE	AEHLOSSS	ASSHOLES
AEHIPPSS	PAPISHES	AEHLOSST	SHOALEST
AEHIPPST	EPITAPHS	AEHLOSTT	LOATHEST
	HAPPIEST	AEHLPPRT	THRAPPLE
	PEATSHIP	AEHLPRSS	SPLASHER
AEHIPRRS	PHRASIER	AEHLPSSS	SPLASHES
AEHIPRRT	RATHRIPE	AEHLPSST	PATHLESS
AEHIPRSS	PARISHES		PLASHETS
	SHARPIES	AEHLPSTU	SULPHATE
AEHIPRTT	THREAPIT	AEHLPSTY	STAPHYLE
AEHIPSSW	PEISHWAS	AEHLRRTU	URETHRAL
AEHIPSTZ	ZAPTIEHS	AEHLRSSS	SLASHERS
AEHIQSSU	QUASHIES	AEHLRSST	HARSLETS
AEHIRRRS	HARRIERS		SLATHERS
AEHIRRSS	ARRISHES	AEHLSSTT	STEALTHS
AEHIRRST	TRASHIER	AEHLSSTW	THAWLESS
AEHIRRSV	RAVISHER	AEHLSTTY	STEALTHY
AEHIRRTW	WRATHIER	AEHMMRSS	SHAMMERS
AEHIRSST	SHERIATS	AEHMNNPY	NYMPHEAN
AEHIRSSV	RAVISHES	AEHMNOPR	MORPHEAN
AEHIRSSW	SWASHIER	AEHMNORS	HORSEMAN
AEHIRSTW	SWATHIER		MENORAHS
	WATERISH		SHOREMAN
AEHIRSTY	HYSTERIA	AEHMNOST	HOASTMEN
AEHIRSWY	HAYWIRES	AEHMNOSU	HOUSEMAN
AEHISSST	STASHIES	AEHMNPRU	PREHUMAN

AEHMNSTU	HUMANEST
AEHMOPRT	METAPHOR
AEHMOPST	APOTHEMS
AEHMPRST	HAMPSTER
AEHMRSSS	SMASHERS
AEHMRSST	HAMSTERS
AEHMRSTU	MAUTHERS
AEHMRSTW	MAWTHERS
AEHMSSSU	SHAMUSES
AEHMSTTY	AMETHYST
AEHMSUZZ	MEZUZAHS
AEHNNPRU	NENUPHAR
AEHNNPSU	UNSHAPEN
AEHNNSUV	UNSHAVEN
AEHNNSUW	UNWASHEN
AEHNOOPT	HANEPOOT
AEHNOPRT	HAPTERON
AEHNOPST	PHAETONS
	PHONATES
	STANHOPE
AEHNOPSW	WANHOPES
AEHNOPXY	XENOPHYA
AEHNOQTU	HAQUETON
AEHNORSS	HOARSENS
AEHNPRSS	SHARPENS
AEHNPRST	PANTHERS
AEHNPSSU	UNSHAPES
AEHNRSSS	RASHNESS
AEHNRSTU	HAUNTERS
	UNEARTHS
	UNHEARTS
	URETHANS
AEHNSSTT	THATNESS
AEHNSSTW	WHATNESS
AEHNSTUW	UNSWATHE
AEHOORST	TOHEROAS
AEHOPPRS	PROPHASE
AEHOPRSS	PHAROSES
AEHOPSST	PATHOSES
	POTASHES
	SPATHOSE
AEHOPSTT	HEATSPOT
AEHORRSV	OVERRASH
AEHORSST	ASTHORES
	HAROSETS
	HOARSEST
AEHORSTT	RHEOSTAT
AEHORSTX	THORAXES
AEHORSUV	HAVEOURS
AEHORSVW	OVERWASH
AEHORSWY	HORSEWAY
AEHPRRSS	PHRASERS
	SHARPERS
AEHPRSST	SHARPEST
	SPARTHES
AEHPRSUX	HARUSPEX
AEHPRSUY	EUPHRASY
AEHQRSSU	SQUASHER
AEHQSSSU	SQUASHES
AEHRRSTU	URETHRAS
AEHRRSTY	TRASHERY
AEHRRTTW	THWARTER
AEHRSSST	SHASTERS
AEHRSSSW	SWASHERS
AEHRSSTT	SHATTERS
AEHRSSTV	HARVESTS
AEHRSTTY	SHATTERY
AEHRSTUU	HAUTEURS
AEHSSTUX	EXHAUSTS

AEIIINTT	INITIATE
AEIIIRRT	RETIARII
AEIIKLNT	KALINITE
AEIIKNRS	KAISERIN
AEIIKNSS	AKINESIS
AEIIKNST	KAINITES
AEIIKRTY	TERIYAKI
AEIILLMR	MILLIARE
AEIILLRS	RAILLIES
AEIILLST	TAILLIES
AEIILLTV	ILLATIVE
AEIILMNN	MAINLINE
AEIILMNS	ALIENISM
AEIILMPR	IMPERIAL
AEIILMTT	MILITATE
AEIILNNS	ANILINES
AEIILNQU	AQUILINE
AEIILNRR	AIRLINER
AEIILNRS	AIRLINES
	SNAILIER
AEIILNRT	INERTIAL
AEIILNST	ALIENIST
	LITANIES
AEIILPRT	LIPARITE
AEIILRSS	LAIRISES
AEIILRST	LAIRIEST
AEIILRSV	RIVALISE
AEIILRSZ	LAIRIZES
AEIILRTT	LITERATI
AEIILRVZ	RIVALIZE
AEIILSSS	SILESIAS
AEIILSST	SAILIEST
AEIILSTV	VITALISE
AEIILSTX	LAXITIES
AEIILSTZ	TAILZIES
AEIILTVZ	VITALIZE
AEIIMMRT	MARITIME
AEIIMMSX	MAXIMISE
AEIIMMXZ	MAXIMIZE
AEIIMNST	MINIATES
AEIIMNTT	INTIMATE
AEIIMNTU	MINUTIAE
AEIIMNTV	VITAMINE
AEIIMRST	AIRTIMES
	SERIATIM
AEIIMSTT	IMITATES
AEIINNRS	SIRENIAN
AEIINNSS	INSANIES
AEIINNTV	INNATIVE
AEIINPRT	PAINTIER
AEIINPST	PIANISTE
AEIINQSU	EQUINIAS
AEIINRRV	RIVERAIN
AEIINRSS	AIRINESS
AEIINRST	INERTIAS
	RAINIEST
AEIINRSY	YERSINIA
AEIINSST	ISATINES
	SANITIES
	SANITISE
AEIINSSX	SIXAINES
AEIINSTV	VANITIES
AEIINSTX	AXINITES
AEIINSTZ	SANITIZE
AEIINSVV	INVASIVE
AEIINTTT	TITANITE
AEIINTTU	UINTAITE
AEIIPRRS	PRAIRIES
AEIIPRST	PARITIES
AEIIPRSW	PAIRWISE

AEIIPRZZ	PIZZERIA
AEIIPSST	EPITASIS
AEIIRRST	RARITIES
AEIIRRSV	RIVIERAS
AEIIRRTT	IRRITATE
AEIIRSSS	SIRIASES
AEIIRSST	IRISATES
	SATIRISE
AEIIRSTV	VAIRIEST
AEIIRSTW	WISTERIA
AEIIRSTZ	SATIRIZE
AEIIRSVV	VIVARIES
AEIIRTTT	TRITIATE
AEIIRTVZ	VIZIRATE
AEIISTTV	VITIATES
AEIITTTV	TITIVATE
AEIITTVV	VITATIVE
AEIJKNSS	JANSKIES
AEIJLNSV	JAVELINS
AEIJLOPS	JALOPIES
AEIJLOSU	JALOUSIE
AEIJMMST	JAMMIEST
AEIJMNSS	JASMINES
AEIJNRST	NARTJIES
AEIJNRTU	JAUNTIER
AEIJNSTT	JANTIEST
AEIJNSTU	JAUNTIES
AEIJORST	JAROSITE
AEIJPSSS	JASPISES
AEIJSTZZ	JAZZIEST
AEIKKLLW	LIKEWALK
AEIKKLPR	PARKLIKE
AEIKKMNO	KAKIEMON
AEIKLLSS	KILLASES
AEIKLNNP	PANNIKEL
AEIKLNOS	KAOLINES
AEIKLNSS	SEALSKIN
AEIKLNST	LANKIEST
AEIKLNSW	SWANLIKE
AEIKLNSY	SNEAKILY
AEIKLOST	KEITLOAS
AEIKLPSS	KALPISES
AEIKLRSS	SERKALIS
AEIKLRST	LARKIEST
	STALKIER
	STARLIKE
AEIKLRSV	KLAVIERS
AEIKLSSS	SAIKLESS
AEIKMMSS	MISMAKES
AEIKMNRS	RAMEKINS
AEIKMNST	MANKIEST
	MISTAKEN
AEIKMPRS	RAMPIKES
AEIKMPSS	MISSPEAK
AEIKMSST	MISTAKES
AEIKMSTW	MAWKIEST
AEIKNPRR	PRANKIER
AEIKNRST	KERATINS
	NARKIEST
AEIKNRSW	SWANKIER
AEIKNRTW	KNITWEAR
AEIKNSST	SNAKIEST
AEIKNSSW	SWANKIES
AEIKNSSY	KYANISES
AEIKNSTV	KISTVAEN
AEIKNSTY	KYANITES
AEIKNSYZ	KYANIZES
AEIKPRST	PARKIEST
AEIKPSTW	PAWKIEST
AEIKQSTU	QUAKIEST

AEIKRSST	ASTERISK
	SARKIEST
AEILLLMO	MALLEOLI
AEILLLNY	LINEALLY
AEILLMNS	MANILLES
AEILLMSY	MESIALLY
AEILLNNO	LANOLINE
AEILLNNS	NAINSELL
AEILLNNU	UNLINEAL
AEILLNOP	APOLLINE
AEILLNOR	ALLERION
AEILLNPS	SPLENIAL
AEILLNQU	QUINELLA
AEILLNRY	LINEARLY
AEILLNSS	SENSILLA
AEILLNVY	VENIALLY
AEILLOTV	VOLATILE
AEILLPPR	APPERILL
AEILLPSS	ILLAPSES
AEILLPST	PALLIEST
	PASTILLE
AEILLPSV	LIPSALVE
AEILLQTU	TEQUILLA
AEILLRRS	RALLIERS
AEILLRRY	RAILLERY
AEILLRSS	RAILLESS
AEILLRST	LITERALS
	TALLIERS
AEILLRSU	RUELLIAS
AEILLRSY	SERIALLY
AEILLRTU	TAILLEUR
AEILLSSS	SAILLESS
AEILLSST	TAILLESS
AEILLSTW	WALLIEST
AEILLSUV	ALLUSIVE
AEILLSYZ	SLEAZILY
AEILLTUZ	LAZULITE
AEILMMNS	MELANISM
AEILMMNT	IMMANTLE
AEILMMNY	IMMANELY
AEILMMOR	MEMORIAL
AEILMMOT	IMMOLATE
AEILMMRS	SMALMIER
AEILMMRT	TRILEMMA
AEILMMSS	MELISMAS
AEILMNNO	MINNEOLA
AEILMNNP	IMPANNEL
AEILMNNS	LINESMAN
	MELANINS
AEILMNOS	MINEOLAS
	SEMOLINA
AEILMNPS	IMPANELS
	MANIPLES
AEILMNRS	MARLINES
	MINERALS
AEILMNRT	TERMINAL
AEILMNRU	LEMURIAN
AEILMNSS	ISLESMAN
AEILMNST	AILMENTS
	ALIMENTS
	MANLIEST
AEILMOPR	PROEMIAL
AEILMORS	MORALISE
AEILMORZ	MORALIZE
AEILMOST	LOAMIEST
AEILMPRS	IMPEARLS
	LEMPIRAS
AEILMPRV	PRIMEVAL
AEILMPST	IMPLATES
	PALMIEST

	PALMIETS	AEILNSTW LAWNIEST	AEILRSVV REVIVALS	AEIMPRRS RAMPIRES
	PETALISM	AEILNSUV UNVAILES	AEILRSVY VIRELAYS	AEIMPRRT IMPARTER
	SEPTIMAL	AEILNSUW LAUWINES	AEILRTTY ALTERITY	AEIMPRSS IMPRESAS
AEILMPTY PLAYTIME	AEILNSUY UNEASILY	AEILRTUZ LAZURITE	SAMPIRES
AEILMQRU QUALMIER	AEILNTVY NATIVELY	AEILRTVV TRIVALVE	AEIMPRST PRIMATES
AEILMRRS LARMIERS	VENALITY	AEILSSSV VESSAILS	AEIMPRSV VAMPIRES
AEILMRSS REALISMS	AEILNUVV UNIVALVE	AEILSSTT SALTIEST	AEIMPRSW SWAMPIER
AEILMRST LAMITERS	AEILOORV OVARIOLE	SLATIEST	AEIMPRTU APTERIUM
MARLIEST	AEILOPPT OPPILATE	AEILSSTW SWALIEST	AEIMPSSS IMPASSES
AEILMRSY SMEARILY	AEILOPRS PELORIAS	AEILSTTW WALTIEST	AEIMPSST IMPASTES
AEILMRTT REMITTAL	POLARISE	AEILSTVY VILAYETS	PASTIMES
AEILMRUV VELARIUM	AEILOPRT EPILATOR	AEIMMNNT IMMANENT	AEIMQRSU MARQUISE
AEILMSSX SMILAXES	PETIOLAR	AEIMMNOT AMMONITE	AEIMRRRS MARRIERS
AEILMSTT MALTIEST	AEILOPRZ POLARIZE	AEIMMNSS MISNAMES	AEIMRRSS SIMARRES
SMALTITE	AEILOPST SPOLIATE	AEIMMPRS SPAMMIER	AEIMRSST ASTERISM
AEILMSTU SIMULATE	AEILORSS SOLARISE	AEIMMPST PSAMMITE	MAISTERS
AEILMSTY LAYTIMES	AEILORST SOTERIAL	AEIMMRSS SMARMIER	MISRATES
STEAMILY	AEILORSV OVERSAIL	AEIMMRST MARMITES	SEMITARS
AEILMTTU MUTILATE	VALORISE	AEIMMRTU IMMATURE	SMARTIES
ULTIMATE	VARIOLES	AEIMMSST MISMATES	AEIMRSSY EMISSARY
AEILNNOS SOLANINE	VOLARIES	AEIMMSZZ MIZMAZES	AEIMRSTT MISTREAT
AEILNNRT INTERNAL	AEILORSY ROYALISE	AEIMNNOT NOMINATE	TERATISM
AEILNNSY INSANELY	AEILORSZ SOLARIZE	AEIMNNRS REINSMAN	AEIMRSTU MURIATES
AEILNNTY INNATELY	AEILORTT LITERATO	AEIMNNST MANNITES	SEMITAUR
AEILNOPS OPALINES	AEILORVZ VALORIZE	AEIMNOPT PTOMAINE	AEIMRSTW WARTIMES
AEILNOPT ANTIPOLE	AEILORYZ ROYALIZE	AEIMNORS MORAINES	AEIMRSTX MATRIXES
AEILNOPU POULAINE	AEILOSST ISOLATES	AEIMNORW AIRWOMEN	AEIMRSTY SYMITARE
AEILNORS AILERONS	AEILOSSX OXALISES	AEIMNORZ ARMOZINE	AEIMRSWW SWIMWEAR
ALERIONS	AEILOSTT TOTALISE	AEIMNOSU MOINEAUS	AEIMSSST ASTEISMS
ALIENORS	AEILOSTV VIOLATES	AEIMNOSW WOMANISE	MASSIEST
AEILNORT ORIENTAL	AEILOTTV VOLITATE	AEIMNOTZ MONAZITE	AEIMSSTT MASTIEST
RELATION	AEILOTTZ TOTALIZE	AEIMNOWZ WOMANIZE	MISSTATE
AEILNORV OVERLAIN	AEILPPQU APPLIQUE	AEIMNPRT TRIPEMAN	AEIMSSTZ MESTIZAS
AEILNOST ELATIONS	AEILPPRS APPERILS	AEIMNQRU RAMEQUIN	AEIMSTYZ AZYMITES
INSOLATE	AEILPPTU PUPILATE	AEIMNRRS MARINERS	AEIMTTUV MUTATIVE
TOENAILS	AEILPRRS REPRISAL	AEIMNRRV RIVERMAN	AEINNNOX ANNEXION
AEILNOTT TONALITE	AEILPRRT PALTRIER	AEIMNRSS SEMINARS	AEINNOPV PAVONINE
AEILNPRS PEARLINS	AEILPRST PILASTER	SIRNAMES	AEINNORS RAISONNE
PRALINES	PLAISTER	AEIMNRST MINARETS	AEINNORT INORNATE
AEILNPRT TRIPLANE	PLAITERS	RAIMENTS	AEINNOST ENATIONS
AEILNPSS PAINLESS	AEILPRSV PREVAILS	AEIMNRSU ANEURISM	AEINNOTT INTONATE
SPANIELS	AEILPRSW SLIPWARE	AEIMNRSY SEMINARY	AEINNOTV INNOVATE
AEILNPST PANTILES	AEILPRXY PYREXIAL	AEIMNRTT MARTINET	VENATION
PLAINEST	AEILPSST PALSIEST	AEIMNRTU RUMINATE	AEINNPRS PANNIERS
AEILNPSX EXPLAINS	AEILPSSY PAISLEYS	AEIMNRTW WARIMENT	AEINNPST PANTINES
AEILNRRS SNARLIER	AEILPSTT PLATIEST	AEIMNRTY TYRAMINE	AEINNRRT INERRANT
AEILNRSS RAINLESS	AEILPSTY PTYALISE	AEIMNSSS SAMISENS	AEINNRSS INSNARES
AEILNRST ENTRAILS	AEILPSUV PLAUSIVE	AEIMNSSZ MAZINESS	AEINNRST ENTRAINS
LATRINES	AEILPTYZ PTYALIZE	AEIMNSUV MAUVEINS	TRANNIES
RATLINES	AEILQRSU SQUAILER	AEIMNTTU MATUTINE	AEINNRSU ANEURINS
TRENAILS	AEILQRTU QUARTILE	AEIMNTVZ VIZAMENT	UNARISEN
AEILNRSU LUNARIES	REQUITAL	AEIMOOPS IPOMOEAS	AEINNRSW SWANNIER
AEILNRSV RAVELINS	AEILQSTU LIQUATES	AEIMOPSX APOMIXES	AEINNSST INSANEST
AEILNRSX RELAXINS	TEQUILAS	AEIMOPTT OPTIMATE	AEINNSSV VAINNESS
AEILNRSY INLAYERS	AEILQSUY QUEASILY	AEIMORRS ARMOIRES	AEINNSTT ANTIENTS
SNAILERY	AEILQTUY EQUALITY	ARMORIES	STANNITE
AEILNRTT RATTLINE	AEILRRST RETIRALS	AEIMORST AMORTISE	AEINNTUV UNNATIVE
AEILNRTU RETINULA	RETRIALS	ATOMISER	AEINOPPT ANTIPOPE
TENURIAL	TRAILERS	AEIMORTT AMORETTI	AEINOPRT ATROPINE
AEILNRTV INTERVAL	AEILRRSU RURALISE	AEIMORTZ AMORTIZE	AEINOPST SAPONITE
AEILNRTY INTERLAY	AEILRRTY LITERARY	ATOMIZER	AEINOPSZ EPIZOANS
AEILNSST EASTLINS	AEILRRUZ RURALIZE	AEIMOSST AMITOSES	AEINOPTZ TOPAZINE
ELASTINS	AEILRSST REALISTS	AMOSITES	AEINOQTU EQUATION
SALIENTS	SALTIERS	ATOMISES	AEINORRT ANTERIOR
STANIELS	SALTIRES	OSMIATES	AEINORRW IRONWARE
AEILNSSU INULASES	SLAISTER	AEIMOSTZ ATOMIZES	AEINORSS ERASIONS
AEILNSSZ LAZINESS	AEILRSSV REVISALS	AEIMOTTV MOTIVATE	AEINORST ANOESTRI
AEILNSTU ALUNITES	RIVALESS		ARSONITE
INSULATE	AEILRSTT TERTIALS		NOTARIES
AEILNSTV VENTAILS	AEILRSTU URALITES		NOTARISE

	ROSINATE	AEINSSSV VINASSES	SWARTIER	AEKNRSSW SWANKERS
AEINORSV	AVERSION	AEINSSTT INSTATES	AEIRRTTT RETRAITT	AEKNRSTZ KRANTZES
AEINORTT	TENTORIA	NASTIEST	AEIRRTTY TERTIARY	AEKNSSTW SWANKEST
AEINORTZ	NOTARIZE	SATINETS	AEIRRVWY RIVERWAY	AEKNSSWY SWANKEYS
AEINOSST	ASSIENTO	AEINSSVW WAVINESS	AEIRSSST TIRASSES	AEKOPSTU OUTSPEAK
	ASTONIES	AEINSSWX WAXINESS	AEIRSSSZ ASSIZERS	AEKORRSS ROSAKERS
AEINOSSV	EVASIONS	AEINSTTV TASTEVIN	AEIRSSTT ARTISTES	AEKORRWW WORKWEAR
AEINOSSX	SAXONIES	AEINSTTT NATTIEST	ARTSIEST	AEKORSSS KAROSSES
AEINOSTV	STOVAINE	AEINSTTW TAWNIEST	STRIATES	AEKORSTV OVERTASK
AEINOSTX	SAXONITE	AEINSTWY YAWNIEST	AEIRSSTV TRAVISES	AEKORTUY EUKARYOT
AEINOSXZ	OXAZINES	AEINSUVV VESUVIAN	AEIRSSTW WAISTERS	AEKOSTTU OUTTAKES
AEINOTVX	VEXATION	AEINTTUU AUTUNITE	WAITRESS	AEKPPSSU UPSPEAKS
AEINPPRS	SNAPPIER	AEIOPPST APPOSITE	WASTRIES	AEKPSSSY PASSKEYS
AEINPPST	NAPPIEST	AEIOPRRT PRIORATE	AEIRSTTT RATTIEST	AEKQRSUW SQUAWKER
AEINPRRT	TERRAPIN	AEIOPRSV VAPORISE	TARTIEST	AEKRRSST STARKERS
AEINPRRU	UNREPAIR	AEIOPRTX EXPIATOR	TITRATES	AEKRSSTT STARKEST
AEINPRST	PAINTERS	AEIOPRVZ VAPORIZE	AEIRSTTW WARTIEST	AELLLORY LOYALLER
	PANTRIES	AEIOPSST SOAPIEST	AEIRSTTX EXTRAITS	AELLLRTU TELLURAL
	PERTAINS	AEIOPTTV OPTATIVE	AEIRSTUZ AZURITES	AELLLSUV VULSELLA
	PINASTER	AEIOQSSU SEQUOIAS	AEIRSTVY VESTIARY	AELLMNOZ MANZELLO
	REPAINTS	AEIORRRS ARRIEROS	AEIRSWWY WAYWISER	AELLMNST STALLMEN
AEINPRSU	UNPRAISE	AEIORRSS ROSARIES	AEISSSST SASSIEST	AELLMNTY MENTALLY
AEINPRTT	TRIPTANE	AEIORRST ROARIEST	AEISSSTW TISWASES	TALLYMEN
AEINPRTU	PAINTURE	ROTARIES	AEISSSTY ESSAYIST	AELLMORR MORALLER
AEINPRTX	EXPIRANT	AEIORSSV SAVORIES	AEISSTTT TASTIEST	AELLMORT MARTELLO
AEINPSTT	PATIENTS	AEIORSTV VOTARIES	AEISSTTU SITUATES	AELLMOTY TOMALLEY
AEINPSTU	PETUNIAS	AEIORSVW AVOWRIES	AEISSTTV VASTIEST	AELLMPUU PLUMULAE
	SUPINATE	AEIORTTV ROTATIVE	AEISSTWZ TIZWASES	AELLMRSY MERSALYL
AEINPSTY	EPINASTY	AEIOSSTT TOASTIES	AEISTTTT TATTIEST	AELLMSST SMALLEST
AEINPTTY	ANTITYPE	AEIOSSTZ AZOTISES	AEISTTTU ATTUITES	AELLMSWX MAXWELLS
AEINQRTU	QUAINTER	AEIOSTZZ AZOTIZES	AEISTTTW TAWTIEST	AELLNOPS PALLONES
AEINQSTU	ANTIQUES	AEIPPPST PAPPIEST	AEJLNSUV JUVENALS	AELLNOPV VOLPLANE
	QUANTISE	AEIPPRRT TRAPPIER	AEJLOSSU JALOUSES	AELLNORS LLANEROS
AEINQTTU	EQUITANT	AEIPPRRZ APPRIZER	AEJLOSUY JEALOUSY	AELLNOSV NOVELLAS
AEINQTUZ	QUANTIZE	AEIPPRSS APPRISES	AEJLOSUZ AZULEJOS	AELLNOWW ENWALLOW
AEINRRST	RESTRAIN	AEIPPRST PERIAPTS	AEJNORSZ ZANJEROS	AELLNPRU PRUNELLA
	RETRAINS	AEIPPRSZ APPRIZES	AEKKLLWY LYKEWALK	AELLNPSS PLANLESS
	STRAINER	AEIPPSST SAPPIEST	AEKKMNOO KAKEMONO	AELLNPTT PLANTLET
	TERRAINS	AEIPPSTZ ZAPPIEST	AEKKOSSS SAKKOSES	AELLNPTU PLANTULE
	TRAINERS	AEIPQRTU PRATIQUE	AEKLLSTU KELLAUTS	AELLNRUY UNREALLY
	TRANSIRE	AEIPRRSS PRAISERS	AEKLMRUW LUKEWARM	AELLNRVY VERNALLY
AEINRRTV	VERATRIN	AEIPRRSY SPRAYIER	AEKLMRUY YARMULKE	AELLNSST TALLNESS
AEINRRTW	INTERWAR	AEIPRSST PASTRIES	AEKLNNSS LANKNESS	AELLNSTT TALLENTS
AEINRRUW	UNWARIER	PIASTRES	AEKLNOSY ANKYLOSE	AELLNTTY LATENTLY
AEINRSST	RESIANTS	RASPIEST	AEKLNPPS KNAPPLES	AELLNTUU LUNULATE
	RETSINAS	TRAIPSES	AEKLNPRS PRANKLES	AELLOPRS REPOSALL
	SNARIEST	AEIPRSSU UPRAISES	AEKLOPTY KALOTYPE	AELLOPRW WALLOPER
	STAINERS	AEIPRSSV PARVISES	AEKLORSW SALEWORK	AELLORRY ROYALLER
	STARNIES	AEIPRSTV PRIVATES	AEKLORSY ROKELAYS	AELLORRS ROSELLAS
	STEARINS	AEIPRSTW WIRETAPS	AEKLORTV OVERTALK	AELLORST REALLOTS
AEINRSSU	SENARIUS	AEIPRSTY ASPERITY	AEKLOSST SKATOLES	AELLORSV OVERALLS
AEINRSSW	WARINESS	AEIPRSVY VESPIARY	STALKOES	AELLORSW SALLOWER
AEINRSSX	XERANSIS	AEIPRSXY PYREXIAS	AEKLPRRS SPARKLER	AELLORWW WALLOWER
AEINRSTT	INTREATS	AEIPSSST PASTISES	AEKLPRSS SPARKLES	AELLOSUV ALVEOLUS
	NITRATES	AEIPSSSV PASSIVES	AEKLPRST SPARKLET	AELLPSTY PLAYLETS
	STRAITEN	AEIPSSTT PASTIEST	AEKLRSST STALKERS	AELLQRSU SQUALLER
	TARTINES	AEIPSSTW WASPIEST	AEKMMNRS MARKSMEN	AELLRRSU ALLURERS
	TERTIANS	AEIPSZZZ PIZAZZES	AEKMNRSU UNMASKER	AELLRRTY RETRALLY
AEINRSTU	RUINATES	AEIPTTUV PUTATIVE	AEKMOPRT TOPMAKER	AELLRRTY LATTERLY
	URANITES	AEIQRRRU QUARRIER	AEKMORTW TEAMWORK	AELLRTVY TREVALLY
	URINATES	AEIQRRSU QUARRIES	AEKMPRRV VERKRAMP	AELLRWYY LAWYERLY
AEINRSTW	TINWARES	AEIQRRTU QUARTIER	AEKMPRSU UPMAKERS	AELLSSST SALTLESS
AEINRSUV	VAURIENS	AEIRRRST STARRIER	AEKNNRSS RANKNESS	TASSELLS
AEINRSUZ	AZURINES	TARRIERS	AEKNORRV OVERRANK	AELLSSTW SETWALLS
	SUZERAIN	AEIRRSST TARSIERS	AEKNORUY EUKARYON	SWALLETS
AEINRSVV	VERVAINS	AEIRRSSY SISERARY	AEKNOTTU OUTTAKEN	AELLSSTY TASSELLY
AEINRSZZ	SNAZZIER	AEIRRSTT RETRAITS	AEKNPPRS KNAPPERS	AELLSTUU ULULATES
AEINRTTU	TAINTURE	STRAITER	AEKNPRSS SPANKERS	AELLSUVV VALVULES
AEINSSST	SAINTESS	TARRIEST	AEKNPSSU UNSPEAKS	AELLSUXY SEXUALLY
	SESTINAS	AEIRRSTW STRAWIER	AEKNRSST STARKENS	AELMMNOS MAMELONS

AELMMOSY	MYELOMAS	AELNORTT	TETRONAL	AELORUUX	ROULEAUX	AEMMNRRY	MERRYMAN
AELMMRSS	SLAMMERS		TOLERANT	AELOSSTV	SOLVATES	AEMMNRTU	RAMENTUM
AELMMRST	STRAMMEL	AELNORTU	OUTLEARN	AELOSSTY	ASYSTOLE	AEMMORSS	MARMOSES
	TRAMMELS	AELNORTY	ORNATELY	AELOSSVY	SAVELOYS	AEMMORST	MARMOSET
AELMMSST	STAMMELS	AELNOSTV	VOLANTES	AELOSTTU	TOLUATES	AEMMRSST	STAMMERS
AELMMSSY	MALMSEYS	AELNPRST	PANTLERS	AELOSTUV	OVULATES	AEMMRTUY	MAUMETRY
AELMNNOU	NOUMENAL		PLANTERS	AELOSTUY	AUTOLYSE	AEMMRTWY	MAWMETRY
AELMNNRY	MANNERLY		REPLANTS	AELOTUUV	OUTVALUE	AEMMSSTU	SUMMATES
AELMNNTU	UNMANTLE	AELNPRSU	PURSLANE	AELOTUYZ	AUTOLYZE	AEMMSSUW	WAMMUSES
AELMNOPS	NEOPLASM		SUPERNAL	AELPPRSS	SLAPPERS	AEMNNOPW	PENWOMAN
	PLEONASM	AELNPRTY	PLENARTY	AELPPSST	STAPPLES	AEMNNORT	ORNAMENT
AELMNORS	ALMONERS	AELNPSSS	SPANLESS	AELPPSSU	APPULSES	AEMNNOSS	MANNOSES
AELMNOST	SALMONET	AELNPSSU	SPANSULE	AELPRRSW	SPRAWLER	AEMNNRST	MANRENTS
AELMNOSU	MELANOUS	AELNPSTX	EXPLANTS	AELPRRTT	PRATTLER		REMNANTS
AELMNOYY	YEOMANLY	AELNPTTU	PETULANT	AELPRSST	PLASTERS	AEMNOORR	MAROONER
AELMNPRS	LAMPERNS	AELNPTTY	PATENTLY		PSALTERS	AEMNOORT	ANTEROOM
AELMNRSU	MENSURAL	AELNQSUU	UNEQUALS		STAPLERS	AEMNOORY	AERONOMY
	NUMERALS	AELNRRSS	SNARLERS	AELPRSSU	PERUSALS	AEMNOOTZ	METAZOON
AELMNSTT	MANTLETS	AELNRRTY	ERRANTLY	AELPRSSY	PARSLEYS	AEMNOPRS	PROSEMAN
AELMNSTU	NUTMEALS	AELNRRUV	NERVULAR		SPARSELY	AEMNOPRT	EMPATRON
AELMOOPT	OMOPLATE	AELNRSST	SALTERNS	AELPRSTT	PARTLETS	AEMNOPRW	MANPOWER
AELMOPRR	PREMOLAR	AELNRSTT	SLATTERN		PLATTERS	AEMNORRS	RANSOMER
AELMOPRS	PLEROMAS		TRENTALS		PRATTLES	AEMNORST	MONSTERA
AELMOPRT	PROMETAL	AELNRSTU	NEUTRALS		SPLATTER		STOREMAN
	TEMPORAL	AELNRSTV	VENTRALS		SPRATTLE	AEMNORSU	ENAMOURS
AELMOPSU	AMPOULES	AELNRSUV	UNRAVELS	AELPRSTU	APLUSTRE		NEUROMAS
AELMOPSX	EXOPLASM	AELNRSVY	SYLVANER	AELPRSTY	PLASTERY	AEMNORSV	OVERMANS
AELMOPSY	MAYPOLES	AELNRSXY	LARYNXES		PSALTERY		OVERSMAN
	PLAYSOME	AELNRUWY	UNWARELY	AELPSSSS	PASSLESS	AEMNORSY	ROMNEYAS
AELMOPTT	PALMETTO	AELNSSST	SALTNESS	AELPSSSU	LAPSUSES	AEMNORTT	MARTENOT
AELMORST	MOLERATS	AELNSSTY	STANYELS	AELPSSTT	PELTASTS	AEMNORTU	ROUTEMAN
AELMORSU	RAMULOSE	AELNSTUV	ENVAULTS	AELPSSTU	PULSATES	AEMNORTY	MONETARY
AELMORSV	REMOVALS	AELNSUUX	UNSEXUAL		SPATULES	AEMNORYY	YEOMANRY
AELMORTU	EMULATOR	AELNTTUX	EXULTANT	AELPSUUV	UPVALUES	AEMNOSTU	NOTAEUMS
AELMOSSS	MOLASSES	AELOOPRZ	ZOOPERAL	AELQRRSU	QUARRELS		OUTNAMES
AELMOSST	MALTOSES	AELOORSS	AEROSOLS	AELQRSUY	SQUARELY		SEAMOUNT
AELMOSTT	MATELOTS		ROSEOLAS	AELQSTTU	SQUATTLE	AEMNPRSS	PRESSMAN
AELMOSTY	ATMOLYSE	AELOORTZ	ZOOLATER	AELQSTUZ	QUETZALS	AEMNPRSU	SUPERMAN
AELMOTYZ	ATMOLYZE	AELOPPRS	PROLAPSE	AELRRSTT	RATTLERS	AEMNPSST	ENSTAMPS
AELMPRRT	TRAMPLER		PROPALES		STARTLER		PASSMENT
AELMPRSS	SAMPLERS		SAPROPEL	AELRRSTW	TRAWLERS	AEMNPSTY	PAYMENTS
AELMPRST	TRAMPLES	AELOPPSU	PAPULOSE	AELRRTVY	VARLETRY	AEMNQSUW	SQUAWMEN
AELMPRSY	LAMPREYS	AELOPPTU	POPULATE	AELRSSST	STARLESS	AEMNRRSU	MANURERS
	SAMPLERY	AELOPPXY	APOPLEXY	AELRSSTT	SLATTERS	AEMNRRUY	NUMERARY
AELMQSUU	SQUAMULE	AELOPQUY	OPAQUELY		STARLETS	AEMNRSST	SARMENTS
AELMRSTT	MALTSTER	AELOPRRV	REPROVAL		STARTLES		SMARTENS
	MARTLETS	AELOPRSS	REPOSALS	AELRSSTU	SALUTERS	AEMNRSSU	SURNAMES
AELMRSTY	MASTERLY	AELOPRST	PETROSAL	AELRSSTW	WARTLESS	AEMNRSSW	WARMNESS
AELMRTUY	MATURELY		PROLATES		WASTRELS	AEMNRSTU	ANESTRUM
AELMSSST	MASTLESS	AELOPRSU	LEAPROUS	AELRSSUW	WALRUSES		MENSTRUA
AELNNNPU	UNPANNEL	AELOPRSV	OVERLAPS	AELRSTTT	TARTLETS		TRANSUME
AELNNOOP	NAPOLEON	AELOPRVY	OVERPLAY		TATTLERS	AEMNRSTV	VARMENTS
AELNNOXO	NALOXONE	AELOPSSS	SOAPLESS	AELRSTTU	LUSTRATE	AEMNRSTW	TRANSMEW
AELNNORU	NEURONAL	AELOPSST	APOSTLES		TUTELARS		TREWSMAN
AELNNOSU	ANNULOSE	AELOPSSU	ESPOUSAL	AELRSTTY	SLATTERY	AEMNRSUY	ANEURYSM
AELNNPRS	PLANNERS		SEPALOUS	AELRSTUV	VAULTERS	AEMNSTWY	WAYMENTS
AELNNPSU	UNPANELS	AELOPSSX	EXPOSALS		VESTURAL	AEMOOPST	POMATOES
AELNNRSS	ENSNARLS	AELOPSTT	PALETOTS	AELRSTWZ	WALTZERS	AEMOORSW	WOOMERAS
AELNNRST	LANTERNS	AELOPSTU	OUTLEAPS	AELRSUVY	SURVEYAL	AEMOORTT	AMORETTO
AELNNRSU	UNLEARNS		PETALOUS	AELRTTTW	TWATTLER	AEMOOSST	MAESTOSO
AELNNRTU	UNLEARNT	AELOPTTU	OUTLEAPT	AELRTTUX	TEXTURAL		OSTEOMAS
AELNNSST	STANNELS	AELORRST	REALTORS	AELRTTUY	TUTELARY	AEMOOSSV	VAMOOSES
AELNNSTU	ANNULETS		RELATORS	AELSSSTU	SALTUSES	AEMOOSTT	TOMATOES
AELNOOTZ	ENTOZOAL	AELORSTU	ROSULATE	AELSSSTY	STAYLESS	AEMOOSTU	AUTOSOME
AELNOPRS	PERSONAL	AELORSTV	LEVATORS	AELSSWZZ	SWAZZLES	AEMOPPRS	PAMPEROS
AELNOPST	LAPSTONE	AELORSTY	ROYALETS	AELSTTTW	TWATTLES	AEMOPRTW	POMWATER
	PLEONAST	AELORSUU	ROULEAUS	AELSTTUY	ASTUTELY		TAPEWORM
	POLENTAS	AELORSVY	OVERLAYS	AEMMMOTU	OMMATEUM	AEMOQSSU	SQUAMOSE
AELNORSU	ALEURONS	AELORTTV	VARLETTO	AEMMMRTY	MAMMETRY	AEMORRRU	ARMOURER
AELNORSV	VERONALS	AELORTYZ	ZEALOTRY	AEMMNPRS	RAMPSMEN	AEMORRST	REARMOST

AEMORRSY	ROSEMARY	AENORSTV	VENATORS
AEMORSSS	MORASSES	AENORSUV	RAVENOUS
AEMORSST	MAESTROS	AENORTTX	TETRAXON
AEMORSSY	MAYORESS	AENORTTY	ATTORNEY
AEMORSTV	OVERMAST	AENOSSTU	SOUTANES
AEMORSVW	OVERSWAM	AENOSSTZ	STANZOES
AEMORTTU	TAUTOMER	AENOSSUU	NAUSEOUS
AEMOSSTT	EASTMOST	AENOSSVW	WAVESONS
AEMOSSTW	TWASOMES	AENPPRSS	PARSNEPS
AEMOSSUZ	ZAMOUSES		SNAPPERS
AEMOSSWY	SOMEWAYS	AENPPRST	PARPENTS
AEMOSTTZ	MOZETTAS	AENPPRSU	UNPAPERS
AEMOTTZZ	MOZZETTA	AENPRRST	PARTNERS
AEMPRRST	TRAMPERS	AENPRSST	PASTERNS
AEMPRRSY	SPERMARY	AENPRSSW	SPAWNERS
AEMPRSST	STAMPERS	AENPRSTT	PATTERNS
AEMPRSSW	SWAMPERS		TRANSEPT
AEMPRSTT	TRAMPETS	AENPRSTU	PERSAUNT
AEMPRSTU	TEMPURAS	AENPRSUV	PARVENUS
	UPSTREAM	AENPSSSY	SYNAPSES
AEMPSSUW	MAWPUSES	AENPSSTU	PESAUNTS
	WAMPUSES	AENPSSTW	STEWPANS
AEMPSTTT	ATTEMPTS	AENPSSTY	SYNAPTES
AEMQRSSU	MARQUESS	AENPSSTZ	SPETSNAZ
	MASQUERS	AENPSTZZ	SPETZNAZ
AEMRRSSW	SWARMERS	AENQRRTU	QUARTERN
AEMRRTUV	VERATRUM	AENQSTTU	QUESTANT
AEMRSSSU	MASSEURS	AENRRRTY	ERRANTRY
AEMRSSTT	MATTRESS	AENRRSTT	TRANTERS
	SMARTEST	AENRSSST	SARSNETS
	SMATTERS	AENRSSTT	TARTNESS
AEMRSSTY	MAYSTERS	AENRSSTU	ANESTRUS
AEMRSTTU	MATUREST		SAUNTERS
	TESTAMUR	AENRSSTV	SERVANTS
AEMRTUUX	TRUMEAUX		VERSANTS
AEMSTTTU	TESTATUM	AENRSSUW	UNSWEARS
AENNNPST	PENNANTS	AENRSTTU	TAUNTERS
AENNNTTU	UNTENANT	AENRSTUV	VAUNTERS
AENNOPRT	PATRONNE	AENRSTUW	UNWATERS
AENNOPST	PENTOSAN	AENRSTWY	STERNWAY
AENNOPUW	UNWEAPON	AENRTUVY	VAUNTERY
AENNORST	RESONANT	AENRTUWY	UNWATERY
AENNORSU	UNREASON	AENSSSTV	VASTNESS
AENNORTW	WANTONER	AENSSSTW	WASTNESS
AENNORVY	NOVENARY	AENSSTTU	TAUTNESS
AENNOSSU	UNSEASON		UNSTATES
AENNOSTU	TONNEAUS	AENSSTTX	SEXTANTS
AENNPRSS	SPANNERS	AENSSTXY	SYNTAXES
AENNPSSU	PANNUSES	AEOOPPPS	PAPPOOSE
AENNQSTU	QUANNETS	AEOOPPSS	PAPOOSES
AENNRSTT	ENTRANTS	AEOOPRRT	OPERATOR
AENNRSTY	TYRANNES	AEOOPRSS	OROPESAS
AENNRSWY	SWANNERY	AEOOPSTT	POTATOES
AENNRTTY	TENANTRY	AEOORRST	SORORATE
AENOOPST	TEASPOON	AEOORTTT	TATTOOER
AENOORRT	RATOONER	AEOORTTV	ROTOVATE
AENOPPRS	PROPANES	AEOPPRRV	APPROVER
AENOPRSS	PERSONAS	AEOPPRSS	APPOSERS
	RESPONSA	AEOPPRSV	APPROVES
AENOPRST	OPERANTS	AEOPQRTU	PAROQUET
	PRONATES	AEOPQSTU	OPAQUEST
AENOPRTT	PATENTOR	AEOPRRRT	PARROTER
AENOPRWY	WEAPONRY	AEOPRRST	PRAETORS
AENOPSSU	POSAUNES		PRORATES
AENORRRW	NARROWER	AEOPRRTV	OVERPART
AENORRST	ANTRORSE	AEOPRRUV	VAPOURER
AENORSST	ASSENTOR	AEOPRRVW	WRAPOVER
	SENATORS	AEOPRSST	ESPARTOS
	TREASONS		PORTASES
AENORSTT	ORNATEST		PROTASES

	SEAPORTS	AEQRTTTU	QUARTETT
AEOPRSSU	ASPEROUS	AERRSSSU	ASSURERS
AEOPRSSV	OVERPASS	AERRSSTT	RESTARTS
AEOPRSTT	PROSTATE		STARTERS
AEOPRSTU	APTEROUS	AERRSTTU	SERRATUS
AEOPRSTV	OVERPAST	AERRSSTY	STRAYERS
AEOPRSVY	OVERPAYS	AERRSTUY	TREASURY
AEOPRSWY	ROPEWAYS	AERSSSST	STRASSES
AEOPSSST	POTASSES	AERSSSTY	SATYRESS
AEOPTTUY	AUTOTYPE	AERSSTTU	STATURES
AEOQRSTU	EQUATORS	AERSSTTW	SWATTERS
	QUAESTOR	AERSSTUX	SURTAXES
AEOQRSUV	VAQUEROS	AERSSTXY	STYRAXES
AEOQRTTU	TORQUATE	AERSTTUU	VETTURAS
AEOQRTUZ	QUATORZE	AERSTTVY	TRAVESTY
AEORRRST	ARRESTOR	AERTTUXY	TEXTUARY
AEORRSST	ASSERTOR	AESSTTTU	ASTUTEST
	ORATRESS		STATUTES
	ROASTERS	AFFFFINN	NIFFNAFF
AEORRSSU	AROUSERS	AFFFGILN	FLAFFING
AEORRSTT	ROSTRATE	AFFGGINR	GRAFFING
AEORRTUV	AVOUTRER	AFFGGINS	GAFFINGS
AEORRTZZ	TERRAZZO	AFFGHIRT	AFFRIGHT
AEORSSSS	ASSESSOR	AFFGIINP	PIAFFING
AEORSSTT	STRATOSE	AFFGIINX	AFFIXING
	TOASTERS	AFFGIIRT	GRAFFITI
AEORSSTV	VOTARESS	AFFGILMN	MAFFLING
AEORSSTX	STORAXES	AFFGILNR	RAFFLING
AEORSTTT	ATTESTOR	AFFGILNW	WAFFLING
	TESTATOR	AFFGIMRS	MISGRAFF
AEORSTTU	OUTRATES	AFFGINNY	NYAFFING
	OUTSTARE	AFFGINQU	QUAFFING
AEORSTUW	OUTSWEAR	AFFGINST	STAFFING
	OUTWEARS	AFFGINUW	WAUFFING
AEORSTVY	OVERSTAY	AFFGIORT	GRAFFITO
AEORSUVW	WAVEROUS	AFFHIKSU	KUFFIAHS
AEORTUWY	OUTWEARY	AFFHILNS	HAFFLINS
AEORTVXY	VEXATORY	AFFHILST	FLATFISH
AEPPPSSU	PAPPUSES	AFFHILTU	FAITHFUL
AEPPRRST	STRAPPER	AFFIINTY	AFFINITY
	TRAPPERS	AFFILMNS	MAFFLINS
AEPPRRSW	WRAPPERS	AFFILSUX	SUFFIXAL
AEPPRSSU	UPSPEARS	AFFIMSST	MASTIFFS
AEPPRSSW	SWAPPERS	AFFINORR	FORFAIRN
AEPQRSTU	PARQUETS	AFFINOSU	AFFUSION
AEPRRRSS	SPARRERS	AFFINRSU	FUNFAIRS
AEPRRSSY	RESPRAYS		RUFFIANS
	SPRAYERS	AFFIORRS	FORFAIRS
AEPRRSTU	PARTURES	AFFIPSTT	TIPSTAFF
	RAPTURES	AFFIRRSU	FURFAIRS
AEPRSSST	SPARSEST	AFFLLOOT	FOOTFALL
	TRESPASS	AFFLLTUU	FAULTFUL
AEPRSSTT	SPATTERS	AFFLOOOT	FOALFOOT
	TAPSTERS	AFFLORTU	FORFAULT
AEPRSSTU	PASTURES	AFFLRRUU	FURFURAL
	UPSTARES	AFFNORSS	SAFFRONS
AEPRSSTY	YAPSTERS	AFFNORST	AFFRONTS
AEPRSTTU	STUPRATE	AFFNORSY	SAFFRONY
AEPRSTTY	TAPESTRY	AFFNRRUU	FURFURAN
AEPRSTUX	SUPERTAX	AFGGGILN	FLAGGING
AEPRTUVY	PYRUVATE	AFGGGINS	FAGGINGS
AEPSSSSU	PASSUSES	AFGGILNN	FANGLING
AEQRRSSU	SQUARERS		FLANGING
AEQRRSTU	QUARTERS	AFGGINOR	FORAGING
AEQRSSTU	SQUAREST	AFGGINOT	FAGOTING
AEQRSTTU	QUARTETS	AFGGINRT	GRAFTING
	SQUATTER	AFGHIINT	FAITHING
AEQRSTUZ	QUARTZES	AFGHILLN	HALFLING
		AFGHILNS	FLASHING
		AFGHILNT	FANLIGHT

AFGHILPS	FLAGSHIP	AFHILSTT	FLATTISH	AFINQTUY	QUANTIFY		SNAGGING
AFGHINRT	FARTHING	AFHIMNST	MANSHIFT	AFINRSTX	TRANSFIX	AGGGINRS	RAGGINGS
AFGHINRW	WHARFING	AFHIMNSU	HAFNIUMS	AFINSSTU	FAUNISTS	AGGGINSS	SAGGINGS
AFGHINST	SHAFTING	AFHINOSS	FASHIONS		FUSTIANS	AGGGINST	STAGGING
AFGHIOST	GOATFISH	AFHINSTU	UNFAITHS	AFIORSTU	FAITOURS	AGGGINSU	GAUGINGS
AFGHLLUU	LAUGHFUL	AFHIOSSU	FASHIOUS	AFIORSTZ	SFORZATI	AGGGINSW	SWAGGING
AFGHLSTU	FLAUGHTS	AFHIRSST	STARFISH	AFIRSTTY	STRATIFY	AGGGIYZZ	ZIGZAGGY
	GHASTFUL	AFHKLNTU	THANKFUL	AFISSSTT	SITFASTS	AGGHIILS	GHILGAIS
AFGHRSTU	FRAUGHTS	AFHKORSX	FOXSHARK	AFKLNOTU	OUTFLANK	AGGHILNU	LAUGHING
AFGIILLN	FLAILING	AFHKORSY	HAYFORKS	AFKLNPRU	PRANKFUL	AGGHILST	GASLIGHT
AFGIILNS	FAILINGS	AFHKRSTU	FUTHARKS	AFKLNSTU	TANKFULS	AGGHILSY	SHAGGILY
AFGIIMNN	INFAMING	AFHLLOTU	LOATHFUL	AFKLOSWY	FOLKWAYS	AGGHIMNO	HOMAGING
AFGIINNT	FAINTING	AFHLOSTU	OUTFLASH	AFKLRSSU	SARKFULS	AGGHIMNS	GINGHAMS
AFGIINRS	FAIRINGS	AFHLOSTY	HAYLOFTS	AFKMOORT	FOOTMARK	AGGHINNP	PHANGING
	FRAISING	AFHLRTUW	WRATHFUL	AFLLLORY	FLORALLY	AGGHINNS	GNASHING
AFGIINTX	FIXATING	AFHNOOST	FANTOOSH	AFLLLUWY	LAWFULLY		HANGINGS
AFGIKLNN	FANKLING	AFHOOPST	POOFTAHS	AFLLMNUY	MANFULLY	AGGHINNW	WHANGING
	FLANKING	AFHOOPTT	FOOTPATH	AFLLMORY	FORMALLY	AGGHINPR	GRAPHING
AFGIKNNR	FRANKING	AFHOPSTU	POUFTAHS	AFLLMPSU	PALMFULS	AGGHINST	GHASTING
AFGIKORT	KOFTGARI	AFIIKMRS	FAKIRISM	AFLLNOSW	SNOWFALL	AGGHINUW	WAUGHING
AFGILLNS	FALLINGS	AFIILLLY	FILIALLY	AFLLNUUW	UNLAWFUL	AGGIIJJS	JIGAJIGS
AFGILLNT	FLATLING	AFIILLNU	UNFILIAL	AFLLOSTU	OUTFALLS	AGGIILNN	ALIGNING
AFGILMMN	FLAMMING	AFIILMMS	FAMILISM	AFLLRTUY	ARTFULLY	AGGIILNR	GLAIRING
AFGILMNO	FLAMINGO	AFIILMNS	FINALISM	AFLLSTUW	WASTFULL	AGGIILNS	SILAGING
AFGILNOS	LOAFINGS	AFIILNRU	UNIFILAR	AFLMNORU	UNFORMAL	AGGIILNT	LIGATING
AFGILNOT	FLOATING	AFIILNST	FINALIST	AFLMOPRT	PLATFORM		TAIGLING
AFGILNPP	FLAPPING	AFIILNTY	FINALITY	AFLMORRU	FORMULAR	AGGIILNV	GINGIVAL
AFGILNST	FATLINGS	AFIILRST	AIRLIFTS	AFLMORSU	FORMULAS	AGGIIMNS	IMAGINGS
AFGILNTT	FLATTING	AFIIMRSY	FAIRYISM	AFLMORSW	WOLFRAMS	AGGIINNR	GRAINING
AFGILNTU	FAULTING	AFIINNOS	SAINFOIN	AFLMORTU	FOULMART	AGGIINNS	AGNISING
AFGILORW	GAIRFOWL		SINFONIA	AFLMORTW	FLATWORM		GAININGS
AFGILSSY	GLASSIFY	AFIINOTX	FIXATION	AFLMOSST	FLOTSAMS	AGGIINNZ	AGNIZING
AFGIMNOS	FOAMINGS	AFIIORRT	TRIFORIA	AFLMOSUY	FAMOUSLY	AGGIINRS	AGRISING
AFGIMNRS	FARMINGS	AFIKLNNR	FRANKLIN	AFLNOPRU	APRONFUL	AGGIINRZ	AGRIZING
	FRAMINGS	AFIKLORT	FORKTAIL	AFLNORST	FRONTALS	AGGIINST	AGISTING
AFGIMNTU	FUMIGANT	AFIKNRST	RATFINKS	AFLNRTUU	UNARTFUL	AGGIINSU	AGUISING
AFGIMORS	GASIFORM	AFILLLOT	FLOTILLA	AFLNTUUV	VAUNTFUL	AGGIINUZ	AGUIZING
AFGIMRST	MISGRAFT	AFILLMSS	MISFALLS	AFLNTUUY	UNFAULTY	AGGIJJOS	JIGAJOGS
AFGINNNS	FANNINGS	AFILLNPU	PLAINFUL	AFLOOSTW	WOOLFATS	AGGIJLNN	JANGLING
AFGINNSW	FAWNINGS	AFILLPST	PITFALLS	AFLORSSU	FUSAROLS	AGGILLNS	GINGALLS
AFGINORV	FAVORING	AFILLPSU	PAILFULS	AFLORSUV	FLAVOURS	AGGILLNU	ULLAGING
AFGINORY	FORAYING	AFILLSUV	VIALFULS	AFLOSSSU	FOSSULAS	AGGILLNY	GALLYING
AFGINPPR	FRAPPING	AFILLTUY	FAULTILY	AFLOSTUU	FLATUOUS	AGGILMNN	MANGLING
AFGINRST	INGRAFTS	AFILMNOR	FORMALIN	AFLPRSTY	FLYTRAPS	AGGILMNO	GLOAMING
	STRAFING		INFORMAL	AFLRSTTU	STARTFUL	AGGILMNU	GLAUMING
AFGINRSW	SWARFING	AFILMOPR	PALIFORM	AFLRSTUY	TRAYFULS	AGGILNNO	GANGLION
AFGINRSY	FRAYINGS	AFILMSSS	FALSISMS	AFMNNORT	FRONTMAN	AGGILNNR	GNARLING
AFGINRTU	FIGURANT	AFILNORT	FLATIRON	AFMNORST	FORMANTS	AGGILNNS	ANGLINGS
AFGINSST	FASTINGS		INFLATOR	AFMOOPRR	PROFORMA		SLANGING
AFGINSTW	WAFTINGS	AFILNPPT	FLIPPANT	AFMORSTU	FOUMARTS	AGGILNNT	GNATLING
AFGINSUY	SANGUIFY	AFILNRUY	UNFAIRLY	AFMORTUY	FUMATORY		TANGLING
AFGKNOPS	PAKFONGS	AFILNSTU	FLUTINAS	AFNORRSW	FORWARNS	AGGILNNW	WANGLING
AFGKORST	KOFTGARS		INFLATUS	AFOOPPRS	APPROOFS	AGGILNOP	GALOPING
AFGLLNOT	FLATLONG	AFILORTY	FILATORY	AFOOPRRT	RATPROOF	AGGILNOT	GLOATING
AFGLLRUU	FULGURAL	AFILRSTU	FISTULAR	AFOORSTZ	FORZATOS		GOATLING
AFGLLRUY	FRUGALLY	AFILSSTU	FISTULAS		SFORZATO	AGGILNPU	PLAGUING
AFGLLSSU	GLASSFUL	AFILSTTU	FLAUTIST	AFOOSTWY	FOOTWAYS	AGGILNPY	GAPINGLY
AFGLLSTU	GASTFULL	AFIMMNOR	MANIFORM	AFORSTTW	FORSWATT	AGGILNRY	GRAYLING
AFGLNNOO	GONFALON	AFIMMORR	RAMIFORM	AFORSTTW	FORSWATT		RAGINGLY
AFGLNORU	GROANFUL	AFIMNOPR	NAPIFORM	AFOSSTUU	FASTUOUS	
AFGLNOUW	WAGONFUL	AFIMNORR	RANIFORM	AGGGGILN	GAGGLING	AGGILNSS	GLASSING
AFGNNNOO	GONFANON	AFIMNORT	NATIFORM	AGGGHILN	HAGGLING	AGGILNSZ	GLAZINGS
AFGOORTZ	ZOOGRAFT	AFIMNOSU	INFAMOUS	AGGGHINS	SHAGGING	AGGINNOR	GROANING
AFHIILRS	FRAILISH	AFIMORRU	AURIFORM	AGGGILNN	GANGLING	AGGINNOT	TANGOING
AFHIIMST	MISFAITH	AFIMORRV	VARIFORM	AGGGILNR	GARGLING	AGGINNOW	WAGONING
AFHIINST	FAINTISH	AFIMORSV	VASIFORM		RAGGLING	AGGINNPR	PRANGING
AFHIKSUY	KUFIYAHS	AFINNORS	FRANIONS	AGGGILNS	LAGGINGS	AGGINNPS	SPANGING
AFHILLNS	HALFLINS	AFINNOTU	FOUNTAIN		SLAGGING	AGGINNRR	GNARRING
AFHILLSW	WALLFISH	AFINNRTY	INFANTRY	AGGGILNW	WAGGLING	AGGINNRT	GRANTING
AFHILLSY	FLASHILY	AFINOPSY	SAPONIFY	AGGGINNS	GANGINGS	AGGINNRU	RAUNGING
						AGGINNST	STANGING

```
AGGINNTU GAUNTING    AGHINNTY ANYTHING             TRAILING    AGIKNOST GOATSKIN
AGGINNTW TWANGING    AGHINOST HOASTING    AGIILNRV VIRGINAL    AGIKNPRS PARKINGS
AGGINOVY VOYAGING    AGHINPPW WHAPPING    AGIILNSS AISLINGS             SPARKING
AGGINPRS GRASPING    AGHINPPY HAPPYING             SAILINGS    AGIKNPTU UPTAKING
         SPARGING    AGHINPRS HARPINGS    AGIILNST TAILINGS    AGIKNQSU QUAKINGS
AGGINPSS GASPINGS             PHRASING    AGIILNSW WAILINGS    AGIKNRSS SARKINGS
AGGINPUZ UPGAZING             SHARPING    AGIILNTT LITIGANT    AGIKNRST KARTINGS
AGGINRSS GRASSING    AGHINPSS SHAPINGS    AGIILNTV VIGILANT             STARKING
         SIRGANGS    AGHINPSW PSHAWING    AGIILOSV VILIAGOS    AGIKNSST SKATINGS
AGGINRST GRATINGS    AGHINQSU QUASHING    AGIILPST PIGTAILS             TASKINGS
AGGINRSU SUGARING    AGHINRRU HURRAING    AGIILTVY VAGILITY    AGILLLNS LALLINGS
AGGINRSV GRAVINGS    AGHINRRY HARRYING    AGIIMMNS MAIMINGS    AGILLMNS SMALLING
AGGINRSZ GRAZINGS    AGHINRSS SHARINGS    AGIIMMSS IMAGISMS    AGILLMNU MULLIGAN
AGGINRTY GYRATING    AGHINRST TRASHING    AGIIMNNR INARMING    AGILLMNY MALIGNLY
AGGINRUU AUGURING    AGHINRTW THRAWING    AGIIMNOW MIAOWING    AGILLMSU GALLIUMS
AGGINRYZ AGRYZING             WRATHING    AGIIMNPV IMPAVING    AGILLNOW ALLOWING
AGGINSSS GASSINGS    AGHINSST HASTINGS    AGIIMNSS AMISSING    AGILLNOY ALLOYING
AGGINSST STAGINGS             STASHING    AGIIMNST GIANTISM    AGILLNPS SPALLING
AGGIRTUZ ZIGGURAT    AGHINSSV SHAVINGS    AGIIMNTT MITIGANT    AGILLNRU ALLURING
AGGLLLOY LOLLYGAG    AGHINSSW SWASHING    AGIIMORS ORIGAMIS             LINGULAR
AGGLLOOY ALGOLOGY             WASHINGS    AGIIMSST IMAGISTS    AGILLNRY NARGILLY
AGGLMOOR LOGOGRAM    AGHINSTT HATTINGS    AGIINNPS SPAINING             RALLYING
AGGLOORY AGROLOGY    AGHINSTW SWATHING    AGIINNPT PAINTING    AGILLNST STALLING
AGGLRSTY STRAGGLY             THAWINGS    AGIINNRS INGRAINS    AGILLNSU LINGULAS
AGGMORRS GROGRAMS    AGHINUZZ HUZZAING    AGIINNRT TRAINING    AGILLNSW WALLINGS
AGGNUWZZ ZUGZWANG    AGHIPRRT TRIGRAPH    AGIINNRV RAVINING    AGILLNSY SALLYING
AGHHIILT HIGHTAIL    AGHIRSTT STRAIGHT    AGIINNST SAINTING             SIGNALLY
AGHHISWY HIGHWAYS    AGHISSTW SIGHTSAW             SATINING             SLANGILY
AGHHLOTU ALTHOUGH    AGHKOSSW GOSHAWKS             STAINING    AGILLNTY TALLYING
AGHIILNN INHALING    AGHLLMPU GALLUMPH    AGIINNSW SWAINING    AGILLOOR GILLAROO
AGHIINNS HAININGS    AGHLMOOR HOLOGRAM    AGIINNTT TAINTING    AGILLOPT GALLIPOT
AGHIIRTT AIRTIGHT    AGHLMPSU GALUMPHS    AGIINOPT OPIATING    AGILLORS GORILLAS
AGHIJNRT NIGHTJAR    AGHLNOSU SHOGUNAL    AGIINORS SIGNORIA    AGILLOST GALLIOTS
AGHIKNNS SHANKING    AGHLNSUY NYLGHAUS    AGIINPRS ASPIRING    AGILLPRY PLAYGIRL
AGHIKNNT THANKING    AGHLOOSS GASOHOLS             PAIRINGS    AGILLPUY PLAGUILY
AGHIKNRS SHARKING    AGHMMOOY HOMOGAMY             PRAISING    AGILLSSU LUGSAILS
AGHIKNSS SHAKINGS    AGHMOOPY OMOPHAGY    AGIINPRT PIRATING    AGILLSSY GLASSILY
AGHIKNSW HAWKINGS    AGHMOPRY MYOGRAPH    AGIINRRV ARRIVING    AGILMMNS LAMMINGS
AGHILLNO HALLOING    AGHNNSTU SHANTUNG    AGIINRSS RAISINGS             SLAMMING
AGHILLNS HALLINGS    AGHNOORS SHAGROON    AGIINRTT ATTIRING             SMALMING
AGHILLNT ALLNIGHT    AGHNORST STAGHORN    AGIINSSZ ASSIZING    AGILMNNT MANTLING
AGHILMTY ALMIGHTY    AGHNOSTU HANGOUTS    AGIINSTV VISTAING    AGILMNPS SAMPLING
AGHILNOO HOOLIGAN    AGHNPRSY SYNGRAPH    AGIINSTW WAITINGS    AGILMNQU QUALMING
AGHILNOS SHOALING    AGHNTTUU UNTAUGHT    AGIISSTV VISAGIST    AGILMNRS MARLINGS
AGHILNOT LOATHING    AGHOPSSW SWAGSHOP    AGIJMNOR MAJORING    AGILMNST MALTINGS
AGHILNPS PLASHING    AGHRSTTU STRAUGHT    AGIJNNSU JAUNSING    AGILMOPR LIPOGRAM
AGHILNRS HARLINGS    AGIIILNS LIAISING    AGIJNNTU JAUNTING    AGILMORS ALGORISM
         RINGHALS    AGIIINNS INSIGNIA    AGIJNRRS JARRINGS    AGILMPSU PLAGIUMS
AGHILNRY NARGHILY    AGIIKLNS SKAILING    AGIKLMOR KILOGRAM    AGILNNNP PLANNING
AGHILNSS HASSLING    AGIIKNRT TRAIKING    AGIKLNNP PLANKING    AGILNNOP PANGOLIN
         LASHINGS    AGIILLOV VILLAGIO    AGIKLNNR RANKLING    AGILNNOS LOANINGS
         SLANGISH             VILLIAGO    AGIKLNOS OAKLINGS    AGILNNPT PLANTING
         SLASHING    AGIILMNP IMPALING    AGIKLNST SKLATING    AGILNNRS SNARLING
AGHILNST HALTINGS    AGIILMNS MAILINGS             STALKING    AGILNNSS LINSANGS
         LATHINGS    AGIILMNU MIAULING             TALKINGS             SLANTING
AGHILNSU LANGUISH    AGIILNNP PLAINING    AGIKLNSW WALKINGS             TANLINGS
AGHILNSW SHAWLING    AGIILNNS NAILINGS    AGIKLNTY TAKINGLY    AGILNNUW UNLAWING
         WHALINGS             SNAILING    AGIKLNUW WAULKING    AGILNNUY UNGAINLY
AGHILRSY GARISHLY    AGIILNNU INGUINAL    AGIKMNNU UNMAKING             UNLAYING
AGHILRTY GRAITHLY    AGIILNNY INLAYING    AGIKMNPU UPMAKING    AGILNOOO OOGONIAL
AGHILSUY AGUISHLY    AGIILNOR ORIGINAL    AGIKMNRS MARKINGS    AGILNOOS ISOGONAL
AGHIMMNS SHAMMING    AGIILNOT INTAGLIO    AGIKNNPP KNAPPING    AGILNOPR PAROLING
AGHIMMNW WHAMMING             LIGATION    AGIKNNPR PRANKING    AGILNOPS GALOPINS
AGHIMNSS MASHINGS             TAGLIONI    AGIKNNPS SPANKING    AGILNOPT PLOATING
         SMASHING    AGIILNOX GLOXINIA    AGIKNNRR KNARRING    AGILNORT TRIGONAL
AGHIMNTY THINGAMY    AGIILNPT PLAITING    AGIKNNRS RANKINGS    AGILNOSS GLOSSINA
AGHIMPRU GRAPHIUM    AGIILNQU QUAILING    AGIKNNRU UNRAKING             LASSOING
AGHINNSS SNASHING    AGIILNRS GLAIRINS    AGIKNNST TANKINGS    AGILNOST ANTILOGS
AGHINNST TANGHINS             RAILINGS    AGIKNNSW SWANKING             SALTOING
AGHINNTU HAUNTING    AGIILNRT RINGTAIL    AGIKNOSS SOAKINGS    AGILNOTY ANTILOGY
```

AGILNPPP	PLAPPING
AGILNPPS	LAPPINGS
	SLAPPING
AGILNPPY	APPLYING
AGILNPRS	SPARLING
	SPRINGAL
AGILNPSS	SAPLINGS
AGILNPST	PLATINGS
	SPALTING
	STAPLING
AGILNPSW	LAPWINGS
	SPAWLING
AGILNPSY	PALSYING
	SPLAYING
AGILNPTT	PLATTING
AGILNPUY	UPLAYING
AGILNRST	RATLINGS
	STARLING
AGILNRSU	SINGULAR
AGILNRSW	WARLINGS
	WARSLING
AGILNRTT	RATTLING
AGILNRTW	TRAWLING
AGILNRVY	RAVINGLY
AGILNRWW	WRAWLING
AGILNRWX	WRAXLING
AGILNSST	ANGLISTS
	LASTINGS
	SALTINGS
	SLATINGS
AGILNSSV	SALVINGS
AGILNSSW	SWALINGS
AGILNSTT	SLATTING
AGILNSTU	SALUTING
AGILNSUV	AVULSING
AGILNSUW	WAULINGS
AGILNSVY	SAVINGLY
AGILNSWW	WAWLINGS
AGILNSWY	SWAYLING
AGILNTTT	TATTLING
AGILNTTW	WATTLING
AGILNTUV	VAULTING
AGILNTUX	LUXATING
AGILNTWZ	WALTZING
AGILOORS	GLORIOSA
AGILOOXY	AXIOLOGY
AGILOPST	GALIPOTS
AGILORSS	GIRASOLS
AGILOSST	SALIGOTS
AGILSYYZ	SYZYGIAL
AGIMMNRS	SMARMING
AGIMMOSY	MISOGAMY
AGIMNNOS	MASONING
AGIMNNOW	WOMANING
AGIMNNRU	MANURING
	UNARMING
AGIMNNTU	UNTAMING
AGIMNOOV	AMOOVING
AGIMNORS	ORGANISM
AGIMNORU	ORIGANUM
AGIMNORY	AGRIMONY
AGIMNOSV	VAMOSING
AGIMNPRT	TRAMPING
AGIMNPSS	SPASMING
AGIMNPST	STAMPING
	TAMPINGS
AGIMNPSV	VAMPINGS
AGIMNPSW	SWAMPING
AGIMNRRY	MARRYING
AGIMNRST	MIGRANTS
	SMARTING
AGIMNRSW	SWARMING
	WARMINGS
AGIMNRSY	MYRINGAS
AGIMNRTU	MATURING
AGIMNSSU	ASSUMING
AGIMNSTT	MATTINGS
AGIMNTTU	MUTATING
AGIMORRT	MIGRATOR
AGIMORSS	ISOGRAMS
AGIMORSU	GOURAMIS
AGIMQRUY	QUAGMIRY
AGIMRRST	TRIGRAMS
AGINNNNY	NANNYING
AGINNNOY	ANNOYING
AGINNNPS	PANNINGS
	SPANNING
AGINNNST	TANNINGS
AGINNNSV	VANNINGS
AGINNOOP	NAPOOING
AGINNOPR	APRONING
AGINNOPT	POIGNANT
AGINNORT	IGNORANT
AGINNOST	ASTONING
AGINNOTT	NOTATING
AGINNPPS	SNAPPING
AGINNPRW	PRAWNING
AGINNPST	PANTINGS
AGINNPSW	SPAWNING
	WINGSPAN
AGINNPUY	UNPAYING
AGINNQTU	QUANTING
AGINNRRS	SNARRING
AGINNRSS	SNARINGS
AGINNRST	STARNING
AGINNRSW	WARNINGS
AGINNRTT	TRANTING
AGINNRTU	NATURING
AGINNRTY	TRAYNING
	TYRANING
AGINNSTU	SAUNTING
	UNSATING
AGINNSTW	WANTINGS
AGINNSTY	STAYNING
AGINNSUY	UNSAYING
AGINNSWY	YAWNINGS
AGINNTTU	ATTUNING
	NUTATING
	TAUNTING
AGINNTUV	VAUNTING
AGINNTUX	UNTAXING
AGINNVVY	NAVVYING
AGINOORT	ROGATION
AGINOPPS	APPOSING
AGINOPQU	OPAQUING
AGINOPRV	VAPORING
AGINORRS	GARRISON
	ROARINGS
AGINORRW	ARROWING
AGINORSS	ASSIGNOR
	SIGNORAS
	SOARINGS
AGINORST	ORGANIST
	ROASTING
AGINORSU	AROUSING
AGINORSV	SAVORING
AGINORTT	ROTATING
	TROATING
AGINORTV	GRAVITON
AGINORTY	GYRATION
	ORGANITY
AGINOSST	AGONISTS
AGINOSSU	SAGOUINS
AGINOSTT	TANGOIST
	TOASTING
AGINPPRS	RAPPINGS
AGINPPRT	TRAPPING
AGINPPRW	WRAPPING
AGINPPST	STAPPING
	TAPPINGS
AGINPPSW	SWAPPING
AGINPPTU	PUPATING
AGINPPUY	APPUYING
AGINPRRS	SPARRING
AGINPRRY	PARRYING
AGINPRSS	PARSINGS
	RASPINGS
AGINPRST	PARTINGS
	PRATINGS
AGINPRSW	WARPINGS
AGINPRSY	PRAYINGS
	SPRAYING
AGINPRTT	PRATTING
AGINPRTU	UPRATING
AGINPRTY	PARTYING
AGINPSSS	PASSINGS
AGINPSST	PASTINGS
AGINPSSU	PAUSINGS
AGINPSTT	SPATTING
AGINQRSU	SQUARING
AGINRRST	STARRING
	TARRINGS
AGINRRTY	TARRYING
AGINRSST	GASTRINS
	STARINGS
AGINRSSU	ASSURING
AGINRSSY	SYRINGAS
AGINRSTT	RATTINGS
	STARTING
AGINRSTV	STARVING
AGINRSTW	STRAWING
	WRASTING
AGINRSTY	STRAYING
AGINRSVW	SWARVING
AGINRSVY	VARYINGS
AGINRSWY	RINGWAYS
AGINSSTT	TASTINGS
AGINSSTW	WASTINGS
AGINSSTY	STAYINGS
AGINSSWY	SWAYINGS
AGINSTTT	TATTINGS
AGINSTTW	SWATTING
AGINSVVY	SAVVYING
AGINSWWX	WAXWINGS
AGIOORSU	ORAGIOUS
AGIOORSZ	GRAZIOSO
AGIOORTU	AUTOGIRO
AGIOPPRT	AGITPROP
AGIORRTT	GRATTOIR
AGIORSST	AGISTORS
	ORGIASTS
AGIRSSTU	SASTRUGI
AGIRSTUZ	ZASTRUGI
AGIRTTUY	GRATUITY
AGJLRSUU	JUGULARS
AGJNOORS	JARGOONS
AGKMMORY	KYMOGRAM
AGKMNOPS	KAMPONGS
AGKNOPST	PAKTONGS
AGKORRSW	RAGWORKS
AGLLLNOW	LONGWALL
AGLLMOPW	GLOWLAMP
AGLLNOOS	GALLOONS
AGLLRUVY	VULGARLY
AGLMOOTY	ATMOLOGY
AGLMOPSY	POLYGAMS
AGLMOPYY	POLYGAMY
AGLMORSU	GLAMOURS
AGLNORSU	LANGUORS
AGLNOSST	GLASNOST
AGLNOSWY	LONGWAYS
AGLNPSUY	GUNPLAYS
AGLNRUUV	UNVULGAR
AGLNSSTU	SUNGLASS
AGLNSTUY	YGLAUNST
AGLOOPST	GOALPOST
AGLOOTUY	AUTOLOGY
AGLOPRSS	LOPGRASS
AGLORSSY	GLOSSARY
AGLPSSYY	SPYGLASS
AGLRTTUU	GUTTURAL
AGLSTUUY	AUGUSTLY
AGMMNOOR	MONOGRAM
	NOMOGRAM
AGMMNOOY	MONOGAMY
AGMMOORT	TOMOGRAM
AGMMORSY	MYOGRAMS
AGMNNOSW	GOWNSMAN
AGMNOOPR	PORNOMAG
AGMNOORY	AGRONOMY
AGMNORST	ANGSTROM
AGMNSSTU	MUSTANGS
AGMNSSTY	GYMNASTS
AGMOOOSU	OOGAMOUS
AGMOOPRY	POROGAMY
AGMOPRSS	PROGRAMS
AGMOPRSU	GOPURAMS
AGMORRSW	RAGWORMS
AGMRSSSU	GRASSUMS
AGNNNOOS	NONAGONS
AGNNOOPT	POONTANG
AGNNOQTU	QUANTONG
AGNORRST	GRANTORS
AGNPRSSU	UPSPRANG
AGOORRTY	ROGATORY
AGOORTUY	AUTOGYRO
AGORRSST	GROSSART
	ROTGRASS
AGORRSTW	RAGWORTS
AGORRTYY	GYRATORY
AGORSTTY	GYROSTAT
AHHIKLSS	SHASHLIK
AHHILNPT	PHTHALIN
AHHILOST	HAILSHOT
AHHILPSW	WHIPLASH
AHHIMMSS	MISHMASH
AHHIMNSU	HAHNIUMS
AHHIPRSS	SHARPISH
AHHISSTT	SHITTAHS
AHHLMRTY	RHYTHMAL
AHHLNOPT	NAPHTHOL
AHHMPRRU	HARRUMPH
AHHNORTW	HAWTHORN
AHHOPRSS	SHOPHARS
AHHOPSTU	APHTHOUS
AHIIKRSS	SHIKARIS
AHIILNPS	PLAINISH
AHIILOST	HALIOTIS
AHIILRTY	HILARITY

AHIIMNOT	HIMATION	AHIORSTV TOVARISH	AIIILLVX LIXIVIAL	AIIMOPSX APOMIXIS
AHIIMNST	ISTHMIAN	AHIORSUV HAVIOURS	AIIILMST MILITIAS	AIIMORTT IMITATOR
	THIAMINS	AHIOSTWY HOISTWAY	AIIILNST INITIALS	TIMARIOT
AHIIMSSS	SASHIMIS	AHIPPSST SAPPHIST	AIIILRVZ VIZIRIAL	AIIMOSST AMITOSIS
AHIINPRS	HAIRPINS	AHIPRSST HARPISTS	AIIIMRSS SAIMIRIS	AIIMPPRS PRIAPISM
AHIINPST	ANTISHIP	AHIPRSSW WARSHIPS	AIIIRSSS SIRIASIS	AIIMPRTY IMPARITY
AHIINSST	SAINTISH	AHIQRSSU SQUARISH	AIIJKMOT KOMITAJI	AIIMRSST SIMITARS
AHIINSSW	SWAINISH	AHIRRSST STIRRAHS	AIIJNRTX JANITRIX	AIIMRUVV VIVARIUM
AHIINSTU	HUITAINS	AHIRSSTT STARTISH	AIIKKSUY SUKIYAKI	AIIMSSTT MASTITIS
AHIIOPST	HOSPITIA	AHIRSSTW TRISHAWS	AIIKLNRR LARRIKIN	AIINNOPS PIANINOS
AHIIPRSS	AIRSHIPS	AHISSSTU SHIATSUS	AIIKMMSS SKIMMIAS	AIINNOSV INVASION
AHIKLNRS	RINKHALS	AHISSTTW WHATSITS	AIIKMNNN MANNIKIN	AIINNQTU QUINTAIN
AHIKLRSY	RAKISHLY	AHISTTWW WHITTAWS	AIIKMNNS MANIKINS	AIINNSTY INSANITY
AHIKMNSS	KHAMSINS	AHKMORRS MARKHORS	AIIKNNNP PANNIKIN	AIINOOSV AVOISION
AHIKMRSS	KASHMIRS	AHKMRSTU MUKHTARS	AIILLLMT MILLTAIL	AIINOPSS SINOPIAS
AHIKNPRS	PRANKISH	AHLLNOOS SHALLOON	AIILLMRY MILLIARY	AIINORST INTARSIO
AHIKPRSS	SPARKISH	AHLLNOSS SHALLONS	AIILLNNV VANILLIN	AIINORTT TRITONIA
AHILLMPS	PHALLISM	AHLLNOSY HALLYONS	AIILLNOP POLLINIA	AIINOSTT NOTITIAS
AHILLMSS	SMALLISH	AHLLNOUW UNHALLOW	AIILLNOT ILLATION	AIINPRSS ASPIRINS
AHILLMTU	THALLIUM	AHLLOPSS SHALLOPS	AIILLNSV VILLAINS	AIINPSST PIANISTS
AHILLNOS	HALLIONS	AHLLOSST SHALLOTS	AIILLNVY VILLAINY	AIINRRTT IRRITANT
AHILLNPS	PHALLINS	AHLLOSSW SHALLOWS	AIILLPRS SLIPRAIL	AIINRSTV VITRAINS
AHILLNRT	INTHRALL	AHLLOSTU THALLOUS		AIINSTTV NATIVIST
AHILLNTW	WANTHILL	AHLLPRYY PHYLLARY	SPIRILLA	VISITANT
AHILLSST	TALLITHS	AHLMMOPY LYMPHOMA	AIILLQSU QUILLAIS	AIINTTVY NATIVITY
AHILLSVY	LAVISHLY	AHLMMSSU MASHLUMS	AIILLWWW WILLIWAW	AIIORRST SARTORII
AHILMMSS	MASHLIMS	AHLMNOOR HORMONAL	AIILMNOS MONILIAS	AIIORSTT AORTITIS
AHILMNSS	MASHLINS	AHLMOOPS OMPHALOS	AIILMNOT LIMATION	AIIORSTV OVARITIS
AHILMOPT	PHILAMOT	AHLMOPTY POLYMATH	MILTONIA	AIIORTTV VITIATOR
AHILMOST	HALIMOTS	AHLNNORT LANTHORN	AIILMNPS ALPINISM	AIIPRRST AIRSTRIP
AHILMQSU	QUALMISH	AHLNOPRS ALPHORNS	AIILMNPT PALMITIN	AIIPRSST PIARISTS
AHILNOPS	SIPHONAL	AHLNORST ALTHORNS	AIILMNTT MILITANT	AIIPRVVY VIVIPARY
AHILNOPT	OLIPHANT	AHLORRTY HARLOTRY	AIILMPUV IMPLUVIA	AIIPSTTU PITUITAS
AHILNORT	HORNTAIL	AHLOSTUU OUTHAULS	AIILMRST MISTRIAL	AIIRSSTT SATIRIST
AHILNRST	INTHRALS	AHLRSTUY LATHYRUS	TRIALISM	AIISSSTY SYSSITIA
AHILOPST	HOSPITAL	AHLRTTWY THWARTLY	AIILMRTY LIMITARY	AIJKKNOU KINKAJOU
AHILOSTU	HALITOUS	AHMMMOST MAMMOTHS	MILITARY	AIJLLOOR JILLAROO
AHILPPSS	SHIPLAPS	AHMMMSUU HUMMAUMS	AIILMSTV VITALISM	AIJLLOVY JOVIALLY
AHILPSSY	PHYSALIS	AHMNNSTU HUNTSMAN	AIILNOPV PAVILION	AIJLNTUY JAUNTILY
AHILRSTY	TRASHILY	MANHUNTS	AIILNOSS LIAISONS	AIJMORTY MAJORITY
AHILRTWY	WRATHILY	AHMNOPST PHANTOMS	AIILNOSV VISIONAL	AIJNNRTU INJURANT
AHIMMNSU	HUMANISM	AHMNOPTY PHANTOMY	AIILNPST ALPINIST	AIJNOPPY POPINJAY
AHIMMORZ	MAHZORIM	AHMOOPSS SHAMPOOS	PINTAILS	AIJNORST JANITORS
AHIMMOSV	MOSHAVIM	AHMOORSW WASHROOM	AIILNSTY SALINITY	AIKKNOTY KANTIKOY
AHIMNOST	HOISTMAN	AHMOOSSS SAMSHOOS	AIILOPPS PAPILIOS	AIKKRTUZ ZIKKURAT
AHIMNOSW	WOMANISH	AHMORRSU MORRHUAS	AIILORSV RAVIOLIS	AIKLLMRR RILLMARK
AHIMNSTU	HUMANIST	AHMORSST HARMOSTS	AIILQSSU SILIQUAS	AIKLMPSU LAMPUKIS
AHIMNTUY	HUMANITY	AHMORSTY HARMOSTY	AIILRSTT TRIALIST	AIKLMPTU KALUMPIT
AHIMOPRS	APHORISM	AHMOSTTW MOSTWHAT	AIILRTTY TRIALITY	AIKLNPST LANTSKIP
MORPHIAS	AHMPSTYY SYMPATHY	AIILRTVY RIVALITY	AIKLOTTW KILOWATT
AHIMOPST	OPSIMATH	AHMQSSUU MUSQUASH	AIILSTTV VITALIST	AIKLRSTT TITLARKS
AHIMPPSS	SAPPHISM	AHMRSSTY THRYMSAS	AIILTTVY VITALITY	AIKLSSSY SKYSAILS
AHIMSTUZ	AZIMUTHS	AHNNSTYY SYNANTHY	AIIMMNNY MINYANIM	AIKMMNOO MAKIMONO
AHIMSTVZ	MITZVAHS	AHNOOPRS HARPOONS	AIIMMNSS ANIMISMS	AIKMORSS KOMISSAR
AHINNNSY	NANNYISH	AHNOOPSU APHONOUS	AIIMMNSX MAXIMINS	AIKNNOOS NAINSOOK
AHINNOPT	ANTIPHON	AHNOORRY HONORARY	AIIMMNTY IMMANITY	AIKNORST SKIATRON
AHINNSTX	XANTHINS	AHNOPPSW PAWNSHOP	AIIMMSTX MAXIMIST	AIKNOSTT STOTINKA
AHINOPRU	OPHIURAN	AHNOPPSY PANSOPHY	AIIMNNOS INSOMNIA	AIKRSSTY SATYRISK
AHINORST	TRAHISON	AHNOPSST SNAPSHOT	AIIMNPSS PIANISMS	AILLLNOO LINALOOL
AHINORSS	ASTONISH	AHNORSSX SAXHORNS	SINAPISM	AILLMMSY SMALMILY
AHINOSTZ	HOATZINS	AHNORTWW WANWORTH	AIIMNPST IMPAINTS	AILLMNQU QUILLMAN
AHINPPSS	SNAPPISH	AHNOSTTW WHATNOTS	AIIMNPSX PANMIXIS	AILLMOST MAILLOTS
AHINPRST	TRANSHIP	AHNOSTUX XANTHOUS	AIIMNRST MARTINIS	MISALLOT
AHINQSUV	VANQUISH	AHNPPSUU PUPUNHAS	AIIMNSST ANIMISTS	AILLMOTY MOLALITY
AHINRSTY	RHYTINAS	AHOOPTYZ ZOOPATHY	SAINTISM	AILLMPRY PRIMALLY
AHINSSTU	INHAUSTS	AHOOSSTY SOOTHSAY	SAMNITIS	AILLMUUV ALLUVIUM
AHIOOPPT	PHOTOPIA	AHOPSTTW TOWPATHS	AIIMNSTT IMITANTS	AILLNNOS LANOLINS
AHIOPRST	APHORIST	AHOPSTUW SOUTHPAW	AIIMNSTV NATIVISM	AILLNOPP PAPILLON
AHIOPSXY	HYPOXIAS	AHOSSTUY SOUTHSAY	VITAMINS	AILLNOPS PAILLONS
		AHRSTUWY THRUWAYS	AIIMNTTU TITANIUM	AILLNOST STALLION

AILLNOSU	ALLUSION	AILNNPSU	PINNULAS	AILRSTTY	STRAITLY	AINNQSTU	QUINNATS
AILLNOUV	ALLUVION	AILNNPTU	UNPLIANT	AILRSUVV	SURVIVAL	AINNRSTT	INTRANTS
AILLNPTY	PLIANTLY	AILNNSTU	INSULANT	AILRTTUY	TITULARY	AINNRSTU	INSURANT
AILLNSST	INSTALLS	AILNOOPT	OPTIONAL	AILSSTUW	LAWSUITS	AINNRSTY	TYRANNIS
AILLORSY	SAILORLY	AILNOOST	SOLATION	AIMMMNOU	AMMONIUM	AINNSSTT	INSTANTS
AILLORTT	LITTORAL	AILNOPRU	UNIPOLAR	AIMMNORT	MORTMAIN	AINNSSTU	UNSAINTS
	TORTILLA	AILNOPSY	POLYNIAS	AIMMNSTU	MANUMITS	AINOOPTT	POTATION
AILLOSTY	LOYALIST	AILNORTZ	TRIZONAL	AIMMORSS	AMORISMS	AINOORRS	ORARIONS
AILLPPSU	SUPPLIAL	AILNOSSS	SASSOLIN	AIMMOSST	ATOMISMS	AINOORST	ORATIONS
AILLPRSY	SPIRALLY	AILNOSUV	AVULSION		SOMATISM	AINOORTT	ROTATION
AILLPRTY	PALTRILY	AILNOSVY	SYNOVIAL	AIMMOSSU	MIASMOUS	AINOOSTT	OSTINATO
AILLPSUV	PLUVIALS	AILNOTTV	VOLITANT	AIMMRRSY	MISMARRY	AINOOSTV	OVATIONS
AILLPSWY	SPILLWAY	AILNOTTY	TONALITY	AIMMRSUU	MASURIUM	AINOOTTV	OTTAVINO
AILLRSTY	RALLYIST	AILNOTUX	LUXATION	AIMNNOSS	MANSIONS	AINOPPRT	PARPOINT
AILLRTUY	RITUALLY	AILNPPSY	SNAPPILY		ONANISMS	AINOPPST	APPOINTS
AILLRTWY	WILLYART	AILNPRSU	PURSLAIN	AIMNNOTU	MOUNTAIN	AINOPPTU	PUPATION
AILLSTWW	WITWALLS	AILNPRSW	PRAWLINS	AIMNNOTY	ANTIMONY	AINOPRSS	PARISONS
AILLSUVY	VISUALLY	AILNPRUV	PULVINAR		ANTINOMY	AINOPRST	ATROPINS
AILMMNOO	MONOMIAL	AILNPSTU	NUPTIALS	AIMNNRTU	RUMINANT	AINOPRTV	PROVIANT
AILMMNUU	ALUMINUM		PATULINS	AIMNOOOZ	ZOONOMIA	AINOPSSS	PASSIONS
AILMMORS	MORALISM		UNPLAITS	AIMNOPRS	RAMPIONS	AINOPSTU	OPUNTIAS
AILMMORT	IMMORTAL	AILNPSTY	PTYALINS	AIMNOPST	MAINTOPS		UTOPIANS
AILMMRSY	SMARMILY	AILNPSUU	NAUPLIUS		TAMPIONS	AINOQRSU	NARQUOIS
AILMMSSY	MYALISMS	AILNPTTU	TULIPANT	AIMNOQRU	MAROQUIN	AINORRSW	WARRISON
AILMMSUU	ALUMIUMS	AILNQRTU	TRANQUIL	AIMNORSU	MAINOURS	AINORRTU	URINATOR
AILMNNOS	NOMINALS	AILNQSTU	QUINTALS	AIMNORTY	MINATORY	AINORSST	ARSONIST
AILMNNOT	MANNITOL	AILNQTUY	QUAINTLY	AIMNOSST	STASIMON	AINORSSW	WARISONS
AILMNNTU	LUMINANT	AILNRSTT	RATTLINS	AIMNOSTU	MANITOUS	AINORSTT	STRONTIA
AILMNOOP	PALOMINO	AILNRSTU	LUNARIST		TINAMOUS	AINORSTU	SUTORIAN
AILMNOOR	MONORAIL	AILNRTTU	RUTILANT	AIMNOTTU	MUTATION	AINORSTX	TRIAXONS
AILMNOOS	MOONSAIL	AILNRUWY	UNWARILY	AIMNPRYY	PAYNIMRY	AINORTVY	VANITORY
AILMNOOT	MOTIONAL	AILNSSTU	STUNSAIL	AIMNPSTU	SUMPITAN	AINOSSSU	SUASIONS
AILMNOPR	PROLAMIN		UNALISTS	AIMNRRSU	MURRAINS	AINOSSTT	STATIONS
AILMNOPS	LAMPIONS	AILNSTTU	LUTANIST	AIMNRSSU	URANISMS	AINOSSVY	SYNOVIAS
AILMNOPY	PALIMONY	AILNSTUU	NAUTILUS	AIMNRSTT	TRANSMIT	AINOSTTU	TITANOUS
AILMNORT	TORMINAL	AILOOPRT	TROOPIAL	AIMNRSTU	NATRIUMS	AINPPRSS	PARSNIPS
AILMNOSS	MALISONS	AILOORRS	SORORIAL		NATURISM	AINPPRTT	TRIPPANT
AILMNPSS	PLASMINS	AILOORST	ISOLATOR	AIMNRSTV	VARMINTS	AINPRSST	SPIRANTS
AILMNPST	IMPLANTS	AILOORSW	WOORALIS	AIMNRSUU	URANIUMS		SPRAINTS
AILMNPTU	PLATINUM	AILOORTV	VIOLATOR	AIMNSSTU	TSUNAMIS	AINPRSTU	PURITANS
AILMNRSU	MURLAINS	AILOPRRV	PROVIRAL	AIMNSSYZ	ZANYISMS		UPTRAINS
AILMNRUY	LUMINARY	AILOPRTU	TROUPIAL	AIMOPRSS	PROSAISM	AINPSSSY	SYNAPSIS
AILMNSTU	SIMULANT	AILOPRTY	POLARITY	AIMOPRST	ATROPISM	AINPSSTU	PUISSANT
AILMOORT	MOTORAIL	AILOPRUY	POLYURIA	AIMOPSST	IMPASTOS	AINQTTUY	QUANTITY
	MOTORIAL	AILOPSST	APOSTILS	AIMOPSSY	SYMPOSIA	AINRSSTT	STRAINTS
AILMOPRX	PROXIMAL		TOPSAILS	AIMORRST	ARMORIST		TRANSITS
AILMORSS	SOLARISM	AILOPSTT	TALIPOTS	AIMORRSU	ORARIUMS	AINRSTTU	NATURIST
AILMORST	MORALIST	AILORSST	SOLARIST		ROSARIUM	AINRSTTY	TANISTRY
AILMORSU	SOLARIUM	AILORSTU	SUTORIAL	AIMORRUV	VARIORUM	AINSSSTU	SUSTAINS
AILMORSY	ROYALISM	AILORSTY	ROYALIST	AIMORSST	AMORISTS	AIOOORRT	ORATORIO
AILMORTY	MOLARITY		SOLITARY	AIMORSSU	OSSARIUM	AIOORSUV	OVARIOUS
	MORALITY	AILORSUW	WOURALIS	AIMORSUZ	ZOARIUMS	AIOPRRST	AIRPORTS
AILMOSTU	SOLATIUM	AILORTTU	TUTORIAL	AIMOSSTT	ATOMISTS		PARITORS
AILMOSTV	VOLTAISM	AILORTUV	OUTRIVAL		SOMATIST	AIOPRRTT	PORTRAIT
AILMPPSY	MISAPPLY	AILOSSTU	OUTSAILS	AIMPPRUU	PUPARIUM	AIOPRSST	AIRSTOPS
AILMPRSU	PRIMULAS	AILOTTTY	TOTALITY	AIMPPSST	MAPPISTS		PROSAIST
AILMPSST	PALMISTS	AILPPRUY	PUPILARY	AIMPRSTY	PARTYISM		PROTASIS
	PSALMIST	AILPRSSU	UPRISALS	AIMRSSST	TSARISMS	AIOPRSTT	PATRIOTS
AILMPSSY	MISPLAYS	AILPRSTU	STIPULAR	AIMRSSTY	SYMITARS	AIOPRSUV	PAVIOURS
AILMPSTY	PTYALISM	AILPSSWY	SLIPWAYS	AIMRSTTU	STRIATUM	AIOPSTTU	UTOPIAST
AILMRRSU	RURALISM	AILPSTUY	PLAYSUIT	AIMRTTUY	MATURITY	AIORRRSW	WARRIORS
AILMRSST	MISTRALS	AILQSTTU	QUITTALS	AIMSSSST	STATISMS	AIORRSTT	TRAITORS
AILMRSSU	SIMULARS	AILRRSTU	RURALIST	AINNNOST	SANTONIN	AIORRSTV	VARISTOR
	SURMISAL	AILRRSTY	STARRILY	AINNOOTT	NOTATION	AIORRTWY	RYOTWARI
AILMRSTU	ALTRUISM	AILRRTUY	RURALITY	AINNOOTV	NOVATION	AIORSSTU	SAUTOIRS
	MURALIST	AILRSSTU	TRISULAS	AINNOOTZ	ZONATION	AIORSSUV	SAVIOURS
	ULTRAISM	AILRSSTY	TRYSAILS	AINNOPSS	SAPONINS	AIORSTTV	VOTARIST
AILNNOOT	NOTIONAL	AILRSTTU	ALTRUIST	AINNOSST	ONANISTS	AIORSTUV	VIRTUOSA
AILNNOSU	UNISONAL		TITULARS	AINNOTTU	NUTATION	AIOSSSTY	ISOSTASY
AILNNOTU	LUNATION		ULTRAIST	AINNPSTU	UNPAINTS	AIPPRSTY	PAPISTRY

AIPRSSTU	UPSTAIRS	ALNRRTUU	NURTURAL	AMORTTUY	MUTATORY	BBCEILRS	CRIBBLES
AIPRSSTY	SPARSITY	ALOOPPRS	PROPOSAL	AMPRSSUW	UPSWARMS		SCRIBBLE
AIRRSTTY	ARTISTRY	ALOOPRTU	UPROOTAL	AMRRSSTU	RASTRUMS	BBCEIOST	COBBIEST
AIRRSTZZ	RIZZARTS	ALOORSUV	VALOROUS	ANNOORST	SONORANT	BBCEKKOS	KEBBOCKS
AIRSSSTT	TSARISTS	ALOORTYZ	ZOOLATRY	ANNOSSTU	STANNOUS	BBCEKKSU	KEBBUCKS
AIRSSTTT	ATTRISTS	ALOPPRSU	POPULARS	ANOOPRRT	PRONATOR	BBCEKLUU	BLUEBUCK
AISSSTTT	STATISTS	ALOPPRRY	POLYPARY	ANOOPRSS	SOPRANOS	BBCELORS	CLOBBERS
AJKMNSTU	MUNTJAKS	ALOPPSSU	SUPPOSAL	ANOOPRST	PATROONS		COBBLERS
AJKNNOOU	JUNKANOO	ALOPPSUU	PAPULOUS	ANOORSTT	ARNOTTOS	BBCELORY	COBBLERY
AJLNORSU	JOURNALS	ALOPPRRSU	PARLOURS	ANOORSUU	ANOUROUS	BBCEMNOU	BUNCOMBE
AJMRSTUY	JURYMAST		SPORULAR	ANOPRRSS	SPORRANS	BBCERRSU	SCRUBBER
AJORRTUY	JURATORY	ALOPRSTT	PORTLAST	ANOPRTTU	TRAPUNTO	BBCGIINR	CRIBBING
AKKLRSSY	SKYLARKS	ALOPRSTU	POSTURAL	ANOPSSTU	OUTSPANS	BBCGILNO	COBBLING
AKLNNOPT	PLANKTON		PULSATOR	ANOQRSSU	SQUARSON	BBCGILNU	CLUBBING
AKLOPRSW	LAPWORKS	ALOPRSTY	PASTORLY	ANORSSTU	SANTOURS	BBCGINSU	CUBBINGS
AKLOSTTU	OUTTALKS	ALOPSSSU	SPOUSALS	ANORSTVY	SOVRANTY	BBCHILSU	CLUBBISH
AKLOSTUW	OUTWALKS	ALOPSSUV	VOLUSPAS	ANPPSSUW	SUPPAWNS	BBCHKOOS	BOSCHBOK
AKLPRRSU	LARKSPUR	ALOPSTUU	PATULOUS	ANPRSSTU	SUNTRAPS	BBCILMSU	CLUBBISM
AKMMNOOR	MONOMARK	ALOPSTUY	OUTPLAYS		UNSTRAPS	BBCILRSY	SCRIBBLY
AKMNRSTU	TRANKUMS	ALOQRRSU	RORQUALS	ANPRSTUU	PURSUANT	BBCILSTU	CLUBBIST
AKMOORST	MOOKTARS	ALOQRSSU	SQUALORS	ANRRTTUY	TRUANTRY	BBDDEEMO	DEMOBBED
AKMOPRST	POSTMARK	ALORRSUY	SURROYAL	ANRSSTYY	SYNASTRY	BBDDEILR	DRIBBLED
AKMQSTUU	KUMQUATS	ALORSUVY	SAVOURLY	AOOOPRTZ	PROTOZOA	BBDDENUU	UNDUBBED
AKNOORST	OSTRAKON	ALORTUWY	OUTLAWRY	AOOPPRSY	APOSPORY	BBDEEGIR	GIBBERED
AKNOPSTW	SWANKPOT	ALOSSTTU	OUTLASTS	AOOPRSSU	SAPOROUS	BBDEEGIT	GIBBETED
AKNORSTU	OUTRANKS	ALPPSTUY	PLATYPUS	AOOPRSTT	TAPROOTS	BBDEEIJR	JIBBERED
AKOPRRTW	PARTWORK	ALPRSSUU	PURSUALS	AOOPRSTU	ATROPOUS	BBDEEIST	DEBBIEST
AKORRSTW	ARTWORKS	ALPRSTUU	PUSTULAR	AOOPRSTW	SOAPWORT		EBBTIDES
AKORSWWX	WAXWORKS	AMMNOORT	MOTORMAN	AOOPRSUV	VAPOROUS	BBDEEMNU	BENUMBED
ALLLPRUY	PLURALLY	AMMNPTUY	TYMPANUM	AOOPRTTY	POTATORY	BBDEENUW	UNWEBBED
ALLMNORY	NORMALLY	AMMOORRS	MAORMORS	AOORRSTT	ROTATORS	BBDEEOPP	BEBOPPED
ALLMNOSY	ALLONYMS		MORMAORS	AOORRSTU	OUTROARS	BBDEERRU	RUBBERED
ALLMOPSX	SMALLPOX	AMMOPSTU	POMATUMS	AOORRTTY	ROTATORY	BBDEFILR	FRIBBLED
ALLMORTY	MORTALLY	AMMNOOSX	MONAXONS	AOORSSTU	OUTSOARS	BBDEGLRU	GRUBBLED
ALLMOUWY	MULLOWAY	AMNNOOTT	MONTANTO	AOORSSUV	SAVOROUS	BBDEHORT	THROBBED
ALLMPRUU	PLUMULAR	AMNNORSW	MANSWORN	AOPPRRST	RAPPORTS	BBDEHRSU	SHRUBBED
ALLMTUUY	MUTUALLY	AMNNORSY	MANSONRY	AOPPRSST	PASSPORT	BBDEILLN	BELLBIND
ALLNORSS	LASSLORN	AMNNOSTT	MONTANTS	AOPRRRTY	PARROTRY	BBDEILQU	QUIBBLED
ALLOOSTX	AXOLOTLS	AMNNOSTW	TOWNSMAN	AOPRRSSW	SPARROWS	BBDEILRR	DRIBBLER
ALLOPRSY	PAYROLLS	AMNNOSTY	ANTONYMS	AOPRRSTY	PORTRAYS	BBDEILRS	DIBBLERS
ALLORTWW	WALLWORT	AMNNOSUW	UNWOMANS	AOPRRTUY	POURTRAY		DRIBBLES
ALLOSSWW	SWALLOWS	AMNNOTTU	MOUNTANT	AOPRSSTT	STARSPOT	BBDEILRT	DRIBBLET
ALLRUUVY	UVULARLY	AMNNPSTU	PUNTSMAN	AOPRSTTU	OUTPARTS	BBDEILRU	BLUEBIRD
ALMMNRUU	NUMMULAR	AMNNSTTU	STUNTMAN	AOPRSTTY	PYROSTAT	BBDEINOR	RIBBONED
ALMMORTW	MALTWORM	AMNOOPPS	POMPANOS	AOPRSTUY	OUTPRAYS	BBDEINRU	UNRIBBED
ALMNOOPS	LAMPOONS	AMNOOSTT	OTTOMANS	AORRSTTW	STARWORT	BBDEIRRS	DRIBBERS
ALMNORTY	MATRONLY	AMNOOSTZ	MATZOONS	AORRTTWW	WARTWORT		RIBBERDS
ALMNOSSU	SOLANUMS	AMNOOTUY	AUTONOMY	AORSSTTU	STRATOUS	BBDEKLNO	KNOBBLED
ALMOOPRY	PLAYROOM	AMNOOTWY	TOYWOMAN	AORSSTTY	STAROSTY	BBDEKLNU	KNUBBLED
ALMOPPST	LAMPPOST	AMNOOTXY	TAXONOMY	AOSSTTUY	OUTSTAYS	BBDELOSS	BOBSLEDS
ALMOPRST	MARPLOTS	AMNOPRSY	PARONYMS	APPRRSUU	PURPURAS	BBDELSTU	STUBBLED
ALMORSUU	RAMULOUS	AMNOPRYY	PARONYMY	APRSSTTU	UPSTARTS	BBDENRUU	UNRUBBED
ALMOSTTU	MULATTOS	AMNOPSTU	PANTOUMS	BBBCEOWY	COBWEBBY	BBEEERSU	BEBEERUS
ALMRTUUY	TUMULARY	AMNORSST	TRANSOMS	BBBDEEOR	BEROBBED	BBEEHINS	NEBBISHE
ALMSSSUY	ALYSSUMS	AMNORSTU	ROMAUNTS	BBBEILRU	BUBBLIER	BBEEHLOW	BOBWHEEL
ALNNOOPR	NONPOLAR	AMNOSTUY	AUTONYMS	BBBEILSU	BUBBLIES	BBEEIIRR	BERIBERI
ALNNOTWY	WANTONLY	AMNOTTUY	TAUTONYM	BBBEINOT	BOBBINET	BBEEILPR	PEBBLIER
ALNNRSSU	UNSNARLS	AMNRSTTU	TANTRUMS	BBBELRSU	BLUBBERS		PLEBBIER
ALNOOPRS	POLARONS	AMOOORSS	AMOROSOS	BBBGILNO	BLOBBING	BBEEIRRS	BEBERRIS
ALNOOPRT	PORTOLAN	AMOOPRST	TAPROOMS		BOBBLING	BBEEISTW	WEBBIEST
	PRONOTAL	AMOORRTY	MORATORY	BBBGILNU	BLUBBING	BBEELLLU	BLUEBELL
ALNOOPST	PLATOONS	AMOORSTZ	SMORZATO		BUBBLING	BBEFILRR	FRIBBLER
ALNOOPXY	POLYAXON	AMOORTWY	MOTORWAY	BBBHNOOY	HOBNOBBY	BBEFILRS	FRIBBLES
ALNOOPYZ	POLYZOAN	AMOOSSTU	ASTOMOUS	BBBHOOUU	HUBBUBOO	BBEFISTU	FUBBIEST
ALNOORST	ORTOLANS	AMOOTTUY	AUTOTOMY	BBCCIKOS	BIBCOCKS		
ALNOPRST	PLASTRON	AMOPRSXY	PAROXYSM	BBCDEILR	CRIBBLED		
ALNOPRTU	PORTULAN	AMOPSSTT	TOPMASTS	BBCDERSU	SCRUBBED		
ALNOPSYY	POLYNYAS	AMOQSSUU	SQUAMOUS	BBCDIMOY	BOMBYCID		
ALNORRWY	NARROWLY	AMORRTUY	MORTUARY	BBCEHINS	NEBBICHS		
ALNPPSTU	SUPPLANT	AMORSTTU	OUTSMART	BBCEHIRU	CHUBBIER		

BBEGIIST	GIBBSITE	BBGIILNN NIBBLING	BCDEEHOU DEBOUCHE	BCEEMNRU ENCUMBER
BBEGILNP	PEBBLING	BBGIINNS SNIBBING	BCDEEILR BICKERED	BCEEMRRU CEREBRUM
BBEGILRS	GRIBBLES	BBGIINRS RIBBINGS	BCDEEILR CREDIBLE	CUMBERER
BBEGILRY	GLIBBERY	BBGIJNOS JOBBINGS	BCDEEILS DECIBELS	BCEENORS OBSCENER
BBEGILST	GLIBBEST	BBGILMNO MOBBLING	BCDEEILU EDUCIBLE	BCEENRSU CRUBEENS
BBEGINNS	SNEBBING	BBGILMNU BUMBLING	BCDEEINT BENEDICT	BCEERSTU SUBERECT
BBEGIRRU	GRUBBIER	BBGILNNO NOBBLING	BCDEEIPS BESPICED	BCEFFIIR FEBRIFIC
BBEGLORS	GOBBLERS	BBGILNNU NUBBLING	BCDEEIRS DESCRIBE	BCEFILOR FORCIBLE
BBEGLRSU	GRUBBLES	BBGILNOW WOBBLING	ESCRIBED	BCEGHILN BELCHING
BBEGRRSU	GRUBBERS	BBGILNOY LOBBYING	BCDEEIST BISECTED	BCEGHINN BENCHING
BBEHLORS	HOBBLERS	BBGILNRU BURBLING	BCDEEJOT OBJECTED	BCEGIINO BIOGENIC
BBEHMSTU	BETHUMBS	BBGILNSU SLUBBING	BCDEEKMO BEMOCKED	BCEGIMNO BECOMING
BBEIILRS	RIBIBLES	BBGINNSU SNUBBING	BCDEEKNO BECKONED	BCEGLNOO CONGLOBE
BBEIIMRS	IMBIBERS	BBGINOSW SWOBBING	BCDEEKTU BUCKETED	BCEHIIRT BITCHIER
BBEIIRST	RIBBIEST	BBGINRSU RUBBINGS	BCDEELRU BECURLED	BCEHIMRS BESMIRCH
BBEIKNOR	KNOBBIER	BBGINSSU SUBBINGS	BCDEEMRU CUMBERED	BCEHIMRU CHERUBIM
BBEIKNRU	KNUBBIER	BBGINSTU STUBBING	BCDEEORV BEDCOVER	BCEHINRU BUNCHIER
BBEILLNO	BONIBELL	TUBBINGS	BCDEEOTT OBTECTED	CHERUBIN
BBEILNRS	NIBBLERS	BBHIMOSY HOBBYISM	BCDEHINS DISBENCH	BCEHIORS BRIOCHES
BBEILNRU	NUBBLIER	BBHINOSS SNOBBISH	BCDEHLOT BLOTCHED	BCEHIORT BOTCHIER
BBEILORS	SLOBBIER	BBHINSSU SNUBBISH	BCDEHOOR BROOCHED	BCEHIRST BRITCHES
BBEILORW	WOBBLIER	BBHIOOSY BOOBYISH	BCDEIIOS BIOCIDES	BCEHIRTY BITCHERY
BBEILOST	BIBELOTS	BBHIORTY HOBBITRY	BCDEIITU DECUBITI	BCEHLOST BLOTCHES
BBEILOSW	WOBBLIES	BBHIOSTY HOBBYIST	BCDEIKRR REDBRICK	BCEHLRSU BLUCHERS
BBEILPRS	PRIBBLES	BBHIRSUY RUBBISHY	BCDEIKST BEDTICKS	BCEHMSTU BESMUTCH
BBEILQRU	QUIBBLER	BBHOOSUW WHOOBUBS	BCDEILRY CREDIBLY	BCEHNRSU BRUNCHES
BBEILQSU	QUIBBLES	BBHRSSUU SUBSHRUB	BCDEIMNO COMBINED	BCEHOORS BROOCHES
BBEILRRU	RUBBLIER	BBIIILMS BILIMBIS	BCDEKORS BEDROCKS	BCEHORRU BROCHURE
BBEILRRY	BILBERRY	BBIILSST BIBLISTS	BCDEKOSS BEDSOCKS	BCEHORSS BORSCHES
BBEILRST	STIBBLER	BBIKLLOO BILLBOOK	BCDELMRU CRUMBLED	BCEHORST BOTCHERS
	TRIBBLES	BBIKLNOO BOBOLINK	BCDELMSU SCUMBLED	BCEHORTY BOTCHERY
BBEILRSU	SLUBBIER	BBILLOYY BILLYBOY	BCDELOSU BECLOUDS	BCEHRSTU BUTCHERS
BBEILSST	STIBBLES	BBILOSTY LOBBYIST	BCDEMNOU UNCOMBED	BCEHRTUY BUTCHERY
BBEIMOST	BOMBSITE	BBILOSUU BIBULOUS	BCDENRUU UNCURBED	BCEHSTTU BUTCHEST
BBEIMRSU	BRUMBIES	BBIMNOSS SNOBBISM	BCDEORSU OBSCURED	BCEIIKLN ICEBLINK
BBEINORS	SNOBBIER	BBIMOOSY BOOBYISM	BCDESSUU SUBDUCES	BCEIIKRR BRICKIER
BBEINOST	NOBBIEST	BBINORRY RIBBONRY	BCDHIRSU BRUCHIDS	BCEIIKRS BRICKIES
BBEINRSU	SNUBBIER	BBKLOOSU BLOUBOKS	BCDHOOSU CUBHOODS	BCEIILMS MISCIBLE
BBEINSTU	NUBBIEST	BBKOOOOS BOOBOOKS	BCDIIMOR BROMIDIC	BCEIILNV VINCIBLE
BBEIRSTU	STUBBIER	BBNOORSU BOURBONS	BCDIIPSU BICUSPID	BCEIIMRS IMBRICES
	SUBTRIBE	BBNORSTU STUBBORN	BCDIKLLU DUCKBILL	BCEIINRS INSCRIBE
BBEISSTU	STUBBIES	BCCDEILY BICYCLED	BCDILMOY MOLYBDIC	BCEIKLMS LIMBECKS
BBEISTTU	TUBBIEST	BCCDHIKO DOBCHICK	BCDINRUU RUBICUND	BCEIKLOO BOOKLICE
BBEKLNOS	KNOBBLES	BCCDIKOR COCKBIRD	BCDIORSW COWBIRDS	BCEIKLOR BLOCKIER
BBEKLNSU	KNUBBLES	BCCEEIRR CEREBRIC	BCDKORSU BURDOCKS	BCEIKSST BESTICKS
BBEKLOSS	BLESBOKS	BCCEHIRU CHERUBIC	BCDSSTUU SUBDUCTS	BCEILMRS CLIMBERS
BBEKLSUU	BUBUKLES	BCCEIIIS CICISBEI	BCEEEFIN BENEFICE	RECLIMBS
BBEKNOOT	BONTEBOK	BCCEIILO LIBECCIO	BCEEEFKN NECKBEEF	BCEILNOS BINOCLES
BBEKNORS	KNOBBERS	BCCEIIOS CICISBEO	BCEEEHRS BREECHES	BCEILNRU RUNCIBLE
BBELLRUY	LUBBERLY	BCCEILOS ECBOLICS	BCEEENRS BESCREEN	BCEILORS BRICOLES
BBELNORS	NOBBLERS	BCCEILRU CRUCIBLE	BCEEERSU BERCEUSE	CORBEILS
BBELORSW	WOBBLERS	BCCEILSU CUBICLES	BCEEFILN FENCIBLE	BCEILOTU TUBICOLE
BBELORSY	LOBBYERS	BCCEILSY BICYCLES	BCEEGIRS ICEBERGS	BCEILPRU REPUBLIC
	SLOBBERY	BCCEMRUU CUCUMBER	BCEEHKSU BUCKSHEE	BCEIMNOS COMBINES
BBELRSSU	SLUBBERS	BCCIIMOR MICROBIC	BCEEHLNS BLENCHES	BCEIMORS CROMBIES
BBELSSTU	STUBBLES	BCCILMOU COLUMBIC	BCEEHLRS BELCHERS	MICROBES
BBENORSY	SNOBBERY	BCCILOOR BROCCOLI	BCEEHNRS BENCHERS	BCEIMOST COMBIEST
BBENRSSU	SNUBBERS	BCCILOSU BUCOLICS	BCEEHNRU UNBREECH	BCEIMOSW COMBWISE
BBEORSSW	SWOBBERS	BCCIRTUU CUCURBIT	BCEEHOSU BOUCHEES	BCEIMRRU CRUMBIER
BBFGILNU FLUBBING	BCCMOOSX COXCOMBS	BCEEIILM IMBECILE	BCEINORU BOUNCIER
BBGGILNU GLIBBING	BCCMSSUU SUCCUMBS	BCEEINOT CENOBITE	BCEINOVX BICONVEX
BBGGIILN GLIBBING	BCCSSUUU SUCCUBUS	BCEEIOSX ICEBOXES	BCEINRSU BRUCINES
BBGGILNO GOBBLING	BCDDEEEK BEDECKED	BCEEIPSS BESPICES	BCEIOOPS BIOSCOPE
BBGGINRU GRUBBING	BCDDEEKU BEDUCKED	BICEPSES	BCEIORRS CRIBROSE
BBGHILNO HOBBLING	BCDDEHIL CHILDBED	BCEEIRSS ESCRIBES	BCEIORST BISECTOR
BBGIIIMN IMBIBING	BCDDESUU SUBDUCED	BCEEIRTT BRETTICE	BCEIRRSS SCRIBERS
BBGIIJNS JIBBINGS	BCDEEEHR BREECHED	BCEEKNSU BUCKEENS	BCEIRSTU BRUCITES
BBGIIKLN KIBBLING	BCDEEHLN BLENCHED	BCEELLOT BELLCOTE	BCEJOORT OBJECTOR
BBGIILMN BLIMBING	BCDEEHNR BEDRENCH	BCEELOOR BORECOLE	BCEJSSTU SUBJECTS
			BCEELRTU TUBERCLE	BCEKLNOT BLONCKET

BCEKLNUU	UNBUCKLE	BCIKOSTT	BITTOCKS
BCEKLORS	BLOCKERS	BCILLPUY	PUBLICLY
BCEKLRSU	BUCKLERS	BCILMOSY	SYMBOLIC
BCEKMSTU	STEMBUCK	BCILMPSU	UPCLIMBS
BCEKOORU	BUCKEROO	BCILNOUY	BOUNCILY
BCEKORST	BROCKETS	BCINORSU	RUBICONS
BCEKORSU	ROEBUCKS	BCINOSSU	SUBSONIC
BCEKOSTY	BYCOKETS	BCINOSTU	SUBTONIC
BCELLOSW	COWBELLS	BCINOSUU	INCUBOUS
BCELMOSS	COMBLESS	BCIOORST	ROBOTICS
BCELMRSU	CLUMBERS	BCIORSST	CROSSBIT
	CRUMBLES	BCJKMSUU	JUMBUCKS
BCELMSSU	SCUMBLES	BCKLLOOS	BOLLOCKS
BCELORSU	COLUBERS	BCKLLOSU	BULLOCKS
BCELORTU	CLOTEBUR	BCKLNOSU	SUNBLOCK
BCELRSSU	CURBLESS		UNBLOCKS
BCEMRSSU	SCUMBERS	BCKMMOSU	BUMMOCKS
BCENORSU	BOUNCERS	BCKOOOPY	COPYBOOK
BCEORRSU	OBSCURER	BCKOSTTU	BUTTOCKS
BCEORRWY	COWBERRY	BCLMOORU	CLUBROOM
BCEORSSU	OBSCURES	BCLMOOSU	COULOMBS
BCFIIMOR	MORBIFIC	BCLOORTU	CLUBROOT
BCFIIORT	FIBROTIC	BCLORSTU	CLOTBURS
BCFILORY	FORCIBLY	BCMORSUU	CUMBROUS
BCFIMORU	CUBIFORM	BCMOSSTU	COMBUSTS
BCFSSSUU	SUBFUSCS	BCOORSSW	CROSSBOW
BCGHIINR	BIRCHING	BCOOSTTY	BOYCOTTS
BCGHIINT	BITCHING	BCORSTTU	OBSTRUCT
BCGHINNU	BUNCHING	BDDDEEEM	EMBEDDED
BCGHINOT	BOTCHING	BDDDEEIM	IMBEDDED
BCGHINTU	BUTCHING	BDDDEEIR	DEBRIDED
BCGIIKNR	BRICKING	BDDDEENU	UNBEDDED
BCGIILMN	CLIMBING	BDDDENUU	UNBUDDED
BCGIINRS	SCRIBING	BDDEEELL	DEBELLED
BCGIKLNO	BLOCKING	BDDEEESS	SEEDBEDS
BCGIKLNU	BUCKLING	BDDEEFLU	BEFUDDLE
BCGIKNSU	BUCKINGS	BDDEEGGU	DEBUGGED
BCGIMNOR	CROMBING	BDDEEGIL	BEGILDED
BCGIMNOS	COMBINGS	BDDEEGIR	BEGIRDED
BCGIMNRU	CRUMBING	BDDEEGNU	BEDUNGED
BCGINNOU	BOUNCING	BDDEEGTU	BUDGETED
	BOUNCOING	BDDEEHOS	DEBOSHED
BCGINORU	COURBING	BDDEEIMM	BEDIMMED
BCHIILTY	BITCHILY	BDDEEIMO	EMBODIED
BCHIIOST	COHIBITS	BDDEEINR	REBIDDEN
BCHIISSU	HIBISCUS	BDDEEINT	INDEBTED
BCHIKLOS	BLOCKISH	BDDEEINW	BINDWEED
BCHIKOSU	CHIBOUKS	BDDEEIRS	BIRDSEED
BCHIOORY	CHOIRBOY		DEBRIDES
BCHIOPRS	PIBROCHS	BDDEEISS	BEDSIDES
BCHKNORU	BUCKHORN	BDDEEKNU	DEBUNKED
BCHKOSTU	BUCKSHOT	BDDEELMU	BEMUDDLE
BCHNOORS	BRONCHOS	BDDEELNO	BOLDENED
BCHNORSU	BRONCHUS	BDDEENNU	UNBENDED
BCHORSST	BORSCHTS	BDDEENOT	OBTENDED
BCHORSTT	BORTSCHT	BDDEENRU	BURDENED
BCIIILMU	UMBILICI	BDDEEORR	BORDERED
BCIIKLNS	NIBLICKS	BDDEEORS	DESORBED
BCIILMRU	LUMBRICI	BDDEESSU	DEBUSSED
BCIILMSU	BULIMICS	BDDEESTU	BEDUSTED
BCIILORS	COLIBRIS	BDDEGINS	BEDDINGS
BCIIMNOO	BIONOMIC	BDDEIIMO	IMBODIED
BCIIMORU	CIBORIUM	BDDEILNR	BRINDLED
BCIIMRSS	SCRIBISM	BDDEILOO	BLOODIED
BCIINORV	VIBRIONC	BDDEINNU	UNBIDDEN
BCIISSTU	BISCUITS	BDDEINOU	UNBODIED
BCIISTUY	BISCUITY	BDDEINRU	UNDERBID
BCIKKNSU	BUCKSKIN	BDDEIORS	DISORBED
BCIKLOOT	BOOTLICK		
BCIKORRW	CRIBWORK		

	DISROBED	BDEEHLNO	BEHOLDEN
BDDEISSU	SUBSIDED	BDEEHLOR	BEHOLDER
BDDEISTU	BUDDIEST	BDEEHLOW	BEHOWLED
BDDELMRU	DRUMBLED	BDEEHOOV	BEHOOVED
BDDENOTU	OBTUNDED	BDEEHORT	BOTHERED
BDDEORTU	OBTRUDED	BDEEHORW	BEWHORED
BDDGIINS	BIDDINGS	BDEEHOSS	DEBOSHES
BDDGILNU	BUDDLING	BDEEIILR	BIELDIER
BDDGINOR	BRODDING	BDEEIIPT	BEPITIED
BDDGINSU	BUDDINGS	BDEEIKRS	KERBSIDE
BDDGOOSY	DOGSBODY	BDEEIKSS	BEKISSED
BDDHIIRY	DIHYBRID	BDEEILLL	LIBELLED
BDDINOOW	WOODBIND	BDEEILLT	BILLETED
BDDINPUU	PUDIBUND	BDEEILLU	ELUDIBLE
BDEEEEMS	BESEEMED	BDEEILMO	BEMOILED
BDEEEEMT	BETEEMED		EMBOILED
BDEEEGIS	BESIEGED	BDEEILMR	LIMBERED
BDEEEGMM	BEGEMMED	BDEEILNV	VENDIBLE
BDEEEGNO	EDGEBONE	BDEEILOR	REBOILED
BDEEEGRU	BUDGEREE	BDEEILOS	OBELISED
BDEEEHTU	HEBETUDE	BDEEILOT	BETOILED
BDEEEILV	BELIEVED	BDEEILOZ	OBELIZED
BDEEEINS	BENISEED	BDEEILRW	BEWILDER
BDEEELLR	REBELLED	BDEEILSV	BEDEVILS
BDEEELLV	BEVELLED	BDEEILTT	BETITLED
BDEEELMM	EMBLEMED	BDEEIMNR	BRIDEMEN
BDEEELPT	BEPELTED	BDEEIMOS	EMBODIES
BDEEELRS	BLEEDERS	BDEEIMRT	TIMBERED
BDEEELUW	BLUEWEED	BDEEIMST	BEDTIMES
BDEEEMMR	MEMBERED	BDEEIMSU	EMBUSIED
BDEEEMNS	BEDESMEN	BDEEINOS	EBONISED
BDEEEMRW	EMBREWED	BDEEINOT	OBEDIENT
BDEEENTT	BENETTED	BDEEINOZ	EBONIZED
BDEEEPSS	BESPEEDS	BDEEINRS	INBREEDS
BDEEERRS	BREEDERS	BDEEINST	BENDIEST
BDEEERRV	REVERBED	BDEEINSW	BENDWISE
BDEEERTT	BETTERED	BDEEINSZ	BEDIZENS
BDEEERTV	BREVETED	BDEEIORU	BOUDERIE
BDEEETTW	BEWETTED	BDEEIRRU	REBURIED
BDEEFFPU	BEPUFFED	BDEEIRST	BEDRITES
BDEEFFRU	BUFFERED		BESTRIDE
	REBUFFED	BDEEKNRU	BUNKERED
BDEEFFTU	BUFFETED	BDEELLOW	BELLOWED
BDEEFGGO	BEFOGGED		BOWELLED
BDEEFGIT	BEGIFTED	BDEELLRU	BULLERED
BDEEFILR	BELFRIED	BDEELMNO	EMBOLDEN
BDEEFINR	BEFRIEND	BDEELMOR	REBELDOM
BDEEFIRS	DEBRIEFS	BDEELMPU	BEPLUMED
BDEEFIRU	RUBEFIED	BDEELMRT	TREMBLED
BDEEFITT	BEFITTED	BDEELMRU	LUMBERED
BDEEFLOO	BEFOOLED	BDEELNNO	ENNOBLED
BDEEFLOU	BEFOULED	BDEELNRS	BLENDERS
BDEEFOOR	FOREBODE	BDEELNST	BENDLETS
BDEEFSUU	SUBFEUED	BDEELNTU	UNBELTED
BDEEGGIW	BEWIGGED	BDEELORU	REDOUBLE
BDEEGGMO	EMBOGGED	BDEELORW	BOWLERED
BDEEGGNU	UNBEGGED	BDEELOSU	BESOULED
BDEEGGRU	BEGRUDGE	BDEELOSV	BELOVEDS
	BUGGERED	BDEELRTU	BUTLERED
BDEEGHIS	BESIGHED	BDEEMNOT	BODEMENT
BDEEGILN	BLEEDING		ENTOMBED
BDEEGILU	BEGUILED	BDEEMNOW	ENWOMBED
BDEEGIMR	BEGRIMED	BDEEMNRU	NUMBERED
BDEEGINR	BREEDING	BDEEMORR	EMBORDER
BDEEGINW	BEDEWING	BDEEMOSS	EMBOSSED
BDEEGINY	BEDYEING	BDEEMPRU	BUMPERED
BDEEGKNU	BEGUNKED	BDEEMRTU	EMBRUTED
BDEEGLNO	BELONGED	BDEEMSSU	EMBUSSED
	ENGLOBED	BDEENNOT	BONNETED
BDEEGMOU	EMBOGUED		

BDEENOUY	UNOBEYED	BDEILORT	TRILOBED	BDENNOUY	YBOUNDEN
BDEENPRS	PREBENDS	BDEILORV	LOVEBIRD	BDENNRUU	UNBURDEN
BDEEOPRS	BEPROSED	BDEILOSS	BODILESS		UNBURNED
BDEEOPRW	BEPOWDER	BDEILOSW	DISBOWEL	BDENOOTU	UNBOOTED
BDEEORRR	BORDERER	BDEILRRS	BRIDLERS	BDENOOTW	BENTWOOD
BDEEORRS	RESORBED	BDEILRST	BRISTLED	BDENORSU	BOUNDERS
BDEEORSS	BEDSORES		DRIBLETS		REBOUNDS
BDEEORST	BESORTED	BDEILRSU	BUILDERS		SUBORNED
	BESTRODE		REBUILDS	BDENOTTU	BUTTONED
BDEEORSV	OBSERVED	BDEILSTU	BLUDIEST	BDENRSUU	UNBRUSED
BDEEORTU	OUTBREED	BDEIMNOT	INTOMBED	BDENRUUY	UNDERBUY
BDEEORTV	OBVERTED	BDEIMNSU	NIMBUSED	BDENSSTU	SUBTENDS
BDEEOSSS	OBSESSED	BDEIMNUU	UNIMBUED	BDEOORRS	BROODERS
BDEEOSST	BETOSSED	BDEIMORR	IMBORDER	BDEOORRW	BORROWED
BDEEOSTT	BESOTTED	BDEIMORS	BROMIDES	BDEOOTUX	OUTBOXED
	OBTESTED	BDEIMOSS	IMBOSSED	BDEOPSST	BEDPOSTS
BDEEOSTW	BESTOWED	BDEIMRSU	IMBURSED	BDEORRSU	BORDURES
BDEERSUW	BURWEEDS	BDEIMRTU	IMBRUTED		BOURDERS
BDEERTTU	BUTTERED	BDEINOOS	NOBODIES		SUBORDER
	REBUTTED	BDEINOOW	WOODBINE	BDEORRTU	OBTRUDER
BDEESSSU	DEBUSSES	BDEINOSU	BEDOUINS	BDEORRUW	BURROWED
BDEFIIRU	RUBIFIED	BDEINRSU	BURNSIDE	BDEORSTU	DOUBTERS
BDEFILRS	FILBERDS	BDEINRTU	TURBINED		OBTRUDES
BDEFINRR	FERNBIRD		UNDERBIT		REDOUBTS
BDEFIORS	FIBROSED	BDEINRUU	UNBURIED	BDERSSUU	SUBDUERS
BDEFOORS	FORBODES	BDEINTTU	UNBITTED	BDERSTUU	SUBTRUDE
BDEGHILT	BLIGHTED	BDEIOORR	BROODIER	BDFGNOOU	FOGBOUND
BDEGHIRT	BEDRIGHT	BDEIORRS	BROIDERS	BDFIIORS	FIBROIDS
BDEGHIST	BEDIGHTS	BDEIORRY	BROIDERY	BDFILLLO	BILLFOLD
BDEGIINT	BETIDING	BDEIORSS	DISROBES	BDFINORU	UNFORBID
	DEBITING	BDEIORST	DEBITORS	BDFINRUU	FURIBUND
BDEGILNN	BLENDING	BDEIORSV	OVERBIDS	BDFLOTUU	DOUBTFUL
BDEGILNO	IGNOBLED	BDEIOSSY	DISOBEYS	BDGGIINR	BRIDGING
	INGLOBED	BDEIOSUX	SUBOXIDE	BDGGILNU	BLUDGING
BDEGINNS	BENDINGS	BDEIRSSU	DISBURSE	BDGIILNN	BLINDING
BDEGINOS	OBSIGNED	BDEISSSU	SUBSIDES	BDGIILNR	BRIDLING
BDEGLMRU	GRUMBLED	BDEISSTU	SUBEDITS	BDGIILNU	BUILDING
BDEGLNOU	BLUDGEON	BDEKNOOU	UNBOOKED	BDGIINNS	BINDINGS
BDEGLRSU	BLUDGERS	BDELLOOR	BORDELLO	BDGIINRS	BIRDINGS
BDEGORRY	DOGBERRY		DOORBELL	BDGIINRW	BIRDWING
BDEGORSU	BUDGEROS	BDELLOUZ	BULLDOZE	BDGILNNU	BUNDLING
BDEGORUW	BUDGEROW	BDELMOOS	BLOOSMED	BDGILNOO	BLOODING
BDEHIKOS	KIBOSHED	BDELMRSU	DRUMBLES	BDGILNOU	DOUBLING
BDEHILMT	THIMBLED	BDELMRUU	DELUBRUM	BDGINNOS	BONDINGS
BDEHIOPS	BISHOPED	BDELMSTU	STUMBLED	BDGINNOU	BOUNDING
BDEHKOSY	KYBOSHED	BDELNNOU	UNNOBLED		UNBODING
BDEHLMOW	WHOMBLED	BDELNNUU	UNBUNDLE	BDGINOOR	BROODING
BDEHLSUV	BUSHVELD	BDELNOSS	BOLDNESS	BDGINOOY	BOODYING
BDEHORSY	HERDBOYS	BDELNOST	BLONDEST	BDGINORS	SONGBIRD
BDEIIKTZ	KIBITZED	BDELNOTU	UNBOLTED	BDGINORU	OBDURING
BDEIILRU	BLUIDIER	BDELNOUU	UNDOUBLE	BDGINOTU	DOUBTING
BDEIILTY	DEBILITY	BDELNOUW	UNBLOWED	BDGINSUU	SUBDUING
BDEIIMOS	IMBODIES	BDELNRSU	BLUNDERS	BDGLLOSU	BULLDOGS
BDEIKMOS	IMBOSKED	BDELOORV	OVERBOLD	BDGLOOST	DOGBOLTS
BDEIKNOR	BRODEKIN	BDELORSU	BOULDERS	BDGNRUUY	BURGUNDY
BDEIKNSU	BUSKINED		DOUBLERS	BDHIIPRW	WHIPBIRD
BDEILLMU	BDELLIUM	BDELORSW	BOWLDERS	BDHIMOOR	RHOMBOID
BDEILLOW	BILLOWED	BDELORTU	TROUBLED	BDHIMORT	BIRTHDOM
BDEILMSU	SUBLIMED	BDELOSST	BESTSOLD	BDHINOPS	HOPBINDS
BDEILNOU	UNILOBED	BDELOSTU	DOUBLETS	BDHIORST	BIRDSHOT
BDEILNOY	BODYLINE	BDELPSUU	SUBDUPLE	BDHIOSSU	BUSHIDOS
BDEILNRS	BLINDERS	BDEMNNOS	BONDSMEN	BDHMOOOS	HOBODOMS
	BRINDLES	BDEMNOSU	EMBOUNDS	BDHNRSUU	UNSHRUBD
BDEILNRU	UNBRIDLE	BDEMNOTU	UNTOMBED	BDHOOOSY	BOYHOODS
BDEILNST	BLINDEST	BDEMNSSU	DUMBNESS	BDIIINRS	BRINDISI
BDEILNVY	VENDIBLY	BDEMOORS	BEDROOMS	BDIIKNOS	BODIKINS
BDEILOOR	BLOODIER		BOREDOMS	BDIILMSS	DISLIMBS
BDEILOOS	BLOODIES	BDEMOOSY	SOMEBODY	BDIILOQU	OBLIQUID
BDEILOPU	UPBOILED	BDEMOOTT	BOTTOMED	BDIIMRUU	RUBIDIUM
BDEILOQU	OBLIQUED	BDEMSSUU	SUBSUMED		

BDIKNORS	BRODKINS		
BDILLOOY	BLOODILY		
BDILMORY	MORBIDLY		
BDILNNSU	UNBLINDS		
BDILNOWW	WINDBLOW		
BDILNPRU	PURBLIND		
BDILNSUU	UNBUILDS		
BDILPSUU	UPBUILDS		
BDILRTUY	TURBIDLY		
BDIMNORU	MORIBUND		
BDIMNPSU	DUMPBINS		
BDIMOOSS	DISBOSOM		
BDIMOSTU	MISDOUBT		
BDINNRUW	WINDBURN		
BDINOORS	BRIDOONS		
BDINRTUU	UNTURBID		
BDINSSTU	DUSTBINS		
BDIOORSU	BOUDOIRS		
BDIOORTY	BOTRYOID		
BDIORSSW	WOSBIRDS		
BDIRSSTU	DISTURBS		
BDKNOOOR	DOORKNOB		
BDKNOOSU	BUNDOOKS		
BDKOOORW	WORDBOOK		
BDKOORWY	BODYWORK		
BDLLSTUU	BULLDUST		
BDLNOOOU	DOUBLOON		
BDLNOOUY	UNBLOODY		
BDLNOOWW	BLOWDOWN		
BDLOOOSX	OXBLOODS		
BDMOORRS	SMORBROD		
BDNNOOTU	BUNODONT		
BDNOORSU	BOURDONS		
BDNOOSWW	DOWNBOWS		
BDNOOTUU	OUTBOUND		
BDNORSTU	TURBONDS		
BDNORSUW	RUBDOWNS		
BDOOOSWX	BOXWOODS		
BEEEEFLN	ENFEEBLE		
BEEEEFRS	FREEBEES		
BEEEEKSS	BESEEKES		
BEEEEMST	BETEEMES		
BEEEENRT	TEREBENE		
BEEEENRZ	EBENEZER		
BEEEFIRS	FREEBIES		
BEEEFIST	BEEFIEST		
BEEEFLSS	FEBLESSE		
BEEEFLST	FEEBLEST		
BEEEGILN	BELEEING		
BEEEGINS	BESEEING		
BEEEGIRS	BESIEGER		
BEEEGISS	BESIEGES		
BEEEGRTT	BEGETTER		
BEEEHIST	BHEESTIE		
BEEEHISV	BEEHIVES		
BEEEHLRT	HERBELET		
BEEEHLWW	WEBWHEEL		
BEEEHNSS	SHEBEENS		
BEEEILLL	LIBELLEE		
BEEEILRV	BELIEVER		
BEEEILSV	BELIEVES		
BEEEINST	EBENISTE		
BEEEIRRZ	BREEZIER		
BEEEIRST	BEERIEST		
BEEEJLSW	BEJEWELS		
BEEELLRR	REBELLER		
BEEELLRT	BELLETER		
BEEELLRV	BEVELLER		
BEEELMNS	ENSEMBLE		
BEEELMRS	RESEMBLE		

BEEELMSY	BESEEMLY
BEEELMZZ	EMBEZZLE
BEEELPRS	BLEEPERS
BEEEMMRR	REMEMBER
BEEEMNSU	UNBESEEM
BEEEMRSW	EMBREWES
BEEENNSZ	BENZENES
BEEENSST	SEBESTEN
BEEENSTW	BETWEENS
BEEEPPPR	BEPEPPER
BEEEPRST	BEPESTER
BEEERSST	BRETESSE
BEEERSTT	BESETTER
BEEESSST	TSESSEBE
BEEFFLMU	BEMUFFLE
BEEFGILN	FEEBLING
BEEFGINR	BEFRINGE
BEEFHILS	FEEBLISH
BEEFILLT	LIFEBELT
BEEFILLX	FLEXIBLE
BEEFILNU	UNBELIEF
BEEFILRS	BELFRIES
BEEFINST	BENEFITS
BEEFIRST	BRIEFEST
BEEFIRSU	RUBEFIES
BEEFLORW	BEFLOWER
BEEFNORR	FREEBORN
BEEFNRTU	UNBEREFT
BEEGGNSU	GEEBUNGS
BEEGHLMR	BERGMEHL
BEEGIILL	ELIGIBLE
BEEGIILX	EXIGIBLE
BEEGILLR	GERBILLE
BEEGILNP	BLEEPING
BEEGILNT	BEETLING
BEEGILOS	OBLIGEES
BEEGILRU	BEGUILER
BEEGILSU	BEGUILES
BEEGIMNT	BEMETING
BEEGIMRS	BEGRIMES
BEEGINNR	BEGINNER
	BENIGNER
BEEGINNS	BEGINNES
BEEGINRR	BREERING
BEEGINRS	BIGENERS
BEEGINRZ	BREEZING
BEEGINST	BEIGNETS
BEEGINSU	BEGUINES
BEEGINSW	BEESWING
BEEGKLUY	KEYBUGLE
BEEGLNOR	BELONGER
BEEGLNOS	ENGLOBES
BEEGMNOS	GOMBEENS
BEEGMOSU	EMBOGUES
BEEGMRSU	SUBMERGE
BEEGNOOW	WOBEGONE
BEEGNOTT	BEGOTTEN
BEEGNSTU	UNBEGETS
BEEHHMOT	BEHEMOTH
BEEHINSS	BESHINES
	NEBISHES
BEEHIRST	HERBIEST
BEEHISST	BHISTEES
BEEHKSSU	BUKSHEES
BEEHLOOR	BOREHOLE
BEEHLOVY	BEHOVELY
BEEHLRSS	HERBLESS
BEEHLRST	BLETHERS
	HERBLETS
BEEHNNOS	HEBENONS
BEEHNRRT	BRETHREN
BEEHOOSV	BEHOOVES
BEEHORSW	BEWHORES
BEEHRSST	SHERBETS
BEEHRSSW	BESHREWS
BEEIILNZ	ZIBELINE
BEEIINOS	EBIONISE
BEEIINOZ	EBIONIZE
BEEIINRT	BENITIER
BEEIIPST	BEPITIES
BEEIIRRR	BRIERIER
BEEIISTU	UBIETIES
BEEIJLSU	JUBILEES
BEEIJSTU	BEJESUIT
BEEIKSSS	BEKISSES
BEEILLLR	LIBELLER
BEEILLNO	LOBELINE
BEEILLTT	BELITTLE
BEEILMOS	EMBOLIES
BEEILMPR	PERIBLEM
BEEILNNS	BLENNIES
BEEILNRS	BERLINES
BEEILNSS	SENSIBLE
BEEILNST	STILBENE
	TENSIBLE
BEEILNSU	NEBULISE
BEEILNUZ	NEBULIZE
BEEILOSS	OBELISES
BEEILOSZ	OBELIZES
BEEILOTV	LOVEBITE
BEEILRRT	TERRIBLE
BEEILRSU	BLUESIER
BEEILRYZ	BREEZILY
BEEILSTT	BETITLES
BEEIMRRU	UMBRIERE
BEEIMRTT	EMBITTER
BEEIMSSU	EMBUSIES
BEEINNSS	BEINNESS
BEEINNSZ	BENZINES
BEEINORT	TENEBRIO
BEEINOSS	EBONISES
BEEINOST	BETONIES
	EBONITES
BEEINOSZ	EBONIZES
BEEINPRS	PEBRINES
BEEINRSS	NEBRISES
BEEINRTT	REBITTEN
BEEINSTT	BENTIEST
BEEIOQSU	OBSEQUIE
BEEIORSS	SOBERISE
BEEIORSW	BOWERIES
BEEIORSZ	SOBERIZE
BEEIORTV	OVERBITE
BEEIQSUZ	BEZIQUES
BEEIRRSU	REBURIES
BEEIRRSV	BREVIERS
BEEIRRTT	BITTERER
BEEIRSSU	SUBERISE
BEEIRSSW	BREWISES
BEEIRSTU	UBERTIES
BEEIRSUZ	SUBERIZE
BEEKMOPR	PEMBROKE
BEEKNOPS	BESPOKEN
BEEKNOST	BETOKENS
	STEENBOK
BEEKRRSS	BERSERKS
BEEKRRSU	REBUKERS
BEELLORW	BELLOWER
	REBELLOW
BEELLOST	LOBELETS
BEELLSST	BESTSELL
BEELMMOP	BEPOMMEL
BEELMNNO	NOBLEMEN
BEELMOSW	EMBOWELS
BEELMRRT	TREMBLER
BEELMRRU	LUMBERER
BEELMRST	TREMBLES
BEELNNOS	ENNOBLES
BEELNOSS	BONELESS
	NOBLESSE
BEELNOSU	BLUENOSE
BEELNOSZ	BENZOLES
BEELNSSU	BLUENESS
BEELNTUY	BUTYLENE
BEELOOST	OBSOLETE
BEELOQRU	BRELOQUE
BEELORVW	OVERBLEW
BEELOSTW	STEELBOW
BEELOSTY	EYEBOLTS
BEELPRUV	BUPLEVER
BEELRSSV	VERBLESS
BEELRSUZ	ZEBRULES
BEELSSTU	TUBELESS
BEELSTTU	BLUETTES
BEEMNRRU	NUMBERER
	RENUMBER
BEEMOPRT	OBTEMPER
BEEMORSS	EMBOSSER
BEEMORSW	EMBOWERS
BEEMOSSS	EMBOSSES
BEEMQSUU	EMBUSQUE
BEEMRRSU	UMBRERES
BEEMRSSU	SUBMERSE
BEEMRTTU	UMBRETTE
BEEMRTUZ	ZERUMBET
BEEMSSSU	EMBUSSES
BEENORTU	BOUNTREE
BEENOSST	BONESETS
BEENPRST	BESPRENT
BEENRSTT	BRENTEST
BEENRSTW	BESTREWN
BEENRTTU	BRUNETTE
BEENSSTU	SUBTEENS
	SUBTEENE
BEEOORRT	BOORTREE
BEEOORRV	OVERBORE
BEEOORTT	BEETROOT
	BOOTTREE
BEEOPRSS	BEPROSES
BEEORRSU	BOURREES
BEEORRSV	OBSERVER
	VERBOSER
BEEORRTU	BOURTREE
BEEORSST	SOBEREST
BEEORSSU	SUBEROSE
BEEORSSV	OBSERVES
	OBVERSES
BEEORSTU	TUBEROSE
BEEORSTW	BESTOWER
BEEORSWY	EYEBROWS
BEEOSSSS	OBSESSES
BEEOSSST	BETOSSES
BEEPRRSU	SUPERBER
BEEPRRSV	PREVERBS
BEEPRSTY	PRESBYTE
BEEQSSTU	BEQUESTS
BEERRSTW	BREWSTER
BEERRTTU	REBUTTER
BEERSSSU	SUBSERES
BEERSSTW	BESTREWS
	WEBSTERS
BEERSSUV	SUBSERVE
	SUBVERSE
BEERSTTU	BURETTES
BEESTTUV	BUVETTES
BEFFLRSU	BLUFFERS
BEFFLSTU	BLUFFEST
BEFGIILL	FILLIBEG
BEFGIILS	FILIBEGS
BEFGIINR	BRIEFING
BEFGIRSU	FIREBUGS
BEFHILSU	BLUEFISH
BEFHIRSU	BUSHFIRE
BEFIIRSU	RUBIFIES
BEFILLXY	FLEXIBLY
BEFILMOR	FORELIMB
BEFILOST	BOTFLIES
BEFILRST	FILBERTS
BEFINORS	BONFIRES
BEFIORSS	FIBROSES
BEFIORTT	FOREBITT
BEFIRSST	FIBSTERS
BEFISSTU	FUBSIEST
BEFLLLUY	BELLYFUL
BEFLLSTY	FLYBELTS
BEFLMRSU	FUMBLERS
BEFLORUW	FURBELOW
BEFLSTUU	TUBEFULS
BEFNOORR	FORBORNE
BEFNOSSY	FYNBOSES
BEFORRXY	FOXBERRY
BEGGGINS	BEGGINGS
BEGGIINN	BINGEING
BEGGIOST	BOGGIEST
BEGGLORS	BOGGLERS
BEGGOOOS	GOOSEGOB
BEGHHIST	BEHIGHTS
BEGHIILP	PHILIBEG
BEGHILRT	BLIGHTER
	THERBLIG
BEGHINOR	NEIGHBOR
BEGHINOT	BEHOTING
BEGHINOV	BEHOVING
BEGHINRT	BERTHING
	BRIGHTEN
BEGHINST	BENIGHTS
BEGHIRRT	BRIGHTER
BEGHNOTU	BOUGHTEN
BEGHOSTU	BESOUGHT
BEGHOSUU	BUGHOUSE
BEGHRRSU	BURGHERS
BEGIIISS	SIGISBEI
BEGIILLY	ELIGIBLY
BEGIILST	BILGIEST
BEGIIMNR	BEMIRING
BEGIIMNT	BETIMING
BEGIINNS	INBEINGS
BEGIINRT	REBITING
BEGIINRZ	ZINGIBER
BEGIIOSS	SIGISBEO
BEGIKMNO	KEMBOING
BEGIKNRU	REBUKING
BEGILLLU	GULLIBLE
BEGILLNU	BULLGINE
BEGILLNY	BELLYING
BEGILMNR	REMBLING
BEGILMNS	SEMBLING
BEGILNNY	BENIGNLY
BEGILNOR	IGNOBLER

BEGILNOS	IGNOBLES	BEHIOOPR	BIOPHORE
	INGLOBES	BEHIRRST	REBIRTHS
BEGILNOV	BELOVING	BEHIRRSU	BRUSHIER
BEGILNOW	ELBOWING	BEHIRSST	HERBISTS
BEGILNRT	TREBLING	BEHIRSSU	HUBRISES
BEGILNSS	BLESSING	BEHIRSSY	HYBRISES
	GLIBNESS	BEHISSTU	BUSHIEST
BEGILNST	BELTINGS	BEHKOSSY	KYBOSHES
BEGILNSU	BLUEINGS	BEHLLOOT	BOLTHOLE
	BULGINES	BEHLLOOW	BLOWHOLE
BEGILNTT	BLETTING	BEHLLOPS	BELLHOPS
BEGILNUW	BLUEWING	BEHLLPSU	BELLPUSH
BEGILNZZ	BEZZLING	BEHLMOSW	WHOMBLES
BEGILRST	GILBERTS	BEHLMSTU	HUMBLEST
BEGILSTU	BULGIEST	BEHLOOPY	HYPOBOLE
BEGIMNOW	EMBOWING		LYOPHOBE
BEGIMNOX	EMBOXING	BEHLOOST	BOTHOLES
BEGIMNRU	EMBRUING	BEHLORST	BROTHELS
	UMBERING	BEHLOSSU	SLOEBUSH
BEGIMNSU	BEMUSING	BEHLRRSU	BURRHELS
BEGIMOST	MISBEGOT	BEHLRSSU	BLUSHERS
BEGIMOSY	BOGEYISM	BEHLSSTU	BLUSHETS
BEGINNNR	BRENNING	BEHMNOTY	BOTHYMEN
BEGINNNU	UNBENIGN	BEHMOSTU	BEMOUTHS
BEGINNOR	ENROBING	BEHMPSTU	BETHUMPS
	RINGBONE	BEHNNOUY	HONEYBUN
BEGINNSU	UNBEINGS	BEHNRSTU	BURTHENS
BEGINOOS	BESOGNIO	BEHOOOST	BOOTHOSE
BEGINORR	REBORING	BEHOORST	THEORBOS
BEGINORS	SOBERING	BEHOOSUY	HOUSEBOY
BEGINORW	BOWERING	BEHORRST	BROTHERS
BEGINRRS	BRINGERS	BEHORSTT	BETROTHS
BEGINRRY	BERRYING	BEHRRSSU	BRUSHERS
BEGINRSW	BREWINGS	BEIIKRTZ	KIBITZER
BEGINSTT	BETTINGS	BEIIKSTZ	KIBITZES
BEGKMOSS	GEMSBOKS	BEIILMMO	IMMOBILE
BEGLLOSU	GLOBULES	BEIILMOS	MOBILISE
BEGLLOTU	GLOBULET	BEIILMOZ	MOBILIZE
BEGLMOOS	BEGLOOMS	BEIILMSU	BULIMIES
BEGLMRRU	GRUMBLER	BEIILNRS	RINSIBLE
BEGLMRSU	GRUMBLES	BEIILOPR	PERIBOLI
BEGLNOUW	BLUEGOWN	BEIILRST	TRILBIES
BEGLNRSU	BLUNGERS	BEIILRTT	LIBRETTI
	BUNGLERS	BEIILRUZ	BRUILZIE
BEGLOOSS	GLOBOSES	BEIILSSV	VISIBLES
BEGLOOST	BOOTLEGS	BEIILSTT	STILBITE
BEGLRSTY	BERGYLTS	BEIIMNNR	RENMINBI
BEGNOORU	BOURGEON	BEIIMNOS	EBIONISM
BEGNORSU	BURGEONS	BEIIMRTT	IMBITTER
BEGNORTU	BURGONET	BEIINORS	BRIONIES
BEGNSSUU	SUBGENUS	BEIINRST	BRINIEST
BEHHKOST	KHOTBEHS	BEIINSST	STIBINES
BEHIISTX	EXHIBITS	BEIINSTT	STIBNITE
BEHIKNST	BETHINKS	BEIIOPSS	BIOPSIES
BEHIKOSS	KIBOSHES	BEIIORST	ORBITIES
BEHILLOS	SHOEBILL	BEIIOSTT	BIOTITES
BEHILLTY	BLITHELY	BEIIRSST	BIRSIEST
BEHILMRW	WHIMBREL	BEIISSTT	BITSIEST
BEHILMST	THIMBLES	BEIISTTT	BITTIEST
BEHILNPY	BIPHENYL	BEIJLMRU	JUMBLIER
BEHILORR	HORRIBLE	BEIJMOSU	JUMBOISE
BEHILORS	BOLSHIER	BEIJMOUZ	JUMBOIZE
BEHILOSS	BOLSHIES	BEIJNORW	BIJWONER
BEHILRST	BLITHERS	BEIKLNRS	BLINKERS
BEHILRTU	THURIBLE	BEIKLOSS	OBELISKS
BEHILSTT	BLITHEST	BEIKLOTY	KILOBYTE
BEHIMNOO	BONHOMIE	BEIKLSTU	BULKIEST
BEHIMRTU	THUMBIER	BEIKMNNR	BRINKMEN
BEHINOPS	HOPBINES	BEIKNRRY	INKBERRY
BEHINOSW	WISHBONE		

BEIKNRSS	BRISKENS	BEIMPSTU	BUMPIEST
BEIKOORS	BOOKSIER	BEIMRSSU	IMBURSES
BEIKOORT	BROOKITE	BEIMRSTU	IMBRUTES
BEIKOOST	BOOKIEST		RESUBMIT
BEIKOSST	BOSKIEST		TERBIUMS
BEIKRSST	BRISKEST	BEINNOSS	BENISONS
	BRISKETS		BONINESS
BEILLMSS	LIMBLESS	BEINNOST	BONNIEST
BEILLMSU	SEMIBULL	BEINNOSZ	BENZOINS
BEILLNTU	BULLETIN	BEINNRYZ	ZEBRINNY
BEILLORS	BROLLIES	BEINORRW	BROWNIER
BEILLOSX	BOLLIXES	BEINORRZ	BRONZIER
BEILLSST	BESTILLS	BEINORST	BORNITES
BEILLSTU	BULLIEST		RIBSTONE
BEILMMOS	EMBOLISM	BEINORSW	BROWNIES
BEILMNOU	NOBELIUM	BEINORSY	BRYONIES
BEILMNRU	UNLIMBER	BEINORTZ	BRONZITE
BEILMNST	NIMBLEST	BEINOSST	EBONISTS
BEILMNUU	NEBULIUM	BEINOSSX	BOXINESS
BEILMOOR	BLOOMIER	BEINOSTT	BOTTINES
BEILMORS	EMBROILS	BEINOSTU	BOUNTIES
BEILMPTU	PLUMBITE	BEINRRSY	NISBERRY
BEILMRRU	RUMBLIER	BEINRRSU	SUBERINS
BEILMRSS	BRIMLESS	BEINRSTT	BITTERNS
BEILMRST	TIMBRELS	BEINRSTU	TRIBUNES
BEILMRSU	SUBLIMER		TURBINES
BEILMRSW	WIMBRELS	BEINRSUU	UNBURIES
BEILMSSU	SUBLIMES	BEINSSSU	BUSINESS
BEILNNTU	BUNTLINE	BEINSTTU	BUNTIEST
BEILNOOS	OBELIONS	BEIOORST	ROBOTISE
BEILNOPS	BONSPIEL	BEIOORTZ	ROBOTIZE
BEILNOSW	BOWLINES	BEIOOSSV	OVIBOSES
BEILNSSY	SENSIBLY	BEIOOSTZ	BOOZIEST
BEILNSTZ	BLINTZES	BEIOPSTY	BIOTYPES
BEILOORV	OVERBOIL	BEIOQTUU	BOUTIQUE
BEILOOST	LOOBIEST	BEIORRST	ORBITERS
BEILOPPW	BLOWPIPE	BEIORRSU	BOURSIER
BEILOPSS	POSSIBLE	BEIORRTU	ROBURITE
BEILOQRU	OBLIQUER	BEIORSTY	SOBRIETY
BEILOQSU	OBLIQUES	BEIOSSST	BOSSIEST
BEILORRS	BROILERS	BEIOSSSU	SOUBISES
BEILORST	STROBILE	BEIOSSTU	BOUSIEST
	TRILOBES	BEIOTTZZ	BOZZETTI
BEILORSW	BLOWSIER	BEIQRSTU	BRIQUETS
BEILORTT	BLOTTIER	BEIRRSSU	BRISURES
	LIBRETTO		BRUISERS
BEILORWZ	BLOWZIER	BEIRRSTU	BURRIEST
BEILOSTW	BLOWIEST	BEIRRTTU	TRIBUTER
BEILRRTT	BRITTLER	BEIRSSTU	BUSTIERS
BEILRRTY	TERRIBLY	BEIRSTTU	TRIBUTES
BEILRSST	BLISTERS	BEIRSTTY	TREYBITS
	BRISTLES	BEISSTTU	BUSTIEST
BEILRSTT	BRITTLES	BEISTUZZ	BUZZIEST
	TRIBLETS	BEJKOOST	JESTBOOK
BEILRSTU	BURLIEST	BEJLMRSU	JUMBLERS
	SUBTILER	BEKLNORY	BROKENLY
BEILRSTY	BLISTERY	BEKLNRSU	BLUNKERS
BEILRSUY	BRULYIES	BEKLOOOR	BOOKLORE
BEILRSUZ	BRULZIES	BEKLOORT	BROOKLET
BEILRTTY	BITTERLY	BEKLOOSS	BOOKLESS
BEILSTTU	SUBTITLE	BEKLOOST	BOOKLETS
BEIMMRRS	BRIMMERS	BEKLORUV	OVERBULK
BEIMNORS	BROMINES	BEKMOOPS	SPEKBOOM
BEIMNSSU	NIMBUSES	BEKMOSST	STEMBOKS
BEIMNSTU	BITUMENS	BEKNNORU	UNBROKEN
BEIMOORR	BROOMIER	BEKNOOOT	NOTEBOOK
BEIMOORS	RIBOSOME	BEKNOPRU	UPBROKEN
BEIMORSW	IMBOWERS	BEKOOORV	OVERBOOK
BEIMORTY	BIOMETRY	BEKOORST	BOOKREST
BEIMOSSS	IMBOSSES	BEKOORTU	OUTBROKE

BEKOOTTX	TEXTBOOK	BEMOSTUX	BUXOMEST
BELLMORT	MORTBELL	BEMOSTUY	MYOTUBES
BELLMORU	UMBRELLO	BEMSSSUU	SUBSUMES
BELLMRUY	LUMBERLY	BENNNOTU	UNBONNET
BELLNTUY	TUNBELLY	BENNOOTU	BOUTONNE
BELLORTW	BELLWORT	BENOORSU	SUBORNER
BELLRRSU	BURRELLS	BENORRUV	OVERBURN
BELMMOOS	EMBLOOMS	BENORSST	SORBENTS
BELMMRSU	MUMBLERS	BENORSTU	RUBSTONE
BELMNOSU	NELUMBOS	BENORSTW	BESTROWN
BELMOORS	BLOOMERS		BROWNEST
	REBLOOMS	BENORSTY	RENTBOYS
BELMOORY	BLOOMERY	BENORSUU	BURNOUSE
BELMOOSS	BLOOSMES	BENORSWY	BYWONERS
BELMOPRS	PROBLEMS	BENORTTU	REBUTTON
BELMORSY	SOMBRELY	BENOSSUZ	SUBZONES
BELMORUW	RUMBELOW	BENOSSWY	NEWSBOYS
BELMOSST	TOMBLESS	BENSSSUY	BUSYNESS
BELMOSSY	SYMBOLES	BEOORRRW	BORROWER
BELMPRSU	PLUMBERS	BEOORRVW	OVERBROW
BELMPRUY	PLUMBERY	BEOORSST	BOOSTERS
BELMRRSU	RUMBLERS	BEOORSTY	BOTRYOSE
BELMRRUY	MULBERRY	BEOOSTUX	OUTBOXES
BELMRSSU	SLUMBERS	BEOOTTZZ	BOZZETTO
BELMRSTU	STUMBLER	BEOPRRSV	PROVERBS
	TUMBLERS	BEOPSSTU	BESPOUTS
	TUMBRELS	BEOQSTUU	BOUQUETS
BELMRSUY	SLUMBERY	BEORRSTU	ROBUSTER
BELMSSTU	STUMBLES	BEORSSSU	SORBUSES
BELNNOSU	UNNOBLES	BEORSSUU	SUBEROUS
BELNOOSY	BOLONEYS	BEORSTUU	TUBEROUS
BELNOSUU	NEBULOUS	BEORSUVY	OVERBUSY
BELNSSTU	SUNBELTS		OVERBUYS
BELNSTTU	BLUNTEST	BEOSSTTU	OBTUSEST
BELNSTUU	UNSUBTLE	BEPRRSTU	PERTURBS
BELOOPRS	BLOOPERS	BEPSSTUY	SUBTYPES
BELOORVW	OVERBLOW	BEQRRSUU	BRUSQUER
BELOOSST	BOOTLESS	BERRSSTU	BURSTERS
BELOOTUV	OBVOLUTE	BERRSTUU	SURREBUT
BELORRTU	TROUBLER	BERSSTTU	BUTTRESS
BELORSST	BOLSTERS	BERSSTUV	SUBVERST
	LOBSTERS		SUBVERTS
BELORSSW	BROWLESS	BESSSSUY	BYSSUSES
BELORSTT	BLOTTERS	BESSTTUX	SUBTEXTS
	BOTTLERS	BFFGILNU	BLUFFING
BELORSTU	BOULTERS	BFFNOOSU	BUFFOONS
	TROUBLES	BFFNOSUX	SNUFFBOX
BELOSTUY	OBTUSELY	BFGILMNU	FUMBLING
BELPRSUY	SUPERBLY	BFGIORST	FROGBITS
BELRSSTU	BLUSTERS	BFGLLORU	BULLFROG
	BUSTLERS	BFHLLSUU	BLUSHFUL
BELRSTUY	BLUSTERY	BFIINORS	FIBROINS
BELSSTTU	SUBTLEST	BFIIORSS	FIBROSIS
BELSSTUY	SUBSTYLE	BFILLSSU	BLISSFUL
BELSTTUY	SUBTLETY	BFIMNORU	NUBIFORM
BEMMOOSS	EMBOSOMS	BFIMORTU	TUBIFORM
BEMMORRS	BROMMERS	BFINORYZ	BRONZIFY
BEMMRRSU	BRUMMERS	BFIORSTT	FROSTBIT
BEMNOORT	TROMBONE	BFKLOOSY	FLYBOOKS
BEMNORSW	EMBROWNS	BFKSSSUU	SUBFUSKS
BEMNORSY	EMBRYONS	BFLLOSWY	FLYBLOWS
BEMNSTTU	BUTMENTS	BFLOORSU	SUBFLOOR
BEMNTTUY	BUTTYMEN	BFOOOSTY	FOOTBOYS
BEMOORRS	SOMBRERO	BGGGILNO	BOGGLING
BEMORSST	BESTORMS	BGGGINOR	BROGGING
	MOBSTERS	BGGGINSU	BUGGINGS
	SOMBREST	BGGIILNN	BINGLING
BEMORSSU	MORBUSES	BGGIILNY	GIBINGLY
BEMORSWW	WEBWORMS		

BGGIINNO	BOINGING	BGILNOSU	BLOUSING
BGGIINNR	BRINGING	BGILNOSW	BOWLINGS
BGGIINRU	BRIGUING	BGILNOTT	BLOTTING
BGGILNNU	BLUNGING		BOTTLING
	BUNGLING	BGILNOTU	BOULTING
BGGILNRU	BURGLING	BGILNRRU	BLURRING
BGGINOOT	TOBOGGIN	BGILNRTU	BLURTING
BGGINOSY	BYGOINGS	BGILNSTU	BUSTLING
BGHHIORW	HIGHBROW	BGILNTTU	BUTTLING
BGHHIOSY	HIGHBOYS	BGILOORS	OBLIGORS
BGHILMNU	HUMBLING	BGILRSSU	BUSGIRLS
BGHILNSU	BLUSHING	BGIMNOOR	BROOMING
BGHILRTY	BRIGHTLY	BGIMNOOS	BOOMINGS
BGHIMNTU	THUMBING		BOSOMING
BGHINORS	BIGHORNS	BGIMNORS	SOMBRING
BGHINRSU	BRUSHING	BGIMOSSY	BOGYISMS
BGHNORSU	HORNBUGS	BGINNNOU	UNBONING
BGHNOTUU	UNBOUGHT	BGINNORU	UNROBING
BGHOOPTU	BOUGHPOT	BGINNORW	BROWNING
BGHOORSU	BOROUGHS	BGINNORZ	BRONZING
BGIIJLNR	JIRBLING	BGINNOUX	UNBOXING
BGIIKLNN	BLINKING	BGINNRSU	BURNINGS
BGIIKMNO	KIMBOING	BGINNRTU	BRUNTING
BGIIKNNO	BOINKING	BGINNSTU	BUNTINGS
BGIIKNRS	BRISKING	BGINOOST	BOOSTING
BGIILLNS	BILLINGS	BGINORSW	BROWSING
BGIILMNW	WIMBLING	BGINPRSU	UPBRINGS
BGIILNNN	BLINNING	BGINRSTU	BRUSTING
BGIILNOR	BROILING		BURSTING
BGIILNOS	BOILINGS	BGINSSSU	BUSSINGS
BGIILNPP	BLIPPING	BGINSSTU	BUSTINGS
BGIILNRS	BIRLINGS	BGINSUZZ	BUZZINGS
	BIRSLING	BGKNOOOS	SONGBOOK
	BRISLING	BGKORSSY	GRYSBOKS
BGIILNSS	SIBLINGS	BGLNOOSW	LONGBOWS
BGIILNTZ	BLITZING	BGLNOSUW	BLOWGUNS
BGIIMMNR	BRIMMING	BGLOORXY	GLORYBOX
BGIIMNRS	BRIMINGS	BGLOORYY	BRYOLOGY
BGIIMNRU	IMBRUING	BGMOOSTU	GUMBOOTS
BGIINNOR	INORBING	BGNOOSWY	GOWNBOYS
BGIINNRS	INBRINGS	BGOPRSUU	SUBGROUP
BGIINORT	ORBITING	BGORSTUW	BUGWORTS
BGIINRST	RINGBITS	BHIIINST	INHIBITS
BGIINRSU	BRUISING	BHIIKRSS	BRISKISH
BGIINRTU	BRUITING	BHIILMPS	BLIMPISH
BGIINSTU	BUISTING	BHIIMRST	MISBIRTH
BGIINVVY	BIVVYING	BHIIOPRT	PROHIBIT
BGIJLMNU	JUMBLING	BHIIPSSS	SIBSHIPS
BGIJNORU	OBJURING	BHIKLLOO	BILLHOOK
BGIKLNNU	BLUNKING	BHILLNOR	HORNBILL
BGIKNNOU	BUNKOING	BHILLSTU	BULLSHIT
BGIKNOOR	BROOKING	BHILNSTU	BLUNTISH
BGIKNOOS	BOOKINGS	BHILORRY	HORRIBLY
BGIKNORS	BROKINGS	BHILOSTU	HOLIBUTS
BGIKNSSU	BUSKINGS	BHILOSYY	BOYISHLY
BGILLNOU	GLOBULIN	BHIMNORT	THROMBIN
BGILLNUY	BULLYING	BHIMOOPR	BIOMORPH
BGILMMNU	BUMMLING	BHIMOOSS	HOBOISMS
	MUMBLING	BHIMOPSS	PHOBISMS
BGILMNOO	BLOOMING	BHIMSSTU	BISMUTHS
BGILMNPU	PLUMBING	BHINOPSU	UNBISHOP
BGILMNRU	RUMBLING	BHINORSW	BROWNISH
BGILMNTU	TUMBLING	BHIOOPRS	BIOPHORS
BGILMORY	GORBLIMY	BHIOPSST	PHOBISTS
BGILMOSU	GUMBOILS	BHIRSTTU	TURBITHS
BGILNNOS	SNOBLING	BHKNOOOR	HORNBOOK
BGILNNTU	BLUNTING	BHKOOOPS	BOOKSHOP
BGILNOOP	BLOOPING	BHLOOOTT	TOLBOOTH
BGILNOST	BILTONGS	BHLRSUUY	BULRUSHY
	BOLTINGS	BHMOPTTU	THUMBPOT

BHMORSTU	THROMBUS
BHOOSSTW	BOWSHOTS
BIIKLOST	KILOBITS
BIIKNOOT	BOOTIKIN
BIILLMOR	MORBILLI
BIILLNOS	BILLIONS
BIILLOSU	BOUILLIS
BIILLSTW	TWIBILLS
BIILMOTY	MOBILITY
BIILNNRS	BIRLINNS
BIILNOOV	OBLIVION
BIILNOTY	NOBILITY
BIILNQSU	QUIBLINS
BIILNTUY	NUBILITY
BIILORST	STROBILI
BIILOSSU	SIBILOUS
BIIMMOSZ	ZOMBIISM
BIIMNOSU	NIOBIUMS
BIIMNSSU	MINISUBS
BIIMSSTU	STIBIUMS
BIINRSTU	BURINIST
BIIQTUUY	UBIQUITY
BIIRSSTU	BURSITIS
BIJNOSSU	SUBJOINS
BIKLNOSY	LINKBOYS
BIKMNPSU	BUMPKINS
BIKOOUUZ	BOUZOUKI
BIKORRSW	RIBWORKS
BILLMSUY	BULLYISM
BILLNOOU	BOUILLON
BILLNOSU	BULLIONS
BILLRSWY	WRYBILLS
BILLSTUY	SUBTILLY
BILMMPSU	PLUMBISM
BILMNORS	NOMBRILS
BILMOSTU	BOTULISM
BILMRSTU	TUMBRILS
BILNOSTU	NUBILOUS
BILOORST	SORBITOL
BILOPSSY	POSSIBLY
BILORSST	BRISTOLS
BILOSSSU	SUBSOILS
BILSSTTU	SUBTLIST
BILSTTUY	SUBTILTY
BIMMOSSS	IMBOSOMS
BIMNORSW	IMBROWNS
BIMNOSSY	SYMBIONS
BIMNOSTY	SYMBIONT
BIMNRUUV	VIBURNUM
BIMOSSTY	SYBOTISM
BIMRSSUX	BRUXISMS
BINOORST	ISOBRONT
BINORSST	RIBSTONS
BINRRSTU	INBURSTS
BINSSTUU	SUBUNITS
BIOPRRSU	SUBPRIOR
BIOPRSTW	BOWSPRIT
BIORRSTW	RIBWORTS
BIORSSTT	BISTORTS
BIORSTTU	BITTOURS
BIORSTUY	BISTOURY
BIOSTTUY	OBTUSITY
BIRSSTTU	SUBTRIST
BISSSSTU	SUBSISTS
BKKOOORW	BOOKWORK
	WORKBOOK
BKMOOORW	BOOKWORM
BKMOORUZ	ZOMBORUK
BLLLLOOY	LOBLOLLY
BLMMPSUU	PLUMBUMS
BLMNPSUU	UNPLUMBS
BLMOOOST	TOMBOLOS
BLMOOOTY	LOBOTOMY
BLMOORSW	LOBWORMS
BLMOOSSS	BLOSSOMS
BLMOOSSY	BLOSSOMY
BLNOOSSU	BLOUSONS
BLOOSSTY	SLYBOOTS
BLOPSSTU	SUBPLOTS
BLORSTUY	ROBUSTLY
BLOSTUUU	TUBULOUS
BMNOOSSU	UNBOSOMS
BMNORSUW	MOWBURNS
BMNORTUW	MOWBURNT
BMOOORSX	BOXROOMS
BMOORSSU	SOMBROUS
BMORSSTU	STROMBUS
BNNOTTUU	UNBUTTON
BNNRSSUU	SUNBURNS
BNNRSTUU	SUNBURNT
BNOOOSUY	SONOBUOY
BNOORTUW	BROWNOUT
BNORRUUW	UNBURROW
BNRSSTUU	SUNBURST
BORSTTUU	OUTBURST
BPRSSTUU	UPBURSTS
CCCDIILY	DICYCLIC
CCCEEILT	ECLECTIC
CCCEGOSY	COCCYGES
CCCEIIRT	ECCRITIC
CCCEILNY	ENCYCLIC
CCCEILUY	EUCYCLIC
CCCHIORY	CHICCORY
CCCIINSU	SUCCINIC
CCCILNOY	CYCLONIC
CCCILOPY	CYCLOPIC
CCCINSTU	SUCCINCT
CCCIOORS	SCIROCCO
CCCNOOST	CONCOCTS
CCDDEENO	CONCEDED
CCDDEEOT	DECOCTED
CCDDELOU	OCCLUDED
CCDDENOU	CONDUCED
CCDEEENR	CREDENCE
CCDEEHLN	CLENCHED
CCDEEILN	LICENCED
CCDEEINS	SCIENCED
CCDEEIOS	ECOCIDES
CCDEEKOR	COCKERED
CCDEEKOY	COCKEYED
CCDEELRY	RECYCLED
CCDEENOR	CONCEDER
CCDEENOS	CONCEDES
CCDEESSU	SUCCEEDS
CCDEHHRU	CHURCHED
CCDEHIKT	TCHICKED
CCDEHILN	CLINCHED
CCDEHIPU	HICCUPED
CCDEHKLU	CHUCKLED
CCDEHLTU	CLUTCHED
	DECLUTCH
CCDEHNRU	CRUNCHED
CCDEHORS	SCORCHED
CCDEHORT	CROTCHED
CCDEHORU	CROUCHED
CCDEHOST	SCOTCHED
CCDEHRTU	CRUTCHED
CCDEHSTU	SCUTCHED
CCDEIINO	COINCIDE
CCDEIIST	DEICTICS
CCDEILOS	SCOLECID
CCDEINOR	CORNICED
CCDEINOS	CONCISED
CCDEINOT	OCCIDENT
CCDEIOPP	COPPICED
CCDEIOPU	OCCUPIED
CCDEKNOU	UNCOCKED
CCDELNOU	CONCLUDE
CCDELOSU	OCCLUDES
CCDELOTU	OCCULTED
CCDENOOO	COCOONED
CCDENOSU	CONDUCES
CCDEORRU	OCCURRED
CCDEORSU	SUCCORED
CCDEOSTU	STUCCOED
CCDHIIKP	DIPCHICK
CCDHIILO	CICHLOID
CCDHIILS	CICHLIDS
CCDHIORR	DICHROIC
CCDHINOO	CONCHOID
CCDIILOS	CODICILS
CCDIILSU	CULICIDS
CCDIINOO	CONOIDIC
CCDIINOS	SCINCOID
CCDIINST	DISCINCT
CCDIIORS	CRICOIDS
CCDIIORT	DICROTIC
CCDILOSY	CYCLOIDS
CCDINOTU	CONDUCTI
CCDKLOSU	CUCKOLDS
CCDKLOUY	CUCKOLDY
CCDKOOOW	WOODCOCK
CCDNOORS	CONCORDS
CCDNOSTU	CONDUCTS
CCEEELMN	CLEMENCE
CCEEGINR	RECCEING
CCEEGNOS	COGENCES
CCEEHIKR	CHECKIER
CCEEHINZ	ZECCHINE
CCEEHKRS	CHECKERS
	RECHECKS
CCEEHLNS	CLENCHES
CCEEHORS	ECORCHES
CCEEHOSU	COUCHEES
CCEEHRSY	SCREECHY
CCEEIILS	CICELIES
CCEEIIST	CECITIES
CCEEILNR	ENCIRCLE
CCEEILNS	LICENCES
CCEEILNT	ELENCTIC
CCEEILPY	EPICYCLE
CCEEILRT	ELECTRIC
CCEEIMNU	ECUMENIC
CCEEINOR	CICERONE
CCEEINOV	CONCEIVE
CCEEINSS	SCIENCES
CCEEIORV	COERCIVE
CCEEIPSS	SPECCIES
CCEEIRSS	ECCRISES
CCEEIRSV	CRESCIVE
	CREVICES
CCEEITTU	EUTECTIC
CCEEKLOR	COCKEREL
CCEEKOSY	COCKEYES
CCEELMNY	CLEMENCY
CCEELOSS	SCOLECES
CCEELRSY	RECYCLES
CCEEMMNO	COMMENCE
CCEEMMOR	COMMERCE
CCEEMOPS	COMPESCE
CCEENNOS	ENSCONCE
CCEENORT	CONCRETE
CCEENRST	CRESCENT
CCEERSSU	CERCUSES
CCEFIIPS	SPECIFIC
CCEFIRRU	CRUCIFER
CCEFLLOU	FLOCCULE
CCEFLOOS	FLOCCOSE
CCEFNOST	CONFECTS
CCEGHIKN	CHECKING
CCEGHIOR	CHOREGIC
CCEGIKLN	CLECKING
CCEGILOO	ECOLOGIC
CCEGILRY	GLYCERIC
CCEGINOR	COERCING
CCEGINRY	RECCYING
CCEGNOOS	COGNOSCE
CCEHHINS	CHINCHES
CCEHHRSU	CHURCHES
CCEHIIMR	CHIMERIC
CCEHIIMS	ISCHEMIC
CCEHIINZ	ZECCHINI
CCEHIKNS	CHICKENS
CCEHIKSU	CHUCKIES
CCEHILNR	CLINCHER
CCEHILNS	CLINCHES
CCEHILOR	CHOLERIC
CCEHILOY	CHOICELY
CCEHINOR	CORNICHE
	ENCHORIC
CCEHINOS	CONCHIES
CCEHINOZ	ZECCHINO
CCEHINST	TECHNICS
CCEHIORT	RICOCHET
CCEHIOST	CHOICEST
CCEHIRSS	SCREICHS
	SCRIECHS
CCEHKLSU	CHUCKLES
CCEHKNSU	UNCHECKS
CCEHLMOR	CROMLECH
CCEHLNNU	UNCLENCH
CCEHLNSU	CLUNCHES
CCEHLRSU	CLERUCHS
CCEHLRUY	CLERUCHY
CCEHLSTU	CLUTCHES
	CULTCHES
CCEHNRSU	CRUNCHES
CCEHORRS	SCORCHER
CCEHORSS	SCORCHES
CCEHORST	CROCHETS
	CROTCHES
CCEHORSU	CROUCHES
CCEHORTT	CROTCHET
CCEHOSST	SCOTCHES
CCEHRSTU	CRUTCHES
	SCUTCHER
CCEHRTUY	CUTCHERY
CCEHSSTU	SCUTCHES
CCEIIKLN	NICKELIC
CCEIILNT	ENCLITIC
CCEIILST	SCILICET
CCEIILTU	LEUCITIC
CCEIILNU	CULICINE
CCEIINNR	ENCRINIC
CCEIINOR	CICERONI

CCEIIRRT	CIRCITER	CCENORSW	CONCREWS	CCILNOOS	COLONICS	CDDEEKNU	UNDECKED
CCEIIRSS	ECCRISIS	CCENORTY	CORNETCY	CCILNOSU	COUNCILS	CDDEEKOT	DOCKETED
CCEIIRST	ICTERICS	CCENRRUY	CURRENCY	CCILOOPS	PICCOLOS	CDDEEKUW	DUCKWEED
CCEIIRTT	RECTITIC	CCEOOORR	COROCORE	CCILORUU	CURCULIO	CDDEELPU	DECUPLED
CCEIIRTU	EUCRITIC	CCEOORSU	CROCEOUS	CCILOSSY	CYCLOSIS	CDDEELSU	SECLUDED
CCEIKLRS	CLICKERS	CCEOOSTT	COCOTTES	CCILSSTY	CYCLISTS	CDDEELUX	EXCLUDED
CCEIKLRU	CLUCKIER	CCEOPRUY	REOCCUPY	CCIMNSUU	SUCCINUM	CDDEELUY	DEUCEDLY
CCEIKLST	CLICKETS	CCEORRST	CORRECTS	CCINOOST	COCTIONS	CDDEENOS	SECONDED
CCEIKORS	COCKSIER	CCEORSSU	CROCUSES	CCINOPRT	PROCINCT	CDDEENSS	DESCENDS
CCEIKOST	COCKIEST	CCEORSTU	STUCCOER	CCINOPSY	SYNCOPIC	CDDEEORR	RECORDED
CCEIKRST	CRICKETS	CCESSSUU	CUSCUSES	CCINORSY	CRYONICS	CDDEEORS	DECODERS
CCEILMOO	COELOMIC	CCFIINOR	CORNIFIC	CCINOSTV	CONVICTS	CDDEERUV	DECURVED
CCEILMOP	COMPLICE	CCFIIRUX	CRUCIFIX	CCIOOPST	SCOTOPIC	CDDEESUW	CUDWEEDS
CCEILNOR	CORNICLE	CCFILLOU	FLOCCULI	CCIOORSS	SIROCCOS	CDDEFIIO	CODIFIED
CCEILNUY	UNICYCLE	CCFILNOT	CONFLICT	CCIOOTXY	OXYTOCIC	CDDEFINO	CONFIDED
CCEILOSS	SCOLICES	CCFKLOOT	COCKLOFT	CCIOPSTU	OCCIPUTS	CDDEGIIN	DECIDING
CCEILRRS	CIRCLERS	CCFLOOOO	LOCOFOCO	CCIRSSUY	CIRCUSSY	CDDEGINO	DECODING
CCEILRRU	CURRICLE	CCGHHIOU	HICCOUGH	CCJNNOTU	CONJUNCT	CDDEGINU	DEDUCING
CCEILRST	CIRCLETS	CCGHIINN	CINCHING	CCKKLMUU	MUCKLUCK	CDDEHIOW	COWHIDED
CCEILRTY	TRICYCLE	CCGHIKNO	CHOCKING	CCKMMORU	CRUMMOCK	CDDEIINT	INDICTED
CCEILRUU	CURLICUE	CCGHIKNU	CHUCKING	CCKMOOOR	MOORCOCK	CDDEIISS	DISCIDES
CCEILSTU	CUTICLES	CCGHINOS	GNOCCHIS	CCKNORTU	TURNCOCK	CDDEIKOS	DOCKISED
CCEIMNOO	ECONOMIC	CCGHINOU	COUCHING	CCKOPRSU	COCKSPUR	CDDEIKOZ	DOCKIZED
CCEIMOST	COSMETIC	CCGIIKLN	CLICKING	CCKOSSTU	CUSTOCKS	CDDEILLO	COLLIDED
CCEIMRRU	MERCURIC	CCGIIKNR	CRICKING	CCLLOTUY	OCCULTLY	CDDEILNU	INCLUDED
CCEINNOS	INSCONCE	CCGIILNR	CIRCLING	CCLMOOPU	COCOPLUM	CDDEILOR	CLODDIER
CCEINNOV	CONVINCE	CCGIKLNO	CLOCKING	CCLNOOOR	CONCOLOR	CDDEILRU	CUDDLIER
CCEINOOR	COERCION		COCKLING	CCLOOOSZ	ZOCCOLOS	CDDEINTU	INDUCTED
CCEINOPT	CONCEPTI	CCGIKLNU	CLUCKING	CCLOORSU	OCCLUSOR	CDDEIORV	DIVORCED
CCEINORS	CONCISER	CCGIKNOR	CROCKING	CCMOOORS	MOROCCOS	CDDEIRRU	CRUDDIER
	CORNICES	CCGILLOY	GLYCOLIC	CCNOOPSU	PUCCOONS	CDDEIRSU	DISCURED
CCEINORT	NECROTIC	CCGILNOY	GLYCONIC	CCNOORSU	CONCOURS	CDDEKNOU	UNDOCKED
CCEINOSS	CONCISES	CCGILNSY	CYCLINGS	CCNOOSTU	COCONUTS	CDDELLOU	COLLUDED
CCEINOST	CONCEITS	CCGILOSU	GLUCOSIC	CCOOOORR	COROCORO	CDDELNOO	CONDOLED
CCEINOTT	CONCETTI	CCGINNOS	SCONCING	CCOOSSUU	COUSCOUS	CDDELOOR	CROODLED
	TECTONIC	CCGKOORS	GORCOCKS	CCOOTTUU	TUCOTUCO	CDDELRSU	CRUDDLES
CCEINOTY	CONCEITY	CCHHILSS	SCHLICHS	CCORSSTU	CROSSCUT	CDDELSSU	SCUDDLES
CCEINPRT	PRECINCT	CCHHINOT	CHTHONIC	CCORSSSU	SUCCOURS	CDDEMNOU	DUNCEDOM
CCEINRTU	CINCTURE	CCHHLRUY	CHURCHLY	CCOTTUUU	TUCUTUCO	CDDENNOO	CONDONED
CCEINSTY	SYNECTIC	CCHHNRUU	UNCHURCH	CCRSUUUU	SURUCUCU	CDDENOOR	CORDONED
CCEIOORT	CROCOITE	CCHIINUZ	ZUCCHINI	CDDDEETU	DEDUCTED	CDDENORU	UNCORDED
CCEIOOTZ	ECTOZOIC	CCHIIORT	ORCHITIC	CDDDEIIS	DISCIDED	CDDEOORR	CORRODED
CCEIOPPS	COPPICES	CCHIKMPU	CHIPMUCK	CDDDELRU	CRUDDLED	CDDEOORT	DOCTORED
CCEIOPRT	ECTROPIC	CCHIKSST	SCHTICKS	CDDDELSU	SCUDDLED	CDDEOPRU	PRODUCED
CCEIOPRU	OCCUPIER	CCHINORS	CHRONICS	CDDDIIIO	DIDDICOI	CDDERSSU	SCUDDERS
CCEIOPSU	OCCUPIES	CCHINOSU	SCUCHION	CDDDIIOY	DIDDICOY	CDDGHILO	GODCHILD
CCEIORST	CORTICES	CCHINSSU	SCUCHINS	CDDEEEEX	EXCEEDED	CDDGILNO	CLODDING
CCEIPSST	SCEPTICS	CCHIPSSY	PSYCHICS	CDDEEEFN	DEFENCED		CODDLING
CCEIRSSU	CIRCUSES	CCHKLOSS	SCHLOCKS	CDDEEEFT	DEFECTED	CDDGILNU	CUDDLING
CCEJNOST	CONJECTS	CCHKMOSS	SCHMOCKS	CDDEEEIV	DECEIVED	CDDGINSU	SCUDDING
CCEKLORS	CLOCKERS	CCHKMSSU	SCHMUCKS	CDDEEEJT	DEJECTED	CDDHIIRY	DIHYDRIC
CCEKNOST	CONTECKS	CCHKOOST	COCKSHOT	CDDEEENR	DECERNED	CDDHILOS	CLODDISH
CCEKNOSY	COCKNEYS	CCHKOPTU	PUTCHOCK	CDDEEENT	DECEDENT	CDDHIORS	DICHORDS
CCEKOPST	PETCOCKS	CCHKOSTU	COCKSHUT	CDDEEEPR	PRECEDED	CDDIIOIS	DIDICOIS
CCEKORRY	CROCKERY	CCHKSSTU	SCHTUCKS	CDDEEERS	SCREEDED	CDDIIOSY	DIDICOYS
CCEKORST	CROCKETS	CCHLNTUU	UNCLUTCH	CDDEEERW	DECREWED	CDDIISTY	DYTISCID
CCEKORSU	COCKSURE	CCHNRSUY	SCRUNCHY	CDDEEETT	DETECTED	CDDIKOPS	PIDDOCKS
CCELLOST	COLLECTS	CCIIKNPY	PICNICKY	CDDEEFOR	DEFORCED	CDDIORSS	DISCORDS
CCELMOPT	COMPLECT	CCIIMNSY	CYNICISM	CDDEEHIS	DEHISCED	CDDKOPSU	PUDDOCKS
CCELNOSY	CYCLONES	CCIINNSU	CICINNUS	CDDEEHNR	DRENCHED	CDDKORSU	RUDDOCKS
CCELOPSY	CYCLOPES	CCIINORZ	ZIRCONIC	CDDEEIIS	DEICIDES	CDDMMOUU	MOCUDDUM
CCELOSSY	CYCLOSES	CCIIRSTU	CIRCUITS	CDDEEIKR	DICKERED	CDEEEFFT	EFFECTED
CCELSSUY	CYCLUSES	CCIIRTUY	CIRCUITY	CDDEEILN	DECLINED	CDEEEFHL	FLEECHED
CCENNORS	CONCERNS	CCIKKLOP	LOCKPICK	CDDEEILP	PEDICLED	CDEEEFNS	DEFENCES
CCENNOST	CONCENTS		PICKLOCK	CDDEEIOV	DEVOICED	CDEEEFRT	REFECTED
	CONNECTS	CCIKLOSW	COWLICKS	CDDEEIPT	DEPICTED	CDEEEHHW	WHEECHED
CCENOORT	CONCERTO	CCIKNOPR	PRINCOCK	CDDEEIRS	DECIDERS	CDEEEHLR	LECHERED
CCENOOTT	CONCETTO	CCIKOPRS	CROPSICK		DESCRIED	CDEEEHMS	SMEECHED
CCENOPST	CONCEPTS	CCIKOPST	COCKPITS	CDDEEIRT	CREDITED	CDEEEHPS	DEPECHES
CCENORST	CONCERTS				DIRECTED		SPEECHED

CDEEEHRS	CREESHED		DECIPHER	CDEEINPR	PINCERED	CDEENNTU	UNDECENT
CDEEEHST	TEDESCHE	CDEEHIPS	CEPHEIDS	CDEEINPS	DISPENCE	CDEENNTY	TENDENCY
CDEEEHSW	ESCHEWED	CDEEHIRR	CHERRIED	CDEEINPT	DEPEINCT	CDEENOOS	COOSENED
CDEEEINP	PIECENED		DREICHER		INCEPTED	CDEENORR	CORNERED
CDEEEINV	EVIDENCE	CDEEHISS	DEHISCES		PEINCTED	CDEENORS	CENSORED
CDEEEIPS	EPICEDES	CDEEHIST	TEDESCHI		PENTICED		NECROSED
CDEEEIRV	DECEIVER	CDEEHITW	ITCHWEED	CDEEINTV	INVECTED		SECONDER
	RECEIVED	CDEEHKST	SKETCHED	CDEEIORV	DIVORCEE	CDEENORT	CENTRODE
CDEEEISV	DECEIVES	CDEEHKTV	KVETCHED	CDEEIOSS	DIOCESES	CDEENOSS	SECONDES
CDEEEJRT	REJECTED	CDEEHLMO	LEECHDOM	CDEEIOSV	DEVOICES	CDEENOVX	CONVEXED
CDEEEKNW	NECKWEED	CDEEHLQU	QUELCHED	CDEEIPRS	PRECISED	CDEENOVY	CONVEYED
CDEEELLX	EXCELLED	CDEEHLSU	SCHEDULE	CDEEIPRT	DECREPIT	CDEENPRU	PRUDENCE
CDEEELST	DESELECT	CDEEHMTU	HUMECTED		DEPICTER	CDEENRSU	CENSURED
	SELECTED	CDEEHNQU	QUENCHED	CDEEIPRU	PEDICURE	CDEENRUV	VERECUND
CDEEELUX	EXCLUDEE	CDEEHNRR	DRENCHER	CDEEIPST	PECTISED	CDEENSST	DESCENTS
CDEEEMNT	CEMENTED	CDEEHNRS	DRENCHES	CDEEIPTZ	PECTIZED	CDEENSSU	CENSUSED
CDEEEMPR	EMPERCED	CDEEHNRT	TRENCHED	CDEEIQSU	QUIESCED	CDEENSTY	ENCYSTED
CDEEENNT	TENDENCE	CDEEHNRW	WRENCHED	CDEEIRRS	DECRIERS	CDEEOOPR	COOPERED
CDEEENOS	SECONDEE	CDEEHNST	STENCHED	CDEEIRRT	DIRECTER	CDEEOOTV	DOVECOTE
CDEEENRS	RECENSED	CDEEHNUW	UNCHEWED		REDIRECT	CDEEOPPR	COPPERED
	SCREENED	CDEEHORS	COSHERED	CDEEIRSS	DESCRIES	CDEEOPRS	PROCEEDS
	SECERNED	CDEEHORT	HECTORED	CDEEIRST	DISCREET	CDEEOPRU	RECOUPED
CDEEENRT	CENTERED		TOCHERED		DISCRETE	CDEEORRR	RECORDER
	DECENTER	CDEEHPRU	CHERUPED	CDEEIRSU	DECURIES	CDEEORRS	RESCORED
CDEEEPRS	PRECEDES	CDEEHPRY	CYPHERED	CDEEIRSV	DESCRIVE	CDEEORRU	RECOURED
CDEEEPTX	EXCEPTED	CDEEHQTU	QUETCHED		SCRIEVED	CDEEORST	CORSETED
	EXPECTED	CDEEHRTW	WRETCHED		SERVICED		ESCORTED
CDEEERRS	SCREEDER	CDEEHSSU	DUCHESSE	CDEEIRTU	CUITERED		SECTORED
CDEEERSS	RECESSED	CDEEIILT	ELICITED	CDEEJKOY	JOCKEYED	CDEEORTT	DETECTOR
	SECEDERS	CDEEIIMN	MEDICINE	CDEEKLNO	ENLOCKED	CDEEORTV	CORVETED
CDEEERST	DECREETS	CDEEIIMP	EPIDEMIC	CDEEKLPS	SPECKLED		VECTORED
	RESECTED	CDEEIINT	INDICTEE	CDEEKMRU	MUCKERED	CDEEOSST	CESTODES
	SECRETED	CDEEIIST	EIDETICS	CDEEKNOR	RECKONED		COSSETED
CDEEERSV	SCREEVED	CDEEIISV	DECISIVE	CDEEKNRS	REDNECKS	CDEEOSTT	ESCOTTED
CDEEERTX	EXCRETED	CDEEIITT	DIETETIC	CDEEKNRU	UNRECKED	CDEEPRST	SCEPTRED
CDEEESTX	EXSECTED	CDEEIJNT	INJECTED	CDEEKOPT	POCKETED	CDEERRRU	RECURRED
CDEEETUX	EXECUTED	CDEEIJOR	REJOICED	CDEEKORT	ROCKETED	CDEERRSU	REDUCERS
CDEEFFOR	COFFERED	CDEEIKMY	MICKEYED	CDEEKORW	ROCKWEED	CDEERRUV	RECURVED
	EFFORCED	CDEEIKNR	NICKERED	CDEEKOST	SOCKETED	CDEERSSU	SEDUCERS
CDEEFHLN	FLENCHED	CDEEIKNS	SICKENED	CDEEKPRU	PUCKERED	CDEERSUV	DECURVES
CDEEFHLT	FLETCHED	CDEEIKNV	INVECKED	CDEEKRSU	SUCKERED	CDEERSUX	EXCURSED
CDEEFIIS	EDIFICES	CDEEIKPT	PICKETED	CDEEKRTU	TUCKERED	CDEERTTU	CURETTED
CDEEFIIT	FETICIDE	CDEEIKRW	WICKEDER	CDEELLPU	CUPELLED	CDEERTUV	CURVETED
CDEEFINT	INFECTED		WICKERED	CDEELMOW	WELCOMED	CDEFFINO	COFFINED
CDEEFKLR	FRECKLED	CDEEIKRY	YICKERED	CDEELNOS	ENCLOSED	CDEFFISU	SUFFICED
CDEEFKOR	FOREDECK	CDEEIKTT	TICKETED	CDEELNPU	PEDUNCLE	CDEFFLSU	SCUFFLED
CDEEFLST	DEFLECTS	CDEEILNP	PENDICLE	CDEELNTY	DECENTLY	CDEFHILN	FLINCHED
CDEEFNNU	UNFENCED	CDEEILNR	RECLINED	CDEELNUW	UNCLEWED	CDEFHIMO	CHIEFDOM
CDEEFNOR	ENFORCED	CDEEILNS	DECLINES	CDEELOPU	DECOUPLE	CDEFHIRT	FRICHTED
CDEEFORS	DEFORCES		LICENSED	CDEELORS	RECLOSED	CDEFIIIL	FILICIDE
	FRESCOED		SILENCED	CDEELORV	CLOVERED	CDEFIIIT	CITIFIED
CDEEFORT	DEFECTOR	CDEEILNT	DENTICLE	CDEELORY	RECOYLED	CDEFIIOR	CODIFIER
CDEEGIIR	REGICIDE	CDEEILNU	NUCLEIDE	CDEELOST	CLOSETED	CDEFIIOS	CODIFIES
CDEEGINO	GENOCIDE	CDEEILOR	RECOILED	CDEELOTU	ELOCUTED	CDEFIIST	DEFICITS
CDEEGINR	RECEDING	CDEEILPS	ECLIPSED	CDEELPRU	PRECLUDE	CDEFINNO	CONFINED
CDEEGINS	SECEDING		PEDICELS	CDEELPSU	DECUPLES	CDEFINNU	INFECUND
CDEEGIOS	GEODESIC		PEDICLES	CDEELRTU	LECTURED	CDEFINOR	CONFIDER
CDEEGIOT	GEODETIC	CDEEILRS	SCLEREID		RELUCTED		INFORCED
CDEEGNOR	CONGREED	CDEEILRT	DERELICT	CDEELSSU	SCEDULES	CDEFINOS	CONFIDES
CDEEHHSU	SHEUCHED	CDEEILRU	RECUILED		SECLUDES	CDEFINOX	CONFIXED
CDEEHHTT	THETCHED	CDEEIMNR	ENDERMIC	CDEELSUX	EXCLUDES	CDEFKORS	DEFROCKS
CDEEHILN	LICHENED	CDEEIMNS	ENDEMICS	CDEEMOPR	COMPERED	CDEFLNOU	FLOUNCED
CDEEHILP	CHELIPED	CDEEIMOR	MEDIOCRE	CDEEMOPT	COMPETED	CDEFLORY	FORCEDLY
CDEEHINR	ENRICHED	CDEEIMOS	COMEDIES	CDEEMORT	ECTODERM	CDEFNORU	FROUNCED
	INHERCED	CDEEIMPR	PREMEDIC	CDEEMSTU	TUMESCED		UNFORCED
	NICHERED	CDEEIMRS	MISCREED	CDEENNOS	CONDENSE	CDEFNSTU	DEFUNCTS
	RICHENED	CDEEIMRV	DECEMVIR	CDEENNOU	DENOUNCE	CDEFOSSU	FOCUSSED
CDEEHIOS	ECHOISED	CDEEINNS	INCENSED		ENOUNCED	CDEGHORU	GROUCHED
CDEEHIOZ	ECHOIZED	CDEEINNT	INDECENT	CDEENNOV	CONVENED		
CDEEHIPR	CIPHERED	CDEEINOS	CODEINES	CDEENNPY	PENDENCY		

CDEGHRTU	GRUTCHED	CDEIIKLS	SICKLIED	CDEILORU	CLOUDIER	CDEISSSU	DISCUSES
CBEGIINN	INCEDING	CDEIIKMM	MIMICKED	CDEILORV	COVERLID	CDEJNORU	CONJURED
CDEGIINX	EXCIDING	CDEIIKNR	CIDERKIN	CDEILOSS	DISCLOSE	CDEKKLNU	KNUCKLED
CDEGIKNO	DECKOING	CDEIIKNW	INWICKED	CDEILOST	DOCILEST	CDEKLMOR	CLERKDOM
	DECOKING	CDEIIKRS	DRICKSIE	CDEILPPR	CRIPPLED	CDEKLMOU	DUCKMOLE
CDEGIKNS	DECKINGS	CDEIIKRT	DICKTIER	CDEILPSU	CLUPEIDS	CDEKLNOU	UNLOCKED
CDEGILSU	CLUDGIES	CDEIIKST	DICKIEST	CDEILRTY	DIRECTLY	CDEKLNRU	CRUNKLED
CDEGINNO	ENCODING		STICKIED	CDEILSTU	DULCITES	CDEKLOPU	UPLOCKED
CDEGINNS	SCENDING	CDEIILMO	DOMICILE		LUCIDEST	CDEKLORY	YELDROCK
CDEGINOS	COGNISED	CDEIILNN	INCLINED	CDEILSXY	DYSLEXIC	CDEKLOSW	WEDLOCKS
CDEGINOY	DECOYING	CDEIILNO	INDOCILE	CDEILTTU	CUITTLED	CDEKLRTU	TRUCKLED
CDEGINOZ	COGNIZED	CDEIILOT	IDIOLECT	CDEIMMOX	COMMIXED	CDEKNOOU	UNCOOKED
CDEGINRU	REDUCING	CDEIILPS	DISCIPLE	CDEIMOOW	WOODMICE	CDEKNOOV	CONVOKED
CDEGINRY	DECRYING	CDEIILPU	PULICIDE	CDEIMORT	MORTICED	CDEKNORU	UNCORKED
CDEGINSU	SEDUCING	CDEIILRU	RIDICULE	CDEIMOST	DOMESTIC	CDEKNSUU	UNSUCKED
CDEGINSY	DYSGENIC	CDEIIMOS	DIOECISM	CDEIMPRS	SCRIMPED	CDEKNTUU	UNTUCKED
CDEGNORU	CONGRUED	CDEIIMRT	DIMETRIC	CDEINNOU	UNCOINED	CDELLNUU	UNCULLED
CDEGOORS	SCROOGED	CDEIINNT	INCIDENT	CDEINNOV	CONNIVED	CDELLOOP	CLODPOLE
CDEGORSU	SCOURGED	CDEIINOS	DECISION	CDEINOOS	COOSINED	CDELLORS	SCROLLED
	SCROUGED		ICONISED	CDEINOOZ	ENDOZOIC	CDELLORU	COLLUDER
CDEGORSW	SCROWDGE	CDEIINOV	INVOICED	CDEINORR	CORDINER	CDELLOSU	COLLUDES
CDEHIILO	HELICOID	CDEIINOZ	ICONIZED	CDEINORS	CONSIDER	CDELLOTU	CLOUDLET
CDEHIILS	CEILIDHS	CDEIINRT	INDIRECT	CDEINORT	CENTROID	CDELMNOO	MONOCLED
CDEHIIMO	HOMICIDE	CDEIIRUV	VIRUCIDE		DOCTRINE	CDELMNOU	COLUMNED
CDEHIINO	ECHINOID	CDEIISSU	SUICIDES	CDEINORU	DECURION	CDELMPRU	CRUMPLED
CDEHIIVV	CHIVVIED	CDEIISTT	DICTIEST	CDEINOST	DEONTICS	CDELNOOS	CONDOLES
CDEHIKOS	HOICKSED	CDEIJNOO	COJOINED	CDEINOSU	DOUCINES		CONSOLED
CDEHIKRW	HERDWICK	CDEIJSST	DISJECTS	CDEINOTU	EDUCTION	CDELNOSS	COLDNESS
CDEHILMR	MERCHILD	CDEIKLNO	INLOCKED	CDEINOUV	UNVOICED	CDELNOSU	ENCLOUDS
CDEHILNR	CHILDREN	CDEIKLNR	CRINKLED	CDEINOVV	CONVIVED		UNCLOSED
CDEHILOR	CHLORIDE	CDEIKLNU	UNLICKED	CDEINPRS	PRESCIND	CDELNOSY	CONDYLES
CDEHILOS	CHELOIDS	CDEIKLOS	SIDELOCK	CDEINPRU	UNPRICED		SECONDLY
CDEHILRT	ELDRITCH	CDEIKLPR	PRICKLED	CDEINPSY	DYSPNEIC	CDELNOTU	UNCOLTED
CDEHIMOT	METHODIC	CDEIKLRT	TRICKLED	CDEINRRU	INCURRED	CDELNOUW	UNCOWLED
CDEHIMRS	SMIRCHED	CDEIKLST	STICKLED	CDEINRSS	DISCERNS	CDELNRUU	UNCURLED
CDEHINNR	INDRENCH	CDEIKLWY	WICKEDLY		RESCINDS	CDELOORS	CROODLES
CDEHINOS	HEDONICS	CDEIKMSU	MUSICKED	CDEINRSU	INDUCERS		DECOLORS
CDEHINQU	QUINCHED	CDEIKNPU	UNPICKED	CDEINRUV	INCURVED	CDELOORU	COLOURED
CDEHINST	SNITCHED	CDEIKNTU	TUNICKED	CDEINSSX	EXSCINDS		DECOLOUR
CDEHIOOR	OCHIDORE	CDEIKOSS	DOCKISES	CDEINSTY	SYNDETIC	CDELOPSU	UPCLOSED
CDEHIOSW	COWHIDES	CDEIKOSY	YOICKSED	CDEIOORS	CORODIES	CDELOPTU	OCTUPLED
CDEHIOTY	THEODICY	CDEIKOSZ	DOCKIZES	CDEIOPRT	DEPICTOR	CDELORSS	CORDLESS
CDEHIQTU	QUITCHED	CDEIKRRS	DERRICKS	CDEIOPST	DESPOTIC		SCOLDERS
CDEHIRST	DITCHERS	CDEIKSTU	DUCKIEST	CDEIORRT	CREDITOR	CDELORSU	CLOSURED
CDEHISTT	STITCHED	CDEILLOS	CODILLES		DIRECTOR	CDELORSW	CLOWDERS
CDEHISTW	SWITCHED		COLLIDES	CDEIORRV	DIVORCER		SCROWLED
CDEHITTW	TWITCHED	CDEILLOU	LODICULE	CDEIORSS	DISCOERS	CDELORTU	CLOTURED
CDEHKLSU	SHELDUCK	CDEILLPU	PELLUCID	CDEIORST	CORDITES	CDELOSSU	DULCOSES
CDEHKSUY	HEYDUCKS	CDEILMMS	SCLIMMED	CDEIORSU	DISCOURE	CDELOSTU	LOCUSTED
CDEHLOOS	DESCHOOL	CDEILMOP	COMPILED	CDEIORSV	DISCOVER	CDELPRSU	SCRUPLED
	SCHOOLED		COMPLIED		DIVORCES	CDELPRUU	UPCURLED
CDEHLORT	CHORTLED	CDEILMOS	MELODICS	CDEIORSW	CROWDIES	CDELPSTU	SCULPTED
CDEHLOSU	SLOUCHED	CDEILMPR	CRIMPLED	CDEIORSY	DECISORY	CDELRSSU	SCUDLERS
CDEHMOOS	SMOOCHED	CDEILMRU	DULCIMER	CDEIORTU	OUTCRIED	CDELRSUY	CURSEDLY
CDEHMOSU	SMOUCHED	CDEILMSY	DYSMELIC	CDEIOSST	CESTOIDS	CDELRTUU	CULTURED
CDEHMSTU	SMUTCHED	CDEILNOS	INCLOSED	CDEIOSTT	COTTISED	CDELSSTU	DUCTLESS
CDEHNORS	CHONDRES	CDEILNOU	UNCOILED	CDEIPRSS	DISCERPS	CDELSTTU	SCUTTLED
CDEHNRSU	CHUNDERS	CDEILNRY	CYLINDER	CDEIPRST	PREDICTS	CDEMMNOO	COMMONED
CDEHOOOR	RHEOCORD	CDEILNSU	INCLUDES		SCRIPTED	CDEMMNOS	COMMENDS
CDEHORSU	CHORUSED		NUCLIDES	CDEIPRSY	CYPRIDES	CDEMMNOU	COMMUNED
CDEHORSW	CHOWDERS	CDEILOOW	WOODLICE	CDEIPRTU	PICTURED	CDEMMOOS	COMMODES
	COWHERDS	CDEILOPU	CLUPEOID	CDEIPSST	DISCEPTS	CDEMMOOV	COMMOVED
CDEHOSSU	HOCUSSED		UPCOILED	CDEIRRSU	SCURRIED	CDEMMOTU	COMMUTED
CDEHOSSW	COWSHEDS	CDEILORS	SCLEROID	CDEIRSSU	DISCURES	CDEMMRSU	SCRUMMED
CDEHSSSU	SCHUSSED			CDEIRSTU	CRUDITES	CDEMNNOS	CONDEMNS
CDEIIILS	SILICIDE				CURDIEST	CDEMNOOW	COMEDOWN
CDEIIIMT	MITICIDE				CURTSIED	CDEMNOPS	COMPENDS
CDEIIIOS	IDIOCIES			CDEIRSTV	VERDICTS	CDEMNOSU	CONSUMED
CDEIIIRV	VIRICIDE			CDEISSST	DISSECTS	CDEMNOTU	DOCUMENT
CDEIIITV	VITICIDE					CDEMNSUU	SECUNDUM

CDEMOOPS	COMPOSED	CDHIISST	DISTICHS	CDLOOOTW	COLTWOOD	CEEELLSU	ECUELLES
CDEMOPTU	COMPUTED	CDHILNSU	UNCHILDS	CDLOOPSY	LYCOPODS	CEEELRRV	CLEVERER
CDEMORSU	DECORUMS	CDHILOOS	DOLICHOS	CDLOORTY	DOCTORLY	CEEELRST	RESELECT
CDEMOSTU	COSTUMED	CDHIMOSU	DOCHMIUS	CDLOOSTU	OUTSCOLD	CEEELRTT	ELECTRET
	CUSTOMED	CDHINNOR	CHONDRIN	CDMNOOPU	COMPOUND		TERCELET
CDEMPRSU	SCRUMPED	CDHIOOPW	WOODCHIP	CDMNORUU	CORUNDUM	CEEELSST	CELESTES
CDENNOOS	CONDONES	CDHIOORS	CHOROIDS	CDMOSSUW	MUDSCOWS	CEEEMNRT	CEREMENT
CDENNOOT	CONNOTED	CDHIOORT	TROCHOID	CDNNOOOT	CONODONT	CEEEMPRS	EMPERCES
CDENNOST	CONTENDS	CDHIOPRW	WHIPCORD	CDNNOSTU	CONTUNDS	CEEEMRTY	CEMETERY
CDENNOUY	UNCOYNED	CDHIOPRY	HYDROPIC	CDOOOPST	OCTOPODS	CEEENNPT	TENPENCE
CDENOORT	CREODONT	CDHIOPSY	PSYCHOID	CDOORRUY	CORDUROY	CEEENNST	SENTENCE
CDENOOST	SECODONT	CDHIORRT	TRICHORD	CDOOSTUW	WOODCUTS	CEEENNPRS	PRESENCE
CDENOOTT	COTTONED	CDHIOSUV	DISVOUCH	CDOPRSTU	PRODUCTS	CEEENPRT	PRETENCE
CDENOOVY	CONVOYED	CDHIPSTY	DIPTYCHS	CEEEEHLS	LEECHEES	CEEENQSU	SEQUENCE
CDENORSS	CORSNEDS	CDHKOORS	HORDOCKS	CEEEEPRS	PRECEESE	CEEENRRS	SCREENER
CDENORSW	DECROWNS	CDHLOOPY	COPYHOLD	CEEEFFIR	EFFIERCE	CEEENRRT	RECENTER
CDENORTU	CORNUTED	CDHNORSU	CHONDRUS	CEEEFFRT	EFFECTER		RECENTRE
	TROUNCED	CDHOORRU	UROCHORD	CEEEFHLS	FLEECHES	CEEENRSS	RECENSES
CDENOSTU	CONTUSED	CDIIIMNU	INDICIUM	CEEEFILR	FLEECIER	CEEENNSS	ESSENCES
CDENRSUU	UNCURSED	CDIIIORT	DIORITIC	CEEEFINR	ENFIERCE	CEEENSST	CENTESES
CDENRTUU	UNDERCUT	CDIILMOS	DOMICILS	CEEEFLRS	FLEECERS	CEEEPRRS	CREEPERS
CDEOOPPS	COPEPODS	CDIILOTY	DOCILITY	CEEEFNOR	CONFEREE	CEEEPRTX	EXPECTER
CDEOOPRS	SCROOPED	CDIILTUY	LUCIDITY	CEEEGIMN	EMCEEING	CEEERRST	ERECTERS
CDEOOPST	POSTCODE	CDIIMNOU	CONIDIUM	CEEEGINS	EGENCIES	CEEERRSV	SCREEVER
CDEOORRS	CORRODES		ONICDIUM	CEEEGINX	EXIGENCE	CEEERSST	RECESSES
CDEOORSU	DECOROUS	CDIINOOS	ISODICON	CEEEGITX	EXEGETIC	CEEERSST	SECRETES
CDEOORSV	VOCODERS		ONISCOID	CEEEGMNR	MERGENCE		SESTERCE
CDEOOSTV	DOVECOTS	CDIINORS	CRINOIDS	CEEEGNRS	REGENCES	CEEERSSV	SCREEVES
CDEOPRRU	PROCURED	CDIINOST	DICTIONS	CEEEHIKR	CHEEKIER	CEEERSTX	EXCRETES
	PRODUCER	CDIINSTT	DISTINCT	CEEEHIRR	CHEERIER	CEEERTUX	EXECUTER
CDEOPRSU	PRODUCES	CDIIOORS	SORICOID		REECHIER	CEEESSSX	EXCESSES
CDEOQSTU	DOCQUETS	CDIIOPRT	DIOPTRIC	CEEEHIRS	CHEESIER	CEEESTUX	EXECUTES
CDEORRSW	CROWDERS	CDIIORSU	SCIUROID	CEEEHLRV	CHEVEREL	CEEFFNOS	OFFENCES
CDEORSST	DOCTRESS	CDIIOSSS	CISSOIDS	CEEEHLSS	SLEECHES	CEEFFORS	EFFORCES
CDEORSSU	SCOURSED	CDIIPTUY	CUPIDITY	CEEEHMSS	SMEECHES	CEEFFORT	EFFECTOR
CDEORSSW	SCOWDERS		PUDICITY	CEEEHNNP	PENNEECH	CEEFGILN	FLEECING
CDEORSTU	EDUCTORS	CDIIRSTT	DISTRICT	CEEEHNRS	ENCHEERS	CEEFHIKR	KERCHIEF
	SEDUCTOR	CDIJNSTU	DISJUNCT	CEEEHPRS	CHEEPERS	CEEFHIRY	CHIEFERY
CDEORSUU	DOUCEURS	CDIKKNOW	KICKDOWN	CEEEHPSS	SPEECHES	CEEFHISS	CHIEFESS
CDEOSSTU	CUSTODES	CDIKNORS	DORNICKS	CEEEHRRS	CHEERERS	CEEFHIST	CHIEFEST
CDEPRSTY	DECRYPTS	CDIKNOSW	WINDOCKS	CEEEHRSS	CREESHES		FETICHES
CDEPRUUV	UPCURVED	CDILLOOS	COLLOIDS		SECESHER	CEEFHLNS	FLENCHES
CDERSTTU	DESTRUCT	CDILLOTU	DULCITOL	CEEEHRVY	CHEVERYE	CEEFHLRT	FLETCHER
CDFIILSU	FLUIDICS	CDILLOUY	CLOUDILY	CEEEHSSS	SECESHES	CEEFHLRU	CHEERFUL
CDFIKORS	DISFROCK	CDILOOPS	PODSOLIC	CEEEIJTV	EJECTIVE	CEEFHLST	FLETCHES
CDFNNOOU	CONFOUND	CDILOORT	LORDOTIC	CEEEIKRR	CREEKIER	CEEFHRST	FECHTERS
CDGHIILN	CHILDING	CDILOOTY	COTYLOID	CEEEILNN	LENIENCE	CEEFIINT	INFICETE
CDGHIINS	CHIDINGS	CDILOSST	DISCLOST	CEEEILNS	LICENSEE	CEEFILRY	FIERCELY
CDGHIINT	DICHTING	CDIMMOSU	MODICUMS	CEEEILNT	TELECINE	CEEFINPP	FIPPENCE
	DITCHING	CDIMOORT	MICRODOT	CEEEILRS	CELERIES	CEEFINRT	FRENETIC
CDGHINNU	DUNCHING	CDINNQUU	QUIDNUNC	CEEEILRT	ERECTILE	CEEFIPRT	PERFECTI
CDGHINOU	DOUCHING	CDINOOOR	CORONOID	CEEEILTV	CLEVEITE	CEEFIRST	FIERCEST
CDGIINNU	INDUCING	CDINORSW	DISCROWN		ELECTIVE	CEEFKLRS	FLECKERS
CDGIKLNU	DUCKLING	CDINORTU	INDUCTOR	CEEEIMNN	EMINENCE		FRECKLES
CDGIKLOR	GRIDLOCK	CDINOSTU	CONDUITS	CEEEIMPR	EMPIERCE	CEEFKLSS	FECKLESS
CDGIKNOS	DOCKINGS		DISCOUNT	CEEEIMRR	REREMICE	CEEFLNOR	FLORENCE
CDGIKNSU	DUCKINGS		NOCTUIDS	CEEEINNT	ENCEINTE	CEEFLNSU	FLUENCES
CDGILNOS	CODLINGS	CDIOOPRS	PROSODIC	CEEEINPR	PIECENER	CEEFLNTU	FECULENT
	SCOLDING	CDIOORRR	CORRIDOR	CEEEINPS	EPICENES	CEEFLRST	REFLECTS
CDGILNOU	CLOUDING	CDIOOSTT	COTTOIDS	CEEEINRS	CERESINE	CEEFNORR	CONFRERE
CDGILNRU	CURDLING	CDIOPRSU	CUSPIDOR	CEEEINSS	ESNECIES		RENFORCE
CDGINORS	CORDINGS	CDIOSSTY	CYSTOIDS	CEEEIPPR	CREEPIER	CEEFNORS	ENFORCES
CDGINORW	CROWDING	CDIOSTUV	OVIDUCTS	CEEEIPRS	CREEPIES	CEEFNRVY	FERVENCY
CDHHIILS	CHILDISH	CDJLNOUY	JOCUNDLY	CEEEIPRV	PERCEIVE	CEEFOPRR	PERFORCE
CDHIILTW	TWICHILD	CDKMMORU	DRUMMOCK	CEEEIRRV	RECEIVER	CEEFOPRT	PERFECTO
CDHIINST	CHINDITS	CDKNNOSU	DUNNOCKS	CEEEIRSV	RECEIVES	CEEFORRS	FRESCOER
CDHIIOOR	CHORIOID	CDKOOORW	CORKWOOD	CEEEIRSX	EXERCISE	CEEFORSS	FRESCOES
CDHIIORT	HIDROTIC	CDLLLOOP	CLODPOLL	CEEEIRTV	ERECTIVE	CEEFORTW	CROWFEET
	TRICHOID	CDLNOSUU	UNCLOUDS	CEEEJRRT	REJECTER	CEEFPRST	PERFECTS
CDHIIOSZ	SCHIZOID	CDLNOUUY	UNCLOUDY	CEEEKNNP	PENNEECK		PREFECTS

CEEGHIKN CHEEKING	CEEHIOSZ ECHOIZES	CEEIINVV EVINCIVE	CEEINORX EXOCRINE
CEEGHILN LEECHING	CEEHIPRT HERPETIC	CEEIIPRS EPICIERS	CEEINOSS SENECIOS
CEEGHINP CHEEPING	CEEHIQRU CHEQUIER	CEEIIRST SERICITE	CEEINOST SEICENTO
CEEGHINR CHEERING	CEEHIRRR CHERRIER	CEEIJNOT EJECTION	CEEINOTV EVECTION
REECHING	CEEHIRRS CHERRIES	CEEIJORR REJOICER	CEEINPRT PRENTICE
CEEGHINS CHEESING	CEEHIRRT CHERTIER	CEEIJORS REJOICES	CEEINPST PECTINES
CEEGIJNT EJECTING	CEEHIRRS RICHESSE	CEEIJRUV VERJUICE	PENTICES
CEEGIKLN CLEEKING	CEEHIRST CHESTIER	CEEIKSS KECKSIES	CEEINPSX SIXPENCE
CEEGILNP CLEEPING	HERETICS	CEEIKLNN NECKLINE	CEEINRRS SINCERER
CEEGILNT ELECTING	CEEHIRTT TETCHIER	CEEIKLPR PICKEREL	CEEINRSS CERESINS
CEEGILOT ECLOGITE	CEEHIRTU HEURETIC	CEEIKNRS SICKENER	SCRIENES
CEEGILRS CLERGIES	CEEHIRTV VETCHIER	CEEIKNST NECKTIES	CEEINRST CENTRIES
CEEGILRT TELERGIC	CEEHISTT ESTHETIC	CEEIKPRS PICKEERS	ENTERICS
CEEGIMNS MISCEGEN	TECHIEST	SPECKIER	ENTICERS
CEEGINOO COOEEING	CEEHISTW CHEWIEST	CEEIKPRT PICKETER	SCIENTER
CEEGINOR EROGENIC	CEEHKLRS HECKLERS	CEEILLLP PELLICLE	SECRETIN
CEEGINPR CREEPING	CEEHKNPS HENPECKS	CEEILLMS MICELLES	CEEINRSU INSECURE
CEEGINRS CREESING	CEEHKRST SKETCHER	CEEILLNT LENTICEL	SINECURE
GENERICS	CEEHKRTV KVETCHER	LENTICLE	CEEINRTT RETICENT
CEEGINRT ERECTING	CEEHKSST SKETCHES	CEEILMOR COMELIER	CEEINRTU CEINTURE
GENTRICE	CEEHKSTV KVETCHES	CEEILMPS SEMPLICE	ENURETIC
CEEGINST GENETICS	CEEHLNOS ECHELONS	CEEILNNT CENTINEL	CEEINSST CENTESIS
CEEGINSU EUGENICS	CEEHLNOT ENCLOTHE	CEEILNNY LENIENCY	CEEIOPPR PERICOPE
CEEGINXY EXIGENCY	CEEHLNPU PENUCHLE	CEEILNOS CINEOLES	CEEIOPPS EPISCOPE
CEEGIORX EXOERGIC	CEEHLNSU ELENCHUS	CEEILNOT COTELINE	CEEIOPST ECTOPIES
CEEGLLOR COLLEGER	CEEHLORT RECLOTHE	ELECTION	PICOTEES
CEEGLLOS COLLEGES	CEEHLOSS ECHOLESS	CEEILNOV VIOLENCE	CEEIORST COTERIES
CEEGLNST NEGLECTS	CEEHLOSW COWHEELS	CEEILNRR RECLINER	ESOTERIC
CEEGLOSU ECLOGUES	CEEHLQSU QUELCHES	CEEILNRS LICENSER	CEEIORSX EXORCISE
CEEGMMOR COMMERGE	CEEHLRSW WELCHERS	RECLINES	CEEIORTT EROTETIC
CEEGMNOO ONCOGENE	CEEHLSSS CHESSELS	SILENCER	CEEIORTX EXOTERIC
CEEGNNOR CONGENER	CEEHMNSS CHESSMEN	CEEILNRU CERULEIN	CEEIORXZ EXORCIZE
CEEGNNPU PUNGENCE	MENSCHES	CEEILNRV VERNICLE	CEEIOSTV COVETISE
CEEGNORS COGENERS	CEEHMORT COMETHER	CEEILNSS ENCLISES	CEEIPPRT PRECEPIT
CONGREES	CEEHMRSS SCHEMERS	LICENSES	CEEIPPTU EUPEPTIC
CEEGNORT CONGREET	CEEHMRST MERCHETS	SILENCES	CEEIPRRS PIERCERS
CEEGNORV CONVERGE	CEEHNNOW NOWHENCE	CEEILNSU LEUCINES	PRECISER
CEEGNOTY ECTOGENY	CEEHNNRT ENTRENCH	CEEILORR RECOILER	CEEIPRSS PRECISES
CEEGNRSU URGENCES	CEEHNORT COHERENT	CEEILOSS SOLECISE	CEEIPRST CREPIEST
CEEGNRVY VERGENCY	CEEHNORV CHEVERON	CEEILOSZ SOLECIZE	RECEIPTS
CEEGORST CORTEGES	CEEHNPSU PENUCHES	CEEILPSS ECLIPSES	CEEIPRSU EPICURES
CEEGQRSU GRECQUES	CEEHNQRU QUENCHER	CEEILQSU LIQUESCE	CEEIPSST PECTISES
CEEHHMNN HENCHMEN	CEEHNQSU QUENCHES	CEEILRST RETICLES	CEEIPSTZ PECTIZES
CEEHHSTT THETCHES	CEEHNRRT RETRENCH	SCLERITE	CEEIQSSU QUIESCES
CEEHIIST ETHICISE	TRENCHER	TIERCELS	CEEIRRSS CERRISES
CEEHIITZ ETHICIZE	CEEHNRST TRENCHES	CEEILRSU CISELEUR	CRESSIER
CEEHIKLY CHEEKILY	CEEHNRSW WENCHERS	CISELURE	CEEIRRST RECITERS
CEEHIKNW CHEEWINK	WRENCHES	RECUILES	CEEIRRSW SCREWIER
CEEHILLN CHENILLE	CEEHNSST STENCHES	CEEILRSV VERSICLE	CEEIRRTU URETERIC
CEEHILLV CHEVILLE	CEEHOPRY CORYPHEE	CEEILRTU RETICULE	CEEIRSSV SCRIEVES
CEEHILRT TELECHIR	CEEHOPTT POCHETTE	CEEILRTY CELERITY	SERVICES
CEEHILRV CHEVERIL	CEEHORRS COHERERS	CEEILSSV CLEVISES	CEEIRSTU CERUSITE
CEEHILRW CLERIHEW	COSHERER	VESICLES	CUTESIER
CEEHILRY CHEERILY	CEEHORRT HECTORER	CEEILSTT TELESTIC	EUCRITES
CEEHILSV VEHICLES	TORCHERE	TESTICLE	CEEIRSTV VERTICES
CEEHILSW SWELCHIE	CEEHORSS ORCHESES	CEEILSTU LEUCITES	CEEIRSTX EXCITERS
CEEHIMMS CHEMMIES	CEEHORST TROCHEES	CEEIMMRS MESMERIC	CEEIRSVX CERVIXES
CEEHIMRS CHIMERES	CEEHOSUV VOUCHEES	CEEIMNNY EMINENCY	CEEISSST CITESSES
CEEHIMRT HERMETIC	CEEHPRRS PERCHERS	CEEIMNPS SPECIMEN	CEEISTTZ ZETETICS
CEEHIMSS CHEMISES	CEEHPRSU UPCHEERS	CEEIMNST CENTIMES	CEEISUVX EXCUSIVE
CEEHINPR ENCIPHER	CEEHPSST SPETCHES	CEEIMORT METEORIC	CEEJKOTT JOCKETTE
CEEHINPT PHENETIC	CEEHQRSU CHEQUERS	CEEINNOT NEOTENIC	CEEJORRT REJECTOR
CEEHINRS ENRICHES	CEEHQSTU QUETCHES	CEEINNRS INCENSER	CEEJORST EJECTORS
INHERCES	CEEHRSTW WRETCHES	CEEINNRT INCENTRE	CEEKKNPS KENSPECK
CEEHINST SITHENCE	CEEHRTTU TEUCHTER	CEEINNSS INCENSES	CEEKLNST NECKLETS
CEEHINSX CHENIXES	CEEHSTTU TEUCHEST	NICENESS	CEEKLPSS SPECKLES
CEEHINTT ENTHETIC	CEEIIMPR EPIMERIC	CEEINNST NESCIENT	CEEKLRSS CLERKESS
CEEHIORS CHEERIOS	CEEIIMRT EREMITIC	CEEINORT ERECTION	RECKLESS
CEEHIOSS ECHOISES	CEEIINRT ICTERINE	NEOTERIC	CEEKNORR RECKONER
CEEHIOSV COHESIVE	CEEIINST NICETIES	CEEINORV OVERNICE	CEEKNRSU SUCKENER

CEEKORRT	ROCKETER	CEENNORV	CONVENER		SUFFICER	CEFNOSTU	CONFUTES
CEEKOSSY	SOCKEYES	CEENNOSU	ENOUNCES	CEFFISSU	SUFFICES	CEFORRST	CROFTERS
CEEKPRSY	RYEPECKS	CEENNOSV	CONVENES	CEFFLORU	FORCEFUL	CEFORSTU	FRUCTOSE
CEEKRRSW	WRECKERS	CEENNRST	CENTNERS	CEFFLRSU	SCUFFLER	CEFOSSSU	FOCUSSES
CEELLLSU	CELLULES	CEENOPST	POTENCES	CEFFLSSU	SCUFFLES	CEGGHIRS	CHIGGERS
CEELLMOU	MOLECULE	CEENOPTW	TWOPENCE	CEFFORSS	SCOFFERS	CEGGILOO	GEOLOGIC
CEELLNOS	COLLEENS	CEENORSS	NECROSES	CEFFORST	COFFRETS	CEGGILOR	CLOGGIER
CEELLNOU	NUCLEOLE	CEENORSV	CONSERVE	CEFGHINT	FECHTING		COGGLIER
CEELLORT	RECOLLET		CONVERSE		FETCHING	CEGGILRS	SCRIGGLE
CEELLPSU	PUCELLES	CEENORSZ	COZENERS	CEFGIKLN	FLECKING	CEGGINNO	CONGEING
CEELLRRU	CRUELLER	CEENORTT	TRECENTO	CEFGINNS	FENCINGS	CEGGINOO	GEOGONIC
CEELLRVY	CLEVERLY	CEENORVY	CONVEYER	CEFGLNUY	FULGENCY	CEGGIORS	GEORGICS
CEELLSSU	CLUELESS		RECONVEY	CEFHIIMS	MISCHIEF		SCROGGIE
CEELMOOS	COELOMES	CEENOSVX	CONVEXES	CEFHILNR	FLINCHER	CEGGLNOY	GLYCOGEN
CEELMOPT	COMPLETE	CEENPPTU	TUPPENCE	CEFHILNS	FLINCHES	CEGGLORS	CLOGGERS
CEELMORW	WELCOMER	CEENPRSS	SPENCERS	CEFHILRS	FILCHERS	CEGHHINT	HECHTING
CEELMOST	TELECOMS	CEENPSSU	SUSPENCE	CEFHILRT	FLICHTER	CEGHIINY	HYGIENIC
CEELMOSW	WELCOMES	CEENRSSU	CENSURES	CEFHILST	FLITCHES	CEGHIKLN	HECKLING
CEELMRTU	ELECTRUM	CEENRSTU	UNSECRET	CEFHINSU	FUCHSINE	CEGHIKNT	KETCHING
CEELNNOP	PENONCEL	CEENSSSU	CENSUSES	CEFHISTT	FITCHETS	CEGHILNT	LETCHING
CEELNNOT	CENTONEL	CEENSTTU	CUNETTES	CEFHISTU	FUCHSITE	CEGHILNW	WELCHING
CEELNOPU	OPULENCE	CEEOORRW	ORECROWE	CEFHISTW	FITCHEWS	CEGHILST	GLITCHES
CEELNORS	ENCLOSER	CEEOORST	CREOSOTE	CEFHLSSY	FLYSCHES	CEGHIMNS	SCHEMING
CEELNORT	ELECTRON	CEEOPRRT	RECEPTOR	CEFHLSTU	CHESTFUL	CEGHINNW	WENCHING
CEELNORU	ENCOLURE	CEEOPRTX	EXCEPTOR		FUTCHELS	CEGHINOR	COHERING
CEELNOSS	ENCLOSES	CEEOPSST	PECTOSES	CEFIIIST	CITIFIES		OCHERING
CEELNPTU	CENTUPLE	CEEOPSTY	ECOTYPES	CEFIILRT	CLIFTIER	CEGHINPR	PERCHING
CEELNRST	LECTERNS	CEEOQTTU	COQUETTE	CEFIILST	FELSITIC	CEGHINRT	RETCHING
CEELNRSU	LUCERNES	CEEORRRS	SORCERER	CEFIILTY	FELICITY	CEGHINRU	EUCHRING
CEELNRTU	RELUCENT	CEEORRSS	RESCORES	CEFIIOPR	OPIFICER	CEGHINST	ETCHINGS
CEELNRTY	RECENTLY	CEEORRST	ERECTORS	CEFIIORS	ORIFICES	CEGHINVY	CHEVYING
CEELNSTU	ESCULENT	CEEORRSU	RECOURES	CEFIIPRT	PETRIFIC	CEGHIRSS	SCREIGHS
CEELORSS	CORELESS		RECOURSE	CEFIIRRT	FERRITIC	CEGHIRTU	THEURGIC
	RECLOSES		RESOURCE		TERRIFIC	CEGHISTU	GUICHETS
	SCLEROSE	CEEORRSV	RECOVERS	CEFIKLOR	FIRELOCK	CEGHMRUY	CHEMURGY
CEELORST	CORSELET	CEEORRSW	RECOWERS	CEFIKLRS	FLICKERS	CEGHNORS	GROSCHEN
	ELECTORS	CEEORRVY	RECOVERY	CEFIKLST	FICKLEST	CEGHORSU	CHOREGUS
	ELECTROS	CEEORSTX	CORTEXES	CEFILLLO	FOLLICLE		COUGHERS
	SELECTOR	CEEORTTV	CORVETTE	CEFILMRU	CRIMEFUL		GROUCHES
CEELORSY	RECOYLES	CEEORTUX	EXECUTOR		MERCIFUL		GRUTCHES
CEELORTV	COVERLET	CEEOSTTT	OCTETTES	CEFILNOT	FLECTION		GUTCHERS
CEELOSSU	COLEUSES	CEEPPRST	PERCEPTS	CEFILNST	INFLECTS	CEGIILNR	CLINGIER
CEELOSTU	ELOCUTES		PRECEPTS	CEFILNSU	FUNICLES	CEGIILNS	CEILINGS
CEELOSTV	COVELETS	CEEPPRSU	PREPUCES	CEFILOUV	VOICEFUL		CIELINGS
CEELPRST	PLECTRES	CEEPRRSU	PRECURSE	CEFILRSU	LUCIFERS	CEGIILNT	GENTILIC
	PRELECTS	CEEPRSST	RESPECTS	CEFIMOST	COMFIEST	CEGIILOP	EPILOGIC
CEELRRTU	LECTURER		SCEPTRES	CEFINNOR	CONFINER	CEGIILOS	LOGICISE
CEELRSST	LECTRESS		SPECTERS	CEFINNOS	CONFINES	CEGIILOZ	LOGICIZE
CEELRSSU	CURELESS		SPECTRES	CEFINORS	CONIFERS	CEGIINNT	ENTICING
	RECLUSES	CEEPRSTX	EXCERPTS		FORENSIC	CEGIINNV	EVINCING
CEELRSTU	LECTURES	CEERRSST	RECTRESS		FORINSEC	CEGIINPR	PIERCING
CEELRSTY	SECRETLY	CEERRSSU	RESCUERS		INFORCES	CEGIINRT	RECITING
CEELRSUY	SECURELY		SECURERS	CEFINORT	INFECTOR	CEGIINSS	GNEISSIC
CEELSTTU	LETTUCES	CEERRSTW	SCREWERS	CEFINOSX	CONFIXES	CEGIINSX	EXCISING
CEEMMNTU	CEMENTUM	CEERRSUV	RECURVES	CEFINOTT	CONFETTI	CEGIINTV	EVICTING
CEEMMORS	COMMERES	CEERRTUZ	CREUTZER	CEFIOPRS	FORCIPES	CEGIINTX	EXCITING
CEEMNORR	CREMORNE	CEERSSST	CRESSETS	CEFIORTY	FEROCITY	CEGIIOST	EGOISTIC
CEEMNORW	NEWCOMER	CEERSSTU	SECUREST	CEFIRRSU	SCURFIER	CEGIJLOU	LOGJUICE
CEEMNORY	CEREMONY	CEERSSUX	EXCURSES	CEFIRSTU	FRUTICES	CEGIKKLN	KECKLING
CEEMNOYZ	COENZYME		EXCUSERS	CEFKLLOS	ELFLOCKS	CEGIKLNR	CLERKING
CEEMNRSU	CERUMENS	CEERSTTU	CURETTES	CEFKLOOR	FORELOCK		RECKLING
CEEMOORV	OVERCOME	CEERTUXY	EXECUTRY	CEFKLOST	FETLOCKS	CEGIKNNS	NECKINGS
CEEMOORW	OWRECOME	CEESSSTU	CESTUSES	CEFKLRUW	WRECKFUL		SNECKING
CEEMOPRS	COMPEERS	CEESTTUV	CUVETTES	CEFLLOSU	FLOSCULE	CEGIKNPS	PECKINGS
	COMPERES	CEFFHIRU	CHUFFIER	CEFLNOSU	FLOUNCES		SPECKING
CEEMOPST	COMPETES	CEFFIILR	CLIFFIER	CEFLNRUU	FURUNCLE	CEGIKNRT	TRECKING
CEEMOSSS	COSMESES	CEFFIORS	OFFICERS	CEFLNSTU	SCENTFUL	CEGIKNRW	WRECKING
CEEMSSTU	TUMESCES	CEFFIORU	COIFFEUR	CEFMORSY	COMFREYS	CEGIKSTU	GUCKIEST
CEENNORT	CRETONNE		COIFFURE	CEFNORSU	FROUNCES	CEGILMMN	CLEMMING
CEENNORU	RENOUNCE	CEFFIRSU	SCUFFIER	CEFNOSSU	CONFUSES	CEGILNOO	NEOLOGIC

CEGILNOS	ECLOSING
CEGILNRS	CLINGERS
	CRINGLES
CEGILNRU	RECULING
	ULCERING
CEGILNRY	GLYCERIN
CEGILNSU	LUCIGENS
CEGILNSY	GLYCINES
CEGILNTU	CULTIGEN
CEGIMNOY	MYOGENIC
CEGIMNSU	MUCIGENS
CEGIMNUY	GYNECIUM
CEGINNOR	ENCORING
CEGINNOZ	COZENING
CEGINNRS	SCERNING
CEGINNRT	CENTRING
CEGINNST	SCENTING
CEGINNSY	ENSIGNCY
CEGINOOP	GEOPONIC
CEGINOOR	OROGENIC
CEGINOOY	COOEYING
CEGINOOZ	ZOOGENIC
CEGINOPR	COPERING
CEGINOPY	PYOGENIC
CEGINORT	GERONTIC
CEGINORV	COVERING
CEGINORW	COWERING
CEGINOSS	COGNISES
CEGINOSZ	COGNIZES
CEGINOTV	COVETING
CEGINRRS	CRINGERS
CEGINRRU	RECURING
CEGINRST	CRESTING
CEGINRSU	RECUSING
	RESCUING
	SCUNGIER
	SECURING
CEGINRSW	SCREWING
CEGINRSY	SYNERGIC
CEGINRTU	ERUCTING
CEGINSUX	EXCUSING
CEGIRSTU	SCUTIGER
CEGKLORS	GROCKLES
CEGLLOOU	COLLOGUE
CEGLLORY	GLYCEROL
CEGLLRYY	GLYCERYL
CEGLNOTY	COGENTLY
CEGLOOOY	OECOLOGY
CEGLOOTY	CETOLOGY
CEGLOSSU	GLUCOSES
CEGLOSSY	GLYCOSES
CEGMNNOO	COGNOMEN
CEGNNOOS	ONCOGENS
CEGNNPUY	PUNGENCY
CEGNOOTY	GONOCYTE
CEGNORSS	CONGRESS
CEGNORSU	CONGRUES
	SCROUNGE
CEGNORSY	CRYOGENS
CEGNORYY	CRYOGENY
CEGNOSST	CONGESTS
CEGOORSS	SCROOGES
CEGORRSU	SCOURGER
	SCROUGER
CEGORSSU	SCOURGES
	SCROUGES
CEHHIIRT	HITCHIER
CEHHINPY	HYPHENIC
CEHHIRST	HITCHERS
CEHHNORU	HURCHEON

CEHHOOST	HOOTCHES
CEHHOPTY	HYPOTHEC
CEHIIKNR	CHINKIER
CEHIIKNS	CHINKIES
CEHIILLR	CHILLIER
CEHIILLS	CHILLIES
CEHIILMO	HEMIOLIC
CEHIILNN	LICHENIN
CEHIILNT	LECITHIN
CEHIILOT	EOLITHIC
CEHIIMOP	HEMIOPIC
CEHIIMOS	ISOCHEIM
	ISOCHIME
CEHIIMPT	MEPHITIC
CEHIIMST	ETHICISM
CEHIINST	ICHNITES
CEHIIPPR	CHIPPIER
CEHIIPPS	CHIPPIES
CEHIIPRR	CHIRPIER
CEHIIPRT	PITCHIER
CEHIIRST	CHRISTIE
CEHIIRTT	CHITTIER
	TRICHITE
CEHIISTT	CHITTIES
	ETHICIST
	ITCHIEST
	THEISTIC
	TICHIEST
CEHIISVV	CHIVVIES
CEHIKLPT	KLEPHTIC
CEHIKLRS	CLERKISH
CEHIKLSU	SUCHLIKE
CEHIKMOS	HOMESICK
CEHIKNRU	CHUNKIER
CEHIKNST	KITCHENS
	KNITCHES
	THICKENS
CEHIKNSW	CHEWINKS
CEHIKOOS	CHOOKIES
CEHIKOSS	HOICKSES
CEHIKOST	CHOKIEST
	THICKOES
CEHIKRSS	KIRSCHES
	SHICKERS
	SKRIECHS
CEHIKRSW	WHICKERS
CEHIKSST	CHEKISTS
	KITSCHES
CEHIKSTT	THICKEST
	THICKETS
	THICKSET
CEHIKTTY	THICKETY
CEHILLRS	CHILLERS
	SCHILLER
CEHILLST	CHILLEST
CEHILMMS	SCHIMMEL
CEHILMSY	CHIMLEYS
CEHILMTY	METHYLIC
CEHILNOP	PHENOLIC
	PINOCHLE
CEHILNOR	CHLORINE
CEHILNOS	CHOLINES
CEHILNPY	PHENYLIC
CEHILNSS	CHINLESS
CEHILNST	LINCHETS
	TINCHELS
CEHILORT	CHLORITE
	CLOTHIER
CEHILORY	HEROICLY
CEHILPRS	PILCHERS

CEHILPTY	PHYLETIC
CEHILRSV	CHERVILS
CEHILSTT	LICHTEST
CEHILSTW	SWITCHEL
CEHILTTY	TETCHILY
CEHIMMRU	CHUMMIER
CEHIMMSS	CHEMISMS
CEHIMMSU	CHUMMIES
CEHIMNNW	WINCHMEN
CEHIMNOP	PHONEMIC
CEHIMNOR	CHOIRMEN
CEHIMNPT	PITCHMEN
CEHIMNSY	CHIMNEYS
CEHIMORS	MORICHES
CEHIMORT	CHROMITE
	TRICHOME
CEHIMOSS	ECHOISMS
CEHIMRSS	SMIRCHES
CEHIMSST	CHEMISTS
CEHINNRT	INTRENCH
CEHINOOS	COHESION
CEHINOPS	CHOPINES
CEHINOPT	PHONETIC
CEHINOPU	EUPHONIC
CEHINORS	CHORINES
CEHINORT	NOTCHIER
CEHINORU	UNHEROIC
CEHINOSY	HYOSCINE
CEHINOTY	ONYCHITE
CEHINPRS	PINCHERS
CEHINPRU	PUNCHIER
	UNCIPHER
CEHINPSU	PENUCHIS
CEHINQSU	QUINCHES
CEHINRSS	RICHNESS
CEHINRST	CHRISTEN
	CITHERNS
	SNITCHER
CEHINRTU	RUTHENIC
CEHINSST	SNITCHES
CEHINSTW	WITCHENS
CEHINSTZ	CHINTZES
CEHIOORS	CHOOSIER
	ISOCHORE
CEHIOPPR	CHOPPIER
CEHIOPRS	SOPHERIC
CEHIOPRU	EUPHORIC
	POUCHIER
CEHIOPSS	HOSPICES
CEHIOPST	POSTICHE
	POTICHES
CEHIORRT	RHETORIC
CEHIORSS	CHORISES
	ORCHESIS
	ORCHISES
CEHIORST	ROTCHIES
	THEORICS
CEHIORSW	CHOWRIES
CEHIORTT	TROCHITE
CEHIORTU	COUTHIER
	TOUCHIER
CEHIOSST	ECHOISTS
	TOISECHS
CEHIPRRS	CHIRPERS
CEHIPRSS	SPHERICS
CEHIPRST	PITCHERS
	SPITCHER
CEHIQSTU	QUITCHES
CEHIRSST	STRICHES
CEHIRSTT	CHITTERS

	RICHTEST
	STITCHER
CEHIRSTY	HYSTERIC
CEHIRTTW	TWITCHER
CEHIRTWY	WITCHERY
CEHISSTT	STITCHES
CEHISSTU	CUSHIEST
CEHISSTW	SWITCHES
CEHISTTW	TWITCHES
CEHKKRSU	CHUKKERS
CEHKLLOS	SKELLOCH
CEHKLMOS	HEMLOCKS
CEHKORSS	SHOCKERS
CEHKPSTU	KETCHUPS
CEHKRSSU	SHUCKERS
CEHKRSTU	HUCKSTER
CEHLLMOS	MOCHELLS
CEHLLMSU	MUCHELLS
	SCHELLUM
CEHLLOSY	YELLOCHS
CEHLLOUY	LOUCHELY
CEHLMNOU	HOMUNCLE
CEHLMSUY	CHUMLEYS
CEHLNNOU	LUNCHEON
CEHLNNSU	CHUNNELS
CEHLNOST	NOTCHELS
CEHLNOTU	UNCLOTHE
CEHLNRSU	LUNCHERS
CEHLNSTY	LYNCHETS
CEHLOOSS	SCHOOLES
CEHLORST	CHORTLES
CEHLORSU	SLOUCHER
CEHLORTY	HECTORLY
CEHLOSSU	SLOUCHES
CEHLOSTU	SELCOUTH
CEHLPPSS	SCHLEPPS
CEHLPPSY	SCHLEPPY
CEHLQSUY	SQUELCHY
CEHLRRSU	LURCHERS
CEHLSTUY	LECYTHUS
CEHMNRSU	MUNCHERS
CEHMNRTU	TRUCHMEN
CEHMNSSU	MUCHNESS
CEHMOORS	MOOCHERS
CEHMOOSS	SMOOCHES
CEHMOOSZ	SCHMOOZE
CEHMORSU	MOUCHERS
CEHMORUV	OVERMUCH
CEHMOSSU	SMOUCHES
CEHMSSTU	SMUTCHES
CEHNNNOU	NUNCHEON
CEHNNOPU	PUNCHEON
CEHNNOSU	NONESUCH
	UNCHOSEN
CEHNNRSU	CHUNNERS
CEHNOORS	COEHORNS
	SCHOONER
CEHNORSV	CHEVRONS
CEHNORTU	CHOUNTER
CEHNORVY	CHEVRONY
CEHNPRSU	PUNCHERS
CEHNRSTU	CHUNTERS
CEHNSSSU	SUCHNESS
CEHNSSTU	CHESNUTS
CEHNSTTU	CHESTNUT
CEHNSTUY	CHUTNEYS
CEHOOORZ	ZOOCHORE
CEHOORSS	CHOOSERS
	SOROCHES

CEHOORST	CHEROOTS	CEIILSSS	SCISSILE
CEHOORSU	OCHEROUS	CEIIMNOT	EMICTION
	OCHREOUS	CEIIMOPT	EPITOMIC
CEHOOSUW	COWHOUSE	CEIIMORS	ISOMERIC
CEHOPPRS	CHOPPERS	CEIIMOST	COMITIES
CEHOPPRY	PROPHECY		SEMIOTIC
CEHOPRST	POTCHERS	CEIIMPRR	CRIMPIER
CEHOPRSY	CORYPHES	CEIIMPRS	EMPIRICS
CEHORRST	TORCHERS	CEIIMPSS	EPICISMS
CEHORSSU	CHORUSES	CEIIMRRT	TRIMERIC
CEHORSSZ	SCHERZOS	CEIIMRST	MERISTIC
CEHORSTU	SCOUTHER		TRISEMIC
	TOUCHERS	CEIINNOP	NEPIONIC
CEHORSTW	SCOWTHER	CEIINNOR	IRENICON
CEHORSUV	VOUCHERS	CEIINNOS	CONIINES
CEHOSSSU	HOCUSSES		OSCININE
CEHOSTTU	COUTHEST	CEIINNOT	NICOTINE
CEHOTTUZ	ZUCHETTO	CEIINNRT	INTRINCE
CEHPRSTU	PUTCHERS	CEIINNST	INSCIENT
CEHPSSTU	PUTSCHES	CEIINOPS	EPINOSIC
CEHRRSSU	CRUSHERS	CEIINOPT	EPITONIC
CEHRSSTY	SCYTHERS	CEIINORS	RECISION
CEHRSTTY	STRETCHY		SORICINE
CEHSSSSU	SCHUSSES	CEIINOSS	ICONISES
CEIIILSV	CIVILISE	CEIINOSV	INVOICES
CEIIILVZ	CIVILIZE	CEIINOSX	EXCISION
CEIIIMNT	CIMINITE	CEIINOSZ	ICONIZES
CEIIINSS	SINICISE	CEIINOTV	EVICTION
CEIIINSV	INCISIVE	CEIINPSS	PISCINES
CEIIINSZ	SINICIZE	CEIINRSS	SERICINS
CEIIJSTU	JUICIEST	CEIINRST	CITRINES
CEIIKLMR	LIMERICK		CRINITES
CEIIKLRS	SICKLIER		INCITERS
CEIIKLRT	TICKLIER	CEIINRSU	INCISURE
CEIIKLSS	SICKLIES		SCIURINE
CEIIKMMR	MIMICKER	CEIINRTU	NEURITIC
CEIIKNRZ	ZINCKIER	CEIINSSU	CUISINES
CEIIKNSS	KINESICS	CEIINSTU	CUTINISE
CEIIKNST	KINETICS	CEIINSTY	CYTISINE
CEIIKPST	PICKIEST		SYENITIC
CEIIKQSU	QUICKIES	CEIINSTZ	CITIZENS
CEIIKRRT	TRICKIER		ZINCIEST
CEIIKRST	STICKIER		ZINCITES
CEIIKSST	EKISTICS	CEIINTUZ	CUTINIZE
	STICKIES	CEIIOPRS	IRISCOPE
CEIILLMT	MELLITIC	CEIIOPRT	PERIOTIC
CEIILLOP	POLLICIE	CEIIOPTT	PICOTITE
CEIILLPT	ELLIPTIC	CEIIOSTV	SOVIETIC
CEIILLSS	SILICLES	CEIIPRRS	CRISPIER
CEIILLSU	SILICULE	CEIIPRST	PICRITES
CEIILMNT	LIMNETIC		PRICIEST
CEIILMOT	CIMOLITE	CEIIPSST	EPICISTS
CEIILNNS	INCLINES		SPICIEST
CEIILNOS	ISOCLINE	CEIIQRTU	CRITIQUE
	SILICONE	CEIIRSSU	CRUISIES
CEIILNQU	CLINIQUE	CEIIRSTT	RECTITIS
CEIILNSS	ENCLISIS	CEIIRSTV	VERISTIC
CEIILOPP	EPIPLOIC	CEIISSST	CISSIEST
	EPIPOLIC	CEIISTVV	VIVISECT
CEIILOPS	POLICIES	CEIJNORT	INJECTOR
CEIILORT	ELICITOR	CEIJNOUV	CUNJEVOI
CEIILOTZ	ZEOLITIC	CEIJRSTU	JUSTICER
CEIILPPS	CLIPPIES	CEIJSSTU	JUSTICES
CEIILPRT	PERLITIC	CEIKKNRS	KNICKERS
CEIILPRU	PIRLICUE	CEIKKRRS	SKERRICK
CEIILPTX	EXPLICIT	CEIKLNPS	SPICKNEL
CEIILPTY	PYELITIC	CEIKLNRS	CLINKERS
CEIILQRU	CLIQUIER		CRINKLES
CEIILRSU	SLUICIER	CEIKLNSS	SLICKENS
CEIILRTV	VERTICIL	CEIKLOSV	LOVESICK
CEIKLPRS	PICKLERS	CEILNNOT	CONTLINE
	PRICKLES	CEILNNSU	NUCLEINS
CEIKLPRU	PLUCKIER	CEILNNSY	SYNCLINE
CEIKLRSS	SLICKERS	CEILNOOS	COLONIES
CEIKLRST	STICKLER		COLONISE
	STRICKLE		ECLOSION
	TICKLERS	CEILNOOZ	COLONIZE
	TRICKLES	CEILNOPR	PERCOLIN
CEIKLRSY	SICKERLY	CEILNOPS	PINOCLES
CEIKLRTT	TRICKLET	CEILNOPT	LEPTONIC
CEIKLSST	SLICKEST	CEILNORS	INCLOSER
	STICKLES		LICENSOR
CEIKLSTU	LUCKIEST	CEILNOSS	CONSEILS
CEIKMNOR	MONICKER		INCLOSES
CEIKMOPT	IMPOCKET	CEILNOST	LECTIONS
CEIKMORS	OCKERISM	CEILNOSX	LEXICONS
CEIKMRSS	SMICKERS	CEILNPRY	PRINCELY
CEIKMRSU	MUSICKER	CEILNRTU	LINCTURE
CEIKMSST	SMICKETS	CEILNRUV	CULVERIN
CEIKMSTU	MUCKIEST	CEILNSST	STENCILS
CEIKNNSU	INSUCKEN	CEILNSTU	CUTLINES
CEIKNQSU	QUICKENS		TUNICLES
CEIKNRSS	SNICKERS	CEILNSUU	UNSLUICE
CEIKNRST	STRICKEN	CEILOPRT	PETROLIC
CEIKNRSU	UNSICKER	CEILOPRV	PROCLIVE
CEIKNSSS	SICKNESS	CEILOPST	TOECLIPS
CEIKNSST	SNICKETS	CEILOPTU	EPULOTIC
CEIKOPST	POCKIEST		POULTICE
CEIKORRS	ROCKIERS	CEILOPTY	EPICOTYL
CEIKORST	CORKIEST	CEILORST	CLOISTER
	ROCKIEST		COISTREL
	STOCKIER		CORTILES
CEIKOSSY	YOICKSES		COSTLIER
CEIKPRRS	PRICKERS		CREOLIST
CEIKPRST	PRICKETS	CEILORTT	CLOTTIER
CEIKPSST	SKEPTICS	CEILORTY	CRYOLITE
	SPICKEST	CEILOSSS	OSSICLES
CEIKQSTU	QUICKEST	CEILOSST	SOLECIST
	QUICKSET		SOLSTICE
CEIKRRST	TRICKERS	CEILOSSU	COULISSE
CEIKRRTY	TRICKERY	CEILOTVY	VELOCITY
CEIKRSST	STICKERS	CEILPPRS	CLIPPERS
CEIKRTTY	RICKETTY		CRIPPLES
CEIKSTUY	YUCKIEST	CEILPRSU	SURPLICE
CEILLNOS	LIONCELS	CEILPRUU	PURLICUE
CEILLNOU	NUCLEOLI	CEILPSSU	SPICULES
CEILLOPS	POLLICES	CEILRRSU	SCURRILE
CEILLOQU	COQUILLE	CEILRSTT	CLITTERS
CEILLORS	COLLIERS	CEILRSTU	CURLIEST
	ORSELLIC		UTRICLES
CEILLORY	COLLIERY	CEILSSSS	SCISSELS
CEILLOTU	COUTILLE	CEILSTTU	CUITTLES
CEILLRTU	TELLURIC	CEIMMNNO	MNEMONIC
CEILLSST	CELLISTS	CEIMMNOU	ENCOMIUM
CEILLSSU	CULLISES		MECONIUM
CEILMMUY	MYCELIUM	CEIMMORT	RECOMMIT
CEILMNOP	COMPLINE	CEIMMOSX	COMMIXES
CEILMNOT	MONTICLE	CEIMMRRS	CRIMMERS
CEILMOPR	COMPILER	CEIMMRRU	CRUMMIER
	COMPLIER	CEIMMRSU	CRUMMIES
CEILMOPS	COMPILES		SCUMMIER
	COMPLIES	CEIMMRSY	MERYCISM
	POLEMICS	CEIMNNOO	ENCOMION
CEILMOSS	SOLECISM	CEIMNNOS	MECONINS
CEILMOSU	COLISEUM	CEIMNNOY	NEOMYCIN
CEILMPRS	CRIMPLES	CEIMNOPT	PENTOMIC
CEILMPRU	CLUMPIER	CEIMNORS	CREMOSIN
CEILMPUU	PECULIUM		INCOMERS
CEILMRSU	CLUMSIER		SERMONIC
CEILMTUU	LUTECIUM	CEIMNORT	INTERCOM

CEIMNRST	CENTRISM	CEIOOPRS	OPORICES
CEIMNSSU	MENISCUS	CEIOOTUV	OUTVOICE
CEIMOOST	COOMIEST	CEIOOTXX	EXOTOXIC
CEIMOOUZ	ZOOECIUM	CEIOPPRS	CROPPIES
CEIMOPRS	COMPRISE	CEIOPPSY	EPISCOPY
CEIMOQSU	COMIQUES	CEIOPRRU	CROUPIER
CEIMORRS	MORRICES	CEIOPRSS	PERSICOS
CEIMORRT	MORTICER	CEIOPRST	PERSICOT
CEIMORST	MORTICES	CEIOPRSU	PRECIOUS
CEIMORSX	EXORCISM	CEIOPRTU	EUTROPIC
CEIMORSY	ISOCRYME		OUTPRICE
CEIMORTY	EMICTORY	CEIOPSST	COPSIEST
CEIMOSSS	COSMESIS	CEIOPSSU	SPECIOUS
CEIMOSTV	VICOMTES	CEIORRSS	CROSIERS
CEIMPRRS	CRIMPERS	CEIORRSU	COURIERS
CEIMPRRU	CRUMPIER	CEIORRSZ	CROZIERS
CEIMRRSU	SCRIMURE	CEIORRTU	COURTIER
CEIMRRTU	TURMERIC	CEIORRUZ	CRUZEIRO
CEIMRSST	CRETISMS	CEIORRSSU	SCOURIES
CEIMSSTY	SYSTEMIC	CEIORSSV	CORSIVES
CEINNNOT	INNOCENT	CEIORSSW	SCOWRIES
CEINNNOU	INCONNUE	CEIORSSX	SIXSCORE
CEINNORS	INCENSOR	CEIORSTT	COTTIERS
CEINNORV	CONNIVER	CEIORSTU	CITREOUS
CEINNOSV	CONNIVES		OUTCRIES
CEINNOTU	CONTINUE	CEIORSTV	EVICTORS
CEINOOST	COONTIES		VORTICES
CEINOOTZ	ENTOZOIC	CEIORSTX	EXCITORS
	ENZOOTIC		EXORCIST
CEINOPPR	CORNPIPE	CEIORSVY	VICEROYS
CEINOPRS	CONSPIRE	CEIORTTU	TOREUTIC
	INCORPSE	CEIOSSSV	VISCOSES
CEINOPRT	INCEPTOR	CEIOSSTT	COTTISES
CEINOPTU	UNPOETIC	CEIOSSTU	COITUSES
CEINOPRV	PROVINCE	CEIPQSTU	PICQUETS
CEINOPTT	ENTOPTIC	CEIPRRSS	CRISPERS
CEINORRS	RESORCIN	CEIPRRST	RESCRIPT
CEINORRT	TRICORNE	CEIPRSST	CRISPEST
CEINORSS	NECROSIS	CEIPRSTU	CREPITUS
	SERICONS		CUPRITES
CEINORST	CORNIEST		PICTURES
	RECTIONS		PIECRUST
CEINORSU	NOURICES	CEIPSSST	CESSPITS
	ROUNCIES	CEIRRRSU	CURRIERS
CEINORTT	CONTRITE		SCURRIER
	CORNETTI	CEIRRSSU	CRUISERS
CEINORTU	NEUROTIC		SCURRIES
CEINORTV	CONTRIVE		SUCRIERS
CEINOSSS	CESSIONS	CEIRRSTT	CRITTERS
	COSINESS		RESTRICT
CEINOSST	SECTIONS		STRICTER
CEINOSSX	COXINESS	CEIRRSTU	CRUSTIER
CEINOSTT	CENTOIST		RECRUITS
	STENOTIC	CEIRRSUV	SCURVIER
CEINOSTU	COUNTIES	CEIRSSSU	CUISSERS
CEINOSTX	EXCITONS		SCISSURE
CEINOSTY	CYTOSINE	CEIRSSTT	TRISECTS
CEINOSUV	UNVOICES	CEIRSSTU	CITRUSES
CEINOSVV	CONVIVES		CURTSIES
CEINPRSS	PRINCESS		RICTUSES
CEINPSST	INSPECTS	CEIRSSTV	VICTRESS
CEINPSTY	PYCNITES	CEIRSSUV	SCURVIES
CEINRSST	CISTERNS	CEIRSTTU	TUTRICES
CEINRSTT	CENTRIST	CEIRSTUV	CURVIEST
	CITTERNS	CEIRSTUY	SECURITY
CEINRSTU	CURNIEST	CEISSSTU	CISTUSES
CEINRSUV	INCURVES	CEISTTTU	CUTTIEST
CEINRSVV	CRIVVENS	CEJLOOSY	JOCOSELY
CEINRTTU	INTERCUT	CEJNORRU	CONJURER
	TINCTURE	CEJNORSU	CONJURES

CEJNRTUU	JUNCTURE	CELNOSSU	CLONUSES
CEJNSSUU	JUNCUSES		COUNSELS
CEJOPRST	PROJECTS		UNCLOSES
CEKKLNSU	KNUCKLES	CELNOSTU	NOCTULES
CEKKNORS	KNOCKERS	CELNOSUV	CONVULSE
CEKLLOOV	LOVELOCK	CELNOSVY	SOLVENCY
CEKLLOPS	PELLOCKS	CELNOVXY	CONVEXLY
CEKLLSSU	LUCKLESS	CELNPTUU	PUNCTULE
CEKLMNOS	LOCKSMEN	CELNRSTU	LECTURNS
CEKLNOSS	SLOCKENS	CELOOPSS	CESSPOOL
CEKLNOST	STENLOCK	CELOORRU	COLOURER
CEKLNRSU	CRUNKLES	CELOORVY	OVERCLOY
CEKLOPST	LOCKSTEP	CELOPRSU	COUPLERS
CEKLPRSU	PLUCKERS	CELOPSSU	OPUSCLES
CEKLRRTU	TRUCKLER		UPCLOSES
CEKLRSSU	SUCKLERS	CELOPSTU	COUPLETS
CEKLRSTU	TRUCKLES		OCTUPLES
CEKMNOST	STOCKMEN	CELOPSUU	OPUSCULE
CEKMNRTU	TRUCKMEN	CELOPTTU	OCTUPLET
CEKNNSSU	UNSNECKS	CELORSST	CORSLETS
CEKNOOSV	CONVOKES		COSTRELS
CEKNOPST	PENSTOCK		CROSSLET
CEKNORST	CRONKEST	CELORSSU	CLOSURES
CEKNORTU	COKERNUT		SCLEROUS
CEKNOSTU	UNSOCKET	CELORSSW	SCROWLES
CEKNRSTU	STRUCKEN	CELORSSY	SCROYLES
CEKNRSWY	WRYNECKS	CELORSTT	CLOTTERS
CEKOOPRS	PRECOOKS		CROTTLES
CEKOOPSW	COWPOKES	CELORSTU	CLOTURES
CEKOORST	CROOKEST		CLOUTERS
CEKOPRST	SPROCKET		COULTERS
CEKORRTY	ROCKETRY	CELORSTY	COYSTREL
CEKORRST	RESTOCKS	CELORSUU	ULCEROUS
CEKRRSTU	TRUCKERS		URCEOLUS
CEKRSSUU	RUCKUSES	CELORSUY	CROUSELY
CELLMOSU	COLUMELS	CELORTTU	COURTLET
CELLNOOS	COLONELS	CELORTVY	COVERTLY
CELLNSUU	NUCELLUS	CELOSTTU	CULOTTES
CELLNTUU	LUCULENT	CELPRRSU	SCRUPLER
CELLOOQU	COLLOQUE	CELPRSSU	SCRUPLES
CELLORSS	ESCROLLS	CELPRSUY	SPRUCELY
CELLOSSY	CLOYLESS	CELRSSTU	CLUSTERS
CELLRRSU	CRULLERS		CUSTRELS
CELLRSSU	SCULLERS	CELRSSTY	CLYSTERS
CELLRSUY	SCULLERY	CELRSTTU	CLUTTERS
CELMNOOS	MONOCLES		SCUTTLER
CELMNOTY	CLOYMENT	CELRSTUU	CULTURES
CELMNOUY	UNCOMELY	CELRSTUV	CULVERTS
CELMNTUU	MUCULENT	CELRSTUY	CLUSTERY
CELMOOOT	LOCOMOTE	CELSSTTU	SCUTTLES
CELMOOSY	CLOYSOME	CELSSTUU	CULTUSES
CELMOPSU	COMPULSE	CEMMNOOR	COMMONER
CELMOPSY	SYMPLOCE	CEMMNOOS	CONSOMME
CELMOSUU	CUMULOSE	CEMMNOOY	COMMONEY
CELMPRSU	CRUMPLES	CEMMNOST	COMMENTS
CELMPRTU	PLECTRUM	CEMMNOSU	COMMUNES
CELMPSUU	SPECULUM	CEMMOOST	COMMOTES
CELMSSUU	SECULUMS	CEMMOOSV	COMMOVES
CELNNOSU	NUCLEONS	CEMMORTU	COMMUTER
CELNNOTY	NOCENTLY	CEMMOSTU	COMMUTES
CELNNOUV	UNCLOVEN	CEMMRSSU	SCUMMERS
CELNOORS	CONSOLER	CEMMNOST	CONTEMNS
CELNOORU	ENCOLOUR	CEMMNOOR	CROMORNE
CELNOOSS	CONSOLES	CEMMNOOTY	MONOCYTE
	COOLNESS	CEMMNOPTT	CONTEMPT
CELNOOVV	CONVOLVE	CEMMNRSU	CONSUMER
CELNOPRT	PLECTRON		MUCRONES
CELNOPUU	UNCOUPLE	CEMMNOSSU	CONSUMES
CELNORTW	CROWNLET		MUSCONES
CELNORWY	CLOWNERY	CEMNRSTU	CENTRUMS

CEMOOPRS	COMPOSER	CEOPPRRS	CROPPERS	CFIINORT	FRICTION	CGHIKNOS	SHOCKING
CEMOOPSS	COMPOSES	CEOPPRST	PROSPECT	CFIINOST	FICTIONS	CGHIKNSU	SHUCKING
CEMOOPST	COMPOTES	CEOPRRRU	PROCURER	CFIKLSTU	STICKFUL	CGHILMNU	MULCHING
CEMOORSY	SYCOMORE	CEOPRRSS	SCORPERS	CFIKNNOS	FINNOCKS	CGHILNNU	LUNCHING
CEMOOSSS	COSMOSES	CEOPRRST	PORRECTS	CFIKOSSS	FOSSICKS	CGHILNNY	LYNCHING
CEMOOSTU	OUTCOMES	CEOPRRSU	CROUPERS	CFIKPSTU	PUCKFIST	CGHILNOT	CLOTHING
CEMOPRSS	COMPRESS		PROCURES	CFILMOOR	COLIFORM	CGHILNRU	LURCHING
CEMOPRST	COMPTERS	CEOPRSTT	PROTECTS	CFIMNOOR	CONIFORM	CGHIMMNU	CHUMMING
CEMOPRTU	COMPUTER	CEOPRSTW	SCREWTOP	CFIMNORS	CONFIRMS	CGHIMNNU	MUNCHING
CEMOPSTU	COMPUTES	CEOPRSUU	COUPURES	CFIMNORU	UNCIFORM	CGHIMNOO	MOOCHING
CEMORSSU	CORMUSES		CUPREOUS	CFINNOTU	FUNCTION	CGHIMNOP	CHOMPING
CEMORSTU	COSTUMER	CEOQRSTU	CROQUETS	CFKKLOOR	FOLKROCK	CGHIMNOR	CHROMING
	CUSTOMER		ROCQUETS	CFKLLOSU	LOCKFULS	CGHIMNOU	MOUCHING
CEMOSSTU	COSTUMES	CEOQRTUY	COQUETRY	CFLLOPRU	CROPFULL	CGHIMPSY	SPHYGMIC
CEMPRSTU	CRUMPEST	CEORRSSS	SCORSERS	CFLMRSUU	FULCRUMS	CGHINNOS	CHIGNONS
	CRUMPETS	CEORRSSU	CURSORES	CFLNOORT	CORNLOFT	CGHINNOT	NOTCHING
	SPECTRUM		SCOURERS	CFLNORSU	SCORNFUL	CGHINNPU	PUNCHING
CENNOORV	CONVENOR	CEORRSSW	SCOWRERS	CFLOOPSU	SCOOPFUL	CGHINNRU	CHURNING
CENNOOST	CONNOTES	CEORRSTY	CORSETRY	CFLOPRSU	CROPFULS	CGHINNSY	SYNCHING
CENNORTU	NOCTURNE	CEORSSST	CROSSEST	CFMNOORS	CONFORMS	CGHINOOS	CHOOSING
CENNOSST	CONSENTS	CEORSSSU	SUCROSES	CFMOORST	COMFORTS	CGHINOPP	CHOPPING
CENNOSTT	CONTENTS	CEORSSTU	SCOUTERS	CFNNOORT	CONFRONT	CGHINOPT	POTCHING
CENNOSTV	CONVENTS	CEORSSUV	CORVUSES	CFOOORTW	CROWFOOT	CGHINOPU	POUCHING
CENNRSSU	SCUNNERS	CEORSTUU	COUTURES	CFRSTUUU	USUFRUCT	CGHINORT	TORCHING
CENOOOTZ	ECTOZOON	CEORSTUV	COUVERTS	CGGGHINU	CHUGGING	CGHINOSU	CHOUSING
CENOOORS	CORONERS	CEORSTUY	COURTESY	CGGGILNO	CLOGGING		HOCUSING
	CROONERS	CEOSSSTU	COSTUSES		COGGLING	CGHINOTU	TOUCHING
CENOORST	CORONETS	CEPPRRSU	CRUPPERS	CGGGINOS	SCOGGING	CGHINOUV	VOUCHING
CENOORSU	CORNEOUS	CEPPRSSU	SCUPPERS	CGGGINSU	SCUGGING	CGHINPSY	PSYCHING
CENOORTT	CORNETTO	CEPPRTUU	UPPERCUT	CGGHILNU	GULCHING	CGHINPTU	PINCHGUT
CENOORVY	CONVEYOR	CEPRSSTU	SPRUCEST	CGGHINOU	COUGHING	CGHINRRU	CHURRING
CENOPRSY	NECROPSY	CEPRSTUU	CUTPURSE	CGGIILNN	CLINGING	CGHINRSU	CRUSHING
CENOPSSY	SYNCOPES	CEPSSSTU	SUSPECTS	CGGIINNO	COIGNING		RUCHINGS
CENOPSTU	POUNCETS	CERSSSUU	CURSUSES	CGGIINNR	CRINGING	CGHINSTY	SCYTHING
CENOQRSU	CONQUERS		RUSCUSES	CGGIINRS	GRICINGS	CGHNOOSU	SOUCHONG
CENOQSTU	CONQUEST	CERSSTTU	SCUTTERS	CGGILRSY	SCRIGGLY	CGHOORST	TORGOCHS
CENORRSS	SCORNERS	CERSSTUY	CURTSEYS	CGGINNSU	SCUNGING	CGIIILNT	LIGNITIC
CENORRSW	CROWNERS	CERSSUUX	EXCURSUS	CGGINOOS	SCOOGING	CGIIINNS	INCISING
CENORRTU	TROUNCER	CFFGILNU	CUFFLING	CGGINOSU	SCOUGING	CGIIINNT	INCITING
CENORSST	CONSTERS	CFFGINOS	SCOFFING	CGHHIILN	HILCHING	CGIIKLNN	CLINKING
CENORSTT	CORNETTS	CFFGINSU	SCUFFING	CGHHIINT	HITCHING	CGIIKLNP	PICKLING
CENORSTU	CONSTRUE	CFFHINOS	CHIFFONS	CGHHINNU	HUNCHING	CGIIKLNS	LICKINGS
	CORNUTES	CFFIRTUY	FRUCTIFY	CGHHINOT	HOTCHING		SLICKING
	COUNTERS	CFFMOSSU	OFFSCUMS	CGHHINTU	HUTCHING	CGIIKLNT	TICKLING
	RECOUNTS	CFGHIILN	FILCHING	CGHIIKNN	CHINKING	CGIIKMMS	GIMMICKS
	TROUNCES	CFGIIKLN	FICKLING	CGHIIKNO	HOICKING	CGIIKMMY	GIMMICKY
CENORSTV	CONVERTS		FLICKING	CGHIIKNR	CHIRKING	CGIIKNNS	SNICKING
CENORSTW	CROWNETS	CFGIKLNO	FLOCKING	CGHIIKNT	THICKING	CGIIKNNZ	ZINCKING
CENORSUU	CERNUOUS	CFGIKNOR	FROCKING	CGHIILLN	CHILLING	CGIIKNOY	YOICKING
CENORSUV	UNCOVERS	CFGIKNSU	FUCKINGS	CGHIILNR	CHIRLING	CGIIKNPR	PRICKING
CENORSUY	CYNOSURE	CFGINORT	CROFTING	CGHIILNT	LICHTING	CGIIKNPS	PICKINGS
CENOSSTT	CONTESTS	CFGINOSU	FOCUSING	CGHIIMNR	CHIRMING	CGIIKNRS	SCRIKING
CENOSSTU	CONTUSES	CFHIINOO	FINOCHIO	CGHIIMNS	MICHINGS	CGIIKNRT	TRICKING
	COUNTESS	CFHIIORR	HORRIFIC	CGHIIMNT	MITCHING	CGIIKNRW	WRICKING
CENOSTTX	CONTEXTS	CFHIMOSS	SCOMFISH	CGHIINNP	PINCHING	CGIIKNST	STICKING
CENPRSTY	ENCRYPTS	CFHIMSSU	SCUMFISH	CGHIINNW	WINCHING		TICKINGS
CENPRTUU	PUNCTURE	CFHLOPUU	POUCHFUL	CGHIINOR	CHOIRING	CGIILLOS	ILLOGICS
CENPSTUX	EXPUNCTS	CFHORSTU	FUTHORCS	CGHIINPP	CHIPPING	CGIILNOP	POLICING
CENRRSTU	CURRENTS	CFIIILSY	SILICIFY	CGHIINPR	CHIRPING	CGIILNPP	CLIPPING
CENRSSTU	CURTNESS	CFIIKNYZ	ZINCKIFY	CGHIINPT	PITCHING	CGIILNPS	SPLICING
	ENCRUSTS	CFIILNST	INFLICTS	CGHIINQU	QUICHING	CGIILNSS	SLICINGS
CENRSSUU	UNCURSES	CFIILNUU	FUNICULI	CGHIINRR	CHIRRING	CGIILNSU	SLUICING
CENRSSUW	UNSCREWS	CFIILOPR	PROLIFIC	CGHIINRT	CHIRTING	CGIILOST	LOGISTIC
CEOOOPST	OTOSCOPE	CFIILPSU	PULSIFIC		RICHTING	CGIILRTU	LITURGIC
CEOOPRRV	OVERCROP	CFIIMNOS	SOMNIFIC	CGHIINTT	CHITTING	CGIIMNNO	INCOMING
CEOOPRSS	SCOOPERS	CFIIMORT	MORTIFIC	CGHIINTW	WITCHING	CGIIMNNS	MINCINGS
CEOOPSWX	COWPOXES	CFIINOPT	PONTIFIC	CGHIINVV	CHIVVING	CGIIMNPR	CRIMPING
CEOORRVW	OVERCROW			CGHIINVY	CHIVYING	CGIIMNPU	PUMICING
CEOORSST	SCOOTERS					CGIIMNSU	MISCUING
CEOOSTUV	COVETOUS					CGIINNOS	COININGS

CGIINNOT	NOTICING		UNCOPING	CHIKNNOP	PHINNOCK	CHNORSTU	COTHURNS
CGIINNPR	PRINCING	CGINNORS	SCORNING	CHIKNOOS	CHINOOKS	CHOOORYZ	ZOOCHORY
CGIINNSU	INCUSING	CGINNORW	CROWNING	CHIKOPTY	KYPHOTIC	CHORSTTU	SHORTCUT
CGIINNSW	WINCINGS	CGINNOSS	CONSIGNS	CHIKORST	TROCHISK	CIIIKNTU	CUITIKIN
CGIINNTT	TINCTING	CGINNOTU	COUNTING	CHIKOSST	STOCKISH	CIIILMPT	IMPLICIT
CGIINOOS	ISOGONIC	CGINOOPS	SCOOPING	CHIKPSSY	PHYSICKY	CIIILMSU	SILICIUM
CGIINOPT	PICOTING	CGINOOST	SCOOTING	CHILLMSU	CHILLUMS	CIIILPST	SPILITIC
CGIINORT	TRIGONIC	CGINOOTV	COGNOVIT	CHILLOOT	OILCLOTH	CIIILSTV	CIVILIST
CGIINOST	COTISING	CGINOPPR	CROPPING	CHILMOPS	COMPLISH	CIIILTVY	CIVILITY
CGIINOSV	VOICINGS	CGINOPRS	CORPSING	CHILMOSU	SCHOLIUM	CIIIMNSV	INCIVISM
CGIINPRS	CRISPING	CGINOPRU	CROUPING	CHILNNPY	LYNCHPIN	CIIINNOS	INCISION
CGIINRSU	CRUISING	CGINOPSU	SCOUPING	CHILNOOS	SCHOLION	CIIINTVY	VICINITY
CGIINRSV	SCRIVING	CGINOPSW	SCOWPING	CHILNOSU	ULICHONS	CIIJRSTU	JURISTIC
CGIJNNOU	JOUNCING	CGINORSS	CROSSING	CHILNOSW	CLOWNISH	CIIKKLLS	KILLICKS
CGIKKNNO	KNOCKING		SCORINGS	CHILOOOZ	HOLOZOIC	CIIKLLSY	SICKLILY
CGIKLNNO	CLONKING		SCORSING	CHILOOPT	HOLOPTIC	CIIKLOPT	POLITICK
CGIKLNNU	CLUNKING	CGINORSU	COURSING	CHILOSYY	COYISHLY	CIIKLPST	LIPSTICK
CGIKLNOR	ROCKLING		SCOURING	CHILOTUY	TOUCHILY	CIIKLRTY	TRICKILY
CGIKLNPU	PLUCKING		SOURCING	CHIMMORU	CHROMIUM	CIIKLSTY	STICKILY
CGIKLNRU	RUCKLING	CGINORTU	COURTING	CHIMNOOR	HORMONIC	CIIKMMMS	MIMMICKS
CGIKLNSU	SCULKING	CGINOSTU	SCOUTING	CHIMNOSU	INSOMUCH	CIIKMNNS	MINNICKS
	SUCKLING	CGINPPSU	CUPPINGS	CHIMNOUY	ONYCHIUM	CIIKNOOT	COOTIKIN
CGIKMNOS	MOCKINGS	CGINPRSU	SPRUCING	CHIMOORU	MOUCHOIR	CIIKNSTU	CUTIKINS
	SMOCKING	CGINRRSU	SCURRING	CHIMORSS	CHRISOMS	CIILLNOP	POLLINIC
CGIKNOOR	CROOKING	CGINRRUY	CURRYING	CHIMORST	CHRISTOM	CIILMOPY	IMPOLICY
CGIKNORS	ROCKINGS	CGINRSSU	CURSINGS	CHIMPSSY	PSYCHISM	CIILMOSS	SCIOLISM
CGIKNORT	TROCKING	CGINRSSY	SCRYINGS	CHIMSSTY	TYCHISMS	CIILMQSU	CLIQUISM
CGIKNORW	CORKWING	CGINRSTU	CRUSTING	CHINOORT	ORTHICON	CIILMRSY	LYRICISM
CGIKNOST	STOCKING	CGINRSUZ	SCRUZING	CHINOPTY	HYPNOTIC	CIILNOPS	CIPOLINS
CGIKNPSU	KINGCUPS	CGINSTTU	CUTTINGS		PYTHONIC	CIILNOSS	SILICONS
CGIKNRTU	TRUCKING	CGKNOSTU	GUNSTOCK		TYPHONIC	CIILOOPT	POLITICO
CGIKNSSU	SUCKINGS	CGLLOSYY	GLYCOSYL	CHINORTU	COTHURNI	CIILOOTZ	ZOOLITIC
CGIKNSTU	GUNSTICK	CGLMOOYY	MYCOLOGY	CHINOSSU	CUSHIONS	CIILOPPT	POPLITIC
CGILLNOS	COLLINGS	CGLNOOOY	ONCOLOGY	CHINOSTZ	SCHIZONT	CIILOPST	POLITICS
CGILLNOY	COLLYING	CGLOOOTY	TOCOLOGY	CHINOSUY	CUSHIONY		PSILOTIC
CGILLNSU	CULLINGS	CGLOOTYY	CYTOLOGY	CHINSTTU	UNSTITCH	CIILORST	CLITORIS
	SCULLING	CGMNNOOR	MONGCORN	CHIOOPPT	PHOTOPIC		COISTRIL
CGILLNUY	CULLYING	CGMNNORU	MUNGCORN	CHIOOPRS	POCHOIRS	CIILOSST	SCIOLIST
CGILMNPU	CLUMPING	CGOORRSW	GORCROWS	CHIOORSS	ISOCHORS		SOLICITS
CGILMNSU	MUSCLING	CHHIIKST	THICKISH	CHIOORSU	ICHOROUS	CIILOSTY	SOLICITY
CGILMNTU	MULCTING	CHHIILTY	HITCHILY	CHIOORSZ	CHORIZOS	CIILOSVV	SLIVOVIC
CGILMNUU	CINGULUM	CHHIIPST	PHTHISIC	CHIOORTT	ORTHOTIC	CIILRSTY	LYRICIST
	GLUCINUM	CHHIKORS	CHIKHORS	CHIOPRST	STROPHIC	CIILRTUU	UTRICULI
CGILNNOW	CLOWNING	CHHILRSU	CHURLISH	CHIOPSTY	HYPOCIST	CIILSSSS	SCISSILS
CGILNOOR	COLORING	CHHIMRTY	RHYTHMIC	CHIORSSS	CROSSISH	CIIMNOST	ISONOMIC
CGILNOOY	COOINGLY	CHHNORSU	RHONCHUS	CHIORSST	CHORISTS	CIIMNOST	MICTIONS
CGILNOPP	CLOPPING	CHHOOPTT	HOTCHPOT	CHIPRRSU	CHIRRUPS		MONISTIC
CGILNOPU	COUPLING	CHIIKLST	TICKLISH	CHIPRRSY	PYRRHICS		NOMISTIC
CGILNORU	CLOURING	CHIIKNNS	KINCHINS	CHIPRRUY	CHIRRUPY	CIIMORST	TRISOMIC
CGILNOSS	CLOSINGS	CHIIKRST	TRICKISH	CHIPRTTY	TRIPTYCH	CIIMOSST	MISTICOS
CGILNOSW	COWLINGS	CHIILLLY	CHILLILY	CHIPSSTY	PSYCHIST		STOICISM
	SCOWLING	CHIILMSY	HYLICISM	CHIRRSSU	SCIRRHUS	CIIMOSTY	MYOSITIC
CGILNOTT	CLOTTING	CHIILNNP	LINCHPIN	CHISSTTU	CHUTISTS	CIIMRSTY	MYRISTIC
CGILNOTU	CLOUTING	CHIILOST	HOLISTIC	CHKLOOOS	HOOLOCKS	CIINNSTT	INSTINCT
CGILNPSU	SCULPING	CHIILPRY	CHIRPILY	CHKMMOOS	HOMMOCKS	CIINNSTU	TUNICINS
CGILNRSU	CURLINGS	CHIILQSU	CLIQUISH	CHKMMOSU	HUMMOCKS	CIINOOST	COITIONS
CGILOORU	UROLOGIC	CHIILSTY	HYLICIST	CHKMMOUY	HUMMOCKY		ISOTONIC
CGILORSW	COWGIRLS	CHIIMPRU	PICHURIM	CHKNOOSS	SCHNOOKS	CIINOOTZ	ZOONITIC
CGILPSTU	GILTCUPS	CHIINNPS	INCHPINS	CHKNORSU	CORNHUSK	CIINOPSU	OPINICUS
CGILPSTY	GLYPTICS	CHIINOPS	SIPHONIC	CHKOOOPS	COOKSHOP	CIINORSS	INCISORS
CGIMMNSU	SCUMMING	CHIINORT	ORNITHIC	CHKOOSST	SCHTOOKS	CIINORSY	INCISORY
CGIMNNOO	GNOMONIC	CHIIORSS	CHORISIS	CHKPSTUU	PUTCHUKS	CIINOSSS	SCISSION
	ONCOMING	CHIIORST	HISTORIC	CHLNOOOP	COLOPHON	CIINOTTY	TONICITY
CGIMNOPT	COMPTING		ORCHITIS	CHLOORSU	CHLOROUS	CIINPRSS	CRISPINS
CGIMNPRU	CRUMPING	CHIIPPRU	HIPPURIC	CHLOPSTY	SPLOTCHY	CIINPSTU	SINCIPUT
CGIMRRUY	MICRURGY	CHIIRSTT	TRISTICH	CHLORTUY	CHOULTRY	CIIOOPST	ISOTOPIC
CGINNNOS	CONNINGS	CHIKLLOS	HILLOCKS	CHMNORRU	CRUMHORN	CIIOPRST	PORISTIC
CGINNNSU	CUNNINGS	CHIKLLOY	HILLOCKY	CHNNOORS	CHRONONS	CIIOQTUX	QUIXOTIC
CGINNOOR	CROONING	CHIKMNPU	CHIPMUNK	CHNOORST	TORCHONS	CIIORRWW	WIRRICOW
CGINNOPU	POUNCING	CHIKMNTU	MUTCHKIN	CHNORRSS	SCHNORRS	CIIOTTXY	TOXICITY

CIIPRRTU PRURITIC
CIIPRSTU PURISTIC
CIIRSTTU TRUISTIC
CIISSTTY CYSTITIS
CIJNNOOS CONJOINS
CIJNNOOT CONJOINT
CIJNNOTU JUNCTION
CIJNNSTU INJUNCTS
CIJOOSTY JOCOSITY
CIKKLLOS KILLOCKS
CIKLLOPR KILLCROP
CIKLLOPS PILLOCKS
CIKLLORS ROLLICKS
CIKLLOSS SILLOCKS
CIKLLOSW KILLCOWS
CIKLLPUY PLUCKILY
CIKLMSSU MISLUCKS
CIKLNOST LINSTOCK
CIKLOSTY STOCKILY
CIKMNNOS MINNOCKS
CIKMOORS SICKROOM
CIKMOPST MOPSTICK
CIKNNOPS PINNOCKS
CIKNNOSW WINNOCKS
CIKNSSTU UNSTICKS
CIKOPPST POCKPITS
CIKOSSTT STOCKIST
CIKOSTUW OUTWICKS
CIKPSSTU STICKUPS
CILLMSUY CLUMSILY
        CULLYISM
CILLNOOT COTILLON
CILLNORS INSCROLL
CILLNOSU CULLIONS
        SCULLION
CILLOOOT OCOTILLO
CILLOORS CRIOLLOS
CILMNOPS COMPLINS
CILMNOPU PULMONIC
CILMNOUU INOCULUM
CILMNUUV VINCULUM
CILMOPSY OLYMPICS
CILMPRSY SCRIMPLY
CILMPSUU SPICULUM
CILMSSTU CULTISMS
CILNOORS ORCINOLS
CILNOORU UNICOLOR
CILNOOSS CLOISONS
CILNOOST COLONIST
CILNOOTU LOCUTION
CILNOPRS PILCORNS
CILNOSTU LINOCUTS
CILNOSUY COUSINLY
CILNPSSU INSCULPS
        SCULPINS
CILNPSTU INSCULPT
CILOOPST COPILOTS
CILOOPYZ POLYZOIC
CILOORRT TRICOLOR
CILOORST CORTISOL
CILOORSU COULOIRS
CILOOSSU SCIOLOUS
CILOPPRY PROPYLIC
CILOPRSW PILCROWS
CILOPSSW COWSLIPS
CILORSTY COYSTRIL
CILOSSTU OCULISTS
CILOSSTY SYSTOLIC
CILOSSUU LUSCIOUS
CILPRSTU CULPRITS

CILPSSTU SCULPSIT
CILRSTTY STRICTLY
CILRSTUY CRUSTILY
CILRSUVY SCURVILY
CILSSTTU CULTISTS
CIMMOSSS COSMISMS
CIMNOOOZ ZOONOMIC
CIMNOORS OMICRONS
CIMNOORU CORONIUM
CIMNOPRT COMPRINT
CIMNORSS CRIMSONS
CIMNORSY CRONYISM
CIMNOSTU MISCOUNT
CIMNOSUY SYCONIUM
CIMOOOTZ ZOOTOMIC
CIMOORSS MORISCOS
CIMOPSSY COPYISMS
CIMOSSST COSMISTS
CIMOSTUU MUTICOUS
CIMOSTUY MUCOSITY
CIMOSTYZ ZYMOTICS
CINNNOSU INCONNUS
CINNOOSS SCOINSON
CINNOOST SCONTION
CINNOOTU CONTINUO
CINNORSU UNICORNS
CINNOSTU UNCTIONS
CINNOSTY SYNTONIC
CINNQUUX QUINCUNX
CINOOOTZ ZOONOTIC
CINOOPRS SCORPION
CINOOPRT PROTONIC
CINOOSUV COVINOUS
CINOOTXY OXYTOCIN
CINOPSTY SYNOPTIC
CINORRST TRICORNS
CINORSST CISTRONS
        CORNISTS
CINORSTT CONTRIST
CINORSTU RUCTIONS
CINORSUY COUSINRY
CINOSSST CONSISTS
CINOSSTU SUCTIONS
CINOSTUV VISCOUNT
CINRSSTU INCRUSTS
CINRSTTU INSTRUCT
CINRSTUY SCRUTINY
CIOOPRSS SCORPIOS
CIOOPRST PORTICOS
        PROOTICS
CIOOPTYZ ZOOTYPIC
CIOOQSTU COQUITOS
CIOORRSW WORRICOW
CIOORSSU SCORIOUS
CIOPSSTY COPYISTS
CIORRSTU CURSITOR
CIORSSSS SCISSORS
CIPPRRUU PURPURIC
CIPSSTTY STYPTICS
CIRRSTTU CRITTURS
CJNOORRU CONJUROR
CJOOORSU JOCOROUS
CJRSUUUU SUCURUJU
CKKNOOTU KNOCKOUT
CKKOORRW ROCKWORK
CKLLMOSU MULLOCKS
CKLLOOPS POLLOCKS
CKLLOORS ROLLOCKS
CKLLORSU RULLOCKS
CKLMMOSU SLUMMOCK

CKLOOOSY OLYCOOKS
CKLOORSW ROWLOCKS
CKLOOSTU LOCKOUTS
CKLOPSTU PUTLOCKS
CKMMMOSU MUMMOCKS
CKMOOOOR COOKROOM
CKNOSSTU UNSTOCKS
CKNRSTUU UNSTRUCK
CKOOOSTU COOKOUTS
CKOORSSU SOUROCKS
CKOPSTTU PUTTOCKS
CKOSSSTU TUSSOCKS
CKOSSTUY TUSSOCKY
CLLLOOPT CLOTPOLL
CLLMOSSU MOLLUSCS
CLLOOPSS SCOLLOPS
CLLOOQUY COLLOQUY
CLMMNOOY COMMONLY
CLMOOOTY COLOTOMY
CLMOOPST COMPLOTS
CLMOPSTU PLUMCOTS
CLMOSSUU OSCULUMS
CLNOORST CONTROLS
CLNOORTU CONTROUL
        COUNTROL
CLNOSSTU CONSULTS
CLNOSTUY UNCOSTLY
CLOOOPRT PROTOCOL
CLOORTUY LOCUTORY
CLOOSSSU COLOSSUS
CLOPRSTU SCULPTOR
CLRSSUUU SURCULUS
CMMNNOOU UNCOMMON
CMNOOOST MONOCOTS
CMNOOOTY ONCOTOMY
CMNOORRW CORNWORM
CMNOPSTU CONSUMPT
CMOOPRST COMPORTS
CMOOPSST COMPOSTS
CMORSSTU SCROTUMS
CMORSTUW CUTWORMS
CNNOOORT CONTORNO
CNNORSTU NOCTURNS
CNNORSUW UNCROWNS
CNOOOORT OCTOROON
CNOOPPRS POPCORNS
CNOOPRSU CROUPONS
CNOOPSSU SOUPCONS
CNOORRTY CRYOTRON
CNOORSST CONSORTS
CNOORSTT CONTORTS
CNOORSTU CONTOURS
        CORNUTOS
        CROUTONS
        OUTSCORN
CNOOSTTW COTTOWNS
CNOPRSTY CRYPTONS
CNOSTUUU UNCTUOUS
COOOPSYZ ZOOSCOPY
COOPRRST PROCTORS
COOPRSTU OUTCROPS
COOPRSUU CROUPOUS
COOPRSUY UROSCOPY
COORRWWY WORRYCOW
COORSSTU OUTCROSS
COOSSTTY OTOCYSTS
COPRRSTU CORRUPTS
DDDEEIIR DIDDERED
DDDEEOOR DODDERED
DDDEEEFN DEFENDED

DDDEEENP DEPENDED
DDDEEENR REDDENED
DDDEEENU UNDEEDED
DDDEEFOR FODDERED
DDDEEGIS DISEDGED
DDDEEHRS SHREDDED
DDDEEIST STEDDIED
DDDEEJRU JUDDERED
DDDEELRT TREDDLED
DDDEENOR REDDENDO
DDDEENOS SODDENED
DDDEENUW UNWEDDED
DDDEEORR DODDERER
DDDEEPRU PUDDERED
DDDEERTU DETRUDED
DDDEGNOU UNGODDED
DDDEHIRT THRIDDED
DDDEIINV DIVIDEND
DDDEIIST STIDDIED
DDDEILNU UNLIDDED
DDDEILNW DWINDLED
DDDEILQU QUIDDLED
DDDEILRS DIDDLERS
DDDEILTW TWIDDLED
DDDEIMOS DISMODED
DDDEINOR DENDROID
DDDEINNU UNDERDID
DDDEIOST DODDIEST
DDDEIQSU SQUIDDED
DDDEISTU DUDDIEST
DDDENORW DROWNDED
DDDGIILN DIDDLING
DDDIIOOR DORIDOID
DDEEEEMR REDEEMED
DDEEEENP DEEPENED
DDEEEFLX DEFLEXED
DDEEEFNR DEFENDER
DDEEEFRR DEFERRED
DDEEEGLR LEDGERED
DDEEEGMR DEMERGED
DDEEEGNR DEGENDER
        GENDERED
DDEEEGRR REGREDED
DDEEEGRT DETERGED
DDEEEHLW WHEEDLED
DDEEEHNU UNHEEDED
DDEEEIMR REMEDIED
DDEEEIST DEEDIEST
        STEEDIED
DDEEELLV DEVELLED
DDEEELNW WEDELLED
DDEEELPT DEPLETED
DDEEELSS DEEDLESS
DDEEELTW TWEEDLED
DDEEEMNT DEMENTED
DDEEEMRS DEMERSED
DDEEENNU UNNEEDED
DDEEENPX EXPENDED
DDEEENRR RENDERED
DDEEENRT TENDERED
DDEEENSU UNSEEDED
DDEEENTX EXTENDED
DDEEENUW UNWEEDED
DDEEERRT DETERRED
DDEEERST DESERTED
DDEEERSV DESERVED
DDEEESTT DETESTED
DDEEESTV DEVESTED
DDEEFFIR DIFFERED
DDEEFFNO OFFENDED

DDEEFGIT	FIDGETED
DDEEFINR	FRIENDED
DDEEFINU	UNDEFIDE
	UNDEFIED
DDEEFLNO	ENFOLDED
DDEEFLOU	DEFOULED
DDEEFMOR	DEFORMED
DDEEFNRU	REFUNDED
	UNDERFED
DDEEFORR	FODDERER
DDEEGGOR	DOGGEDER
DDEEGHNU	UNHEDGED
DDEEGILN	ENGILDED
DDEEGINR	ENRIDGED
DDEEGINS	DESIGNED
	SEIGNED
DDEEGIRV	DIVERGED
DDEEGISS	DISEDGES
DDEEGIST	DIGESTED
DDEEGJRU	REJUDGED
DDEEGLNO	GOLDENED
DDEEGMMU	DEGUMMED
DDEEGOPS	GODSPEED
DDEEGRRS	DREDGERS
DDEEGSTU	DEGUSTED
DDEEHILS	SHIELDED
DDEEHINR	HINDERED
DDEEHIRT	DITHERED
DDEEHISS	EDDISHES
DDEEHNOR	DEHORNED
DDEEHNSU	DUDHEENS
DDEEHORT	DEHORTED
DDEEHRRS	SHREDDER
DDEEHRSS	SHEDDERS
DDEEIINT	INEDITED
DDEEIIRV	REDIVIDE
DDEEILLV	DEVILLED
DDEEILMN	MILDENED
DDEEILMW	MILDEWED
DDEEILRW	WILDERED
DDEEIMNP	IMPENDED
DDEEIMNR	REMINDED
DDEEIMOR	MOIDERED
DDEEIMSS	MISDEEDS
DDEEIMST	DEMISTED
DDEEIMTT	DEMITTED
DDEEINNR	DINNERED
DDEEINNT	INDENTED
	INTENDED
DDEEINRT	DENDRITE
DDEEINST	DESTINED
DDEEINTU	UNEDITED
DDEEIOPR	PERIODED
DDEEIPPR	REDIPPED
DDEEIPRS	PRESIDED
DDEEIPRV	DEPRIVED
DDEEIPSS	DEPSIDES
	DESPISED
DDEEIRRS	DERIDERS
DDEEIRST	REDDIEST
DDEEIRSV	DIVERSED
DDEEIRTV	DIVERTED
DDEEISST	DESISTED
	STEDDIES
DDEEISTV	DIVESTED
DDEEITTW	DEWITTED
DDEEJLLO	JODELLED
DDEEKNSU	DUSKENED
DDEELLMO	MODELLED
DDEELLOW	DOWELLED
DDEELLOY	YODELLED
DDEELMPU	DEPLUMED
DDEELMRS	MEDDLERS
DDEELNOU	LOUDENED
DDEELOPR	DEPLORED
	POLDERED
DDEELOPX	EXPLODED
DDEELOPY	DEPLOYED
DDEELORS	SOLDERED
DDEELOSU	DELOUSED
DDEELOVV	DEVOLVED
DDEELPRS	PEDDLERS
DDEELPRU	PRELUDED
DDEELRST	TREDDLES
DDEELRSU	DELUDERS
DDEEMNOR	ENDODERM
	MURDERED
DDEENNOR	DONNERED
DDEENNOY	ENDODYNE
DDEENNTU	UNTENDED
DDEENOPR	PERDENDO
	PONDERED
DDEENOPW	PONDWEED
DDEENORS	ENDORSED
DDEENORW	WONDERED
DDEENOSS	ENDOSSED
DDEENPRS	SPREDDEN
DDEENRSU	SUNDERED
DDEENRTU	RETUNDED
DDEEOPRT	DEPORTED
DDEEOPRW	POWDERED
DDEEORRW	REWORDED
DDEEORTT	DETORTED
DDEEORTU	DETOURED
DDEEORUV	DEVOURED
DDEEORVY	OVERDYED
DDEEPRRU	PERDURED
DDEEPRSS	SPREDDES
DDEERRUV	VERDURED
DDEERSTU	DETRUDES
DDEERTUX	EXTRUDED
DDEFFISU	DIFFUSED
DDEFIIIN	NIDIFIED
DDEFIILM	MIDFIELD
DDEFIILR	FIDDLIER
DDEFIIMO	MODIFIED
DDEFIIMW	MIDWIFED
DDEFILNO	INFOLDED
DDEFILRS	FIDDLERS
DDEFILSY	FIDDLEYS
DDEFLNOU	UNFOLDED
DDEFLRSU	FUDDLERS
DDEFLRUU	UDDERFUL
DDEFNNUU	UNFUNDED
DDEGGINR	DREDGING
DDEGGLOY	DOGGEDLY
DDEGGNOO	DOGGONED
DDEGHILN	HEDDLING
DDEGIINR	DERIDING
DDEGIIST	GIDDIEST
DDEGILMN	MEDDLING
DDEGILNP	PEDDLING
DDEGILNR	REDDLING
DDEGILNS	SLEDDING
DDEGILNU	DELUDING
	INDULGED
	UNGILDED
DDEGILOS	DISLODGE
DDEGILRS	GRIDDLES
DDEGILRY	GLIDDERY
DDEGILST	GLIDDEST
DDEGILUV	DIVULGED
DDEGIMOS	DEMIGODS
DDEGINNS	SNEDDING
DDEGINNU	DENUDING
DDEGINRS	REDDINGS
DDEGINRU	UNGIRDED
DDEGINST	STEDDING
DDEGINSW	SWINDGED
	WEDDINGS
DDEGINUU	UNGUIDED
DDEGIOST	DODGIEST
DDEGIQSU	SQUIDGED
DDEGLOPS	SPLODGED
DDEGNORU	GROUNDED
	UNDERDOG
DDEGNOSS	GODSENDS
DDEGNOSU	DUDGEONS
DDEGORSS	GORSEDDS
DDEGRRSU	DRUDGERS
DDEGRRUY	DRUDGERY
DDEHILNY	HIDDENLY
DDEHILOO	IDLEHOOD
DDEHIMOS	DISHOMED
DDEHINNU	UNHIDDEN
DDEHINOR	DIHEDRON
DDEHIORS	SHODDIER
DDEHIOSS	SHODDIES
DDEHIRSS	SHIDDERS
DDEHIRSW	WHIDDERS
DDEHIRSY	HYDRIDES
DDEHNOOU	UNHOODED
DDEHNPUU	UPHUDDEN
DDEHNRSU	HUNDREDS
DDEHOOOO	HOODOOED
DDEHOOSW	WOODSHED
DDEHORSU	SHROUDED
DDEHRSSU	SHUDDERS
DDEHRSUY	SHUDDERY
DDEIIIRS	IRIDISED
DDEIIIRZ	IRIDIZED
DDEIIKLS	DISLIKED
DDEIIKRS	KIDDIERS
DDEIILNR	DIELDRIN
DDEIILOZ	IDOLIZED
DDEIILRT	TIDDLIER
DDEIILST	TIDDLIES
DDEIIMSS	SMIDDIES
DDEIIMVW	MIDWIVED
DDEIINRT	NITRIDED
DDEIINTU	UNTIDIED
DDEIIOPS	DIOPSIDE
	DIPODIES
DDEIIOST	ODDITIES
DDEIIOSX	DIOXIDES
DDEIIOXZ	OXIDIZED
DDEIIRSV	DIVIDERS
DDEIISST	STIDDIES
DDEIISTT	TIDDIEST
DDEIKNRS	KINDREDS
DDEIKOSY	DISYOKED
DDEILMOP	IMPLODED
DDEILMOV	DEVILDOM
DDEILNPS	SPLENDID
DDEILNRT	TRINDLED
DDEILNRU	UNRIDDLE
DDEILNSW	DWINDLES
	SWINDLED
DDEILOPS	DISPLODE
DDEILOSY	DYSODILE
DDEILPRS	PIDDLERS
DDEILPRU	PUDDLIER
DDEILQRU	QUIDDLER
DDEILQSU	QUIDDLES
DDEILRRS	RIDDLERS
DDEILRSS	SLIDDERS
DDEILRST	STRIDDLE
	TIDDLERS
DDEILRSY	SLIDDERY
DDEILRTW	TWIDDLER
DDEILRZZ	DRIZZLED
DDEILSTW	TWIDDLES
DDEILSTY	LYDDITES
	TIDDLEYS
DDEIMMNU	UNDIMMED
DDEIMNNU	UNMINDED
DDEIMNSU	MUEDDINS
DDEIMNUV	VIDENDUM
DDEIMORS	DERMOIDS
DDEIMOSU	MEDUSOID
DDEIMSTU	MUDDIEST
DDEINNRU	UNRIDDEN
DDEINNTU	UNDINTED
DDEINOPS	DISPONED
DDEINORS	INDORSED
DDEINOSW	DISENDOW
	DISOWNED
DDEINOWW	WINDOWED
DDEINPPU	UNDIPPED
DDEINPSS	DISPENDS
DDEINRST	STRIDDEN
DDEINRTU	INTRUDED
DDEINSST	DISTENDS
DDEINSSW	SWIDDENS
DDEINSTU	DISTUNED
DDEIOPRS	DROPSIED
DDEIOPRV	PROVIDED
DDEIOPSS	DISPOSED
DDEIOPST	PODDIEST
DDEIORRS	DISORDER
	SORDIDER
DDEIOSST	SODDIEST
DDEIOSTW	DOWDIEST
DDEIPRSS	DISPREDS
DDEIPRSU	SPUDDIER
DDEIPSTU	DISPUTED
DDEIRSSU	DRUIDESS
DDEIRSTU	RUDDIEST
	STURDIED
DDEKMOSU	DUKEDOMS
DDELLNUU	UNDULLED
DDELMRSU	MUDDLERS
DDELNORU	UNLORDED
DDELNRTU	TRUNDLED
DDELNSUY	SUDDENLY
DDELOORS	DOODLERS
DDELOPRS	PLODDERS
DDELORST	STRODDLE
	STRODLED
DDELOSYY	DYSODYLE
DDELPRSU	PUDDLERS
DDELSSTU	STUDDLES
DDEMMSSU	SMEDDUMS
DDEMNOOU	UNDOOMED

DDEMNOST	ODDMENTS
DDEMNOUU	DUODENUM
DDEMNPUU	PUDENDUM
DDEMOOTU	OUTMODED
DDENNORS	DENDRONS
DDENNOSU	UNSODDEN
DDENOOUW	UNWOODED
DDENOPSS	DESPONDS
DDENORSU	REDOUNDS
DDENORTU	ROTUNDED
DDENORUW	UNWORDED
DDENOSTU	STOUNDED
DDENOSTW	STOWNDED
DDENOSUW	SWOUNDED
DDENSTUY	SUDDENTY
DDEOOOOV	VOODOOED
DDEOORSW	REDWOODS
DDEOORWW	ROWDEDOW
DDEOOUUV	VOUDOUED
DDEORTUU	OUTDURED
DDFGIILN	FIDDLING
DDFGILNU	FUDDLING
DDFIIOSU	FIDDIOUS
DDFMNOUU	DUMFOUND
DDGGIINY	GIDDYING
DDGGILNU	GUDDLING
DDGGINRU	DRUDGING
DDGHIINW	WHIDDING
DDGHILNO	HODDLING
DDGHILNU	HUDDLING
DDGHINTU	THUDDING
DDGHOOOS	GODHOODS
DDGIIINV	DIVIDING
DDGIIKNS	SKIDDING
DDGIIKNY	KIDDYING
DDGIILMN	MIDDLING
DDGIILNN	DINDLING
DDGIILNP	PIDDLING
DDGIILNR	RIDDLING
DDGIILNT	TIDDLING
DDGIILNW	WIDDLING
DDGILMNU	MUDDLING
DDGILNNO	NODDLING
DDGILNOO	DOODLING
DDGILNOP	PLODDING
DDGILNOT	TODDLING
DDGILNPU	PUDDLING
DDGILNRU	RUDDLING
DDGIMNUY	MUDDYING
DDGIMRSU	DRUDGISM
DDGINNOS	NODDINGS
	SNODDING
DDGINOPR	PRODDING
DDGINOQU	QUODDING
DDGINORS	RODDINGS
DDGINPSU	PUDDINGS
	SPUDDING
DDGINPUY	PUDDINGY
DDGINRUY	RUDDYING
DDGINSTU	STUDDING
DDGOOOSW	DOGWOODS
DDHILOSY	SHODDILY
DDHIORSY	HYDROIDS
DDHIOSWY	DOWDYISH
DDHLLOOO	DOLLHOOD
DDIIIIVV	DIVIDIVI
DDIILOPY	DIPLOIDY
DDIIMMUY	DIDYMIUM
DDIIMRSU	DRUIDISM
	SIDDURIM
DDIINOPU	DUPONDII
DDIIQSTU	QUIDDITS
DDIIQTUY	QUIDDITY
DDILORSY	SORDIDLY
DDILOSSY	DYSODILS
DDIMOSUY	DIDYMOUS
DDIMOSWY	DOWDYISM
DDINNOWW	DOWNWIND
DDINOOOT	ODONTOID
DDLLMOOS	DOLLDOMS
DDLMORSU	DOLDRUMS
DDMNOORS	DROMONDS
DDOORWWY	ROWDYDOW
DDORSSTY	DROSTDYS
DEEEEFRR	REFEREED
DEEEEFRZ	DEFREEZE
DEEEEGKR	KEDGEREE
DEEEEHLR	REHEELED
DEEEEKMN	MEEKENED
DEEEELTY	EYELETED
DEEEEMMS	MESEEMED
DEEEEMRR	REDEEMER
DEEEEMST	ESTEEMED
DEEEENRV	VENEERED
DEEEERTT	TEETERED
DEEEFFIR	EFFEIRED
DEEEFINR	FINEERED
	REDEFINE
DEEEFIPT	TEPEFIED
DEEEFIRW	FIREWEED
DEEEFLLR	REFELLED
DEEEFLPT	DEEPFELT
DEEEFLRT	FELTERED
DEEEFLRX	REFLEXED
DEEEFLSX	DEFLEXES
DEEEFMNR	FREEDMEN
DEEEFNRT	DEFERENT
DEEEFNSS	DEFENSES
DEEEFNST	ENFESTED
DEEEFORV	OVERFEED
DEEEFRRR	DEFERRER
	REFERRED
DEEEFRRT	FERRETED
DEEEFRST	FESTERED
DEEEFRTT	FETTERED
DEEEFRTW	FEWTERED
DEEEGHNW	WHEENGED
DEEEGILS	ELEGISED
DEEEGILZ	ELEGIZED
DEEEGIPR	PEDIGREE
DEEEGIRR	GREEDIER
DEEEGISS	DIEGESES
DEEEGISW	EDGEWISE
DEEEGLPS	PLEDGEES
DEEEGLSS	EDGELESS
DEEEGLSV	SELVEDGE
DEEEGMRR	DEMERGER
	REMERGED
DEEEGMRS	DEMERGES
DEEEGNNR	ENGENDER
DEEEGNRU	RENEGUED
DEEEGNRV	REVENGED
DEEEGQSU	SQUEEDGE
DEEEGRRS	REGREDES
DEEEGRST	DETERGES
DEEEGRTT	GETTERED
DEEEHKRS	SHREEKED
DEEEHLMT	HELMETED
DEEEHLPW	WHEEPLED
DEEEHLRW	WHEEDLER
DEEEHLSS	HEEDLESS
DEEEHLSW	WHEEDLES
DEEEHLWZ	WHEEZLED
DEEEHMMS	EMMESHED
DEEEHMNS	ENMESHED
DEEEHRTT	TETHERED
DEEEILNR	NEEDLIER
DEEEILNS	SELENIDE
DEEEILRV	RELIEVED
DEEEILTV	DELETIVE
DEEEILVW	WEEVILED
DEEEIMNS	INSEEMED
DEEEIMRS	REMEDIES
DEEEINRR	REINDEER
DEEEINST	NEEDIEST
DEEEINSX	ENDEIXES
DEEEINTV	EVENTIDE
DEEEIPRS	SPEEDIER
DEEEIPTX	EXPEDITE
DEEEIRRR	DERRIERE
DEEEIRSS	DIERESES
DEEEIRST	REEDIEST
DEEEIRSZ	RESEIZED
DEEEIRTW	TWEEDIER
DEEEIRVW	REVIEWED
DEEEISST	SEEDIEST
	STEEDIES
DEEEISSV	DEVISEES
DEEEISTW	WEEDIEST
DEEEJLLW	JEWELLED
DEEEJNRU	DEJEUNER
DEEEJNSU	DEJEUNES
DEEEKNSW	WEEKENDS
DEEEKOPW	POKEWEED
DEEEKRST	STREEKED
DEEEKRSW	RESKEWED
	SKEWERED
DEEELLLV	LEVELLED
DEEELLNT	DENTELLE
DEEELLNV	NEVELLED
DEEELLNW	NEWELLED
DEEELLPR	REPELLED
DEEELLPT	PELLETED
DEEELLPX	EXPELLED
DEEELLRT	TELLERED
DEEELLRV	REVELLED
DEEELMOS	SOMEDELE
DEEELNPU	UNPEELED
DEEELNRS	NEEDLERS
DEEELNRT	RELENTED
DEEELNRU	UNREELED
DEEELNSS	LESSENED
	NEEDLESS
	SELDSEEN
DEEELNSU	UNSEELED
DEEELOPV	DEVELOPE
DEEELPRT	PELTERED
	REPLETED
DEEELPST	DEPLETES
	STEEPLED
DEEELRSS	REDLESS
DEEELRST	DEERLETS
	STREELED
DEEELRTT	LETTERED
DEEELRTW	WELTERED
DEEELSSS	SEEDLESS
DEEELSSW	WEEDLESS
DEEELSTW	TWEEDLES
DEEELTVV	VELVETED
DEEEMNNT	NEEDMENT
DEEEMNSS	DEMESNES
	SEEDSMEN
DEEEMPRT	TEMPERED
DEEEMPTX	EXEMPTED
DEEEMRSS	DEMERSES
DEEEMRST	DEEMSTER
DEEENNRT	ENTENDER
DEEENNUW	UNWEENED
DEEENOPR	REOPENED
DEEENORS	ENDORSEE
DEEENPRT	REPENTED
	REPETEND
DEEENPRU	UNPEERED
DEEENPRV	PREVENED
DEEENPRX	EXPENDER
DEEENPSS	DEEPNESS
DEEENRRR	RENDERER
DEEENRRT	TENDERER
DEEENRRV	REVEREND
DEEENRST	RESENTED
DEEENRTT	TENTERED
DEEENRTU	NEUTERED
DEEENRTX	EXTENDER
DEEENRUV	REVENUED
	UNREEVED
DEEENSSS	SEEDNESS
DEEENSTT	DETENTES
DEEENSTU	DETENUES
DEEENSTX	DENTEXES
DEEENSUV	VENDEUSE
DEEEOPRR	PEDERERO
DEEEOPRT	DEPORTEE
DEEEORST	STEREOED
DEEEORSW	OREWEEDS
DEEEORVY	OVEREYED
DEEEOSTV	DEVOTEES
DEEEPPPR	PEPPERED
DEEEPRSS	SPEEDERS
DEEEPRST	ESTREPED
	PESTERED
DEEEPRSZ	SPREEZED
DEEEPRTX	EXPERTED
DEEEQRRU	REQUERED
DEEEQSUZ	SQUEEZED
DEEERRRV	VERDERER
DEEERRST	DESERTER
DEEERRSV	DESERVER
	RESERVED
	REVERSED
DEEERRTV	REVERTED
DEEERSSV	DESERVES
DEEERSTT	RESETTED
	SETTERED
	STREETED
DEEERSTV	REVESTED
DEEERSTW	WESTERED
DEEERSTX	EXSERTED
DEEERSUW	SERUEWED
DEEERSVW	SERVEWED
DEEERTTT	TETTERED
DEEERTTV	REVETTED
DEEESTTU	SUEDETTE
DEEESTTV	VEDETTES
DEEFFGLU	EFFULGED
DEEFFGOR	GOFFERED
DEEFFINR	NIFFERED
DEEFFINS	EFFENDIS
DEEFFINT	INFEFTED
DEEFFNOR	OFFENDER

	REOFFEND		REJIGGED	DEEGIRST	DIGESTER	DEEHLNPU	UNHELPED
DEEFFRSU	SUFFERED	DEEGGINR	GINGERED		ESTRIDGE	DEEHLORV	OVERHELD
DEEFGILR	FLEDGIER		NIGGERED	DEEGIRSU	GUDESIRE		VERDELHO
DEEFGINR	FINGERED		RENIGGED	DEEGIRSV	DIVERGES	DEEHLPPS	SHLEPPED
DEEFGINS	FEEDINGS	DEEGGIRR	DREGGIER	DEEGISST	SEDGIEST	DEEHLSTU	SLEUTHED
DEEFGIPS	PIGFEEDS	DEEGGLOR	DOGGEREL	DEEGJPRU	PREJUDGE	DEEHMNRS	HERDSMEN
DEEFGIUW	GUDEWIFE	DEEGGNOR	ENGORGED	DEEGJRSU	REJUDGES	DEEHMORT	MOTHERED
DEEFGLNU	ENGULFED	DEEGGNPU	UNPEGGED	DEEGLLRU	GRUELLED	DEEHNOPY	PHONEYED
DEEFHIMU	HUMEFIED	DEEGGORR	REGORGED	DEEGLLUY	GULLEYED	DEEHNORR	DEERHORN
DEEFHINT	HINDFEET	DEEGGQSU	SQUEEGED	DEEGLNOR	GOLDENER		DEHORNER
DEEFHLOR	FREEHOLD	DEEGGRRU	RUGGEDER	DEEGLNOU	ENGOULED	DEEHNORT	DETHRONE
DEEFHLRS	FELDSHER	DEEGHHIR	HIGHERED	DEEGLNOZ	LOZENGED		THRENODE
DEEFHORT	FOTHERED	DEEGHHSU	SHEUGHED	DEEGLNRY	LEGENDRY	DEEHNPRS	PREHENDS
DEEFIILN	FEDELINI	DEEGHHUW	WHEUGHED	DEEGLOPR	PLEDGEOR	DEEHNSTU	ENTHUSED
	LENIFIED	DEEGHILS	SLEIGHED	DEEGLOPS	DOGSLEEP	DEEHOORV	HOOVERED
DEEFIINT	DEFINITE	DEEGHIST	HEDGIEST	DEEGLORW	GLOWERED	DEEHOPRT	POTHERED
DEEFIIRS	DEIFIERS	DEEGHITW	WEIGHTED	DEEGLOSY	GOLDEYES	DEEHORRT	DEHORTER
	EDIFIERS	DEEGHNRU	HUNGERED	DEEGLPRS	PLEDGERS	DEEHORSU	REHOUSED
	FIRESIDE	DEEGHOPR	GOPHERED	DEEGLPST	PLEDGETS	DEEHORSW	SHOWERED
DEEFIIRV	VERIFIED	DEEGHOPS	SHEEPDOG	DEEGLRSS	SLEDGERS	DEEHORTT	HOTTERED
DEEFILLR	REFILLED	DEEGHORW	HEDGEROW	DEEGMNRU	DUNGMERE	DEEHORTX	EXHORTED
DEEFILLT	FILLETED	DEEGHOSW	HOGWEEDS	DEEGNNOS	ENDOGENS	DEEHRRSW	SHREWDER
DEEFILMS	MEDFLIES	DEEGHOTT	DOGTEETH	DEEGNNOY	ENDOGENY	DEEHRTUW	WUTHERED
DEEFILNX	INFLEXED	DEEGIINN	INDIGENE	DEEGNORV	GOVERNED	DEEIILRV	LIVERIED
DEEFILPR	PILFERED	DEEGIISS	DIEGESIS	DEEGNPRU	REPUGNED	DEEIILRW	WIELDIER
DEEFILRS	DEFILERS	DEEGIKST	KEDGIEST	DEEGNPUX	EXPUNGED	DEEIIMRS	DIMERISE
	FIELDERS	DEEGILMO	LIEGEDOM		EXPUNGED	DEEIIMRZ	DIMERIZE
DEEFILRT	FILTERED	DEEGILMP	IMPLEDGE	DEEGOSTU	OUTEDGES	DEEIIMST	ITEMISED
DEEFIMTU	TUMEFIED	DEEGILMT	GIMLETED	DEEGOTUW	GOUTWEED	DEEIIMTZ	ITEMIZED
DEEFINRR	INFERRED	DEEGILNN	NEEDLING	DEEGPRUX	EXPURGED	DEEIINST	DIETINES
DEEFINRS	DEFINERS	DEEGILNO	ELOIGNED	DEEGRRSU	RESURGED	DEEIINSX	ENDEIXIS
DEEFINRZ	FRENZIED		LEGIONED	DEEGRSTU	GESTURED	DEEIIPRS	EPEIRIDS
DEEFINSS	FINESSED	DEEGILNR	ENGIRDLE	DEEGRTTU	GUTTERED	DEEIIRSS	DIERESIS
DEEFINST	FENDIEST		LINGERED	DEEGSSTU	GUSSETED	DEEIIRST	SIDERITE
	INFESTED		REEDLING	DEEHHIRT	HITHERED	DEEIIRSV	DERISIVE
DEEFIORS	FORESIDE	DEEGILNS	SEEDLING	DEEHHNPY	HYPHENED	DEEIIRSW	WEIRDIES
DEEFIORT	FOETIDER	DEEGILNT	DELETING	DEEHHPRS	SHEPHERD	DEEIISSS	DISSEISE
DEEFIPRX	PREFIXED	DEEGILRS	LEIDGERS	DEEHHRST	THRESHED	DEEIISSW	SIDEWISE
DEEFIRRV	FERVIDER	DEEGILRW	WEREGILD	DEEHHRSU	HUSHERED	DEEIISSZ	DISSEIZE
DEEFIRTT	REFITTED	DEEGILRY	GREEDILY	DEEHIKRS	SHREIKED	DEEIJNNO	ENJOINED
DEEFISTT	FETIDEST	DEEGILST	GELIDEST		SHRIEKED	DEEIJNOR	REJOINED
DEEFLLNU	UNFELLED		LEDGIEST	DEEHIKSV	KHEDIVES	DEEIJRTT	JITTERED
DEEFLNOR	FORELEND	DEEGIMMR	IMMERGED	DEEHILNS	ENSHIELD	DEEIKKRY	YIKKERED
DEEFLNSU	UNSELFED	DEEGIMNN	EMENDING	DEEHILRS	RELISHED	DEEIKLLR	KILLDEER
DEEFLNTU	DEFLUENT	DEEGIMRU	DEMIURGE		SHIELDER	DEEIKLLS	KILLDEES
DEEFLORW	DEFLOWER	DEEGINNR	ENRINGED	DEEHILSV	DISHEVEL		SKELLIED
	FLOWERED	DEEGINNS	ENSIGNED	DEEHIMMS	IMMESHED	DEEIKLNN	ENKINDLE
	REFLOWED	DEEGINNT	TEENDING	DEEHIMNS	INMESHED		ENLINKED
DEEFLOST	FEEDLOTS	DEEGINNW	ENDEWING	DEEHIMRT	MITHERED	DEEIKLNR	REKINDLE
DEEFLPSU	SPEEDFUL	DEEGINOP	PIGEONED	DEEHINRR	HINDERER	DEEIKLNS	SILKENED
DEEFLRUX	REFLUXED	DEEGINPS	SPEEDING	DEEHINRS	DRISHEEN	DEEIKLSW	SILKWEED
DEEFMNOR	ENFORMED	DEEGINRS	DESIGNER	DEEHINST	DISTHENE	DEEIKNRS	DEERSKIN
DEEFMNOT	FOMENTED		ENERGIDS	DEEHINTW	WHITENED	DEEIKNRT	TINKERED
DEEFMORR	DEFORMER		REDESIGN	DEEHIORS	HEROISED	DEEIKNTT	KITTENED
	REFORMED		REEDINGS	DEEHIORZ	HEROIZED	DEEIKOSV	DOVEKIES
DEEFMORS	FREEDOMS		RESIGNED	DEEHIPRS	HESPERID	DEEIKPPR	KIPPERED
DEEFMPRU	PERFUMED	DEEGINSS	DINGESES		PERISHED	DEEIKRSU	DUKERIES
DEEFNORZ	DEFROZEN		EDGINESS	DEEHIRRS	REDSHIRE	DEEIKRSV	SKIVERED
DEEFNOST	SOFTENED		SDEIGNES	DEEHIRRT	DITHERER	DEEIKSTT	DISKETTE
DEEFNRRU	REFUNDER		SEEDINGS	DEEHIRSV	SHIVERED	DEEILLMP	IMPELLED
DEEFNSST	DEFTNESS	DEEGINST	INGESTED		SHRIEVED		MILLEPED
DEEFOORT	REFOOTED		SIGNETED	DEEHIRTW	WITHERED	DEEILLNO	NIELLOED
DEEFORST	DEFOREST		STEEDING	DEEHIRTY	HEREDITY	DEEILLOR	ORIELLED
	FORESTED	DEEGINSW	WEEDINGS	DEEHKNOS	KEESHOND	DEEILLPR	PERILLED
	FOSTERED	DEEGINSX	DESEXING	DEEHKNRU	HUNKERED	DEEILLRT	TILLERED
DEEFPRSU	PERFUSED	DEEGINZZ	GIZZENED	DEEHLLOR	HOLLERED		TREDILLE
DEEFRRTU	RETURFED	DEEGIORS	GEORDIES	DEEHLLOV	HOVELLED	DEEILLRV	RIVELLED
DEEGGHHO	HEDGEHOG	DEEGIOST	EGOTISED	DEEHLMMW	WHEMMLED	DEEILLWY	WILLEYED
DEEGGHIP	HEDGEPIG	DEEGIOTZ	EGOTIZED	DEEHLMNU	UNHELMED	DEEILMOS	MELODIES
DEEGGIJR	JIGGERED	DEEGIPSW	PIGWEEDS	DEEHLMSW	WELDMESH		MELODISE

DEEILMOZ MELODIZE	DEEIMSSU MEDIUSES	DEEIPRRT TREPIDER	DEELLOTW TOWELLED
DEEILMPT IMPLETED	DEEINNRS SINNERED	DEEIPRRV REPRIVED	DEELLOTX EXTOLLED
DEEILNOS ESLOINED	DEEINNRT INDENTER	DEEIPRRZ REPRIZED	DEELLOVV VOWELLED
DEEILNOT DELETION	INTENDER	DEEIPRSS DESPISER	DEELLOVY VOLLEYED
ENTOILED	INTERNED	DISPERSE	DEELLOWY YELLOWED
DEEILNPP LIPPENED	DEEINNRU UNREINED	PRESIDES	DEELLPUW UPWELLED
DEEILNRU UNDERLIE	DEEINNRV INNERVED	DEEIPRST PRIESTED	DEELLRSU DUELLERS
DEEILNSS IDLENESS	DEEINNST DENTINES	RESPITED	DEELLRSW DWELLERS
LINSEEDS	DESINENT	DEEIPRSU DUPERIES	DEELLSSW WELDLESS
DEEILNST ENLISTED	DEEINNSZ DENIZENS	DEEIPRSV DEPRIVES	DEELLSUX DUXELLES
LINTSEED	DEEINNTV INVENTED	PREVISED	DEELMMPU EMPLUMED
LISTENED	DEEINNTW ENTWINED	DEEIPRTT PITTERED	DEELMNOO MELODEON
DEEILNSY DYELINES	DEEINNUV UNENVIED	DEEIPRTX EXTIRPED	DEELMNOS LODESMEN
DEEILNTT ENTITLED	DEEINOPS DISPONEE	DEEIPSSS DESPISES	DEELMNTU UNMELTED
DEEILNUV UNVEILED	DEEINORS ORDINEES	DEEIPSST DESPITES	DEELMNTW WELDMENT
DEEILOPT LEPIDOTE	DEEINORT ORIENTED	DEEIPSTT TEPIDEST	DEELMOOS DOLESOME
PETIOLED	DEEINPPR NIPPERED	DEEIPSTU DEPUTIES	DEELMOPR EMPOLDER
DEEILORT DOLERITE	DEEINPSS DISPENSE	DEPUTISE	DEELMOPY EMPLOYED
LOITERED	PIEDNESS	DEEIPTUZ DEPUTIZE	DEELMORS REMODELS
DEEILOTT TOILETED	DEEINPST PENTISED	DEEIQRRU REQUIRED	DEELMOST MOLESTED
DEEILPSS SEEDLIPS	DEEINPSU UNESPIED	DEEIQRTU REQUITED	DEELMOSU DUELSOME
DEEILPST EPISTLED	DEEINQRU ENQUIRED	DEEIQRUV QUIVERED	DEELMPSU DEPLUMES
DEEILPSU EPULIDES	INQUERED	DEEIQTUU QUIETUDE	DEELMRUY DEMURELY
DEEILPSY SPEEDILY	DEEINRRT INTERRED	DEEIRRSS DERRISES	DEELNOOS LOOSENED
DEEILRSU LEISURED	TRENDIER	DESIRERS	DEELNOLT REDOLENT
DEEILRSV DELIVERS	DEEINRRV REDRIVEN	DRESSIER	DEELNORV OVERLEND
DESILVER	DEEINRST INSERTED	RESIDERS	DEELNOSS LESSONED
SILVERED	RESIDENT	DEEIRRST DESTRIER	DEELNOSU ENSOULED
SLIVERED	SINTERED	DEEIRRSU RUDERIES	DEELNOSY ESLOYNED
DEEILRSW WIELDERS	TRENDIES	DEEIRRSV REDRIVES	DEELNPRS RESPLEND
DEEILRSY YIELDERS	DEEINRSU UREDINES	DEEIRRTV VERDITER	DEELNPST SPLENTED
DEEILRTT LITTERED	DEEINRSV INVERSED	DEEIRRWW WIREDREW	DEELNRTU UNDERLET
RETITLED	DEEINRSW WIDENERS	DEEIRRZZ RIZZERED	DEELNRTY TENDERLY
DEEILRVY DELIVERY	DEEINRSX INDEXERS	DEEIRSST EDITRESS	DEELNSSW LEWDNESS
DEEILSSS IDLESSES	DEEINRTU REUNITED	RESISTED	DEELNSTY ENSTYLED
DEEILSST TIDELESS	DEEINRTV INVERTED	SISTERED	DEELOORT RETOOLED
DEEILSSV DEVILESS	DEEINRTW WINTERED	DEEIRSSU DIURESES	DEELOPPR LOPPERED
DEEILSTU DILUTEES	DEEINRTX DEXTRINE	REISSUED	DEELOPRS DEPLORES
DEEILSTV DEVILETS	DEEINSST DESTINES	RESIDUES	DEELOPRX EXPLODER
DEEILSUV DELUSIVE	DEEINSSV VENDISES	DEEIRSSV DEVISERS	EXPLORED
DEEILTUY YULETIDE	DEEINSSW DEWINESS	DISSERVE	DEELOPRY REDEPLOY
DEEIMMNS ENDEMISM	WIDENESS	DISSEVER	DEELOPSV DEVELOPS
DEEIMMRS IMMERSED	DEEINSTT DINETTES	DIVERSES	DEELOPSX EXPLODES
SIMMERED	DEEINSTU DETINUES	DEEIRSTT TIREDEST	DEELORRS SOLDERER
DEEIMMSS MISDEEMS	DEEINSTV EVIDENTS	DEEIRSTU ERUDITES	DEELORSU URODELES
DEEIMNOR DOMINEER	INVESTED	SURETIED	DEELORSV RESOLVED
DEEIMNOS DEMONISE	DEEINSUZ UNSEIZED	DEEIRSTW WEIRDEST	DEELORTT DOTTEREL
DEEIMNOZ DEMONIZE	DEEINTUV DUVETINE	DEEIRTTT TITTERED	TOLTERED
DEEIMNPT PEDIMENT	DEEINUVW UNVIEWED	DEEIRTTV RIVETTED	DEELORTV REVOLTED
DEEIMNRR REMINDER	DEEIOPRT PERIDOTE	DEEIRTTW WITTERED	DEELORTY DELETORY
DEEIMNRV VERMINED	DEEIOPRX PEROXIDE	DEEISSSU DISEUSES	DEELORUV LOUVERED
DEEIMNSS DESMINES	DEEIOPSS EPISODES	DEEISTTV VIDETTES	DEELORVV REVOLVED
SIDESMEN	DEEIOPST EPIDOTES	DEEJKNTU JUNKETED	DEELOSSU DELOUSES
DEEIMNST DEMENTIS	POETISED	DEEJPRRU PERJURED	DEELOSTV DOVELETS
SEDIMENT	DEEIOPSX EPOXIDES	DEEJPTTU UPJETTED	DEELOSVV DEVOLVES
DEEIMNTT MITTENED	DEEIOPTZ POETIZED	DEEKLNOS SLOKENED	DEELOTUV EVOLUTED
DEEIMOST TEDISOME	DEEIORRV OVERRIDE	DEEKLNST SKLENTED	DEELPPRU REPULPED
DEEIMPRR PERIDERM	DEEIORSV OVERSIDE	DEEKLRSS SKELDERS	DEELPRSS SPELDERS
REPRIMED	DEEIORTU ETOURDIE	DEEKMNOY MONKEYED	DEELPRSU PRELUDES
DEEIMPRS DEMIREPS	DEEIOTVX VIDEOTEX	DEEKNNNU UNKENNED	REPULSED
PREMISED	DEEIPPQU EQUIPPED	DEEKNOTW KNOTWEED	DEELPRTU DRUPELET
SIMPERED	DEEIPPRZ ZIPPERED	DEEKNOTY KEYNOTED	DEELPRUV PULVERED
DEEIMPRX PREMIXED	DEEIPPST PEPTIDES	DEEKORRW REWORKED	DEELPSUX DUPLEXES
DEEIMPSS SEMIPEDS	PEPTISED	DEEKRUVY KURVEYED	EXPULSED
DEEIMRSS DERMISES	DEEIPPTT PIPETTED	DEELLMOR MODELLER	DEELPTTY PETTEDLY
DEEIMRST DEMERITS	DEEIPPTZ PEPTIZED	DEELLMOW MELLOWED	DEELRSTU LUSTERED
DEMISTER	DEEIPQRU REPIQUED	DEELLNOP POLLENED	RESULTED
DIMETERS	DEEIPQTU PIQUETED	DEELLNOR ENROLLED	ULSTERED
MISTERED	DEEIPRRS REPRISED	DEELLORW ROWELLED	DEELRSTW LEWDSTER
DEEIMRTT REMITTED	RESPIRED	DEELLORY YODELLER	WRESTLED

DEELRSTY RESTYLED	DEENRRTU RETURNED	DEERRTTU TURRETED	DEFIILNS INFIDELS
DEEMMORS MESODERM	DEENRSSU RUDENESS	DEERRTUX EXTRUDER	INFIELDS
DEEMMRRU DUMMERER	DEENRSTU DENTURES	DEERSSST DESSERTS	DEFIILRW WILDFIRE
DEEMMRSU SUMMERED	SEDERUNT	STRESSED	DEFIILSU FLUIDISE
DEEMNNRU UNDERMEN	UNDERSET	DEERSSSU DURESSES	DEFIILTY FIDELITY
DEEMNNTU TENENDUM	UNDESERT	DEERSSTU RUSSETED	DEFIILUZ FLUIDIZE
DEEMNOOS MOONSEED	DEENRSUU UNDERUSE	DEERSSTY DYESTERS	DEFIIMNO OMNIFIED
DEEMNOQU QUEENDOM	DEENRSUV UNVERSED	DEERSSUV SUVERSED	DEFIIMNU MUNIFIED
DEEMNORR MODERNER	DEENRTUV VENTURED	DEERSTUV VESTURED	DEFIIMOR MODIFIER
DEEMNORS SERMONED	DEENSSSY SYNDESES	DEERSTUX EXTRUDES	DEFIIMOS MODIFIES
DEEMNORT ENTODERM	DEENSTTU UNTESTED	DEERSUVW SURVEWED	DEFIIMRS MISFIRED
DEEMNOSS DEMONESS	DEENTTUW UNWETTED	DEERSUVY SURVEYED	DEFIIMSS FIDEISMS
ENMOSSED	DEENTUVY DUVETYNE	DEERTTUX TEXTURED	DEFIIMSW MIDWIFES
DEEMNOUY EUDEMONY	DEEOORRV OVERDOER	DEFFHILW WHIFFLED	DEFIINOT NOTIFIED
DEEMOORT ODOMETER	OVERRODE	DEFFHLSU SHUFFLED	DEFIINTU FINITUDE
DEEMOPPY POMPEYED	DEEOORSV OVERDOES	DEFFHORS SHROFFED	DEFIINTY IDENTIFY
DEEMOPRV PREMOVED	OVERDOSE	DEFFILNS SNIFFLED	DEFIIOSS OSSIFIED
DEEMOPST DEEPMOST	DEEOPPST ESTOPPED	DEFFILOV FIVEFOLD	DEFIIOTV VIDEOFIT
DEEMOQRU QUEERDOM	DEEOPRRR PREORDER	DEFFIORS OFFSIDER	DEFIIPRU PURIFIED
DEEMORST MODESTER	DEEOPRRS PEDREROS	DEFFIOSS OFFSIDES	DEFIIPSS FISSIPED
DEEMORSX EXODERMS	DEEOPRRT REPORTED	DEFFIRSU DIFFUSER	DEFIIPTY TYPIFIED
DEEMORTU MOUTERED	DEEOPRRV REPROVED	DEFFISSU DIFFUSES	DEFIIRRT DRIFTIER
UDOMETER	DEEOPRSS DEPOSERS	DEFFISUX SUFFIXED	DEFILLNU UNFILLED
DEEMPRST DEMPSTER	DEEOPRST POSTERED	DEFFLNSU SNUFFLED	DEFILLPU UPFILLED
DEEMPRSU PRESUMED	REEDSTOP	DEFFLRTU TRUFFLED	DEFILMNU FULMINED
DEEMPRTU PERMUTED	REPOSTED	DEFFNORS FORFENDS	UNFILMED
DEEMRRRU DEMURRER	DEEOPRTT POTTERED	DEFFSSUU SUFFUSED	DEFILNNO NINEFOLD
MURDERER	REPOTTED	DEFFSTUY DYESTUFF	DEFILNRS FLINDERS
DEEMRSTU DEMUREST	DEEOPRTW POWTERED	DEFGGILN FLEDGING	DEFILNRU UNRIFLED
MUSTERED	DEEOPRTX EXPORTED	DEFGHILT FLIGHTED	URNFIELD
DEEMRTTU MUTTERED	DEEOPRUZ DOUZEPER	DEFGHIRT FRIGHTED	DEFILNRY FRIENDLY
DEEMSSTY SYSTEMED	DEEOPSST POSSETED	DEFGIILN DEFILING	DEFILOPR PROFILED
DEENNNOP PENNONED	DEEOPSSU ESPOUSED	FIELDING	DEFILORU FLUORIDE
DEENNNPU UNPENNED	DEEOQRTU REQUOTED	DEFGIILU UGLIFIED	DEFILORR FLORIDER
DEENNOPT DEPONENT	ROQUETED	DEFGIINN DEFINING	DEFILOTU OUTFIELD
DEENNOPU UNOPENED	DEEORRRS ORDERERS	DEFGIINY DEIFYING	DEFILPRU PRIDEFUL
DEENNORS ENDERONS	REORDERS	EDIFYING	DEFILPTU UPLIFTED
DEENNORW RENOWNED	DEEORRRV VERDEROR	DEFGIIRR FRIGIDER	DEFILRRU FLURRIED
DEENNOSS DONENESS	DEEORRST RESORTED	DEFGILNU INGULFED	DEFILRVY FERVIDLY
DEENNOST SONNETED	RESTORED	DEFGILTY GIFTEDLY	DEFILRZZ FRIZZLED
DEENNOSY DOYENNES	ROSTERED	DEFGINSU DEFUSING	DEFIMNOR INFORMED
DEENNPST PENDENTS	DEEORRSV OVERREDS	FEUDINGS	DEFIMORY REMODIFY
DEENNRTU UNTENDER	DEEORRTT RETORTED	DEFGINTU UNGIFTED	DEFIMRRU DRUMFIRE
DEENNRUV UNNERVED	DEEORRTU REROUTED	DEFGINUZ DEFUZING	DEFINNRU REINFUND
DEENNSSU NUDENESS	RETOURED	DEFGIOOW GOODWIFE	UNFRIEND
UNSENSED	DEEORRVW OVERDREW	DEFGIORS FIREDOGS	DEFINOPR FORPINED
DEENNSTU UNNESTED	DEEORSST OERSTEDS	DEFGJORU FORJUDGE	DEFINORW FOREWIND
DEENNTTU UNNETTED	DEEORSTT ROSETTED	DEFGNORU UNFORGED	DEFINSTU UNSIFTED
UNTENTED	TETRODES	DEFGOOSX DOGFOXES	DEFINTTU UNFITTED
DEENNTUV UNVENTED	DEEORSTX DEXTROSE	DEFHIIMU HUMIFIED	DEFIOORW FIREWOOD
DEENOORT ENROOTED	DEEORSTY STOREYED	DEFHIINS FIENDISH	DEFIOPRT PROFITED
DEENOORV OVERDONE	DEEORSUV OVERUSED	FINISHED	DEFIORSU FOUDRIES
DEENOORW WOODENER	DEEORSVY OVERDYES	DEFHILLO LIFEHOLD	DEFIOTXY DETOXIFY
DEENOPRR PONDERER	DEEORTTT TOTTERED	DEFHILSS DISFLESH	DEFIRRST DRIFTERS
DEENOPSS SPONDEES	DEEORTTX EXTORTED	DEFHINSU UNFISHED	DEFIRSSU FISSURED
DEENOPST PENTODES	DEEORTUV DEVOUTER	DEFHIOOW WIFEHOOD	DEFISSTU FEUDISTS
DEENORRS ENDORSER	DEEOSSUX EXODUSES	DEFHLOOS ELFHOODS	DEFKLORY FORKEDLY
DEENORRW WONDERER	DEEOSTUW OUTWEEDS	SELFHOOD	DEFLLOOR FOLDEROL
DEENORSS ENDORSES	DEEOSTUX TUXEDOES	DEFHLOSU FLOUSHED	DEFLLOOW FOLLOWED
DEENORST ERODENTS	DEEPPRSU SUPPERED	DEFHOOOR FORHOOED	DEFLMPRU FRUMPLED
DEENORSW ENDOWERS	DEEPRRSU PERDURES	DEFHOORS SERFHOOD	DEFLNOOU UNFOOLED
WORSENED	DEEPRRVY REPRYVED	DEFHOORW FORHOWED	DEFLNOPS PENFOLDS
DEENORTU DEUTERON	DEEPRSTU PERTUSED	DEFIIILV VILIFIED	DEFLNORS FONDLERS
DEENOSSS ENDOSSES	DEEPRSUW PURSEWED	DEFIIIMN MINIFIED	FORLENDS
DEENOSST STENOSED	DEEPRSUY PSEUDERY	DEFIIINS NIDIFIES	DEFLNORU FLOUNDER
DEENPPRS PERPENDS	DEEPRTTU PUTTERED	DEFIIIVV VIVIFIED	UNFOLDER
DEENPRSS SPENDERS	DEEPRUVY PURVEYED	DEFIILLN INFILLED	DEFLNRUU UNFURLED
DEENPRST PRETENDS	DEERRSSU DRESSERS	DEFIILLP FILLIPED	DEFLNSSU FUNDLESS
DEENRRSU ENDURERS	DEERRSUV VERDURES	DEFIILLW WILDLIFE	DEFLOORS FORSLOED
SUNDERER		DEFIILMS MISFILED	DEFLOORT FORETOLD

DEFLOORV	OVERFOLD	DEGHIORU	DOUGHIER
DEFLOOSS	FOODLESS	DEGHIPST	DESPIGHT
DEFLOPUW	UPFLOWED		SPIGHTED
DEFLORSU	FOULDERS	DEGHIQTU	QUIGHTED
DEFLPRUU	UPFURLED	DEGHITTW	TWIGHTED
DEFLRSUU	SULFURED	DEGHLNOR	HORNGELD
DEFMNORU	UNFORMED	DEGHLOOS	DOGHOLES
DEFMOOOR	FOREDOOM		GOLOSHED
DEFMORSS	SERFDOMS		SHOOGLED
DEFNNORT	FRONDENT	DEGHLOPU	PLOUGHED
DEFNNOSS	FONDNESS	DEGHLOSU	SLOUGHED
DEFNOORS	FRONDOSE	DEGHMOSU	GUMSHOED
DEFNOORU	UNROOFED	DEGHMPRU	GRUMPHED
DEFNOORV	OVERFOND	DEGHNORT	THRONGED
DEFNOOTU	UNFOOTED	DEGHNORY	HYDROGEN
DEFNOPRS	FORSPEND	DEGHORRS	DROGHERS
DEFNORRU	FRONDEUR	DEGHPSUU	UPGUSHED
DEFNORSU	FOUNDERS	DEGIIIRS	RIGIDISE
	REFOUNDS	DEGIIIRZ	RIGIDIZE
DEFNORTU	FORTUNED	DEGIIIST	DIGITISE
DEFNOSSW	DOWFNESS	DEGIIITZ	DIGITIZE
DEFNRRUU	UNDERFUR	DEGIILNR	GRIDELIN
	UNFURRED	DEGIILNS	EILDINGS
DEFNRTUU	UNTURFED		SIDELING
DEFOORRW	FOREWORD	DEGIILNT	DILIGENT
DEFOOTUX	OUTFOXED	DEGIILNV	DEVILING
DEFORRUW	FURROWED	DEGIILNW	WIELDING
DEFORSST	DEFROSTS	DEGIILNY	YIELDING
DEFORSTW	FROWSTED	DEGIILTY	GELIDITY
DEGGGIIT	GIGGITED	DEGIIMNP	IMPEDING
DEGGGILN	GLEDGING		IMPINGED
DEGGHINS	HEDGINGS	DEGIIMNS	DEMISING
DEGGHLOS	SHOGGLED	DEGIIMSU	MISGUIDE
DEGGHRSU	SHRUGGED	DEGIINNR	NIDERING
DEGGIINN	DEIGNING	DEGIINNS	DESINING
DEGGILNP	PLEDGING		SDEINING
DEGGILNS	GELDINGS	DEGIINNT	ENDITING
	SLEDGING		INDIGENT
	SNIGGLED		TEINDING
DEGGILNU	DELUGING	DEGIINNW	INDEWING
DEGGILRW	WRIGGLED		WIDENING
DEGGINNU	UNEDGING	DEGIINNX	INDEXING
DEGGINRU	UNRIGGED	DEGIINNZ	DIZENING
DEGGINSW	WEDGINGS	DEGIINOS	INDIGOES
DEGGINUW	UNWIGGED	DEGIINOV	VIDEOING
DEGGIORS	DISGORGE	DEGIINRS	DESIRING
DEGGIOST	DOGGIEST		RESIDING
DEGGIPRS	SPRIGGED		RINGSIDE
DEGGIRST	STRIGGED	DEGIINRT	DIRIGENT
DEGGLMSU	SMUGGLED	DEGIINRV	DERIVING
DEGGLNSU	SNUGGLED		VIRGINED
DEGGLORS	DOGGRELS	DEGIINRW	WEIRDING
DEGGLRUY	RUGGEDLY	DEGIINST	DINGIEST
DEGGNORU	UNGORGED		INDIGEST
DEGGNOSU	GUDGEONS	DEGIINSV	DEVISING
DEGGRRSU	DRUGGERS	DEGIIRST	RIDGIEST
DEGGRSTU	DRUGGETS		RIGIDEST
DEGHIILL	GHILLIED	DEGIISSU	DISGUISE
DEGHIINS	DINGHIES	DEGIJMSU	MISJUDGE
DEGHIKNT	KNIGHTED	DEGIKKNO	DEKKOING
DEGHILNS	HINDLEGS	DEGIKLNU	DUKELING
	SHINGLED	DEGIKNNU	UNKINGED
DEGHILOU	OUGHLIED	DEGILLNU	DUELLING
DEGHILPT	PLIGHTED	DEGILLNW	DWELLING
DEGHILST	DELIGHTS	DEGILMPS	GLIMPSED
	SLIGHTED	DEGILNNO	OLDENING
DEGHINNS	SHENDING	DEGILNNS	LENDINGS
DEGHINNU	UNHINGED	DEGILNOP	DIPLOGEN
DEGHIOOS	SHOOGIED	DEGILNOS	GLENOIDS
DEGHIOPS	DOGESHIP		SIDELONG
DEGILNPS	SPELDING	DEGINSTU	DUNGIEST
DEGILNRU	INDULGER	DEGINTTU	DUETTING
DEGILNRY	YELDRING	DEGIOORS	GOODSIRE
DEGILNSU	INDULGES	DEGIOOST	GOODIEST
DEGILNSV	DEVLINGS	DEGIOPRR	PORRIDGE
DEGILNSW	SWINGLED	DEGIOPSS	GOSSIPED
	WELDINGS	DEGIOPST	PODGIEST
DEGILNWY	WINGEDLY	DEGIORRU	GOURDIER
DEGILOOR	GOODLIER	DEGIORST	STODGIER
DEGILOOY	IDEOLOGY	DEGIPSTU	PUDGIEST
DEGILOST	GODLIEST	DEGIQSSU	SQUIDGES
	GOLDIEST	DEGIRSTU	DURGIEST
DEGILOSZ	GOLDSIZE	DEGISSST	DISGESTS
DEGILPSU	PULSIDGE	DEGJMNTU	JUDGMENT
DEGILRRS	GIRDLERS	DEGLLNOY	GOLDENLY
DEGILRSU	GUILDERS	DEGLLOOP	GOLLOPED
	SLUDGIER	DEGLLOSS	GOLDLESS
DEGILRSW	WERGILDS	DEGLMNOT	LODGMENT
DEGILRZZ	GRIZZLED	DEGLMOOY	DEMOLOGY
DEGILSUV	DIVULGES	DEGLNOUV	UNGLOVED
DEGIMNNS	MENDINGS	DEGLNRTU	GRUNTLED
DEGIMNOS	SMIDGEON	DEGLOOPY	PEDOLOGY
DEGIMNOT	DEMOTING	DEGLOOUU	DUOLOGUE
DEGIMNPU	IMPUGNED	DEGLOPRS	PLEDGORS
DEGIMNRU	DEMURING	DEGLOPSS	SPLODGES
DEGIMNSS	SMIDGENS	DEGLPRSU	SPLURGED
DEGIMOOT	GOODTIME	DEGMMNUU	UNGUMMED
DEGIMOOY	GEOMYOID	DEGMRSSU	SMUDGERS
DEGIMRSU	SMUDGIER	DEGNNORU	GROUNDEN
DEGINNNU	UNENDING	DEGNNOSU	DUNGEONS
DEGINNOP	DEPONING	DEGNNOUW	UNGOWNED
DEGINNOT	DENOTING	DEGNOORS	DRONGOES
DEGINNOW	ENDOWING	DEGNOOSS	GOODNESS
DEGINNOZ	DOZENING	DEGNOOST	STEGODON
DEGINNPS	SPENDING	DEGNOPPU	OPPUGNED
DEGINNRT	TRENDING	DEGNORRU	GROUNDER
DEGINNRU	ENDURING		REGROUND
	UNRINGED	DEGNORSU	GUERDONS
DEGINNSS	SENDINGS	DEGNORTU	TRUDGEON
DEGINNST	STENDING	DEGNORUU	UNROUGED
DEGINNSU	UNSIGNED	DEGNORYY	GYRODYNE
DEGINNSY	DESYNING	DEGNPRUU	UNPURGED
DEGINNTU	UNTINGED	DEGNRSTU	TRUDGENS
DEGINNUW	UNWINGED	DEGORSST	STODGERS
DEGINOPR	PROIGNED	DEGORSTU	DROGUETS
DEGINOPS	DEPOSING	DEGPRSUU	UPSURGED
	DISPONGE	DEGRRSTU	TRUDGERS
	PIDGEONS	DEHHILTW	WITHHELD
DEGINORR	ORDERING	DEHHISTW	WHISHTED
DEGINORS	NEGROIDS	DEHHMRTY	RHYTHMED
DEGINORU	GUERIDON	DEHHOOSW	WHOOSHED
DEGINORV	DOVERING	DEHIILLS	HILLSIDE
DEGINORW	DOWERING	DEHIILLW	WHILLIED
DEGINOSW	WENDIGOS	DEHIILSV	DEVILISH
	WIDGEONS	DEHIIMMS	SHIMMIED
DEGINOTV	DEVOTING	DEHIIMNS	MINISHED
DEGINPRS	SPRINGED	DEHIIMRU	MUDIRIEH
DEGINPRY	PREDYING	DEHIIMST	DITHEISM
DEGINPSU	DISPUNGE		SMITHIED
DEGINPTU	DEPUTING	DEHIINNS	SHINNIED
DEGINRRS	GRINDERS	DEHIINNW	WHINNIED
	REGRINDS	DEHIINSS	SHINDIES
DEGINRRY	GRINDERY	DEHIIRRW	WHIRRIED
DEGINRSS	DRESSING	DEHIIRST	DISHERIT
DEGINRST	STRINGED	DEHIISST	DISHIEST
DEGINRSW	REDWINGS	DEHIISTT	DITHEIST
DEGINRSY	SYNERGID		STITHIED
	SYRINGED	DEHIJMNO	DEMIJOHN
DEGINSSU	DINGUSES	DEHIKMOS	SHEIKDOM
DEGINSSW	SWINDGES	DEHIKPSU	DUKESHIP

DEHILLOP	PHELLOID	DEHMMRTU	THRUMMED
DEHILLRS	SHRILLED	DEHMNOOY	HOMODYNE
DEHILLRT	THRILLED	DEHMNRUY	UNRHYMED
DEHILMOS	DEMOLISH	DEHMOORW	WHOREDOM
DEHILMPW	WHIMPLED	DEHMOOSS	SHMOOSED
DEHILMSS	DISHELMS	DEHMOOST	SMOOTHED
DEHILMTY	DIMETHYL	DEHMOOSZ	SHMOOZED
DEHILNOR	INHOLDER	DEHMOPRY	HYPODERM
DEHILNPY	DIPHENYL	DEHMORUU	HUMOURED
DEHILOOR	HELIODOR	DEHNNTUU	UNHUNTED
DEHILOOS	DHOOLIES	DEHNOOPU	UNHOOPED
DEHILOPS	POLISHED	DEHNOORU	HONOURED
DEHILPSU	SULPHIDE	DEHNOOSW	HOEDOWNS
DEHILPSY	SYLPHIDE	DEHNOPSY	SYPHONED
DEHILRTW	WRITHLED	DEHNORSU	ENSHROUD

DEIIMMRS DIMERISM ... DEIISSTT DIETISTS

DEHILSTW	WHISTLED		UNHORSED
DEHILTTW	WHITTLED	DEHNORSY	ENHYDROS
DEHIMNOS	HEDONISM	DEHNORTY	THRENODY
DEHIMORS	HEIRDOMS	DEHNOSTZ	DOZENTHS
DEHIMOSS	DISHOMES	DEHNOSUU	UNHOUSED
DEHIMPRS	SHRIMPED	DEHNRSTU	THUNDERS
DEHIMPSY	DEMYSHIP	DEHNRTUY	THUNDERY
DEHIMSTU	HUMIDEST	DEHOOOPP	POPEHOOD
DEHIMSTY	MYTHISED	DEHOOPRT	THEROPOD
DEHIMTYZ	MYTHIZED	DEHOOSSW	SWOOSHED
DEHINOOP	INHOOPED	DEHOPRST	POTSHERD
DEHINOPR	NEPHROID	DEHORRST	REDSHORT
DEHINOPS	DIPHONES	DEHORTUY	OUTHYRED
	SIPHONED	DEHOSSTU	STOUSHED
	SPHENOID	DEHPRSSU	SPRUSHED
DEHINORS	HORDEINS	DEHPRSUU	UPRUSHED
DEHINOST	HEDONIST	DEHRSTTU	THRUSTED
DEHINPSS	ENDSHIPS	DEIIIMST	DIMITIES
DEHINPSU	PUNISHED	DEIIINSV	DIVINISE
DEHINSUW	UNWISHED	DEIIINVZ	DIVINIZE
DEHIOOVW	WIVEHOOD	DEIIIRSS	IRIDISES
DEHIOPRS	SPHEROID	DEIIIRSZ	IRIDIZES
DEHIOPRT	TROPHIED	DEIIIRTV	VIRIDITE
DEHIORRR	HORRIDER	DEIIISVV	DIVISIVE
DEHIORSS	DISHORSE	DEIIKLMS	MISLIKED
	HIDROSES	DEIIKLNR	KINDLIER
DEHIORTU	OUTHIRED	DEIIKLNS	DISLIKEN
DEHIORTW	WORTHIED	DEIIKLNV	DEVILKIN
DEHIORTY	THYREOID	DEIIKLSS	DISLIKES
DEHIOSSU	DISHOUSE	DEIIKNST	DINKIEST
DEHIOSTU	HIDEOUTS	DEIILLMP	MILLIPED
DEHIPSSU	PSEUDISH	DEIILLMT	TIDEMILL
DEHIQSSU	SQUISHED	DEIILLST	DILLIEST
DEHIRRSU	DHURRIES	DEIILMPR	DIMPLIER
DEHIRSTT	THIRSTED	DEIILMRU	DELIRIUM
	THRISTED	DEIILMST	DELIMITS
DEHIRTWW	WITHDREW		LIMITED
DEHKLNOU	ELKHOUND	DEIILMSV	DEVILISM
DEHKNOOU	UNHOOKED		MISLIVED
DEHKNSUU	UNHUSKED	DEIILNNU	INDULINE
DEHLLOOW	HOLLOWED	DEIILNOS	LIONISED
DEHLLOPY	PHYLLODE	DEIILNOZ	LIONIZED
DEHLMMOW	WHOMMLED	DEIILNPV	VILIPEND
DEHLMMUW	WHUMMLED	DEIILNVY	DIVINELY
DEHLMORY	HYDROMEL	DEIILORS	IDOLISER
DEHLOORV	HOLDOVER	DEIILORZ	IDOLIZER
	OVERHOLD	DEIILOSS	IDOLISES
DEHLOOSS	HOODLESS	DEIILOSZ	IDOLIZES
DEHLOPRU	UPHOLDER	DEIILPRT	TRIPLIED
DEHLOPSS	SPLOSHED	DEIILRST	REDISTIL
DEHLORSU	SHOULDER	DEIILSTU	UTILISED
DEHLPRUU	UPHURLED	DEIILSTV	LIVIDEST
DEHLRRSU	HURDLERS	DEIILTUY	TUILYIED
DEHLRSWY	SHREWDLY	DEIILTUZ	TUILZIED
DEHLSTTU	SHUTTLED		UTILIZED

DEIIMMRS	DIMERISM	DEIISSTT	DIETISTS
DEIIMMST	MISTIMED	DEIISTVV	VIVIDEST
DEIIMMTT	IMMITTED	DEIISTZZ	DIZZIEST
DEIIMNOS	DOMINIES	DEIJNORS	JOINDERS
DEIIMNRT	DIRIMENT	DEIJNSSU	DISJUNES
DEIIMNTU	MUTINIED	DEIKKLNO	KLONDIKE
DEIIMPRU	PERIDIUM	DEIKLLSS	DESKILLS
DEIIMSST	MISDIETS	DEIKLMMS	SKLIMMED
DEIIMSTT	TIMIDEST	DEIKLMNU	UNMILKED
DEIIMSVW	MIDWIVES	DEIKLNNU	UNLINKED
DEIINNOP	PINIONED	DEIKLNRS	KINDLERS
DEIINNPP	PINNIPED	DEIKLNRW	WRINKLED
DEIINNTW	INTWINED	DEIKLNSS	KINDLESS
DEIINNUV	UNDIVINE	DEIKLNTW	TWINKLED
DEIINORS	DERISION	DEIKLSTT	SKITTLED
	IRONISED	DEIKMOSY	MISYOKED
	RESINOID	DEIKMPRS	SKRIMPED
DEIINORZ	IRONIZED	DEIKNNPU	UNPINKED
DEIINOST	EDITIONS	DEIKNNRU	UNKINDER
	SEDITION	DEIKNNSS	KINDNESS
DEIINOSV	VISIONED	DEIKNORV	OVERKIND
DEIINPPW	WINDPIPE	DEIKNORW	INWORKED
DEIINPRS	INSPIRED	DEIKNRRS	DRINKERS
DEIINPRT	INTREPID	DEIKNRSS	REDSKINS
DEIINPRY	PYRIDINE	DEIKNSSU	UNKISSED
DEIINPTU	UNPITIED	DEIKORSS	DROSKIES
DEIINQRU	INQUIRED	DEIKOSSY	DISYOKES
DEIINQSU	QUINSIED	DEIKPRSU	SPRUIKED
	SQUINIED	DEIKRRSU	SKURRIED
DEIINRSS	INDRISES	DEIKSSTU	DUSKIEST
	INSIDERS	DEILLMNU	UNMILLED
DEIINRST	DISINTER	DEILLNSW	INDWELLS
	INDITERS	DEILLNTU	UNTILLED
	NITRIDES	DEILLNUW	UNWILLED
	RINDIEST	DEILLOOV	LIVELOOD
DEIINRSU	DISINURE	DEILLOPW	PILLOWED
	URIDINES	DEILLORR	LORDLIER
DEIINRSV	DIVINERS	DEILLORS	DOLLIERS
DEIINRTU	UNTIDIER	DEILLOSV	LIVELODS
DEIINSST	INSISTED	DEILLOWW	WILLOWED
	TIDINESS	DEILLRRS	DRILLERS
DEIINSTU	DISUNITE	DEILLRSV	DREVILLS
	NUDITIES	DEILLSTU	DUELLIST
	UNITISED		DULLIEST
	UNTIDIES	DEILMNOO	MELODION
DEIINSTV	DIVINEST	DEILMNSS	MILDNESS
DEIINSTW	WINDIEST		MINDLESS
DEIINTTU	INTUITED	DEILMNSU	MUSLINED
DEIINTTY	IDENTITY	DEILMOOT	DOLOMITE
DEIINTUZ	UNITIZED	DEILMOPR	IMPLORED
DEIIOPRS	PRESIDIO		IMPOLDER
DEIIOPRT	DIPTEROI	DEILMOPS	IMPLODES
DEIIOPZZ	PEZIZOID	DEILMORU	LEMUROID
DEIIORST	DIORITES		MOULDIER
DEIIORSX	OXIDISER	DEILMOST	MELODIST
DEIIORTX	TRIOXIDE	DEILMOSU	EMULSOID
DEIIORTY	IODYRITE	DEILMPPU	PLUMIPED
DEIIORXZ	OXIDIZER	DEILMPSU	DISPLUME
DEIIOSSX	OXIDISES	DEILMPTU	MULTIPED
DEIIOSXZ	OXIDIZES	DEILMRRU	DRUMLIER
DEIIPPRR	DRIPPIER	DEILMRSU	MISRULED
DEIIPPST	DIPPIEST	DEILMSSY	DEMISSLY
DEIIPRST	RIPTIDES	DEILNNOT	INDOLENT
	SPIRITED	DEILNOOS	SOLENOID
DEIIPRSZ	DISPRIZE	DEILNORS	DISENROL
DEIIPTTY	TEPIDITY	DEILNOSS	SONDELIS
DEIIQSTU	DISQUIET	DEILNOSU	DELUSION
DEIIRRSU	DIURESIS		INSOULED
DEIIRSTT	DIRTIEST		UNSOILED
	TRITIDES	DEILNOTU	OUTLINED

DEILNOVV	INVOLVED	DEIMNOST	DEMONIST
DEILNPRS	SPELDRIN	DEIMNOTW	DOWNTIME
DEILNPRU	UNDERLIP	DEIMNPRU	UNPRIMED
DEILNPSS	SPELDINS	DEIMNPSS	MISSPEND
	SPINDLES	DEIMNPTU	IMPUDENT
DEILNPST	SPLINTED	DEIMNRTU	RUDIMENT
DEILNRSS	RINDLESS	DEIMNSSS	MISSENDS
DEILNRST	SNIRTLED	DEIMNSST	MINDSETS
	TENDRILS	DEIMNSSU	UNMISSED
	TRINDLES	DEIMNSSW	MISWENDS
DEILNRSW	SWINDLER	DEIMNSTU	MISTUNED
DEILNSSV	VILDNESS	DEIMOORS	MOIDORES
DEILNSSW	SWINDLES	DEIMOOSS	SODOMIES
	WILDNESS		SODOMISE
	WINDLESS	DEIMOOST	DOOMIEST
DEILNSTU	DILUENTS		MOODIEST
	INSULTED		SODOMITE
	UNLISTED	DEIMOOSZ	SODOMIZE
DEILNTTU	UNTITLED	DEIMOPRS	PROMISED
DEILNTUY	UNITEDLY	DEIMOPRT	IMPORTED
DEILNUWY	UNWIELDY	DEIMOPRV	IMPROVED
DEILOOPS	POOLSIDE	DEIMORRR	MIRRORED
DEILOPPY	POLYPIDE	DEIMORRS	MISORDER
DEILOPRU	PRELUDIO		MORRISED
DEILOPSS	DESPOILS	DEIMORSS	MISDOERS
	SOLIPEDS	DEIMORST	MORTISED
DEILOQRU	LIQUORED	DEIMORSU	DIMEROUS
DEILORSS	SOLDIERS		ERODIUMS
DEILORST	STOLIDER		SOREDIUM
DEILORSU	SOULDIER	DEIMORUX	EXORDIUM
DEILORSY	SOLDIERY	DEIMOSST	MODISTES
DEILOSST	SOLIDEST	DEIMOSTT	DEMOTIST
DEILOSSV	DISSOLVE	DEIMPRST	DIREMPTS
DEILOSTT	DOILTEST	DEIMPSTU	DUMPIEST
DEILOSTU	SOLITUDE	DEIMQRSU	SQUIRMED
DEILOTUV	OUTLIVED	DEIMRSSU	SURMISED
DEILPPRT	TRIPPLED	DEIMRSUU	RESIDUUM
DEILPPST	STIPPLED	DEINNNOU	INNUENDO
DEILPPSU	SUPPLIED	DEINNNPU	UNPINNED
DEILPPTU	PULPITED	DEINNNSU	NUNDINES
DEILPSTT	SPLITTED	DEINNNTU	UNTINNED
DEILPSTU	STIPULED	DEINNOOT	NOONTIDE
DEILPSUY	SPULYIED	DEINNORS	ENDIRONS
DEILPSUZ	SPULZIED	DEINNORU	UNIRONED
DEILPTTU	UPTILTED	DEINNOWW	WINNOWED
DEILRSTU	DILUTERS	DEINNPRU	UNDERPIN
	LURIDEST	DEINNRUU	UNINURED
DEILRSVY	DIVERSLY	DEINNRUV	UNDRIVEN
DEILRSZZ	DRIZZLES	DEINNSTU	DUNNIEST
DEILRTVY	DEVILTRY		DUNNITES
DEILSSTY	DISTYLES	DEINNTUW	UNTWINED
	STYLISED	DEINOOPS	POISONED
DEILSTUY	SEDULITY	DEINOOSZ	OZONISED
DEILSTYZ	STYLIZED	DEINOOTV	DEVOTION
DEILSWZZ	SWIZZLED	DEINOOZZ	OZONIZED
DEILTWZZ	TWIZZLED	DEINOPPR	PROPINED
DEIMMNOS	DEMONISM	DEINOPPW	DOWNPIPE
DEIMMOST	IMMODEST	DEINOPRS	DISPONER
DEIMMPST	MISDEMPT		POINDERS
DEIMMSTU	DUMMIEST		PRISONED
DEIMNNOS	MISDONNE	DEINOPRV	PROVINED
DEIMNNOU	UNMONIED	DEINOPRY	PYRENOID
DEIMNNSU	MINUENDS	DEINOPSS	DISPONES
DEIMNOOS	DOMINOES		SPINODES
	MONODIES	DEINOPSU	UNPOISED
DEIMNOOT	DEMOTION	DEINOPTW	DEWPOINT
	MOTIONED	DEINORSS	INDORSES
DEIMNOOX	MONOXIDE		SORDINES
DEIMNOPT	PIEDMONT	DEINORSU	DOURINES
DEIMNORT	DORMIENT		

	SOURDINE		WORDIEST
DEINORSW	WINDORES	DEIORSWW	WIDOWERS
	WINDROSE	DEIORTUV	OUTDRIVE
DEINORTT	INTORTED	DEIOSSTU	OUTSIDES
DEINORVW	OVERWIND	DEIOSSTX	EXODISTS
DEINOSST	DONSIEST	DEIOSTTT	DOTTIEST
DEINOSSV	VOIDNESS	DEIOSTUZ	OUTSIZED
DEINOSSZ	DOZINESS	DEIPPRST	STRIPPED
DEINOSTU	OUNDIEST	DEIPRRTU	IRRUPTED
DEINOSTW	DOWNIEST		PUTRIDER
DEINOTTU	DUETTINO	DEIPRSSU	DISPURSE
DEINPPRU	UNRIPPED		SUSPIRED
DEINPPUZ	UNZIPPED	DEIPRSTU	DISPUTER
DEINPRST	SPRINTED		STUPIDER
DEINPRSY	INSPYRED	DEIPSSTU	DISPUTES
DEINPRTU	TURNIPED		PUDSIEST
DEINPRUZ	UNPRIZED	DEIPTTTU	TITTUPED
DEINPSST	STIPENDS	DEIQRRSU	SQUIRRED
DEINQSTU	SQUINTED	DEIQRSTU	SQUIRTED
DEINRRTU	INTRUDER	DEIRRSTU	STURDIER
DEINRSSU	SUNDRIES	DEIRSSST	DISSERTS
DEINRSTT	STRIDENT		DISTRESS
	TRIDENTS	DEIRSSTU	DIESTRUS
DEINRSTU	INTRUDES		DRUSIEST
DEINRSTX	DEXTRINS		STUDIERS
DEINRTUW	UNDERWIT		STURDIES
DEINSSST	DISNESTS	DEIRSSWY	DYSURIES
	DISSENTS	DEIRSTTU	DETRITUS
DEINSSSY	SYNDESIS	DEIRSTUX	DRUXIEST
DEINSSTT	DENTISTS	DEIRSUVV	SURVIVED
DEINSSTU	DISTUNES	DEISSSTU	SUDSIEST
DEINSTUU	UNSUITED	DEISSTTU	DUSTIEST
DEINTTUW	UNWITTED	DEISTTTU	DUETTIST
DEIOOPRR	DROOPIER	DEJLOOOR	JORDELOO
DEIOORSW	WOODSIER	DEJOOPPY	POPJOYED
DEIOOSTW	WOODIEST	DEKKLNOY	KLONDYKE
DEIOOSVV	VOIVODES	DEKLNOOU	UNLOOKED
DEIOOSWW	WOIWODES	DEKLOOPU	UPLOOKED
DEIOPRRV	PROVIDER	DEKLRSSU	SKUDLERS
DEIOPRSS	DISPOSER	DEKLSTTU	SKUTTLED
	DROPSIES	DEKMPRSU	SKRUMPED
DEIOPRST	DIOPTERS	DEKNORUW	UNWORKED
	DIOPTRES	DEKNRSTU	DRUNKEST
	DIPTEROS	DEKNRSUY	UNDERSKY
	PERIDOTS	DEKNSSSU	DUSKNESS
	PROTEIDS	DEKOOPRV	PROVOKED
	RIPOSTED	DEKOOTWW	KOWTOWED
DEIOPRSV	DISPROVE	DELLLOOP	LOLLOPED
	PROVIDES	DELLMOSW	SWELLDOM
DEIOPRSW	DROPWISE	DELLNOPU	UNPOLLED
DEIOPSSS	DISPOSES	DELLNORU	UNROLLED
DEIOPSST	DEPOSITS	DELLNORW	ROWNDELL
	TOPSIDES	DELLNPUU	UNPULLED
DEIORRRT	TORRIDER	DELLNSSU	DULLNESS
DEIORRSS	DROSSIER	DELLOPRS	REDPOLLS
DEIORRSW	DROWSIER	DELLOPRU	UPROLLED
DEIORRSY	DERISORY	DELLOPTU	POLLUTED
DEIORRTU	OUTRIDER	DELLORRY	DROLLERY
DEIORRTW	WORRITED	DELLORSS	LORDLESS
DEIORRZZ	RIZZORED	DELLORST	DROLLEST
DEIORSSS	DOSSIERS		STROLLED
DEIORSST	STEROIDS	DELLOSVW	LOWVELDS
DEIORSSU	DESIROUS	DELLOTUW	OUTDWELL
DEIORSSV	DEVISORS	DELMNOOV	NOVELDOM
DEIORSTT	DORTIEST	DELMNORY	MODERNLY
DEIORSTU	IODURETS	DELMNOSU	UNSELDOM
	OUTRIDES	DELMNOTW	MELTDOWN
	OUTSIDER	DELMNPUU	PENDULUM
	SUITORED		UNPLUMED
DEIORSTW	ROWDIEST	DELMOOSW	ELMWOODS

DELMORSS	SMOLDERS	DEMOOPRS	PREDOOMS
DELMORSU	MOULDERS	DEMOOPRT	PROMOTED
	REMOULDS	DEMOORST	DOOMSTER
	SMOULDER	DEMOORSU	DORMOUSE
DELMOSTY	MODESTLY	DEMOORTY	ODOMETRY
DELMRTUU	MULTURED	DEMOOSTU	OUTMODES
DELMTTUU	TUMULTED	DEMOOTUV	OUTMOVED
DELNOOSU	NODULOSE	DEMOPPRT	PROMPTED
	UNLOOSED	DEMOPSSU	POSSUMED
DELNOOSZ	SNOOZLED	DEMORRUU	RUMOURED
DELNOOWY	WOODENLY	DENNNSUU	UNSUNNED
DELNOPPU	UNLOPPED	DENNORST	TENDRONS
DELNOPRS	SPLENDOR	DENNORSU	ENROUNDS
DELNORSU	LOUNDERS	DENNOTUW	UNWONTED
	NOURSLED	DENNPRUU	UNPRUNED
	ROUNDELS	DENNRRUU	UNDERRUN
	ROUNDLES	DENNRTUU	UNTURNED
	UNSOLDER	DENOOOVW	OVENWOOD
DELNORTU	ROUNDLET	DENOOPPR	PROPONED
DELNORYY	YONDERLY	DENOOPRS	PRODNOSE
DELNOSSU	LOUDNESS	DENOOPSY	POYSONED
DELNOSUU	UNDULOSE	DENOORTU	UNROOTED
	UNSOULED	DENOOSSW	WOODNESS
DELNOSUV	UNSOLVED	DENOOSTU	DUOTONES
DELNPRSU	PLUNDERS	DENOPPRS	PROPENDS
DELNRSTU	RUNDLETS	DENOPRSS	RESPONDS
	TRUNDLES	DENOPRST	PORTENDS
DELNSUZZ	SNUZZLED		PROTENDS
DELOOPPS	PLEOPODS	DENOPRSU	POUNDERS
DELOORRV	OVERLORD	DENOPRSV	PROVENDS
DELOORSS	LORDOSES	DENOPRUV	UNPROVED
DELOORSV	OVERSOLD	DENOPSTU	OUTSPEND
DELOORSW	WOOLDERS		UNPOSTED
DELOORTY	ROOTEDLY	DENOPSTW	STEWPOND
DELOOSSW	WOODLESS	DENOPSUX	EXPOUNDS
DELOPPRS	DROPPLES	DENOQTUU	UNQUOTED
DELOPPST	STOPPLED	DENORRSU	RONDURES
DELOPRST	DROPLETS		ROUNDERS
DELOPRSU	POULDERS		UNORDERS
	POULDRES	DENORRSW	DROWNERS
DELOPSTU	POSTLUDE	DENORRTU	ROTUNDER
DELORSST	OLDSTERS	DENORRUU	ROUNDURE
	STRODLES	DENORSSU	DOURNESS
DELORSSW	WORDLESS		RESOUNDS
DELORSTT	DOTTRELS		SOUNDERS
DELORSUY	DELUSORY	DENORSTU	ROUNDEST
DELOSSUU	SEDULOUS		TONSURED
DELOSTTT	DOTTLEST		UNSORTED
DELOTTUW	OUTDWELT	DENORSUU	UNROUSED
DELOTUVY	DEVOUTLY		UNSOURED
DELRSSTU	STRUDELS	DENORSUW	WOUNDERS
DELSSSTU	DUSTLESS	DENORTTU	UNROTTED
DEMMNOMO	MONOMODE	DENORTUW	UNDERTOW
DEMMNOOS	DOOMSMEN	DENOSSTU	SOUNDEST
DEMMNOSU	SUMMONED	DENOSTUW	UNSTOWED
DEMMNSUU	UNSUMMED	DENOTUUV	UNDEVOUT
DEMMRRSU	DRUMMERS	DENPRSTU	UPTRENDS
DEMMRRUU	MURMURED	DENPRSUU	UNPURSED
DEMMRSTU	STRUMMED	DENPRTUU	UPTURNED
DEMNOOOP	MONOPODE	DENPSSSU	SUSPENDS
DEMNOORU	UNMOORED	DENRRTUU	NURTURED
DEMNOOSW	WOODSMEN	DENRSTTU	STRUNTED
DEMNORST	MORDENTS	DENSSTTU	STUDENTS
DEMNORSW	SWORDMEN	DENSTUVY	DUVETYNS
DEMNORSY	SYNDROME	DEOOORSW	ROSEWOOD
DEMNORUW	UNWORMED	DEOOOSWW	WOODWOSE
DEMNOSTU	DEMOUNTS	DEOOPPRS	PROPOSED
	MUDSTONE	DEOOPPRT	PTEROPOD
DEMOOPPS	POPEDOMS	DEOOPRRV	PROVEDOR
DEMOOPRR	PRODROME		

DEOOPRST	DOORSTEP	DFILNOPS	PINFOLDS
	TORPEDOS	DFIMOOOR	IODOFORM
DEOOPRTU	UPROOTED	DFIMORSS	DISFORMS
DEOOPWWW	POWWOWED	DFINRSUW	WINDSURF
DEOORRSW	SORROWED	DFIOOPRS	DISPROOF
DEOORRVW	OVERWORD	DFLNOOWW	DOWNFLOW
DEOORRWW	OWREWORD	DFNOOPRU	PROFOUND
DEOORTUV	OUTDROVE	DFOOOSTW	SOFTWOOD
DEOOTTUV	OUTVOTED	DGGGIINS	DIGGINGS
DEOPPRRS	DROPPERS	DGGGINOS	DOGGINGS
DEOPPRST	STROPPED	DGGGINRU	DRUGGING
DEOPPRSU	PURPOSED		GRUDGING
DEOPPSSU	SUPPOSED	DGGHIINT	DIGHTING
DEOPRRTU	PROTRUDE	DGGIILNR	GIRDLING
DEOPRSTU	POSTURED		RIDGLING
	PROUDEST	DGGIILNS	GILDINGS
	SPROUTED		GLIDINGS
DEOPRSUU	POURSUED	DGGIINNR	GRINDING
	UPROUSED	DGGIINNW	WINGDING
DEORRSST	RODSTERS	DGGIINRS	GIRDINGS
DEORRSSW	SWORDERS		RIDGINGS
DEORRTTU	TORTURED	DGGIINSU	GUIDINGS
DEORSSTW	WORSTEDS	DGGILNOS	GODLINGS
DEORSSTY	DESTROYS		LODGINGS
DEORSTTU	STROUTED	DGGIMNSU	SMUDGING
DEORSTUU	OUTDURES	DGGINNSU	SNUDGING
DEORSTUV	OVERDUST	DGGINOST	STODGING
DEORSTUX	DEXTROUS	DGGINRTU	TRUDGING
DEOSSSYY	ODYSSEYS	DGGIRSTU	DRUGGIST
DEOSSTTU	TESTUDOS	DGHHOOOS	HOGHOODS
DEPPSSYY	DYSPEPSY	DGHIILNS	HIDLINGS
DEPRRTUU	RUPTURED		HILDINGS
DEQRSUUY	SURQUEDY	DGHIIMNT	MIDNIGHT
DERSTTTU	STRUTTED	DGHIIMST	MISDIGHT
DFFGINSU	DUFFINGS	DGHIINPS	SPHINGID
DFFIILUY	FLUIDIFY	DGHIINRT	THIRDING
DFFIIMRS	MIDRIFFS	DGHIINSS	DISHINGS
DFFIIRST	TRIFFIDS		SHINDIGS
DFFIIRTY	FRIFFIDY	DGHIISST	DISSIGHT
DFFLOORU	FOURFOLD	DGHIKNOO	KINGHOOD
DFFOORUW	WOODRUFF	DGHILNOS	HOLDINGS
DFGGHIOT	DOGFIGHT	DGHILNRU	HURDLING
DFGGIINR	FRIDGING	DGHILNSY	HYLDINGS
DFGHILOS	GOLDFISH	DGHILOOR	GIRLHOOD
DFGIIIRY	RIGIDIFY	DGHILPSY	DIGLYPHS
DFGIILRY	FRIGIDLY	DGHINNOU	HOUNDING
DFGIINNS	FINDINGS	DGHINNSU	DUNSHING
DFGIINRT	DRIFTING	DGHINSTU	UNDIGHTS
DFGILNNO	FONDLING	DGHIOPSS	DOGSHIPS
DFGILNOO	FLOODING		GODSHIPS
DFGILNOS	FOLDINGS	DGHNOTUU	DOUGHNUT
DFGINNOU	FOUNDING	DGHOORST	DROUGHTS
DFGINNSU	FUNDINGS	DGHORTUY	DROUGHTY
DFGINOOR	FORDOING	DGIIIMRS	DIRIGISM
DFGMOOSY	FOGYDOMS	DGIIINNT	INDITING
DFHIIMUY	HUMIDIFY	DGIIINNV	DIVINING
DFHILSSU	DISHFULS	DGIIINOS	IODISING
DFHIMRSU	DRUMFISH	DGIIINOZ	IODIZING
DFHINOOT	HINDFOOT	DGIIIRTY	RIGIDITY
DFHLOOOT	FOOTHOLD	DGIIKLNN	KINDLING
DFHNOOUX	FOXHOUND	DGIIKLNS	KIDLINGS
DFIIINVY	DIVINIFY	DGIIKNNR	DRINKING
DFIILMTU	MULTIFID	DGIILLNR	DRILLING
DFIILOSY	SOLIDIFY	DGIILLNS	DILLINGS
DFIILTUY	FLUIDITY	DGIILLNU	ILLUDING
DFIINPRT	DRIFTPIN	DGIILLOU	LIGULOID
DFIKNOOS	SKINFOOD	DGIILMNP	DIMPLING
DFILLOOT	FLOODLIT	DGIILNNN	DINNLING
DFILLORY	FLORIDLY	DGIILNOR	DROILING
DFILMMOS	FILMDOMS		

DGIILNOS	DISLOIGN	DGINOOPR	DROOPING	DHIORSWY	ROWDYISH	DIIOPRTY	PITYROID
DGIILNPS	DISPLING	DGINOOPS	SPONGOID	DHIPRSSY	SYRPHIDS	DIIORSSV	DIVISORS
DGIILNSS	SLIDINGS	DGINOOTU	OUTDOING	DHJOPRSU	JODHPURS	DIJOSSTU	JUDOISTS
DGIILNSW	WILDINGS	DGINOPPR	DROPPING	DHKMNOOO	MONKHOOD	DIKLMOOW	MILKWOOD
DGIILNTU	DILUTING	DGINOPPS	DOPPINGS	DHLLOPYY	PHYLLODY	DIKLNNUY	UNKINDLY
DGIIMNNS	MINDINGS	DGINORSW	DROWSING	DHLMOOSU	HOODLUMS	DIKLNORS	LORDKINS
DGIIMNOS	MISDOING		SWORDING	DHLOOORT	ROOTHOLD	DIKLRUUU	DURUKULI
DGIIMNOU	GONIDIUM		WORDINGS	DHLORXYY	HYDROXYL	DIKNORSV	DVORNIKS
DGIIMNSS	SMIDGINS	DGINOSSW	DISGOWNS	DHLOSSTU	SHOULDST	DIKNORTU	OUTDRINK
DGIIMPUY	PYGIDIUM	DGINOSUY	DIGYNOUS	DHMMRSUU	HUMDRUMS	DIKOOSTU	DITOKOUS
DGIINNOP	POINDING	DGINSTUY	STUDYING	DHMNOOOT	HOMODONT	DILLMNOP	MILLPOND
DGIINNRW	WINDRING	DGISSSTU	DISGUSTS	DHMORTUY	DRYMOUTH	DILLOSTY	STOLIDLY
DGIINNSS	SINDINGS	DGLOOOPY	PODOLOGY	DHNNOOSU	NUNHOODS	DILMNOOS	SMILODON
DGIINNSW	WINDINGS	DGLOOOSW	LOGWOODS	DHNORSUU	UNSHROUD	DILMNORW	LINDWORM
DGIINORR	GRIDIRON	DGLOOOSY	DOSOLOGY	DHNORSUW	DOWNRUSH	DILMNRSU	DRUMLINS
DGIINORS	DORISING	DGLOOOXY	DOXOLOGY	DHOOOPRT	ORTHOPOD	DILMOOSU	MODIOLUS
DGIINORZ	DORIZING	DGMOPRSU	GUMDROPS	DHOOORTX	ORTHODOX	DILMOSSU	SOLIDUMS
DGIINOSV	VOIDINGS	DGMOPSYY	GYPSYDOM	DHOOPRSU	UPHOORDS	DILMOSSY	ODYLISMS
DGIINOSW	WINDIGOS	DGMORSUU	GURUDOMS	DHOPRSSU	PUSHRODS	DILNOPST	DIPLONTS
DGIINOTT	DITTOING	DGNNORUU	UNGROUND	DHOPRSYY	HYDROPSY	DILNOPSU	LISPOUND
DGIINOWW	WIDOWING	DGNOOORS	GODROONS	DIIILLQU	ILLIQUID	DILNOQSU	QUODLINS
DGIINPPR	DRIPPING	DGNOOSTW	DOGTOWNS	DIIILTVY	LIVIDITY	DILNOUWY	WOUNDILY
DGIINPPS	DIPPINGS	DGNOOTYZ	ZYGODONT	DIIIMOST	IDIOTISM	DILNPSSU	LISPUNDS
DGIINRST	STRIDING	DGOORSTT	DOGTROTS	DIIIMRSU	IRIDIUMS	DILOOPPY	POLYPOID
DGIINRTY	DIRTYING	DHHILOTW	WITHHOLD	DIIIMTTY	TIMIDITY	DILOOPRY	DROOPILY
DGIINSSU	DISUSING	DHIIIMNS	DIMINISH	DIIINOSV	DIVISION	DILOORSS	LORDOSIS
DGIINTTY	DITTYING	DHIIIOST	HISTIOID	DIIINTVY	DIVINITY	DILOOSUY	ODIOUSLY
DGIINVVY	DIVVYING		IDIOTHIS	DIIIPRST	DISPIRIT	DILOOTUV	VOLUTOID
DGIINYZZ	DIZZYING	DHIILOSS	SOLIDISH	DIIIRTVY	VIRIDITY	DILOPRTY	TORPIDLY
DGIKLOOY	KIDOLOGY	DHIIMNOO	HOMINOID	DIIITVVY	VIVIDITY	DILORSTU	DILUTORS
DGIKMNOS	KINGDOMS	DHIIMNOS	HOMINIDS	DIIJNOSS	DISJOINS	DILORSWY	DROWSILY
DGIKNOOR	DROOKING	DHIIMPSS	MIDSHIPS	DIIJNOST	DISJOINT	DILOSSTY	STYLOIDS
DGIKNOOW	KINGWOOD	DHIIMTUY	HUMIDITY	DIIKLLNY	KINDLILY	DILPRTUY	PUTRIDLY
DGIKNORU	DROUKING	DHIINPSW	WINDSHIP	DIIKLNSS	DISLINKS	DILPSTUY	STUPIDLY
DGIKNOSS	DOGSKINS	DHIINRSU	HIRUDINS	DIIKNOST	DOITKINS	DILRSTUY	STURDILY
DGILLNOR	DROLLING	DHIINTWW	WITHWIND	DIILLMNR	MILLRIND	DIMMNORY	MYRMIDON
	LORDLING	DHIIOPRU	OPHIURID	DIILLMNW	WINDMILL	DIMMOOSU	ISODOMUM
DGILLNOY	DOLLYING	DHIIORSS	HIDROSIS	DIILLMPY	LIMPIDLY	DIMMOSST	MIDMOSTS
DGILLOOW	GOODWILL	DHIIORSZ	RHIZOIDS	DIILLQUY	LIQUIDLY	DIMNNOOS	MIDNOONS
DGILMNOU	MOULDING	DHIKNOOW	HOODWINK	DIILLSST	DISTILLS	DIMNNOSS	DONNISMS
DGILMNPU	DUMPLING	DHIKORSY	HYDROSKI	DIILLSTY	IDYLLIST	DIMNNOST	DINMONTS
DGILMSUY	SMUDGILY	DHILLNOW	DOWNHILL	DIILMNSS	DISLIMNS	DIMNOOOS	ISODOMON
DGILNNOO	NOODLING	DHILLOPY	PHYLLOID	DIILMOSS	IDOLISMS	DIMNOOST	MONODIST
DGILNNOU	LOUNDING	DHILLORS	DROLLISH		SOLIDISM	DIMNOPSU	IMPOUNDS
DGILNNOW	LOWNDING	DHILLOST	TOLLDISH	DIILMOTY	MYTILOID	DIMNOSTU	DISMOUNT
DGILNOOR	DROOLING	DHILMOPY	LYMPHOID	DIILMUUV	DILUVIUM	DIMNOSUW	UNWISDOM
DGILNOOW	WOOLDING	DHILMOSY	MODISHLY	DIILNOTU	DILUTION	DIMOOPRR	PRODROMI
DGILNORS	GIRLONDS	DHILNOPS	DOLPHINS	DIILNOUV	DILUVION	DIMOOPRY	MYRIOPOD
	LORDINGS	DHILOPRS	LORDSHIP	DIILNOXY	XYLOIDIN	DIMOORTW	MODIWORT
DGILNORY	YOLDRING	DHILOPSS	SLIPSHOD	DIILNTUY	UNTIDILY	DIMOPRSU	MISPROUD
DGILNPUY	DUPLYING	DHILORRY	HORRIDLY	DIILOPRT	TRIPLOID	DIMOPSSU	SPODIUMS
DGILOOTW	GILTWOOD	DHILPSSU	LUDSHIPS	DIILOPSY	YPSILOID	DIMORSSW	MISWORDS
DGILOSTY	STODGILY	DHILPSSY	SYLPHIDS	DIILORSU	SILUROID	DIMORSWY	ROWDYISM
DGILRTUY	TURGIDLY	DHIMNOST	HINDMOST	DIILOSST	IDOLISTS	DIMOSTUY	DUMOSITY
DGIMMNRU	DRUMMING	DHIMNOSU	UNMODISH		SOLIDIST	DIMRSTUU	TRIDUUMS
DGIMMNUY	DUMMYING	DHIMOOOY	OMOHYOID	DIILOSTY	SOLIDITY	DIMRSUUV	DUUMVIRS
DGIMNNOU	MOUNDING	DHIMOOSS	MISSHOOD	DIILQSUU	LIQUIDUS	DINNOORS	RONDINOS
DGIMNOOY	MOODYING	DHIMOPPY	HIPPYDOM	DIILRSSU	SILURIDS	DINNOOST	TONDINOS
DGINNNSU	DUNNINGS	DHIMOPRS	DIMORPHS	DIIMNNOO	DOMINION	DINOOORW	IRONWOOD
DGINNOOS	SNOODING	DHIMORSU	HUMIDORS	DIIMNNSU	UNDINISM	DINOOPSU	DIPNOOUS
DGINNOPU	POUNDING		RHODIUMS	DIIMNORS	MIDIRONS	DINOORST	TORDIONS
DGINNOPW	POWNDING	DHINOORS	DISHONOR	DIIMNSUU	INDUSIUM	DINOORSU	NIDOROUS
DGINNORU	ROUNDING	DHINOPSS	DONSHIPS	DIIMOPRS	PRISMOID	DINOOSST	ISODONTS
DGINNORW	DROWNING	DHINORSS	DISHORNS	DIIMORSS	DIORISMS	DINOOSTT	ODONTIST
	ROWNDING	DHINORSU	ROUNDISH	DIIMPUXY	PYXIDIUM	DINOOSTY	NODOSITY
DGINNOSU	SOUNDING	DHIOOPRZ	RHIZOPOD	DIIMRUUV	DUUMVIRI	DINORSTU	STURNOID
	UNDOINGS	DHIOPRSU	PROUDISH	DIIMTTUY	TUMIDITY		TURDIONS
DGINNOSW	SOWNDING	DHIOPSTY	TYPHOIDS	DIINNOSU	DISUNION	DINORSWW	WINDROWS
DGINNOUW	WOUNDING	DHIORSTY	THYROIDS	DIINOSSU	SINUSOID	DINOSSTW	SITDOWNS
DGINNSSY	SYNDINGS		THYRSOID	DIINSTUY	DISUNITY	DINOSTUW	OUTWINDS

DINPRTUY	PUNDITRY	EEEEGSTX	EXEGETES	EEEGNSTT	GENETTES		EMPERISE
DINRSTUY	INDUSTRY	EEEELLPX	EXPELLEE	EEEGOPRT	PROTEGEE		PREEMIES
DIOOPRRT	PRODITOR	EEEELMST	TELESEME	EEEGRRST	REGREETS	EEEIMPRZ	EMPERIZE
DIOOPRRV	PROVIDOR	EEEENRRV	VENEERER	EEEGRSSS	EGRESSES	EEEIMRRS	MISERERE
DIOORSST	DISROOTS	EEEEPPSW	PEESWEEP	EEEGRSUX	EXERGUES	EEEIMRST	EREMITES
DIOORSTT	RIDOTTOS	EEEEPPRV	REPREEVE	EEEHILRW	EREWHILE	EEEIMRTT	REMITTEE
DIOPRSST	DISPORTS	EEEEPTTW	PEETWEET		WHEELIER	EEEINNNT	NINETEEN
DIOPSSST	DISPOSTS	EEEFFFOS	FEOFFEES	EEEHILSW	WHEELIES	EEEINNRT	INTERNEE
DIORRSST	STRIDORS	EEEFFLOR	FOREFEEL	EEEHINRS	SHEENIER	EEEINQTU	QUEENITE
DIORSSTT	DISTORTS	EEEFFLTY	EFFETELY	EEEHINSS	SHEENIES	EEEINRRS	SNEERIER
DIOSSTUU	STUDIOUS	EEEFFNRT	EFFERENT	EEEHIPRS	SHEEPIER	EEEINRSS	EERINESS
DIPRSSTU	DISRUPTS	EEEFFORS	OFFEREES	EEEHIRSS	HERESIES	EEEINRST	ETERNISE
DIRSSTTU	DISTRUST	EEEFFORV	FOREFEET	EEEHIRST	ETHERISE		TEENSIER
DKNORTUU	OUTDRUNK	EEEFFRVW	FEVERFEW		SHEETIER	EEEINRSV	VENERIES
DKOOORWW	WOODWORK	EEEFGRSU	REFUGEES	EEEHIRTZ	ETHERIZE	EEEINRSZ	SNEEZIER
DKORSTUW	STUDWORK	EEEFHRSS	SHEREEFS	EEEHIRWZ	WHEEZIER	EEEINRTT	REINETTE
DLLNORUY	UNLORDLY	EEEFIPRR	REPRIEFE	EEEHKLNO	KNEEHOLE		TEENTIER
DLMNOOSY	MYLODONS	EEEFIPST	TEPEFIES	EEEHLMNW	WHEELMEN	EEEINRTZ	ETERNIZE
DLMNOOTY	MYLODONT	EEEFIRRT	FREETIER	EEEHLNSW	ENWHEELS	EEEINSSW	SWEENIES
DLMNOSUU	UNMOULDS	EEEFLRRS	FLEERERS	EEEHLNTV	ELEVENTH	EEEINSTT	TEENIEST
DLMORSUY	SMOULDRY	EEEFLRSX	REFLEXES	EEEHLNTY	ETHYLENE	EEEINSTW	TWEENIES
DLNOOPRU	POULDRON	EEEFLSST	FEETLESS	EEEHLNXY	HEXYLENE		WEENIEST
DLNOOSUU	NODULOUS	EEEFLSST	FLEETEST	EEEHLOPW	WEEPHOLE	EEEINTUX	EUXENITE
DLNOPRSU	PULDRONS	EEEFNNPY	PENNYFEE	EEEHLPSW	WHEEPLES	EEEIPRRV	REPRIEVE
DLNOPSSY	SPONDYLS	EEEFNORS	FORESEEN	EEEHLRSW	WHEELERS	EEEIPRST	PEERIEST
DLNORTUY	ROTUNDLY	EEEFNRRT	REFERENT	EEEHLSWZ	WHEEZLES		STEEPIER
DLNOSUUU	UNDULOUS	EEEFNRRS	FREENESS	EEEHMMSS	EMMESHES	EEEIPRSW	SWEEPIER
DLOOOORS	DOLOROSO	EEEFNRTT	ENFETTER	EEEHMNSS	ENMESHES	EEEIPSST	SEEPIEST
DLOOORSU	DOLOROUS	EEEFNRUZ	UNFREEZE	EEEHMNTV	VEHEMENT	EEEIPSTW	WEEPIEST
DLOOPPSY	POLYPODS	EEEFORRV	OVERFREE	EEEHMRSS	HERSEEMS	EEEIQSUX	EXEQUIES
DLOOPPUW	PULPWOOD	EEEFORSS	FORESEES	EEEHNNPT	NEPENTHE	EEEIRRST	REESTIER
DLOOPPYY	POLYPODY	EEEFRRRT	FERRETER	EEEHNNQU	HENEQUEN		RETIREES
DLOOPSTY	TYLOPODS	EEEFRRSZ	FREEZERS	EEEHNPRS	ENSPHERE	EEEIRRSV	REREVISE
DLOOPSWY	PLYWOODS	EEEGGILN	NEGLIGEE	EEEHNRSS	HERENESS		REVERIES
DMNNOOOT	MONODONT	EEEGGIRS	EGGERIES	EEEHNRVW	WHENEVER	EEEIRRTV	RETRIEVE
DMNOOSTW	DOWNMOST	EEEGHINT	EIGHTEEN	EEEHNRVW	WHEREVER	EEEIRRVW	REVIEWER
	TOWMONDS		TEHEEING	EEEHRSST	SEETHERS	EEEIRSST	STEERIES
DMOOORWW	WOODWORM	EEEGHNSW	WHEENGES		SHEEREST	EEEIRSSV	SEVERIES
	WORMWOOD	EEEGILMN	LIEGEMEN	EEEHSSST	ESTHESES	EEEIRSSZ	RESEIZES
DMOPPPUU	PUPPODUM	EEEGILNV	ENVEIGLE	EEEHSSTT	ESTHETES	EEEIRTVX	EXERTIVE
DMOPPPUY	PUPPYDOM		LEVEEING	EEEIKLMS	MISLEEKE	EEEISSTW	SWEETIES
DMORSTUW	MUDWORTS	EEEGILPS	ESPIEGLE	EEEIKLRS	SKEELIER	EEEJLLRW	JEWELLER
DNNOOPRU	PUNDONOR	EEEGILRT	GLEETIER		SLEEKIER	EEEJNPSY	JEEPNEYS
DNNORSUU	UNROUNDS	EEEGILSS	ELEGISES	EEEIKLSW	WEEKLIES	EEEKLLSU	UKELELES
DNNORSUW	RUNDOWNS	EEEGILSZ	ELEGIZES	EEEIKRRS	SKEERIER	EEEKLNNR	ENKERNEL
DNNORTUW	DOWNTURN	EEEGIMNX	EXEEMING	EEEIKRST	REEKIEST	EEEKLNRS	KNEELERS
DNNOSSUW	SUNDOWNS	EEEGINNR	ENGINEER	EEEILLRV	REVEILLE	EEEKLNSS	SLEEKENS
DNNRSTUU	TURNDUNS	EEEGINRR	GREENIER	EEEILMRS	SEEMLIER	EEEKLPSW	EKPWELES
DNOOPPRU	PROPOUND	EEEGINRS	ENERGIES	EEEILNNO	EOLIENNE	EEEKLRSS	SLEEKERS
DNOOPRSW	SNOWDROP		ENERGISE	EEEILNPR	PELERINE	EEEKLSST	SLEEKEST
DNOOPRUW	DOWNPOUR	EEEGINRV	ENGRIEVE	EEEILNRY	EYELINER	EEEKMNSS	MEEKNESS
DNOORSUW	WONDROUS	EEEGINRZ	ENERGIZE	EEEILNST	SELENITE	EEEKMRSS	KERMESSE
DNOOSTWW	STOWDOWN	EEEGIPRS	PERIGEES	EEEILPRS	SLEEPIER	EEEKNNSS	KEENNESS
DNOOTUUW	OUTWOUND	EEEGISSX	EXEGESIS	EEEILRRV	RELIEVER	EEEKNORS	KEROSENE
DNORRSUU	SURROUND	EEEGISTV	EGESTIVE	EEEILRST	LEERIEST	EEEKNORV	OVERKNEE
DNORSSUY	UNDROSSY	EEEGITVV	VEGETIVE		SLEETIER	EEEKNPST	KEEPNETS
DOOOPRST	DOORPOST	EEEGLMOS	GLEESOME		STEELIER	EEEKNRSS	SKREENES
	DOORSTOP	EEEGLNRT	GREENLET	EEEILRSV	RELIEVES	EEEKOPRV	OVERKEEP
DOOORSTU	OUTDOORS	EEEGMNRT	EMERGENT	EEEILRSZ	SLEEZIER	EEEKRSST	SKEETERS
DOOOSTTU	OUTSTOOD	EEEGMORT	GEOMETER	EEEILSST	SEELIEST	EEELLLRV	LEVELLER
DOOPSWWY	POWSOWDY	EEEGMRRS	REMERGES	EEEILSSW	ELSEWISE	EEELLLSW	SEWELLEL
DOORRSTU	DORTOURS	EEEGNNRS	SENGREEN	EEEILSTV	TELEVISE	EEELLNQU	QUENELLE
DOORRSSU	ORDUROUS	EEEGNPRS	EPERGNES	EEEILTVW	TELEVIEW	EEELLPRR	REPELLER
DOORSSUU	SUDOROUS	EEEGNPRS	RENEGERS	EEEIMNRU	MEUNIERE	EEELLRRT	RETELLER
EEEEFNRZ	ENFREEZE	EEEGNNRU	RENEGUER	EEEIMNST	EMETINES	EEELLRRV	REVELLER
EEEEFRRS	REFEREES	EEEGNRRV	REVENGER	EEEIMPRR	PREMIERE	EEELMNST	ELEMENTS
EEEEFRRZ	REFREEZE	EEEGNRRY	GREENERY	EEEIMPRS	EMPERIES	EEELMOPP	EMPEOPLE
	GREEGREE	EEEGNRST	GREENEST			EEELMOPY	EMPLOYEE
	SQUEEGEE	EEEGNRSU	RENEGUES			EEELMOTT	OMELETTE
	EXEGESES	EEEGNRSV	REVENGES	EEEIMPRS	EMPERIES	EEELMPSX	EXEMPLES

EEELMRTU	MULETEER		VENERERS
EEELMSSS	SEEMLESS	EEENRRSW	RENEWERS
EEELMSST	TEEMLESS	EEENRRTU	RETURNEE
EEELNOPV	ENVELOPE	EEENRRTV	REVERENT
EEELNOSV	NOVELESE	EEENRSSS	SERENESS
EEELNQTU	QUEENLET	EEENRSST	SERENEST
EEELNRSW	NEWSREEL	EEENRSSU	ENURESES
EEELNRSY	SERENELY	EEENRSSZ	SNEEZERS
EEELNRTV	NERVELET	EEENRSTV	EVENTERS
EEELOPPR	REPEOPLE	EEENRSTX	EXTERNES
EEELORST	SLOETREE	EEENRSTY	YESTREEN
EEELPRSS	PEERLESS	EEENRSUV	REVENUES
	SLEEPERS		UNREEVES
	SPEELERS	EEENSSTW	SWEETENS
EEELPRST	REPLETES		TWEENESS
EEELPRSY	SLEEPERY	EEENSSWY	SWEENEYS
EEELPSST	STEEPLES	EEEOPRRV	OVERPEER
EEELRRTT	LETTERER	EEEORRSV	OVERSEER
EEELRSST	TREELESS	EEEORSST	EROTESES
EEELRSSV	SLEEVERS	EEEORSSV	OVERSEES
EEELRSTT	RESETTLE	EEEORSSY	EYESORES
EEELRSTV	LEVERETS	EEEORSVY	OVEREYES
	VERSELET	EEEPPPRR	PEPPERER
EEELRSVY	SEVERELY	EEEPPRST	PESTERER
EEELRTVV	VELVERET	EEEPPRSU	REPERUSE
EEELSSTW	WEETLESS	EEEPRRSV	PERVERSE
EEELSTVY	STEEVELY		PRESERVE
EEELTTTX	TELETEXT	EEEPRRTW	PEWTERER
EEEMMNRS	MERESMEN	EEEPRSST	ESTREPES
EEEMMRUZ	MEZEREUM		STEEPERS
EEEMNNTT	TENEMENT	EEEPRSSW	SWEEPERS
EEEMNORZ	MEZEREON	EEEPRSSZ	SPREEZES
EEEMNPRT	PETERMEN	EEEPSSTT	STEEPEST
EEEMNRST	ENTREMES	EEEPSTTT	SEPTETTE
EEEMNSST	MEETNESS	EEEQRRSU	REQUERES
EEEMORRV	EVERMORE	EEEQRRUV	VERQUERE
EEEMORST	EROTEMES	EEEQRSTU	QUEEREST
	STEREOME	EEEQRSUZ	SQUEEZER
EEEMORTV	OVERTEEM	EEEQSSUZ	SQUEEZES
EEEMPRRT	TEMPERER	EEERRRSV	REVERERS
EEEMPRSS	EMPRESSE		REVERSER
EEEMPSSY	EMPYESES	EEERRSST	STEERERS
EEEMRRTX	EXTREMER	EEERRSSV	RESERVES
EEEMRSST	SEMESTER		REVERSES
EEEMRSTX	EXTREMES	EEERRSTT	RESETTER
EEENNOPR	NEOPRENE	EEERRSTV	SEVEREST
EEENNPST	PENTENES	EEERSSUV	REVEUSES
EEENNRST	ETRENNES	EEERSSUW	SERUEWES
EEENNRUV	UNEVENER	EEERSSVW	SERVEWES
EEENNSSV	EVENNESS	EEERSTTW	TWEETERS
EEENNSTT	ENTENTES	EEERSTWZ	TWEEZERS
EEENOPRR	REOPENER	EEESSTTT	SESTETTE
EEENORSV	OVERSEEN	EEESSTTV	STEEVEST
EEENORVW	OVERWEEN	EEESSTTW	SWEETEST
EEENORVY	EVERYONE	EEESTTTX	SEXTETTE
EEENPPRS	PREPENSE	EEFFFGLU	GEFUFFLE
EEENPRRT	REPENTER	EEFFFKLU	KEFUFFLE
EEENPRST	PRETENSE	EEFFFNOS	ENFEOFFS
	TERPENES	EEFFFORS	FEOFFERS
EEENPRSV	PREVENES	EEFFGIIS	EFFIGIES
EEENPSST	ENSTEEPS	EEFFGINR	EFFERING
	STEEPENS	EEFFGIRR	GREFFIER
EEENPSSW	ENSWEEPS	EEFFGLSU	EFFULGES
EEENPSSX	EXPENSES	EEFFHIKY	KEFFIYEH
EEENRRSS	SNEERERS	EEFFINST	FIFTEENS
EEENRRST	ENTERERS	EEFFISUV	EFFUSIVE
	RESENTER	EEFFLNTU	EFFLUENT
	TERREENS	EEFFLORT	FOREFELT
	TERRENES	EEFFLSUX	EFFLUXES
EEENRRSV	RENVERSE	EEFFNOSS	OFFENSES

EEFFORRS	OFFERERS	EEFILRRT	FERTILER
EEFFORSX	FORFEXES	EEFILRSS	FIRELESS
EEFFRRSU	SUFFERER	EEFILRST	FERLIEST
EEFFSSTU	SUFFETES	EEFILRSU	FUSILEER
EEFGIILR	FILIGREE	EEFILSST	FELSITES
EEFGILNR	FLEERING	EEFILSSW	WIFELESS
EEFGILNS	FEELINGS	EEFIMORT	FORETIME
EEFGILNT	FLEETING	EEFIMRST	FEMITERS
EEFGINNP	PFENNIGE	EEFIMSTU	TUMEFIES
EEFGINRR	REFRINGE	EEFINNSS	FINENESS
EEFGINRS	FEERINGS	EEFINNST	FENNIEST
	REEFINGS	EEFINORV	OVERFINE
EEFGINRV	FEVERING	EEFINRRS	REFINERS
EEFGINRZ	FREEZING	EEFINRRY	REFINERY
EEFGIRRU	REFIGURE	EEFINRSS	FINESSER
EEFGLMNU	FUGLEMEN		RIFENESS
EEFGLNRY	GREENFLY	EEFINRST	FERNIEST
EEFGLNUV	VENGEFUL	EEFINRSU	REINFUSE
EEFGLORS	FORELEGS	EEFINRSZ	FRENZIES
EEFGMNOR	FORGEMEN	EEFINSSS	FINESSES
EEFGNOOR	FOREGONE	EEFINSTT	FEINTEST
EEFGOORR	FOREGOER	EEFIORRV	OVERFIRE
EEFGOORS	FOREGOES	EEFIORSX	ORIFEXES
EEFHILRS	FLESHIER	EEFIPRSX	PREFIXES
	SHELFIER	EEFIRRST	FERRITES
EEFHIMSU	HUMEFIES	EEFIRRTT	FRETTIER
EEFHIRSV	FEVERISH	EEFIRSTT	FRISETTE
EEFHISST	FETISHES	EEFIRSTY	ESTERIFY
EEFHISSY	FISHEYES	EEFKNORW	FOREKNEW
EEFHISTT	HEFTIEST	EEFLLNSS	FELLNESS
EEFHLLWY	FLYWHEEL	EEFLLORT	FORETELL
EEFHLMOT	HOMEFELT	EEFLLORV	OVERFELL
EEFHLRSS	FLESHERS	EEFLLRSU	FUELLERS
EEFHMNRS	FRESHMEN	EEFLLRXY	REFLEXLY
EEFHMORR	HEREFROM	EEFLLSSS	SELFLESS
EEFHNORT	FOREHENT	EEFLMNSU	MENSEFUL
EEFHNRSS	FRESHENS	EEFLMORU	FUMEROLE
EEFHORRT	THEREFOR	EEFLNNOS	ENFELONS
EEFHORRW	WHEREFOR	EEFLNORT	FORELENT
EEFHORSW	FORESHEW	EEFLNORW	ENFLOWER
EEFHRRSS	FRESHERS	EEFLNOST	FELSTONE
EEFHRSST	FRESHEST	EEFLNRTU	REFLUENT
	FRESHETS	EEFLNSSS	SELFNESS
EEFIIKLL	LIFELIKE	EEFLNSSU	SENSEFUL
EEFIIKRS	FIKERIES	EEFLNTUV	EVENTFUL
EEFIILMT	LIFETIME	EEFLOOSV	FOVEOLES
EEFIILNS	LENIFIES	EEFLOPTT	POLTFEET
EEFIILRW	WIFELIER	EEFLORRW	FLOWERER
EEFIIMNN	FEMININE		REFLOWER
EEFIIMNS	FEMINISE	EEFLORSS	FORLESES
EEFIIMNZ	FEMINIZE	EEFLORTW	FLOWERET
EEFIINRS	FINERIES	EEFLORVW	OVERFLEW
EEFIIRRT	FREITIER	EEFLORWW	WEREWOLF
	FERITIES	EEFLOSUX	FLEXUOSE
	FIERIEST	EEFLRRSU	FERRULES
EEFIIRSV	VERIFIES	EEFLRSTT	FETTLERS
EEFIKNNP	PENKNIFE	EEFLRSTU	FLEURETS
EEFILLMT	TELEFILM	EEFLRSUX	FLEXURES
EEFILLSS	LIFELESS		REFLUXES
EEFILMNR	RIFLEMEN	EEFMNORT	FOMENTER
EEFILMOS	LIFESOME	EEFMNRRY	FERRYMEN
EEFILMST	FISTMELE	EEFMNRST	FERMENTS
EEFILNOS	FELONIES	EEFMORRR	REFORMER
	OLEFINES	EEFMOSTT	MOFETTES
EEFILNSS	FINELESS	EEFMPRRU	PERFUMER
EEFILNUV	NIEVEFUL	EEFMPRSU	PERFUMES
EEFILORS	FORELIES	EEFMSTTU	FUMETTES
EEFILPRR	PILFERER	EEFNNORS	ENFROSEN
		EEFNNORZ	ENFROZEN
		EEFNORRZ	REFROZEN

EEFNORST ENFOREST
SOFTENER
EEFNORTU FOURTEEN
EEFNORTW FOREWENT
EEFNOSTT OFTENEST
EEFNQRTU FREQUENT
EEFNRTTU UNFETTER
EEFORRST FORESTER
FOSTERER
EEFORRSU FERREOUS
EEFORRSV FOREVERS
EEFORRTY FERETORY
EEFORSUV FEVEROUS
EEFOSSTT FOSSETTE
EEFOSSTU FOETUSES
EEFOSTTU FOUETTES
EEFPRSSU PERFUSES
EEFRRSSU REFUSERS
EEFRRSTU REFUTERS
EEGGGLST GLEGGEST
EEGGHLLS EGGSHELL
EEGGHLOR HOGGEREL
EEGGHMSU MESHUGGE
EEGGHSTU THUGGEES
EEGGIJRR REJIGGER
EEGGIKLN GLEEKING
EEGGILNR LEGERING
EEGGILNS NEGLIGES
EEGGILNT GLEETING
EEGGILST LEGGIEST
EEGGIMNR EMERGING
EEGGINNP PEENGING
EEGGINNR GREENING
RENEGING
EEGGINRS GREESING
EEGGINRT GREETING
EEGGINST EGESTING
EEGGINSU SEGUEING
EEGGKRSS SKEGGERS
EEGGLOOR GEOLOGER
EEGGNORS ENGORGES
EEGGORRS REGORGES
EEGGORSU GOUGERES
EEGGPRRS PREGGERS
EEGGPRSU PUGGREES
EEGGQRSU SQUEGGER
EEGHHINT HEIGHTEN
EEGHIIST EIGHTIES
EEGHIKNT THEEKING
EEGHIKRS SKEIGHER
EEGHILNS HEELINGS
SHEELING
EEGHILNW WHEELING
EEGHINNS SHEENING
EEGHINPS PHEESING
EEGHINPT PHENGITE
EEGHINPZ PHEEZING
EEGHINRS GREENISH
SHEERING
EEGHINST SEETHING
SHEETING
EEGHINSY HYGIENES
EEGHINTT TEETHING
EEGHINWZ WHEEZING
EEGHIOTT GOETHITE
EEGHIRSW REWEIGHS
WEIGHERS
EEGHISST SIGHTSEE
EEGHISTY EYESIGHT
EEGHLNNT LENGTHEN

EEGHMNOY HEGEMONY
EEGHNNRU ENHUNGER
EEGHNOOP GEOPHONE
EEGHNOPS PHOSGENE
EEGHNOPY HYPOGENE
EEGHNRST GREENTHS
EEGHNRSY GREYHENS
EEGHNSSU HUGENESS
EEGHOPTY GEOPHYTE
EEGHORTT TOGETHER
EEGHOSTT GHETTOES
EEGHSTTU TEUGHEST
EEGIILNR LINGERIE
EEGIILNV INVEIGLE
EEGIIMNS GEMINIES
EEGIINTV GENITIVE
EEGIIOST EGOITIES
EEGIJLNY JEELYING
EEGIJNRS JEERINGS
EEGIKLNN KNEELING
EEGIKLNS KEELINGS
SLEEKING
EEGIKLOT EKLOGITE
EEGIKMNS SMEEKING
EEGIKNNS KEENINGS
EEGIKNPS KEEPINGS
EEGIKNRS KREESING
SKEERING
EEGIKNST STEEKING
EEGILNOR ELOIGNER
EEGILNPS PEELINGS
SLEEPING
SPEELING
EEGILNRR LINGERER
EEGILNRS LEERINGS
REELINGS
EEGILNRU REGULINE
EEGILNRV LEVERING
EEGILNSS SEELINGS
EEGILNST GENTILES
SLEETING
STEELING
EEGILNSV SLEEVING
EEGILNSW SWEELING
EEGILNTW TWEELING
EEGILNTX TELEXING
EEGILOPU EPILOGUE
EEGILOSS GELOSIES
EEGILOSU EULOGIES
EULOGISE
EEGILOUZ EULOGIZE
EEGILQSU SQUILGEE
EEGILRSU REGULISE
EEGILRSV VELIGERS
EEGILRTV VERLIGTE
EEGILRTY LEGERITY
EEGILRUZ REGULIZE
EEGILSST ELEGISTS
EEGIMMNW EMMEWING
EEGIMMRS IMMERGES
EEGIMMST GEMMIEST
EEGIMNNS MENINGES
EEGIMNNW ENMEWING
EEGIMNRS REGIMENS
EEGIMNRT METERING
REGIMENT
EEGIMNRU MERINGUE
EEGIMNRY EMERYING
EEGIMNSS SEEMINGS
EEGIMNST MEETINGS

STEEMING
EEGIMNSU EUGENISM
EEGINNPR PREENING
EEGINNQU QUEENING
EEGINNRS ENGINERS
INGENERS
SERENING
SNEERING
EEGINNRT ENTERING
EEGINNRV ENERVING
EEGINNRW RENEWING
EEGINNRY ENGINERY
RENEYING
EEGINNST STEENING
EEGINNSU INGENUES
UNSEEING
EEGINNSV EEVNINGS
EVENINGS
EEGINNSW ENSEWING
EEGINNSZ SNEEZING
EEGINNTV EVENTING
EEGINOOS OOGENIES
EEGINOPR PERIGONE
EEGINOPS EPIGONES
EEGINORR ERIGERON
EEGINORS ERINGOES
EEGINORV VIROGENE
EEGINOST EGESTION
EEGINPRS SPEERING
SPREEING
EEGINPRT PETERING
EEGINPRU PUREEING
EEGINPRV PREEVING
EEGINPST STEEPING
EEGINPSW SWEEPING
WEEPINGS
EEGINQRU QUEERING
EEGINQUU QUEUEING
EEGINRRS RESIGNER
EEGINRRV REVERING
EEGINRSS GREISENS
EEGINRST GENTRIES
INTEGERS
REESTING
STEERING
STREIGNE
EEGINRSU SEIGNEUR
EEGINRSV SEVERING
VEERINGS
EEGINRSW SEWERING
EEGINRTU GENITURE
EEGINRTV EVERTING
EEGINRTW TWEERING
EEGINRTX EXERTING
GENETRIX
EEGINSSS GNEISSES
EEGINSSU GENIUSES
EEGINSTT GENTIEST
EEGINSTU EUGENIST
EEGINSTV STEEVING
VENTIGES
EEGINSTW SWEETING
EEGINSTX EXIGENTS
EEGINTTV VIGNETTE
EEGINTTW TWEETING
EEGINTUX TEGUEXIN
EEGINTWZ TWEEZING
EEGIOPSU EPIGEOUS
EEGIORST ERGOTISE
EEGIORTZ ERGOTIZE

EEGIORVV OVERGIVE
EEGIOSST EGOTISES
EEGIOSTZ EGOTIZES
EEGIPRST PRESTIGE
EEGIRRST REGISTER
EEGIRRSV GRIEVERS
EEGIRSTT GRISETTE
TERGITES
EEGISSTV VESTIGES
EEGJORSU GOUJEERS
EEGKNORS KEROGENS
EEGKNRSU GERENUKS
EEGLMMSU GEMMULES
EEGLMNOP EMPLONGE
EEGLMNTU EMULGENT
EEGLMOSS GLOSSEME
EEGLNNTU UNGENTLE
EEGLNOPY POLYGENE
EEGLNOSU EUGENOLS
EEGLNOSZ LOZENGES
EEGLNOTY TELEGONY
EEGLNSTT GENTLEST
EEGMMOSU GEMMEOUS
EEGMNOST EMONGEST
GEMSTONE
EEGMNSST SEGMENTS
EEGMNTTU TEGUMENT
EEGMORSU GRUESOME
EEGMORTY GEOMETRY
EEGNNORT ROENTGEN
EEGNNOSS GONENESS
EEGNNOSV EVENSONG
EEGNOORV ENGROOVE
OVERGONE
EEGNOPTY GENOTYPE
EEGNORST ESTROGEN
EEGNORSU GENEROUS
EEGNORSY ERYNGOES
EEGNPRUX EXPUNGER
EEGNPSUX EXPUNGES
EEGNRSSY GREYNESS
EEGNRSUY GUERNSEY
EEGNSSTU GUESTENS
EEGOOPSY POOGYEES
EEGOORSV OVERGOES
EEGOPRST PROTEGES
EEGORRST OSTREGER
EEGORRVW OVERGREW
EEGORSSS OGRESSES
EEGORSTU UROSTEGE
EEGORSTV OVERGETS
EEGPRSUX EXPURGES
EEGRRSSU RESURGES
EEGRSSSU GUESSERS
EEGRSSTU GESTURES
EEHHIPSS SHEEPISH
EEHHIRTW HEREWITH
EEHHLRST THRESHEL
EEHHRRST THRESHER
EEHHRSST THRESHES
EEHHSSTW WHEESHTS
EEHIIKLV HIVELIKE
EEHIKLMO HOMELIKE
EEHIKLRW WHELKIER
EEHIKRRS SHRIEKER
EEHILLMS SHLEMIEL
EEHILLNP HELPLINE
EEHILLRS HELLIERS
SHELLIER
EEHILMOR HOMELIER

EEHILNOP	NEOPHILE	
EEHILORT	HOTELIER	
EEHILOSS	HELIOSES	
EEHILRSS	HEIRLESS	
	RELISHES	
EEHILRSV	SHELVIER	
EEHILSST	LEISHEST	
	SHELTIES	
EEHILSSV	HIVELESS	
EEHILWYZ	WHEEZILY	
EEHIMMSS	HIMSEEMS	
	IMMESHES	
	MISHMEES	
EEHIMNOS	HEMIONES	
EEHIMNRS	SHIREMEN	
EEHIMNSS	INMESHES	
EEHIMPRS	EMPERISH	
EEHIMPST	EPITHEMS	
	HEMPIEST	
EEHIMQUV	VEHMIQUE	
EEHIMRST	ERETHISM	
	ETHERISM	
EEHIMRTT	THERMITE	
EEHIMSST	MESHIEST	
EEHINNQU	HENEQUIN	
EEHINNRS	ENSHRINE	
EEHINNRT	INHERENT	
EEHINNSS	SNEESHIN	
EEHINNST	HENNIEST	
EEHINORS	HEROINES	
EEHINORT	ETHERION	
EEHINPRS	INSPHERE	
EEHINPRT	NEPHRITE	
	PREHNITE	
	TREPHINE	
EEHINRRS	ERRHINES	
EEHINRTT	THIRTEEN	
EEHINRTW	WHITENER	
EEHIOPPS	HOSEPIPE	
EEHIORSS	HEROISES	
EEHIORST	ISOTHERE	
	THEORIES	
	THEORISE	
EEHIORSZ	HEROIZES	
EEHIORTZ	THEORIZE	
EEHIPPST	PSEPHITE	
EEHIPPTY	EPIPHYTE	
EEHIPRRS	PERISHER	
	SPHERIER	
EEHIPRSS	PERISHES	
EEHIPRST	TREESHIP	
EEHIPRTT	PERTHITE	
	TEPHRITE	
	THREEPIT	
EEHIPSST	STEEPISH	
EEHIPSTT	EPITHETS	
EEHIPSUU	EUPHUISE	
EEHIPUUZ	EUPHUIZE	
EEHIQRSU	QUEERISH	
EEHIRRSS	SHERRIES	
EEHIRRSW	WHERRIES	
EEHIRSST	HEISTERS	
EEHIRSSV	SHRIEVES	
EEHIRSSX	RHEXISES	
EEHIRSTT	ETHERIST	
EEHIRTVY	THIEVERY	
EEHISSST	ESTHESIS	
EEHISSTW	SWEETISH	
EEHISTTW	THEWIEST	
EEHISTWY	WHEYIEST	

EEHKLOSY	KEYHOLES	
EEHKOOSY	EYEHOOKS	
EEHLLMPS	PHELLEMS	
EEHLLMSS	HELMLESS	
EEHLLLMSS	ENSHELLS	
EEHLLORV	HOVELLER	
EEHLLPSS	HELPLESS	
EEHLLRSS	SHELLERS	
EEHLMMNS	HELMSMEN	
EEHLMMSW	WHEMMLES	
EEHLMOOS	HOLESOME	
EEHLMOSS	HOMELESS	
EEHLNOTT	TELETHON	
EEHLOPSS	HOPELESS	
EEHLORST	HOSTELER	
EEHLORSV	SHOVELER	
EEHLOSSS	SHOELESS	
EEHLPRST	TELPHERS	
EEHLPRSU	SPHERULE	
EEHLRSST	SHELTERS	
EEHLRSSW	WELSHERS	
EEHLRSTY	SHELTERY	
EEHLSSTW	THEWLESS	
EEHMMOPR	MORPHEME	
EEHMMORT	OHMMETER	
EEHMNOOS	MOONSHEE	
EEHMNOPS	PHONEMES	
EEHMNORS	HORSEMEN	
	SHOREMEN	
EEHMNOSU	HOUSEMEN	
EEHMNOSW	SOMEWHEN	
EEHMNRSU	ENRHEUMS	
EEHMNRSY	MYNHEERS	
EEHMOORT	RHEOTOME	
EEHMOOSS	HOMEOSES	
EEHMORST	THEOREMS	
EEHMORVW	WHOMEVER	
EEHMRSUX	EXHUMERS	
EEHMSSTY	METHYSES	
EEHNNORT	ENTHRONE	
EEHNNPPU	UNHEPPEN	
EEHNNSSS	NESHNESS	
EEHNNSTU	UNNETHES	
EEHNOPRU	HEREUPON	
EEHNOPST	POSHTEEN	
	POTHEENS	
EEHNOPTY	HYPNOTEE	
	NEOPHYTE	
EEHNORST	HONESTER	
EEHNORSW	HERONSEW	
	NOWHERES	
EEHNORTU	HEREUNTO	
EEHNORTV	OVERHENT	
EEHNPRSU	UNSPHERE	
EEHNRTTU	UNTETHER	
EEHNSSTU	ENTHUSES	
EEHNSSTV	SEVENTHS	
EEHOOPRS	OOSPHERE	
EEHOOPSW	WHOOPEES	
EEHOORSV	OVERSHOE	
EEHOPRSU	EUPHROES	
EEHORRTX	EXHORTER	
EEHORSSU	REHOUSES	
EEHORSVW	WHOSEVER	
EEHORTTU	THEREOUT	
EEHORTUW	WHEREOUT	
EEHPRSST	HEPSTERS	
	SPERTHES	
EEHPRSTU	SUPERHET	
EEHRRSTW	WHERRETS	

EEHRSSSU	RHESUSES	
	USHERESS	
EEHRSSTW	WERSHEST	
EEHRSTTW	WHETTERS	
EEIIKLLR	LIKELIER	
EEIIKLPP	PIPELIKE	
EEIIKLSW	LIKEWISE	
EEIILLMT	MILLIEME	
EEIILLMT	MELILITE	
	MELINITE	
EEIILMRT	TIMELIER	
EEIILMSS	EMISSILE	
EEIILNPP	PIPELINE	
EEIILNST	LENITIES	
EEIILNTV	LENITIVE	
EEIILORS	OILERIES	
EEIILRST	TILERIES	
EEIILRSV	LIVERIES	
EEIILSTV	LEVITIES	
	VEILIEST	
EEIILSTW	LEWISITE	
EEIIMMTT	MIMETITE	
EEIIMNOT	MEIONITE	
EEIIMNST	ENMITIES	
EEIIMOST	MOIETIES	
EEIIMPRS	RIEMPIES	
EEIIMRSS	MISERIES	
EEIIMSST	ITEMISES	
EEIIMSSV	EMISSIVE	
EEIIMSTZ	ITEMIZES	
EEIINNST	NINETIES	
EEIINORT	ERIONITE	
EEIINPPR	PIPERINE	
EEIINPRS	PINERIES	
EEIINPRV	VIPERINE	
EEIINRRV	RIVERINE	
EEIINRST	RESINISE	
EEIINRST	ERINITES	
	NITERIES	
EEIINRSV	VINERIES	
EEIINRSW	WINERIES	
EEIINRSZ	RESINIZE	
EEIINRTT	INTERTIE	
	RETINITE	
EEIINSSV	INESSIVE	
EEIINSTT	ENTITIES	
EEIINSTV	INVITEES	
	VEINIEST	
EEIIORSS	OSIERIES	
EEIIPRSX	EXPIRIES	
EEIIPRTT	EPITRITE	
EEIIQSTU	EQUITIES	
EEIIQTUV	QUIETIVE	
EEIIRRST	REISTIER	
EEIIRRSV	RIVIERES	
EEIIRRTV	TIRRIVEE	
EEIIRSTV	VERITIES	
EEIISSTV	VISITEES	
EEIISTVW	VIEWIEST	
EEIJKRST	JERKIEST	
EEIJLNNU	JULIENNE	
EEIJLNRT	JETLINER	
EEIJLNUV	JUVENILE	
EEIJMMST	JEMMIEST	
EEIJNNOR	ENJOINER	
EEIJSTTT	JETTIEST	
EEIKLLRS	SKELLIER	

EEIKLLRY	KYRIELLE	
EEIKLLSS	SKELLIES	
EEIKLNSS	LIKENESS	
EEIKLORS	ROSELIKE	
EEIKLORT	LORIKEET	
EEIKLPST	PIKELETS	
	SPIKELET	
EEIKLRST	TRISKELE	
EEIKMRSS	KERMISES	
EEIKNORS	KEROSINE	
EEIKNRST	KERNITES	
EEIKOQUV	EQUIVOKE	
EEIKPPRR	KIPPERER	
EEIKPRST	PERKIEST	
EEIKPSST	PESKIEST	
EEIKRRSS	SKERRIES	
EEIKSSTY	SKIEYEST	
EEIKSTTT	TEKTITES	
EEILLMPR	IMPELLER	
EEILLMRS	SMELLIER	
EEILLMRU	REILLUME	
EEILLMST	MELLITES	
EEILLNOR	LONELIER	
EEILLNSY	SENILELY	
EEILLNVV	VENVILLE	
EEILLORS	ORSEILLE	
EEILLORV	LOVELIER	
EEILLOSV	LOVELIES	
EEILLPSS	ELLIPSES	
EEILLPSY	SLEEPILY	
EEILLRSS	LEISLERS	
EEILLRST	TREILLES	
EEILLSSV	VEILLESS	
EEILLSTV	EVILLEST	
EEILLTVY	VELLEITY	
EEILLVVY	WEEVILLY	
EEILMNNS	LINESMEN	
EEILMNNU	ENLUMINE	
EEILMNOP	PEMOLINE	
EEILMNRS	ERMELINS	
EEILMNRU	LEMURINE	
	RELUMINE	
EEILMNSS	ISLESMEN	
EEILMNSU	SELENIUM	
	SEMILUNE	
EEILMOPS	POLEMISE	
EEILMOPZ	POLEMIZE	
EEILMORT	MOTELIER	
EEILMOST	MESOLITE	
	MISLETOE	
EEILMPST	IMPLETES	
EEILMPSX	IMPLEXES	
EEILMRST	TERMLIES	
EEILMRSV	VERMEILS	
EEILMSST	TIMELESS	
EEILMSUV	EMULSIVE	
EEILNNST	LENIENTS	
	SENTINEL	
EEILNNSV	ENLIVENS	
EEILNOPR	LEPORINE	
EEILNORS	ELOINERS	
EEILNOST	NOSELITE	
EEILNOSV	NOVELISE	
EEILNOVZ	NOVELIZE	
EEILNPPZ	ZEPPELIN	
EEILNPRS	PILSENER	
EEILNPRU	PERILUNE	
EEILNPRV	REPLEVIN	
EEILNPST	PLENTIES	
EEILNRSS	REINLESS	

```
EEILNRST LISTENER      EEIMNORS EMERSION               WENNIEST      EEINSTTW TENTWISE
         SILENTER      EEIMNORT TIMONEER      EEINOPPR PEPERINO               TWENTIES
EEILNRTY ENTIRELY      EEIMNORV VOMERINE               PEPERONI      EEINSTTX EXISTENT
         LIENTERY      EEIMNOST MONETISE      EEINOPRS ISOPRENE      EEIOPPRS EPISPORE
EEILNRUV UNVEILER               SEMITONE               PIONEERS               POPERIES
EEILNSSV EVILNESS      EEIMNOTX XENOTIME      EEINORRT REORIENT      EEIOPRRS ROPERIES
         VILENESS      EEIMNOTZ MONETIZE      EEINORSS ESSOINER      EEIOPRRT PORTIERE
EEILNSTT ENTITLES      EEIMNPRT TRIPEMEN      EEINORST SEROTINE      EEIOPRRV OVERRIPE
EEILNSTV VEINLETS      EEIMNPRU PERINEUM      EEINORSV EVERSION      EEIOPRST POETRIES
EEILOPRS PELORIES      EEIMNPST SEPIMENT      EEINORTT TENORITE      EEIOPSST POETISES
EEILOPST PETIOLES      EEIMNQSU MESQUINE      EEINORTX EXERTION      EEIOPSTZ POETIZES
EEILORRT LOITERER      EEIMNRRT TERMINER      EEINOSST ESSONITE      EEIORRRS ORRERIES
EEILORRV OVERLIER      EEIMNRRV RIVERMEN      EEINOSTT NOISETTE      EEIORRSS ROSERIES
EEILORRW LOWERIER      EEIMNRSV MINEVERS               TEOSINTE               ROSIERES
EEILORST LITEROSE      EEIMNRTU MUTINEER      EEINPPSS PEPSINES      EEIORRTV OVERTIRE
         TROELIES      EEIMNRTV VIREMENT      EEINPRRS REPINERS      EEIORRTW TOWERIER
EEILORSV OVERLIES      EEIMNSSW MISWEENS      EEINPRSS EREPSINS      EEIORRTX EXTERIOR
         RELIEVOS      EEIMNSTT MINETTES               RIPENESS      EEIORRUV OUVRIERE
         VOLERIES      EEIMOPRS PROMISEE      EEINPRSU PENURIES      EEIORSST EROTESIS
EEILORSW OWLERIES               REIMPOSE               RESUPINE      EEIORSSX OREXISES
EEILORVV OVERLIVE      EEIMOPSS EPISOMES      EEINPRTX INEXPERT      EEIORSVW OVERWISE
         OVERVEIL      EEIMOPST EPITOMES      EEINPSST PENTISES      EEIORSVZ OVERSIZE
EEILOSST ESTOILES               EPSOMITE      EEINPSTT INEPTEST      EEIORVVW OVERVIEW
EEILOSTW OWELTIES      EEIMORSS ISOMERES               SPINETTE      EEIORVWW WIREWOVE
EEILOSTZ ZEOLITES      EEIMORST TIRESOME      EEINQRRU ENQUIRER      EEIPPPRR PREPPIER
EEILOSVW VOWELISE      EEIMORTV OVERTIME      EEINQRSU ENQUIRES      EEIPPPRS PREPPIES
EEILOTTT TOILETTE      EEIMORTX OXIMETER               INQUERES      EEIPPPST PEPPIEST
EEILOVWZ VOWELIZE      EEIMOSSW SOMEWISE               SQUIREEN      EEIPPRRS PERSPIRE
EEILPPSS PIPELESS      EEIMOSSX EXOMISES      EEINQSTU QUIETENS      EEIPPRTY PERIPETY
EEILPPSY EPILEPSY      EEIMPPRS EPISPERM      EEINQSUY QUEYNIES      EEIPPSST PEPTISES
EEILPRRS REPLIERS      EEIMPRRS PREMIERS      EEINRRSS RESINERS      EEIPPSTT PIPETTES
EEILPRSS SPIELERS               REPRIMES      EEINRRST INSERTER      EEIPPSTZ PEPTIZES
EEILPRST EPISTLER               SIMPERER               REINSERT      EEIPQRSU PERIQUES
         PELTRIES      EEIMPRSS EMPRISES               REINTERS               REPIQUES
         PERLITES               IMPRESSES              RENTIERS      EEIPRRRS PERRIERS
         REPTILES               IMPRESSE               TERRINES      EEIPRRSS REPRISES
EEILPSSS PELISSES               MESPRISE      EEINRRSU REINSURE               RESPIRES
EEILPSST EPISTLES               PREMISES      EEINRRSV VERNIERS      EEIPRRSV REPRIVES
EEILPSSU EPULISES               SPIREMES      EEINRRTV INVERTER      EEIPRRSZ REPRIZES
EEILPSSV PELVISES      EEIMPRST EMPTIERS      EEINRRTX INTERREX      EEIPRRTT PRETERIT
EEILPSTY EPISTYLE      EEIMPRSX PREMIXES      EEINRSST INTERESS               PRETTIER
EEILQRSU RELIQUES      EEIMPRSZ MESPRIZE               SENTRIES      EEIPRSST RESPITES
EEILRRSV RELIVERS      EEIMPSST SEPTIMES               TRENISES      EEIPRSSV PREVISES
         REVILERS      EEIMPSSY EMPYESIS      EEINRSSU ENURESIS      EEIPRSTT PRETTIES
EEILRSST LEISTERS      EEIMPSTT EMPTIEST      EEINRSSV VERSINES      EEIPRSTY PERSEITY
         RITELESS      EEIMQRSU REQUIEMS               VERSINES      EEIPRSVW PREVIEWS
         TIRELESS      EEIMQSTU MESQUITE      EEINRSTT INERTEST      EEIPRSZZ PREZZIES
EEILRSSU LEISURES      EEIMRRST MERRIEST               INTEREST      EEIPRTUV ERUPTIVE
EEILRSSV SERVILES               TRIREMES               STERNITE      EEIPSSSS SPEISSES
EEILRSSW WIRELESS      EEIMRRTT REMITTER      EEINRSTU ESURIENT      EEIPSSTW SPEWIEST
EEILRSTT RETITLES               TRIMETER               NEURITES               STEPWISE
EEILSSTW WITELESS      EEIMRSST TRISEMES               RETINUES      EEIPSTTT PETTIEST
EEILSSTX SEXTILES      EEIMRSSV VERMISES               REUNITES      EEIQRRRU REQUIRER
EEILSSVW VIEWLESS      EEIMRSTT TERMITES      EEINRSTV NERVIEST      EEIQRRSU REQUIRES
EEILSTTX TEXTILES      EEIMRSTU EMERITUS               REINVEST      EEIQRRTU REQUITER
EEILSTVY STIEVELY      EEIMRTTY TEMERITY               SERVIENT      EEIQRRUV VERQUIRE
EEIMMNRS IMMENSER      EEIMSSST MESSIEST               SIRVENTE      EEIQRSSU ESQUIRES
EEIMMORS MEMORIES               METISSES      EEINRSTX INTERSEX      EEIQRSTU QUIETERS
         MEMORISE      EEINNNPS PENNINES      EEINRSTY SERENITY               REQUITES
EEIMMORZ MEMORIZE      EEINNPTT PENITENT      EEINRSUV UNIVERSE      EEIQRSTW QWERTIES
EEIMMOST SOMETIME      EEINNRST INTENSER      EEINRTTY ENTIRETY      EEIQRTUY QUEERITY
EEIMMRSS IMMERSES               INTERNES               ETERNITY      EEIQSSSU ESQUISSE
EEIMMRST MERISTEM      EEINNRSU NEURINES      EEINSSST SESTINES      EEIQSTTU QUIETEST
         MIMESTER      EEINNRSV INNERVES      EEINSSSW WISENESS      EEIRRRST RETIRERS
         MISMETRE               NERVINES      EEINSSSX SEXINESS               TERRIERS
EEIMMRSU EUMERISM      EEINNRTT RENITENT      EEINSSTW NEWSIEST      EEIRRSST TRESSIER
EEIMMSSS MISSEEMS      EEINNRUX XENURINE      EEINSSTX SIXTEENS      EEIRRSSV REVERSIS
EEIMNNOS NOMINEES      EEINNSST TENNISES      EEINSSTY SYENITES               REVISERS
EEIMNNRS REINSMEN      EEINNSTT SENTIENT      EEINSTTT NETTIEST      EEIRRSTV REVERIST
EEIMNOPS EPISEMON      EEINNSTW ENTWINES               TENTIEST               RIVERETS
```

```
           RIVETERS
EEIRRSTW   REWRITES
EEIRRSVV   REVIVERS
EEIRRTTT   TITTERER
EEIRSSSU   REISSUES
EEIRSSSV   IVRESSES
EEIRSSTT   RESTIEST
EEIRSSTU   SURETIES
EEIRSSTV   SIEVERTS
           TREVISES
           VESTRIES
EEIRSSUZ   SEIZURES
EEIRSTVV   VETIVERS
EEIRSTVY   SEVERITY
EEIRTTTZ   TERZETTI
EEISSSTT   TESTIEST
EEISSTTU   SUETIEST
EEISSTTV   STIEVEST
EEISSTTW   STEWIEST
EEISSTTZ   ZESTIEST
EEISTTTX   TETTIXES
EEISTUXZ   ZEUXITES
EEJJLNUY   JEJUNELY
EEJKMOOS   JOKESOME
EEJLLMSU   JUMELLES
EEJLPSTU   PULSEJET
EEJNOORS   REJONEOS
EEJNORSY   ENJOYERS
EEJPRRRU   PERJURER
EEJPRRSU   PERJURES
EEJQRRSU   JERQUERS
EEKKOSTV   VETKOEKS
EEKKRRST   TREKKERS
EEKLLNRY   KERNELLY
EEKLLNSV   KNEVELLS
EEKLLSUU   UKULELES
EEKLNNNU   UNKENNEL
EEKLNOSS   KEELSONS
EEKLNOST   SKELETON
EEKLNOSV   VELSKOEN
EEKLRSST   KESTRELS
           SKELTERS
EEKNOPRS   RESPOKEN
EEKNOSTY   KEYNOTES
           KEYSTONE
EEKNSSTU   NETSUKES
EEKOORST   KREOSOTE
EEKOPRTV   OVERKEPT
EEKORSTV   OVERKEST
EEKRRTUZ   KREUTZER
EELLMORW   MELLOWER
EELLMPTU   PLUMELET
EELLMRSS   SMELLERS
EELLMRSV   VERMELLS
EELLNORR   ENROLLER
EELLNOUV   NOUVELLE
EELLNPRU   PRUNELLE
EELLNRSU   SULLENER
EELLNSST   SNELLEST
EELLNSTU   ENTELLUS
EELLOPSS   ELLOPSES
EELLORSS   ROSELLES
EELLORST   SOLLERET
EELLORSV   OVERSELL
EELLORSZ   ROZELLES
EELLORTX   EXTOLLER
EELLORWY   YELLOWER
EELLOSSV   LOVELESS
EELLOSUV   LEVULOSE
EELLPRSS   RESPELLS

           SPELLERS
EELLQRSU   QUELLERS
EELLRSSU   RULELESS
EELLRSSW   SWELLERS
EELLSSTW   SWELLEST
EELMMPSU   EMPLUMES
EELMMPUX   EXEMPLUM
EELMNOOS   LONESOME
           OENOMELS
EELMNORS   SOLEMNER
EELMNSUY   UNSEEMLY
EELMNTTU   TEMULENT
EELMNTUY   UNMEETLY
EELMOOSV   LOVESOME
EELMOPRS   PLEROMES
EELMOPRY   EMPLOYER
EELMOPST   LEPTOMES
EELMOPSY   POLYSEME
EELMORST   MOLESTER
EELMORSW   EELWORMS
EELMORTY   MOTLEYER
           REMOTELY
EELMOSSV   MOVELESS
EELMOTVW   TWELVEMO
EELMPPRU   EMPURPLE
EELMPSST   SEMPLEST
           STEMPELS
           STEMPLES
EELMPSTT   TEMPLETS
EELMRRTU   MURRELET
EELMRSST   SMELTERS
           TERMLESS
EELMRSTY   SMELTERY
EELMRTUX   LUXMETER
EELMSSST   STEMLESS
EELMSSTT   STEMLETS
EELNNOSS   LONENESS
EELNNUVY   UNEVENLY
EELNOORS   LOOSENER
EELNOPPU   UNPEOPLE
EELNOPRT   PETRONEL
EELNOPSV   ENVELOPS
EELNOPTY   POLYTENE
EELNOQTU   ELOQUENT
EELNORST   ENTRESOL
EELNORTT   TELETRON
EELNORTV   OVERLENT
EELNOSSS   NOSELESS
           SOLENESS
EELNOSST   NOTELESS
           TONELESS
EELNOSSU   SELENOUS
EELNOSSY   ESLOYNES
EELNOSSZ   ZONELESS
EELNOSTT   NOTELETS
EELNOSTU   TOLUENES
EELNOTVV   EVOLVENT
EELNRSTT   LETTERNS
EELNRSUV   NERVULES
EELNSSTU   TUNELESS
           UNSTEELS
EELNSSTY   ENSTYLES
EELNSSUV   UNSELVES
EELNSTTU   LUNETTES
           UNSETTLE
EELOPPSS   PEPLOSES
EELOPPST   ESTOPPEL
EELOPRRX   EXPLORER
EELOPRSX   EXPLORES
EELOPSTU   EELPOUTS

           OUTSLEEP
EELOQRUY   REQUOYLE
EELORRSV   RESOLVER
EELORRTV   REVOLTER
EELORRUV   OVERRULE
EELORRVV   REVOLVER
EELORSSS   ROSELESS
EELORSSV   RESOLVES
EELORSTT   LORETTES
EELORSTU   RESOLUTE
EELORSVV   REVOLVES
EELORTTU   ROULETTE
EELORTUV   REVOLUTE
EELOSSST   OSSELETS
EELOSSSU   SOLEUSES
EELOSSTT   TELEOSTS
EELOSSTV   VOTELESS
EELOSTTX   SEXTOLET
EELOSTUV   EVOLUTES
           VELOUTES
EELPPSSU   PEPLUSES
EELPPSTU   SEPTUPLE
EELPQRSU   PREQUELS
EELPRSST   SPELTERS
EELPRSSU   REPULSES
EELPRSTZ   PRETZELS
EELPRSUX   PLEXURES
EELPRTXY   EXPERTLY
EELPSSUX   EXPULSES
           PLEXUSES
EELPSTUX   SEXTUPLE
EELRRSTW   WRESTLER
EELRSSST   RESTLESS
           TRESSELS
EELRSSTT   SETTLERS
           STERLETS
           TRESTLES
EELRSSTW   SWELTERS
           WRESTLES
EELRSSTY   RESTYLES
           TYRELESS
EELRSSTZ   SELTZERS
EELRSTWY   WESTERLY
EELSSTTV   SVELTEST
EELSSTUY   EUSTYLES
EEMMNOOP   MENOPOME
EEMMNOST   MEMENTOS
EEMMNOTV   MOVEMENT
EEMMNRRY   MERRYMEN
EEMMOORS   MEROSOME
EEMMOSSU   MOUSMEES
EEMMNNOPW  PENWOMEN
EEMMNNOSV  ENVENOMS
EEMNOOSS   SOMEONES
EEMNOOSY   MOONEYES
EEMNOPRS   PROSEMEN
EEMNORRS   SERMONER
EEMNORST   SERMONET
           STOREMEN
EEMNORSU   MOUNSEER
EEMNORSV   OVERSMEN
EEMNORSY   MONEYERS
EEMNORTU   ROUTEMEN
EEMNPRSS   PRESSMEN
EEMNPRSU   SUPERMEN
EEMNPRTU   UNTEMPER
EEMNRSTW   TREWSMEN
EEMNSSTU   MUTENESS
           TENESMUS
EEMNSTTV   VESTMENT

EEMOORRV   MOREOVER
EEMOORTT   ROOMETTE
EEMOOSSX   EXOSMOSE
EEMOPRRS   EMPERORS
           PREMORSE
EEMOPRSV   PREMOVES
EEMOPRSW   EMPOWERS
EEMOQTTU   MOQUETTE
EEMORRSS   REMORSES
EEMORRSU   UROMERES
EEMORRSV   REMOVERS
EEMORRTU   MOUTERER
           OUTREMER
EEMORSST   SOMERSET
EEMORSTT   REMOTEST
EEMORSTU   TEMEROUS
EEMOTTTU   TEETOTUM
EEMPRRSU   PRESUMER
           SUPREMER
EEMPRSST   SEMPSTER
EEMPRSSU   PRESUMES
           SUPREMES
EEMPRSTT   TEMPTERS
EEMPRSTU   PERMUTES
EEMPSSTT   TEMPESTS
EEMPSSTY   EMPTYSES
EEMRRSTU   MUSTERER
EEMRRSUU   REMUEURS
EEMRRTTU   MUTTERER
EEMSSTTU   MUSETTES
EENNNOSS   NONSENSE
EENNNPTY   TENPENNY
EENNOORT   ROTENONE
EENNOPSS   OPENNESS
EENNOPTX   EXPONENT
EENNORRW   RENOWNER
EENNORST   TENONERS
EENNORSU   NEURONES
EENNOSTT   NONETTES
EENNQSUU   UNQUEENS
EENNRSUV   UNNERVES
EENNSSSU   UNSENSES
EENNSSTX   NEXTNESS
EENOORST   ROESTONE
EENOORTV   OVERTONE
EENOPPRS   PROPENES
           PROPENSE
EENOPPST   PEPTONES
EENOPRSS   RESPONSE
EENOPRST   PROTENSE
EENOPRSU   PERONEUS
EENOPRTT   ENTREPOT
EENOPRXY   PYROXENE
EENOPSST   PENTOSES
           POSTEENS
EENORRSV   OVERRENS
EENORRTT   ROTTENER
EENORSSS   SORENESS
EENORSSU   NEUROSES
EENORSTT   ONSETTER
EENORSTV   OVERNETS
EENORSTX   EXTENSOR
EENORSVW   OVERSEWN
EENORTVW   OVERWENT
EENOSSST   STENOSES
EENOSSSY   ESSOYNES
EENPPRST   PERPENTS
EENPRSST   PERTNESS
           PRESENTS
           SERPENTS
```

Code	Word	Code	Word
EENPRSSU	PURENESS	EEPRRSSS	PRESSERS
EENPRSTT	STREPENT	EEPRRSSU	PERUSERS
EENPRSTV	PREVENTS		PRESSURE
EENPSSSU	SUSPENSE	EEPRRSTV	PERVERTS
EENPSSTY	STEPNEYS	EEPRRSVY	REPRYVES
EENPSTTU	PETUNTSE	EEPRSTTU	UPSETTER
EENPTTUZ	PETUNTZE	EEPRSTTX	PRETEXTS
EENQSSTU	SEQUENTS	EEPSSTTT	SEPTETTS
EENRRSSU	ENSURERS	EEQRSSTU	QUESTERS
EENRRSTV	RENVERST	EERRSSTU	TRESSURE
	REQUESTS	EERRSSTW	STREWERS
EENRRSUV	NERVURES		WRESTERS
EENRRTUV	VENTURER	EERRSTTU	REUTTERS
EENRSSSU	SURENESS		UTTERERS
EENRSSTT	STERNEST	EERRSTUV	VESTURER
	TESTERNS	EERRSTVY	REVESTRY
EENRSSTU	TRUENESS	EERRSUVY	RESURVEY
EENRSSTW	WESTERNS	EERSSSST	STRESSES
EENRSSTY	STYRENES	EERSSSTU	ESTRUSES
EENRSTUV	VENTURES	EERSSSUY	SEYSURES
EEOOPRSX	EXOSPORE	EERSSTTU	TRUSTEES
EEOOPRTZ	ZOETROPE	EERSSUVW	SURVEWES
EEOORRVW	OVERWORE	EERSTTTU	UTTEREST
EEOPPRSS	PORPESSE	EERSTTUX	TEXTURES
EEOPPSTU	OUTPEEPS	EESSSTTT	SESTETTS
EEOPRRRT	REPORTER	EESSTTTX	SEXTETTS
EEOPRRRV	REPROVER	EFFFGINO	FEOFFING
EEOPRRSU	REPOUSER	EFFFILRU	FLUFFIER
EEOPRRSV	REPROVES	EFFFISTU	FUFFIEST
EEOPRRTT	POTTERER	EFFFOORS	FEOFFORS
EEOPRRTX	EXPORTER	EFFGILRU	GRIEFFUL
EEOPRSSS	ESPRESSO	EFFGINOR	OFFERING
EEOPRSST	PORTESSE	EFFGINSU	EFFUSING
EEOPRSSU	ESPOUSER	EFFGRSTU	GRUFFEST
	REPOUSSE	EFFHIIRW	WHIFFIER
EEOPRSSX	EXPOSERS	EFFHIISW	FISHWIFE
	EXPRESSO	EFFHIITT	FIFTIETH
EEOPRSTT	TREETOPS	EFFHIKSU	KUFFIEHS
EEOPRSTU	OUTPEERS	EFFHIKUY	KUFFIYEH
EEOPRSTV	OVERSTEP	EFFHILRW	WHIFFLER
EEOPRSTY	SEROTYPE	EFFHILSW	WHIFFLES
EEOPRSUX	EXPOSURE	EFFHIRSS	SHERIFFS
EEOPSSSU	ESPOUSES	EFFHIRSW	WHIFFERS
	POSEUSES	EFFHISTU	HUFFIEST
EEOPSTUW	OUTWEEPS	EFFHISTW	WHIFFETS
EEOQRSTU	REQUOTES	EFFHLRSU	SHUFFLER
EEOQRTTU	ROQUETTE	EFFHLSSU	SHUFFLES
EEORRRST	RESORTER	EFFHOORS	OFFSHORE
	RESTORER	EFFIIMST	MIFFIEST
	RETRORSE	EFFIINRS	SNIFFIER
EEORRRTT	RETORTER	EFFIINST	NIFFIEST
EEORRSST	RESTORES	EFFIIPRS	SPIFFIER
EEORRSSV	REVERSOS	EFFIKLSS	SKIFFLES
EEORRSTU	REROUTES	EFFILNRS	SNIFFLER
EEORRSTX	EXTRORSE	EFFILNSS	SNIFFLES
EEORRTTT	TOTTERER	EFFILORT	FORELIFT
EEORRTUV	OVERTURE	EFFILPRS	PIFFLERS
	TROUVERE	EFFILPRU	PLUFFIER
EEORSSST	OSSETERS	EFFILRRS	RIFFLERS
EEORSSTT	ROSETTES	EFFINOSU	EFFUSION
EEORSSTV	ESTOVERS	EFFINRSS	SNIFFERS
	OVERSETS	EFFINRSU	SNUFFIER
EEORSSUV	OVERUSES	EFFINSST	STIFFENS
EEORSSVW	OVERSEWS	EFFIOPRS	PIFFEROS
EEORSTVX	VORTEXES	EFFIORST	FORFEITS
EEORTTTZ	TERZETTO	EFFIOSTT	TOFFIEST
EEOSSSVW	VOWESSES		
EEOSSTTT	SESTETTO		
EEPPRSST	STEPPERS		
EEPPSSUW	UPSWEEPS		
EEPQRRUU	PERRUQUE		

Code	Word	Code	Word
EFFIPSTU	PUFFIEST	EFGINRSU	GUNFIRES
EFFIQRSU	SQUIFFER		REFUSING
EFFIRSTU	STUFFIER	EFGINRSW	SWERFING
EFFISSTT	STIFFEST	EFGINRTT	FRETTING
EFFISSUX	SUFFIXES	EFGINRTU	FEUTRING
EFFLMNUU	UNMUFFLE		REFUTING
EFFLMRSU	MUFFLERS	EFGINRTY	GENTRIFY
EFFLNRSU	SNUFFLER	EFGIOOST	GOOFIEST
EFFLNRUU	UNRUFFLE	EFGIOPTT	PETTIFOG
EFFLNSSU	SNUFFLES	EFGIORSV	FORGIVES
EFFLOSSU	SOUFFLES	EFGIRRST	GRIFTERS
EFFLRRSU	RUFFLERS	EFGLOOVX	FOXGLOVE
EFFLRSTU	TRUFFLES	EFGLORST	FROGLETS
EFFNRSSU	SNUFFERS	EFGLRSUU	SURGEFUL
EFFOOORT	FOREFOOT	EFGLSSTU	SLUGFEST
EFFOOORS	OFFERORS	EFGNOSST	SONGFEST
EFFOPRRS	PROFFERS	EFGNSSUU	FUNGUSES
EFFORRUV	OVERRUFF	EFGORRSU	FERRUGOS
EFFRSSTU	STUFFERS	EFGORSTU	FOREGUTS
EFFSSSUU	SUFFUSES	EFHHIRSS	FRESHISH
EFGGGILN	FLEGGING	EFHIILRT	FILTHIER
EFGGIINN	FEIGNING	EFHIILST	TILEFISH
EFGGILOS	SOLFEGGI	EFHIIMSU	HUMIFIES
EFGGINRU	REFUGING	EFHIINRS	FINISHER
EFGGIORR	FROGGIER	EFHIINSS	FINISHES
EFGGIOST	FOGGIEST	EFHIIPPS	PIPEFISH
EFGGIRRS	FRIGGERS	EFHIIPRS	FIRESHIP
EFGGISTU	FUGGIEST	EFHIIRST	SHIFTIER
EFGGORRY	FROGGERY	EFHIISST	FISHIEST
EFGHILNS	FLESHING	EFHILRSU	FLUSHIER
	SHELFING	EFHIOOOR	FORHOOIE
EFGHINRS	FRESHING	EFHIOPRS	FORESHIP
EFGHINRT	FRIGHTEN	EFHIORRT	FROTHIER
EFGHIRST	FIGHTERS	EFHIORRS	ROSEFISH
	FREIGHTS	EFHIORSV	OVERFISH
EFGHNOTU	FOUGHTEN	EFHIORTT	FORTIETH
EFGIILNU	FIGULINE	EFHIPRSS	SERFSHIP
EFGIILSU	UGLIFIES	EFHIPRSU	FURPHIES
EFGIIMNS	MISFEIGN	EFHIRRTU	THURIFER
EFGIINNR	ENFIRING	EFHIRRST	SHIFTERS
	INFRINGE	EFHISSTU	SHUFTIES
	REFINING	EFHKLNOU	FUNKHOLE
EFGIINNT	FEINTING	EFHLLLSU	SHELLFUL
EFGIINNX	ENFIXING	EFHLNORS	HORNFELS
EFGIINRX	FRINGIER	EFHLOOSS	HOOFLESS
EFGIINRU	FIGURINE	EFHLOOSX	FOXHOLES
EFGIINRY	REIFYING	EFHLOPSU	HOPEFULS
EFGIINRZ	FRIEZING	EFHLORSY	HORSEFLY
EFGIITUV	FUGITIVE	EFHLOSSU	FLOUSHES
EFGIKNOR	FOREKING	EFHLOSUU	HOUSEFUL
EFGILLNO	LIFELONG	EFHLRSSU	FLUSHERS
EFGILLNU	FUELLING	EFHLSSTU	FLUSHEST
EFGILLUU	GUILEFUL	EFHLSTTW	TWELFTHS
EFGILMOR	FILMGOER	EFHNORST	FORHENTS
EFGILNNS	FLENSING	EFHOORSW	FORESHOW
EFGILNOR	FLORIGEN	EFHORRTY	FROTHERY
EFGILNRS	FLINGERS	EFHRRSTU	FURTHERS
EFGILNRY	FERLYING	EFHRSTTU	FURTHEST
EFGILNST	FELTINGS	EFIIILRV	VILIFIER
EFGILNTT	FETTLING	EFIIILSV	VILIFIES
EFGILSTU	GULFIEST	EFIIIMNS	MINIFIES
EFGIMNST	FIGMENTS	EFIIINNT	INFINITE
EFGIMRUU	REFUGIUM	EFIIIRVV	VIVIFIER
EFGINNNP	PFENNING	EFIIISTX	FIXITIES
EFGINNPS	PFENNIGS	EFIIISVV	VIVIFIES
EFGINNRS	FERNINGS	EFIIKLRS	FLISKIER
EFGINORV	FORGIVEN	EFIIKRRS	FRISKIER
EFGINORW	FOREWING	EFIILLRR	FRILLIER
EFGINPUY	PINGUEFY	EFIILLRS	FRILLIES
EFGINRRY	FERRYING	EFIILMRS	FLIMSIER

Key	Word(s)	Key	Word(s)
EFIILMSS	FLIMSIES / MISFILES	EFILMSUY	EMULSIFY
EFIILMST	FILMIEST	EFILNNTU	INFLUENT
EFIILNRT	FLINTIER / INFILTER	EFILNORU	FLUORINE
EFIILNTY	FELINITY / FINITELY	EFILNOSU	NOISEFUL
EFIILOQU	FILIOQUE	EFILNOSX	FLEXIONS
EFIILRRT	FLIRTIER	EFILNRTT	FLITTERN
EFIILRSU	FUSILIER	EFILNSUX	INFLUXES
EFIILSTT	FITLIEST	EFILNUWY	UNWIFELY
EFIIMMNS	FEMINISM	EFILOOSS	FLOOSIES
EFIIMNOS	FISNOMIE / OMNIFIES	EFILOOSZ	FLOOZIES
EFIIMNRR	INFIRMER	EFILOPPR	FLOPPIER
EFIIMNST	FEMINIST	EFILOPRR	PROFILER
EFIIMNSU	MUNIFIES	EFILOPRS	PROFILES
EFIIMNTY	FEMINITY	EFILORRU	FLOURIER
EFIIMRSS	MISFIRES	EFILORSS	FLOSSIER
EFIINNST	FINNIEST	EFILORST	FLORIEST / TREFOILS
EFIINORR	INFERIOR	EFILORTU	FLUORITE
EFIINORT	NOTIFIER	EFILOSSX	SEXFOILS
EFIINOST	NOTIFIES	EFILOSTT	LOFTIEST
EFIINPSV	FIVEPINS	EFILOSTU	OUTFLIES
EFIINPSX	SPINIFEX	EFILPPRS	FLIPPERS
EFIINRST	SNIFTIER	EFILPPST	FLIPPEST
EFIINRSU	UNIFIERS	EFILPPSU	PIPEFULS
EFIINRSY	RESINIFY	EFILPRTU	UPLIFTER
EFIINSTT	NIFTIEST	EFILPSTU	SPITEFUL
EFIINSUV	INFUSIVE	EFILRRST	TRIFLERS
EFIIOSSS	OSSIFIES	EFILRRSU	FLURRIES
EFIIPRRU	PURIFIER	EFILRSST	RIFTLESS / STIFLERS
EFIIPRST	SPITFIRE	EFILRSTT	FLITTERS
EFIIPRSU	PURIFIES	EFILRSTW	FEWTRILS
EFIIPRTY	TYPIFIER	EFILRSVV	FLIVVERS
EFIIPSTY	TYPIFIES	EFILRSZZ	FRIZZLES
EFIIRRST	FIRRIEST	EFILRTTU	FRUITLET
EFIIRRTU	FRUITIER	EFILSSST	SELFISTS
EFIIRRZZ	FRIZZIER	EFILSSTT	LEFTISTS
EFIIRSTT	RIFTIEST	EFILSTTU	FLUTIEST / FUTILEST
EFIIRTUV	FRUITIVE	EFILSTTW	SWIFTLET
EFIIRVVY	REVIVIFY	EFIMMRSU	FERMIUMS
EFIISSTT	FISTIEST	EFIMNORR	INFORMER
EFIISTZZ	FIZZIEST	EFIMNORS	ENSIFORM / FERMIONS
EFIJLORS	FRIJOLES	EFIMNRSS	FIRMNESS
EFIJLOST	JETFOILS	EFIMNSTT	FITMENTS
EFIKLNSU	FLUNKIES	EFIMORRT	RETIFORM
EFIKLORS	FOLKSIER	EFIMORRW	FIREWORM
EFIKLSTU	FLUKIEST	EFIMOSTT	OFTTIMES
EFIKNNOS	FINNESKO	EFIMPRRU	FRUMPIER
EFIKNORS	FORESKIN	EFIMRSTU	FREMITUS
EFIKNRSU	REFUSNIK	EFINNORS	INFERNOS
EFIKNSTU	FUNKIEST	EFINNSTU	FUNNIEST
EFIKORRW	FIREWORK	EFINOPRS	FORPINES
EFIKORST	FORKIEST	EFINOPTX	PONTIFEX
EFIKRRSS	FRISKERS	EFINORRT	FRONTIER
EFIKRSST	FRISKETS	EFINORSU	REFUSION
EFILLLNU	FLUELLIN	EFINORSX	FORNIXES
EFILLMSU	SMILEFUL	EFINOSSX	FOXINESS
EFILLOOS	FOLIOLES	EFINOSSZ	FOZINESS
EFILLORV	OVERFILL	EFINRSST	SNIFTERS
EFILLRUY	IREFULLY	EFINRSSU	INFUSERS
EFILLSTY	STELLIFY	EFINRTTU	UNFITTER
EFILLTUY	FUTILELY	EFIOOPST	POOFIEST
EFILMNSU	FULMINES	EFIOORST	ROOFIEST
EFILMOST	FILEMOTS	EFIOOSTT	FOOTIEST
EFILMRSS	FIRMLESS	EFIOOSTW	WOOFIEST
EFILMSSS	SELFISMS	EFIOPRRS	PORIFERS
EFILMSST	FILMSETS / LEFTISMS		

Key	Word(s)	Key	Word(s)
EFIOPRRT	PROFITER	EFLOORRS	FLOORERS
EFIOPRST	FIREPOTS	EFLOORSS	FORSLOES / ROOFLESS
EFIORRST	FROSTIER / ROTIFERS	EFLOORSW	FORESLOW
EFIORRSW	FROWSIER	EFLOORSZ	FOOZLERS
EFIORRTT	RETROFIT	EFLOORTU	FOOTRULE
EFIORRWZ	FROWZIER	EFLOORVW	OVERFLOW
EFIORSST	FOISTERS	EFLOOSST	FOOTLESS
EFIORSTW	FROWIEST	EFLOPRUW	POWERFUL
EFIPPRRS	FRIPPERS	EFLORSTT	FORTLETS
EFIPPRRY	FRIPPERY	EFLORSTW	FELWORTS
EFIPRRUY	REPURIFY	EFLORSUY	YOURSELF
EFIPRTTY	PRETTIFY	EFLORSVY	FLYOVERS
EFIRRRSU	FURRIERS	EFLOSUUX	FLEXUOUS
EFIRRRUY	FURRIERY	EFLPRSSU	PRESSFUL
EFIRRSSU	FRISEURS / FRISURES	EFLPRSUU	PURSEFUL
EFIRRSTT	FRITTERS	EFLRSSTU	FLUSTERS
EFIRRSTU	FRITURES / FRUITERS / FURRIEST	EFLRSTTU	FLUTTERS
EFIRRTUV	FURTIVER	EFLRSTUU	FRUSTULE
EFIRRTUY	FRUITERY	EFLRSTUY	FLUSTERY
EFIRSSSU	FISSURES	EFMNNORT	FRONTMEN
EFIRSSTU	SURFEITS / SURFIEST	EFMNORTY	FROMENTY
EFIRSSTW	SWIFTERS	EFMNRTUY	FRUMENTY / FURMENTY
EFIRSTTU	TURFIEST / TURFITES	EFMOORST	FOREMOST
EFIRSTUX	FIXTURES	EFMOORSU	FOURSOME
EFIRSTUZ	FURZIEST	EFMOPRRS	PERFORMS / PREFORMS
EFISSSTU	FUSSIEST	EFMOPRST	POMFRETS
EFISSTTU	FUSTIEST	EFNNOOOR	FORENOON
EFISSTTW	SWIFTEST	EFNNORST	FORNENST
EFISTTTU	TUFTIEST	EFNNORUZ	UNFROZEN
EFISTUZZ	FUZZIEST	EFNOOOTT	FOOTNOTE
EFKLLOOR	FOLKLORE	EFNOOPRT	PENTROOF
EFKLMNOS	MENFOLKS	EFNOOSST	EFTSOONS / FESTOONS
EFKLMORS	MERFOLKS	EFNOPRST	FORSPENT
EFKLNSUY	FLUNKEYS	EFNORRST	RENFORST
EFKLOPSU	POKEFULS	EFNORRSU	FORERUNS
EFKLORUW	FLUEWORK	EFNORSTU	FORTUNES
EFKLPSSU	SKEPFULS	EFNOSSST	SOFTNESS
EFKNOORW	FOREKNOW	EFOOORST	FOOTSORE
EFKOOPRS	FORSPOKE	EFOOPRRS	REPROOFS
EFKORRTW	FRETWORK	EFOOPRSS	SPOOFERS
EFLLLOOW	WOOLFELL	EFOOPRST	FORETOPS / POOFTERS
EFLLLOWY	FELLOWLY	EFOOPRSY	SPOOFERY
EFLLLPSU	SPELLFUL	EFOOPSTT	FOOTSTEP
EFLLOORW	FOLLOWER	EFOORRSW	FORSWORE
EFLLORUV	OVERFULL	EFOORRST	FOOTREST
EFLLOUWY	WOEFULLY	EFOOSTUX	OUTFOXES
EFLLRUUY	RUEFULLY	EFOPRRSU	PROFUSER
EFLLSUUY	USEFULLY	EFORRSST	FORTRESS
EFLMMRUY	FLUMMERY	EFORRSTW	FROWSTER
EFLMORRY	FORMERLY	EFORRSTY	FORESTRY
EFLMORSS	FORMLESS	EFORRSUV	FERVOURS
EFLMORSU	FULSOMER	EFORRTTU	FROTTEUR
EFLMPRSU	FRUMPLES	EFORSSST	FOSTRESS
EFLNOOSU	FELONOUS	EGGGIILR	GIGGLIER
EFLNORSU	FLEURONS	EGGGILNS	LEGGINGS
EFLNORTT	FRONTLET	EGGGILOR	GOGGLIER
EFLNOSSU	FOULNESS	EGGGILRS	GIGGLERS
EFLNOSTT	FLETTONS / FONTLETS	EGGGINPS	PEGGINGS
EFLNSSUY	SYNFUELS	EGGGIORR	GROGGIER
EFLNSTTU	TENTFULS	EGGGLORS	GOGGLERS
EFLNSUUU	UNUSEFUL	EGGGNNOR	RONGGENG
		EGGGOOOS	GOOSEGOG
		EGGGORRY	GROGGERY
		EGGHIINN	NEIGHING

EGGHIINW	WEIGHING		EGGLORUY	GURGOYLE
EGGHILRS	HIGGLERS		EGGLPRSU	PLUGGERS
EGGHINSS	GHESSING		EGGLRSSU	SLUGGERS
EGGHIRST	THIGGERS		EGGLRSTU	STRUGGLE
EGGHLOSS	SHOGGLES		EGGMNTUY	NUTMEGGY
EGGHRTUY	THUGGERY		EGGMSSTU	SMUGGEST
EGGIILNR	NIGGLIER		EGGNOOST	GEOGNOST
EGGIILRW	WIGGLIER		EGGNOOSY	GEOGNOSY
EGGIINNN	ENGINING		EGGNORST	GONGSTER
EGGIINNR	GREINING		EGGNRSUY	SNUGGERY
	REIGNING		EGGNSSTU	SNUGGEST
EGGIINNS	SINGEING		EGGOORSU	GORGEOUS
EGGIINNW	WINGEING		EGGSSSTU	SUGGESTS
EGGIINRV	GRIEVING		EGHHILTY	EIGHTHLY
	REGIVING		EGHHINSS	HIGHNESS
EGGIIPST	PIGGIEST		EGHHOSSW	SHOWGHES
EGGIIRTW	TWIGGIER		EGHIILLS	GHILLIES
EGGIKNOS	GINGKOES		EGHIILNR	HIRELING
	GINKGOES		EGHIILNS	SHEILING
EGGILLNY	GINGELLY			SHIELING
EGGILMNU	EMULGING		EGHIIMRT	MIGHTIER
EGGILMSS	LEGGISMS		EGHIINNR	INHERING
EGGILNNO	LONGEING		EGHIINRT	THINGIER
EGGILNNT	GENTLING		EGHIINST	HEISTING
	GLENTING			NIGHTIES
EGGILNNU	LUNGEING			THINGIES
EGGILNRS	NIGGLERS		EGHIINSV	INVEIGHS
	SNIGGLER		EGHIINTV	THIEVING
EGGILNRY	GINGERLY		EGHIIRST	TIGERISH
EGGILNSS	SNIGGLES		EGHIKNRS	GHERKINS
EGGILNSU	LUGEINGS		EGHIKRSS	SKREIGHS
EGGILOOS	GOOGLIES			SKRIEGHS
EGGILQSU	SQUIGGLE		EGHILLNO	HELLOING
EGGILRRW	WRIGGLER		EGHILLNS	SHELLING
EGGILRSW	WIGGLERS		EGHILMNW	WHELMING
	WRIGGLES		EGHILNNU	UNHELING
EGGIMNNU	EMUNGING		EGHILNOV	HOVELING
EGGIMORS	SMOGGIER		EGHILNPS	HELPINGS
EGGIMSTU	MUGGIEST		EGHILNPT	PENLIGHT
EGGINNNR	GRENNING		EGHILNPW	WHELPING
EGGINNOR	ENGORING		EGHILNRS	HERLINGS
EGGINNSS	GINSENGS			SHINGLER
EGGINORR	GORGERIN		EGHILNSS	SHINGLES
	ROGERING		EGHILNST	ENLIGHTS
EGGINRRU	GRUNGIER			LIGHTENS
	REURGING		EGHILNSV	SHELVING
EGGINRSS	GRESSING		EGHILNSW	WELSHING
	SNIGGERS		EGHILNUW	GLUHWEIN
EGGINSSU	GUESSING		EGHILORT	REGOLITH
EGGINSTT	GETTINGS		EGHILOSU	OUGHLIES
EGGINSTU	GUESTING		EGHILPRT	PLIGHTER
	GUNGIEST		EGHILPST	PIGHTLES
EGGIOSST	SOGGIEST		EGHILRST	LIGHTERS
EGGIPRRS	PRIGGERS			RELIGHTS
EGGIPRRY	PRIGGERY			SLIGHTER
EGGIPSTU	PUGGIEST		EGHILSST	SLEIGHTS
EGGIRRST	TRIGGERS		EGHILSTT	LIGHTEST
EGGIRSTT	TRIGGEST		EGHIMNNS	MENSHING
EGGIRSTU	RUGGIEST		EGHIMNSS	MESHINGS
	STUGGIER		EGHIMNUX	EXHUMING
EGGIRSTW	TWIGGERS		EGHIMPRU	GRUMPHIE
EGGISTUV	VUGGIEST		EGHIMSTT	MIGHTEST
EGGJLRSU	JUGGLERS		EGHINNOY	HONEYING
EGGJLRUY	JUGGLERY		EGHINNSS	NIGHNESS
EGGLMOOY	GEMOLOGY		EGHINNST	SENNIGHT
EGGLMRSU	SMUGGLER		EGHINNSU	UNHINGES
EGGLMSSU	SMUGGLES		EGHINORT	THROEING
EGGLNSSU	SNUGGLES		EGHINORV	HOVERING
EGGLORSS	SLOGGERS		EGHINOSS	SHOEINGS
			EGHINOST	HISTOGEN

EGHINOSU	GINHOUSE		EGIILNNU	LINGUINE
EGHINPRS	SPHERING		EGIILNNV	LIVENING
EGHINPSS	SPHINGES		EGIILNOR	RELIGION
EGHINQTU	QUETHING		EGIILNPS	SPIELING
EGHINRRS	HERRINGS		EGIILNRS	RESILING
EGHINRRU	HUNGRIER		EGIILNRT	GIRTLINE
EGHINRRY	HERRYING			RETILING
EGHINRST	RIGHTENS			TINGLIER
EGHINRSU	USHERING			TIRELING
EGHINRSW	SHREWING		EGIILNRV	RELIVING
	WHINGERS			REVILING
EGHINRTW	WRETHING		EGIILNST	LIGNITES
EGHINSTT	SHETTING			LINGIEST
	TIGHTENS		EGIILNSV	VEILINGS
EGHINTTW	WHETTING		EGIILNSW	WISELING
EGHIOOSS	SHOOGIES		EGIILRRS	GRISLIER
EGHIOPSU	PISHOGUE		EGIILRTU	GUILTIER
EGHIORST	GHOSTIER		EGIILRTZ	GLITZIER
EGHIORSU	ROUGHIES		EGIIMMNW	IMMEWING
EGHIOSTT	GOTHITES		EGIIMNNU	INGENIUM
EGHIOSTU	TOUGHIES		EGIIMNOS	IGNOMIES
EGHIOSTV	EIGHTVOS		EGIIMNPS	IMPINGES
EGHIOTUW	OUTWEIGH		EGIIMNRS	REMISING
EGHIQRTU	REQUIGHT		EGIIMNRT	MERITING
EGHIRRST	RIGHTERS			MITERING
EGHIRRUY	HIERURGY		EGIIMNST	MINGIEST
EGHIRSST	SIGHTERS		EGIIMNSV	MISGIVEN
EGHIRSTT	RIGHTEST		EGIIMNTT	EMITTING
	STREIGHT		EGIIMOPT	IMPETIGO
EGHISSTU	GUSHIEST		EGIIMORR	GRIMOIRE
EGHISTTT	TIGHTEST		EGIIMRST	GRIMIEST
EGHLMNOP	PHLEGMON			TIGERISM
EGHLNORS	LEGHORNS		EGIIMSSV	MISGIVES
EGHLNPSU	ENGULPHS		EGIINNPR	REPINING
EGHLNRUY	HUNGERLY			RIPENING
EGHLOOOR	HOROLOGE		EGIINNRS	RESINING
EGHLOORY	RHEOLOGY		EGIINNSS	INSIGNES
EGHLOOSS	GOLOSHES			SEININGS
	SHOOGLES		EGIINNST	STEINING
EGHLOOTY	ETHOLOGY		EGIINNSV	VEININGS
	THEOLOGY		EGIINNSW	SINEWING
EGHLOPRU	PLOUGHER		EGIINNVW	VINEWING
EGHMNOOY	HOMOGENY		EGIINNWZ	WIZENING
EGHMNOSU	HUMOGENS		EGIINOPR	PEIGNOIR
EGHMOPUY	HYPOGEUM		EGIINORS	SEIGNIOR
EGHMOSSU	GUMSHOES		EGIINPRS	SPEIRING
EGHNOOPT	PHOTOGEN		EGIINPRV	PRIEVING
EGHNOOTY	THEOGONY		EGIINPRX	EXPIRING
EGHNORSU	ENROUGHS		EGIINPSS	PIGSNIES
	ROUGHENS		EGIINQTU	QUIETING
EGHNORUV	OVERHUNG		EGIINRRT	RETIRING
EGHNOSTU	TOUGHENS		EGIINRRW	REWIRING
EGHNRSTT	STRENGTH		EGIINRST	GIRNIEST
EGHOOOSW	HOOSEGOW			IGNITERS
EGHORRSU	ROUGHERS			REISTING
EGHORRTW	REGROWTH			STINGIER
EGHORSTU	ROUGHEST			STRIGINE
EGHOSTTU	TOUGHEST		EGIINRSU	SIGNIEUR
EGHPSSUU	UPGUSHES		EGIINRSV	REVISING
EGIIINSV	VISIEING		EGIINRSW	RINGWISE
EGIIJLNR	JINGLIER		EGIINRTU	INTRIGUE
EGIIKLLO	KILLOGIE		EGIINRTV	RIVETING
EGIIKLNN	LIKENING		EGIINRTX	GENITRIX
EGIIKLNR	KINGLIER		EGIINRVV	REVIVING
EGIILMMN	IMMINGLE		EGIINSSZ	SEIZINGS
EGIILMST	LEGITIMS		EGIINSTW	WINGIEST
EGIILNNO	ELOINING		EGIINSTX	EXISTING
EGIILNNR	RELINING		EGIINSTZ	ZINGIEST
EGIILNNS	ENISLING		EGIINSVW	VIEWINGS
	ENSILING		EGIIPPRR	GRIPPIER

EGIIPRSW PERIWIGS	EGILNPRY REPLYING	GORMIEST	SPETTING
EGIIPSST PIGSTIES	EGILNPSS SPIGNELS	EGIMOSST EGOTISMS	EGINQRUY QUERYING
EGIIRRTT GRITTIER	EGILNPST PELTINGS	EGIMOSTW TWIGSOME	EGINQSTU QUESTING
EGIITUXY EXIGUITY	PESTLING	EGIMPRRU GRUMPIER	EGINQSUU QUEUINGS
EGIJKNRS JERKINGS	EGILNPSY YELPINGS	EGINNNOT TENONING	EGINRRST RESTRING
EGIJLLNY JELLYING	EGILNPTT PETTLING	EGINNNOZ ENZONING	RINGSTER
EGIJLNRS JINGLERS	EGILNRRU RULERING	EGINNNRS RENNINGS	STRINGER
EGIJLNRU JUNGLIER	EGILNRRY ERRINGLY	EGINNNST STENNING	EGINRRSW WRINGERS
EGIJLNST JINGLETS	EGILNRSS RINGLESS	EGINNNUY ENNUYING	EGINRRSY SERRYING
EGIJNNOY ENJOYING	SLINGERS	EGINNOOR RONEOING	EGINRRTY RETRYING
EGIJNQRU JERQUING	EGILNRST LINGSTER	EGINNOPR REPONING	EGINRSST RESTINGS
EGIJNSST JESTINGS	RINGLETS	EGINNOPS OPENINGS	STINGERS
EGIKKLNS LEKKINGS	STERLING	EGINNORT NITROGEN	EGINRSSV SERVINGS
EGIKKNRT TREKKING	TINGLERS	EGINNORV VIGNERON	VERSINGS
EGIKLLNN KNELLING	TRINGLES	EGINNPSU PENGUINS	EGINRSSW SWINGERS
EGIKLNPS SKELPING	EGILNRSW NEWSGIRL	EGINNRRS GRINNERS	EGINRSSY SYRINGES
EGIKLNSS KINGLESS	EGILNRUV VELURING	EGINNRRU UNERRING	EGINRSTT GITTERNS
EGIKLNST KINGLETS	EGILNSSS SIGNLESS	EGINNRST STERNING	EGINRSTV STERVING
EGIKMNPS KEMPINGS	EGILNSST GLISTENS	EGINNRSU ENSURING	EGINRSTW STREWING
EGIKNNNS KENNINGS	SINGLETS	EGINNRTU RETUNING	WRESTING
EGIKNNOT TOKENING	EGILNSSW SWINGLES	EGINNRTV VENTRING	EGINRSVW SWERVING
EGIKNNSY ENSKYING	WINGLESS	EGINNSSS SENSINGS	EGINRTTU UTTERING
EGIKNORV OVERKING	EGILNSTT LETTINGS	EGINNSTT NETTINGS	EGINSSTT SETTINGS
REVOKING	SETTLING	STENTING	TESTINGS
EGIKNPPS SKEPPING	EGILNSTW SWELTING	TENTINGS	EGINSSTV VESTINGS
EGIKNRRS SKERRING	WINGLETS	EGINNSTV VENTINGS	EGINSSTW STEWINGS
EGIKNRSU RESKUING	EGILNSUV EVULSING	EGINNSUW UNSEWING	WESTINGS
EGILLMNS SMELLING	EGILNTUX EXULTING	EGINNSUX UNSEXING	EGINSTTT STETTING
EGILLNNS SNELLING	EGILNVXY VEXINGLY	EGINNSVY ENVYINGS	EGIOOPST GOOPIEST
EGILLNOS LOGLINES	EGILOOOS OOLOGIES	EGINOORV INGROOVE	EGIOORRV GROOVIER
EGILLNOV LIVELONG	EGILOOSU ISOLOGUE	EGINOPRS PERIGONS	EGIOOSST GOOSIEST
EGILLNPS SPELLING	EGILOOTY ETIOLOGY	REPOSING	EGIOPRSU GROUPIES
EGILLNQU QUELLING	EGILORRW GROWLIER	SPONGIER	PIROGUES
EGILLNST STELLING	EGILORSS GLOSSIER	EGINOPRW POWERING	EGIOPRTU PORTIGUE
TELLINGS	EGILOSSS GLOSSIES	EGINOPRY PIGEONRY	EGIORRTT GROTTIER
EGILLNSW SWELLING	EGILOSST ELOGISTS	EGINOPST PONGIEST	EGIORRTU GROUTIER
WELLINGS	EGILOSTU EULOGIST	EGINOPSX EXPOSING	EGIORSST GORSIEST
EGILLNSY YELLINGS	EGILPPRS GRIPPLES	EGINOPSY POESYING	STRIGOSE
EGILLNTU GLUTELIN	EGILRRZZ GRIZZLER	EGINORRS IGNORERS	EGIORSSU GRISEOUS
EGILLOOR GLORIOLE	EGILRSST GLISTERS	EGINORST SIGNORES	EGIORSTU GOUSTIER
EGILMMNS LEMMINGS	GRISTLES	GENITORS	EGIORSTV VERTIGOS
EGILMMRS GLIMMERS	EGILRSTT GLITTERS	ROSETING	OYSTRIGE
EGILMMRY GLIMMERY	EGILRSTU GURLIEST	EGINORSY SEIGNORY	EGIORSTZ ZORGITES
EGILMNNO LEMONING	EGILRSUV VIRGULES	EGINORTT OTTERING	EGIORSUV GRIEVOUS
EGILMNPU IMPLUNGE	EGILRSZZ GRIZZLES	EGINORTU OUTREIGN	EGIOSSTT EGOTISTS
EGILMNRS GREMLINS	EGILRTTY GLITTERY	ROUTEING	EGIOSTTU GOUTIEST
MERLINGS	EGIMMNOV EMMOVING	EGINORTW TOWERING	EGIOSTUV OUTGIVES
MINGLERS	EGIMMNST STEMMING	EGINORTX OXTERING	VOGUIEST
EGILMNRU RELUMING	EGIMMRST GRIMMEST	EGINORTZ ROZETING	EGIOSUUX EXIGUOUS
EGILMNST MELTINGS	EGIMMSTU GUMMIEST	EGINORVW OVERWING	EGIPPRRS GRIPPERS
SMELTING	GUMMITES	EGINOSTT TENTIGOS	EGIPRSUU GUIPURES
EGILMNSU LEGUMINS	EGIMNNNO MIGNONNE	EGINOTUV OUTGIVEN	EGIRRSST GRITTERS
EGILMOOR GLOOMIER	EGIMNNOV ENMOVING	EGINPPPR PREPPING	EGIRRSTY REGISTRY
EGILMORS GOMERILS	VENOMING	EGINPPRS REPPINGS	EGIRSSTU SURGIEST
EGILMOSU ELOGIUMS	EGIMNNUW UNMEWING	EGINPPST STEPPING	EGIRSTTT GRITTEST
EGILMOUU EULOGIUM	EGIMNORS NEGROISM	EGINPPRS SPERRING	EGISSTTU GUSTIEST
EGILMPRU GLUMPIER	EGIMNORV REMOVING	SPRINGER	GUTSIEST
EGILMPSS GLIMPSES	EGIMNOST MITOGENS	EGINPRRU REPURING	EGISSYYZ SYZYGIES
EGILNNST NESTLING	EGIMNOSU GEMINOUS	EGINPRSS PRESSING	EGJLNORU JONGLEUR
EGILNNTT NETTLING	EGIMNOSY MOSEYING	SPERSING	EGJLNOTU JELUTONG
EGILNOPP PEOPLING	EGIMNPRS IMPREGNS	SPRINGES	EGKLORSW LEGWORKS
POPELING	EGIMNPRU IMPUGNER	EGINPRST PRESTING	EGLLMORW GROMWELL
EGILNORS RESOLING	EGIMNPST PIGMENTS	EGINPRSU PERSUING	EGLLOOPY PELOLOGY
EGILNORW LOWERING	EGIMNPTT TEMPTING	PERUSING	EGLMMSTU GLUMMEST
EGILNOSU LIGNEOUS	EGIMNPTY EMPTYING	SUPERING	EGLMNOOS ENGLOOMS
EGILNOSW LONGWISE	EGIMNRSS GRIMNESS	EGINPRTU ERUPTING	LONGSOME
EGILNOVV EVOLVING	EGIMNRSU RESUMING	REPUTING	EGLMNOOY MENOLOGY
EGILNPRS PINGLERS	EGIMNRUY ERYNGIUM	EGINPRYY PERIGYNY	EGLMNORS MONGRELS
SPERLING	EGIMORST ERGOTISM	EGINPSSY PIGSNEYS	
SPRINGLE		EGINPSTT PETTINGS	

EGLMNSSU	GLUMNESS	EGOOPRRU	PROROGUE
EGLMOORS	LEGROOMS	EGOORRVW	OVERGROW
EGLMOPRU	PROMULGE	EGOORSTT	GROTTOES
EGLMORSS	GORMLESS	EGOORSTU	OUTGOERS
EGLNNOOR	LONGERON	EGOPPRSS	PROGRESS
EGLNNOSS	LONGNESS	EGOPRRSU	GROUPERS
EGLNNTUY	UNGENTLY		REGROUPS
EGLNOOOY	OENOLOGY	EGOPSSUY	GYPSEOUS
EGLNOOPR	PROLONGE	EGORRSST	GROSERTS
EGLNOOPY	PENOLOGY	EGORRSSU	GROUSERS
EGLNOORV	OVERLONG	EGORSSST	GROSSEST
EGLNOPYY	POLYGENY	EGPRSSUU	UPSURGES
EGLNORSU	LOUNGERS	EHHIIPRS	HEIRSHIP
EGLNORUU	LONGUEUR	EHHIISTV	THIEVISH
EGLNOSSS	SONGLESS	EHHILMNT	HELMINTH
EGLNOSUV	UNGLOVES	EHHIOPRS	HEROSHIP
EGLNOSXY	LOXYGENS	EHHIORTT	HITHERTO
	XYLOGENS	EHHIPRSS	HERSHIPS
EGLNPRSU	PLUNGERS	EHHIPSST	PHTHISES
EGLNRSTU	GRUNTLES	EHHIRSSW	SHREWISH
EGLNRTUY	URGENTLY	EHHIRSTW	WHITHERS
EGLOOORY	OREOLOGY	EHHISSTU	HUSHIEST
EGLOOPRU	PROLOGUE	EHHNOORS	SHOEHORN
EGLOOPTY	LOGOTYPE	EHHOOPST	THEOSOPH
EGLOORSY	SEROLOGY	EHHOOSSW	WHOOSHES
EGLOOSXY	SEXOLOGY	EHHOOSTU	HOTHOUSE
EGLOPRTU	GROUPLET	EHHORSTU	SHOUTHER
EGLORRSW	GROWLERS	EHHRSSTU	THRUSHES
EGLORRWY	GROWLERY	EHIIKLPT	PITHLIKE
EGLORSSS	GLOSSERS	EHIIKLPW	WHIPLIKE
EGLORSUU	RUGULOSE	EHIIKSSW	WHISKIES
EGLORSUY	RUGOSELY	EHIILLST	HILLIEST
EGLPRSSU	SPLURGES	EHIILLSW	WHILLIES
EGLRSUZZ	GUZZLERS	EHIILMOS	HOMILIES
EGLSSUUV	VULGUSES	EHIILOSS	HELIOSIS
EGMMORST	GROMMETS	EHIILRSV	LIVERISH
EGMMOSSU	GUMMOSES	EHIILSTT	LITHITES
EGMMRSTU	GRUMMEST	EHIIMMRW	WHIMMIER
	GRUMMETS	EHIIMMSS	SHIMMIES
EGMNNOOY	MONOGENY	EHIIMNOS	HOMINIES
	NOMOGENY	EHIIMNSS	MINISHES
EGMNNOSW	GOWNSMEN	EHIIMPST	MEPHITIS
EGMNOOOS	MONGOOSE	EHIIMRSW	WHIMSIER
EGMNOORY	MEROGONY	EHIIMSST	SMITHIES
EGMNOOSU	MUNGOOSE	EHIIMSSW	WHIMSIES
EGMNORSU	MURGEONS	EHIINNOS	INHESION
EGMNOSYZ	ZYMOGENS	EHIINNQU	HENIQUIN
EGMNRRSU	GRUMNESS	EHIINNRS	INSHRINE
EGMNSSSU	SMUGNESS	EHIINNRW	WHINNIER
EGMORSTU	GOURMETS	EHIINNSS	SHINNIES
EGNNOOTY	ONTOGENY	EHIINNSW	WHINNIES
EGNNORST	RONTGENS	EHIINRRT	HIRRIENT
EGNNOSTU	GUNSTONE	EHIINRST	INHERITS
EGNNOTTU	UNGOTTEN	EHIINRSZ	RHIZINES
EGNNSSSU	SNUGNESS	EHIINSST	SHINIEST
EGNNSTTU	TUNGSTEN		SHINTIES
EGNNSTUU	UNGUENTS	EHIINSTW	WHINIEST
EGNOORRV	GOVERNOR	EHIINSVX	VIXENISH
EGNOPPRU	OPPUGNER	EHIIPPRW	WHIPPIER
EGNOPRSS	SPONGERS	EHIIPPST	HIPPIEST
EGNOPRSY	PYROGENS	EHIIPRSV	VIPERISH
EGNORRST	STRONGER	EHIIPSTT	PITHIEST
EGNORRSW	WRONGERS	EHIIRRST	SHIRTIER
EGNORSST	SONGSTER	EHIIRRSW	WHIRRIES
EGNORSSU	SURGEONS	EHIIRRTX	HERITRIX
EGNORSTU	STURGEON	EHIIRSSU	HUISSIER
EGNORSTW	WRONGEST	EHIIRSSW	SWISHIER
EGNOSTUY	YOUNGEST	EHIIRSTT	SHITTIER
EGNRRSTU	GRUNTERS		THIRTIES
	RESTRUNG	EHIISSST	STISHIES

EHIISSTT	STITHIES	EHILRSTT	THRISTLE
EHIISTTW	WHITIEST	EHILRSTU	LUTHIERS
	WITHIEST	EHILRSTW	WHIRTLES
EHIISTTX	SIXTIETH		WHISTLER
EHIJNNOS	JOHNNIES	EHILRSTY	SLITHERY
EHIKLOSY	YOKELISH	EHILRTTW	WHITTLER
EHIKLOTY	LEKYTHOI	EHILRTTY	TRIETHYL
EHIKLSTU	HULKIEST	EHILSSTT	THISTLES
EHIKMNST	METHINKS	EHILSSTU	LUSHIEST
EHIKNRRS	SHRINKER	EHILSSTW	WHISTLES
EHIKNRST	RETHINKS	EHILSTTU	THULITES
	THINKERS	EHILSTTW	WHITTLES
EHIKNSTU	HUNKIEST	EHIMMNUY	HYMENIUM
EHIKOOST	HOOKIEST	EHIMMRSS	SHIMMERS
EHIKOPRS	POKERISH	EHIMMRSY	SHIMMERY
EHIKRRSS	SHIRKERS	EHIMNOPR	MORPHINE
EHIKRSSW	WHISKERS	EHIMNORT	THERMION
EHIKRSWY	WHISKERY	EHIMNOST	HOISTMEN
EHIKSSTU	HUSKIEST	EHIMNOSU	HEMIONUS
EHIKSSTW	WHISKETS	EHIMNOTT	MONTEITH
EHIKSSWY	WHISKEYS	EHIMNPRS	PHRENISM
EHILLLMO	MOLEHILL	EHIMNPST	SHIPMENT
EHILLMOY	HOMELILY	EHIMNRRU	MURRHINE
EHILLNOS	HELLIONS	EHIMNRRY	MYRRHINE
EHILLNSS	INSHELLS	EHIMNRSU	RHENIUMS
EHILLOPY	LYOPHILE	EHIMNSTY	THYMINES
EHILLPTY	PHYLLITE	EHIMOOSS	HOMEOSIS
EHILLRRS	SHRILLER	EHIMOOST	SMOOTHIE
EHILLRRT	THRILLER	EHIMOPRS	SOPHERIM
EHILLRST	THILLERS	EHIMOPSS	PHIMOSES
EHILLRTY	LITHERLY	EHIMORSS	HEROISMS
EHILLSSW	SWELLISH	EHIMORST	ISOTHERM
EHILLSTU	HULLIEST		MOITHERS
EHILMOOR	HEIRLOOM		
EHILMOST	HELOTISM	EHIMORSZ	RHIZOMES
EHILMPSW	WHIMPLES	EHIMORTU	MOUTHIER
EHILMPSY	SYMPHILE	EHIMOSTT	MOTHIEST
EHILMQUU	UMQUHILE	EHIMPPSS	PSEPHISM
EHILMSTT	MELTITHS	EHIMPRRS	SHRIMPER
EHILNOOP	OENOPHIL	EHIMPRSU	MURPHIES
EHILNOPS	PINHOLES	EHIMPRSW	WHIMPERS
EHILNORU	UNHOLIER	EHIMPSTU	HUMPIEST
EHILNOSS	HOLINESS		HUMPTIES
EHILNOST	NEOLITHS		TUMPHIES
EHILNOSV	NOVELISH	EHIMPSUU	EUPHUISM
EHILNOTX	XENOLITH	EHIMPTTU	UMPTIETH
EHILNPSY	SYLPHINE	EHIMRSST	SMITHERS
EHILOOPZ	ZOOPHILE	EHIMRSSU	HEURISMS
EHILOOST	HOOLIEST	EHIMRSTY	SMITHERY
EHILOPRS	PILHORSE	EHIMSSTU	MUSHIEST
	POLISHER	EHIMSSTY	METHYSIS
EHILOPRT	HELIPORT		MYTHISES
EHILOPSS	POLISHES	EHIMSSWY	WHIMSEYS
EHILOPST	HELISTOP	EHIMSTTY	THYMIEST
	HOPLITES	EHIMSTYZ	MYTHIZES
	ISOPLETH	EHINNRST	THINNERS
EHILORSS	SLOSHIER	EHINNSST	THINNESS
EHILORTY	RHYOLITE	EHINNSTT	THINNEST
EHILPRST	PHILTERS	EHINOPPR	HORNPIPE
	PHILTRES	EHINOPRT	TRIPHONE
EHILPRSU	PLUSHIER	EHINOPST	PHONIEST
EHILPSSS	SHIPLESS		SIPHONET
EHILPSST	PITHLESS		
	THLIPSES	EHINORRT	THORNIER
EHILPSTU	SULPHITE	EHINORSS	HERISSON
EHILRRSW	WHIRLERS	EHINORST	HORNIEST
EHILRSST	SLITHERS	EHINOSST	HISTONES
	THRISSEL	EHINOSTU	OUTSHINE
EHILRSSU	SLUSHIER	EHINPPSS	SHIPPENS
EHILRSSV	SHRIVELS	EHINPRSU	PUNISHER
		EHINPSSU	PUNISHES

EHINPSSX SPHINXES	EHLMMSUW WHUMMLES	EHNOOSTU OUTSHONE	EIIKLNRS SLINKIER
EHINRSSU INRUSHES	EHLMNOST MENTHOLS	EHNOPRSY HYPERONS	EIIKLNRT TINKLIER
EHINRSTZ ZITHERNS	EHLMNOSY HOMELYNS	EHNOPSSS POSHNESS	EIIKLPSS PLISKIES
EHINSSST THISNESS	EHLMNOUY UNHOMELY	EHNOPSSY HYPNOSES	EIIKLRTT KITTLIER
EHINSSUW UNWISHES	EHLMORTY MOTHERLY	EHNORRST NORTHERS	EIIKLSST SILKIEST
EHIOORTT TOOTHIER	EHLNNOPU UNHOLPEN	EHNORRST SHORTENS	EIIKMPRS SKIMPIER
EHIOOSST STOOSHIE	EHLNOPSU SULPHONE	EHNORSSU ONRUSHES	EIIKMRRS SMIRKIER
EHIOPPPS POPESHIP	EHLNORSS HORNLESS	UNHORSES	EIIKMRST MIRKIEST
EHIOPPRS SHOPPIER	EHLNORST HORNLETS	EHNORSTT THORNSET	EIIKNNRS SKINNIER
EHIOPPST HOPPIEST	EHLNOSTY HONESTLY	EHNORSTU SOUTHERN	EIIKNNSS INKINESS
POETSHIP	EHLNRSTU LUTHERNS	EHNOSSUU UNHOUSES	EIIKNPST PINKIEST
EHIOPRST TROPHIES	EHLNSSSU LUSHNESS	EHNOSTUU NUTHOUSE	EIIKNSST SINKIEST
EHIORRST HERITORS	SHUNLESS	EHNRSSTU HUNTRESS	EIIKNSTZ ZINKIEST
EHIORSST HOISTERS	EHLOOPRT PORTHOLE	SHUNTERS	EIIKPSST SPIKIEST
HORSIEST	POTHOLER	EHNSSSTU THUSNESS	EIIKQRRU QUIRKIER
HOSTRIES	EHLOOPST POTHOLES	EHOOPRSW WHOOPERS	EIIKRSST RISKIEST
SHORTIES	EHLOOPTY HOLOTYPE	EHOOPRTY ORTHOEPY	EIIKSSTV SKIVIEST
EHIORSTT THEORIST	EHLOPPRT THROPPLE	EHOOPSTU HOUSETOP	EIIKSSVV SKIVVIES
THORITES	EHLOPRTY PROTHYLE	POTHOUSE	EIILLLVY LIVELILY
EHIORSTU OUTHIRES	EHLOPSSS SPLOSHES	EHOOPSTY OOPHYTES	EIILLMMS MILLIMES
EHIORSTV OVERHITS	EHLORSST HOLSTERS	EHOOPTYZ ZOOPHYTE	EIILLMNR MILLINER
EHIORSTW WORTHIES	HOSTLERS	EHOORSST ORTHOSES	EIILLMNS SLIMLINE
EHIORTUY YOUTHIER	EHLORSTT THROSTLE	SHOOTERS	EIILLMNU ILLUMINE
EHIORTWZ HOWITZER	EHLORSTY HOSTELRY	SOOTHERS	EIILLNST NIELLIST
EHIOSSTT TOSHIEST	EHLORTTT THROTTLE	EHOORSTV OVERSHOT	EIILLNSU SUILLINE
EHIOSSTW SHOWIEST	EHLOSSTT SHOTTLES	EHOOSSSW SWOOSHES	EIILLNSV VILLEINS
EHIOSSTY ISOHYETS	EHLOSSTW THOWLESS	EHOOSSTT SOOTHEST	EIILLNTV VITELLIN
EHIPPRSS SHIPPERS	EHLOSSTY THYLOSES	EHOOSTUU OUTHOUSE	EIILLPSS ELLIPSIS
EHIPPRSW WHIPPERS	EHLPSSTU PLUSHEST	EHOPPRSS SHOPPERS	EIILLRST STILLIER
EHIPPSSU HIPPUSES	EHLRSSTU HURTLESS	EHOPPRST PROPHETS	EIILLSST SILLIEST
EHIPPSTW WHIPPETS	HUSTLERS	EHOPPRSW WHOPPERS	EIILLSTT TILLIEST
EHIPQSUY PHYSIQUE	RUTHLESS	EHOPPRSY PROPHESY	TILLITES
EHIPRSST HIPSTERS	EHLSSTTU SHUTTLES	EHOPRRSY ORPHREYS	EIILLSTW TWILLIES
THRIPSES	EHMMRRTU THRUMMER	EHOPRSST STROPHES	EIILLSUV ILLUSIVE
EHIPRSSW WHISPERS	EHMMSSUU HUMMUSES	EHOPRSTU POUTHERS	EIILMNNT LINIMENT
EHIPRSTW WHIPSTER	EHMNNSTU HUNTSMEN	EHOPRSTY TROPHESY	EIILMNOT LIMONITE
EHIPRSWY WHISPERY	EHMNOORS HORMONES	EHOPRTUY EUTROPHY	EIILMNSS LIMINESS
EHIPSSTU PUSHIEST	MOORHENS	EHOPSSTY PHYTOSES	EIILMOPT IMPOLITE
EHIPSTUU EUPHUIST	EHMNOOST SMOOTHEN	EHORRSTW THROWERS	EIILMPPR PIMPLIER
EHIQSSSU SQUISHES	EHMNOOTY THEONOMY	EHORSSTT SHORTEST	EIILMPRS IMPERILS
EHIRRSSV SHRIVERS	EHMNOPSU HOMESPUN	EHORSSTU SHOUTERS	EIILMPST LIMEPITS
EHIRRSTT THIRSTER	EHMNPSTY NYMPHETS	SOUTHERS	EIILMRSS SLIMSIER
EHIRRSTV THRIVERS	EHMNSTTU HUTMENTS	EHORSTUY OUTHYRES	EIILMRST LIMITERS
EHIRRSTW WHIRRETS	EHMOOOTZ ZOOTHOME	EHOSSSTU STOUSHES	MIRLIEST
EHIRRTTU TRUTHIER	EHMOOPTY HOMOTYPE	EHPRSSSU SPRUSHES	EIILMRZZ MIZZLIER
EHIRSSSW SWISHERS	EHMOORST SMOOTHER	EHPRSSUU UPRUSHES	EIILMSSS MISSILES
EHIRSSTU RUSHIEST	EHMOOSSS SHMOOSES	EHPRSTTU TURPETHS	EIILMSST ELITISMS
EHIRSSTW SWITHERS	EHMOOSST SMOOTHES	EHPSSTUY TYPHUSES	SLIMIEST
EHIRSTTW WHITRETS	EHMOOSSZ SHMOOZES	EHRRSTTU THRUSTER	EIILMSSV MISLIVES
WHITSTER	EHMOPRSW MORPHEWS	EHRSSSTY SHYSTERS	EIILMSTT MISTITLE
WHITTERS	EHMORSST SMOTHERS	EHRSSTTU SHUTTERS	EIILMSTY MYELITIS
EHIRSWZZ WHIZZERS	EHMORSTU MOUTHERS	EIIILMSS SIMILISE	EIILNNOT LENITION
EHIRTTTW WHITTRET	EHMORSTY SMOTHERY	EIIILMSZ SIMILIZE	EIILNOSS ELISIONS
EHISSSTU STUSHIES	EHMORTUV VERMOUTH	EIIILPPR LIRIPIPE	ISOLINES
EHISSSTW SWISHEST	EHMOSSTY MYTHOSES	EIIIMMNS MINIMISE	LIONISES
EHISSTUW THUSWISE	EHMOTUZZ MEZUZOTH	EIIIMMNZ MINIMIZE	OILINESS
EHISSUVW HUSWIVES	EHMPRSTU THUMPERS	EIIIRRTV TIRRIVIE	EIILNOST ETIOLINS
EHKLOSTY LEKYTHOS	EHMRRSTU MURTHERS	EIIIRSST IRITISES	EIILNOSV OLIVINES
EHKMOORW HOMEWORK	EHMRTUYY EURYTHMY	EIIJKNRT JIRKINET	EIILNOSZ LIONIZES
EHKMORSU HUMORESK	EHMSSTUY MYTHUSES	EIIJMPST JIMPIEST	EIILNOTT TOILINET
EHKNNRSU SHRUNKEN	THYMUSES	EIIJNRSU INJURIES	EIILNQTU QUINTILE
EHKOPSSY KYPHOSES	EHNNOPRS NEPHRONS	EIIKKLLM MILKLIKE	EIILNRST NIRLIEST
EHLLMOPY PHYLLOME	EHNNOPSY HYPNONES	EIIKKNST KINKIEST	NITRILES
EHLLNSSU UNSHELLS	EHNNORRT NORTHERN	EIIKLLMN LIMEKILN	EIILNSSW WILINESS
EHLLNSTU NUTSHELL	EHNNORTU UNTHRONE	EIIKLLRS SKILLIER	EIILNSTT LINTIEST
EHLLOOOP LOOPHOLE	EHNNOSTU UNHONEST	EIIKLLSS SKILLIES	EIILNSTY SENILITY
EHLLOORW HOLLOWER	EHNOOPTY HONEYPOT	EIIKLMRS MISLIKER	EIILNSVY SYLVIINE
EHLMMOSW WHOMMLES	EHNOORRU HONOURER	EIIKLMSS MISLIKES	EIILNTTU INTITULE
	EHNOORSS SOREHONS	EIIKLMST MILKIEST	EIILNTUV VITULINE
	EHNOORSW WHORESON	EIIKLNPS SPELIKIN	EIILOPST PISOLITE

```
         POLITIES        EIIMSSTT MISTIEST   EIIPRSST SPIRIEST   EIKLSSTT SKITTLES
EIILORST ROILIEST        EIINNNPS NINEPINS   EIIPRSTT RISPETTI   EIKLSSTU SULKIEST
EIILORTT TROILITE        EIINNOSU UNIONISE   EIIPRSTU PURITIES   EIKLSTTT KITTLEST
EIILOSST SOILIEST        EIINNOSV ENVISION   EIIPRSTV PRIVIEST   EIKMMORS MIRKSOME
EIILOTVV VOLITIVE        EIINNOUZ UNIONIZE   EIIPRSTY PYRITISE   EIKMMRRS KRIMMERS
EIILPPRR RIPPLIER        EIINNPSS SPINNIES   EIIPRSVV SPIVVIER   EIKMMRSS SKIMMERS
EIILPPRS SLIPPIER        EIINNQSU QUININES   EIIPRTYZ PYRITIZE   EIKMNORS MONIKERS
EIILPPST LIPPIEST        EIINNRTV INVERTIN   EIIPSSTT PIETISTS   EIKMNOST TOKENISM
EIILPRST TRIPLIES        EIINNSST TININESS            STIPITES   EIKMNOSU MOUSEKIN
EIILPRSU PLURISIE        EIINNSSW INSINEWS            TIPSIEST   EIKMOPSS MISSPOKE
EIILPSST PITILESS        EIINNSTT TINNIEST   EIIPSSTW SWIPIEST   EIKMOSST SMOKIEST
         SPILITES        EIINNSTW INTWINES            WISPIEST   EIKMOSSY MISYOKES
EIILPSTY PYELITIS        EIINOPRS RIPIENOS   EIIPSTTT PITTIEST   EIKMRSTU MURKIEST
EIILPSUZ SPUILZIE        EIINOPRT POINTIER   EIIPSTTU PITUITES   EIKMSSSU KUMISSES
EIILQSSU SILIQUES        EIINOPTT PETITION   EIIQSTTU QUIETIST   EIKMSSTU MUSKIEST
EIILRRSW SWIRLIER        EIINORRT INTERIOR   EIIRRSTW WRISTIER   EIKNNOST INKSTONE
EIILRRTW TWIRLIER        EIINORSS IONISERS   EIIRRSTV REVISITS   EIKNNPSS PINKNESS
EIILRSTT STILTIER                 IRONISES            VISITERS   EIKNNRSS SKINNERS
EIILRSTU UTILISER        EIINORSV REVISION   EIIRSTTU UTERITIS   EIKNOORS ROOINEKS
EIILRTUZ UTILIZER                 VISIONER   EIIRSTTW TWISTIER   EIKNOOST NOOKIEST
EIILSSTT ELITISTS        EIINORSZ IONIZERS   EIIRSTTZ RITZIEST   EIKNORTT KNOTTIER
         SILTIEST                 IRONIZES   EIISSSST SISSIEST   EIKNOSTW WONKIEST
EIILSSTU ULITISES        EIINOSST NOISIEST   EIISSTTV STIVIEST   EIKNPRSU SPUNKIER
         UTILISES        EIINOSTV NOVITIES   EIISTTTW WITTIEST   EIKNPRTU TURNPIKE
EIILSTUY TUILYIES        EIINPPRS SNIPPIER   EIJJNTUY JEJUNITY   EIKNPSSU SPUNKIES
EIILSTUZ TUILZIES        EIINPPST NIPPIEST   EIJKNSTU JUNKIEST   EIKNRSST STINKERS
         UTILIZES        EIINPRRS INSPIRER   EIJLLOST JOLLIEST   EIKNRSTT KNITTERS
EIIMMNNT IMMINENT        EIINPRSS INSPIRES   EIJLOSTT JOLTIEST            TRINKETS
         MINIMENT        EIINPRST PRISTINE   EIJMNPSS JIMPNESS   EIKNSSSU UNKISSES
EIIMMNSU IMMUNISE        EIINPSST SNIPIEST   EIJMPSTU JUMPIEST   EIKNSSST SKINTEST
EIIMMNUZ IMMUNIZE                 SPINIEST   EIJNORST JOINTERS   EIKOOPRS SPOOKIER
EIIMMPRU IMPERIUM        EIINPTUV PUNITIVE   EIJNORTU JOINTURE   EIKOPPRW PIPEWORK
EIIMMRSW SWIMMIER        EIINQRRU INQUIRER   EIJNOSTT JETTISON   EIKOPRST PORKIEST
EIIMMSSS SEISMISM        EIINQRSU INQUIRES   EIJNPRSU JUNIPERS   EIKOPRSV OVERSKIP
EIIMMSST MISTIMES        EIINQSSU SQUINIES   EIJNRRSU INJURERS   EIKORRWW WIREWORK
EIIMNOPT PIMIENTO                 SQUINIES   EIJSSSUV JUSSIVES   EIKPPRSS SKIPPERS
EIIMNORT MINORITE        EIINQSTU INQUIETS   EIKKLNRS KLINKERS   EIKPPSST SKIPPETS
EIIMNOSS EMISSION        EIINQTUY EQUINITY   EIKKNRSS SKINKERS   EIKPRRSU SPRUIKER
         SIMONIES                 INEQUITY   EIKKOOST KOOKIEST   EIKRRSST SKIRTERS
EIIMNOSV VISNOMIE        EIINRRTW WINTRIER   EIKKSTUY YUKKIEST            SKIRRETS
EIIMNOTV MONITIVE        EIINRSST SINISTER   EIKLLMSS MILKLESS            STRIKERS
EIIMNPRS PRIMINES        EIINRSSW WIRINESS   EIKLLNSW INKWELLS   EIKRRSSU SKURRIES
EIIMNRSS MIRINESS        EIINRSTT NITRITES   EIKLLNUY UNLIKELY   EIKRSSTT SKITTERS
EIIMNRST INTERIMS                 STINTIER   EIKLLORV OVERKILL   EIKRSSTU TURKISES
         MINISTER        EIINRSTU NEURITIS   EIKLLOSS SKOLLIES   EIKSSTTU TUSKIEST
EIIMNRSV MINIVERS        EIINRSTV INVITERS   EIKLLSSS SKILLESS   EILLLOVY LOVELILY
EIIMNRTT INTERMIT                 VINTRIES   EIKLLSST SKILLETS   EILLLPUV PULVILLE
EIIMNRTX INTERMIX                 VITRINES   EIKLMNOS MOLESKIN   EILLMNOU LINOLEUM
EIIMNSTT MINTIEST        EIINSSSZ SIZINESS   EIKLMNRS KREMLINS   EILLMNQU QUILLMEN
EIIMNSTU MUTINIES        EIINSSTU UNITISES   EIKLNOOR OERLIKON   EILLMNSU MULLEINS
EIIMNSTV MINIVETS        EIINSTTT NITTIEST   EIKLNOSW SNOWLIKE   EILLMOPS PLIMSOLE
EIIMOPRX MIREPOIX                 TINTIEST   EIKLNPRS SPRINKLE   EILLMOST MELILOTS
EIIMOPST OPTIMISE        EIINSTTW TWINIEST   EIKLNRRU KNURLIER   EILLMPSS MISSPELL
EIIMOPTZ OPTIMIZE        EIINSTUZ UNITIZES   EIKLNRSS SLINKERS            PSELLISM
EIIMOSSV OMISSIVE        EIIOPRRS PRIORIES   EIKLNRST LINKSTER   EILLMPTU MULTIPLE
EIIMOSTY MOYITIES        EIIOPSTV POSITIVE            STRINKLE   EILLMSST MISTELLS
EIIMOSUX EXIMIOUS        EIIORRST RIOTRIES            TINKLERS   EILLMUVX VEXILLUM
EIIMOTVV VOMITIVE        EIIORSST RIOTISES   EIKLNRSW WINKLERS   EILLNOPY EPYLLION
EIIMPRSS MISPRISE        EIIORSTZ RIOTIZES            WRINKLES   EILLNOST STELLION
         PISMIRES        EIIOSSTT OSTEITIS   EIKLNRTW TWINKLER   EILLNOTU LUTEOLIN
EIIMPRSZ MISPRIZE                 OTITISES   EIKLNSSS SKINLESS   EILLNPUU LUPULINE
EIIMPSST PIETISMS        EIIOSSTZ ZOISITES   EIKLNSST LENTISKS   EILLNSTY SILENTLY
EIIMPSTW WIMPIEST        EIIOTTTV TOTITIVE   EIKLNSSY SKYLINES            TINSELLY
EIIMQSTU QUIETISM        EIIPPPST PIPPIEST   EIKLNSTT KNITTLES   EILLNSVY SNIVELLY
EIIMRRRS SMIRRIER        EIIPPRRS RIPPIERS   EIKLNSTW TWINKLES   EILLNUVY UNLIVELY
EIIMRSTT METRITIS        EIIPPSTT TIPPIEST   EIKLOOPR PLOOKIER   EILLOORW WOOLLIER
EIIMRSTW MISWRITE        EIIPPSTZ ZIPPIEST   EIKLOORT ROOTLIKE   EILLOOSW WOOLLIES
EIIMSSSS MISSISES        EIIPPRSS PRISSIER   EIKLOPRU PLOUKIER   EILLOPTY POLITELY
EIIMSSST MISSIEST        EIIPPRST STRIPIER   EIKLOPRW PILEWORK   EILLORST TRILLOES
EIIMSSSV MISSIVES                            EIKLOSTY YOLKIEST            TROLLIES
```

```
EILLORSZ ZORILLES
EILLOSSS SOILLESS
EILLOSST TOILLESS
EILLOSTW LOWLIEST
EILLPRSS SPILLERS
EILLQSTU QUILLETS
EILLRSST STILLERS
EILLRSSW SWILLERS
EILLRSTT TESTRILL
EILLRSVY SILVERLY
EILLSSST LISTLESS
EILLSSTT STILLEST
EILLSTTT LITTLEST
EILLSTUV VITELLUS
EILMMNOS MOLIMENS
EILMMPRU PLUMMIER
EILMMRSS SLIMMERS
EILMMRSU SLUMMIER
EILMMSST SLIMMEST
EILMMSTU LUMMIEST
EILMNOSU EMULSION
EILMNOSV NOVELISM
EILMNOTU MOULINET
EILMNOTY MYLONITE
EILMNPSU SPLENIUM
EILMNRST MINSTREL
EILMNSSS SLIMNESS
EILMNSSU EMULSINS
EILMNSTU MUSLINET
EILMNTUY MINUTELY
         UNTIMELY
EILMOOPS LIPOSOME
EILMOORS SLOOMIER
EILMOOST TOILSOME
EILMOPRR IMPLORER
EILMOPRS IMPLORES
         PELORISM
EILMOPST POLEMIST
EILMORRS LORIMERS
EILMOSTT MOTLIEST
EILMPPRU IMPURPLE
EILMPPRS SIMPLERS
EILMPRSU SLUMPIER
EILMPRUY IMPURELY
EILMPSST MISSPELT
         SIMPLEST
EILMPSSU IMPULSES
EILMPSTU LUMPIEST
         PLUMIEST
EILMRSSU MISRULES
EILMRSSY REMISSLY
EILMRSTU MURLIEST
EILMRSTY LYMITERS
EILMSSTU LITMUSES
EILMSUUV ELUVIUMS
EILMTTUU LUTETIUM
EILMTTUY MULTEITY
EILNNOST INSOLENT
EILNNOSW SNOWLINE
EILNNOTV VINOLENT
EILNNPSU PINNULES
EILNNTTY INTENTLY
EILNOOPP EPIPLOON
EILNOOPS POLONIES
         POLONISE
EILNOOPZ POLONIZE
EILNOOST LOONIEST
         OILSTONE
EILNOOSV VIOLONES
EILNOPPS PLENIPOS

EILNOPPY POLYPINE
EILNOPRS PROLINES
EILNOPSS EPSILONS
EILNOPST POINTELS
EILNOPTU UNPOLITE
EILNORRS LORINERS
EILNORRT RITORNEL
EILNORST RETINOLS
EILNORTT TROTLINE
EILNOSSU ELUSIONS
EILNOSSW LEWISSON
EILNOSTU ELUTIONS
         OUTLINES
EILNOSTV NOVELIST
         VIOLENTS
EILNOSTW TOWLINES
EILNOSUV EVULSION
EILNOSVV INVOLVES
EILNOTUV INVOLUTE
EILNOTXY XYLONITE
EILNOTYZ ZYLONITE
EILNPRSS PILSNERS
EILNPRST SPLINTER
EILNPRSU PURLINES
EILNPSST PLENISTS
EILNPSSU SPINULES
         SPLENIUS
EILNPSUY SUPINELY
EILNQUUY UNIQUELY
EILNRRUU UNRULIER
EILNRSST SNIRTLES
EILNRSTU INSULTER
         LUSTRINE
EILNRSTY TINSELRY
EILNRTUV VIRULENT
EILNRTWY WINTERLY
EILNSSTT TINTLESS
EILNSSTU UTENSILS
EILNSSVY SYLVINES
EILNSTTU LUTENIST
EILNSUWY UNWISELY
EILOOPRR POORLIER
EILOOPST LOOPIEST
EILOOPTZ ZOPILOTE
EILOORST TROOLIES
EILOORTV OVERTOIL
EILOOSST OSTIOLES
         STOOLIES
EILOOSTZ ZOOLITES
EILOPPPR POPPLIER
EILOPPRS SLOPPIER
EILOPPTY POLYPITE
EILOPRRT PORTLIER
EILOPRSS SPOILERS
EILOPRST POITRELS
EILOPRSU PERILOUS
EILOPRSV OVERSLIP
EILOPRTW PILEWORT
EILOPSSS PSILOSES
EILOPSST PISTOLES
         PTILOSES
         SLOPIEST
EILOPSSV PLOSIVES
EILOPSTT PISTOLET
         PLOTTIES
         POLITEST
EILOPSTX EXPLOITS
EILOPSUV PLUVIOSE
EILORRTU ULTERIOR
EILORSSS RISSOLES

EILORSSU SOILURES
EILORSST TRIOLETS
EILORSTU LOURIEST
         OUTLIERS
EILORSZZ SOZZLIER
EILORTTY TOILETRY
EILOSSST LOSSIEST
EILOSSTU LOUSIEST
EILOSTTT STILETTO
EILOSTUV OUTLIVES
         SOLUTIVE
EILPPRRS RIPPLERS
EILPPRRT TRIPPLER
EILPPRSS SLIPPERS
EILPPRST RIPPLETS
         STIPPLER
         TIPPLERS
         TRIPPLES
EILPPRSU PERIPLUS
         SUPPLIER
EILPPRSY SLIPPERY
EILPPRTU PULPITER
EILPPSST STIPPLES
EILPPSSU SUPPLIES
EILPPSSW SWIPPLES
EILPPSTU PULPIEST
EILPRSST SPIRTLES
EILPRSTT SPLITTER
         TRIPLETS
EILPRSTY PRIESTLY
         SPRITELY
EILPRSUU PURLIEUS
EILPRSUY PLEURISY
EILPRTTY PRETTILY
EILPSSTT SPITTLES
EILPSSTU STIPULES
EILPSSUY SPULYIES
EILPSSUZ SPULZIES
EILQRRSU SQUIRREL
EILQRSTU QUILTERS
EILQRSUU LIQUEURS
EILQRSUY SQUIRELY
EILQSTUU LUSTIQUE
EILRRSSU SLURRIES
EILRRSTU SULTRIER
EILRRSTW TWIRLERS
EILRRTWY WRITERLY
EILRSSST STIRLESS
EILRSSTT SLITTERS
         STILTERS
         TESTRILS
EILRSSTU SURLIEST
EILRSSTY SISTERLY
EILRSSZZ SIZZLERS
EILRSTTU SURTITLE
EILRSTTW WRISTLET
EILRSTTZ STRELITZ
EILRSTUV RIVULETS
EILRSUUX LUXURIES
EILSSSTY STYLISES
EILSSTTU LUSTIEST
EILSSTTY STYLITES
EILSSTUU LITUUSES
EILSSTVY SYLVITES
EILSSTYZ STYLIZES
EILSSWZZ SWIZZLES
EILSTWZZ TWIZZLES
EIMMMNOT IMMOMENT
EIMMNNOT MONIMENT
EIMMNNTU MUNIMENT

EIMMNORS MISNOMER
EIMMOPRU EMPORIUM
EIMMOPST METOPISM
EIMMOSTT TOTEMISM
EIMMPRST PRIMMEST
EIMMPRSU PREMIUMS
EIMMRRST TRIMMERS
EIMMRSST MISTERMS
EIMMRSSW SWIMMERS
EIMMRSTT TRIMMEST
EIMMRSTU RUMMIEST
EIMMSSTU MUMSIEST
EIMMSTUY YUMMIEST
EIMNNOPT IMPONENT
EIMNNOST MENTIONS
EIMNNOTT OINTMENT
EIMNNOUY EUONYMIN
EIMNOOPS EMPOISON
EIMNOORS IONOMERS
         MOONRISE
EIMNOORT REMOTION
EIMNOORV OMNIVORE
EIMNOOSS MONOSIES
EIMNOOST EMOTIONS
         MOONIEST
EIMNOOSX EXOMIONS
EIMNOPRT ORPIMENT
EIMNOPSS PEONISMS
EIMNOPST EMPTIONS
         NEPOTISM
         PIMENTOS
EIMNOPTT IMPOTENT
EIMNORSS MERSIONS
         MINORESS
EIMNORSU MONSIEUR
EIMNORSW WINSOMER
EIMNORTY ENORMITY
EIMNOSST MOISTENS
EIMNOSTU MOUNTIES
EIMNPRSS PRIMNESS
EIMNPSST MISSPENT
EIMNRSST ENTRISMS
         MINSTERS
         TRIMNESS
EIMNRSSU NEURISMS
EIMNRSTU TERMINUS
EIMNRSTY ENTRYISM
         MISENTRY
EIMNSSSS SENSISMS
EIMNSSSU SENSUISM
EIMNSSTU MISTUNES
EIMNSTTU MINUTEST
EIMNSUZZ MUEZZINS
EIMOORST MOORIEST
         MOTORISE
         ROOMIEST
EIMOORTZ MOTORIZE
EIMOPPRR IMPROPER
EIMOPPST MOPPIEST
EIMOPRRS PRIMEROS
         PRIMROSE
         PROMISER
EIMOPRRT IMPORTER
         REIMPORT
EIMOPRRV IMPROVER
EIMOPRSS IMPOSERS
         PROMISES
EIMOPRST IMPORTES
EIMOPRSV IMPROVES
EIMOPRUU EUROPIUM
```

```
EIMOPSTY PEYOTISM
EIMOQSTU MISQUOTE
EIMORRSS MORRISES
EIMORRST MORTISER
         STORMIER
EIMORRTT REMITTOR
EIMORSST EROTISMS
         MORTISES
         TRISOMES
EIMORSSV VERISMOS
EIMORSTT OMITTERS
EIMORSTU MOISTURE
EIMORSTW MISWROTE
         WORMIEST
EIMORSTY ISOMETRY
EIMORSVW OVERSWIM
EIMOSSST MOSSIEST
EIMOSSTT MOISTEST
EIMOSSTU MOUSIEST
EIMOSSTZ MESTIZOS
EIMOSTTT MOTTIEST
         TOTEMIST
EIMOSTTU TITMOUSE
EIMPRRSU PRIMEURS
EIMPRSST IMPRESTS
EIMPRSSU PRIMUSES
EIMPRSTU IMPUREST
         IMPUTERS
         STUMPIER
EIMPSSST MISSTEPS
EIMPSSTU SPUMIEST
         STUMPIES
EIMPSSTY EMPTYSIS
EIMQSSTU MESQUITS
EIMQSTUY MYSTIQUE
EIMRRRSU SMURRIER
EIMRRSSU SURMISER
EIMRSSST MISTRESS
EIMRSSSU MISUSERS
         SURMISES
EIMRSSTT METRISTS
EIMRSSTY SMYTRIES
EIMRSSUU MIURUSES
EIMRSTTU SMUTTIER
EIMRSTUV VITREUMS
EIMRSTUX MIXTURES
EIMSSSSU MISSUSES
EIMSSSTU MUSSIEST
EIMSSTTU MUSTIEST
EIMSTUZZ MUZZIEST
EINNOPSS PENSIONS
EINNOQSU QUINONES
EINNORST INTONERS
         TERNIONS
EINNORSU REUNIONS
EINNORSV ENVIRONS
EINNORTT TONTINER
EINNORTU NEUTRINO
EINNORTV INVENTOR
         NOVERINT
EINNORWW WINNOWER
EINNOSSS NOSINESS
EINNOSST TENSIONS
EINNOSSV VENISONS
EINNOSTT TINSTONE
         TONTINES
EINNOSTU NOUNIEST
EINNPRSS SPINNERS
EINNPRST ENPRINTS
EINNPRSY SPINNERY

EINNPSST SPINNETS
EINNPSSU PUNINESS
EINNPSSY SPINNEYS
EINNPSXY SIXPENNY
EINNRSTU RUNNIEST
         STURNINE
EINNRSTV VINTNERS
EINNRTTU NUTRIENT
EINNSSTU SUNNIEST
EINNSSUW UNSINEWS
EINNSTUW UNTWINES
EINOOPRS POISONER
         SPOONIER
EINOOPSS SPOONIES
EINOORSS EROSIONS
EINOORST SNOOTIER
EINOORSZ OZONISER
EINOORZZ OZONIZER
EINOOSST ISOTONES
EINOOSSZ OOZINESS
         OZONISES
EINOOSTZ ZOONITES
EINOOSZZ OZONIZES
EINOOTXX EXOTOXIN
EINOPPRS POPERINS
         PROPINES
EINOPRRS PRISONER
EINOPRSS PORINESS
         PRESSION
         ROPINESS
EINOPRST POINTERS
         PROTEINS
         REPOINTS
EINOPRSU PRUINOSE
EINOPRSV OVERSPIN
         PROVINES
EINOPRTU ERUPTION
EINOPSTT NEPOTIST
EINOQSTU QUESTION
EINOQTTU QUOTIENT
EINORRST INTRORSE
         SNORTIER
EINORRTV INVERTOR
EINORSSS ROSINESS
EINORSST TERSIONS
EINORSSU NEUROSIS
         RESINOUS
EINORSSV VERSIONS
EINORSTT SNOTTIER
         TENORIST
         TRITONES
EINORSTU ROUTINES
         SNOUTIER
EINORSTV INVESTOR
EINORSTY TYROSINE
EINORSTZ TRIZONES
EINORSUV SOUVENIR
EINORTTU RITENUTO
EINOSSSS SESSIONS
EINOSSST SONSIEST
         STENOSIS
EINOSSTT SNOTTIES
         STONIEST
EINOSSTW SNOWIEST
EINOSTTT TOTIENTS
EINOSTTW TOWNIEST
EINOSTUU TENUIOUS
EINOSTVY VENOSITY
EINPPRSS SNIPPERS
EINPPSST SNIPPETS

EINPPSTY SNIPPETY
EINPRRST PRINTERS
         REPRINTS
         SPRINTER
EINPRRTU PRURIENT
EINPRSST SPINSTER
EINPRSSY INSPYRES
EINPRSTU UNPRIEST
         UNRIPEST
EINPRTTU INPUTTER
EINPSTTX SPINTEXT
EINPSTTY TINTYPES
EINQRSTU SQUINTER
EINQSSTU INQUESTS
EINQSTTU QUINTETS
EINQSTUU UNIQUEST
         UNQUIETS
EINQTTTU QUINTETT
EINRRSSU INSURERS
EINRSSST INSTRESS
EINRSSSU SUNRISES
EINRSSTT ENTRISTS
         STINTERS
EINRSSXY SYRINXES
EINRSTTU RUNTIEST
EINRSTTW TWINTERS
EINRSTTY ENTRYIST
EINRSTUV UNRIVETS
         VENTURIS
EINRSTUW UNWRITES
EINRTUUV UNVIRTUE
EINSSSST SENSISTS
EINSSSTU SENSUIST
EINSSTTW ENTWISTS
EINSSTUW UNWISEST
EINSSTUX UNSEXIST
EINSSTXY SYNTEXIS
EINSTTTU NUTTIEST
EINSTTTW TWITTENS
EIOOPPRS PORPOISE
EIOOPPST OPPOSITE
EIOOPRST PORTOISE
         ROOPIEST
EIOOPSST ISOTOPES
EIOOPSTV POOVIEST
EIOORRSS SORORISE
EIOORRSZ SORORIZE
EIOORSTT ROOTIEST
         TORTOISE
EIOOSSTT SOOTIEST
         TOOTSIES
EIOOSTWZ WOOZIEST
EIOPPRTW PIPEWORT
EIOPPSST SOPPIEST
EIOPRRSS PRIORESS
EIOPRRST PIERROTS
         SPORTIER
EIOPRRSU SUPERIOR
EIOPRRTV OVERTRIP
EIOPRSST PERIOSTS
         PROSIEST
         REPOSITS
         RIPOSTES
         TRIPOSES
EIOPRSTT PORTIEST
         RISPETTO
         SPOTTIER
EIOPRSTU ROUPIEST
         SPOUTIER
EIOPRSTV PIVOTERS

         SPORTIVE
EIOPRSUV PERVIOUS
         PREVIOUS
         VIPEROUS
EIOPRTTT TRIPTOTE
EIOPRTTY PETITORY
EIOPRTUZ OUTPRIZE
EIOPSSST SEPIOSTS
EIOPSSTU SOUPIEST
EIOPSSTY ISOTYPES
EIOPSTTT POTTIEST
EIOPSTTU POUTIEST
EIOPSTTY PEYOTIST
EIOPSTUW WIPEOUTS
EIOQRSTU QUOITERS
EIORRRST ERRORIST
EIORRRSW WORRIERS
EIORRRTU ROTURIER
EIORRSST RESISTOR
         ROISTERS
         SORRIEST
EIORRSSV REVISORS
EIORRSTT RORTIEST
EIORRSTU STOURIER
EIORRSTV SERVITOR
EIORRSUV OUVRIERS
EIORRSVV REVIVORS
EIORRSVY REVISORY
EIORRTTU TROUTIER
EIORSSTT STOITERS
EIORSSTY SEROSITY
EIORSTTU TUTORISE
EIORSTTV VIRETOTS
EIORSTUV VIRTUOSE
         VITREOUS
         VOITURES
EIORTTUZ TUTORIZE
EIOSSSTT TOSSIEST
EIOSSTTU TOUSIEST
EIOSSTTW TOWSIEST
EIOSSTUZ OUTSIZES
EIOSTTTT TOTTIEST
EIOSTTTU TOUTIEST
EIPPRRST STRIPPER
         TRIPPERS
EIPPRRTY TRIPPERY
EIPPRSTT TRIPPETS
EIPQRSTU QUIPSTER
EIPRRRSU SPURRIER
EIPRRSSU SPURRIES
         SURPRISE
EIPRRSTZ SPRITZER
EIPRSSST PERSISTS
EIPRSSSU SUSPIRES
EIPRSSTT SPITTERS
         TIPSTERS
EIPRSSTU PURSIEST
EIPRSTTU PURTIEST
         PUTTIERS
EIPRSUVW PURVIEWS
EIPRSVVY SPIVVERY
EIPSSTXY PTYXISES
EIQRRSTU SQUIRTER
EIQRSSSU SQUIRESS
EIQRSSTU QUERISTS
EIQRSTTU QUITTERS
EIQRSUZZ QUIZZERS
EIQRUYZZ QUIZZERY
EIRRRSST STIRRERS
EIRRSSTV STRIVERS
```

EIRRSTTU	TRUSTIER	ELLMNOSY	SOLEMNLY
EIRRSSTU	SUITRESS	ELLMNOTY	MOLTENLY
EIRSSTTU	RUSTIEST	ELLMNPUY	LUMPENLY
	TRUSTIES	ELLMOORS	MORELLOS
EIRSSTTW	TWISTERS	ELLMPSUU	PLUMULES
EIRSSUVV	SURVIVES	ELLNNOST	TONNELLS
EIRSSUVW	SURVIEWS	ELLNNSSU	NULLNESS
EIRSTTTU	RUTTIEST	ELLNOORV	LOVELORN
EIRSTTTW	TWITTERS	ELLNOOSW	WOOLLENS
EIRSTTUX	TUTRIXES	ELLNOPRU	PRUNELLO
EIRTTTWY	TWITTERY	ELLNOSSU	NOUSELLS
EIRTTUWZ	WURTZITE	ELLNOSVY	SLOVENLY
EISSSSTU	TUSSISES	ELLNOSXY	XYLENOLS
EJLOPSTU	PULSOJET	ELLNOUVY	UNLOVELY
EJMOPRUV	OVERJUMP	ELLNPSSU	UNSPELLS
EJNORRSU	REJOURNS	ELLOOSSW	WOOSELLS
EJNORSUY	JOURNEYS	ELLOPRRS	PROLLERS
EJNRSTUU	UNJUSTER	ELLOPRST	POLLSTER
EJNSSSTU	JUSTNESS	ELLOPRTU	POLLUTER
EJOORSVY	OVERJOYS	ELLOPRUV	PULLOVER
EJORSSTU	JOUSTERS	ELLOPSST	PLOTLESS
EJOSSTTU	OUTJESTS	ELLOPSTU	POLLUTES
EKKLOOSY	OLYKOEKS	ELLORRST	STROLLER
EKKLRSSU	SKULKERS		TROLLERS
EKKMORSY	KROMESKY	ELLORSTY	TROLLEYS
EKLLMSSU	SKELLUMS	ELLOSSSU	SOULLESS
EKLLOSSY	KYLLOSES	ELLOSSTU	OUTSELLS
EKLNOOOR	ONLOOKER	ELLOSTTU	OUTTELLS
EKLNOPRS	PLONKERS	ELLOSTUW	OUTSWELL
EKLNORSS	SNORKELS		OUTWELLS
EKLNOSST	KNOTLESS	ELLPSSUW	UPSWELLS
EKLNPRSU	PLUNKERS	ELLSSSTU	LUSTLESS
EKLOOORV	OVERLOOK	ELMMNOTU	LOMENTUM
EKLOOPSW	SLOWPOKE	ELMMNOTY	MOMENTLY
EKLORSSW	WORKLESS	ELMMORST	TROMMELS
EKLSSSTU	TUSKLESS	ELMMRSSU	SLUMMERS
EKLSSTTU	SKUTTLES	ELMMRSTU	STRUMMEL
EKMMORSU	MURKSOME	ELMMRSUY	SUMMERLY
EKMMRSSU	SKUMMERS	ELMMSSTU	STUMMELS
EKMNOSSU	MUSKONES	ELMNNOSU	UNSOLEMN
EKMOORSW	WORKSOME	ELMNOOOP	MONOPOLE
EKMOOSSS	KOSMOSES	ELMNOOSS	MOONLESS
EKMRSTUY	MUSKETRY	ELMNOOST	MOONLETS
EKNNOPSU	UNSPOKEN	ELMNOPSU	PULMONES
EKNOORSS	SNOOKERS	ELMNPPSU	PLUMPENS
EKNOORST	STROOKEN	ELMNPSUU	UNPLUMES
EKNOPPSU	UPSPOKEN	ELMNUUZZ	UNMUZZLE
EKNORSST	STONKERS	ELMOOPPS	POMPELOS
EKNORSTT	KNOTTERS	ELMOOPSY	POLYSOME
EKNORSTW	NETWORKS	ELMOORST	TREMOLOS
EKNORSUY	YOUNKERS	ELMOORSY	MOROSELY
EKNRSTUY	TURNKEYS	ELMOOSSY	LYSOSOME
EKOOORTV	OVERTOOK	ELMOPRSY	POLYMERS
EKOOPRRV	PROVOKER	ELMOPRTY	METOPRYL
EKOOPRRW	ROPEWORK	ELMOPRYY	POLYMERY
EKOOPRSV	PROVOKES	ELMOPSYY	POLYSEMY
EKOOPRSY	SPOOKERY	ELMORSSU	EMULSORS
EKOOPSTU	OUTSPOKE	ELMOSYYZ	LYSOZYME
EKOORRVW	OVERWORK	ELMPPRSU	PLUMPERS
EKOORSST	STOOKERS	ELMPPSTU	PLUMPEST
	STROOKES	ELMPRSSU	RUMPLESS
EKOPRSTU	UPSTROKE	ELMRRTUU	MULTURER
EKORRSST	STROKERS	ELMRSTUU	MULTURES
EKORRUVY	KURVEYOR	ELMRSUZZ	MUZZLERS
EKORSSTU	KURTOSES		
EKPPSSUU	SEPPUKUS		
ELLLMOWY	MELLOWLY		
ELLLNSUY	SULLENLY		
ELLLORRS	LORRELLS		
ELLMNOOS	MOELLONS		

ELNOOSSZ	SNOOZLES	EMMNNOTU	MONUMENT
ELNOOSTZ	SOLONETZ	EMMNOORS	MONOMERS
ELNOPTTY	POTENTLY	EMMNOORT	MOTORMEN
ELNORSSU	NOURSLES	EMMNORSU	SUMMONER
ELNORSTU	TURNSOLE	EMMNOSTY	METONYMS
ELNORSVY	SLOVENRY	EMMNOTTU	TOMENTUM
ELNORTTY	ROTTENLY	EMMNOTYY	METONYMY
ELNOSSSW	SLOWNESS	EMMOOORS	ROOMSOME
	SNOWLESS	EMMOPRRS	PROMMERS
ELNOSSTV	SOLVENTS	EMMOPTTY	POMMETTY
ELNOSSTW	WONTLESS	EMMRRRUU	MURMURER
ELNOSTUZ	ZONULETS		REMURMUR
ELNPPSUU	UNSUPPLE	EMMRSTYY	SYMMETRY
ELNPRTUU	PURULENT	EMNNNOOU	NOUMENON
ELNSSUZZ	SNUZZLES	EMNNOOOT	MONOTONE
ELOOPRSS	SPOOLERS	EMNNOSTW	TOWNSMEN
ELOOPRUW	OWERLOUP	EMNNPSTU	PUNTSMEN
ELOOPSSS	SESSPOOL	EMNNSTTU	STUNTMEN
ELOORSST	ROOTLESS	EMNOOPST	METOPONS
ELOORSTT	ROOTLETS	EMNOOPTY	MONOTYPE
ELOORSTU	TORULOSE	EMNOORST	MESOTRON
ELOORSUV	OVERSOUL		MONTEROS
ELOOSSST	SOOTLESS	EMNOORSU	ENORMOUS
ELOOSSTU	OUTSOLES		NEMOROUS
ELOOSSWY	WOOLSEYS	EMNOORSW	NEWSROOM
ELOPPRRY	PROPERLY	EMNOORTY	NOOMETRY
ELOPPSST	STOPPLES	EMNOOSST	MOONSETS
ELOPRRSU	PROULERS	EMNOOSUV	VENOMOUS
ELOPRRSW	PROWLERS	EMNOOTTY	TENOTOMY
ELOPRRSY	PYRROLES	EMNOOTUV	OUTVENOM
ELOPRRTY	PORTERLY	EMNOOTWY	TOYWOMEN
ELOPRSSS	PLESSORS	EMNORRSU	MOURNERS
ELOPRSSU	SPORULES	EMNORSST	MONSTERS
ELOPRSTT	PLOTTERS	EMNORSTT	SORTMENT
ELOPRSTU	PLOUTERS		TORMENTS
	POULTERS	EMNORSTU	MONTURES
ELOPRSTW	PLOWTERS		MOUNTERS
ELOPRSTY	PROSTYLE		REMOUNTS
	PROTYLES	EMNORSUU	NUMEROUS
ELOPRSUV	OVERPLUS	EMNOSSST	STEMSONS
ELOPRSYY	PYROLYSE	EMNOSUUY	EUONYMUS
ELOPRXYY	PYROXYLE	EMNRSSTU	MUNSTERS
ELOPRYYZ	PYROLYZE		STERNUMS
ELOPSSST	SPOTLESS	EMOOPRRT	PROMOTER
	STOPLESS	EMOOPRST	PROMOTES
ELOPSSUU	OPULUSES	EMOOPRSY	POMEROYS
ELOPSTTU	OUTSLEPT		PYROSOME
ELORSSTT	SETTLORS	EMOOPRSZ	ZOOSPERM
	SLOTTERS	EMOOPSSU	ESPUMOSO
ELORSTUY	SOUTERLY	EMOORSST	MOROSEST
	UROSTYLE	EMOORSSU	UROSOMES
ELORTTTU	TROUTLET	EMOORTYZ	ZOOMETRY
ELOSSSTY	SYSTOLES	EMOOSSTW	TWOSOMES
ELOSSWZZ	SWOZZLES	EMOOSSTY	MYOSOTES
ELPPRSTU	PURPLEST	EMOOSTUV	OUTMOVES
ELPPSSTU	SUPPLEST	EMOPPRRT	PROMPTER
ELPRSSSU	SPURLESS	EMOPRSSU	SPERMOUS
ELPRSSTU	SPURTLES		SUPREMOS
ELPRSTTU	SPLUTTER	EMORRRUU	RUMOURER
ELPRSTUU	PULTURES	EMORRSSU	MORSURES
ELPRSUZZ	PUZZLERS	EMORSSSU	SMOUSERS
ELPSSTUU	PUSTULES	EMORSSTU	OESTRUMS
ELRRSSTU	RUSTLERS		STRUMOSE
ELRRSTTU	TURTLERS	EMORSUVW	OVERSWUM
ELRSSSTU	RUSTLESS	EMOSSTTW	WESTMOST
ELRSTTUY	SLUTTERY	EMOSSTVZ	ZEMSTVOS
ELRSTUUV	VULTURES	EMPRRTUY	TRUMPERY
ELSSSTUY	STYLUSES	EMPRSSTU	STUMPERS
ELSSSTYY	SYSTYLES		SUMPTERS
EMMMNOTU	MOMENTUM	EMPRSSUU	RUMPUSES

EMPRSTTU	STRUMPET
	TRUMPETS
EMRRSSTU	STURMERS
ENNOOORT	TENOROON
ENNOOOTZ	ENTOZOON
ENNOOPPT	OPPONENT
ENNOOSTT	NONETTOS
ENNOPRSU	UNPERSON
ENNOPRUV	UNPROVEN
ENNOPTWY	TWOPENNY
ENNORSST	STERNSON
ENNORSTU	NEUTRONS
ENNORSTY	SONNETRY
ENNORTTU	UNROTTEN
ENNOSSTU	NEUSTONS
	SUNSTONE
ENNPPTUY	TUPPENNY
ENNRSSTU	STUNNERS
ENOOOSSZ	ZOONOSES
ENOOPPRS	PROPONES
ENOOPPST	POSTPONE
ENOOPRSS	POORNESS
	SNOOPERS
ENOOPSSY	SPOONEYS
ENOOPSTT	POTSTONE
ENOORRVW	OVERWORN
ENOORSSZ	SNOOZERS
ENOORSVW	OVERSOWN
ENOOSSTT	TESTOONS
ENOOSTXY	OXYTONES
ENOPPRRU	UNPROPER
ENOPRRSU	PRONEURS
ENOPRSST	POSTERNS
ENOPRSTT	PORTENTS
ENOPSSST	STEPSONS
ENOPSSSY	SYNOPSES
ENOPSTTU	OUTSPENT
ENOQSTUU	UNQUOTES
ENORRSST	SNORTERS
ENORRSTT	TORRENTS
ENORRSUV	OVERRUNS
ENORRTUU	TOURNURE
ENORRTUV	OVERTURN
	TURNOVER
ENORSSSU	SOURNESS
ENORSSTT	SNOTTERS
	STENTORS
ENORSSTU	TONSURES
ENORSTTU	STENTOUR
ENORSTTY	SNOTTERY
ENORSTUV	VENTROUS
ENORSTUY	TOURNEYS
ENOSSSUU	SENSUOUS
ENOSSTTU	STOUTENS
ENPRRSSU	SPURNERS
ENPRSSSY	SPRYNESS
ENPRSSTU	PUNSTERS
ENPRSSUU	UNPURSES
ENPRTTUY	UNPRETTY
ENRRRTUU	NURTURER
ENRRSTUU	NURTURES
ENRRSSTU	ENTRUSTS
ENRSSTTU	UNSUREST
ENRSTTUU	UNTRUEST
EOOOPRSS	OOSPORES
	SOPOROSE
EOOOPRSZ	ZOOSPORE
EOOOPRTZ	ZOOTROPE
EOOPPRRS	PROPOSER
EOOPPRSS	OPPOSERS
	PROPOSES
EOOPPRSV	POPOVERS
EOOPRRSS	SPOORERS
EOOPRRST	TROOPERS
EOOPRRTU	OUTROPER
	UPROOTER
EOOPRSST	STOOPERS
EOOPRSTU	OUTROPES
	PORTEOUS
EOOPRSTV	OVERPOST
	OVERTOPS
EOOPRSTW	TOWROPES
EOOPRTUW	OUTPOWER
EOOPSTYZ	ZOOTYPES
EOORRRSW	SORROWER
EOORRSST	ROOSTERS
EOORSSVW	OVERSOWS
EOORSTUW	OUTSWORE
EOORTTUV	OUTVOTER
EOOSTTUV	OUTVOTES
EOPPRRSS	PROSPERS
EOPPRRTY	PROPERTY
EOPPRSST	STOPPERS
EOPPRSSU	PURPOSES
	SUPPOSER
EOPPRSSW	SWOPPERS
EOPPSSSU	SUPPOSES
EOPRRSST	PORTRESS
	SPORTERS
EOPRRSTU	POSTURER
	TROUPERS
EOPRRUVY	PURVEYOR
EOPRRSTT	PROTESTS
	SPOTTERS
EOPRSSTU	POSTURES
	SEPTUORS
	SPOUTERS
EOPRSSUU	POURSUES
	UPROUSES
EOPRSSUW	POURSEWS
EOPSSTTU	OUTSTEPS
EOPSSTTW	STEWPOTS
EOQRSSTU	QUESTORS
EORRRTTU	TORTURER
EORRSSST	STRESSOR
	TROSSERS
EORRSSTU	ROUSTERS
	TROUSERS
EORRSSTW	STROWERS
	TROWSERS
EORRSSTY	ROYSTERS
EORRSTTT	TROTTERS
EORRSTTU	TORTURES
	TROUTERS
EORRSUVY	SURVEYOR
EORRTUUV	TROUVEUR
EORSSSTU	TUSSORES
EORSSTTT	STOTTERS
EORSSTTU	TUTORESS
EORSSTTW	SWOTTERS
EORSSTUX	SEXTUORS
EORSTTUW	OUTWREST
EORSTUUV	VERTUOUS
EOSSSTXY	XYSTOSES
EOSSTTTU	STOUTEST
EPPPRTUY	PUPPETRY
EPPPRSUU	PURPURES
EPPRSSUU	SUPPRESS
EPRRRSSU	SPURRERS
EPRRSSUU	PURSUERS
	USURPERS
EPRRSSUY	SPURREYS
EPRRSTUU	RUPTURES
EPRSSTTU	SPUTTERS
EPRSTTUY	SPUTTERY
EQRRTUUU	TRUQUEUR
ERRSSSTU	TRUSSERS
ERRSSTTU	TRUSTERS
ERRSSTTY	TRYSTERS
ERRSTTTU	STRUTTER
ERSSTTTU	STUTTERS
ESSSTUXY	XYSTUSES
FFFGILNU	FLUFFING
FFFMOOTU	FOOTMUFF
FFGHIINW	WHIFFING
FFGHINOU	HOUFFING
FFGHINOW	HOWFFING
FFGHIRSU	GRUFFISH
FFGIIKNS	SKIFFING
FFGIILNP	PIFFLING
FFGIILNR	RIFFLING
FFGIILNS	SIFFLING
FFGIINNS	SNIFFING
FFGIINPS	SPIFFING
FFGIINRS	GRIFFINS
FFGIINST	STIFFING
	TIFFINGS
FFGIKNOS	SKOFFING
FFGILMNU	MUFFLING
FFGILNPU	PLUFFING
FFGILNRU	RUFFLING
FFGINNSU	SNUFFING
FFGINORS	GRIFFONS
FFGINOSW	SOWFFING
FFGINPSU	PUFFINGS
FFGINSTU	STUFFING
FFHIISST	STIFFISH
FFHIISTY	FIFTYISH
FFHIKNSU	HUFFKINS
FFHIOPSS	SPOFFISH
FFHOOOST	OFFSHOOT
FFIILMOR	FILIFORM
FFIILNSY	SNIFFILY
FFIILNTY	FLINTIFY
FFIINOOS	SOFFIONI
FFIKLRSU	FRISKFUL
FFILLOPP	FLIPFLOP
FFILLTUY	FITFULLY
FFILRTUU	FRUITFUL
FFILSSTU	FISTFULS
FFILSTUY	STUFFILY
FFIMORSU	FUSIFORM
FFINOPRT	OFFPRINT
FFINOPST	PONTIFFS
FFLLOOSU	LOOFFULS
FFLMNOOU	MOUFFLON
FFLNOTUU	FOUNTFUL
FFLORRUU	FURFUROL
FFNORSTU	TURNOFFS
FFNSTUUY	UNSTUFFY
FGGGIINR	FRIGGING
FGGGILNO	FLOGGING
FGGGINOR	FROGGING
FGGHIINT	FIGHTING
FGGHIISS	FISHGIGS
FGGHINTU	GUNFIGHT
FGGIILNN	FLINGING
FGGIINNR	FRINGING
FGGIINRT	GRIFTING
FGGIINRU	FIGURING
FGGIISZZ	FIZZGIGS
FGGILNOR	FROGLING
FGGILNOS	GOLFINGS
FGGINOOR	FORGOING
FGGINORS	FORGINGS
FGHIIKNS	KINGFISH
FGHIINSS	FISHINGS
FGHIINST	SHIFTING
FGHILLTU	LIGHTFUL
FGHILMTU	MIGHTFUL
FGHILNSU	FLUSHING
FGHILRTU	RIGHTFUL
FGHINORT	FROTHING
FGHINRSU	FRUSHING
FGHIOTTU	OUTFIGHT
FGHLORUU	FURLOUGH
FGHNOORS	FOGHORNS
FGHNOTUU	UNFOUGHT
FGIIINNX	INFIXING
FGIIKLNS	FLISKING
FGIIKNNS	KNIFINGS
FGIIKNRS	FRISKING
FGIILLNR	FRILLING
FGIILLNS	FILLINGS
FGIILMNP	FLIMPING
FGIILNOS	FOILINGS
FGIILNPP	FLIPPING
FGIILNRS	RIFLINGS
FGIILNRT	FLIRTING
	TRIFLING
FGIILNSS	FISSLING
FGIILNST	STIFLING
FGIILNTT	FLITTING
FGIILNZZ	FIZZLING
FGIINNST	SNIFTING
FGIINNSU	INFUSING
FGIINNUX	UNFIXING
FGIINNUY	UNIFYING
FGIINOQU	QUOIFING
FGIINOST	FOISTING
FGIINRRS	FIRRINGS
FGIINRST	FRISTING
FGIINRTT	FRITTING
FGIINRTU	FRUITING
FGIINRZZ	FRIZZING
FGIINSST	SIFTINGS
FGIINSTT	FITTINGS
FGIINSTW	SWIFTING
FGIINSZZ	FIZZINGS
FGIIRSTU	FIGURIST
FGIKLNNU	FLUNKING
FGILLNOW	WOLFLING
FGILLNOY	FOLLYING
FGILMNPU	FLUMPING
FGILNNTU	GUNFLINT
FGILNOOR	FLOORING
FGILNOOS	FOOLINGS
FGILNOOT	FOOTLING
FGILNOOZ	FOOZLING
FGILNOPP	FLOPPING
FGILNOPS	FOPLINGS
FGILNORU	FLOURING
FGILNOST	SOFTLING
FGILNOSU	FLOUSING
FGILNOSW	FOWLINGS
	WOLFINGS
FGILNOTU	FLOUTING

	OUTFLING	FIILLMSY	FLIMSILY	FLNOOTUW	OUTFLOWN	GGHIINRT	GIRTHING
FGILNPRU	PURFLING	FIILLMTU	MULTIFIL	FLOOOPTT	POLTFOOT		RIGHTING
FGILNRRU	FLURRING	FIILLNTY	FLINTILY	FLOOPTTY	TOPLOFTY	GGHIINST	SIGHTING
FGILNSTU	FLUTINGS	FIILMNRY	INFIRMLY	FLOORSSW	FORSLOWS	GGHIINTW	WIGHTING
FGILNSTY	FLYTINGS	FIILMOPR	PILIFORM	FLOOSTUW	OUTFLOWS	GGHIIPRS	PRIGGISH
FGILNUZZ	FUZZLING	FIILMPSY	SIMPLIFY	FLOPRSTU	SPORTFUL	GGHILNPU	GULPHING
FGIMNORS	FORMINGS	FIILNOST	TINFOILS	FLORTTUU	TROUTFUL	GGHILSSU	SLUGGISH
FGIMNPRU	FRUMPING	FIIMOSTY	MOISTIFY	FLRSTTUU	TRUSTFUL	GGHIMSTU	THUGGISM
FGIMOSSY	FOGYISMS	FIINNOSU	INFUSION	FMRSSTUU	FRUSTUMS	GGHINORU	ROUGHING
FGINNORT	FRONTING	FIINORTU	FRUITION	FNNOOORT	FRONTOON	GGHINOST	GHOSTING
FGINNORW	FROWNING	FIINOSSS	FISSIONS	FNNOORST	FRONTONS	GGHINOSU	SOUGHING
FGINOOPR	PROOFING	FIINTUXY	UNFIXITY	FNOOORTW	FOOTWORN	GGHINOTY	HOGTYING
FGINOOPS	SPOOFING	FIIQUYZZ	QUIZZIFY	FNOOPRSU	SUNPROOF	GGIIILNS	GINGILIS
FGINOORS	ROOFINGS	FIKKLNOS	KINFOLKS	FNOORRSW	FORSWORN	GGIIINNT	IGNITING
FGINOOST	FOOTINGS		KINSFOLK	FNOORTUW	OUTFROWN	GGIIJLNN	JINGLING
FGINORST	FROSTING	FIKLNOSW	WOLFKINS	FOOOPSTT	FOOTPOST	GGIIKLNN	KINGLING
FGINRRSU	FURRINGS	FIKLNSSU	SKINFULS	FOOORSTT	FOOTROTS	GGIILLNR	GRILLING
FGINRSSU	SURFINGS	FIKNORSW	FORSWINK	FOOOSTTU	OUTFOOTS	GGIILLNY	GILLYING
FGINRSTU	TURFINGS	FILLLUWY	WILFULLY	FOORSTTX	FOXTROTS	GGIILMNN	MINGLING
FGINSTTU	TUFTINGS	FILLNUUW	UNWILFUL	GGGGIILN	GIGGLING	GGIILMNY	GINGLYMI
FGIORSTW	FIGWORTS	FILLOPPY	FLOPPILY	GGGGIINR	GRIGGING	GGIILNNP	PINGLING
FGISSTUU	FUGUISTS	FILLOPSU	SPOILFUL	GGGGILNO	GOGGLING	GGIILNNS	SINGLING
FGLLMOOU	GLOOMFUL	FILMNOOS	MONOFILS	GGGGILNU	GLUGGING		SLINGING
FGLLNSUU	LUNGFULS	FILMOPRS	SLIPFORM		GUGGLING	GGIILNNT	GLINTING
FGLNORSU	FURLONGS	FILMORRY	LYRIFORM	GGGGINOR	GROGGING		TINGLING
FGLNORUW	WRONGFUL	FILMOSSU	MOFUSSIL	GGGHIILN	HIGGLING	GGIILNPS	PIGLINGS
FGLOOOST	FOOTSLOG	FILNOSUX	FLUXIONS	GGGHIINT	THIGGING	GGIILNRS	RIGLINGS
FGLORSUU	FULGOURS	FILOOSTW	WITLOOFS	GGGHIINW	WHIGGING	GGIIMNOS	MISGOING
FGNOORSU	FOURGONS	FILORSST	FLORISTS	GGGHINOS	HOGGINGS	GGIIMNPU	GUIMPING
FGNOORTU	UNFORGOT	FILORSTU	FLORUITS		SHOGGING	GGIIMPRS	PRIGGISM
FHHOORST	SHOFROTH	FILORSTY	FROSTILY	GGGIIJLN	JIGGLING	GGIINNNR	GRINNING
FHIIKLMS	MILKFISH	FILRSTTU	TRISTFUL	GGGIIJNS	JIGGINGS	GGIINNOR	GROINING
FHIIKNSS	FISHSKIN	FILSSTTU	FLUTISTS	GGGIILNN	GINGLING		IGNORING
FHIILLTY	FILTHILY	FILSTTUY	STULTIFY		NIGGLING	GGIINNOS	INGOINGS
FHIILRST	FLIRTISH	FIMMNOOR	OMNIFORM	GGGIILNS	LIGGINGS	GGIINNRS	RINGINGS
FHIILSTY	SHIFTILY	FIMMORRU	MURIFORM	GGGIILNW	WIGGLING	GGIINNRW	WRINGING
FHIKLLLO	HILLFOLK	FIMMORSS	MISFORMS	GGGIINNS	SNIGGING	GGIINNSS	SINGINGS
FHIKMNOS	MONKFISH	FIMNORSU	UNIFORMS	GGGIINPR	PRIGGING	GGIINNST	STINGING
FHIKNORT	FORTHINK	FIMOPRRY	PYRIFORM	GGGIINPS	PIGGINGS	GGIINNSW	SWINGING
FHILLOOT	FOOTHILL	FIMORTUY	FUMITORY	GGGIINRS	RIGGINGS	GGIINNTW	TWINGING
FHILMPSU	LUMPFISH	FIMOSTUY	FUMOSITY	GGGIINRT	TRIGGING	GGIINNUV	UNGIVING
FHILMRTU	MIRTHFUL	FIMRSTUU	FUTURISM	GGGIINSW	SWIGGING	GGIINPPR	GRIPPING
FHILORSU	FLOURISH	FINORSSS	FRISSONS		WIGGINGS	GGIINPSY	GIPSYING
FHILORTY	FROTHILY	FINORSUY	INFUSORY	GGGIINTW	TWIGGING	GGIINRST	RINGGITS
FHILPSSU	SHIPFULS	FIOORSSU	FURIOSOS	GGGIJLNO	JOGGLING	GGIINRTT	GRITTING
FHIMPRSU	FRUMPISH	FIORTTUY	FORTUITY	GGGIJLNU	JUGGLING	GGIINSTU	GIUSTING
FHINOSSU	FUSHIONS	FIRSTTUU	FUTURIST	GGGIJNOS	JOGGINGS	GGIIRSSS	GRISGRIS
FHINRTTU	UNTHRIFT	FIRTTUUY	FUTURITY	GGGIKNSU	SKUGGING	GGILLNUY	GULLYING
FHIOOPTT	PHOTOFIT	FJLLOUYY	JOYFULLY	GGGILNOO	GOOGLING	GGILLOOW	GOLLIWOG
FHIOPSSX	FOXSHIPS	FJLNOUUY	UNJOYFUL	GGGILNOS	LOGGINGS	GGILMMNO	GLOMMING
FHIORSTY	FORTYISH	FKKLOORW	WORKFOLK		SLOGGING	GGILMNOO	GLOOMING
FHKORSTU	FUTHORKS	FKKOORTW	KOFTWORK	GGGILNOT	TOGGLING	GGILNNOP	PLONGING
FHLLLOTU	LOTHFULL	FKLMOOOT	FOLKMOOT	GGGILNPU	PLUGGING	GGILNNOS	LONGINGS
FHLLOSTU	SLOTHFUL	FKLNRTUU	TRUNKFUL	GGGILNRU	GURGLING	GGILNNOU	LOUNGING
FHLMOTUU	MOUTHFUL	FKMOORRW	FORMWORK	GGGILNSU	SLUGGING	GGILNNPU	PLUNGING
FHLNORSU	HORNFULS	FKNORSUW	FORSWUNK	GGGIMNSU	MUGGINGS	GGILNNUU	UNGLUING
FHLOOSTU	SOOTHFUL	FKOOORTW	FOOTWORK		SMUGGING	GGILNORW	GROWLING
FHLOOTTU	TOOTHFUL	FLLOOPUW	UPFOLLOW	GGGINNOS	NOGGINGS	GGILNORY	GLORYING
FHLOPSSU	SHOPFULS	FLLRSTUY	STRYFULL		SNOGGING	GGILNOSS	GLOSSING
FHLORTTU	TROTHFUL	FLMNOOSU	MOUFLONS	GGGINNSU	SNUGGING		GOSLINGS
FHLORTUW	WORTHFUL	FLMNORUU	MOURNFUL	GGGINOPR	PROGGING	GGILNOSZ	GLOZINGS
FHLORTUY	FOURTHLY	FLMOOORW	MOORFOWL	GGGINORT	TROGGING	GGILNOTU	GLOUTING
FHLOSTUU	OUTFLUSH	FLMOOOST	TOMFOOLS	GGGINOSS	SOGGINGS	GGILNTTU	GLUTTING
FHLOTUUY	YOUTHFUL	FLMOORSU	ROOMFULS	GGGINPSU	PUGGINGS		GUTTLING
FHLRTTUU	TRUTHFUL	FLMORSTU	STORMFUL	GGGINRSU	RUGGINGS	GGILNUZZ	GUZZLING
FHOOORST	FORSOOTH	FLNOOPSU	SPOONFUL	GGGINSTU	TUGGINGS	GGILQSUY	SQUIGGLY
	HOOFROTS	FLNOORRS	FORLORNS	GGHHIINT	HIGHTING	GGIMMNSU	GUMMINGS
FIIINNTY	INFINITY	FLNOOSTU	SNOOTFUL	GGHHINOU	HOUGHING	GGIMNOOR	GROOMING
FIIKLRSY	FRISKILY			GGHIILNT	LIGHTING	GGINNNSU	GUNNINGS
FIILLMOS	MILFOILS			GGHIINPT	PIGHTING	GGINNOOS	ONGOINGS

GGINNOPR	PRONGING	GHIINRTV	THRIVING	GHINOPSS	GINSHOPS	GIIKKNNS	SKINKING
GGINNOPS	SPONGING	GHIINRTW	WRITHING	GHINORSS	HORSINGS	GIIKKNRS	KIRKINGS
GGINNORW	WRONGING	GHIINSSS	HISSINGS		SHORINGS	GIIKLLNS	KILLINGS
GGINNOSS	SINGSONG	GHIINSST	INSIGHTS	GHINORST	SHORTING		SKILLING
GGINNOTU	TONGUING	GHIINSSW	SWISHING	GHINORSV	SHROVING	GIIKLMNS	MILKINGS
GGINNRTU	GRUNTING		WHISSING	GHINORSW	SHROWING	GIIKLNPP	PLINKING
GGINNUVY	UNGYVING		WISHINGS	GHINORTT	TROTHING	GIIKLNNS	INKLINGS
GGINOORV	GROOVING	GHIINSTT	SHITTING	GHINORTW	INGROWTH		SLINKING
GGINOOST	STOOGING		TITHINGS		THROWING	GIIKLNNT	TINKLING
GGINOOTU	OUTGOING	GHIINSTW	WHISTING		WORTHING	GIIKLNRS	SKIRLING
GGINOPRS	PROGGINS		WHITINGS	GHINOSST	HOSTINGS	GIIKLNST	KITLINGS
GGINOPRU	GROUPING	GHIINSVV	SHIVVING	GHINOSSU	HOUSINGS	GIIKLNTT	KITTLING
GGINOPSU	UPGOINGS	GHIINWZZ	WHIZZING	GHINOSSW	SHOWINGS	GIIKMMNS	SKIMMING
GGINORSS	GROSSING	GHIIORSV	VIGORISH	GHINOSTT	SHOTTING	GIIKMNPS	SKIMPING
GGINORSU	GROUSING	GHIIRSTT	RIGHTIST		TONIGHTS	GIIKMNRS	SMIRKING
GGINORSW	GROWINGS	GHIKLNTY	KNIGHTLY	GHINOSTU	SHOUTING	GIIKNNNS	SKINNING
GGINORTU	GROUTING	GHIKLSTY	SKYLIGHT		SOUTHING	GIIKNNOV	INVOKING
GGINPRSU	PURGINGS	GHIKNNTU	UNKNIGHT	GHINOSTW	SOWTHING	GIIKNNPR	PRINKING
GGINPSYY	GYPSYING	GHIKNSSU	HUSKINGS	GHINOSUY	YOUNGISH	GIIKNNPS	PINKINGS
GGINRSSU	SURGINGS	GHILLNOO	HOLLOING	GHINOTTU	OUTNIGHT	GIIKNNSS	SINKINGS
GGLLOOWY	GOLLYWOG	GHILLNOU	HULLOING	GHINPSSU	GUNSHIPS	GIIKNNST	STINKING
GHHIILST	LIGHTISH	GHILLSTY	SLIGHTLY	GHINRRUY	HURRYING	GIIKNNSW	SWINKING
GHHIINSW	WHISHING	GHILMNSU	MULSHING	GHINRSTU	UNGIRTHS		WINKINGS
GHHIISTT	TIGHTISH	GHILMPSU	GLUMPISH		UNRIGHTS	GIIKNNTT	KNITTING
GHHILOSU	GHOULISH	GHILNOOS	SHOOLING	GHINSSTU	HUSTINGS	GIIKNNTW	TWINKING
GHHIMNPU	HUMPHING	GHILNOPP	HOPPLING	GHINSTTU	HUTTINGS	GIIKNPPS	SKIPPING
GHHIMOST	HIGHMOST	GHILNOPY	HOPINGLY		SHUTTING	GIIKNPSS	PIGSKINS
GHHINOOS	HOOSHING	GHILNOSS	SLOSHING	GHIORTTU	OUTRIGHT	GIIKNQRU	QUIRKING
GHHINSSU	SHUSHING	GHILNOST	SLOTHING	GHIOSTTU	OUTSIGHT	GIIKNRRS	SKIRRING
GHHIOSTU	TOUGHISH	GHILNOSU	HOUSLING	GHIPRSST	SPRIGHTS	GIIKNRSS	GRISKINS
GHHIRSST	SHRIGHTS	GHILNOSW	HOWLINGS	GHIPRSTU	UPRIGHTS	GIIKNRST	SKIRTING
GHHOORTU	THOROUGH	GHILNPSU	INGULPHS	GHIPRSUU	GURUSHIP		STRIKING
GHHOSTTU	THOUGHTS	GHILNRSU	HURLINGS	GHLMOOOS	HOMOLOGS	GIIKNSSV	SKIVINGS
GHIIJNOS	JINGOISH	GHILNRTU	HURTLING	GHLMOOOY	HOMOLOGY	GIILLMNS	MILLINGS
GHIIKNNT	THINKING	GHILNRUY	HUNGRILY	GHLNNOOR	LONGHORN	GIILLMNU	ILLUMING
GHIIKNPS	KINGSHIP	GHILNSSU	SLUSHING	GHLNOORU	HOURLONG	GIILLNOS	GILLIONS
GHIIKNRS	SHIRKING	GHILNSTU	HUSTLING	GHLNORSU	SLUGHORN	GIILLNPR	PRILLING
	SHRIKING		SUNLIGHT	GHLNOTYY	YONGTHLY	GIILLNPS	SPILLING
GHIIKNSW	WHISKING	GHILORSW	SHOWGIRL	GHLOOORY	HOROLOGY	GIILLNQU	QUILLING
GHIILLNO	HILLOING	GHILPRTY	TRIGLYPH	GHLORTUU	TURLOUGH	GIILLNRT	TRILLING
GHIILLNS	SHILLING	GHIMMNSU	HUMMINGS	GHMORSSU	SORGHUMS	GIILLNST	STILLING
GHIILMST	MISLIGHT	GHIMNOPU	GUMPHION	GHMOSSTU	MUGSHOTS		TILLINGS
GHIILMTY	MIGHTILY	GHIMNORU	HUMORING	GHMPSSUY	SPHYGMUS	GIILLNSW	SWILLING
GHIILNPR	HIRPLING	GHIMNOTU	MOUTHING	GHNOPRSY	GRYPHONS	GIILLNTT	LITTLING
GHIILNRS	HIRLINGS	GHIMNPTU	THUMPING	GHNOPYYY	HYPOGYNY	GIILLNTW	TWILLING
	HIRSLING	GHIMNRTY	RYTHMING	GHNOSSTU	GUNSHOTS	GIILLNWY	WILLYING
GHIILNRT	THIRLING	GHIMNSTU	GUNSMITH		SHOTGUNS	GIILLOPW	POLLIWIG
GHIILNRW	WHIRLING	GHIMRSSU	SIMURGHS	GHNOSTUU	UNSOUGHT	GIILLPSW	PIGSWILL
GHIILNST	TINGLISH	GHINNNSU	SHUNNING	GHNOSTUY	YOUNGSTH	GIILLTUY	GUILTILY
GHIILNTW	WHITLING	GHINNOOR	HONORING	GHOOOSSW	HOOSGOWS	GIILMMNP	PLIMMING
GHIILTTW	TWILIGHT	GHINNOPY	PHONYING	GHOORTUY	YOGHOURT	GIILMMNS	SLIMMING
GHIIMMNW	WHIMMING	GHINNORS	HORNINGS	GHOPRTUW	UPGROWTH	GIILMNNU	LUMINING
GHIIMNNU	INHUMING	GHINNORT	NORTHING	GHORSTUY	YOGHURTS		UNLIMING
GHIIMNST	SMITHING		THORNING	GIIILMNT	LIMITING	GIILMNOS	SMOILING
GHIINNNS	SHINNING		THRONING	GIIILNNS	INISLING	GIILMNPS	LIMPINGS
GHIINNNT	THINNING	GHINNOST	NOTHINGS	GIIILNNU	LINGUINI		SIMPLING
GHIINNNY	HINNYING	GHINNSSU	SNUSHING	GIIILOTV	VITILIGO	GIILMNPW	WIMPLING
GHIINNRS	SHRINING	GHINNSTU	HUNTINGS	GIIIMMNX	IMMIXING	GIILMNPY	IMPLYING
GHIINNST	NITHINGS		SHUNTING	GIIINNOS	IONISING	GIILMNSS	SMILINGS
GHIINNSW	WHININGS	GHINOOPT	PHOTOING	GIIINNOT	IGNITION	GIILMNST	MISTLING
GHIINNUV	UNHIVING	GHINOOPW	WHOOPING	GIIINNOZ	IONIZING	GIILMNZZ	MIZZLING
GHIINOST	HOISTING	GHINOOST	SHOOTING	GIIINNTV	INVITING	GIILMPRS	PILGRIMS
GHIINPPS	HIPPINGS		SOOTHING	GIIINSTV	VISITING	GIILMPSU	PUGILISM
	SHIPPING	GHINOOSW	WOOSHING	GIIJMMNY	JIMMYING	GIILNNNU	UNLINING
GHIINPPW	WHIPPING	GHINOOTT	TOOTHING	GIIJMNOS	JINGOISM	GIILNNPP	NIPPLING
GHIINRRS	SHIRRING	GHINOOTW	WHOOTING	GIIJNNOS	JOININGS	GIILNNPS	SPLINING
GHIINRRW	WHIRRING	GHINOPPS	HOPPINGS	GIIJNNOT	JOINTING	GIILNNTU	UNTILING
GHIINRST	SHIRTING		SHOPPING	GIIJNNRU	INJURING	GIILNNTW	TWINLING
GHIINRSV	SHRIVING	GHINOPPW	WHOPPING	GIIJNOST	JINGOIST		WINTLING
					JOISTING	GIILNNUV	UNLIVING

GIILNOPS SPOILING
GIILNOPT PILOTING
GIILNORS LIGROINS
GIILNOSS SOILINGS
GIILNOST TOILINGS
GIILNPPR RIPPLING
GIILNPPS SIPPLING
         SLIPPING
GIILNPPT TIPPLING
GIILNPRS SPIRLING
GIILNPRT TRIPLING
GIILNPSS LISPINGS
         SPILINGS
GIILNQSU QUISLING
GIILNQTU QUILTING
GIILNRSW SWIRLING
GIILNRTW TWIRLING
GIILNRVY VIRGINLY
GIILNSST LISTINGS
GIILNSTT SLITTING
         STILTING
         TILTINGS
         TITLINGS
GIILNSTU LINGUIST
GIILNSTW WITLINGS
GIILNSTY STINGILY
GIILNSZZ SIZZLING
GIILNTTT TITTLING
GIILNTTU TITULING
GIILNTTW TWILTING
GIILOSST OLIGISTS
GIILPSTU PUGILIST
GIILRSST STRIGILS
GIIMMNPR PRIMMING
GIIMMNRT TRIMMING
GIIMMNRU IMMURING
GIIMMNSW SWIMMING
GIIMNNOP IMPONING
GIIMNNOY IGNOMINY
GIIMNNTU MINUTING
         MUNITING
         MUTINING
GIIMNOPS IMPOSING
GIIMNOST MOISTING
GIIMNOTT OMITTING
GIIMNOTV MOTIVING
         VOMITING
GIIMNPPR PRIMPING
GIIMNPRS PRIMINGS
GIIMNPRU UMPIRING
GIIMNPTU IMPUTING
GIIMNRRS SMIRRING
GIIMNSST MISTINGS
GIIMNSSU MISUSING
GIIMNSSW SWINGISM
GIIMNSTT SMITTING
GIIMNSTU MUISTING
GIIMNSTY STIMYING
GIIMORRS RIGORISM
GIINNNOO ONIONING
GIINNNOT INTONING
         NOINTING
GIINNNPS PINNINGS
         SPINNING
GIINNNRU INURING
GIINNNST TINNINGS
GIINNNSW WINNINGS
GIINNNTW TWINNING
GIINNOPR PROINING
GIINNOPS PIONINGS

GIINNOPT POINTING
GIINNOQU QUOINING
GIINNORS IRONINGS
         ROSINING
GIINNORT IGNITRON
GIINNPPS SNIPPING
GIINNPRT PRINTING
GIINNPSS SNIPINGS
GIINNPSU PINGUINS
GIINNRSS RINSINGS
GIINNRSU INSURING
         RUININGS
GIINNRTU UNTIRING
GIINNRUW UNWIRING
GIINNSSW INSWINGS
GIINNSTT STINTING
         TINTINGS
GIINNSTU UNITINGS
GIINNSTW TWININGS
GIINNUVW UNWIVING
GIINOPST POSITING
         SOPITING
GIINOPTV PIVOTING
GIINOQTU QUOITING
GIINORSS SIGNIORS
GIINORST RIOTINGS
         ROISTING
         ROSITING
GIINORSV VISORING
GIINORTZ ROZITING
GIINORVZ VIZORING
GIINOSTT STOITING
GIINPPQU QUIPPING
GIINPPRT TRIPPING
GIINPPST TIPPINGS
GIINPRSS RISPINGS
GIINPRST SPIRTING
         STRIPING
GIINPRSU SIRUPING
         UPRISING
GIINPSTT PITTINGS
         SPITTING
GIINPTTU TITUPING
GIINQRSU SQUIRING
GIINQRTU QUIRTING
GIINQTTU QUITTING
GIINQUZZ QUIZZING
GIINRRST STIRRING
GIINRSTV STRIVING
GIINRSTW WRITINGS
GIINSSSW SWISSING
GIINSSTT SITTINGS
GIINSSTU SUITINGS
         TISSUING
GIINSTTW TWISTING
         WITTINGS
GIINTTTW TWITTING
GIIORRST RIGORIST
GIIPRSTZ SPRITZIG
GIJKLNOY JOKINGLY
GIJLLNOY JOLLYING
GIJLNOST JOSTLING
GIJLNSTU JUSTLING
GIJNOSTT JOTTINGS
GIJNOSTU JOUSTING
GIJNTTUY JUTTYING
GIKKLNSU SKULKING
GIKKNNSU SKUNKING
GIKLLNNO KNOLLING
GIKLNNOP PLONKING

GIKLNNPU PLUNKING
GIKLNNRU KNURLING
         RUNKLING
GIKLNNUY UNKINGLY
GIKLNOOS LOOKINGS
GIKLNOPR PORKLING
GIKLNRSU LURKINGS
GIKMNOSS SMOKINGS
GIKNNOSS SNOOKING
GIKNNOQU QUONKING
GIKNNOSW SNOWKING
GIKNNOTT KNOTTING
GIKNNOTU KNOUTING
GIKNNOUY UNYOKING
GIKNNPSU SPUNKING
GIKNNRTU TRUNKING
GIKNOOPS SPOOKING
GIKNOOTW KOTOWING
GIKNOPST KINGPOST
GIKNORRW RINGWORK
GIKNORST STROKING
GIKNORSW WORKINGS
GILLMOOY GLOOMILY
GILLNNSU NULLINGS
GILLNOPR PROLLING
GILLNOPS POLLINGS
GILLNORS ROLLINGS
GILLNORT TROLLING
GILLNOST TOLLINGS
GILLNOSY LOSINGLY
GILLNOVY LOVINGLY
GILLNPUY PULINGLY
GILLNSUY SULLYING
GILLOOPW POLLIWOG
GILLOPSS LIPGLOSS
GILLOPWY POLLYWIG
GILLORVY GILLYVOR
GILLOSSY GLOSSILY
GILMMNSU SLUMMING
GILMNOOS SLOOMING
GILMNOPY MOPINGLY
GILMNORS MORLINGS
GILMNORT MORTLING
GILMNOSS MOSLINGS
GILMNOSU MOUSLING
GILMNOSY SMOYLING
GILMNOTT MOTTLING
GILMNOTU MOULTING
GILMNOUV VOLUMING
GILMNOVY MOVINGLY
GILMNPPU PLUMPING
GILMNPRU RUMPLING
GILMNPSU SLUMPING
GILMNSUY MUSINGLY
GILMNUZZ MUZZLING
GILMOOSY MISOLOGY
GILMPRUY GRUMPILY
GILNNOOS GLONOINS
         LOONINGS
         SNOOLING
GILNNOSU NOUSLING
GILNNOTW TOWNLING
GILNNOUV UNLOVING
GILNNRSU NURSLING
GILNNSSU UNSLINGS
GILNNUZZ NUZZLING
GILNOOPS LOOPINGS
         SPOOLING
GILNOORT ROOTLING

GILNOOST STOOLING
         TOOLINGS
GILNOOTT TOOTLING
GILNOOVY VINOLOGY
GILNOOWY WOOINGLY
GILNOPPP PLOPPING
         POPPLING
GILNOPPS LOPPINGS
         SLOPPING
GILNOPPT TOPPLING
GILNOPRU PROULING
GILNOPRW PROWLING
GILNOPSU SOUPLING
GILNOPSY POSINGLY
         SPONGILY
GILNOPTT PLOTTING
GILNORSU LOURINGS
GILNORTU TROULING
GILNORVY ROVINGLY
GILNOSSW SLOWINGS
GILNOSTT SLOTTING
GILNOSTU TOUSLING
GILNOSVW WOLVINGS
GILNOSWY YOWLINGS
GILNOSZZ SOZZLING
GILNOTUY OUTLYING
GILNOTUZ TOUZLING
GILNPPRU PURPLING
GILNPPSU SUPPLING
GILNPRSU PURLINGS
         SLURPING
         SPURLING
GILNPRYY PRYINGLY
GILNPSSU PLUSSING
GILNPUZZ PUZZLING
GILNRRSU SLURRING
GILNRSTU LUSTRING
         RUSTLING
GILNRTTY TRYINGLY
GILNSSTU SINGULTS
         TUSSLING
GILNSTTU SUTTLING
GILNTUUY UNGUILTY
GILNUWZZ WUZZLING
GILOOORS ROSOGLIO
GILOOOST OOLOGIST
GILOORSS GIROSOLS
GILOORSU GLORIOUS
GILOORVY VIROLOGY
GILOOSSS ISOGLOSS
GILOOSTY SITOLOGY
GILORSTT TRIGLOTS
GILOSTUY GULOSITY
GIMMMNSU MUMMINGS
GIMMMNUY MUMMYING
GIMMNOTY TOMMYING
GIMMNSSU SUMMINGS
GIMMNSTU STUMMING
GIMMOSSU GUMMOSIS
GIMNNORS MORNINGS
GIMNNORU MOURNING
GIMNNOTU MOUNTING
GIMNNOUV UNMOVING
GIMNNSTU MUNTINGS
GIMNOOOU OOGONIUM
GIMNOOPS SPOOMING
GIMNOORS MOORINGS
         SMOORING
GIMNOORT MOTORING

GIMNOORV	VROOMING	GINOPPQU	QUOPPING
GIMNOOSS	OSMOSING	GINOPPSS	SOPPINGS
GIMNOOST	MOOTINGS	GINOPPST	STOPPING
	SMOOTING		TOPPINGS
GIMNOPST	STOMPING	GINOPPSW	SWOPPING
GIMNOPTU	GUMPTION	GINOPRSS	PROSINGS
GIMNORRU	RUMORING	GINOPRST	SPORTING
GIMNORRW	RINGWORM	GINOPRSU	INGROUPS
GIMNORST	STORMING		POURINGS
GIMNORSU	ROUMINGS	GINOPRTU	TROUPING
GIMNOSST	GNOMISTS	GINOPSST	POSTINGS
GIMNOSSU	MOUSINGS		SIGNPOST
	SMOUSING		STOPINGS
	SOUMINGS	GINOPSSU	SPOUSING
GIMNOSTU	MOUSTING	GINOPSTT	SPOTTING
	SMOUTING	GINOPSTU	POUTINGS
GIMNOSYY	MISOGYNY		SPOUTING
GIMNPRTU	TRUMPING	GINOPTTY	TYPTOING
GIMNPSTU	STUMPING	GINORRWY	WORRYING
GIMNRRSU	SMURRING	GINORSST	SORTINGS
GIMNSTTU	SMUTTING	GINORSSU	SOURINGS
GIMNSTYY	STYMYING	GINORSTU	ROUSTING
GIMPSSYY	GYPSYISM		ROUTINGS
GIMRSSUU	GURUISMS		TOURINGS
GINNNOOS	NOONINGS	GINORSTW	STROWING
GINNNOST	STONNING		WORSTING
GINNNPSU	PUNNINGS	GINORSTY	ROYSTING
GINNNRSU	RUNNINGS		STORYING
GINNNSTU	STUNNING		STROYING
	TUNNINGS	GINORTTT	TROTTING
GINNNTUU	UNTUNING	GINORTTU	TROUTING
GINNOOPS	SNOOPING		TUTORING
	SPOONING	GINOSSST	SOSSINGS
GINNOOST	SNOOTING	GINOSSSU	SOUSINGS
GINNOOSW	SWOONING	GINOSSSW	SOWSSING
GINNOOSZ	SNOOZING	GINOSSTT	SOTTINGS
GINNOPPU	UNPOPING	GINOSSTU	TOUSINGS
GINNOPRU	UNROPING	GINOSSTV	STOVINGS
GINNOPRY	PROYNING	GINOSSTW	STOWINGS
GINNOPSS	SPONGINS	GINOSTTT	STOTTING
	SPONSING		TOTTINGS
GINNOPSY	PYONINGS	GINOSTTW	SWOTTING
GINNOPTY	POYNTING	GINOSTUW	OUTSWING
GINNORSS	SNORINGS		OUTWINGS
	SORNINGS	GINOTUVY	OUTVYING
GINNORST	SNORTING	GINPPPUY	PUPPYING
GINNORSU	GRUNIONS	GINPPRSU	UPSPRING
GINNOSST	STONINGS	GINPPRRSU	PURRINGS
GINNOSTT	SNOTTING		SPURRING
GINNOSTU	SNOUTING	GINPRSTU	SPURTING
	STOUNING	GINPRSUU	PURSUING
GINNOSTY	STONYING		USURPING
GINNOSUW	SWOUNING	GINPRSUY	SYRUPING
GINNPRSU	PRUNINGS	GINPSSUW	UPSWINGS
	SPURNING	GINPSTTU	PUTTINGS
GINNRSTU	TURNINGS	GINPTTUY	PUTTYING
	UNSTRING	GINRSSTU	RUSTINGS
GINNSTTU	NUTTINGS		TRUSSING
	STUNTING	GINRSTTU	RUTTINGS
GINNSTUY	UNTYINGS		STURTING
GINOOPPS	OPPOSING		TRUSTING
GINOOPRS	SPOORING	GINRSTTY	TRYSTING
GINOOPRT	TROOPING	GINRSTUU	SUTURING
GINOOPSS	SOOPINGS	GIOOPRRS	PORRIGOS
GINOOPST	STOOPING	GIOORRSU	RIGOROUS
GINOOPSW	SWOOPING	GIOORSTU	GOITROUS
GINOORST	ROOSTING	GIOORSUV	VIGOROUS
	ROOTINGS	GIOPRRSU	PRURIGOS
GINOORTW	WROOTING	GIOPRSSY	GOSSIPRY
GINOPPPR	PROPPING		

GIOPRSTU	GROUPIST	HIIKSSTT	SKITTISH
GIORSTUY	RUGOSITY	HIILMMSS	SLIMMISH
GJOORSTT	JOGTROTS	HIILMOST	HOMILIST
GKLOOOTY	TOKOLOGY	HIILMPSU	SILPHIUM
GLLOOPSY	POLYGLOT	HIILMPSY	IMPISHLY
GLLOOPWY	POLLYWOG	HIILMSTU	LITHIUMS
GLLOOXYY	XYLOLOGY	HIILMSWY	WHIMSILY
GLMNOOOT	MONOGLOT	HIILMTUY	HUMILITY
GLMNOOOY	MONOLOGY	HIILPSST	THLIPSIS
	NOMOLOGY	HIILPSSY	SYPHILIS
GLMOOOPY	POMOLOGY	HIILRSTT	TRILITHS
GLMOOORS	MOORLOGS	HIILSSTT	STILTISH
GLMOOYYZ	ZYMOLOGY	HIIMNSTT	TINSMITH
GLMORSUW	LUGWORMS	HIIMOPSS	PHIMOSIS
GLNNOORS	LORGNONS	HIIMSSTT	SHITTIMS
GLNOOOSY	NOSOLOGY	HIINORST	HISTRION
GLNOOOTY	ONTOLOGY	HIINPSTW	TWINSHIP
GLNOOPRS	PROLONGS	HIIORSST	HISTRIOS
GLNOOPSY	POLYGONS	HIIPPQSU	QUIPPISH
GLNOOPYY	POLYGONY	HIKNNORS	INKHORNS
GLNOPYYY	POLYGYNY	HIKNNSTU	UNTHINKS
GLNORSTY	STRONGLY	HIKNOTTU	OUTTHINK
GLNORTUW	LUNGWORT	HIKOOPSS	SPOOKISH
GLNOSSUW	SUNGLOWS	HIKOPSSY	KYPHOSIS
GLNOSTTU	GLUTTONS	HILLMSUY	MULISHLY
GLNOTTUY	GLUTTONY	HILLNOUY	UNHOLILY
GLOOOPSY	POSOLOGY	HILLOPST	HILLTOPS
GLOOOPTY	OPTOLOGY	HILMMOSU	HOLMIUMS
	TOPOLOGY	HILMNOOT	MONOLITH
GLOOORUY	OUROLOGY	HILMOOPT	PHILOMOT
GLOOPSSY	GOSSYPOL	HILMOPSY	MOPISHLY
GLOOPTYY	TYPOLOGY	HILMOSSW	WHOLISMS
GLOORSUU	ORGULOUS	HILMPPSU	PLUMPISH
GMMPSUUW	MUGWUMPS	HILMPSYY	SYMPHILY
GMNNOOOY	MONOGONY	HILMSTUU	THULIUMS
GMNNOOYY	MONOGYNY	HILNOPSU	UNPOLISH
GMNOORSU	GUNROOMS	HILNOSTY	TONISHLY
GMNOORSW	MORWONGS	HILOOPYZ	ZOOPHILY
GMORSTUW	MUGWORTS	HILOOSTT	OTOLITHS
GNNPRSUU	UNSPRUNG	HILOOSTZ	ZOOLITHS
GNNRSTUU	UNSTRUNG	HILOPPSY	POPISHLY
GNOOORSS	GORSOONS	HILORSTU	UROLITHS
GNOOOSSS	GOSSOONS	HILORTWY	WORTHILY
GNOOORSW	WRONGOUS	HILOSSTY	HYLOISTS
GNOORTUW	OUTGROWN		THYLOSIS
GNOPRSTU	GUNPORTS	HILOSTWW	WHITLOWS
GNPPRSUU	UPSPRUNG	HILOSTYY	TOYISHLY
GOORSTUW	OUTGROWS	HILPPRSU	PURPLISH
GOORTTUW	GOUTWORT	HILPPSUY	UPPISHLY
HHIINNST	THINNISH	HILPRSUW	UPWHIRLS
HHIIPSTS	PHTHISIS	HILSSTTU	SLUTTISH
HHILPSSY	SYLPHISH	HIMMOPRU	PHORMIUM
HHIMNPSY	NYMPHISH	HIMMSSTY	MYTHISMS
HHIMPSSU	SUMPHISH	HIMNOPRX	PHORMINX
HHINOOSW	NOHOWISH	HIMNOPSY	PHISNOMY
HHIORSST	SHORTISH	HIMNSSTY	HYMNISTS
HHKKSSUU	KHUSKHUS	HIMOOPRS	ISOMORPH
HHMRSTUY	RHYTHMUS	HIMOPRWW	WHIPWORM
HHOOPPRS	PHOSPHOR	HIMOPSSS	SOPHISMS
HHOOSSTT	HOTSHOTS	HIMOPSST	PHOTISMS
HIIILMNS	NIHILISM	HIMORSTU	HUMORIST
HIIILNST	NIHILIST		THORIUMS
HIIILNTY	NIHILITY	HIMOTTVZ	MITZVOTH
HIIINRST	RHINITIS	HIMPRSTU	TRIUMPHS
HIIKMNST	MISTHINK	HIMPSTUY	PYTHIUMS
HIIKMRSS	SKIRMISH	HIMRSSTY	RHYMISTS
HIIKNPSS	KINSHIPS	HIMSSTTY	MYTHISTS
HIIKOPRS	PIROSHKI	HINNORST	TINHORNS
HIIKOPRZ	PIROZHKI	HINNPSSU	NUNSHIPS
HIIKQRSU	QUIRKISH	HINNSSUY	SUNSHINY

HINOORST HORNITOS	IIIKMNNS MINIKINS	IIMNNOOT MONITION	IKMNPPSU PUMPKINS
HINOORSZ HORIZONS	IIIKMNSS MINISKIS	IIMNNOSU UNIONISM	IKMNRSTU TRINKUMS
HINOPPSS SHIPPONS	IIILLMNP MINIPILL	IIMNNOTU MUNITION	IKNNRSTU TURNSKIN
HINOPSSS SONSHIPS	IIILLMNU ILLINIUM	IIMNOOSS OMISSION	IKNOOPRT PINKROOT
HINOPSSY HYPNOSIS	IIILLNOS ILLISION	IIMNOPRS IMPRISON	IKNOORRW IRONWORK
HINOPSTW TOWNSHIP	IIILMRSV VIRILISM	IIMNOPST MISPOINT	IKNOOSST ISOKONTS
HINORSST HORNISTS	IIILMUVX LIXIVIUM	IIMNORTT INTROMIT	IKNOPSST INKSPOTS
HINORTXY THYROXIN	IIILRTVY VIRILITY	IIMNORTY MINORITY	IKNOPSTW TOWNSKIP
HIOOPRTT POORTITH	IIIMMMNS MINIMISM	IIMNOSSS MISSIONS	IKNPSSTU SPUTNIKS
HIOORSST ORTHOSIS	IIIMMNST INTIMISM	IIMNOSST SIMONIST	IKORSSTU KURTOSIS
HIOOSSTT SHOOTIST	MINIMIST	IIMNOSTX MIXTIONS	IKORSTTU OUTSKIRT
HIOPRSSW WORSHIPS	IIIMMPRS IMPRIMIS	IIMNPRST IMPRINTS	ILLLMOPS PLIMSOLL
HIOPRSUZ RHIZOPUS	IIIMNSTT INTIMIST	MISPRINT	ILLLMPPU PULPMILL
HIOPSSST SOPHISTS	IIIMNTTY INTIMITY	IIMNPTUY IMPUNITY	ILLLOOPP LOLLIPOP
HIOPSSTU UPHOISTS	IIINORRS IRRISION	IIMNRSTY MINISTRY	ILLMNOSU MULLIONS
HIOPSSTY PHYTOSIS	IIINPRST INSPIRIT	IIMOPSTT OPTIMIST	ILLMOORS MOORILLS
HIORRSSY SORRYISH	IIINQTUY INIQUITY	IIMOSSTY MYOSITIS	ILLMOPRW PILLWORM
HIOSSTTU STOUTISH	IIINSSTU SINUITIS	IIMOTTVY MOTIVITY	ILLMPTUY MULTIPLY
HIPPPSUY PUPPYISH	IIIOSTTU OUISTITI	IIMPRTUY IMPURITY	ILLNOQSU QUILLONS
HKMNORRU KRUMHORN	IIISSTTW WISTITIS	IIMRRTUV TRIUMVIR	ILLNORSU RULLIONS
HKNOORRW HORNWORK	IIJMNOSS MISJOINS	IIMRSTTU TRITIUMS	ILLNPSUU LUPULINS
HKOOOPST POTHOOKS	IIJNNOST INJOINTS	IIMRSTUV TRIVIUMS	ILLOOPRW POORWILL
HKOOPRSW WORKSHOP	IIKLLNOS SKILLION	IIMSSSTU MISSUITS	ILLOORSZ ZORILLOS
HLLLOOWY HOLLOWLY	IIKLMNPS LIMPKINS	IIMSSTUW SWIMSUIT	ILLOPPSS SLIPSLOP
HLLMNOOU MONOHULL	IIKLMPSY SKIMPILY	IINNOOPS OPINIONS	ILLOPPSY SLOPPILY
HLLOPPRY PROPHYLL	IIKLNOSS OILSKINS	IINNOPTU PUNITION	ILLOPRTW PILLWORT
HLMOOSTY SMOOTHLY	IIKMNORS KIRIMONS	IINNOSTU INUSTION	ILLOPRXY PROLIXLY
HLMORRSY MYRRHOLS	IIKMNPSS SIMPKINS	UNIONIST	ILLORSUY ILLUSORY
HLNOOPPY POLYPHON	IIKNOSTT STOTINKI	UNITIONS	ILLOSTXY XYLITOLS
HLOPRSTY PROTHYLS	IILLLPUV PULVILLI	IINNPSST TINSNIPS	ILLOTTWY WITTOLLY
HLPRSSUU SULPHURS	IILLMNOS MILLIONS	IINNSTTU TINNITUS	ILLRSTUY SULTRILY
HLPRSUUY SULPHURY	IILLMRTU TRILLIUM	IINOOPST POSITION	ILMNOOPS POLONISM
HMMNOOSY HOMONYMS	IILLNOOR ORILLION	IINOPSSS ISOSPINS	ILMNOOPU POLONIUM
HMMNOOYY HOMONYMY	IILLNOPS PILLIONS	IINORSST IRONISTS	ILMNOSUU LUMINOUS
HMMOORSU MUSHROOM	IILLNORT TRILLION	IINORSTT INTROITS	ILMOPPSU POPULISM
HMMRSTUU HUMSTRUM	IILLNOST STILLION	IINOSTTU TUITIONS	ILMORSTU TURMOILS
HMNOOOST MOONSHOT	IILLNOSU ILLUSION	IINOSTVY VINOSITY	ILMORSTY STORMILY
HMNOOOTY HOMOTONY	IILLNOSZ ZILLIONS	IINRTTUY TRIUNITY	ILMOSTUV VOLUMIST
HMNOORRW HORNWORM	IILLNSST INSTILLS	IINSSTTW INTWISTS	ILMOSTUY TIMOUSLY
HMNOOSTU UNSMOOTH	IILLNSTT LITTLINS	IIOOPSTV OVIPOSIT	ILMPPTUU PULPITUM
HMNOPSYY HYPONYMS	IILLOPUV PULVILIO	IIOOSTTY OTIOSITY	ILMPSSTU PLUMISTS
SYMPHONY	IILMMPSS SIMPLISM	IIOPPRTY PRIORITY	ILMPSTUY STUMPILY
HMOOOPRZ ZOOMORPH	IILMMSUU SIMULIUM	IIOPRSSS PISSOIRS	ILMSSTTU STIMULUS
HMOOORSW SHOWROOM	IILMNORT MIRLITON	IIORRRSY IRRISORY	ILMSTTUY SMUTTILY
HMOOPTYY HOMOTYPY	IILMNOSS LIONISMS	IIORSSTV IVORISTS	ILNOOPSS PLOSIONS
HMOORSUU HUMOROUS	IILMNSTU LUMINIST	VISITORS	ILNOOPSV VOLPINOS
HNOOOOPR OOPHORON	IILMORSS SIMILORS	IIORSTUV VIRTUOSI	ILNOOPSY SPOONILY
HNOOPRSW SHOPWORN	IILMORST TROILISM	IIOSSTTU OUSTITIS	ILNOOSST SOLITONS
HNOOPSTY TYPHOONS	IILMOTTY MOTILITY	IIPRSSTU SPIRITUS	ILNOOSTU SOLUTION
HNOORRTW HORNWORT	IILMPSST SIMPLIST	IJKLLOSY KILLJOYS	ILNOOTUV VOLUTION
HNOORSTU SOUTHRON	IILMRSSY MISSILRY	IJLNOQSU JONQUILS	ILNOPRSU PURLOINS
HNOOSSTU UNSHOOTS	IILNNOOT NOLITION	IJNNOSTU UNJOINTS	ILNOPSSU UPSILONS
HNOPRTUW UPTHROWN	IILNNSSU INSULINS	IKKLNORW LINKWORK	ILNOPSSW SNOWSLIP
HNORSTUW UNWORTHS	IILNOOST INOSITOL	IKKLNOSY KOLINSKY	ILNOPSSY YPSILONS
HNORTUWY UNWORTHY	IILNOOTV VOLITION	IKKMNOSU KIKUMONS	ILNOPSTU UNSPOILT
HNOSSTUU UNSHOUTS	IILNORSS SIRLOINS	IKKNORST KIRKTONS	ILNORSST NOSTRILS
HNRSTTUU UNTRUTHS	IILOOPPR LIRIPOOP	IKKNORTW KIRKTOWN	ILNORSSU SURLOINS
HOOOSTTU OUTSHOOT	IILOOPRST TRIPOLIS	IKLLOOTV KILOVOLT	ILNORSTU TORULINS
HOOPPSTY PHOTOPSY	IILOPSSS PSILOSIS	IKLLOSSY KYLLOSIS	ILNORTXY NITROXYL
HOOPRRST PORTHORS	IILOPSST PTILOSIS	IKLMNPSU LUMPKINS	ILNOSSTW STOWLINS
HOOPSSTU UPSHOOTS	IILOPSTY PILOSITY	IKLMORSW SILKWORM	ILNOSTTY SNOTTILY
HOOPSSTY TOYSHOPS	IILORSTT TROILIST	IKLMORTW MILKWORT	ILNOSTUV VOLUTINS
HOORTTUW OUTWORTH	IILORSTV VITRIOLS	IKLNOOST KILOTONS	ILNPSUUV PULVINUS
HOOSSTTU OUTSHOTS	IILOSSTV VIOLISTS	IKLNPSSU SKULPINS	ILOOORSS ROSOLIOS
HOPPRRYY PORPHYRY	IILRSSTU SILURIST	IKLOOPSY SPOOKILY	ILOOPPRS PROPOLIS
HOPRRSUY PYRRHOUS	IILSTUUV UVULITIS	IKLOOSTT TOOLKITS	ILOOPSST POLOISTS
HOPRSTUW UPTHROWS	IILSTUVV VULVITIS	IKLOSSSU SOUSLIKS	ILOORSTU RISOLUTO
HPRSTTUU UPTHRUST	IIMMNTUY IMMUNITY	IKMNNOSW MISKNOWN	ILOOSSST SOLOISTS
IIIJJLNS JINJILIS	IIMMOPST OPTIMISM	IKMNOOOS OKIMONOS	ILOPPSTU POPULIST
IIIKLNPS SPILIKIN	IIMMSTTU MITTIMUS	IKMNOSSW MISKNOWS	ILOPRSTY SPORTILY

ILOPSTTY SPOTTILY	SPONSION	IOQRTUXY QUIXOTRY	MMOPSSTY SYMPTOMS
ILOPSUUV PLUVIOUS	INNOOPSU UNPOISON	IORRSUVV SURVIVOR	MNNOOOSS MONSOONS
ILOQRTUU LOQUITUR	INNOORST NOTORNIS	IORSSTTU TOURISTS	MNNOOOTY MONOTONY
ILPPRTUY PULPITRY	INNOPRSU UNPRISON	IORSSUUU USURIOUS	MNNOSSYY SYNONYMS
ILRSTTUY TRUSTILY	INNOSSTU NONSUITS	IORSTTUY TOURISTY	MNNOSTUU UNMOUNTS
ILRSTUUX LUXURIST	INOOOSSZ ZOONOSIS	YTTRIOUS	MNNOSYYY SYNONYMY
ILSSSTTY STYLISTS	INOOOTXZ ZOOTOXIN	IORSTUUV VIRTUOUS	MNOOOPPS POMPOONS
IMMNOSSU MUSIMONS	INOOPRST PORTIONS	IPRRSSTU STIRRUPS	MNOOORTW MOONWORT
IMMNOSUU MUONIUMS	POSITRON	IPRRSTUU PRURITUS	MNOOORXY OXYMORON
IMMOORTU MOTORIUM	SORPTION	IPRRSTUU PURSUITS	MNOOPRTU PRONOTUM
IMMRSTUY SUMMITRY	INOOPSSS POISSONS	JLNSTUUY UNJUSTLY	MNOOPSTY TOPONYMS
IMMSSSTU SUMMISTS	INOOPSST POSITONS	JLOOSUYY JOYOUSLY	MNOOPTYY TOPONYMY
IMNNNOSU MUNNIONS	INOOPSTT SPITTOON	JMOPSTUU OUTJUMPS	MNOOSTTW TOWMONTS
IMNNOORS NORIMONS	INOOPTTU OUTPOINT	JNNOORRU NONJUROR	MNORSSTU NOSTRUMS
IMNNOOTT MONOTINT	INOORSST ISOTRONS	JNOORSSU SOJOURNS	MNORSTUU SURMOUNT
IMNNOSUU NUMINOUS	TORSIONS	JNOOSUUY UNJOYOUS	MOOOPRRT PROMOTOR
IMNOOPPS POMPIONS	INOORSTY SONORITY	KKNOORTW KNOTWORK	MOOORRTW TOMORROW
IMNOOPST TOMPIONS	INOPPSST TOPSPINS	KKOOSSUU KOUSKOUS	MOOPSSSU OPOSSUMS
IMNOOPSU OPSONIUM	INOPRTUY PUNITORY	KLLMNSUU NUMSKULL	MOORRSUU RUMOROUS
IMNOORRS MORRIONS	INOPSSSU POUSSINS	KLLMOSSU MOLLUSKS	MOORSTUU TUMOROUS
IMNOORST MONITORS	INOPSSSY SYNOPSIS	KLNORSTY KLYSTRON	MORRSSTU ROSTRUMS
TROMINOS	INOPSSTU SPINOUTS	KLOOORWW WOOLWORK	MORSSTUU STRUMOUS
IMNOORTY MONITORY	INORSSUV UNVISORS	KLOOOSTU LOOKOUTS	NNOOOPST PONTOONS
IMNOORVY OMNIVORY	INPPRRUU PURPURIN	OUTLOOKS	SPONTOON
IMNOOSUX OXONIUMS	INPRSSTU UNSTRIPS	KLOOPRSW SLOPWORK	NNOOPRSU PRONOUNS
IMNOPPSU PUMPIONS	INPRSSTY TRYPSINS	KMOOORRW WORKROOM	NNOOPSSS SPONSONS
IMNORRSU MURRIONS	INPRSTTU TURNSPIT	KNNNOSUW UNKNOWNS	NOOOPPRS PROSOPON
IMNORSTY TRIONYMS	INRSSTTU INTRUSTS	KNOOPSTT TOPKNOTS	NOOORSTU SONOROUS
IMNOSTUU MUTINOUS	INSSSTUU SUNSUITS	KNOPRSTY KRYPTONS	NOOPRSSS SPONSORS
IMNRSTUU UNTRUISM	INSSTTUW UNTWISTS	KOOPRSTW WORKTOPS	NOORSSTU UNROOSTS
IMOOPRRS PROMISOR	IOOPRRSV PROVISOR	KOORSTUW OUTWORKS	NOORSTUW OUTSWORN
IMOOPRST IMPOSTOR	IOOPRSSV PROVISOS	KORSTTUW TUTWORKS	NOPSSSTU SUNSPOTS
IMOOQSTU MOSQUITO	IOOPRSSY ISOSPORY	LLLMMSUU MULMULLS	NORSTTUU OUTTURNS
IMOORSTT MOTORIST	IOOPRSTY ISOTROPY	LLMOOPRS ROLLMOPS	NRSSTTUU UNTRUSTS
IMOORSTU SUMOTORI	POROSITY	LLOOPRST TROLLOPS	NRSTTUUY UNTRUSTY
TIMOROUS	IOORRSTY SORORITY	LLOOPRTY TROLLOPY	OOOOPRST POTOROOS
IMOORSTY MOROSITY	IOORRTTT TROTTOIR	LLOSUUVV VOLVULUS	OOOPRSSU SOPOROUS
IMOORTVY VOMITORY	IOORSSTT RISOTTOS	LMNOOOPY MONOPOLY	OOOPRSTU OUTROOPS
IMOOSSTY MYOSOTIS	IOORSSUV VOUSSOIR	LMNOOPYY POLYONYM	OOORSTTU OUTROOTS
IMOPRRSY PRIMROSY	IOORSTTU TORTIOUS	LMOOOORT TOOLROOM	OOPRSSTV PROVOSTS
IMOPRSST TROPISMS	IOORSTUV VIRTUOSO	LMOOPSYY POLYSOMY	OOPRSTTU OUTPORTS
IMOPRSTU PROTIUMS	IOORSUUX UXORIOUS	LMOOSSSU MOLOSSUS	OUTSPORT
IMOPSSTU UTOPISMS	IOOSSTTU STOTIOUS	LMOPPRTY PROMPTLY	OOPRSTUU OUTPOURS
IMORSSTU TOURISMS	IOPRRSUV PROVIRUS	LMRSSTUU LUSTRUMS	OOPSSSTT TOSSPOTS
IMORSTTU TUTORISM	IOPRSSTT PROTISTS	LNOOOPRT POLTROON	OOPSSSTU OUTPOSTS
IMPPPSUY PUPPYISM	TROPISTS	LNOOOPYZ POLYZOON	OORSTTUU TORTUOUS
IMRSSTTU MISTRUST	IOPRSSUU SPURIOUS	LNOOPPRY PROPYLON	OPPRRSTU PURPORTS
IMRSSTTY MISTRYST	IOPRSTTU OUTSTRIP	LNOOPSTU PULTOONS	OPPRSSTU SUPPORTS
IMRSTTUY YTTRIUMS	IOPRSTUU POURSUIT	LNRSTUUV VULTURNS	OPRSSSUU SOURPUSS
INNNORSU RUNNIONS	IOPRSTUY PYRITOUS	LOOOORSS OLOROSOS	ORSSTTUU SURTOUTS
INNNORTU TRUNNION	IOPRSUVX POXVIRUS	LOOPPSUU POPULOUS	RRSSSUUU SUSURRUS
INNNOSTY SYNTONIN	IOPSSTTU UTOPISTS	LOOPPSUY POLYPOUS	
INNOOPSS OPSONINS	IOQRSTTU QUITTORS	LORSSTUU LUSTROUS	